D1709818

HACKH'S
CHEMICAL
DICTIONARY

OTHER BOOKS BY JULIUS GRANT

Books and Documents
Science for the Prosecution
Cellulose Pulp and Allied Products
Fluorescence Analysis in Ultra-Violet Light
Laboratory Handbook of Pulp and Paper Manufacture

HACKH'S
CHEMICAL
DICTIONARY

[American and British Usage]

*Containing the Words Generally Used in Chemistry,
and Many of the Terms Used in the Related
Sciences of Physics, Astrophysics, Mineralogy,
Pharmacy, Agriculture, Biology,
Medicine, Engineering, etc.*

Based on Recent Chemical Literature

FOURTH EDITION
Completely Revised and Edited by

JULIUS GRANT
M.SC., PH.D., F.R.I.C.   CHEMICAL CONSULTANT

McGRAW-HILL BOOK COMPANY
New York   San Francisco   Toronto   London   Sydney

PREFACE

The unprecedented advances in science in general and chemistry in particular during the 25 years that have elapsed since the third edition of this Dictionary was completed have created some special problems in the preparation of this new edition. The advances referred to have, of course, produced many new words, which have had to be defined. Coping numerically with these is a problem in itself, though by no means an insuperable one. The author started "collecting" as soon as the manuscript of the third edition left his hands; and although he does not presume to have recorded every new word which has appeared, he feels fairly safe in claiming the inclusion of most new words of any importance. A Dictionary of this nature must define new, old, and even many obsolete terms (indicating, of course, that they are obsolete), and as a result the total number or words now defined, is nearly 55,000. Due attention has, of course, been given to the fact that the Dictionary is intended to include words from related sciences, as well as from chemistry.

Since new organic compounds are being recorded in the literature at the rate of many thousands a year, it is obvious that relatively few of them can be included in this Dictionary. With compounds of minor importance however, a "definition" need be little more than a chemical formula and a list of a few physical properties, and these are easily obtainable from the chemical literature.

An explanation of the policies adopted in dealing with some special problems is desirable. Often, a commonly accepted or abbreviated name for a chemical compound or preparation has, in the course of years, become a registered trade name; and vice versa. Thus difficulties have occurred in the second and third editions of the Dictionary when a company has wished to register a trade name, because the question may arise whether the name is already accepted as a common description of the compound concerned. Since the Dictionary has been widely quoted as an authority in arriving at decisions of this nature, it should be made clear that the listing of a word as a free chemical term does not necessarily mean that it has not been adopted as a trade name; and that there is no intention to use a term in a generic sense if it is in fact a trade name.

In the present edition, product names have been given an initial capital letter and described as trademarks when such information has been available. Other products have been shown similarly and identified as proprietary or trade names where this information is known. The use of a general designation does not therefore exclude the possibility that a more specific designation may properly apply. It has always been the policy of the author not to mention by name individual companies owning or associated with trade-name entries, registered or otherwise, and this policy is still followed.

It has also been necessary to make a firm decision on definitions and data contained in standard publications which are revised at regular intervals, and in particular the Pharmacopoeias. The policy adopted has therefore been to include, and to define according to the published data, all terms given in the United States Pharmacopoeia and the British Pharmacopoeia current in July, 1968. Subsidiary publications such as the National Formulary and the British Pharmacopoeia Codex have been dealt with rather less comprehensively. Many of the terms they contain are, of course, included in the two above Pharmacopoeias, but of the remainder only the more important are defined in the Dictionary.

Preparations such as germicides, insecticides, detergents, plastics, man-made fibers, and agricultural chemicals call for similar discretionary treatment. It is obviously impossible to include all the names concerned, whether chemical, abbreviated, or trade names. Some such products have as many as 12 different trade names, and their full chemical names would occupy at least two lines of the Dictionary. Here again, it has been necessary to make a selection, and it is believed that the more important compounds and trade names have been included. A number of British Standards contain recommended names for such compounds, and the International Organization for Standardization (ISO) is at present drawing up definitions of chemical terms covering a wide range of industries. All this work is, however, far from complete, and it is subject to revision as new words appear and others become obsolete.

Chemical nomenclature and notation, especially of organic chemicals, present another difficult problem. The first essential is uniformity throughout the Dictionary, but the whole question of the standardization of chemical nomenclature is continuously under consideration by the International Union of Pure and Applied Chemistry. Unfortunately, this is a never-ending task, because the rulings of the Union have to be adapted to changes in chemical custom. So far as possible therefore, those rulings of the Union up to 1968 which are accepted by U.S. and U.K. chemical organizations, are used in this Dictionary. This policy applies particularly to the definitions of radicals. However, it must be appreciated that there are some classes of compounds for which no rules have yet been published. Further details are given under the definitions of nomenclature, symbols, and units, and in the Explanatory Notes.

It is inevitable that the full implementation of the above improvements and additions would have involved a considerable increase in both the number and lengths of many of the definitions, so much so that it was apparent that the Dictionary would become unwieldly. A considerable increase in selling price, would in turn, have resulted. After serious consideration it was therefore decided to deal with the situation not by reducing the number of definitions, but by rewording them more precisely, deleting a certain amount of relatively trivial matter, and adopting a more concise style of expression and nomenclature. The photographs of eminent chemists and many of the illustrations and diagrams have unfortunately been victims of this policy, but the definitions have been modified so as to minimize the loss where illustrations were formerly used to amplify the text. This policy has enabled the price of the Dictionary to be kept within reasonable bounds without material detriment to its efficiency and scope.

Despite the above considerations, the objects and scope of this Dictionary remain the same as stated by Ingo Hackh in the Preface to the first edition: ". . . not to make a mere compilation or collection of facts, but to restate and redefine in simple modern terms the phenomena of science, and to connect these phenomena with one another . . . A chemical dictionary should state clearly and precisely the theories, laws, and rules; describe accurately the elements, compounds, minerals, drugs, vegetable and animal products; list concisely the important reactions, processes, and methods; mention briefly the chemical apparatus, equipment, and instruments; and, finally, should note the names of the investigators who have built up the science. As chemistry reaches into nearly every branch of human endeavor it should not forget to bring in the collateral vocabulary of physics, astrophysics, geology, mineralogy, botany, zoology, medicine, and pharmacy and, also, the pertinent jargon of industry, mining, and commerce."

It is obvious, that a dictionary of this magnitude and status, involves the author in a considerable measure of responsibility. Even in scientific work, the art of definition becomes at times an expression of personal opinion, although accuracy, current usage, and conciseness should always be the guiding principles. Adherence as closely as possible to standard procedures (and preferably to international standards where these exist and are accepted), and to customary usage in America and Great Britain in other instances will, it is hoped, maintain for the Dictionary the authoritative position it has been privileged to occupy for so many years.

As in previous editions, special care has been taken to balance the treatment betweeen the American and British points of view. The desirability of such balance has always been felt strongly in the past, but in our present-day world every line of approach to community of thought among the English-speaking nations has a special significance. The increasing use of English as a language of science has in fact been an important feature of the years since the publication of the third edition, and at the same time American and British usages have drawn closer together. Since both are covered in this Dictionary it is hoped that this new edition will make a modest contribution to the international amity which so markedly distinguishes science from politics.

A publication of this nature and magnitude calls for rather more than the usual degree of cooperation from the publishers. The author has pleasure in recording his appreciation of this cooperation, and in particular that afforded by Mrs. Winifred C. Eisler who was responsible on their behalf for the purely editorial work involved in preparing the manuscript for the printers.

Finally, it is hoped that future editions will benefit in the same way as in the past, from readers' suggested additions, deletions, and corrections.

London, England

JULIUS GRANT

EXPLANATORY NOTES

Spelling. American usage is given precedence, but British forms are also listed: e.g., "sulfur" and sulphur," respectively.

Capitals are always used in the definitions for the initial letter of the first word of a sentence.

Nomenclature, notation, symbols, and spelling generally follow the system adopted in the American Chemical Society publications (see *Chemical Abstracts*, July, 1968); but British renderings, where they differ, are also included in all instances, and cross-references are given where necessary (see "Symbols, Signs, and Abbreviations," The Royal Society, London, 1967).

Nomenclature recommended by the International Union of Pure and Applied Chemistry is included in most instances. See under the definitions of *international, nomenclature, notation, symbols, units*. An asterisk indicates an internationally accepted name; but its absence does not mean that the rendering is unacceptable. The most recent rulings on certain of these matters are summarized in "Fifty Years of I.U.P.A.C., 1918–1968," August, 1968.

Tables. Ordinarily, capitalized initials are used for the first words. Exceptions are, however, made in the tables of SI units and Symbols, where lowercase letters are used so as to conform with the procedure adopted in the official publications.

Ring systems are represented by one of the three following methods, and are numbered as shown.

Line formula	Square formula	Geometric formula

Synonyms are given under each definition in order of approximate importance. Most of them are also listed separately in the Dictionary, with a cross-reference to the entry under which the actual definition is to be found in the form of the word itself only. Thus, "**brassil**. Pyrite" means "for 'brassil,' 'see pyrite' " or "same as 'pyrite'."

Commercial names are referred to the scientific synonym, unless the compound is of special commerical importance. E.g., "soda ash" is defined under that heading.

In the case of a few complex organic compounds having abbreviated or trade names for which a full definition is not justified or is unobtainable, the only definition given under the shorter name is the full chemical name.

Italics are used only as follows: (1) according to custom (thus "*Acacia*" the plant, but "acacia" the gum); (2) for cross-reference (e.g., "**acaricide**. A mite killer. Cf. *insecticide*"); (3) for the titles of publications, etc.; (4) for some subheadings of the definitions, usually a subdivision of the boldface subentry immediately preceding; (5) for alternative ring numberings of organic compounds; (6) for the letters *o-*, *m-*, *p-* used as abbreviations for ortho, meta, and para, respectively; (7) for certain symbols, where custom demands (see table under symbols).

Where a cross-reference consists of a double word, the portion of the word under which the definition is to be found is italicized if it is not the first portion. This applies also to synonym cross-references. E.g., "chromone, 3-phenyl. Iso*flavone*."

Compound words should be sought under the heading of the first of the words, in the first instance. Thus "soda ash" is to be found under "soda," and not under "ash." Cross-references are, however, usually given under the second word, and in some cases where importance and general custom demand, the actual definition will be found under the latter, and a cross-reference under the former. Thus "high-speed ferrotungsten" is defined under "ferrotungsten" with a cross-reference under "high-speed."

Wheret he word defined is continuously repeated in its main definition or subdefinitions, it is represented by its initial lowercase letter followed by a period, so long as the meaning is not thereby obscured.

Trade names and registered trademarks have a capital initial letter, and are so described where known. The listing of a word as a free chemical term does not necessarily mean that it has not been adopted as a trade name or trademark. However, there is no intention to use a term in a generic sense if it is in fact a trade name or trademark (see Preface).

Where an entry is both a trademark or trade name and a generic name, the entry generally has a capitalized initial, and is folllowed by the trademark or trade name definition first, and then, after "(not cap.)," by the generic definition.

Letters in parentheses in or at the end of a word defined indicate an alternative method of spelling. Thus, "flavin(e)."

Hyphens in boldface represent a repetition of a main boldface entry; or, when used in an italic subentry, a repetition of an immediately preceding boldface entry. Otherwise hyphens are used only when necessary to avoid ambiguity and where custom demands, e.g., "pyrogallin-P."

Water of crystallization is shown: e.g., $Na_2SO_4 \cdot 10H_2O$.

Ambiguous terms and spelling are avoided: e.g. "bromethane" which could mean either "bromoethane" or "bromomethane."

Derivatives of organic compounds are generally to be found under the parent compound. Thus, *p*-nitrophenol" is under "phenol." The positional letters, *o-*, *m-*, and *p-*, etc., are listed in this order; thus, "orthoanisidine" is under "anisidine, *o-*." Similarly for α-, β-, and γ-.

Substituents of organic compounds are listed in alphabetical order, but compound radical names are treated as units, the alphabetical order also being applied to the compound radical.

Official drugs listed in the American or British Pharmacopoeia current in July, 1968 are indicated thus: (U.S.P.) or (B.P.), respectively.

The usual order of presenting or describing a compound is:

Name. Formula = molecular weight. Synonyms. Occurrence, preparation or type of substance. Color, crystalline form, density (of more important compounds), melting point (of solids), boiling point (of liquids), solubility in water; chemical, industrial, and medicinal uses.

Symbols are defined in the appropriate places (see especially the first entries under each letter of the alphabet), and under *constants, notation, nomenclature, SI units,* and *symbols*; they follow the commonly accepted conventions.

Data such as atomic weights are dated 1967; world production of commodities, etc., are approximate and are usually dated 1967, though some 1967 data are estimates.

Abbreviations commonly used in the definitions are:

Å for angström unit.

α for specific rotation. E.g., $[\alpha]_D^{20}$ is the value of α for the D line at 20°C.

Ac for acetyl, CH_3CO—. E.g., AcOH is acetic acid.

Am for ammonium, NH_4—. E.g., AmCl is ammonium chloride. Sometimes Am for amyl, C_5H_{11}—.

    i-Am for isoamyl.

at. for atomic.   E.g., at. wt., at. no.

b. for boiling point in °C.   E.g., b_{600mm} 60 means, boils at 60°C under a pressure of 600 mm of mercury.

Bu for butyl, C_4H_9—; i-Bu for isobutyl.

Bz for benzoyl, PhCO—.   E.g., BzOH is benzoic acid.

Cf. for compare.

cryst. for crystalline or crystallizing.

d. for density at room temperature. $d_{0°}$ for density at 0°C; $d_{air=1}$ for density compared to air.

decomp. for decompose, -osing, -oses, or -osed.   E.g., decomp. 20 means decomposes at 20°C.

Et for ethyl, C_5H_5—.   E.g., EtOH is ethyl alcohol.

m. for melting point in °C (used similarly to b., boiling point).

M for monovalent metal.

Me for methyl, CH_3—.   E.g., MeOH is methyl alcohol.

mol. for molecular.   E.g., mol. wt.

n for refractive index.   E.g., $[n]_D^{20}$ is the value for the D line at 20°C.

no. for number.   E.g., at. no.

Ph for phenyl, C_6H_5—.   E.g., PhOH is phenol.

pl. for plural.

Pr for propyl, C_3H_7—. i-Pr for isopropyl.

q.v. for (1) which see (in cross-references);

      (2) as much as desired (in prescriptions, etc.).

R for any monovalent radical; R′, R″, etc., for different monovalent radicals.

sapon. for saponification.   E.g., sapon. val.

unsap. for unsaponifiable.   E.g., unsap. matter.

val. for value.   E.g., iodine val.

vol. for volume.

wt. for weight.   E.g., at. wt.

X for any halogen or monovalent anion.

A

A. (1) Abbreviation for: (*a*) ampere, (*b*) anode, (*c*) alternate, (*d*) year, (*e*) atomic weight, (*f*) angström. (2) Symbol for argon (obsolete). **A acid.** 1,7-Dihydroxynaphthalene-3,6-disulfonic acid.

A. Symbol for mass number.

°A. Symbol for degree absolute.

Å. Abbreviation for angström.

a. Abbreviation for: (1) asymmetric, (2) ana position, (3) area. **a-, an-** Prefix indicating without or not, as anhydrous.

a. A constant in van der Waals' equation, q.v. [*a*]. Symbol for specific rotation; [*a*]$_D$ for the D line; [*a*]$_D^t$ at temperature *t*.

A$_n$. Abbreviation for normal atmosphere. 760 mm Hg (d.13.59509), or 1.013249 × 10⁶ dynes/cm². [written as 1.013249×10^6]

α. Greek alpha, abbreviation for: (1) alpha position, (2) alpha particles, (3) a mutation isomer of a sugar; as, α-glucose. [α]. See [*a*]. **α acid.** 2,8-Naphthylaminesulfonic acid.

abaca Manila hemp. The inner fiber of *Musa textilis*, a banana species of the Philippine Islands.

Abasin. Trademark for a brand of acetylcarbromal.

abati drying oven. A constant-temperature oven with xylene bath (100–200°C.).

abaxial. Not in the line of axis.

Abbe, Ernst. 1840–1905. German physicist. **A. condenser.** An arrangement of lenses to increase the illumination of an object under the microscope. **A. refractometer.** A device for rapid, direct determination of refractive index. **A. theory.** The limit of microscopic visibility is determined by $w = \lambda/2n \sin\mu$, where w is the width of the object, $n \sin\mu$ the aperture, and λ the wavelength of the light.

abbreviations. See *atomic weight, electrical units, notation, quantum, radical*, etc. Many international standardizing bodies maintain the general principle that symbolic abbreviations for units shall not carry a full stop as part of the abbreviation. See table, pp. 2–3.

Abderhalden, Emil. 1877–1950. Dutch-born German chemist, noted for physiological and pathological research. **A. reaction, A. test.** A serum reaction for diagnosis of pregnancy. Cf. *complement fixation, ninhydrin, placentin*.

Abegg, Richard. 1869–1910. German chemist noted for his theory of valence.

Abel, Sir Frederick Augustus. 1827–1902. English chemist noted for research on explosives and petroleum. **A. fuse.** See *fuse*. **A. heat test.** A test for the stability of nitroglycerin; the sample is heated with a potassium iodide–starch paper which must not be colored by the products evolved within a certain time. **A. reagent.** A 10% solution of chromium iodide used for etching steel in microanalysis. **A. tester.** An apparatus for the determination of the flash point of oils.

abelmoschus. See *musk* seed.

aberration. Deviation from the normal. **astronomical-** The apparent angular displacement of light from a star. **chromatic-** The unequal refraction of white and multicolored light. **spherical-** The deviation of light passing through a lens, or reflected from a mirror, caused by the inequality in the degree of convergence. See aplanatic *focus*.

abhesive. Nonadhesive.

abienic acid. Abieninic acid.

abieninic acid. $C_{13}H_{20}O_2 = 208.2$. Abienic acid. An acid resin from *Abies pectinata*, European silver fir.

Abies. A genus of evergreen trees, the Coniferae (Pinaceae) or firs, which yield turpentine, resin, and pitch.

abietene. $C_{19}H_{30} = 258.3$. Diterebentyl. A liquid hydrocarbon, b.340–345, from the resin of *Pinus sabiniana*. Cf. *colophene*. **a. sulfonic acid.** Black paste produced by the slow action of sulfuric acid on a. at 10°C. A textile industry wetting agent.

abietic acid. $C_{19}H_{29}COOH = 302.32$. Sylvic acid. An acid from the resin of pine species (colophony). Yellow leaflets, m.161, insoluble in water, used in varnishes and driers. Cf. *pimaric acid, Steele acid.* **dehydro-** $C_{19}H_{27}COOH = 300.21$. An oxidized resinic acid produced by treating a. with sulfur. **dihydro-** $C_{19}H_{31}COOH = 304.21$. A reduced resinic acid produced by heating a. with hydrogen under pressure.

a. anhydride. $C_{44}H_{26}O_4 = 654.6$. The anhydride (?) of abietic acid; the chief constituent of colophony.

abietin. (1) $C_{53}H_{76}O_8 = 841.8$. A crystalline resin from the pitch of European silver fir. (2) Abietene. (3) Coniferin.

abietinic acid. $C_{19}H_{28}O_2 = 288.3$. A crystalline acid from rosin; 3 isomeric forms.

abietinolic acid. $C_{16}H_{24}O_2 = 248.2$. An acid resin from the pitch of European silver fir.

abietite. $C_4H_8O_6 = 152.1$. A tetrose sugar from the needles of European silver fir.

abiogenesis. Autogenesis. The spontaneous generation of life from inanimate or lifeless matter. Cf. *biogenesis*.

abiosis. Absence of life.

ablation. The wearing of solid surfaces by hot gases at high speeds, e.g., of meteorites or long-range missiles entering the earth's atmosphere.

Abney clinometer. A pocket altimeter for measuring heights or slopes.

abnormal. Irregular; different from normal.

abradant. Abrasive.

abrasion. Mechanical wearing away.

abrasive. A grinding or polishing material.

abrastol. $Ca(SO_3C_{10}H_6OH)_2 \cdot 3H_2O = 540.3$. Asaprol, calcium β-naphthol-α-monosulfonate. Pink scales, decomp. 50, soluble in water, darkens on

ABBREVIATIONS (U.S. AND U.K. USAGE)

The following abbreviations are not obligatory. The same abbreviations are used for the singular and plural forms of nouns.

Where two abbreviations are given for the same term and separated by a semicolon, the first is the preferred U.S. and the second the preferred U.K. usage.

absolute	abs.
alternating current	a-c; a.c.
ampere	amp; A
angström unit	A; Å
anhydrous	anhyd.
approximate, -ly	approx.
aqueous	aq.
Assignee (patent titles only)	Assee.
atmospher(e),(es),(ic),	atm.
atomic	at.
atomic number	at. no.
atomic weight	at. wt.
Baumé	Bé
biochemical oxygen demand	B.O.D.
boiling point	b.p. or b.
British thermal unit	Btu; BThU.
calculat(e),(ed),(ion)	calc.,(d.)(n.)
Calorie (large)	kcal
calorie (small)	cal
centimeter	cm
centimeter-gram-second system	cgs, CGS
centipoise	cp; cP
centistoke	cs; cS
coefficient	coeff.
concentrat(e),(ed),(ion)	conc.,(d.),(n.)
constant[1]	const.
corrected[2]	corr.
critical[1]	crit.
crystal,-lize,(d)	cryst.,(d.)
crystalli(ne),(zation)	crystn.
cubic centimeter	cc or cm^3

cubic meter	cu m or m^3
Curie	C; c.
current density	c.d.
cycles per second	cps; c/s
decimeter	dm
decompos(e),(ing),(ed),(ition)[3]	decomp.,(d.),(n.)
density	d, ρ
deriv(ative),(ed),(ation)[4]	deriv.,(d.),(n.)
diameter	diam.; dia.
dilut(e),(ed),(ing),(ion)	dil.,(td.),(tg.),(n.)
direct current	d-c; d.c.
electromagnetic unit	emu, EMU
electromotive force	emf
electron volt	ev; eV
electrostatic unit	esu, ESU
equal to	=
equivalent	equiv.
equivalent to	≡
ethylenediaminetetraacetic acid	EDTA
feet, foot	ft
feet per minute	fpm, ft/min
for example	e.g.
freezing point	f.p.
gallon	gal
gram	g; gm
hectare	ha
horsepower	hp
hour	hr; h
hydrogen-ion concentration	[H^+]
inch	in.
indefinite	indef.

[1] Used only to qualify a physical constant.
[2] Used only to qualify a numerical value.

[3] Used only in connection with m.p. or b.p.
[4] Used only in a chemical sense.

exposure to light; a germicide, antipyretic, and antirheumatic.

abraum salts. (German abräumen—to put away.) The potash salts of Strassfurt, e.g., kainite. See *Stassfurt* salts.

abrazite. Gismondite.

abriachanite. Amorphous blue asbestos.

abric acid. $C_{21}H_{24}NO_3 = 334.3$. An acid from the abrus seeds or prayer beads of *Abrus precatorius*.

abrin. Jequiritin. A poisonous mixture of albumose and paraglobulin from abrus seeds; an ophthalmic irritant.

abrodil. Sodium monoiodomethane sulfonate, used for intravenous injections to obtain X-ray pictures of the body.

abrotanum. Southern wood. The leaves are used as an aromatic.

abrotine. $C_{21}H_{22}NO_2 = 318.19$. An alkaloid from southern wood, *Artemisia abrotanum* (Compositae).

abrus root. Indian licorice. The roots of *A. precatorius* (Leguminosae) of India, tropical Africa, and Brazil; a licorice substitute. **a. seeds.** Jequirity, prayer or jumble beads, love peas, crab's eye. Used in ophthalmology, and in India as a weight (rati).

abs. Abbreviation for absolute (temperature).

abscess. An inflammation or collection of pus in the tissues of the body.

abscissa. The distance of any point measured perpendicularly to a horizontal scale (the ordinate); *x* axis. See *coordinates*.

ABS copolymers. Generic term for copolymers made from acrylonitrile, butadiene, and styrene; light in weight and resistant to chemicals and tensile stress.

absinthe. (1) Absinthium. (2) A strong alcoholic beverage containing anise and wormwood oil. **a. oil.** Wormwood oil.

absinthic acid. An acid of wormseed and related to succinic acid.

absinthiin. $C_{15}H_{20}O_4 = 264.15$. A crystalline, poisonous principle, m.68, from absinthium.

absinthin, absynthin. $C_{40}H_{56}O_8 \cdot H_2O = 682.6$. A glucoside from the dried leaves and flowering tops of *Artemisia absinthium*, wormwood. Brown powder, m.122, insoluble in water.

absinthium. Vermouth, wormseed, matterwood. The bitter dried leaves and flowering tops of *Artemisia absinthium* (Compositae). **oil of-** Wormwood oil.

absinthol. Thujol.

absolute. (1) An actual condition, independent,

ABBREVIATIONS (*continued*)

infrared	IR, i.r.	per cent, percentage	%
inorganic	inorg.	potential difference	p.d.
insoluble	insol.	pounds per square inch	psi
iso[5]	*i-*	pounds per square inch absolute	psia
kilogram	kg	pounds per square inch gage	psig
kilovolt	kv; kV	precipitat(e),(ed),(ing),(ion)	ppt,(d.),(g.),(n.)
kilowatt	kw; kW	qualitative,-ly	qual.
kilowatt-hour	kwhr; kWh	quantitative,-ly	quant.
liter	l	recrystalliz(e),(ed),(ing),(ation)	recryst.,(d.),(g.),(n.)
maximum, maxima	max.	refractive index	n
megacycle	Mc; mc	relative humidity	R.H.
melting point	m.p. or m.	respiratory quotient	R.Q.
meter	m	revolutions per minute	rpm
meter-kilogram-second system	mks, MKS	Roentgen unit	r
microgram	μg or γ	saponification value	sap. val.
micron	μ	second (time only)	sec
microsecond	μsec	secondary[5]	*s-, sec-*
milliampere	ma; mA	soluble[4]	sol.
milligram	mg	specific[1]	sp.
milliliter	ml	specific gravity	sp. gr.
millimeter	mm	square centimeter	sq cm or cm^2
millimicron	mμ	standard (normal) temperature	
millisecond	msec	and pressure	S.T.P.
millivolt	mv; mV	temperature	temp.
minimum, minima	min.	tertiary[5]	*t-, tert-*
minute	min	Twaddell	Tw.
molecul-e, -ar	mol.	ultraviolet	UV; uv
molecular solution	M	vacuum	vac.
molecular weight	mol. wt.	value[7]	val.
namely	viz.	vapor density	v.d.
normal solution	N	vapor pressure	v.p.
number	no.	viscosity	η
observ(e),(ed),(ation)	obs.,(d.),(n.)	volt	v; V
organic[4]	org.	volume	vol.
ounce	oz	watt	w; W
part(s)[6]	pt.(s.)	wavelength	λ
part(s) per million	ppm	weight	wt.

[5] Used only in organic names.
[6] Used for relative weights or volumes.

[7] Used only in physical constants.

unrestrained, and nonrelative. (2) Pure, refined. **a. alcohol.** Ethanol(100%). **a. boiling point.** Critical temperature. The temperature above which the liquid phase cannot exist. **a. density.** The density or specific gravity reduced to standard conditions; with gases, e.g., 760 mm pressure and 0°C. **a. humidity.** The water-vapor content of the atmosphere in grams per cubic meter. **a. temperature.** °A. The degree of heat based upon the standard temperature scale which begins with absolute zero = −273°C. Indicated by K (abbreviation for Kelvin). **a. units.** The 3 simplest and fundamental units of all measurements, viz., the centimeter, gram, and second in the cgs system, or the foot, pound, and second in the fps system. **a. zero.** The temperature at which molecular movement ceases. Absolute zero, 0°K (also T) or 0°A = −273.09°C = −459.4°F = −219°R.

absorbate. The absorbed phase in chromatography, q.v.

absorbent. (1) Able to take up gases or liquids. (2) An agent which imbibes or attracts moisture or gases. **light-** Any transparent solid, liquid, or gaseous substance which retains certain radiations falling on it. **medicinal-** A purified fat-free cotton.

absorbing power. See *absorption* coefficient.

absorptiometer. (1) An apparatus (bunsen) to measure the absorption of a gas by a liquid. (2) A device for regulating the thickness of a liquid in spectrophotometry.

absorption. The apparent disappearance of one or more substances or forces by being taken into another substance or transformed into another form of energy. Cf. *adsorption.* (1) *Chemical.* Holding by cohesion or capillary action in the pores of a solid. (2) *Physical.* Retention of waves of heat or light by a solid, liquid, or gas. The radiations may be transformed into either kinetic energy when the temperature rises; or excited atoms or molecules when the substance becomes fluorescent. (3) *Physiological.* The transformation of nonliving into living matter, i.e., food to protoplasm. **heat of-** The number of calories evolved when a gas is absorbed by a liquid.

a. apparatus. An absorptiometer or other device for the absorption of gases or vapors. **a. band.** A group of light waves which are absorbed by molecules. Cf. *a. spectrum.* **a. cell.** A small glass or quartz cup with parallel walls filled with a colored solution for the production of absorption spectra. **a. coefficient.** (1) *Chemical.*

The amount of a gas at standard temperature and pressure, which will saturate a quantity of a liquid solvent. Ostwald a.c.: ratio of the concentration of a gas in the liquid to its concentration in the gas phase. (2) *Light*. The constant k in the equation $I = I_0 \cdot e^{-kcd}$, where I_0 and I are the intensities of the incident and transmitted light, respectively; and c is the concentration, d the thickness of the solution, and e the base of natural logarithms. (3) *X rays*. The constant k in the formula $I = I_0 \cdot e^{-kd}$. **a. of food.** See *metabolism*. **a. of gases.** See *absorption* (1). **a. law.** See *Beer's law, Dalton's law* (3), *Henry's law*. **a. of light.** See *absorption* (2). **a. lines.** See *a. spectrum*. **a. paper.** A fat-free filter paper used for the Adams determination of fat in milk. **a. ray.** A light ray transformed into heat by passing through matter. **a. spectrum.** The image produced by rays when passing in succession through an absorbing medium and a spectroscope. In general, *molecules* absorb groups of wavelengths, giving *bands*; *atoms* absorb single wavelengths, giving *lines*. Cf. *spectrum*. **a. tube.** Glass apparatus used in the laboratory for the absorption of gases by liquids or solids. **a. value.** Iodine value.

absorptive power. Capacity to absorb, expressed numerically.

absorptivity. Extinction coefficient.

abstergent. Detergent.

abstract. A summary of essential features.

absynthin. Absinthin.

abundance of elements. The estimated relative proportions of chemical elements in the earth. See table below.

A.C. Abbreviation for alternating current.

Ac. (1) Symbol for actinium. (2) Abbreviation for: (1) acetyl, (2) acetate, (3) acyl radical.

ac- Prefix indicating substitution in an *alicyclic* nucleus. Cf. *ar-*.

acacatechin. $C_{15}H_{14}O_6 = 290.11$. 4-Catechol-3,5,7-trihydroxychroman. A constituent of *catechu*.

acacia. Gum arabic. The dried, gummy exudation of *Acacia senegal* (Leguminosae). Cf. *babool, catechu*. Oval beads used extensively in pharmacy and in adhesives.

acacin. $C_{15}H_{16}O_6 = 291.1$. A catechin present in *Anacardium occidentale*, Lin. See *kauri* gum.

acacipetalin. $C_{11}H_{19}NO_6 = 261.16$. A cyanogetic glucoside, m.176, from *Acacia* species.

acadialite. A variety of chabazite.

acajou. The fragrant heartwood of *Cedrela brasiliensis* (mahogany). **a. balsam.** An extract of the seeds of *Anacardium occidentale* (mahogany nuts); a blistering agent. **a. nut.** Semecarpus.

acalypha. The Indian herb *A. indica*; a substitute for ipecac.

Acanthaceae. A family of tropical plants comprising 175 genera and 1,400 species. Cf. *adhatotic acid, ibogaine*.

acanthite. Ag_2S_4. Native, black needles, d.7.2.

acari. A mite from grain, with 4 pairs of walking legs.

acaricide. A mite killer. Cf. *insecticide*.

acaroid resin. Earth shellac, yellow resin, grass tree

PERCENTAGE ABUNDANCE OF CHEMICAL ELEMENTS

Order of abundance	Lithosphere		Hydrosphere		Atmosphere		Meteorites			
							Iron		Stone	
1	O	47.33	O	85.79	N	75.53	Fe	72.06	O	35.43
2	Si	27.74	H	10.67	O	23.02	O	10.10	Fe	23.32
3	Al	7.85	Cl	2.07	Ar	1.40	Ni	6.50	Si	18.03
4	Fe	4.50	Na	1.14	H	0.02	Si	5.20	Mg	13.60
5	Ca	3.47	Mg	0.14	C	0.01	Mg	3.80	S	1.80
6	Na	2.46	Ca	0.05	Kr	0.01	S	0.49	Ca	1.72
7	K	2.46	S	0.05	Xe	0.005	Ca	0.46	Na	1.64
8	Mg	2.24	K	0.04	Remainder	0.005	Co	0.44	Al	1.53
9	Ti	0.46	N	0.02	—		Al	0.39	Ni	1.52
10	H	0.22	Br	0.01	—		Na	0.17	Cr	0.32
11	C	0.19	C	0.01	—		P	0.14	Mn	0.23
12	P	0.12	I	0.006	—		Cr	0.09	K	0.17
13	S	0.12	Fe	0.002	—		C	0.04	C	0.15
14	Mn	0.08	Remainder	0.002	—		K	0.04	Co	0.12
15	Ba	0.08	—		—		Mn	0.03	Ti	0.11
16	F	0.07	—		—		Ti	0.01	P	0.11
17	Cl	0.06	—		—		Cu	0.01	H	0.09
18	Cu	0.03	—		—		Remainder	0.03	Cl	0.09
19	N	0.02	—		—		—		Cu	0.01
20	Sr	0.02	—		—		—		Remainder	0.01
	Remainder	0.48	—		—		—		—	

gum, botany bay gum, accroides gum, yacca gum. The exudation of the stems of *Xanthorrhoea hastilis* (Liliaceae) of Australia.

acceleration. (1) *Chemical.* An increase or a decrease in the speed of a chemical reaction. Cf. *catalysis.* (2) *Physical.* The increase in velocity per second, in centimeters per second per second. Cf. *force.*

accelerator. A substance which increases the speed of a chemical reaction. Cf. *catalyst, retarder.* **catalyst-** Promoter. **impregnation-** Introfier. **rubber-** A compound which hastens and improves the curing of rubber, e.g., thiocarbanilide. Cf. *vulcanization.* **super-** A quick-acting vulcanizing agent, e.g., thiuram. **ultra-** Super-.

acceptable explosives. Unstable chemicals and mixtures which may be transported on railways and steamers subject to certain restrictions.

acceptor. See *induced* reactions.

accessory. Supplementary in function. **a. food factors.** Vitamins.

accident frequency rate. The number of time-costing accidents per 100,000 man-working hours.

accretion. The increase in size of a body by external addition.

accroides gum. Acaroid resin.

accumulator. A device for storing electricity; usually based on a reversible chemical reaction. **steam-** An iron vessel in which steam is stored under pressure in contact with hot water.
   a. metal. An alloy: Pb 90, Sb 75, Sn 9.25%.

accuracy. The systematic bias which is the difference between the "true" value and that obtained from a very large number of tests.

ace- (1). Prefix indicating relationship to acetylene (or the ethylene radical). (2). The group, —C—C—, attached to a bicyclic system; as the atoms 7 and 8 in acenaphthalene. Cf. *aci-.*

Acecoline. Trade name for a brand of acetylcholine hydrochloride.

acedicon. An alkaloidal isomer of acetylated codeine, m.152.

acenaphthene. $C_{10}H_6(CH_2)_2 = 154.1.$ Ethylene-naphthalene. A hydrocarbon from coal-tar distillates. Colorless needles, m.95, insoluble in water; used in organic synthesis. **bi-** Biacene. **7,8-diketo-** Acenaphthenequinone.
   a. dione. Acenaphthenequinone.

acenaphthenequinone. $C_{12}H_6O_2 = 182.2.$ Diketoacenaphthene. Colorless crystals, m.261, soluble in alcohol.

acenaphthenone. $C_{12}H_8O = 168.2.$ Colorless crystals, m.121, soluble in alcohol.

acenaphthenyl. The radical $C_{12}H_9—$, from acenaphthene.

acenaphthylene. $C_{12}H_8 = 152.1.$ An unsaturated hydrocarbon from acenaphthene. Colorless crystals, m.92, insoluble in water. **7,8-dihydro-** Acenaphthene.

acene. Describing a group of condensed ring aromatic compounds of the anthracene type.

Acer. The maples. **A. saccharum.** Sugar maple.

acerdese. Manganite.

acerdol. Calcium permanganate.

aceric acid. Impure malic acid from the sap of the maple (*Acer rubrum*).

aceritol. See *acertannin.*

aceroides gum. Misnomer for *acaroid resin.*

acertannin. $C_{20}H_{20}O_{13}(+2$ or $4H_2O) = 468.2.$ A pyrogallol tannin, q.v. Hydrolysis by tannase produces gallic acid and aceritol.

acet. (1) The radical $CH_3C\equiv$; as in *acetals,* MeCH(OR)$_2$. The radical Me·CO—, from acetic acid (aceto).

acetal. MeCH(OEt)$_2$ = 118.14. Diethylacetal, 1,1-diethoxyethane*, acetol. Liquid, b.103, slightly soluble in water; a hypnotic and solvent. Cf. *acetals, hydrins.* **amino-** Aminoacetal. **dichloro-** Dichloroacetal. **trichloro-** Trichloroacetal.
   a. diethyl. MeCH(OEt)$_2$ = 118.2. Colorless liquid, d.0828, b.105; an intermediate in chemical synthesis. **a. resin.** See *resin.*

acetaldehyde. $CH_3·CHO$ = 44.04. Ethanal*, aldehyde, ethyl aldehyde, acetic aldehyde. Colorless aromatic liquid, b.20.8, soluble in water, alcohol, or ether. Used as a solvent, reducing agent (silvering mirrors), and in the manufacture of organic compounds. *meta-* Metaldehyde. *para-* Paraldehyde. **amino-** Glycinaldehyde. **amyl-** Heptaldehyde. **benzal-** Cinnamaldehyde. **benzol-** Benzoyl. **hydroxy-** Glycolaldehyde. **keto-** Pyruvic aldehyde. **met-** Metaldehyde. **phenyl-** α-Tolualdehyde. **tribromo-** Bromal. **trichloro-** Chloral. **trimethyl-** Pivaldehyde.
   a. ammonia. $CH_3·CHOH·NH_2$ = 61.08. 1-Aminoethanol. Addition compound of aldehyde and ammonia. Solid, m.97; soluble in water. **a. cyanohydrin.** $CH_3·CHOH·CN$ = 71.06. Liquid, b.183 (decomp.), soluble in water. **a. semicarbazone.** Me·CH:N·NHCONH$_2$ = 101.1. Solid, m.162.

acetaldol. Aldol.

acetaldoxime. Aldoxime.

acetaldoxine. Me·CHNO = 58.05. Colorless crystals or liquid, d.0.9645, m.13, b.114; soluble in alcohol.

acetalphenaphthylamine. Acetnaphthalide.

acetals. (1) Dialkyl ethers of the hypothetical ethylidene glycol $CH_3·CH(OR)_2$ = 1,1-diethoxyethane (acetal). (2) Analogous ethers of higher or lower glycols; as, formal. Cf. *hydrins.* **ketone-** Ketals.

acetamide. Me·CO·NH$_2$ = 59.05. Ethanamide. Colorless crystals, m.82; soluble in water; used in organic synthesis. **acetyl-** Diacetamide. **benzal-** Cinnamamide. **benzyl-** α- is hydrocinnamamide; *N-* is benzylacetamide. **bromo-** Acetbromamide. **bromodiethyl-** Neuronal. **cyan-** CN·CH$_2$·CO·NH$_2$ = 84.1. Colorless crystals, m.118. **di-** Diacetamide. **dichloro-** CHCl$_2$·CO·NH$_2$ = 127.98. Colorless crystals, m.98, soluble in water. **hydroxy-** Glycolamide. **methylphenyl-** Exalgin. **phenyl-** *N-* Acetanilide. α- α-Toluamide.
   a. chloride. Me·CCl$_2$·NH$_2$ = 113.0, b.90. **a. nitrate.** MeCO·NH$_3$·ONO$_2$ = 121.1. Colorless crystals, formed by the action of nitric acid on a.

acetamidine. $C_2H_6N_2$ = 58.1. Ethanamidine, m.166.

acetamido. Acetamino. **a. ethylsalicylic acid.** Benzacetin. **a. phenetol.** Phenacetin.

acetamino. Acetamido. Containing the $CH_3·CO·NH—$ radical. **a. naphthol.** $C_{12}H_{11}NO_2$ = 201.16. *1,2-* White leaflets, m.235; *1,4-* White needles, m.187. **a. phenol.** $C_6H_4(OH)·NH·CO·Me$ = 151.12. *1,2-* White leaflets, m.201. *1,3-* Colorless needles, m.149. *1,4-* Colorless monoclinic crystals, m.168. **a. salol.** Salophen.

acetanilide. $PhNH \cdot CO \cdot Me = 135.12$. Acetylamino-benzene, antifebrin. Colorless leaflets, m.114, soluble in water; an antipyretic, antirheumatic, and preservative. **aceto-** $MeCOCH_2 \cdot CONHPh = 177.15$. Colorless crystals, m.85. **acetyl-** Diacet-anilide. **amino-** $NH_2C_6H_4 \cdot NH \cdot CO \cdot Me = 150.14$. *para-* Colorless crystals, m.160. **bromo-** Acet-bromoanilide. **di-** $PhN(MeCO)_2 = 177.1$. Colorless leaflets, m.37. **ar-ethoxy-** Acetphenetide. **p-ethoxy-** Phenacetin. **ar-methoxy-** Acetaniside. **N-methyl-** Exalgin. **ar-methyl-** Acetotoluide. **oxy-methyl-** Methacetin. **α-phenyl-** α-Toluanilide.
   a. bromide. Antisepsin.

acetaniside. $C_6H_4(OMe)NH \cdot COMe = 165.14$. Meth-oxyacetanilide, **ortho-** Colorless crystals, m.80, soluble in water. **meta-** Methacetin.

acetannin. $C_{14}H_8(COCH_3)_2O_9 = 406.2$. Tannyl acetate, tannigen. The acetic acid ester of tannin, m.160.

acetarsol. $C_6H_3 \cdot OH \cdot (NHCOMe)AsO \cdot (OH) = 275.05$. Stovarsol, acetarsone, acetylaminohydroxyphenyl-arsonic acid. White powder, slightly soluble in water; used to treat amebic dysentery. Cf. *car-barsone, tryparsamide.*

acetarsone. Acetarsol.

acetate. Ac. A salt of acetic acid containing the CH_3COO- radical. A. are readily decomp. by strong acids or heat.

acetazolam(ide). $C_4H_6O_3N_4S_2 = 222.30$. White crystals, m.258, slightly soluble in water.

acetbromamide. $CH_2Br \cdot CONH_2 = 138.0$. Brom-acetamide. Colorless leaflets, m.108, soluble in ether. **N-** $CH_3CONHBr$. **diethyl-** Neuronal.

acetbromanilide. $BrC_6H_4NHCOCH_3 = 214.0$. **para-** Antisepsin, asepsin. Colorless needles, m.165.5; antipyretic and antiseptic.

acetene. Ethylene.

acetenyl. Ethinyl. The radical $HC \vdots C-$, from acetylene.

acet extract. See *extract.*

acethydrazide. A compound containing the $NH_2 \cdot NH \cdot CO \cdot CH_2-$ radical. Cf. *hydrazide.*

acetic. Describing compounds containing acetyl, CH_3CO-. **a. acid.** Acetic acid. **a. aldehyde** Acetaldehyde. **a. anhydride.** Acetic acid anhy-dride. **a. ester, a. ether.** Ethyl acetate. **a. peracid.** Peracetic acid. **a. peroxide.** $(CH_3CO)_2-O_2$. An explosive derivative of a. anhydride.

acetic acid. $CH_3 \cdot COOH = 60.04$. Ethanoic acid*, ethylic acid, vinegar acid, acetone carboxylic acid (B.P.). (1) 99.5% or glacial-. Clear, colorless liquid or crystalline mass miscible with water or alcohol, d.1.048, m.16, b.118. A reagent, solvent, precipitant, and general neutralizing and acidifying agent. (2) 36% (common-). A clear colorless liquid, d.1.049, miscible with water or alcohol. (3) $5.2-6.3\%$ (dilute-). An official test solution of the U.S.P. A. is produced by the oxidation of alcohol (vinegar), and in the pyrolig-neous acid resulting from the destructive distillation of wood. **aceto-** Acetoacetic acid. **acetyl-** Aceto-acetic acid. **activated-** The acetyl derivative of coenzyme A, a key intermediate in carbohydrate and fat metabolism. **allyl-** γ-Pentenoic acid. **m-amidophenyl-** $NH_2 \cdot C_6H_4 \cdot CH_2 \cdot COOH$. Colorless crystals m.149. **amino-** Glycine. **aminobutyl-** Norleucine. **benzal-** Cinnamic acid. **benzamino-** Hippuric acid. **benzoyl-** $C_9H_8O_3 = 164.06$. β-

Ketohydrocinnamic acid, 3-oxo-3-phenylpropanoic acid, $PhCOCH_2COOH$. Colorless needles, m.103. **benzyl-** Hydrocinnamic acid. **bromo-** $C_2H_3O_2Br = 139.0$. Bromoethanoic acid*. Colorless hexa-gons, m.50, soluble in water. **butyl-** Caproic acid. **carbamido-** Hydantoic acid. **carbazyl-** Carbazol-acetic acid. **chloro-** $C_2H_3O_2Cl = 94.5$. Chloro-ethanoic acid*. Rhombic crystals, m.51. **cyano-** Cyanacetic acid. **di-** (1) Acetoacetic acid. (2) Diacetic acid. **diacetyl-** Diacetic acid. **dibromo-** $C_2H_2O_2Br_2 = 217.9$ Dibromoethanoic acid*. Colorless crystals, m.48. **dicarbamido-** Allantoic acid. **dichloro-** $C_2H_2O_2Cl_2 = 128.9$. Dichloroethanoic acid*. Colorless liquid, b.190. **diethyl-** $Et_2CH \cdot COOH = 116.1$. 3-Carboxypen-tane. Colorless liquid, b.190. **dihydroxy-** Glyoxylic acid. **diiodo-** $C_2H_2O_2I_2 = 311.97$. Diiodoeth-anoic acid*. Yellow crystals, m.110. **dimethyl-** Isobutyric acid. **dimethylene-** $EtCMe_2 \cdot COOH = 116.13$. Colorless liquid, b.187; an isomer of caproic acid. **dioctyl-** Isostearic acid. **diphenyl-** $Ph_2CHCOOH = 212.17$. Colorless needles, m.148. **diphenylene-** Fluorenecarboxylic acid. **ethoxy-** Ethylglycollic acid. **ethyl-** Butyric acid. **formyl-** Malonaldehydic acid. **furfuryl-** Furoic acid. **guanido-** Glycocyamine. **hydrazi-** $CH \cdot COOH (NH)_2 = 88.0$. **hydroxy-** Glycolic acid. **imino-** $NH(CH_2COOH)_2 = 133.1$. Rhombic crystals, m.227. **iodo-** $C_2H_3O_2I = 185.9$. Iodoethanoic acid. Yellow crystals, m.82. **isoamyl-** $C_7H_{14}O_2 = 130.1$. Colorless liquid, d.0.910, b.209. **isobutyl-** Iso-*caproic* acid. **isopropyl-** Isovaleric acid. **iso-propylidene-** Senecioic acid. **keto-** Pyruvic acid. **mercapto-** $HS \cdot CH_2COOH = 92.09$. 2-Mercapto-ethanoic acid, thioglycollic acid. Colorless liquid, m. -16.5. **methoxy-** $MeOCH_2COOH = 90.05$. Methylglycollic acid. Colorless liquid, d.1.1768. **methyl-** Propionic acid. **methylamino-** Sarcosine. **nitro-** See *nitro acids.* **oxybis-** Diglycollic acid. **per-** Peracetic acid. **phenyl-** Toluic acid. **pyro-** Pyroligneous acid. **sulfo-** $HSO_3 \cdot CH_2 \cdot COOH = 140.1$. Sulfoethanoic acid. Colorless crystals, m.86. **thiol-** $MeCOSH = 76.09$. Ethanethiolic acid, thioacetic acid. Colorless liquid, b.93. **trimethyl-** Pivalic acid. **triphenyl-** $Ph_3C \cdot COOH = 240.2$. Colorless crystals, m.264. **ureido-** Hydan-toic acid. **vinyl-** β-Butenic acid.
   a. acid amide. Acetamide. **a. acid amine.** Acetamide. **a. aldehyde.** Acetaldehyde. **a. an-hydride.** $(MeCO)_2O = 102.05$. Acetyl oxide, ethanoic anhydride*. Colorless liquid, b.137, soluble in alcohol; a reagent. **a. ester.** Ethyl acetate. **a. ether.** Ethyl acetate. **a. oxide.** A. anhydride. **a. peracid.** Peracetic acid.

acetidin. Ethyl acetate.

acetifier. An apparatus to hasten acetification, the production of vinegar from fermented liquids by atmospheric oxidation.

acetimeter. Hydrometer (obsolete).

acetimetry. The determination of acetic acid in vinegar by titration with alkali.

acetimido[yl]. The radical acetylimino.

acetin. Esters obtained by reaction of glycerol and acetic acid; e.g., **mono-** Acetin, $C_3H_5(OH)_2-(O \cdot COMe) = 134.11$. Colorless liquid, b.240. Used in the manufacture of dynamite and as a solvent for dyes. **di-** See *diacetin.* **tri-** See *triacetin.*

acetnaphthalide. $MeCONHC_{10}H_7 = 185.16$. 1-Acet-α-naphthylamine. Colorless crystals, b.159. 2-Acet-β-naphthylamine. Colorless leaflets, m.132.

aceto. Acet.

acetoacetate. A salt containing the $MeCOCH_2COO-$ radical, derived from acetoacetic acid.

acetoacetic acid. $Me\cdot CO\cdot CH_2\cdot COOH = 102.07$. Acetylacetic acid, diacetic acid. Colorless liquid, decomp. 100, miscible with water, Derived from β-hydroxybutyric acid in the body and increases during diabetes. Cf. *acetone.* **a. ester.** (1) Acetoacetic ether. (2) Compounds derived from acetoacetic acid by replacing the acid hydrogen by an organic radical. Two isomeric forms: enolic form, $R-CH_2\cdot CO\cdot CH_2\cdot COO-R$; ketonic form, $R-CH_2\cdot C(OH):CH\cdot COO-R$. **a. ester condensation.** The formation of a. esters by metallic sodium from the corresponding alkyl ester. **a. ester decomposition.** The decomposition of a. esters. Strong acids or weak alkalies split the ester to a ketone alcohol and carbon dioxide; strong bases decompose it to acids (acetic acid, etc.). **a. ester synthesis.** The formation of organic compounds by hydrolyzing their a. esters. **a. ether** $MeCOCH_2COOEt = 130.11$. Ethylacetoacetate, ethyl-3-oxobutanoate*. Colorless liquid, b.181; used in organic synthesis.

acetoamidophenol. Acetaminophenol.

acetobenzoic anhydride. Benzoyl acetate.

acetobrom-. Acetbrom-.

acetocaustin. Trichloroacetic acid.

acetochloral. Chloral.

acetocinnamene. Benzylidene *acetone.*

acetoglyceral. $C_5H_{10}O_3 = 118.08$ Glycerol-ethylidene ether. Colorless liquid, d.1.081, b.184.

acetoin. $MeCO\cdot CHOH\cdot Me = 98.1$. 3-Hydroxy-2-butanone*, methylacetylcarbinol, a condensation product of 2 molecules of acetic acid. Colorless liquid, b.141.

acetol. $MeCOCH_2OH = 74.06$. Acetylcarbinol, 1-hydroxy-2-propanone*. Colorless liquid, b.145, soluble in water; a reducing agent.

acetoluide. Acetotoluide.

acetolysis. The breaking up of an organic molecule by acetic anhydride or acetic acid.

acetomenaph(thone). $C_{15}H_{14}O_4 = 258.31$. Menadiol diacetate. White crystals, m.114. Used medicinally for its vitamin K effect, and to treat neonatal hemorrhage, and obstructive jaundice.

aceton acid. Acetonic acid.

acetonamine. Organic compounds containing the NH_2- and $CO-$ radicals. di- $NH_2\cdot CMe_2\cdot CH_2\cdot CO\cdot Me$.

acetonaphthone. Naphthyl methyl ketone. **1-hydroxy-2-** $MeCOC_{10}H_6OH = 186.08$. 1-Hydroxy-2-naphthyl methyl ketone, 2-acetyl-1-naphthol. Yellow needles, m.100.

acetone. $CO\cdot Me_2 = 58.06$. Dimethyl ketone, 2-propanone*, methylacetal, dimethylketal. Colorless ethereal liquid, d.0.792, b.57, miscible with water; a constituent of wood spirit and produced by fermentation and in the body during diabetes by decarboxylation of acetoacetic acid. A solvent, precipitant for albumin, reagent, and anthelmintic and tonic. **acetonyl-** See *acetonyl.* **acetyl-** Acetylacetone. **allyl-** Allyllactone. **amido-** Aminoacetone. **benzal-** $PhCH:CH\cdot COMe = 146.08$. 4-Phenyl-3-butene-2-one*, benzylidene a., acetocinnamene,

methyl styryl ketone. Colorless crystals, m.41; used in organic synthesis. **benzylidene-** Benzal a. **bromo-** $CH_2Br\cdot CO\cdot Me = 136.98$. Monobromacetone. Colorless liquid, b.140. **chloro-** $CH_2Cl\cdot CO\cdot Me = 92.51$. Monochloracetone. Colorless liquid, b.119. **diamido-** $CO(CH_2NH_2)_2 = 88.1$. **dibenzal-** Styryl ketone. **dichloro-** $alpha$-$CHCl_2\cdot CO\cdot CH_3 = 126.95$. Colorless liquid, b.190. $beta$-$CH_2Cl\cdot CO\cdot CH_2Cl = 126.95$. Colorless liquid, b.120. **diethoxy-** $CO(CH_2OEt)_2$. **diisonitroso-** $CO(CH:NOH)_2$. Colorless crystals, m.144, **dimethoxy-** $CO(CH_2OMe)_2$. **dioxy-** $CO(CH_2OH)_2$. A constituent of suntan lotions. **ethoxy-** See *ethoxyacetone.* **ethylidene** 3-Penten-2-one*. **hydroxy-** Acetol. **meta-** Diethyl ketone. **monobromo-** See *bromo-.* **monochloro-** See *chloro-.* **oxalyldi-,** $Me\cdot CO\cdot CH_2\cdot CO\cdot CO\cdot CH_2\cdot CO\cdot Me$. Colorless crystals, m.120, insoluble in water. **sulfocyan-** $MeCO\cdot CH_2\cdot SCN$. Colorless liquid, d.1.180, soluble in water.

a. acid. Acetonic acid. **a. alcohol.** Acetol. **a. bodies.** The aliphatic ketones in blood and urine. **a. bromoform.** $CBr_3\cdot COHMe_2 = 331.1$. Brometone, Colorless crystals; a sedative. **a. carboxylic acid.** Acetic acid. **a. chloride.** $Me\cdot CCl_2Me = 112.98$. 2,3-Dichloropropane*, b.69. **a. chloroform.** $CCl_3\cdot CMe_2OH = 177.1$. Chloretone, chlorbutanol, aneson, anesin. Colorless crystals, m.80; an antiseptic, hypnotic and anesthetic. **a. collodium.** Collodion. **a. cyanhydrin.** $Me_2C\cdot OH\cdot CN = 85.1$, b.120. **a. diacetic acid.** Hydrochelidonic acid. **a. dicarboxylic acid.** $CO\cdot(CH_2COOH)_2 = 146.1$. β-Ketoglutaric acid, 3-oxopentanedioic acid*. Colorless crystals, m.130. **a. oil.** The oily residue from the distillation of crude a. Used as a solvent, a denaturating agent and in the purification of anthracene. **a. phenylhydrazone.** $Me_2:C:N\cdot NPh = 148.2$. Crystals, m.16. **a. semicarbazone.** $Me_2:C:N\cdot NH\cdot CONH_2 = 115.12$, m.190. **a. sodium bisulfite.** $NaSO_3\cdot CMe_2OH$. Colorless crystals, soluble in water. **a. sugar.** Isopropylidine sugar. A condensation compound of sugar and a. containing a $-O\cdot CMe_2\cdot O-$ group.

acetonic acid. $Me_2C(OH)COOH = 104.1$. Acetone acid, butyllactic acid, α-hydroxyisobutyric acid. Colorless crystals, m.79, soluble in water.

acetonitrile. $CH_3\cdot CN = 41.1$. Methyl cyanide, ethane nitrile*, cyanomethane, from coal tar and the residue of molasses. Colorless liquid, d.0.783, b.81, soluble in water; used in organic synthesis and perfumery. **allyl-** See *allyl.* **amino-** Glycinonitrile. **benzoyl-** $PhCOCH_2CN = 145.06$. Cyanoacetophenone, β-ketohydrocinnamonitrile. White leaflets, m.80. **phenyl-** α-Tolunitrile. **triethoxy-** $(EtO)_3C\cdot CN$. Cyanoformic ester, oxalnitrilic ethyl ester. Colorless liquid, b.160. **trinitro-** $CN\cdot C(NO_2)_3 = 176.03$. Trinitroethanenitrile*. (1) Colorless crystals, m.41. (2) White leaflets, m.42. **vinyl-** Allyl cyanide.

acetonitrolic acid. $Me(NO_2)C:NOH = 104.04$. Ethylnitrolic acid. Yellow rhombs, m.88 (decomp.), soluble in water.

acetonyl. The radical $CH_3\cdot CO\cdot CH_2-$ **a. acetone.** $MeCO(CH_2)_2\cdot CO\cdot Me = 114.1$. Hexan-2,5-dione, g-diketohexane, 2,5-hexanedione*, γ-diketohexane. Colorless liquid of pleasant odor, b.188; used as a solvent. **a. amine.** 1-Amino-2-propanone. **a. urea.** $C_5H_8O_2N_2 = 123.1$, b.175, soluble in water.

acetonylidene. The radical MeCOCH=.

acetophenitide. $1,4\text{-EtO}\cdot\text{C}_6\text{H}_4\cdot\text{NH}\cdot\text{COMe} = 179.16$. **ortho-** N-Acetyl-o-phenetidine. Colorless leaflets, m.79. **para-** Phenacetin, acetphenetidine. Crystalline powder, m.134; an antipyretic, analgesic, and antirheumatic. **amino-** Phenacol.

acetophenetidin. Acetophenetide.

acetophenine. $\text{C}_{24}\text{H}_{19}\text{N} = 321.3$. Colorless crystals, m.135, slightly soluble in alcohol.

acetophenone. $\text{Me}\cdot\text{CO}\cdot\text{Ph} = 120.1$. Phenyl methyl ketone, hypnone. Transparent crystals, m.21; a hypnotic and orange perfume. **allyl-** $\text{Ph}\cdot\text{CO}\cdot\text{CH}_2\cdot\text{CH}_2\cdot\text{CH}:\text{CH}_2$. Colorless liquid, b.236. **amido-** Amidoacetophenone. **benzal-** Chalcone. **benzyl-** Phenyl propiophenone. **chloro-** See tear gases. **cyano-** Benzoyl acetonitrile. **ar-hydroxy-** See hydroxy. **ω-hydroxy-** $\text{PhCOCH}_2\cdot\text{OH}$. Phenacyl alcohol. Colorless crystals, m.86. **nitroso-** Benzoylformoxime. **phenyl-** A. acetone.
  a. acetone. $\text{PhCO}\cdot\text{CH}_2\cdot\text{CH}_2\cdot\text{COMe} = 176.1$. Phenylacetylacetone. **a. carboxylic acid.** Acetylbenzoic acid. **a. oxime.** $\text{Me}\cdot\text{C(NOH)}\cdot\text{Ph} = 135.2$. Colorless crystals, m.59.

acetophenones. The homologs of acetophenone:
$\text{PhCOCH}_2\text{—R}$ . . . . . Acetylated benzenes.
Ph—R—COMe . . . . Phenylated fatty ketones.
R—$\text{C}_6\text{H}_4\cdot\text{COMe}$ . . . Nucleus substituted phenones.

acetopiperone. $\text{C}_9\text{H}_8\text{O}_3 = 164.1$. 3,4-Methylenedioxy-1-methylketobenzene. Colorless crystals, m.87.

acetopyrine. $\text{C}_{11}\text{H}_{12}\text{N}_2\text{O}\cdot\text{C}_2\text{H}_7\text{OOC}_6\text{H}_4\text{COOH}$. Acopyrin. A combination of antipyrine and acetylsalicylic acid, used to treat fevers and rheumatism.

acetosalicylic acid. Acetylsalicylic acid.

acetothienone. Thienyl methyl ketone.

acetotoluide. $\text{Me}\cdot\text{C}_6\text{H}_4\cdot\text{NHCOMe} = 149.09$. Acetotoluide. **ortho-** Colorless crystals, m.107; an antipyretic. **meta-** Colorless crystals, m.65. **para-** Colorless needles, m.151; an antipyretic. Cf. exalgin. **N-methyl-** $\text{MeCON(Me)}\cdot\text{C}_6\text{H}_4\text{Me} = 163.11$. N-Acetyl-N-methyl-o-toluidine. White crystals, m.56.

acetoveratrone. $\text{C}_{10}\text{H}_{12}\text{O}_3 = 180.1$. 3,4-Dimethoxy-1-methylketobenzene. Colorless crystals, m.48; used in perfumery.

acetoxime. $\text{Me}_2\text{C}:\text{NOH} = 73.08$. Propanoxime, 2-propanone oxime*. Colorless prisms, m.58.

acetoximes. A group of ketoximes derived from acetoximes; two isomeric forms,

$$
\begin{array}{cc}
\text{N}\cdot\text{OH} & \text{HO}\cdot\text{N} \\
\| & \| \\
\text{R}'\text{—C—R} & \text{R}'\text{—C—R} \\
\text{anti-} & \text{syn-}
\end{array}
$$

where R′ has a greater radical weight than R.

acetoxy. The radical $\text{CH}_3\text{COO—}$.

acetoxylide. $\text{MeCONHC}_6\text{H}_3\text{Me}_2 = 163.11$. Aceto-as-m-xylide, 2,4-dimethylacetanilide. White needles, m.129.

acetozone. Acetylbenzoyl peroxide. An unstable compound, is marketed as a 50% mixture with an inert substance as a disinfectant and antiseptic.

acetphenetid. Acetophenetide.

acetrizoic acid. $\text{C}_9\text{H}_6\text{I}_3\text{NO}_3 = 556.88$. 3-Acetamido-2,4,6-triiodobenzoic acid. White powder, m.280 (decomp.). The sodium salt is a radiopaque (urographic) injection (B.P.).

acet-theocin sodium. Soluble theocine, theophylline sodium acetate. A white powder; a diuretic.

acettoluide. Acetotoluide.

acetum. Latin for vinegar.

aceturic acid. Acetylglycine.

acetyl. Symbol: Ac. The acyl radical $\text{CH}_3\text{CO—}$. **a. hydrate.** Acetic acid. **a. number.** A measure of the amount of oxyacids and alcohols in a vegetable or animal fat. The number of milligrams of potassium hydroxide to neutralize the acetic acid obtained by saponification of one gram of a fat which has been acetylated with acetic anhydride. Cf. Cook formula. **a. value.** A. number.

acetylacetonate. $\text{M[CH(COMe)}_2]_3$. A compound of acetylacetone with aluminum, beryllium, or rare earth.

acetylacetone. $\text{MeCO}\cdot\text{CH}_2\cdot\text{COMe} = 100.09$. Pentane-2,4-dione, 2,4-pentane dione*. Colorless liquid, b.137; used in organic synthesis.

acetylamine. (1) The radical $\text{CH}_3\cdot\text{CO}\cdot\text{NH—}$, derived from acetamide. (2) Acetamide.

acetylamino. Acetylamine. **a. acetic acid.** Acetyl glycine. **a. benzoic acid.** $\text{MeCONH—C}_6\text{H}_4\text{—COOH} = 179.13$. **ortho-** Colorless needles, m.185. **meta-** Colorless crystals, m.243 (decomp.). **para-** Colorless needles, m.250. **a. phenetole.** Acetphenetid. **a. salol.** Salophen.

acetylate, acetylation. Introducing an acetyl radical into an organic molecule; e.g., by boiling glacial acetic acid.

acetylbenzene. Acetophenone.

acetylbenzoate. Benzoyl acetate.

acetylbenzoic acid. $\text{MeCO}\cdot\text{C}_6\text{H}_4\text{COOH} = 164.11$. Acetophenone carboxylic acid. **ortho-** Crystals, m.114. **para-** Crystals, m.205 (sublimes).

acetylbiuret. $\text{MeCO}\cdot\text{NH}\cdot\text{CO}\cdot\text{NH}\cdot\text{CO}\cdot\text{NH}_2 = 145.11$. Colorless needles, m.193.

acetyl bromide. $\text{Me}\cdot\text{COBr} = 122.95$. Ethanoyl bromide*. Colorless fuming liquid, b.77, decomp. in water. **bromo-** $\text{CH}_2\text{Br}\cdot\text{COBr} = 201.85$. Bromoethanoyl bromide*. Colorless liquid, b.148, decomp. in water.

acetylcannabinol. $\text{MeCO}\cdot\text{O}\cdot\text{C}_{21}\text{H}_{29}\text{O}$. Obtained by heating cannabinol with acetic acid anhydride.

acetylcarbamide. Acetylurea.

acetylcarbazole. $\text{C}_{12}\text{H}_8\text{N}\cdot\text{COCH}_3 = 209.2$. Crystals, m.70.

acetylcarbinol. Acetol.

acetylcarbromal. $\text{BrCEt}_2\cdot\text{CO}\cdot\text{NH}\cdot\text{CO}\cdot\text{NH}\cdot\text{COMe} = 279.03$. Abasin, acetylbromdiethylacetylcarbamid. White crystals; a sedative.

acetyl chloride. $\text{Me}\cdot\text{COCl} = 78.49$. Ethanoyl chloride*. Colorless fuming liquid, b.55, decomp. in water; a. reagent. **chloro-** $\text{CH}_2\text{Cl}\cdot\text{COCl} = 112.93$. Chloroethanoyl chloride*. Colorless liquid, b.107, decomp. in water. **dichloro-** $\text{CHCl}_2\cdot\text{COCl} = 147.37$. Dichloroethanoyl chloride*. Colorless liquid, b.105, decomp. in water. **trichloro-** $\text{CCl}_3\text{COCl} = 181.83$. Colorless liquid, b.118, decomp. in water. **trimethyl-** Pivalyl chloride.

acetylcholine. $\text{CH}_3\cdot\text{CO}\cdot\text{OCH}_2\cdot\text{CH}_2\cdot\text{NMe}_3\cdot\text{OH} = 163.2$. Acetylethanoltrimethylammonium hydroxide Vagusstoff. An alkaloid from ergot which lowers blood pressure and increases peristalsis. **a. hydrochloride.** $\text{Me}_3\text{NClC}_2\text{H}_4\text{COOMe}$. Acecoline. White hygroscopic crystals; a vasodilator.

acetyl cyanide. $\text{Me}\cdot\text{COCN} = 69.1$. Pyruvonitrile A colorless liquid, b.93.

acetylene. (1) A member of the a. series. (2) $C_2H_2 = 26.03$. Ethine, ethyne*. The simplest compound containing a triple bond, $HC\equiv CH$. Colorless gas with garlic odor, d.0.91. b.-83; slightly soluble in water, soluble in alcohol. Uses: A general anesthetic; for oxyacetylene welding, and cutting of metals; in organic synthesis; and as an illuminant. Produced by the action of water on calcium carbide. (3) The radical$=CH\cdot CH=$. **butyl-** Hexyne*. **carboxy-** Propiolic acid. **di-** Diacetylene.* **dimethyl-** Crotonylene. **diphenyl-** Tolane. **ethyl-** Butyne*. **hexyl-** Caprilidene. **methyl-** Allylene. **pentyl-** Heptyne*. **phenyl-** PhC$\equiv$CH. Acetenylbenzene. Colorless liquid, b.139. **phenylmethyl-** PhC$\equiv$CMe. Phenylallylene. Colorless liquid, b.185. **propyl-** Pentine. **vinyl-** Vinylacetylene.

a. acids. $C_nH_{2n-3}COOH$. Tetrolic acids which contain the $-C\vdots C-$ group; as, propiolic acid, propynoic acid*, $HC\vdots C\cdot COOH$. **a. alcohols.** Organic compounds which contain both an OH$-$ and a $-C\vdots C-$ group; as, propin-3-ol, 2-propyn-1-ol*, $HC\vdots C\cdot CH_2OH$. **a. carboxylic acid.** Propiolic acid. **a. dicarboxylic acid.** $HOOC\cdot C\vdots C\cdot COOH = 114.0$. Butynedioic acid*. Colorless crystals, m.178, insoluble in water. Cf. *glutinic* acid, *muconic* acid. *di-* Diacetylene dicarbonic acid. *tetra-* Tetracetyl dicarbonic acid. **a. dichloride.** $CHCl=CHCl = 96.95$. Dioform, dichloroethylene. *cis-* b.48. *trans-* b.60. Colorless liquids, immiscible with water. **a. dinitrile.** $NC\cdot C\vdots C\cdot CN = 76.0$. Carbon subnitride. **a. diurein.** Glycoluril. **a. series.** C_nH_{2n-2}. Alkines, ethines. Unsaturated hydrocarbons which contain a triple bond, $-C\vdots C-$; e.g., ethyne*, ethine, acetylene, C_2H_2. **a. stones.** Acetylith. **a. tetrabromide.** $CHBr_2\cdot CHBr_2 = 345.71$. Tetrabromoethane, Muthmann's liquid. Yellow oil, b$_{36\,mm}$136, insoluble in water. Used to separate mineral mixtures and in microscopy. **a. tetrachloride.** Tetrachloroethane. **a. urea.** $C_2H_2(CON_2H_2)_2 = 142.11$. A liquid, decomp. 300.

acetyl fluoride. $MeCOF = 62.03$. Ethanoyl fluoride*. Colorless liquid, d.1.0369, b.10; used in organic synthesis. **a. iodide.** $MeCOI = 169.16$. Ethanoyl iodide*. Brown fuming liquid, d.1.98, b.107; used for acetylation. **a. peroxide.** $(MeCO)_2O_2 = 118.07$. Ethanoyl peroxide*. Colorless leaflets, m.30, slightly soluble in water.

acetylformic acid. Pyruvic acid.

acetylglycine. $MeCO\cdot NH\cdot CH_2\cdot COOH = 117.09$. Acetylaminoacetic acid, aceturic acid. Colorless crystals, m.206.

acetylide. A derivative of acetylene with the H atoms replaced by metals; as, cuprous acetylide, Cu_2C_2.

acetylidene. The hypothetical isomer of acetylene, $C=CH_2$, in which one atom is divalent.

acetylimino. Acetimido(yl). The radical $CH_3\cdot CO\cdot N=$.

acetylith. Acetylene stones. Sugar-coated granules of calcium carbide used to generate acetylene.

acetylization. Acetylation.

acetylize. Acetylate.

acetylphenol. $PhO\cdot COCH_3 = 136.10$. Colorless liquid, b.193.

acetylphenylenediamine (p). $Me\cdot CO\cdot NH\cdot C_6H_4NH_2 = 150.14$. Aminoacetanilide. Colorless needles, m.159, slightly soluble in water. Used medicinally and in organic synthesis.

acetylphenylhydrazine. Pyrodin.

acetylpropyl alcohol. $MeCO\cdot CH_2CH_2\cdot CH_2OH = 102.11$. Colorless liquid, d.1.0159, b.208, miscible with water; a solvent.

acetylrosaniline. $C_{20}H_{18}N_3COMe = 343.3$. Red crystals, m.218, insoluble in water.

acetylsalicylate. A compound containing the $MeCO\cdot C_6H_4COO-$ radical, from acetylsalicylic acid.

acetylsalicylic acid. $MeCOO\cdot C_6H_4\cdot COOH = 180.06$. Aspirin, xaxa, acid aceticosalicylas, acetophen, salacetin. Colorless crystals, m.135, slightly soluble in water; an antirheumatic and antipyretic. **a. methyl ester.** Methyl acetyl salicylate.

acetylsalol. Spiroform.

acetyltannin. Tannigen.

acetylthymol. $C_{12}H_{16}O_2 = 192.1$. Thymylacetate. Yellow liquid, b.244; an antiseptic.

acetyltropeine. $MeCO\cdot C_8H_{14}ON = 183.2$. A syrup, b.236, soluble in water.

acetylurea. $MeCO\cdot NH\cdot CONH_2 = 102.08$. Acetylcarbamide. Colorless crystals, m.218, slightly soluble in water.

Achard, Franz Karl. 1753–1821. A German pioneer in the manufacture of beet sugar.

achilleic acid. Aconitic acid obtained from *Achillea millefolium*.

achilleine. $C_{20}H_{38}O_{15}N_2 = 546.4$. An alkaloid from *Achillea millefolium*, yarrow, or milfoil. Brownish-red bitter masses, soluble in water; an antipyretic.

achilletin. $C_{11}H_{17}O_4N = 227.0$. A split product produced from achilleine by sulfuric acid.

achmatite, achmite. An epidote (Ural Mountains).

achondrite. A meteorite containing chondrules, of variable composition, but usually of low metal content. See *chondrite*.

achrodextrins. Achroodextrins.

achroite. A colorless tourmaline from Elba.

achromatic. Transmitting white light without breaking it up into colored rays. Cf. *apochromatic*. **a. lens.** A combination of lenses of different refractive indices to correct chromatic aberration by bringing two spectral color rays to a common focus. A combination of a convex lens of crown glass with a concave lens of flint glass. **a. objectives.** A system of lenses which brings light of different wavelengths to a common focus; i.e., avoids chromatic aberrration. **a. substage.** A device for microscopes to correct chromatic aberration. **a. system.** A combination of prisms or lenses with a common focus for different colors; e.g., an achromatic lens.

achromic. Without color. **a. method.** The evaluation of diastase preparations from the a. period. **a. period.** The time for a 1% starch solution to reach the a. point; i.e., become transformed into achroodextrin. **a. point.** The stage in the hydrolysis of starch by enzymes when iodine no longer produces a blue color.

achromobacteria. Small Gram-negative bacteria, usually motile. They produce no pigment or gas on gelatin, but a brown color on potato.

achroodextrins. $C_{36}H_{62}O_{31} = 990.7$. Intermediate split products formed after erythrodextrin by the hydrolysis of starch or dextrin; termed alpha-, beta, etc. They are not colored blue by iodine, and are converted into glucose by boiling with dilute acid.

aci- Prefix indicating acid character, as in aci-phenylnitromethane, PHCH : NO(OH). Cf. α-*phenylnitromethane*, PhCH₂·NO₂; *ace-*.

acicular. Slender, needlelike or hairlike in shape, as crystals or bacteria. **a. oxylepidine.** Dibenzoyl *stilbene.*

acid. (1) A chemical compound which yields hydrogen ions when dissolved in water; whose hydrogen can be replaced by metals or basic radicals; or which reacts with bases to form salts and water (neutralization). Antonym: base. (2) An extension of the term includes substances dissolved in media other than water. Cf. *base, ammonia system.* (3) A substance which gives up protons (*proton donor*) or reacts as A ⇌ B + H⁺, where A is acid and B is base, e.g., HAc ⇌ Ac⁻ + H⁺. **A-, α-, β-.** See *A* and *sulfonic acids.* **acrylic-** $C_nH_{2n-2}O_2$. **alcohol-** See *alcohol.* **aldehyde-** An organic a. containing aldehyde and carboxyl radicals. **aliphatic-** An a. derived from chain compounds; e.g., fatty acids. **amic-** Amido a. **amido-** An organic a. containing the —CONH₂ group and the carboxyl radical. **amino-** An organic a. containing the —NH₂ and —COOH groups. **aromatic-** An organic compound containing a closed chain (e.g., benzene ring) and the carboxyl group. **battery-** Electrolyte a. Sulfuric a. of d.1.150–1.835. **bromo-** An organic a. containing bromine. **carboxylic-** See *organic acid.* **carbylic-** See *carbylic acid.* **chloro-** An organic a. containing chlorine. **diatomic-** A. containing 2 H atoms which are replaceable by metals or basic radicals. Cf. *oxalic acid, fumaric acid.* **dibasic-** Diatomic. **dihydric-** Diatomic. **dihydroxy-** An organic a. containing 2 hydroxy groups and one or more carboxyl groups. **effective-** See *acidity.* **electrolyte-** Battery a. **fatty-** $C_nH_{2n}O_2$. An organic a. **halogen-** An inorganic a. containing a halogen; as, HCl, HClO₃. **haloid-** An inorganic a. containing a halogen element and no oxygen: e.g., HCl. **hexabasic-** Hexatomic. **hexatomic-** An a. containing 6 H atoms replaceable by metals or basic radicals. **hydrogen-** Hydracid. **hydroxy-** An organic a. containing one hydroxy group and one or more carboxyl groups. Cf. *phenol.* **inorganic-** A compound of hydrogen with a non-metal other than carbon, or an acid radical containing no carbon. **labile-** A grouping, as —SO₃H or —OSO₃H, the acidic properties of which depend on the other groups present. **meta-** (1) An inorganic a. of a trivalent nonmetal containing one replaceable H; e.g., HPO₃. (2) An organic, aromatic a. with the radical in the meta position. **mineral-** Inorganic a. **mixed-** A mixture of nitric and sulfuric acids used for nitration. **monamino-** An organic a. containing one amino group and carboxyl group(s). **monatomic-** An a. having 1 H atom replaceable by metals or basic radicals. **mono- amino-** Monamino a. **mono-atomic-** monobasic-, monohydric-** Monatomic. **monohydroxy-** An organic a. containing 1 OH group and carboxyl group(s). **nitro-** See *nitro* acid, *nitroic* acid, etc. **normal-** (1) Inorganic ortho- a. (2) A straight-chain fatty a. (3) A solution con-

taining one gram-equivalent a. per liter; as, N-HCl. **organic-** A carbon compound containing carboxyl group(s) —COOH; indicated by the prefix *carboxy-*, or the suffixes *carboxylic, carbonyl*; or simply *-oic* or *-oyl.* For classification, see *acids.* **ortho-** (1) An inorganic a. of trivalent elements containing 3 H atoms replaceable by basic radicals; e.g., H₃PO₄. (2) An organic a. containing a closed chain (e.g., benzene ring) and radicals in the ortho position. **oxy-** (1) An inorganic a. containing oxygen, thereby differing from the haloid or hydrogen acids. Those having least oxygen have the suffix *-ous*; those having most oxygen, the suffix *-ic.* (2) An organic a. containing an ether or oxy group in addition to the carboxyl radical. **oxygen-** Oxy a. (inorganic). **oxyhalogen-** An a. containing oxygen and a halogen; as, HClO₃. **para-** An organic a. derived from aromatic hydrocarbons with the radicals in the para position. **pentatomic-** An a. containing 5 H atoms replaceable by metals or basic radicals. **pentabasic-** Pentatomic. **phenol-** Phenol acids. **plant-** A. derived from vegetable sources. **polyatomic-** An a. containing more than 1 H atom replaceable by metals or basic radicals. **polybasic-** Polyatomic. **pseudo-** (1) A tautomeric form of an organic a. (2) An a. containing hydroxyl radicals:

$$\left(O{=}Pt\!\!\diagup_{\!\!O}^{\!\!O}\right)H_2 \rightleftarrows O{=}Pt\diagdown_{\!OH}^{\!OH}$$

True a.   Pseudo a.

pyro- An a. produced by the action of heat; usually an intermediate compound between acids and acid anhydrides. **racemic-** An organic a. consisting of a molecular mixture of optically active dextro and levo compounds. Cf. *tartaric acid.* **resin-** A. derived from resins, q.v. **rubber-** q.v. **soldering-** Hydrochloric a. of suitable strength used for soldering. **Spekker-** A mixture of equal volumes of sulfuric a. (d.1.84) and phosphoric a. (d.1.75) used to dissolve iron alloys for analysis, particularly with the Spekker photoelectric absorptiometer. **Steele-** q.v. **sulfinic-** An acidic organic compound in which an H atom is replaced by the —SO₂H group. Named from the hydrocarbon; as, ethanesulfinic acid*, EtSO₂H. **sulfo-** An organic a. in which sulfur replaces the C atom of the carboxyl group. Cf. *thioacids.* **sulfonic-** An acidic organic compound in which an H atom is replaced by the SO₂OH group. Named from the hydrocarbon; as, ethanesulfonic acid*, EtSO₃H. **tetrabasic-** Tetratomic. **tetrahydric-** Tetratomic. **tetrahydroxy-** An organic a. containing 4 OH groups and carboxyl group(s). **tetratomic-** An a. containing 4 H atoms replaceable by a metal or basic radical. **thio-** An a. in which one or more S atoms replaces the oxygen of the acid radical; e.g., thiosulfuric acid. Cf. *sulfoacids.*

a. of air. Carbon dioxide. **a. albuminate.** A metaprotein soluble in weak alkali. **a. of amber.** Succinic a. **a. amide.** An organic compound containing the formamyl radical, —CONH₂. Cf. *a. imide.* **a. anhydride.** An a. from which one or more molecules of water have been removed; e.g., SO₃ is the anhydride of H₂SO₄, MeCO·O·OCMe is the anhydride of MeCOOH. **a. of ants.** Formic a. **a. of apples.** Malic a. **a. of benzoin.** Benzoic a.

a. bordeaux. Bordeaux B. **a. brown.** Naphthylamine brown. **a. capacity.** The number of OH^- ions which a molecule of a base yields in an aqueous solution; thus, NaOH one, $Ca(OH)_2$ two. **a. chloride.** A compound containing the —COCl radical; e.g., acetyl chloride, MeCOCl. **a. dye.** A dye which acts as a base and is used in an acid bath. **a. egg.** An earthenware jar for storing acids. **a. esters.** The derivatives of polyvalent organic acids of which some of the acid H atoms are replaced by a radical (R); hence they contain the COOH and COOR groups. **a. fuchsin.** A. magenta II, a. rosein. The di- and trisulfonic acids of rosaniline and pararosaniline; a stain and indicator. **a. function.** Hydrogen ion. **a. group.** The carboxyl radical —COOH, present in all organic acids. **a. halide.** An organic compound containing the —COX radical in which X is a halogen (Cl, Br, I, or F); as, acid chlorides, R-oyl chloride*, R—COCl. **a. hydrazide.** An organic compound containing the —$CONHNH_2$ radical; as, acethydrazide, $MeCONHNH_2$. **a. hydrogen.** The hydrogen of the —COOH group in organic compounds replaceable by metals, alkyls, aryls, or basic radicals. **a. imide.** A compound containing the —C(: NH)-OH radical. Cf. *a. amide.* **a. infraprotein.** An acid metaprotein. **a. ion.** A negatively charged atom (e.g., Cl^-) or radical (e.g., $SO_4^=$). See table. **a. of lemon.** Citric a. **a. of milk.** Lactic a. **a. mordant dye.** An a. dye requiring a mordant to fix it on fibers. **a. nitriles.** Nitriles. **a. number.** A measure of free fatty acids in animal and vegetable fats. The number of milligrams of KOH necessary to neutralize the free fatty acids in one gram of fat. **a. peroxide.** An organic compound containing the —CO·O—O·CO— radical; e.g., acetyl peroxide $(C_2H_3O)_2O_2$. Cf. *a. anhydride.* **a. proof material.** Any substance resisting the corroding effect of a.; as, stoneware. **a. proof stain.** See *table*top impregnation. **a. pump.** A pressure pump used to draw a. or ammonia from carboys. **a. radical.** (1) A mono- or polyvalent radical derived from a mono- or polyvalent a. by subtracting one or more H atoms. See table. (2) The acyl radical is sometimes known as the acid radical, and has the suffix *carbonyl* or *-oyl*; as, benzoyl, PhCO—. **a. rock.** A rock containing more than 60% Si. **a. salt.** A compound derived from a. and bases in which only a part of the hydrogen of the a. is replaced by a basic radical; e.g., an acid sulfate $NaHSO_4$. They are usually designated with the prefix *bi-*; e.g., bisulfate. **a. solution.** An aqueous solution containing more hydrogen ions than hydroxyl ions (see *hydrogen-ion concentration*). **a. of sugar.** Oxalic acid. **a. sulfate.** Bisulfate, disulfate. An inorganic compound containing the —HSO_4 radical derived from sulfuric a. **a. value.** (1) Acidity expressed in terms of normality. (2) A. number.

acidamide. An organic compound containing the radical —$CONH_2$. Cf. *acid imide.*

acidation. (1) Acidylation. Conversion into an acid. (2) Acidification; making a solution acidic.

acidify. To add an acid to a solution until the pH value falls below 7.0.

acidimeter. Hydrometer (obsolete).

acidimetry. The titration of an acid with a standard alkali solution. See *quantitative analysis.*

acidity. (1) Sourness. See *taste.* (2) An excess of hydrogen ions in aqueous solution; measured by: (a) the intensity or *degree* of acidity, expressed as pH value, q.v.; (b) the *amount* of acidity, expressed as normality, q.v. Antonym: Alkalinity. (3) The power of a base to unite with one or more equivalents of an acid. Antonym: Basicity. **amount of-** The normality or percentage of an acid as determined by titration (effective acid). **degree of-** The strength of an acid expressed by its hydrogen-ion concentration. Cf. *pH value.*

acidol. $C_5H_{11}O_2N \cdot HCl = 153.6$. Betaine hydrochloride. Colorless crystals, soluble in water. A substitute for hydrochloric acid in digestive disturbances.

acids. See table, pp. 12–14.

acidulate. Acidify.

acidulation. Acidation.

acidum. Latin for acid; e.g., **a. aceticum.** See *acetic acid*; **a. benzoicum.** See *benzoic acid*; etc.

acidylation. Acylation. The process of introducing an acid radical into an organic compound; e.g., acetylation (acetyl radical).

acieral. An aluminum alloy containing Cu 3–6, Fe 0.1–1.4, Mn 0–1.5, Mg 0.5–0.9, Si 0–0.4%. Cf. *aerometal.*

acinitro compound. Isonitro c. A colored isomer of a nitro compound containing the OH(O:)N group.

acitrin. $C_{18}H_{15}O_2N = 277.1$. 2-Phenylcinchonic acid ethyl ester. Yellow crystals, m.61, soluble in water; used to treat gout and rheumatism.

acivinil alcohols. Unsatured *ketols.*

Ackermann automatic reckoner. A device to determine the dry substance of milk from its specific gravity and fat content.

Acker process. The manufacture of sodium hydroxide by electrolysis of molten salt using molten lead as cathode.

acme burner. A bunsen burner with regulators for gas and air, constructed so that the flame cannot strike back.

acmite. $NaFeSi_2O_6$. Aegirite. A rock-forming monoclinic pyroxene, d.3.53, hardness 6–6.5, mol. vol. 65.5; occurs as a brownish, greenish, or black *silica* mineral, q.v., in Norway, and in boiler scales.

acne bacillus vaccine. A vaccine containing the acne bacillus, used to treat acne.

acocantherin. A crystalline glucoside from *Acocanthera abyssinica.* The active principle of the shashi arrow poison of Eastern Africa, related to ouabain.

acoin. Di-p-anisylphenetylguanidine chlorhydrate. White crystals, m.176, soluble in water; a local anesthetic.

acolytine. Lyaconine. An alkaloid of *Aconitum.*

aconic acid. $C_5H_4O_4 = 128.06$. Formylsuccinic acid lactone, 4,5-dihydro-5-keto-3-furan carboxylic acid. Colorless, triclinic crystals, m.164, sparingly soluble in water.

aconine. $C_{26}H_{21}NO_{11} = 523.17$. An amorphous alkaloid from the root of aconite. **acetylbenzoyl-** Aconitine. **pseudo-** Pseudaconine.

aconitase. An enzyme which catalyzes the conversion of aconitates into citrates.

aconite. Aconitum, monkshood, wolf's bane, blue rocket, friar's cowl, *Aconitum napellus*

(Ranunculaceae), whose root and leaves are used medicinally. **a. alkaloids.** Alkaloids from *Aconitum* species, e.g.:

Aconine	$C_{26}H_{21}O_{11}N$
Indaconine	$C_{27}H_{47}O_9N$
Pyraconitine	$C_{32}H_{41}O_9N$
Aconitine	$C_{34}H_{47}O_{11}N$
Japaconitine	$C_{34}H_{49}O_{11}N$
Indaconitine	$C_{34}H_{47}O_{10}N$
Pseudaconitine	$C_{36}H_{51}O_{12}N$

a. leaves. The dried leaves of *A. napellus*, used similarly to a. *root*. **a. root.** The dried tuberous roots of aconite (not less than 0.5% alkaloids); an antineuralgic, sudorific, and sedative.

aconitic acid. $COOH \cdot CH_2 \cdot C(COOH):CH \cdot COOH = 174.1$. Citridic acid, achilleic acid, adonic acid, 1,2,3-propenetricarboxylic acid*. Colorless crystalline leaflets, m.190, obtained from *Aconitum*, *Equisetum* (horsetail), *Adonis* and *Achillea* species, or made from citric acid. It occurs also in beets and sugar-cane.

COMMON ACIDS, RADICALS, AND SALTS

Acid	*Radical or ion*	*Salt*
Acetic	$CH_3COO—$	Acetate
Adipic	$—OOC(CH_2)_4COO—$	Adipate
Anisic	$C_6H_4 \cdot OCH_3 \cdot COO—$	Anisate
Arsenic	$AsO_4\equiv$	Orthoarsenate
	$AsO_3—$	Metaarsenate
Arsenous	$AsO_3\equiv$	Orthoarsenite
	$AsO_2—$	Metaarsenite
	$As_2O_5\equiv$	Pyroarsenite
Benzoic	$PhCOO—$	Benzoate
Boric	$BO_3\equiv$	Orthoborate
	$B_4O_7=$	Pyroborate
	$BO_2=$	Metaborate
	$BO_3—$	Perborate
Bromic	$BrO_3—$	Bromate
Bromous	$BrO_2—$	Bromite
Butyric (*n*)	$Me(CH_2)_2COO—$	Butyrate
Capric	$Me(CH_2)_8COO—$	Caprate
Caproic (*n*)	$C_5H_{11}COO—$	Caproate
Carbonic	$CO_3=$	Carbonate
	$HCO_3—$	Bicarbonate
Chloric	$ClO_3—$	Chlorate
Chlorous	$ClO_2—$	Chlorite
Chromic	$CrO_4=$	Chromate
	$Cr_2O_7=$	Dichromate
Chromous	$CrO_3=$	Chromite
Cinnamic	$PhCH:CHCOO—$	Cinnamate
Citraconic	$—OOCMeC:CHCOO—$	Citraconate
Citric	$C_3H_4(OH)(COO)_3\equiv$	Citrate
Cresotinic	$C_6H_3(OH)MeCOO—$	Cresotinate
Cyanacetic	$NC \cdot CH_2 \cdot COO—$	Cyanacetate
Cyanic	$CNO—$	Cyanate
Elaidic	$C_{14}H_{29}CH:CHCH_2COO—$	Elaidinate
Ferricyanic	$Fe(CN)_6\equiv$	Ferricyanide
Ferrocyanic	$Fe(CN)_6\equiv$	Ferrocyanide
Fluosilicic	$SiF_6=$	Fluosilicate
Formic	$HCOO—$	Formate
Fumaric	$—OOCCH:CHCOO—$	Fumarate
Gallic	$C_6H_2(OH)_3COO—$	Gallate
Glutaric	$—OOC(CH_2)_3COO—$	Glutarate
Glycolic	$HOCH_2COO—$	Glycolate
Hydrobromic	$Br—$	Bromide
Hydrochloric	$Cl—$	Chloride
Hydrocyanic	$CN—$	Cyanide
Hydrofluoric	$F—$	Fluoride
Hydroiodic	$I—$	Iodide
Hypochloric	$ClO—$	Hypochlorite
Iodic	$IO_3—$	Iodate
Iodous	$IO_2—$	Iodite
Lactic	$MeCH(OH)COO—$	Lactate
Lauric	$C_{11}H_{23}COO—$	Laurate
Levulinic	$MeCO(CH_2)_2COO—$	Levulinate

aconitine. $C_{34}H_{47}O_{11}N = 645.4$. Acetylbenzoylaconine. An extremely poisonous alkaloid from the root of *Aconitum napellus*. Colorless prisms, or amorphous powder, m.195, slightly soluble in water; a circulatory sedative. Cf. *aconite alkaloids*. **pseudo-** Pseudaconitine.
  a. arsenate. Colorless crystals, soluble in water.
a. hydrobromide. $C_{34}H_{47}O_{11}N \cdot HBr \cdot 2\frac{1}{2}H_2O = 771.5$. Colorless crystals, m.163, soluble in water. A cardiac, respiratory or spinal sedative, vasodilator, diuretic, antipyretic, and diaphoretic. **a. hydro-**

chloride. $C_{34}H_{47}O_{11}N \cdot HCl \cdot 3H_2O = 736.1$. Colorless, *l*-rotatory crystals, soluble in water; used as the hydrobromide. **a. nitrate.** $C_{34}H_{47}O_{11}N \cdot HNO_3 \cdot 5H_2O = 798.65$. Colorless, *l*-rotatory crystals, soluble in water. Used instead of the hydrobromide for hypodermic medication. **a. phosphate.** $C_{34}H_{47}O_{11}N \cdot H_3PO_4 = 743.4$. White crystals, soluble in water. **a. salicylate.** $C_{34}H_{47}O_{11}N \cdot C_7H_6O_3 = 783.5$. White crystals, soluble in water. **a. sulfate.** $(C_{34}H_{47}O_{11}N)_2 \cdot H_2SO_4 = 1389.02$. Colorless *l*-rotatory crystals, soluble in water.

COMMON ACIDS, RADICALS, AND SALTS (*continued*)

Acid	Radical or ion	Salt
Maleic	—OOCCH:CHCOO—	Maleate
Malic	—OOCCH₂CHOHCOO—	Malate
Malonic	—OOC·CH₂·COO—	Malonate
Molybdic	$MoO_4=$	Molybdate
Nitric	NO_3—	Nitrate
Nitrous	NO_2—	Nitrite
Oleic	$C_{17}H_{33}COO$—	Oleate
Oxalic	—OOC·COO—	Oxalate
	HOOC·COO—	Bioxalate
Oxybenzoic	HOC_6H_4COO—	Oxybenzoate
Palmitic	$C_{15}H_{31}COO$—	Palmitate
Perchloric	ClO_4—	Perchlorate
Periodic	IO_4—	Periodate
Phosphoric	$PO_4\equiv$	Orthophosphate (triphosphate)
	PO_3—	Metaphosphate
	$P_2O_7=$	Pyrophosphate
	H_2PO_4—	Acid phosphate
	HPO_4—	Phosphate
	$P_2O_7\equiv$	Pyrophosphate
Phosphorous	$PO_3\equiv$	Orthophosphite
	PO_2—	Metaphosphite
	$P_2O_5\equiv$	Pyrophosphite
Phthalic	$C_6H_4(COO)_2=$	Phthalate
Picric	*trinitrophenol*	
Propionic	C_2H_5COO—	Proprionate
Pyrogallic	*trihydroxybenzene*	
Pyruvic	MeCO·COO—	Pyruvate
Salicylic	HOC_6H_4COO—	Salicylate
Selenic	$SeO_4=$	Selenate
Selenous	$SeO_3=$	Selenite
Silicic	$SiO_4\equiv$	Orthosilicate
	$SiO_3=$	Metasilicate
Stearic	$C_{17}H_{35}COO$—	Stearate
Suberic	$C_6H_{12}(COO)_2=$	Suberate
Succinic	—OOC·CH₂CH₂·COO—	Succinate
Sulfonic acid	—SO₂OH	(see *sulfonic* acids)
Sulfanilic	$NH_2C_6H_4SO_3$—	Sulfanilate
Sulfuric	$SO_4=$	Sulfate
	HSO_4—	Bisulfate
Sulfurous	$SO_3=$	Sulfite
	HSO_3—	Bisulfite
Tannic	$C_{14}H_9O_9$—	Tannate
Tartaric	$(CHOH)_2—(COO)_2=$	Tartrate
	$C_2H_2(OH)_2COOH \cdot COO$—	Bitartrate
	—OOC·CHMe·CH₂·COO—	Pyrotartrate
Telluric	$TeO_6\equiv$ and $TeO_4=$	Tellurate
Tellurous	$TeO_3=$	Tellurite
Thioacetic	MeCOS—	Thioacetate
Thiocyanic	SCN—	Thiocyanate
Titanic	$TiO_3=$	Titanate
Tungstic	$W_2O_7=$ or $WO_4=$	Tungstate

$C_nH_{2n+1}COOH$	Fatty acids
$C_nH_{2n-1}COOH$	Acrylic acids, alicyclic acids
$C_nH_{2n-3}COOH$	Acetylene acids, fatty acids
$C_nH_{2n-7}COOH$	Aromatic acids (1)
$C_nH_{2n}(COOH)_2$	Oxalic acids
$C_nH_{2n-2}(COOH)_2$	Fumaric acids
$C_nH_{2n-4}(COOH)_2$	Acetylenedicarboxylic acids
$C_nH_{2n-8}(COOH)_2$	Aromatic acids (2)
$HO \cdot R \cdot COOH$	Alcohol acids, phenol acids
$R(CO)COOH$	Ketone acids
$NH_2 \cdot R \cdot COOH$	Amino acids
$R \cdot SO_3H$	Sulfonic acids
$H_xS_yO_z$	Sulfuric acids
$R \cdot COSH$	Thiocarbonic acids

Aconitum. A genus of poisonous plants of the Ranunculaceae family. See *aconite*.

aconitylphenetidine. Apolysin.

acopyrin. Acetopyrin.

acoretin. A neutral resin obtained by the oxidation of the aqueous extract of sweet flagroot, *Acorus calamus*.

acorin. $C_{36}H_{60}O_6 = 588.6$. A glucoside from calamus; the rhizome of *Acorus calamus*, sweet flag (Araceae); used in perfumery.

acorn. The fruit of the oak, *Quercus robur*; an astringent for treating diarrhea. **a. flour.** Racahout. **a. sugar.** Quercitol. **a. tube.** A small thermionic valve.

acoustics. The study of sound and its effects.

acovenoside. Venenatin. A cardiac glycoside from the bark and wood of *Acokanthera venenata*, G. Don. Crystalline plates, m.222; or prisms, m.163.

ACP. Calcium acid phosphate for use in foods, e.g., baking powders.

acqua. Italian for water.

acquired immunity. The resistance of an organism resulting from an attack by an infectious disease. Also artificially produced by treatment with a vaccine or serum.

acraldehyde. Acrolein.

acre. A surface measure, 1 acre = 0.4047 hectare = 4 rods = 160 poles = 1/640 sq mile.

Acree-Rosenheim reaction. The test solution plus dilute formaldehyde is layered on concentrated sulfuric acid; a purple ring indicates proteins.

acrid. Pungent, bitter, burning, or irritating; as from a drug or sensation.

acridic acid. $C_9H_5N(COOH)_2 = 217.0$. Acridinic acid. α,β- or 2,3-quinolinedicarboxylic acid. Colorless crystals, decomp. 130; an oxidation product of acridine.

acridine. $(C_6H_4)_2N \cdot CH = 179.15$. A tricyclic, heterocyclic hydrocarbon obtained from coal tar. Colorless leaflets, m.109, soluble in water. Used in the synthesis of dyes and drugs and to treat trypanosomiasis. Cf. *chrysaniline*, *rivanol*. **diaminosulfate.** Proflavine. **diamino--chloride.** Acriflavine. **diaminodimethyl-** A yellow dyestuff. **dihydro-** Acridan. **dihydroketo-** Acridone. **diphenanth-** Diphenanthacridine.

    a. dye. Dyestuff derived from a.; as, *acriflavine*, characterized by fluorescent solutions.

acridinic acid. Acridic acid.

acridol. An oxidation product of acridine, probably acridine-10-oxide.

acridone. $(C_6H_4)_2NH \cdot CO = 195.08$. Ketodihydro-

acridine. Colorless crystals, m.354, insoluble in water.

acridyl. The radical $C_{13}H_8N$—, derived from acridine.

acriflavine. $C_{14}H_{14}N_3Cl = 261.8$. 4,8-Diamino-1-methylacridine chloride, trypaflavine,

Brown crystals, soluble in water (fluorescent solution); an antiseptic and disinfectant. **a. hydrochloride.** A more soluble a. containing 1 mole HCl. **a. neutral.** A less soluble a. without HCl.

acrifoline $C_{16}H_{23}O_2N = 261.03$. A minor alkaloid from *L. annotinum*.

Acrilan. Trademark for a synthetic fiber made from acrylonitrile.

acrimonious. Bitter, caustic, sharp; as, a taste.

acrinyl. *p*-Hydroxybenzyl. The C_7H_7O— radical. $(HO \cdot C_6H_4 \cdot CH_2$—). **a. isothiocyanate.** $C_7H_7O \cdot NCS = 165.1$. Occurs in white mustard oil and is a split product of sinalbin. **a. sulfocyanate.** $C_7H_7O \cdot CNS = 165.13$. Oily colorless liquid in white mustard oil; insoluble in water.

Acrocomia. The coyol palm of S. America.

acrodextrin. Achroodextrin.

acrol. The $CH_2:CH \cdot CH=$ radical, from acrolein. Cf. *aeryl*.

acrolactic acid. Glucic acid.

acroleic acid. Acrylic acid.

acrolein. $CH_2:CH \cdot CHO = 56.05$. Acrylic aldehyde, propenal*, allyl aldehyde. A decomposition product of glycerol and glycerides. A yellow, irritant pungent liquid, d.0.84, b.52.4, soluble in water; used in organic synthesis. Flammable. Cf. *acrol*, *acryl*. **dimethyl-** Tiglaldehyde. **furfur-** Furfuracrolein. **met-** See *metacrolein*. **methyl-** Crotonaldehyde. **2-naphthyl-** $C_{13}H_{10}O = 182.1$. Yellow needles, m.48. **phenyl-** Cinnamaldehyde.

acrolite. A synthetic resin from phenol and glycerol.

acromelin. $C_{17}H_{16}O_9 = 364.12$. A lactone obtained from *Physcia acromela*.

acrometer. A hydrometer for determining the specific gravity of oils.

acronarcotic. A drug which is both acrid and narcotic; as, aconite.

acronize. A preparation of chlortetracycline used to preserve poultry and fish.

Acronol. Trademark for basic dyestuffs.

acropeptides. Complex amino acids produced by the action of hot glycerol on gelatin.

acrose. $C_6H_{12}O_6 = 180.09$. A synthetic carbohydrate obtained by the action of dilute sodium hydroxide on glycerose. α- i-Fructose.

acrosite. Pyrargyrite.

acryl. The radical C_3H_3O— from acrolein. **alpha-** The radical $CH_2:C(CHO)$— **beta-** A monovalent radical occurring in two isomeric forms:

acrylaldehyde. Acrolein.

acrylate. A salt of acrylic acid containing the $C_3H_3O_2$— radical.

acrylic acid. $CH_2:CH\cdot COOH = 72.05$. Acroleic acid, propenoic acid, propene acid, ethylenecarboxylic acid. An oxidation product of acrolein. A pungent colorless liquid, m.10, b.140, soluble in water. **dimethyl-** α,β- See *angelic* and *tiglic acid*. β,β- Senecioic acid. β-**ethyl-** α-Pentenic acid. α-**hydroxy-** Pyruvic acid. **imidoazole-** Urocanic acid. **methyl-** α- $CH_2:CMe\cdot COOH = 80.05$. Methacrylic acid. An isomer of butenic acid, m.16. β- See *crotonic* and *isocrotonic acid*. **phenyl-** α- Atropic acid. β- Cinnamic acid. **propyl-** Hexenoic acid.

acrylic acids. Olefin acids. A series of unsaturated aliphatic acids of the general formula, $C_nH_{2n-2}O_2$; as acrylic acid, $C_2H_3\cdot COOH$; butenic acids (crotonic, isocrotonic, vinylacetic, and methylacrylic acid), $C_3H_5\cdot COOH$.

acrylic aldehyde. Acrolein.

acrylonitrile. Vinylcyanide.

acrylophenone. $CH_2:CH\cdot COPh = 132.06$. Phenylvinyl ketone. An isomer of cinnamaldehyde. β-**phenyl-** Chalcone.

acrylyl. The radical $CH_2:CH\cdot CO$—, from acrylic acid.

Actaea. A genus of ranunculaceous herbs.

acterol. An irradiated ergosterol, q.v.

actidione. An antifungal antibiotic (which has no antibacterial properties) from *Streptomyces griseus*.

actiduins. A group of antibiotics from the *Streptomycetes*. They are yellow to red in color, and fluoresce yellow, especially in organic solvents. They contain C, H, N, and S, and sometimes Cl; m. exceeds 350 (decomp.). Sparingly soluble in water.

actin. A fibrous protein constituent of muscle material. See *actomyosin*.

actiniasterol. A sterol, m.145, from sea anemone, *Anemonia sulcata*.

actinic. Pertaining to radiations; especially light that produces a chemical change. **a. rays.** Rays in the violet and ultraviolet regions which produce chemical changes. Cf. *irradiation, ultraviolet*.

actinides. Elements having the same electronic structure in that the $5f$ shell is filled. The 14 elements of at. no. 90–103. The theoretical analogues of the lanthanons, e.g., neptunium, plutonium, americium, curium.

actinine. $C_{13}H_{24}O_5N_2 = 288.3$. An alkaloid from *Actinea equina*.

actinism. The study of chemical changes produced by radiations. Cf. *photochemistry*, *excitation*, *activation*.

actinium. Ac = 227. A radioactive element, at. no. 89, discovered (1899) by DeBierne in pitchblende, and identical with the anemium of Giesel (1902). It is trivalent, an isotope of mesothorium 2, and the predecessor of the a. series. See *radioactive substances*. **a. emanation.** Actinon. **a. K.** Element 87. **a. series.** A series of radioactive disintegration products derived from uranium II.

actinodaphnine. $C_{19}H_{19}NO_4 = 325.15$. An alkaloid from *Actinodaphne* species (Lauraceae), resembling laurotetanine. Cf. *bulbocapnine*.

actinogram, actinograph. Skiagram.

actinolite. $Ca(MgFe)(SiO_4)_3$. A green, rock-forming amphibole resembling tremolite; fibrous variety is asbestos.

actinometer. (1) A screen which fluoresces in radioactive rays, used as a photometer. (2) A device for measuring the power of actinic rays. Cf. *uroxameter*.

actinomycetin. An antibiotic substance from cultures of *Streptomyces albus*.

actinomycin. $C_{41}H_{56}O_{11}N_8(?)$. A bright red crystalline quinonoid-type antibiotic from cultures of *Streptomyces antibioticus*; 2 fractions A and B; decomp. 250.

actinon. An = 222. Actinium emanation, Act-Em, an isotope of niton, Nt, at. no. 86. See *radon*. Cf. *radioactive series*.

actinouranium. An isotope of uranium and a primary radioelement, at. no. 92. Cf. *radioactive series*.

actinozoa. The phylum Coelenterata, or jellyfish, which have starlike structures.

action. The physical concept of activity, or work performed in unit time; hence: *action* = *energy* $\times$ *time* or *momentum* $\times$ *distance*; hence $a = mv^2t$, where m is the mass, v the velocity, t the time. **chemical-** A reaction in which the atoms of a molecule or molecules are rearranged. **electronic-** The change of an electron from one to another energy level. Cf. *excitation*. **physical-** A transformation of matter which does not affect molecular structure.

activated. Rendered active, reactive, or excited. **a. atom.** See *atom*. **a. carbon.** Charcoal produced by the destructive distillation of vegetable matter; as, nutshells; with or without the addition of chemicals. Used in powdered form to decolorize sugar solutions, oils, etc., or in granular form as an adsorbent in gas masks and for the recovery of solvent vapors; a general-purpose antidote (U.S.P.). Cf. *Norit, revivification*. **a. molecule.** A molecule with one or more excited atoms. Cf. *irradiation, excitation*. **a. sludge.** The oxidized and flocculent sediment of sewage which contains bacteria. **a. s. process.** Sewage is agitated in contact with air, thereby causing oxidation and flocculation by bacterial action; it is left to settle in separation tanks, and yields a harmless effluent.

activation. (1) A method by which a metallic catalyst is rendered active or is regenerated; as, heating platinum sponge. Cf. *revivification*. (2) The transformation of an inactive enzyme (zymogen) into an active enzyme by a kinase; e.g., pepsinogen (the *zymogen*) is transformed by hydrochloric acid (the *kinase*) into pepsin (the *active enzyme*). (3) Excitation. (4) Irradiation. (5) A. of carbon, e.g., by heating with steam, or sulfuric acid.

activator. (1) A catalyst. (2) A substance used in flotation to produce a coating having metallic properties; as, sodium sulfide for lead carbonate ores.

activatory. See *phase.*

active. (1) Dynamic or working, as opposed to static or inert. (2) Having optical properties, as an asymmetric carbon atom. Cf. *optical activity.* **surface-** See *surfactant.*

    a. deposit. The formation of a radioactive layer on a substance exposed to radio elements. **a. immunity.** The stimulation of an organism to produce substances protective against infection by bacteria. **a. immunization.** The processes by which the protective agencies of an organism are made resistant to bacterial invasion. **a. mass.** The number of moles (gram-molecules) in a unit volume (1 liter). **a. oxygen test.** A test for rancidity in fats, by the liberation of iodine from potassium iodide in acetic acid. **a. principle.** The substance responsible for the physiological action of a drug: e.g., an alkaloid.

activin. An organic iodine compound of casein used medicinally.

activity. (1) The rate in watts at which work is performed. Cf. *action.* (2) The ratio of the escaping tendency (*fugacity*) of two phases at the same temperature. A correction applied to the concentration of a strong electrolyte, to satisfy Ostwald's dilution law, q.v. (3) A measure of interionic forces. Cf. *a. coefficient.* **amylolytic-** Digestive power of amylase. **excited-** Active deposit. **ionic-** Thermodynamic concentration. In a dilute solution which obeys the gas laws, the i.a. equals the concentration; in other solutions the value which ensures that the gas laws hold. **optical-** The capacity of a substance to rotate the plane of polarized light. **peptic-** Digestive power of pepsin. **radio-** See *radioactivity.* **tryptic-** Digestive power of trypsin.

    a. of activated carbon. The percentage of carbon disulfide vapor absorbed by carbon (generally 50%). **a. coefficient.** The ratio a/c; see *activity* (2).

actol. Silver lactate.

actomyosin. A combination of actin and myosin, q.v., which comprises the tractile muscle system.

acton. Ethyl orthoformate.

actor. A compound which takes part in both primary and secondary reactions. See *induced reactions.*

acute. Quick, short, or sharp. Cf. *chronic.* **a. poisoning.** See *poisoning.*

acyclic. Describing organic compounds which contain no ring system; as, the methane series. Synonym: Aliphatic (chains). Antonym: Cyclic, aromatic (rings).

acyl. An organic radical derived from an organic acid by the removal of the hydroxyl group; e.g., $R \cdot CO-$ is the a. radical of $R \cdot CO \cdot OH$. See *acetyl, benzenesulfonyl, benzoyl,* etc. **a. derivative.** An organic compound containing an a. radical; e.g., amides, $R \cdot CO \cdot NH_2$. **a. radical.** Acyl.

acylation. Acidylation. The formation or introduction of an acyl radical in or into an organic compound.

acyloin. $R \cdot CO \cdot CHOH \cdot R$. An organic compound formed by condensation of aldehydes, as, $Ph \cdot CO \cdot CHOH \cdot Ph$, benzoin.

aczol. An ammoniacal solution of zinc and copper phenolates; a wood preservative.

adaline. $Et_2CBr \cdot CO \cdot NH \cdot CO \cdot NH_2 = 237.1$. Carbromal, α-bromo-α-ethylbutyrylurea. White crystals, m.116, slightly soluble in water; a hypnotic and sedative.

adamant. A hard mineral; as, diamond.

adamantine. Diamond. **a. boron.** See *boron.* **a. spar.** A dark gray, smoky variety of corundum from India; green in transmitted light.

adamellose. An igneous andesite-diorite rock containing hornblende, feldspar, quartz, chlorite, agnetite, apatite, and rutile (Pigeon Point, Minn.).

Adam galactometer. A graduated buret with two glass bulbs, used in milk analysis.

adamine. Adamite.

adamite. Zn_2HAsO_5. Adamine. A native arsenate; yellow orthorhombic crystals (Chile, Greece).

Adamkiewicz reaction. Protein solutions give a violet ring when layered on glacial acetic acid and concentrated sulfuric acid.

adamon. Dibromodihydrocinnamic acid ester of borneol; a sedative and anaphrodisiac.

adamsite. (1) A greenish-black mica. (2) Diphenylamine chlorarsine. Adansonia. *Adansonia digitata* (Bombacaceae), the baobab tree of Africa, yields edible boui or monkey bread. The bark is an emollient; the dried leaves, lalo, are an antipyretic; the fibers are suitable for paper.

adansonine. An alkaloid from the bark and leaves of *Adansonia digitata.* Colorless white crystals; a febrifuge.

adaptation. The advantageous adjustment of an organism to a change in its surrounding.

adapter. A tapered glass tube used to connect a retort or condenser with the receiving vessel.

adatom. An atom adsorbed on a surface so that it will migrate over the surface like a two-dimensional gas. Cf. *adion.*

addiction. Devotion to or the habitual use of a substance or practice. **a.-producing drugs.** Drugs subjected to international control by the World Health Organization because of their a.-producing powers.

addition. A chemical reaction which involves no change of valency; usually the union of two binary molecules to form a more complex compound; as, $HCl + NH_3 = NH_4Cl$. **a. compound.** Adduct. An inorganic compound formed by addition; e.g., NH_4Cl.

additive. Added to. **a. compound.** An organic compound formed by the saturation of one or more double or triple bonds of an unsaturated compound; e.g., benzene hexachloride, $C_6H_6Cl_6$, is an additive compound of benzene. **a. property.** A property of a molecule which is the sum of the individual properties of the atoms or linkages composing it; thus, when the molecular refractivity of a molecule is the sum of the atomic refractivities of its atoms.

adduct. Addition group or compound.

adduction. Oxidation.

adelgesin. $C_{23}H_{28}O_{15} = 544.3$. Light brown needles, m.205. A glucosidal constituent of the bark of "pineapple" gall, produced by *Adelges abietes.*

adelite. $MgCaHAsO_5$. A native arsenate of the wagnerite group; monoclinic gray crystals.

adelomorphic cell. Any living cell of uncertain or indefinite shape; e.g., an ameba.

adenantherine. A crystalline alkaloid resembling physostigmine, obtained from *Adenanthera pavonia* (Leguminosae).

adenase. A deamidizing enzyme in animal tissues which hydrolyzes adenine to hypoxanthine.

adenine. $C_5H_5N_5 = 135.12$. 6-Aminopurine. A purine base derived from nucleic acid and found in the pancreas and spleen. White needles, m.360, slightly soluble in water. **a. nucleotide.** Adenosinetriphosphoric acid, the primary constituent of resting muscle.

adenocarpine. $C_{19}H_{24}ON_2 = 296.8$. An alkaloid from the *Adenocarpus* species, and an optical isomer of santiognine; m.(hydrochloride) approx. 140.

adenoid. Resembling or pertaining to glands.

adenos. A fine quality of cotton from Asia Minor.

adenosine. $C_{10}H_{13}N_5O_4 = 267.1$. Adenine riboside. A glucoside from nucleic acid consisting of adenine and *d*-ribose. Colorless needles, m.229, soluble in water. **a. phosphoric acid.** Adenylic acid. **a. triphosphoric acid.** Adenine nucleotide.

adenylic acid. $C_{10}H_{13}N_5O_4 \cdot HPO_3 = 347.18$. Adenosinephosphoric acid. A nucleotide from red blood corpuscles and yeast, consisting of adenine, ribose, and phosphoric acid. White needles, m.197. It lowers the blood pressure and intestinal motion. Cf. *adenine nucleotide, guanylic acid.*

adeps. Any animal grease or fat, e.g., lard. **a. lanae.** Lanolin. **a. mineralis.** Petrolatum.

adermin. The antidermatitic vitamin B_6, obtained from yeast extract by dialysis.

adfluxion. Affluxion.

adglutinate. Agglutinate.

adhatotic acid. An organic acid from the leaves of *Adhatoda vasica* (Acanthaceae). Cf. *vasicine.*

adhere. To be attached to or to stick to another substance. Cf. *cohere.*

adhesion. The attraction or force which holds unlike molecules together. Cf. *cohesion, wetting, adsorption.*

adhesive. Any substance that sticks or binds materials together. **a. meter.** An apparatus to determine the relative viscosity of road materials.

adiabatic. A change occurring without a loss or gain of heat. Cf. *Reech's theorem.* **a. calorimeter.** An instrument for the study of reactions in which there is a minimum loss of heat; *Riehe calorimeter.* **a. elasticity.** The modulus of elasticity of a gas undergoing a change in volume without transfer of heat; e.g., in explosions. **a. expansion.** The expansion of a gas without the production of a cooling effect. **a. processes.** An experiment carried out so that no heat can leave or enter the system.

adiactinic. A substance which does not transmit photochemically active radiations.

adicity. Valency.

adinole. A mineral consisting of metallic silver and albite.

adion. An adsorbed ion. Cf. *adatom.*

adipaldehyde. $CHO(CH_2)_4CHO = 114.08$. Hexanedial*, adipic dialdehyde. Oily liquid, b.94.

adipamide. $NH_2CO(CH_2)_4CONH_2 = 144.11$. Adipic diamide, hexanediamide*. An isolog of succinamide, m.220.

adipic acid. $COOH(CH_2)_4COOH = 146.11$. Adipinic acid, hexanedioic acid*. Colorless needles, m. 149, sparingly soluble in water. Used principally in nylon manufacture and for plasticizers. **tetrahydroxy-** See *saccharic acids.* **a. dialdehyde.** Adipaldehyde. **a. diamide.** Adipamide. **a. ketone.** Cyclopentanone*.

adipinic acid. Adipic acid.

adipoin. $C_6H_{10}O_2 = 114.08$. β-Hydroxycyclohexanone. White powder, m.91, slightly soluble in water.

adipyl. The radical $-OC(CH_2)_4CO-$, from adipic acid. **a. chloride.** $C_6H_8O_2Cl = 192.98$. Hexanedioyl chloride*. Colorless liquid, $b_{10mm}113$.

adjacent (position). Adjoining, near. The consecutive arrangement of radicals in an organic ring compound; as, the 1,2,3-position in the benzene ring.

adjective. Supplemental or accessory. **a. dyes.** Dyes requiring a mordant.

adjoining. Adjacent.

adjuvant. An auxiliary drug which assists the action of another drug.

Adler benzidine reaction. A sensitive test for blood in urine. Cf. *benzidine test.*

adlumine. $C_{21}H_{21}NO_6 = 383.17$. An alkaloid from *Adlumia fungosa* (Papaveraceae). Cf. *bicuculline.*

adnephrine. Adrenaline.

adnic. Admiralty nickel. An alloy: Cu 70, Ni 29, Sn 1%.

adobe. A soil of arid regions, formed by the disintegration of rocks, consisting essentially of CaO, SiO_2, CO_2, and Fe_2O_3. Brown, claylike masses used in Egypt and New Mexico for building and pottery.

adonic acid. $C_3H_3(CO_2H)_3 = 174.2$. An acid in *Adonis vernalis*, probably identical with aconitic acid.

adonidin. $C_{24}H_{42}O_9 = 474.3$. A glucoside from *Adonis vernalis*. A hygroscopic, yellow, very bitter powder; a heart stimulant and diuretic. Cf. *picroadonidin.*

adonin. $C_{24}H_{40}O_9 = 472.3$. A glucoside from *Adonis vernalis*; a heart stimulant.

adonis. False hellebore, pheasant's eye. The dried over-ground leaves and stems of *A. vernalis* (Ranunculaceae). The fluid extract is a heart stimulant.

adonite. $C_5H_{12}O_5 = 152.12$. Adonitol. A pentatomic alcohol, from *Adonis vernalis*. Colorless prisms, m.102, soluble in water.

adonitol. Adonite.

adrenal cortex. A sterile solution in dilute alcohol of a mixture of the endocrine principles from the cortex of the adrenal glands of healthy domestic animals used as food by man; a source of hormones.

adrenal gland. A small gland above each kidney.

Adrenalin. Trademark for adrenaline, epinephrine.

adrenaline. $C_6H_3(OH)_2 \cdot CHOH \cdot CH_2 \cdot NHMe = 183.1$. Adrenine, adrine, adrenamine (U.S. usage), epinephrine, hemostatin, suprarenaline, *l*-methylaminoethanol catechol. Brown microcrystalline powder, m.205, slightly soluble in water. Obtained from the suprarenal glands of animals, and used as intravenous injections to raise the blood pressure, and as an astringent, hemostatic, and heart tonic. **d-.** Dextro-. Is 6.7% as active as the *l*-. **i-.**

Inactive-. Is 50% as active as the *l*-. **l-.** Levo-. The natural or synthetic, physiologically active compound (see above). **a. acid tartrate.** The B.P. name for epinephrine bitartrate (U.S.P.), q.v. **a. hydrochloride.** The epinephrine of the trade, used for adrenaline. **a. bitartrate.** The suprarenine of the trade.

Adrenalone. $C_9H_{11}O_3N = 181.1$. Trade name for methylaminoacetocatechol. The ketone of adrenaline.

Adrenine. Trade name for epinephrine.

adrenolutine. A fluorescent oxidation product of adrenaline.

adsorbate. That which is adsorbed.

adsorbent. A substance that adsorbs; as, charcoal. Cf. *absorbent.* **crystallogenetic-** A crystalline substance which when dehydrated without losing its shape, becomes porous and thus, absorbent; as, chabazite.

adsorption. The ability of a substance (*adsorbent*) to hold or concentrate gases, liquids, or dissolved substances (*adsorbate*) upon its surface; cf. *adhesion, sorption, absorption, desorption, persorption, wetting.* **anomal-** A. which does not follow the a. isotherm; as, with certain colloidal dyes. **apolar-** Nonpolar a. **co-** A. in which two substances are held on a surface, which adsorbs neither alone. **differential-** See *differential* a. **heat of-** The calories liberated during a. **negative-** A. in which the surface concentration of the adsorbate is lowered by preferential a. of the liquid. **nonpolar-.** Apolar- a. in which nonelectrolytes or equivalent ions of electrolytes are held on a surface. **oriented-** A. in which the molecules are grouped on the surface in a definite direction. Cf. *mono*molecular film. **polar-** A. in which definite anions or cations are held in nonequivalent amounts. **positive-** A. in which the surface concentration of the adsorbate is relatively high. **preferential-** Pronounced a. of one substance compared with another of similar physical properties; e.g., chemosorption. **specific-** (1) Preferential-. (2) The quantity of adsorbate on one square centimeter surface. **a. analysis.** Separation of mixtures by the different absorbability of the components. Cf. *chromatographic analysis.* **a. catalysis.** A chemical reaction in which the adsorbent acts as a catalyst. **a. coefficient.** The quantity x of the a. isotherm. **a. colorimetry.** The a. of colored substances from solution on a white adsorbent, and comparison of the separated and dried colored powders with standards, similarly prepared, in visible or in ultraviolet light (a. fluorimetry); e.g., the estimation of atebrin in urine using silica gel. **a. displacement.** The replacement of one adsorbate on a surface by another. **a. equilibrium.** The distribution of molecules on a surface and in the surrounding medium. Cf. *a. isotherm.* **a. exponent.** The quantity $1/n$ of the a. isotherm. **a. fluorimetry.** See *a. colorimetry.* **a. isotherm.** The approximate, empirical relationship existing between the concentration x, held upon the surface and the amount c, which is not adsorbed: $x/m = \alpha \cdot c^{1/n}$, where m is the amount of adsorbent, and α and $1/n$ are experimental constants. **a. potential.** The work obtainable when an adsorbate is brought into the a. space.

adsorptive. Adsorbate.

adstringent. Astringent.

adubiri. A fish poison from *Paulowilhelmia speciosa*, used in Ghana.

adularia. A variety of *orthoclase*.

adularin. A potassium silicate of uncertain composition.

adulterant. A substance of cheaper or inferior quality, sometimes harmful, added to an article, compound, or food.

adulteration. (1) The fraudulent addition of a foreign substance, especially harmful preservatives, to food products. (2) The removal of an essential constituent of a substance, as cream from milk.

advection. Heating or cooling effects due to horizontal currents in air or water. Cf. *convection.*

adventitious. Not typical or normal; accidental.

advitant. Vitamin (obsolete).

æ- See: (1) *ae-*; (2) also under *e-*.

aegerite. Wurtzite.

aegirite. Acmite.

aenigmatite. Black, triclinic, amphibole metasilicate of sodium and ferrous iron, containing some titanium instead of silicon, d.3.8.

aeolotropic. Anisotropic.

aeonite. Wurtzite.

aequum. The amount of food just sufficient to support an organism doing work.

aer. Atmos.

aerated water. A water artificially impregnated with oxygen or carbon dioxide; as, soda water.

aerobe. An organism that requires an atmosphere of oxygen for respiration. Cf. *anaerobe.*

aerobic bacteria. Certain protophyta which require gaseous oxygen for the maintenance of their vitality. Cf. *anaerobic.*

aerobioscope. A device to determine the number of bacteria in air.

aerobiosis. Life sustained in an atmosphere containing oxygen.

aerodynamics. Pneumatics. The study of the motion of gases.

Aerofloat. Trademark for flotation agents of the dithiophosphoric acid type.

aeroklinoscope. An air cell used to float algae on water.

aerolite. A meteoric stone of silicates. Cf. *siderolite.*

aerometal. An alloy: Al, with Cu 0.2–4, Fe 0.3–1.3, Mn 0–1.2, Mg 0–3, Zn 0–3, Si 0.5–1.0%. Cf. *acieral.*

aerometer. An instrument to determine the density of gases.

aeron. An aluminum alloy with Cu 1.5–2.0, Si 1.0, Mn 0.75%.

aeronomy. The study of the upper atmosphere, and especially its radiation and electromagnetic properties.

aerophone. An apparatus to amplify sound waves.

aeroplankton. Organisms (pollen, bacteria, etc.) carried by air.

aeroscope. A glass apparatus to obtain bacteria from air.

aerosiderite. An iron meteorite. Cf. *siderite.*

aerosite. Pyrargyrite.

Aerosol. (1) Trade name for a powerful wetting agent of the sulfonated bicarboxy acid ester type; e.g., **A.-OT** is dioctyl sodium sulfosuccinate. (2) (not cap.) A colloidal system, q.v., with gas as the surrounding medium; as, smokes and fogs. **a.**

pressure packaging. A method of dispensing cosmetics, medicaments, and similar products in the form of a gas-liquid aerosol spray. A homogeneous mixture of the product and a liquefied gas (e.g., dichlorofluoroethane) in the pack under pressure is released by opening a valve.

aerosphere. Atmosphere.

Aerosporin. Trademark for polymixin-A.

aerostatics. The study of gases in mechanical equilibrium. Cf. *hydrostatics*.

aerotherapeutics. Therapy by varying the pressure or composition of the atmosphere in which the patient lives.

aerotonometer. An instrument to determine the pressure of gases in blood.

aerotropic. Attracted by air; as, of an organism.

aerugo. (1) Cupric subacetate. (2) The oxide or rust of a metal.

aeschynite. Resinous, black, orthorhombic native columbates of calcium, iron, cerium, lanthanum, titanium, and thorium.

aescigenin. $C_{12}H_{20}O_2 = 196.2$. A glucoside from the horse chestnut *Aesculus hippocastanum*.

aescinic acid. $C_{24}H_{40}O_2 = 360.32$. Capsuloesic acid. A monobasic acid from the seeds of *Aesculus hippocastanum*, horse chestnut.

aescorcin. $C_9H_8O_4 = 180.1$. Escorcin. A split product of aesculin. Brown powder, soluble in alkalies; used to detect corneal defects.

aesculetin. Esculetin.

aesculetinic acid. Esculetinic acid.

aesculin. Esculin.

aesculinic acid. Esculin.

aethan. Ethane (German).

aether. (1) Official Latin (also German) for ether; formerly also for ester. (2) The hypothetical universal medium through which electromagnetic waves (e.g., light and heat) are propagated.

aetherische oel. German for essential oil.

aethusine. A volatile alkaloid from *Aethusa cynapium*, believed identical with coniine.

aethyl. Ethyl (German).

aethyleni. Official Latin for ethylene.

aethylis. Official Latin for ethyl.

aetioporphyrin. $C_{31}H_{36}N_4 = 464.5$. A split product of hemoglobin or chlorophyll.

Afcodur. Trade name for a polyvinyl chloride plastic, m. approx. 120. It is 5.5 times lighter than steel, and resistant to corrosion and flame.

Afenil. $CaCl_2 \cdot 4(NH_2)_2CO$. Trade name for calcium chloride–urea, used in calcium therapy.

affination. A centrifugal filtration process in which most of the molasses contaminating raw sugars is removed.

affinity. The selective tendency of elements to combine with one, rather than another element, when physicochemical conditions are equal or slightly in favor of the "rejected" element. See *affinity curve, reaction isotherm*. **electro-.** See *electroaffinity*. **electron-.** See *electron*. **residual-.** See *residual bond*.

a. bond. See *bond*. **a. constant.** The ratio, F_a/F_b, where F_a is the intrinsic tendency of substance a to decompose, and F_b the tendency of substance b to combine. See *dissociation constant*. **a. curve.** A graph obtained when the heat of formation is plotted against the types of combining atoms. The peak shown by C:C is con-

sidered to be due to affinity and thus explains the many carbon compounds.

affluxion. Adfluxion. Flowing or coming together.

African kino. Kino. **A. pepper.** Capsicum. **A. saffron.** Carthamus.

afridol. $Hg(OH) \cdot C_6H_3Me \cdot COONa = 351.7$. Sodium mercuric hydroxytoluylate. White powder, used to treat parasitic skin diseases.

afsal. Urasol.

after. Behind; following in point of time. **a. contraction, a. expansion.** The percentage change in length of a brick or refractory after 2 hr at 1410°C.

aftitalite. $KNaSO_4$. A mineral from Italy.

Ag. Symbol for silver (argentum).

agalmatolite. Pyrophyllite.

agamy. Agamogenesis. Asexual reproduction. Cf. gamogenesis (sexual reproduction).

agaphite. A Persian turquoise.

agar (-agar). Agal-agal, Bengal isinglass, Japanese gelatin, Japanese isinglass. The dried mucilaginous substance from marine algae or seaweeds as, *Gelidium corneum, Gracilaria lichenoides, Gigartina speciosa* (Rhodophyceae). Bundles of thin, transparent membranes insoluble in cold water, and slowly swelling and soluble in hot water. Used as a culture medium; as a glue; and to make silk and paper transparent. **glucose-** See *glucose agar*. **glycerin-** See *glycerin agar*. **lactose-** See *lactose agar*. **litmus-** See *litmus agar*. **plain-** A culture medium; 15 gm agar-agar, 10 gm peptone, 5 gm sodium chloride, and 1,000 ml bouillon stock solution, neutralized with sodium hydroxide, and filtered white hot.

agaric. *Agaricus albus*, touchwood, spunk, tinder. The dried fruit body of the fungus, *Polyporus officinalis* (Polyponaceae), which grows on the *Larix* species. **fly-.** See *Amanita*. **surgeon's-.** Amadonu. **white-.** Agaric.

a. acid. $C_{19}H_{36}(OH)(COOH)_3 \cdot 1\frac{1}{2}H_2O = 443.45$. Laricic acid, agaricic acid, agaricinum. Colorless microcrystals, m.140, slightly soluble in water; the active principle of agaric, used as a local irritant. **a. mineral.** Rock milk. A soft, white deposit of microscopic crystals of calcite.

Agaricaceae. Mushrooms or toadstools (4,600 species); some are poisonous (*Amanita*), others edible (*Agaricus, Cantharellus*).

agaricic acid. Agaric acid.

agaricin. An alcoholic extract of white *Agaric* or *Polyporus officinalis*. Brown powder, soluble in water, containing impure agaric acid; used as a purgative and antiperspirant.

agaricinum. Agaric acid.

agaricol. $C_{10}H_{16}O = 152.1$. A monoatomic alcohol in white agaric; colorless powder, m.223.

agarose. A neutral galactose polymer, responsible for the gel strength of agar.

agarythrine. Yellow, bitter alkaloid in the fungus *Agaricus rubra*, oxidized to the red coloring matter of fungi.

agate. SiO_2. A cryptocrystalline quartz or chalcedony, composed of colored layers or clouds. Used as a semiprecious stone, for ornaments, for pebbles in ball mills, and for the knife-edges of chemical balances. **blood-** Hemachate. **Iceland-** An obsidian. **oriental-** A translucent gem variety. **white-** chalcedony.

agathin. $HO \cdot C_6H_4CH : N \cdot NMePH = 226.2$. Cosmin. Salicyl- α-methylphenylhydrazine. Yellow crystals, m.74, insoluble in water; used to treat neuralgia.

Agathis. A conifer of Australia and Malaya; source of kauri resin.

Agave. American aloe. A genus of Central American plants (Amaryllidaceae). The fibers are used for threads and ropes; the leaves and juice as a diuretic and in adhesives. The fermented juice (pulque) is popular in Mexico; from it is distilled a spirit (mescal). Cf. *henequen, sisal.*

agedoite. Asparagine.

ageing. Aging.

Agene process. The bleaching of flour with nitrogen trichloride. It can produce a crystalline toxic peptide, and is prohibited in some countries.

agent. A substance or force that effects a change. Cf. *reagent.* **balancing-** See *buffer* and *poiser.* **catalytic-** See *catalyst.* **emulsifying-** See *emulsifier.* **freezing-** See *freezing mixtures.* **frothing-** See *frother.* **oxidizing-** See *oxidizing agent.* **reducing-** See *reducing agent.* **refrigerating-** The gases ammonia, sulfur dioxide, or methyl chloride, used in refrigerators. **refining-** Substances, e.g., sulfuric acid or caustic soda, used to purify organic compounds. **vulcanizing-** See *vulcanization.* **warning-** An odorous substance used to indicate danger in mines, or to detect leakage in pipes.

AgeRite. Trademark for aldo-α-naphthylamine; an anti-aging agent for rubber. Cf. *ohmoil.*

Agfa. Trade name for dyes, fine chemicals, etc. (Aktien Gesellschaft für Anilin Farben). **A. silk.** A viscose rayon.

agglomeration. A cluster or accumulation of particles or substances.

agglutinant. A substance which causes agglomeration.

agglutinate. (1) To cause agglutination. (2) The product of agglutination.

agglutination. The clumping together of cells or bacteria by the interaction of bacteria and the corresponding immune serum; used in sero-diagnosis.

agglutinins. A group of substances formed in the blood as a result of bacterial infection or inoculation which cause the clumping together of the bacteria. Cf. *hemagglutinin.*

agglutinogen. A substance in bacteria which stimulates the production of agglutinins in animals.

aggregate. In concrete, the mixed rock and sand; as distinct from the binder (cement).

aggregation. The gathering of units into a whole; the clustering together of particles. **state of-** The physical form of matter; as, solid, liquid, gaseous, or colloidal.

aggressivity. Describing a soil which has a corrosive action on metals.

aging, ageing. (1) Any irreversible change in living matter which occurs as a function of time. (2) Natural or artificial maturing or ripening; as of cheese. **a. test.** A test involving exaggerated conditions of a.; used to determine rapidly how a material will behave over a period of time.

agitator. A device to keep liquids in motion.

aglucone. The nonsugar part of a glucoside.

aglycone. That component of a glycoside, e.g., plant pigment, which is not a sugar.

agmatine. $NH_2C(NH) \cdot NH(CH_2)_4NH_2 = 130.2$. Aminobutylguanidine. An amine isolated from herring spawn and ergot. Cf. *synthalin.*

agnetite. A mineral constituent of adamellose.

agnin. Lanolin.

agon. The active radical of an enzyme. Cf. *pheron.*

agoniadin. $C_{21}H_{26}O_{12} = 470.2$. Plumierin. The active principle of the bark of *Plumeria succuba,* pagoda tree; an antipyretic, anthelmintic, and emmenagogue.

Agricola, Georg Bauer. 1490–1555. German physician and alchemist.

agriculture. The study of the cultivation of the soil.

agrimonia oil. The volatile oil of agrimony.

agrimony. A rosaceous plant, *Agrimonia eupatoria;* a tonic and astringent.

Agrinite. Trade name for a tankage, q.v., containing $8\frac{1}{4}\%$ nitrogen.

Agripol. Norepol. Trademark for a rubber substitute made by condensing a polyhydroxy alcohol with polymerized vegetable oil acids.

agrochemistry. The study of soil nutrition chemistry, and fertility, as distinct from its formation and classification.

agrostemma. Corncockle. The poisonous plant *A. githago* (Caryophyllaceae). **a. saponin.** $C_{35}H_{54}O_{10}$ (*Brandl*) or $C_{29}H_{44}O_4$ (*Wedekind & Schicke*). A hemolytic substance, m.286. It causes paralysis.

agroxone. Methoxone.

agucarina. Saccharin.

ague tree. Sassafras.

aguilarite. Ag_4SSe. A black mineral sulfoselenide.

aguirin. Theobromine sodium acetate.

Agulhon's reagent. A 0.1 N solution of chromic acid in dilute nitric acid, used to titrate primary alcohols.

agurin. Aguirin.

Aich's metal. An alloy containing Cu 56, Zn 42, Fe 1%, which is very malleable at red heat.

aikinite. $CuPbBiS_3$. Aikenite. A black, orthorhombic mineral.

ailanthic acid. A bitter, nitrogenous acid from the bark of *Ailanthus excelsa,* "tree of heaven" (Simarubaceae).

air. The mixture of gases that forms the earth's atmosphere, q.v. **alkaline-** Ammonia. **azotic-** Nitrogen. **dephlogisticated-** Oxygen (obsolete). **enriched-** A. to which oxygen has been added. **expired-** Warm a. coming from the lungs having less oxygen and more carbon dioxide and moisture than normal a. **fixed-** Carbon dioxide (obsolete). **inspired-** A. which is taken into the lungs. **liquid-** A clear liquid obtained by alternate compression and expansion of refrigerated a., b.-181. Used commercially for manufacturing oxygen, in the production of low temperatures, and as an external cure for poison ivy or poison oak inflammations. **mephitic-** Carbon dioxide (obsolete). **phlogisticated-** A. from which oxygen has been removed by a burning substance (obsolete). **reserve-** A. that can still be exhaled after an ordinary expiration. **residual-** (1) A. that remains in the lungs after the most complete expiration possible. (2) A. that remains in an evacuated container, e.g., an incandescent lamp bulb. **tidal-** A. taken in and given out at each respiration. **vital-** Oxygen.

a. bath. A drying oven utilizing a current of heated air for maintaining a desired temperature.

a. compressor. A pump which compresses the atmosphere. **a. conditioning.** The control of humidity and temperature of air by filtering and washing with water of definite temperature, either for human comfort (45–55% humidity) or for industries (viscose, paper). **a. dry.** To expose to air without heating. **a. gas.** Producer gas. **a. liquefying apparatus.** An arrangement of high-pressure pump, valves, and expansion orifices for the liquefaction of air. **a. meter.** Anemometer. **a. pump.** A mechanical device to compress or withdraw air, e.g., blowers, vacuum pumps. **a. proof.** Hermetically sealed, or gastight. **a. salt.** An early term for the efflorescence of bricks. **a. sampler.** A device to take samples of dust and bacteria from air. **a. showers.** Showers, mainly of electrons and protons, with some more penetrating particles, which occur in the air.

airofmor. Airol.

Airol. Trademark for a bismuth oxyiodide–subgallate compound used as a local antiseptic.

airosol. Aerosol.

ajacine. $C_{15}H_{21}O_4N = 279.17$. An alkaloid, m.143, from larkspur, *Delphinium ajacis*. **a. hydrochloride.** $C_{15}H_{21}O_4N \cdot HCl = 315.64$. Colorless crystals, m.93, soluble in water.

ajakol, ajacol. Thanatol.

ajava. The ripe fruit of *Ammi* or *Carum copticum*, (Umbelliferae) of India; a carminative.

Ajax metal. A bearing alloy: Ni 25–50, Fe 30–70, Cu 5–20%.

ajmaline. $C_{20}H_{26}O_2N_2 = 326.22$. An alkaloid from the roots of *Rauwolfia serpentina*.

ajowan. Ajava. **a. oil.** The essential oil from the seeds of *Carum copticum*, ajava. It resembles caraway seed oil, d.0.900–0.930, $[\alpha]_D + 1.3$; contains thymol and cymene.

akazgine. An alkaloid from the bark and leaves of African *Strychnos akazga* (Loganiaceae). Colorless crystals resembling strychnine in therapeutic effect.

akcethin. Thioacetin.

akee oil. A nondrying, yellow fat from *Blighia sapida* (Sapindaceae) from Jamaica.

åkermanite. $2CaO \cdot MgO \cdot 2SiO_2$. A melilite.

akuammine. $C_{22}H_{28}O_4N_2 = 382.23$. An alkaloid from the seeds of *Picralima kleineana* (Apocynaceae) of Gaboon. Cf. *ditaine*.

Akulon. Trade name for a polyamide synthetic fiber.

akund. See *Calotropis* floss.

akundarol. $C_{38}H_{61}O \cdot OH = 550.5$. A sterol from akanda, *Calotropis gigantea* (Asclepiadaceae). Cf. *calotropin*.

Al. (1) Symbol for aluminum. (2) Alkyl radical.

-al. Suffix indicating an aldehyde structure.

A.L.63. An antilouse powder containing naphthalene 50, rotenone (derris root) 1, high-boiling tar acids 2, kaolin 47%.

alabamine. Ab. Ekaiodine. The original name for astatine, element 85 discovered in monazites and by the magneto-optic method by Allison et al. (1931); a homotope of iodine. Cf. *anglohelvetium*.

alabandite. MnS. Manganblende. A black, isometric, native sulfide.

alabaster. $CaSO_4 \cdot 2H_2O$. A fine-grained, colorless, compact gypsum. See *selenite*.

alabastrine. Naphthalene.

alacreatine. $C_4H_9O_2N_3 = 131.2$. Lactylguanidine. Guanidopropionic acid. An isomer of creatine, formed by the union of alanine and cyanamide.

alamandite. Almandite.

alangine. An alkaloid from the bark of *Alangium lamarckii* (Cornaceae) of India; a febrifuge and emetic.

alanine. $C_3H_7O_2N = 89.08$. α-Aminopropionic acid, lactamine, 2-aminopropanoic acid*. White crystals, **dl-** or **i-.** m.295. **d-** m.297, **l-** 295 (subl, 200), soluble in water. Synthesized from acetaldehyde, ammonia, and hydrochloric acid; a constituent of many proteins. See *polypeptides*. Stereoisomers:

levo-   dextro-

β- or **beta-** 3-Aminopropanoic acid*. **benzoyl-** $PhCONH \cdot CHMe \cdot COOH = 193.09$. α-Benzamidopropionic acid. Colorless crystals, m.163. **dithiobis-** Cystine. **hydroxy-** Serine. **hydroxyphenyl-** Tyrosine. **imidazolyl-** Histidine. **indyl-** Tryptophan. **mercapto-** Cysteine. **phenyl-** Phenylalanine. **salicyl-** *o*-Tyrosine. **sulfo-** Cysteic acid.

alant acid anhydride. See *helenin*. **a. camphor.** Helenin. **a. root.** Inula. **a. starch.** Inulin.

alantic acid. $C_{15}H_{22}O_3 = 250.2$. Inulic acid. A monobasic acid from the roots of *Inula elecampane*. **a. anhydride.** $C_{15}H_{20}O_2 = 232.2$. Colorless crystals or incrustation from the roots of *Inula elecampane*.

alantin. Inulin.

alantol. $C_{10}H_{16}O = 152.1$. Pinguin. Yellow oil, b.200, soluble in alcohol, obtained from the roots of *Inula elecampane*; an internal antiseptic.

alantolactone. See *helenin*.

alanyl. (1) The radical $Me \cdot CHNH_2 \cdot CO-$. (2) The radical $-NH \cdot CHMe \cdot CO-$, from alanine. **a. alanine.** $C_6H_{12}N_2O_3 = 160.11$. A dipeptide. White needles, m.276, slightly soluble in water.

alaskite. An igneous rhyolite-granite rock containing quartz and feldspar (aplite).

alaskose. A rhyolite containing phenocrysts of quartz and feldspar.

Alastra. Trade name for a viscose fiber.

alaterite. Mineral caoutchouc.

albahaca oil. See *tolu* oil.

albamine. Alabamine.

albane. $C_{10}H_{16}O = 152.1$. A crystalline resin obtained by boiling gutta-percha in alcohol.

albanose. A leucitic rock containing melilite, diopside, and magnetite.

albargin. Silver gelatose. A colloidal silver preparation used medicinally.

albarium. A white lime obtained by burning marble; used for stucco.

albaspidin. $C_{25}H_{32}O_8 = 460.2$. A crystalline principle in *Aspidium*, resembling *albopannin*.

albata. Nickel silver. White alloy of Cu, Ni, and Zn.

albedo. The degree of whiteness of a reflecting surface, expressed as the ratio of the reflected light to the incident light: e.g.,

Black velvet	0.004
Moist earth	0.08
Blue paper	0.26
Pinewood	0.40
White paper	0.60
Snow	0.78

Cf. *brightness*.

Albene. (1) Trade name for a cellulose fiber. (2) (not cap.) An insoluble white precipitate obtained by boiling melam in water.

alberene. A fine grade of soapstone used for electrical insulation.

albertite. Albert coal. A black, brittle, asphaltum-like hydrocarbon with conchoidal fracture, d.1.1; a fuel.

Albertol. Trade name for a phenolformaldehyde plastic. Cf. *Bakelite*.

Albertus, Magnus. 1203–1280. Albrecht Graf von Bollstädt. German alchemist noted for his writings.

albite. $NaAlSi_3O_8$. Pericline. A white, triclinic soda-feldspar common in granite and other rocks, d.2.605, hardness 6–6.5, mol. vol. 101.1. Cf. *anemonsite*.

albocarbon. Naphthalene.

alboferrin. Phosphoalbuminate of iron. Brown powder; a ferruginous tonic.

Albolene. A brand of medicinal Russian mineral oil. Cf. *petrolatum*.

albopannin. $C_{21}H_{24}O_7 = 388.2$. White needles, m.147, from the rhizome of *Aspidium*, male fern.

albumate. Albuminate. **tannin-** Tannalbin.

albumen. White of egg. The liquid white of fresh eggs; chiefly albumin.

albumin. (1) $C_{72}H_{112}N_{18}O_{22}S$. A protein in the white of egg, blood, lymph, chyle, and many other animal and vegetable tissues and fluids, soluble in water, coagulates on heating, and hydrolyzes to amino acids; white or yellow scales. (2) A simple protein, q.v., insoluble in pure water or dilute salt solution and coagulable by heat. Cf. *globulin*. **blood-** Serum a. A. prepared from blood and used to manufacture photographic papers, in textile printing, the leather industry, and as a clarifying agent. **egg-** Ovalbumin. A. prepared from eggs, used in foodstuffs and as a clarifying agent. **milk-** Whey albumin. A. prepared from milk by coagulating the casein, used in the manufacture of adhesives, varnishes, and ivory substitutes. **nucleo-** See *nucleo*albumin. **osso-** A protein from ossein. **ov-** Egg a. **phospho-** An albuminous substance which contains phosphorus. **serum-** Blood a. **whey-** Milk a. **a. tannate.** Tannalbin.

albuminate. A compound of albumin with another substance (often basic); as, metals, creosote, quinine, tannin. **acid-** A meta protein soluble in weak alkali. **alkali-** A compound of albumin and alkali metals.

albuminoid. (1) Resembling albumin. (2) Scleroproteins. Simple proteins, insoluble in neutral solvents, e.g., gelatin.

albuminometer. A graduated glass tube for the quantitative determination of albumin in urine.

albuminose. A decomposition product of fibrin.

albuminuria. The presence of albumin in the urine, and the resulting pathological condition.

albumoscope. A U-shaped glass tube for the detection of albumin in urine. One arm is filled with nitric acid and the other with urine; at the point of contact a white ring forms.

albumose. A cleavage product of albumin formed during its hydrolysis. Cf. *artose*.

albumosease. An enzyme from the stomach secretions, which hydrolyzes albumin to albumose.

alburnitas. A disease of trees, which hinders the transformation of sapwood into hardwood.

alburnum. The sapwood of a tree.

alcahest. Alkahest.

alcamines. Alkamines.

alcapton. Alkapton.

alchemical. Pertaining to alchemy. **a. symbols.** See *alchemistic* symbols.

alchemistic period. About 300–1550 A.D. **a. symbols.** The characters or ideographs used by the alchemists. They indicate the relationship of astrological and alchemical speculations. See figure.

Alchemical and chemical symbols.

alchemy. The empirical stage of chemical knowledge, characterized by speculative theories. The chief aim of alchemy was the transmutation of base metals into gold, and the search for the alkahest or philosopher's stone which was supposed to confer eternal youth.

Alcian. Trade name for dyestuff onium salts, made by reacting a tertiary amine with the chloromethyl derivatives of insoluble phthalocyanine colors. Used in textile printing.

Alclad. Trademark for a strong, light aluminum alloy coated with pure aluminum to resist corrosion.

alcohol. (1) Ethanol, ethyl a. (2) See *alcohols.* **absolute-** See *ethanol*, 100%. **acetone-** See *acetol.* **allyl-** See *allyl alcohol.* **amyl-** See *amyl alcohol.* **benzyl-** See *benzyl alcohol.* **butyl-** See *butanol.* **butyric-** See *butanol.* **capryl-** See *octyl alcohol.* **cetyl-** See *cetyl alcohol.* **cinnamyl-** See *cinnamic alcohol.* **dehydrated-** See *ethanol*, 100%. **denatured-** See *ethanol.* **ethyl-** See *ethanol.* **ethylene-** See *glycol.* **ethylic-** See *ethanol.* **glycyl-** See *glycerol.* **grain-** See *ethanol*, 95%. **hexadecatylic-** See *cetyl alcohol.* **isobutyl-** See *isobutanol.* **isopentylic-** See *amyl alcohol.* **isopropyl-** See *isopropanol.* **methyl-** See *methanol.* **octoic-** See *caprylic alcohol.* **octylic-** See *caprylic alcohol.* **palmityl-** See *cetyl alcohol.* **phenylallyl-** See *cinnamic alcohol.* **solid-** A gelatinous mixture of ethanol with solid fatty acids or with soaps; a household fuel. **sulfur-** See *carbon disulfide.* **wood-** See *methanol.*

a. acid. Compounds containing the carboxyl and hydroxyl radicals. **a. aldehyde.** HO·R·CHO; as, aldol. **a. amide.** HO·R·CONH$_2$. Hydroxyamide; as, glycolamide. **a. amine.** HO·R·NH$_2$. Hydroxyamine; as, ethoxyamine. **a. ether.** R·O·-R·OH. Hydroxy ether; as, diethyline, Cellosolve. Cf. *lacquer.* **a. fuel.** A blend of ethyl, methyl, or butyl alcohol with benzol, petrol, acetone, and/or ether. **a. ketone.** R·CO·R·OH. Hydroxyketone; as, ketol. **a. phenols.** *ar*-Hydroxyphenols. Compounds containing hydroxy groups attached to both a ring and a side chain, as o-hydroxybenzyl a., salicyl a., C$_6$H$_4$OH·CH$_2$OH.

alcohol acids. Aliphatic, monohydroxy, monobasic acids; as, carbonic acid, hydroxyformic acid, HO·COOH. Aliphatic, dihydroxy, monobasic acids; as, glyoxylic acid, dihydroxyacetic acid, (HO)$_2$CH·COOH. Aliphatic, polyhydroxy, monobasic acids; as, erythric acid, CH$_2$OH(CHOH)$_2$-COOH. Aliphatic, monohydroxy, dibasic acids; as, tartronic acid, hydroxymalonic acid, HOOC·-CHOH·COOH. Aliphatic, dihydroxy, dibasic acids; as, tartaric acid, dihydroxysuccinic acid, HOOC·(CHOH)$_2$COOH. Aliphatic, polyhydroxy, dibasic acids; as, trihydroxyglutaric acid, HOOC(CHOH)$_3$COOH. Aliphatic, monohydroxy, tribasic acids; as, citric acid, (OH·COOH):C:-(CH$_2$:COOH)$_2$. Aromatic, monohydroxy, monobasic acids; as, mandelic acid, PhCHOHCOOH.

alcoholate. A compound derived from an alcohol by replacing the hydroxyl —H by a base; as, sodium ethylate, EtONa.

alcoholic. (1) Describing a preparation containing an alcohol (usually ethanol); as, a. extract. (2) Describing a reaction which forms an alcohol; e.g., a fermentation. (3) Dissolved in alcohol; as, a. potash.

alcoholometer. An apparatus for estimating the alcohol content of a liquid; e.g., a hydrometer.

alcohols. R·OH. Alkyloxides. Alkyl compounds containing a hydroxyl group. Classified according to: (1) relation of the carbon atom: primary a.,

R·CH$_2$OH; secondary a., R$_2$CHOH; tertiary a., R$_3$COH; (2) the number of OH groups; as,

		Prefix		Suffix
R·OH	mono-	-hydroxy		ol
R·(OH)$_2$	di-	-atomic		diol
R(OH)$_3$	tri-	-basic	a. or	triol
R(OH)$_4$	tetra-	-hydric		tetrol
R(OH)$_5$	penta-	-valent		pentol
R(OH)$_x$	poly-			—

See *aromatic alcohol, a. phenols,* and *a. acid.* **aldehyde-** A compound containing the —CHO and —OH groups. **aromatic-** A cyclic compound containing the —OH group in a side chain; cf. *phenols.* **diatomic-** or **dihydric-** An aliphatic compound containing 2 —OH groups. **hexatomic-** or **hexahydric-** An aliphatic compound containing 6 —OH groups derived from hexoses. **keto-** A compound containing the ═CO and —OH groups. **monatomic-, monobasic-,** or **monohydric-** A compound containing one —OH group. **nitrated-** A compound containing the —ONO$_2$ group. **pentatomic-, pentabasic-,** or **pentahydric-** A compound containing 5 —OH groups. **primary-** A compound containing the carbinol group, —CH$_2$-OH. **secondary-** A compound containing the ═CHOH group. **tertiary-** A compound containing the ≡COH group. **triatomic-, tribasic-,** or **trihydric-** A compound containing 3 —OH groups. **a. of crystallization.** The a. contained in a crystalline salt in a molecule; e.g., KOH·2C$_2$H$_6$O.

alcoholysis. The cleavage of a C—C bond by the addition of an alcohol: R·CH$_2$·R' + R''OH → R''OCH$_2$R + R'H. Cf. *hydrolysis.*

alcopol. Trade name for a surfactant of the dioctylsulfosuccinate type.

alcosol. A sol in alcohol.

alcumite. A corrosion-resistant alloy: Cu 88–90, Al 7.5, Fe 28.35, Ni 1%.

alcyl. Alicyclic. An aliphatic-cyclic radical; a saturated aromatic radical.

aldalcoketose. A carbohydrate containing the aldehyde (—CHO), alcohol (—OH), and ketone (═CO) radicals.

aldarsone. Phenarsone sulfoxylate; used to treat *Trichomonas vaginalis vaginitis* and syphilis.

aldebaranium. Ad. A rare-earth metal, isolated (1907) by Auer von Welsbach; identical with thulium, q.v.

aldehydase. An oxydase (cf. *enzymes*) which forms acids from aldehydes.

aldehyde. (1) Acetic a. or acetaldehyde. (2) See *aldehydes.* **acetic-** Acetaldehyde. **anisic-** Anisaldehyde. **cinnamic-** Cinnamaldehyde. **cuminic-** Cumic a. **heptylic-** Oenanthal. **meta-** Metaldehyde. **oenanthic-** Oenanthal. **para-** See *paraldehyde.* **propionic-** Propionic a. **pyromucic-** Furfural. **salicylic-** Salicylaldehyde.

a. ammonia. (1) A compound formed by the combination of an a. and ammonia. Crystalline, decomp. on warming with dilute acid; used for the purification of aldehydes. (2) (CH$_3$·CHO·NH$_3$)$_3$ = 183.24. Colorless crystals, m.70–80, soluble in water. **a. condensation.** See *aldol* condensation. **a. group.** The —CHO radical, in which the H is not replaceable by a positive radical, but can be replaced by negative atoms or groups. Cf. *alde-hydes*. **a. ketone.** R·CO·R·CHO. Ketoaldehyde.

aldehydene. Acetylene.

aldehydes. Organic compounds containing the —CHO radical, oxidized to acids and reduced to alcohols. A. are indicated by the prefix *oxo-*, *aldo-* (for O of CO), or *formyl-* (for CHO); or by the suffix *-al**, *-dial**, *-trial**, etc. **amido-** Compounds containing the amido and a. groups. **di-** Compounds containing 2 a. groups. **olefin-** Compounds containing a double bond and the a. group. **paraffin-** Compounds containing the a. group attached to a saturated aliphatic chain. **thio-** Compounds containing the —CHS group. **vitamin A-** Axerophthol.

aldehydic hydrogen. The H atom of the aldehyde group; not readily replaced by metals.

aldehydine. C_5H_3NMeEt = 121.14.   2-Ethyl-5-methylpyridine. Colorless liquid, d_{23}°0.9918, b.173, insoluble in water,

aldime. R—CH(:NH). An acid imide.

aldobionic acids. Oxidized trisaccharides; as, gluco-β-glycuronic acid, from the hydrolysis of flaxseed mucilage.

aldohexose. A hexose containing the aldehyde group; as glucose. Cf. *ketohexose, sugars*.

aldoketenes. RHC:CO. A group of homologs of ketene; see *ketoketene*. It comprises ketene, and monoalkylated derivatives of carbon suboxide.

aldol. Me·CHOH·CH$_2$·CHO = 88.08. (1) β-Hydroxy-butyric aldehyde, 3-hydroxybutanal*. A condensation product of acetaldehyde. Colorless liquid, d.1.109, soluble in hot water. Its solution leaves a polymer, paraldol, on evaporation; a hypnotic and sedative. Cf. *paraldehyde, metaldehyde, paraldol*. (2) One of a class of condensation products formed from an aldehyde.

a. condensation. The polymerization of an aldehyde in presence of dilute acid or alkali, e.g., aldol formation. The aldol polymer is stabler than the meta and para polymers. Three types: (1) true aldol condensation $R_2CO + H·CH_2·COR \rightarrow R_2C(OH)·CH_2·COR \rightarrow R_2C=CH·COR$. (2) Cannizzaro reaction: $2R·CHO \rightarrow R·COOCH_2·RR·COOCH_2R + H_2O \rightarrow R·COOH + R·CH_2OH$. (3) Claisen condensation: $2R·COOR' \rightarrow RC(OH):-CHCOOR' + R'OH$.

aldopentose. A pentose containing the aldehyde group; as, arabinose.

aldose. A carbohydrate containing the aldehyde group. Cf. *ketose, sugars*.

aldoxime. C_2H_5ON = 59.05. Acetaldoxime. Colorless liquid, b.115, soluble in water; used in organic synthesis. Isomeric forms:

N·OH   HO·N
‖   ‖
MeCH   MeCH

syn- or trans-   anti- or cis-

aldoximes. Organic compounds containing the —CHNOH or =C·NOH group. Stereoisomers:

HO·N   N·OH
‖   ‖
R·C·H·   R·C·H·

anti-   syn-

N·OH   N·OH   N·OR'   O—N·R'
‖   ‖   ‖   \ /
R'·C·R"   R"·C·R'   H·C·R"   H·C·R"

anti-C-   syn-C-   N-Alkyl-   O-Alky-
Alkyl-   Alkyl-   oximes   oximes
oximes   oximes

The alkyl is replaceable by the aryl radical.

aldrey. A noncorroding aluminum alloy, used for transmission lines: Mg 0.4, Si 0.6, Fe 0.3%.

aldrin. A chlorinated dimethanonaphthalene. White crystals, m.104; a pesticide.

alembic. (1) Ancient name for a retort. (2) Figuratively, anything that purifies.

aletris. False unicorn, starwort, blazing star, colic root, star grass, bitter grass, devil's bit. The dried rhizomes of *Aletris farinosa* (Hæmodoraceae) of the United States; a tonic. Cf. *helonoid*.

aletroid. Aletrin. A resinoid from the rhizome of *Aletris farinosa*; a uterine stimulant.

Aleurites. (1) The Chinese wood or tung oil plant. (2) A genus of trees (Euphorbiaceae) of the warmer zones of Asia which yield oil; as, *A. cordata*, tung oil.

aleuritic acid. $C_{16}H_{32}O_5$ = 304.3. A trihydroxy-palmitic acid, m.102, from the shellac of *Aleurites montana*.

aleurometer. A cylinder for testing the baking capacity of flour from the expansion of its gluten.

aleuronate. A vegetable protein food for diabetics; a tasteless, yellow powder. **a. powder.** Baked flour mixed with cooked starch for injection into the pleural cavity of animals (rabbits) to stimulate the production of leucocytes. Cf. *leucocyte* extract.

aleurone. Protein grains in the endosperm of ripe seeds.

Alexander tester. An apparatus to determine the gel strength of glue.

alexandrite. Al_2O_3·BeO. A green variety of chrysoberyl with red fluorescence.

alexandrolite. A clay containing chromium.

alexin. Complement, cytase. A defense protein in body fluids, leucocytes, and serum that partly destroys pathogenic microorganisms. It can combine with the antigen antibody. See *immunity, Ehrlich's theory, antilysin*.

alfa. Halfa. Local name for esparto grass, q.v., from Algeria and Tunisia.

alfalfa. Lucerne. The plant *Medicago sativa* (Leguminosae); a fodder.

alfalfone. $C_{21}H_{42}O$ = 310.3. A ketone from alfalfa.

alferric. Containing alumina and ferric oxide. **a. minerals.** Igneous rocks containing aluminum and iron; intermediate between the salic and femic groups.

alga. (Pl. algae.) Unicellular or polycellular plants (Thallophytae), a class of cryptograms, which live in fresh or salt water and are distinguished from fungi by the presence of chlorophyll and response to photosynthesis; as, seaweeds, kelps, agar-agar. Cf. *lichens*. Classification by color: Cyanophyceae (blue-green or fission a.), Phaeophyceae (brown), Chlorophyceae (green), Rhodophyceae (red), Bacillariophyceae (yellow a., diatoms). **calcareous-** A. containing calcium as *Lithothamnium*, whose skeletons consist of calcite 95, magnesite 5%. **siliceous-** Slimy ooze (Si 70%) formed on the seabed by diatoms, radiolarians, and algae skeletons. Cf. *oceanic* sediments.

algarites. The naturally occurring protobitumins formed during the acid hydrolysis of algae. They consist of algarose with metallic salts, sulfur, and nitrogen derivatives.

algaroba. Algarobilla. The sweet pods of *Prosopsis dulcis*, of S. America; used for tanning and to prepare a gum.

algarose. A protobitumen formed by acid hydrolysis of carbohydrates.

algaroth. Antimony oxychloride. White powder; a purgative and emetic.

Algil. Trade name for a mixed-polymer fiber.

algin. Alginic acid, norgine. A protein of marine algae, a by-product in the preparation of iodine from kelps, principally *Laminaria digitata*. Used as a fabric dressing, for thickening jellies, and in mucilages. **a. fiber.** $(C_6H_2O_6)_n$. Seaweed rayon. A polymer of d-mannuronic acid, mol. wt. 48,000–185,000.

Alginate. (1) Trade name for an algin synthetic fiber. (2) (not cap.) Any of the salts of algin, as sodium alginate; used as protective colloids, for thickening solutions, for forming films on drying, for textile dressing, and for synthetic fibers.

alginic acid. Algin.

algiron. Iron alginate; used to treat anemia.

algodonite. Cu_6As. A steel-gray native arsenide.

algorithmic. Describing the language used to express computation processes.

algulose. Almost pure cellulose obtained in the extraction of iodine from kelp.

alibate. To cover with a protective layer of aluminum.

alicyclic. Aliphatic-cyclic. The group of cyclic organic compounds derived from the corresponding aliphatic compounds by ring formation, and having a saturated ring; as, the cycloparaffins. **a. acids.** A group of acids whose molecules contain a saturated ring; as, cyclopropanecarboxylic acid, $CH_2 \cdot CH \cdot CH \cdot COOH$. **a. compound.** A compound containing a carbon ring whose properties are aliphatic rather than aromatic.

alignment chart. Nomograph.

aliphatic. Acyclic. Pertaining to an open-chain carbon compound; as, paraffins. Cf. *aromatic*, *alicyclic*. **a. acids.** Fatty acids. The organic acids derived from the a. hydrocarbons. See *acids*. **a. amino group.** The NH_2 radical, when attached to a chain. **a. amino group apparatus.** Van Slyke apparatus. **a. compounds.** See *organic* compounds. **a. hydrocarbon.** A compound of carbon and hydrogen having an open chain, as in the methane series. See *hydrocarbons, nomenclature, organic compounds*.

alipin. Alypine.

alipite. A nickel mineral containing silicates, magnesium, and free silica.

aliquot. A part which when multiplied makes a whole without leaving any remainder; thus 4 is an a. of 12, but 7 is not.

alismin. A principle extracted from *Alisma plantago*, the water plantain.

alite. $8CaO \cdot SiO_2Al_2O_3(?)$. The primary crystalline constituent of Portland cement clinker, also found native. Cf. *belite*.

alival. $CH_2I \cdot CHOH \cdot CH_2OH = 202.3$. Iodopropylene glycol. Colorless powder; an iodoform substitute.

alizaramide. $C_6H_4 \cdot (CO)_2 \cdot C_6H_2 \cdot OH = 239.1$. Amidoxyanthraquinone, derived from alizarin by heating with ammonia water. Brown needles, sublime 150, insoluble in water.

alizarate. (1) A derivative of alizarin in which the H of both OH groups is replaced by a metal. Cf. *lake*. (2) Phthalate.

alizaric acid. Phthalic acid.

alizarin. $C_{14}H_8O_4 = 240.13$. Anthraquinonic acid, 1,2-dihydroxyanthraquinone.

$$C_6H_4 \begin{matrix} CO \\ \\ CO \end{matrix} C_6H_2 \begin{matrix} OH \\ \\ OH \end{matrix}$$

The red color of *Rubia tinctorium*, dyers' madder. Synthetically prepared from anthracene and the hydrolysis of ruberythric acid. Orange crystals, m.290, insoluble in cold water; used to dye fabrics and in the manufacture of dyestuffs; also as a reagent and indicator (alkalies—red, acids—yellow, changing at pH 9.5). **a. black.** Naphthazarine. A black a. dye, made by the reduction of α-dinitronaphthalene. **a. blue.** $C_{17}H_9O_4N = 291.1$. Anthracene blue. Brown-violet needles, m.270, soluble in alcohol. Blue coloring matter, dye and pH indicator (acids—green, alkalies—blue, changing at pH 12. **a. blue amide.** $C_{17}H_{10}O_3N_2 = 290.1$. Aminohydroxyanthraquinone quinoline. A derivative of a. blue in which one —OH is replaced by a NH_2 group; a dye. **a. bordeaux, a. brown.** See *a.* dyes. **a. carboxylic acid.** $C_{14}H_7O_4 \cdot COOH = 284.14$. 2-Carboxyl a. Red triclinic crystals, m.305, soluble in water; used to manufacture dyestuffs. **a. carmine.** Sodium a. sulfonate. **a. dyes.** Dyes derived from anthraquinone (see table); used as sodium salts of their sulfonic acids. **a. red.**

ALIZARIN DYES (ANTHRAQUINONES)

Alizarin	1,2-Dihydroxyanthraquinone
Quinizarin	1,4-Dihydroxyanthraquinone
Anthrarufin	1,5-Dihydroxyanthraquinone
Chrysazin	1,8-Dihydroxyanthraquinone
Anthraflavin	2,6-Dihydroxyanthraquinone
Anthragallol	1,2,3-Trihydroxyanthraquinone
Purpurin	1,2,4-Trihydroxyanthraquinone
Quinalizarin	1,2,5,8-Tetrahydroxyanthraquinone
Alizarin cyanin	1,2,4,5,8-Pentahydroxyanthraquinone
Alizarin brown (anthragallol)	1,2,3-Trihydroxyanthraquinone

Sodium sulfalizarate, a. sodium monosulfonate. Brown powder, soluble in water; an indicator for titrating acids (yellow) and bases (red); changes at pH 5.5. **a. sulfonate.** Any salt of a. sulfonic acid. **a. sulfonic acid.** $C_{14}H_7O_4 \cdot SO_3H = 320.1$. 1,2-Dihydroxy-7-sulfonic anthraquinone. Orange crystals, soluble in water; used to manufacture dyes. **a. yellow.** Sodium p-nitraniline salicylate. An indicator changing at pH 11.1 from yellow (acid) to purple (basic).

alizarinic acid. Phthalic *acid*.

Alk. Abbreviation for: (1) alkaloid, (2) alkyl.

alkahest. See *alchemy*.

alkalamides. Organic compounds derived from ammonia by replacing H atoms by acid or basic radicals.

alkalescent. Slightly alkaline.

alkali. [Pl. alkalies (U.S.), alkalis (U.K.).] Usually a hydroxide of lithium, sodium, potassium, rubidium or cesium; but also the carbonates of these metals and ammonia, and the amines. **mineral-** An inorganic base. **vegetable-** An organic base. **volatile-** Ammonia.
    a. albuminate. A compound of albumin and an alkali metal. A water-soluble, alkaline powder used for culture media. **a. blue.** The sodium salt of a triphenylrosanilinesulfonic acid, used as indicator, changing at pH 12.5 from blue (acid) to red (basic), and in dyeing wool. **a. cell.** See *photoelectric* cell. **a. earth metals.** The elements Ca, Sr, Ba of the second group in the periodic system. **a. earths.** The oxides of Ca and Ba (lime, baryta). **a. metals.** The elements of the first group of the periodic system: Li, Na, K, Rb, Cs. All are strongly electropositive, have a low specific gravity and melting point, are silver-white and ductile, and react vigorously with water, liberating hydrogen and forming hydroxides. **a. metaprotein.** A protein cleavage product, soluble in alkalies. **a. reaction.** Basic reaction. See *alkaline* reaction. **a. series.** See *quantum* numbers. **a. waste.** Waste calcium sulfide from the LeBlanc process.

alkalimeter. An apparatus to determine carbon dioxide in carbonates, e.g., Schrötter's apparatus.

alkaline. Producing hydroxyl ions in an aqueous solution; as, any base. **a. reaction.** The color changes caused by alkalies, or the hydroxyl ion; as, red litmus turning blue, colorless phenolphthalein turning red. See *indicators*. **a. solution.** A solution containing more hydroxyl ions than hydrogen ions. See *hydrogen-ion* concentration. **a. tide.** The reduced acidity of tissue fluids and urine which follows eating.

alkalinity. Having an excess of hydroxyl ions in aqueous solution. Cf. *bases, acidity, hydrogen ion*.

alkalize. To make alkaline or basic. Antonym: acidify.

alkaloid. An organic nitrogenous base. Many a. of great medical importance occur in the animal and vegetable kingdoms, and some have been synthesized. **acylindole-** A. from apocyanaceous plants (genus *Tabernaemontana*), derived from tetracyclic 2-acylindoles; as, vobasine. **animal-** A base derived from animals; as, xanthine. **cadaveric-** A cleavage product from putrefaction of animal tissues; as, betaine. See *ptomaines*. **putrefactive-** Cadaveric a. **vegetable-** An a. from vegetable tissues.

alkaloidal. Pertaining to alkaloids.

alkalometry. (1) The medication of alkaloids for therapeutic purposes. (2) The determination of alkaloids.

alkamine. Amino alcohol. An organic compound containing the amino and alcohol groups. **a. ester.** An organic compound formed by the esterification of an acid with an alcohol containing the amino group.

alkanes. Alkynes (preferred term). A group of aliphatic hydrocarbons, C_nH_{2n+2}. Cf. *methane series*.

alkanet. Alkanna root. The root of *Alkanna tinctoria* (Boraginaceae); a red coloring for oils or fats.

alkanization. The combination of isobutane and butenes from petroleum, in presence of sulfuric acid, to form isooctane and trimethylbutene.

alkannin. $C_{15}H_{14}O_4 = 258.19$. Anchusin. Red powder, softening at 100, insoluble in water. A color for fats or oils, and an indicator. **a. extract.** Extract alkanet. A crude a. **a. paper.** Boettger's paper. A filter paper stained with a. and used as

CHEMICAL CLASSIFICATION OF ALKALOIDS

	Derivatives of	Example	Occurring in
1.	Pyridine	Piperine	Pepper
		Coniine, trigonelline	Hemlock
		Arecoline, arecaidine	Arecanut
		Nicotine	Tobacco
2.	Pyrrolidine	Atropine, hyoscyamine, sparteine	Solanaceae
		Cocaine	Coca leaves
3.	Quinoline	Quinine, cinchonine, quinidine, cinchonidine	Cinchona
		Strychnine, brucine	Nux vomica
4.	Isoquinoline	Papaverine, morphine, codeine, thebaine	Morphium
		Narcotine, hydrastine	Hydrastis
		Laudanosine	Opium
5.	Purine	Caffeine, theobromine, xanthine	Coffee, tea, beets
6.	Glyoxaline	Pilocarpine, ergotoxine, ergometrine	Jaborandus, ergot
7.	Amines	Asparagine, leucine, betaine, choline	
8.	Glucosides	Solanine	
9.	Unknown constitution	Aconitine, veratrine, yohimbine	

See also *aconite, Areca, opium, quinine, Solanaceae, spartium* and *staphisagrine* alkaloids.

a test for alkalies (green), carbonates (blue), and acids (red).

Alkanol. Trademark for a group of wetting agents.

alkanolamine. Alkylolamide.

alkapton. $C_6H_4(OH)_2$. A protein decomposition product found in the urine as crystals (alkaptonuria) or cerebrospinal fluid. Cf. *homogentisic acid.*

alkargen. Cacodylic acid.

alkarsin. A mixture of cacodyl and its oxidation products.

alkasal. A mixture of aluminum salicylate and potassium acetate.

Alkathene. Trademark for a polyethylene plastic.

alkazid process. The removal of sulfur dioxide from coal gas by absorption in cold α-aminopropionic acid solution, and subsequent liberation by heat as a source of sulfur. Cf. *Thylox.*

alkenes. C_nH_{2n}. Aliphatic unsaturated hydrocarbons; cf. *ethylene series.*

alkenyl. An unsaturated, univalent aliphatic radical.

alkines. C_nH_{2n-2}. Aliphatic, unsaturated hydrocarbons which contain triple bonds; the *acetylene series*, q.v.

Alkon. Trade name for an acetal copolymer proposed to replace metals.

alkone. C_nH_{2n-4}. See *hydrocarbon series.*

alkoxides. Organic compounds in which the H of the hydroxyl group is replaced by a metal; as, in alcoholates.

alkoxy. An alkyl radical attached to the remainder of the molecule by oxygen; as, methoxy.

alkyd resins. A group of adhesive resins made from unsaturated acids (phthalic anhydride) and glycerol; protective and decorative coatings and bonding materials.

alkyl. C_nH_{2n+1}—. Alphyl, aphyl. A monovalent radical derived from an aliphatic hydrocarbon by removal of 1 H; as, methyl-. Cf. *alkyle, alkylene.* **a. halide.** $R·Cl.$ **a. nitrite.** $R·NO_2.$ **a. oxide.** See *ethers.* **a. sulfide.** See **mercaptan.**

alkylamine. An amine-containing alkyl group attached to aminonitrogen.

alkylation. Substitution of an aliphatic hydrocarbon radical for a H atom in a cyclic compound; as, the introduction of a side chain into an aromatic compound. **acid-** or **hot-** Introducing the alkyl into the amino or hydroxy group by heating under pressure with alcohol in presence of mineral acid. **basic-** or **cold-** Treatment with alkyl sulfate in presence of sodium hydroxide.

alkylbenzaldoxime. Compounds derived from benzaldoxime by replacing a hydrogen atom of the aldoxime group by another radical; 4 series of isomeric compounds and 8 stereoisomers:

anti-C-Alkylbenzaldoxime . . . . PhCHON—R
syn-C-Alkylbenzaldoxime . . . . PhCHON—R
N-Alkylbenzaldoxime . . . . PhCHON—R
O-Alkylbenzaldoxime . . . . PhCHNO—R
Cf. *aldoxime.*

alkyle. (1) C_nH_{2n+1}. An unsaturated hydrocarbon. (2) Alkylide. A compound of a metal (Al, Pb, Hg, Zn, etc.) and an alkyl radical; as, tetraethyllead.

alkylene. C_nH_{2n}—. An organic radical derived from an unsaturated aliphatic hydrocarbon; as, ethylene-. **a. oxides.** (1) Alcohol ethers. The aliphatic compounds that contain both the carbinol and ether groups; as, diethyline. (2) Epihydrins. Alicyclic compounds which are the inner anhydrides (ethers) of glycols; as, ethylene oxide.

alkyl halides. $C_nH_{2n+1}X$. Alkylogen. A combination of an alkyl and halogen grouping.

alkylide. See *alkyle* (2).

alkylidene. C_nH_{2n}—. A divalent organic radical derived from an aliphatic hydrocarbon; as, ethylidene, in which 2 H atoms are taken from the same C atom.

alkylogens. Alkyl halides.

alkylolamide (-ine). Alkanolamine. A compound of an amide and an alkyl group; in particular, ethanol amines and lauric or coconut fatty acids. The di-a. are stabilizers in liquid detergents.

alkyls. See (1) *alkyl*, (2) *alkyle.*

alkynes. Preferred term for *alkanes.*

allanic acid. $C_4H_5O_5N_5 = 203.2$. A monobasic crystalline acid obtained by the oxidation of allantoin with nitric acid.

allanite. Bagrationite. Orthite. A dark monoclinic orthite of the zoisite group which resembles epidote, in which a rare-earth metal partly replaces the aluminum and iron.

allantal. Sheet aluminum coated with an Al-Cu alloy.

allantoic acid. $(NH_2CONH)_2CHCOOH = 176.2$. Dicarbamidoacetic acid. A crystalline monobasic acid obtained by boiling allantoin in alkaline solution.

allantoin. $C_4H_6O_3N_4 = 158.11$. Glyoxyl diureide. Glyoxuric acid diureide. Colorless crystals, m.227 (decomp.), soluble in hot water. Produced by the oxidation of uric acid and widely distributed in nature (urine of animals, seeds and roots of plants). It hastens epithelial formation.

allantoxanic acid. $C_3H_3O_4N = 117.0$ Colorless crystals obtained by the action of potassium ferricyanide on allantoin.

allanturic acid. $NH·CO·NH·(CO)·CHOH = 116.1$. Glyoxalylurea. A pentacyclic, heterocyclic compound. On reduction and hydrolysis it yields hydantoin, hydantoic acid, and finally glycine and ammonium carbonate.

allelomorph. (1) One of a mixture of isomers in a solution which will first separate or crystallize out. (2) One of the many character units existing in the germ plasm of hybrids which may appear in their offspring.

allelomorphism. Desmotropism.

allelotrope. A member of a system of 2 isomeric or desmotropic substances in equilibrium.

allelotropism. The existence of 2 isomeric or desmotropic substances in an unstable equilibrium, so that either rearrangement of the atoms may occur.

allemontite. $SbAs_3$. A rhombohedric, gray or reddish native arsenide.

allene. Propadiene*. **ethyl-** 1,2-Pentadiene*. **methyl-** 1,2-Butadiene*.

Allen's test. A modification of Fehling's test for sugar in urine.

allergen. Anaphylactin. A toxic substance which causes anaphylaxis.

allergia. The hypersensitivity of an organism to a later reinjection of the same serum. Cf. *anaphylaxis.*

allergic protein. An extract prepared from a vegetable or animal substance, used for diagnosis or desensitization; e.g., pollen extract in hay fever.

allergy. The hypersusceptibility or increased resistance of an organism to a certain antigen.

allethrin. A synthetic allyl homologue of cinerin, q.v.; an insecticide, similar to, but more efficient than, pyrethrin.

allicine. $C_6H_{10}OS_2 = 162.42$. A water-soluble oil; the principal antibacterial constituent of onion oil.

alligation. If two substances when mixed retain their specific values (A and B) of a property, the value for the mixture can be calculated from the formula $(aA + bB)/(a + b)$, where a and b are the proportions. Cf. *additive*.

Allihn condenser. A condenser with a condensing surface of glass bulbs.

Allium. A genus of plants (Liliaceae) which contain a pungent, volatile oil (allyl sulfide). Their bulbs are used as a food, condiment, and aid to digestion; as, *A. cepa* (common onion), *A. porrum* (leek), *A. sativum* (garlic).

allo- Prefix (Greek "other") applied to the stabler form of 2 isomers.

allochroite. A green to black manganese garnet, q.v.

allochromy. A phosphorescence or radiation effect, q.v., in which the wavelength of the emitted light differs from that of the incident light.

allocinnamic acid. $C_9H_8O_2 = 148.11$. White crystals; 3 allotropic forms, m.42, 58, and 68.

alloclasite. A steel-gray sulfide of cobalt, bismuth, and arsenic with some iron.

allocyanine. Neocyanine.

alloisomerism. Stereoisomerism.

allomaleic acid. Fumaric acid.

allomerism. Similarity of crystalline form with a difference of chemical composition.

allomerization. The dehydrogenation of chlorophyll in alcoholic solution by the action of atmospheric oxygen.

allomorphism. Similarity of chemical composition but difference in crystalline form, especially of minerals; as, $CaCO_3$ in calcite and aragonite.

allomucic acid. $HOOC(CHOH)_4COOH = 200.1$. An optically inactive acid derived from d- and l-allose, m.166–171, soluble in hot water.

Allonal. $C_{10}H_{14}O_3N_2 = 210.12$. Trademark for 5-allyl-5-isopropylbarbiturate of phenyldimethyldimethylaminopyrazolon; a soporific. Cf. *barbital*.

allopalladium. See *palladium*.

allophanamide. Biuret.

allophane. $Al_2SiO_5 \cdot 4H_2O$. An amorphous, native hydrated calcium silicate from Grafenthäl, Germany.

allophanic acid. $NH_2 \cdot CONH \cdot COOH = 104.1$. Ureacarbonic acid, carbamyl carbamic acid. A hypothetical acid known as its esters. **a. amide.** Biuret.

allose. $C_6H_{12}O_6 = 180.15$. A synthetic hexose, isomeric with glucose.

allotelluric acid. See *telluric acid* (anhydrous).

allotoxin. A substance formed by living tissue, which tends to counteract the toxic effect of bacteria.

allotrope. One of two or more isomeric forms of an element; as, red and white phosphorus.

allotropic. Occurring in 2 or more isomeric forms; e.g., carbon as graphite, diamond, or charcoal.

a. modification. Allotrope.

allotropism. Allotropy.

allotropy. Allotropism. A change in the properties of an element without a change of state, q.v.; isomerism of a chemical element which occurs in different amorphous and crystalline forms; as, with sulfur. Cf. *monotropy*, *pseudomonotropy*. **dynamic-** Tautomerism.

alloxan. $CO(NH \cdot CO)_2 \cdot CO = 142.1$. Mesoxalylurea, pyrimidinetetrone, "erythric acid" (Brugnatelli). Two crystalline forms: 1 mole H_2O, small, colorless crystals; 4 moles H_2O, large, colorless, efflorescent prisms; decomp. 170, soluble in water. It appears in the intestinal mucus during diarrhea. **oxime-** Violuric acid.

alloxanic acid. $NH_2 \cdot CO \cdot NH \cdot CO \cdot CO \cdot COOH = 160.1$ Tetrahydro-4-hydroxy-2,5-diketo-4-imidazolecarboxylic acid. Colorless crystals obtained from alloxan by treatment with alkalies; decomp. by heat.

alloxanthin. Alloxantin.

alloxantin. $C_8H_4O_7N_4 = 286.2$. A purine base. Colorless prisms or rhombs, soluble in water. **tetramethyl-** Amalinic acid.

alloxazin. $C_{10}H_6N_4O_2 = 214.12$. A heterocyclic compound in some plant pigments. **iso-** Flavin.

alloxuric bodies. Purine bases.

alloy. A mixture of two or more metallic elements (or nonmetals, as C, Te, P) which has a metallic appearance and which is either:

1. A molecular mixture, microscopically homogeneous; as,

(a) A solid solution of A in B or B in A, in which case the properties are intermediate between those of A and B; or

(b) A metallic compound, A_xB_y, with properties differing from A and B; or

(c) A combination of (a) and (b); as, A in A_xB_y.

2. A colloidal mixture, microscopically heterogeneous; as, two or more phases consisting of crystals:

(d) of metallic elements, $[A] + [B]$

(e) of metallic compounds, $[A_xB_y] + [AB_z]$

(f) of solid solutions $[A \text{ in } B] + [B \text{ in } A]$

(g) of combinations of d, e, and f; as, $[A] + [A_xB_y] + [A \text{ in } B]$, etc. Generally the m. of an alloy is lower than that of its highest-melting constituent. A. are usually described in terms of their constituents, in decreasing order of amounts present, as Heusler's a., q.v., as a copper-manganese-aluminum a. Cf. *intermediate compounds*.

antifriction- A. which are sufficiently plastic to fit themselves to the shape of a shaft; usually Sn or Pb alloyed with Cu or Sb. **coinage-** A. used for coins. Cf. *gold a.*, *silver a.* **eutectic-** An a. which has the lowest constant melting point; i.e., whose constituents are present in such proportions that it solidifies completely at the *eutectic* temperature, q.v. **fusible.** Low-fusing a. **heavy-** An a. of W 90, Ni 7.5, Cu 2.5%. It has a high density (16.5–17.0 gm/ml) and tensile strength equal to that of steel. **Heussler's-** A nonferrous magnetic a. which contains nonmagnetic metals; as, Cu 60, Mn 20, Al 14 pts. **light-** An a. containing Al as distinct from Mg. Cf. *ultralight a.* **low-** An a. containing a large proportion of one constituent. **low-fusing-** Fusible a. An a. melting below the m. of tin. The lowest-melting a. (15°C) consists of Ga 88, Sn 12%. Others are: Newton's, Bi 8, Pb 5, Sn 3% (m.94); Lipowitz's, Bi 5, Pb 2.7, Sn 1.3, Cd 1.0% (m.65). Cf. *D'Arcet* metal a., *Wood's* a., *Rose* metal. **master-** An a. containing a known amount of a particular metal, used instead of the pure metal for making alloys. **mercury-** Amalgam. **pyrophoric-** Fe–Ce a. which spark when rubbed with a file. **ultralight-** An a. containing magnesium, as distinct from aluminum. Cf. *light* a.

alloying. To produce an alloy.

allspice. Pimenta.

allulose. $CH_2OH \cdot CO \cdot (CHOH)_3 \cdot CH_2OH = 180.0$. *d*-Ribo-2-ketohexose, *d*-piscose. An epimer of *d*-fructose. A reducing, nonfermentable constituent of cane-sugar molasses, cf. *glutose*.

alluvium. The deposit carried down by a river.

allyl. The radical $—C_3H_5$. α- or Δ^2- $—CH_2 \cdot CH:CH_2$, β- or Δ^1-iso-, (propenyl), $—C(CH_3):CH_2$. γ- or Δ^1-, (isopropenyl), $—CH:CH \cdot CH_3$. **a. acetate.** $MeCOOC_3H_5 = 100.09$. Colorless liquid, b.103, slightly soluble in water. **a. acetic acid.** $C_3H_5 \cdot CH_2 \cdot COOH = 100.09$. Colorless liquid, b.187, slightly soluble in water. **a. acetone.** $C_3H_5 \cdot CH_2 \cdot CO \cdot CH_3 = 98.11$. Colorless liquid, b.129, insoluble in water. **a. acetonitrile.** $C_3H_5CH_2CN = 81.09$. Colorless liquid, b.140, insoluble in water. **a. alcohol.** $CH_2:CH \cdot CH_2OH = 58.06$. Propenol, propenyl alcohol. Colorless liquid, b.96, insoluble in water. Used in organic synthesis, in chemical warfare; an antiseptic. **a. aldehyde.** Acrolein. **a. amine.** $CH_2:CH \cdot CH_2NH_2 = 57.08$. 2-Propenylamine*. Yellow oil, b.53, miscible with water; prepared from mustard oil. *methyl-* $C_3H_5 \cdot NH \cdot CH_3 = 71.10$. Colorless liquid, b.65, miscible with water. *phenyl-* Allylaniline. **a. aniline.** $C_3H_5 \cdot NH \cdot C_6H_5 = 133.14$. Phenylallylamine. Colorless liquid, b.208, slightly soluble in water. **a. benzene.** $CH_3 \cdot CH:CH \cdot C_6H_5 = 118.13$. **n-,** Phenylallylene. Colorless liquid, b.160, soluble in alcohol. **iso-** Benzylethylene, $BzCH:CH_2$. Colorless liquid, b.155. **a. benzoate.** $C_6H_5 \cdot COOC_3H_5 = 162.13$. Colorless liquid, b.228. **a. bromide.** $CH_2:CH \cdot CH_2Br = 120.98$. Bromallylene. Colorless liquid, b.70, insoluble in water. **a. butyrate.** $CH_3(CH_2)_2COOC_3H_5 = 128.13$. Colorless liquid, b.142, miscible with alcohol. **a. carbinol.** $CH_2:CH \cdot CH_2 \cdot CH_2 \cdot OH = 72.1$. Colorless liquid. *methyl-* $CH_2:CH \cdot CH_2 \cdot CH(OH)CH_3 = 86.11$. Colorless liquid, b.115, soluble in water. **a. chloride.** $CH_2:CH \cdot CH_2Cl = 76.52$. Chlorallylene, 3-chloropropene*. Colorless liquid, b.46; insoluble in water. **a. cinnamate.** $C_6H_5 \cdot CH:CH \cdot COOC_3H_5 = 188.16$. Colorless crystals, b.285, insoluble in water. **a. cyanamide.** Sinamin. **a. cyanide.** $CH_2:CH \cdot CH_2CN = 67.07$. 3-Butanenitrile. A colorless liquid, b.119; soluble in alcohol. **a. disulfide.** $C_3H_5 \cdot S \cdot S \cdot C_3H_5 = 146.02$. Colorless liquid, b.138, in garlic. **a. ether.** $(CH_2:CH \cdot CH_2)_2O = 98.11$. Diallyloxide. Colorless liquid, b.94.3, slightly soluble in water. *methyl-* $CH_2:CH \cdot CH_2 \cdot O \cdot CH_3 = 72.08$. Colorless liquid, b.46, slightly soluble in water. **a. ethyl ether.** $C_3H_5 \cdot O \cdot C_2H_5 = 86.11$. A colorless liquid, b.64. **a. fluoride.** $CH_2:CH \cdot CH_2F = 60.04$. 3-Fluoropropene. Colorless gas, b.—10, slightly soluble in water. **a. formate.** $HCOOC_3H_5 = 86.07$. Colorless liquid, b.82, insoluble in water, soluble in alcohol. **a. iodide.**

$CH_2:CH \cdot CH_2I = 167.98$. 3-Iodopropene. Yellow liquid, b.101, insoluble in water. **a. isoamyl ether.** $C_3H_5 \cdot O \cdot C_5H_{11} = 128.17$. Allylisoamyl ether. Colorless liquid, b.120, slightly soluble in water. **a. isocyanide.** $CH_2:CH \cdot CH_2NC = 67.07$. Colorless liquid, b.100, slightly soluble in water. **a. isothiocyanate.** A mustard oil. **a. malonic acid.** $C_3H_5 \cdot CH:(COOH)_2 = 144.09$. Colorless crystals, m.103, (decomp.), soluble in water. **a. mercaptan.** $CH_2:CH \cdot CH_2SH = 74.12$. 2-Propene-2-thiol*. Yellow liquid, b.90, miscible with alcohol. **a. mustard oil.** $CH_2:CH \cdot CH_2NCS = 99.13$. A. isothiocyanate. Colorless liquid, b.151, slightly soluble in water. It occurs in mustard seeds (*Sinapis nigra*) as potassium myronate, q.v., combined in the form of glucoside, and in horseradish; a vesicant. **a. oxalate.** $(COOC_3H_5)_2 = 170.12$. Colorless liquid, b.217, insoluble in water. **a. phenylcinchonine ester.** Antiquinol. **a. phenyl ether.** $C_6H_5 \cdot O \cdot C_3H_5 = 134.13$. Colorless liquid, b.192, insoluble in water. **a. phenylmethyl ether.** Anethol. **a. phenylurea.** $Ph \cdot NH \cdot CO \cdot NH \cdot C_3H_5 = 176.16$. Colorless crystals, m.115. **a. pyridine.** $C_5H_4N \cdot C_3H_5 = 119.12$. Colorless liquid, b. 190. **a. pyrocatechol methylene ester.** Safrole. **a. sucrose.** A substance formed by the action of a. chloride with sucrose at 85°C. Used in heat-, water-, and grease-resistant coatings. **a. sulfhydrate.** A. mercaptan. **a. sulfide.** $(C_3H_5)_2S = 114.17$. 3-(2-Propenylthio)-propene*, 2-propenyl sulfide*, diallyl sulfide. Yellow liquid, b.138, slightly soluble in water; a constituent of garlic used medicinally. **a. sulfocarbamide.** $C_3H_5 \cdot NH \cdot CS \cdot NH_2 = 116.16$. A. thiourea. Colorless monoclinic crystals of garlic odor, m.74, soluble in water. Used to treat scar tissue, in photography, and as a reagent. Cf. *a. mustard oil.* **a. sulfocyanide.** $CH_2:CH \cdot CH_2SCN = 99.13$. A. thiocyanate. Colorless liquid, b.161, insoluble in water. **a. sulfourea.** A. sulfocarbamide. **a. thiocarbimide.** A. mustard oil. **a. thiocyanate.** A. sulfocyanide. **a. thioether.** A. sulfide. **a. thiourea.** A. sulfocarbamide. **a. tribromide.** $(CH_2Br)_2 \cdot CHBr = 280.9$. Tribromoallylene, 1,2,3-tribromopropane*. Colorless crystals or oil, m.18, b.219, soluble in alcohol; an antispasmodic and sedative. **a. trisulfide.** $(C_3H_5)_2S_3 = 178.26$. Diallyl trisulfide. Colorless liquid, b.140, insoluble in water.

allylene. $CH_3 \cdot C:CH = 40.05$. Propyne*, methyl acetylene. Colorless gas, b.— 24, soluble in ether. Cf. *propadiene*. **dimethyl-** Methylbutine. **methyl-** Butine. **phenyl-** See *phenylmethyl*acetylene. **a. dichloride.** $CH_3 \cdot CCl:CHCl = 110.97$. 1,2-Dichloropropene*, b.55. **a. oxide.** $(CH_3 \cdot C:CH)_2O = 56.05$. 1,2-Epoxypropene*. Colorless liquid, b.62, slightly soluble in water.

allylin. $CH_2:CH \cdot CH_2 \cdot O \cdot CH_2 \cdot CHOH \cdot CH_2OH = 132.1$. Allyloxyglycerol. Heavy liquid, b.230, formed on heating glycerol with oxalic acid.

almadina. Euphorbia gum.

almandine. Almandite.

almandite. (1) $Fe_3Al_2Si_3O_{12}$. Almandine. An isometric, red-brown to black garnet, d.3.9–4.2, mol. wt. 499.1, mol. vol. 118.0. (2) A violet variety of spinel, q.v.

Almen test. The detection of carbohydrates by the reduction of alkaline bismuth ions.

almond. The dried ripe seeds of *Prunus amygdalus*,

communis (Rosaceae) of S. Europe and California.
bitter- The seeds of variety *amara*, used in the manufacture of a. oil, amygdalin and for flavoring; **sweet-** The seeds of variety *dulcis*, used in the manufacture of oil.
    a. cake. Crude a. meal. **a. camphor.** Benzoin. **a. furnace.** A remelting furnace of the reverberatory type, q.v. **a. meal.** The residue remaining after the expression of oil from almonds; used in cosmetics, cooking, confectionery, and perfumes **a. oil.** *artificial-* Benzaldehyde. *artificial bitter-* Nitrobenzene. *bitter-* An oil obtained from bitter a. by maceration with water and distillation. Colorless liquid, d.1.045–1.060, b.180, soluble in water; a flavoring. *sweet-* An oil obtained by expressing sweet a. Yellow liquid, d.0.915–0.920, soluble in alcohol; a perfume, and a lubricant for delicate mechanisms. **bitter a. water.** A solution containing hydrocyanic acid, ammonium cyanide, and mandelic acid nitrile.

alneon. An alloy of Al with Zn (10–20%) and small amounts of Cu and Ni; used for castings.

alnuoid. An extract from the bark of *Alnus serrulata*, American alder; a tonic.

Alnus. Alnus bark. The astringent bark of the American alder, *A. serrulata* (Betulaceae); contains tannic acid.

alochrysine. $C_{15}H_8O_5 = 268.1$. An oxidation product of barbaloin, obtained with chromic acid.

aloe(s). (1) A genus of plants (Lilaceae); the juices are the aloes of commerce, and the fibers are used for cords and nets. (2) An extremely bitter, black, shining resin from the juice of the leaves of several a. species; a cathartic. **American-** Agave. **Barbados-** The resin from *A. vulgaris* of Jamaica and Barbados. **Cape-** The resin from *A. ferox* and other species of S. Africa; used in the manufacture of a brown dye. **hepatic-** The resin from *A. chinensis* and other species from the Dutch Indies. **Socotrine-** The resin from *A. perryi* from Socotra.   **a. emodin.** $C_{15}H_{10}O_5 = 270.1$. A crystalline constituent of aloes, cascara sagrada, frangula, and senna leaves. Yellow crystals, m.224; a cathartic.

aloeresic acid. $C_{30}H_{32}O_{14} = 616.3$. A yellow-brown, microcrystalline powder from Cape aloes.

aloetic acid. $C_{14}H_4O_{10}N_4 = 388.2$. Tetranitroanthraquinone. Orange powder obtained by treating aloin with nitric acid.

aloewood. Eaglewood, lignum, aloe. A fragrant resinous heartwood from *Aquilaria agallocha* (Asia). A tonic, stimulant, diuretic, incense, and perfume.

aloin. $C_{20}H_{18}O_9 = 402.14$. A neutral, bitter, purgative principle of aloes. Yellow prisms, m.147, soluble in water, named according to its origin: barbaloin, nataloin, etc.

Aloxite. Trademark for artificial aluminum oxide products made by fusing materials high in alumina (as bauxite). White to red crystals; used as abrasives, filters and refractories. Cf. *Alundum*.

alpaca. The long, silky, lustrous wool from the alpaca llama (*Auchenia paco*).

alpax. A light Al eutectic alloy with Si 13%; used for molding, as it has a low shrinkage.

alpha. α. First letter of the Greek alphabet. **a. acid.** 2,8-Naphthylaminesulfonic acid. **a. cellulose.** See *cellulose*. **a. derivatives.** (1) Substitution products of straight-chain compounds in which the substituting atom or radical is attached to the

same C atom as the principal group; e.g., α-hydroxypropionic acid, $CH_3 \cdot CHOH \cdot COOH$. (2) A substitution product of a polycyclic compound, in which the substituting atoms or radicals are attached to the C atom closest to the C atom shared by both rings; e.g., in naphthalene, the 1-, 4-, 5-, or 8-position. (3) Substitution products of heterocyclic compounds in which the substituting atom or radical is attached to the C atom closest to the heterocyclic atom; e.g. in pyridine, the 2- or 6-position. (4) The first of a series of derivatives to be discovered; no structural significance. (5) An even rotational quantum number; as, α-hydrogen (or para-H). (6) A stereoisomer of a sugar; as, α-glucoside. *Note.* For compounds beginning with *alpha-* see under the main heading. **a. flock.** Finely divided, purified wood cellulose; used as a filler for rubber. **a. particles.** Positively charged helium nuclei emitted from radioactive substances at 20,000 miles/sec. Their mass equals that of a helium atom; when their charge is neutralized by the capture of 2 negative electrons, they form helium atoms. Cf. *alphatopic* change. **a. position.** See a. derivatives. **a. rays.** A. particles.

alphatopic. Pertaining to 2 radioactive elements or isotopes which differ by an α particle and an atomic weight of 4.00. **a. change.** The spontaneous disintegration of certain radioactive elements in which an α particle is emitted and the element thereby moves 2 places lower in the periodic table. See *radioactive* elements.

alphazurine. An indicator changing at pH 6.0 from purple (acid) to green (alkaline), used to improve the end point of methyl red.

alphol. $C_{17}H_{12}O_3 = 264.09$. α-Naphthylsalicylate. White powder, m.83, insoluble in water; used medicinally. Cf. *betol*.

alphyl. Alkylphenyl. A radical having both aromatic and aliphatic structures; as, benzyl. Cf. *aralkyl*.

alpinin. $C_{17}H_{12}O_6 = 312.1$. A crystalline constituent of galangal, the rhizome of *Alpinia officinarum* (Zingiberaceae).

alquifou. Potters' lead. Black lead ore. A mineral zinc sulfide; produces a green pottery glaze.

Alsace gum. Dextrin.

alsol. Aluminum acetotartrate.

Alstonia. A genus of trees and herbs (Apocynaceae) of India and Malaya, which yield dita bark, q.v.

alstonine. $C_{21}H_{20}N_2O_4 \cdot 3\frac{1}{2}H_2O = 427.4$. Chlorogenine. An alkaloid from the bark of *Alstonia constricta* (Apocynaceae), of Asia. Colorless crystals, m.195, insoluble in water; an antipyretic and antiperiodic. Cf. *ditaine, porphyrine*.

alstonite. $BaCO_3 \cdot CaCO_3$. Neotype. Barytocalcite. Bromlite.

altaite. PbTe. Occurs native in tin ores as white isometric crystals (Central Asia).

Alter, David. 1807–1881. An American physician, discoverer of spectrum analysis.

alterative. A drug that stimulates the nutritive functions of the body.

alternaric acid. $C_{21}H_{30}O_8 = 410.27$. An antifungistatic substance from *Alternaria solani*, Ell.

alternating current. A.C. An electric, pulsating current, the direction of flow of which changes rapidly. Cf. *alternator, commutator, rectifier.* **pure-** An A.C. which is constant in frequency and output, and gives a correct sine-wave curve.

alternation. (1) A series of changes following periodically or in turn. **a. of generations.** (2) The successive change from asexual to sexual reproduction and back again, observed in low forms of life, as mosses. **a. law.** The arc spectra of the elements have alternately odd and even multiplicities when passing from the first to the higher groups of the periodic table. **a. rule.** Pauli's principle.

alternator. A dynamo with a large number of poles producing 120 or more alternations or cycles of current per second.

althes, althaea. Marshmallow, hollyhock, q.v. The dried roots, flowers and leaves of *Altheae officinalis* (Malvaceae): an emollient and demulcent.

altheine. Asparagine.

althionic acid. Ethylsulfuric acid.

altimeter. An instrument to measure heights.

altiscope. Periscope.

altitude. The vertical elevation above any given point, cf. *coordinates*; in particular above sealevel. **a. gage.** A barometer for determining a.

altrose. $C_6H_{12}O_6 = 180.10$. A hexose, isomeric with glucose, talose, and allose.

aludel. A pear-shaped vessel open at each end used to connect other vessels. **a. furnace.** A furnace used to reduce mercurial ores.

alum. (1) Generic for double salts of the general formula $M_2'SO_4 \cdot M_2'''\text{-}(SO_4)_3 \cdot 24H_2O$, or $M'M'''\text{-}(SO_4)_2 \cdot 12H_2O$. M' is monovalent and may be Na, K, Rb, Cs, NH_4, Tl, Ag, hydroxylamine, or the radical of an organic quaternary base, (e.g. NMe_4), M''' is trivalent and may be Fe, Cr, Al, Mn, In, Tl, Ga, V, Co, Ti, Rh, etc. SeO_4 or TeO_4 may replace SO_4. (2) Double salts of aluminum sulfate and the sulfate of a monovalent metal (M'), hence; $M_2'SO_4 \cdot Al_2(SO_4)_3 \cdot 24H_2O$. (3) The original name of ammonium alum, $(NH_4)_2SO_4 \cdot Al_2(SO_4)_3 \cdot 24H_2O$. Cf. pseudo*alum*. (4) Erroneously, aluminum sulfate; as, papermaker's a. (5) Generally, potassium aluminum sulfate. **ammonium-** Ammonium minum sulfate. **ammonium chrome-** Ammonium chromic sulfate. **ammonium iron-** Ferriammonium sulfate. **burnt-** Aluminum potassium sulfate, dehydrated at 200°. **cesium-** Aluminum cesium sulfate. **chrome-** Sodium chromic sulfate. **common-** Aluminum potassium sulfate. **copper-** Cupric aluminate. **iron-** A native ferric potassium sulfate. **manganese-** Manganous ammonium sulfate. **neutral-** Alunite. **official-** Either ammonium or potassium alum (B.P.). **pearl-** Specially prepared a. for paper manufacture. **pickle-** A. prepared for canneries. **porous-** Aluminum sodium sulfate. **potassium-** Aluminum potassium sulfate. **potassiumchrome-** Chromic potassium sulfate. **potassium manganese.** Potassium manganic sulfate. **pseudo-** A. containing a divalent in place of the univalent metallic sulfate; as, $MnSO_4 \cdot Al_2 \cdot (SO_4)_3 \cdot 24H_2O$; not isomorphous with the alums. **roman-** A native aluminum and iron sulfate from Tolfar, Italy. **rubidium-** Aluminum rubidium sulfate. **sodium-** Aluminum sodium sulfate. **thallium-** Aluminum thallium sulfate. **true-** A. containing aluminum.

a. flour. Aluminum potassium sulfate. **a. hematoxylin solution.** A stain (1 pt. hematoxylin, 100 pts. saturated aqueous ammonium alum, 0.5 pt. thymol, 300 pts. water). **a. meal.** Aluminum potassium sulfate. **a. root.** The root of *Heuchera americana*, which contains gallic and tannic acids; an astringent. **a. shale.** A clay containing iron pyrites and aluminum silicate; source of ammonium alum. **a. stone.** Alunite.

Alumel. Trademark for an alloy: Ni 94, Mn 2.5, Al 2.0, Si 1.0, Fe 0.5%; used in thermocouples.

alumian. $Al_2O(SO_4)_2$. A white, native, basic aluminum sulfate.

alumina. Aluminum oxide, Al_2O_3. α-Corundum. **ferric-** A colloidal solution of $Al(OH)_3$ and $FeCl_3$; a coagulant in water purification. **lime-** Essonite. **natural-** Corundum. Cf. *ruby, sapphire*.

a. cream. The hydroxides of aluminum. A clarifying agent, used in optical experiments. **a. mordans.** A fixing agent used in dyeing; usually aluminum compounds. **a. white.** Soluble a., transparent a., a. hydrate; a white pigment in paints and inks.

aluminate. (1) *ortho-* M_3AlO_3. A salt of aluminic acid, q.v., or compound derived from $Al(OH)_3$; as, Na_3AlO_3, sodium aluminate. (2) *meta-* $MAlO_2$. Salts existing only in solution; as, AlO_2^- ion. (3) A combination of Al_2O_3 with a metallic oxide; as, $MgAl_2O_4$, spinel.

aluminic acid. H_3AlO_3. A tautomer of aluminum hydroxide, $Al(OH)_3 \rightleftharpoons H_3AlO_3$; reacts as acid toward an alkaline solution.

aluminiferous. A rock yielding or containing Al.

aluminite. $Al_2(SO_4)(OH)_4 \cdot 7H_2O$. Native, soft, white, monoclinic hydrous aluminum sulfate. Cf *websterite*.

aluminium. Aluminum (U.K. usage).

aluminoferric. A mixture of aluminum sulfate and a ferrous salt, used to coagulate sewage.

aluminum. Al $= 26.98$. Aluminium. An earth metal and element of at. no. 13. One of the most abundant metals, isolated in an impure form by Oersted (1825), and in the pure form by Wöhler (1827) from sodium and aluminum trichloride. Silver-white, light, ductile metal, $d_{20°} \cdot 2.70$, m. 658.5, b. 1800; soluble in acids or alkalies; readily oxidized and covered with a fine protective film of aluminum oxide. Used extensively for cooking utensils, airships, airplanes, boats, automobiles. A. foil is used as a substitute for silver foil in the printing and glass industry. A. forms many important alloys; as, *magnalium, electron, duralumin*. World production (1967), 7.2 million tons. A. has a valency of 3 and forms one series of compounds. Aluminates are derived from aluminum hydroxide (aluminum valency 3):

Aluminum ion . . . . Al^{3+}
ortho-Aluminate ion . . . . AlO_3'''
meta-Aluminate ion . . . . AlO_2''
Alums . . . . $M_2'Al_2(SO_4)_4 \cdot 24H_2O$

primary- Virgin a. A. obtained direct from ore. **secondary-** A. from scrap metal. **virgin-** Primary a.

a. acetate. $(CH_3COO)_3Al = 204.17$. Amorphous white powder, decomp. by heat, soluble in water. A 5% aqueous solution is used as a gargle, astringent, or antiseptic. **a. a. solution.** See *Burow's* solution (U.S.P.). **a. acetate, basic.** $Al(C_2H_3O_2)_2 \cdot OH = 162.1$. White crystals; used as a mordant,

disinfectant, and for embalming. **a. acetoglycer-
inate.** White antiseptic powder. **a. acetotartrate.**
$AlC_2H_3O_2 \cdot C_4H_4O_6$. Alsol. White crystals, soluble in water; an antiseptic. **a. ammonium sulfate.**
$Al_2(NH_4)_2(SO_4)_4 \cdot 24H_2O = 906$. Ammonium alum.
a. alkyls. Compounds of aluminum and alkyl
radicals, e.g., trimethylaluminums. **a. alloys.**
Some m. (in °C) are:

With	90% Al 10%	80% Al 20%	70% Al 30%	60% Al 40%	50% Al 50%
Ag	625	615	600	590	580
Au	675	740	800	855	915
Cu	630	600	560	540	580
Fe	860	1015	1110	1145	1145
Sb	750	840	925	945	950
Sn	645	635	625	620	605

a. arsenate. $AlAsO_4 = 166.02$. White powder,
soluble in acids. **a. benzoate.** $Al(C_7H_5O_2)_3 =$
390.15. White crystals, soluble in water. **a. bifluoride.** $(Al_2F_6)_3(HF)_4 \cdot 10H_2O$. A. acid fluoride.
White crystals, soluble in water. **a. borate.**
$2Al_2O_3 \cdot B_2O_3 \cdot 3H_2O = 338.4$. White granules, soluble in water; used in glass and porcelain. **a.
boroformate.** $Al_2O_3B(OH)_3H_2CO_3 \cdot 5H_2O = 316.2$.
Transparent crystals, soluble in water; an antiseptic
and astringent. **a. borotannate.** Cutal, lutol.
Brown powder; a disinfecting dusting powder.
a. borotartrate. Boral. Colorless crystals, soluble in water; an astringent. **a. bromate.** Al-
$(BrO_3)_3 \cdot 9H_2O = 573.00$. Colorless hygroscopic
crystals, m.62.3, decomp. 100, soluble in water.
a. bromide. $AlBr_3 \cdot 6H_2O = 374.96$. Colorless or
yellow hygroscopic crystals, m.93, soluble in water;
used in organic synthesis. *anhydrous-* $AlBr_3 =$
266.86. Yellow fuming scales; used in organic
synthesis. **a. bronze.** An alloy: Cu 90, Al 10%,
m.1050. **a. butoxide.** $Al(OC_4H_9)_3 = 246.18$.
White powder, m.102, decomp. in water. **a. carbide.** $Al_4C_3 = 144.4$. Yellow hexagons, decomp.
in water; used to generate methane. **a. carbonate.**
$Al_2(CO_3)_3 = 234.2$. White lumps, insoluble in
water; a mild antiseptic. **a. caseinate.** Yellow
powder, insoluble in water. **a. cesium sulfate.**
$AlCs(SO_4)_2 \cdot 12H_2O = 568.2$. Cesium alum. Colorless crystals, m.117, slightly soluble in water. **a.
chloride.** $AlCl_3 \cdot 6H_2O = 231.54$. Colorless crystals, soluble in water. *anhydrous-* $AlCl_3 = 133.48$.
Yellow crystals, m.180, soluble in water. Used in
Friedel-Crafts reaction; medicinally in locomotor
ataxia; industrially as a catalytic agent and in
refining petroleum; and as a reagent for naphthalene. **a. dichromate.** $Al_2(Cr_2O_7)_3 = 702.2$. Red
crystals, soluble in water. **a. ethoxide.** Al-
$(OC_2H_5)_3 = 162.09$. Triethoxyaluminum. White
powder, m.134, soluble in hot water; a reagent for
water. **a. ethyl.** $Al(C_2H_5)_3 = 114.2$. Triethyl-
aluminum. Colorless liquid, b.190, decomp. explo-
sively in water. **a. fluoride.** $AlF_3 \cdot 3\frac{1}{2}H_2O = 147.2$.
Colorless crystals, slightly soluble in water, losing
$2H_2O$ at 120. *anhydrous-* $AlF_3 = 84.1$. White
powder, soluble in water; used in the glass industry.
a. fluosilicate. $Al_2(SiF_6)_3 = 480.12$. A silicofluoride. White powder, insoluble in water, used in

the glass and enamel industries. **a. gallate.** Gal,
lal. **a. gluconate.** See *gluconate.* **a. hydrate.**
a. hydroxide. **a. hydroxide.** $Al(OH)_3 = 78 \cdot 0$.
White powder, insoluble in water; occurs native as
gibbsite, hydrargylite, and zirlite. With bases it
forms salts; see *aluminic* acid. Used as an astringent, dusting powder, mordant, filter aid, and
neutralizing agent. *basic-* Includes: $AlO(OH)$, e.g.,
boehmite, $Al_2O(OH)_4$, e.g., *bauixite;* also mixtures
with the normal hydroxide. **a. h. gel.** An aqueous
suspension of a. h. and alumina equivalent to
3.6–4.4% $Al(OH)_3$, with preservative and flavoring; an antacid. **a. hypophosphite.** $Al(H_2-
PO_2)_3 = 223.3$. Colorless crystals, soluble in
water. **a. iodide.** $AlI_3 \cdot 6H_2O = 515.9$. White
crystals, soluble in water. *anhydrous-* $AlI_3 =$
407.9. Brown crystals, m.180, soluble in water;
used in organic synthesis. **a. lactate.** $Al(C_3H_5-
O_3)_3 = 294.09$. Yellow powder, soluble in
water. **a. methyl.** $Al(CH_3)_3 = 72.1$. A. methide,
trimethylaluminum. Colorless liquid, b.130; decomp. by water. **a. minerals.** A. is the most
abundant metal and is present in all rocks
(except the limestones and sandstones), chiefly in
silicates; as, feldspar, clays, micas, sillimanite,

Classification: mineral		U.S. usage	U.K. usage
Al_2O_3	Carborundum	α	α
Al_2O_3	. . . .	γ	γ
Al_2O_3, H_2O	Diaspore	β	α
Al_2O_3, H_2O	Bauxite ⎫ Boehmite⎭	α	γ
$Al_2O_3, 3H_2O$	Bayerite	β	α
$Al_2O_3, 3H_2O$	Hydrargillite⎫ Gibbsite ⎭	α	γ

andalusite, cyanite. The principal ores are: corundum, Al_2O_3; bauxite, $Al_2O_3 \cdot 2H_2O$; cryolite,
$AlF_3 \cdot 3NaF$. **a. naphtholsulfonate, a. β-naphtholsul-
fonate.** Alumnol. **a. nitrate.** $Al(NO_3)_3 \cdot 9H_2O = 375.3$.
Colorless, rhombs, m. 73, decomp. 150, soluble in
water; an astringent. *anhydrous-*$Al(NO_3)_3 =$
213.1. White powder, soluble in water; used in the
textile and leather industries. **a. nitride.** $AlN =$
41.1. Yellow crystals, m.2150, decomp. by water.
a. oleate. $Al(C_{18}H_{33}O_2)_3 = 870.8$. White powder,
soluble in alcohol. Used as an antiseptic, in the
manufacture of waterproofing materials, and as a
paint drier. **a. oxalate.** $Al_2(COO)_6 = 318.2$.
White powder, insoluble in water. **a. oxide.**
$Al_2O_3 = 102$. Alumina, corundum. White powder, or colorless hexagons, d.3.75, m.2020, insoluble
in water. Crystalline forms: α- or artificial corundum (the common form); β-, made by heating the
hydroxide to 500–1000°C; γ-, by heating to 900–
1100°C, and ζ-, by heating in molten Li_2O. An
abrasive, refractory, and filtering material. Cf.
Alundum, borolon. **a. palmitate.** $Al(C_{16}H_{31}O_2)_3 =$
789.9. White granules, insoluble in water; a
lubricant and waterproofing material. **a. phenolate.** $Al(OC_6H_5)_3 = 306.09$. A phenoxide. Colorless powder, m.265, decomp. in water; an antiseptic.
a. p-phenolsulfonate. $Al(C_6H_4(OH)SO_3)_3$. Aluminum sulfophenylate, sozal. Pink powder, soluble, in
water; a dusting powder. **a. phosphate.** $AlPO_4 =$

122.1. Colorless hexagons or white powder, insoluble in water. Occurs in native variscite, sphaerite, and turquoise. Used in pharmacy, as a cement, and in ceramics. **a. potassium chloride.** $AlCl_3$. $KCl = 208.0$. White crystals, soluble in water, **a. potassium phenolsulfonate.** $AlK(C_6H_4 \cdot OH \cdot SO_3)_4$. Pink crystals, soluble in water; an astringent, antiseptic, and styptic. **a. potassium sulfate.** Al_2K_2-$(SO_4)_4 \cdot 24H_2O = 948.74$. Potassium alum, potash alum, common alum, kalinite. White powder or transparent cubes, m. 84, soluble in water; used as a mordant, in glue and cements; and as an astringent, emetic, or styptic. **a. potassium tartrate.** $KAl(C_4H_4O_6)_3 = 362.13$. White powder, soluble in water. **a. propoxide.** $Al(OC_3H_9)_3 = 204.13$. White powder, m.106, b.248, decomp. in water. **a. rectifier.** An apparatus to convert an alternating current into a pulsating direct current when the former is connected to 2 aluminum plates in sodium bicarbonate solution. **a. resinate.** $Al(C_{44}H_{63}O_5)_3 = 2041.5$. Brown soft mass, insoluble in water; used for waterproofing and as a drier in varnish. **a. rhodanate.** $Al(CNS)_3 = 201.4$. A. sulfocyanide, rhodanide, or thiocyanate. Yellow powder, slightly soluble in water; used in the textile industry. **a. rubidium sulfate.** $AlRb(SO_4)_2$-$12H_2O = 520.85$. Rubidium alum. Colorless crystals, m.99, slightly soluble in water. **a. salicylate.** $Al(C_6H_4OH \cdot COO)_3 = 438.2$. Salamin. Pink powder, insoluble in water, soluble in alkalies; an antiseptic. **a. silicate.** $Al_2(SiO_3)_3 = 282.4$. White masses, insoluble in water; used in the glass industry as a refractory lining. Natural forms are cyanite, andalusite, sillimanite, mullite. Cf. *kaolin*. **a. silicofluoride.** A. fluosilicate. **a. sodium chloride.** $AlCl_3 \cdot NaF = 191.94$. Colorless crystals, m.183, soluble in water. **a. sodium fluoride.** AlF_3-$3NaF = 210.10$. Colorless crystals, sparingly soluble in water. **a. sodium sulfate.** $AlNa(SO_4)_2$-$12H_2O = 458.42$. Sodium alum. Colorless rhombs. m. 61, soluble in water; used for water purification, **a. stearate.** $Al(C_{18}H_{35}O_2)_3 = 877.2$. Obtained by saponifying animal fat and treatment of the soap with alum. Gray mass, soluble in warm water. Used in lubricating and waterproofing compounds. **a. sulfate.** $Al_2(SO_4)_3 \cdot 18H_2O = 666.5$. Colorless monoclinic crystals, decomp. by heat, soluble in water; used as alum. *anhydrous-* $Al_2(SO_-)_3 = 342.4$. White crystals, decomp. 77, soluble in water. Used as a reagent for dyes; in wine; as an antiseptic, caustic, or astringent; and in the leather paper, and dye industries. **a. sulfide.** $Al_2S_3 = 150.4$. Yellow crystals, m.1100, decomp. by water or acids. **a. sulfocyanate.** A. rhodanate. **a. sulfocyanide.** A. rhodanate. **a. sulfophenylate.** A. phenylsulfonate. **a. tannate.** Tannal. Brown powder; an antiseptic and astringent. **a. tartrate.** $Al_2(C_4H_4O_6)_3 = 498.2$. White powder, insoluble in water, soluble in ammonia or acids. **a. thallium sulfate.** $AlTl(SO_4)_2 \cdot 12H_2O = 639.4$. Thallium alum. Colorless crystals, slightly soluble in water. **a. triethide.** $AlEt_3 = 114.09$. Triethyl a. Colorless liquid, decomp. by water to ethane and a. hydroxide. **a. trimethide.** $AlMe_3 = 72.04$. Trimethyl a. Colorless liquid, decomp. in water to methane and a. hydroxide. **a. zinc sulfate.** $Al_2Zn(SO_4)_4 = 503.8$. Zinc alum. Colorless crystals, powder, or sticks, soluble in water; a caustic.

alumite. Alunite.
alumnol. $Al_2[C_{10}H_6OH(SO_3)_2]_3$. Aluminum β-naphtholsulfonate. White powder, soluble in water; an astringent and antiseptic.
alums. See *alum*.
Alundum. Trademark for a pure, crystalline, granular aluminum oxide, d.3.9–4.0, m.2050. Used as reagent for the determination of carbon in steel, as an abrasive, a basic refractory, filtering material, and for chemical apparatus. **A. cement.** A carrier for catalysts prepared by heating Al_2O_3 90, SiO_2 5, CaO 5 pts. **A. crucible.** (1) A highly refractive crucible for the electric furnace, used for melting platinum. (2) A porous filtering crucible. **A. filter cone.** An A. filter cone which fits into a funnel. **A. muffle.** An A. muffle for metal assay.
alunite. $K_2SO_4 \cdot Al_2(SO_4)_3 \cdot 4Al(OH)_3(?)$. Alumite. Neutral alum. Alum stone. Native, white rhombic hexagons; hardness 3.5–4.0; sparingly soluble in water.
alunogen. $Al_2(SO_4)_3 \cdot 18H_2O$. Native, silky-white monoclinic crystals.
Alurate. Trademark for a brand of allylisopropylbarbituric acid; an oral sedative-hypnotic.
alva marina. A prepared seaweed for stuffing mattresses or chairs.
alveograph. An instrument for evaluating the qualities of baking dough. A disk of nonyeasted dough is clamped across an air inlet, and the pressure required to burst it is measured.
alveolar air. Respirated air.
alvite. $(ZnHfTh)SiO_4$. A mineral.
alypine. $C_{15}H_{26}O_2 \cdot N_2HCl = 302.6$. 2-Benzoxy-2-dimethylaminomethyl-1-dimethylaminobutane hydrochloride. White hygroscopic crystals, m.169; a local anesthetic.
Am. Abbreviation for: (1) NH_4 group (ammonium); (2) C_5H_{11} radical (amyl). (3) Symbol for *americium*.
amadou. Surgeons' agaric, punk, tinder. The fungus *Boletus igniarius*, found on old tree trunks; used as tinder, for surgical pads, and as a styptic.
amalgam. (1) An alloy of mercury, generally solid or semiliquid; as, sodium a. (2) An alloy of silver and mercury. **native-** An alloy of mercury with silver or gold; e.g., $AuHg_3$, occurring as minerals, as *arquerite*.
amalgamation. The formation of an alloy of a metal with mercury. **a. process.** A method of extracting noble metals from ores by alloying them with mercury.
amalgamator. An apparatus to extract gold from ores.
amalic acid. Amalinic acid.
amalinic acid. $C_{12}H_{12}O_7N_4 = 324.3$. Amalic acid, tetramethylalloxantin. Colorless crystals, m.245, soluble in hot water.
amandin. A globulin from fruit kernels, e.g., peach seeds.
Amanita. A genus of fungi (mushrooms), many of which are poisonous; as, *A. phalloides*, Death head fungus, death cup, containing phallin, q.v.; *A. muscaria*, fly agaric, fly amanita, containing muscarufin; *A. verna*, the "destroying angel." **a. toxin.** A protein from *A. phalloides*, death-head fungus; a cause of mushroom poisoning.
amanitine. $Me_3N(OH)CHOH \cdot Me = 121.1$. (1) An alkaloid of *Amanita* species; as, *A. pantherina* and

A. muscaria, identical with neurine. (2) $Me_3N\cdot(OH)CH_2CH_2OH = 121.1$. Isocholine. An alkaloid from mushrooms (*Agaricus muscaria*), oxidized to muscarine. Cf. *choline*.

amaranth. $NaSO_3\cdot C_{10}H_5\cdot N:N\cdot C_{10}H_4(SO_3Na)_2OH = 604.50$. A red aniline dye used as a food color (F. D. & C. Red No. 2).

Amaranthaceae. A family of plants comprising 40 genera and 500 species of weeds, pot plants, and fodder plants.

amaranthus. The fresh root of the shrub *A. spinosa*, used in India as a specific for gonorrhea.

amarbital. A brand of phenylethylbarbituric acid.

amargosa bark. The root bark of the goatbush, *Castela nicholsoni* (Simarubaceae); a source of castelamarin.

amarine. $C_{21}H_{18}N_2\cdot\frac{1}{2}H_2O = 307.28$. Triphenyldihydroglyoxalin. Bitter, colorless prisms, anhydrous at 130, insoluble in water, formed by the action of ammonia on benzoic acid; occurs in oil of bitter almonds.

amaroid. Bitter principles, in plants other than alkaloids, glucosides, or tannins; as, quassin, chamomillin.

amaron. $C_{28}H_{20}N_2 = 384.32$. Tetraphenyl-*p*-pyrimidine, benzoin imide. Colorless needles, m.245, insoluble in water.

Amaryllidaceae. A family of plants comprising about 75 genera and 700 species. Many are ornamental tropical and subtropical plants; as narcissus, agave. Cf. *lycorine*.

amatol. An explosive (80 pts. ammonium nitrate, 20 pts. trinitrotoluene) used in coal mines.

amazonite. Amazon stone, microcline. A bright green potassium aluminum silicate; precious stone.

amber. $C_{10}H_{16}O$ (?). Electrum, succinum. A fossilized, bituminous resin, d.1.1; brittle, transparent brown masses. Used as a precious stone and in experiments on static electricity. It occurs as succinite and gedanite. **artificial-** Colophony. **Baltic-** Succinite. **Canadian-** Chernawinite. **synthetic-** A formaldehyde-phenol or -urea resin.

a. acid. Succinic acid. Cf. *ambreic* acid. **a. oil.** A brown essential oil of empyreumatic and balsamic odor distilled from a., d.0.915–0.975, miscible with alcohol. **a. seed.** Musk seed.

ambergris. The opaque, gray wax formed in the intestines of the sperm whale, d.0.7–0.92, m.60, b.100, soluble in alcohol or ether; used in perfumery. Cf. *ambrein, spermaceti*.

Amberg swimming cup. A perforated porcelain tumbler with cork stopper, used for washing microscope specimens by floating them in a solvent.

amberite. (1) A smokeless powder composed of guncotton, paraffin, and barium nitrate. (2) Compressed amber scrap used for electrical insulation.

Amberlite. Trademark for certain ion-exchange resins.

amblygonite. $LiAlFPO_4$. Native green triclinic crystals from California.

amblystegite. Enstatite.

amboceptor. Fixator. A heat-resisting substance in blood with 2 haptophore groups (cytophile and complementophile); it unites the cell body with the complement. Cf. *polyceptor, complement* fixation, *Ehrlich's* side-chain theory.

amboyna wood. A wood, *Pterospermum indicum*, used in East India for inlay work.

ambreic acid. Yellow substance derived from amber, probably identical with cholesteric acid.

ambrein. $C_{23}H_{40}O = 332.34$. A cholesterin from ambergris.

ambrette. Musk seed.

ambrettolic acid. $Me(CH_2)_7CH:COH\cdot(CH_2)_5\cdot COOH = 270.25$. ζ-Hydroxy-ζ-hexadecenic acid. **dihydro-** Juniperic acid.

ambrion. An insulating material; asbestos impregnated with pitch.

ambrite. A fossilized resin (New Zealand); greasy, yellow masses, sometimes used for semiprecious stones.

Ambrosia. A genus of composite-flowered herbs, whose pollen causes hay fever, as *A. artemisifolia*, or ragweed.

ameba. Amoeba. A unicellular animal without definite shape, resembling a mass of moving jelly, with all the features of life; as, growth reproduction, metabolism, locomotion.

amebicide. An agent that destroys ameba.

ameboid. Assuming various shapes, like a moving ameba.

amelairoside. Piceoside. A glucoside from *Amelancher vulgaris* (Rosaceae).

American aloe. Agave. **A. colombe.** Fraserin. **A. ginseng.** Ginseng. **A. hellebore.** Veratrum. **A. ipecac.** Gillenia. **A. melting point.** An arbitrary value for the m. of paraffin wax which is 3°F. higher than the standard m. as determined by the ASTM method. **A. saffron.** Carthamus. **A. valerian.** See *Cypripedium*. **A. veratrum.** Veratrum. **A. wormseed oil.** Chenopodium oil.

American Chemical Society. Organized in 1876, Publishers of the *Journal of the Am. Chem. Soc.*, *Chemical Abstracts*, and the *Journal of Industrial and Engineering Chemistry*. Secretary, 1155 16th St., N.W., Washington, D.C. **A. Society for Testing and Materials.** See *ASTM*.

americium. Am. Proposed name for element 95 (Seaborg), which has six $5f$ electrons. Cf. *curium*. The stablest isotope has mass no. 241.

amesite. A ferromagnesium aluminum silicate.

Ames moisture tester. A paraffin-jacketed container for the determination of moisture in butter.

amethocaine hydrochloride. $C_{15}H_{24}O_2N_2\cdot HCl = 300.82$. White crystals, m.148, soluble in water; a local anesthetic.

amethyst. A purple, quartz precious stone from India, Brazil. **oriental-** Al_2O_3. A purple, native alumina. **true-** Oriental-.

ametryne. Common name for 6-ethylamino-4-isopropylamino-2-methylthio-1,3,5-triazine. A pesticide.

amianthus. Earth flax, mountain flax. A fine, silky asbestos.

amicron. A particle of diameter less than 5 mμ. See *micron*.

amidase. A hydrolytic enzyme which splits ammonia from urea.

amidation. The process of forming an amide, by: (1) heating the corresponding ammonium salt, (2) reaction of ammonia on an acid chloride, (3) reaction of ammonia with an ester. Cf. *amination*.

amide. (1) An organic compound containing the $-CO\cdot NH_2$ radical; as, formamide, $H\cdot CO\cdot NH_2$; benzamide, $Ph\cdot CO\cdot NH_2$. A. are derived from acids by replacement of $-OH$ by $-NH_2$; as,

—COOH → —CONH$_2$; or from ammonia by the replacement of H by an acyl group: NH$_3$ → NH$_2$·-OCR. (2) **Ammonobases.** Compounds in which H of NH$_3$ is replaced by a metal; as, sodamide, NaNH$_2$. **alkyl-** R·C:O·NHR. Compounds obtained by treating an acid chloride or acid anhydride with an amine and sodium hydroxide. Cf. *anilide.* **keto-** A compound containing the radical —CO·CONH$_2$. **oxy-** A compound containing both, the —OH and —CONH$_2$ groups. **thio-** A compound containing the —CSNH$_2$ group.

a. chloride. A chlorinated amide, R·C:Cl$_2$·NR$_2$ derived from an alkyl a., which changes readily to the imide chloride, R·C:NH·Cl. **a. group.** The formamyl group, —CO·NH$_2$ which confers weakly basic properties.

amidin. A transparent solution of starch in water.

amidines. Compounds containing the radical —C:NH·NH$_2$; as, formamidine, H·C(:NH)NH$_2$. Derived from the amides by replacement of O by the amido residue, >NH or >NR. Cf. *benzimidazole, phasotropy.* **di-** A compound containing 2 amidine groups; e.g., oxalamidine, NH$_2$(HN:)-C—C(:NH)NH$_2$.

amidino. Guanyl. The radical NH$_2$·C:NH—.

amido. The —NH$_2$ radical when present in a compound with the —CO radical; otherwise termed *amino.* **a. acetophenone.** C$_6$H$_4$NH$_2$·COMe. Colorless crystals, m.106, soluble in water; a reagent in Ehrlich's diazo reaction. **a. aldehyde.** A compound containing both the amino and aldehyde radical; as, NH$_2$—CH$_2$—CHO, a. acetaldehyde. **a. benzoylformic acid.** Isatinic acid. **a. F acid.** β-Naphthylamine-7-sulfonic acid. **a. ketone.** A compound containing both the amino and keto groups; as, NH$_2$·CH$_2$COMe, amidoacetone. **a. mandelic acid.** Hydrindic acid. **a. mandelic acid lactame.** Dioxindole. **a. naphtholdisulfonic acid.** H acid. **a. oximes.** Amidoximes. **a. phosphoric acid.** Phosphamic acid. The compound, PO(NH$_2$)O$_3$. **a. pyrine.** Pyramidone. **a. thiazole.** C$_3$H$_4$N$_2$S = 100.1. α-*methyl-* NH$_2$·C$_4$-HNS·Me. Colorless crystals, m.42. **a. triazulfole.** CH$_2$N$_4$S = 102.2. Amidotriazosulfole. *methyl-* CN$_3$S·NHMe. Colorless crystals, m.96. **a. urea.** Semicarbazide.

amidogen. Amido.

amidol. (NH$_2$)$_2$C$_6$H$_3$OH·HCl = 160.5. 3,4-Diaminophenol hydrochloride. Colorless crystals, slightly soluble in water; a photographic developer.

amidone. Me·CH(NMe$_2$)·CH$_2$·C(Ph)$_2$COMe = 295.20. Hoechst-10820. White solid, m.73, slightly soluble in water; an analgesic.

amidopyrine. C$_{13}$H$_{17}$ON$_3$ = 231.16. Dimethylaminoantipyrine, ampydin. White crystals, m.108, soluble in water; an analgesic (U.S.P.).

amidoxalyl. Oxamyl.

amidoxime. Oxamidine. A compound containing the amidoxime group, —C(:NOH)NH$_2$; e.g., methenyl- or formamidoxime, HC(NOH)NH$_2$.

Amidoxyl. Hydroxylamino. Trademark for a compound containing the amidoxyl group, —NHOH.

amidrazone. A compound containing the C$_6$H$_5$·-NH·N:C(NH$_2$) radical; e.g., methyl-C$_6$H$_5$·NH·N:-C(NH$_2$)·CH$_3$. See *hydrazidines.*

amigen. A protein hydrolysis product used in amino acid therapy.

Amilan. Trade name for a polyamide synthetic fiber.

Amilar. Trade name for a polyester synthetic fiber.

amination. The formation of an amine by: (1) reduction of a nitro compound, (2) reduction of a cyanide, (3) oxidation of an amide, (4) treating isocyanate with ammonia. Cf. *amidation.*

amine. (1) See *amines.* (2) Suffix indicating an —NH$_2$ group.

amines. A group of compounds derived from ammonia by substituting organic radicals for the hydrogens; as, H$_2$NR, primary- (amines); RHNR, secondary- (imines); R$_2$NR, tertiary- (nitriles); R$_4$NOH, quaternary- (ammonium). Cf. *amino, amide, arsine, phosphine.* **di-** A. containing 2NH$_2$ groups. **filming-** A. which form monomolecular films on hot surfaces, thereby promoting drop-type condensation; e.g., the use of *n*-octadecylamine inside drying cylinders. **metallic-** An amide (2), q.v. **neutralizing-** A. used to neutralize boiler-feed water, the excess being steam-volatile; as, cyclohexamine. **pressor-** A protein casein derivative having vasoconstrictory effects; as, tyramine. **primary-** Amino bases. Compounds in which 1 H is replaced by a radical; e.g., NH$_2$CH$_3$. **quaternary-** Tetraalkyl ammonium bases. Compounds derived from ammonium hydroxide containing 4 radicals; e.g., N(CH$_3$)$_4$OH. **secondary-** Imino bases. Compounds in which 2 H are replaced by a radical; e.g., NH(CH$_3$)$_2$. **tertiary-** Nitrile bases. Compounds in which 3 H are replaced by radicals; e.g., N(CH$_3$)$_3$. **thionyl-** A compound containing the —N:SO radical. **tri-** A compound containing 3 NH$_2$ groups. Cf. *semidines.*

aminic acid. Formic acid.

amino. The —NH$_2$ group indicated by the prefix *amino-* or suffix *amine**; as, aminomethane or methylamine. **a. acetal.** NH$_2$·CH$_2$·CH(OEt)$_2$ = 133.16. Colorless needles m.163, soluble in water. Cf. *glycinaldehyde.* **a. acetanilide.** NH$_2$·C$_6$H$_4$·-NHCOMe = 150·14. Acetylphenylenediamine. Colorless needles, *ortho-* m.165, *meta-* m.90, *para-* m.160, slightly soluble in water. **a. acetic acid.** Glycine. **a. acetone.** NH$_2$CH$_2$COMe = 73.08. Colorless needles, m.188, (decomp.), soluble in water. **a. acetphenetidine.** See *phenocoll.* **a. acetophenone.** NH$_2$·C$_6$H$_4$·COMe = 135.1. *p*-Aminophenyl methyl ketone. Yellow powder, m.105, soluble in water. *ortho-* b.251. **a. acid.** See *amino acids.* **a. alcohols.** Alkamines. **a. anthraquinone.** See *anthraquinone.* **a. azobenzene.** Ph·N:NC$_6$H$_4$NH$_2$ = 197.2. Aniline yellow. Yellow needles, m.125, slightly soluble in water. An intermediate in the preparation of dyes and medicinals; an indicator changing at pH 2.5 from orange (acid) to yellow (alkaline). **a. azobenzene chlorhydrate.** C$_{12}$H$_{11}$N$_3$·HCl. Blue needles, slightly soluble in water; used in dye manufacture. **a. azobenzene-β-naphthol.** Sudan red III. **a. azonaphthalene.** C$_{10}$H$_7$N:NC$_{10}$H$_6$NH$_2$ = 297.25. *alpha-* Red needles, m.174, slightly soluble in alcohol. *beta-* Red needles, m.159. **a. azotoluene.** MeC$_6$H$_4$N:NC$_6$H$_3$(NH$_2$)Me. Red crystals, m.100, insoluble in water; used to treat ulcers. **a. azotoluene hydrochloride.** Me-C$_6$H$_4$N:NC$_6$H$_3$(NH$_2$)Me·HCl. Colorless crystals, soluble in water. Its 4 isomeric forms are used in

organic synthesis. **a. barbituric acid.** Uramil. **a. benzaldehyde.** See *benzaldehyde.* **a. benzamide.** See *benzamide.* **a. benzene.** Aniline. **a. benzenesulfonic acid.** *ortho-* Orthanilic acid. *meta-*Metanilic acid. *p-*Sulfanilic acid. **a. benzoic acids.** See *benzoic acid.* **a. caproic acid.** Leucine. **a. dracilic acid.** See *p-aminobenzoic acid.* **a. diphenyl** Xenylamine. **a. ethanol.** Ethanolamine. **a. ethionic acid.** Taurine. **a. formic acid.** See *formic acid.* **a. G acid.** 2-Naphthylamine-6,8-disulfonic acid. **a. glutaric acid.** See *glutaric acid.* **a. guanidine.** See *guanidine.* **a. phenol.** NH_2·$C_6H_4OH = 109.1$. *1,2-,* or *ortho-* Aminophenol base. Colorless rhombs, m.179, slightly soluble in water. *1,3-,* or *meta-* Colorless crystals, m.123, slightly soluble in water. *1,4-,* or *para-* Rodinol. Colorless leaflets, m.184 (decomp.), slightly soluble in water. A developer in photography and reducing agent in the dye industry. **a. phthalhydrazide.** Luminol. **a. propionic acid.** Alanine. **a. purine.** Adenine. **2-a pyridine.** $C_5H_6N_2 = 94.0$. Yellow lumps, m.55 (sublimes), soluble in water; an intermediate in organic syntheses. **a. quinoline.** C_9H_6N·$NH_2 = 144.13$. *alpha-* Colorless crystals, m.125, slightly soluble in water. *beta-* Colorless crystals. decomp. 280, insoluble in water. **a. R acid.** 2-Naphthylamine-3,6-disulfonic acid. **a. succinamic acid.** Asparagine. **a. sulfonic acid.** Sulfamic acid. **a. thiophen.** Thiophenine. **a. toluene.** Toluidine. **a. xylol.** Xylidine.
amino acids. NH_2—R—COOH. R is an aliphatic radical. A. have both basic and acidic properties and form the units of peptides and proteins. The first 3 letters are accepted as abbreviations, as ala for alanine (IUPAC). **alpha- or primary-** NH_2·CHR·COOH. The commoner amino acids. **beta- or secondary-,** NH_2·CHR·CH_2·COOH. **gamma- or tertiary-** NH_2·CHR·CH_2·CH_2·COOH. **delta-** or **quaternary-** NH_2CHR·CH_2·CH_2·CH_2·COOH.

aminoacrine hydrochloride. $C_{13}H_{10}N_2$·HCl·$H_2O = 248.7$. 5-Aminoacridine hydrochloride. Yellow, bitter crystals, slightly soluble in water.
aminohippuric acid. $C_9H_{10}N_2O_3 = 194.19$. White crystals, discolor in light, m.198, soluble in water; a pharmaceutic aid (U.S.P.).
aminoid. A protein hydrolysis product used in amino acid therapy.
aminoketones. Aromatic compounds containing the —NHCHO radical; e.g., formanilide, C_6H_5·NHCHO. Cf. *peptides.*
aminophenols. Aromatic compounds containing both, the —OH and —NH_2 groups attached to the benzene ring; e.g., aminophenol, HO·C_6H_4·NH_2.
aminopherases. A group of intracellular desmolase-type enzymes described by the name of the amino acid they transaminate; e.g., aspartic a. catalyzes the transamination between *l-*aspartic acid and acipyruvic acid.
aminophylline. $C_{16}H_{24}N_{10}O_4$·2HO = 456.68. Theophylline ethylenediamine. Euphylline. Yellow, bitter powder, with ammoniacal odor, soluble in water (decomp.). Loses carbon dioxide in air to form theophylline; a diuretic, blood coagulant, and muscle relaxant (U.S.P.).
Aminosol. Trademark for a mixture of free amino acids (70–80%) with glucose and mineral salts prepared by enzymic degradation of casein followed by dialysis; an infant food.
amiodoxyl benzoate. $C_6H_4(IO_2)COONH_4 = 305.1$. Ammonium *o-*iodoxybenzoate. Crystals, soluble in water: an antiarthritic.
amiton. $C_{10}H_{24}O_3NSP = 389.28$. *o,o-*Diethyl-*S*-2,-diethylaminoethylphosphorthiolate. Colorless liquid, b.$_{0.04mm}$88. Soluble in cold water (sparingly soluble at 25); an acaricide and sealicide, especially against spiders.
amitosis. Cell division with no apparent change in the structure of the cell nucleus. Cf. *mitosis.*

AMINO ACIDS

1. *Monoaminomonocarboxylic acids:* NH_2—R—COOH

Carbamic acid	NH_2·COOH
Glycine, aminoacetic acid	NH_2·CH_2·COOH
Glycin, N-*p*-hydroxyphenylaminoacetic acid	$C_6H_4(OH)$·$NHCH_2$·COOH
Alanine, α-aminopropionic acid	NH_2·CHMe·COOH
Valine, α-aminoisovaleric acid	NH_2·CH·COOH(CHMe$_2$)
Leucine, α-aminoisocaproic acid	NH_2·CH·COOH(CH$_2$·CHMe$_2$)
Isovaline, α-amino-α-methylbutyric acid	NH_2·CMe·COOH(CH$_2$Me)
Phenylalanine, α-amino-β-phenylpropionic acid	NH_2·CH·COOH(CH$_2$·Ph)
Tyrosine, α-amino-β-parahydroxyphenylpropionic acid	NH_2·CH·COOH(CH$_2$·PhOH)
Serine, α-amino-β-hydroxypropionic acid	NH_2·CH·COOH(CH$_2$OH)
Cysteine, α-amino-β-thiopropionic acid	NH_2·CH·COOH(CH$_2$SH)
Methionine, α-amino-γ-methylthiobutyric acid	NH_2·CH·COOH(CH$_2$)$_2$·SMe

2. *Monoaminodicarboxylic acids:* NH_2·R(COOH)$_2$

Aspartic acid, α-aminosuccinic acid	NH_2·CH·COOH(CH$_2$·COOH)
Glutamic acid, α-aminoglutaric acid	NH_2·CH·COOH(CH$_2$)$_2$·COOH

3. *Diaminomonocarboxylic acids:* $(NH_2)_2$R·COOH

Arginine, α-amino-δ-guanidinevaleric acid	NH_2·CH·COOH(CH$_2$)$_3$·NH·CNH·NH$_2$
Lysine, α,ε-diaminocaproic acid	NH_2·CH·COOH(CH$_2$)$_4$·NH$_2$
Ornithine, α,δ-diaminovaleric acid	NH_2·CH·COOH(CH$_2$·CH$_2$·CH$_2$·NH$_2$)
Asparagine, α-aminosuccinamic acid	NH_2·CH·COOH(CH$_2$·CONH$_2$)
Citrulline, α-amino-δ-ureylvaleric acid	NH_2·CH·COOH(CH$_2$)$_3$NH·CO·NH$_2$

4. *Heterocyclic amino acids*

Histidine, α-amino-β-imidazolepropionic acid	NH_2·CH·COOH·CH$_2$·(C$_3$H$_3$N$_2$)
Tryptophan, α-amino-β-indolepropionic acid	NH_2·CH·COOH·CH$_2$·C·CH(C$_6$H$_4$)NH
Proline, α-pyrrolidinecarboxylic acid	NH·CH·COOH·CH$_2$·(CH$_2$)CH$_2$

amitriptiline hydrochloride. $C_{20}H_{23}N \cdot HCl = 313.93$. White, bitter powder, soluble in water; an antidepressant (B.P.).

Ammate. (1) Trademark for a weedicide based on ammonium sulfamate. (2) (not cap.) Common name for the ammonium salt of sulfamic acid; a weedicide.

ammelide. $N \vdots (C \cdot OH \vdots N)_2 \vdots C \cdot NH_2 = 128.1$. Cyanin monamide, aminocyanuric acid, cyanuramide, 6-amino-s-triazine-2,4-diol. Colorless powder, decomp. if heated, insoluble in water. **iso-** See *isocyanurimide*.

ammeline. $N:(CNH_2:N)_2:C \cdot OH = 127.1$. Diaminocyanuric acid, cyanurodiamide, cyanin, diamide, 4,6-diamino-s-triazin-2-ol. Colorless, deliquescent needles, decomp. by heat, insoluble in water. **ethyl-** See *ethyl*. **iso-** Isocyanurimide.

ammeter. *Ampere* meter.

ammines. Ammoniates, ammonates, ammino compounds, metal ammines, ammono. Complex inorganic metal-ammonia compounds which may be regarded as metal salts with ammonia; with a role analogous to that of "water" of crystallization; e.g., $CoCl_3 \cdot 6NH_3$ Cf. *aquo* ions, *ammonia* system, *crystal* ammonia, tetrammines.

ammino- Prefix indicating the presence of NH_3 in a coordinate compound; as in *ammines*.

ammiolite. A native antimonate of mercury.

ammite. A sandstone or oolite.

ammoidin. Xanthotoxin.

ammonate. See *crystal* ammonia.

ammonchelidonic acid. Chelidamic acid.

ammonia. (1) $NH_3 = 17.01$. Colorless gas, $d_{air=1}$ 0.5971, m.-77.7. b.-35.5; very soluble in water, forming ammonium hydroxide. It has a strong characteristic odor and is used in ice machines as a refrigerant, as a fertilizer applied directly to irrigation water, and as a reagent in the chemical industries. (2) Incorrect term for a solution of a. in water (NH_4OH); see *a. water*. **anhydrous-** Liquid a. Colorless liquid, $d_{-32°}$ 0.6382, m.-77.56. b.-33.3. Used in organic synthesis, as a solvent, and in refrigeration. **cracked-** Catalytically decomposed a. vapor (N and H); used to provide an inert atmosphere. **crystal-** See *crystal*. **hydroxy-** Hydroxylamine. **liquid-** Anhydrous a. **substituted-** See *amine*, *amide*, *ammines*, *amino*, *ammonium*. World production (1967) 33.5 million tons.

a. absorption apparatus. A device for absorbing a.; as Folin's tubes. **a. amalgam.** An amalgam of mercury and ammonium. **a. liquor.** Gas liquor; obtained by scrubbing coke plant gases with water and used in the Solway process, q.v., and in the manufacture of a. and ammonium salts. **a. nitrogen.** The nitrogen in an organic compound especially proteins, which is in the form of a NH_2 or $>NH$ radical (amino- or imino-nitrogen, respectively). **a. soda process.** A process (Brunner and Mond, 1874) for the manufacture of sodium carbonate from salt, ammonia, limestone, and coke. Cf. *Solvay* process. **a. spirit** A solution of ammonium carbonate, ammonium hydroxide, and flavoring agents; a reflex stimulant. **a. system.** A system of acids, bases, and salts with liquid a. as solvent instead of water. Thus

$$M \cdot NH_2 + HX \underset{\text{ammonolysis}}{\overset{\text{neutralization}}{\rightleftharpoons}} MX + H \cdot NH_2$$

Ammonio Ammonio   Ammonio
base   acid   salt

a. tube. Faraday tube. **a. water.** $NH_4OH = 35.1$. Ammonium hydroxide, spirits of hartshorn. An aqueous solution of ammonia. (1) 35%. *Concentrated* ammonium hydroxide. Clear, colorless liquid, d.0.880, of strong, characteristic odor and alkaline reaction; a reagent, solvent, precipitant, and neutralizing agent; used in pharmacy as 31.5–33.5% strength (B.P.). (2) 28%. d.0.900; used as (1) (U.S.P.). (3) 20%. d.0.925; used as (1). (4) 10%. *Dilute* ammonium hydroxide, d.0.960. The test solution of the U.S.P., and a common reagent; used as (1).

ammoniac. Ammoniacum. **sal-** Ammonium chloride. **a. oil.** Dark, yellow essential oil from ammoniacum, d.0.891, b.250–290, slightly dextrorotatory.

ammoniacal. Pertaining to ammonia; as, its odor.

ammoniacum. Gum ammoniac. A resinous gum from *Dorema ammoniacum*, (Umbelliferae) of Persia and Northern India. Used as a sedative and tonic in hysteria, externally in plasters, and as a porcelain cement.

ammoniate. (1) Ammine. (2) An organic nitrogen fertilizer.

ammoniated iron. Ferric ammonium chloride. **a. mercury.** See *mercury*. **a. superphosphate.** A superphosphate treated with (1) ammonia or (2) dissolved bone and nitrogenous compounds; a fertilizer.

ammonification. The enrichment of the soil with ammonia or ammonium compounds; e.g., the production of NH_3 from proteins and decaying organic matter by soil bacteria.

ammonifying. (1) Producing or (2) adding ammonia.

ammonio. (1) Ammono. (2) Prefix indicating a double salt of ammonium and a metal; as, a. cupric chloride (see *cupric*).

ammonite. A fossil shell.

ammonium. Am. The radical $-NH_4$, which has basic properties and resembles an alkali metal radical. Cf. *ammono*, *ferriammonium*, *tetraethylammonium*, *americium*. **a. acetate.** $CH_3COONH_4 = 77.08$. Colorless hygroscopic crystals, m.89, very soluble in water. Used as an antipyretic and diaphoretic antidote in formaldehyde poisoning, a reagent, and in separating Pb, Ca, Ba, and Sr sulfates. **a. aldehyde.** See *aldehyde* ammonia. **a. alum.** $Al_2(NH_4)_2(SO_4)_4 \cdot 24H_2O = 906.90$. Aluminum a. sulfate. Colorless, regular crystals, m.94.5. soluble in water. Used for water purification, in baking powder, foam fire extinguishers, and electroplating, an astringent, diuretic, emetic, and purgative. **a. aluminum sulfate.** A. alum. **a. aminosulfonate.** $NH_4SO_3NH_2 = 114.2$. Deliquescent crystals, soluble in water. **a. anacardate.** Brown syrup, used to color hair. **a. antimonate.** $NH_4SbO_3 \cdot 2H_2O = 222.27$. Colorless crystals, decomp. by heat, soluble in water. **a. arsenate.** $(NH_4)_3AsO_4 \cdot 3H_2O = 247.2$. Colorless crystals, soluble in water. *acid-* $(NH_4)_2HAsO_4 = 176.0$. White crystals, soluble in water; used to treat skin diseases. **a. arsenite.** $NH_4AsO_2 = 125.0$. Colorless prisms, soluble in water. **a. atreolate.** Atreol. **a. aurichloride.** $NH_4AuCl_4 = 357.10$. Yellow plates, decomp. 100, soluble in water. **a. auricyanide.** $NH_4Au(CN)_4 \cdot H_2O = 337.32$. Yellowish plates, decomp. 200, soluble in water. **a. aurocyanide.** $NH_4Au(CN)_3 = 293.3$. Colorless plates, decomp. 150, soluble in water. **a. benzoate.**

$NH_4 \cdot C_7H_5O_2 = 139.1$. White crystals, decomp. 198, soluble in water; an antipyretic, diuretic, and alterative. **a. biarsenate.** A. arsenate, acid- **a. biborate.** $NH_4HB_2O_4 \cdot 1\frac{1}{2}H_2O = 132.1$. Colorless crystals, soluble in water. **a. bicarbonate.** $NH_4\cdot HCO_3 = 79.1$. Colorless rhombs, decomp. 40–60, soluble in water. Used to neutralize hyperacidity of the stomach, and in manufacturing ammonium salts. **a. bichromate.** $(NH_4)_2Cr_2O_7 = 252.2$. Orange crystals, decomp. by heat, soluble in water. Used as a reagent, and in the manufacture of inks, glass, leather, and fireworks. **a. bifluoride.** $NH_4F \cdot HF = 57.1$. A. acid fluoride, matt salt, a. hydrogen fluoride. Colorless hexagons, soluble in water. Used in the analysis of silicates, in the glass and porcelain industry for etching and as a preservative. **a. bimalate.** $NH_4H(C_4H_4O_5) = 131.1$. White crystals, soluble in water. **a. bioxalate.** $HOOC \cdot COONH_4 = 107.1$. A. acid oxalate, binoxalate. Colorless crystals, soluble in water; an ink eraser and reagent. **a. biphosphate.** $NH_4H_2PO_4 = 115.1$. Monoammonium phosphate, diacid a. phosphate. Colorless tetragons, soluble in water. Used as a reagent, and with sodium bicarbonate in baking powder. **a. bisulfate.** $NH_4HSO_4 = 115.11$. Monoammonium sulfate, a. acid sulfate. Colorless crystals, soluble in water; a reagent. **a. bisulfite.** $NH_4HSO_3 = 99.11$. Monoammonium sulfite, sulfite acid. Colorless crystals, soluble in water; a preservative. **a. bitartrate.** $NH_4HC_4H_4O_6 = 167.1$. Monoammonium tartrate, a. acid tartrate. Colorless crystals, soluble in water. Used to detect calcium, and in baking powders. **a. borate.** $(NH_4)BO_3 = 113.1$. Colorless crystals, soluble in water. **a. borobenzoate.** White powder, soluble in water; an antiseptic. **a. borofluoride.** $NH_4BF_4 = 105.04$. Colorless regular crystals, soluble in water. **a. borocitrate.** White antiseptic powder, soluble in water. **a. bromide.** $NH_4BF_4 = 97.96$. Colorless crystals, sublime on heating, soluble in water; used as a reagent, to treat neuralgia, and in the manufacture of photographic plates. **a. bromoplatinate.** A platinic bromide. **a. camphorate.** $NH_4C_{10}H_{15}O_4 \cdot 3H_2O = 271$. Colorless crystals, soluble in water; a sedative. **a. carbamate.** $NH_2 \cdot COONH_4 = 78.1$. A. carbaminate. White crystals, soluble in water; a stimulant. Cf. *a. carbonate carbamate*. **a. carbazotate.** A. picrate. **a. carbonate.** $(NH_4)_2CO_3 \cdot H_2O = 114.1$. Colorless plates, decomp. 85, soluble in water; a reagent. **a. carbonate acid.** A. bicarbonate. **a. carbonate carbamate.** $NH_4HCO_3 \cdot NH_4NH_2CO_2 = 157.1$. Hartshorn salt. The a. carbonate of commerce. Colorless crystals, m.85 (sublimes), soluble in water; contains 30–32% ammonia. Used as a reagent in separating the alkaline earth metals from magnesium; as a heart stimulant; in lotions; in the manufacture of cocoa, baking powder, rubber goods; and in the dye industry. **a. carnallite.** The mineral $MgCl_2 \cdot NH_4Cl \cdot 6H_2O$. **a. caseinate.** Eucasin. White powder, soluble in water, either *mono-* or *di-* (0.011 or 0.022% NH_3, respectively). **a. chlorate** $NH_4ClO_3 = 101.50$. Colorless explosive, monoclinic crystals, soluble in water. **a. chloraurate.** a. aurichloride. **a. chloride.** $NH_4Cl = 53.5$. Sal ammoniac, salmiac, ammoniak. Colorless, regular or tetragonal crystals, or

white granules, dissociates 350, sublimes without melting, soluble in water. Used as a reagent in qualitative analysis, as an expectorant, stimulant, diuretic or diaphoretic, and externally, as a cooling and stimulating wash for contusions; also for filling dry batteries, for soldering flux, and in textile printing. **a. chloroiridate.** A. iridichloride. **a. chloropalladate.** $(NH_2)_2PdCl_6 = 355.54$. A. palladic chloride. Brown crystals, decomp. by heat. sparingly soluble in water. **a. chloropalladite.** $(NH_4)_2PdCl_4 = 284.62$. A. palladous chloride. Red crystals, soluble in water. **a. chloroplatinate.** $(NH_4)_2PtCl_6 = 444.1$. Yellow regular crystals, decomp. by heat, slightly soluble in water; a reagent. **a. chloroplatinite.** $(NH_4)_2PtCl_4 = 373.12$. Yellow, regular crystals, slightly soluble in water. **a. chlorostannate.** $(NH_4)_2SnCl_6 = 367.5$. White crystals, soluble in water. **a. chromate.** $(NH_4)_2CrO_4 = 152.1$. Yellow needles, decomp. 185, soluble in water; a reagent and mordant. *acid-* see *a. bichromate*. **a. chromic sulfate.** $Cr_2(SO_4)_3(NH_4)_2SO_4, 24H_2O = 956.71$. Green octagons, soluble in water. **a. citrate.** $(NH_4)_3C_6H_5O_7 = 243.2$. White deliquescent powder, soluble in water; a reagent. **a. cuprate.** A. carbonate carbamate. **a. cuprate.** Deep blue ammoniacal solution of cupric hydroxide, used for waterproofing fabrics. **a. cyanate.** $NH_4CNO = 60.1$. Colorless crystals, soluble in cold water, decomp. in hot water. **a. cyanide.** $NH_4CN = 44.1$. Colorless, regular crystals, decomp. 37, soluble in water. **a. dichromate.** A. bichromate. **a. dithiocarbamate.** $NH_2 \cdot CS \cdot CNH_4 = 90.1$. Yellow prisms, soluble in water. **a. dithiocarbonate.** $NH_4S \cdot CO \cdot SH = 111.1$. Yellow crystals, a substitute for hydrogen sulfide in qualitative analysis. **a. dithionate.** $(NH_4)_2S_2O_6 = 196.20$. Colorless, monoclinic crystals, soluble in water. **a. embeliate.** $NH_4C_9H_{13}O_3 = 187.1$. Violet-gray powder, soluble in water; a taeniacide. **a. ethyl sulfate.** $(NH_4)(C_2H_5)SO_4 = 143.1$. Colorless crystals, m.99, soluble in water. **a. ferrichloride.** Ferric a. chloride. **a. ferricitrate.** Ferric a. citrate. **a. ferric oxalate.** $(NH_4)_3Fe(C_2O_4)_3 \cdot 4H_2O = 446.06$. Gray crystals, decomp. 165, soluble in water. **a. ferricyanide.** $2(NH_4)_3Fe(CN)_6 \cdot H_2O = 550.05$. Red crystals, soluble in water; a reagent. **a. ferrocyanide.** $(NH_4)_4Fe(CN)_6 \cdot 3H_2O = 338.20$. Green-yellow crystals, soluble in water; a reagent. **a. fluoride.** $NH_4F = 37.0$. Malt salt. Colorless hexagons, sublime if heated, soluble in water. Used as a reagent, an alterative or antiperiodic, and for etching glass. **a. fluoride acid.** A. bifluoride. **a. fluosilicate.** $(NH_4)_2SiF_6 = 158.18$. Colorless rhombs, soluble in water. **a. formate.** $H \cdot COONH_4 = 63.06$. Colorless crystals, m.116, decomp. 180, soluble in water; an antiseptic. **a. gallate.** $NH_4C_7H_5O_5 \cdot H_2O = 205.13$. Yellow crystals, soluble in water. **a. glycerophosphate.** $(NH_4)_2PO_4C_3H_5(OH)_2 = 206$. Colorless crystals, soluble in water; used to treat influenza. **a. heptamolybdate.** A. molybdate basic. **a. hippurate.** $NH_4H(C_9H_8O_3N)_2 \cdot H_2O = 393.3$. Colorless crystals, soluble in water. **a. hydrogen fluoride.** A. bifluoride. **a. hydrogen phosphate.** A. phosphate. **a. hydrosulfide.** $NH_4HS = 51.1$. Colorless crystals, soluble in water; a reagent for metals. **a. hydrosulfide solution.** A solution prepared by passing hydrogen sulfide through a. hydroxdie. Yellow alkaline liquid; a reagent. **a. hydroxide.** $NH_4OH = 35.1$. A hydrate of ammonia, crystalline below -79, otherwise only known in solution as ammonia water, q.v. Cf. *quaternary amines, hydroxylammonium compounds.* **a. hypophosphite.** $NH_4H_2PO_2 = 83.10$. White rhombs, decomp. 240, soluble in water; a nerve tonic. **a. hyposulfide.** A. thiosulfite. **a. hyposulfite.** $(NH_4)_2S_2O_3 = 148.2$ A. thiosulfate. Colorless crystals, soluble in water; an antiseptic. **a. ichthyolsulfonate.** Ichthyol. **a. iodate.** $NH_4IO_3 = 192.96$. Colorless rhombs, decomp. 125, soluble in water. **a. iodide.** $NH_4I = 144.96$. Colorless regular crystals or powder, sublimes when heated, soluble in water. A reagent for acetone; used to treat syphilis and leprosy, and in photography. **a. iodoxylbenzoate.** Amiodoxylbenzoate. **a. iridichloride.** $(NH_4)_2IrCl_6 = 441.9$. A. chloroiridate, a. iridic chloride. Red powder, slightly soluble in water. **a. iron chloride.** Orange powder, soluble in water; a mixture of 2.5% $FeCl_3$ and 97.5% NH_4Cl. Used to treat anemia, chlorosis, and scrofulosis. **a. lactate.** $NH_4C_3H_5O_3 = 107.1$. Colorless syrup, miscible with water. **a. linoleate.** $C_{17}H_{31}COONH_4 = 297.2$. Soft mass; an emulsifier for fats, and a waterproofing, glazing, and polishing agent. **a. magnesium arsenate.** $MgNH_4AsO_4 \cdot 6H_2O = 289.4$. Colorless tetragons, decomp. by heat, slightly soluble in water. **a. magnesium phosphate.** $MgNH_4PO_4, 6H_2O = 245.6$. Colorless tetragons, slightly soluble in water. **a. malate.** $NH_4C_4H_5O_5 = 151.08$. Rhombic crystals, m.161, soluble in water. **a. monomagnesium phosphate.** $Mg(NH_4)_4(PO_4)_2 = 286.3$. **a. mellitate.** $C_6(COONH_4)_6 \cdot 9H_2O = 606$. Colorless crystals, soluble in water. An emulsifier for fats and waxes, and a waterproofing, glazing, and polishing agent. **a. metaborate.** A. biborate. **a. metaphosphate.** See *a. phosphate.* **a. metavanadate.** A. vanadate. **a. molybdate.** $(NH_4)_2MoO_4 = 196.1$. Colorless monoclinic crystals, decomp. by water. Used as a reagent, and in the manufacture of pigments. *basic-* $(NH_4)_6Mo_7O_{24} \cdot 4H_2O = 1236.6$. A. heptamolybdate. Green-yellow crystals, decomp. by heat, soluble in a. chloride solution. Used as a reagent and in the preparation of pigments. **a. molybdate solution** (6%). Yellow liquid, with a slight odor of nitric acid; a reagent for orthophosphates and arsenates. **a. mucinate.** $(NH_4)_2C_6H_8O_8 = 244$. Colorless crystals, soluble in water. **a. muriate.** A. chloride. **a. nickel sulfate.** Nickelammonium sulfate. **a. nitrate.** $NH_4NO_3 = 80.1$. German saltpeter, Norway saltpeter. Colorless tetragons, m. 170, decomp. 200, soluble in water. Used as an oxidizing agent, as a flux for metals, in the preparation of laughing gas, in freezing mixtures, and in explosives. **a. nitrite.** $NH_4NO_2 = 64.1$. Colorless crystals, decomp. by heat, into water and nitrogen, soluble in water. **a. nitrosophenylhydroxylamine.** Cupferron. **a. oleate.** $(NH_4)_2C_{18}H_{33}O_2 = 317$. Ammonia soap. Colorless gel, soluble in alcohol; a cleanser. **a. oxalate.** $(COONH_4)_2 \cdot H_2O = 142.1$. Colorless prisms, soluble in water. A reagent used in the separation of Ca; as a precipitant for Ba, Zn, Pb; and in determination of quinine. **a. oxalate acid.** A. bioxalate. **a. oxalurate.** $NH_4C_3H_3N_2O_4 = $ 149. Yellow crystals, soluble in hot water. **a. oxaminate.** $NH_2 \cdot CO \cdot COONH_4 = 106.1$. Colorless crystals, soluble in water. **a. pallidichloride.** A, chloropalladate. **a. palmitate.** $NH_4C_{16}H_{31}O_2 = 274$. Soft masses, soluble in water; a cleanser. **a. perchlorate.** $NH_4ClO_4 = 117.5$. White prisms, decomp. by heat, soluble in water; used in explosives. **a. perchromate.** $(NH_4)_3CrO_8 = 234.13$. Yellow rhombs, decomp. 50, soluble in water. **a. permanganate.** $NH_4MnO_4 = 137.1$. Purple rhombs, decomp. by heat, soluble in water; used in pyrotechnics. **a. persulfate.** $(NH_4)_2S_2O_8 = 228.2$. Colorless monoclinic crystals, decomp. by heat, soluble in water. A disinfectant, deodorant, and preservative, a reagent for albumen and indican; an oxidizing agent in analysis; used in photography, as a reducer; and in electroplating. **a. phenolsulfonate.** $C_6H_4(OH)SO_3 \cdot NH_4 = 191.14$. White crystals, soluble in water. **a. phenylate.** $C_6H_5O \cdot NH_4 = 111.1$. White crystals soluble in water; an antiseptic and antipyretic. **a. phosphate.** $(NH_4)_2HPO_4 = 132.2$. Diammonium orthophosphate, ammonium diphosphate. Colorless monoclinic crystals, soluble in water. A precipitant for Mg, Zn, Ni, and U; an antirheumatic, fertilizer, and fireproofing material. *mono-* A. biphosphate; *tri-* A. phosphate, tribasic. *meta-* $NH_4PO_3 = 97.8$. A. metaphosphate. Colorless crystals, soluble in water. **a. phosphate monobasic.** $NH_4H_2PO_4 = 115.2$. Monoammonium phosphate, Ammo-Phos. Colorless powder, soluble in water; a fertilizer. **a. phosphate tribasic.** $(NH_4)_3PO_4 = 149.1$. Triammonium phosphate. Colorless crystals, soluble in water; a culture medium. **a. phosphite.** (1) *mono-* $NH_4H_2PO_3 = 99.10$. Colorless crystals, m.123, decomp. 50, soluble in water. (2) *di-* $(NH_4)_2HPO_3 = 116.1$. Diammonium phosphite. Colorless crystals, soluble in water; a reducing agent. **a. phosphomolybdate.** $(NH_4)_3PO_4 \cdot 12MoO_3 \cdot 3H_2O = 1931.2$. Yellow crystals, slightly soluble in water; a reagent for alkaloids. **a. phosphotungstate, a. phosphowolframate.** $(NH_4)_3PO_4 \cdot 12WO_3 \cdot 3H_2O = 2795$. White powder, soluble in water; a reagent. **a. phthalate.** $C_6H_4(COONH_4)_2 = 200.2$. Colorless crystals, soluble in water. **a. picramate.** $C_6H_2NH_2(NO_2)_2 \cdot ONH_4 = 216.09$. Brown crystals, soluble in water, used in bacteriology. **a. picrate.** $NH_4C_6H_2O(NO_2)_3 = 246$. A. carbazotate, ammonium picronitrate. Yellow, explosive crystals, decomp. by heat, soluble in water or alcohol. **a. picrocarminate solution.** Red staining solution used to differentiate the nucleus and cytoplasm of cells. **a. picronitrate.** A. picrate. **a. platinic bromide.** $(NH_4)_2PtBr_6 = 710.80$. A. bromoplatinate. Red, regular crystals, decomp. by heat, slightly soluble in water. **a. platinic chloride.** $(NH_4)_2PtCl_6 = 444.0$. Yellow hygroscopic crystals, soluble in water; a reagent. **a. purpurate.** Murexide. **a. pyrophosphate.** $(NH_4)_4P_2O_7 = 246.3$. White crystals, soluble in water. **a. rhodanate.** A. thiocyanate. **a. salicylate.** $NH_4C_7H_5O_3 = 155.1$. White monoclinic crystals, soluble in water; an antirheumatic, antipyretic, expectorant, and bactericide. **a. selenate (acid).** $NH_4HSeO_4 = 162.2$. Colorless crystals, soluble in water. **a. selenate (normal).** $(NH_4)_2SeO_4 = 179.28$. White crystals, soluble in water. **a. selenite.** $(NH_4)_2SeO_3 = 163.2$. White crystals, soluble in water used as a reagent for alkaloids and in red glass. **a. sesquicarbonate.** $2NH_4CO_3\cdot(NH_4)_2CO_3H_2O = 272.2$. White crystals, decomp. by heat. **a. silicofluoride.** $(NH_4)_2SiF_6 = 178.07$. Colorless crystals, soluble in water; an antiseptic. **a. silvinate.** $NH_4C_{20}H_{29}O_2 = 319$. Yellow microcrystals, slightly soluble in water. **a. stannic chloride.** A. chlorostannate. **a. stearate.** $C_{17}H_{35}\cdot COONH_4 = 301$. White, soaplike mass, soluble in hot alcohol. **a. succinate.** $C_2H_4(COONH_4)_2 = 152.2$. Colorless crystals, soluble in water; used in gynecology. **a. sulfate.** $(NH_4)_2SO_4 = 132.2$. Colorless rhombs, m.140, decomp. 280, soluble in water. Used as a precipitant for proteins, to separate Ca and Sr, and in the manufacture of fertilizers. *acid-* A. bisulfate. **a. sulfhydrate.** A. hydrosulfide. **a. sulfide.** $(NH_4)_2S = 68.2$. White crystals, decomp. by heat, soluble in water; a reagent. **a. sulfide solution.** An aqueous solution of a. hydrosulfide. **a. sulfite.** $(NH_4)_2SO_3\cdot H_2O = 134.2$. White monoclinic crystals, decomp. by heat, soluble in water; an antiseptic. *acid-* A. bisulfite. **a. sulfocarbonate solution.** A liquid prepared from a. carbonate and carbon disulfide; an insecticide and parasiticide. **a. sulfocyanate.** A. thiocyanate. **a. sulfoichthyolate.** Ichthyol. **a. sulfophenylate.** $C_6H_4OH\cdot SO_3NH_4 = 191$. A sulfocarbolate. Colorless crystals, soluble in water; an antiseptic. **a. sulphate.** A. sulfate. **a. tartrate.** $C_2H_4O_2(COONH_4)_2 = 184$. Colorless monoclinic crystals. Two forms: refractive indices $\alpha = 1.55$ and $\beta = 1.581$, soluble in water; an expectorant. *acid-* $NH_4HC_4H_4O_6 = 167.08$. A. bitartrate; a. hydrogen tartrate. Monoclinic prisms: refractive indices 1.519, 1.561, and 1.591; soluble in water. **a. tellurate.** $(NH_4)_2TeO_4 = 227.2$. White powder, soluble in acids; a reagent for glucosides and alkaloids. **a. thioacetate.** $CH_3COSNH_4 = 93.2$. Yellow crystalline masses, soluble in water; a reagent. **a. thioacetate solution.** A 30% aqueous solution; a reagent in organic analysis and substitute for hydrogen sulfide. **a. thiocarbonate.** $(NH_4)_2CS_3 = 144.27$. Yellow crystals, soluble in water. **a. thiocyanate, -ide.** $NH_4CNS = 76.1$. A. rhodanate. Colorless, deliquescent, monoclinic crystals, m.159, at 170 it changes to thiourea, soluble in water. A reagent; also used in the dye and textile industry. **a. thionurate.** $(NH_4)_2C_4H_3N_3SO_6 = 257$. White crystals, soluble in water. **a. thiostannate.** $(NH_4)_2SnS_3 = 251$. **a. thiosulfate.** $(NH_4)_2S_2O_3 = 148.21$. A. hyposulfite. Colorless rhombs, decomp. 150, soluble in water. **a. triborate.** $NH_4\cdot H(BO_2)_2 = 105.1$. A. acid borate. Colorless crystals, soluble in water. **a. tungstate.** $(NH_4)_2WO_4 = 284.1$. Colorless crystals, soluble in water. *ortho-* $(NH_4)_2W_2O_{18}\cdot 8H_2O = 3276.2$. Colorless crystals, soluble in water. *meta-* $(NH_4)_2W_4O_{18}\cdot 8H_2O = 1204.4$. Colorless, octahedra, soluble in water. *para-* $(NH_4)_6W_7O_{24}\cdot 6H_2O = 1888.3$. Colorless rhombs, slightly soluble in water. Used to prepare a. phosphotungstate. **a. uranate.** $(NH_4)_2U_2O_7 = 627.2$. Yellow-red powder used for coloring porcelain. **a. uranylcarbonate.** *Uranyl*ammonium carbonate. **a. uranylfluoride.** *Uranyl*ammonium fluoride. **a. urate.** $(NH_4)C_5H_3N_4O_3 = 185.1$. Colorless crystals, soluble in water; an antiseptic. **a. valerate.** $C_4H_9\cdot COONH_4 = 119.1$. Colorless,

hygroscopic crystals, soluble in water; a hypnotic, sedative, and tonic. **a. valerianate.** A. valerate. **a. vanadate.** $NH_4VO_3 = 155.2$. White powder, soluble in water; used in the textile industry, in the manufacture of vanadium catalysts, photographic dyes, indelible ink, and ceramics. **a. wolframate.** A. tungstate.

ammono. Pertaining to the *ammonia* system, q.v. **a. base.** MNH_2. An inorganic amide. Cf. *base*, *ammonio.* **a. salt.** Cf. *ammonia* system.

ammonocarbonous acid. Hydrocyanic acid.

ammonolysis. (1) A reaction which corresponds with hydrolytic dissociation: $NH_3 \rightarrow H^+ + NH_2^-$. (2) The cleavage of a bond by the addition of ammonia; $R-R' + NH_3 \rightarrow RNH_2 + HR$. (3) Treatment (of oils) with hot ammonia gas under pressure.

Ammo-Phos. Trademark for ammonium phosphate fertilizer containing ammonia 13 and available phosphorus pentoxide 48%.

amniotin. Estrone.

amobarbital. $C_{11}H_{18}N_2O_3 = 226.28$. 5-Ethyl-5-isoamylbarbitone, amylobarbital. White, bitter, crystals, m.157, slightly soluble in water; a central depressant (U.S.P.). **a. sodium.** $C_{11}H_{17}N_2O_3Na = 248.26$. White, hygroscopic, bitter granules; used as a.

amodiaquine (hydrochloride). $C_{20}H_{22}ON_3Cl\cdot 2HCl = 464.8$. Yellow, bitter crystals m.158, soluble in water, an antimalarial (B.P.).

amoeba. Ameba.

amoeboid. Resembling an ameba. **a. cell.** A leucocyte. **a. movement.** The rolling movement of the protoplasmic jelly of a unicellular organism.

amoil. Amyl phthalate used for high-vacuum pumps.

amorphism. The noncrystalline condition of a solid substance; due to an irregular molecular assembly.

amorphous. (1) Unorganized. (2) Describing a solid substance which does not crystallize and is without definite geometrical shape. (3) In bacteriology, any bacteria without visible differentiation in structure.

amosite. A long-fibered variety of Transvaal asbestos.

amoxy. Amyloxy. The radical $Me(CH_2)_4O-$ from amyl alcohol.

ampelite. A graphite schist containing SiO_2 53.8, Al_2O_3 23.5%, and sulfur (Pyrenees). Used as refractory up to 1850°C.

Ampère, Andre Marie. 1775–1836. French physicist; developed molecular theory.

ampere. The unit of amount of electric current. One ampere passing through silver nitrate solution deposits 0.001118 gm of silver per second. The strength of a current with an electromotive force of one volt passing through a resistance wire (or solution) of one ohm. 1 amp = 1 coulomb/sec = 1 volt through 1 ohm = 10^{-1} emu (cgs) = 3×10^9 esu. **international-** 1 int. a. = 0.9999 absolute a. **micro-** One-millionth of an a. **milli-** One-thousandth of an a. **a. meter.** Ammeter. An instrument for measuring electric current. Cf. *voltammeter*, *ohmammeter.* **a. volt.** A volt-ampere or a watt.

amperometer. Ampere meter.

amperometry. Chemical analysis by methods which involve measurements of electric currents. Cf. *conductometric analysis, polarography, potentiometry.*

amphenone. $NH_2\cdot C_6H_4CMe\cdot C:OMe$. *p*-Aminopropiophenone. A specific inhibitor of the adrenal cortex.

amphetamine. $C_6H_5 \cdot CH_2 \cdot CH(NH_2)Me = 135.2$. Benzedrine. Racemic 1-phenyl-2-aminopropane. Colorless liquid. Its vapors shrink nasal mucosa. **a. sulfate.** $(C_9H_{13}N)_2 \cdot H_2SO_4 = 368.50$. Benzedrine sulfate. White, bitter powder; used for its vasomotor, respiratory, and stimulatory effects.

amphi- Prefix (Greek) meaning "on both sides" or "both." **a. position.** The 2,6-hydrogen atoms in 2 condensed hexatomic rings; as, naphthalene.

amphiboles. $M_x(SiO_3)_y$. Rock-forming minerals with occluded water; M is Ca, Mg, Fe, or the alkali metals, e.g., crocidolite. Elongated, fibrous black or dark green crystals. Cf. *silica* minerals.

amphibolites. Metamorphic rocks derived from argillaceous limestones and related to the glaucophane schists.

amphichroic, amphichromatic. Describing mixed indicators whose color changes neutralize each other; e.g., litmus and congo red.

amphigene. Leucite.

amphiphatic. Describing a detergent or wetting agent which greatly reduces the surface tension of water. Part of the molecule is hydrophilic, and the other consists of straight or branched long hydrocarbon chains; e.g., cetyl trimethyl bromide, $[C_{16}H_{33}Me_3N]^+Br^-$.

amphiphile. A substance containing both polar water-soluble and hydrophobic water-insoluble groups; e.g., $C_{12}H_{25} \cdot OH$, where $C_{12}H_{25}$ is hydrophobic.

amphiprotic. Able to lose or gain a proton. Cf. *acid, base.*

ampholyte. Amphoteric electrolyte. A substance which in solution yields H^+ or OH^-, i.e., donates or accepts a proton, according as it is in an acid or basic solution. Cf. *isoelectric* point, *zwitterion.*

ampholytoid. Amphoteric colloid. A particle in suspension capable of adsorbing H^+ or OH^-, depending on the pH value.

amphoteric. Describing substances having both acid and basic properties; as, the amino acids, $NH_2 \cdot R \cdot COOH$. **a. hydroxides.** The hydroxides of some metals which may dissociate to H^+ or OH^- ions; as, $2Al(OH)_3 \rightleftharpoons H^+ + AlO_2 + H_2O$ (acid) or $Al^{3+} + 3OH^-$ (base). **a. sulfides.** The sulfides of the metallic nonmetals, which may react as weak acids or weak bases; e.g., $H_3(AsS_3) \rightleftharpoons As(SH)_3$.

amphotericin B. A patented polyene antibiotic, produced by *Streptomyces nodosus.* Orange powder, insoluble in water (U.S.P.).

amphotropine. $[(CH_2)_6N_4]_2 \cdot C_8H_{14}(COOH)_2 = 480$. Hexamethylenamine camphorate. Colorless crystals.

ampicillin. $C_{16}H_{19}O_4N_3S = 349.36$. 2-(Aminobenzyl) penicillin. White, bitter crystals, soluble in water; an antibiotic (B.P.). Also used as the sodium salt and trihydrate (B.P.).

amplifier. (1) A magnifier. (2) A vacuum tube acting as an electric valve, by which weak electric impulses are strengthened; as in radio reception.

amplitude. The maximum displacement of an oscillation, vibration, or wave.

ampoule, ampul. A small, sealed, glass vial, e.g., for a sterilized hypodermic injection.

amrad gum. A gummy exudation from elephant apple. *Feronia elephantum* (Rutaceae), of India.

amyctic. An irritating stimulant, especially for skin.

amygdala. The seeds of *Prunus amygdalus*, containing emulsin and amygdalin. **a. amara.** See bitter *almond.* **a. dulcis.** See sweet *almond.*

amygdalic acid. (1) Mandelic acid. (2) $C_{20}H_{28}O_{13} = 476.22$. Gentiobioside. A glucoside from almonds.

amygdalin. $C_{20}H_{27}O_{11}N \cdot 3H_2O = 511.37$. d- Mandelonitrile glucoside, amygdaloside. A glucoside from bitter almonds and wild cherry-bark. Colorless crystals, m.210, soluble in water. Hydrolyzes to 2 moles glucose, hydrocyanic acid, and benzaldehyde; an expectorant and source of oil or bitter almonds.

amygdalinic acid. Mandelic acid.

amygdaloid. Shaped like an almond.

amygdophenin. $H_4O \cdot C_2H_5NH \cdot CO \cdot CHOH \cdot C_6H_5 = 271.2$. Phenetidine amygdalate. Gray crystals; an analgesic.

amyl(o). Am. Pentyl (preferred usage). The $-C_5H_{11}$ radical, from pentane. **iso-** *i*-Am. The $-C_5H_{11}$ radical, from isopentane. **tert-** The radical $C \colon Me_2 \cdot MeCH_2$, from pentane. **a. acetate.** $MeCOOC_5H_{11} = 130.13$. Isoamyl acetate, isoamylacetic ester, banana oil, pear oil, pentyl acetate, amylacetic ester. Colorless, flammable liquid, b.148, sparingly soluble in water, miscible with alcohol. Used in making fruit flavors; as a solvent for nitrocellulose, varnishes, and lacquers; for waterproofing materials, metallic paints, and liquid bronzes; and as fuel for the Hefner standard candle. **a. acetic ether.** Amyl acetate. **a. alcohol.** $CH_3(CH_2)_4OH = 88.11$. Fusel oil, grain oil, potato spirit, fermentation amyl alcohol. Colorless liquid, d.0.870, b.137.5, miscible with alcohol. A mixture of isomeric alcohols used as a solvent, reagent, in pharmaceuticals, artificial silk, varnishes, lacquers, mercury fulminate, and photography. See table. *active-* See iso- or secondary-. *alpha-* See secondary-. *beta-* See tertiary-. *dextro-* See iso- or secondary-. *iso-* $CH_3 \cdot CH_2 \cdot CH(CH_3) \cdot CH_2OH$. Isobutylcarbinol, 2-methylbutanol,

AMYL ALCOHOLS

Primary:

1-Pentanol, d.0.817, m. -78.5, b.137.9...............	$CH_3 \cdot CH_2 \cdot CH_2 \cdot CH_2 \cdot CH_2OH$
3-Methyl-1-butanol, d.0.812, m. -117.2, b.130.5	$CH_3CHMe \cdot CH_2 \cdot CH_2OH$
2-Methyl-1-butanol, d.0.816, m.128...................	$CH_3 \cdot CH_2 \cdot CHMe \cdot CH_2OH$
2,2-Dimethylpropanol, m.53, b.114	$CH_3 \cdot CMe_2 \cdot CH_2OH$

Secondary:

2-Pentanol, d.0.809, b.119..........................	$CH_3 \cdot CH_2 \cdot CH_2 \cdot CHMeOH$
3-Pentanol, d.0.815, b.115.6	$CH_3 \cdot CH_2 \cdot CHOH \cdot CH_2 \cdot CH_3$
3-Methyl-2-butanol, d.0.819, b.114....................	$CH_3 \cdot CHMe \cdot CHMeOH$

Tertiary:

2-Methyl-2-butanol, d.0.809, m. -11.9, b.101.8	$CH_3CH_2 \cdot CMe_2OH$

active amyl alcohol. Occurs in *d*- and *l*- stereoisomeric forms. Colorless liquid, d.0.825, b.132, the chief constituent of fusel oil. *levo*- See iso- or secondary-, *normal*- See primary-. *primary*-Butylcarbinol, normal amyl alcohol, 1-pentanol*. Colorless liquid, d.0.817, b.137, soluble in water. *secondary*-α-Amyl alcohol, secondary butylcarbinol, 1-methylbutanol*, 2-pentanol*; occurs in *d*- and *l*-forms. Colorless flammable liquid, d.0.8169, b.118, miscible with water; used in organic synthesis and as a solvent. *tertiary*- Amylene hydrate, dimethylethylcarbinol, 1-dimethylpropylalcohol. Colorless, flammable liquid, b.102, soluble in water; used in fruit ethers. **a. aldehyde.** Valeraldehyde. **a. amine.** $C_5H_{11}NH_2 = 87.14$. *n*- Normal amylamine, pentylamin*, 1-aminopentane. Colorless liquid, b.104, miscible with water. *iso*- Colorless liquid, b.95, soluble in water. Used as an emulsifier and in dye manufacture. Cf. *diamyl*amine, *triamyl*amine. *methyl*- Isohexylamine. **a. amine hydrochloride.** $C_5H_{11}NH_2 \cdot HCl = 123.5$. Colorless crystals, soluble in water; an antipyretic. **a. aniline** (iso). $PhNHC_5H_{11} = 163.20$. A liquid, b.260. **a. benzene.** $C_5H_{11} \cdot C_6H_5 = 148.18$. Phenylpentane. Colorless liquid, b.201, soluble in alcohol. **a. benzoate.** $C_6H_5COOC_5H_{11} = 192.19$. *n*- Colorless liquid, b.260, soluble in alcohol. *iso*- Colorless liquid, b.262, insoluble in water. **a. bromide.** $C_5H_{11}Br = 151.03$. *n*-, 1-Bromopentane*. Colorless liquid, b.$_{740mm}$ = 128.7, soluble in alcohol. *iso*-β-Bromopentane. Colorless liquid, b.120, insoluble in water; an antiseptic. **a. butyrate.** $C_3H_7COOC_5H_{11} = 158.19$. *isoamyl n*-*butyrate.* Isoamylbutyric ester. Colorless liquid, b. 179, slightly soluble in water; used in fruit ethers. *n-amyl isobutyrate.* Colorless liquid, b.154, slightly soluble in water. Used in organic synthesis and in artificial fruit essences. *isoamyl isobutyrate.* Colorless liquid, b.169, miscible with alcohol. **a. carbamate.** $C_5H_{11}CO_2NH_2 = 131$. Amylcarbamic ester, amyl urethane. Colorless crystals, m.60, soluble in alcohol. Cf. *aponal, hedonal.* **a. carbinol.** Hexyl alcohol. **a. carbylamine.** $C_5H_{11}NC = 97.13$, b.137, insoluble in water. **a. chlorcarbonate.** $ClCOOC_5H_{11} = 150.58$. *iso*- Colorless liquid, b.100, insoluble in water. **a. chloride.** $C_5H_{11}Cl = 106.57$. *n*- 1-Chloropentane*. Colorless liquid, b.$_{740mm}$107, miscible with alcohol. *iso*- β-Chloropentane. Colorless liquid, b.100, insoluble in water. **a. cyanide.** $C_5H_{11}CN = 97.13$. Capronitrile. Colorless liquid, b.163, insoluble in water. *iso*- Isocapronitrile. Colorless liquid, b.155. **a. ether.** $(C_5H_{11})_2O = 158.23$. *n*- Pentyloxypentane*. Yellow liquid, b.169, insoluble in water. *iso*- Isoamyl oxide. Colorless liquid, b.173, insoluble in water; a solvent. **a. ethyl ketone.** $C_2H_5COC_5H_{11} = 128.17$. 3-Octanone, b.164. **a. formate.** $HCOOC_5H_{11} = 116.13$. *n*- Colorless liquid, b.123, slightly soluble in water. *iso*- Colorless liquid, b.130, slightly soluble in water; used in fruit essences. **a. furoate.** $C_4H_3O \cdot COOC_5H_{11} = 182.11$. *n*- Colorless liquid, b.233; used in perfumery and lacquers. *iso*- b.$_{25mm}$136. **a. hydrate.** See *amyl* alcohols. **a. hydride.** Pentane. **a. hydrosulfide.** Amyl mercaptan. **a. iodide.** $C_5H_{11}I = 198.03$. *n*- 1-Iodopentane*. Colorless liquid, b.$_{739mm}$155, miscible with alcohol. *iso*-

Isoiodopentane. Colorless liquid, b.148, insoluble in water; a sedative and antiseptic. **a. isobutyrate.** Amyl isobutyrate. **a. isocyanide.** $Me(CH_2)_4CN = 97.09$. Pentylcarbylamine*. Colorless liquid, b.155. **a. ketone.** 6-Hendecanone. **a. mercaptan.** C_5H_{11}-$SH = 104.14$. 1-Pentanethiol*. A liquid, b.116. Used as an odorant for natural gas and in organic synthesis. Cf. *diamyl* sulfide. **a. methyl ether.** $C_5H_{11}OCH_3 = 102.14$. A liquid, b.92. **a. mustard oil.** $C_5H_{11}NCS = 129.21$. *iso*- Isoamyl isothiocyanate. Colorless liquid, d.0.942, b.184, sparingly soluble in water. **a. nitrate.** $C_5H_{11}NO_3 = 133.16$. *iso*- Colorless liquid, b.147, slightly soluble in water; an antimalarial. **a. nitrite.** Amyl nitrite. **a. nitrite.** $C_5H_{11}NO_2 = 117.15$. Pentyl nitrite*. *n*- Yellow, flammable liquid, b.96, insoluble in water. *iso*- Colorless liquid, b.94, slightly soluble in water. Used as vasodilator and antispasmodic, as a reagent for phenols and wormseed oil, and in perfumes. **a. oxide.** Amyl ether. **a. oxyhydrate.** Amyl alcohol. **a. phenol.** $C_5H_{11} \cdot C_6H_4OH = 164.18$. Isoamyl-*p*-phenol. White needles, m.94, slightly soluble in water. Used in the manufacture of synthetic resins, varnishes, and antiseptic emulsions. **a. phenylhydrazine.** $NH_2 \cdot NPhC_5H_{11} = 178.16$. Colorless liquid, b.175; a reagent for aldehydes. **a. phenylketone.** $C_5H_{11}COC_6H_5 = 176.19$. Colorless liquid, b.242, insoluble in water. **a. phthalate.** $C_6H_4(COOC_5H_{11})_2 = 306.46$. Amoil. Colorless crystals, b.$_{11mm}$205, used in vacuum pumps, instead of mercury. **a. propionate.** $C_2H_5COOC_5H_{11} = 144.17$. Colorless liquid, b.160, sparingly soluble in water. **a. rhodanate.** A. thiocyanate. **a. salicylate.** $C_6H_4(OH)COOC_5H_{11} = 208.19$. *n*- Colorless liquid, b.277, soluble in water. *iso*- Colorless liquid, b.270, insoluble in water; an antirheumatic and fruit flavor. **a. sulfate.** $(C_5H_{11})_2SO_4 = 238.23$. Pentylsulfate. Colorless liquid, b.$_{2.5mm}$117, decomp. by water. **a. sulfide.** $(C_5H_{11})_2S = 174.18$. *n*- Colorless liquid, b.204. *iso*- Colorless liquid, b.215, insoluble in water. **a. sulfocyanate.** A. thiocyanate. *iso*- Amyl rhodanate. Colorless liquid, b.197, miscible with alcohol or ether. **a. thiocyanate.** $C_5H_{11}CNS = 129.21$. Amyl mustard oil. **a. urea.** NH_2-$CONHC_5H_{11} = 130.16$. White crystals, m.90, slightly soluble in water. **a. urethane.** C_5H_{11}-$OCONH_2 = 131.14$. Amyl carbamate. Crystals, m.65, soluble in water. **a. valerate.** $C_4H_9COOC_5$-$H_{11} = 182$. *iso*- Isoamylvaleric ester, apple essence. Colorless liquid, b.196, insoluble in water. Used in fruit ethers, and as a sedative. **a. xanthate.** The amyl ester of xanthic acid; a flotation reagent.

amylan. A levorotatory gum in malt and barley; does not reduce Fehling's solution.

amylase. An amylolytic enzyme in blood, hempseed, or malt which hydrolyses polysaccharides to glucose. **pancreatic-** Amylopsin. **salivary-** Ptyalin. **vegetable-** Diastase.

amylate. A compound of starch.

amylene. $MeCH_2CH_2CH:CH_2 = 70.11$. **n-** or **1-** Propylethylene, Δ¹-pentene, 1-pentene*. Colorless flammable liquid, b.40, insoluble in water. **iso-** or **2-** Ethylmethylethylene, Δ²-pentene, 2-pentene*. Colorless flammable liquid, b. 37, insoluble in water. Three forms:

$$\begin{array}{ccc} \text{Et·CH} & \text{Et·CH} & \text{Et·C·Me} \\ \parallel & \parallel & \parallel \\ \text{HC·Me} & \text{Me·CH} & \text{HCH} \\ \text{trans-} & \text{cis-} & \text{asymmetric} \end{array}$$

β-iso- Pental.

a. alcohol. A. alcohol, tertiary-. **a. bromide.** $C_5H_9Br = 149.0$. Yellow liquid, b.105 (decomp.). **a. carbamate.** Aponal. **a. chloral.** Dormiol. **a. diamine.** Cadaverine. **a. ether.** A. oxide. **a. glycol.** Pentanediol. **a. hydrate.** See tert-*amyl* alcohol. **a. hydride.** Amylene. **a. iodide.** $C_5H_9I = 196.00$. Yellow liquid, b.132 (decomp.). **a. oxide.** (1) $(C_5H_9)_2O$. A. ether. (2) Pentamethylene oxide, pentahydropyran. The ring compound $C_5H_{10}O$, b.82. **a. oxide linkage.** In sugars and related compounds, the formation of a ring by an O atom connecting the first and fifth C atom. Cf. *pyranose.*

amylenum. Official Latin for amylene.

amyl hydrate. Amyl alcohol.

amyl hydride. Pentane.

amylic alcohol. Amyl alcohol.

amylidene. Pentylidene. The radical $Me(CH_2)_3\text{-}$ $CH=$, from pentane.

amyline. The cellulose membrane of starch granules.

amylis. Official Latin for amyl.

amylit. A diastatic enzyme of malt, used in the textile industry.

amylo-. (1) Pertaining to starch. (Greek amylum.) (2) Synonym for amyl- (B.P. usage).

amylobacter. A bacillus acting on starch and causing butyric acid fermentation.

amylobarbital. $C_{11}H_{18}O_3N_2 = 226.3$. Amobarbital, amylobarbitone, 5-ethyl-5-(3-methylbutyl)barbituric acid. White, bitter crystals, m.156, insoluble in water; used as barbituric acid.

amylobarbitone. Amylobarbital (B.P.).

amylocellulose. A starch-cellulose complex which encloses the starch granulose of plants.

amyloclastic. Amylolytic.

amylodextrin. Soluble *starch.*

amyloform. An antiseptic mixture of starch and formaldehyde.

amylogen. A soluble starch.

amylograph. An instrument to measure the baking quality of starch in terms of its viscosity at various temperatures.

amyloid. (1) $(C_6H_{10}O_5)_x = (162.11)_x$. An explosive, m.42, slightly soluble in water. (2) Colloidal cellulose, Guignet cellulose. Parchment paper formed by the action of sulfuric acid on cellulose. (3) An intermediate in the lignification of woody tissues.

amyloin. Maltodextrin.

amylolysis. The conversion of starch into sugar by boiling dilute acids (hydrolysis) or by enzymes.

amylolytic. Amyloclastic. Capable of transforming starch into sugar. **a. activity.** The digestive power of amylase. **a. enzyme.** Amylase. **a. fermentation.** See *fermentation.*

amylopectin. The gel constituent of starch paste. It comprises 75% of starch substance, and has a branched or laminated structure. Its shorter 1,4-glucose chains are linked laterally by α-1,6-glycosidic bonds. Cf. *amylose.*

amylopsase. See *amylopsin.*

amylopsin. Amylopsase. An amylase in pancreatic juice, splitting starch to glucose.

amylose. (1) The sol constituent of starch paste. It comprises about 25% of starch substance and consists of unbranched chains of glucose residues, members of which are linked internally by α-1,4-glycosidic bonds. Cf. *amylopectin.* (2) Polysaccharide. α-, β- See *starch.*

amylum. (1) Latin name for starch. (2) Corn starch. Cf. *paramylum.*

amyrin. $C_{24}H_{39}O = 343.4$. A crystalline resin in elemi and other gums. A decomposition product of basseol. α- $C_{30}H_{50}O$. Ilicic alcohol.

Amyris. A genus of tropical trees and shrubs producing fragrant resins and gums, e.g., *A. elemifera* (elemi) of Mexico.

Amytal. $C_{11}H_{18}O_3N_2 = 226.16$. Trademark for 5-ethyl-5-isoamylbarbituric acid. Colorless crystals, m.156; an anesthetic and sedative. Cf. *barbital.*

an- Prefix indicating, without or not.

-an. Suffix indicating a sugar body, glucoside, or gum.

An. Symbol for *actinon.*

ana- Prefix (Greek) indicating, again, along, over, through, without, or against. **a. position.** The positions of the 2 H atoms attached to the first and fifth C atom of two condensed hexatomic rings; as, naphthalene.

anabasine. $C_{10}H_{14}N_2 = 162.12$. Neonicotine, 1,2-(3-pyridyl)piperidine. An isomer of nicotine from *Anabasis aphylla* (Chenopodiaceae) of Central Africa. Colorless liquid, d.1.048, b.28, soluble in water; an insecticide.

anabolism. Synthetic metabolism. The processes by which food constituents are transformed into living matter.

Anacardiaceae. The cashew family, 60 genera and 500 species of trees or shrubs with gummy, milky, or resinous juices often poisonous; e.g., *Rhus toxicodendron,* poison ivy, poison oak; *Anacardium occidentale,* cashew nuts. See also *Rhus, quebracho, mangiferin.*

anacardic acid. $C_{22}H_{32}O_3 = 344.3$. An acid from the seeds of *Anacardium occidentale.* Brown crystals, m.26, soluble in alcohol; an anthelmintic.

anacardin. $C_{15}H_{14}O_6 = 290.06$. A catechin present in *Anacardium occidentale* Lin. Cf. *kauri* gum.

anacardium. Cashew nut, caje nut. The dried, edible fruit of *A. occidentale,* a shrub of tropical America. Cf. *acajou* balsam, *cardol.*

anaclastic. Having refracting powers.

anaerobe. A bacterium which can grow in an oxygen-free atmosphere and derives the oxygen it requires from other compounds. **facultative-** A bacterium which prefers an atmosphere containing oxygen, but is not dependent on oxygen gas for its metabolism. **obligatory-** A bacterium which cannot live in an atmosphere containing oxygen.

anaerobic. Able to grow in an oxygen-free atmosphere. **a. culture apparatus.** A glass container for growing bacteria, from which the atmospheric oxygen is removed by chemicals, e.g., pyrogallic acid.

anaesthesia. Anesthesia.

anaesthesin(e). Benzocaine.

anagyrine. $C_{15}H_{18}ON_2 = 242.2$. An alkaloid from

the seeds of *Anagyris foetida* (Leguminosae). A brittle, resinlike mass, b.245. It resembles cytisine and sparteine in structure. **a. hydrobromide.** $C_{15}H_{18}ON_2 \cdot HBr = 323.3$. Yellow crystals, m.265, soluble in water; a heart stimulant.

anahemin. A liver polypeptide responsible for the maturation of the red blood cells in the bone marrow.

analcime. Analcite.

analcite. $NaAlH_2Si_2O_7$. Analcine. A white, isometric native sodium aluminum silicate zeolite, deposited in high-pressure boilers.

analeptic. (1) A drug that restores health. (2) More specifically, a drug that stimulates the central nervous system, and especially the respiratory and vasomotor centers.

analgen(e). (1) $C_7H_5O \cdot NHC_6H_2(OEt):C_3H_3N = 292.24$. 5-Benzamido-8-ethoxyquinoline, benzanalgen, quinalgene, labordin. Colorless crystals, m.208, insoluble in water; an antipyretic, antirheumatic, and analgesic. (2) $C_{13}H_{14}O_2N_2 = 230.12$. 5-Acetylamino-8-ethoxyquinoline. Colorless crystals, m.155.

analgesic. A drug that relieves pain without causing loss of consciousness, either by direct action on nerve centers (brain), or by diminishing the conductivity of the sensory nerve fibers; e.g., the use of nitrogen dioxide in obstetrics.

analgesine. Antipyrine.

analgic. Painless.

analgin. Creolin.

anallachrom. Esculin.

analogs, analogues. Analogous series. Compounds with similar electronic structures but different atoms; as, *isosteres* and *isologs*.

analogy. A similarity or a likeness in properties. Cf. *homology, isology.*

Analoids. Patented tablets containing exact quantities of reagents, used in chemical analysis. Cf. *Fixanol.*

analyser. Analyzer.

analysis. (1) Assay. The determination, detection, or examination of a substance. (2) Breaking down or splitting into simpler constituents. (3) The reverse of synthesis. **bio-** (1) The detection of substances with the aid of microorganism; e.g., by the selective action of yeasts on sugars; or by ascertaining the minimum amount of the sample under test that will inhibit growth of an organism or produce specific disease symptoms in an experimental animal. (2) The determination of the strength of substances (as, hormones) from their effects on animals. **activation-** The identification of elements from the characteristic radiations they emit on returning to their normal states after bombardment by high-energy fast neutrons. **biochemical-** The chemical examination of biological material. **blowpipe-** The detection of metallic elements and acid radicals by means of the blowpipe. **chromatographic-** See *chromatographic*. **clinical-** The examination of body fluids and tissues for the diagnosis of diseases. **colorimetric-** The quantitative a. of substances by means of the color intensity of their reaction products. **complexometric-** See *complexometric*. **conductometric-** See *conductometric analysis*. **differential thermal-** Following a chemical reaction from the difference in temperature between the substance being

examined and a thermally inert standard when both are heated similarly. **diffusion-** See *diffusion*. **dry-** A. without the use of solutions. **electro-** See *electrodeposition* analysis. **elementary-** The determination of the constituents of an organic compound by combustion; e.g., C as CO_2, H as H_2O. **gas-** A. of gas mixtures by measuring the volumes before and after treatment with selective absorbing agents. **gravimetric-** The determination of the composition of a substance by weighing its constituents directly or indirectly. **iodimetric-** Titration of oxidizing substances with a standard sodium thiosulfate and acid potassium iodide solutions. **mechanical-** See *mechanical*. **mechanochemical-** Qualitative microanalysis based on the color produced when solid reactants are rubbed together in a mortar. **micro-** (1) Identification of substances under the microscope, e.g., starch. (2) The identification of characteristic reaction products (precipitates, crystals) with the microscope. (3) Modifications on the small scale of the processes of quantitative analysis. **m.biological-** q.v. **narco-** q.v. **nephelometric-** Measurements of turbidity to determine the amounts of precipitates. **organic-** *Elementary* analysis. **proximate-** The determination of the chemical nature of the active constituents of a sample; e.g., the alkaloids in drugs. **qualitative-** The detection of the kind or nature of an element or compound in a substance. **quantitative-** The determination of the amount or quantity of an element or compound in a substance. **rational-** See *rational*. **screen-** See *screen*. **spectroscopic-** See *spectroscopic*. **spectrum-** The detection of elements and binary compounds by their characteristic radiations as observed through the spectroscope. **spot-** See *spot*. **submicro-** A. concerned with quantities of 20–50 γ. **technical-** Practical or empirical methods used in industry for evaluating materials. **thermodynamic-** The measurement of a component of a gas mixture by passing the mixture through a calibrated orifice for a known time, into an evacuated vessel, and measuring the increase in pressure in the latter. **ultimate-** Elementary a. **volumetric-** The determination of elements and compounds in a substance by titration with standard solutions. **wet-** An a. made with solutions. See also *bead tests, biological assay, calorimetry, chromatography, colorimetry, electrolysis, flame tests, reactions, spectroscopy, thermal, titration.*

analytical. Pertaining to analysis. **a. balance.** See *balance*. **a. chemistry.** See *chemistry*. **a. metabolism.** Catabolism. **a. reactions.** The characteristic reactions of elements or ions, used for their identification or determination; e.g., precipitate formation, color changes. **a. weights.** The standardized weights of an analytical balance.

analyzer. (1) A device which indicates a certain condition, change, or phenomenon. (2) The nicol prism of a polariscope nearest to the eyepiece. (3) The first tower of a coffee still. **curve-** A device for determining the slope of a graph. **micropolar-** An optical attachment for a microscope for the determination of polarization in crystals. **polarization-** The nicol prism in a polariscope nearest to the eye. Cf. *polarizer.*

anamirtin. (1) $C_{10}H_{26}O_{10}$. A glucoside from the fruits of *Anamirta paniculata*. (2) $C_{19}H_{24}O_{10}$. A glyceride from fishberries, *Cocculus indicus.* Cf. *cocculin.*

anamorphism. A change caused by the action of pressure, water, or heat on rock. Cf. *catamorphism.*

anamorphoscope. A mirror which corrects distorted images.

anamorphosis. The distortion of objects by mirrors.

anaphase. A stage of cell division following the division of the nucleus.

anaphe. A wild silk, resembling tussah.

anaphrodisiac. A drug which diminishes sexual desire.

anaphoresis. The antonym of cataphoresis, q.v.

anaphylactin. Allergen.

anaphylatoxin. A poison produced in anaphylaxis caused by the injection of proteins.

anaphylaxis. The increased sensitiveness of an organism to second and subsequent protein injections. Cf. *allergia, immunity.*

anarcotine. A non-narcotic alkaloid in Indian opium.

anasthol. A mixture of methyl chloride and ethyl chloride; a local anesthetic in dentistry.

anatase. TiO_2. Octahedrite. A native titanium oxide.

Anaxagoras. 500–428 B.C. The first Greek scientist. He distinguished physical from psychical phenomena, and assumed indivisible parts of matter.

anayodin. $HI·OH·C_9H_7N·HSO_3$. Iodoxyquinolinesulfonic acid. Yellow powder, soluble in water; an amebicide.

anchietine. An alkaloid from the root of *Anchietea salutaris* (Violaceae).

anchoic acid. Azelaic acid.

anchored compound. An organic compound attached to certain cells by a characteristic radical. See *chemotherapy.*

anchoring group. (1) An organic radical which connects the compound to which it belongs with cell tissue. (2) The salt-forming radical of a dyestuff.

anchovy. A small edible fish of the herring family. **a. pear.** The fruit of a Jamaican tree used in the manufacture of pickles.

anchusic acid. An acid from the root of *Alkanna tinctoria* (Boraginaceae).

anchusin. $C_{35}H_{40}O_8 = 588.4$. A red coloring matter from the root of *Alkanna tinctoria*. Cf. *alkanet, alkannin.*

andalusite. Al_2SiO_5. A native aluminum silicate, gray or pink rhombic prisms, used for gems; decomp. at 1410 to mullite. Cf. *silica.*

andesine. $NaCaAl_3Si_5O_{16}$. A native triclinic feldspar. Cf. *andose.*

andesite. A rock-forming mineral consisting of andesine with hornblende and mica.

andirin. (1) $C_{40}H_{43}O_3N = 585.5$. Yellow coloring matter from the bark of the cabbage tree. (*Andira inermis*). (2) Rhatanin. Cf. *yaba* bark, *goa.*

andorite. $AgPbSb_3S_6$. A native, orthorhombic sulfostibide.

andose. A volcanic rock of andesite with diorite.

andradite. An iron garnet, q.v.

Andrews, Thomas 1813–1885. Irish worker on the critical temperature and pressure of gases.

androkin. Androsterone.

andromedotoxin. A poisonous principle of mountain laurel, *Kalmia latifolia* (Ericaceae).

andrometoxin. A poisonous principle from *Andromeda, Azalea,* and *Rhododendron* species. Colorless crystals, m.228, soluble in alcohol.

Andropogon. A genus of grasses, some of which yield essential oils used in perfumery; e.g., *A.* (or *Cymbopogon*) *citratus*, lemongrass oil.

androstane. $C_{19}H_{32} = 260.0$. A solid hydrocarbon, parent substance of sex hormones, bile acids, sterols, etc. See *cholane* derivatives. **a. ring.** A saturated four-ring complex in many important biochemical compounds. See *cholane* derivatives.

androsterone. $C_{19}H_{30}O_2 = 290.13$. Androtin, androkin, 3-*cis*-hydroxy-17-ketoandrostane. The male sex hormone, from urine, testes, plants, or synthetically prepared. Colorless crystals, m.178, soluble in benzene Cf. *Theelin, cholane* ring. **dehydro-** $C_{19}H_{28}O_2 = 288.13$. A male hormone from urine, or synthetically prepared. Colorless crystals, m.148, soluble in water.

androtin. Androsterone.

-ane. Suffix indicating: (1) a saturated methane hydrocarbon, (2) a deoxy compound; as, quinane.

anechoic. Acoustically neutral; without echoes.

anemium. Actinium.

anemometer. An apparatus to measure wind velocity or pressure. Cf. *pitot* tube.

anemone camphor. A principle from pulsatilla (*Anemone pulsatilla*), which splits into anemonin and anemonic acid.

anemonic acid. $C_{10}H_{10}O_5 = 210.1$. Yellow crystals from anemone camphor.

anemonin. $C_{10}H_8O_4 = 192.1$. Pulsatilla camphor. Yellow crystals m.152 (decomp.); insoluble in water; an antispasmodic, sedative, and anodyne. **hydro-** $C_{10}H_{12}O_4 = 196.1$. Large, colorless scales, m.78.

anemoninic acid. $C_{10}H_{12}O_6 = 228.1$. Colorless crystals derived from anemonic acid, m.189, soluble in water.

anemosite. A mixed feldspar; sodium anorthite with albite.

aneroid. See *barometer.* **a. battery.** Dry cell.

anesthesia. Loss of feeling. **local-** Loss of feeling at a definite part of the body.

anesthesin. Benzocaine.

anesthesiophore radical. The benzoyl group, $PhCO^-$, which produces anesthetic effects.

anesthetic, anaesthetic. A drug which causes loss of feeling. **general-** A. which affects the consciousness, hence affects the feelings of the whole organism; as, ether. **local-** Local analgesic. A. which is applied only to a particular part of the body, e.g., cocaine.

a. gas. Nitrous oxide.

anesthetizing valve. A device for mixing an anesthetic with air for respiration in animal experiments.

anethole. $MeO·C_6H_4·CH:CHMe = 148.21$. Anethol, *p*-allyl phenyl methyl ether, anise camphor, *p*-propenylanisole. A constituent of anise and fennel oils. Colorless leaflets, or aromatic liquid with fragrant odor, m.22, slightly soluble in water. Used as a reagent for lignin, flavoring agent, carminative, and antiseptic, and in microscopy. **a. dibromide.** Needles, m.67. **a. glycol.** $C_{10}H_{14}O_3 = 182.10$. α-form, m.31; β-form, m.115. **a. picrate.** Orange needles, m.70 (decomp.).

anethoquinine. Quinine anisate.

anethum. Garden dill, dill seeds. The fruits of *Paucedanum* (*Anethum*) *graveolens* (Umbelliferae); a carminative, and condiment.

aneurin(e) hydrochloride. $C_{12}H_{17}ON_4S = 304.80$. Thiamine hydrochloride, vitamin B_1, 3-(4-amino-2-methyl-5-pyrimidylmethyl-5,2-hydroxyethyl-4-methylthiazonium chloride hydrochloride. White, bitter crystalline powder, soluble in water.

angelic acid. $MeCH:CMeCOOH = 100.08$. Angelicic acid, 1,2-dimethylacrylic acid, *cis*-2-methyl-2-butenoic acid*. Colorless monoclinic crystals, m.46, sparingly soluble in water. A constituent of the roots *Angelica, Chamomile*, and *Arnica* species, used as a flavoring; isomer of *liglic* acid. **cinnamenyl-** See *cinnamenyl*. **hydro-** α-Methylbutyric acid. **iso-** Tiglic acid.

angelica. The dried herb of *A.* or *Archongelica officinalis* (Umbelliferae).
a. lactone. $C_5H_6O_2 = 98.1$. *alpha-* Colorless crystals, m.18, or colorless liquid, b.167. *beta-* Colorless liquid, b.83; a flavoring. **a. root.** The rhizomes and roots of *Angelica* species; the fluid extract is a diuretic, diaphoretic, and stimulant. **a. root oil.** Colorless, essential oil, b.60–70. Its chief constituents are phellandrene and valeric acid; a flavoring. *Japanese-* Colorless crystals, m.62; a flavoring. **a. seed.** The ripe, dried fruits of *Angelica* species; a carminative and stimulant. **a. seed oil.** An essential oil from angelica seeds. Its chief constituents are phellandrene and valeric acid; a flavoring. **a. tree.** The shrub *Xanthoxylum americanum* (Rutaceae) of the United States. The crushed bark smells like angelica; a purgative and emetic.

angelicic acid. Angelic acid.

angelicin. $C_{18}H_{30}O = 262.3$. A constituent of the roots of *Angelica officinalis*. Colorless crystals, m.127, insoluble in water.

angico gum. Brazilian gum, Para gum. A mucilaginous secretion of *Piptadenia rigida* (Leguminosae) of Brazil. Cf. *cebil* gum.

angiology. The science of blood and lymph vessels.

angioneurosin. *Nitroglycerin*.

angiosperm. A flowering plant whose seeds are enclosed in a fruit; e.g., the peapod. Cf. *gymnosperm*.

angle. The figure formed by two converging lines where they meet. **acute-** An a. less than 90°. **adjacent-** An a. which has one line common with another a. **complementary-** The complement of an a. is 90° less the a. **critical-** See *critical*. **meter-** See *meter*. **oblique-** An a. opposite to a right a. **obtuse-** An a. greater than 90°. **right-** An a. of 90°. **supplementary-** The supplement of an a. is 180° less the a. **a. thermometer.** An L-shaped thermometer.

anglesite. $PbSO_4$. Occurs native in colored orthorhombic crystals. Cf. *sardinianite*.

anglohelvetium. Astatine. The name proposed by Leigh-Smith and Minder for element no. 85 discovered by them in 1940, and isolated in 1943 from monazite sand.

angora. A long, silky, curly goat's wool.

angostura. A S. American tree, *Galipea cusparia, Cusparia febrifuga*, (Rutaceae). **a. alkaloids.** The alkaloids of a.; as, angosturine. **a. bark.** Cusparia bark, carony bark. The bark of a.; a bitter tonic and stimulant. **a. oil.** An essential

oil from the bark of a. Yellow aromatic liquid, d.0.930–0.960, soluble in alcohol. It contains galipene, galipol, cadinene, and pinene; used in flavorings.

angosturine. $C_{19}H_{40}O_{14}N = 398.4$. An alkaloid from angostura bark. Colorless crystals, m.85; a tonic.

Ångström, A. J. 1814–1874. Swedish optical physicist.

ångström. a, Å, A.U., or A (preferred). A unit of wavelength: $1 A = 10^{-7}$ mm $= 10^{-10}$ m $= 0.000,000,000,1$ meter $= 1$ am. (atom meter). Also $10 A = 1 \mu\mu = 1 m\mu = 10^{-6}$ mm. **international A.** I.A. The wavelength of the red line of cadmium $= 6438.4696$ I.A. in air at 15°C. Thence the I.A. $= 10^{-10}$ m. Cf. λ (*lambda*) and kX.

angular. Having sharp angles. **a. acceleration.** Angular acceleration: $a = (v_t - v_0)/t$, where v_t is the velocity after time t, and v_0 the initial velocity; unit, one radian per second per second. **a. aperture.** The largest angle subtended by a wave surface transmitted by an objective. **a. momentum.** Spin. The product of the a. velocity and moment of inertia of a body expressed in grams per centimeter-second. **a. motion.** The motion of a line, fixed at one end in one plane, relative to a straight line through the center of rotation. **a. velocity.** The ratio $v = \theta/t$, where θ is the angle traversed in the time t; unit, one radian per second.

angustione. $C_{11}H_{16}O_3 = 196.11$. A cyclohexane triketone isolated from the oil of *Backhousia angustifolia* (Myrtaceae). Colorless liquid, $b_{15mm}129$.

anhalamine. $C_9H_7(OCH_3)_2OH \cdot NH = 209.1$. An alkaloid from *mescal* buttons, q.v.

anhaline. $C_{10}H_{17}ON = 167.15$. An alkaloid from *Anhalonium fissuratum*.

anhalonidine. $C_{12}H_{15}O_3N = 221.19$. 1,2-Dihydro-6-hydroxy-7,8-methoxy-1-methylquinoline. An alkaloid from mescal buttons. Colorless octahedra, m.154, soluble in water.

anhalonine. $C_{12}H_{15}O_3N = 221.19$. 1,2,3,4-Tetrahydro-6-methoxy-1-methyl-7,8-methylenedioxy quinoline. An extremely poisonous alkaloid from *Anhalonium* species (Cactaceae). Colorless needles, m.254, soluble in water. **methoxy-** Iopophorine.

$$
\begin{array}{ccc}
 & CH & CH_2 \\
MeO \cdot C & C & CH_2 \\
| & \| & \| \\
O—C & C & NH \\
 & C & HCMe \\
CH_2—O & &
\end{array}
$$

a. hydrochloride. $C_{12}H_{15}O_3N \cdot HCl = 257.7$. Colorless crystals, soluble in water; a heart tonic.

Anhalonium. A Mexican cactus species, *A. lewinii* (peyotl), containing narcotic alkaloids. Cf. *mescal* buttons. **a. alkaloids.** See *anhalamine, anhalonine, lophophorine, mexaline, pellotine*.

anhidrotic. Antihidrotic. A drug which reduces perspiration.

anhydride. A compound (usually an acid) from which water has been removed; as, $H_2XO_3 - H_2O = XO_2$. **acid-** The oxides of nonmetals, which form acids with water. **basic-** The oxides of metals, which yield bases with water. **inner-** A ring compound formed by the abstraction of water; as, lactones. Cf. *acetic-, chromic-, osmic-,* etc.

Anhydrite. (1) Trade name for a desiccant containing chiefly anhydrous calcium sulfate. (2) (not cap). $CaSO_4$. A native anhydrous calcium sulfate; gray, orthorhombic masses. Cf. *muriacite, tripestone, vulpinite.*

anhydro- Prefix to compounds from which one or more molecules of hydrogen have been removed, making them less saturated. Cf. *anhydrous.*

anhydroecgonine. $C_9H_{13}O_2N = 167.55$. Ecgonidine. Colorless crystals, m.235, soluble in water. **a. hydrochloride.** $C_9H_{13}O_2N \cdot HCl = 203.63$. Colorless needles, m.241, soluble in water.

anhydroformaldehyde aniline. $PhN:CH_2 = 105.01$. A solid, m.120, insoluble in water.

anhydroglycochloral. Chloralose.

anhydrohydroxyprogesterone. U.S.P. name for ethisterone.

Anhydrone. Trade name for anhydrous, magnesium perchlorate prepared by igniting the trihydrate; a powerful desiccant.

anhydrosynthesis. The theoretical coupling of a functioning group, q.v., with another compound, with the subsequent elimination of water. Cf. *derivative.*

anhydrotimboine. Timbonine.

anhydrous. Describing a compound that has lost all its water. Cf. *anhydro-.*

anibine. 4-Methoxy-6(3'-pyridyl)-α-pyrone. An alkaloid from the wood of the S. American rosewood, *Aniba duckei.*

anilides. (1) Compounds containing the C_6H_5NH— radical, from aniline, e.g., benzanilide, $Ph \cdot NH \cdot CO \cdot Ph$. (2) Sometimes applied to compounds containing the $NH_2C_6H_4$— group (anilinate); as, arsenic acid anilide (=arsanilic acid). **acet-** Acetanilide. **form-** $C_6H_5N:CHO$. Colorless crystals, m.46. **methylacet-** Exalgin.

anilidothiobiazole. 1,2,3-Thiodiazole.

anilinate. $NH_2C_6H_4M$. A compound of aniline and a metal. Cf. *anilides.*

aniline. $C_6H_5NH_2 = 93.10$. Phenylamine, aminobenzene, aniline oil, benzidam. A pale brown liquid, darkening with age, m.—6, b.184.4, slightly soluble in water. Used as a reagent, for aldehydes, chloroform, fusel oil, phenols, etc.; in bacteriology, for preparing staining solutions; in medicine, as an antiseptic; and extensively in the dye and rubber industries for organic synthesis and in the manufacture of resins and varnishes. Cf. *anilide, anilinate, nitrobenzene* reduction. **acetyl-** Acetanilide. **allyl-** See *allyl.* **amino-** Phenylenediamine. **aminodimethyl-** Dimethylphenylenediamine. **benzal-** Benzalaniline. **benzilidene-** See *benzalaniline.* **benzoyl-** Benzanilide. **benzyl-** See *benzyl.* **bi-** Benzidine. **bromo-** $NH_2C_6H_4Br = 172.0$. Aminobromobenzene. *ortho-* Colorless crystals, m.31, soluble in alcohol. *meta-* Colorless crystals, m.18, soluble in alcohol. *para-* Colorless rhombs, m.66 (decomp.), insoluble in water. **chloro-** $NH_2C_6H_4Cl = 127.57$. Aminochlorobenzene. *ortho-* Colorless liquid, b.207, soluble in water. *meta-* Colorless liquid, b.230. *para-* Rhombs, m.70, soluble in hot water. **cyano-** Cyananilide. **diacetyl-** Diacetanilide. **dibenzyl-** See *benzyl.*

dichloro- $NH_2C_6H_3Cl_2 = 162.01$. Aminodichlorobenzene. *2,4-* Colorless needles, m.63. soluble in alcohol. *3,4-* Colorless needles, m.72, soluble in alcohol. *3,5-* Colorless needles, m.63, soluble in alcohol. **diethyl-** $C_6H_5N(C_2H_5)_2 = 149.21$. Yellow liquid, m.38, sparingly soluble in water. **dimethyl-** $C_6H_5N(CH_3)_2 = 121.17$. Yellow liquid, m.2.5, slightly soluble in water. **dimethyl-** *ar-* Xylidine. *N-* See *dimethyl.* **dimethylamino-** Dimethylphenylenediamine. **dinitro-** Dinitraniline. **diphenyl-** Triphenylamine. **ethoxy-** Phenetidine. **ethyl-** $C_6H_5NH(C_2H_5) = 121.17$. Colorless liquid, b.205, sparingly soluble in water. **formyl-** Formanilide. **hexahydro-** Cyclohexylamine. **hydroxy-** *ar-* Aminophenol. *N-* Phenylhydroxylamine. **iodo-** NH_2C_6-$H_4I = 219.01$. Aminoiodobenzene. *ortho-* Colorless needles, m.60, sparingly soluble in water. *meta-* Colorless leaflets, m.26, insoluble in water. *para-* Colorless needles, m.63, insoluble in water. **isopropyl-** Cumidine. **methenyltri-** Leucaniline. **methoxy-** Anisidine. **methyl-** *ar-* Toluidine. *N-* $C_6H_5NHCH_3 = 107.12$. Yellow liquid, m.196, slightly soluble in water. **nitro-** $NH_2 \cdot C_6H_4 \cdot NO_2 = 138.06$. Aminonitrobenzene. *N-* Phenylnitramine, nitranilide. Yellow crystals, m.46 (explode 98), soluble in water. *ortho-* or *1,2-* Yellow rhombs, m.72. *meta-* or *1,3-* Yellow needles, m.112. *para-* or *1,4-* Yellow needles, m.147. **nitroso-** $NH_2C_6H_4NO = 122.10$. *para-* Steel-blue needles, m.173, soluble in alcohol. **p-nitrosodiethyl-** $(C_2H_5)_2N \cdot C_6H_4NO = 178.18$. Colorless needles, m.84, slightly soluble in water. **p-nitrosodimethyl-** $(CH_3)_2N \cdot C_6H_4NO = 150.14$. Green scales, m.88, slightly soluble in water. **pentachlor-** $NH_2C_6Cl_5 = 265.36$. Colorless needles, m.232, soluble in alcohol. **phenyl-** *ar-* Biphenylamine. *N-* Diphenylamine. *para-* Xenylamine. **propionyl-** Propioanilide. **thio-** Thioaniline. **thionyl-** Thionylaniline. **tribromo-** Tribromoaniline. **trimethyl-** See *mesidine, pseudocumidine.* **trinitro-** Picramide.

a. acetate. $C_8H_5N \cdot CH_3COOH = 153.1$. Colorless liquid, soluble in water; a reagent for furfural. **a. azo-β-naphthol.** *Sudan* yellow. **a. black.** Nigrosine. **a. blue.** A mixture of the salts of triphenylrosanilinesulfonic acids. Blue powder, soluble in water; a dye for cotton and silk. **a. brown.** Triaminoazobenzene. **a. camphorate.** $(C_6H_5NH_2)_2 \cdot C_{10}H_{16}O_4 = 386.3$. Yellow crystals, sparingly soluble in water; an antispasmodic. **a. chloride.** a. hydrochloride. **a. colors.** a. dyes. **a. dyes.** (1) Artificial or synthetic coloring matters. (2) Those derived from benzene or aniline. **a. fluoride.** a. hydrofluoride. **a. hydrobromide.** $C_6H_5NH_2 \cdot HBr = 174.2$. Gray crystals, soluble in water. **a. hydrochloride.** $C_6H_5NH_2 \cdot HCl = 129.6$. A. salt. Colorless crystals, m.198, soluble in water. Used as reagent for chlorates, and for preparation of dyestuffs. **a. hydrofluoride.** $C_6H_5NH_2 \cdot HF = 113.1$. Colorless crystals, soluble in water. **a. hydroiodide.** $C_6H_5NH_2 \cdot HI = 221.07$. Yellow crystals, soluble in water. **a. hydrosilicofluoride.** $(C_6H_5NH_2)_2 \cdot H_2SiF_6 = 330.1$. Colorless crystalline powder, soluble in water; a reagent. **a. nitrate.** $C_6H_5NH_2 \cdot HNO_3 = 156.1$. Colorless crystals, decomp. 190, soluble in water. **a. oil.** Crude a. **a. orange.** *Victoria* orange. **a. oxalate.** $(C_6H_5NH_2)_2C_2H_2O_4 = 276.1$. Colorless crystals, soluble in water. **a. point.** The critical solution temperature of a mixture of a. and a water-insoluble liquid; used to determine petroleum in mixtures by comparing their a.p. with those of known mixtures. **a. printing.** A flexographic printing process, with transparent inks. **a. purple.** Mauvein. The first a. dye (W. H. Perkin, 1856). **a. red.** Fushsin. **a. salt.** a. hydrochloride. **a. sulfate.** $(C_6H_5NH_2)_2$·$H_2SO_4 = 294.1$. White crystals, soluble in water; a stimulant. **a. sulfonic acid.** *ortho-* Orthanilic acid. *meta-* Metanilic acid *para-* Sulfanilic acid. **a. tribromide.** Tribromoaniline. **a. yellow.** (1) Spirit yellow, amidoazobenzene hydrochloride. Blue needles, soluble in water used to color lacquers. (2) Uranine yellow II.

anilino. The radical C_6H_5NH—.

anilipyrine. A compound of acetanilide and antipyrine. Colorless crystals, m.75, soluble in water; an antipyretic and antineuralgic.

anilism. (1) Poisoning produced by aniline vapors. (2) Specifically, cyanotic TNT poisoning.

aniluvitonic acid. $C_{11}H_9O_2N = 187.08$. Methylcinchoninic acid. Colorless crystals, m.241.

animal. A living organism, capable of locomotion and requiring organic food. **a. alkaloids.** Basic organic compounds formed by the decomposition of animal matter. See *leucomaine, ptomaine.* **a. charcoal.** See *charcoal.* **a. dyes.** Coloring matters of a. origin; as, cochineal. **a. fibers.** Textile fibers of a. origin; as, silk. **a. oil.** (1) A fat or oil of a. origin. (2) Bone oil. **a. poisons.** Toxic substances of a. origin; as, the toxins from snakes. **a. products.** Substances of a. species; as, secretions (e.g., lanolin from sheep) and tissues (e.g., sponge from *Spongia* species).

animalcule. A protozoon or microscopically small animal in ponds or stagnant water. Cf. *ameba, paramecia.*

anime. *Animi* resin.

animi resin. A fossil copal from E. Africa, used for varnishes and lacquers.

animikite. Ag_9Sb, occurring native in the Lake Superior region.

aninsulin. An antigenic, nonhypoglycemic substance made by heating insulin with formaldehyde.

anion. The negatively charged atom or radical liberated at the anode during electrolysis; as, Cl⁻. Cf. *cation, ion.*

anionotropy. A case of *ionotropy*, q.v., in which a OH⁻ or X⁻ group breaks off from a molecule and leaves a positive ion in a state of dynamic equilibrium. Cf. *prototropy.*

anisacetone. $MeO·C_6H_4CH_2COMe = 164.09$. *p*-Methoxyphenylacetone. A constituent of anise oil.

anisal. Anisylidene. The radical $MeOC_6H_4CH=$, from anisaldehyde.

anisalcohol. $MeO·C_6H_4·CH_2OH = 138.1$. Anisylalcohol. Colorless needles, m.45, insoluble in water.

anisaldehyde. $MeO·C_6H_4·CHO = 136.1$. Anisyl aldehyde, *p*-methoxybenzaldehyde. A colorless liquid, b.245, sparingly soluble in water; used in perfumery. **3-hydroxy-** Isovanillin. **ortho-** *o*-Methoxybenzaldehyde.

anisaldoxime. $MeO·C_6H_4·CH:NOH = 151.1$. *p*-Methoxybenzaldoxime. α- Colorless crystals, m.64. β- Colorless crystals, m.133.

anisate. $MeO·C_6H_4·COOM$. Any salt of anisic acid.

anise. Aniseed, a. fruit. The dried ripe fruit of *Pimpinella anisum* (Umbelliferae). A condiment, expectorant, and carminative. **star-** The seeds of *Illicium verum* (Magnoliaceae), the source of anise oil.

a. bark oil. An essential oil from the bark of a Madagascar tree. Yellow spicy oil, soluble in alcohol chief constituent, methylchavicol. **a. camphor.** Anethole. **a. fruit.** Anise. **a. oil.** The essential oil from the seeds of *Pimpinella anisum* (Umbelliferae). Yellow liquid, b.210, soluble in alcohol; a flavoring and carminative. It contains anethole and methyl chavicol. **star-** Illicium oil. An essential oil from the seeds of *Illicium verum* (Magnoliaceae). Colorless liquid, m.14–18, soluble in alcohol; a flavoring containing anethole and methyl chavicol. **a. seed oil.** A. oil **a. water.** Aqua anisi. A saturated solution of a. oil in water.

anisic acid. $MeO·C_6H_4·COOH = 152.1$. *p*-Methoxybenzoic acid, umbellic acid, draconic acid. Colorless monoclinic crystals, m.184, slightly soluble in water; an antiseptic and antipyretic. **4-hydroxy-** Vanillic acid. **hydroxymethyl-** Everninic acid. **3-methoxy-** Veratric acid.

a. alcohol. Anisalcohol. **a. aldehyde.** Anisaldehyde.

anisidine. $NH_2C_6H_4OMe = 123.1$. Methoxyaniline, methyloxyaniline. **ortho-** Brown oil, m.6, b.224, slightly soluble in water. **meta-** Volatile liquid, b.251. **para-** Colorless needles, m.58, soluble in alcohol. **acet-** Methacetin. **di-** Dianisidine.

anisil. $MeOC_6H_4CO·COC_6H_4OMe = 270.1$. Bianisaldehyde. Colorless crystals, m.133.

anisole. $C_6H_5·OMe = 108.1$. Methoxybenzene*, methyl phenyl ether. Colorless liquid, b.155, insoluble in water; used in perfumery. **acetamido-** Acetaniside. **p-allyl-** Estragole. **amino-** Anisidine. **azoxy-** Azoxyanisole. **bromo-** Br-$C_6H_4OMe = 186.97$. Bromomethoxybenzene*, bromophenyl methyl ether. *ortho-* or *1,2-* An oil, b.222. *para-* or *1,4-* Colorless crystals, m.11. **dinitro-** $(NO_2)_2·C_6H_4OMe = 198.06$. Dinitromethoxybenzene. Yellow leaflets, m.89. **hydroxy-** Guaiacol. **iodo-** Iodanisole. **methoxy-** Veratrole. **nitro-** Nitroanisole. **propenyl-** Anethole. **trinitro-** $(NO_2)_3C_6H_4OMe = 243.06$. Methyl picrate. Yellow crystals, m.68, insoluble in water; an explosive. **vinyl-**$C_9H_{10}O = 134.08$. Methoxystyrene, CH_2:-$CH·C_6H_4·OMe$. *ortho-* or *1,2-* Colorless liquid, b.195. *meta-* or *1,3-* An oil, b.90. *para-* or *1,4-* Colorless liquid, b.204, insoluble in water.

anisomeric. Not isomeric.

anisonitrile. $MeO·C_6H_4·CN = 133.06$. Methoxybenzonitrile. **1,4-** or **para-** Colorless crystals, m.60.

anisotonic. Not isotonic.

anisotropic. (1) Having different physical properties in different directions, as crystals. (2) Doubly refractive; not optically homogeneous. Antonym: isotropic. **a. liquid.** *Liquid* crystal.

anisoyl. The radical $MeO·C_6H_4·CO$—, from anisic acid. **di-** Anisil.

a. chloride. $MeO·C_6H_4·COCl = 170.6$. Anisyl chloride. Colorless needles, m.26; insoluble in water.

anisum. Anise.

anisyl. The radical $MeO·C_6H_4$—, or methoxyphenyl (preferred U.K. usage); derived from anethole; 3 isomers: ortho- (-guaiacyl), meta-, and para-, **a.**

alcohol. Anisalcohol. **a. amine.** Anisidine. **a. chloride.** Anisoyl chloride.

anisylidene. Anisal.

anitin. Anytin.

anitol. Anytol.

ankerite. $(CaMgFeMn)CO_3$. A native carbonate.

annabergite. $Ni_3As_2O_2 \cdot 8H_2O$. Nickel bloom, nickel ocher. Occurs as green, monoclinic crystals in Nevada.

annaline. A native calcium sulfate.

annatto. Annotto, annotta, arnotta, orleana, roucou. The orange coloring matter from the pulp of the fruit seeds of the evergreen *Bixa orellana* (Bixaceae). Used to color cheese and milk, and to dye textiles. Cf. *bixin*.

anneal. To temper by heating.

annealing. The tempering of glass or metals by heating, then cooling, to render them less brittle. See *tempering*. **a. color.** The tints of steel during a. a. cup. A fine clay crucible for silica fusions.

annerodite. A native uranium and yttrium columbate; as, black orthorhombic crystals.

annidalin. *Thymol* iodide.

annotto. Annatto.

annular. A ring-shaped enclosed space.

annulene. Generic name for large, ring-conjugated, aromatic compounds.

anode. Posode. The positive pole of electrode of a battery, vacuum tube, or electrolyzing circuit.

anodic. Pertaining to the anode. **a. oxidation.** The protection of metals, as, aluminum, against corrosion by producing a thin surface film of oxide on the metal, which is made the anode in a chromic acid bath.

anodyne. A drug which relieves pain; as, opium.

anodynin. Antipyrine.

anodynon. Ethyl chloride.

anogen. Mercurous iodobenzene-*p*-sulfonate.

anol. $MeCH{:}CH{\cdot}C_6H_4{\cdot}OH = 134.08$. *p*-Propenylphenol. Crystals, m.98; a constituent of essential oils.

anolyte. The liquid in the immediate neighborhood of the anode during electrolysis. Cf. *catholyte*.

anomalous. Contradictory. Cf. a. *liquid*, a. *viscosity*.

anomaly. An abnormal or irregular type or form.

anomite. Biotite, containing lithium.

anonaceine. An alkaloid from *Hylopeia aethiopica* (Anonaceae).

anorganic. Inorganic.

anorthic. Triclinic.

anorthite. $CaAl_2Si_2O_8$. A triclinic feldspar. **sodium-** A. containing albite. Cf. *silica*, *anemonsite*.

anorthoclase. A triclinic sodium-potassium feldspar.

anorthosite. An igneous gabbro feldspar.

anoxemia. Lack of blood oxygen, as in mountain sickness.

anoxyscope. An apparatus to demonstrate the necessity for oxygen for plant growth.

anserine. $C_{10}H_{16}O_3N_4 = 240.14$. N-β-alanyl-1-methylhistidine. A dipeptide in the muscles of birds, reptiles, and fishes, m.238; a homolog of carnosine.

ant amber, a. butter, a. incense. A dirty-white resin collected by ants in their nests, chiefly in European conifer woods.

Antabuse. Trademark for tetraethylthiuram di-sulfide, a nontoxic drug used to treat alcoholism.

antacid. A substance that neutralizes acids or relieves acidity; e.g., milk of magnesia.

antacidin. Calcium saccharate.

antagonism. Counteraction or opposition. **biological-** Inhibition of the toxic effect of certain substances by other substances, e.g., certain ions.

antagonist. Physiological *antidote*.

antalkaline. A substance that neutralizes alkalies or relieves alkalinity; e.g., acetic acid.

antarcticite. $CaCl_2 \cdot 6H_2O$. Crystals found in an antarctic lake, believed to prevent its freezing.

antazoline hydrochloride. $C_{17}H_{19}N_3 \cdot HCl = 301.83$. 2-(N-benzylanilinomethyl)-2-imidazoline hydrochloride. White, odorless crystalline powder, m.239 (decomp.), soluble in water; an antihistaminic (U.S.P., B.P.). Also used to distinguish between nitrates and nitrites (red and yellow color, respectively, in presence of sulfuric acid).

Anthallan. Trade name for di-1-(*n*-butyl)aminomethyltrihydroxybenzofuraneone); used to treat hay fever and asthma.

anthelmintic. Helminthic. A drug that expels intestinal worms. Cf. *vermicide*.

anthemane. $C_{18}H_{38} = 254.4$. Octodecane, a paraffin in chamomile flowers.

anthemene. $C_{18}H_{38} = 252.4$. Octadecylene. A hydrocarbon, m.18, from *anthemis*, q.v.

anthemidine. An antispasmodic alkaloid from mayweed (*Anthemis cotula*).

anthemis. Roman chamomile, ground apple. The flower heads of *Anthemis nobilis*, (Compositae); a tonic and antispasmodic.

anthemol. $C_{10}H_{16}O = 152.1$. Chamomile camphor. A constituent of anthemis.

anther. The pollen-bearing part of a flower.

antheraxanthin. $C_{20}H_{58}O_3(?)$. A carotenoid, m.211, from the anthers of *Lilium tigrinum* (Liliaceae).

anthesterol. Taraxasterol.

anthion. Potassium persulfate.

antho- Prefix (Greek "flower") indicating a relationship to flowers.

anthocyanidins. Derivatives of 3,5,7-trihydroxyflavylium chloride occurring in the red, blue, and purple colorings of flowers. Cf. *flavones*.

anthocyanins. Glucosides comprising the soluble colors of blue, red, and violet flowers; as, delphinin. Cf. *flavylium*.

anthocyans. A group of red, blue, or violet plant colors.

anthophyllite. $MgFe(SiO_3)$. A brown orthorhombic amphibole.

anthoxanthins. Glucosides comprising the colors of yellow flowers; as, quercetin.

anthracene. $C_{14}H_{10} = 178.15$. Anthracin, *p*-naphthalene, anthracene oil. A hydrocarbon

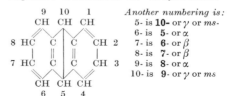

	Another numbering is:
	5- is **10-** or γ or *ms*-
	6- is **5-** or α
	7- is **6-** or β
	8- is **7-** or β
	9- is **8-** or α
	10- is **9-** or γ or *ms*

from coal-tar distillation. Colorless, blue-fluorescent needles, m.216.5, insoluble in water; used in the manufacture of alizarin dyes. Commercial a. contains carbazole and phenanthrene. **amino-** Anthramine. **diamino-** Anthradiamine. **dibromo*-** $C_6H_4 \cdot C_2Br_2C_6H_4 = 335.97$. *9,10-* or *ms-* Yellow crystals, m.221, insoluble in water. **dichloro*-** $C_6H_4 \cdot C_2Cl_2 \cdot C_6H_4 = 247.05$. *9,10-* or *ms-* Yellow needles, m.209, insoluble in water. **dihydro*-** $C_6H_4(CH_2)_2C_6H_4 = 180.17$. Hydroanthracene, diphenylene dimethylene. Colorless triclinic crystals, m.109, insoluble in water. **dihydrodiketo-** Anthraquinone. **dihydroketo-** Anthranone. **dihydroxy-** See *anthradiol, rufol, flavol, chrysazol.* **dimethyl-** $C_{14}H_8(CH_3)_2 = 206.20$. *2,3-* Colorless leaflets, m.246. *2,4-* Colorless needles, m.71. **ethyl*-** $C_{16}H_{14} = 206.11$. *9-* or *ms-* Colorless leaflets, m.59, insoluble in water. **hexahydro-** $C_{14}H_{16} = 184.20$. Colorless leaflets, insoluble in water. **hydro-** Dihydro-. **hydroxy-** See *anthranol, anthrol.* **ketohydroxy-** Oxanthrol. **methyl-** C_{14}-$H_9CH_3 = 192.17$. *alpha-* Colorless scales, m.200, soluble in alcohol. *beta-* White crystals, m.25, slightly soluble in water. **nitro-** $C_{14}H_9NO_2 = 223.15$. α-Nitrosoanthrone. Yellow needles, m.146, insoluble in water. **peri-** Chrysazol. **tetradecahydro-** A. perhydride. **tetrahydroxy-** Anthratetrol. **trihydroxy-** See *anthratriol, anthrarobin.*

a. blue. Alizarin blue. **a. carboxylic acid** Anthroic acid. **a. diol.** Anthradiol. **a. dione.** Anthraquinone. **a. oil.** A product of coal-tar distillation (above 270° C) containing a. with carbazole, phenanthrene, etc. **a. perhydride.** $C_6H_8 \cdot (CH_2)_2 \cdot C_6H_8 = 192.2$. Saturated anthracene. Colorless needles, m.88, soluble in alcohol **a. sulfonic acid.** Anthraquinonesulfonic acid. **a. tetrol.** Anthrotetrol **a. tetrones.** Anthradiquinones. A group of ketone derivatives containing 4 O atoms attached to the a. ring. **a. triol.** Anthratriol. **a. violet.** Gallein.

anthracenol. Anthrol.

anthracenone. Anthrone.

anthrachrysone. $C_{14}H_8O_6 = 272.13$. Anthraquinone 1,3,5,7-tetrol, anthrachrysazin. Orange crystals, m.360, insoluble in water.

anthracine. (1) A ptomaine produced by the anthrax bacillus. (2) Anthracene. Cf. *anthrazine.*

anthracite. Stone coal. A bright, lustrous, hard, brittle, mineral coal, q.v., containing 2–8% volatile carbon, d.1.3–1.8. **meta-** Contains less than 2% volatiles. **semi-** Contains 8–14% volatiles.

anthracometer. A device to determine the amount of carbon dioxide in gas mixtures.

anthraconite. Stinkstone. An earthy amorphous form of bituminous calcium carbonate.

anthracyl. The $C_{14}H_7$— radical, derived from anthracene; 3 isomers: α-, β-, and γ-.

anthradiamine. $C_{14}H_8(NH_2)_2 = 208.11$. Anthracenediamine*. Yellow needles, m.160.

anthradiol. $C_{14}H_{10}O_2 = 210.15$. Anthrahydroquinone, oxanthranol, *9,10*-anthracenediol*. Yellow needles, m.180, insoluble in water. 1,6- or *1,5-* Rufol. 1,9- or *1,8-* Chrysazol. 2,6- Flavol. **1,2-** *1,2*-Anthracenediol*. Green leaflets, m.160.

anthradiquinone. Anthracene tetrone.

anthraflavic acid. $C_{14}H_8O_4 = 240.13$. *2,6-* or 2,7-dihydroxyanthraquinone. Yellow needles, m.330, insoluble in water. **iso-** See *isoanthraflavic* acid.

anthragallol. $C_{14}H_8O_5 = 256.03$. 1,2,3-Trihydroxyanthraquinone, alizarin brown. Brown needles,

m.310, soluble in alkalies (green color); a dye, and dye intermediate.

anthraglucorhein. A cathartic glucoside from *Rheum* species; a brown powder, soluble in alcohol.

anthraglucosagradin. A glucoside from *Cascara sagrada.* Brown powder, soluble in alcohol; a cathartic.

anthraglucosennin. A glucoside from *Cassia angustifolia.* Brown powder, soluble in alcohol; a cathartic.

anthrahydroquinone. Anthradiol.

anthraldehyde. $C_{14}H_9 \cdot CHO = 208.08$.

anthramine. $C_{14}H_{11}N = 193.17$. Aminoanthracene, anthrylamine. β- or **2-** Yellow needles, m.237, sparingly soluble in water. γ- or **5-** Yellow crystals, m.146, soluble in alcohol; a dye intermediate.

anthranil. $C_6H_4 \cdot CO \cdot NH = 119.09$. Anthroxan, *o*-aminobenzoic acid lactam, anthranilic acid lactam. Colorless crystals or liquid, m.18, soluble in alkalies; **iso-** iso-*o*-aminobenzoic acid lactam.

a. aldehyde. *o*-Aminobenzaldehyde. **a. carbonic acid.** Isatoic acid.

anthranilate. A salt of anthranilic acid.

anthranilic acid. $NH_2 \cdot C_6H_4 \cdot COOH = 137.1$. *o*-Aminobenzoic acid. Yellow crystals, m.144, soluble in water; used in the manufacture of dyes and perfumes. Cf. *anthranoyl.* *N*-**carboxy-** Isatoic acid. **dinitro-** See *chrysalic* acid, *chrysanisic* acid. **oxalyl-** Kynuric acid.

a. di-N-propylaniline. An indicator changing at pH 5.5 from red (acid) to yellow (basic).

anthranilo. The radical C_6H_4 :CO·N—, from anthranil. **a. nitrile.** $NH_2 \cdot C_6H_4 \cdot CN = 118.08$. *o*-Aminophenyl cyanide. Yellow prisms, m.50.

anthranol. $C_{14}H_{10}O = 194.15$. 9-Hydroxyanthracene*. Yellow needles, decomp. 160, soluble in ether. Cf. *anthrone.* **dioxy-** Anthrarobin.

anthranone. $C_6H_4 \cdot CO \cdot CH_2 \cdot C_6H_4 = 194.15$. Anthrone. An isomer of anthranol. **10-hydroxy-** Oxanthrone. **nitroso-** Nitro*anthracene.*

anthranoyl. The radical $H_2N \cdot C_6H_4 \cdot CO—$, from anthranilic acid.

anthranthrenes. $C_{26}H_{16} = 328.11$. Hexacyclic hydrocarbons, consisting of 2 fused anthracene rings.

anthranylamine. Anthramine.

anthraparazene. $C_{30}H_{18}N_2 = 406.2$. The compound

anthrapurpurin. $C_{14}H_8O_5 = 256.13$. **1,2,7-** or 1,2,8-Trihydroxyanthraquinone. Orange needles, m.325, slightly soluble in water. Used in the manufacture of dyes. **a. diacetate.** Purgatol.

anthrapyridine. **alpha-** 6,7-Benzoquinoline. **beta-** 6,7-Benzoisoquinoline. Colorless crystals, m.280, soluble in water.

anthraquinol. Anthradiol.

anthraquinoline. $C_{17}H_{11}N = 229.2$. Naphthoquinoline. Colorless crystals, m.170, insoluble in water.

anthraquinone. $C_6H_4 \cdot (CO_2) \cdot C_6H_4 = 208.1$. Dihydrodiketoanthracene. Yellow needles, insoluble in water. A constituent of *Cassia, Aloe,*

Mirabilis, and *Rumex* species; manufactured by oxidation of anthracene. Used in the manufacture of alizarin and other dyes. **amino-** $C_{14}H_7O_2NH_2 =$ 223.15. Anthraquinoylamine *1-* or *α-*, Red, iridescent needles, m.242, insoluble in water; used in dystuff synthesis. *2-* or *β-* Red needles, m.302, insoluble in water, soluble in alcohol; used in organic synthesis. **2-amino-1-hydroxy-** $NH_2 \cdot C_{14}$-$H_6O_2 \cdot OH = 239.08$. *β*-Alizarinamide. Brown needles. m.226. **bromo-**$C_{14}H_6O_2Br = 286.97$. Yellow crystals. *1-* m.188. *2-* m.204. **chloro-** $C_{14}H_6O_2Cl = 242.51$. Yellow needles. *1-* m.162. *2-* m.211, insoluble in water. **dihydroxy-** *1,2-* Alizarin. *1,3-* Xanthopurpurin. *1,4-* Quinizarin. *1,5-* or *1,6-* Anthrarufin. *1,8-* or *1,9-* Chrysazin. *2,3-* Hystazarin. *2,6-* or *2,7-* Anthraflavic acid. *2,7-* or *2,8-* See *isoanthraflavic acid*. **4,6,2-di-hydroxymethyl-** Chrysophanic acid. **dioxy-** *Alizarin* blue. **hexahydroxy-** Rufigallic acid. **hydroxy-** $C_{14}H_7O_2 \cdot OH = 224.1$. Yellow leaflets, m.302, soluble in water. **methyl-** $C_{14}H_7O_2Me = 222.2$. Yellow crystals, m.177, soluble in alcohol. **nitro-** $C_{14}H_7O_2 \cdot NO_2 = 253.1$. Yellow needles, m.228, insoluble in water. **pentahydroxy-** Alizarin cyanine. **tetrahydroxy-** *1,2,5,6-* Rufiopin. *1,2,5,8-* Quinalizarin. *1,3,5,7-* Anthrachrysone. **tetra-hydroxymethyl-** Fisetin. **trihydroxy-** *1,2,3-* Anthragallol. *1,2,4-* See *purpurin*. *1,2,6-* or *1,2,7-* Flavopurpurin. *1,2,7-* or *1,2,8-* Anthrapurpurin. **trihydroxymethyl-** See *morin* and *emodin*. **trioxy-** Trihydroxy-.

   a. acridine. Naphthacridinedione. **a. acridone.** Naphthacridinetrione. **a. aldehyde.** 5,10-Dihydro-5,10-diketoanthraldehyde. **a. methide.** 5-Methyleneanthrone. **a. sulfonic acid.** Beta acid, alizarinsulfonic acid. An intermediate in the manufacture of alizarin. Cf. *silver* salt. **a. tetrol.** Tetrahydroxy a. **a. triol.** Trihydroxy a.

anthraquinonic acid. Alizarin.

anthrarobin. $C_{14}H_{10}O_3 = 226.1$. Dioxyanthraleucoalizarin, desoxyalizarin, dithranol. Yellow granules, insoluble in water. Used to treat skin diseases, and as a substitute for chrysarobin.

anthrarobinate. A salt of anthrarobin.

anthrarufin. $(C_6H_3 \cdot OH)_2(CO)_2 = 240.1$. 1,5- or 1,6-Dihydroxyanthraquinone. Yellow leaflets, m.280, soluble in water.

anthrasol. A colorless coal tar used in ointments.

anthratetrol. $C_{14}H_6(OH)_4 = 242.15$. Tetrahydroxyanthracene. A group of tetraatomic hydroxy derivatives of anthracene.

anthratriol. $C_{14}H_7(OH)_3 = 196.15$. Trihydroxyanthracene. A group of triatomic hydroxy derivatives of anthracene; as, anthrarobin.

anthraxolite. A metamorphic coal resembling anthracite, the end product in the metamorphosis of petroleum.

anthraxylon. A layer formation in coal corresponding with the larger pieces of woody peat. Similar to, and sometimes confused with, vitrain; see *coal.*

anthrazine. $(C_{14}H_8)_2N_2 = 380.2$. Anthracenediazine. Cf. *anthracine.*

anthroic acid. $C_{14}H_9 \cdot COOH = 226.16$. Anthracene carboxylic acid*. **α-** or **1-** Yellow needles, m.260 (sublime), insoluble in water. **β-** or **2-** Yellow leaflets m.280 (sublime), insoluble in water. **γ-** or **5-** Yellow needles, decomp. 206, soluble in water, or

alcohol. A. acids are used in organic synthesis and in the manufacture of dyes.

anthrol. $C_{14}H_{10}O = 194.15$. Hydroxyanthracene. **1-** Colorless needles, m.153. **3-** or **2-** Colorless needles, decomp. 200, soluble in alcohol. **γ-** or **5-** (or **9-**). Anthranol.

anthrone. Anthranone.

anthroxan. Anthranil. **a. aldehyde.** $C_8H_5O_2N = 147.1$. Colorless crystals, m.72. Cf. *anthranilaldehyde.*

anthryl. The 5 isomeric radicals $C_{14}H_9$—, derived from anthracene. **a. amine.** Anthramine.

anthrylene. The 11 isomeric radicals $—C_{14}H_8$—, derived from anthracene.

anti- Prefix (Greek) indicating: (1) against or opposed, (2) anti position. **a. position.** Opposite to the syn position, q.v. Cf. *stereoisomerism.*

antiabrin. A substance formed in the blood after the injection of abrin.

antiagglutinin. A blood substance which prevents agglutination.

antiaggressin. A substance formed in the body counteracting the action of aggressins.

antialbumid. A decomposition product of albumin formed during gastric and pancreatic digestion.

antialbuminate. Antialbumate, parapeptone. An incompletely digested albumin. Cf. *syntonin.*

antialexin. A blood substance opposing the action of alexin.

antiallpecia vitamin. See *vitamin.*

antiamboceptor. A substance given off by protoplasm in order to combine with the cytophilic group of an amboceptor. Cf. *Ehrlich* side-chain theory.

antianaphylactin. A substance counteracting anaphylactin. Cf. *allergen.*

antiantibody. A substance formed in the blood of an organism after injection of an antibody.

antiantidote. A substance which opposes the action of an antidote.

antiantienzyme. A substance which opposes the action of an antienzyme.

antiar. The milky juice of the upas (Javanese) or ipoh (Malayan) tree, *Antiaris toxicaria* (Malacca, Java); an arrow poison.

antiarin. (1) $C_{14}H_{20}O_5 = 268.16$. A glucoside of antiar. An East Indian arrow muscle poison. (2) $C_{14}H_{20}O_5 \cdot 2H_2O = 304.2$. The active principle of antiar.

antiarthrin. A condensation product of gallic acid and saligenin. Brown powder, soluble in alcohol, used in uric acid diathesis.

antiarthritic. A drug that prevents or relieves arthritis; as, atophan. Cf. *antipodagric.*

antiasthmatic. A drug relieving asthma; e.g., atropine.

antibacterial. Antimycotic. A substance that checks the growth of bacteria. Cf. *antiseptic, disinfectant.*

antiberberin. A black liquid prepared from rice and used to treat beriberi.

antiberiberi. See *vitamin B.*

antibilious. A drug that relieves a bilious condition.

antibiote. An early term for antibiotic (1), q.v.

antibiotic. (1) A substance destructive to life; a poison. (2) A chemical inhibitor of the growth of organisms produced by a microorganism, e.g., penicillin. It can be antibacterial or antifungal.

antibiotics. See table, p. 52.

INTERNATIONAL STANDARDS FOR ANTIBIOTICS

Substance	Defined potency, I.U./mg	Equivalence of 1 I.U. to American μg	Calculated purity of Standard on basis of American μg%
Penicillin (sodium salt)	1,670	Not used	99*
Phenoxymethylpenicillin (free acid)	1,695	Not used	99*
Streptomycin (sulfate)	780	1 μg of base	97.5
Dihydrostreptomycin (sulfate)	760	1 μg of base	95.1
Bacitracin	55	Not used	Not known
Tetracycline (hydrochloride)	990	1 μg hydrochloride	99.0
Chlortetracycline (hydrochloride)	1,000	1 μg hydrochloride	100
Oxytetracycline (base dehydrate)	900	1 μg anhydrous base	97.1
Erythromycin (base)	950	1 μg anhydrous base	95
Polymixin B	7,874	Not used	Not known

* Independent estimate (Lightbown, 1961).

antiblennorrhagic. A drug used to prevent or treat gonorrhea; e.g., methylene blue.

antibody. A substance formed in the body fluids of animals after an injection; it counteracts the effects of the injected substance; as, antitoxins and precipitins.

anticachectic. A drug used to treat malnutrition.

anticatalase. A substance opposing the action of a catalase.

anticatalyzer. A substance that inhibits the action of a catalyst.

anticatarrhals. A drug subduing the inflammation of mucuous membranes.

anticathode. Target. An electrode in a vacuum tube placed relative to the cathode so that the rays from the latter impinge on it. See vacuum *tubes, X-ray* tube.

antichlor. A chemical used to remove excess chlorine after bleaching; as, sodium thiosulfate.

anticholerin. A substance derived from cultures of cholera bacillus; used to treat cholera.

anticoagulin. A substance that prevents the coagulation of blood or milk.

anticol. A colloidal antimony solution used as parasiticide.

anticomplement. A substance formed by using cells to combine with the haptophore group of the complement. See *Ehrlich* side-chain theory.

anticrotin. The antitoxin of crotonallin.

anticytolisis. *Complement* fixation.

anticytotoxin. A substance opposing the action of cytotoxins.

antidiabetic. A drug used to treat diabetes.

antidimmer. A preparation which prevents moisture from accumulating on glass.

Antidolorin. A proprietary brand of ethyl chloride.

antidote. An agent counteracting or neutralizing the action of a poison. **chemical-** A substance which precipitates or alters a poison; as, oils, soaps, egg white. **mechanical-** A means of removing a poison from the system; e.g., stomach pump. **physiological-** A drug which counteracts a poison by having an opposite effect. **universal-** (1) A solution of 2 pts. magnesia and 1 pt. iron sulfate in water. (2) A mixture of 2 pts. charcoal, 1 pt. magnesium oxide, and 1 pt. tannic acid in water.

antidysenteric. A substance which checks or prevents diarrhea; e.g., bismuth salts.

antiemetic. A substance which prevents vomiting; e.g., bismuth subnitrate.

antienzyme. A substance that inhibits enzyme action.

antierrhine. A drug which diminishes nasal discharges.

Antifebrin. A proprietary brand of acetanilide.

antiformin. Hychlorite. A strongly alkaline solution of sodium hypochlorite; a disinfectant.

antifreeze. A substance added to the radiator water of automobiles to prevent freezing; e.g., ethylene glycol.

antifungin. Magnesium borate used as a gargle.

antigalactic. A drug to diminish milk secretion; e.g., atropine.

antigen. An injection which causes the formation of antibodies; as, (1) *toxins:* (*a*) bacterial (diphtheria); (*b*) vegetable (ricin); (*c*) animal (snake); (2) *ferments* or *enzymes* (lipase), (3) *precipitinogens* (animal proteins); (4) *agglutinogens* (bacteria); (5) *opsogens* (aggresins), (6) *lysogens* (animal cells).

antiglobulin. A precipitin that coagulates globulin.

antihemolytic. An agent that prevents hemolysis.

antihidrotic. Anhidrotic.

antihistaminic. A substance that counteracts the effects of an excess of histamine in the body; as, chlorcyclizine hydrochloride.

antihypo. Potassium percarbonate, used in photography.

antiknock. See *knock.*

antilab. Antirennin.

antilithic. A drug that prevents the formation of urinary stones; e.g., colchicine.

antiluetic. Antisyphilitic.

antiluetin. $SbO(C_4H_4O_6)_2K(NH_4)_2 \cdot H_2O$. Potassium ammonium antimonic bitartrate; used to treat syphilis.

antilysin. A substance formed in blood which destroys bacterial lysins; e.g., alexins.

antilyssic. A drug used to treat rabies.

antimalarial. A drug relieving or preventing malaria; e.g., quinine.

antimalum. A mixture of essential oils, chiefly camphor oil, used externally for rheumatism.

antimellin. A glucoside from the bark of *Eugenia jambolana* (Myrtaceae) used to treat diabetes.

antimers. Enantiomers, optical antipodes. A pair of isomers having structures like an object and

its mirror image; they are identical in all properties except those that can be described as right and left.
antimonate. Antimoniate, stibnate, stibiate, stibate. A salt of antimonic acids, q.v., viz; *ortho*-antimonate, M_3SbO_4; *meta*-, $M_4Sb_2O_5$ or $MSbO_3$; *pyro*-, $M_4Sb_2O_7$.
antimonial glass. Antimonous sulfide. **a. lead.** Hard lead. An alloy: Pb 85, Sb 15%; resistant to sulfuric acid. **a. nickel sulfide.** Ullmannite. **a. silver.** Ag_3Sb. Dycrasite. Native silver antimonide. **a. saffron.** Antimonous oxysulfide.
antimoniate. Antimonate.
antimonic. A compound of pentavalent antimony, $=Sb\equiv$. **a. acid.** *ortho*- $H_3SbO_4 = 187.2$. White powder, d.6.6, decomp. by heat, slightly soluble in water. *meta*- $HSbO_3 = 169.21$. White powder, sparingly soluble in water. *pyro*- $H_4Sb_2O_7 = 356.43$. Colorless powder, slightly soluble in water. **a. chloride.** $SbCl_5 = 295.5$. Antimony pentachloride. Fuming yellow liquid, $b_{30mm}92$, decomp. in water, soluble in acids; a reagent for alkaloids. **a. fluoride.** $SbF_5 = 215.2$. Antimony pentafluoride. An oil, $d_{22}°2.99$, soluble in water. **a. oxide.** $Sb_2O_5 = 320.4$. A. acid anhydride, antimony peroxide. Yellow powder, insoluble in water. **a. oxychloride.** $SbOCl_3 = 243.28$. Yellow powder, decomp. by heat, insoluble in water. **a. sulfide.** $Sb_2S_5 = 400.8$. Antimony pentasulfide. Orange powder, $d_0°4.120$, insoluble in water; a diaphoretic, emetic, and expectorant.
antimonide. Stibide. A binary compound of antimony, analogous to arsenides.
antimonii. Official Latin for "of antimony"; antimonic or antimonous compounds.
antimonine. *Antimony* lactate.
antimonious. Antimonous.
antimonite. (1) A salt of antimonous acids, q.v.; as, Na_3SbO_3. (2) Antimony glance. **sulf-** A salt of sulfantimonous acid containing the radical $\equiv SbS_3$; as, $(NH_4)_3SbS_2$.
antimonium. Antimony.
antimono. The divalent group —Sb:Sb—.
antimonous. Stibous, stibious, stibnous, antimonious. Describing compounds of trivalent antimony, $Sb\equiv$. **a. acid.** *ortho*- $H_3SbO_3 = 171.4$. *meta*- $HSbO_2 = 153.21$. A hypothetical acid which forms salts. *pyro*- $H_4Sb_2O_5 = 327.5$. White solid, forms the trioxide when heated. **a. arsenate.** A mixture of a. oxide and arsenic acid, used to treat skin diseases. **a. arsenite.** A mixture of a. oxide and arsenous acid, used to treat skin diseases. **a. basic chloride.** Antimony oxychloride. **a. bromide.** $SbBr_3 = 361.3$. Yellow rhombs, m.94, hydrolyzes in water. **a. chloride.** $SbCl_3 = 228.3$. Butter of antimony. White rhombs, m.73, sparingly soluble in water. *Antimony butter* is a fuming acid. Used as a caustic, a mordant, for manufacturing antimony salts, and for staining iron and copper articles. **a. fluoride.** $SbF_3 = 178.97$. Grayish octahedra, m.292, soluble in water; Cf. *DeHaën's* salt. Used in ceramics and as a mordant. **a. fluoride and ammonium sulfate.** De Haën's salt. **a. hydride.** $SbH_3 = 124.79$. Stibine. Colorless poisonous gas, b. —18, sparingly soluble in water. **a. iodide.** $SbI_3 = 502.97$. 3 allotropes. (1) Red *hexagonal* crystals; (2) red *monoclinic* crystals; (3) yellow *rhombic* crystals, m.171, decomp. in water. An

alterative, and skin ointment. **a. nickel.** NiSb. A native alloy. **a. oxalate.** $SbO \cdot (C_2O_4)_2 = 313.77$. Antimonyl oxalate. White powder, soluble in acids; a mordant. **a. oxide.** $Sb_2O_3 = 291.24$. Valentinite, antimony bloom. a. glass, Sb_4O_6. Colorless rhombs, m. 655, insoluble in water. A powerful reducing agent, an expectorant and emetic. **a. oxychloride.** $SbOCl = 173.47$. Algaroth, mercurius vitae, basic antimony chloride. White regular crystals, insoluble in water. Used in the manufacture of tartar emetic and as an emetic and purgative. **a. oxyiodide.** $SbOI = 262.8$. Yellow crystals, insoluble in water. **a. oxysulfide.** $Sb_2S_3 \cdot Sb_2O_3 = 630.6$. Antimony flowers, a. red, a. vermilion, antimonial saffron. A double salt of a. sulfide and oxide, containing some $SbOS_2$ (crocus metallorum). Brown powder, vulcanizer for rubber. **a. sulfate.** $Sb_2(SO_4)_3 = 528.0$. White powder, soluble in acids. **a. sulfide.** $Sb_2S_3 = 340.0$. Stibnite, antimony red, black antimony sulfide. Black powder or red crystals, m.555, insoluble in water; a diaphoretic alterative, pigment for the manufacture of safety matches, and opacifier, q.v.

antimony. Sb = 121.75. Stibium. A metal of the arsenic or nitrogen family and element at. no. 51. A rhombohedral, blue-white, brittle, lustrous substance, d.6.62, m.630, b.1440, soluble ·in concentrated sulfuric acid or aqua regia. Basilius Valentinus described its preparation and properties in 1450. Occurs native, as metal, as sulfide (stibnite), and as antimonides and sulfantimonides of the heavy metals. Allotropes: (1) ordinary metallic or β-antimony, Sb_1; (2) an unstable, yellow or α-antimony, Sb_4; (3) amorphous, black antimony, Sb_2, d.5.3, which heat changes to (1). A. is tri- and pentavalent, and resembles arsenic and phosphorus in chemical behavior. Compounds derived from trivalent antimony:

Antimonous (stibnous)	Sb^{3+}
Stibines	SbR_3
Antimonites	SbO_2^-
Antimonyl	SbO^+
From pentavalent antimony:	
Antimonic (stibnic)	Sb^{5+}
Stibonium	R_4SbX
Metaantimonate	SbO_3^-
Orthoantimonate	SbO_4^{3-}

A. is used extensively in alloys (Britannia metal, type metal, pewter) and to prepare antimony compounds used in medicine and as pigments.
black- Antimonous sulfide. **butter of-** Antimonous chloride. **flowers of-** Antimonous oxysulfide. **gray-** A. glance. **red-** (1) Kermesite. (2) Antimonous oxysulfide. **white-** Valentinite.
  a. anhydride. See *antimonous* or *antimonic* oxide. **a. arsenide.** Allemontite. **a. ash.** See *a. oxides.* **a. black.** Antimonous sulfide. **a. blende.** Antimony glance. **a. bloom.** Antimonous oxide. **a. butter.** Antimonous chloride. **a. chlorides.** See *antimonous(ic)* chloride and oxychloride. **a. crocus.** Antimonous oxysulfide formed by the deflagration of equal parts of antimonous sulfide and saltpeter. **a. flowers.** Antimonous oxysulfide. **a. fluoride.** See *antimonous(ic)*

fluoride. **a. glance.** Antimonite, stibnite, a. blende, gray a. A native antimonous sulfide. **a. glass.** Antimonous oxide. **a. lactate.** Sb-$(C_3H_5O_3)_3$ = 389.97. Antimonine. Yellow crystals, soluble in water; a dye mordant. **a. minerals.** A. is closely associated with arsenic and bismuth minerals; also occurs as the antimonides and sulfantimonides of the heavy metals, and as stibnite, kermesite, valentinite, and cervantite. Cf. *plagionite. antimonous* nickel. **a. mordants.** See *antimonous* fluoride, a. lactate and a. potassium tartrate. **a. needles.** Antimonous sulfide. **a. ocher.** Stibiconite. **a. oxides.** See *antimonous* oxide, *antimony tetroxide, antimonic* oxide. **a. pentachloride.** Antimonic chloride. **a. pentafluoride.** Antimonic fluoride. **a. pentamethyl.** $Sb(CH_3)_5$ = 197.17. Pentamethylstibine. Colorless liquid, b.97, insoluble in water. **a. pentasulfide.** Antimonic sulfide. **a. pentoxide.** Antimonic oxide. **a. peroxide.** Antimonic oxide. **a. persulfide.** Antimonic sulfide. **a. potassium oxalate.** $SbK_3(C_2O_4)_3 6H_2O$ = 611.97. White powder, soluble in water; a dye mordant. **a. potassium tartrate.** $[SbOK(C_4H_4O_6)]_2 \cdot H_2O$ = 667.82. Tartar emetic, antimonyl potassium tartrate, tartar stibiatus. Colorless octahedra, soluble in water. Used as an emetic, expectorant, and diaphoretic; as a dye mordant for textiles and leather; and as an analytical reagent. **a. red.** Antimonous oxysulfide. **a. regulus.** Metallic a. **a. salt.** DeHaën's salt. **a. sodium sulfate.** $SbF_3 \cdot Na_2SO_4$. A. trifluoride sodium sulfate. **a. sodium thioglycollate.** White powder; a trypanosomicide. **a. sulfide.** Antimonous sulfate. **a. sulfide.** See *antimonous(ic)* sulfide. **a. sulfuret.** Antimonous sulfide. **a. tetroxide.** Sb_2O_4 = 307.54. Cervanite. Cervantite. Colorless powder, insoluble in water. **a. thioglycollamide.** $Sb(S \cdot CH_2CONH_2)_3$ = 392.06. White crystals, m.139, slightly soluble in water; a trypanosomicide. **a. tribromide.** Antimonous bromide. **a. trichloride.** Antimonous chloride. **a. triethyl.** $Sb(C_2H_5)_3$ = 209.12. Triethylstibine. Colorless liquid, b.159, insoluble in water. **a. trifluoride.** Antimonous fluoride. **a. trifluoride sodium sulfate.** $SbF_3 \cdot Na_2SO_4$ = 320.8. White crystals, soluble in water. **a. trimethyl.** $Sb(CH_3)_3$ = 167.00. Trimethylstibine. Colorless liquid, b.80.6, insoluble in water. **a. trioxide.** Antimonous oxide. **a. triphenyl.** Triphenyl*stibine*. **a. trisulfate.** Antimonous sulfate. **a. trisulfide.** Antimonous sulfide. **a. vermillon.** Antimonous oxysulfide. **a. white.** Antimonous oxide. **a yellow.** Basic *lead* antimonate.

antimonyl. The radical SbO—. **a. aniline tartrate.** Yellow crystals, a trypanosomicide. **a. compound.** A basic substance containing the a. radical. **a. oxalate.** Antimonous oxalate. **a. potassium tartrate.** Antimony potassium tartrate. **a. sulfate.** $(SbO)_2SO_4$ = 375.27. White powder. *basic*-$(SbO)_2SO_4 \cdot Sb_2(OH)_4$ = 676.89. White powder.

ntimosan. Potassium antimonyl pyrocatechol di-·lfonate. White powder, used to treat schistoso-·is.

·n. An antibiotic.

·. Antibacterial.

A drug used to treat neuralgia; e.g.,

·n. Vitamin B.

antinonnin. $C_6H_2(NO_2)_2CH_3ONa$. Sodiumo- dinitrocresolate. Victoria yellow. Yellow, odorless germicide and plant spray.

antinosin. $C_6H_2I_2ONa_2 \cdot CO \cdot O_6H_4O$. Sodium tetraiodophenolphthalein. Nosophen sodium. Blue powder, soluble in water. Used as an antiseptic and to render the gall bladder visible in X rays.

antioxidant. Age resistor, antioxygen. A substance to retard deterioration by oxidation, e.g., of rubber (hydroquinone), or of food.

antioxygen. Antioxidant.

antiparasite. Antiparasitic.

antiparasitic. A drug that inhibits the growth of vegetable and animal parasites.

antipepsin. A substance that opposes the action of pepsin.

antiperiodic. A drug to treat malaria; e.g., quinine.

antiphlogistic. A drug that inhibits the progress of inflammation; e.g., aconite, mercury (internal), and glycerin (local). **a. theory.** A theory (Lavoisier) contradicting the older phlogiston theory, q.v.

antipodagric. A drug used to treat gout; e.g,. colchicum.

antipode. An antimeter, q.v.

antipyonin. Sodium tetraborate.

antipyrene. Antipyrine.

antipyretic. A drug relieving fever; as, aconite.

antipyreticin. Resalgin.

antipyrine. $C_{11}H_{12}ON_2$ = 188.17. Antipyrene, analgesine, phenazone, 2,3-dimethyl-1-phenyl-5(2)-pyrazolone, anodynin, sedatine, methozan, parodyn, phenylon, oxydimethyl quinizine, dimethyloxyquinizine, pyrazin, metozine. White powder, m.113, soluble in water. An antipyretic, sedative, antineuralgic, antirheumatic; and reagent for nitrous and nitric acid. **amido-** $C_{11}H_{13}ON_3$ = 203.2. 1-Phenyl-2,3-dimethyl-4-aminopyrazolone. Colorless crystals, m.109, soluble in water. **chloral-** Hypnal. **dimethylamino-** Pyramidon. **homo-** *Homo*antipyrine. **methyl-** $C_{12}N_{14}ON_2$ = 202.2. 1-Phenyl-2,3,4-trimethylpyrazolone. Colorless crystals, m.82. **methylenedi-** Salubrol. **methylethylglycol-** Astrolin. **monobromo-** Bromopyrine. **nitroso-** $C_{11}H_{11}O_2N_2$ = 217.2. 1-Phenyl-2,3-dimethyl-4-nitrosopyrazolone.

a. benzoate. Benzopyrine. **a. camphorate.** A compound of a. and camphor. **a. carbolate.** Phenopyrine. **a. mandelate.** Tusol. **a. monobromide.** Bromopyrine. **a. phenate.** Phenopyrine. **a. resorcylate.** Resalgin. **a. salicylate.** Salipyrine. **a. tannate.** A compound of a. and tannic acid. Yellow powder, insoluble in water.

antipyrotic. A drug to treat burns.

antipyryl. A radical derived from antipyrine.

$$OC \cdot NPh \cdot NMe \cdot CMe : C—$$
$$5 \quad 1 \quad 2 \quad 3 \quad 4$$

antiquinol. Allylphenyl cinchonine ester. Yellow crystals, m.30, insoluble in water; an antiseptic and analgesic.

antirachitic. Effective against rickets; as, cod-liver oil.

antirennin. A constituent of blood serum opposing the enzyme rennin.

antirheumatic. A compound that relieves rheumatism; e.g., colchicine.

antirheumatin. A compound of sodium saliyclate and methylene blue. Blue crystals, soluble in water; an antirheumatic.

antiricin. A substance formed in the blood after injection of ricin.

antirobin. A substance formed in the blood after injection of robin.

antiscorbutic. A compound to treat scurvy by virtue of its ascorbic acid content; e.g., lime juice.

antisepsin. $C_8H_8ONBr = 213.99$. Asepsin, acetanilide bromide, acetbromanilide. Colorless crystals; an antipyretic and antiseptic.

antiseptic. A substance that opposes sepsis, putrefaction, or decay by inhibiting or destroying microorganisms; e.g., alcohol, boric acid, chlorine, mercuric chloride, phenol. Cf. *antibiotic, disinfectant, germicide.*

antiseptin. A mixture of boric acid, zinc iodide, and thymol; a dusting powder.

antiseptol. Cinchonine iodosulfate. A red dusting powder for skin diseases.

antispasmin. $C_{23}H_{28}O_9NNa \cdot 3NaC_7H_5O_3$. Narcein sodium salicylate. An unstable white hygroscopic powder; an antispasmodic, sedative, and hypnotic.

antispasmodic. A drug relieving convulsions or spasms; e.g., valerian.

antistat. A substance that prevents the formation of static electricity, e.g., on film.

antisudorific. A drug that prevents excessive perspiration. Cf. *anhidrotic.*

antisyphilitic. Antiluetic. A drug to treat syphilis; e.g., arsenic, mercury.

antitetrazin. An antineuralgic quinine derivative.

antithermin. $C_{11}H_{14}O_2N_2 = 206.2$. Phenylhydrazinelevulinic acid. Colorless crystals, m.108, insoluble in water; an analgesic, antipyretic, or antiseptic.

antithrombin. The blood substance which prevents coagulation.

antidote. A mixture of equal parts of magnesia, charcoal, and ferric hydroxide; a poison antidote. Cf. *antidote.*

antitoxic. Antidote.

antitoxin. A protein defensive antibody developed in the blood after the injection of a poison. **diphtheria-** A preparation from the blood serum of animals infected with diphtheria. **streptococcus-** A preparation from the serum of animals infected with *Streptococcus bacillus.* **tetanus-** A preparation from the serum of animals infected with tetanus. Cf. *antigen, antibody.*

antitussin. $(C_6H_4F)_2 = 190.1$. Difluorodiphenyl. Colorless crystals, m.87, used to treat whooping cough.

antivenin. A globulin antivenom from the serum of the Heloderma snake.

antivenom. An antitoxin against snake venom.

antiviral. Describing a substance used to combat virus diseases.

antodyne. *Phenoxy*propandiol.

ant oil. Furfural.

antozone. Monoatomic oxygen.

antrycide. 4-Amino-6-(2'-amino-6'-methylpyrimidyl-4'-amino)quinaldine-1,1'-bimethosulfate. White crystals, soluble in water. Used to protect cattle against the tsetse fly.

antrypol. Germanin.

ANTU. Abbreviation for α-naphthylthiourea; a rat bait.

anysin. Ichtyol.

anytin. Anitin. Brown-black germicidal sulfurated hydrocarbon derived from ichthyol.

anytol. Anitol. A compound of anitin and aromatic phenols and alcohols. **cresol-** Metasol, metacresolanytol a germicide, **eucalyptol-** Eucasol; a germicide and disinfectant.

AOAC. Association of Official Agricultural Chemists.

APA. Antipernicious enemic factor; see *vitamin B$_{12}$.*

apa- Apo-.

apaconitine. An alkaloid derived from aconitine.

apagallin. Mercury tetraiodophenolphthalein; an antiseptic and indicator. Cf. *Mercurochrome.*

apatite. $3Ca_3(PO_4)_2CaF_2$. A native crystalline calcium fluophosphate fertilizer from Norway and Canada. Cf. *phosphorite, fluorapatite.*

apatropine. Apoatropine.

aperient. A laxative or mild purgative.

aperiodic. See *balance.*

aperture. (1) An opening into or through a body. (2) The diameter of the open part of an objective or lens.

apex. The highest point of a cone, curve, or orbit.

aphalerite. See *wurtzite.*

aphanesite. $2CuO \cdot As_2O_3 \cdot 4H_2O$. Native copper arsenate.

aphelion. (1) The position of a celestial body when farthest from the sun. Cf. *perihelion.* (2) Figuratively, the position of an electron in an elliptical orbit when farthest from the nucleus. Cf. *apogee.*

aphicide. A substance to kill *Aphis.* Cf. *insecticide.*

aphrite. Earth foam, foam spar. A white pearly variety of calcite.

aphrizite. Black *tourmaline,* q.v.

aphrodine. Yohimbine.

aphrodisiac. A drug which arouses sexual desires: e.g., nux vomica.

aphrodite. $4MgO \cdot SiO_{10}H_6$. A native basic silicate; meerschaumlike masses.

aphrosiderite. $(Fe,Al)Si_4O_{20} \cdot 5H_2O$. Olive-green, soft, hexagonal scales.

aphthitalite. $NaKSO_4$. Native, colorless hexagons. Cf. *glaserite.*

aphthonite. A gray tetrahedritic silver ore.

aphyl. Alkyl.

apigenin. $C_{15}H_{10}O_5 = 270.08$. 4',5,7-Trihydroxyflavone. A plant flavone.

apiin. $C_{27}H_{32}O_{16} = 612.3$. A glucoside from the seeds of *Apium petroselinum.* Yellow crystals, m.228, soluble in hot water.

apinol. $C_{10}H_{18}O = 154.14$. Apinolum, levomenthone. An amber-colored oil from pine-wood, b.182, insoluble in water. An antiseptic, germicide, and local anesthetic.

apiole. $C_{12}H_{14}O_4 = 222.2$. Parsley camphor, 2,5-dimethoxy-3,4-methenedioxy-1²-propenylbenzene, occurring in the seeds of *Petroselinum* (parsley) and *Apium* (celery). Colorless needles of parsley odor, m.30, insoluble in water; an emmenagogue and antiperiodic. **iso-** Colorless crystals, m.56, **liquid-** The green oily oleoresin of parsley seeds, soluble in alcohol.

apiolic acid. $C_{10}H_{10}O_6 = 226.08$. Colorless crystals, m.175.

apionol. $C_6H_2(OH)_4 = 142.1$. Phentetrol, v-tetrahydroxybenzene. Colorless crystals, m.161. **dimethyl-** $C_6H_2(OH)_2(OMe)_2 = 170.1$. 1,2-Dimethoxy-3,4-dihydroxybenzene. Colorless crystals, m.106, soluble in alcohol. **tetramethyl-** $C_6H_2(OMe)_4 = 198.2$. v-Tetramethoxybenzene. Colorless crystals m.81.

apionone. $(HO)_2C_6H_2 \cdot O \cdot O \cdot CH_2 = 154.1$. 1,2-Methenedioxy-3,4-dihydroxybenzene. Colorless crystals, m.69.

apiose. $C_5H_{10}O_5 = 150.07$. A methyl tetrose from the glucoside of celery.

aplite. (1) A pink or red cobalt-silver ore from Canada. See **alaskite.** (2) SiO_2 60, Al_2O_3 24, CaO 6, Na_2O 6, K_2O 3, Fe_2O_3 0.2%. A ceramic composed chiefly of plagioclase.

aplome. A yellow-green manganese garnet.

aplotaxene. $C_{17}H_{28}(?)$. An aliphatic hydrocarbon from costus oil.

APNS. Thorin.

apo-, apa- Prefix (Greek "from") indicating a derived compound, e.g., apomorphine derived from morphine.

apoatropine. $C_{17}H_{21}O_2N = 271.3$. Apatropine, atropamine. An alkaloid derived from atropine by the action of nitric acid. Colorless prisms. m.61, insoluble in water. **a. hydrochloride.** $C_{17}H_{21}O_2N \cdot HCl = 307.7$. White leaflets, m.238, soluble in water. **a. sulfate.** $(C_{17}H_{21}O_2N)_2 \cdot H_2SO_4 = 640.5$. Colorless crystals, soluble in water.

apobiotic. Reducing vital activity.

apocamphoric acid. Campho acid.

apocholic acid. $C_{24}H_{38}O_4 = 390.27$. A dehydration product of cholic acid.

apochromatic. A lens combination to correct chromatic aberration by bringing color rays to a common focus. Cf. *achromatic.*

apocodeine. $C_{18}H_{19}O_2N = 281.3$. An alkaloid derived from codeine; colorless gum, sparingly soluble in water. **a. hydrochloride.** $C_{18}H_{19}O_2N \cdot HCl = 317.7$. Yellow, hygroscopic powder, soluble in water; an expectorant, hypnotic, and emetic.

apocrenic acid. $C_{24}H_{12}O_{12} = 492.1$. Brown solid derived from humus by oxidation.

apocyanines. A group of cyanine dyes with directly linked nitrogen rings; as; **erythro-** 3:4′ link. **xantho-** 3:2′ link.

Apocynacae. Dogbanes. Tropical and subtropical plants with a milky juice, often poisonous; e.g., roots: *Apocynum cannabinum* (Canadian hemp), *Apocynum androsaemifolium* (dogbane); barks: *Aspidosperma quebracho blanco* (quebracho), *Alstonia scholaris* (chlorogenin); leaves: *Nerium odorum* (karabin), *Urechites suberecta* (urechitine); seeds: *Strophanthus kombe* (strophanthus), *Acocanthera venenata* (ouabain).

apocynamarin. $C_{14}H_{18}O_3 = 234.1$. A glucoside from the rhizome of *Apocynum cannabinum*; a cardiac tonic. Cf. *cynotoxin.*

apocynein. An active glucoside, from *Apocynum cannabinum*, Canadian hemp. White crystals, soluble in alcohol Cf. *apocynin.*

apocynin. A resinoid from *Apocynum cannabinum*. Brown amorphous powder which contains apocynein.

apocynoid. The combined active principles of *Apocynum cannabinum*; a tonic, emetic, and cathartic.

apocynum. Canadian hemp, black Indian hemp, Indian physic, dogbane. The dried rhizome and roots of *Apocynum cannabinum*; a heart tonic.

apogee. (1) The point in its orbit at which the moon is farthest from the earth; Cf. *perigee.* (2) The point in the orbit of an electron farthest from the nucleus. Cf. *aphelion.*

Apollinaris water. A German mineral water.

apolysin. $C_{14}H_{17}O_7N = 311.2$. Phenetidin citric acid, aconitylphenetidine, 1-ethoxy-4-citrylaminobenzene. White crystals, m.72, soluble in hot water; an antipyretic, antineuralgic, and antiseptic.

apomorphine. $C_{17}H_{17}O_2N = 267.23$. An alkaloid derived from morphine. Colorless mass, becoming green on exposure, sparingly soluble in water an expectorant and emetic. **a. hydrochloride.** $C_{17}H_{17}O_2N \cdot HCl = 303.71$. Gray monoclinic prisms, m.270, soluble in water; a hypnotic, emetic, and expectorant.

apomyelin. A phosphatide prepared from brain matter.

aponal. $NH_2COOCMe_2Et = 131.09$. **tert-** Amylcarbamate. Colorless crystals; a hypnotic. Cf. *hedonal.*

apophylite. $KCa_4H_{16}Si_8O_{28}$. Native white or pinkish octahedra.

apopinol. Apiole.

apoquinamine. $C_{19}H_{22}ON_2 = 294.4$. An alkaloid derived from quinamine.

apoquinine. Homoquinine.

aporetin. A resin from the roots of rhubarb. Brown powder, insoluble in ether, soluble in alkalies.

aporphine. $C_{17}H_{17}N = 235.12$. A morphine derivative.

aposafranone. $C_{18}H_{12}ON_2 = 272.11$. Benzene indone, 3-aminophenylphenazine. Red crystals m.242, soluble in water; a dye.

apothecaries' weight. A system of weights and measures used in compounding medicines. The troy pound of 5,760 grains is the standard, and is subdivided into 12 ounces; the ounce into 8 drams; the dram into 60 grains. For fluid measure the quart of 42 fluid ounces is subdivided into 2 pints; the pint into 16 fluid ounces, the fluid ounce into 8 drams, and the dram into 60 minims. Abbreviations:

♏	minim	= 0.0616 ml
gtt	gutta, a drop	
Э	scruple = 20 grains	= 1.296 gm
Ʒ	dram = 60 grains	= 3.8888 gm
℥	ounce = 480 grains	= 31.103 gm
		= 8 drams = 29.573 ml
lb	libra, pound = 5,760 grains	= 373.2417 gm
O	octarius, pint = 7,680 minims	= 473.16 ml

See *weights, conversion* factors.

apothesine. $Ph \cdot CH : CHCOO(CH_2)_4NEt_2 \cdot HCl = 297.74$. γ-Diethylaminopropylcinnamate hydrochloride. Colorless crystals, m.136, soluble in water; a local anesthetic.

apotoxicarol. $C_{18}H_{16}O = 248.12$. A colorless, phenolic hydrolysis product, m.247, from toxicarol.

apparatus. An instrument or device used for experiments, operations, or manufacture.

apple acid. Malic acid. **a. oil.** Amyl valerate.

Appleton, Sir Edward Victor. 1893–1965. British scientist, Nobel Prize winner (1947); established the existence of the Heaviside layer. **A. layer.** An ionized layer in the atmosphere which reflects downward any short radio waves that have penetrated the Heaviside layer below it.

applicator. A device for the local administration of a remedy; e.g., a radium applicator.

Approved Name. A short name selected for a drug by the British Pharmacopoeia Commission with the intent that if the drug is eventually included in the Pharmacopoeia, the A.N. shall be its official title. A.N. do not conflict with registered trademarks. Cf. *U.S. Adopted Names.*

approximate. Near; not exact.

aprotic. Not yielding or accepting a proton. **a. substance.** One which acts as neither an acid nor a base. Cf. *acid. base.*

apyonin. Auramine.

apyron. Lithium acetyl salicylate.

aq. Abbreviation for aqueous.

aqua. Water (Latin). Cf. *aquo.* Denotes: (1) water, (2) an aqueous solution or infusion, (3) in formulas (+*aqua*) a variable amount of water, (4) water of crystallization. **a. anethyl.** See *dill* water. **a. carui.** See *caraway* water. **a. compound.** Hydrate. **a. destillata.** Distilled *water.* **a. fervens.** Hot water. **a. fluvialis.** River water. **a. fontana.** Spring or well water. **a. fortis.** Nitric acid. **a. laurocerasi.** *Cherry laurel* water. **a. marina.** Sea water. **a. nivialis.** Snow water. **a. pluvialis.** Rainwater. **a. pura.** Pure water. **a. regia.** A mixture of 3 pts. HCl and 1 pt. HNO_3. A solvent for noble metals. **a. tepida.** Warm water. **a. vitae.** Brandy or whisky.

Aquadag. Trademark for a colloidal suspension of graphite in water; a lubricant and an electrically conductive coating.

aquamarine. A sea-green beryl.

aquation. The formation of aquo ions. Cf. *hydration, solvation.*

aquatone. A printing process similar to collotype.

aqueous. Watery. **a. solution.** A solution with water as solvent.

aquifer. A subterranean water-bearing formation.

aquinite. Chloropicrin.

aquo. Pertaining to water. **a. ions.** Complex ions which contain several molecules of water; as, $[M(H_2O)_8]^{++}$, where M is a divalent metal. Cf. *hydration, ammonia system, hydrogen ion, base.*

A.R. Abbreviation for analytical reagent.

Ar. Symbol for argon.

ar- Prefix indicating substitution in the *aromatic* nucleus. Cf. *ac-.*

araban. $(C_5H_{10}O_5)n = 150.11n.$ An arabinose polysaccharide in the mucilage of Malvaceae.

arabate. A salt of arabic acid.

arabic acid. $C_5H_{10}O_6 \cdot H_2O = 184.2.$ Arabitic acid, *d*-tetrahydroxyvaleric acid. White powder precipitated from gum arabic solution by alcohol; soluble in water.

arabin. $C_{10}H_{18}O_9 = 282.19.$ Amorphous powder, soluble in water, from gums. **a. water.** A solution of the water-soluble constituents of gums in hydnocarpus oil.

arabinogalactan. An adhesive obtained by leaching larch wood.

arabinose. $CHO_2(CHOH)_3 \cdot CH_2OH = 150.11.$ Pectin sugar, pectinose, gum sugar. The pentoses obtained by hydrolysis of acacia. **d-** White rhombs, m.160, soluble in water; a culture medium for certain bacteria.

arabinulose. $C_5H_{10}O_5 = 150.11.$ The ketopentose corresponding with arabinose.

arabite. Arabitol.

arabitic acid. Arabic acid.

arabitol. $CH_2OH \cdot (CHOH)_3 \cdot CH_2OH = 152.13.$ Arabite. An alcohol derived from arabinose. Colorless, sweet *d*- and *l*-form crystals, m.102, soluble in water.

arabonic acid. $CH_2OH \cdot (CHOH)_3 \cdot COOH = 166.11.$ A hydroxy acid, derived from arabinose. Colorless crystals, m.89, soluble in water.

Araceae. Aroideae.

arachic acid. $Me(CH_2)_{18}COOH = 312.42.$ Arachidic acid, eicosanoic acid*, *n*-eicosoic acid. White leaflets, m.77.5, insoluble in water; a constituent of butter.

arachidic acid. Arachic acid. **a. alcohol.** Eicosyl alcohol.

arachidonic acid. $C_{20}H_{32}O_2 = 304.25.$ A liquid. unsaturated acid, b.245, in lard and mammal fat.

arachin. A globulin from peanuts (24%), *Arachis hypogoea.* Contains chiefly arginine and glutamic acid with other amino acids; a source of Ardil, q.v,

arachis. See *peanuts.* **a. oil.** Peanut oil, groundnut oil. A fixed oil from peanuts, $d_{25}°0.913.$ World production (1964) 3 million tons. See *Bellier's test.*

arachnidism. Poisoning from the bite of the black widow spider, *Latrodectus mactans.*

arachnolysin. A hemolytic principle of spider poison.

arack. Arrack.

araeometer. Areometer. See *hydrometer.*

aragonite. $CaCO_3.$ Pisolite. Needle spar. A native calcium carbonate. Cf. *calcite.*

Aralac. Trade name for a fibrous product made from skim milk casein. Cf. *lanital.*

Araldite. Trademark for an epoxy resin, used for adhesives, lamination, and surface coatings and castings.

aralia. Nard, American spikenard. The dried rhizomes and roots of *A. racemosa* (Araliaceae); an alterative and diaphoretic.

Araliaceae. Aromatic plants which yield: *Panax quinquefolium* (ginseng), *Aralia nudicaulis* (false sarsaparilla), *Aralia racemosa* (American spikenard), *Aralia hispida* (dwarf elder).

aralin. A glucoside from the fresh leaves of *Aralia* species.

aralkyl. Arylated alkyl. A radical in which an alkyl H atom is substituted by an aryl group. Cf. *alphyl.*

aranein. A homeopathic liquid from spider abdomens.

araphite. A magnetic basalt from Colorado.

araroba. *Goa* powder.

Arasan. Trademark for tetramethyl thiuram disulfide; a seed disinfectant.

arbacin. A protein in the sperm of the sea urchin (*Arbacia*).

arbor. Official Latin for tree. **a. Dianae.** Silver tree. Arborescent silver formed on adding mercury to a silver salt solution. **a. Saturni.**

Leadtree. Arborescent lead formed on adding zinc to a lead salt solution. **a. vitae.** Thuja.

arborescent. A branched, treelike growth of bacteria or crystals.

arbusterol. A fat from *Arbutus* species.

arbutin. $[C_{12}H_{16}O_7]_2 \cdot H_2O = 562.4$. Ursin, arbutoside. A glucoside from the leaves of *Arbutus* and other Ericaceae and Pyrolaceae. Colorless crystals, m.195, soluble in water, hydrolyzed to hydroquinone and glucose; a diuretic and urinary disinfectant. **monobenzoyl-** Cellotropin.

Arbutus. A genus of shrubs and trees (Ericaceae): *A. menziesii* (madrone), *A. unedo* (European arbutus), *A. Arctostaphylos uvaursi* (bearberry, arbutin).

arc. (1) A portion of a curved line. (2) a. lamp. **electric-** The discharge of an electric current between electrodes. **mercury-** An electric a. in mercury vapor. **oscillating-** A discharge which changes its position.

    a. furnace. See *furnace.* **a. lamp.** A luminous discharge between two electrodes. **a. resistance.** Tracking. **a. spectrum.** The spectrum produced by arcing between electrodes of the element under investigation. Cf. spark *spectrum, alternation law.*

arcadian nitrate. Sodium nitrate made from synthetic ammonia and soda; a fertilizer. **a. sulfate.** Ammonium sulfate fertilizer.

arcaine. $NH_2 \cdot C(:NH)NH \cdot (CH_2)_4 \cdot NH \cdot C(:NH) \cdot NH_2 = 172.14$. Tetramethylenediguanidine. An animal base from the mussel Noah's Ark (*Areca Noae*), which lowers the sugar content of the blood.

arcanite. Glaserite.

arcanum. (1) A nostrum or secret medicine. (2) Potassium sulfate.

arceine. Aercoline hydrobromide.

archaeometry. The application of the physical sciences to archaeology.

archil. Orchil.

Archimedes. 300 B.C. Greek mathematician of Syracuse. **A. bridge.** A wooden platform across the pan of a balance, used for weighing solids immersed in a liquid. **A. principle.** A body immersed in a liquid will lose weight equal to that of the liquid it displaces. Used to determine the specific gravity of dense, irregular bodies.

archon. The poisonous radical of proteins.

archyl. Protyl.

arciform. Curved, bow-shaped.

arcilla. Argol.

arcing. The conversion of electric energy into light by a current between two electrodes. It differs from sparking in that it depends on ionization of the vapor of the electrodes, and not on that of the gas between them; Cf. *sparking.*

arconium. A hypothetical element, at. wt. 2.9, similar to nebulium and coronium, q.v.

Arcton. Freon (U.K. usage).

arcual. Arc-shaped or arched.

ardennite. $M_4Al_4H_5VSi_4O_{22}$. A native vanadosilicate. Brown orthorhombic crystals.

Ardil. Trademark for a wool-like protein synthetic fiber, made by extruding a solution of an alkaline extract of peanut protein into a coagulating bath. Production of it has now ceased. Cf. *arachin.*

ardometer. An optical pyrometer, q.v.

are. (1) Latin for area. (2) The metric unit of surface: 1 are = 100 square meters = 119.6 square yards.

area. A region or surface S enclosed by boundaries. $S = CL^2$, where C is a constant depending on the contour of the surface (1, if square; $\pi/4$, if round) and L its length (or diameter, if circular).

areametric. Pertaining to area measurement. **a. analysis.** Chemical analysis by forming precipitates in definite areas, which are matched with precipitates similarly produced from standards.

Areca. A genus of Asiatic and Australasian palms, as *A. catechu pinang,* the areca nut, betel nut, or catechu palm. **a. alkaloid.** Betel-nut alkaloids; e.g., arecoline ($C_8H_{13}O_2N$), homoarecoline ($C_9H_{15}O_2N$), arecaine ($C_7H_{11}O_2N \cdot H_2O$), arecaidine ($C_7H_{11}O_2N \cdot H_2O$), guvacoline ($C_7H_{11}O_2N$), coniine ($C_8H_{17}N$). **a. nut.** Pinang, betel nut q.v. The dried seeds of *A. catechu,* an E. Indian palm. It is a tonic, astringent, and anthelmintic, and contains alkaloids, an orange coloring matter (arecin), and chavicol. **a. red.** Arecin.

arecaidine. $C_7H_{11}O_2N = 141.1$. *N*-Methyltetrahydronicotinic acid. An alkaloid from arecoline. Colorless scales, m.223, soluble in water. Cf. *arecoline.*

arecaine. $C_7H_{11}O_2N = 141.1$. *N*-Methylguvacine. An alkaloid from the seeds of *Areca catechu* (betel nuts). Colorless crystals, m.213, soluble in water; an anthelmintic.

arecaline. Arecoline.

arecane. Arecoline.

arecin. $C_{23}H_{26}ON_2 = 346.3$. Areca red. A red coloring matter from betel nuts. Cf. *aricine.*

arecoline. $C_8H_{13}O_2N = 155.1$. Arekane, arecaline. An alkaloid in betel nuts, the methyl ester of methyltetrahydronicotinic acid (arecaidine). Yellow oil, d.2.02, insoluble in water; an anthelmintic. *homo-* See *homo.*

    a. hydrobromide. $C_8H_{13}O_2N \cdot HBr = 236.08$. Arceine. Colorless prisms, m.167, soluble in water; an anthelmintic and miotic. **a. hydrochloride.** $C_8H_{13}O_2N \cdot HCl = 191.5$. Colorless crystals, m.158, soluble in water; an anthelmintic and miotic.

arecolineserine. A mixture of arecoline hydrobromide and eserine sulfate, used in ophthalmology.

arekane. Arecoline.

arendalite. A microcrystalline epidote.

arene. A hydrocarbon containing at least one aromatic ring.

arenolite. An artificial stone.

areometer. Hydrometer. **a. scales.** See *hydrometer* scales.

areometry. Hydrometry.

arepycnometer. A pycnometer for viscious liquids.

areusin. A benzalcoumarone pigment, q.v.

Arfvedson, Johann August. Afzelius. 1792–1841. Swedish chemist and mineralogist, discoverer of lithium (1817).

arfvedsonite. A black soda amphibole.

argal. Argol.

Argand, Aimé. 1755–1803. Swiss physicist, noted for: **A. burner.** A gas or oil burner with a chimney and regulated air supply.

argatoxyl. $C_6H_7O_3NAg$. Silver *p*-aminophenyl arsenate, silver atoxylate.

argein. A colloidal silver protein, used to treat gonorrhea.

argemonine. $C_{20}H_{15}O_4N$ (?). An alkaloid of prickly poppy (*Argemone mexicana*), probably identical with protopine, and related to sanguinarine.

argenol. Argyrol.

argental. Landsbergite.

argentamine. A colorless solution of 8% silver phosphate and 15% ethylenediamine; an antiseptic, astringent, and disinfectant.

argentan. Nickel silver.

argenti. Official Latin for "of silver".

argentic. Containing silver.

argentiferous. Containing silver. **a. lead.** (1) An alloy of silver and lead. (2) A lead-silver sulfide.

argentiform. Silver hexamethylenamine. A white antiseptic powder.

argentimetry. Argentometry.

argentine. Finely divided tin sponge obtained by precipitation of a tin salt solution with zinc; used in printing.

argentite. Ag_2S. Silver glance, argyrite, vitreous silver ore. Native vitreous silver sulfide. Black isometric crystals. Cf. *acanthite*.

argentol. $C_9N_5N \cdot OH \cdot SO_3Ag = 231.94$. Silver quinaseptol, silver oxyquinoline sulfonate. An antiseptic and astringent; used to treat venereal diseases.

argentometer. A hydrometer to determine the silver content of photographic solutions.

argentometry. Volumetric analysis involving the precipitation of insoluble silver salts; as chlorides, chromates.

argentopyrites. $3FeS \cdot 3FeS_2 \cdot Ag_2S$. Native silver and iron sulfide.

argentous. Containing monovalent silver. See *silver*.

argentum. Official latin for silver. Cf. *argenti*. **a. cornu.** Horn silver, chlorargyrite, cevargyrite. A native silver chloride. **a. virum.** Native mercury (Pliny). **a. vitellinum.** Argyrol.

argil. Argol.

argilla. Kaolin.

argillaceous. Containing clay.

arginase. An enzyme of the intestine, mammalian liver, or spleen which transforms arginine to ornithine and urea.

arginine. $NH_2 \cdot CH(COOH) \cdot CH_2 \cdot CH_2 \cdot CH_2 \cdot NH \cdot C:$ $NH \cdot NH_2 = 174.3$. An amino acid from animal and vegetable proteins (albumin and seeds). Colorless crystals, m.238, soluble in water. Cf. *arginase*.

argochrome. A bactericidal compound of methylene blue and silver.

argoflavine. The silver salt of acriflavine; a bactericide.

argol. $KH(C_4H_4O_6)$. Argal, argil. Crude potassium acid tartrate deposited by grapejuice during fermentation; a raw material for the manufacture of tartaric acid; a reducing agent; and an assay flux.

argon. $Ar = 39.948$. A gaseous element, at. no. 18, in the atmosphere and fumaroles, discovered (1894) by Ramsay and Rayleigh. **gaseous-** $d_{air=1}1.38$, m.-189, b.83.81°K. **liquid-** $d_{-186°C}405$. A. from fumaroles and spring water; 2 isotopes: Ar^{36} and Ar^{40}. A. is absolutely inert, possesses no valency, and belongs to the zero group of the periodic system. Obtained by fractionation of liquid oxygen, and used to fill incandescent lamps, rectifiers, and vacuum tubes.

argonin. Silver caseinate. White powder, soluble in water; an ophthalmological antiseptic.

argyria. Poisoning by silver or its compounds.

argyrine. An alkaloid from horse chestnuts.

argyrite. Argentite.

argyrodite. $4Ag_2S \cdot GeS_2$. Native, monoclinic, steel-gray germanium silver sulfide.

Argyrol. Vitellin silver, argenol. Trade name of a brand of silver protein (20% Ag). Brown glistening, hygroscopic scales, soluble in water; an antiseptic in the treatment of inflamed mucous membranes.

arheol. $C_{15}H_{24}O = 220.2$. Santalol. A sesquiterpene alcohol from sandalwood oil. A colorless, oil, d.0.979, b.300, insoluble in water; a urinary antiseptic.

arhovin. A compound of thymolbenzoic acid ester and diphenylamine used to treat gonorrhea.

aribine. $C_{12}H_{10}N_2 = 182.09$. Harman, loturine. An alkaloid from the bark of *Sickingia* (or *Arariba*) *rubra* (Rubiaceae) and the seeds of *Peganum harmala* (Rutaceae). Colorless crystals, m.237.

aricine. $C_{23}H_{26}O_4N_2 = 394.22$. Cusconine, cinchovatine. An alkaloid from the barks of *cusco* and *Cinchona cuprea*. Colorless crystals, m.188, insoluble in water; an antimalarial. Cf. *arisin*.

aristin. A constituent of various Aristolochia species.

aristochin. Aristoquin, diquinine carbonic ester. White powder, insoluble in water, sparingly soluble in alcohol.

Aristol. A brand of thymol iodide.

Aristolochia. The birthwort family (*Aristolochiaceae*). See *serpentaria*, *guacine*, *aristolochine*. **a. yellow.** The coloring matter of the roots and seeds of *A.* species; e.g., *A. clematitis*.

aristolochine. $C_{32}H_{22}O_{13}N_2 = 642$. An alkaloid from the roots or seeds of *A. serpentaria* and *Bragantia wallichii*; a kidney poison and abortive.

aristoquin. Aristochin.

arithmetical means. Half the sum of two quantities. **a. progression.** A series of numbers with equal differences d between consecutive terms. Let a be the first and z the last term, d the difference, and n the number of terms. Then $z = a + (n - z)d$. The sum of n terms is $n(a + z)/2$.

arkansite. Brookite.

arkite. An igneous leucite-syenite rock.

arkusite. Chiolite.

armature. The rotating coil and core of a dynamo.

Armon. Trade name for a viscose synthetic fiber.

armoracia. The fresh root of *Cochlearia armoracia*, horse radish; a condiment.

armored thermometer. A thermometer in a metal case.

Armstrong, Henry Edward. 1847–1937. English organic chemist and educator. **A. acid.** (1) Schäffer's acid. (2) Naphthalene-1,5-disulfonic acid. **A. metal.** An alloy of Mn 4–6, C 0.10, Ni 80, Cr 17.5, Cu 2.9%; used for corrosion-resisting drawn or pressed shapes.

arnatto. Annatto.

Arnaudon's green. Chromic phosphate.

Arndt alloy. Mg 60, Cu 40%. Used in analysis to reduce nitrates to ammonia in neutral solution. **A. Schulz rule.** *Weak* stimuli greatly accelerate life processes; the *strongest* destroy them. Cf. *Kötschau* hypothesis. **A. tube.** A bent glass tube with 4 bulbs used for the determination of hydrogen.

Arnel. Trademark for a cellulose acetate synthetic fiber.

Arnica. Aster. A genus of the composite flowered plants. **a. flowers.** The dried flower heads of *A. montana*, leopard's bane, wolf's bane, mountain tobacco. A depressant and feeble rubefacient. **a. oil.** An essential oil from arnica flowers. Yellow aromatic liquid, d.0.906, acid val. 75.1, sapon. val. 29.9, soluble in alcohol; used in liniments. **a. root oil.** Yellow oil from arnica root, d.0.990, $[\alpha]_D - 2$.

arnicin. $C_{20}H_{30}O_4 = 334.3$. A glucoside from arnica roots and flowers. Yellow, bitter powder.

arnicine. $C_{35}H_{54}O_7 = 586.43$. A resinous, basic principle from arnica flowers.

arnotta. Annatto.

Aroclors. Trademark for: (1) the polychlorine derivatives of biphenyl; used as lubricants; (2) the chlorobiphenyl resins, which are odorless and resistant to light and flame; (3) yellow liquids or brown solids; nonoxidizing and thermoplastic, and not hydrolyzed by water or alkalies.

Aroideae. Arum. A family of herbs with an acrid, colorless juice; fleshy corm or rhizome; and berry fruit. The principal species yield drugs; e.g., *Acorus calamus* (sweet flag, calamus). *Symplocarpus foetidus* (skunk cabbage, symplocarpus), *Arisaema triphyllum* (Indian turnip, arum).

aromadendral. A mixture of cuminaldehyde, phellandral, and *l*-cryptal from eucalyptus.

aromatic. (1) A spicy, fragrant, agreeable odor or taste. (2) A benzene derivative whose molecule contains one or more C rings. **a. acids.** A. compounds which contain one or more carboxyl groups; e.g., benzoic acid (PhCOOH); phthalic acids $[C_6H_4(COOH)_2]$; mellitic acid $[C_6(COOH)]_6$. **a. alcohols.** A. compounds which contain a hydroxyl group in a side chain; e.g., C_7H_8O, benzyl alcohol, phenylcarbinol (PhCH$_2$OH); $C_8H_{10}O$, tolyl alcohol, methylphenylcarbinol $(C_6H_4Me·CH_2OH)$; $C_9H_{12}O$, xylyl alcohol, dimethylphenylcarbinol $(C_6H_3Me_2·CH_2OH)$; $C_{10}H_{14}O$, pseudocumene alcohol, trimethylphenyl carbinol $(C_6H_2Me_3·CH_2OH)$; $C_{11}H_{16}O$, mellityl alcohol $(C_6HMe_4·CH_2OH)$. **a. compound.** A organic compound containing a closed, saturated homocyclic or heterocyclic ring. See *organic* compounds. **a. hydrocarbon.** A compound of carbon and hydrogen with a closed saturated ring of C. atoms; e.g., benzene. **a. series.** A series of a. compounds. **a. tincture.** An alcoholic solution of cinnamon, ginger, cardamom, cloves, and galangal; a carminative. **a. vinegar.** A mixture of acetic acid and essential oils, used to relieve headaches.

aromatics. Spicy, fragrant, and stimulating drugs, with agreeable taste due to an essential oil.

aromatin. A gentian root substitute for hops.

aroxyamines. α-Hydroxyl amines.

aroyl. The radical R·CO—; R is an aromatic (benzoyl, naphthoyl) group.

arphoalin. An albumin preparation containing arsenic and phosphorus.

arquerite. $Ag_{12}Hg$. A native silver amalgam. (Arqueros, Chile) in isomeric crystals.

arrack. A liquor distilled from fermented rice.

arrhenal. *Sodium* methyl arsenite.

arrhenate. MeHAsO·OM. A salt of arrhenic acid, used in medicine instead of *cacodylates*.

arrhenic acid. Me·H·AsO·OH = 123.98. Monomethyl arsenic acid. Used in organic synthesis. *Cf. cacodylic acid.*

Arrhenius, Svante August. 1859–1927. Swedish chemist and physicist, Nobel Prize winner (1903); noted for his theories of ions and ionization (1883) and of cosmics. **A. law.** A solution of high osmotic pressure conducts an electric current. **A. theory.** When an electrolyte dissolves it splits into ions (ionization) to an extent that increases with a decrease in the concentration, and is indicated by the deviation of the solution from the van't Hoff laws. **A. viscosity formula.** $\log x = \theta c$, where x is the viscosity of a solution, c the volume of the suspended particles present, and θ a constant.

arrow poison. A poisonous plant juice (e.g., curare q.v.) or venom of an animal (e.g., snake, etc.) used for poisoning arrowheads. See *acocantherin, antiar, bufagin.*

arrowroot. Maranta. The starch from the rhizomes of the arrowroot plant, *Maranta arundinaceae* (Marantaceae). White powder from Bermuda, used as a nonirritating food in the treatment of fever, and commercially as an adhesive and in laundries. **Bahia-, Para-, Rio-.** Tapioca.

arrowwood. (1) Frangula. (2) Euonymus.

arsabenzol. Arsphenamine.

arsacetin. Acetylatoxyl, sodium *p*-acetylaminophenyl arsonate. Colorless crystals; an antisyphilitic.

arsamin. Atoxyl.

Arsaminol. A Japanese brand of arsphenamine

arsanilate. $M_2(C_6H_8O_3NAs)$. Atoxylate. A salt of arsanilic acid.

arsanilic acid. $NH_2·C_6H_4·AsO(OH)_2 = 217.2$. Atoxylic acid, *p*-aminobenzenearsonic acid, *p*-aminophenylarsinic acid, arsenic acid anilide, *m*-arsenous acid anilide. Colorless crystals, m.232, soluble in ether; used in organic synthesis. The meta and ortho acids are also known. **acetylhydroxy-** Stovarsol. **N-carbamyl-** Carbarsone. **N-carbamylmethyl-** The sodium salt is tryparsamide.

Arsem furnace. An electric vacuum furnace.

arsenate. A salt of arsenic acid containing the $AsO_4' \equiv$ radical; as, Na_3AsO_4. **acid-** An a. containing hydrogen. **basic-** An a. containing a metal oxide or hydroxide. **diacid-** A salt containing the radical $H_2AsO_4^-$. **dihydric-** Diacid a. **meta-** An a. containing the AsO_3^- radical. **monoacid-** A salt containing the radical $HAsO_4^=$. **monohydric-** Monoacid a. **pyro-** An a. derived from $H_4As_2O_7$. **triethyl-** $(EtO)_3·AsO = 226.08$. Colorless liquid, d.1.326, b.238.

arsenhemol. A brown, amorphous compound of arsenic and hemol; an alterative and hematinic.

arsenic. As = 74.92. An element of the phosphorus group, at. no. 33. A rhombohedral, gray, brittle nonmetal of metallic character, $d_{14}°5.727$, m. (under pressure) 450 (sublimes), b.450, insoluble in water, alcohol, or acids. It occurs widely in nature as the sulfide, arsenide, and sulfarsenides of the heavy metal, and in a number of allotropic modifications analogous to those of phosphorus: (1) Metallic arsenic, γ-As, d.5.727. The common stable form. (2) Gray or black arsenic, β-As, d.4.64 which changes at 303 to γ-As. (3) Yellow arsenic, α-As$_4$, d.3.7, the nonmetallic form formed at 500 by rapid condensation of arsenic vapor. It is soluble in carbon disulfide, resembles phosphorus, is photosensitive and unstable, and changes to gray arsenic on exposure to light. (4) Brown arsenic, As_8, d.2.03, an allotrope of (3) deposited from yellow arsenic solutions; changes at 180 to gray arsenic. Arsenic may be tri- or pentavalent. Compounds: derived from trivalent, negative As (arsenides, M_3As); derived from trivalent, positive As (arsenous, As^{3+}); derived from pentavalent, positive As (arsenic, As^{5+}). Orpiment (arsenic sulfide) was known to the ancients as arsenicon (the "masculine one"); used to paint the sunburnt faces of men. A. is used in medicine, especially as cacodylates, and a. compounds are used as germicides, insecticides, pigments, and for the preparation of arsenic salts. **butter of-** Arsenous chloride. **dimethyl-** Cacodyl. **flowers of-** Arsenous oxide. **red-, ruby-** Realgar. **triethyl-** Triethyl-*arsine*. **white-** Arsenolite, arsenite. A native arsenous oxide. World production (1966) 52,000 tons **yellow-** Orpiment.

    a. acid. *ortho-* $H_3AsO_4 \cdot \frac{1}{2}H_2O = 151.0$. Colorless crystals, m.35.5, soluble in water; used to manufacture arsenates. *meta-* $HAsO_3 = 124.0$. White powder, soluble in water to form ortho- a. acid. *pyro-* $H_4As_2O_7 = 264.89$. Colorless powder, decomp. 208, soluble in water, forming ortho- a. acid. **a. apparatus.** See *Marsh* test. **a. bromide.** Arsenous bromide. **a. butter.** Arsenous chloride. **a. chloride.** Arsenous chloride. **a. diethyl.** $AsEt_2 = 133.06$, b.186, insoluble in water. **a. diiodide.** $AsI_2 = 328.80$. White crystals, decomp. 136. **a. dimethyl.** $AsMe_2 = 105.02$. Colorless liquid, b.150, insoluble in water. **a. disulfide.** $As_2S_2 = 214.1$. Realgar, red a. sulfide, red orpiment, a. ruby, red a. glass. Brown monoclinic crystals, m.307, insoluble in water. Used in textile printing, in pyrotechnics, in tanneries and in the manufacture of shots. **a. fluoride.** $AsF_5 = 169.96$. Colorless, poisonous gas, d.$(H_2=1)$5.964, m.-80. b.-53, soluble in water. **a. glass.** (1) An indefinite term for a. compounds; e.g., a. sulfides. (2) Arsenous oxide. **a. hydride.** (1) Arsenous hydride. (2) As_4H_2, AsH_2 or $(AsH)_x$. An ill-defined solid hydride, formed from water and sodium arsenide. **a. iodide.** (1) A. diiodide. (2) Arsenous iodide. **a. minerals.** A. is usually associated with antimony and bismuth minerals and occurs in many sulfide minerals; e.g., realgar (As_2S_2), orpiment (As_2S_3); also in the arsenides and sulfoarsenides of the heavy metals. **a. oxide.** (1) $As_2O_5 = 229.9$. A. pentoxide, a. acid anhydride. Colorless powder, d.4.086, decomp. by heat, soluble in water. (2) See *arsenous* oxide. **a. oxychloride.** See *arsenous* oxychloride. **a. pentafluoride.** A. fluoride. **a. pentasulfide.** A. sulfide. **a. pentoxide.** A. oxide. **a. phosphide.** Arsenous phosphide. **a. ruby.** A. disulfide. **a. selenide.** Arsenous selenide. **a. sulfide.** (1) $As_2S_5 = 310.4$. A. pentasulfide. Yellow crystals, insoluble in water; a pigment. (2) See a. disulfide. (3) Arsenous sulfide. **a. thiocyanate.** $As(SCN)_3 = 249.0$. **a. tribromide.** Arsenous bromide. **a. trichloride.** Arsenous chloride. **a. trifluoride.** Arsenous fluoride **a. triethide.** Triethyl*arsine*. **a. triiodide.** Arsenous iodide. **a. trimethyl.** Trimethyl*arsine*. **a. trioxide.** Arsenous oxide. **a.**

trisulfide. Arsenous sulfide.
arsenical. Pertaining to arsenic. **a. nickel.** Niccolite. **a. pyrites.** Mispickel.
arsenicals. Drugs, fungicides, or insecticides whose effects depend primarily on their arsenic content; e.g., cacodylates.
arsenicum. Latin for arsenic.
arsenide. A binary compound of negative trivalent As; e.g., H_3As. Cf. *speise*.
arsenidine. $CH_2 \cdot (CH_2)_4 \cdot AsH = 146.0$. Arsepidine. A heterocyclic analog of piperidine.
arsenii. Official Latin for arsenic
arsenious. Arsenous.
arsenite. (1) A salt of a hypothetical arsenous acid; orthoarsenites, K_3AsO_3; metaarsenites, $KAsO_2$; pyroarsenites, $Ca_2As_2O_5$. (2) White *arsenic*. **triethyl-** $(EtO)_3As = 210.08$. Colorless liquid, b.166.
arsenium. The element arsenic.
arseniuretted hydrogen. Arsine.
arsenius. See *arsenous*.
arseno. The group —As:As—, isologous with the azo group.
arsenobenzene. PhAs:AsPh. An analog of azobenzene.
Arsenobenzol. A brand of arsphenamine.
arsenoferratin. An iron albuminate containing arsenic.
arsenofuran. C_4H_5As. Arsenophen. An analog of pyrrole.
arsenogen. A compound of iron, phosphorus, arsenic, and paranucleic acid.
arsenohemol. Arsenhemol.
arsenolite. White arsenic.
arsenophen. Arsenofuran.
arsenophenol. $HO \cdot C_6H_4 \cdot As : As \cdot C_6H_4 \cdot OH = 336.00$. Dihydroxyarsenobenzene. **diamino-** Arsphenamine.
arsenopyrite. FeAsS. Mispickel. A native sulfarsenide.
arsenoso. The group —OAs.
arsenous. Describing a compound of trivalent arsenic. **a. acid.** H_3AsO_3 or $HAsO_2$. A monobasic acid, from which the arsenites, q.v., are derived; in particular, arsenous oxide, As_2O_3. **a. acid anhydride.** a. oxide. **a. bromide.** $AsBr_3 = 314.72$. Arsenic tribromide. Yellow crystals, m.31, soluble in water. **a. chloride.** $AsCl_3 = 181.3$. Arsenic trichloride, arsenic butter. Yellow liquid d.2.205, b.130, soluble in water. **a. fluoride.** $AsF_3 = 131.96$. Yellow liquid, d.2.73, b.63, decomp. by water. **a. hydride.** $AsH_3 = 78.0$. Arsine. Hydrogen arsenide. Poisonous gas with strong garlic odor. $d_{(air=1)}2.695$, soluble in water; used in organic synthesis. **a. iodide.** $AsI_3 = 455.72$. Arsenic triiodide. Arsenic iodide. Orange crystals, m.146, (sublimes), soluble in water; an antiseptic. **a. oxide.** As_4O_6 or $As_2O_3 = 197.9$. Arsenic trioxide, "arsenic," a. acid anhydride, white arsenic. White, octahedral or amorphous mass, sublimes 218, soluble in water. Used in the pharmacy, glass, leather, and pigment industries; as a poison for noxious animals and plants, in the manufacture of shots and arsenic salts. Antidotes; Stomach pump, emetics, iron hydroxide. **a. oxychloride.** $AsOCl = 126.42$. Brown mass, decomp. by water or heat. **a. phosphide.** $AsP = 106.0$. Brown fragments, decomp. by water or

heat. **a. selenide.** $As_2Se_3 = 386.52$. Arsenic triselenide. Brown crystals, m.360, insoluble in water. **a. sulfide.** $As_2S_3 = 246.1$. Arsenic trisulfide, yellow arsenic sulfide, orpiment, auripigment, king's yellow. Orange monoclinic crystals or amorphous powder, m.310, insoluble in water; a pigment.

arsenyl. Sodium methylarsenate.

arsepidine. Arsenidine.

arsine. (1) $AsH_3 = 78.0$. See *arsenous* hydride, *arsyl*, and *Arsylene*. (2) See *arsines*. **alk-** Me_2-$As \cdot O \cdot AsMe_2$. Cacodylic oxide. Colorless liquid, b.120. Cf. *alkarsin*. **diethyl-** (1) Et_2AsH or $C_4H_{11}As = 134.05$. (2) Tetraethylarsine. **dimethyl-** $Me_2AsH = 106.07$. Cacodylhydride. Colorless liquid, b.36, miscible with alcohol. **diphenylene-** Dibenzoarsenole. **ditertiary-** The

compound ⬡ $\begin{array}{c}AsMe_2 \\ AsMe_2\end{array}$ **ethyl-** $EtAsH_2 = 105.98$

Arsinoethane. Colorless liquid, b.36. **methyl-** $CH_5As = 91.97$. Arsinomethane, $MeAsH_2$. A gas, b.2, soluble in alcohol. **methyldichloro-** $CH_3Cl_2As = 160.87$. Methylarsenic dichloride, $MeAsCl_2$. Colorless liquid, b.133. **mono-R-** $RAsH_2$. **tetraethyl-** $Et_2As \cdot AsEt_2$. Ethylcacodyl. Colorless liquid, b.188. **tetramethyl-** Cacodyl. **tri-R-** R_3As. **triethyl-** $C_6H_{15}As = 162.08$. Arsenic triethyl, $AsEt_3$. Colorless liquid, decomp. 141. **trimethyl-** $AsMe_3 = 120.03$. Arsenic trimethyl, arsenous methide. Colorless liquid, b.5.3, soluble in water.

arsines. Arsine analogs of amines, phosphines, stibines in which the hydrogen is replaced by a hydrocarbon radical, as R_2AsH, dialkylarsine.

arsinic acid. (1) An organic compound derived from trivalent arsenic; as R_2AsO_2H, diaryl or dialkyl a. acid. (2) U.K. usage an "arsinic" acid, as well as an "arsonic" acid (U.S. usage). **aminophenyl-** Arsanilic acid. **dimethyl-** Cacodylic acid. **methyl-** Methane arsonic acid.

arsino- (1) The H_2As- group. (2) Prefix indicating the —As:As— group. (3) The radical $(OH)OAs=$ derived from arsinic acid. **a. salicylic acid.** Colorless crystals, used as atoxyl.

arsinoso. (1) The $(HO)_2As=$ group. (2) The $HO \cdot As=$ group. (3) Less correctly, the radical $O:As$—, isologous with nitroso.

arso. The O_2As— group.

arsonate. A salt of arsonic acid containing the $RAsO_2$—radical.

arsone. The compound $AsO(OH)_2$.

arsonic acid. An organic compound derived from pentavalent arsenic; as, $R_2AsO_2(OH)$, diaryl or dialkyl a. acid. **p-carbaminophenyl-** Carbasone. **phenyl-** Benzenearsonic acid.

arsonium. The radical AsH_4—, an isolog of ammonium and phosphonium. **a. compounds.** $AsH_3 \cdot HX$, or AsH_4X. Arsine addition compounds. **a. hydroxide.** AsH_4OH. An isolog of ammonium hydroxide and parent substance of, e.g., R_4AsOH, tetra-R-arsonium hydroxide.

arsono. The arsonic acid radical $(HO)_2OAs$—.

arsonoso. (1) The $HOOAs$— group. (2) The $HO \cdot OAs$— group.

Arsonval, Jacques Arsene d'. 1951–1940. French physicist, pioneer in high-frequency electric therapy.

arsphenamine. $As_2(C_6H_3 \cdot OH \cdot NH_2)_2 \cdot 2HCl = 437.2$. Salvarsan, diarsenol, arsphenolamine hydrochloride, arsaminol, arsenobenzol, 3-diamino-4-dihydroxylarsenobenzene, kharsivan, Ehrlich 606, S.O.S.

$$\begin{array}{cc} HO & OH \\ >C_6H_3 - As:As—C_6H_3< & \\ (HCl)NH_2 & NH_2(HCl) \end{array}$$

Yellow, hygroscopic, crystals, unstable in air, soluble in water; used to treat syphilis and relapsing fever. **neo-** *Neo*arsphenamine.

arsphenoxide. Mapharsen.

arsycodile. Sodium cacodylate.

arsyl. The radical H_2As—, from arsine.

Arsylene. Trademark for the radical $HAs=$, from arsine.

arsynal. Sodium methyl arsenite.

artabotrine. $C_{36}H_{55}O_6N = 597.42$. An alkaloid, m.187, from the stems and roots of *Artabotrys suaveolens* (Anonaceae).

artarine. $C_{21}H_{23}O_4N = 353.2$. An alkaloid from artar root; a heart stimulant.

artar root. A drug from the root of *Zanthoxylum senegalense* (Rutaceae); W. Africa.

Artemisia. A genus of plants belonging to the aster family (Compositae); e.g., *A. absinthium*, wormwood; *A. maritima*, wormseed, santonica. **a. oil.** Wormwood oil.

artemisin. $C_{15}H_{18}O_4 = 262.2$. Oxysantonin. From the seeds of *Artemisia* species. White crystals, m.200, soluble in hot water; a gastric stimulant.

arterin. A red pigment of arterial blood. Cf. *oxyhemoglobin*.

arteriograph. An instrument to trace and record the pulse.

arteriosclerosis. Abnormal hardening of the artery walls.

artery. The blood vessels in which the blood passes from the heart to the organs of the body.

arthranitin. $C_{63}H_{110}O_{32} = 1376.90$. Cyclamin. A glucoside from arthanite (*Cyclamen europaeum*). White powder, soluble in water; a purgative and emetic.

arthriticin. (1) $(C_2H_5O)C_6H_4 \cdot N(CH_3) \cdot NH \cdot CH_2$-$CO \cdot NH_2$. A disinfectant used to treat arthritis. (2) Piperazine.

arthropods. Invertebrate animals with jointed limbs, e.g., spiders and crustaceans.

Artic. Trademark for methylchloride used in refrigerators.

artificial. Made by man as opposed to natural. Cf. *synthetic*.

artolinantipeptone. Artose.

artose. $C_{185}H_{288}O_{58}N_5 9S = 4036.5$. A water-soluble albumose produced from wheat gliadin. Cf. *deutero*artrose, *hetero*artrose.

artotype. Collotype.

aruba acid. A naphthenic acid extracted from Colombian gas oil by alkali.

arum. (1) A genus of plants (Aroidae) whose corms yield starchy products; e.g., sago from *A. maculatum*. (2) An edible starch similar to sago from *A. maculatum* (Southern Europe).

aryl. A organic radical derived from an aromatic hydrocarbon by the removal of one atom; e.g., phenyl from benzene. Cf. *alkyl*.

arylarsonate. A compound of arsenic containing aryl radicals; e.g., salvarsan.

aryle, arylide. A compound of a metal containing an aryl radical; as, PbR_4.

arznei. German term for drugs.

as- Abbreviation for asymmetric.

As. Symbol for arsenic.

ASA. Abbreviation for American Standards Association, founded in 1918; now United States of America Standards Institute (USASI).

asafetida. Asafoetida. A gum resin obtained by incising the rhizomes of *Ferula asafetida* and other *Ferula* species (Umbelliferae). Soft mass of garlic odor; acrid, bitter taste; emulsifies with water; a carminative and sedative. Cf. *ferulic* acid. **milk of-** See *milk*.
a. oil. Yellow, volatile oil distilled from asafetida, d.0.975–0.990, $[\alpha]_D + 16$.

asaprol. Abrastol.

asarin. Asarone.

asarite. Crude asarone.

asarone. $(MeO)_3C_6H_2 \cdot CH:CHMe = 208.1$. Asarum camphor, asarin, propenyl-2,4,5-trimethoxybenzene, from the roots of *A. europaeum*. Colorless crystals, m.67, soluble in alcohol; a tonic and antiseptic. Cf. *calamus oil.*

asaronic acid. $(MeO)_3C_6H_2COOH = 212.09$. 2,4,5-Trimethoxybenzoic acid. Colorless crystals, m.144.

Asarum. (1) A genus of plants of the birthwort family (Aristolochiaceae). (2) Canada snakeroot, wild ginger. The dried rhizomes and roots of *A. canadense*; a carminative and flavoring agent. **a. camphor.** Asarone. **a. oil.** An essential oil from asarum species. *Canadian-* From the roots of *A. canadense*. Colorless liquid, d.0.95, $[\alpha]_D - 3.5$, soluble in alcohol. The chief constituents are arasol and methyleugenol; used in perfumery. *European-* From the roots of *A. europaeum*, soluble in alcohol.

asaryl. The radical $(MeO)_3C_6H_2$—, from asarone.

asbestine. A short-fibered asbestos paint extender.

asbestos. Amianthus, earth flax, mountain cork stone flax; fibrous actinolite. A native magnesium calcium silicate. Two types: (1) Chrysotile (white-). (2) Amphiboles (e.g., crocidolite, blue-). World production (1966), 3.8 million tons. Gray masses, either compact or long, silky fibers. It is acid- and heat-resisting, and may be spun or woven; used for Gooch filters, fireproof objects, e.g., curtains, packings. Cf. *erocidolite, chrysotile, hornblende.* **blue-** Crocidolite. Abriachanite. **Canadian-**Chrysotile. White a.
a. board. Sheets of pressed a. fibers used for fireproofing or insulating. **a. cord.** A. string to support crucibles. **a. filter.** (1) A Gooch crucible with a. fibers to filter analytical precipitates. (2) A filter containing a. with a proportion of cellulose fibers; used to filter beer, etc. **a. magnesia mixture.** A mixture of a. and magnesia used for steam packings. **a. sponge.** A. impregnated with platinum salt solution and ignited; a catalyst. **a. stopper.** A stopper made from a.-magnesia mixture, for high temperatures and corrosive chemicals.

asbolane. Asbolite.

asbolin. Yellow oil from the distillation of pine roots, which contains pyrocatechin; used to treat tuberculosis.

asbolite. Asbolane, earthy cobalt. An earthy psilomelane or wad, q.v., containing cobalt oxide.

ascaricide. A drug which destroys *Ascaris* parasites (intestinal worms).

ascaridic acid. Ascaridolic acid.

ascaridol. $C_{10}H_{16}O_2 = 168.1$. A terpene peroxide, the active constituent of chenopodium oil. Explosive liquid, $d_{21°}0.9985$, $b_{8\ mm}97$. **a. glycol.** $C_{10}H_{18}O_3 = 186.1$. Colorless crystals, m.63.

ascaridolic acid. $C_{10}H_{16}O_5 = 216.2$. Cineolic acid, ascaridic acid. The oxidation product of ascaridol glycol; *d-* and *l-*forms, m.130, *dl-*, m.117.

Ascaris. A genus of round worms; some are intestinal parasites.

Ascarite. Trade name for a solid absorbent for carbon dioxide made from sodium hydroxide and asbestos. It changes from white to gray, when saturated.

ascaryl alcohol. $C_{33}H_{68}O_4 = 528.48$. A dihydric alcohol, m.84, from the fat of *Ascaris* species.

ascharite. $3Mg_2B_2O_5 \cdot H_2O$. A native borate (Stassfurt).

aschistic process. A process in which work is converted directly into heat.

Asclepiadaceae. The milkweed family. A group of herbs, usually with a milky juice which contains caoutchouc; e.g., *Asclepias tuberosa*, asclepias root; *Gonolobus condurango*, condurango bark.

asclepiadin. A bitter principle of asclepias.

asclepias. Pleurisy root. The dried roots of *A. tuberosa* (Asclepiadaceae); a diaphoretic, diuretic, expectorant, and tonic.

asclepidin. A concentration of asclepias principles.

asclepidoid. The combined principles of asclepias.

asclepin. A resinoid from asclepias; a cathartic and diaphoretic.

ascelpion. $C_{20}H_{34}O_3 = 322.3$. A camphor-like principle of *A. syriaca*.

Ascomycetes. A group of fungi (molds) e.g., Aspergillus, Penicillium.

ascorbic acid. $C_5H_8O_6 = 176.05$. Preferred name for cevitamic acid, hexuronic acid, 3-keto-*l*-gulonolactone, antiscorbutin, vitamin C (U.S.P., B.P.), antiscorbutic principle. The *l-*form is the δ-lactone of 2,4,5,6-tetrahydroxy-3-ketohexanoic acid. The enolic form of 3-keto-*l*-gulofuranolactone, m.192, $[\alpha]_D + 21.0$, soluble in alcohol. **d-** Has no vitamin effect. **iso-** Erythorbic acid. Isovitamin C. An antioxidant, used to prevent beer haze.

```
    CO—           CO—           CO—
   |    |         |    |         |    |
  HOC  |        HOC  |        HCOH  |
   ‖     O       ‖     O       |     O
  HOC  |        HOC  |         CO   |
   |    |         |    |         |    |
  HC—           HC—           CH—
   |             |             |
  HOCH          HCOH          HCOH
   |             |             |
  CH_2OH        CH_2OH        CH_2OH
    l-            d-            iso-
(Vitamin C)                 (Isovitamin C)
```

ascorbigen. Bound ascorbic acid, usually associated with an indole group.

ascus. A cell in which spores are formed.

-ase. Suffix indicating: (1) an enzyme; e.g., diastase; usually of vegetable origin, but applicable to animal enzymes, the names of which usually end in -in; thus pepsase rather than pepsin; (2) certain ores; e.g., orthoclase.

asebotin. A glucoside from the leaves of mountain laurel (Kalmia latifolia).

asebotoxin. A glucoside from Andromeda japonica (Ericaceae).

asellin. $C_{25}H_{32}N_4 = 388.5$. An alkaloid from cod-liver oil.

asepsin. Bromoacetanilide.

asepsis. Freedom from infection.

aseptol. $C_6H_4 \cdot OH : HSO_3 = 174.7$. o-Phenolsulfonic acid, sulfophenol, sozolic acid, o-sulfocarbolic acid. Red oil, d.155, soluble in water; an antiseptic, and reagent for albumin, bile pigments, nitrites, and nitrates.

aseptoline. Pilocarpine.

asexual. Without sex, as the lower forms of plants and animals.

asferryl. Iron arsenotartrate. A green-yellow powder, used to treat anemia and chlorosis.

ash. (1) The incombustible mineral residue remaining after a substance has been incinerated. (2) See Fraxinus. **caustic-** Sodium carbonate. **causticized-** A mixture of sodium carbonate and sodium hydroxide. **light-** A by-product of oil combustion containing silica, alumina, iron oxide, and small amounts of alkaline oxides and carbonates. **poison-** Ischionanthus. **pot-** Potash. **prickly-** Xanthoxylum. **soda-** Commercial sodium carbonate.

Ashcroft paper tester. A device to determine approximately the bursting strength of paper.

ashing. The process of burning organic matter, especially in analysis.

ashphalt. Asphalt.

asiatic acid. $C_{31}H_{52}O_5(?)$. The aglycone of asiaticoside, q.v. Dextrorotatory needles, m.225.

asiaticoside. $C_{54}H_{90}O_{23}(?)$. A glycoside from Centella asiatica (Umbelliferae), m.231 (decomp.); used to treat leprosy.

asiminine. An alkaloid from the seeds of papaw, Asimina triloba (Anonaceae); a narcotic.

asiphyl. Mercuric atoxylate.

askarel. Generic name for a chlorinated diphenyl; a liquid dielectric.

asonidin. Plumierin.

asparacemic acid. dl-Aspartic acid.

asparagic acid. Aspartic acid.

asparagine. $NH_2 \cdot CH \cdot (COOH) \cdot (CH_2CONH_2) \cdot H_2O = 150.10$. Aspargine, asparamide, agedoite, altheine, aminosuccinic acidamide, α-aminosuccinamic acid, aspartamic acid. An alkaloid in the sprouts of dicotyledons and in many seeds. White rhombs m.230, soluble in hot water; a constituent of many proteins, and an isomer of malamide. **a. hydrargyrate.** A mercury compound of aspargine; used to treat syphilis. **a. sulfate.** $C_4H_8O_3N_2 \cdot H_2SO_4 = 230.1$. White powder, soluble in water.

asparaginic acid. Aspartic acid.

asparagus. The root of Asparagus officinalis (Liliaceae); an aperient and diuretic. Cf. chrysoidin.

asparagyl. The radical, $NH_2 \cdot CO \cdot CH_2 \cdot CHNH_2 \cdot CO—$, from aspargine.

asparamide. Aspargine.

aspargine. Asparagine.

aspartamic acid. Asparagine.

aspartase. An enzyme from Escherichia coli and other organisms, which catalyzes the reversible splitting of ammonia from aspartic acid to form fumaric acid.

aspartic acid. $NH_2 \cdot CH \cdot (COOH) : (CH_2 \cdot COOH) = 133.09$. Aminosuccinic acid, asparaginic acid, asparagic acid. **dl-** Asparagine acid. White monoclinic prisms, m.278. **d-** Colorless leaflets m.251. **l-** Rhombic leaflets, m.270, slightly soluble in water; used in organic synthesis.

aspartyl. The radical —CO·CH₂·CHNH₂·CO—, from aspartic acid.

aspasiolite. A partly decomposed iolite.

aspergillic acid. $C_{12}H_{20}O_2N_2 = 320.08$. An antibiotic produced by Aspergillus molds.

aspergillin. (1) Vegetable hematin. The black coloring matter of the spores of various Aspergillus species (molds). (2) Also used to describe at least 4 of the antibiotics obtained from Aspergillus, including flavicin, flavicidin, and gliotoxin, q.v.

Aspergillus. A genus of molds; many are parasitic. Cf. mycogalactan, tané-koji, aspergillin.

asphalt. Jews' pitch, petrolene, mineral pitch, earth pitch, Trinidad pitch, petroleum pitch. Native mixtures of hydrocarbons; amorphous, solid or semisolid, brownish-black pitch or bitumen, produced from the higher-boiling-point mineral oils by the action of oxygen; divided into asphaltenes and carbenes, q.v. Used for pavements, roofing, and waterproofing materials. Cf. parintité. **a. base.** See petroleum. **a. sludge.** A nonconducting sludge of oxygenated bodies of high molecular weight in electric transformers. **a. stone.** Natural a. A limestone naturally impregnated with bitumen. **a. testing apparatus.** See penetrometer, viscosimeter. **a. thermometer.** An armored thermometer graduated from 200 to 450°F.

asphaltenes. That portion of asphalt or bitumen which is soluble in carbon disulfide but insoluble in paraffin oil or in ether. Cf. carbenes, kerotenes.

asphaltic bitumen. A more accurate term for asphalt.

asphyxia. Suffocation due to a deficiency of oxygen.

aspidin. $C_{23}H_{32}O_7 = 420.3$. A poisonous constituent of malefern, Aspidium.

aspidinol. $C_{12}H_{16}O_4 = 224.2$. An alcohol, m.161, from aspidium.

Aspidium. Marginal fern (U.S.P.). (1) A genus of ferns. Filices. (2) Male fern, the dried rhizome of Dryopteris filix-mas (Poldiaceae). An anthelmintic and teniacide. It contains filicic acid, filmaron, and aspidin. Cf. pannol, filix, fustin.

aspidosamine. $C_{22}H_{28}O_2N_2 = 352.4$. An alkaloid from quebracho bark. Brown powder, m.100, soluble in alcohol; an emetic. **a. hydrochloride.** $C_{22}H_{28}O_2N_2 \cdot HCl = 387.8$. Brown powder, soluble in water; an emetic.

aspidosperma. Quebracho. The bark of Aspidosperma quebracho (Apocynaceae) of S. America. It contains quebrachine and other alkaloids; an antiperiodic and respiratory tonic.

aspidospermine. $C_{22}H_{30}O_2N_2 = 354.26$. (1) An alkaloid from the bark of Aspidosperma quebracho. White needles, m.206, soluble in alcohol; used to treat dyspnea, asthma. (2) Brown powder, which consists of a mixture of quebracho alkaloids. **a. citrate.** $C_{22}H_{30}O_2N_2 \cdot C_6H_8O_7 = 546.32$. Orange powder, soluble in water, comprising the citrates of quebracho alkaloids. **a. hydrochloride.** $C_{22}H_{30}$-$O_2N_2 \cdot HCl = 390.82$. Orange powder, soluble in water. **a. sulfate.** $(C_{22}H_{30}O_2N_2)_2H_2SO_4 = 806.61$. Colorless crystals, soluble in water, used to treat typhoid fever and dyspnea. **a. sulfate, amorphous.** The sulfate of quebracho alkaloids. Orange-yellow powder, soluble in water.

aspirator. A suction apparatus. **a. bottle.** A bottle containing liquid, with an airtight stopper, a short inlet tube, and an outlet at the bottom. The flow of liquid from the outlet draws in air or gas from a source connected to the inlet tube. Cf. *siphon*.

aspirin. *Acetyl*salicylic acid. **methyl-** See *methylacetylsalicylate*.

aspirochyl. Mercuric atoxylate.

assafetida. Asafetida.

assay. (1) Originally the analysis of ores or alloys. (2) Analysis in general; of pharmaceutical and official drugs in particular. **dry-.** Assaying by dry methods. **wet-.** Assaying by wet methods. **a. balance.** A very delicate analytical balance. **a. combination furnace.** A combination of 3 furnaces for roasting sulfides, fusing in a crucible, and cupellation. **a. crucibles.** Fireclay crucibles for the analysis of ores and alloys. **a. flasks.** A glass vessel of shape intermediate between that of a tall beaker and an Erlenmeyer flask. **a. mill.** A small crusher for pulverizing ores. **a. ton.** A.T. = 29.1667 gm. **a. ton system.** In the analysis of gold and silver ores, the number of milligrams of gold or silver obtained from an assay ton equals the number of ounces per short ton of 2,000 lb of ore. For a ton of 2,240 lb A.T. = 32.6667 gm. **a. ton weights.** A set of weights (4 A.T. to $\frac{1}{20}$A.T.) used in mineralogical analysis and gold assay.

asselline. A leucomaine from cod-liver oil.

assimilation. Constructive metabolism, or the transformation of nonliving matter (food) into living matter (tissues).

associating. Forming complexes, e.g., by polar molecules. Cf. *solvent*. **non-** Describing nonpolar molecules which do not form complexes.

association. The combination, connection, or correlation of substances or functions. **molecular-** The aggregation of similar molecules, especially in solutions. Cf. coordinate *bond*, *dissociation*, *liquids*.

astacin, astacene. $C_{40}H_{48}O_4 = 592.34$. A carotenoid produced by the oxidation of astaxanthin, q.v.; a pigment from the lobster, *Astacus gammarus*.

astatic. Describing forces in equilibrium. **a. couple.** See *astatic* galvanometer. **a. current.** An electric circuit so arranged as to be unaffected by the earth's electric field. **a. galvanometer.** A galvanometer in which an astatic couple effect is produced by two equally strong magnets. **a. needle.** Two magnetic needles placed above one another with reversed poles (N over S).

astatine. At = 210. Alabamine, q.v., ekaiodine, virginium. A member of the halogen element family, at. no. 85. It has no stable isotopes, the stablest being At^{211}. Obtained from monazite sands and (Allison, etc., 1931) by bombarding bismuth with high-energy particles and evaporating off the bismuth; obtained mainly as At^{211}, soluble in benzene or chloroform. Forms compounds of the types At^-, AtO_2^-, and AtO^-.

astaxanthin. $C_{40}H_{52}O_4 = 596.4$. See *astacin*.

asteriasterol. A sterol, m.70, from starfish.

asterism. An arrangement of silk, q.v., in gems, giving a starlike effect.

asterium. A supposed element in the hottest stars. Cf. *nebulium*.

asterubin. $Me_2NC(:NH) \cdot NH \cdot (CH_2)_2SO_3H \cdot = 195.2$. A guanidine derivative, from the starfish, *Aster rubens*.

asthenics. Cerebrospinal neurotics. A drug which produces muscular weakness; e.g., aconite.

astigmatism. The inability of the eye to focus light rays from different meridians on the same point.

ASTM. American Society for Testing and Materials. An organization to promote knowledge of engineering materials and to develop standards, specifications, and methods of testing for various materials. Cf. *BSI*.

Aston, Francis William. 1877–1946. English physicist who developed mass spectra; Nobel Prize winner (1922). **A. rule.** Not more than 2 isotopes are known for any element of odd atomic number, except among the radioactive elements. **A. spectrum.** A mass spectrum, from which the isotopic weights of an element are determined.

astorism. The star-shaped appearance of a Laue pattern of a distorted crystal.

astrakanite, astrochanite. $MgSO_4 \cdot Na_2SO_4 \cdot 4H_2O$. Blödite. Native magnesium sodium sulfate (Stassfurt).

astral oil. Kerosine.

astringency. Sour taste with contracting power, as in tannins.

astringent. A drug that contracts tissues, and thereby lessens secretions. Used to treat diarrhea and externally to check bleeding; e.g., alum.

astrolin. $C_5H_{10}O_3 \cdot C_{11}H_{12}ON_2 = 306.2$. Methylethylglycolic antipyrine. Colorless with pleasant acid taste, m.64, soluble in water; relieves neuralgic headaches.

astronautics. The study of voyaging through space.

astronomical unit. (1) The mean distance from the sun to the earth: 149,500,000 km. (2) See *parsec*, *light year*, and *magnitudes*.

astronomy. The study of the cosmos, and the characteristics of celestial bodies.

astrophyllite. $H_4(K,Na)_2(Fe,Mn)_5(SiTiZr)_7O_{22}$. A native silicate; bronze-yellow orthorhombic crystals.

astrophysics. The interpretation of spectral lines which indicate the movement, velocity, composition, temperature, and other characteristics of a celestial body.

asymmetric. (1) Unsymmetric; e.g., the 1,2,4-position of benzene. (2) Pertaining to an asymmetric atom. (3) Triclinic. **a. atom.** An atom that has each of its bonds united to a different atom or radical. Thus an a. N atom has 3 different radicals. **a. carbon.** A C atom which has 4 different radicals or atoms attached to it. Compounds containing one or more a. carbon atoms are optically active. **a. compound.** A compound that contains one or more asymmetric atoms. Cf. *stereoisomerism*. **a. molecule.** See *asymmetric*.

asymmetry. Absence of symmetry.

asymptotes. Rectilinear or curvilinear lines which continually approach a curve or line without touching it.

A.T. See *assay* ton.

At. Symbol for the element astatine.

at. wt. Abbreviation for atomic weight.

Atabrine hydrochloride. $C_{23}H_{30}ON_3Cl\cdot 2HCl\cdot 2H_2O =$ 508.7. Atebrin(e), hepacrine, mepacrine (B.P.), quinacrine hydrochloride (U.S.P.), chinacrin. Trademark for the dihydrochloride of methoxy-chlorodiethylaminopentylaminoacridine, an antimalarial. Cf. *atebrin(e)*.

atacamite, atakamite. $CuOCl\cdot Cu(OH)_2$. Remolinite. A native, green hydrous copper oxychloride.

atactic. See *polyvinyl* chain.

atalpo clay. A Cornish colloidal china clay; a soap filler and a catalyst.

atanasin. $C_{20}H_{18}O_8 = 386.02$. A flavonoid from *Brickellia squarrosa*, of Puerto Rico.

ataraxic. A sedative drug.

-ate. Suffix for compounds: (1) which contain a nonmetal in its higher positive valence (cf. *-ite*); (2) which are formed from an acid and base (salts).

atebrin[e]. $C_6H_3(NH_2)_2Me = 122.1$. Mecaprine hydrochloride. An antimalarial. Cf. *Atabrine*, *plasmoquin*.

athamantin. $C_{24}H_{30}O_7 = 430.3$. A bitter principle from the roots and seeds of *Athamanta oreoselinum* (Umbelliferae).

athermal. A cool spring or mineral water.

atherospermine. $C_{30}H_{20}O_5N = 474.2$. An alkaloid from the bark of *Atherosperma moschatum* (Monimiaceae) of Australia; sometimes used as tea and as an antirheumatic.

atisine. $C_{22}H_{31}NO_2 = 341.25$. Colorless powder, m.85, slightly soluble in water.

Atkinson hemin test. A method of preparing blood crystals (hemin) for microscopical examination and identification.

atm. Abbreviation for *atmosphere*.

atmolysis. The separation of gases by diffusion through porous walls; see *Graham's* law. **fractional-** A method for continuous diffusion of a gas, used to separate isotopes.

atmometer. An instrument to determine the amount of water passing into the air by evaporation.

atmos. Aer. A unit of air pressure on one square centimeter; equal to a column of 760 mm of mercury.

atmosphere. (1) The air or the gases surrounding the earth. (2) The pressure exerted by the air at sea level. (3) A unit of pressure. (*a*) Correctly, the pressure which equals the weight of mercury, d.13.5951, 760 mm high (at 0°C and $g = 980.665$ cm/sec²) $= 29.922$ in. $=$ a pressure of 14.6974 psi or 1.0333 kg/cm² $= 1,013,249$ dynes/cm². (*b*) The bar, 10^{-6} dynes/cm²; 75.006 cm mercury, used in Europe. **standard-** An a. used for the graduation of altitude instruments: gravity, 980.62 cm/sec² at all heights; pressure at zero height, 1,013.25 mb; temperature at zero height, 288°K; lapse rate of temperature, 6.5°C/km to 11 km, and zero above.

atmospheric gases. The carbon dioxide varies in quantity (approx. 0.03% by vol.), and the per-centage volumes of the other gases (on the moisture- and carbon dioxide–free air) are: nitrogen 78.03, oxygen 20.99, argon 0.94, neon 0.0012, helium 0.0004, krypton 0.0001, xenon 0.00001%, and carbon monoxide usually less than 5 ppm.

atmotherapy. Medical treatment with vapors; as, atomizers in respiratory disorders.

atom. The smallest part of an element that remains unchanged during chemical reaction, and is thus chemically indestructible and indivisible. It may undergo physical changes, as, excitation, disinte-gration, and transformation to other atoms. Cf. *radioactive* elements, *matter*. An a. has three fundamental numbers: (1) Mass number, giving the number of protons and neutrons. ($=isotopic$ *weight*). (2) Atomic number, giving the number of extranuclear electrons. (3) Packing fraction, which is an indication of the forces binding nuclear particles together. See also *atomic* structure. **activated-** Excited. **asymmetric-** See *asymmetric atom*. **Bohr-** The concept of a dynamic atom derived from phenomena of radiations. Cf. *atomic* structure 5. **chemist's-** Lewis. **cubical-** Lewis. **dark-** An a. that does not emit radiations. **dynamic-** Bohr. **excited-** Activated. An a. in which the electrons are moving in elliptical orbits or on a higher *energy level*, q.v. Such a. occur in sun and stars, and are produced by exposing vapors and gases to strong electric fields or radiations. **exploding-** An a. that rapidly disintegrates and releases much energy. Cf. *a. energy*. **fluctuating-** Schrödinger. **giant-** An entity which surrounds all matter and fills space. **ionized-** An a. from which some of the valence electrons are removed (positive ion), or which has captured additional electrons (negative ion). **irradiated-** See *irradiation*. **kinetic-** Bohr. **labeled.-** *Radioactive* indication. **Langmuir-** An elaborated concept of Lewis a. Cf. *atomic* structure 4. **Lewis-** The concept of a static a. based on crystal structure and chemical bonds. Cf. *atomic* structures 3 and 4. **neutral-** An a. in which the positive nuclear charge is balanced by the negative electrons, in either the normal or excited state. Cf. *stripped a., ionized a.* **normal-** An a. which is neither excited nor ionized; the electrons are in their lowest energy levels. **nuclear-** Stripped. **physicist's-** Bohr. **planetary-** Rutherford. **pulsating-** Schrödinger. **radiating-** An a. in which the electrons pass from a higher to a lower energy level and thereby emit radiations. Cf. *quantum*. **recoil-** An a. from which an α particle is rejected and which thereby recoils with a speed corresponding with its mass. Cf. *radioactivity*. **Rutherford's-** The original concept (1911) of a planetary a. which resembled a solar system. Cf. *atomic* structure 1. **Schrödinger-** The pulsating a., consisting of an electric field of different intensities. Cf. *atomic* structure 6. **static-** Lewis. **stripped-** An a. whose electrons have been removed by strong electric fields or extremely high temperature; supposed to exist in the interior of celestial objects and to account for their extreme densities. Cf. *spectral* classification. **tetrahedral-** An a. in which pairs of electrons are supposed to oscillate around the 4 corners of a tetrahedron. Cf. *atomic* structure 4. **tracer-** Radioactive indicator.

a. annihilation. The destruction of matter by its complete transformation into radiation; e.g., stellar energy. **a. bomb.** A device for producing explosively a large amount of energy·in a very short time. Two pieces of uranium (U^{235}) or plutonium (Pu^{239}) are contacted rapidly, e.g., by firing one into the other, so that together they exceed the critical mass. The mass is bombarded with thermal neutrons, which cause it to disinte-grate. The first a. b. was exploded in New Mexico July 16, 1945. First used in warfare at Hiroshima and Nagasaki in August, 1945; and equivalent to

RELATIVE ATOMIC WEIGHTS (1967)

International Union of Pure and Applied Chemistry
Based on the Atomic Mass of $^{12}C = 12$

The values apply to elements as they exist in nature, without artificial alteration of their isotopic composition; and to natural mixtures that do not include isotopes of radiogenic origin.

Name	Symbol	Atomic Number	Atomic Weight	Name	Symbol	Atomic Number	Atomic Weight
Actinium	Ac	89	....	Mercury	Hg	80	200.59
Aluminum	Al	13	26.9815	Molybdenum	Mo	42	95.94
Americium	Am	95	....	Neodymium	Nd	60	144.24
Antimony	Sb	51	121.75	Neon	Ne	10	20.179†
Argon	Ar	18	39.948	Neptunium	Np	93	....
Arsenic	As	33	74.9216	Nickel	Ni	28	58.71
Astatine	At	85	....	Niobium	Nb	41	92.906
Barium	Ba	56	137.34	Nitrogen	N	7	14.0067
Berkelium	Bk	97	....	Nobelium	No	102	....
Beryllium	Be	4	9.0122	Osmium	Os	76	190.2
Bismuth	Bi	83	208.980	Oxygen	O	8	15.9994*
Boron	B	5	10.811*	Palladium	Pd	46	106.4
Bromine	Br	35	79.904†	Phosphorus	P	15	30.9738
Cadmium	Cd	48	112.40	Platinum	Pt	78	195.09
Calcium	Ca	20	40.08	Plutonium	Pu	94	....
Californium	Cf	98	....	Polonium	Po	84	....
Carbon	C	6	12.01115*	Potassium	K	19	39.102
Cerium	Ce	58	140.12	Praseodymium	Pr	59	140.907
Cesium	Cs	55	132.905	Promethium	Pm	61	....
Chlorine	Cl	17	35.453†	Protactinium	Pa	91	....
Chromium	Cr	24	51.996†	Radium	Ra	88	....
Cobalt	Co	27	58.9332	Radon	Rn	86	....
Copper	Cu	29	63.546†	Rhenium	Re	75	186.2
Curium	Cm	96	....	Rhodium	Rh	45	102.905
Dysprosium	Dy	66	162.50	Rubidium	Rb	37	85.47
Einsteinium	Es	99	....	Ruthenium	Ru	44	101.07
Erbium	Er	68	167.26	Samarium	Sm	62	150.35
Europium	Eu	63	151.96	Scandium	Sc	21	44.956
Fermium	Fm	100	....	Selenium	Se	34	78.96
Fluorine	F	9	18.9984	Silicon	Si	14	28.086*
Francium	Fr	87	....	Silver	Ag	47	107.868†
Gadolinium	Gd	64	157.25	Sodium	Na	11	22.9898
Gallium	Ga	31	69.72	Strontium	Sr	38	87.62
Germanium	Ge	32	72.59	Sulfur	S	16	32.064*
Gold	Au	79	196.967	Tantalum	Ta	73	180.948
Hafnium	Hf	72	178.49	Technetium	Tc	43	....
Helium	He	2	4.0026	Tellurium	Te	52	127.60
Holmium	Ho	67	164.930	Terbium	Tb	65	158.924
Hydrogen	H	1	1.00797*	Thallium	Tl	81	204.37
Indium	In	49	114.82	Thorium	Th	90	232.038
Iodine	I	53	126.9044	Thulium	Tm	69	168.934
Iridium	Ir	77	192.2	Tin	Sn	50	118.69
Iron	Fe	26	55.847†	Titanium	Ti	22	47.90
Krypton	Kr	36	83.80	Tungsten	W	74	183.85
Lanthanum	La	57	138.91	Uranium	U	92	238.03
Lawrencium	Lr	103	....	Vanadium	V	23	50.942
Lead	Pb	82	207.19	Xenon	Xe	54	131.30
Lithium	Li	3	6.939	Ytterbium	Yb	70	173.04
Lutetium	Lu	71	174.97	Yttrium	Y	39	88.905
Magnesium	Mg	12	24.305	Zinc	Zn	30	65.37
Manganese	Mn	25	54.9380	Zirconium	Zr	40	91.22
Mendelevium	Md	101	....				

*Variable because of natural variations in isotopic composition.
Observed ranges:

Boron	±0.003	Oxygen	±0.0001
Carbon	±0.00005	Silicon	±0.001
Hydrogen	±0.00001	Sulfur	±0.003

†Likely experimental uncertainties:

Bromine	±0.001	Copper	±0.001
Chlorine	±0.001	Iron	±0.003
Chromium	±0.001	Silver	±0.001

20,000 tons of TNT. **a. building.** The formation of atoms from $+$ and $-$ electrons, a process assumed to occur in interstellar space, where pressure, temperature, and density are extremely low. It generates the highly penetrating cosmic rays. **a. creation.** The creation of matter by the complete transformation of energy as a link in the mass-energy cycle. **a. energy.** The disintegration of atoms, either naturally, as in natural radio-activity, or artificially, as by the bombardment of atomic nuclei with protons, deuterons, α particles, neutrons, or photons, whereby new atoms are formed and energy is liberated. **a. of electricity.** Electron. **a. fragment.** The disintegration product of an atom that has been split by an α particle Cf. *Wilson* method. **a. meter.** *Angström* unit. **a. model.** (1) Atomic model. (2) A model depicting certain properties of atoms, especially valency and isomerism. (3) An electrical or magnetic device which illustrates the structure and properties of the a.

atomic. Pertaining to the ultimate electrical unit of an element. **a. bomb.** See *atom* bomb. **a. diameter.** The imaginary line connecting the extreme electron orbits through the center of the a. **a. disintegration.** See *atom energy.* **a. distance.** The average or equilibrium length between the centers of 2 atoms as determined from crystal structure and band-spectra data, or calculated from a. radii. **a. domain.** The imaginary sphere occupied by the a. structure. **a. energy.** The force which holds the a. together; the energy liberated when an atom disintegrates or is transformed. 1 gm Ra $\equiv$ 2 billion calories. Cf. *packing* effect. **a. excitation.** See excited *atom, excitation.* **a. evolution.** Cf. *spectral* classification, *"old* age" theory. **a. field.** The space around an atom which cannot normally be penetrated by other atoms. See *molecular* diagram, *magnetic* field. **a. fragment.** Cf. *atom* fragment. **a. frequency.** Characteristic K radiations. Cf. Moseley *spectrum* and a. number. **a. group.** Radical. **a. heat.** The heat required to raise the temperature of one gram atom of an element 1°C; the product of the specific heat and the atomic weight of an element $=$ 6.4. Cf. *heat* capacity. **a. kernel.** An atom stripped of its valence electrons; Cf. *a. nucleus.* **a. mass.** The quantity of matter, q.v., contained in an atom. For hydrogen, the ratio $m/e = 1.04 \times 10^{-4}$, where m is the mass of H atom, and e the electric charge $= 1.57 \times 10^{-20}$. Hence $m = 1.64 \times 10^{-24}$ gm, and the mass of any other atom is its a. weight multiplied by this quantity. **a. meter.** Angström unit. **a. migration.** *Molecular* rearrangement. **a. model.** The concept of a. structure; as, Bohr's atom. **a. nucleus.** The central, positively charged part of an atom consisting of I positive charges and $I - N$ negative charges, where I is the isotopic weight and N the atomic number. Cf. *neutron, proton, kernel.* **a. number.** Ordination number, N or Z (zahl). It indicates the order of the elements in the periodic system, and represents the number of negative electrons outside the a. nucleus. It is related to the frequency ν and wavelength λ of the X-ray spectrum of an element by $c/\lambda = \nu = C(A - b)^2$, where C and b are constants, A is the a. number, and c the velocity of light. It is shown

as a prefix subscript, thus, $_{16}$S. Cf. *mass number.* *equivalent a. n.* EAN. The atomic number of an element, less the number of electrons lost on ionization, plus the number of electrons gained by coordination. **a. orbital.** a. o. The region, for a given electronic state, over which the electron is distributed in an atom. **a. oscillations.** The vibrations of a. nuclei or atoms within a molecule. Cf. *activated* molecule. **a. percentage.** The percentage by weight of a mixture, or system of compounds divided by the atomic weight. **a. plane.** The imaginary surface which passes through a set of atoms in a space lattice indicated by the Miller indices 100, 110, 111, etc. See figure. **a. potential.** *Ionization* potential. **a. properties.**

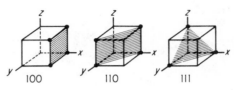

Atomic planes.

Those characteristics of an element that depend on a. structure, q.v., as opposed to molecular structure. **a. radius.** (1) The distance from the a. nucleus to the valence electrons. (2) The halfway distance between like atoms. Thus the a. r. for the single bond C is 0.77, for single bond N is 0.70; hence the distance C—C is 1.54, C—N is 1.47. **a. refraction.** The product of the specific refraction and the a. weight of an element. **a. species.** (1) Atoms of the known elements, q.v. (2) Isotopic species. The a. structure of an isotope. Thus chlorine consists of the a. species Cl^{35} and Cl^{37}, or isotopes with isotopic weights 35 and 37. **a. structure.** The composition of atoms, based upon a speculative interpretation of chemical and physical properties of the elements. See table at top of facing page.

1. The atom in its ground or normal (i.e., unexcited) state consists of an extremely small, positively charged nucleus containing the mass of the atom, surrounded by a number of electrons sufficient in number to neutralize the electric charge. The number of positive charges on the nucleus varies from 1 to 102 and corresponds with the a. number; the number of total charges varies from 1 to 238, and corresponds with the isotopic weight (Rutherford et al.) Cf. *periodic* system.

2. The nucleus itself, 10^{-12} cm. in diameter, consists of neutrons and protons which are closely bound together (Prout, Harkins.) Cf. *packing* effect, *isotopes.*

3. The electrons are distributed in successive shells containing 2, 8, 18, 32, etc. (i.e., $2n^2$) electrons, respectively (Kossel, Lewis.) Cf. *orbits, shells, periodic* system, *Stoner* quanta, *Pauli's* principle.

4. The electrons oscillate in shells, usually pairs, around centers corresponding with the corners of a cube or tetrahedron; as, in crystals (Lewis, Langmuir.) Cf. *octet, kernel, valency.*

5. The electrons exist in orbitals, which may be either spherical or dumbbell-shaped, and at

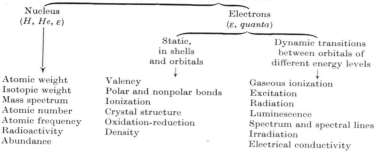

ATOMIC STRUCTURE

Nucleus (H, He, ε)

Electrons (ε, quanta)

Static, in shells and orbitals

Dynamic transitions between orbitals of different energy levels

Atomic weight
Isotopic weight
Mass spectrum
Atomic number
Atomic frequency
Radioactivity
Abundance

Valency
Polar and nonpolar bonds
Ionization
Crystal structure
Oxidation-reduction
Density

Gaseous ionization
Excitation
Radiation
Luminescence
Spectrum and spectral lines
Irradiation
Electrical conductivity

different energy levels; as, in luminous gases (Bohr, Sommerfeld). Cf. *orbits, quantum, excitation*.

6. The spatial distribution of an electron in its orbital is defined by a wavelike property ("wave function"). When this is substituted in the Schrödinger wave equation, it gives the energy of the orbital. Cf. *wave mechanics*.

7. In ions and sigma bonds, the electrons are localized in the region of their particular atoms; in pi bonds, they are less localized, being shared by several atoms; in metals, they are completely delocalized ("free"), being shared by all atoms ("electron gas").

a. theory. (1) The concept of a. structure. (2) The idea of finite particles of matter, as conceived by Democritus (400 B.C.), and established by Dalton (1808) and others. Cf. *kinetic* theory. **a. transformation.** The building up of atoms from those of lower a. weight. **a. transmutation.** An artificial process for changing one atom into another. Cf. *nuclear* chemistry. **a. units.** The definition of standards in terms of atomic dimensions; e.g., of the meter in terms of the wavelength of a standard mercury line in air. **a. volume.** The space occupied by one gram atom of an element; the quotient of the atomic weight and the density of the solid or liquid element. **a. weight.** A number indicating the relative weight of an element as compared with hydrogen ($=1.0080$) or oxygen ($=16.000$). It is the mean of the isotopic weights. In 1960 it was agreed internationally to adopt a new scale of a. based on the whole number 12.000 as the a. w. of the dominant natural isotope of carbon, instead of $O = 16.000$. Cf. *nucleidic mass*. This "unified" a. w., therefore, differs from the previous chemical and physical scales by 43 and 317 ppm, respectively. *absolute*- The actual weight of an atom. *chemical*- The a. w. determined by chemical methods and *weight* relations; they are based on oxygen gas $= 16.000$. *physical*- (1) The a. w. determined by physical methods and *mass* relations. Thus *chem. a. w. = phys. a. w.*/1.00022. (2) More correctly, the a. w. based on $O^{16} = 16$. *rational*- The a. w. in vacuo, corrected for buoyancy in air; used in highly accurate analytical work.

atomicity. Valency.

atomization. Breaking up a liquid into a fine spray or fog.

atomizer. A device for atomization; a nebulizer.

atommeter. Angström unit.

atomology. The study of atomic structure.

atomsite. A green slag produced on the ground surrounding the first atom bomb, q.v., site in New Mexico.

atophan. $Ph \cdot C_9H_5N \cdot COOH = 249.1$. Phenylquinolinecarboxylic acid, phenylcinchoninic acid, quinophen, agotan, cinchophen. Colorless crystals, sublime 200; an antirheumatic. Cf. *acitrin*.

atopite. $Ca_2Sb_2O_7$. A native, yellow, isometric antimonite.

Atoquinol. $C_{19}H_{15}O_2N = 289.1$. Trademark for phenylcinchoninic acid. A yellow powder, insoluble in water; an antirheumatic.

atoxyl. $NaC_6H_7O_3NAs = 239.1$. Sodium *m*- arsenite anilide, arsamin, sodium arsanilate. White powder, used in hypodermic medication. Cf. *maretin*. **acetyl-** Arsacetin. **a. mercury.** Mercuric atoxylate.

atoxylate. $MH_2 \cdot C_6H_4AsO_3 =$. Arsanilate. A salt of arsanilic acid.

atoxylic acid. Arsanilic acid.

A to Z. Trade name (Linen Industry Research Association, Belfast) for a range of yarns produced from any one type of man-made fiber.

atractylene. $C_{15}H_{24} = 204.19$. A sesquiterpene, d.0.927, b$_{14 mm}$141, from the essential oil of Asian *Atractylis* (Compositae).

atractylol. $C_{15}H_{26}O = 222.2$. A solid alcohol, m.59, from the essential oil of *Atractylis*.

atreol. Ammonium atreolate. An aqueous solution of a mixture of ammonium salts derived from organic acids, in which the N is in the sulfonic radical. A black syrup, soluble in water; a mild antiseptic.

atroglyceric acid. $CH_2OH \cdot C(OH)Ph \cdot COOH = 182.1$. α-Phenylglyceric acid. White crystals, m.146.

atrolactic acid. $Me \cdot C(OH) \cdot Ph \cdot COOH \cdot H_2O = 166.1$. α-Phenyllactic acid, α-methylmandelic acid, hydroxyhydratropic acid, atrolactinic acid. Colorless crystals, m.90, soluble in water.

atromentin. $C_{20}H_{16}O_6 = 352.12$. 2,5-Dihydroxy-3,6-bis(*p*-methoxyphenyl)quinone. A plant pigment.

Atromid. Trademark for a compound of androsterone and ethyl-*p*-chlorophenoxyisobutyrate. Used to control the concentration of blood cholesterol and to treat hardening of the arteries.

atronene. $C_{16}H_{14} = 206.11$. Atronol, phenyldihydronaphthalene. Colorless crystals, m.326, insoluble in water.

atronic acid. $C_{17}H_{14}O_2 = 250.21$. Colorless prisms, m.164, soluble in water.

atropamine. Apoatropine.

atropic acid. CH_2:$CPh\cdot COOH = 148.1$. α-Phenyl-acrylic acid, α-methylene-α-toluic acid. Colorless scales, m.106, sparingly soluble in water. **iso-** Isatropic acid. **methyl-** $C_6H_5\cdot C(NCH\cdot CH_3)COOH = 176.1$. Colorless crystals, m.135.

atropine. $C_{17}H_{23}O_3N = 289.28$. Coromegine, daturine, isotropine, tropyl tropate, tropin tropic ester, *dl*-hyoscyamine. An alkaloid from *Atropa belladonna*, deadly nightshade, or *Datura stramonium*. Colorless needles, m.115, slightly soluble in water. An antispasmodic, mydriatic, and antidote for morphine, pilocarpine, and prussic acid. The antidotes of atropine are emetics, stomach pump, pilocarpine, morphine. **a. arsenate.** $(C_{17}H_{23}O_3N)_2H_3AsO_4 = 720.56$. Colorless crystals, soluble in water. **a. borate.** $(C_{17}H_{23}O_3N)_2B_4O_7 = 733.6$. White crystals, soluble in water. **a. gold hydrochloride.** $C_{17}H_{23}O_3N\cdot HAuCl_4 = 629.33$. Yellow leaflets, m.136, slightly soluble in water. **a. hydrobromide.** $C_{17}H_{23}O_3N\cdot HBr = 370.2$. Colorless crystals, soluble in water. **a. hydrochloride.** $C_{17}H_{23}O_3N\cdot HCl = 325.78$. White crystals, soluble in water. **a. hydroiodide.** $C_{17}H_{23}O_3N\cdot HIO_3$. Colorless crystals, soluble in water. **a. iodate.** $C_{17}H_{23}O_3N\cdot HIO_3 = 465.21$. Colorless crystals; soluble in water. **a. methylbromide.** $C_{16}H_{20}O_3N(CH_3)_2Br = 384.1$. White crystals, m.222, soluble in water. **a. methylnitrate.** $C_{16}H_{20}O_3N(CH_3)_2NO_3 = 366.1$. Eumydrine. White crystals, soluble in water. **a. nitrate.** $C_{17}H_{23}O_3N\cdot HNO_3 = 352.28$. Colorless crystals, soluble in water. **a. salicylate.** $C_{17}H_{23}O_3N\cdot C_7H_5O_2 = 410.3$. Colorless, deliquescent powder, soluble in alcohol. **a. santonate.** $C_{17}H_{23}O_3N\cdot C_{15}H_5O_4 = 553.3$. Colorless crystals, soluble in water. **a. stearate.** $C_{17}H_{23}O_3N\cdot C_{18}H_{36}O_2 = 573.3$. Colorless powder, used in ointments. **a. sulfate.** $C_{17}H_{23}O_3N\cdot H_2SO_4 = 387.36$. Colorless crystals, m.192, soluble in water; used in ophthalmology. **a. valerate.** $C_{17}H_{23}O_3N\cdot C_5H_{10}O_2\cdot\frac{1}{2}H_2O = 400.33$. Colorless crystals, m.42, soluble in water.

atroscin. Hyoscine hydrobromide.

atroscine. $C_{17}H_{21}O_4N\cdot H_2O = 321.27$. Isohyoscine, Isoscopolamine. An alkaloid from *Scopolia atropoides* (Solanaceae). Transparent crystals, soluble in water.

atroxindole. $C_9H_9ON = 147.1$. Methyloxindole. Colorless crystals, m.119.

attapulgite. Palygorskite. The active element in montmorillonite clay, responsible for its catalytic polymerization of unsaturated compounds, and its ion-exchange properties. A. is very absorbent and thixotropic; used in paints, to condition fertilizers and clarify oils; minute, rectangular, hollow needles.

attar of roses. An essential oil from damascene and cabbage roses, used in perfumery.

attemperator. A pipe through which water flows at a constant temperature; used for temperature control.

attenuation. (1) Weakening the toxicity of a microorganism or virus. (2) The extent to which the specific gravity of a liquid is lowered by alcoholic fermentation.

atto- Prefix for 10^{-18} (IUPAC).

attraction. The force that holds molecules together. **chemical-** Affinity. **capillary-** The force that raises or depresses a fluid in a capillary tube. **electric-** The force that draws oppositely charged bodies

together. **electron-** The force exerted by an atomic nucleus on the electron pair; a *bond*. **gravitational-** Gravitation. **magnetic-** The action of a magnet on iron particles. **mechanical-** See *adhesion* and *cohesion*. **radiant-** See *relativity* (general).

attritus. A botanical constituent of coal.

Atwater calorimeter. A bomb calorimeter for determining the energy- heat value of foods.

A.U. (1) Obsolete abbreviation for Angström unit. (2) Abbreviation for atomic units.

Au. Symbol for gold (aurum).

aubepine. Anisaldehyde.

aucubin. A glucoside from greater plantain, *Plantago major*. White needles, m.180, soluble in water.

audiometer. An apparatus to test hearing. Cf. *eudiometer*.

audion. *Electric* valve.

audiphone. A device to increase sound volume.

auerbachite. Native, amorphous zirconium silicate.

auerlite. Thorium silicophosphate (North Carolina). Cf. *monazite*.

Auer metal. A mixture of mischmetal 65, Fe 35%, used as pyrophoric alloy in gas lighters and for tracer bullets.

Auer von Welsbach. See *Welsbach*.

augelite. A natural, basic aluminum phosphate.

augite. $CaMg_2Al_2Si_3O_{10}$. Malacolite. A dark aluminum pyroxene in basalt. Cf. *sahlite*.

augustione. Angustione.

aura. (1) The current of air or breeze produced by the discharge of static electricity from a point. (2) A peculiar radiation said to emanate from living organisms. Cf. *scotography*.

auramine. $Me_2N\cdot C_6H_4\cdot C(NH_2)$:$C_6H_4$:$NMe_2Cl = 267.28$. Tetramethyl-*p*-diamidoimidobenzophenone, yellow pyoktannin. Yellow scales, m.136, insoluble in water; a dye. **a. hydrochloride.** The a. of commerce. A yellow powder, soluble in water; a dye and antiseptic.

aurentia. An orange aniline dye; used in light filters and biological stains.

Aurantiacea. The orange family. See *Citrus*.

aurantiin. Naringin.

aurantine. An orange extract.

aurantium. Orange (Latin).

aurate. A salt of auric acid containing the AuO_3= radical.

aureolin. Primulin. **a. yellow.** Potassium cobaltic nitrite; a yellow paint pigment.

Aureomycin. Trademark for chlortetracycline. An antibiotic metabolic product of *Streptomyces aureofaciens*. Yellow solid. **A. hydrochloride.** See *chlortetracycline* hydrochloride (U.S.P.).

aureotracin. An antibiotic prepared by precipitation of a dilute solution of Aureomycin or bacitracin.

auri. Gold (Latin).

auribromhydric acid. $HAuBr_4\cdot 5H_2O = 607.96$. Yellow crystals, m.27, soluble in water.

auribromide. Bromaurate. A salt of the type $MAuBr_4$.

auric. Describing compounds of trivalent gold, $Au\equiv$. **a. acid.** $H_3AuO_3 = 248.2$. Auric hydroxide. Brown powder, decomp. 150, insoluble in water. **a. bromide.** $AuBr_3 = 436.96$. Brown powder, soluble in water; an antiepileptic. **a. chloride.** $AuCl_3 = 303.58$. Red leaflets, decomp. 180, soluble in water; used in photography. **a. chloride**

acid. $AuCl_3 \cdot HCl \cdot 4H_2O = 412.11$. Aurochlorohydric acid. Yellow crystals, soluble in water. **a. chloride cryst.** $AuCl_3 \cdot 2H_2O = 339.61$. Orange leaflets, soluble in water. **a. chloride fused.** $AuCl_3 \cdot HCl \cdot xH_2O$. Brown masses, soluble in water. Used in electroplating and as an alterant. **a. cyanide.** $Au(CN)_3 \cdot 6H_2O = 383.33$. White hygroscopic crystals, soluble in water; used to treat tuberculosis. **a. hydroxide.** $Au(OH)_3 = 248.22$. Auric acid. Brown powder, decomp. 150, insoluble in water. **a. iodide.** $AuI_3 = 577.96$. Green powder, decomp. by heat, insoluble in water. **a. nitrate acid.** $Au(NO_3)_3 \cdot HNO_3 \cdot 3H_2O = 500.30$. Yellow triclinics, decomp. by heat, soluble in water. **a. oxide.** $Au_2O_3 = 442.2$. Black powder, losing oxygen on heating; insoluble in water. **a. potassium bromide.** $KAuBr_4 \cdot 2H_2O = 592.4$. Potassium bromaurate. Yellow needles, soluble in water; an antiepileptic. **a. potassium chloride.** $KAuCl_4 \cdot 2H_2O = 414.4$. Potassium chloraurate. Yellow needles, soluble in water; a ceramic pigment. **a. potassium cyanide.** $KAu(CN)_4 \cdot 2H_2O = 376.5$. Yellow crystals, soluble in water. **a. potassium iodide.** $KAuI_4 = 743.8$. Potassium iodoaurate. Black crystals, decomp. by heat, soluble in water. **a. sodium bromide.** $NaAuBr_4 \cdot 2H_2O = 576.2$. Sodium bromaurate. Black crystals, soluble in water; an antiepileptic. **a. sodium chloride.** $NaAuCl_4 = 362.2$. Sodium chloraurate. Yellow crystals, soluble in water; an alterant. **a. sulfate.** $Au_2O_3 \cdot 2SO_3 \cdot H_2O = 620.54$. Yellow deliquescent crystals, decomp. by heat, soluble in water. **a. sulfide.** $Au_2S_3 = 490.58$. Brown powder, insoluble in water.

aurichalcite. The mineral $2(ZnCu)CO_3 \cdot 3(ZnCu)(OH)_2$.

aurichloride. A salt containing the $AuCl_4-$ radical.

aurichlorohydric acid. *Auric chloride acid.*

auricyanhydric acid. $HAu(CN)_4 = 302.24$. Colorless crystals, soluble in water.

auricyanide. A salt containing the $Au(CN)_4-$ radical.

auriferous. Containing gold.

auriiodide. A compound containing the $-AuI_4$ radical.

aurin. $(HOC_6H_4)_2 = C = C_6H_4 : O = 290.22$. Pararosolic acid, coralline. A triphenylmethane dye. Red needles, m.220 (decomp.), insoluble in water; a textile dye and indicator; yellow (acid) to magenta (basic) at pH 7.5. Cf. *rosolic acid.* **a. carboxylic acid.** Aluminon.

auripigment. Arsenous sulfide.

auro. Aurous.

auroauric. A compound containing divalent gold or 1 atom each of mono- and trivalent gold. **a. bromide.** $AuBr_2 = 357.04$ or $Au_2Br_4 = 714.08$. A black powder, insoluble in water. **a. chloride.** $AuCl_2 = 268.12$, $Au_2Cl_4 = 536.24$. Gold dichloride. Red crystals, insoluble in water. **a. oxide.** $AuO = 213.2$. Brown powder, insoluble in water. **a. sulfide.** $Au_2S_2 = 458.5$. Black powder, decomp. by heat, insoluble in water.

aurobromide. $MAuBr_2$. Bromaurite.

aurochin. Quinine *p*-amidobenzoate.

aurochloride. A double chloride containing the $AuCl_2-$ radical.

aurocyanide. A cyanide containing the $Au(CN)_2-$ radical.

aurodiamine. $AuHN \cdot NH_2 = 228.3$. Fulminating gold. Green powder, explodes if struck or heated.

auroglaucin(e). $C_{19}H_{22}O_3 = 298.1$. A pigment produced on textiles by the action of *Aspergillus glaucus*, m.152.

auromine. $C_{17}H_{23}N_3 = 269.30$. Rose needles, m.96, insoluble in water.

aurone. $C_{15}H_{10}O_5 = 270.02$. A dibenzylidene coumarone, the coloring matter of yellow dahlia, *D. variabilis*. Orange solid, m.312 (decomp.).

aurora. Aurora Borealis. A display of variously colored lights in the atmosphere, above 87 km, with a conspicuous green line, 5577.3 Å., due to oxygen. **a. tube.** A vacuum discharge tube of uranium glass.

aurorium. A hypothetical element said to produce the characteristic lines of the aurora (obsolete). Cf. *nebulium.*

aurosulfide. A salt containing the $AuS-$ group.

aurothioglucose. $C_6H_{11}AuO_5S = 392.18$. Glucosylthiogold. Yellow powder, soluble in water; an antirheumatic (U.S.P.).

aurous. Describing compounds of monovalent gold, $Au-$. **a. bromide.** $AuBr = 277.14$. Green powder, decomp. 115, insoluble in water. **a. bromide acid.** $AuBr \cdot HBr \cdot 5H_2O = 448.2$. Red crystals, soluble in water. **a. chloride.** $AuCl = 232.66$. Yellow crystals, decomp. by heat or water. **a. cyanide.** $AuCN = 223.22$. Yellow crystals, decomp. by heat, insoluble in water, soluble in potassium cyanide solutions. **a. hydroxide.** $AuOH = 214.2$. Brown crystals, decomp. 250. **a. iodide.** $AuI = 324.12$. Gold monoiodide. Green powder, decomp. 120, slightly soluble in water; an alterant. **a. oxide.** $Au_2O = 410.4$. Violet powder, decomp. 250, insoluble in water. **a. potassium cyanide.** $KAu(CN)_2 = 288.4$. Potassium cyanaurite. White crystals, soluble in water; used as an antiseptic and in electroplating. **a. sodium cyanide.** $NaAu(CN)_2 = 272.2$. Sodium cyanaurite. White crystals, soluble in water; used in electroplating. **a. sulfide.** $Au_2S = 426.46$. Black powder, insoluble in water.

aurum. Gold (Latin). **a. vegetable.** Pipitzahoic acid.

ausonium. See *ekarhenium* and *esperium*.

austempering. The tempering of steel by the transformation of the austenite, q.v., at a temperature within the martensitic zone.

austenite. A carbon-iron γ-ferrite formed in highly carbonized steel. Cf. *martensite.*

australene. Pinene.

austrium. A supposed element (Przibram, 1900) shown to be gallium.

auto- Prefix (Greek) meaning "self-."

autoactivation. Activation of a gland by its own secretions.

autoantibiosis. Inhibition of a culture medium by the previous growth of the organism.

autocatalysis. Catalysis produced by the products of a catalytic reaction.

autoclave. An apparatus for heating liquids, or sterilizing at high steam pressure.

autocoid. Hormone (obsolete).

autocollimation spectroscope. A comparison spectroscope.

autocytolysis. Autolysis.

autocytotoxin. A body toxin formed by absorbed degenerated cells.

autodecomposition. A decomposition autocatalysis, q.v.

autolysate, autolyzate. The product of the self-liquefaction of organic cells or tissues.

autolysis. The dissolution of cells by their own serum. Cf. *heterolysis.*

autolyze, autolyse. To liquefy organic cells.

automatic. Self-working. **a. buret.** A buret with an overflow at the zero point. **a. pipet.** A pipet with an overflow at its mark for rapid use.

automation. The replacement of routine labor by instrumentation, control techniques, and power-driven equipment.

automolite. Gahnite.

autooxidation. (1) Oxidation by the unaided atmosphere. (2) An oxidation reaction initiated only by an inductor. See induced *reaction.*

autophytes. Plants that can live on inorganic matter. Cf. *saprophytes.*

autoprotolysis. Transfer of a proton from one molecule to another of the same substance.

autoradiography. The use of radioactive tracer isotopes to record activity distribution on a surface by means of contact photographic film.

autotrophic. Describing an organism deriving its energy by oxidation of inorganic substances.

autoxidation. Autooxidation.

autunite. $CaO \cdot 2UO_3P_2O_5 \cdot 8H_2O = 915.1$. Native, yellow orthorhombic crystals (Utah and South Dakota).

auvergnose. A diorite (North Carolina).

auximone. An agent that stimulates the growth of seedlings and plants; as, pantothenic acid.

auxin. Phytohormone. General term for the growth-regulating constituent of plants. Cf. plant *hormone.* **a.A.** $C_{18}H_{32}O_5 = 328.25$. A monocyclic trihydroxycarboxy acid plant hormone from *Avena,* m.196. **a.B.** $C_{18}H_{30}O_4 = 310.23$. A monocyclic hydroxyketocarboxy acid plant hormone from maize germ.

auxiometer. A device to measure the magnifying power of lenses.

auxochrome. A group of atoms that intensifies the color of a chromophore, develops a color from a chromogen, or enhances the violet shade of a compound. Cf. *bathochrome.*

auxogluc. An atom or radical which combined with glucophores yields sweet compounds.

auxograph. A device to record plant growth rate.

auxotox radical. The methylimine group $=N \cdot CH_3$, associated with liver degeneration.

av. Avoirdupois.

ava. Kava.

available. Utilizable in a chemical reaction. **a. acidity.** Hydrogen-ion concentration; **a. nitrogen.** The soluble nitrogen of fertilizers.

avalite. A claylike silicate containing chromium.

Avcoset. Trade name for a viscose synthetic fiber.

Avena. A genus of grasses which yield important cereals; as, *A. sativa* (common oat).

avenacein. $C_{25}H_{44}O_7N_2(?)$. An antibiotic pigment produced by *Fusaria.*

avenin. Legumin. A protein from oats. A yellow powder; a general stimulant.

avenine. $C_{56}H_{21}O_{18}N = 995.4$. An alkaloid from oats; a nerve stimulant.

aventurine. (1) A brown venetian glass with embedded brass filings. (2) A feldspar containing iron. **a. quartz.** Micaceous quartz (Urals). Cf. *imperial* jade.

avenyl. A constituent of hydnocarpus oil, used to treat leprosy.

average. Mean.

avertin. $CBr_3CH_2OH = 282.77$. Bromatol, ethobrome. Colorless crystals, m.80; a rectal anesthetic.

Avicenna [**Abu Ali en Hosein Ben Abdallah**]. 980–1037. Persian mathematician and alchemist.

avidin. A protein-carbohydrate complex in egg white, which inactivates the biotin present; it can produce dermatitis.

Avisco. Trade name for a viscose synthetic fiber.

avitaminosis. A deficiency disease due to lack of a vitamin; as, scurvy. Cf. *hypovitaminosis.*

avocado. The fruit of *Persea gratissima,* avocado or alligator pear, a staple food in Latin America. The seed yields a black, indelible ink. **a. oil.** An oil from a. containing vitamins A, D, and E, and phytosterol and lecithin; used as an emollient. **a. sugar.** A mannoketoheptose from avocado. Cf. *sugars.*

Avogadro, Amadeo (**Conte di Quaregna**). 1776–1856. Italian scientist who formulated the gas laws. **A. constant.** A. number. **A. hypothesis.** A. law. **A. law.** Equal volumes of all gases at the same pressure and temperature contain the same number of molecules. **A. number.** A. constant, N. The number of molecules contained in 1 mole (gram molecule), determined from the spectral line structure. **A. theory.** A. law.

avoirdupois. The English system of weights and measures. See *weights.*

awaruite. A native nickel-iron (67% Ni).

axerophtol. $C_{20}H_{29} \cdot OH = 286.2$. Vitamin A_1, vitamin A alcohol (more correctly, aldehyde). The alcohol of which vitamin A is the fatty-acid ester; the hydrolysis product of β-carotene.

axestone. A hard variety of jade from Cornwall.

axial. Pertaining to an axis. **a. angle apparatus.** Goniometer. **a. ratio.** The ratio of the length to the basal side of the close-packed hexagonal structure of certain metals; usually 1.57–1.64, but 1.9 for Zn and Cd. **a. symmetry.** The transform of an organic compound. See *stereoisomerism.*

axin. A varnish from Mexican cochineal, *Lacus axinus,* containing axinic acid.

axinic acid. $C_{18}H_{28}O_2 = 276.3$. See *axin.*

axinite. $H_2(Ca \cdot Fe \cdot Mn)_4(BO) \cdot Al_2(SiO_4)_5$. A plum-colored gem mineral.

axiom. A self-evident proposition. Cf. *postulate.*

axis. A line, imaginary or real, passing through an object, around which all parts of the object are symmetrical. Cf. *coordinate, crystal* system, *pinakoids.* **electric-** The direction of a crystal that offers least resistance to an electric current. **principal,** See *principal.* **optic-** An imaginary line passing through the center of a lens system. x-, y-, z-. See *coordinates.*

axonometry. Measurement of crystal axes.

Az. French symbol for nitrogen (azote).

aza- See *tetraarylaza.*

azacyclo- Prefix indicating an NH— group in a saturated carbon ring.

azadarach. Azadarichta, margosa bark, neem bark. The bark of the Indian lilac tree or bead tree,

Melia azadarichta (Meliaceae) of Asia; an anthelmintic and emetic.

azafrin. $C_{28}H_{40}O_4 = 440.28$. A carotenoid pigment, m.212, from the roots of azafranilla, *Escobedia scrabifolia* (Scrophulariaceae) of S. America.

azaleine. Fuchsin.

azarin. $C_{16}H_{17}O_4N_3S = 347.3$. Red aniline dye.

azedarine. An alkaloid from the roots of *Melia azedarach* (Asia). See *margosine*.

azelaic acid. $HOOC(CH_2)_7COOH = 188.17$. Anchoic acid, lepargylic acid. An oxidation product of oleic acid. Colorless leaflets, m.106, soluble in water. **a. acid value.** A chemical constant of fats; the potassium salts of the azelaic glycerides formed.

azeotropes. Any one of two or more compounds which form mixtures of constant boiling point whose distillates have the same composition as the original mixture. **negative-A.** with minimum boiling mixtures. **positive-A.** with maximum boiling mixtures.

azeotropy. The property of azeotropes. Cf. *hylotropy*.

azerin. The digestive enzyme of insectiverous plants.

azete. $(CH)_3 \cdot N$. A heterocyclic compound.

azide. (1) A compound containing the —N_3 group. (2) Triazo.

azidinblue. Trypan blue.

azido. Triazo.

azimid. $C_2H_2N_6 = 110.08$. Osotriazol.

azimide. Benzoylazide.

azimido. Azimino. The —$NH \cdot N : N$— group. **a. benzene.** Benzotriazole.

azimino. Azimido.

azimuth. The angle between the meridian and the vertical plane through an object. Cf. *coordinates*.

azine. Pyridine.

azino. The radical $=N \cdot N=$.

azipeten. $NH : C : O$. The basic group of polypeptide formation.

azlon. Generic name for a synthetic protein fiber.

azo- Prefix indicating the radical —$N : N$—. Cf. *azote, azino, diazo, trisazo, tetrazo, hydrazo, oxyazo*.

Azobacter. Aerobic soil bacteria that oxidize atmospheric nitrogen. See *Azotobacter*.

azobenzene. $PhN : NPh = 182.08$. Nitrogen benzide, diphenyldiimide. Orange leaflets, m.68, insoluble in water; used in organic synthesis. **p-amino-** $C_{12}H_9N_2 \cdot NH_2 = 197.2$. **p-diamino-** $C_{12}H_8N_2(NH_2)_2 = 212.2$. Colorless crystals, m.241; its hydrochloride is chrysoidine. **dihydroxy-** Azophenol. **dimethyl-** Azotoluene. **diphenyl-** Coupier's blue. **hydroxy-** See *benzene*. *o-* or *2-* Golden crystals, m.123 its hydrochloride is spirit (aniline) yellow. *m-* or *3-* Orange needles, m.57. *p-* or *4-* Yellow monoclinic crystals, m.126.

azobenzide. Azobenzene.

azobenzoic acid. $(: N \cdot C_6H_4 \cdot COOH)_2 = 270.23$. **ortho-** Dark yellow needles, decomp. 237, sparingly soluble in water. **meta-** Amorphous powder, decomp. by heat, soluble in water. **para-** Red amorphous powder, decomp. by heat, insoluble in water.

azocholoramid. N,N-Dichloroazodicarbonamidine. A bactericide, soluble in water.

azocyanide. A compound containing the —$N : N \cdot CN$ radical.

azodermine. Acetylamidoazotoluene. Red powder that stimulates epithelial growth.

azodicarbonamide. $NH_2 \cdot CON_2 \cdot CONH_2 = 116.08$. Azoformamide, decomp. 180, soluble in water.

azodiphenyl. *Coupier's* blue.

azoflavin. Azoacid yellow, Indian yellow. A mixture of nitrated diphenylamine orange and nitrodiphenylamine; a textile dye.

azoisobutyronitrile. $CN \cdot CMe_2 : N : N \cdot CMe_2 \cdot CN = 164.2$. Colorless crystals, m.105.

azoles. Pentatomic heterocyclic ring compounds; e.g., pyrrole.

azolitmin. $C_7H_7O_4N = 169.1$. The coloring matter of litmus indicator. Violet scales, soluble in water (acids red, alkalies blue).

azonaphthalene. $C_{10}H_7N : N \cdot C_{10}H_7 = 282.30$. Naphthyldiimide. α- or **1,1'-** Red needles, m.190, insoluble in water. β- or **2,2'-** m.204. αβ- or or **1,2'-** m.136.

azonium. R_3N_2X.

azophenetole. $(C_6H_4OEt)_2N_2 = 270.16$. Diethoxyazobenzene. **ortho-** m.131, insoluble in water. **para-** m.167, insoluble in water.

azophenol. $HO \cdot C_6H_4 \cdot N : N \cdot C_6H_4 \cdot OH = 214.22$. Dihydroxyazobenzene. **ortho-** or **2,2'-** Yellow leaflets, m.171 (sublimes), insoluble in water. **meta-** or **3,3'-** Brown scales, m.205, sparingly soluble in water. **para-** or **4,4'-** Brown triclinics, decomp. 216, slightly soluble in water. Dyestuff intermediates.

azophenyl. The $PhN : N$— group. Cf. *phenylazo, oxyazo*. **a. ethane.** $PhN : NEt = 133.2$. Benzene azoethane. Colorless liquid, b.280. **a. methane.** $PhN : NMe = 119.2$. Colorless liquid, b.150.

azophenylene. Phenazine.

azorite. $ZrSiO_4$. A native silicate.

azosulfonic acid. A compound containing the —$N : N \cdot SO_3H$ radical.

azotate. Nitrate.

azote. French for nitrogen, Az.

Azotobacter. Soil bacteria which convert atmospheric nitrogen to nitrates. Cf. *Azobacter*.

azotoluene. $MeC_6H_4N : N \cdot C_6H_4Me = 210.27$. Ditolyldiimide, **oo-** or **2,2'-** Red prisms, m.55, insoluble in water. **mm-** or **3,3'-** Orange rhombs, m.54, insoluble in water, **pp-** or **4,4'-** Yellow needles, m.114, insoluble in water.

azotometer. An apparatus to determine nitrogen gasometrically.

azovan blue. $C_{34}H_{24}O_{14}N_6S_4Na_4 = 960.9$. Evans blue. Blue hygroscopic powder; used in the determination of blood and plasma volumes.

azoxazole. Furazan.

azoxy. The —NON— radical.

azoxyanisole. p-$(MeO \cdot C_6H_4N)_2O = 258.20$. White crystals, m.117, soluble in alcohol.

azoxybenzene. $Ph \cdot NON \cdot Ph = 198.22$. Zinin. Yellow needles, m.36 (decomp.), insoluble in water.

azoxybenzoic acid. $(C_6H_4COOH)_2NON = 286.23$. **ortho-** or **1,1'-** Yellow leaflets, m.248 (decomp.), sparingly soluble in water. **meta-** or **2,2'-** Yellow needles, decomp. 320, insoluble in water. **para-** or **3,3'-** Yellow amorphous powder, decomp. 240, insoluble in water.

azoxynaphthalene. $C_{10}H_7 \cdot NON \cdot C_{10}H_7 = 298.23$. **1,1'-** or α- Red rhombs, m.127, insoluble in water. **2,2'-** or β- m.167, insoluble in water.

azoxytoluidine. Diaminoazotoluene.

azulene. $C_{16}H_{26}O = 234.3$. A dehydrogenated azulogen. The blue coloring matter of some essential oils. Oily liquid, b.170, insoluble in water. Cf. *cerulein*.

azulin. A blue dye formed by heating aniline with corallin.

azulmic acid. $C_4H_5ON_5$ = 139.2. Azulmin. A brown decomposition product of cyanogen.

azulogens. Sesquiterpenes in many essential oils. They give a blue color (azuline) with bromine in chloroform.

azurine. (1) Theobromine sodium acetate; a diuretic.

(2) A bluish-black aniline dye.

azurite. $CuCO_3 \cdot Cu(OH)_2$. Blue malachite, chessylite, lazulite, lapis lazuli. A monoclinic mineral used in paints and ceramics. Cf. *malachite*.

azylase. A diastatic enzyme which degrades the amides of substituted acids but not true peptides.

azymic. Describing: (1) a reaction not caused by fermentation; (2) an enzyme that does not cause fermentation.

azymous. Unfermented.

B

B. Symbol for boron.

⁰B. Symbol for Baumé scale density, q.v.

b. Abbreviation for "boils at." **b**$_{x}$mm. Boils at x mm pressure.

b. The covolume or volume occupied by the molecules in van der Waals' equation.

c. Greek "beta." (1) Symbol for the specific heat constant. (2) Bohr magneton. (3) In chemical names, substitution at the *second* C atom. See *beta.* **β acid.** Anthraquinone-2-sulfonic acid.

Ba. Symbol for barium.

bababudanite. $4NaFe(SiO_3)_2 \cdot 2FeSiO_3 \cdot 3MgSiO_3$. A soda amphibole (Mysore).

babassu oil. Oil from the fruit kernel of the Brazilian palm tree, *Orbignya martiana* (Palmae).

babbitt (metal). A bearing alloy: Sn 65–95, Sb 8–12, Cu 1 pt. **genuine b.** The b. of Isaac Babbitt (1839): Sn 89.3, Sb 8.9, Cu 1.8%.

Babcock, Stephen Moulton. 1843–1931. American chemist. **B. bottle.** A graduated glass flask for the determination of fat in milk. **B. milk tester.** A centrifuge used in milk-fat analysis. **B. pipet.** A pipet used in milk analysis.

babingtonite. $(Ca,Fe,Mn)6Fe_2Si_9O_{27}$. A vitreous, greenish-black, triclinic pyroxene.

babitt. Babbitt.

Babo, Clement Heinrich Lambert Freiherr von. 1818–1899. German chemist. **B. absorption tube.** A glass cylinder filled with glass beads, used for the absorption of gases by liquids. **B. law.** The relative lowering of the vapor pressure of a solvent by a solute is the same at all temperatures.

babool, babul. *Acacia arabica.* Its bark is a tannin; its gum is *gum arabic.*

babussu. An edible oil from a Brazilian nut used for detergents.

bacca. Latin for berry.

baccarine. An alkaloid from mio-mio, *Baccharis cordifolia* (Compositae) of S. America.

baccatin. An antibiotic from *Gibberella baccata.* White solid, m.141, insoluble in water.

bacciform. Berry-shaped.

Bachoune, Arnold (Villanovanus). 1235–1315. French alchemist who noted the dangers of putrefaction and of copper utensils in cooking.

Bacillus. A nonsporing rod-shaped bacterium (Bacteriaceae). Cf. *bulgara, Lactobacillus, tetanus.* **B. Calmette.** Guérin vaccine (B.P.), B.C.G. A relatively nonpathogenic B. which sensitizes man to tuberculosis.

bacitracin. An antibiotic polypetpide produced by certain strains of *Bacillus subtilis.* White, bitter, hygroscopic powder, soluble in water (U.S.P.). **zinc-** Hygroscopic, buff powder, slightly soluble in water; an antibacterial (U.S.P.).

backscatter. The scattering of β-particles from a radioisotope (as Kr^{85}), by a film toward a detector; used to measure film thickness.

Bacon, Francis (Baron Verulam). 1561–1626. Eng-lish philosopher and exponent of the inductive method in science. **B., Roger.** 1214–1294. English alchemist who studied gunpowder and combustion.

bacteria. (Sing. bacterium.) Small unicellular fungi (Schizomycetes). They contain proteins 8–15, fats 0.5–4, ash 0.5–3, water 80–85%. **acetic acid-** *Bacillus aceti.* A b. that oxidizes alcohol to acetic acid. **ammonifying-** A soil b. that reduces nitrogen to ammonia. **butyric acid-** *Bacillus butyricus.* A b. found in milk, water, dust, etc., that produces butyric acid from fats. **chromogenic-chromoparous-, chromophorous-** B. producing colored products. **denitrifying-** A soil b. that oxidizes ammonia to nitrogen. **lactic acid-** A b. in air that produces lactic acid. **nitrifying-** A soil b. that oxidizes nitrogen to nitrites and nitrates. **photo-** A b. that causes phosphorescence, in decaying fish. **soil-** B. essential for plant growth.

b. membrane. A scum or pellicle which consists of b. Cf. *bacterial* membrane.

Bacteriaceae. A family of unicellular plants (Schizomycetes). Cf. *bacteria.*

bacterial. Pertaining to bacteria. **b. action.** The effects of bacteria or their metabolism; e.g., hydrolyzing, deaminizing, decarboxylating, etc. **b. forms.** The shapes of bacteria (see figures). **b. membrane.** The cell walls of a bacterium. Cf. *bacteria* membrane. **b. poisons.** See *poison.* **b. precipitation.** (1) Precipitins. (2) Deposition of inorganic salts by the action of bacteria.

| Streptococci | Diplococci | Tetrads | Sarcinae |

Round bacteria—cocci.

Rod-shaped bacteria—bacilli.

Spiral-shaped bacteria—spirillae.

bactericide. An agent that kills bacteria.

bactericidin. A bactericidal antibody of the blood serum.

bacterin. Bacterial vaccine. A sterile suspension of dead pathogenic bacteria in physiological salt solution. Used to produce immunity by stimulating the production of antibodies.

bacteriofluorescin. Fluorescent compounds produced by bacteria.

bacteriological. Pertaining to bacteriology. **b. fermentation tube.** A glass U tube with a closed arm to collect gases formed by bacterial action. **b. filter apparatus.** A filter for bacteria which renders the solution sterile. See *Berkefeld* f. **b. incubator.** A closet at a definite temperature, in which cultures of bacteria are grown.

bacteriology. The study of bacteria.

bacteriolysin. A blood antibody which promotes the disintegration of bacteria.

bacteriolysis. Destruction of bacteria by dissolution.

bacteriophage. Phage. An ultramicroscopic, transmissible, filter-passing, and lytic agent of bacteria. Believed to be a virus composed of genetically active deoxyribonucleic acid in a protein shell; used therapeutically.

bacteriopurpurin. A purple color produced by bacteria.

bacteriostatic. An antibiotic, q.v., which inhibits, as distinct from killing, bacteria.

bacterium. Latin (sing.) for *bacteria*.

baddeckite. A ferric iron muscovite.

baddeleyite. ZrO_2. Brazilite. Zirconium oxide (Ceylon, Brazil).

baden acid. 2,8-Naphthylaminesulfonic acid.

badische acid. 2,8-Naphthylaminesulfonic acid.

Badouin's reagent. See *Baudouin..*

Baekeland, Leo Hendrik. 1863–1944. Belgian-born American chemist; developed Bakelite and photographic processes.

bael. Bengal quince, Indian bel. The fresh unripe fruit of *Aegle marmelos* (Rutaceae); a specific for dysentery.

baeumlerite. $KCl \cdot CaCl_2$. Native calcium-potassium chloride (Germany).

Baeyer, J. F. W. Adolf von. 1835–1917. German pioneer in the organic synthesis of arsenicals, and organic compounds. **B. acid.** *Bayer* acid. **B. strain theory.** A theory that explains the relative stabilities of penta- and hexamethylene ring compounds in terms of the angles between the C atom valencies.

baffle. An obstruction in the path of a gas or fluid.

bagasscocis, bagassosis. A respiratory disease due to the dust from dried bagasse.

bagasse. Sugarcane from which the juice has been extracted; used for paper pulp and fuel.

bagrationite. Allanite.

bahama white wood. Canella.

Bahia arrowroot. Tapioca.

baicalein. $C_{15}H_{10}O_5 = 270.08$. 5,6,7-Trihydroxy-flavone. A flavone from baicalin. Produced when the camphor used in the manufacture of Celluloid was replaced by nitroglycerin (Nobel).

baicalin. A glucoside from the roots of *Scutelaria baicalensis* (Labiatae).

baikalite. $MgO \cdot CaO \cdot 2SiO_2$. Diopside. A native silicate.

baikiain. *l*-1,2,3,6-Tetrahydropyridine-2-carboxylic acid. An amino acid from the heartwood of Rhodesian teak, *Baikiaea plurijuga*. Colorless needles, decomp. 110, soluble in water.

bainite. α-Ferrite, q.v., saturated with carbon; similar to martensite.

Bakelite. Trademark for a synthetic resin obtained by the condensation of formaldehyde with phenols.

Baker, Herbert Brereton. 1862–1935. British chemist and educator who studied the effect of intensive drying on chemical reactions.

bakerite. $8CaO \cdot 5B_2O_3 \cdot 6SiO_2$. Calcium borosilicate from the Mohave Desert.

baking powder. A powder containing sodium bicarbonate, tartaric (or other) acid, and starch filler. A substitute for yeast to produce carbon dioxide in breadmaking. **b. soda.** *Sodium* bicarbonate.

BAL. Common name for dimercaprol (U.S.P., B.P.), British antilewisite, dithioglycerol(2,3-dimercapto-propanol). Used to treat mercury poisoning and arsenical dermatitis. **BAL intrav.** Trade name for dithioglycerol glucoside. Injected intravenously to increase the excretion of copper from man.

balaban. The hydrocarbon of chicle.

balance. (1) A device for weighing. (2) The harmonious adjustment of related parts; as, *nitrogen* balance. **analytical-** A b. of sensitivity 0.1–0.01 mg. **aperiodic-** Damped b. **assay-** An analytical b. for metallurgy. **automatic-** A damped b. with a single pan and built-in counterpoise, which gives an immediate scale reading without the use of weights. **chain-** A b. in which the effects of weights are produced by altering the length of a metal chain hanging from one of the beams. **cloth testing-** A specially constructed torsion b. for weighing textiles. **coin-** A sensitive b. used in mints. **counter-,counterpoise-** A fixed weight, used as a tare or balance for a piece of apparatus or balance pan. **cream test-** A torsion b. for milk testing. **damped-** Aperiodic. A b. in which the equilibrium position is rapidly attained by the damping action of a piston in a cylinder. **gas-** A b. for the specific gravity of gases. **micro-** A highly sensitive b. utilizing the torsion of a quartz fiber, sensitivity 0.001–0.000004 mg. **Mohr-** A b. for specific gravities of solids. **moisture-** A b. whose pan, with the sample to be weighed, hangs in an insulated oven. **projection.-** A b. in which beam movement is magnified optically. **specific gravity-** Westphal b. **spring-** A pan suspended by a vertical wire coil with a scale to indicate the strain. **torsion-** A balance which measures the twisting force to turn a suspension thread or wire through a given angle. **Westphal-** See *Westphal.*

b. pans. Pairs of counterpoised watch glasses or metal dishes for weighing powders. **b. rider.** A small platinum U-shaped wire with hook, which slides along the b. beam. **b. weights.** Standardized weights of brass or aluminum, nickel- or gold-plated.

balanced. In equilibrium. **b. reaction.** A reaction that proceeds in either direction by a variation of temperature, pressure, or concentration of the reactants. Cf. *equilibrium.*

Balard, Antoine Jerôme. 1802–1876. French chemist; discovered bromine (1826) and the nature of bleaching powder.

balas ruby. Spinel. Cf. *ballas.*

balata. (1) The dried juice of *Mimusops globosa* (Spotaceae) of W. Indies. A substitute for gutta-percha. Cf. *chicle.* (2) The hard, dense heartwood of the bully tree, *Bumelia retusa* (Sapotaceae).

baleen. *Whalebone.*

balkhas(h)ite. A fossil hydrocarbon wax (Lake Balkhash, Central Asia). It resembles torbanite.

ballas. A mineral intermediate between carbon and diamond with a radial crystalline structure. Cf. *balas.*

ball clay. A white, high-plasticity burning clay originally mined in balls. **b. mill.** A spherical container with balls of iron or quartz for fine grinding. Cf. *pebble* mill.

Balling, Carl Joseph Napoleon. German fermentation chemist. **B. degree.** A specific gravity scale for liquids. (1) $x°$ Balling = specific gravity (17.5° C) $= 200/(200 \pm x)$; $x = +$ or $-$ according as the liquid is heavier or lighter than water, respectively. (2) Brix degree. See *hydrometers.*

ballistic galvanometer. A device to indicate small or intermittent electric currents, based on the accumulation of static electricity, which is suddenly released from a capacitor to deflect a needle.

balloelectric. Pertaining to the electric charge of atomized liquids.

ballometer. An instrument to measure the balloelectric charges by means of a metal plate connected to a quadrant electrometer.

ballotini. Very small glass beads; a heating medium in fluid-bed drying.

balm. (1) Melissa, (2) Balsam. **bee-** Monarda. **Indian-** Trillium.

b. of Gilead (Mecca). (1) Poplar buds. (2) The exudation of *Commiphera (Balsamodendron) opobalsamum* (Burseraceae.) **b. oil.** Melissa oil, lemon. Yellow essential oil, d. 0.90, from the leaves and flowering tops of *Melissa officinalis;* a flavoring.

Balmer formula. The wavelength λ of the lines in the hydrogen spectrum $= 3616.14 \, m^2/(m^2 - 4)$, where m is an integer from 3 to 16. **B. series.** A series of related lines in the hydrogen spectrum deduced from the quantum theory, and corresponding with an orbital electron transition. Cf. *energy* levels, *Lyman* series, *Paschen* series, *quantum* number.

balneology. The study of therapy of natural waters.

balsam. A plant exudate mixture of resins, essential oils, cinnamic and benzoic acid. **b. apple.** The fruit of *Momordica balsamina* (Cucurbitaceae). **b. of Peru.** *Peru* b. **b. tree.** Mastic.

baltimoriase. Calcium, aluminum, and magnesium silicate (Baltimore County).

Baly, Edward Charles Cyril. 1871–1948. British physicist. **B. spectrum tube.** A graduated tube in which slides another tube. The intermediate adjustable space is filled with the solution whose absorption spectrum is to be examined.

bamboo. (1) A tropical genus of treelike grasses, with woody, light cylindrical stems, growing in clumps. (2) The hollow, siliceous, coated stems of bamboo species, used as a building material, for fishing rods and paper pulp. Cf. *tabashis.* **sacred-** *Nandina domestica* (Japan); it yields domesticine and nandinine.

b. oil. Vinifera palm oil from the fruit of *Gentiliana raphia;* used to soften leather.

banalsite. $BaNa_2Al_4Si_4O_{16}.$ A barium feldspar (Wales).

banana. The fruit of *Musa sapientum.* Cf. *plantain, pisang* wax. **b. oil.** An alcoholic solution of amyl acetate.

bancoul nuts. The seeds of *Aleurites ambina,* source of an oil resembling castor oil. Cf. *tung* oil.

Bancroft, Wilder Dwight. 1867–1953. American colloid chemist.

band. A compact series of spectral lines due to molecules. **b. head.** The wavelength of the sharpest edge of a spectral b. **b. spectrum.** See *spectrum.*

bandoline. A hair gloss from tragacanth and quince seeds.

bandose. A quartz-mica-hornblende diorite (Cecil County).

Bandrowski's base. $(NH_2)_2C_6H_3 \cdot N \cdot C_6H_4 \cdot N \cdot C_6H_3 \cdot (NH_2)_2 = 290.1.$ Bisdiaminophenyl-*p*-phenylene-diamine. Used in organic synthesis.

bane. A pest or poison; e.g., dogbane.

Bang method. The determination of glucose in urine by titration with alkaline cupric thiocyanate solution.

banisterine. $C_{13}H_{12}ON_2 = 212.1.$ An alkaloid, m.257 from *Banisteria* species (Malpighiaceae) of America. It stimulates respiration.

Banting, Sir Frederick. 1891–1941. Canadian biochemist, associated with the discovery of insulin.

baobab. See *Adansonia.*

baphiin. $C_{12}H_{10}O_4 = 218.08.$ Colorless crystals, decomp. by heat.

baptisia. Wild indigo. The dried roots of *Baptisia tinctoria* (Leguminosae); an astringent.

baptisin. $C_{26}H_{32}O_{14} = 540.3.$ A glucoside, m.240, from the roots of *Baptisia tinctoria;* a purgative. Cf. *rhamnomannoside.*

baptisoid. The total active principles of baptisia; a cathartic.

baptitoxine. (1) An alkaloid from the root of *Baptisia tinctoria.* (2) Cytisine.

bar. (1) The international unit of pressure. See *atmosphere.* Cf. *barye.* 1 bar $= 10^6$ dynes/cm$^2 = 1.013$ kg/cm$^2 = 0.987$ atm. (2) Hectopieze.

baras-camphor. Bornel.

barbados nuts. Purging nuts. The poisonous seeds of *Jatropha curcas* (Euphorbiaceae) of W. Indies, Brazil. See *curcin.*

barbaloin. $C_{16}H_{18}O_7 = 322.1.$ A constituent of Barbados aloes, m.148.

barban. Common name for 4-chlorobut-2-ynyl N-(3-chlorophenyl)carbamate; a pesticide.

barbatic acid. $C_{19}H_{20}O_7 = 360.14.$ A depside from *Usnea* lichens. Colorless prisms, m.186.

barberry. The fruit of *Berberis vulgaris* used in pickles. See *berberis, berberine, oxyacanthine.*

barbierite. A soda orthoclase (Norway).

barbital. Barbitone.

barbitone. $C_8H_{12}O_3N_2 = 184.1.$ Diethylbarbituric acid, 2,4,6-trioxy-5-diethyl-pryimidine, veronal, malonurea, diethyl malonyl urea, barbital. **sodium-** $C_8H_{11}O_3N_2Na = 206.20.$ Calmine. White, bitter powder, m.190, soluble in water; a hypnotic.

barbituric acid. $C_4H_4O_3N_2 = 128.09.$ Malonyl urea, 2,4,6-trioxypyrimidine, pyrimidinetrione. Colorless rhombs, m.245, decomp. 260, slightly soluble in water. Cf. *hydantoin, uramil.* There are numerous derivatives. Cf. *Allonal, barbitone, Dial, embutal.*

barcenite. A native mercury antimonite.

Bardach reaction. Acetone and iodopotassium iodide form yellow needles, (instead of hexagonal iodoform crystals) in presence of proteins.

bardana. Lappa.

bardane oil. A semisolid oil from the seeds of burdock, *Arctium lappa.*

Barff boroglycerin. A saturated solution of boric acid in glycerin; a preservative for specimens.

Barfoed, Christian Theodor. 1816–1889. Danish analyst. **B. solution.** A solution of 13.3 gm cupric acetate in 200 ml dist. water and 5 ml 38% acetic acid. **B. test.** A test for dextrose (in presence of maltose), which is reduced by B. solution.

baric. Barium (obsolete).

barilla. The fused ash of seaweeds which consists of sodium carbonate and sulfate; formerly used to make soap, glass. etc. Cf. *kelp* ash. **b. de cobre.** Nodules of native copper in ores.

barite. $BaSO_4$. Barytes, cawk, heavy spar. A native crystalline barium sulfate; white crystals, sometimes colored. Used in pigments, lithopones, and paper fillers.

barium. $Ba = 137.34$. An element of the calcium family, at. no. 56. Baryum plutonium. A white soft metal, d.3.46, m.850, soluble in water. Widely distributed in feldspars and micas, and as sulfate and carbonate; but never native. B. is divalent and forms one series of compounds; soluble compounds are poisonous. Discovered by Scheele (1774) in barytes, and isolated by Davy (1808). **b. acetate.** $Ba(C_2H_3O_2)_2 \cdot H_2O = 273.4$. White prisms, decomp. by heat, soluble in water. A reagent for sulfates or chromates. **b. aluminate.** White powder, a water softener. **b. amylsulfate.** $Ba(C_5H_{11}SO_4)_2 \cdot 2H_2O = 507.5$. Colorless crystals, soluble in water. **b. arsenate.** $Ba_3(AsO_4)_2 = 690.1$. Black powder; insoluble in water. *acid-*$BaHAsO_4 \cdot H_2O = 295.35$. B. biarsenate. Opaque crystals, anhydrous at 150. **b. benzoate.** $Ba(C_7H_5O_2)_2 \cdot 2H_2O = 415.4$. Colorless leaflets, soluble in water. **b. benzosulfonate.** $Ba(C_6H_5SO_3)_2 \cdot H_2O = 487.1$. Colorless crystals soluble in water. **b. biarsenate.** B. arsenate (acid). **b. bichromate.** $BaCr_2O_7 = 353.57$. Red prisms, soluble in water. *crystalline-* $BaCr_2O_7 \cdot 2H_2O = 389.58$. Orange needles. **b. binoxalate.** B. bioxalate. **b. binoxide.** B. peroxide. **b. bioxalate** $Ba(HC_2O_4)_2 \cdot 2H_2O = 351.4$. B. dioxalate, acid b. oxalate. Colorless crystals, soluble in water. **b. bioxide.** B. peroxide. **b. bisulfate.** B. sulfate (acid). **b. borate.** $BaB_2O_4 \cdot 7H_2O = 349.5$. White powder, soluble in water. **b. boride.** $BaB_6 = 203.37$. Black, regular crystals, insoluble in water. **b. borotungstate.** $2BaO \cdot B_2O_3 \cdot 9WO_3 \cdot 18H_2O = 2788.74$. B. borowolframate, colorless crystals, soluble in water. **b. bromate.** $Ba(BrO_3)_7(H_2O) = 411.2$. Monoclinic crystals, decomp. 260; slightly soluble in water. **b. bromide.** $BaBr_2 = 297.21$. Colorless crystals, m.880; soluble in water. *crystalline-* $BaBr_2 \cdot 2H_2O = 333.24$. White, monoclinic crystals, m.880; soluble in water. **b. butyrate.** $Ba(C_4H_7O_2)_2 \cdot 2H_2O = 347.55$. Colorless powder, soluble in water. **b. carbide.** $BaC_2 = 161.38$. Gray crystals, decomp. by water, yielding acetylene. **b. carbonate.** $BaCO_3 = 197.4$. Color-

less rhombs, m.795, decomp. 1450, insoluble in water; occurs native as witherite. Used as a reagent, rat poison, in water purification, sugar refining, case hardening, manufacture of glass, enamel ware, and ceramics. **b. chlorate.** $Ba(ClO_3)_2 \cdot H_2O = 322.3$. White monoclinic crystals, m.414; soluble in water. Used as a reagent, and in pyrotechnics for green fires. **b. chloride.** $BaCl_2 \cdot 2H_2O = 244.32$. White rhombs, m.960; soluble in water; a reagent for sulfuric acid. Used in veterinary medicine, as a rat poison, and for water purification. **b. chloroplatinate.** $BaPtCl_6 \cdot 4H_2O = 617.4$. Platinic b. chloride. Red monoclinic crystals, soluble in water. **b. chloroplatinite.** $BaPtCl_4 \cdot 3H_2O = 528.46$. Platinous b. chloride. Orange rhombs, sparingly soluble in water. **b. chromate.** $BaCrO_4 = 253.5$. Yellow ultramarine, lemon yellow. Yellow scales, d.4.498; insoluble in water. Used as a pigment and in safety matches. **b. citrate.** $Ba_3(C_6H_5O_7)_2 \cdot 7H_2O = 918.23$. Colorless powder, soluble in water. **b. cyanate.** $Ba(CNO)_2 = 221.40$. Colorless crystals, sparingly soluble in water. **b. cyanide.** $Ba(CN)_2 = 189.40$. Colorless crystals, soluble in water, used in metallurgy. **b. cyanoplatinite.** $BaPt(CN)_4 \cdot 4H_2O = 508.69$. B. platinocyanide. Yellow crystals with bluish fluorescence, soluble in water; used in X-ray screens. **b. dichromate.** B. bichromate. **b. dioxalate.** B. bioxalate. **b. dioxide.** B. peroxide. **b. diphenylamine sulfonate.** An oxidation-reduction indicator. **b. diphosphate.** See *b. phosphates.* **b. dithionate.** $BaS_2O_6 \cdot 2H_2O = 333.52$. B. hyposulfate. White rhombs, d.5.6, soluble in water. **b. ethylsulfate.** $Ba(C_2H_5SO_4)_2 \cdot 2H_2O = 423.5$. Colorless crystals, soluble in water; used in organic synthesis. **b. feldspar.** Celsian. **b. ferrate.** $BaFeO_4 = 257.4$. Purple powder, insoluble in water. **b. ferrocyanide.** $Ba_2Fe(CN)_6 \cdot 6H_2O = 594.77$. Yellow prisms; soluble in water. **b. fluobromide.** $BaBr_2 \cdot BaF_2 = 472.58$. White plates, decomp. by water. **b. fluochloride.** $BaCl_2 \cdot BaF_2 = 383.66$. White plates, decomp. by water. **b. fluoiodide.** $BaI_2 \cdot BaF_2 = 566.68$. Colorless plates, d.5.21 decomp. by water. **b. fluoride.** $BaF_2 = 175.4$. White powder, m.1280, insoluble in water; used for embalming and in enamels. **b. fluosilicate.** $BaSiF_6 = 279.67$. White powder, insoluble in water; an insecticide. **b. formate.** $Ba(HCOO)_2 = 227.4$. B. formiate. Colorless crystals, soluble in water. **b. hexanitride.** $BaN_6 \cdot H_2O = 239.45$. White crystals, explode when heated; soluble in water. **b. hydrate.** B. hydroxide. **b. hydride.** $BaH_2 = 139.39$. White crystals, m.1200, decomp. by water. **b. hydrogen phosphate.** B. phosphate (acid). **b. hydrogen sulfide.** B. sulfhydrate. **b. hydroxide.** $Ba(OH)_2 \cdot 8H_2O = 315.5$. Caustic baryta, hydrated b. Colorless tetragons, m.78, soluble in water. Used for fusing silicates, saponifying fats, refining oils, and in sugar manufacture. **b. hypophosphate.** $Ba_2P_2O_6 = 432.82$. White needles, soluble in water. **b. hypophosphite.** $Ba(H_2PO_2)_2 \cdot H_2O = 285.50$. Colorless crystals, soluble in water, decomp. by heat. **b. hyposulfate.** B. dithionate. **b. hyposulfite.** B. thiosulfate. **b. iodate.** $Ba(IO_3)_2 \cdot H_2O = 505.2$. White crystals, decomp. by heat, sparingly soluble in hot water or alcohol. **b. iodide.** $BaI_2 \cdot 2H_2O = 427.24$. Heavy rhombs, m.740, soluble in water; an alterant. **b. lactate.** $Ba(C_3H_5O_3)_2 = 315.5$.

Colorless crystals, soluble in water. **b. malate.** $BaC_4H_4O_5 = 269.42$. White powder; slightly soluble in water. **b. malonate.** $BaC_3H_2O_4 \cdot H_2O = 257.42$. White powder; slightly soluble in water. **b. manganate.** $BaMnO_4 = 256.4$. Mangan green, Casseler green, Rosenstiel green. A green nontoxic pigment. **b. mercuryiodide.** See *Rohrbach's* solution. **b. metasilicate.** B. silicate. **b. metatungstate.** $BaW_4O_{13} \cdot 9H_2O = 1243.5$. White tetragons, soluble in water. **b. methylsulfate.** $Ba(CH_3SO_4)_2 \cdot 2H_2O = 401.5$. Colorless crystals, soluble in water. **b. molybdate.** $BaMoO_4 = 297.4$. White powder, insoluble in water. **b. monophosphate.** See *b. phosphate*. **b. monosulfide.** B. sulfide. **b. monoxide.** B. oxide. **b. nitrate.** $Ba(NO_3)_2 = 261.4$. White crystals, m.575, (decomp.), soluble in water. Occurs native as nitrobarite. Used as a reagent and precipitant, for standardizing soap solutions and in pyrotechnics for green lights. **b. nitrite.** $Ba(NO_2)_2 \cdot H_2O = 247.4$. Colorless hexagons, decomp. 115, soluble in water. **b. oleate.** $Ba(C_{18}H_{33}O_2)_2 = 700.1$. White granules, insoluble in water. **b. oxalate.** $Ba(C_2O_4) \cdot H_2O = 243.4$. White powder, insoluble in water. **b. oxide.** $BaO = 153.4$. Baryta, b. monoxide, b. protoxide. White powder or crystals, m.1923, soluble in water. Used in the glass industry, and to manufacture b. salts. **b. perchlorate.** (1) *anhydrous-* $Ba(ClO_4)_2$. Desicchlora. (2) *tetrahydrate,* $Ba(ClO_4)_2 \cdot 4H_2O = 408.35$. Colorless hexagons, m.505; soluble in water; used in pyrotechnics. **b. periodate.** $Ba_5(IO_6)_2 = 1137.6$. White powder, insoluble in water. **b. permanganate.** $Ba(MnO_4)_2 = 375.3$. Violet crystals, soluble in water; used to manufacture permanganates. **b. peroxide.** $BaO_2 = 169.4$. B. dioxide, b. superoxide, b. binoxide. White powder, insoluble in water, decomp. acids produce hydrogen peroxide. Formerly used to prepare oxygen (Brin's method), as a bleach, as reagent for iodine and indican in urine, and in the glass industry. $BaO_2 \cdot 8H_2O = 313.45$. Colorless crystals; insoluble in water. **b. persulfate.** $Ba(SO_4)_2 \cdot 4H_2O = 401.55$. White crystals, decomp. by water. **b. phosphate.** *di-*$BaHPO_4 = 233.4$. Acid b. phosphate. Colorless rhombs, insoluble in water. *mono-* $BaH_4(PO_4)_2 = 331.5$. Colorless triclinic crystals, decomp. by water. *pyro-* $Ba_2P_2O_7 = 448.8$. White rhombs, insoluble in water. *tri-* $Ba_3(PO_4)_2 = 602.2$. Colorless crystals, insoluble in water. **b. phosphide.** $BaP_2 = 199.4$. Gray masses, decomp. by water to PH_3. **b. phosphite.** $BaHPO_3 \cdot 1\frac{1}{2}H_2O = 244.4$. Colorless powder, soluble in hot water. **b. platinic chloride.** B. chloroplatinate. **b. platinic rhodanate.** $BaPt(CNS)_6 = 680.8$. Platinic b. thiocyanate. Red needles, soluble in water. **b. platinocyanide.** B. cyanoplatinite. **b. platinous chloride.** B. chloroplatinite. **b. platinous cyanide.** B. cyanoplatinite. **b. potassium chlorate.** $BaK(ClO_3)_3 = 426.8$. Colorless crystals, soluble in water; used in pyrotechnics. **b. propionate.** $Ba(C_3H_5O_2)_2 \cdot H_2O = 301.50$. Colorless powder, soluble in water. **b. protoxide.** B. oxide. **b. pyrophosphate.** See *b. phosphate*. **b. rhodanate, b. rhodanide.** B. thiocyanate. **b. salicylate.** $Ba(C_7H_5O_3)_2 \cdot H_2O = 429.6$. Colorless needles, soluble in water. **b. selenate.** $BaSeO_4 = 280.57$. White amorphous powder, insoluble in water. **b. selenite.** $BaSeO_3 = 264.57$.

White powder, used in the glass industry. **b. silicate.** $BaSiO_3 = 213.67$. B. metasilicate. Colorless rhombs, m.1470, soluble in water. **b. silifluoride.** $BaSiF_3 = 279.5$. White powder, soluble in water. **b. stearate.** $Ba(C_{18}H_{35}O_2) = 704.12$. White unctuous mass; packing for pump bearings for alkalies. **b. succinate.** $BaC_4H_4O_4 = 253.5$. Colorless crystals, soluble in water. **b. sulfate.** $BaSO_4 = 233.4$. Synthetic blanc fixe. Rhombic crystals, decomp. 1580, insoluble in water. A reagent for colloidal metals. Used in X-ray meals and (as "blanc fixe") in white pigments and printing inks. Cf. *lithopone. acid-* $Ba(HSO_4)_2 = 331.51$. B. bisulfate. White powder. **b. sulfhydrate.** $Ba(SH)_2 = 203.51$. B. hydrosulfide. Yellow powder, soluble in water; decomp. 250. **b. sulfide.** *mono-* $BaS = 169.4$. Colorless rhombs, or yellow, phosphorescent powder, decomp. by heat. Used as a depilatory and alterant, for the preparation of arsenic-free hydrogen sulfide gas and in making luminous paint. Cf. *Bologna* phosphorus. *tri-* $BaS_3 = 233.55$. Yellow crystals; soluble in water. *tetra-* $BaS_4 = 265.61$. Red rhombs, soluble in water. **b. sulfite.** $BaSO_3 = 217.43$. White powder, insoluble in water. **b. sulfocyanate, b. sulfocyanide.** B. thiocyanate. **b. sulfophenylate.** $Ba(C_6H_5SO_4)_2 = 483.1$. B. phenylsulfate. White crystals, soluble in water; an antiseptic. **b. sulfovinate.** B. ethylsulfate. **b. tannate.** Yellow powder, soluble in water. **b. tartrate.** $BaC_4H_4O_6 \cdot H_2O = 303.41$. White powder, very slightly soluble in water. **b. tetrasulfide.** B. sulfide. **b. thiocyanate.** $Ba(CNS)_2 \cdot 2H_2O = 289.55$. B. sulfocyanide. Colorless crystals, soluble in water; used in photography and dyeing. **b. thiosulfate.** $BaS_2O_3 \cdot H_2O = 267.51$. White powder, soluble in water. **b. titanate.** $BaTiO_3 = 233.5$. White powder; a pigment. **b. triphosphate.** See *b. phosphate*. **b. trisulfide.** See *b. sulfide*. **b. trithionate.** $BaS_2O_6 \cdot 2H_2O = 365.6$. Colorless scales, soluble in water. **b. tungstate.** $BaWO_4 = 385.4$. Tungsten white. White powder, insoluble in water; a pigment. **b. value.** The equivalent of the saponification value of an oil or fat (as BaO). **b. white.** B. sulfate. **b. wolframate.** B. tungstate.

bark. Any portion of a stem or root of a tree outside the cambium circle. Many are used medicinally.

Barker Index. An identification system for crystal forms.

barkevite. Berkevilite. A black amphibole.

Barkhausen effect. The magnetization of a ferromagnetic material changes discontinuously with the magnetic field strength.

barkometer. A Baumé hydrometer for tanning liquids.

barley. The seeds of *Hordeum distichum*. **hulled-** B. grain deprived of husk. **Indian-** Sabadilla. **pearl-** The polished and rounded b. seed rich in starch but not protein.

    b. gum. Mainly pentosans, isolated from barley.

barm. A suspension of yeast in a fermenting liquid.

barn. (1) b. SI unit of area. (2) Unit of cross section in radioactivity studies: 10^{-24} cm²/nucleus.

barograph. A self-registering barometer.

baroluminescence. Luminescence induced by high pressures.

barometer. An instrument to indicate atmospheric pressure. **alcohol-** A b. using colored alcohol. **aneroid-** A b. whose action depends on the changes in shape of an evacuated metal box, magnified by levers. **Fortin-** A mercury b. in which the base of the scale is the point of an ivory pin adjusted so as just to touch the mercury surface of the reservoir. **glycerin-** A b. using colored glycerin. **mercury-** A b. using mercury.

b. tube. A narrow tube closed at one end and more than 32 in. (760 mm) long.

barometograph. A photographic record of baroscope pressure changes.

barophoresis. Interaction. Diffusion at a speed dependent on extraneous forces; e.g., gravity.

baroscope. A U tube with a liquid to show pressure changes.

Barosma. A genus of South Africa evergreen plants (Rutaceae). **B. betulina.** The source of *buchu*.

barosmin. (1) A concentration from *Barosma betulina* or *B. crenulata;* a diuretic. (2) $C_{27}H_{32}O_{16} = 612.2$. Rutin, rutoside, eldrin. A rhamnoglucoside from buchu, m.183. Cf. *sophorin*.

barosmoid. The total principles from the leaves of *Barosma betulina;* a diuretic and stimulant.

barotaxis. An apparent correlation between the barometric pressure and the activity of an organism.

barotropism. The reaction of living cells to changes in pressure.

barra. Burra gokero.

barrandite. A native iron phosphate.

barrel. bbl. (1) A unit of weight or volume whose magnitude varies (in gallons for liquids, pounds for solids);

Wine	31
Ale	36
Petroleum	42
Rosin	180
Flour	196
Butter	224
Pork, beef	200
Cement	376

(2) A cylinder-shaped wood or sheet-metal container.

barreter lamp. A device to smooth out fluctuating voltages.

barrier. A packaging material (e.g., paper, film) which acts as a b. to a specific agent (e.g., water vapor).

barringtonin. $C_{18}H_{28}O_{10} = 404.2$. A colorless amorphous glucoside from *Barringtonia speciosa* (Myrtaceae); a cardiac poison.

baru. The seeds of *Hibiscus tiliaceus* (Malvaceae), a Malayan musk seed substitute.

barutin. A compound of theobromine and barium sodium salicylate.

barye. The cgs unit of pressure; 1 barye = 1 dyne/cm^2 = 1.019 mg/cm^2. Also a measure of noise. Cf. *bar*, *decibel*.

barylite. $2BaO \cdot SiO_2$. Native barium silicate (Franklin, N.J.).

baryon. A fundamental particle of mass equal to or greater than that of a nucleon.

barysilite. $Pb_3Si_2O_7$. Native lead silicate; white hexagons.

baryta. Barium oxide. **calcined-** Barium oxide. **caustic-** Barium hydroxide. **hydrated-** Barium hydroxide.

b. mixture. A mixture of saturated $Ba(NO_3)_2$ and $Ba(OH)_2$ (1:2) used in urine analysis. **b. water.** A saturated solution of barium hydroxide; an absorbent for carbon dioxide.

baryto- Prefix indicating barium in a mineral. **b. calcite.** Alstonite.

baryum. Barium

basalt. Igneous rock composed of particles of feldspar, augite, and iron. Cf. *diabase*.

basaluminite. $2Al_2O_3 \cdot SO_3 \cdot 10H_2O$. A white mineral coating on joint faces in quarries in Northamptonshire (U.K.).

basanite. Jasper used in the streak test for gold. Cf. *touchstone*.

base. (1) A compound which yields hydroxyl ions in aqueous solution; and which reacts with an acid to form water and a salt. (2) More generally, it includes solvents other than water. Cf. *ammono-*, *hydrocarbo-*. (3) A substance whose molecules can take up protons. **ammono-** A metallic amine that yields NH_2^- ions in liquid ammonia. **aquo-** A compound that yields OH^- ions in water. **hydrocarbo-** A metallic aryl- or alkyl compound which dissociates in hydrocarbons. **inorganic-** The hydroxide of a metal. **leuco-** Leucobase. **nitrogenous-** An amine, characterized by the ending *-ine*. Cf. *diamine*. **organic-** A carbon compound containing trivalent nitrogen. **primary-, secondary-, tertiary-** See *amines*.

b. exchange. The replacement of one cation adsorbed on a colloidal particle (e.g. soil) by another. **b. goods.** A mixture of fertilizers, usually superphosphates and nitrogen. **b. metal.** (1) A metal whose hydroxide is soluble in water. (2) A metal which oxidizes rapidly. Cf. *noble* metal. **b. unit.** The smallest possible repeating unit of a polymer. Cf. *mer*.

basic. Having properties of a base. **di-** A base having *two;* **mono-** *one;* **tetra-** *four;* **tri-** *three* replaceable H atoms.

b. anhydride. The oxide of a metal. **b. capacity.** Basicity. The H atoms in an acid that can be replaced by a monovalent metal. **b. dyes.** Salts of colorless bases and an acid. In dyeing, the free base combines with the acid constituent of an animal fiber or the acid constituent of the mordant of a vegetable fiber, thereby fixing the color. **b. hearth.** See *Thomas* process. **b. lime phosphate.** A superphosphate neutralized with 6% excess of calcium carbonate. **b. nitrogen.** The nitrogen of a protein (basic amino acids and cystine) precipitable by phosphotungstic acid. **b. phosphate slag.** B. slag. **b. principle.** An alkaloid. **b. rocks.** Igneous rocks consisting of free basic oxides; e.g., corundum. **b. salt.** A compound of a base and acid in which not all the hydroxide of the base has been replaced by an acid radical; e.g., $Bi(OH)_2Cl$. **b. slag.** Thomas slag (phosphate). A finely ground by-product of steel manufacture: P_2O_5 12–25, CaO 40–50, SiO_2 5–15%, (80% of the phosphoric acid soluble in 2% citric acid).

basicity. (1) Basic capacity. (2) The reciprocal of acidity: (*a*) hydroxyl-ion concentration (effective alkalinity); (*b*) normality (free alkalinity). Cf. *acidity.*

basil. (1) Sweet basil. The plant *Ocimum basilicum* (Labiatae); a flavoring. (2) A tanned sheepskin. **b. oil.** The essential oil from the leaves of *Ocimum basilicum.* Yellow, aromatic liquid, d.0.945–0.987, soluble in alcohol. Chief constituents cineol, chavicol, linalool; a flavoring.

Basil Valentine. A 15th-century monk of Erfurt (Germany) and alchemist who described antimony salts; the nitrates of bismuth, tin, mercury; the preparation of hydrochloric acid and sugar of lead; and the manufacture of sulfuric acid and ammonia.

basophil. Stainable by basic dyestuffs.

bass. Bast. **b. wood.** Linden.

bassic acid. $C_{30}H_{46}O_5 = 486.41.$ A trihydroxytriterpene acid.

bassisterol. $C_{27}H_{46}O = 383.3.$ An unsaponifiable alcohol in illipé *butter.*

bassora gum. A mixture of colored tragacanth gums (India), partly soluble in water.

bassorin. $C_6H_{10}O_5 = 262.1.$ Tragacanthose. A carbohydrate from tragacanth gum. Colorless powder, producing a stiff gel and viscous paste with water.

bast. Bass. The fibrous inner part of Russian *Calotropis gigantea* (Asclepiadaceae); used for ropes, mats, shoes. **b. fiber.** See *fiber.*

bastite. An altered pyroxene, resembling serpentine.

bastnasite. $[(Ce·La·Di)F]CO_3.$ Hamartite. A rare-earth carbonate.

bastose. Jute cellulose (obsolete).

basylous. Basic (obsolete).

Bates polariscope. A sugar polariscope.

bat guano. Bodies and droppings of bats; a fertilizer.

bath. A vessel or device for keeping objects at a desired temperature. **air-** A b. containing air of definite temperature. **metal-** A b. of molten metal. **oil-, paraffin-** A b. of molten paraffin. **sand-** A shallow metal dish filled with sand. **steam-** A device heated by steam. **water-** A metallic container for keeping water at a desired temperature. Cf. *thermostat.*

bathochrome. An organic radical which displaces the absorption spectrum of an organic molecule toward the red. Cf. *auxochrome.*

bathochromic. Describing a change in color to a shorter wavelength.

bathocuproine. $C_{26}H_{20}N_2 = 360.36.$ 2,9-Dimethyl-4,7-diphenyl-1,10-phenanthroline. A reagent for copper (purple color extractable in amyl alcohol).

batholite. A fused granite having permeated sedimentary layers.

bathophenanthroline. 4,7-Diphenyl-1,10-phenanthroline, Snyder's reagent. A reagent for copper (cf. *bathocuproine*) and ferrous iron (red color).

batik. An ancient Oriental method of printing calico, using a wax resist.

bating. Puering.

batrachiolin. A vitellin from frogs' eggs.

batracin. A S. American arrow poison from the skin of an amphibian, *Phyllobates chocoensis.*

Battersea. A brand of fire-resisting ware.

battery. Electrical cells, dynamos, or couples connected to function as a single supply. **storage-** Accumulator.

batyl alcohol. $C_{18}H_{37}O{-}C_3H_5(OH)_2 = 344.3.$ A

glyceryl ether from shark liver oils. Lustrous crystals, m.69. Cf. *chimyl* and *selachyl* alcohols.

Baudouin test. Cane sugar and boiling hydrochloric acid give a red color with sesame oil.

Baumann, Eugen. 1846–1896. German chemist. **B.- Schotten reaction.** Alcohols and acid chlorides in alkaline solution give an ester.

Baumé, Antoine. 1728–1804. French pharmacist. **B. hydrometer.** See *hydrometers.*

bausteine. German for building stone. The amino acids of proteins, the "building stones" of protoplasm. Cf. *polypeptides.*

bauxite. $Al_2O(OH)_4.$ Beauxite. Native aluminum hydroxide. A gray-red claylike mineral which often contains iron; used to manufacture alum, aluminum, and firebricks. World production (1964) 36 million tons. Cf. *boehmite.* **red-** A b. from Var, France (40–45% alumina).

bay. The sweet bay or laurel tree; *Laurus nobilis* (Lauraceae). **Indian-** *L. indica.* **red-** *Persea carolinesis.* Cf. *bayberry.*
    b. leaves oil. The essential oil distilled from bay leaves, *L. nobilis.* **b. oil.** Myrcia oil. An essential oil from *Pimenta acris.* Yellow liquid, d.0.980. Chief constituents: chavicol, eugenol, myrcene. **b. rum.** See *bay rum.* **b. salt.** Crude sodium chloride from the evaporation of seawater. **b. wood.** Honduras (Campeche Bay) mahogany.

bayberry. (1) The fruit of *Laurus nobilis,* European laurel, sweet bay. (2) The fruit of *Myrica cerifera,* wax myrtle. (3) The fruit of *Pimenta acris,* allspice or pimenta. **b. bark.** Myrica, candleberry, waxberry. The dried bark of the root of *Myrica cerifera* (Myricacea); a digestive. **b. wax.** Myrtle wax, laurel wax, bayberry tallow. A fat mixture, chiefly palmitin, from myrica fruits.

baycurine. An alkaloid from the roots of *Statice braziliensis* (baycuru root) (Plumbaginaceae) of Brazil.

baycuru root. The roots of *Statice braziliensis* (Plumbaginaceae). A powerful astringent.

Bayer acid. (1) *2,8-* or 2,7-Naphthylaminesulfonic acid. (2) *β-*Naphtholsulfonic acid. **B. 205.** Germanin.

bayerite. $Al(OH)_3.$ A native aluminum hydroxide similar to boehmite.

bayldonite. Native lead vanadate.

bay rum. Bay-rum, spiritus myrciae. An aromatic liquid containing bay oil 8, orange oil 0.5, pimenta oil 0.5, alcohol 610, water 320 ml/liter. A refreshing ablution cosmetic.

BBC. Brombenzyl cyanide.

bbl. Abbreviation for barrel(s).

B.C.G. See *Bacillus* Calmette.

bdella. Hirudo.

bdellium. An aromatic gum resin from *Balsamodendron africanum.* Cf. *Burseraceae.*

Be. Symbol for beryllium.

Bé. Abbreviation for Baumé.

beaded. Describing a disjointed line of bacteria along the line of inoculation.

beading. The formation of bead-shaped drops by solvent vapor.

beading oil. A mixture of sweet almond oil and ammonium sulfate, used to produce artificial beading.

bead test. A crystal of microcosmic salt or borax is melted to a bead in the loop of a platinum wire, dipped in the substance to be analyzed, and held in the oxidizing (O.F.) or reducing (R.F.) part of the bunsen or blowpipe flame. The color of the clear flux indicates the metals shown in the table.

Metal	Microcosmic salt		Borax	
	O.F.	R.F.	O.F.	R.F.
Cr	Green	Green	Green	Green
Co	Blue	Blue	Blue	Blue
Cu	Blue	Red	Greenish-blue	Red
Fe	Brown	Colorless	Yellow	Green
Mn	Violet	Colorless	Violet	Colorless
Mo	Colorless	Green	Colorless	Brown
Ni	Yellow	Yellow	Brown	Gray
Ti	Colorless	Violet	Colorless	Yellow
W	Colorless	Blue	Colorless	Brown
U	Green	Green	Red	Green
V	Yellow	Green	Colorless	Green

beaker. A quartz, porcelain, aluminum. or copper vessel used to hold liquids. **b. flask.** A wide-lipped conical beaker or flask.

Beale's stain. An aqueous carmine solution containing alcohol, ammonia, and glycerin, for staining tissue.

beans. Seeds (usually of Leguminosae plants) of the bean family. **bog-, buck-** Menyanthes. **broad-, common-** Seeds of *Vicia* (*Faba*) *vulgaris*. **calabar-** Physostigma. **castor-** See *castor*. **French-, kidney-, navy-** Seeds of *Phaseolus vulgaris*. **lima-** Seeds of *Phaseolus lunatus*. **ordeal-** Physostigma. **soja- ,soya-** See *soy*. **St. Ignatius-** Strychnos. **vanilla-** See *vanilla*.

bearberry. Uva ursi. **b. bark.** Cascara sagrada.

bearing. The stationary support of an axle or rotating shaft. **b. metal solution.** A solution containing conc. HCl 400, conc. HNO_3 200 ml, KCl 40 gm, water 1 liter.

bearsfoot. The root of *Polymnia uvedalia* (Compositae), N. America; an alterative. **English-** The plant *Helleborus foetidus* (Ranunculaceae).

bearsweed. Eriodictyon.

bearswood. Cascara sagrada.

beater. An oval-shaped vessel used in papermaking, having a roll with blunt knives which circulates, cuts, fibrillates, and hydrates the pulp.

Beaudouin's reagent. See *Baudouin*.

Beaumé. See *Baumé*.

beauxite. Bauxite.

beaverite. A highly hydrated lead sulfate (Utah).

bebeerine. $C_{18}H_{21}O_3N = 299.30$. Bauxine, bebirine, cissampeline, pelosine. An alkaloid from bebeeru, the bark of Guiana *Nectandra rodiaei* (Lauraceae). White powder, m.214, soluble in alcohol. An antipyretic. **b. hydrochloride.** $C_{18}H_{21}O_3N \cdot HCl = 335.76$. Red scales, m.259, soluble in water. **b. sulfate.** $(C_{18}H_{21}O_3N)_2 \cdot H_2SO_4 = 696.6$. Brown crystals, soluble in water.

bebeeru. The bark of the greenheart tree, *Nectandra rodiaei* (Lauraceae) of tropical America; used like cinchona bark. Cf. *chondroine*.

bebirine. Bebeerine.

beccarite. ZrO_2. An olive-green, vitreous zirconium oxide.

beche-de-mer. Trepang. A coral reef slug; a Chinese delicacy

Becher, Johann Joachim. 1635–1682. German physician, adventurer, and alchemical writer; founded the phlogiston theory.

Bechhold filter. An ultrafiltration apparatus to separate colloids by disks impregnated with nitrocellulose.

bechilite. Borocalcite.

beckelite. Calcium silicate containing cerium, lanthanum, and didymium.

Beckmann, Ernst. 1853–1923. German organic chemist. **B. apparatus.** A glass apparatus to determine the molecular weight by (1) lowering the freezing point or (2) raising the boiling point of a solution. **B. burner.** A glass tube supported over a dish in which vapors or gases are evolved; used to produce colored flames. **B. reaction. B. rearrangement.** An intramolecular rearrangement, in which a ketoxime forms its isomeric amide when treated with phosphorus pentachloride. **B. thermometer.** Ultrathermometer. A thermometer for the B. apparatus to read temperatures to 0.01°C over a range of about 6°C.

Becquerel, Antoine Henri. 1852–1908. French physicist, Nobel Prize winner (1903). **B. rays.** The radiations emitted from uranium and similar substances which affect the photographic plate. Cf. *radioactive* rays.

becquerelite. $2UO_3 \cdot 3H_2O$. A hydrous, highly radioactive mineral (Congo).

beda nuts. The dried ripe seeds of *Terminalia belerica* (cf. *myrobalan*) from India; a tan and black dye.

bee balm. Monarda.

beech. A genus of trees, *Fagus sylvatica*. Cf. *fagine*. **b. nut.** The seeds of b.; a source of oil and b. nut cake. **b. wood creosote.** The distillation product of b. wood; an antiseptic and preservative.

beef extract. An aqueous extract of lean beef, partly desiccated. It contains the soluble fibrin and proteins; used in culture media.

beegerite. $Pb_6Bi_2S_9$ or $6PbS \cdot Bi_2S_3$. Native lead sulfobismuthide.

beehive. A small, circular glass shelf with a hole for collecting gases in pneumatic troughs.

beemerose. A nephelite rock (New Jersey).

beer. A beverage containing 3–7% alcohol; a fermented infusion or decoction of malted barley with hops. Cf. *brewing wort*. **near-** B. containing less than 0.5% alcohol, used during prohibition in the United States.

beerbachose. A diorite from California.

Beer's law. The intensity of an emergent ray of light is inversely proportional to the depth of liquid through which it travels. Cf. *Lambert's* law.

beeswax. (1) Wax from the honeycomb of bees. It contains cerolein, cerotic acid, myricyl alcohol, melissic acid, and alkanes. (2) White wax, cera alba. The bleached wax from the honeycomb of bees, d.0.966, m.63; used in pharmacy and industry.

beet. *Beta vulgaris* (Chenopodiaceae), cultivated for its root (sugar beet) containing up to 20% sugar. **b. slop.** The liquid product remaining after extraction of b. sugar; a fertilizer. **b. sugar.** Sugar extracted from beet. See *sucrose*.

Beggiatoaceae. A family of bacteria; motile cells in sheathless threads containing sulfur granules.

behenic acid. $Me(CH_2)_{20}COOH = 340.44$. Docosanoic acid.* A constituent of ben oil and the roots of *Centaurea behen*. Colorless needles, m.84, insoluble in water.

behenolic aicd. $Me(CH_2)_7 \vdots C.C(CH_2)_{11}COOH = 336.43$. 1,3-Docosynoic acid*. White needles, m.58, insoluble in water.

behenolyl. The radical $C_{21}H_{39}CO$—, from behenolic acid. **b. amide.** $C_{22}H_{41}ON = 335.3$. Colorless crystals, m.90. **b. chloride.** $C_{22}H_{39}OCl = 342.3$. Colorless crystals, m.29.

beidellite. $Al_2O_3 \cdot 3SiO_2 \cdot 4H_2O$. An inactive base-exchange clay (Colorado).

Beilby layer. The amorphous, atomic surface layer formed on a metal when it is polished, or when crystal surfaces are rubbed together.

Beilstein, Friedrich Konrad. 1838–1906. Russian-born German chemist; compiler of **B.'s Handbuch**, a general reference book of organic compounds. Cf. *Prager*-Jacobson classification.

bel. A unit of comparative loudness. The log of the ratio of the intensities of two sounds. The smallest change in loudness that the ear of a young and healthy person can detect. Cf. *decibel, sound, loudness*.

Belastran. Trade name for a viscose synthetic fiber.

belcherose. A pyroxenite rock (Massachusetts).

beldongrite. Native manganese iron oxide.

Belimat. Trade name for a viscose synthetic fiber.

belite. $2CaO \cdot SiO_2$. A crystalline constituent of portland cement clinker. Cf. *alite*.

Bell, Jacob. 1810–1950. British pharmacist, founder of the Pharmaceutical Society of Great Britain and the *Pharmaceutical Journal*.

bell. A hollow, cup-shaped vessel. **b. glass.** B. jar. A glass b. with or without tubulations, to cover specimens and for vacuum experiments. **b. metal.** A b. alloy: Cu 80, Sn 20%, d.8.7, m.890. **b. metal ore.** Stannite.

belladonna. Deadly nightshade, banewort, poison cherry, death's herb. *Atropa belladonna* (Solanaceae). **b. leaves.** The dried leaves of *A. belladonna;* a narcotic, antispasmodic, anodyne. **b. roots.** The roots of *A. belladonna;* an antispasmodic.

belladonnine. $C_{17}H_{21}O_2N = 271.26$. An alkaloid from belladonna. Cf. *atropine*.

Bellier's test. A means of detecting over 2% of arachis oil in a saponified oil, by the formation of arachidic acid, q.v.

belonesite. $MgO \cdot MoO_3$. A molybdenum ore; needle-shaped crystals.

belonites. Small needle-shaped crystals in volcanic rock.

Bemberg silk. Trademark for an artificial fiber made by a cuprammonium process.

bemegride. $C_8H_{13}NO_2 = 155.22$. **beta-** Ethyl-β-methylglutarimide. White, bitter flakes, m.127, soluble in water; a respiratory stimulant (U.S.P., B.P.).

Benadryl. Trademark for β-dimethylaminoethylbenzhydryl ether hydrochloride. Used to treat hay fever and asthma.

Bence-Jones protein. A protein in the urine of patients with myeloma.

bendrofluazide. $C_{15}H_{14}O_4N_3F_3S_2 = 421.46$. White crystals, m.225, insoluble in water; a diuretic (B.P.).

bene. Sesame.

Benedict, Stanley Rossiter. 1884–1936. American biochemist. **B.'s solution.** A solution of sodium and potassium tartrate, sodium carbonate, and copper sulfate; used to detect and determine reducing sugars.

beneficiation. The improvement or refining of ores, e.g., by grinding, screening, concentration, etc.

Bengal isinglass. Agar. **b. kino.** *Butea* gum. **b. lights.** A mixture of sulfur, sugar, and potassium nitrate to which either barium or strontium salts are added to give a green or red light; used in pyrotechnics.

benitoite. $BaTiSi_3O_9$. A mineral found only at San Benito, Calif.

benjamin. Benzoin gum.

ben oil. The expressed oil from the seeds of *Moringa pterygosperma* and *M. oleifera* (Moringaceae). It is a bland laxative used for extracting odors. Cf. *benne* oil.

benne oil. Sesame oil.

bensylidyne. The radical $\equiv CPh$.

benthal decomposition. The over-all stabilization of sludge deposits in streams due to combined aerobic and anaerobic mechanisms.

benthonics. The study of the ocean floor.

bentonite. Sodium montmorillonite. A clay (Pacific Coast States) which swells 12-fold when wetted with water and has strong adsorbing properties. Used in pharmacy (U.S.P., B.P.). **b. magna.** A pharmaceutical suspending agent, made by stirring b. into 20 times its weight of hot water.

benz- Benzo-.

benzacetin. (1) $C_{11}H_{13}O_4N = 223.11$. Acetamido-ethylsalicylic acid. Colorless crystals, m.190. Cf. *phenacetin*. (2) $C_{10}H_{11}O_4N = 209.09$. Acetamido-methylsalicylic acid. Colorless crystals, m.205.

benzaconine. $C_{32}H_{43}O_{10}N = 601.1$. Picraconitine, napelline. An alkaloid produced by the partial hydrolysis of aconitine, m.130.

benzacridine. $C_{10}H_6 \cdot N(CH) \cdot C_6H_4 = 229.1$. Phenonaphthacridine. **dihydro- b.** Tetrophan.

benzal. Benzilidene, benzenyl. The radical $Ph \cdot CH<$ derived from toluene. Cf. *benzylidene, benzenyl*.

benzalacetone. $PhCH:CH \cdot CO \cdot Me = 146.1$. Acetocinnamone. Colorless crystals, m.41, with a coumarin odor, soluble in alcohol; used in organic synthesis.

benzalacetophenone. $PhCH:CH \cdot CO \cdot Ph = 208.17$. Cinnamyl phenyl ketone. Colorless crystals, m.62, insoluble in water.

benzalagen. Analgen.

benzalaniline. $PhCH:NPh = 181.1$. Colorless crystals, m.45; used in organic synthesis.

benzalazine. $PhCH:N \cdot N:CHPh = 208.1$. Dibenzalhydrazine. Yellow prisms, m.93 (decomp.), insoluble in water.

benzalbromide. $PhCHBr_2 = 249.87$. α-Dibromotoluene. A fuming oil, b.140.

benzalchloride. $PhCHCl_2 = 160.99$. Chlorobenzal. Colorless liquid, b.206, insoluble in water. Used in chemical warfare and in dye manufacture.

benzalcohol. Benzyl alcohol.

benzalcoumarones. Plant pigments responsible for the golden yellow of certain plants.

benzalcyanhydrin. $PhCH(OH)CN = 133.11$. Mandelonitrile. Colorless liquid, m. -10, decomp. 170; insoluble in water.

benzaldehyde. $C_6H_5 \cdot CHO = 106.09$. Phenylaldehyde, benzene carbonal, benzene methylal, benzoylhydride, artificial almond oil. Colorless liquid of bitter almond odor, b.179, sparingly soluble in water. Used in dye manufacture, perfumes, and drugs; a reagent for alkaloids and fusel oil. **amino-** *ortho-* $NH_2 \cdot C_6H_4CHO = 121.1$. Anthranilaldehyde. Colorless leaflets, m.39 (decomp.), slightly soluble in water. *meta-* Yellow amorphous powder. *para-* scales, m.70, soluble in water. **α-bromo-** Benzoyl bromide. **α-chloro-** Benzoyl chloride. **cyano-** Benzoyl cyanide. See *diethyl-*, **dihydroxy-** *2,3-* Pyrocatechualdehyde. *2,4-* β-Resorcylaldehyde. *2,5-* Gentisaldehyde. *3,4-* Protocatechuic aldehyde. **dimethoxy-** Veratraldehyde. **dinitro-** $(NO_2)_2C_6H_4CHO = 196.05$. Dinitrobenzene carbonal*. Yellow crystals. *2,4-* m.72. *2,6-* m.123, slightly soluble in water. **3-ethoxy-4-hydroxy-** Bourbonal. **ethoxymethoxy-** Vanillin ethyl ether. **hexahydro-** Cyclohexane aldehyde. **hydroxy-** *ortho-* Salicylaldehyde. *meta-* Colorless needles, m.104, soluble in water. *para-* Colorless needles, m.115 (sublimes), sparingly soluble in water. **hydroxymethoxy-** Vanillin. **isopropyl-** Cumaldehyde. **p-methoxy-** Anisaldehyde. **methyl-** Tolyl aldehyde. **methylenedioxy-** Piperonal. **nitro-** *ortho-* $NO_2 \cdot C_6H_4 \cdot CHO = 151.09$. Yellow needles, m.44, slightly soluble in water. *meta-* Colorless needles, m.58, slightly soluble in water. *para-* Colorless prisms, m.106, insoluble in water. **3,4,5-trihydroxy-** Gallaldehyde. **trimethyl-** Durylaldehyde. **trinitro-** $(NO_2)_3C_6H_3CHO = 241.05$. Trinitrobenzene carbonal. *2,4,6-* Yellow scales, m.119, insoluble in water. **b. azine.** Benzalazine. **b. cyanhydrin.** See *benzalcyanhydrin.* **b. green.** Malachite green. **b. hydrazone.** Benzalhydrazine. **b. oxime.** Benzaldoxime. **b. phenylhydrazone.** $PhCH:N \cdot NHPh = 196.18$. Benzalphenylhydrazone, benzilidenephenylhydrazine. Colorless crystals, m.155.

benzaldoxime. $PhCH:NOH = 121.10$. Several isomeric forms, each giving two series of derivatives:

$$\underset{\text{α-anti-}}{\overset{\begin{array}{c}N \cdot OH \\ \| \\ Ph \cdot CH\end{array}}{}} \qquad \underset{\text{β-syn-}}{\overset{\begin{array}{c}N \cdot OH \\ \| \\ HC \cdot Ph\end{array}}{}}$$

alpha- Benzantialdoxime, antibenzaldoxime. Colorless leaflets, m.35. **beta-** Isobenzaldoxime. Colorless needles, m.125, insoluble in water. Substitution products:

$$\underset{\substack{O\text{-}syn\text{-}\\ \beta\text{-}O}}{\overset{\begin{array}{c}N-OR \\ \| \\ HCPh\end{array}}{}} \quad \underset{\substack{O\text{-}anti\text{-}\\ \alpha\text{-}O}}{\overset{\begin{array}{c}N-OR \\ \| \\ PhCH\end{array}}{}} \quad \underset{\substack{N\text{-}syn\text{-}\\ \beta\text{-}N}}{\overset{\begin{array}{c}R-N:O \\ \| \\ HCPh\end{array}}{}} \quad \underset{\substack{N\text{-}anti\text{-}\\ \beta\text{-}N}}{\overset{\begin{array}{c}R-N:O \\ \| \\ PhCH\end{array}}{}}$$

p-methoxy- $PhCHOHMe = 135.08$. Anisaldoxime. Colorless crystals, m.45. **methyl-** *N-* Benzantialdoxime N-methyl ether. *O-* (1) $PhCN:NOMe = 135.8$. Benzantialdoxime O-methyl ether. Colorless liquid, b.191. (2) Benzsynaldoxime O-methyl ether. Colorless crystals, m.82. **N-phenyl-** $PhCH:NOPh = 197.08$. Colorless crystals. m.109. **nitro-α-** *meta-* Colorless crystals, m.117. *para-* Colorless crystals, m.129. **nitro-β-** *ortho-* Colorless crystals, m.136. *meta-* Colorless crystals, m.118. *para-* Colorless crystals, m.174.

b. acetate. $PhCH:NO \cdot COCH_3 = 163.08$. **anti-** Colorless crystals, m. 15, soluble in water. **b. acetic acid.** $PhCH:NO \cdot CH_2COOH = 179.09$. Anti-O-acetic acid. Colorless crystals, m.98. *anti-N-acetic acid.* $PhCH(ON)CH_2COOH = 179.09$. Colorless crystals, m.183. **b. carboxylic anhydride.** $C_8H_5O_2N = 147.09$. A ring compound which, at $145°C$, becomes $C_6H_4(CN) \cdot COOH$.

benzalethylamine. $PhCH:NC_2H_5 = 133.1$. Colorless liquid, b.195.

benzal green. Malachite green.

benzalhydrazine. $PhCH:N \cdot NH_2 = 120.1$. Colorless crystals, m.16.

benzalkonium. $[C_6H_5 \cdot CH_2 \cdot N, Me_2R]^+$. A radical which forms antibiotics and/or surfactants with Cl, saccharinate, and phthalimidate structures. **b. chloride.** $[C_6H_5CH_2N(Me)_2R]Cl$. A mixture of alkyldimethylbenzylammonium chlorides. R is a mixture of alkyls from C_8H_{17} to $C_{18}H_{37}$; an antibacterial and detergent.

benzalphthalide. $C_{15}H_{10}O_2 = 222.1$. Colorless crystals, m.99.

benzamarone. $PhCH(CHPh \cdot COPh)_2 = 480.7$. Colorless crystals, m.219, slightly soluble in hot water.

benzamide. $PhCONH_2 = 121.14$. Benzene carbon amide*. Colorless monoclinic tablets, m.128, slightly soluble in water. **amino-** *ortho-* $NH_2 \cdot C_6H_4 \cdot CONH_2 = 136.12$. Aminobenzene carbon amide*. Colorless leaflets, m.108, soluble in water. *meta-* Yellow leaflets, m.70, slightly soluble in water. *para-* Yellow crystals, m.179, slightly soluble in water. **benzoyl-** Dibenzamide. **bromo-** $C_7H_6NOBr = 199.97$. Colorless crystals. *ortho-* m.156. *meta-* m.150. *para-* m.190. **chloral-** See *chloral.* **chloro-** $C_7H_6NOCl = 155.56$. Colorless crystals. *ortho-* m.141. *meta-* m.135. *para-* m.178. **di-** Dibenzamide. **fluoro-** $C_7H_6NOF = 139.05$. Colorless crystals. *ortho-* m.116. *meta-* m.130. *para-* m.155. **hydro-** See *hydrobenzamide.* **hydroxy-** *ortho-* $HO \cdot C_6H_4 CONH_2 = 137.10$. Yellow leaflets, m.140, soluble in water. *meta-* Colorless leaflets, m.170, soluble in water. *para-* Colorless needles, m.158, sparingly soluble in water. **iodo-** $C_7H_6NOI = 246.99$. Colorless crystals. *ortho-* m.184. *meta-* m.187. *para-* m.128. **methyl-** Toluamide. **nitro-** *ortho-* $NO_2C_6H_4CONH_2 = 166.10$. White needles, m.174, soluble in water. *meta-* Yellow needles, m.141, sparingly soluble in water. *para-* Colorless needles, m.153, sparingly soluble in water. **n-phenyl-** Benzanilide. **m-semicarbazido-** Cryogenin. **silver-** $PhCONHAg = 227.94$. **sodium-** $PhCONHNa = 143.06$. **tri-** $(PhCO)_3N = 329.13$. Tribenzalamine. Colorless crystals, m.202. **thio-** See *thiobenzamide.* **b. oxime.** Benzamidoxime.

benzamidine. $PhC(NH_2):NH = 120.14$. Colorless crystals, m.75, soluble in water. **b. urethane.** $PhC(:NH)NHCO \cdot OC_2H_5 = 192.12$. Colorless crystals, m.38.

benzamido. The radical $PhCONH—$, from benzamide.

benzamidoxime. $PhC(:NOH)NH_2 = 136.08$. White crystals, m.80, slightly soluble in water.

benzamine. β-Eucaine. **b. lactate.** $C_{15}H_{21}O_2N \cdot C_3H_6O_3 = 337.24$. Benzoyl vinyl diacetone alkamine lactate. Colorless crystals, soluble in water.

benzaminic acid. *m-Aminobenzoic acid.*

benzamino acids. Amino*benzoic acids.* **b. acetic acid.** Hippuric acid.

benzanalgen. Analgen.

benzanilide. $Ph \cdot CO \cdot NH \cdot Ph = 197.2$. Benzoylaniline. White crystals, m.160, insoluble in water; an antipyretic. **ethoxy-** Benzophenetide. **hydroxy-** $HO \cdot C_6H_4 \cdot CONH_2 = 137.06$. Colorless crystals, *ortho-* m.140. *meta-* m.170. *para-* m.162. Used in organic synthesis. **methoxy-** Benzaniside. **methyl-** Benzotoluide. **nitro-** See *nitrobenzanilide.* **thio-** See *thiobenzamide.*

benzanthene penicillin G (B.P.). See *penicillin.*

benzanthracenes. $C_{18}H_{11} = 227.1$. Hydrocarbons in which a benzene and anthracene ring have a double bond in common. Cf. **benzopyrene.**

benzantialdoxime. See *benzaldoxime.*

benzaurine. $PhC:C_6H_4:O \cdot C_6H_4OH = 274.21$. Yellow crystals, m.100, insoluble in water.

benzazide. Benzoylazide.

benzazimide. $C_7H_5ON_3 = 147.1$. Colorless crystals, m.212.

benzazine. (1) Quinoline. (2) *Iso*quinoline.

benzazole. **1-** Indole. **2-** *Iso*indole. **iso-** Indolenine.

benzdiazine. Benzodiazine.

benzdifuran. Benzodifuran.

benzdioxazine. Benzodioxazine.

Benzedrine. $C_6H_5 \cdot CH_2 \cdot CHNH_2 \cdot CH_3$. Trademark for a brand of amphetamine. Colorless liquid, slightly soluble in water. **B. sulfate.** White powder, soluble in water.

benzene. $C_6H_6 = 78.08$. Benzol (German), benzole (French), phenylhydride, cyclohexatriene, phene. Colorless crystals, m.5.4°, insoluble in water, miscible with organic solvents. Used as a solvent in organic synthesis, in the manufacture of dyes, in photography, as a motor fuel, and in electrotechnics; it is a narcotic and destroys leucocytes. Cf. *b. structure.* **acetenyl-** Phenyl*acetylene.* **acetyl-** Acetophenone. **allyl-** See *allyl.* **amino-** Aniline. **aminoethoxy-** Phenetidine. **aminoethoxy-** $C_6H_4NH_2 \cdot C_2H_6 = 121.14$. *ortho-* Colorless liquid, b.215. *meta-* Colorless liquid, b.214. *para-* White leaflets, m.5. **amyl-** $PhC_5H_{11} = 148.18$. Colorless liquid, b.129, soluble in alcohol. **anilino-** Diphenylamine. **arsenobis-** Arsenobenzene. **azimino-** Benzotriazole. **azo-** Azobenzene. **azoxy-** Azoxybenzene. **benzoyl-** Benzophenone. **benzyl-** Diphenylmethane. **bromo-** Phenyl bromide. **bromochloro-** $BrC_6H_4Cl = 191.40$. *1,3-* or *m-* Colorless liquid, b.196. *1,4-* or *p-* White prisms, m.67. **bromofluoro-** $BrC_6H_4F = 174.95$. *1,4-* or *p-* Colorless liquid, b.153. **bromoiodo-** $BrC_6H_4I = 282.86$. *1,2-* or *o-* Colorless liquid, b.258. *1,3-* or *m-*Oily liquid, b.252. *1,4-* or *p-* White needles, m.92. **bromonitro-** $Br \cdot C_6H_4 \cdot NO_2 = 201.96$. *ortho-* Colorless crystals, m.38, insoluble in water. *meta-* Colorless crystals, m.52.6, insoluble in water. *para-* White monoclinic crystals, m.125, insoluble in water. **chloramido-** Chloraniline. **chloro-*** Phenyl chloride. **chloronitro-** $ClC_6H_4NO_2 = 157.55$. *ortho-* Colorless needles, m.32.5, insoluble in water. *meta-* Colorless rhombs, m.44.2, insoluble in water. *para-* White monoclinic prisms, m.83, insoluble in water. **chlorotrinitro-** Picryl chloride. **cyano-** Benzonitrile. **diamino-** Phenylenediamine. **diaminoazo-** $(NH_2)_2C_6H_3 \cdot N:NPh = 212.20$. *2,4-*Yellow needles, m.118, slightly soluble in water. **2,4-diaminoazob. hydrochloride.** Chrysoidine orange. **diazo-** See *diazo.*

diazoamino- $PhN:N \cdot NHPh = 197.27$. Yellow leaflets, m.96, insoluble in water. **dibromo-** $C_6H_4Br_2 = 235.98$. *ortho-* Colorless needles, m.-1, insoluble in water, *meta-* Colorless crystals, m.1, insoluble in water. *para-* White monoclinic crystals, m.89, insoluble in water. **dichloro-** $C_6H_4Cl_2 = 146.96$. *ortho-* Colorless liquid, b.179, insoluble in water. A solvent, insecticide, and sweeping compound. *meta-* Colorless liquid, b.173, insoluble in water. *para-* Paradow. White needles, m.53, insoluble in water; an antiparasitic. **dicyano-** *ortho-* Phthalonitrile. *meta-m-*Phthalonitrile. *para-* Terephthalicnitrile. **diethoxy-** $C_6H_4(OCH_3)_2 = 166.11$. *1,2-.* White crystals, m.166. *1,3-.* White prisms, m.12. *1,4-* Hydroquinone diethyl ether. White scales, m.71. **diethyl-** $C_6H_4(C_2H_5)_2 = 134.17$. *ortho-* Colorless liquid, b.-185, insoluble in water. *meta-* Colorless liquid, b.181, miscible with alcohol. *para-* Colorless liquid, b.183, insoluble in water. **difluoro-** $C_6H_8F_2 = 114.03$. *para-* Colorless liquid, b.89, insoluble in water. **dihydro-** Cyclohexadiene. **dihydrodiketo-** Quinine. **dihydroimino-** Benzenimine. **dihydroketo-** Benzenone. **dihydroxy-** $C_6H_4(OH)_2$. *1,2-* or *o-* Catechol. *1,3-* or *m-* Resorcinol. *1,4-* or *p-* Hydroquinol. **diiodo-*** $C_6H_4I_2 = 330.01$. *1,2-,* or *o-.* Colorless prisms, m.23, insoluble in water. *1,3-,* or *m-.* White rhombs, m.34, insoluble in water. *1,4-* or *p-.* White leaflets, m.129, insoluble in water. **dimethoxy-** *1,2-* Veratrole. *1,4-* Hydroquinoldimethyl ether. **dimethyl-** Xylene. **dimethylethyl-** $C_6H_3(CH_3)_2C_2H_5 = 134.17$. Colorless liquid, b.183, insoluble in water. **dinitro-** $C_7H_4(NO_2)_2 = 168.14$. *1,2-,* or *o-* Colorless scales, m.117, sparingly soluble in water. *1,3-* or *m-* Yellow needles, m.90, sparingly soluble in water. Used in the manufacture of explosives. *1,4-* or *p-* White needles, m.171, sparingly soluble in water. **diphenyl-** $C_6H_4Ph_2 = 230.21$. *para-* Terphenyl. White leaflets, m.205, insoluble in water. **ethenyl-** Styrolene. **ethoxy-** Phenetole. **ethyl-** $PhC_2H_5 = 106.12$. Colorless liquid, b. 137, insoluble in water. **ethylmethyl-** $MeC_6H_4Et = 120.1$. *1,2-* or *o-* Colorless liquid, b.159. *1,3-* or *m-* Colorless liquid, b.159, *1,4-* or *p-* Colorless liquid, b.162. **fluoro-** See *fluobenzene.* **formamido-** Formanilide. **hexachloro-** $C_6Cl_6 = 284.73$. White monoclinics, m.229, insoluble in water; Cf. b. hexachloride. **hexaethyl-** $C_6(C_2H_5)_6 = 246.53$. Colorless monoclinics, m.129, insoluble in water. **hexahydro-** Cyclohexane. **hexahydrohexahydroxy-** Inosite. **hexahydropentahydroxy-** Pinite. **hexahydroxy-** $C_6(OH)_6 = 174.13$. B. hexol. Colorless needles, decomp. 200, slightly soluble in water. **hexaiodo-** $C_6I_6 = 833.55$. Brown needles, decomp. 150. **hexamethyl-** $C_6(CH_3)_6 = 162.21$. Mellitene. White rhombs, m.164. **hexaoxy-** See *triquinoyls.* **hydrazino-** Phenylhydrazine. **hydrazo-** $PhNH \cdot NHPh = 184.24$. Colorless crystals, m.131, sparingly soluble in water. **hydroxy-** Phenol. **hydroxyazo-** $HO \cdot C_6H_4N:NPh = 198.16$. *1,2-* or *o-* White needles, m.83, slightly soluble in water. *1,4-* or *p-* White prisms, m.152, slightly soluble in water. **inorganic-** $B_3H_6N_3 = 80.77$. The substance formed by the action of ammonia on borane. It resembles benzene in physical properties. **iodo-** $PhI = 203.99$. Colorless liquid, b.188, insoluble in water. **iodoso-** $PhIO = 219.99$. White powder, explodes 210, soluble in water. **iodoxy-** $PhIO_2 =$

235.99. Colorless needles, explode 230, sparingly soluble in water. **isocyano-** Phenyl isocyanide. **isopropyl-** Cumene. **isopropylmethyl-** Cymene. **methoxy-** Anisole. **methoxypropenyl-** Anethole. **methyl-** Toluene. **methylethyl-** See *ethylmethyl-*. **methylisopropyl-** Cymene. **nitro-** $PhNO_2 = 123.08$ Yellow liquid, b.210, with almond odor, slightly soluble in water. Tautomeric forms: $PhNO_2$ and PhONO. **nitroso-** $PhNO = 107.08$. Colorless prisms, m.68, insoluble in water. **nitroxy-** $PhNO_3$. Phenyl nitrate. **octa-** Cyclooctatetraene. **penta-amino-** See *pentamino-*. **pentabromo-** $C_6HBr_5 = 472.64$. Colorless needles, m.160, insoluble in water. **pentachloro-** $C_6HCl_5 = 250.34$. Colorless needles, m.85, insoluble in water. **pentaethyl-** $C_6H(C_2H_5)_5 = 218.21$. Colorless liquid, b.277; insoluble in water. **pentamethyl-** $C_6H(CH_3)_5 = 148.21$. White crystals, m.53, insoluble in water. **pentamino-** $C_6H(NH_2)_5 = 153.17$. Colorless needles, soluble in water. **phenyl-** Biphenyl. **propenyl-** Allyl b. **tetrahydro-** Cyclohexene. **tetrahydroxy-** Apinol. **tetramethyl-** $C_6H_2Me_4 = 134.3$. *1,2,3,4-* Prehnitene. *1,2,3,5-* Isodurene. *1,2,4,5-* Durene. **trihydroxy-** $C_6H_3(OH)_3 = 126.2$. *1,2,3-* Pyrogallol. *1,2,4-* Benzenetriol. *1,2,5-* Phloroglucinol. **trimethyl-** $C_6H_3Me_3$. *1,2,3-* Hemimellitene. *1,2,4-* Pseudocumene. *1,3,5-* Mesitylene. **trinitro-** See *trinitrobenzene*. **trinitrotriazido-** $C_6(NO_2)_3(N_3)_3 = 336.09$. Yellow solid, m.131, insoluble in water, soluble in acetone; a detonator and substitute for mercury fulminate. **vinyl-** Styrene.

b. arsonic acid. $PhAsO(OH)_2 = 201.01$. A reagent for Sn, Zr, and Th. *amino-* Arsanilic acid. **b. azimide.** See *benzotriazole*. **b. azoaniline.** See *diazoaminobenzene*. **b. azobenzene.** See *azobenzene*. **b. azo-α-naphthylamine.** $PhN:NC_{10}H_6NH_2 = 247.21$. Red needles, m.123. **b. carbinol.** Benzyl alcohol. **b. carbonal*.** Benzaldehyde. **b. carbonamidine*.** Benzamidine. **b. carbonitrile*.** Benzonitrile. **b. carboxylic acid*.** Benzoic acid. **b. diamine.** Phenylenediamine. **b. diazonium chloride.** $Ph·NClN$. Formed by diazotizing aniline with acid nitrous acid; explosive when dry. **b. diazonium hydroxide.** $PhN:N·OH$. An intermediate in the formation of diazoaminobenzene from aniline. **b. dibromide.** See *dibromobenzene*. **b. dicarbinol.** Xylenediol. **b. dicarbonal*.** Phthalaldehyde. **b. dicarbonitrile*.** Phthalonitrile. **b. dicarboxylic acid*.** $C_6H_4(COOH)_2$. *1,2-* or *o-* Phthalic acid. *1,3-* or *m-* Isophthalic acid. *1,4-* or *p-* Terephthalic acid. **b. dichloride.** Dichlorobenzene. **b. diol*.** $C_6H_4(OH)_2$. *1,2-* or *o-* Pyrocatechol. *1,3-* or *m-* Resorcinol. *1,4-* or *p-* Hydroquinol. **b. disulfochloride.** $C_6H_4(SO_2Cl)_2 = 275.10$. Colorless, viscous liquid, b.80, slightly soluble in water. **b. disulfonic acid.** $C_6H_4(SO_3H)_2$. Three isomers used in organic synthesis. **b. disulfoxide.** $PhSO·SOPh = 250.1$. Colorless crystals, m.45. **b. dithiol.** Phenylene dimercaptan. **b. hexabromide.** $C_6H_6Br_6 = 457.84.*$ White monoclinic crystals, m.212. Cf. *hexabromobenzene*. **b. hexacarboxylic acid.** $C_6(COOH)_6$. Mellitic acid. **b. hexachloride.** $C_6H_6Cl_6 = 290.78$. Hexachlorocyclohexane*. BHC. Gammexane. Lindane. Colorless prisms, m.112, soluble in water. The gamma isomer has highly insecticidal properties, especially toward lice, flies, and mosquitoes, and is a scabicide (U.S.P.). Cf. *hexachloro-*

Benzene ring.

Substitutions are designated by

ortho-	*o-*	1,2-	*vicinal*	*v-*	1,2,3-
meta-	*m-*	1,3-	*symmetric*	*s-*	1,3,5-
para-	*p-*	1,4-	*asymmetric*	*a-*	1,2,4-

benzene. **b. indone.** Aposafranone. **b. induline.** Aposafranine. **b. methylal.** Benzaldehyde. **b. monosulfonic acid.** B. sulfonic acid. **b. nucleus.** See *b. ring*. **b. pentacarboxylic acid.*** $C_6H(COOH)_5 = 298.05$. Colorless crystals, decomp. 238, soluble in water. **b. pentamine*.** $C_6H(NH_2)_5 = 153.1$. Colorless needles, soluble in water. **b. positions.** See *b. ring*. **b. ring.** The graphical representation of b. structure as a hexagon with numbers representing the C atoms (see figure). **b. series.** C_nH_{2n-6}. Aromatic hydrocarbons and homologs of b. **b. siliconic acid*.** $C_6H_5SiOOH = 138.11$. Silicobenzoic acid. Glassy scales, m.92, insoluble in water. **b. structure.** Theories of the arrangement of the C atoms in the b. molecule; i.e., plane formula (Kekulé, 1865), diagonal formula (Claus, 1867), prism formula (Ladenburg, 1869), bridge formula (Claus, 1870), centric formula (Armstrong and Baeyer, 1892), partial valence formula (Thiele, 1899); the modern conception of a dynamic formula. See *Pauling* structure. *geometrical-* Tetrahedra illustrating the arrangement of the atoms in the b. molecule. **b. sulfamide.** See *b. sulfonic* amide. **b. sulfide.** Phenyl sulfide. **b. sulfinic acid.** $PhSO·OH = 142.1$. Colorless prisms, m.83, decomp. 100, soluble in water, isomeric with b. sulfonyl. **b. sulfochloride.** B. sulfonic chloride. **b. sulfonanilide.** $Ph·SO_2·NH·Ph = 233.3$. **b. sulfone amide*.** See *b. sulfonic amide*. **b. sulfone chloride.** See *b. sulfonic chloride*. **b. sulfonic acid*.** $PhSO_2·OH = 185.2$. Colorless leaflets, m.65, soluble in water. **b. sulfonic amide.** $PhSO_2NH_2 = 157.2$. B. sulfamide. White plates, m.156 (decomp), soluble in water. **b. sulfonic chloride.** $PhSO_2Cl = 176.6$. Colorless oil, m.14, insoluble in water; a reagent for amines. **b. sulfonic hydroxamide.** $PhSO_2NHOH = 173.2$. Colorless crystals, m.126. **b. sulfonitramide.** $PhSO_2NHNO_2 = 202.2$. **b. sulfonyl.** The acyl radical derived from b. sulfonic acid, $Ph·SO_2-$. The isomer of b. sulfinic acid. **b. sulfoxide.** $Ph_2SO_2 = 218.14$. Colorless crystals, m.128,

BENZENE SERIES

	Formula
Benzene, phenylhydride	PhH
Toluene, methylbenzene	PhMe
Xylene, dimethylbenzene	$C_6H_4Me_2$
Mesitylene, hemimellitene, Ψ'-cumene, trimethylbenzene	$C_6H_3Me_3$
Durene, tetramethylbenzene	$C_6H_2Me_4$
Pentamethylbenzene	C_6HMe_5
Hexamethylbenzene	C_6Me_6

insoluble in water. **b. tetracarboxylic acid***. C_6H_2-(COOH)$_4$. *1,2,3,4-* or *v-* Prehnitic acid. *1,2,3,5-* or *a-* Mellophanic acid. *1,2,4,5-* or *s-* Pyromellitic acid. **b. tetrol.** Tetrahydroxybenzene. **b. tricarboxylic acid*.** $C_6H_3(COOH)_3$. *1,2,3,-* or *v-* Hemimellitic acid. *1,2,4-* or *a-* Trimellitic acid. *1,3,5-* or *s-* Trimesic acid. **b. triol*.** $C_6H_3(OH)_3 = 126.2$. Hydroxyquinol, hydroxyhydroquinone. *1,2,4-* or *a-* Colorless crystals, m.140. *1,2,3-* or *v-* Pyrogallol. *1,3,5-* or *s-* Phloroglucinol. **b. trisulfonic acid*.** $C_6H_3(SO_2OH)_3 = 318.3$. Colorless, deliquescent crystals, used in organic synthesis.

benzenoid. (1) Related structurally to benzene. (2) A suggested structure for benzene involving 6 carbonoids, q.v.

benzenone. $C_6H_6O = 94.05$. Dihydroketobenzene. 1,2- and 1,4-isomers exist. **hydroxy-** Quinol. **imino-** Quinonimine. **methyl-** Toluenone.

benzenyl. The radical $PhC\equiv$, from toluene.

benzenylamidine. Benzamidine.

benzenylamidothiophenol. $C_{13}H_9NS = 211.1$. Phenylbenzothiazole. Yellow needles, with rose odor, m.115, soluble in alcohol; a perfume.

benzenylamidoxime. $PhC(NH_2){:}NOH = 136.20$. It occurs in syn and anti forms. Colorless crystals, m.89. **acetyl-** $PhC(NH_2){:}NO{\cdot}COMe$. Colorless liquid, m.16.

benzenylamino- Benzenylamido-

benzenyltetrazoic acid. Phenyltetrazole.

benzenyl trichloride. Benzotrichloride.

benzethonium chloride. $C_{27}H_{42}O_2NCl{\cdot}H_2O = 466.11$. Colorless, bitter crystals, soluble in water.

benzfuran. The ring structure

benzhexol hydrochloride. $C_{20}H_{31}ON{\cdot}HCl = 337.0$. White, bitter powder, m.250(decomp.), soluble in alcohol.

benzhydrazoin. $C_{19}H_{16}N_2 = 272.2$. Colorless crystals, m.55.

benzhydrol. Benzohydrol. **b. ether.** $(Ph_2CH)_2O = 350.31$. Colorless crystals, m.109, sparingly soluble in water.

benzhydroxamic. See *benzohydroxamic.*

benzidam. Aniline.

benzidine. $NH_2C_6H_4{\cdot}C_6H_4NH_2 = 184.1$. Bianiline. Gray scales, m.133, slightly soluble in water, soluble in boiling water. A reagent for sulfates, blood, and small quantities of higher-valency metals. **dimethoxy-** Dianisidine. **dimethyl-** Tolidine.

b. conversion. The formation of b. from hydrazobenzene by boiling mineral acids. **b. dicarboxylic acid.** Diaminophenic acid. **b. sulfate.** $C_{12}H_{12}N_2{\cdot}H_2SO_4 = 282.3$. White crystals, soluble in water; used similarly to benzidine. **b. sulfone.** $(NH_2C_6H_3)_2{\cdot}SO_2 = 246.22$. Colorless crystals, m.350, insoluble in water. **b. test.** Adler's reaction. B. produces a purple color with an acetic acid–ether extract of blood. Certain metals also react.

benzidino. The radical $NH_2{\cdot}C_6H_4C_6H_4{\cdot}NH{-}$, from benzidine.

benzil. $PhCO{\cdot}COPh = 210.15$. Dibenzoyl, diphenyldiketone. Yellow needles, m.95.2, insoluble in water; a reagent. **bisazo-** See *bisazobenzil.* **bishydrazi-** See *bishydrazibenzil.* **dimethoxy-** Anisil. **dimethyl-** Tolil. **p-hydroxy-** Yellow needles, m.130, soluble in alkali.

benzilamphioxime. γ-Benzildioxime.

benzilaniline. Benzylaniline.

benzilantioxime. α-Benzildioxime.

benzildianil. $PhC{:}N(Ph){\cdot}(Ph)N{:}CPh = 360.2$. Colorless crystals, m.142.

benzildioxime. $C_{14}H_{12}O_2N_2 = 240.1$.

HO·N ‖ Ph·C·C·Ph ‖ N·OH	N·OH ‖ Ph·C·C·Ph ‖ HO·N	N·OH ‖ Ph·C·C·Ph ‖ N·OH
α- or *b. antidioxime* m.237	β- or *b. syndioxime,* m.207	γ- or *b. amphidioxime* m.165

Crystalline solids, decomp. by heat, insoluble in water: a reagent for nickel. **b. peroxide.** $Ph_2C_2N_2O_2 = 238.2$. Colorless crystals, m.114.

benzilic acid. $Ph_2C(OH)COOH = 228.17$. Diphenylglycolic acid. White monoclinic crystals, m.150, slightly soluble in water.

benzilidene. Benzal. **b. acetophenone.** $PhCH{:}CH{\cdot}COPh = 208.1$. Colorless crystals, m.58. **b. aniline.** Benzalaniline. **b. hydrazine.** Benzalhydrazine. **b. phthalide.** Benzalphthalide.

benzilmonoxime. $C_{14}H_{10}N_2O = 225.17$.

Crystals in isomeric forms: *alpha-* m.137; *beta-* m.114; insoluble in water.

benzilsynoxime. β-Benzildioxime.

benzimidazole. $C_6H_4{\cdot}N{:}CH{\cdot}NH = 118.2$. *o*-Phenyleneformamidine. Colorless crystals, m.167. Cf. *naphthimidazole.* **benzylene-** Pseudoisoindolebenzimideazole. **methyl-** $C_7H_5N_2{\cdot}CH_3 = 132.1$. *o*-Phenyleneacetamidine. Colorless crystals, m.176.

benzimidazolone. $C_6H_4(NH)_2{:}CO = 134.2$. *o*-Phenyleneurea. Colorless crystals, m.308. **thio-** Phenylenesulfone.

benzimidazolyl. The radical $C_7H_5N_2{-}$, from benzimidazole.

benzimidoyl. The radical $PhC({:}NH){-}$.

benzin, benzine. Benzoline, gasoline, petroleum b. A mixture of hydrocarbons obtained from the second distillate of crude petroleum, b.70–90. Clear colorless liquid, d.0.640–0.675, insoluble in water, miscible with organic solvents. A solvent for oils, resins, alkaloids, and rubber; a textile cleaner and a fuel. Cf. *benzene.*

benzinduline. Aposafranine.

benzisodiazole. $C_7H_6N_2 = 118.2$. **1,2-** Indiazene.

benzisosulfonazole. Saccharin.

benzisoxazole. $C_7H_5ON = 119.1$. Indoxazene, isoindoxazene.

$C_6H_4\!\!\begin{smallmatrix}O\\CH\end{smallmatrix}\!\!N$. β,γ- Anthranil.

benzisoxdiazole. Benzofurazan.

benzo- Prefix indicating the radical $C_6H_4=$, from benzene.

benzoate. PhCOOR or PhCOOM. A salt of benzoic acid. **b. of soda.** See *sodium benzoate*.

benzoazimidole. $C_6H_5ON_3 = 135.1$. Colorless crystals, m.157.

benzobis-m-methylimidazole. $C_{10}H_{10}N_4 = 186.3$. Colorless crystals, m.145.

benzocaine. $NH_2C_6H_4COOEt = 165.2$. Anesthesin. Colorless crystals, m.90, insoluble in water; a local anesthetic.

benzocarbolic acid. Phenylbenzoate.

benzocinnoline. *5,6*-Naphthisodiazine.

benzocoumaran. Naphthofuran.

benzodianthrone. Helianthin.

benzodiazine. $C_8H_6N_2 = 130.06$. Benzdiazine. Nine isomers with 2 N atoms in positions: **1,2-**

Cinnoline. **1,3-** Quinazoline. **1,4-** Quinoxaline. **1,5-** Pyridopyridine. **1,8-** Naphthyridine. **2,3-** Phthalazine. **alpha-** Cinnoline. **beta-** Phthalazine. **para-** Quinoxaline.

benzodiazole. $C_7H_6N_2 = 118.1$. **1,2-** Isoindazole. **2,1-** Indazole. **1,3-** Benzimidazole.

benzodiazthine. $C_6H_4\cdot(NH)\cdot(S\cdot CH):N = 150.1$. Phenylsulfocarbizine. Colorless crystals, m.129.

benzodifuran. $C_{10}H_6O_2 = 158.0$. Five isomers. The

and

numerals indicate the positions of 2 O atoms and 2 CH groups: **o-alpha-** Oxygen at 6 and 8, CH groups at 5 and 7. **m-alpha-** Oxygen at 1 and 3, CH groups at 2 and 4. **m-beta-** Oxygen at 5 and 7, CH groups at 6 and 8. **p-alpha-** Oxygen at 6 and 7, CH groups at 5 and 8. **p-beta-** Oxygen at 2 and 3, CH groups at 1 and 4.

benzodioxazine. $C_7H_5O_2N = 135.1$. Benzodiazine derivatives containing 2 O atoms and 1 N atom.

benzodioxdiazine. $C_6H_4N_2O_2 = 136.1$. Heterocyclic compounds, similar to benzodiazine, but with 2 O and 2 N atoms.

benzodioxtriazine. $C_5H_3O_2N_3 = 137.1$. Heterocyclic compounds, similar to benzodiazine, but with 2 O and 3 N atoms.

benzodisulfole. Benzodithiole.

benzofluorenes. $C_6H_4\cdot CH_2\cdot C_{10}H_6 = 216.1$ A group of aromatic hydrocarbons. **1,2-** Chrysofluorene.

benzofuran. Coumarone. **dihydro-** Coumaran. **dihydroketo-** Benzofuranone.

benzofurancarboxylic acid. Coumarilic acid.

benzofuranone. $C_8H_6O_2 = 134.1$.

$$1(2)\text{-}C_6H_4\cdot O\cdot CO\cdot CH_2.$$

$$2(1)\text{-} \text{Coumaranone.} \ C_6H_4\cdot CO\cdot O\cdot CH_2.$$

benzofuryl. The radical C_8H_5O-, from coumarone.

benzoglycolic acid. Amygdalic acid.

benzoglyoxaline. Benzimidazole.

benzohydrol. $Ph_2CHOH = 184.09$. Diphenylcarbinol. Colorless needles, m.68, insoluble in water, **tetramethyldiamino-** *Michler's* hydrol.

benzohydroxamic acid. $C_7H_7NO_2 = 137.11$. Two isomers:

anti- or α-   *syn-* or β-

benzohydryl. The radical $(C_6H_5)_2CH-$, from diphenyl methane. **b. amine.** $Ph_2CH\cdot NH_2 = 138.18$. Colorless liquid, b.288. **b. benzoic acid.** $Ph\cdot CHOH\cdot C_6H_4COOH = 288.2$. Crystals, m.164 (decomp.), slightly soluble in water. **b. hydroxylamine.** $Ph_2CH\cdot NH\cdot NHOH = 214.11$. Colorless crystals, m.78.

benzohydrylidene. Diphenylmethane.

benzoic acid. $Ph\cdot COOH = 122.09$. Phenylformic acid, benzenecarboxylic acid. White needles, m. 121, sparingly soluble in water, soluble in alcohol or ether; in benzoin and cranberries. An antipyretic, antiseptic, or expectorant; used in calico printing, in the manufacture of aniline dyes, and to standardize bomb calorimeters. **acetylamino-** $CH_3CONH\cdot C_6H_4COOH = 179.13$. Acetamidobenzoic acid. *ortho-* Colorless needles, m.185. *meta-* White crystals, decomp. 248. *para-* Colorless needles, decomp. 250. **aldehyde-** $CHO\cdot C_6H_4COOH = 150.09$. *ortho-* White leaflets, m.97. *meta-* White needles, m.164. *para-* Colorless needles, m.246. **amino-** $NH_2\cdot C_6H_4\cdot COOH = 137.09$. *ortho-* Anthranilic acid. Yellow leaflets, m.144. *meta-* Benzaminic acid. Yellow crystals, m.174. *para-* Dracilic acid, vitamin B_x, anticanitic factor. Part of the vitamin B complex, q.v., in yeast; a deficiency causes prematurely gray hair. Yellow crystals, m.186. **4-amino-3,5-dinitro-** Chrysanisic acid. **azo-** See *azo*. **azodi-** Azobenzoic acid. **azoxy-** See *azoxybenzoic acid*. **bromo-** $Br\cdot C_6H_4\cdot COOH = 201.04$. *ortho-* Colorless needles, m.150. *meta-* White needles, m.155. *para-* Colorless prisms, m.251. **carbamyl-** Phthalamic acid. **carbamylphenyl-** Diphenamic acid. **carboxyformyl-** Phthalonic acid, terephthalonic acid. **chloro-** $ClC_6H_4COOH = 156.53$. *ortho-* Rhombic crystals, m.137. *meta-* White crystals, m.153. *para-* Colorless monoclinic crystals, m.236. **dichloro-** $Cl_2C_6H_3COOH = 190.97$. *2,5-* or *a-* Colorless needles, m.156. *2,6-* or *v-* White needles, m.127. *3,4-* or *s-* White needles, m.203. **dihydroxy-** $(OH)_2C_6H_3COOH = 154.09$. *2,3-* Pyrocatechoic acid. $(+2H_2O = 190.12)$. Colorless needles, m.204. *2,4-*$(+3H_2O = 208.14)$. β-Resorcylic acid. White needles, m.206. *3,5-*$(+1\frac{1}{2}H_2O = 181.12)$. α-Resorcylic acid. Colorless prisms, m.232 *2,5-* Gentisic acid. Colorless needles m.199. *3,4-* Protocatechuic acid. *2,6-* γ-Resorcylic acid. Colorless needles, m.167. **dihydroxymethyl-** Orsellic acid. **dimethoxy-** Veratric acid. **dimethoxy-formyl-** Opianic acid. **dimethoxyhydroxy-** Syringic acid. **dimethyl-** $Me_2C_6H_3COOH = 150.13$. *2,3-v-*Xylic acid. Colorless prisms, m.144. *2,4-* Xylic acid. Colorless monoclinic crystals, m.126. **2,5-**Isoxylic acid. White needles, m.132. *2,6-* White needles. m.116. *3,4-* White prisms, m.163. *3,5-*1,3,5-Mesitylinic acid. White monoclinic crystals, m.166. **dinitro-** $(NO_2)_2C_6H_3COOH = 212.15$. *2,3-*Colorless crystals, m.201. *2,4-* Colorless prisms m.179. *2,5-* Colorless needles, m.177. *2,6-*Colorless needles, m.202. *3,4-* Colorless needles, m.163. *3,5-* Colorless crystals, m.203. **ethoxy-**$EtO·C_6H_4·COOH = 166.13$. *ortho-* Colorless liquid or crystals, m.19. *meta-* Colorless needles, m.137. *para-* Colorless needles m.195. **ethyl-**$EtC_6H_4COOH = 150.13$. *ortho-* Colorless needles, m.68. *meta-* Colorless needles, m.47. *para-*Colorless leaflets, m.112. **formyl-** Phthalaldehydic acid. **formyldimethoxy-** Opianic acid. **disulfo-**Dithiobenzoic acid. **fluoro-** Fluobenzoic acid. **hexahydro-** $C_6H_{11}COOH = 128.14$. Naphthenic acid, cyclohexane carboxylic acid. Colorless monoclinic crystals m.30. **hydrazinehydroxy-**Orthin. **hydrazine-** $NH_2NH·C_6H_4COOH = 152.08$. *ortho-* Colorless crystals, m.155. *meta-* Colorless crystals, m.231. *para-* Colorless needles, m.258. **hydrazo-** $(NH·C_6H_4COOH)_2 = 272.25$. *ortho-*Colorless leaflets, m.205. **hydroxy-** $HO·C_6H_4·COOH = 138.08$. *ortho-* Salicylic acid. *meta-*Colorless rhombic crystals, m.201. *para-* Colorless monoclinic crystals, m.213. **hydroxydimethoxy-**Syringic acid. **hydroxymethoxy-** Vanillic acid. **hydroxymethyl-** Cresotic acid. **isopropyl-** Cumic acid. **methoxy-** $MeO·C_6H_4COOH = 152.19$. *ortho-*White leaflets, m.99. *meta-* White needles, m.102. *para-* Anisic acid. **methyl-** Toluic acid. **methylenedioxy-** Piperonylic acid. **nitro-** $NO_2C_6H_4·COOH = 167.08$. *ortho-* Colorless needles, m.148. *meta-* Silky needles, m.141. *para-* White scales, m.242. **pentamethyl-** $C_6Me_5COOH = 192.19$. Colorless needles, m.210. $PhC_6H_4COOH = 198.15$. *ortho-* Colorless needles, m.111. *meta-* White leaflets, m.160. *para-* White needles, m.219. **sulfamine-** $NH_2SO_2C_6H_4COOH = 201.1$. *ortho-*Colorless crystals, m.167. The anhydride is saccharin. *meta-* Colorless crystals, m.238. *para-*Colorless crystals, decomp. 280. **sulfo-** $HOSO_2·C_6H_4COOH·3H_2O = 266.18$ *ortho-* Colorless crystals, m.250. *meta-* $(+2H_2O = 236.16)$. Colorless crystals, m.141. *para-* Colorless needles, m.259. **tetrahydro-** $C_6H_9COOH = 126.08$. A solid, d.1.072. **tetramethyl-** $MeC_6HCOOH = 178.1$. *2,3,4,5-* Colorless crystals, m.165. *2,3,5,6-* Colorless crystals, m.127. **trihydroxy-** *2,3,4-* See trihydroxy. *3,4,5-* Gallic acid. **trimethoxy-** Asaronic acid. **trimethyl-** $Me_3C_6H_2COOH = 164.1$. *2,3,4-* Prehnitilic acid. Colorless crystals, m.167. *3,4,5-*α-Isodurylic acid. Colorless crystals, m.215. *2,3,5-*γ-Isodurylic acid. Colorless crystals, m.127. *2,4,5-*Durylic acid. Colorless crystals, m.150. *2,4,6-* β-Isodurylic acid, mesitylenecarboxylic acid. Colorless crystals, m.152.

b. acid anhydride. $PhCO·O·COPh = 226.14$. Colorless crystals, m.42, b.360; a strong antiseptic. **b. alcohol.** Benzyl alcohol. **b. aldehyde.** Benzaldehyde. **b. amide.** Benzamide. **b. anhydride.** Benzoic acid anhydride. **b. ether.** Ethylbenzoate.

b. sulfimide, b. sulfinide. Saccharin. **b. trichloride.** Benzotrichloride.

benzoin. (1) $PhCO·CH(OH)Ph = 212.17$. Oxyphenyl benzoyl ketone, phenyl benzoyl carbinol, bitter almond oil camphor. White hexagons, m.132, b.343, absent from gum b.; an antiseptic for ointments. (2) Benzoinum, gum b. The balsamic resin *Styrax* species. See *b. gum*. **diisopropyl-** Cuminoin. **dimethoxy-** Anisoin. **hydro-**$PhCH(OH)CH(OH)Ph = 214.19$. White leaflets, m.138. **isohydro-** Colorless monoclinic crystals, m.120.

b. condensation. A reaction between 2 aromatic aldehydes under the influence of KCN to form water and a compound $X·CH(OH)·CO·X$. Cf. *aldol* condensation. **b. gum.** Benjamin gum benzoinam, kemenian (Malay), luban jawi (Arabic). *Siam-* The resin from *Styrax benzoin* and other species (chief constituents: benzoic acid, an essential oil, vanillin); used in perfumery and cosmetics. *Sumatra-* The resin from *Styrax* species (chief constituents: cinnamic and benzoic acids); used for varnishes and in the manufacture of cinnamic acid. **b. oxime** $C_{14}H_{13}NO_2 = 227.2$. Phenyl-α-oxybenzyl ketoxime, $Ph·CHOH·C:-NOH·Ph$. (1) *d-* Colorless needles, m.132. (2) *l-*White powder, m.174. (3) *syn-d, l-* or β- crystals, m.99. (4) *anti-d, l-* or α- crystals, m.152; a sensitive reagent for copper or molybdenum.

benzoiodohydrin. $PhCOOC_3H_5ClI = 324.4$. Chloriodoglycerin benzoic ether. Brown fat, soluble in alcohol.

benzol. See *benzene.* **b. bichloride.** See *benzene,* dichloro-. **b. bromide.** See *benzene,* bromo-. **b. chloride.** See *benzene,* chloro-.

benzoline. Benzine.

benzomorpholine. $C_6H_4·O·NH(CH_2)_2 = 135.1$. Colorless oil, b.268.

benzonaphthacene. alpha- Dibenzanthracene. **beta-**Pentacene.

benzonaphthene. $C_{13}H_{10} = 166.07$.

$$
\begin{array}{ccc}
& CH_2-CH=CH & \\
& \| & | \\
CH=C & C & C=CH \\
| & \| & | \\
CH=C & C & C=CH
\end{array}
$$

benzo-α-naphthindole. $C_{16}H_{11}N = 217.1$. Phenyl-α-naphthylcarbazole. An isomer of hydrindochroman.

benzonaphthol. Naphthol-benzoate.

benzonitrile. $C_6H_5·CN = 103.08$. Phenyl cyanide, benzenecarbonitrile*, Colorless liquid, m. — 13, b.191. It resembles bitter almond oil in odor; used in the synthesis of dyes and drugs. **amino-**$NH_2C_6H_4CN = 118.10$. Anthranilo nitrile. *meta-*Colorless needles, m.53. *para-* Colorless needles, m.86. **dimethyl-** Xylonitrile. **hydroxy-** Salicylonitrile. **methoxy-** Anisonitrile. **methyl-** Tolunitrile. **nitro-** $NO_2C_6H_4CN = 148.09$. *ortho-* White silky needles, m.109. *meta-* Colorless needles, m.117. *para-* White leaflets, m.147.

benzoparadiazine. Quinoxaline.

benzoparoxazine. $C_8H_7ON = 133.1$.

$$
C_6H_4 \underset{NH-CH}{\overset{O-CH}{<}} \|
$$

2-phenyl- Colorless crystals, m.103.

benzopentazole. $C_4H_3N_2 = 79.1$. Heterocyclic compounds of the type:

$$\begin{array}{c} 6-7-C-1 \\ | \quad\quad | \quad\quad \rangle 2 \\ 5-4-C-3 \end{array}$$

with 5 N atoms in the 2 rings.

benzoperoxide. Commercial benzoyl peroxide.

benzophenanthrazine. Dibenzophenazine.

benzophenanthrene. *a-* Chrysene. *def-* Pyrene. *l-* Triphenylene.

benzophenazine. $C_2H_6 \cdot N:N \cdot C_6H_4 = 230.2$. Naphthophenazine, phenonaphthazine. Yellow needles, m.143.

benzophenid. Phenyl benzoate.

benzophenol. Phenyl benzoate.

benzophenone. $Ph \cdot CO \cdot Ph = 182.12$. Diphenyl ketone, benzoylbenzene. Colorless prisms; 4 allotropic forms: *alpha-* m.48.5; *beta-* m.26.5; *gamma-* m.46; *delta-* m. −51. A mild hypnotic; used in organic synthesis. **benzoyl-** Phthalophenone. **di- amino-, dihydroxy-** See *di-*. **nitro-** $NO_2 \cdot C_6H_4COPh = 227.15$. *ortho-* Orthonitrobenzophenone. Colorless crystals, m.105. *meta-* Metanitrobenzophenone. Colorless needles, m.94. *para-* Paranitrobenzophenone. White leaflets, m.138. **pentahydroxy-** Maclurin. **tetramethyldiamino-** *Michler's* ketone. **thio-** Thiobenzophenone. **trihydroxy-** $C_{13}H_{10}O_4 = 230.08$. Benzophloroglucinol. **2,6,2-** White solid, m.133.

b. carboxylic acid. Benzoylbenzoic acid. **b. dicarboxylic acid.** $C_6H_4COOH \cdot CO \cdot C_6H_4 = 270.16$. **2,2-** or **0,0-** Ortho-ortho-b. Colorless crystals m.150–200. **b. dicarboxylicdilactone.** $C_{15}H_8O_4 = 252.1$. The spiro compound $C(O \cdot C_6H_4 \cdot CO)_2$. Colorless crystals, m.212. **b. oxime.** Benzophenoxime. **b. sulfide.** Thioxanthone.

benzophenoxime. $Ph_2C:N \cdot OH = 197.16$. Benzophenone oxime. White crystals, m.140.

benzophloroglucinol. $C_{13}H_{10}O_4 = 230.12$. **2,4,6-** $Ph \cdot CO \cdot C_6H_2(OH)_3$.

benzophosphinic acid. $HOOC \cdot C_6H_4PO(OH)_2 = 202.13$. Colorless crystals, m.300.

benzopinacol. $Ph_2COH \cdot COH \cdot Ph_2 = 366.31$. Tetraphenylethylglycol, benzopinacone. Colorless crystals, m.185.

benzopinacone. Benzopinacol.

benzopseudoxazole. Anthranil.

benzopurpurin. Ozamin 4B. The soluble sodium salt of *o*-toluidinedisazobinaphthylaminesulfonic acid. Used to dye cotton red, and as a biological stain and indicator, changing at pH 4.0 from purple (acid) to scarlet (alkali).

benzopyran. $C_9H_8O = 132.06$. Heterocyclic compounds; *e.g.,*

$$C_6H_4 \langle \begin{array}{c} O \cdot CH_2 \\ CH \end{array} \rangle CH \quad\quad C_6H_4 \langle \begin{array}{c} O \cdot CH \\ CH_2 \end{array} \rangle CH$$

1,2-   **1,4-**

$$C_6H_4 \langle \begin{array}{c} CH_2 \cdot O \\ CH \end{array} \rangle CH$$

2,1-

dihydro- Chroman. **keto-** *1,2-* Coumarin. *1,-4* Chromone.

benzopyranyl. The radical C_9H_7O-, from benzopyran.

benzopyrazine. Quinoxaline.

benzopyrazole. Isoindazole.

benzopyrazolon(e). Indazolone.

benzopyrene. $C_{20}H_{11} = 251.1$. An anthracene ring with a naphthalene ring attached in the 1,2-position; the principal carcinogen in coal-tar pitch. Cf. *benzanthracenes, benzopyrine.*

benzopyridine. Quinoline.

benzopyrilium. Compounds derived from benzopyran, containing tetravalent oxygen.

benzopyrine. $Ph \cdot COOH \cdot C_{11}H_{12}ON_2 = 310.16$. Antipyrine benzoate. Cf. *salipyrine, benzopyrene.*

benzopyrone. **1,2-** Coumarin. **1,4-** Chromone. **2,1-** Isocoumarin. **dihydrophenyl-** Flavonone. **phenyl-** Flavone.

benzopyrrole. Indole.

benzopyrylium. Benzopyrilium.

benzoquinol. Quinol.

benzoquinoline. $C_{10}H_6 \cdot N:(CH)_3 = 179.2$. **6,7-** α-Anthrapyridine. Colorless crystals, m.275. **6,7- iso-** β-Anthrapyridine. Colorless crystals, m.166. **4,5-** or **meso-** $C_{12}H_9N = 167.2$.

$$\begin{array}{c} NH-CH-CH \\ | \quad\quad | \quad\quad | \\ CH=C \quad\quad C-C=CH \\ | \quad\quad | \quad\quad | \\ CH=CH-C-C=CH \end{array}$$

3,4- Phenanthridine.

benzoquinone. Quinone.

benzosalin. $C_6H_4(OMe)COO(PhCO) = 256.1$. Methyl benzoyl salicylate, benzoylsalicylic acid methyl ester. White, aromatic crystals, m.85; an antiseptic.

benzoselenazole. $C_6H_6 \cdot SeN \cdot CH = 182.1$. **iso-** Benzisoselenazole. **pseudo-** Benzopseudoselenazole.

benzoselenodiazole. $C_6H_4Se \cdot N:N = 183.1$. Isopiaselenol. **iso-** Benzisoselenodiazole, piaselenol. Colorless crystals, m.76.

benzoselenofuran. $C_6H_4 \cdot Se \cdot CH:CH = 181.1$. Selenonaphthene. **iso-** Benzoisoselenofuran.

$$C_6H_4 \langle \begin{array}{c} CH \\ | \\ CH \end{array} \rangle Se$$

benzosol. $PhCOOC_6H_4OMe = 228.09$. Guaiacol benzoate. Colorless solid, m.61; a disinfectant.

benzosulfinide. Saccharin.

benzosulfonazole. $C_7H_5O_2NS = 167.1$.

$$\text{1-} \quad C_6H_4 \langle \begin{array}{c} SO_2 \\ CH \end{array} \rangle N; \quad\quad \text{2-} \quad C_6H_4 \langle \begin{array}{c} SO_2 \\ N \end{array} \rangle CH_2$$

benzosulfonazolone. Saccharin.

benzotetrazine. $C_6H_4 \cdot (N:N)_2 = 132.2$.

benzotetrazole. $C_5H_4N_4 = 120.2$. Heterocyclic compounds containing 4 N atoms, one of which is NH. **1,3,4,6-** Purine.

$$\begin{array}{c} 7 \\ 6 \quad C-1 \\ | \quad || \quad \rangle 2 \\ 5 \quad C-3 \\ 4 \end{array}$$

benzothiazine. $C_8H_7NS = 149.2.$ Heterocyclic compounds; as: **1,4,2-**

$$C_6H_4 \diagup^{S \cdot CH_2}_{N} \diagdown CH$$

benzothiazole. $C_6H_4 \cdot S \cdot N : CH = 135.1.$ Methenyl-amidothiophenol. Colorless liquid, b.234. **bis-** Bisbenzothiazole. **dihydro-** Benzothiazoline. **iso-isopseudo-** Benzisothiazole. **phenyl-**Benzenyl-amidothiophenol. **pseudo-** Benzopseudothiazole.

benzothiodiazole. $C_6H_4 \cdot S \cdot N : N = 136.1.$ Isopiazthiole, diazosulfide, phenylene diazosulfide, iso-piazothiole. **iso-** Benzisothiodiazole, piazthiole.

benzothiofuran. Thionaphthene.

benzothiophene. Thionaphthene.

benzothiopyran. $C_9H_8S = 148.1.$ Heterocyclic compounds; e.g.: **1,2-** Thiochromene.

$$C_6H_4 \diagup^{S \cdot CH_2}_{CH = CH}$$

dihydro- Thiochroman. **2-keto-** Thiocoumarin. **4-keto-** Thiochromone.

benzothiopyrone. $C_9H_6OS = 162.1.$ Thiochromone. Heterocyclic compounds; as,

$$C_6H_4 \diagup^{S \cdot CO}_{CH : CH} \qquad C_6H_4 \diagup^{S \cdot CH}_{CO \cdot CH}$$

1,2-	**1,4-**
Thiocoumarin	Thiochromone

hydroxy- Thiochromonol. **phenyl-** Thioflavol.

benzotoluide. $PhCONH \cdot C_6H_4Me = 211.3.$ Methyl-benzanilide, N-benzoyltoluidine. **ortho-** Rhombic needles, m.146. **meta-** Monoclinic prisms, m.125. **para-** Rhombic needles, m.158, b.232.

benzotriazepine. The ring system:

(structure: cyclohexane ring with NH—H and N=N)

benzotriazine. $C_7H_5N_3 = 131.2.$ Heterocyclic compounds; as

$$C_6H_4 \diagup^{N:N}_{CH:N} \qquad C_6H_4 \diagup^{N:N}_{N:CH}$$

1,2,3-	**1,2,4-**
Phentriazin	Phenpyrrodiazole

benzotriazole. $C_6H_5N_3 = 119.2.$ Heterocyclic compounds; as: **1,2,3-** Benzisotriazole. Colorless crystals m.99.

$$C_6H_4 \diagup^{NH}_{N} \diagdown N$$

benzotrichloride. $C_6H_5 \cdot CCl_3 = 195.4.$ Toluene trichloride, α-trichlorotoluene, phenylchloroform.

Yellowish liquid of penetrating odor, m. -21, b.214, decomp. in water; used in the synthesis of aniline dyes.

benzotrifluoride. $C_6H_5CF_3 = 108.04.$ Colorless liquid, b.102; an intermediate in the manufacture of dyestuffs and pharmaceuticals.

benzotrifuran. $C_{12}H_6O_3 = 198.04.$ **1,3,5-** The heterocyclic compound:

(structure diagram)

benzotropine methanesulfonate. $C_{21}H_{25}NO \cdot MeSO_3H = 403.54.$ 3-Diphenylmethoxytropanemethane-sulfonate. White, bitter crystals, m.143, soluble in water; a parasympatholytic (B.P.).

benzoxanthene. $C_{10}H_6 \cdot CH_2 \cdot O \cdot C_6H_4 = 232.1.$ Naphthoxanthene, phenonaphthoxanthene. Cf. *naph-thoxanthine.*

benzoxazine. $C_8H_7ON = 133.1.$ Heterocyclic compounds; e.g.:

$$C_6H_4 \diagup^{O—CH_2}_{CH=N} \qquad C_6H_4 \diagup^{O—CH_2}_{N=CH}$$

1,3- or **1,3,2-**	**1,4-** or **1,4,2-**

dihydro- Phenomorpholine. **b. dione.** Isatoic anhydride.

benzoxazole. $C_6H_4 \cdot O \cdot N : CH = 119.09.$ Methenyl-amidophenol. Colorless crystals, m.32. Cf. *benz-isoxazole.* **amino-** $C_7H_6ON_2 = 134.1.$ Colorless crystals, m.130; 2 isomers. **anilido-** $C_7H_4ON \cdot NHPh = 210.13.$ Colorless crystals, m.137. **methyl-** Ethenylamidophenol. **phenyl-** $C_7H_4ON \cdot Ph = 195.1.$ Colorless crystals, m.103. **thio-** Thiobenzoxazole.

benzoxazolon(e). $C_6H_4 \cdot O \cdot NH \cdot CO = 135.05.$ **N-ethyl-** $C_7H_4EtO_2N = 163.07.$ Colorless crystals, m.29.

benzoxazolyl. The radical $C_7H_4ON—$, derived from benzoxazole.

benzoxdiazine. $C_7H_6ON_2 = 134.07.$ Heterocyclic compounds, similar to benzodiazine, which contain 1 O and 2 N atoms in the ring.

benzoxdiazole. $C_6H_4 \cdot O \cdot N : N = 120.05.$ Cf. *naph-thoxdiazole.*

benzoxtetrazine. $C_5H_4ON_4 = 136.07.$ Heterocyclic compounds, similar to benzodiazine, which contain 1 O and 4 N atoms in the ring.

benzoxtriazine. $C_6H_5ON_3 = 135.07.$ Heterocyclic compounds containing 1 O and 3 N atoms in the ring; as: **1,4,2,3-**

$$C_6H_4 \diagup^{O—N}_{NH} \diagdown N$$

benzoxy. Benzoyloxy.

benzoyl. The aryl radical $C_6H_5CO—$, Bz, from benzoic acid. Cf. *chlorobenzoyl, nitrobenzoyl.* **b. acetaldehyde.** $PhCOCH_2 \cdot CHO = 148.11.$ Colorless crystals. **b. acetate.** $PhCO \cdot O \cdot OCMe = 164.06.$ Acetyl benzoate, acetobenzoic acid anhydride. **b.**

acetic acid. PhCO·CH$_2$·COOH = 164.11. Phenyl ketoacetic acid. Colorless needles, m.61, decomp. 103; used in organic synthesis. **b. acetic ethyl ester.** Ph·CO·CH$_2$·COOEt = 192.10. Oily liquid, b.148. **b. acetone.** Ph·CO·CH$_2$·CO·Me = 162.13. Acetylacetophenone. A homolog of b. acetaldehyde. Colorless liquid, b.260; used in organic synthesis. **b. acetonitrile.** Ph·CO·CH$_2$·CN = 145.1. Cyanacetophenone. Colorless crystals, m.80. **b. acetyl.** Ph·CO·CO·Me = 148.1. Colorless oily liquid, b.214. **b. amide.** Benzamide. **b. aniline.** Benzanilide. **b. anthraquinone.** C$_6$H$_4$:(CO)$_2$:C$_6$H$_3$COPh = 312.20. White crystals, m.182. **b. azide.** C$_6$H$_5$·CO·N$_3$ = 147.2. Azimide, benzazide, benzoyl nitride. Colorless crystals or liquid, m.20. **b. benzoic acid.** PhCOC$_6$H$_4$COOH = 226.08. Benzophenonecarboxylic acid. Colorless crystals. *ortho-* m.127. *meta-* m.162. *para-* m.194. **b. benzoate.** C$_{14}$H$_{12}$O$_2$ = 212.25. Colorless oil, d.1.118, insoluble in water; a scabicide (U.S.P.). **b. benzylamine.** PhCO·NHCH$_2$Ph = 211.11. Colorless crystals, m.105. **b. bromide.** C$_6$H$_5$·COBr = 185.04. α-Bromobenzaldehyde, benzene carbonyl bromide. Colorless liquid, b.218, decomp. in water. **b. butylcarbinol.** PhCO(CH$_2$)$_4$OH = 178.11. Colorless crystals, m.49. **b. carbinol.** PhCOCH$_2$OH = 136.06. Colorless crystals, m.83. **b. carbinolacetate.** PhCOCH$_2$O·COMe = 178.08. Colorless crystals, m.49. **b. chloride.** C$_7$H$_5$OCl = 140.53. α-Chlorobenzaldehyde, benzene carbonyl chloride. Colorless liquid, b.198; decomp. with water. A reagent for alcohol and lysidine, and used in organic synthesis. **b. cyanide.** C$_6$H$_5$·CO·CN = 131.12. α-Cyanobenzaldehyde. Colorless scales, m.32. **b. cyclobutane.** C$_6$H$_5$·CO·CH(CH$_2$)$_3$ = 160.15. Colorless liquid, b.258. **b. cyclopropane.** C$_6$H$_5$·CO·CH(CH$_2$)$_2$ = 146.13. B. trimethylene. Colorless liquid, b.239. **b. disulfide.** PhCOSSCOPh = 274.2. Dibenzoyl disulfide. Colorless prisms, m.128 (decomp.). **b. ecgonine.** Cocaine. **b. fluoride.** C$_7$H$_5$OF = 128.08. Benzene carbonyl fluoride. Colorless liquid, b.161.5. **b. formaldehyde.** C$_8$H$_6$O$_2$ = 134.1. (1) *anhydrous.* PhCO·CHO. Phenylglyoxal. Colorless liquid, b$_{125mm}$ 142. (2) *hydrated.* PhCO·CH(OH)$_2$. Colorless crystals, m.73. **b. formic acid.** C$_6$H$_5$·CO·CO$_2$H = 150.1. Phenyl glyoxylic acid. Colorless crystals, m.65. **b. formoxine.** C$_6$H$_5$·CO·CH:NOH = 149.1. Isonitrosoacetophenone. Colorless crystals, m.127; a reagent for ferrous salts. **b. glycine.** Hippuric acid. **b. glycocoll.** Hippuric acid. **b. glycolic acid.** PhCO·OCH$_2$·COOH = 180.1. Colorless prisms. **b. hydrazine.** PhCONHNH$_2$ = 136.1. α-Hydrazinobenzaldehyde. Colorless crystals, m.112. *di-* (PhCONH)$_2$ = 270.3. Dibenzoylhydrazine. Colorless crystals, m.233. **b. hydride.** Benzaldehyde. **b. hydrogen peroxide.** PhCO·O$_2$H = 138.05. Colorless crystals, m.41. **b. hydroxide.** Benzoic acid. **b. iodide.** C$_7$H$_5$OI = 231.95. Benzene carbonyl iodide, α-iodobenzaldehyde. Colorless leaflets, m.3 (decomp.), decomp. in water. **b. methane.** Acetophenone. **b. naphthol.** Naphthol benzoate. **b. oxide.** Benzoic anhydride. **b. peroxide.** (PhCO)$_2$O$_2$ = 242.15. Benzoperoxide, luzidol. Colorless rhombic crystals, m.103. A flour "improver," and a bleaching agent. **b. phenylhydrazine.** PhCONHNHPh = 212.17. Colorless crystals, m.145; an antiseptic. **b.**

propionaldehyde. PhCO(CH$_2$)$_2$CHO = 162.1. Colorless liquid, b.245. **b. propionic acid.** PhCO·(CH$_2$)$_2$COOH = 178.1. Colorless needles, m.116. **b. pseudotropeine.** Tropacocaine. **b. pyrocatechol.** *Dihydroxy* benzophenone. **b. salicin.** Populin. **b. sulfide.** PhCO·S·COPh = 242.1. Colorless crystals, m.48. **b. sulfonic imide.** Saccharin. **b. thiourea.** PhCONH·CS·NH$_2$ = 180.14. Small colorless prisms, m.170. **b. trimethylene.** B. cyclopropane. **b. urea.** PhCONH·CO·NH$_2$ = 164.12. Crystalline solid, m.215.

benzoylation. The introduction of the PhCO— radical into a molecule.

benzoylene. The radical —C$_6$H$_4$·CO—. **b. guanidine.** C$_8$H$_7$ON$_3$ = 161.2. Benzglycocyanidine. **b. urea.** C$_8$H$_6$O$_2$N$_2$ = 162.2. Diketotetrahydroquinazoline.

benzoyles. A group of organic aromatic compounds containing the benzoylene radical.

benzoyloxy. Preferred term for benzoxy. The radical C$_6$H$_5$COO—, from benzoic acid.

benzpinacone Benzopinacol.

benzpyrazole Isoindazole.

benzpyrene. Benzopyrene.

benzseleno-. See *benzoseleno-.*

benzsulfhydroxamic acid. Benzenesulfonic hydroxamide.

benzsulfo-. See *benzosulfo-.*

benzsynaldoxime. Benzaldoxime.

benzthiophen. Thionaphthene.

benztrioxazine. C$_6$H$_5$O$_3$N = 139.1. A group of heterocyclic compounds with 3 O and 1 N atoms in the ring; as: **8-** or **8,2,3,4-**

benzyl. The aryl radical C$_7$H$_7$— or PhCH$_2$, derived from toluene. **b. acetamide.** C$_9$H$_{11}$ON = 149.01. *N*-PhCH$_2$NHCOMe. α-Hydrocinnamamide. Colorless crystals, m.60. **b. acetate.** MeCOOCH$_2$Ph = 150.13. Colorless liquid. b.206. Cf. *methyl benzoate.* **b. acetoacetic ether.** C$_2$H$_3$O·CHCH$_2$Ph·COOEt = 220.20. Colorless liquid, b. 287. **b. acetophenone.** Propiophenone. **b. acrylic acid.** CH$_2$:C(PhCH$_2$)$_2$COOH = 162.08. Methylenehydrocinnamic acid, Colorless crystals, m.69. **b. alcohol.** PhCH$_2$OH = 108.10. Phenylcarbinol, benzalcohol, phenmethylol, α-hydroxytoluene. Colorless aromatic liquid with a sharp burning taste, b.204.7, slightly soluble in water. Used as a local anesthetic and in perfumery. *hydroxy-* C$_6$H$_4$(OH)CH$_2$OH = 124.10. *ortho-* Saligenin. *meta-* m-Oxybenzyl alcohol. Colorless needles, m.67, decomp. 300. *para-* Colorless needles, m.110. *hydroxymethoxy-* Vanillic alcohol. *isopropyl-* Cuminol. *methoxy-* Anisyl alcohol. *methyl-* Homosaligenin. *methylaminoethyl-* Ephedrine. *methylenedioxy-* Piperonyl alcohol. *methylisopropyl-* Thymotic alcohol. *nitro-* NO$_2$C$_6$H$_4$CH$_2$OH = 153.10. *ortho-* Colorless needles, m.74. *meta-* White, rhombic crystals, m.27. *para-* Colorless needles m.93, b.179. *oxy-* See *hydroxybenzyl alcohol.* **b. amine.** PhCH$_2$NH$_2$ = 107.15. Phenylmethylamine. Colorless liquid, b.184; used in organic synthesis. *di-* (PhCH$_2$)$_2$NH = 197.13. Diphenylmethylimine. Colorless liquid, b.300. *imino-* Benzamidine. *tri-* $(PhCH_2)_3N = 287.17$. Colorless crystals, m.91. **b. aniline.** $PhCH_2NHPh = 183.2$. Colorless prisms, m.32, used in organic synthesis. *di-* $(PhCH_2)_2NPh = 285.3$. Colorless crystals, m.67.7 **b. azide.** $PhCH_2N_3 = 133.12$. A liquid, $b_{25mm}108$. **b. benzene.** Diphenylmethane. **b. benzoate.** $Ph\cdot COOCH_2\cdot Ph = 212.27$. Colorless oily, aromatic liquid with a sharp burning taste, m.18.5; an antispasmodic. **b. benzoic acid.** Diphenylmethanecarboxylic acid. **b. bichloride.** Benzalchloride. **b. bromide.** $PhCH_2Br = 171.06$. α-Bromotoluene, Colorless liquid, b.198.5. A poison gas in chemical warfare. **b. carbamate.** $C_8H_9O_2N = 151.12$. $PhCH_2O\cdot CO\cdot NH_2$. Colorless liquid, b.198. **b. carbamide.** B. urea. **b. carbinol.** $PhCH_2CH_2OH = 122.10$. Phenyl ethyl alcohol. phenylethanol, α-hydroxy-β-phenyl ether. Colorless liquid, b.212; A constituent of oil of rose, geranium, etc.; used in perfumes. *iso-* PhCHMeOH. Phenylmethylcarbinol. Colorless liquid, b.203. **b. carbonimide.** $PhCH_2NC$, isomeric with b. cyanide. **b. chloride.** $PhCH_2Cl = 126.55$. α-Chlorotoluene. Colorless liquid, b.178. Used in the synthesis of bitter almond oil and aniline dyes. **b. cinnamate.** $C_8H_7COOCH_2Ph = 238.11$. Cinnamein. Colorless prisms, m.39; used in perfumery. **b. cyanamide.** $PhCH_2NHCN = 132.12$. Crystalline solid, m.33. **b. cyanide.** $PhCH_2CN = 117.15$. Phenylacetonitrile, α-tolunitrile. Colorless liquid, b.233.5; used in organic synthesis. *iso-* B. carbonimide. *nitro-* $NO_2\cdot C_6H_4\cdot CH_2CN = 162.11$. *ortho-* Colorless needles, m.83. *para-* Colorless prisms, m.115. **b. dichloride.** Benzal chloride. **b. diphenyl.** $PhCH_2\cdot C_6H_4Ph = 244.15$. *ortho-* Monoclinic needles, m.54. *para-* Colorless leaflets, m.85. **b. diphenylamine.** $PhCH_2\cdot NPh_2 = 259.15$. Colorless crystals, m.87. **b. disulfide.** $PhCH_2S\cdot SCH_2Ph = 246.30$. Colorless leaflets, m.71. **b. ether.** $(PhCH_2)_2O = 198.19$. Benzyl oxide. Colorless, oily liquid, b.297. **b. ethylaniline.** $Ph\cdot N\cdot Et(CH_2\cdot Ph) = 208.2$. Yellowish liquid, b.286 (decomp.). **b. ethylbenzene.** $PhCH_2C_4H_6\cdot Et = 196.20$. Colorless liquid, b.194. **b. formamide.** $PhCH_2\cdot NH\cdot CHO = 135.1$. *o-nitro-* $NO_2\cdot C_6H_4\cdot CH_2\cdot NHCHO = 181.10$. Colorless crystals, m.89. **b. fumarate.** $(PhCH_2OOC\cdot CH=)_2 = 326.14$. Dibenzyl fumarate. White, odorless solid; an antispasmodic. Cf. *b. succinate.* **b. hydrazine.** $PhCH_2\cdot NHNH_2 = 122.2$. Colorless liquid, $b_{35mm}135$. *di-* $PhCH_2NHNHCH_2Ph = 212.3$. Colorless crystals, m.65; used in organic synthesis. **b. hydroxylamine.** $C_7H_9ON = 123.09$. *alpha-* $PhCH_2ONH_2$. Colorless liquid, b.123. *beta-* $PhCH_2NHOH$. Colorless crystals, m.57. *di-* $PhCH_2NHOCH_2Ph = 213.14$. *tri-* $(PhCH_2)_2NOCH_2Ph = 303.19$. **b. idene.** Benzylidene. **b. iodide.** $PhCH_2I = 218.08$. α-Iodotoluene. Colorless liquid, m.24 (decomp.). Used in the manufacture of drugs and dyes. **b. isocyanide.** B. carbimide. **b. isosulfocyanide.** B. sulfocyanide. **b. isothiocyanate.** B. mustard oil. **b. ketone.** $(PhCH_2)_2CO = 210.19$. White crystals, m.34. **b. mercaptan.** $PhCH_2SH = 124.16$. B. sulfhydrate, b. thiol. Colorless liquid, b. 196. **b. morphine.** Peronine. **b. mustard oil.** $PhCH_2NCS = 149.19$. Benzyl isothiocyanate. Colorless liquid, b.243. **b. naphthalene.** $C_{10}H_7CH_2Ph = 218.20$. Monoclinic prisms. *alpha-* m.58.6. *beta-* m.35. **b. naphthyl ketone.** $PhCH_2COC_{10}H_7 = 246.11$.

Colorless scales, m.57. **b. nitrile.** B. cyanide. **b. oxethylamine.** $C_9H_{13}ON = 151.2$. Picrate. Colorless crystals, m.136. **b. penicillin.** See *penicillin.* **b. phenanthracene.** $PhCH_2C_6H_3(CH)_2C_6H_4 = 268.13$. Colorless needles, m.155. **b. phenol.** $PhCH_2C_6H_4OH = 184.1$. *para-* Colorless crystals, m.84. **b. phenylamine.** B. aniline. **b. phthalimidine.** $C_6H_4\cdot N(CH_2)\cdot Ph\cdot CO\cdot NH = 224.1$. Colorless crystals, m.137. **b. pyridine.** $PhCH_2\cdot C_5H_4N = 169.11$. *alpha-* b.276. *beta-* m.34. **b. succinate.** $(PhCH_2OOC\cdot CH_2)_2 = 328.14$. Dibenzyl succinate. White, odorless powder; an antispasmodic. Cf. *b. fumarate.* **b. sulfhydrate.** B. mercaptan. **b. sulfide.** $(PhCH_2)_2S = 214.22$. B. thioether. Colorless scales, m.49; used in organic synthesis. **b. sulfine.** $(PhCH_2)\cdot O:S:O = 246.24$. An isomer of b. sulfone. **b. sulfinic acid.** $PhCH_2SO\cdot OH = 124.12$. **b. sulfocyanide.** $PhCH_2CNS = 149.19$. B. rhodanide, b. thiocyanate. Colorless prisms, m.41. *iso-* B. isorhodanide, b. isothiocyanate. Colorless liquid, b.240. **b. sulfone.** $Ph(CH_2)_2O_2S = 246.24$. Colorless needles, m.150. **b. sulfonic acid.** $PhCH_2\cdot (OH)\cdot O_3S = 172.1$. **b. sulfoxide.** $Ph(CH_2)_2SO = 230.21$. Colorless leaflets, m.132. **b. tartronic acid.** $PhCH_2(OH)\cdot (COOH)_2 = 210.1$. Colorless crystals, m.143 (decomp.). **b. thiourea.** $PhCH_2NH\cdot CS\cdot NH_2 = 166.2$. B. sulfocarbamide. Colorless crystals, m.162. **b. thiocyanate.** B. sulfocyanide. **b. urea.** $PhCH_2NH\cdot CO\cdot NH_2 = 150.20$. B. carbamide. Colorless needles, m.147 (decomp.).

benzylation. The introduction of the benzyl radical into an organic molecule.

benzylcarbamide. See *benzyl.*

benzylene. The radical $-C_6H_4CH_2-$, usually in bicyclic compounds. **b. chloride.** Benzachloride. **b. glycol.** Hydrobenzoin. **b. pseudothiourea.** Coumothiazone. **b. ψ-thiourea.** Imidocoumothiazone. **b. thiurea.** B. pseudothiurea.

benzylidene. The PhCH= radical, in which the 2 valencies are usually attached to 1 atom of another radical, thus forming a double bond. Cf. *benzal, bensylidyne.* **b. acetone.** $PhCH:CHCOMe = 146.1$. Benzalacetone, methyl cinnamyl ketone, acetocinnamone, methyl styryl ketone. Colorless crystals with coumarin odor, m.42; used in organic synthesis. *di-* Styryl ketone. **b. bromide.** $PhCHBr_2 = 249.94$. A liquid, $b_{20mm}130$. **b. chloride.** Benzal chloride.

benzylmorphine. Peronine.

benzylphenylamine. Benzylaniline.

BEPO. British experimental pile. An atomic pile, q.v., designed to develop 6,000 kw of heat in its uranium metal bars; used to produce radioactive isotopes.

beraunite. A native iron phosphate.

Berberidaceae. Barberry. Herbs, shrubs, or trees with a watery juice. Several yield drugs.

berberine. $C_{20}H_{17}O_4N\cdot 6H_2O = 443.34$. An alkaloid from the roots of *Hydrastis canadensis* (golden seal), *Berberis vulgaris,* and other Ranunculaceae. Orange crystals, m.145. Cf. *bebeerine.* **b. bisulfate.** B. sulfate. **b. carbonate.** $C_{20}H_{17}N\cdot H_2CO_3\cdot 2H_2O = 395.15$. Yellow crystals, soluble in hot water. **b. hydrochloride.** $C_{20}H_{17}O_4N\cdot HCl\cdot 2H_2O = 407.61$. Yellow powder, soluble in water. A tonic, stomachic, and gentle laxative. **b. sulfate.** $C_{20}H_{17}O_4N\cdot H_2SO_4 = 433.32$. Orange needles, soluble in water; an antiperiodic, stomachic, and tonic.

berberis. The dried stems of *Berberis aristata* or *B. vulgaris.* The fluid extract is a tonic and purgative. See *barberry.*

berberonic acid. $C_5H_5N(COOH)_3 = 250.1$. 2,4,5-Pyridinetricarboxylic acid*. Colorless, triclinic crystals, decomp. 235.

berengelite. A Peruvian pitch, used for caulking.

beresovite. A native mixed chromate and carbonate of lead.

bergamot oil. A yellow-green, volatile essential oil from the rind of *Citrus bergamia* (Rutaceae), d.0.880–0.885. It contains linalyl acetate, limonene, and linalol. Used in perfumery, and as a histological clearing agent.

bergaptol. A constituent of lime oil.

bergblau. A native copper carbonate.

bergenin. $C_{14}H_{16}O_9 = 328.14$. Vakerin. A constituent of the barks of many tropical trees. Colorless needles, m.226.

bergenine. $C_6H_3O_3 \cdot H_2O = 141.1$. A bitter principle from *Saxifraga crassifolia;* m.140.

bergenose. An ilmenite-norite (Norway).

bergenization. See *Bergius* process (1).

Bergius, Friedrich. 1884–1949. German industrial chemist, Nobel Prize winner (1931). **B. process.** (1) Berginization. Production of motor fuel by the hydrogenation and liquefaction of coal at 400–450°C in hydrogen at 120–200 atm. (2) The manufacture of sugar from wood by treating sawdust with 40% hydrochloric acid and removing the acid by vapors from hot mineral oil.

Bergman, Torbern Olof. 1735–1784. Swedish chemist; who (in 1783) adapted the alchemical symbols of circles and arcs to represent compounds by joining them together.

beriberi. A vitamin B deficiency disease.

Berkefeld filter. A porous porcelain cylinder for the filtration of toxins and sera or the preparation of sterile solutions.

berkelium. Bk. An element, at. no. 97, having a short life owing to radioactive decay. Prepared, by irradiation, by Cunningham and Thompson (Lawrence Radiation Laboratory) in 1959.

berkevilite. Barkevite.

Berkshire sand. Purified sea sand for filtration.

Berlin blue. Ferric ferrocyanide.

bernstein. Amber. **b. säure.** Succinic acid.

Berthelot, Marcellin Pierre Eugène. 1827–1907. French statesman and physical chemist: "All chemical reactions are dependent upon physical forces." Cf. *Berthollet.*

berthierine. Iron ore (Alsace) consisting of magnetite and chamosite.

berthierite. $FeSb_2S_4$. A native sulfantimonide.

Berthollet, Count Claude Louis. 1748–1822. French chemist; discovered the compositions of ammonia and hydrogen sulfide and developed industrial chemistry. Cf. *Berthelot.*

berthollide. Bertollide. Proposed name for a compound of variable proportions; e.g., an alloy. Cf. *daltonide.*

bertrandite. $H_2Be_4Si_2O_9$. A native beryllium silicate; colorless, transparent, orthorhombic crystals.

beryl. $Al_2Be_3Si_6O_{18}$. A native beryllium, aluminum silicate. Hexagonal crystals, d.2.7, hardness, 7.5–8. The transparent varieties are gems; e.g., *aquamarine, emerald.*

beryllia. Beryllium oxide.

beryllium. Be = 9.01 (formerly glucinum, Gl). An element of the magnesium group, at. no. 4. A hard, noncorrodible, grayish black metal in hexagons, d₂₀ol.85, m.1285, soluble in acids or alkalies. B. ores generally occur in granite rocks, e.g., beryl. B. is divalent and forms one series of compounds. It was discovered (1797) by Vauquelin in beryl, and isolated (1828) by Bussy and Woehler. Used as a moderator in nuclear reactions, in fuel "cans" for atomic fuels, in lightweight structures to impart strength and hardness to aluminum alloys, and with silver to form untarnishable alloys; also for windows in X-ray tubes. **b. acetate.** $(CH_3COO)_2Be = 127.07$. Colorless plates, decomp. 285. *basic*- $BeO \cdot 3Be(C_2H_3O_2)_2 = 406.22$. White octahedra, m.284, decomp. in water. **b. acetylacetonate.** $Be(C_5H_7O_2)_2 = 207.13$. Monoclinic crystals, m.108. **b. alkyls.** The organic compounds of b., containing aliphatic radicals; e.g., b. ethide. **b. bromide.** $BeBr_2 = 168.94$. White, hygroscopic needles, m.601. **b. carbide.** $Be_2C = 30.21$. Yellow hexagons, decomp. by water. **b. carbonate.** $BeCO_3 \cdot 4H_2O = 141.2$. White powder, decomp. by acids; occurs also in basic salts of variable composition. *basic*- $(BeO)_5CO_2 \cdot 5H_2O = 259.59$. White powder, decomp. by acids. **b. chloride.** (1) $BeCl_2 = 80.9$. White, deliquescent needles, m.400. (2) $BeCl_2 \cdot 4H_2O$. Yellow syrup, miscible with water. **b. ethide, b. ethyl.** $BeEt_2 = 67.20$. Colorless liquid, b.185–188. **b. fluoride.** $BeF_2 = 47.1$. White powder, d₁₅₀· m.800. **b. hydroxide.** $Be(OH)_2 = 48.1$. White powder, decomp. by heat, insoluble in water. **b. iodide.** $BeI_2 = 252.92$. White needles, m.510, decomp. by water. **b. nitrate.** $Be(NO_3)_2 \cdot 3H_2O = 187.2$. Colorless, deliquescent crystals, soluble in water; a reagent and hardener for gas mantles. **b. oxalate.** $Be(C_2O_4) \cdot 3H_2O = 151.07$. Rhombic crystals, m.(−2H₂O)100, (−H₂O)220. **b. oxide.** $BeO = 25.1$. Beryllia. Amorphous white powder, infusible, insoluble in water. Used to manufacture b. salts, and as a refractory. **b. oxychloride.** $Be_2OCl_2 = 105.12$. White hexagons, infusible, insoluble in water. **b. phosphate.** Beryllonite. **b. potassium fluoride.** $BeF_2 \cdot 2KF = 163.30$. White crystals. **b. silicate.** Be_2SiO_4. White powder, used as refractory, for sparking plug porcelain and in making b. compounds. Cf. *beryl.* **b. sodium fluoride.** $BeF_2 \cdot 2NaF = 131.10$. Gray crystals; used to prepare metallic b. **b. sulfate.** (1) $BeSO_4 \cdot 4H_2O = 177.2$. White tetragons; loses 2 molecules of water at 100; decomp. by further heat. (2) $BeSO_4 \cdot 7H_2O = 231.28$. White monoclinic crystals.

beryllonite. $NaBePO_4$. Yellow, transparent crystals, d.2.845, hardness 5.5–6.

berzelianite. Cu_2Se. A native selenide; thin white crusts. Cf. *crookesite, umangite.*

berzeliite. $(Mg \cdot Ca \cdot Mn)_3As_2O_8$. A native arsenate of magnesium, calcium, and manganese; red waxy masses.

berzelium. A supposed element of at. wt. 212 (Baskerville).

Berzelius, Baron Jöns Jakob. 1779–1848. Swedish chemist, the investigator of atomic weights, using oxygen as standard; worked on electrochemical analysis, isomerism, and the gas laws; discovered selenium and thorium, and isolated silicon.

Bessemer, Sir Henry. 1813–1898. English metallurgist, inventor of the B. process (1856). **B. converter.** A large egg-shaped retort used in the B. process. **B. iron.** Iron made by the B. process. **B. process.** Making steel by pouring molten cast iron in a specially designed converter and passing a stream of air through the molten mass to oxidize manganese, silicon, and carbon.

Bestuscheff's tincture. An ethereal tincture of iron chloride.

beta. Second letter of the Greek alphabet. **b. acid.** 2,6-Naphthylaminesulfonic acid. **b. chlora process.** A method of bleaching flour with nitrosyl chloride and chlorine. **b. eucane.** Betaeucaine, **b. gauge.** A nucleonic gauge, q.v., which uses b. rays. **b. hydrogen.** See *hydrogen molecule*. **b. position.** Substitution of the 2d, 3d, 6th, or 7th H atom of a dicyclic compound or of the H atom attached to the C atom next but one to the principal group of a straight-chain compound. **b. particles.** A stream of electrons emitted from radioactive substances with the velocity of light. **b. ray.** See *b. particles*.

Beta. Beets (Chenopodiaceae). The juice of *B. vulgaris* yields sugar, betaine, and an indicator.

betacaine. Betaeucaine.

betaeucaine. $C_{15}H_{21}NO_2 = 247.2$. Trimethyl-benzoyl-oxypiperidine. Its hydrochloride is a local anesthetic. **b. hydrochloride.** $C_{15}H_{21}O_2N\cdot HCl = 283.65$. White odorless powder, soluble in water; a local anesthetic.

betaimidazolethylamine. Histamine.

betaimineazolylethylamine. Ergamine.

betaine. $MeNCO(CH_2):O(+H_2O) = 117.11$. Lycine, oxyneurine, dimethylsarcosine, trimethylglycocoll. An alkaloid, from beets, or synthetic. Colorless monoclinic crystals, m.293 (decomp.), soluble in water or alcohol. **nicotine methyl-** Trigonelline. **thio-** Thetine. **trimethyloxybutyn-** Carnitine.

b. hydrochloride. $C_{15}H_{11}O_2N\cdot HCl = 153.57$. Acidol. Colorless crystals, m.235; used to neutralize tetanus toxin.

betaines. Organic bases characterized by the $=NMe_3$ group; e.g., glycine betaine, $Me_3N\cdot CH_2\cdot CO$,

$$Me_3N\cdot CH_2\cdot CO$$
$$\vert\!\!-\!\!O\!\!-\!\!\vert$$

carnitine, $Me_3N\cdot CH_2\cdot CHOH\cdot CH_2\cdot CO$. Cf. *stachydrine, trigonelline*.

$$\vert\!\!-\!\!\!-\!\!O\!\!-\!\!\!-\!\!\vert$$

betaisoamylene. Amylene.

betamethasone. $C_{22}H_{29}O_5F = 392.50$. White, bitter crystals, m.246 (decomp.), insoluble in water; an adrenocortical steroid (B.P.).

betamethylethylpyridine. Collidine.

betamethylindole. Skatole.

betanaphthol. See *naphthol*. **b. benzoate.** See *β-naphthol benzoate*. **b. orange.** Tropaeolin. **b. salicylate.** Betol.

betanaphthyl. Naphthyl. **b. amine.** *β*-Naphthylamine. **b. benzoate.** *β*-Naphthol benzoate. **b. salicylate.** Betol.

betanin. An anthocyanin from beetroot.

beta-oxybutyric acid. *β*-Oxybutyric acid.

betaquinine. Quinidine.

betaterpineol. *β*-Terpineol.

betatopic. Pertaining to a radioactive substance which differs from one of its isotopes by 1 orbital electron and 1 integer in atomic number (cf. *alphatopic*). **b. change.** The transformation of a radioactive substance when it loses an orbital electron, and thereby becomes an isotope of an element with an atomic number higher by 1.

betatron. An X-ray generator operating at up to 300 million volts, in which electrons are accelerated by spinning them in a circular field surrounding an alternating magnetic field. They will penetrate atomic nuclei.

betaxin. Vitamin B_1.

betel. (1) Originally the betel vine. Cf. *betel leaf*. (2) A fragment of betelnut rolled up in a betel leaf, with some lime or gambir, for chewing (E. Indies). A tonic and stimulant. (3) Pinang. The Areca or catechu palm of the East Indies. **b. leaf.** The dried leaves of *Piper betle* (Piperaceae). **b. nut.** Areca nut, buyo, semen arecae. The dried seed of *Areca catechu*, an E. Indian palm. It contains many alkaloids (e.g., arecoline); an astringent, anthelmintic, tonic, and stimulant. Cf. *areca nut*. **b. phenol.** Chavibetol.

bethanechol chloride. $C_7H_{17}N_2O_2Cl = 196.69$. Carbamethylcholine chloride. White crystals having a slight ammoniacal odor; a parasympathomimetic (U.S.P.).

bethroot. Trillium.

betol. $C_{10}H_7COO\cdot C_6H_4OH = 264.2$. Salinaphthol, naphthalol, *β*-naphthyl salicylate. White, amorphous powder, m.95; an intestinal antiseptic, antirheumatic, and antizymotic. Cf. *alphol*.

Bettendorf test. A test for arsenic in presence of bismuth and antimony compounds. A freshly prepared stannous chloride solution is added to the sample; a brownish tint indicates arsenic.

Betts' process. Refining lead from the fluosilicate with gelatin as electrolyte.

betula. A genus of the oak family (Cupuliferae). See *birch*. **b. camphor.** Betulinol. **b. oil.** See *birch oil*.

betulin. Betulinol. **b. amaric acid.** $C_{36}H_{52}O_{16} = 740.5$. An oxidation product of betulinol.

betulinic acid. $C_{36}H_{54}O_6 = 582.6$. A dibasic acid, m.195, formed by oxidation of betulin.

betulinol. $C_{24}H_{40}O_2 = 360.4$. Betula camphor, betulin. A diatomic alcohol from the bark of betula species. Colorless crystals, m.258.

beudantite. Biereite, corkite. A native sulfate and phosphate of iron and lead; dark green or black rhombohedra.

Beutel buret float. A hydrometer-like closed glass tube, used to facilitate buret readings.

bev. Abbreviation for billions of electron volts. A unit of atomic anergy.

Bexan. Trade name for a polyvinyl chloride synthetic fiber.

beyrichite. Ni_3S_4. Native in metallic, gray hexagons.

bhang. An intoxicating preparation made from the flowering tops of hemp. Cf. *hashish*.

BHC. See benzene hexachloride. **gamma-** Lindane. The *γ* isomer of BHC. An insecticide.

Bi. Symbol for bismuth.

bi- (1) Prefix indicating 2 or double. Cf. *di-* and *bis-*. (2) Misnomer for acid salt; as, bisulfate.

biacenaphthylidene. Biacene.

biacene. $C_{10}H_6\cdot CH_2\cdot C:C\cdot CH_2\cdot C_{10}H_{16} = 304.2$. Red-yellow crystals, m.271, which show distinct dichroism when dissolved in concentrated sulfuric acid; indigo blue in transmitted light, red in incident light.

biacetyl. MeCO·COMe = 86.05. 2,3-Butanedione*, diacetyl. Colorless liquid of pungent, sweet odor, d.0.9793, b.88, slightly soluble in water. **b. dioxime.** Dimethylglyoxime. **b. monoxime.** MeCO·C(NOH)Me.

biacetylene. HC≡C—C≡CH = 50.0. Butadiine, butadiyne*.

Bial's reagent. A solution of orcin in acidic ferric chloride, used to detect pentoses in urine.

biallyl. Diallyl.

bianiline. **N-** Hydrazobenzene. **para-** Benzidine.

bianisaldehyde. Anisil.

bianisidine. Dianisidine.

bianthryl. $C_{28}H_{18}$ = 354.29.

$$ HC \underset{C_6H_4}{\overset{C_6H_4}{<}} C - C \underset{C_6H_4}{\overset{C_6H_4}{>}} CH. $$

Colorless leaflets, m.300.

biarsine. $H_2As{-}AsH_2$ = 153.94. Diarsine, diarsyl. Cf. *arsines.* **tetraethyl-** As_2Et_4 = 266.03. Ethylcacodyl. Colorless liquid, igniting in air, b.187. **tetramethyl-** Cacodyl.

biaxial. Having 2 axes. **b. crystals.** A crystal with 2 optical axes.

bibasic. Dibasic; having 2 H atoms which can be replaced by metals.

bibenzal. Stilbene.

bibenzenone. Diphenoquinone.

bibenzenyl. Tolane.

bibenzil. (1) Dibenzil, (2) Dibenzyl.

bibenzohydrol. Benzopinacol.

bibenzoic acid. Diphenic acid.

bibenzoyl. (1) Benzil. (2) Dibenzoyl; prefix indicating 2 benzoyl radicals.

bibenzyl. $C_{14}H_{14}$ = 182.19. Dibenzyl. **asymmetric-** Me·CHPh$_2$. Colorless liquid, b.209. **symmetric-.** PhCH$_2$·CH$_2$Ph. Diphenylethane. Colorless needles, m.52. **b. alcohol.** Hydrobenzoin.

biberine. Bebeerine.

biborate. An acid borate; as, NaHBO$_3$. Cf. *diborate.*

bibulous. Absorbing moisture. **b. paper.** Blotting or filter paper.

bicarbonate. Dicarbonate, acid carbonate. A salt containing the —HCO$_3$ radical. **b. of potash.** Potassium b. **b. of soda.** Sodium b.

bicarbureted hydrogen. Ethylene (obsolete).

bichloride. A salt containing 2 atoms of chlorine.

bicholestatriene. $C_{54}H_{82}(?)$. A derivative of provitamin D$_3$.

bichromate. Dichromate, acid chromate. A salt containing the =Cr$_2$O$_7$ radical. **b. cell.** See *cell.*

bichrome. Potassium dichromate.

biconcave. See concave *lens.*

biconvex. See convex *lens.*

bicuculline. $C_{22}H_{17}O_6N$ = 367.15. An alkaloid from *Dicentra cucullaria, Corydalis sempervirens,* and *Adlumia fungosa.* (Fumaraceae.) Dimorphic crystals m.177 and 196. *Adlumine* has two CH$_3$O— groups instead of the first CH$_2$O$_2$.

bicyclic. Containing 2 rings; as naphthalene.

bicyclodecane. Decalin.

bicycloheptane. **1,2,3-** Norpinane. **1,2,2-** Norcamphane. **0,1,4-** Carane. **2:4-** Pinane.

bicycloheptene. **0,1,4-** Carene. **1,1,4-** Norcarene. **1,1,3-** Pinene.

bidesyl. PhCO·CHPh·CHPh·COPh = 390.2. Dibenzoyldibenzyl. Colorless crystals, m.255.

bidiphenyleneethane. $(C_6H_4)_2CH·CH(C_6H_4)_2$ = 330.2. Colorless crystals, m.246. Cf. *tetraphenylene.* **b.** Bifluorene.

bieberite. CoSO$_4$·7H$_2$O. Native in red monoclinic crystals.

Biebrich red. Scarlet R.

biethylene. 1,3-Butadiene.

biflavonyl. The structure

Cf. *ginkgetin.*

bifluorene. $(C_6H_4)_2·C:C·(C_6H_4)_2$ = 328.2. Bidiphenylene ethylene. Red needles, m.188.

biformyl. Glyoxal.

bihexyl. Dodecane*.

bihydrazine. NH$_2$·NH·NH·NH$_2$ = 62.2. Buzane, dihydrobuzylene, tetrazane. Cf. *tetrazanes.*

biindoxyl. Indigo white.

biindyl. $C_6H_4·CH_2CH:C·C:CHCH_2·C_6H_4$ = 230.1. Cf. *diindyl.*

bikhaconitine. $C_{36}H_{51}O_{11}N$ = 673.40. Bikh. An alkaloid from the root of *Aconitum ferox,* m.113.

bilateral. Pertaining to 2 or both sides.

bile. Gall, chola. The yellow, brown, or greenish secretion of the liver (solids 14, water 86%), d.1.026–1.032. **b. acids.** Acids found in b.; e.g., glycocholic acid, $C_{26}H_{43}O_6NS$. See *cholane, porphin.* **b. pigments.** The coloring matter of b.; as, bilirubin, XO$_6$ (red); biliverdin, XO$_8$ (green); bilicyanin, XO$_9$ (blue); bilipurpurin, XO$_{10}$ (purple); bilixanthin, XO$_{12}$ (brown); X is C$_{32}$H$_{36}$N$_4$. **b. salts.** The sodium salts of b. acid which aid digestion.

bilharziasis. Schistosomiasis. A helminth disease in tropical countries.

bilicyanin. $C_{32}H_{36}O_9N_4$ = 620.3. A blue pigment obtained by oxidation of biliverdin.

biliflavin. A yellow pigment derived from biliverdin.

bilifulvin. Bilirubin.

bilifuscin. $C_{16}H_{20}O_4N_2$ = 304.6. Brown, insoluble powder from bile pigments; used as a reagent. **meso-** A brown pigment formed by the decomposition of hemoglobin.

bilin. A mixture of sodium taurocholate and sodium glycocholate; the main constituent of bile.

bilineurine. Choline.

bilinigrin. A black oxidation product of bilirubin.

biliphain. Bilirubin.

biliprasin. A green pigment derived from biliverdin.

bilipurpurin. Cholohematin. A purple bile pigment,

bilirubin. $C_{32}H_{36}O_6N_4$ = 572.5. Bilifulvin, biliphain. hematoidin. The red insoluble coloring matter of bile which is structurally related to hematoporphyrin and hematin and is derived from hemoglobin. Red-yellow needles, m.192. Cf. *porphin ring, cholothallin.* **hydro-** Urobilin.

bilirubinic acid. $C_{17}H_{24}O_3N_2$ = 304.16. A monobasic acid containing 2 attached pyrrole rings, formed from bilirubin and hemin by reduction.

bilisoidanic acid. $C_{24}H_{32}O_9$ = 464.6. An acid obtained from bile by treatment with nitric acid.

biliverdic acid. $C_8H_9O_4N = 183.08$. Crystals, m.114.

biliverdin. $C_{32}H_{36}O_8N_4 = 604.5$. An oxidation product of bilirubin. Green, amorphous powder, soluble in alcohol. It occurs in some fish scales and fins, and yields the pigment biliflavin.

bilixanthin. $C_{32}H_{36}O_{12}N_4 = 668.3$. Brown oxidation product of bile pigments, q.v.

billion. (1) A million millions; 10^{12} (British and German usage). (2) A thousand millions; 10^9 (Continental Europe and U.S.A. usage). Cf. *milliard*.

Billroth's mixture. An anesthetic: chloroform 3, alcohol 1, ether 1 pts.

biloidanic acid. $C_{22}H_{32}O_{12} = 488.25$. Norsolanellic acid. An oxidation product of bile.

bimetal. A sheet made of 2 metal layers and having special properties; as, corrosion resistance.

bimolecular. Pertaining to 2 molecules. **b. reaction.** See *reactions, 2d order*.

binaphthalene. $C_{10}H_7—C_{10}H_7 = 254.22$. Naphthyl naphthalene. α,α'- or **alpha-** m.160, b.365. β,β'- or **beta-** m.187, b.452. α,β'- or **gamma-** m.70.

binaphthyl. (1) The radical—$C_{20}H_{13}$, from binaphthalene. (2) Dinaphthyl.

binarite. Marcasite.

binary compound. A compound containing only 2 elements with 2 or more atoms; e.g., $NaCl$, $FeCl_3$. **b. mixture.** A mixture of any 2 substances. **b. salt.** A salt containing 2 bases; as, $NaKSO_4$. **b. system.** Any combination possible with 2 metals; cf. *phase rule*, *alloy*.

binder. A material used to hold solid substances together; as, bitumen.

bindheimite. Native hydrous lead antimonate.

binding. Holding together. **b. energy.** The force that holds together the negatively and positively charged portions of an atom or molecule. Cf. solution *energy*.

bing. Spoil bank. Colliery refuse consisting of pyritic fine coal and shale.

biniodide. (1) Diiodide. (2) In pharmacy: (*a*) mercuric iodide, (*b*) mercuric potassium iodide.

binitro. See *dinitro-*

binnite. $2As_2S_3 \cdot 3Cu_2S$. A native copper-arsenic sulfide.

binocular microscope. A microscope with 2 eyepieces giving a stereoscopic effect.

binoxalate. Bioxalate.

binoxide. Dioxide.

bio- Prefix (Greek "bios") meaning life. **Bio.** Bismuthyl.

bioanalysis. The determination of small quantities of substances by means of protozoa or bacteria.

bioassay. The determination of the activity of drugs from their effects on animals.

biocatalyst. (1) Enzyme. (2) Ergine.

biocatalyzator. A protoplasmic substance that promotes growth.

biochanin A. $C_{15}H_{14}O_5 = 239.20$. 2,4,6-Trihydroxyphenyl,4-methoxybenzyl ketone, m.192. An estrogenic flavone from red clover.

biochemical. Pertaining to the matter changes within an organism. **b. oxygen demand.** B.O.D. A chemical measure of the deoxygenating power of an effluent in terms of the difference between the Winkler oxygen value in contact with oxygen-saturated water before and after 5 days at 17.8°C.

biochemistry. A branch of chemistry dealing with the changes occurring in living organisms and cells.

biocolloid. A gluelike organic substance; as the glutin of bone glue.

bioctyl. Hexadecane*.

biodegradable. Describing a substance that can be decomposed by biological action, e.g., a soft detergent.

biodyne. A natural, cellular respiratory factor.

bioelement. An element essential to life. Principally those most abundant in organisms. Cf. *abundance*, *periodic chain*.

DISTRIBUTION OF BIOELEMENTS (PER CENT)

	Mammals		Gymnosperms
O	62.43	C	53.96
C	21.15	O	38.65
H	9.86	H	6.18
N	3.10	Al	0.065
Ca	1.90	Si	0.057
P	0.95	S	0.052
K	0.23	Fe	0.030
S	0.16	N	0.030
Cl	0.08	Ca	0.007
Na	0.080	K	0.006
Mg	0.027	P	0.005
I	0.014	Mg	0.003
F	0.009	Cl	0.002
Fe	0.005	Na	0.001
Br	0.002	F	0.001
Al	0.001	Mn	0.001
Si	0.001		
Mn	0.001		
	100.00		100.00

biogen. The inactive parent compound of bios.

biogenesis. The theory that all life comes only from life. Antonym: abiogenesis.

biogenic. See *bioelement*.

biogeochemistry. See *geochemistry*.

biognosis. The study of life.

biological assay. The determination of the active principles of a drug from the smallest quantity that will produce certain symptoms in animals or organisms. It can supplement or replace chemical methods of analysis. **b. oxygen demand.** Biochemical oxygen demand.

biologics. Preparations derived from living organisms, used in therapy:

1. *Antiserums*, producing passive or temporary immunity.
   A. *Antitoxic*, used to neutralize specific toxins; as, diphtheria.
   B. *Antibacterial;* as, antidysenteric.
2. *Vaccines*, producing active or permanent immunity; bacterial suspensions; as, rabies *vaccine*.

Energy transformation		Biophysics
Matter changes		Biochemistry
MORPHOLOGY	Cells	Cytology
	Tissues	Histology
	Organs	Anatomy
	Organisms	Taxonomy
PHYSIOLOGY	Generative	Embryology
	Sustentative	Metabolism
	Correlative	Circulation and nerves
PATHOLOGY	Plants	Phytopathology
	Animals	Zoopathology
	Man	Pathology
ETIOLOGY	The race	Phylogeny
	The individual	Ontogeny
CHOROLOGY	Plants	Flora
	Animals	Fauna
	Plants and animals	Ecology
PALEONTOLOGY	Plants	Paleobotany
	Animals	Paleozoology
	Man	Ethnology

3. *Bacterial antigens,* derived from bacteria and having immunizing power.
  A. *Bacterial vaccines,* killed bacteria in suspension.
  B. *Ectoantigens,* or washings from live pathogenic bacteria; as, gonococcus, *immunogen.*
  C. *Toxoids* and *filtrates;* as, gonococcus filtrate.
4. *Pollen and protein extracts,* used for diagnosing and treating hay fever, asthma, dermatitis, etc.

biology. The science of living matter, its forms, functions, occurrence, behavior, and evolution. See table above.
Branches:
1. Botanical (plants)
2. Zoological (animals)
3. Anthropological (man)

bioluminescence. The phosphorescence of living vegetable or animal organisms.

biomechanics. The study of the application of mechanics and engineering to the human body and to man-machine relationships; e.g., artificial joints. Cf. *cybernetics.*

biometry. The application of statistics to biological science.

biomolecule. A molecule of protoplasm; a unit of living substance. Cf. *idioblast, protoplasm.*

biomone. A particle of living matter made up of biomolecules.

bionergy. The "vital" force generated in living cells.

bionomy. The measurement of life phenomena.

bio-osmosis. The osmotic pressure of living cells.

biophage. A cell or organism feeding on living cells or organisms.

biophore. Biomone. The smallest particle of living matter.

bioplasm. Protoplasm.

bioplast. Micelle.

biorization. Pasteurization at 1–3 atm.

bios. $C_5H_{11}O_3N = 133.2$. A crystalline substance similar in character to a vitamin, which was found to be essential for the growth of certain types of yeast, m.223. Now known to consist principally of *i*-inositol, vitamin B_1, nicotinic acid, and pantothenic acid, q.v. Cf. *biogen.* **b.IIa.** The fraction of b. containing pantothenic acid and biotin. **b.IIb.** Vitamin H. **b.VIII.** Pyridoxine.

biose. (1) A carbohydrate containing 2 hydroxyl groups; as, $C_2H_4O_2$. Cf. *tetrose, pentose, hexose.* (2) Disaccharide.

biosphere. The air, land, sea, and water immediately surrounding mankind.

biosterin. (1) A vitamin (obsolete). (2) Biosterol.

biosterol. $C_{22}H_{44}O_2 = 340.7$. An alcohol resembling cholesterol, with the growth-stimulating property of vitamin A.

biota. The flora and fauna of a region.

biotic. (1) Pertaining to life or living organisms. (2) Suggested alternative name for vitamin.

biotin. (1) $C_{10}H_{16}O_3NS(?)$. Vitamin H, coenzyme R, 2-keto-3,4-imidazolido-2-tetrahydrothiophene-*n*-valeric acid, m.231, soluble in water. A growth-promoting cyclic urea derivative from agar. (2) $C_{11}H_{18}O_3N_2S(?)$. A very active constituent of bios in wild yeasts and egg yolk, isolated as the crystalline methyl ether.

biotite. A brown-black ferrous mica.

biotoxin. A toxin formed in the tissues of the living body.

bioxalate. Binoxalate, acid oxalate. A salt containing the $—HC_2O_4$ radical.

bioxindol. Iso*indigotin.* **dihydroxy-** Isatide. **hydroxy-** Isatan.

bioxyl. Bismuthyl chloride.

biozeolite. A zeolitic biological slime from sewage filters.

biphenyl. (1) $(C_6H_5)_2 = 154.14$. Phenylbenzene. Colorless scales, m.71, insoluble in water. (2) Diphenyl. **amino-** *ortho-* Biphenylamine. *para-* Xenylamine. **diamino-** $NH_2C_6H_4·C_6H_4NH_2$. *o,o'-* or *2,2'-* Colorless crystals, m.81. *o,p'-* or *2,4'-* Diphenyline. *p,p'-* or *4,4'-* Benzidine. **difluoro-** Antitussin. **dimethyl-** Ditolyl. **methyl-** Ph·C₆H₄·Me = 168.10. Phenyl tolyl. *m-* or *3-* Colorless liquid, b.275. *p-* or *4-* Colorless liquid, b.265.

b. amine. $Ph \cdot C_6H_4 \cdot NH_2 = 169.10$. *ar-* Phenylaniline, aminobiphenyl. Cf. *diphenylamine*. *o-* or *2-* Colorless crystals, m.45. *p-* or *4-* Xenylamine. **b. diamine.** *o,o'-* Diamino b. *p,p'-* Benzidine. **b. mercury.** $(PhC_6H_4)_2Hg = 506.75$. White scales, m.216.

biphenylene. (1) The hypothetical compound $C_6H_4:$-C_6H_4. (2) The radical $-C_6H_4 \cdot C_6H_4-$. **b. disazo.** The radical $-N:NC_6H_4 \cdot C_6H_4N:N-$. **b. oxide.** Dibenzofurane. **b. sulfide.** Dibenzothiophen.

BIPP. A mixture of bismuth iodoform and paraffin; an antiseptic which is harmless to tissues.

bipropargyl. $C_6H_6 = 78.05$. Dipropargyl, 1,5-hexadiyne*, 1,5-hexadine, $CH\equiv C \cdot CH_2 \cdot CH_2C\equiv CH$. Colorless liquid, b.85.4.

bipropenyl. 2,4-Hexadiene*.

bipseudoindoxyl. Indigotin.

birch. A tree of the genus Betula. **b. camphor.** Betulinol. **b. oil.** Sweet b. oil, betula oil. The essential oil from the bark of *Betula lenta*, black birch. Colorless oil, d.1.127–1.182, b.218–222 (chief constituent methylsalicylate); a flavoring. antirheumatic, and antipyretic. **b. tar oil.** A tarry oil from the wood of *Betula alba*, white birch. Brown oil with empyreumatic odor, d.886–0.950, soluble in alcohol, (chief constituents phenols and cresols). Used as a disinfectant, antiparasitic, and in leather dressing. **b. wood carbon.** Norit.

birdlime. A viscid substance from the bark of the Ilex species and mistletoe; contains viscin, viscum, and ilicic alcohol.

birectification. Analysis of fermented liquors by fractional distillation.

birefractive. Doubly refracting.

birefringence. Double *refraction*. **electrical-** *Kerr* effect.

birotation. Mutarotation. The exceptionally high or low optical activity of a freshly prepared aqueous solution of a sugar which, on standing or after boiling or the addition of ammonia, is reduced to a normal value.

birthwort. Serpentaria.

bis- Prefix indicating *twice*, generally applied to molecules made up of 2 similar halves.

bisabolene. $C_{15}H_{24} = 204.21$. A monocyclic sesquiterpene from bisabol myrrh and star anise oil. Colorless liquid, d.0.8727, b.103.

bisacodyl. $C_{22}H_{19}O_4N = 361.36$. White crystals, m.134, insoluble in water; a laxative (B.P.).

bisazimethylene. Ketazine.

bisazo- Tetrazo-.

bisazobenzil. $Ph \cdot CN_2 - CN_2 \cdot Ph = 232.2$, A homocyclic azide.

bisbenzimidazole. $C_{14}H_{10}N_4 = 234.2$. A heterocyclic system related to indigo. Colorless crystals, m.305.

bischofite. $MgCl_2 \cdot 6H_2O$. A native magnesium chloride.

biscuit ware. An unglazed, porous porcelain, which has been fired twice.

bisdiazo- Tetrazo-. **b. amine.** $NH:N \cdot NH \cdot N:NH = 73.06$. A hypothetical compound known as its derivatives. Cf. *hydronitrogen*. **b. hydrazine.** $HN:N \cdot NH \cdot NH \cdot N:NH = 88.08$. A hypothetical compound known as its derivatives.

bisethylxanthate. Ethylxanthogenate.

bisglyoxaline. Glycosine.

bishydrazicarbonyl. Diurea.

bishydroxycoumarin. $C_{19}H_{12}O_6 = 336.30$. 3,3'-Methylenebis(4-hydroxycoumarin). White bitter crystals, m.290; an anticoagulant.

bismal. $4C_{15}H_{12}O_{10} \cdot 3Bi(OH)_3 = 2188.46$. Bismuth methylene digallate. Gray-brown powder, soluble in alkalies; an astringent.

bismarck brown. Triaminoazobenzene.

Bismarsen. $C_{21}H_{21}O_{12}As_3Na_3S_3N_3Bi$. Trademark for bismuth sulfarsphenamine. Brown powder; used to treat syphilis.

bismethylbenzoylcarbinol. $PhC \cdot (OCH_2)_2 \cdot PhC = 240.2$. Colorless crystals, m.92.

bismite. $Bi_2O_3 \cdot 3H_2O$. Native bismuth ocher.

bismon. Colloidal bismuth metahydroxide.

bismuth. $Bi = 208.98$. An element of the arsenic group, at. no. 83. Bismutum, wismuth. A pink, silvery, brittle metal resembling antimony, $d_{20°}9.78$, m.269.2, b.1435.5, insoluble in water, soluble in acids. It occurs native, as sulfide (bismuthinite), and in a few rare minerals; as, sulfobismuthide, Isotopes: radium $E = 210.4$, thorium $C = 212.4$, actinium $C = 212(?)$, radium $C = 214.4$. B. is tri- and pentavalent, and forms 2 series of compounds:

Derived from trivalent b.:

Bismuthides . . . . M_3Bi
Bismuthous compounds . . . . Bi^{3+}
Bismuthyl compounds . . . . BiO^-
Bismuthines . . . . BiR_3

Derived from pentavalent b.:
Bismuthic compounds . . . . Bi^{5+}

B. (discoverer unknown) is mentioned by Basil Valentine (1450) as a "bastard of tin." Its name comes probably from the Arabic, "wiss majat," a metal which easily melts, or German, "wismuth," wiesen matte, a meadow. Used commercially in alloys of low melting point (wood metal), in type metal, and in the manufacture of b. compounds and drugs; its insoluble salts cast X-ray shadows (b. meal); the soluble salts are very toxic. B. is very diamagnetic. Cf. *Lipowitz alloy, rose metal, D'arcet metal.* **tribromphenol-** Xeroform. **triiodophenol-** Neoform. **trimethyl-** Bismuthine.

b. acetate. $Bi(OOCMe)_3 = 381.1$. White powder, soluble in acetic acid. **b. albuminate.** An additive compound of albumin with 9% b.; used to treat cholera and colics. **b. ammonium citrate.** White scales, soluble in water. **b. benzoate.** $Bi(OOCPh)_3 = 572.15$. Gray powder, used to treat stomach disorders. **b. borate.** $BiBO_3 = 267.9$. Gray powder soluble in acids; an intestinal antiseptic. **b. borosalicylate.** Gray powder, decomp. in water. **b. bromide.** $BiBr_3 = 448.8$. Yellow crystals, m.210, decomp. in water. **b. camphorate.** $Bi_2(C_{10}N_{14}O_4)_3 = 1014$. White powder, insoluble in water. **b. carbolate.** B. phenylate. **b. carbonate.** Bismuthyl carbonate. **b. chloride.** $BiCl_3 = 315.5$. White crystals, m.232, insoluble in water. **b. chromate.** $Bi_2O_3 \cdot 2CrO_3 = 666.0$. Yellow powder, insoluble in water; is a pigment. Hetoform. **b. cinnamate.** B. **b. citrate.** $BiC_6H_5O_7 = 398.04$. White crystals, insoluble in water; a stomachic and astringent. **b. chrysophanate.** $BiC_{15}H_9O_4 \cdot 2Bi_2O_3 = 1394.07$. Dermol. Yellow powder, insoluble in water; used to treat skin diseases. **b. dichloride.** $BiCl_2 =$

278.9. Black needles, m.163, decomp. by water. **b. dithiosalicylate** (basic). Thioform. **b. gallate.** $Bi(OH)_2C_7H_5O_5 = 412.06$. Dermatol, b. subgallate. Yellow powder (55% b.), insoluble in water, soluble in alkalies; an internal and external antiseptic and astringent. **b. glance.** Bismuthinite. **b. gold.** Au_2Bi. Occurs naturally. **b. hydroxide.** $Bi(OH)_3 = 260.0$. White powder, insoluble in water; used in the manufacture of b. salts. **b. iodate.** $Bi(IO_3)_3 = 733.76$. Heavy white powder, insoluble in water. **b. iodide.** $BiI_3 = 589.76$. Gray crystals, m.408, insoluble in water, soluble in potassium iodide solution. **b. iodosubgallate.** B. oxyiodogallate. **b. lactate.** $Bi(C_3H_5O_3)C37H_4O_3 = 386.07$ White crystals, slightly soluble in water; an antiseptic. **b. loretinate.** A surgical dusting powder. **b. meal.** A meal containing an insoluble bismuth salt given before an X-ray examination, to render the digestive organs visible. **b. methylene digallate.** Bismal. **b. minerals.** The commonest are: native b., Bi; bismuthinite (b. glance), Bi_2S_3; tetradymite, Bi_2Te_3; bismite, $Bi(OH)_3$; b. ocher (bismuthite), Bi_2O_3; bismutite- $Bi_2H_2CO_6$; b. telluride, $Bi_2(S \cdot Te)_2$. **b. molybdate.** $Bi_2(MoO_4)_3 = 898.1$. Yellow powder, insoluble in water. **b. naphtholate, b. β-naphtholate.** Orphol. **b. nickel.** A native mixture of b. and nickel sulfides. **b. nitrate.** $Bi(NO_3)_3 \cdot 5H_3O = 485.1$. B. ternitrate. White, triclinic, deliquescent crystals, m.74 (decomp.), decomp. in water; an astringent, antiseptic, Cf. b. subnitrate. **b. ocher.** See b. minerals. **b. oleate.** $Bi(C_{17}H_{33}COO)_3 = 1053.2$. Yellow granules; used to treat skin diseases. **b. organic compound.** A compound with aliphatic or aromatic hydrocarbon radicals attached to b.; e.g., b. trimethyl. **b. oxalate.** $Bi_2(COO)_6 = 682.03$. White granules, soluble in acids. **b. oxide.** (1) Commonly, bismuthous oxide. (2) One of.: $Bi_2O_3 = b$. trioxide, bismuthous oxide. $Bi_2O_4 = b$. tetroxide. $Bi_2O_5 = b$. pentoxide. bismuthic oxide. **b. oxybromide.** Bismuthyl bromide. **b. oxychloride.** Bismuthyl chloride. **b. oxyfluoride.** Bismuthyl fluoride. **b. oxyiodide.** Bismuthyl iodide. **b. oxyiodogallate.** $BiI(OH)(C_7H_4O_4) = 504.98$. B. iodosubgallate, Airol, Airoform. A voluminous, gray-green tasteless powder, insoluble in water; an iodoform substitute, **b. pentoxide.** Bismuthic oxide. **b. permanganate.** $Bi(MnO_4)_3 = 566.5$. Black powder, insoluble in water; a dusting powder. **b. peroxide.** $Bi_2O_4 = 482.0$. Brown powder, liberating oxygen at 150. **b. phenol sulfonate.** B. sulfocarbolate. Pink powder, soluble in water; an antiseptic. **b. phenylate.** $Bi(OH)_2OPh = 336.6$. B. phenol, -phenate, -carbolate. Gray powder (80% b.), insoluble in water; an intestinal antiseptic. **b. phosphate.** $BiPO_4 = 304.0$. White powder, decomp. by heat. **b. phospholactate.** White, crystals, slightly soluble in water, decomp. by heat; an intestinal antiseptic. **b. potassium iodide.** $BiI_3 \cdot 4KI = 1253.9$. Yellow crystals, soluble in water. Cf. Dragendorff's reagent. **b. potassium tartrate.** $BiK(C_4H_4O_6)_2 = 545.1$. Colorless crystals, soluble in water; a reagent for glucose in urine. **b. propionate.** $Bi(C_3H_5O_2)_3 = 428.19$. White powder, insoluble in water. **b. pyrogallate.** $Bi(OH)C_6H_3(OH)O_2 = 350.04$. B. gallate, helcosol. Yellow powder (60% b.), insoluble in water; an intestinal antiseptic and

dusting powder. **b. salicylate.** $Bi(C_7H_5O_3)_3 \cdot Bi_2O_3 = 1744.04$. B. subsalicylate. White microcrystals, insoluble in water; an intestinal antiseptic, and dusting powder. **b. selenide.** $Bi_2Se_3 = 655.6$. Black crystals, decomp. by heat, insoluble in water. **b. silver.** Native silver, containing 16% b. **b. sodium iodide.** $BiI_3 \cdot 4NaI = 1190.1$. Red crystals, decomp. in water; an antiseptic and alterant. **b. subcarbonate.** Bismuthyl carbonate. **b. subgallate.** B. gallate. **b. subnitrate.** B. basic nitrate. A mixture of $Bi(OH)_2NO_3$ and $BiOH(NO_3)_2$ or of $(BiO)NO_3$ and $(BiO)OH$. An antiseptic, astringent white powder (79–82% b.), insoluble in water, decomp. 260. Used in stomach and intestinal disorders; as a b. meal, q.v.; and as a dusting powder. Cf. pearl white(3). **b. subsalicylate.** B. salicylate. **b. sulfate.** $Bi_2(SO_4)_3 = 706.2$. White crystalline powder, decomp. by water or heat. **b. sulfide.** $Bi_2S_3 = 514.2$. Brown rhombic crystals or powder, decomp. by heat, insoluble in water. **b. sulfite.** $Bi_2(SO_3)_3$, White powder of variable composition. **b. sulfocarbolate.** B. phenoisulfonate. **b. tannate.** Yellow powder resulting from action of tannic acid on b. hydroxide, insoluble in water; an antiseptic and astringent. **b. tartrate.** $Bi_2(C_4H_4O_6)_3 \cdot 6H_2O = 970.0$. White powder, insoluble in water or glycerol; used to treat Vincent's angina. **b. telluride.** See b. minerals. **b. tetraiodophenolphthalein.** Eudoxine. **b. tetroxide.** B. peroxide. **b. thiosalicylate.** Thioform. **b. tribromide.** B. bromide. **b. tribromphenylate.** Xeroform. **b. trichloride.** B. chloride. **b. triethyl*.** $BiEt_3 = 296.15$. Colorless oil, b.107, insoluble in water, miscible with alcohol. **b. trimethyl*,** $BiMe_3 = 254.07$. Trimethyl bismuthine. Colorless liquid, d.2.300, b.110. **b. triphenyl*.** $BiPh_3 = 440.16$. Triphenyl bismuthine. Colorless crystals, m.78. **b. trisulfide.** B. sulfide. **b. tungstate.** $BiWO_3 = 441.5$. B. wolframate. White powder, decomp. in water. **b. valerate.** $Bi(C_5H_9O_2)_3 = 512.22$. White powder, insoluble in water; a sedative and antispasmodic. **b. violet.** A triphenylmethane dye combined with b.; a nontoxic antiseptic.

bismuthi. Official Latin for bismuth.

bismuthic. Describing compounds of pentavalent bismuth. **b. oxide.** $Bi_2O_5 = 498.0$. Bismuth pentoxide. Brown powder, liberates oxygen at 150, insoluble in water.

bismuthide. (1) M_3Bi. Analogous to arsenide, stibnide. (2) Bismuth osmaltide. **sulfo-** Beegerite.

bismuthine. (1) BiR_3, An organic bismuth compound, analogous to arsine and stibine. (2) Bismuthinite. **ethyl-** $C_6H_{15}Bi = 296.12$. Triethyl bismuth, $BiEt_3$. Colorless liquid, $b_{80mm}107$. **methyl-** $BiMe_3 = 254.07$. A liquid, d.2.300, b.110. **phenyl-** $BiPh_3 = 440.16$. A solid, m.78.

bismuthinite. Bi_2S_3. Bismuthine. Bismuth glance. Native bismuth sulfide.

bismuthiol. Mercaptosulfothiobiazole. A reagent for bismuth salts (red precipitate). Cf. mercaptophenyldithiodiazolone.

bismuthite. $(BiO)_2CO_3 \cdot H_2O$. Native bismuth carbonate; green earthy masses.

bismuthosmaltite. $Co(As,Bi)_3$. Native cobalt bismuthide; or smaltite containing bismuth.

bismuthosphaerite. $(BiO)_2CO_3$. Native bismuth carbonate; yellow fibrous masses.

bismuthous. Describing compounds of trivalent bismuth, comprising the common bismuth compounds. **b. oxide.** $Bi_2O_3 = 466.0$. Bismuth trioxide. Yellow tetragons, m.850, insoluble in water. Used as bismuth subnitrate.

bismuthyl. The radical BiO—, from trivalent bismuth. **b. bromide.** $BiOBr = 305.92$. Bismuth oxybromide. Brown powder, insoluble in water; used to treat dyspepsia and hysterics. **b. carbonate.** $(BiO)_2CO_3 = 527.02$. Bismuth subcarbonate. White powder, insoluble in water. Used in ointments and face powders and internally for stomach disorders. **b. chloride.** $BiOCl = 260.50$. Bismuth oxychloride. White powder, decomp. at red heat, insoluble in water; an astringent and antiseptic. **b. dichromate.** $(BiO)_2 \cdot Cr_2O_7 = 666.01$. Orange crystals, insoluble in water. **b. fluoride.** $BiOF = 244.04$. Bismuth oxyfluoride. White crystals, insoluble in water. **b. hydroxide.** $(BiO)OH$. Basic bismuth hydroxide. **b. iodide.** $BiOI = 352.4$. Bismuth oxyiodide. White powder, insoluble in water. **b. nitrate.** $(BiO)NO_3 \cdot H_2O = 305.03$. Basic bismuth nitrate. The main constituent of bismuth subnitrate, q.v.

bismutite. Bismuthite.

bismutosmaltite. Bismuthosmaltite.

bisphenol. p,p'-Dihydroxydiphenyldimethylmethane; mol. wt. 228.1. Brown crystals, m.152, insoluble in water; used in the manufacture of phenolic and epoxy resins. World output (1964) 54 million pounds.

bistetrazole. $C_2H_2N_8 = 138.3$. Ditetrazyl:

$$\begin{array}{ccc} N{=\!=}N & & N{=}N \\ | & \diagup C{-}C \diagdown & | \\ NH{-}N & & N{-}NH \end{array}$$

bistort. Snakeweed adderwort. The root of *Polygonum bistorte;* an astringent.

bistriazole. $C_4H_4N_6 = 136.3$. Ditriazolyl:

$$\begin{array}{ccc} CH{=}N & & N{=}CH \\ | & \diagup C{-}C \diagdown & | \\ NH{-}N & & N{-}NH \end{array}$$

Colorless liquid, b. 300.

bisulfate. Acid sulfate. A compound containing the HSO_4- radical, from sulfuric acid.

bisulfide. Disulfide. A binary compound containing 2 atoms of sulfur.

bisulfite. Acid sulfite. An oxy salt containing the HSO_3- radical, from sulfurous acid. **b. compounds.** $R_2C \cdot (OH) \cdot (SO_3Na)$. Addition compounds of sodium bisulfite and an aldehyde or ketone.

bit. Abbreviation for binary digit.

bitartrate. Acid tartrate. A salt containing the $C_4H_5O_6-$ radical, from tartaric acid.

bithionol. $C_{12}H_6O_2SCl_4 = 356.07$. 2,2'-Thiobis(4,6-dichlorophenol). White crystals, m.168, insoluble in water.

bithiophene. Thiophthene.

bitter. (1) See *bitters*. (2) An astringent taste, as of magnesium sulfate. **b. almond oil.** An essential oil from the seeds of *Prunus amygdala amara*, b. almond. Pale yellow liquid, d.1.038–1.060 (chief constituents: benzaldehyde, hydrocyanic acid, phenoxyacetonitrile); a flavoring. **b. almond oil camphor.** Benzoin. **b. apple.** Colocynth. **b. ash.**

Quassia. **b. bark.** Cinchona. **b. cucumber.** Colocynth. **b. cups.** Colocynth. **b. damson.** Simaruba. **b. herb.** Erythraea. **b. principle.** Generic term for the bitter-tasting principle of a drug, e.g., due to alkaloids or glucosides. **b. root.** Gentian. **b. salt.** Magnesium sulfate. **b. spar.** A ferruginous dolomite. **b. stick.** Chirata. **b. wintergreen.** Chimaphila. **b. wood.** Quassia.

bittern. Waste liquid from the solar salt industry; contains magnesium salts and bromides from seawater.

bitters. (1) A group of drugs which includes gentian, quassia etc. (2) Mineral waters characterized by a bitter or saline taste, (e.g., due to magnesium sulfate). (3) A preparation which contains the bitter principles of plants; as, Angostura b.

bittersweet. Dulcamara. **American-, false-** Waxwort. The root and bark of *Celastrus scandens* (Celastraceae); a diaphoretic.

bitumens. Native solid or semisolid hydrocarbons (naphtha or asphalt) soluble in carbon disulfide; rich in C and H. Cf. *asphaltenes, carbenes, kerotenes, protobitumen.* **albino-** A petroleum resin. **asphaltic-** Asphalt.

bituminous. Having the qualities of bitumen. **b. coal.** A coal rich in hydrocarbons (50–80% C). **b. materials.** B. substances used for pavings and roofings; as, asphalt, shales, tars. **b. resins.** Red, transparent fossil resins from brown coals (80% wax). Cf. *retinite resins.*

biurate. Acid urate. A salt of uric acid.

biurea. $(NH_2 \cdot CO \cdot NH-)_2 = 118.08$. Cf. *diurea.*

biuret. $NH_2 \cdot CO \cdot NH \cdot CO \cdot NH_2 = 121.19$. Allophanamide, dicarbamylamine, carbamylurea. Colorless needles, decomp. 190, soluble in hot water. A condensation product of urea; a reagent. **acetyl-** $MeCO \cdot NH \cdot CO \cdot NH \cdot CONH_2 = 145.11$. Colorless needles, m.193, soluble in water.

b. reaction. Pitrowsky reaction. A test for protein compounds which contain the —CO·NH— group. Drops of copper and potassium hydroxide solutions give a violet color.

bivalence, bivalent. The capacity of an element to combine with 2 univalent (or 1 divalent) atoms or radicals; as, ferrous, oxygen. Cf. *divalent.*

bivinyl. $CH_2 : CH \cdot CH : CH_2 = 54.1$. Erythrene, 1,3-butadiene*, vinyl ethylene. Colorless gas, b.−3; an anesthetic. **2-methyl-** Isoprene.

Bixaceae, Bixineae. Trees and shrubs; some yield important drugs; as, *Gynocardia odorata*, chaulmoogra oil; *Bixa orellana*, annato.

bixin. $MeOOC(CH : CHCMe : CH)_4CH : CH \cdot COOH = 394.2$. A red, crystalline coloring matter from annatto, m.196. soluble in hot alcohol.

bixol. $Me_2C{=}C \cdot CH \cdot _2(CMe {=} CHCH_2)_2 \cdot CH_2OH = 249.3$. Dark green oil with a parsley taste, from the seeds of *Bixa orellana*, d.0.8845.

Bjerrum, Niels. 1879–1959. Danish physical chemist, noted for his work on the theory of electrolytic dissociation; the thermodynamic anomalies of strong electrolytes are due to interionic forces.

Bk. Symbol for the element berkelium.

Black, Joseph. 1728–1799. Scottish chemist and physicist, pioneer in experimental research. He introduced the term "fixed air" for the gas (carbon dioxide) given off from carbonates; opposed the phlogiston theory, q.v.; and developed the concept of latent heat.

black. Describing a substance that reflects no colored rays of light; hence absence of color. **chemical-, gas-, impingement-** A very fine grade of carbon b. produced from the flame of natural gas; particle size, 10–30 mμ. Used in rubber, paints, and lacquers. **b. alum.** A mixture of aluminum sulfate and activated carbon used in water treatment. **b. antimony.** Antimonic sulfide. **b. ash.** Impure sodium carbonate with some unburnt carbon and incombustible mineral matter produced in the sodawood-pulp recovery process. **b. balsam.** Peru balsam. **b. berry.** See *rubus*. **b. body.** A material that absorbs all radiant energy and transforms it into heat. Cf. *Stefan-Boltzmann equation*. **b. boy.** Grass-tree gum. A resin from *Xanthorrhoea hastilis* (Liliaceae), of Australia; a varnish and sealing wax. **b. cobalt.** An earthy native cobalt. **b. cohosh.** Cimicifuga. **b. copper.** Copper oxide. **b. damp.** Choke damp. **b. dogwood.** Frangula. **b. drops.** Opium vinegar. **b. dyes.** See *aniline b., chrome b., sedan b.* **b. flux.** A reducing agent used in assaying; made by burning together potassium carbonate 1, argol 3 pts. **b. fish oil.** Malon oil. **b. haw.** *Viburnum prunifolium.* **b. hellebore.** The rhizomes of *Helleborus niger;* the fluid extract is a cathartic or diuretic. **b. henbane.** Hyoscyamus. **b. Indian hemp.** Apocynum. **b. jack.** Sphalerite. **b. lead.** (1) Plumbago. (2) Alquifou. **b. leg.** Anthrax. **b. lotion.** See *lotion.* **b. manganese.** Pyrolusite. **b. metal.** A black electrolytic deposit of certain metals, e.g., platinum. **b. mustard.** Sinapis nigra. **b. pigments.** See *bone b. graphite, ivory b., lampblack.* **b. potassium.** Suint ash. **b. powder.** An explosive: potassium nitrate 62–75, Sulfur 10–19, charcoal 12–5%. **b. precipitate.** Mercurous nitrate. **b. silver.** Stephanite. **b. tellurium.** (Pb, Au)(Te·S). A native telluride. **b. tin.** Cassiterite. **b. willow bark.** The bark of *Salix nigra;* the fluid extract is a bitter tonic, anaphrodisiac, and antiperiodic.

Blackmar oil thief. A device for taking oil samples from tank cars.

blackstrap. An inedible grade of molasses from sugar refining; a source of alcohol.

Blagden's law. The lowering of the freezing point of a solution is in proportion to the amount of dissolved substance present. Cf. *Raoult's law, Coppet's law.*

blairmorite. A rock containing 71% analcite. (Alberta, Canada).

Blaise reaction. A Grignard reaction, q.v.

blanc fix(e). Synthetic barium sulfate produced by the action of barium chloride on aluminum sulfate; a pigment for coating paper.

blanch. (1) A lead ore embedded in rocks. (2) To bleach. (3) A heat treatment of foodstuffs before preserving them, to destroy enzymes which cause deterioration. **b. liquor.** A solution of calcium hypochlorite.

blancophore. See optical *bleaching.*

blangel. Silica gel dehydrating agent, impregnated with a cobalt salt to indicate by a color change when it is hydrated.

blast. (1) To smash to pieces by an explosive. (2) To subject a material to a hot firing. (3) A current of hot gases. (4) A nucleated red blood corpuscle. **b. burner.** A large blowpipe with compressed air

blown into the gas flame. **b. furnace.** A smelting oven, with an air current, used in the manufacture of pig iron. **b. lamp.** B. burner.

blasting. The process of loosening natural deposits of rocks and other materials by explosives. **b. gelatin.** A plastic high explosive; a 5–10% solution of collodion cotton in nitroglycerin; cf. *gelignite.* **b. oil.** Nitroglycerin. **b. powders.** Nondetonating explosives, deflagrating powders. The black granular powders used for mining and road building; as *black* powder. Cf. *soda* powder.

blastokolin. The natural inhibitor to ripening in apples; probably associated with maleic acid.

blastomycin. A sterile, red-dyed concentrate of the soluble growth products of *Blastomyces dermatitidis;* a dermal reactivity indicator (U.S.P.).

Blau gas. A fuel gas produced by cracking gas oil at 550°C, comprising saturated paraffin hydrocarbons with some hydrogen and ethylene.

bleaching. The whitening and removal of natural impurities by chemical or physical agents, e.g., chlorine or exposure to sunlight. **optical-** The use of blancophores, certain organic compounds (e.g., derivatives of diaminostilbenesulfonic acid), which have a short-wavelength fluorescence (blue or violet) in visible light, to enhance the whiteness of (e.g.,) paper or textiles when present in very small quantities. **b. materials.** Oxidizing or reducing agents; as, sulfur dioxide, sodium acid sulfite, hydrogen peroxide, calcium hypochlorite, chlorine water, oxides of nitrogen. **b. powder.** Chloride of lime, formed by passing chlorine gas over dry slaked lime; principally calcium oxychloride; but when it absorbs moisture it is converted into a mixture of the chloride and hypochlorite of calcium.

Bleeker method. The reduction of vanadium compounds by electrolysis.

blende. (1) Sphalerite, zinc blende. Cf. *Sidot's b.* (2) A sulfide ore; as, antimony b. Cf. *glance.*

blennostasin. $C_{19}H_{22}ON_2 \cdot 2HBr = 456.05.$ Cinchonidine dihydrobromide. Yellow crystals; a vasoconstrictor.

blick. The brightening of a noble metal during cupellation by adsorption of the outer layer of lead oxide.

blister steel. A finely granulated steel. Cf. *cementation.*

blistering beetle. Cantharides.

blocking. The tendency of a film to adhere to itself.

block tin. An alloy of tin with iron, cobalt, lead, antimony and arsenic.

blodite. bloedite, blödit. Astrakanite.

Blondlot rays. n-*Rays.*

blood. A red homogeneous liquid that circulates in vertebrates through the body channels; d.1.045–1.075. pH = 7.35, constituting 0.05% of the body weight and containing solids 2.2 and water 98% in a delicately adjusted equilibrium of salts, proteins, enzymes, and organized particles (b. corpuscles, plasma, serum, fibrin, q.v.). B. carries nutritive materials from the intestines to cells and tissues, and oxygen from the lungs to the tissues; removes the waste products from the tissues, and carries them to the kidneys, lungs, intestines, or skin; distributes internal secretions from one organ to another: defends an organism against infection and maintains its isotonic condition. B. consists of a liquid (plasma, q.v.) and cellular elements.

The plasma contains the serum, q.v., and fibrinogen; the cellular elements are the red and white b. corpuscles and the b. plates. The main constituents of the serum are albumin, globulin, glucose, and salts. The red b. corpuscles contain the oxyhemoglobin, lecithin, and some salts; the enzyme fibrin is in the white b. corpuscles. Cf. *porphin, fibrin, hemoglobin.* **arterial-** Bright-red b. rich in oxygen or oxyhemoglobin. **beaten-** Defibrinated b. **citrated-** Whole human b. drawn under aseptic conditions and protected from coagulation by addition of an acid citrate-dextrose solution. Hemoglobin value, not less than 66%. **clotted-** A thick, semisolid mass of blood corpuscles embedded in a network of precipitated fibrin. **concentrated-** Whole human b. containing not less than 5.5 million red corpuscles per cubic millimeter. **defibrinated-** A red homogeneous liquid, consisting of blood corpuscles and serum. **dried-** B. of slaughtered animals, dried and ground; a fertilizer (not less than 12% organic nitrogen). **venous-** Dark red b., rich in carbon dioxide or reduced hemoglobin. Cf. *b. gases.*

b. alkalinity. The buffering property of b. B. is nearly neutral (pH = 7), but it can neutralize acidity because of its dissolved alkalies; see *buffer solution.* **b. amylase.** A b. enzyme converting glycogen or starch to a reducing sugar. **b. apparatus.** A device for determining the oxygen and carbon dioxide in b. **b. capsules.** Wright's capsules. A glass capillary tube used to take b. samples for microscopical examination. **b. cast.** The b. fibers observed in urine by microscopical examination. **b. clot.** A clump of coagulated b. which contains the fibrin and b. corpuscles. **b. collector.** An evacuated ampul with which b. is withdrawn (Keidel). **b. count.** The determination of the number of b. cells in a definite volume of b. **b. crystals.** Hemin. **b. elder.** Ebul. **b. enzymes.** Amylase, invertin, glycolytic enzymes, proteolytic enzymes, cholesterases, and lipases. **b. gases.** Carbon dioxide, oxygen, and nitrogen. E.g., b. of cats contains, vol. %:

	CO_2	O	N_2
arterial b.	25.07	13.60	1.00
venous b.	40.83	9.93	0.77

b. glycolysis. The breakdown by b. plasma of glucose into decomposition products, of uncertain nature. **b. groups.** The classification of types of human b. in terms of the agglutinating behavior (clumping) of the red corpuscles, in presence of the serum of a different b. The agglutinins in the b. serum of one group will not agglutinate with their own corpuscles, but only with the agglutinogens from a foreign b. Principal agglutination reactions:

Serum of group (agglutinin)	Corpuscles of blood group			
	A	B	AB	O
A	—	+	+	—
B	+	—	+	—
AB	—	—	—	—
O	+	+	+	—

Used to establish paternity; to identify bloodstains; and to ascertain the suitability of blood for transfusion. Cf. *agglutinins, Rh factor.* **b. hemoglobin.** The coloring matter (chromoprotein) of b. which breaks down to hematin and hemin, q.v., and these, in turn, to hematoporphyrin, q.v., which is isomeric with bilirubin. **b. hydrogen ion concentration.** Mean value at $18°C$, 6×10^{-8} to 2×10^8; pH = 7.2–7.7. **b. osmotic pressure.** 7.3 atm (freezing-point method). **b. pigment.** Hemoglobin. Cf. *cytochrome.* **b. plasma.** The liquid portion of the b. Composition (gm per 1,000 gm):

Water..............................	901.51
Total solids	98.49
Albumin.............................	81.92
Fibrin...............................	8.06
Sodium chloride	5.546
Sodium carbonate	1.532
Calcium phosphate...................	0.298
Potassium chloride...................	0.359
Potassium sulfate....................	0.281
Sodium phosphate	0.271
Magnesium phosphate................	0.218

b. platelets. Thrombocytes. A structural element of the b. containing cytozyme which stops bleeding by coagulation. **b. root.** Sanguinaria. **b. serum.** The liquid portion of the b. after removal of the fibrin, d.1.0292. Composition (gm per 1,000 gm):

Water..............................	908.84
Total solids	91.16
Albumin, etc........................	82.59
Sodium chloride	5.591
Sodium carbonate	1.545
Potassium chloride...................	0.362
Calcium phosphate...................	0.300
Potassium sulfate....................	0.283
Sodium phosphate	0.273
Magnesium phosphate................	0.220

b. serum, artificial. Loeffler's mixture. A culture medium (250 ml glucose bouillon, 750 ml horse or beef serum). **b. sugar.** The carbohydrates of b.; as, glucose. **b. stone.** (1) Hematite. (2) Jasper.
bloom. (1) The fluorescence of lubricating oils. (2) The delicate coating which covers fresh fruit or leaves. (3) The cloudy appearance produced by aging on the surface of varnish. (4) The crystallization of a component on the surface of a material; as fat or sugar, on chocolate.
blowdown. The sludge and/or concentrated feed-water removed periodically from the inside of the boiler of a steam-raising plant.
blown. Describing canned foods that have expanded or burst their cans by liberation of gas (e.g., hydrogen) inside.
blowpipe. (1) A metal tube tapering to a fine point, used to blow air into a flame and to direct it as a fine conical tongue in qualitative or mineralogical analysis, soldering, melting in dentistry or jewelry manufacture. (2) A blast burner. **b. analysis.** Qualitative analysis of minerals, alloys, or inorganic materials by observing their behavior in the b. flame, bead test; and reactions on charcoal or plaster of paris.

blown oils. Polymerized oils, oxidized oils. An oil which has been oxidized by a stream of air, which converts it into a fast-drying oil; used for paints and varnishes.

Bloxam, Charles. 1831–1887. British analytical chemist noted for his writings.

blubber oil. Whale oil.

blue. A spectrum of wavelength 0.000047 cm, between those of green and violet. **Chinese-** Ferric ferrocyanide in pigment form. **Egyptian-** Powdered glass pigment consisting of copper oxide dissolved in a melt containing quartz sand, lime and soda. Cf. *smalt*. **heteropoly-** See molybdenum b.

   b. cohosh. Caulophyllum. **b. copper.** CuS. A native amorphous copper sulfide. **b. copperas.** Copper sulfate. **b. cross.** Ph_2AsCl. Diphenylchlorarsine, D.A. A nose irritant, m.39; a war poison gas. **b. dyes.** See *alizarin b., alkali b., anthracene b., cyanin b., methyl b., methylene b.,* etc. **b. ground.** Kimberlite. **b. gum.** Eucalyptus. **b. iron ore.** Vivianite. **b. john.** A native, crystalline copper sulfate with fluorspar. **b. mass.** Mercury ointment. **b. print.** A photographic copy made on ferriferrocyanide paper. **b. powder.** Zinc dust. **b. salt.** Crystallized *nickel sulfate*. **b. stone.** A native, crystalline copper sulfate. Cf. *b. john*. **b. unit.** An expression of vitamin A potency in terms of the intensity of the b. color produced with antimony trichloride. Cf. *Carr-Price value*. **b. verdigris.** Copper acetate. **b. verditer.** Basic *copper carbonate*. **b. vitriol.** (1) Chalcanthite, native copper sulfate. (2) Crystallized copper sulfate.

blushing. The turbidity of lacquers and varnishes due to the precipitation of the resins by moisture or evaporation. Cf. *bloom* (3).

board. A thick paper which usually exceeds 0.009 in. in thickness (U.S. usage) or 220 gm/sq. meter of weight (U.K. usage). **fiber-** B. made by disintegrating vegetable matter into its elemental fibers and reassembling them as b. **intermittent-** B. made in sheets instead of in a continuous web. **paper-** B. made in a web on a continuous wire, as with paper, but with a greater thickness of pulp. **particle-** B. made by disintegrating vegetable matter into particles or fiber aggregates (as distinct from individual fibers), and then reassembling them as a board with the aid of a binding agent, e.g., a synthetic resin. **paste-** A b. made by pasting sheets of paper together. **V-** See *V*. **W-** See *W*.

   b. foot. A unit of volume of boards sawn from logs; the volume of a b. 1 in. thick and 1 ft^2 in area, i.e., $\frac{1}{12}$ ft.^{3} Cf. *cunit, cord, fastmeter*.

Board of Trade unit. B.T.U. The British unit of electric energy. 1 B.T.U. = 1 khwr. = 3.6 × 10^6 watt-sec. Cf. *British Thermal Unit*, BThU.

boart. Bort.

Boas reagent. A solution of 5 gm resorcinol and 3 gm sugar in 100 gm dilute alcohol. A test for hydrochloric acid in gastric juice; a rose-red color develops on boiling.

boat. A small elongated vessel of porcelain, quartz, or platinum which can be inserted in a combustion tube.

bobierite. $Mg_2P_2O_7\cdot8H_2O$. A native crystalline phosphate in guano.

Bobina rayon. Trade name for a viscose synthetic fiber.

Bobol. Trade name for a viscose synthetic fiber.

B.O.D. Biochemical oxygen demand.

bodies. (1) Biochemical substances of similar structure. (2) Cellular structures in protoplasm. **acetone-** Substances, as acetone, acetoacetic acid, or β-oxybutyric acid, in urine. **alloxur-** A compound of uric acid and alloxan, secreted in the urine; as, the purine b. **Buchner-** A defensive protein of the organism. **purine-** A derivative of uric acid; as, xanthine.

body. (1) The trunk of an animal or plant. (2) The largest part of an organ. (3) The consistency or viscosity of a liquid. (4) A limited portion of matter. (5) The strength of a liquid; as, wine. **black-** See *Stefan-Boltzmann equation, black body*. **b. fluids.** See *blood, lymph*, internal *secretions*. **b. tube.** The portion of the microscope which carries the objective, and inside which slides the draw tube.

boehmite. Al_2O_3,H_2O. A form of bauxite.

Boerhaave, Herman. 1668–1738. Dutch pioneer of modern chemistry, noted for his textbook.

bog. A marsh or morass. **b. berry.** The fruit of *Vaccinium oxycoccus*, cranberry. **b. butter.** Butyrelite. A soft mineral occurring in marshes. **b. iron ore.** Bogore. **b. manganese.** Wad. **b. ore** Bogore.

Bogert, Marston Taylor. 1868–1957. American chemist, noted for his work on organic synthesis.

boghead. A carbonaceous rock, or cannel with a high iron carbonate content. **b. naphtha.** Photogen.

bog iron ore. Bogore.

bog-manganese. Wad.

bogore. $2Fe_2O_3\cdot3H_2O$. Bog iron ore, marsh ore, brown iron ore, brown hematite, brown ocher, limonite. A hydrous ferric oxide with some ferrous carbonate, from marshy places; a source of iron.

bohemium. Bo. The element, at. no. 75. The Bohemian scientists J. Heyrowsky and Doleysek (1925), claimed its discovery as an impurity in magnesium, but it is identical with *rhenium* previously discovered by Naddack, Tacke, and Berg.

Bohr, Niels. 1885–1962. Danish physicist; Nobel prize (1922) for his theory of atomic structures. **B. atom.** A hypothesis of atomic structure, q.v.; the electrons move in circular or elliptical orbits around a positive nucleus, resembling a very small solar system. **B. and Coster notation.** See *quantum numbers*. **B. formula.** For the hydrogen series, $N = [2\pi^2me^4(M + m)]/Mh^3$, where e = charge and m = mass of an electron, M = atomic weight of hydrogen and h = Planck's constant; $N = 109,678.7$. **B. formula for Rydberg's constant.** $R_\infty = [2\pi^2e^5]/[h^3c^2e/m]$. Cf. *Lewis-Adams formula, constants*. **B.s. theory.** Spectrum lines are produced: (1) by emission of radiation (energy) when electrons drop from an orbit of greater to lower energy (energy levels); or (2) by absorption of radiation (energy) when the electrons move from an orbit of lower to higher energy. Cf. *quantum, spectrum series, Stoner quanta, correspondence principle*.

boil. Quick ebullition or vaporization of a liquid by heat and/or low pressure.

boiled oil. Linseed oil which has been heated to 210–260°C, and thereby hardens more readily; used in varnishes and lacquers.

boiler. An open or closed vessel for evaporating liquids, cooking food, or generating steam. **vacuum-** A closed b. in which evaporation of a liquid is caused by low pressure, with or without heat. **b. compound.** A substance used to prevent the formation of b. scale. Cf. *water softening.* **b. fluid.** A solution which prevents the formation of a compact b. incrustation. **b. incrustation.** The insoluble mass, deposited on the bottom and sides of a vessel in which hard water has been evaporated, of calcium and magnesium carbonates and sulfates. **b. mud.** A loose deposit of b. incrustations. **b. scale.** A compact, thick layer of successive deposits. **b. stone.** B. scale.

boilers. Group name for nitrocellulose and lacquer solvents, q.v., arranged in order of their boiling points: **low-** B. below 100°C. **medium-** B. near 125°C. **high-** B. from 150–200°C.

boiling. The state of ebullition; the brisk change from the liquid to the vapor state. **b. point.** B.p., b. The temperature at which, under a specified pressure, a liquid is transformed into a vapor; i.e., at which the vapor pressure of the liquid equals that of the surrounding gas or vapor. Cf. *condensation point, Clapeyron equation.* **absolute b. point.** The b. on the absolute scale; $(x°C + 273)°A.$ **b.p. apparatus.** A device to determine the b.p. of a liquid under a definite pressure. **lowering of b.p.** A decrease in pressure lowers the b.p.; e.g., by lowering the pressure 10 mm water will boil 0.37°C lower. **b.p. elevation.** The presence of a dissolved substance raises the b.p. of a liquid. The rise is a function of its molecular weight and may be used to determine it. Cf. *Raoult's Law, Beckmann apparatus.*

Boisbaudran, Paul Émile Lecoq de. 1838–1912. French scientist, discoverer of gallium, samarium, and dysprosium.

boldine. $C_{19}H_{21}NO_4 = 327.17.$ An alkaloid from the leaves of *Peumus boldus* (Monimiaceae). Gray powder, insoluble in water; a hypnotic. Cf. *laurotetanine.* **b. hydrobromide.** $C_{30}H_{53}O_8 \cdot HBr = 621.34.$ White crystals, soluble in water; a hypnotic and local anesthetic.

boldo. The dried leaves of *Peumus boldus* (Monimiaceae) of Chile; a tonic, antirheumatic, and antipyretic.

boldoglucin. $C_{30}H_{53}O_8 = 541.5.$ A glucoside from the leaves of *Peumus boldus.* A thick syrup; a narcotic and hypnotic.

bole. (1) A fine clay, colored by iron. (2) The trunk or stem of a tree. (3) A measure of corn; 6 bushels. **red-** Ocher. **white-** Kaolin.

boleite. A native hydrous oxychloride of lead, silver, and copper; blue crystalline masses (Boleo, Lower California).

Boletus. A genus of fungi or mushrooms (Basidiomycetes).

Bologna phosphorus. Luminescent barium sulfide.

bolometer. A device for measuring minute quantities of radiant heat from the change in the conductivity of a black body.

Boltaflex. Trade name for a mixed-polymer synthetic fiber.

bolting cloth. A fabric of unsized silk, used for sieves.

boltonite. $Mg_2SiO_4.$ A native variety of fosterite.

Boltzmann's constant. $k = 1.380 \times 10^{-61}$ erg/°C. The gas constant, R, expressed per molecule. If m is the number of molecules, $R = PV/Tm.$ Cf. *Maxwell-B.* law. **B. equation.** See *molecular free path.* **B's law.** The law of equipartition of energy: The total kinetic energy of a system, due to translation, rotation, vibration, etc., is equally divided among all the degrees of freedom. The energy per degree of freedom is $0.5RT$ per gram molecule.

bolus. (1) Masticated food ready to be swallowed. (2) Kaolin. (3) A small rounded mass. **silver-** Silver in edible form for internal administration as a germicide; e.g., colloidal silver, or silver-kaolin pills. **b. alba.** Kaolin.

bomb. (1) A projectile of iron or steel filled with explosive, poisonous, or incendiary substances, and used in chemical warfare. (2) A heavy iron tube containing a substance which is to be oxidized for the determination of its calorific value. (3) Radium in concentrated form (1–5-gm units) used for intensive local treatment, e.g., of cancer. **atomic-** q.v. **cobalt-** q.v. **hydrogen-** q.v. **b. calorimeter.** See *calorimeter..*

bombard. To expose to rays, e.g., of radioactive substances, or converging cathode rays.

bombardment. Exposure to a radioactive substance; e.g., to cathode rays focused on a point as in the X-ray tube; or the hitting of atomic nuclei by high-speed α particles and the disruption of the hydrogen subatoms composing it.

bombazine. A fabric having a silk warp and a cotton, linen, or woolen weft; similar to, but lighter than, poplin.

bombiosterol. $C_{27}H_{46}O = 386.32.$ A sterol, m.148, in chrysalis oil.

bonanza. A rich vein of ore.

bond. The linkage between atoms, thought to consist of an electron pair rotating between 2 kernels and forming an electromagnetic vector along axis *ab:*

$$+ \; \frac{\quad : \quad}{a \qquad b} \; +$$

I. *Atomic b.* Each atom contributes one electron:
  1. *Homopolar b.* (**nonpolar**). The electron pair is held equally by both kernels, neither of which becomes negative with respect to the other, $a = b$; as in H_2, CH_4.
  2. *Heteropolar b.* (**polar**). The electron pair is held unequally; hence one kernel becomes negative and the other positive, $a > b$; as in HCl.
II. *Molecular b.* One atom contributes both electrons:
  3. *Coordinate b.* (**semipolar**). An unshared electron-pair of an octet on a kernel (as of N, O, F) is shared by a kernel having an incomplete octet (generally H, also Li, Be, B, etc.).

In *electronic* structure symbols dots represent the electrons of the particular b. However, it is more strictly correct to represent the bonds by orbits, q.v. Cf. *valence, linkage, associated liquids, combination, compounds, atomic radius, molecular diagram, chelate, fiber.* **π-** A 3-dimensional b. produced by the overlap of 2 bonds at right angles, giving rise to double and single bonds. **σ-** A b. produced by the overlap of 2 directional orbitals in one plane. Types: bonding and antibonding. Two electrons in the same state will oscillate between these states.

bonded fiber. Web. Generic term to describe materials produced by assembling fibers (especially textile fibers) together without weaving. Bonding is achieved by chemical action, extraneous adhesives, or thermoplastic fibers. Used for diapers and filter cloths. See *Bonlinn.*

bonducin. $C_{14}H_{15}O_5 = 263.1$. A bitter principle of bonduc seeds, *Caesalpinia crista* (Leguminosae). White, bitter powder, insoluble in water; a febrifuge.

bondur. A corrosion-resisting aluminum alloy: Cu 2–4, Mn 0.3–0.6, Mg 0.5–0.9%. Cf. *acieral.*

bone. The skeletal material of the vertebrates. **b. ash.** Impure calcium phosphate. The remains of burnt animal bones; a fertilizer (35–38% P_2O_5). **b. black.** A usually impure charcoal made from bones and blood; used to refine sugar, oil, etc. **b. earth.** B. ash. **b. meal.** Finely ground animal bones used as fertilizer (N 3.3–4.1, P_2O_5 20–25%). *steamed-* Finely ground bones, previously steamed under pressure to remove the glue (N 1.6–2.5, P_2O_5 25%). **b. oil.** Animal oil, Dippel's oil. A tarry oil obtained by dry distillation of bones, d.0.900–0.980, soluble in water; chief constituent, pyridine. Used as an insecticide and in organic synthesis. **b. phosphate.** Calcium phosphate. **b. tallow.** Soft grease obtained by boiling fresh bones; used to make cheap soaps. **b. turquoise.** Fossil bones, or teeth colored with $Fe_3P_2O_8$. **b. wax.** See *wax.*

bongkrekik acid. $C_{12}H_{18}O_3$, produced by the action of certain bacteria on coconuts.

Bonlinn. Trademark for a bonded synthetic fiber web.

Bonney's blue paint. A 1% solution of brilliant green and/or crystal violet in a mixture of equal parts of rectified spirit and water. Used to treat caustic soda burns.

boost. (1) To overload or place an excessive strain on an engine, or when charging an accumulator. (2) See *synergist.*

Boot density bottle. A specific-gravity bottle, capacity about 5 ml, having double walls with a vacuum between. Used to determine specific gravities at constant temperature.

boracic acid. Boric acid.

boracite. $Mg_7Cl_2B_{16}O_{30}$. White transparent isometric crystals (Stassfurt); hardness 7, d.2.9–3.

boracium. Original name of boron (Davy).

Boraginaceae. Borage family, a group of herbs, some of which yield drugs; e.g., *Alkanna tinctoria,* alkannin; *Borago officinalis,* borage; *Pulmonaria officinalis,* lungwort.

boral. Aluminum borotartrate; an antiseptic and astringent.

boranate. Borohydride. Tetrahydrido borate. A salt containing the BH_4^- ion.

borane. Boron hydride.

borate. A salt of boric acid. **bi-** MH_2BO_3. Acid borate. **di-** Pyro-b. **hypo-** MH_3BO. **meta-** A

salt containing the —BO_2 radical. **ortho-** Borate. **per-** A salt containing the —BO_3 radical. **pyro-** A salt containing the $>B_4O_7$ radical. **tetra-** Pyro-.

boratto. A silk and wool fabric.

borax. $Na_2B_4O_7 \cdot 10H_2O$. Zala, tinkal. A native sodium tetraborate, found in California and Asia Minor; a cleaning agent, antiseptic, flux, etc. **b. bead.** A crystal of borax, melted in the loop of a platinum wire until it is transparent, is colored by metallic oxides. **b. carmine.** See *Grenacher stain, Nikiforoff stain.* **b. glass.** (1) Fused borax, used as a flux. (2) See *glass.* **b. methylene blue.** Sahli stain.

borazine. $(HB=NH)_x$. An unstable intermediate compound produced in the preparation of borazole.

borazole. $B_3N_3H_6 = 80.53$. Inorganic benzene

An isostere of benzene prepared by heating ammonia and diborane at 200°. Colorless mobile liquid, m.−58 b.55.

borazon. A form of boron nitride having extremely high abrasive properties. Made by heating boron under high pressure with lithium nitride.

bordeaux B. Acid B, α-naphthalene-azo-β-naphthol-3,6-disulfonic acid. An indicator for pH 10.5 (pink) to 12.5 (orange). **colors.** Artificial coloring matters for foodstuffs. **b. mixture.** Insecticides: (1) A mixture of equal weights of copper sulfate and lime in water; (2) a solution of copper arsenate and phenols.

Bordet test. An agglutination test to differentiate human and animal bloods.

borethyl. Triethyl borine.

boric acid. $B(OH)_3 = 62.9$. Boracic acid, fumarole acid. Triclinic white crystals, m.185, soluble in water. Used as a reagent, and to manufacture borates. Found in the volcanic lagoons of Tuscany. **meta-** HBO_2. **ortho-** B. acid. **per-** HBO_3. **pyro-** $H_2B_4O_7$. **benzyl-** $C_7H_7B(OH)_2 = 135.89$. Benzylboron dihydroxide. White crystals, m.161. **ethyl-** $C_2H_4B(OH)_2 = 73.87$. Ethylboron dihydroxide. Colorless crystals, sublime 40.

borickite. Anhydrous phosphate of iron.

boride. M_3B or BR_3. A binary compound of negative boron with a more positive element or radical.

boriding. Boronzing.

borine. BR_3. A compound of boron with an acyl or aryl radical. **triethyl-** BEt_3. Borethyl. Colorless liquid, b.95. **trimethyl-** BMe_3. Bormethyl. Cf. *methyl borate, ethyl borate.* **triphenyl-** BPh_3. Borphenyl.

borium. Boron.

bormethyl. Trimethyl *borine.*

borneene. $C_{10}H_{16} = 136.18$. **n-** or $\Delta^{5 \cdot 6}$-Borneene. An isomer of bornylene. **iso-** or $\Delta^{6 \cdot 7}$-Borneene

n- or $\Delta^{5 \cdot 6}$-   *i-* or $\Delta^{6 \cdot 7}$-

Borneo camphor. d-Borneol. **B. tallow.** See *tallow*.

borneol. $C_{10}H_{18}O = 154.20.$ **d-** Camphyl alcohol, Borneo camphor, baras camphor, sumatras camphor, bornyl alcohol, 2-hydroxycamphane, 2-camphanol,

$$\begin{array}{cc}
\text{dextro-} & \text{iso-}
\end{array}$$

A terpene from *Dryobalanops camphora*, or prepared synthetically. Transparent leaflets, m.203. slightly soluble in water. **epi-** Epiborneol. **iso-** 4-Hydroxycamphane. Transparent crystals, m.-210. Used in perfumery, Celluloid manufacture, as an antiseptic and stimulant. **b. acetate.** Bornyl acetate. **b. salicylate.** Bornyl salicylate. **b. valerate.** Gynoval.

bornesitol. Quebrachitol.

Born-Haber cycle. The relationship of $U =$ lattice energy of crystals, $I =$ ionization potential, $E =$ electron affinity, $S =$ heat of sublimation, $D =$ heat of dissociation, and $Q =$ chemical heat of formation, can be expressed by the diagram:

$$\begin{array}{l}
+U_{MX} \\
[MX] \longrightarrow (M)^+ + (X)^- \\
\text{Crystal} \qquad \text{Gaseous ions} \\
-Q_{MX} \uparrow \qquad \downarrow \quad -I_M + E_X \\
[M] + \tfrac{1}{2}(X_2) \longleftarrow (M) + (X) \\
\text{At standard} \quad -S_M + \tfrac{1}{2}D_{X2} \quad \text{Monoatomic} \\
\text{state} \qquad\qquad\qquad\qquad \text{gas}
\end{array}$$

bornite. $FeS \cdot 2Cu_2S \cdot CuS.$ Peacock copper, purple copper. A native copper iron sulfide. Red-brown brittle, isometric crystals, d.5.0.

bornyl. The $-C_{10}H_{17}$ radical derived from borneol by removing the hydroxyl group. **b. acetate.** $MeCOOC_{10}H_{17} = 196.22.$ d-Borneol acetic ester. Colorless crystals, m.29, slightly soluble in water. **b. amine.** $C_{10}H_{17}NH_2 = 153.25.$ 2-Aminocamphane. White crystals, m.163, soluble in water. **b. chloride.** $C_{10}H_{17}Cl = 172.65.$ Pinene hydrochloride 2-chlorocamphane. Colorless crystals, m. 158 decomp. by water at 49. **b. salicylate.** C_6H_4-$(OH)COOC_{10}H_{17} = 274.18.$ Salit, d-borneol salicylic ester. Colorless solid used externally mixed with equal parts of olive oil, for rheumatism.

bornylene. $C_{10}H_{16} = 136.18.$ $\Delta^{5 \cdot 6}$-Camphane, 1-methyl-1(4)isopropyl-$\Delta^{5 \cdot 6}$-hexamethylene, an isomer of borneene:

Colorless crystals, m.113, insoluble in water.

bornyval. Gynoval.

borobutane. See *boron hydrides*.

borocaine. $C_{13}H_{20}O_2N_2 \cdot 5HBO_2.$ Ethocaine borate. White crystals; an antiseptic.

borocalcite. $CaB_4O_7 \cdot 4H_2O.$ Bechilite. A native borate.

borofluohydric acid. Borofluoric acid.

borofluoric acid. $HBF_4 = 88.01.$ Hydroborofluoric acid, fluoboric, borofluohydric acid. Colorless liquid, b.130, miscible with water.

borofluoride. Fluoboride. A salt of borofluoric acid containing the BF_4- radical.

borofluorin. A mixture of boric acid, benzoic acid, sodium fluoride, and formaldehyde; an antiseptic and germicide.

boroglyceride. Glyceryl borate. An antiseptic paste of boric acid and glycerin.

borohydride. Boranate.

borol. Sodium and potassium borosulfate. Colorless transparent masses, soluble in water; a disinfectant and antiseptic.

borolon. An artificial aluminum oxide; white or brown-red crystalline masses, d.3.9–4.0, obtained by fusing bauxite. An abrasive, refractory, or filtering material.

boron. $B = 10.81.$ A metal of the aluminum group, at. no. 5, analogous to carbon; 3 modifications: (1) *Crystalline* b. Colorless tetragons of great hardness, d.2.51, sometimes variously colored by impurities; insoluble in acids, and alkalies, and slowly soluble in molten alkali carbonates. (2) *Amorphous* b. Gray powder, d.2.45, m. above 2000, b. about 3500; it burns in air at about 700; insoluble in water, soluble in acids (decomp.). (3) *Adamantine* b. Clear and colorless or brown crystals having the crystal shape of diamond. B. occurs widely distributed in small quantities in several silicates (tourmaline) and as borates (borax, ulexite), and in many alkaline lakes (California, Tibet). B. forms only one (trivalent) series of compounds.

Boron X-ides	BX_3
Borates	$B(OM)_3$
Borines	BR_3
Boranes	B_xH_y

B. was discovered (1807) independently by Davy and Gay-Lussac and Thenard. Crystalline b. was first prepared by Woehler (1856). Metallic b. is used as an industrial catalyst; in metallurgy to give hardness; and because it absorbs neutrons, in atomic reactors. **tetraphenyl-** A chemical reagent, particularly for the gravimetric determination of potassium. **b. alkyls.** See *borine*. **b. bromide.** $BBr_3 = 250.8.$ A colorless, fuming liquid, d.2.69, b.90, decomp. by water. **b. carbide.** $B_4C = 76.92.$ Black crystals, d.2.51; m.2350, insoluble in water. **b. chloride.** $BCl_3 = 117.2.$ Colorless liquid, d.1.434, b.18, decomp. by water. **b. fluoride.** $BF_3 = 67.82.$ Colorless gas, $d_{(air-1)}2.3$, b.$-101.$ **b. hydrides.** $BH_3 = 13.84$ or $B_2H_4 = 27.7.$ Borane, boroethane. Colorless gas, b.-87, decomp. by alcohol. B_2H_6 only is known: BH_3 is analogous to CH_3. B. forms numerous other hydrides (hydroborons); as, B_4H_{10} (borobutane), $B_{10}H_{14}$ (borodecane), analogous to the hydrocarbons and silanes. They have high calorific values and are used in high-energy fuels. **b. hydroxide.** Boric acid. **b. iodide.** $BI_3 = 391.8.$ Colorless crystalline scales, m.43, decomp. by water. **b. minerals.** Chiefly: borax, $Na_2B_4O_7 \cdot$ $10H_2O$; ulexite, $Na_2B_4O_7Ca_2B_6O_{11} \cdot 16H_2O$; borocalcite, $CaB_4O_7 \cdot 4H_2O$; sassolite, H_3BO_3; boracite,

$2Mg_3B_8O_{15} \cdot MgCl_2$. **b. nitride.** $BN = 24.8$. Colorless, infusible, crystals, insoluble in acids or alkalies (decomp. by hydrofluoric acid). **b. oxide.** $B_2O_3 = 69.64$. Colorless powder, m.577, slightly soluble in water or acids. **b. phosphide.** $BP = 42.0$. Red powder, burns at 200, insoluble in water. **b. sulfide.** $B_2S_5 = 117.83$. Colorless crystals, m.310, decomp. in water. *penta-* $B_2S_2 = 182.3$. Colorless crystals, d.1.85, m.390. **b. tribromide.** B. bromide. **b. trichloride.** B. chloride. **b. triethoxy-** Ethyl borate. **b. triethyl-** Borine. **b. trimethoxy-** Methyl borate. **b. trimethyl-** Borine. **b. trisulfide.** B. sulfide.

boronatrocalcite. Ulexite.

boronium. $Ph_2 \cdot B \cdot X \cdot Y$. The negatively charged ion derived from a tetrahedrally substituted boron atom.

boronzing. Boriding. The production of a hard surface layer of boride on a metal object by a process involving diffusion of boron.

borophenylic acid. Phenylboric acid. A mixture $PhBO_2$, phenyl borate, and PhB_3O_5, phenyl triborate. White or pink crystals, m.204, soluble in water; an antiseptic.

borosalicylates.

$$C_6H_4 \diagup \begin{matrix} O \\ \diagdown \\ CO \cdot O \end{matrix} B—B \diagup \begin{matrix} O \cdot CO \\ \diagdown \\ O \end{matrix} C_6H_4$$

borosilicate. Silicoborate. A salt of boric and silicic acids.

borotungstic acid. $(WO_3)_9 B_2O_3 \cdot 24H_2O$. Yellow liquid, d.3.0, soluble in water. Used to determine the density of minerals.

borowolframic acid. Borotungstic acid.

borphenyl. Triphenylborine.

Borrel grinder. A device for grinding organic tissues by means of flexible steel leaves which rotate at a high speed in a steel cylinder.

borsal, borsyl. Sodium borosilicate.

bort. Anthracite diamond, carbonado. A dark, lustrous conglomerate of minute diamonds from Brazil; used for cutting stones and in boring machines.

boryl. (1) The radical —BO. (2) Ethyl borosalicylate. White powder; an antiseptic and antirheumatic.

boss. Clampholder.

boswellic acid. $C_{32}H_{52}O_4 = 500.5$. An acid constituent of African olibanum, the resinous exudate of *Boswellia papyrifera* (Burseraceae).

botany. (1) The science of the structure, function, occurrence, and classification of plants and vegetable organisms. (2) Waste jute cuttings for paper manufacture. Cf. *hessian.*

Botany Bay gum. Acaroid resin.

botryolite. Datolite.

Böttcher chamber. A counting apparatus for blood corpuscles and bacteria; a microscope slide with ruled squares.

Böttger test. A test for glucose in urine; a black precipitate results with sodium carbonate and bismuth subnitrate.

bottle. A vessel with a narrow neck. **aspirator-** See *aspirator.* **balsam-** A small, wide-necked b.

with a loosely fitting glass cover. **density-** See specific gravity. **b. dropping-** A b. with a pipet fitted into its stopper. **gas-** A b. used for generating or washing gases, which usually has a two-hole stopper for the inlet and outlet tubing. **graduated-** A graduated b. used for mixing liquids. **hard rubber-** A b. made of rubber and used for certain acids. **immersion oil-** B.'s of various shapes, with a glass rod attached to the stopper. **milk testing-** Babcock b. Gerber b. **oil sample-** A long narrow b. **paraffin-** A b. made of paraffin for holding hydrofluoric acid. **percolator-** A widemouthed b., graduated in milliliters, pints, or ounces. **reagent-** A glass b. with the name and symbol of a reagent etched on. **specific gravity-** A small, light, accurately counterpoised and graduated b. used to determine the weight of a given volume of liquid. **specimen-** A widemouthed b. with a closure, for holding specimens. **washing-** A glass b. fitted with an inlet and outlet tube. The latter reaches to the bottom and at the other end has a small jet. Used for washing precipitates, or as a bubbler for washing gases. **weighing-** A small, light, glass-stoppered container, used for weighing liquids or solids. **Woulfe-** A glass b. with 2 or 3 necks, used as a washing or gas-generating bottle. **b. brush.** A length of stiff, woven, galvanized wire with bristles on the end portion and tip.

bottlenose oil. An inferior sperm oil from the blubber of the bottlenose whale, used in soap making.

botulin. A ptomaine produced by bacteria (*Bacillus botulinus*) and sometimes found in tinned and preserved meats.

botulism. Food poisoning due to *Clostridium botulinum*, the only microorganism with spores having a high heat resistance; it occurs in canned foods.

Bouchardat, Alexander. 1806–1886. French pharmacist noted for methods of urine analysis **B. reagent.** A solution of 1 pt. iodine and 2 pts. potassium iodide in 20 pts. water gives a brown precipitate with alkaloids.

bougie. (1) A filter cylinder made of porous porcelain. Cf. Berkefeld. (2) A taper-shaped pharmaceutical preparation for introduction into the rectum or urethra. (3) A narrow tube for introduction into the urethra or other body orifice. **b. unit.** The French photometric standard; 0.05% of the light emitted by 1 cm² of platinum at its solidifying point.

bouillon. Meat broth, used as food or culture medium. **glycerin-** Koch's culture medium: 10 gm Liebig meat extract, 10 gm peptone, 20 ml glycerin, 1,000 ml water, and sufficient sodium carbonate solution to make alkaline to litmus. Cf. *glucose b.* **plain-** A culture medium: 10 gm peptone, 5 gm sodium chloride, and 1,000 ml bouillon stock solution, neutralized with sodium hydroxide. **b. stock.** A solution of 500 gm lean beef in 1,000 ml water, used for culture media.

Bouin's fluid. A preservative for embryological and histological material: 75 ml saturated picric acid, 25 ml 40% formaldehyde, and 5 ml glacial acetic acid.

boulangerite. $3PbS \cdot 2Sb_2S_3$. A native lead sulfantimonate. Gray needles or feathery masses, d.6.18. Cf. *epiboulangerite.*

bourbonal. $CHO \cdot C_6H_3(OH) \cdot OEt = 166.07$. Ethyl vanillin-3-ethoxy-4-hydroxybenzaldehyde. A synthetic substitute for vanillin, stronger in flavor.

bournonite. $CuPbSbS_3$. Bluish-gray, brittle native copper lead sulfantimonite.

boussingaultite. $(NH_4)_2Mg(SO_4)_2 \cdot 6H_2O$. A native magnesium sulfate (Tuscany).

Bouveault-Blanc reaction. The reduction of esters to alcohols by metallic sodium.

B.O.V. Brown oil of vitriol. Commercial sulfuric acid (77–78% H_2SO_4 by weight).

bowenite. Serpentine.

Bowen tube. Bowen potash bulb. A tube with bulbs for the absorption of gases.

Boyce burner. An adjustable burner which regulates the gas and air flows.

Boyle, The Hon. Robert. 1627–1691. English pioneer in the investigation of gas laws. **B.'s law.** If the temperature is constant, the pressure of a given quantity of a gas is inversely proportional to the voume it occupies $PV = $ constant.

B.P. Abbreviation for: (1) the beriberi-preventing factor of vitamin B; (2) boiling point; (3) British Pharmacopoeia, B.Ph.

b.p. Abbreviation for boiling point.

B.Ph. Abbreviation for British Pharmacopoeia (obsolete).

B powder. Soda powder.

Br. Symbol for bromine. $Br_2 = $ bromine molecule. $Br^- = $ bromide ion. $Br^* = $ excited bromine atom.

brachydome. See *dome.*

brackish. Describing water having a chloride content exceeding 2,000 ppm. Cf. *water.*

Bragg, Sir William Henry. 1862–1942. British chemist, Nobel Prize winner (1915); noted for research on crystal structure. **B. crystallogram.** The photographic record obtained by B.'s method. **B. crystal model.** Crystalline structure as determined by the diffraction of monochromatic X rays. **B. method.** If a crystal is placed in the path of a narrow X-ray beam, the layers of atoms in the crystal act as reflection planes for the incident ray and a series of lines, corresponding with the several orders of spectrum, will be produced on the photographic plate. $\lambda = 2d \sin \theta$, where θ is the glancing angle, d the spacings between atomic planes, and λ the wavelength. Cf. *X-ray spectrograph, crystal structure, Laue pattern.*

brain. The nerve tissues in the skull which consist, chemically, of: (1) white b. substance (cephalins, lecithins, paramyelins, myelins, cholesterol, phrenosterol, cerebrin and cerebrosides); (2) buttery substance (cephaloidin, lecithin, myelin, paramyelin, aminomyelin, sphingomyelin, phrenosin and aminolipins); (3) aqueous b. extract, containing alkaloids (hypoxanthine, etc.), amino acids, inositol, organic and inorganic acids and salts. **b. sugar.** Cerebrose.

bran. The husk or outer covering of the grain of wheat. **b. oil.** Furfural.

branched chain. A forked atomic chain; as,

$$\cdots\; C\!-\!C \underset{\displaystyle C\!-\!C\;\cdots}{\overset{\displaystyle C\!-\!C\;\cdots}{\Big\langle}} \qquad \text{See } chain.$$

Brand, Hennig. An alchemist of Hamburg; discovered the first nonmetallic element (phosphorus) in 1669.

Brandt, Georg. 1694–1768. Swedish mineralogist; discovered the first metallic element (cobalt) in 1735.

brandy. An alcoholic beverage distilled from wine. Cf. *cognac.*

brasan. Brazan.

brasileic acid. $Me(CH_2)_7(CHOH)_2(CH_2)_{12}COOH = 386.4$. Isodihydroxybehenic acid. Yellow crystals, m.99, soluble in hot alcohol. Cf. *brasilic, brassylic,* and *brazilic acids.*

brasilein. Brazilein.

brasilic acid. $C_{12}H_{12}O_6 = 252.09$. Colorless crystals, m.129. Cf. *brasileic, brassylic,* and *brassidic acids.*

brasilin. Brazilin.

brass. A copper-base alloy containing zinc. In the classics, an alloy of copper and tin. **alpha-** B. containing less than 40% Cu. **beta-** B. containing more than 40% Cu. **aluminum-** An alloy: Cu 55–76, Zn 25–45, Al 1–4%. **calamine-** Marcasite. **cartridge-** An alloy: Cu 70, Zn 30%. **coal-** Roman b. **iron-** B. containing 1–9% Fe. **naval-** An alloy: Cu 61, Zn 38, Sn 1%. **Roman-** B. made by heating charcoal, copper, and calamine below 1000°C. **yellow-** Muntz metal.

90% Cu, 10% Zn, red brass	. . . .	m.	1040
80% Cu, 20% Zn, Dutch metal	. . . .	m.	995
67% Cu, 33% Zn, yellow, ordinary b.	. . . . .	m.	940
60% Cu, 40% Zn, Muntz metal	. . . .	m.	900

b. stone. $FeCO_3$. A native carbonate of iron.

brassic. See *brassidic.*

brassicasterol. $C_{28}H_{46}O = 398.35$. A sterol, from rape oil, m.148.

brassidic acid. $Me(CH_2)_7CH{:}CH(CH_2)_{11}COOH = 338.45$, *12*-Docosenoic acid*, isoerucic acid. Colorless leaflets, m.65, slightly soluble in water. An isomer of erucic acid and cetoleic acid. Cf. *brasilic* and *brasileic* acids.

brassil. Pyrite.

brassylic acid. $HOOC(CH_2)_{11}COOH = 244.19$. 1.11-Hendecanedicarboxylic acid. Colorless crystals, m.114, slightly soluble in water. Cf. *brasileic, brasilic,* and *brazilic acids.*

brattice. A coarse hessian which has been treated successively with bitumen and wood flour; used in mines for partitions and ventilation.

Brauner, Bohuslav. 1855-1935. Czechoslovakian chemist; noted for inorganic research and atomic-weight determinations.

braunite. $MnSiO_3 \cdot 3Mn_2O_3$. A native manganese silicate. Brown or gray lustrous tetragons.

Braun tube. (1) A potash bulb. (2) A special type of cathode-ray tube used in television.

bravaisite. Glauconite.

Bravais lattice. Space lattice.

Bray, William Crowell. 1879–1946. American chemist, noted for research in catalysis, qualitative analysis, and chemical kinetics.

Brayera. A genus of Rosaceae. See *brayerin. kousso.*

brayerin. $C_{31}H_{38}O_{10} = 570.3$. A bitter, resinous principle from *Brayera* species.

brazan. $C_6H_4OC_{10}H_6 = 218.2$. Brasan, phenylenaphthylene oxide.

braze. To solder with an alloy of Cu and Zn. Cf. *solder.*

Brazil. B. gum. Angico gum. **B. nut.** The edible seeds of *Bertholletia excelsa* (Myrtaceae). **b. nut oil.** Castanhao oil. **b. wax.** Carnauba wax. **b. wood.** See *brazilwood*.

brazileïn. $C_{16}H_{12}O_5 = 284.1$. Dark-red crystals obtained by oxidation of brazilin; it resembles hematoxylin.

brazilianite. $Na_2Al_6P_4O_{16}(OH)_8$. A monoclinic gemstone, similar to chrysoberyl in appearance (Brazil).

brazilic acid. Brasilic acid.

brazilin. $C_{16}H_{14}O_5 \cdot 1\frac{1}{2}H_2O = 313.21$. Brasilin. The coloring matter of brazilwood. Colorless or yellow needles, m.250, soluble in water. Used as a dye and indicator (acids—yellow, alkalies—purple).

brazilite. Baddeleyite.

brazilwood. (1) The heartwood of *Peltophorum dubium* (Leguminosae) of S. America. A source of brazilin. (2) A redwood of *Caesalpinia* species of S. America. **yellow-** Morus tinctoria.

brazing. Brazeing. A process for joining metals in which a molten filler metal is drawn by capillary attraction into the space between closely adjacent surfaces of the parts to be joined. The m. of the filler usually exceeds 500°C. Cf. *soldering*.

break point. See *chlorination*.

breccia. Angular rock fragments in a finer matrix.

breeze. Coke, 0.75–1 in. in size, from which no further size-graded product is removed. Used for steam raising, gas producers, briquetting, wall making, and for breaking up heavy soils.

bregenin. $C_{40}H_{87}O_5N = 661.71$. A phosphatide from brain substance.

breithauptite. NiSb. A native antimonide.

Bremen blue. Blue *copper carbonate*. **B. green.** $Cu(OH)_2$. Verdite. A green pigment produced by the weathering of copper; or artificially, by the action of alkali with copper sulfate.

bremsstrahlung. Radiation produced when β particles are stopped. They are similar in properties to low-energy X rays, and are a body hazard.

Brenkona. Trademark for a continuous-filament luster rayon yarn.

brenzcaïn. $C_6H_4(OMe)OCH_2Ph = 214.11$. Brenzcatechin methyl ether, guaiacol benzylic ether. Colorless crystals, m.62, insoluble in water; a local anesthetic.

brenzcatechin. Catechol. **b. dimethyl ether.** Veratrol. **b. methyl benzyl ether.** Brenzcaïn.

breunnerite. $MgFe(CO_3)$. A native mixture of siderite and magnesite.

brevium. $Bv = 234$. The radioactive element uranium X_2, at. no. 91. It is an isotope of ekatantalum, q.v., and has a half period of 1.65 min; hence the name (Fajans). Now known as protactinium.

brewing. The process by which malted grain is treated with hot water to produce an extract (wort). This is boiled with hops, filtered, and fermented with yeast.

brewsterite. A rock-forming zeolite mineral.

Brewster's angle. The particular angle of incidence p at which the reflection of approximately monochromatic plane-polarized light from a surface is a minimum. Its tangent equals the refractive index n of the material. **B. law.** Tan $p = n(\sin p)/(\cos p)$.

brick. A baked clay molded in various, generally rectangular, shapes. **fire-** A b. used for furnace linings. **silica-** A b. used as lining for high-temperature appliances. **Sil-O-Cel.** Trademark for an insulating b.

bridge. (1) A connecting atom or atoms within a ring of atoms. Cf. *ring structure*. (2) A connecting device; as, *Kelvin b.*, *Wheatstone b.*

brightening. Subjecting dyed material to 5 lb steam pressure brightens the color.

brightness. The intensity of light or color, q.v.; hence, the amount of light emitted or reflected by an object. Surface brightness is measured in *lamberts*. **absolute-, apparent-,** and **photographic-** See *spectral* classification.

Briglo. Trade name for a viscose synthetic fiber.

brilliance. Brightness.

brilliant. Intensely bright. **b. cresyl blue.** A dye used as a stain for blood. **b. crocein.** Sodium amino-azobenzeneazo-β-naptholdisulfonate. Brown powder, soluble in water; a deep red dye. **b. green.** $C_{27}H_{34}O_4N_2S = 482.70$. Viride nitens (B.P.). Di-(p-diethylamino)triphenylcarbinol anhydride sulfate. Small, golden crystals, soluble in water or alcohol. Used in pharmacy as an epithelial stimulant in minor skin injuries and affections; also as an indicator, changing at pH 2.0 from yellow (acid) to green (alkaline). **b. yellow.** A dye indicator, changing at pH 0.5 from blue (acid) to yellow, and at pH 8.0 from yellow to scarlet (alkaline).

Bri-lon. A brand of Bri-nylon, q.v.

brimstone. Sulfur.

brine. (1) Water which is nearly saturated with salts; e.g., sodium chloride. (2) General term for solutions of a chloride of sodium, calcium, or magnesium, used in cooling systems.

Brinell, Johan August. 1849–1925. Swedish engineer. **B. hardness.** The area of indentation produced by a hardened steel ball (10 mm diameter) under a pressure of 3000 or 500 kg. B.h. = $P/\pi t D$, where P is the pressure, kg; t the depth of indentation, mm; and D is the diameter of ball, mm. **B. tester.** A device for determining the B. hardness.

Brinton Reishauer bottle. A specific gravity bottle which holds 100 ml of liquid.

Brin process. The preparation of oxygen gas by heating barium oxide which, at 500°, forms barium peroxide. This gives off oxygen at about 1000°C.

Bri-Nylon. Trade name for a polyamide synthetic fiber, which has triangular facets to produce a sparkling effect.

briquet, briquette. A brick of compressed solid fuel; as, coal, lignite, sawdust, or waste materials.

brisance. The violence or shattering effect of an explosive, measured in terms of its detonation velocity.

britannia metal. A hard silver-white alloy: Sn 80–90, Sb 10–20 pts., and small quantities of copper, and sometimes lead, bismuth, or zinc. Similar to pewter, but spun from rolled sheets instead of being cast. Used in household utensils as it takes a high polish.

Britenka. Trademark for a continuous-filament rayon yarn.

britholite. $(Na_2Ca_7Ce_{11})(F \cdot OH)_4[SiO_4]_9(PO_4)_3]$. A cerium silicate apatite.

British Chemical Societies. (1) Chemical Society.

Organized 1841. Publishers of *Journal and Proceedings*. Secretary: Burlington House, London W.1. (2) Society of Chemical Industry. Organized in 1881. Publishers of a weekly, *Chemistry and Industry;* and monthly, *Journal of Food and Agriculture,* and *Journal of Applied Chemistry.* Secretary: 14, Belgrave Square, London, S.W.1. These two societies also publish Annual Reports on the Progress in Pure and Applied Chemistry, respectively; and Society of Chemical Industry publishes Abstracts.

British gum. Dextrin. **B. plate.** See *nickel* silver.

British Standards Institution. See *BSI.*

British thermal unit. Btu (U.S. usage). BThU (U.K. usage). (Cf. *Board of Trade Unit,* B.T.U.). 100,000 Btu = 1 therm. A measure of energy in the English system, which corresponds with the calories of the metric system. The heat required to raise one pound of water from 39 to 40°F; hence, the heat required to raise the temperature of one pound water at its temperature of maximum density by one degree Fahrenheit. It varies with the temperature:

60.5°F	1054.54 joules
32–212°F (mean)	1055.79
39°F	1059.52
Steam tables	1055.06

mean- The $\frac{1}{180}$ part of the heat required to raise the temperature of one pound water from 32 to 212°F = 252 cal; 1 Btu/lb = 1.8 cal/gm.

brittle. (1) Easily broken or pulverized. (2) In bacteriology, the dry growth of bacteria, which is friable under a platinum needle. **b. silver ore.** Stephanite.

Brix hydrometer. A hydrometer graduated with the Brix scale. **B. degree.** The per cent by weight of soluble solids in a syrup at 68°F (UK. official usage.) An arbitrary scale for the direct conversion of the saccharometer reading of a sugar solution into its specific gravity; (1) $x°$ Brix indicates that the solution to which it refers contains x gm of sugar in 100 ml. (2) At 15.6°C, specific gravity = 400/(400 ± $x°$ Brix), where x is + or − according as the liquid is heavier or lighter than water, respectively. See *hydrometers.*

broach. A mixture of diamond dust, bentonite, and a silicate, used for watch bearings.

brochanite. $Cu_2(OH)_2SO_4$. Warringtonite. A native, basic copper sulfate, occurring in emerald-green vitreous masses. The green patina of copper.

Brocillin. See *penicillin.*

Brodie coagulometer. A device for measuring the coagulation of the blood under the microscope. **B. kymograph-.** An apparatus for recording blood pressure. **B. solution.** A solution of salt of such a specific gravity that a column 10,000 mm high is equivalent to a pressure of 1 atm; used in manometers.

broggerite. A variety of pitchblende.

Broglie, Maurice, Duc de. 1875–1960. French physicist, noted for his work on corpuscular physics and X-ray spectra. **B., Louis Victor, Prince de.** b. 1892. French physicist noted for work on wave mechanics; Nobel Prize winner (1929). **B.**

formula. An expression connecting wavelength λ with momentum mv accelerated by volts V.

$$\lambda = h/mv = \sqrt{150/V} \text{ A}$$

brom- Bromo-. **b. acetone.** Bromoacetone.

bromacetanilide. See *acetanilide.*

bromacetate. A salt of bromacetic acid containing the $CH_2Br\cdot COO-$ radical.

bromacetic acid. $CH_2Br\cdot COOH = 138.95$. Bromoacetic acid. Colorless hexagons, m.49, soluble in water.

bromacetol. 2,2-Dibromopropane*.

bromal. $CBr_3CHO = 280.9$. Tribromoacetaldehyde, 2,2,2-tribromoethanol*. Yellow liquid, d.2.65, b.174, decomp. in water; a hypnotic and anodyne. **b. hydrate.** $CBr_3\cdot CH(OH)_2 = 298.9$. Tribromaldehyde hydrate, 2,2,2-tribromo-1,1-ethanediol*. Colorless crystals, m.53, soluble in water; a hypnotic, antispasmodic, and sedative.

bromalin. $C_6H_{12}N_4\cdot C_2H_5Br = 249.2$. Bromethylformin, hexamethylenetetramine bromethylene. Colorless crystals, m.200; soluble in water; an antiepileptic and sedative.

bromalonic acid. See *malonic acid.*

bromamide. Aniline tribromide.

bromaniline. See *aniline.*

bromargyrite. Bromyrite.

bromate. A salt of bromic acid containing the $-BrO_3$ radical; as sodium bromate, $NaBrO_3$.

bromated. Brominated. (1) Combined with or containing bromine. (2) The introduction of bromine into a molecule. **di-** A molecule containing 2 Br atoms. **mono-** A molecule containing 1 Br atom.

b. camphor. See *camphor.*

bromation. Bromination.

bromatology. The science of food and diet.

bromaurate. $MAuBr_4$. A salt derived from auric bromide and a metallic bromide, MBr.

brombenzamide. See *benzamide.*

brombenzene. See *benzene.*

bromcamphor. See *camphor, monobromated.*

bromchlorphenol blue. $C_{19}H_{10}Br_2Cl_2O_2S = 580.6$. Dibromodichlorosulfonphthalein. Yellow powder, soluble in water or alcohol. An indicator, changing from yellow (pH 4.5) to blue (pH 5.5).

bromcresol green. $C_{21}H_{14}Br_4O_5S = 700.0$. 2,3,6,7-Tetrabromo-*m*-cresolsulfonephthalein. Gray powder, soluble in water or alcohol; a pH indicator between 4.5 (yellow) and 5.5 (blue). **b.c. purple.** $C_{21}H_{16}Br_2C_5S = 540.41$. Dibromo-o-cresolsulfonphthalein. Yellow powder; a pH indicator between pH 5.2 (yellow) and 6.8 (purple).

bromelia. $C_{10}H_7OEt = 172.1$. Ethoxynaphthalene, β-naphthyl ethyl ether. Colorless crystals, m.38, insoluble in water. Used in perfumery.

Bromeliaceae. The pineapple family.

bromelin. A proteolytic enzyme in pineapples, which converts proteins into proteoses and peptones.

bromeosin. See *eosin.*

bromethane. Misnomer for: (1) bromomethane; (2) bromoethane.

bromethyl. (1) Ethyl bromide. (2) Bromomethyl. (3) Bromoethyl.

bromethylene. Ethylene bromide.

bromethylformin. Bromalin.

brometone. $CBr_3\cdot CMe_2OH = 310.9$. Acetone

bromoform, 2,2,2-tribromo-1-methyl-1-propanol*.
White prisms, with camphor-like odor and taste,
m.167, slightly soluble in water; a sedative.
bromhydrin. Br—R—OH. An organic compound.
Cf. *halohydrin, chlorhydrin.* **tri-** Allyl tribromide.
bromic acid. $HBrO_3 = 128.97$. Colorless crystals,
decomp. about 100, slightly soluble in water. Its
salts are bromates. **hydro-** See *hydrobromic acid.*
b. ether. Ethyl bromide.
bromide. A binary salt containing negative monovalent bromine; e.g., sodium bromide, NaBr.
Bromides are usually soluble in water. **hydro-**
An addition compound of HBr and an organic
base, e.g. an alkaloid.
brominated. Bromated.
bromination. (1) To treat with bromine. (2) To
introduce Br into an organic molecule. Bromation,
bromization.
bromine. $Br = 79.90$. An element of the chlorine
group, at. no. 35. A dark brown liquid, fuming
halogen, $d_0°3.19$, m. -7.5, b.58.78, soluble in water,
alcohol, chloroform or ether. Gaseous b. has a
density of 5.524 (air = 1) and molecular weight
(Br_2) 159.84. Elementary b. never occurs native,
and is found mainly as the bromides of alkali
metals, in natural waters, brines, and seawater.
Solid ores are carnallite and silver bromide. B. is
mainly monovalent, but in some compounds it is
tri-, penta-, or heptavalent and forms the compounds:

—1 bromides	Br^-
+1 hypobromites	BrO^-
+3 bromites	BrO_2^-
+5 bromates	BrO_3^-
+7 perbromates	BrO_4^-

B. was discovered (1826) by Balard in the mother
liquors of seawater. Greek "bromos" (stench).
Liquid b. is a reagent, and oxidizing agent, in
organic synthesis. **b. chloride.** $BrCl·10H_2O =$
295.6. Yellow crystals or liquid, m.7, decomp.
readily, very soluble in water or ether. **b. cyanide.**
$BrCN = 106.01$. Cyanogen bromide. Colorless
needles, m.52, soluble in water. **b. fluoride.**
$BrF = 98.92$. Colorless prisms, m.50, decomp.
by water. **b. hydrate.** $Br·10H_2O = 260.01$. Red
octahedra, decomp. 15, soluble in water. **b.
hydride.** Hydrobromic acid. **b. iodide.** $BrI =$
206.85. B. monoiodide. Colorless crystals, m.36,
soluble in carbon disulfide. **b. monochloride.** B.
chloride. **b. monoiodide.** B. iodide. **b. pentachloride.** $BrCl_5 = 257.21$. Colorless liquid, used
in organic synthesis. **b. sulfide.** $Br_2S_2 = 223.96$.
Red liquid, d.2.629, b.195, decomp. by water. **b.
water.** A saturated aqueous solution of bromine
(about 3% Br); a reagent.
Brominol. Registered trademark for a brominized
olive oil (33% Br); an X-ray contrast medium.
bromipin. 10% brominated sesame oil. Yellow oil;
a sedative, nervine, and antiepileptic. 33% b. is
used as an X-ray contrast medium.
bromite. Bromyrite.
bromization. Bromation. To saturate with bromine. Cf. *bromination.*
bromilite. Alstonite.
brommalonic acid. $CHBr(COOH)_2 = 183.01$. Colorless needles, soluble in water.

bromnaphthalene. See *naphthalene.*
bromo- Brom-. Prefix indicating a bromine atom
in an organic compound. **di-** A compound containing 2 Br atoms. **tri-** A compound containing
3 Br Atoms.
bromoacetic acid. See *bromacetic acid.*
bromoacetone. $BrCH_2COMe = 136.95$. Mono-
bromomethyl ketone. Colorless liquid, d.1.603,
b.127; a poison gas.
bromobenzamide. See *benzamide.*
bromobenzene. See *benzene.*
bromobenzyl cyanide. $BrC_6H_4CH_2CN = 195.97$.
o-Bromophenylacetonitrile, 2-bromo-7-cyanotolu-
ene. Colorless liquid, m.26; a lacrimatory poison
gas (BBC).
bromocaffeine. $C_8H_9O_2N_4Br = 272.1$. White
powder, m.206, slightly soluble in water.
bromocamphor. Camphor, monobromated.
bromocyanogen. Cyanogen bromide.
bromoethyl. (1) Ethyl bromide. (2) The radical
$BrC_2H_4—$.
bromoform. $CHBr_3 = 252.90$. Tribromomethane*,
formyl bromide, methenyl bromide. Colorless
liquid, d.2.904, m.7.7, b.150.4, slightly soluble in
water. Used for separation of minerals, and as
local anesthetic, antispasmodic, and sedative.
nitro- $CBr_3NO_2 = 297.78$. Bromopicrin, tri-
bromonitromethane. Colorless liquid, m.10, b118mm
127; insoluble in water.
bromoformin. Bromalin.
bromoketone. $BrCH_2·COEt = 150.98$. Bromomethyl ethylketone; used in chemical warfare.
bromol. Tribromphenol.
bromomethane. Methyl bromide. **tri-** Bromoform.
bromomethyl. (1) Methyl bromide. (2) The radical
$BrCH_2—$.
bromometry. The determination of the halogen-
absorbing capacity of unsaturated compounds or
of materials containing them, e.g., fats; usually
expressed in terms of iodine.
bromonaphthalene. See *naphthalene.*
bromophenol. See *bromphenols.* **b. blue.** See *brom-
phenols.*
bromophosgene. Carbonyl bromide.
bromopicrin. Nitrobromoform.
bromoprene. $CH_2:CBr·CH:CH_2 = 134.0$. 2-
Bromobutadiene-1,4. An intermediate in the
polymerization of synthetic rubber. Cf. *isoprene,
duprene.*
bromopyrine. $C_{11}H_{11}ON_2Br = 267.0$. Mono-
bromantipyrine. White crystals, m.114, soluble in
hot water; an antipyretic and antiseptic.
bromothymol blue. Bromthymol blue. See *indicators.*
bromotoluene. See *toluene.*
bromphenols. $Br·C_6H_4·OH = 173.0$. A series of
compounds, formed by the action of bromine on
phenol: **ortho-** A liquid, b.194, sparingly soluble in
water. **meta-** A solid, m.32. **para-** A solid,
m.63, sparingly soluble in water. **tri-** $C_6H_3OBr_3 =$
330.9. The solid, $1,2,4,6-C_6H_2·OH·Br_3$, m.96;
sparingly soluble in water.
  b. blue. $C_{19}H_{10}Br_4O_5S = 673.75$. 2,3,6,7-
Tetrabromophenolsulfonphthalein. Yellow powder, soluble in water; a pH indicator from pH
3.0 (yellow) to 4.6 (blue). **b. red.** $C_{19}H_{12}Br_2O_5S =$
511.9. Dibromophenolsulfonphthalein. Yellow
powder, a pH indicator from 6.0 (yellow) to 7.0 (red).

bromphenyl acetylcystein. Phenylmercapturic acid.

bromthymol blue. $C_{27}H_{38}Br_2O_5S = 624$. Dibromothymolsulfonphthalein. Brown crystals with green luster; a pH indicator from pH 6.0 (yellow) to 7.6 (blue).

bromum. Official Latin for bromine.

Bromural. $MeCHMe(CHBrCO)NH \cdot CONH_2 = 223.03$. Trade name for 2-monobromoisovaleryl urea. Colorless needles, m.145, soluble in water; a nerve sedative and hypnotic.

Bromwell apparatus. A graduated glass cylinder of special shape for fusel oil determination.

bromyrite. AgBr. Bromargyrite, bromite. An unctuous native silver bromide. Yellow or green transparent or opaque isometric crystals.

bronchography. A method of rendering the tracheobronchial tree visible by means of a radiopaque.

brongniardite. $Ag_2PbSb_2S_5$. A native silver-lead-sulfoantimonite, which occurs in isometric crystals.

Brönner acid. 2,6-Naphthylaminesulfonic acid.

bronze. A copper-base alloy usually containing up to 30% tin; e.g.:

90% Cu 10% Sn, gunmetal m.1005
80% Cu 20% Sn, bell metal . . . . m. 890
70% Cu 30% Sn, speculum . . . . m. 755

acid- An alloy containing Cu 82–88, Pb 2–8, Sn 8–10, Zn 0–2%. **aluminum-** An alloy: Cu 90, Al 10%. **carbon-** An alloy used for bearings. **coinage-** See *coinage*. **jewelry-** An alloy: Cu 87.5, Zn 12.5%. **manganese-** An alloy: Cu 88, Sn 10, Mn 2%. **phosphor-** See *phosphor*. **saffron-** Orange *tungsten*. **silicon-** A noncorrosive alloy of copper and tin, with 1–4% silicon. **Sillmann-** An alloy: Cu 86, Al 10, Fe 4%. **Tobin-** An alloy: Cu 55, Zn 43, Sn 2%. **tungsten-** Tungsten bronze. **uchatius-** A gear and bearing alloy containing Cu 92, Sn 8%.
b. blue. Prussian blue. **b. disease.** The formation of light green spots of basic cupric chloride on old b., e.g., in museums.

bronzite. Schillerspar. A rhombic native pyroxene consisting of $MgSiO_3$ with 10% $FeSiO_3$ with a bronze luster.

brookite. Arkansite. A reddish-brown to black orthorhombic variety of rutile, d.4.0, hardness 6–6.5.

broom. Scoparius. **Spanish-** Spartium. **b. corn-** Sorghum.

brown. Describing a pigment or color made by mixing red, yellow, and black. **b. coal.** Lignite. **b. dyes.** See *aniline* b., *bismarck* b., *resorcin* b., *spirit* b. **b. hematite.** See *hematite*. **b. iron ore.** See *limonite, bog iron ore, ocher, hematite*. A hydrous iron oxide with some iron carbonate. **b. ocher.** B. iron ore. **b. oil of vitriol.** B.O.V. **b. pigments.** See *Cassel* b. *chrome* b., *ocher, sepia, vandyke* b., *zinc*. b. **b. spar.** Pearl spar. A variety of dolomite, q.v., with a brown tinge due to ferric or manganic oxide.

Brown, Alexander Crum. 1869–1908. Scottish chemist noted for organic research. **Crum B. rule.** If the hydrogen of an aromatic compound can be converted by direct oxidation into a hydroxyl compound, substitution will take place in the meta position. If not, the substituting radical enters the ortho or para position. **B., Robert,** 1773–1858. British botanist, discoverer of Brownian movement.

Brownian movement. Pedesis. The rapid vibratory motion of extremely small particles suspended in a liquid, caused by the bombardment of the particle by the moving molecules of the liquid. The velocity varies inversely with the size of the particles, and depends also upon the viscosity of the medium. Cf. *Svedberg's equation*.

browning. The formation of off-color in foods during processing.

Brownite cupel. A shallow vessel used in silver analysis.

brownmillerite. $4CaO \cdot Al_2O_3 \cdot Fe_2O_3$. A phase in the stabilization of dolomite by calcination with silica.

Broxil. Trade name for potassium 6-(α-phenoxypropionamido)penicillanic acid, a high-potency oral penicillin.

brucealin. The active glycosidic principle of the seeds of *Brucea javanic*, Merr. A chinese antiamebic drug, decomp. 140.

brucine. $C_{23}H_{26}O_4N_2 \cdot 4H_2O = 466.41$. Dimethoxy-strychnine.

An alkaloid from the seeds of *Strychnos* species (nux vomica, ignatia, etc.). Colorless crystals, m.178, slightly soluble in water; a nerve tonic. **b. hydrobromide.** $C_{23}H_{26}O_4N_2 \cdot HBr = 479.31$. White crystals, soluble in water; used as brucine. **b. hydrochloride.** $C_{23}H_{26}O_4N_2 \cdot HCl = 430.81$. White crystals, soluble in water; a tonic. **b. nitrate.** $C_{23}H_{26}O_4N_2 \cdot HNO_3 \cdot 2H_2O = 493.39$. White crystals, decomp. 230, soluble in water. **b. phosphate.** $(C_{23}H_{26}O_4N_2)_2H_3PO_4 = 886.78$. White crystals, soluble in water. **b. sulfate.** $(C_{23}H_{26}O_4N_2)_2 \cdot H_2SO_4 \cdot 7H_2O = 1012.86$. Colorless needles, soluble in water. **b. test.** A solution of 0.5 gm in 200 ml concentrated sulfuric acid; a test for nitric acid.

brucite. $Mg(OH)_2$. Nemalite. A native magnesium hydroxide.

Bruehl receiver. Receivers for a condenser in an airtight container; a number of distillates may be collected separately by revolving the apparatus so that each receiver comes under the end of the condenser in turn.

Brunck, Heinrick von. 1847–1911. German chemist who developed organic chemical industry.

brunfelsia. Manaca.

Bruninghaus optimum. The concentration of an activator of luminescence which produces the maximum effect.

Brünner acid. 2,6-Naphthylaminesulphonic acid.

brunswick green. (1) Green *copper carbonate*. (2) A basic copper carbonate having the same composition as atacamite, q.v.

brushite. $CaHPO_4 \cdot 2H_2O$. A native acid calcium phosphate.

Brussels nomenclature. A classification of chemical products of commercial importance. Used in Europe for Customs and similar purposes, proposed by the Customs Cooperation Council.

bryoidin. $C_{20}H_{38}O_3 = 326.30$. A bitter principle of elemi gum.

bryonane. $C_{20}H_{42} = 282.3$. A saturated hydrocarbon, m.69, b.400, from the leaves of *Bryonia dioica* (Cucurbitaceae), possibly identical with laurane.

bryonia. English mandrake, white bryony. The dried roots of *Brionia* species (Cucurbitaceae) containing bryonin, alkaloids, and resin; a cathartic. **black-** Blackeye root. The root of *Tamus communis* (Dioscoraceae) a rubefacient and diuretic. **white-** Bryonia.

bryonin. $C_{48}H_{80}O_{19}(?)$. A glucoside from the root of *Bryonia* species (Cucurbitaceae). An amorphous brown powder, soluble in water or alcohol; a cathartic.

Bryophyta. A division of Cryptogamia, including liverworts (Hepatica) and mosses (Musci).

B.S. See *Bureau of Standards*.

BSI. British Standards Institution. An organization which issues specifications, methods of testing materials, and glossaries of terms for a number of chemical products and industries. Cf. *ASTM*.

BTB. (1) Abbreviation for bromthymol blue. (2) A mixture of boric acid, tar oil, and bentonite, used as a spray for sheep against blowfly.

BThU. Abbreviation for British thermal unit (U.K. usage).

B.T.U. Abbreviation for Board of Trade unit (U.K. usage).

Btu. Abbreviation for British thermal unit (U.S. usage). See *BThU*.

Bu. Symbol for butyl. **i-Bu.** Symbol for isobutyl.

BuOH. Butyl alcohol.

bu. Abbreviation for bushel.

bubble. (1) A small air droplet. (2) To pass gas through a liquid. **b. counter.** A device to measure the volume of a gas. A capillary tube through which the gas bubbles escape, connected with a U tube partly filled with mercury; each b. makes an electric contact. **b. gage.** A small glass vessel containing a liquid through which the gas bubbles; used to indicate gas flow.

Bubblfil. Trade name for a viscose synthetic fiber.

bubulin. A compound of cow's dung.

bucco. Buchu.

Buchner, Eduard. 1860–1917. German chemist. Nobel Prize winner (1907), who found that enzyme action is purely chemical. **B. funnel.** A porcelain funnel with a cylindrical top, containing a perforated porcelain plate, on which a filter paper is placed. **B. number.** The number of milliliters of normal alcoholic potassium hydroxide solution required to neutralize 2.5 gm of wax dissolved in 80% alcohol.

bucholzite. A variety of fibrolite.

buchu. Bucco, bucku. The dried leaves of *Barosma betulina* (Rutaceae) of S. Africa; a diuretic, anticatarrhal, used as fluid extract. Cf. *rutin*, *barosmin*. **b. camphor.** See *diosphenol*.

buckbean. Menyanthes.

Buck mortar. A specially shaped mortar for grinding gold ore with mercury.

buckram. A stiffening fabric, made by impregnating an open-weave cotton cloth with an adhesive.

buckthorn. Rhamnus. **b. bark.** Frangula. **b. berries.** Rhamnus cathartica. The dried, ripe fruit of *Rhamnus cathartica* (Rhamnaceae). A cathartic, used as fluid extract. Cf. *xanthorhamnin*.

buckwheat. The seeds of *Fagopyrum esculentum*, (Polygonaceae); a food.

Bucky rays. Grenz rays.

Budde effect. The expansion in volume of chlorine or bromine vapor when exposed to light.

buddeized. Sterilized by warm hydrogen peroxide.

budding. A form of cell division in which the new cell is an outgrowth of the parent cell, from which it subsequently becomes detached; as, yeast.

buddling. The process of crushing an ore and washing it in a stream of water.

budiene. Bivinyl.

Bueb process. A method for making ferrous ferrocyanide from iron sulfate, ammonia, and hydrocyanic acid.

buergerite. A species of tourmaline.

bufagin. $C_{24}H_{32}O_5 = 380.3$. A neutral, digitalis-like principle in the skin-gland venom of the toad, *Bufo agua*. A Brazilian arrow poison. Cf. *sterols*.

bufanolide. Bufogenan. Describing the fully saturated system of the squill-toad poison group of lactones; the configuration at the 20-position is the same as in cholesterol. Cf. *steroid*.

buffer. A substance which, when added to a solution, resists a change in hydrogen ion concentration on addition of acid or alkali. **oxidation-reduction-** A mixture of compounds which resists a change in oxidation-reduction potential and so enables selective oxidation and reduction to be carried out. Cf. *redox*. **b. action.** The capacity to neutralize, within limits, either acids or bases, without changing the original acidity or alkalinity; as, of blood, soil, plant juices. **b. capacity.** (1) The millimoles of H^+ which a unit volume of the solution in question will neutralize when an excess of standard acid is added. (2) B. index. The number of moles of strong acid or base required to change the pH by one unit when added to 1 liter of the buffer solution. **b. index.** B. capacity. **b. salts.** Salts which behave as buffers, generally those of acids with a low dissociation; e.g., the carbonates and phosphates of the blood, which maintain a pH of 7.35, notwithstanding the absorption of carbon dioxide or the introduction of acids. **b. solution.** A solution of a weak acid or base and its salts, such as acetates, borates, phosphates, phthalates, which behave as buffers. The following is a "universal" b. solution from pH 2.5 to pH 11.5 (Prideaux and Ward). A 0.1 N solution is made containing phosphoric, phenylacetic, and boric acids, 0.02 N to the hydrogen ion in each case. If V is the number of milliliters of 0.2 N hydrochloric acid and 0.2 N sodium hydroxide which is added to 100 ml of this solution with subsequent dilution to 200 ml, then pH = $3.1 \pm 0.1185V$ (sodium hydroxide is +, hydrochloric acid is −). **b. value.** The amount of standard solution (acid or alkali) to bring about a specified change in the hydrogen ion concentration of a solution.

bufogenan. Bufanolide.

bufonin. $C_{34}H_{54}O_2 = 494.43$. A poisonous principle in the secretion of toads and lizards, e.g., *Bufo vulgaris;* slightly soluble in water or alcohol. Cf. *phrynin.*

bufotalin. $C_{24}H_{30}O_3 = 266.23$. A split product of bufotoxin, which resembles digitaligenin.

bufotanine. $C_{14}H_{18}O_2N_2 = 246.16$. An alkaloid from the secretion of the parotoid gland of *Bufo vulgaris.*

bufotenine. $C_{12}H_{16}ON_2 = 204.20$. N,N-dimethyl-5-hydroxytryptamine. An amine from the skin of the common toad.

bufotoxin. $C_{34}H_{46}O_{10} = 614.37$. A poisonous, acidic skin secretion of toads.

bugleweed. The herb of *Lycopus virginicus* (Labiatae); an astringent and sedative.

bulb. A spherical or bulb-shaped apparatus.

bulbocapnine. $C_{19}H_{19}O_4N = 325.16$. An alkaloid from the bulbs of *Corydalis cava, Bulbocapnus cavus* (Papaveraceae). White crystals, m.199, soluble in alcohol. **b. hydrochloride.** $C_{19}H_{19}O_4N \cdot HCl = 361.6$. White crystals, soluble in hot water.

bulgara. *Bacillus lactis bulgaricus* in intestinal flora; used to treat intestinal toxemia.

bulgur. Dried, precooked wheat.

bulk. (1) The increase in the volume of a solvent by the dissolved substance. Cf. *cut.* (2) The ratio of the thickness to the weight per unit area of a paper: a measure of the air space present.

bullate. A bacterial growth resembling a blistered surface.

bullion. (1) Coinage metal in mass form. (2) Metal money, as distinct from paper money. (3) Any metal in bar form.

bull's-eye condenser. A mounted concave lens for the illumination of opaque objects under the microscope.

bully tree. See (1) *chicle,* (2) *balata,* (3) *sapota.*

bumping. Uneven boiling of a liquid, due to superheating: avoided by adding an inert solid; e.g., glass beads, pumice.

buna. A German rubber substitute prepared by the polymerization of butadiene.

Bundesmann test. A test for the water resistance of fabrics, which are sprayed with water and rubbed on the underside.

Bunsen, Robert Wilhelm Eberhard von. 1811–1899. German chemist. **b. burner.** A gas burner with adjustable air supply. **B. cell.** An electrolytic element with a constant potential of 1.9 volt. An anode of amalgamated zinc in 10% sulfuric acid and a cathode of carbon in conc. nitric acid. Cf. *Grove's* cell. **B. clamp.** A clamp with cylindrical, rubber-covered jaws, for holding glassware. **B. eudiometer.** A graduated glass tube with platinum electrodes to pass an electric discharge through a combustible gas mixture; the volume changes, and thence the composition may be determined. **B. flame.** See *flame.* **B. funnel.** A glass funnel with long stem at an angle of 60°. **B. gas bottle.** A cylindrical glass bottle with outlet and inlet tubes for washing gases. **B. reactions.** Flame reactions. The behavior in the Bunsen flame: e.g., substances imparting characteristic color. Cf. *analysis, bead* test. **B. -Roscoe law.** Reciprocity law. The amount of substance decomposed by radiant energy is proportional to the amount of energy absorbed. **B. valve.** See *valve.*

bunsenite, bunsenine. NiO. Krennerite. Native nickel oxide; green isometric crystals.

bunt. A seed-borne fungus disease of wheat.

Bunte, Hans. 1848–1925. German chemist. **B. gas buret.** A buret with a two-way stopcock at one end.

buoyancy. Capacity to float in a liquid or gas. **b. correction.** True weight $= g(1 - K + g'/d)$, where g is the observed weight; $g' = 0.0012$, the weight of 1 ml air; d is the density of the body being weighed; and $K = 0.00014$. the ratio of the densities of air and brass weights.

buphane. Candelabra flower. Cape poison bulb, gifbol. *Buphane distidia* and *B. toxicaria* (Amaryllidaceae), S. Africa; an antiseptic.

buphanine. An alkaloid from the bulb of buphane.

buphanitine. $C_{23}H_{24}N_2O_6 = 424.20$. An alkaloid from buphanine, m.240.

burbonal. Bourbonal.

Burchard-Liebermann reaction. Acetic anhydride produces a blue-green color with cholesterol in chloroform containing concentrated sulfuric acid.

burdock. Lappa.

Bureau of Standards. The U.S. official institution for maintaining standards of quality for apparatus and chemicals.

buret, burette. A graduated glass tube with a stopcock, used in volumetric analysis to measure volumes of liquids. **automatic-** A b. with a device for rapidly refilling to the zero point. **certified-** A b. which has been officially tested for accuracy. **chamber-** A b. in which drainage errors are minimized by a wide upper chamber containing the bulk of the liquid, and a small bottom graduated tube, with a tap. **gas-** A b. used in gas analysis, e.g., *Bunsen* b. **Schellbach-** A b. with a milk-glass scale and a central blue line which facilitates reading by giving the meniscus the appearance of a cusp.

b. cap. A small glass cup that fits loosely over the top of a b. **b. clamp.** A pinchcock attached to the rubber tubing outlet of a b. **b. float.** A float inside the b., facilitating readings. **b. reader.** A lens or device clamped on the b. to facilitate readings.

Burger's vector. A measure of the magnitude and direction of slip in a crystal lattice. It is unity when it equals the interatomic distance.

Burgundy mixture. A substitute for bordeaux mixture containing copper sulfate and sodium carbonate.

burkeite. $Na_2CO_3 \cdot 2Na_2SO_4$. **sesqui-** $2Na_2CO_3 \cdot 3Na_2SO_4$. By-products from the cocrystallization of sodium sulfate and carbonate in the isolation of potassium from the Trona deposits, q.v.

Bürker chamber. A counting chamber for hemocytometers; essentially an accurately ruled microscope slide.

burlap. Coarse jute fabric, used in linoleum manufacture and as a wrapping.

burling. A process for removing burrs and other impurities from woolen felt.

burner. A device to obtain a flame by the combustion of solids, liquids, or gases. **acme-** A b. for gas or gasoline vapor. **alcohol-** A wick-type b. for alcohol. **Argand-** A b. with an inner tube to supply air to the flame. **blast-** A b. in which compressed air is blown into the flame. **Boyce-Acme** b. **bunsen-** See *Bunsen.* **Chaddock-** A noncorrodible b. made from refractory. **combustion tube-** A bunsen b. with wing tops. **evaporating-** A round cast-iron disk with holes to fit the top of a bunsen b. **Fletcher-** Hollow, cast-iron rings with holes or slits, for rapidly heating large vessels. **gauze top-** A bent iron tube with gauze top. **Jansen-** A blast b. for glass blowing with air and gas regulation. **Mekker-** A bunsen b. with a top grid which mixes the gases and prevents "striking back." **micro-** A very small gas b. **multiple tube-** A gas b. with several tubes arranged in a circle or line. **pilot light-** A b. with a small inside tube producing a small flame burning continuously. **porcelain-** Chaddock- **rose-** An evaporating b. which enables very small flames to be obtained. **spectrum-** A b. with platinum holders, for producing colored or monochromatic light from solids. **Teclu-** See *Teclu b.*

b. attachments. See *crown top, gauze top, wing top, chimney, star, tripod.*

burnettizing. The preservation of wood by treatment with creosote under pressure.

burning. See *calcination, firing.*

burnt. Calcined, or strongly heated. **b. alum.** Anhydrous *potassium aluminum sulfate.* **b. lime.** Calcium oxide.

Burow's solution. A solution containing 4.8–5.8 gm aluminum acetate per 100 ml; an external astringent (U.S.P.).

burra gokero. Barra gokhru. The seeds of *Pedalium murex*, Pedaliaceae (tropical Africa and Asia); an antispasmodic and diuretic.

Burseraceae. A group of tropical trees and shrubs that secrete resins and oils; e.g. *Commiphora myrrha*, myrrh.

bursine. An alkaloid from *Capsella bursapastoris* (shepherd's purse), Cruciferae.

bursting disk. A metal disk of standard composition and thickness which ruptures above a specified pressure. Used as a safety valve on pressure vessels. **b. strength tester.** A device for testing the resistance of paper to bursting. A rubber diaphragm is forced through a clamped circular area of paper by means of air or glycerin, and the pressure at the bursting point is measured.

burtonization. The addition of calcium salts to a water supply. Used in brewing, where a water similar to that of Burton-on-Trent (England) is required.

busbar. The conducting metal rod which carries objects to be plated or otherwise treated in electrolytic deposition plants.

bushel. 1 bu (British) = 0.35239 hectoliter or 35.2 liters = 8 gal or 2219.36 ± 17 cu in. **imp.-** British bu. **U.S.A.-** = 2150.42 cu in. **Winchester-** U.S.A. b.

busulfan. $Me \cdot SO_2 \cdot O \cdot (CH_2)_4 \cdot O \cdot SO_2 Me = 246.32$. Tetramethylene-di(methane sulfonate). White crystals, m.117, soluble in water; a cytotoxic agent used to treat leukemia (B.P.).

butacaine sulfate. Butyn, (q.v.).

butadiene-* Bivinyl. **bromo-*** Bromoprene. **chloro-*** Chloroprene. **methyl-*** Isoprene. **b. dicarboxylic acid.** Muconic acid.

butadiine, butadiyne*. Biacetylene.

Butagas. Trademark for compressed butane, used for domestic lighting and heating.

butalanin. α-Amino-i-*valeric acid.*

butalastic. A general term for synthetic rubbers, in which the repeating unit of the polymer was originally a diene.

butaldehyde. Butyraldehyde.

Butamen process. The catalytic isomerization of normal butane.

butamin. Tutocaine.

butanal*. Butyraldehyde.

butanamide*. Butyramide.

butane. $MeCH_2 \cdot CH_2 Me = 58.1$. Tetrane. Colorless gas, b.1, insoluble in water, a constituent of natural and illuminating gas. **bromo-*** Butyl bromide. **chloro-*** Butyl chloride. **dibromo-*** Butylene bromide. **dihydroxy-** Butanediol*. **diphenyl-** Dibenzylethane. **hydroxy-** Butyl alcohol. **iodo-*** Butyl iodide. **iso-** $CHMe_3$. Trimethylmethane. Colorless gas, b.−11, insoluble in water **nitro-*** $C_4H_9NO_2 = 103.08$. Butyl nitrite. Colorless liquid, b.151, slightly soluble in water. **phenyl-** Butylbenzene.

b. diamine. Putrescine. **b. dicarboxylic acid*.** Adipic acid.

butanedial*. Succinaldehyde.

butanediamide*. Succinamide.

butanediamine*. Putrescine.

butanediol*. $C_4H_{10}O_2 = 90.1$. Butylene glycol, dihydroxybutane. **α-** or **1,2-** Colorless liquid, b.191. **β-** or **1,3-** Colorless liquid, b.204. **γ-** or **1,4-** Tetramethylene glycol. Colorless liquid, m.16. **ψ-** or **2,3-** Colorless liquid, b.184. **dimethyl-** Pinacol.

butanedione*. $C_4H_6O_2 = 86.1$. A group of diketones: **1,3-** $HCO \cdot CH_2 \cdot COMe$. **2,3-** Biacetyl.

butane-ol. Butyl alcohol.

butanoic acid. Butyric acid.

butanol*. Butyl alcohol. **chlor-** See *chlor*butanol.

butanone*. Methyl ethyl ketone. **dimethyl-** Pinacoline. **hydroxy-** $Me \cdot CO \cdot CHOH \cdot Me$. Acetoin. An ethereal liquid formed during fermentation by yeast.

butanoyl*. Butyryl.

Butaprene. Trademark for a buna-type synthetic rubber having a high flexibility at low temperatures.

butea gum. Bengal kino. The dried, red astringent juice of the dhak or pallas tree, *Butea frondosa* (Leguminosae) of India; an astringent.

butenal*. Crotonaldehyde.

butene*. (1) $C_4H_4 = 52.04$. Cyclobutylene. A homocyclic hydrocarbon. (2) Butylene (butene*).

butenic acid. $C_4H_6O_2 = 86.05$. Butenoic acid*. **alpha-** See *crotonic* and *isocrotonic acid.* **beta-** $CH_2 : CH \cdot CH_2 \cdot COOH$. Vinylacetic acid. Colorless liquid, b.163, soluble in water. **iso-** Methyl *acrylic acid.* **α-methyl-** See *angelic* and *tiglic acid.* **β-methyl-** Senecioic acid.

butenoic acid*. Butenic acid.

butenol*. $C_4H_8O = 72.05$. **1-** 1-buten-1-ol, Me-$CH_2 \cdot CH : CHOH$. **2-** 2-buten-1-ol. $CH_3 CH : CH \cdot CH_2 \cdot OH$. Crotonyl alcohol. **3-** 3-buten-1-ol, $CH_2 : CH \cdot CH_2 \cdot CH_2 OH$.

butenyl. The radical $C_4H_7—$, derived from butylene. **Δ-** But-1-enyl.

Butesin. $NH_2 C_6 H_4 COOC_4 H_9 = 193.12$. Trademark for *n*-butyl-*p*-aminobenzoate. White crystals, m.57, insoluble in water; a local anesthetic. **iso-** m.65.

B. picrate. Yellow powder; an analgesic combination of trinitrophenol and B.

butine. $C_4H_6 = 54.05$. Butyne*. An unsaturated hydrocarbon containing a triple bond; as: **T1-** CH:C·CH$_2$Me. Ethylacetylene. Colorless crystals, m.18. **T2-** Crotonylene.

butobarbitone. $C_{10}H_{16}O_3N_2 = 212.30$. 5,N-Butyl-5-ethylbarbituric acid. Fine, white slightly bitter powder, m.123, soluble in water; used as barbituric acid.

butopyronoxyl. $C_{12}H_{18}O_4 = 226.28$. Pale brown aromatic liquid, b.258, miscible with water; an insect repellent (U.S.P).

butoxy. The radical Me(CH$_2$)$_3$O—, derived from butanol.

butter. (1) A food prepared by churning cheese. It contains not less than 80% of milk fat, water, vitamins, proteins, lactose, and mineral salts. World production (1964), 4.5 million tons. (2) A soft inorganic chloride, e.g., b. of antimony (antimonic chloride). (3) A low-melting vegetable fat, vegetable b.; as, illipé b. from *Bassia* species. **b. fat.** The oily portion of mammal's milk composed of 88% of the glycerides of oleic, stearic, and palmitic acids, and 6% of the glycerides of butyric, caproic, caprylic, and capric acids; d.0.912, m.32. **b. rock.** A soft greasy exudate of iron and aluminum from rocks. **b. yellow.** (1) A yellow dye often used for tinting butter. (2) *p*-Diaminoazobenzene. (3) *4*-dimethylaminobenzene-1-azonaphthalene. (4) *N*, *N'*-Dimethyl-*p*-aminoazobenzene.

butternut. Tuglans. **b. tree.** A tree of the genus Bassia (Sapotaceae). The seeds yield a fat used for soap or lamp oil.

button. A small round lump of metal left in the crucible after fusion, or on charcoal after reduction of an ore.

Butvar. Trademark for a butyryl polyvinyl plastic, q.v.

butyl. Bu. **normal-** The hydrocarbon radical C_4H_9— or CH$_3$·CH$_2$·CH$_2$·CH$_2$—. **iso-** *i*-Bu. The hydrocarbon radical iso- C_4H_9—, or (CH$_3$)$_2$CH·CH$_2$—. **secondary-** The radical CH$_3$·CH$_2$·CH·Me—. **tertiary-** The hydrocarbon radical (CH$_3$)$_3$·C—. According to British nomenclature: Bu^n = *n*-butyl. Bu^i = isobutyl. Bu^s = sec-butyl. Bu^t = *tert*-butyl.

b. acetate. $C_6H_{12}O_2 = 116.13$. Colorless liquid, b.125, slightly soluble in water; a solvent. **b. alcohol.** Butyl alcohol (below). **b. aldehyde.** Butyraldehyde. **b. amine.** $C_4H_{11}N$ or BuNH$_2$ = 73.15. *normal-* Colorless liquid, b.78, soluble in alcohol. *iso-* *i*-BuNH$_2$. Colorless liquid, b.66, miscible with water. **b. benzene.** $C_{10}H_{14} = 134.14$. *iso-* Colorless liquid, b.167. *sec-* Colorless liquid, b.171. **b. benzoate.** $C_{11}H_{14}O_2 = 178.18$. PhCOOBu. Colorless oil, b.248.5; insoluble in water. *iso-* Colorless liquid, b.237, insoluble in water. **b. bromide.** $C_4H_9Br = 137.05$. *normal-* Colorless oil, b.101, insoluble in water. *iso-* Colorless oil, b.90, insoluble in water. **b. butyrate.** PrCOOBu = 144.17. *normal-* Colorless liquid, b.165, slightly soluble in water. *iso-* Colorless liquid, b.157, slightly soluble in water. *iso-iso-* Colorless liquid, b.146, insoluble in water. **b. carbamate.** NH$_2$COOBu = 117.12. Colorless crystals. *iso-* Colorless crystals, m.55, insoluble in water. **b. carbinol.** Me$_3$C·CH$_2$OH = 88.13. Colorless crystals, m.52, slightly soluble in water. **b. Carbitol.** see *Carbitol*. **b. Cellosolve.** See *Cello-*

solve. **b. chloral.** MeCHClCCl$_2$·COH = 175.43. Croton chloral. Colorless liquid, b.165, soluble in water. **b. chloral hydrate.** $C_4H_7O_2Cl_3 = 193.46$. Colorless crystals, m.78, soluble in water; an analgesic and hypnotic. **b. chloride.** $C_4H_9Cl = 92.54$. *normal-* Colorless liquid, b.78, insoluble in water. *iso-* Me$_2$CHCH$_2$Cl. Colorless liquid, b.69, insoluble in water. *tert-* Me$_3$C·Cl. Colorless liquid, b.51. **b. cyanide.** $C_5H_9N = 83.06$. Valeronitrile. Colorless liquid, b.141, insoluble in water. *iso-* Me$_2$CHCH$_2$CN. Colorless liquid, b.127, slightly soluble in water. *tert-* Me$_3$CCN. Crystalline solid, m.15. **b. ether.** $C_8H_{18}O = 130.19$. B. oxide. Colorless liquid, b.141, soluble in water. *iso-* Colorless liquid, b.122°C, slightly soluble in water. **b. formate.** HCOOBu = 102.11. *normal-* Tetrylformate. Colorless liquid, b.107, slightly soluble in water. *iso-* Colorless liquid, b.98.5, miscible with alcohol. **b. hydrate.** B. alcohol. **b. hydride.** Butane. **b. iodide.** BuI = 184.06. 1-Iodobutane*. *normal-* Colorless liquid, b. 130, insoluble in water. *iso-* 1-Iodo-2-methylpropane*. Colorless liquid, b.120, insoluble in water. *sec-* Me·CH$_2$·CHIMe. Colorless liquid, b.118. *tert-* Me$_3$CI. Colorless liquid, b.99. **b. isobutyrate.** See *b. butyrate.* **b. isocyanide.** BuNC = 83.10. Butylcarbylamine*. Colorless liquid, m.115, slightly soluble in water. **b. isovalerate.** See *b. valerate*. **b. ketone.** Bu·CO·Bu = 142.20. Colorless liquid, b.181, slightly soluble in water. **b. mercaptan.** $C_4H_9SH = 90.16$. 1-Butanethiol*. Colorless liquid, b.92; occurs in the odorous skunk secretion. **b. methoxyphenol.** Butylated hydroxyanisole. **b. mustard oil.** BuNCS = 115.19. B. sulfocyanide. Colorless liquid, b.167, insoluble in water. *iso-* Isobutylsulfocyanide. Colorless liquid, b.162, insoluble in water. *sec-* Me·CH$_2$·CH(NCS)Me. Colorless liquid, b.160. *tert-* Me$_3$C·NCS. An oil, b.140. **b. nitrate*.** BuNO$_3$ = 119.13. Colorless liquid b.123, insoluble in water. **b. nitrite*.** BuNO$_2$ = 103.10. Colorless liquid, b.67, soluble in alcohol, also occurs as the tautomer BuONO. **b. oxide.** B. ether. **b. oxide linkage.** A bond linking the first and fourth C atom of a chain through an O atom. Cf. *sugar*, *furanose.* **b. phenylate.** B. phenyl ether. **b. phenyl ether.** $C_{10}H_{14}O = 150.14$. Butyl phenylate, Colorless liquid, b.198, insoluble in water; an antiseptic. **b. phenyl ketone.** BuCO·Ph = 162.17. Phenylpentanone. *normal-* Colorless liquid, b.240, insoluble in water. *iso-* Colorless liquid, b. 225, insoluble in water. **b. phthalate.** C$_6$H$_4$(COOBu)$_2$. Colorless liquid, b$_{20mm}$ 204, used instead of mercury in diffusion pumps. **b. propionate.** EtCOOBu = 130.14. Colorless aromatic liquid, b.136, soluble in alcohol. Used in fruit essences. **b. rhodanate.** B. mustard oil. **b. sulfide.** Bu$_2$S = 146.24. *normal-* Colorless liquid, b.182, insoluble in water. *iso-* (Me$_2$CH·CH$_2$)$_2$S. *sec-* (MeCH$_2$CHMe)$_2$S. Colorless liquid, b.165. **b. sulfocyanide.** B. mustard oil. **b. valerate.** $C_9H_{18}O_2 = 158.18$. *normal-* BuCOOBu. Colorless liquid, b.184, soluble in alcohol; a fruit flavor. *iso-* Me$_2$CHCH$_2$COOCH$_2$CHMe$_2$. Colorless liquid, b.169, insoluble in water.

butyl alcohol. $C_4H_{10}O$ or BuOH = 74.10. Butanol, butyl hydroxide, hydroxybutane. **iso-** Me$_2$CH·CH$_2$OH. Colorless liquid, d$_{33}$0.7980, m.—108, b.107.87, slightly soluble in water. It can be produced by fermentation (Fernbach's process). **normal-** See *primary*. **primary-** Me·CH$_2$·CH$_2$·CH$_2$OH. 1-Butanol, propylcarbinol. (normal-) Colorless liquid, b.117.7, miscible with alcohol or ether; a solvent, defrother, dehydrator, and penetrant. **secondary-** MeCH$_2$CHMeOH. Ethylmethylcarbinol. Colorless liquid, b.99.52, soluble in water. **tertiary-** Me$_3$COH. Colorless liquid or rhombic crystals, m.25, b.83, miscible with water. **tribromo-** Brometone. **trichloro-** Chloretone.

butylated hydroxyanisole. C$_{11}$H$_{16}$O$_2$ = 180.16. 2-Butyl-4-methoxyphenol. White crystals, m.64, insoluble in water; an antioxidant (B.P.). **b. hydroxytoluene.** C$_{15}$H$_{24}$O = 220.24. Dibutyl-*p*-cresol. White crystals, insoluble in water; an antioxidant (B.P.).

butylene. (1) C$_4$H$_8$ = 56.06. α-, Δ^1-, or 1-Butene, ethylethylene, CH$_2$:CHCH$_2$Me, b. −18. β-, Δ^2-, or 2-Butene, Ψ-butylene, dimethylethylene, Me-CH:CHMe, b.1; an anesthetic. γ-, iso-, or 2-methylpropene, Me$_2$C:CH$_2$. b. −6. ψ- or *pseudo*-β-Butylene. (2) The C$_4$H$_8$ = radical, derived from butane. **diiso-** CMe$_3$·CH$_2$·CH:CH$_2$ = 112.12. 2,2,4-Trimethyl-1-pentene. **triiso-** C$_{12}$H$_{24}$ = 168.18. The hydrocarbon CMe$_3$·CH$_2$·CMe:CHCH$_3$. 2,2,4,6,6-Pentamethyl-3-heptene. **methyl-** Pental. **b. bromide.** Me$_2$CBr·CH$_2$Br = 215.90. Yellow liquid, b.158, miscible with alcohol. *pseudo*-MeCHBr·CHBrMe. β-Butylene bromide. Yellow liquid, b.158, soluble in alcohol. **b. glycol.** Butanediol. **b. oxide.** C$_4$H$_8$O = 72.08. Tetrahydrofurane. An intermediate, and the only solvent known for polyvinyl chloride.

butylidene. The divalent radical, Me(CH$_2$)$_2$CH=.

butyl rubber. (1) Generic name for vulcanizable elastic copolymers of isobutylene and small amounts of diolefins. (2) A mixture of isobutylene 98 and butadiene or isoprene 2% (U.S. usage). World production, excluding U.S.S.R. bloc (1961), 141,000 tons.

Butyn. (C$_{18}$H$_{30}$N$_2$)$_2$·H$_2$SO$_4$ = 646.5. Trademark for butacaine sulfate. Colorless crystals, m.99, soluble in water; a cocaine substitute.

butyne*. Butine.

butyraldehyde. PrCHO = 72.08. Butanal*. butal. Colorless liquid, b.77. **iso-** Me$_2$CH·CHO. Colorless liquid, b.63, miscible with water. **hydroxy-**Aldol. **trichloro-** Butyl chloral.

butyramide. PrCONH$_2$ = 87.13. Butanamide*. Colorless scales, m.115, slouble in water. **iso-** Me$_2$CH·CONH$_2$. Crystalline solid, m.118, soluble in water.

butyrase. An esterase. See *enzymes*.

butyrate. A salt or ester of butyric acid containing the C$_4$H$_7$O$_2$— radical.

butyrelite. Bog butter. A fat in peat.

butyric acid. Me·CH$_2$·CH$_2$·COOH = 88.80. Butanoic acid*, ethylacetic acid. The fourth member of the fatty-acid series, **normal-** Colorless liquid of unpleasant odor, b.162.5, miscible with water; produced in the decay of cheese. See b. *fermentation*. Used as a bacteriological reagent, as a food flavor, and in fruit essences. **iso-** Me$_2$CHCOOH. Colorless liquid, m.80, slightly soluble in water. **amino-** C$_4$H$_9$O$_2$N = 103.77. Aminobutanoic acid*. **α-** or **1-** NH$_2$·CHEt·COOH.

Crystals, m.285. **β-** or **2-** NH$_2$CHMe·CH$_2$COOH. Crystals, m.184. **γ-** or **3-** NH$_2$(CH$_2$)$_3$COOH. Crystals, m.193. *iso-* NH$_2$·CMe$_2$·COOH. Liquid b.280. **α-amino-β-hydroxy-** NH$_2$·CH(CHOH·Me)-COOH. A constituent of proteins. Cf. *amino acids*. **aminomethyl-** Isovaline. **chloro-** C$_4$H$_7$O$_2$Cl = 122.51. **α-** or **1-** EtCHCl·COOH. b$_{15mm}$101. **β-** or **2-** MeCHCl·CH$_2$·COOH. m.44, b$_{13mm}$100. *β(dl)-* or *2(dl)-* m.16, b$_{22mm}$116. **α-** or **3-** Cl(CH$_2$)$_3$-COOH. m.16, b$_{22mm}$196. **hydroxy-** EtCHOHCOOH = 104.08. Colorless crystals, m.43, b.255 (decomp.), soluble in water. **hydroxyethyl-** Diethoxalic acid. **keto-** Acetoacetic acid. **methyl-** *alpha-* Hydroangelic acid. *beta-* Isovaleric acid. **oxy-** See *hydroxy-b*. **trihydroxy-** Erythric acid.

b. aldehyde. Butyraldehyde. **b. amide.** Me$_2$CH··CONH$_2$ = 87.13. Colorless leaflets, m.129, soluble in water. **b. anhydride.** C$_8$H$_{14}$O$_3$ = 158.16. *normal-* PrCO·O·OCPr. Colorless liquid b.192, decomp. by water to form the acid. *iso-* Me$_2$CHCO·O·OCHMe$_2$. Colorless liquid, b.182.5, decomp. in water. **b. diisonitroso peroxide.** C$_4$H$_4$O$_4$N$_2$ = 144.06. Peroxide diisonitrosobutyric acid. Colorless crystals, m.92. **b. fermentation.** The production of b. acid by fermentation of sugar or starch by *B. butyricus*, in presence of calcium carbonate.

butyrin. (PrCOO)$_3$C$_3$H$_5$ = 302.28. Tributyrin. Yellow liquid, b.285, insoluble in water; a constituent of butterfat. Cf. *glycerides*.

butyrinase. An enzyme of blood serum which hydrolyzes butyrin to glycerol and butyric acid.

butyrobetaine. The base Me$_3$N·(CH$_2$)$_3$CO(:O) = 145.07. m.130. Occurs in mussels (*Arca noae*), snakes (*Python moluris*), and anthrozoans (*Actinia equina*).

butyrolactone. C$_4$H$_6$O$_2$ = 86.6. Butanolide. The internal anhydride of butyric acid. Colorless liquid, b.204.

butyrometer. An instrument to determine the amount of butterfat in milk.

butyrone. Pr·CO·Pr = 114.11. Dipropyl ketone. Colorless liquid, b.143.5; a solvent.

butyronitrile. Propyl cyanide.

butyrophenone. PhCOCH$_2$CH$_2$Me = 148.09. Phenyl *n*-propyl ketone. Colorless liquid, b.233; used in organic synthesis. **iso-** PhCOCHMe$_2$. Phenyl isopropyl ketone. A liquid, b.217.

butyrous. Butter-like in consistency.

butyrum. Latin for butter. **b. antimonii.** Antimonous chloride.

butyryl. **normal-** The −C$_4$H$_7$O radical, derived from *n*-butyric acid. **iso-** The Me$_2$CHCO= radical, derived from isobutyric acid. **b. chloride.** C$_4$H$_7$OCl = 106.53. *normal-* Butanoyl chloride. Colorless liquid, b.101. *iso-* Me$_2$CH·COCl. Colorless liquid, d.1.0174.

buxidine. Colorless prisms; an alkaloid from the leaves of *Buxus sempervirens*.

buxine. C$_{19}$H$_{21}$O$_3$N = 311.22. An alkaloid from the leaves of *Buxus sempervirens*, Buxaceae. **pseudo-** C$_{24}$H$_{48}$ON$_2$ = 380.50. Ψ-Buxine. An alkaloid from the leaves of *Buxus sempervirens*.

Buxton's fluid. A mixture of 50 ml water 20 ml glycerin, 40 gm gum arabic, 50 gm chloral hydrate, and 0.5 gm cocaine hydrochloride; a microscopical mountant.

buyo. Betel nut.

buzane. Bihydrazine.

buzylene. (1) $HN:N\cdot NH\cdot NH_2$. Isotetrazene, diazo-hydrazine. Cf. *tetrazone.* (2) The $=N:N\cdot NH\cdot NH=$ radical. **dihydro-** Bihydrazine.

byerite. A bituminous coal resembling albertite.

byerlite. A substance resembling asphalt, made by heating petroleum residues with sulfur in air.

bynin. Hordenin. A malt gliadin. Cf. *proteins.*

by-product. A product other than the principal material from a manufacturing process.

byssinosis. A pulmonary disease due to inhalation of cotton dust. Cf. *siderosis.*

byssochlamic acid. $C_{18}H_{20}O_6 = 332.1$. A di-anhydride produced by the action on a tetrabasic acid of *Byssochlamis fulva.*

byssus. (1) Flax. (2) Lint. (3) The protein threads which attach the edible sea mussel, *Mytilus*, to rocks.

bythium. Ekatellurium. A supposed element of the sulfur group.

bytownite. A triclinic anorthite feldspar. Cf. *silica minerals.*

Bz. (1) The benzoyl radical, PhCO—. (2) The benzene ring. See *quinoline.*

BzH. Benzaldehyde.

BzOH. Benzoic acid.

C

C (1) Symbol for carbon. (2) Abbreviation for constant. **°C.** Symbol for degree Celsius (the international standard) and degree centigrade. **C acid.** Naphthylamine-4,8-disulfonic acid.

C. Abbreviation for concentration. C_v, C_p. Symbols for molecular heat at constant volume and pressure, respectively. C_H. Hydrogen ion concentration.

c. Symbol for: (1) velocity of light in a vacuum: $c = (2.99796 \pm 0.00004) \times 10^{10}$ cm/sec; (2) specific heat.

Ca. (1) Symbol for calcium. (2) Abbreviation for cathode.

ca. Abbreviation for candle, centare, and circa.

cabasite. Chabazite.

cabbage. The vegetable *Brassica oleracea* (Cruciferae). **c. seed oil.** The edible fatty oil from the seeds of *Brassica oleracea* (Cruciferae); used in soaps, ointments, liniments, and to substitute for olive oil. **c. sugar.** A triose from c. leaves. **c. tree bark.** Yaba bark.

cabrerite. $(Ni \cdot Co)_3 As_2O_8 \cdot 8H_2O$. A green, fibrous native arsenate of nickel and cobalt.

cacaine. Theobromine.

cacao. Cocoa. Cf. *coca.* **c. butter.** Oil of theobroma. A yellow oil expressed from the seeds of *Theobroma cacao*. It has a low m. and is used for receptacles for drugs (U.S.P., B.P.). **c. red.** $(C_{17}H_{16}O_7)_x$. The red pigment of c., soluble in ether or alcohol. **c. syrup.** A pharmaceutical flavoring containing c., sucrose, glucose, glycerin, a little sodium chloride, vanillin, and a preservative, in water (U.S.P.).

cacaorin. $C_{60}H_{84}N_4O_{15}$. A glucoside from cacao beans; oxidized to cacao red.

cachet. A container, usually of molded rice paste, to hold dry powders and to administer dry medicaments in a tasteless form.

cacodiliacol. Guaiacol cacodylate.

cacodyl. (1) Dicacodyl. (2) The radical C_2H_6As—, derived from arsine. **di-** $Me_2As \cdot AsMe_2 = 210.1$. Dicacodyl, tetramethylarsine. Colorless poisonous liquid, b.170. **ethyl-** $Et_2As \cdot AsEt_2 = 275.9$. Tetraethylarsine. Colorless liquid, b.185. (2) Diethylarsine.

    c. chloride. $AsClMe_2 = 140.56$. Dimethylarsenic chloride. Colorless liquid, b.100. **c. cyanide.** $AsMe_2CN = 131.06$. Dimethylarsenic cyanide. Colorless crystals, m.33. **c. hydride.** $AsMe_2H = 106.07$. Dimethylarsine. Colorless volatile liquid, b.36, miscible with alcohol. **c. oxide.** $AsMe_2 \cdot O \cdot AsMe_2 = 226.1$. Alkarsine. Colorless liquid, b.120.

cacodylates. Salts of cacodylic acid, containing the $AsO \cdot Me_2 \cdot O$— radical; soluble in water, and used for hypodermic injections. **thio-** Salts of thiocacodylic acid containing the $Me_2AsO \cdot S$— radical; insoluble in water.

cacodylic acid. $Me_2AsO \cdot OH = 138.1$. Dimethyl-

arsinic acid, alkargen. A monobasic acid. Colorless crystals, m.200, soluble in water; used in the manufacture of cacodylates. **ethyl-** Diethylarsinic acid.

cacotheline. $C_{20}H_{22}N_2O_5(NO_2)_2 = 462.2$. A red product of the action of nitric acid on brucine; a reagent for tin and sulfur dioxide.

cacoxenite. A yellow iron phosphate occurring with limonite.

cactine. An alkaloid from *Cereus grandiflorus*, night-blooming cactus.

cactoid. The combined principles from the leaves and stems of *Cereus grandiflorus*; a heart stimulant.

cactus. Cactaceae family with succulent stems and thorny leaves, including the genera: *Anhalonium*, *Cereus*, and *Opuntia*. Cf. *prickly pear*, *mescal buttons*, *cochineal*. **c. alkaloids.** See *anhalonium alkaloids, cactine, pectenine, pilocerine.*

cadalene. $C_{15}H_{18} = 198.14$. 3,8-Dimethyl-5-isopropylnaphthalene. A reduction product of cadinene and zingiberene.

cadaverine. $NH_2(CH_2)_5NH_2 = 102.1$. Pentamethylene diamine, amylenediamine. A ptomaine formed by the hydrolysis of proteins; an isomer of sapin. Colorless liquid, m.9.

cadaverines. Ptomaines.

cade oil. Juniper tar oil. Yellow oil from the dry distillation of *Juniperus oxycedrus;* d.0.980-1.055, soluble in alcohol; chief constituent, cadinene. Used in soaps, ointments, and pharmaceuticals.

Cadet's liquid. A solution containing principally cacodyl and cacodyl oxide; used medicinally.

cadinene. $C_{15}H_{24} = 204.2$. 3,8-Dimethyl-1,4,7-trihydro-5-isopropylnaphthalene(?). A sesquiterpene, b.275; a constituent of essential oils from juniper species and cedars.

cadion. $C_{18}H_{13}O_2N_6 = 346.3$. *p*-Nitrobenzenediazoaminoazobenzene. Brown powder, insoluble in water; a reagent for cadmium (pink) and magnesium (blue). **c.2D.** 4-Nitronaphthalenediazoaminoazobenzene. A reagent for cadmium.

cadmia. An ancient name for zinc carbonate.

cadmium. Cd = 112.40. An element of the zinc family, at. no. 48. White, ductile metal, d.8.625, m.321.6, b.778, insoluble in water. Obtained from zinc ores, and as a by-product in zinc distillation. C. is generally divalent, but monovalent (cadmous) compounds are known. C. compounds are poisonous, and its salts are little ionized. Discovered (1817) simultaneously by Strohmeyer and Herman. Used for electrodes and in low-melting-point alloys. **c. acetate.** $Cd(OOCMe)_2 \cdot 3H_2O = 284.5$. White monoclinics, soluble in water. A reagent for sulfur, selenium, or tellurium in steel; used in dentistry. **c. alloys.** A mixture of c. usually with Ag, Na, Tl, or Zn; used to reduce the m. **c. amalgam.** An amalgam of c. and mercury, used in dentistry and the c. cell, q.v. **c. borotungstate.** $Cd_2B_2W_9O_{32} \cdot 18H_2O = 2739.1$. Yellow crystals, soluble in water, used to separate minerals mechanically. See *Klein's liquid*. **c. bromate.** $Cd(BrO_3)_2 = 368.2$. Colorless crystalline powder, soluble in water. **c. bromide.** $CdBr_2 = 272.2$. Colorless crystals, m.568, soluble in water. *cryst-* $CdBr_2 \cdot 4H_2O = 344.3$. White crystals, soluble in water; used in photography. **c. carbonate.** $CdCO_3 = 172.4$. Otavite. White rhombs, decomp. by heat, insoluble in water. **c. cell.** C. normal element. **c. chlorate.** $Cd(ClO_3)_2 = 279.2$. White crystals, soluble in water. **c. chloride.** $CdCl_2 = 183.3$. White crystals, soluble in water. *cryst-* $CdCl_2 \cdot 2H_2O = 219.3$. White monoclinics, soluble in water; a reagent for pyridine bases, and used in photography, the dye industry, and textile printing. **c. chloroacetate.** (1) *mono-* $(CH_2Cl \cdot COO)_2Cd \cdot 6H_2O = 407.45$. Colorless crystals. (2) *di-* $(CHCl_2 \cdot COO)_2Cd \cdot H_2O = 386.27$. Colorless crystals. (3) *tri-* $(CCl_3 \cdot COO)_2Cd \cdot 1\frac{1}{2}H_2O = 464.18$. Rhombic crystals. **c. cinnamate.** $(C_6H_5 \cdot CH:CHCOO)_2Cd = 406.52$. White powder, insoluble in water. **c. cyanide.** $Cd(CN)_2 = 164.1$. Colorless powder, soluble in water. **c. diethyl*.** $Cd(C_2H_5)_2 = 170.49$. Ethyl cadmium. Colorless liquid, b$_{20mm}$64. **c. dimethyl*.** $Cd(CH_3)_2 = 142.16$. Methyl cadmium. Colorless liquid, b.106. **c. ferricyanide.** $Cd_3[Fe(CN)_6]_2 = 972.7$. Brown crystals, soluble in water. **c. ferrocyanide.** $Cd_2Fe(CN)_6 = 436.2$. Yellow crystals, soluble in water. **c. fluoride.** $CdF_2 = 150.4$. White crystals, m.520, soluble in water or alcohol. **c. fluosilicate.** $CdSiF_6 = 254.47$. C. silicofluoride. White hexagons, soluble in water. **c. formate.** $Cd(OOCH)_2 = 202.1$. Colorless powder, soluble in water. **c. fumarate.** $Cd_2C_4H_2O_4 = 338.84$. White powder, insoluble in water. **c. hydroxide.** $Cd(OH)_2 = 146.4$. White hexagons, slightly soluble in water. **c. iodate.** $Cd(IO_3)_2 = 462.27$. White crystals decomp. by heat, slightly soluble in water. It forms the hydrate $Cd(IO_3)_2 \cdot H_2O = 480.20$; and the ammonate $Cd(IO_3)_2 \cdot 4NH_3 = 530.4$, which explodes on heating. **c. iodide.** $CdI_2 = 366.27$. Colorless scales; two water-soluble allotropes: *alpha-* m.388. *beta-* m.404. Soluble in water. Used as a reagent for alkaloids and nitrous acid; in photography; and as an antiseptic. **c. lactate.** $Cd(C_3H_5O_3)_2 = 290.2$. Colorless powder, slightly soluble in water. **c. line.** The red radiation from c. vapor, a fundamental standard of length; (1,533,164.14 waves/meter). **c. lithopone.** See *lithopone*. **c. malate.** $Cd_2C_4H_2O_4 \cdot 2H_2O = 374.87$. White powder, slightly soluble in water. **c. methide.** $Cd(CH_3)_2 = 142.4$. Dimethyl cadmium. Used in Grignard's reaction. **c. minerals.** C. is associated with zinc, though in small quantities. Its chief ores are greenockite (CdS) and the carbonate and oxide. **c. nitrate.** (1) $Cd(NO_3)_2 = 236.42$. Colorless powder, m.350. (2) Hydrate: $Cd(NO_3)_2 \cdot 4H_2O = 308.49$. Colorless prisms, m.5.94, soluble in water. A reagent for zinc and ferrocyanides; used in the manufacture of yellow and orange glazes. **c. normal element.** C. cell, Weston element. An H-shaped glass vessel with a c. amalgam cathode, a mercury anode, and a saturated c. sulfate solution electrode. It has a reproducible potential of 1.0186 volt, at 18°C. **c. oxalate.** (1) $CdC_2O_4 = 200.41$. White powder, m.340. (2) Hydrate: $CdC_2O_4 \cdot 3H_2O = 254.46$. White powder, insoluble in water. **c. oxide.** (1)

$CdO = 128.41$. Amorphous brown powder, insoluble in water. (2) $Cd_2O = 240.82$. Cadmous oxide. Yellow powder, decomp. by heat. (3) $Cd_4O = 465.64$. C. suboxide. Brown amorphous powder, decomp. by water. (4) C. peroxide, insoluble in water. CdO_2, Cd_3O_5 or Cd_5O_8. **c. oxybromide.** $CdO \cdot CdBr_2 \cdot H_2O = 418.67$. Yellow powder, decomp. by water. **c. oxychloride.** $CdO \cdot CdCl_2 \cdot H_2O = 329.75$. Colorless powder, decomp. 280; slightly soluble and slowly decomp. by hot water. **c. permanganate.** $Cd(MnO_4)_2 = 350.0$. Purple crystals, soluble in water. **c. peroxide.** C. oxide (4). **c. phosphate.** $Cd_3(PO_4)_2 = 526.0$. White powder, insoluble in water. **c. plating.** A rustproofing coating of c. on iron or steel. **c. potassium cyanide.** $Cd(CN)_2 \cdot 2KCN = 294.5$. White crystals, soluble in water. **c. potassium iodide.** $CdI_2 \cdot 2KI \cdot H_2O = 716.31$. White powder, yellows on aging, soluble in water; a reagent for alkaloids. **c. red.** (1) A mixture of c. selenide, sulfide, and barite. (2) A mineral pigment: Cd 60, S 25, and Se 15%. **c. salicylate.** $Cd(C_7H_5O_3)_2 \cdot H_2O = 404.1$. White needles, soluble in water; an astringent. **c. selenate.** $CdSeO_4 = 255.1$. Colorless crystals, soluble in water. **c. selenide.** $CdSe = 191.6$. Red powder, insoluble in water; used in rubber manufacture for abrasion resistance. **c. silicofluoride.** C. fluosilicate. **c. suboxide.** $Cd_4O = 465.64$. C. oxide (3). **c. succinate.** $CdC_4H_4O_4 = 228.0$. White powder, slightly soluble in water. **c. sulfate.** $CdSO_4 = 208.0$. White rhombs, m. 1000, soluble in water. *cryst-* (1) $CdSO_4 \cdot 4H_2O = 280.5$. White crystals, soluble in water. (2) $3CdSO_4 \cdot 8H_2O = 769.5$. White monoclinics, soluble in water. Used in c. cells, and as an antiseptic and astringent in eye-washes. **c. sulfide.** $CdS = 144.5$. Greenockite. (1) *Orange*. Insoluble in water; used as a pigment and in pyrotechnics. (2) *Light yellow*. C. yellow, jaune brilliant. Hexagonal crystals, insoluble in water; used as a pigment for coloring soaps, ceramics, rubber, and in pyrotechnics. **c. sulfite.** $CdSO_3 = 192.0$. White powder, slightly soluble in water. **c. tartrate.** $Cd(C_4H_4O_6)(H_2O)$. White crystalline powder, slightly soluble in water. **c. tungstate.** $CdWO_4 = 360.0$. Colorless powder, insoluble in water. **c. valerate.** $Cd(C_5H_9O_2)_2 = 314.2$. Colorless scales, soluble in water; an antispasmodic. **c. wolframate.** C. tungstate. **c. yellow.** C. sulfide.

cadmous. Describing a compound of monovalent Cd.

cadoxen. $[Cd(en)_3](OH)_2$. Triethylenediamine cadmium hydroxide. A stable solvent for cellulose.

cae- See *ce-*.

Caesalpinia. A genus of subtropical trees (Leguminosae); e.g.: *C. coriaria*, dividivi; *C. sappan*, brazilwood.

caesium. See *cesium*.

caferana. Tachia. The dried roots of *Tachia guianensis* (Gentianaceae), Brazil; a tonic and antiperiodic.

caferanine. A crystalline principle in caferana.

caffalic acid. $C_{34}H_{54}O_{15} = 702.4$. An acid in coffee.

caffeic acid. $C_9H_8O_4 \cdot \frac{1}{2}H_2O = 189.12$. 3,4-Dihydroxycinnamic acid. Yellow prisms in black fir resin, m.195, decomp., soluble in water. **dimethylhydro-** $C_{11}H_{14}O_4 = 210.11$. Colorless crystals, m.96.

hydro- $C_9H_{10}O_4 = 182.08$. 3,4-Dioxyphenylpropionic acid. Colorless crystals, m.213.

caffeine. $C_8H_{10}O_2N_4 \cdot H_2O = 212.30$. Theine, methyltheobromine, 1,3,7-trimethylxanthine, guaranine, psoraline. A diureide in coffee, tea, and cola nuts. White bitter needles, m.230, soluble in water; a diuretic and heart stimulant. **bromo-** See *bromo c.* **chloral-** See *chloral c.* **ethoxy-** See *ethoxy c.* **hydroxy-** $C_8H_{10}O_3N_4 = 210.2$. 1,3,7-Trimethyluric acid. White needles, m. 345, soluble in hot water; a diuretic. **phenoxy-** See *phenoxy c.*

c. arsenate. $C_8H_{10}N_4O_2 \cdot H_3AsO_4 = 336.1$. White powder, soluble in hot water. **c. benzoate.** $C_8H_{10}N_4O_2 \cdot C_7H_6O_2 = 316.23$. White, crystalline powder, soluble in water. **c. citrate.** $C_8H_{10}O_2N_4 \cdot C_6H_8O_7 = 386.25$. White, crystals, soluble in water; used similarly to caffeine. **c. hydrate.** $C_8H_{10}O_2N_4 \cdot H_2O = 212.21$. White, bitter needles, soluble in water; a central nervous-system stimulant (B.P.). **c. hydrobromide.** $C_8H_{10}O_2N_4 \cdot HBr = 275.03$. White crystals, soluble in water. **c. hydrochloride.** $C_8H_{10}O_2N_4 \cdot HCl + 2H_2O = 266.56$. White crystals, soluble in water. **c. nitrate.** $C_8H_{10}O_2N_4 \cdot HNO_3 = 257.30$. White, crystals, soluble in water. **c. phenylate.** $C_8H_{10}O_2N_4 \cdot C_6H_6O \cdot H_2O = 306.35$. White crystals, soluble in water. **c. salicylate.** $C_8H_{10}O_2N_4 \cdot C_7H_6O_3 = 332.33$. White crystals, soluble in water. **c. sodium benzoate.** A mixture of c. and sodium benzoate, soluble in water; a hypodermic medication. **c. sodium bromide.** A mixture of 60% c. and 40% sodium bromide; white powder, soluble in water. **c. sodium citrate.** A mixture of 50% c. and 50% sodium citrate; white powder, soluble in water. **c. sodium salicylate.** A mixture of 45% c. and 55% sodium salicylate; white powder, soluble in water. **c. sulfate.** $(C_8H_{10}O_2N_4)_2 \cdot H_2SO_4 = 486.65$. White, crystals, decomp. by water. **c. sulfonate.** Symphorol. **c. triiodide.** $C_8H_{10}O_2N_4I_2 \cdot 2HI = 703.98$. Green prisms, m.171, decomp. by water; an alterant and diuretic. **c. valerate.** $C_8H_{10}O_2N_4 \cdot C_5H_{10}O_2 = 296.34$. White, crystals, decomp. by alcohol; used to treat hysteria.

caffetannic acid. $C_{15}H_{18}O_9 = 342.14$. Chlorogenic acid. A tannin in coffee, nux vomica, St. Ignatius beans, as its calcium or magnesium salt. Amorphous powder, soluble in water.

cahinca. David's root. The dried roots of *Chiococca racemosa* (Rubiaceae). See *chiococceine.*

cahincic acid. $C_{40}H_{64}O_{18} = 832.6$. Caincic acid. The glucoside active principle of cahinca root. White, bitter crystals, soluble in water; a purgative and diuretic. Cf. *chiococcic acid.*

Cailletet, Louis. 1832–1913. French ironmaster noted for work on liquefaction of gas.

caincic acid. Cahincic acid.

caincin. Cahincic acid.

cairngorm. A variety of quartz.

cajeput. Cajuput, tree tea, swamp tea. Leaves of *Melaleuca leukadendron* (Myrtaceae), E. India. **c. oil.** The colorless essential oil of cajeput; chief constituents cineol and terpineol. $[a]_D = -10°$ to $-4°$.

cajeputene. Terpene.

cajuput. Cajeput.

cajuputol. Eucalyptol.

cake. A solid crystalline mass. **niter-** Sodium sulfate

containing about 33% sulfuric acid. A by-product of nitric acid manufacture. **salt-** Sodium sulfate.

caking. Transformation of a powder into a solid mass by moisture, heat, or pressure.

Cal. Abbreviation for large calorie: kg-cal, Calorie.

cal. Abbreviation for small calorie: gm-cal, calorie.

calabar bean. Physostigma. **false-** Pseudophysostigma.

calabarine. An alkaloid from calabar bean.

Calais sand. Very fine sand from Calais, France; an abrasive.

calamene. $C_{15}H_{24} = 204.19$. A sesquiterpene from calamus oil.

calamine. (1) $Zn(OH)_2 \cdot Zn_3Si_2O_7 \cdot H_2O$. Native zinc silicate. (2) Obsolete name for zinc carbonate (smithsonite). (3) Natural zinc carbonate; also a suspension of zinc carbonate in water, used medicinally (U.K. usage). **electric-** See electric. **c. brass.** Brass.

calaminth. Basil thyme, mountain minth. *Calamintha officinalis* (Labiatae); a diaphoretic and expectorant.

calaminthone. $C_{10}H_{16}O = 152.2$. A ketone in French oil of marjoram, distilled from the leaves of *Calamintha nepeta* (Labiatae).

calamus. Sweet flag, sweet grass, sweet cane. Dried rhizomes of *Acorus calamus* (Araceae); a stimulant and carminative. Cf. *acorin, acoretin.* **c. oil.** The brown oil from calamus; chief constituents, asarone and eugenol. Used in perfumes, and flavors.

calaverite. $(Au,Ag)Te_2$. Native gold telluride containing 40% Au (Colorado, California).

calaya. An extract from the fruit of *Anneslea febrifuga* (Theaseae); an antiperiodic.

calc. Abbreviation for calculated.

calcareous, calcarious. Containing calcium. **c. algae.** Limestone from the algae of *Lithothamnium*, whose skeletons contain calcium carbonate 95% and magnesium carbonate 5%. Cf. *coccolith.* **c. sinter.** Travertine, onyx. Tufa deposits of calcium carbonate formed by the evaporation of water containing calcium bicarbonate.

calcariuria. The abnormal elimination of calcium salts in the urine.

calcarone, calcarella. A Sicilian sulfur furnace.

calcein. Fluorescein complexone. A fluorescent indicator for the determination of calcium by titration with EDTA; color change green to pink.

calcemic dose. Vitamin D equivalent to 50,000–1,000,000 I.U. per day which mobilizes calcium from the skeleton; as distinct from the antirachitic dose of 700–1,000 I.U. per day.

calcic. Pertaining to calcium.

calciferol. Ergocalciferol. $C_{28}H_{44}O = 396.74$. Vitamin D_2 (B.P.). White, odorless, tasteless crystals, m. 115–118, insoluble in water. The antirachitic vitamin. **pre-** The substance from which c. and ergosterol are produced reversibly by heat h and irradiation i, respectively:

$$\begin{array}{cc}
\text{Ergosterol} & \text{Lumisterol} \\
i \uparrow\downarrow & \uparrow\downarrow i \\
\text{Precalciferol} & \\
i \uparrow\downarrow & \uparrow\downarrow h \\
\text{Tachysterol} & \text{Calciferol}
\end{array}$$

calcification. Hardening of tissue by calcium salt formation.

calcii. Official Latin genitive of calcium.

calcimeter. An apparatus to determine carbonates by liberating carbon dioxide with acid and absorbing it in alkali.

calcination. Roasting. (1) Oxide formation by heating oxy salts, e.g., calcium oxide from calcite. (2) Expelling the volatile portions of a substance by heat. Cf. *roasting.*

calcined. Heated to a high temperature. **c. phosphate.** A fertilizer obtained by roasting finely ground phosphate rock with potassium salts.

calcinol. Calcium iodate.

calcioferrite. Iron phosphate in sedimentary beds of limonite.

calciovolborthite. Native copper and calcium vanadate.

calcite. $CaCO_3$. Calcspar. Crystalline: Iceland spar (birefringent), corn spar, satin spar; amorphous: chalk, stalactite, baryte; spongy: mountain milk; flaky: schiefer spar. **baryto-** Alstonite. **chloro-** Hydrophilite.

calcitization. Conversion of marble to calcite.

calcium. $Ca = 40.08$. An element of the magnesium family, at. no. 20. White crystals, d.1.415, m.810, soluble in water forming the hydroxide and in acids forming salts. The third most abundant metal, occurring as carbonates (limestone), sulfates (gypsum), fluorides (fluorspar), phosphates (apatite), and complex silicates (feldspar). Man's daily requirement of 0.7 gm should be supplied by milk (1.5 lb) or cheese (0.25 lb), as no other foods are adequate. Isolated by Davy (1808) by electrolysis; made by electrolyzing a fused mixture of fluorspar and c. chloride. C. is divalent, and forms one series of compounds. Used in organic synthesis, as a deoxidizer in alloys, in the preparation of metals, as reducing agent, as a purifier for argon, and, with lead, in antifriction alloys. The radioactive isotope Ca^{47} (half-life, 4.7 days) has a great metabolic similarity to, without the undesirable qualities of, Sr^{90}. It emits gamma radiation, and is used for biological and medical purposes. **c. acetate.** $Ca(OOCMe)_2 \cdot H_2O = 176.1$. White needles decomp. by heat, soluble in water. Used in the manufacture of acetic acid, acetone, and dyes. **c. albuminate.** A light brown, granular compound of c. and albumin, slightly soluble in water; an alterant and nutrient. **c. aminosalicylate.** $C_{14}H_{12}N_2O_6Ca \cdot 3H_2O = 398.35$. White crystals with bitter-sweet taste, soluble in water; a tuberculostatic antibacterial (B.P.). **c. arsenate.** $Ca_3(AsO_4)_2 = 398.0$. Tricalciumorthoarsenate. White powder; slightly soluble in water; an insecticide. **c. arsenite.** $Ca_3(AsO_3)_2 = 366.0$. White granules, soluble in water. **c. behenate.** $Ca(C_{22}H_{43}O_2)_2 = 718.6$. Colorless crystals. *dibromo-* Sabromin. *monoiodo-* Sajodin. **c. benzoate.** $Ca(C_7H_5O_2)_2 \cdot 3H_2O = 336.3$. Colorless crystals, soluble in water; an antiseptic. **c. biarsenate.** $CaH_4(AsO_4)_2 = 322.1$. White powder, soluble in water; an insecticide. **c. bichromate.** $CaCr_2O_7 = 256.1$. Brown hygroscopic crystals, soluble in water. **c. bimalate.** $CaH_2(C_4H_4O_5)_2 \cdot 6H_2O = 408.2$. White powder, sparingly soluble in water. **c. biphosphate.** See *c. phosphate.* **c. bisulfite.** $Ca(HSO_3)_2 = 202.8$. Used as an antiseptic, a gargle, and to prevent fermentation. **c. bitartrate.** $CaH_2(C_4H_4O_6)_2 = 338.1$. White crystals, soluble

in hot water. **c. borate.** $Ca(BO_2)_2 \cdot 2H_2O = 161.7$. White crystals, soluble in hot water; an antiseptic and astringent. **c. borocitrate.** White powder, slightly soluble in water. **c. bromide.** $CaBr_2 = 199.9$. White granules, m.760, soluble in water. A sedative, and substitute for potassium bromide; used in photography. *cryst-* $CaBr_2 \cdot 6H_2O = 308.1$. White needles, m.38, soluble in water. **c. bromiodide.** $CaBr_2 \cdot CaI_2 = 493.6$. Yellow powder, soluble in water; a sedative. **c. butyrate.** $Ca(C_4H_7O_2)_2 \cdot H_2O = 232.2$. Colorless crystals, soluble in water. **c. cacodylate.** $Ca(Me_2AsO_2)_2 \cdot H_2O = 332.1$. White powder, soluble in water; a hypodermic medication. **c. carbide.** $CaC_2 = 64.0$. Gray crystals, decomp. by water, soluble in alcohol; used to prepare acetylene gas. Cf. *acetylith.* **c. carbonate.** $CaCO_3 = 100.0$. A widely distributed rock (calcite). Rhombohedra, or white rhombs, or an amorphous fine white powder, d.2.7–2.949, decomp. 825, insoluble in water. Used medicinally as an antacid, and in toothpaste, white paint, cleaning powder, paper fillers, and for the preparation of carbon dioxide. *gamma-* Vaterite. **c. chinate.** C. quinate. **c. chinovate.** A compound of c. and chinovose. Yellow powder used to treat malaria. **c. chlorate.** $Ca(ClO_3)_2 \cdot 2H_2O = 242.9$. White monoclinics, decomp. by heat, soluble in water. Used in photography, pyrotechnics, manufacturing soda water, and as a weedicide. **c. chlorhydrophosphate.** C. chlorphosphate. **c. chlorhydrosulfate.** C. chlorsulfate. **c. chloride.** $CaCl_2 = 111.1$. White deliquescent granules, m.774, soluble in water. Used as an additive for concrete (2% accelerates setting, and imparts strength and frost resistance), as a drying agent in desiccators, to raise the boiling point of solutions, to preserve meat, in freezing mixtures, for making textiles less flammable, as a dust preventer on roads (halophilite), and in the manufacture of hydrochloric acid, alizarin, and sugars. *ammonia-* The unstable compound $CaCl_2 \cdot 8NH_3$. *cryst-* $CaCl_2 \cdot 6H_2O = 219.1$. $CaCl_2 \cdot 2H_2O$ also exists. Colorless hexagons, m.29.5, soluble in water. Used to stop bleeding; and in breweries and soda-water manufacture. *fused-* C. chloride. **c. chloride tube.** A glass vessel filled with c. chloride to dry gases or for the quantitative absorption of water. **c. chlorophosphate.** C. chlorhydrophosphate. Yellow powder, soluble in water; a tonic. **c. chlorosulfate.** White powder, almost insoluble in water. **c. chromate.** $CaCrO_4 \cdot 2H_2O = 192.2$. Yellow crystals slightly soluble in water. **c. cinnamate**, or **c. cinnamylate.** $Ca(C_9H_7O_2)_2 \cdot 3H_2O = 388.25$. White crystals, soluble in hot water. **c. citrate.** $Ca_3(C_6H_5O_7)_2 \cdot 4H_2O = 570.51$. White crystals, slightly soluble in water. **c. cyanamide.** $CaCN_2 = 80.1$. White powder, decomp. by water; an intermediate in atmospheric nitrogen fixation; a catalyst in ammonia manufacture. See *cyanamide, nitrolim.* **c. cyanide.** $Ca(CN)_2 = 92.1$. Calcyanide, "powdered cyanic acid." Colorless crystals, decomp. in moist air to form cyanic acid; a fumigant. **c. cyclamate.** $C_{12}H_{24}O_6N_2S_2Ca_2H_2O = 432.61$. White, very sweet crystals, soluble in water; a sweetening agent (B.P.). **c. dibrombehenate.** Sabromin. **c. disodium edetate.** $C_{10}H_{12}O_8N_2Na_2Ca \cdot (xH_2O) = 374.28$. The mixed di- and trihydrates of c. disodium ethylenediaminetetraacetate. White crystals, soluble in water; a metal-complexing agent (U.S.P.). **c. ethylsulfate.** $Ca(EtSO_4)_2 \cdot H_2O = 308.33$, C. sulfovinate. White crystals, soluble in water. **c. ferricyanide.** $Ca_3[Fe(CN)_6]_2 \cdot H_2O = 562.4$. Red deliquescent needles, soluble in water. **c. ferrocyanide.** $Ca_2Fe(CN)_6 = 292.2$. Yellow crystals, soluble in water. **c. ferrophospholactate.** White powder, soluble in hot water; used medicinally in syrups. **c. fluoride.** (1) $Ca_2F_6 = 154.07$. Colorless regular crystals, m.1378; sparingly soluble in water, soluble in water containing carbon dioxide. Used to etch glass and in the preparation of enamels and hydrofluoric acid. (2) Fluorite. **c. fluosilicate.** $CaSiF_6 \cdot 2H_2O = 218.17$. C. silicofluoride. Hexagons, slightly soluble in water. **c. formate.** $Ca(OOCH)_2 = 130.0$. White crystals, soluble in water. **c. fumarate.** $CaC_4H_2O_4 \cdot 3H_2O = 208.14$. Rhombic, white crystals, soluble in water. **c. gluconate.** $(C_5H_{11}O_5COO)_2Ca = 430.39$. White, odorless powder, soluble in water, used as an electrolyte replenisher. **c. glycerinate.** $Ca(C_3H_5O_4)_2 \cdot 2H_2O = 286.20$. White powder, soluble in water. **c. glyceroborate.** Colorless crystalline crust; an antiseptic. **c. glycerophosphate.** $CaPO_4C_3H_5(OH)_2 \cdot 2H_2O = 246.18$. Neurosin. White crystals, soluble in water; a nervine tonic. **c. glycollate.** $Ca(C_2H_3O_3)_2 \cdot H_2O = 208.1$. White crystals, slightly soluble in water. **c. hippurate.** $Ca(C_9H_8O_3N)_2 = 396.1$. White crystals, soluble in water; an antiarthritic. **c. hydride.** $CaH_2 = 42.0$. Hydrolith. Colorless powder, insoluble in water; used in organic synthesis. **c. hydroxide.** $Ca(OH)_2 = 74.1$. Hydrated lime, slaked lime. White hexagonal crystals or powder, decomp. by heat, slightly soluble in water, soluble in ammonium chloride solution. Used in water softeners and mortar. **c. hypochlorite.** $Ca(OCl)_2 \cdot 4H_2O = 215$, or $CaOCl_2 \cdot xHO$. White powder, used as disinfectant, bleaching and oxidizing agent, and to prepare chlorine. Cf. *bleaching powder.* **c. hypophosphate.** $Ca(H_2PO_2)_2 = 170.2$. Monoclinic white crystals, decomp. at red heat, soluble in water. Used for nutritive disturbances. **c. hyposulfite.** See (1) *c. bisulfite* or (2) *c. thiosulfate.* **c. iodate.** $Ca(IO_3)_2 \cdot 6H_2O = 498.8$. Calcinol. White prisms, decomp. by heat, slightly soluble in water; an antiseptic and iodoform substitute. **c. iodide.** $CaI_2 = 293.9$. A yellow powder, m.631, soluble in water; a substitute for potassium iodide. *cryst-* $CaI_2 \cdot 6H_2O = 402.0$. Colorless plates, m.42, very soluble in water; used in photography. **c. isobutyrate.** $Ca(C_4H_7O_2)_2 \cdot 5H_2O = 304.1$. Colorless needles, soluble in water. **c. lactate.** $Ca(C_3H_5O_3)_2 \cdot 5H_2O = 308.3$. White crystals, soluble in water; used to treat rachitis and scrofula. **c. larsenite.** (Pb,Ca)ZnSiO_4. A rare mineral having a vivid yellow fluorescence (Franklin Furnace, N.J.) **c. lime.** Quicklime containing 75% or less of CaO. **c. linoleate.** $Ca(C_{18}H_{31}O_2)_2 = 598.56$. White powder, insoluble in water. **c. loretinate.** White powder, used in antiseptic gauze. **c. magnesium phosphate.** Mixed c. and magnesium phosphates. White powder, insoluble in water. **c. malate.** $CaC_4H_4O_5$. (1) *active-* $2H_2O = 208.14$. (2) *racemic-* $3H_2O = 226.16$. Colorless rhombs, slightly soluble in water. **c. maleate.** $Ca_4H_2O_4 = 172.11$. Colorless rhombs, soluble in water. **c. malonate.** $CaC_3H_2O_4 \cdot 4H_2O = 214.16$. White powder, in-

soluble in water. **c. mandelate.** $C_{16}H_{14}CaO_6 = 342.37$. White powder, slightly soluble in water; a urinary tract anti-infective. **c. manganite.** $CaO \cdot MnO_2 = 143.02$. See *Weldon process.* **c. meconate.** $CaC_7H_2O_7 \cdot H_2O = 256.12$. Yellow powder, sparingly soluble in water. **c. metabisulfite.** C. bisulfite. **c. metaphosphate.** C. phosphate (2). **c. methyl sulfate.** $Ca(MeSO_4)_2 = 262.0$. White crystals, soluble in water. **c. minerals.** C. is one of the most abundant metals and a main constituent of many rocks; e.g.: limestone, $CaCO_3$; gypsum, $CaSO_4$; apatite, $3Ca_3(PO_4)_2 \cdot CaF_2$. **c. monoiodo behenate.** Sajodin. **c. monophosphate.** See *c. phosphate* (3). **c. nitrate.** $Ca(NO_3)_2 \cdot 4H_2O = 236.1$. Colorless monoclinics, m.43, very soluble in water; a fertilizer (Norway saltpeter), and explosive. Cf. Baldwin's *phosphorus.* **c. nitride.** $Ca_3N_2 = 148.0$. Brown mass, m.900, decomp. by water. **c. nitrite.** $Ca(NO_2)_2 = 132.1$. Colorless prisms, soluble in water. **c. oleate.** $Ca(C_{18}H_{33}O_2)_2 = 602.6$. Yellow granules, soluble in alcohol. **c. oxalate.** $CaC_2O_4 \cdot H_2O = 146.0$, or $Ca(OOC)_2 = 128.0$. White microcrystals, insoluble in water. See *raphides.* **c. oxide.** CaO = 56.0. Lime, burnt lime, quicklime, caustic lime, calx. White masses, d_5° 3.306, m.1995; sparingly soluble in water (limewater), soluble in acids. Used as a reagent, and as an antacid and mild caustic. Commercial grades are used in mortar, fertilizers and for causticizing soda ash. **c. oxychloride.** $CaOCl_2$ Bleaching powder. **c. oxysulfide.** CaO·CaS = 128.0. Yellow powder, used to treat skin diseases. **c. palmitate.** $Ca(C_{16}H_{31}O_2)_2 = 550.6$. Yellow crystals, insoluble in water. **c. pantothenate.** (U.S.P.). See *vitamin.* **c. permanganate.** $Ca(MnO_4)_2 \cdot 4H_2O = 330.0$. Acerdol. Purple hygroscopic prisms, decomp. by heat, soluble in water. An antiseptic and disinfectant; used in dentistry and disinfecting drinking water. **c. peroxide.** $CaO_2 = 72.0$. Cream-colored powder, decomp. by water; an antacid, detergent, bactericide, and antiseptic. **c. phenate.** $Ca(OPh)_2 = 226.1$. C. carbolate, c. phenylate, c. phenolate. Pink powder, slightly soluble in water; an antiseptic. **c. phenolsulfonate.** $Ca(SO_3C_6H_4OH)_2 = 354.4$. C. sulfophenate, c. sulfocarbolate. Pink powder, soluble in water; an intestinal antiseptic. **c. phosphate.** There are:

$CaHPO_4$ = dicalcium phosphate, A.C.P.
$Ca(PO_3)_2$ = calcium metaphosphate
$CaH_4(PO_4)_2$ = monocalcium phosphate as salts of phosphoric acid
$Ca_2P_2O_7$ = calcium pyrophosphate
$Ca_3(PO_4)_2$ = tricalcium phosphate

Naturally occurring phosphates include: monetite, $2CaO \cdot P_2O_5 \cdot H_2O$; fluorapatite, $CaF_2 \cdot 9CaO \cdot 3P_2O_5$; dahllite, $CaCO_3 \cdot 6CaO \cdot 2P_2O_5$. (1) *di-* $CaHPO_4 \cdot 2H_2O = 172.1$. Secondary-, dibasic-, diacid-. Colorless plates, slightly soluble in water, soluble in ammonium citrate solution; used in dentistry and as a c. replenisher (U.S.P.). (2) *meta-* $Ca(PO_3)_2 = 198.0$. White powder, insoluble in water. (3) *mono-* $CaH_4(PO_4)_2 \cdot H_2O = 252.1$. Primary-, acid-. Colorless rhombs, soluble in water; used in baking powders. (4) $Ca_2P_2O_7 \cdot 4H_2O = 328.3$. *pyro-* Colorless crystals, slightly soluble in water. (5) *tri-*

$Ca_3(PO_4)_2 \cdot H_2O = 328.3$. Normal-, tertiary-, neutral-, tribasic-. White powder, insoluble in water. Used as a food for bone tissues, and in the manufacture of enamels, cleansing agents, and phosphorus. **c. phosphide.** (1) $Ca_2P_2 = 142.0$. Gray granules, decomp. by water to form flammable phosphine; used in chemical warfare. (2) $Ca_3P_2 = 182.27$. Tricalcium diphosphide. Yields nonflammable phosphine in water. **c. phosphite.** $2Ca\text{-}HPO_3 \cdot 3H_2O$. White crystals, slightly soluble in water, decomp. by heat, forming phosphine, PH_3. **c. phthalate.** $CaC_8H_4O_4 \cdot H_2O = 222.1$. Colorless prisms, soluble in water. **c. plumbate.** $Ca(PbO_3)_2$ or $Ca_2PbO_4 = 350.9$. Orange crystals, insoluble in cold water, decomp. by hot water. Used as an oxidizing agent, in accumulators, pyrotechnics, glass, and matches. **c. plumbite.** $CaPbO_2 = 278.9$. Colorless crystals, slightly soluble in water. **c. propionate.** $Ca(C_3H_5O_2)_2 = 186.1$. White powder, soluble in water. **c. pyrophosphate.** See *c. phosphate* (4). **c. quinate.** $CaC_{14}H_{22}O_{12} = 426.24$. C. chinate, $[C_6H_7(OH)_4COO]_2Ca$. **c. rhodanide.** C. thiocyanate. **c. saccharate.** Antacedin. Colorless scales, soluble in water; an antacid. **c. salicylate.** $Ca(OOC \cdot C_6H_4 \cdot OH)_2 \cdot 2H_2O = 350.20$. Colorless crystals, soluble in carbonated water. **c. santoninate.** $Ca(C_{15}H_{19}O_4)_2 = 566.39$. White crystals, sparingly soluble in water; an anthelmintic. **c. selenate.** $CaSeO_4 = 183.1$. White crystals, sparingly soluble in water. **c. selenite.** $CaSeO_3 \cdot 2H_2O = 219.30$. White powder, soluble in water. **c. silicate.** $CaSiO_3 = 116.17$. Okonite. White mass, insoluble in water. **c. silicofluoride.** Lapis albus. **c. silicotitanite.** Sphene. **c. stearate.** $Ca(C_{18}H_{35}O_2)_2 = 606.6$. White granules, insoluble in water. **c. succinate.** $CaC_4H_4O_4 \cdot H_2O = 174.1$. White crystals, soluble in water. **c. sulfate.** (1) *Anhydrite-* $CaSO_4 = 136.1$. White rhombs, m.1360, insoluble in water, soluble in ammonium salts; a desiccant and absorbent, for gases. (2) *Sesquihydrate-* $CaSO_4 \cdot \frac{1}{2}H_2O = 145.1$. Plaster of paris. White powder containing 5% water made by heating gypsum to 120–130°C. It quickly solidifies with water; used for castings and molds. (3) *Dihydrate-* $CaSO_4 \cdot 2H_2O = 172.1$. Gypsum. White monoclinic crystals; used as a paper filler (pearl hardening, mineral white), as pigment, fertilizer, a retarder for portland cement, and a cleaning agent. **c. sulfide.** $CaS = 72.1$. Hepar calcis, sulfurated lime. Yellow powder, used for luminous paints. **c. sulfite.** $CaSO_3 \cdot 2H_2O = 156.16$. White powder soluble in dilute sulfurous acid. Used as a disinfectant in breweries, as an antichlor in bleaching, and in manufacturing cellulose pulp. **c. sulfocarbolate.** C. phenolsulfonate. **c. sulfocyanide.** C. thiocyanate. **c. superoxide.** C. peroxide. **c. tannate.** Yellow powder, insoluble in water. **c. tartrate.** $CaC_4H_4O_6 \cdot 4H_2O = 260.2$. White powder, sparingly soluble in water. **c. thiocyanate.** $Ca(CNS)_2 = 156.0$. C. rhodanide. White crystals, soluble in water; it dissolves silk from mixed textiles; a vasodilator. **c. thiosulfate.** $CaS_2O_3 \cdot 6H_2O = 260.1$. White rhombs, decomp. by water and heat. **c. tungstate.** $CaWO_4 = 288.0$. C. wolframate, artificial scheelite. Tetragonal scales or white powder, insoluble in water; used in luminous pigments. **c. urate.** $Ca(C_5H_3O_3N_4)_2 = 374.22$. White powder, sparingly soluble in water.

c. valerate. $Ca(C_5H_9O_2)_2 \cdot 3H_2O = 296.28$. White crystals, soluble in water; a sedative. **c. wolframate.** C. tungstate.

calcothar. Colcothar.

calcspar. Calcite.

calculus. (1) An abnormal deposit of mineral salts. **biliary-** Gallstones. Solid deposits occurring either as (*a*) *cholesterol-*, consisting of cholesterol; (*b*) *pigment-* consisting of bile pigments, bilirubin, and calcium salts; (*c*) *inorganic-*, consisting of carbonates and phosphates of calcium. **urinary-** Solid masses of urinary sediment in the urinary tract. (*a*) *uric acid-* consisting of uric acid and urates; (*b*) *phosphate-* consisting of the triple phosphates; (*c*) *oxalate-* consisting of calcium oxalate crystals. (2) The mathematical laws of continuously varying quantities, which can be graphically expressed in curves. Cf. *diagram.*

calcyanide. Calcium cyanide.

Caldwell crucible. A silica crucible having an open bottom to hold a platinum or porcelain disk.

Caledon. Trade name for anthraquinone vat dyestuffs.

caledonite. Native basic lead and copper sulfates.

calefacient. A drug applied externally to induce a sense of warmth.

calender. A machine which presses moist cloth, paper, etc., between heavy rollers, to glaze its surface.

calendula. Marigold. The flowering tops of *Calendula officinalis* (Compositae); a stimulant.

calendulin. An amorphous substance from calendula.

caleometer. An electrical instrument to measure the heat loss of a coil of wire at constant temperature.

calglucon. Calcium gluconate.

Calgon. Trademark for a glassy form of sodium hexametaphosphate containing a small amount of sodium pyrophosphate. It forms a soluble complex with calcium carbonate; used to soften water. See *threshold treatment.*

caliber, calibre. The inside diameter or bore of a tube.

calibration. (1) The graduation of a measuring instrument; (2) the determination of its error.

caliche. Chile saltpeter. Crude sodium nitrate (20–50%, with sodium iodate) in the deserts of Atacama and Tarapaca (Northern Chile).

calico. A plain, heavy cotton cloth.

californite. Massive vesuvianite, resembling jade.

californium. Cf. An element, at no. 98, probably originally in the earth but disappeared by radioactive decay. Prepared by irradiation, by Cunningham and Thompson (Lawrence Radiation Laboratory) in 1959; compounds with oxygen and chlorine exist.

calipers. A device to measure the diameter of a tube. **micrometer-** An instrument to measure with an accuracy up to 0.01 mm. **vernier-** An instrument to determine the inside or outside diameter of a tube.

calisaya. Cinchona.

callainite. Turquoise.

callaite. Turquoise.

calliandrein. A glucoside from *Calliandra grandiflora.* (Leguminosae). White, odorless, powder resembling saponin; an antipyretic.

callicrein. A circulatory pancreatic hormone.

callistephin. An anthocyanin from strawberries and

the purple aster (*Callistephus chinensis*), isolated as the hydrochloride, $C_{21}H_{21}O_{10}Cl$.

callitrol. The alkali-soluble fraction, $b_{6mm}118$, of the wood oil of *Callitris glauca*, Australian cypress; chiefly *d*-citronellic acid.

callitrolic acid. $C_{64}H_{82}O_5(OH)COOH$. A resinous acid in sandarac.

callophane. A portable instrument utilizing daylight as a source of ultraviolet light.

calmine. Barbital sodium.

calnitro. A fertilizer made from ammonium nitrate and chalk containing 16–20% nitrogen.

calomel. (1) Native mercurous chloride of secondary origin. (2) Mercurous chloride (pharmaceutical).
c. electrode. A standard half-cell or electrode whose emf is that of mercury and calomel in contact with a solution of potassium chloride. At 20°C:

Saturated potassium chloride . . . . . . 0.2492 volt
1.0 *M* potassium chloride 0.2860
0.1 *M* potassium chloride 0.3379

calorgas. A compressed mixture of hydrocarbon for heating and lighting purposes (by-products of coal hydrogenation 21,000 BThU/lb).

caloric. Alchemical term for fire, which was supposed to possess weight.

calorie. The former unit of quantity of heat. The heat required to raise the temperature of 1 gm of water from $t°$ to $(t + 1)°C$. Hence the 15° cal, the 20° cal, etc., where $t = 15$, 20 etc. The international unit of heat is now the joule, q.v., and the c. is defined in terms of it (1948). **gram-** Small c. **great-** Large c. **I.T.-** International steam table c.; 1000 I.T.C. = 1/860 international kilowatt-hour. **kilo-** Large c. **large-** Millithermil. *Cal.* or kilogram-calorie. The heat required to raise the temperature of 1 kg water from 14.5 to 15.5°C. **mean-** The $\frac{1}{100}$ part of the heat required to raise 1 gm water from 0 to 100°C at atmospheric pressure. **micro-** Small c. Microthermil. **small-** cal or gram-calorie. The quantity of heat required to heat 1 gm water from 14.5 to 15.5°C. At 18°C, 1 cal = 1 therm = 0.001 Cal = 4.183 joules = 4.181×10^7 ergs = 3.086 ft-lb = 0.426 kg-meter = 1.162×10^{-6} kwhr = 0.003968 BThU.

I.T.c. . . . . 4.1868 joules
15° c. 4.1855
4° c. 4.2045
Thermochemical c. 4.1840
Mean c. (0–100°C) 4.1897

calorifacient. A substance which produces warmth.

calorific. Carrying or holding warmth. **c. value.** (1) Technical: the number of large calories obtained by the combustion of fuels or gases. (2) Physiological: The number of small calories derived from consuming foods or the daily diet. **gross c.v.** The number of heat units liberated when a fuel is completely burnt in oxygen saturated with water vapor, with the formation of liquid water. **net c.v.** The number of heat units liberated when a fuel is completely burnt in oxygen saturated with water vapor, with the formation of water vapor. It is less than the gross c.v. by the latent heat of the water present originally or formed by combustion of hydrogen (usually 1060 BThU/lb).

calorimeter. An instrument to measure the amount of heat liberated or absorbed. **adiabatic-** A c. kept at constant temperature. **bomb-** An enclosed steel bomb for determination of the calorific power of fuels. **Emerson-** A c. for determining the heat value of fuels. **Féry-** A c. for determining the heat value of foods. **flame-** A c. to measure heats of combustion of gases or vapors in oxygen at constant pressure. **isothermal-** A c. which operates by transferring the heat of reaction to a surrounding liquid, which is simultaneously cooled by bubbling through it an inert gas, so that the heat production is just balanced. Cf. *colorimeter.*

calorimetric. Pertaining to measuring heat quantities. Cf. *colorimetric.*

calorimetry. The measurement of heat. Cf. *colorimetry.*

caloriscope. A device to demonstrate the release of heat in the respiration of an organism.

caloritropic. Thermotropic.

calorizing. A process for the production of aluminum coatings. Cf. *sherardizing.*

calotropin. A glucoside from *Calotropis procera* (Asclepiadaceae) which acts similarly to digitalis; an arrow poison. Cf. *akundarol.*

Calotropis floss. Akund. The seed hair of *Calotropis procera* and *C. gigantea.* A fine, soft, lustrous but weak fiber, used in textiles.

calotype. An early photograph (1840). Silver halide was formed on a sheet of paper by soaking it successively in appropriate reagents.

Calsolene. Trademark for a highly sulfonated castor oil used as a detergent.

calumba. Columba. The roote of *Jateorhiza calumba* (*J. palmata*) (Menispermaceae), E. Africa. A bitter stomachic tonic. **American c.** Fraserin.

calumbic acid. Colombic acid. An acid principle from calumba. Cf. *columbic.*

calumbin. $C_{28}H_{30}O_2 = 398.23$. Columbin. A glucoside from calumba. Yellow crystals, m.182, slightly soluble in water; a bitter tonic.

calutron. An electromagnetic isotope separator (University of California).

calx. (1) Latin for lime or calcium oxide. (2) The alchemical name for an oxide or dross.

calycanthine. $C_{22}H_{26}N_4 = 346.27$. An alkaloid from *Calycanthus fertilis*, Carolina allspice.

calyx. The violet sheath around the flame of an air–coal-gas mixture burning at a small hole.

calyxanthine. Calycanthine.

camariphen hydrochloride. $C_{18}H_{27}NO_2 \cdot HCl = 325–393$. White, bitter crystals, m. 144, soluble in water; a parasympatholytic (B.P.).

cambium. A layer of growing tissue between the wood and bast of a tree.

cambogia. Gamboge.

cambopinic acid. $C_{11}H_{18}O_2 = 182.14$. A crystalline acid from the resin of *Pinus cambodgiana.*

cambric. A stiffened, plain light fabric of cotton or linen, originally from Cambrai, Belgium.

camelina. The plant *C. satina* (Cruciferae), Mediterranean, which yields an oil, oil cake, and fiber.

camellin. $C_{53}H_{84}O_{19} = 1024.81$. A glucoside from the seeds of *Camellia japonica* (Theaceae). A red, bitter powder, soluble in water; a cardiac stimulant.

camel's hair brush. A small brush used in microoperations.

camenthol. A mixture of camphor and menthol for inhalation.

camera. (1) A lightproof box, compartment, or chamber. (2) An optical device for taking photographs. **ciné-** A c. taking more than 15 pictures per second. **ultrarapid-** 128 per second. **chronoteine-** (q.v.) 3,200 per second. **stereoscopic-** A c. taking two pictures at slightly different angles simultaneously to bring out perspective. Cf. *binocular.*

camera lucida. A prism attachment for the eyepiece of a microscope, which throws a magnified image of the object onto paper for tracing.

camomile. See *anthemis, calendula, chamomile, matricaria.*

camouflet. A space formed by an underground explosion; usually contains carbon monoxide.

Campden tablets. A domestic preservative, containing sodium or potassium metabisulfite.

campeachy wood. Logwood.

camphane. $C_{10}H_{18} = 138.2$. 1,7,7-Trimethylnorcamphane. White crystals, m.154, soluble in alcohol. **2-amino-** Bornyl amine. **2-chloro-** Bornyl chloride. **2,3-dihydroxy-** Camphene glycol. **2-hydroxy-** Borneol. **3-hydroxy-** Epiborneol. **4-hydroxy-** Isoborneol. **2-keto-** Camphor. **3-keto-** Epicamphor.

c. carboxylic acid. Camphocarboxylic acid.

camphanic acid. $C_{10}H_{14}O_4 = 198.11$. α-Hydroxycamphoric acid lactone. Colorless crystals, m.201.

camphanol. **2-** Borneol. **3-** Epiborneol. **4-** Isoborneol.

camphanone. **2-** Camphor. **3-** Epicamphor.

camphanyl. The group $C_{10}H_{17}—$, derived from camphane.

camphene. $C_{10}H_{16} = 136.17$. 3,3-Dimethyl-2-methylenenorcamphane.

CH
H₂C | C = CH₂ 1
| CH₂ | 6 2—8
H₂C | CMe₂ 7
CH 5 3—9
4 10

It occurs in three isomeric forms: (1) **i-** Inactive c. Colorless needles, m.47, insoluble in water. (2) **d-** Dextro-c. Colorless needles, m.51, soluble in alcohol. (3) **l-** Levo-c. Colorless needles, m.52, soluble in alcohol. **chloro-** See *chlorocamphene.* **8-Δ¹-pentenyl-** Sesqui-camphene.

c. camphonic acid. Camphoric acid. **c. glycol.** $C_{10}H_{18}O_2 = 170.15$. 2,3-Dihydroxycamphane.

camphenilene. The radical $C_9H_{15}—$, derived from camphenilane.

camphenilidene. The radical $C_9H_{14}=$, derived from camphenilane.

camphenilone. $C_9H_{14}O = 138.17$. 3-Ketocamiphanilane. **1-methyl-** Camphenone.

camphenone. $C_{10}H_{16}O = 150.11$. 1-Methylcamphenilone. Colorless crystals, m.168.

campho acid. $C_{10}H_{14}O_6 = 230.11$. Carboxylapocamphoric acid. Colorless crystals, m.196.

camphocarboxylic acid. $C_{11}H_{16}O_3 = 196.2$. 2-Keto-3-carboxycamphane. Colorless crystals, soluble in water.

camphogen. Cymene.

camphol. Borneol.

campholactone. $C_9H_{14}O_2 = 154.1$. Colorless crystals, m.50.

campholene. $C_8H_{14} = 110.1$. 3-Isopropyl-Δ³-cyclo-

pentene. A pentacyclic hydrocarbon. Cf. *camphoceenic acid.*

campholenic acid. $C_{10}H_{16}O_2 = 168.2$. Colorless liquid, d.0.992, b.256.

campholic acid. $C_{10}H_{18}O_2 = 170.2$. 1,2,2,3-Tetramethylcyclopentanecarboxylic acid. Colorless prisms, m.95, slightly soluble in water.

campholide. $C_{10}H_{16}O_2 = 168.2$. White crystals, m.211.

camphonanic acid. $C_9H_{16}O_2 = 156.2$. 1,2,2-Trimethylcyclopentanecarboxylic acid. Colorless crystals, soluble in alcohol.

camphor. (1) $C_{10}H_{16}O = 152.2$. 2-Ketocamphane, 2-camphanone, Japan, laurel. A stearoptene from the leaves of Laurus or *Cinnamomum camphora,*

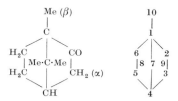

S.E. Asia. Large crystalline plates, easily broken when moistened with ether, d.0.879, m.175, [a]D + 44°; insoluble in water. An antispasmodic, carminative, diaphoretic, antiseptic, and plasticizer for synthetic resins. Cf. *menthol, thymol.* (2) A group name for odorous principles of plants. See *camphors.* **alant-** Helenin. **amido-** $C_{10}H_{17}ON = 167.2$. Colorless oily liquid. b.244. **anemone-** Anemonin. **anise-** Anethole. **artificial-** Terpene monochlorhydrate. **asarum-** Asarone. **azo-** $C_{10}H_{16}N_2O = 180.2$. Monoketazocamphorquinone. **beta-** Epicamphor. **betula-** Betulinol. **bitter almond-** Benzoin. **Borneo-** Borneol. **cantharides-** Cantharidin. **champaca-** Champacol. **cyan-** $C_{11}H_{15}ON = 177.2$. White crystals, m.127. **cyanmethylene-** $C_{12}H_{15}ON = 189.2$. Colorless crystals, m.46, b.280. **dextro-** Camphor. **diketo-** C. quinone. **elecampane-** Helenin. **epi-** Epicamphor. **isonitroso-** $C_{10}H_{15}O_2N = 181.12$. Colorless crystals, m.153. **Japanese-** Camphor. **keto-** Camphorquinone. **laurel-** Camphor. **ledum-** Ledum camphor. **Malayan-** Borneol. **oxymethylene-** $C_{11}H_{16}O_2 = 180.2$. White crystals, m.77. **parsley-** Apiol. **peppermint-** Menthol. **pernitroso-** $C_{10}H_{16}O_2N_2 = 197.2$. White crystals, m.43. **pine-** Pinol. **pulsatilla-** Anemonin. **Sumatra-** Borneol. **tar-** Naphthalene. **Tonka-** Coumarin. **thyme-** Thymol.

c. chlorated. $C_{10}H_{15}OCl = 186.6$. Yellow crystals, m.106, soluble in alcohol; an antiseptic. **c. dibromated.** $C_{10}H_{14}OBr_2 = 310.2$. Yellow crystals, m.115, soluble in alcohol or ether; an antiseptic. **c. imide.** See *camphorimide.* **c. monobromated.** $C_{10}H_{15}BrO = 231.2$. Colorless crystals, m.76 soluble in alcohol; an antispasmodic, antineuralgic, and soporific. **c. oil.** The essential oil from the leaves of *Cinnamomum camphora.* Colorless liquid, d.0.87–1.04, of strong odor; an antiseptic and rubefacient. **c. wood oil.** Oil distilled from the branches. Yellow oil of strong odor, d.1.155, containing camphor, safrole, pinene, phellandrene, cadinene; a liniment for rheumatism, bruises, and sprains. See *antimalum, camphorated oil.*

camphoramic acid. $C_5H_4Me_3\cdot(CONH_2)\cdot COOH = 198.13$. Camphoramidic acid. White crystals. **alpha-** m.177, **beta-** m.183, soluble in water.

camphoranic acid. $C_9H_{12}O_6 = 216.1$. Colorless crystals, m.209.

camphorated oil. Camphor liniment. A rubefacient mixture of camphor 1, cottonseed or olive oil 4 pts.

camphoric acid. $C_8H_{14}(COOH)_2 = 200.2$. *cis*-1,2,2-Trimethyl-1,3-cyclopentanedicarboxylic acid. Colorless prisms, m.187, decomp., soluble in water. **c. a. amide.** Camphoramic acid. **c. a. diamide.** $C_{10}H_{18}O_2N_2 = 198.6$. White crystals, m.197.

camphorimide. $C_{10}H_{15}O_2N = 181.2$. Camphoric imide. Colorless crystals, m.248.

camphormethylenecarboxylic acid. $C_{12}H_{16}O_3 = 208.2$. White crystals, m.101.

camphormethylimide. $C_{11}H_{17}O_2N = 195.2$. White crystals, m.40.

camphormethylisoimide. $C_{11}H_{17}O_2N = 195.2$. White crystals, m.134.

camphornitrilo acid. $C_{10}H_{15}O_2N = 181.2$. Cyanlauronic acid. Colorless crystals, m.152.

camphoronic acid. $CH_2COOH\cdot CMeCOOH\cdot CMe_2\cdot COOH = 218.1$. α,α,β-Trimethylcarballylic acid. Microcrystals, m.135. **camphoroxime.** $C_{10}H_{17}ON = 167.2$. Colorless needles, m.118, insoluble in water.

camphoroyl. The radical $C_8H_{14}:(CO)_2=$, derived from camphoric acid.

camphors. A group of odoriferous plant principles, solid volatile substances (stearoptenes), Cf. *terpenes.* Camphor, menthol, and thymol are official.

camphoryl. The monovalent radical $C_{10}H_{15}O-$, derived from camphor. **c. hydroxylamine.** $C_{10}H_{15}-O_3N = 197.1$. Colorless crystals, m.225.

camphorylidene. The radical $C_{10}H_{14}O=$, derived from camphor.

camphyl. The radical $C_{10}H_{16}=$, derived from camphor. **c. alcohol.** Borneol. **c. amine.** $C_{10}H_{17}NH_2 = 153.2$. A solid, $d_{37}°0.93$, b.198.

camptonide. A variety of diorite.

camptonose. A variety of basalt.

camwood. A red dye wood from *Baphia nitida* (Leguminosae), W. Africa. Cf. *sandalwood, santalin.*

canada asbestos. Chrysotile. **c. balsam.** A turpentine-like balsam exuded from incisions in the bark of *Abies balsamea*, of Canada and Maine. Yellow liquid, with a pleasant odor and bitter taste, dries in air to a transparent resin. Used as a microscope cement and varnish. Its refractive index equals that of glass. **c. snakeroot.** Asarum. **c. turpentine.** The essential oil of *Pinus maritima.* (Coniferae).

canadase. Anorthosite from Maine.

canadine. $C_{20}H_{21}O_4N = 339.17$. *l*-Tetrahydroberberine. An alkaloid from *Hydrastis canadensis.* Silky needles, m.133, insoluble in water.

canadium. A supposed element of the platinum group.

canadol. Impure hexane from petroleum; a local anesthetic.

canaigre. The roots of *Rumex hymenosepalis* (Polygonaceae), Texas and Mexico; contains 25–30% tannin.

canal rays. Positive rays. The positively charged molecules of gas emerging behind the perforated cathode of a high-vacuum tube at about 3.2×10^9 cm/sec. They produce ionization, photographic action, fluorescence, and disintegration of certain substances. Cf. *ray, mass spectra, positive-ray analysis.*

cananga. Ylang ylang.

canavalia bean. The urease-rich seeds of *Canavalia* species.

canavalin. A globulin of jack beans, the seed of *Canavalia* species (Leguminosae).

cancer. An abnormal growth of malignant tissue.

cancerine. $C_8H_5O_3N = 163.1$. A ptomaine found as colorless crystals in pathological urine.

cancrinite. (1) $Na_4Al_3HCSi_3O_{15}$. Yellow, hexagonal rock, d.2.4, hardness 5–6. (2) $4Na_2O\cdot CaO\cdot 4Al_2O_3\cdot 9SiO_2\cdot 2(CO_2\cdot SO_3)\cdot 3H_2O$. A constituent of steam-boiler scales.

candela. New candle.

candelilla wax. Gama wax. Brown wax, d.0.983, m.67, from the candelilla plant (Mexico); used in candles, cements, polishes, varnishes, leather dressings, and dentistry.

candle. ca. International unit of luminous intensity. Cf. *photometric units.* **new-** Candela. The 1948 international unit of luminous intensity. The brightness of a full blackbody radiator at the solidification temperature of platinum is taken as 60 new c. per cm.[2] **c. balance.** A balance to determine the burning rate of a c. **c. nut oil.** Lumbang oil. **c. power.** The luminous intensity of a standard c. 1 candle = 1.11 Hefner units = 0.104 carcel unit. 1 candle per cm² = 3.1416 lamberts = 3141.6 millilamberts. 1 candle per in.² = 0.4968 lambert. = 496.8 millilamberts. **c. standard.** C. made of sperm wax, weight $\frac{1}{6}$lb, which burns 120 grains per hour. See *standard c., foot-c., meter-c.*

candoluminescence. Luminescence due to incandescent heat, i.e., temperatures exceeding 1000°C.

canella. Whitewood, cinnamon bark. The bark of *Winterana canella* (Canellaceae), W. Indies; a condiment. **c. oil.** The essential oil of c. Colorless liquid, d.0.920–0.935, containing eugenol, cineol, and caryophyllin.

cane sugar. Sucrose made from sugarcane.

canfieldite. Ag_8SnS. A rare, native sulfide.

cannabane. $C_{18}H_{22} = 238.2$. Cannabene hydride. A volatile hydrocarbon in hemp oil. Cf. *cannibene.*

cannabene. $C_{18}H_{20} = 236.2$. A hydrocarbon in hemp oil.

cannabidiol. $C_{21}H_{30}O_2 = 314.27$. An isomer of cannabol in hemp resins.

cannabin. (1) A glucoside, or (2), a resin, from *Cannabis indica.*

cannabine. An alkaloid from cannabis; a hypnotic.

cannabinol. $C_{21}H_{26}O_2 = 310.23$. The active principle of *Cannabis sativa.* Yellow oil, d.1.042, b_{100mm} 315, insoluble in water, green fluorescence in glacial acetic acid. **acetyl-** See *acetyl-c.*

cannabis. Indian hemp, Indian c., the flowering tops of the female plant of *C. indica* or *C. sativa*, hemp (Urticaceae); a narcotic. See *bhang, ganja, hashish.*

cannaboid. The combined principles of *Cannabis indica*; an antispasmodic and sedative.

cannabol. $C_{21}H_{30}O_2 = 314.27$. An isomer of cannabidiol in hemp resins, m.66.5.

cannel coal. A hard bituminous coal with a luminous flame, a smooth conchoidal fracture, and a high volatiles content. Used for gas production. Cf. *boghead, torbanite.*

cannibene. $C_{15}H_{24}$ = 204.19. A sesquiterpene, d.0.897, b.259, from hemp oil. Cf. *cannabane.*

cannizzarization. The Cannizzaro reaction.

Cannizzaro, Stanislao. 1826–1910. Italian chemist noted for his work on organic chemistry and the amplification and application of Avogadro's hypothesis to the atomic theory. **C. number.** The number of milligrams of potassium hydroxide which react with 1 gm aldehyde in C. reaction. **C. reaction.** The decomposition of aromatic aldehydes by alcoholic potash, with the formation of acids and alcohols; e.g.:

$$2RCHO + KOH \rightarrow R \cdot CH_2OH + R \cdot COOK$$

cannonite. A high-explosive nitrocellulose-nitroglycerin mixture.

cannula. A glass or metal tube for insertion into or to connect arteries.

cantharene. C_8H_{12} = 108.1. Dihydro-*o*-xylene. Colorless liquid, b.135.

cantharides. Blistering beetle, cantharis, Russian fly, Spanish fly, *Lytta* or *Cantharis vesicatoria*; a blistering agent. **c. camphor.** *Sodium cantharidate.*

cantharidic acid. Cantharidin.

cantharidin(e). $C_{10}H_{12}O_4$ = 196.1. 2,3-Dimethyl-7-oxybicyclo[2.2.1]heptane-2,3-didicarboxylic anhydride, cantharidin. Colorless crystals, slightly soluble in water, m.210; a blistering agent, diuretic, and stimulant.

Cantharis. A genus of beetles, now *Lytta.*

Canton phosphorus. A luminescent mixture of oystershells 2, sulfur 1 pt.

canula. Cannula.

canvas. A strong close hemp or flax fabric used in filter presses and sacking.

caoutchouc. (Malayan, "weeping tree"). Rubber. **Gaboon-** Dambonite. **mineral-** q.v. **oil of-** Terpene.

CAP. Abbreviation for *chloracetophenone.*

capacitance. The amount of electricity required to raise a body to a given potential. An isolated capacitor has unit c. when unit electrical quantity will charge it to unit potential. Units: (1) international farad—the c. of a capacitor charged to 1 volt by 1 coulomb; (2) microfarad—one-millionth farad. **electromagnetic-** 10^9 farads.

capacity. (1) The ability to hold or contain a force or energy. (2) Volume. (3) The amount of matter; as compared with intensity. Thus, the c. factor of acidity is *normality.* Cf. *intensity.* **electrostatic-** Capacitance. **heat-** Thermal c. **specific inductive-** Dielectric constant. **thermal-** Heat c. The number of calories required to raise the temperature of an insulated body one degree centigrade.

caparrosa. The leaves of *Nea theifera* (Nyctaginaceae), S. America; a tea.

capers. The green flower buds of *Capparis spinosa* (Capparidaceae), Mediterranean; a pickle and condiment.

capillaries. The network of delicate blood vessels or other small tissue connecting tubes.

capillarity. The attractive force between two unlike molecules as shown by a meniscus formation (see figure).

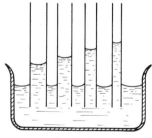

Capillarity.

capillary. A tube with a very small inside diameter. **c. analysis.** (1) Early name for chromatographic analysis. (2) A filter paper dipped into a *negative* colloid absorbs both the dispersed and external phase; but in a *positive* colloid only the external phase. Cf. *adsorption.* **c. correction.** A correction for the capillarity of mercury applied to mercury thermometers of diameter above 25 mm. **c. electrode.** see *Lippmann* electrode. **c. electrometer.** See *electrometer.* **c. pipet.** A pipet for measuring fractions of a milliliter. **c. tubing.** Glass tubing with inside diameter less than 1 mm.

capillator. An apparatus for the colorimetric determination of pH values in which the solutions are compared in capillary tubes, to reduce the effect of color or turbidity.

capnometry. The measurement of smoke density. Cf. *nephelometry.*

caporit. A disinfectant mixture of calcium hypochlorite and sodium chloride containing about 50% active chlorine.

capraldehyde. $C_{10}H_{20}O$ = 156.15. Capric aldehyde, decanal, *n*-decyl aldehyde. Colorless liquid, d.0.828, b.209, from essential oils. **iso-** A liquid, d.0.830, b.169.6.

capramide. (1) Caproyl amide. (2) $Me(CH_2)_8 \cdot CONH_2$ = 171.17. *n*-Decylic amide. White crystals, m.108.

caprate. A salt of capric acid, containing the radical $C_9H_{19}COO-$.

capric acid. $Me(CH_2)_8COOH$ = 172.21. Octylacetic acid, *n*-decoic acid, *n*-decanoic acid, decyclic acid, decatoic acid. A fatty acid in animal fats. Colorless needles, m.31, slightly soluble in water. Cf. *rutic acid.* **c. aldehyde.** Capraldehyde. **c. amide.** Capramide. **c. anhydride.** $[Me(CH_2)_8CO]_2O$ = 326.30. White crystals, m.239, insoluble in water. **c. nitrile.** Caprinitrile.

Caprifoliaceae. Honeysuckle family. Shrubs or twining plants, some yielding drugs. Flowers: *Sambucus canadensis*, elder; bark: *Viburnum opulus*, cramp bark; roots: *Triosteum perfoliatum*, fever root; fruits: *Lonicera xylosteum*, xylostein.

caprilic acid. Caprylic acid.

caprin. A compound of capric acid and glycerin, e.g., dicaprin (glyceryl dicaprate).

caprine. Norleucine.

caprinitrile. $Me(CH_2)_8CN$ = 153.16. Decane nitrile, *n*-nonyl cyanide. Colorless liquid, b.243.7, insoluble in water.

caproaldehyde. $(CH_2)_4CHO = 100.09$. Hexanal, *n*-hexoic aldehyde. Colorless liquid, b.131.

caproate. A salt of caproic acid, containing the radical $C_5H_{11}COO—$.

caproic acid. $Me(CH_2)_4COOH = 116.13$. Butylacetic acid, *n*-hexoic acid, *n*-hexylic acid, pentylformic acid. A fatty acid in animal fats. Colorless liquid, b.205.7, slightly soluble in water. **α-amino-** Norleucine. **α,ε-diamino-** Lysine. **α-hydroxy-** Leucinic acid. **iso-** $Me_2CH(CH_2)_2COOH$. Dimethylbutyric acid. A liquid d.0.925, b.208. **γ-keto-** Homolevulinic acid. **pseudo-**$MeCMe_2 \cdot CH_2COOH$. *tert-* Butylacetic acid. A liquid, m.—11, b.190. **secondary-** $Et_2CHCOOH$. Diethylacetic acid. A liquid, b.197. **secondary active-** $Me(CH_2)_2 \cdot CH-MeCOOH$. Methylpropylacetic acid. A liquid, b.193.5. **tertiary-** $Me_2CEtCOOH$. Dimethylacetic acid. A liquid, b.187.

caproin. A compound of glycerin and caproic acid; e.g., glyceryl tricaproate, dicaproin (glyceryl dicaproate).

Caprokol. $C_6H_3(OH)_2C_6H_{13} = 194.2$. Trademark for 4-hexylresorcinol. Colorless crystals; a urinary antiseptic having 40 times the germicidal power of phenol.

caprolactam. The monomer for nylon 6.

caprone. $C_{11}H_{22}O = 170.2$. 6-Hen-decanone*. A volatile ketone from butter.

capronic acid. Caproic acid.

capronitrile. Amyl cyanide.

capronium. Ytterbium.

capronyl. The radical $C_5H_{11}CO—$, from caproic acid. **c. chloride.** $C_6H_{11}OCl = 134.6$. Colorless liquid, b.138.

caprophyl. Dung bacteria.

caproyl. The radical $C_7H_{15}CO—$, from caprylic acid. **c. acetate.** Octyl acetate. **c. alcohol.** Octyl alcohol. **c. aldehyde.** Capraldehyde. **c. chloride.** $C_7H_{15}COCl = 162.57$. Colorless liquid, b.196.

capryl. Hexyl. The radical $C_6H_{13}—$, from hexane. **c. alcohol.** Hexyl alcohol. **c. amine.** $C_6H_{13}NH_2 = 101.1$. Hexylamine. A poisonous ptomaine from decomposed yeast or rancid animal oils. **c. hydride.** Hexane.

caprylate. A salt of caprylic acid.

caprylene. Octene.

caprylic acid. $Me(CH_2)_6COOH = 144.17$. Hexylacetic acid, *n*-octoic acid, octylic acid. A fatty acid in butter. Colorless leaflets, m.16, slightly soluble in water. **iso-** CEt_3COOH. Triethylacetic acid. A solid, m.39.5, b.202. **c. alcohol.** Octyl alcohol. **c. aldehyde.** $Me(CH_2)_6CHO = 128.12$. Octanal. Colorless liquid, b$_{32mm}$81; in citron.

caprylidene. $Me(CH_2)_5C\ddot{.}CH = 110.11$. Octine, *n*-hexylacetylene. A liquid, b.125.

caprylin. A compound of glycerin and caprylic acid, e.g., tricaprylin (glyceryl tricaprylate).

capryryl. Octanoyl. The radical $Me(CH_2)_6CO—$, from caprylic acid. **c. chloride.** $C_7H_{15}COCl = 162.57$. Octanoyl chloride. Colorless liquid, b. 163.

capsaicin. $C_{18}H_{27}O_3N = 305.3$. A bitter principle, m.65, from capsicum. Cf. *zingerone*.

capsanthin. $C_{40}H_{58}O_3 = 586.4$. The red carotinoid pigment of paprika, m.175.

capsic acid. An active principle of pimenta.

capsicin. An oleoresin from capsicum. Brown masses, soluble in alcohol; a stimulant, anodyne, and rubefacient.

capsicine. An alkaloid from capsicum.

capsicol. The essential oil of capsicum.

capsicum. Cayenne pepper, chili, pepper red. The unripe fruits of *Capsicum fastigiatum, C. annuum*, and other Solanaceae; a local stimulant and condiment. Cf. *paprika*. **c. resin.** An oleoresin from *Capsicum*; a circulatory stimulant and heart tonic.

capsularin. $C_{22}H_{36}O_8 = 428.3$. A glucoside in jute leaf, *Corchorus capsularis* (Tiliaceae). Colorless needles m.175.

capsule. (1) A membranous sac enclosing a structural part of an organism. (2) A small sealed container for volatile compounds. (3) More specifically, in pharmacy, a medicament in a closed shell, e.g., methylcellulose or gelatin, which is soluble in water at 37°.

capsuloesic acid. Aescinic acid.

captan. *N*-(Trichloromethylthio)tetrahydrophthalimide. A fungicide, particularly against apple scab.

caput. Pl. capita. A head. **c. mortuum.** (1) Early name for the earthy residue from distillation or incineration. (2) Calcothar.

caracolite. $PbOHCl \cdot Na_2SO_4$. An orthorhombic native double salt.

caraguata. The fiber from *Eryngium pandanifolium* (Umbelliferae), S. America; used for ropes, matting, and bags.

carajura. A red pigment from *Begonia chica*; a source of carajurin.

carajurin. $C_{17}H_{14}O_5 = 298.11$. The principal colored constituent of carajura.

carajutin. $C_{15}H_{10}O_5 = 270.08$. A derivative of carajurin. Scarlet needles.

caramel. $(C_{12}H_{18}O_9)x$. Obtained by heating sugar to about 200, in presence of ammonium salts. A dark brown soluble mass; a coloring matter for food and beverages.

caramelan. A brown amorphous constituent of caramel. It forms soluble salts with lead and alkalies; is hydrolyzed by dilute acids to dextrose, furfural, and levulic acid; and reduces Fehling's solution.

carana. Mararo, caranna, gum carana. A gray resin, *Urotium carana* (Rutaceae), S. America.

caranda wax. A wax from *Copernical australis*, Brazil; m.82, d$_{25}$°0.984, acid val. 2.7, iodine val. 10.5; similar to carnauba wax.

carane. $C_{10}H_{18} = 138.2$. 3,7,7-Trimethylbicyclo-[0.1.4]heptane. A constituent of essential oils. $Δ^3$- Carene. **amino-** Carylamine. **hydroxy-** Carol. **keto-** Carone.

c. amine. Carylamine. **c. diol.** $C_{10}H_{18}O_2 = 170.2$. Dihydroxycarane, in Indian turpentine. **c. ol.** Carol.

caraneol. Carol.

caranna. Carana.

carase. Papain.

carat. Karat. A unit of weight of precious stones and the fineness of gold. Based on the ancient use of seeds of the locust pod tree, *Ceratoria siliqua*, which are remarkably uniform in weight. Standard of pure gold is 24 c.; e.g., 15 c. gold contains 9 pts. base metal: i.e., 37.5% of gold. 1 c. = 205 mg or 3.163 troy grains. **English-** 3.1683 gm = 205.31 mg. Defined by the British Board of Trade in

1888. **metric-** The international c., weighing 0.200 gm. 200.000 mg = 3.086 grains. It is subdivided into points (1 point = 0.01 c.) and pearl grains (1 p.g. = 0.25 c.). Compulsory in the U.K. in 1914.

caraway. The fruits of *Carum carvi* (Umbelliferae); an aromatic, stimulant and flavoring. **c. oil.** The essential oil of c. seeds, d.0.907–0.915, b.180–230; used for flavoring. **c. water.** Aqua carum: Water flavored with c. oil.

carbachol. (U.S.P.). $C_6H_{15}N_2O_2Cl$ = 182.66. Carbamylcholine chloride (B.P.), choryl, moryl. White, hygroscopic crystals, m.203, soluble in water; used in ophthalmology.

carbacidometer. Air tester.

carbagel. Calcium chloride on porous carbon; a desiccant.

carbamamidine. Guanidine.

carbamase. An enzyme, splitting proteins to amines.

carbamate. A salt of carbamic acid; it contains the NH_2COO- radical. **ethyl-** Urethane.

carbamic. The radical $-NH \cdot COO-$, from carbamic acid. **c. esters.** Urethanes.

carbamic acid. NH_2COOH. Amidocarbonic acid, aminoformic acid. The simplest amino acid, known as its salts (carbamates). Cf. *thionamic acid*. **amino-** Carbazic acid. **carbamyl-** Allophanic acid. **cyano-** See *cyano c*. **dithio-** See *dithio c*. **nitro-** See *nitro c*. **phenyl-** Carbanilic acid.

carbamide. An isomer of urea, q.v. **c. chloride.** Carbamyl chloride.

carbamidine. Guanidine.

carbamido. Ureido (U.K. usage), uramido, uramino. The radical NH_2CONH-, from urea. **phenyl-** The radical $PhNH \cdot CO \cdot NH-$.

carbaminate. Carbamate.

carbamonitrile. Cyanamide.

carbamoyl. The radical NH_2CO- from carbamic acid. **c. carbamic acid.** Allophanic acid. **c. chloride.** NH_2COCl = 79.48. Carbamide chloride. Colorless needles, m.50, insoluble in water. Cf. *Friedel-Crafts reaction*. **c. cyanide.** Oxamonitrile.

carbamylic ester. Phenylurethane.

carbanil. Phenyl cyanate. **c. aldehyde.** Formanilide.

carbanilide. $PhNH \cdot CO \cdot NHPh$ = 212.25. Diphenylurea. Colorless needles, m.236, slightly soluble in water.

carbanilino- Phenylcarbamyl. Prefix for the radical $PhNHCO-$.

carbanilo- Prefix for the radical $PhNH-$. **c. nitrile.** Cyanoanilide.

carbanion. (1) Carbonate ion, $CO_3^=$ (obsolete). (2) The ion R_3C^-.

carbarsone. $C_7H_9N_2O_4As$ = 260.08. *N*-Carbamylarsanilic acid, *p*-carbaminophenylarsonic acid. White powder, insoluble in water; an antiprotozoan. Cf. *tryparsamide, acetarsol*.

carbates. General name for the substituted dithiocarbamates.

carbazide. A compound containing the $-NH \cdot NH \cdot CO \cdot NH \cdot NH-$ radical. **semi-** A compound containing the $NH_2CO \cdot NH \cdot NH-$ radical. **sulfo-** A compound containing the $-NH \cdot NH \cdot CS \cdot NH \cdot NH-$ radical. **sulfosemi-** A compound containing the $NH_2CS \cdot NH \cdot NH-$ radical.

carbazole. $C_{12}H_9N$ = 167.1. Dibenzopyrrole, di-

phenylenimide. $C_6H_4 \diagdown \overset{NH}{\diagup} C_6H_4$. Colorless crystals, m. 245; an explosives stabilizer. **acetyl-** See *acetyl c*. **N-ethyl-** $C_{14}H_{14}N$ = 196.2. Colorless crystals, m.68. **hexahydro-** $C_{12}H_{15}N$ = 173.2. Colorless crystals, m.99. **N-methyl-** $C_{13}H_{12}N$ = 182.1. Colorless crystals, m.87. **naphthopheno-** See *naphthophenocarbazole*. **tetrahydro-** $C_{12}H_{13}N$ = 171.12. Colorless crystals, m.119.

carbazone. A compound containing the $-N:N \cdot CO \cdot NH \cdot NH-$ radical. **sulfo-** A compound containing the $-N:N \cdot CS \cdot NH \cdot NH-$ radical.

carbazotate. Picrate.

carbazyl. The radical $C_{12}H_8N-$ from carbazole; 5 isomers.

carbazylic acid. An organic acid of the type $RC(:NH)NH_2$.

carbene. (1) Cuprene. (2) The radical R_2C. (3) Methylene.

carbenes. Constituents of bitumen, insoluble in carbon tetrachloride, soluble in carbon disulfide. Cf. *asphaltenes*.

carbenoid. Describing the properties of a carbene.

carbenzol. A phenolic distillate from shale tar containing phenols; used to treat skin diseases.

carbethoxy. The radical $-COOEt$. Cf. *carbomethoxy*.

carbethoxymino. Urethane. The radical $-NH \cdot CO_2Et$.

carbethylic acid. Ethyl carbonate.

carbide. Carbonide, carburet. Cf. *acetylide*. A binary carbon compound of a metal. With water, carbides give acetylene (Li_4C); methane (Al_2C); hydrogen and methane (MgC_2); or a mixture of hydrogen, methane, and acetylene (rare-earth carbides). Carbides of the rare metals form solid, liquid, or gaseous compounds; some carbides (as SiC, Ti_xC_y) are extremely stable. Cf. *Crystolon, Carboloy*.

carbimazole. $C_7H_{10}O_2N_2S$ = 186.20. 1-Ethoxycarbonyl-2,3-dihydro-3-methyl-2-thioimidazole. White bitter crystals, with characteristic odor, m.123, slightly soluble in water; an antibiotic (B.P.).

carbimide. Isocyanic acid.

carbinol. Primary alcohol. General formula $R \cdot CH_2 \cdot OH$. (1) The radical $-CH_2OH$, of primary alcohols. (2) Methanol. (3) Acetylmethylcarbinol, responsible for the flavor of butter. **acetyl-** Acetol. **allyl-** Δ^3-*l*-Butenol. **anthryl-** Anthracene carbinol. **benzyl-** Phenethyl alcohol. **butyl-** *primary-* Amyl alcohol *secondary-* 2-Methyl-1-butanol *tertiary-* 2-Dimethylpropanol. **diethyl-** 3-Pentanol. **dimethyl-** *secondary-* Propanol. **diphenyl-** Benzohydrol. **ethyl-** Propanol. **hexamethyl-** 2-Octanol. **methyl-** Ethanol. **phenyl-** Benzyl alcohol. **propyl-** *n*-Butyl alcohol, *n*-butanol. **triethyl-** 3-Ethyl-3-pentanol. **trimethyl-** *tert*-Butyl alcohol, *tert*-butanol.

Carbitol. $EtO(CH_2)_2 \cdot O \cdot (CH_2)_2OH$ = 134.11. Trademark for diethylene glycol ethyl ether. Colorless liquid, b.195, soluble in water; used as a solvent and in cosmetics. **butyl-** $BuO(CH_2)_2OCH_2CH_2OH$ = 162.2. Diethylene glycol butyl ether. Colorless liquid, b.222; a solvent.

carbo. Charcoal. **c. animalis.** Charcoal from animal matter; a decolorizing agent. **c. lignius.** Wood charcoal. Used for decolorizing solutions, and in blowpipe analysis. **c. sanguinarius.** Blood coal. Charcoal from animal blood.

carbobenzoyl. A compound containing the radical —CO·C$_6$H$_4$COOH. **c. acetic acid.** Colorless, m.90. **c. formic acid.** Phthalonic acid. **c. propionic acid.** Colorless, m. 137.

carbocinchomeronic acid. Cinchomeronic acid.

carbocyanines. Dyes used as photographic sensitizers; e.g., pinacyanol. Cf. *cyanine.*

carbocyclic. Describing a homocyclic ring compound in which all the ring atoms are carbon, e.g., benzene.

carbodiazone. A compound containing the radical —N:N·CO·N:N—. **sulfo-** A compound containing the radical —N:N·CS·N:N—.

Carbofrax. Trademark for certain silicon carbide refractories bonded by other ceramics.

carbohydrase. An enzyme which splits carbohydrates.

carbohydrates. C$_x$(H$_2$O)$_y$. Organic compounds synthesized by plants. They contain C, with H and O in the proportion of water. Monosaccharides: x and y are 2, 3, 4, 5, 6, or 7; e.g., glycerose. Disaccharides: x is 12, y is 11; e.g., lactose. Trisaccharides: x is 18, y is 16; e.g., raffinose. Polysaccharides: x and y exceed 18; e.g., dextrin, cellulose. Natural c. are generally dextrorotatory, except fructose and inosite. Conjugated saccharides: (1) gums and mucilage group (saccharides and acids); (2) glucosides, q.v. (saccharides and another compound); (3) tannins, q.v. (saccharides and tannins).

carbohydrazidine. See *oxidiimide dihydrazide.*

carbohydrazones. Carbazides.

carbohydride. Hydrocarbon.

carboids. Kerotenes.

carbolate. Phenate. A phenol ester; contains the radical PhO—.

carbolfuchsin. Ziehl's stain: fuchsin 5, phenol 25, alcohol 50, water 500 pts.

carbolic acid. Phenol. **c. liquid.** Cresylic acid. **c. oil.** The phenolic fraction of coal tar, b.180–230.

carbolmethyl violet. A microscope stain: 10 pts. alcoholic methyl violet 6B, 90 pts. of 5% aqueous phenol solution.

Carbolon. Trademark for silicon carbide.

Carboloy. Trademark for cemented tungsten carbide; used for high-speed machine tools and second in hardness to diamond.

carbolxylene. A clearing solution: 3 pts. xylene, 1 pt. phenol.

carbometer. A device to measure carbon dioxide in air.

carbomethene. Ketene.

carbomethoxy. The radical —COOMe. Cf. *carbethoxy.*

carbon. C = 12.011. At. no. 6. A nonmetallic bioelement; 3 allotropes: amorphous (coal), graphite, and crystalline (diamond). It occurs native as coal, graphite, and diamond; in combination with hydrogen as petroleum, with oxygen as c. dioxide. The isotope C^{14} (half-life period, 5,750 years) is produced by irradiation of tellurium nitride, and is a source of labeled organic compounds used as tracer compounds, e.g., in medicine, and for dating geological and archeological specimens; e.g., the Dead Sea Scrolls were dated 20 B.C. C^{12}, the natural dominant isotope of c. is now the basis of the scale of atomic weights of the elements; i.e., C^{12} = 12. Cf. *isotopes.* C. is an element essential to vegetable and animal life. Its principal valency is 4, but a few compounds of mono-, di-, and trivalent c. have been prepared. Its atoms have a greater affinity for one another than for other atoms, and give rise to numerous different (organic) compounds, owing to its valency of 4. The binary compounds are: carbides, M$_x$C$_y$; hydrocarbons, C$_x$H$_y$; carbon-x-ides, C$_x$H$_y$; carbonyls, CO$^-$. **amorphous-** C. as minute graphite-like crystallites **graphitic-** The loss on ignition of graphite below its fusion point in air. **whetlerized-** C. containing 5–12% Cu, to increase its absorbency. Cf. *activated c., gas c., charcoal, graphite, diamond, lampblack.*

c. apparatus. An instrument to determine total c. in fuels. **c. atom.** Tetrahedronal c. *asymmetric-* C. linked to 4 different types of atoms or radicals. *primary-* C. having one bond satisfied by c. *quaternary-* C. surrounded by 4 c. atoms. *secondary-* C. linked to 2 c. atoms. *tertiary-* C. linked to 3 c. atoms. **c. bisulfide.** C. disulfide. **c. black.** Lampblack. **c. bond.** The nonpolar electronic linkage between 2 c. atoms. It may be electrically neutral, negative, or positive. **c. bronze.** An alloy for bearings. **c. chains.** A succession of linked c. atoms in a compound. *closed-* Aromatic compounds. *open-* Aliphatic compounds. **c. compounds.** See *organic compounds.* Characteristics: (1) nonpolarity: they do not ionize; their reactions are molecular and have a low velocity; (2) polymerism; (3) isomerism and asymmetry; (4) combustibility: all c. atoms are oxidized to c. dioxide and other products. **c. cycle.** The circulation of c. between a living organism and the surrounding environments:

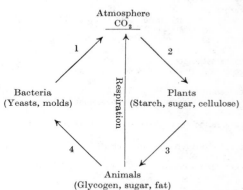

Atmosphere
CO$_2$

Bacteria (Yeasts, molds)

Respiration

Plants (Starch, sugar, cellulose)

Animals (Glycogen, sugar, fat)

(1) *Bacterial action,* (2) *photosynthesis,* (3) *metabolism,* (4) *decay.*

c. dichloride. C$_2$Cl$_4$ = 165.84. Ethylene perchloride. Colorless liquid, b.122. **c. dioxide.** CO$_2$ = 44.01. Carbonic acid gas, carbonic anhydride. Heavy, colorless incombustible gas, d$_{air}$1.53, m.−65, b.$_{.5.3atm}$−56, soluble in water. Shipped as compressed liquid in steel tanks, and used for carbonating beverages, in refrigerators and fire extinguishers, for destruction of vermin, and as a fertilizer. Cf. Dry Ice. **c. disulfide.** CS$_2$ = 76.13.

Colorless liquid with characteristic odor, b.46.2, slightly soluble in water; a local anesthetic, and a solvent for sulfur, iodine, rubber. **c. group.** The fourth group of the periodic system, q.v. **c. hexachloride.** $C_2Cl_6 = 236.77$. C. trichloride, ethyl perchloride, hexachloroethane. Colorless crystals, m.182, b.187, insoluble in water. **c. isotopes.** C. has 5 isotopes of atomic weights 10–14; C^{12} and C^{13} only are stable. C^{13} is used as a tracer element in nutritional work. **c. light.** An electric arc light with C. electrodes. **c. monosulfide.** $CS = 44.04$. Colorless gas, b.–130, very unstable and polymerizes to a red solid. **c. monoxide.** $CO = 28.01$. Colorless poisonous gas, b.–190, slightly soluble in water, formed during incomplete combustion of C. **c. oxysulfide.** $COS = 60.07$. Carbonyl sulfide. Colorless gas, b.50.2, slightly soluble in water, explosive in air. **c. paper.** A tissue paper coated with a mixture of a wax and a black pigment (often c. black); used to make copies of writing. **c. print.** A photographic process for artistic reproductions of negatives. **c. residue.** Conradson c. The amount of c. produced from a lubricating oil heated in a closed crucible under standard conditions. **c. subnitride.** Acetylene dinitrile. **c. suboxide.** $O:C:C:C:O = 68.02$. A pungent lacrimatory colorless gas, b.7, decomp. by water to malonic acid. **c. subsulfide.** $C_3S_2 = 100.0$. Red pungent liquid, m.–0.5, polymerized by heat. **c. tetrabromide.** $CBr_5 = 331.85$. Tetrabromomethane*. Colorless scales, d.3.42, m.92, insoluble in water. **c. tetrachloride.** $CCl_4 = 153.84$. Tetrachloromethane*, phenoxin, Pyrex. Colorless liquid, b.76, slightly soluble in water. A local anesthetic, fire extinguisher, nonflammable solvent, cleaning agent, (benzene substitute), and reagent. **c. tetrafluoride.** $CF_4 = 88.0$. Tetrafluoromethane*, fluoromethane, Colorless gas, b.–126, by-product in the manufacture of aluminum from cryolite. **c. tetraiodide.** $CI_4 = 519.84$. Tetraiodomethane*. Red crystals. $d_{20}°4.32$, decomp. by heat, insoluble in water. **c. trichloride.** Hexachloroethane.

carbonaceous. Containing carbon.

carbonado. Bort. A hard, black cutting diamond.

carbonatation. Formation of carbonates by carbon dioxide. Cf. *carbonation*.

carbonate. A salt of the theoretical carbonic acid, containing the radical $CO_3=$. Carbonates are readily decomposed by acids. The carbonates of the alkali metals are water-soluble; all others are insoluble. **bi-** Acid c. A salt containing the radical $HCO_3—$. **chloro-** See *chloro-c.* **c. minerals.** Rock-forming minerals; as, calcite, $CaCO_3$; dolomite, $CaMg(CO_3)_2$; magnesite, $MgCO_3$; siderite, $FeCO_3$.

carbonation. (1) Carbonization. (2) The precipitation of lime by carbon dioxide, e.g., in sugar refining. (3) The saturation of water with carbon dioxide, e.g., in soda-water manufacture.

carbonic. A compound containing tetravalent carbon. Cf. *carbonium.*

carbonic acid. (1) $HO·COOH$. *m*-Carbonic acid, hydroxyformic acid. The hypothetical acid of carbon dioxide and water; known only as its salts (carbonates), acid salts (bicarbonates), amides (carbamic acid) and acid chlorides (carbonyl chloride). (2) An old term for carboxylic acid.

ortho- $C(OH)_4$. Exists only as compounds, e.g., esters.

c. acid ester. An organic compound in which the H of c. acid is substituted by a radical. *meta*-Compounds of the general formula $RO·CO·OR$. *ortho*- Compounds of the general formula $C(OR)_4$.

c. acid hydrate. $CO_2·6H_2O$.

carbonic anhydrase. An intracellular enzyme occurring in high concentrations in red-blood corpuscles. It catalyzes the reversal of the reaction $CO_2 + H_2O \rightleftharpoons H_2CO_3$.

carbonic anhydride. Carbonic acid.

carbonic ester. Carbonic acid ester. **ethyl-** $CO(OEt)_2 = 118.1$. Colorless liquid, b.126. **ethylene-** $CO(OC_2H_3)_2 = 114.1$. Colorless crystals, m.39. **methyl-** $CO(OMe)_2 = 90.1$. Colorless liquid, b.91. **methylethyl-** $EtO·CO·OMe = 104.1$. Colorless liquid, b.109. **methylpropyl-** $PrO·CO·OMe = 118.1$. Colorless liquid, b.131.

carbonic ether. Ethyl carbonate.

carbonide. Carbide.

carboniferous. (1) Containing carbon. (2) Belonging to the coal age; see *geologic era*.

carbonite. (1) Small charcoal briquettes. (2) A high explosive: nitroglycerin 17–30, sodium nitrite 24–30, flour 37–44%.

carbonitrile. Cyanide, nitrile. The radical —CN, indicated by the prefix *cyano-*, or the suffix *-nitrile* or *-carbonitrile*.

carbonium. Describing: (1) a compound with divalent or trivalent carbon, associated with chemical color and reactivity; (2) the ion R_3C^+.

carbonization. (1) The transformation of organic matter into charcoal. (2) The distillation of coal, as in gas manufacture. **high temperature-** Heating coal out of air at 1000–1300°C, with the formation of gas, tar, oil, ammonia, and coke. **low temperature-** Heating coal at 450–700°C, with the formation of gas, petroleum (hydrocarbons from pentane to octane, and amylene to octene), and coke.

carbonize. To convert to carbon by charring or burning incompletely.

carbonizer. Concentrated aluminum chloride solution; removes cellulose from wool.

carbonoid. A suggested tetragonal structure of carbon, with 4 faces, one for each valency. Cf. *benzenoid.*

carbonometer. A device to determine the carbonic acid content of blood. Cf. *carbometer.*

carbonoxysulfide. Carbon oxysulfide.

carbon rheostat. An electrical resistance consisting of a number of carbon plates mounted so that pressure can be placed on them by a screw and their total resistance thus altered.

carbonyl. The radical =CO. Cf. *carbonyls, thionyl*. **c. amidophenol.** Oxybenzoazole. **c. bromide.** $COBr_2 = 187.83$. Bromophosgene. Poisonous liquid, b.64.5. **c. chloride.** $COCl_2 = 98.92$. Phosgene. Poisonous gas, b.8.2, decomp. by water; an important chemical intermediate, e.g., in the manufacture of polyurethane resins. World production (1960), 10,000 tons. **c. dioxy.** The radical —O·CO·O—. **c. diurea.** $(NH_2·CO·NH)_2·CO = 146.06$. Triuret. White crystals, m.232, insoluble in water. Cf. *biuret.* **c. hemoglobin.** A highly poisonous combination of carbon monoxide and hemoglobin. **c. pyrrole.** $CO(C_4H_4N)_2 = 160.1$.

Colorless crystals, m.63. **c. sulfide.** Carbon oxysulfide. **c. thiocarbonanilide.** $C_2ON_2SPh = 254.1$. Colorless crystals, m.87. **thio-c. thiocarboanilide.** $C_2N_2S_2Ph_2 = 270.1$. Colorless crystals, m.79.

carbonyles. Carboxides. Compounds of carbon monoxide and metals, some volatile; as, nickel carbonyl.

carboraffin. An activated charcoal, used chiefly for decolorizing sugar solutions.

Carborundum. Trademark for certain silicon carbide and other abrasives.

carbosant. $(C_{15}H_{23})\cdot O\cdot COO(C_{15}H_{23}) = 466.37$. Santalyl carbonate. Carbonic acid ester of sandalwood oil. Yellow oil, insoluble in water.

Carbosorb. A grade of Ascarite.

carbostyril. $C_9H_7ON = 145.15$. 2-Hydroxyquinoline, 2(1)-quinolone. Colorless prisms, m.199, slightly soluble in water. **ethyl-** See *ethyl-c.* **hydro-** $C_9H_9ON = 147.15$. Colorless crystals, m.163. **hydroiso-** $C_9H_9ON = 147.15$. Crystals, m.71. **iso-** $C_9H_7ON = 145.15$. Crystals, m.208. **methyl-** Lepidone. **nitro-** $C_9H_6O_3N_2 = 190.2$. Colorless crystals, m.168. **octohydro-** $C_9H_{15}ON = 153.19$. Crystals, m.151. **oxy-** $C_9H_7O_2N = 161.16$. Colorless crystals, m.300. **pseudo-** $C_9H_7ON = 145.15$.

carbostyrilic acid. Kynuric acid.

Carboxide. (1) Trademark for a mixture of ethylene oxide 1 and carbon dioxide 9 pts; a fumigant for insects in grain, tobacco, etc. (2) (not cap.) Carbonyl (obsolete). (3) (not cap.) The keto group.

carbox metal. The alloy: Pb 84, Sb 14, Fe 1, Zn 1%.

carboxy. Carboxyl.

carboxyhemoglobin. A compound of carbon monoxide and hemoglobin formed in the blood by carbon monoxide poisoning.

carboxyl. Oxatyl, carboxy. The acidic —COOH group. It determines the basicity of an organic acid. **c. nitrogen.** See *nitrogen.*

carboxylase. A yeast enzyme which splits the carboxyl group into carbon dioxide. **co-** Vitamin B_1 pyrophosphate.

carboxylic acid. A compound of the type R—COOH. See *acids, carbazylic* acid. Cf. *carbylic acid.*

carboxymethylcellulose. See *sodium c.m.c.*

carboy. Demijohn. A 10- to 13-gal glass flask protected by wickerwork; used for acids, etc. **c. inclinator.** A support to enable a c. to be inclined and emptied easily.

carbromal. Adaline.

carbro process. A method of making color prints from color photographs.

Carbrosolide. Trade name for silicon carbide.

carburation. (1) Carbonization as applied to internal combustion engines. (2) Carburization.

carburet. Carbide.

carburetor, carburettor. (1) A device for making illuminating gas by spraying oil on hot surfaces over which water gas passes. (2) The part of the internal combustion engine where full vaporization occurs.

carburite. A mixture of equal parts carbon and iron, for recarburizing steel in the electric furnace.

carburization. The dissolution of carbon in molten metals; as, steel produced by heating in a stream of carbon monoxide. **case-** Carburization on the surface.

c. gas. The production of a toughened surface layer of high-carbon steel by heating steel components in a carbon-rich gas.

carburizing. Carburization.

carburolith. A solid safety fuel which excludes flammable vapor under pressure. It consists of petroleum with 3% of a stabilizer (sodium silicate mixed with copper alginate and an excess of ammonia).

carbylamine*. (1) Isocyanide. (2) Ethylisocyanide.

carbylic acid. An organic acid which has carbon in its acid radical; as: **ammonia-** $R\cdot CNH\cdot NH_2$, carbazylic. **aquo-** $R\cdot COOH$, carboxylic. **thio-** $R\cdot CSSH$, dithionic. Cf. *siliconic acid, stannonic acid.*

carcel unit. The brightness of the carcel lamp, burning 42 gm of colza oil per hour. 1 carcel unit = 9.6 candles = 7.5 German standard candles, q.v.

carcinogen. A substance which produces cancer in living tissues; as, benzopyrene.

carcinolipin. A crystalline lipoid factor in egg yolk having carcinogenic properties.

carcinoma. A tumor originating from malignant epithelial cells, e.g., skin cancer (epithelioma).

carcinomic acid. An unsaturated fatty acid in cancerous serum and tissue.

cardaissin. A substance extracted from suprarenal glands of cows; a heart stimulant.

cardamom. The seeds of *Elettaria cardamomum* (Zingiberaceae), tropical Asia; an aromatic and a spice. **c. oil.** The essential oil of c., d.0.895–0.905; it contains terpinene, dipentene, and limonene. **Malabar-** d.0.933–0.943; contains cineol. **Siam-** d.0.905; contains borneol.

Cardanol. $C_{20}H_{32}O = 288.30$. m-$C_{14}H_{27}\cdot C_6H_4\cdot OH$. Trademark for a liquid obtained by the distillation of cashew-nut juice, $b_{10mm}225$. Its esters are plasticizers.

cardanolide. Cardogenan. Describing the fully saturated system of digitaloid lactones; the configuration at the 20-position is the same as in cholesterol. Cf. *steroid.*

cardiac. Pertaining to the heart ($\chi\alpha\rho\delta\iota\alpha$ = heart). **c. sedative.** A drug which lessens the frequency of heart action, as, aconite. **c. stimulant.** A drug which increases the force and frequency of the heartbeat, as, digitalis.

cardiazole. Pentamethylenetetrazole.

carding. An operation in the manufacture of woolen felts which opens up the material, mixes the fibers, and removes foreign matter, by the action of wire brushes.

cardiogram. The tracing produced by a cardiograph. **electro-** A photographic record of the electric heart currents, which deflect a galvanometer mirror that reflects light onto photographic paper.

cardiograph. A device to record the movement of the heart, especially its force and character; a small diaphragm placed over the heart or artery transmits the heartbeat by air pressure to a recording diaphragm. **electro-** A sensitive galvanometer to measure the electric pulsations of the heart.

cardioid. Heart-shaped. **c. condenser.** A device to concentrate light in the ultramicroscope.

cardogenan. Cardanolide.

Cardol. $C_{21}H_{30}O_2 = 314.3$. Trademark for an irritant phenolic oil liquid from the shell of *Anacardium occidentale*, cashew nuts.

carene. $C_{10}H_{16} = 136.2$. 4,7,7-Trimethyl-Δ^3-norcarene. A terpene group in essential oils. **d-** Colorless, sweet-smelling oil, d.0.8586, b.170; in Indian turpentine.

Carex. Red couch grass. A perennial grasslike herb (Cyperaceae).

Cargau. Trade name for a protein synthetic fiber.

cargentos. Colloidal silver oxide containing a little casein; a germicide.

Carica. The papaw or melon tree. *Carica papaya* (Caricacae), S. America. Cf. *papaya.* **c. xanthin.** Kryptoxanthin.

caricin. (1) A glucoside from the seeds of carica. Cf. *papain.* (2) A protease, papain.

cariogenetic. Producing dental caries. Cf. *carcinogenetic.*

Carissa. A genus of spiny shrubs (Apocynaceae), Asia and Australia.

carissin. A glucoside from *Carissa ovata*, a cardiac stimulant.

caritinoid. Carotenoid.

Carius, Georg Ludwig. 1829–1875. German chemist. **C. furnace.** A combustion furnace with 5 iron tubes.

carlic acid. $C_{10}H_{10}O_6 = 226.1$. An acid from the mold *Penicillium Charlesii.* Cf. *carolic acid.*

carlosic acid. $C_{10}H_{12}O_6 = 228.1$. An acid from the fungus. *Penicillium Charlesii.*

Carlsbad salt. (1) Natural. Sal carolinum genuinum, sal thermarum carolinarum. The salts obtained by evaporation of the water of the springs at Karlovy Vary (Carlsbad), Czechoslovakia. (2) Artificial. Sal carolinum factitium. Sal carlsbadense. A mixture of thenardite 44, potassium sulfate 2, sodium chloride 18, sodium carbonate 36%.

Carl's solution. An insect preservative: 170 ml 95% alcohol, 60 ml 40% formaldehyde, 20 ml glacial acetic acid, 280 ml water. Cf. *fixative.*

carminative. A drug relieving colic, and promoting gas expulsion from the gastrointestinal tract.

carmine. Coccinellin. Natural Red 4 (Color Index). A mixture of carminic acids, c. red, and other substances obtained by precipitating a decoction of cochineal with alum. Bright red, friable pieces, soluble in ammonia water; a microscopical stain. **ammonia-** A solution of c. in ammonia water. **blue-** See *indigo* c. **borax-** An alkaline c. strain containing borax, to stain the cell nuclei. **indigo-** See *indigo* c. **lithium-** See *Orth's* stain. **c. lake.** A compound of c. and alumina. **c. red.** $C_{11}H_{12}O_7 = 256.1$. Purple lustrous crystals, a split product of carminic acid; a microscope stain.

carminic acid. $C_{22}H_{20}O_{13} = 492.15$. Cochinilin. A glucosidal hydroxyanthrapurpurin derivative from cochineal. Purple crystals, m.136, soluble in water; a reagent for albumin and aluminum, a microscope stain, and pH indicator changing at pH 5.5 red (acid) to magenta (alkaline).

carminite. A lead ore containing phosphates, arsenates, and vanadates.

carmoisine. A carmine-red dye used in foodstuffs.

carnallite. $KCl \cdot MgCl_2 \cdot 6H_2O = 277.85$. A native, potassium, magnesium chloride (Stassfurt, Germany). Cf. *sylvine.* **ammonium-** The mineral $MgCl_2 \cdot NH_4Cl \cdot 6H_2O$.

carnauba. (1) The Brazilian wax palm, *Copernicia ceriferai;* or (2) its root; an alternative. **c. wax.** Brazil wax. A wax mainly myricyl cerotate, obtained from the young leaves of c. Yellow masses, m.83–88; a polish (U.S.P.).

carnaubic acid. $C_{23}H_{47}COOH = 368.37$. In carnauba wax and beef kidney, m.72.

carnaubyl alcohol. $C_{24}H_{49}OH = 354.39$. A constituent of carnauba wax and wool fat, m.69, insoluble in water.

carnegieite. $Na_2Al_2Si_2O_8$. A sodium feldspar.

carnegine. $C_{13}H_{19}O_2 = 221.15$. An alkaloid from Cactaceae; a dimethyl derivative of salsoline, q.v. Cf. *dioscorine.*

carnelian. Cornelian.

carneol. Cornelian (obsolete).

carnine. $C_7H_8O_3N_4 \cdot H_2O = 214.2$. A crystalline alkaloid from muscles, meat extract, yeast, and certain fishes; slightly soluble in water. Cf. *xanthine.*

carnitine. $Me_3 \cdot N \cdot CH_2 \cdot CHOH \cdot CH_2 \cdot CO = 161.2$.

Novain, vitamin B_T, γ-trimethyl-β-oxybutyrobetaine. A base found in the muscle tissue of cephalopods. Soluble in water or alcohol. Its absence affects the development of flour beetles. Cf. *crotonbetaine.*

carnomuscarine. A nitrogeneous extractive of muscles.

carnosine. $C_9H_{14}O_3N_4 = 226.3$. Ignotine, β-alanyl-histidine. Colorless crystals, from meat extracts, m.219 (decomp.). Cf. *anserine.*

Carnot, Sadi. 1796–1832. French engineer. **C. function.** The ratio between the lost and utilized heat of a living body. **C. theorem.** The work obtainable from a given quantity of heat absorbed in a machine that is working in a reversible cycle depends only on the temperatures of the source of heat and refrigerator.

carnotite. A radioactive mineral vanadate of uranium and potassium, (23% V).

Carnoy's fluid. A mixture of absolute alcohol and glacial acetic acid used to fix animal tissues before staining.

Caro, Heinrich. 1834–1910. German industrial chemist. **C.'s acid.** See *Caro's.*

carob beans. St. John's bread. The pods of *Ceratonia siliqua* (Leguminosae), rich in sugar and gum; a fodder. Its seeds were the "carats," q.v., of jewelers. Cf. *tragon.* **c. gum.** The gum of c. beans; an emulsifier and traganth substitute.

caroba. The Brazilian caraiba tree, *Jacaranda procera* (Bignoniaceae).

carobic acid. A crystalline acid from caroba leaves.

carobine. A caroba alkaloid.

carobone. A balsamic resin from caroba leaves.

carol. $C_{10}H_{18}O = 154.2$. Caraneol, 5-hydroxy-carane. A monobasic alcohol, from carane, in many essential oils.

carolic acid. $C_9H_{10}O_4 = 182.1$. An acid from the mold *Penicillium Charlesii.* Cf. *carlic acid.*

carolinium. A supposed element in thorium minerals.

carolite. Carrollite.

caronamide. 4'-Carboxyphenylmethanesulfonanilide. A constituent of tissues which inhibits the renal secretion of penicillin.

carone. $C_{10}H_{16}O = 152.2$. 5-Ketocarane. A ketone of essential oils, derived from carane. Colorless oil b.210.

carony bark. Angostura bark.

Caro's acid. Permonosulfuric acid. Made by dissolving potassium persulfate in concentrated sulfuric acid, or by heating the acid with an oxidizing agent, as hydrogen peroxide. A powerful oxidizing agent; converts aniline into nitroglycerin.

carotenase. A liver enzyme which splits carotene, producing vitamin A.

carotene. $C_{40}H_{56} = 536.6$. Carotin; caritol, primary vitamin A precursor. A lipochrome, m.174, in foodstuffs; associated with chlorophyll, animal tissues, blood serum, milk fat, etc. Isomeric forms: **alpha-** The smaller portion, optically active, m.187, maximum absorption bands at 521 and 485 mμ. **beta-** The larger portion, optically inactive, m.184, maximum absorption bands at 511 and 478 mμ. Cf. *xanthophyll, carotenoids.* β-**c. epioxide,** β-**c. oxide.** Constituents of provitamin A; cf. *mutatochrome.* Other associated plant pigments are neo-c., ψ-c., and γ-c. m.178. **red-** Lycopin.

carotenoids. Carotinoids, polyenes. Lipochromes or carotene-like plant pigments deposited in animal tissues. They may be hydrocarbons, alcohols, ketones, or acids, with alternate double bonds; e.g., polyene hydrocarbons ($C_{40}H_{56}$), α-carotene; polyene alcohols ($C_{20}H_{29}OH$), vitamin A; polyene ketones ($C_{40}H_{50}O_2$), rhodoxanthin; polyene acids ($C_{20}H_{24}O_4$), crocetin. Cf. *cholane ring, cerebrosides.*

carotin. Carotene.

carotinoids. Carotenoids.

carpaine. $C_{14}H_{25}O_2N = 239.3$. An alkaloid from the leaves of *Carica papaya* (Caricaceae). Colorless crystals, m.119, soluble in alcohol; a diuretic and heart stimulant, resembling digitalis in action. **c. hydrochloride.** $C_{14}H_{25}O_2N \cdot HCl = 275.67$. White crystals m. 225, soluble in water; used in hypodermic medication.

carpamic acid. $C_{14}H_{27}O_3N = 257.2$. An acid formed by hydrating carpaine.

Carpenter, Sir Harold. 1875–1940. British metallurgical chemist.

carposide. Caricin.

carrageen, carragheen. Irish moss.

carrageenin. A water-soluble extractive from carragheen. Used as a stabilizer, for suspending cocoa in chocolate manufacture, and to clarify beverages.

Carrel-Dakin solution. An isotonic sodium hypochlorite solution, for bathing wounds. Cf. *Dakin solution.*

carrene. Methylene chloride.

carrollite. Co_2CuS_4. A rare, native cobalt-copper sulfide.

carron oil. An emulsion of linseed oil in limewater, for burns. First used at the Carron ironworks, Scotland.

carrotin. Carotene.

carroting. The preparation of hair for felting by treating the tips of the fibers on the skin with a solution of mercuric nitrate in nitric acid.

carstone. A ferruginous sandstone (Norfolk, England).

carthamein. An oxidation product of carthamin.

carthamic acid. Carthamin.

carthamin. $C_{14}H_{16}O_7 = 296.2$. The red color of safflower, *Carthamus tinctorius.* Dark red scales, insoluble in water; a dye.

carthamus. African saffron. Composite plants, as *C. tinctorius,* false or American saffron or safflower, cultivated in Asia; a dye, condiment, and for making rouge.

Cartier scale. A hydrometric scale for determining ethyl alcohol based on 12.5°C; used in S. America.

cartilagin. Chondrigen. The protein of cartilage; the white, elastic substance of the bone surface.

carubinose. *d*-Mannose.

carum. Caraway. Cf. *ajava.*

carvacrol. Me·$C_6H_3(OH)C_3H_7 = 150.16$. 2-Hydroxy-*p*-cymene, isopropyl-*o*-cresol, 2-cymophenol, oxycymol. An aromatic constituent of essential oils, camphor, origanum, caraway, savory and other Labiatae. A thick, colorless, oil, d.0978, m.0, b.236; insoluble in water. Used in perfumery, and as a vermifuge and fungicide. **c. iodide.** $C_{10}H_{13}OI = 276.06$. Iodocrol. An almost odorless iodoform substitute.

carvacrotic acid. A colorless crystalline acid derived from carvacrol.

carvacryl. The radical $Me(Me_2CH)C_6H_3—$, from carvacrol. **c. amine.** Cymidine.

carvene. *d*-Limonene.

carveol. Me·$C_6H_7(OH)C_3H_5 = 152.16$. 2-Hydroxylimonene. A constituent of essential oils of the Labiatae, b.232.

carvol. Carvone.

carvomenthane. $C_{10}H_{18} = 138.14$. Δ^1-terpene, 1-methyl-4-isopropyltetrahydrobenzene. Colorless liquid from carvone, d.0.806, b.175.

carvomenthol. $C_{10}H_{20}O = 156.2$. 2-*p*-Menthanol. An isomer of menthol in essential oils, d.0.904, b.222, soluble in alcohol.

carvomenthyl. The radical $—C_{10}H_{17}$, from carvomenthane. **c. amine.** $C_{10}H_{17}NH_2 = 153.2$. Tetrahydrocarvylamine. Colorless liquid, b.212.

carvone. $C_{10}H_{14}O = 150.16$. $\Delta^{6,8}(9)$-Terpadienone-2 in the oils of caraway, cumin, and dill. Colorless liquid, b.225. **c. anil.** $C_{10}H_{13}O \cdot NHPh = 241.2$. Yellow oil, b.180, which darkens with age.

carvylamine. tetrahydro- Carvomenthylamine.

Carya. The hickory tree, *Carya tomentosa* (Juglandaceae), N. America, cultivated for its wood and fruits (pecans).

caryin. A crystalline compound from the bark of carya.

caryinite. A native phosphate and arsenate of lead.

caryl- The radical $C_{10}H_{17}—$, from carane.

caryocinesis. Karyokinesis.

caryophyllin. $C_{30}H_{48}O_3 = 456.4$. Oleanolic acid. A ketone from oil of cloves, soluble in alcohol.

caryophyllinic acid. $C_{20}H_{32}O_8 = 400.3$. An acid from caryophyllin.

caryophyllum. Cloves. The brown, fragrant flower heads of *Eugenia caryophyllata* (Myrtaceae) which contain an oil used as a flavoring and aromatic stimulant.

casca. Spanish and Portuguese for "bark." **c. bark.** Erythrophloeum.

cascara amarga. Honduras bark. The bark of *Picramnia antidesma* (Simarubaceae), tropical America; a tonic. **c. sagrada.** Sacred bark. Chittem bark, bearwood. The bark of *Rhamnus purshiana,* a shrub (Western U.S.). A cathartic, stimulant, and laxative. See *peristaltin, cascarin, anthraglucosagradin.*

cascarilla. The bark of various *Croton* and *Cinchona* species, especially *Croton eluteria.* The fluid extract or tincture is a stomachic tonic.

cascarillic acid. $C_{11}H_{20}O_2 = 184.14$. An acid from the oil of cascarilla. Colorless liquid, b.270.

cascarilline. $C_{12}H_{18}O_4 = 226.2$. Colorless bitter crystals from the bark of *Croton eluteria.*

cascarin. A colorless crystalline glucoside from Cascara sagrada; a hypodermic purgative.

casease. A bacterial ferment that dissolves casein. Cf. *caseinase.*

caseate. Caseinate.

caseation. The curdling of milk into a cheesy mass.

case-harden. To harden wrought iron by heating it in contact with carbon or potassium ferrocyanide; to produce a surface layer of steel. See *carburization, cementation.*

casein. The protein of milk (1 ton from 1,000 gal), and principal constituent of cheese. White solid, soluble in acids. Used as food; in combination with formaldehyde, as a plastic: in the leather industry; as a substitute for linseed oil in making pigments; for making albumin, rubber, and gelatin for films; and as an adhesive when mixed with lime. The composition of a typical casein is:

Carbon	53%
Hydrogen	7%
Oxygen	22.65%
Nitrogen	15.7%
Sulfur	0.8%
Phosphorus	0.85%

Its isoelectric point is pH 4.7; hence it occurs as neutral casein, metal caseinate, casein salt. **animal-** Casein. **blood-** Albumose (obsolete). **fibrous-** See *Aralac, lanital.* **gluten-** Vegetable casein. **milk-** Casein. **saliva-** Ptyalin. **vegetable-** A protein from cereal seeds, forming 10-20% of flour gluten.

caseinase. Rennase.

caseinate. Caseate. A compound of casein with a metal.

caseinic acid. $C_{12}H_{24}O_5N_2 = 276.21$. An acid from casein.

caseinogen. A compound protein of milk which yields casein by enzyme action.

Casella acid. 2,7-Naphtholsulfonic acid.

Casenka. Trade name for a protein synthetic fiber.

cashew. The nut of *Anacardium occidentale*, tropical America, Cf. *anacardium, anacardic acid, Cardanol, Cardol.* **c. apples.** Peduncles or pseudostems of the c. tree; a rich source of ascorbic acid. **c. oil.** Yellow oil, used in lacquers and paints. Cf. *harvel coating.*

cashmere. A fine, soft textile fiber from the coat of the Kashmir goat.

casimirin. A glucoside from the seeds of white sapota, *Casimiroa edulis* (Rutaceae), Mexico, a hypnotic.

Caslen. Trade name for a protein synthetic fiber.

casoid. A synthetic plastic made from a casein basis.

Casolana. Trade name for a protein synthetic fiber.

cassareep. The evaporated juice of bitter cassava (W. Indies), a meat preservative.

cassava. Manioc, mandioc, manihoi (Euphorbiaceae), S. and Central America; as, **bitter-** *Manihot utilissima* and **sweet-** *Manihot aipi.* Their large tuberous roots contain starch, used to prepare tapioca and Brazilian arrowroot.

cassel brown. A brown pigment found near Cassel, Germany; a fossilized, tertiary period humus. **c. yellow.** Lead oxychloride.

Casseler green. Barium manganate.

casseliase. A mica peridotite (Kentucky).

casselose. A nephelite-mellite basalt (Texas).

casserole. A laboratory porcelain dish with handle.

Cassia. (1) Sweet-smelling trees (obsolete). (2) A genus of leguminous herbs and trees. (3) An inferior cinnamon from *Cinnamomum cassia*, a spice and source of oil. **purging-** The pod pulp of *Cassia fistula.* **c. bark.** Chinese cinnamon. **c. buds.** The unripe fruit of cinnamon species. **c. leaves.** Senna. **c. oil.** Chinese oil of cinnamon, from the bark of *Cassia chinensis.* It is darker, less agreeable, and heavier than true cinnamon oil. **c. seeds.** The fruits of *Cassia fistula*, E. India; a laxative and poultice.

cassina. Holly from coastal Southern U.S.; its leaves are used in a beverage.

cassiopeium. Cp. The name given to lutecium, q.v., by Auer von Welsbach, who separated it from ytterbium in 1905.

cassiterite. SnO_2. Tinstone, block tin, tin spar, stream tin. Brown, black, red or yellow tetragons, d.6.9, hardness 6-7, found as pebbles in streams (Malaya).

cast. (1) To form a molten substance into a definite shape by allowing it to cool in a mold. (2) Cf. *casts.* **dip-** A c. formed by dipping a solid mold in molten metal, and withdrawing it so that a shell of metal is left on the mold. **slush-** A c. formed by filling a hollow mold with molten metal, and then emptying it so that a solid metal lining remains in the mold.

castable. A dry, premixed blend of refractory cement (or bond) to which a liquid is added immediately before use for casting or lining plant.

castanea. The leaves of *Castanea vulgaris*, the chestnut tree (U.S.); used as fluid extract for whooping cough.

castanhao oil. Brazil nut oil. A liquid fat from the seeds of *Bertholletia* species.

castelamarin. $C_9H_{14}O_3 = 170.11$. A bitter principle, m.269, from *Castela nicholsoni* (Simarubaceae). Cf. *amargosa bark.*

castine. An alkaloid from *Vitex Agnus castus* (Verbenaceae).

castonin. A globulin from European chestnut.

castor. (1) The beaver, *Castor fiber*, an amphibious rodent. (2) Castoreum. A brown, strong-smelling solid from the preputial follicles of the beaver; an antispasmodic and stimulant. **c. beans.** The seeds of *Ricinus communis.* **c. oil.** Ricinus oil from the c. bean. Yellow liquid, $d_{25}°$ 0.945-0.965; purgative. Cf. *dericin, ricinolein.* **c. pomace.** The solid residue after extraction of c. oil from c. bean. A fertilizer: nitrogen 4.1-6.6, phosphorus oxide 1-1.5, potassium oxide 1-1.5%. **c. seeds.** C. beans.

castoreum. Castor. **c. oil.** Essential castor oil. Yellow liquid, obtained by distillation of castoreum.

casts. Cylindrical structures in uriniferous tubules, and sediments. **blood-** C. consisting of erythrocytes, indicating renal hemorrhage. **epithelial-** C. consisting of epithelial cells, indicating acute nephritis. **fatty-** C. consisting of fat globules or fatty acids, indicating degeneration of the kidney. **granular-** C. consisting of granular material, indicating an inflammatory kidney. **hyaline-** C. consisting of the basic material of casts, found in kidney disorders. **pus-** C. consisting of pus cells or leucocytes, indicating renal suppuration. **waxy-** C. consisting of the yellow basic material found in amyloid disease.

cata- Prefix from the Greek κατα, meaning down, against, back, or of a lower order. Cf. *ana-.*

catabiotic. Capable of using up or dissipating. **c.**

force. Energy derived by an organism from the metabolic effects of its food.

catabolism. Disintegration or the breaking down of tissues; the destructive metabolism by which living matter is transformed into waste materials and eliminated from the body. Cf. *anabolism*.

catadyn. An oligodynamic catalyst; as, silver.

catalase. (1) An oxidizing enzyme of blood and the tissues which splits peroxides to oxygen and water; isolated from bacterial cultures as octahedra. (2) The oxidizing enzyme of fresh tobacco leaves. Cf. *peroxidase*.

catalasometer. An instrument to measure catalase activity from the change in level of a liquid in a graduated tube passing through the stopper of the vertical cylinder in which the reaction occurs.

catalinite. Beach pebbles of Santa Catalina Island; a green, red, or brown variety of quartz.

catalysant. A substance which is catalyzed. Cf. *substrate*.

catalysate. The product of catalysis.

catalysis. Contact action or cyclic action. The effect produced by a small quantity of a substance (catalyst) on a chemical reaction, after which the substance appears unchanged. Due to: formation of an intermediate compound (*chemical*); adsorption (*mechanical*); excitation by light (*photochemical*). **heterogeneous-** Acceleration of a chemical reaction is a heterogeneous system. **homogeneous.** Acceleration of a chemical reaction in a homogeneous mixture. **iso-** The coexistence of two catalytic influences in the same system. **isomeric-** The catalytic transformation of a substance to an isomeric form. **negative-** (1) The catalytic retardation of a reaction; e.g., mannitol reduces the oxidation of phosphorus. (2) The catalytic halting of a reaction; e.g., oxygen stops the reaction of hydrogen and chlorine. **photo-** Acceleration of a reaction by light. **photochemical-** The action of light as a catalyst. **pseudo-** Acceleration of a chemical reaction by a chemical catalyst.

catalyst. Catalyzator, catalyzer. A substance which effects catalysis. **chemical-** A substance which changes the speed of a chemical reaction, but is present in its original concentration at the end of the reaction; e.g., nitric acid in the lead-chamber process for sulfuric acid. **inducing-** Promoter. A substance which stimulates or aids catalysis. **mechanical-** A substance which influences the speed of a chemical reaction without itself undergoing a change, e.g., the reaction of $2H_2O_2 = 2H_2O + O_2$ is accelerated by colloidal Pt, or Au. **negative-** Retarder. A c. which retards a chemical reaction. **positive.** Accelerator. A c. which accelerates a chemical reaction. Cf. *enzyme, ferment, sensitizer*. **stereoscopic-** A c. used in polymerization processes to predetermine the final spatial configuration, and hence the physical and chemical properties, of large polymeric molecules.

catalytic. Pertaining to catalysis. **c. action.** Catalysis. **c. agent.** Catalyst. **c. force.** The mechanical expression of the change in the speed of a chemical reaction due to a catalyst. **c. poison.** Anticatalyzers, paralyzers. A substance which counteracts the effect of a catalyst.

catalyzer. Catalyst.

catamorphism. The chemical and physical changes produced on rock by the action of wind and water.

Cf. *anamorphism*.

cataphoresis. Kataphoresis. The downward motion of electrically charged particles suspended in a medium under the influence of an electric field. Cf. *endosmosis*. Its antonym *anaphoresis* implies upward motion.

catapleiite. A complex zirconium silicate.

catechin. $C_{15}H_{14}O_6 = 290.01$. An acid from catechu, mahogany wood, and kino. Yellow powder, soluble in water; used for tanning and calico printing. **c.a.** $+3H_2O$. *dl*-Catechol, acacatechin. The principal constituent of *Acacia catechu*. Thin needles, m.214. **c.b.** $+4H_2O$. *d*-Catechol, gambir catechin. Thin needles, m.94, soluble in alcohol. **c.c.** $+4H_2O$. *d*-Epicatechol. Thin needles: anhydrous at 274.

catechol. (1) Pyrocatechol. (2) Catechin. Condensed tannin. **benzoylpyro-** Dihydroxybenzophenone. **dimethoxy-** Veratrol. **methyl-** Guaiacol.

catechu. Cutch, cashoo, black catechu. An extract of the dark heartwood of *Acacia catechu;* an astringent. Cf. *japonic acid*. **pale-** Gambir. **c. palm.** Areca.

catechuic acid. Catechin.

catechuretin. $C_{38}H_{28}O_{12} = 676.22$. Produced from catechu by the action of sulfuric acid.

catechutannic acid. A red, amorphous anhydride of catechuic acid from catechu.

catelectrode. Cathode (obsolete).

catenane. A compound composed of large interlocking rings, which are otherwise unbonded.

catenary. The curve assumed by a chain suspended at each end.

catenation. The formation of polymers based on a chain or ring of atoms of one kind.

catgut. An aseptic cord prepared from animal intestines; used for ligatures.

cathartic. A drug which causes the evacuation of the bowels, e.g., castor oil. Cf. *purgative, laxative, aperient, hydragogue*.

cathartic acid. $C_{180}H_{96}O_{82}N_2S$. The glucosidal and active principle of senna.

cathartin. (1) A bitter principle of senna (Lassaigne and Feneulle). (2) A compound from the ripe fruits of *Rhamnus cathartica* (Winkler). (3) A compound from jalap.

cathartomannite. $C_{21}H_{44}O_{19}$. A nonfermentable carbohydrate-like substance from senna.

cathetometer. A precision instrument to measure small vertical displacements. It consists usually of a microscope with cross wires and scale mounted on a rigid vertical rod.

cathidine, cathine, cathinine. Three alkaloids from African tea, the leaves of *Catha edulis* (Celastraceae), N. Africa. Cf. *katine*.

cathine. $C_9H_{13}ON = 151.11$. *d*-Norisoephedrine. A crystalline alkaloid, m.77, soluble in water, from bushman's tee (boesmanstee), the leaves of *Catha edulis* (Celastraceae), S. Africa. Cf. *celastrine, katine*.

cathode. Kathode, negode, katode. The negative pole or electrode of an electric device. **c. deposit.** (1) A metal precipitate produced by electrolysis. (2) A metallic mirror formed on a vacuum tube near the cathode. See *cathodic sputtering*.

cathode rays. Negative rays. A stream of negatively charged electrons issuing from the cathode of a vacuum tube perpendicular to the surface, with velocities (10^9 to 10^{10} cm/sec) depending upon the existing potential difference. When they are stopped by a solid substance, they produce heat, phosphorescence, X rays, pressure, or photographic action. C. rays are analogous to the β rays of radioactive matter.

cathodic sputtering. Disintegration of the cathode in an electric discharge tube, covering the surrounding glass with a mirror of cathode metal.

catholyte. The liquid close to the cathode. Cf. *anolyte.*

cation. Kathion, cathion, negion. (1) A positively charged atom, radical, or group of atoms, which travels to the cathode or negative pole during electrolysis. (2) A positively charged gas molecule. Cf. *anion, ion.*

cationotropy. A case of ionotropy, q.v., in which a H^+ or M^+ breaks off a molecule and leaves a negative ion in dynamic equilibrium. Cf. *prototropy.*

catlinite. Pipestone. A red clay (Upper Missouri); used for pipes.

catoptric. An optical system with metallic reflectors instead of glass mirrors.

catoptrics. The study of mirrors and reflected light.

catoptron. A mirror.

catoptroscope. A device to examine objects by reflected light.

caulobacters. Stalk-shaped bacteria.

caulophyllin. A resinous precipitate obtained by pouring concentrated tincture of caulophyllum into water.

caulophylline. An alkaloid from blue cohosh, *Caulophyllum thalictroides.* Colorless, crystals.

caulophylloid. The combined principles from caulophyllum, used to relieve congestive and spasmodic conditions of generative organs.

caulophyllosapogenin. $C_{56}H_{88}O_9 = 904.68$. A glucoside, m.315, from caulophyllum.

caulophyllum. Squawroot, blue cohosh. The rhizome and roots of *C. thalictroides* (Beriberidaceae), N. America; a sedative, diuretic and antispasmodic.

caulosaponin. $C_{54}H_{38}O_{17} = 1008.7$. Leontin. A glucoside, m.255, from caulophyllum.

caustic. (1) Corrosive or burning. (2) The hydroxide of a light metal, e.g., caustic soda. (3) Describing a curve or surface of maximum brightness produced by the concentration of rays of light after reflection or refraction. (4) A drug which destroys soft body tissues, used to destroy pathological tissues; an escharotic. **lunar-** Silver nitrate. **Vienna-** Potash fused with lime. Cf. *soda lime.* **volatile-** Ammonium hydroxide.

    c. cracking. C. embrittlement. A form of metallic failure of steam-raising plant, not yet fully explained. Very fine cracks develop in the overlaps of riveted seams on the dry side of the boiler. Associated with high localized stresses and high concentrations of c. soda produced by the evaporation of alkaline waters. **c. curve.** The line produced by the intersection of a number of reflected or refracted rays of light. **c. embrittlement.** C. cracking (more correctly). **c. lime.** Calcium oxide. **c. potash.** Potassium hydroxide. **c. soda.** (1) Sodium hydroxide. (2) Sodium hydroxide containing 76–78% sodium oxide, used in the manufacture of soap, paper, paints, leather, chemicals, and drugs; also for softening water, mercerizing cotton, refining oils, and in the prepar-

ation of cleaners. World production (1966) 17.5 million tons.

causticity. The extent to which a substance is caustic (as a percentage): $100(2x - y)/y$, where x and y are the milliliters of hydrochloric acid necessary to make a solution of the substance neutral to phenolphthalein and methyl orange, respectively. It expresses the relative proportions of carbonate and hydroxide.

causticized ash. A mixture of soda ash (Na_2CO_3) and caustic soda (NaOH), containing 15–45% NaOH. Used as water softener, for cleansers, and in the manufacture of leather.

Cavendish, Henry. 1731–1810. English philosopher and chemist, a pioneer in studies of specific heat and eudiometry and the discoverer of hydrogen. He determined the compositions of water, air, and nitric acid.

Caventou, Joseph Bienaimé. 1795–1877. French pharmacist; discoverer of brucine and strychnine, and (with Pelletier) of quinine.

cavitation. The production of emulsions by disruption of a liquid into a two-phase system of liquid and gas, when the hydrodynamic pressure in the liquid is reduced to the vapor pressure.

cawk. Barytes.

cayaponine. A purgative alkaloid from *Cayaponia globosa* (Cucurbitaceae), Brazil.

cayenne pepper. Capsicum.

Cb. Symbol for columbium.

cc. Abbreviation for cubic centimeter. **cc test.** A unit of evaluation of hydrogen peroxide. The number of cubic centimeters of 0.1 N potassium permanganate equivalent to 2 cc of sample.

Cd. Symbol for cadmium.

c.d. Abbreviation for current density.

Ce. Symbol for cerium.

ceanothine. An alkaloid from New Jersey tea, the root of *Ceanothus americanus* (Rhamnaceae), Eastern U.S.; a purgative.

ceara rubber. The coagulated latex of *Manihot glaziovii* (Euphorbiaceae), Brazil and Argentine.

cebil gum. The reddish yellow tears from *Piptadenia cebil* (Leguminosae), Brazil. Cf. *angico.*

cebur balsam. Tagulaway.

cecidomin. $C_{23}H_{28}O_{15} = 544.2$. A glucosoidal constituent of gall from *Cecidomyia tiliae.* Orange needles, m.227–231.

cecilose. A pyroxenite (Maryland).

cedar. A group of trees of the pine family. **red-** Juniperus. **white-** Thuja.

    c. gum. Yellow tears from *Cedrela toona,* Indian mahogany (Meliaceae), Queensland. **c. leaves oil.** C. oil. **c. oil.** The essential oil, d.0.870–0.890, from *Juniperus virginiana;* used in microscopy as clarifying agent and for oil-immersion lenses. It contains limonene, cadinene, and borneol. **c. wood oil.** Oil from *Cedrela odorata,* W. Indies and S. America. Odorous liquid, d.0.945–0.960, soluble in alcohol; contains cedrene and cedrol.

cedarite. Chemavinite.

cedrarine. Orexin.

cedrene. $C_{15}H_{24} = 204.2$. An oil from red cedar, $d_{15}°0.984$, b.237. **c. camphor.** Cedrol.

cedrin. An active principle of cedron. Colorless bitter crystals, soluble in water; an antiperiodic.

cedrol. $C_{15}H_{26}O = 222.2$. Cedrene camphor. The crystalline portion of oil of red cedar, m.87, b.294.

cedron. The seeds of *Simaba cedron* (Simarulbaceae), Central America; a febrifuge.

cedronella. Lemongrass.

cedronine. An alkaloid from cedron.

cel. The velocity imparted by 1 dyne in 1 sec to 1 gm.

celadonite. A glauconite.

Celafibre. Trade name for a cellulose acetate synthetic fiber.

Celafil. Trademark for a ruptured, continuous-filament acetate yarn.

celandin. Chelidonium.

celandine. Pilewort. **greater-** Chelidonium. **lesser-** Pilewort.

Celanese. Trademark for a cellulose acetate synthetic fiber.

Celaperm. Trademark for a cellulose acetate synthetic fiber.

celastin. Menyanthin.

celastrine. An alkaloid from the seeds of Celastraceae. White crystals; a stimulant causing an increase in body temperature. Cf. *cathine.*

Celbenin. See *penicillin.*

Celcos. Trade name for a cellulose acetate synthetic fiber.

celcure salts. A 10% solution of chalcanthite 50, sodium dichromate 45, chromous acetate 5 pts. Used to impregnate wood to protect it against fungal and insect attack.

Celechrome. Trade name for a cellulose acetate synthetic fiber.

celery. The vegetable *Apium graveolens* (Umbelliferae), Cf. *apiole, apigenin.* **c. seeds.** Used as a spice and for making **c. seed oil,** which contains selinene and apiol. A colorless liquid, d.0.870–0.895.

celestine, celestite. SrSO$_4$. Strontium sulfate, deposited in sedimentary rocks.

Celite. Trademark for certain diatomaceous earth products, particularly filter aids, fillers, abrasives, heat-insulating materials, insulating plasters and cements.

cell. (1) *Biological.* The anatomical unit of life from which all living matter is constituted, and develops. It consists essentially of a small protoplasmic mass which is a changing colloidal chemical system of proteins, and is differentiated into a nucleus and cell body. This protoplasm is divided into cytoplasm (cell body), containing spongioplasm (solid) and hyaloplasm (liquid); and nucleoplasm (cell nucleus), containing linin (solid) and nucleoplasm. (2) *Galvanic.* An electrical element; or device for transforming chemical into electric energy. Its action is due to the passage of ions through an electrolyte. It usually consists of a metal in an electrolyte containing ions of that substance, connected by a tube containing an electrolyte, to a second electrode similar to but not identical with the first. Cf. *galvanic battery.* (3) *General.* A small container with two parallel transparent sides. **air-** The air-containing chambers of the lungs or of vegetable tissues. **alkali-** Photoelectric c. **amoeboid-** A c. resembling an amoeba, e.g., a leucocyte. **animal-** A c. of animal tissue. **asexual-** A c. which reproduces itself without external stimulus. **bichromate-** An electric amalgamated zinc-carbon c. (2.0 volts) in. a 12% solution of potassium dichromate containing (approximately) 9% sulfuric acid. **blood-** See

blood. **Bunsen-** See *Bunsen.* **cadmium-** See *cadmium.* **carrier-** Leucocyte. **chromatophore-** A biological unit containing coloring matter. **Clark's-** See *Clark.* **columnar-** An elongated c., a number of which form part of the epithelial tissue. **concentration-** A galvanic combination of 2 electrodes of the same substance immersed in solutions containing ions of the substance differing only in the concentrations of the ions. **Daniell-** An electrical zinc-copper c. (about 4 volts). **daughter-** A c. produced by the division of another (mother) c. **dead-** A c. which has ceased to perform vital functions; it may serve for mechanical protection, e.g., horn. **diffusion-** A percolator for extracting sugar from beets. **dry-** See *dry.* **electrical-** (1) An accumulator. (2) A voltaic c. (3) An electrolytic c. **electrolytic-** (1) A c. used for electroplating. (2) Galvanic c. **electroresponsive-** See *electroresponse.* **embryonic-** A c. from which tissues develop. **epithelial-** A c. of the skin. **galvanic-** See *cell* (2) and *galvanic.* **giant-** An abnormally large c. **Leclanché-** An electrical zinc-carbon c. (about 1.5 volts). **load-** An electric transducer for transforming weights into electric currents; used for weighing and based on the change in electrical resistance when the internal structure of a steel billet is distorted under load. **locomotive-** A c. capable of independent movement. **optical-** See *selenium.* **oxidation-reduction-** An electrolytic c. utilizing an oxidation-reduction reaction. **photoconductive-** Photoelectric, photoemissive, photovoltaic. See *photo.* **reversible-** An electrolytic c. in which the energy spent in reversing the chemical changes in the c. is approximately equal to that given out by the direct operation of the c. **secondary-** *biological-* A c. formed by the coalescence of other cells. *electrical-* An accumulator. **selenium-** See *selenium.* **solar-** A device to convert solar energy into chemical power by the action of solar photons on a semiconductor (e.g., silicon) junction. **standard-** A c. giving a definite voltage. See *cadmium* c. **transition-** *biological-* A c. whose characteristics are between 2 well-defined types of cells, and which is supposed to change from one type to the other. *electrical-* A voltaic c. which contains an electrolyte undergoing a definite change with temperature; e.g., ZnSO$_4$·7H$_2$O changes at 39°C to ZnSO$_4$·6H$_2$O, with corresponding change in the emf. **voltaic-** See *cell* (2). **Weston-** Cadmium c. **c. constant.** Resistance capacity. **c. division.** See *karyokinesis.*

cellase. Cellulosase. An enzyme which digests cellulose.

cellit. Technical acetylcellulose.

cellobiose. C$_{12}$H$_{22}$O$_{11}$ = 342.17. Cellose. A disaccharide, glucose-β-glucoside, m.225; an intermediate product in the hydrolysis of cellulose; and a bacteriological reagent.

cellodextrin. Cellulose dextrin. The water-soluble constituent formed by the prolonged action of concentrated mineral acids on cellulose; precipitated by alcohol.

celloidin. Collodion wool. A concentrated solution of pyroxylin. Used in microscopy for embedding specimens or section cutting.

cellon. Tetrachlorethane.

Cellophane. (1) Trade name and mark of British Cellophane Ltd. for sheets of transparent cellulose and cellulose wrappings. In particular, for the film obtained by the precipitation of a viscose solution with ammonium salts. Used as a wrapping (2) (not cap.). In the U.S., a generic name for film produced from wood pulp by the viscose process.

cellose. Cellobiose.

Cellosize. Trademark for a mixture of glyoxal and hydroxyethylcellulose, used to impart wet strength to paper.

Cellosolve. $EtOCH_2CH_2OH = 90.08$. Trademark for glycol ethyl ether, hydroxy ether, 2-ethoxyethanol*, Colorless liquid, d.0.935, b.135.1, soluble in water; a lacquer solvent. **butyl-** $BuO \cdot CH_2 \cdot CH_2OH = 118.11$. Glycol butyl ether, 2-butoxyethanol*. Colorless liquid, b.171.2; a solvent for brushing lacquers. **ethyl-** Cellosolve. **methyl-** $MeO(CH_2)_2 \cdot OH = 76.01$. Ethylene glycol monomethyl ether, methoxyethanol*. Volatile liquid, b.124; miscible with toluene; a solvent for nitrocellulose.

c. acetate. $MeCOO(CH_2)_2OH = 104.0$. Hydroxyethyl acetate, glycol monoacetate. Colorless volatile liquid, b.153, soluble in toluene; used for lacquers. **c. butylate.** $C_6H_{14}O_2 = 118.1$. Colorless liquid, b.170; a solvent for nitrocellulose.

cellotriose. Procellose.

cellotropin. $C_6H_4O \cdot Ph \cdot COO \cdot C_6H_{11}O_5 = 376.16$. Monobenzoylarbutin. White powder, insoluble in water, used to treat scrofula.

Celluloid. Trade name for zylonite, Xylonite (U.K.). A malleable substance prepared from nitrocellulose (pyroxylin or nitrated cotton, usually containing 10.8–11.1% nitrogen) and camphor, pressed into various shapes and rendered less flammable by the addition of ammonium phosphate and other ingredients. Used in the manufacture of many articles, and in dentistry and surgery.

cellulosans. Pentosans associated with cellulose in wood.

cellulosase. Cellase.

cellulosate. Sodium cellulose formed by the action of sodium in liquid ammonia, on cellulose; analogous to alcoholates.

cellulose. $(C_6H_{10}O_5)x = (162)x$. A carbohydrate polymer of glucose residue units in the walls and skeletons of vegetable cells.

A *c. micelle* contains 1,500–2,000 such units arranged in 40–60 *cellobiose* chains, each containing 15 to 20 pairs of glucose residues. It is almost pure in pith, absorbent cotton, and filter paper, and is a colorless, transparent mass, insoluble in water or other solvents, but soluble in copper ammonium hydroxide, and in sulfuric acid with the formation of amyloid (vegetable parchment). See *collodion, Celluloid, pyroxylin.* Sources:

1. Seed fibers (87–91%); as, cotton.
2. Woody fibers (58–62%); as, coniferous and deciduous woods.

3. Bast fibers (32–37%); as, flax.
4. Leaf fibers; as, sisal.
5. Fruit fibers; as, coconut.

C. is divided into the following fractions by digestion with 17.5% sodium hydroxide: **alpha-** Long-chain c. molecules, insoluble in cold 17–18% sodium hydroxide solution under specified conditions; not a chemical entity, but a convenient measure of the "true" c. present in a plant or pulp. **beta-** The fraction precipitated by acid from sodium hydroxide solution. Cf. *alpha-c.* **gamma-** The fraction that is not precipitated by acid from sodium hydroxide solution. Cf. *alpha-c., beta-c.* **amino-** A red, water-soluble powder formed by the action of sodium amide on c. nitrate; each NO_3 group is replaced by NH_2. **B-** Bacterial c. C. produced by bacterial synthesis from sugars. It consists of long glucose anhydride chains. Cf. *beta-c.* **colloidal-** Amyloid. **Cross and Bevan-** C. isolated from vegetable material by successive chlorination and alkali treatments. **Guignet-** amyloid. **hemi-** See *hemicellulose.* **holo-** See *holo.* **oxidized-** A white, gauze lint local hemostate (U.S.P.). Soluble in dilute alkalies; contains 16–24% COOH. **pseudo-** Hemicellulose.

c. acetate. The esters of c. and acetic acid, used extensively in industry and as rayon, imitation leather, fabrics, yarns, bristles, lacquers. *mono-* $C_6H_9O_4 \cdot COOMe = 205.00$. C. monoacetate. *di-* $C_6H_8O_3(COOMe)_2 = 246.11$. C. diacetate. *tri-* $C_6H_7O_2(COOMe)_3 = 288.19$. C. triacetate. Colorless, amorphous mass, insoluble in water. *tetra-* $C_6H_6O(COOMe)_4 = 330.17$. C. tetraacetate. White, amorphous mass, softening 150, insoluble in ordinary solvents. *penta-* $C_6H_5(COOMe)_5 = 372.24$. C. pentacetate. White amorphous mass, insoluble in water. **c. dextrin.** Cellodextrin. **c. gum.** Carboxymethyl-c. **c. nitrate.** The esters of cellulose and nitric acid, used extensively in explosives and in lacquers. Cf. *nitrocellulose.* There exist, according to the degree of nitration: *tri-* $C_{12}H_{17}O_7(NO_3)_3 = 459.23$. C. trinitrate. *tetra-* $C_{12}H_{16}O_6(NO_3)_4 = 504.23$. C. tetranitrate. Both are white amorphous masses., insoluble in ordinary solvents, and are the principal constituents of collodion. *penta-* $C_{12}H_{15}O_5(NO_3)_5 = 549.23$. C. pentanitrate. White amorphous mass, soluble in mixed alcohol and ether. *hexa-* $C_{12}H_{14}O_4(NO_3)_6 = 594.23$. C. hexanitrate. The principal constituent of guncotton. White amorphous mass, ignites about 160. insoluble in ordinary solvents.

Celotex. Trademark for an insulating wallboard produced by pressing bagasse or other fibers.

celsian. $BaO \cdot Al_2O_3 \cdot 2SiO_2$. A barium feldspar refractory.

Celsius, Anders. 1701–1744. Swedish astronomer. **C. scale.** See *centigrade* scale. The international temperature scale since 1948.

Celta. Trade name for a cellulose acetate synthetic fiber.

celtium. Early name for hafnium in zirconium minerals (Urbain and Dauvillier).

cement. (1) A plastic material which hardens to form a connecting medium between solids. (2) Portland cement. A fine gray powder (probably $3CaO \cdot SiO_2$, $3CaO \cdot Al_2O_3$, and $2CaO \cdot SiO_2$). Made by heating a calcareous (limestone, marl or chalk) with an argillaceous material (clay or shale,

$Al_2O_3 \cdot SiO_2$) at 1350–1800°C to vitrification. The resulting clinker is mixed with 2% gypsum and ground. Composition: lime 62–67, chalcedony 18–20, alumina 4–8, iron 2–3, magnesium 1–4, potassium and sodium 0.5%, titanium and manganese traces. Used for concrete (cement 1, sand 2, gravel 4 pts, and for each 100 lb cement, 6 gal water). **adamantine-** Mixed powdered pumice stone with silver amalgam; used to fill teeth. **aluminous-** Ciment fondu. A strong acid-resistant hydraulic c. Made by grinding the clinker of monocalcium aluminate and dicalcium silicate formed by fusing bauxite and line. **bituminous-** C. prepared from natural pitch. **chalcedony-** C. made from chalcedony. **clinker-** Uncrushed portland c. **copper-** Dental c. **dental-** See *dental* c. **glass-** A mending material for broken glass, e.g., a mixture of resins. **glycerin-** A glue containing glycerin. **Hensler's-** A mixture of litharge 3, quicklime 2, china clay 1 pts., ground with oil; used to fill cracks in stoneware. **hydraulic-** A c. that sets under water; as, portland c. **portland-** A hydraulic c. made by calcining limestone with clay or river mud. **quick-setting-** A mixture of alkyd resin 11–20, nitrocellulose solution 35, solvent 11–21, and plasticizer 4–8%. **refractory-** See *refractory* c. **Roman-** A quick-setting c. made by mixing burnt clay with lime and sand. **rubber-** A coating mixture of unvulcanized rubber and sulfur dissolved in oil. **silicate-** See *dental* c. **zinc oxide-** See *dental* c.

cementation. (1) The setting of a plastic material. (2) Heating wrought iron in a bed of charcoal or hematite, to convert it into steel (blister steel). (3) Heating one metal in contact with another to coat it.

cementing. Binding together. c. electron. Electrons of the atomic nucleus which hold protons together.

cementite. Fe_3C. Iron carbide in steel.

cementum. The bonelike covering of the root *dentine*, q.v., of teeth, consisting of calcium salts deposited in a collagenous matrix.

cenospheres. Hollow, spherical coal structures.

cent. Abbreviation for the Latin centum (a hundred), or centesimus (a hundredth).

cental. 100 lb weight.

Centaurea. A genus of herbs, containing 470 species, e.g., *C. behen* behenic acid.

centaureidin. $C_{18}H_{18}O_8 = 362.2$. A flavone decomposition product of centaurin.

centaurin. A glucoside from the roots of *Centaurea jacea*.

centaurine. An alkaloid from *Erythrea centaurium*.

centaury. The *Erythraea* species, used for tonic preparations. **American-** Sabbatia.

centelloside. A triterpene-sugar constituent of *Centella asiatica*, Ceylon. Yellow, neutral gum, soluble in water, and similar in properties to asiaticoside.

centesimal. Centigrade.

centi- Prefix denoting 1/100.

centigrade. °C. Centesimal. A thermometer scale based on the freezing point (0°) and boiling point (100°) of water; originated by Celsius.

centigram. The one-hundredth part of a gram (= 0.154 grain troy).

centiliter, centilitre. The one-hundredth part of a liter (0.61 in.³).

centimeter, centimetre. The one-hundredth part of a meter (0.3937 in.). **cubic-** A cube whose edge is 1 cm long. It differs from the milliliter which is 1/1,000 part of a liter; thus 1/1,000 liter = 1 ml = 1.00027 cc. Cf. *cubic centimeter*. **reciprocal-** Kaiser.

centimeter-cube. Cubic centimeter.

centinormal. 0.01 *N*. See *normal* solution.

centipoise. 0.01 poise, q.v. A unit of viscosity or fluidity (water at 20°C as unity). Cf. *rhe*.

centner. (1) A German standard weight of 50 kg. (2) A drachm weight divided into 100 equal portions.

centrifugal. Tending to move outward, away from a center. **c. force.** The tendency of one body moving round another to leave its axis of motion.

centrifugalization. Centrifugation.

centrifugation. Separation of solids from liquids, or liquids of different specific gravity, by subjecting them to fast rotation.

centrifuge. A machine for centrifugation consisting of a rapidly rotating container, holding test tubes or bottles containing the mixture. **c. tube.** A heavy-walled glass container, often graduated, used in a c.

centrifuging. Centrifugation.

centripetal. Tending to move toward the center.

centron. The positive nucleus of an atom. Cf. *proton*.

centrosome. A small highly refractive body of protoplasm between nucleus and cell body, taking an active part in cell division. See *karyokinesis*.

cephaëline. $C_{14}H_{19}O_2N = 233.2$. An alkaloid from the root of *Cephaelis ipecacuanha*, Rio ipecac, and *Cephaelis acuminata*, Carthagena ipecac. White crystals, sparingly soluble in water; an emetic. **c. hydrochloride.** $C_{14}H_{19}O_2N \cdot HCl = 269.67$. White crystals, soluble in water; an emetic.

Cephaëlis. A genus of Rubiaceae (Central and S. America) which yields ipecacuanha.

cephalanthin. A glucoside from *Cephalanthus occidentalis*, buttonbush (Rubiaceae), N. America.

cephaletin. An amorphous, bitter principle from swamp dogwood, *Cephalanthus occidentalis*, (Rubiaceae) N. America.

cephalin. (1) Kephalin. (2) A white crystalline acid principle from *Cephalanthus occidentalis*.

cephaloridine. An antibiotic related to penicillin, produced by *Cephalosporium acremonium*.

cephalosporin. $C_{32}H_{48}O_8 = 560.48$. A tetracyclic, steroidal monocarboxylic acid isolated from strains of *Cephalosporium*; an antibotic similar to penicillin.

Ceporin. Trade name for an antibiotic from *Cephalosporium* mold; has the widest bactericidal range of any known antibiotic.

ceptor. A characteristic of an organism responsible for its transformation, e.g., amboceptor.

cera. Wax. **c. alba.** Bleached beeswax. c. flava. Unbleached beeswax.

ceramels. Mixtures of refractory oxides or carbides embedded in a metallic base, which combine the properties of metals and ceramics.

ceramic ink. A ground mixture of potassium carbonate 1, borax 1, litharge 2, cobalt salt 2 pts., mixed with oil, written on glass or procelain, and burnt in with the bunsen burner.

ceramics. The art of making objects (vases, pottery) from clay, and burning metallic colors into them.

See diagram.

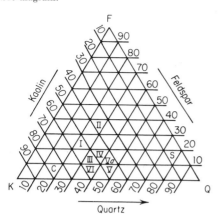

Ceramic ware.

I Hard porcelain.   Va German whiteware.
II Soft porcelain.   VI Calcareous whiteware.
III Japanese porcelain.   C Clay.
IV Stoneware.   S Sand.
V Whiteware.   F Feldspar.

cerane. $C_{26}H_{54} = 366.42$. Isohexacosane. Colorless crystals, m.61, insoluble in water.

cerargyrite. $AgCl$. Hornsilver, argentum cornu. A native isomer of silver chloride.

cerasein. Cerasin. A resin from the bark of *Prunus* (*Cerasus*) *sarotina*, wild cherry; a diuretic and antipyretic.

cerasin. (1) Kerasin. (2) Cerasein. (3) Cerasinose.

cerasinose. A carbohydrate produced from cherry gum by boiling with dilute sulfuric acid.

cerasite. A Japanese variety of iolite.

cerate. (1) A pharmaceutical compound of oil or lard with wax, resin, or spermaceti. (2) A soap or metallic salt made from lard. (3) Cerotate.

ceratin. Keratin.

ceratinase. A hydrolytic enzyme from carob beans.

ceratum. A mixture of white wax 3, lard 7 pts.

cerberetin. $C_{19}H_{26}O_4 = 318.3$. A decomposition product of cerberin. Yellow powder, m.85.

cerberidin. A digitalis substitute from *Thevetia cerbera*. Yellow powder, soluble in water.

cerberin. $C_{27}H_{40}O_8 = 492.4$. A glucoside from the seeds of *Cerbera odallam* and *Thevetia neriifolia*, (Apocynaceae) E. Indies. A senna substitute. Cf. *odallin*.

cereal. (1) An edible seed of Gramineae; e.g., wheat, rye, oats, rice, maize, barley. (2) A preparation of (1).

cerealin. A (diastatic) enzyme in bran.

cerebral. Pertaining to the brain. **c. depressants.** Drugs which temporarily depress brain functions. **c. excitants.** Drugs which stimulate brain activity.

cerebric acid. A fatty acid from the white substance of brain tissue.

cerebrin. $C_{17}H_{33}O_3N = 299.4$. A colorless, fatty principle, obtained from brain tissue by boiling with barium hydroxide.

cerebrine. Cerebrum siccum. Dried brain substance, used to treat neurasthenia.

cerebron. $C_{40}H_{81}O_6N = 671.8$. An amino lipotide from the white brain tissue.

cerebronic acid. $C_{25}H_{50}O_3 = 478.5$ and $C_{24}H_{48}O_3 = 466.5$. A mixture of α-hydroxypentacosanic acid and α-hydroxytetracosanic acid, m.80.5, obtained by hydrolysis of the white brain substance.

cerebrose. $C_6H_{12}O_6$. Brain sugar. Galactose from brain tissue.

cerebrosides. Galactosides. Nitrogeneous, fatty substances containing galactose in white brain matter.

cerebrospinal. Pertaining to the brain and spinal cord.

cerebrospinase. An oxidizing ferment in cerebrospinal fluid.

Cerenkov effect. The residual fluorescence shown by certain liquids after exposure to, and then removal of, a radioactive substance.

ceresin. Earth wax, ozocerite. A purified mineral wax, m.58; a beeswax substitute.

cerevisin. A dried brewer's yeast derived from the yeast *Saccharamyces cerevisae*.

cerevisterol. A sterol from yeast, m.265.3. Cf. *ergosterol*.

ceria. Cerium dioxide.

ceric. (1) A compound of tetravalent cerium, C^{4+}. (2) Pertaining to wax. **c. acid.** Cerotic acid. **c. ammonium nitrate.** $Ce(NO_3)_4 \cdot 2NH_4NO_3 = 548.3$. Orange crystals, soluble in water, readily reduced to cerous compounds. **c. fluoride.** $CeF_4 \cdot H_2O = 224.13$. White powder, insoluble in water, used in ceramics. **c. hydroxide.** $Ce(OH)_4 = 208.0$. Yellow powder, insoluble in water. **c. nitrate.** $Ce(NO_3)_4 = 388.3$. Orange, hygroscopic crystals, soluble in water. **c. oxide.** $CeO_2 = 172.3$. Cerium dioxide, ceria. Yellow powder, m.1950, insoluble in water; used in ceramics and gas mantles. **c. sulfate.** $Ce(SO_4)_2 \cdot 4H_2O = 404.5$. Yellow needles, forming a basic salt with excess water. Used as reducer in photography, and as oxidizing agent in analytical chemistry.

ceride. A tertiary lipid formed from higher monovalent alcohols and fatty acids.

ceridin. Cerolin.

cerin. (1) $C_{30}H_{50}O_2 = 442.3$. A sterol constituent of cork; colorless, acicular crystals. (2) Cerotic acid.

cerinic acid. Cerotic acid.

ceriometry. Volumetric analysis with ceric sulfate solution.

cerite. A rare-earth hydrous silicate found in gneiss (Bastnaes, Sweden). **fluo-** Fluocerite.

cerium. $Ce = 140.12$. A rare-earth element, at. no. 58. A gray, malleable metal, d.7.042, m.623, b.1400; it burns in air like magnesium, decomp. in water. Occurs as silicate (cerite and allanite) and phosphate (monazite), with other rare-earth metals. Discovered by Klaproth (1803), independently by Berzelius and Hisinger, and first isolated by Mosander (1839). C. forms two series of compounds with valencies 3 (cerous, Ce^{3+}) and 4 (ceric, Ce^{4+}). C. is prepared by electrolysis of the fused chloride, and is used in alloys for lighter flints (misch metal), for machine-gun tracer bullets, as a "getter" of noble gases in radio tubes, as scavenger in steelmaking, and for flashlight powders. The compounds are poisonous, and are used for incandescent gas mantles. **c. compounds.** See *ceric cerous*. **c. dioxide.** Ceric oxide.

cermet. A material in which a ceramic is heat-bonded to a metal.

cerodi- Prefix indicating the heptacyclic ring structure:

$$14—15—C—16—C—1—2$$
$$| \quad | \quad | \quad |$$
$$13—C—C—C—C—4—3$$
$$| \quad | \quad |$$
$$11—12—C—C—C—C—5$$
$$| \quad | \quad | \quad |$$
$$10—9—C—8—C—7—6$$

cerolein. A constituent of beeswax, soluble in cold alcohol.

cerolin. Ceridin. A fatty constituent of yeast, used to treat acne.

ceromel. Honeycomb; a mixture of wax and honey.

ceromelissic acid. $C_{33}H_{66}O_2 = 494.6$. An acid, m.94, from lardacein.

ceropic acid. $C_{36}H_{68}O_{30} = 980.7$. White microcrystals from the needles of *Pinus sylvestris* (Coniferae).

ceroplastic acid. $C_{33}H_{70}O_2 = 498.6$. An acid, m.97, from lardacein.

cerosate. A compound containing the radical $C_{23}H_{47}COO—$, from cerosic acid.

cerosic acid. $C_{23}H_{47}COOH = 368.5$. Tetracosanic acid, m.85, from cerosin.

cerosin. Cerosinyl cerosate. A wax found as coating on sugarcane.

cerosinyl. The radical $C_{24}H_{49}—$, from cerosic acid.

cerotate. A compound containing the radical $C_{26}H_{53}COO—$, from cerotic acid. Cf. *carnauba wax*.

cerotene. $C_{27}H_{54} = 378.5$. An unsaturated hydrocarbon from wax. Cf. *cerylene, carotene*.

cerotic acid. (1) $C_{26}H_{53}COOH = 410.5$. Cerotinic acid, heptacosanoic acid*, cerotin, cerinic acid. The monobasic, fatty acid of wax. White powder, m.82.5, insoluble in water. Cf. *neocerotic acid*. (2) $C_{25}H_{51}COOH = 396.41$. Hexacosanoic acid*. White needles, m.88, insoluble in water.

cerotin. Ceryl cerotate.

cerotinate. Cerotate.

cerotinic acid. Cerotic acid.

cerotol. Ceryl alcohol.

cerous. Containing trivalent cerium. **c. acetate.** $Ce(C_2H_3O_2)_3 \cdot H_2O = 335.2$. White crystals, m.115, soluble in water. **c. ammonium nitrate.** $Ce(NO_3)_3 \cdot 3NH_4NO_3 \cdot 10H_2O = 681.56$. Large crystals, soluble in water; used in the manufacture of gas mantles. **c. benzoate.** $Ce(C_7H_5O_2)_3 = 503.3$. White powder, soluble in hot water. **c. bromate.** $Ce_2(BrO_3)_6 \cdot 9H_2O = 1070.4$. White crystals, soluble in water. **c. bromide.** $CeBr_3 \cdot 7H_2O = 506.1$. White, hygroscopic crystals, soluble in water. **c. carbonate.** $Ce_2(CO_3)_3 \cdot 5H_2O = 550.4$. White powder, insoluble in water. **c. chloride.** $CeCl_3 = 246.6$. White crystals, m.848, soluble in water. *cryst-* $CeCl_3 \cdot 7H_2O = 372.7$. Pink crystals, soluble in water; used in the manufacture of gas mantles. **c. citrate.** $CeC_6H_5O_7 = 329.4$. White powder, insoluble in water. **c. fluoride.** $CeF_3 = 197.13$. Colorless crystals, m.1324, slightly soluble in water. **c. hydroxide.** $Ce(OH)_3 = 191.2$. Yellow

powder, insoluble in water. **c. hypophosphite** $Ce(H_2PO_2)_3 \cdot H_2O = 353.3$. White powder, insoluble in water; used to treat phthisis. **c. iodide.** $CeI_3 \cdot 9H_2O = 682.7$. Pink crystals, soluble in water. **c. lactate.** $Ce(C_3H_5O_3)_3 = 407.5$. White powder, sparingly soluble in water. **c. malate.** $Ce_2(C_4H_4O_5)_3 = 676.5$. White powder, soluble in water. **c. nitrate.** $Ce(NO_3)_3 \cdot 6H_2O = 434.5$. White crystals, soluble in water; used to make gas mantles. **c. oxalate.** $Ce_2(C_2O_4)_3 \cdot 9H_2O = 706.8$. Pink crystals, usually containing lanthanum and praseodymium salts, insoluble in water. A raw material in the preparation of rare earths, and a sedative. **c. oxide.** $Ce_2O_3 = 328.5$. Gray powder, d.6.9, insoluble in water. **c. phosphate.** $CePO_4 = 235.3$. Yellow rhombs, insoluble in water. **c. salicylate.** $Ce(C_7H_5O_3)_3 = 551.5$. White powder, insoluble in water. **c. sulfate.** $Ce_2(SO_4)_3 = 568.7$. Monoclinic crystals, soluble in water. *cryst-* $Ce_2(SO_4)_3 \cdot 8H_2O = 713.1$. Pink crystals, soluble in water; used to prepare aniline black. **c. valerate.** $Ce(C_5H_9O_2)_3 = 443.5$. White powder, soluble in water.

ceroxane. The ring structure

ceroxylin. $C_{20}H_{32}O = 288.26$. Crystals in the waxy exudation of *Ceroxylon andicola*, wax palm (S. America).

Certification (Trade) Mark. A trademark certified by the British Standards Institution.

cerulean blue. Ceruleum.

cerulein. $C_{20}H_{12}O_7$, or $C_{20}H_{10}O_6 \cdot H_2O = 364.14$. Coerulein. An acidic or internal anhydride coloring matter from gallein.

ceruleum. A blue pigment: cobaltous stannate and calcium sulfate.

cerulic acid. An oxidation product of coffee.

cerulignone. $C_{16}H_{16}O_6 = 304.0$. Coerulignone, cedriret. Blue needles, obtained by treating crude pyroligneous acid with potassium dichromate. **hydro-** Hydroceruliignone.

cerumen. Human ear wax.

cerusa, ceruse, cerussa. White lead.

cerussite. $PbCO_3$. White lead carbonate produced by the action of carbon dioxide and water on lead ores.

cervantite. Sb_2O_4. A secondary mineral formed by the oxidation of antimony sulfide.

ceryl. The radical $C_{26}H_{53}—$, from ceryl alcohol. **c. alcohol.** $C_{26}H_{54}O = 382.43$. 1-Hexacosanol*, cerotin. A monatomic alcohol from Chinese wax and wool fat. Colorless crystals, m.79, insoluble in water. *iso* An isomeric alcohol from Java wax. White crystals, m.62, insoluble in water. **c. cerotate.** $C_{26}H_{53}OOC \cdot C_{26}H_{53} = 774.80$. An ester of ceryl alcohol and cerotic acid. Colorless crystals, m.84, in Chinese wax. **c. palmitate.** $C_{15}H_{31}COO \cdot C_{26}H_{53} = 620.8$. An ester of ceryl alcohol and palmitic acid, in opium wax.

cerylate. A compound containing the radical $C_{27}H_{55}O$—, from ceryl alcohol.

cerylene. $C_{27}H_{54} = 378.54$. A hydrocarbon from Chinese wax. Cf. *cerotene.*

cerylic. Ceryl.

cesiated. Coated with cesium.

cesium, caesium. Cs = 132.91. A rare element of the alkali family, at. no. 55. A silver, soft, metal, d.187, m.26.4, b.670, which reacts violently with water. It is the most electropositive element (valency 1). C. occurs in mineral waters and minerals and in the ashes of a few plants, and is prepared by the distillation of c. hydroxide with magnesium powder in hydrogen. Discovered spectroscopically by Kirchhoff and Bunsen (1860); isolated by Setterberg (1881). C. metal is a rubidium substitute, its salts are microchemical reagents, gas absorbents in radio tubes, a source of metallic vapor in power tubes, and a sensitive coating in photoelectric cells. **c. acetate.** $CsC_2H_3O_2 = 191.93$. Deliquescent white crystals, m.194, soluble in water. **c. alum.** C. aluminum sulfate. **c. aluminum sulfate.** $Cs_2Al_2(SO_4)_4$·$24H_2O = 1136.50$. C. alum. Colorless crystals, soluble in water. **c. ammonium bromide.** $CsBr$·$NH_4Br = 309.68$. White crystals, soluble in water; a nerve sedative. **c. ammonium chloride.** $CsCl$·$3NH_4Cl = 328.75$. White crystals, soluble in water. **c. antimonous chloride.** $Cs_6SbCl_9 = 1131.5$. Antimony c. chloride, c. chlorostibate. Yellow crystals, soluble in water. **c. benzoate.** $CsC_7H_5O_2 = 253.85$. White powder, soluble in water. **c. bicarbonate.** $CsHCO_3 = 193.8$. White crystals, soluble in water. **c. bisulfate.** $CsHSO_4 = 229.8$. C. acid sulfate. White crystals, soluble in water. **c. bitartrate.** $CsHC_4H_4O_6 = 281.85$. C. acid tartrate. White rhombs, soluble in water. **c. bromate.** $CsBrO_3 = 260.8$. White crystals, soluble in water. **c. bromide.** $CsBr = 212.7$. White crystals, soluble in water; used to treat nervous heart disturbances. **c. carbonate.** $Cs_2CO_3 = 325.6$. White hygroscopic crystals, soluble in water; used in soda-water manufacture. **c. carbonate, acid.** C. bicarbonate. **c. chlorantimonate.** C. antimonous chloride. **c. chloride.** $CsCl = 168.3$. White regular crystals, m.646 (sublimes), soluble in water; used in soda-water manufacture. **c. chloroplatinate.** $Cs_2PtCl_6 = 674.0$. Yellow octahedra, soluble in water. **c. chromate.** $Cs_2CrO_4 = 381.7$. Yellow crystals, soluble in water. **c. cyanide.** $CsCN = 158.8$. White crystals, soluble in water. **c. dichromate.** $Cs_2Cr_2O_7 = 481.8$. Yellow crystals, soluble in water. **c. fluosilicate.** $Cs_2SiF_6 = 407.4$. White crystals, soluble in water. **c. formate.** $CsCHO_2 = 177.82$. Deliquescent white powder, m.265, soluble in water. The *monohydrate* loses water at 41°C. **c. hydroxide.** $CsOH = 149.8$. A gray, deliquescent mass, m.275, soluble in water. **c. iodate.** $CsIO_3 = 307.6$. White crystals, soluble in water. **c. iodide.** $CsI = 259.7$. White crystals, m.621, soluble in water; used medicinally to substitute potassium iodide. **c. ion.** Cs^+, present in solutions of c. salts in water. **c. manganese chloride.** $2CsCl$·$MnCl_2$·$3H_2O = 512.51$. Pink crystals, soluble in water. **c. nitrate.** $CsNO_3 = 194.8$. Colorless prisms, m.414, decomp., soluble in water; used in pyrotechnics. **c. nitrite.** $CsNO_2 = 178.8$. White crystals, soluble in water. **c.**

oxalate. $Cs_2C_2O_4 = 353.62$. White powder, soluble in water. **c. oxide.** (1) $Cs_2O = 281.6$. Normal c. oxide, c. monoxide. Orange crystals, soluble in water. (2) $Cs_2O_2 = 297.6$. C. dioxide. (3) $Cs_2O_3 = 313.6$. C. trioxide. (4) $Cs_2O_4 = 329.6$. C. tetroxide, c. peroxide. **c. perchlorate.** $CsClO_4 = 232.2$. White cyrstals, soluble in water. **c. periodate.** $CsIO_4 = 323.6$. White crystals, soluble in water. **c. permanganate.** $CsMnO_4 = 251.8$. Violet prisms, soluble in water. **c. peroxide.** $Cs_2O_4 = 329.6$. C. tetroxide. Yellow granules, decomp. violently in water. **c. platinic chloride.** C. chloroplatinate. **c. rubidium alum.** C. rubidium aluminum sulfate. **c. rubidium aluminum sulfate.** $CsRbAl_2(SO_4)_4$·$24H_2O = 1064.93$. C. rubidium alum. Colorless crystals, soluble in water. **c. rubidium ammonium bromide.** $CsBr$·$RbBr$·$6NH_4Br$. White, crystals, soluble in water; a nerve sedative. **c. rubidium bromide.** $CsBr$·$RbBr = 378.10$. White crystals, soluble in water; used medicinally to substitute potassium bromide. **c. rubidium chloride.** $CsCl$·$RbCl = 289.18$. Yellowish, crystals, soluble in water. **c. salicylate.** $CsC_7H_5O_3 = 269.85$. White powder, soluble in warm water. .**c. silicofluoride.** C. fluosilicate. **c. sulfate.** $Cs_2SO_4 = 361.7$. Colorless .needles, soluble in water; used in soda-water manufacture. **c. sulfide.** (1) $Cs_2S = 297.6$. C. monosulfide. (2) $Cs_2S_2 = 329.6$. C. disulfide. (3) $Cs_2S_3 = 361.6$. C. trisulfide. (4) $Cs_2S_5 = 425.6$. C. pentasulfide. **c. sulfite.** $Cs_2SO_3 = 345.6$. White crystals, soluble in water. **c. tartrate, acid.** C. bitartrate. **c. tetroxide.** C. peroxide. **c. trinitride.** $CsN_3 = 175.0$. Used as a "getter" in radio tubes. **c. trisulfide.** See *c. sulfide.*

cespitine. $C_5H_{13}N = 87.1$. An isomer of amylamine from coal tar.

cetaceum. Spermaceti.

cetane. $C_{16}H_{34} = 226.25$. Hexadecane. Colorless solid, m.20.

cetavlon. $C_{16}H_{33}NMe_3Br$. CTAB. Cetyltrimethylammonium bromide, a cationic detergent, bactericide, and analytical spot-test reagent.

cetene. CH_2:$CH(CH_2)_{13}CH_3 = 224.33$. Cetylene, 2-hexadecyne. A hydrocarbon, m.4, from cetyl alcohol.

cetenylene. $C_{16}H_{30} = 222.23$. An unsaturated hydrocarbon heptine homolog. Cf. *hexadecine.*

cetic. Indicating the radical $C_{16}H_{33}$—.

cetic acid. $C_{15}H_{30}O_2 = 242.23$. A fatty acid from spermaceti.

cetin. $C_{15}H_{31}COOC_{16}H_{33}$. Cetyl cetylate. The principal constituent of spermaceti. Colorless crystals, m.50, insoluble in water.

cetoleic acid. $Me(CH_2)_9CH$:$CH(CH_2)_9COOH = 338.4$. An isomer of erucic acid in marine animal oils.

cetostearyl alcohol. A mixture chiefly of cetyl and stearyl alcohols, m. below 43; used in ointments (B.P.).

Cetraria. (1) A genus of lichens. (2) Iceland moss: *C. vulpina*, vulpic acid; *C. islandica*, island moss, cetrarin.

cetraric acid. $C_{18}H_{16}O_8 = 360.2$. A crystalline dibasic acid from Iceland moss.

cetrarin. $C_{30}H_{30}O_{12} = 582.3$. Cetrarinic acid. A white, crystalline, bitter principle of Iceland moss, insoluble in water. A blood-forming agent, stomachic, and expectorant. **c. base.** A brown, amorphous mixture of cetrarin, cetraric acid, stearic acid, and other substances from Iceland moss; used similarly to cetrarin.

cetrarinic acid. Cetrarin.

cetrimide. A mixture of do-, tetra-, and hexadecyl trimethylammonium bromides. White, bitter powder, soluble in water; a bacteriostatic.

cetyl. Hexadecyl. The radical $C_{16}H_{33}$,— isomer of the cetic radical. **c. alcohol.** $C_{16}H_{33}OH = 242.35$. Ethal, 1-hexadecanol*, cetol. Colorless wax, m.40, insoluble in water; used to treat eczema. A solution in kerosine forms a film on water surfaces, used to reduce losses due to evaporation. **c. amine.** $C_{16}H_{33}NH_2 = 241.26$. Hexadecylamine. Colorless solid, insoluble in water. **c. cyanide.** Margaronitrile. **c. ether.** $(C_{16}H_{33})_2O = 466.51$. 1-Hexadecyl oxyhexadecane*. White leaflets, m.55, soluble in water. **c. iodide.** $C_{16}H_{33}I = 352.3$. 1-Iodohexadecane*. Colorless scales, m.22, insoluble in water. **c. trimethylammonium bromide.** Cetavlon.

cetylate. (1) A salt of palmitic acid containing the radical $C_{15}H_{31}COO—$. (2) A compound derived from cetyl alcohol containing the radical $C_{16}H_{33}O—$.

cetylene. Cetene.

cetylic acid. Palmitic acid.

cetylide. $(C_{16}H_{31}O_2)_3C_{16}H_{18}(OH)_3 = 1026.01$. A hydrolysis-product of cerebrin.

cevadic acid. $C_5H_8O_2 = 100.01$. Methyl crotonic acid, tiglic acid. A constituent of cevadine.

cevadilla. Sabadilla.

cevadilline. Sabadilline.

cevadine. $C_{32}H_{49}O_9N = 591.5$. Veratrine (Merck). An alkaloid from the seeds of sabadilla. Colorless needles, m.205, insoluble in water.

cevilline. $C_{29}H_{47}O_7N = 521.5$. An alkaloid saponification product of cevadilline.

cevine. $C_{27}H_{43}O_8N = 509.5$. An alkaloid hydrolysis product of cevadine.

cevitamic acid. Vitamin C.

cevollite. A fibrous zeolite alteration product of melilite.

ceyssatite. A white absorbent earth of almost pure silica (Ceyssat, France); used to treat eczema.

Cf. (1) Symbol for californium. (2) Abbreviation for confer or compare.

Cg. Abbreviation for centigram.

c.g. Abbreviation for center of gravity.

cgs, CGS. Abbreviation for centimeter-gram-second units.

Ch. Abbreviation for chain.

chabazite. $CaAl_2Si_4O_{12} \cdot 6H_2O$. Phacolite, cabazite. A zeolite, produced artifically by the action of water on cement. Cf. *acadialite, gmelinite.*

Chaddock burner. A small pottery furnace. **C. clamp.** A wooden test-tube holder. **C. support.** A buret stand with wire springs to hold two burets.

chaetomin. An antibiotic from cultures of *Chaetomium cochliodes.*

Chaga's disease. A form of trypanosomiasis in S. America.

chain. (1) A series of connected successive events or substances; as in c. reaction, or periodic c. (2) Similar atoms linked by homopolar bonds, as a carbon c. (3) A measure of length: 1 chain = 4 rods = 100 links = 20.11684 m. **bacterial-** A chainlike bacterial growth. *long-* A c. of more than

8 bacteria. *short-* A c. of 2–8 bacteria. **branched-** See (1) *lateral-* (2) *forked-.* **carbon-** A series of connected carbon atoms. **closed-** A ring formed by a c. of atoms, e.g., the benzene ring. **forked-** A branch of two small chains at the end atom of a long c. **lateral-** A branch c. in the middle of a longer c. **nuclear-** A reaction resulting from some types of nuclear fission. Cf. *atomic* bomb. Thus, 1 neutron + $U^{235} \rightarrow$ fission products + 2 neutrons + gamma rays. Then, 2 neutrons + $U^{235} \rightarrow$ fission products + 4 neutrons + gamma rays. The 4 neutrons react similarly, and so on. **open-** A number of atoms joined in a line. **periodic-** See *periodic system.* **side-** (1) Lateral c. (2) Usually a c. attached to a ring. (3) An atomic group of protoplasm which reacts with a nonprotoplasmic group. **straight-** Open c.

c. reaction. A series of successive reactions, each of which depends on the preceding one.

chainomatic. Describing an analytical balance with no separate weights less than 0.1 gm. Weights are determined by adjusting and measuring the length of the fine chain that hangs from one of the arms to balance the substance.

chaksine. $C_{11}H_{21}O_3N_3OH = 260.22$. A quaternary base in *Cassia absus.*

chalcacene. $C_{30}H_{20} = 380.15$. A pyrolytic product of acenaphthene. Red needles m.359, isomeric with rhodacene.

chalcanthite. $CuSO_4 \cdot 5H_2O$. Blue crystals, formed by the evaporation of cupriferous mine waters.

chalcedony. A cryptocrystalline, amorphous quartz, which occurs as a variety of semiprecious stones: agate (banded), cornelian (opaque), chrysoprase (green opaque), bloodstone (dark opaque, red spots), jasper, silicified wood moss agate (milky with dendritic manganese oxide), onyx (agate with alternating light and dark bands), plasma (green mottled), prase (gray-green), sardonyx (golden or blood-red).

chalcedonyx. White and gray layered agate.

chalcocite. Cu_2S. A native copper sulfide.

chalcogen(-ide)s. (Approved internationally.) Chalkogen. The elements oxygen, sulfur, selenium, tellurium, and polonium. Cf. *halogenide.*

chalcomorphite. A native, hydrous aluminum silicate.

chalcone. (1) $Ph \cdot CH:CH \cdot CO \cdot Ph = 208.10$. Phenyl styryl ketone, β-phenyl acrylophenone. (2) Aralkylic ketones. Natural yellow and orange substituted benzalacetophenone derivatives of the type $Ar \cdot CO \cdot CH:CHAr$. Cf. *flavones.*

chalcophanite. $ZnO \cdot 2MnO_2 \cdot 2H_2O$. A metallic, bluish black zinc manganite.

chalcophyllite. $Cu_7As_2O_{12} \cdot 14H_2O$. An oxidation-product of enargite; hexagonal, green, transparent crystals.

chalcopyrite. $CuFeS_2$. A metallic, yellow ore.

chalcopyrrhotite. $CuFe_4S_6$. A brown ore.

chalcose. A hexose component of the antibiotic chalcomycin.

chalcosiderite. $CuFe_6(PO_4)_4 \cdot 8H_2O$. A green ore.

chalcostibite. $CuSbS_2$. Wolfsbergite. A native, metallic, gray copper sulfantimonide, d.4.8–5.0.

chalcuite. A bluish green turquoise (New Mexico).

chaldron. An obsolete unit of dry measure; equals 36 bushels.

chalk. $CaCO_3$. Creta, calcite. Amorphous shell

residues, deposited from ocean oozes. See *calcium carbonate*. **French-** A grade of talc.

chalking. (1) To treat with chalk, e.g., in dyeing by passing cotton through a 0.6% suspension of chalk. (2) To form a powder which is easily rubbed off, e.g., from paints.

chalkogen(-ide)s. Chalcogens.

chalmersite. $CuFe_2S_3$. A native copper iron sulfide.

chalybeate. A drug or natural water containing iron salts; a blood tonic.

chalybite. Spathic iron ore. Native ferrous carbonate. Cf. *siderite*.

chamaeliretin. A resin-like substance from chamaelirin.

chamaelirin. The bitter principle of false unicorn root, *Chamaelirium luteum* (Liliaceae); poisonous saponin-like glucoside. Cf. *helonoid*.

chamazulene. $C_{15}H_{18}$ = 198.14. A blue hydrocarbon from chamomile oil.

chamber. (1) A boxlike receptacle. **cloud-** A c. making traveling particles visible. **fog-** Cloud c. **ionization-** A partly evacuated box, with galvanometer for detecting rays. (2) The leaded c. used in sulfuric acid manufacture, q.v. **c. acid.** Impure 60–70% sulfuric acid from the c. process. **c. crystals.** Nitrosyl sulfate. **c. process.** The manufacture of sulfuric acid in lead chambers from the interaction of sulfur dioxide, air, steam, and oxides of nitrogen.

Chamberland, Charles Edouard. 1851–1908. French bacteriologist. **C. filter.** A porous clay cylinder for filtering bacteria from solutions. **C. flask.** A glass flask with side tube, for growing bacteria.

chamelirin. Chamaelirin.

chamomile. A genus of composite plants; especially *Anthemis* species. **common-, English-, or Roman-** The flowers of *Anthemis nobilis* a tonic and febrifuge. **German-** See *Matricaria*. **wild-** Stinking mayweed, *Anthemis cotula*. See *anthemidine*.

c. oil. Essential oil from the *Anthemis nobilis* flowers. Blue liquid, d.0.910; contains esters of butyric, angelic, and tiglic acids. **German-** The essential oil of *Matricaria*, d.0.930–0.940; it contains esters of caproic acid, azulene, and chamazulene.

chamomillin. A bitter principle of chamomile.

chamosite. A constituent of berthierine.

champacol. $C_{17}H_{30}O$ = 250.24. Camphor from the wood of *Michelia champaca* (Magnoliaceae), Java. Colorless needles, m.87, insoluble in water.

chandoo. Chundoo. The best quality of raw opium, prepared for smoking. Cf. *mudat yenshee*. **c. dross.** Yenshee.

change of state. Passing from the solid to the liquid or from the liquid to the gaseous state; or the reverse. See *condensation, freezing, fusion, vaporization, sublimation*.

Chaperon cell. A voltaic cell consisting of amalgamated zinc and copper in a solution of potassium hydroxide; 0.98 volt.

char. (1) To carbonize or burn incompletely. (2) Charcoal.

charas. A drug from hemp resin.

charcoal. Amorphous carbon from the incomplete combustion of animal or vegetable matter, e.g., wood. Used to adsorb gases or coloring matters, in blowpipe analysis, and as a pigment (c. black). **activated-** See *activated carbon*. **animal-** C. pre-

pared from bone or blood. **vegetable- or wood-** C. from the incomplete combustion of wood, nutshells or fruit stones. Used medicinally, for hyperacidity and some forms of indigestion; commercially, as clarifying and decolorizing agent, and in gas masks. Cf. *carbonization, Norit*.

Chardin filter paper. A paper for the filtration of agar-agar solution for culture media.

Chardonize. Trade name for a cellulose acetate synthetic fiber.

Chardonnet silk. A viscose rayon, q.v.

charge. (1) A load or burden, e.g., the c. of ore in a furnace, the c. of electricity in a capacitor. (2) In physics, a definite quantity of electricity. **atomic-** The electricity carried by an atom or ion, which depends on the number of valence electrons. 1 electron ≡ 1.1×10^{-19} coulomb. Cf. Faraday. **elementary-** The c. of an electron, e = 4.770×10^{-10}. **fictitious-** The quantity of electricity contained in the material of a capacitor as distinct from the true c. of the plates. **ionic-** See *ionic c*. **nuclear-** See *atomic structure*. **residual-** The quantity of electricity remaining in a capacitor after discharge. **specific-** The ratio e/m_0. Cf. *electron*.

charging rod. (1) A piece of sealing wax, hard rubber, or glass used for charging electroscopes. (2) A device in which a Celluloid tube is rubbed over flannel to charge electroscopes.

Charles, Jacques Alex Caesar. 1746–1823. French chemist. **C. law.** Dalton's law, Gay-Lussac law. The volume of a gas at 0°C increases with each degree centigrade by $\frac{1}{273}$ if the pressure is constant. The pressure of a gas increases with each degree centigrade by $\frac{1}{273}$, if the volume is constant. Hence the ratio between the increase in pressure per degree and the pressure at 0°C (pressure coefficient) is the same for all gases.

Charleston phosphate. A soft phosphate mineral (27% phosphorus pentoxide).

charlock. The seeds of *Sinapis* (*Brassica*) *arvensis*, field mustard; condiment.

Charlton white. Lithopone.

charpie. Lint.

Charpy test. A measure of the effect of impact on sheet material. It is the dynamic analog of the Brinell test, q.v.

charring. Carbonizing.

Chatterton's compound. A cement for glass.

chaulmestrol. Ethyl chaulmoograte used to treat leprosy.

chaulmoogra oil. A yellow oil from the seeds of *Taraktogenos Kurzii* (Bixineae), India, d.0.946–0.951, m.5–20, iodine no. 103.5. It contains chaulmoogric, gynocardic and hydnocarpic acids. Used medicinally to treat leprosy and skin diseases.

chaulmoogrene. $C_{18}H_{34}$ = 250.3. *n*-Docecyl-Δ^4 cyclopentane, from chaulmoogric acid.

chaulmoogric acid. $C_{18}H_{32}O_2$ = 280.3. Cyclopentenyl tridecoic acid. Colorless crystals from chaulmoogra oil, m.68, soluble in alcohol.

chaulmugra. Chaulmoogra.

chavibetol. $C_{10}H_{12}O_2$ = 165.9. 1-Hydroxy-2-methoxy-5-allylbenzene. Colorless liquid, b.254. **iso-** Betelphenol, a constituent of essential oils. Cf. *eugenol*.

chavicic acid. An amorphous acid from chavicine.

chavicine. An alkaloid from black pepper.

chavicol. $C_6H_4\cdot(OH)C_3H_5 = 134.1.$ *p*-Allylphenol. A colorless constituent of betel oil, b.237. **methyl-** Estragole.

chavosot. *p*-Allylphenol, a dental bactericide.

chebulinic acid. (1) $C_{28}H_{20}O_{19}.$ A principle from the seeds of *Terminalia chebula*, E. Indies; an intestinal antiseptic. (2) $C_{41}H_{34}O_{27} = 958.0.$ An acid derived from tannin. (3) $C_{34}H_{30}O_{23} = 806.2.$ Eutannin. An acid from myrobalans. Rhombic prisms, decomp.234, soluble in hot water.

checkerberry. Gaultheria.

cheddite. A high explosive: potassium chlorate 70–90, aromatic nitro compounds 0–20, paraffin 0–15%.

cheese. A food prepared from the casein of skimmed or unskimmed milk, and flavored by the activity of certain bacteria.

cheiramidine. $C_{22}H_{26}O_4N_2\cdot H_2O = 400.24.$ An alkaloid from *Remijia puridieana* (Rubiaceae).

cheiramine. A secondary alkaloid from *Remijia purdieana*.

Cheiranthus. Wallflower. The herb *C. cheiri* (Cruciferae), which yields alkaloids, glucosides, and acids.

cheirantic acid. An oleic-type acid from the oil of *Cheiranthus*.

cheirantin. A glucoside from *Cheiranthus*.

cheirin. A digitalis-like glucoside from *Cheiranthus*,

chierinine. $C_{18}H_{35}O_{17}N_3 = 567.4.$ An alkaloid from the leaves of *Cheiranthus*. Colorless crystals, sparingly soluble in water.

chekan, cheken. The shrub *Myrtus cheken* (Myrtaceae) Chile; its bark is an astringent.

chekenetin. $C_{11}H_7O_6\cdot H_2O = 253.1.$ Olive crystals from *Myrtus* (*Eugenia*) *cheken* (Myrtaceae), Chile.

chekenine. $C_{13}H_{11}O_3 = 215.1.$ A volatile alkaloid from *Mytrus cheken*. Rhombic yellow scales.

chekenone. $C_{40}H_{44}O_8 = 652.4.$ A crystalline principle from *Myrtus cheken*.

chelafrin. Adrenalin.

chelate. (Greek *chele*—a crab's claw.) Pertaining to a molecular structure in which a ring can be formed by the residual valencies (unshared electrons) of neighboring atoms. **c. compound.** An organic compound in which atoms of the same molecule are coordinated; e.g., coordinate compounds of metals with ethylenediamine

$$\begin{array}{c} CH_2\cdot NH_2 \\ | \qquad\qquad\searrow M \\ CH_2\cdot NH_2 \nearrow \end{array}$$

c. groups. Atomic groups capable of forming rings by one or two coordinate bonds.

chelation. See *sequestration, complexing* agent.

chelatometry. Complexometric titration.

chelen. Ethyl chloride.

chelerythrine. $C_{21}H_{17}O_4N = 347.2.$ A narcotic alkaloid related to sanguinarine from the seeds of *Chelidonium majus* (Papaveraceae). Red crystals, m.203, slightly soluble in alcohol.

chelidonate. A salt of chelidonic acid containing the radical $C_7H_2O_6^-$.

chelidonic acid. $C_7H_4O_6 = 184.0.$ Pyronedicarboxylic acid from *Chelidonium majus* resembling meconic acid.

chelidonine. $C_{20}H_{19}O_5N = 353.2.$ An alkaloid from *Chelidonium majus* and opium. Colorless tablets, m.130, insoluble in water, a narcotic. **homo-** See *homochelidonine*.

c. hydrochloride. $C_{20}H_{19}O_5N\cdot HCl = 388.67.$ White crystals, soluble in water; a narcotic. **c. phosphate.** White crystals, a mild narcotic. **c. sulfate.** $(C_{20}H_{19}O_5N)_2\cdot H_2SO_4 = 804.49.$ White crystals, soluble in water; a sedative (small doses) and stimulant (larger doses).

Chelidonium. (1) Papaveraceous plants, e.g., *C. majus*, greater celandine. (2) Celandin. The leaves and stems of *C. majus*, used as a cathartic and for skin diseases.

chelidonoid. The combined principles of *Chelidonium majus*: chelidonine, chelerythrine, protopine, and other alkaloids.

chelidoxanthine. A yellow, crystalline bitter principle from *Chelidonium majus*.

chelonin. A brown, bitter, amorphous powder from *Chelone glabra*, snakehead (Scrophulariaceae); a tonic.

chelonoid. The combined principles of *Chelone glabra*; an irritant and anthelmintic.

chemavinite. Cedarite, Canadian amber. A mineral resin from Hudson Bay.

chemical. (1) Pertaining to chemistry. (2) See *chemicals*. **c. action.** A change in the molecular composition of a substance produced chemically or by heat, light, or electricity. See *reaction*. **c. activity.** Reactivity. **c. affinity.** See *affinity*. **c. antidote.** A c. used to counteract the effect of a poison, e.g., soaps. **c. burns.** The corrosive effect of chemicals on the skin. **c. change.** Reaction. **c. compound.** See *compounds*. **c. constitution.** See *structure*. **c. denudation.** The process by which salts in the soil are dissolved by water and carried to the sea. **c. energy.** The energy relations of c. reactions. Intensity is expressed by c. affinity or c. potential; capacity is expressed by the equivalent weight or the active mass. **c. entities.** The fundamental concepts of chemistry; as, atoms, ions, molecules, and free radicals. **c. equation.** The expression of a reaction in terms of c. formulas, e.g., reacting substances $(A + B) =$ reaction products $(C + D)$. *ionic-* The general statement of a c. reaction which shows only those substances actually undergoing change; thus: $Ba^{++} + SO_4^= = BaSO_4$. *molecular-* The specific statement of a c. reaction showing the relative proportions of substances involved; thus: $BaCl_2 + H_2SO_4 = BaSO_4 + 2HCl$. **c. microscopy.** The utilization of the microscope in chemistry, e.g., for identification of substances. **c. pulp.** Plant material treated by the soda, sulfite, or sulfate process for papermaking. **c. reaction.** See *reaction*. **C. Reference Substance.** A substance of established purity prepared for use in official (e.g., B.P. and B.P. Codex) assays. **c. societies.** The largest are, in order of foundation:

Chemical Society of London.............. 1841
Société Chimique de Paris 1858
Chemische Gesellschaft, Berlin............ 1867
American Chemical Society, Washington.... 1876

c. solvents. See *solvents*. **c. system.** An equilibrium characterized by definite proportions of reacting substances and reaction products. Cf. *phase rule, system*.

chemicals. Compounds or substances of definite molecular composition. Generally restricted to a single molecular species; whereas *drug* refers to a substance derived from a vegetable or animal source and often a mixture of substances. The grades of purity of chemicals are:

C.P. .... Chemically pure, the highest grade
U.S.P. or B.P. . Tested to conform with the requirements of the U.S. or British Pharmacopoeia, respectively
A.R........... Analytical reagent
Pure.......... For general work
Tech.......... For technical work
Crude .... An impure grade

kinetic-. Refrigerants.

chemiluminescence. Visible light produced during a chemical reaction without apparent temperature increase. See *luminescence*.

chemistry. The science of the fundamental structure of matter, the composition of substances, their transformation, analysis, synthesis, and manufacture. **analytical-** C. dealing with the detection (qualitative) and determination (quantitative) of substances. **animal-** C. dealing with the composition of animal tissues and fluids. Cf. *bio-*. **applied-Chemical technology.** C. applied to some useful end, either directly (through industry), or for the welfare of man. **astro-** The c. of the composition of celestial objects, as stars, and nebulae. **bio-** The c. of life; c. dealing with the composition of animal and vegatable matter, the changes occurring in the living organism, the transformation of food into living material, and the elimination of waste products. **biological-** Biochemistry. **commercial-** The compounding of substances for some utilitarian purpose. **electro-** C. dealing with the relation between electrical and chemical energy and their transformation. Cf. *electrolysis*. **empirical-** Chemical knowledge obtained by uncorrelated and unsystematic experimentation. **engineering-** C. applied to the composition and properties of engineering materials. **fermentation-** A branch of biochemistry dealing with the catalytic changes produced by enzymes. **food-** C. dealing with the quality, composition, and examination of foods. **forensic-** The application of chemical knowledge to legal matters. **galvano-** Electro-. **geo-** The c. of the earth's surface and the changes occurring in the atmosphere, hydrosphere, and lithosphere. **geological-** Geochemistry. **histo-** The c. of the composition of and chemical changes occurring in the tissues of plants and animals. **histological-** Histochemistry. **historical-** The study of the evolution of chemical thought through the ages. **inorganic-** The c. of polar compounds, usually those not containing carbon. **judicial-** Forensic. **legal-** Forensic. **manufacturing-** C. applied to the large-scale preparation of substances. **mechano-** A branch of physical c. dealing with the mechanical properties of substances, e.g., surface tension. **medical-** C. applied to medicine, to diagnose and combat disease. **meta-** The study of the subatomic or characteristically atomic properties of matter; as, adsorption. **micro-** See *micro, chemical microscopy.* **microscopical-** Microchemistry. **mineral-** Mineralogical or inorganic. **mineralogical-** C. dealing with the composition and formation of minerals. **organic-** The c. of carbon compounds; generally

those which are nonpolar. **pathological-** The c. of the composition of abnormal tissues and body fluids, and the changes caused by disease. **pharmaceutical-** C. applied to the preparation, testing, and composition of drugs. **photo-** The study of the relations of radiant and chemical energy and their transformation. **photographic-** C. applied to photography. **physical-** A branch of theoretical c. which deals with the transformation of physical and chemical energies. **physiological-** The c. of the composition of and chemical changes in the healthy animal or vegetable organism. **phyto-** The c. of plants and plant functions. **pure-** A branch of theoretical c. that deals with chemical forces alone. **radio-** A branch of theoretical c. which studies the composition and structure of the atom as revealed by the radioactive elements. **stereo-** The theoretical c. of the spatial structure of molecules. **stoichiometric-** C. dealing with chemical force as expressed by atomic weight and valency, the proportions in which substances react, and the distribution of atoms of a molecule. **structural-** A branch of stereochemistry dealing with the internal molecular arrangement of carbon compounds. **synthetic-** The building up of compounds from simpler substances. **technical-** C. applied to technology. **theoretical-** The deduction of laws which govern the experimentally established facts of c. **therapeutical-** A branch of medical c. dealing with the effect of drugs on the living organism. **thermo-** Physical c. dealing with the relation of heat and heat radiations during chemical changes. **topo-** See under *topochemistry.* **toxicological-** C. dealing with the composition and detection of poisons. **vegetable-** The biochemistry of the composition of plants and the changes occurring during their normal functions. **zoö-** The c. of animals and animal functions, excluding man.

chemoceptor. The anchoring group in the protoplasm of a cell which unites with the haptophore of drugs and renders them active.

chemo-immunology. The study of the chemical changes occurring in the immunization of an organism.

chemokinesis. The increase in activity of an organism due to a chemical substance.

chemology. An obsolete alternative term for chemistry.

chemolysis. The dissolution of organic matter during decay, due to chemical (not bacteria) action.

chemoreceptor. Chemoceptor.

chemoresistance. The specific resistance of a cell due to a chemical substance.

chemosmosis. Chemical reactions taking place through an intervening semipermeable membrane.

chemostat. A device to control the composition of the medium in the continuous culture of organisms.

chemosynthesis. A chemical reaction due to oxidation by bacteria; as, $H_2S \rightarrow H_2SO_4$. Cf. *photosynthesis*.

chemotaxis. Chemotropism. The attraction or repulsion of cells or organisms by chemicals.

chemotherapy. The action of certain molecules on protoplasm, certain radicals having selective affinity for parts of the cells. Cf. *chemoceptor*.

chemotropism. Chemotaxis, **negative-** The repulsion of microorganisms by chemicals. **positive-** The attraction of microorganisms by chemicals.

Chemstrand. Trade name for a mixed-polyester synthetic fiber.

chemurgic. Chemistry applied to farming. **C. Council.** An organization of Dearborn, Mich., U.S.A., to advance the industrial use of American farm products through applied science.

chenopodin. A bitter principle from *Chenopodium album*.

chenopodium. (1) The goosefoot family. (2) American wormseed, Mexican tea. The fruit of *C. anthelminticum*; used as a mild cardiac stimulant. **c. oil.** American wormseed oil. The essential oil from the seeds of *C. ambrosioides*; an anthelmintic. **c. seeds.** The fruits of *C. ambrosioides* or *C. anthelminticum*, American wormseed; an anthelmintic.

chernawinite. Canadian amber. A resinous mineral similar to amber.

chernozem. A black earth from semiarid steppe lands. The top layer is rich in humus; the bottom layers are rich in calcium carbonate.

cherry. A tree of the subgenus *Cerasus* of *Prunus* (Rosaceae). Cf. *cerasinose*. **wild-** See *wild*. **c. juice.** Succus cerasi. A sour, aromatic liquid from the ripe fruit of *Prunus cerasus*. Contains not less than 1% of malic acid; a pharmaceutical flavor.

cherry laurel. *Prunus laurocerasus* (Rosaceae); a sedative. **c. oil.** The essential oil of c., d.1.054–1.066, soluble in alcohol; contains hydrogen cyanide and benzaldehyde. **c. water.** The distillate of crushed c. leaves; an insecticide.

chert. Petrosilex. A mainly quartz splintering rock from sedimentary strata.

Cherwell. See *Lindemann*.

Cheshunt mixture. A substitute for bordeaux mixture, in which the lime is replaced by ammonium carbonate.

chessylite. Azurite.

chestnut. Castanea.

chevkinite. A complex mixture of hydrated oxides of K, Na, Fe, Ca, Mn, La, and Ce.

Chevreul, Michael Eugéne. 1786–1889. French chemist noted for work on fats and textile dyeing.

chi. The Greek letter χ, indicating 22nd C atom.

chibou. The resin of *Bursera gummifera*, Florida and tropical America; used in plasters.

chicle. Gum chicle, balata, tuno gum. The dried juice of the bully tree, *Mimusops balata* (Sapotaceae), northern S. America. Soft, gray masses, tasteless, m.49; used in chewing gum.

chicory. The root of *Cichorium intybus*, Europe and Asia, naturalized in the U.S.; a coffee substitute or adulterant.

chile. Capsicum. **c. niter.** Sodium nitrate. **c. saltpeter.** Caliche. Sodium nitrate in large deposits in Chile.

chilenite. Ag_6Bi. A silver bismuthide.

chilli, chilly. Capsicum.

chilte. A rubber tree, *Jatropha tepiquensis*, Mexico. It yields a latex, and a chicle used as a chewing gum base.

Chimaphila. Pipsissewa. The dried leaves of *C. umbellata* (Ericaceae); an antiperiodic and astringent.

chimaphilin. $C_{24}H_{21}O_4 = 373.1$. Yellow needles obtained from the leaves of *Chimaphila umbellata*, m.114, insoluble in water; a diuretic.

chimaphiloid. The combined principles from the leaves of *Chimaphila umbellata*; a stimulant and diuretic.

chimosis. See *gastric digestion*.

china. (1) Cinchona bark. (2) Porcelain. **c. clay.** The product obtained by leaching weathered deposits of granitic rocks to remove quartz and mica. Cf. *kaolin*. **c. grass.** Ramie. **c. jute.** The fiber from *Abutilon avicennae* (Malvaceae) China. **c. root.** (1) Smilax. (2) Galangal. **c. stone.** A mixture of feldspathic minerals, micas, and quartz; a flux for ceramic glazes. **c. tallow tree.** *Sapium sebiferum* (Euphorbiceae), whose seeds are rich in oil. **c. wood oil.** Tung oil.

chinacrin. Atebrin.

chinaldine. Quinaldine.

chinaphenine. $Et \cdot O \cdot C_6H_4NH \cdot CO \cdot OC_{20}H_{23}ON_2 = 485.29$. Quinine carbophenetidine. White powder, soluble in water; an antipyretic and antineuralgic.

chinaphthol. Quinanaphthol.

chinaroot. The dried rhizome of *Smilax china*, S. China, resembling sarsaparilla.

chinaseptol. Diaphtol.

chinazoline. Quinazoline.

chinchona. Cinchona bark.

chindoline. Quindoline.

chinese blue. Prussian blue. **c. cinnamon.** Cassia bark. **c. green.** Lokao. Green dye from the bark of Eurasian buckthorns, *Rhamnus utilis* and *R. globosa*. **c. oil.** Tung oil. **c. wax.** Ceryl cerotate formed on *Fraxinus chinensis* from the secretions of *Coccus ceriferus*.

chinic acid. Quinic acid.

chinidine. Cinchonidine.

chinindoline. Quinindoline.

chinine. Quinine.

chiniofon. $C_9H_6ONIS + Na_2CO_3$. Yatren, a mixture of 7-iodo-8-oxyquinoline-5-sulfonic acid with its sodium salt and sodium bicarbonate. Yellow crystals, effervescing in water to form sodium iodoxyquinoline sulfonate; an antidysenteric and amebicide (U.S.P.). **c. sodium.** $C_9H_5O_4NIS \cdot Na = 373.10$.

chinioidina. Quinoidine.

chinoform. Quinoform.

chinoidine. Quinoidine.

chinol. Hydroquinol.

chinoline. Quinoline.

chinopyrine. Quinopyrine.

chinoral. Quinoral. A compound of quinine and chloral; a hypnotic and antiseptic.

Chinosol. $C_9H_6ON \cdot SO_3K \cdot H_2O$. Trademark for for quinosol. Oxyquinoline potassium sulfonate. White powder; an antiseptic, styptic, and antipyretic.

chinothein. A mixture of quinine, caffeine, and antipyrine.

chinotoxine. Quinotoxine. A synthetic drug resembling curare.

chinotropine. Quinotropine.

chinovate. (1) A salt of quinovatic acid. (2) A compound of chinovase.

chinovin. Quinovin.

chinovose. A carbohydrate from cinchona bark.

chinwood. Taxus.

chiococcine. An alkaloid from the roots of *Chiococca racemosa*, cahinca, resembling emetine.

chiolite. $2NaF \cdot AlF_3$. Arksutite. A mineral resembling cryolite.

chionanthin. $C_{22}H_{28}O_{10} = 452.22$. A resin from *Chionanthus virginica*, the poison ash or fringe tree (N. America); a tonic and sedative. Cf. *chionanthus*.

chionanthoid. The combined principles from the bark of *Chionanthus virginica;* a hepatic stimulant and cholagogue.

chionanthus. The bark of *C. virginica*, poison ash, Virginia snow flower, mist tree (Oleaceae), southern U.S.; an aperient and diuretic.

chipboard. A low-grade board made from waste paper. **wood c.** A rigid constructional material made from wood particles bonded with a synthetic resin.

chipmunk crusher. A grinding machine for ores and rocks.

chiquito. A fat from *Combretum butyrosum* (Combretaceae), tropical Africa.

chirata. Chiretta. The dried herb of *Swertia* (*Ophelia*) *chirata* (Gentianaceae), India; a bitter tonic.

chiratin. $C_{26}H_{48}O_{15} = 600.5$. A glucoside from chirata. Yellow, hygroscopic powder, hydrolyzed to ophelic acid and chiratogenin.

chitenidine. $C_{19}H_{22}ON_2 = 294.2$. An oxidation product of quinine.

chitenine. $C_{19}H_{22}O_4N_2 = 342.19$. An oxidation product of quinine, used to treat malaria.

chitin. $C_{15}H_{26}O_{10}N_2 = 394.3$. The horny framework of invertebrates (crabs, lobsters, beetles); the animal analog of plant cellulose.

chitosamin. Glucosamine.

chitosan. A split product of chitin, related to mucin and chondrosin, and thus supporting the theory that the arthropods are ancestors of the vertebrates.

chittim bark. Cascara sagrada.

chlamydobacteria. Bacteria having various shapes; as, streptothrix.

chlamydozoa. A minute animal organism in a rigid sheath or capsule.

chlor- See *chloro-*.

chloracetamide. See *acetamide*.

chloracetate. A salt of chloracetic acid; contains the radical $CH_2ClCOO—$.

chloracetic acid. $CH_2ClCOOH = 94.49$. Carboxymethyl chloride. Colorless, rhombs, m.63, soluble in water. **tri-** See *trichlor-*.

chloracetone. $CH_2 \cdot Cl \cdot CO \cdot CH_3 = 92.51$. Acetyl methyl chloride. Colorless liquid, $d_{16°}1.162$, b.119, insoluble in water; liable to spontaneous combustion if not stored carefully.

chloracetophenone. $C_6H_5 \cdot COCH_2Cl = 154.5$. C.A.P. Phenacyl chloride. Rhombic crystals, m.59; a tear gas.

chloracetyl. Chloroacetyl. The radical $CH_2Cl \cdot CO—$, from chloracetic acid. **c. chloride.** $CH_2Cl \cdot COCl = 112.93$. Colorless liquid, b.105, decomp. by water.

chloracid. An organic acid containing chlorine.

chloracrylate. A salt of chloracrylic acid containing the radical $C_2H_2Cl \cdot COO—$.

chloral. $CCl_3 \cdot CHO = 147.37$. Trichloroacetic aldehyde, trichloroethanal*. Colorless, oily liquid, $d_{20°}$ 1.512, b.98, soluble in water; a hypnotic.

amylene- Dormiol. **anhydrogluco-** Chloralose. **butyl-** See *butyl*. **poly-** Hydronal. **urethan-** Uralin.

c. alcoholate. $CCl_3 \cdot CHOH \cdot OEt = 193.46$. Trichloroethylate. Colorless crystals, m.46, soluble in water; a hypnotic. **c. amide.** $CCl_3CHON \cdot NH_2 = 164.4$. C. ammonium. White crystals, m.71, soluble in alcohol; a hypnotic and analgesic. **c. ammonia.** C. amide. **c. antipyrine.** Hypnal. **c. benzamide.** $CCl_3CHOH(C_6H_5CONH) = 268.4$. Colorless crystals; a hypnotic. **c. betaine.** $C_7H_{12}O_3NCl_3 \cdot H_2O = 281.61$. White crystals, m.128, soluble in water; a hypnotic (B.P.). **c. caffeine.** A molecular mixture of caffeine and chloral, soluble in water. **c. cyanhydrin.** $CCl_3 \cdot CHOH \cdot CN = 174.4$. Trichloroacetonitrile. Colorless crystals, m.60, soluble in water; a substitute for bitter almond water. **c. hydrate.** $CCl_3CH(OH)_2 = 165.39$. Hydrated c., crystalline c. Colorless deliquescent needles, m.47.4, b.97 (decomp.), soluble in water, alcohol, or ether. A hypnotic, antispasmodic, antiseptic; a reagent for ergosterol; and a clearing agent for microscopy. **c. uric acid.** Chloraluric acid.

chloralbine. $C_6H_6Cl_2 = 148.9$. Colorless crystals from trichlorphenol.

chloralide. A compound of chloral.

chloralimide. $CCl_3CH:NH = 146.4$. Colorless crystals, m.155, soluble in alcohol; a hypnotic and analgesic.

chlorallyl. The radical $C_3H_4Cl—$, from allyl.

chlorallylene. Allyl chloride.

chloraloin. $C_{34}H_{30}O_{14}Cl_6 = 874.92$. Yellow precipitate from the action of chlorine on aloes.

chloralose. $C_8H_{11}O_6Cl_3 = 309.4$. Anhydroglucochloral. Colorless crystals, m.185, soluble in water; a hypnotic. **para-** An isomeric by-product obtained by the action of chloral on glucose. Colorless crystals, m.227; without therapeutic effect.

chloralurethane. Uralin.

chloraluric acid. $C_{14}H_{22}O_{11}N_{12}Cl_2 = 651.5$. Colorless crystals, obtained by the action of chlorous acid on uric acid.

chlorambucil. $C_{14}H_{19}NO_2Cl_2 = 304.21$. α-4-Di-(2-chloroethyl)aminophenylbutyric acid. White crystals, m.66, insoluble in water; used to treat leukemia (U.S.P., B.P.).

chloramide. Chloral amide.

chloramidobenzene. Chloraniline.

chloramine. $NH_2Cl = 51.53$. Monochloramine. Colorless, unstable, pungent liquid. An intermediate in the preparation of hydrazine from chlorine and ammonia. **chloramine-T.** Chlorazene.

chlorammine process. Chlorinating water by injecting chlorine and ammonia.

chloramphenicol. (U.S.P., B.P.). Chloromycetin.

chloranil. $C_6Cl_4O_2 = 245.84$. Tetrachlorquinone. Yellow scales, m.290 (sublime), slightly soluble in alcohol; an oxidizing agent in the dye industry, and seed protectant.

chloranilate. A salt of chloranilic acid containing the radical $C_6Cl_2O_4—$.

chloranilic acid. $C_6Cl_2O_2(OH)_2 = 209.0$. 2,5-Dichloro-3,6-dihydroxyquinone. Red leaflets, m.283, insoluble in water.

chloraniline. See *aniline*.

chloranion. The chlorate ion.

chloranol. $C_6H_2O_2Cl_4 = 247.85$. Tetrachloro-quinol. Pale yellow crystals; used as a reagent and in the dye industry.

chlorantimoniate. A double salt of a chloride with antimony trichloride.

chlorargentate. A double salt of a metal chloride with silver chloride.

Chlorargyrite. Argentum cornu.

chlorarsine. Cacodyl chloride.

chlorastrolite. A variety of jade.

chlorate. A salt of chloric acid which contains the radical $ClO_3—$. **c. ion.** The ion $ClO_3—$, from chloric acid.

chlorated. A substance containing readily available chlorine; as in chloride of lime. C.f. *chlorinated*.

chloraurate. (1) A double salt of auric chloride with another chloride. (2) A salt containing the radical $AuCl_4—$.

chlorauric acid. $HAuCl_4 = 340.0$. Yellow crystals, formed on evaporation of a solution of gold in aqua regia.

chlorauride. Auric chloride.

chloraurite. (1) A double chloride of the type $AuCl \cdot MCl$. (2) A compound containing the radical $AuCl_2—$.

Chlorazene. $MeC_6H_4SO_2Na:NCl \cdot 3H_2O = 281.5$, Trademark for sodium *p*-toluenesulfochloramine, mianine, activin, tochlorine, chloroamine, tolamine, chloramine-T. Dakin's antiseptic. A by-product of the manufacture of saccharin. Colorless crystals, soluble in water. Used as an antiseptic for irrigating wounds, and for the volumetric analysis of nitrites.

Chlorazol. $C_4H_3O_4NCl_3 = 235.4$. Trademark for a proprietary line of direct dyestuffs. An acrid, oily liquid obtained from proteins by distilling with nitric and hydrochloric acid.

chlorbenz-. Chlorobenz-.

chlorbenzamide. Benzamide.

chlorbenzene. See *benzene*, chloro-.

chlorbutanol, chlorbutol. Chloretone.

chlorcyclizine hydrochloride. $C_{18}H_{21}N_2Cl \cdot HCl = 337.30$. White crystals, m.225, soluble in water; an antihistaminic.

chlordane. Chlordom. A chlorinated hexahydro-methanoindene. Odorless liquid, $b_{2mm}17$; an insecticide (U.S. usage).

chlordiazepoxide hydrochloride. $C_{16}H_{14}ON_3Cl \cdot HCl = 336.22$. White, bitter crystals, soluble in water; a tranquilizer (B.P.).

chlordom. Chlordane.

chlorellin. An antibiotic produced by unicellular species of *Chlorella*.

chlorethanal alcoholate. Somnol.

chlorethane. See *ethane*.

chlorethanol. $ClCH_2 \cdot CH_2OH = 80.50$. Chlor-carbinol. Colorless liquid, d.1.213, b.129.

chlorethene. Ethylene.

chlorethyl. Ethyl chloride.

chlorethylene. See *ethylene*.

chlorethyl ether. $(ClCH_2 \cdot CH_2)_2O = 142.98$. Chlorex, Colorless liquid, d.1.213, b.178; a solvent.

chlorethylidene. Ethylidene.

chloretone. $CCl_3 \cdot CMe_2OH = 177.4$. Acetone chloroform, chlorobutanol, anesin, aneson. Color-less, odorous, deliquescent crystals, m.80, sparingly soluble in water; an anesthetic, antiseptic, and hypnotic.

Chlorex. Trademark for a solvent consisting pri-marily of dichloroethyl ether. **C. process.** A method of refining lubricating oils with C.

chlorhexidine hydrochloride. $C_{22}H_{30}N_{10}Cl_2 \cdot 2HCl = 578.40$. 1,6-Di-(4-chlorophenyldiguanido)hexane dihydrochloride. White, bitter crystals, m.225 (decomp.), soluble in water; an antiseptic (B.P.).

chlorhydrate. Hydrochloride.

chlorhydrin. A compound containing the radicals —Cl and —OH.

chloric acid. $HClO_3$. An acid of pentavalent chlorine, existing only in solution and as salts (chlorates). **per-** $HClO_4$. An acid of hepta-valent chlorine, existing only in dilute solution and as perchlorates.

chloride. A salt containing the Cl^- ion, usually a binary compound in which chlorine is the negative constituent. **c. of lime.** Bleaching powder. **c. of soda.** Sodium c. **c. ion.** Chlorion. A neg-atively charged atom Cl^-, formed from a soluble chloride in water.

chloridion. Chloride ion.

chloridization. (1) Chlorination. (2) The treatment of ores with chlorine or hydrochloric acid, to produce the chloride of the principal metal present.

chloridometer. Chlorometer. A device for esti-mating chlorides in urine.

chlorimetry. The determination of available or free chlorine in compounds.

chlorin. Crude dinitroresorcinol.

chlorinate. To introduce chlorine into a compound.

chlorinated. Treated with chlorine. Cf. *chlorated*. **c. lime.** Bleaching powder containing not less than 30% available chlorine. **c. solvents.** Non-flammable, stable, noncorrosive liquids formed by the action of chlorine on acetylene; e.g.: dieline, $C_2H_2Cl_2$, b.52; perchloroethane, C_2Cl_6, b.185.

chlorination. (1) The introduction of chlorine into a compound, especially by the substitution of H atoms. (2) The sterilization of water by chlorine. **break-point-** The optimum chlorine content of water in water, which produces no residual odor. When successive doses of chlorine are added to water, the residual chlorine rises to a maximum, then falls to a minimum (the break point), and then rises linearly. **exhaustive-** The successive substitution of all H atoms by Cl. **super-** See *super*.

chlorine. Cl = 35.453. A halogen element, at. no. 17. Greenish-yellow, poisonous, gas with suf-focating odor, m. -102.0, b. -33.60, d. (liquid Cl) 1.4, d. (gaseous Cl_2) 71.63 ($H_2 = 2$), or 2.49 (air = 1), soluble in water. After fluorine it is the most electronegative element. It is the most abundant halogen, and occurs as chlorides (seawater, salt deposits) in many minerals, and in all vegetable and animal tissues. It is a by-product from soda manufacture, or from electrolysis of chlorides. World output (1965), 18.2 million tons. Discovered by Scheele (1774). It consists of two isotopes: Cl^{35} and Cl^{37}; and is mono-, tri-, or pentavalent, giving:

−1 chloride..................	Cl^-	(NaCl)
+1 hypochlorite...............	ClO^-	(NaOCl)
+3 chlorites...................	ClO_2^-	$(NaClO_2)$
+5 chlorates	ClO_3^-	$(NaClO_3)$
+7 perchlorates	ClO_4^-	$(NaClO_4)$

A bleaching agent for textiles, straw, and sponges

a poison gas in chemical warfare; a gold extractant; a disinfectant, germicide, and insecticide; an oxidizing and reducing agent. **available-** (1) The c. that can be liberated from a substance, e.g., bleaching powder, by acids. (2) The c. equivalent of the active oxygen of an oxidizing agent, e.g., a hypochlorite. **eu-** A mixture of c. and c. dioxide produced by the action of hydrochloric acid on potassium chlorate. **c. cyanide.** Cyanogen chloride. **c. dioxide.** $ClO_2 = 67.5$. C. peroxide. A yellow irritating gas, b.9.9; or red liquid, d.1.5; soluble in water, decomp. in alcohol; a strong oxidizing agent forming hypochlorites or peroxides. It explodes in contact with ammonia, methane, phosphine, or hydrogen sulfide. **c. heptoxide.** $Cl_2O_7 = 182.9$. The anhydride of perchloric acid. Colorless oil, b.82, readily explodes. **c. hydrate.** $Cl \cdot 8H_2O = 179.6$ or $Cl \cdot 5H_2O = 86.91$. Yellow octahedra, stable below 9. **c. hydride.** Hydrochloric acid. **c. monoxide.** $Cl_2O = 86.9$. Anhydride of hypochlorous acid. Yellow liquid or gas, b.5, soluble in water, decomp. by alkalies. **c. oxides.** $Cl_2O =$ c. monoxide, anhydride of hypochlorous acid. $ClO_2 =$ c. dioxide. $Cl_2O_7 =$ c. heptoxide, anhydride of perchloric acid. $ClO_7 =$ c. tetroxide. The existence of Cl_2O_3 and Cl_2O_5 is doubtful. **c. water.** A pale green liquid of strong odor, obtained by passing c. through water. It contains 0.4 gm c. per 100 ml, and on keeping, it decomposes to hydrochloric and hypochlorous acid. A reagent to determine iodine, bromine, quinine, uric acid, or xanthine; an oxidizing and bleaching agent and antiseptic.

chlorinity. The weight of halides (as grams of Cl) in 1 kg seawater. Salinity $= 0.03 + 1.805 \times$ chlorinity.

chloriodic acid. Iodine monochloride.

chloriodide. A double salt of an iodide and chloride.

chloriodoform. $CHCl_2I = 210.8$. Formyl dichloroiodide. Yellow aromatic liquid.

chlorion. Chloride ion.

chlorisatide. $C_{16}H_{10}O_4N_2Cl_2 = 365.1$. A chlorine-substituted isatin. White insoluble powder.

chlorite. (1) A salt containing the radical $ClO_2{}^-$, from chlorous acid. (2) A group of rock-forming minerals; e.g., clinochlore.

chlorition. $ClO_2{}^-$ formed by ionization of chlorous acid and chlorites.

chloritoid. $Al_2O_3 \cdot FeO \cdot SiO_2 \cdot H_2O$. Phyllite mineral.

chlorknallgas. An explosive mixture of chlorine and hydrogen.

chloro- Describing an organic compound which contains chlorine atoms substituted for hydrogen atoms. The prefixes chlor- and chloro- are often interchangeable, but the former indicates a closer relationship of chlorine to the compound which it prefixes. E.g., chloracetate, $CH_2ClCOO-R$, is derived from chloracetic acid; chloroacetate, $CH_3 \cdot COO-R-Cl$, is derived from acetic acid and chlorine.

chloroacetophenone. Chloracetophenone.

chlorobenzaldehyde. $Cl \cdot C_6H_4 \cdot CHO = 140.5$. Chlorobenzene carbonal*. **o-** or **2-** m.11. **m-** or **3-**. m.17. **p-** or **4-** m.47.

chlorobenzoate. A salt of chlorobenzoic acid containing the radical $C_6H_4Cl \cdot COO-$.

chlorobenzoic acid. See *benzoic acid, chloro-*.

chlorobenzoyl. $C_7H_5OCl = 140.5$. Colorless liquid. **c. chloride.** $ClCO \cdot C_6H_4Cl$. ortho- b.238. meta- b.117. *para-* b.119.

chlorobenzyl. The radical C_7H_6Cl-; 10 isomers are possible.

chloroboric acid. Boron trichloride.

chlorobromacetate. A salt of chlorbromacetic acid of the type $CHClBr \cdot COOM$.

chlorobromopropane. Trimethylene chlorobromide.

chlorobutadiene. Chloroprene.

chlorobutanol. Chloretone.

chlorobutyric acid. Butyric acid.

chlorobutyryl. The radical $C_3H_2Cl \cdot CO-$.

chlorocalcite. Hydrophilite.

chlorocamphene. $C_{10}H_{12}Cl_4 = 273.8$. Colorless liquid from the action of chlorine on terebenthene.

chlorocarbinol. $CH_2Cl \cdot CH_2OH = 80.5$. Chlorethanol.

chlorocarbonate. Chloroformate. A compound containing the radical $ClCO \cdot O-$.

chlorocarbonic acid. Chloroformic acid.

chlorochromic acid. The compound $HCrO_3Cl$. See *chromyl chloride*.

chlorocinnamoyl. The radical $C_6H_4Cl \cdot CH:CH \cdot CO-$.

chlorocinnose. $C_9H_4OCl_4 = 269.8$. Colorless crystals, obtained by distillation of a mixture of cinnamic acid with phosphorus pentoxide.

chlorocitraconyl. $C_5H_4O_2Cl_2 = 166.9$. An addition product of citraconyl and chlorine.

chlorocitric acid. See *citric acid*.

chlorocosane. A liquid chlorinated paraffin containing chlorine in stable combination.

chlorocresol green. $C_{21}H_{14}Cl_4O_5S = 521.9$. 2,3,6,7-Tetrachloro-*m*-cresolsulfonphthalein. Gray powder; a pH indicator between 4.0 (yellow) and 6.0 (blue).

chlorocruorin. A respiratory, dichroic, red-green pigment related to hemoglobin; found in the blood of certain molluscs and especially marine worms.

chlorocyanide. A double salt of a chloride and cyanide: $MCl \cdot MCN$.

chlorocyanogen. Cyanogen chloride.

chlorodifluoromethane. $CHClF_2 = 86.5$. Colorless gas, b. -39.8; an anesthetic and refrigerant. Cf. *Freon*.

chlorodracylic acid. *p*-Chlorobenzoic acid.

chlorofluoride. A double salt of a chloride and fluoride: $MCl \cdot MF$.

chloroform. $CHCl_3 = 119.37$. Trichloromethane*. Colorless liquid, $d_{15}°1.499$, m.-63.2, b.61.2, almost insoluble in water; used as a general solvent, cleanser, anesthetic, anodyne, and antispasmodic. **aceton-** Chloretone. **colloidal-** Desalgin. **crystal-** Chloroformate. **germanium-** See *germanium*. **methyl-** $MeCCl_3 = 133.4$. Colorless liquid; an anesthetic. **nitro-** Chloropicrin. **phenyl-** Benzotrichloride.

c.-d. $CDCl_3 = 120.37$. Deuterochloroform, CH^bCl_3. White solid, m.64.2–64.7, formed from CCl_3CHO and D_2O. **c. of crystallization.** Chloroformate.

chloroformate. (1) A crystal with chloroform in its crystal structure. Cf. *water of crystallization*. (2) Chlorocarbonate. An ester of chloroformic acid; as palite.

chloroformic acid. $Cl \cdot COOH = 80.5$. Chlorocarbonic acid. A hypothetical acid; esters are known.

chlorofumaryl. Fumaryl chloride.

chlorogenic acid. $C_{16}H_{18}O_9 \cdot H_2O$. An acid in coffee and other plants. A depside of caffeic and quinic acid, m.208.

chlorogenine. $C_{21}H_{20}O_4N_2 \cdot 3\frac{1}{2}H_2O = 434.73$. Alstonine. An alkaloid from the bark of *Alstonia constricta*. Brown powder, m.195, insoluble in water; an antipyretic and antiperiodic resembling quinine.

chlorogriseofulvin. $C_{17}H_{18}O_6 = 318.16$. A neutral, crystalline, antibiotic product of the metabolism of *Penicillium griseofulvin*, Diercke, m.180.

chlorolactic acid. See *lactic acid*.

chloromalonic acid. See *malonic acid*.

chloromenthene. $C_{10}H_{17}Cl = 172.6$. A substitution product of menthol; a yellow oil.

chloromercuriphenol. $C_6H_4(OH)ClHg = 329.11$. Colorless crystals, m.152, soluble in alkalies.

chlorometer. Chloridometer.

chloromethane. Methyl chloride.

chloromethapyrilene. Chlorothen.

chloromethyl. The radical CH_2Cl—, from methyl chloride. **di-** The radical —$CHCl_2$. **tri-** The radical —CCl_3.

 c. chloroformate. Palite. **c. silicane.** $MeSiH_2Cl = 80.56$. Methylchlorosilane. Colorless gas, b.7.

Chloromycetin. $C_{11}H_{12}O_5N_2Cl_2 = 323.06$. Trademark for chloramphenicol (U.S.P.). *(1)*-ψ-1-*p*-Nitrophenyl-2-dichloroacetamide propane-1,3-diol. A stable, crystalline antibiotic from soils. Yellow needles, m.150; used to treat typhus.

chloronaphthalene. See *naphthalene*.

chloronitric acid. (1) Nitroxylchloride. (2) Aqua regia.

chloronitrobenzene. See *nitrobenzene*.

chloronitrophenol. See *nitrophenol*.

chloronitrous acid. Nitrogen oxychloride.

chlorophane. CaF_2. A mineral from Virginia.

chlorophenesic acid. Dichlor*phenol*.

chlorphenesin. $C_9H_{11}O_3Cl = 202.62$. 3-(4-Chlorophenoxypropane)-1,2-diol. White, bitter crystals, m.81, soluble in water; an antiseptic (B.P.).

chlorophenic acid. Monochlor*phenol*.

chlorophenisic acid. Trichlor*phenol*.

chlorophenol. See *phenol*. **c. indophenol.** An oxidation-reduction indicator. **c. red.** $C_{19}H_{12}Cl_2O_5S = 423.0$. Dichlorophenolsulfonphthalein. Yellow powder; a pH indicator between 5.5 (yellow) and 6.5 (red).

chlorophenothane. $C_{14}H_9Cl_5 = 354.51$. Dicophane, 1,1,1-trichloro-2,2-bis(*p*-chlorophenyl)ethane. White powder, congeals at 89, soluble in water; the insect toxicant of DDT.

chlorophenusic acid. Pentachloro*phenol*.

chlorophoenicite. $(Zn \cdot Mn)_3As_2O_8 \cdot 7(Zn \cdot Mn)(OH)_2$. It is green by reflected, and purple by transmitted light. **magnesium-.** C. with Mg in place of Zn.

chlorophorin. $C_{25}H_{30}O_4(?)$. A stilbene phenolic derivative, m.158, from iroko, *Chlorophora excelsa*, a decay-resistant African tree.

chlorophyll. The chromoprotein green coloring matter of plants. Soft, green mass, insoluble in water. Solutions in organic solvents fluoresce blue or green and are colloidal. C. contains

 70% chlorophyll *a*, $C_{55}H_{72}MgN_4O_5 = 892.9$
 30% chlorophyll *b*, $C_{55}H_{70}MgN_4O_6 = 908.9$

both of which have been synthesized (1960) from monocyclic pyrroles, by a 30-step process. Split

products are phtopyrrole (cf. *hemopyrrole*) and aetiophyllin, $C_{31}H_{34}N_4Mg$. A nonpoisonous coloring matter and deodorant, for oils, cosmetics, etc.; marketed as copper or zinc compounds. **alpha-** The purified chlorophyll $(C_{31}H_{29}N_3Mg)NH \cdot CO \cdot (COOMe)COOC_{22}H_{33}$. Cf. *phylloerythrin, phylloporphyrin*.

chlorophyllide. An ester of chlorophyllin; e.g., chlorophyll is the c. of phytol.

chloropicrin. $CCl_3NO_2 = 164.39$. Nitrochloroform, aquinite, trichloronitromethan*, P.S. Colorless liquid, $d_9°1.692$, b.112, insoluble in water; an insecticide and emetic gas.

chloroplast. A green protoplasmic granule containing the chlorophyll of vegetable cells; diameter 4–5μ.

chloroplatinate. Platinichloride. A double salt of platinic chloride and another chloride; or a salt of chlorplatinic acid containing the radical $PtCl_6=$.

chloroplatinic acid. $H_2PtCl_6 = 410.0$. The platinum chloride of commerce.

chloroplatinite. Platinochloride. A double salt of platinous chloride and anbther chloride; a salt of platinous acid containing the radical $PtCl_4=$.

chloroplatinous acid. $H_2PtCl_4 = 339.0$. A dibasic acid containing divalent Pt.

chloroprene. $CH_2:CH \cdot CCl:CH_2 = 88.5$. 2-Chloro-1,3-butadiene*. Colorless liquid, d.0.9583, b.59, synthesized from acetylene. It polymerizes to form: **alpha-** A plastic resembling unvulcanized rubber. **beta-** 2 volatile, fragrant products, $b_{27mm}92$–97 and 114–118. **micro-** A transparent product resembling vulcanized rubber. **omega-** A granular, balata-like, amorphous product, becoming plastic at 60°C. Used to manufacture duprene.

chloroprocaine hydrochloride. $C_{13}H_{19}O_2N_2Cl \cdot HCl = 307.22$. White crystals, m.174, soluble in water; a local anesthetic (U.S.P.).

chlorpropamide. $C_{10}H_{13}O_3N_2SCl = 276.74$. White crystals, m.127, insoluble in water; a hypoglycemic (U.S.P.).

chloropyridine. See *pyridine*.

chloroquine phosphate. $C_{18}H_{28}N_3Cl \cdot 2H_3PO_4 = 515.58$. Bitter, white crystals, darkening in light, soluble in water. Two forms: m.194 or 216. An antimalarial (U.S.P.); c. sulfate (B.P.).

chlororaphin. An antibiotic from *Chromobacterium*.

chlorosalol. $C_6H_4(OH)COOC_6H_4Cl = 248.53$. Chlorphenol salicylate. Colorless, crystals; an external antiseptic.

chlorosis. (1) Anemia, due to a deficiency of hemoglobin; or, with plants, of magnesium. (2) The use of chlorine and chlorides in agriculture.

chlorothen citrate. $C_{14}H_{18}N_3SCl \cdot C_8H_8O_7 = 487.98$. Chloromethapyrilene citrate. White crystals, slightly soluble in water; an antihistaminic.

chlorothiazide. $C_7H_6O_4N_3ClS_2 = 295.70$. White crystals, insoluble in water; a diuretic (B.P.).

chlorotoluene. Benzyl chloride.

chlorotrianisene (B.P.). Tri-*p*-anisylchloroethylene.

chlorotrinitrobenzene. Picryl chloride.

chlorous. Describing a compound containing trivalent chlorine $Cl\equiv$. **c. acid.** $HClO_2 = 68.5$. Known only in solution and as its salts (chlorites).

chlorovaleric acid. Monochlorovaleric acid.

chlorovalerisic acid. Trichlorovaleric acid.

chlorovalerosic acid. Tetrachlorovaleric acid.

chloroxalic acid. Chloroxalethyline.

chloroxalovinic acid. $C_4HO_4Cl_5 = 290.3$. Pentachlorethyloxalic acid. Colorless, hygroscopic crystals, soluble in water.

chloroxone. DCP (U.S.P.), 2-methyldichlorophenoxyacetic acid. A plant hormone weed killer, selective for charlock cereal crops.

chloroxyl. Trademark for a brand of cinchophen hydrochloride.

chloroxylene. Xylyl chloride.

chloroxylenol. $C_8H_9OCl = 156.60$. Trademark for parachlorometaxylenol, 2-chloro-5-hydroxy-1,3-dimethylbenzene. White crystals m.114, insoluble in water; a local antiseptic.

chloroxylonine. $C_{22}H_{23}O_7N = 413.3$. An alkaloid from satinwood of *Chloroxylon swietenia* (Rutaceae), E. Indies.

chlorphenasic, chlorphenesic, chlorphenic, chlorphenisic, chlorphenosic. See *chlorophen-*.

chlorphenesin. $C_9H_{11}O_3Cl = 202.55$. 3-(4-Chlorophenoxy) propane-1,2-diol. White, bitter crystals, m.80, soluble in water; used to treat fungal infections (B.P.).

chlorpheniramine maleate. $C_{16}H_{19}N_2Cl·C_4H_4O_4 = 390.88$. White crystals, m.132, soluble in water; an antihistaminic (B.P.).

chlorphenol. See *phenol*.

chlorproguanil hydrochloride. $C_{11}H_{15}N_5Cl_2·HCl = 324.64$. White bitter crystals, soluble in water; an antimalarial (B.P.).

chlorpromazine hydrochloride. $C_{17}H_{19}N_2ClS·HCl = 355.30$. Largactil, 3-chloro-10-(3'-dimethylamino-*n*-propyl)phenothiazine hydrochloride. White, pungent crystals, discoloring in light, m. approx. 195, soluble in water; a hypnotic which lowers body temperature (B.P.).

chlorpropamide. $C_{10}H_{13}O_3N_2ClS = 276.68$. N-4-Chlorobenzenesulfonyl-N'-propyl urea. White crystals, m.128, insoluble in water; an oral hypoglycemic (B.P.).

chlortetracycline hydrochloride. $C_{22}H_{23}O_8N_2Cl·HCl = 515.36$. Aureomycin hydrochloride. Bitter, yellow crystals, soluble in water; an antibiotic (B.P.).

chloryl. (1) The radical ClO_2—, as in $Cl_2O_5·3SO_3$. (2) Carbachol.

chlorylene. $CHCl—CCl_3 = 131.38$. Trichloroethylene. Colorless liquid, b.88; an antineuralgic.

chocolate. (1) A flavored beverage made from cocoa, milk, and sugar. (2) Theobroma paste. Ground cocoa; a basis for certain drugs.

choke damp. Black damp. A mixture of carbon dioxide and other gases in mines.

chola. Bile.

cholagogue. A drug that stimulates the flow of bile, e.g., salicylates.

cholalic acid. Cholic acid.

cholane. $C_{24}H_{42} = 328.39$. A hydrocarbon parent substance of sterols, hormones, bile acids, and toad poisons, is related to the carotenoids and cerebrosides by ring fracture. **c. ring.** Androstane ring. The tetracyclic, saturated ring system (the numbers are C atoms).

cholanthrene. $C_{20}H_{14} = 254.0$. A pentacyclic strongly carcinogenic hydrocarbon.

cholate. (1) A salt or ester of cholic acid, indicated by the radical $C_{24}H_{41}COO$—. (2) Taurocholate. A salt of taurocholic acid, indicated by the radical $C_{23}H_{39}O_3·COO$—.

choleate. A salt or ester of choleic acid containing the radical $C_{25}H_{44}O_5NS·COO$—. Cf. *taurocholate*.

cholecalciferol. Vitamin D_3.

cholecyanin. Bilicyanin.

choleic acid. (1) Taurocholic acid. (2) $C_{25}H_{42}O_4 = 392.31$. From bile, m.190. **glyco-, tauro-** See *bile acids*.

cholesterase. An enzyme that hydrolyzes cholesterol.

cholesterate. A salt or ester of cholesteric acid, containing the radical $C_8H_8O_5$—.

cholesterilene. $C_{26}H_{42} = 354.7$. An unsaturated hydrocarbon derived from cholesterol. White crystals.

cholesterin. Cholesterol.

cholesterinic acid. Cholesteric acid.

cholesterol. $C_{27}H_{45}OH = 386.35$. Cholesterin. A monoatomic alcohol in blood, brain tissue, spleen, liver, bile; the principal constituent of gallstones and certain cysts; prepared from wool grease. Pearly scales, m.148, insoluble in water. An antiseptic, an antidote to saponins and important in metabolism. See *cholane*. **7-dehydro-** Provitamin D_3. **iso-** Lanosterol. **thio-** $C_{27}H_{46}SH$. A solid, m.191. Cf. *lanisterol*.

cholestrophan. $NMe·CO·NMe·CO·CO = 142.06$. Dimethylparabanic acid. Pearly leaflets, m.145, soluble in water.

choletelin. $C_{16}H_{18}N_2O_6$. A yellow oxidation product of biliverdin.

cholic acid. $C_{24}H_{40}O_5 = 408.32$. Cholalic acid, formed by the hydrolysis of bile acids. White crystals, m.198, insoluble in water. Cf. *cholane*. **desoxy-** See *desoxycholic acid*. **glyco-** See *glycocholic acid*. **litho-** See *lithocholic acid*. **rhizo-** An oxidation product of cholic acid. **tauro-** See *taurocholic acid*.

choline. $Me_3N(OH)CH_2CH_2OH = 121.26$. Bilineurine, sinkaline, trimethylethanolammonium hydroxide. A ptomaine in many animal and vegetable tissues. Viscous liquid, soluble in water. **acetyl-** See *acetyl*. **hydroxy-** Muscarine. **iso-** Amantine.

c. bases. A group of quarternary amines containing pentalent nitrogen, and derived from ammonium hydroxide by replacing the hydrogen atoms by radicals: choline, neurine, muscarine, betaine, sinapine. **c. chloride.** $C_5H_{14}ClO_2N = 155.5$. Colorless, hygroscopic crystals, soluble in water. **c. hydrochloride.** C. chloride. **c. theophyllinate.** $C_{12}H_{21}O_3N_5 = 283.28$. White crystals, m. 190, soluble in water; a bronchodilator (B.P.).

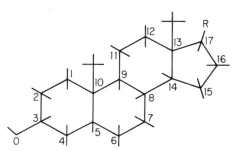

The androstane or cholane ring.

cholohematin. Bilipurpurin. A brown bile pigment.

chololic acid. Cholic acid.

cholophaein. $C_{16}H_{18}O_4N_2 = 302.16$. A brown biliary pigment in feces. Cf. *choletelin*.

chondrigen. Cartilagin.

chondrin. A mixture of mucin and gelatin from cartilage. A transparent, gelatinous mass, soluble in water.

chondrite. A stone meteorite containing rounded constituents (chondrules): iron and nickel 8–16, marcasite 5%, with silicates. Cf. *achondrite*.

chondrodite. Humite.

chondrodystrophy. Abnormal skeleton formation in the embryo.

chondroine. $C_{18}H_{21}O_4N = 315.2$. An alkaloid from *Nectandra rodiaci* (Lauraceae), tropical America. Cf. *bebeerine*.

chondroitin. $C_{18}H_{27}O_{14}N = 481.22$. A mucus-like constituent of chondrin.

chondrometer. An instrument to determine the weight of a bushel of grain.

chondromucoid. A cartilage albuminoid containing conjugated chondroitic acids.

chondroprotein. A group of mucoids in the connective tissues.

chondrosamine. $C_6H_{12}O_5N = 178.11$. 2-Amino-*d*-galactose. A widely distributed polysaccharide.

chondrule. See *chondrite*.

chorionic gonadotrophin. A dry, sterile preparation of the gonad-stimulating substance from the urine of pregnant women (B.P.).

choritoid. $Al_2O_3 \cdot FeO_2 \cdot SiO_2 \cdot H_2O$. A mica-type mineral.

choroid. The layer below the retina of the eye.

chrithmene. Crithmene.

chroatol. $C_{10}H_{16}2HI = 391.8$. Terpene iodohydrate. A green oil, obtained by the action of iodine on turpentine.

chroma. The degree of saturation of a color.

chroman. $C_6H_4 \cdot O \cdot CH_2 \cdot CH_2 \cdot CH_2 = 134.13$. Dihydrobenzopyran. Its derivatives are coronary vasodilators. **hydrindo-** Hydrindochroman. **thio-** Thichroman.

chromastrip. The strip of paper used in paper chromatography q.v.

chromate. A salt of chromic acid containing the radical $CrO_4=$. **bi-, Di-, di-** An acid salt derived from chromic acid containing the radical $Cr_2O_7=$, which makes aqueous solutions orange. **per-** See *perchromate*.

c. cell. See *cell*. **c. green.** A mixture of chrome yellow and prussian blue. Cf. *chrome green*. **c. ion.** The $CrO_4=$ ion, yellow in aqueous solutions.

chromatic. Pertaining to colors. *iso-* or *ortho-* 3500–6000 A. *tri-* 3500–6500 A. *pan-* 3500–7000 A.

c. aberration. The refraction of the constituent rays of white light by a lens, to different extents; it produces an image fringed with color. **c. plate.** A photographic plate used in conjunction with color screens to produce a contrasting colored image. Cf. *photosensitizer*.

chromatin. The structural part of the cell nucleus that is most deeply stained.

chromatographic analysis. The analysis of mixtures of solutions by selective adsorption on materials such as gelatin, alumina. The analytical process based on differences in the distribution ratios of the components of mixtures between a mutually immiscible mobile and a fixed phase. In particular, the formation of isolated bands which can be separated mechanically and further examined. The mobile phase (sample and carrier) can be a gas, liquid, or solid in solution, but the stationary phase (the column) can be only a liquid or solid. Hence the combinations: liquid:liquid (paper); liquid:solid (conventional separation); gas:liquid (partition); gas:solid (adsorption). There are no theoretical differences among these methods. **gas-** C. in which the mobile phase is a gas; e.g., the gas mixture is passed through the column. **reversed phase-** Column c. in which the stationary phase is less polar than the mobile phase. **thin-film-** The use of thin films (as silica) deposited on glass, for the separating column in c. **vapor-phase-** Gas c.

chrome. (1) Chromium. (2) Chromium ore. (3) Chromium oxide. (4) Lead chromate. **c. alum.** Ammonium chromic sulfate. **c. green.** A mixture of chromic oxide and cobalt oxide. **c. ore.** Chromite. **c. red.** Lead chromate. **c. violet.** Aurine tricarboxylic acid. **c. yellow.** Lead chromate.

Chromel. Trademark for alloys highly resistant to heat, oxidation, and acids. They contain Ni 80–90, Cr 10–20, with or without Fe 24–66%.

chromic. Describing a compound containing trivalent chromium, $Cr\equiv$. **c. acetate.** $Cr(C_2H_3O_2)_3 \cdot H_2O = 247.09$. Green powder, soluble in water. **c. acid.** (1) $H_2CrO_4 = 118.1$. The hydrate of CrO_3; exists only in solution or as salts. (2) CrO_3. Chromium trioxide. **c. anhydride.** Chromium trioxide. **c. arsenide.** Chromium arsenide. **c. boride.** Chromium boride. **c. bromide.** (1) $CrBr_3 = 291.76$. Green hexagons, soluble in water. (2) $CrBr_3 \cdot 6H_2O = 399.85$. C.b. hexahydrate. Green scales, insoluble in water. **c. carbide.** $Cr_3C_2 = 180.06$. Black powder, d.5.62, insoluble in water. **c. carbonate.** $Cr_2(CO_3)_3$. Black powder containing some hydroxide; insoluble in water. **c. chloride.** (1) $CrCl_3 = 158.38$. Purple crystals, soluble in water. (2) $CrCl_3 \cdot 6H_2O = 266.48$. Green or purple scales, soluble in water. **c. fluoride.** $CrF_3 \cdot 4H_2O = 181.1$. Green crystals, m.1,000, soluble in water; used in dyeing and printing cotton, and coloring white marble. **c. hydroxide.** $Cr(OH)_3 \cdot 2H_2O = 139.1$. A green pigment, insoluble in water. **c. iodide.** $CrI_3 \cdot 9H_2O = 437.9$. Black powder, soluble in water. **c. nitrate.** $Cr(NO_3)_3 \cdot 9H_2O = 400.2$. Purple prisms, m.36.5, soluble in water; a reagent. It crystallizes also with $7H_2O$ and with $6NH_3$. **c. oxide.** $Cr_2O_3 = 152.0$. Chrome green. Green hexagons, m.2059, insoluble in water; a pigment for calico printing, ceramics and glass. **c. oxychloride.** Chromyl chloride. **c. phosphate.** $CrPO_4 = 147.1$. Plessy's green, Arnaudon's green. Green powder, insoluble in water; a pigment. It crystallizes with 3 and $6H_2O$. **c. potassium alum.** Potassium c. sulfate. **c. potassium cyanide.** Potassium chromicyanide. **c. potassium oxalate.** $K_3Cr(C_2O_4)_3 \cdot 3H_2O = 487.35$. Purple crystals, soluble in hot water. **c. potassium sulfate.** Potassium c. sulfate. **c. silicide.** $Cr_3Si_2 = 212.1$. Black crystals, insoluble in water. **c. sulfate.** $Cr_2(SO_4)_3 = 392.2$. Green powder, soluble in water; used to manufacture c. compounds. It crystallizes with $6H_2O$ (green) or

$15H_2O$ (violet). *cryst-* $Cr_2(SO_4)_3 \cdot 18H_2O = 716.5$. Violet crystals, anhydrous at 100, soluble in water; used to manufacture green inks and chromium compounds. **c. sulfide.** $Cr_2S_3 = 200.6$. Green powder, insoluble in water. **c. sulfite.** $Cr_2(SO_3)_3 = 344.2$. Green crystals, d.2.2. **c. tartrate.** $Cr_2(C_4H_4O_6)_3 = 548.5$. Purple scales, soluble in water.

chromicyanide. The radical $Cr(CN)_6 \equiv$. **c. ion.** The $Cr(CN)_6{}^{3-}$ ion; it imparts a yellow color to solutions.

chromising. Chromizing.

chromite. (1) An oxide of iron and chromium containing 68% of chromic oxides. Black streaked masses (Asia Minor), d.4.3–4.6, hardness 5.5. Used to make refractory bricks and cements, chromium compounds or ferrochrome, and to color glass and tiles green. (2) A salt of chromous acid containing the radical CrO_2-. **thio-** A compound of the type $M_2Cr_2S_4$. **c. ion.** The $CrO_3{}^{=}$ ion, derived from chromous acid or the chromites.

chromitite. The mineral Fe_2O_3, Cr_2O_3.

chromium. $Cr = 51.996$. An element, at no. 24, silver-white, hard, brittle, d.7.1, m.1615, insoluble in water, but dissolved rhythmically by acids (active and passive c.); discovered by Vauquelin (1797); occurs principally in chromite. C. is prepared from ores by reduction with metallic aluminum (thermite process), and is used in corrosion-resistant alloys and heavy duty steels. C. compounds are poisonous and variously colored. They are di-, tri-, or hexavalent:

+2 chromous (blue) .... Cr^{++}
+3 chromic (purple) .... Cr^{3+}
   chromites (green) .... $CrO_2{}^-$
+6 chromyl (red) .... $CrO_2{}^{++}$
   chromates (yellow) .... $CrO_4{}^=$
   dichromates (orange) .... $Cr_2O_7{}^=$

In acid solution   *In alkaline solution*

Reduction $\left\{ \begin{array}{c} Cr^{3+} \\ \text{green or} \\ \text{violet} \\ \uparrow \\ Cr_2O_7{}^{3-} \\ \text{orange} \end{array} \right.$ $\rightleftharpoons$ $\left. \begin{array}{c} CrO_2{}^- \\ \text{green} \\ \downarrow \\ CrO_4{}^= \\ \text{yellow} \end{array} \right\}$ Oxidation

Cr^{51}. A radioactive isotope made by neutron irradiation of Cr. **c. acetate.** See *chromous*. **c. arsenide.** $CrAs = 127.1$. Black crystals, d.6.35, insoluble in water. **c. boride.** $CrB = 63.1$. Black powder, insoluble in water. **c. chloride.** See *chromic, chromous, chromyl*. **c. dioxide.** $CrO_3 = 84.1$. Black powder obtained on reducing potassium dichromate by sodium thiosulfate, and regarded as chromic chromate, $Cr_2O_3 \cdot CrO_3 = 3CrO_2$. **c. minerals.** C. is common in magnesium and other rocks: e.g., chromite, $FeCr_2O_4$; crocoite, $PbCrO_4$; knoxvillite, $CrSO_4$. **c. mordants.** C. used in tanning and dyeing; chrome alum. **c. oxides.** See *chromous oxide, chromic oxide (green), c. dioxide (black), c. trioxide (red).* **c. phosphide.** $CrP = 83.2$. Black powder, insoluble in water. **c. plating.** The electrolytic coating of metals with a layer of c. 0.00001 in. thick, over a layer of nickel, which produces a noncorrodible surface. **c. potassium oxalate.** $K_3Cr(C_2O_4)_3 \cdot H_2O = 487.36$. Violet

crystals, soluble in water. **c. tetrasulfide.** $Cr_3S_4 = 284.27$. Gray powder. **c. trioxide.** $CrO_3 = 100.01$. Chromic acid anhydride. Crimson needles, m.190, soluble in water, readily reduced to the green oxide. A powerful oxidizing agent. **c. tungsten steel.** A heat- and chemical resistant steel containing 5 Cr and 1% W.

chromizing. Forming a protective surface layer of c.; e.g., on steel by ion exchange, by heating it in c. vapor at 800–900°C.

chromo. A paper coated with a mixture of a white pigment (e.g., china clay, blanc fixe, etc.) and an adhesive (e.g., casein), to obtain fine color prints.

chromoform. Methylhexaminetetramine dichromate; a urinary antiseptic.

chromogen. (1) The parent substance of a dyestuff, or of a compound which produces a colored substance. (2) A substance in biological life which, on oxidation, forms colored compounds; as, sepia. Cf. *chromophore, auxochrome.* **c.-I.** Chromotropic acid.

chromogene. A light-resistant acid dye.

chromogenic. Pertaining to a chromogen. **c. bacteria.** Bacteria which produce colored substances.

chromoisomerism. Chromotropy.

chromoisomers. Differently colored modifications of a substance. Cf. *chromotropy.*

chromolipoid. Lipochrome.

chromomere. A structural unit of a chromosome containing a gene.

chromometer. Colorimeter.

chromone. $C_6H_4 \cdot CO \cdot CH \cdot O = 146.05$. 1,4-Benzopyrone. White needles, m.59, insoluble in water; present in many vegetable pigments. Some derivatives are coronary vasodilators. **2-phenyl-** Flavone. **3-phenyl-** Iso*flavone*.

chromonucleic acid. Desoxyribosenucleic acid.

chromophilic. Having an affinity for colors.

chromophore. A structural arrangement of atoms in many colored organic substances, e.g., —N=N—. Cf. *resonator,*

chromophoric. Having properties of a chromophore. **c. group.** The nitro, azo, quinoid, and —C:CH·CO— radicals, having the possibility of a shifting double bond. See *chromophore, auxochrome.*

chromophotometer. Colorimeter.

chromoplast(id). The micelles of coloring matter in plant cells, usually other than chlorophyll.

chromoprotein. A conjugated protein (or protein compound) and a chromophore; as, hemoglobin. Cf. *cytochrome.*

chromosaccharometer. A device to determine sugar in urine colorimetrically.

chromosan. A mixture of sodium dichromate and ammonium phosphate; a dye mordant.

chromoscope. A colorimeter.

chromosome. A differentiated protoplasm formed from the chromatin of the nucleus during cell division. Their number is constant for each animal species, but may differ between species.

chromosomin. The principal protein of chromosomes.

chromosphere. A gaseous upper "atmosphere" surrounding the sun, composed mainly of hydrogen, helium, and calcium vapors, and responsible for the Fraunhofer lines. Cf. *photosphere, corona.*

chromotrope-B. p-Nitrobenzeneazo-1,8-dihydroxy-naphthalene-3,6-disulfonic acid. A colorimetric reagent for boron. **c.-2B.** p-Azonitrobenzene.

chromotropic acid. $C_{10}H_6O_2(SO_3H)_2 = 320.18$. Chromotrope acid, chromogen-I, 1,8-dihydronaphthalene-3,6-disulfonic acid; an intermediate and analytical reagent.

chromotropy. Chromoisomerism. The property of certain substances of the same chemical composition, of occurring in differently colored forms (chromoisomers).

chromous. Describing a compound of divalent chromium, $Cr =$. **c. acetate.** $Cr_2(C_2H_3O_2)_6 \cdot 2H_2O = 494.24$. A blue mass, soluble in water; used in calico printing and as a stain. **c. acid.** $HCrO_2$ or $HO \cdot CrO$. A blue powder; a weak acid which yields chromites. **c. chloride.** $CrCl_2 = 123.0$. White crystals, soluble in water to form a blue solution which absorbs oxygen. **c. hydroxide.** $Cr(OH)_2 = 86.0$. Brown powder, decomp. by heat, insoluble in water. **c. iodide.** $CrI_2 = 306.0$. White crystals, soluble in water. **c. oxalate.** $Cr(OOC)_2 = 140.1$. Green scales, soluble in hot water. **c. oxide.** $CrO = 68.04$. Chromium monoxide. Stable only in the hydrated state. **c. sulfate.** $CrSO_4 \cdot 7H_2O = 274.2$. Blue crystals, soluble in water.

Chromspun. Trademark for a cellulose acetate synthetic fiber.

chrom-X. A high-carbon ferrochromium steel.

chromyl. The radical $CrO_2 =$ containing hexavalent chromium. **c. amide.** $CrO_2(NH_2)_2 = 116.1$. **c. chloride.** $CrO_2Cl_2 = 155.0$. Chromic oxychloride, chlorochromic acid. Red fuming liquid, d.1.96, b.116, decomp. in water; a powerful oxidizing agent.

chronic. Long-continued. Cf. *acute*.

chronograph. An instrument to record small time intervals.

chronopotentiometry. Electroanalysis based on the time after which a rapid change in potential of a working electrode occurs; this is a measure of the concentration of the electroactive substance present.

chronoscope. A device to measure short time intervals.

chronoteine. A high-speed moving picture camera for the study of rapid-moving machinery or phenomena. Cf. *stroboscope*.

chrysalicic acid. $C_7H_5O_6N_3 = 227.06$. Dinitro-o-aminobenzoic acid. Isomer of chrysanisic acid.

chrysamine. $Na_2C_{18}H_{16}O_6N_4 = 430.17$. Flavophenine. A yellow azo dye, obtained from benzidine and toluidine.

chrysammic acid. $C_{14}H_2(NO_2)_4(OH)_2O_2 = 420.14$. Chrysamminic acid. A constituent of aloes prepared by the action of nitric acid on chrysophanic acid. A solid, insoluble in water.

chrysamminic acid. Chrysammic acid.

chrysanilic acid. A decomposition product of indigo blue.

chrysaniline. $C_{19}H_{15}N_3 = 285.2$. ms-p-Amidophenyl-2-amidoacridine. Yellow crystals, m.268.

chrysanisic acid. $NH_2 \cdot C_6H_2(NO_2)_2COOH = 227.06$. 3,5-Dinitro-4-aminobenzoic acid. Colorless crystals, m.259. Isomer of chrysalic acid.

chrysanthemin. An anthocyanin from elderberries.

chrysanthemum monocarboxylic acid. $C_{10}H_{16}O_2 = $ 168.13. Colorless crystals, m.18.5. **c. dicarboxylic acid.** Colorless lozenges, m.168. Certain esters are the active principles of pyrethrum flowers.

chrysarobin. $C_{15}H_{12}O_4 = 256.1$. A neutral principle from goa powder, the exudates of *Andira* (*Vouacapoua*) *araroba* (Leguminosae), Brazil. Yellow crystals, insoluble in water. A gastrointestinal antiseptic, antiparasitic, and alterant. **c. tetraacetate.** Lenirobin. **c. triacetate.** Eurobin.

chrysatropic acid. Scopoletin.

chrysazin. $C_{14}H_6O_2(OH)_2 = 240.13$. 1,8-Dihydroxyanthraquinone. A solid, m.280, slightly soluble in alcohol. **tetranitro-** Chrysammic acid.

chrysazol. $C_{14}H_{10}O_2 = 210.1$. 1,9-Dioxyanthracene, 1,8-anthradiol. A phenol derived from anthracene; used in the dye industry.

chryseam. $C_4H_5N_3S_2 = 159.8$. White crystals; reagent for nitrites (red color).

chrysene. $C_{18}H_{12} = 228.19$. Benzophenanthrene. Red fluorescent scales from coal tar, m.250, slightly soluble in alcohol.

chrysin. $C_{15}H_{10}O_4 = 254.1$. 5.7-Dihydroxyflavone, in poplar buds, m.275.

chrysoberyl. $BeAl_2O_4$. A golden yellow gem, d.3.5–3.8. Cf. *alexandrite*.

chrysocolla. $CuH_2SiO_4 \cdot H_2O$. A green mineral, d.2.0–2.2.

chrysofluorene. $C_{10}H_6 \cdot C_6H_4 \cdot CH_2 = 216.1$. Naphthylenephenylenemethane. Colorless crystals, m.180.

chrysoidin. $C_7H_{22}O_4 = 170.2$. A yellow pigment in asparagus berries.

chrysoidine. $C_{12}H_{13}N_4Cl = 248.66$. Diaminoazobenzene. **c. orange.** Brown powder, soluble in water. A disinfectant, dye, and indicator at pH 7.0; orange (acid), yellow (basic).

chrysoketone. $C_{10}H_6 \cdot C_6H_4 \cdot CO = 230.1$. Crystals, m.130.

chrysolepic acid. Picric acid.

chrysolite. Olivine.

chrysophanic acid. $C_{15}H_{10}O_4 = 254.1$. 4,5-Dihydroxy-2-methylanthraquinone, parietic acid. A constituent of rhubarb root, senna leaves, goa powder and the wood of *Vouacapoua araroba*. Yellow crystals; a mild laxative. Cf. *rhein*.

chrysophanin. $C_{20}H_{20}O_9 = 404.2$. A glucoside in rhubarb and senna.

chrysophanol. Chrysophanic acid.

chrysophyscin. Physcion.

chrysopicrin. Vulpic acid.

chrysoprase. A green opaque gem variety of chalcedony.

chrysoquinone. $C_{10}H_6 \cdot C_6H_4 \cdot CO \cdot CO = 258.1$. Chrysene quinone. Red needles, m.235.

chrysorrhetin. A yellow coloring matter of senna.

chrysotile. $3MgO \cdot 2SiO_2 \cdot 2H_2O$. Canada asbestos; comprises 90% of world asbestos output, as it blends with textile fibers.

chrysotoxin. An active principle of ergot.

chuchuarine. $C_{20}H_{15}O_2N_{12} = 455.2$. An alkaloid from *Semecarpus anacardium* (Anacardiaceae), E. Indies. It resembles strychnine.

chum. The sediment in fatty oils.

chundoo. See *chandoo*.

churning. The slow stirring of milk or cream by which the fat globules aggregate to form butter.

chyazic acid. Hydrocyanic acid.

chyle. An emulsion of lymph and fat formed in the small intestines during digestion, and passing into the veins as blood.

chymase. An enzyme coagulating casein.

chyme. Liquid partly-digested food, passing from the stomach into the intestines.

chymia. An obsolete term for chemistry.

chymification. Gastric digestion.

chymogen. Rennase.

chymosin. Rennase.

chymotrypsin. An enzyme that coagulates milk.

chymotrypsinogen. A protein in beef pancreas. The precursor of chymotrypsin; it can be purified to the stage of complete homogeneity.

C.I. Abbreviation for Color Index.

Cibazol. Trademark for sulfanilamidothiazole.

ciceric acid. A mixture of oxalic and malic acid from *Cicer arietinum*, *Vicia sativa*, and other vetches.

Cicuta. A genus of poisonous umbelliferous plants; as *C. virosa*, water hemlock.

cicutoxine. $C_{17}H_{22}O_2 = 258.20$. A conjugated alcohol, and the active principle of *Cicuta virosa* (Umbelliferae), W. Europe, m.54. A convulsant poison, and isomer of oenanthotoxin.

cider. Fermented expressed apple juice. Cf. *perry.*

C.I.E. (Commission Internationale de l'Éclairage.) Units which define colors in terms of 3 hypothetical primary colors corresponding with the wavelengths 700.0, 546.1, and 435.8mμ.

cigar burning. Decomposition in a hot, defined reaction zone moving through a solid bed with characteristic velocity.

Cignolin. A brand of dioxyanthranol.

cilia. The hairlike protuberances on the surface of microorganisms, used chiefly for locomotion.

CIL-n. Trade name for a polyamide synthetic fiber.

ciment fondu. A hydraulic cement, formed by the complete fusion of bauxite and lime to form monocalcium aluminate and dicalcium silicate. Cf. aluminous *cement.*

cimicic acid. $C_{15}H_{28}O_2 = 240.3$. A monobasic acid from bedbugs, *Cimex lectularius*. Yellow crystals, m.44.2.

Cimicifuga. Macrotis, black cohosh, black snakeroot. The rhizome of *C. racemosa;* a tonic and antispasmodic.

cimicifugin. Macrotin. A resinoid from the rhizome of *Cimicifuga racemosa*. Brown powder, insoluble in water; an antispasmodic and nerve tonic.

cimifuga. Cimicifuga.

cimmol. Cinnamyl hydride.

cina. Santonica.

cinaebene. $C_{10}H_{16} = 136.2$. A hydrocarbon from the essential oil of *Artemisia santonica*.

cincaine. Percaine.

cinchaine. $C_{22}H_{30}O_2N_2 = 330.3$. Isopropylhydrocupreine. A cinchona alkaloid anesthetic.

cinchamidine. $C_{19}H_{24}ON_2 = 296.3$. Hydrocinchonidine. An alkaloid from cinchona bark. White leaflets, m.230, insoluble in water.

cinchene. $C_{19}H_{24}N_2 = 276.3$. An alkaloid obtained from cinchonine by boiling with alcoholic potash.

cinchocaine hydrochloride. $C_{20}H_{29}O_2N_3 \cdot HCl = 379.9$. White, slightly bitter hygroscopic crystals, soluble in water. A prolonged-action local anesthetic (B.P.).

cinchofulvic acid. Cinchona red.

cincholepidine. Lepidine.

cincholine. An alkaloid from cinchona bark.

cinchomeronic acid. $C_7H_5O_4N = 167.14$. 2,3-Pyridinedicarboxylic acid. Colorless crystals m.266. **carbo-** 1,2,3-Pyridinetricarboxylic acid. Colorless crystals, m.250. **iso-** 1,4-Pyridinedicarboxylic acid. Colorless leaflets, m.236, slightly soluble in water. **methyl-** Picolinedicarboxylic acid.

cinchona. (1) Quina, china, Jesuit's bark, loxa bark, huanco bark, Peruvian bark, fever bark. The bark of *Cinchona* species containing at least 3% cinchona alkaloids; a tonic and febrifuge. (2) A genus of trees of the Rubiaceae found in the Andes and cultivated in Ceylon and Java; e.g.: *C. callisaya*, callisaya bark; *C. cordifolia*, Cartagena bark; *C. officinalis*, crown or loxa bark. **c. alkaloids.** The more important are quinine, cinchonine, cinchonidine. **c. tannin.** Quinotannic acid.

cinchonamine. $C_{19}H_{24}ON_2 = 296.3$. An alkaloid from the bark of *Remijia purdieana* (Rubiaceae). Yellow crystals, m.184, insoluble in water. **c. hydrochloride.** $C_{19}H_{24}ON_2 \cdot HCl \cdot H_2O = 350.78$. Yellow crystals, soluble in water. **c. nitrate.** $C_{19}H_{24}ON_2 \cdot HNO_3 = 359.32$. Yellow crystals, soluble in water. **c. sulfate.** $C_{19}H_{24}ON_2 \cdot H_2SO_4 = 394.39$. Colorless crystals, soluble in water; said to have 6 times the therapeutic effect of quinine sulfate.

cinchonane. $C_{19}H_{22}N_2 = 278.19$. Desoxycinchonine. Colorless crystals, m.92.

cinchonate. A salt of cinchonic acid, containing the radical $C_{11}H_{12}O_9 \equiv$.

cinchonicine. Cinchotoxine.

cinchonidine. $C_{19}H_{22}ON_2 = 294.3$. Chinidine. The *levo* isomer of cinchonine; an alkaloid from cinchona bark. White crystals, m.205, insoluble in water; an antiperiodic. **hydro-** Cinchamidine.

 c. borate. $C_{19}H_{22}ON_2 \cdot H_3BO_3 = 356.31$. White powder, soluble in alcohol. **c. dihydrobromide.** Blennostasin. **c. hydrobromide** $C_{19}H_{22}ON_2 \cdot 2HBr = 456.15$. Yellow prisms, soluble in water. **c. hydrochloride.** $C_{19}H_{22}ON_2 \cdot HCl + H_2O = 348.8$. Colorless prisms, soluble in water, alcohol. **c. hydroiodide.** $C_{19}H_{22}ON_2 \cdot HI \cdot 2H_2O = 458.23$. Yellow crystals, soluble in water. **c. salicylate.** $C_{19}H_{22}ON_2 \cdot C_7H_6O_3 = 432.34$. White crystals, soluble in alcohol. **c. sulfate.** $(C_{19}H_{22}ON_2)_2 \cdot H_2SO_4 \cdot 3H_2O = 740.7$. Colorless crystals, soluble in water; similar to quinine sulfate. **c. tannate.** Yellow powder of variable composition, soluble in alcohol. **c. tartrate.** $(C_{19}H_{22}ON_2)_2 \cdot C_4H_6O_6 \cdot 2H_2O = 774.66$. White crystals soluble in hot water.

cinchonine. $C_{19}H_{22}ON_2 = 294.29$. An alkaloid from cinchona bark; the *dextro* isomer of cinchonidine. Colorless crystals, m.240–250, slightly soluble in water; an antiperiodic and bitter tonic: a quinine substitute, and a spot reagent for bismuth (orange-red). **hydro-** Cinchotine. **hydroxy-** Cupreine. **pseudo-** Cinchotine.

 c. benzoate. $C_{19}H_{22}ON_2 \cdot C_7H_6O_2 = 416.34$. Yellow crystals, slightly soluble in water. **c. bisulfate.** $C_{19}H_{22}ON_2 \cdot H_2SO_4 \cdot 4H_2O = 464.43$. Colorless, cubic crystals, soluble in water. **c. ferrocitrate.** Yellow scales, soluble in water. **c. hydrobromide.** $C_{19}H_{22}ON_2 \cdot HBr = 375.22$. Colorless crystals, soluble in water. **c. hydrochloride.**

$C_{19}H_{22}ON_2\cdot HCl\cdot 2H_2O = 366.79$. Colorless needles, soluble in water. **c. iodosulfate.** Antiseptol, iodochinchonine sulfate. Brown powder, insoluble in water; contains 50% I. A dusting powder and iodoform substitute. **c. nitrate.** $C_{19}H_{22}ON_2\cdot$-$HNO_3\cdot H_2O = 375.32$. White crystals, soluble in water. **c. salicylate.** $C_{19}H_{22}ON_2\cdot C_7H_6O_3 = 432.34$. Pink crystals, soluble in hot water; used to treat rheumatism. **c. sulfate.** $(C_{19}H_{22}ON_2)_2\cdot$-$H_2SO_4\cdot 2H_2O = 722.69$. Colorless rhombs, m.198, slightly soluble in water. Used as an antiperiodic and tonic; as a reagent for bismuth, hydrochloric acid, or sulfite cellulose; in leather manufacture.

cinchoninic acid. $C_{10}H_7O_2N = 173.1$. α-Quinoline-monocarboxylic acid. Colorless, crystals obtained by oxidation of cinchonine. **methyl-** Aniluvitonic acid. **2-phenyl-** Atophan.

cinchophen. Atophan.

cinchotannic acid. Quinotannic acid.

cinchotenicine. $C_{18}H_{20}O_3N_2 = 312.4$. An amorphous alkaloid from cinchona bark; isomeric with cinchotenine.

cinchotenidine. $C_{28}H_{20}O_3N_2\cdot 3H_2O = 366.4$. A colorless crystalline alkaloid from cinchona bark; isomeric with cinchotenine.

cinchotenine. $C_{18}H_{20}O_3N_2\cdot 3H_2O = 366.4$. A colorless crystalline alkaloid produced by oxidation of cinchonine.

cinchotine. $C_{19}H_{24}ON_2 = 296.4$. Hydrocinchonine, ψ-cinchonine. An alkaloid, m.286, from cinchona and cuprea barks; prepared artificially by the oxidation of quinine.

cinchotoxine. $C_{19}H_{22}ON_2 = 294.19$. Cinchonicine. An alkaloid, m.59, obtained by heating cinchonine or cinchonidine.

cinene. Terpene.

cineole. Eucalyptole.

cineolic acid. $C_{10}H_{16}O_5 = 216.12$. **levo-** Colorless crystals, d.0.92, m.196, decomp. in water. **1,4-** Ascaridolic acid.

cinerin. A cyclopropane carboxy acid derivative; an insecticidal active principle of pyrethrum.

cinnabar. HgS. A native red mercuric sulfide.

cinnaldehyde. Cinnamaldehyde.

cinnamal. Cinnamilidene. The radical PhCH:CH·-CH=.

cinnamaldehyde. PhCH:CHCHO $= 132.11$. β-Phenylacrolein, benzalacetaldehyde, 3-phenyl-propenal. Yellow volatile liquid, $d_4°1.050$, b.245. Chief constituent of oil of cinnamon, cinnaldehyde, and cassia. Used as an itch remedy, and artificial flavor. **hydroxy-** Coumaraldehyde. **hydroxy-methoxy-** Ferulaldehyde.

cinnamamide. PhCH:CHCONH$_2 = 147.1$. Benzal-acetamide. Colorless crystals, m.141.5, soluble in alcohol. **hydro-** Hydrocinnamamide.

cinnamate. A salt of cinnamic acid containing the radical $C_9H_7O_2$—.

cinnamein. $C_9H_7O_2\cdot C_7H_7 = 238.11$. Benzylcin-namate. A colorless liquid ester from Peru and tolu balsams.

cinnamene. Styrene. **aceto-** Benzylidene acetone.

cinnamenyl. Styryl. The radical Ph·CH:CH—, from cinnamene. **c. acetone.** $C_8H_7CH:CHCOMe = 172.1$. Colorless crystals, m.68. **c. acrylic acid.** $C_8H_7CH:CHCOOH = 174.1$. Colorless crystals, m.165.

cinnamic. Describing a compound containing the radical Ph·CH:CH—.

cinnamic acid. PhCH:CHCOOH $= 148.11$. Benzal-acetic acid, β-phenylacrylic acid, styrylformic acid. A constituent of balsams and storax; *trans* and *cis* forms. Colorless monoclinic scales, m.133, slightly soluble in water; a reagent for indole. **allo-** The *cis* form of c. **amino-** $NH_2C_9H_7O_2 = 163.26$. *ortho-* Colorless needles, decomp. 160, slightly soluble in water. *meta-* Yellow needles, m.180, slightly soluble in water. *para-* Yellow needles, decomp. 175, sparingly soluble in water. **3,4-dihydroxy-** Caffeic acid. **3,4-dioxy-** Caffeic acid. **hydro-** PhCH$_2$CH$_2$COOH $= 150.13$. β-Phenyl-propionic acid. Colorless needles, m.49, sparingly soluble in water. **hydroxy-** Coumaric and umbellic acids. **hydroxymethoxy-** See *ferulic acid, isofe-rulinic acid*. **methoxy-** MeOC$_9$H$_7$O$_2 = 179.09$. *o-2-Methoxy-*. Colorless crystals, m.182, soluble in alcohol. **nitro-** NO$_2$C$_9$H$_7$O$_2 = 193.11$. *ortho-* White needles, m.249, insoluble in water. *meta-* Yellow needles, m.197, slightly soluble in water. *para-* Colorless prisms, m.285, sparingly soluble in water. **oxy-** Coumaric acid.

cinnamic alcohol. PhCH:CHCH$_2$OH $= 134.13$. Styryl alcohol, peruvin, styrene, styrolene alcohol, 3-phenyl-2-propen-1-ol, from balsam, storax, and cinnamon bark. White needles, m.33, slightly soluble in water; an artificial flavor, deodorant, and antiseptic. **hydroxymethoxy-** Coniferyl alcohol.

cinnamic aldehyde. Cinnamaldehyde. **c. anhydride.** (PhCH:CHCO)$_2$O $= 278.2$. White crystals, m.127, slightly soluble in hot water.

cinnamide. Cinnamamide. **hydro-** Cinnhydramide.

cinnamilidene. (1) PhCH:CH·CH:CH$_2 = 130.1$. (2) Cinnamal. **c. acetic acid.** PhCH:CH·CH:CH·-COOH $= 174.08$. **c. malonic acid.** PhCH:CH·-CH:C(COOH)$_2 = 218.08$.

Cinnamomum. A genus of trees (Lauraceae) which yield important drugs; as, *C. camphora*, camphor; *C. cassia*, cassia bark; *C. zeylanicum*, cinnamon.

cinnamon. The dried inner bark of *Cinnamomum* species, Ceylon, and *C. cassia*, q.v., China. A carmin-ative, astringent, and condiment. **wild-** Canella. **c. oil.** The essential oil from the bark of cinnamon species. *Cassia-*, from *C. cassia*, d.1.045–1.063, b.240–260, contains 70–85% cinnamaldehyde. *Ceylon-*, from *C. zeylanicum*, d.1.024–1.040, contains cinnamaldehyde and eugenol. *leaf-*, d.1.044–1.065, contains, eugenol, sapol, and cin-namaldehyde. **c. stone.** A mineral of the garnet group.

cinnamone. Styryl ketone.

cinnamoyl. The radical PhCH:CHCO—.

cinnamyl. (1) Cinnamoyl. (2) Correctly the radical Ph·CH:CH·CH$_2$—. **c. acetate.** CH$_3$COOC$_9$H$_9$, in many essential oils. **c. alcohol.** Cinnamic alcohol. **c. chloride.** PhCH:CHCOCl $= 166.51$. Chlor-cinnamyl. Colorless crystals, m.36. **c. cinnamate.** Styracin. **c. cocaine.** An alkaloid, m.121, from cocoa leaves. **c. eugenol.** $C_8H_7COOC_9H_{11}O = 282.14$. Eugenol cinnamate. Colorless needles; an antiseptic. **c. guaiacol.** Styracol. **c. hydride.** Allylbenzene. **c. methyl ketone.** Benzalacetone. **c. phenyl ketone.** Benzalacetophenone.

cinnitraniside. Nitranisyl cinnamide.

cinnoline. $C_6H_4 \cdot N{:}N{\cdot}CH{:}CH = 130.2$. α-Phenol-1,2-benzodiazine. Colorless crystals, m.390. **dihydro-** $C_8H_8N_2 = 132.2$. Colorless crystals, m.88, soluble in alcohol.

cinnyl. Cinnamyl.

cinobufagin. $C_{25}H_{32}O_6 = 428.2$. A cardiac poison from Ch'an-Su, the dried venom of the Chinese toad.

circle. A ring or a plane figure bounded by a uniformly curved line. Let r be the radius, d the diameter and π a constant (3.14159). Then diameter $= 2r$, circumference $= 2\pi r$, area $= \pi r^2$. Cf. *pi*. **great-** In crystallography, a c. which passes through 2 diametrically opposite points on the surface of a sphere. **small-** A c. whose diameter is less than that of the great c.

circonium. Zirconium.

circuit. The continuous path of an electric current.

circular. Round. **c. inch.** The area of a circle 1 in. in diameter $= 0.7854$ in.$^2 = 507$ mm^2.

circulation. A continuous movement in a regular course, as of the blood through the blood vessels.

circulatory equalizer. A drug that restores the equilibrium of the circulatory system.

circumference. The outline of a more or less circular body. Cf. *circle*.

circumflux. Flowing or winding around.

circumfusion. Pouring or fusing around; as, a low-melting-point flux.

circumpolar. Around a pole.

cis. Describing a form of isomerism of organic compounds in which the hydrogen atoms attached to two carbon atoms with double bonds are substituted adjacently on the same side of the molecule. Thus, with $\overset{a}{\underset{b}{>}}C{=}C\overset{c}{\underset{d}{<}}$ $a{:}c$ is the cis position, $a{:}d$ is the trans position.

Cisalfa. Trade name for a viscose-protein synthetic fiber combination.

cissampeline. $C_{18}H_{21}O_3N = 299.3$. An alkaloid from pareira root, *Cissampelos pareira* (Menispermaceae), Brazil; a diuretic.

cistus. Labdanum.

Citicide. Trade name for a chlorinated turpentine insecticide.

citraconic acid. $COOH{\cdot}Me{\cdot}C{:}CH{\cdot}COOH = 130.0$. Methylmaleic acid, methylbutenedioic acid*. A dibasic acid isomeric with itaconic acid. **c. anhydride.** $C_5H_4O_3 = 112.0$. An intramolecular anhydride of citraconic acid; a colorless oil.

citraconyl. The radical $C_5H_4O_4{-}$, from citraconic acid.

citral. $Me_2C{:}CH{\cdot}CH_2{\cdot}CH_2{\cdot}CH{:}CMeCHO = 152.18$. **alpha-** Geranial. An aldehyde of several essential oils (citron oil) in 4 isomers; *cis-* and *trans-*terpinolene and *cis-* and *trans-*limonene. Yellow volatile liquid, d.0.897, b.225, insoluble in water; used in perfumery and as a flavoring. **beta-** Neral. Colorless liquid, d.0.888, b$_{12mm}$104.

citramalic acid. $HOOC{\cdot}CMeOH{\cdot}CH_2{\cdot}COOH = 148.1$. 2-Hydroxy-2-methylbutanedioic acid*, derived from citraconic acid and isomeric with itamalic acid. **dl-** Monoclinic prisms, m.119.

citramide. $C_6H_{11}O_4N_3 = 189.11$. Colorless crystals, m.215, derived from ethyl citrate by the action of ammonia.

citramin. Citarin.

citrate. A salt containing the radical $C_6H_5O_7{\equiv}$, from citric acid. **c. soluble.** The phosphates in a fertilizer that are soluble in ammonium citrate solution.

Citratus. A fertilizer brand of dicalcium phosphate.

citrene. $C_{10}H_{16} = 136.2$. *d*-Limonene. A terpene of lemon oil, b.168. **c. terpin.** $C_{10}H_{20}O_2 = 172.16$. Citrene dihydrate. Colorless crystals, formed by the action of water on citrene.

citresia. Magnesium acid citrate.

citric acid. $C_3H_4(OH)(COOH)_3 \cdot H_2O = 210.11$. 2-Hydroxy-1,2,3-propanetricarboxylic acid*, in fruit juices. Colorless crystals, m.153, decomp., soluble in water. A reagent in analysis, and constituent of soda-fountain mixtures and pharmaceuticals (B.P.). Cf. *citromyces*. **phenetidin-** Apolysin. **c. a. cycle.** Krebs cycle. The main sequence of carbohydrate oxidation in the body tissues: pyruvate → oxalacetate → citrate → *isocitrate* → oxalsuccinate → α-ketoglutarate → succinate → formate → malate → oxalacetate → $CO_2 + H_2O$. It has respiratory and biosynthetic functions, e.g., the synthesis of amino acids.

citridic acid. Aconitic acid.

citrin. (1) Cucurbo citrin. A hypotensor glucoside from watermelon seeds. (2) Hesperidin.

citrine. (1) A yellow variety of quartz. (2) A yellow mercury ointment.

citrinin. $C_{13}H_{14}O_5 = 250.05$. Notalin. A yellow pigment from *Penicillium citrinum*, m.171 (decomp.); inhibits the growth of *Staphylococcus aureus*.

citrometer. A hydrometer graduated in percentages of citric acid.

citromin. Citarin.

Citromyces. A mold fungus, *C. pfefferianus*, which ferments glucose to citric acid.

citromycetin. $C_{14}H_{10}O_7 \cdot 2H_2O = 308.07$. A yellow flavone from the fungus *Citromyces*, m.205 (decomp.), probably identical with frequentic acid, an antibiotic from the mold *Penicillium frequentans*, Westling.

citronella. Lemongrass. **c. oil.** The essential oil of *Andropogon* or *Cymbopogon* species (lemongrass). A perfume and mosquito repellant. **Batu-** d.0.900–0.920, **Singapore-** d.0.886–0.900. Both contain geraniol and citronellal.

citronellal. $C_{10}H_{18}O = 154.19$. Two isomers from many essential oils: limonene form; $MeC{:}CH(CH_2)_3{-}CHMeCH_2CHO$; terpinolene form, $CH_2{:}CMe(CH_2)_3{-}CHMeCH_2CHO$. Colorless liquid, d$_{17}$0.854, b.207, slightly soluble in water; used in perfumery and as a flavoring.

citronellaldehyde. Citronellal.

citronellic acid. $C_{10}H_{18}O_2 = 170.14$. Colorless liquid, d.0.931, b.257.

citronellol. $CH_2{:}CMe(CH_2)_3CHMe{\cdot}CH_2{\cdot}CH_2OH = 156.21$. 2,6-Dimethyloctene-1-ol-8. An isomer of rhodinol; two stereoisomers. An unsaturated alcohol constituent of many essential oils; colorless liquid, d.0.856, b$_{17mm}$118, slightly soluble in water.

citronin. Dinitrodiphenylamine.

citronyl. Citronella oil.

citrophen. $(EtO{\cdot}C_6H_4{\cdot}NHCO)_3C_3H_4OH$. A compound of citric acid and *p*-phenetidine. White crystals, m.181, soluble in water. An antipyretic, sedative, and antineuralgic.

citrulline. (1) A resinoid of colocynth. Yellow amorphous powder, insoluble in water; a laxative. (2) $C_6H_{13}N_3O_3 = 175.11$. An amino acid from casein and watermelon, *Citrullis vulgaris*, m.220; an intermediate in urea formation.

Citrus. Aurantiaceae. A genus of trees (Rutaceae), whose fruits are edible and yield juice, rinds, oils, and acids; e.g.:

C. aurantium .... Sweet orange
C. aurant. var: *bigarardia* .... Bitter (Seville) orange
C. medica .... Citron
C. med. var. *limonum* .... Lemon
C. med. var. *acida* .... Lime
C. decumana .... Grapefruit (shaddock)

citryl. Lemon oil.

civet. A soft fat of strong musklike odor from the civet cat, *Viverra civetta*, E. Indies. It contains an essential oil and ammonia. An antispasmodic and perfume.

civetane. $CH_2 \cdot CH:CH \cdot CH_2 \cdot (CH_2)_{13} = 236.2$. Cycloheptadecene. Colorless crystals, m.47, b.120.

civetone. $(CH_2)_7 \cdot CH:CH \cdot (CH_2) \cdot_7 CO = 250.3$. 9-
Cycloheptadecen-1-one*. Extracted from glands of the civet cat.

C.K. wax. See *wax*.

Cl. Symbol for chlorine, Cl^- chloride ion, Cl^* excited chlorine atom, Cl_2 chlorine molecule, Cl_2^+ ionized chlorine molecule, Cl_2^* excited chlorine molecule.

cl. Abbreviation for centiliter.

cladding. A thin veneer of metal (usually nickel) to protect steel plate from corrosion.

cladonic acid. An acid from *Cladonia rangiferina*, reindeer moss.

Cladothrix. A quasi-branched form of Schizo-mycetes. **C. ochracea.** A C. which oxidizes ferrous salts to ferric hydroxide and causes brown deposits in springs.

Claisen, Ludwig. 1851–1930. German chemist. **C. condensation.** Claisen reaction. **C. flask.** A distillation flask with a U-shaped, tubulated neck. **C. reaction.** A reaction of an aldehyde with an aldehyde or ketone in the presence of alkali or sodium ethoxide: $R \cdot CHO + CH_3 \cdot CO \cdot R' = R \cdot CH:-CH \cdot CO \cdot R' + H_2O$.

clamp. A device to hold an instrument in position or to control the flow of a gas or liquid.

Clapeyron, Benoit-Paul Emile. 1799–1864. French engineer. **C. equation.** $dp/dT = \lambda/T(v_2 - v_1)$, where p = pressure, T = absolute temperature, λ = heat of vaporizing 1 gm of liquid, v_2 = specific volume of vapor, v_1 = specific volume of liquid. Cf. *Clausius equation*.

clarain. A constituent of coal, q.v.

clarificant. A substance for clearing a solution.

clarification. A process by which a liquid is clarified, e.g., filtration. Cf. *defecation*.

Clark cell. A standard cell giving 1.433 volts at 15°C. It consists of a mercury anode and a cathode of amalgamated zinc in a saturated solution of zinc sulfate. **C. degree.** See *hardness* (water).

Clarke, Frank Wigglesworth. 1847–1931. American chemist, noted for geochemical research.

Classen, Alexander. 1843–1934. German chemist. **C. switchboard.** A switchboard and worktable for quantitative electrolysis.

classification of compounds. See *compounds, chemicals, organic compounds, ring systems*. **-of drugs.** See *drug*. **-of elements.** See *periodic system*. **-of reactions.** See *reactions*.

clathrates. Substances which fix gases or liquids as inclusion complexes (up to 15% by weight), so that the complex may be handled in solid form and the included constituent subsequently released by the action of a solvent or by melting. Used to handle radio active gaseous isotopes.

Claude, Georges. 1871–1900. French inventor. **C.'s method.** Air is liquefied in stages by passage through an orifice under pressure; and the expanding gas cooled by doing work externally in a piston engine. Cf. *Linde, nitrogen fixation*.

claudetite. A native arsenious oxide.

Claus, Adolf. 1840–1900. German chemist noted for his benzene formula.

Clausius, Rudolf Julius. 1822-1888. German physicist. **C. equation.** Clausius-Clapeyron equation: $\log P = -L/4.58T + C$, where P is the vapor pressure at the absolute temperature T, L the molecular heat of vaporization, and C a constant of integration. Its integrated form is

$$2.303 \log \frac{P}{760} = \frac{L}{R}\left(\frac{1}{T_{760}} - \frac{1}{T_p}\right)$$

where T_{760} and T_p are the boiling points at 760 and p mm pressure, respectively; R is 1.985 gm-cal. See also *Clapeyron equation*. **C. law.** The specific heat of a gas is independent of temperature at constant volume. **C.- Mosotti equation.** The polarization of the dielectric per mole = $m(D - 1)/d(D + 2)$ where D is the dielectric constant, m the molecular weight, d the density, and P the molal polarization.

clausthalite. PbSe. A native selenide (Klausthal, Czechoslovakia).

clavacin. An antibiotic from fungi, identical with clavatin, claviformin, and patulin.

clavatin. Clavicin from *Aspergillus clavatus*.

clavicepsin. $C_{18}H_{34}O_{16} = 506.26$. An inert glucoside m.198, in ergot.

clavicin. $(C_7H_6O_4)_x$. Clavatin. Anhydro-3-hydroxy-methylenetetrahydro-γ-pyrone-2-carboxylic acid. An antibiotic from *Aspergillus clavatus* and *Penicillium claviforme*, m.110. Probably identical with patulin.

claviforme. Clavicin from *Penicillum claviforme*.

claviformin. Clavacin.

clavine. $C_{11}H_{22}O_4N_2 = 246.18$. An alkaloid of ergot, m.263.

clay. $H_4Al_2Si_2O_9$. A plastic, soft, variously colored earth, formed by the decomposition of aluminum minerals. In true clay 30% by weight of solid particles are of diameter less than 0.002 mm. Used for pottery. Cf. *ceramics*. **American-** C. made from quartz feldspar, whitening, ball clay, and kaolin, and glazed at 1300°. **bone-** A hard, translucent c. containing approximately 50% of kaolin and calcined animal bones (U.K. usage). **china-** See *china clay*. **feldspathic-** Porcelain.

fire- q.v. **hydrogen-** A c. with zeolitic properties with respect to hydrogen ions. **japan-** Montmorillonite. **pipe-** q.v. **potters'-** q.v.
c. ironstone. Siderite. **c. substance.** Kaolinite.

cleaning solution. Mixed concentrated sulfuric acid and sodium dichromate, used to clean chemical glassware.

clearing. (1) Clarification. (2) Freeing cotton fiber from grease by boiling in a weak solution of sodium carbonate. (3) In photography, removal of fog from a plate. (4) In microscopy, removal (e.g., by chloral hydrate) of extraneous matter from plant material to render the essential plant structure visible.

cleavage. (1) Separation as layers, e.g., the splitting of crystals. (2) Biology: segmentation. Cf. *amitosis.*

clebrium. A noncorrosive alloy of iron with Cr 13–19, Ni 2–4, Mo 0–3.2, C 0–2, Mn 0.8–2.8%.

cleiophane. Sphalerite.

clematine. An alkaloid from *Clematis vitalba* (Ranunculaceae).

Clematis. A climbing, ranunculaceous plants.

Clemmensen reduction. The reduction of certain aldehydes and ketones to hydrocarbons (as, acetophenone to styrene) by activated zinc and acid.

Clerget inversion. The determination of sucrose polarimetrically after inversion of 100 ml solution with 5 ml strong hydrochloric acid at 69° for 7.5 min. Sucrose = $100(a - b)/(142.66 - 0.5t)$, where a and b are the polarizations originally and after inversion at t°C.

Clerici solution. A molar mixture of thallium malonate and thallium formate, d.4.27; a mineralogical flotation agent for density determinations.

Cleve, Per T. 1840–1905. Swedish chemist, co-discoverer of helium and rare-earth metals. **C.'s acid.** 1-Naphthylamine-6-sulfonic acid. **C.'s salts.** $[Pt(NH_3)_3Cl_x]Cl$; $x = 1$ or 3.

Cleveland tester. A flash-point apparatus.

climacteric. Pertaining to a critical period or stage, e.g., in the ripening of fruit.

clinical analysis. The diagnostic examination of body fluids and waste products.

clinker. The hard, partly vitrified residue after combustion of coal, also produced by volcanic action; used to manufacture cement. Cf. *slag.*

clinochlore. Ripidolite. A green chlorite or aluminum magnesium silicate, d.2.65–2.78.

clinohedrite. $H_2CaZnSiO_5$. An orange-colored mineral from Franklin, N.J.

clinometer. A device to measure slopes.

clinostat. A moving disk apparatus to determine the phototropism of a plant.

Clorarsen. Trademark for dichlorophenarsine hydrochloride.

closed chain. A ring compound. See *chain.*

clot. A solid concretion of a jellylike mass.

cloth. A fabric woven of cotton. **cheese-** Loosely woven, thin cotton cloth used for straining. **filter-** A canvas used in filter presses.

clotting. The coagulation of blood, lymph, or milk.

cloud point. The temperature at which a solid starts to precipitate from solution in an oil when cooled under standard conditions.

cloudy. (1) Containing a diffused precipitate. (2) Describing a bacterial culture which does not contain pseudozoogleae.

clove(s). Caryophyllus. The dried flower buds of *Caryophyllus aromaticus* (Myrtaceae); a spice. **c. oil.** Essential oil of cloves. Yellow, volatile liquid, d.1.079, b.243; consists mainly of eugenol.

clovene. $C_{15}H_{24} = 204.19$. A terpene from clove oil. Colorless liquid, d.0.93, b.263.

cloxacillin sodium. $C_{19}H_{17}O_5N_3ClSNa\cdot H_2O = 475.90$. White, bitter crystals, soluble in water; an antibiotic (B.P.).

clupanodonic acid. $C_{22}H_{34}O_2 = 330.27$. Docosa-4,7,11-trien-18-ynoic acid, in fish blubber. Yellow oil, d.0.9410, b5mm 236, soluble in ether.

clupein. A protein from herring, *Clupea harengus:* C 47.93, H 7.59, O 12.78, N 31.68%.

Clymocol. A germicide brand of monochloromethylisopropylphenol.

Cm. Symbol for curium.

cm. Centimeter. **cm².** Square centimeter. **cm³.** Cubic centimeter = cc.

C.N. Coordination number.

cnicin. $C_{42}H_{56}O_{15} = 800.5$. A glucoside from Canada thistle, *Cnicus arvenis,* or *Carduus benedicta* (Compositae). White crystals, soluble in cold water.

Co. Symbol for cobalt.

coacervate. The liquid product of coacervation.

coacervation, coazervation. The reversible collection of emulsoid particles into liquid droplets preceding flocculation. An intermediate stage between sol and gel formations. Cf. *coagulation.*

coagel. The gel formed by coagulation.

coagulability. The capacity to clot.

coagulase. An enzyme that clots and precipitates proteins.

coagulation. The precipitation of colloids in a soft mass.

coagulator. An incubator for keeping test-tubes at blood temperature.

Coagulem. Trademark for a lipoid obtained by fractionally centrifuging blood. Brown powder, soluble in water, and rich in thrombokinase; used to stop bleeding by coagulating the blood.

coagulometer. A device to determine the speed of coagulation of blood.

coal. A native, black or brown, brittle or soft substance from the degradation of ancient forests, consisting chiefly of carbon, with hydrogen, nitrogen, oxygen, and other elements. Coals are classified according to their state of mineralization (% carbon); as, *lignites, bituminous c.,* and *anthracites;* or microscopically as:

  1. *Clarain,* a lustrous mixture of leaves, wood, resinous bodies, etc., in a structureless matrix.

  2. *Vitrain,* lustrous thin bands with conchoidal fracture, in which the wood structure is destroyed.

  3. *Durain,* a dull variety of c. which contains microspores and megaspheres and a high ash.

  4. *Fusain,* thin bands of soft dull coal containing no volatile matter.

Calorific values are, in BThU per pound:

Anthracite	13,350
Coke	12,000
Charcoal	13,000
Bituminous A	14,260
Cannel	13,700
Lignite	6,000
Peat	1,900
Wood	7,600

World resources: bituminous and anthracites

4,017,000 million; brown and lignites 707,000 million tons. **brown-** Lignite. **cannel-** A hard c. for gas production. **char-** See *charcoal*. **hard-** Anthracite. **mother of-** Fusain. **soft-** Bituminous c. **Standard C. Unit.** S.C.U. The thermal energy of 1 ton of c. **white-** Waterpower.

    c. brass. Marcasite. **c. gas.** The gaseous product of the distillation of c. The average composition is:

Hydrogen	43–55%	Nonilluminating but heating
Methane	25–45%	
Carbon monoxide	4–11%	
Olefines, acetylenes and benzene	2– 5%	Illuminants
Nitrogen	2–12%	Impurities
Carbon dioxide	0– 3%	
Oxygen	0–1.5%	

c. oil. (1) Kerosene. (2) Petroleum. **c. tar.** The condensed liquid from the distillation of c., containing hydrocarbons (benzene), phenols, basic substances (pyridine), finely divided free carbon. **c. unit.** See *Standard c. unit*.

coalite. Trademark for an open-structure smokeless fuel made by low-temperature carbonization of coal at 620°C; volatile matter 10%.

coarse metal. A fusible silicate of iron produced in the reverberatory furnace.

coazervate. Coacervate.

coazervation. Coacervation.

cobalamin. Internationally approved collective name for vitamins possessing vitamin B_{12} activity (1952).

cobalt. Co = 58.93. An element of the iron group, at. no. 27, discovered by G. Brandt (1733). A steel-gray, pinkish, ductile metal, d.8.718, m.1465, insoluble in water. It occurs as metal in meteorites, as sulfide and arsenide in smaltite and cobaltite. It is prepared by reduction of its oxides in hydrogen. World production (1967) 17,800 tons (W. bloc). C. is bi- and trivalent and forms two series of compounds: cobaltous, Co++; cobaltic, Co³⁺. It forms many colored double salts. Its complex ions include: cobaltous hexahydrate, $Co(H_2O)_6^{++}$; cobaltous hexacyanide (cobaltocyanide), $Co(CN)_6^{4-}$. The cobaltous compounds are the more stable, and are pink when hydrated, and green when anhydrous. Metallic c. is used in alloys and in ceramics The radioactive isotope Co⁶⁰ is used to detect flaws in small metal articles. **black-** An earthy native c. **earthy-** Asbolite. **red-** Erythrite. **speiss-** An impure smaltite.

    c. acetate. Cobaltous acetate. **c. aluminate.** Thenard's blue. **c. bloom.** The mineral $Co_3(AsO_4)_2$, $8H_2O$. **c. blue.** A dark blue mineral pigment containing cobaltous oxide 35, zinc oxide 20, and chalcedony 25%. **c. bomb.** A hydrogen bomb enclosed in c. to serve as a neutron absorber, which produces radioactivity and Co⁶⁰; 500 tons deuterium reacting inside 10⁵ tons c. would give sufficient Co⁶⁰ to kill the population of the earth in a few years. **c. carbonyl.** C. tetracarbonyl **c. chlorides.** See *cobaltichloride, cobaltic,* and *cobaltous chloride*. **c. cyanide.** Cobalticyanide. **c. green.** Cobalt zincate, Rinman's green. A solid solution of cobaltous oxide and zinc oxide; a green pigment. **c. minerals.** C. is usually associated with nickel and found as sulfide, or arsenide; e.g., jaipurite, CoS; linnaeite, Co_3S_4;

smaltite, $CoAs_2$. **c. nitride.** Co_2N = 132.0. Black crystals. **c. nitrites.** Cobaltinitrite. **c. oxides.** CoO = cobaltous oxide. Co_2O_3 = cobaltic oxide, Co_3O_4 = cobalto cobaltic oxide; a blue pigment for ceramics and glass. **c. phosphide.** Co_2P = 149.0. A black, metallic substance. **c. sulfates.** See *cobaltic sulfate, cobaltous sulfate*. **c. tetracarbonyl.** $Co(CO)_4$ = 171.0. C. carbonyl. Black crystals, m.43, insoluble in water. **c. violet.** A c. phosphate pigment for oil paints. **c. yellow.** Cobaltic potassium nitrite. **c. zincate.** C. green.

cobaltammine compounds. Ammonates. Compounds of ammonia and cobalt, e.g., purpureocobalt chloride $[Co(NH_3)_5Cl]Cl_2$.

cobaltic. Containing trivalent cobalt, Co≡. **c. chloride.** $CoCl_3$ = 165.4. Blue crystals, d.2.94, decomp. on heating, soluble in water. See *cobaltichloride*. **c. hydroxide.** $Co(OH)_3$ = 110.0. Black powder, insoluble in water. **c. oxide.** Co_2O_3 = 166.0. Cobalt sesquioxide. Black powder, decomp. at red heat, insoluble in water. **c. potassium cyanide.** Potassium cobalticyanide. **c. potassium nitrite.** $K_3Co(NO_2)_6 \cdot xH_2O$. Potassium cobaltinitrite, cobalt yellow, potassium c. hexanitrite. Yellow precipitate obtained by adding potassium nitrite to c. nitrate acidified with acetic acid. **c. sulfate.** $Co_2(SO_4)_3$ = 406.2. Blue crystals, decomp. in water. **c. sulfide.** Co_2S_3 = 214.0. Black powder, insoluble in water.

cobaltichloride. luteo- $[(NH_3)_3 \cdot Co \cdot (NH_3)_3]Cl_3$. Hexammine c. Orange-yellow crystals, soluble in water. Reagent for pyrophosphoric acid. **praseo-** $[(NH_3)_2 \cdot Co \cdot (NH_3)_2]Cl_3$. Tetrammine c. Green crystals, soluble in water. **purpureo-** $[(NH_3)_3 \cdot Co \cdot (NH_3)_2 \cdot Cl]Cl_2$. Chloropentammine c. Purple crystals, soluble in water. **roseo-** $[(NH_3)_3 \cdot Co \cdot (NH_3)_2 \cdot H_2O]Cl_3$. Aquapentammine c. Red crystals, decomp. by water.

cobalticyanic acid. $H_3Co(CN)_6$ = 216.1. Colorless needles, decomp. above 100, soluble in water.

cobalticyanide. Salts of cobalticyanic acid containing the $Co(CN)_6^{3-}$, yellow in aqueous solution.

cobaltinitrite. Salts containing the trivalent complex ion $Co(NO_2)_6^{3-}$, imparting a yellow color to the aqueous solution.

cobaltite. The mineral (CoFe)SAs. Cf. *sehta*.

cobaltocobaltic oxide. Co_3O_4 = 240.9. Black-crystals, insoluble in water.

cobaltosic oxide. Cobaltocobaltic oxide.

cobalto sulfate. A salt containing the $Co(SO_4)_2^=$ ion which imparts a red color to the aqueous solution.

cobaltous. Containing divalent cobalt, Co++. **c. acetate.** $Co(C_2H_3O_2)_2 \cdot 4H_2O$ = 249.1. Purple crystals, soluble in water; used in invisible inks. **c. ammonium sulfate.** $Co(SO_4)_2(NH_4)_2SO_4 \cdot 6H_2O$ = 491.29. Red crystals, soluble in water. **c. arsenate.** $Co_3(AsO_4)_2 \cdot 8H_2O$ = 599.1. Erythrite, cobalt bloom. Purple monoclinic crystals, insoluble in water; a light blue pigment for porcelain and glass. **c. benzoate.** $Co(C_6H_5COO)_2 \cdot 4H_2O$ = 373.08. Red leaflets, dehydrated at 115, soluble in water. **c. bromate.** $Co(BrO_3)_2 \cdot 6H_2O$ = 423.0. Red crystals, soluble in water. **c. bromide.** $CoBr_2 \cdot 6H_2O$ = 326.9. Red hygroscopic crystals, soluble in water; used to fill hygrometers. **c. butyrate.** $Co(C_4H_7O_2)_2$ = 233.2. Purple granules, soluble in water. **c. carbonate.** $CoCO_3$ = 119.0.

Rose powder, decomp. by heat, insoluble in water; used to prepare cobalt pigments. **c. chlorate.** $Co(ClO_3)_2 \cdot 6H_2O = 334.0$. Purple crystals, m.50, decomp. 100, very soluble in water. **c. chloride.** $CoCl_2 = 129.9$. Blue crystals, sublime on heating, soluble in water. It crystallizes also as; hexahydrate, $CoCl_2 \cdot 6H_2O$; tetrammonate, $CoCl_2 \cdot 4NH_3$; pentammonate, $CoCl_2 \cdot 5NH_3$. $cryst$-$CoCl_2 \cdot 6H_2O = 238.0$. Ruby monoclinic crystals, m.87, soluble in water; used in hygrometers, invisible inks, chemical barometers, and electroplating. **c. chromate.** $CoCrO_4 = 174.9$. Brown powder containing some c. hydroxide, insoluble in water. **c. citrate.** $Co_3(C_6H_5O_7)_2 = 555.2$. Pink powder, sparingly soluble in water. **c. cyanide.** $Co(CN)_2$, and $Co(CN)_3 \cdot 3H_2O = 165.1$. Red powder, anhydrous at 250°C, decomp. 300, insoluble in water, soluble in potassium cyanide solution. **c. fluosilicate.** $CoSiF_6 \cdot 6H_2O = 309.09$. Trigonal pink crystals, soluble in hot water. **c. formate.** $Co(OOCH)_2 = 149.0$. Red crystals, soluble in water. **c. hydroxide.** $Co(OH)_2 = 93.0$. Rose-red crystals, insoluble in water. **c. iodide.** $CoI_2 \cdot 6H_2O = 420.83$. Brown crystals, soluble in water. **c. linoleate.** $Co(C_{18}H_{31}O_2)_2 = 617.42$. Brown powder, insoluble in water. **c. nickelous sulfate.** $NiSO_4 \cdot CoSO_4 = 309.72$. A double salt of cobaltous and nickelous sulfates. **c. nitrate.** $Co(NO_3)_2 \cdot 6H_2O = 291.1$. Red crystals, m.56, decomp. at red heat, very soluble in water. Used as an antidote for cyanide poisoning, for the preparation of cobalt pigments, for secret ink, and as a reagent in blowpipe analysis. **c. oleate.** $Co(C_{17}H_{33}COO)_2 = 621.4$. Brown masses, insoluble in water. **c. oxalate.** $Co(OOC)_2 \cdot H_2O = 165.0$. Pink powder, insoluble in water. **c. oxide.** $CoO = 75.0$. Brown powder, decomp. 2850, insoluble in water. **c. phosphate.** $Co_3(PO_4)_2 \cdot 2H_2O = 403.3$. Red powder, insoluble in water; used for light blue pigments, in ceramics and glass. **c. propionate.** $Co(C_3H_5O_2)_2 \cdot 3H_2O = 259.06$. Red crystals, m.ca.250, soluble in water. **c. silicate.** $Co_2SiO_4 = 209.8$. Purple crystals, insoluble in water. **c. sulfate.** $CoSO_4 \cdot 7H_2O = 281.2$. Rose vitriol. Cf. *bieberite*. Red crystals, m.97, anhydrous at 450, soluble in water. Used to prepare cobalt salts and cobalt oxides for ceramic pigments, and in galvanostegy for cobalting metals. **c. stannate.** $CoSnO_3$. Blue pigment. Cf. *ceruleum*. **c. sulfide.** $CoS = 91.0$. Brown powder, m.1100, insoluble in water. **c. tartrate.** $Co(C_4H_9O_6) = 212.0$. Pink powder, sparingly soluble in water.

cobefrin. $(OH)_2C_6H_3 \cdot CHOH \cdot CHMe \cdot NH_2 = 183.1$. 3,4-Dihydroxyaminopropanol benzene, corbasil. White crystals; a vasoconstrictor.

cobra. A poisonous snake of India, *Naja tripudians*, whose venom contains ophiotoxin and cobralysin. **c. lecithid.** A hemolytic compound of lecithin and cobra toxin formed in the blood.

cobralysin. The hemolytic substance of cobra venom.

cobric acid. White microcrystals, from cobra venom, containing calcium sulfate.

coca. Erythroxylon. The dried leaves of the S. American shrub *Erythroxylum coca*; a source of cocaine. **c. alkaloids.** A group of related alkaloids; as cocaine, $C_{17}H_{21}NO_4$; ecgonine, $C_9H_{15}NO_3$.

cocaine. $C_{17}H_{21}O_4N = 303.26$. Erythroxylon, methylbenzoylecgonine. An alkaloid from the leaves of *Erythroxylum coca*. White monoclinic scales, m.98, slightly soluble in water; used chiefly as the hydrochloride as a local anesthetic and cerebrospinal stimulant. **isatropyl-** See *isatropyl-cocaine*. **methyl-** Cocainidine. **tropa-.** See *tropacocaine*.

c. benzoate. $C_{17}H_{21}O_4N \cdot C_7H_6O_2$. White crystals, soluble in water. **c. bitartrate.** d-ψ-Psicaine. **c. borate.** White crystals, soluble in water; used for eyewashes. **c. chloride.** C. hydrochloride. **c. citrate.** $(C_{17}H_{21}O_4N)_2C_6H_8O_7 = 798.58$. White crystals, soluble in water; a dental anesthetic. **c. hydrobromide.** $C_{17}H_{21}O_4N \cdot HBr = 384.19$. White crystals, soluble in water. **c. hydrochloride.** $C_{17}H_{21}O_4N \cdot HCl = 339.73$. Colorless prisms, m.186, soluble in water; an anesthetic, stimulant, antipruritic, and sedative. **c. hydroiodide.** $C_{17}H_{21}O_4N \cdot HI = 431.19$. Yellow crystals, soluble in water. **c. lactate.** $C_{17}H_{21}O_4N \cdot C_3H_6O_3 = 393.31$. A syrupy mass, soluble in water; an anesthetic, sedative, and antiseptic. **c. nitrate.** $C_{17}H_{21}O_4N \cdot HNO_3 = 366.28$. White crystals, soluble in water. **c. oleate.** A solution of cocaine in oleic acid, used externally. **c. salicylate.** $C_{17}H_{21}O_4N \cdot C_7H_6O_3 = 441.31$. Colorless crystals, soluble in water. **c. sulfate.** $C_{17}H_{21}O_4N \cdot H_2SO_4 = 401.35$. White crystals, soluble in water. **c. tannate.** $C_{17}H_{21}O_4N \cdot C_{14}H_{10}O_9 = 625.4$. White powder, soluble in alcohol. **c. tartrate.** $(C_{17}H_{21}O_4N)_2 \cdot C_4H_6O_6 = 756.57$. Colorless crystals, soluble in water.

cocainidine. $C_{18}H_{23}O_4N = 317.3$. Methylcocaine. An alkaloid from coca leaves, similar to cocaine.

cocatannic acid. $C_{17}H_{22}O_{10} \cdot 2H_2O(?)$. Yellow microcrystals, from the leaves of *Erythroxylum coca*.

Coccaceae. Spherical Schizomycetes (bacteria), which includes Coccus, Diplococcus, Staphylococcus, and Streptococcus.

coccalinic acid. Menispermic acid.

cocceric acid. $C_{31}H_{62}(OH)COOH = 496.49$. White crystalline mass from cochineal wax, m.92.5.

coccerin. $C_{30}H_{60}(C_{31}H_{61}O_3)_2 = 1382.11$. A wax derived from cochineal.

cocceryl. The radical $C_{30}H_{60}=$ from c. alcohol. **c. alcohol.** $C_{30}H_{62}O_2 = 454.6$. A dibasic alcohol from cochineal wax. White crystals, m.102.

coccerylic acid. Cocceric acid.

cocci. Plural of coccus.

Coccidium. A genus of sporozoa.

coccinellin. Carmine.

coccognin. A glucoside from the fruits of *Daphne gnidium* (Thymelaceae).

coccolith. The minute calcareous skeleton of floating marine algae.

coccon. Pomegranate seeds.

cocculin. $C_{19}H_{26}O_{10} = 414.3$. A crystalline constituent of *Cocculus indicus*, fishberry; a narcotic. Cf. *kukoline*.

cocculus. The fruit of menispermaceous plants. **c. indicus.** Fishberry, Indian berry, Oriental berry, Levant berry. The fruit of *Anamirta paniculata* (Menispermaceae), a climbing shrub, E. Indies; a verminicide. See *cocculin, kukoline*.

coccus. (1) A spherical bacterium. (2) Insects of the family Coccidae, scale insects, that yield cochineal, Chinese wax, kermes, lac, manna.

cocethyline. $C_{18}H_{23}O_4N = 317.5$. Ethylbenzoyl-ecgonine. Colorless crystals, m.109, soluble in alcohol; a cocaine substitute.

cochineal. The female insect, *Coccus cacti*, reared on several species of cactus (*Opuntia*) in tropical America. Its chief constituent is carmine; used to color pharmaceutical preparations, and as an indicator. **c. solution.** An indicator prepared by macerating 3 gm of unbroken c. for 4 days in 250 ml of a mixture of 1 pt. alcohol and 3 pts. water (alkalies—violet; acids—yellowish red). **c. wax.** Coccerin.

cochinilin. Carminic acid.

cochlear, cochleare. A spoon. A pharmaceutical measure: cochlear magnum (tablespoon) = 15 ml = $\frac{1}{2}$ fluid ounce; cochlear medium (dessertspoon) = 8 ml = 2 fluid drachms; cochlear parvum (teaspoon) = 4 ml.

Cochlearia. (1) A genus of cruciferous plants. (2) Scurvy grass. *C. officinalis*; a stimulant, diuretic, and antiscorbutic. (3) *C. armoracia*, horseradish, q.v.

cochrome. An alloy of Co and Cr. Cf. *Nichrome*.

cocinic acid. $C_{11}H_{22}O_2 = 186.17$. A fatty acid from coconut oil.

cocinin. An ester of cocinic acid; the chief constituent of coconut oil.

coclaurine. An alkaloid from the leaves and bark of *Cocculus laurifolius* (Menispermaceae).

cocoa. Cacao, q.v. Cf. *coca, coconut.* (1) C. tree. The tropical shrub *Theobroma cacao* (Sterculiaceae). (2) C. seeds. (3) Brown, finely ground seeds of *Theobroma cacao*, after expression of their fat. (4) The beverage made from (3). (5) Cf. *coca, coconut.* **c. butter.** Cacao butter, oleum theobromatis, theobroma oil. Brown·fat obtained by compression of cacao seeds between hot or cold plates, d.0.976–0.995, sapon. val. 192–200, iodine no. 32–37.7, m.30–35, soluble in ether. **c. nut.** (1) Cocoa. (2) Coconut. Cf. *coca.* **c. nut oil.** See *coconut oil.* **c. oil.** Cocoa butter. **c. red.** $C_{17}H_{12}(OH)_{10}$. A dihydroxyhydroflavonol derivative, and the pigment of c.; 2.5–5% is formed during the drying of the white beans, by enzyme action. **c. seeds.** Cacao. The dried and fermented seeds of the cocoa tree, *Theobroma cacao*, tropical and S. America. Used to make a beverage; contains cocoa butter 50, albumin 18, starch 10, theobromine 1.5%. World consumption (1961), 1 million tons. **c. shell meal.** The ground husks of c. seeds; a fertilizer: nitrogen 2.5, phosphorus pentoxide 1, potassium oxide 2.5%.

coconut. Cocoanut. The fruit of *Cocos nucifera*, a palm (Pacific and Australian Islands and E. and W. Indies). Cf. *copra, coir.* **c. butter.** Coconut oil. **c. cake.** The material remaining after the expression of c. oil. **c. oil.** A fixed oil expressed from the fruit of *Cocos nucifera* or copra (dried coconut, the coconut palm). Used in the manufacture of margarine, food products, and soap. Yellow oil, d.0.9259, m.14. Sapon. val. 246–268, iodine no. 8–9.5, acid val. 5–50. Cf. *cocoa butter.*

cod. The cod fish, *Gadus morrhua.* **c. ichthulin.** A vitellin from cod eggs. **c. liver oil.** See *codliver oil.*

codamine. $C_{20}H_{25}O_4N = 343.20$. An alkaloid of opium, isomeric with laudanine, m.121.

codeine. $C_{18}H_{21}O_3N \cdot H_2O = 317.28$. Methylmor-phine. A levorotatory alkaloid from opium (0.2–0.8%). Colorless crystals, anhyd. 155, soluble in water; a mild narcotic. **c. citrate.** $(C_{18}H_{21}O_3N)_3$-$C_6H_8O_7 = 1089.84$. Colorless crystals soluble in water. **c. hydrobromide.** $C_{18}H_{21}O_3N \cdot HBr$-$2H_2O = 434.24$. Colorless crystals soluble in water; used medicinally for whooping cough. **c. hydrochloride.** $C_{18}H_{21}O_3N \cdot HCl \cdot 2H_2O = 371.77$. White needles, m.264, soluble in water. **c. methyl bromide.** Eucodeine. **c. phosphate.** $C_{18}H_{21}O_3N$-$H_3PO_4 \cdot 1.5H_2O = 424.40$. White crystals, anhydrous at 235, soluble in water; a sedative. **c. salicylate.** $C_{18}H_{21}O_3N \cdot C_7H_6O_3 = 455.31$. Colorless, crystals, soluble in water; used in rheumatic disorders. **c. sulfate.** $(C_{18}H_{21}O_3N)_2 \cdot H_2SO_2$-$5H_2O = 786.69$. White rhombs, decomp. 278, soluble in water.

codeinone. $C_{18}H_{21}O_3N$. The quinone form of codeine. **dihydro-** Dicodide. **dihydrohydroxy-** Eucodal.

codethyline. $C_{19}H_{23}O_3N = 313.19$. Morphine ethylate, m.93. **c. hydrochloride.** Dionine.

Codex Alimentaris. An international compendium of food standards, compositions, and analytical methods.

codliver oil. Oleum morrhuae, banks oil. A fixed oil from the liver of *Gadus morrhua.* Yellow oil, $d_{25}°0.915–0.925$, soluble in alcohol: contains: gaduin, olein, morrhuic acid, phosphorus, iodine, and sulfur compounds. An alterative, and nutritive in tuberculous diseases, malnutrition, and malassimilation, since it contains several vitamins. **artificial-** An irradiated ergosterol or cholesterol. **c.o. emulsion.** An emulsion of c.o. with various pharmaceutical ingredients which mask its unpleasant taste (peppermint oil) or enhance its value (phosphates).

codol. Retinol.

coeff. Abbreviation for coefficient.

coefficient. A numerical factor by which the value of one quantity is multiplied to give the value of another; or to indicate its rate of range. **activity-** q.v. **distribution-** q.v. **c. of absorption.** See *absorption.* **c. of compressibility.** *A.* The relative deviation of a gas from Boyle's law, q.v.: $p_1v_1/p_0v_0 = 1 - A$, where p_1, p_0, v_1, and v_0 are 2 sets of measurements of p and v between 1 atm and zero pressure. **c. of conductivity.** A number indicating the amount of heat or electricity that passes through a unit of thickness of substance in a unit of time, when the temperature, and potential difference is 1°C or 1 volt, respectively. **c. of expansion.** A number indicating the expansion of a substance for a temperature increase of 1°C. Cf. *Charles's law.*

coenzyme. A catalyst for the activation of an enzyme. Cf. *coferment.* **c. —Q.** Ubiquinone. **c. —II.** The c. of dehydrogenase, in horse erythrocytes.

coer-. See *cer-*.

coesite. Synthetic crystalline silica. It is 15% denser than quartz and is very abrasive.

coferment. A substance that increases the activity of a ferment or enzyme, e.g., calcium for thrombin. Cf. *coenzyme.*

coffee. The dried seeds of the coffee tree, *Coffea arabica, C. liberica*, etc. (Rubiaceae), Asia, Africa, Central or S. America. Contains (unroasted): fat

13.27, water 11.23, albuminoids 12.07, sugar 8.55, fiber 3.92, caffeine 1.21%. World production (1960), 3 million tons.

coffeic acid. Caffeic acid.

coffeine. Caffeine.

coffinite. $U(SiO_4)_{1-x}(OH)_{4x}$. A primary constituent of radioactive siltstones, from S. Island, New Zealand.

cognac. A high-grade brandy. **c. essence.** (1) Ethyl nonylate or (2) ethyl chloride, used to imitate the c. flavor. **c. oil.** (1) A brandy adulterant; coconut oil, alcohol, and sulfuric acid. (2) The essential oil of cognac, containing the esters of caprinic and caprilic acids. (3) Ethyl oenanthate; a flavoring.

Cohen, Ernst Julius. 1869–1944. Dutch chemist noted for research in physical chemistry. **C., Julius Berend.** 1859–1935. British chemist, noted for his work on optical activity and the laws of aromatic chemistry.

cohere. To hold together; as, molecules of the same type. Cf. *adhere*.

coherer. An electrical-resistance tube filled with a granulated conductor by which electromagnetic waves are detected from the change in resistance produced by the corresponding variations in the coherence of the particles.

cohesion. The attractive force which holds the molecules of a substance together. Cf. *adhesion*.

cohesive. Sticking together.

cohoba. A snuff used in Haiti.

cohobation. Repeated distillations, the distillate being returned each time to the residue in the distillation vessel. It was believed formerly to result in a higher degree of purity.

cohosh. An Indian (Algonkian) name for various medicinal plants; e.g.: **black-** *Cimicifuga racemosa.* **blue-** *Caulophyllum thalictroides,* **red-** *Actaea spicata.* **white-** *Actaea alba.*

cohydrol. A colloidal solution of graphite. Cf. *Aquadag.*

coil. A loop or spiral made of wire, tubing, glass, or other material. **induction-** A transformer for inducing an electric current, consisting of a coarse wire c. (primary c.) wound around an iron core and surrounded by a long insulated c. of fine wire in which the induced current is produced. **primary-** See *induction-*. **resistance-** A series of wire coils of known electrical resistance, used to reduce the strength of a galvanic current or to test the resistance of an object by comparison (bridge). **Ruhmkorff-** An induction apparatus, in which the secondary c. is a very fine, long wire permanently mounted and connected to a condenser. **secondary-** The outer coil of an induction c. **Tesla-** An induction c. without the iron c. used for Tesla discharges.

coinage metals. See table at head of next column.

coir. The fibers of the coconut husk, made by retting the husks in seawater and crushing between rollers; used for cables and cordage.

coke. The carbonaceous residue (70–80%) of coal after the volatile constituents have been distilled off. **native-** Carbonite. **c. oven.** A retort in which coal is converted to c. **c. oven gas.** The fuel and illuminating gas distilled from coal.

coking. Making coke by heating coal for about 12 hr.

Cola. A genus of sterculiaceous plants; a source of caffeine. **c. nut.** Kola.

COINAGE METALS

U.S.:	"silver"	Ag 90, Cu 10
	others: before 1942	Cu 75, Ni 25
	1942–1945	Cu 56, Ag 35, Mn 9
	1946–present ...	Cu 75, Ni 25
	proposed	a bimetallic composite (Cu between Cu–Ni)
U.K.:	bronze	Cu 95.5, Sn 3, Zn 1.5
	gold (sovereign)	Au 91.66, Cu 8.34
	nickel-brass (threepenny piece) .	Cu 79, Zn 20, Ni 1
	"silver": before 1920 .	Ag 92.5, Cu 7.5
	1920–1927 ..	Ag 50, Cu or Ni 50
	1927–1946..	Ag 50, Cu 40, Ni 5, Zn 5
	1946–present	Cu 75, Ni 25 (cupronickel)

colamine. $NH_2 \cdot CH_2 \cdot CH_2 \cdot OH = 61.06$. 2-Aminoethanol. Colorless liquid, b.171.

colatannin. $C_{16}H_{20}O_8 = 340.15$. Colatin. The tannin from cola; crystals m.148, soluble in alcohol.

colatin. Colatannin.

colatorium. A strainer or sieve.

Colcesa. Trade name for a cellulose acetate synthetic fiber.

colchiceine. $C_{21}H_{23}O_6N \cdot H_2O = 403.19$. An alkaloid from colchicum. Yellow needles, m.172, soluble in water.

colchicine. $C_{22}H_{25}O_6N = 399.45$. An alkaloid from the seeds of *Colchicum autumnale*, meadow saffron. Yellow crystals, m.135–150, soluble in water; an antineuralgic. **c. salicylate.** $C_{22}H_{25}O_6N \cdot C_7H_6O_3 = 537.26$. Cholchisal. Yellow powder, soluble in water. **c. tannate.** $C_{22}H_{25}O_6N \cdot C_{14}H_{10}O_9 = 721.45$. Yellow powder containing 38–40% colchicine; soluble in alcohol.

Colchicum. (1) A genus of liliaceous plants. (2) The plant, *C. autumnale*, meadow saffron, autumn crocus, wild saffron (Europe and N. Africa); a specific for gout. **c. corm.** The root or bulb of *C. autumnale*, meadow saffron, which contains colchicine; a cathartic and local stimulant. **c. flowers.** The blossoms of *C. autumnale*. **c. seeds.** The seeds of *C. autumnale*, containing less colchicine than the corm.

colchinine. $C_{22}H_{15}O_6N = 389.12$. An alkaloid, m.146.

colchisal. Colchicine salicylate.

Colcord. Trade name for a cellulose acetate synthetic fiber.

colcothar. Prussian red, rouge. Caput mortuum, crocus martis. Red ferric oxide obtained by heating ferrous sulfate in air; a styptic and tonic, a polishing material for lenses, and a pigment.

cold. Relatively low degree of heat; lacking warmth. **c. cream.** A white, scented ointment cosmetic, consisting of wax, spermaceti, olive oil, or other fat emulsified with rose water. **c. flow.** The very slow flow of an apparently solid substance, e.g., pitch. **c. storage.** See *refrigeration*.

cole. Rape.

colemanite. $Ca_2B_6O_{11} \cdot 5H_2O$. A native calcium borate, (California).

Coleoptera. An order of insects which includes the beetles. Cf. *Cantharis*.

colibacterin. A vaccine from *Bacillus coli*.

colicine. A bactericidal substance produced by certain strains of Enterobacteriaceae. C. resemble bacteroiophages but, unlike them, do not multiply in the cells they kill.

coliform. An adjective meaning like *Bacterium coli* in morphology and staining reactions, but not necessarily in cultural and biochemical characteristics. Incorrectly used as a noun, or to define any particular group of organisms.

colistin sulfate. The sulfate of a mixture of antimicrobial peptides, produced by a strain of *Bacillus polymyxa*. White, bitter powder, soluble in water; an antibiotic (B.P.).

coliston. Mixed polypeptides produced by strains of *Bacillus polymyxa* var. *colistinus*.

colla. Glue. **c. animalis.** Gelatin. **c. glutinum.** Gluten. **c. piscium.** Ichthyol. **c. taurina.** Gelatin.

collagen. Ossein. A hydroxyproline, glycine-type protein, the chief organic constituent of connective tissue and bones: C 50.75, H 6.47, N 17.86%; yields gelatin in boiling water.

collargol. (1) Colloidal silver and silver oxide formed by reduction and stabilized by egg albumen. (2) A dialyzed and evaporated alkaline solution of colloidal silver (93% Ag).

collateral. Side by side.

collector. A substance used in flotation; increases the capacity of the air bubbles to carry mineral particles; as, xanthates.

colletin. A glucoside from *Colletia spinosa* (Rhamnaceae), S. America.

collidine. $C_8H_{11}N = 121.17$. **alpha-** 4-Ethyl-2-methylpyridine*. Colorless liquid, in coal tar, b.179, soluble in water. **beta-** 3-Ethyl-4-methylpyridine*. Colorless liquid, b.198, insoluble in water. Obtained from the decomposition of cinchonine or coal tar. **gamma-** 2·4·6-Trimethylpyridine*. Colorless liquid from coal tar, b.172, sparingly soluble in water. **hydro-** A ptomaine in putrefying fish.

colligate. To connect together.

colligative. Connected. **c. properties.** Properties related by a mathematical function. **c. p. of solutions.** Those properties which depend quantitatively on the solute. E.g., 1 mole/liter causes:

Vapor pressure	Lowering 0.5 mm
Boiling point	Raising 0.54°C
Freezing point	Lowering 1.85°C
Osmotic pressure	22.4 atm

collimator. A lens system to produce parallel rays.

collinsics. The relationship between molecular weight M, density D, and refractive index μ (H. Collins): $M/\Sigma V_r = D$, and $(\mu - 1)(\Sigma V_r) = \Sigma R_0$, where ΣV_r is the sum of the relative volumes, and ΣR_0 is the sum of the optical refractivities. Cf. *Lorentz-Lorenz equation.*

collinsoniod. The combined principles from the root of *Collinsonia canadensis*, stoneroot (Labiatae); a diuretic and diaphoretic.

collision. Interaction between material systems (molecule, atom, or electron), or electromagnetic induction, resulting in a change in molecular energy. Cf. *induction, chain reaction.* **molecular-** The mechanical contact of molecules is thought to be essential for reaction.

collochemistry. Colloidal chemistry.

collodion. A solution of pyroxylin (gun cotton, nitrated cellulose) in a mixture of alcohol and ether. Colorless, opalescent, thick liquid containing not less than 5% dissolved matter. A reagent for differentiating phenol and creosote; a protective film for wounds, burns, or ulcers; and an airtight seal. **c. cotton.** Pyroxylin.

collodium. Collodion.

colloid. A state of subdivision of matter which comprises either single large molecules (*molecular c.*; as, proteins) or aggregations of smaller molecules (*association c.*; as, gold). The particles of ultramicroscopic size (*dispersed phase*) are surrounded by different matter (*dispersion medium* or *external phase*); both phases may be solid, liquid, or gaseous. See table. The size and electrical charge of the particles determine the properties of c., e.g., Brownian movement, etc. Sizes range from 1×10^{-7} to 1×10^{-5} cm (or 0.1 to 0.001 μ). The smallest particle (colloidal gold) was 1.7×10^{-7} cm (Zsigmondy). **association-** A compound whose molecules aggregate to form colloidal particles. **dispersion-** A dispersoid or finely divided substance. **emulsion-** Emulsoid. A liquid dispersoid, e.g., finely divided droplets of one liquid suspended in another. **eu-** A c. whose molecules are over 2,500 A long. **hemi-** A c. whose molecules are 50–250 A long. **heteropolar-** A c. which consists of polar molecules; as salts. Cf. *heteropolar bond.* **homopolar-** A c. of nonpolar molecules; as hydrocarbons. **hydrophilic-** See *hydrophile.* **hydrophobic-** See *hydrophobe.* **irreversible-** A c. which once coagulated, cannot be readily returned to the colloidal state. **lyophilic-** See *lyophile.* **lyophobic-** See *lyophobe.* **meso-** A c. whose molecules are 250–2,500 A long. **molecular-** A compound whose molecule is of colloidal size; e.g. 100–500 $m\mu$ long and 0.2–1 $m\mu$ thick. **protective-** A substance which promotes stability of the colloidal state by enveloping the particles. **reversible-** A c. which, when coagulated can readily be converted to the colloidal state. **suspension-** Suspensoid. A solid dispersoid, e.g., finely divided solid particles of ultramicroscopic size in a liquid.

c. equivalent. The number of atoms sharing a free electric charge. **c. mill.** A grinding mill for making emulsions and suspensions, or for the disintegration and dispersion of solids or liquids. **c. zone.** See *orientation, zone.*

colloidal. Pertaining to colloids. **c. metal.** Finely divided metal particles of 1 to 100 $m\mu$. They expose a large surface and are very reactive, e.g., as industrial catalysts. **c. movement.** *Brownian movement.* **c. system.** See *colloid* and table on facing page.

collose. An intermediate stage in liquefaction of woody tissues.

collosol. A colloidal solution of a drug or metal, used in ampul medication.

collotype. Artotype. A method of printing from a gelatin surface on a glass plate sensitized with potassium dichromate and exposed under a negative.

colloxylin. Collodion.

Colnova. Trade name for a cellulose acetate synthetic fiber.

colocynth. Bitter apple. Bitter cups. The fruit of *Citrullus colocynthis* (Cucurbitaceae), Asia Minor; a cathartic.

colocynthin. $C_{56}H_{84}O_{23} = 1124.8$. A glucoside from the fruit of *Citrullus colocynthis*; a strong purgative.

COLLOIDAL SYSTEMS

	In solid	In liquid (**hydrosols**)	In gas (**aerosols**)
Solid.........	*Solid sols* Alloys, colored glass, certain precious stones, paper	*Suspensions* Paints, milk of magnesia, collargol	*Smokes* Iodine vapor, cement dust, hydrochloric acid, ammonia
Liquid	*Gels* Celluloid, jellies, green leaves, glue	*Emulsions* Milk, blood, liniments, crankcase oil, protoplasm	*Fogs* Sprays, mists, clouds, visible steam
Gas..........	*Solid foams* Rubber, pumice, plaster, fire foam, lungs, adsorbed gases, aerogels	*Foams* Lather, froths, mayonnaise, whipped cream	No example

colog. Abbreviation for cologarithm. Colog $x = -\log x = \log 1/x$.

Colomal. Trade name for a cellulose acetate synthetic fiber.

colombic acid. Calumbic acid. Cf. *columbic*.

colonial spirit. Methanol.

colonies. Clusters of bacteria visible to the eye.

colophene. $C_{20}H_{32} = 272.3$. A turpentine hydrocarbon; a colorless liquid.

colopholic acid. Colophonic acid.

colophonic acid. Colopholic acid. An acid derived from turpentine; used in plasters, soaps, or cements. Cf. *abietene*.

colophonite. (1) An amber-colored andralite (iron garnet q.v.). (2) A soil colophony. Cf. *copals*.

colophonium. Rosin.

colophony. Rosin.

color, colour. (1) The visual sensation caused by light. (2) Light of a definite wavelength or group of wavelengths which is emitted, reflected, refracted, or transmitted by an object. A c. is defined by three properties; *hue*, the wavelength of the monochromatic light, i.e., shade; *saturation*, the percentage of the light of the above wavelength present, i.e., strength; *brightness*, the amount of light reflected as compared with a standard under the same conditions, i.e., luminosity. Cf. *C.I.E.* units, *dye*. **artists'-** The finely ground pigments used by artists. **basic-** The three colors: red, yellow, and blue. **complementary-** Any two colors of the spectrum which produce white light when blended as rays of colored light; e.g., red and green, blue and orange. **compound-** A c. produced by

PRIMARY COLORS

Wavelength, λ in μ	Color
0.410	Violet
0.470	Blue
0.520	Green
0.580	Yellow
0.600	Orange
0.650	Red

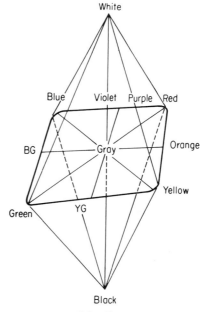

Color diagram.

mixing 2 or more primary pigment colors; as, orange, from yellow and red. **contrast-** Complementary. **primary-** (1) The seven hues of the rainbow or solar spectrum: red, orange, yellow, green, blue, indigo, and violet. (2) The basic colors: red, green, violet, or (pigments) red, yellow, blue. Cf. *Helmholtz's theory.* **secondary-** Compound c.

c. diagram. A chart to illustrate the relationship of the principal colors. Colors opposite each other are complementary; if subtracted, they produce darker shades and finally black; if combined (as with beams of colored light), they produce lighter tints and finally white. **c. filter.** Light filter. A solid, liquid, or gaseous layer which absorbs certain wavelengths. **C. Index.** Colour Index. A numbered list of synthetic dyestuffs and inorganic pigments compiled by the Society of Dyers and Colourists (Yorkshire, England), which gives the scientific and commercial names, components, formulas, methods of preparation, discoverers, literature references, and descriptions of properties and methods of application; 2d ed., 1958 (American Association of Textile Chemists and Colorists, Lowell, Mass.). **c. photography.** Photographically recording the form and c. of an object. Negatives from exposures through differently colored screens are printed on films stained in the complementary colors. Superimposing the prints gives a transparency in natural colors. In practical c. film, 3 differently sensitized emulsions are superimposed on the same support, each producing on exposure an appropriate image in a different c. The combined effect is a c. transparency. **c. reaction.** A chemical change in which a change of c. occurs. **c. scale.** (1) See *c. diagram, spectrum.* (2) C. as an indication of temperature; e.g.:

Incipient red heat	500– 600°C
Dark red heat	600– 800°C
Bright red heat	800–1000°C
Yellowish red heat	1000–1200°C
Incipient white heat	1200–1400°C
White heat	1400–1600°C

c. screen. A c. filter used in photography to render colored objects more contrasting in a black and white print; or to reduce glare. **c. screen law.** The photographic intensity of a c. is increased by a screen of the complementary c.; and decreased by a screen of the same c. **c. theory.** (1) C. of solutions of certain compounds may be due to: (*a*) Solvation, q.v.; the dehydrated compound is colorless. (*b*) Association; the c. changes on dilution. (*c*) Ionization; the un-ionized molecule is differently colored. (*d*) Tautomerism; see *leuco salts.* (2) The emission of a certain wavelength of light is due to electrons which oscillate from one atomic orbit to the other. See also *Helmholtz's theory, Beer's law.*

coloradoite. HgTe. A telluride from Colorado.

Colorado-9. Trade name for 1-trichloro-2,2-bis(*p*-bromophenyl)ethane; an agricultural insecticide.

Coloray. Trade name for a cellulose acetate synthetic fiber.

colorimeter. A device to measure the intensity and shade of colored solutions; or to compare standard color solutions (comparator) in quantitative analysis. Cf. *comparator, tintometer.*

colorimetric analysis. The quantitative analysis of a substance by comparing the intensity of the color produced by a reagent with a standard color, e.g., produced similarly in a solution of known strength. Cf. *Nessler solution.*

colorimetry. (1) Colorimetric analysis. (2) Color measurement. Cf. *calorimetry.* **adsorption-** q.v. **kinetic-** C. based on the rate of development (as distinct from depth) of color in standard and sample.

coloring matter. A substance which produces the sensation of color. See *colors, dyes, pigments.* **c. tablet.** A soluble tablet containing a definite amount of a pure color; to color pharmaceutical preparations.

colors. Pigments or dyes, q.v. To indicate the shade of a color or dye, letters are sometimes used, thus:

G =	gelb (German) = yellow
J =	jaune (French) = yellow
JJ =	intense yellow
O =	orange
OOO =	very intense orange
R =	reddish tint
RR =	very red
S =	black or sulfonated

colostrum. (1) The first secretion of the mammary glands; a thin milk. (2) Orange-colored fat, m.28–38, similar to lard, obtained from top milk by the action of 3–4 times its volume of hydrochloric acid, d.1.12, at 92°C, for 90 min.

columba. Calumba.

columbate. Niobate.

columbian spirits. Methanol.

columbic. Niobic.

columbin. $C_{21}H_{22}O_7 = 386.2$. A glucoside from the root of *Jateorrhiza calumba.* Yellow crystals. m.182, sparingly soluble in water; a bitter tonic.

columbite. The mineral $(Fe \cdot Mn)(Cb \cdot Ta)_2O_4$. Cf. *tantalite.*

columbium. Cb. An element, at. no. 41. In 1949 it was officially renamed niobium, Nb, q.v.

columbo. Calumba. **American-** Fraserin.

columbous. Niobous.

columboxy. Nioboxy.

columbyl. Nioboxy.

column. A pillar. **c. still.** A still for fractional distillation.

colza. Rape seed oil.

comanic acid. $C_6H_4O_4 = 140.1$. Pyrone-α-carboxylic acid. An acid from chelidonic acid, m.250, slightly soluble in water.

combination. (1) The union of 2 or more substances; to form a new substance. (2) A chemical reaction in which two elements combine and form a binary compound; or two binary compounds combine and form a complex compound. **molecular-** The union or aggregation of molecules by chemical or coordinate bonds, q.v.; as: *equilibrium* c. of 2 molelules of odd molecular number; *irreversible* c. or polymerization, q.v.; *reversible* c. or association, q.v. Cf. *liquids, bonds.*

c. principle. The frequency, q.v., of a radiation may be represented by the difference between two terms.

combining. Uniting or joining together. **c. weight.** Equivalent weight.

combustible. Flammable. **c. gases.** The fuel gases of industry; as, hydrogen, hydrocarbons, carbon monoxide, and their mixtures.

combustion. Burning; a chemical change accompanied by the liberation of heat, sound, and/or light. **fractional-** q.v. **heat of-** See *heat.* **organic-** The decomposition of organic compounds, and the collection of the products for *elementary analysis,* q.v. **slow-** (1) The slow oxidation of a substance. (2) The combination of two gases by means of a heated wire. **spontaneous-** (1) Accelerated c. effecting a sudden outburst of heat and light (explosion). (2) Self-ignition, q.v. **wet-** Oxidation by strong oxidizing agents; as, sulfuric acid–dichromate mixture.

c. boat. A small tray of refractory material

for burning organic compounds in a c. tube.
c. capsule. A small porcelain crucible used in coal analysis. **c. furnace.** A heating appliance used in the elementary analysis of organic compounds, consisting of a row of burners or electric heating units, under a gutter in which are placed the c. tube, with means for regulating the temperature. **c. train.** The arrangement of apparatus for elementary organic analysis: usually hydrogen, oxygen, and air tanks; potash bulb, calcium chloride tube, c. tube and furnace, potash bulb, and calcium chloride or sulfuric acid tube. **c. tube.** A wide glass, silica, or porcelain tube, resistant to high temperatures. **c. tube furnace.** (1) C. furnace. (2) An electrically heated, refractory-lined, hollow spool, used for c. work.

commensal. Living in close association with man; as certain rodents.

comminute. To bring to a state of fine division.

comminution. The process of grinding or breaking into small fragments, e.g., cutting, rasping, slicing, levigating, pulverizing, triturating.

common salt. Sodium chloride.

commutator. A device to interrupt or reverse an electric current. **dynamo-** A transformer of alternating into direct current, attached to a dynamo.

comolised. Highly aggregated.

comosic acid. An acid substance derived from the bulbs of *Muscari comosum* (Liliaceae).

comparator. (1) An electrical device to calibrate a-c instruments. (2) See *colorimeter*.

comparison spectroscope. A spectroscope in which 2 spectra can be produced simultaneously side by side for comparison.

comparison tubes. A set of test tubes of the same glass and dimensions, used in colorimeters to compare colors.

comparoscope. A device attached to a microscope for comparing separate slides simultaneously.

compatibility. The retention of the respective properties of 2 or more drugs when administered together. **in-** The impairing influence of 2 or more substances on one another when mixed. Cf. *incompatible*.

compatible. Describing 2 drugs that do not interfere or react chemically, physically, or therapeutically with each other.

compensation apparatus. Potentiometer.

complement (1) To supply a missing part. (2) Alexin, cytase, end body. See *Ehrlich's side-chain theory*. (3) The difference between an acute angle and 90°. **c. fixation.** C. deflection, c. deviation. The combining of the zymophore group of the c. to make it inert. See *Ehrlich's side-chain theory, Wassermann reaction*. (4) A hypothetical substance in fresh serum which can cause hemoglobin to escape from red cells that have combined with an antibody.

complementary color. See *color*. **c. c. screens.** (1) Copper ruby glass (red) and copper glass (blue); (2) uranium glass (yellow) or chromium glass (greenish yellow) and cobalt glass (blue).

complex. Complicated; not simple. **normal-** A c. ion or compound which in solution dissociates reversibly into its component parts, e.g., $Cd(CN)_4''$. **penetration-** A c. ion or compound which is sufficiently stable to retain its identity in solution, e.g., $Fe(CN)_6''$. **II-** (di- or oligo-olefin)$_m MX_n$, where M

is a transition metal and X a singly charged atom; as ferrocene.

c. acid. A combination of 2 or more nonmetallic compounds or acid radicals, e.g., 2HF and SiF_4 give H_2SiF_6. **c. compound.** A combination of 2 or more compounds or ions, e.g., 4KCN and $Fe(CN)_2$ give $K_4Fe(CN)_6$. **c. ion.** A c. electrically-charged radical or group of atoms, e.g., $Cu(NH_3)_2{}^{++}$. **c. reaction.** A chemical change in which 2 or more reactions occur simultaneously.

complexan. Complexone.

compleximetry, -ometry. Titration with, or of, a substance forming a slightly dissociated soluble complex.

complexing agent. Chelating agent.

complexometric titration. A method of volumetric analysis in which the formation of a colored complexone is used to indicate the end point; e.g., the use of EDTA, q.v., to determine the hardness of water.

Complexon. Trade name for certain compounds of ethylenediaminetetraacetic acid. **C.-I.** Trade name for trimethylaminotricarboxylic acid, a complexone.

complexone. (1) The sodium salt of ethylenediaminetetraacetic acid (EDTA). Used in complexometric titration, q.v. (German: komplexon.) (2) Complexan. In general, one of a group of polyaminopolycarboxylic acids which form anionic complexes.

component. (1) An ingredient or part of a mixture (as distinct from the *constituent* of a compound). (2) The smallest number of chemical substances capable of forming all the constituents, q.v., of a system in whatever proportions they may be present. See *phase rule*.

Compositae. Composite family. A group of herbaceous or woody plants, rarely shrubs, with many florets arranged in compact heads as a compound flower on a common receptacle. Many yield important drugs; e.g.: Roots; *Taraxacum officinale*, dandelion; *Cichorium intybus*, chicory; *Arnica montana*, arnica root. Leaves: *Ambrosia artemisiaefolia*, ragweed. Herbs: *Tanacetum vulgare*, tansy; *Artemisia absinthium*, wormwood; *Senecio aureus*, ragwort. Flowers: *Anthemis nobilis*, English chamomile; *Carthamus tinctorius*, safflower. Seeds: *Helianthus annuus*, sunflower seeds. Fruits: *Arctium lappa*, burdock fruit. Juice: *Lactuca virosa*, lactucarium.

composition. The elements or compounds comprising a material or produced from it by analysis. Cf. *constitution*.

compost. A mixed organic manure produced by the natural decomposition of waste organic matter, by means of mesophilic and thermophilic organisms.

compound (1) A substance whose molecules consist of unlike atoms, and whose constituents cannot be separated by physical means. A c. differs from a physical mixture by reason of the definite proportions of its constituent elements which depend on their atomic weights, by the disappearance of the properties of the constituent elements, and, by entirely new properties characteristic of the c. formed. (2) To mix drugs, or make up a prescription. **acyclic-** An organic c. in which the C atoms are arranged in an open chain. **addition-** A c. formed by the union of 2 simpler or binary compounds: $NH_3 + HCl = NH_4Cl$. **additive-** A c. formed by the saturation of double or triple bonds. **aliphatic-** An acyclic c. or paraffin. **amino-** An organic c. containing the radical NH_2-. **aromatic-** An organic c. in which the C atoms form a ring or closed chain, e.g., benzene series. **asymmetric-** A c. containing one or more optically active C atoms. **azo-** An organic c. containing the —N:N— group. **binary-** A c. whose molecules consist of only 2 kinds of atoms. **carbon-** See *organic c.* **chain-** A cyclic c. **closed chain-** Aromatic c. **coal tar-** A c. derived from coal tar, especially aromatic organic c. **condensation-** A c. formed by the union of 2 or more molecules, especially organic compounds, in which one or more molecules of water are usually liberated. **coupling** A c. which substitutes another atom, generally hydrogen. **cyclic-** Aromatic c. **diazo-** A c. containing the —N:N— group. **endothermic-** A c. formed with the absorption of heat; they are usually explosive. **exothermic-** A c. formed with the liberation of heat; they are usually stable. **fatty-** Aliphatic c. **homocyclic-** An aromatic c. with only C atoms in its ring, e.g., benzene. **heterocyclic-** An aromatic c. with atoms other than C atoms in its ring, e.g., pyridine. **index-** A c. from which another is derived by substitution; thus methane is the i. c. for chloromethane. **inorganic-** A c. containing no C atoms. The majority are polar. **metameric-** Metamers. **molecular-** (1) Addition c. (2) See *combination, association, polymerization.* **nonpolar-** A relatively unstable c. of elements having weak electrical forces, e.g., carbon compounds. See *compounds.* **open-chain-** Aliphatic c. **organic-** A c. containing C and H atoms, with or without other atoms in the molecule. The majority are nonpolar (except metallic salts of organic acids). **organometallic-** Organic c. in which an H is replaced by a metal. **paraffin-** A saturated aliphatic hydrocarbon. **polar-** A fairly stable c. of elements of strong electromotive force, e.g., NaCl. See *compounds.* **quaternary-** (1) A c. with 4 different atoms, e.g., $NaHSO_4$. (2) A combination of a fully substituted ammonium radical with a halogen, e.g। $N(C_2H_5)_4 \cdot I$. **ring-** See *aromatic c.* **series of-** Compounds containing the same positive or negative radical; e.g.: ferrous compounds, ferric compounds, ferrates; sulfides, sulfites, sulfates. **saturated-** A c. in which all the C bonds are satisfied. **spiro-** An organic ring c. in which one C atom is common to 2 rings. **substitution-** A c. formed by the replacement of certain atoms by other atoms or group of atoms. Cf. *index c.* **sulfur-** A c. containing sulfur, especially organic compounds containing divalent sulfur. **ternary-** A c. of 3 different atoms, e.g., KCN. **tertiary-** Ternary c. **unsaturated-** A carbon c. with double or triple bond.

c.E. Cortisone. **c. ethers.** Esters. **c. microscope.** See *microscope.* **c. molecule.** A molecule consisting of more than kind of atom. **c. protein.** See conjugate proteins.

compounds, classes of. nonpolar- Do not ionize or conduct an electric current; are relatively inert; do not associate, but may polymerize; have a frame structure; exhibit isomerism; have a low dielectric constant; are generally known as organic substances. **polar-** Ionize and conduct an electric current; are very reactive; form double molecules and complex ions; possess a condensed structure; exhibit tautomerism; have a high dielectric constant; are generally known as inorganic substances.

Compral. Cyrinal. Trade name for pyramidon and trichloroethanol urethane; an analgesic.

compregnation. The combined application of impregnation and high pressure; e.g., in the lamination of wood veneers with plastics.

compressed gas. A g. stored at high pressure in a steel cylinder for shipment; as, carbon dioxide. Fuel gases are used in cylinders under various trade names; as, Calorgas. Cf. *cylinders.*

compressibility. The resistance offered by substances to high pressure. **coefficient of-** See *coefficient.* Cf. *piezometer.*

Compton, Arthur Holly. b. 1892. American physicist and Nobel prize winner (1927). **C., Karl Taylor.** 1887–1954. American physicist. **C. effect.** Scattered homogeneous X rays give rise to a change of wavelength (fluorescence) which depends on the direction of observation. Cf. *Raman effect.* **C. rule.** Atomic weight multiplied by heat of fusion equals twice the absolute melting point.

computer. A calculating device (usually electronic) which receives readings from a recording instrument and converts them into means (usually electric impulses) of operating a controlling or correcting unit. **analog-** A c. which represents the magnitude of numbers by a physical quantity such as length or voltage, e.g., a slide rule. **digital-** A c. based on numbers, e.g., a calculating machine.

conalbumin. A noncrystalline albumin of egg white.

conamarin. A glucoside from the root of hemlock, *Conium maculatum* (Umbelliferae). Cf. *conine.*

conarachin. A globulin in peanuts (8.7%), consisting principally of arginine, lysine, and cysteine.

conc., concn. Abbreviations for *concentrated* and *concentration.*

concanavalin. A globulin from jack beans.

concave. Presenting a depressed or hollow surface. **c. lens.** See *lens.* **c. mirror.** See *mirror.*

concentra(te), (tion). (1) Chemistry: (*a*) Increasing the amount of a dissolved substance by evaporation of the solvent or by adding more of the substance. (*b*) The strength of a solution, expressed as:
Percentage, %, or gm per 100 ml
Molarity, M, or moles per liter
Molality, M, or moles per 1,000 gm
Normality, N, or equivalents (in grams) per liter
(2) Physics: Gathering together that which is diffused, e.g., light, sound, or heat. **absolute-** The c. of the active ion of a substance; e.g., the H^+ of an acid. **hydrogen-ion-** The number of H^+ in grams per liter. See *hydrogen ion.* **ionic-** The number of gram ions in a unit volume of solution. **molal-** The number of moles (gram molecules) in a unit volume (liter). Cf. *molality.* **normal-** *N.* The number of equivalent moles per liter.
c. limit. The minimum c. of a substance detectable by a particular chemical reaction.

concentrator. A mechanical device to increase concentration. Cf. *separator.*

concentric. Describing a number of rings with a common center.

concha. A shell.

conche. Shell-like pots with granite bottoms and heavy rolls, used in chocolate manufacture.

conching. The rolling of chocolate mixes, to develop flavor.

conchinine. Quinidine.

conchiolin. $C_{30}H_{48}O_{11}N_9 = 710.8$. A protein from mollusk shells, resembling keratin. It is the fine organic network matrix of natural pearl in which calcium carbonate crystals are distributed.

concrete. A mixture of gravel, broken rock, and sand held together by cement, q.v. (2) A concentrated or clotted extract of a plant. **post-stressed-** C. in which tension is induced in the reinforcement after hardening and transferred externally by anchorages into the structure. **prestressed-** C. in which cracking is prevented by applying pressure to the structural member before it is loaded to neutralize the tension caused by the working load. **reinforced-** C. formed around iron bars, rods, or wire.

condensation. (1) Conversion to a more compact form. (2) Transformation from the gaseous to the liquid state. (3) A combination of similar molecules to form a more complex compound (polymerization, etc.). (4) A union of like or unlike molecules, usually with elimination of molecules of (e.g.) water, acid. (5) An accumulation of electrons, e.g., in a condenser. (6) The formation of a pencil of parallel or convergent light rays from convergent rays, e.g., by a convex lens. **retrograde-** The deposition of hydrocarbon gases as liquids, from the high-pressure state, when pressure is appreciably reduced.

condensed. (1) Reduced in volume. (2) Liquefied from a gas or vapor. **c. nucleus.** See *nucleus*.

condenser. (1) A device to concentrate matter or energy. (2) An apparatus for cooling vapors to liquids, e.g., Liebig. (3) A device for the polymerization of organic compounds. (4) A series of insulated conductors for the accumulation of electricity. See *electrical*. (5) A system of lenses or mirrors, e.g., Abbé, q.v. **bull's-eye-** A convex lens c. **electrical-** Sheets of tin foil separated by paraffin, with the alternate tin foils connected to a common terminal, for storing electrons. **high potential-** Alternating brass sheets and glass plates in an oil-filled box. **Liebig-** Generally 2 straight concentric glass tubes with cold water passing through the outer, and the vapor to be condensed through the inner tube. **paraboloid-** q.v. **reflux-** q.v. **substage-** Abbé. **c. flask.** A large spherical flask filled with liquid, to absorb the heat from a source of light and to concentrate its intensity. **c. tube.** The inner tube of a c.

condiment. A spicy or stimulating vegetable product, used for its flavor.

condistillation. The separation of organic substances by distilling with another liquid. Cf. *steam distillation*.

conductance. (1) The capacity to convey energy, as heat or electricity. (2) The ratio between an electric current flowing through a unit cube and the difference in potentials between its ends; the reciprocal of resistance, q.v.

conduction. The property of transmitting matter or energy. **air-** C. by a current of air. **electrolytic-** The passage of electrons by means of ions. **sound-** The passage of sound waves in air. **thermal-** The transmission of heat by materials.

conductivity. (1) The degree of conduction; the capacity for transmitting electricity, heat, light, or sound. (2) The quantity of electricity transmitted per unit area per unit potential gradient per unit time, Λ. **coefficient of-** See *coefficient*. **electrical-** See *electrical*. **equivalent-** The ratio of the measured specific c. to the number of gram equivalents of salt in 1 ml solution. Cf. degree of *ionization*. **heat-** Thermal-. **limiting-.** The c. of a solution at infinite dilution, i.e., when ionization is complete. **molal-** or **molecular-** The c. in reciprocal ohms of a solution containing 1 mole of solute placed between electrodes 1 cm apart, i.e., the specific c. multiplied by the number of milliliters containing 1 mole of solute. **specific-** The reciprocal, in mhos, of the specific resistance of an electrolyte. **super-** The abnormally high c. of metals at temperatures near absolute zero. **supra-** Super-c. **thermal-** The number of gram calories passing through a 1-cm cube in 1 sec, with a temperature difference of 1°C; or BThU passing through 1 in. of an area of 1 ft² in 1 hr, with a temperature difference of 1°F. **unilateral-** See *valve effect*. **unit of-** Mho, the reciprocal ohm; ohm^{-1}.

  c. apparatus. A device to determine the c. of solutions. **c. cell.** A glass vessel containing 2 electrodes at a definite distance apart, and filled with a solution whose c. is to be determined. **c. bridge.** A modified Kelvin bridge for measuring very low resistances, on which the c. is read directly from the slide wire. **c. water.** A very pure water of specific c. 0.4×10^{-6} ohm^{-1} cm^{-1} in a vacuum, at 18°C. Cf. *water*.

CONDUCTIVITY

Electrical	Metal	Thermal (relative)
681,200	Silver	1.000
640,600	Copper	0.7198
186,000	Zinc	0.2653
141,000	Iron	0.1665
50,400	Lead	0.0877
10,630	Mercury	0.0148

conductometric. Pertaining to conductivity measurements. **c. analysis.** Analysis in which the progressive change in conductivity determines the end point of a reaction. Cf. *potentiometric titration*.

conductophore. The molecular structure associated with a toxophore, q.v.

conductor. A medium which conducts. **electrical-** Metals, solutions of salts, molten substances, or ionized gases which transmit electrons, and allow an electric current to pass. **non-** See *insulator*.

condurangin. A glucoside from condurango bark. **alpha-** $C_{20}H_{32}O_6 = 368.3$. White powder, m.60, insoluble in water. **beta-** $C_{18}H_{28}O_7 = 356.3$. Amorphous yellow powder, sparingly soluble in water; a stomachic.

condurango. Candurangu, condorvine. The vine, *Gonolobus condurango* (Asclepiadaceae), Colombia. **c. bark.** A bitter tonic and stomachic.

Condy's fluid. A liquid disinfectant claimed to produce ozone by oxidation.

cone. A body having a circular base and tapering point. **filtering-** A hollow c. of porous material, e.g., alundum, which fits into a support, for rapid filtration of solutions. **measuring-** A slightly tapered ruler to measure inside diameters. **pyrometer-** Seger c., q.v.

conedendrin. $C_{20}H_{20}O_6 = 356.16$. A constituent of many coniferous trees, m.255, insoluble in water.

conessine. $C_{24}H_{40}N_2 = 356.5$. Wrightine. An alkaloid from the bark of *Wrightia zeylanica* (Apocynaceae), Ceylon. Colorless, deliquescent needles, m.121, slightly soluble in water; an astringent and anthelmintic.

confection. Pharmaceutical term for a soft paste compounded with a sweet mucilaginous liquid.

configuration. The spatial arrangement of elements (e.g., atoms in a molecule); or of parts, in a particular form of figure. Thus dextrose and levulose differ in *structure* but coincide in c. with respect to the three asymmetric C atoms; *d-* and *l-*sugars coincide in *structure* but differ in c. **electronic-** Constellation.

congealing. (1) Freezing. (2) The setting of cement or solidification of a liquid. **c. point.** The temperature at which a liquid freezes.

congelation. Freezing, solidification. The transformation from the liquid to the solid state, by low temperature, hydration, or chemical reaction.

conglomerate. An aggregation or a mass of units.

conglutin. A protein from the seeds of leguminous plants.

conglutinin. A protein of beef serum which clumps blood cells. See *agglutinin*.

congo blue. Trypan blue. **c. paper.** A filter paper stained with congo red solution. **c. red.** $C_{32}H_{22}O_6N_6S_2Na_2 = 696.69$. Benzidinedisazo-*m*-aminobenzenesulfonic acid-1-naphthylamino-4-sulfonate of sodium. A red azo dye; used as indicator (alkalies—red, acids—blue); and to detect free mineral acids in organic acids. **c. solution.** A solution of 1 gm c. red in 90 ml water and 10 ml alcohol. **c. yellow.** $C_{24}H_{18}O_4N_5SNa$. An orange-yellow dye.

conhydrine. $C_8H_{17}ON = 143.2$. Oxyconiine, hydroxyconiine, α-methyl-2-piperidineëthanol. An alkaloid from the seeds of *Conium maculatum*, poison hemlock. Colorless crystals, m.98, soluble in water; a narcotic, antiseptic, and anodyne. **pseudo-** 2-α-Hydroxypropylpiperidine. Colorless crystals, m.118, soluble in water.

conic acid. Coniic acid.

coniceine. $C_8H_{15}N = 125.13$. **alpha-** Colorless liquid, d.0.893, b.158. **beta-** 2-Allylpiperidine. White needles, d.0.852, m.40. **gamma-** 1,2,3,4-Tetrahydro-6-propylpyridine. Colorless liquid, d.0.872, b.172. **delta-** Piperolidine. **epsilon-** Methylconidine. Colorless liquid, d.0.8856, b.151.

conicic acid. Coniic acid.

conicine. Coniine.

Coniferae. Pinales; pine family. Trees or shrubs, usually with a resinous juice and awl- or needle-shaped leaves, which bear cones. It includes the old families Pinaceae and Taxaceae.

coniferaldehyde. Ferulaldehyde.

coniferin. $C_{16}H_{22}O_8 \cdot 2H_2O = 378.2$. A glucoside from the cambium of coniferous trees and asparagus. Gray powder, m.185, soluble in hot water; used to manufacture vanillin.

coniferol. $C_{10}H_{12}O_3 = 180.1$. Coniferyl alcohol, *m*-methoxy-*p*-oxystyrone. Colorless crystals, m.73, slightly soluble in water. It oxidizes to vanillin. Cf. *lignin*.

coniferyl. The radical $HO \cdot (MeO)C_6H_3CH:CH-$. **c. alcohol.** Coniferol. **c. aldehyde.** Ferulaldehyde. **c. benzoate** $C_{17}H_{16}O_4$. The chief constituent of of Siamese gum benzoin. Colorless needles, m.73.

coniic acid. Conicic acid. An acid constituent of conium.

coniine. Conine.

conine. $C_8H_{17}N = 127.2$. Cicutine, 2-propyl-piperidine, coniine. An alkaloid from the seeds of *Conium maculatum*, poison hemlock (Umbelliferae). Yellow oil, d.0.862, b.166, insoluble in water; narcotic. Cf. *conhydrine*. **hydroxy-** Conhydrine. **para-** Paraconine.
    c. hydrobromide. $C_8H_{17}N \cdot HBr = 208.01$. White crystals, m.210, soluble in water; an antispasmodic and antineuralgic. **c. hydrochloride.** $C_8H_{17}N \cdot HCl = 163.66$. Colorless rhombs, m.211, soluble in water.

conium. The seeds of *Conium maculatum*, poison hemlock (Umbelliferae); a narcotic and sedative. Cf. *conine, conamarin*.

conjugate. Paired or coupled. **c. double bonds.** Two double bonds in the relative positions indicated by the formula —CH=CH—CH=CH— They form additive compounds by saturation of the 1 and 4 carbons, so that a double bond is produced between the 2 and 3 carbons. **c. foci.** The anterior and posterior foci of a lens. **c. proteins.** Polypeptides or proteins which contain a prosthetic group; e.g., hemoglobin which contains hematin.

conjugation. (1) The linking together of centers of unsaturation. (2) The combination of large molecules, (e.g., proteins) with another compound.

conophor oil. A substitute for linseed oil from a W. African weed.

Conradson test. A destructive distillation method for the estimation of carbon residues in fuel and lubricating oils. It ranges from 0% (gasoline) to 4.5% (steam-cylinder oils).

consecutive. Following in an uninterrupted sequence or order. **c. position.** Adjacent position.

conservation. Protection from loss, decay, or deterioration. **c. of energy.** The principle that energy is never created or lost, but is always transformed into some other form of energy. Cf. *mass-energy cycle*. **c. of matter.** The principle that matter is never created or lost but is always transformed into some other form of matter, e.g., the radioactive elements.

conservative. Preservative. **c. motion.** In metallurgy, the movement of a dislocation on the slip plane as opposed to **non-c.m.,** when the dislocation moves out of the slip plane.

consistence. The viscosity or solidity of a fluid.

consistency. (1) The degree of solidity or fluidity. Cf. *dissipation, penetration*. (2) The percentage of solid matter in a mixture, e.g., of pulp. **c. meter.** A device to determine the solidity of a semisolid or syrupy substance, e.g., gelatin; usually a disk rotating in the substance, driven by a constant force.

consistometer. An apparatus to determine the hardness or consistency of semiliquids, and hard, brittle, bituminous materials, usually a plunger dropping at constant force onto the material to be tested. The depth of penetration is measured

consolute. (1) A liquid or solution which is completely miscible with another. (2) Miscible in all proportions.

const. Abbreviation for *constant*.

constant. (1) That which is unchangeable, permanent, or invariable. (2) Physics: a property which remains numerically the same. (3) Mathematics: a quantity having a definite and fixed value. **basic-** The numerical value of a permanent property which can be determined directly. **cell-** Specific resistance. **conventional-** The numerical value of a physical property generally accepted as normal. **derived-** The numerical value of an unchanging physical property which is indirectly determined. **experimental-** The numerical value of a physical property determined by experiment and accepted as standard. See table, pp. 176–177.
 c. proportions. A fundamental law of chemistry: Every chemical compound always contains the same percentage by weight of its constituent elements (Proust).

constantan. Constantin.

constantin. Constantan. A thermocouple alloy: Cu60, Ni40%, d.8.4, m.1290.

constellation. Obsolete term for the configuration or arrangement of electrons in a molecule which gives rise to certain properties; as, color. Cf. *resonator*.

constituent. (1) An element or part of a compound. Cf. *component* of a mixture. (2) An element or compound formed from the components, q.v., of a system. Thus, in a system $CaCO_3 = CaO + CO_2$ there are 3 *constituents* ($CaCO_3$, CaO, and CO_2), but only 2 *components*, as any 2 will determine the amount of the third.

constitution. The structure in which elements are arranged in a material. Cf. *configuration*.

constitutional formula. See *formula*.

contact. (1) The touching of bodies. (2) An electric switch. **c. action.** Catalysis. **c. difference.** C. potential. **c. potential.** The difference in potential of two metallic plates in close c. **c. process.** The catalytic manufacture of sulfuric acid from sulfur dioxide and oxygen. **c. series.** Electromotive series. **c. substance.** Catalyst.

container. See *shipping, storage*.

contamination. Infection by accidental contact. Cf. *infection*.

contoured. An irregular, smooth, undulating surface, as a relief map; used to describe bacterial cultures.

contractile. Capable of being drawn together.

contraction. (1) Chemistry: The drawing together of atoms in the molecule, depending partly upon their mutual electromotive forces $= 100 - (100M/A' - A'' \ldots)$, where M is the molecular volume, A' A'', etc., the atomic volumes of the constituents. (2) Physiology: The shortening of muscles in response to a stimulus.

Contramine. $NEt_2 \cdot CS \cdot SNH_2ET_2 = 322.1$. Trademark for diethylammonium diethylthiocarbamate. A softener of fibrous tissue used to treat chronic infections.

contrast. A comparison made by accentuating points of difference. **c. stain.** A double stain, in which only the special feature to be examined takes one color.

contravalence. Covalence.

control. A blank test or standard, e.g., an experiment performed simultaneously with another to

study the relative effects of different conditions.

conus. Cone.

convallamaretin. $C_{20}H_{36}O_8 = 404.4$. A decomposition product of convallamarin.

convallamarin. $C_{23}H_{44}O_{12} = 512.4$. A glucoside from *Convallaria majalis*, lily of the valley (Liliaceae). Yellow powder, soluble in water; a cardiac stimulant and diuretic, similar to digitalis.

convallaretin. $C_{14}H_{26}O_3 = 242.2$. A resinoid from convallaria; an emetic.

Convallaria. Lily of the valley. The flowers and roots of *C. majalis;* an antispasmodic, sternutatory, and diuretic.

convallarin. $C_{34}H_{62}O_{11} = 646.6$. A glucoside from the root of Convallaria. Colorless prisms, sparingly soluble in water; a purgative.

convection. The transmission of heat by the rise of heated liquids or gases, and the fall of colder parts which in turn become heated.

convergent. Inclining toward one point.

conversion. (1) The change from one isomer to another. (2) The change from one unit or system of measurement to another. **c. factor.** A numeral by which a quantity must be multiplied in order to express it in other units. C. factors are given under the definitions of individual units.

converter. A device used to change (1) energy or (2) matter into another form; as, (1) phase c., or (2) digester.

convex. A rounded or bulging exterior surface; opposed to concave. **c. lens.** See *lens*. **c. mirror.** See *mirror*.

convicin. $C_{20}H_{28}O_{16}N_6 = 608.24$. A hexose glucoside of pyrimidine, in *Vicia* species.

Convolvulaceae. A family of twining herbs, some with a milky juice; e.g.: *Exogonium purga*, jalap; *Convolvulus scammonia*, scammony.

convolvulin. $C_{31}H_{50}O_{16} = 678.5$. Rhodeorhetin. A glucoside from jalap. Yellow mass, soluble in alcohol; drastic purgative.

convolvulinic acid. $Me(CH_2)_3 \cdot CHOH(CH_2)_9COOH = 258.3$. Colorless crystals, m.50, from jalap resin.

convolvulinolic acid. Convolvulinic acid.

convolvulus. The root of *C. panduratus*, manroot (Convolvulaceae), N. America; a diuretic and laxative.

convulsant. A drug causing convulsions.

conydrine. Conhydrine.

conyrine. $C_8H_{11}N = 121.09$. α-Propylpyridine. Colorless crystals, m.167, from the reduction of conine by zinc dust.

Cook formula. The acetyl number, q.v.: $(S' - S)/(1 - 0.00075S)$, where S and S' are the saponification values before and after acetylation.

Coolidge, William David. b. 1873 American physical chemist. **C. tube.** (1) A modified X-ray tube; the cathode is a tungsten spiral in a molybdenum tube. (2) Electron tube. An evacuated cathode tube with a thin nickel window and a cathode consisting of a wire made incandescent by a secondary electric current. On passing a high voltage, a stream of electrons passes out of the window and produce effects similar to the β rays of radium.

cooling. Depriving of heat; as, freezing. **air-** C. by means of air currents. **water-** C. by means of cold water.

Cooper-Hewitt lamp. An incandescent mercury-vapor lamp; an exhausted glass tube, 3–4 ft long, containing a little mercury to which is applied an electric potential.

Quantity	Symbol	Value	Error $\times 10^x$
Meter............................	m =	1,650,763.73 wavelengths in vacuo of the unperturbed transition $2p_{10}$—$5d_5$ in Kr^{86}	
Kilogram..........................	kg =	mass of the international kilogram at Sevres, France	
Second...........................	sec =	1/31,556,925.974,7 of the tropical year at 12 hr ET, 0 January 1900	
Degree Kelvin......................	°K =	defined in the thermodynamic scale by assigning 273.16°K to the triple point of water (freezing point, 273.15°K = 0°C)	
Unified atomic mass unit..............	$u = \frac{1}{12}$	the mass of an atom of the C^{12} nuclide	
Mole.............................	mole =	amount of substance containing the same number of atoms as 12 gm of pure C^{12}	
Standard acceleration of free fall	$g_n =$	9.806,65 m/sec², 980.665 cm/sec²	
Normal atmospheric pressure	atm =	101,325 N/m², 1,013,250 dynes/cm²	
Thermochemical calorie	$cal_{th} =$	4.1840 joules, 4.1840 × 10⁷ ergs	
International Steam Table calorie	$cal_{IT} =$	4.1868 joules, 4.1868 × 10⁷ ergs	
Liter	l =	0.001,000,028 m³, 1,000.028 cm³	
Inch.............................	in =	0.0254 m, 2.54 cm	
Pound (avdp.)	lb =	0.453,592,37 kg, 453.592,37 gm	
Atomic weight of oxygen.............	O =	16.000	
Mass of 1 ml water at 4°C	gm =	1.0000	
Density of water at 4°C	$d_4° =$	1.0000	
Temperature of freezing water at 1 atm .		0°C	
Temperature of boiling water at 1 atm ..		100°C	
Normal atmospheric pressure		760 mm Hg of d.13.5951	

BASIC CONSTANTS (BY OBSERVATION)

Velocity of light	$c =$	2.99796×10^{10} cm/sec	±0.00004
Gravitational constant................	$G =$	6.664×10^{-8} cm³/(gm)(sec²)	±0.002
Electronic charge	$e =$	4.803×10^{-10} esu	±0.005
	$e/c =$	1.6021×10^{-20} emu	±0.0016
Electronic ratio	$e/m =$	1.761×10^7 emu/gm.......................	±0.001
	$(e/m)c =$	5.279×10^{17} esu/gm.....................	±0 003
Faraday	$F =$	9.6487×10^4 coulombs	±0.00005
Volume of 1 mole gas at 0°C and normal atmosphere......................	$v_0 =$	22.4141×10^3 cm³/mole	±0.0008
Absolute zero (ice-point)	$T_0 =$	273.18	±0.03°K
Planck's constant	$h =$	6.547×10^{-27} erg sec	±0.008
Rydberg wave number...............	$R_\infty =$	109737.42 cm⁻¹	±0.06

cooperite. A native sulfarsenide containing Pt 64, Pd 9%.

coordinate. Related. **c. bond.** See *bond*. **c. paper.** A sheet of paper ruled with horizontal and vertical lines, used to draw graphs and curves. **c. valence.** See *bond valence*.

coordinates. Means by which the position of a point, particle, object, or star is defined by reference to base lines or base planes. Cf. *diagram*, *abscissa*, *ordinate*, *crystal c.*

Polar c. give the latitude and longitude on a sphere of known radius.

Rectangular c. (*Cartesian* c.) give the distances of a point from each of 2 or 3 perpendicular lines or planes.

Vector c. Straight lines in definite directions and of definite length.

coordination. The harmonious linking of parts of the same rank or order. **ç. number.** The valence number of the central atom of addition compounds indicating the number of molecules or atoms linked to that atom. Thus with $[PtX_6]R_2$ where X may or may not be the same radical as R the c. n. is 6. Cf. *Werner's theory.*

copahene. $C_{20}H_{27}Cl = 302.7$. Colorless crystals insoluble in water.

copahin. A resinoid from copaiba balsam.

copahuvic acid. Copaivic acid.

copaiba. Balsam of copaiba copaiva. An oleoresin from leguminous trees of tropical America especially *Copaifera officinalis.* Grades: **Bahia-** refr. index 1.508, acid val. 110–150. **Maracaibo-** refr. ind. 1.517, acid val. 120–160. **Maranham-** refr. ind. 1.515, acid val. 140–170. **mixture-** q.v. **Para-** refr. ind. 1.510, acid val. 100–160. Insoluble in water; a stimulant, diuretic, and laxative.

c. oil. A sesquiterpene essential oil from c. d.0.895–0.905 b.250–275. **c. resin.** The resin remaining after distillation; mainly copaivic acid.

copaiva. Copaiba.

copaivic acid. $C_{20}H_{30}O_2 = 302.3$. Copahuvic acid. A monobasic acid from the resin of copaiba.

copalchi. The barks of *Strychnos pseudoquina, Croton niveus*, S. America; used as a febrifuge.

copalin. Kopalin. The resin exuded from the sweet gum tree, *Liquidambar styraciflua.*

copals. Hard resin exudations from E. Indies, S. America, and Africa trees used in varnish manufacture. **E. African-** Animi resin. **fossil-** High-grade c. from the ground where trees yielding it have disappeared. **fresh-** Inferior c. from living trees. **kauri-** Kauri gum. **Manila-** See *Manila.* **semifossil-** C. collected from the ground near living trees.

Avogadro's number	$N_0 = 6.023 \times 10^{23}$ mole^{-1}	± 0.006
Loschmidt's number	$n_0 = 2.705 \times 10^{19}$ cm^{-3}	± 0.003
Gas constant	$R_0 = 8.3136 \times 10^7$ erg/(deg)(mole)	± 0.001
	$R_0' = 1.9864$ cal/(deg)(mole)	± 0.0004
	$R_0'' = 8.246 \times 10^{-2}$ (liter)(atm)/(deg)(mole)	± 0.0009
	$R_0''' = 82.048$ (cm^3)(atm)/(deg)(mole)	± 0.009
Molecular gas constant................	$k_0 = 1.3708 \times 10^{-16}$ erg	± 0.0014
Mass of hydrogen atom	$m_H = 1.6608 \times 10^{-24}$ gm	± 0.0017
Mass of electron	$m_0 = 8.994 \times 10^{-28}$ gm	± 0.014
Mass of electron (spectroscopic)	$m_0 = 9.035 \times 10^{-28}$ gm	± 0.010
Mass of α particle	$m_a = 6.597 \times 10^{-24}$	± 0.007
Distance nucleus to electron (normal H)	$a_0 = 0.5284 \times 10^{-8}$ cm	± 0.0004
Radius of Bohr (K) orbit (normal H) ...	$a_0' = 0.5291 \times 10^{-8}$ cm	± 0.0004
Speed of electron (normal H)	$v_0 = 2.1824 \times 10^8$ cm/sec	± 0.0017

CONVENTIONAL CONSTANTS

Atmosphere (normal)	$A_n = 1.013250 \times 10^6$ dyne/cm^2	
Aberration constant	$20.47''$	
Wavelength of red Cd line.............	$\lambda_{Cd} = 6438.4696$ A	
Gravity constant (normal).............	$g = 980.665$ cm/sec^2	

EXPERIMENTAL CONSTANTS

Atomic weight of hydrogen...........	H = 1.0078	
Grating space in calcite	3.028 A	
Gram calorie (mean)...................	cal$_m$ = 4.186 joules	
British Thermal Unit (mean)	BThu = 1054.8 joules	
International Ohm	1.00052 absolute ohm	± 0.00002
International Ampere................	0.99995 absolute amp	± 0.00005

c. balsam. Liquid ambar.

Copel. Trademark for an alloy: Cu 55, Ni 45%; used in thermocouples.

copernik. The alloy: Fe 50, Ni 50%.

copiapite. $Fe_4S_5O_{18} + H_2O$. Yellow copperas.

copis. A white transparent shell (Philippine Islands) used to manufacture screens, lamps, etc.

Coplin jar. A glass box with internal perpendicular grooves to hold microscopic slides during staining.

copolymer. ABS- q.v.

copper. (1) Cu = 63.55. Cuprum. A metallic element, at. no. 29. An orange, ductile, malleable metal, d.8.90, m.1083, b.2840, insoluble in water. World production (1966) 5.1 million tons. It occurs in nature as metal, oxide (cuprite), sulfide (c. glance, chalcopyrite), or carbonate (malachite, etc.) and was known in prehistoric times (c. age). It is prepared or refined by electrolysis of crude c. in c. sulfate solution and forms 2 series of compounds, cuprous compounds, e.g., CuCl; cupric compounds, e.g., $CuCl_2$. The cupric compounds are the more stable; they are blue when hydrated, and grayish when anhydrous; they are poisonous and ionize in aqueous solution. Metallic c. is used extensively for wires, plates, coins, utensils, etc., and is a constituent of many alloys (brass, bronze, bell metal, gunmetal, etc.). (2) A general term suggested for alloys containing 98% or more of c. **black-** Cupric oxide. **blue-** A native c. sulfide. **indigo-** Covellite. **peacock-, purple-** Dornite. **rose-** See *rosette*. **scale-** C. in thin flakes. **silicon-** The alloy: Cu 70–80, Si 30–20%. **wood-** Olivenite. **yellow-** Chalcopyrite.

c. acetoarsenite. Paris green. **c. alloys.** See *aluminum bronze, bell metal, brass, constantan, Dutch metal, nickeline, Muntz metal, speculum.* **c. ammonium chloride.** See *cupric ammonium*

chloride. **c. arsenite.** See *cupric arsenite.* **c. blue.** Azurite. **c. bromide.** See *cuprous, cupric.* **c. carbonate.** Verditer. Cf. *Bremen. basic-* See *cupric c.* **c. chloride.** See *cupric, cuprous chloride.* **c. froth.** Tyrolite. A native copper arsenate. **c. green.** A native pigment of lead chromate and c. oxide. **c. lazur.** Azurite. **c. minerals.** The chief ores of copper are: Native c., Cu; covellite, CuS; chalcopyrite, $CuFeS_2$: berzelianite, Cu_2Se; algodonite, Cu_6As; klaprotholite, $Cu_6Bi_4S_9$; cuprite, Cu_2O; malachite, $Cu_2(OH)_2CO_3$; azurite (chessylite), $Cu_3(OH)_2(CO_3)_2$. **c. mordant.** Cupric sulfate or cupric acetate. **c. number.** The number of milligrams of c. obtained by the reduction of Fehling's or Benedict's solution by 1 gm of a carbohydrate. **c. orthosilicate.** Dioptase. Chrysocolla. **c. peroxide.** Cu_2O_3 and $CuO_2 \cdot H_2O$. Yellow powder, decomp. in water. **c. phosphide.** See *cuprous p.* and *cupric p.* $Cu_5P_2H_2O$ also exists. **c. shavings.** Small shavings of metallic c., used as a catalyst and to prepare cuprammonium reagent. **c. sulfate.** Cupric sulfate. **c. vitriol.** Cupric sulfate.

copperas. $FeSO_4$. Native ferrous sulfate. **blue-** Cupric sulfate. **green-** Ferrous sulfate. **yellow-** Copiapite. **white-** Zinc sulfate.

copperon. Cupferron.

Coppet, Louis Cas de. 1841–1911. French physicist. **C's law.** The depression in the freezing point of a solution below 0°C is proportional to the amount of solute. Cf. *Raoult's law.*

copra. Dried coconut kernels from which oil is expressed.

copraol. A fat from coconut oil.

coprecipitation. See *precipitation.*

coprolite. The fossil dung of prehistoric animals; a fertilizer (25–30% phosphorus pentoxide).

coprophilia. Bacteria in dung.

coproporphyrin. The coloring matter of bottom-fermentation yeasts.

coprostanol. Coprosterol.

coprosterol. $C_{27}H_{48}O = 388.37$. Dihydrocholesterol, stercorol, coprostanol. Colorless crystals, m.98, from feces. Cf. *cholane ring*.

copro-yeast. See *yeast*.

coptine. A colorless, crystalline alkaloid from *Captis trifolia*, golden thread (Ranunculaceae).

copyrine. $C_8H_6N_2 = 130.06$.   2,7-Pyridopyridine, 2,7-benzodiazine, q.v.; an isomer of quinoxaline. **dibenzo-** See *dibenzocopyrine*.

corajo. Vegetable ivory, tagna. A hard, white substance from the tagud nut. Cf. *phytelephas*.

coral. The solid calcareous skeletons of the coral animal, *Polyps anthozoa;* chiefly calcium carbonate colored by ferric oxide. **c. bean.** Sophora. **c. root.** Crawley. The root of *Corallorhiza odontorhiza* (Orchidaceae); a powerful diaphoretic.

corallin. (1) Peonin, aurine R. A reagent and dye from resolic acid. (2) A pigment in *Streptothrix* species. **c. solution.** A 1% solution of c. in 10% alcohol; an indicator for ammonia and weak bases (alkalies—red; acids—yellow). **c. yellow.** Sodium rosolate.

corallinate. Rosolate.

coralline. (1) Corallin. (2) Rosolic acid.

corallite. Carrolite.

Coramine. Nikethamide. Trademark for a cardiac stimulant pyridine derivative.

corbefrin. Cobefrin.

corbyn. A glass bottle of 1,200 ml. capacity, shaped like a winchester, q.v.

corchorin. Strophanthidin.

corchularin. $C_{22}H_{36}O_8 = 428.28$. A crystalline bitter principle from the seeds of *Corchorus capsularis*, Linn. (jute), m.174.

cord. The volume occupied by an orderly pile of logs 8 ft long, 4 ft wide, and 4 ft high, the logs being laid as near parallel to the ground and to one another as possible. Maximum value 128 ft³, (3.625 m³), but more usually 90 to 95 ft³ of solid wood because of the spaces between the logs. Cf. *cunit, board foot, fast meter*.

cordein. Methyl *cordol*.

cordial. (1) An elixir. (2) A liqueur.

cordierite. Iolite.

cordite. General name for smokeless powders; in particular, a c. sporting powder: nitroglycerin 30–58, nitrocellulose 65–37, mineral jelly 5–6%.

cordol. $C_6H_4OH \cdot COOC_6H_2Br_3 = 450.82$. Tribromsalol. White powder, insoluble in water; an intestinal antiseptic and hemostatic. **acetyl-** Cordyl, acetyltribromsalol. White needles; an analgesic, hypnotic, intestinal antiseptic, and antispasmodic. **methyl-** Cordein methyltribromsalol. Colorless needles; an antiseptic and analgesic.

Cordura. Trade name for a cellulose acetate synthetic fiber.

cordyl. Acetyl *cordol*.

core. The central part. **c. oil.** A semisolid mixture, usually of a drying oil, a carbohydrate, and sand; used to line iron foundry molds to facilitate removal of the finished casting.

coreductase. The coenzyme of reductase, q.v.

Corfam. Trade name for a polyester fiber with a microporous resinous binder of the methane type.

coriaceous. Describing a tough leathery growth of bacteria.

corialgin. $C_{27}H_{22}O_{18} = 634.18$. 1-Galloyl-3,6-hexahydroxydiphenyl-β-D-glucopyranose. The natural coloring matter of *Caesalpina coriaria*.

coriamin. A 25% aqueous solution of pyridine-β-carbonic acid diethylamide $NC_5H_4 \cdot CON(C_2H_5)_2$.

coriamyrtin. $C_{30}H_{36}O_{10} = 556.3$. A glucoside from the leaves, flowers, and seeds of *Coriaria myrtifolia*, curriers sumach (Coriariaceae). Colorless crystals, m.220, sparingly soluble in water; a tetanic poison. Cf. *picrotoxin*.

coriander. The seeds of *Coriandrum sativum* (Umbelliferae); a carminative. **c. oil.** The essential oil from coriander, d.0.863–0.875, containing linalol and pinene; a flavoring agent.

coriandrol. Linalool.

coriarine. An alkaloid from *Coriaria myrtifolia*. Cf. *coriamyrtin*.

coridine. $C_{10}H_{15}N = 149.1$. A homolog of pyridine obtained by distillation of animal matter. **hydro-** Hydrocoridine.

Coriester. Glucose-1-phosphoric acid. See *sugar phosphates*.

cork. Suber. (1) The exterior layers of the bark of certain oaks; e.g., *Quercus suber* and *Qu. occidentalis*. See *cerin, corticinic acid, phellonic acid, suberic acid*. (2) A stopper made from c. **c. borer.** A set of metallic tubes for boring holes in c. stoppers. **c. press, c. tongs.** Devices for pressing and softening c. stoppers.

corm. A thick underground plant stem that has the character of a tuber and bulb. See *colchicum*.

corn. (1) General term for cereals. (2) Maize. (3) A hard mass of tissue. **Indian-** Maize. **c. oil.** Oil of *maize*. **c. silk.** The stigmas of maize; a diuretic. **c. spar.** Crystalline calcite. **c. starch.** See *starch*. **c. sugar.** *d*-Glucose. **c. syrup.** A mixture of dextrins, dextrose and maltose.

cornelian. A bright red chalcedony.

cornflower. Bluebottle. The blossoms of *Centaurea cyanus* (Compositae), containing cyanidin. Cf. *anthocyanins, flavones*.

cornic acid. Cornin.

cornification. Rendering hard and brittle by drying.

cornin. Cornic acid. A crystalline substance from the bark of *Cornus florida;* dogwood (Cornaceae). Cf. *cornuoid*.

cornine. An alkaloid from *Cornus florida;* an antiperiodic.

Corning filter. A filter made by the Corning Co. for isolating ultraviolet light.

cornstone. Impure clay containing limestone.

cornuoid. The combined principles from the bark of *Cornus florida;* an antimalarial and febrifuge.

Cornu prism. A quartz prism composed of two 30°-angle right and left quartz prisms in optical contact. Cf. *Littrow prism*.

cornutine. An alkaloid of ergot. **c. citrate.** The citrate of cornutine; used to treat spermatorrhea.

cornutol. A liquid extract of ergot containing the water- and alcohol-insoluble constituents.

coromegine. Atropine.

corona. The incandescent gases surrounding the sun seen during total eclipse. Its light is partly polarized and yields unknown bright lines, and continuous (Fraunhofer) spectra. **c. discharge.** The c. produced at electrodes during a high-voltage discharge. See *Cottrell precipitator.* **c. spectrum.** The reversed spectrum of the sun c.

coronillin. $C_7H_{12}O_5 = 176.1.$ A glucoside from the seeds of *Coronilla scorpioides* (Leguminosae). Yellow powder, soluble in water; a cardiac poison, diuretic, and heart stimulant.

coronium. Protofluorine. A hypothetical element from the spectrum of the sun's corona.

corononene. $C_{24}H_{12} = 300.11.$

A dyestuff base, obtained from anthracite.

corporin. Progesterone.

corpse light. The blue flame inside the miners' safety lamp, which indicates the presence of firedamp (methane).

corpus. (1) The body. (2) The main part of an organ. (3) A dried organ, used therapeutically. **c. ciliariae.** An extract of the ciliary or vitreous body; used to treat ophthalmia. **c. luteum.** The dried corpora lutea from the ovaries of cows or hogs. Yellow powder, slightly soluble in water. It contains hormones, e.g., progesterone. Cf. *lutein, ovarian substance.*

corpuscle. (1) A small particle. (2) A free electron. **blood-** See *blood.* **light-** See *photon.* **negative-** See *electron.* **positive-** See *proton.*

corr. Abbreviation for corrected.

correlation. Reciprocal relationship; interdependence. **c. coefficient.** The quantity

$$\sqrt{(1 - p^2)/(n - 1)}$$

where n is the number of values obtained for a given determination, and p is the true value.

correlogram. A graph or diagram correlating 2 or more variables.

correspondence principle. The relation between the orbits of an electron in an atom and the characteristic radiation. Cf. *Bohr's theory, Pauli's principle.*

corresponding state. If the pressure, volume and temperature are expressed for each substance (whether solid liquid, or gaseous) by the critical constants P_c, V_c, and T_c, then the (Van der Waals) equation of state will hold for all substances, in the liquid or gaseous state, for they will then correspond. **c. temperatures.** Those temperatures of 2 or more substances which are equal fractions of the critical temperatures.

corrigent. A drug which favorably influences the action. of another drug.

corrin. $C_{19}H_{22}N_4 = 306.22.$ The tetracyclic ring, system in members of the cobalamin group; see vitamin B_{12}.

corrinoid. Generic name for compounds containing the corrin nucleus.

corroborant. Tonic.

corrode. To disintegrate slowly by chemical action.

corronel. An alloy: Ni 70, Cu 30%.

corrosion. Gradual electrochemical disintegration or decomposition; e.g., of iron by acid rocks in natural water. Cf. *surrosion, erosion.* **fretting-** C. caused by the oscillatory slipping movement of two closely fitting metal surfaces e.g., due to vibration.

corrosive. (1) A drug that destroys organic tissues by chemical means or inflammation. (2) An agent that causes corrosion. **c. poison.** See *poison.* **c. sublimate.** Mercuric chloride.

corrosives. The irritant poisons, which locally destroy organic tissues.

corrugation. Wrinkling.

corsite. Napoleonite. A banded or spotted diorite (Corsica); an ornamental stone.

cortepinitannic acid. $C_{32}H_{34}O_{17} = 690.2.$ Bright red powder from the bark of Scotch fir, *Pinus sylvestris.* Cf. *pinicortannic acid.*

cortex. The bark of a tree, root, or fruit.

cortexin. The sexual-differentiation hormone of the germ cell. It is a secondary sex hormone and induces femaleness. Cf. *medullarin.*

corticalin. The hormone of the cortex of the suprarenal gland. It regulates the recreative phase of carbohydrate metabolism.

corticin. Bark tannin.

corticinic acid. $C_{12}H_{10}O_6 = 250.08.$ A colorless crystalline substance from cork.

corticoles. A group of lichens.

corticosterone. 11,21-Dihydroxyprogesterone, a steroid hormone from adrenal cortex extracts.

corticotrophin. ACTH. The active principle of the anterior lobe of the pituitary gland (B.P.).

corticrocin. $C_{14}H_{14}O_4 = 246.04.$ Tetradecahexa-enedicarboxylic acid. The yellow pigment of the fungus *Corticium croceum*, red needles decomp. 310, soluble in water.

cortin. An extract of adrenal cotex.

cortisone. Kendall's compound E, 17(α)-hydroxy-11-dehydrocorticosterone. A hormone in the adrenal gland, and in the seeds of *Strophanthus sarmentosus*, a W. African tropical vine; used to treat arthritis. It can be synthesized from ergosterol, or from hecongenin obtained from sisal waste and from ox bile. **c. acetate.** $C_{23}H_{30}O_6 = 402.90.$ A white, odorless crystalline powder, m.240 (decomp.), insoluble in water; an adrenocortical hormone (U.S.P., B.P.).

corundum. α-Alumina. Oriental topaz. A hard native or artificial aluminum oxide, used as an abrasive and refractory. *Emery* is impure c. Cf. *adamantine, sapphire, oriental c.*

coruscation. The emission of sparks or flashes.

corybulbine. $C_{21}H_{25}O_4N = 355.20.$ An alkaloid from *Corydalis cava*; colorless crystals, insoluble in water.

corycavine. $C_{23}H_{23}O_6N = 409.20.$ An alkaloid from *Corydalis cava*, m.218.

corydaline. $C_{22}H_{27}O_4N = 369.22.$ An alkaloid from *Corydalis cava* and *C. tuberosa*, holewort (Fumariaceae). Colorless crystals; an alterative, and diuretic.

corydalis. Turkey corn, holewort. The root of *C. cava* (*Bulbocapnus cavus*) (Fumariaceae). Used for menstrual disorders, as a malarial tonic and vermifuge. It contains a number of isoquinoline alkaloids.

corylin. A globulin from hazel nuts.

corynin. $C_{50}H_{100}O_4 = 764.7$. A hydroxy acid, m.70, from the fat of the diphtheria bacillus.

corynine. Yohimbine.

cosanates. A group of salts or esters derived from fatty acids, with 20–29 C atoms; as: eicosanate, $C_{19}H_{39}COO$—; pentacosanate $C_{24}H_{49}COO$—.

cosanic acids. A group of fatty acids with 20–29C atoms; as: eicosanic acid, $C_{20}H_{40}O_2$, m.76; tetraeosanic (cerosic) acid, $C_{24}H_{48}O_2$, m.85; heptacosanic (cerotic) acid, $C_{27}H_{54}O_2$, m.89.

cosanols. A group of aliphatic alcohols of the methane series with 20–29 C atoms; as: eicosanol $C_{20}H_{42}O$, m.65.

cosaprin. Sodium acetsulfanilate.

cosine. The ratio of the base to the hypotenuse of a right-angled triangle is the c. of the angle subtended by these sides.

cosmetic. A pharmaceutical preparation to preserve, restore, or simulate beauty.

cosmic. Pertaining to the universe. **c. rays.** Ultra-γ rays. A radiation of extremely short wavelength (around 0.0005 A), frequency, and penetration, which reaches the surface of the earth from all directions of space (cosmos). First noted by Gockel (1910–11) up to 4,500 m height, and by Kohlhörster (1912–14) up to 9,200 m. They result from violent atomic disintegration and comprise: (1) a soft component (+ or − electrons); (2) a hard component (penetrating mesons); (3) a very penetrating component of low intensity (probably nucleons).

cosmin. Agathin.

cosmotron. A proton synchrotron which produces protons having energy comparable with that of cosmic radiations, i.e., 3 Bev.

costunolide. $C_{15}H_{20}O_2 = 232.18$. A sesquiterpene lactone having a 10-C ring; a primary constituent of costus root oil; m.106.

costus oil. A perfumery oil extracted from the root of the costus, *Aplotaxis saussurea lappa*. It consists mainly of sesquiterpenes with 20% aplotaxene; $n_D 1.5159$.

cosyl. Radicals derived from the methane series of hydrocarbons with 20–29 C atoms; e.g.: eicosyl, $C_{20}H_{41}$—; nonocosyl, $C_{29}H_{57}$—.

cotarnic acid. $C_{11}H_{12}O_5 = 224.09$. A dibasic acid oxidation product of cotarnine.

cotarnine. $C_{12}H_{15}O_4N = 237.13$. An alkaloid oxidation product of narcotine; a sedative and astringent. Cf. *cuprine, cupronine*. **c. hydrochloride.** Stypticine. **c. phthalate.** Styptol.

cotein. $C_{22}H_{18}O_6 = 378.15$. Cotoin. A crystalline principle from coto bark; a skin irritant.

coto. The bark from a Bolivian tree. Two varieties: Coto verum, containing cotein; and para-coto, containing paracotoin, cotoin, and essential oil.

cotoin. $C_{14}H_{12}O_4 = 244.09$. 4-Methoxy-2,6-dihydroxybenzophenone. A constituent of para-coto bark. Yellow crystals, m.129, soluble in water; an irritant. **hydro-** $C_{15}H_{14}O_4 = 258.1$. 2,4-Dimethoxy-6-oxybenzophenone, m.95.5. **para-** $C_{12}H_8O_4 = 216.05$. Dioxymethylene phenyl coumaline. An active principle from para-coto bark. Yellow crystals, m.152 soluble in alcohol. **proto-** $C_{16}H_{14}O_4 = 292.11$.

cotonetin. $C_{20}H_{16}O_5 = 336.1$. Colorless scales, from coto bark.

cotton. (1) The hairs of the seeds of *Gossypium* species (Malvaceae): cellulose 91, moisture 7%. (2) A textile material spun from c. fibers. Cf. *linter*. (3) Pyroxylin or freshly nitrated c. **absorbent-** A purified and fat-free c. **gun-** Pyroxylin. **soluble-** Nitrocellulose. **styptic-** C. impregnated with ferric chloride and dried; used to stop bleeding. **c. gum tree.** See *gum tree*. **c. oil.** C. seed oil; **c. root bark.** The dried root bark of the c. plant. an emmenagogue. Cf. *gossypoid*. **c. seed meal.** The residue after extracting c. oil, finely ground and used as cattle feed and fertilizer; it contains nitrogen 6.7–7.4, potassium 1.5–2, and phosphorus pentoxide 2–3%. **c. seed oil.** Oleum gossypii seminis. The yellow, viscid fixed oil expressed from the seeds of various Gossypium species. The refined oil is colorless and has a nutty odor, $d_{15}°0.9264$. Used extensively in pharmaceutical preparations, and as a substitute for olive oil. See *Halphen's test*.

cottonization. The disintegration of (e.g., bast) fibers, without damage to their structural characteristics. The product is used in conjunction with cotton for spinning fabrics.

Cottrell, Frederick Gardner. 1877–1948. American chemist. **C. precipitator.** A device to deposit the fine particles of a fog or smoke on a series of wires at a different electric potential from their surroundings. Used to recover materials where dust or smoke is a waste product.

cotyledon toxin. An amorphous, colorless substance from *Cotyledon orbiculata*, pig's ear or honde oor (Crassulaceae), S. Africa; used to treat epilepsy.

couepic acid. $Me(CH_2)_3CH:CH(CH_2)_7COOH = 278.21$. ε-Eleostearic acid, from the seed oil of *Couepia grandiflora* (Rosaceae) S. America.

Coulomb, Charles Augustin de. 1736–1806. French physicist. **C. electromagnetic law.** The force between 2 similar magnetic poles varies inversely as the square of the distance between them. **C. electrostatic law.** The force between 2 electric charges varies: (1) inversely as the squares of their distance apart; and (2) directly as the product of their electric charges. **C. unit.** See *coulomb*.

coulomb. Coul. Weber. A unit of electrical quantity. The amount of electricity transferred by a current of 1 amp in 1 sec. $1 \text{ coul} = 10^{-1}$ emu $= 10^9 \times 3$ esu $= 1$ (volt)(sec)/ohm $= 1$ amp/ sec $= 1/96,487$ faraday. **international-** 1 Int. coul $= 0.9999$ abs. coul.

coulometer. Voltameter.

coulometric analysis. A conductometric (q.v.) method, in which the change of intensity of a current passing through an electrolyzed solution is used as an end-point indicator, or to follow a change in composition of the solution.

coumalic acid. $C_6H_4O_4 = 140.03$. 2-Keto-1,2-pyran-5-carboxylic acid, 2-oxo-1,2-pyran-5-carboxylic acid*. Colorless crystals m.206. **dimethyl-** $C_8H_8O_4 = 168.07$. Isodehydracetic acid. Colorless crystals, m.155.

coumalin. $C_5H_4O_2 = 96.03$. α-Pyrone. Colorless liquid or crystals, m.5. **dimethyl-** $C_7H_8O_2 = 124.05$. Mesitene lactone. Colorless crystals, m.51.5. **phenyl-** $C_2H_3PhO_2 = 172.07$. 1-Phenyl-α-pyrone. Colorless crystals, m.68. Cf. para-*cotoin*.

coumaraldehyde. $C_9H_8O_2 = 148.06$. o-Oxycinnamaldehyde. Colorless crystals m.133, sparingly soluble in water.

coumaran. $C_8H_8O_3 = 152.07$. Dihydrocoumarone. Colorless liquid, b.189.

coumaranone. 2(1)-Benzofuranone.

coumaric acid. $C_9H_8O_3 = 164.11$. Coumarinic acid. An acid from the leaves of *Melilotus*. **ortho-** o-Hydroxycinnamic acid. Colorless needles, m.208, slightly soluble in water. **meta-** Colorless prisms, m.191, sparingly soluble in hot water. **para-** White needles, m.206 slightly soluble in water. **acetyl-** Tylmarin. **hydro-** $HO \cdot C_6H_4 \cdot CH_2 \cdot CH_2 \cdot COOH = 166.13$. β-Phenolpropionic acid. White monoclinics, m.128, soluble in water. Cf. *melilotic acid*. **hydroxy-** Umbellic acid.
 c. aldehyde. Coumaraldehyde. **c. lactone.** Coumarin.

coumarilic acid. $C_8H_5O \cdot COOH = 162.1$. 1-Benzofurancarboxylic acid. **alpha-** Colorless crystals, m.190. **beta-** Colorless crystals. **β-methyl-α-** $C_9H_7O \cdot COOH$. Colorless crystals, m.189.

coumarin. $C_9H_6O_2 = 146.05$. 1,2-Benzopyrone. The anhydride of o-coumaric acid in tonka beans, sweet clover, and other plants; also prepared synthetically. Colorless rhombs, m.67, soluble in hot water; a flavoring agent. **bishydroxy-** See *bis-*. **6,7-dihydroxy-** Esculetin. **7,8-dihydroxy-** Daphnetin. **dimethyl-** $C_{11}H_{10}O_2 = 174.1$. 4,7-Dimethyl-1,2-benzopyrone. Colorless crystals, m.148. **ethyl-** $C_{11}H_{10}O_2 = 174.1$. Colorless crystals, m.71. **7-hydroxy-** Umbelliferone. **iso-** 2,1-Benzopyrone. Colorless crystals, m.47. **isopropyl-** $C_{12}H_{12}O_2 = 188.1$. Colorless crystals. m.54. **7-methoxy-** Herniarin. **α-methyl-** $C_{10}H_8O_2 = 160.1$. Colorless crystals, m.90. **β-methyl-** $C_{10}H_8O_2 = 160.1$. Colorless crystals, m.125, **3-oxy-** $C_9H_6O_3 = 162.1$. Colorless crystals, m.282. **4-oxy-** Umbelliferone. **4-oxy-β-methyl-** Resocyanin. **5-oxy-** $C_9H_6O_3 = 162.1$. Colorless crystals, m.249.

coumarinic acid. Coumaric acid.

coumarketone. A compound containing the radical $C_6H_4(OH)CH:CH \cdot CO$—. **methyl-** $C_{10}H_{10}O_2 = 162.1$. o-Oxybenzal ketone. Colorless crystals, m.139.

coumarone. $C_8H_6O = 118.09$. Benzofuran. Colorless liquid, b.169,

$$C_6H_4 \underset{CH}{\overset{O}{\diagdown \diagup}} CH$$

insoluble in water. **dihydro-** Coumaran. **dihydro-keto-** Benzofuranone. **dimethyl-** $C_{10}H_{10}O = 146.15$. 1,2-Dimethylbenzofuran. Colorless liquid, b.210. **hydro-** See *hydrocoumarone*. **ketodihydro-** See ketocoumaran. **methyl-** $C_8H_8O = 133.12$. 2-Methylbenzofuran, β-methylcoumarine. Colorless liquid, b.189.

coumazonic acid. $C_{10}H_{11}ON = 161.09$. **methyl-** $C_{11}H_{13}ON = 175.1$. Benzotrimethylmethoxazine. Colorless crystals, m.218.

coumothiazone. imido- $C_8H_8N_2S = 164.1$. Benzylene-ψ-thiourea. Colorless crystals, m.137.

counterirritant. A superficial irritant, used to make the effects of other irritants or abnormal processess; e.g., cantharides.

counterstain. A microscope stain used to contrast structures already colored by another stain.

counting apparatus. A device for counting bacteria or blood corpuscles. **c. chamber.** A c.a. microscope slide with rectangular rulings. **c. pipet.** A graduated capillary glass tube, to make milk or blood smears for bacteria counts.

coupeic acid. An active principle of oiticica oil.

Coupier's blue. $Ph \cdot C_6H_4N : N \cdot C_6H_4 \cdot Ph = 334.16$. Azodiphenyl, m.250.

couple. (1) A pair of galvanic cells. Cf. *thermocouple*, *zinc-copper c.* (2) To condense or unite 2 molecules.

coupling. Condensation between the N of a diazo group and a C of a ring compound. **oxidative-** Dehydrogenation (usually of a phenol) by electron transfer, to produce a free radical which dimerizes internally, couples, or reacts with another compound. Used in the synthesis of natural products.

courare. Curare.

Courlene. Trade name for a polythene synthetic fiber.

Courlose. Trade name for sodium carboxymethylcellulose.

Courpleta. Trade name for a cellulose acetate synthetic fiber.

Courtaulds. Trade name for a protein synthetic fiber.

Courtelle. Trade name for a polyacrilonitrile synthetic fiber.

Courtois, Bernard. 1777–1838. French chemist; discoverer of iodine.

cousso. See *kousso*.

C.O.V. Concentrated oil of vitriol; 95–96% sulfuric acid by weight.

Covadur. Trade name for a viscose synthetic fiber.

covalence. See *valence*. **dative-.** C. in which one of the two atoms concerned contributes both electrons. Cf. *electrovalence*. **normal-** C. in which each of the atoms concerned contributes one electron.

covelline, covellite. CuS. Native copper sulfide.

covolume. The quantity b in Van der Waals' equation, q.v.

Coward unit. A vitamin unit, q.v.

Cowper stove. Tall iron cylinders lined with firebrick to produce a hot blast for iron smelting.

coxanthin. $C_{40}H_{56}O_6 = 632.4$. A carotenoid pigment of brown algae.

coyol palm. A tropical palm, *Acrocomia*, yielding an oil.

CP. Abbreviation for chemically pure.

Cp. (1) Symbol for cassiopeium. (2) Abbreviation for molecular heat at constant pressure.

Cr. Symbol for chromium.

cracca. Tephrosia.

cracked. Broken, as of a molecule split into component parts. **c. kerosine.** A gasoline substitute obtained by superheating kerosine under pressure, and distilling a volatile fraction at the boiling point of gasoline.

crackene. Proposed name for the hydrocarbon mixture obtained by cracking low-temperature tars.

cracking. A process of making gasoline by superheating hydrocarbons with a catalyst in a gas, e.g.,

hydrogen. Cf. *hydrogenation, Bergius's process*.
c. patterns. The characteristic spectra of hydrocarbons given by the mass spectrometer.

cradin. A peptic ferment from the leaves and twigs of the common fig, resembling papain in its action.

Crafon. Trade name for bundles of fibers, each comprising a core of polymethyl methacrylate with a plastic sheath of lower refractive index. The bundles are jacketed in polyethylene, and transmit light even when flexed or bent.

Crafts, James Mason. 1839–1917. American chemist, noted for organic syntheses. Cf. *Friedel-Crafts reaction*.

cramp bark. High cranberry. The bark of *Viburnum opulus* (Caprifoliaceae); an antispasmodic.

Crane, Evan Jay. b. 1889 American chemist, noted for work on nomenclature and chemical literature.

crateriform. A round depressed cone in a solid culture medium, due to liquefaction by bacteria.

crawley. Coral root.

cream. The thick, yellow fatty layer formed on the surface of milk. **cold-** Cold c. **ice-** A frozen food prepared from milk and flavorings.

creaming. The gradual rise or fall of the disperse phase of an emulsion, according as its specific gravity is less or greater than that of the continuous phase. Cf. *colloids, churner*.

cream of tartar. Potassium bitartrate.

creasote. Creosote.

creatinase. An enzyme which transforms creatine to creatinine.

creatine. $NH_2 \cdot C:NH \cdot NMe \cdot CH_2 \cdot COOH = 131.12$. Methylglycocyamine. An alkaloid or amino acid from the muscular tissue of vertebrates. Colorless monoclinics, decomp. 300, sparingly soluble in water; a tonic. Cf. *alacreatine*.

creatinine. $C_4H_7ON_3 = 113.20$. Methylglycocyamidine,

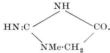

An anhydride of creatine, present in urine. White prisms, decomp. 270, slightly soluble in water. Cf. *phosphagen*. **xantho-** See *xanthocreatinine*.

creatotoxin. A meat poison, or ptomaine.

creep. The 3-phase continuous deformation which occurs when a metal is subjected to a constant load; viz. primary (transient); secondary (steady state or quasi-viscous); tertiary.

creepage. Tracking.

creeping. Describing the behavior of: (1) a precipitate rising on the walls of a wet glass container; (2) a solution which deposits crystals during crystallization on the sides and top of its container; (3) a liquid which passes through the packing of machinery; (4) flow; a nonrecoverable strain; the elongation of a metal under a stress considerably less than that required to break it.

Cremona. Trade name for a polyvinyl alcohol synthetic fiber.

crenic acid. $C_{24}H_{12}O_{16} = 556.1$. Apocrenic acid. An acid produced by molds in the soil.

crenilabrin. A protamine from the sperm of the cunner fish, *Crenilabrus pavo*.

creolin. Analgin. A black, syrupy liquid derived from coal tar, consisting of saponifiable acids and resins; an emulsifier, antiseptic, deodorant, and hemostatic.

creosal. Tannosal.

creosol. $MeO \cdot C_6H_3(OH)Me = 138.12$. 2-Methoxy-1-hydroxy-4-methylbenzene. Colorless oil from beech wood cresols, b.220, slightly soluble in water; an antiseptic.

creosotal. Creosote carbonate.

creosote. An oily distillate from wood tar: chiefly cresol, oxycresol, and methylcresol, b.200, soluble in water; an antiseptic, local anesthetic, and caustic. **heavy-** Green oil. **methylene-** Pneumin. **oleo-** C. oleate
    c. carbonate. Creosotal. An antiseptic, oily derivative of creosote. **c. oleate.** Oleocreosote. A yellow oil, insoluble in water; an antiseptic.

cresalol. $C_6H_4(OH)COOC_6H_4Me = 228.10$. A mixture of the ortho, meta, and para compounds. A white antiseptic dusting powder.

Cresatin. $MeC_6H_4OOCMe = 150.08$. Trademark for *m*-cresyl acetate. Colorless oil, insoluble in water; an antiseptic.

cresegol. See *egol*.

cresidine. $NH_2 \cdot C_6H_3Me \cdot OH = 123.08$. Aminocresol. **5,3-** m.79.

Creslan. Trademark for an acrylic synthetic fiber.

cresol. Cresylic acid. **amino-** Credine-ll. **p-chlor-m-** $C_7H_7OCl = 142.06$. Colorless crystals with a characteristic odor, m.65, slightly soluble in water. **iodo-** Traumatol. **isopropyl-o-** Caryacro. **6-isopropyl-m-** Thymol. **ortho-** Colorless liquid, m.30, sparingly soluble in water. **meta-** Colorless liquid, m.4, slightly soluble in water. **2-methoxy-p-** Creosol. **methyl-** Xylenol. **para-** Colorless prisms, m.36, sparingly soluble in water. Commercial c. is a brown-red syrupy liquid from coal tar, and contains a mixture of the three cresols; a disinfectant. **triiodo-** Losophan. **trinitro-** See *trinitrocresol*.

cresolphthalein. $C_6H_4(CO)_2(C_6H_3OHMe)_2 = 346.14$. Colorless crystals, m.216, slightly soluble in water; an indicator, pH 8.2 (colorless) to 9.2 (red).

cresol purple. $C_{21}H_{18}O_5S = 382.27$. *m*-Cresolsulfonphthalein. Brown powder; an indicator, pH 1.5 (red) to 2.5 (yellow). **brom-** See *bromocresol purple*.

cresol red. $C_{21}H_{18}O_5S = 382.27$. *o*-Cresolsulfonphthalein. Brown powder; an indicator, pH 7.2 (yellow) to 8.8. (red).

cresolsulfonic acids. $C_6H_3Me(OH)(SO_2OH) = 188.13$. Monobasic acids derived from the cresols; used as antiseptics and in organic synthesis. **a-** or **1,2,4-** Colorless crystals, m.188. **v-** or **1,2,3-** Colorless crystals, m.118.

cresorcin. $C_{22}H_{16}O_5 = 360.14$. 2,7-Dimethylfluorescein. A yellow dye indicator.

cresorcinol. 2,4-Dihydroxytoluene.

cresorcyl. The $-C_6H_2(OH)_2Me$ radical.

cresotic acids. $C_6H_3Me(OH)(COOH) = 152.06$. Isomeric acids designated by the positions of the hydroxy group (first numeral) and the methyl group (second numeral), e.g., 2,3- or 2-hydroxy-*m*-toluic acid, m.160.

cresotinic acid. Cresotic acid.

cresoxy. Toloxy.

crestmorite. $2CaO \cdot 2SiO_2 \cdot 3H_2O$. A constituent of boiler scales.

cresyl. (1) The radical $HOC_6H_3(CH_3)$—, from cresol. Ten isomers, derived from o-, m-, and p-cresols. (2) Tolyl, q.v. Cf. *cresotic acid.* **c. acetate.** Kresatin. **c. alcohol.** Cresol. **c. blue.** An oxidation-reduction indicator, q.v. **c. hydrate.** Cresol. **c. hydride.** Toluene. **c. phosphate.** Tricresyl phosphate. **c. violet.** A vital stain for blood.

cresylate. Homologs of the phenates containing the radical $C_6H_4(CH_3)O$—, from cresol.

cresylene. Tolylene.

cresylic acid. Mixed o-, m-, and p-cresols.

cresylite. An explosive: picric acid 60, trinitro-m-cresol 40%.

creta (praeparata). Chalk.

cretaceous. Describing a chalky growth of bacteria.

cretaform. Oxymethylcresol tannin; an internal astringent and antiseptic.

crill. Fine fiber debris in wood pulp.

Crinovyl. Trade name for a polyester synthetic fiber.

criogenine. 1-Phenylsemicarbazide. A reagent for cupric ions (pink color).

cristal. Crystal.

cristallisation. Crystallization.

cristobalite. A crystalline form of silica, formed on heating quartz to 1200. Two forms: α- and β-; transition temperature 200–275°C. Cf. *silica.*

crit. Abbreviation for critical.

crith. Krith.

crithmene. $C_{10}H_{16} = 132.12$. A terpene from samphire, *Crithmum maritimum* (Umbelliferae).

critical. Pertaining to: (1) a turning point or abrupt change; (2) the safe point of nuclear interaction. **c. air-blast test.** A test made under standard conditions for the minimum airflow required to keep a fuel burning after ignition. Values: low-temperature coke (coalite) 0.017, anthracite 0.039, high-temperature coke 0.053. **c. angle.** The angle of incidence i of a ray of light at which it is refracted through a prism so that its angle of emergence is 90°: $\sin i = 1/n$, where n is the refractive index. **c. coefficient.** RTd/p, where R is the gas constant, T the c. absolute temperature, d the c. density, p the c. pressure. **c. conditions.** The c. temperature and c. pressure. **c. constant.** A magnitude relating to the c. state. **c. density.** The density of the liquid and vapor at the c. temperature and c. pressure. **c. hygrometric state.** $100p/P$, where p and P are the vapor pressures of the system and of water, respectively. It determines whether a substance will deliquesce or effloresce. **c. path planning.** A method of scheduling plant construction in which each job is represented by an arrow on a time scale; the planned sequence of the project is denoted by joining appropriate arrows. **c. point.** The conditions at which 2 phases are just about to become 1 phase. **c. pressure.** The pressure necessary to condense a gas at the c. temperature, q.v. See table. **c. solution temperature.** The temperature at which a mixture of 2 liquids, immiscible at ordinary temperatures, just ceases to separate into 2 phases. It is altered considerably by impurities. **c. temperature.** The temperature, T_c, at which a gas can be liquefied by the c. pressure; above this temperature the gas cannot be liquefied at any

pressure. See table. **c. volume.** The volume of 1 gm of substance at the c. temperature and c. pressure.

CRITICAL TEMPERATURES AND
PRESSURES OF SOME COMMON GASES

Substance	Critical temperature, °C	Critical pressure, atm.
Helium............	−267.75	2.26
Hydrogen.........	−234.5	13.4
Oxygen	−118	49.3
Nitrogen	−145	33.65
Chlorine...........	141	79.6
Carbon monoxide....	−113.7	34.6
Carbon dioxide......	31	72.85
Nitrous oxide	36.5	71.65
Ammonia..........	133	112.3
Water.............	374	217.5

croceic acid. 2-Naphthol-8-sulfonic acid.

crocetin. $C_{20}H_{22}O_4 = 328.15$. **alpha-** The aglucone of crocin. Orange crystals, insoluble in water. Cf. *carotenoids, crocin.* **beta-** $C_{21}H_{23}O_4 = 341.15$. The monomethyl ester of α-c. **gamma-** $C_{22}H_{25}O_4 = 354.15$. The dimethyl ester of α-c.

crocic acid. Croconic acid.

crocidolite. $NaFe(SiO_3)_2 \cdot FeSiO_3 \cdot H_2O$. A lavender, acid-resistant asbestos.

crocin. $C_{44}H_{70}O_{28} = 1046.56$. The coloring matter of saffron, *Crocus sativa.* Red powder, soluble in water; a yellow dye. Cf. *carotenoids, crocose.*

crocoisite. $PbCrO_4$. Crocolite, crocoite, Siberian red lead. Red, native lead chromate.

crocoite, crocolite. Crocoisite.

croconic acid. $C_5H_2O_5 = 142.04$. Crocic acid. A dibasic ketonic acid. Yellow crystals, m.180, soluble in water. **c. acid hydride.** $C_5H_5O_5 = 145.03$. A tribasic ketonic acid. Cf. *leuconic acid.*

crocose. $C_6H_{12}O_6 = 180.05$. A sugar and split product of crocin. Colorless crystals, soluble in water. Cf. *gentiobiose.*

crocus. (1) Saffron. (2) Red ferric oxide used for polishing. **antimony-** See *antimony.* **meadow-** Colchicum.

c. martis. Colcothar.

Cronstedt, Axel, Frederik. 1722–1765. Swedish metallurgist, noted for his discovery of nickel and ore classification.

Crookes, Sir William. 1832–1919. English physicist and chemist, founder of *Chemical News.* **C. glass.** An optical glass which eliminates many solar ultraviolet rays. **C. radiometer.** An evacuated glass bulb containing a shaft with 4 vanes; each vane, which revolves, has one side black, the other silvered. **C. space.** A dark space around the cathode of a low-pressure high-voltage X-ray tube. **C. tube.** A highly exhausted vacuum tube.

crookesite. A mineral containing Tl (17%), Se, Cu, and Ag.

crotaconic acid. $C_5H_6O_4 = 130.05$. An isomer of itaconic acid derived from crotonic acid.

crotaline. A protein in rattlesnake venom; used to treat epilepsy.

crotalotoxin. $C_{34}H_{54}O_{21} = 798.42$. A crystalline principle from rattlesnake venom, *Crotalus adamanteus.*

Croton. A genus of euphorbiaceous plants, yielding, e.g.: *C. lacciferus,* lac; *C. cascarilla,* cascarilla bark; *C. tiglium,* croton oil. **c. oil.** A yellow oil from the seeds of *C. tiglium,* d.0.940–0.955, insoluble in water; a drastic purgative and local irritant. Cf. *tiglic acid, tiglium.*

crotonal. The radical $C_4H_6=$, from crotonaldehyde.

crotonaldehyde. $C_3H_5 \cdot CHO = 70.07$. Propylene aldehyde: cis- and trans- forms. Colorless liquid, b.104, soluble in water; a solvent for fats and resins.

crotonallin. A tonic albumin from the seeds of *Croton tiglium.*

crotonarin. The solid part of croton oil.

crotonbetaine. $C_7H_{13}NO_2 = 143.12$. A base from beef-muscle extract. Cf. *carnitine.*

crotonic acid. $C_3H_5 \cdot COOH = 86.046$. α-Butenic acid. Colorless monoclinics, m.72, soluble in water. Cf. *isocrotonic acid.* α-**methyl-** Tiglic acid. β-**methyl-** Senecioic acid. γ-**methyl-** α-Pentenic acid. **c. aldehyde.** Crotonaldehyde. **c. anhydride.** $(MeCH:CH \cdot CO)_2O = 154.08$. 2-Butenoic anhydride*. Colorless liquid, b.247.

crotonoid. An atomic arrangement in which an atom with free electrons (e.g., O or N) is bound by a double bond to carbon adjacent to an ethylene linkage; as $R \cdot CH:CH \cdot HC:O$. It forms coordinate compounds. Cf. *conjugate bond.*

crotonol. Crotonolic acid.

crotonolic acid. $C_9H_{14}O_2 = 154.11$. A purgative monobasic acid from croton oil.

crotonyl. (1) The radical $MeCH:CHCO—$; or (2) the monovalent radical $CH_3 \cdot CH:CH—$, from crotonaldehyde. It is isomeric with propenyl and allyl and occurs in the cis- and trans- forms. **c. alcohol.** $CH_3 \cdot CH:CH \cdot CH_2OH = 72.08$. 3-Buten-1-ol. Colorless liquid, b.117, soluble in water.

crotonylene. $MeC:CMe = 54.05$. Dimethylacetylene. A colorless mass from coal gas, m.27. Isomeric with ethylacetylene.

crotoxin. An active protein, containing sulfur, from snake venom. It contains 18 common amino acids.

crottel. A vegetable dye resembling cudbear, from Scotland.

crotyl alcohol. Butenol*.

crown filler. $CaSO_4 \cdot 2H_2O$. Hydrated calcium sulfate; a paper filler. **c. glass.** Glass. **c. top.** Rose burner.

crucible. (1) A conical vessel with rounded base for fusing or incinerating. (2) The hearth of a blast furnace. **assay-** A small porcelain c. for the combustion of drugs or of precipitates, in quantitative analysis. **Gooch-** A c. with a perforated bottom for filtrations in analysis. **Hessian-** A large clay c. for metallurgical work. **Munroe-** A c. similar to a Gooch c. with spongy platinum deposited on filter paper as filtering medium. **nickel-** A fusion c. **platinum-** A small platinum c. used in chemical analysis. **quartz-** A c. of transparent quartz, used for high-temperature combustion. **Rose-** A c. lid fitted with an inlet tube for burning a substance in a current of coal gas. **sillimanite-** A superior assay c. **sintered glass-** A c. with a base of sintered glass as filtering medium.

c. etching. Diamond *ink.* **c. furnace.** An electrically heated resistance wire embedded in a refractory material, which attains temperatures of 1000°C. in 30 min. **c. holder.** A rubber ring in a glass funnel for holding Gouch crucibles. **c. steel.** Pot steel; made by the c. process. **c. tong.** Scissorlike metal tongs for handling crucibles. **c. triangle.** A wire or pipeclay triangle for supporting a c. over a burner. **c. tubing.** Rubber tubing fitting over a c. to connect it with a flask in vacuum filtration.

Cruciferae. The mustard family; herbs with pungent, watery juice and flowers of 4 petals and sepals, crosswise arranged; e.g.: *Brassica (Sinapis) alba,* white mustard seeds; *B. napus,* rape seed oil; *Cochlearia armoracia,* horseradish; *Isatis tinctoria,* indican, woad.

crude. Unrefined or raw; e.g., drugs (roots, leaves, etc.), c. chemicals (technical and unrefined substances, the hydrocarbons obtained from coal tar). Cf. *intermediates.*

Crum Brown rule. See *Brown.*

cruorine. Early name for hemoglobin; cf. *erythro-c.*

crurin. $(C_9H_7N \cdot HSCN)_3Bi(SCN)_3 = 947.60$. Quinoline bismuth sulfocyanate. Brick-red crystals; an antiseptic and astringent.

crushing. Hammering to pieces; as, opposed to grinding, q.v.

crutcher. A mixing machine used in the soap industry.

Crylor. Trade name for a polyamide synthetic fiber.

cryofine. Kryofine.

cryogenics. Low-temperature operations, generally below −100°C.

cryogenin. (1) A substance producing a low temperature. (2) Cryogenine.

cryogenine. *m-*Benzaminosemicarbazide. White, odorless, bitter crystals, slightly soluble in water; an antiseptic and antipyretic.

cryohydrate. Cryosel. A salt that contains water of crystallization only at a low temperature; e.g., a eutectic mixture of salt and ice.

cryohydric point. The temperature at which a cryohydrate crystallizes from a freezing mixture.

cryolac number. The proportion of the freezing-point depression of milk accounted for by the chloride and lactose present. It indicates addition of water.

cryolite. Na_3AlF_6. A pale-gray mineral, d.3.0; a source of aluminum, alum, and caustic soda. Cf. *Thomsen process.* **c. glass.** Milk *glass.*

cryometer. A thermometer for low temperatures.

cryoscope. A device to determine the freezing point of a liquid. Cf. *Hortvet's c.*

cryoscopic method. The determination of the molecular weight of an organic substance from the depression of the freezing point of a solution containing it. Cf. *Raoult's law.*

cryoscopy. The study of physical and chemical phenomena at low temperatures; especially the depression of freezing point. Cf. *kryoscopy.*

cryosel. Cryohydrate.

cryostat. A low-temperature thermoregulator.

cryothod. Podzol.

cryptal. $C_{10}H_{16}O = 152.12$. 4-Isopropylcyclohexene aldehyde. A constituent of the oil from *Eucalyptus hemiphloia.*

cryptidine. $C_{11}H_{11}N = 157.09$. An alkaloid formed by the dry distillation of quinine. Cf. *kryptidine.*

cryptocarine. An alkaloid from the bark of *Crypto-carya australis* (Lauraceae), Queensland.

cryptocrystalline. Microcrystalline.

cryptocyanine. Kryptocyanine.

cryptogamia. A division of plants characterized by having no true flowers and propagated by spores; e.g.: Thallophyta (algae, lichen, fungi); Bryophyta (mosses, liverworts); Pteridophyta (filices, ferns). Cf. *Phanerogamia.*

cryptohalite. An ammonium fluosilicate; a white efflorescence at the mouth of fumaroles and burning coal mines.

cryptometer. An optical wedge to determine the covering power of paint.

cryptophanic acid. $C_5H_9O_5N = 163.07$. A dibasic acid constituent of urine.

cryptopine. $C_{21}H_{23}O_5N = 369.2$. An alkaloid of opium, m.217; a hypnotic and anodyne.

cryptopyrrole. $C_8H_{13}N = 123.08$. A base derived from hemin and chlorophyllin. Colorless liquid, $b_{13mm}85$.

cryptoscope. Fluoroscope.

cryptovalency. Abnormal valency, e.g., tetravalent oxygen.

cryptoxanthin. $C_{40}H_{55}OH = 552.38$. A carotenoid, m.169, from the berries of the *Physalis* species. It is the precursor of vitamin A and is similar in effect.

cryst. Abbreviation for *crystalline.*

crystal. A homogeneous and angular solid of definite form which is characterized by geometrically arranged plane surfaces (faces) and a symmetrical internal structure. See *c. structure.* General types: homopolar, ionic, and metallic. See figures

A.[3] (5) Measured density D_m, number Z of molecules in unit cell, and calculated density D_c. (6) $F(000)$. (7) Type(s) of X rays used, absorption coefficient μ, and experimental methods. (8) Space group, and molecular symmetry implied. (9) Optical data. **acicular-** A needle-shaped c. **arborescent-** A slender and branching c. resembling a tree. **blood-** Hemin. **complex-** A c. with dissimilar faces. **double-** Twin crystals. **hemihedral-** A c. having half as many faces as the geometrical pattern demands. **holohedral-** A c. having all the faces that the geometrical pattern demands. **homopolar-** Nonpolar. A c. having a space lattice of atoms in which all valencies are satisfied; characteristic of organic compounds. **ionic-** Polar. A c. consisting of a space lattice of ions; as, Na^+ and Cl^-. Hence the entire c. is a giant molecule; characteristic of inorganic compounds. **lead chamber-** Nitrosyl sulfate. **liquid-** A liquid which has the optical properties of a c. **metallic-** Coordinate. A c. consisting of a space lattice of positive ions and electrons in which the electrons conduct an electric current. **micro-** A c. of microscopic size. **mixed-** A c. that contains 2 or more isomorphous substances, as, aluminum chromium sulfate. **nonpolar-** Monopolar. **polar-** Ionic. **racemic-** A c. composed of 2 optically compensating isomers. **seed-** Crystallon. A c. introduced into a saturated solution as a nucleus for crystallization. **simple-** A c. that belongs to a definite c. system. **Teichmann's-** The hemin crystals of blood smears. **twin-** Two crystals grown together along a common face.

c. alcohol. Alcohol molecules in a c. structure. **c. ammonia.** The ammonia of crystallization in the ammonates. Per molecule of substance x, there are: monammonate, $x\cdot NH_3$; hexammonate, $x\cdot 6NH_3$. **c. axis.** An imaginary line through the center of a plane of a c. See *c. system.* **c. carbonate.** $Na_2CO_3\cdot H_2O$. The monohydrate of sodium carbonate. **c. chloroform.** Chloroform or molecules in c. structure. **c. coordinates.** The designation of the axes of a c. as derived from a crystallogram. See figure and *c. system.* **c. detector.** A crystal which transmits electric current in one

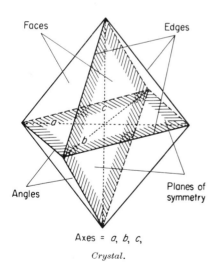

Faces

Edges

Angles

Planes of symmetry

Axes = $a, b, c,$

Crystal.

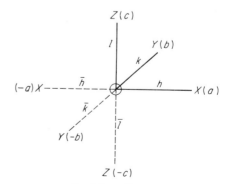

$Z(c)$

$Y(b)$

l

k

$(-a)X$ ----- $\bar{h}$ ----- h ----- $X(a)$

$\bar{k}$

$\bar{l}$

$Y(-b)$

$Z(-c)$

Crystal coordinates.

h, k, l are the integers indicating the number of atomic planes on that axis.

and *c. structure.* The Chemical Society (U.K.) recommends that c. data be presented in the sequence and as set out below: (1) Molecular formula and formula weight M. (2) Melting point, m.p. (3) System and point group. (4) Unit cell parameters (translations in A.) and volume of cells, direction only, used to rectify alternating currents; as galena. **c. ether.** Ether molecules in a c. structure. **c. face.** A plane surface of a c. **c. form.** The external geometrical shape of a c. See *c. system.* **c. overgrowth.** The growth of one c. around another, shown chiefly by isomorphous crystals. **c. pattern.** Space lattice, q.v. **c. structure.** The internal structure of a c. as revealed

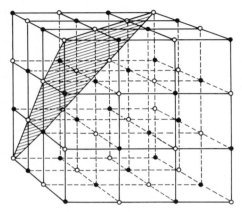

Crystal structure (sodium chloride).

by X-ray diffraction measurements. The individual atoms are arranged in a definite pattern (space lattice), and the rows of atoms act as a diffraction grating for the very short X rays. See figure. Cf. *atomic planes.* **c. system.** The 7 fundamental systems of crystallography. The simplest means of classifying crystals is in terms of their axes. See figure. **c. violet.** $C_{25}H_{30}N_3Cl = 408.00$. Hexane-*p*-rosaniline hydrochloride. Green crystals, slightly soluble in water; an indicator, pH 0 (green) to pH 2.0 (blue); a bacteria stain and antiseptic. Cf. *gentian violet.* **c. water.** Water of crystallization; the water molecules which are part of the crystalline structure of a substance; e.g., monohydrate, $X \cdot H_2O$; octohydrate, $X \cdot 8H_2O$.

crystalbumin. An albuminoid in the crystalline lens of the eye.

crystallin. (1) A solution of pyroxylin 1 pt. in methanol 4 and amyl acetate 15 pts.; used similarly to collodion. (2) A soluble protein from the eye lens. **alpha-** Coagulating at 72. **beta-** Coagulating at 63.

crystalline. Pertaining to crystals. **micro-** Pertaining to crystals of microscopic size.

crystallite. An imperfectly formed crystal.

crystallization. The change from the dissolved, molten, liquid, or gaseous state to a solid state of ordered and characteristic shape. **fractional-** Repeated c. for the purification of a substance. **heat of-** See *heat.* **liquid of-** The molecules of solvent which enter into the space lattice of crystals.

crystallize. (1) To assume crystalline shape. (2) To cause crystallization.

crystallized. Formed into crystals.

crystallogram. The photographic record obtained when X rays are diffracted by a crystal. Cf. *X-ray spectrometer, halo, corona.* **Bragg-.** De-Broglie. Siegbahn. A spectrumlike pattern produced when monochromatic X rays pass through a slit and a rotating crystal. Cf. *Moseley spectrum.* **Clark-.** Duane. A curve obtained by plotting the ionization current at different angles when X rays pass through a stationary crystal. **DeBroglie-** Bragg. **Debye-** Scherer. Hull. A spectrumlike pattern of curved and concentric lines, produced on a film surrounding a crystal, which diffracts a beam of monochromatic X rays. **Duane-** Clark. **Hull-** Debye. **Laue-** The original c., in which polychromatic X rays pass through a pinhole and a single stationary crystal, behind which is a plane photographic plate. **modified Laue-** Monochromatic pinhole. **monochromatic pinhole-** A modified Laue method using monochromatic X rays. **Polyani-** Siegbahn. **Scherer-** Debye. **Schiebold-** Siegbahn. **Siegbahn-** Polyani. Schiebold. A Laue pattern produced by monochromatic X rays and a slowly rotating single crystal.

crystallographic apparatus. A device to measure the angles and optical properties of crystals; e.g., goniometer.

Crystal systems.

System	Interaxial angles	Length of axes		System	Interaxial angles	Length of axes
1. Isometric (cubic)	$\alpha = \beta = \gamma = 90°$	$a = b = c$				
2. Tetragonal	$\alpha = \beta = \gamma = 90°$	$a = b \lessgtr c$	5.	Triclinic	$\alpha \lessgtr \beta \lessgtr \gamma \lessgtr 90°$	$a \lessgtr b \lessgtr c$
3. Orthorhombic (rhombic)	$\alpha = \beta = \gamma = 90°$	$a \lessgtr b \lessgtr c$	6.	Hexagonal	$\alpha = \beta = 90°$ $\gamma = 60°$ and $120°$	$a = b \lessgtr c$
4. Monoclinic	$\alpha = \gamma = 90°$ $\beta \lessgtr 90°$	$a \lessgtr b \lessgtr c$	7.	Trigonal	$\alpha = \beta = \gamma \lessgtr 90°$	$a = b \lessgtr c$

crystallography. The study of crystals.

crystalloids. Noncolloidal substances which pass through a semipermeable membrane (obsolete).

crystalloluminescence. Light emitted during crystallization, e.g., by arsenic oxide.

crystallon. Seed *crystal*.

crystallose. A soluble sodium salt of saccharin; a diabetic sweetening agent.

Crystolon. Trademark for silicon carbide.

crystule. A unit cell of a crystal.

CTAB. Cetavlon, q.v.

CTS. Anhydrous sodium aluminum sulfate, a cream of tartar substitute.

cubanite. $CuFe_2S_4$. A copper ore.

cube. (1) A regular solid bounded by 6 equal square plane faces, the opposite faces being parallel. Cf. *space lattice*. **hydrogen-** A c.-shaped alloy, Na 35, Pb 65%, for the rapid preparation of hydrogen (hydrone). **oxygen-** Cubes of sodium peroxide, with a trace of cupric oxide, for the rapid preparation of oxygen (ozone). (2) Cubé. An extract from c. root, *Lonchocarpus nicou* (Leguminosae), Peru; a fish poison and insecticide. It contains rotenone, toxicarol, and tephrosine. Cf. *derris, deguelin.*

cubeb(s). The dried unripe fruit of *Piper cubeba* (Piperaceae), Java; a stimulant and diuretic. **c. camphor.** $C_{15}H_{20}O = 222.22$. The solid portion of oil of c. **c. oil.** Essential oil of c.; an aromatic, colorless liquid d.0.905–0.925, b.175–180; contains cadinene, cubebene, and c. camphor.

cubebene. $C_{15}H_{26} = 206.22$. A liquid hydrocarbon from cubeb oil.

cubebic acid. $C_{13}H_{14}O_7 = 282.10$. An amorphous resinous acid from cubeb.

cubebin. $C_{20}H_{20}O_6 = 356.15$. 3,4-Dimethylenoxy-*p*-oxystyrone. Colorless needles, m.132.

cubic. Pertaining to a cube. **c. centimeter.** A unit of volume in the metric system: the space occupied by a cube whose side is 1 cm long. 1 cc = 1 cm.^{3} = 0.99996 ml = 0.06102336 cu in. The volume occupied by 1 kg water at 4°C. is the liter = 1,000 ml = 1000.028 cc. **c. decimeter.** 1 cu dm = 1 dm^3 = 1,000 cm^3 = 61.023 in.- **c. foot.** 1 cu ft = 28317.016 cm^3. **c. inch.** 1 cu in. = 1 in.^{3} = 16.387 cm^3. **c. meter.** 1 m^3 = 1,000,000 cm^3 = 1.308 yd^3 = 25.314 cu ft. **c. system.** See *crystal system.* **c. yard.** 1 cu yd = 1 yd^3 = 0.765 m^3.

cubical. Relating to a cube or to three dimensions. **c. atom.** A theory of atomic structure (G. N. Lewis). In a stable atom or compound there are 8 valence electrons situated at the corners of a cube. **c. expansion.** Volume expansion. The enlargement of a solid in 3 planes. **c. system.** The isometric or regular crystal system, q.v.

cubit. An obsolete linear measure; 1 c. = 18 in. **Bible-** 21.8 in.

cucaivite. AgCuSe. Native silver selenide.

cucoline. $C_{19}H_{23}O_4N = 329.2$. An alkaloid from the root of *Cocculus* or *Sinomenium diversifolius* (Menispermaceae). White needles, m.162, insoluble in water. **hydro-** $C_{19}H_{25}O_4N = 331.2$. Colorless crystals, m.198.

cucumber. (1) The vine, *Cucumis sativus* (Cucurbitaceae). (2) C. fruit used as food. **bitter-** Colocynth. **oil of-** Gourd oil.

Cucurbitaceae. The gourd family of succulent herbs, generally creeping and climbing by tendrils. A source of drugs: e.g.: Roots: *Bryonia alba (dioica)*, bryony; fruits: *Citrullus colocynthis*, colocynth; seeds: *Cucurbita pepo*, pumpkin seed, cucurbitine; resin: *Ecballium elaterium*, elaterium.

cucurbitine. An alkaloid from the seeds of *Cucurbita pepo.*

cucurbitol. $C_{24}H_{40}O_4 = 392.32$. An alcohol from the seeds of the watermelon, *Cucumis citrullus* (Cucurbitaceae). Colorless crystals, m.260.

cucus oil. Vetiveria oil

cudbear. Persio, orchil. A purple coloring matter from lichens; or, made by the action of ammoniacal substances (e.g., urine) and air on certain lichens. Known in classical times, but the name is derived from a manufacturer, Cuthbert Gordon (1758). Used as a food color for pharmaceutical preparations.

cuinoline. Cinnoline.

cullet. Crushed or broken glass.

culture. (1) A growth of microorganisms. (2) C. media, q.v. (3) To breed, incubate, or grow microorganisms. **direct-** A growth obtained from a natural source (tissue, sputum, etc.), and directly transferred to a c. medium. **pure-** A growth obtained from a single species.

c. apparatus. A device for growing microorganisms. **c. dish.** A Petri, q.v., or similar dish. **c. flask.** A glass flask for growing microorganisms in liquid c. media. **c. media** (sing. **c. medium**). The substances on which bacteria are grown; e.g.: agar glucose, bouillon, gelatin glucose, blood serum. **c. slide.** A microscope slide with cavities to hold a small quantity of liquid. **c. tube.** A plain-rim test tube for c. media.

cumal. Cumylene. The radical $C_3H_7 \cdot C_6H_4 \cdot CH=$, from cumic aldehyde.

cumaldehyde. Cumic aldehyde.

cumalin. Coumalin.

cumanilide. Cumophenamide.

cumaric acid. Coumaric acid.

cumarin. Coumarin.

cumenamic acid. Cuminamic acid.

cumene. $PhCHMe_2 = 120.15$. Isopropylbenzene. Colorless liquid, b.153, insoluble in water; a constituent of cumin oil. **methyl-** Cymene. **pseudo-** See *pseudocumene.*

cumenol. Cuminol.

cumenuric acid. Cuminuric acid.

cumenyl. Cumyl. The radical $C_3H_7 \cdot C_6H_4—$, from cumene; several isomers. **c. acrylic acid.** $C_{12}H_{14}O_2 = 190.1$. A monobasic homolog of cinnamic acid. **c. amine.** Cumidine. **c. angelic acid.** $C_{14}H_{18}O_2 = 218.15$. A monobasic acid. **c. crotonic acid.** $C_{13}H_{16}O_2 = 204.12$. A monobasic acid. **c. cyanide.** Cumonitrile. **c. sulfurous acid.** $C_9H_{11} \cdot HSO_3 = 200.20$. A monobasic acid, derived from cumene by the action of sulfuric acid.

cumic. Pertaining to the acid derived by oxidation from oil of cumin, q.v. **c. acid.** $C_{10}H_{12}O_2 = 164.15$. *p*-Isopropylbenzoic acid. Colorless triclinics, m.116.5, sparingly soluble in water. **c. alcohol.** Cuminol. **c. aldehyde.** $Me_2CH \cdot C_6H_4 \cdot CHO = 148.15$. *p*-Isopropylbenzaldehyde. Colorless liquid, b.235, insoluble in water. **c. amide.** Cuminamide.

cumidic acid. $C_{10}H_{10}O_4 = 194.08$. Dimethylphthalic acid. A dibasic acid oxidation product of durene. Colorless crystals, m. exceeds 320.

cumidine. $C_9H_{13}N = 135.16$. *p*-Isopropylaniline. Colorless liquid, b.225, insoluble in water. **pseudo-** See *pseudocumidine.*

cumidino. The radical $Me_2CH \cdot C_6H_4 \cdot NH—$, from cumidine.

cumin. The fruits of *Cuminum cyminum* (Umbelliferae), Europe; a stimulant, aromatic, and sedative. **c. oil.** Roman c. oil. A limpid liquid with a sharp taste, from c. seeds, d.0.900–0.930, containing cymene and cumic aldehyde.

cuminal. (1) Cumal. (2) Cumic aldehyde. **di-** Cuminil.

cuminalcohol. Cuminol.

cuminaldehyde. Cumic aldehyde.

cuminic acid. Cumic acid. **c. alcohol.** Cuminol. **c. aldehyde.** Cumic aldehyde.

cuminil. $C_{20}H_{22}O_2$ or $C_9H_{11}CO \cdot COC_9H_{11} = 294.18$. Dicuminoketone. Colorless crystals, m.84.

cuminol. $C_3H_7 \cdot C_6H_4CH_2OH = 150.11$. Isopropylbenzyl alcohol. Colorless liquid, from cumin seeds.

Cummings apparatus. A glass apparatus for the determination of ammonia in illuminating gas. **c. pump.** A mercury-vapor vacuum pump.

cumobenzyl alcohol. See *phenylparaffin alcohols.*

cumol. (1) Pseudocumene. (2) An oily mixture of trimethyl benzenes from coal tar, b.168–178.

cumulated double bonds. Two double bonds on the same carbon atom: $\geq C = C = C \leq$ Cf. *conjugated.*

cumulative. Storing up; increasing progressively. **c. poison.** See *poison.*

cumyl. Cumenyl.

cumylene. Cumal.

cumylic acid. Durylic acid.

cunene. Cupriethylenediamine solution; a solvent in cellulose viscosity determinations.

cunit. Cubic unit. A measure of volume, especially of wood, equal to 100 cu ft of solid unbarked wood. Cf. *cord, board foot.*

cuorin. $C_{71}H_{125}O_{21}NP_2 = 1389.01$. A phospholipin from the cow's heart.

cupal. Copper-plated aluminum.

cupel. A flat crucible of bone ash, used in cupellation. **c. mold, mould.** A brass cup with pestle for making cupels. **c. rake.** An iron shovel or spatula for handling cupels. **c. tongue.** A steel tong for removing cupels from the oven.

cupellation. The separation of silver or gold. Unrefined metal is mixed with lead and placed in a cupel in the muffle furnace, where the impurities are volatilized or absorbed by the cupel; a button of noble metal is left.

cupferron. $NH_4O \cdot NO \cdot NPh = 155.09$. Nitrosophenylhydroxylamine, copperon. Yellow crystals, m.164. Its acid solution is a quantitative precipitant reagent for aluminum, titanium, zirconium, etc. **styryl-** 4-Stilbenzylnitrosohydroxylamine. Used similarly to c., but gives less soluble metal complexes.

cupola. A dome-shaped furnace for melting pig iron.

cupra. Abbreviation for cuprammonium, e.g., c. rayon.

Cuprador. Trade name for a mixed cuprammonium and polyacrylonitrile synthetic fiber.

Cupralon. Trade name for a mixed cuprammonium and polyurethane synthetic fiber.

cupraloy. The alloy Cu 99.4 and $(Cr + Ag)$ 0.6%, having high strength and electrical conductivity.

cuprammonia. A solution of cupric hydroxide in ammonia water; a solvent for cellulose.

cuprammonium ion. The $Cu(NH_3)_4^{++}$ ion having the characteristic deep blue color obtained by adding excess ammonia to a cupric salt solution. **c. rayon, c. silk.** See *rayon.* **c. sulfate.** The solution $CuSO_4 + 4NH_3 + H_2O$. **c. viscosity.** The viscosity of a solution of cellulose in c. measured under standard conditions; it measures the degree of polymerization of cellulosic materials.

cuprase. A nontoxic colloidal cupric hydroxide, used to treat cancer.

cuprate silk. Cuprammonium rayon, q.v.

cuprea bark. The bark of *Remijia*, tropical America, which yields cinchona alkaloids.

cupreane. Desoxycupreine, cupreidane, desoxycupreidine. Alkaloids from cuprea bark.

cupreidine. $C_{19}H_{22}O_2N_2 = 310.17$. The *d*- isomer of cupreine; a cinchona alkaloid from cuprea bark. **desoxy-** Cupreidane.

cupreine. $C_{19}H_{22}O_2N_2 = 310.17$. *l*-Cupreidine. A cinchona alkaloid from cuprea bark. Colorless crystals, m.198, slightly soluble in water. **desoxy-** Cupreane. **ethylhydro-** Optochine. **methyl-** Quinine.

cuprene. $(C_{11-15}H_{10})_x$. Carbene. A brown, solid polymerization product of heating acetylene in presence of copper.

cupreol. $C_{20}H_{34}O = 290.35$. A cholesterol-like substance from the bark of *Cinchona calisaya* (Rubiaceae).

cupreous. Cuprous.

Cupresa. Trade name for a cuprammonium synthetic fiber.

cupressin. An oil, *Cypress* species, used to treat whooping cough.

cupressus. Cypress.

cupric. Describing compounds of divalent copper, which give the cupric Cu^{++} ion in aqueous solution. **c. abietinate.** $Cu(C_{19}H_{27}O_2)_2 = 638.01$. Green scales, insoluble in water, soluble in oils (greencolored solution); an anthelmintic, vermifuge, and wood preservative. **c. acetate.** $Cu(C_2H_3O_2)_2 \cdot H_2O = 199.6$. Verdigris, cryst. aerugo, crystals of Venus. Bluish green crystals, m.250 decomp., soluble in water; an astringent, mordant, porcelain paint, and enamel. **sub-** C. subacetate. **c. aluminate.** Copper alum, lapis divinus. A compound of c. sulfate, aluminum sulfate, and potassium nitrate. Bluish green sticks, soluble in water, used in ophthalmology and as a mild caustic. **c. ammonium chloride.** $CuCl_2 \cdot 2NH_4Cl \cdot 2H_2O = 277.53$. Ammonio-c. chloride. Blue crystals, soluble in water; a reagent for carbon in steel. **c. ammonium sulfate.** $Cu(NH_3)_4SO_4 \cdot H_2O = 245.8$. Dark blue rhombs, decomp. at 150, soluble in water. **c. arsenate.** $Cu_3(AsO_4)_2 \cdot 4H_2O = 540.7$. Bluish green crystals, insoluble in water; an alterative. **c. arsenite.** $CuHAsO_3 = 187.5$ or $Cu(AsO_3)_2 = 309.5$. A mixture of the neutral and acid salt. Green crystals, insoluble in water; an intestinal antiseptic. **c. benzoate.** $Cu(PhCOO)_2 \cdot 2H_2O = 341.6$. Blue crystals, insoluble in water. **c. borate.** $CuB_4O_7 = 219.6$. Green crystalline powder, insoluble in water; used in ceramics and paints. **c. bromide.** $CuBr_2 = 223.4$. Gray crystals, de-

comp. by heat, soluble in water. **c. butyrate.**
$Cu(C_4H_7O_2)_2 \cdot 2H_2O = 273.6$. Green monoclinics,
slightly soluble in water; a reagent for essential
oils. **c. carbonate.** Only basic carbonates are
known, e.g., $3CuO \cdot 2CO_2 \cdot H_2O$, copper lasur,
mountain blue. Used to control seed wheat,
smut, as a pigment, and in ceramics. **c. cement.**
See *dental cement.* **c. chlorate.** $Cu(ClO_3)_2 \cdot 6H_2O =$
338.0. Blue, hygroscopic crystals, soluble in
water; a mordant. **c. chloride.** $CuCl_2 = 134.5$.
Anhydrous copper chlorde. Brown crystals, m.498
(decomp.), soluble in water; a mordant. *cryst-*
$CuCl_2 \cdot 2H_2O = 170.5$. Blue rhombs, losing 2
moles water at 100°C, and decomp. at red heat;
soluble in water. Used as a reagent, as a mordant,
for manufacturing sympathetic inks, and as a
disinfectant. **c. chromate.** $CuCrO_4 = 179.7$.
Yellow liquid. *basic-* $CuCrO_4 \cdot 2Cu(OH)_2 = 374.9$.
Basic copper chromate. Brown powder, insoluble
in water; a mordant. **c. citrate.** $Cu_2C_6H_4O_7 \cdot$
$2\frac{1}{2}H_4O = 360.2$. Green powder, soluble in water;
a reagent for glucose. **c. cyanide.** $Cu(CN)_2 =$
115.6. Green powder, soluble in water. Cf.
cuprocupric cyanide. **c. dichromate.** $CuCr_2O_7 \cdot$
$2H_2O = 315.8$. Brown crystals, soluble in water.
c. ferrocyanide. $Cu_2Fe(CN)_6 \cdot 7H_2O = 465.2$.
Brown powder, insoluble in water, soluble in
potassium cyanide solution. **c. fluoride.** $CuF_2 \cdot$
$2H_2O = 137.6$. Blue crystals, sparingly soluble
in water. **c. fluosilicate.** C. silicofluoride. (1)
tetrahydrate. $CuSiF_6 \cdot 4H_2O = 277.69$. Blue
prisms, soluble in water. (2) *hexahydrate.* $CuSiF_6 \cdot$
$6H_2O = 313.72$. Blue octahedra, soluble in water.
Used to color and harden marble, as a disinfectant
and plant spray. **c. formate.** $Cu(HCOO)_2 = 153.6$.
Blue monoclinics, soluble in water. **c. hydroxide.**
$Cu(OH)_2 = 97.6$. Blue crystals, decomp. by
heat, insoluble in water. **c. hyposulfite.** C. thiosulfate. **c. iodide.** $CuI_2 = 317.3$. Brown powder,
soluble in water. **c. ion.** The Cu^{2+} ion. **c.
lactate.** $Cu(C_3H_5O_3)_2 \cdot 2H_2O = 277.6$. Green
crystals, slightly soluble in water. **c. nitrate.**
(1) $Cu(NO_3)_2 \cdot 3H_2O = 241.6$. Blue prisms,
m.114.5, decomp. 170, soluble in water; a reagent
for detecting oxygen, an astringent, and used to
prepare photosensitive papers. (2) $Cu(NO_3)_2 \cdot$
$6H_2O = 295.7$. Blue crystals, m.26.4 (decomp.),
very soluble in water. Used as (1). **c. nitrite.**
$Cu(NO_2)_2 = 155.6$. Green unstable powder of
variable composition, soluble in water. **c. nitroprussiate.** $CuFe(CN)_5(NO) = 279.6$. Green,
granular photosensitive powder, insoluble in
water. **c. nucleinate.** Cuprol. Green powder,
soluble in water; an astringent. **c. oleate.** Cu-
$(C_{18}H_{23}O_2)_2 = 626.2$. Green wax, insoluble in
water; an antiseptic. **c. oxalate.** $Cu(OOC)_2 =$
151.6. Green powder, insoluble in water. **c.
oxide.** $CuO = 79.6$. Black crystals, d.6.4, m.1064,
insoluble in water or potassium cyanide solution.
Used as a reagent, a teniafuge, and in ceramics
and glass to produce blue and green colors. **c.
oxychloride.** $CuO \cdot CuCl_2 = 214.1$. Green powder,
soluble in ammonia or acids; a green pigment.
c. palmitate. $Cu(C_{16}H_{31}O_2)_2 = 594.2$. Blue
powder, m.115, insoluble in water. **c. phosphate.**
$Cu_3(PO_4)_2 \cdot 3H_2O = 434.8$. Blue rhombs, slightly
soluble in water. *acid-* $CuHPO_4 = 159.6$. Green
powder, insoluble in water. An antituberculotic,

and a reagent for carbon dioxide in water. **c.
phosphide.** $Cu_3P_2 = 252.8$. Metallic powder,
insoluble in water; used to manufacture phosphorus bronze. **c. potassium chlorate.** $Cu(ClO_3)_2 \cdot$
$2KClO_3 = 475.61$. Green crystals, soluble in
water. **c. potassium chloride.** $CuCl_2 \cdot 2KCl \cdot 2H_2O$
$= 319.910$. Green crystals, soluble in water. **c.
potassium cyanide.** $Cu(CN)_2 \cdot 2KCN \cdot 2H_2O =$
281.74. Green crystals, soluble in water. **c.
potassium ferrocyanide.** $K_2CuFe(CN)_6H_2O =$
371.60. Brown powder, insoluble in water. **c.
potassium tartrate.** $K_2Cu(C_4H_4O_6)_2 = 437.83$.
Blue scales, soluble in water. **c. rhodanide.** C.
thiocyanate. **c. salicylate.** $Cu(C_7H_5O_3)_2 \cdot H_2O =$
409.7. Green needles, soluble in water. **c.
selenate.** $CuSeO_4 \cdot 5H_2O = 296.8$. Blue crystals,
slightly soluble in water. **c. silicate.** $CuSiO_3 =$
139.7. Green crystals, insoluble in water. **c.
silicofluoride.** C. fluosilicate. **c. sodium chloride.**
$CuCl_2 \cdot 2NaCl \cdot 2H_2O = 287.44$. Green crystals,
soluble in water. **c. stearate.** $Cu(C_{18}H_{35}O_2)_2 =$
630.2. Blue, amorphous powder, insoluble in
water; a bronze for plaster. **c. subacetate.** Verdigris, aerugo. Greenish-blue powder, soluble in
water. The blue variety has the average composition $CuO \cdot Cu(C_2H_3O_2)_2$; the green variety
$CuO \cdot 2Cu(C_2H_3O_2)_2$. Used in the manufacture of
pigments (Schweinfurt green), as a mordant, and
in cotton printing. **c. subcarbonate.** $CuCO_3 \cdot$
$Cu(OH)_2 = 221.2$. C. carbonate. Blue monoclinics, decomp. by heat, insoluble in water. A
reagent for glucose, an astringent, antidote, and a
pigment. **c. sulfate.** *anhydrous-* $CuSO_4 = 159.6$.
White, amorphous powder, d.3.516, decomp. 621,
soluble in water. Used to dehydrate liquids, and
to detect traces of water (turns blue). *basic-*
$CuSO_4 \cdot 3Cu(OH)_2 = 452.40$. Blue powder, slightly
soluble in water. *cryst-* $CuSO_4 \cdot 5H_2O = 249.71$.
Copper sulfate, Roman vitriol, blue vitriol, blue-
stone. Blue, triclinic crystals, $d_{16°}2.286$, loses 4
moles water at 100 and 5 moles at 250, soluble in
3.5 pts cold and 1 pt boiling water, insoluble in
alcohol. A reagent for glucose, peptones, and
picric acid; a caustic, styptic, emetic, and alternative. Used in the dye industry, the manufacture of green and blue pigments, electroplating,
manufacturing plant sprays. **c. sulfide.** $CuS =$
95.8. Black powder or hexagons, d.3.98, insoluble
in water; an antiparasitic paint for ships. **c.
sulfite.** $CuSO_3 \cdot H_2O = 161.6$. Blue crystals,
soluble in water. **c. sulfocarbolate.** C. sulfophenate. **c. sulfocyanate.** C. thiocyanate. **c.
sulfophenate.** $Cu(PhSO_4)_2 \cdot 6H_2O = 517.81$. C.
phenylsulfonate. Green crystals, soluble in water;
a bactericide and antiferment. **c. tannate.** Brown
powder of variable composition, made by treating
tannin with cupric salts; insoluble in water. **c.
tartrate.** $CuC_4H_4O_6 \cdot 3H_2O = 265.7$. Blue powder,
soluble in water; a reagent for glucose. **c. thiocyanate.** $Cu(SCN)_2 = 179.6$. Blue powder,
insoluble in water, soluble in ammonia. **c. thiosulfate.** $CuS_2O_3 = 175.6$. Blue crystals, sparingly
soluble in water.

cupricyanide. A compound containing the radical
$Cu(CN)_4 =$.

cupriethylenediamine. $Cu[(CH_2NH_2)_2]_2(OH)_2$. A
solution of ethylenediamine saturated with cupric
hydroxide in which the ratio $Cu:(CH_2NH_2)_2$ is 1:2.

Used as solvent for cellulose, in place of cuprammonium, for viscosity determinations.

cuprine. $C_{11}H_7O_3N = 201.05$. An alkaloid derived from cotarnine.

cupri sulphas. An early name for copper sulfate, used medicinally as an emetic.

cuprite. Cu_2O. Ruberite, ruby copper, tile ore. Native cuprous oxide.

cuprocupric. A complex copper salt: a mixture of cuprous and cupric salts. **c. cyanide.** $Cu_3(CN)_4$·-$5H_2O = 384.83$. Green powder; insoluble in water, soluble in potassium cyanide solution.

cuprocyanide. A compound containing the radical $Cu(CN)_4\equiv$.

cuproine. $C_{18}H_{12}N_2 = 256.32$. 2:2 -Diquinolyl. A reagent for copper (purple complex, soluble in isopentyl alcohol).

cuprol. A copper salt of nucleic acid.

cupron α-Benzoinoxime. A quantitative precipitant for copper.

Cupro Nickel. (1) Brand name for an alloy containing Cu 88.35, Ni 10, Fe 1.25, and Mn 0.40%, used for condenser plates and tubes for evaporators and heat exchangers. (2) (not cap.) An alloy used in British *coinage*, q.v.

cuproxine. $C_{20}H_{18}O_3N_2 = 334.13$. An alkaloid derived from cotarnine.

cuprophane. Transparent film made by the cuprammonium process. Cf. *rayon*.

cuprosulfate. A double salt of copper sulfate and another sulfate.

cuprotungstite. $CuWO_4$. A tungsten ore.

cuprous. Describing a compound of monovalent copper; generally less common, and less stable than the corresponding cupric compounds. **c. acetylide.** $CuC_2H_2O = 169.16$. Amorphous, explosive, red powder; formed from acetylene and a cupric solution. **c. bromide.** $Cu_2Br_2 = 287.0$. Brown powder, m.484, insoluble in water. **c. carbonate.** $Cu_2CO_3 = 123.5$. Yellow powder, decomp. by heat, insoluble in water. **c. chloride.** $Cu_2Cl_2 = 198.2$. Resin of copper. Nantokite. Green tetrahedra, m.422, insoluble in water. A reagent in gas analysis, and for detecting arsine and antimonous hydride. **c. cupric cyanide.** Cuprocupric cyanide. **c. cyanide.** $Cu_2(CN)_2 = 179.4$. Colorless amorphous powder, decomp. red heat, insoluble in water. **c. fluosilicate.** $Cu_2SiF_6 = 269.20$. C. silicofluoride. Red powder. **c. hydroxide.** $Cu_2(OH)_2 = 161.2$. Yellow powder, insoluble in water. **c. iodide.** $Cu_2I_2 = 381.0$. Brown crystals, m.606, insoluble in water, soluble in potassium iodide solution; when mixed with equal parts of mercuric iodide, it indicates temperature of parts of machines in frictional contact. **c. ion.** The monovalent Cu^+ ion. **c. oxide.** $Cu_2O = 143.1$. Brown granular powder, d.5.88, insoluble in water; used in red ceramics and glass. **c. phosphide.** $Cu_3P = 221.71$. Metallic powder insoluble in water; used to manufacture phosphorus bronze. **c. potassium cyanide.** $CuCN·3KCN = 285.1$. White crystals, soluble in water. **c. rhodanide.** C. thiocyanate. **c. sulfate.** $Cu_2SO_4 = 223.20$. White powder, decomp. by water. **c. sulfide.** $Cu_2S = 159.2$. Chalcocite. Black powder, m.1100, insoluble in water. **c. sulfite.** $Cu_2SO_3H_2O = 225.2$. Brown crystals, insoluble in water. **c. thiocyanide.** $Cu_2(CNS)_2 = 243.4$.

C. sulfocyanate. C. sulfocyanide. C. rhodanide, **c. rhodanate.** Gray powder, m.1080, insoluble in water.

cuproxide. CuO. A native copper oxide.

cuprum. Latin for copper. See *cupric*.

Cupuliferae. A family of trees comprising Betulaceae (birches) and Fagaceae (oaks, chestnuts, beeches), that yield woods and drugs; e.g.: *Quercus alba*, white oak; *Q. species*, nutgalls; *Q. suber*, cork; *Betula lenta*, sweet birch oil; *Ostrya virginica*, ironwood. Cf. *quercitron, fagin*.

curangin. $C_{43}H_{77}O_{20} = 973.63$. Glucoside from *Curanga amara* (Scrophulariaceae), S. Asia. Febrifuge and vermifuge.

curare. Woorara, urari, curara, curari, S. American arrow poison. A black, brittle resin of various *Strychnos* species; a motor nerve paralyzant, containing the active principles curarine and curine.

curarine. $C_{19}H_{26}O_2N = 300.15$. A crystalline alkaloid from curare; a paralyzant. **proto-** An alkaloid from curare. **pseudo-** Pseudocurarine. **tubo-** $C_{19}H_{26}ON_2 = 314.21$. An amorphous, brown alkaloid from curare.

curcas oil. An oil from the seeds of *Jatropha curcus*, *Linn.*, physic nut (Siam and E. Indies), d.0.919; a drying oil, emetic, and purgative.

curcin. A toxic albumin of Barbados nuts, the seeds of *Curcas purgans* (Euphorbiaceae), W. Indies; resembles ricin.

curcuma. Turmeric.

curcumene. Terpenes from the volatile oil of the rhizomes of *Curcuma aromatica*.

curcumin. (1) $C_{10}H_{10}O_3 = 178.08$. Coloring matter of tumeric, the rhizome of *Curcuma longa*. Deep yellow, lustrous crystals, sparingly soluble in water, soluble in alcohol; an indicator, pH 7.4 (yellow) to 8.6 (brown); a reagent for beryllium; and a dye. (2) $[MeO(HO)C_6H_3CH{:}CHCO]_2CH_2 = 368.16$. 1,7-Bis-(4-hydroxy-3-methoxyphenyl)-1,6-heptadiene-3,5-dione*. Orange-yellow needles, m.183, insoluble in water.

curdling. Coagulation (of milk).

curds. The precipitate obtained by curdling.

Curie, Irene. See *Joliot*. **C., Marie Sklodowska.** 1867–1934. The French codiscoverer of radium, polonium, and radioactivity. **C., Pierre.** 1859–1906. The French codiscoverer of radium and husband of Madame C. **C. electroscope.** An electroscope to detect minute amounts of radioactive substances. **C. point.** The temperature above which the molecular forces of magnetism of paramagnetic bodies cease to exist. **electrical C.p.** The temperature above which the increase in dielectric constant of certain crystals (e.g., phosphates) ceases. **lower C.p.** The point at which dielectric measurements in an alternating field show a rapid decrease in the magnitude of the reversible polarization with decreasing temperature. **c. therapy.** Radium therapy. **c. unit.** Curie.

curie. (1) A unit of radioactivity; the amount of emanation from, or in equilibrium with $1\text{ Ci} = 3.700 \times 10^{10}$ disintegrations/sec. It equals 0.663 mm^3 or 6.56×10^{-6} gm of emanation (radon) and maintains an air ionization of 2.75×10^4 esu (0.92 ma). (2) It is now more usual, and more convenient and accurate to base the c. on the number of α particles emitted, i.e., by comparing the number emitted by a sample with the emission from 1 gm of radium or the emanation in equilibrium with it, namely 3.6×10^{10} α particles/sec. The c. is now being replaced by the rutherford, q.v. **international c.** The international unit of radioactivity, which is equivalent to 3.7×10^{10} disintegrations/sec. **micro-** The millionth part of a c., 10^{-6} c. **milli-** The one-thousandth part of a c., 10^{-3} c. **millimicro-** 10^{-9} c. Cf. *eman, mache.*

curiegraph. A photograph of a tissue injected with a radium emanation (obsolete).

curiescopy. The visual examination in a dark chamber on a fluorescent screen of the emanations emitted by a radium preparation injected into a tissue.

curine. $C_{18}H_{19}O_3N = 297.2$. A paralyzant alkaloid from curare. Colorless microcrystals, m.161, soluble in water.

curite. $PbO_5 \cdot UO_3 \cdot 4H_2O$. A radioactive mineral (Congo).

curium. Cm. Suggested name for element 96, in the last place in the periodic table.

curled. Describing typical growths of bacteria in parallel chains or weavy strands; as, anthrax colonies.

curling factor. Griseofulvin.

current. (1) A stream or flow. (2) Electric c., which moves along a conductor; its unit is the *ampere*; its quantity the *coulomb*; its potential difference the *volt.* **alternating-** (A.C.) A periodically reversing electric c. **d'Arsonval-** The highvoltage discharge of a capacitor through a wire solenoid, producing high-frequency alternations. **direct-** (D.C.). A c. whose direction is always the same. **eddy-** The c. set up around a conductor. See *eddy.* **Foucault-** Electric c. induced in a mass of metal by a magnetic field of varying intensity. **high-frequency-** An alternating c. changing its direction many times per second. **induced-** The c. produced in an induction apparatus by a primary c. **primary-** The c. that produces an induced c. **secondary-** Induced c.

  c. breaker. A device to interrupt the electric c., e.g., a commutator or switch. **c. capacitor.** A device to store electricity, e.g., accumulator. **c. changer.** A device to reverse an electric c., e.g., a commutator. **c. condenser.** C. capacitor. **c. density.** See *density.* **c. regulator.** A device to regulate electric c., e.g., a rheostat.

curry. The powdered leaves of *Murraya koenigii* (Tutaceae), India, sometimes flavored with other spices; used to season food.

currying. The incorporation of oil and grease into leather.

curtisite. $C_{24}H_{18}(?)$. A native, solid hydrocarbon (California).

Curtius, Theodor. 1857–1928. German organic chemist. **C. reaction.** The preparation of amines and urethanes by the action of water and alcohol on acid azides.

curve. A continuous line, which is not straight. In a graphic diagram (cf. coordinate system) a line connecting points whose positions are defined by their abscissas and ordinates, and therefore expressing a relationship. **c. analyzer.** A table with 2 moveable scales, used to measure curves.

cuscamidine. Amorphous alkaloid from cusco bark.

cuscamine. Crystalline alkaloid, m.218, from cusco bark.

cusco bark. Red bark from *Cinchona succirubra* (Rubiaceae).

cuscohygrine. Hygrine.

cusconidine. Yellow amorphous alkaloid from cusco bark.

cusconine. $C_{23}H_{26}O_4N_2 = 394.3$. An alkaloid, m.110, from cusco bark. Cf. *aricine.*

cuscus oil. Vetiver oil.

cusp. The point formed at the discontinuous join of two curves.

cusparia bark. Angostura bark.

cusparidine. $C_{19}H_{17}O_3N = 307.2$. An alkaloid from angostura bark, *Cusparia officinalis.* White crystals, m.78, sparingly soluble in water.

cusparine. $C_{19}H_{17}O_3N = 307.14$. 2-Homopiperonyl-4-methoxyquinoline. An alkaloid from angostura bark. Colorless crystals, m.90, insoluble in water.

cusso. Kousso.

cut. (1) The weight in pounds of resin added to each gallon of solvent. (2) A fraction of crude petroleum.

cutal. Aluminum borotannate.

cutch. Catechu.

cutin. The waxy protective coating of plants.

cutinite. The petrographic component from leaf cuticle.

cutting. (1) Etching. (2) Lubricating. (3) Mixing. **c. fluid.** A liquid used to keep working parts cool, e.g., in drilling. (4) Dissolving casein, e.g., in ammonia. Cf. *cut.*

cuttlefish. A mollusk, genus *Sepia*, order Cephalopoda; it discharges a pigment from a gland near the liver (painter's sepia).

cwt. Abbreviation for hundredweight.

Cy. Abbreviation for cyanide radical, CN—.

cyamelide. $(HNCO)_3 = 129.05$. *s*-Trioxanetriimine. White amorphous powder, insoluble in water.

cyamethine. Cyanomethine.

Cyan. (1) Prefix indicating the trademark of a group of blue or green phthalocyanine pigments, q.v. (2) (not cap.) Cyano-

Cyana. Trademark for a mixed-polymer synthetic resin.

cyanacetic acid. $CN \cdot CH_2 \cdot COOH = 85.09$. Nitrilmalonic acid. Colorless crystals, m.70, soluble in water.

cyanalcohol. Cyanhydrin.

cyanaldehyde. $CN \cdot CH_2 \cdot CHO = 69.02$. Nitrilmalonaldehyde. Colorless crystals, soluble in water.

Cyanamid. Trade name for a mixture of calcium cyanamide 65–70, calcium hydroxide 15–20%, and free carbon, used as fertilizer.

cyanamide. $NH:C:NH = 42.11$. Urea anhydride. Colorless needles, m.46, soluble in water. **allyl-**Sinamine. **benzyl-** See *benzyl* **calcium-** CaNCN. An intermediate in synthesizing ammonia from air. **diethyl-** See *diethyl.* **dimethyl-** See *dimethyl.* **diphenyl-** Phenylcyananilide. **phenyl-** Cyananilide.

  c. process. A method of nitrogen fixation. Limestone and coke are heated to form calcium carbide over which (at 1000°C) a current of nitrogen passes and produces calcium cyanamide which is treated in autoclaves by high-pressure steam to give ammonia.

cyanamil. Cinnamyl cinnamate.

cyananilide. PhNHCN = 118.05. Phenylcyanamide, carbanilonitrile. Colorless crystals, m.47, soluble in alcohol. **phenyl-** $Ph_2N \cdot CN$ = 194.09. Diphenylcyanamide. Colorless crystals, m.73.

cyanate. A salt of cyanic acid containing the radical —CNO. **iso-** Carbimide. A salt of isocyanic acid containing the radical —N:C:O. **pseudo-** The radical —O·N:C. **sulfo-** Thio-. **tauto-** The radical —O·C:N. **thio-** The radical —CNS.

cyanation. (1) Introduction of the radical —CN into a molecule. (2) Formation of a nitrile.

cyanaurite. $MAu(CN)_2$. A double salt of a metal cyanide and aurous cyanide.

cyanethine. $C_9H_{15}N_3$ = 165.10. 2,6-Diethyl-5-methyl-4-amido-1,3-pyrimidine. Colorless crystals, m.189.

cyanetholin. Ethyl cyanate.

cyanethylamide. Ethyl cyanamide.

cyanic acid. HCNO = 43.06. Cyanohydroxide. Colorless poisonous liquid, d.1.140, which polymerizes to cyamelide and fulminuric acid; its salts are cyanates. **hydro-** HCN = 27.06. Prussic acid. Colorless poisonous liquid, $d_{18}°$ 0.697, m. —11, b.25, miscible with alcohol, water, or ether. Its salts are cyanides. **iso-** HNCO = 43.06. A monobasic acid; its salts are isocyanates. **pseudo-** HONC = 43.06. A monobasic acid; its salts are pseudocyanates. **pseudoiso-** Tauto-. **sulfo-** Thio-. **tauto-** HOCN = 43.06. Pseudoiso-, fulminic acid. A monobasic acid; its salts are fulminates. **thio-** See *thiocyanic acid.* **trihydro-** Cyanidine.

cyanide. A compound containing the radical —CN, from hydrocyanic acid. **azo-** The radical —N:N·CN. **chloro-** q.v. **cupri-** q.v. **ferri-, ferro-** See *ferricyanide, ferrocyanide.* **hydro-** A compound containing a HCN molecule. **iso-** The radical —NC, from isocyanic acid, HNC. **sulfo-, thio-** Thiocyanate.

 c. process. The extraction of gold from ores by leaching with potassium c. solution.

cyanidin. $C_{15}H_{10}O_6 \cdot HCl$ = 322.53. An anthocyanidin, q.v., from the flowers of *Centaurea* species.

cyanidines. (1) A group of compounds derived from the hypothetical trihydrocyanic acid. They contain the ring radical $C_3N_3\equiv$. (2) An anthocyanidin, q.v. (3) *sym-*Triazine, q.v. **di-amido-** Formoguanine. **triphenyl-** Cyanophenine. **trioxy-** Cyanuric acid.

cyanilide. Cyananilide.

cyanin. (1) $C_{27}H_{30}O_{16}$ = 610.23. A glucoside from cornflower and other flowers, which hydrolyzes to cyanidin. (2) Anthocyanin. A group of blue pigments found in certain flowers, as cornflower. **carbo-** Carbocyanin. **di-** See *dicyanine.* **iso-** Isocyanin. **phyco-** See *phycocyanin.* **syn-** See *syncyanin.*

 c. dyes. A group of aniline dyes derived from cyanine; photographic sensitizers; e.g.: kryptocyanin (1,1'-diethyl-4,4'-carbocyanin iodide), cyanin (1,1'-diisoamylcyanin iodide), pinachrome (1,1'-diethyl-6-ethoxy-6'-methoxyisocyanin iodide).

cyanine. (1) $C_{29}H_{35}N_2I$ = 538.1. Quinoline blue, Iodcyanin. Green metallic crystals, soluble in warm water; an indicator and photographic sensitizer. (2) Cyanin.

 c. hydroiodide. $C_{29}H_{35}N_2I \cdot HI$ = 665.9. Yellow needles, soluble in water.

cyanite. $(AlO)_2$, SiO_3. Kyanite, rhoetzite, disthene. A blue or white silicate (India), decomp. above 1100°C to mullite and siliceous glass; a refractory for high-temperature furnace linings. Cf. *sillimanite, andalusite, mullite, fibrolite.*

cyan(o)- Cy. The radical N∶C—. It acts like a halogen (forming cyanides) and like ammonia, forms many complex salts. See *cyanides.* **di-** Cyanogen. **hexa-** A cyclic polymer. **iso-** The radical —N∶C. See *isocyanides.* **thio-** The radical —NCS. *iso-* The radical —CNS.

 c. salts. A group of addition compounds in which the c. radical forms part of the complex ion; as, $ZnCy_3^-$, $CuCy_3^=$, $FeCy_6^{4-}$.

cyanoaniline. Cyananilide.

cyanobenzene. See *benzene.*

cyanobenziline. $C_{24}H_{21}N_3$ = 351.20. Colorless crystals, m.106.

cyanobenzyl. The radical $CN \cdot CH_2 \cdot C_6H_4$—, from α-benzyl cyanide. **c. cyanide.** $CN \cdot CH_2 \cdot C_6H_4 \cdot CN$ = 142.1. **ortho-** *o*-α-Homophthalonitrile. Colorless crystals, m.81. **meta-** Colorless crystals, m.88. **para-** Colorless crystals, m.100.

cyanocarbonic acid. Cyanoformic acid. **c. ester.** $CN \cdot COOC_2H_5$ = 99.07. A liquid, b.115, insoluble in water.

cyanocobalamin. $C_{63}H_{88}O_{14}N_{14}PCo$. APA (antipernicious anemia factor). Vitamin B_{12} (U.S.P., B.P.). Dark red crystals, soluble in water or alcohol. A hematopoietic. Co^{57-}, Co^{54-}, Co^{60-}. Produced by the growth of certain organisms on media containing the respective cobaltous ion isotopes; used to follow c. absorption (Co^{57}, Co^{58}: B.P.; Co^{58}, Co^{60}: U.S.P.).

cyanoconine. $C_9H_{14}N_2$ = 150.10. 2.6-Diethyl-5-methyl-1,3-pyrimidine. Colorless liquid, b.205.

cyanocoumarin. $C_9H_5O_2 \cdot CN$ = 161.05. 3-Cyanocoumarin. Colorless crystals, m.182.

cyanoform. $H \cdot CN:C:(CN)_2$ = 91.03. Tricyanomethane, m.93.

cyanoformate. A salt of cyanoformic acid containing the radical $CN \cdot COO$—.

cyanoformic acid. $CN \cdot COOH$ = 71.03. A monobasic acid known only as its salts, the cyanoformates.

Cyanogas. Trade name for a crude powdered calcium cyanide, used as rodent killer, being sprinkled where the moisture of the earth causes slow evolution of hydrocyanic acid gas.

cyanogen. (1) NC·CN = 52.03. Cyanocyanide ethane dinitrile*, prussite, dicyanogen, oxalonitrile. Colorless poisonous gas with odor of bitter almonds $d_{(air)}1.806$, m.—34, b.—21, soluble in water, alcohol or ether. (2) Originally, the radical —CN. **amido-** Cyanamide. **bromo-** C. bromide. **chloro-** C. chloride. **di-** Cyanogen. **mono-** CN = 26.02. A compound produced by the decomposition of c. at high temperature; believed to be present in stellar bodies. **oxo-** See *oxomonocyanogen.*

 c. bromide. NCBr = 106.01. Bromine cyanide. Colorless needles, m.52, soluble in water. **c. chloride.** (1) NCCl = 61.50. Chlorine cyanide. Colorless poisonous gas or liquid, m.—5, b.15, soluble in water. (2) $C_3N_3Cl_3$ = 184.43. Solid, m.145. **c. disulfhydrate.** $NH_2 \cdot CS \cdot CS \cdot NH_2$ = 120.2. Rubeane. **c. halides.** Compounds having the general formula NCX; X is a halogen. They tend to polymerize to $N_3C_3X_3$. **c. iodide.** $NCI = 152.9$. Iodine cyanide. Colorless needles, soluble in water. **c. monosulfhydrate.** Flavean hydride. **c. sulfide.** $(CN)_2S = 84.1$. Colorless scales, m.60, soluble in water.

cyanogenetic. Yielding cyanogen; as, certain glucosides, amygdalin. Cf. *syncyanin.*

cyanohematin. A compound of hematin and cyanogen.

cyanohydride. Cyanohydrin.

cyanohydrin. Cyanalcohol. A compound containing the radicals —CN and —OH. **c. synthesis.** Addition of a carbon atom by the reaction $R\cdot HC:O + HCN \rightarrow R\cdot CHOH\cdot CN$. Cf. *Wohl's reaction.*

cyanol. Aniline.

cyanomaclurin. (1) $C_{15}H_{12}O_6 = 288.08$. A tannin from the wood of *Arctocarpus integrifolia.* Colorless crystals, m. exceeds 290. (2) A synthetic anthocyanidin.

cyanomethine. $C_6H_9N_3 = 123.07$. Cyamethine. 2,6-Dimethyl-4-amidopyrimidine. Colorless crystals, m.180.

cyanophenyl. Pseudo-*carbostyril.*

Cyanophyceae. A group of blue algae. See *phycocyanin.*

cyanotype. Blueprint.

cyanoximide. A compound containing the radical $NC\cdot C(NOH)—$.

cyanoximidoacetic acid. $NC\cdot C(:NOH)\cdot COOH = 114.03$. Colorless crystals, m.129. **c. acetic ester.** $NC\cdot C(N:OH)COOEt = 142.08$. Colorless crystals, m.127.

cyanur. Indicating the trivalent cyanidine ring:

c. amide. C. tetramide. **c. diamide.** $C_3H_5ON_5 = 127.3$. Ammeline. Colorless crystals, decomp. by heat, insoluble in water. **c. monoamide.** $C_3H_4O_2N_4 = 128.2$. Ammelide. Colorless crystals, insoluble in water. **c. tetramide.** $C_3H_6N_6 = 126.3$. Melamine. Colorless prisms, decomp. by heat, sparingly soluble in water.

cyanuric acid. $HO\cdot C:(N\cdot C\cdot OH)_2:N\cdot 2H_2O = 165.21$. Pyrolithic acid, trioxycyanidine, *s*-triazinetriol, trihydroxycyanidine, pyrouric acid, pyruric acid. Colorless monoclinics, sparingly soluble in water. Cf. *cyanur, melem, melamide.* **iso-** Tricarbimide. The ketone form of cyanuric acid.

```
      NH—CO
     /       \
   OC         NH
     \       /
      NH—CO
```

Cf. *mellimide.* **thio-** q.v. **c. chloride.** Tricyanogen chloride.

cyanuric azide. $C_3N_3(N_3)_3 = 204.12$. Colorless crystals, m.94, insoluble in water; a detonating explosive.

cyanuric chloride. Tricyanogen chloride.

cyanuric ester. A derivative of cyanuric acid containing the cyanur radial $C_3N_3O_3\Equiv$. **ethyl-**

$C_3N_3(OEt)_3 = 213.14$. Colorless crystals, m.29, b.275. **ethyliso-** $C_3O_3N_3Et_3 = 213.14$. Ethyl tricarbimide. Colorless crystals, m.96. **iso-** A derivative of isocyanuric acid, containing the isocyanur radical, $C_3H_3N_3\Equiv$. **methyl-** $C_3N_3(OMe)_3 = 171.10$. Colorless crystals, m.135, soluble in alcohol. **methyliso-** $C_3O_3N_3Me_3 = 171.10$. Methyl tricarbimide. Colorless crystals, m.175.

cyanurin. A blue compound produced in urine containing indican on addition of an acid.

cybernetics. The study of the interrelationships among humans, machines, and social organization. Cf. *biomechanics.*

cybotactates. Aggregates of molecules in liquids, generally oriented. Cf. *zones.*

cybotactic. Pertaining to end-to-end or side-to-side arrangements of molecules. Cf. coordinate *bond, association.*

cybotaxis. The cubic space arrangement of the molecules of noncrystalline substances.

cyclamic acid. $C_6H_{11}\cdot NH\cdot SO_3H = 179.21$. Cyclohexylsulfamic acid. White, sweet crystals, m.179, soluble in water; a sweetening agent (B.P.). Cf. *calcium cyclamate, sweetness.*

cyclamin. Arthranitin.

cyclamiretin. $C_{15}H_{22}O_2 = 234.2$. A decomposition product of cyclamin.

cycle. (1) Varve. Any periodic repetition of a phenomenon; nitrogen cycle. (2) A ring or closed atomic chain; as, homocycle. **mega-c. per sec.** Mc/sec. A unit of wavelength frequency.

cycleine. $C_{27}H_{31}O_4N_2 = 447.4$. An alkaloid from *Cyclea peltata* (Menispermacea), E. India; used to treat diarrhea and hemorrhoids.

cyclic. Arranged in a ring. Cf. *acyclic, aromatic.* **carbo-** Indicating a ring of carbon atoms, e.g., benzene. **di-** An atomic structure containing 2 rings, e.g., naphthalene. **hepta-** (1) An atomic structure containing 7 rings. (2) A ring of 7 atoms. **hetero-** A ring composed of 2 or more different kinds of atoms, e.g., pyridine. **hexa-** (1) An atomic structure containing 6 rings. (2) A ring of 6 atoms, e.g., benzene nucleus. **homo-** A ring composed of one kind of atom. **mono-** An atomic structure containing one ring only. **penta-** (1) An atomic structure containing 5 rings, e.g., morphine. (2) A ring of 5 atoms, e.g., cyclopentane. **poly-** An atomic structure containing 2 or more rings. **tetra-** (1) An atomic structure containing 4 rings. (2) A ring of 4 atoms. **tri-** (1) An atomic structure containing 3 rings. (2) A ring of 3 atoms, e.g., cyclopropane. **c. action.** See *catalysis.* **c. compound.** A compound that contains a ring of atoms, or a closed homocyclic or heterocyclic chain of atoms in its molecule. See *rings.* **c. hydrocarbons.** A compound of hydrogen and carbon, which contains a ring of carbon atoms. Cf. *benzene series, cycloparaffins.*

cyclite. Benzyl bromide.

cyclization. Ring formation.

cyclizine hydrochloride. $C_{18}H_{22}N_2\cdot NCl = 302.91$. Marezine. White, bitter crystals, m.285 (decomp.), soluble in water; an antihistamine and anti-travel-sickness remedy (B.P.).

cyclo- Prefix indicating a ring compound.

cyclobarbital. Phanodorn. 5-Δ^1-Cyclohexenylethylbarbituric acid; a sedative.

cyclobarbitone. $C_{12}H_{16}O_3N_2 = 236.27$. White, odorless, slightly bitter crystals, m.172, slightly soluble in water; a sedative (used as **c. calcium,** B.P.).

cyclobutane. $C_4H_3 = 56.1$. Tetramethylene, q.v.

Cf. *picean nucleus.*

$$CH_2 \diagdown CH_2 \diagup CH_2 \diagdown CH_2$$ Colorless

gas, b.11. **ethyl-** $C_6H_{12} = 84.1$. Colorless liquid b.72. **methyl-** $C_5H_{10} = 70.1$. Colorless liquid, b.39.

c. carboxylic acid. See *alicyclic acids.*

cyclobutanol. $C_4H_8OH = 72.1$. Colorless liquid, b.123.

cyclobutanone. $C_4H_6O = 70.1$. Colorless liquid, b.99.

cyclobutene. $(CH_2 \cdot CH)_2 = 54.1$. Colorless gas, b.3.

cyclobutyl. The radical $CH_2 \cdot CH_2 \cdot CH_2 \cdot CH—$.

cyclobutylene. $C_4H_4 = 52.1$. Tetramethyldiene, $\Delta^{1 \cdot 3}$-tetramethylene, butene.

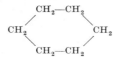

cyclofenchene. $C_{10}H_{16} = 136.12$. A tricyclic terpene. Colorless liquid, b.144.

cyclogallipharic acid. $C_{21}H_{34}OH \cdot COOH = 348.32$. Hydroginkolic acid, m.87; from commercial tannins.

cyclogeranic acid. $C_{10}H_{16}O_2 = 168.2$. Colorless crystals, m.106.

cycloheptadecene. Civetane.

cycloheptadecenone. Civetone.

cycloheptane. Suberane.

cycloheptanol. Suberol.

cycloheptanone. Suberone.

cycloheptene. $C_7H_{12} = 96.09$. Suberene. Colorless oil, b.115, insoluble in water.

cyclohexadiene. $C_6H_8 = 80.06$. Dihydrobenzene. A group of partly saturated benzenes: 1,2-dihydrobenzene, b.78.5; 1,3-dihydrobenzene, b.80.5; 1,4-dihydrobenzene, b.85.5.

cyclohexandiol. Cyclohexanediol.

cyclohexane. $C_6H_{12} = 84.13$. Hexamethylene,

$$CH_2—CH_2 \diagup \diagdown CH_2 \quad CH_2 \diagdown \diagup CH_2—CH_2$$

Colorless hydrocarbon (1–2%) in Austrian and Caucasian petroleum, d.0.780, m.6.4, b.81; insoluble in water, soluble in alcohol or ether. Synthesized by hydrogenation of benzene. A starting point for nylon derivative manufacture. **dimethyl-** $C_8H_{16} = 112.1$. *1,2-* Hexahydro-*o*-xylene. Colorless liquid, b.124. *1,3-* Hexahydro-*m*-xylene. Colorless liquid, b.120. *1,4-* Hexahydro-*p*-xylene. Colorless liquid, b.119. **ethyl-** $C_8H_{16} = 112.1$. Hexahydroethylbenzene. Colorless liquid, b.132. **hexahydroxy-** See *inosite, phenose.* **hydroxy-** Cyclohexanol. **isopropyl-4-methyl-** $Me_2CH \cdot C_6H_{10} \cdot Me =$

140.2. *p-* Methane. Colorless liquid, b.167. **methyl-** Hexahydrotoluene. **pentahydroxy-** See *quercitol, pinite.* **propyl-** $C_9H_{18} = 126.1$. Colorless liquid, b.140. **tetramethyl-** $C_{10}H_{20} = 140.2$. Hexahydrodurene. Colorless liquid, b.161. **trihydroxy-** Phloroglucitol. **trimethyl-** $C_9H_{18} = 126.2$. *1,2,4-* Hexahydro-Ψ-cumene. Colorless liquid, b.142. *1,3,5-* Hexahydromesitylene. Colorless liquid, b.137.

cyclohexanediol. **1,2-** Hexahydrocatechol. **1,3-** See *quinitol.* **1,4-** See *quinitol.*

cyclohexanehexol. Inositol.

cyclohexanepentol. Quercitol.

cyclohexanol. $PhH_6OH = 100.1$. Hexalin. Colorless crystals, m.15; a solvent for gums, waxes, rubber, and nitrocellulose and emulsifier. **trimethyl-** $C_9H_{18}O = 142.1$. A liquid, b_{760mm} 198, soluble in most organic solvents; a mutual solvent for water-immiscible liquids.

cyclohexanone. $C_6H_{10}O = 98.1$. Pimelinketone. Colorless liquid, b.155; a solvent. **2-methyl-** $C_7H_{12}O = 112.1$. Colorless liquid, b.166. **3-methyl-** Colorless liquid, b.164. **4-methyl-** Colorless liquid, b.163. **2,4,5-trimethyl-** $C_9H_{16}O = 140.1$. Colorless liquid, b.191. **3,5,5-trimethyl-** Dihydroacetophenone. Colorless liquid, b.189.

cyclohexatriene. Benzene.

cyclohexene. $C_6H_{10} = 82.1$. Tetrahydrobenzene. Colorless liquid, b.83. Cf. *carveol, dambonite.*

c. trione*. Urinoid.

cyclohexenol. $C_6H_{10}O = 98.1$. Colorless liquid, b.163.

cyclohexenyl. The radical $C_6H_9—$, from cyclohexene; 3 isomers.

cyclohexyl*. The radical $C_6H_{11}—$, from cyclohexane. **bi-** $C_6H_{11}—C_6H_{11} = 166.2$. Dodecahydrodiphenyl. Colorless liquid, b.240.

c. sulfamic acid. Cyclamic acid.

cyclohexylidene. The ring radical $CH_2 \cdot CH_2 \cdot CH_2 \cdot CH_2 \cdot CH_2 \cdot C=$, from cyclohexane.

cyclol. The hypothetical space-enclosing arrangement of diazine and triazine rings in globular proteins.

cyclomethycaine sulfate. $C_{22}H_{33}O_3N \cdot H_2SO_4 = 457.55$. White, bitter crystals, m.164, soluble in water; local anesthetic (B.P.).

cyclone. A static reaction vessel of circular cross-section in which fluids under pressure form a vortex.

cyclonite. Cyclotrimethylenetrinitramine.

cyclonium. Proposed name for illinium, q.v.

cyclononane. $C_9H_{18} = 126.2$. Colorless liquid, b.170.

cycloöctadiene. $C_8H_{12} = 108.1$. A hydrocarbon constituent of rubber.

cycloöctane $(CH_2)_8 = 112.1$. Octomethylene, m.9.5.

cycloöctotetraene. $C_8H_8 = 104.1$. Octabenzene. Yellow liquid, b. about 40.

cycloölefin(e). A ring compound with double bonds and $=CH_2$ groups. General formula, C_nH_{2n-2}.

cycloparaffin. Polymethylene, naphthene. A completely saturated carbocyclic ring compound consisting of $=CH_2$ groups. General formula, C_nH_{2n}.

cyclopentadecanone. $C_{15}H_{28}O = 224.2$. Exaltone. Synthetic musk perfume, m.65.6. **8-methyl-** Muscone.

cyclopentadiene. $C_5H_6 = 66.0$. Cyclopentylene. Colorless liquid, b.41. **methylene-** Fulvene. **pentamino-** Pentaminopentol.

cyclopentadienylide. Metallocene.
cyclopentamethylene. Cyclopentane.
cyclopentane. $C_5H_{10} = 70.1$. Pentene. A ring hydrocarbon in Caucasian petroleum. Colorless liquid, b.51. **diethyl-** $C_9H_{18} = 126.2$. Colorless liquid, b.93. **dimethyl-** $C_7H_{14} = 98.1$. *1,1-* b.83. *1,2-* b.92. *1,3-* b.91. **ethyl-** $C_7H_{14} = 98.1$. Colorless liquid, b.101. **methyl-** $C_6H_{12} = 84.1$. Colorless liquid, m.141, **pentaketo-** Leuconic acid. **trimethyl-** $C_8H_{16} = 112.1$. Colorless liquid, b.114.
  c. acetic acid. $C_5H_{10} \cdot CH_2COOH = 129.1$. Colorless liquid, b.140. **c. carboxylic acid*.** See *alicyclic acids*. **c. formic acid.** $C_5H_{10}COOH = 115.1$. Colorless liquid, b.214.
cyclopentanol*. $C_5H_{10}O = 86.1$. Colorless liquid, b.139.
cyclopentanone*. $C_5H_8O = 84.1$. Adipinketone. Colorless liquid, b.130.
cyclopentene*. $(CH_2)_3 \cdot CH{:}CH = 68.1$. Δ^1-Pentamethylene. Colorless liquid, b.45. Cf. *camphoceenic acid.* **trimethyl-** Laurolene.
  c. tridecoic acid. Chaulmoogric acid. **c. undecylic acid.** Hydnocarpic acid.
cyclopentenyl. The radical C_5H_7— from cyclopentene.
cyclopentyl. The radical C_5H_9—, from cyclopentane.
cyclopentylene. Cyclopentadiene.
cyclophosphamide. $C_7H_{15}O_2N_2Cl_2P \cdot H_2O = 279.10$. White crystals, m.51, soluble in water; a cycotoxic agent (B.P.).
cyclopia. *C. vogelii* (Leguminosae), S. Africa. Source of bush tea, used for lung disorders. **c. fluorescin.** $C_{14}H_{18}O_{12} = 378.4$. A pigment from *C. genistoides.* **c. red.** $C_{25}H_{32}O_{10} = 492.25$. A pigment from *C. genistoides.*
cyclopin. $C_{25}H_{28}O_{13} = 536.3$. A glucoside from *Cyclopia* species.
cyclopropane*. $C_3H_6 = 42.1$. Trimethylene, pro-

CH₂

pene. CH_2——CH_2 Colorless gas, b.—35, insoluble in water; an anesthetic. **benzoyl-** See *benzoyl.* **dimethyl-** $C_5H_{10} = 70.1$. Colorless liquid, b.21. **ethyl-** $C_5H_{10} = 70.1$. A liquid, m.21. **methyl-** $C_4H_8 = 56.1$. Colorless gas, b.4. **trimethyl-** $C_6H_{12} = 84.1$. Colorless liquid, b.57.
  c. carboxylic acid*. See *acyclic acids.*
cyclopropyl. The radical $CH_2 \cdot CH_2 \cdot CH$—, from cyclopropane.
cyclopropylene. Cyclopropene.
cyclopterin. A protein from the sperm of the lumpsucker, *Cyclopterus lumpus.*
cycloserine. $C_3H_6O_2N_2 = 102.08$. 4-Aminoisoxazolid-3-one. Yellow, bitter crystals produced by *Streptomyces orchidaceus*, soluble in water; an antibiotic.
cyclotetraene. An 8-membered ring, the vinyl analog of benzene. An intermediate in the manufacture of hydrogenated products.
cyclotrimethylenetrinitramine. $C_3H_6O_6N_6 = 222.11$. Cyclonite, hexogen. White crystals, insoluble in water, m.204; an explosive.
cyclotron. A device to produce atomic particles and high-speed gas atoms for nuclear bombardments, by accelerating ionized gas particles in a high-frequency field. It comprises a heavy magnet surrounding an expansion chamber, and can weigh over 300 tons and generate 15 million electron volts. Cf. *rhumbatron.*
cyclural. Hexobarbitone, q.v.
cydonin. $C_{18}H_{25}O_{14} = 468.3$. A gum or mucilaginous carbohydrate from quince seeds, *Cydonia vulgaris.*
cylinder. A glass tube, closed at one end, used to hold liquids. **filter-** A c. of porous material used to filter solutions. **graduated-** A c. with a measuring scale. **steel-** A steel c., used to ship compressed gases.
cylindrite. $Pb_3FeSn_4Sb_2O_{14}$. A gray ore.
cymag. A mixture of crude sodium cyanide and magnesium sulfate monohydrate. It evolves hydrogen cyanide on exposure to air; a vermin poison.
cymarigenin. Apocynamarin.
cymarin. $C_{30}H_{48}O_{14} = 568.35$. A glucoside from *Apocynum cannabinum*, which hydrolyzes to cymarigenin and cymarose. Colorless prisms, m.137, slightly soluble in water; therapeutically similar to strophanthin. Cf. *apocynamarin.*
cymarose. $C_7H_{14}O_4 = 162.08$. Digitose methyl ether. A sugar, m.91, from cymarin.
Cymbopogon. A genus of aromatic grasses. Cf. *Andropogon.*
cymene. $C_{10}H_{14} = 134.17$. *p*-Isopropyltoluene. A colorless liquid constituent of the oils of eucalyptus, cumin, and thyme, insoluble in water. **ortho-** b.157. **meta-** m.25, b.175–176. **hexahydro-** Methane. **hydroxy-2-** Carvacrol. **3-** Thymol.
  c. alcohol. 7-Cymol.
cymenol. Carvacrol.
cymenyl. Cymyl. The radical $C_{10}H_{13}$—, from cymene.
cymograph. Kymograph.
cymol. **2-** Carvacrol. **3-** Thymol. **7-** Cymene alcohol.
cymyl. Cymenyl. **2,p-** Carvacryl. **3,p-** Thymyl.
cynapine. An alkaloid from *Aethusa cynapium*, fool's parsley (Umbelliferae). Colorless crystals.
cyneol. Cineol(e); obsolete.
cynoctonine. $C_{36}H_{34}O_{13}N_2 = 702.28$. An amorphous alkaloid, m.137, from *Aconitum septentrionale* (Ranunculaceae).
cynodine. An alkaloid from *Cynodon dactylon* (Gramineae), dog's tooth, Bermuda grass or dooba grass (India).
cynoglossine. An alkaloid from the root of hound's tongue. *Cynoglossum officinale* (Boraginaceae).
cynotoxin. $C_{20}H_{28}O_{16} = 524.3$. Colorless crystalline principle from *Apocynum cannabinum.*
cynurenic acid. $C_{20}H_{14}O_6N_2 \cdot 2H_2O = 395.14$. Oxychinolin carbonic acid. A protein split product in dog's urine.
cyopin. Coloring matter of blue pus. Cf. *pyocyanin.*
cyperone. $C_{15}H_{22}O = 218.18$. A sesquiterpene ketone from the oil of *Cyperus rotundus.*
cypressene. $C_{15}H_{24} = 204.19$. A hydrocarbon from cypress oil, d.0.9647. Cf. *cupressin.*
cypress oil. Oleum cupressi. An essential oil from *Cypressus sempervirens.* Yellow liquid, $d_{15}°0.88$. Cf. *cupressin, cypressene.*
cypripedium. Lady's slipper. The dried rhizome of *C. pubescens* or *C. parvifolium*, American valerian (Orchidaceae); used medicinally.
cypripedoid. The combined principles of the root of

Cypripedium pubescens; a stimulant, antispasmodic, and diaphoretic.

cyprite. Chalcocite.

cyproheptadine hydrochloride. $C_2H_{21}N \cdot HCl \cdot 1.5H_2O$ = 350.90. Yellow crystals, slightly soluble in water; an antihistamine (B.P.).

cysteine. $NH_2 \cdot H \cdot C \cdot COOH \cdot CH_2 \cdot SH$ = 121.13. Amidothiolactic acid, β-mercaptoalanine. A cystine amino acid in proteins and urinary calculi.

cystine. $C_6H_{12}O_4N_2S_2$ = 240.26. *o*-Diamidopropionic acid. An amino acid found in keratin, and as minute hexagons in urine.

cystopurin. $(CH_2)_6N \cdot_4 2NaC_2H_3O_2 \cdot 6H_2O$. A molecular compound of hexamethylenetetramine and sodium acetate.

cytase. (1) Alexin. (2) A cytohydrolytic carbohydrase enzyme.

cytidine. $C_9H_{13}N_3O_5$ = 243.13. Ribosylcystosine. Colorless needles, m.220; hydrolyzed by intestinal juice. **c. phosphoric acid.** $C_9H_{12}N_3O_5 \cdot PO(OH)_2$. A pyrimidine nucleotide from cell nuclei. Cf. *solurol*.

cytidylic acid. $C_9H_{14}N_3O_8P$ = 323.16. A pyrimidine mononucleotide from yeast nucleic acid, composed of cytosine, *d*-ribose, and phosphoric acid; used to control blood pressure and flow.

cytisine. $C_{11}H_{14}ON_2$ = 190.12. Ulexine, baptitoxine, sophorine. Alkaloid from the seeds of *Cytisus*, *Laburnum*, and *Ulex* species (Leguminosae). Colorless crystals, m.152. soluble in water; a local antiseptic and diuretic. Cf. *anagyrine, sparteine*. **c. hydrochloride.** $C_{11}H_{14}ON_2 \cdot HCl$ = 226.59. Colorless crystals, soluble in water; a nerve tonic, **c. nitrate.** $C_{11}H_{14}ON_2 \cdot HNO_3$ = 253.24. Yellow crystals, soluble in water; a nerve tonic.

cytochemistry. The study of the chemical properties of living cells.

cytochrome. (1) The intracellular respiratory pigment. Cf. *chlorophyll, hemoglobin*. See table. (2) A pigment of bacteria, *e.g.*, tuberculosis, related to chlorophyll but containing Fe and Cu. Cf. *porphin ring*. **c.-c.** A red secondary pigment from meat.

Pigment	Color	Metal occurrence
Chlorophyll	Green	Mg plants
Hemoglobin	Red	Fe vertebrata
Hemocyanin	Blue	Cu crustacea
Chlorocruorin	Green	Fe worms
Achroglobin	Colorless	Mn mollusks

cytoclasis. The destruction of living cells.

cytoglobin. A protein from white blood corpuscles.

cytoligneous substances. The cytolytic vegetable (bacteria) or animal (erythrocytes, spermatozoa, tissue) cells.

cytology. The study of living cells.

cytolysis. The destruction or dissolution of living cells.

cytoplasm. The protoplasm of the cell body, excluding the nucleus.

cytosine. $C_4H_5ON_2$ = 111.07. 2-Oxy-6-aminopyrimidine, derived from nucleic acid. Colorless plates, sparingly soluble in water.

cytotoxin. An antibody having a specific action on the cells of certain organs; *e.g.*, nephrotoxin.

cytozyme. Thrombokinase. A substance of the body cells that coagulates blood. See *coagulen*.

D

D. (1) Symbol for deuterium, the hydrogen isotope of mass $2 = H^2$. (2) Abbreviation for density of gases. $D(H_2)$— Density compared with hydrogen gas as unity. $D(O_2)$— Density compared with oxygen gas as 32 (molecular weight). $D_{(air)}$— Density compared with air as unity. (3) The characteristic line of sodium. See *Fraunhofer lines*. (4) Abbreviation for diameter.

d. (1) Abbreviation for specific gravity or density of solids and liquids. d_4° = density at 4°C. d_{50}° = density at 50°C. d_c = critical density. (2) Abbreviation for dextro- or dextrorotary. (3) Differential, as in dy/dx.

d = dextro. $d(l)$ = dextro- or levo-. (dl) = dextro- and levo-, i.e., inactive.

δ. Greek letter delta. (1) Symbol for the fourth C atom in a chain. (2) A *rate* of change, as in $\delta x/\delta y$.

Δ. Greek capital letter D (delta). (1) A double bond, as Δ^1 between the first and second C atoms, $\Delta^{2\cdot4}$- between the second-third and the fourth-fifth C atoms. It is now preferable to denote unsaturation by means of a numeral before the syllable indicating an unsaturated group, e.g., hex-2-ene. (2) Difference between two values, hence a *ratio*; as, $\Delta x/\Delta y$.

2,4-D. $C_8H_6O_3Cl_2 = 221.05$. Common name for 2,4-dichlorophenoxyacetic acid. Yellow crystals having a slight odor, m.142, soluble in water; a herbicide and pesticide.

D.A. Blue cross.

dacite. An igneous rock classed between the monazites and the quartz diorites; it consists chiefly of plagioclase, feldspar, mica, and hornblende (Yellowstone Park and California).

Dacron. Trademark for a polyester synthetic fiber.

dacryagogue. A substance that stimulates tears. Cf. *lacrimatory*.

dacryolin. The albuminous matter of tears.

dactylin. $C_{23}H_{28}O_{15} = 544.2$. A glucoside from the pollen of orchard grass, *Dactylis glomerata*. Yellow needles, m.184, soluble in hot water.

Dag. Trademark for a brand of colloidal dispersions.

Daguerre, Louis Jacques Mandé. 1789–1851. French physicist and painter; inventor of photography. **D. process.** A polished silver plate is made light-sensitive by exposure to iodine vapor. The exposed silver iodide is developed by means of mercury vapor and thiosulfate.

daguerrotype. A photograph made by Daguerre's process (1839).

dahlia. Composite plants whose bulbs yield inulin and a purple color. **d. paper.** A test paper impregnated with the coloring matter of d. (acids— red, alkalies—green). **d. violet.** See *pyoktanin*.

dahlin. (1) A purple aniline dye derived from mauveine. (2) Inulin.

dahllite. $Ca_6(PO_4)_4 \cdot CaCO_3$. A white, fibrous calcium phosphate–carbonate.

Dahl's acid. 2,5-Naphthylaminesulfonic acid. **D.a.II.** 1-Naphthylamine-4,6-disulfonic acid. **D.a.III.** 1-Naphthylamine-4,7-disulfonic acid.

dahmenite. An explosive: ammonium nitrate 91, naphthalene 6.5, potassium dichromate 2.5%.

daidzin. A pigment from soybean meal.

dakeite. Schroeckingerite. A fluorescent uranium mineral (Wyoming).

Dakin, Henry Drysdale. 1880–1952. English-born American biochemist. **D. antiseptic.** Chlorazene. **D. solution.** A solution of 0.5% sodium hypochlorite with sodium bicarbonate; used to treat infected wounds.

Dalen Martens machine. A device to measure the tensile strength and elasticity of rubber.

Dalmatian flowers. Pyrethrum.

Dalton, John. 1766–1844. English chemist, mathematician, and physicist; founder of the atomic theory. **D's law.** (1) The pressure of a gas mixture equals the sum of the partial pressures of the constituent gases. Cf. *Charles's law*. (2) Laws of proportion. See *proportion*. (3) Absorption of gases: The solubility of different gases in a mixture is unaffected by the presence of other gases so long as no chemical reaction occurs.

dalton. A unit of mass; $\frac{1}{16}$ of the mass of an oxygen atom, approximately 1.65×10^{-24} gm.

daltonide. Early name for a chemical compound of constant proportions; as opposed to berthollide.

damar. Dammar.

damascenine. $C_{10}H_{13}O_3N = 195.1$. An alkaloid from the seeds of *Nigella damascena* (Ranunculaceae).

dambonite. $C_6(OH)_4(OMe)_2 = 202.1$. *p*-Dimethoxy-tetrahydroxybenzene. Colorless crystals from Gaboon caoutchouc.

dambose. $C_6H_{12}O_6 \cdot 2H_2O = 216.16$. Isoinositol. A sugar from caoutchouc. Colorless hexagons, m.220, soluble in water.

damiana. The dried leaves of *Turnera diffusa* (Turneraceae), Mexico; an aromatic nervine and tonic.

dammar. Dammara. An oleoresin from Coniferae (Asia, Australia, S. America), resembling copal. Yellow masses, m.115–125, soluble in hot alcohol; used in varnishes and plasters. **true-** The resin from *Dammara orientalis* (E. Indies) or *D. australis* (New Zealand).

damourite. A yellow olivine-type muscovite.

damping. Slowing-down motion, as of the swing of a balance, q.v. Cf. *Pregl*. **d. period.** The time needed for an excited electron to drop to the normal orbit and emit the characteristic radiations of the atom. Cf. *lingering period*.

danain. $C_{14}H_{14}O_5 = 262.24$. A glucoside from the root of *Danais fragrans* (Rubiaceae), Madagascar.

danaite. (Fe·Co)AsS. A native sulfoarsenide.

danalite. $(Zn \cdot Mn \cdot Fe \cdot Be)_7SSi_3O_{12}$. A rare native silicate and sulfide.

danburite. $CaB_2Si_2O_8$. Yellow, orthorhombic calcium borosilicate, d.2.95, hardness 7.

dandelion. Taraxacum.

Daniell, John Frederic. 1790–1845. English chemist and physicist. **D. cell.** A voltaic cell (1.08 volts) consisting of an amalgamated zinc electrode in dilute sulfuric acid (1:12) and a copper electrode in saturated copper sulfate solution.

dannemorite. A rare amphibole.

daphnandrine. $C_{36}H_{38}O_6N_2 = 594.32$. An alkaloid from the bark of *Daphnandra micrantha* (Monimiaceae), Australia; a cardiac and muscular paralyzant.

daphnetin. $C_9H_6O_4 = 178.3$. 7,8-Dihydroxycoumarin. Yellow crystals, m.255, soluble in water.

daphnin. $C_{15}H_{17}O_9 \cdot 2H_2O = 376.2$. A glucoside from the bark of the bay or laurel, *Daphne mezereum* (Thymelaceae). Prisms, m.200.

daphniphylline. An alkaloid from *Daphniphyllum bancanum* (Euphorbiaceae), Dutch E. Indies; a cardiac poison.

daphnite. $H_{56}Fe_{27}Al_{29}Si_{18}O_{121}$. A hydrous iron-aluminum chlorite.

dapsone. $C_{12}H_{12}O_2N_2S = 248.32$. 4,4′-Diaminodiphenylsulfone. White, bitter crystals, m.180, slightly soluble in water; used as a bacteriostatic and to treat leprosy (U.S.P.,B.P.).

darak. Tikitiki. Philippine rice bran.

Daraprim. Pyrimethamine. Trademark for 2,4-diamino-5-*p*-chlorophenyl-6-ethylpyrimidine. A tasteless and nontoxic antimalarial.

darapskite. $NaNO_3 \cdot Na_2SO_4 \cdot H_2O$. A native sodium nitrate and sulfate (Chile, California).

D'Arcet metal. (1) Mellot's metal. An alloy: Bi 8, Pb 5, Sn 3 pts.; m.100; used to fill teeth. (2) An alloy: Bi 50, Pb 25, Sn 25%; m.94; used in fire sprinklers and fusible plugs.

dari. A grain similar to millet; a source of fermentation alcohol.

Darlan. Trademark for a nitrile copolymer of vinyl acetate and vinylidene dinitrate. It is chemically unique in that it has two CN groups directly attached to the same C atom.

dasymeter. An instrument to measure the heat loss of a furnace by analysis of the waste gases.

date palm. Its fruit is used as food, its fiber for ropes, and its sap to make sugar.

datiscin. $C_{21}H_{22}O_{12} = 466.2$. A glucoside from the roots of *Datisca cannabina* (Datiscaceae); used to treat fevers and stomachic troubles.

dative bond. See co-*valence*.

datolite. $2CaO \cdot B_2O_3 \cdot 2SiO_2 \cdot H_2O$. A rare zeolite. Colorless or green, monoclinic masses, d.2.9, hardness 5–5.5.

Datura. Thorn apple, Jamestown weed. A genus of Solanaceae; e.g., *D. stramonium*.

daturic acid. Margaric acid.

daturine. Hyoscyamine. *dl*-Atropine.

daubreeite. BiOCl. Amorphous, white, native bismuth oxychloride.

daubreelite. $FeCr_2S_4$. A black constituent of meteorites.

daucine. An alkaloid from wild carrot, *Daucus carota* (Umbelliferae); a diuretic.

daughter cell. A cell formed by division of a single cell.

daviesite. A colorless, orthorhombic, native lead oxychloride.

Davitamon-K. Trade name for menaphthone.

Davy, Sir Humphry. 1778–1829. English chemist who isolated metals by electrolysis, and devised:

D.'s lamp. See *miner's* lamp.

davyum. A supposed element in platinum ores, and a possible precursor of rhenium, q.v.

Dawbarn. Trade name for a mixed-polymer synthetic fiber.

dawsonite. $NaAlCO_3(OH)_2$. White, monoclinic crystals.

Daxad. Trademark for a group of dispersing agents.

day. A unit of time. **mean solar-** The average period from noon to noon $= 1,440$ min $= 86,400$ sec $= 1.0027379$ sidereal days. **sidereal-** 86,164.10 sec. The interval between successive passages of a star through the meridian.

Dayan. Trademark for a mixed-polymer synthetic fiber.

Db. Symbol for dubhium, q.v.

db. Abbreviation for *decibel*.

D.C. Abbreviation for direct current.

DCP. Chloroxone (U.S. usage).

DCPA. Abbreviation for 2,4-dichlorophenoxyacetic acid, a growth-promoting substance, used for control of weeds in turf.

DD. 1,3-Dichloropropane. An insecticide, resembling DDT, q.v.

DDD. DTE, 2,2-bis-(*p*-chlorphenyl)-1,1-dichloroethane, m.111. An insecticide resembling DDT; a specific inhibitor of the adrenal cortex.

DDM. G-4, dichlorophene, 2,2′-dihydroxy-5,5′-dichlorodiphenylmethane. An insecticide resembling DDT.

DDNP. Abbreviation for diazodinitrophenol.

DDT. Geigy 33. Common name for a mixture of insecticidal isomers with the general formula

$$X\!\!-\!\!\langle\;\rangle\!\!-\!\!\underset{\underset{CCl_3}{|}}{CH}\!\!-\!\!\langle\;\rangle\!\!-\!\!X.$$

The $=CH\!-\!CCl_3$ group is associated with their great contact and stomach insecticidal activity. X is usually Cl. Technical DDT contains not less than 50% *p,p*′-dichloro-2,2-diphenyl-1,1,1-trichloroethane. Yellow crystals, m. exceeds 104. **fluorine-** Gix. **o,p′-** Colorless plates, m.74. **p,p′-** Colorless needles, m.109.

DDX. 2,2′-bis-(*p*-Chlorophenyl)-1,1,1-trichloroethane. An insecticide resembling DDT.

De. Symbol for denedium, q.v.

de- Prefix indicating removal, e.g., of atoms, radicals, or water; as, dehydro-.

Deacon process. A method of making chlorine by passing a hot mixture of hydrochloric acid gas with atmospheric oxygen over a cuprous chloride catalyst.

deactivation. (1) Rendering inactive, e.g., a catalyst. (2) Loss of the radioactivity of a preparation.

dead. A quiet, molten alloy (as steel) which does not evolve gas.

dealcoholizing. Removal of alcohol from liquids.

deamidation. Substitution of the amino group by another radical.

deamidizing. Splitting off the amino group, e.g., adenase.

deamination. Removal of the amino group by hydrolysis:

$$R \cdot NH_2 + H_2O \rightarrow R \cdot OH + NH_3$$

oxidative-:

$$R{\cdot}CHNH_2{\cdot}COOH \to R{\cdot}CO{\cdot}COOH + NH_3$$

reductive-:

$$R{\cdot}CHNH_2COOH \to R{\cdot}CH_2{\cdot}COOH + NH_3$$

deaminizing. Splitting off ammonia from amino acids and proteins with formation of the corresponding fatty acids.

deanol. $OH(CH_2)_2{\cdot}NMe_2$. 2-Methylaminoethanol. An antidepressant.

deaquation. Dehydration.

Debierne, Abdré. 1874–1949. French physicist, noted for work in radioactivity.

de Broglie. See *Broglie.*

Debye, Peter. 1884–1966. Dutch physicist. **D. crystallogram.** A spectrum-like pattern produced by refracting monochromatic X rays by a crystal. **D.-Hückel theory.** The distribution of ions in a small volume at distance r from a chosen ion is $ne(r + e\psi)KT$, where n is the number of molecules of salt in 1 ml, e the elementary electric charge, ψ the potential due to the ion, K the Boltzmann constant, and T the absolute temperature.

deca- Ten (Greek); prefix denoting 10 times. Cf. *deci-.*

decagram. Ten grams.

decahydronaphthalene. Dekalin.

decalcify. To remove lime salts from a tissue or bone.

decalescent. Absorbing heat, at a certain temperature, by a bar of steel during heating, due to allotropic changes. Cf. *recalescent.* **d. outfit.** A device to determine the hardening temperature of high-carbon steel from its decalescence.

Decalin. Trademark for decahydronaphthalene.

decaliter. Ten liters, or 10,000 ml.

decal process. Decalomania. A process for transferring lithographed designs on the surface of a specially coated paper to another surface by moistening the paper.

decameter. Ten meters.

decane*. $C_{10}H_{22} = 142.23$. **normal-** The tenth hydrocarbon of the methane series. Colorless liquid, $d_{20}{}^\circ 0.730$, b.173, insoluble in water. **amino-** $Me(CH_2)_9NH_2$. Decylamine*. White crystals, m.17. **iodo-*** $C_{10}H_{21}I = 268.08$. *n*-Decyliodide. Colorless liquid, $b_{15mm}132$.
   d. carboxylic acid*. Undecylic acid. **d. dioic acid*.** Sebacic acid. **d. diol*.** $CH_2OH(CH_2)_8{\cdot}CH_2OH = 174.17$. Decamethylene glycol. White crystals, m.71.5. **d. nitrile*.** Capronitrile. **d. oic acid*.** Capric acid.

decanoic acid*. Capric acid.

decanol*. Decyl alcohol.

decant, decantation. Separation of a sediment (liquid or solid) by pouring or syphoning off the top liquid layer.

decarbonization. Removing carbon.

decarboxylating. Splitting off carbon dioxide from amino acids and proteins by bacterial action, with formation of amines.

decarboxylizing. Removal of carboxyl group(s) from an organic acid; as, carbon dioxide, e.g. by yeast carboxylase.

decarboxyrissic acid. $C_{10}H_{12}O_5 = 192.08$. 3,4-Methoxyphenoxyacetic acid. Colorless crystals, m.116.

decarburization. Removal of carbon from iron and steel.

decarburize. Decarbonize.

decatizing. A steam or hot-water finishing process for woolen piece goods, designed to reduce and fix the luster produced on pressing, to render the fabric nonshrinking, and to produce a full and firm handle.

decatoic acid. Capric acid.

decatyl. Decyl.

decavitamin capsules (tablets). A U.S.P. formulation containing vitamins A and D, ascorbic acid, calcium pantothenate, cyanocobalamin, folic acid, nicotinamide, pyridoxine hydrochloride, riboflavin, and thiamine hydrochloride.

decay. (1) The progressive decomposition of organic matter, generally due to aerobic bacteria. Cf. *putrefaction.* (2) The progressive disintegration of radioactive substances. Cf. *disintegration, period of decay.*

decene*. $C_{10}H_{20} = 140.21$. Decylene, octylethylene. **normal-** $CH_2{:}CH(CH_2)_7Me$. Diamylene. Colorless liquid, b.172, insoluble in water.

Deceresol OT. Trademark for the dioctyl ester of sodium sulfosuccinic acid; a wetting agent.

dechenite. $PbV_2O_6(?)$. A rare mineral named after von Dechen.

Decholin. Trademark for dehydrocholic acid.

deci- Ten (Latin). Prefix denoting one-tenth. Cf. *deca-.*

decibel. db. One-tenth of a bel, q.v.; a measure of noise. See table. Cf. *barye.*

NOISE VALUES

0 db = 0.0002 barye (threshold of hearing, around 1,500 cps)
40 db = 0.02 barye (quiet flat)
60 db = 0.2 barye (typing office)
80 db = 2 baryes or 2 dynes/cm² (noisy workshop)
120 db = 200 baryes (jet engine)
160 db = 20,000 baryes, or 20.38 gm/cm² (Pimonov siren, the noisiest apparatus so far devised; its sound energy can kill a small animal)

Decicain. Trade name for amethocaine hydrochloride.

decigram. One-tenth of a gram.

deciliter. One-tenth of a liter, or 100 cc, or 3.38 U. S. fluid ounces, or 3.52 English fluid ounces.

decilog. dL. The expression of a ratio on a logarithmic basis.

decimal. A fraction of ten; a tenth part. **d. classification.** A universal system in which the whole of human knowledge, taken as unity, is divided into 10 domains represented by decimal fractions:

0.0 Generalities	0.5 Pure science
0.1 Philosophy	0.6 Applied science
0.2 Religion	0.7 Art
0.3 Social sciences	0.8 Literature
0.4 Philology	0.9 History and geography

The system proceeds from the general to the particular by continued subdivision of the numbers into decimal fractions corresponding with the subdivisions of the subject. Thus, every concept in the domain of pure science is represented by a decimal fraction greater than 0.5 or less than 0.6.

Thus:

0.50 General	0.55 Geophysics
0.51 Mathematics	0.56 Palaeontology
0.52 Astronomy	0.57 Biology
0.53 Physics	0.58 Botany
0.54 Chemistry and	0.59 Geology
crystallography	

For convenience, the first decimal point is omitted. To indicate a work dealing independently with 2 or more subjects, the numbers corresponding with those subjects are connected by a + sign. A functional relationship between 2 or more concepts is expressed by the appropriate numbers linked by a colon. Thus:

537.531	X rays
535.4	Diffraction
548.0	Crystals

Thence: 537.531:535.4:548.0 X-ray diffraction by crystals. Further symbols indicate form, place, language, etc. See British Standard 1,000.

decimeter. One-tenth meter = 10 cm = 3.937 in.

decimolar. One-tenth of the molecular weight, in grams. **d. solution.** A solution containing, in 1 liter, 1/10 gm molecule; e.g., a 0.1 M sodium hydroxide solution contains 4.01 gm NaOH per liter.

decinormal. One-tenth of the normal or equivalent strength. **d. solution.** A solution containing, in 1 liter, 1/10 gm of the equivalent weight of a substance; e.g., a 0.1 N solution of sulfuric acid contains 4.905 gm H_2SO_4 per liter.

declination. Deviation, bending; e.g., magnetic d., the variation of the compass needle from the true north.

decoction. The solution made on boiling a solute with a solvent. Cf. *infusion.*

decoctum. A soluble pharmaceutical made by boiling vegetable drugs with water and straining.

decoic acid. Capric acid.

decolorant. A substance which absorbs or destroys a color.

decoloration. Bleaching by natural means.

decolorization, decolorizing. Bleaching or destroying a color artificially.

decomp. Abbreviation for decomposed, decomposing, or decomposition.

decompose. (1) To break down, split up, or analyze a substance. (2) To rot.

decomposition. The breaking down of a substance into simpler constituents. **double-** Metathesis. A chemical change in which 2 molecules exchange one or more of their constituents. **hydrolytic-** Decomposition, especially of rocks, by water. Cf. *hydrolysis.* **single-** Analysis. A chemical change breaking a molecule into its constituents.

d. apparatus. A device for water electrolysis. **d. of rocks.** The disintegration of rocks in the successive stages: solution, hydration, disintegration, mechanical sorting.

decortication. Stripping the bark, hull or other outer layer from a plant.

decoylamide. Caprylamide.

decrepitate. (1) To crackle. (2) To roast a moist material.

decrepitation. Flying apart with a cracking sound when heated, e.g., crystals.

decyl. Decatyl. The radical $C_{10}H_{21}$—, from decane. **d. alcohol.** $C_{10}H_{22}O = 158.23.$ *normal-* Me(CH$_2$)$_8$-CH$_2$OH. Decatyl alcohol, nonylcarbinol, 1-decanol*. Colorless oil, b.231, soluble in alcohol. **d. aldehyde.** Decanal. **d. amine*.** Amino*decane.* **d. hydride.** Decane.

decylene. Decene*.

decylenic acid. $C_{10}H_{18}O_2 = 170.14.$ An unsaturated acid in butter; m. 0.

decylethylene. Dodecylene.

decylic acid. Capric acid.

decyne*. Decine.

deduction. (1) A conclusion drawn from established facts and data. Cf. *speculation.* (2) An inference from general to particular. Cf. *induction.*

Deenate. Trademark for an insecticide based on DDT, q.v.

defecation. The industrial clarification of sugar solutions.

defervescence. Cessation of boiling.

defibrinated. Rendered free of fibrin. **d. blood.** Blood d. by shaking with lead bullets, beating, or chemical precipitation.

definite proportions law. The proportion of elements by weight is always constant for the same compound.

deflagration. Sudden combustion, usually accompanied by a flame and crackling sound. **d. spoon.** A metal spoon with long handle, used to burn substances in gases.

deflect. To turn from a straight course.

deflocculation. Removal or reversal of flocculation.

deformability. The property of a substance by which its shape, flow, or elasticity may be altered without rupture, as with pitch.

defrother. An agent which destroys or prevents foam.

deg. Abbreviation for degree.

degasification. Elimination of gases from metals previous to coating or plating.

degauss. See *gauss.*

degeneration. (1) The deterioration of cells; the loss of race characteristics by an organism. (2) Degeneracy. A measure of the number of equivalent levels of energy of an atomic or molecular orbital.

Degener's indicator. Phenacetolin.

degradation. Conversion of an organic compound to a compound containing a smaller number of carbon atoms. **energy-** See *thermodynamics.* **mass-** See *mass-energy cycle.*

degras. Wool fat. A dark brown grease from sheep wool, used in the leather industry.

degreaser. A solvent that removes fat or oil; as, dichloroethylene.

degree. A position or a unit: generally a difference in temperature (as, °C), density (as °B), or direction (as ° angle). **d. of freedom.** Variance. Each of the 3 variables: pressure, temperature, and specific volume, one or more of which must be fixed in order to define the state of a system. See *phase rule.* **d. of hardness.** The hardness, q.v., of a mineral is indicated by its position in an arbitrary scale. See *Moh's scale.* **d. of ionization.** The percentage of ionized molecules in a solution.

d. of polymerization. D.P. The number by which the simplest formula expressing the percentage composition of a polymeric substance must be multiplied in order to give the molecular weight. Usually applied to cellulose, $(C_6H_{12}O_5)_n$, which varies considerably in its d.p., according to the state in which it occurs. Cf. *cuprammonium*. **d. of temperature.** A division of the thermometer scale, q.v., usually expressed in degrees centigrade, °C.

deHaën salt. $SbF_3\cdot(NH_4)_2SO_4 = 310.8$. A double salt of antimony trifluoride and ammonium sulfate; a textile mordant.

dehydracetic acid. $C_8H_8O_4 = 168.04$. Methylacetopyronone. Colorless, rhombic scales, m.108, slightly soluble in hot water. **iso-** Dimethylcoumalic acid.

dehydrant. A therapeutic dehydrater, q.v.

dehydrated food. Foodstuffs from which water has been removed to reduce bulk (for convenience of transport) and to ensure their keeping properties. On addition of water the original state is substantially restored.

dehydrater. (1) A device to dry tissues for histological work. (2) Dehydrator. A substance that removes water; as, sulfuric acid. Cf. *desiccant.*

dehydration. (1) Removal of water from compounds and crystals. (2) Removing of hydrogen from organic compounds by reducing agents (dehydrogenation).

Dehydrite. $Mg(ClO_4)_2\cdot 2H_2O$. Trademark for magnesium perchlorate; used as a desiccant. Cf. *Anhydrone.*

dehydro- Prefix for an organic compound indicating the presence of less hydrogen; e.g., dehydrocorydaline.

dehydroangustione. $C_{11}H_{14}O_3 = 194.09$. A bicyclic diketone from the oil of *Backhousia angustifolia*, d.1.103, $b_{11mm}127$.

$$CH_2-CO-\ CMe-C\!:\!CH_2$$
$$CO-CMe_2-CH-O$$

Cf. *angustione.*

dehydrocholesterol-7 (activated). Vitamin D_3 (U.S.P.) $C_{27}H_{44}O = 384.65$. White, odorless crystals, m.86, insoluble in water, soluble in fixed oils; an antirachitic vitamin.

dehydrocholic acid. $C_{24}H_{34}O_5 = 402.54$. A split product of cholic acid, obtained with nitric acid. White fluffy, bitter powder, m.231–242, slightly soluble in water; a choleretic.

dehydrogenase. A dehydrogenating enzyme in the cell walls of *B. coli.*

dehydrogenation. Removal of hydrogen from organic compounds by reducing or oxidizing agents in presence of a catalyst.

dehydroisynolic acid. The synthetic estrogenic hormone

dehydrolysis. Removal of hydrogen and oxygen in the proportions of water from organic substances. Cf. *dehydration.*

dehydrolyzing agent. A chemical which removes water from organic compounds, e.g., phosphorus pentoxide. Cf. *desiccant.*

dehydromucic acid. $C_6H_4O_5 = 156.0$. 2,5-Furandicarboxylic acid. Colorless crystals from the dry distillation of mucic acid.

dehydroperillic acid. Thujic acid.

dehydrothiotoluidine. $C_{14}H_{13}N_3S = 255.1$. Aminobenzenyl-*o*-aminothiocresol. Yellow needles, m.191, insoluble in water. Its solutions have a violet fluorescence; a dye.

dehydrothioxylidene. $C_{16}H_{16}N_2S = 268.2$. Aminotoluenyl-*o*-aminothioxylenol. Yellow prisms, m. 107, insoluble in water; a dye.

deionization. Demineralization.

Dekalin. $(CH_2)_4\cdot CH\cdot CH\cdot(CH_2)_4 = 138.2$. Trade name for decahydronaphthalene, bicyclo[0.4.4]decane. A saturated aromatic hydrocarbon. Colorless liquid, d.0.8747, b.188, insoluble in water, miscible with ether; a cleaning fluid, solvent, and substitute for turpentine and lubricating oil. Cf. *Tetralin.*

de Khotinsky. See *Khotinsky.*

delanium. A strong, compact form of carbon, made from coal by the controlled heating of a gelatinous carbonaceous mass; used to construct chemical plant.

delcosine. $C_{21}H_{33}NO_6 = 395.3$. An alkaloid, m.198, isomeric and occurring with deltaline in *Delphinium consolida.*

delessite. $(Mg,Fe)_4Al_4H_{10}Si_4O_{22}$. A green, hydrous silicate, related to chlorite.

deliquescence. Gradual liquefaction by absorption of atmospheric moisture; as by calcium chloride. Cf. *hygroscopic.*

deliquescent. Having the property of deliquescence.

deliriant. A cerebrospinal nerve drug which produces confusion of will power and delirium; as, belladonna.

delphin blue. $C_{20}H_{17}O_6N_3S$. A blue dye made by heating aniline with gallocyanin and sulfating.

delphine. Delphinine.

delphinic acid. An acid from the oil of *Delphinium* species (Ranunculaceae).

delphinidin. $C_{15}H_{10}O_7\cdot HCl = 338.53$. An anthocyanidin from the flowers of *Delphinium* species.

delphinin. $C_{41}H_{38}O_{21}Cl = 901.8$. A glucoside from larkspur, *Delphinium consolida*; hydrolyzes to delphinidin and *p*-hydroxybenzoic acid.

delphinine. $C_{22}H_{35}O_6N = 409.28$ or $C_{34}H_{47}NO_9 = 577.37$. An alkaloid from the seeds of *Delphinium staphisagria* (Ranunculaceae), Europe and Asia Minor. Colorless crystals, decomp. 120, soluble in alcohol; an antispasmodic, anticonvulsive, and antineuralgic. Cf. *staphisagria alkaloids.*

Delphinium. A genus of Ranunculaceae, larkspurs, which yield staphisagria alkaloids, q.v.

delphinoidine. $C_{22}H_{35}O_6N = 409.3$. An alkaloid from the seeds of larkspur, *Delphinium consolida* (Ranunculaceae), Europe and America.

delphisine. $C_{54}H_{46}O_8N_2 = 850.5$. An alkaloid from the seeds of stavesacre, *Delphinium staphisagria* (Ranunculaceae).

delphocurarine. $C_{23}H_{33}NO_7 = 435.3$. An alkaloid from the seeds of *Delphinium scopulorum*. Amorphous white powder, m.185, resembling curare in effect. Cf. *delcosine.*

Delrin. Trade name for a linear polyoxymethylene-type acetal resin, made by the polymerization of formaldehyde and having a high strength and solvent resistance. It is moldable and is used in aerosol containers; m.180.

delta. Greek letter δ or Δ. δ symbol for (1) difference; (2) the fourth C atom in a chain; Δ for double bond, q.v. **d. acid.** δ-acid. 2,7-Naphthylaminesulfonic acid. **d. metal.** A tough alloy: Cu 60, Zn 38.2, Fe 1.8%. **d. point.** See *helium*.

deltaline. $C_{21}H_{33}NO_6 = 395.3$. An alkaloid, m.180, from *Delphinium occidentale*. Cf. *delcosine*.

Delustra. Trademark for a matt continuous-filament rayon yarn.

delvauxite. A hydrous, ferric vanadium phosphate.

delvinal sodium. Sodium ethyl (1-methyl-1-butenyl) barbiturate. A rapidly acting sedative.

demagnetization. Destruction of magnetic properties.

demal. A solution containing 1 gm equivalent of solute per cubic decimeter (1 dm^3 = 1.000027 liter). Suggested in place of *normal* in electrical conductivity measurements.

demargarinate. To separate solid glycerides from an edible oil by cooling.

dematoid. A green andralite (iron garnet, q.v.).

demecarium bromide. $C_{32}H_{52}O_4N_4Br_2 = 716.61$. White crystals, soluble in water, m.165; a cholinesterase inhibitor (U.S.P.).

Demerol. Trademark for dolantin, dolantol, pethedine hydrochloride. A plant constituent associated with opium alkaloids. The ethyl ester of 1-methyl-4-phenylpiperidine-4-carbonic acid; a powerful analgesic.

demethylation. Removal of the methyl group.

demethylchlortetracycline hydrochloride. $C_{21}H_{21}O_8$-$N_2Cl\cdot HCl = 501.30$. Yellow, bitter crystals, soluble in water; an antibiotic (B.P.).

demethylene. Prefix used to denote the replacement of CH_2 by 2 H atoms.

demi. (French) Half. See *semi* (Latin) and *hemi* (Greek). A glass carboy-shaped vessel, holding 4 gal.

demineralization. Deionization. (1) Removal of inorganic constituents. (2) Removal of dissolved solids from water, e.g., boiler feed, without use of heat. Double-exchange methods are used to convert the salts into the corresponding acids, which are subsequently absorbed in plastic substances. Cf. *base* exchange, *zeolite*. **mixed-bed-** D. by means of an intimate mixture of cation- and anion-exchange resins, which act as numerous cation- and anion-exchange columns in series.

Democritus of Miletus. (Greek, Demokritos.) 460–370 B.C. An early Greek philosopher of Thrace, noted for his speculations on atoms and cosmology.

demolization. The purely physical dispersion of a molecular system by highly superheated steam.

demulcent. An oily or mucilaginous drug, which soothes or protects an inflamed tissue.

demuriation. The removal of hydrochloric acid from organic chlorine derivatives.

denaturation. Addition of unpleasant or inert substances to a product, e.g., alcohol, to make it unfit for human consumption. (2) The production of suspensoid properties in albumins and globulins.

dendrite. (1) Dentrite. A treelike or arborescent crystalline structure; as, in geology the black designs found in the division planes of rocks (moss agate); due to infiltration and subsequent evapora-

tion of solutions of iron and manganese salts. (2) A protoplasmic protuberance on a nerve cell.

dendrobine. $C_{16}H_{25}NO_2 = 263.2$. An alkaloid from Chin-shih-hu, *Dendrobium* (Orchidaceae); a tonic and antipyretic.

dendrology. Dating trees from growth rings.

denebium. De. A supposed element (Eder, 1916), identical with thulium.

denier. The thickness of a thread or yarn expressed as the weight in grams of 9,000 meters. Cf. *tex*.

Denigè's reagent. A solution of 5 gm yellow mercuric chloride in 20 ml concentrated sulfuric acid and 100 ml water; a test for citric acid.

denim. A strong, fairly heavy, usually cotton fabric, with diagonal stripes due to 2 differently colored threads.

denitration, denitrification. Removal of nitrates or nitrogen; as, the d. of soils by growing plants.

denitrify. To remove nitrogen or nitrates.

Dennstedt furnace. An electrically heated combustion furnace for elementary organic analysis.

densimeter. A hydrometer.

densi-tensimeter. An apparatus for the simultaneous determination of vapor pressure and vapor density.

densitometer. An optical device to measure optical density.

density. (1) In chemistry and physics, the weight of matter per unit volume of a substance. For solids and liquids: d. = specific gravity. For gases (M = molecular weight):

$$D_{(air)} = \text{d. in relation to air} = 1$$
$$D_{(O_2)} = \text{d. in relation to } O_2 = 32 = M$$
$$D_{(H_2)} = \text{d. in relation to } H_2 = 1 = M/2$$

Cf. *hydrometer* scales, normal and relative *density*, *specific gravity*. (2) In photography, the blackness of the image on an exposed plate, measured photometrically. Cf. *optical* d. (3) In physics, *current density*, c.d., or J, the number of amperes passing per square centimeter of an electrode. **limiting-** The d. of a gas corresponding with the pressure at which it becomes an ideal gas and obeys Boyle's law. The ratio of the l. d. of 2 gases equals the ratio of their molecular weights. **normal-** The limiting d. at atmospheric pressure; the weight in grams of a liter of substance measured at STP, the weights being adjusted to sea level at latitude 45°. **relative-** The weight of a volume of substance compared with that of a standard measured under the same conditions. For solids and liquids 1 ml of water at 4°C is the standard; for gases and vapors, an equal volume of hydrogen. **vapor-** The ratio of the weight of a given volume of a gas or vapor to that of the same volume of hydrogen measured at STP; 1 cc hydrogen weighs 0.00009 gm = 0.5 mol wt. See *Avogadro's law*.

d. comparator. A photoelectric densitometer, q.v. **d. fluids.** Fluids for separating minerals by flotation; as:

d.5.3.........	Thallium mercury nitrate solution
d.4.27.......	Clerici solution
d.3.5.........	Rohrbach solution
d.3.33.......	Methylene iodide
d.3.17.......	Toulet's solution
d.2.97.......	Acetylene tetrabromide
d.2.90.......	Bromoform
d.1.94.......	Ethyl iodide

densograph. A graph showing the relation between the intensity of illumination and the density of the image on a photographic plate.

dental alloy. A mixture of Ag 66–69, Cu 5, Zn 0.5–1.7, Sn 26–26.5%, amalgamated with Hg. **d. cement.** A quick-setting mixture of finely powdered (1) zinc oxide (= *zinc cement*), (2) copper oxide (= *copper cement*), or (3) aluminum calcium silicate (= *silicate cement*); mixed before use with orthophosphoric acid containing suitable amounts of Al, Zn, and Na phosphates

dentifrice Toothpaste.

dentin(e). The hard substance of teeth, giving elasticity. Root d. and crown d. are covered with cementum and enamel, q.v., respectively. Composition: water 5, hydroxyapatite and inorganic constituents 75, collagen 20%, with citric acid, insoluble proteins, mucopolysaccharides, and fats.

dentists' amalgam. An alloy: Hg 70, Cu 30%.

dentrite. Dendrite.

denudation. Stripping or making bare. Cf. *erosion.* **chemical-** The loss of nutritive salts from agricultural land.

deodorant. An agent which removes, corrects, or represses undesirable odors.

deoxidation. Reduction, the removal of oxygen from a compound; or reduction of the oxygen content (as in steel manufacture).

deoxycortone acetate. $C_{23}H_{32}O_4 = 372.52$. DOCA. 21-Acetoxypregn-4-ene-3,20-dione. Colorless crystals, m.158, insoluble in water. Used to treat Addison's disease (B.P.)

deoxyribose. See *deoxyribose.*

Department of Scientific and Industrial Research. DSIR. A British government department which provides funds for scientific research on a national scale, and subsidizes 49 trade research organizations.

dephlegmator. Fractionating column.

dephlogisticated. Without phlogiston (obsolete). **d. air.** Oxygen (obsolete). **d. marine acid.** Chlorine.

dephraden. Dexamphtetamine sulfate.

depilation. Removal of hairs and epidermis from hides.

depilatory. A substance that removes hairs from skin, e.g., barium sulfide.

depolarization. The prevention or removal of polarization. **electrical-** The prevention of electrical polarization, *e.g.*, by separating electrodes by a porous diaphragm. **optical-** The effect produced by placing a depolarizer between the analyzer and polarizer of a polarization apparatus.

depolarizer. An optical device to refract polarized rays into ordinary and extraordinary rays.

deposit. A concentration of matter at a particular place; e.g., a geologic location, test tubes (precipitate), tissues, or electrodes.

deposition. The formation of a deposit. Cf. *electro-d., electroless d.*

depressant. A cerebrospinal nerve drug which diminishes the functional activity of an organ or organism, *e.g.*, cocaine.

depression. A lowering effect. **molecular-** The lowering of the freezing point below 0°C of a solution containing a mole of a substance per liter. Cf. *Raoult's law.*

depressor. (1) A negative catalyst, q.v. (2) A

buffer. (3) Depressant. A substance used in flotation to reduce the tendency of gangue materials to be carried along with the froth, as, cyanides. **d. effect.** The resistance of a solution to a change in pH value. Cf. *buffer effect.*

depsides. Ester-like anhydrides of phenolcarboxylic acids, from lichens or synthetic.

depsiphore. A structural arrangement of atoms common to many tanning agents. Cf. *chromophore.*

Dequalinium. Trade name for decamethylenebis-4-aminoquinaldinium. Its acetate and chloride are antiseptics (B.P.) used to treat seborrhea and dandruff.

derbylite. An antimoniotitanate of iron.

derby red. Basic *lead* chromate.

dericin. A light-colored, viscous oil from castor oil; a solvent.

derinatol. Basic *bismuth* gallate.

derivant. Derivative.

derivate. Derivative.

derivation. (1) The preparation of one organic substance from another. (2) The theoretical connection between the molecular structures of related organic compounds.

derivative. (1) A compound, usually organic, obtained from another compound by a simple chemical process; *e.g.*, acetic acid is a d. of alcohol. (2) An organic compound containing a structural radical similar to that from which it is derived, *e.g.*, benzene derivatives containing the benzene ring. Cf. *anhydrosynthesis.* **additive-** Additive compound. **functional-** A d. which contains a radical whose hydrogen is capable (theoretically) of further replacement. Cf. functioning *group.* **nonfunctional-** A d. which contains a radical without replaceable hydrogen. Cf. nonfunctioning *group.* **nuclear-** A d. with substitution on the carbon stem. Cf. stem *nucleus.* **side chain-** A d. with substitution in the side chain, q.v.

derived units. Units. q.v., of physical measurements which can be deduced fundamentally. Thus, the fundamental unit of length l will give the unit of area l^2 and the unit of volume l^3.

dermatitant. A substance that irritates or inflames the skin.

dermatol. Bismuth subgallate.

dermatoscope. A binocular microscope.

dermatosome. (1) The smallest fiber or fibril detected microscopically. (2) The small fiber debris produced by the action of hydrochloric acid on cellulose (obsolete).

dermics. A drug used for skin diseases.

dermol. $Bi(C_{15}H_9O_4)_3 \cdot Bi_2O_3$. Basic bismuth chrysophanate. Amorphous yellow powder; a skin antiseptic.

derric acid. $C_{10}H_{14}O_7 = 243.09$. An oxidation product of derrisic acid from derris root, m.170, soluble in water. Cf. *risic acid.*

derrid. A resin from *Derris elliptica* (Leguminosae), E. Indies; a Malay arrow poison.

derrin. Early name for rotenone.

derris. The leaves of *D. uliginosa* (Leguminsae), S. Sea Islands; a Fijian fish poison. It contains rotenone, toxicarol, and deguelin but is not toxic to man. Cf. *cube.* **d. extract.** An infusion of d.; an insecticide. **d. root.** Tuba root. The dried root of *D. elliptica* (Leguminosae), Indonesia, Sarawak; an insecticide.

derritol. $C_{21}H_{24}O_6 = 372.19$. An alcohol derived from rotenone. Yellow needles, m.161.

desamidase. An enzyme which splits off the $—NH_2$ group.

desamidization. Deamidization.

desaulesite. A rare nickel-magnesium silicate.

Descartes, René. 1596–1650. French philosopher, physicist, and chemist.

desclizite. $Pb·Zn_4V_2O_4·H_2O$. A native zinc-lead vanadate; green masses, d.6.1, hardness 3.5.

desensitization. (1) Photography: rendering silver salts less sensitive to light. (2) Biochemistry: destruction of immune bodies.

desensitizer. A substance which renders a photographic emulsion less sensitive, *e.g.*, pinakryptol. Cf. *sensitizer*.

desertomycin. $C_{33}H_{60-62}O_{14}N$. An antibiotic from *Streptomyces flavofungini*, in African desert sands, m.189, slightly soluble in water.

deshydro- Prefix indicating containing less hydrogen; hence, unsaturated.

deshydroxy- Prefix indicating containing less hydroxyl. **d. cholic acid.** A constituent of bile.

desiccant. A drying agent. Weights of residual moisture in one liter of saturated air at 25°C after passing through the d. are, in milligrams:

P_2O_5	Practically none
$Mg(ClO_4)_2$	Practically none
KOH	0.003
H_2SO_4(95 %)	0.003
NaOH	0.16
CaO	0.2
$CaCl_2$	0.36
$ZnCl_2$	0.8
$CuSO_4$	1.4

chemical- A d. which acts by absorption, e.g., reacts with water; as, phosphorus pentoxide. **physical-** A d. which acts by adsorption; as, silica gel.

desiccated. Dried.

desiccation. The process of drying.

desiccator. A device for drying substances, e.g., a closed glass vessel containing a deliquescent substance. **vacuum-** A d. which may be evacuated.

desicchlora. An anhydrous, granulated barium perchlorate: a regenerable desiccant and absorbent for ammonia.

desivac process. A process of freezing and dehydrating aqueous preparations.

deslanoside. $C_{47}H_{74}O_{19} = 943.11$. Desacetyl lanatoside C. White, hygroscopic crystals, m.220–235, slightly soluble in water; a very poisonous cardiotonic.

desmin. $(Na_2-Ca)Al_2Si_6O_{16}·6H_2O$. A sodium-calcium aluminum silicate; hardness 3.5–4.

desmolases. Enzymes whose actions liberate energy; as, reductases.

desmotrope. One of a pair of tautomeric compounds. The most important types are:

1. Keto-enol tautomerism:

$$=CH·CO— \rightleftharpoons =C:C(OH)—$$

2. Keto-cyclo tautomerism:

$$—CO—...—C(OH)= \rightleftharpoons —C(OH)....C—$$
$$\underset{O}{\underline{\hspace{1.5cm}}}$$

3. Imino-amino tautomerism:

$$=CH·C(:NH)— \rightleftharpoons =C:CNH_2—$$

4a. Nitroso-isonitroso- and
4b. Oxime-isoxime tautomerism:

$$=CH·NO· \rightleftharpoons =C:NOH \rightleftharpoons =C—NH$$
$$\underset{nitroso-}{\quad} \underset{isonitroso-}{\quad} \underset{oxime-}{\quad} \underset{\substack{O \\ isoxime-}}{\diagdown\diagup}$$

5. Nitro-isonitro tautomerism:

$$=CH·NO_2 \rightleftharpoons =C:N(:O)OH$$

6. Nitrosamine-isodiazo tautomerism:

$$—NH·N:O \rightleftharpoons —N:N·OH$$

7. Azo-hydrazone tautomerism:

$$=CH·N:N— \rightleftharpoons =C:N·NH—$$

desmotropism. Allelomorphism, dynamic allotropy. A form of isomerism (tautomerism) of organic compounds between 2 molecules containing the same number and kind of atoms of like valency, in the same position, but with different linkages, e.g., shifting of the double bond. See *isomerism*, *tautomerism*.

desogen. A mixture of the methosulfates of trimethylammonium bases; a disinfectant.

desorption. (1) The reverse of adsorption, q.v. (2) The evolution or liberation of a volatile material from solution. (3) In chromatography, the removal of an absorbate from an absorbent.

desoxalic acid. $C_5H_6O_8 = 194.1$. 1,2-Dihydroxy-1,1,2-ethane tricarboxylic acid. Colorless liquid, decomp. by heat, slightly soluble in water.

desoxy- Prefix indicating the removal of oxygen. **d. compounds.** Organic compounds in which the OH group has been replaced by H. Their names end in -ane; thus, desoxyquinine becomes quinane. **d. sugar.** A group of carbohydrates occurring in nature, which by adding water, form a sugar; as, digitalose.

desoxyalizarin. Anthrarobin.

desoxybenzoin. $Ph·CH_2·CO·Ph = 196.1$. Phenylbenzylketone. Colorless scales, m.60, slightly soluble in water.

desoxycholic acid. $C_{24}H_{40}O_4 = 392.32$. A bile acid. Cf. *cholane*.

desoxycodeine. Codeinane.

desoxycorticosterone. 21-Hydroxyprogesterone, a steroid hormone from adrenal cortex extracts. **d. acetate.** $C_{23}H_{32}O_4 = 372.51$. White crystals, m.158, insoluble in water; an adrenocortical hormone.

desoxydation. Removal of oxygen; reduction.

desoxyephedrine. $C_6H_5·CH_2·CH(CH_3)·NH(CH_3) = 149.23$. Desoxyn, methedrine, pervitine, methylamphetamine hydrochloride. A vasoconstrictor and cerebral stimulant; used as the hydrochloride.

desoxymorphine. Morphane.

desoxyn. Desoxyephedrine.

desoxyquinine. Quinane.

desoxyribonucleic acid. Chromosomic acid, thymus nucleic acid. A constituent of nuclear cell material, associated with the transmission of the characteristics of the cell and largely responsible for cell division.

desoxyribose. A combined sugar in desoxyribonucleic acid and cellular nuclear material. Cf. *Feulgen* and *Dische* tests.

dessertspoon. A measure; 2 fluid drams, about 8 ml.

destructive distillation. Decomposition of organic compounds by heat out of contact with air; as, the production of wood tar.

desulfuration. (1) Removal of sulfur. (2) Reduction of sulfur content; as, in steel manufacture. (3) Precipitation of sulfides with lead or mercury cyanide. See *cyanidization*.

desyl. The radical $PhCO \cdot C(H—) \cdot Ph$, from desoxybenzoin. **bi-** See *bidesyl*.

detaline. Deltaline.

detection. Qualitative identification. Cf. *determination*. **d. limit.** The smallest quantity detectable by a chemical reaction.

detector. A device to detect electric waves; as, a valve.

detergent. A cleansing agent. Synonym: abstergent. Cf. *surfactant*. A substance that cleans. Typical constituents are surfactants, EDTA, carboxymethylcellulose, silicates, sulfates, chlorides, perborates, fluorescent dyes, pigments, perfume, water. The principal classes of synthetic detergents contain as the principal constituent:

    Fatty acid (natural, e.g., pine oil, or purified), fatty alcohol, rosin and naphthenic acid hydrophobic group, an ether linkage, and an anionic hydrophilic group, e.g., carboxylate, sulfate, sulfonate.

    Hydrocarbon (from petroleum, alkylbenzenes, alkylnaphthenyl compounds) as hydrophobic group, an ester linkage, and an amino or quaternary ammonium hydrophilic group.

    Ether (polyoxypropylene) hydrophobic groups, with amido linkage, and an ampholytic (aminosulfonic or aminocarboxylic) hydrophilic group. **soft-** A biodegradable d. that does not give rise to frothing in sewage disposal works.

determinism. The principle that all properties of the atom may be related and determined. Cf. *indeterminancy, uncertainty*.

detonation. An explosion produced by a chemical change.

detonator. Primer. A compound which ignites an explosive mixture.

detonics. The study of detonation reactions.

detoxication. The reduction in toxicity of poisons due to chemical changes caused by body metabolism.

deuteranope. A dichromat, q.v., having a normal appreciation of brightness throughout the spectrum. Cf. *deuteronope*.

deuterate. (1) To convert the H atom or atoms in a molecule into deuterium. (2) A substance containing heavy water of crystallization (obsolete).

deuteric acid. An acid containing deuterium; as $R \cdot COOD$. Cf. *deuterobenzoprotic acid*.

deuterium. $D_2 = 4.02712$. Heavy hydrogen, deuteronium, diplogen. The isotope of hydrogen, at. wt. 2.01356, H^2 or H^b. **d. oxide.** $D_2O = 20.03$. Heavy water, $H^2{}_2O$ or $H^b{}_2O$. Colorless liquid, d.1.1056, m.3.8, b.101.42, $n_{20}^D1.3281$; it inhibits plant and animal growth.

deutero- Prefix meaning: (1) second in order, (2) derived from, (3) containing heavy hydrogen (deuterium).

deuteroalbumose. An albumose derivative. Yellow powder, soluble in water.

deuteroammonia. The compound ND_3 or $NH^2{}_3$. It differs from ammonia as follows:

%D ...	NH_3	NH_2D	NHD_2	ND_2
	0	68	90	99
m.	195.2°A	197.9°A	198.6°A	199°A
b.	239.75°A	241.7°A	242.1°A	242.3°A
		mono-	di-	tri-

deuteroammonium. The radical $ND_4{}^+$. There are mono-, di-, tri-, and tetra- derivatives.

deuteroartose. $C_{156}H_{244}N_{40}O_{56}S$. A secondary artose.

deuterochloroform. Chloroform-*d*.

deuterofibrinose. A product formed from fibrin during digestion.

deuteroglobulose. A product formed from globulin during digestion.

deuteron. Deuton, diplon. A deuterium nucleus; a particle of mass 2.0 with one positive charge. Cf. *proton*.

deuteronium. Deuterium.

deuteronope. A person who is blind to the color green. Cf. *deuteranope*.

deuteroproteose. Deuteroalbumose.

deuteroxyl. The OD^- or OH^{2-} ion.

deuton. A deuteron.

Deutscher Normenausschus. DNA. The German standards organization.

Devarda's alloy. An alloy: Cu 50, Al 45, Zn 5%; a strong reducing agent in alkaline solution.

developed dyes. Colors produced from colorless substances by chemical reactions.

developer. A reducing liquid to render the image on an exposed photographic plate visible, usually by formation of black silver.

development. (1) Biology: the growth and differentiation in the structure of an organism, and acquisition of new, favorable characteristics. (2) Photography: the action of a developer. (3) Chromatography: separation of ions absorbed on an absorbent into bands, by passing a solution through the column of absorbent. Cf. *elution*.

deviation. The bending or turning of a direction or course.

devil's apple. Stramonium.

devitrifaction. Removal of transparency due to crystallization.

devitrification. Devitrifaction.

dew. Moisture precipitated on a surface from an atmosphere saturated with water vapor. **d. point.** The temperature of the atmosphere at which the saturation vapor pressure equals the actual (partial) vapor pressure of the water vapor in the air, and dew begins to form; an indication of the humidity of the air, q.v.

Dewar, Sir James. 1842–1923. British chemist. **D. flask.** Vacuum flask. A silvered, double-walled, glass vessel, evacuated between the walls; used as container for liquefied gases or cold liquids.

deweylite. $Mg_4Si_3O_{10} \cdot 6H_2O$. An amorphous, white silicate related to talc.

dexamed. Dexamphetamine sulfate.

dexamethasone. $C_{22}H_{29}O_5F = 392.54$. White crystals, m.255, insoluble in water; an adrenocortical steroid (B.P.).

dexamphetamine sulfate. $(C_9H_{13}N)_2 \cdot H_2SO_4 = 368.51$. Dephraden, dexamed, dexedrine. White bitter, saline crystals, soluble in water; a sympathomimetic (B.P.).

dexedrine. Dexamphetamine sulfate.

dextran. $(C_6H_{10}O_5)_x = (162.1)_x$. A gummy, fermentable carbohydrate from growths of *Leuconostoc mesenteroides* on sucrose. A polymerized glucose in which the glucose units are joined through 1,6-glucoside links. Used as a plasma substitute and blood anticoagulant (B.P.); it causes ropiness in wines. **d. sulfate.** Used similarly to d.

dextrase. An enzyme converting dextrose to lactic acid.

dextrin. $(C_6H_{10}O_5)_x$. British gum, starch gum, amylin, gummeline. A carbohydrate intermediate between starch and the sugars produced from starch by hydrolysis by dilute acids, diastase, or dry heat. An amorphous, yellow powder, soluble in water, precipitated by strong alcohol. It gives a reddish color with starch and is not fermentable, but is converted to maltose by the action of enzymes (diastase), and to dextrose by acids. Used as an adhesive, in printing and in inks and water colors. **achroo-** See *achroo*-dextrin. **alpha-** $(C_6H_{10}O_5)_6$. Schardinger d. **amylo-** See *amylo*-dextrin. **animal-** Glycogen. **beta-** $(C_6H_{10}O_5)_7$. A crystalline degradation product of starch. **erythro-** See *erythro*dextrin. **pyro-** See *pyro*dextrin.

dextrinose. Gentiobiose.

dextro- *d-.* Prefix meaning toward the right; e.g., d.-rotatory. Cf. *levo-*.

dextrocarvol. Carvone.

dextrocompound. A dextrorotatory compound; an optically active compound that turns the plane of polarized light clockwise.

dextrogyric. Dextrorotatory.

dextromethorphan hydrobromide. $C_{18}H_{25}ON$, HBr· $H_2O = 370.31$. 3-Methoxy-N-methylmorphinan hydrobromide. White, bitter crystals, m.127, soluble in water; a cough suppressant (B.P.).

dextronic acid. Gluconic acid.

dextropropoxyphene hydrochloride. $C_{22}H_{29}O_2N \cdot HCl = 375.95$. White, bitter powder, m.165, soluble in water; an analgesic (B.P.).

dextrorotary. Dextrorotatory.

dextrorotatory. Turning to the right (clockwise). **d. compound.** Dextrocompound. See *optical activity, asymmetric carbon atom.*

dextrosans. Glucosans.

dextrosazone. Glucosazone.

dextrose. Glucose. **d. monohydrate.** $C_6H_{12}O_6 \cdot H_2O = 198.21$. Medical glucose (B.P.), made by the hydrolysis of starch.

deyamittin. $C_{18}H_{12}O_3N$. A glucoside from *Cissampelos pareira.* Colorless crystals. Cf. *dyamettin, cissampeline.*

DFP. Common name for diisopropylfluorophosphonate, developed during World War II as a poison affecting the nervous system. Now used as a remedy for postoperational intestinal paralysis.

dg. Abbreviation for decigram, 0.1 gm.

dhurrin. $C_{14}H_{17}NO_7 = 311.14$. A glucoside from millet and sorghum, which hydrolyzes to glucose,

hydrogen cyanide, and p-hydroxybenzaldehyde. Colorless needles, m.196.

Di. Symbol for didymium, a mixture of neodymium and praseodymium.

di- Prefix meaning two, or twice. Cf. *bi-*.

dia- Prefix meaning through, or opposite.

diabantite. $H_{18}(Mg, Fe)_{12}Al_4Si_9O_{45}$. A chlorite-type silicate.

diabase. Dolerite. An igneous rock formed in the transition from basalt to granitoid gabbros; it consists of plagioclase, magnetite, augite, and sometimes olivine.

diabetin. Fructose.

diacetamide. $Me \cdot CO \cdot NH \cdot CO \cdot Me = 101.11$. N-acetylacetamide. Colorless needles, m.78, soluble in water. **phenyl-** Diacetanilide.

diacetanilide. $Me \cdot CO \cdot NPh \cdot CO \cdot Me = 177.15$. N-Acetylacetanilide, N-phenyldiacetamide, acetoacetanilide. Colorless leaflets, m.37.5, soluble in water.

diacetate. (1) A salt of diacetic acid. (2) A salt containing 2 acetoxy groups, CH_3COO-.

diacetenyl. The radical $-C\vdots C-C\vdots C-$. **d. benzene.** Diphenyldiacetylene.

diacetic acid. (1) $(MeCO)_2CH \cdot COOH = 144.1$. Diacetylacetic acid. Colorless liquid in diabetic urines. (2) Acetoacetic acid. (3) Succinic acid. **acetone-** Hydrochelidonic acid. **ethidene-** β-Methylglutaric acid. **phenylene-** Phenylenediacetic acid. **propidene-** β-Ethylglutaric acid. **d. ester.** $(MeCO)_2CHCOOEt = 172.1$. Ethyldiacetate, ethyldiacetic ester. Colorless liquid, decomp. 200, slightly soluble in water.

diacetin. $(MeCOOCH_2)_2CHOH = 176.14$. Glyceryl diacetate. Colorless liquid, m.40, soluble in water.

diacetonamine. $C_6H_{13}ON = 115.08$. β-Amino-isopropylacetone. Formed by the action of ammonia on acetone. Yellow liquid. Cf. *acetonamine.*

diacetone. Acetylacetone. **d. alcohol.** $MeCOCH_2C-Me_2OH = 116.1$. Colorless liquid, b.164; a solvent for nitrocellulose and resins.

diacetyl. (1) Biacetyl. (2) Prefix indicating 2 acetyl radicals. **methyl-** See *methyldiacetyl*. **d. amide.** Diacetamide. **d. anilide.** Diacetanilide. **d. glucose.** $C_{10}H_{16}O_8 = 264.2$. Colorless crystals, m. exceeds 100, soluble in water. **d. morphine.** Heroine. **d. peroxide.** $MeCO \cdot O \cdot O \cdot COMe = 118.08$. Yellow liquid; an antiseptic. **d. tannin.** Tannigen. **d. urea.** $MeCO \cdot NH \cdot CO \cdot NH \cdot COMe = 144.2$. Colorless crystals, soluble in water.

diacetylene. $HC \cdot C \cdot C \vdots CH = 50.0$. Butadiine. Colorless gas. **d. glycol.** $CH_2OH \cdot C \vdots C \cdot C \vdots C \cdot CH_2OH = 110.1$. Hexadiindiol. Colorless crystals, m.111.

diacetylenes. C_nH_{2n-6}. Unsaturated hydrocarbons containing 2 triple bonds.

diacid. A compound containing 2 OH groups; as, $Ca(OH)_2$.

diacolation. Extraction in presence of sand, sometimes used for pharmaceutical tinctures.

diad. An element or radical with valency 2.

diadochite. $H_{24}Fe_4P_2S_2O_{29}$. Yellow monoclinics, d.38, hardness 3.5–4.5.

diagnostic. Means of recognition. **d. reactions.** Chemical tests for a pathological condition, e.g., Ehrlich reaction. **d. test.** Biochemical experiments to detect pathological conditions, e.g., Wassermann test.

DIAGRAM 207 **DIAMINOPHOSPHATIDES**

diagram. A graph showing the relation of one or more properties of one or more substances. Cf. *coordinates*.

Diakon. Trademark for a methyl methacrylate plastic.

Dial. (1) Trademark for diallyl barbitone. (2) (not cap.) Term suggested for a dialdehyde. **d. uramide.** Uramil.

dialdehyde. Dial. A compound containing 2 aldehyde groups. **d. starch.** A product of the oxidation of starch with periodic acid. Used to improve the strength of paper.

dialin. $C_{10}H_{10} = 130.08$. Dihydronaphthalene. **1,2-** Colorless liquid, b.84.5. **1,4-** Colorless liquid, m.15.

dialkene. Diolefine.

dialkyl. A compound containing 2 alkyl radicals.

dialkylene. A compound containing 2 alkylene radicals.

diallag. $(Mg,Fe)CaSi_2O_6$. A calcium silicate, sometimes containing alumina, d.3.2, hardness 4.

diallyl. (1) $CH_2:CH\cdot CH_2\cdot CH_2\cdot CH:CH_2 = 82.1$. $\Delta^{1,5}$-Hexadiene*. Colorless liquid, b.59.5, insoluble in water. (2) A compound containing 2 allyl radicals. $(CH_2:CH\cdot CH_2)_2NH = 97.09$. Di-2-propenylamine*. Colorless liquid, b.111. **d. barbitone.** $C_{10}H_{12}O_3N_2 = 208.2$. Dial. Shining scales, m.170, slightly soluble in water; a hypnotic and sedative. **d. sulfide.** Allyl sulfide. **d. urea.** Sinapolin.

dialozite. $MnCO_3$. Native manganous carbonate.

dialuramide. Uramil.

dialurate. A salt of dialuric acid.

dialuric acid. $OC(NH\cdot CO)_2\cdot CHOH = 144.1$. Tartronylurea, 5-hydroxybarbituric acid. A monobasic heterocyclic acid from alloxan. Colorless prisms, slightly soluble in water.

dialysate. Dialyzate.

dialysed. Dialyzed.

dialysis. Utrafiltration. Microfiltration by a semipermeable membrane, which separates crystalloids (molecules) from colloids of ultramicroscopic size.

dialyzate. The crystalloid which is dialyzed through a membrane. Cf. *diffusate*. Incorrectly used to describe the portion which does not pass through the membrane. Cf. *tenate*.

dialyzator. An apparatus for dialysis.

dialyzed. Separated by dialysis. **d. iron.** Colloidal ferric hydroxide solution.

dialyzer. The semipermeable membrane used in dialysis, e.g., collodion. Cf. *diffusion shell*.

diamagnetic. Repelled by a magnet; taking a position at right angles to the field of an electromagnet; having magnetic permeabilities less than 1. Cf. *paramagnetic*.

diameter. (1) A straight line passing through the center of a body or figure. Cf. *circle, caliber*. (2) The number of times the d. of a magnified object is increased.

diamide. (1) Oxamide. (2) A compound containing 2 —$CONH_2$ groups.

diamidine. (1) Oxalamidine. (2) A compound containing 2 amidine groups.

diamido-. Prefix indicating 2 amido radicals. **d. cyanidine.** Formoguanine.

diamidogen. Hydrazine.

diamine. (1) Hydrazine. (2) See *diamines*. **amylene-** $C_5H_{14}N_2 = 102.2$ Pentamethylenediamine,

cadaverine, 1,5-diaminopentane. **butylene-** $C_4H_{12}N_2 = 88.2$. Tetramethylenediamine, putrescine, 1,4-diaminobutane. **diethylene-** $NH\cdot(CH_2)_2\cdot(CH_2)_2\cdot NH = 86.2$. Cyclic tetramethylenediamine. **dimethylene-** Ethylenediamine. **ethylene-** $NH_2CH_2CH_2NH_2 = 60.1$. Dimethylenediamine. Colorless liquid, b.116. **hexamethylene-** Triethylenediamine. **pentamethylene-** Amylenediamine. **phenylene-** $C_6H_7N_2 = 107.1$. *ortho-* 1,2-Diaminobenzene. *meta-* 1,3-Diaminobenzene. *para-* 1,4-Diamino*benzene*. **propylene-** $NH_2(CH_2)_3NH_2 = 74.2$. Trimethylenediamine. Colorless liquid, b.119. **tetramethylene-** Butylenediamine. *cyclic-* Piperazine. **triethylene-** Cyclic hexamethylenediamine. **trimethylene-** Propanediamine.

d. blue. Trypan blue.

diamines. Compounds containing 2 —NH_2 groups. **aliphatic-** Compounds containing 2 amino groups attached to a carbon chain, e.g., ethylenediamine. **aromatic-** Compounds containing 2 amino groups attached to a carbon ring, e.g., phenylenediamene. **heterocyclic-** Saturated ring compounds with the amino group in the ring, e.g., diethylenediamine. **homocyclic-** Aromatic diamines.

diamino- Prefix indicating 2 amino groups (—NH_2). **d. anthraquinone.** $C_{14}H_{10}O_2N_2 = 238.2$. *alpha-* or 1,4- Red needles, m.236, slightly soluble in water. *beta-* or 2,3- Brown needles, sublime on heating, soluble in water. *ortho-* or 1,2- Blue crystals, decomp. 130, insoluble in water. **d. azobenzene.** Azobenzene. **d. azobenzene hydrochloride.** Chrysoidine. **d. azotoluene.** $C_{14}H_{16}N_4 = 240.16$. Isomers include 2,2'-diamino-4,4'-azotoluene, m.203; 3,3'-diamino-2,2'-azotoluene, m.145. **d. benzene.** See *benzene*. **d. benzoic acid.** See *benzoic acid*. **d. benzophenone.** $C_{13}H_{12}ON_2 = 212.2$. **alpha-,** *para-*, or 4,'4-$NH_2\cdot C_6H_4\cdot CO\cdot C_6H_4\cdot NH_2$. Colorless needles, m.172, soluble in water. *beta-, meta-*, or 3,3'- Yellow needles, m.237, soluble in water. **d. diphenic acid.** $C_{14}H_{12}O_4N_2 = 272.2$. Benzidine dicarboxylic acid. Colorless crystals, insoluble in water. **d. diphenyl.** Benzidine. **d. diphenylamine.** $NH_2C_6H_4\cdot NH\cdot C_6H_4NH_2 = 199.3$. Colorless scales, m.158, insoluble in water; used in organic synthesis. **d. diphenylethylene.** Diaminostilbene. **d. diphenylmethane.** $C_{13}H_{14}N_2 = 184.19$. *para-* or 4,4'- Colorless scales, m.87, soluble in water; used in organic synthesis. **d. naphthalene.** Naphthylenediamine. **d. naphthalenesulfonic acid.** $C_{10}H_4(NH_2)_2(SO_3H)_2 = 318.24$. *1,5,3,7-* Colorless crystals, insoluble in water. *1,8,3,6-* Colorless prisms, soluble in water; used to make H acid. **d. naphthalenesulfonic acid.** $C_{10}H_5(NH_2)_2SO_3H = 238.17$. 1,3,6- Colorless crystals, slightly soluble in water. 1,4,2- Colorless crystals, slightly soluble in water; used in organic synthesis. **d. phenol.** See *phenol*. **d. phenol hydrochloride.** Amidol. **d. stilbene.** $NH_2C_6H_4\cdot CH:CH\cdot C_6H_4\cdot NH_2 = 210.2$. Diaminodiphenylethylene. Colorless scales, m.170, slightly soluble in water. **d. stilbene disulfonic acid.** $C_{14}H_{12}N_2(SO_3)_2 = 370.23$. 1,2,4- or α- Yellow crystals, insoluble in water. **d. triphenylmethane** $C_{19}H_{18}N_2 = 274.26$. *para-* or 4,4'- Colorless crystalline beads, m.139, slightly soluble in water; an intermediate.

diaminophosphatides. Fatty substances containing 2N atoms to one P atom, e.g., aminomyeline.

diaminodiphosphatides. Phosphatides containing 2N atoms and 2P atoms, e.g., assurin. **diamino-monophosphatides.** Diaminophosphatides.

diammonium. (1) $NH_4 \cdot NH_4' = 36.08$. Cf. *hydrazinium*. (2) Prefix indicating the presence of 2 ammonium radicals. **mercur-** See *mercuridiammonium*.

diamond. $C = 12.001$. Crystalline carbon, colorless or tinted isomeric crystals, d.3.53, hardness 10, insoluble and nonfusible, burning to carbon dioxide. Used as a precious stone, for cutting glass, and as bearings for delicate mechanisms. **industrial-** 1. *Carbons, carbonado, black Brazilian,* d. in porous clusters of fine-grained microcrystals. 2. *Ballas,* nonporous, mostly round, minute d. crystals. 3. *Boarts, borts.* Translucent crystals which cleave in layers. 4. *Synthetic,* made by heating graphite and carbon black with a tantalum catalyst at 1600°C and 95,000 atm. They differ from natural diamonds in having spiral growth forms. **d. black.** $C_6H_3(OH)(COONa) \cdot N : N \cdot C_{10}H_6N : N \cdot C_{10}H_5(OH)SO_3Na$. A black azo wool dye. (1) Waste from d. cutting and polishing. (2) Finely powdered glass, used as a polish or filter. **d. flavin.** $C_6H_4(OH) \cdot C_6H_3N : N \cdot C_6H_3(OH)COOH$. A yellow azo dye. **d. mortar.** A small, hard steel mortar.

diamorphine hydrochloride. $C_{21}H_{23}O_5N \cdot HCl \cdot H_2O = 423.86$. Diacetylmorphine hydrochloride. White, bitter crystals, m.231, soluble in water; a narcotic analgesic (B.P.).

diamyl. (1) Decane. (2) Indicating a compound containing 2 amyl radicals. **d. amine.** $C_{10}H_{23}N = 157.3$. Colorless liquid, b.187, soluble in alcohol. **d. ketone.** 6-Hendecanone*. **d. phthalate.** See *phthalate*. **d. sulfide.** $(C_5H_{11})_2S = 174.3$. Colorless liquid; and odorant for natural gas. Cf. *amylmercaptan*.

diamylene. (1) Decene. (2) Indicating a compound containing 2 amylene radicals. (3) Terpene.

dianiline. Prefix indicating 2 aniline molecules. **d. fluosilicate.** $(C_6H_5NH_2)_2 \cdot H_2SiF_5 = 330.20$. White plates, subliming 230, soluble in water.

dianisidine. $C_{14}H_{16}O_2N_2 = 244.2$. Dimethoxybenzidine, bianisidine. Colorless needles, m.170, slightly soluble in water. **ortho-** A microreagent for copper (green color in presence of acetic acid and a thiocyanate. Sensitivity 1:10⁶).

dianthryl. Bianthryl.

diaphanometer. An instrument to measure transparency.

diaphanoscope. (1) A darkened box with a source of light to view transparent objects. (2) An instrument to illuminate body cavities.

diaphorase. See yellow *enzyme*.

diaphoretic. A drug stimulant of sweat gland secretions, e.g., pilocarpine. Cf. *sudorific*.

diaphorite. $(Ag_2Pb)_5Sb_4S_{11}$. A metallic, orthorhombic sulfoantimonite.

diaphragm. (1) A disk, with one or more holes, of variable size, to regulate the amount of light passing through a lens. (2) The porous wall of a galvanic cell separating the 2 liquids. (3) A semipermeable partition or wall.

diaphthol. $C_9H_5N(OH)SO_3H = 225,14$. Quinaseptol, *o*-oxyquinoline-*m*-sulfonic acid. Yellow crystals, m.295, slightly soluble in water; an antiseptic.

diarabinose. $C_{10}H_{18}O_9 = 282.14$. A disaccharide of arabinose, m.260.

diarsenate. A salt containing 2 arsenate radicals.

diarsenide. A compound containing 2 arsenic atoms.

diarsenite. A salt containing 2 arsenite radicals.

diarsenous acid. Pyroarsenic acid.

diarsine. Biarsine.

diarsonium. Cacodyl.

diarsyl. Biarsine.

diascope. Portable X-ray tube for visual diagnosis by insertion into body cavities.

diasone. Diazone.

diaspore. $Al_2O_3 \cdot H_2O$. A hydrous aluminum oxide decomposition product of rocks.

diastase. (1) Vegetable amylase. (2) Amylase. A malt enzyme hydrolyzing below 75°C into maltose, dextrin, and maltodextrins. Yellow powder, soluble in water. Cf. *ptyalase*.

diastasic action. The action of diastase.

diastasimetry. Measuring diastatic power.

diastatic action. Diastasic action.

diathermy. Slow penetration of heat.

diathesin. $C_7H_8O_2 = 124.1$. Salicyl alcohol, *o*-oxybenzyl alcohol. Colorless crystals, m.86, soluble in water. Used to treat rheumatism.

Diatol. Brand name for diethylcarbonate.

diatom. A unicellular alga, usually with 2 symmetric halves. **d. ooze.** Ocean sediments (about 1,500 fathoms deep) of empty shells of diatoms (23% Ca).

diatomaceous earth. Kieselguhr.

diatomic. (1) A molecule of 2 atoms, e.g., a binary compound. (2) A substance containing 2 replaceable H atoms. **d. acid.** An acid containing 2 replaceable H atoms. **d. alcohol.** An organic compound having 2OH groups. **d. base.** A base containing 2 active OH groups.

diatomite. Kieselguhr.

diazacyclo- Prefix indicating the presence of 2 NH groups in a large ring.

diazene. Diazete.

diazete. $C_2H_4N_2 = 56.0$. Diazene. The heterocyclic system, $CH_2 \cdot N : N \cdot CH_2$.

diazines. (1) Hydrocarbons, consisting of a hexatomic ring with 2 N atoms and 4 C atoms. *1,2-* or *o-* Pyridazine. *1,3-* or *m-* Pyrimidine. *1,4-* or *p-* Pyrazine. (2) Suffix indicating a ring compound with 2 N atoms; as, benzodiazine.

diazo- Prefix indicating the radical —N:N—. Cf. *diazonium*. **d. compounds.** Very reactive organic nitrogen compounds formed when nitrous acid acts at low temperatures on the salts of primary aromatic amines. Usually explosive; and therefore used in solution as intermediates in dyestuff manufacture. Cf. *disazo compounds*. **d. test.** Pathological urine turns red on addition of diazobenzenesulfonic acid.

diazoacetate. A salt of diazoacetic acid. **ethyl-** $C_4H_6O_2N_2 = 114.07$. Colorless liquid, $b_{120mm}143$.

diazoamino. Azimino. The radical —N:N·NH—. **d. benzene.** $Ph \cdot N : N \cdot NH \cdot Ph = 197.27$. 1,3-Diphenyltriazene*. Yellow leaflets, m.98, decomp., insoluble in water. **d. naphthalene.** $C_{20}H_{15}N_3 = 297.3$. 1,3-Di-1-naphthyltriazine*. Yellow leaflets, explode on heating insoluble in water.

diazoate. A salt of the type $Ar \cdot N : NO \cdot OM$, from diazoic acid. Cf. *diazotate*.

diazobenzene. See *benzene.* **d. acid.** Nitranilide. **d. chloride.** $C_6H_5N_2Cl = 140.60$. Benzenediazonium chloride*. Colorless needles, decomp. by heat, soluble in water. **d. cyanide.** $C_7H_5N_3 = 158.21$. Yellow prisms, m.69, slightly soluble in water. **d. hydroxide.** Diazonium hydroxide. **d. imide.** $C_6H_5N_3 = 119.20$. Yellow oil, d.1.098, explodes when heated, insoluble in water. **d. nitrate.** $C_6H_5O_3N_3 = 167.19$. Colorless needles, explode on heating, soluble in water. **d. sulfonic acid.** $C_6H_4O_3N_2S = 184.18$. Benzeneazosulfuric acid. Red prisms, decomp. by heat, insoluble in water. Cf. *diazo test.*

diazodinitrophenol. $C_6H_2N_4O_5 = 210.1$. DDNP, dinol, 4,6-dinitrobenzene-2-diazo-1-oxide. Yellow needles; a detonator for percussion caps.

diazoethane. $CH:N\cdot N:CH = 54.0$. Aziethylene,

aziethane. **dimethyl-** $C_4H_6N_2 = 82.0$. Colorless crystals, m.270.

diazohydrates. Compounds containing the —N:NO— group.

diazohydroxide. The radical —N:NOH; 2 isomers

anti- $\overset{\text{NOH}}{\underset{\text{R—N}}{\|}}$ syn- $\overset{\text{HON}}{\underset{\text{R—N}}{\|}}$

diazoic acid. An isomer, $Ph\cdot N:NO\cdot OH$, of phenylnitramine, from which diazoates are derived.

diazoimide. Hydrazoic acid.

diazoimido compounds. Compounds containing the radical —N:N:N, from diazoimide. **d. phenyl.** Diazobenzeneimide.

diazoles. Pentacyclic hydrocarbons with 2N atoms. **1,2-** Pyrazole. **1,3-** Imidazole. **iso-** See *isodiazole.* **oxa-** See *oxadiazole.* **thio-** See *thiodiazole.*

diazomethane. $N:N\cdot CH_2 = 42.04$. Azimethylene, azimethane. Poisonous, yellow, explosive, odorless gas, used for methylation.

diazone. The disodium formaldehyde sulfoxylate derivative of 4,4'-diaminophenylsulfone; used to treat tuberculosis.

diazonium. The radical $=N:N$. **d. compounds.** Aromatic nitrogen compounds containing the group $ArN(:N)$—. **d. hydroxide.** The unstable base $PhN:NOH$ which is ionized into 90% $PhNN^+$ and OH^- and forms salts of the type $PhNNX$. Cf. *tyrotoxin.* **d. ion.** The basic radical $PhNN^+$. **d. salts.** Compounds of the type $R\cdot X\cdot N:N$, where X is an acid radical; as diazobenzene chloride, $PhNNCl$.

diazoöxyamido. The radical —N:N·N(OH)—. **d. benzene.** $C_{12}H_{11}ON_3 = 213.1$. Colorless crystals, m.127.

diazoparaffins. Aliphatic hydrocarbons containing the diazo group; as, diazomethane.

diazophenol. (1) $C_6H_4ON_2 = 120.1$. *p*-Diazophenol, furo-[*ab*]diazole. Colorless crystals, explode 38. (2) Internal diazo oxides formed from true diazophenols by dehydration, e.g., $C_6H_4\cdot O\cdot N:N$.

diazosalt. A compound of the type $Ar\cdot N:N\cdot X$, where Ar is an aromatic radical and X an acid radical or a halogen.

diazosplit. The decomposition of a diazosalt and formation of an aryl compound; e.g., $ArNNX = ArX + N_2$, where X is an acid or halogen radical. Cf. *Sandmeyer's reaction.*

diazotate. An acidic metal salt and tautomer of diazonium hydroxide, containing the radical $ArN:NO$—. Cf. *diazoate.* Isomers: cis (syn or normal) and trans (anti or iso); either may occur ionized or un-ionized in solution, and form salts of the type ArNNOM, where M is a monovalent metal. **d. ion.** The acid $PhNNO^-$ ion; exists in 2 isomers. **d. split.** The decomposition of a d. to a phenol and nitrogen: $ArNNOH = ArOH + N_2$.

diazotetrazole. $CN_6 = 96.06$. A heterocyclic compound. Colorless, explosive crystals.

diazotization. Diazo compound formation.

diazotizing. Primary amines are treated with nitric oxides or nitrites (Griess, 1860); used to manufacture analine dyes.

diazoxy. The radical —N(:O)=N—.

diazthines. Thiodiazines.

dibasic. (1) Describing compounds which contain 2 H atoms replaceable by a monovalent metal; or an acid which furnishes 2 H ions. (2) Diatomic, dihydric. Describing an alcohol containing 2 OH groups; as, ethylene glycol.

dibenzacridine. $C_{10}H_6\cdot N\cdot C_{10}H_6\cdot CH = 279.1$. Naphthacridine; 6 possibilities: $\alpha\alpha'$-, $\alpha\beta'$-, $\alpha\gamma'$-, $\beta\beta'$-, and $\gamma\gamma'$-.

dibenzamide. (1) $(PhCO)_2NH = 225.09$. Benzoylbenzamide, dibenzoylamine. Colorless crystals, m.148. (2) A compound with 2 —NH·CO·Ph radicals. **ethidine-** $(PhCONH)_2CHMe = 268.2$. Colorless crystals, m.204. **ethylene-** $(PhCONH\cdot CH_2)_2 = 268.2$. Colorless crystals, m.249. **methylene-** $C_{15}H_{14}O_2N_2 = 254.2$. Colorless crystals, m.221.

dibenzanthracene. $C_{22}H_{14} = 278.1$. Naphthophenanthrene, benzonaphthacene. A homocyclic hydrocarbon; as, $C_{10}H_6\cdot CH\cdot C_{10}H_6\cdot CH$. Cf. *pentacene.*

dibenzenyl. (1) Tolane. (2) Prefix indicating the presence of 2 benzenyl radicals, $\equiv C\cdot Ph$. **d. azoxime.** $C_{14}H_{10}ON_2 = 222.2$. Colorless crystals, m.108.

dibenzo- Prefix indicating the presence of 2 benzo groups, $(>C_6H_4)_2$. **d. furane.** $C_6H_4\cdot O\cdot C_6H_4 = 168.1$. Dibenzofurfurane, diphenylene oxide. Colorless crystals, m.81. **d. furane-p-oxazine.** Phenoxazine. **d. furfurane.** D. furane. **d. pyrene.** $C_{24}H_{14} = 302.1$.

(structural diagram)

d. pyrone. Xanthone. **d. pyrrole.** Carbazole. **d. quinoline.** Phenanthroquinoline. **d. thiophen.** $C_6H_4\cdot S\cdot C_6H_4 = 186.1$. Diphenylene sulfide. Colorless crystals, m.97. **d. thioxine.** Phenothioxin.

dibenzoyl. (1) Benzil. (2) Prefix indicating 2 benzoyl radicals, PhCO—. **d. catechol.** $C_{20}H_{14}O_4 = 318.21$. Colorless crystals, m.84. **d. ethane.** $PhCO\cdot CH_2\cdot CH_2\cdot COPh = 238.1$. Diphenazyl. Colorless crystals, m.145. **d. furazane.** $PhCO\cdot C:N\cdot N:C\cdot O\cdot COPh = 278.3$. Colorless crystals, m.118. **d. glucoxylose.** A glucoside, m.148, from *Danielia latifolia* (Bignoniaceae), Brazil. **d. ketone**

Diphenyl triketone. **d. malonitrile.** (PhCO·C:-
NH)$_2$CH$_2$ = 278.3. Colorless crystals, m.130. **d.
methane.** (Ph·CO)$_2$CH$_2$ = 224.1. Colorless crystals, m.81. **d. peroxide.** Benzoyl peroxide. **d.
styrene.** PhCO·CH:CPh·COPh = 312.2. Anhydro-
acetophenone benzil. Colorless crystals, m.129.
dibenzyl. (1) Bibenzyl. (2) Prefix indicating 2
benzyl radicals, PhCH$_2$—. **d. amine*** C$_{14}$H$_{15}$N =
197.2. Colorless liquid, b.300, insoluble in water.
d. diethyl stannane. (C$_6$H$_5$CH$_2$)$_2$SnEt$_2$ = 358.89.
Colorless liquid, b.223, soluble in alcohol. **d.
ethane.** Ph(CH$_2$)$_4$Ph = 210.14. Diphenylbutane.
Colorless crystals, m.52, soluble in alcohol. **d.
glycolic acid.** Oxatolic acid. **d. hydrazine.**
(PhCH$_2$NH—)$_2$ = 207.3. Colorless crystals, m.65;
used in organic synthesis. **d. ketone.** Ph·CH$_2$·-
CO·CH$_2$·Ph = 210.09. Colorless crystals, m.33.9,
insoluble in water. **d. mercury.** Hg(C$_6$H$_5$CH$_2$)$_2$ =
382.72. Colorless needles, soluble in alcohol.
dibenzylidene. A compound containing 2 C$_6$H$_5$·CH—
radicals. **d. acetone.** Styryl ketone.
diborane diphosphine. B$_2$H$_6$·2PH$_3$ = 96.1. White
crystalline solid, dissociates above − 30 into diborane and phosphine.
dibrom-, dibromo- Prefix indicating 2Br atoms. **d.
acetic acid.** C$_2$H$_2$O$_2$Br$_2$ = 217.95. Colorless crystals, m.48, soluble in water. **d. anthracene.**
C$_{14}$H$_8$Br$_2$ = 336.0. 5, -10 or γ-. Yellow needles,
m.221, insoluble in water. **d. anthraquinone.**
C$_{14}$H$_6$O$_2$Br$_2$ = 366.05. alpha- Yellow needles,
m.237, soluble in alcohol. beta- Yellow needles,
m.275, sparingly soluble in alcohol. **d. barbituric
acid.** Dibromine. **d. benzene.** See benzene. **d.
indigo.** C$_{16}$H$_8$O$_2$N$_2$Br$_2$ = 319.93. Tyrian purple.
Purple crystals in Murex and Purpura species.
d. isethionate. C$_{17}$H$_{18}$O$_2$N$_4$Br$_2$·2C$_2$H$_6$O$_4$S = 722.42.
White, bitter crystals, m.190, soluble in water; an
antiseptic (B.P.). **d. quinone chloroimide.** A reagent for phenols. **d. thymolsulfonphthalein.** An
indicator, changing at pH 7.0 from yellow (acid)
to blue (alkaline).
dibromide. A salt ionizing to 2 bromide ions.
dibucaine hydrochloride. C$_{20}$H$_{29}$O$_2$N$_3$·HCl = 379.94.
White crystals, m.98, soluble in water (U.S.P.).
dibutyl. (1) Prefix indicating 2 butyl (C$_4$H$_9$) radicals
joined through a third atom or group. (2) Octane.
d. beryllium. Be(C$_4$H$_9$)$_2$ = 123.16. Colorless
liquid, b$_{25mm}$170, decomp. in water. **d. cadmium.**
Cd(C$_4$H$_9$)$_2$ = 226.55. An oil, d.1.306, b$_{12.5mm}$103.
d. phthal(ate.) See phthalate. **d. tin bromide.**
(C$_4$H$_9$)$_2$SnBr$_2$ = 392.67. White needles, m.20.
d. tin chloride. (C$_4$H$_9$)$_2$SnCl$_2$ = 303.75. Colorless
needles, m.43.
di-i-butyl- Prefix indicating 2 isobutyl radicals.
d. cadmium. Cd(C$_4$H$_9$)$_2$ = 226.55. An oil, d.1.269,
b$_{20mm}$90.5. **d. mercury.** Hg(C$_4$H$_9$)$_2$ = 314.75.
Colorless liquid, d.1.835, b.205, slightly soluble in
water.
dibutyrin. C$_3$H$_5$(OH)(OOC·C$_3$H$_7$)$_2$ = 232.15. Glyceryl dibutyrate. Colorless liquid, d.1.803, b.282;
formed from butyrin by pancreatic lipase.
dicacodyl. See cacodyl.
dicarbazyl. C$_{24}$H$_{16}$N$_2$ = 332.3. The heterocyclic
ring system,

C$_6$H$_4$
| 〉N—N〈 C$_6$H$_4$
C$_6$H$_4$ | C$_6$H$_4$

dicarbonate. Bicarbonate.
dicarboxyl. Oxalic acid.
dicarboxylic acid. A compound with 2 —COOH
groups.
Dicel. Trademark for a continuous-filament cellulose
acetate yarn.
dicentrine. C$_{20}$H$_{21}$O$_4$N = 339.3. An alkaloid from
Dicentra pusilla (Fumariaceae). Cf. glaucine.
dicetyl. Me(CH$_2$)$_{30}$Me = 450.5. Dotriacontane;
m.70.
dichlone. C$_{10}$H$_4$O$_2$Cl$_2$ = 327.28. 2,3-Dichloro-1,4-
naphthoquinone; a foliage spray.
dichlor-, dichloro- Prefix indicating the presence of
2 Cl atoms in an organic molecule. **d. acetal.**
C$_6$H$_{12}$O$_2$Cl$_2$ = 187.09. Colorless liquid, b.180–185.
d. acetamide. See acetamide. **d. acetic acid.** See
acetic acid. **d. acetone.** See acetone. **d. ace-
tylchloranilide.** Cl$_2$CH·CO·NCl$_2$Ph = 258.5. A
chlorinating agent. **d. acetyl chloride.** C$_2$HOCl$_3$
= 147.37. Colorless liquid, b.107; hydrolyzed by
water or alcohol. **d. aldehyde.** See acetaldehyde.
d. amide T. CH$_3$·C$_6$H$_4$·SO$_2$NCl$_2$ = 240.06. p-
Toluene dichlorosulfamine. Yellow crystals of
strong chlorine odor, m.78–83, insoluble in water;
an antiseptic. **d. aniline.** See aniline. **d. anthracene.** See anthracene. **d. benzene.** See benzene.
d. diethyl ether. 2,2'-Dichloroethyl ether. **d.
diethyl sulfide.** Mustard gas. **d. difluoromethane.**
CCl$_2$F$_2$ = 121.0. Kinetic 12, F-12, Freon. Colorless gas, d.1.40, b.−30; a refrigerant. **d. ethyl
ether.** C$_4$H$_8$OCl$_2$ = 142.98. Dichloroether. 1,2-
or α,β- CH$_2$Cl·CHCl·OEt. Colorless liquid, d.1.174,
b.142, soluble in alcohol. 2,2- or β,β'- (CH$_2$Cl·-
CH$_2$)$_2$O. Dichlorodiethyl ether. Colorless liquid,
d.1.213, b.178, insoluble in water; a solvent for
fats and pectins. **d. ethylene.** CHCl:CHCl =
96.93. 1,2-Acetylene dichloride, dieline, dioform.
Colorless liquid of pleasant odor, d.1.278, b.55.
A mixture of the 2 stereoisomers: cis, d.1.265,
b.48.4; trans, d.1.291, b.60.3. Used as rubber
solvent, for extraction, as a metal degreaser,
anesthetic, and refrigerant. **d. hydrin.** C$_3$H$_6$OCl$_2$
= 128.97. alpha- Dichloroisopropyl alcohol. 1,3-
dichloro-2-propanol*. Colorless, ethereal liquid,
d$_{19}$°1.367, b.174, miscible with alcohol; a solvent.
beta- Dichloropropyl alcohol, 2,3-dichloro-1-pro-
panol*. Colorless liquid, d$_{17}$°1.355, b.182. **d. methane.** Methylene chloride. **d. naphthalene.** See
naphthalene. **d. nitrohydrin.** C$_3$H$_5$O$_3$NCl$_2$ = 186.0.
1,3-Dichloro-2-propanol nitrate*. Colorless liquid,
d.1.459, insoluble in water. **d. phenolindo-o-cresol.**
An oxidation-reduction indicator. **d. phenolindo-
phenol.** Tillmans' reagent. **d. phenosulfonphthal-
ein.** A pH indicator, changing at 6.0 from yellow
(acid) to red (alkaline). **d. quinone chloroimide.**
A reagent for phenols.
dichloralphenazone. C$_{15}$H$_{18}$O$_5$N$_2$Cl$_6$ = 519.00. A
complex of chloral hydrate and phenazone. White
crystals, m.66, soluble in water; a hypnotic (B.P.).
dichloricide. p-Dichlorobenzene.
dichloride. An inorganic salt containing 2 chloride
atoms.
dichlorophen(e). C$_{13}$H$_{10}$O$_2$Cl$_2$ = 269.10. White
powder, m.175, insoluble in water; used to treat
tapeworm. **d. amide.** C$_6$H$_6$O$_4$N$_2$Cl$_2$S$_2$ = 305.16.
4,5-Dichloro-m-benzene disulfonamide White
crystals, m.237, slightly soluble in water; a carbonic
anhydrase inhibitor (U.S.P., B.P.).

dichlorophenamide. $C_6H_6O_4N_2Cl_2S_2 = 305.26$. 4,5-Dichlorobenzene-1,3-disulfonamide. White crystals, m.240, insoluble in water; used to treat glaucoma (B.P.).

dichlorophenarsine hydrochloride. $C_6H_3ClAsCl\cdot(NH_2)(OH)\cdot HCl = 290.41$. Clorarsen, holarsol, phenarsen, 3-amino-4-hydroxyphenyldichloroarsine hydrochloride. White powder, soluble in water; an antisyphilitic.

dichlorvos. DDVP. Dimethyl-2,2-dichlorovinyl phosphate. Clear mobile liquid, d.1.43; an insecticide.

dichroine. $C_{16}H_{21}O_3N_3(?)$. An antimalarial alkaloid from the roots and leaves of *Dichroa febrifuga*, Lour., m.237, slightly soluble in water.

dichroism. (1) The property by which certain crystals exhibit different colors when viewed in different directions, or when viewed by reflected or refracted light. (2) The property of showing different colors when viewed through different thicknesses, e.g., certain indicator solutions.

dichroite. Iolite.

dichromat. A person having reduced color discrimination, and requiring a mixture of only two radiations when matching colors. Cf. *deuteranope, protanope.*

dichromate. (1) A salt containing the radical $=Cr_2O_7$ (bichromate). (2) Sodium dichromate.

dichromatic. Having different colors according to the thickness of the layer through which the solution (e.g., dyestuffs) is viewed. Cf. *dichroism.*

dichromic acid. The hypothetical acid, $H_2Cr_2O_7$ or $2CrO_3\cdot H_2O$, from which dichromates are derived.

dichroscope. An instrument to determine the refractive power of crystals.

dicinchonine. $C_{38}H_{44}O_2N_4 = 588.5$. An alkaloid from cinchona bark.

dick. Ethyldichlorarsine.

dickite. A form of kaolin.

Dick test. An antitoxin test for scarlet fever (B.P.).

dicodeine. $C_{72}H_{84}O_{12}N_4$. A polymer of codeine.

dicodide. $C_{18}H_{21}O_3N = 299.15$. Dihydrocodeinone. A codeine derivative.

diconchinine. Diquinidine.

diconic acid. $C_9H_{10}O_6 = 214.1$. A citric acid derivative.

dicophane. Chlorophenothane.

dicoumarin. 3,3'-Methylenebis-4-hydroxycoumarin. The active agent responsible for sweet clover disease of cattle; an anticoagulant in the treatment of thrombosis and embolectomy.

dicyan(o). (1) Indicating a compound containing 2 cyano radicals. (2) Cyanogen. **d. acetylene.** $CN\cdot C \vdots C\cdot CN = 76.09$. Colorless crystals, m.21. **d. diamide.** $NH_2\cdot C(:NH)\cdot NHCN = 84.18$. Cyanoguanidine, param. An isolog of guanylurea. Colorless scales, m.205, soluble in water. **d. diamidine.** $NH_2\cdot C(:NH)\cdot NH\cdot CONH_2 = 102.2$. Guanylurea. The amide of guanidinecarboxylic acid. Colorless crystals, m.105, soluble in water. Cf. *Grossmann reagent.*

dicyanide. A salt containing 2 cyanide radicals.

dicyanin(e). An aniline-dye, infrared photosensitizer. **d. A.** $C_{21}H_{27}N_2O_2I = 466.2$. 1,1'-Diethyl-4,2'-dimethyl-6,6'-diethoxy-2,4'-carbocyanin iodide. A quinoline dye infrared photosensitizer. Cf. *cyanin* dyes.

dicyanodiamide. Dicyandiamide.

dicyanogen. CN—CN $= 52.0$. Oxalonitrile, ethane dinitrile. Colorless, poisonous gas, b. -25. Cf. *cyanogen.*

dicyclic. Describing a system of 2 fused rings; as, naphthalene, but not biphenyl.

dicyclomine hydrochloride. $C_{19}H_{35}O_2N\cdot HCl = 346.05$. White bitter crystals, m.173, soluble in water; an antispasmodic (B.P.).

Didial. Trademark for a combination of diallyl-barbituric acid and ethylmorphine.

didiphenylamine- Prefix indicating 2 diphenylamine radicals. **d. fluosilicate.** $[(C_6H_5)_2NH]_2\cdot H_2SiF_6 = 482.26$. White crystals, m.169.

didiphenylene ethylene. Difluorene.

didymia. Didymium oxide.

didymium. Di. A supposed element discovered by Mosander (1841) in the earth didymia; it is a mixture of neodymium and praseodymium. "D. salts," by-products of the manufacture of gas mantles, are mixtures of neodymium and praseodymium salts; hence, the symbol Di below means Nd and Pr. **d. carbonate.** $Di_2(CO_3)_6\cdot 6H_2O$. Pink powder, insoluble in water. **d. chloride.** $Di_2Cl_6\cdot 12H_2O$. Purple crystals, soluble in water, a germicide. **d. nitrate.** $Di_2(NO_3)_6\cdot 12H_2O$. Purple, asymmetric crystals, soluble in water; an antiseptic. **d. oxide.** Di_2O_3. Gray powder, insoluble in water. **d. salicylate.** $Di_2(C_7H_5O_3)_6$. Dymal. White powder; an antiseptic. **d. sulfate.** $Di_2(SO_4)_3\cdot 6H_2O$. Red crystals, slightly soluble in water; a disinfectant.

die casting. Producing a shape by forcing a measured quantity of molten aluminum into a hardened alloy steel die (2–10 tons/in.^{2}).

dieldrin. $C_{12}H_8OCl_6 = 380.88$. A chlorinated dimethanonaphthalene. White crystalline solid, m.175; an insecticide. Cf. *eldrin.*

dielectric. A nonconductor of electricity. **d. constant.** ϵ. Permittivity. Inductivity. Specific capacitance: $\epsilon = ee'/fr^2$, where f is the force of repulsion between 2 point charges of electricity e and e', which are at a distance r apart in a uniform medium. For practical purposes the relative permittivity is used; i.e., the ratio of the capacitance of a capacitor, when the dielectric is the substance under investigation, and air. **d. strength.** The potential (volts) at which an insulator breaks down, divided by the thickness (in 0.001 in.). Cf. *Clausius-Mosotti equation, Helmholtz equation.*

dieline. Dichloroethylene.

Diel's hydrocarbon. $C_{18}H_{16}$. The theoretical basis of the sterol molecule.

Dien. Trade name for a polyester synthetic fiber.

diene. Suffix indicating 2 double bonds. **d. series.** Diolefines.

dienestrol. $C_{18}H_{18}O_2 = 266.34$. 3,4-Bis(p-hydroxyphenyl)-2,4-hexadiene, $OH\cdot Ph(C\cdot CHMe)_2PhOH$. An estrogen (B.P.), m.233.

dienol. Catalytically dehydrated castor oil; a drying oil for paints.

Diesel fuel. Heavy fuel oil in which combustion is started by spontaneous ignition due to compression.

diet. The customary or prescribed food of an individual.

dietary. A systematic diet repeated at definite time intervals. **d. standard.** The amount of nourishment required per day by a man, corresponding with 3000 cal approximately, and varying according to the work performed by the individual; e.g., 120 gm protein (429 cal), 500 gm carbohydrates (2050 cal), 50 gm fat (465 cal), mineral matter and vitamins. Cf. *pelidisi*.

Dieterici's rule. Total latent heat $M\lambda =$ external work $P(V_2 - V_1) +$ internal latent heat CRT ln (V_2/V_1), where V_2 is the molal fraction of the liquid, V_1 that of the vapor, M the molecular weight, λ the latent heat.

diethacetic acid. Diethylacetic acid.

diethanolamine. $NH(CH_2 \cdot CH_2OH)_2 = 105.09$. Dihydroxydiethylamine. Colorless liquid, d.1.10, $b_{150mm}217$; a solvent, emulsifying agent, and detergent. Cf. *triethanolamine*.

diethazine hydrochloride. $C_{18}H_{22}N_2S \cdot HCl = 334.90$. 10-(2-Diethylaminoethyl) phenothiazine hydrochloride. White, bitter crystals, m.153, soluble in water; a parasympatholytic (B.P.).

diethoxalic acid. $C_6H_{12}O_3 = 132.1$. 1-Hydroxy-1-ethylbutyric acid. Colorless triclinics, m.80, soluble in water.

diethyl- Prefix indicating 2 ethyl radicals. **d. acetal.** Acetal. **d. acetic acid.** See *acetic acid*. **d. aldehyde.** Acetal. **d. amine*.** $Et_2NH = 73.12$. A secondary amine in putrefying fish. Colorless liquid, $d_{15°}$, 0.712, b.56, soluble in water. **d. aminobenzaldehyde.** $C_{11}H_{15}ON = 177.2$. Colorless needles, m.78. **d. aminophenol.** $C_{10}H_{15}ON = 165.18$. Colorless crystals, m.74. **d. aniline.** See *aniline*. **d. arsine.** (1) $Et_2AsH = 134.04$. Ethyl cacodyl. (2) $(AsEt_2)_2 = 266.02$. Colorless liquid, b.186. **d. barbituric acid.** Veronal. **d. benzene.** See *benzene*. **d. beryllium.** $BeEt_2 = 67.10$. Colorless liquid, m.12. **d. cadmium.** $CdEt_2 = 170.49$. An oil, d.1.656, $b_{19.5mm}640$. **d. carbamazine.** $C_{16}H_{29}O_8N_3 = 391.43$. White, hygroscopic crystals, m.136, soluble in water; an anthelmintic (U.S.P., B.P.). **d. carbinol.** $CHEt_2 \cdot OH = 88.13$. Colorless liquid, b.116, sparingly soluble in water. **d. carbonate.** $Et_2CO_3 = 118.1$. Diatol. Colorless, flammable liquid, d.0.975, b.126; a solvent for nitrocellulose. **d. carbonic ether.** Ethyl carbonate. **d. cyanamide.** $C_5H_{10}N_2 = 98.08$. Colorless liquid, b.186. **d. dioxide.** $EtO \cdot OEt = 90.1$. Ethyl peroxide. Colorless liquid, d.0.825, b.65, slightly soluble in water. **d. disulfide.** $EtS \cdot SEt = 122.21$. Ethyl dioethane, ethyl disulfide. Colorless liquid, d.0.993, b.153, soluble in water. It is toxic to *Ascaris*. Cf. *dithiene*. **d. ether.** Ether (2). **d. glycerol.** $CH_2OEt \cdot CHOH \cdot CH_2OEt = 148.2$. Colorless liquid, b.191; a solvent. Cf. *diethyline*. **d. glycol ether.** Ethylene diethylate. **d. hydrine.** Diethyline. **d. ketone.** $EtCOEt = 86.09$. 3-Pentanone. Colorless liquid, d.0.814, b.103, soluble in water; a hypnotic. **d. malate.** $EtOOC \cdot CHOH \cdot COOEt = 190.1$. Colorless liquid, b.250, soluble in water; a lacquer solvent. **d. malonic acid.** See *malonic acid*. **d. malonylurea.** Veronal. **d. mercury.** $HgEt_2 = 258.69$. Colorless liquid, d.2.44, b.159, insoluble in water. **d. nitramine.** See *nitramine*. **d. nitrosamine.** Nitrosodiethyline. **d. oxalic acid.** Diethoxalic acid. **d. oxamide.** $EtNH \cdot CO \cdot CO \cdot NHEt = 144.21$. Oxal ethyline. A nicotine alkaloid. Colorless needles, m.175, slightly soluble in water. **d. peroxide.** D. dioxide. **d. phosphate.** Ethyl phosphate. **d. phosphine.** $Et_2PH = 90.11$. Colorless liquid, b.85. **d. phosphoric acid.** $(EtO)_2PO \cdot OH = 154.12$. Colorless

liquid, soluble in water. **d. phthalate.** See *phthalate*. **d. propylcarbinol.** Octanol*. **d. stilbestrol** (U.S.P.), **d. stilboestrol** (B.P.), $C_{18}H_{20}O_2 = 286.36$. White crystals, m.170, insoluble in water; an estrogen. **d. sulfate.** Ethyl sulfate. **d. sulfide.** Ethyl sulfide. *dichloro-* Mustard gas. **d. sulfine.** The radical $>SEt_2$. **d. sulfone.** Ethylsulfone. **d. sulfone diethylmethane.** Tetronal. **d. sulfone dimethylmethane.** Sulfonal. **d. sulfone ethylmethylmethane.** Trional. **d. sulfone methylethylmethane.** Trional. **d. tartrate.** $EtOOC \cdot (CHOH)_2 \cdot COOEt = 206.1$. Colorless liquid, b.280, soluble in water; a solvent for nitrocellulose and resins. **d. telluride.** Ethyl telluride. **d. thiurea.** Ethylthiourea. **d. tin.** $SnEt_2 = 176.78$. Yellow oil d.1.654, b.150, insoluble in water. **d. tin dibromide.** $Et_2SnBr_2 = 336.61$. White needles, m.63. **d. tin dichloride.** $Et_2SnCl_2 = 247.69$. White crystals, m.84. **d. tin difluoride.** $Et_2SnF_2 = 214.78$. White plates, m.229. **d. tin diiodide.** $Et_2SnI_2 = 430.62$. White crystals, m.45. **d. tin oxide.** $Et_2SnO = 192.78$. White powder, insoluble in water. **d. toluamide.** An insect repellent. **d. toluene.** See *toluene*. **d. toluidine.** $Me \cdot C_6H_4 \cdot NEt_2 = 163.22$. *para-* Colorless liquid, b.229. **d. urea.** See *urea*. **d. zinc.** $ZnEt_2 = 123.46$. Colorless liquid, b.118; ignites in air.

diethylene. (1) Cyclobutane. (2) Prefix indicating 2 ethylene radicals. **d. diamine.** Piperazine. **d. dioxide.** Dioxan. **d. disulfide.** $S \cdot (CH_2)_2 \cdot S(CH_2)_2 =$

120.20. Dithiane. Colorless crystals, m.111, insoluble in water. **d. glycol.** $CH_2OH \cdot CH_2 \cdot O \cdot CH_2 \cdot CH_2OH = 106.1$. 2,2′-Oxybisethanol. Colorless liquid, d.1.1175, b.224, miscible with water or acetone. A solvent for gums and nitrocellulose; a hygroscopic agent; an antifreeze; a softener for glues, paper, and cork. **d. glycol butyl ether.** Butylcarbitol. **d. glycol ethyl ether.** Carbitol. **d. oxide.** Dioxan.

diethylethylene. Δ^3-Hexylene.

diethylidene. (1) 2-Butylene. (2) Prefix indicating 2 ethylidene radicals, $>CHMe$.

diethylin. (1) The radical $-NEt_2$, from diethylamine. (2) Diethyline.

diethyline. $CH_2OEt \cdot CHOEt \cdot CH_2OH = 148.1$. 1.2-Diethylglycerinester. Colorless liquid. Cf. *diethylglycerol*. *nitroso-* $Et_2N \cdot NO = 102.09$. Nitrosodiethylamine. Colorless liquid, d.0.951, b.177; used in organic synthesis.

dietics, dietetics. The science of the regulation of food.

dietzeite. $7Ca(IO_3)_2 \cdot 8CaCrO_4$. A native calcium chromate and iodate, in Chilean nitrate.

differential. By selective increments. **adsorption-** The selective adsorption of dyestuffs. See adsorption *indicators*.

  d. reduction. Selective reduction by metals of one component of a mixture.

differentiation. (1) Mathematics: Defining an infinitesimal increment of a quantity. (2) Biology: The development of new characteristics of a cell or organism; the specialized division of labor among the various cells, tissues, or organs.

diffraction. The bending of a ray of light at the edge of an object. Cf. *refraction*. Interference color fringes result when a number of parallel light waves strike a number of closely spaced parallel edges (a grating), e.g., rows of atoms in a crystal. **crystal-** See *X-ray spectrograph, crystal.*

d. formula. The wavelength of a radiation is $\lambda = s \sin d/n$, when the angle of incidence is 90°; or $(s/n)(\sin i - \sin d)$, where i is the angle of incidence, d the angle of diffraction, s the distance between the lines of the grating, and n the order of the spectrum. **d. grating.** A glass, film, or metal plate with fine rulings, used to produce a series of spectra, and for spectroscopic measurements.

diffusate. That which passes through a dialyzer, q.v.

diffuse. (1) Hazy in appearance. (2) Passing through a membrane. (3) Spreading through a gas, liquid, or solid. **d. series.** See *series.*

diffused. (1) Widely scattered, without definite limits. (2) Spreading or passing through an object, e.g., diffused poison. **d. reflection.** The ratio of reflected to incident light at a surface. See *albedo.*

diffusion. The spreading, or scattering of a material (gas, liquid), or energy (heat, light). **d. analysis.** Determination of particle size and molecular weight by d. **d. constant.** $D = Sx/qct$, where S is the weight of substance diffusing in t sec through a cylinder of length x and cross section q, and c is its concentration in grams per milliliter. **d. of energy.** The irregular reflection of light or heat waves from a surface, part being absorbed. **d. law.** The velocity of d. of 2 substances is in inverse proportion to the square root of the vapor density or molecular weight. Cf. *Graham's law, atmolysis.* **d. of matter.** The spreading or intermixing movement of gaseous or liquid substances, due to molecular movement. **d. shell.** A membrane for dialysis (dialyzer).

diflavine. The monohydrochloride of 2,7-diaminoacridine; an antiseptic.

difluor(o)- Prefix indicating 2F atoms. **d. benzene.** Benzene. **d. dichloromethane.** Dichlorodifluoromethane.

difluoroamino. The radical $-NF_2$ produced in the synthesis of tetrafluorohydrazine, N_2F_4.

difluoroethylene. $C_2H_{16} = 328.2$. Colorless prisms, m.218. Cf. *difluorene, dihydrorubicene.*

difluoride. A compound containing 2F atoms.

diformyl. Glyoxal.

digallic acid. $C_6H_2(OH)_3 \cdot COOC_6H_2(OH)_2COOH = 322.08$. White needles, m.275 (decomp.), slightly soluble in water; occurs in Chinese tannin and plant galls.

digentisic acid. $C_6H_3(OH)_2 \cdot COO \cdot C_6H_3(OH)_2COOH = 290.08$. Occurs in tannins. Needles, m.204, slightly soluble in water.

digestant. A digestion aid.

digester. A large iron vessel with cover and safety valve, used to decompose, soften, or cook substances at high pressure and temperature. See *autoclave.*

digesting shelf. A rack to hold Kjeldahl flasks.

digestion. (1) In physiology, the metabolic transformation of food into living matter, by ferments. (2) The treatment of substances with chemicals under heat and pressure, e.g., wood to make wood pulp. (3) The disintegration of substances by strong chemical agents as in the Kjeldahl determination. **artificial-** D. of food by ferments outside

the living body. **gastric-** D. in the stomach, e.g., by pepsin. **intestinal-** D. in the intestines. **oral-** Salivary d. **peptic-** Gastric d. **primary-** D. in the mouth, e.g., by diastase. **secondary-** Assimilation of food by body cells.

Digifolin. Trademark for a solution of glucosides from digitalis leaves.

digilanid. One of the 3 natural glucosides of *Digitalis lanata*, specifically designated d. A, d. B, and d. C; more properly called lanatosides. Enzyme hydrolysis yields the glucosides digitoxin, gitoxin, and digoxin, respectively, together with a molecule of glucose; the glucosides are further hydrolyzed by acid to digitoxigenin, gitoxigenin, and digoxigenin, with 3 molecules of digitoxose from each.

digipoten. A mixture of glucosides from digitalis leaves.

digit. (1) Three-fourths of an inch. (2) A measure of the extent of an eclipse; one-twelfth of the apparent diameter of the sun or moon. (3) An integer under 10.

digitalein. $C_{22}H_{33}O_9 = 446.4$. A glucoside of digitalis leaves. White powder, soluble in water; a diuretic and cardiac tonic.

digitaligenin. $C_{24}H_{32}O_3 = 368.24$. A split product from the glucoside of digitalis seeds.

digitalin. $(C_5H_3O_2)_x$. A glucoside from digitalis leaves. **amorphous-** Crude d. **crude-** Amorphous d. A mixture of digitoxin, digitalin, and digitalein. Amorphous, yellow powder, soluble in water or alcohol giving foaming solutions. **crystalline-** Digitonin. **French-** Homolle's-. A mixture of glucosides from digitalis leaves prepared by Homolle's method. Yellow, amorphous powder, m.100. **German-** A mixture of glucosides from digitalis leaves, mainly digitonin. Yellow powder, soluble in water. **true-** $C_{35}H_{56}O_{14} = 680.3$. D. verum, Schmiedeberg's d., from the seeds and leaves of digitalis. White powder, m.217, soluble in water.

digitalis. The leaves of *Digitalis purpurea*, foxglove (Scrophulariaceae); a narcotic, cardiac, and stimulant. Contains many glucosides and active principles.

digitalose. A methyl pentose from digitalis.

digitogenin. $C_{26}H_{42}O_5 = 434.3$. A split product of digitonin.

digitonin. $C_{54}H_{92}O_{28} = 1188.7$. A glucoside from digitalis leaves. Colorless crystals, decomp. by heat, insoluble in water. Physiologically inactive, and hydrolyzes to glucose, galactose, and digitogenin.

digitoxigenin. $C_{24}H_{36}O_4 = 388.3$. Colorless crystals, m.245, physiologically active. **anhydro-** $C_{24}H_{34}O_3 = 370.3$. Colorless crystals, m.184, physiologically inactive.

digitoxin. $C_{41}H_{64}O_{13} = 764.96$. A glucoside from digitalis leaves; the chief active principle. White leaflets, with bitter taste, m.240, slightly soluble in water. A cardiotonic (U.S.P., B.P.).

digitoxose. $C_6H_{12}O_4 = 148.09$. *3,4,5*-Trihydroxyhexanal. A crystalline split product of digitoxin and gitoxin.

diglyceride. A compound of the type $HO \cdot C_3H_5(OR)_2$. Cf. *glyceride.*

diglycerin. $C_6H_{14}O_5 = 166.12$. Colorless liquid, b.225, soluble in water.

diglycol- Prefix indicating 2 $-CH_2OH$ groups. **d.**

laurate. Odorless yellow oil, emulsible in water, soluble in hydrocarbons.

diglycolamic acid. $C_4H_7O_4N = 133.08$. Colorless prisms, m.150 (decomp.), soluble in water.

diglycolic acid. $(CH_2 \cdot COOH)_2O = 134.07$. Oxy-diethanoic acid*. Colorless prisms, m.148, soluble in water. d. anhydride. $O \cdot CH_2 \cdot CO \cdot O \cdot CO \cdot CH_2 =$ 116.0. Colorless crystals, m.97, soluble in alcohol. diglycolide. $O \cdot CH : C \cdot OH \cdot O \cdot C \cdot OH : CH = 116.0$.

Colorless crystals, m.86.

diglycoloimide. Diglycolamide anhydride.

digoxigenin. $C_{23}H_{34}O_5 = 390.3$. A hydrolysis product of digoxin, m.220.

digoxin. $C_{41}H_{64}O_{14} = 780.96$. An optically active glucoside, from digitalis. White powder, m.265 (decomp.), insoluble in water; a cardiotonic (U.S.P., B.P.). Hydrolyzes to 3 molecules of digitoxose and digoxigenin.

dihexyl. (1) Two hexyl radicals. (2) Dodecane*.

dihydracrylamic acid. Dilactamic acid.

dihydracrylic acid. $C_6H_{10}O_5 = 162.09$. Colorless crystals, decomp. by heat; soluble in water.

dihydranol. $C_6H_3(OH)_2 \cdot CH_2(CH_2)_5CH_3$. n-Heptyl-resorcinol. Used to treat intestinal putrefaction.

dihydrate. (1) A compound containing 2 OH groups. (2) A crystal containing 2 molecules of water of crystallization.

dihydric. Dibasic.

dihydride. A binary compound containing 2 H atoms, e.g., calcium hydride.

dihydro- Prefix indicating 2 additional H atoms in an organic compound. d. anthracene. $C_6H_4 \cdot CH_2 \cdot CH_2 \cdot C_6H_4 = 180.10$.

Diphenylene dimethylene. d. benzene. See benzene. d. bromide. An organic compound containing 2 molecules of hydrobromic acid, e.g,. morphine dihydrobromide. d. carveol. $C_{10}H_{18}O = 154.16$. 8(9)-Terpene-ol-2. Colorless liquid, b.225. d. carvone. $C_{10}H_{16}O = 152.16$. 8(9)-Terpene-ol-2. Colorless liquid, b.222. d. cholesterol. Formed from cholesterol in the body, and excreted in the gut. d. cymene. $C_{10}H_{16} = 136.12$. The terpadienes: limonene, phellandrene, terpinene, etc. d. lutidine. $C_7H_{11}N = 109.07$. A ptomaine from cod-liver oil. d. morphinone hydrochloride. $C_{17}H_{19}O_3N \cdot HCl = 321.81$. White crystals, soluble in water; an analgesic. d. naphthalene. Dialin. d. pentine. $C_5H_8 = 68.06$. 2,4- $MeCH:CH \cdot CH:CH_2$. Piperylene. 2,3- $MeCH:C:CHMe$. d. propene. $CH_2 \cdot CH_2 \cdot CH_2 = 42.1$. Cf. cyclopropane. d. quinazoline. See orexin, quinazoline. d. quinoline. $C_9H_9N = 131.08$. Colorless liquid, b.223. d. resorcinol. $C_8H_8O_2 = 112.07$. Colorless prisms, decomp. 105, soluble in water. d. rubicene. $C_{26}H_{14} = 326.1$. The octocyclic hydrocarbon

$$C_6H_3 > CH—CH < C_6H_3$$
$$C_6H_3 \qquad\qquad C_6H_3.$$

Colorless needles, m.296. Cf. difluorene, difluorenylene. d. streptomycin sulfate. $(C_{21}H_{41}O_{12}N_7)_2 \cdot 3H_2SO_4 = 1461.48$. White powder, slightly soluble in alcohol; an antibiotic.

dihydrol. A supposed polymer of water, $(H_2O)_2$, in equilibrium with the normal molecule. Cf. trihydrol, hydrone theory.

dihydroxy- Prefix indicating 2 OH groups. d. acetone. $(CH_2OH)_2CO = 90.1$. White solid, m.70; converted by alkali into fructose. d. acetic acid. Glyoxalic acid. d. anthraquinones. Dibasic phenols derived from anthraquinone: 1,2- Alizarin. 1,3- Xanthopurpurin. 1,4- Quinizarin. 1,5- Anthrarufin. 1,8- Chrysazin. 2,3- Hystazarin. 2,6- Anthraflavic acid. 2,7- Isoanthraflavic acid. b. benzene. 1,2- Catechol. 1,3- Resorcinol. 1,4- Quinol. d. benzoic acid. See benzoic acid. d. benzophenone. $HO \cdot C_6H_4 \cdot CO \cdot C_6H_4 \cdot OH = 214.08$. Isomers: 2,5- m.122; 2,2'- m.59, b.340; 2,3'- m.126; 3,4'- m.197; 4,4'- m.210. d. cholenic acid. $C_{24}H_{38}O_4 = 582.3$. An isomer of apocholic acid. Cf. sterols. Long needles, m.260. d. cinnamic acid. Caffeic acid. d. disulfonic acid. Chromatropic acid. d. fluorescein. Gallein. d. naphthalene. $C_{10}H_8O_2 = 160.11$. 1,4- alpha-. 1,5- ana-. 1,6- epi. Colorless prisms, m.134, soluble in alcohol. 1,7- kata-. Colorless needles, m.178, soluble in water. 1,8- peri. Colorless needles, m.140, slightly soluble in water. 2,3- beta-. Rhombic crystals, m.159, soluble in hot water. 2,6- amphi-. 2,7- pros-. Colorless needles, m.261, slightly soluble in water. d. palmitic acid. $C_{16}H_{32}O_4 = 288.0$. White needles, m.125; in cod-liver oil. d. phthalophenone. Phenolphthalein. d. propionic acid. Glyceric acid. d. stearic acid; $C_{18}H_{36}O_4 = 316.28$. Rhombic crystals, m.126.5, in castor oil; 10 isomers. d. succinic acid. Tartaric acid.

dihydroxyl. Dihydroxy. d. amine. $HO \cdot NH \cdot OH$. A hypothetical hydroxyhydroxylamine. d. nicotine. Pilocarpidine.

diimide. (1) The hypothetical compound $HN:NH$, known only as its organic derivatives. (2) A compound containing 2 $—C:NOH$ groups; as glyoxime.

diimines. Organic compounds containing 2 imine, $=NH$, radicals.

diimino- Prefix indicating 2 imino groups. d. hydrazine. N_4H_2. The hypothetical compound $HN:N \cdot N:NH$, known only as its derivatives. Cf. hydronitrogen.

diindogen. Indigotin.

diine. Suffix indicating 2 triple bonds. See diacetylenes.

diiod-, diiodo- Prefix indicating 2 I atoms in an organic compound. d. acetic acid. $C_2H_2O_2I_2 = 311.97$. Diiodo- acetic acid. Yellow crystals, m.110, slightly soluble in water. d. acetylene. $C_2I_2 = 277.7$. Small needles, insoluble in water. d. hydrine. Diiodo- isopropanol. d. tyrosine. $C_9H_9NO_3I_2 = 432.96$. White crystals, m.205, slightly soluble in water. An amino acid in gorgonin, spongin, and thyroglobulin.

diiodide. A compound containing 2 I atoms.

diiodoacetic acid. Diiodacetic acid.

diiodobenzene. $C_6H_4I_2 = 329.90$. ortho- m.23, soluble in water. meta- m.34, soluble in alcohol. para- m,129, soluble in alcohol.

diiodoeosin. See Rose Bengal.

diiodoform. $I_2C:CI_2 = 531.4$. Tetraiodoethylene, ethylene periodide. Yellow needles, insoluble in water; decomp. by light; an antiseptic.

diiodohydroxyquinoline. $C_9H_5ONI_2 = 397.00$.

Yellow crystals, insoluble in water; an amebicide (B.P.).

diisatogen. $C_{16}H_8O_4N_2 = 292.3$. The heterocyclic system

diisoamyl. (1) 2,7-Dimethyloctane. (2) Prefix indicating the presence of 2 isoamyl groups. **d. amine.** $C_{10}H_{23}N = 157.27$. Colorless liquid, d.0.788, b.190, slightly soluble in water. **d. ketone.** $C_{11}H_{22}O = 170.24$. Yellow liquid, b.226, insoluble in water, miscible with alcohol or ether.

diisobutyl. (1) 2,5-Dimethylhexane. (2) Prefix indicating 2 isobutyl groups. **d. amine.** $C_8H_{19}N = 129.24$. Colorless liquid, b.140, sparingly soluble in water. **d. ketone.** $Me_3 \cdot C \cdot CO \cdot CMe_3 = 142.23$. Valerone. Colorless liquid, b.181, insoluble in water.

diisonitrosoanethol peroxide. $C_9H_8O_2N_2 = 176.2$. Colorless crystals, m.97.

diisopropenyl. (1) $CH_2 :CMe \cdot CMe :CH_2 = 82.078$. 2,3-Dimethylbutadiene. Colorless liquid, b.69.6. Cf. *hexine, hexadiene.* (2) Prefix indicating 2 isopropenyl groups.

diisopropyl. (1) Prefix indicating 2 isopropyl radicals. (2) An isomer of hexane (2,3-dimethylbutane or dimethylisopropylmethane). **d. ketone.** $C_7H_{14}O = 114.12$. Colorless liquid, b.124, soluble in alcohol.

dika fat. The fat of *Irvingia gabonensis* (Simarubaceae), Sierra Leone.

diketo- Prefix indicating 2 $=CO$ groups. **d. hydrindene.** Indandione.

diketone. A compound containing 2 —CO radicals. **α-** or **1,2-** A compound containing the radical —CO·CO—. **β-** or **1,3-** A compound containing the radical —CO·CH₂·CO—. **γ-** or **1,4-** A compound containing the radical —CO·CH₂·CH₂·CO—.

diketopurine. Xanthine.

diketotriazolidine. Urazole.

diketotrimethylpurine. Caffeine.

dil. Abbreviation for dilute.

dilactamic acid. $MeCHOH \cdot COO \cdot CHMe \cdot CONH_2 = 161.2$. Colorless crystals, soluble in water.

dilactic acid. $C_6H_{10}O_5 = 162.1$. (1) Lactyl lactate, lactolactic acid. $MeCHOH \cdot COO \cdot CHMe \cdot COOH$. (2) Lactic anhydride, lactic acid anhydride. $MeCHOH \cdot CO \cdot O \cdot CO \cdot CHOHMe$.

dilantin. Diphenylhydantoin. **d. sodium.** $C_{15}H_{11}N_2O_2Na = 274.25$. Diphenylhydantoin sodium, an antiepileptic.

dilatancy. Inverse thixotropy. A form of thixotropy, q.v., in which a viscous suspension sets solid under the influence of pressure.

dilatation. Distention or expansion.

dilatometer. An instrument for measuring expansion (dilation) due either to a change in temperature or to chemical action.

diatometry. The measurement of small volume changes in liquids, due to physical or chemical actions.

dilaudide. $C_{17}H_{19}O_3 \cdot HCl$. Dihydromorphinone hydrochloride. White powder, soluble in water; a heroin substitute.

dilituric acid. 5-Nitrobarbituric acid.

dill. Anetum. The dried ripe fruit of *Peucedanum*

graveolens (Compositae); a spice and carminative. **d. oil.** The essential oil of d., d.0.895–0.915, soluble in alcohol. It contains phellandrene, terpinene, and carvone. **d. water.** A filtered solution of 20 ml of d. oil in 600 ml of 90% alcohol, to which is added 1,000 ml of water and 50 gm of powdered talc (B.P.).

diloxanide fuorate. $C_{14}H_{11}O_4NCl_2 = 328.21$. 4-(N-Methyldichloroacetamido)phenyl 2-fuorate. White crystals, m.115, slightly soluble in water; used to treat amebiasis (B.P.).

diluent. (1) An inert solid or liquid, used to increase the bulk of another substance. (2) An inert substance used to increase the bulk of a solution; not necessarily a solvent for solute. (3) A liquid added to lacquer to increase flow and evaporation.

dilution. (1) The process of diluting. (2) The state of being diluted or diffused; as, a solute in a solvent. **heat of-** The heat, in gram calories, liberated or absorbed on diluting infinitely one gram molecule of a substance with water.

d. law. Ostwald's law. **d. ratio.** A measure of the solvent power of a diluent (definition 2). The volume of diluent to produce incipient precipitation of a solute, divided by the total volume of solvent. **d. rule.** To mix or dilute a with b to give c, use the diagram;

and take x parts of a and y parts of b, where a, b, and c are expressed in the same unit.

dimazon. $C_{18}H_{19}O_4N_3 = 341.3$. Diacetylaminoazotoluene. A red dye, related to Scarlet R. Red crystals, m.75, insoluble in water; promotes growth of epithelial tissue.

dimefox. $(Me_2N)_2P:O \cdot F = 154.33$. Tetramethylphosphorodiamidic fluoride. A systemic insecticide.

Dimenformon. Trademark for estradiol monobenzoate.

dimenhydrin(ate). $C_{17}H_{21}ON \cdot C_7H_7O_2N_4Cl = 470.00$. 8-Chlorotheophylline diphenhydramine, containing 54% 5-diphenhydramine $(C_{17}H_{21}ON)$ and 46% 8-chlorotheophylline $(C_7H_7O_2N_4Cl)$. White, bitter crystals, m.104, soluble in water; an antihistamine (U.S.P., B.P.).

dimension. A magnitude in one direction. **four-** The concept of space and time; as, length, width, height, and duration. **three-** The concept of space.

dimensional equation. A mathematical expression showing dimensions in terms of fundamental units, q.v., thus: energy $= ML^2T^{-2}$, where M is mass, L length, and T time.

dimer. A condensation product or polymer of 2 molecules. Cf. *trimer, dimeric.*

dimercaprol. $C_3H_8OS_2 = 124.23$. BAL. Colorless liquid with mercaptan odor, $b_{15mm}122$, soluble in water; antidote for arsenical and mercury poisoning (U.S.P., B.P.).

dimercurammonium. The radical HgN—. **d. chloride.** $HgNCl = 250.1$. Yellow powder. **d. oxide.** $(HgN)_2O = 445.2$. White powder.

dimercuriammonium. Dimercurammonium.

dimercurous ammonium. The radical —HgNH₂.

dimeric. Able to form twofold polymers.

dimethacetic acid. Dimethylacetic acid.

dimethano- Prefix indicating 2 —CH_2— bridges in a ring.

dimethoxalic acid. Isobutyric acid.

dimethoxy- Prefix indicating 2 OMe radicals. **d. catechol.** Veratrol. **d. ethane.** $MeOCH_2 \cdot CH_2OMe$ = 90.08. Glycol dimethyl ether. Colorless liquid, b.84.5; a lacquer solvent. **d. phthalaldehydic acid.** Opianic acid.

dimethsterone. $C_{23}H_{32}O_2 \cdot H_2O$ = 358.28. White crystals, m.100, insoluble in water; a progestational steroid (B.P.).

dimethyl. (1) Ethane. (2) Prefix indicating 2 Me radicals. **d. acetal.** $(MeO)_2CH \cdot Me$ = 90.1. Ethylidene dimethyl ether. Colorless liquid, d_0°0.879, b.62.5, miscible with water; an anesthetic substituting chloroform. **d. acetic acid.** Isobutyric acid. **d. acetylene.** Crotonylene. **d. allylene.** 3-Methylbutine. **d. amine*.** $Me_2 \cdot NH$ = 45.11. Volatile liquid, b.7, soluble in water; a bait for boll weevils. **d. aminoazobenzene.** $C_{14}H_{15}N_3$ = 225.13. Butter yellow. Yellow scales, used as an indicator (acids—rose-red, alkalies—yellow) and oil coloring matter. **d. aminoazobenzenesulfonic acid.** Sulfobenzeneazodimethylaniline. **d. aminobenzal rhodanine.** $C_{12}H_{12}NOS_2$. A colorimetric reagent for copper, mercury, and silver. **d. aminobenzene.** Dimethylaniline. **d. aniline.** $Ph \cdot NMe_2$ = 121.14. Brown oil, b.193.3, soluble in water. Used in organic synthesis, as reagent for nitrates, and to manufacture methyl violet. **d. anilinesulfonic acid.** $C_8H_{11}O_3NS$ = 201.22. *ortho-* or *2-* Yellow masses, m.229, soluble in alcohol. *para-* or *4-* Brown scales, m.257, insoluble in water. **d. anthracene.** $C_{16}H_{14}$ = 206.12. *α-* or *1,4-* Colorless scales, m.225, insoluble in water. *β-* or *1,3-* Colorless leaflets, m.204, insoluble in water. *2,3-* m.246. *2,4-* m.71. *2,6-* m.231. **d. arsenic acid.** Cacodylic acid. **d. arsine.** Me_2AsH = 106.07. Colorless liquid, b.36, miscible with alcohol. **d. benzene.** Xylene. **d. benzoic acids.** $C_6H_3 \cdot Me_2 \cdot COOH$ = 150.13. Xylic acids. **d. beryllium.** $BeMe_2$ = 39.07. White needles, sublime 200, decomp. by water to methane. **d. cadmium.** $CdMe_2$ = 142.46. An oil, b.106. **d. carbinol.** Isopropyl alcohol. **d. carbonate.** Methyl carbonate. **d. cyclooctadiene.** See *cyclooctadiene.* **d. diamidotoluphenazine.** Neutral red. **d. ether.** Methyl ether. **d. ethylcarbinol.** *tert-*Iso*amyl alcohol.* **d. ethylene.** Butylene. **d. ethylmethane.** Isopentane. **d. diethyltin.** $Me_2 SnEt_2$ = 206.82. Colorless liquid, b.145, soluble in alcohol. **d. glyoxime.** $C_4H_8O_2N_2$ = 116.10. Diacetyldioxime. White needles, m.234, insoluble in water; a reagent for nickel or palladium. **d. hexane.** Octane. **d. hydantoin.** $C_5H_8N_2O$ = 128.1. White solid, m.178 (sublimes), very soluble in water; a plasticizer. **d. hydrazine.** See *hydrazine.* **d. hydrazone.** See *hydrazone.* **d. hydroxybenzenesulphonphthalein.** Xylenol blue. **d. ketone.** Acetone. **d. mercury.** $HgMe_2$ = 230.66. Colorless liquid, b.94. **d. nitrosamine.** $C_2H_6ON_2$ = 74.11. Nitrosodimethylin. Yellow oil, b.153, insoluble in water. **d. naphthalene.** See *naphthalene.* **d. octane.** $C_{10}H_{22}$ = 142.17. Isomeric liquid hydrocarbons of the methane series. *2,6-* b.159. *2,7-* b.160. *l-3,6-* b.162. *d-3,6-* b.160. **d. oxalate.** $C_4H_6O_4$ =

118.07. Colorless prisms, m.54. **d. oxamide.** $C_4H_8O_2N_2$ = 116.16. *asymmetric-* $NH_2 \cdot OC \cdot CO \cdot$. NMe_2. Oxalmethylin. Colorless leaflets, m.104, soluble in water. *symmetric-* $MeNH \cdot OC \cdot CO \cdot NHMe$. Colorless needles, m.209, slightly soluble in water. **d. oxyquinizine.** Antipyrine. **d. phenol.** Xylenol. **d. phenylenediamine.** $NH_2C_6H_4NMe_2$ = 136.2. Aminodimethylaniline. *ortho-* b.218. *meta-* b.270. *para-* Brown crystals, m.41, insoluble in water; a reagent for cellulose. **d. phenylenediamine hydrochloride.** $C_8H_{12}N_2 \cdot HCl$ = 172.6. *para-* Hygroscopic crystals, soluble in water. **d. phenylenediamine sulfate.** $C_8H_{12}N_2 \cdot H_2SO_4$ = 234.29. *para-* Brown crystals, soluble in water. **d. phosphine.** Me_2PH = 62.07. Colorless liquid, b.25, insoluble in water. **d. phosphinic acid.** $(CH_3)_2PO \cdot OH$ = 94.07. Colorless crystals, m.76, soluble in water. **d. phosphoric acid.** $(MeO)_2PO \cdot (OH)$ = 126.07. **d. phthalate.** $C_{10}H_{10}O_4$ = 194.19. $o-C_6H_4(COOMe)_2$. Colorless, aromatic oil, d.1.190, b.280, insoluble in water; used to compound calamine lotion (U.S.P., B.P.), and as an insect repellent. **d. piperazintartrate.** Lycetol. **d. propylcarbinol.** Hexyl alcohol (4). **d. propylmethane.** 2-Methylpentane. **d. pyrazine.** Ketine. **d. pyrazole.** $C_5H_8N_2$ = 96.1. A precipitant for cobalt salts. **d. pyridine.** Lutidine. **d. pyrrole.** C_6H_9N = 95.07. Colorless oil, b.165, slightly soluble in water. **d. silicane.** SiH_2Me_2 = 60.12. Colorless gas, b.—20.1. **d. sulfate.** $(CH_3O)_2SO_2$ = 126.12. Colorless liquid, b.188, soluble in water; a reagent for coal-tar oils. **d. sulfine.** The radical C_2H_6S—. **d. sulfoxide.** $Me_2 \cdot S:O:SMe_2$ = 110.41. An analgesic and fungicide prepared from cellulose lignin. **d. thetine.** $C_3H_8O_2S$ = 120.07. Colorless crystals, decomp. by heat, soluble in water. **d. thiophen.** C_6H_8S = 112.12. *2,3-* $HC \cdot S \cdot CMe \cdot CMe \cdot CH$. Colorless liquid, b.136.

2,4- $HC \cdot C \cdot CMe \cdot CH \cdot CMe$. Colorless liquid, b.138.

2,5- $MeC \cdot S \cdot C \cdot Me : CH \cdot CH$. Colorless liquid, b.135, insoluble in water. **d. urea.** See *urea.* **d. yellow.** Dimethylaminoazobenzene. **d. xanthine.** Theobromine.

dimethylene. (1) Ethylene. (2) Prefix indicating 2 methylene radicals. **d. diamine.** Ethylenediamine. **d. imine.** $CH_2 \cdot NH \cdot CH_2$ = 43.1. Ethyleneimine, vinylimine. Colorless liquid b.55, insoluble in water. **d. oxide.** Ethylene oxide. **d. sulfide.** Ethylene sulfide. **d. trisulfide.** Ethylene sulfide.

dimethyline. The radical —NMe_2. **nitroso-** Nitrosodimethylamine.

dimetric. Tetragonal. Cf. *crystal systems.*

dimidium bromide. Phenanthridium 1553.

dimine. Cyclohexylethylamine dithiocarbamate, m.93, decomp. 100; a catalyst in rubber vulcanization.

diminution. (1) Proposed term for reduction. Cf. *augmentation.* (2) A lessening or decrease.

dimorphic. Occurring in 2 crystalline forms having different melting points.

dimorphism. The property of being dimorphic. Cf. *polymorphism.*

dimsylsodium. Abbreviation for the sodium derivative of dimethyl sulfoxide. It forms the ion

$CH_3·SO·CH_2Na^+$; used in analytical chemistry for the titration of very weak acids.

dinaphthacridine. $C_{14}H_8·N·C_{14}H_8·CH = 379.2$. Six isomers. Cf. *dibenzacridine.*

dinaphthanthracene. Dibenzanthracene.

dinaphthazine. Dibenzophenazine.

dinaphtho- Prefix indicating 2 $C_{10}H_6$= groups. Cf. *naphthalene.*

dinaphthofluorene. Dibenzofluorene.

dinaphthol. $HO·C_{10}H_6·C_{10}H_6OH = 286.22$. **alpha-** Colorless rhombic crystals, m.300, insoluble in water. **beta-** White needles, m.218, insoluble in water.

dinaphthoxanthene. $C_{21}H_{14}O = 282.1$. Colorless crystals, m.199.

dinaphthyl. (1) Binaphthyl. (2) Prefix indicating 2 naphthyl radicals, $C_{10}H_7$—. **d. mercury.** Hg-$(C_{10}H_7)_2 = 329.68$. Rhombic crystals, m.243, insoluble in water. **d. methane.** $C_{10}H_7·CH_2·C_{10}H_7 = 268.2$. *alpha-* Colorless prisms, m.109, soluble in hot alcohol. *beta-* Small needles, m.92, soluble in alcohol. **d. tin.** $Sn(C_{10}H_7)_2 = 372.81$. White powder, m.200.

dinaphthylene- Prefix indicating 2 naphthylene groups, $C_{10}H_6$=. **d. methane.** See *picene* and *fluorene.* **d. thiophen.** $C_{10}H_6·S·C_{10}H_6 = 284.1$ Colorless crystals, m.147.

dindevan. Phenylindanedione.

dindyl. Diindyl.

dineric. Having 2 liquid layers (phases). Cf. *dimer.*

dinex. DNOCHP. Common name for the insecticide 2,4-dinitro-6-cyclohexylphenol.

Dingler, Emil Maximilian. 1806–1874. German technical chemist and editor. **D., Johann Gottfried.** 1778–1855. German apothecary and founder of *Polytechnischen Journal* (1820).

dinicotinic acid. $C_7H_5O_4N = 167.1$. **2,4-** or **3,5-** pyridinedicarboxylic acid*. Colorless crystals, m.314.

dinitramidobenzoic acid. **ortho-** Chrysalicic acid **para-** Chrysanisic acid.

dinitraniline. Dinitroaniline.

dinitril. Zetek.

dinitro- Prefix indicating 2 nitro groups. **d. amidobenzene.** Dinitraniline. **d. aniline.** Dinitroaniline. **d. anthraquinone.** $C_{14}H_6O_6N_2 = 298.07$. *alpha-* Yellow crystals, m.356, slightly soluble in water. *beta-* Yellow needles, m.280, sparingly soluble in water. **d. benzaldehyde.** $C_7H_4O_5N_2 = 196.08$. *2,4-* Yellow prisms, m.72, slightly soluble in water. **d. benzene.** See *benzene.* **d. benzoic acid.** See *benzoic acid.* **d. chlorobenzene.** $C_6H_3-O_4N_2Cl = 202.55$. *1,2,3-* Colorless needles, m.38.8, soluble in alcohol. *1,2,4-* Colorless, monoclinics, m.37, soluble in alcohol. *1,3,2-* Colorless crystals, m.42, slightly soluble in alcohol. *1,3,4-* Colorless crystals, m.50, soluble in alcohol. *1,3,5-* Colorless needles, m.59, soluble in alcohol; a reagent for mercaptans. **d. cresol.** $C_7H_6O_5N_2 = 198.2$. Saffron substitute. An orange, poisonous coal-tar dye, m.104. **d. glycerin, d. glycerol.** $C_3H_6(NO_2)_2 = 182.06$. Glycerol-1,3-dinitrate. An oil, d.1.47, b_{15mm}148; a high explosive. **2-methyl-*n*-propyl-** Dinosel. **d. naphthalene.** $C_{10}H_6O_4N_2 = 218.2$. Yellow crystals, m.153, insoluble in water. *1,2-* m. 103. *1,3-* m.145. *1,4-* m.129. *1,5-* m.216. *1,6-* m.162.

1,7- m.156. *1,8-* m.170. **d. naphthol.** $C_{10}H_6O_5N_2 = 234.06$. Intermediates in organic synthesis: *2,4-* α- m.138. *4,5-α-* decomp. 230. *4,8-α-* decomp. 235. *1,6-β-* m.195. *1,8-β-* m.198. **d. orthocresol.** DNC. **d. phenamic acid.** Picramic acid. **d. phenol.** $C_6H_4O_5N_2 = 184.14$. Hydroxydinitrobenzene. *2,3-* Yellow needles, m.144, slightly soluble in alcohol; a pH indicator. *2,4-* Yellow scales, m.114, slightly soluble in water. *2,6-* Yellow needles, m.62, slightly soluble in water. *3,4-* Colorless needles, m.134, *3,5-* Colorless leaflets, m.122. *2,5-* or *3,6-* Colorless leaflets, m.104. **d. phenylhydrazine.** $(NO_2)_2C_6H_3NH·NH_2 = 198.08$. Red needles, m.197 (explode); a reagent for aldehydes and malic acid. **d. resorcinol.** $C_6H_4O_6N_2 = 200.10$. *2,4,1,3-* Yellow scales, m.142, soluble in hot water. *crude-* Solid green, dark green, chlorin, diquinoyldioxime. Brown mass, sparingly soluble in water; a green pigment in calico printing, and in dyeing iron mordanted textiles. **d. salicylic acid.** $C_6H_2-(OH)(NO_2)_2COOH$. A reagent for glucose. **d. toluene.** $C_7H_6O_4N_2 = 182.17$. *2,4-* Colorless needles, m.71, slightly soluble in water. *2,3-* m.63. *2,5-* Colorless needles, m.48, soluble in alcohol. *2,6-* Colorless needles, m.66, soluble in alcohol. *3,4-* Colorless needles, m.59, insoluble in water. *3,5-* Colorless needles, m.92, sparingly soluble in water. **d. xylene.** $C_8H_8O_4N_2 = 196.18$. *2,4,1,3-* Colorless prisms, m.93, soluble in hot alcohol. *2,3,1,4-* Colorless needles, m.124, sparingly soluble in alcohol. *2,5,1,4-* Colorless hexagons, m.93, soluble in alcohol.

dinitroaniline. $C_6H_3NH_2(NO_2)_2 = 183.19$. *2,3-* m.127. *2,4-* Yellow, monoclinics, m.181, insoluble in water. *2,5-* m.137. *2,6-* Yellow needles, m.138, soluble in alcohol. *3,4-* m.154. *3,5-* m.159. **d. fluosilicate.** $(C_6H_4NH_2NO_2)_2SiF_6 = 420.2$. Rhombic crystals, m.200.

dinitrogen tetroxide. See *nitrogen* tetroxide.

dinitroso-. Prefix indicating 2 —NO groups; as, **d. resorcinol**, used as reagent for iron.

dinol. Diazodinitrophenol.

dinonylphthalate. $C_6N_4(COOC_9H_{19})_2 = 418.38$. Bis-(3,5,5-trimethylhexyl) phthalate. Pale viscous liquid, d.0.972; a plasticizer for cellulose and polymer plastics, especially for water resistance.

dinoseb. $C_{10}H_{12}O_5N_2 = 240.12$. DNPB, DNSPB, DNOSPB. Common name (U.K. usage) for 2,4-dinitro-6-*sec*-butylphenol, m.41; a weedicide.

dinoxam. DNAP, DNSAP, DNOSAP. Common name for 2,4-dinitro-6-*sec*-amylophenol; an insecticide.

dinucleotide. A compound formed from 2 purine bases: as, adenine-uracil.

dioctyl. (1) Hexadecane. (2) Prefix indicating 2 octyl radicals. **d. acetic acid.** Isostearic acid. **d. sodium sulfosuccinate.** $C_{20}H_{37}O_7SNa = 444.57$. White wax, soluble in water. A wetting agent; used in compounding calamine lotion (U.S.P.).

diodone. Diodrast, perabrodil, iodopyracet (U.S. usage). 3,5-diiodo-4-pyridone-*N*-acetic acid. An X-ray contrast medium (B.P.).

diodoquin. $C_9H_5ONI_2 = 397.0$. Diiodohydroxyquinoline (U.S.P.). Yellow crystals, insoluble in water; an amebecide.

diodrast. Diodone.

dioform. $CHCl=CHCl = 96.93$. Acetylene

dichloride. Colorless liquid of chloroform-like odor, d.1.29, b.55. It is a mixture of *cis*-, d.1.265, b.48, and *trans*-, d.1.291, b.60.

-dioic. Suffix indicating 2 —COOH groups.

diol. Glycol. An organic compound with 2 OH groups. Cf. *glycols*.

diolefin(e). Diene series. An unsaturated aliphatic hydrocarbon with the general formula C_nH_{n-2} and 2 double bonds, e.g., allene (propadiene), C_3H_4.

diolein. $C_{37}H_{72}O_5 = 596.5$. Glycerol dioleate. The dioleic ester of glycerol, formed from triolein by action of lipase.

Diolen. Trade name for a polyester synthetic fiber.

diondiacids. Organic acids containing 2 keto and 2 carboxyl groups, e.g., hexan-3,4-diondiacid, $HOOC·CH_2·CO·COCH_2·COOH$ (ketipic acid).

-dione. Suffix indicating 2 keto groups, $>CO$; as, butadione.

dionine. $C_{19}H_{23}O_3N·HCl = 349.66$. Ethylmorphine hydrochloride. Colorless crystals, soluble in water; a substitute for morphine and codeine. Cf. *codethyline*.

diophane hydrochloride. A local anesthetic, more powerful than procaine, but damaging tissue.

diopside. $CaMgSi_2O_6$. A monoclinic, yellow, rock-forming pyroxene, d.3.2, hardness 5–6. Cf. *baikalite*.

dioptase. CuH_2SiO_4. A greenish, hexagonal hydrous copper silicate, d.3.3, hardness 5.

diopter. The unit of "power" of a lens. The reciprocal of the focal length in meters.

dioptra. An optical device to measure heights and angles.

dioptrics. The study of light refraction.

diorite. An igneous rock containing quartz, plagioclase, and small amounts of femic minerals; as, malchite.

diorsellinic acid. Lecanoric acid.

dioscin. $C_{24}H_{38}O_9·3H_2O = 524.4$. A saponin from the roots of *Dioscorea japonica* (Dioscoraceae). White, silky needles, m.248, insoluble in water.

dioscorea. Yam root. Tropical shrubs with edible tubers (yams). That of *Dioscorea villosa* (wild yam) is an antispasmodic and diaphoretic. **d. sapotoxin.** $C_{23}H_{28}O_{10} = 464.3$. A toxic principle from *Dioscorea* species.

Dioscorides. Greek philosopher of Anazarba, Asia Minor, who made mercury from cinnabar (A.D. 50).

dioscorine. $C_{13}H_{19}O_2N = 221.2$. An alkaloid from the rhizome of *Dioscorea hirsuto* (Dioscoreaceae), Java.

dioscoroid. The combined principles from the root of *Dioscorea villosa*, wild yam. The fluid extract is an antispasmodic.

diose. A monosaccharide containing 2 C atoms. Cf. *biose, carbohydrates*.

diosmeleoptene. $C_{10}H_{18}O = 154.2$. A terpene of peppermint-like odor; an isomer of borneol from the essential oil *Diosma* (or *Barosma*) *betulina*. Cf. *buchu*.

diosphenol. $C_{10}H_{16}O_2 = 168$. Buchu camphor, 2-Hydroxy-Δ^1-3-*p*-methenone. Crystals, from the essential oil of *Diosma betulina*.

Diothane. $C_{22}H_{27}O_4N_3 = 397.3$. Trademark for piperidinopropanediol diphenylurethane. Colorless needles, m.195–200, soluble in hot water; a local anesthetic.

dioxadiene. *p*-Dioxin.

dioxane. $O·(CH_2)_2·O·(CH_2)_2$. Diethylene dioxide, dihydro-*p*-dioxin. Colorless liquid, d.1.038, m.11, b.101, soluble in water. A solvent used in the silk and varnish industries and as a dehydrant in histology. Cf. *dithiane*.

dioxazole. $C_2H_3O_2N = 73.1$. Heterocyclic compounds with 1 N and 2 O atoms; as, 1,2,3- CH:CH·-NH·O·O. Cf. *dithiazole*.

dioxdiazine. $C_2H_2O_2N_2 = 86.1$. Heterocyclic hydrocarbons with 2 N and 2 O atoms in the hexatomic ring. Isomers: 1,2,3,4-; 1,2,3,5-; 1,2,3,6-; 1,2,4,5-; 1,3,2,4-; 1,3,2,5-; 1,3,4,5-; 1,3,4,6-; 1,4,2,3-; 1,4,2,5-; 1,4,2,6-. First 2 numbers indicate positions of O atoms; last 2 of N atoms.

dioxdiazole. $CH_2O_2N_2 = 74.1$. Heterocyclic hydrocarbons with 2 N and 2 O atoms in the pentatomic ring. Isomers: 1,2,3,4-; 1,2,3,5-; 1,3,2,4-; 1,3,4,5-. The O atoms occupy the positions indicated by the first 2 numbers. Cf. *dithiodiazole*.

dioxide. A compound containing 2 O atoms: (1) normal or true dioxides in which the valency of oxygen is 2; as, manganese d., O:Mn:O; (2) abnormal dioxides or peroxides, such as barium d. (peroxide), Ba⟨^O_O⟩|. The true dioxides, only, give oxygen with concentrated acids, and chlorine with concentrated hydrochloric acid. Peroxides, only, give hydrogen peroxide.

dioxime. The radical —HC:NOH, occurring in a syn- and anti-form.

dioximes. Compounds containing 2 dioxime radicals. **alpha-** Glyoximes. **beta-** Glyoxime peroxides. **gamma-** Compounds in which the 2 oxime radicals are separated by the ethylene radical; e.g., succinaldehyde dioxime, HON:CHCH_2·CH_2·CH:NOH.

dioxindole. $C_6H_4·NH·CO·CHOH = 149.08$. o-Aminomandelic acid lactame. Colorless prisms, m.180, decomp. 195, soluble in water.

dioxine. $C_{10}H_7O_2N = 173.1$. β-Oxynaphthoquinoxime. A yellow dye.

dioxins. $C_4H_6O_2 = 86.1$ and $C_4H_4O_2 = 84.1$. Heterocyclic hydrocarbons, e.g., *ortho*- or *1,2*-O·O·CH:CH·CH:CH. **dihydro-*p*-** Dioxan.

Dioxogen. A brand of hydrogen peroxide.

dioxolan(e)s. $C_3H_6O_2 = 74.04$. Heterocyclic compounds with 3 C and 2 O atoms.

dioxtriazine. $CHO_2N_3 = 87.1$. Aromatic hydrocarbons with 3 N and 2 O atoms in the hexatomic ring. Isomers: 1,2,3,4,5-; 1,2,3,4,6-; 1,3,4,5,6-; 1,3,2,4,5-; 1,3,2,4,6-; 1,4,2,3,5-;. The N atoms occupy the last 3 positions.

dioxy- (1) Prefix indicating 2 additional O atoms in an organic compound. (2) Incorrectly used for dihydroxy. **d. anthracene.** See *chrysazol, rufol*. **d. anthranol.** Dithranol. **d. benzene.** See *catechol, resorcinol, quinol*. **d. ethylene.** Dioxan. **d. phthalaldehydic acid.** Noropianic acid. **d. quinoline.** See *quinoline*. **d. tetrazotic acid.** $CH_2O_2N_4$. A structural arrangement, known only in combination. **d. xanthone.** 1,7- Euxanthone.

dipalmitate. A compound containing 2 palmitic acid radicals.

dipalmitin. $C_{33}H_{68}O_5 = 568.5$. Glycerol dipalmitate. A dipalmitic acid ester of glycerin formed from triplamitin by the action of lipase.

diparalene. Chlorcyclizine hydrochloride.

dipentene. Terpene. **d. glycol.** Terpine.

dipeptide. A peptide of the type, $NH_2RCO\cdot NH\cdot R\cdot COOH$; as anserine.

diphenate. (1) A salt of diphenic acid. (2) Diphenylate.

diphenazyl. Dibenzoylethane.

diphenhydramine. See *dimenhydrinate*. **d. hydrochloride.** $C_{17}H_{21}ON\cdot HCl = 291.83$. White, crystalline powder, m.168, soluble in water; an antihistaminic (U.S.P., B.P.).

diphenic acid. $(C_6H_4\cdot COOH)_2$. Colorless crystals, m.229, soluble in hot water. **d. anhydride.** $C_{14}H_8O_3 = 224.09$. Colorless crystals, m.213.

diphenide. $C_{14}H_{10}O_2 = 210.1$.

diphenimide. $C_{14}H_9O_2N = 223.1$. Colorless crystals, m.219.

diphenol. A compound containing 2 phenolic OH— groups.

diphenoquinone. $O:C_6H_4:C_6H_4:O = 184.1$. Bibenzenone.

diphenydranimechlorotheophyllinate. Dramamine.

diphenyl. (1) Biphenyl. (2) Prefix indicating 2 phenyl radicals. **d. acetic acid.** $C_{14}H_{12}O_2 = 212.17$. Colorless needles, m.148, soluble in hot water. **d. acetonitrile.** $C_{14}H_{11}N = 193.2$. Colorless crystals, m.72. **d. acetylene.** Tolane. **d. amine.** See *diphenylamine**. **d. aniline.** Triphenylamine. **d. anthrone.**

$$Ph\cdot C_6H_3\cdot CO\cdot C_6H_3\cdot Ph\cdot CH_2 = 346.2.$$

Colorless crystals, m.192. **d. benzene.** See *benzene*. **d. benzidine.** $C_{24}H_{20}N_2 = 336.14$. A sensitive reagent for nitrates, zinc, etc. **d. benzylsultam.** $C_{19}H_{15}O_2NS = 321.2$. Colorless crystals, m.210. **d. carbazide.** $CO(NH\cdot NHPh)_2 = 214.08$. Phenylhydrazine urea. White powder, m.170. An indicator (alkalies—pink, acids—colorless), and reagent for cadmium (blue-violet), chromium (red), and mercury (blue). **d. carbinol.** Benzohydrol. **d. chlorarsine.** Blue cross. **d. cyanarsine.** $Ph_2AsCN = 255.0$. D.C. Colorless prisms, m.32, with odor of bitter almonds. A nose-irritant poison gas. **d. diacetylene.** $Ph\cdot C\vdots C\cdot C\vdots C\cdot Ph = 202.08$. Diacetenylbenzene. Colorless needles, m.88, soluble in alcohol. **d. dicarboxylic acid.** Diphenamic acid. **d. diethylene.** $Ph\cdot CH:CH\cdot CH:CH\cdot Ph = 206.1$. Colorless crystals, m.148. **d. diketone.** Compounds containing 2 phenyl and 2 keto groups. **d. dimethylethane.** $Ph\cdot CHMe\cdot CHMe\cdot Ph = 210.2$. Colorless crystals, m.123. **d. endoanilodihydrotriazole.** Nitron. **d. ethane.** Dibenzyl. **d. ether.** Phenyl ether. **d. ethylene.** Stilbene. **d. guanidine.** $(PhNH)_2C:NH = 211.2$. Melaniline. White needles, m.147, slightly soluble in water; a standard in acidimetry. **d. hydantoin sodium.** $C_{15}H_{11}O_2N_2Na = 274.26$. Phenyltoin sodium. White powder, soluble in water; an anticonvulsant. **d. hydrazine.** $PhNH\cdot NHPh = 184.24$. Yellow triclinics, m.34.5, slightly soluble in water; a reagent for aldehydes and ketones. **d. hydrazone.** Osazone. **d. imide.** Carbazole. **d. ketone.** Benzophenone. **d. methane.** $Ph\cdot CH_2\cdot Ph = 168.17$. Methylene-diphenyl, ditan, benzylbenzene. Colorless needles,

m.26.5, insoluble in water; used in organic synthesis. **d. nitrogen.** $C_{12}H_{10}N = 182.09$. The free radical Ph_2N. **4,5-d. octan-2,7-dione.** $MeCO\cdot CH_2\cdot CHPh\cdot CHPh\cdot CH_2\cdot COMe = 294.2$. Colorless crystals, m.161. **d. oxide.** Phenyl ether. **d. pentadienone.** Styryl ketone. **d. phosphine.** Ph_2PH. **d. sulfide.** Phenylsulfide. **d. tetraketone.** $Ph\cdot CO\cdot CO\cdot CO\cdot CO\cdot Ph = 266.1$. Colorless crystals, m.87. **d. tetraketoxime.** $C_{16}H_{11}O_4N = 295.2$. Colorless crystals, m.176. **d. thiocarbazone.** Dithizone. A reagent for lead; produces a compound soluble in certain organic solvents enabling the lead to be separated. **d. thiourea.** Sulfocarbanilide. **d. tin.** $SnPh_2 = 272.78$. Yellow, amorphous powder, m.226, insoluble in water. **d. triketone.** $PhCO\cdot CO\cdot COPh = 238.1$. Dibenzoyl ketone. Colorless crystals, m.70. **d. urea.** Carbanilide.

diphenylamine. $Ph_2NH = 169.19$. Phenylaniline. Colorless leaflets, m.54, sparingly soluble in water. A reagent for nitrates in water, milk, etc., and an indicator in iron dichromate titrations. **3-hydroxy-** $C_{12}H_{11}ON = 185.10$. *m*-Phenylaminophenol. Colorless crystals, m.82. **4-hydroxy-** $C_{12}H_{11}ON = 185.10$. *p*-Phenylaminophenol. Colorless crystals, m.70. **seleno-** Phenoselenazine. **thio-** Phenothiazine. **d. blue.** Diphenylbenzidine. An oxidation product of d.; an oxidation-reduction indicator. **d. chlorarsine.** $NH\cdot(C_6H_4)_2\cdot AsCl = 277.5$. Adamsite, D.M. Yellow crystals m.195, insoluble in water. The vapors are a nose irritant.

diphenylate. A compound containing 2 phenoxy groups, $PhO—$.

diphenylene. (1) The radical $(C_6H_4)_2=$. (2) A compound with $2\ C_6H_4<$ radicals. **d. acetic acid.** Fluorenecarboxylic acid. **d. dimethylene.** Dihydroanthracene. **d. dioxide.** Dibenzodioxin. **d. diphenylethylene.** $C_{26}H_{18} = 330.2$. Yellow crystals, m.229. Cf. *difluorene*. **d. ether.** Benzofuran. **d. glycolic acid.**

$$\begin{array}{c} HO\cdot C(COOH) \\ \diagup \qquad \diagdown \\ C_6H_4\text{———}C_6H_4 \end{array} = 226.1.$$

Mesoöxyfluorenecarboxylic acid. Colorless crystals, m.162. **d. imide.** Carbazole. **d. ketone.** Fluorenone. **d. methane.** Fluorene. **d. oxide.** Dibenzofurane. *methylene-* Xanthene. **d. oxycarbinol.** Xanthydrol. **d. phenylmethane.** $(C_6H_4)_2\cdot CHPh = 242.1$. Colorless crystals, m.146. **d. sulfide.** Dibenzothiophen. *methylene-* Thioxanthene.

diphenyleneimide. Carbazole.

diphenyl. Xenyl. The radical $—C_6H_4Ph$.

diphosgene. $Cl\cdot COOCCl_3 = 198.00$. A lung irritant, d.166, m.-57, b. 128, used in World War I.

diphosphate. (1) A compound containing 2 phosphoric acid radicals, $\equiv PO_4$. (2) A compound containing the radical $=HPO_4$.

diphosphenyl. $Ph\cdot P:P\cdot Ph = 216.2$. Yellow crystals.

diphosphoglyceric acid. $[(HO)_2PO\cdot O]_2C_2H_3\cdot COOH = 266.0$. m.174. Occurs in blood.

diphosphoric acid. Pyrophosphoric acid. **anhydrooxymethylene-** $C_2H_8O_9P_2 = 238.09$. A constituent of green plants (see *phytin*); 26% phosphorus.

diphthalyl. $C_{16}H_8O_4 = 264.1$. A heterocyclic ketone. Colorless crystals, m.234.

dipicolinic acid. $C_7H_5O_4N = 167.1$. 1,5- or 2,6-Pyridinedicarboxylic acid. Colorless needles, m.225, slightly soluble in water.

dipicrylamine. Hexanitrodiphenylamine.

dipipanone hydrochloride. $C_{24}H_{31}ON \cdot HCl \cdot H_2O = 404.03$. 4,4-Diphenyl-6-piperidinoheptan-3-one. White, bitter crystals, m.125, soluble in water; a narcotic analgesic (B.P.).

dipiperidyls. Compounds formed by reduction of pyridine or dipyridyl. Soluble in water, giving strongly alkaline solutions which absorb carbon dioxide readily and regenerate it if heated.

diplococcin. An antibiotic from certain strains of milk streptococci; used to treat bovine mastitis.

diplogen. Deuterium.

diploid. Describing cells having a normal duplicate number of chromosomes. d. number. The 46 chromosomes normally present in the nuclei of human cells, established at fertilization by the union of sperm and ovum, each of which carries the haploid number of 23 chromosomes.

diplomethane. Methane d.

diplon. Deuteron.

diplosal. $HO \cdot C_6H_4COOC_6H_4COOH = 258.08$. Salicylosalicylic acid. Colorless crystals, m.148; used in medicine.

dipole. (1) A coordinated valence link between 2 originally neutral atoms, whereby one loses, and the other gains a share of 2 electrons. Cf. *covalence*. (2) The electrical symmetry of a charge of positive electricity very close to an equal negative charge; measured by the d. moment. d. moment. A molecular constant, μ, indicating the distribution of electrical charges in a neutral molecule. It is zero if they are symmetrically distributed. Cf. *Debye equation, association*.

Dippel, Johann Konrad. 1673–1734. German alchemist. D.'s oil. The distillation product of bones and other animal matter, chiefly containing pyridine and bases. Formerly used to denature alcohol.

dipping refractometer. See *refractometer*.

dipropargyl. (1) Bipropargyl. (2) Prefix indicating 2 propargyl radicals.

dipropyl- Prefix indicating 2 propyl radicals. d. amine. $(MeCH_2CH_2)_2NH = 101.19$. Colorless liquid, b.110, soluble in water. d. beryllium. $Be(C_3H_7)_2 = 95.1$. Colorless liquid, b.245. d. cadmium. $Cd(C_3H_7)_2 = 198.52$. Colorless liquid, $b_{21mm}84$. d. carbinol. $(MeCH_2CH_2)_2CHOH = 116.2$. Heptane-4-ol, 3-propylbutanol. Colorless liquid, b.154, soluble in alcohol. d. ether. Propyl ether. d. ketone. Butyrone. d. mercury. $Hg(C_3H_7)_2 = 286.73$. Colorless liquid, b.190, insoluble in water. d. tin. $Sn(C_3H_7)_4 = 204.8$. Colorless liquid. d. tin dibromide. $Sn(C_3H_7)_2Br_2 = 364.64$. Yellow crystals, m.54. d. tin dichloride. $(C_3H_7)_2SnCl_2 = 275.72$. White crystals, m.81.

diprotocatechuic acid. $C_{14}H_{10}O_7 = 290.08$. Needles, m.237, soluble in alcohol; occurs in tannins. Cf. *diresorcylic acid*.

dipsomania. Acute craving for alcohol.

dipyrazolone. A compound containing 2 pyrazolone groups.

dipyridine. $C_{10}H_{10}N_2 = 158.22$. Nicotyrine. Colorless needles, m.108, soluble in water.

dipyridyl. $C_5NH_4 - C_5NH_4 = 156.21$. Bipyridine. See Table.

	m.	b.	Water solubility
α–α	70	272	Slight
α–β	Liquid	288	Insoluble
β–β	68	291	Very soluble
γ–γ	114	305	Hot only
β–γ	61	297	Very soluble
α–γ	Liquid	281	Slight

diquinidine. Diconchinine. An alkaloid from cinchona.

diquinoline. $C_{18}H_{14}N_2 = 258.29$. Yellow needles, m.114, insoluble in water. alpha- $C_{18}H_{12}N_2 = 256.27$. Monoclinic scales, m.175, insoluble in water. beta- Monoclinic leaflets, m.191, insoluble in water.

diquinolyl, 2,2'-

$= 256.31$.

Brown crystals, m.94; reagent for cuprous ions (purple complex soluble in many solvents; sensitivity 0.2 ppm).

direct dyes. Substantive dyes.

direct-vision spectroscope. A spectroscope with prisms arranged so that the emergent rays follow the direction of the incident rays.

diresorcinol. $C_{12}H_{10}O_4 \cdot 2H_2O = 254.17$. White crystals, m.310, soluble in hot water.

diresorcylic acid. $(HO)_2 \cdot C_6H_3 \cdot COO \cdot C_6H_3(OH)COOH = 290.08$. An isomer of digentisic acid. Microneedles, decomp. 215, soluble in hot water; occurs in tannins.

disaccharides. Carbohydrates yielding 2 simple sugars (monosaccharides) on hydrolysis. See *carbohydrates*.

disagglomeration. The chemical transformation of compact masses into a fine powder.

disalicylic acid. (1) Salicylic anhydride. (2) Diplosal. acetylmethylene- Urasol.

disassimilation. Oxidation of assimilated material, which liberates energy.

disassociation. The splitting of a molecule into simpler constituents. electrical- The splitting of molecules into ions; *e.g.*, ionization. photo- The disarrangement of molecules under the influence of light; e.g., with silver salts. thermal- Commonly, dissociation. D. by the action of heat; often reversed by lowering the temperature. Cf. *dissociation*.

disazo compound. A compound containing 2 azo groups, $R \cdot N:N \cdot R \cdot N:N \cdot R$, including many dyes. Cf. *diazo compounds*.

disc. Disk.

discharge. (1) The sudden escape or liberation of stored or accumulated energy; e.g., electricity (spark discharge), or chemical energy (explosion). (2) Any waste liquid from a manufacturing plant. (3) The output of a pump. disruptive- A crackling d. of electric energy. silent- A gradual loss of electric energy due to the conductivity of air. Cf. *saturation current*.

Dische reaction. The development of a blue color when a substance is heated with diphenylamine under standard conditions. A stain reaction for nuclear substances in cells, due to the presence of desoxyribose. Cf. *Feulgen reaction.*

Discol. Trade name for an internal-combustion fuel: alcohol 50, benzol 25, hydrocarbons 25%.

discrasite. Dyscrasite.

discutient. A drug which dissipates morbid matter.

diselenide. A compound of the type R·Se·Se·R.

disgregation. Dispersion. Cf. *aggregation.*

dish. A shallow or flat glass or metal vessel. **crystallizing-** A shallow glass d. used for evaporation and crystallization. **culture-** A shallow flat-bottom d. of heavy glass; used to grow bacteria cultures (petri d.). **filtering-** A d.-shaped cone of porous material. **incineration-** q.v. **moisture-** A d. with a ground glass stopper.

disilane. See *silanes.* **hexafluoro-** $Si_2F_6 = 170.1$. A gas, m. -18.7.

disilicic acid. Silicic acid.

disiloxane. $(SiH_3)_2O = 106.95$. Colorless, odorless combustible gas, b. -15.2.

disinfect(ion). To free from infection, by destroying harmful microorganisms. Cf. *sterilize.*

disinfectant. An agent that disinfects, and usually destroys microorganisms but not bacterial spores, e.g., phenol.

disinfest. To free from infesting insects, rodents, or other small animals. Cf. *disinfect.*

disintegration. (1) Decomposition. (2) See *atomic d.* **artificial-** See *radioelements.*

disintoxicate. Detoxicate.

disk. A round plate. **alundum-** A porous alundum d. used as a filter. **bursting-** A diaphragm designed to rupture at a predetermined pressure, to safeguard against excessive pressure the apparatus in which it is fitted.

　　d. assay. The assay of antibiotics using disks dipped in different strengths of test solution and incubated in a medium with the active bacterium. The antibiotic concentration is estimated from the size of the inhibited growth zone around each d.

dislocation. The plastic deformation of metals. **edge-** D. in which the d. line is at right angles to the direction of slip. **screw-** D. in which the d. line is parallel to the direction of slip.

　　d. line. A crystal defect, which marks the boundary between the regions of slip and nonslip.

dismutation. The conversion of one substance into two; as, Cannizzaro's aldehyde reaction.

disoxidation. Deoxidation.

dispensary. A place where medicines are dispensed.

dispensatory. A book giving information on drugs in more detail than a Pharmacopoeia. Cf. *formulary.*

dispensing. The compounding of medicines. **d. dose.** See *dosage.*

dispergator. A peptizing agent. Cf. *peptizator.*

dispersed. Finely divided. Colloidal. **d. phase** Colloidal matter. Cf. *colloids.* **d. system.** An apparently homogeneous substance which consists of a microscopically heterogeneous mixture of 2 or more finely divided phases (solid, liquid, or gaseous), e.g., liquid and liquid (milk); solid and gas (smoke). See *colloids.*

dispersimeter. A device to measure the average grain of optically heterogeneous media, e.g., autochrome plate.

dispersion. (1) Scattering of light, which depends on the size of particles present. (2) Separation by

refraction of the constituent rays of a beam of nonhomogeneous light, i.e., the angle between the extreme rays of the spectrum produced. **coefficient of-** The constant B in the formula $\mu - 1 = A(1 + B/\lambda^2)$, where μ is the refractive index for the wavelength λ, and A a constant.

　　d. curve. A curve relating d. (2) and the wavelength of the light used. **d. medium.** The material surrounding dispersed matter.

dispersivity. The difference between the refractivities of a substance for rays of different wavelengths. **specific-** The d. expressed in terms of refractive index and density.

dispersoid. A finely divided substance.

displacement. (1) A chemical change in which one element, molecule, or radical is removed by another. (2) An ionic change in which one element exchanges charges with another element by oxidation or reduction. **electron-** D.(2).

　　d. law. The first enhanced spark spectrum of an element has a structure similar to that of the element preceding it in the periodic table. **d. reaction.** Metals: $M + YX = MX + Y$; the metal M, being more positive than the metal Y, is oxidized. Nonmetals: $N + YX = YN + X$; the nonmetal N, being more electronegative than the nonmetal X, is reduced. **d. series.** Electromotive series, Volta series, constant series. The elements in decreasing order of their negative potentials: (negative) F, Cl, O, N, Br, I, S, Se, Te, P, V, W, Mo, C, B, Au, Os, Pt, Ir, Ta, Pd, Ru, Sb, Bi, As, Hg, Ag, Cu, Si, Ti, H (zero), Sn, Pb, Ge, Zr, Ce, Ni, Co, Tl, Nb, Cd, Fe, Cr, Zn, Mn, U, Gd, In, Ga, Al, rare earths, Be, Sc, Y, Mg, Li, Ca, Sr, Ba, Na, K, Rb, Ce (positive).

disproportionation. The conversion of like into 2 or more unlike molecules. Cf. *dismutation.*

disruption. Tearing apart suddenly.

dissection. Cutting to pieces; as, the removal of tissues from an animal.

dissemination. (1) Dispersion. (2) The natural scattering of seeds.

dissipation. The transformation of mechanical into heat energy. **d. constant.** $Q = E/\omega\mu$, where E is Young's modulus, $\omega = 2\pi f$, and μ is the internal viscosity, Q measures internal friction; e.g., quartz 100,000, silver 6,000, lead 30.

dissociated. Split into simpler constituents. **electrolytically-** Ionized.

dissociation. The physical breaking apart of a molecule. **electrolytic-** Ionization. **photo-** See *disassociation.* **thermal-** D. of a molecule of solid, liquid, or gas into simpler molecules or atoms by heat, and reversal at low temperatures. Cf. *disassociation.*

　　d. constant. See *mass action.* **d. pressure.** The sum of the partial pressures of dissociated molecules in a system.

dissolution. (1) Solution. (2) Hydrolysis of organic tissues.

dissolve. To bring a solid into solution.

dissolved. In a state of solution. **d. substance.** Solute.

dissolvent. Solvent.

dissonance. (1) Discord. (2) A combination of sounds which produces beats.

dissymmetry. Absence of complete symmetry. Cf. *asymmetry.*

dist. Abbreviation for distilled.

distance. The length between 2 points. Cf. *magnitudes*.

Distaval. Trademark for *thalidomide*.

distearin. $C_{39}H_{75}O_5 = 623.7$. Glycerol distearate. The distearic ester of glycerin, m.74.5.

disthene. Cyanite.

distilland. That which undergoes distillation.

distillate. A liquid produced by condensation from its vapor during distillation. Cf. *tenate*.

distillation. Purification of a liquid by boiling it and condensing and collecting the vapors. **cold-** D. at low temperatures, e.g., in a vacuum. **con-** See *condistillation*. **destructive-** D. of complex organic matter, e.g., wood, into a number of split and oxidation products. **fractional-** Slow d. of a mixture and separate collection of the distillates at each boiling point, or after temperature intervals. **isothermal-** The transfer of water vapor from a weak to a strong solution in a closed space, owing to the difference in vapor pressures. **molecular-** D. carried out at a residual gas pressure below 1 micron, where the mean free path of the residual gas molecules is greater than the width of the distilling gap. **repeated-** Cohobation. **steam-** D. by the passage of steam through a liquid.

    d. apparatus. A device for d.; generally a closed vessel connected through a condenser to a receiver. **d. flask.** A flask having a long neck with tubular outlet. **d. value.** The ratio of the concentration of a substance in the vapor of its boiling solution, to that (y) in the liquid: $\log (1 - y)/(\log (1 - x)$, where x is the volume of the distillate. Cf. *Henry's law*.

distilled. Describing a liquid that has been vaporized and condensed. **d. water.** Vaporized and condensed water, used extensively in the laboratory. *double-* Water that has been distilled twice, the second time in a glass or platinum still. Used in medicine.

distillery. A place where distillation occurs; generally a factory making alcohol from fermented sugars. **d. waste.** The residue from the stills of an alcohol d.; used as a fertilizer.

distribution. (1) The occurrence of a substance on the earth's surface. Cf. *abundance*. (2) The assimilation or spread of a substance in the animal organism. **d. coefficient.** Partition coefficient, Overton coefficient. The ratio of solubility in protoplasm to solubility in water, which measures the diffusibility of a substance into the cell protoplasm. **d. law.** If a substance is dissolved in 2 immiscible liquids, a and b, then the ratio of its concentrations in each is constant. Cf. *partition*, *Nernst's law*. **d. principle.** Michael's rule. If HX adds onto an olefin linkage, where X is a halogen, it unites with the C atom having the lesser number of hydrogens. Cf. *Markownikoff's rule*.

distyrene. (PhCH:CH—)$_2$ = 206.11. White crystals, m.124.

disulfate. (1) A pyrosulfate, $M_2S_2O_7$. (2) A bisulfate, $MHSO_4$.

disulfide. A compound containing 2 sulfide atoms. **alkyl-** An organic compound containing a C chain and the —S·S— radical. **ethyl-** $Et_2S_2 = 122.22$. Colorless liquid, b.151. **methyl-** $Me_2S_2 = 94.19$. Colorless liquid, b.112.

disulfo- Prefix indicating 2 S atoms, as sulfide or sulfuric acid. **d. acid** 1-Naphthylamine-4,8-disulfonic acid. **d. benzoic acid.** See *benzoic acid*. **d. chloride.** Sulfur monochloride. **d. cyanate.** Dithionate. **d. cyanic acid.** Dithionic acid. **d. metholic acid.** Methionic acid. **d. naphtholic acid.** Naphthalenedisulfonic acid.

disulfole. Dithiole.

disulfonic acid. See *sulfonic acids*.

disulfuric acid. Pyrosulfuric acid.

dita bark. Alstonia, Australian quinine. Australian fever bark, from *Alstonia scholaris* (Apocynaceae), Australia; a febrifuge. It yields ditaine, ditamine, echicerin, echitenine. Cf. *alstonine*.

ditaine. $C_{22}H_{28}O_4N_2 = 384.23$. Echitamine. An alkaloid from dita bark. Colorless crystals, m.206, soluble in water; used medicinally like curare. **d. sulfate.** $C_{22}H_{28}O_4N_2 \cdot H_2SO_4 = 700.48$. Colorless needles, soluble in water.

ditamine. $C_{16}H_{19}O_2N = 257.2$. An alkaloid from *Alstonia scholaris*. Colorless crystals, m.75, insoluble in water.

ditan. Diphenylmethane.

diterpenes. A group of compounds of general formula $C_{20}H_{32}$. See *terpenes*.

dithanol. Dioxyanthrarobin.

dithiane. (1) Diethylene disulfide. (2) Heterocyclic hydrocarbons with 2 S atoms in a hexatomic ring.

dithiazamine iodide. $C_{23}H_{23}N_2S_2I = 518.49$. Green crystals, slightly soluble in organic solvents; an anthelmintic (U.S.P.).

dithiazine. $C_3H_3NS_2$. Heterocyclic hydrocarbons with 2 S and 1 N atom in the hexatomic ring.

dithiazol. $C_2H_3NS_2$. Heterocyclic hydrocarbons with 2 S and 1 N atom in the pentatomic ring.

dithiene. Heterocyclic hydrocarbons with 2 S atoms in the hexatomic ring.

dithienyl. $C_8H_6S_2 = 166.1$. **alpha-** Colorless crystals, m.33. **beta-** Colorless crystals, m.83. **d. ketone.** $C_9H_6OS_2 = 194.1$. Thienone. Colorless crystals, m.88. **d. methane.** $C_9H_8S_2 = 180.1$. $(C_4H_3S)_2CH_2$. Colorless crystals, m.43. **d. phenylmethane.** $(C_4H_3S)_2 \cdot CH \cdot Ph = 257.2$. Colorless crystals, m.75.

dithiobisalanine. Cystine.

dithiocarbamic acid. $NH_2 \cdot CS \cdot SH = 93.2$. Colorless needles, decomp. by water.

dithiocarbonic acid. $HO \cdot CS \cdot SH = 100.00$. Theoretical acid. Cf. *xanthic acid*.

dithiodiazole. $CH_2N_2S_2$. Heterocyclic hydrocarbons with 2 S and 2 N atoms in the pentatomic ring.

dithioethidene. A compound containing the bivalent —S·CH(CH$_3$)·S— radical. **ethylene-** $C_4H_8S_2 = 120.1$. Colorless liquid, b.173.

dithiol. (1) Toluene-3,4-dithiol-4-methyl-1,2-dimercaptobenzene; reagent for tin, tungsten, and molybdenum. (2) British anti-*lewisite*.

dithiole. $C_3H_4S_2 = 104.0$. Disulfole. Erroneously called dithiazole. Heterocyclic hydrocarbons with 2 S atoms in the pentatomic ring.

dithion. A mixture of sodium dithiosalicylates. Yellow powder, soluble in water; used in veterinary medicine.

dithionate. A salt of the type $M_2S_2O_6$.

dithionic acid. (1) $HO \cdot SO_2 \cdot SO_2 \cdot OH = 162.1$. Known only in solution and as salts (hyposulfates). (2) The organic acid $R \cdot CS \cdot SH$. Cf. *thio acid*.

dithionite. Hyposulfite. A salt of the type $M_2S_2O_4$.

dithionous acid. $HO\cdot SO\cdot SO\cdot OH = 130.1$. Hyposulfurous acid. Known only in solution, and as salts (hyposulfites).

dithiosalicylate. Thioform.

dithiosalicylic acid. See *thioform*.

dithiourazole. $C_2H_3S_2N_3 = 133.2$. Colorless crystals, m.245. Cf. *urazole*.

dithiourethane. $NH_2\cdot CS\cdot SEt$. Ethyl dithiocarbamate.

dithiozone. Dithizone.

dithizone. $PhN:N\cdot CS\cdot NH\cdot NHPh = 360.09$. Diphenylthiocarbazone, dithizone. Blue crystals, soluble in carbon tetrachloride (green color), alkalies (red color), and sulfuric acid (blue color). A microreagent for lead (red), copper (brown), and zinc (purple); also used to separate these from other metals.

dithranol. $C_{14}H_{10}O_3 = 226.20$. Dioxyanthrenol anthrarobin. 1,8-Dihydroxyanthranol. Yellow powder, m.176, insoluble in water; used to treat skin infections.

ditolyl. $Me\cdot C_6H_4\cdot C_6H_4\cdot Me = 182.19$. Dimethyldiphenyl. **2,2'-** or **o,o-** Colorless liquid, b.272, insoluble in water. **2,3'-** or **o,m-** Colorless liquid, b.228, insoluble in water. **3,3'-** or **m,m-** Colorless liquid, b.286, insoluble in water. **4,4'-** or **p,p-** Colorless prisms, m.121.

  d. amine. $(MeC_6H_4)_2NH = 197.23$. Nine isomers; as: *ortho-* Colorless liquid, b.313, sparingly soluble in water. *meta-* Colorless liquid, b.319, insoluble in water. *para-* Colorless needles, m.79, insoluble in water. **d. tin.** $Sn(C_6H_4Me)_2 = 300.81$. Yellow amorphous powder, m.111, soluble in benzene.

ditophal. $C_{12}H_{14}O_2S_2 = 254.42$. Diethyldithiophthalate. Yellow, viscous liquid, d. 1170–1185; used to treat leprosy (B.P.).

diurea. $(CO\cdot NH\cdot NH\cdot)_2 = 116.1$. Biurea, *p*-urazine, bishydrazicarbonyl. Colorless crystals, m.270. Cf. *urazine*, *biuret*. **acetylene-** Glycol uril.

diureide. A compound that contains 2 —NH·CO·NH— radicals.

diuretic. A drug that increases discharge of urine, e.g., caffeine.

divalent. (1) Describing an element occurring in 2 states of oxidation; as, mercury (1 and 2). (2) Bivalent.

divanadyl. The radical $V_2O_2^{4+}$.

divaric acid. $C_{10}H_{12}O_4 = 196.09$. 6-Propyl-β-resorcylic acid, from the lichen *Evernia divaricata*.

diversine. $C_{20}H_{27}O_5N = 361.3$. An alkaloid in *Sinomenium acutum* (Menispermaceae). Yellow powder, m.85, insoluble in water. Cf. *sinomenine*.

divi-divi. The pods of *Caesalpinia coriaria*, used for tanning.

divinyl. (1) Bivinyl. (2) Prefix indicating 2 vinyl radicals. **d. acetylene.** $CH_2:CH\cdot C:C\cdot CH:CH_2 = 78.05$. 1,5-Hexadien-3-yne*. An oil, d.0.785, b.84; basis for synthetic rubber. **d. ether.** $(CH_2: CH_2)_2O = 72.05$. Vinyl ether, vinesthine, vinethine, ethenoxyethene*. Colorless liquid, b.29; an anesthetic. **d. ketone.** Pentedienone.

dixanthylurea. $[O(C_6H_4)_2CHNH]_2CO$. The alcohol-insoluble product of xanthydrol and urea; used to determine the latter in urine.

dixylyl. Two xylyl radicals, $C_6H_3Me_2$—. **d. tin.** $Sn(C_6H_3Me_2)_2 = 328.84$. Colorless crystals, m.157.

djalmaite. Yellow to black radioactive crystals (Brazil), containing 72% tantalum oxide.

djenkol bean. See *jenkolic acid*.

djenkolic. Jenkolic.

djenkolik acid. See *jenkolic*.

dkg. Abbreviation for dekakilogram—10 kg.

dkl. Abbreviation for dekaliter—10 liters.

dkm. Abbreviation for dekameter—10 m. **dkm².** Abbreviation for square dekameter—100 m².

dkm³. Abbreviation for cubic dekameter—1,000 m³. **dl.** Abbreviation: (1) for deciliter—0.1 liter; (2) decilog.

dl- A dextro- *and* levo- compound, e.g. inactive (*i*-) or racemic (*r*-).

d(l)- A dextro- *or* levo-compound.

D.M. Diphenylaminechlorarsine.

dm. Abbreviation for decimeter—0.1 m. **dm².** Abbreviation for square decimeter—100 cm². **dm³.** Abbreviation for cubic decimeter—1,000 cm³.

D.N.A. Abbreviation for Deutscher Normenausschus.

DNAP. Dinosan.

DNBP. Dinosel.

DNC. $C_7H_6O_5N_2 = 189.06$. DNOC. Recommended common name for 3,5-dinitrocresol, m.86; pesticide, especially against aphis.

DNOC. Common name for dinitroörthophenol; used as an insecticide.

DNOCHP. Dinex.

DNOSAP. Dinosam.

DNOSBP. Dinosel.

DNSAP. Dinosam.

DNSBP. Dinoseb.

Dobell solution. An antiseptic: sodium borate 1.5, sodium bicarbonate 1.5, carbolic acid 0.3%, and glycerin.

Döbereiner, Johann Wolfgang. 1780–1849. German chemist. **D.s matchbox or lamp.** A portable lamp producing a flame by passing hydrogen gas over platinum sponge in contact with air. **D.'s rule.** The atomic weights of similar elements, A, B, and C, is approximately $2B = A + C$. See *triads*.

Döbner's violet. See *violet*.

DOCA. Deoxycortone acetate.

docosane*. $Me(CH_2)_{20}Me = 310.5$. m.44.

docosanoic acid*. Behenic acid.

docosoic acid. Behenic acid.

doctor solution. Sodium plumbite solution containing flowers of sulfur. **d. test.** Gasoline is mixed with d. solution; sulfur is shown by the formation of lead sulfide. **d. treatment.** Petroleum is agitated with sodium plumbite solution and free sulfur.

dodecahedron. A solid with 12 equal surfaces.

dodecanal*. Lauricaldehyde.

dodecane*. $Me(CH_2)_{10}Me = 170.28$. Colorless liquid, b.214.5, insoluble in water.

dodecanic acid. Lauric acid. **hydroxy-** Sabinic acid.

dodecanoic acid*. Lauric acid.

dodecanol*. Dodecyl alcohol.

dodecenal*. $Me(CH_2)_9CH:CH\cdot CHO = 182.20$. An aldehyde in the oil from *Eryngium foetidum* (Umbelliferae).

dodecene*. Dodecylene.

dodecoaldehyde. Lauric aldehyde.

dodecoic acid. Lauric acid.

dodecyl. The radical $C_{12}H_{25}$—. Cf. *lauryl.* **d. alcohol.** $Me(CH_2)_{11}OH$ = 186.20. *n*- or *l*-Dodecanol*. Colorless crystals, m.24. **d. amine*.** $C_{12}H_{27}N$ = 185.22. Aminododecane. Colorless crystals, m.28. **d. gallate.** $C_{19}H_{30}O_5$ = 338.34. 3,4,5-Trihydroxybenzoate. White powder, m.97, insoluble in water; an antioxidant (B.P.).

dodecylene. $CH_2\!:\!CH(CH_2)_9Me$ = 168.27. Decylethylene, *l*-dodecene*. Colorless liquid, b.213, insoluble in water.

dodine. The accepted generic name for *n*-dodecylguanidine acetate; used to control fungus fruit diseases.

dog grass. Triticum.

dogwood. (1) A genus of trees and shrubs. (2) Cornus. The dried roots of *C. florida* of Eastern U.S.; an astringent. Cf. *cornuoid.* **alder-**Frangula. **Jamaica-** Piscidia. **pond-** or **swamp-**See *cephaletin.*

Dolan. Trade name for a polyacrylonitrile synthetic fiber.

Dolantal. Pethidine hydrochloride.

dolerite. Diabase. A coarse-grained basalt.

dolerophanite. Cu_2SO_5. A copper persulfate in volcanic sublimates.

Dolezalek electrometer. A quadrant electroscope.

dolichol. A very long-chain isoprenoid alcohol in tobacco; mol. wt. approx. 1,200.

Dolime. Trademark for the dolomitic lime made by burning dolomite.

dolomite. $CaMg(CO_3)_2$. An important calcium-magnesium carbonate, which forms mountain ranges as a white, grayish, or yellowish rock, d.2.85–2.95, hardness 3.5–4.

dolomol. $Mg(C_{18}H_{35}O_2)_2$ = 590.8. Magnesium stearate, containing small amounts of the oleate and 7% magnesium oxide. A soft, white, unctuous dusting powder, insoluble in water.

dome. A d.-shaped crystal face, chiefly in the rhombic system. **d. faces.** Prism faces developed parallel to a lateral axis, and intersecting the other 2 axes. *Brachy-* A d. face parallel to the brachy (shorter) axis. *Macro-* A d. face parallel to the macro (longer) axis.

domesticine. $C_{19}H_{19}O_4N$ = 325.15. An alkaloid from the sacred bamboo of Japan, *Nandina domestica* (Berberidaceae). Cf. *nandinine.*

domeykite. Cu_3As. A rare copper arsenide.

domingite. $Pb_3Sb_4S_9$. Warrenite. A lead sulfostibate.

domiphen bromide. $C_{22}H_{40}BrNO$ = 413.95. Yellow, bitter flakes, m.108, soluble in water; an antiseptic detergent (B.P.).

donarite. An explosive: ammonium nitrate 70, trinitrotoluol 25, nitroglycerin 5%.

donaxine, Gramine.

Donnan, Frederick George. 1870–1956. English physical chemist. **D. equilibrium.** If a non-diffusible substance is separated from diffusible substances by a semipermeable membrane, the ions will pass through in different amounts, and establish an electrostatic difference (membrane potential); the osmotic pressure within being greater than that of the outer solution.

donor. See *induced reactions.*

dope. $C_9H_{11}NO_4$ = 197.08. 3,4-Dihydroxyphenyl-alanine. An amino acid, precursor of melanin.

dope. (1) Formerly a colloquialism, now an accepted term for any drug that affects the speed of action, stamina, or courage of an animal or human being. (2) A substance, or lacquer, used to stiffen fabrics, e.g., aircraft wings.

Doppler principle. (1842). Wave-type radiations emitted by a moving object decrease and increase in wavelength as the object approaches and recedes from the observer, respectively.

dopplerite. $C_{12}H_{14}O_6$. Masses of humus embedded in peat: C 56.5, H 5.5%.

dormiol. $CCl_3\!\cdot\!CHOH\!\cdot\!OMe_2Et$ = 233.49. Amylene chloral. Colorless liquid, d.1.24, insoluble in water; a hypnotic.

doron. Trade name for a glass wool fiber bonded with a plastic or woven nylon; used to make "bulletproof" suits.

dorosmic acid. $C_{17}H_{34}O_2$ = 270.27. Margaric acid. A fatty acid from the oil of *Dorosma nesus*, needles, m.55, soluble in hot alcohol.

dose. The quantity of medicine given at one time. **fatal-** The minimum d. to cause death. **lethal-** Fatal d. **maximum-** The largest d. that can be given with safety. **median lethal-** LD_{50}. The expression of toxicity in milligrams per kilogram of body weight. The dose that kills 50% of a group of 30 or more animals receiving equal amounts of the substance. **minimum-** The smallest d. to produce a physiological action. **poisonous-** Toxic d. **safe-** A d. between the minimum and maximum d. **toxic-** The minimum d. that will produce poisonous and harmful effects.

dotriacontane*. Diacetyl.

double bond. Δ. A condition that exists in unsaturated compounds where 2 single valence bonds connect 2 atoms. They are readily saturated by addition of 2 other atoms. Cf. *unsaturated.*

double salt. A compound which crystallizes as a single substance but which, in solution ionizes as 2 substances.

doublet. See *multiplet, duplet.*

double weighing. Elimination of irregularities in the balance arm by weighing a substance first on one pan of the balance and then on the other.

doubling. The conversion of spun yarn into thread, by twisting a single yarn, or by twisting together 2 or more single yarns.

douglasite. $K_2FeCl_4\!\cdot\!2H_2O$. An ore from Stassfurt, Germany, producing miner's damp by reaction to form hydrogen.

DOV. Distilled oil of vitriol (approx. 96% sulfuric acid).

Dover's powder. A mixture of morphine, emetine, and camphor: an anodyne and hypnotic.

Dowicide-H. Trademark for sodium tetrachlorophenolate containing an excess of alkali; a wood preservative.

Dowtherm. Trademark for a eutectic mixture of phenyl ether and 26.5% diphenyl, m.12, b.258; used for controlled heating.

doxylamine succinate. $C_{21}H_{28}O_5N_2$ = 388.47. Doxaminium succinate. White powder with a characteristic odor, m.102, soluble in water; an antihistaminic.

DP. Abbreviation for: (1) degree of polymerization; (2) diastatic power; (3) difference in pressure.

dr. Abbreviation for dram. **dr. ap.** Apothecaries' dram, =3. **dr. av.** Avoirdupois dram. **dr. fl.** Fluid dram.

dracaenic acid. $C_{12}H_{12}O_3 = 204.09$. An acid from *Dracaena draco*, the dragon tree of Teneriffe.

drachm. Dram.

dracilic, dracylic acid. (1) Obsolete term for benzoic acid. (2) *p*-Aminobenzoic acid.

dracoalban. $C_{20}H_{40}O_4 = 344.4$. White powder, m.200, from dragon's blood.

dracone. A large flexible container towed in water, for transporting oil in bulk.

dracoresin, dracoresene. $C_{26}H_{44}O_2 = 388.34$. A yellow resin from dragon's blood.

draconic acid. Anisic acid.

draconis sanguis. Dragon's blood.

draconyl. $C_{14}H_7 = 175.1$. A hydrocarbon distilled from dragon's blood.

draconylic acid. Anisic acid.

dracylic acid. See *dracilic acid*.

Dragendorff, Johann Georg Noel. 1836–1898. German analyst. **D. reaction.** The sulfates of many alkaloids give an orange-red precipitate with D. reagent. **D. reagent.** Suspend 1.5 gm bismuth subnitrate in 20 ml hot water; add 7 gm potassium iodide and 20 drops of dilute hydrochloric acid.

dragon's blood. Sanguis draconis. The resinous exudation from the fruits of rattan palms (India, E. Indies). Odorless, tasteless masses, insoluble in water, soluble in alcohol, giving a red solution. **d. gum.** Tragacanth.

Draka-Saran. Trade name for a mixed-polymer synthetic fiber.

Dralon. Trade name for a polyacrylonitrile synthetic fiber.

dram. Drachm. A unit of apothecaries weight, ℨ. One dram = 0.16 ounce = 3 scruples = 60 grains = 3.8879351 gm. **fluid-** One-eighth of a fluid ounce: 60 minims.

Dramamine. Registered trademark for a brand of β-dimethylaminoethyl ether 8-chlorotheophyllinate. A preventive for sea- and other forms of sickness.

Draper effect. Photochemical induction observed when a mixture of hydrogen and chlorine is exposed over water to diffused daylight. **D. law.** Absorption law. Only rays which are absorbed by a system can produce a chemical change in it.

drastic. Describing a drug having powerful irritant and purgative action.

draught. A current of air or gas. **d. tube.** A glass tube used in qualitative analysis to heat a substance in a current of air.

drawinella. Trade name for a cellulose acetate synthetic fiber.

draw tube. A tube sliding within another; as, the d.t. of a microscope carrying the eyepiece.

Drierite. A brand of anhydrous calcium sulfate dessicant.

driers, dryers. (1) Siccatives. Oxidizing substances which hasten the drying of varnishes, paints, etc.; as, lead resinates. (2) Usually, dryers. Mechanical devices to remove moisture by heat and/or air currents.

drift. (1) The uncertain motion of an indicating pointer, e.g., of a galvanometer. (2) The passage of an electron from its normal position without complete transfer. Cf. *bonds*.

drikold. Dry Ice.

drimin. $C_{13}H_{14}O_4 = 234.1$. A crystalline substance,

m.256, from *Drimys winteri* (Magnoliaceae), S. America. Cf. *winter's bark*.

drimol. $C_{28}H_{58}O_2 = 426.6$. A wax from *Drimys granatensis* (Magnoliaceae), S. America.

drip. Liquid expressed from the muscle substance; in particular, the red serum that oozes from frozen meat during thawing due to the failure of the fiber to reabsorb it.

driped. Hide steeped in chrome alum, dried, and soaked in melted paraffin wax.

dripping. An unbleached, untreated cooking fat containing not less than 99% saponifiable matter and not more than 1.5% free fatty acids. It excludes premier jus.

dropping bottle. A small glass bottle with pipet, or special stopper, enabling the contents to be delivered dropwise. **d. funnel.** A separatory funnel with long stem and glass stopcock. **d. pipet.** A small glass tube drawn out at one end, with a rubber bulb at the other.

drop reaction. Spot test.

drops. Portions of liquid, ordinarily 0.1–0.3 ml. **Prince Rupert-** Solidified glass d. with tips, under great internal strain, which shatter to a fine powder when the tips are broken off.

drosera. Sundew. *Drosera rotundifolia*, or other Droseraceae; used as a mild astringent.

dross. Scum, scurf. The impurities floating on molten metals. **opium-** Yenshee.

Druce, F. G. R. English chemist noted as codiscoverer of the element dvimanganese (rhenium).

drug. A medicinal substance. See *anchoring group*, *pharmacophore*. Drugs are classified according to composition or constituents, structure or physical features, effect and use, origin and source. See *Approved Name*. **addiction-producing-** See *addiction*. **crude-** A commercial d. before refining. **inorganic-** Inorganic salts, acids, or bases used as medicines. **organic-** Organic compounds used as medicines.

drumine. An alkaloid from the sap of *Euphorbia drummondii* (Euphorbiaceae), Australia; a local anesthetic.

Drummond, Sir Jack Cecil. 1891–1952. British chemist noted for his work on nutrition, especially in connection with wartime rationing. **D., Thomas.** 1797–1840. English engineer who invented the calcium light, q.v.

dry. (1) Free from liquid. (2) Evaporate. **air-** Dry in air. **bone-** Completely free from water. **d. battery.** Set of d. cells. **d. box.** *Glove* box. **d. cell.** An electric cell containing moist paste instead of a liquid electrolyte. See *Gassner cell*. **D. Ice.** Drikold. Trademark for solid carbon dioxide used as a refrigerant. **d. method.** Analysis by heat, e.g., blowpipe analysis.

dryers. Driers.

drying. Removal of liquid by heat, vacuum, or chemical agents. Cf. *dehydration*. **fluid bed-** See *fluid*. **d. agent.** (1) Drier. (2) An agent that removes water, as, heat or chemicals; e.g., metallic sodium used to dry alcohol. Cf. *desiccant*. **d. oil.** A liquid fat, e.g., tung oil, which absorbs oxygen and becomes hard and resinous; usually the glycerides of linoleic and linolenic acids. **d. oven.** A receptacle for d. by heat. **d. tube.** A U-shaped glass tube filled with a d. agent, e.g., calcium chloride, sulfuric acid; used for d. gases and vapors.

drypophantin. $C_{23}H_{18}O_{15}$ = 544.2. A glucoside from *Dryophanta divisa*. Red needles, m.220.

Ds. Symbol for dysprosium. More accurately, Dy.

DSIR. *Department* of Scientific and Industrial Research.

DTE. DDT.

dualin. An explosive: nitrogen 50, nitrated sawdust 50%.

dubhium. Db. A supposed element (Eder, 1916), identical with ytterbium.

duboisine. $C_{17}H_{23}O_3N$ = 289.2. *l*-Hyoscyamine. An alkaloid from the leaves of *Duboisia myoporoides*, corkwood (Solanaceae), New South Wales. White needles, m.107, sparingly soluble in water; a sedative mydriatic. **d. hydrobromide.** $C_{17}H_{23}O_3N \cdot$HBr = 370.13. Yellow hygroscopic powder, soluble in water. **d. hydrochloride.** $C_{17}H_{23}O_3N \cdot$HCl = 325.67. Yellow, deliquescent powder, soluble in water. **d. sulfate.** $(C_{17}H_{23}O_3N)_2H_2 \cdot$SO$_4$ = 676.4. Yellow powder, soluble in water; an atropine substitute.

Duboscq colorimeter. See *colorimeter*.

Ducilon. Trade name for a polyamide synthetic fiber.

ductile. Capable of being drawn out into a fine wire.

ductility. The extent to which a solid is ductile. Cf. *chew*.

ductless glands. Glands of the mammalian body that secrete enzymes into the blood and perform important chemical reactions. Cf. *hormones*.

Dudley apparatus. A glass apparatus to determine sulfur in iron and steel by the bromine method. **D. pipet.** A pipet to deliver 100 ml water at 10°C in 35 sec. Used for viscosity tests.

duff. A low-grade, small-size, high-ash anthracite.

dufrenite. $H_3Fe_2PO_7$. A fibrous, green, hydrous iron phosphate.

dufrenoysite. $Pb_2As_2S_5$. A gray, orthorhombic, brittle lead sulfarsenide.

dugaldine. A glucoside from *Helenium* (*Dugaldia*) *hoopesii*, western sneezewood (Compositae).

dugong oil. A cod-liver oil substitute from the superficial fat of the sea cow, *Halicore australis*, a herbiverous aquatic mammal.

dulcamara. Bittersweet, woody nightshade, scarlet berry, felonwood, violet bloom. The stems of *Solanum dulcamara* (Solanaceae). It contains glucosides. Cf. *dulcamarin*.

dulcamarin. $C_{22}H_{34}O_{10}$ = 458.3. A glucoside from *Solanum dulcamara*.

dulcamarrhetin. $C_{16}H_{26}O_6$ = 314.2. A brown resin split product of dulcamarin.

dulcin. (1) Sucrol. (2) Dulcitol.

dulcine. Dulcitol.

dulcite. Dulcitol.

dulcitol. $HOCH_2(CHOH)_4CH_2OH$ = 182.15. Euonymin, dulcin, 1,2,3,4,5,6-hexanehexol*, dulcite, dulcose, melampyrine, hexahydrohexane; from the sap of *Melampyrum*, *Scrophularia*, and *Euonymus* species. Colorless needles, m.189, soluble in water; a sweetening for diabetics. **iso-** Rhamnose.

dulcose. Dulcitol.

Dulin rotarex. A centrifuge to determine mineral matter in asphalts.

Dulkona. Trademark for a matt continuous-filament rayon yarn.

Dulong, Pierre Louis. 1745–1838. French chemist. **D. and Petit law.** Elementary atoms or molecules have an equal atomic heat capacity. Thus, atomic weight × specific heat is approximately 6.2 for all elements (at constant pressure). Certain elements of low atomic weight and high melting point obey the law only at high temperatures, e.g., Be.

Dumas, Jean Baptiste André. 1800–1884. A French chemist noted for research on atomic weights, the gravimetric decomposition of water and the composition of air. **D. bulb.** A thin glass bulb drawn out to a fine opening; used in vapor-density determinations.

dumasin. An isomer of mesitone obtained on dry distillation of calcium acetate.

dumortierite. $Al_8HBSi_3O_{20}$. A dark orthorhombic rock.

dumosa oil. An oil from *Eucalyptus dumosa*. Cf. *lerp*.

dundakine. An alkaloid from the bark of *Sarcocephalus esculentus*, dundaki (Rubiaceae), Cameroons.

dundasite. A rare aluminum and lead carbonate.

dunder. Waste saccharin liquors from sugar factories and distilleries.

dung bacteria. Caprophyl. Bacteria which occur normally in manure.

dunite. A green peridotite rock, consisting of chrysolite and olivine (Corundum Hill, N.C.).

Dunning colorimeter. An instrument for the colorimetric estimation of phenolsulfonephthalein excreted with urine in the renal function test.

dunninone. 2-Hydroxynaphthaquinone, m.98.

duotal. Guaiacol carbonate.

duplet. Doublet. A pair of electrons shared by 2 atoms, corresponding with a single, nonpolar bond.

Duponal. Trademark for a group of surface-active fatty alcohol sulfates.

Dupont nitrometer. An arrangement of gas burets for the determination of nitrogen in explosives.

Duprene. Trade name for a synthetic rubber made by polymerization of chloroprene. Cf. *rubber*.

durain. A constituent of coal, q.v.

duralium. An alloy: Al 93–95, Cu 3.5–5.5%, and small amounts of Mg and Mn; used for chemical equipment.

Duralumin. Trademark for an alloy: Mg 0.5, Mn 0.25–1.00, Cu 3.5–4.5, Al 93–95%, with traces of Fe and Si. It can be machined and resists dilute acids and seawater.

durangite. $AlNaFAsO_4$. An orange, monoclinic mineral.

durene. $C_6H_2Me_4$ = 134.16. α- or **s-**. Durol 1,2,-4,5-tetramethylbenzene. Colorless, monoclinics, m.79, insoluble in water. **β- or iso-** 1,2,3,5-Tetramethylbenzene. Colorless liquid, b.195. **γ- or v-** Prehnitene, 1,2,3,4-tetramethylbenzene. Colorless liquid, b.204. **hexahydro-** Tetramethyl*cyclohexane*.

Duriron. Trade name for a resistant alloy: Fe 84.5, Si 14, other elements 1.5%.

Durite. Trademark for a phenol-formaldehyde plastic.

durol. Durene.

durra. Kaffir corn, broom corn, shallu. *Sorghum vulgare* (*Andropogon sorghum*), S. Africa.

durrin. $C_{14}H_{17}NO_7$ = 311.14. A cyanogenetic glucoside from durra.

duryl. The radical Me_4C_6H— from durene.

durylene. The radical

$$\begin{array}{c} \text{CMe—CMe} \\ —C\diagup \qquad \diagdown C— \\ \text{CMe}=\text{CMe} \end{array}$$

durylic acid. $C_6H_2Me_3 \cdot COOH$ = 164.1. 2,4,5-Trimethylbenzoic acid. cumylic acid. Colorless crystals, m.150, soluble in water. **iso-** 2,4,6,-Trimethylbenzoic acid.

dust. A finely powdered earth or waste material. The average size of outdoor d. is 0.5 micron; industrial d. 1.5 micron. Average d. content (million particles per cubic foot): outdoor air in rain 0.3, cement plant 26, coal mine 112. **cosmic-** Finely divided matter in the outer atmosphere; supposed to originate from meteors and comets. **d. chamber.** An enlargement in a gas flue in which solid particles can collect. **d. precipitator.** A d. chamber with charged high-voltage wires, to precipitate suspended solid particles. See *Cottrell precipitator*. **d. reticulation.** See pneumoconiosis.

dusting. Applying a fine powder. **d. powders.** The fine-grained solids sprinkled over wounds or on the skin; as, talcum powder. *B.P.*: A white, free-flowing absorbable powder containing up to 2.0% magnesium oxide, with maize starch which has been modified so that it will not gel on steam sterilization.

Dutch liquid. Ethylene dichloride. **D. metal.** An alloy: Cu 80, Zn 20%. **D. process.** The preparation of white lead by the slow action on lead of carbon dioxide evolved from fermenting bark. **D. white.** A white lead pigment containing 66% barium sulfate.

dvi. Two or second (Sanskrit). Applied to the second undiscovered element of a group in the periodic system. Cf. *eka-elements*.

dvicesium. Francium.

dvimanganese. Rhenium.

dvitellurium. Polonium.

dwi. Dvi.

dwt. Abbreviation for: (1) pennyweight; (2) deadweight (of ships); see *ton*.

Dy. Symbol for dysprosium.

dyad. A divalent element or radical.

dyamettin. A glucoside from the root of *Cissampelos pareira*. Cf. *deyamettin*.

dye. A natural or synthetic coloring matter used in solution to stain materials, as opposed to pigments which are used in suspension. A d. consists of a chromophore group and a salt-forming group (anchoring group). Cf. *dyes*. **d. bath.** A solution of a d. for dyeing. **d. stuff.** Dye. **d. wood.** A wood that yields a coloring matter on extraction. Cf. *brazilwood, hematoxylon*.

Dyer, Bernard. 1856–1948. British chemist noted for his work on the analysis of foodstuffs and agricultural products.

dyes. Dyestuffs. Synthetic d. are usually coal tar or aniline colors. *Classification* (based on application):
1. Substantive or direct d.: dye by immersion in *acid* or *basic* bath.
2. Adjective or mordant d.: require a fixing agent.
3. Sulfur d: need a sodium sulfide bath followed by oxidation.
4. Vat d.: applied in their soluble, colorless, reduced (leuco) state and oxidized afterward to an insoluble color.
5. Ingrain colors: deposited on formation of an insoluble dye by chemical reaction. The fiber is immersed successively in the reagents.

acid- (1) D. which color the acidophile or basic granules of the protoplasm (generally the cytoplasm); as, eosin. (2) D. which color fibers in acid solution; e.g., nitro and azo d. **acid-mordant-** D. which color animal fibers in acid solution with a mordant. **adjective-** Mordant d. **artificial-** Synthetic as opposed to natural coloring matters, e.g., coal tar. **azine-** D. containing the $=N-N=$ group. **azo-** D. containing the azo group. **bacteriological-** D. used to stain protoplasm; they may be acid, basic, neutral, or specific. **basic-** (1) D. which color the basophile or acid granules of the protoplasm (generally the nucleus and nucleoproteins); as, hematin. (2) D. used for dyeing in alkaline solution. **cationic-** A generalized name for basic d. It includes fast and fugitive d. having a pentavalent N atom, usually in the triphenylmethane structure

where R is an alkyl or aryl group, and X is the anion of a mineral or organic acid. Used to dye acrylic fibers with fast shades. **direct-** Substantive dyes. **leuco-** Vat dyes. **mineral-** Inorganic substances used in dyeing; e.g., iron salts. **mixed-** Polygenetic d. **monogenetic-** Substances that dye only in one color. **mordant-** Substances that require an additional substance for fixation on the fiber. **natural-** Coloring matters of vegetable or animal origin, e.g., carmine. **neutral-** D. which color both the acidophile and basophile portions of protoplasm. **nitro-** D. containing the nitro radical. **nitroso-** D. containing the nitroso group. **oxazine-** D. containing the $-R(O \cdot N \cdot)R-$ group. **oxyazo-** D. containing azo and oxy groups. **oxyketone-** D. containing the quinone group. **polygenetic-** D. that produce 2 or more colors, e.g., alizarin. **provisional-** See writing *ink*. **pyronine-** D. containing the $-R(O \cdot C)R-$ group. **specific-** D. which color protoplasm selectively. **Stenhouse-** Deeply colored d. made by the interaction of furfural, an aromatic amine, and the salt of a mineral acid. **substantive-** Substances which stain fibers directly, without use of a mordant. **sulfide-** Insoluble d. used in a sodium sulfide bath and oxidized afterward. **sulfite-** D. used in sodium sulfite solution. **thiazine-** D. containing the $-R(S \cdot N)R-$ group. **triphenylmethane-** D. derived from triphenylmethane. **vat-** See *classification*. **vegetable-** D. derived from plants; as, alkanet, litmus, madder, rouge, turkey red (red and purple); fustic, gamboge, saffron (yellow and orange); indigo, wood (blue and green).

dymal. Didymium salicylate.

dyn. Abbreviation for *dyne*.

dynad. The intraatomic field of force.

Dynafuel. Trade name for a fuel claimed to be 50% superior to 100-octane fuel.

Dynalkol. Trade name for a motor fuel containing gasoline 70, alcohol 26, benzene 4%.

dynambin. A papaverine-yohimbine tartrate, used to treat pyorrhea and endocrine disturbances.

dynamic. Describing forces not in equilibrium, and resulting in motion; opposed to static. **d. allotropy.** Desmotropy. **d. formula.** See *benzene ring.* **d. isomerism.** Tautomerism.

dynamics. The study of forces not in equilibrium. Classification: Electrodynamics (electrons), thermodynamics (atoms, molecules), gravitation mechanics (masses).

dynamites. A class of explosives, usually a mixture of trinitroglycerin with an absorbing inert material. E.g.:

Kieselguhr d..... TNG 72–75, kieselguhr 28–25%
Pittsburgh d..... TNG 40, sodium nitrate 44, wood pulp 15, calcium carbonate 1%
U.S.A. straight d. TNG 15–75, sodium nitrate 5–66, combustible material 5–20, calcium carbonate 1%

dynamo. A machine converting mechanical into electric energy. Cf. *electric motor.*

dynamometer. An apparatus to measure the force or power developed by an engine.

dyne. Dyn. The cgs unit of force. The force which, acting for 1 sec, gives to 1 gm a velocity of 1 cm/sec; hence: 1 dyne = 1 gm/gravity acceleration, cm/sec² = 1/980.665 gm = 1.02 mg; and 980.665 dynes = 1 gm. **mega-** Bar. 10^6 or 1,000,000 dynes = 1.013 kg.

d. centimeter. The work done by a force of 1 dyne exerted along a distance of 1 cm; e.g., the work required to raise 1.02 mg by 1 cm. 1 dyne-cm = 1 erg.

Dynel. Trade name for a high-melting-point synthetic fiber comprising a copolymer of vinyl chloride 60, acrylonitrile 40%, m.115.

dypnone. $PhCO \cdot CH{:}CMePh$ = 221.11. A condensation product of 2 molecules of hypnone, $b_{22mm} 225$.

dysalbumose. An albumose obtained from fibrin by the action of pepsin. Brown powder, insoluble in water.

dyscrasite. Ag_3Sb. A gray, mineral, rhombic d.9.6, hardness 3.5.

dyslysin. (1) $C_{24}H_{36}O_3$ = 372.4. A resinous, dehydrated split product of choline acids. (2) An anhydrous decomposition product of bile acids.

dysprosium. Dy = 162.50. Atomic number 66. A rare-earth metal discovered in holmia (Lecoq de Boisbaudran, 1886). It is trivalent, forms yellow or greenish salts, and occurs in small amounts in samarskite and gadolinite. **d. acetate.** $Dy(C_2H_3O_2)_3 \cdot 4H_2O$ = 411.59. Yellow needles, decomp. 120, soluble in water. **d. chloride.** $DyCl_3$ = 268.9. Green crystals, m.680, soluble in water. **d. nitrate.** $Dy(NO_3)_3 \cdot 5H_2O$ = 438.5. Yellow crystals, m.88, soluble in water. **d. oxalate.** $Dy_2(C_2O_4)_3 \cdot 10H_2O$ = 769.08. Yellow prisms, insoluble in water. **d. oxide.** Dy_2O_3 = 373.0. Colorless powder, d.7.81, insoluble in water. **d. sulfate.** $Dy_2(SO_4)_3 \cdot 8H_2O$ = 757.0. Yellow crystals, soluble in water.

dystectic mixture. An alloy or mixture containing those proportions of constituents which produce the highest constant-melting point. Cf. *eutectic mixture.*

E

E. Symbol for: (1) electromotive force. (2) electrode potential. **E₀.** Symbol for electroaffinity.
E. *Einstein:* 6.06×10^{23} quanta. Cf. *faraday.*
E 605. Parathion. Diethyl-*p*-nitrophenylthiophosphate. A potent insecticide, especially to aphides.
e. (1) The base of natural logarithms: $e = 2.718,281,828...$ See *exponential.* (2) Symbol for an electron; as in H = H⁺ + *e.* (2) The elementary electric charge on an electron: half the charge on an α particle: $e = 4.770 \times 10^{-10}$ esu = 1.591×10^{-20} emu = 1.591^{-19} coulomb. *e/m.* The ratio of charge to mass of an electron: 1.765×10^{7} emu/gm. e^{-1}. A mathematical constant: $e^{-1} = 0.367,879,441...$
ε. Greek letter epsilon. (1) An ergon or quantum, q.v. (2) An etheron, q.v. (3) Symbol for dielectric constant. (4) Electrode potential: ϵ_c to a normal calomel electrode, ϵ_h to a normal hydrogen electrode.
η. Greek letter eta. Symbol for viscosity.
EAN. Equivalent *atomic* number.
earth. (1) Soil. (2) The solid portion of the globe, or lithosphere. See *abundance.* (3) The globe, as distinguished from other heavenly bodies. **diatomaceous-** Kieselguhr. **Fuller's-** *Fuller's* earth. **green-** Terra verde. **infusorial-** Kieselguhr. **rare-** See *rare-earth metals.* **red-** Ocher. **siliceous-** Kieselguhr.
e. age. The period of existence of the e., i.e., the 4 stages:

1.	Gaseous	
2.	Fluid surface	.... 10^{5} years
3.	Intermediate	.... $\pm 10^{5}$ years
4.	Solid	.... 2.3×10^{9} years

e. alkali metals. The elements of the second group of the periodic system: Mg, Ca, Sr, Ba, Ra. **e. constants.**

Equatorial radius 6,378,388 meters = 3,963.2 miles
Polar radius 6,356,911 meters = 3,949.8 miles
One degree latitude at equator = 68.70 miles
One degree latitude at pole = 69.41 miles
Mean density 5.5247
Mean density of continental surface....... 2.67
Rigidity................... 8.6×10^{11} cgs units
Viscosity .... 10.9×10^{16} cgs units
Volume.................... 1,083,319 × 10⁶ km³
Area...................... 510,100,934 km²
Area of land .... 148,847,000 km²
Area of ocean .... 361,254,000 km²
Mean distance from earth to sun =
149,500,000 km = 92,900,000 miles
Mean distance from earth to moon =
384,393 km = 238,854 miles

First man-made earth satellite 1957
e. flax. Amianthus. **e. inductor.** An electric coil, which rotates in a frame. **e. metals.** The elements of the third group of the periodic system: Al, Sc, Y, La. *rare-* The elements of the fifth sub-period from Ce (at. no. 58) to Hf (at. no. 72). **e. nut oil.** Arachis oil. **e. oil.** Petroleum or asphalt. **e. shellac.** Acaroid resin. **e. wax.** Ozocerite.
earthenware. An opaque porous ceramic made from kaolin, ball and flint clays, and china stone.
East Indian oil. An essential oil from *Anethum sowa* (Umbelliferae), containing limonene and apiol.
Eastman Cellulose Acetate. Trademark for a cellulose acetate synthetic fiber.
Easton syrup. A pharmaceutical preparation containing iron, quinine, and strychnine phosphates.
eau. French for water. **e. de cologne.** Cologne *water.* **e. de javelle.** A bleaching solution of potassium hypochlorite. **e. de labarraque.** A bleaching solution of sodium hypochlorite.
eblanin. Paraxanthine.
Ebner fluid. A mixture of 2.5 ml hydrochloric acid, 2.5 gm sodium chloride, 100 ml water, and 500 ml alcohol, for decolorizing bacteriological specimens.
ebonite. Black, vulcanized, hard rubber. Cf. *vulcanite.*
ebony. A hard, dark, heavy wood from *Diospyros* species (Ebenaceae).
ebul, ebulus. The dwarf elder, *Pilea grandis* (Urticaceae), W. Indies. The berries are used for an alcoholic beverage.
ebullient. Bubbling or boiling.
ebulliometry. Ebullioscopy.
ebullioscope. An apparatus to determine boiling points.
ebullioscopic equation. Mol. wt. = $p(d/t)$, where p is weight in grams of a substance per 100 gm solvent, d the molecular rise in boiling point, and $t°$C the observed rise in boiling point.
ebullioscopy. The determination of molecular weights from the increase in boiling point of a solution. Cf. *Raoult's law.*
ebullition. Bubble formation.
ecbalin. Elateric acid.
ecballium. Elaterium.
ecbolics. Oxytocics.
ecboline. An alkaloid of ergot.
eccentric. (1) Not concentric. (2) Not circular, e.g., an orbit. (3) With the axis away from the center. (4) Away from the center.
ecgonidine. *dl*-Anhydroecgonine.
ecgonine. $C_9H_{15}O_3N \cdot H_2O = 203.19$. Tropinecarboxylic acid. A split product of cocaine. White, monoclinic prisms, m.198, soluble in water. **anhydro-** See *anhydro.* **ethylbenzoyl-** Cocethyline. **methylbenzoyl-** Cocaine.
e. hydrochloride. $C_9H_{15}O_3N \cdot HCl = 239.66$. Colorless, triclinic leaflets, m.246, soluble in water.
echelon cell. A wedge-shaped glass cell used in

absorption spectroscopy for different thicknesses of absorbing liquid.

echicaoutchin. $C_{25}H_{40}O_2 = 372.4$. An elastic resin-like substance from dita bark, q.v.

echicerin. $C_{30}H_{48}O_2 = 440.5$. Colorless needles from dita bark, m.157, insoluble in water.

echiine. An alkaloid from *Echium vulgare* (Boraginaceae), which produces tetanic convulsions.

echinacea. The dried rhizome of *Brauneria pallida* (*Echinacea angustifolia*) (Compositae), N. America; an alterative and "systemic" antiseptic.

echinacoid. The dry combined principles of echinaceae.

echinochrome. A brown respiratory pigment in sea urchins. Cf. *porphin derivatives*. **e.-A.** 2-Ethyl-pentahydroxynaphthaquinone. A pigment derived from a leuco compound in the ripe eggs of certain marine invertebrates. Cf. *fertilizin*.

echinopsine. $C_{10}H_9ON = 159.1$. An alkaloid from *Echinops* species, globe thistle (Compositae); similar in action to strychnine.

echinulate. A growth of bacteria characterized by toothed outgrowths.

echinulin. $C_{28}H_{39}O_2N_3 = 449.38$. A colorless substance formed with the pigments auroglaucin and flavoglaucin in the mycelium of the mold *Aspergillus glaucus.*

echitamine. $C_{22}H_{29}O_4N_2Cl = 420.74$. Ditaine. The major alkaloid of *Alstonia scholaris.*

echitenine. $C_{20}H_{27}O_4N = 345.0$. An alkaloid from dita bark. Brown powder, m.120, soluble in alcohol.

echitin. $C_{32}H_{52}O_2 = 468.51$. An acid from dita bark. Colorless leaflets, m.170, soluble in hot alcohol.

echothioptate iodide. $C_9H_{23}O_3NIPS = 383.23$. White hygroscopic crystals, m.120 (decomp.), soluble in water; an ophthalmic cholinergic (U.S.P.).

echtgelb. Eger's yellow.

echugin. $(C_5H_8O_2)_x$. A glucoside from *Adenium boehmianum*, and active principle of African arrow poisons, which arrests the heart in systole. Colorless, rhombic scales, soluble in water.

eclogite. A rock chiefly of augite and hornblende.

ecology. A branch of biology dealing with the habits of organisms in relation to their surroundings.

ectohormone. Pheromone.

ectolyte. A substance that destroys warts.

ectoplasm. The outer compact hyaline layer of cell protoplasm.

eddy currents. The electric currents set up by alternating currents in metal near or in an electric circuit. Cf. *Foucault current.*

edenite. Hornblende containing iron.

Eder's solution. A solution of mercuric chloride and ammonium oxalate, used to measure the intensity of X radiation in terms of the amount of Hg precipitated.

edestan. A protean from slightly denatured edestin.

edestin. A globulin, mol. wt. 29,000, from hemp, rye, and cotton seeds, deficient in cystine and lysine.

edetate. A salt of ethylenediamine tetraacetate. **disodium-** $C_{10}H_{14}O_8N_2Na_2 \cdot 2H_2O = 372.24$. White crystals, soluble in water; a metal complexing agent (U.S.P.).

edetic acid. Ethylenediaminetetraacetic acid.

edge filtration. *Streamline* filtration.

edingtonite. $BaAl_2Si_3O_{10} \cdot 4H_2O$. A gray, rhombic silicate, d.2.7. hardness 4–4.5.

edinol. $C_7H_9O_2N = 139.08$. *p*-Aminosaligenin; a photographic developer.

Edison, Thomas Alva. 1847–1931. American physicist and inventor. **E. cell.** An accumulator; iron and nickel oxide electrodes in 20% potassium hydroxide solution. **E. effect.** An electrode opposite a glowing filament becomes negatively charged. **E. Lelande cell.** A cell (0.7 volt) consisting of an amalgamated zinc electrode and copper electrode in a solution of potassium hydroxide.

edrophonium chloride. $C_{10}H_{16}ONCl = 201.66$. Ethyl-(3-hydroxyphenyl)dimethylammonium chloride. White, bitter, saline crystals, m.168, soluble in water; an anticholinesterase (B.P.).

EDTA. Ethylenediaminetetraacetic acid.

effervescence. The bubbling of a liquid due to escape of gas, not to boiling.

effervescent. Having the property of effervescence. **e. mixture.** A mixture of substances which form a gas when moistened, e.g., baking powder. **e. salts.** Medicinally active substances mixed with sodium bicarbonate and citric or tartaric acid.

efficiency. (1) The ratio: useful work to energy supplied. (2) Statistics: The proportion of the total available data that is relevant according to the theory of probability.

efflorescence. The property of crystals becoming anhydrous and crumbling when exposed to air, e.g., washing soda.

efflorescent. Tending to effloresce.

effluent. (1) A waste product discharged from a process. (2) Emergent, e.g., radiations.

efflux. The flow of a fluid.

effuse. Describing a veil-like growth of bacteria.

effusiometer. An instrument (Bunsen) to determine the molecular weights of gases from effusion measurements.

effusion. (1) Pouring out; discharge. (2) The escape of a gas under pressure through an aperture. The relative e. rates of gases into air are inversely proportional to the square roots of their molecular weights.

efylon. Trade name for a polyamide synthetic fiber.

e.g. Abbreviation for exempli gratia (for example.)

Eger's yellow. E.Y. Echtgelb. The yellow dye $HSO_3 \cdot C_6H_4 \cdot N = N \cdot C_6H_3 \cdot (SO_3H) \cdot NH_2$.

egg. An ovum of shell, egg white, and yolk. **acid-** A closed storage tank for strong acids. **storage-** An e. kept in water-glass solution or in a frozen condition. **e. albumen.** A crystallizable protein, mol. wt. 33,800, from egg-white. **e. magma.** A frozen mixture of churned yolks and whites of selected eggs, used in cookery.

eglantine. $Ph \cdot CH_2COOC_4H_9 = 192.12$. Isobutyl-$\alpha$-toluate. Colorless liquid, b.254, insoluble in water; a flavoring.

eglestonite. Hg_4Cl_2O. A rare, native, mercuric chloride–oxide (Thomas Egleston, 1832–1900).

egols. Antiseptic substances consisting of the *o*-nitro-*p*-sulfonates of phenol, cresol, or thymol, with mercury and potassium; e.g.: cresegol, from cresol; phenegol, q.v.; thymegol, from thymol.

egonol. An unsaturated alcohol in ego oil from the seeds of *Styrax japonica.*

EGTA. Ethylene glycol bis(β-aminoethyl ether)

N,N,N',N'-tetraacetic acid. A complexone, analogous to EDTA; used to determine calcium in presence of magnesium.

Ehrlich, Paul. 1854–1915. German biochemist. **E. 606.** Arsphenamine. **E. diazo reaction.** The red color produced by pathological urine with the diazo reagent. **E. diazo reagent.** $A = 1$ gm sodium nitrite in 200 ml water. $B = 5$ gm sulfanilic acid, 50 ml hydrochloric acid, and 950 ml water. Mix 1 of A and 50 of B. **E. side-chain theory.** See *E. theory*. **E. solution.** A 2% solution of p-dimethylamidobenzaldehyde in 50% hydrochloric acid; used to detect urobilinogen in urine. **E. theory.** Side-chain theory. Immunity is due to antibodies (synonyms: immune substance, haptins, free receptors) which unite with and make harmless the antigen (synonyms: poisonous substance, invading substance, toxin, etc.) and thereby prevent it from attaching itself to the chemical system of the protoplasm. To affect a living cell, poisonous substance must enter the protoplasm by combining with certain atomic groups (the side chains or receptors). In direct action, the antigen has a haptophoric group which anchors the toxin to the protoplasm, and toxophoric group which causes the toxic disturbances. In indirect action, the antigen consists of: (1) the *complement, addiment* (Ehrlich), *cytase* (Bordet and Metchnikoff), or *alexin* (Buchner), a zymphoric group, containing the poisonous radical, and a haptophoric group, with which it is anchored to the amboceptor. (2) the *amboceptor, fixateur* (Metchnikoff), *preparateur* (Müller), *immune body* (Pfeiffer), *sensitizer* or *intermediate* body, the link between the complement and the receptor. **E. triacid stain.** A mixture of Orange G, Acid Fuchsine, and Methylene Green in aqueous alcohol and glycerin; used for differentially staining white blood corpuscles.

eicosane*. $C_{20}H_{42} = 282.4$. A saturated methane hydrocarbon in petroleum. Colorless liquid, m.37, insoluble in water.

eicosanic acid. $C_{20}H_{40}O_2 = 312.28$. White solid, m.74, in Japan wax. Cf. *arachidic acid*.

eicosanic acid*. Arachidic acid.

eicosanol*. Eicosyl alcohol.

eicosinene. Icosinene.

eicosyl. The radical—$C_{20}H_{41}$. **e. alcohol.** $Me(CH_2)_{18}$-$CH_2OH = 298.32$. Arachidic alcohol, eicosanol*. Colorless solid, m.71, in Madagascar palm wax.

eigenfunction. Characteristic function (German). If when an operator operates on an operand, the result can be expressed as the product of a constant and the operand. then the constant is known as the eigenvalue (eigenwert), and the operand as the eigenfunction. See *quantum numbers*.

eigons. Compounds of iodine or bromine which, as antiseptics, liberate iodine or bromine in the alimentary canal or in wounds.

eikonogen. $NH_2C_{10}H_5OH \cdot SO_3Na \cdot 2\frac{1}{2}H_2O$. Sodium amido-$\beta$-naphthol monosulfate. White crystals; a developer in photography.

eikonometer. A measuring scale on a microscope eyepiece seen superimposed on the image of the object.

eikosane. Eicosane.

-ein, -eine. A suffix, often indicating an internal anhydride.

Einstein, Albert. 1879–1955. German-born, American physicist and mathematician, Nobel Prize winner (1921). **E. equation for diffusion.** The diffusion coefficient $D = RT/6\pi Nr\eta$, where N is Avogadro's number, r the radius of the molecule, RT the gas constants, and η the viscosity. **E. formula.** $Mc^2 = E$, where M is the mass in grams, c the velocity of light in centimeters per second, and E the energy in ergs. Cf. *mass-energy cycle*. **E. law.** In a photochemical reaction one quantum of energy affects one molecule of matter, thus: $HI + h\nu = H + I$. **E. particle equation.** The motion of a particle in a liquid is related to the radius of the particle and the viscosity of the liquid. **E. theory.** See *relativity*. **E. unit.** Einstein. **E. viscosity formula.** $\eta = \eta_0(1 + k\phi)$, where η is the viscosity of a colloidal solution, η_0 the viscosity of the pure suspending medium, ϕ the total colloid per unit volume, and k a constant (1.5 to 4.75).

einstein. A unit of energy, $E = 6.06 \times 10^{23}$ quanta, analogous to the faraday (6.06×10^{23} electrons). The amount of absorbed radiation to activate 1 gm molecule of matter.

einsteinium. Es. Element 99, at. wt. 247. Known as its 5 isotopes, 248–252, produced by the bombardment of californium and berkelium in a cyclotron (University of California, 1954). It is radioactive and nonfissible.

eka- One or first (Sanskrit). Prefix applied to the first undiscovered element in a group of the periodic system. Cf. *dvi-*.

eka-elements. The missing elements of the periodic table. Cf. *eka-*, *dvi-*. E.g.: gallium (formerly e.-aluminum), germanium (formerly e.-silicon).

ekaosmium. Eo. Element 94, obtained by neutron bombardment of uranium (Enrico Fermi, 1936), and named esperium; half-life 90 min.

ekarhenium. Er. Element 93, obtained by neutron bombardment of uranium (Enrico Fermi, 1936), and named ausonium; half-life 13 min.

ekatantalum. Et. Element 91. Isotopes:

Protactinium (Pa)	32,000 years
Uranium Z (UZ)	9.7 hr
Brevium (Bv)	1.65 min

e. pentoxide. Et_2O_5. White powder, forming salts with acids.

ektebin. An antigen ointment containing concentrated tuberculin (dead human and bovine tubercle bacilli) used to treat tuberculosis.

El. Symbol for eline.

elae- Elae-, ele-,

elaeodic acid. Ricinoleic acid.

elaeolite. Nephelite.

elaeomargaric acid. Eleostearic acid.

elaeometer. A hydrometer for oils.

elaeostearic acid. Eleostearic acid.

elaidic acid. $C_{18}H_{34}O_2 = 282.37$. *trans*-9-Octadecenoic acid. A trans- isomer of oleic acid. Colorless leaflets, m.51.5, insoluble in water.

elaidin. $C_{57}H_{104}O_6 = 885.1$. The alaidic ester of glycerin in many nondrying oils other than fish oils; an isomer of olein.

elain. Ethylene (obsolete).

elaoptene. The liquid part of an essential oil. Cf. *stereoptene*.

elastase. A pancreatopeptidase enzyme.

elastic. Describing a substance that assumes its original shape after a force, causing distortion, is removed. **e. coefficient.** Young's modulus. **e. constants.** The numerical expressions of the force to which a solid, liquid, or gas can be subjected without deformation of its shape or condition after the force has ceased to act. **e. fluid.** A gas, as compared with a liquid. **e. limit.** The stress or force which produces a permanent change of 0.001% of the length of a substance. **e. modulus.** Modulus of elasticity.

elastica. Rubber.

elasticity. The property of being elastic. **adiabatic-** See *adiabatic*, **cubical-** The bulk modulus, or the hydrostatic pressure divided by the resulting decrease in volume per unit volume. **limit of-** The smallest value of stress that produces permanent alteration. **longitudinal-** Young's modulus. **modulus of-** Rigidity modulus. The ratio of stress intensity to percentage strain. **shear-** See *rigidity*. **torsional-** See *rigidity*.

elasticum. A carbohydrate layer between the epithelium and cortex of wool, responsible for the shrinkage of the latter.

elastin. A protein of yellow, elastic tissue, partly attacked by pepsin and digestible by trypsin.

elastomer. A generic term (Fisher) for all substances having the properties of natural, reclaimed, vulcanized, or synthetic rubber, q.v., in that they stretch under tension, have a high tensile strength, retract rapidly, and recover their original dimensions fully. Typical elastomers contain long-polymer chains. See table of elastomers below. **synthetic-** Rubber substitutes produced by: (1) polymerization of butadiene alone or with styrene (Ameripol, Buna, Hycar, Perbunan); (2) interaction between sodium polysulfides and dihalides (Thiokol); (3) polymerization of chloroprene

Elastomer	Trade names (examples)	Composition and manufacture
Natural rubber	....	*cis*-1,4-polyisoprene
Homopolymers		
Polychlorobutadiene............	Neoprene, Perbunan C	Emulsion polymerization of chloroprene (2-chloro-1,3-butadiene)
Polybutadiene	Buna 85, Diene, Philprene-*cis*-4, etc.	Ionic polymerization (in solution) of butadiene
Polyisoprene..................	Coral Rubber, Ameripol SN, etc.	Ionic polymerization (in solution) of isoprene
Copolymers		
Styrene-butadiene rubber	Buna S, Buna Hüls, SBR, Krylene, etc.	Emulsion polymerization of butadiene with styrene
Butyl rubber	Enjay Butyl, etc.	Ionic polymerization (in solution) of isobutylene with small amounts of isoprene
Nitrile rubber.................	Perbunan, Butaprene, Hycar, etc.	Emulsion polymerization of butadiene with acrylonitrile
Ethylene-propylene copolymer...	C 23	Ionic polymerization (in solution) of ethylene with propylene
Fluorine elastomers............	Kel F	Polymerization of monochloro-trifluorethylene with vinylidene fluoride
	Viton A	Polymerization of hexafluoro-propylene with vinylidene fluoride
Polyacrylates.................	Lactoprene	Copolymerization of methyl or ethyl acrylate with small amounts of chloroethyl vinyl ether
	Acrilan	Copolymerization of acrylic ester with acrylonitrile
Polycondensation products		
Polyurethanes	Vulcollan, Vulcaprene, etc.	Polycondensation of diisocyanates with polyesters
Silicone rubber................	G. E. Silicone R, Siloprene, etc.	Polycondensation of hydrolyzed dimethyldichlorosilane
Polysulfide rubber.............	Thiokol	Condensation of sodium polysulfides with aliphatic dihalogen compounds
Chemical conversion of high polymers		
Halogen substituted rubber	Hypalon	Chlorosulfonation (in solution) of polyethylene

From *Chemistry and Industry*, 1959, p. 1498.

(Duprene, Neoprene); (4) polymerization of iso-butylene (Vistanex); (5) polymerization and plasticization of vinyl chloride (Koroseal).

Elastoplast. Trademark for: (1) a substance having both elastic and plastic properties; (2) a boracic acid–plaster first-aid dressing.

elateric acid. $C_{20}H_{28}O_5 = 348.27$. Ecbalin. An acid of elaterium, m.200.

elaterin. $C_{20}H_{28}O_5 = 348.22$. Memordicin, from the juice of *Ecballium elaterium* and *Memordica balsamina* (Cucurbitaceae). White crystals. **alpha-** m.232. **beta-** m.195. Insoluble in water; a drastic purgative.

elaterite. $(CH_2)_x$. Mineral caoutchuc, elastic bitumen. A flammable elastic, brown mineral resin, d.0.8–1.23.

elaterium. Ecballium. Sediment from the juice of *Ecballium elaterium* (squirting cucumber) containing chiefly elaterin; a powerful cathartic.

elaterone. $C_{24}H_{30}O_5 = 398.23$. A ketone from elaterium. Colorless crystals, m.300.

elatic acid. $C_8H_{12}O_2 = 140.09$. An acid from colophony.

elayl. Ethylene. **e. chloride.** Ethylene dichloride.

Elbon. $C_{16}H_{14}O_3N_2 = 282.2$. Trademark for cinnamyl-*p*-oxyphenylurea. White needles, m.204, insoluble in water; used medicinally to treat respiratory disorders.

elder. Sambucus. **dwarf-** (1) Ebulus. (2) *Aralia hispida.*

Eldred's wire. Nickel-steel wire with a copper jacket and a platinum sheath, which may be sealed into glass.

eldrin. Barosmin.

elecampane. Inula.

elecampin. Inulin.

electret. The electrical equivalent of a permanent magnet. Thus carnauba wax, when solidified in a strong electric field acquires an orientation of molecules in the direction of this field, which can be retained for several years. The charges are on the surface and may amount to 5 esu/cm².

electric. Charged with or capable of developing electricity. Cf. *electrical.* **e. arc.** The luminous arc produced by the passage of electricity at high voltage from one electrode to another. **e. attraction.** The force by which oppositely charged bodies are drawn together. **e. axis.** The axis of a crystal that offers least resistance to the passage of an electric current. **e. battery.** A series of dry cells (q.v.) or galvanic (q.v.) elements. **e. calamine.** $ZnSiO_4 \cdot H_2O$. A native zinc silicate (U.K. usage). **e. charge.** A definite quantity of electricity, q.v. **e. conductivity.** See *conductivity.* **e. current.** The quantity of electricity; or the number of electrons flowing per unit time. In esu units it is the amount of electricity transferred in 1 sec; in emu units it is a current of such strength that 1 cm of the wire experiences a side thrust of 1 dyne, if at right angles to a magnetic field of unit intensity. The practical unit is the ampere, q.v.; its quantity the coulomb, q.v.; and its potential difference the volt, q.v. **e. double layer.** See *electrolytic solution pressure.* **e. eye.** A photoelectric cell used to indicate a null point or end point, or to control a process automatically. Cf. *sectrometer.* **e. field.** The forces around an electrically charged body. **e. field intensity.** A unit of force; the ratio of the force acting on a quantity of electricity at a point, to that quantity of electricity. **e. furnace.** A furnace, q.v., for heating or processing molten electrolytes. **e. lines of forces.** Imaginary curves radiating from a positive toward a negative charge. **e. potential.** Electromotive force. **e. radiation.** See *electromagnetic radiation.* **e. spark.** A luminous discharge produced by the disruptive passage of electricity at high voltage from one electrode to another. **e. surface density.** The number of electrons per unit area. **e. tension.** Electromotive force. **e. transformer.** See *transformer.* **e. valve.** A device that allows an e. current to pass in one direction only; as, a rectifier.

electrical. Pertaining to electricity. **e. birefringence.** Kerr effect. **e. capacitance.** See *capacitance.* **e. capacitor.** See *capacitor.* **e. capacity.** E. capacitance. **e. cell.** Voltaic cell. **e. condenser.** E. capacitor. **e. conductivity.** Molal (molecular) conductivity. (1) The quantity of electricity transmitted by a unit area in unit time under a unit potential gradient. (2) The conductivity (in mhos) of one gram equivalent of electrolyte, in solution, between electrodes 1 cm apart. **e. Curie point.** See *Curie.* **e. current.** Electric c. **e. elements.** Voltaic cells. **e. flux.** The flow of an electric current. **e. pressure.** Electromotive force. **e. units.** See table below. Conductivity is the reciprocal of resistance. Unit, reciprocal ohm, mho. emu = electromagnetic units, based on the strength of magnetic poles. esu = electrostatic units, based on the strength of electric charges.

electricity. A form of energy that produces magnetic, chemical, thermal, and radiant effects, generated by friction or induction or chemically. (1) *Material conception:* All-pervading negative electrons; their continuous motion is a "current," their abrupt motion a "discharge," their absence a "positive charge." (2) *Dynamic conception:* A stress or strain in the ether resulting in "electric waves" and "radiation." (3) *Magnetic conception:* A field of force. **acid-** Positive e. **atmospheric-** The e. of the atmosphere, e.g., from charged clouds.

Unit of	Practical emu	cgs emu	cgs esu
Resistance......................	1 ohm	10^9	1.1124×10^{-12}
Current (strength)...............	1 ampere	10^{-1}	2.998×10^9
Electromotive force (potential)	1 volt	10^8	0.0033349
Capacity	1 farad	10^{-9}	8.9892×10^{11}
Quantity	1 coulomb	10^{-1}	2.998×10^9
Inductance	1 henry	10^9	1.1124×10^{-12}
Work	1 joule	10^7	10^7

chemical- Galvanic e. **dynamic-** Current or galvanic as opposed to static e. It indicates electrons in movement. It may be generated by chemical reaction (voltaic), induction (faradic), or magnets (magnetic). **faradic-** Induced e. A current of high voltage produced in a secondary coil when a galvanic current passes through the primary coil of an induction machine. **frictional-** Static e. obtained by friction, e.g., rubbing a glass rod with fur. **galvanic-** Dynamic. **induced-** Faradic. **negative-** A current of electrons passing from anode to cathode outside, and from cathode to anode inside, a galvanic cell. **photo-** See *photoelectricity*. **positive-** (1) An absence or deficiency of negative electrons. (2) A current in the direction opposite to negative. According to this convention, a current flows from negative to positive. **static-** Frictional, as opposed to dynamic. It indicates electrons accumulated at rest, and their sudden escape from the surface of an insulated conductor. **thermo-** (1) E. produced by heat. (2) The heating effects of e. **tribo-** E. produced by friction. **voltaic-** A current produced by an electric battery.

electrification. Charging with electricity or electrons.

electrify. To charge with electricity.

electrion. Early name for electron.

electroaffinity. E or E_0. Electrolytic potential. The electrode potential, q.v., for a concentration corresponding with 1 gm ion/liter of ions liberated from an electrode. See *electromotive force*.

electroanalysis. Analytical methods based on electrolysis or conductometry; as, electrometric titration.

electrochemical. Pertaining to both chemistry and electricity. **e. constant.** Faraday. **e. deposition.** The formation of a metallic layer by electrolysis for: (1) recovery of metals from ores, or refining metals; (2) electroplating, to produce a protective or ornamental coating, or for reproduction, e.g., in photoengraving. **e. equivalent.** E. The mass in grams of any element deposited from an electrolytic cell by an electric current of 1 coulomb: $E = (A/V)0.000,010,36$, where A is the atomic weight, and V the valency of the element. Cf. *Faraday's law*. **e. machining.** Finishing an article by making it an e. anode, the cathode being shaped to impart the required form when material is transferred to it from the anode by electroplating in reverse. **e. series.** Displacement series. **e. spectrum.** A current-voltage graph produced by the polarograph, q.v.

electrochemistry. The science of transforming chemical into electrical energy, and vice versa.

electrocratic. Describing a colloid stabilized by an electric charge.

electrode. The device by which an electric current passes into or out of a cell, apparatus, or body. It may be a simple wire or complex device, (hydrogen e.) or the container of the cell itself. **auxiliary-** A standard e. used during electrodeposition to measure the potential at which this occurs. **calomel-** See (1) *calomel e.*, (2) *Hildebrand e.* **capillary-** See *Lippmann e.* **dropping-** A standard e. formed by a stream of mercury falling in fine droplets through a capillary tube into the electrolyte. A fresh surface is thus obtained continuously. Cf. *polarograph, Heyrovsky.* **gas-** See *gas e.* **gas-jet-** See *sprudel effect.* **glass-** A thin glass membrane

separating solutions of known and unknown pH value, the potential difference between the 2 sides being measured. **Hildebrand-** q.v. **hydrogen-** q.v. **negative-** The cathode, negode, or negatively charged pole, by which the current "passes out," and to which anions are attracted. **positive-** The anode, posode, or positively charged pole, by which the current "enters," and to which cations are attracted. **quinone-** q.v. **reversible-** An e. which owes its potential to reversible ionic changes as $H_2 \rightleftharpoons 2H^+ + 2e^-$.

e. potential. The tendency, expressed in volts, of a metal to dissolve in a solution containing its ions. The algebraic difference of the 2e. potentials of the electrodes gives the voltage E of the cell $= E_0 \mp (0.058/n) \log C$, where C is the concentration in gram ions per liter of the ions given off by the e., E_0 the electroaffinity, n the valency of the ion.

electrodeposition. The precipitation of a metal on an electrode. **e. analysis.** The quantitative e. of an element from a solution. The electrode is weighed before and after deposition.

electrodynamics. The study of moving charges.

electrodynamometer. An instrument to measure the intensity of faradic and alternating currents.

electroencephalogram. An electrical record of the waveform of electric currents developed in the human brain.

electroendosmosis. The production of endosmosis, q.v., by an electric potential.

electroforming. The production of metallic tubes, sheets, or patterns by electrolysis.

electrographic analysis. The qualitative analysis of a metallic surface by placing it in contact with a gelatin-coated paper saturated with an electrolyte and making it the anode of an applied electric current. After removal of the electrolyte, a suitable reagent is added to the paper. Any suitable other metal may be used as electrode on the other side of the paper.

electroless deposition. The deposition of a metal in solution on another solid metal by chemical means, instead of by means of an electric current as in electrodeposition, e.g., by the reducing action of hypophosphites in nickel plating.

electroluminescence. Electrophotoluminescence. The adiabatic emission of light by certain substances when placed in an electric field.

electrolysis. The separation of the ions of an electrolyte hence, the decomposition of a compound, liquid, molten, or in solution, by an electric current. Cf. *electrochemical decomposition*. **internal-** The separation of a metal in the presence of a much more electropositive (i.e., baser) metal, by inserting an anode of the baser metal in the solution, and connecting it directly with a platinum cathode on which the metal is deposited. No external current is required; e.g., Cu on Zn immersed in $CuSO_4$ solution.

electrolyte. (1) A substance that dissociates into 2 or more ions, to some extent, in water. Solutions of e. thus conduct the electric current and can be decomposed by it (*electrolysis*). (2) Sulfuric acid, d.1.150–1.835, used in batteries and accumulators. **non-** A substance that does not dissociate into ions. **strong-** An e. that is highly dissociated even at moderate dilutions, and does not obey Ostwald's dilution law. **weak-** An e. that is fully or partly dissociated only at high dilution, and obeys the dilution law.

electrolytic. Pertaining to decomposition by an electric current. **e. apparatus.** An ammeter, voltmeter, rheostat, and rotating platinum anode for quantitative electrodeposition. **e. dissociation.** Ionization. **e. gas.** A mixture of hydrogen (2 vol.) and oxygen (1 vol.) obtained by electrolysis of water. **e. potential.** Electroaffinity. **e. separation.** The graded electrodeposition, q.v., of metals from a solution, by varying the applied potential according to the electrode potentials of the metals. **e. solution tension theory.** Nernst theory.

electrolyze, electrolyse. To subject to electrolysis.

electromagnet. Soft iron around which is wound an insulated wire; while an electric current passes through the wire, the iron is magnetized.

electromagnetic. Pertaining to electricity and magnetism. **e. field.** The area of force surrounding an electromagnet or a conductor through which a current flows. The intensity of the magnetic field at the center of a circular conductor of radius r is $2i/r$, where i is the current. **e. law.** See *Coulomb.* **e. radiation.** See *radiation.* **e. separation.** The separation of the magnetic constituents of ores by means of an electromagnet. **e. units.** emu. A system of electrical units based on dynamics; it includes the practical units (volts, ampere, ohm, etc.) which are multiples or fractions of the cgs e. units. See *electrical units* (table).

electromerism. Mobile electron tautomerism shown by a set of compounds, the electron constellations of which vary in position, although the atomic kernels do not. Cf. *chelate bond.*

electromers. Isomers that differ in the distribution of electrons among their atoms.

electrometer. An instrument to measure the quantity or intensity of an electric current. **absolute-** Galvanometer. Ammeter. **capillary-** A null-point e. which detects 1 mv by the motion, in a capillary tube, of a dilute sulfuric acid–mercury interface. **emanation-** See *emanation.* **photo-** Photogalvanometer. **quadrant-** Galvanoscope.

electromotion. Mechanical action produced by electricity.

electromotive. In motion produced by electricity. **e. force.** e, emf. Electric pressure, voltage. The work, in volts per unit quantity of electricity flowing through a cell.

1 international volt = 1.00043 absolute volts

1 absolute volt = 0.99957 international volt

= 1 practical emu

= 10^8 cgs emu

= 0.0033349 esu

For molar concentrations the emf of an electrolytic cell is the algebraic difference between the electroaffinities, q.v., of the ions of the metals forming the electrodes. See *electrode potential.* **e. series.** Displacement series.

electron. (1) An alloy: Mg 90, Al 5%, and a little Zn, Mn, or Cu. (2) Negatron, β particle. An elementary unit of electricity, or a negatively

charged corpuscle, whose accumulation on an insolated conductor produces static electricity, and whose flow through a conductor produces an electric current. Electrons are in the atomic nucleus and atomic shell, and their number and arrangement account for valency and other properties. Electrons are liberated from the atom by radioactive disintegration, and transferred from one atom to another in oxidation-reduction reactions (electronation). They are made visible by the Wilson track method, and Millikan's fog chamber. Their mass changes with their velocity. Constants are:

Mass . . . . 9.035×10^{-28} gm
Charge . . . . 4.8029×10^{-10} esu
                     or 1.602×10^{-20} emu
Spin (angular momentum) . . . 9.02×10^{-28} erg-sec

Cf. *e, atom.* **Auger-** See secondary electron *spectroscopy.* **binding-** An e. which holds together the positive charges in the atomic nucleus. **cementing-** An e. which is assumed to hold together the 2 H nuclei of the helium atom. **free-** (1) A corpuscle or charge of negative electricity (mass 9.01×10^{-28} gm). (2) An e. in an atom which is not shared by another atom. **heavy-** Yukawa particle. A penetrating component of cosmic rays, having an electronic charge greater than that of an e., but less than that of a proton. **metastasic-** An e. which changes its position in the atom owing to radioactive changes; generally moving from the valence orbit into the interior. **negative-** Negatron or free e. Cf. *positive e.* **nuclear-** E. of the atomic nucleus. **orbital-** E. in the orbit of an atom. **paired-** One of 2 electrons constituting a nonpolar bond, q.v. Cf. *twin e.* **phoretic-** E. which conduct by passing freely from atom to atom when their outer orbits are in contact. **photo-** E. liberated from a surface by exposure to light. **piezo-** A supposedly disk-shaped e. in the helium nucleus. **positive-** (1) A heavy small corpuscle associated with a mass more than that of hydrogen; is assumed to be an H nucleus or atom from which an e. has been removed. (2) Positron, q.v. A particle of nearly zero mass with a positive charge. **recoil-** E. scattered by bombardment of a substance with α or β rays. **secondary-** Auger- E. emitted by a metal surface irradiated with X rays of 150–200 kv frequency. They affect photographic film to extents that depend on the atomic number of the surface metal and are used in qualitative analysis. **twin-** See *paired* e. **valency-** The 1 to 8 electrons in the outer orbit of an atom which are responsible for valency. They can pass from one atom to the other (polar bond) or be held in common by 2 atoms (nonpolar bond). See *bond, valency.*

e. affinity. The capture by a substance, e.g., an oxidizing agent, of the electrons of other substances. See *electronate.* **e. beam.** A stream of electrons, as in a cathode tube. **e. compounds rule.** The position of the phase boundaries, at room temperature, in the equilibrium diagram of a binary alloy depends on the e. concentration. **e. diffraction.** The diffraction of a stream of electrons by a surface. Cf. *e. microscope.* **e. displacement.** A shift of an e. pair held in common between 2 atomic nuclei, toward one nucleus. See *Lucas theory.* **e. distribution curve.** A curve showing the e. distribution among the different available energy levels. **e. exchange polymer.** See *polymer*. **e. eye.** Iconoscope. **e. formula.** A chemical notation depicting the e. displacement in an organic compound. **e. fugacity.** The tendency to lose electrons by an electrode in a solution. **e. gas.** A system consisting of free electrons shared by all atoms, as in a metal; see *atomic structure*. **e. lens.** The electrostatic field surrounding an aperture in a charged conductor. A circular hole will focus electrons with a focal length of $2V/(G_2 - G_1)$, where V is the energy of incident particles in volts, and G_1, G_2 are the potential gradients on the 2 sides of the plate. See *microscope*. **e. microscope.** See *microscope*. **e. optics.** The control of e. motion by means of charged electric fields. Cf. *lens* effect on light. **e. pair.** A pair of electrons which are held in common by 2 atoms. **e. probe analysis.** Quantitative analysis by comparison of the characteristic X-ray intensities from the sample and from a standard. **e. replacement.** Electronation. Cf. *displacement*. **e. screening effect.** See *screening effect*. **e. spin resonance.** A spectroscopic technique analogous to nuclear magnetic resonance, q.v., in which radiation of measurable frequency and wave length is used to supply energy to protons instead of to electrons. **e. transfer.** The passage of one or more electrons from atom or to atom or ion in an oxidation-reduction reaction. **e. tube.** A device for an electric discharge; as, thermionic valve. **e. volt.** ev. eV. Equivalent volt = 1.59×10^{-12} erg. The energy acquired by an e. when it falls through a potential of one volt.

electronate. To cause electronation or reduction. **de-** To cause de-electronation or oxidation.

electronation reactions. Oxidation-reduction reactions.

electronegative. (1) Having a negative charge or excess of electrons. (2) Capable of capturing electrons. **e. element.** An element with more than 3 valence electrons located on the left side of the periodic table, especially the nonmetals. **e. ion.** Anion, or negative ion. **e. radical.** An acid radical or a group of atoms having a negative charge.

electronic. Pertaining to electrons. **e. charge.** A quantity of electricity numerically equal to the charge on an electron = $(4.770 \pm 0.005) \times 10^{-10}$ absolute esu. **e. formula.** See *formula*. **e. mass.** The mass of a negative electron moving with a velocity much less than that of light. **e. number.** The number of peripheral electrons in the elements of a compound. **e. ratio.** The ratio of e. charge to e. mass: $e/m = 5.305 \times 10^{17}$ esu = 1.769×10^7 emu. **e. structure symbol.** A notation showing the distribution of electrons in the molecule. See *bonds, molecular diagram*.

electronics. Radionics. The study of the applications of vacuum tubes (valves) in electric circuits.

electronyl. The atomic entity that is active by virtue of the number of electrons in excess of or less than the nuclear charge.

electroosmosis. The flow of a liquid through a capillary when an electric field is applied parallel to its axis. **e. pressure.** The pressure developed between the ends of a capillary when the e. flow of a liquid through it is prevented.

electropainting. Electrolytic deposition of paint in

a thin layer on a metal surface, which is made the anode.

electrophilic. Nucleophilic. Describing chemical reactions having the characteristics of electronic processes.

electrophoresis. The migration of suspended particles in an electric field. In particular, the accelerated chromatographic separation of compounds by immersing each end of the medium in an electrolyte and applying an electric potential. Cf. *ionophoresis*.

electrophorogram. A paper chromatogram produced by electrophoresis.

electrophorus. Insulated disks of ebonite and brass, used to produce frictional electricity.

electrophotography. A method of photocopying in which a zinc oxide–coated paper is negatively charged by a corona discharge, exposed to light via the document which dissipates the charge locally, and developed by contact with a positively charged resinous toning powder, which is subsequently fixed by fusion.

electroplating. The formation of a metallic coat on a baser metal by electrolysis.

electropolishing. The production of a highly polished and chemically clean surface on a stainless steel object by making it the anode in an electrolyte, to reverse the process of electroplating; about 0.0005 in. is removed.

electropositive. (1) Having a positive charge or a deficiency of electrons. (2) Capable of losing or giving up electrons. **e. elements.** The elements on the right-hand side of the periodic table, especially the light metals. **e. ion.** Cation. An atom which has lost one or more negative electrons and has become positive. **e. radical.** A basic radical or a group of atoms having a positive charge; as, NH_4^+

electropotential. Electrode potential.

electrorefining. The purification of metals by electrolysis.

electroresponse. The increase in resistance of certain cells with increase of current.

electroscope. A device to detect electric charges or gaseous ions. **gold-leaf-** Two strips of gold leaf suspended from an insulated conductor and in a glass vessel. **measuring-** A gold-leaf e. which can be rotated so that an electrostatic and gravitational balance is established. The position of the leaf is read in a low-focus microscope.

electroscopy. The measurement of the degree of ionization of a gas in terms of the rate of fall of the leaf of a charged gold electroscope.

electrosol. A colloidal solution of a metal obtained by passing an electric discharge between metal electrodes in distilled water. See *collosol*.

electrostatic. Pertaining to electric charges at rest. **e. capacity.** The ratio of quantity of electricity to difference of potential. **e. law.** See *Coulomb*. **e. mixing.** See *mixture*. **e. series.** Triboelectric series. **e. units.** esu, ESU. A system of electrical units based on static data. See *electrical units* (table).

electrostenolysis. The precipitation of metals in the pores of a membrane by electrolysis.

electrostriction. (1) The contraction of the solvent of a solution due to the attractions of the water dipoles by the ions of the solute. (2) Mechanical deformation due to the application of an electric charge. Cf. *piezelectricity*.

electrosynthesis. Synthetic reactions produced by an electric current.

electrotaxis. Electrotropism. The motion of living cells caused by an electric current.

electrotropism. Electrotaxis.

electrotyping. The reproduction of type, reliefs, etc., by copper electrodeposited on the layer of graphite with which a mold or object has been covered.

electrovalence. A fundamental atomic linkage due to transfer as distinct from sharing of electrons. Cf. *polar bonds*.

electroviscosity. The increase in the effective viscosity of a solid suspension due to the double layer on the particle present.

electrowinning. The separation of metals from their ores by electrolysis. Cf. *electrorefining*.

electrum. (1) Amber (2) An alloy: Au 80, Ag 20 %, d.13.0–16.0, hardness 2.5–3.0.

elemecin. $C_6H_2 \cdot (OMe)_3C_3H_5 = 208.10$. 3,4,5-Trimethoxypropenylbenzene. Aromatic ether, b.153, from elemi.

elemene. $C_{15}H_{26} = 206.2$. A hydrocarbon, $b_{10mm}119$ from elemi.

element(s). Matter consisting of atoms of one type; a substance that cannot be further decomposed by chemical means; a chemical unit; an ultimate constituent of matter. There are 103 known elements, from H to Lr, inclusive. The atoms of an e. may consist of a mixture of 2 or more atoms of different mass which have similar chemical properties, but different atomic weights (isotopes). The atomic weight is the mean of those of the isotopes calculated in the proportions present. The elements of higher atomic weight are radioactive. **abundance of-** See *abundance*. **alkaline-** E. of the first group of the periodic system: Li, Na, K, Rb, Cs. **basylous-** E. of the first, second, and third groups of the periodic system, located in the upper right half of the periodic table, whose oxides form bases with water. **bio-** See *bioelements*. **biogenic-** A chemical element contained in living organisms. **bridge-** E. in the lower half of the periodic table (especially the rare-earth metals), which show a gradation of properties. *Bunsen-Bunsen cell*. **chemical-** Element. **dvi-** See *dvi-*. **earthy-** E. of the third group of the periodic system; *e.g*, Al, Sc. **eka-** See *eka-element*. **electrical-** Galvanic, or voltaic cell. An electrolytic cell. **electronegative-** E. whose atoms have more than 4 valency electrons, on the left of the periodic table. **electropositive-** E. whose atoms have less than 4 valence electrons, on the right of the periodic table. **extinct-** Supposed e. of very low atomic weight, which may have formerly existed on the earth. See *nebulium*. **group-** E. belonging to the same group in the periodic system; as opposed to period elements. **haloid-** E. of the seventh group of the periodic table: F, Cl, Br, I. **heating-** Resistance wire, used in heating apparatus. **inert-** E. of the zero group of the periodic table; noble gases He, A, Kr, Xe, Nt, which are electrically inert; few compounds are known. **metallic-** E. of the lower half and right upper half of the periodic table, e.g., the light and heavy metals. **negative-** Electronegative. **nonmetallic-** E. in the left upper half of the perio-

dic table. **normal-** Standard cell. **period-** An e. whose properties are closely related to e. in the same period of the periodic table; e.g., Mn, Fe, Co, Ni. Cf. *group* e. **primal-** The original, nebulous form of matter from which all are supposed to have evolved: the protyle, pantagon, or urstoff. **principal-** The 14 most common, abundant, and important e.; viz., Al, Ca, C, Cl, H, Fe, Mg, N, O, P, K, Si, Na, S. Cf. *abundance*. **radio-** An e. made artificially radioactive by bombardment with particles; as radiosodium. **radioactive-** Those e. of at. no. 82 to 103. **terminal-** E. of the zero group of the periodic system which form the terminals of each period, i.e., the noble gases. **transition-** (1) E. of the fourth group of the periodic system which form the transition from light metal to nonmetal, light metal to heavy metal, and heavy metal to nonmetal: i.e., elements of the carbon group. (2) The triads Fe, Co, Ni; Ru, Rh, Pd; and Os, Ir, Pt; which connect the seventh and first groups. (3) The e. from Ti to Ni, Zr to Pd, and Hf to Pt, which connect the A series in the periodic system. **transuranic-** The radioactive e., Np, Pu, Am, Cm, Bk, Cf having half-life periods of 25 min to 24,000 years. **typical-** The e. of the second period of the periodic system, which show the typical characters of each group: Ne, Na, Mg, Si, P, S, Cl.

For alphabetical list of elements giving *atomic weights* and *atomic numbers*, see *atomic weights* (table).

For numerical list of atomic numbers including *valency* and *atomic structure* of elements, see *periodic chain*.

See also, *ions, ionic numbers, radioactive elements*.

For a list of *isobars, isotopes*, see *abundance, displacement series, isomorphs*.

elementary. (1) Ultimate, simple, fundamental. (2) Pertaining to elements. **e. analysis.** The determination of carbon and hydrogen in organic compounds. Cf. *analysis*. **e. charge.** The charge on an electron, $e = 4.770 \times 10^{-10}$ esu. **e. molecule** An association of similar atoms; as, O_2. **e. space.** The space surrounding the positively charged nucleus, in which the electrons are arranged in patterns. Cf. *dynad*.

elementide. A group of atoms or elements transferred as whole complexes in a chemical reaction.

elemi. (1) Gum elemi. A soft, yellow aromatic resin from *Canarium commune* (Burseraceae), Philippines. Used in ointments, and to toughen varnishes (2) Originally the resin of *Amyris elemifera*. **e. oil.** An essential oil, d.0.870–0.910, from e.

elemicin. $C_{12}H_{16}O_3 = 208.1$. 1-Allyl-3,4,5-trimethoxybenzene. Colorless liquid, b.144, from elemi oil. **iso-** Elemecin.

elemin. $C_{40}H_{68}O = 564.7$. A crystalline resin in elemi.

elemol. $C_{15}H_{26}O = 222.2$. A camphor from elemi. **alpha-** m.46. **beta-** $b_{10mm}144$.

elemonic acid. An acid, m.220.5, from elemi.

eleonorite. $Fe_6P_4O_{19} \cdot 8H_2O$. Brown, rhombic masses, d.2.52–2.59, hardness 7.

eleoptene. The liquid terpene or hydrocarbon of an essential oil. Cf. *stearoptene*.

eleostearic acid. $Me(CH_2)_7(CH:CH)_3(CH_2)_3COOH = 280.27$. Octadeca-9,11,13-trienoic acid.* From

HISTORICAL TABLE OF ELEMENTS

Prehistoric and Archaic Time

	Carbon	
	Sulfur	
	Gold	
	Silver	
4000 B.C.	Copper	Egypt
3500 B.C.	Iron	
?	Lead	
1600 B.C.	Tin	Chaldea
1000 B.C.	Antimony	
300 B.C.	Mercury	Theophrastus

Alchemistic Period

1220	Arsenic	Albertus Magnus
1450	Bismuth	Basil Valentine
1520	Zinc	Paracelsus
1669	Phosphorus	Brand

Beginnings of Chemistry

1733	Cobalt	Brandt
1750	Platinum	Wood
1751	Nickel	Cronstedt
1758	Sodium in salts	Marggraf
	Potassium in salts	Marggraf

Founding of Chemistry

1766	Hydrogen	Cavendish
1772	Nitrogen	Rutherford
1774	Oxygen	Priestley
	Chlorine	Scheele
	Manganese	Scheele, Gahn
	Barium	Scheele
1782	Tellurium	Müller
	Molybdenum	Hjelm
1783	Tungsten	d'Elhujar
1787	Strontium	Cruickshank
1789	Zirconium	Klaproth
	Uranium	Klaproth
	Titanium	Gregor
1794	Yttrium	Gadolin
1797	Chromium	Vauquelin
	Beryllium	Vauquelin
1801	Columbium	Hatchett
1802	Tantalum	Ekeberg
1803	Cerium	Klaproth
	Osmium	Tennant
	Iridium	Tennant
1804	Palladium	Wollaston
	Rhodium	Wollaston

Beginnings of Electrochemistry

1808	Calcium	Davy
	Magnesium	Davy
	Boron	Davy
1812	Iodine	Courtois
1817	Selenium	Berzelius
	Lithium	Arfvedson
	Cadmium	Strohmeyer
1823	Silicon	Berzelius
1826	Bromine	Balard
1827	Aluminium	Wöhler
1828	Thorium	Berzelius

Beginnings of Electrochemistry (continued)

1830	Vanadium	Sefström
1839	Lanthanum	Mosander
1841	(Didymium)	Mosander
1843	Erbium	Mosander
1845	Ruthenium	Claus

Beginnings of Spectroscopy

1860	Cesium	Bunsen
1861	Rubidium	Bunsen
	Thallium	Crookes
1863	Indium	Reich, Richter

Beginnings of Systematization

1872	Eka-elements	Mendeleyeev
1875	Gallium	Boisbaudran
1878	Terbium	Delafontaine
	Ytterbium	Marignac
	Holmium	Soret
	Thulium	Cleve
1879	Samarium	Boisbaudran
	Scandium	Nilson
1880	Gadolinium	Marignac
1885	Praseodymium	Welsbach
1886	Dysprosium	Boisbaudran
	Neodymium	Welsbach
	Germanium	Winkler
	Fluorine	Moissan

Modern Chemistry

1894	Argon	Ramsay and Rayleigh
1895	Helium	Clove, Ramsay
1898	Neon	Ramsay and Travers
	Krypton	Ramsay and Travers
	Xenon	Ramsay and Travers
	(radioactivity)	
	Polonium	Curie
	Radium	Curie
	Actinium	Debierne, Giesel
	Radon (niton)	Curie, Dorn
1900	Europium	Demarcay
1907	Lutetium	Urbain, Welsbach
1913	Brevium	Fajans
	(mass spectrograph)	
1923	Hafnium	Coster and Hevesy
	(technetium)	
1925	Masurium	Noddack and Tacke
	Rhenium	Noddack and Tacke
1926	Illium	Hopkins
	(magneto-optic method)	
1930	Virginium	Allison and Murphy
1931	Alabamine (astatine)	Allison, etc.
1935	Ekarhenium	Rolla
	Ekaosmium	Rolla
	(artificially produced)	
1939	Francium	Perey
1940	Neptunium	Abelson and McMillon
	Plutonium	Seaborg, etc.
1944	Americium	Seaborg, James, Morgan, and Ghiorso
	Curium	Seaborg, James
	(artificially produced)	Morgan, and Ghiorso

HISTORICAL TABLE OF ELEMENTS (*continued*)

Modern Chemistry (*continued*)

1949	Berkelium . . . . (artificially produced)	Seaborg, Thompson, and Ghiorso
	Californium	as berkelium
1952	Einsteinium	University of California, Argonne National Laboratory, Los Alamos Scientific Laboratory
1953	Fermium . . . . (from fission debris)	as einsteinium
1955	Mendelevium . . . . (artificially produced)	Ghiorso
1957	Nobelium . . . . (artificially produced)	International team (Nobel Institute for Physics, Stockholm)
1961	Lawrencium (artificially produced)	Ghiorso, Sikkeland, Larsh, and Latimer, University of California

the oil of the seeds of *Elaeococca vernicia*. Colorless scales. **alpha-** m.48. **beta-** m.71. Insoluble in water; both occur in tung oil. **epsilon-** Couepic acid. A solid, m.75, from the fat of the seeds of *Couepia grandiflora* (Rosaceae), S. America.

elimination. The expulsion of waste from the body.

eline. El. Ekaiodine. Early name for astatine, At. Insoluble in ordinary solvents; widely distributed, but in small quantities; found in the water of Great Salt Lake and in some deserts oils of Western U.S. **e. chlorides.** El_xCl_y. White waxy masses or crystalline fibers, soluble in water, alcohol, or ether. **e. nitrate.** $ElNO_3$ (?). Yellowish-white solid, soluble in water or carbon tetrachloride. **e. sulfate.** $El(SO_4)_2$ (?). White, hygroscopic solid, soluble in water, alcohol, or ether.

elinvar. An alloy of Fe, Ni, and Cr, used to manufacture watch hairsprings (*elasticity invari*able).

elixir. (1) A liquid preparation for the administration of drugs in a pleasant form. Usually sweetened and aromatized alcoholic liquids or cordials. (2) The alchemical principle of everlasting life and youth, and the means of converting the baser metals into gold, (philosopher's stone). **simple, aromatic-** A suspension of talc in an aqueous-alcoholic solution of a syrup, with orange flavoring (U.S.P.).

elkerite. Pseudofucosan. A native fucose pentosan bitumen formed by the slow oxidation of crude oil. Cf. *fucosan*.

Elkosin. Trademark for sulfisomidine.

ellagene. $C_{20}H_{14} = 254.12$ A hydrocarbon produced by the reduction of ellagic acid. Small plates, m.197, soluble in warm benzene.

ellagic acid. $C_{14}H_6O_8 = 302.05$. Gallogen. Yellow crystals, decomp. by heat, sparingly soluble in hot water. It occurs or is produced by hydrolysis of many tannins; as, myrobalans.

ellagitannic acid. $C_{14}H_{10}O_{10} = 338.1$. A tannin-like substance from the pods of *Caesalpinia coriaria*, (Leguminosae) and the root bark of *Punicia granatum* (Punicaceae); slightly soluble in water.

ellagitannin. A tannin giving ellagic acid on hydrolysis. Two types, derived from myrabolans and from galloyl derivatives of ellagic acid.

Elliot tester. An apparatus to determine the flash-point of illuminating oil.

elliptone. $C_{20}H_{16}O_6 = 352.0$. A toxic constituent of derris root, *D. elliptica*.

elm bark. Ulmus, elm bark, slippery elm. The bark of *Ulmus campestri* or *U. fulva*, (Urticaceae); a demulcent, and adulterant for cassia. Cf. *ulmin*, *ulmic acid*.

Elon. Trademark for monomethyl-*p*-amino-phenol-sulfonate, a photographic developer.

elpidite. $Na_2ZrSi_6O_{15}\cdot 3H_2O$. A red, pearly, silicate d.2.5, hardness 7.

eluant. A liquid used for the extraction of one solid from another, e.g., in chromatography.

eluate. The solution resulting from elution.

elution. A process of extracting one solid from another.

elutriation. The process of washing and separating suspended particles by decantation.

elwotite. A hard alloy of tungsten containing not more than 30% titanium.

Em. Symbol for emanation. See *radon*.

em. The cgs electromagnetic unit of quantity of electricity.

emamium. Early name for actinium.

eman. A radioactive unit for the radon content of the atmosphere; 10^{-10} curie per liter. Cf. *mache unit*.

emanation. Em. An element, at. no. 86, consisting of the isotopes radon, thoron, and actinon. A gaseous disintegration product of radioactive substances. **actinium-** AcEm, Actinon. An isotope of radon, a disintegration product of AcX, and the parent substance of AcC'. **radium-** RaEm, radon, Rn. Disintegration product of radium and the parent substance of RaC'. **thorium-** ThX. Thoron. An isotope of radon. The gaseous disintegration product of ThX, and the parent substance of ThC'. See *radioactive*, *isotopes*.

e. electroscope. An electroscope (Rutherford) to measure the emanation of radioactive bodies.

Embden ester. A glucose–phosphoric acid ester in muscle.

embedding. The fixing of tissues in a solid mass, so that they can be cut into thin sections. **e. bath.** A device for heating paraffin wax and placing tissues in the molten liquid. **e. oven.** An incubator with drawers.

embeliate. A salt of embelic acid.

embelic acid. $C_{18}H_{28}O_4 = 308.22$. Embelin. The active principle, m.142, from the berries of *Embelia ribes* (Myrsinaceae); used to treat tapeworms.

embelin. Embelic acid.

embellic acid. Embelic acid.

embequin. Diiodohydroxyquinoline.

embinal. Barbitone-sodium.

embolite. $2AgBr\cdot 3AgCl$. A rare mineral; gray masses, d.5.8, hardness 1.5.

embrocation. Pharmaceutical term for a preparation applied by rubbing.

embryology. The study of the development of an organism.

embutal. Pentobarbital.

emdite. Abbreviation for ethylammonium ethyldiethylcarbamate; an alternative to hydrogen sulfide in qualitative inorganic analysis.

emerald. A green variety of beryl; a precious stone. **oriental-** A green variety of corundum. **e. green.** Paris green.

emergent column. The portion of the thread of a thermometer which is not immersed in the substance whose temperature is being measured. Correction for its contraction (mercury in glass) $N(T - t) \times 0.000156$, where N is the number of degrees on the emergent stem, T the temperature as read, and t the temperature halfway up the emergent column given by a second similar thermometer.

emeri. Emery.

emery. Impure crystalline corundum mixed with oxides of iron; a polishing, grinding, and abrasive material. **e. cloth.** An abrasive fabric coated with glue and e. **e. paper.** Paper coated with glue and e. used in place of sandpaper.

emetamine. $C_{29}H_{36}O_4N_2 = 476.29.$ An alkaloid from ipecac. Colorless crystals, m.156.

emetic. A drug that causes vomiting; used especially in cases of poisoning; e.g. 12% common salt, or 0.8% zinc sulfate, in warm water. **mechanical-** Causing vomiting by tickling the throat with a feather.

emetine. $C_{24}H_{40}O_4N_2 = 480.66.$ An alkaloid related to cephaeline from the root of *Cephaelis ipecacuanha*, ipecac. Colorless crystals, m.74, sparingly soluble in water; a specific agent against ameba. **iso-** $C_{29}H_{44}O_4N_2 = 480.32.$ An alkaloid from ipecac, m.98. **e. hydrochloride.** $C_{29}H_{40}O_4N_2 \cdot 2HCl = 553.58.$ White crystals, m.53, soluble in water; an antiprotozoan (U.S.P.).

emetoid. A 10% trituration of the alkaloids of ipecac, containing emetine and cephaeline hydrochlorides; an expectorant and eliminant.

emf. EMF. Abbreviation for electromotive force.

emission. The liberation of energy, especially as radiations. **e. spectrum.** See *spectrum*.

emitron. Iconoscope. An electron tube used in television (obsolete).

emmenagogue. A drug that produces or increases menstrual flow; e.g., ergot.

emmenin. A crystalline female sex hormone, related to estrone.

emmer. A variety of wheat, formerly abundant in Central Europe and the Near East.

Emmerling tube. A cylinder filled with glass beads for the absorption of gases by liquids.

emodin. $C_{15}H_{10}O_5 = 270.09.$ 1,3,8-Trihydroxy-6-methylanthraquinone. A purgative principle in many *Rhamnus* species. Orange prisms, m.234, sparingly soluble in water. **aloe-** 1,9-Dioxy-3-carbinolanthraquinone. An isomer of emodin and constituent of aloes, cascara, senna, and frangula.

emollient. A drug applied externally to soothe skin, e.g., talcum.

empiric(al). Describing knowledge gained by experience, without theoretical considerations. Cf. *scientific*.

empirical formula. A chemical formula which shows the number and variety of atoms, but does not indicate the way in which they are linked together; e.g., $Fe_2S_3O_{12}$ is the e.f. for $Fe_2(SO_4)_3.$

emplastrum. An adhesive plaster.

emplectite. $CuBiS_2.$ Gray masses, d.6.4, hardness 2.5.

empyreal air. See *oxygen*.

empyreumatic. Any odorous substance formed by the destructive distillation of vegetable or animal matter. **e. oils.** Oily e., e.g., creosote.

emu, EMU. Abbreviation for electromagnetic units.

emulgator. Emulsifier.

emulsification. Making an emulsion from 2 immiscible liquids by agitation with addition of an emulsifier to prevent the droplets coalescing. **de-** The breaking up of an emulsion; e.g., by addition of an excess of the dispersed phase, heating, freezing, or centrifuging.

emulsifier. Emulsifying agent, emulgator. A substance which makes an emulsion more stable (as, ammonium lineolate), by reducing the surface tension or protecting the droplets with a film.

emulsify. To make an emulsion.

emulsifying wax. A B.P. preparation containing cetostearyl alcohol 90, sodium lauryl sulfate 10, and water 4 pts., heated at $115°C.$

emulsin. Synaptase. An enzyme in almonds, and the seeds of Rosaceae. White, albuminous powder, soluble in water, and containing C 48.7, H 7.1, O 28.7, N 14.1, S $1.25\%.$ It hydrolyzes glucosides.

emulsion. Emulsoid. A fluid consisting of a microscopically heterogeneous mixture of 2 normally immiscible liquid phases, in which one liquid forms minute droplets suspended in the other liquid. Cf. *colloids*, *emulsifier*, *Aerosol*. **invert-** water in oil e.

en-, -en. (1) Greek prefix meaning in, on, or at. (2) Prefix indicating a C:C bond; as, enamic, enolic. Cf. *ene-*. (3) Suffix often indicating a hydrocarbon or cyclic compound, e.g., thiophen.

enamel. (1) A gloss paint. (2) A vitreous, opaque, or transparent glaze, fused over metal or pottery. **dentine-** The mainly inorganic covering of the crown of teeth. When mature, it is the hardest body tissue, being as hard as sapphire. **grayware-** A mixture of feldspar 50, borax 30% with anhydrous sodium carbonate, sodium nitrate, and cryolite. **jewelry-** A mixture of silica 14, boric acid 20, sodium nitrate 10, potassium nitrate $23\%.$ **white cover-** A mixture of quartz 10–22, feldspar 18–33, borax 18–34, soda 3–10, sodium nitrate 2–5, cryolite 3–17$\%$; colored with a metallic oxide, generally triplumbic tetroxide.

enamic form. The ammine form of an imine, characterized by the radical $>C:CH \cdot NO—$; cf. *enimization*.

enamine. A tautomeric form of Schiff's base. Cf. *keto-inol* equilibrium.

enanth. A synthetic polymer (U.S.S.R. origin) made by the high-pressure polymerization of ethylene and certain amino acids.

enanthaldehyde. $C_6H_{13}CHO = 114.1.$ Heptylic aldehyde, heptanal, oenanthal. Colorless liquid, b.155, slightly soluble in water.

enanthic acid. Heptoic acid. **e. aldehyde.** Enanthaldehyde. **e. ether.** $C_6H_{13} \cdot O \cdot C_2H_5 = 158.2.$ Cognac oil, oenanthylic ethylether, ethyl pelargonate. Colorless oil, insoluble in water; a flavoring.

enanthine. Heptine.

enantho. Heptyl alcohol.

enanthotoxin. $C_{17}H_{22}O_5 = 306.17$. A poisonous resin from the rhizomes of *Oenanthe* (five-finger root).

enanthyl. The radical $C_2H_{13}-$, derived from hexane.

enanthylic acid. Enanthic acid.

enantiomers. Optical isomers related as object and nonsuperimposable image. Cf. *enantiomorph*.

enantiomorph. (1) A crystal which corresponds with another crystal as an object with its image. (2) The opposite optically active substance, e.g., the dextro- and levo- forms.

enantiomorphus. Related as enantiomorphs.

enantiotropic, enantiotropy. Existing in 2 crystal forms, one stable above, the other below, the transition-point temperature.

enargite. Cu_3AsS_4. Gray, metallic rhombs, d.4.3–4.5, hardness 3.

endiol. The grouping $-C(OH){=}C(OH)-$.

endo- Prefix indicating a "bridge" linkage joining 2 nonadjacent atoms in a ring of an organic molecule.

endocrine. Pertaining to the secretion of ductless glands. See *hormones*.

endogenous. Generated or orginiating within. **e. purines.** The purine waste products of metabolism in excretions. Cf. *exogenous*.

endomorph. A mineral enclosed within another (the perimorph).

endoscope. A device to render internal organs or surfaces visible.

endosmosis. The diffusion of a liquid through an organic membrane. Cf. *exosmosis*.

endothermic. Absorbing heat. Antonym: exothermic. **e. compound.** A compound absorbing heat during formation, and liberating heat on decomposition. **e. reaction.** A slow chemical change which absorbs a definite number of calories; the stable exothermic compounds are transformed into unstable e. compounds.

endotoxin. Bacterial poisons set free by autolysis after cell death.

endoxerosis. The internal decline of a plant.

endoxy- Prefix indicating oxygen in a ring.

end point. (1) The stage in titration when the reaction is complete. (2) The point of balance between 2 forces.

endrin. $C_{12}H_8OCl_6 = 373.94$. White crystals, m. exceeds 200 (decomp.), insoluble in water; a pesticide stereoisomer of dieldrin, having similar properties.

-ene. Suffix indicating: (1) Hydrocarbons of the ethylene and benzene series. Cf. *-diene, -yl.* (2) A cyclic compound; as, terpene, menthene. (3) A bivalent radical with points of attachment on separate C atoms; as, ethylene. Cf. *-idene.*

enema. A liquid preparation for rectal injection.

energetics. (1) The study of forces at work. (2) A philosophy which denies the existence of passive inert matter and conceives the universe as arrangements of energies in space.

energon. An indivisible unit of energy. See *quantum*.

energy. Capacity to do work; e.g., heat, light, electricity, chemical action, or mechanical energy. The work done by the force which produces a change in the velocity of a body or a change in its shape and configuration, or both. It can be defined by *force* $\times$ *distance*, or *one-half mass* $\times$ *square of velocity.* **atomic-** See *atomic*. **available-** Free. **chemical-** E. involved in chemical changes. See *thermodynamics.* **conservation of-** E. may be transformed from one form to another, but cannot be destroyed or created. **creation of-** E. is created when matter is annihilated; as, in a star. Cf. *mass-energy cycle.* **degradation of-** The tendency for e. always to be changing to a lower form, e.g., into heat (Kelvin). **destruction of-** The conversion of e. into matter. **dissipation of-** Degradation of. **dynamic-** Kinetic. **electric-** Electricity. **free-** The amount of e. which can be utilized for work. The change in the free e. of a reacting substance is a measure of its affinity. **ionization-** Ionization potential. **kinetic-** The power of a body due to its motion $= 0.5$ mass $\times$ (velocity)^2. Cf. *kinetics.* **latent-** Potential e. **lattice-** The forces which hold the atoms together in a crystal. **mechanical-** E. manifesting itself in mechanical work. **medial-** The e. of a medium or solvent on which its dielectric powers and its ionization, tautomerism, etc., depend. **potential-** Static, latent e. The unreleased e. in a body due to its position, composition. or condition; as, a lifted weight, an endothermic compound, or a compressed gas. p.e. $=$ mass $\times$ distance $\times$ acceleration due to gravity. **radiant-** See *radiations.* **solution-** The e. forces between the molecules of solute and solvent. Cf. *bond.* **specific-** The power of a body due to its relative position (potential e.) and motion (kinetic e.). **thermal-** See *heat*, standard *coal* unit. World energy resources of fossil fuels (as coal equivalent, million tons):

Coal	3,000,000
Oil shales and sands	200,000
Peat	100,000
Natural gas	90,000
Petroleum	90,000

e. change of atom. The change of voltage, V, where λ is the wavelength; $V = 12,336/\lambda$. **e. diagram.** A figure giving a relative picture of the stationary states of a radiating atom. Cf. *quantum, hydrogen atom.* **e. levels.** The stationary states or orbits of an atom. An electron changing from one to ano.ner will absorb (excitation) or emit (radiation) energy. See *mass energy cycle.* **e. quanta.** See *quantum theory, Stoner quanta.* **e. units.** Units of e. are based on the work to produce a change in velocity (kinetic energy), or of condition or shape (potential energy), or both. See table, p. 243.

Unit of velocity: $v = LT^{-1}$

Unit of acceleration: a $= 981$ cgs units

Unit of force: $F = Ma$

Unit of pressure: $p =$ dyne/cm^2 (981 cgs units)

$\quad p =$ atmosphere (1,013,663, cgs units)

Unit of work: erg $=$ dyne/cm.

$\quad$ 1 kg-meter $= 981 \times 10^5$ ergs

Practical conversion factors: 1 international joule $= 1.00034$ absolute joules. 1 absolute joule $= 0.99966$ international joule $= 10^7$ ergs $= 0.101972$ kg-meter $= 0.737560$ ft-lb $= 0.277778 \times 10^{-6}$ kwhr.

enesol. Mercury salicylarsenite.

enfleurage. Removal of the perfume from picked flowers (e.g., jasmine), by placing them near an odorless mixture of tallow and lard, which absorbs the perfume to give a pomade from which the perfume is subsequently extracted.

engineering. Utilizing the physical properties of matter in inventing, designing, constructing, building, and managing structures and machines. **chemical-** The branch of e. concerned with chemical plants.

Engler, Carl. 1842–1925. German chemist noted for his work on petroleum. **E. degree.** A relative unit of viscosity.

enhanced. Intensified, e.g., enhanced spectrum lines.

eniac. Abbreviation for electronic numerical integrator, an automatic calculator. It transforms quantities into electric pulses which are counted at 100,000 per second.

enimization. An intramolecular rearrangement of amines and imines analogous to the keto-enol equilibrium: (enamic form)—C:CH·NH—⇌CH·-CH:N— (enimic form).

enim. A glucosidal coloring matter of black grape skins.

-enine. Suffix indicating a hydrocarbon with a double and triple bond; e.g., butenine.

Enka, Enkalon. Trade names for polyamide synthetic fibers.

Enkalene. Trade name for a polyester-terylene synthetic fiber.

enndecane. Nonadecane.

ennea- Prefix indicating nine. See *Greek*.

enneadekane. Nonadecane.

enniatin. A Gram-positive antibacterial (but not antifungal) antibiotic from *Fusarium orthoceras*.

enol form. The alcohol form of a ketone characterized by the radical =C:(OH)·R. See *isomerism*.

enolic ester type. A compound of the enol form, $R_2C=C(OH)R$.

Enovid. Norethynodrel. Trade name for 17-ethinyl-17-hydroxy-5(10)-estren-3-one, a 19-nor steroid structurally similar to progesterone. An oral contraceptive.

ensilage. (1) Silage, or fodder preserved in a silo. (2) The process of making silage.

ensmartis. Ferriammonium chloride.

enstatite. $MgSiO_3$. A gray, rhombic silicate, in meteors, d.3.1, hardness 5.5.

Entepas. Trade name for a sodium aminosalicylate.

enterokinase. An activating enzyme of the intestinal epithelium, which transforms trypsinogen to trypsin.

enthalpimetry. The use of heat-change measurements to indicate a reaction end point.

enthalpy. The heat content H per unit mass in BThU per pound, $H = E + PV/J$, where E is internal energy, P absolute pressure in pounds per square foot, V specific volume in cubic feet per pound, and J = joules equivalent (778 ft-lb/BThU).

entropy. The unavailable energy of a substance due to the internal motion of the molecules. Cf. *free energy*. The degree of molecular chaos of a system (Gibbs), or the extent to which an energy system has "rundown" (Tolman). Entropy is directly proportional to the quantity of heat contained in a body, and inversely proportional to its temperature; at absolute zero, e. vanishes.

-enyl. Suffix indicating a bivalent unsaturated hydrocarbon radical; as, ethenyl.

enzyme(s). Ferment. A catalyst, usually a protein, produced by living cells; it has a specific action and optimum activity at a definite pH value. Classification is based on the type of reaction, or the material (substrate) acted upon. The first e. crystallized was *urease* (Sumner 1926). Common enzymes and their pH optima:

Amylase, salivary	6.1–6.9
Amylase, pancreatic	7.0
Amylase, malt	4.6–5.2
Catalase	7.0
Lipase, pancreatic	8.0
Lipase, gastric	4–5
Lipase, salivary	7.6–7.8
Maltase	6.1–6.8
Maltase, *Solanum indicum*	5.5
Papain	4–7
Pepsin (on egg albumin)	1.2–1.6
Pepsin (on gelatin)	3.0–3.5
Phosphatase, bone	9.5
Phosphatase, plasma	8.8–9.2
Phosphatase, red blood cells	6.0–6.8
Phosphatase, plant sources	3.4–6.0
Protease, autolytic (kidney, liver)	4.5
Rennin	4.5
Sucrase, intestinal	6.8
Sucrase, yeast	4.4–4.6
Sucrase, *Solanum indicum*	6.0
Trypsin, pancreatic	8.0
Trypsin, synthetic action	5.7
Urease	7.0

The Report of the Commission on Enzymes of the International Union of Biochemistry, 1961, classifies and gives the nomenclature and properties of over 700 e. **amylolytic-** E. hydrolyzing starch to dextrin and maltose; e.g., amylase. **anti-** A substance which inhibits e. action. **apo-** See *holo-*. **blood-** E. of the blood, q.v. **co-** A catalyst formed in the body from pantothenic acid. Cf. activated *acetic acid.* **coagulating-** E. changing soluble proteins to insoluble products, e.g., thrombin. **cytohydrolytic-** The e. which render cellulose soluble, e.g., cytase. **deamidizing-** E. hydrolyzing amines to ammonia and hydroxy acids or purine bodies, e.g., deamidase. **decarboxylizing-** E. splitting carbon dioxide from organic acids, e.g., carboxylase. **desmo-** An insoluble e. linked to insoluble cell constituents. Cf. *lyo-.* **glycolytic-** E. hydrolyzing glucosides to glucose and residue, e.g., glucosidase. **holo-** The whole e. which is divided into the apoenzyme (protein carrier) and the coferment. **hydrolytic-** E. hydrolyzing carbohydrates to simple sugars, e.g., inulase. **inactive-** A nonreactive e. **inverting-** E. which change optically inactive sugars to optically active carbohydrates, or dextrorotary to levorotary or vice versa, e.g., invertase. **lipolytic-** E. hydrolyzing esters (fats, etc.) to fatty acids and alcohols, e.g., lipases. **lyo-** The soluble form of an e. which can be dissolved from the cell. Cf. *desmo-.* **old yellow-** An enzyme in brewers' yeast which oxidizes the reduced form of coenzyme. **oxidizing-** E. oxidizing alcohols or aldehydes to acids, or phenols to quinones, e.g., oxidase. **pro-** Zymogen, **proteolytic-** E. hydrolyzing proteins to albumoses and peptones, e.g., pepsin. **Q-** An e- from potato, which converts

ENERGY CONVERSION FACTORS

	joule	cal	BThU	kwhr	atm
1 joule =	1	0.239006	0.947831×10^{-3}	2.77778×10^{-7}	9.86896×10^{-3}
1 cal =	4.1840	1	3.96573×10^{-3}	1.162220×10^{-6}	4.12917×10^{-2}
1 BThU =	1.055040×10^3	2.52161×10^2	1	2.93067×10^{-4}	10.41215
1 kwhr =	3.6×10^6	8.60422×10^5	3412.19	1	35,528.2
1 atm =	101.3278	24.2179	9.60417×10^{-2}	2.8147×10^{-5}	1

ENERGY CONVERSION FACTORS FOR MOLAR AND MOLECULAR QUANTITIES

	ergs/molecule	cal/mole	ev/molecule	cm^{-1}
1 erg/molecule =	1	1.43965×10^{16}	6.2422×10^{11}	5.0362×10^{15}
1 cal/mole =	6.9461×10^{-17}	1	4.3359×10^{-5}	0.34982
1 ev/molecule =	1.60199×10^{-12}	2.30631×10^4	1	8.0679×10^8
1 wave number =	1.98562×10^{-16}	2.85861	1.23947×10^{-4}	1

amylose into amylopectin. **reducing-** E. which reduce oxidizing agents, e.g., peroxidase. **yellow-** Diaphorase. A compound of protein with lactoflavin phosphate, from yeast.

e. elixir. A palatable preparation of pepsin and rennet; a gastric tonic. **e. unit.** The amount of an e. that will catalyze the transformation of 1 micromole of substrate per minute under standard conditions.

enzymolysis. A chemical change produced by enzyme action.

enzymosis. Enzymolysis, with special reference to fermentation.

eosin, eosine. $C_{20}H_8O_5Br_4 = 648.84$. Tetrabromfluorescein, bromeosin. Red, triclinic needles, insoluble in water; a dye and indicator (alkalies—green fluorescence, acids—yellow). **soluble-** (1) Commercial e. (2) E. Yellowish.

E. Bluish. Erythrosin. **e. dyes.** Dyestuffs for wool and silk derived from fluorescein, e.g., eosin.
e. soluble. E. Yellowish. **E. Yellowish.** $C_{20}H_6O_5$-$Br_4K_2 = 724.83$ or $C_{20}H_6O_5Br_4Na_2 = 691.83$. A red powder, soluble in water; a dye.

eosins. A group of dyestuffs derived from triphenylmethane.

epanorin. $C_{25}H_{25}O_6N = 435.24$. A yellow constituent of the lichen *Lecanora epanora*.

epanutin. Phenytoin-sodium.

ephedrine. $C_6H_5 \cdot CH(OH) \cdot CH(NH \cdot Me) : Me = 165.32$. 2-Methylamino-α-phenylpropanol. An alkaloid from *Ephedra* species (Gnetaceae), Europe; or synthetic. **levo-** An alkaloid from the Chinese drug MaHuang from *Ephedra equisetina* (Gnetaceae). White, bitter crystals, m.41, soluble in water; used similarly to e. hydrochloride. **pseudo-** The dextro isomer of α-phenyl-β-methyl-β-methylaminoethanol. An alkaloid from *Ephedra vulgaris* (Gnetaceae), Japan. Colorless crystals, m.115, insoluble in water. Cf. *adrenaline*.

e. hydrochloride. $C_{10}H_{15}ON \cdot HCl = 201.72$. Odorless, bitter white crystals, m. 218, soluble in water or alcohol (B.P.). Used as a mydriatic, and in ophthalmology as an atropine substitute. *levo-* Colorless crystals, readily soluble in water. Used as an adrenalin substitute to raise blood pressure; also in bronchial asthma and hay fever. *pseudo-* Yellow crystals, m.175, soluble in water or alcohol. Used in ophthalmology as 10% solution. **e.**

sulfate. $(C_{10}H_{15}ON)_2 \cdot H_2SO_4 = 428.56$. Fine, white, odorless crystals, darkened in light. Soluble in water or alcohol; a sympathomimetic (U.S.P.).

epi- (1) Greek prefix indicating upon, through, or toward. (2) Prefix indicating a bridge or intramolecular connection; as,

$$R \cdot C \cdot C \cdot C \cdot R$$
$$\diagdown O \diagup$$

epi-position. ε- The 1,6-position of naphthalene or other condensed rings. Cf. *epoxy*.

epiborneol. $C_{10}H_{18}O = 154.20$. 3-Camphanol, 3-hydroxycamphane. An isomer of borneol, q.v.

epiboulangerite. $Pb_3Sb_2S_8$. A metallic sulfantimonide of lead.

epicaine. A vasopressor and local anesthetic, said to be α-(3,4-dihydroxyphenyl)-β-(p-aminobenzoyl-β-diethylaminoethanol)-α-ethanone hydrochloride.

epicamphor. $C_{10}H_{16}O = 152.2$. 3-Camphanone, 3-ketocamphane, β-camphor. An isomer of camphor in which the keto group is in the 3-position.

epicatechol. $C_{15}H_{14}O_6 = 290.11$. **dextro-** or Catechol-c. Colorless prisms, m.245, from gambir catechu. **levo-** Thick white prisms, m.245. **dextro- levo-** Colorless needles, m.225. A constituent of the green tea leaf.

epichlorite. A basic, aluminum-iron silicate of the chlorite group.

epichlorohydrin. $C_3H_5OCl = 92.51$. Chloropropylene oxide, 1-chloro-2,3-epoxypropane,

$$CH_2 \overset{O}{\diagup\diagdown} CH \cdot CH_2Cl$$

A colorless liquid, $d_0°1.203$, b.117, insoluble in water, miscible with alcohol or ether. Used as a solvent for resins and nitrocellulose, and in the manufacture of varnishes, lacquers, and cements for celluloid articles. Cf. *epihydrin*.

epicyanohydrin. $C_3H_5OCN = 83.07$. Cyanopropylene oxide, β,γ-expoxybutyronitrile. Colorless prisms, m.162, soluble in hot water or alcohol.

epidemiology. The scientific study of epidemics.

epidermin. A fibrous protein of the epidermis.

epidichlorohydrin. $C_3H_4Cl_2 = 110.95$. 2,3-Dichloropropene*. Colorless liquid, b.96, insoluble in water; a solvent.

epididymite. $Na_2O\cdot2BeO\cdot6SiO_2\cdot H_2O$. Rhombic crystals, d.3.55.

epidioxide. Indicating a substance containing 2 O atoms attached to different C atoms of the same skeleton. Cf. *epoxide*.

epidosite. A crystalline schist derived from diabase.

epidote. $HCa_2(Al\cdot Fe)_3Si_3O_{16}$. Pistacite. A crystalline schist in gneisses, garnet rock, amphibolite, etc. Green, monoclinic masses, d.3.3–3.5, hardness 6–7.

epidotization. The disintegration of feldspar, hornblende, augite, and biotite into epidote.

epiethylin. $O\cdot CH_2\cdot CH\cdot CH_2OC_2H_5 = 86.07$. Glycidyl ethyl ether, 2,3-epoxy-1-ethoxypropane. Colorless liquid, b.124; a solvent for varnishes.

epigenite. $Cu_7As_2S_{12}$. A copper sulfoarsenide containing iron.

epiguanine. $C_6H_7ON_5 = 165.1$. 2-Amino-6-methyl-8-oxypurine, methylguanine. A purine in the urine, especially during leukemia.

epihydric acid. Glycidic acid. **e. alcohol.** Glycidol.

epihydrin. $CH_2\cdot O\cdot CHMe = 58.1$. Propylene epoxide. Colorless liquid, d.0.859, m.35, soluble in water. **e. alcohol.** Glycidol. **e. carboxylic acid.** $C_4H_6O_3 = 102.1$. Colorless crystals, m.225.

epihydrinic acid. Glycidic acid.

epiiodohydrin. $C_3H_5OI = 183.89$. 1,2-Epoxy-3-iodopropane. Colorless liquid, b.160, insoluble in water; a solvent.

Epikote. Trade name for a class of condensation polymers prepared from epichlorhydrin and diphenyloylpropane; used in coatings and varnishes.

epimeric. Having the character of epimerides.

epimerides. Epimers. Isomers differing only in the arrangement of H and OH on the last asymmetric C atom of a chain; as, *d*-glucose and *d*-mannose.

epimers. Epimerides.

epinephrine. U.S.P. name for adrenaline. **e. bitartrate.** $C_9H_{13}O_3N\cdot C_4H_6O_6 = 333.30$. Adrenaline bitartrate, suprarenin. Gray crystals, darkening on exposure, m.149, soluble in water; a sympathomimetic (U.S.P., B.P.).

epinine. $(HO)_2C_6H_3(CH_2)_2NHMe = 167.1$. 3,4-Dihydroxyphenylethylamine. Colorless crystals; synthetic substitute for epinephrine.

epiosin. $C_{16}H_{12}N_2 = 232.2$. Methyldiphenylenamidoazol. Prisms, m.195, insoluble in water. An anodyne.

epipastic. A dusting powder.

epiphenylin. $O\cdot CH_2\cdot CHCH_2OPh = 150.08$. Glycidyl phenyl ether, 2,3-epoxy-1-phenoxypropane. Colorless liquid, $b_{22mm}131$; a solvent for varnishes.

epiphyte. An organism living on, but not feeding on, another organism, e.g., orchid.

epipolic. Fluorescent.

episol. A brand of sodium morrhuate used as a sclerosing agent.

epispastic. Vesicant.

episperm. The membrane between the shell and kernel of a seed.

epistilbite. $Ca_2Al_4Si_{11}O_{30}$. Colorless, monoclinics d.2.24–2.36, hardness 3.5–4.

epithelium. See *carcinoma*.

epm. Abbreviation for equivalents per million = parts per million per equivalent weight in milligrams.

e.p.n.s. Abbreviation for electroplate on nickel-silver.

epidoxation. A oxidizing reaction in which an unsaturated olefin link is converted to a cyclic 3-membered ether;

epoxide. Oxirane. A product of epoxidation. E. have many uses in plastics (see *epoxy resins*), plasticizers, insecticides, and drugs.

epoxy- Prefix indicating an —O— bridge in a molecule attached to different C atoms, which are otherwise united. See *epoxidation*. **e. propanol.** Glycidol. **e. propionic acid.** Glycidic acid. **e. resins.** A group of synthetic resins containing the group $(—O—C_6H_4\cdot CMe_2\cdot C_6H_4\cdot O\cdot CH_2\cdot CH—OH\cdot CH_2)_n$, where n is 0 to 9. They adhere to smooth surfaces, and resist weather and chemicals.

EPR. Trademark for ethylenepropylene rubber, which has the special qualities of resistance to heat and oxidation.

epsilon. (Greek). Symbol for ergon, etheron, dielectric constant, electrode potential, epiposition. ϵ. **acid.** 3,6-Naphthylaminedisulfonic acid.

epsomite. $MgSO_4$. Colorless, rhombic prisms, d.1.7, hardness 2.

Epsom salts. Magnesium sulfate.

eptoin. Phenytoin-sodium.

epuration. The purification of sugary liquors by defecation, etc.

epuré. A bituminous constructional mixture from Trinidad.

eqn. Abbreviation for equation.

equanil. Meprobamate.

equation. (1) A symbolical expression of equality. (2) An expression of a chemical reaction. The formulas of the reacting substances are placed on the left, those of the reaction products on the right, with the equality sign between. This indicates that the total number of atoms of each kind on each side balance. The molecular equation, $2NaOH + H_2SO_4 = Na_2SO_4 + 2H_2O$, states that 2 molecules of sodium hydroxide and one molecule of sulfuric acid give one molecule of sodium sulfate and 2 molecules of water. **analytical-** An e. showing the decomposition of a compound into simpler constituents. See *analysis*. **electronic-** Ionic. **ionic-** An e. expressed in terms of ions as, $2OH^- + 2H^+ = 2H_2O$. **metathetical-** An e. expressing a metathesis. **molecular-** An e. expressed in terms of molecules. Many molecular equations can be expressed in ionic form (see above). **numeric-** A mathematical e., each term of which is dimensionless. **transmutation-** An e. which indicates the disintegration or synthesis of elements. Thus, $_1H^1 + _5B^{11} \rightarrow 3_2He^4$ means that element no. 5 (boron, isotopic weight 11) is bombarded by a proton (element no. 1, hydrogen, weight 1) and forms 3 atoms of element 2 (helium, weight 4). The sum of the atomic numbers (prefixed subscripts), and also the sum of the isotopic weights (suffixed superscript), is the same on both sides.

e. of state. A group of mathematical expressions derived from the equation $pv = RT$, which define the physical conditions of a homogeneous liquid or gaseous system by relating concentration or volume, pressure, and absolute temperature for a given mass of substance. See *Ramsay-Young, Van der Waals, Dieterici*, and *Clausius* equations.

equilenin. $C_{18}H_{18}O_2 = 266.2$. 3-Hydroxy-17-keto-estrapentaene. A sterol, q.v., sex hormone produced by the biological degradation of cholesterol in urine during pregnancy. See *cholane*.

equilibrium. A condition in which contending forces are balanced. Cf. *triple point diagram*. **chemical-** The balanced state reached when chemical reaction apparently stops; decomposition and recombination proceed with equal speed. See *mass action*. **disturbed-** The result of the removal of one or more reaction products or reacting substances from a chemical e., causing it to shift. **heterogeneous-** A chemical e. between 2 (or more) phases. **homogeneous-** A chemical e. in a single phase. **invariant** An e. in which the quantity of one component approaches zero. **ionic-** An e. that involves a balanced condition of ions. **kinetic-** The balanced state of 2 opposite reactions. Cf. *static e.* **molecular-** An e. in which the components are molecules. **monophase-** Homogeneous. **polyphase-** Heterogeneous. **stable-** A mobile condition which, after a casual displacement, is again restored. **static-** The equilibrium attained when all reaction ceases. **e. constant.** Dissociation constant.

equilin. $C_{18}H_{20}O_2 = 268.2$. 3-Hydroxy-17-keto-estratetraene. A female sex hormone produced by the biological degradation of cholesterol. See *cholane*.

equipartition. (1) The orderly arrangement of atoms, e.g., in a crystal. (2) The condition of molecules in a gas, where the molecules keep the same average distance apart under the same pressure. **e. of energy.** The total energy of a molecule is divided equally among its different degrees of freedom.

equisetic acid. Aconitic acid.

Equisetum. A genus of herbaceous, spore-producing plants (horsetail, scouring rush, bottlebrush) which are rich in silica.

equiv. Abbreviation for equivalent.

equivalence. The relative combining powers of a set of atoms or radicals. **e. point.** Stoichiometric point. The point of a titration where the amounts of titrant and substance being titrated are chemically equivalent.

equivalent. (1) The weight in grams of an element that combines with or displaces 1 gm of hydrogen. (2) The weight of a substance contained in one liter of a normal solution: determined by: (*a*) dividing the atomic weight of an element by its valency; (*b*) dividing the molecular weight of a compound by the valency of its principal atom or radical; (*c*) calculating the quanity of a substance that combines with 1 gm of hydrogen or with 8 gm of oxygen. (3) Having the same valency. **electrochemical-** See *electrochemical*. **gram-** Equivalent weight. **milli-** The weight of a substance in grams contained in 1 ml of a normal solution. **toxic-** The lethal dose, q.v.

e. charge. The amount of electricity in a gram-e. of substance, i.e., 6.06×10^{23} electrons or 96,494 international coulombs. Cf. *Faraday*. **e. conductivity.** See *conductivity*. **e. weight.** Gram-equivalent; the equivalent of a substance in grams, calculated by dividing its formula weight by its valency. With *acids*, the number of replaceable H atoms, with *bases* the number of OH groups.

equiviscous temperature. An expression of viscosity in terms of the temperature at which a substance has a standard viscosity.

Er. Symbol for erbium.

era. See *geologic era*.

erbia. Erbium oxide.

erbium. Er = 167.26; at. no. 68. A rare-earth metal, discovered in 1879 by Cleve in the erbia of Marignac (1878) and Berlin (1860). (The erbia discovered and named in 1843 by Mosander was actually terbium.) A metallic substance, d.4.77, insoluble in water, soluble in acids; trivalent and forms red salts. It has been suggested for use in incandescent lamp filaments to produce a selective emission of visible rays. **e. acetate.** $Er(C_2H_3O_2)_2$. $4H_2O = 416.77$. Pink triclinic crystals, soluble in water. **e. nitrate.** $Er(NO_3)_3 \cdot 6H_2O = 461.8$. Pink crystals, soluble in water. **e. oxalate.** $Er_2(C_2O_4)_3 \cdot 10H_2O = 779.44$. Red powder, decomp. 575. **e. oxide.** $Er_2O_3 = 383.4$. Erbia. Orange powder, insoluble in water. At high temperature it glows green. **e. sulfate.** $Er_2(SO_4)_3 \cdot 8H_2O = 767.6$. Red crystals, soluble in water.

Erdmann, H. 1862–1910. German chemist noted for analytical methods. **E., Otto Linneé.** 1804–1869. German chemist noted for atomic weight determinations. **E. float.** A small, partly filled, sealed glass tube for obtaining accurate buret readings. **E. reagent.** (1) Concentrated sulfuric acid containing 2 drops of conc. nitric acid per 100 ml; a reagent for alkaloids. (2) A solution of 1,8-aminonaphthol-4,6-disulfonic acid gives a red color with nitrites.

erdschreiber. A culture medium made by autoclaving earth with solutions of sodium nitrate and sodium dihydrogen phosphate.

eremophilone. $C_{15}H_{22}O = 218.15$. A ketone, m.42, in the wood oil of *Eremophila mitchelli* (Myoporaceae), Australia.

erepsin. A proteolytic enzyme in animal and vegetable tissues.

ereptase. Erepsin.

erg. The cgs unit of work or energy: the force necessary to overcome the resistance of one dyne acting through one centimeter.

$$1 \text{ joule} = 10^7 \text{ ergs}$$
$$1 \text{ foot-poundal} = 4.214 \times 10^5 \text{ ergs}$$
$$1 \text{ gram-calorie (20°C)} = 4.184 \times 10^7 \text{ ergs}$$

ergamine. Histamine.

ergine. (1) $C_{16}H_{17}N_3O = 267.14$. A base obtained by hydrolysis of ergotoxine. (2) Erogone. A categorical name for substances which exert biological catalytic effects in small quantities, e.g., vitamins.

ergobasine. Ergometrine.

ergocalciferol. Vitamin D_2. See *calciferol*.

ergochrysin. $C_{28}H_{28}O_{12} = 556.2$. Yellow pigment, m.366, from ergot.

ergocornine. $C_{31}H_{39}O_5N_5 = 561.40$. A constituent of commercial ergotoxine, obtained by fractional crystallization of the tartrate derivatives.

ergocristine. $C_{35}H_{39}O_5N_5 = 609.40$. A constituent of commercial ergotoxine associated with ergocornine.

ergodic. Having the same average value of a specific

property, whether derived from a large number of small samples or small number of large samples.

ergoflavine. $C_{15}H_{14}O_7 = 306.1$. Yellow pigment, m.344, from ergot.

ergokryptine. A constituent of commercial ergotoxine, associated with ergocornine.

ergometrine. $C_{19}H_{23}N_3O_2 = 329.2$. Ergobasine, ergotocin, ergotetrine. An alkaloid from ergot; colorless crystals, m.159, soluble in water with blue fluorescence. Used in obstetrics, and (as its salts) as an oxytoxic. The maleate (ergotrate) and tartrate are official (B.P.).

ergon. (1) ϵ. or $h\nu$. An energy quantum, q.v. $\epsilon = 6.554 \times 10^{-27}$ erg. sec $= h\nu$. (2) Vitazyme.

ergonomics. The scientific study of the relationship between man and his environment; the science of fitting the occupation to the worker.

ergonovine. Ergometrine (U.S.P.).

ergosinine. $C_{30}H_{35}N_5O_5 = 545.3$. An alkaloid, decomp. 228, from ergot.

ergosterin. Ergosterol.

ergosterol. Ergosterin. An inert alcohol derived from ergot; occurs in yeast and is the provitamin of vitamin D. See *sterols*. It is a mixture of $C_{26}H_{40}O = 368.31$, white solid, m.154, and $C_{27}H_{42}O = 383.32$, colorless solid, m.165. Cf. *irradiation*. **irradiated-** Viosterol.

ergotetrine. Ergometrine.

ergot. Ergota, spurred rye, *Secale cornutum*. The dried sclerotium of *Claviceps purpurea* (Hypocreaceae), Spain, a fungus on numerous grasses, especially replacing the grain of rye, *Secale cereale* (Gramineae). Hard, black, shining, elongated mycelia. Its active principles include: ergometrine, ergotoxine, histamine, tyramine, and acetylcholine. Inert constituents are: ergotinine, ergothioneine, secalonic acid, schlererythrin, clavicepsin, ergosterol, fungisterol, vernine, amino acids, and secale aminosulfonic acid. See *ergotine*.

ergotamine. See *gynergen*. **e. tartrate** tablets are official (B.P.).

ergothioneine. $C_9H_{15}O_2N_3S\cdot2H_2O = 265.44$. See *ergot*.

ergotine. A brown extract of ergot; an emmenagogue, oxytocic, vasoconstrictor, and hemostatic. **E. Bombelon, E. Bonjean, E. Denzel, E. Keller, E. Kohlmann.** Extracts of e. prepared by different methods. **E. Wernich.** A dialyzed extract of e. previously purified by alcohol or ether. **E. Wiggers.** A dried extract of fat-free e. **E. Yvon.** An extract of e. made with tartaric acid.

ergotinine. $C_{35}H_{39}O_5N_5 = 609.6$. The anhydride of ergotoxine and an alkaloid inactive of ergot. Yellow needles, darkening in air, m.219–229, insoluble in water. **amorphous-** Ergotoxine. **hydro-** Ergotoxine.

    e. citrate. An amorphous, gray powder, slowly soluble in water. **e. Kraft.** Ergotoxine. **e. Tanret.** Ergotoxine.

ergotocin. Ergometrine.

ergotoxine. $C_{35}H_{41}O_6N_5 = 627.8$. Ergotinine Kraft or Tanret. Hydroergotinine, amorphous ergotinine. Yellow powder, m.138, sparingly soluble in water: physiologically inactive. **e. ethanesulfonate.** $C_{31}H_{39}O_5N_5\cdot C_2H_5SO_3H = 671.63$. A standardized derivative of e., used as color comparison standard in the assay of ergot and its preparations.

ergotrate. Ergometrine maleate.

Ericaceae. Heather family; shrubs or trees with bell-shaped flowers. Many contain glucosides or drugs; e.g.: *Arctostaphylos uva ursi* bearberry; *Ledum latifolium*, Labrador tea.

ericin. Mesotan.

ericinol. $C_{10}H_{16}O = 152.2$. An alcohol of *Ledum palustris*, wild rosemary (Ericaceae). Colorless oil with a peculiar odor; darkens and yellows on exposure.

ericolin. $C_{35}H_{56}O_{21} = 806.6$. A glucoside from *Ledum palustris*, wild rosemary (Ericaceae). A brown, soft mass, soluble in water.

erigeron. Fleabane, colts-tail, prideweed. The herb or seeds of *E. canadense* (Compositae); an astringent and tonic. **e. oil.** The essential oil of e., d.0.845–0.865, containing *d*-limonene.

erilite. A plastic made from casein and formaldehyde. Cf. *galalith*.

erinite. $Cu_3(AsO_4)_3\cdot2Cu(OH)_2$. An emerald green, native, copper arsenate; it is a decomposition product of enargite.

eriochrome. Omega chrome. One of a class of dyestuffs used as indicators in titration with EDTA, q.v.

eriodictin. A flavone dyestuff present with hesperidin, in citrin (vitamin P).

eriodictyol. A chalcone of phloroglucinol occurring as glucoside in eriodictyon.

eriodictyon. Mountain balsam. Yerba santa. The dried leaves of *Eriodictyon californicum* (Hydrophyllaceae); an aromatic and expectorant or syrup. **e. oil.** The essential oil of e., d.0.937.

eriophyesin. $C_{23}H_{18}O_{15} = 544.21$. A glucosidal coloring matter of nail gall from *Eriophyes macrotrichus*. Brown needles, m. 259.

Erlangen blue. Prussian blue. Emil.

Erlenmeyer, R. A. K. E. 1825–1909. German chemist. **E. flask** or **erlenmeyer.** A conical glass flask with flat bottom.

ergone. Ergine (2).

erose. Describing the bacterial growths of certain irregularly toothed margins.

erosion. Denudation. The wearing away, especially of rocks, due to weather or chemicals, e.g., alkaline waters. Cf. *corrosion, surrosion*.

errhine. A drug which increases nasal secretions. Cf. *sternutatory*.

error. (1) Deviation from the truth. (2) The principle that the accuracy of a determination depends on the accuracy of the data on which it is based. **cavitation-** Damage characterized by pitting in hydraulic systems under extreme conditions of high-speed liquid flow; believed to be due to the collapse of vapor-filled cavities. **mean-** The quantity $\pm\sqrt{\Sigma\ d^2/(n-1)}$; where $\Sigma\ d$ is the sum of the deviations of individual values from the mean, n the number of determinations. **mean- of the mean.** The quantity $\pm\sqrt{\Sigma\ d^2/n(n-1)}$. **protein-** See *protein*. **standard-** The standard deviation of a mean of sets of experiments. **standardized-** *t* function. The e. of a series of tests, expressed as a fraction of the standardized e. See *standard*.

erucic acid. $C_{22}H_{42}O_2 = 338.45$. *cis*-13-Docosenoic acid*, found in the oil of grape seeds. Colorless needles, insoluble in water; an isomer of brassidic and cetoleic acids.

erucidic acid. Brassic acid.

eryodiction. Eriodictyon.

erysicine. A mixture of erysodine and erysovine, q.v., from *Erythrina* alkaloids.

erysimin. A glucoside from the seeds of *Erysimum* species (Cruciferae); resembles digitalis physiologically.

erythorbic acid. $CH_2OH \cdot CHOH \cdot O \cdot O:C:C \cdot OH:C \cdot OH \cdot CH = 176.03$. Isoascorbic acid. An antioxidant, preventing beer haze.

erythraea. Bitter herb, canchalaqua. The herb of *Erythraea chilensis* (Gentianaceae), resembling centaurea, q.v.; a bitter tonic.

erythrene. Bivinyl.

erythric acid. (1) $CH_2OH(CHOH)_2COOH = 136.1$. *d*-Trihydroxybutyric acid. (2) Erythrin. (3) E. of Brugnatelli. Alloxan.

erythrin. (1) $C_{20}H_{22}O_{10} = 422.20$. Colorless microcrystals, m.13, sparingly soluble in water, found in *Roccella tinctoria*. (2) A native cobaltous arsenate. Cf. *erythrine*.

erythrina. (1) The coral tree (Papilionaceae), W. and E. Indies, Central America, and Malaysia. (2) A genus of Leguminosae.

erythrine. An alkaloid from the seeds of *Erythrina broteroi*, E. Indies; *E. carraloides*, Mexico; *E. corallodendron*, Brazil; an antidote to strychnine, and a hypnotic.

erythrite. (1) Phycsite, red cobalt. A native cobalt arsenate. (2) Erythritol.

erythritic acid. Erythric acid.

erythritol. $H(CHOH)_4H = 122.09$. Erythrite, phycite, tetrahydroxybutane, lichen sugar, from the lichen, *Protococcus vulgaris;* a split product of erythrine. Tetragonal prisms, m.112, soluble in water. **nitro-** E. tetranitrate. **penta-** $C_5H_{12}O_4 = 136.1$. Colorless crystals, m.250. Cf. *penta-erythritol*.

e. benzene. Fuchsin. **e. tetraacetate.** $C_{12}H_{18}O_8 = 290.14$. White crystals; a plasticizer for cellulose acetate, to increase ultraviolet light transmission. **e. tetranitrate.** $C_4H_6(NO_3)_4 = 302.3$. Tetranitroerythrol, tetranitrol. Yellow crystals, m.61 (explode), slightly soluble in water; a vasodilator and explosive.

erythrocentaurin. $C_{17}H_{24}O_8 = 476.2$. The red coloring matter of *Erythraea centaurium* and *Sabbatia angularis*. Needles, darkening in light, m.136, insoluble in water.

erythrocephaelin. The coloring matter of ipecac.

erythrocruorin. Hemoglobin from invertebrates. The hemoglobin of vertebrates has a higher molecular weight and lower isoelectric point.

erythrocyte. A red blood corpuscle.

erythrodextrin. A dextrin split product of starch, giving a red color with iodine. Cf. *achroodextrin*.

erythroglucin. Erythrol (2).

erythrol. (1) Erythritol. (2) $CH_2OH \cdot CHOH \cdot CH:CH_2 = 88.04$. 3-Butene-1,2-diol. White crystals, m.197.

erythrolaccin. The alkali-soluble coloring matter of shellac.

erythrolitmin. $C_{26}H_{23}O_{13} = 543.2$. Red crystals derived from *Corona solis*.

erythromin. Rio.

erythromycin. $C_{37}H_{67}O_{13}N = 733.56$. An antibiotic from *Streptomyces erythreus*, Waksman. White,

bitter, hygroscopic crystals, insoluble in water (U.S.P., B.P.).

erythronium. The name given by del Rio (1804) to vanadium; rediscovered by Sefström (1831).

erythrooxyanthraquinone. $C_{14}H_8O_3 = 224.08$. Oxyanthraquinone. Orange needles, m.190, soluble in alcohol.

erythrophloeine. An alkaloid from the bark of *Erythrophloeum guinense* (Leguminosae), Guinea; an ordeal poison. Yellow syrup, sparingly soluble in water. Cf. *sassy bark*.

Erythrophloeum, Erythrophloeum. Leguminous trees (W. Africa) furnishing sassy bark; an ordeal poison.

erythroprotid. $C_{13}H_8O_5N = 258.1$. A red product obtained by boiling proteins with concentrated alkali.

erythroquine reaction. A characteristic color is formed on adding to an alkaloid, in succession, chloroform, bromine water, and potassium ferrocyanide.

erythroretin. $C_{38}H_{36}O_{14} = 716.4$. A red coloring matter from rhubarb.

erythrose. $CHO \cdot (CHOH)_2 \cdot CH_2OH = 120.1$. Trihydroxybutyricaldehyde. A tetrose sugar derived from erythrol, in dextro- and levo- forms. Isomers: threose, erythrulose.

erythrosiderite. K_2FeCl_5. A rare potassium–ferric chloride mineral.

erythrosin. (1) $C_{13}H_{18}O_6N_2 = 298.2$. A red compound obtained by treating tyrosine with nitric acid. (2) $C_{20}H_8O_5I_4 = 835.84$. Tetraiodofluorescein, pyrosin. Yellow crystals, insoluble in water; a dye. (3) $C_{20}H_6O_5I_4Na_2 = 879.82$. Eosin. Bluish, sodium iodoeosin, sodium tetraiodofluorescein. Brown powder, soluble in water; a dye, and hydrogen ion indicator, changing at pH 2.0 from orange (acid) to magenta (basic). Cf. *iodeosin*.

erythroxyline Cocaine.

erythroxylon. Coca.

erythrytol.. Erythritol.

Esbach, George Hubert. 1843–1890. French physician. **E. reagent.** A solution of 1 gm trinitrophenol and 2 gm citric acid in 100 ml water, for determining albumin in urine.

escalation. A mathematical device used in the pricing of chemical plant and processes which compensates for increases in the costs of mechanical and electrical engineering and of labor.

escharotic. A substance that produces a crust of dead tissue.

eschatin. An extract of lipoids from the suprarenal cortex; used to treat Addison's disease.

Eschka mixture. A mixture of 2 pts. magnesium oxide and 1 pt. dried sodium carbonate; a fusion reagent for determining sulfur in coal.

eschwegite. $5Y_2O_3 \cdot 5(Ta, Nb)_2O_5 \cdot 10TiO_2 \cdot 7H_2O$. A reddish gray, isotropic rare-earth mineral.

esciorcin, aesciorcin. Escorcin.

escoquinine. Quinine aesculinate.

escorcin. $C_9H_8O_4 = 180.1$. Escorcinal, aescorcin. Brown powder derived from aesculetin; used in ophthalmology.

esculetin. $C_9H_6O_4 = 178.1$. Aesculetin, 6,7-dihydroxycoumarin. A split product of esculin. **methoxy-** Gelseminic acid. **methyl-** Scopoletin.

esculetinic acid. $C_9H_8O_5 = 196.06$. Aesculetinic acid. Colorless crystals, m.168.

esculin. $C_{15}H_{16}O_9 = 340.20$. Aesculin, aesculinic acid, anallachrom, polychrom, bicolorin. A glucoside from the seeds of *Aesculus hippocastanum*, horse chestnut. Colorless needles, slightly soluble in water, giving fluorescence; an antimalarial.

-ese. Suffix denoting a substance formed by a synthesizing enzyme.

esenbeckic acid. An acid from the bark of *Esenbeckia febrifuga* (Rutaceae), tropical America.

eseridine. $C_{15}H_{23}O_3N_3 = 293.2$. An alkaloid in calabar beans. Colorless crystals, m.132, soluble in alcohol; a veterinary laxative.

eserine. Physostigmine.

Esmarch bottle. A device for sampling water at any depth by removing and replacing a stopper mechanically.

eso- Prefix indicating substitution for a hydrogen atom attached to a ring atom.

esoxin. A ptomaine from the sperm of white, freshwater fish.

esparto. A tall grass, *Stipa tenacissima* or *Lygeum spartum* (Gramineae), N. Africa; a source of paper pulp.

esperium. Es. See *ekaosmium*.

essence. (1) A solution of a volatile or essential oil in alcohol. (2) The active principle of a plant. (3) A fruit essence, q.v. **e. niobe.** Methyl benzoate.

essential. Pertaining to an essence. **e. oils.** Volatile ethereal oils of characteristic odors, distilled from plants. Distinguished from fatty oils by their volatility, nongreasiness, and nonsaponifying property. They exist in plants, as such, imparting the characteristic odor to flowers, leaves or woods; as terpenes (oil of turpentine, juniper, etc.); or are developed from plant constituents by enzyme action (oil of mustard) or heat (cade). They are flammable, soluble in alcohol or ether, slightly in water, and can contain hydrocarbons, alcohols, phenols, ethers, aldehydes, ketones, acids, and esters. **e. salt.** A salt obtained by evaporating plant juices.

essonite. $6CaO \cdot 3SiO_2 + 2Al_2O_3, 3SiO_2$. Garnet lime-alumina, wolfsbergite. Calcium garnet. A pale yellow mineral.

ester. (1) Ethereal salt. An organic salt formed from an alcohol (base) and an organic acid by elimination of water:

$$R \cdot OH + R' \cdot COOH = R'COO \cdot R + H_2O$$
alcohol   acid   ester   water

(2) Compounds of the type R_2SO_4 or $R \cdot COOM$ are erroneously called esters. (3) The ethyl esters of an acid; e.g., diacetic ester is ethyl diacetyl diacetate. **acid-** Ether acid. Compounds of polybasic acids in which not all the carboxyl hydrogen atoms are replaced by alcohol radicals, e.g., $R \cdot OOC \cdot R \cdot COOH$. **alkamine-** See *alkamine ester*. **basic-** Compounds of polyhydric alcohols in which not all the hydroxyl groups are replaced by acid radicals, e.g., $R \cdot COO \cdot R \cdot OH$. **imido-** See *imido ester*. **mixed-** An e. in which the radicals R of $R \cdot COOR$ are different. **Robison-** Hexosemonophosphoric acid; formed in the fermentation of sugar by yeast. **rosin-** Ester gum.

e. gum. Rosin ester. A compound obtained by esterifying colophony, with a polyhydric alcohol, e.g., glycerol. **e. number.** The difference between the saponification number and acid number, i.e.,

the number of milligrams of potassium hydroxide to saponify the neutral esters in 1 gm of a fat, oil, or wax. **e. oils.** Pale edible oils produced by esterification of refinery acids with glycerol.

esterase. An enzyme saponifying esters.

esterification. Formation of an ester by dehydration or catalytic agents. **inter-** The controlled rearrangement of fatty acids between the glycerol molecules of a fat, e.g., by heating at 45–95°C with a Na-K alloy; e.g., to improve the creaming properties of lard.

e. law. Meyer's law. Esterification of aromatic acids is retarded and prevented in presence of 1- and 2-ortho-substituents, respectively.

Esterol. A brand of benzyl succinate used as an antispasmodic.

estersil. An ester of $Si(OH)_4$.

estigyn. Ethinylestradiol.

estimation. An approximate evaluation. Cf. determination.

estopen. Penethamate hydriodide.

estoral. Menthyl borate.

estradiol. $C_{18}H_{24}O_2 = 272.2$. Oestradiol, Dimenformon, Ovocylin, Progynon-DH, 3,17-dihydroxy-1,3,5-estratriene. Cf. *estrone*.

estradiovalerate. $C_{23}H_{32}O_3 = 356.51$. White crystals, m.147, insoluble in water; an estrogen (U.S.P.).

estragole. $MeO \cdot C_6H_4 \cdot C_5H_{11} = 178.14$. Methyl chavicol, *p*-allylanisole, *p*-methoxyallyl benzene. An ether of anise odor, in estragen oil.

estragon oil. Tarragon oil. An essential oil, d.0.9–0.94, from *Artemisia dracunulus* (Compositae).

estrane. $C_{18}H_{17} = 233.14$ Oestrane, 2-methyl-1,2-cyclopentanoperhydrophenanthrene. A tetracyclic hydrocarbon parent substance of steroidal female sex hormones.

e. diol. $C_{18}H_{30}O_2 = 278.2$. 3,17-Dihydroxyestrane. Cf. *estrone*. **e. triol.** $C_{18}H_{30}O_3 = 294.2$. 3,16,17-Trihydroxyestrane.

estratriene. $C_{18}H_{24} = 240.2$. $\Delta^{1,3,5}$-estratriene. The parent compound of estrone. Cf. *androstane*, *cholane*.

estrin. Estrone. Adiol benzoate.

estriol. $C_{18}H_{24}O_3 = 288.2$. Oestriol, Theelol, trihydroxyestrin. A trihydroxy alcohol from pregnancy urine. White needles, m.218, insoluble in water. Cf. *cholane*.

estrogen. Any drug inducing estrus.

estrone. $C_{18}H_{22}O_2 = 270.37$. Oestrone, Theelin, emmenin, thelykinine, folliculin, oestrane, Progynon, Menformon. The female sex hormone from the placenta and urine of pregnant women and ovarian follicles. A monoatomic keto alcohol. See *cholane*. White, monoclinic crystals, m.260, insoluble in water. Cf. *androsterone*.

esu, ESU. Abbreviation for electrostatic units. See *electromagnetic units*. **Et.** (1) Abbreviation for the ethyl radical, $-C_2H_5$. (2) Symbol for ekatantalum.

-et. A suffix. See *-uret.*

eta. η (Greek). Symbol for viscosity.

Étard's reaction. The oxidation of methyl to aldehyde radicals by chromyl chloride: $R \cdot CH_3 + Cr(OCl)_2 = R \cdot CHO + H_2O + CrCl_2$. **E. salt.** The complex potassium chromium sulfate, $K_3[Cr(SO_4)_3]$.

etch figure. The characteristic pattern produced when a polished metallic surface is etched by a suitable reagent.

eteline. See *chlorinated* solvents.

ethacetic acid. *n*-Butyric acid.

ethal. Cetyl alcohol.

ethaldehyde. Cetyl aldehyde.

ethalic acid. Palmitic acid.

ethamine. Ethylamine.

ethamolin. Ethanolamine.

ethanal*. Acetaldehyde. **hydroxy-*** Glycolaldehyde. **trichloro-*** Chloral. **e. acid.** Glyoxalic acid.

ethanamide*. Acetamide.

ethanamidine*. Acetamidine.

ethane*. $C_2H_6 = 30.05$. Methylmethane, dimethyl, ethylhydride. An alkane or a saturated hydrocarbon of the methane series. Colorless gas, $d_{air=1}1.049$, m.-172, b.-86, slightly soluble in water; a constituent of natural and illuminating gas. The ethyl (C_2H_5-), ethylene ($-CH_2 \cdot CH_2-$), ethenyl ($\equiv C \cdot Me$), and acetylene ($=CH \cdot CH =$) radicals are derived from ethane. Unsaturated hydrocarbon derivatives include ethene* (ethylene), $CH_2 : CH_2$, and ethyne* (ethine or acetylene), $CH : CH$. **amino-** Ethylamine*. **bromo-*, chloro-*,** etc. See *ethyl bromide, ethyl chloride,* etc. **dibenzoyl-** Diphenazine. **dibenzyl-** Diphenylbutane. **dibromo-*, dichloro-*,** etc. See *ethylene bromide, ethylene chloride,* etc. **dihydroxy-** Glycol. **diphenyl-** Dibenzyl. **hexabromo-*** Hexabromoethane. **hexachloro-*** Hexachloroethane. **hydroxy-** Ethanol*. **nitro-** See *nitroethane.* **nitroso-** See *nitrosoethane.* **perchloro-** Hexachloro-. **phenyl-** Ethylbenzene. **triethoxy-*** Ethenyl trimethyl ether. **e. dial*.** Glyoxal. **e. diamide*.** Oxamide. **e. diamine*.** Ethylenediamine. **e. dinitrile*.** Cyanogen. **e. dioic acid*.** Oxalic acid. **e. diol*.** Glycol. **e. dioyl chloride*.** Oxalyl chloride. **e. dithiol*.** Dithioglycol. **e. nitrile*.** Acetonitrile. **e. sulfinic acid*.** Ethylsulfinic acid. **e. sulfonic acid*.** Ethylsulfonic acid. **e. thiol*.** Ethyl mercaptan. **e. thiolic acid*.** Thio*lacetic acid.* **e. thionamide*.** Thioacetamide.

ethanite. A synthetic rubber, prepared by subjecting natural gas to a heating and cooling process.

ethano- Prefix indicating a $-CH_2 \cdot CH_2-$ bridge.

ethanoic acid*. Acetic acid. **oxo-*.** Glyoxylic acid **e. anhydride*.** Acetic anhydride.

ethanol*. $C_2H_6O = 46.046$. Ethyl alcohol, alcohol, spirit, spirit of wine, grain alcohol, absolute alcohol, ethyl hydrate, etc. (1) Et·OH. Absolute alcohol, dehydrated alcohol. Colorless liquid, $d_4^{25}0.78505$, m.-117.3, b.78.32, miscible with water or ether; a reagent and solvent. (2) 99% alcohol. The "absolute alcohol" of the U.S.P. and B.P., used extensively for tinctures and pharmaceutical preparations, as a solvent and preservative, as an antiseptic, and in perfumery. (3) Grain alcohol, cologne spirits. Colorless liquid (ethanol 90, water 10%). (4) Diluted alcohol, proof spirit. Colorless liquid, ethanol about 49, water 51% (by weight). (5) Denatured alcohol. Alcohol made unpotable by the addition of substances such as methanol, pryidine, formaldehyde, sublimate, or other denaturant. Used in industry, the arts and commerce, principally as a solvent or fuel. See also *methylated spirits.* **amino-*** Colamine. **butoxy-*** Butyl *Cellosolve.* **chloro-*** Ethylene chlorohydrin. **cyano-** Ethylene cyanohydrin. **ethoxy-*** Cellosolve. **imino-** See *iminoethanol.* **oxybis-** Diethylene glycol. **phenyl-** Benzyl carbinol. **tribromo-*** Avertin. **trichloro-*** See *trichloroethanol.* **trimethyl-** Butyl carbinol

ethanolamine. $NH_2(CH_2)_2 \cdot OH = 61.09$. 2-Aminoethanol, β-hydroxyethylamine, monoethanolamine. Colorless liquid, d.1.04 $b_{150mm}171$, soluble in gasoline; used for pharmaceutical injections and dry cleaning. **di-** Diethanolamine. **tri-** Triethanolamine.

ethanoyl*. Acetyl.

ethene*. $C_2H_4 = 28.04$. (1) Ethylene, olefiant gas. Colorless, flammable gas of peculiar odor, $d_{air=1}$ 0.978, b.-102.7, slightly soluble in water. From ethene the radicals vinyl, $-CH : CH_2$, and vinylene, $-CH : CH-$, are derived. A dental anesthetic and source of polyethylene, ethanol, styrene monomer, and e. dichloride. (2) The radical ethylene, q.v. **e. dichloride.** Ethylene chloride. **e. series.** Olefins. The homologs of ethene; or a group of aliphatic hydrocarbons, q.v., C_nH_{2n}.

etheno- Prefix indicating a $-CH : CH-$ bridge. Cf. *ethano-.*

ethenol. Vinyl alcohol.

ethenone. Ketene.

ethenyl. The radical $H_3C \cdot C \equiv$, from ethane. **e. amide.** Acetamidine. **e. amine*.** Vinylamine. **e. aminophenol.** $C_8H_7ON = 133.06$. Colorless liquid, b.201, insoluble in water. **e. aminothiophenol.** $C_8H_7SN = 149.20$. Colorless liquid, b.238, insoluble in water. **e. bromide.** Vinyl bromide. **e. chloride.** Trichloroethane. **e. diphenylamidine.** $C_{14}H_{14}N_2 = 210.13$. Colorless needles, m.131, sparingly soluble in water. **e. triethyl ether.** $C_8H_{18}O_3 = 162.17$. Triethoxyethane. Colorless liquid, b.142, decomp. by hot water. **e. tricarboxylic acid.** $C_5H_6O_6 = 162.07$. Colorless prisms, decomp. by heat, insoluble in water.

ethenylidene. The radical $=CH \cdot CH_2-$. **e. chloride.** β-Trichloroethane.

ether. (1) An alkyl or aryl oxide (general type R·O·R·), derived from an alcohol by replacing the hydroxyl hydrogen: $R \cdot OH + R \cdot OH = R \cdot O \cdot R + H_2O$. See *ethers.* (2) $C_4H_{10}O = 74.10$. Ethylic ether, ethyl oxide, ethoxyethane*, diethyl ether, sulfuric ether. Colorless liquid, d.0.720, b.35, slightly soluble in water, miscible with alcohol. A reagent and solvent for fats, resins, alkaloids, and an anesthetic. (3) Physics: AEther. A hypothetical, all-pervading medium of the universe, for the transmission of radiations, light, heat, and electricity. Cf. *etherons.* **acetic-** Ethyl acetate. **aldehyde-** Crotonic aldehyde. **allophanic-** Ethyl allophanate. **anesthetic-** Ether (2). **anhydrous-** Ethyl ether which has been distilled over sodium; a reagent and solvent. **decachlor-** Perchlor ether. **dichloro-** Dichlorethyl ether. **diethyl-** Ether (2). **dimethyl-** See *methyl ether.* **formic-** Ethyl formate. **hydrobromic-** Ethyl bromide. **hydrochloric-** Ethyl chloride. **hydrocyanic-** Ethyl cyanide. **hydroiodic-** Ethyl iodide. **isopropyl-** See *propyl-* **methyl-** Methyl ether. **mixed-** An e. in which the radicals present differ. **petroleum-** Distilled petroleum. The 50–60°C fraction. **simple-** An e. in which both radicals are alike. **sulfuric-** Ether (2).

e. acid. An acid ester, q.v. **e. alcohol.** A compound of the type R·O·R·OH; as, the diether of a glycol. **e. of crystallization.** The molecules of e. as a component part in a crystal lattice.

ethereal. Resembling or made with ether. **e. fruit oil.** See fruit *oil.* **e. liquid.** A highly volatile liquid. **e. oil.** Essential oil. **e. salt.** Ester.

etherene. Ethylene.

etheric acid. Acetoacetic acid.

etheride. A compound containing the radical —COX; X is a halogen.

etherification. The process of making an ether from an alcohol. Cf. *ethers.*

etherin. Obsolete name for ethylin. **e. theory.** A theory of the constitution of organic compounds (Dumas and Boullay, 1828).

etherion. A supposed element, atomic weight 0.001, expelled from substances at high temperatures and low pressures.

etheron. Aetheron. A supposed particle of ether, smaller and faster than an electron; a mass of $\frac{1}{47} \times 10^9$ that of hydrogen, speed 294,000 miles/sec.

etherophosphoric acid. Ethylphosphoric acid.

etherosulfuric acid. Ethylsulfuric acid.

ethers. (1) Ether (1). Named R-oxides, or indicated by the prefix R-oxy- or alkoxy- (2) The halogen derivatives of alkyl and aryl radicals are sometimes called ethers, e.g., R·Cl. (3) The esters of inorganic or organic acids are sometimes called ethers; e.g., R·NO₂. **complex-** Compound. **compound-** (1) Alkyl or aryl oxides in which 2 different radicals are joined by the oxygen, R·O·R.′ (2) Esters. **cyclic-** E. in which the initial C atom in the series is limited directly to the oxide O; as, ethylene oxide, CH₂·CH₂·O. **haloid-** Alkyl or aryl halides.

mixed- Compound. **simple-** Alkyl or aryl oxides having 2 like radicals, R·O·R. **thio-** Alkyl or aryl sulfide, e.g., e. in which the oxygen is replaced by sulfur. See *mercaptans.*

ethide. A compound of ethyl radical and a metal; as, lead ethide, PbEt₄.

ethidine. Ethylidene.

Ethidol. Trade name for ethinylestradiol.

ethine. Acetylene. **e. series.** Acetylene series, q.v. A group of unsaturated aliphatic hydrocarbons with one triple bond; general formula, CₙH₂ₙ₋₂.

ethinyl. Acetenyl. ethynyl, acetylenyl. The radical CH⫶C—, from acetylene. **e. bromide.** C₂₀H₂₄O₂ = 296.41. Bromoacetylene, e. estradiol. White crystals, m.144, insoluble in water; an estrogen (U.S.P.). Used to treat menopausal symptoms and to suppress lactation.

Ethiodan. Trade name for ethyliodophenylundecanoate.

ethionic acid. HO·SO₂·CH₂·CH₂·SO₂OH = 206.1. Ethylenesulfonic acid, known only in solution. Cf. *isethionic acid.* **amino-** Taurine.

ethiops mineral. Black mercurous sulfide.

ethisterone. C₂₁H₂₈O₂ = 312.46. Pregneninolone,

anhydrohydroxyprogesterone. White crystals, darkening in light, m.271 (decomp.) insoluble in water; a progestational hormone (B.P.).

ethocaine. Procaine **e. borate.** Borocaine.

Ethocel. Trademark for ethylcellulose.

ethodin. Rivanol.

ethohexadiol. C₈H₁₈O₂ = 146.23 Ethyl hexanediol. Colorless oil, soluble in water, distils 240–250; an insect repellent.

etholide. A tertiary lipid formed from alcohol acids by the esterification of the hydroxyl group of one with the carboxyl groups of the other molecule.

ethopropazine hydrochloride. C₁₉H₂₄N₂S·HCl = 348.91. White, bitter crystals, slightly soluble in water (B.P.).

ethosuximide. C₇H₁₁O₂N = 141.21. White powder, m.46, soluble in water; an anticonvulsant (B.P.).

ethotoin. C₁₁H₁₂O₂N₂ = 204.15. 3-Ethyl-5-phenylhydantoin. White crystals, m.90, insoluble in water; an anticonvulsant.

ethoxalyl. The radical EtOOC·CO—.

ethoxide. Ethylate.

ethoxy. The radical C₂H₅O—, from ethanol. Cf. *oxethyl.* **e. acetic acid.** Ethylglycolic acid. **e. acetone.** MeCOCH₂OEt = 102.1. Colorless liquid. b.128; a solvent. **e. aniline.** C₈H₁₁ON = 137.10. Colorless liquid, d₀₀1.11, b.286, sparingly soluble in water. **e. butyric acid.** Hydroxyethylbutyric acid. **e. caffeine.** C₁₀H₁₄O₃N₄ = 238.51. Colorless crystals, m.140. Slightly soluble in water; a narcotic. **e. catechol.** C₈H₁₀O₂ = 138.1. A homolog of guaiacol.

ethoxyl. Ethoxy.

Ethyl. (1) Trademark for an antiknock compound to prevent or reduce knocking in internal-combustion engines, and for the resultant fuel. Also a trademark for other products not necessarily associated with fuels or internal-combustion engines. See *Ethyl gas.* (2) (not cap.) The radical C₂H₅— or Et—, from ethane. **e. acetamide.** MeCONHEt = 87.08. Colorless liquid; used in organic synthesis. **e. acetate.** Me·COOEt = 88.06. Acetic ether, acetic ester, acetidin. Colorless liquid, m.−82.4, b.77, slightly soluble in water. Used as a stimulant and antispasmodic, as a reagent in organic synthesis, as a solvent for lacquers, and in the separation of dyes. **e. acetoacetate.** MeCOCH₂COOEt = 130.11. Acetoacetic ester, diacetic ether. Colorless liquid, b.181, slightly soluble in water; a solvent. **e. acetylene.** Butine. **e. acid phosphate.** See *e. phosphate.* **e. acid.** E. arsenic acid. **e. acid sulfate.** E. sulfuric acid. **e. acrylate.** C₅H₈O₂ = 100.09. Colorless liquid, b.99. **e. alcohol.** Ethanol*. **e. aldehyde.** Acetaldehyde. **e. allyl.** (1) C₅H₁₀ = 70.09 Colorless liquid, b.70. (2) Prefix indicating an ethyl and allyl radical. **e. allyl ether.** EtOCH₂CH⫶CH₂ = 86.11. 3-Ethoxypropylene. Colorless liquid, b.66, insoluble in water. **e. amine*.** EtNH₂ = 45.11. Ethamine, aminoethane. A ptomaine from putrefying yeast and wheat flour. Colorless liquid, b.17, miscible with water. **e. aminoacetate.** NH₂CH₂COOEt = 103.1. Ethylglycine, e. glycol. **e. aminobenzoate.** Benzocaine. **e. aminobenzoic acid.** EtNH·C₆H₄·COOH = 165.20. Colorless prisms, m.112, slightly soluble in water. **e. amyl.** (1) Me(CH₂)₄CH⫶CH₂ = 98.108. Δ¹-Heptane. Colorless liquid, b.99. (2) Prefix indicating an ethyl and amyl radical. **e. amylaniline.** Et·N·-(C_5H_{11})·Ph = 191.2.   Amylethylphenylamine. Colorless oil, b.262, soluble in alcohol. **e. amyl ketone.** $C_8H_{16}O$ = 128.17. Colorless liquid, almost insoluble in water, miscible with alcohol or ether. *normal-* Et·CO·(CH$_2$)$_4$Me. 3-Octanone*. d.0.825, b.165. *active-* Me·CH$_2$·CHMe·CH$_2$·CO·Et. 5-Methyl-3-heptanone*. b.161. *tert-* Me·CH$_2$·-CMe$_2$·CO·Et. 4,4-Dimethyl-3-hexanone*. d.0.825, b.151. **e. aniline.** See *aniline.* **e. anthracene.** $C_{16}H_{14}$ = 206.12. Colorless scales, m.60, insoluble in water. *dihydro-* $C_{16}H_{16}$ = 208.14. Colorless oil, m.320, insoluble in water. **e. arsen.** See *arsine.* **e. antimonide.** Acid antimony ethide. **e. arsen.** See *arsine.* **e. azotide.** E. nitrate. **e. azotite.** E. nitrite. **e. benzene.** See *benzene.* **e. benzoate.** PhCOOEt = 150.13. Colorless liquid, b.213, slightly soluble in water. **e. benzoic acid.** See *benzoic acid.* **e. benzoyl acetate.** PhCOCH$_2$COOEt = 192.16. Benzoyl-acetic ester. Colorless liquid, b.267, insoluble in water. **e. benzylaniline.** Ph·N·Et·(CH$_2$Ph) = 211.2. Ethylbenzylphenylamine. b$_{710mm}$285. **e. benzylate.** E. benzyl ether. **e. benzyl ether.** Et·OCH$_2$Ph = 136.15. E. benzylate, benzyl e. oxide. Colorless liquid, b.186, insoluble in water. **e. benzyl ketone.** Et·CO·CH$_2$Ph = 148.15. 1-Phenylbutan-2-one. Colorless liquid, b.223, insoluble in water. **e. biscoumacetate.** $C_{22}H_{16}O_8$ = 408.4. 4,4'-Dihydroxydicoumarin-3,3'-yl acetate. Bitter, yellow crystals, slightly soluble in water; an oral anticoagulant. **e. borate.** A salt of ethanol and boric acid. *ortho-* B(OEt)$_3$ = 146.2. E. orthoborate, boron triethoxide, triethylic borate. Colorless, flammable liquid. *meta-* (EtO)$_2$(BO)$_2$ = 144.1. E. metaborate. Colorless, heavy liquid. *pyro-* $C_2H_5B_3O_5$ = 141.4. E. borate. A colorless, gummy mass. **e. boric acid.** Et$_2$B-(OH)$_2$ = 73.87. White crystals, sublime 40, soluble in water. Boryl. **e. borosalicylate.** Boryl. **e. bromacetate.** $C_4H_7O_2Br$ = 167.04. Colorless liquid, b.159, insoluble in water. **e. bromide.** C_2H_5Br = 109.01. Aethylium bromatus, aether bromatus, monobromoethane, bromic ether, bromo-ethane*. Colorless liquid, d.1.450, m.—116, b.39, almost insoluble in water; a local anesthetic. Cf. *ethylene bromide.* **e. butyl ether.** EtOBu = 102.15. Colorless liquid, b.92, insoluble in water. **e. butyl ketone.** Et·CO·Bu = 114.16. Heptan-3-one. Colorless liquid, b.147, insoluble in water. **e. butyrate.** PrCOOEt = 116.11. Ethylbutyric ester. Colorless liquid, b.121, insoluble in water; a pineapple flavoring. *iso-*Me$_2$CHCOOEt. Color-less liquid, b.110, sparingly soluble in water. **e. cacodyl.** Diethylarsine. **e. cacodylic acid.** Diethylarsinic acid. **e. caproate.** Me(CH$_2$)$_4$-COOEt = 144.2. E. caproic ester. Colorless liquid, m.167, soluble in alcohol. **e. caprylate.** $C_{10}H_{20}O_2$ = 172.17. Ethylcaprylic ester. Colorless liquid, b.30, soluble in alcohol. **e. carbamate.** Urethane. **e. carbazole.** $C_{14}H_{13}N$ = 195.13. Colorless scales, m.68, soluble in hot alcohol. **e. carbimide.** E. isocyanate. **e. carbinol.** Propanol. **e. carbonate.** Et$_2$CO$_3$ = 118.11. Carbethylic acid, carbonic ester, diethylcarbonic ether, diatol. Colorless liquid, d.0.978, b.126, insoluble in water. Used in organic synthesis; a solvent for nitro-cellulose and resins. *ortho-* C(OEt)$_4$ = 192.2.

Tetraethyl carbonate, tetraethoxymethane. Color-less, aromatic liquid. **e. carbonic acid.** Propi-onic acid. **e. carbostyril.** $C_{11}H_{11}ON$ = 174.12. Colorless crystals, m.168. **e. carbylamine.** EtNC. E. isocyanide. **e. cellulose.** Ethocel, lumarith E.C. Made by heating ethyl chloride, with alkali cellulose produced by treating cellulose pulp with sodium hydroxide. It has film-forming properties, good strength, and grease resistance; used for transparent rigid containers. **e. chaulmoograte.** The e. esters of the mixed acids of chaulmoogra oil; clear, yellow liquid, d.0.904. **e. chloracetate.** CH$_2$Cl·COOEt = 122.53. Colorless liquid, b.145, insoluble in water. **e. chloracetoacetate.** Me-COCHClCOOEt = 164.55. Colorless liquid, b.197, slightly soluble in water; used in organic synthesis. **e. chloralurethane.** Somnal. **e. chloride.** C_2H_5Cl = 64.50. Monochlorethane, hydrochloric ether, aethylium chloratus, aether, chloratus, kelene, chloroethane*, chelen, anodynon. Colorless liquid, d$_0$0.921, m.—141.2, b.12.2, slightly soluble in water; a topical anesthetic (U.S.P.), constituent of cognac essence, refrigerant, and ethylating agent. **e. chlorocarbonate.** E. chloroformate. **e. chloroformate.** ClCCOOEt = 108.52. E. chlorocarbonate. Colorless liquid with a pungent odor, d.1.135, b.93, decomp. in water. **e. chloro-propionate.** MeCHClCOOEt = 136.55 Ethyl-chlorpropionic ester, aether chlorpropionicus. Colorless liquid, b.146, slightly soluble in water. **e. cinnamate.** PhCH:CH·COOEt = 176.16. Eth-ylcinnamic ester, aether cinnamylicus. Color-less oil, m.12, insoluble in water; a strawberry flavoring. **e. crotonic acid.** MeCH:CEt·COOH = 114.09. Colorless monoclinic crystals, m.40 (sublime), sparingly soluble in water; a peppermint flavoring. **e. cyanacetate.** CN·CH$_2$·COOEt = 113.13. Ethylcyanacetic ester, aether cyanaceti-cus. Colorless liquid, b.207, insoluble in water. **e. cyanate.** EtOCN = 71.1. Cyanetholin. Colorless, unstable liquid, insoluble in water. *iso-* EtNCO = 71.1 E. carbimide. Colorless liquid, b.60, soluble in alcohol. **e. cyanide.** C_3H_5N = 55.10. Propionitrile, hydrocyanic ether, ether cyanatus, propane nitrile*. Colorless liquid, b.97.1, soluble in water. *iso-* E. isocyanide. **e. cyanuramide.** E. cyanamide. **e. diacetoacetate.** (MeCO)$_2$CHCOOEt = 172.14. Colorless liquid, d.1.101, b.200, slightly soluble in water. **e. di-bromoacetate.** Br$_2$CHCOOEt = 246.0. Ethyldi-bromoacetic ester. Colorless liquid, miscible with alcohol or ether. **e. dibromocinnamate.** Zebromal. **e. dichloroacetate.** Cl$_2$CHCOOEt = 156.97. Ether dichloraceticus, ethyldichloracetic ester. Colorless liquid, b.156, slightly soluble in water. **e. di-chlorarsine.** $C_2H_5AsCl_2$ = 175.0. Dick. A liquid, d.1.66, b.155. A vesicant and lung irritant. **e. dichloride.** Ethylene chloride. **e. diethyl aceto-acetate.** MeCO·CEt$_2$·COOEt = 186.19. Diethyl-acetoacetic e. ester. Colorless liquid, b.218 insoluble in water. **e. diethylmalonate.** Et$_2$C-(COOEt)$_2$ = 216.22. Colorless liquid, b.223, insoluble in water. **e. diiodobrassidate.** Lipo-iodine. **e. diiodosalicylate.** $C_2H_2I_2(OH)$-COOC$_6$H$_4$ = 417.8. Ether diiodosalicylicus. Colorless crystals, m.132, sparingly soluble in water; an iodoform substitute. **e. dimethyl malonate.** Me$_2$·C·(COOEt)$_2$ = 188.18. Colorless liquid, b.197, insoluble in water. **e. dioxythiocarbonate.** $C_5H_{10}O_2S = 134.1$. Colorless, strongly refractive liquid, soluble in alcohol. Cf. *xanthic acid.* **e. diphenylamine.** $EtNPh_2 = 197.25$. Diphenylethylamine. Colorless liquid, b.296, insoluble in water. **e. diphenylphosphine.** $EtPPh_2 = 214.2$. Diphenylethylphosphine. Colorless liquid, b.293, insoluble in water. **e. diselenide.** $EtSe\cdot SeEt = 216.3$. Diethyl selenide, e. perselenide. A heavy, brown, pungent liquid, b.186. **e. disilicate.** $[(EtO)_3Si]_2O = 346.6$. Colorless, oily, flammable liquid with peppermint odor. **e. disulfide.** $EtS\cdot SEt = 122.21$. E. persulfide, e. dithioethane*. Colorless liquid with garlic odor, $d_{22}0.993$, b.153, sparingly soluble in water. **e. dithidethane.** Diethyl sulfide. **e. dithiocarbonate.** $CO(SEt)_2 = 150.23$. Dithiourethane, d.1085, b.197. **e. ene.** Ethylene. **e. ether.** $Et_2O = 74.08$. Colorless liquid, b.35, slightly soluble in water; a solvent and anesthetic. **e. fluoride.** $EtF = 48.05$. Fluoroethane*. Colorless gas, b.-32, soluble in water. **e. formamide.** $EtNH\cdot CHO = 73.1$. Colorless liquid, b.199, soluble in alcohol. **e. formate.** $HCOOEt = 74.07$. Ethylformic ester. Colorless liquid, b.54.4, slightly soluble in water; a flavoring. **e. furoate.** $C_4H_3\cdot COOEt = 124.07$. Colorless liquid, m.34; a solvent and industrial perfume. **E. Gas, E. Gasoline.** E. petrol, "Ethyl." When used as a trademark, Ethyl designates a gasoline mixed with a fluid containing tetraethyllead, halogens and other constituents of an antiknock compound. **e. glycerate.** $CH_2OH\cdot CHOH\cdot COOEt = 134.11$. Colorless liquid, b.235, slightly soluble in water. **e. glycine.** $EtNH\cdot CH_2\cdot COOH = 103.08$. Colorless scales, decomp. 160, soluble in water. **e. glycol ether.** Cellosolve. **e. glycolate.** $HOCH_2COOEt = 104.07$. E. hydroxyacetate. Colorless liquid, b.160, soluble in alcohol; a solvent for nitrocellulose and resins. **e. glycolic acid.** $EtO\cdot CH_2\cdot COOH = 104.07$. Ethoxyacetic acid. Colorless liquid, b.206, soluble in alcohol. e. **green.** Ethylated crystal violet, q.v. **e. hydrate.** Ethanol. **e. hydrazine.** $NH_2\cdot NHEt = 60.15$. Colorless liquid, b.100, soluble in water. **e. hydride.** Ethane. **e. hydrine.** Ethylin. **e. hydrobromide.** E. bromide. **e. hydrochloride.** E. chloride. **e. hydrocupreine.** Optochine. **e. hydrogen sulfate.** Ethylsulfuric acid. **e. hydroperoxide.** $EtO\cdot OH = 62.06$. Colorless liquid, b$_{150mm}$26, soluble in water. **e. hydroselenide.** E. selenomercaptan. **e. hydrosulfide.** E. mercaptan. **e. hydroxyacetate.** E. glycolate. **e. hydroxylamine.** $C_2H_7ON = 61.11$. *alpha-* NH_2OEt. Ethoxyamine. Colorless liquid, b.68, soluble in water. *beta-* $EtNHOH$. Hydroxylethylamine. Colorless leaflets, m.60, soluble in water. **e. hydroxypropionate.** $C_5H_{10}O_3 = 118.1$. *alpha-* E. lactate. *beta-* $CH_2OH\cdot CH_2\cdot COOEt$. Colorless liquid, b.187, soluble in water; a solvent for resins. **e. iodide.** $C_2H_5I = 156.02$. Iodoethane*, hydroiodic ether, e. hydroiodic ester, ether iodatus. Colorless liquid, ethereal odor, d.1.92, b.72.3, slightly soluble in water. Used for mineral separation and in iodine therapy. **e. iodoacetate.** $CH_2I\cdot COOEt = 214.0$. K.S.K. Colorless heavy oil, d.7.44, b.179; a lacrimatory. **e. isoamyl ether.** $EtOC_5H_{11} = 116.17$. Colorless liquid, b.112, insoluble in water. **e. isobutyl**

ether. $EtOC_4H_9 = 102.15$. Colorless liquid, b.78, insoluble in water. **e. isobutyl ketone.** $EtCOC_4H_9 = 114.16$. 2-Methylhexane-4-one. Colorless liquid, b.136, insoluble in water. **e. isobutyrate.** $Me_2CH\cdot COOEt = 116.13$. Ethyl dimethyl acetate. Colorless liquid, $d_{20}0.869$, b.110, slightly soluble in water. **e. isocyanate.** See *e. cyanate.* **e. isocyanide.** $EtNC = 55.1$. E. carbylamine*. Colorless liquid, b.79, soluble in water. **e. isophthalate.** $C_6H_4(COOEt)_2 = 222.2$. Colorless oil, b.285. **e. isopropyl acetoacetate.** $MeCO\cdot CH(CHMe_2)\cdot COOEt = 172.18$. Colorless liquid, b.200, slightly soluble in water. **e. isopropyl ether.** $Me_2CHOEt = 88.13$. Isopropyl ethoxide. Colorless liquid, b.54, soluble in water. **e. isopropyl ketone.** $Me_2CH\cdot CO\cdot Et = 100.13$. 2-Methylpentan-3-one. Colorless liquid, b.115, slightly soluble in water. **e. isosuccinate.** $MeCH(COOEt)_2 = 174.15$. Colorless liquid, b.198, sparingly soluble in water. **e. isosulfocyanate.** See *e. thiocyanate.* **e. isothiocyanate.** See *e. thiocyanate.* **e. isovalerate.** $Me_2CHCH_2COOEt = 130.16$. Colorless liquid, d.0.972, b.134, insoluble in water. **e. kairine.** See *kairine.* **e. ketone.** Diethyl ketone. **e. lactate.** $MeCH(OH)COOEt = 118.1$. Ethyl-α-hydroxypropionate. Colorless liquid, b.154, soluble in water; a solvent for nitrocellulose and resins. **e. malate.** $EtOOC\cdot CH_2\cdot CHOH\cdot COOEt = 190.15$. Colorless liquid, b.248, miscible with water; used in lacquers. **e. malonate.** $CH_2(COOEt)_2 = 160.14$, Colorless liquid, d.1.061, b.198, slightly soluble in water; a plasticizer for cellulose acetate. **e. malonic acid.** $EtCH(COOH)_2 = 132.07$. Colorless, prisms, m.111, decomp. 160, soluble in water; isomeric with dimethylmalonic, methyl succinic, and glutaric acids. **e. mannite.** $C_{10}H_{10}O_5 = 210.1$. A substitution product of mannite; a colorless syrup. **E. melamine.** E. cyanamide. **e. mercaptan.** $EtSH = 62.11$. Thioethyl alcohol, e. hydrosulfide, ethanethiol*. Colorless liquid, b.37, slightly soluble in water; an odorous constituent of feces. **e. mercaptide.** A compound of the type $Et\cdot S\cdot M$, where M is a monovalent metal. **e. mercuric chloride.** $EtHgCl = 265.11$. Silvery, iridescent leaflets, d.3.5, m.192.5, insoluble in water. **e. mercuric hydroxide.** $EtHgOH = 246.66$. Silvery, iridescent leaflets, m.190, insoluble in water. **e. methylether.** $Et\cdot O\cdot Me = 60.1$. Ethyl methyl oxide. Colorless liquid; an anesthetic. **e. monotartrate.** $C_6H_{10}O_6 = 178.11$. Colorless rhombs, m.90, soluble in water. **e. morphinehydrochloride (U.S.P.).** Dionine. **e. mustard oil.** E. isothiocyanate. See *e. thiocyanate.* **e. naphthalene.** $C_{10}H_7\cdot C_2H_5 = 156.16$. Naphthylethane. *alpha-* Colorless liquid, b.256, insoluble in water. *beta-* Colorless liquid, b.251, insoluble in water. **e. naphthylamine.** $EtNH\cdot C_{10}H_7 = 171.21$. Ethylaminenaphthalene. *alpha-* Colorless liquid, b.303. *beta-* Colorless liquid, b.305. **e. naphthyl ether.** $C_{10}H_7(OEt) = 172.16$. Ethoxynaphthalene. *alpha-* Colorless liquid, m.6, insoluble in water. *beta-* Bromelia. Colorless crystals, m.37, insoluble in water. **e. nitramine.** See *nitramine.* **e. nitrate.** $C_2H_5O_3N = 91.09$. Aether nitricus. Colorless liquid, d.1.116, m.-112, b.87.6, insoluble in water. **e. nitrite.** $C_2H_5O_2N = 75.09$. Aether nitrosus, sweet spirits of niter. Colorless liquid, d.0.900, b.17, slightly soluble in water; a diuretic and diaphoretic. Cf. *nitroethane*. **e. nitrobenz-oate.** $NO_2 \cdot C_6H_4COOEt = 195.16$. *ortho-* Colorless triclinic crystals, m.30, soluble in alcohol. *meta-* Colorless prisms, m.48, insoluble in water. *para-* Colorless crystals, m.57, soluble in alcohol. **e. nitrocarbamate.** Urethane. **e. nitrolic acid.** $MeC(NOH) \cdot NO_2 = 104.12$. Yellow rhombs, m.86 (decomp.), soluble in water. **e. nonylate.** $C_8H_{17} \cdot COOEt = 186.2$. E. perlargonate, oenanthic ether. Colorless liquid with strong vinous odor and acrid taste, $d_{17} 0.8635$, b.277, insoluble in water; a flavoring. **e. oenanthate.** $C_6H_{13}COOEt = 158.2$. Cognac oil. A colorless oil in old wines; a flavoring. **e. oleate.** $C_{20}H_{38}O_2 = 310.50$. Yellow oil with unpleasant taste, $d_{20} 0.870$, iodine val. 75–84. **e. orthophosphate.** See *e. phosphate*. **e. orthosilicate.** See *e. silicate*. **e. oxalurate.** $(COOEt)_2 = 146.10$. Colorless liquid, b.186. slightly soluble in water. **e. oxide.** Ether. **e. oxydithio-carbonic acid.** Xanthic acid. **e. palmitate.** $C_{15}H_{31} \cdot COOEt = 284.39$. Colorless needles, m.24.2, insoluble in water. **e. pelargarate.** E. norylate. **e. perchlorate.** $C_2H_5ClO_4 = 128.5$. Perchloric ether. Colorless, explosive liquid with a sweet odor. **e. perchloride.** Hexachloroethane. **e. peroxide.** Diethyl dioxide. **e. persulfide.** E. disulfide. **e. phenacetin.** See *phenacetin*. **e. phenate.** Phenetol. **e. phenol.** $Et \cdot C_6H_4OH = 122.12$. *ortho-* Phlorol. Colorless liquid, $d_0 1.037$, b.206.8, soluble in alcohol. *para-* 1,4-. Colorless needles, b.214, insoluble in water. **e. phenyl acetate.** $PhCH_2CO \cdot OEt = 164.15$. Colorless liquid, b.229, insoluble in water. **e. phenylacetylene.** $PhC \vdots CEt = 130.10$. Colorless liquid, $d_{21} 0.923$, b.202, soluble in alcohol **e. phenyl carbamate.** Phenylurethane. **e. phenyl-carbinol.** $(Ph \cdot Et) \vdots CHOH = 136.11$. Ethylphenyl-kydroxymethane. Colorless liquid, b.212, insoluble in water. **e. phenyl cinchonate.** Acitrin. **e. phenyl ether.** Phenetole. **e. phenylhydraz-ine.** $PhNEt \cdot NH_2 = 136.16$. *alpha-* Colorless oil, b.237, soluble in alcohol. *beta-* Colorless oil, sparingly soluble in water. **e. phenyl ketone.** $Ph \cdot COEt = 134.13$. Colorless leaflets, d.1.015, m.15, b.218, insoluble in water. **e. phenyl sulfone.** $PhSO_2Et = 170.21$. Colorless scales, m.42, sparingly soluble in water. **e. phenylurea.** $PhNH \cdot CO \cdot NHEt = 164.23$. Colorless needles, m.99, insoluble in water. **e. phosphate.** E. phosphoric acids: (1) *mono-* $C_2H_5 \cdot H_2PO_4 = 126.06$. Colorless oil, forming metallic salts (e. phosphates). (2) *di-* $(C_2H_5)_2 \cdot HPO_4 = 154.09$. Colorless syrup, forming salts (diethyl phosphates). (3) *normal-* or *tri-* $(C_2H_5)_2PO_4 = 182.15$. Colorless aromatic liquid, b.215, decomp. in water. (4) *pyro-* or *tetra-* $(C_2H_5)_4P_2O_7 = 290.16$. Colorless, odorous oil. **e. phosphine.** $EtPH_2 = 62.11$. Colorless liquid, b.25. **e. phosphinic acid.** $Et \cdot PO(OH)_2 = 110.1$. An isomer of e. phosphite (1). **e. phosphite.** E. phosphorous acids: (1) $C_2H_5H_2PO_3 = 110.06$. Acid e. phosphite, forming e. phosphites. (2) $(C_2H_5)_2 \cdot HPO_3 = 138.09$. Diethyl phosphite, forming diethyl phosphites. (3) $(C_2H_5)_3PO_3 = 166.12$. Normal e. phosphite, triethyl phosphite. Colorless liquid of disagreeable odor. (4) $(C_2H_5)_4H_2P_2O_5 = 202.10$. E. pyrophosphorous acid, forming e. pyrophosphites. **e. phosphoric acid.** See *e. phosphate*. **e. phosphorus acid.** See *e. phosphite*. **e. phthalate.** $C_6H_4(COOEt)_2 = 222.17$. Colorless

liquid, $d_{20} 1.118$, b.295, insoluble in water. *iso-* See *e. isophthalate*. *meta-* See *e. isophthalate*. *para-* See *e. terephthalate*. *tere-* See *e. terephthalate*. **e. propiolate.** $HC \vdots COOEt = 98.07$. Colorless liquid, b.119, insoluble in water. **e. propionate.** $EtCOOEt = 102.11$. Colorless liquid, d.0.896, b.98, slightly soluble in water; used in perfumery. **e. propyl.** Pentane. **e. propylcarbinol.** $Pr \cdot CHOH \cdot Et = 102.15$. Hexan-3-ol. Colorless liquid b.135, miscible with alcohol. **e. propylene.** Amylene. **e. propyl ether.** $Et \cdot O \cdot Pr = 88.13$. E. propyl oxide. Colorless liquid, b.60, slightly soluble in water. **e. propyl ketone.** $Et \cdot CO \cdot Pr = 100.13$. Hexan-3-one. Colorless liquid, b.122, sparingly soluble in water. **e. pseudocyanate.** E. isocyanate. **e. pyoctanin.** See *pyoktanin*. **e. pyr-role.** See *pyrrole*. **e. pyruvate.** $MeCO \cdot COOEt = 116.1$. Colorless liquid, d.1.060, b.144; a solvent for nitro-cellulose. **e. racemate.** An optically active isomer of e. tartrate. **e. red.** $C_{23}H_{23}N_2I$. 1,1-Diethyl isocyanine iodide. A quinoline dye; a photosensi-tizer. **e. rhodanate.** E. thiocyanate. **e. salicy-late.** $HO \cdot C_6H_4 \cdot COOEt = 166.13$. Sal ethyl. Colorless liquid of pleasant odor and taste, $d_{20} 1.132$, b.231, insoluble in water: an antiseptic and solvent. **e. selenide.** $Et_2Se = 137.1$. Diethyl selenide. Colorless oil, b.107. *di-* E. selenide. *per-* E. selenide. **e. silicate.** (1) $(C_2H_5)_4SiO_4 = 208.6$. E. orthosilicate. Colorless, flammable liquid; isolog of e. orthocarbonate. (2) $(C_2H_5)_2SiO_3 = 134.4$. E. metasilicate. Colorless liquid, b.165, decomp. by water; isolog of e. carbonate. (3) $(C_2H_5)_6Si_2O_7 = 342.8$. E. disilicate. **e. silicon.** The radical $EtSi \equiv$, silicon monoethide. **e. stannic acid.** $EtSnO \cdot OH = 180.75$. White powder, insoluble in water. **e. strychnine.** See *strychnine*. **e. succinate.** $EtOOC(CH_2)_2COOEt = 174.16$. Colorless liquid, d.1.044, b.216.5, insoluble in water; a plasticizer. *iso-* E. succinate. **e. succinic acid.** $HOOC \cdot CH_2 \cdot CHEt \cdot COOH = 146.11$. Color-less prisms, m.98, soluble in water. **e. succinyl succinate.** $C_{12}H_{16}O_6 = 256.2$. Green prisms, soluble in water (blue fluorescence). **e. sulfas.** E. sulfate. **e. sulfate.** $(C_2H_5)_2SO_4 = 154.15$. Normal e. sulfate, diethyl sulfate. Colorless oil with peppermint odor, d.1.184, b.208, insoluble in water. *acid-* E. sulfuric acid. *di-* E. sulfate. *mono-* E. sulfuric acid. **e. sulfide.** $(C_2H_5)_2S = 90.15$. Diethyl sulfide, ethylthioethane*. Color-less liquid, $d_{20} 0.837$, $b_{754mm} 92$, insoluble in water. *di-* E. sulfide. *dichloro-* Mustard gas. *penta-* E. pentasulfide. *per-* E. disulfide. **e. sulfinic acid.** $Et \cdot SO \cdot OH = 94.11$. Ethane sulfinic acid*. Colorless syrup, an isolog of propionic acid. **e. sulfite.** $(C_2H_5)_2SO_3 = 138.15$. Colorless liquid, b.161, decomp. by water; isolog of e. carbonate. **e. sulfocarbonate.** E. thiocarbonate. **e. sulfo-chloride.** $C_2H_5 \cdot SOOCl = 128.60$. Colorless liquid, m.29, decomp. by water. **e. sulfocyanate, -ide.** E. thiocyanate. **e. sulfohydrate.** E. mercaptan. **e. sulfone.** $C_4H_{10}O_2S = 122.15$. Ethylsulfonyl-ethane*. Colorless rhombs, m.73, sparingly soluble water. **e. sulfonic acid.** $EtSO_2 \cdot OH = 110.11$. Ethane sulfonic acid*. Colorless, deliquescent crystals, soluble in water. **e. sulfonic chloride.** $EtSO_2Cl = 128.55$. Ethane sulfonyl chloride*. Colorless liquid, b.177, decomp. by water. **e. sulfonic oxide.** E. sulfoxide. **e. sulfoxide.** $Et_2SO =$

106.20.   Ethyl sulfinylethane*.   Colorless liquid, $b_{15mm}88$, miscible with alcohol.   **e. sulfuric acid.** $EtHSO_4 = 126.09$.   Acid e. sulfate, sulfovinic acid, e. hydrogen sulfate.   Colorless, syrup decomp. by heat or water.   Used medicinally as its salts, and for precipitating casein from milk.   **e. tartrate.** $EtOOC(CHOH)_2COOEt = 206.16$.   E. racemate, diethyl tartrate.   Colorless liquid, b.280, slightly soluble in water; a solvent for nitrocellulose, gums and resins.   **e. tartronic acid.** $C_5H_6O_5 = 146.05$.   Colorless scales, m.116 (decomp), soluble in water.   **e. telluride.** $Et_2Te = 185.5$.   Tellurium ethyl.   A heavy red oil, giving off yellow fumes. di- $Et_2Te_2 = 313.1$.   Diethyl telluride, e. pertelluride.   A dark-red liquid, decomp. by water.   **e. terephthalate.** C_6H_4- $(COOEt)_2 = 222.17$.   E. p-phthalate.   Colorless liquid, b.119, insoluble in water.   **e. thioalcohol.**   E. mercaptan.   **e. thiocarbimide.**   E. isothiocyanate.   **e. thiocarbonate.**   (1) $CS(EtO)_2 = 134.14$.   A liquid, d.1.028, b.162.   (2) $(EtS)_2CS = 166.1$.   Yellow oil of unpleasant odor; isolog of e. carbonate and e. sulfite.   **e. thiocyanate.** $C_2H_5SCN = 87.15$.   E. sulfocyanide.   Colorless liquid, b.148, insoluble in water. iso- $C_2H_5 \cdot NCS = 87.15$.   E. mustard oil.   Colorless liquid, $b_{753mm}131$, insoluble in water.   **e. tin tribromide.** $EtSnBr_3 = 387.49$.   Colorless needles, m.310, soluble in water.   **e. toluate.** $MeC_6H_4COOEt = 164.15$. $ortho$- E. 1,2-toluate.   Colorless liquid, b.221, insoluble in water. $meta$- E. 1,3-toluate.   Colorless liquid, b.228, insoluble in water. $para$- E. 1,4-toluate.   Colorless liquid, b.229, insoluble in water.   **e. toluene.**   E. methyl$benzene$.   **e. urea.**   See $urea$.   **e. urethane.**   See $urethane$.   **e. valerate.** $BuCOOEt = 130.16$.   E. valeriate, e. valerinate.   Colorless liquid, b.145, insoluble in water.   **e. vanillate.** $C_{10}H_{12}O_4 = 196.15$.   Colorless crystals, m.44, insoluble in water.   **e. vanillin.**   See $vanillin$.   **e. vinyl ether.** $C_2H_5 \cdot O \cdot C_2H_3 = 72.08$.   Colorless liquid, b.36, soluble in water.   **e. violet.**   An indicator changing at pH 2.0 from blue-green (acid) to purple (alkali).   **e. xylene.**   Dimethylethyl$benzene$.

ethylal.   Acetaldehyde.

ethylamine.   See $ethyl\ amine$.

ethylate.   An alcoholate or ethoxide.   A compound derived from ethanol by replacing the hydrogen of the hydroxy group by a monovalent metal (M) e.g., MOEt.   Cf $ethoxide$, $alcoholate$.

ethylation.   The introduction of an ethyl group into a compound.

ethylene.   (1) Ethene.   (2) Acetene.   Elayl.   The radical $-CH_2 \cdot CH_2-$.   World production (1967) 9 million tons.   Chiefly used as a source of polyethylene.   Cf $ethylidene$.   **azi**- Diazoethane.   **bromo**- Vinyl bromide.   **chloro**- Vinyl chloride.   **di**- See $diethylene$.   **dichloro**- Acetylene chloride.   **diethyl**- Δ^3-Hexylene.   **dimethyl**- ψ-Butylene.   **diphenyl**- Stilbene.   **keto**- Ketene.   **pentyl**- Heptene.   **perchloro**- See $tetrachloroethylene$.   **phen**-, **phenyl**- Styrolene.   **tetrachloro**- q.v.   **tetraiodo**- Diiodoform.   **tetraphenyl**- q.v.   **trimethyl**- Pental.   **vinyl**- Bivinyl.

e. acetate. $MeCOOCH_2 \cdot CH_2OOCMe = 146.11$.   Colorless liquid, b.186, soluble in water.   **e. alcohol.**   E. glycol.   **e. aldehyde.**   Acrolein.   **e. benzoate.** $Ph \cdot COO \cdot CH_2 : CH_2 \cdot OOC \cdot Ph = 270.1$.   Colorless

prisms, m.73, insoluble in water.   **e. bichloride.**   E. chloride.   **e. bromide.** $BrCH_2 \cdot CH_2Br = 187.96$.   Glycol dibromide, bromoethylene, 1,2-dibromoethane.   Colorless liquid, b.131, slightly soluble in water.   Used as an anesthetic in organic synthesis, and added to Ethyl Gasoline, q.v.   **e. bromohydrin.**   Glycol bromohydrin.   **e. carboxylic acid.**   Acrylic acid.   **e. chlorohydrin.** $ClCH_2 \cdot CH_2OH = 80.06$.   Chloroethyl alcohol, 2-chlorethanol, 1-hydroxy-2-chlorethane.   Colorless liquid, b.128, miscible with water.   Used in organic synthesis, and to force the sprouting of plants. $commercial$- A 40% solution, d.1.097, b.96, used to introduce the OEt group into a molecule.   **e. chloride.** $ClCH_2 \cdot CH_2Cl = 98.94$.   Glycol dichloride, elayl chloride, 1,2-dichloroethane, vinylene chloride, Dutch liquid.   Colorless liquid, b.83.7, slightly soluble in water.   Used in organic synthesis; as a solvent for lacquers and fats; as a textile cleanser; and as a fumigant for foodstuffs.   Cf $dichloroethylene$. $1,1$-Ethylidene chloride.   **e. cyanohydrin.** $C_3H_5ON = 71.07$.   2-Cyanoethanol, 1-hydroxy-2-cyanoethane.   Colorless liquid, m.221, miscible with water.   **e. cyanide.** $C_4H_4N_2 = 80.07$.   Succinonitrile, glycol dicyanide, 1,2-dicyanoethane.   Colorless crystals, m.54, soluble in water.   **e. diamine.** $NH_2CH_2 \cdot CH_2NH_2 = 60.09$.   Diaminoethane, 1,2-ethanediamine*, in ptomaines.   Colorless crystals, m.10, soluble in water.   Cf $sublamine$.   **e. d. monohydrate.**   Colorless liquid with an ammoniacal odor; a muscle relaxant (B.P.).   **e. d. tetraacetic acid.**   EDTA, versenic acid.   White crystals, slightly soluble in water, decomp. above 160; made from an alkali cyanide, formaldehyde, and e.d.   It forms slightly ionized complexes with alkaline earths and other elements.   Used as the more soluble sodium salt, as an analytical reagent., e.g., to titrate the hardness salts of water with Eriochrome Black T as indicator; also in detergents, rubber processing, and scale prevention.   Cf $chelation$.   **e. dibenzamide.**   See $dibenzamide$.   **e. dibromide.**   See $e. bromide$.   **e. dicarbonitrile.**   E. cyanide.   **e. dicarboxylic acid.** cis- Maleic acid. $trans$- Fumaric acid.   **e. dichloride.**   E. chloride.   **e. dicyanide.**   E. cyanide.   **e. diethylate.** $EtO \cdot CH_2 \cdot CH_2OEt = 118.1$.   Diethyl glycol ether.   **e. dihydrate.**   E. glycol.   **e. diiodide.**   E. iodide.   **e. dinitrate.**   E. nitrate.   **e. dinitrite.**   E. nitrite.   **e. dioxide.**   Dioxan.   **e. dioxy.**   The radical $-OCH_2 \cdot CH_2O-$.   **e. diphenate.**   E. diphenyl ether.   **e. diphenyldiamine.** $C_{14}H_{16}N_2 = 212.17$.   Colorless crystals, m.59, insoluble in water.   **e. diphenyl ether.** $C_{14}H_{14}O_2 = 214.19$.   E. diphenate.   Colorless crystals, m.98.5, sparingly soluble in water.   **e. disulfhydrate.**   E. mercaptan.   **e. disulfonic acid.**   E. sulfonic acid.   **e. glycol.**   Glycol.   **e.g. dinitrate.**   E. nitrate.   **e.g. ethyl ether.**   Cellosolve.   **e. hydride.**   Ethane.   **e. iodide.** $(CH_2I)_2 = 281.98$.   Diiodoform.   e. diiodide, 1,2-diiodoethane*.   Yellow prisms, m. 8.1. slightly soluble in water; an iodoform substitute.   **e. mercaptan.** $HSCH_2 \cdot CH_2 \cdot SH = 94.20$.   Glycol sulfohydrate, e. disulfhydrate.   dithioethylene glycol.   Colorless liquid, b.146, soluble in alcohol.   **e. monoacetate.**   Glycol acetate.   **e. naphthalene.**   Acenaphthalene.   **e. nitrate.** $(CH_2NO_3)_2 = 152.12$.   EGDN, e. dinitrate.   Yellow liquid, exploded by heat or impact, insoluble in water.   **e. nitrite.** $(CH_2NO_2)_2 = 120.12$.   Glycol dinitrite.   Colorless liquid, b.96, insoluble in water. **e. oxide.** $(CH_2)_2$:O $= 44.04$. Dimethylene oxide, 1,2-epoxy-ethane*. Colorless gas, b_{746mm}14, soluble in water; an insecticide and weedicide. Cf. *Carboxide*. E. (di)oxide is used to make e. glycol and thence Terylene. **e. perchloride.** Carbon dichloride. **e. periodide.** Diiodoform. **e. rhodanate.** E. sulfocyanide. **e. series.** C_nH_{2n}. Olefins, ethene series, alkenes. Unsaturated hydrocarbons with one double bond; as, ethylene, ethene* (C_2H_4), and melene, triacontylene* $(C_{30}H_{60})$. **e. sulfate.** *acid-* $C_2H_4(HSO_4)_2 = 222.1$. E. sulfuric acid. A colorless syrup. *basic-* $(OH)C_2H_4(HSO_4) = 142.1$. E. hydroxysulfuric acid; known only as its compounds. **e. sulfide.** $(C_2H_4S)_2 = 60.06$. A solid, m.110, sublimes 200, insoluble in water. **e. sulfocyanide.** $C_2H_4(SCN)_2 = 144.21$. E. thiocyanate. Colorless rhombs, m.90, sparingly soluble in water. **e. sulfonic acid.** Ethionic acid. **e. sulfuric acid.** See *e. sulfate*. **e. tetrabromide.** Tetrabromoethane. **e. tetrachloride.** Tetrachloroethane. **e. thiocyanate.** E. sulfocyanide. **e. trichloride.** Trichloroethylene. **e. urea.** $C_3H_6ON_2 = 86.09$. Colorless needles, m.131, soluble in water.

ethylene glycol. See *glycol*.

ethylic acid. Acetic acid.

ethylidene. Ethidene. The radical $CH_3 \cdot CH =$, from ethane; isomeric with ethylene. **e. acetone.** MeCO·CH:CH·Me $= 84.09$. A liquid, b_{741mm}122. **e. bichloride.** E. chloride. **e. bromide.** MeCHBr$_2$ $= 187.96$. 1,1'-Dibromoethane. Colorless liquid, b.112, insoluble in water. **e. chloride.** $C_2H_4Cl_2 = 98.94$. Ethylidene perchloride, 1,1'-dichloroethane, chlorinated hydrochloric ether. Colorless liquid, b.59, sparingly soluble in water. **e. cyanhydrin.** MeH·C·(OH)CN $= 71.08$. 1-Cyanoethanol, lactonitrile, 1-hydroxy-1'-cyanoethane. Colorless liquid, b.182 (decomp.), miscible with water. **e. dichloride.** E. chloride. **e. diiodide.** E. iodide. **e. glycol.** Me·CH(OH)$_2$. Known only in its derivatives, e.g., chloral hydrate. **e. iodide.** MeCHI$_2 = 281.98$. 1,1-Diiodoethane*. Colorless liquid, b.178, insoluble in water. **e. lactic acid.** Lactic acid. **e. perchloride.** E. chloride. **e. urea.** $C_3H_6ON_2 = 86.15$. Colorless needles, m.126, decomp. 165, slightly soluble in water. **e. urethane.** $C_8H_{16}O_4N_2 = 204.2$. Colorless needles, m.125(decomp.), soluble in water.

ethylin. A compound derived from glycerol by substituting one or more ethoxy groups for hydroxy groups: **mono-** $C_3H_5(OH)_2OEt = 118.1$. Colorless liquid, b.230. **di-** $C_3H_5 \cdot OH \cdot (Et)_2 = 146.1$. 1,2-Diethylin. 1,3-Diethylglycerol. **tri-** $C_3H_5(OEt)_3 = 174.2$. Colorless liquid, b.185.

ethylogen. A complex carbide, from which water liberates ethylene slowly.

ethyloic- Prefix indicating the radical $-CH_2 \cdot \cdot CO-OH$ as a side chain.

ethylol. Oxethyl. The radical $CH_2OH \cdot CH_2-$

ethyne*. Acetylene.

ethynyl*. Ethinyl. **e. bromide.** Bromoacetylene.

etianic acid. Testane-17-carboxylic acid. Cf. *steroid*.

eticyclin. Ethinylestradiol.

etiline. Tetrachloroethane.

etiography. The study of phenomena which destroy solid material; e.g., corrosion, thermal and mechanical stresses.

etiology. The study of the origin of a disease.

etiophyllin. $C_{31}H_{34}N_4Mg = 486.62$. Aetiophyllin. The decarboxylated magnesium base of chlorophyll. Blue tablets, m.205. See *porphin*.

etioporphyrin. $C_{31}H_{34}N_4 = 462.26$. A tetrapyrrole derivative from chlorophyll and hemoglobin. Violet crystals, m.280. See *porphin*.

Etisul. Trade name for diethyl dithiol isophthalate; used to treat leprosy.

Ettinghausen effect. The galvanomagnetic change in temperature of a plate through which a current flows. Cf. *Hall, Leduc, Nernst effects*.

ettringite. $Ca_{12}Al_4(OH)_{24}(SO_4)_6 \cdot 5H_2O$. A mineral found in contact zones of chalk and dolomite (Eire).

Eu. Symbol for europium.

eubacteria. The true bacteria, as distinct from the myxobacteria, q.v.

eucaine A. $C_{19}H_{27}O_4N = 333.3$. Tetramethyl-N-methyl-β-benzoxypiperidine-γ-carboxylic ester, α-eucaine. Colorless crystals, m.103; substitute for cocaine. **e. B.** $C_{15}H_{21}O_2N = 247.17$. β-Eucaine, benzamine, betacaine, trimethylbenzoyloxypiperidine. Colorless crystals, m.91; a local anesthetic.
  e. hydrochloride. *alpha-* $C_{19}H_{27}O_4N \cdot HCl = 368.8$. Colorless crystals, m.200, soluble in water; an anesthetic. *beta-* $C_{15}H_{22}O_2NCl = 283.64$. Colorless crystals, m.268.

eucairite. CuAgSe. A white, metallic, isometric, native selenide.

eucalin. $C_{12}H_{12}O_6 = 252.1$. A nonfermentable disaccharide from the hydrolysis of melitose, resembling inositol. Cf. *eucalyptolene*.

eucalyptene. $C_{10}H_{16} = 136.2$. A terpene derived from eucalyptol. Colorless liquid, b.170, soluble in alcohol; an antiseptic.

eucalyptol. $C_{10}H_{18}O = 154.25$. Cineol, cajeputole. Colorless liquid, $d_20.927$, b.176, insoluble in water, miscible with alcohol. A chief constituent of eucalyptus and cajeput oils; an antiseptic, antispasmodic, antiperiodic, and expectorant.

eucalyptolene. $C_{10}H_{16} = 136.2$. An isomer of eucalyptene, in eucalyptus oil. Yellow liquid, b.300, miscible with alcohol.

eucalyptus. (1) A genus of trees (Myrtaceae). Cf. *lerp, mallee bark, marri kino*. (2) Blue gum tree. The dried leaves of *Eucalpytus globulus* (Myrtaceae), originally Australia; an antiperiodic, tonic, and antipyretic. **e. oil.** The essential oil of e. leaves, varying from peppermint to turpentine in odor. Chief constituents: eucalyptole, pinene, capronaldehyde, valeraldehyde, butyraldehyde. Yellow liquid, d.0.91–0.93, miscible with alcohol; an antiseptic and flavoring.

eucasin. Ammonium caseinate.

eucasol. Anytol.

eucatropine. Euphthalmine. **e. hydrochloride,** $C_{17}H_{25}O_3N \cdot HCl = 327.86$. White granules, m.184. soluble in water.

eucazulene. $C_{15}H_{18} = 198.14$. A blue hydrocarbon from eucalyptus oil.

euchinine. Quinine ethyl carbonate.

eu-chlorine, euchlorine. A mixture of chlorine and chlorine dioxide obtained from potassium chlorate and concentrated hydrochloric acid.

euchroite. $Ca_4As_2O_9$. Green rhombs, d.3.4, hardness 3.

eucodal. $C_{18}H_{21}O_4N = 315.02$. Dihydrohydroxycodeinone. White powder, a hypnotic.

eucodeine. $C_{18}H_{21}O_3N\cdot CH_3\cdot Br = 396.2$. Methyl-codeinebromide. White powder, m.261, soluble in water; a sedative.

eucol. Guaiacol acetate.

eucolloid. A colloid, with satisfied primary valencies, forming particles of chain length over 2500 A (mol. wt. over 1,000). Cf. *mesocolloid*.

eucryptite. $LiAlSiO_4$. Transparent, native hexagonal lithium aluminum silicate.

euctolite. A basaltic rock from Italy.

eucupine. $C_{24}H_{34}O_2N_2 = 282.41$. Isoamylhydrocupreine. A quinine alkaloid, q.v. White powder, insoluble in water. **e. hydrochloride.** Colorless crystals, soluble in water; a powerful bactericide.

eudalene. $C_{14}H_{16} = 186.11$. 7-Iso-propyl-1-methyl-naphthalene. A hydrocarbon obtained from eudesmol and selinene by treatment with sulfur.

eudeiolite. A native calcium–iron–cerium columbate–titanate–thorate. Brown, shining mass, d.3.44, hardness 4.

eudialite. $Na_{13}(Ca\cdot Fe)_6(Si\cdot Zr)_{20}O_{52}Cl$. A native silicate-chloride.

eudiometer. A graduated glass tube with platinum electrodes, closed at one end, used to measure volume changes during combination of gases.

eudiometry. Gasometry.

eudoxine. $(C_6H_2I_2OBi_2)_3\cdot COC_6H_4O$. Bismuth tetra-iodophenolphthalein, bismuth nosophene. Yellow powder, insoluble in water; used to treat intestinal irritations.

euflavine. $C_{14}H_{14}N_3Cl = 261.8$. 2,8-Diamino-10-methylacridinium chloride. A dye similar to acriflavine.

eugallol. Pyrogallol monoacetate.

eugenic acid. (1) Eugetinic acid. (2) Eugenol.

eugenin. $C_{10}H_{12}O_2 = 164.1$. An isomer of eugenol, from oil of cloves.

eugenol. $C_{10}H_{12}O_2 = 164.21$. Allyl-4,3-guaiacol, 2-methoxy-1-hydroxy-4-allylbenzene, in many essential oils; as, oil of cloves; isomer of chavibetol and eugenin. Colorless liquid, d_{18}c1.063, b.253, slightly soluble in water. Used as a dental analgesic (B.P.), antiseptic, and antituberculosic; in perfumery and for manufacturing vanillin. **iso-**Propenylguaiacol. An isomer with the side chain —CH:CH·Me. Colorless liquid, b.240. **cinnamyl-**E. cinnamate. **methyl-** $C_{11}H_{14}O_2 = 178.17$. Eugenol methyl ether, 1,2-methoxy-4-allylbenzene. Colorless liquid, b.244, insoluble in water.

e. acetamide. $C_{12}H_{15}O_3N = 221.2$. Colorless scales, m.110, soluble in water; an anesthetic. **e. benzoate.** Benzoeugenol. **e. cinnamate.** $C_{18}H_{18}O_3 = 282.14$. Cinnamyleugenol. Colorless needles; an antiseptic.

eugetic acid. Eugetinic acid.

eugetinic acid. $C_6H_2(OH)(OMe)\cdot C_3H_5\cdot COOH = 208.10$. Eugenic acid, eugetic acid. Colorless prisms, m.124, sparingly soluble in water.

euglenarhodon. A xanthophyll carotenoid from certain flagellates.

eukairit. CuAgSe. A native selenide.

eukinase. The desiccated and powdered pancreatic juice of pigs; mainly trypsin.

eulachon oil. Candlefish oil. The oil of *Thaleichthys pacificus*, candlefish; a cod-liver oil substitute.

eulissin. Decamethonium iodide.

eulysin. $C_{24}H_{36}O_5 = 404.3$. A yellow split product of decacrylic acid.

eulytin. $Bi(SiO_4)_3$. A yellow silicate, d.6.1, hardness 5–6.

eumenol. A fluid extract emmenagogue from the root of Chinese tang-kui, man-mu (Araliaceae).

eumydrine. Methyl atropine nitrate. White crystals, soluble in water; a mydriatic, antihidrotic, and antispasmodic.

eunatrol. Sodium oleate.

euonymin. Euonymus. A glucoside from the bark and root of *Euonymus* species. Yellow powder; a cholagogue and cathartic.

euonymit. Dulcite.

euonymoid. The combined principle from *Euonymus*. Green powder, soluble in alcohol; a hepatic stimulant and mild cathartic.

euonymus. (1) *Euonymus*. A genus of shrubs (Celastraceae). (2) Indian arrowroot, wahoo, spindle tree, burning bush. The dried bark of the root of *E. atropurpureus* (Celastraceae); a laxative, cathartic, and diuretic.

euosmite. $C_{34}H_{29}O_2 = 469.3$. A fossil resin.

euparal. A synthetic resin, n.1.53, substituting Canada balsam in microscopy.

euparin. $C_{12}H_{11}O_3 = 203.1$. Yellow crystals from the leaves of *Eupatorium purpureum* (Compositae), purple brown; an aromatic.

eupatheoscope. An instrument to measure the cooling effect of air currents. Cf. *katathermometer*.

eupatirin. Stevioside.

eupatorin. A glucoside from the leaves of *Eupatorium perfoliatum*, boneset, thoroughwort, and *Eupatorium cannabinum*, hempweed (Compositae), Europe, America, Asia.

eupatorium. (1) *Eupatorium*. A genus of Compositae; as, *E. cannabinum*, hemp. (2) Indian page, boneset, thoroughwort. The leaves and flowering tops of *Eupatorium perfoliatum*; a diaphoretic tea, tonic, and laxative.

euphorbain. A protease in the latex of certain Euphorbiaceae, e.g., *E. lathyris*.

Euphorbia. A genus of plants characterized by a milky juice. **e. gum.** Potato gum. A latex gum from the W. African *E.*: rubber 10, resins 50%. Cf. *euphorbium*. **e. pilulifera.** Pill-bearing spurge, *E. pilulifera* (Euphorbiaceae), Antilles, Australia; an antibronchitic.

Euphorbiacea. The spurge family: a group of herbs, shrubs, or trees, often with a milky acrid juice yielding rubber; e.g., roots: *Euphorbia resinifera* (euphorbium); herbs: *Mercurialis perennis* (mercurialis); barks: *Croton eluteria* (cascarilla bark); seeds: *Ricinus communis* (castor oil), *Croton tiglium* (croton seed); glands: *Mallotus philippinensis* (kamala); plant products: *Hevea brasiliensis* (para rubber).

euphorbin. $C_{30}H_{48}O = 424.5$. A bitter principle from the resinous juice of *Euphorbia* species.

euphorbium. A resin from *Euphorbia resinifera*, Morocco; an emetic and aperient. Cf. *euphorbia gum*.

euphorine. Phenylurethane.

euphthalmine. $C_{17}H_{25}O_3N\cdot HCl = 327.7$. Eucatropine. A synthetic alkaloid, the mandelic acid derivative of eucaine. White powder, m.113, soluble in water; a mydriatic.

euphurbin. $C_{15}H_{24}O = 220.2$. A crystalline principle from the resinous juice of *Euphorbia resinifera*.

euphylline. Aminophylline.

eupion. An antiseptic constituent of wood tar.

eupittone. Eupittonic acid.

eupittonic acid. $C_{19}H_8O_3(OMe)_6 = 470.3$. Pitacol, eupittone, hexamethoxyaurine. A hexamethoxylated amino dye. Orange needles, decomp. 200, soluble in alkalies, with blue coloration.

eupurpuroid. The combined principles from *Eupatorium purpureum*, purple boneset, Joe-Pye weed; a diuretic and renal tonic.

eupyrine. $C_{18}H_{18}O_5N = 328.15$. Vanillin ethyl carbonate p-phenetidine. Green crystals, m.87, sparingly soluble in water; an antipyretic.

euquinine. Quinine ethyl carbonate.

eureka burner. A self-lighting bunsen-type burner.

Euresol. $C_8H_8O_3 = 152.06$. Trade name for resorcin monoacetate. Yellow oil, b.283, insoluble in water: a skin antiseptic.

eurobin. Chrysarobin triacetate. Yellow powder; a skin antiseptic.

europhen. $C_{22}H_{29}O_2I = 452.1$. Diisobutyl cresol iodide. Yellow, amorphous powder of saffron-like odor, m.110, insoluble in water; an iodoform substitute, antiseptic, antisyphilitic, and dusting powder.

europium. Eu $= 151.96$; at. no. 63. A rare-earth metal discovered (1896) by Demarcay in cerium minerals. Principal valency 3; its compounds are rose-colored. **e. nitrate.** $Eu(NO_3)_3 = 338.0$. Colorless crystals, soluble in water. **e. oxide.** $Eu_2O_3 = 352.00$. White powder, insoluble in water. **e. sulfate.** $Eu_2(SO_4)_3 \cdot 8H_2O = 736.2$. Colorless crystals, soluble in water.

eurybin. A glucoside from *Eurybia* (or *Olearia*) *moschata*, New Zealand.

eurythrol. An aqueous extract of ox spleen; used to treat anemia and chlorosis.

euscopol. $C_{17}H_{21}O_4N \cdot HBr = 384.11$. Optically inactive scopolamine hydrobromide. Colorless crystals, m.181, soluble in water; a hypnotic.

eustenin. Theobromine sodium iodide.

eutannin. $C_{28}H_{20}O_{19} = 660.2$. Colorless crystals; an intestinal antiseptic. Cf. *chebulinic acid*.

eutectic. An alloy of metals in proportions such that it has the lowest possible melting point. **e. alloy.** A mixture of metals which solidifies completely at the e. temperature. **e. mixture.** A mixture of substances which has the lowest possible constant melting point. Cf. *dystectic mixture*. **e. temperature** The melting point of a eutectic mixture. Cf. *diagram*.

eutropic series. A series in which crystalline form and physical constants show a regular variation.

eutropy. The progression of the isomorphism of crystals of salts of an element, with its atomic number.

euxanthic acid. $C_{19}H_{18}O_{11} \cdot H_2O = 440.16$. Purreic acid, hamathionic acid. Yellow crystals from E. Indian yellow (purree), decomp. 160, soluble in hot water. Cf. *coccinic acid*.

euxanthin. $C_{19}H_{16}O_{10} = 404.2$. The principal constituent of E. Indian yellow (purree). Yellow crystals.

euxanthinic acid. Euxanthic acid.

euxanthone. $(HO \cdot C_6H_3)_2CO \cdot O = 228.06$. Purrone, purrenone, porphyric acid, 1,7-dihydroxyxanthone. Yellow crystals, m.237, **iso-** 3,6-Dioxyxanthone. Yellow crystals, soluble in alkalies with fluorescence. **methoxy-** Gentisin.

euxanthonic acid. $C_{13}H_{10}O_5 = 246.08$. Yellow needles, decomp. 200; soluble in hot water.

euxantogen. Mangiferin.

euxenite. $(Y \cdot Er \cdot Ce)_2(Ti \cdot Nb)_6Fe(UO)O_{16}(?)$. Polycrase. A mineral containing helium, germanium, and uranium.

ev, eV. Abbreviation for electron volt.

evacuant. A cathartic.

evacuate. To remove a gas from a container; to produce a vacuum.

Evans blue (U.S.P.). *Azovan* blue.

evansite. $H_6Al_3PO_{10}$. A hydrous aluminum phosphate.

evaporate. (1) To convert a liquid into its vapor by heat or low pressure. (2) To concentrate a solution by removing part of the solvent as gas or vapor.

evaporation. The process of converting a liquid into a vapor. **direct-** E. by means of flame. **indirect-** E. by means of steam, water, oil bath, or other indirect sources of heat. **latent heat of-** The amount of heat energy absorbed by a unit weight of substance as it passes from the liquid to the vapor state. If T is the absolute boiling point, and E the molecular elevation of boiling point of a solution, then the latent heat of e. $= 0.02T^2/E$. See *latent heat*. **spontaneous-** E. without artificial heat, e.g., by sun heat or air currents. **vacuum-** E. by exposure to low pressure.

e. burner. A gas burner with a perforated disk top to heat a large area. **e. dish.** A shallow dish to contain evaporating solutions.

evaporator. A device to volatilize liquids. **solar-** An appliance heating a liquid from above, by infrared radiation.

evaporimeter. An instrument to measure the rate of evaporation of a liquid in terms of the rate of fall of its level.

evaporite. Natural deposits of mineral salts produced by evaporation of large volumes of water.

Everitt's salt. Potassium ferrous ferrocyanide.

evernesic acid. Everninic acid.

evernic acid. $C_{17}H_{16}O_7 = 332.13$. Colorless needles, m.164, insoluble in water. A homolog of lecanoric acid, from *Evernia prunastri*, a lichen.

everniine. $C_{16}H_{14}O_7 = 318.11$. Yellow powder, from gums and lichens, soluble in water.

everninic acid. $C_9H_{10}O_4 = 182.09$. Evernesic acid, 4-methoxy-6-methylsalicylic acid, from lichens. Colorless crystals, m.157, soluble in hot water. **ethyl ester of-** Lichenol. **methyl ester of-** Sparassol.

evipal. Hexobarbitone, q.v. **e. sodium.** E. soluble; sodium hexobarbitone.

evipan. Hexobarbitone, q.v.

evodene. A terpene from *Evodia rutaecarpa*.

evodiamine. $C_{19}H_{17}ON_3 = 303.14$. An alkaloid from *Evodia rutaecarpa*. Colorless crystals, m.278.

evolution. (1) Chemistry: the escape or liberation of a gas. (2) Biology: the gradual development of a species through many generations, by which new species are formed and develop into more specialized organisms. **atomic-** See *spectral* classification.

evonymin. Euonymin.

Ewer and Pick's acid. Naphthalene-1,6-disulfonic acid.

ex. An inscription on a pipett or measuring vessel, indicating that it is to be used to deliver (not to contain) its nominal volume (U.K. usage). Cf. *in*.

ex- Prefix (Greek) indicating, out of, or out from.

exalgin. $Ph·N·Me(COMe) = 149.1$. Methylacetanilide, methylphenylacetamide. Colorless crystals, m.101, sparingly soluble in water; an analgesic and antipyretic.

exaltation. The amount by which the molecular refractivity of a compound exceeds the sum of the refractivities of its atoms; an indication of constitution.

exalton(e). Cyclopentadecanone.

exanthema. A copper deficiency pathological condition of certain citrus fruits.

excelsin. A globulin, mol. wt. 14,738, from brazil nuts.

excidants. Stimulants.

excipient. An inert carrier for a medicinal agent; as, starch in tablets.

excitation. Activation. The passage of an electron from its normal orbit to one of higher energy content due to absorption of radiations. On its return to the normal state the absorbed radiation is emitted, e.g., as fluorescence. Cf. *atom, energy levels.* **photochemical-** Excitation. **thermal-** See *thermal*.

excitomotors. Drugs that excite the nerve activities.

exciton. The energy of an electron, which can be passed from one to another.

excitonic. Describing a molecule (as found in silicon) which is a stable complex of 2 pairs of electrons and unoccupied energy levels ("holes") that electrons can fill.

exclusion principle. Pauli's principle.

excretin. $C_{20}H_{36}O = 292.4$. A cholesterol-like substance in human feces. Yellow needles, m.96, insoluble in water.

exinite. A perhydrous constituent of coal with preserved protective plant structures, e.g., cuticles.

exo- Prefix indicating, substitution in a side chain. Cf. *endo-*.

exobiology. The study of life in space.

exocondensation. Ring formation.

exocyclic. Pertaining to a cyclic compound with substitution or a double bond in the side chain.

exogenous. Produced outside. **e. purines.** The purine bodies of excretions which have passed through the system and have their origin in food. Cf. *endogenous*.

exograph. An X radiograph on a film outside the body.

exosmosis. The diffusion of salts through the plant membrane from the protoplasm into water. Antonym: endosmosis.

exothermic. Indicating liberation or escape of heat. **e. compound.** A stable compound formed with liberation of heat, as result of an e. reaction. **e. reaction.** A reaction in which heat is liberated; usually rapidly and sometimes explosively. Cf. *endothermic*.

expansion. An increase in dimension. **adiabatic-** The rapid e. of a gas, with a cooling effect. **cubical-** Volume e.; increase in 3 dimensions. **linear-** Increase in length. **thermal-** The increase in volume due to increase in temperature. It depends on the coefficient of e., which is relatively small for solids and liquids, but large for gases **e. equations.** (1) *Linear* e. of solids: If l_0 is the length at 0°C, x the coefficient of e., then the

length at t°C is: $l_t = l_0(1 + xt)$. The coefficient of e. is $(l_t - l_0)/l_t·l_0$. (2) *Cubical* e. of solids: $l_t = l_0(1 + at + bt)$, where a and b are the first and second coefficients of e. (3) *Volume* e. of solids or liquids (approximately): $V_t = V_0(1 + 3xt)$. (4) E. *of gases:* The volume V_t of a gas at temperature t°C is (at constant temperature) for an original volume V_0 at 0°C: $V_t = V_0(1 + 0.00367t)$. Cf. *Charles's law, gas laws.* **e. regulators.** Thermoregulators.

expectorant. A drug that promotes the secretion of mucus from the respiratory tract, e.g., ipecac.

experiment. A test or trial to illustrate natural phenomena, or to determine some unknown fact by careful observation and variation of the operating conditions. Cf. *observation,* which involves acceptance of the conditions of nature.

experimental. Pertaining to knowledge obtained by actual tests, or based on facts, not speculation.

experimentation. The performance of experiments.

expired air. Air from the lungs of living organisms; it has less O_2, but more CO_2 and moisture than normal air.

exploding atom. An atom undergoing radioactive change by the spontaneous emission of electrons or helium nuclei.

explosion. A sudden, violent, and noisy, exothermic chemical change in which heat, light, and gases are produced. Cf. *implosion.* **e. forming.** The formation of metal shapes by the action of an e. on molten metal in a mold. **e. spectrum.** See *spectrum*.

explosives. A group of endothermic compounds or mixtures which cause explosions. They are characterized by chemical stability and sensitiveness to ignition and detonation, and have a high detonation velocity and explosive strength, Generally applied to mixtures used for ordnance, pyrotechnics or mining operations, approximately 1 lb of e. being used for every 4.2 tons of coal mined. Classification by composition:

1. Gunpowders (mixtures of potassium nitrate, sulfur, and charcoal)

2. Nitrate mixtures (as, class 1, with barium or sodium nitrate in place of potassium nitrate)

3. Potassium chlorate mixtures

4. Dynamites (nitroglycerin)

5. Guncottons (nitro compounds)

6. Picric acid or its derivatives

7. Spreng e. (not explosive, but becoming so on addition of an oxidizing substance and detonator)

8. Miscellaneous and fulminating mixtures

9. Atomic e. (atom bomb, q.v.) Cf. *propellant*.
Classification by chemical properties:

1. N—O bonds: (*a*) Nitrates and nitric esters (e.g., ammonium nitrate, nitrocellulose); (*b*) carbon-nitro groups (e.g., tetranitromethane, picric acid)

2. Peroxides and ozonides (e.g., hydrogen peroxide)

3. Chlorine compounds (e.g., methyldichloramine)

4. Self-linked nitrogen compounds (contain N—N, N=N, and N≡N linkages; e.g., hydroazoic acid, lead azide)

blasting- E. used in mining. **compound-** E. that are a mixture of substances, e.g., gunpowder. **detonating-** High e. **high-** Detonating e. E. that are more sudden than gunpowder. They have high brisance and shattering power, but little propelling power. **low-** E. that can be fired by flame. **nondetonating-** E. that explode like gunpowder. **permissible-** E. that pass the safety tests of a government agency; as, Bureau of Mines, Ordnance Dept.: class A, less than 53 liters; class B, 53–106 liters; class C, 106–158 liters of poisonous gases from 680 gm explosive. **propulsive-** E. used in shells and guns, e.g., cordite. **simple-** Explosive pure or single substances, e.g., nitroglycerin.

exponential. If the base of the napierian system of logarithms, e (0.43429) is raised to the power indicated by the variable x, then e^x is the exponential of x.

expressed. Squeezed out. **e. oil.** A fatty oil, q.v., as compared with essential oil (distilled).

expression. (1) The squeezing out of a liquid, e.g., oils. (2) A mathematical symbol or equation.

expt. Abbreviation for experiment.

extender. (1) A material added as a diluent or to adjust the physical condition of a product; e.g., china clay in paints. (2) A substance added to synthetic resins to adjust the viscosity to a desired value.

extinction. Fading out. Cf. *optical density.* **e. coefficient.** E. The quantity $1/cy$ (log I_0/I), where I_0 and I are the intensities of light, respectively, *falling on* and *transmitted by* a solution y cm thick and of molar concentration c. Characteristic curves relate E and the wavelength of light used.

Exton reagent. A reagent for albumin (a solution of 200 gm $Na_2SO_4 \cdot 10H_2O$ and 50 gm sulfosalicylic acid in 1 l. water).

extract. (1) A dried plant juice; e.g., of aloes, kino, opium. (2) A pharmaceutical preparation made from vegetable tissues by expression, maceration, digestion, or infusion with a solvent. **acet-** E. prepared by macerating a drug with acetic acid. **alcoholic-** E. prepared by exhaustively extracting the drug with alcohol. **aqueous-** E. prepared by infusing or percolating a powdered drug with water. **dry-** Powdered. **fluid-** An e. of such

strength that 1 ml represents 1 gm of the active principles of the drug. **nitrogen-free-** The difference between the weight of a vegetable material and the combined weights of its moisture, ash, fat, protein, and crude fiber; e.g., mainly carbohydrates. **powdered-** An evaporated and powdered e. **solid-** A thick, semisolid e.

extractant. The liquid phase used to remove a solute from another liquid phase.

extraction. Dissolution and removal of one constituent of a mixture in a solvent. **alcohol-** See fluid *extract, tincture.* **back-** Stripping. **dilute acetic acid-** See *vinegar.* **ether-** See *oleoresin.* **liquid-liquid-** The transfer of a solute from one liquid phase to another liquid (immiscible) phase. **water-** See *decoction, infusion.* **wine-** See *wine.*

e. apparatus. Apparatus used for the extraction of fats, oils, or waxes from substances, preparatory to or as part of analysis. See *Soxhlet.* **e. coefficient.** The ratio of the concentrations of a solute in the organic and aqueous phases. **e. flasks.** Small round flasks of high-resistance glass. **e. thimble.** A cup made of some fat-free porous material (filter paper, Alundum) in which substances are extracted. **e. tube.** A tube holding e. thimbles, so that the solution flows downward into the container, and the solvent vapors pass above the thimbles to the condenser; e.g., Soxhlet tube.

extractive. Unspecified substance(s) extracted with a specific solvent in chemical analysis, e.g., ether extractives.

extrusion. Forcing a substance through an aperture.

exudate. A material that has filtered through the walls of living cells and accumulates in the adjacent tissues. **vegetable-** (1) Soluble in water, insoluble in alcohol—gums. (2) Soluble in alcohol, insoluble in water—resins.

exude. Oozing out, under heat or pressure, of a soft or fusible substance from a harder or less fusible material.

E.Y. Eger's yellow.

eyebright. The herb of *Euphrasia officinalis* (Scrophulariaceae); an eye lotion.

F

F. (*a*) Symbol for fluorine. (*b*) Abbreviation for: (1) magnetomotive force, (2) faraday, (3) Fahrenheit, (4) degree of freedom, (5) free energy, (6) force.

F-12. Freon.

f. Abbreviation for: (1) farad (cf. *faraday*), (2) force, (3) acceleration.

f. Function: thus $x = f(t)$, x is a function of t. φ, ϕ, Φ. Greek phi. (1) Abbreviation for phenyl. (2) Symbol for fluidity.

Fa. Symbol for francium (obsolete). Cf. *Fr.*

faba. Latin for bean. **f. physostigma.** See *physostigma*.

fabiana. The dried leaves of *F. imbricata* (Solanaceae), S. America. **f. resin.** $(C_{18}H_{30}O_2)_3$. F. tannoid. A crystalline resin from f. Cf. *crocin*, *pichi*.

fabianol. $C_{54}H_{90}O_2 = 771.0$. A volatile oily liquid from *Fabiana imbricata*.

fabric. General term for a cloth material of fibrous structure. Cf. *textile*, *staple* fiber. Types: *Felt*, made by interlocking fibers by the combined action of physical entanglement, chemical action, moisture, and heat, usually from animal fibers, e.g., wool. *Knitted* f., made by interlooping the fibers. *Woven* f., made by interlacing spun yarns, or continuous filaments containing one or more filaments, in 2 directions at right angles. **bonded-** F. made by applying a synthetic resin, by spraying, impregnating, or printing, in the form of fiber, powder, or liquid, a web or sheet of fibers, and subjecting the resulting product to heat or an organic solvent to complete the binding action; and finally to curing. The binder may be a thermoplastic fiber comprising 100% of the web. **needled-** A f. of improved strength and closeness made by punching projecting fibers into the mesh. **nonwoven-** Bonded.

Fabrikoid. Trademark for pyroxylin-treated fabrics, used for bookbinding, etc.

fabulite. Synthetic strontium nitrate used for imitation diamonds.

face-centered cube. A unit of crystal structure: a space lattice, q.v., in which a fifth atom is located centrally to the 4 corners of a plane.

F acid. (1) 2,7-Naphthylaminesulfonic acid. (2) 7-Amino-2-naphthalenesulfonic acid. (3) β-Naphthol-8-sulfonic acid.

facing. The addition of a coloring matter to food to improve its appearance; as in flour.

fact. Anything that has real existence. Known to be true. A result established by repeated experiment.

Factice. Trademark to designate a line of vulcanized vegetable oils.

factitious. Made artificially.

factor. (1) A reacting substance (reactant) which takes part in a chemical change. (2) When two quantities are multiplied together, each is a f. of the multiplication. (3) Vitamin, q.v. **accessory food-** Vitamin. **analytic-** Gravimetric or volumetric. **conversion-** See *conversion*. **filtrate-** Obsolete name for vitamin B_3. **gravimetric-** A quantity which, multiplied by the weight of precipitate obtained in gravimetric analysis, gives the amount of the related substance being determined. **round-** See *inch*. **volumetric-** A quantity which, multiplied by the number of milliliters of a standard solution, gives the amount of the corresponding substance that is being determined in volumetric analysis. **volumetric correction-** A quantity (determined by experiment) which, multiplied by the number of milliliters of a volumetric solution, gives the number of milliliters of a normal solution.

f. quantity. An aid to rapid calculation in quantitative analysis. E.g., in the determination of carbon in steel as CO_2 the f. quantity is 2.73; if 2.73 gm of steel is taken for analysis, the number of decigrams of CO_2 gives the percent of carbon present.

factors. See *conversion* factors.

facultative. Permissive or optional. **f. aerobe.** A bacterium which prefers anaerobic conditions, but can live in an atmosphere containing oxygen. **f. anaerobe.** A bacterium which prefers an oxygen atmosphere, but can live in its absence.

fadeometer. An instrument for comparing the fading properties of dyed fabrics, etc., which are exposed under standard conditions to a carbon arc.

faecal. See *fecal*.

faeces. See *feces*.

fagacid. An acid resin from beech wood, soluble in alkalies; an antiseptic in soaps and plasters.

fagarine. The 3 alkaloids of *Fagara coco*, a tree of Argentina; they are differentiated by the prefixes α, β, γ. The α-fagarine $(C_{19}H_{23}NO_4)$ is a possible substitute for quinidine; β-fagarine is identical with skimmianine; γ-fagarine is a methoxydictamine.

fagopyrisin. Photogenic injury to animals which results from the eating of buckwheat. Cf. *hypericism*.

fahlerz. Tetrahedrite.

Fahr. Abbreviation for Fahrenheit.

Fahrenheit, Gabriel Daniel. 1686–1736. German physicist. **F. scale.** A thermometer scale invented by F. based on the lowest temperature he could obtain by freezing mixtures. Water freezes at 32°F, and boils at 212°F. See *thermometer scales*.

faience. Glazed pottery.

faille. A plain weave used for dress or shirt fabrics, with a pronounced rib.

Fairbanks cement testing machine. A lever device resembling a balance for testing the tensile strength of cement blocks.

Fajans, Kasimir. b. 1887. German physicist noted for his work on radioactive substances and the discovery of brevium. **F.-Soddy law.** When an α-particle is expelled from a radioactive substance, the product is 2 places lower in the periodic table. A β-ray change, (expulsion of an electron) produces a rise of one place.

fallout. The radioactive debris from a nuclear explosion. It enters the human body mainly with food, and the principal radioactive elements, the foods conveying them and the organs affected are: iodine-131 (milk, thyroid gland), strontium-90 (all foods, bones), cesium-137, and carbon-14 (all foods, reproductive cells). See *radioactive.*

false body. A term that describes a marked decrease in viscosity resulting from an increase in shear rate, followed by rapid recovery on release of the shear. Applied to inks, paints, coating mixes, etc. Cf. *thixotropy.*

false hellebore. Adonis.

false unicorn. Aletris. **f. u. root.** See *chamaelirin, helonias.*

Fament's process. The removal of phosphorus and sulfur from iron by a current of hydrogen in heated retorts.

family. (1) A group, or a part of a period of elements that have similar properties. See *periodic system.* (2) Order. A biological division higher than genus.

fanghi di sclefani. A fine, yellow, volcanic powder, mainly sulfur, with small amounts of manganese, iron, and calcium.

farad. f. A unit of electric capacitance; the capacitance of a capacitor charged to a potential of one volt by one coulomb of electricity; 10^{-9} cgs unit. Cf. *faraday.* **international-** 0.99951 absolute f. (1948). **micro-** The one-millionth part of a f.; the practical unit.

Faraday, Michael. 1791–1867. English chemist and physicist. **F. cell.** A system in which 2 crystalline quartz prisms each acts as a disperser, and as a polarizer or analyzer. **F. effect.** A beam of polarized light passed through a magnetic field is rotated in the direction of the lines of magnetic force. **F. laws.** (1) The weight of an ion deposited electrolytically is proportional to the strength of the current passing through the solution. (2) 96,489 coulombs (1 faraday) liberate 1 gm equivalent of an ion by electrolysis. See *electrochemical equivalent.* **F. tube.** Ammonia tube. A V-shaped tube of hard glass, which, inverted, is used for distillation and crystallization of liquids under pressure. **F. unit.** Farad. **F. washing bottle.** Washing bottle.

faraday. F. The quantity of electricity which liberates one gram equivalent of a metal by electrolysis. 1 faraday = 96,489 coulombs = 9648.9 ± 0.7 emu = $(2.89270 \pm 0.00021) \times 10^{14}$ esu = 6.06×10^{23} electrons/mole. Cf. *farad, Faraday's law.*

faradiol. $C_{30}H_{50}O_2 = 442.39.$ A diatomic alcohol from colt's foot, *Tussilago farfara* (Compositae).

faradization. The therapeutic use of induced high-voltage currents.

farina. (1) Flour, or fine meal. (2) A starch, usually from potato.

farinaceous. Containing or consisting of flour.

farinose. The substance of which the cell walls of starch granules are composed.

farnesene. $C_{15}H_{24} = 204.2.$ 3,7,11-Trimethyl-2,6,10-dodecatetrene. A sesquiterpene from citronella oil.

farnesol. $CMe_2:CH(CH_2)_2CMe:CH(CH_2)_2CMe:CH-\cdot CH_2OH = 222.2.$ Isomer of nerolidol, d.0.895, $b_{0.2mm}120$, from the flowers of *Acacia farnesiana*, oil of cassia, ambrette seed oil, etc.; has a floral odor; used in perfumery.

Farrar's process. Pig iron is treated with ammonium chloride, potassium ferrocyanide, and manganese dioxide.

fastness. The extent to which a dye or dyed fabric, etc., resists change of color on exposure to light and/or air.

fast red. Azo-β-naphthol-α-naphthylaminosulfonic acid. A red indicator dye, pH 10.5–12.1.

fat. (1) A solid or liquid oil, the glycerol esters of the higher fatty acids, e.g., tristearin. See *fats.* (2) Abounding, rich. Cf. *lean.* **animal-** A f. of animal origin. **mineral-** See mineral oil. **vegetable-** A f. of vegetable origin. **wool-** Degras. **f. asphalt.** An asphalt of low gravel content. **f. clay.** A clay of good plasticity. **f. coal.** Coal rich in volatile matter. **f. ore.** A high-grade ore. **f. sand.** A sand for molding, containing large amounts of clay and alumina. **f. soluble.** A substance soluble in oils; as, vitamin A.

fatal. Causing death. **f. dose.** The quantity of a drug that causes death.

fatigue. The local deformation of metals by repeated stresses.

fats. (1) Greasy or oily substances. (2) Fixed oils, fatty oils, expressed oils. The glyceryl ester of a fatty acid, or of a mixture of fatty acids. Generally odorless, colorless, and tasteless if pure, but they may be flavored according to origin. F. are insoluble in water, soluble in most organic solvents. They occur in animal and vegetable tissue and are generally obtained by heating or boiling or by extraction under pressure. World production of principal vegetable oils and fats (1966), 21.6 million tons. Cf. *oil, wax, sterol.*

fatsin. $C_{31}H_{53}O_{20} = 745.4.$ A glucoside from *Fatsia japonica* (Araliaceae), Japan.

fatty acids. (1) Organic, monobasic acids derived from hydrocarbons by the equivalent of oxidation of a methyl group to an alcohol, aldehyde, and then acid:

$$R \rightarrow CH_3 \rightarrow R\cdot CH_2OH \rightarrow R\cdot CHO \rightarrow R\cdot COOH$$

(a) Saturated: $C_nH_{2n+1}COOH$ (as, acetic acid, CH_3COOH); (b) unsaturated: $C_nH_{2n-1}COOH$ (see *acrylic acids*); (c) unsaturated: $C_nH_{2n-3}COOH$ (see *acetylene acids*); (d) unsaturated: $C_nH_{2n-5}COOH$ (as, linolinic acid, $C_{17}H_{29}COOH$). (2) The three acids occurring most frequently in fats as glyceryl esters: palmitic, stearic, and oleic acids.

fatty compounds. Aliphatic compounds.

fatty series. See *aliphatic series, methane series.*

fault finder. An instrument for measuring the resistance of conductors; used to locate faults.

fayalite. (1) $Fe_2SiO_4.$ A ferrous orthosilicate olivine (Fayal, Madeira).

Fe. Symbol for iron (ferrum).

Feather. Trade name for a viscous synthetic fiber. **f. ore.** Jamesonite.

febrifacient. A drug that produces fever.

febrifuge. A drug that reduces or prevents fever, e.g., an antipyretic.

feces, faeces. Excrements or alimentary refuse.

feedback. The measurement of how much a particular property (as temperature) differs from a required value, and the use of this measurement to restore the latter.

feedstock. Crude oil, as fed to a refinery.

Fehling, Herman von. 1812–1885. German chemist. **F. solution.** A mixture for the determination of reducing sugars: solution A (copper sulfate 34.639 gm in 500 ml water), and solution B (sodium–potassium tartrate 173, sodium hydroxide 60 gm, in 500 ml water), mixed in equal parts before use. The copper produced by reduction at the boiling point is weighed or measured volumetrically. Cf. *Benedict's Pavy's solution.*

Feic. Abbreviation for the ferricyanide ion, $Fe(CN)_6\equiv$.

feints. The impure portion of the second distillate of fermentation alcohol.

Feiser solution. A solution of sodium hydrosulfite 16, sodium hydroxide 6.6, and sodium anthraquinone β-sulfonate 2 gm, in 100 ml water; used to absorb oxygen in gas analysis.

feldspar. Felspar. (1) Igneous crystalline rocks, chiefly silicates of alumina with soda, potash, or lime. (2) The mineral $K_2O, Al_2O_3, 6SiO_2$.

felite. A form of belite.

fellmongering. The operation of separating the wool of sheep from the pelt.

felspar. Feldspar.

femergin. Trade name for ergotamine tartrate (B.P.C.).

femic. Containing iron and magnesium. **f. minerals.** Igneous rocks richer in iron than in aluminum.

femto- Prefix for 10^{-15}(IUPAC).

-fen, -phen. Suffix indicating a sulfur-containing hydrocarbon.

fenamate. A *N*-arylanthranilic acid derivative; an analgesic, antipyretic, and anti-inflammatory substitute for aspirin.

fenchane. $C_{10}H_{18} = 138.2.$ 2,7,7-Trimethylbicyclo-[1.2.2]-heptane. An isomer of camphane, pinane, and carane. Cf. *terpenes.*

fenchanol. Fenchyl alcohol.

fenchanone. Fenchone.

fenchene. $C_{10}H_{16} = 136.2.$ 7,7-Dimethyl-2-methylenenorcamphane. A terpene constituent of essential oils; isomers:

α-(alpha-) γ-(gamma-)

β-(beta-)

Colorless liquid, soluble in alcohol. **alpha-** d.0.866, b.155. **beta-** d.0.860, b.152. **gamma-** d.0.854, b.146.

fenchol. Fenchyl alcohol.

fencholic acid. $C_{10}H_{16}O_2 = 170.5.$ Colorless crystals, m.19, soluble in alcohol.

fenchone. $C_{10}H_{16}O = 152.1.$ 1,3,3-Trimethyl-2-norcamphanone. A ketone in essential oils. Colorless liquid, d.0.9465, b.192, insoluble in water. Cf. *pinone.*

fenchoxime. $C_{10}H_{17}ON = 167.2.$ Colorless crystals, m.161, insoluble in water.

fenchyl. The radical $C_{10}H_{17}$—, derived from fenchane. **f. alcohol.** $C_{10}H_{18}O = 154.3.$ 1-Hydroxyfenchane. Colorless crystals, m.39, in pine oil.

fenchyval. The isovaleric ester of fennel oil.

fennel. Foeniculum. The dried fruit of *Foeniculum vulgare* (Umbelliferae); an aromatic, carminative, and spice. **water-** The oil, d.0.85–0.89, from *Oenanthe aquatica.*

f. oil. Oleum foeniculi. The essential oil from *F. vulgare.* Colorless, aromatic liquid, d.0.965–0.075, containing chiefly pinene, phellandrene, and anethole; a carminative, antispasmodic, and flavoring (U.S.P.).

Fenton's reagent. Hydrogen peroxide containing some Fe++; used for oxidizing sugars and alcohols.

fenugreek. The seeds of *Trigonella foenum greekum* (Leguminosae); Morocco, India; a condiment, emollient, and poultice.

Feoc. Abbreviation for the ferrocyanide ion. $Fe(CN)_6\equiv$.

ferbam. $(Me_2N\cdot C\colon S\cdot)_3Fe.$ Fermate. Official name for ferric dimethyldithiocarbamate, a fungicide.

ferberite. $FeWO_4.$ A metallic iron tungstate, containing less than 20% manganese tungstate. Cf. *hubnerite.*

fergusonite. $Y(Cb\cdot Ta)O_4.$ A native, brown yttrium columbate and tantalate, d.5.8–5.9, hardness 5.5–6.

fermate. Ferbam.

ferment. (1) A substance that causes chemical changes, especially fermentation, without participating in them. See *catalyst.* Used interchangeably with enzyme, but more correctly when describing organized catalysts not removable from the cell. Enzymes, or unorganized catalysts are removable and exist in filtered solutions. **active-** A f. produced from a zymogen with or without the aid of an activator. **co-** Coferment. **organized-** A ferment. **pro-** Zymogen. **unorganized-** An enzyme. (2) Undergoing fermentation,

fermentation. The anerobic breakdown of organic compounds by microorganisms, to simpler products. **acetic-** The production of vinegar from alcoholic liquids by f. **alcoholic-** The conversion of sugar to alcohol and carbon dioxide by the ferment of yeast cells. **amylolytic-** The hydrolysis of starch to dextrins by saliva. **butyric-** The formation of butyric acid. **lactic-** The souring of milk; e.g., the formation of lactic acid from sugars. **malolactic-** The conversion of malic acid (e.g., in wines) into lactic acid by f. (e.g., by lactobacilli). **panary-** The f. processes in bread manufacture. **vinous-** The production of wine by f.

f. alcohol. Ethanol made by f. **f. chemistry.** Zymurgy. **f. tube.** A bent glass tube with bulb, used in tests for f. to collect the gases evolved.

Fermi, Enrico. 1902–1954. Italian-born physicist noted for his synthesis of trans-uranium, element

93, by bombarding uranium with neutrons. Cf. *ausonium, fermium.*

fermium. Fm = 253. An actinide radioelement, at. no. 100. Discovered (1953) by ion-exchange separation of the debris from the thermonuclear explosion "Mike" (Pacific, 1952). Its known isotopes have mass numbers of 250 to 254; none is stable. It forms trivalent positive ions in solution.

fern. See *Filices.* **male-, marginal-** Aspidum.

ferrate. (1) A deep red salt of the unknown acidic oxide, FeO₃, ferric acid, containing the radical =FeO₄, as in Na₂FeO₄, sodium ferrate. (2) Erroneously applied to ferrite, q.v.

ferratogen. Ferric nucleinate.

ferret. A device that is passed through a pipeline to scrape and wash it.

ferri- (1) Prefix indicating the presence of a ferric ion, Fe³⁺, in a compound. (2) Official Latin for iron; in particular, ferrous iron.

ferriammonium- Prefix indicating the presence of both trivalent iron, Fe³⁺, and ammonium, NH₄⁺. **f. chloride.** (NH₄)FeCl₄ = 215.6. Ammoniated iron, ammonio chloride of iron, ammonium ferratum chloratum, flores martialis, aes martis. Orange crystals of styptic taste, soluble in water; used to treat epilepsy and scrofula. **f. chromate.** (NH₄)-Fe(CrO₄)₂ = 305.0. Brown crystals, soluble in water. **f. citrate.** Fe(NH₄)₃(C₆H₅O₇)₂ = 488.2. Ferric ammonium citrate. Brown scales, soluble in water; used to treat anemia. *green-* Ferric ammonium citrate green, green iron, and ammonium citrate. Green scales, turning brown in light, soluble in water; used in hypodermic medication. **f. oxalate.** (NH₄)₃Fe(C₂O₄)₃·3H₂O = 427.8. Green cyrstals, soluble in water. Used in photography and blueprint paper. **f. sulfate.** (NH₄)Fe(SO₄)₂·12H₂O = 482.01. Iron and ammonium alum. Violet octahedra, soluble in water. Used as a styptic, astringent, reagent, and indicator, and in the dye industry. **f. tartrate.** NH₃Fe-(C₄H₄O₆)₂ = 368.86. Iron and ammonium tartrate. Brown crystals, soluble in water: a styptic.

ferric. Ironic (obsolete). A compound of trivalent iron, Fe≡ or Fe³⁺, usually more stable than the corresponding ferrous salt; yellow, brown, or red in color. **f. acetate.** Fe(C₂H₃O₂)₃ = 288.8. Brown scales, soluble in water; a tonic and a dye mordant. *basic-* Fe(OH)(C₂H₃O₂)₂ = 190.9. Red, amorphous powder, sparingly soluble in water; used in the dye industry. **f. albuminate.** Cinnamon-colored powder, soluble in water; used as a tonic and to treat beriberi. **f. alginate.** Fe₃C₇₆H₇₇O₂₂N₂· Brown scales, insoluble in water; a hematinic. **f. ammonium.** Ferriammonium. **f. ammonium citrate.** Red deliquescent scales, prepared by evaporating together solutions of citric acid and ferric hydroxide. Soluble in water; a hematinic. **f. arsenate.** FeAsO₄·2H₂O = 230.9. Brown powder, insoluble in water. See *ferrous arsenate.* **f. arsenite.** 4Fe₂O₃·As₂O₃·5H₂O = 926.72. Brown powder. **f. benzoate.** Fe₂(PhCOO)₆ = 353.78. Brown powder, used to make ferrated cod-liver oil. **f. bromide.** FeBr₃ = 295.6. Red crystals, decomp. by heat, soluble in water. **f. cacodylate.** Fe-(Me₂AsO₂)₃ = 467.2. Yellow powder, slowly soluble in water. Used hypodermieally to treat

anemia, chlorosis, tuberculosis, syphilis. **f. camphorate.** Yellow powder, insoluble in water; used to treat chlorosis. **f. carbonate.** A mixture of Fe₂(CO₃)₃, Fe(OH)₃ and Fe(OH)₂. Brown powder, insoluble in water; a hematinic. *saccharated-* See *ferrous carbonate.* **f. chloride.** FeCl₃ = 162.2. Ironic chloride, iron 3-chloride. Brown crystals m.298, soluble in water. *hydrous-* FeCl₃·xH₂O. Orange crystals (x = 5, 6, or 12), soluble in water; used in the dye industry and as a styptic. **f.chromate.** Fe₂(CrO₄)₃·xH₂O. A brown solution miscible with water; a mordant. *acid-* Fe₂(Cr₂O₇)₃ = 759.7. Brown granules, soluble in water; used in pigments. **f. citrate.** FeC₆H₅O₇·3H₂O. Ferri citras. Red scales, slowly soluble in water; a hematinic. *green-* Ferriammonium citrate. **f. citrate (Fe⁵⁹).** An injection for investigating hematological disorders (B.P.). **f. dimethyldithiocarbamate.** Ferbam. **f. ferricyanide.** Fe[Fe(CN)₆] = 267.7. Ironic ferricyanide. Red solid, soluble in water. **f. ferrocyanide.** Fe₄[Fe(CN)₆]₃ = 859.1. Ironic ferrocyanide, insoluble. Prussian blue, q.v.; Turnbull's blue. Dark blue crystals, insoluble in water; a tonic and antiperiodic, pigment (Prussian blue, Berlin blue, Paris blue), and blue ink (with oxalic acid). α- or *soluble-* Potassium f. ferricyanide. **f. fluosilicate.** Fe₃(SiF₆)₃ = 537.86. A flesh-colored gel, soluble in water. **f. formate.** Fe(HCOO)₃ = 190.9. Red crystals, soluble in water. **f. glycerophosphate.** Fe₂[C₃H₅(PO₄)(OH)₂]₃ = 616.2. Yellow scales, soluble in water; a tonic. **f. hydroxide.** Fe(OH)₃ = 106.9. Ironic hydroxide. Brown powder, insoluble in water; a hematinic and antidote for arsenic, and used in the rubber industry. **f. hypophosphite.** Fe(H₂PO₂)₃ = 250.9. Dihydric f. hypophosphite. Gray powder, sparingly soluble in water; a tonic. **f. iodate.** Fe(IO₃)₃. Brown powder, usually containing f. iodide, decomp. by heat; an alterant. **f. iodide.** FeI₃ = 436.8. Black crystals, soluble in water. **f. lactate.** Fe(C₃H₅O₃)₃ = 322.9. Brown powder; a tonic. **f. malate.** Fe₂(C₄H₄O₅)₃ = 507.7. Brown, deliquescent scales, soluble in water; a tonic and alterant. **f. nitrate.** Fe(NO₃)₃·9H₂O = 404.0. Colorless rhombs, m.47, soluble in water. *-solution.* An aqueous solution (33% f. nitrate). Red liquid; used in dyeing, calico printing, tanning, and in iron pigments. **f. nucleinate.** Ferratogen, ferrinol. Yellow powder obtained from yeast grown in ferruginous media, soluble in water; a tonic. **f. oleate.** Fe(C₁₈H₃₃O₂)₃ = 899.9. Red, soft mass, used in paints. **f. oxalate.** Fe₂(COO)₆ = 375.7. Ironic oxalate. Yellow scales, decomp. 100, soluble in water. **f. oxide.** Fe₂O₃ = 159.7. Ironic oxide, red iron oxide. Pompeian red, iron sesquioxide; in nature: red hematite, martite. Red hexagons or powder, m.1541, insoluble in water; a pigment and abrasive for polishing metals. *magnetic-* Ferriferrous oxide; used in tape recorders. **f. peptonate.** Brown powder or red scales (5 or 25% f. oxide), soluble in water; a nonastringent hematinic. **f. perchlorate.** Fe(ClO₄)₃ = 354.2. Brown crystals, soluble in water. **f. perchloride.** Ferriferrous chloride. **f. persulfate.** Ferriferrous sulfate. **f. phenate.** Compounds of f. iron and phenol of variable composition; purple, deliquescent masses, soluble in water. **f. phosphate.** FePO₄·-2H₂O = 186.91. Ironic phosphate. Yellow rhombs, insoluble in water; used in dentistry. *green-* Ferriammonium phosphate. **f. potassium ferrocyanide.** Potassium f. ferrocyanide. **f. pyrophosphate.** $Fe_4(P_2O_7)_3 = 745.5$. White powder, soluble in carbonated water; a tonic. *green-* Compounds of f. pyrophosphate with ammonium citrate, sodium citrate, magnesium citrate, or potassium citrate; used in hypodermic medication. **f. pyrosulfate.** $FeS_2O_7 = 231.9$. White, microcrystalline powder. **f. rhodanate.** F. thiocyanate. **f. subcarbonate.** Sesquioxide of iron, saffron of mars, red oxide of iron, hydras ferricus, crocus martis. A precipitate from iron solutions of variable mixtures of f. oxide and f. hydroxide; a tonic. **f. subsulfate.** $Fe_4O(SO_4)_5$ or $Fe_2(SO_4)_3 \cdot Fe_2(SO_4)_2O = 719.49$. Monsel's salt. Brown scales, soluble in water; a styptic. **f. succinate.** $FeC_4H_4O_4(OH)$. Brown powder, slightly soluble in water; a tonic. **f. sulfate.** $Fe_2(SO_4)_3 \cdot 9H_2O = 562.1$. Yellow rhombs, soluble in water. **f. sulfide.** $Fe_2S_3 = 207.9$. Yellow crystals, decomp. heat or solvents. **f. sulfocyanate.** F. thiocyanate. **f. tannate.** $Fe_2(OH)_3C_{14}H_7O_9 = 481.78$. Brown powder, insoluble in water; used medicinally. **f. tartrate.** $Fe_2(C_4H_4O_6)_3 \cdot H_2O = 573.9$. Brown scales, soluble in water; an emmenagogue and tonic. **f. thiocyanate.** $Fe(CNS)_3 \cdot 3H_2O = 284.1$. Ironic sulfocyanide, f. rhodanate. Brown granules, soluble in water. **f. valerianate.** $Fe(OH)_2C_5H_9O_2 = 190.9$. Brown powder, insoluble in water; a tonic and emmenagogue. **f. vanadate.** $Fe(VO_3)_3 = 352.8$. Ironic metavanadate. Brown powder, insoluble in water.

ferricyanic acid. The hypothetical acid, $H_3Fe(CN)_6$, from which the ferricyanides are derived.

ferricyanide. A salt of ferricyanic acid containing the radical $Fe(CN)_6 \equiv$. **ferric-** Ferric ferricyanide. **ferrous-** Ferrous ferricyanide. Cf. *nitroprusside*.

ferriferous. (1) Containing iron in the ferric state. (2) Containing iron.

ferriferrous. Ferrosoferric. Describing a compound containing both divalent and trivalent iron: $Fe=$ and $Fe\equiv$. **f. chloride.** Fe_3Cl_8 or $FeCl_2 \cdot 2FeCl_3 = 451.2$. Yellow, deliquescent crystals, soluble in water. **f. cyanide.** (1) Ferric ferrocyanide. (2) Ferrous ferricyanide. **f. hydroxide.** $Fe_3(OH)_8 = 303.61$. Black powder, soluble in hydrochloric acid. **f. oxide.** Fe_3O_4 or $FeO \cdot Fe_2O_3$ or $Fe:(FeO_2)_2 = 231.5$. Magnetic iron oxide, martial ethiops, black iron oxide. Black, regular crystals, m.1537, insoluble in water. **f. sulfate.** $Fe_3(SO_4)_4 = 551.7$. Several derivatives; some occur as minerals. **f. sulfide.** Fe_3S_4 or $FeS \cdot Fe_2S_3 = 295.7$. Black powder, insoluble in water.

ferrimagnesium citrate. $FeMg_3(C_6H_5O_7)_3 \cdot (H_2O)_3$. Iron and magnesium citrate, ironic magnesium citrate. Brown scales, soluble in water; a hematinic and tonic.

ferrimanganese. An alloy of iron and manganese, used to deoxidize and desulfurize molten steel.

ferrimanganic. A compound containing both, trivalent iron, $Fe\equiv$, and manganese, $Mn\equiv$. **f. citrate.** $FeMn(C_6H_5O_7)_2$. Brown scales, slowly soluble in water; a hematinic. **f. pyrophosphate.** $Fe_2Mn_2(P_2O_7)_3 \cdot (H_2O)_x$. Yellow powder of variable composition; a tonic. **f. tartrate.** $FeMn(C_4H_4O_6)_3$. Brown scales, soluble in water.

ferrinol. Ferric nucleinate.

ferripotassium. A double salt containing potassium and trivalent iron. **f. citrate.** $FeK_3(C_6H_5O_7)_2 \cdot (H_2O)_x$. Brown scales, soluble in water; a tonic and hematinic. **f. cyanide.** Potassium ferricyanide. **f. oxalate.** $K_3Fe(COO)_3 \cdot 3H_2O = 359.3$. Green crystals, soluble in water. **f. sulfate.** Potassium ferric sulfate.

ferripyrine. $2FeCl_3 \cdot 3C_{11}H_{12}ON_2$. Contains ferric chloride 36, antipyrine 64%. Red crystals, soluble in water; a styptic and hematinic.

ferrisodium. A double salt containing sodium and trivalent iron. **f. benzoate.** A mixture of equal parts ferric benzoate and sodium benzoate. **f. citrate.** $FeNa_3(C_6H_5O_7)_2(H_2O)_x$. Brown leaflets, soluble in water; a tonic and astringent. **f. oxalate.** $Na_3Fe(COO)_3 \cdot 4\frac{1}{2}H_2O = 338.0$. Green crystals, soluble in water; a tonic, astringent, and emmenagogue, and used in photography. **f. pyrophosphate.** $Na_3Fe(P_2O_7)_2 \cdot 7H_2O = 599.1$. Gray granules, soluble in water; a tonic. **f. sulfate.** $NaFe(SO_4)_2 \cdot 12H_2O$. Sodium iron alum. Brown octahedra, soluble in water.

ferrite. (1) An unstable compound of ferric oxide with a strong base (as, $NaFeO_2$) which exists in strongly alkaline solutions. Cf. *ferrate*. (2) α-, β-, or γ- An allotrope of iron, q.v. **ferrous-** Fe_3O_4. Magnetic iron oxide.

ferritin. A protein, containing iron, from the spleen, liver, and marrow; believed to regulate blood circulation.

ferro- Prefix indicating metallic iron (as in ferroaluminum) or divalent iron (as in ferrocyanide). **f. prussiate.** Potassium ferrocyanide.

ferroaluminum. An alloy: Fe 80, Al 20%, d.6.30, m.1480.

ferroammonium. Describing a compound containing divalent iron and ammonium. **f. bromide.** $FeBr_2 \cdot 2NH_4Br = 411.8$. Brown powder, soluble in water. **f. chloride.** Ferriammonium chloride. **f. cyanide.** Ammonium ferrocyanide. **f. sulfate.** $(NH_4)_2Fe(SO_4)_2 \cdot 6H_2O = 392.0$. Ammonium ferrosulfate, ironous ammonium sulfate. Mohr's salt. Green crystals, soluble in water; used in photography, and as a volumetric standard.

ferrocarbon titanium. An alloy obtained by the reduction of titanium oxide with carbon; used to deoxidize molten steel.

ferrocene. $(CH_2)_5Fe(CH_2)_5 = 196.04$. Dicyclopentadienyl iron. Orange crystals, m.173, soluble in ether; notable for its stability.

ferrocerium. A pyrophoric alloy made by fusing cerium chloride and iron; used as flint for automatic lighters.

ferrochrome. Ferrochromium.

ferrochromium. An alloy: Fe 50, Cr 50%, d.6.9, m.1458.

ferroconcrete. Reinforced concrete.

ferrocyanic acid. $H_4Fe(CN)_6$. A hypothetical acid from which ferrocyanides are derived.

ferrocyanide. A compound containing the radical $Fe(CN)_6 \equiv$. **ferric-** Ferric ferrocyanide. **ferrous-** See *ferrous ferrocyanide*.

ferrodolomite. The mineral $CaFe(CO_3)_2$.

ferroferric. Ferriferrous.

ferroferricyanide. Ferrous ferricyanide.

ferroferrocyanide. Ferrous ferrocyanide.

ferromagnesium. (1) An alloy of magnesium and iron. (2) A compound containing divalent iron and magnesium. **f. lactate.** Iron and magnesium lactate. Yellow powder, soluble in water; a tonic. **f. sulfate.** $MgFe(SO_4)_2 \cdot 6H_2O = 380.2$. Iron and magnesium sulfate. Green crystals, soluble in water; a tonic.

ferromagnetism. Magnetism due solely to magnetic iron.

ferromanganese. The alloy: Fe 50, Mn 50%, d.7.0, m.1325; used for tough steels.

ferromanganic. Describing a compound containing divalent iron and trivalent manganese.

ferromanganous. Describing a compound containing divalent iron and divalent manganese. **f. chloride.** $MnFeCl_4 = 252.6$. Orange crystals, soluble in water. **f. iodide.** $MnFeI_4 = 618.2$. Brown prisms, soluble in water. **f. lactate.** Iron and manganese lactate. White powder, soluble in water; a tonic. **f. sulfate.** $MnFe(SO_4)_2 \cdot 12H_2O = 518.8$. Iron and manganese sulfate. Yellow crystals, soluble in water; a tonic.

ferromolybdenum. A steel containing about 2% Mo; used for high-speed lathe tools.

ferron. 7-Iodo-8-hydroxyquinoline-5-sulfonic acid; a reagent.

ferronickel. The alloy: Fe 74.2, Ni 25, C 0.8%, d.8.1, m.1500; used for steel and tools. **valve steel-** The alloy: Fe 67.8, Ni 32, C 0.2%, d.8.0, m.1480.

ferrophosphorus. A by-product of heating phosphate rock, silica, and coke; used to increase fluidity during steel casting.

ferropotassium. Describing a compound of divalent iron and potassium with another radical. **f. cyanide.** Potassium ferrocyanide. **f. tartrate.** A mixture of iron tartrates and potassium tartrates of variable composition; used for medicinal baths.

ferropyrine. Ferripyrine.

ferrosilicon. A hard steel alloy: Fe 97.6, Si 2, C 0.4%; used in deoxidized steel. **f. zirconium.** An alloy of iron, silicon, and zirconium, used to purify molten steel and improve shock resistance.

ferrosilite. Clinoferrosilite. Acicular crystals of $FeSiO_3$ in obsidian.

ferrosoferric. Ferriferrous. **f. oxide.** Ferriferrous oxide.

ferrosoferro- Ferrous ferro-.

ferrotitanium. An alloy made by reducing titanium dioxide with powdered aluminum and iron; used to deoxidize molten steel.

ferrotungsten. Tungsten steel. A tool alloy: Fe 94.5, W 5, C 0.5%. **high speed-** High-speed tool steel. The alloy: Fe 75, W 18, Cr 6, V 0.3, C 0.7%.

ferrous- Ironous (obsolete). Prefix indicating compounds containing divalent iron, $Fe=$. They have generally a green color, give the f. ion Fe^{++} in aqueous solution, and are reducing agents. **f. acetate.** $Fe(CH_3COO)_2 = 114.0$. Green crystals, used in solution as iron liquor (printer's liquor), and as a mordant. **f. ammonium.** Ferroammonium. **f. ammonium gluconate.** $C_{12}H_{22}O_{14}Fe \cdot 2H_2O = 482.19$. Yellow powder with caramel odor, soluble in water; a hematinic (U.S.P., B.P.). **f. arsenate.** $Fe_3(AsO_4)_2 \cdot 6H_2O = 553.6$. Green, amorphous powder, insoluble in water or alcohol, soluble in ammonia or hydrochloric acid; used as an insecticide (iron arsenate). **f. bromide.** $FeBr_2 \cdot 6H_2O = 323.8$. Red crystals, soluble in water; used medicinally. **f. carbonate.** $FeCO_3 = 115.8$. Green rhombohedra, decomp. by heat, soluble in

carbonated water; used in carbonated "ferruginous" waters. **f. chloride.** $FeCl_2 \cdot 4H_2O = 198.8$. Green, monoclinic crystals, soluble in water. Used as a reducing and adsorbing reagent, in calico printing, as a stain, and in the extraction of copper from ores. **f. ferricyanide.** $Fe_3[Fe(CN)_6]_2 = 591.3$. Ferroferricyanide. Blue powder, decomp. by heat, insoluble in water; a pigment. **f. ferrite.** $Fe_3O_4 \cdot$ Magnetic iron oxide. **f. ferrocyanide.** $Fe_2[Fe(CN)_6] = 323.6$. Ferrosoferrocyanide. White powder, insoluble in water. **f. fluoride.** $FeF_2 = 93.84$ and $FeF_2 \cdot 8H_2O = 237.97$. White powder, sparingly soluble in water. **f. fluosilicate.** $FeSiF_6 \cdot 6H_2O = 305.99$. Colorless crystals, soluble in water. **f. fumarate.** $C_4H_2FeO_4 = 169.91$. Brown powder, slightly soluble in water; a hematinic (U.S.P.). **f. hydroxide.** $Fe(OH)_2 = 89.8$. White powder, rapidly oxidizes to brown, insoluble in water. **f. hypophosphite.** $Fe(H_2PO_2)_2 = 185.8$. Dihydric f. hypophosphite. White powder, rapidly oxidizes. **f. hyposulfite.** $FeS_2O_3 = 167.8$. White powder, soluble in water; rapidly oxidizes. **f. iodide.** $FeI_2 \cdot 4H_2O = 381.7$. Green, deliquescent scales, anhydrous at 177, soluble in water. **f. lactate.** $Fe(C_3H_5O_3)_2 \cdot 3H_2O = 287.8$. Green needles or scales, with slight odor, soluble in water; used medicinally. **f. nitrate.** $Fe(NO_3)_2 \cdot 6H_2O = 288.0$. Green crystals, m.61, soluble in water. **f. oxalate.** $Fe(COO)_2 = 143.8$. Yellow powder, soluble in water. **f. oxide.** $FeO = 71.84$. Black iron oxide, iron monoxide. Black powder, m.1419, insoluble in water. **f. perchlorate.** $Fe(ClO_4)_2 \cdot 6H_2O = 362.86$. Soluble green powder. **f. phosphate.** $Fe_3(PO_4)_2 \cdot 8H_2O = 501.7$. Blue monoclinic crystals, insoluble in water; native as vivianite. **f. phosphide.** $FeP = 86.86$. Black powder. Also: Fe_2P, Fe_2P_2, Fe_3P, Fe_3P_4. **f. platinichloride.** $FePtCl_6 = 463.8$. **f. structure.** The crystal structure of cast iron. **f. sulfate.** (1) *heptahydrate-* or *crystallized-* $FeSO_4 \cdot 7H_2O = 278.0$. Iron sulfate, green vitriol, green copperas, Ferri sulphas. Blue-green, monoclinic crystals, d.1.875, m.64 (decomp.), soluble in water; native as melanterite. Used for mordanting wool, as a disinfectant, and in the manufacture of ink and prussian blue. (2) *pentahydrate-* $FeSO_4 \cdot 5H_2O = 241.9$. Green crystals, d.2.2; native as siderotilate. (3) *tetrahydrate-* $FeSO_3 \cdot 4H_2O = 223.9$. (4) *monohydrate-* $FeSO_4 \cdot H_2O = 169.9$. White powder, obtained by heating iron sulfate to 140; native as szomolnokite. (5) *anhydrous-* $FeSO_4 = 151.8$. White powder obtained by heating iron sulfate to 300. **f. sulfide.** $FeS = 87.9$. Pyrite. Black crystals, m.1197, insoluble in water; used for making hydrogen sulfide. **f. sulfocyanide.** F. thiocyanate. See *tantalate.* **f. tartrate.** $FeC_4H_4O_6 = 203.9$. White crystals, soluble in water. **f. thiocyanate.** $Fe(CNS)_2 \cdot 3H_2O = 226.04$. Green crystals, soluble in water. **f. titanate** $FeTiO_3$. Ilmenite. **f. tungstate.** See *ferberite, wolframite.*

ferrovanadium. An alloy of iron and vanadium, used in the manufacture of steel for automobile parts.

ferroverdin. $C_{30}H_{24}O_8NFe$. Green pigment produced by streptomycetes, insoluble in water.

ferrox process. A process for dissolving hydrogen sulfide from industrial gases in a suspension of ferric hydroxide in alkali.

ferroxyl indicator. A jelly of potassium ferrocyanide and phenolphthalein in agar-agar, used to test for the corrosion of iron. Iron wire electrodes will turn it red (cathode) and blue (anode).

ferrugineous. Ferruginous.

ferruginous. (1) Containing iron. (2) Describing a drug whose therapeutic effect depends on the presence of iron, e.g., chalybeates.

ferrum. Official Latin for iron in certain E. European Pharmacopoeias. **f. reductum.** Frary's metal, ferry metal. A mixture of iron and ferriferrous oxide obtained by the reduction of ferric oxide in hydrogen.

fertiliser. Fertilizer.

fertilizer. (1) A plant food added to soil; as, nitrates. (2) Manure. **f. grade.** The minimum guaranteed plant food expressed in terms of *nitrogen*, available *phosphoric acid*, and water-soluble *potash*. World production (1967), 54 million tons.

fertilizin. A substance secreted by certain marine invertebrates which fertilizes their ripe eggs; related to echinochrome A, q.v.

Ferula. A genus of Umbelliferae, yielding asafetida, galbanum, sagapenum, and sumbul.

ferulaldehyde. $C_{10}H_{10}O_3 = 178.08.$ *p*-Coniferaldehyde, hadromal. Colorless crystals, m.83, used in perfumery. It occurs in woody tissues, and gives a red color with phloroglucinol in hydrochloric acid.

ferulene. $C_{15}H_{26} = 206.20.$ A dihydrosesquiterpene from fennel, $b_{7mm}126.$

ferulic acid. $C_{10}H_{10}O_4 = 194.1.$ Ferulaic acid, *m*-methoxy-*p*-hydroxycinnamic acid. A constituent of asafetida and black fir resin. Colorless needles, m.169 (decomp.), soluble in hot water. Cf. *coniferol.* **hydro-** $C_{10}H_{12}O_4 = 196.1.$ Colorless crystals, m.89, soluble in water. **iso-** Hesperitinic acid.

fervanite. A vanadium mineral similar to steigerite.

fervorization. The process of heating soil or culture media at 137° for one hour to stimulate the germination of seeds immersed therein.

Féry calorimeter. A thermoelectric device for determining the calorific power of foods. **F. refractometer.** An instrument for the direct reading of the refractive index of a transparent liquid.

fetron. A mixture: stearic acid 3, petrolatum 97%; a base for ointments.

fetuin. A globulin of low molecular weight in the fetal serum of cows, sheep, and other mammals.

Feulgen reaction. The restoration of color to Schiff reagent; a stain test for nuclear material in cells, due to the presence of deoxyribose. Cf. *Dische* reaction.

feverbark. See (1) *Alstonia*, (2) *Cinchona.*

feverfew. The herb of *Pyrethrum parthenium* (Compositae): a carminative. Cf. *pyrethrum camphor.*

fiber. A long ribbon or threadlike cell or tissue of vegetable or animal origin, used for paper (cf. *tracheid*), textiles, cordage, wickerwork and brushes. **animal-** A f. obtained from animals, as alpaca, silk, wool. **artificial-** (1) F. made from mineral matter; as, spun glass, metallic threads. Cf. *mineral f.* (2) F. imitating natural f.; as, rayon. **bast-** A f. from the bast of plants; as, hemp, jute. **bonded-** q.v. **conjugate-** Hybrid f. A synthetic f.

made by injecting 2 different f. -forming solutions into the same spinneret. **cordage-** A f. used for making ropes; e.g., hemp, sisal. **crude-** The residue after boiling fat-free ground plant successively for $\frac{1}{2}$ hour in 1.25% sulfuric acid and 1.25% caustic soda. **hard-** The leaf or structural f. from tropical and subtropical plants, used for cordage, mats, and sacking; e.g., agave, manila hemp, *Phormium*. **high wet-modulus-** Synthetic cellulose f. having high tensile strength, wet strength, and dimensional stability. **horn-** Vulcanized f., leatheroid. A hard, tough, substance made by compressing layers of paper treated with acids or zinc chloride. **hybrid-** Conjugate. **linen-** F. used for making threads or yarn from flax. **man-made-** Synthetic. **mineral-** Asbestos f. Cf. *artificial f.* **polynosic-** A high wet-modulus f. having a high degree of polymerization, alkali resistance, and crystallinity. **soft-** Bast or stem f.; e.g., flax, hemp, or jute. **split-** F. made by heating and stretching polymer sheets under conditions which split them into fibers. **staple-** F., natural or synthetic, in comparatively short and uniform lengths, from which it is spun alone or in admixture into continuous threads. Natural fibers usually occur in this form, but f. made as a continuous filament, e.g., rayon, must be cut if used to make cotton-type fabrics. Cf. *filament yarn.* **sugarcane-** Bagasse. **synthetic-** See under individual names. World output (1967): polyamide 1.3, polyester 0.8, acrylic 0.6, total 6.5 million pounds. **vegetable-** F. from plants: (1) Hair fibers (from seed hairs), e.g., *Gossypium*, cotton. (2) Bast fibers (from stalks and stems), e.g. *Linum* (Linaceae), flax. (3) Cordage fibers (from vascular bundles), e.g., Agave (Amaryllidaceae), sisal. (4) Paper fibers (from gramineae and coniferae), e.g., cereal straws, pine, fir, wood f. **vulcanized-** Horn f.

    f. fineness value. See *tex, denier, micronaire.*

    Dimensions of fibers, in millimeters: see table.

Fiber	Length	Diameter
Cotton	20–30	0.019
Linen	8–70	0.020
Hemp...............	5–55	0.025
Jute	0.8–6	0.018
Cereal straw	0.3–2.0	0.015
Bamboo..............	0.8–4.0	0.012
Coniferous wood.......	5	0.040
Deciduous wood.......	2	0.025
Silk.................	—	0.013
Wool................	20–150	0.060
Asbestos.............	1.0	0.003

Fibestos. Trademark for a cellulose acetate synthetic fiber.

Fibramine. Trade name for a cellulose-viscose synthetic fiber.

fibre. Fiber. **f.V.** Dacron.

Fibrelta. Trade name for a cellulose-viscose synthetic fiber.

fibrid. A fluffy synthetic material having the physical properties of both fibers and films. Used for nonwoven fabrics.

fibril. A small fiber or filament.

fibrin. A protein from blood (0.1–0.4%) and muscle

tissue, formed from fibrinogen by the action of ferments., e.g., thrombin. Colorless or yellow, horny masses, insoluble in water, but swelling in dilute acid to a gel. Used technically in photography; the dye, textile, and leather industries; also in foods. **muscle-** Syntonin. **vegetable-** Gluten. Gluten f. A by-product in the manufacture of starch. Yellow, horny masses, insoluble in water. It has a high food value.

f. foam. Artificial foam made by clotting foamed human fibrinogen with thrombin; freezing, drying, and heating at 130 for 3 hours (B.P.).

fibrinogen. A globulin of the blood plasma which gives fibrin by the action of paraglobulin or of the fibrin enzyme, thrombin, and essential for the coagulation of blood. Cf. *fibroinogen*.

fibrinolysin. A substance formed in the blood that causes fibrin clots to dissolve.

fibrinolysis. The hydrolysis of fibrin.

Fibro. Trade name for a cellulose viscose, synthetic staple fiber.

Fibroceta. Trade name for a cellulose acetate synthetic fiber.

Fibrogen. Trademark for a highly purified lung tissue, rich in fibrinogen; a hemostatic.

fibroin. $(C_{15}H_{23}O_6N_5)_x = (369.2)x$. A protein constituent of silk and spider webs.

fibroinogen. Renatured fibroin, e.g., produced by neutralization of a solution of fibroin in cupriethylenediamine solution. Cf. *fibrinogen*.

Fibrolan. Trademark for cellulose dyes.

Fibrolane. Trade name for a protein synthetic fiber.

fibrolite. Al_2O_3,SiO_2. Sillimanite. A yellow, native silicate.

fibrolysin. A sterilized 15% solution of thiosinamine and sodium salicylate; used to break up fibrous tissue.

fibroplastin. Paraglobulin.

Fibrovyl. Trade name for a polyvinyl chloride synthetic fiber.

fibrox. A fibrous variety of siloxicon, q.v.; a heat insulator.

F.I.C. Abbreviation for Fellow of the Institute of Chemistry; revised in 1943 to F.R.I.C., Fellow of the Royal Institute of Chemistry.

fichtelite. $C_{18}H_{22} = 248.25$. White, crystals, m.46, in peat beds (Fichtelgebirge, Bavaria).

ficin. A proteolytic, crystalline enzyme; the active principle of oje, the milky sap of the *Ficus* species, which dissolves live parasitic worms.

F.I.D. Abbreviation for "Food Inspection Division" of the Department of Agriculture, U.S.A.

fiducial error limit. A statistical expression of the limits of error based on a certain reference figure, e.g., as in 10 ± 0.1.

field. (1) The region or space within which a phenomenon occurs. (2) In optics, the area visible at any one time through an instrument, e.g., a microscope. **atomic-** The space surrounding an atom which cannot normally be penetrated by other atoms. **electric-** The space surrounding an electrically charged body in which its action is perceptible. **electromagnetic-** q.v. **gravitational-** The region surrounding the earth in which bodies are attracted towards its center. **intraatomic-** Dynad. **interatomic-** The space between dynads. Cf. *molecular diagram, atomic radius.* **magnetic-** The space surrounding a magnet, in which its

action is perceptible. **molecular-** The space surrounding a molecule which is impenetrable by other molecules.

field intensity. The intensity of the energy of a limited region or space. **electric-** The energy of an electric field, $H = q/r^2$, measured by the force exerted on unit charge at a point distant r from an electric charge q in a vacuum. For a dielectric, $H = q/Kr^2$. where K is the dielectric constant of the medium. **magnetic-** The energy of a magnetic field, measured by the force exerted at a point at a distance r from an isolated magnetic pole of strength m: $H = m/\mu r^2$, where μ is the magnetic permeability.

fig. The dried fruit of *Ficus carica* (Urticaceae); a food and laxative. Cf. *cradin*.

figwort. Scrophularia.

filament. A fine threadlike body or structure. **carbon-** A fine thread of graphite or carbon, used in electric bulbs. **nuclear-** The threadlike chromatin in the nucleus of a cell. **protoplasmic-** A threadlike protoplasm, as cilia. **tungsten-** A fine thread of tungsten, used in electric bulbs.

f. yarn. Reeled filaments of synthetic fiber, e.g., rayon, as distinct from staple fiber.

filamentous. (1) Having the shape of a filament. (2) A growth of bacteria composed of long, interwoven threads.

filar micrometer. A scale attachment for microscopes; 0.001 mm can be estimated.

file. A very hard steel tool with a rough surface of fine sharp ridges; used for smoothing or shaping objects. **rattail-, round-** A tool for smoothing out round holes, as in a cork stopper. **triangular-** A tool for cutting glass tubing by making a sharp cut with one edge, and then breaking the tube.

Filices. (sing., filix, q.v.) Ferns. An order of Pteridophytae or spore-bearing plants which yield aspidium, polystichum, filicin, etc.

filicic acid. (1) $C_{14}H_{14}O_5 = 262.2$. Colorless crystals, decomp. 185, insoluble in water; a constituent of *Aspidium* species, and a decomposition product of filicin. (2) $C_{36}H_{42}O_1 = 682.32$. White crystals, m.125, from *Aspidium* species. Cf. *filixic acid, filicinic acid.*

filicin. $C_{35}H_{40}O_{12} = 652.4$. Filicic acid anhydride. A constituent of the root of *Aspidium filix-mas*; a vermifuge.

filiform. Describing a uniform growth of bacteria along the line of inoculation.

filitannic acid. The tannin of the male fern.

filix. (Pl. Filices, q.v.) A fern, as filix-mas, the male fern. **f. extract.** A fluid extract made from the root of the male fern, *Aspidium filix-mas*. It contains filicic acid, filicin, albaspidin, aspidinol, and filmaron.

filixic acid. $C_{35}H_{38}O_{12} = 650.29$. An acid, m.183, from filix extract. Cf. *filicic acid, filicinic acid.*

fillers. Materials used (1) to close the pores of paper; (2) to increase the bulk or weight of substances (loading); (3) to modify the properties of synthetic substances or insulating compositions.

film. (1) A membrane or covering layer. (2) A light-sensitive, flexible, transparent sheet coated with opaque silver salts for making photographs. (3) The transparent developed form of (2). **f. slide.** A greatly reduced photograph of printed matter,

Filter	Time to pass 100 ml water	Pore sizes of materials retained
Coarse	1–10 sec	$0.5-3\,\mu$ (kaolin)
Medium	10–30 sec	$0.1-1\,\mu$ (bacteria)
Fine	30–100 sec	$0.05-0.5\,\mu$ (colloidal gold)
Ultrafine (colloidal):		
Fast	1–5 min	Fine colloids
Medium	6–30 min	Benzopurpurin dyes
Fine	50–150 min	Albumen
Finest	> 150 min	Congo red dyes

which can be read by magnified projection; facilitates storage of scientific literature.

filmaron. $C_{47}H_{54}O_{16} = 874.5$. An amorphous substance, m.60; the anthelmintic principle of filix extract.

filter. (1) A strainer or purifier. (2) Chemistry: a porous material through which a liquid passes for the purpose of (a) removing a precipitate or suspended matter, or (b) clarifying the liquid. Cf. *membrane.* (3) Physics: an absorbing, semitransparent substance, e.g., light f. **asbestos-** A mixture of asbestos and glass wool used for filtration. **Berkefeld-** A tube made of diatomaceous earth, used for filtering and sterilizing water. **Chamberland-** A tube made of porous clay, used for the filtration and sterilization of liquids, vaccines, or serums. **folded-** F. paper, folded in alternate directions, used for rapid filtration. **gas-** A device for removing solid or liquid impurities from gases. **gel-** The use of gel as a molecular sieve, q.v. **glass-** (1) A glass Gooch-type crucible having a sintered glass base of appropriate pore size. Used in quantitative analysis. (2) Glass wool. **Gooch-** A platinum, glass or porcelain crucible with a perforated bottom covered by asbestos fibers, in which a precipitate may be heated and weighed. **Kelly-** A leaf f. for filtering slurries under pressure. **light-** Color screen. **membrane-** A disk of nitrocellulose (porosity 0.03–3 microns) used in analytical and bacteriological work. **paper-** F. paper. **paper pulp-** F. paper moistened and pulped for use similar to glass wool. **Pasteur-** A tube of unglazed porcelain for filtration by pressure or vacuum. **streamline-** See *streamline filtration.* **ultra-** See *ultrafiltration, membrane f.* **vacuum-** See *vacuum.*

f. aid. A powder, e.g., kieselguhr, added to the solution to be filtered to form a porous bed on the f. and facilitate filtration. **f. bag.** A sack of fiber for straining liquids. **f. cloth.** Strong canvas for a f. press. **f. cone.** A cone of porous material; as, Alundum, for filtration. **f. crucible.** Gooch crucible. **f. cylinder.** A porous tube used as a f. **f. flask.** A conical flask with side neck made of heavy glass, for vacuum filtration. **f. mantle.** A glass or metal tube around a f. cylinder. **f. paper.** Unsized, porous paper used for filtration. made in various textures and grades of purity. *qualitative-* A common f. paper used for straining, clearing, and purifying solutions or the collection of suspended matter. *quantitative-* A high-grade f. paper, resistant to dilute acids and consisting of pure cellulose with a small ash prepared by repeated acid and water washings of the paper pulp. **f. paper analysis.** (1) Identification of substances

by a spot test or f. paper test, q.v. (2) Capillary analysis. (3) The germination of seeds on moist f. paper and examination of the exudation from the rootlets, e.g., by fluorescence methods. **f. paper test.** A color reaction made with minute quantities of materials and reagents, with which a f. paper is successively moistened. **f. press.** A frame on which perpendicular iron plates are suspended and pressed together by a screw. Liquid to be filtered is pumped into canvas bags between the plates, and the tightening of the screw furnishes the pressure for filtration. **f. pump.** A pressure or vacuum pump used for filtration. Laboratory pumps are usually small vacuum pumps connected to the water faucet and operated by the water current drawing the air from a container. **f. tube.** (1) A glass tube to connect a Gooch crucible to a filter flask. (2) Bougie.

filtrate. The clear liquid that has passed through a filter. Cf. *tenate.* **f. factor.** Vitamin B_3.

filtration. The process of separating a solid from a liquid by a porous substance through which only the liquid passes. **centrifugal-** The separation of filtrate from precipitate by centrifuging. **direct-** The usual gravity separation of a solid from a liquid through a filter. **edge-** Streamline f. **forced-** Centrifugal, pressure, or vacuum f. **meta-** See *metafiltration.* **pressure-** F. by forcing the liquid by air pressure through the filter. **streamline-** See *streamline.* **vacuum-** F. by drawing the liquid by suction through the filter.

Filtros. Brand name for a porous acidproof filter material.

fimbriate. Describing a growth of bacteria characterized by large and extremely long filaments on the borders of the colonies.

fineness. (1) The state of subdivision of a powder or granulated substance, determined by sieves. (2) The purity of a gold alloy, expressed in parts per 1,000. See *gold.*

finings. Substances added to a fermented beverage to clear it from suspended matter, e.g., yeast, and render it brilliant, e.g., isinglass. **blue-** Potassium ferrocyanide, used to remove iron from wine; now prohibited in many countries.

finishing material. A substance used in industry for the last or finishing stage of manufacture; as, of textiles: (1) Substances making fibers soft, hygroscopic, and pliable, e.g., glycerin. See *plasticizers.* (2) Coloring substances, e.g., dyes. (3) Waterproofing substances, e.g., plastics. (4) Fireproofing substances, e.g., water glass. (5) Antiseptic substances, e.g., phenol. (6) Inert substances added as loadings or fillers; e.g., barytes, gypsum, chalk, clay.

finn oil. Tall oil.

Finsen lamp. A mercury-vapor arc lamp in a quartz container; a source of ultraviolet rays to treat skin diseases.

Fioco. Trade name for a viscose cellulose synthetic fiber.

Fiolax. Trade name for an alkali-free glass resistant to sudden temperature changes; used for chemical glassware.

fir. (1) A coniferous tree of the *Abies* genus. (2) Same as firkin. (3) A *Pinus* species. **balsam of-** Canada balsam. **oil of-** Pine oil.

fire. A bright flame caused by combustion. **f. air.** Scheele's name for oxygen. **f. brick.** A fire-resistant brick for lining furnaces, containing mullite, cristobalite, and tridymite as crystalline phases. **f. clay.** Stowbridge clay. A refractory clay containing more silica and alumina than basic oxides. **f. damp.** An explosive mixture of methane and air in coal mines; detected by the "corpse light" in a Davy lamp. **f. extinguisher.** An agent that extinguishes fires by cooling the burning substance, e.g., by water; or by covering it with a medium in which combustion cannot occur, as, carbon tetrachloride, fire foam. **f. foam.** A colloidal blanket of alumina and carbon dioxide to extinguish fires, e.g., in oil tanks, produced by spraying interacting solutions containing alum, and sodium carbonate and glue. **f. point.** The minimum temperature at which an oil will burn continuously. Cf. *flash point.* **f. proofing.** See *fireproofing.*

fire polishing. Smoothing the sharp edges of glass by slightly fusing them in a flame.

fireproofing. Coating or impregnation with a substance that reduces combustibility, as, water glass for textiles.

firkin. (1) Fir. An obsolete volumetric measurement: 9 gal = 34.06799 liters. (2) A wooden vessel.

firn. Granular, compressed snow, 200 ft below the surface in Arctic regions.

Fischer, Emil. 1852–1919. German chemist noted for his synthesis of polypeptides and carbohydrates. **F., Hans.** 1881–1945. German biochemist noted for his work on blood chlorophyll and bile pigments and for the synthesis of hemin (Nobel prize 1940).

fisetic acid. Fisetin.

fisetin. $C_{15}H_{10}O_6 = 285.1$. Fisetic acid. Tetraoxymethylanthraquinone. A yellow coloring matter from the wood of *Quebracho colorado*, fustic, or *Rhus cotinus.* Yellow needles, m.360. Cf. *fustin.* **iso-** Luteolin.

fish bean. See *tephrosia.* **f. berry.** Cocculus indicus, Indian berry, oriental berry. The dried fruit of *Anamirta cocculus* (Menispermaceae); a narcotic poison. **f. glue.** See *isinglass.* **f. guano.** F. scrap, f. tankage. A fertilizer made from non-edible fish and offal by cooking, expressing the oil, drying, and grinding (nitrogen 6–10, phosphorus pentoxide 0.4–8%). **f. oil.** Liquid fats obtained from fishes, characterized by great absorption of oxygen without drying to a varnish. They are colored dark red by concentrated acids and yield little or no elaidin. **f. poison.** (1) A ptomaine produced by decaying f. proteins. (2) A poison produced by certain species of fishes, as, fugu

toxin, or ichthyotoxin. (3) A poison used by natives to stupefy f. before catching them; usually derived from *Derris, Cracca,* and *Lonchocarpus* species. **f. scrap.** F. guano. **f. tankage.** F. guano.

fissile. Describing material that undergoes atomic fission.

fission. A division. (1) Biology: the separation of a single cell into 2 or more equal parts, capable of developing to the original size of the parent cell. Cf. *karyokinesis.* (2) Astronomy: the separation of a spherical and semiliquid body into 2 parts that revolve around each other, as, double stars formed by f. from a single star. (3) Atomic chemistry: the splitting of an atom into 2 atoms of nearly identical weight; e.g., the capture of a neutron by a nucleus of U^{235} forming a highly excited U^{236} nucleus, which at once divides into 2 fragments of approximately equal weights and at the same time emits 1 to 3 neutrons and gamma radiation. The energy of motion of the fragments is transformed into heat, and the reaction may be propagated from atom to atom as a chain reaction, as in the atomic bomb. Cf. nuclear *fusion.*

fistelin. The aglucone of the glucoside fustin.

Fittig, Rudolf. 1835–1910. German organic chemist. **F. reaction.** F. synthesis. **F. synthesis.** The formation of an aromatic homolog from an aryl iodide or bromide by means of an alkyl iodide or bromide and metallic sodium, e.g., RBr + R'Br + 2Na = R—R' + 2NaBr.

five finger grass. Cinquefoil. The herb of *Potentilla reptans* (Rosaceae); a febrifuge and astringent. **American-** The herb of *P. canadensis* used similarly. Cf. *tormentil.*

Fixanal. Trade name for an analytical chemical, accurately weighed and sealed in a glass ampul for the rapid preparation of volumetric solutions.

fixation. The process of rendering permanent. (1) Photography: the dissolving of light-sensitive silver salts from plates, films, or paper, to make them insensitive to the further action of light. (2) Microscopy: the preparation of minute structures in their original form on a slide. (3) Immunology: the prevention of hemolysis by the complement, q.v. (4) Industry: the combining of atmospheric nitrogen in the form of a useful compound. See *nitrogen fixation.* **complement-** See *complement fixation.* **nitrogen-** See *nitrogen fixation.*

fixative. A substance used to make an object permanent, as: (1) a mordant used in dyeing; (2) a varnish for pastel paintings; (3) an agent (Formalin and acetic acid) used in biology to make permanent tissues; (4) a f. used in perfumery to make an odorous substance less volatile; as, methyl anisate.

fixator. Amboceptor.

fixed. Made permanent or definite. **f. air.** Early name for carbon dioxide. **f. oil.** A liquid fat which absorbs oxygen and becomes resinous (drying oil) or remains liquid (nondrying oil) as compared with evaporating (essential or volatile) oil. **f. proportions, Law of.** See *constant proportions.* **f. white.** Barium sulfate.

fixing. The act of rendering permanent. **f. bath.** A 20% solution of sodium thiosulfate; used to fix photographic plates, films, or papers.

Fizeau, Armand, Hippolyte, Louis. 1819–1896.

French physicist noted for research on the interference of light and heat, and the determination of the velocity of light and electricity.

Fl.   Abbreviation for fluorine, F (obsolete).

fl.   Abbreviation for fluid.   **fl. dr.**   A fluid dram or drachm.   **fl. oz.**   A fluid ounce.

flag.   See *calamus*.

flagstaffite. $C_{12}H_{24}O_3$.   An orthorhombic mineral, m.99–105.

flame.   A source of heat; essentially a stream of gas or vapor heated as the result of chemical reaction, usually oxidation.   Its luminosity may depend on glowing solid particles; e.g., dust, carbon, etc. **acetylene-** The hot, ignited gases emerging from a blowpipe fed with acetylene and compressed air or oxygen.   **augmented-** A f., the energy of combustion of which has been increased by subjecting it to a diffuse electric discharge.   **Bunsen-** The f. produced by a gas bunsen burner; either nonluminous (with air), or luminous (without air).   **dark-** A nonluminous f., e.g., produced by burning pure hydrogen in oxygen.   **hydrogen-** A bluish, nonluminous f. produced by the oxidation of hydrogen in air.   **luminous-** A bright or pale, colored f., e.g., sodium light.   **nonluminous-** Dark.   **oxidizing-** The nonluminous f. of a gas burner, used in blowpipe analysis for oxidation.   **oxyhydrogen-** The hot gas mixture from a blowpipe fed with compressed hydrogen and oxygen.   **reducing-** The luminous blowpipe f., due to the presence of solid particles of carbon.   **solar-** Protuberances on the sun due to hydrogen flames or luminousgases.

   f. coloration.   A qualitative analytical test performed by placing the substance, moistened with hydrochloric acid on a platinum wire, in the nonluminous bunsen flame, and observing the resulting color.

Bright yellow	Sodium
Brick red	Calcium
Crimson	Strontium
Red	Lithium
Green-yellow	Molybdenum, Boron
Green	Barium
Blue	Indium
Blue-white	Lead, Arsenic, Antimony
Purple	Potassium
Blue, changing to green	Copper

   f. cutting.   Cutting ferrous metals by oxidation. The metal is heated at 1500°F by oxyacetylene jets in the cutting torch, and a stream of oxygen is applied through a central jet.   **f. hardening.**   The surface hardening of iron by heating a thin surface layer to the hardening temperature with an oxyacetylene f., followed by rapid cooling.   **f. photometer.**   An instrument for the photoelectric measurement of the concentration of an element in a solution from the intensity of the characteristic color produced when it is sprayed into a f. under standard conditions; especially suitable for the alkali metals.   **f. reactions.**   See *Bunsen, f. tests*. **f. spectra.**   Spectra produced by the vapors of elements; used for spectroscopic analysis. The characteristic lines of f. spectra are due to electrons falling back to normal orbits from the easily excited levels.   Cf. arc and spark *spectrum*.   **f. temperature.**   In degrees centigrade:

Alcohol and air	1705
Gas bunsen burner:	
No air	1712
Half air	1812
Full air	1871
Hydrogen and air	1900
Gas and oxygen	2200
Hydrogen and oxygen	2420
Acetylene and air	2458
Acetylene and oxygen	3000
Thermite (Al + Fe)	3000

   f. tests.   Qualitative test made with the bunsen burner, such as f. colorations, bead tests, and blowpipe tests.

flame-ionization detector.   A device in which the change in conductivity of a standard (usually hydrogen) flame due to the inclusion of another gas or vapor is used to detect or determine the latter, as in gas chromatography.

flameproof.   Describing that which cannot be ignited.   **f. group.**   The maximum gap dimensions in electrical apparatus that will prevent a surrounding gas from being ignited: ammonia, methane, 1; *n*-butane, carbon monoxide, ethane, propane, vinyl chloride, 2; α- and β-butylene, ethylene, propylene, coal gas, 3; acetylene, hydrogen, water gas, 4 (maximum gap too small to be practical).

flame-resistant.   Resistant to ignition, but capable of being ignited.

flammable.   (U.S. and U.K. usage.) Inflammable. Combustible; able to be set on fire.

flash.   (1) A sudden, luminous, temporary flame. (2) A volatile mixture, thrown on the fires of a kiln to produce a colored glaze on bricks or tiles that are being baked; thus: **black-** containing manganese.   **zinc-** containing zinc salts (yellow and green shades).

flashlight.   A mixture of combustible solids used in photography; as, magnesium powder.

flashpoint.   The lowest temperature at which the vapors of a liquid decompose to a flammable gaseous mixture.   It is a constant of oils.   It is below the burning point (the lowest temperature at which the gas will burn steadily).   Cf. *autoignition, Abel*.   **closed-** F. p. determined in a vessel which is exposed to air only at the moment of application of the flame.   **open-** F. p. determined with the sample exposed to air during preliminary heating.

flash spectrum.   The reversal of the Fraunhofer lines of the solar spectrum as a bright line spectrum immediately before a total eclipse.

flask.   A glass, metal, paraffin, plastic, or rubber receptacle or vessel for holding solids, liquids, or gases.   **Abderhalden-** A glass vessel intermediate in shape between a beaker and an erlenmeyer f. **acetylation-** A small pear-shaped f. used in menthol determinations.   **assay-** A conical glass beaker used for precipitation.   **boiling-** A spherical glass vessel with long neck.   **delivery-** A f. graduated to deliver a specified volume of liquid as distinct from containing this volume.   Cf. *volumetric* f. **Dewar-** A vacuum f., with side tube in its neck. **erlenmeyer-** A conical-shaped f. with narrow neck and wide flat bottom.   **filtering-** An erlenmeyer f. with heavy walls and side tube.   **mercury-** The commercial unit of measurement of mercury

equivalent to 75 lb. **silica-** A f. of semiopaque silica.
vacuum- Dewar vessel. A double-walled glass vessel of appropriate shape for holding liquefied gases. **volumetric-** A f. with a long graduated neck. **Wurtz-** Distillation f-.

flavacidin. An antibiotic from fungi, probably identical with gliotoxin.

flavaniline. $C_{16}H_{14}N_2 = 234.28$. α-Aminophenyl-γ-methylquinoline. Colorless prisms, m.97, insoluble in water.

flavanol. $C_{15}H_{10}O_3 = 238.1$. 3-Hydroxyflavone. Yellow needles, m.170, soluble in alcohol.

flavanols. Vegetable dyes derived from flavonol. See table.

FLAVANOLS

A. Anthocyanidins

Pelargonidin	5,7,4'-Trihydroxy-*f*.
Fisetinidin	7,3',4'-Trihydroxy-*f*.
Cyanidin	5,7,3',4'-Tetrahydroxy-*f*.
Delphinidin	5,7,3',4'5'-Pentahydroxy-*f*.
Peonidin	3'-Methoxy-5,7,4'-trihydroxy-*f*.
Oenidin	3',4'-Dimethoxy-5,7,5'-trihodroxy-*f*.
Myrtillidin	7-Methoxy-5,3',4',5'-tetrahydroxy-*f*.

B. Anthocyanins

Chrysanthemin . . .	3-Glucosidylcyanidin
Pelargonenin	5-Glucosidylpelargonidin
Oenin	3-Glucosidyloenidin
Pelargonin	3,5'Diglucosidylpelargonidin

flavatin. See *flavacidin*.

flavazine. $C_{16}H_{13}N_4O_4SNa$. The sodium salt of 1-*p*-sulfophenylmethyl-4-phenyldiazonium-5-pyrazolone; a yellow acid dye.

flavazole. A combination, in equimolecular proportions, of proflavine base and sulfathiazole; an antiseptic.

flavianic acid. $C_{10}H_6N_2O_8S = 314.0$. 2,4-Dinitro-1-naphthol-7-sulfonic acid. Yellow crystals, used in the separation of amines, and as a selective precipitant for zirconium.

flavicid. $C_{18}H_{22}N_3Cl = 315.5$. 2,7-Dimethyl-3-dimethylamino-6-amino-10-methyl acridinium chloride. Brown, water-soluble powder; an antiseptic.

flavicidin. Flavacidin.

flavicin. See *flavacidin*.

flavin(e). (1) $C_{10}H_6N_4O_2 = 214.05$. Isoalloxazine.

(2) Quercetin. (3) A yellow plant pigment; as, lactoflavin (the free yellow pigment), lumiflavin (a cleavage product formed on irradiation of lactoflavin), protein flavin (united to proteins), carbohydrate flavin (united to carbohydrates as in vitamin G).

flavinduline. 9-Phenyl-9-α,γ-dibenzophenazonium.

flavine. (1) Acriflavine. (2) Flavin.

flavoglaucin(e). $C_{19}H_{28}O_3 = 304.23$. A yellow pigment, m.109, isolated from growing cultures of *Aspergillus glaucus* and other molds.

flavol. 1,3-Anthradiol. Cf. *flavanol*.

flavone. $C_{15}H_{10}O_2 = 222.1$. 2-Phenylbenzo-1,4-pyrone, 2-phenylchromone,

Colorless needles, m.97, insoluble in water. In many flower colors. Cf. *flavones*. **dihydro-** Flavanone.

flavones. Vegetable coloring matters; the hydroxy or methoxy derivatives of flavone. See table. Cf. *anthoxanthin*.

Flavone (in *iso*flavone the phenyl group is at 3). *h*. = hydroxyflavone.

Flavanol	3-*H*.
Chrysin	5,7-Di-*h*.
Quercetin	2,3',4'-Tri-*h*.
Apigenin	3,7,4-Tri-*h*.
Luteolin	5,7,3,4-Tetra-*h*.
Quercitin	3,5,7,3,4-Penta-*h*.
Morin	3,5,7,2',4'-Penta-*h*.
Myricetin	3,5,7,3,4,5-Hexa-*h*.
Quercetagin . .	3,4,5,6,7,3',4'-Hepta-*h*.
Rhamnetin . .	7-Methoxy-3,5,2,4-tetra-*h*.
Genistin	7-Glucosidyl genistein
Daidzin	7-Glucosidyl daidzin.

flavopannin. $C_{21}H_{26}O_7 = 390.2$. A monobasic acid from the root of *Aspidium athamanticum*.

flavophenine. Chrysamine. Cf. *pannol*.

flavopurin. $C_{14}H_8O_5 = 256.13$. 1,2,7-Trihydroxyanthraquinone, alizarin X, alizarin R.G., C.A., S.D.G., and I.O. A yellow dye.

flavopurpurin. $C_{14}H_8O_5 = 256.13$. 1,2,6-Trihydroxyanthraquinone. Yellow needles, m.459, slightly soluble in hot water; a dye.

flavoxanthin. $C_{40}H_{56}O_3 = 584.5$. A carotinoid pigment, m.184, from the petals of *Ranunculus acer*.

flavylium. A salt derived from flavones; contains tetravalent oxygen. Cf. *anthocyanidin*.

flax. Byssus. The bast fiber of *Linum usitatissimum*, flax plant, grown in Europe and Egypt for the fiber, in the U.S., Russia, and Argentine for the seeds (linseed oil). Unbleached flax is used for ropes, twine, and coarse fabrics. Bleached flax is used for linen, lace, etc.: linen rags for high-quality paper. **earth-** Asbestos. **mountain-** (1) A fine silky asbestos. (2) The herb of *Linum catharticum*, purging flax; a laxative. **New Zealand-** See New Zealand *hemp*. **stone-** Asbestos.

Flaxedil. Trademark for gallamine triethoxide (B.P.C.).

flaxseed. Linseed.

fleabane. The herb or seeds of *Erigeron Canadense* (Compositae); a diuretic and tonic.

Fleischl hemometer. An optical instrument to determine hemoglobin in the blood by comparison with blood-colored glass wedges.

Fleming, Sir Arthur. 1881–1960. British physicist, pioneer in the development of the thermionic valve, radio, and radar.

Fleming tube. A glass apparatus for the absorption of carbon dioxide in the determination of carbon in steel.

Flemming's solution. A fixative and preservative for small organisms: 25 ml 1% chromic acid, 10 ml 1% osmic acid, 5 ml glacial acetic acid, 60 ml water.

Fletcher furnace. A laboratory gas or gasoline furnace for metals or ceramics. **F. burner.** A gas ring burner.

flex. Flexible insulated copper wire, for electrical connections.

flexibility. (1) Ability to bend without breaking. (2) Adaptability.

flexography. Relief-type printing with quick-drying inks containing volatile solvents. Cf. *aniline* printing.

flexure. Any curved or bent portion or section.

flint. SiO_2. Flintstone. An opaque quartz in chalkstone, resembling chalcedony. Used in the ceramic, glass, and road-making industries. **f. brick.** A firebrick made of powdered f. **f. glass.** Potash-lead glass. A highly refractive and easily fusible glass; used in optical and chemical apparatus **f. stone.** Flint.

float. A buoyant, sealed glass tube used in burets for easier reading. **f. stone.** A light, porous quartz that floats on water.

floats. A finely ground phosphate rock; a fertilizer.

floccose. Describing a growth of bacteria in short, curved chains, resembling wool threads.

flocculation. Coagulation (of a finely divided precipitate).

flocculent. (1) Woolly or cloudy, flakelike, and non-crystalline. (2) Describing a growth of bacteria characterized by pseudozooglea, e.g., small, adherent masses of bacteria of various shapes floating in the culture medium.

Florence test. The formation of brown needles or plate-shaped crystals by a solution of iodine in potassium iodide in presence of semen.

florentium. Ft (originally Fr). The element, at. no. 61, claimed to be discovered (1924) by Rolla and Fernandez; now named promethium, Pm.

flores. (1) The flowers or blossoms of a plant. (2) A chemical obtained by sublimation. See *flower*. **f. martiales.** Ferriammonium chloride.

Floridin. Trademark for a variety of fuller's earth from Florida.

floss. (1) A fluffy silky thread, e.g., *Calotropis f.*, q.v. (2) The floating scum of oxides produced in the puddling of iron; a catalyst, e.g., for the polymerization of unsaturated styrenes.

flotation. The concentration of ores by grinding with a frothing agent, floating them on water, and agitating the mixture by compressed air. The wet gangue settles, and the concentrated ore is skimmed off. Cf. *density fluids*, *Owen process*. **f. activator.** A reagent producing a metallic coat; as, sodium sulfide or copper sulfate. **f. collector.** An agent that increases the carrying capacity of air bubbles;

e.g., xanthates. **f. depressor.** An agent preventing the gangue from being carried by the air bubble; as, cyanides. **f. frother.** A reagent producing a foam of stable air bubbles; as, f. oils. **f. oils.** Petroleum and wood oils (pine oil, creosote) used to wet the metallic particles. **f. regulator.** A reagent that controls pH value; as, lime.

flour. (1) Wheat f., farina tritici. The white starchy powder made by bolting wheat. (2) A powdered cereal or seed used for food. **baker's-** Second-grade wheat f. **bleaching-** See *Agene*, *beta-chlora*, and *Golo* processes. **buckwheat-** Powder made from buckwheat. **enriched-** Plain white f., to which vitamin concentrates and calcium salts, or a proportion of the wheat germ, have been added. **graham-** Unbolted wheat meal. **National-** A war-time enriched f., q.v. **patent-** High-grade, white, wheat meal, which has been bolted and all bran removed. **rye-** Powdered rye.

flouve oil. A mixture containing principally esters and coumarin from the sweet-scented vernal, *Anthoxanthum odoratum*. L., d.1.1291; used in perfumes.

flow. The motion of a fluid. Cf. *flux*, *nernst unit*. **cold-** See *cold*. **molecular-** The relative number of gas molecules which pass through a fine orifice: $Q = p_2 - p_1/(W \sqrt{\rho})$, where Q is the quantity of gas in milliliters per second which flows through an opening at a difference of pressure $(p_2 - p_1)$, ρ is the density of the gas at 1 barye pressure, and W is the resistance overcome. **f. sheet.** The diagrammatic representation of an industrial process, showing the sequence and interdependence of the successive stages.

flowers. (1) A chemical obtained by sublimation; usually a metallic oxide; as f. of sulfur. (2) The blossoming portion of a plant, consisting normally of a calyx (composed of sepals), corolla (composed of petals), and stamens and pistils. Many flowers contain coloring materials, essential oils, odoriferous substances and drugs.

Flox. Trade name for a viscose cellulose synthetic fiber.

floz. Fl. oz. Abbreviation for fluid ounce.

fluavil. $C_{20}H_{32}O = 288.3$. A resin from gutta-percha, m.42, soluble in alcohol.

fluctuate. To vary or move within certain limits.

fluctuation. Successive rises and falls.

fludrocortisone acetate. $C_{23}H_{31}O_6F = 422.51$. White crystals, m.225, soluble in water; an adrenocortical steroid (B.P.).

flue. A channel for gases or liquids.

fluellite. $AlF_3 \cdot H_2O = 102.67$. Hydrous aluminum fluoride. Orthorhombic crystals, d.2.17, hardness 3.

fluid. A form of matter that cannot permanently resist any shearing force, which causes flow. **elastic-** A gas, e.g., a condition of matter in which the molecules flow apparently without resistance. **inelastic-** A liquid, e.g., a condition of matter in which the molecules move freely but are restricted by gravitation. **Newtonian-** A f. which obeys Newton's law; an increase in pressure or rate of shear increases the velocity gradient (and therefore the rate at which a f. passes through a tube) in the same proportion. **non-Newtonian-** Heterogeneous f., e.g., sols or gels. **perfect-** A hypothetical state of matter in which the molecules offer no mechanical resistance. **viscous-** A syrup or soft mass which flows slowly.

fluid acetextract. A solution made by extracting a drug in dilute acetic acid.

fluid bed drying. A method of drying (e.g., textiles) in which the drying medium is a bed of sand particles or small glass spheres, 0.1–1.0 mm in diameter. This is fluidized by passing hot air upward through it.

fluid dram. A pharmaceutical measurement. 1 fl dr = 60 minims = 3.69661 cc (U.S.) or 3.55 ml (U.K.).

fluid extract. An alcoholic solution of a drug representing the drug weight by volume, e.g., 1 gm of the drug corresponds with 1 ml of fluid extract. Cf. *tincture.*

fluid friction. Viscosity.

fluidity. The property of flowing easily, measured in ρ = rhe, the reciprocal of poise, q.v. Cf. *viscosity.*

fluidization, fluidizing. The suspension and maintenance in a state of turbulent motion of solid material in a finely divided form in a stream of gas. This increases the surface activity of the particles. Used in catalytic processes, the gasification of brown coal, and the cracking of petroleum.

fluid ounce. A pharmaceutical measure of volume. 1 fl oz = 29.57 ml = 8 fl dr = $\frac{1}{128}$ gal (U.S.); 1 fl oz = 28.41 ml = 8 fl dr = $\frac{1}{160}$ imperial gal (U.K.).

fluid wax. Liquid waxes obtained from the oils of marine animals. They consist of esters of monoatomic alcohols, with traces of glycerides.

fluo- (1) Prefix indicating the presence of fluorine. (2) Prefix indicating the property of fluorescence.

fluobenzene. $C_6H_5F = 96.1.$ Phenyl fluoride. Colorless liquid, d.1.023, b.86, soluble in alcohol.

fluobenzoic acid. $C_7H_5O_2F = 140.1.$ Colorless rhombs, m.182, soluble in hot water.

fluoborate. A salt of fluoboric acid containing the radical BF_4—.

fluoboric acid. $HBF_4 = 87.8.$ The hypothetical parent acid of the fluoborates.

fluocarbon. Fluorocarbon.

fluocerite. $(Ce\cdot La\cdot Nd\cdot Pr)_2OF_4.$ A mineral containing the fluorides of the ceria earths.

fluochromate. A salt of fluochromic acid containing the radical $CrOF$—.

fluocinolone acetonide. $C_{24}H_{30}O_6F_2 = 452.50.$ White crystals, m.275, insoluble in water; an antidermatitic (B.P.).

fluoflavine. $C_{14}H_{10}N_4 = 234.1.$ A fluorescent substance, m.360, soluble in alcohol.

fluoform. See *fluoroform.*

fluogermanate. $M_2GeF_6.$ A salt of fluogermanic acid.

fluogermanic acid. $H_2GeF_6 = 188.6.$ Hydrofluogermanic acid. An acid obtained by passing germanium tetrafluoride into water.

fluohydric acid. Hydrofluoric acid.

fluomethane. Fluoromethane.

fluon. Trade name for polytetrafluoroethylene (U.K. usage).

fluoplumbic acid. $H_2PbF_6 = 323.2.$ Hydrofluoplumbic acid. A white powder obtained by passing lead tetrafluoride into water.

fluoracetamide. Fluoroacetamide.

fluoran(e). $O:(C_6H_4)_2:C:(O\cdot C_6H_4)\cdot CO = 300.20.$

o-Phenolphthalein anhydride. Colorless needles, m.182, soluble in acids; an intermediate in the manufacture of dyes.

fluorandiol. Fluorescein.

fluoranthene. (1) The ring structure

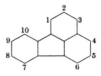

(2) $C_{16}H_{10} = 206.16.$ Idryl. A hydrocarbon in coal tar. Colorless needles m.110, soluble in hot water.

fluoranthraquinone. $C_{15}H_7O_2 = 219.1.$ Colorless crystals, m.188, soluble in alcohol.

fluorapatite. The mineral $CaF_2\cdot 3Ca_3(PO_4)_2.$ Cf. *apatite.*

fluoration. The introduction of fluorine into an organic molecule.

fluorbenzene. See *fluobenzene.*

fluorbenzoic acid. See *fluobenzoic acid.*

fluoremetry. Fluorimetry.

fluorene. $(C_6H_4)_2\cdot CH_2 = 166.15.$ α-Dipheneylenemethane. Fluorescent, colorless scales m.113, insoluble in water. Occurs in coal tar; used in the manufacture of dyes. Its radicals are fluoryl and fluorylidene. **amino-** Fluorylamine. **benzo-** Chrysofluorene. **chryso-** See *chrysofluorene.* **di-** See *difluorene.* **dibenzo-** q.v. **dinaphtho-** Dibenzofluorene. **naphtho-** q.v. **oxo-** Fluorenone*. **ms-phenyl-** Diphenylenedimethylethane. **picene-** q.v.

   f. alcohol. $C_6H_4\cdot CHOH\cdot C_6H_4 = 182.15.$ Diphenylenecarbinol, fluorenol*. Colorless crystals, m.153, soluble in alcohol. **f. carboxylic acid.** $C_{14}H_{10}O_2 = 210.15.$ Diphenyleneacetic acid.

fluorenic acid. $C_{14}H_{10}O_2 = 210.08.$ Colorless crystals, soluble in water.

fluorenol*. Fluorene alcohol.

fluorenone*. $(C_6H_4)_2\cdot CO = 180.15.$ Diphenylene ketone, oxofluorene. An oxidation product of fluorene. Yellow prisms, m.84, soluble in alcohol.

fluores. An early name for fluorite.

fluorescein. $O:(C_6H_3\cdot OH):C:(O\cdot C_6H_4)\cdot CO = 332.20.$ Uranin A, 3,6-dihydroxyfluoran, resorcinolphthalein, fluorandiol, dioxyfluoran. Orange-red powder, soluble in alkalies with orange color and green fluorescence. Used in the manufacture of eosin and other dyes and as an indicator for pH3.6 (yellow) to pH5.6 (fluorescent). **dihydroxy-** Gallein. **dimethyl-** Cresorcin. **sodium-** $C_{20}H_{10}O_5\cdot Na_2 = 376.28.$ Uranin, soluble f. Hygroscopic, orange powder, soluble in water; a diagnostic aid in ophthalmology (U.S.P., B.P.). **tetrabromo-** Eosin. **tetrabromodichloro-** Phloxin. **tetraiodo-** Erythrosin.

   f. paper. Zellner's paper. Paper impregnated with a solution of f. in alcohol; an indicator. *potassium-* Potassium f. *sodium-* Uranin.

fluorescence. The property of certain solids, liquids, or gases when illuminated to radiate unpolarized light of a different (usually greater) wavelength; due to the return of electrons, displaced by the exciting radiation, to a more stable position. Cf. *phosphorescence, luminescence.* **f. analysis.** The examination of substances in ultraviolet light with the object of identifying or determining them or assessing their quality or purity from the color and intensity of the f. produced. **f. efficiency.** The intensity of f. emitted by a substance per absorbed quantum of light. **f. microscopy.** Microscopical examination using ultraviolet instead of visible light; many structures fluoresce. **f. serology.** The diagnosis of disease from the f. of serums. Cf. *fluorometry.*

fluorescent. Epipolic. The property of having fluorescence. **non-** Describing a substance which emits a f. that is invisible to the human eye.

   f. screen. A glass plate covered with a f. substance, e.g., a platinocyanide. Used to make visible rays that are normally invisible to the eye.

   f. unit. The standard luminescence produced by 1 mg of radium element on 1 cm^2 of a barium platinocyanide screen. See *fluorimeter.*

fluorescin. $C_{20}H_{14}O_5 = 334.2$. Yellow powder, insoluble in water; a dye. Cf. *fluorescein.*

fluoric acid. Incorrect term for hydrofluoric acid. The name fluoric acid indicates the nonexistent compound HFO_3.

fluoride. A salt of hydrofluoric acid containing the radical F—. **acid-** MHF_2.

fluorimeter. Fluorometer, photofluorometer. An instrument to measure the intensity of fluorescence, especially the fluorescence caused by X rays, cathode rays, and radium.

fluorimetry. Fluorometry. Measurement of the color and intensity of fluorescence, q.v.

fluorination. The introduction of fluorine into an organic molecule.

fluorine. $F = 19.00$. A halogen element, at. no. 9. A poisonous, pale green gas, $d_{air=1}1.31$, m. -233, b. -187, $d_{liq}1.14$, soluble in water, alcohol, or ether. F. is the most negative element, and more reactive than oxygen. It has a valency of 1, and forms one series of compounds, the fluorides. Discovered (1771) by Scheele in fluorite, cryolite, and other minerals, and isolated (1886) by Moissan. Its compounds with uranium (UF_4 and UF_6) are used in atomic reactors. Liquid f. has a bright yellow color; solid f. is colorless. F. salts are of the types: MF or M_2F_2 (normal fluorides), MHF_2 (acid fluorides). **proto-** Coronium.

   f. DDT. Gix. **f. hydride.** Hydrofluoric acid. **f. iodine.** Fluoriodine. **f. oxide.** (1) $OF_2 = 54.0$. A gas less active than f., having the same odor, sparingly soluble in water. (2) $O_2F_2 = 70.0$. Brown gas. (3) $OF = 35.0$. Colorless gas.

fluorinion. Fluorion.

fluoriodate. A compound derived from the iodates by the partial replacement of the oxygen by fluorine; as difluoriodates, $R \cdot IO_2F_2$.

fluoriodine. $F_5I = 221.8$. Iodine pentafluoride. Colorless fuming liquid, b.97, of great chemical reactivity, decomp. by water.

fluorion. The monovalent fluorine ion, F^-.

fluorite. $CaF_2 = 78.09$. Fluorspar. Siliceous sinter. Native calcium fluoride, variously colored, brittle, d.3.18, hardness 4. Used as flux in the steel and glass industries and in the manufacture of hydrofluoric acid.

fluoroacetamide. $F \cdot CH_2CONH_2 = 77.03$. White crystals, soluble in water, m.109. An arrow

poison and rodenticide from the giftbloor plant (S. Africa); it acts by blocking the citric acid cycle.

fluoroacetanilide. $F \cdot CH_2CONHC_6H_5 = 153.2$. White solid, sparingly soluble in water, m.75; an insecticide.

fluorobenzene. Fluobenzene.

fluorocarbon. A member of the chain system $CF_3 \cdot (CF_2)_n \cdot CF_3$, which forms the most unreactive known substances: as, $C_{10}F_{21}SO_3H$, used to reduce spray in chromium plating, being unaffected by hot chromic acid. The most important fluoropolymer is polytetrafluoroethylene (mol. wt. 400,000–9,000,000), used as a protective coating in the chemical and electrical industries. See *Freon, Teflon.*

fluorochrome. A substance capable of inducing fluorescence in another substance.

fluoroform. $CHF_3 = 70.0$. Fluoform, trifluoromethane*. Colorless gas, d.2.53, b_{40atm} 20, slightly soluble in water.

fluoroformol. A 2.8% solution of fluoroform in water. Colorless, odorless, tasteless, nonirritant liquid, used to treat tuberculosis.

fluorogen. Fluorophore.

fluorography. The taking of miniature snapshots of a fluorescent screen in mass chest radiography; e.g., 200 patients per hour.

fluorometer. Fluorimeter.

fluoromethane. $CF_4 = 88.0$. Carbon tetrafluoride. Colorless gas; a by-product in the manufacture of aluminum from cryolite.

fluorometry. Fluorimetry.

fluorones. A group of compounds of the type

$$C_6H_4 \underset{\underset{R}{\overset{|}{C}}}{\overset{O}{\diagdown}} C_6H_3{:}O, \text{ derived from fluorine.}$$

fluorophore. A group of atoms which confers fluorescence on a compound; as, the oxazine ring. Cf. *chromophore.*

fluorophosphonate. A member of a series of compounds having the general formula $(RO)_2POF$, where R is an alkyl group. They have a high toxicity as lethal inhalants, and were evolved during World War II as possible poison gases. They affect the eyes without producing tears, and death ensues rapidly.

fluoropolymer. See *fluorocarbon.*

fluoroscope. (1) A fluorescent screen used to make visible certain rays, e.g., X rays. (2) An apparatus to determine the fluorescence of a solution by comparison with a standard.

fluorosis. Disease (and in particular mottling of the enamel of the teeth) due to an excess of fluorine ions in the system; usually derived from drinking water.

fluorosulfonic acid. $2OS \cdot OH \cdot F = 168.10$. Colorless liquid, m. -87, b.163; an intermediate in fine chemical manufacture.

Fluorouracil. Trademark for a fluorinated pyrimidine; an antimetabolic in treating carcinomas.

fluorspar. Fluorite.

fluoryl. The radical $C_{13}H_9$—, from fluorene;

isomers. **f. amine.** $C_{13}H_9NH_2 = 181.09$. Amino-fluorene. White crystals, insoluble in water.

fluorylidene. The radical $C_{13}H_8 =$ derived from fluorene.

fluosilicate. Silicofluoride. A salt of the type M_2SiF_6 derived from fluosilicic acid.

fluosilicic acid. $H_2SiF_6 = 144.3$. Hydrofluosilicic acid. A strong acid which exists only in solutions, and decomposes on concentration or heating into hydrofluoric acid and silicon tetrahydride; obtained by the action of silicon tetrafluoride on water.

fluothane. Halothane.

fluotitanic acid. $H_2TiF_6 = 163.9$. Hydrofluotitanic acid. A dibasic acid obtained by passing titanium tetrafluoride into water.

fluoxymesterone. $C_{20}H_{29}O_3F = 336.55$. White crystals, m.278, insoluble in water; an androgen.

flussigas. Calorgas.

flux. (1) A continuous flow or discharge. (2) A substance that causes other substances to melt more readily by dissolving their oxides or surface impurities, e.g., sodium carbonate. (3) The capacity of a nuclear reactor, in neutrons per centimeter per second. **aluminum-** A mixture of the alkali chlorides and fluorides. **black-** A f. and reducing agent used in metallurgy; a mixture of potassium carbonate and charcoal made by heating tartar. **radiant-** The amount of radiant energy (electromagnetic radiation) that flows along a beam per unit of time. **oxidizing-** A mixture of borax glass 30, boric acid 20, silica 5, potassium chlorate 20, sodium perborate 25%. **reducing-** A mixture of borax glass 50, boric acid 15, argol 25, animal charcoal 10%. **soldering-** A mixture of borax glass 55, boric acid 35, silica or dry sodium silicate 10%.

f. density. The radiant f. per unit area. Cf. *intensity*.

fly ash. The fine ash or flue dust carried by the combustion products of pulverized coal plants.

foam. A heterogeneous mixture of a gaseous phase in a liquid phase; finely divided gas bubbles suspended in a liquid. Cf. *flotation, colloids*.

foaming. Describing a liquid which forms a surface foam on heating or on agitation.

focal. Pertaining to a focus.

focus. A point on which rays converge and produce an intensified effect. **acoustic-** The meeting point of waves reflected from a concave surface. **anterior-** A point before an optical system, which corresponds with the posterior focus. **aplanatic-** The point from which rays pass through a lens without spherical aberration. **conjugate-** The mutually convertible anterior and posterior foci of a lens. **posterior-** A point behind an optical system corresponding with the anterior focus. **principal-** The point on which parallel rays passing through a lens converge. **real-** The point at which convergent rays intersect. **virtual-** The point at which rays, if prolonged, would intersect one another.

focusing. The adjustment of lenses or mirrors to produce a distinct image, e.g., in a microscope.

fodder. Dry food for domestic animals, e.g., hay.

fog. A heterogeneous mixture of a liquid phase in a gaseous phase; finely-divided liquid droplets suspended in a gas. See *colloid*. **f. chamber.** Cloud chamber. A small container in which a

haze is produced by sudden pressure changes. Cf. *Wilson tracks*.

fogging. (1) To produce a mist by agitating or heating a liquid in a closed container. (2) In photography, a uniform haze over the plate, due to overexposure or light leakage.

foil. A very thin sheet of metal, e.g., of aluminum; usually not thicker than 0.15 mm.

folia. Latin for leaves.

folic acid.

NH_2—$CH_2\cdot NH\cdot C_6H_4\cdot CO-$
OH $NH:CH(CH_2:CH_2\cdot CO_2H)CO_2H =$
441.42. Pteroylglutamic acid. Orange platelets, slightly soluble in water. The vitamin B complex of the U.S.P. and B.P. It prevents anemia in chicks, is present in green leaves and animal tissues, and is important in yeast nutrition.

Folin, Otto. 1867–1934. American biochemical analyst, born in Sweden. **F. apparatus.** A glass, specially designed absorption tube, used for the rapid determination of nitrogen, urea, or ammonia, in urine or other fluids. **F. diet.** The daily food ration: 500 ml milk, 300 ml cream, 450 gm eggs, 200 gm Horlick's malted milk, 20 gm sugar, 6 gm salt, 2,100 ml water.

folliculin. Estrone.

Folutein. Trade name for chorionic gonadotrophin.

fomometer. A small glass cup attached to a short length of capillary tubing, used for the rapid estimation of surface tension from the equilibrium height of the liquid in the tube when the cup is half-filled and the f. is inverted on a level surface.

fongisterol. $C_{25}H_{40}O\cdot H_2O = 382.39$. Fungisterol. A sterol, q.v., m.144, from ergot.

food. A substance which builds up tissues, repairs waste, and supplies living organisms with heat. The essential constituents are: Water, carbohydrates (starch, glucose, etc.), fats, proteins (albumins, etc.), salts, vitamins.

Daily mineral requirements, in grams:

10	NaCl	0.35	Mg
3	K	0.015	I
1.50	Mn	0.010	Fe
1.30	P	0.002	Cu
0.7	Ca	Traces	Zn, Al, Si, F

In addition, vitamins, q.v.:

A	200 int. units	(0.004 gm haliver oil)
B	200 int. units	(20 gm dried yeast)
C	400 int. units	(40 ml lemon juice)
D	1100 int. units	(0.1 gm haliver oil)
G	450 Sherman units .	(30 gm dried yeast)
E	Doubtful.	

See also *f. sources*. **animal-** F. derived from animals; as, meat, fish, milk, eggs, liver oil. **flesh-forming-** The proteins and salts necessary as tissue builders. **heat-forming-** The carbohydrates and fats which supply bodyheat. **iron-** F. containing iron, from 0.01921% (parsley) to 0.00015% (lemon). **nitrogenous-** The proteins, lecithins, and other foods containing nitrogen. **nonnitrogenous-** The carbohydrates and salts. **protective-** F. which supplies calcium, vitamins A,

BASIC DIETARY ALLOWANCES
Food and Nutrition Board, National Research Council

Subject and weight, kg	Calories, 1000	Protein, gm	Calcium, gm	Iron, gm
Man, 70..............	2.5–4.5	70	0.8	12
Woman, 56...........	2.1–3.0	85–100	1.5–2.0	15
Girls, 49–54	2.4–2.6	75–80	1.0–1.3	15
Boys, 47–64	3.2–3.8	85–100	1.4	15
Children (1–12 years) ...	1.2–2.5	40–70	1.0–1.2	12

C, and G (milk, cheese, and green vegetables), in which common diets are often deficient. **staple-F.** which is most frequently used; as, bread, bacon, rice, etc. **vegetable-** F. from plants; e.g., cereals, nuts, vegetables, fruits, sugars.

f. and drug acts. Legislative measures in force: in the U.S. since Jan. 1, 1907 (now the U.S. Federal Food, Drug and Cosmetic Act, 1936), and in U.K. since 1860 (the Food and Drugs Act, 1955), prohibiting the manufacture, sale, or transportation of adulterated, misbranded, poisonous, or deleterious foods, drugs, medicines or liquors; and designating official names for drugs. See *Approved Names.* **F. Chemical Codex.** Specifications for chemicals for use in food issued by the National Academy of Sciences (U.S.). **f. hormones.** Vitamins. **f. poisons.** Toxic substances, e.g., ptomaines, developed by decomposition of foods. **f. sources.:**

1. CEREALS: seeds of Gramineae; rich in carbohydrates, e.g., *Avena sativa*, oats.
2. PULSES: seeds of Leguminosae; rich in proteins, e.g., *Arachis hypogaea*, peanuts.
3. NUTS: oily seeds of various plants; rich in fats, e.g., *Carya* species, pecan.
4. ROOTS and TUBERS: underground reserves of certain plants; generally rich in carbohydrates, e.g., *Allium cepa*, onion.
5. GREEN VEGETABLES: leaves, inflorescences, stems, and young shoots of certain plants; generally containing vitamins and salts, e.g., *Brassica oleracea*, cabbage, cauliflower.
6. FRUITS used as VEGETABLES: fleshy fruits of various plants, e.g., *Solanum lycopersicum*, tomato.
7. FRUITS and BERRIES: generally containing acids, sugars, and salts, e.g., *Fragaria vesca*, strawberry.
8. MEAT and FISH: rich in proteins.
9. DAIRY PRODUCTS: rich in calcium and vitamins.
10. MISCELLANEOUS: mushrooms and yeast; honey, sugar, and maple syrup; sago, tapioca; spices and condiments.
Cf. *Codex Alimentaris.*

foot. ft. A unit of length. 1 ft = 12 in. = 0.304801 meter. **board-** q.v. **cubic-** cu ft or ft³. A measure of volume. 1 ft³ = 1,728 in.³ = 2,832 cm³. **square-** sq ft or ft². A measure of area. 1 ft² = 144 in.² = 929.03 cm².

foot-candle. A measure of illumination: 1 ft candle = 1 lumen per ft² = the illumination from a standard candle on a surface of 1 ft² 1 ft distant. 1 ft-candle = 1.076 milliphots = 10.76 lux. Cf. *meter-candle.*

foot-pound. ft-lb. A unit of work in the fps system:

the work required to lift 1 lb 1 ft, where $g = 32.2$ ft/sec². 1 ft-lb = 0.1383 kg-meter = 1.356 joules = 0.3240 cal = 0.001285 BThU = 0.3766 × 10⁻⁶ kwhr. 1 hp = 33,000 ft-lb/min of work. **f.p.-second.** Fps system. A system of measurements based on the foot, pound, and second. Cf. *cgs system, mks system.*

foot-poundal. A unit of force in the fps system: the force which during 1 sec will accelerate a mass of 1 lb 1 fps = 1 poundal.

foot powder. A mixture of fine salicylic acid and French chalk; an antiseptic dusting powder.

foots. The sediment which settles from an oil on standing: chiefly albuminous matter.

forbesite. A rare, natural nickel cobalt arsenate.

forbidden explosives. A group of unstable chemicals and mixtures which may not normally be transported or shipped, and which are condemned by the U.S. Bureau of Explosives; e.g., liquid nitroglycerin, dynamite containing over 60% nitroglycerin, nitrocellulose dry and uncompressed in quantity greater than 10 lb, and dry mercury fulminate. **f. lines.** Spectrum lines corresponding with atomic transitions not in harmony with Pauli's principle. When a gas is excited by (e.g.,) electric energy, certain lines only are seen in the absorption spectrum; others (f. lines), never. Thus the line may correspond with the passage of an electron from A to B and B to C, but never from A (the normal state) to C.

force. The rate of change of momentum. The interaction between 2 bodies whereby their state of rest or motion, or their form or size is changed. Cf. *attraction, repulsion.* The unit of force is the dyne (cgs system) or poundal (fps system). Force = (mass × velocity)/time = mass × (velocity/time) = mass × acceleration. **catabiotic-** The heat energy derived by a living organism from food. **catalytic-** The chemical work performed by a catalyst. **centrifugal-** See *centrifugal.* **chemical-** See *affinity.* **cohesive-** See *cohesion.* **electromotive-** See *electromotive f.* **kinetic-** See *kinetic energy.* **latent.** See *latent energy.* **living-** See *vital f.* **vital-** The energy obtainable from a living organism or cell.

forceps. A small V-shaped instrument for grasping objects such as analytical weights.

forensic. Pertaining to courts of law. **f. analysis.** Chemical analysis performed for the purpose of assisting justice. **f. chemistry.** Legal chemistry, judicial chemistry. The application of chemistry for purposes of criminal or civil law, e.g., f. analysis. **f. medicine.** See *medicine.*

forgenin. $HCOONMe_4 = 119.1$. Tetramethylammonium formate. Colorless hygroscopic crystals.

In small doses it stimulates; in large doses it acts similarly to curare.

forked chain. A chain of C atoms linking together 2 smaller chains; as,

$$-C-C-C\begin{smallmatrix}C-\\ \\C-\end{smallmatrix}$$. Cf. *branched chain.*

Forlion. Trade name for a polyacrylonitrile synthetic fiber.

formal. (1) $CH_2(OMe)_2 = 60.1$. Methylal, dimethoxymethane*, methyl aldehyde, formyl aldehyde, oxymethylene. Colorless liquid; an anesthetic and hypnotic. (2) Containing one grammolecular weight in 1 liter. Cf. *molar* (in 1,000 ml) and *molal* (in 1,000 gm).

formaldehyde. $H\cdot CHO = 30.03$. Methanal*, methylene oxide. The simplest aldehyde, derived from methanol. Colorless gas, b.−21, soluble in water; marketed as an aqueous solution. **poly-** See *Delrin.*

  f. solution. A 37% aqueous solution of f. Colorless liquid with characteristic odor. Used as a reagent, preservative (not for foods), antiseptic, and deodorant; industrially in synthesis; and in the formation of plastics.

formaldoxime. $H_2C:NOH = 45.1$. The simplest oxime. Colorless liquid, b.84.

Formalin. Trademark for a 27% (U.S.) or 40% (U.K.) formaldehyde solution.

formaloin. $CH_2:C_{17}H_{16}O_7$. A condensation product of formaldehyde and aloin. Yellow powder, soluble in water; used medicinally.

formamide. (1) A compound containing the radical $H\cdot CONH—$. (2) $H\cdot CO\cdot NH_2 = 45.1$. Formylamine, methanamide*. Colorless, hygroscopic liquid, d.1.337, $b_{10mm}105$, soluble in water. **allyl-** $C_4H_7ON = 85.1$. Colorless liquid, b.109. **ethyl-** $C_3H_7ON = 73.1$. Colorless liquid, b.199. **phenyl-** Formanilide.

formamidine. A compound containing the radical $—N:CH\cdot NH—$. **diphenyl-** $PhN:CH\cdot NHPh = 196.2$. Methenyldiphenyldiamine. Colorless crystals, m.135. **o-phenylene-** Benzimidazole.

formamido. (1) The radical $H\cdot CO\cdot NH—$, from formamide. (2) $HN:CH\cdot NH_2 = 44.05$.

formamine. Hexamethylenetetramine.

formamyl. Amide group. The radical $—CONH_2$. which confers weakly basic properties.

Formanek's indicator. Alizarin green, dihydroxydinaphthazoxonium sulfonate. A green oxazine dye indicator: pH 0.3 (violet), 1.0 (pink), 12.0 (yellow), 14.0 (brown).

formanilide. $C_7H_7ON = 121.14$. Phenylformamide, formamidobenzene, carbanil aldehyde. Yellow prisms, m.50, soluble in water; an antiseptic. **thio-** Thioformanilide.

formate. Formiate. A compound containing the radical $H\cdot COO—$.

formation. (1) The process of being made. (2) Geology: an assemblage of rocks having their origin, age, or composition in common. **heat of-** See *heat.*

formazyl. (1) $Ph\cdot N:N\cdot C:N\cdot NH\cdot Ph = 224.2$. Formazyl hydride. Colorless crystals, m.116. (2) The radical $(PhN:N)_2H\cdot C—$ **f. carboxylic acid.** $PhN:N\cdot C(COOH):N\cdot NHPh = 268.4$. Red needles, m.162 (decomp.), insoluble in water; a colorimetric

reagent for silver. **f. hydride.** Formazyl. **f. methyl ketone.** $PhN:N\cdot C(COMe):N\cdot NHPh = 266.4$. Colorless crystals, m.134.

formcoke. A caclined agglomerate prepared from bituminous coals; used in blast furnaces.

formhydroxamic acid. The theoretical compound $H\cdot CO\cdot NH\cdot OH$.

formiate. Formate.

formic acid. $H\cdot COOH = 46.03$. Formylic acid, methanoic acid*, aminic acid. The first member of the aliphatic series. Colorless liquid, $d_{20\circ}1.218$, m.8.6, b.100.8, miscible with water. Contained in ants, spiders, and various plants; a reagent for nitrates in water and the analysis of essential oils. **acetyl-** Pyruvic acid. **amidobenzoyl-** Isatic acid. **amino-** Carbamic acid. **benzoyl-** Benzoylformic acid. **carbamyl-** Oxamic acid. **carbobenzoyl-** Phthalonic acid. **formyl-** Glyoxylic acid. **hydrazino-** Carbazic acid. **hydrazobis-** Bicarbamic acid. **hydroxy-** Carbonic acid. **phenyl-** Benzoic acid. **styryl-** Cinnamic acid.

  f. aldehyde. Formaldehyde. **f. nitrile.** Hydrocyanic acid.

formin. The glycerol esters of formic acid; e.g., mono- $C_3H_5(OH)_2OOCH$, tri- $C_3H_5(OOCH)_3$. **bromoethyl-** Bromalin.

formine. Hexamethyleneamine. **f. salicylate.** Saliformin.

formohydrazide*. Formylhydrazine.

Formol. Trademark for an antiseptic solution of formaldehyde in methanol and water. **f. nitrogen.** The nitrogen of unsubstituted amino groups in the protein molecule which combines with formaldehyde. **f. titration.** The determination of amino acids by titration with an alkali, with formaldehyde added to annul the alkalinity of the amino group. **f. toxoid.** F.T. A preparation produced by treating a toxin with formaldehyde solution until its specific toxicity has been removed. Used to diagnose diphtheria. Cf. *Schick test.*

Formolide. A commercial antiseptic: alcohol 15, boric acid 2, sodium benzoate 0.5, and formaldehyde 0.25% in water.

formolite. A yellow, nonfusible, solvent-insoluble resin made by the action of aromatic compounds on formaldehyde in presence of concentrated sulfuric acid. Used in paints, inks, and adhesives.

formonitrile. Hydrocyanic acid.

formonitrolic acid. $(NO_2):CH\cdot NOH = 90.03$. Methylnitrolic acid, nitroformoxime. Colorless crystals, m.64, soluble in water.

formose. Isofructose.

formoxime. $HCH:NOH = 45.03$. Formaldoxime, Colorless liquid, b.84, decomp. in hot water. **nitro-** Formonitrolic acid.

formoxyl. Formyl. **f. hydride.** Formic acid.

formoyl. Methanoyl. The $H\cdot COO—$ group.

formula. A combination of chemical symbols expressing the composition of a molecule. Formulas indicate: (1) the kind of elements and the number of atoms, (2) the weight relations of these elements and the molecular weight, (3) the percentage by weight of the elements present, (4) the valency of the elements. Formulas for gases and vapors also indicate (5) the volume relations, (6) the density, (7) the weight of one liter, (8) the volume occupied by one gram. Thus, chemical formula H_2O means: (*a*) A molecule of water consists of 2 atoms of H

FORMULA SIGNS

·   Points in the center of the line separate composite groups or radicals ($CH_3 \cdot COOH$), the constituents of a double salt ($KCl \cdot PtCl_3$).

,   Commas: (1) indicate interchangeable elements; $(Ni,Fe)AsS$ means $FeAsS$ and $NiAsS$ in variable proportion; or separate water of crystallization, e.g., $FeSO_4$, $7H_2O$; (2) separate numbers forming a single chemical series in organic compounds, e.g., 1,2,3-trinitrobenzene. (U.S.P. and B.P. use periods.)

( )   Parentheses group elements together, or indicate radicals, e.g., $(NH_4)_2SO_4$.

+ or ·   Plus signs or upper dots indicate positive charge or cation, K^+ or $NH_4{}^{\cdot}$.

— or ′   Minus signs or primes indicate negative charge or anion, Cl^- or $SO_4{}''$.

→   Arrows indicate direction of reaction.

⇌   Reversible double arrows indicate equilibrium or tendency to react.

*   Asterisks indicate: (1) an excited atom or molecule; (2) a name accepted by the International Union of Pure and Applied Chemistry.

]   Square brackets are used in addition to parentheses, e.g., $Fe_4[Fe(CN)_6]_3$, to indicate radicals; or in coordination formulas, to show the relationship to the central atom.

1, 2, ...   Numeral before a symbol or parenthesis is a multiplier for that symbol; numeral before a formula is a multiplier of the whole formula. Thus $2Al_2(SO_4)_3 \cdot 6H_2O$ means 2 molecules of crystalline aluminum sulfate, together having 6 molecules of water of crystallization.

$A^{1,2,3}$,   Small upper numerals following the symbol of an element indicate the mass number; thus $_1H^2$, $_3Li^6$, etc.

$_{1,2,3}A$ Small lower numerals before the symbol of an element indicate the atomic number: $_1H^2$, $_3Li^6$.

M, X   Letters such as M or X indicate a metal or a halogen. For other abbreviations (not symbols), see *radicals*.

— or = or ≡
. or : or ⋮   Lines or dots, either single, or double, or triple, indicate valence bonds in a structural formula.

:   Double dots also: (1) indicate electron pairs, in the octet formula; (2) separate sets of series of numbers in organic compounds, e.g., 1,2:7,8-dibenzanthrene.

---

and 1 atom of O. (*b*) The molecular weight is the sum of the atomic weights; hence $2 \times 1.0 + 16.0 = 18.0$. (*c*) In 18 pts. by weight water are 2 pts. H (11.11%) and 16 pts. O (88.89%) by weight. (*d*) The valency of H is $+1$; hence 2 atoms are the equivalent of O (valency -2). (*e*) 2 volumes H and 1 volume O combine to give 2 volumes water (vapor). (*f*) The density of water vapor is: (*i*) compared with oxygen, the molecular weight, 18.00; (*ii*) compared with hydrogen, 9.00; (*iii*) compared with air, the molecular weight divided by 28.95; hence 0.622. (*g*) A gram molecule of any gas or vapor occupies 22.4 liters; hence 1 liter water vapor weighs 0.803 gm. (*h*) As 18 gm water vapor occupies 22.4 liters, 1 gm occupies 1.245 liters. Cf. *nomenclature, notation*. See table above.

abbreviated-An abbreviation of radicals; as, Am for ammonium, Ph for phenyl. **atomic-** Structural f. **Beckmann's-** See *Beckmann's reaction*. **coordinate-** An expression indicating the relation of complex compounds to a central atom; thus $[(NH_3)_3 \cdot Co \cdot (NH_3)_2Cl]Cl_2$ shows that 2 Cl atoms are less firmly held by the Co atom. **constitutional-** A notation indicating constitution by valence bonds or the linkage between radicals and atoms, e.g., $C_2H_4 \cdot (COOH)_2$. **dynamic-** See *benzene ring*. **electronic-** A notation that indicates the electropositive or

electronegative character of an atom in a compound. **empirical-** A notation showing the number and kind of atoms without indicating their grouping, e.g., $C_4H_6O_4$. **excitation-** See *excitation*. **general-** An expression representing the formulas of a series of compounds; thus, $M_2X(SO_4)_2 \cdot 12H_2O$ is the general f. for the alums, in which M is a monovalent metal, and X a trivalent metal. C_nH_{2n-2} is the general equation for the methane series. **graphic-** Diagrammatic. A f. showing space relations; as, a tetrahedron for carbon. Cf. *structure, symbol*. **ionic-** The symbol for an electrically charged atom or radical, as Na^+ or $NH_4{}^-$. **molecular-** A formula for a complex compound indicating the participating molecules; thus $NH_3 \cdot HCl$ is the molecular f. for NH_4Cl. **octet-** A f. showing the number of electrons; as $H : \overset{..}{O} : H$. Cf. *Lewis-Langmuir theory*. **polar-** Octet f. **polarity-** A f. which indicates the relative position of the electron pairs held in common between 2 atoms. **rational-** A f. indicating by the use of radicals the intraatomic arrangement; thus $Al_2(SO_4)_3$. **shorthand-** See *structure symbol*. **space-** Stereometric. **stereochemic-** Stereometric f. **stereometric-** A diagram depicting the arrangement of atoms in an optically active compound, e.g.,

Maleic acid

$$H—C—COOH$$
$$\|$$
$$H—C—COOH$$
cis-

Fumaric acid

$$H—C—COOH$$
$$\|$$
$$HOOC—C—H$$
trans-

structural- A f. indicating the spatial structure of a compound and the linkages of its atoms, thus,

$$O=C—O—H$$
$$|$$
$$H—C—H$$
$$|$$
$$H—C—H$$
$$|$$
$$O=C—O—H$$

Cf. *molecular diagram.* **symbolic-** Structure symbol. **transmutation-** See *equation.*

formulary. A selected list of drugs, chemicals, and medicinal preparations with descriptions; tests for identity, purity, and strength; and formulas for preparing them; especially one issued by official authority, and accepted as a standard. Cf. *dispensatory, pharmacopoeia.*

formula symbol. Structure symbol.

formula weight. The molecular weight expressed in grains.

Formvar. Trademark for a polyvinyl formaldehyde plastic.

formyl. (1) The radical HCO—, from formic acid. (2) An obsolete term for methenyl, HC≡. **f. acetic acid.** $C_3H_4O_3 = 88.0$. $CHO \cdot CH_2 \cdot COOH$ **f. aldehyde.** Formaldehyde. **f. amide.** Formamide. **f. bromide.** Bromoform. **f. chloride.** Chloroform. **f. diphenylamine.** $C_{13}H_{11}ON = 197.2$. Colorless crystals, m.73, insoluble in water. **f. hydrazine.** $NH_2NH \cdot CHO = 60.1$. Formohydrazide*. Colorless crystals, m.54, soluble in alcohol. *di-* $C_2H_4O_2N_2 = 88.1$. Colorless crystals, m.106, soluble in alcohol. **f. sulfaldehyde.** $CH_2 \cdot SH \cdot CH_2 \cdot CSSH = 138.2$. Colorless prisms, m.218, sparingly soluble in water. **f. trichloride.** Chloroform. **f. triiodide.** Iodoform.

formylation. The introduction of the formyl radical into an organic compound.

formylene. Methenyl.

formylic acid. Formic acid.

forsterite. Mg_2SiO_4. A white orthorhombic magnesium silicate of the olivine group, containing iron oxide, d.3.2–3.3, hardness 7.

Fortrel. Trademark for a polyester synthetic fiber.

fortified. Strengthened. **f. wine.** (1) Wine to which a fermentable sugar has been added. (2) Wine to which alcohol or wine brandy has been added.

Fortisan. Trademark for regenerated cellulose produced by the simultaneous stretching and deacetylation of cellulose acetate filaments.

fortoin. $CH_2(C_{14}H_{11}O_4)_2 = 500.3$. Methylene dicotoin. Yellow needles of faint cinnamon-like odor, m.211, insoluble in water, soluble in alcohol; an antiseptic and astringent.

foshagite. $5CaO, 3SiO_2, 3H_2O$. A constituent of boiler scale.

fossil. Remains of prehistoric organisms imprinted or entombed in geological formations.

fossil copal. See *copals.*

fossilin. Vaselin.

foto- Photo-.

fotosensin. A condensation product of phthalic acid and resorcinol, with small amounts of copper and iron, used to sensitize plant growth.

fouadin. Fuadin.

Foucault. Jean Bernard Léon. 1819–1868. French physicist. **F. current.** Eddy current. **F. pendulum.** A Galileo pendulum. **F. prism.** A polarizing prism using a thin film of air for reflection. Cf. *nicol prism.*

four-888. Early name for paludrine.

Fourneau 309. Germanin. A complex urea compound used to cure sleeping sickness.

Fowler, Sir Ralph. 1899–1944. British mathematical physicist. **F. solution.** An aromatic solution of potassium arsenite (1% arsenic trioxide); an antiseptic and fur preservative.

fowlerite. (Mn, Fe, Ca, Zn, Mg)SiO_3. A red, brown, or yellow natural triclinic silicate, d.3.4–3.7, hardness 5–6.5.

Fowler's series. For lines of the helium spectrum: $1/\lambda = 4N(1/9 - 1/n^2)$, where n is 4, 5, 6; λ the wavelength; and N a constant.

foxglove. See *digitalis.*

foyaite. A nepheline syelite (Portugal).

f.p. Abbreviation for freezing point.

fps. Abbreviation for foot-pound-second system.

Fr. Symbol for: (1) francium; (2) florentium (obsolete).

fraction. A separated portion of a whole.

fractional. Pertaining to separated parts. **f. column.** Dephlegmator. Same as f. distillation tubes. **f. combustion.** A method of separating gas mixtures by removing one constituent by combustion. **f. condensation.** A method of separating gas mixtures by lowering the temperature or increasing the pressure until one of the gases liquefies. **f. condensation tube.** An air-cooled vertical condenser tube of special shape to promote condensation. **f. crystallization.** A method for separating or purifying compounds in solution by successive slow crystallizations, the mother liquor being removed at each stage for a further crystallization. **f. distillation.** A method of separating volatile substances by collecting separately the distillates evaporating at certain temperatures. **f. distillation tube.** Shaped glass tubes used to collect distillates separately at different temperatures. **f. expression.** The collection of plant oils or juices expressed at different temperatures. **f. filtration.** The filtration of solutions consecutively through coarse, medium, and fine filters. **f. precipitation.** Salting out. **f. weights.** Analytical weights of less than one gram.

fractionating. Separating into parts. **f. column.** Dephlegmator. A device for fractional distillation. Cf. *still head.*

fractionation. Fractional distillation.

fracture. A sharp edge produced on breaking a solid substance. Cf. *cleavage.* **conchoidal-** The irregular fracture of an amorphous body. **crystalline-** A f. producing the plane faces and sharp edges of a crystal, i.e., cleavage.

fragility. Brittleness. The characteristics of easily breaking apart.

francisceine. An alkaloid from the root of *Franciscea uniflora,* Brazilian manaca (Solanaceae); a diuretic and purgative.

francium. Fr = ?. Fa(obsolete). Alabamine.

Actinium-K. The radioelement, at no. 87, formed by the α decay of actinium. Its stablest isotope has a mass number of 223. It is separated from actinium compounds by fractional precipitation with ammonium carbonate on a rare-earth carrier, and its properties are similar to those of cesium. Its longest-lived isotope has a half-life of 21 min. Discovered by Perey (1939); named for France.

Franck-Condon principle. The change in state of an electron in a molecule takes place so rapidly in relationship to the vibrational motion that the separation and velocity of the nuclei are virtually unchanged.

franckeite. $Pb_5FeSn_3Sb_2S_{14}$. A rare, native sulfostibide.

francolite. A calcium phosphite containing calcium carbonate.

frangula. Buckthorn bark, arrow wood. The dried bark of *Rhamnus frangula* (Rhamnaceae); a laxative. **f. emodin.** Emodin.

frangularoside. A rhamnoside from bark of black alder.

frangulic acid. A dihydroxyanthraquinone from frangula.

frangulin. $C_{20}H_{20}O_9 = 404.15$. A glucoside from the bark of *Rhamnus frangula*. Yellow crystals, m.226, insoluble in water.

Frangulineae. Rhamnales. Plants comprising the Rhamnaceae, buckthorn, and Vitaceae, grape, families.

frangulinic acid. Frangulic acid.

frankincense. Olibanum. **American-** An oleoresin from the bark of *Pinus palustris*, common pine. Cf. *colophony, gum thus*.

Frankland, Sir Edward. 1825–1899. British chemist noted for research on organometallic compounds, valency, water supply, the theory of flames; and a co-worker of Lockyer in the discovery of helium in the sun. **F., Percy Faraday.** 1858–1946. British chemist, noted for his work on stereochemistry. **F. notation.** The grouping together of radicals in a formula, and the assumption that certain salts are addition compounds; thus SO_2HO_2 for H_2SO_4. **F. reaction.** The synthesis of hydrocarbons by the zinc-alkyl condensation: $Zn(CH_3)_2 + 2R \cdot Br = 2R \cdot CH_3 + ZnBr_2$.

Franklin, Benjamin. 1706–1790. American statesman and scientist, founder of the American Philosophical Society. **F., Edward Curtis.** 1862–1937. American chemist noted for his theory of the ammonia system, q.v.

franklinic. Static. Cf. *franklinization*.

franklinite. $(Fe,Zn,Mn)Fe_2O_4$. A black, brittle, isometric spinel, d.5–5.1, hardness 6.1–6.5; a source of iron and zinc.

franklinization. The therapeutic application of static electricity.

Frary's metal. An alloy made by electrolytic deposition of barium and calcium in molten lead; used for shrapnel bullets.

Fras fuel. Petroleum in gel form, for flame throwers.

fraserin. The combined principles from the root of *Frasera walteri*, American calumba; a tonic.

Fraude reagent. Perchloric acid.

Fraunhofer, Joseph von. 1787–1826. German physicist. **F. lines.** The dark lines in spectra of the sun and other stars, produced by the absorption of certain rays of the photosphere by incandescent gases of the solar atmosphere. Some 20,000 have been measured, and more than 5,000 identified with chemical elements. F. lines and the corresponding bright emission lines indicate stellar conditions; as, composition, motion, temperature, magnitude, and mass.

fraxetin. $C_{10}H_8O_5 = 208.06$. A crystalline split product of fraxin, m.227.

fraxin. $C_{16}H_{18}O_{18} = 370.14$. A glucoside from the bark of *Fraxinus* and *Aesculus* species, m.190. Colorless needles, soluble in hot water.

fraxinine. $C_{42}H_{36}O_{27} = 972.3$. A bitter, crystalline principle from *Fraxinus excelsior*.

Fraxinus. A genus of trees, including ash. Cf. *manna*.

fraxitannic acid. $C_{26}H_{32}O_{14}(?)$. A tannin from the leaves of the ash, *Fraxinus excelsior*. Brown powder, soluble in water.

free. Uncombined, unattached, or available. **f. acid.** (1) See degree of *acidity*. (2) The hydrochloric acid of stomach juices. **f. charge.** An electric charge on a body, e.g., f. electrons attached to an atom or molecule and not a part of its structure. **f. electron.** An electron taking no part in the chemical constitution of matter. but free to move from one kind of matter to another, as in a galvanic current. **f. energy.** That portion, F, of the total energy which can be utilized for work. $F = (H - TS)$, where H is the heat content (the internal energy + pressure × volume), T the absolute temperature, and S the entropy. **f. path.** The average distance traveled by an electron, ion, or molecule before colliding with another. See *ionization, electron. molecular-* The average distance traveled by a molecule of gas or by an ion in solution between collisions. **f. radical.** An organic compound in which all the valencies are not satisfied, giving an unsaturated molecule; as, triphenyl methyl from hexaphenylethane: $2Ph_3C \rightleftharpoons Ph_3C—CPh_3$. **f. valence.** An unsatisfied bond.

freedom. Variance. In the phase rule: $P + F = C + 2$, where P is the number of phases, C the number of component substances reacting, F the degree of f., an integer which indicates the least number of variable factors (pressure, temperature, or volume) which must be arbitrarily fixed in order to define the state of equilibrium of a chemical system. A one-component solid-liquid-gas system is invariant, i.e., $F = 0$; a one-component liquid-gas system is univariant, $F = 1$; a one-component gas system is bivariant, $F = 2$.

freeness. The extent to which a pulp for the manufacture of paper has not been hydrated by beating, and, therefore, parts with its water by simple drainage. Antonym: *wetness*.

freeze. (1) To lower the temperature until a liquid solidifies. (2) The interlocking of accurately machined and polished steel parts of machinery; it is avoided by chromium plating one part. **deep-** Refrigeration of foods at a very low temperature. **quick-** Rapid refrigeration of foods. The ice crystals formed are relatively small and do not rupture tissues, and the thawed food retains much of the flavor of the original. **f. drying.** A method of drying a substance by freezing it at below 0°C, and removing the water as ice, by sublimation.

freezing. The solidification of a liquid or solution when its temperature is lowered. **f. attachment.** A device attached to microtomes for freezing tissues by liquid or solid carbon dioxide. **f. mixture.** Frigorific mixture. A mixture of substances that absorbs heat and thus lowers the surrounding temperature; e.g.:

Ammonium nitrate 1, anhydrous sodium carbonate 1, water 1 pt.	-10 to $-26°C$
Ammonium chloride 5, powdered ice or snow 10 pts............	-5 to $-18°C$
Sodium chloride 5, ammonium nitrate 5, ice or snow 12 pts......	-15 to $-25°C$
Calcium chloride 3, ice or snow 1 pts........................	-40 to $-70°C$
Sulfuric acid (dilute) 10, ice or snow 8 pts....................	-65 to $-90°C$
Solid carbon dioxide and ether or chloroform..................	$-77°C$

f. point. Solidification or f. temperature. **f. point apparatus.** A device for the accurate determination of f. point, used to determine the concentration of solutions, osmotic pressure, and molecular weight. See *cryoscopy*. **f. point depression.** Solutions freeze at a lower temperature than the pure solvent proportionally to the concentration of the solute. See *Raoult's law*. A solution containing 0.1 gm mole lowers the f. point of water by $-0.186°C$. **f. salt.** Crude sodium chloride.

freibergite. $(Ag,Cu)_3Sb_2S_7 \cdot (Fe,Zn)_4SbS_7$. A gray sulfantimonide, d.4.85–5.

freierslebenite. $(Pb,Ag_2)_5Sb_4S_{11}$. A black, metallic sulfantimonide, d.2–2.5.

Fremy, Edmond. 1814–1894. French chemist noted for developing the manufacture of iron and steel, sulfuric acid, and artificial rubies. **F. salt.** (1) Potassium hydrogen fluoride. (2) Potassium nitrodisulfonate.

French chalk. A hydrated silicate of magnesium.

Freon. Arcton (U.K. usage). Trademark for a group of halogenated hydrocarbons (usually based on methane), containing one or more fluorine atoms; widely used as noncorrosive and nontoxic refrigerants, propellants, and insecticide solvents. **F-2.** Trademark for dichlorofluoromethane. A F. used in heat-transfer tubes. **F-12.** CCl_2F_2. Trademark for dichlorodifluoromethane; used as a refrigerant and propellant.

frequency. (1) The rapidity with which an occurrence, oscillation, or vibration is repeated. (2) The number ν of complete vibrations or waves per unit time, in millicycles per second. Thus $\nu = c/\lambda$, where c is the velocity of light, and λ the wavelength of the ray concerned; e.g., for green light $\nu = 6 \times 10^{14}$ vibrations/sec. F. is related to energy e and mass m by $h\nu = e = mc^2$, and if the energy unit is 9×10^{20} ergs: $F = E = M$. **high-** A rapid vibrating electric current, q.v. **molecular-** The molecular vibrations. See *gas laws*. **radiation-** The f. of the emitted radiation is proportional to the amount of energy radiated; $W_1 - W_2 = E = h\nu$, where W_1 and W_2 are the energy of the atom in the initial and final state, respectively, E is the energy in ergs, and h Planck's constant.

f. curve. "Gauss bell." Histogram. A curve obtained by dividing a number of values obtained for a particular determination into classes differing by a standard amount, and plotting the number of samples in each class against the corresponding values. The maximum gives the most correct result (*median*), and the ends of the series are the *quartiles*; 25 % of the values being in each quartile. Cf. *mean*.

frequentic acid. Citromycetin.

frequentin. $C_{14}H_{20}O_4(?)$. An antibiotic from a strain of *Penicillium frequentans* in heath soils. Colorless needles, m.128, slightly soluble in water.

Fresenius, Karl Remigus. 1818–1897. German chemist. **F. desiccator.** A desiccator with bell-shaped cover. **F. nitrogen bulb.** A conical flask with side tubes having 2 bulbs near the base.

Fresnel, Augustin Jean. 1788–1827. French physicist noted for experiments on light. **f.** A little-used unit of wave frequency, expressed as 10^{12} sec^{-1}.

Freund acid. 3,6,Naphthylaminedisulfonic acid.

Freundlich, Herbert. 1881–1941. German-born chemist, noted for his work on colloid chemistry.

freyalite. A variety of thorite, q.v.

F.R.I.C. Abbreviation for Fellow of the Royal Institute of Chemistry.

friction. The resistance offered to sliding motion by rubbing. **fluid-** Viscosity. **internal-** The resistance to bending of metals due to their crystalline structure. **mechanical-** See *f. coefficient*. **f. coefficient.** f. The relation of the force F necessary just to move an object along a horizontal plane under pressure N: $F = fN$. It depends on the material of the substance, not on the velocity or area of the surface in contact. Cf. *lubricants*.

Friedel, Charles. 1832–1899. French organic chemist.

Friedel-Crafts condensation. The condensation of hydrocarbons and halogen compounds in the presence of anhydrous aluminum chloride according to the F.-C. reaction; e.g., alkyl halides yield hydrocarbons. **F.-C. reaction.** The synthesis of an aromatic hydrocarbon homolog by the catalytic action of aluminum chloride: $R + R'\cdot Cl + AlCl_3 = R \cdot R' + HCl + AlCl_3$.

friedelin. $C_{30}H_{50}O = 426.4$. A sterol from cork related to the hydrocarbon $C_{30}H_{52}$.

Friedrichs condenser. A condensing worm surrounded by a glass or metal tube. **F. gas bottle.** A glass cylinder with a spiral tube for washing gases.

frieseite. $Ag_2Fe_5S_8$. A rare, native sulfide.

frigid. Cold.

frigidity. Coldness.

frigorific. Describing an agent that produces coldness. **f. mixture.** Freezing mixture.

Frilon. Trade name for a polyamide synthetic fiber.

fringes. The dark, parallel, equidistant lines observed in the interferometer.

fringe tree bark. Chionanthus.

frit. (1) Enamel. A complex alkaline borosilicate glass, usually containing fluorine, produced by melting a mixture such as borax, feldspar, quartz, and cryolite. (2) To sinter.

fritted, frittered. Having been heated near the melting point. **f. glass.** Glass powder heated sufficiently for the particles to adhere together without coalescing completely; used in filters. **fritting.** Becoming pasty and beginning to melt; as, some soft coals.

Froehde reagent. A reagent for alkaloids: 5 mg molybdic acid in 1 ml hot concentrated sulfuric acid.

frost. Dew produced in frozen form. **hoar-** F. produced at a dew point of less than 32°F.

froth. Foam. **iron-** Spongy hematite.

frother. A chemical used in the flotation process. Thus, pine oil produces a thin transient foam; cresylic acid, a heavy permanent foam.

frothing. Foaming. **f. agent.** A substance which produces a froth when shaken with a liquid; as, saponin.

F.R.S. Abbreviation for Fellow of the Royal Society of London.

fructigenin. $C_{26}H_{45}O_7N_2 = 497.44$. An antibiotic pigment produced by *Fusaria*.

fructosamine. $CH_2OH(CHOH)_3CONH_2 = 179.11$. *i*-Dextrosamine, *i*-glucosamine. Colorless syrup, insoluble in alcohol.

fructosans. Sugar anhydrides which hydrolyse to fructose. Cf. *hemicellulose*.

fructose. $C_6H_{12}O_6 = 180.13$. Levulose, fruit sugar, *l*-fructose. A carbohydrate in sweet fruits and honey. Colorless needles, m.94, soluble in water, alcohol, or ether; a preservative. **dextro-** *d*-Fructose. **inactive-** *i*-Fructose, acrose, or formose. An unfermentable carbohydrate formed by polymerization of formaldehyde in limewater. **levo-** *l*-Fructose or levulose. **pseudo-** Allulose.

$$
\begin{array}{ccc}
CH_2OH & CH_2OH & CH_2OH \\
| & | & | \\
C\!=\!O & C\!=\!O & C\!=\!O \\
| & | & | \\
HOCH & HCOH & HCOH \\
| & | & | \\
HCOH & HOCH & HCOH \\
| & | & | \\
HCOH & HOCH & HCOH \\
| & | & | \\
CH_2OH & CH_2OH & CH_2OH \\
l\text{-} & d\text{-} & i\text{-}
\end{array}
$$

fructoside. A glucoside which hydrolyzes to fructose.

fruit. The ripened ovary of a plant together with parts of the flower that share in its development. Some used medicinally; e.g.: anise, caraway, fig, hops, orange, pepper, vanilla. See also *seeds*.

fruit essence. An artificial mixture imitating the taste of a fruit, and consisting of esters of alkyl radicals with organic acids, usually in dilute alcoholic solution. **f. oil.** See *oil*. *apple-* Chiefly amyl valerate. *banana-* Chiefly amyl acetate. *pear-* Chiefly amyl acetate. *pineapple-* Chiefly ethyl butyrate.

fruit sugar. Fructose.

ft. Abbreviation for foot. $ft.^2$ = square foot. $ft.^3$ = cubic foot.

fuadin. Fouadin, stibophen, neoantimosan. Sodium antimony-bispyrocatechol-3,5-sodium disulfonate. See *stibophen*.

fuchsin. $C_{20}H_{19}N_3HCl = 337.8$. Magenta red, rosaniline hydrochloride, aniline red, azaleine, harmaline, rosein, erythrobenzene, rubine, solferino. A red dyestuff, a mixture of the hydrochlorides of rosaniline and pararosaniline. Red rhombs, with green fluorescence, soluble in water; a dyestuff, coloring matter for inks and microscopical stains.

acid- A mixture of the disulfonic and trisulfonic acids of pararosaniline; a dye and stain. **English-** A mixture of the acetates of rosaniline and pararosaniline; a dyestuff. **German-** Fuchsin.

fuchsite. $H_2KAl_3(SiO_4)_3Cr$. A variety of muscovite.

fuchsone. $C_{19}H_{14}O = 258.1$. Quinonediphenylmethane. $O:C_6H_4:C(C_6H_5)_2$. An intermediate in the manufacture of rosaniline dyes.

fucitol. $C_6H_{14}O_5 = 166.11$. A sweet alcohol, m.153, from fucus.

fucoiden. A mucilaginous constituent of seaweed, $R-R'-O\cdot SO_3M$, where R is fucose, R' another carbohydrate complex, and M is Na, K, Mg, or Cu.

fucosan. A fucose polymer in the cell walls of marine algae.

fucose. $C_5H_9MeO_5 = 164.09$. 2,3,4,5-Tetrahydroxyhexanal*. Colorless crystals from fucus, m.145, soluble in water; an isomer of rhodeose.

fucosite. The least water-soluble portion of seaweed, containing fucose, algarose, and an oil. **pseudo-** Elkerite.

fucoxanthin. $C_{40}H_{56}O_6 = 632.5$. A carotenoid pigment from brown algae. Red crystals, m.160.

fucus. Bladder wrack, sea wrack. The dried thallus of *Fucus vesiculosus* (Fucaceae), seaweed; an alterative and resolvent.

fucusamide. Fucusine.

fucusine. $C_{15}H_{12}O_3N_2 = 268.2$. Fucusamine. A crystalline alkaloid from fucus.

fucusol. $C_5H_4O_2 = 96.1$. A colorless oil, resembling furfurol, distilled from seaweed.

fuel. A material that furnishes heat on combustion. Classification: *Natural* or *solid f.*; as wood, peat, lignite, coal, q.v. *Prepared* or *dried f.*; as, briquets and compressed fuels. *Liquid f.*; as, petroleum, gasoline. See table. *Gaseous f.*; as, coal or water gas. **fossil-** F. derived from coal, lignite, peat, natural gas, oil, shales, or tar sands. **Fras-** q.v. **metallic-** Finely powdered magnesium or aluminum. Cf. *Thermit*. **spiked-** Plutonium or highly enriched uranium, used to stop the neutron discharge in a nuclear reaction. **standard-** A concept used in costing to make f. of different calorific values comparable. Each pound in a ton of s.f. is equivalent to 10,000 B.Th.U.

　f. cell. A means of converting the energy of a f. directly into electric energy without use of a heat engine; e.g., the catalytic conversion of H and O into water. **f. gases.** The compressed gases used for welding and cutting metals; as, Blaugas, butane, coal gas. **f. oil.** Crude petroleum.

fugacity. The escaping tendency of a substance in a heterogeneous mixture which enables a chemical equilibrium to respond to altered conditions. In a dilute solution obeying the gas laws, the f. equals the osmotic pressure. In others it is the pressure for which these laws are still valid. Cf. *activity*.

fugin. Fugutoxin, tetrodonine. A poisonous protein from the fish *Tetrodon* species (Japan, China).

fugitive. Unstable; not fast (as a color).

fugitometer. An apparatus for rapidly testing colored materials for fastness to light. Cf. *fademeter*.

fugugetin. $C_{17}H_{12}O_6\cdot 5H_2O = 402.5$. The coloring matter of fukugi, *Garcinia spicata* (Japan), m.288. Cf. *garcinin*.

fugutoxin. Fugin.

PROPERTIES OF LIQUID FUELS

Fuel	Specific gravity at 15°C	Viscosity, cgs units at 20°C	Boiling point, °C	Calorific value, cal/gm	Flash point, °C	Composition, %			
						C	H	O	S
Methyl alcohol	0.796	0.0075	64.6	4,762	—	37.5	12.5	50.0	—
Ethyl alcohol	0.794	0.0151	78.3	6,403	—	52.0	13.0	35.0	—
Benzole mixture.....	0.878	0.0072	86.0	9,600	— 9	91.6	8.1	—	0.3
Aviation petrol......	0.720	0.0062	84	10,510	—	85.0	15.0	—	0.01
Petrol no. 1.........	0.740	0.0068	104	10,500	—	85.3	14.7	—	0.02
Petrol no. 3.........	0.745	0.0076	112	10,430	—	85.5	14.5	—	0.03
Tractor oil.........	0.780	0.0140	166	10,420	37	86.3	13.7	—	0.01
Kerosene	0.793	0.0160	196	10,420	40	86.3	13.6	—	0.08
Diesel oil	0.870	0.049	300	10,300	75	86.3	12.8	—	0.9
Light fuel oil.......	0.895	0.50	348	10,050	80	86.2	12.4	—	1.4
Heavy fuel oil.......	0.949	12.0	360	9,880	110	86.0	11.9	—	2.1
Heptane...........	0.691	0.0058	98	10,710	—	84.0	16.0	—	—
Methylated spirit	0.832	0.012	76	7,170	— 8	59.5	11.6	28.9	—
Methylated spirit (commercial)......	0.824	0.011	74	8,190	— 12	70.7	11.5	17.8	—

Fulcher spectrum. That portion of the hydrogen spectrum which consists of many fine lines due to a lower excitation level of the H_2 molecule.

fulgenic acids. The compounds $R_2C{:}C(COOH){\cdot}C(COOH){:}CR_2$, in which R is a hydrogen, alkyl, or aryl radical.

fulgides. Anhydrides of fulgenic acids, of the type

$$\begin{array}{c} R_2C{:}C{\cdot}CO \\ | \qquad\qquad\quad >O. \\ R_2C{:}C{\cdot}CO \end{array}$$

They are phototropic. **diphenyl-** A form (yellow-green) ⇌ B form (blue). **triphenyl-** A form (orange) ⇌ B form (blue).

fulgaration. Melting together, with an electric spark. Cf. *fritting*.

fulgurator. An atomizer of solutions for producing flame spectra.

fulgurite. Fritted sand produced by lightning passing through the soil.

fuller's earth. Calcium montmorillonite. An impure kaolin containing magnesium and iron used for decolorizing solutions and oils, as a substitute for absorbent charcoal, and as a dusting powder.

full gas. A class of combustible gases, consisting of saturated hydrocarbons, e.g., water gas.

fulmar oil. An oil from *Procellaria glacialis*, a seabird (U.K.); a substitute for cod-liver oil.

fulmargin. A colloidal solution of silver.

fulminate. A salt of fulminic acid containing the radical CNO—. **silver.** Ag·CNO = 149.89. White explosive needles.

fulminates. Salts of fulminic acid. General formula: MONC. Used to detonate high explosives.

fulminating. Causing detonation or explosion. **f. caps.** Small amounts of fulminates used to explode the charge of shells, etc.; usually containing mercuric fulminate. **f. gold.** Aurodiamine. **f. powder.** Percussion powder.

fulminic acid. C:N·O·H = 43.0. Paracyanic acid, ψ-isocyanic acid. An isomer of cyanic acid known only as its very explosive salts.

fulminurate. A salt of fulminuric acid.

fulminuric acid. CN·CH(NO₂)·CONH₂ = 129.14. 2-Cyano-2-nitroethanamide*, isocyanuric acid, cyanonitroacetamide. Colorless needles, m.138,

explode 145, soluble in water; a trimer of cyanuric acid.

fulvalene. The theoretical, unknown hydrocarbon

fulvene. (1) C_6H_6 = 78.1. Methylenecyclopentadiene. An isomer of benzene; a yellow oil.

$$\begin{array}{c} CH{=}CH \\ | \qquad\qquad >C{=}CH_2 \\ CH{=}CH \end{array}$$

(2) A general term for colored products formed on exposure of indanthrene resins to light. **benzo-** See *benzofulvene*.

fumaramic acid. NH₂CO·CH:CH·COOH = 115.1. Colorless crystals, m.217.

fumaramide. NH₂CO·CH:CH·CONH₂ = 114.1. Colorless crystals, m.266.

fumarhydrazide. $C_4H_6O_2N_4$ = 142.1. Colorless crystals, m.220.

fumaria. The dried herb of *Fumaria officinalis*, common fumitory; a sedative and alterative.

Fumariaceae. A family of herbs yielding alkaloids; e.g.: *Corydalis tuberosa* (corydaline), *Fumaria officinalis* (fumarine).

fumaric acid. (H·C·COOH)₂ = 116.05. *trans*-Butenedioic acid*, in *Fumaria officinalis*; an isomer of maleic acid. Colorless prisms, m.286, slightly soluble in water. Used to manufacture polyester and alkyd resins, and to replace citric acid in foodstuffs. **ethyl-** $C_6H_8O_4$ = 144.1. Ethylethylenedicarboxylic acid. Colorless crystals, m.194. **methyl-** Mesaconic acid.

f. acid series. $C_nH_{2n-4}O_4$. A group of dibasic acids with a double bond and many isomers. See *maleic*, *glutaconic*, *allylmalonic*, *allylsuccinic*, and *xeronic* acids.

fumarine. $C_{21}H_{19}O_4N$ = 349.2. Protopine. An alkaloid from *Fumaria officinalis* (Papaveraceae). Colorless crystals, m.199, insoluble in water; an antiphlogistic.

FUNGICIDES

Common name or code number	Chemical name	Type of commodity treated	Persistence and site of action
A. Inorganic Compounds			
Bordeaux mixture	Chemical combination of copper sulfate and lime	Growing plants: U.K. and overseas	Persistent; contact
Burgundy mixture..........	Chemical combination of copper sulfate and sodium carbonate in water	Growing plants: U.K. and overseas	Persistent; contact
Copper compounds..........	Various compounds such as copper oxychloride, copper carbonate, and copper oxide	Growing plants, seeds: U.K. and overseas	Persistent; contact
Sulfur.....................	Elemental sulfur in various physical forms	Growing plants, seeds: U.K. and overseas	Persistent; contact
Lime sulfur	Mixture containing calcium polysulfides	Growing plants, seeds: U.K. and overseas	Persistent; contact
Corrosive sublimate........	Mercuric chloride	Growing plants, soils: U.K. and overseas	Persistent; contact
Calomel	Mercurous chloride	Seed: U.K. and overseas	Persistent; contact
B. Dithiocarbamate Compounds			
Ferbam	Ferric dimethyldithio-carbamate	Growing plants: U.K. and overseas	Semipersistent; contact
Ziram.....................	Zinc dimethyldithio-carbamate	Growing plants: U.K. and overseas	Semipersistent; contact
Nabam....................	Disodium ethylenebis-(dithiocarbamate)	Growing plants: U.K. and overseas	Semipersistent; contact
Zineb	Zinc ethylenebis-(dithiocarbamate)	Growing plants: U.K. and overseas	Semipersistent; contact

fumaroid. A structural arrangement of ethylene derivatives characterized by trans-isomerism:

$$\begin{array}{c} H \\ \diagdown \\ X \diagup \end{array} C = C \begin{array}{c} X \\ \diagup \\ \diagdown H \end{array}. \quad \text{Cf. } \textit{malenoid.}$$

fumarole. A small hole from which volcanic gases and vapors escape. **f. acid.** Boric acid. **f. gases.** The vapors escaping from fumaroles; those of Italy contain steam, boric acid, carbon dioxide, ammonia, and hydrogen sulfide.

fumaryl. The radical —OC·CH:CH·CO—, from fumaric acid. **f. chloride.** $C_4H_2O_2Cl_2$ = 152.9. Colorless liquid, d.1.410, b.160.

fume. Visible or invisible particles of solid or liquid suspended in a gas. **f. cupboard.** A safety-glass-enclosed shelf or table, with a ventilating device, for experiments involving poisonous or unpleasant fumes or gases.

fumigacin. Helvolic acid. An antibiotic from strains of *Aspergillus fumigatus.* Cf. *fumigatin.*

fumigant. A gaseous insecticide, or a substance producing one; as, chloropicrin 0.8, ethylene oxide 2.0, trichloroethylene 7.0, vinyl chloride 8.0. The figures indicate the pounds per 1,000 ft³ to destroy all insects and larvae in 24 hr at 75–80°F. **food-**

A f. used to destroy insect pests on foodstuffs; as, ethylene oxide.

fumigate. To disinfect by means of vapors or smokes.

fumigatin. $C_8H_8O_4$ = 168.1. 3-Hydroxy-4-methoxy-2,5-toluquinone. Maroon crystals, m.116, in cultures of *Aspergillus fumigatus*; an antibiotic. Cf. *penicillin.*

fumigation. Disinfection by means of volatile substances.

fuming. Emitting smoke or vapors.

function. (1) Any specific power. (2) Physiology: the work or purpose of an organ. (3) Mathematics: one quantity is a function of another when for each value of the latter, y, there corresponds a definite value of the former, x. Thus $x = f(y)$. **chemical-** (1) *simple-* Describes a substance containing only one type of radical, which may, however, be repeated several times in the same molecule e.g., polyhydroxy alcohol. (2) *complex-* Describes a molecule having 2 or more different types of radicals; as, amino acids.

fundament. The foundation or basis of a structure, either physical or mental.

fundamental. Pertaining to the basis for groundwork. **f. chain.** The longest chain of a branched hydrocarbon. **f. units.** Units of measurement to

FUNGICIDES (continued)

Common name or code number	Chemical name	Type of commodity treated	Persistence and site of action
	C. Organo-mercury Compounds		
PMC....................	Phenylmercuric chloride	Growing plants: U.K. and overseas	Persistent; contact
PMA....................	Phenylmercuric acetate	Growing plants: U.K. and overseas	Persistent; contact
Aliphatic mercury compounds	Various compounds such as ethylmercuric chloride, iodide, and phosphate	Seed: U.K. and overseas	Persistent; contact
Aromatic mercury compounds	Various complex compounds such as hydroxymercuric cresol	Seed: U.K. and overseas	Persistent; contact
	D. Miscellaneous Organic Compounds		
Thiram...................	Bis(dimethylthiocarbamyl) disulfide	Growing plants, soil, seed: U.K. and overseas	Semipersistent; contact
Tecnazene	Tetrachloronitrobenzene	Seed (potatoes): U.K. and overseas	Sprout-depressant
Salicylanilide..............	Salicylanilide	Growing plants: U.K. and overseas	Persistent; contact
Captan...................	N-Trichloromethylthiotetra-hydrophthalimide	Growing plants: overseas	Persistent; contact
341-SC	Heptadecylglyoxalidine	Growing plants: overseas	Persistent; contact
Chloranil	Tetrachloro-p-benzoquinone	Growing plants, seed; overseas	Persistent; contact
Dichloronaphthoquinone.....	2,3-Dichloro-1,4-naphtho-quinone	Growing plants, seed; overseas	Persistent; contact
Formalin	Formaldehyde	Soils: U.K. and overseas	Semipersistent; surface contact

which all physical phenomena may be reduced, i.e.;

L = length; L^2 = surface; L^3 = volume
M = mass; M/L^3 = density
T = time; LMT = velocity, acceleration
K = dielectric constant
μ = magnetic permeability
θ = temperature
Cf. *dimensional equation.*

fungi. Plural of fungus.

fungicide. An agent that destroys spores and fungi. See table, from "Toxic Chemicals in Agriculture, H.M. Stationery Office, London, 1953. Cf. *herbicide, insecticide, rodenticide.*

fungisterin. Fungisterol.

fungisterol. $C_{25}H_{40}O$ = 356.3. Fungisterin. An inert alcohol in ergot; colorless, waxy masses, m.144.

fungizone. A polyene antibiotic from a strain of *Streptomyces nodosus.*

fungus. (Pl. fungi.) (1) A main division of *Thallophyta* or primitive plants, either parasitic or saprophytic, distinguished from *Algae* by the absence of chlorophyll; e.g.: *Eumycetes* (mushrooms), *Schizomycetes* (bacteria), *Phycomycetes* (alga-like fungi), *Blastomycetes* (yeasts), *Hypomycetes* (molds). (2) Popularly, the mushrooms and toadstools. **f. dyestuff.** A pigment obtained from a f.; as litmus.

funnel. A glass tube with one enlarged, and usually conical end. **Buchner-** A porcelain f. having a flat perforated round bottom; used for rapid filtration by suction. **double wall-** A metal f. with 2 walls, between which hot water or steam is circulated. Used for hot filtration. **dropping-** A separatory f., with long stem and glass stopcock. **Hirsch-** A porcelain f. with a fixed porcelain plate. **hot-air-** Double-wall f. **hot-water-** Double-wall f. **separatory-** A f. of varied shape with a stopcock on its stem; used to separate immiscible liquids. **tap-** Separatory f.

funnel tube. A glass tube with a conical or thistle-shaped top; used to convey liquids into a chemical apparatus.

fur. (1) Abbreviation for furlong. (2) The hairy coat of animals.

furac. See *lead* and *zinc dithiofuroates.*

Furacin. Trademark for a brand of nitrofurazone, 5-nitro-2-furaldehyde semicarbazone, an antibacterial; used to treat bovine mastitis.

furacrolein. Furfur acrolein.

furacrylic. Furanacrylic.

fural. Furfural, furfurylidene. The radical $O\cdot CH:CH\cdot CH:C\cdot CH=$, from furfural; 2 isomers.

furaldehyde. Furfural.

furan. $C_4H_4O = 68.05$. Furfuran, tetrol,

HC—O—CH (α).
HC——CH (β)

Colorless liquid, b.31, insoluble in water; in conifer tar. **dimethyl-** $C_6H_8O = 96.1$. Colorless liquid, b.94, soluble in water. A tanning agent and solvent for polyvinyl plastics. **methyl-** Sylvan. **tetrahydro-** Butylene oxide. **thio-** Thiophen. **f. carbinol.** Furfuralcohol. **f. carboxylic acid.** 2- Pyromucic acid. 3- Furoic acid. **f. dione.** Maleic anhydride. **f. methylamine.** Furfurylamine.

furanacrylic acid. $C_7H_6O_3 = 138.05$. β-2-Furylacrylic acid. White crystals, m.141, insoluble in water.

furandione. Maleic anhydride.

furanose. A sugar having a furan ring; as, γ-glucose.

furanoside. A glucoside derived from pentoses, having a furan ring; as, adenosine.

furantin. Nitrofurantoin (B.P.).

furazan. $C_2H_2ON_2 = 70.1$. Azoxazole, oxdiazole. **methylethyl-** $C_6H_8ON_2 = 124.1$. Colorless liquid, b.170. **phenyl-** $C_8H_6ON_2 = 146.2$. Phenyl-1,2,5-oxidazole. Colorless crystals, m.30.
   f. carboxylic acid. $C_3H_2O_3N_2 = 114.2$. Colorless crystals, m.107. **methyl-** $C_4H_4O_3N_2 = 128.2$. Colorless crystals, m.74. **f. dicarboxylic acid.** $C_4H_2O_5N_2 = 158.2$. Colorless crystals, m.178. **f. propionic acid.** $C_5H_6O_3N_2 = 142.2$. Colorless crystals, m.86.

furfuracrolein. $C_7H_6O_2 = 122.1$. Colorless crystals, m.51.

furfural. (1) $C_4H_3O\cdot CHO = 96.06$. α-Furfuraldehyde, furol, furfurol, furfuryl aldehyde, 2-furancarbonal, 2-furaldehyde. Colorless liquid, turning yellow on standing, d_{22}1.159, m.-36, b.161, soluble in water. Used as a reagent for urea, alkaloids, santonin, cholesterol, ketones, or phenols, and in organic synthesis and plastics manufacture. (2) Fural. **3-,** 3-Furancarbonal. A liquid of benzaldehyde odor, d.1.111, b.144.

furfuralcohol. $C_4H_3O\cdot CH_2OH = 98.07$. Furancarbinol. A solid, m.200 (sublimes), soluble in water.

furfuraldehyde. Furfural.

furfuramide. $C_{15}H_{12}O_3N_2 = 268.11$. Furfuryl amide. Colorless crystals, m.121, decomp. 250; an isomer of furfurine.

furfuran. Furan.

furfurine. $C_{15}H_{12}O_3N_2 = 268.1$. Brown rhombs, m.116, insoluble in water. An isomer of furfuramide.

furfuroin. $C_{16}H_8O_3 = 176.1$. Furfuryl-furfural, furfuryl-fural. The compound,

CH—O—C—CO·CH$_2$·C—O—CH
  CH·CH   CH·CH

furfurol(e). Furfural.

furfurostilbene. $C_{10}H_8O_2 = 160.1$. Colorless crystals, m.101.

furfuryl. The radical C_5H_5O—, from furfural; 2

isomers:

HC—O—C·CH$_2$—.   HC—O—CH
  CH·CH   CH·C—CH$_2$—
  alpha-   beta-

f. acetate. $CH_3COO\cdot C_5H_5O$. Colorless liquid, b.176, insoluble in water; a solvent. **f. alcohol.** $C_5H_5O\cdot CH_2OH = 98.08$. Furylcarbinol. Colorless liquid, b.170, soluble in water; a lacquer solvent. **f. aldehyde.** Furfural. **f. amide.** Furfuramide. **f. amine.** $C_5H_7ON = 97.1$ Colorless liquid, b.145. soluble in water. **f. fural.** Furfuroin. **f. methyl ether.** $C_6H_8O_2 = 112.1$. Colorless liquid, b.135.

furfurylidene. Fural.

furil. $C_4H_3O\cdot CO\cdot CO\cdot C_4H_3O = 190.1$. Difurylglyoxal, bipyromucil. Yellow needles, m.165, insoluble in water. Cf. *furoin*. **f. dioxime.** A color reagent for copper.

furlong. An eighth part of one mile.

furnace. An apparatus for heating, fusing, or hardening materials by exposing them to high temperatures. Classification: see table below

Furnace	Fuel	Combustion products
Blast	+	+
Reverbatory	−	+
Muffle	−	−

  + In contact with the charge.
  − Not in contact with the charge.

arc- A device for obtaining high temperatures by an electric arc. **blast-** A tall oven, in which molten iron is produced by heating a mixture of iron ore and coal by a blast of hot air. **combustion-** An oven, elongated to take a horizontal combustion tube, and heated by a row of burners or a coil of resistance wire; used in organic analysis. **crucible-** A device for heating crucibles by gas, oil, or electricity. **electric-** See *arc-* or *resistance-*. **Héroult-** An electric arc f. used for the reduction of iron. **induction-** A f. heated from outside by electrically induced currents. **muffle-** A f. of refractory material, and completely enclosed except for a small air inlet. **reducing-** (1) A shaft f. in which ores are reduced to metals. Cf. *aludel*. (2) A f. in which an atmosphere of reducing gases is maintained. **resistance-** (1) A modified arc f., in which the electrodes dip into the heated material. (2) A wire-wound electrical resistance coil embedded in a refractory material. **reverberatory-** A f. for roasting ores, so constructed that the flame and hot gases are reflected by the curved roof into direct contact with the material to be heated, which is not contaminated by solid fuel. **revolving-** A sloping, revolving metal cylinder lined with firebricks, down which the charge passes and up which the hot gases are driven. **roasting-** q.v. **tank-** A large oil- or gas-heated container in which glass is melted.

furoates. The esters of furoic acid, used in perfumery.

furodiazole. Oxdiazole.

furoic acid. Pyromucic acid. **f. acid esters.** See *furoates*.

furoin. $C_4H_3O \cdot CHOH \cdot CO \cdot C_4H_3O = 192.1$. A condensation product of furfuran. Colorless crystals, m.135.

furol. Furfural.

furomonazole. **a-** Isoxazole. **b-** Oxazole.

Furon. Trade name for a polyamide synthetic fiber.

furonic acid. $C_7H_8O_3 = 140.1$. Furfurylacetic acid. Colorless crystals, soluble in water.

furoyl. **2-** Pyromucyl. **3-** The radical

$$CH:CH \cdot O \cdot CH:C \cdot CO\text{---}.$$

furyl. The radical $\text{---}C_4H_3O$; 2 isomers:

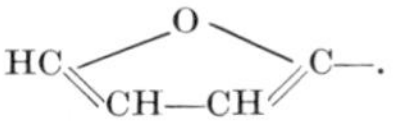

alpha- 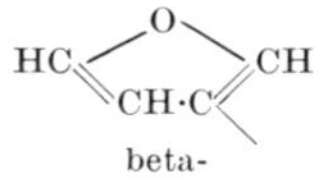   beta-

Cf. *furfuryl.* **f. acrolein.** $(C_4H_3O)CH:CH \cdot CHO = 122.05$. 3(2-Furyl) propenal*. Yellow crystals, m.51, insoluble in water. **f. alcohol.** Furfuralcohol.

furylidene. The radicals:

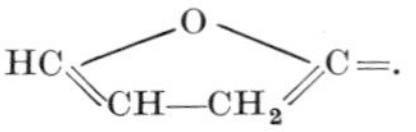

α- or 2(3)- 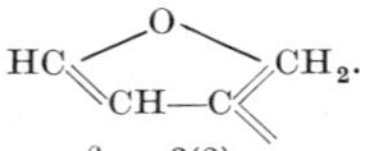   β- or 3(2)-

fusafungine. Locabiotal. An antibiotic from *Fusarium lateritium* 437.

fusain. Mineral charcoal. Mother of coal. See *coal.*

fuschin. Magenta, erythrobenzene.

fuscochlorin. A dark green pigment from algae.

fuscorhodin. A dark red pigment from algae.

fuse. (1) To melt. (2) A safety device for electrical instruments; a fine wire which melts when the electric current becomes too strong. (3) Fuze. A device for igniting an explosive charge. **Abel-** An ignition f. consisting of potassium perchlorate and copper sulfate, and ignited by an electric current. **combination-** A military f. for shells consisting of a time f. and concussion f. **electric-** A device for igniting an explosive charge by electric sparks, e.g., Abel f. **concussion-** An explosive mixture which ignites by concussion, e.g.,

fulminates. **time-** A slow-burning material, which ignites an explosive mixture after a certain time.

fused. Cooled to a compact mass after having been molten or sintered; as slag.

fused ring. A polycyclic compound in which 2 rings have 2 atoms in common, e.g., naphthalene.

fusel oil. Potato spirit, fermentation amyl alcohol. A crude mixture of isoamyl, amyl, butyl, and propyl alcohols, obtained in spiritous fermentation; a source of amyl acetate.

fusibility. The property of becoming liquid when heated.

fusible. Capable of being melted. **f. alloys.** An alloy having a melting point lower than the mean melting poing of the constituents, e.g., Wood's alloy. **f. metals.** A metal or alloy of relatively low melting point.

fusidic acid. An antibiotic from strains of *Fusidium.*

fusing. Melting. **f. point.** Melting point.

fusinites. Highly carbonized cuticular residues in coal. Cf. *exinites.*

fusion. The act of melting or flowing together. **alkaline-** The substitution of the $\text{---}SO_3H$ group of an organic compound by an $\text{---}OH$ group by action of concentrated caustic soda, followed by treatment with acid. **aqueous-** The liquefaction of a substance below 100°C, by solution in its water of crystallization. **false-** Aqueous-. **nuclear-** A process analogous to fission, q.v., in which heat is liberated by the f. of light elements by accelerating them to speeds equivalent to temperatures of over 10^6°C. **watery-** Aqueous.

f. heat. See *heat* of f. **f. mixture.** A mixture of sodium and potassium carbonates; fused with insoluble substances of high melting points to render them soluble as carbonates. **f. point.** Melting point.

fustic. (1) **old-** Yellow brazilwood, fustic wood. The wood of *Morus tinctoria* (Urticaceae), S. America; used to make morin and in drying textiles. (2) **young-** The wood of *Rhus cotinus* (Anacardiaceae). Cf. *morin.*

fustin. (1) $C_{58}H_{46}O_{23} = 1110.4$. A glucoside from the wood of *Rhus cotinus* (Anacardiaceae). Silvery needles, m.218, hydrolyzed to fisetin. (2) The coloring matter of the male fern, *Aspidium filix-mas.* (3) A coloring matter from sumac. (4) The coloring matter of fustic.

fuze. Fuse (3).

G

g. Abbreviation for gram (B.P. usage).

g. A mathematical constant expressing the acceleration of a body due to gravitation. It is calculated for any latitude by Helmert's formula. *g* at sea level and equator = 978.038 cm/sec^2; at latitude 45° = 980.624 cm/sec^2.

G. (1) The newtonian constant of gravitation: $G = (6.65786 \pm 0.0017) \times 10^{-8}$ dyne-cm^2/g^2. (2) Thermodynamic potential.

γ. Greek gamma. Symbol indicating: (1) the third carbon atom of an aliphatic chain; (2) in the naphthalene ring, the position opposite the α-position. (3) 10^{-6} gm. (4) 10^{-4} gauss. *γ* **rays.** See *gamma rays.*

G. Abbreviation for: (1) yellow (gelb) in describing proprietary colors; (2) giga.

G-4. DDM.

Ga. Symbol for gallium.

Gabbet solution. A solution of 2 gm methylene blue in 25 gm sulfuric acid and 75 ml water; a bacteriological stain.

gabbro. Igneous rocks consisting of plagioclase and pyroxenes.

gabianol. A brown oil from natural shale, formerly used to treat diseases of the lung.

G-acid. 2-Naphthol-6,8-disulfonic acid.

gadinine. $C_7H_{16}NO_2$ = 146.1. A ptomaine from putrefying fish.

gadol. Suggested name for vitamin A (from *Gadus,* the cod). Cf. *galol.*

gadoleic acid. $C_{20}H_{38}O_2$ = 310.2. A fatty acid, m.20, from cod-liver oil.

Gadolin, Johann. 1760–1852. Finnish chemist and mineralogist.

gadolinite. Principally $4BeO \cdot FeO \cdot Y_2O_3 \cdot 2SiO_2$. Ytterbite. Yttria. A rare-earth silicate found at Ytterby in black, monoclinic masses, d.4–4.5, hardness 6.5–7; a source of Gd, Ho, and Re.

gadolinium. Gd = 157.25. A rare-earth metal, at. no. 64, discovered (1880) by Marignac in gadolinite, d.1.31. Principal valency 3. It is ferromagnetic below 16°C. On account of its rarity it is of scientific interest only. **g. acetate.** $Gd(C_2H_3O_2)_3 \cdot 4H_2O$ = 406.4. Colorless, crystalline powder, d.1.611, soluble in water. **g. bromide.** $GdBr_3 \cdot 6H_2O$ = 505.4. Colorless crystals, soluble in water. **g. chloride.** $GdCl_3 \cdot 6H_2O$ = 371.8. Colorless crystals, soluble in water. **g. hydroxide.** $Gd(OH)_3$ = 208.3. White powder, insoluble in water. **g. oxalate.** $Gd_2(C_2O_4)_3 \cdot 10H_2O$ = 758.76. Monoclinic crystals, dehydrated 110, slightly soluble in water. **g. oxide.** Gd_2O_3 = 362.6. Colorless crystals, insoluble in water. **g. sulfate.** $Gd_2(SO_4)_3 \cdot 8H_2O$ = 746.8. Colorless crystals, soluble in water.

gadose. A fat from cod-liver oil; a yellow, greasy mass, m.34, slightly soluble in alcohol. **anhydrous-** Pure, anhydrous g. **glycerinated-** G. containing 25% glycerin. **hydrous-** G. containing 25% water.

gadusene. An unsaturated hydrocarbon from cod-liver oil.

gagat. A soft coal.

gage. Gauge (U.K. usage). (1) An instrument for measuring the dimension of an object; or the pressure or flow of a liquid. (2) The diameter of a wire, the thickness of a sheet or plate. **high and low-** A g. that registers both maximum and minimum dimensions. **hot wire-** (1) A resistance wire sealed in a vacuum tube, used to measure very low pressures by determining: (*a*) change of current at constant voltage; (*b*) change of total watts at constant temperature (resistance); (*c*) change of resistance at constant current. (2) A small thermocouple, q.v. **ionization-** A device to measure low pressures from the ionization produced in a gas by a definite electron current. **McLeod-** q.v. **nucleonic-** q.v. **resistance-** Hot-wire g.

Gahn, Johann Gottlieb. 1745–1818. Swedish mineralogist, and discoverer of manganese (1780).

gahnite. $ZnAl_2O_4$. Automolite, zinc-spinel. A vitreous, native zinc aluminate, d.4–4.6, hardness 7.5–8.

gaidic acid. $C_{16}H_{30}O_2$ = 254.3. A monobasic, unsaturated acid, and homolog of elaidic acid. Colorless crystals, m.39.

Gaillard tower. An absorption tower in which a spray of lead-chamber sulfuric acid falls through rising furnace gases and is concentrated.

gaine. An intermediate explosive, used to pass on the action of the detonator to the main, less-sensitive explosive charge.

gaize. A very friable, argillaceous sandstone, converted into a pozzolana when heated.

gal. Abbreviation for gallon.

galactagogue. A drug that increases the secretion of milk.

galactan. $(C_6H_{10}O_5)_x$ = $(162.08)_x$. Gelose. The carbohydrate in the cell wall of algae, e.g., *Irideae, Laminarioides,* obtained as an insoluble dextrorotatory gum from agar-agar. It yields galactose on hydrolysis, and mucic acid on oxidation.

galactase. A proteolytic enzyme of milk, resembling erepsin.

galactolipins. Cerebrosides. Lipin substances of animal and vegetable tissues; as, phrenosin.

galactometer. (1) A graduated glass funnel for determining the fat in milk. (2) A hydrometer for determining the specific gravity of milk.

galactonic acid. $C_6H_{12}O_7$ = 196.1. Pentahydroxy-hexoic acid. A monobasic acid, m.97, derived from galactose. Cf. *lactonic acid.*

galactosan. Galactan.

galactosazone. $C_{18}H_{21}O_4N_4$ = 357.21. Yellow needles, m.192–195.

galactose. $C_6H_{12}O_6$ = 180.03. Dextrogalactose,

cerebrose. **dextro-** A hexose sugar, derived from milk sugar by hydrolysis. Colorless hexagons, m.168, soluble in water. **levo-** Levogalactose, m.162–163, soluble in water.

galactoside. Cerebroside. Glycolipins containing nitrogen, galactose, and a fatty acid, e.g., phrenosin.

Galalith. Trademark for artificial horn prepared by the action of formaldehyde on casein.

galangal. Galanga, India root, chinaroot, kaw-liang ginger, kaw-liang kiang. The dried rhizome of *Alpinia officinarum* (Zingiberaceae), Asia; an aromatic and carminative. **g. oil.** The essential oil, d.0.910–0.940, of g.; it contains *d*-pinene and cadinene.

galangin. (1) $C_{15}H_{10}O_5 = 270.1$. A glucoside from the root of galangal. Cf. *alpinin, kaempferide.* (2) 3,5,7-Trihydroxyflavanol, q.v.

galbanum. A gum resin from *Ferula galbaniflua.* White, yellow, or red tears of waxy consistency, m.100; an expectorant, antispasmodic, and ingredient of plasters.

galega. Goat's rue. The herb *G. officinalis* (Leguminosae); a vermifuge and galactagogue.

galegine. $Me_2C{:}CH{\cdot}CH_2{\cdot}N{:}C{\cdot}(NH_2)_2 = 127.02.$ α-2-Isopentylguanidine. An alkaloid from *Galega officinalis* (Leguminosae); an insulin substitute.

Galen. 130–circ.200 A.D. Iatrochemist who advocated the use of vegetable in place of mineral preparations in medicine. Cf. *galenical.*

galena. PbS. Galenite. A gray, isometric, native lead sulfide, d.7.3–7.6, hardness 2.5. **false-, pseudo-** Sphalerite.

galenical. Medicines of vegetable origin, especially the liquid preparations, e.g., decoctions. Cf. *Galen.*

galenite. Galena.

galenobismuthite. A sulfobismuthide of lead.

galhumic acid. Metagallic acid, q.v.

Galilei, Galileo. 1564–1642. Italian physicist and astronomer, who invented the thermometer and telescope.

galipeine. $C_{20}H_{21}O_3N = 323.2$. An alkaloid from angostura bark; colorless needles, insoluble in water.

galipene. $C_{15}H_{24} = 204.19$. A sesquiterpene from *Galipia officinalis*, the source of angostura bark.

galipidine. $C_{19}H_{19}O_3N = 309.2$. An alkaloid from angostura bark. Lustrous plates, m.110.

galipine. $C_{20}H_{21}O_3N = 323.2$. An alkaloid from angostura bark. Colorless needles, m.116.

galipol. $C_{15}H_{26}O = 222.2$. A sesquiterpene alcohol in the oil of the angostura bark. Colorless crystals, m.89.

galipot resin. The exudation of *Pinus maritima* (Pinaceae); a source of pimaric acid. Cf. *galipot.*

galiquoid. Proposed name for a colloidal system of a gaseous phase dispersed in a liquid phase; e.g., foams.

gall. (1) Bile. (2) Nutgalls.

gallacetophenone. $C_8H_8O_4 = 168.1$. 2,3,4-Trihydroxyacetophenone, methylketotrioxybenzene, Alizarin Yellow C. Yellow powder, m.168, soluble in water; a skin antiseptic.

gallal. An aluminum gallate dusting powder.

gallamine. $C_{30}H_{60}O_3N_3I_3 = 891.68$. Flaxedil, 1,2,-3-tri(2-diethylaminoethoxy)benzene triethiodide. Yellow, bitter, hygroscopic powder, soluble in water.

gallanilide. $PhNHC_6H_2(OH)_3 = 245.09$. Gallanol, 3,4,5-trihydroxybenzanilide. Colorless crystals,

m.205, soluble in hot water; a dusting powder.

gallanol. Gallanilide.

gallate. (1) $C_6H_2(OH)_3COOM$. A salt of gallic acid. (2) A salt of gallic hydroxide; as, $NaGaO_2$.

gallein. $C_{20}H_{10}O_7 = 362.1$. Gallin, pyrogallolphthalein, anthracene violet. Brown powder or green scales, decomp. by heat, sparingly soluble in water. Used as an indicator (alkalies—bright red, acids—pale brown), in the determination of phosphates in urine, and in the manufacture of dyes.

gallic. (1) Describing a trivalent gallium compound. (2) Pertaining to nutgalls. **g. acid.** $C_7H_6O_5{\cdot}H_2O = 188.11$. 3,4,5-Trihydroxybenzoic acid. White, triclinic crystals, m.225, slightly soluble in water. A constituent of nutgalls, mangoes, and other vegetable matter; used as a reagent for detecting ferric salts and mineral acids. **g. bromide.** Gallium bromide. **g. chloride.** Gallium chloride. **g. compounds.** See *gallium.* **g. hydroxide.** Gallium hydroxide. **g. iodide.** Gallium iodide. **g. nitrate.** Gallium nitrate. **g. oxide.** Gallium trioxide. **g. sulfate.** Gallium sulfate.

gallicin. $C_8H_8O_5 = 184.1$. Methyl gallate, methyl gallic ester. Colorless needles, m.202, soluble in hot water; a dusting powder.

gallin. Gallein.

gallinol. Gallanilide.

gallipot. A small glazed earthenware jar used by druggists. Cf. *galipot.*

gallitannic. (1) Galitannic. (2) Gallotannic.

gallium. $Ga = 69.72$. Austrium. A metallic element of the third subgroup of the periodic system, at. no. 31. Gray octahedra, d.5.94, m.29.8. Discovered (1875) by Lecoq de Boisbaudran in zinc blende, after its existence had been predicted by Mendeleev from the periodic system (ekaaluminum). The valencies of g. are 2 and 3; it forms gallous and gallic compounds, the latter being the stabler; it forms alums of the general formula, $MGa(SO_4)_2{\cdot}12H_2O$. Used in quartz thermometers, for brightening optical mirrors, as a substitute amalgam in filling teeth, and for vacuum lamps, in place of mercury. **g. acetate.** $4Ga(C_2H_3O_2)_3{\cdot}2GaO_3{\cdot}5H_2O = 1312.7$. White crystals, m.128, soluble in water. **g. acetyl acetonate.** $Ga(C_5H_7O_2)_3 = 366.88$. White crystals: *alpha-* monoclinic, d.1.42; *beta-* rhombic, d.1.41; m.194, soluble in water. **g. bromide.** $GaBr_3 = 309.9$. G. tribromide, gallic bromide. Colorless, deliquescent crystals, soluble in water. **g. chloride.** See *g. dichloride*, and *g. trichloride.* **g. dibromide.** $GaBr_2 = 229.9$. Gallous bromide. Colorless powder, decomp. by water. **g. dichloride.** $GaCl_2 = 140.9$. Gallous chloride. Colorless crystals, m.164, decomp. by water. **g. diiodide.** $GaI_2 = 323.7$. Gallous iodide. Colorless powder, decomp. by water. **g. hydride.** $Ga_2H_6 = 145.4$. A gas, decomp. 130. **g. hydroxide.** $Ga(OH)_3 = 120.7$. Gallic hydroxide. White powder, insoluble in water. **g. iodide.** $GaI_3 = 450.5$. Gallic iodide. White powder, soluble in water. **g. monoxide.** $GaO = 86.0$. Gallous oxide. Blue mass obtained by heating g. oxide in a stream of hydrogen. **g. nitrate.** $Ga(NO_3)_3 = 256.2$. Colorless crystals, soluble in water. **g. oxalate.** $Ga_2(C_2O_4)_3{\cdot}4H_2O = 475.50$. White crystals, insoluble in water. **g. sulfate.** $Ga_2(SO_4)_3 = 428.0$. Gallic sulfate. Colorless crystals, soluble in water. It forms double salts with alkali sulfates analogous to alums. **g. sulfide.** $Ga_2S_3 = 235.4$. White powder, insoluble in water. **g. tin alloy.** A liquid metal, m.15: Ga 88, Sn 12%. **g. tribromide.** See *g. bromide.* **g. trichloride.** $GaCl_3 = 176.35$. Gallic chloride. Colorless, deliquescent needles, m.76, soluble in water. **g. trioxide.** $Ga_2O_3 = 187.4$. Gallic oxide. Colorless, friable mass, insoluble in water.

gallobromol. $C_7H_4O_5Br_2 = 327.9$. Dibromgallic acid. Brown powder, m.205, slightly soluble in water; used to treat neurasthenia and epilepsy.

gallocyanin. $C_{15}H_{12}O_5N_2 = 300.3$. A purple dye from nitrosodimethylaniline and gallic acid.

galloformin. A condensation product of gallic acid and hexamethylenetetramine. Colorless needles; an internal antiseptic.

gallogen. $C_{14}H_6O_8 = 302.1$. Anhydrous ellagic acid. A constituent of divi-divi, the pods of *Caesalpinia coriaria.* Yellow powder, insoluble in water; an astringent and antidiarrhetic.

gallol. Gallinol.

gallols. A group of compounds of pyrogallol, resorcinol and chrysarobin with various acids; as, eugallol (pyrogallol monoacetate).

gallon. A measure of liquids. 1 U.S. g. = 3.785332 liters = 4 quarts = 8 pints = 0.833 imperial g. = 231 in.^{3}. 1 imperial g. = 4.54596 liters = 277.274 in.^{3} = 1.20032 U.S. g. = volume occuped by 10 lb distilled water at 62°F, bar. 30 in. **Winchester-** q.v. **wine-** A measure of capacity used in the U.S. and U.K. (until 1826), equivalent to 231 in.^{3} or 5 wine bottles.

gallotannic acid. $C_{76}H_{52}O_{46} = 1700.3$. A glucoside from Chinese gallnuts, sumac, tea, etc., which hydrolyzes to glucose and digallic acid. Cf. *tannin.*

gallotannin. Tannic acid.

gallous. Describing a divalent gallium compound. **g. bromide.** Gallium dibromide. **g. chloride.** Gallium dichloride. **g. iodide.** Gallium diiodide. **g. oxide.** Gallium monoxide.

galloyl. The radical $(HO)_3C_6H_2CO—$, from tannin, q.v.

gallulmic acid. Metagallic acid.

galol. A supposed member of the vitamin A_1 group (from Galidae, the shark). Yellow needles, m.59; from shark-liver oil. Cf. *gadol.*

Galvani, Luigi. 1737–1798. Italian physician and anatomist, who accidentally discovered the galvanic current.

galvanic. Voltaic. Pertaining to an electric current produced by chemical action. **g. battery.** A series of voltaic cells. **g. current.** A stream of electrons produced by a displacement reaction. Cf. voltaic *cell.* **g. element.** Voltaic cell. **g. pile.** A pile of disks of 2 different metals, placed alternately and separated by moistened paper; used to produce a g. current.

galvanism. The study of electric currents produced by chemical action (as opposed to heat, friction, or induction).

galvanize, galvanise. To protect a metal with a layer of a less oxidizable metal.

galvanized iron. (1) Iron coated with tin by electrolysis, and then immersed in a zinc bath. (2)

Iron immersed in molten zinc and so coated by that metal without the aid of electricity.

galvanograph. A photographic record from a galvanometer whose mirror deflects a beam of light on to a moving film or paper.

galvanolysis. Electrolysis (obsolete).

galvanomagnetic effect. (1) A g. difference in potential. See *Hall effect.* (2) A g. difference in temperature. See *Ettinghausen effect.*

galvanometer. An instrument to detect and measure the strength of an electric current. A magnetic needle is suspended in a wire coil. The slightest deflection of the needle produced by a current through the coil is measured by an optical system. The coil may be fixed and the magnet movable, or vice versa. **absolute-** An instrument measuring current directly by means of 2 equally strong electromagnets. **astatic-** An instrument with 2 magnetic needles of equal magnetic moment, suspended parallel to each other, with their poles in opposite directions to eliminate terrestrial magnetism. **ballastic-** A g. to determine the capacitance or energy produced in the discharge of a capacitor. **D'Arsonval-** A delicate g.: a magnet and mirror are suspended inside a coil and the deflection of the mirror is read from a reflected light beam on a scale, or the scale may be read in the mirror by means of a telescope. Cf. *galvanograph.* **differential-** An instrument with 2 equal coils through which 2 separate currents are sent and their comparative strengths thus determined. **Einthoven-** String or thread g.: a delicate instrument to detect minute electric currents, consisting of a silvered quartz or platinum thread stretched between the poles of a strong magnet. The magnified shadow of the thread is read on a screen. **Kelvin-** q.v. **mirror-** Reflecting g. **photo-** Galvanograph, q.v. **reflecting-** Mirror g.: a small mirror attached to the galvanic needle. Its deflection is read on a scale by reflected light. **sine-** An obsolete type of g. in which the current passing is proportional to the sine of the angle of deflection. **string-** Einthoven g. **tangent-** The strength of the current through a tangent g. is proportional to the tangent of the angle of deflection. **thread-** Einthoven g.

galvanometry. The measurement of electric currents.

galvanoscope. Quadrant electrometer. An instrument indicating the presence and direction of an electric current, but not its strength. Essentially a magnetic needle inside a wire coil.

galvanostalametry. A method of measuring electrolytic and time parameters by using gas formation at an electrode to indicate an electrode reaction.

galvanostegy. (1) Galvanotropism. (2) Electrolytic tinning to protect against hardening by the nitrite process.

galvanotaxis. The response of a living organism to a galvanic current.

galvanotropism. Galvanostegy. The motion of living cells in a galvanic current.

galyl. $C_{24}H_{22}O_8N_4P_2As_4 = 856.5$. Tetroxydiphosphoaminodiarsenobenzene. An antisyphilitic preparation, said to be less toxic than Salvarsan.

gama wax. Candelilla wax.

gambin. $C_{10}H_7O_2N = 173.1$. **R-** Reddish, β-nitroso-α-naphthol, a nitroso dye. **Y-** Yellowish, nitrosonaphthol, α-nitroso-β-naphthol, a nitroso dye.

gambir. Pale catechu. The dried extract from a decoction of the leaves and twigs of *Ourouparia* or *Uncaria gambir* (Rubiaceae), Asia. Brown powder, insoluble in water; an astringent and tan. **g. catecholcarboxylic acid.** $C_{16}H_{14}O_8$ = 334.11. White solid, from gambir, *d-β-* m.259; *l-β-* m.261, *dl-β-* m.252.

gamboge. Camboge, cambogia, gummi guttae. A gum resin from *Garcinia hanburii* and other Guttiferae. Gray or brown cylinders forming a colloidal solution in water; a hydragogue, cathartic, and pigment.

gamete. A sexual cell capable of uniting with another sexual cell to form a zygote, or fertilized cell.

gamma. (1) Third letter of the Greek alphabet, γ or Γ. (2) A unit of weight, γ = the one-millionth part of a gram (microgram), 0.001 mg or 0.000,000,353 ounce. (3) A unit of magnetic field intensity, γ = 0.000,01 gauss. (4) The g. position. **g. acid.** γ-Acid. 2,5-Naphthylaminesulfonic acid. An intermediate in dyestuff manufacture. **g. benzene hexachloride.** $C_6H_6Cl_6$ = 290.96. Gammexane. Lorexane. The gamma isomer of hexachlorobenzene. White crystals, insoluble in water; a pesticide (B.P.). **g. iron.** An allotropic, nonmagnetic variety of iron existing above 860°C, and crystallizing in the cubic system. **g. particles.** A misnomer for g. rays. **g. position.** (1) The third carbon atom in an aliphatic chain; as, γ-chlorohexane. (2) The third atom of a pentacyclic, or the fourth atom of a hexacyclic compound, as γ-naphthalene substitution, i.e., the position following the β-position and opposite the α-position. **g. radiography.** Radiography in which a small radioactive γ-ray source replaces an X-ray apparatus. **g. rays.** γ-rays. Radiations similar to X rays, but having shorter wavelengths, emitted by radioactive substances as secondary radiation caused by β rays striking matter.

gammagraph. A γ-ray radiograph.

gamone. A substance that acts as a carrier in the interactions between gametes at fertilization.

gangaleodine. $C_{18}H_{14}O_7Cl_2$ = 413.0. A chlorinated depsidone which occurs in lichens of the *Lecanora* species.

ganglion. A nerve cell.

gangue. The earthy portion of an ore. It forms a fusible slag which flows away from the metallic portion on reduction. Cf. *flotation.*

ganister. A fine, compact, hard sandstone, used for grinding and for furnace hearths.

ganja, ganjah. Round, compressed masses of cannabis, as exported from Calcutta.

ganomalite. $(Ca,Mn)Pb_3Si_3O_{11}$. A rare native silicate.

ganomatite. $(Fe,As,Sb)_2O_3$. A gray or brown mineral, d.2.3.

ganophyllite. $Mn_7Al_2Si_8O_{26} \cdot 6H_2O$. A brown, monoclinic silicate.

garage poison. Petromortis. A mixture of carbon monoxide and air from the exhaust of combustion engines.

garancin. A preparation of the coloring matter of madder having 3–4 times its dyeing powers.

Garantose. A brand of saccharin, q.v.

garbage. Refuse from households. **g. tankage.** The dried and ground product obtained by steaming and degreasing g.; a fertilizer.

garcinin. A pigment from fukugi; a dye for silk. Cf. *fugugetin.*

garden celandine. The dried herb of *Chelidonium majus*; a cathartic and diaphoretic.

gardenic acid. $C_{14}H_{10}O_6$ = 274.1. A quinone split product of gardenin.

gardenin. $C_{14}H_{12}O_6$ = 276.1. A yellow crystalline principle from the resin of *Gardenia lucida* (S. Asia).

Gardinol. Trademark for detergent alcohols made by reduction of sulfonated fatty acids, e.g. $HO \cdot R \cdot HSO_3$.

gargle. (1) A disinfecting solution for rinsing the throat. (2) To wash the throat.

garlic. Allium. The fresh bulb of *Allium sativum* (Liliaceae); an irritant, expectorant, and condiment. **g. oil.** The essential oil of g., containing allyl and diallyl disulfide and the compounds $C_6H_{10}S_3$ and $C_6H_{10}S_4$.

garnet. A red, yellow, or green transparent silicate. General type: $A_3B_2Si_3O_{12}$, in which A is a divalent metal, and B a trivalent metal. **aluminum-** $R_3Al_2Si_3O_{12}$: (1) *Grossularite*, $Ca_3Al_2Si_3O_{12}$; varieties: hessonite, succinite, romanzovite, wiluite. (2) *Pyrope*, $Mg_3Al_2Si_3O_{12}$, red to black crystals, d.3.7. (3) *Almandite*, $Fe_3Al_2Si_3O_{12}$, red, d.3.9–4.2. (4) *Spessartite*, $Mn_3Al_2Si_3O_{12}$, red to brown, d.4.2. **calcium-** Essonite. **chromium-** $R_3Cr_2Si_3O_{12}$: (5) *Uvarovite*, $Ca_3Cr_2Si_3O_{12}$, emerald green, d.3.5. *iron-* $R_3Fe_2Si_3O_{12}$: (6) *Andradite*, $Ca_3Fe_2Si_3O_{12}$; varieties (black, amber, or green): topazolite, colophonite, melanite, pyreneite, jelleteite, dematoid. (7) *Manganese g.*, $Mn_3Fe_2Si_3O_{12}$; varieties (black, brown, or green): rothoffite, allochroite, polyadelphite, aplome. (8) *Sodium g.*, $Na_6Fe_2Si_3O_{12}$, lagoriolite. **manganese-** See *iron g.*(7). **sodium-** See *iron g.*(8). **titanium-** $R_3Fe_2(Si,Ti)_3O_{12}$: e.g., schorlomite, $Ca_3(Fe,Ti)_2(Si,Ti)_3O_{12}$.

g. rock. A metamorphic rock containing g. as an accessory mineral, e.g., schists.

garnierite. $(Ni,Mg)SiO_3 \cdot xHO$. Noumeite. A green, amorphous silicate, d.2.5–4, hardness 7.5–8.

garryine. $C_{22}H_{32}O_2N$ = 342.30. An alkaloid from the leaves of *Garrya fremontii*, skunkbush (Cornaceae), California and Oregon. An oil, m.(monohydrate) 75–80.

gas. (1) The vaporous state of matter; a nonelastic fluid, in which the molecules are in free movement, and their mean positions far apart. Gases tend to expand indefinitely, to diffuse and mix readily with other gases, to have definite relations of volume, temperature, and pressure and to condense or liquefy at low temperatures, or under sufficient pressure. 1 cc of any g. contains under standard conditions 27×10^{18} molecules. Cf. *Avogadro's, Charles'* and *Boyle's law.* (2) Illuminating or fuel g. **air-** G. made by blowing air through hydrocarbons. **anesthetic-** The vapors of a volatile anesthetic. **Blau-** q.v. **coal-** An illuminating and fuel g. distilled from coal, consisting of aliphatic hydrocarbons, methane, ethane, etc. **coercible-** Liquefiable g. **combustible-** A flammable g. produced by incomplete combustion, e.g., coke-oven g. **compound-** A gaseous compound, e.g., methane. **compressed-** See *compressed gases.* **electrolytic-** A mixture: 2 vol. H_2, 1 vol.

O_2. **elementary-** An element that is gaseous under ordinarily conditions, e.g., hydrogen. **flammable-** A g. that is able to burn in air, e.g., hydrogen. **fluorine-** Fluorine. **forest-** Producer g. from wood charcoal. **fuel-** A g. used to produce heat by combustion. **full-** A flammable g. consisting of saturated hydrocarbons, e.g., water g. **hydrogen-** Hydrogen. **ideal-** Perfect g. **illuminating-** A g. used to produce light by burning, e.g., coal g. **inert-** (1) Noble g. (2) A g. that does not react readily chemically, e.g., nitrogen. **intestinal-** Gases produced during digestion: nitrogen, hydrogen sulfide, etc. **lacrimatory-, lachrymatory-** G. producing profuse secretion of tears. **laughing-** Nitrous oxide. **lighting-** Illuminating g. **marsh-** Methane. **natural-** (1) The flammable gases from oil wells, used as an illuminant and fuel principally methane, with ethane, propane, butane, and higher hydrocarbons, and small amounts of hydrogen, ethylene, carbon dioxide, and carbon monoxide. Calorific value 530 therms per ton. World consumption (1967), 600,000 million cubic meters (Western bloc). See *fuel*. (2) Helium. **noble-** The members of the zero group of the periodic system consisting of inert elements: He, Ne, Ar, Kr, X, and Nt. **noxious-** Any poisonous g. or a g. with a strong odor. **oil-** Natural g. An illuminating and fuel g. distilled from crude petroleum. **olefiant-** Ethylene. **oxygen-** Oxygen. **perfect-** A fluid that obeys the g. laws. None is known, but it is assumed that as the pressure becomes infinitely small, the g. approaches nearer and nearer to the ideal state, where there is no internal resistance to molecular motion. **permanent-** An obsolete term for gases which are not liquefiable. However, at sufficiently low temperature and high pressure all gases condense. **petroleum-** Oil. **poison-** (1) Lung irritants (phosgene). (2) Lacrimators (bromoacetone). (3) Sternutators (diphenyl cyanarsine). (4) Vesicants (mustard g.). (5) G. which affects body enzymes. **propellant-** A g. used in a pressurized dispenser to expel the contents when a valve is opened. Cf. *aerosol*. **rich-** Full g. **rock-** Natural g. **sewer-** G. from the decay of organic material. **sludge-** A fuel g. (methane 70, carbon dioxide 30%) from the activated sludge sewage treatment process. **sour-** Natural g. containing impurities, chiefly hydrogen sulfide. **sternutatory-** A g. that produces sneezing. **suffocating-** A g. that is nonrespirative, smothering, and finally stops respiration. **sun-** The gaseous constituents of the sun, e.g., hydrogen, helium, carbon dioxide, etc. **toxic-** A g. that causes poisoning. **tracer-** A radioactive g. used as a radioactive indicator, e.g., to detect leaks in underground piping. **two-dimensional-** A layer of adsorbed atoms. Cf. *adatom*. **vesicant-** A g. that blisters the skin. **volcanic-** G. from volcanoes (carbon dioxide, nitrogen, hydrogen, sulfur dioxide, etc.). **war-** Poison g. **water-** An illuminant and fuel prepared by passing steam over glowing coal, and enriching the hydrogen produced by hydrocarbons, and carbon monoxide; as water g.

g. analysis apparatus. See *Haldane, Orsat, etc., apparatus.* **g. bag.** An oval rubber container for holding gases. **g. balance.** A balance for determining the specific gravity of gases. **g. ballons.** A blown spherical glass container with one or more necks, for weighing gases. **g. bath.** Air bath. **g. battery.** G. cell. **g. black.** Lampblack. **g. bleaching.** Bleaching by sulfur dioxide or chlorine. **g. buret.** A graduated glass tube with a stopcock on each end; used in gasometric analysis. **g. calorimeter.** An apparatus to determine the heat value and tar content of g. **g. carbon.** The amorphous, compact residual carbon remaining after distillation of g. from coal; used for electrodes. **g. cell.** An electrolytic cell formed from 2 g. electrodes. **g. chromatography.** See *chromatography* analysis. **g. collecting tube.** An elongated cylinder or bulb with a stopcock at each end. **g. constant.** R in the g. law equation is independent of the chemical nature of a g., but depends on the units of measurement: $R = pv/T$, where p, v, and T are the pressure, volume, and temperature, respectively, under the conditions of an ideal g. If p is grams per square centimeter, and v is cubic centimeters, $R = 84.780$ gm-cm$/T$. If p is atmospheres, and v is liters, $R = 0.08204$ liter-atm$/T$. If p is dynes, and v is cubic centimeters, $R = 8.314 \times 10^7$ ergs/gm mole $= 1.98$ cal. If p is kilograms per square meter, and v is cubic centimeters, $R = 8.48 \times 10^5$ kg-m$^2/T$. Cf. *equations of state*. **g. cylinder.** A steel tank or iron bottle used to ship liquefied gases. **g. electrode.** An electrode (usually a finely divided metal) which holds a g. on its surface, and behaves as a reversible electrode when placed in a solution. Cf. *hydrogen electrode*. **g. engine.** An engine powered by the combustion of a g. or g. mixture. **g. filter.** A device to remove solid or liquid particles from gases. **g. generating bottle.** A device to generate gases in the laboratory. See *Kipp generator*. **g. generator.** A device to manufacture g., e.g., the retort of a g. plant. **g. holder.** A g. storage tank, 2 overlapping halves expanding within each other and sealed by a liquid; or the g. may be displaced from a g.-tight container by allowing water to flow in. **g. integral process.** G.I. A 2-stage water-g. process for producing g. from low-grade coals. Cf. *Lurgi process*. **g. laws.** The combination of Boyle's, Gay-Lussac's, and Charles' laws in the equation $PV = RT$. See *g. constant, equation of state*. **g. liquor.** The liquor from washing g. from the distillation of coal. It contains ammonia, sulfides, and carbonates. **g. manometer.** A steam gage, q.v. **g. mask.** Respirator. **g. meter.** Gasometer. **g. pipet.** A series of glass bulbs mounted on a frame; used in gasometric analysis. **g. regulator.** (1) A device for regulating the pressure of the g. taken from a cylinder in which it is compressed. (2) A device for regulating temperature by controlling the g. supply. **g. thermometer.** A thermometer based on the variation in pressure or volume of a g., generally hydrogen. *constant volume-* Measures the variation in pressure of a g. confined at constant or nearly constant volume. *constant pressure-* Measures the change in volume of a g. confined at constant pressure, generally air pressure.

gaseous. Describing the third state of matter, as opposed to the solid and liquid states.

gasogene. Charcoal gas used as fuel.

gasol. 3-C and 4-C mixed paraffins and olefins produced in the synthesis of oil from carbon monoxide and hydrogen, by the Fischer-Tropsch process, using a metal catalyst.

gasoline, gasolene. Petroleum ether. The third fraction obtained on distillation of petroleum or crude oil, b.75; chiefly paraffins, e.g., hexane. A fuel and solvent. Cf. *Oronite*. **ethyl-** See *ethyl*.

gasoloid. Proposed name for a gaseous dispersed phase in a solid surrounding phase.

gasometer. (1) An instrument to measure gas flow. (2) See *gasholder*.

gasometric. Pertaining to gas analysis.

gasometry. See *gas analysis*.

gassed. Overcome by noxious gas.

Gassner cell. A voltaic dry cell (1.3 volts); zinc and carbon electrodes in a paste of zinc oxide 1, ammonium chloride 1, calcium sulfate 3, zinc chloride 2pts., moistened with water.

gastric. Pertaining to the stomach. **g. content.** Semidigested food mixed with digestive enzymes. **g. digestion.** The decomposition of food materials in the stomach; chiefly the hydrolysis of proteins by pepsin with hydrochloric acid as activator. **g. juice.** The secretions of the stomach glands, containing the digestive enzymes. **g. tonic.** A drug that improves digestion.

gastrin. A hormone in the mucous membrane which excites the secretion of gastric juice.

gatsch. A soft hydrocarbon wax, m.320–460, obtained in the synthesis of oil from carbon monoxide and hydrogen by the Fischer-Tropsch process; a source of edible fatty acids.

gauchamacine. Guachamacine.

gauge. Gage.

gaultheria. The dried leaves of *Gaultheria procumbens*, wintergreen, partridgeberry, or checkerberry (Ericaceae), N. America; a stimulating tea. **g. oil.** Wintergreen oil.

gaultheric acid. Methyl salicylate.

gaultherilene. $C_{10}H_{16} = 136.2$. A terpene in wintergreen oil.

gaultherin. $C_{14}H_8O_8 = 314.4$. Monotropitoside. A glucoside from the bark of *Betula lenta*, black birch; hydrolyzes to methyl salicylate and glucose.

gaultherolin. Methyl salicylate.

Gauss, Karl Friedrich. 1777–1855. German mathematician who developed the conception of the 3 fundamental units: length, mass, and time.

gauss. H. The unit of intensity of a magnetic field (field strength); a force of one dyne on a unit magnetic pole: 1 gauss (emu) $= \frac{1}{3} \times 10^{-10}$ esu. For small measurements: $1 \gamma = 0.00001$ gauss. **de-** To render iron nonmagnetic; e.g., in World War II, coils through which an electric current passed were placed in ships' hulls to protect against magnetic mines. **g. bell.** A normal frequency curve, i.e., conforming to the Gauss law of distribution of results.

Gautier receiver. A glass apparatus for collecting samples during vacuum distillation, q.v.

gauze. A light loosely woven fabric, or fine wire netting. **petrolatum-** Absorbent g. saturated with not less than 4 times its weight of white petrolatum; a protective (U.S.P.). **g. top.** G. covering the top of a bunsen burner to prevent the flame from striking back.

Gay-Lussac, Joseph Louis. 1778–1850. French chemist and physicist. **G.-L. hydrometer.** A hydrometer used for alcoholic liquids, graduated in percentages. **G.-L. law.** The volumes of reacting gases and the volume of the reaction product are in simple proportions, and can be expressed by whole numbers. **G.-L. tower.** A tower used in the chamber process for the manufacture of sulfuric acid to absorb the oxides of nitrogen from the crude acid produced, to form nitrous vitriol (mainly nitrosulfuric acid).

gaylussite. $Na_2Ca(CO_3)_2 \cdot H_2O = 224.03$. A natural carbonate.

gazogene. A fuel gas made by burning charcoal.

Gd. Symbol for gadolinium.

Ge. Symbol for germanium.

Geber. Abu Abdallah Jaber. Arabian alchemist and writer (9th century); the discoverer of sulfuric and nitric acids. Latin writings attributed to him contain speculations on the alchemical "elements."

Gecesa. Trade name for a polyamide synthetic fiber.

gedanite. A fossil resin resembling amber.

gedrite. A variety of anthophyllite containing alumina.

gee-lb. Slug.

gehlenite. $2CaO \cdot Al_2O_3 \cdot SiO_2$. A green, resinous, tetragonal silicate, d.2.9–3, hardness 5.5–6, associated with spinel.

geic acid. Ulmic acid.

Geiger counter tube. A fine axial wire in a metallic cylinder under a gas pressure of 5 cm Hg; used to count electrons, and measure radioactive radiations. Cf. *spinthariscope*.

Geiger-Müller counter. A metal cylinder, charged negatively, in a vacuum tube (0.1 atm), with a center fine wire positively charged. A negative ion produced by radiation moves toward the wire, and by colliding with gas molecules successively ionizes them, causing an avalanche of ions on the wire which can be detected by electrical amplification.

Geigy-33. DDT.

geikielite. Ilmenite.

geissine. $C_{19}H_{24}O_2N_2 \cdot H_2O = 330.3$. Geissospermine. An alkaloid from the bark of *Geissospermium laeve*, pereira bark (Apocynaceae), Brazil.

Geissler Heinrich. 1814–1879. German physicist who determined the coefficient of expansion of water. **G. bulb.** A potash bulb. **G. tube.** A sealed and partly evacuated glass tube, used to study electric discharges through gases and for spectroscopic examination.

geissospermine. Geissine.

gel. (1) Jel., jelly. A colloidal solution of a liquid in a solid. (2) To form a gel. Cf. *coagel*. **alco-** A solid colloidal solution in alcohol. **hydro-** A solid colloidal solution in water. **irreversible-** A g. that cannot be converted into a sol. **reversible-** A g. that becomes a liquid sol on suitable treatment, and can be gelled again. **silica-** See *silica*. **g. filtration.** See *molecular* sieve.

gelate. Gelatinize. To cause solidification of a colloidal solution.

gelatin. $C_{76}H_{124}O_{29}N_{24}S(?)$. An albumin obtained by boiling animal tissue under pressure with water. Yellow films, which soften and swell in cold water; insoluble in alcohol, soluble in hot water; coagulated by tannic acid and hardened by formaldehyde. G. is an amphoteric compound which combines with cations to form "gelatinates," and with anions to form "gelatin salts":

1. Nonionized (isoelectric) . . . . pH   4.7
2. Ionized: (e.g. with sodium chloride)
   A. Metal gelatinate (e.g. sodium
      gelatinate) . . . . pH $<$ 4.7
   B. Gelatin salt (e.g. gelatin chlo-
      ride) . . . . pH $>$ 4.7

G. is used as a nutrient, hemostatic, excipient, culture medium; for photographic papers, films and plates; in glues; as a clarifying agent, adhesive, sizing or stiffening agent, and colloidal protector. Cf. *glue*.   **ana-** One of the 2 constituents of gelatin which produces a gel.   **animal-** Gelatin.   **blasting-** q.v.   **bone-** G. from bones.   **Chinese-** Vegetable g.   **chromatized-** A mixture: 5 pts. 10% g. solution, 1 pt. potassium dichromate.   **Formalin-** Glutolin.   **glycerinated-** A mixture of equal parts of glycerol and g.   **Japanese-** Agar-agar.   **nitro-** A mixture of nitroglycerin and nitrocellulose. Cf. *gelignite*.   **plain-** A culture medium: gelatin 100, peptone 10, sodium chloride 5 gm in 1,000 ml bouillon stock solution, neutralized with sodium hydroxide.   **silk-** Sericin.   **vegetable-** A gelatinous substance from vegetable tissues; as, agar.

   g. culture. A bacterial culture grown on a medium containing g.   **g. disk.** A small disk of medicated g. used to apply drugs to the eye.   **g. filtration.** Filtration through a gel to separate substances of different molecular size.   **g. sugar.** Glycocoll.

gelatinate. A compound of gelatin, q.v., with a positive ion or radical.

gelatinize. (1) To gelate. (2) To convert into gelatin.

gelatinous. Resembling gelatin.

gelation. The formation of a gel.   **con-** See *congelation*.   **re-** See *regelation*.

Gelidium latifolium. A plant (Eire), source of agar.

gelignite. Blasting gelatin, gelatin dynamite. An explosive: nitroglycerin, nitrocellulose, potassium nitrate and wood-meal. Cf. *nitrogelatin*.

gelling point. The concentration and temperature at which semiliquids become solid.

gelometer. An instrument that measures gel strength in terms of the weight of shot, running into a hopper attached to a hard rubber plunger, to force the plunger 4 mm below the gel surface; e.g., the Bloom g. Cf. *penetrometer*.

gelose. Galactan.

gelsemic acid. Scopoletin.

gelsemin. $C_{49}H_{63}N_5O_{14} = 945.9$. A resin from the rhizome of *Gelsemium sempervirens*. Brown powder, insoluble in water; an antipyretic.

gelsemine. $C_{20}H_{22}O_2N_2 = 322.20$. A β,β'-disubstituted oxindole. An alkaloid from the roots of *Gelsemium sempervirens*. White, amorphous powder, m.160, insoluble in water; an analgesic and antispasmodic.

gelseminic acid. $C_{10}H_8O_4 = 192.1$. Scopoletin. 4-Methoxy-5-hydroxycoumarin, m.204.

gelseminine. $C_{42}H_{47}O_{14}N_3 = 819.6$. An alkaloid from the roots of *Gelsemium sempervirens*, yellow jassamine or Carolina jasmine (Loganiaceae), N. America. Colorless crystals, insoluble in water; an antipyretic, antineuralgic, and antispasmodic.   **g. hydrobromide.** $C_{42}H_{47}O_{14}N_3 \cdot HBr = 900.53$.

Colorless crystals, soluble in water.   **g. hydrochloride.** $C_{42}H_{47}O_{14}N_3 \cdot HCl = 856.07$. Colorless crystals, soluble in water.   **g. nitrate.** $C_{42}H_{47}O_{14}N_3 \cdot HNO_3 = 881.61$. Colorless crystals, soluble in water.

Gelsemium. (1) A genus of loganiaceous (de Candolle), apocynaceous (Decaisne) or rubiaceous (Chapman) plants. (2) Yellow jasmine root. The dried rhizome of *Gelsemium sempervirens* (Loganiaceae); a nerve sedative, antispasmodic, and antineuralgic.

gelsemoid. The combined principles from the root of *Gelsemium sempervirens;* an antispasmodic.

gem. A precious stone.   **artificial-, synthetic-** A precious stone made by a chemical process.

gem- Prefix indicating that the radicals in a disubstituted compound are both on the same C atom.

geminal coupling. The H-H linkage of a CH_2 group.

gemmatin. $C_{17}H_{12}O_7 = 328.08$. A coloring matter from the fungus, *Lycoperdon gemmatum*.

-gen. Suffix meaning, to produce or bear; as, hydrogen.

genalkaloid. An alkaloid in which the amino group has been converted into an amino-oxy group. G. have the same therapeutic effect as, but are less toxic than, the parent alkaloid.

gene. A supermolecule or micelle of proteins, considered to be the unit of heredity. Surrounded by colloidal matter, it forms the chromomere, and thence the chromosome.

genease. Maltase.

generate. To produce a gas or electric current.

generator. An apparatus for producing a gas.

generator gas. A fuel gas obtained by blowing air through layers of heated coal or coke; chiefly carbon monoxide and carbon dioxide.

generic test. Reactions of organic compounds which determine their place in Mulliken's classification.

Geneva nomenclature. An international system of naming carbon compounds. See *nomenclature*.

genistein. $C_{15}H_{10}O_5 = 270.08$. Prunetol, 4′,5,7-trihydroxyisoflavone. A plant flavone; the aglucone of genistin.

genistin. $C_{21}H_{20}O_{10} = 432.15$. A glucoside, m.254, from soybean meal. Cf. *plant pigments*.

genoline oil. Linseed oil polymerized by boiling; a lithographic varnish.

genthite. Nickel gymnite.

gentian. Gentian root. The dried rhizome and roots of *Gentiana lutea* (Gentianaceae); a bitter tonic and stomachic. See *aromatin*.   **g. violet.** The hydrochloride, sulfate, or nitrate of triphenylrosaniline and triphenylpararosaniline. Bluish powder, soluble in water; a stain, and disinfectant, very toxic to gram-positive organisms.

Gentianaceae. Gentian family, a group of herbs with a bitter juice, containing little tannin. Thus: roots: *Gentiana lutea* (gentian); herbs: *Swertia chirayita* (chirata).

gentianic acid. Gentisinic acid.

gentianin. (1) An extract containing the bitter principle of the root of *Gentiana* species. (2) Gentisin.

gentianine. $C_{10}H_9O_2N = 175.01$. An alkaloid from *Enicostemma littorale* (Gentianaceae), m.82.

gentianite. $C_{16}H_{32}O_{16} = 480.3$. A carbohydrate in the root of *Gentiana* species.

gentianose. $C_{18}H_{32}O_{16}$ = 504.25. A trisaccharide from gentian.

gentienin. $C_{14}H_{10}O_5$ = 258.1. An isomer of gentisin, m.225.

gentiin. $C_{25}H_{28}O_{14}$ = 552.2. A glucoside from *Gentiana* species, m.274.

gentiobiose. $C_{12}H_{22}O_{11}$ = 342.17. A disaccharide, from the hydrolysis of starch.

gentiopicrin. $C_{16}H_{20}O_2$ = 356.2. A glucoside from the root of *Gentiana* species. Yellow crystals, m.191, soluble in water.

gentisein. $C_{13}H_8O_5$ = 244.1. 1,3,7-Trihydroxy-xanthone. Colorless crystals, m.315.

gentisic acid. $C_7H_6O_4$ = 154.1. Hydroquinone carboxylic acid, gentisinic acid, gentianic acid, 5-hydroxysalicylic acid. Colorless crystals, m.200, soluble in water. A metabolic product of the mold *Penicillium patulum.* Cf. *patulin.*

gentisin. $C_{14}H_{10}O_5$ = 258.1. Gentianin, 1-methoxy-3,7-dihydroxyxanthone. The yellow pigment of the root of *Gentiana.* Yellow needles, m.267, sublimes and decomp. 400, slightly soluble in water. **iso-** 7-Methoxy-1,3-dihydroxyxanthone.

gentisinic acid. Gentisic acid.

genus. (1) A group of related organic compounds (Mulliken). (2) A group of related species of plants or animals.

geochemistry. The study of the chemical changes occurring on the earth's crust. **bio-** The study of the chemical composition of living matter in relationship to organically formed rocks.

geocoronium. A hypothetical element assumed to exist in the upper layers of the atmosphere.

geocronite. $Pb_5Sb_2S_8$ or $5PbS \cdot Sb_2S_3$. A metallic, rhombic sulfide, d.6.4–6.5, hardness 2–3.

geodesy. The science of the form and dimensions of the earth and its surroundings.

geodynamics. The study of the forces and causes which change the earth surface. Cf. *geomorphology.*

geoffrayin. Rhatanin.

geologic(al). Pertaining to geology.

geologic eras. The time intervals during which certain rock strata were formed on the earth's surface. Subdivided into *periods* and into *epochs.* The rocks formed during a period constitute a geologic *system,* those formed during an epoch constitute a *series,* which are subdivided into *formations* many characterized by the remains of life. See table below.

geology. The science of the physical history of the earth and its surface structure. **dynamic-** The study of the causes of geological changes. **economic-** The study of economically important minerals. **eolic-** The study of changes produced by wind. **palaeantologic-** The study of remains of life in relation to rock formations. **stratigraphic-** Historical g.

geometric(al). Pertaining to the principles of geometry. **g. conversion.** The change from one g. isomer to another; as, maleic acid to fumaric acid. **g. isomer.** An optically inactive compound which exists in 2 or more geometrically different atomic arrangements; as, syn- and anti- forms. **g. isomerism.** Describing optically inactive isomeric organic compounds with a double bond, which

GEOLOGIC ERAS

ERA *Period and system* Epoch and series	Time (million years)		
	Era	Period	Epoch
CENOZOIC	60		
Quaternary		1–1.5	
Tertiary		54–63	
Pliocene			6–7.5
Miocene			12–14
Oligocene			16
Eocene			20–26
MESOZOIC	150		
Cretaceous		65–85	
Upper Cretaceous			40–50
Lower Cretaceous			25–35
Jurassic		35–45	
Triassic		35–45	
PALEOZOIC	420		
Carboniferous		100–140	
Permian			25–40
Pennsylvanian			35–50
Mississippian			40–50
Devonian		50	
Silurian		40	
Ordovician		90–130	
Cambrian		70–110	
PROTEROZOIC	850		
Algonkian		?	
Keweenawan			?
Huronian			?
Archean		?	

have a geometrically different spatial arrangement of the atoms. See *isomer.* **g. progression.** A series of numbers related by a constant ratio between successive terms. E.g., the number of possible peptides from 1,2,3, . . . , 6 amino acids is 1,2,6, . . . , 720.

geomorphology. The study of the form of the earth surface. Cf. *geodynamics.*

Geon. Trademark for a polyvinyl chloride and vinylvinylidene copolymer synthetic fiber.

geosote. Guaiacol valerate. An antiseptic compound of guaiacol and valeric acid.

geostatics. The science of the loose sediments of the earth's crust.

geothermic. Referring to heat below the earth's surface. **g. gradient.** The rise in temperature below the earth's crust (average, 1°F per 55 ft of depth).

geranial. Citral.

geranic acid. $C_{10}H_{16}O_2 = 168.2.$ 3,7-Dimethyl-2,6-octadienoic acid*. The oxidation product of citral; oily liquid, $b_{20mm}119.$ **iso-** Colorless crystals, m.103.

geraniol. $Me_2C:CHCH_2 \cdot CH_2 \cdot CMe:CH \cdot CH_2OH = 154.20.$ A constituent of the oils of geranium, eucalyptus, citronella, and ylang. Colorless liquid, d.0.881, b.231, insoluble in water; an insect bait. **dihydro-** Citronellol.

geranium. Cranesbill. The dried rhizome of *Geranium maculatum*; an intestinal astringent. **g. oil.** Occurs in the leaves of *Pelargonium* species, d.0.889–0.906. Contains geranial, citronellol, phellandrene, and tiglates. *Turkish-* Palmarosa oil. The essential oil (70% geraniol) of *Andropogon* (*Cymbogen*) *martini* (Geraniaceae).

geranyl. The radical $C_{10}H_{17}$—, from geraniol. **g. acetate.** $CH_3 \cdot COOC_{10}H_{17} = 196.22.$ Geraniol acetate. Colorless liquid, decomp. 245, slightly soluble in water.

Gerhardt, Charles Friederich. 1816–1856. French chemist. **G. test.** A test for diacetic acid in urine with ferric chloride solution.

gerhardtite. A native, basic copper nitrate.

geriatrics. The study of old age.

germ. (1) An embryonic cell. (2) A bacterium, microbe, or spore.

germanate. A salt of the type M_2GeO_3, from germanium dioxide. **thio-** A salt of the type M_2GeS_3, from germanium disulfide.

germander. Chasse fièvre. The herb of *Teucrium chamaedris* (Labiatae); a tonic and diuretic. **water-** Wood garlic, English treacle. The herb of *T. scordium*; an antiseptic and stimulant.

germane. $GeH_4 = 76.63.$ Germanium hydride. Colorless gas, burning with a blue flame, b.—90. **di-** $Ge_2H_6 = 150.81.$ Germanoethane. A gas, b.29. Cf. *germanium ethide.* **tri-** $Ge_3H_8 = 225.20.$ Germanopropane. A liquid, d.2.20, b.110.

germanic. Describing a compound of tetravalent germanium. **g. chloride.** Germanium tetrachloride. **g. oxide.** Germanium dioxide.

germanin. Bayer 205, naganol, suramin, antrypol, Fourneau 309. The sodium salt of 3,3′-ureidobis [8-(3-benzamido-*p*-toluido)-1,2,5-naphthalenetrisulfonic acid]. A colorless, soluble substance; a specific in the treatment of sleeping sickness.

germanite. A copper sulfarsenide mineral from Tsumeb, S. W. Africa, which contains Ge 5–10,

Ga 0.3–1%, and is a principal source of these metals.

germanium. Ge = 72.59. A metallic element, at. no. 32, of the carbon family, d.5.36, m.958.5, b.2700, insoluble in water. Discovered (1886) by Winkler in argyrodite; predicted (1871) by Mendeleev (ekasilicon). G. is a rare metal, occurring in any quantity only in argyrodite, euxenite, and germanite. Its valency is 2 or 4; hence the compounds: germanous, G^{++}; germanic, Ge^{4+}. G. is used in semiconductor devices; it gives strength to aluminum alloys, hardness to magnesium alloys, and refractive power to glass. **g. alkyls.** Organometallic compounds in which tetravalent g. replaces carbon, e.g., g. ethide. **g. chloroform.** $GeHCl_3 = 179.4.$ Colorless liquid, decomp. by water. **g. dibromide.** $GeBr_2 = 232.46.$ Germanous bromide. Colorless crystals, decomp. by heat. **g. dichloride.** $GeCl_2 = 143.4.$ Germanous chloride. Colorless liquid. **g. diiodide.** $GeI_2 = 326.46$ Yellow crystals. **g. dioxide.** $GeO_2 = 104.5.$ G. oxide, germanic oxide. White powder, m.1025, slightly soluble in water. **g. disulfide.** $GeS_2 = 136.6.$ Germanic sulfide. White powder, decomp. by heat or by water. **g. ethide.** $GeEt_4$ or $C_8H_{20}Ge = 188.5.$ G. tetraethyl. Colorless liquid, b.160. **g. hydride.** Germane. **g. hydroxide.** $Ge(OH)_2 = 106.6.$ Yellow powder, insoluble in water. Cf. *germanoformic acid.* **g. iodide.** See *g. tetraiodide.* **g. monosulfide.** GeS = 104.5. Germanous sulfide. Brown, metallic plates. **g. monoxide.** GeO = 88.5. Germanous oxide. Gray volatile powder, soluble in hydrochloric acid. **g. oxide.** See *g. dioxide* or *g. monoxide.* **g. sulfide.** See *g. disulfide*, or *g. monosulfide.* **g. tetrabromide.** $GeBr_4 = 392.31.$ Germanic bromide. Colorless fuming liquid, m.26. **g. tetrachloride.** $GeCl_4 = 214.4.$ Germanic chloride. Colorless liquid, b.86, decomp. by water. **g. tetraethyl.** G. ethide. **g. tetrafluoride.** $GeF_4 = 146.8.$ Germanic fluoride. Colorless hygroscopic crystals, soluble in water. **g. tetraiodide.** $GeI_4 = 580.2.$ Germanic iodide. Red crystals, m.144, decomp. by water.

germanoformic acid. $H.GeOOH.$ A tautomer of germanium hydroxide obtained by heating $Ge(OH)_2$ with alkali. A red powder and reducing agent.

germanous. Describing compounds of divalent germanium, which are generally less stable than the germanic compounds. **g. chloride.** Germanium dichloride. **g. oxide.** Germanium monoxide. **g. sulfide.** Germanium monosulfide.

german silver. Nickel silver.

germicidal. Destructive to germs.

germicide. An agent that destroys microorganisms, especially disease germs. Cf. *disinfectant.* The strength is measured by the Salle index, a/b, where a is the germ-killing power and b the tissue-destroying effect. Values: iodine 0.09, phenol 12.9, Merthiolate 35.3, Mercurochrome 262.0. Cf. *Rideal-Walker* test.

germination. The sprouting of a seed or spore. **g. capacity.** The percentage of grain, etc., which can be made to germinate. **g. energy.** The g. capacity in a specified time; e.g., for barley, 3 days at 16°C.

germinator. A device to determine the germinating

energy of seeds; a perforated disk holding seeds over water at a definite temperature.

geronic acid. $C_9H_{16}O_3 = 172.10$. 2-Dimethyl-6-ketoheptoic acid. An oxidation product of β-carotene and β-ionone.

gerontin. $C_5H_{14}N_2 = 102.1$. A leukomaine from dog liver.

gerontology. The study of the symptoms and reactions of the decline in physical and organic functions.

gersdorffite. (Ni,Fe)AsS or NiS_2,$NiAs_2$. Plesite. A native, metallic sulfarsenide, d.5.2–6.3, hardness 5.5.

Geryk pump. A vacuum pump. Cf. *Guericke*.

gesarol. An insecticidal spray: 5% DDT and a wetting agent.

gesnerin. The 5-glucoside of 4′,5,7-trihydroxy-flavylium chloride. An anthocyanin from the orange flowers of *Gesneria* species.

gesso. A plaster (whiting and glue) base on the canvases of early paintings.

gestalt. (German for shape). (1) A synergic mental pattern derived from many separate sense impressions. (2) Showing properties other than can be derived from the individual constituents by summation.

gestogens. Sex hormones present in the steroid fraction of oral contraceptives.

getter. (1) A substance that "cleans" gases in vacuum tubes. **absorptive-** or **chemical-** A g. that reacts with the gas; as, Li. **adsorptive-** or **physical-** A g. that binds gases on its surface; as zirconium. (2) A metal (e.g., thallium) coating on the filament of a tungsten lamp, to prolong its life.

gettering. Obtaining and maintaining a high vacuum in a container, e.g., by adding an activated metal which absorbs gas molecules.

geyserite. A hydrous silicic acid sinter produced near geysers.

ghatti gum. Indian gum.

ghee. Indian butterfat, from the seeds of *Bassia butyraceae*; used for soapmaking. **Phalka-** An oil from the seeds of *Bassia* species, used to adulterate ghee.

ghetta acid. $C_{34}H_{68}O_2 = 508.54$. A fatty acid from ghedda, wax (E. India).

Ghosh, Sir Jnan Chandra. 1895–1959. Indian physical chemist, noted for his work on electrolytes and the theory of ionization.

giallioline. Lead antimoniate.

gibberellins. Substances produced from *Gibberalla fujihuroi*, an organism that causes elongation of rice shoots disease; and by fermentation. They promote the growth of trees, cereal crops, and tobacco. White, crystalline, optically active acids. **g.A.** $C_{19}H_{24}O_6$. **g.A₂.** $C_{19}H_{22}O_6$. **g.A₃, g.X.** $C_{19}H_{22}O_6$.

Gibbs, Josiah Willard, 1839–1903. American mathematician and physicist noted for the development of the phase rule, q.v., and thermodynamics. **G. function.** Thermodynamic potential. **G.-Helmholtz equation.** The relationship between the chemical energy transformed and the maximum energy obtainable electrically in a reversible galvanic element:

$$E = Q/nF + T\, dE/dT,$$

where E is the emf of the cell, Q the heat equivalent of the chemical change for molar quantities expressed in electrical units, F 96,540 coulombs, T the absolute temperature at which the cell is working, and n the valency, or the number of charges carried by a mole of the substances undergoing change; dE/dT is the rate of change in emf of the cell with temperature. **G. paradox.** Work results when 2 gases of thermodynamically identical physical properties (e.g., N_2 and CO) are mixed, but not when 2 portions of the same gas are mixed. **G. phase rule.** See *phase rule*.

Gibbs, Oliver Wolcott. 1822–1908. American chemist noted for his work on complex compounds.

gibbsite. $Al_2O_3(H_2O)_3$ Hydrargillite (U.K. usage). A native aluminum hydroxide.

gibrel. $C_{19}H_{21}O_6K = 384.29$. Potassium gibberellate; used to increase the microbial activity of the soil.

Giemsa, Gustav. 1867–1948. German chemotherapist. **G. stain.** A staining for white blood corpuscles: Azur II Eosin 0.3, Azur II Eosin 0.8, glycerin 250 gm; and 250 ml methanol. **G. ultrafilter.** A device for sterilizing and filtering small quantities of biological liquids through a collodion membrane.

giga. G. A unit of 1,000,000,000.

gigacycle. Gc. A unit of frequency. 1 Gc. = 1 kilomegacycle per second = 1×10^9 cycles per second.

gigantic acid. An antibiotic from a species of *Aspergillus giganteus*; similar to penicillin.

gigantolite. A pseudomorph of iolite.

Gilbert, Sir Joseph Henry. 1817–1901. British chemist, noted for agricultural research. **G., Ludwig Wilhelm.** 1769–1824. German chemist, and editor of *Annalen der Physik*. **G., William.** 1540–1603. British natural philosopher, physician to Queen Elizabeth I and a pioneer in magnetism and electricity.

gilbert. An obsolete unit of magnetic quantity. 1 gilbert = 0.7956 ampere-turn. 1 international gilbert = 0.99991 absolute gilbert. **pra-** See *pragilbert*.

Gilead balm. Balm of Gilead, Mecca balsam. An oleoresin from *Balsamodendron gileadense* (Burseraceae). Cf. *poplar buds*.

Giles flask. A volumetric flask with long neck, graduated at x and at $(x + 10\%x)$ of its volume; used to prepare normal solutions.

gill. A liquid measure: 1 gill = 4 fluid ounces = 118.29 ml = 0.25 pint.

gillenia. Indian physic, American ipecac. The root bark of *G. trifoliata* or *G. stipulacea* (Rosaceae); an emetic and cathartic.

gilpinite. Uranvitriol.

gilsonite. Uintaite. A black, brittle, lustrous hydrocarbon mineral.

gin. An alcoholic beverage made by distillation of a fermented extract of grain in the presence of juniper leaves. **artificial-** Fancy g. to which flavoring essences have been added. **fancy-** A mixture of g. and neutral alcohol.

gingelly. Sesame.

ginger. Zingiber. The dried rhizome of *Zingiber officinalis* (Scitaminaceae), Asia, W. Indies, Africa; an aromatic and stimulant. **black-** The crude drug with a black skin. **jamaica-** The yellow roots, with the skin removed. **wild-** Asarum.

g. oil. The essential oil of g., d.0.882–0.900, b.155–300, containing phellandrene and zingiberene.

gingerin. An oleoresin from ginger.

gingerol. An essential oil from ginger.

ginkgetin. $C_{32}H_{22}O_{10} = 566.15$. A yellow biflavonyl pigment from the leaves of *Ginkgo biloba*, maidenhair tree, m.343.

ginkgoic acid. $C_{24}H_{48}O_2 = 368.5$. An unsaturated acid from the fruit of *Ginkgo biloba*.

ginning. The removal of the larger seed hairs from the cotton plant. Cf. *linter*.

ginseng. Panax. The dried roots of *Panax quinque-folium* (Aralia); a tonic and demulcent.

Girard reagents. Quaternary ammonium compounds of the type $Me_3N(Cl).CH_2CONH.NH_2$, which form soluble compounds with substances containing CO groups; these may subsequently be regenerated. Used to separate sex hormones from urine.

gismondine. Gismondite.

gismondite. $CaAl_2Si_4O_{12}$. Gismondine, abrazite. A gray, hydrated, monoclinic zeolite, d.2.4, hardness 5–5.5.

gitalin. $C_{28}H_{48}O_{10} = 544.37$. A glucoside, m.253, from digitalis.

githagin. $C_{28}H_{44}O_4 = 444.4$. The aglycone of **githagin.** A saponin from corn cockle, *Agrostemma githago*; hydrolyzes to githagenin and glucuronic acid.

gitogenic. (1) Having a digitalis-like effect. (2) The structure of digitalis aglucones. See *cholane derivatives*.

gitoxigenin. $C_{24}H_{36}O_5 = 404.3$. A split product of gitoxin.

gitoxin. A glucoside from the leaves of digitalis; it hydrolyzes to 1 mole gitoxigenin and 3 moles digitoxose.

gix. Fluorine–DDT. An insecticide similar in action to DDT. The principal active constituent is 2,2-bis(p-fluorphenyl)-1,1,1-trichloroethylene, m.45.

glacial. Describing a compound of ice-like, crystalline appearance, especially the solid form of a liquid compound; as, glacial acetic acid.

gladiolic acid. $C_{11}H_{10}O_5(?)$. A monobasic acid from *Penicillium gladioli*. Silky needles, m.160; an antibiotic. With ammonia it gives a deep green color, changing after 12 hours to red and then orange.

gladwin. The root of *Iris foetidissima*; an antispasmodic.

glair. Prepared white of egg used for tempera painting.

glance. General term for minerals with a glassy luster, e.g., lead glance.

gland. An organ that separates a specific substance (waste product) from the blood, or that secretes specific substances, e.g., enzymes.

glandula. A group of therapeutic preparations consisting of dried glands.

Glanzstoff. Trade name for a viscose synthetic fiber. Cf. *rayon*.

Glaser furnace. A combustion furnace used for organic elementary analysis.

glaserite. $Na_2SO_4.3K_2SO_4$. Aphthitalite, arcanite. A colorless, vitreous sulfate, d.2.6, hardness 3–3.5 (Stassfurt).

glass. An amorphous, hard, brittle, often transparent material; a fused mixture of the silicates of the alkali and alkaline earth or heavy metals. See table below. Composition: between $(K,Na)_2O$, $(Ca,Pb)O,6SiO_2$ and $5(K,Na)_2O,7(Ca,Pb)O,36SiO_2$. Formula: $(K,Na)O\text{—}Si_nO_{2n-1}O(Ca,Pb)O\text{—}Si_nO_{2n-1}\text{—}O(K,Na)$.

Classification:

1. Potash-lime g.: hard, resistant to water and acids, d.2.4; used for chemical glassware.
2. Soda-lime g.: more fusible and less resistant, d.2.65; used for windows.
3. Potash-lead g.: readily fusible and highly refractive; as, crystal g., d.2.9–3.6; flint g., d.3.3–3.6; paste for artificial gems and lenses; crown g. (containing barium oxide), d.1.5–1.56.
4. Bottle g. (Na, K, Ca, and Al silicates), d.2.73.
5. Opaque g: opacified by barite, smalts, or bone ash.
6. Colored g.:
   - (a) Yellow: antimony, iron, silver, uranium.
   - (b) Red: gold chloride, ocher, cuprous oxide, selenium.
   - (c) Green: ferrous sulfate, copper, chromium oxide.
   - (d) Blue: cobalt oxide, traces of copper.
   - (e) Iridescent: the action of vapors of metallic chlorides on the hot g.
   - (f) Nacreous. Addition of scales of mica.

blown- A g. that is blown into shape. **bohemian-** Potash g. **borax-** A g. with a low expansion coefficient, which contains borax. **borosilicate-** A heat-resistant silicate g. containing at least 5% boric acid, d.2.25, m.730. Cf. *Pyrex*. **bottle-** A g. that is blown into shape in a mold. **bulletproof-** Plate g. sheets cemented together by a transparent medium. **canary-** Uranium g. **cast-** Plate g. **chemical-** An acid- or alkali-resistant g. for chemical apparatus. **chromium-** A g. colored yellow by chromium compounds. **clock-** G. similar in shape to that used for covering clock faces; used to cover beakers, etc., and may contain

TYPICAL GLASS COMPOSITIONS IN PERCENTAGES

Composition		Soda, Window	Flint	Bottle	Borosilicate	Lead	Aluminosilicate	Silica
(A)	SiO_2	71.5	54	74	80.5	35.0	58.7	96.3
	Al_2O_3	1.5	..	0.5	2.4	....	22.4	0.4
	B_2O_3	....	..	....	12.9	....	3.0	2.9
(B)	Na_2O	14.0	..	17	3.8	....	1.4	0.4
	K_2O	....	10	....	....	7.0		
(C)	CaO	13.0	..	5	0.4	....	6.0	—
	PbO	....	36	....	....	58.0		
	MgO	....	..	3.5	....	....	8.5	—

a hole to take a rod. **cobalt-** A g. colored purple-blue by cobalt compounds; a light filter. **conductive-** G. rendered electrically conductive to a desired extent by treatment with tin chloride and heating to produce a layer of tin oxide. **copper-** G. colored blue or red by copper compounds. **cover-** A thin g. square used to cover microscope specimens on the slide. **crown-** A hard optical g. silicate of sodium with calcium and aluminum oxides; formerly made by blowing and spinning, to form a disk, from which small windowpanes were cut. **cryolite-** Milk g. **crystal-** Flint g. **electric bulb-** A lime g. used for electric bulbs. **flint-** A soft optical g. made from sand, potash, and lead oxide. **float-** G. prepared as a continuous ribbon in a bath of molten metal at 1000°C. It has a high surface finish, flatness, and absence of distortion. **frosted-** G. having a roughened surface. **iron-** G. colored yellow, olive green, or pale blue by iron compounds. **Jena-** Optical and heat-resisting g. made at Jena. **laminated-** Safety g. made by cementing thin sheets of g. together with a plastic at 200–260°F and 250–350 psi. It may crack but will not splinter under impact. **lead-** A soft g. with a low melting point, containing lead oxide, e.g., flint g. **lime-** G. containing calcium oxide, e.g., venetian g. **manganese-** G. colored violet by manganese compounds. **milk-** G. colored milky white by cryolite. **Muscovy-** Muscovite. **normal-** A g. of definite chemical composition. **opal-** G. colored milky white by calcium phosphate or bone ash. **optical-** See *crown, flint.* **organic-** Synthetic g. Synthetic resins having the appearance of g., e.g., Perspex. **plate-** A thick g. made by pouring molten g. on iron tables, then rolling and polishing it; used for mirrors or windows. **porous-** G. containing pores of molecular dimensions, made by leaching boric acid from heat-treated borosilicate g. (SiO_2 96, void space 25%). Used in filters and salt bridges. **potash-** Bohemian g. G. containing more potassium than sodium, e.g. crown. **rolled-** Inferior plate g., made by passing molten g. between iron rolls. **ruby-** Dark red g. containing copper compounds or colloidal gold. **safety-** Laminated g. **sheet-** Flat sheets made by blowing long cylinders, splitting them longitudinally, and flattening them out. **silica-** Though not a true g., fused silica is often used for a transparent, resistant g. **silicate-flint-** A Jena g.: SiO_2 29–53, PbO 67–36, K_2O 3–8, Na_2O 0–1, Mn_2O_3 0.04–0.06, As_2O_3 0.2–0.3%; used for optical purposes. **soda-** G. containing more sodium than potassium, e.g., venetian g. **soluble-** Water g. **spun-** G. wool. **synthetic-** Organic g. **thallium-** G. containing Tl in place of Pb. **toughened-** Heat-treated plate g. to prevent splintering under impact. Cf. *laminated g.* **uranium-** A dichroic, greenish yellow glass containing uranium compounds, used for light filters. **watch-** A small clock g., q.v. **water-** Sodium or potassium tetrasilicate. **window-** G. plates made by blowing the molten g. into cylinders, then slitting and flattening them out on tables. **zinc-crown-** An optical g.: SiO_2 65.4, K_2O 15, NaO_2 5, BaO 9.6, ZnO 2.0, As_2O_3 0.4, Mn_2O_3 0.1, B_2O_3 2.5%.

 g. beads. Solid or hollow spheres; used to prevent excessive ebullition of heated liquids or to determine the specific gravity of liquids. **g. colors.**

See *glass* (6). **g. cullet.** (1) Broken g. waste. (2) Powdered waste from g. manufacture; used as abrasive in matches, primers, polishes, soaps, and cements. **g. cutters.** Small mounted diamond fragments, used to cut. **g. drops.** Prince Ruper drops. **g. gage.** A metal disk with round holes, used to measure the outside diameter of g. tubing. **g. marking.** Ceramic ink. **g. of antimony.** The fused mass resulting from the incomplete oxidation of stibnite. **g. paper.** Calico or paper covered with thin glue and sprinkled with powdered g.; used for polishing. **g. tubing.** A hollow g. rod, used in scientific apparatus. *barometer-* Capillary. *capillary-* A thick-walled g. tube having a bore less than 1 mm. **g. tank.** The container lined with aluminum silicate in which g. is melted. **g. wool.** Fine g. threads used for filtering, or in place of cotton wool.

glassine. A thin, hard, and almost transparent paper made from well-beaten chemical wood pulp.

Glauber, Johann Rudolf. 1603–1668. Dutch iatrochemist who prepared many metallic salts. **g. salt.** Crystalline sodium sulfate.

glauberite. $CaSO_4.Na_2SO_4.$ A calcium sodium sulfate (Stassfurt).

glaucine. $C_{21}H_{25}O_4N = 355.3.$ An alkaloid from the sap of *Glaucium flavum*, yellow horned poppy (Papaveraceae). Yellow prisms, m.119.

glauchochroite. $CaMnSiO_4.$ A rare silicate of the olivine group.

glaucodot. $(Fe,Co)S_2, (Fe,Co)As_2.$ A native sulfarsenide. Cf. *alloclasite.*

glauconite. Bravaisite. An amorphous, green, granular iron. potassium, aluminum, magnesium, calcium silicate formed from oceanic sediments of all ages.

glaucophane. $NaAlSi_2O_6.(Fe,Mg)SiO_3.$ An amphibole rock-forming mineral. Gray monoclinic masses, d.3–3.1.

glaucopicrine. An alkaloid from the roots of *Glaucium flavum* and *Chelidonium majus.*

glaze. A glassy coating. **enamel-** A suspension of metallic oxides in a glass which is burned into pottery or ironware. **porcelain-** A mixture of feldspar, lime, and quartz fused into ware. **salt-** A glassy covering of a silicate of sodium and aluminum produced on earthenware by adding salt to the kiln during firing. **transparent-** A glass covering for earthenware.

glazed. Having a glossy appearance. **g. paper.** A paper with a glossy surface, used for transferring precipitates, or for obtaining curves from delicate instruments, e.g., the kymograph, in which the paper is smoked with carbon.

gleditschine. Stenocarpine. An alkaloid from the leaves of *Gleditschia triacanthos*, three-thorned acacia or honey locust tree (Leguminosae), U.S.

GLEEP. Abbreviation for Graphite Low Energy Experimental Pile. A simple atomic pile developing about 100 kw of heat. Cf. *BEPO.*

glendonite. A pseudomorphous calcite (Australia).

gliadin. $C_{685}H_{1068}O_{211}N_{196}S_5 = 15,578.0.$ Prolamin, vegetable protein. Simple proteins or globulins from gluten, the protein of cereals.

glidin. An albuminous nutrient preparation from wheat flour. **arsenic-** Arsan. **bromo-** G. containing bromides. **ferro-** G. containing iron salts. **iodo-** G. containing iodides.

glioma. A malignant tumor of nerve tissue.

gliotoxin. $2C_{13}H_{14}O_2N_2S_2.H_2O = 344.43$. An antibiotic from *Aspergillus fumigatus* and *Gliocladium fimbriatum*, m.221. Cf. *aspergillin, fumigacin.*

globin. $C_{700}H_{1098}O_{196}N_{184}S_2 = 15,283$. An animal protein in hemoglobin. It is a stonelike body, insoluble in water, soluble in acids or alkalies, coagulated by heat, redissolved by acids. **hemo-** See *hemoglobin.* **oxyhemo-** See *hemoglobin.*

globucid. The antibiotic *p*-aminophenylsulfonamide ethylthiodiazole, m.184, sparingly soluble in water.

globularin. $C_{15}H_{20}O_8 = 328.2$. An amorphous glucoside from the leaves of *Globularia alypium*, Globulariaceae (S. Europe).

globulin. A simple protein, coagulated by heat, insoluble in water, soluble in dilute solutions of salts. **acid-** Syntonin. **antihemophilic-** A sterile, white amorphous solid containing normal human plasma; used to accelerate the clotting of blood. **crystalline-** A g. from the eye lens. **gamma-** The antibodies of normal human blood. A yellow powder prepared by the controlled precipitation of the plasma by organic solvents, dissolving the precipitate in saline solution, and drying from the frozen state. **serum-** A simple blood protein. Horse g. has the proposed formula $C_{628}H_{1002}O_{209}N_{160}S_5$.

globulins. Simple proteins, q.v., in vegetable and animal tissues.

globulol. $C_{15}H_{26}O = 222.20$. A sesquiterpene alcohol from eucalyptus oil.

globulose. A split product of globulins produced by peptic digestion.

globulus. A small sphere; e.g., a button of metal.

Glon. Trade name for a vinyl chloride type plastic. **g. insulin.** See *insulin.*

glonoin. Nitroglycerin.

glove box. Dry box. A closed box with a sloping glass front through which air can be drawn. A pair of gloves sealed into it enable operations to be carried out safely (e.g., from radiations) and under observation.

Glover tower. A tower in sulfuric acid manufacture, q.v.

glucagon. A polypeptide in the pancreas glands of domestic mammals. White crystals, soluble in acids; a hyperglycemic (U.S.P.).

glucase. Obsolete term for maltase.

glucic acid. $C_3H_4O_3 = 88.0$. Acrolactic acid, β-hydroxyacrylic acid, 3-hydroxypropenoic acid. Colorless liquid, soluble in water.

glucide. A group term including carbohydrates and glucosides, q.v.

glucin. Sodium aminotriazine sulfonate. A sweetening agent.

glucinic acid. $C_{12}H_{16}O_9.3H_2O = 358.2$. A hexabasic acid formed in the decomposition of glucose by acids or alkalies. Colorless crystals.

glucinum. Gl. Obsolete name for beryllium, q.v.

gluco- See also *glyco-.*

glucochloral. Chloralose.

glucocholic acid. $C_{24}H_{39}O_4.NHCH_2COOH = 465.52$. Colorless needles, m.134, slightly soluble in water.

glucofurone. $C_6H_{10}O_6 = 178.07$. The γ-lactone of gluconic acid. Cf. *glucopyrone.*

glucogen. Glycogen.

glucohydrazones. Intermediate compounds of the osazone reaction (heating aromatic hydrazines and hexoses).

glucokinin. Insulin.

gluconate. A salt of gluconic acid containing the radical $HOCH_2(CHOH)_5COO—$. **aluminum-** A tanning salt—partly a colloidal suspension of aluminum hydroxide in gluconic acid. **calcium-** $[CH_2OH(CHOH)_5COO]_2Ca$. White powder, used medicinally as a source of calcium.

gluconic acid. $C_6H_{12}O_7 = 196.1$. Pentahydroxyhexoic acid, dextronic acid, glycogenic acid. An isomer of mannonic acid, derived from glucose by oxidation. Isomers: **dextro-** Dextronic acid, maltonic acid. White powder, m.125, pleasant sour taste; solutions form lactones and become plastic. Used for fruit jellies, as a sequestrant in paint strippers, and in electroplating. **levo-** $C_5H_6(OH)_5$-COOH. White crystalline solid, soluble in water.

glucophores. Atom groups which form sweet compounds with atoms or radicals (auxoglucs), e.g., $—CHOH·CH_2OH$. Cf. *chromophore.*

glucoprotein. Mucoprotein (obsolete). A conjugated protein having one or more heterosaccharide prosthetic groups with few sugar residues, lacking a serially repeating unit and bound covalently to the polypeptide chain.

glucosamine. $CH_2OH(CHOH)_3CHNH_2CHO = 179.2$. The amine of glucose and a split product of chitin, b.110 (decomp.).

glucosazone. $C_{18}H_{22}O_4N_4 = 358.31$. A reaction product of monosaccharides and aryl hydrazines. Their characteristic crystalline forms and melting points are used to separate and identify monosaccharides.

glucose. $C_6H_{12}O_6 = 180.15$. Dextrose, phlorose, grape sugar, saccharum amylaceum. A monosaccharide carbohydrate constituent of many animal and vegetable fluids (blood, sweet fruits, etc.), formed by hydrolysis of starch, cane sugar, and glucosides. **dextro-** Colorless needles, d.1.562, m.147, soluble in alcohol or water. A reagent to detect carbon dioxide in blood, tellurous acid, etc., and (as glucose liquid or syrup) a nutrient; used in the manufacture of confectionery and the production of beer and alcoholic liquors, curing of tobacco, tanning; and as reducing agent. Isomers:

d- m.147	α-d- m.146	β-d- m.150

medicinal- Dextrose monohydrate.

g. agar-agar. A culture medium: glucose 10, agar 15, peptone 10, sodium chloride 5, bouillon stock 1,000 pts., neutralized with caustic soda.

g. amine. $C_5H_{11}O_5.NH_2 = 179.11$; decomp. 110.

g. bouillon. A culture medium: glucose 10, peptone 10, common salt 5, bouillon stock 1,000 pts., neutralized with caustic soda. **g. evolué.** A reducing bacteriological medium, prepared by heating a 10% solution of g. in 0.1 N caustic soda at 100°C for 15 min. **g. gelatin.** A culture medium: glucose 10, gelatin 100, peptone 10, common salt 5, bouillon stock 1,000 pts., neutralized with caustic soda. **g. imine.** $C_6H_{12}O_5$: NH = 179.11. A solid, m.128. **g. liquid.** Glucosum. A syrup made by the incomplete hydrolysis of starch, and containing glucose and dextrins; a nutrient. **g. oxime.** $C_6H_{12}O_5$:NOH = 195.14. A reaction product of hydroxylamine and glucose, m.138. **g. syrup.** Corn syrup, liquid glucose, starch hydrolysate. A liquid hydrolysis product of edible starch (U.K. usage).

glucosidase. An enzyme which hydrolyzes glucosides.

glucoside. (1) A compound of glucose; as, glucose-α-glucoside or maltose. (2) See *glycosides*. A neutral, non-nitrogenous vegetable constituent decomposed by heat, dilute acids, alkalies, enzymes, bacteria, or fungi, to form a sugar (glucose) and another compound, e.g., salicin. Glucosides are the ethers of monosaccharides; 2 types: alpha- and beta-: **methyl-** $C_7H_{14}O_6$ = 194.11. *alpha-* Long needles, m.168, [a] + 157°. *beta-* Rectangular prisms, m.104, [a] −33°. Natural glucosides have the suffix *-in* and are classified as: ethylene derivatives, e.g., jalapin; benzene derivatives, e.g., arbutin; styrolene derivatives, e.g., daphnin; anthracene derivatives, e.g., digitoxin; cyanogen derivatives, e.g., amygdalin.

glucosimine. Obsolete term for amino sugar.

glucosin. Ptomaine bases obtained by the action of ammonia on carbohydrates.

glucosone. $CH_2OH \cdot (CHOH)_3COCHO$ = 178.1. An osone of glucose and aldehyde ketone; a reaction product from glucosazone.

glucotin. A cement mixture of isinglass, gelatin, and acetic acid.

glucuronic acid. $CHO(CHOH)_4COOH$ = 194.11. Glycuronic acid. An aldehyde–hydroxy acid in urine, m.175.

glue. Colla. Impure gelatin obtained from animal organs by boiling with water, straining and drying as thin, hard, and brittle cakes; an adhesive. **albumen-** G. obtained from flour in starch manufacture. **bone-** Artificial isinglass, from hides and bones. **cartilage-** Chondrin. **casein-** A casein and borax bookbinder's glue. **elastic-** G. containing glycerin; used for printer's rollers and flexible molds. **fish-** Isinglass. **liquid-** G. acidified with acetic or nitric acid. **marine-** Waterproof g. made of caoutchouc or shellac in turpentine. **skin-** G. from hides. **vegetable-** Acacia. **waterproof-** A fish g. dissolved in hot milk.

Glumiflorae. Monocotyledonous plants, comprising the families Cyperaceae and Gramineae.

gluside, glusidum. Official names for saccharin.

glutaconic acid. $HOOC \cdot CH_2CH:CH \cdot COOH$ = 130.1. Propenedicarboxylic acid, pentenedioic acid*. Colorless crystals, m.134. Cf. *fumaric acid*. **g. anhydride.** $O \cdot CO \cdot CH_2 \cdot CH:CH \cdot CO$ = 112.03. Colorless crystals, m.87; an isomer of pyronone.

glutamic acid. $NH_2 \cdot CH(COOH)CH_2 \cdot CH_2 \cdot COOH$ = 147.14. α-Aminoglutaric acid, glutanic acid.

Colorless crystals, decomp. 208, soluble in water. A constituent of proteins in seeds and beets, and the Japanese flavoring, ajinimoto. **g. a. hydrochloride.** A white powder which yields hydrochloric acid with water; used medicinally.

glutamine. $C_3H_5 \cdot NH_2CONH_2 \cdot COOH$ = 146.13; slightly soluble in water.

glutaminic acid. Glutamic acid.

glutamyl. The radical —OC·CHNH₂·CH₂·CH₂·CO—.

glutanic acid. Glutamic acid.

glutaric acid. $COOH(CH_2)_3COOH$ = 132.09. *n*-Pyrotartaric acid, deoxyglutaric acid, pentanedioic acid*. A dibasic acid in sheep wool. Colorless monoclinic crystals, m.97, soluble in water; a constituent of sheep-wool grease. **amino-** Glutamic acid. **dimethyl-** $C_7H_{12}O_4$ = 160.1. Colorless crystals, m.127. **α-ethyl-** $C_7H_{12}O_4$ = 160.1. Colorless crystals, m.60. **β-ethyl-** Propidenediacetic acid. Colorless crystals, m.67. **α-methyl-** $C_6H_{10}O_4$ = 146.1. Colorless crystals, m.76. **β-methyl-** Ethidenediacetic acid. Colorless crystals, m.86.

glutaronitrile. $CN(CH_2)_3CN$ = 94.2. Trimethylene cyanide, pentane dinitrile*. Colorless liquid, b.286.

glutaryl. The radical —OC(CH₂)₃CO—.

glutathione. $(NH_2)_2(C_4H_5O)CONH(C_2H_4S)CONH \cdot CH_2 \cdot COOH$. γ-Glutamylcysteylglycine. A tripeptide in blood, animal organs, and germinating plants. It plays an important part in metabolism.

glutazine. $C_5H_6O_2N_2$ = 126.2. β-Amidoglutarimide. Colorless crystals, m.300.

glutelins. Simple vegetable proteins, coagulated by heat, insoluble in water or dilute salts, soluble in dilute acids or alkalies; as, glutenin.

gluten. A brown, sticky mixture of proteins in the seeds of cereals, and which remains after washing the starch out of wheat flour with water. It confers the toughness on dough. The amino acids of glutens are glutamic acid (12–24%), leucine, proline, and arginine. **animal-** Fibrin.

glutenin. A wheat protein, soluble in dilute alkalies.

glutethimide. $C_{13}H_{15}O_2N$ = 217.26. α-Ethyl-α-phenylglutarimide. White, bitter crystals, m.87, insoluble in water; a hypnotic (B.P.).

glutin. $C_{192}H_{294}N_{60}SO_{70}(?)$ A protein in gelatin.

glutine. Glue of animal origin.

glutinic acid. $HOOC \cdot C:C \cdot CH_2 \cdot COOH$ = 128.09. Pentinedioic acid, propine-1,3-dicarboxylic acid. White solid, m.146.

glutinosin. $C_{48}H_{60}O_{16}(?)$. An antibiotic from the soil fungus *Metarrhizium glutinosum*; a severe skin irritant.

glutol. A reaction product of starch and formaldehyde. Cf. *amyloform*.

Glutolin. $C_{204}H_{336}N_{60}SO_{70}$. Trademark for formaldehyde gelatin. A protein derived from gelatin.

glutose. The unfermentable reducing portion of cane molasses, formerly considered to be a 3-ketohexose. A complex mixture of anhydrofructose; predominantly the compounds formed by the condensation of amino acids and their amides with simple sugars.

glycals. A group of derivatives of sugars obtained by removing hydrogen peroxide; as glucal, from glucose.

glyceraldehyde. $CH_2OH \cdot CHOH \cdot CHO$ = 90.1. 2,3-

Dihydroxypropanal*. Colorless solid, m.132, soluble in water.

glycerals. Compounds derived from glycerol and aldehydes, similar to the acetals.

glyceric acid. $CH_2OH \cdot CHOH \cdot COOH = 106.1$. 2,3-Dihydroxypropanoic acid*. Occurs as d- and l-acids. Colorless syrup, soluble in water, formed during alcoholic fermentation. **α-phenyl-** Atroglyceric acid.

glyceric aldehyde. Glyceraldehyde.

glyceride. An ether or ester derived from glycerol. The fats and oils are mainly triglycerides of fatty acids, e.g., tripalmitin.

glycerin(e). Glycerol. **g. agar-agar.** A culture medium: 60 ml glycerol, 15 gm agar, 10 gm peptone, 5 gm sodium chloride, 1,000 ml bouillon stock, neutralized with caustic soda. **g. trinitrate.** Nitroglycerin.

glycerinate. A salt of glyceric acid, indicated by the radical $C_3H_5O_4$—.

glycerino. Glycero.

glycerinum. Glycerol.

glycero. (1) Glyceryl. (2) The radical —CHO_2·-$CHO \cdot CH_2O$==, from glycerol.

glycerogen. A German wartime substitute for glycerin (glycerol 40, propylene glycol 40, other higher alcohols 20%). Made by hydrogenating inverted sucrose.

glycerol. $(CH_2OH)_2CHOH = 92.08$. Glycerin(e), glycerinum, 1,2,3-propanetriol*, propenyl hydrate. Colorless, sweet syrup, d.1.260, m.17 (solidifies at lower temperature), b.290, soluble in water, insoluble in organic solvents. Obtained by the saponification of fats in the soap industry; used as a mordant, plasticizer, solvent, and reagent, in the manufacture of printer's ink and rolls, and explosives, and for application to the skin. **absolute-** G. free from water. **amyl-** $C_5H_9(OH)_3$. Quintenyl glycerin. **diethyl-** Diethylglycerol. **dithio-** See *BAL.* **mesitylene-** Mesicerin.

g. diacetate. Diacetin. **g. dilaurate.** Dilaurin. **g. dinitrate.** Dinitroglycerin. **g. diphenyl ether.** $C_{15}H_{16}O_3 = 244.2$. 1,3-Diphenoxy-2-propanol*. White crystals, m.80; a plasticizer for nitrocellulose. **g. distearate.** Distearin. **g. ether.** $C_6H_{10}O_3 = 130.2$. Glycerol ether. Colorless liquid, d.0.091, b.169. Cf. *allylin.* **g. monochlorhydrin.** $C_3H_7O_2Cl = 110.51$. *alpha-* 3-Chloro-1,2-propanediol*. Colorless liquid, d.1.322, $b_{0.5mm}81$, miscible with water; used in the synthesis of glycidol. *beta-* 2-Chloro-1,3-dihydroxypropane; $b_{14mm}124$. **g. monophenyl ether.** $C_9H_{12}O_3 = 168.1$. 1-Phenoxy-2,3-propanediol*, autodyne. White solid m.53; a plasticizer. **g. phosphoric acid.** $C_3H_5(OH)_2H_2PO_4 = 172.1$. An oily constituent of lecithins and nerve tissues. **g. sulfuric acid.** $C_3H_5(OH)_2 \cdot HSO_4$. **g. tributyrate.** Tributyrin. **g. trilaurate.** Laurin. **g. trinitrate.** Nitroglycerin. **g. tripalmitate.** Palmitin. **g. tristearate.** Stearin.

glycerophosphate. Lecithin. A salt of glycerolphosphoric acid containing the radical $=PO_4$·-$C_3H_5(OH)_2$.

glycerophosphoric acid. See *glycerolphosphoric acid.*

glycerose. $C_3H_6O_3 = 90.1$. A triose mixture of glyceraldehyde and dioxyacetone, obtained by oxidation of glycerol.

glycerosulfate. A salt of glycerolsulfuric acid containing the radical —$SO_4C_3H_5(OH)_2$.

glycerosulfuric acid. Glycerolsulfuric acid.

glyceryl. Propenyl. The radical —$CH_2 \cdot CH \cdot CH_2$==, from glycerol Cf. *propenyl allyl.* **g. aldehyde.** Glyceraldehyde. **g. chloride.** Trichlorhydrin. **g. ether.** Glycerol ether. **g. hydroxide.** Glycerol. **g. laurate.** Trilaurin. **g. lineolate.** Trilinolein. **g. monostearate.** $C_{20}H_{42}O_4 = 346.32$. A commercial emulsifying and dispersing agent, used mainly in cosmetics. A hard fat, containing 30–40% of the α isomer, m.54–60, dispersible in water. **g. nitrate.** Nitroglycerin.

glycide. Glycidol.

glycidol. $C_3H_6O_2 = 74.05$. Glycide, epihydrin alcohol, 2,3-epoxy-1-propanol*. Colorless liquid, $b_{751mm}162$, miscible with water; used in organic synthesis.

glycin. (1) Glycine. (2) p-Hydroxyphenylaminoacetic acid; a developer. (3) Mannite. (4) Beryllium. (5) Glycyrrhiza.

glycine. $NH_2 \cdot CH_2 \cdot COOH = 75.09$. Glycocoll, aminoacetic acid, aminoethanoic acid*, glycocin, gelatin sugar. Sweet, colorless monoclinic crystals, d.1.575, m.232, slightly soluble in water. **acetyl-** q.v. **benzoyl-** Hippuric acid. **carbamyl-** Hydantoic acid. **glycyl-** The simplest peptide, NH_2-$CH_2CONHCH_2COOH$. **guanylmethyl-** Creatine. **N-methyl-** Sarcosine. **α-methyl-** Alanine. **trimethyl-** Betaine.

g. anhydride. 2,5-Piperazinedione. **g. betaine.** $C_5H_{11}O_2N = 117.08$; occurs in crustaceans, the cephalopods, and octopus.

glycinin. The principal protein of the soybean.

glycirrhiza. Glycyrrhiza.

glycocholate. A salt of glycocholic acid.

glycocholeic acid. $C_{27}H_{45}O_5N = 465.3$. A bile acid compound of glycogen and choleic acid. Colorless prisms, m.175, slightly soluble in hot water.

glycocholic acid. $C_{26}H_{43}O_6N = 465.4$. A bile acid compound of glycine and cholic acid. Colorless needles, m.134, soluble in water.

glycoclastic. Glycolytic.

glycocoll. Glycine. **g. betaine.** Glycine betaine.

glycogen. $(C_6H_{10}O_5)_x$. Animal starch, glucogen, liver sugar, hepatin. A carbohydrate in the animal organism, especially liver. Colorless, tasteless powder, readily hydrolyzed to glucose (red with iodine). Acids hydrolyze it to dextrose, and enzymes to maltose.

glycogenase. A liver enzyme which hydrolyzes glycogen to maltose and dextrin.

glycogenolysis. The successive breaking down of glycogen in animal tissues. Cf. *staircase reaction.* In *normal* tissue, one glucose splits into lactic acid, and one is oxidized; in *cancer* tissue, 13 and 1, respectively.

glycol. (1) See *glycols.* (2) $CH_2OH \cdot CH_2OH = 62.06$. Ethylene g., 1,2-ethanediol, dihydroxyethane, monophenyl ether, phenoxetol. Colorless liquid, d.1.115, $b_{20mm}198$, miscible with water. An antifreeze (60% in water freezes at −49°C); a solvent for cellulose esters; and used to manufacture low-freezing dynamites. **benzylene-** Hydrobenzoin. **butylene-** Butanediol. **diethylene-** Carbitol. **diphenyl-** Hydrobenzoin. **ethylidene-** MeCH(OH)₂. Known only in derivatives; as, acetals. **mesitylene-** Mesitylene g. **phenyl-** Cinnamic alcohol.

propylene- Propanediol. **tetramethylene-** Butanediol. **thiodi-** Dioxyethylene sulfide. **tetramethylethylene-** Pinacone. **tetraphenyl-** Benzopinacol. **trimethylene-** Propanediol.

g. acetate. See *g. monoacetate, g. diacetate*. **g. aldehyde.** $CH_2OH \cdot CHO = 60.04$. Hydroxyaldehyde, glycolal, hydroxyethanal. Colorless plates, m.96, soluble in water. **g. amide.** $CH_2OH \cdot CONH_2 = 75.09$. 2-Hydroxyethane amide. Colorless solid, m.120, soluble in water. **g. bromohydrin.** $CH_2OH \cdot CH_2Br = 124.97$. Ethylene bromhydrin, 2-brom-1-hydroxyethane. Colorless liquid, b.147, soluble in water. **g. chlorohydrin.** $CH_2OH \cdot CH_2Cl = 80.51$. Ethylene chlorhydrin, 2-chloro-1-hydroxyethane. Colorless liquid, b.128, miscible with water. **g. cyanohydrin.** $CH_2OH \cdot CH_2CN = 71.07$. Ethylene cyanhydrin. Colorless liquid, b.222, miscible with water. **g. diacetate.** Ethylene acetate. **g. dibromide.** Ethylene bromide. **g. dichloride.** Ethylene chloride. **g. dicyanide.** Ethylene cyanide. **g. diiodide.** Ethylene iodide. **g. dinitrate.** Ethylene nitrate. **g. dinitrate.** Ethylene nitrite. **g. ethers.** A group of compounds used as laquer solvents; as, g. butyl ether (see *butyl Cellosolve*). **g. leucine.** Norleucine. **g. monoacetate.** Ethylene monoacetate. **g. mercaptan.** $(CH_2SH)_2 = 94.1$. Dithioethylene g. Colorless liquid, b.146, slightly soluble in water. **g. salicylate.** Spirosal. **g. sulfhydrate.** Ethylene mercaptan. **g. thiourea.** $C_3H_4ON_2S = 116.13$. A solid, soluble in water, m.200 (decomp).

glycolal. Glycol aldehyde.

glycoleucine. Norleucine.

glycolic acid. $CH_2OH \cdot COOH = 76.04$. Glycollic acid. Hydroxyacetic acid, hydroxyethanoic acid. Colorless leaflets, m.78 (decomp.), soluble in water. **diphenyl-** Benzilic acid. **phenyl-** See *mandelic acid*.

g. aldehyde. Glycol aldehyde. **g. amide.** Glycol amide. **g. anhydride.** $(CH_2OH \cdot CO)_2O = 134.07$. Colorless powder, m.129, insoluble in water.

glycolide. $(C_2H_2O_2)_x = (58.0)_x$. Glycollide. The anhydride of glycolic acid. Colorless leaflets, m.86, insoluble in water.

glycolipins. Fatty substances, yielding on hydrolysis fatty acids and a carbohydrate, usually glucose. They contain no phosphorus; e.g., kerasin.

glycoloyl. The radical $OH \cdot CH_2 \cdot CO\text{---}$. Cf. *glycolyl*.

glycols. Diols. A group of diatomic, aliphatic alcohols, e.g., aliphatic compounds containing 2 ---OH groups; as, ethandiol (glycol).

glycolyl. (1) The radical $=C_2H_2O$. (2) The radical $HOCH_2 \cdot CO\text{---}$. Incorrect usage. See *glycoloyl*. **g. guanidine.** Glycocyamidine.

glycolysis. The decomposition of glucose and other sugars by enzymes.

glycolytic. Glycoclastic. The degradation of sugar by animal tissue or blood enzymes.

glycophospholipins. Fatty substances which yield a fatty acid, a carbohydrate, and phosphoric acid on hydrolysis.

glycoproteins. Glucoproteins. Conjugated proteins containing a carbohydrate radical and a simple protein; e.g., ichthulin.

Glycosal. Trade name for glycerol salicylate.

glycosamine. $C_6H_{11}O_5NH_2 = 179.2$. A decomposition product of chitin. Colorless crystals, slightly soluble in water.

glycoside. A natural compound of a sugar with another substance, which hydrolyzes to its constituents: *glucosides* yield glucose, *fructosides* yield fructose, *galactosides* yield glactose, etc. Many pigments (as anthocyanins), saponins, and tannins are glycosides. Examples (parent compound in parentheses): sinigrin (ethylene), arbutin (benzene), daphnin (styrolene), quercitrin (flavone, anthoxanthin), cyanin (anthocyanins), frangulin (anthracene), prulaurasin (cyanogen), indican (indoxyl), digitalin (cholane).

glycotropin. A hormone resembling prolactin, q.v.

glycuronate. A salt of glucuronic acid.

glycuronic acid. Glucuronic acid.

glycyl. The radical $NH_2 \cdot CH_2COO\text{---}$, or $\text{---}NH \cdot CH_2 \cdot COO\text{---}$, from glycine. It occurs in peptides, e.g., glycylalanine.

glycyrrhetin. $C_{18}H_{26}O_4 = 306.3$. An amorphous bitter substance from licorice root.

glycyrrhiza. (1) Licorice. The dried aqueous extract of licorice root. Lustrous, black, brittle mass, soluble in water. (2) The rhizome and roots of *Glycyrrhiza glabra typica*, Spanish licorice, and *G. glabra glandulifera*, Russian licorice (Leguminosae).

glycyrrhizic acid. $C_{44}H_{64}O_{19}N = 910.50$. Crystals, m.220, from licorice.

glycyrrhizin. $C_{44}H_{64}O_{19}$ (?). A sweet principle from the roots of licorice. Brown scales, m.205 (decomp.), soluble in water; optically inactive.

glyoxal. $(CHO)_2 = 58.03$. Oxalaldehyde, ethanedial*, diformyl, oxal. Colorless, deliquescent powder or liquid, d.1.14, m.15, b.50.5, soluble in water. **difuryl-** Furil. **dimethyl-** Biacetyl. **diphenyl-** Benzil. **methyl-** Pyruvaldehyde. **phenyl-** Benzoyl formaldehyde. **poly-, trimeric-** $C_{12}H_{18}O_8 = 290.16$. A threefold polymer of g., known only as its acetone derivative.

glyoxalase. An enzyme in all animal tissues, except pancreas and lymph glands. It converts glyoxal or its substituents into glycolic acid or its substituents:

$$R \cdot COCHO + H_2O = R \cdot CHOHCOOH$$

glyoxalene. Imidazole.

glyoxalic acid. (1) $CHO \cdot COOH = 74.0$. Ethanol acid, oxoethanoic acid*, oxaldehydic acid. Colorless rhombs, soluble in water, forming $(HO)_2\text{-}CH \cdot COOH$. Cf. *glyoxylic acid*. **g. hydrate.** Glyoxylic acid.

glyoxaline. $NH \cdot CH : N \cdot CH : CH = 68.13$. Imidel- azole, 1,3-diazole. Colorless prisms, m.88, soluble in water. **bis-** Glycosine. **triphenyldihydro-** Amarine. **g. alkaloids.** Alkaloids containing the imidazole nucleus, e.g., pilocarpine.

glyoxime. $(CH : NOH)_2 = 88.12$. Colorless tablets, m.178, soluble in water. Cf. *dimethylglyoxime, Tschugajew's reaction*.

glyoxyl. Glyoxyloyl (U.K. usage). The radical $CHO \cdot CO\text{---}$, from glyoxal. **g. carboxylic acid.** Glyoxalcarbonic acid.

glyoxylase. Glyoxalase.

glyoxylic acid. $(HO)_2CHCOOH = 92.04$. Dihydroacetic acid, 1,1-dihydroxyethanoic acid*.

The hydrated and crystalline form of glyoxalic acid, q.v.; in unripe fruit. **amino-** Oxamic acid. **aminophenyl-** Isatic acid. **carboxyphenyl-** *ortho*-Phthalonic acid. *para-* Terephthalic acid. **methyl-** Pyruvic acid. **phenyl-** Benzoylformic acid.

glyoxyloyl. Glyoxil.

Glyptal. Trademark for synthetic resins and plasticizers prepared from a polyhydric alcohol and phthalic anhydride.

gm. Abbreviation for gram (gm U.S.P.; g B.P.).

Gmelin, Christian Gottlieb. 1792–1860. German chemist, noted for making artificial ultramarine. **G., Johann Friedrich.** 1748–1804. German physician and writer on chemistry. **G. Leopold.** 1788–1853. German chemist, noted as discoverer of potassium ferricyanide; a prolific author. **G. test.** Nitric acid is dropped on filter paper saturated with urine; concentric rings of various colors appear in presence of bile acids.

gmelinite. $(Ca,Na_2)Al_2Si_3O_{12}$. A native chabazite.

gneiss. Crystalline metamorphic rocks; typically of quartz or feldspar.

gnoscopine. $C_{34}H_{36}O_{11}N_2 = 648.4$. *dl*-Narcotine. An opium alkaloid, m.229, in the mother liquor of narceine; synthesized by dehydration of a molecular mixture of meconine and cotarnine.

goa. Araroba, crude chrysarobin, Brazil powder. Yellow powder from the cavities in the trunks of *Andira araroba*, Leguminosae (Brazil). It contains 80% chrysarobin, and resin, gum, etc., and is used to treat skin diseases (taenifuge) and as a source of chrysarobin. Cf. *yaba bark*, *andirin*.

goaf. The space left in a coal mine after removal of the coal.

Göckel condenser. A Liebig-type condenser with a U-shaped inside tube; at the base the tube is connected with an airtight receiver.

go-devil. A cylindrical brush or scraper used to scrub the interior of pipes by the action of the liquid or gas flowing through.

goethite. $FeO \cdot OH$. Ruby mica. A hydrated oxide of iron. Cf. *göthite*.

Goethlin. See *Göthlin*.

Golay column. A 50-m. long tube, wound on a cylindrical former, to contain the filling used in gas chromatography.

gold. $Au = 196.97$. Aurum. An element, at. no. 79. Yellow, ductile, noble metal, $d_{17.5°}19.32$, m.1064.76, b.2600, insoluble in acid or alkalies, soluble in aqua regia. It occurs in nature as an uncombined metal, has valencies of 1 and 3, and tends to form complex compounds:

Aurus	Au^+
Auric	Au^{3+}
Dicyanoaurate	$Au(CN)_2^-$
Tetroxyaurate	$Au(OH)_4^-$
Tetrachloraurate	$AuCl_4^-$
Disulfoaurate	AuS_2^-

World production (1961), 35 million ounces (troy). **coinage-** An alloy: Au 90, Cu 10%. Cf. *coinage.* **fulminating-** Aurodiamine. **glucosylthio-** Aurothioglucose. **hall-marked-** Standard g. **liquid-** A mixture of an organic g. compound with an adhesive and essential oil, or with oxides of bismuth, chromium, and rhodium, brushed onto ceramics and burned in to produce a pattern. **mosaic-** q.v. **rhodium-** Rhodite. A native alloy: Au 57–66, Rh 34–43%. **rolled-** Describing a mechanically applied surface layer of not less than 9-karat g., at least 10 microns thick (U.K. usage). **standard-** Pure g. (24 karats) and 4 alloys of 22, 18, 14, and 9 karats are legal U.K. standards. Four alloys are used in the U.S.: 22, 18, 14, and 10 karats. **white-** An alloy of g. with 20% Pd; used in jewelry. **yellow-** The alloy: Au 41.67, Cu 38.5, Ag 5.83, Zn 12.83, Ni 1.17%.

g. alloys. See *coinage metal, g. plate, standard g.* The g. content of alloys is indicated in karats, q.v., or by the fineness: parts per 1,000. **g. amalgam.** A fusible, crumbling amalgam of Au 40%, Ag, and Hg. **g. bromide.** See *auric* or *aurous bromide.* **g. chloride.** See *auric chloride.* **g. cyanide.** See *auric,* or *aurous cyanide.* **g. dichloride.** $AuCl_2 = 267.9$. Red crystals, decomp. by water. **g. filled.** Describing a g. surface finish of lower quality than rolled g. **g. foil.** Thin leaves of hammered g., used for gilding or dental work. **g. (Au^{198}) injection.** A sterile gelatin-stabilized, colloidal solution of Au^{198}; used to estimate reticuloendothelial activity (B.P.). **g. iodide.** See *auric iodide* or *aurous iodide.* **g. leaf.** G. foil. **g. monobromide.** Aurous bromide. **g. monochloride.** Aurous chloride. **g. monoiodide.** Aurous iodide. **g. number.** A measure of the protecting action of a colloid. The weight, in milligrams, which when added to 10 ml of a 0.005–0.006% red g. sol, just prevents the color change to blue (due to coagulation) on addition of 1 ml of 10% sodium chloride solution. **g. perchloride.** Auric chloride. **g. plate.** An alloy of gold, silver, and copper; e.g., 18 karats: Au 18, Ag 2, Cu 4 pts.; 20 karats: Au 20, Ag 2, Cu 2 pts. **g. plated.** Describing g. plating equivalent in quality to rolled g., q.v. (U.K. usage). **g. plating.** The electrodeposition of g. from a solution of g. cyanide in potassium cyanide. **g. salt.** G. sodium chloride. **g. size.** A solution of white and red lead and yellow ocher in linseed oil, used to seal permanent microscopical preparations. **g. sodium bromide.** $NaAuBr_4, 2H_2O$. Sodium aurobromide. A yellow, water-soluble salt, used in photography. **g. sodium chloride.** $NaAuCl_4 \cdot 2H_2O = 398.1$. Sodium aurochloride. A yellow, hygroscopic, crystalline mass, soluble in water; used in photography for toning. **g. sodium thiomalate.** $C_4H_3O_4AuNa_2S \cdot H_2O = 408.09$. Yellow powder, soluble in water; an antirheumatic (U.S.P.). **g. sponge.** Spongy metallic g. obtained by precipitating g. solution with oxalic acid, and drying and heating the precipitate. **g. terchloride.** Auric chloride. **g. tribromide.** Auric bromide. **g. trichloride.** Auric chloride. **g. tricyanide.** Auric cyanide. **g. triodide.** Auric iodide. **g. trioxide.** Auric oxide. **g. trisulfide.** Auric sulfide. **g. washed.** Describing a g. surface finish of lower quality than rolled g.

golden. g. rod. Solidago. **g. seal.** Hydrastis. **g. yellow.** Naphthalene yellow.

Goldschmidt's process. Thermite process.

Golgi apparatus. Lipochondria. A homologous, cytoplasmic structure in most animal cells. Spongy structures which mobilize the fat and protein reserves.

Golo process. A process of bleaching flour with nitrosyl chloride.

gomabrea. An exudation from a chilean tree; used as a substitute for gum arabic.

Gomberg, Moses. 1866–1947. American chemist, noted as pioneer in the study of free radicals.

gonadotrophin. An estrogen from mare's serum, used to control ovulation in farm animals.

gonan. The luteinizing sex hormone of pregnancy urine.

gonane. Sterane. The steroid parent structure

gondoic acid. $C_{20}H_{38}O_2 = 310.31$. An eicosenoic acid from the oil of the pilot whale.

goniometer. An optical device for measuring angles, especially of crystals.

Gooch, Frank Austin. 1852–1929. American chemist. **G. crucible.** A crucible with a perforated base; used in analysis for filtering through glass or asbestos.

goosefoot. Chenopodium.

Gore phenomenon. The recalescence of an alloy or steel on cooling, due to transition to another crystalline form.

gorgonin. A scleroprotein from the skeletal tissue of coral. *Gorgonia cavollisa* (sea fans), which contain 9% diiodotyrosine. **gorli oil.** The fixed oil of *Oucoba echinata* (Flacourtiaceae), S. Africa, resembling chaulmoogra oil.

gosio gas. $AsMe_3 = 119.91$. Trimethylarsine. A gas of garlic odor generated by certain molds growing in media containing carbohydrates and arsenic compounds. Discovered by Gosio (1891).

goslarite. $ZnSO_4, 7H_2O$. A mineral zinc sulfate.

gossypetin. $C_{15}H_{10}O_8 = 318.08$. 3,5,7,8,3′,4′-Hexahydroflavone. A flavone, q.v., of gossypium, m.230.

gossypiin. Gossypoid.

gossypin. The cellulose of cotton.

Gossypium. (1) The cotton plant, a genus of Malvaceae. (2) Cotton, or the hairs of the seeds of *G. herbaceum.*

gossypoid. The combined principles from the bark of the root of *Gossypium herbaceum*, cotton root bark; an emmenagogue.

gossypol. The toxic principle of cottonseeds. **bound-** An ether-insoluble product formed from g. in the commercial manufacture of cottonseed meal.

göthite. Fe_2O_3, H_2O. Pyrrhosiderite. A crystalline hydrated ferric oxide. Cf. *goethite.*

Göthlin solution. An artificial serum: sodium chloride 6.5, sodium carbonate 1, potassium chloride 0.1, calcium chloride 0.13 gm, per liter of water.

Göttling, Johann Friedrich August. 1755–1809. German apothecary; the first in Germany to accept Lavoisier's theory.

Göulard's extract. A solution of basic lead acetate, $Pb(OH)_2 \cdot Pb(OAc)_2$; a reagent for phenols.

goutine. Citarin.

Gouy layer. A diffuse layer of positive and negative ions responsible for the stability of colloidal particles.

gr. Abbreviation for grain.

Gräbe. See *Graebe.*

gracilaria. A seaweed from Vancouver, from which agar-agar is made.

grade. The ratio of the rise of a slope to its length; the sine of the angle of slope.

graded. Differentiated. **g. potential.** Analysis by electrodeposition in which metals separate at specific voltages.

grading. Sorting on the commercial scale according to size, quality, rank, etc., by gravity action (air separators), centrifugal force (cyclone separators), or mechanical action (screening).

graduate. (1) A measure for liquids, generally a cone-shaped or cylindrical vessel marked with lines showing the volume. (2) One who has earned a degree from a college or university.

graduated. Divided into units by a series of lines, as a vessel marked for measuring liquids, e.g., thermometers.

Graebe, Carl. 1841–1927. German organic chemist who established the constitution of naphthalene. Cosynthesizer (with Liebermann) of alizarin.

graebite. A natural, organic mineral coloring matter; a derivative of polyhydroxyanthraquinone.

Graetz rectifier. A device for converting alternating to direct current, consisting essentially of 4 electric cells with lead and aluminum plates in a solution of sodium bicarbonate.

grafting. An operation of organic-chemical synthesis, in which a group of elements or a radical is attached to a basic molecular chain, e.g., cellulose.

Graham, Thomas. 1805–1869. Scottish chemist and pioneer in the study of colloids, who introduced bronze coinage. **G. law.** The velocities of diffusion of any 2 gases are inversely proportional to the square roots of their densities. Cf. *diffusion law.* **G. salt.** Calgon. Soluble sodium hexametaphosphate. Prepared by strongly heating monosodium dihydrogen orthophosphate, and cooling the molten mass rapidly.

grain. (1) A unit of the apothecaries, avoirdupois, and troy weights (originally that of an average wheat g.):

1 grain = 64.798918 mg = 0.064798918 gm
$= \frac{1}{20}$ scruple $= \frac{1}{60}$ dram $= \frac{1}{480}$ ounce

(2) The seeds of Gramineae, the cereals. (3) The appearance of a heterogeneous surface. **g. alcohol.** Ethanol. **g. germinator.** Germinator. **g. oil.** Fusel oil. **g. tester.** (1) Germinator. (2) A device for sectioning grains.

graininess. Lack of homogeneity of deposits due to aggregations of particles.

gram. Gramme (gm U.S.P.; g B.P.). A unit of weight in the cgs system; the mass of 1.000027 ml water at 4°C. See *liter.*

1 gm = 1,000 mg = 1,000,000 γ = 1/1,000 kg
= 15.43248 grains = 0.03527 av. oz
= 0.03215 ap. oz

kilo- 1,000 gm, 1 kg. **micro-** The one-millionth part of a g., 1 μg or 1 γ. **milli-** The one-thousandth part of a g., 1 mg.

  g. atom. The atomic weight of an element in grams. **g. calorie.** Small *calorie.* **g. centimeter.**

The gravitational unit of work, g. erg. **g. equivalent.** The equivalent weight of a substance in grams: *n* gm of a substance, where *n* is atomic weight/valency. **g. molecular solution.** Molar solution. **g. molecular volume.** The volume at 0°C and 760 mm pressure occupied by 1 mole of an element. For a gas it equals the volume of 2 gm. hydrogen at STP/limiting density = 22.242 liters. **g. molecular weight.** G. molecule. **g. molecule.** 1 mole: the molecular weight of a substance in grams.

-gram. Suffix indicating a mechanical record; as, spectrogram. Cf. *graph.*

Gram, Hans, C. J. 1853–1938. Danish bacteriologist. **g.-negative.** Describing bacteria that are decolorized by G. stain. **g.-positive.** Describing bacteria that retain the G. stain. **G.'s iodine solution.** A solution: iodine 1, potassium iodide 2 pts. in 200 pts. water; a microscopical stain. **G.'s stain.** A solution: aniline 15, saturated alcoholic solution of methyl violet 7, absolute alcohol 10 ml in 100 ml water; used in bacteriology.

gramicidin. A compound isolated from cultures of certain bacteria in phosphate-enriched soils; toxic to all gram-positive organisms; m.229. **g.-S.** Soviet g. An antibiotic from strains of *Bacillus brevis* from Russian soils. Colorless needles, m.267. Cf. *tyrothricin.*

Graminaceae, Gramineae. The grass family, a group of plants that yield cereals, sugar, starch, and essential oils. E.g.:

Saccharum officinarum	Cane sugar
Agropyron repens	Triticum
Zea mays	Indian corn
Avena sativa	Oatmeal
Tritium vulgare	Wheat
Oryza sativa	Rice
Hordeum distichum	Barley

gramine. (1) β-Dimethylaminomethyl iodide. Colorless plates, m.132. A degradation product of indole alkaloids; an alkylating agent. (2) A protein, m.133, from barley.

gramme. Gram.

granatine. An alkaloid from pomegranate.

granatonine. Pseudo-*pelletierine.*

granatotannic acid. $C_{20}H_{16}O_{13}$ = 464.1. An amorphous substance from the root bark of *Punica granatum,* pomegranate.

granatum. Pomegranate.

grandiflorine. An alkaloid from the fruit of *Solanum grandiflorum.*

granidiorite. A form of granite.

granite. A crystalline, igneous rock, of quartz, orthoclase, with both muscovite and biotite, cooled slowly under great pressure.

granular. Grainlike.

granulated. Made of small particles.

granulation. The process of converting a substance into granules, e.g., by rapidly quenching drops of a molten metal (as with granulated zinc). Cf. *slugging, spheronizing.*

granules. (1) Small grains having in bulk the properties of semifluids. Their flow through an orifice is a function of the orifice area and is practically independent of the head. (2) A medicinal substance in small pellets.

granulose. (1) β-Amylose. A sugar of starch plants, enclosed by an envelope of starch cellulose. It gives a blue color with iodine solution. (2) The product obtained when cotton wool is charred.

grape. (1) Vine, *Vitis vinifera.* (2) The edible fruit of *Vitis* species. **mountain-** The root of *Berberis aquifolium* (Berberidaceae); an alterative and tonic. **Oregon-** Mountain.

g. fruit. The edible fruit of *Citrus maxima,* rich in vitamin C. **g. juice.** The expressed and sterilized, unfermented juice of g.; a beverage. **g. pomace.** A fertilizer. The dried cake remaining after pressing juice from grapes; contains about 1.2% N, small amounts of P and K. **g. seed oil.** An oil expressed from g. seeds; used as lubricant for watches and for coating raisins; d.0.923, sapon. no. 182. **g. sugar.** Glucose.

graph. (1) A record obtained by physical means. (2) A line drawing showing the frequency or periodicity of a phenomenon or relating 2 variables.

-graph. Suffix indicating: (1) a pictorial record, e.g., photograph; (2) an instrument to make mechanical records; as, spectrograph.

graphic. Pertaining to diagrams. **g. formula.** A spatial structural formula, or a geometrical drawing, indicating the isomeric forms of certain carbon compounds. **g. symbol.** See *structure symbol.*

graphite. Black lead, plumbago. A native or artificially made allotropic carbon. Shining amorphous masses or hexagonal lamellae, d.1.9–2.3, hardness 0.5–1.0. Used as pigment; for crucibles, retorts, electrodes and pencils; and as a lubricant. **colloidal-** Deflocculated suspensions of g. in oil (Oildag) or in water (Aquadag), used as lubricants. **pyrolytic-** A light polycrystalline form of carbon produced by gas deposition. Its thermal conductivity is high and low, parallel to and across the plane of deposition, respectively; a coating for missiles and electronic apparatus. **white-** A form of boron nitride used as a refractory and dry lubricant; d.2.2.

graphitic acid. $C_{11}H_4O_5$ = 216.0. Yellow powder produced from native graphite by the action of potassium chlorate and nitric acid. **pyro-** See **pyrographitic acid.**

graphon sulfate. The black substance produced by the slow action on graphite of potassium chlorate and concentrated sulfuric acid.

grappa. A brandy prepared by fermenting pressed pomace, adding grape residues, and distilling.

grasses. See *Graminaceae.* **g. time factor.** A supposed vitamin, q.v., in grass juice, the absence of which affects the optimum growth rates of rats.

grating. A lattice work or screen composed of lines, e.g., a glass, metal, or film with minute fine rulings (often 20,000 per cm); produces a series of spectra by the dispersion of a ray of light. Cf. *diffraction.* **concave-** A slightly concave piece of speculum metal on which the lines are ruled; it focuses the light. **plane-** A g. which requires parallel rays of light; e.g., a slit, and collimator.

g. spectroscope. A spectroscope in which the spectrum is produced by a diffraction grating, and not by a refracting prism.

gratiolin. $C_{20}H_{34}O_7 = 386.3$. A glucoside from *Gratiola officinalis*, hedge hyssop (Scrophulariaceae); yellow needles.

gratiosolin. $C_{46}H_{84}O_{25} = 1036.8$. A glucoside from *Gratiola officinalis*, hydrolyzed by water to gratiosoletin.

graukalk. Technical calcium acetate.

gravimetric. Describing measurement by weight. **g. analysis.** Quantitative analysis by weighing precipitates.

gravimetry. Measurement by weight.

gravitation. (1) The universal attraction between material bodies. Its intensity varies directly with the product of the 2 masses. (2) The tendency of substances to move toward the center of the earth; measured by the g. constant. **g. constant.** g. A measure of the attractive force of the earth. $g = 666.07 \times 10^{-10}$ cm^3/g-sec$^2 = 980.665$ cm/sec^2. **g. formula.** The force f of gravitational attraction between 2 masses, m and m_1, separated by the distance r: gmm_1/r^2, where g is the g. constant $= 6.658 \times 10^{-8}$ dyne-cm^3/g-sec^2.

gravitational. Pertaining to gravitation. **g. constant.** Gravitation constant. **g. effect.** Westling effect. The loss of weight of body A weighed underneath body B on a beam balance. The effect is specific for those pairs of elements whose atomic numbers are related by $B^2/A^2 = n$, where n is an integer. **g. force.** Gravitation formula.

gravity. (1) The attractive force of the earth, measured by the gravitation constant. (2) Specific g. Cf. *Helmert's equation*. **distillation-** The specific g. of 200 ml distillate from 200 ml alcoholic liquor. **original-** O.G. The specific g. of a wort before fermentation as determined from the amount of alcohol in the fermented liquor. It is given by the residual g. plus the g. lost according to the spirit indication, q.v. **present-** The actual specific g. of a fermented liquor. **residual-** The specific g. of the liquid remaining after all the alcohol has been removed by distillation from 200 ml fermented liquor, and the residue is made up to 200 ml. **specific-** See *density* and *specific gravity*. **standard-** 980.665 cm/sec.^{2}

gravure. A process of printing from an inked metal surface which has been etched with acid in such a way that the darker the shade, the deeper the etch, and the more ink it holds available for transfer to the paper.

grax. Whale tissue remaining after extraction of oils, etc.; a fertilizer.

gray, grey. Ash color, a mixture of white and black pigments. **g. oil.** A mixture of 40–50% finely divided mercury in an oil base; an ointment. **g. powder.** A finely divided mixture: mercury 38, chalk 57, honey 10 pts.

grease. (1) A soft fat. (2) A dark, low-grade waste product containing lard, tallow, bone, horse or fish fat, stearins, etc. G. usually has an unpleasant odor, high unsaponifiable matter, and free fatty acids; is used as a lubricant. (3) Oil thickened with soap. Cf. *wax*. **black-** Dark, fatty matter obtained from cottonseed oil; used in candle manufacture. **cup-** An emulsion: mineral oil 80%, lime soaps and water 1%; a lubricant. **Yorkshire-** Lanolin.

Greek alphabet (used in chemistry).

A	α	alpha (*al'-fah*)	a
B	β (β)	beta (*be'tah*)	b
Γ	γ	gamma (*gam'-ah*)	g (hard)
Δ	δ (∂)	delta (*del'-tah*)	d
E	ϵ (ε)	epsilon (*ep-s$\bar{\imath}$'-lon*)	e (short)
Z	ζ	zeta (*ze'-tah*)	z
H	η	eta (*e'-tah*)	e (long)
Θ	θ (ϑ)	theta (*the'-tah*)	th
K	$\varkappa$ (κ)	kappa (*kap'-ah*)	k
Λ	λ	lambda (*lam'-dah*)	l
M	μ	mu (*m$\bar{u}$*)	m
N	ν	nu (*n$\bar{u}$*)	n
Π	π	pi (*p$\bar{\imath}$*)	p
P	ρ (ρ)	rho (*ro*)	r
Σ	σ (ς)	sigma (*sig'-mah*)	s
Φ	φ (ϕ)	phi (*fi*)	ph (f)
Ψ	ψ	psi (*psi; si*)	ps
Ω	ω	omega (*o'-me-gah*)	o (long)

green. (1) Grass color: a hue obtained by mixing yellow and blue pigments. (2) Unused, raw, untreated or incompletely treated. **g. oil.** The anthracene oil fraction of coal tar. A source of vinylcarbazole, m.64; used in the manufacture of polymers. Cf. heavy *creosote*. **g. vitriol.** Ferrous sulfate.

greenockite. CdS. A rare mineral sulfide.

greensalt. A wood-preserving solution of potassium dichromate, copper sulfate, and arsenic acid.

greensand. (1) A sandy deposit containing glauconite. (2) Natural sand dampened for molding.

greenstone. A variety of jade.

Gregory mixture. G. powder. A mixture of rhubarb rhizome, ginger, and magnesium carbonate; used as a stomachic, and formerly as a general panacea. **G. salt.** A mixture of morphine; and codeine hydrochlorides produced in the purification of morphine by the G. process.

greisen. A granite in which feldspar is replaced by quartz.

Grenacher stain. Carmines of alum, borax, and hydrochloric acid, used to stain nuclei and muscle tissues.

Grenet battery. An electrolytic carbon-zinc cell.

grenz rays. Infrarroentgen rays, Bucky rays, longwave X rays. Very soft X rays produced at low voltages and absorbable by glass; used to treat skin diseases. Cf. *radiation*.

GR-I. Abbreviation for government rubber–isobutylene; a synthetic rubber.

Griess, Peter. 1829–1888. German-born British chemist. **G. reaction.** The substitution of amino radicals by hydroxyl, halogen, or cyan radicals by diazotization and treatment with water. **G.-Ilosva reagent.** A solution of sulfanilic acid and α-naphthylamine in acetic acid; a reagent for nitrites.

grifa. Lithium acetyl salicylate.

Griffith white. Lithopone.

Grignard, Victor. 1871–1935. French chemist-Nobel Prize Winner (1912). **G.'s reaction.** Magnesium alkyl condensation: a reaction by which a C atom is introduced into the hydrocarbon radical or a compound by G.'s reagent to pass from a lower to a higher member of a homologous series. **G.'s reagent.** Compounds of the general type R·Mg·X, where R is an organic radical, and X a halogen.

Only one compound in which X is fluorine is known, i.e., C_2H_5MgF.

Typical Grignard reactions:

1. Formation of a *hydrocarbon:*

$$RMgI \xrightarrow[\text{dilute acids}]{\text{hydrolysis in}} Mg\big\langle^I_{OH} + RH$$

2. Preparation of an *acid:*

$$RMgI \xrightarrow{CO_2} R\cdot COOMgI \xrightarrow{\text{hydrolysis}}$$
$$Mg\big\langle^I_{OH} + R\cdot COOH$$

3. Preparation of a *ketone:*

$$RMgI \xrightarrow{R'CN} {}^R_{R'}\!\!\big\rangle C\!:\!NMgI \xrightarrow{\text{hydrolysis}}$$
$$Mg\big\langle^I_{OH} + NH_3 + {}^R_{R'}\!\!\big\rangle CO$$

4. Preparation of: (*a*) a *secondary alcohol,* (*b*) a *ketone,* or (*c*) a *tertiary alcohol.* Polaises reaction:

$$RMgI \xrightarrow{R'CHO} {}^R_{R'}\!\!\big\rangle C\big\langle^{OMgI}_H$$
$$\xrightarrow{\text{hydrolysis}} {}^R_{R'}\!\!\big\rangle C\big\langle^{OH}_H$$
$$(a)$$

$$(a) \xrightarrow{\text{oxidize}} {}^R_{R'}\!\!\big\rangle CO$$
$$(b)$$

$$(b) \xrightarrow{R''MgI} {}^R_{R'}\!\!\big\rangle C\big\langle^{R''}_{OMgI} \xrightarrow{\text{hydrolysis}}$$
$${}^R_{R'}\!\!\big\rangle C\big\langle^{R''}_{OH}$$
$$(c)$$

Grilon. Trade name for a polyamide synthetic fiber.

grindelia. Gum plant, tarweed. The dried leaves and flowering tops of *Grindelia* species (Compositae); an antispasmodic and anticatarrhal.

grindeloid. The combined principles of *Grindelia* species, containing an alkaloid resin and an oil.

grinder. A power-operated device for pulverizing materials by grinding.

grinding. The process of powdering a substance by lateral motion, as opposed to perpendicular motion (crushing).

griphite. $8[(NaAlCaFe)_3Mn(PO_4)_2\cdot 5(OH)_2]$. A native garnet-type hydrophosphate.

grisein. An antibiotic from *Streptomyces griseus;* antibacterial, antirickettsial, but not antifungal.

griseofulvin. $C_{17}H_{17}O_6Cl = 352.77$. Cream powder produced by *Penicillium griseofulvum,* slightly soluble in water; an antifungal (U.S.P.).

griserin. Sodium lorinate.

grog. Broken bricks, or burnt ground fireclay; a refractory.

Grossmann reagent. $(C_2H_6ON_4)_2H_2SO_4$. An ammoniacal solution of dicyandiamidine sulfate; yellow precipitate with nickel.

grossularite. A green calcium aluminum garnet.

Grotthus' law. Radiation must be absorbed to produce a reaction.

ground. Powdered. **g. cherry.** Physalis. **g. nut.** Arachis. **g. nut oil.** Arachis oil. **g. state.** The normal or unexcited state of an atom. **g. wood.** Mechanical wood pulp.

group. (1) A number of elements having similar properties, e.g., the alkali metals. See *periodic system.* (2) A number of atoms that pass through a series of reactions unseparated. See *radical.* (3) A number of elements with similar reactions. See qualitative *analysis.* **functioning-** A g. that has a replaceable hydrogen; as, —OH. **negative-** A negatively ionized atom of an acid radical, e.g. SO_4. **nonfunctioning-** A g. that has no replaceable hydrogen, e.g., —Cl. Cf. *derivative.* **positive-** A positively ionized atom of a metal or radical, e.g., NH_4.

g. precipitant. A reagent that precipitates elements of the same group, e.g., hydrogen sulfide. **g. properties.** The properties of elements belonging to the same g., e.g., of a vertical division of the periodic system. **g. reaction.** The precipitation of elements in a definite analytical g. Cf. *precipitant.* **g. relation.** The relation among elements of a g. (vertical division) of the periodic system.

Grove, Sir William Robert. (1811–1896). British scientist. **G. cell.** A voltaic cell (1.91 volts) of amalgamated zinc in sulfuric acid (d.1.136) and platinum in concentrated nitric acid.

growth. An increase in size. **bacterial-** The appearance of a bacterial colony after incubation. **colloidal-** A phenomenon shown by crystals of a soluble metallic salt (whose silicate is insoluble) in a 50% solution of water glass. Each salt develops characteristic structure due to osmotic pressure and the breaking of the insoluble membrane of metal silicate. **inorganic-** The aggregation of solid particles, by crystallization, periodic precipitation, or colloidal growth.

g. factor. A supposed vitamin, q.v., whose absence hinders the growth of *Lactobacillus casei.*

GR-S. Abbreviation for: Government rubber–styrene (U.S. usage); **SBR:** styrene butadiene rubber (U.K. usage). A synthetic rubber produced by polymerization at 120°F., or cold rubber at 41–55°F.

grumose. Clotted.

grundy. Granulated pig iron.

grunerite. $Fe_7H_2(SiO_3)_8$, from Massachusetts.

gryolite. $CaO\cdot 3SiO_2\cdot 2H_2O$. A constituent of certain boiler scales. Cf. *cryolite.*

G. salt. The sodium or potassium salt of G-acid.

guachamacine. Guachamacine. An alkaloid from guachamaca, the bark of *Malouetia nitida* (Apocynaceae), Venzuela; an arrow poison.

guacin. A resin from the leaves of *Mikania guaco* (S. America); used to cure snakebites.

guaethol. Thanatol.

guaiac. A resin from *Guaiacum officinale* (Zygophyllaceae), S. America. **g. resinic acid.** $C_{20}H_{26}O_4 = 330.3$. An acid of guaiac; yellow crystals. **g.**

wood. Lignum vitae, guaiaci lignum. The heartwood of *Guaiacum* species; a dye. **g. wood oil.** The essential oil of g. d.0.965–0.975, soluble in alcohol. It contains tiglic aldehyde. **g. yellow.** The coloring matter of guaiac wood; yellow crystals.

guaiacene. $C_5H_8O = 84.0$. Tiglic aldehyde. An oil from the distillation of guaiac wood.

guaiaci lignum. Guaiac wood.

guaiacin. $C_{14}H_{24}O = 208.3$. An alcohol, the odorous principle of balsam wood. Colorless crystals, m.91, soluble in alcohol; used in perfumery.

guaiacol. $C_6H_4(OH)OMe = 124.1$. Methylpyrocatechin, *o*-hydroxyanisole, 1-hydroxy-2-methoxybenzene, in wood tar. Colorless prisms, m.32, soluble in water. A reagent to detect lignin, narceine, chelidonine, nitrous acid, and acacia; an antiseptic. **allyl- 4**-Eugenol. **5-** Chavibetol. **cinnamyl-** Styracol. **methyl-** Creosol. **methylenedi-** Pulmoform. **propenyl-** Isoeugenol. **vinyl-** Hesperetol.
  g. acetate. $C_9H_{10}O_3 = 166.1$. Eucol. A liquid, b.238. **g. benzoate.** Benzosol. **g. benzylic ether.** Benzeain. **g. biniodide.** $C_7H_5O_2I_2 = 374.7$. Brown powder, used to treat tuberculosis. **g. cacodylate.** Cacodiliacol. Brown crystals, used medicinally. **g. carbonate.** $(C_7H_7O)_2CO_3 = 274.1$. White crystals, m.87, soluble in ether; a substitute for g. oleate. **g. oleate.** Oleoguaiacol. A mixture of g. and oleic acid in ether. **g. valerate.** Creosote.

guaiaconic acid. $C_{10}H_{24}O_5 = 344.2$. A resinous acid, from guaiac. Brown powder, used in the guaiac test for blood.

guaiacum. Guaiac.

guaiacyl. (1) *o*-Anisyl. (2) $[C_6H_3(OH)(OCH_3)\text{-}SO_3]_2Ca$. Calcium-*o*-guaiacol sulfonate, gujacyl. Gray powder, soluble in water; a local anesthetic.

guaiene. $C_{12}H_{12} = 156.09$. 2,3-Dimethylnaphthalene. Colorless liquid, b.266, insoluble in water. Cf. *guajene*.

guaiol. Tiglic aldehyde.

guaj. Variant of *guai*.

guajene. $C_{15}H_{24} = 204.19$. A hydrocarbon, b.124, from guaiac.

guanamine. A compound containing the group $=N\cdot C(NH_2):N\cdot C(NH_2):N—$; as **acet-** $C_4H_7N_3 = 97.2$. Colorless crystals, m.265.

guanase. An enzyme, converting guanine into xanthine; in adrenals and pancreas.

guanazyl. The radical $—N:NC(:N\cdot NH\cdot CNH\cdot NH_2)—$. **g. benzene.** $Ph_2C_2H_4N_5 = 266.3$. Colorless crystals, m.199.

guanethidine. $C_{10}H_{22}N_4\cdot H_2SO_4 = 296.44$. 1-(2-guanidinoethyl)azacycloöctane. White crystals, m.254, soluble in water; a sympatholytic. **g. sulfate.** $(C_{10}H_{22}N_4)_2\cdot H_2SO_4 = 494.70$. White crystals, soluble in water; an antihypertensive (U.S.P.).

guanidine. $(NH_2)_2C(:NH) = 59.17$. Carbamidine, aminomethanamidine, carbondiamide imide, uramine. Colorless crystals, soluble in water; an isolog of urea. **amidophenol-** See *amidophenolguanidine*. **aminobutyl-** Agmatine. **benzoylene-** q.v. **bi-** Guanylguanidine. **carbamyl-** Guanylurea. $N:C\cdot NH\cdot C(:NH)\cdot NH_2 = 84.06$. Dicyandiamide, param. Colorless crystals, m.205.

decamethylenebis- Synthalin. **diphenyl-** q.v. **guanyl-** Biguanidine. **isopentenyl-** Galegine. **lactyl-** Alacreatine. **nitro-** $CH_4O_2N_4 = 104.2$. Colorless crystals, m.240.
  g. acetic acid. Glycocyamine. **g. phosphoric acid.** Phosphagen.

guanidines. Compounds derived from guanidine, e.g., containing the radical $=N\cdot C(NH)\cdot N=$. See *creatine*.

guanidium. Describing a salt from guanidine, in which 1 N atom is pentavalent: $(NH_2)_2C:NH(R)\text{-}(X)$.

guanidinophosphoric acid. Phosphagen.

guanido. Guanidino (U.K. usage). The radical $—NH\cdot C(:NH)NH$.

guanidoacetic acid. Glycocyamine. **methyl-** Creatine.

guanidopropionic acid. Alacreatine.

guanine. $C_5H_5ON_5 = 151.27$. Imidoxanthine, 2-amino-6-oxypurine, 2-aminohypoxanthine. A leucomain decomposition product of nucleins; in guano, fish scales, human liver, and spleen. Colorless needles, decomp. above 360, insoluble in water.

guanite. Struvite.

guano. Bird manure. The partly decomposed excrements of sea birds from the islands off the western coast of S. America, especially Peru; an excellent fertilizer and a source of guanine.

guanoline. $C_4H_9O_2N_3 = 131.1$. Guanidocarbonic ethyl ester. Colorless crystals, m.114.

guanosin(e). $C_{10}H_{13}N_5O_5 = 283.4$. A pentoside in the pancreas. **g. phosphoric acid.** Guanylic acid.

guanyl. Amidino (U.K. usage). The radical $—C(:NH)NH_2$. **g. urea.** $NH_2\cdot CO\cdot NH\cdot C(:NH)\cdot NH_2 = 100.3$. Dicyandiamidine, carbamylguanidine. An isolog of guanylguanidine.

guanylic acid. $H_2PO_4\cdot C_5H_7O_3\cdot C_5H_4ON_5 = 362.4$. A nucleic acid containing guanosine; in pancreas, ox liver, and yeast.

guanzole. 5-Amino-7-hydroxy-1-IV-triazolo-D-pyrimidine. A substituted protein used to treat plant virus infections.

guar. *Cyamopsis tetragonoloba*. An Indian plant resembling soya, now grown in the U.S. The seeds are a source of mannogalactan mucilage.

guarana. Brazilian cocoa. A paste from the seeds of *Paullinia sorbilis* (Sapindaceae); used to treat migraine. **g. tannin.** Paullinio tannin.

guaranine. $C_8H_{10}O_2N_4 = 194.3$. An alkaloid resembling caffeine, from guarana.

guard tube. A tube which usually contains calcium chloride, to prevent access of atmospheric moisture to gas absorption bulbs during weighing. Cf. *witness*.

guavacine. Guvacine.

guayule. The desert shrub, *Parthenium argentatum* (Compositae), Mexico; cultivated in central California. **g. rubber.** Rubber formerly made from g.

Guericke, Otto von. 1602–1688. German philosopher noted for the Magdeburg hemispheres.

guhr. Trade abbreviation for kieselguhr.

Guignet's green. $3CrO_3, B_2O_3, 4H_2O(?)$. A green pigment resulting from the fusion of potassium dichromate and crystalline boric acid.

guinea green. $C_{37}H_{35}N_2O_6S_2Na$. A dye used as food color and indicator, changing at pH 6.0 from magenta (acid) to green (alkaline).

Guldberg, Cato. 1836–1902. Norwegian chemist. **G. Guye rule.** The critical temperature of a substance is 1.4–1.9 times the absolute boiling point. **G. rule.** The boiling point of a liquid is two-thirds the critical temperature in degrees absolute of gas. **G. and Waage law.** Mass law, law of mass action, law of chemical kinetics. The velocity of a reaction is proportional to the active masses of reacting substances; velocity = amount transformed/time. See *mass law*.

gulose. $C_6H_{12}O_6$ = 180.2. A hexose, isomeric with glucose.

gum. A mucilaginous plant stem excretion; complex carbohydrates yielding sugars on hydrolysis. Gums dissolve or swell in water, and are insoluble in alcohol. Classification: A. Arabin-type: completely soluble in water, e.g., *Acacia senegal* (gum arabic). B. Bassorin type: slightly soluble in water, e.g., *Astragalus gummifer* (tragacanth). C. Cerasin type: swelling in water, e.g., *Prunus cerasus* (cherry gum). Individual gums are dealt with under their respective names. **g. arabic.** Acacia. **g. benjamin.** See *benzoin* (2). **g. cistus.** See *labdanum*. **g. copal.** Copal. **g. dragon** Tragacanth. **g. elastic.** Caoutchouc. **g. plant.** Grindelia. **g. resin.** See *gum resins*. **g. running.** The process of melting gums in varnish manufacture. **g. sugar.** Arabinose. **g. thus.** (1) Olibanum. (2) In naval stores, the crystalline pine oleoresin collected from the scarified faces of trees being worked for turpentine. **g. tragacanth.** Tragacanth. **g. tree.** See *gum-tree*.

gumbotil. A gray, leached deoxidized clay containing tourmaline and epidote, from glacial formations in Kansas.

gummeline. Dextrin.

Gummon. Trade name for an insulating material of tar and asbestos.

gummy. Sticky; resembling gum.

gum resins. Oleoresina. Aromatic exudations of plants; a mixture of various substances (as essential oils) with gum. Commonly used in pharmacy are: ammoniac, asafetida, gambode, myrrh, and scammony. Cf. *resins*.

gum tree. Red gum, sweet gum. A large lumber tree, *Liquidambar styraciflua* (Mississippi swamps). **blue-** Eucalyptus. **cotton-** A timber tree, *Nyssa sylvatica* (Asia), which yields edible fruit.

guncotton. $C_{12}H_{14}O_4(NO_3)_6$ = 594.17. Cellulose hexanitrate. A highly nitrated, sparingly soluble explosive cellulose. **soluble-** Pyroxylin.

gunmetal. Bronze. The alloy: Cu 86–90, Sn, Zn 10, Pb, Ni, Sb, Fe, Al, etc., approximately 2%.

Gunning reagent. A 10% solution of iodine in alcohol. **G. test.** The formation of iodoform by adding G. r. and ammonia to urine indicates the presence of acetone.

gunny. A jute bagging cloth.

gunpowder. A granulated explosive mixture of charcoal about 2, sulfur 3, potassium nitrate 15 pts. Its properties depend largely on the size and shape of the grains, their density and hardness, glazing, and moisture content.

Gunter's chain. A measure of length, 20.1168 meters.

Gunzberg reagent. Phloroglucinol (1:15) and vanillin (1:15), mixed shortly before use, to detect free mineral acids. **G. test.** A drop of G. r. is evaporated; on adding the unknown and again evaporating, a pink color indicates hydrochloric acid.

guoethol. Thanatol.

gur. Jaggery. A crude Indian sugar obtained by evaporating unclarified cane juice in open pans.

gurjun. A balsam varnish, from *Dipterocarpus* species (India). **g. oil.** The essential oil of g., d.0.915–0.925, b.255, containing sesquiterpenes.

gut. Intestines of sheep, cleansed, treated with alkali, and twisted to a cord; corrosion-resistant, and used for fume cupboard sash cords.

gutta. (Pl. guttae.) Latin for drop.

guttameter. A device to measure surface tension by the number of drops formed.

gutta-percha. $(C_{10}H_{16})_2$. Gummi plasticum. The purified, coagulated, milky exudate of *Palaquium* species (Sapotaceae). Yellow masses, sticks, or sheets, with red streaks, insoluble in water, partly soluble in turpentine oil. It contains fluavil, alban, and a volatile oil; softens at 65. Used for insulating, in dentistry, and as a rubber substitute.

Gutzeit, Heinrich Wilhelm. 1845–1888. German chemist. **G. arsenic test.** Zinc and dilute sulfuric acid added to the substance in a test tube, covered with a filter paper moistened with mercuric chloride solution, form a yellow spot on the paper, due to $AsH(HgCl)_2$. This turns black forming $As(HgCl)_3$, then As_2Hg_3.

guvacine. $C_6H_9O_2N$ = 127.1. An alkaloid, m.271, from the betel nut, the fruit of *Areca catechu*, an E. Indian palm; an anthelminthic.

Guyton de Morveau, Louis Bernard. 1737–1816. French lawyer who introduced the first chemical nomenclature.

G.w.a. Grams of water in air. See Mohr *liter*.

gymnemic acid. $C_{32}H_{55}O_{12}$ = 631.4. The active constituent of *Gymnema sylvestre* (Asclepiadaceae); Australia, India, Africa.

gymnosperm. A large group of plants in which the seeds are not enclosed in an ovary, e.g., the conifers. Cf. *angiosperm*.

gynergen. $(C_{33}H_{35}O_5N_5)_2C_4H_6O_6$ = 1313.46. Ergotamine bitartrate. Colorless crystals, decomp. 180, soluble in water; found in ergot. Increases the blood pressure, and is a specific for migraine (U.S.P.). Used to treat psychopathological symptoms arising from war hazards.

gynesin. $C_{19}H_{23}O_3N_3$ = 341.4. A base in female urine.

gynocardic acid. (1) $C_{18}H_{34}O_2$ = 282.2. From the oils of *Gynocardia odorata* and *G. Prainii*, m.67, insoluble in water. (2) A mixture, from gynocardia and chaulmoogra oils, of hydnocarpic, taraktogenic, and gadoleic acids.

gynocardine. $C_{13}H_{19}O_9N$ = 333.15. A glucoside, m.162, from the seeds of *Gynocardia odorata*. It yields on hydrolysis glucose, hydrogen cyanide, and ethylfumaric acid. Cf. *chaulmoogra oil*.

gynoval. $MeCHMeCH_2COOC_{10}H_{17}$ = 238.3. The isovaleric ester of isoborneol. Colorless liquid of aromatic odor, d.0.952–0.957, b.135; a hypnotic and sedative.

gypsum. Selenite. A native hydrated calcium sulfate, q.v. Cf. *anhydrite, plaster of paris*.

gyration. Revolution in a circle.

gyrolite. $H_2Ca(SiO_3)_3,H_2O$. A mineral from Radzein, Bohemia.

H

H. Symbol for: (1) hydrogen, H^+ hydrogen ion, H^* excited hydrogen atom, H_2 hydrogen molecule, H_2^+ ionized hydrogen molecule, H_2^* excited hydrogen molecule, H^1 or H^a hydrogen isotope of mass 1 (protium), H^2 or H^b hydrogen isotope of mass 2 (deuterium), H^3 or H^c hydrogen isotope of mass 3 (tritium); (2) the unit of strength of a magnetic field (gauss); (3) henry, the unit of inductance; (4) enthalpy, q.v. **H-acid.** 8-Amino-1-napthol-3,6-disulfonic acid. **H. ion.** See *hydrogen ion.*
H. lines. (1) Spectrum lines due to hydrogen (Fraunhofer nomenclature in brackets):

$$H_\alpha \,[C] \ldots \ldots 6573\lambda \text{ (red)}$$
$$H_\beta \,[F] \ldots \ldots 4861\lambda \text{ (blue)}$$
$$H_\gamma \,[G] \ldots \ldots 4340\lambda \text{ (blue)}$$
$$H_\delta \,[h] \ldots \ldots 4101\lambda \text{ (violet)}$$

(2) Fraunhofer line H, 3968λ, due to calcium. **H.M.** Abbreviation for heavy metals. **H. rays.** A stream of hydrogen nuclei. **H. salt.** The sodium salt of H-acid.

h. Abbreviation for: (1) hour, (2) height, (3) hundred, (4) hetero-.

h. Planck's constant, q.v.

ha. Abbreviation for hectare.

Haber, Fritz. 1868–1934. German chemist. Nobel Prize winner (1916). **H. process.** The synthesis of ammonia from nitrogen and hydrogen in presence of a catalyst. Cf. *nitrogen fixation.*

habitat. The surroundings in which a living organism is commonly found. **abyssal-** A h. in deep sea. **alpine-** A h. in high mountains. **fossorial-** A h. in burrows and caves. **littoral-** A h. near a shore. **pelagic-** A h. in open sea.

hadal. Describing ocean depths exceeding 20,000 ft.

Hadfield, Sir Robert. 1859–1940. British chemist, noted for development of stainless steels. **H. process.** A metal oxide is reduced by heating with granulated aluminum and fluorspar.

hadromal. Ferulaldehyde.

hæ- See *hae-, he-.*

haem. $C_{34}H_{35}O_3N_4Fe$. The essential unit of cellular and blood pigments, related to aetioporphyrin.

haema-, haemo- Prefix indicating a relationship to blood.

haemanthine. $C_{18}H_{23}O_7N = 365.19$. An alkaloid from buphane.

haematoxylin. Hematoxylin.

Haematoxylon, hematoxylon. (1) A genus of leguminous trees of Central America, specifically *H. campechianum.* (2) The heartwood of *H. campechianum,* logwood, campeachy wood, which contains hematoxylon, an astringent and purple color.

Haeser's coefficient. The number 2.33 by which the last 2 figures of the specific gravity of urine are multiplied in order to obtain the amount of solids in 1,000 ml urine. Cf. *Haine's coefficient.*

haeterolite. The mineral $ZnO \cdot Mn_2O_3$.

hafnium. $Hf = 178.49$. Celtium, Ct. Oceanum An element of the carbon group, at. no. 72, discovered (1924) by Coster and Hevesy in zircon and baddeleyite. Valency 4, d.13.3, m.1700. **h. carbide.** $HfC = 190.6$. Gray powder, m.3887. A mixture of h. carbide 25 and tantalum carbide 75% has the highest known melting point, 4200°C. **h. hydroxide.** $Hf(OH)_4 = 246.6$. White powder, insoluble in water. **h. oxide.** $HfO_2 = 210.6$. White powder, m.3025, insoluble in water, soluble in acids. **h. oxychloride.** $HfOCl_2 = 265.6$. White powder, insoluble in water, soluble in hydrochloric acid. **h. sulfate.** $Hf(SO_4)_2 = 370.6$. White crystalline powder, soluble in water.

Hägglund, Erik. 1888–1959. Swedish authority on the chemistry and technology of wood products.

Hahnemann's mercury. Soluble mercury.

Haine's coefficient. The number 1.1, which when multiplied by the last 2 figures of the specific gravity of urine, gives the amount of solids in grains per fluid ounce. Cf. *Haeser's coefficient.*

hairari root. The roots of *Lonchocarpus* species containing rotenone. Cf. *cube* (2).

halazone. $C_6H_4(SO_2NCl_2) \cdot COOH = 269.9$. Trade name for *p*-sulfondichloraminobenzoic acid. White powder with strong chlorine odor, m.213, soluble in water; used to sterilize water in the field.

half-life, half-period. $t_\frac{1}{2}$. The period in which the activity of a radioactive substance falls to half its initial value. It varies from 3×10^{10} years (Th) to 0.002 sec (AcA).

half-stuff. A pulp intended for papermaking, before it is beaten in preparation for the papermaking machine.

halide. A binary compound of the general type MX, MX_2, or MX_3, in which M is a metal, X a halogen (F, Cl, Br, I). **acid-** A compound of the type $R \cdot COX$. **alkylaryl-** A compound of the type RX, where R is an alkyl or aryl radical. **magnesium-** A compound of the type RMgX, e.g., Grignard's reagent.

  h. lamp. An alcohol torch with copper tube, which ordinarily burns colorless but gives a green flame in presence of organic halides; used to detect leaks of halide refrigerants.

halite. A native sodium chloride.

Haliver oil. Trademark for halibut liver oil, rich in vitamins A and D.

Hall, Sir Arthur Daniel. 1864–1942. British agricultural chemist. **H., Carl von.** 1819–1880. Austrian chemist, noted for work on vanadium compounds. **H., Charles M.** 1863–1914. American chemist, inventor of the H. process. **H. Edwin H.** 1855–1938. American physicist, discovered (1879) H. effect.

H. effect. The production of a voltage across a current-carrying conductor (as indium antimonide) located at right angles to an electric field. Used in computers. **H. formula.** If E is the difference of potential between the lower and upper edge of the metal plate of thickness t, then $E = R(Hi/t)$, where R is a constant specific for different metals, H the magnetic field strength in gausses, and i the electric current in cgs units. **H. process.** The electrolytic process by which metallic aluminum is recovered from aluminum oxide. **H. purinometer.** A graduated glass tube of special construction, for the determination of purines in urine.

halloylite. Halloysite.

halloysite. $Al_2O_3 \cdot 2SiO_2 \cdot 4H_2O$. Halloylite. A refringent, micaceous silicate constituent of clay. **meta-** A clay mineral similar to h., but having the same formula as kaolinite.

Hallwachs effect. Photoelectric effect.

halo. (1) A series of luminous concentric circles around a source of illumination caused by the refraction of light on passing through solid or liquid particles suspended in the atmosphere. (2) A circular photographic image produced when X rays pass through an amorphous substance. Cf. *X-ray crystallogram.*

halo- Prefix indicating presence of a halogen.

halochromism. (1) The formation of colored salts from colorless organic bases by addition of acids. Cf. *solvatochromism.* (2) The production of colorless solutions in some solvents and colored solutions in others.

Halocrin. Trade name for 2,5-dichloro-7-methoxyacridine. A reagent for penicillin.

haloform. A compound of the type CHX_3; as, chloroform. **h. reaction.** A reaction analogous to that by which iodoform is made from alcohol or acetone.

halogen. Halogenide (international usage). The nonmetallic elements of the seventh group of the periodic system: F, Cl, Br, and I. Halogens are multivalent and have valence numbers of -1 (chlorides), 1 (hypochlorites), 3 (chlorites), 5 (chlorates), and 7 (perchlorates). **h. acids.** The hydrogen compounds of the halogens: hydrofluoric, hydrochloric, hydrobromic, and hydroiodic acid.

halogenation. Introduction of a halogen into an organic compound, by addition or substitution; as, chlorination.

halogenide. See *halogen.*

halohydrin. An organic compound of the type $X{-}R{-}OH$, where X is a halogen; as, $Cl{-}CH_2 \cdot CH_2 \cdot OH$.

haloid. Resembling or derived from halogens. **h. acid.** An inorganic acid, HX, containing a halogen but no oxygen. **h. elements.** The halogens.

halophile. A bacterium that can grow in saline media.

halothane. $C_2HBrClF_3 = 197.39$. Colorless liquid, d.1.875, b.50, slightly soluble in water; an inhalation anesthetic (U.S.P.).

Halothene. Trade name for a chlorinated polyethylene.

Halowax. $C_{10}H_7Cl = 762.51$. Trademark for β-chloronaphthalene. Colorless solid, m.56; used in gasoline to lubricate valve stems of internal-combustion engines.

Halphen reagent. A 1% solution of sulfur in carbon disulfide. **H. test.** To 1 ml oil add 1 ml H. reagent and 1 ml amyl alcohol; heat in a brine bath for 30 min; 1% cottonseed oil gives a red color.

hamamelase. An enzyme from *Hamamelis virginiana.* Cf. γ-*hamamelitannins.*

Hamamelidaceae. Witch-hazel family. Shrubs that yield: *Hamamelis virginiana* (witch hazel), *Liquidambar orientalis* (storax), *Liquidambar styraciflua* (sweet gum).

hamamelidin. An extract from *Hamamelis virginiana,* witch hazel; a tonic.

hamamelin. A precipitate from the extract of the bark of *Hamamelis virginiana;* a tonic and astringent.

Hamamelis. Hamamelidaceae.

hamamelitannins. Tannic acids from the bark of witch hazel; 3 forms: **alpha-** $C_{34}H_{36}O_{22}$. Hydrolyzed to gallic acid and glucose. **beta-** $C_{20}H_{20}O_{14} \cdot 6H_2O = 592.23$. The principal form, hydrolyzed to gallic acid and the hexose, hamamelose. Fine white needles, m.115, soluble in water. **gamma-** $C_{27}H_{32}O_{19}$. Yellow crystals, m.222 (decomp.), hydrolyzed by hamamelase to gallic acid, methoxygallose, and glucose.

hamamelose. See γ-*hamamelitannins.*

hamartite. Bastnasite.

hamathionic acid. Euxanthic acid.

Hamilton operator. A special operator equation used to convert the energy equation into the wave equation.

Hanane. Trade name for a mixture of bisdimethylaminofluorophosphine oxide and bisdimethylaminophosphorus anhydride. Colorless liquid, mol.wt. 154, miscible with water. A systemic insecticide to control the W. African cocoa shoot disease.

hand. Obsolete unit of length: 1 hand $= 4$ in. $= 10.16$ cm.

hanfangchine. $C_{36}H_{40}N_2O_6 = 596.4$. An alkaloid from the root of the Chinese plant han-fang-chin, *Cocculus japonicus:* used to treat cholera and pulmonary diseases. Cf. *tetrandrine.*

Hanford pile. See *pile.*

hanksite. $9Na_2SO_4 \cdot 2Na_2CO_3 \cdot KCl$. A mineral from California.

Hanovia lamp. An evacuated quartz tube with 2 mercury reservoir electrodes, used to produce mercury-vapor radiations rich in ultraviolet light.

Hantzsch, Arthur. 1857–1935. German organic chemist noted for studies of the stereochemistry of nitrogen compounds.

Hanus solution. A solution of iodine monobromide in glacial acetic acid, used in the determination of iodine values of oils containing unsaturated organic compounds.

haploid. Describing cells have half the number of diploid chromosomes. **h. number.** The 26 chromosomes normally present in the nucleus of the human sperm and ovum. Cf. *diploid number.*

haptaphore. The chemical group of a drug which unites with the amboceptor. Cf. *chemoreceptor.*

hapten(e). An alcohol-soluble substance present in animal organs which forms antibodies in vitro but has no antigenic properties.

haptin. A receptor in Ehrlich's side-chain theory, q.v.

haptogen. The protein of the membrane of the globules of fat in milk.

haptoglobin. Hp. A serum protein.

harbolite. A carbonaceous asphaltic deposit containing 3% bitumen and coal (Turkey).

hard. (1) Firm; resistant. (2) A condition of water, due to the presence of calcium and magnesium salts. See *hardness.* **biologically-** Resistant to biological decomposition.

h. acid. An a. of high positive charge, whose valence electrons are not readily distorted or removed; as, magnesium. **h. base.** A b. whose valence electrons are not readily distorted, or removed; as, carbonates. **h. salt.** Hartsalz.

Harden, Sir Arthur. 1865–1940. British biochemist. **H.-Young ester.** Fructose diphosphate, produced in the fermentation of sugar by yeast. Cf. *sugar* phosphates.

hardening. A process which makes a material more resistant to cutting, breaking, or bending. **work-** The increase in resistance to deformation produced on cold-working a metal.

h. of fats. Hydrogenation. **h. of steel.** Tempering.

hardness. (1) The state or quality of being hard. Resistance to cutting, bruising, scratching, or grinding. (2) The presence of calcium and magnesium salts in water (usually carbonates and bicarbonates), which incrusts boilers, and impairs the lathering of soap by forming insoluble fatty-acid salts. **Brinell-** See *Brinell hardness.* **Moh's-** See *Moh.* **Shore-** See *Shore.*

h. scale. Moh's scale. **h. of water.** A measure of the calcium and magnesium content of water. *permanent-* magnesium or calcium sulfate or carbonate or other calcium salts (except bicarbonates) in water, which cannot be removed by simple boiling but by chemical treatment. See *permutite.* *temporary-* Magnesium or calcium bicarbonate in water; the water is softened by boiling, insoluble calcium carbonate being formed. *total-* The total amount of calcium and magnesium salts in water, expressed in degrees of hardness. See table below.

hardpan. (1) An accumulation of hard cementing material containing Ca or Fe, in the lower horizon of a topsoil. (2) Erroneously used to describe bedrock underlying surface deposits.

hardware. Colloquialism for made-up electrical (particularly computer) equipment, as distinct from laboratory apparatus.

hardystonite. $Ca_2ZnSi_2O_7$. A mineral from Franklin, N.J.

Hare, Robert. 1781–1858. American chemist noted for work on the oxyhydrogen flame, colorimeter, gas analysis, and artificial graphite.

Hargreaves-Bird cell. An electrolytic cell for the manufacture of chlorine and caustic soda from brine. The cathode is copper gauze, and the anode gas carbon on a lead core.

Harkins, William Draper. 1873–1951. American chemist noted for research on atomic structure. **H. theory.** With the exception of the inert gases, elements of odd atomic number are rarer than adjacent elements of even atomic number.

Harlon. Trade name for a mixed-polymer synthetic fiber.

harmala red. An oriental red dye from harmel.

harmaline. $C_{12}H_{14}ON_2 = 202.09$. Harmine dihydride. An alkaloid from the seeds of *Peganum harmala* (Rutaceae), S. Russia, Turkey. Colorless octahedra, m.238, slightly soluble in water; an anthelmintic and stimulant. Cf. *turkey red.*

harman. Aribine.

harmel. Wild rue, *Peganum harmala,* a common weed of the Russian and Turkish steppes; a vermifuge. Its seeds contain the alkaloids harmaline, harmine, and aribine. Cf. *harmala red.*

harmine. $C_{13}H_{12}ON_2 = 212.0$. Yajeine. An alkaloid from the seeds of *Peganum harmala.* **3,4-dihydro-** Harmaline.

h. dihydride. See *harmaline.*

harminic acid. $C_{10}H_8O_4N_2 = 220.1$. An oxidation product of harmine or harmaline.

harmonic progression. A series whose terms are the reciprocals of an arithmetic progression.

harmony. The adaptation of component parts to a state of equilibrium; fitting together.

harmotome. $(K,Ba)(Al_2Si_5O_{14})\cdot 5H_2O$. A zeolithic mineral having ion-exchange properties.

Harrison Narcotic Act (U.S.). An Internal Revenue regulation to govern the production, importation, manufacturing, compounding, dispensing, selling, or giving away of opium or coca leaves, their salts, derivatives, or preparations.

hartin. $C_{20}H_{34}O_4 = 338.3$. A substance in fossil wood or lignite. Cf. *hartite.*

hartite. $(C_6H_{10})_x$. A hydrocarbon in lignite and fossil wood.

Hartman's solution. A solution: thymol 12.5, ethyl alcohol 10, sulfuric ether 20 gm; used to desensitize dentin selectively.

Hartridge unit. A photoelectric measure of diesel smoke intensity: clean air 0, complete opacity 100.

hartsalz. A mixture of sylvinite and kainite (16% K); a fertilizer.

hartshorn. Spirit of hartshorn. A popular name for ammonia water. **h. salt.** A popular name for ammonium carbonate, q.v.

harvel coating. A waterproof paint made with cashew nut oil.

hashish. The dried leaves and stalks of *Cannabis indica,* q.v.; a narcotic.

hatchettenine. C_nH_{2n+2}. Rock tallow. A yellow, native, waxy hydrocarbon, soluble in ether.

Unit	ppm	Grains per U.S. gal	Clark deg	French deg	German deg
1 ppm	1.0	0.058	0.07	0.10	0.056
1 grain per U.S. gal. . .	17.1	1.000	1.20	1.71	0.958
1 Clark degree	14.3	0.829	1.00	1.43	0.800
1 French degree	10.7	0.583	0.70	1.00	0.560
1 German degree	17.9	1.044	1.24	1.78	1.000

Hatschek, Emil. 1869–1944. Hungarian-born British chemist, noted for his work on colloids.

hausmannite. A native manganese oxide, Mn_3O_4, or manganomanganite, Mn_2MnO_4; brown masses.

hauynite. $3NaAlSiO_4$. A mineral from the Laacher See, Germany.

hawthorn. The fruits of *Crataegus oxycantha* (Rosaceae); a cardiac and tonic.

Hayem solution. Sodium sulfate 5, sodium chloride 1, mercuric chloride 0.5, water 200 pts.; used in the microscopical analysis of blood.

hay-fever extract. Pollen extract.

Haynes alloy. Co 45, Cr 26, W 15, Ni 10, C 0.4, B 0.4%; used for engine rotor blades operating at above 870°C.

hazardous chemicals. Chemicals that may cause loss of life or property by improper handling, shipping, or storing. A labeling guide is issued by the Manufacturing Chemists' Association, Inc., Washington, D.C.

hazen unit. A measure of the color of water.

hb. Abbreviation for hemoglobin.

H.C. A mixture of zinc and hexachloroethane, used to produce artificial smoke.

HCN discoids. Wood pulp disks impregnated with liquid hydrocyanic acid and used in fumigation. Cf. *Zyklon.*

He. Symbol for helium.

heart sugar. Inositol. **h. cut.** The middle fractions of a series of fractionations.

heat. A form of energy that can be transmitted from one body to another: (1) By radiation: vibrations in the ether when stopped by a substance, cause its molecules to vibrate faster, and so produce h. (2) By contact: the molecular vibrations are transmitted directly by conduction and convection. It is supposed that at $-273°C$, the absolute zero, these vibrations cease. **animal-** The h. evolved during the life processes of an animal by oxidation of carbonaceous matter to carbon dioxide. **atomic-** The amount of h. required to raise the temperature of a gram atom of substance from 0 to 1°C. **latent-** The h. absorbed by a substance which does not cause a rise in its temperature; as, h. of evaporation which produces a change of state: liquid to solid. **mechanical equivalent of-.** See *h. equivalent.* **molecular-** The amount of h. required to raise the temperature of one mole of a substance by 1°C, i.e., specific h. × molecular weight. Cf. *Kopp's law.* **radiant-** H. waves transmitted through space. **radioactive-** H. evolved during radioactive decomposition. **sensible-** The h., in BThU per pound, that must be added to a liquid to bring it to its boiling point. **specific-** The amount of h. required to raise one gram of a substance through 1°C under specific conditions. See *calorie.*

h. of absorption. The quantity of h. consumed or liberated when a gas is dissolved. **h. of activation.** H. involved in catalytic processes. **h. of adhesion.** The quantity of h. consumed or liberated in the formation of heterogeneous mixtures. **h. of admixture.** H. of mixing. **h. of adsorption.** The quantity of h. liberated when a substance is adsorbed or condensed on the surface of a solid. **h. of aggregation.** H. involved in the formation of aggregates; as, h. of condensation, crystallization. **h. of association.** The quantity of h. absorbed on the formation of coordinate

compounds. **h. capacity.** The amount of h. required to raise the temperature of a body 1°C. usually expressed in calories. **atomic-** Specific h. Cf. *Dulong and Petit law.* **molecular-** Cf. *Kopp's law.* The molecular h. capacity is the sum of the atomic h. capacities. **h. of combination.** H. of formation, or h. of hydration. **h. of combustion.** The number of calories liberated per gram atom or gram molecule when an element or compound, respectively, is completely oxidized. **h. of compression.** H. produced when a gas is compressed. **h. of condensation.** The reverse of h. of evaporation. **h. conductivity.** The number of calories transmitted per second through a plate 1 cm thick across an area of 1 cm² when the temperature difference is 1°C. *specific-* The constant k in the equation: Conductivity $= k(t_2 - t_1)aT/d$, where t_1 and t_2 are the temperatures of the 2 bodies, a is the area, d the thickness of the conductor, T the time in seconds. **h. of cooling.** The h. liberated at a certain temperature during cooling; it indicates an allotropic rearrangement. **h. of crystallization.** The number of calories liberated or absorbed per mole on crystallization. **h. of decomposition.** The number of calories liberated or absorbed during the complete decomposition of a mole of substance. **h. degree.** The intensity of h. See *thermometer scale.* The entire absence of h. is considered the absolute zero at $-273.13°C$. **h. of dilution.** The quantity of h. consumed or liberated when a liquid is diluted. **h. of dissociation.** The h. involved in the disruption of certain bonds. **h. of dissolution.** H. of solution. **h. effect.** Joule effect. The number of small calories developed by an electric current in a metallic circuit: Watts/4.181 $= ri^2t/4.181$, where r is the internal resistance, i the electric current (equal to the emf divided by the total resistance) and t the time. Cf. *Peltier effect.* **h. engine.** An arrangement for converting h. into work. **h. equivalent.** A factor to convert h. into energy units: 1 mean calorie $= 4.1816 \times 10^7$ ergs; 1 calorie (15°C) $= 4.1809 \times 10^7$ ergs. The conversion factors for the gas constant R, q.v., per degree: 82.07 (cc)(atm), 1.9885 cal, 8.316 joules. **h. of evaporation.** H. of vaporization. The quantity of h. required to convert a definite amount of a liquid at its boiling point into the gaseous state, e.g., 540 cal/gm water at 100°C. Cf. *latent h.* **h. of explosion.** The calories liberated from a mole of explosive. **h. of foods.** See *h. value.* **h. of formation.** The quantity of h. liberated or consumed when a compound is formed from its component elements; it depends on the physical condition (solid, liquid, or gaseous) of the reacting molecules: e.g., S (rhombic) $=$ S (monoclinic) $+$ 77 cal. **h. of fuels.** See *h. value.* **h. function.** When a system passes from one state to another, the h. absorbed is the difference of a function (the heat function W) for the initial and final states. At constant pressure, $W = U + pu$, where U is the intrinsic energy, p the pressure, and u the volume. **h. of fusion.** H. of melting. The quantity of h. required to convert a definite amount of a solid at its melting point into the liquid state, e.g., 79.8 cal/gm water at 0°C. **h. of hydration.** The amount of h. consumed or liberated when a substance takes up water. **h. index.** Maumené number. The temperature in degrees centigrade produced by mixing 50 ml oil with 10 ml concentrated sulfuric acid. **h. of ionization.** The number of calories consumed or liberated when one gram-equivalent of a molecule ionizes. **h. of isomerization.** The h. involved in the formation of isomers. **h. of linkage.** The amount of h. required to form or disrupt certain atomic bonds. **h. of mixing.** For solid and liquid, see *h. of solution;* for liquid and liquid see *h. of dilution;* for gas and liquid see *h. of absorption.* **h. of neutralization.** The number of calories liberated on neutralization: $H^+ + OH^- \rightarrow H_2O + 13{,}700$ cal (at 18°C). **h. number.** H. index. **h. of oxidation.** See *h. of combustion.* **h. quantity.** The amount of h. energy expressed in calories. **h. of racemization.** The quantity of h. consumed or liberated on the change from one stereoisomer to the other. **h. rays.** See *infrared.* **h. of reaction.** The quantity of h. consumed or liberated in a chemical reaction; as, h. of neutralization. **h. regenerators.** Stoves used in the blast-furnace process for iron, which are heated by waste gases, and then cooled by heating up cold gases for the blast. See *Cowper stoves.* **h. shocking.** Preliminary h. treatment to ensure that only the most h.-resistant organisms in a culture survive; the culture has thus increased virility. **h. of solidification.** The quantity of h. liberated on freezing or solidifying. **h. of solution.** H. of dissolution. The quantity of h. liberated or consumed when a solid dissolves in a liquid. **h. of sublimation.** The calories required to convert a solid into a gas at constant temperature. **h. summation.** See *Hess law.* **h. of swelling.** The h. evolved when a colloid, e.g., gelatin, absorbs water. **h. transfer coefficient.** A measure of h.-insulating power: $BThU/(ft^2)(hr)(°F)(in.)$ at 0°C (cork 0.28, polyurethane foam 0.13). **h. of transition.** The quantity of h. liberated or consumed at the transition temperature, when a substance passes from one allotropic form to another. **h. units.** Heat H may be expressed in dynamical units, ML^2T^2; thermal units, $M\theta$; or thermo-metric units, $L^3\theta$. **h. value.** *Foods:* The h. liberated on oxidation of 100 gm food $= 4.1C + 4.1P + 9.3F$ cal/100 gm, where C, P, and F are the percentages of carbohydrates, proteins, and fats, respectively. *Fuels:* The h. obtained on the complete combustion of fuels $= 8{,}149C + 34{,}500H - 3{,}000(O - N)/100$ cal, where C, H, O, and N are respectively the percentages of carbon, hydrogen, oxygen, and nitrogen in the fuel. **h. of vaporization.** See *h. of evaporation.*

heater. A device by which temperature can be raised. **direct-** An open fire or flame. **indirect-** A water, steam, or other bath.

heatronic. Radiotronic.

Heaviside layer. See *Kennelly-Heaviside.*

heavy. (1) Not light. (2) Large in quantity. **h. acids.** Those used in large quantities; as, sulfuric, hydrochloric, and nitric acids. **h. chemicals.** Those formerly manufactured in ton lots; as, sodium carbonate, potassium cyanide, oxalic acid: **h. hydrogen.** Deuterium. **h. metal.** A metal of specific gravity greater than 4. The heavy metals are all located in the lower half of the new periodic table. They have complex spectra, form colored salts and double salts, have a low electrode potential, are mainly amphoteric, yield weak bases and weak acids, and are oxidizing or reducing agents. **h. spar.** Barite. **h. water.** See *water, deuterium.*

hecogenin. A steroid prepared from the juice of the sisal leaf, *Agave sisalana*, by autofermentation followed by hydrolysis; used in the synthesis of cortisone.

hectare. A unit of area in the metric system. 1 hectare $= 100$ ares $= 2.471$ acres $= 10{,}000$ sq. meters.

hecto- In the metric system a prefix indicating hundred, or 100 units.

hectogram. In the cgs system 1 hgm $= 100$ gm $= 3$ oz 230.7 grains (seldom used).

hectoliter. In the cgs system 1 hl $= 100$ liters $= 2.8378$ bushels $= 22$ imperial gal $= 26.4$ U.S. gal.

hectometer. In the cgs system 1 hm $= 0.1$ km $= 100$ meters $= 328$ ft 1 in.

Hector's base. $C_{14}H_{12}N_4S$. An oxidation product of phenylthiocarbamide.

hedenbergite. $CaO \cdot FeO \cdot 2SiO_2$. A silica mineral, q.v., of the pyroxene group, q.v.

hedeoma. The dried leaves and tops of *H. pulegioides*, American pennyroyal, an annual herb of U.S. and Canada; used as a stimulant, carminative, and emmenagogue. **h. oil.** The essential oil of *H. pulegioides*. Colorless or yellowish liquid of pungent odor, used to repel mosquitos and fleas.

hedeomol. $C_{10}H_{18}O = 154.2$. The ketone of the oil from hedeoma. Colorless liquid, b.217. Cf. *pulegone.*

hedera. Ivy.

hederagenin. $C_{31}H_{50}O_4 = 486.5$. A glucoside from the seeds of *Hedera* species, ivy (Araliaceae). Cf. *hederaglucoside.*

hederaglucoside. $C_{32}H_{54}O_{11} = 614.43$. Helexin. A glucoside from *Hedera helix*, common ivy (Araliaceae). White powder, m.233, soluble in alcohol.

hedgehog crystals. Crystals of ammonium urate in urinary deposits.

hedonal. $NH_2 \cdot CO \cdot OCH(Me)Pr = 131.1$. Methyl-propylcarbinolurethane. White crystals, m.74, soluble in water; a hypnotic and diuretic. Cf. *aponal.*

hedyphane. $3Pb_3As_2O_8 \cdot PbCl_2 \cdot (Ca,Ba)O$. A mineral from Franklin, N.J.

Heerwagen pipet. A pipet with piston, for delivering small quantities of mercury.

Hefner lamp. A device for burning amyl acetate with a flame 4 cm high. Used as a German standard for photometric measurements. **H. unit.** The horizontal illuminating intensity of the H. lamp burning at 760 mm in an atmosphere containing 8.8% water vapor. 1 H. unit $\equiv 0.9$ candlepower.

Hehner number. The percentage of water-insoluble fatty acids and unsaponifiable matter in a fat or oil.

Heilbron, Sir Ian. 1886–1959. Scottish chemist, noted for his work on synthetic organic chemistry.

Heim's cage. A metal box for breeding small rodents for experimental purposes.

Heisenberg, Werner. b. 1901. German physical chemist. Nobel Prize winner (1933). **H. principle.** The uncertainty or indeterminism principle. The limit to observational experiments is reached when the observational or determining factors begin to interfere with normal happenings in the experiment under observation.

helcosol. Bismuth pyrogallate.

helenene. $C_{19}H_{26} = 254.2$. A product of distilling crude helenin with phosphoric acid.

helenin. (1) $C_6H_8O = 96.1$. Inula camphor. True helenin. Colorless crystals, m.72, from the roots of *Inula helenium*. (2) $C_{21}H_{28}O_{31} = 776.3$. Crude helenin. A principle from the root of *Inula helenium*: alantol, alant camphor, and alantic anhydride. (3) Inulin. (4) $C_{20}H_{25}O_5 = 345.3$. Bitter crystals from *Helenium autumnale*, sneezewort (Compositae). (5) Helenene.

helenine. An active nucleoprotein antiviral agent from the mycelia of *Penicillium funiculosum*.

helenite. Mineral caoutchouc.

helexin. Hederaglucoside.

helianthic acid. $C_{14}H_9O_8 = 305.1$. An acid from the seeds of *Helianthus annuus*, sunflower (Compositae).

helianthin. $Me_2N \cdot C_6H_4 \cdot N : N \cdot C_6H_4SO_3H$. Dimethylamidoazobenzenesulfonic acid. A red dye. Its sodium salt is methyl orange.

helianthus. Sunflower.

helicin. $C_{13}H_{16}O_7 \cdot \frac{3}{4}H_2O = 297.71$. Salicyl aldehyde glucose. An oxidation product of salicin. Colorless crystals, m.170–175, soluble in water.

helicoprotein. A glucoprotein from the snail, *Helix*.

helictite. A stalactite or stalagmite of irregular shape.

helide. A supposed compound of helium, e.g., $HgHe_{10}$, mercury helide.

heliotrope. A quartz semiprecious stone with a greenish tint and red specks.

heliotropic acid. Piperonylic acid.

heliotropin. (1) Piperonal. (2) A purple diazo dye. (3) The odorous principle of *Heliotropium*.

heliotropine. An alkaloid from *Heliotropium europaeum* (Boraginaceae).

helisterol. $C_{26}H_{44}O_2 = 388.4$. A colorless sterol from plant carotenoids.

helium. He $= 4.003$. A chemically inert gas and element, at. no. 2; a constituent of the atmosphere, of radioactive minerals, and of natural gases. Discovered (1895) by Ramsay and Cleve, after its presence in the sun was indicated spectroscopically (1869) by Lockyer and Frankland. Colorless gas, $d_{air-1}0.137$, m.-272, b.$-4.215°K$. Transported in steel cylinders for filling balloons and airships; also for filling incandescent lamps. When cooled at 2.19°K, it is transformed into He^3 or He^{II}, b.$-450°F$, which has a greater heat conductivity than any other known substance and great creeping properties. Cf. *lambda* phenomenon, *super fluid*. Used also to prevent oxidation in arc welding; in admixture with 20% O as an inhalant (U.S.P., B.P.); and as a diluent for medicinal gases (U.S.P.). World production (1967), 4,800 million ft³. **h. atom.** The h. atom is assumed to consist of a nucleus having 2 positive charges, around which 2 electrons move in orbits whose planes are at 120°. **h. compounds.** H. has a valency of zero, and forms no ordinary compounds. Excited He molecules however, give helides, q.v. **h. nucleus.** The atomic nucleus of He is assumed to be a constituent of all other elements (Harkin's theory), and is itself composed of hydrogen nuclei. Cf. *packing effect.* In radioactive disintegration, q.v.

He nuclei (α rays) are thrown off at high speed. Their positive charge is neutralized by 2 electrons, forming He gas.

helix. (1) The coil of wire in an electromagnet. (2) A spiral arrangement of the periodic system. (3) A snail.

hellebore. A genus of ranunculaceous plants. **American-** *Veratrum viride.* **black-** The root of *Helleborus niger.* **false-** American h. **green-** The root of *H. viridis.* **white-** *Veratrum album.*

helleborein. $C_{37}H_{56}O_{18} = 788.6$. A glucoside from *Helleborus niger* and *H. viridis.* Soluble in water; a local anesthetic and heart stimulant.

helleborin. $C_{26}H_{42}O_6 = 570.4$. A crystalline glucoside from the roots of *Helleborus niger.* Slightly soluble in water; a narcotic.

Helmert's equation. The acceleration due to gravity at sea level is $g = 978.038(1 + 0.005302 \sin^2 H - 0.000007 \sin^2 2I)$, where I is the latitude. Subtract 0.000192 for each meter of height H from the value of g.

Helmholtz, Herman Ludwig Ferdinand von. 1821–1894. German scientist, noted for his generalizations on the conservation of force. H. equation of inductance: $I = (E/R)[1 - t \exp(-R/T)]$, where E is the electromotive force, R the resistance, I the coefficient of self-inductance, T temperature, and t time. **Gibbs-H. equation.** See *Gibbs.* **H. layer.** The electrical double layer of opposite charges formed on the surface of a charged solid in contact with a liquid.

helminth. A worm or intestinal parasite.

helminthiasis. A disease caused by parasitic worms, e.g., bilharziasis.

helminthic. Anthelmintic.

helmitol. $C_7H_8O_7(CH_2)_6N_4 = 344.26$. Hexamethylenetetramine anhydromethylene citrate. Colorless crystals, m.163; a urinary antiseptic. Cf. *cystopurin.*

Helmont, Johann Baptist van. 1577–1644. Belgian alchemist whose work represents the transition from speculative to experimental chemistry. He originated the term gas (chaos).

helonias. False unicorn root, starwort. The root of *H. dioica, Chamaelirium luteum* (Liliaceae); a tonic and diuretic.

helonoid. The combined principles from the root of *Chamaelirium luteum*, false unicorn; a tonic, diuretic, and vermifuge. Cf. *chamaelirin.*

Helvella. A family of cryptograms.

helvellic acid. $C_{12}H_{20}O_7 = 276.2$ A dibasic, poisonous acid from *Helvella esculenta*, which causes hemoglobinuria.

helvetium. An element, at. no. 85, discovered (1940) by Minder of Berne, in the decomposition products of actinium.

helvite. $(BeMoFe)_7Si_9O_{12}S$. A brittle, lustrous, greenish mineral.

helvolic acid. $C_{32}H_{44}O_8 = 556.40$. Fumigacin. A bacteriostatic substance excreted in urine and bile, and similar in action to penicillin, m 205–212, insoluble in water.

hema- Prefix denoting blood. Cf. *haemo-.*

hemachate. Blood agate. A brown agate.

hemacyanin. Hematocyanin. A blue coloring matter in bile. Cf. *hemocyanin.*

hemacytometer. Hemocytometer.

hemaglobinometer. Hemoglobinometer, q.v.

hemaglutination. Hemoglutination.

hemaglutinins. Substances (agglutinins) which cause the clumping of red blood corpuscles.

hemagog. An agent that promotes the menstrual or hemorrhoidal discharge of blood.

hemanthine. An alkaloid of *Haemanthus toxicarus* (Amaryllidaceae); constituent of Australian arrow poisons, resembling scopolamine.

hemase. A blood catalase, q.v.

hematein. $C_{16}H_{12}O_6$ = 300.1. An oxidation product of hematoxylin. Brown powder, insoluble in water; an indicator in alkalimetry.

hematin. $C_{34}H_{32}N_4O_6Fe$ = 648.5. Phenodin, haematin. The prosthetic group of the hemoglobin of blood. Brown powder, soluble in alkalies. **oxy-** $C_{34}H_{32}N_4O_7Fe$ = 664.5. The coloring matter of oxyhemoglobin. It yields on strong oxidation, hematinic acid; on strong reduction, hematoporphyrin; and on heating, pyrrole and pyrrole derivatives. Cf. *porphin*.

hematine crystals. Hematoxylin. **h. extract, h. paste.** Hematoxylin paste; more strictly applied to its oxidation product.

hematinic. An agent that increases the hematin content of blood.

hematinic acids. A group of di- and tribasic acids obtained by the strong oxidation of hematin. Cf. *hematic acid*.

hematite, haematite. Fe_2O_3. Red iron ore. Raddle. An iron ore commonly used for the manufacture of iron and steel **brown-** Hydrated h. or limonite. **red-** Kidney ore. Rhombic or reniform native Fe_2O_3. **spicular-** Specularite.

hematocrit. A small centrifuge, used to separate blood corpuscles in clinical analysis.

hematocrystallin. Oxy*hemoglobin*.

hematocyanin. Hemo*cyanin*.

hematoglobulin. Oxy*hemoglobin*.

hematoidin. Bilirubin.

hematology. The science of the properties and diagnostic indications of blood.

hematolysis. Hemolysis.

hematoporphyrin. (1) $C_{16}H_{18}N_2O_3$ = 286.16. Porporino. A decomposition product of hematin, occurring with hemoporphyrin in urine; m. below 100 (decomp.). (2) $C_{34}H_{38}N_4O_6$. Cruentine. Dark violet powder obtained by adding hemin to glacial acetic acid saturated with hydrobromic acid, and neutralizing with sodium hydroxide. Cf. *porphin*.

hematoxylic acid. Hematoxylin.

hematoxylin. $C_{16}H_{14}O_6 \cdot 3H_2O$ = 356.2. Haematoxylic acid, haematine, logwood crystals, campeachy wood, Jamaica wood, steam black. The coloring principle of *Haematoxylon campechianum*, logwood. Colorless crystals, soluble in water and alkalies (purple color); with acids the color changes to yellow. On exposure it turns black with formation of h. A mordant dye, an indicator in the titration of alkaloids, a microscope stain, and reagent for copper and iron. **h. paste.** Logwood paste, h. extract, logwood extract. A technical grade of h.; a coloring material in the textile and leather industries.

hematoxylon. Haematoxylon.

heme compounds. Derivatives of hemoglobin and chlorophyll; as porphyrins.

hemellitic acid. 2,3-Xylic acid.

hemellitol. Hemimellitene.

hemerythrin. A relatively rare iron-protein compound in living tissue.

hemi- Prefix (Greek) indicating half. See also *semi-* (Latin) and *demi-* (French).

hemialbumose. Propeptone. A decomposition product of albumin, related to peptone.

hemicellulose. (1) A constituent of the cell wall of bacteria. (2) Pseudocellulose. A group of gummy substances intermediate in composition between cellulose and the sugars. (3) A constituent of starch.

hemicolloid. A colloidal particle having a chain length up to 250 Å and a polymerization of 20–100 molecules. Cf. *mesocolloid*.

hemihedral. Describing a crystal which has only half the number of faces that the symmetry of the system requires. Cf. *holohedral*.

hemimellitene. $C_6H_3Me_3$ = 120.1. Hemimellitol, 1,2,3-trimethylbenzene. Colorless liquid, b.175.

hemimellitic acid. $C_6H_3(COOH)_3$ = 210.05. Benzene-1,2,3-tricarboxylic acid. Colorless needles, m.196 (decomp.), slightly soluble in water. Cf. *hemellitic acid*.

hemimellitol. (1) $HO \cdot C_6H_2Me_3$. (2) Hemimellitene.

hemimorphite. Calamine (U.K. usage).

hemin. $C_{34}H_{32}O_4N_4FeCl$ = 658.0. Teichmann's crystals, hematin chloride. The characteristic microcrystals obtained by heating a crystal of sodium chloride, a drop of glacial acetic acid, and blood on a microscope slide; a species identification test for blood.

hemipic acid. Hemipinic acid.

hemipinic acid. $C_6H_2(OMe)_2(COOH)_2$ = 226.1. Hemipic acid. Dimethoxybenzenedicarboxylic acid. Colorless crystals soluble in water; a split product of nicotine. Isomers: First 2 numbers indicate the position of the OMe group; last 2 numbers the COOH groups. **3,4,1,2-** m.185 (decomp.). **4,5,1,2-** m.178. **5,6,1,2-** m.180.

hemiquinoid. Describing the structure

$$R_2C \underset{\diagdown C=C \diagup}{\overset{\diagup C=C \diagdown}{}} C=O$$

Cf. *quinoid*.

hemisotonic. Having an osmotic pressure equal to that of blood. Cf. *isotonic*.

Hemit. Trade name for molded tar and asbestos electrical insulators.

hemiterpenes. Hydrocarbons of the general formula C_5H_8, related to the terpenes, q.v.; as, isoprene.

hemitrope. A twin crystal.

hemlock. (1) The fir tree *Tsuga canadensis* of W. and N. America. (2) The poisonous plants and shrubs of the *Conium* species (Umbelliferae). **poison-, spotted-** Conium. **water-** Cicuta. **h. alkaloids.** Alkaloids from the seeds and bark of *Conium* species: coniine, conhydrine, conicine. **h. bark.** The bark of the h. fir, used in tanning. **h. fir.** The tree, *Tsuga canadensis* of W. and N. America. **h. spruce.** H. fir. **h. tannin.** $C_{20}H_{16}O_{10}$ (?). A tannin from the bark of *Tsuga* species.

hemocuprein. A blue copper-protein compound in the red blood corpuscles and livers of mammals.

hemocyanin. Haemocyanin. A blue coloring matter from the blood of mollusks; related to hematin but contains copper instead of iron. *Cf. hemacyanin, chromoprotein.*

hemocytometer. Hemacytometer, hemameter, etc. A microscope slide with square rulings; used for counting blood corpuscles.

hemodyn. See *periston.*

hemoglobin. Haemoglobin. Hb. A chromoprotein coloring matter of red blood corpuscles of mammals. Brown powder, soluble in water. It consists of hematin combined with the histon, globin. It is the oxygen carrier of the blood of mammals and is related chemically to chlorophyll. Molecular weight: $68,000 \pm 1,000$ (10,000 atoms). **kat-** A compound of denatured globin and hematoxylin, produced by the action of chloroform on methemoglobin. **met-** An oxidation product of h. formed on exposure to air. It contains trivalent iron. **oxy-** Hematocrystallin, hematoglobulin, cruorine. The h. of arterial blood, containing divalent iron. **reduced-** The h. of venous blood. Reactions:

$$O_2 \searrow \qquad \nearrow CO_2$$
$$\text{In lungs}$$

In arterial blood: $\nearrow$ In venous blood:
$[Hb]: Na_3 + CO_2 \rightleftharpoons O_2 + [Hb] \cdot Na_2 + NaHCO_3$
Oxyhemoglobin   Hemoglobin

$$\text{In tissues}$$
$$O_2 \swarrow \qquad \nwarrow CO_2$$

hemoglobinometer. An instrument to determine hemoglobin in blood, e.g., by matching against a color chart, as in the Haldane h.

hemoglutination. The clumping together (agglutination) of red blood corpuscles.

hemolysin. A substance causing hemolysis, as saponin; or the proteins formed in the body by red blood corpuscles from another species, which dissolve the red corpuscles of the host species. **h-** H. from *Helix pomatia.* **l-** H. from *Limulus polyphemus.* **o-** H. from *Octopus vulgaris;* molecular weight, 2,050,000.

hemolysis. Hematolysis. (1) In the living organism, the abnormal loss of hemoglobin by the blood corpuscles, causing the blood to become brighter and clearer; it finally results in death. (2) The dissolution of red blood corpuscles by chemicals, heating, freezing, or biological agents, which causes the blood to become transparent and clear. Used to show the presence of antibodies. See *Wassermann reaction.*

hemolytic. Describing an agent that destroys red blood corpuscles.

hemolyzate. The product of hemolysis.

hemoporphyrin. $C_{16}H_{18}O_3N = 272.2$. A decomposition product of hematin, closely allied to phylloporphyrin; a decomposition product of chlorophyll. *Cf. porphin.*

hemopyrrole. $C_8H_{13}N = 123.2$. A decomposition product of both hemoglobin (hemoporphyrin) and chlorophyll (phylloporphyrin).

hemostatic. An agent which when applied externally checks the flow of blood; as, tannin. *Cf. styptic.*

hemp. The plant *Cannabis indica* or *C. sativa* (Urticaceae): (1) The flowering tops (cannabis) yield a resin (cannabin); (2) the leaves and stalks

are hashish; (3) the seeds yield h. seed oil; and (4) the stems, a fiber used for ropes or paper. **Bombay-Sunn-.** **bow-string-** A tough fiber from *Sanseviera Zeylanica,* (Liliaceae), Ceylon. **Canadian-** *Apocynum cannabinum.* The roots are used medicinally. **china-** See china *jute.* **Deccan-** The fiber from *Hibiscus cannabinus,* (Malvaceae), India. **manila-** Abaca. **Mauritius-** The fiber *Furcraea gigantea* (Amaryllidaceae). **New Zealand-** N.Z. flax. The fiber from *Phormium tenax* **sann-** Sunn h. **sisal-** See *sisal.* **sunn-** Bombay h. A fiber from the stems of *Crotalaria juncea* (Leguminosae), India, Australia.

h. seed. The seeds of *Cannabis* species. **h. seed oil.** A green, nondrying oil, from h. seeds; chief constituent, linolein; $d_{15}0.925-0.932$, m.— 15 to 23. Used for soap, paints, and varnishes.

Hempel, Walther. 1851–1916. German analytical chemist. **H. gas buret.** A glass apparatus used to absorb gases by solid or liquid reagents. The measured gas enters the absorption bulbs through a capillary tube into the leveling bulbs. After absorption the residual gas is pulled back into the buret and measured. **H. palladium tube.** A U-shaped glass tube filled with palladium sponge for use in gas analysis to absorb hydrogen.

henbane. Hyoscyamus.

hendecanal*. $Me(CH_2)_9CHO = 170.17$. Undecylic aldehyde, undecanal*. Colorless liquid, d.0.825, b.117.

hendecane*. Undecane. **h. carboxylic acid.** Lauric acid. **h. dicarboxylic acid.** Brassylic acid.

hendecanoic*. Undecylic.

hendecanol. Hendecyl alcohol.

hendecanone*. $C_{11}H_{22}O = 170.17$. Undecanone. **1-** Hendecanal. **2-** $MeCOC_9H_{17}$. Methyl *n*-nonyl ketone. Colorless liquid, d.0.826, m.121.1, in oils of rue and lime. **6-** $C_5H_{11}COC_5H_{11}$. Diamyl ketone, amyl ketone. Colorless liquid, d.0.826, m.14.6.

hendecene*. $C_{11}H_{22} = 154.17$. Undecylene, undecene*. Unsaturated hydrocarbons; as: **α-** or **1-** $CH_2:CH(CH_2)_8Me$. Colorless liquid, d.0.763, b.188. **β-** or **2-** $MeCH:CH(CH_2)_7Me$. A liquid, d.0.774, b.193. Both are insoluble in water.

hendecoic acid. Undecylic acid.

hendecyl. Undecyl. The radical $Me(CH_2)_{10}$—. **h. alcohol.** $C_{11}H_{24}O = 172.19$. *1-* 1-Hendecanol*, *n*-undecyl alcohol, undecan-1-ol. Colorless liquid, d.0.883, m.19. *6-* 6-Hendecanol*. Colorless liquid. d.0.833, m.16. **h. amine*.** $C_{11}H_{25}$-$N = 171.20$. *n*-Undecylamine. Colorless liquid, m.16.5.

Henderson, George Gerald. 1862–1942. British chemist, noted for his work on terpenes. **H. process.** Roasting copper ores with salt, subsequent leaching of the chlorides, and precipitation of the metals.

heneicosane. $C_{21}H_{44} = 296.4$. A saturated methane hydrocarbon, m.40.5. **h. dicarboxylic acid.** $C_{23}H_{44}O_4 = 384.3$. Colorless crystals, m.124, in japan wax (3 %).

heneicosanic acid. $C_{21}H_{42}O_2 = 326.3$. White needles in fats, m.74.

henequen. The fiber of *Agave fourcroydes* (Mexico, W. Indies); used for ropes. *Cf. sisal.*

henna. The powdered leaves of *Lawsonia inermis*

(Lythraceae), Asia Minor, Egypt, Persia. A brown dye, especially for hair.

Henry, Joseph. 1797–1878. American physicist noted for his research in magnetism. Cf. *henry*. **H., William** 1775–1836. English chemist and co-worker of Dalton. **H.'s law.** The amount of gas dissolved in a liquid is proportional to the pressure of the gas at constant temperature.

henry. *H.* The unit of induction. If the emf induced is 1 volt, and the inducing current varies at the rate of 1 amp/sec, a h. or quadrant, or secohm, $= 10^9$ emu or $1/9 \times 10^{-11}$ esu.

$$1 \text{ international henry} = 1.00049 \text{ absolute henrys}$$
$$1 \text{ absolute henry} = 0.99948 \text{ international h.}$$
$$= 1.1124 \times 10^{-12} \text{ cgs esu}$$
$$= 10^9 \text{ cgs emu}$$
$$= 1 \text{ practical henry}$$

hentriacontane*. $C_{31}H_{64} = 436.6$. A methane hydrocarbon, m.69, from the roots of *Oenanthe crocata* (Umbelliferae), and in beeswax.

hepacrine. Atebrin.

hepar. Greek for liver. **h. antimoni.** Sodium or potassium antimoniate. **h. calcis.** Calcium sulfide. **h. reaction.** A test for sulfur. The compound is reduced with soda and carbon, and the mass moistened on a silver coin. A black stain indicates sulfur. **h. siccum.** The powdered dried liver of animals; diabetes food. **h. sulfuris.** Liver of *sulfur*.

heparin. A blood anticoagulant from the livers or lungs of domestic animals. A conjugated glucuronic acid glucoside, used medicinally (U.S.P., B.P.) as: **h. sodium,** a mixture of the active principles.

hepatica. The dried plant *Hepatica triloba*, liverwort; a mild mucilaginous astringent.

hepatic gas. Hydrogen sulfide.

hepatin. Glycogen.

hepatocuprein. A blue compound containing copper, in mammalian red blood corpuscles and liver.

hepatoflavin. Vitamin B_2 (obsolete).

hepotic acid. Oenanthic acid.

heptachlor. Trade name for the insecticide, 3,4,5,6,7,8,8a-heptachlorodicyclopentadiene.

heptacosane*. $C_{27}H_{56} = 380.5$. A methane hydrocarbon, m.59, in beeswax.

heptad. An element or radical having a valency of 7.

heptadecane*. $C_{17}H_{36} = 240.3$. Dioctylmethane. **h. carboxylic acid*.** Stearic acid. **h. nitrile*.** Margaronitrile.

heptadecanoic acid*. Margaric acid.

heptadecanone*. Pelargone.

heptadecoic acid, heptadecylic acid. Margaric acid.

heptadiene*. $C_7H_{12} = 96.09$. **2,4-** $MeCH:CH\cdot CH:CH\cdot CH_2Me$. Colorless liquid, b.107. **h. one.** Phorone.

heptaldehyde. Heptyl aldehyde.

heptalgin. The hydrochloride of phenodoxone.

heptamethylene. Suberane.

heptanal*. Heptyl aldehyde.

heptane*. $Me(CH_2)_5Me = 100.2$. (1) Normal heptane, methylhexane, dipropylmethane, heptyl hydride, dimethylpentane. Colorless liquid, d.0.690, b.95, insoluble in water, highly flammable; in the needles of *Pinus sabiana*; a solvent and anesthetic. (2) $(CH_3)_2CH(CH_2)_3CH_3$. Dimethyl-

isopentane. Colorless liquid, d.0.680, b.90, soluble in alcohol. (3) $(C_2H_5)_3CH$. Triethylmethane. Colorless liquid, d.689, b.96, soluble in alcohol. (4) $(C_2H_5)_2C(CH_3)_2$. Diethyldimethylmethane. Colorless liquid, d.0.711, b.86, insoluble in water. **bicyclo-** See *carane, fenchane.* **heptahydroxy-** Volemitol.

heptane-1,7-dicarboxylic acid. Azelaic acid.

heptanedioic acid*. Pimelic acid.

heptanoic acid*. Heptoic acid.

heptanol*. Heptyl alcohol.

heptanone*. **2-** Methyl amyl ketone. **3-** Ethyl butyl ketone. **4-** Butyrone.

heptatomic. (1) Heptavalent. (2) Describing a molecule of 7 atoms.

heptavalent. (1) A molecule containing 7 replaceable H atoms or 7 OH groups. (2) Septavalent. An atom that has 7 valence electrons.

heptene*. $CH_2:CH(CH_2)_4Me = 98.2$. Heptylene, pentylethylene. Colorless liquid, d.0.703, b.98, soluble in alcohol.

heptenyl. The radical C_7H_{13}—. **h. methyl carbonate.** Heptine methyl carbonate.

heptenylene. Heptine.

heptine. $HC:C(CH_2)_4Me = 96.1$. Heptenylene, heptyne*, oenanthine, pentyl-acetylene. Colorless liquid d.0.831, b.104, soluble in alcohol. **h. methyl carbonate.** $Me(CH_2)_4C:C\cdot COOMe = 154.11$. Heptenyl methyl carbonate, from the ricinoleic acid of castor oil, d.0.930, insoluble in water; a perfume.

heptoglobin. A protein of blood serum having an inherited gene and therefore, used to establish parenthood.

heptoic acid. $Me(CH_2)_5COOH = 130.2$. *n*-Heptylic acid, amylacetic acid, oenanthic acid, heptanoic acid*. Colorless, oily liquid with an unpleasant odor, d.0.9345, b.223, insoluble in water. **iso-** $Me_2CH(CH_2)_3COOH$. Isoheptylic acid, isooenanthic acid. Colorless liquid, b.210, soluble in alcohol. **h. alcohol.** Heptyl alcohol. **h. aldehyde.** Heptyl aldehyde.

heptols. Pentatomic alcohols, from heptoses.

heptose. A sugar having 7 C atoms. See *carbohydrates*.

hepturonic acid. A pentahydroxy aldehyde acid derived from heptoses; general formula, CHO·· (CHOH)$_5$COOH. Cf. *uronic acids*.

heptyl. The radical $Me(CH_2)_6$—, from heptane. **h. acetate.** $AcOC_7H_{15} = 158.2$. Colorless liquid, d.0.874, b.190, insoluble in water; used in artificial flavorings. **h. alcohol.** $C_7H_{16}O = 116.2$. (1) $C_7H_{15}OH$. Oenanthol, heptylic alcohol, 1-heptanol*, normal hexylcarbinol. Colorless liquid, d.0.830, b.176, soluble in water; used in organic synthesis. (2) $Me(CH_2)_2CHOH(CH_2)_2Me$. Isohexylcarbinol, dipropylcarbinol, 4-heptanol*. Colorless liquid, d.0.814, b.149, soluble in alcohol. (3) $Me_2CH\cdot CHOH\cdot CH\cdot Me_2$. Diisopropylcarbinol, 1,5-dimethyl-3-pentanol*. Colorless liquid, d.0.832, b.131, soluble in water. (4) Et_3COH. Triethylcarbinol, 1,1-diethyl-1-propanol*. Colorless liquid, d.0.860, b.140, soluble in water. (5) $Me_2COH\cdot CH_2\cdot CHMe_2$. Dimethylisobutylcarbinol, 2,5-dimethyl-2-pentanol*. Colorless liquid, b.130, soluble in alcohol. (6) $Me_3C\cdot COHMe_2$. Pentamethylethanol, 2,3,3-trimethyl-2-butanol*. Colorless liquid, b.132, soluble in alcohol. **h. aldehyde.**

$Me(CH_2)_5CHO = 114.1$. Oenanthal, enanthaldehyde*, heptoic aldehyde, normal heptylic aldehyde, heptanal; from castor oil. Colorless, fragrant liquid, d.0.850, b.155, soluble in water; used in organic synthesis. **h. amine***. $Me(CH_2)_6NH_2 = 115.2$. 1-Aminoheptane. Colorless liquid, d.0.78, b.155, slightly soluble in water. **h. ether.** $(C_7H_{15})_2O = 214.3$. Heptylic ether, enanthylic ether, cognac oil, heptyloxyheptane*. Colorless liquid, d.0.815, b.265, insoluble in water. **h. ethyl ether.** $Me(CH_2)_6OEt = 144.2$. Oenanthic ether, cognac oil, heptyl ethyl oxide, ethoxyheptane*. Colorless oil, d.0.840, b.166, insoluble in water; used in flavoring extracts and in organic synthesis. **h. formate.** $HCOOC_7H_{15} = 114.2$. Colorless, aromatic liquid, d.0.894, b.176, insoluble in water; used in organic synthesis. **h. resorcinol.** Dihydranol.

heptylene. Heptene.

heptylic acid. Heptoic acid.

heptyne*. Heptine.

herapathite. $4Qu·3H_2SO_4·2HII_4·6H_2O$. Artificial tourmaline. Quinine sulfate periodide. Produced as optically active crystals when iodine vapor is passed into a solution of quinine sulfate. See *polarizing disk.*

herb. A drug: the leafy, flowering, or fruiting stems of the smaller plants. Many herbs are used as teas (infusions); others in the manufacture of essential oils; e.g.: absinthium, peppermint, tansy. **bitter-** Snakehead. The leaves of *Chelone glabra* (Scrophulaceae); an anthelmintic. Cf. *chelonin.* **blanket-** Mullein. **felon-** Mugwort. **Fuller's-** Saponaria.

herbicide. A chemical substance used in agriculture to destroy unwanted plants, especially grasses. See table (from "Toxic Chemicals in Agriculture," London: H.M. Stationery Office, 1953). Cf. *fungicide, insecticide, rodenticide.*

Hercules stone. Magnetite.

hercynite. $FeAl_2O_4$. Iron spinel. A black mineral, d.3.92, hardness 7.5–8.

herderite. $Be(OH,F)CaPO_4$. A calcium phosphate mineral, d.3.0, hardness 5.

heretine. An alkaloid from *Heritiera javanica* (Sterculiaceae), Dutch Indies.

hermetic. Airtight. **h. art.** Magic or alchemy. **h. casing.** A watertight casing.

Hermite process. The manufacture of hypochlorite bleaching liquor by the electrolysis of sodium chloride 0.5 and magnesium chloride 0.05% in water.

herniarin. $C_{10}H_8O_3 = 176.1$. Methylumbelliferone, 7-methoxycoumarin, from *Herniaria glabra* (Caryophyllaceae).

heroin(e). $C_{21}H_{23}ON_5 = 369.2$. Diacetylmorphine. White powder, m.170, soluble in water. A very toxic narcotic and the most habit forming drug; manufacture in the U.S. is prohibited. **h. hydrochloride.** $C_{21}H_{23}O_5N·HCl = 405.7$. Diacetylmorphine hydrochloride. A more soluble form of heroine used in hypodermic tablets.

herpatite. Herapathite.

herrerite. $(Zn,Cu)CO_3$. A cupriferous smithsonite.

Hertz, Heinrich Rudolf. 1857–1894. German physicist noted for research in theoretical physics.

hertzian waves. Electromagnetic oscillations, resembling light waves but much longer (0.2 cm to 1,000 meters). Cf. *radiations.* **ultra-** Waves in the region between heat waves and radio waves.

herudin. (1) A constituent of leeches which prevents the coagulation of blood. (2) A preparation made from leeches.

Herzberg's stain. (1) A solution of iodine, potassium iodide, and zinc chloride in water, used to stain rag fibers *red*; chemically treated paper pulp *blue*; and groundwood pulp or lignin *yellow*. (2) A solution of potassium iodide in sulfuric acid.

hesion value. A measure of the combined effects of adhesion and cohesion of butter to a solid surface.

hesperetic acid. Hesperitinic acid.

hesperetin. $C_{16}H_{14}O_6 = 302.2$. A split product of hesperidin, and a chalcone of phloroglucinol. Yellow crystals, decomp. 220, soluble in alcohol.

hesperetol. $CH_2:CH·C_6H_4·(OMe)OH = 150.18$. 5-Vinylguaiacol, 3-hydroxy-4-methoxystyrene. Colorless crystals, m.57.

hesperidene. *d*-Limonene.

hesperidin. $C_{22}H_{26}O_{12} = 482.2$. Citrin, vitamin I. A glucoside which occurs with eriodictin in the unripe fruits of *Citrus aurantium*. Yellow powder, decomp. 251, soluble in water. It splits on hydrolysis to hesperitinic acid, glucose, and phloroglucinol.

hesperidine. An alkaloid from the leaves of *Peucedanum galbanum*, wild celery (Umbelliferae).

hesperitinic acid. $C_{10}H_{11}O_4 = 195.1$. Isoferulic acid, *m*-oxy-*p*-methoxycinnamic acid. Yellow needles, m.228.

Hess, Germain Henri. 1802–1850. German-born Russian chemist, and a founder (1840) of thermochemistry. **H., Victor Franz.** b. 1883. German physicist, noted for work on cosmic radiation. Nobel Prize Winner (1936). **H.'s law.** The law of constant heat summation. The net amount of heat liberated or absorbed in a chemical is the same, whether the reaction is performed in one or successive steps. **H. rays.** Ultra-γ rays. Cosmic rays. **H. viscosimeter.** A graduated capillary tube with a rubber bulb, used for determining the viscosity of biological solutions.

hessian. Cuttings from jute cloth, used for paper manufacture. Cf. *botany.* **h. crucible.** (1) A sand crucible. (2) A large clay crucible.

hessite. Ag_2Te. Silver telluride. A black mineral, d.8.3–9, hardness 2.5–3.

hessonite. $Al_2(Ca,Fe)_2Si_8O_{16}$. Cinnamon stone. A garnet, d.3.5, hardness 6.5–7.

Het Acid. Trade name for 1,4,5,6,7,7-hexachlorobicyclo-[2,2,1]-5-heptene-2,3-dicarboxylic acid. Unique among dibasic acids in containing over 54% by weight of stable Cl. Used to impart flame resistance to resins.

hetero- Prefix (Greek) indicating unlikeness or difference.

heteroalbumose. A form of albumose, insoluble in water, precipitated by saturation with sodium chloride.

heteroartose. The protein $C_{74}H_{130}N_{20}O_{24}S$.

hetero atom. A heterocyclic atom.

heterobaric. Possessing different atomic weights; as, isotopes.

heterocycle. A ring of different types of atoms. Antonym: homocycle. Cf. *heterocyclic compound.*

heterocyclic. Pertaining to dissimilar atoms in a ring. **h. atom.** Any atom, other than carbon, C,

HERBICIDES FOR GROWING PLANTS (U.K. AND OVERSEAS)

Common name or code number	Chemical name	Persistence and site of action
Inorganic compounds		
Sodium chlorate.........	Sodium chlorate	Semipersistent; contact
Sodium arsenite.........	Sodium arsenite	Persistent; contact
Oil of vitriol............	Sulfuric acid	Nonpersistent; contact
Organic compounds		
2,4-D.................	2,4-Dichlorophenoxyacetic acid	Persistent; systemic
2,4,5-T................	2,4,5-Trichlorophenoxyacetic acid	Persistent; systemic
MCPA.................	4-Chloro-2-methylphenoxyacetic acid	Persistent; systemic
Propham..............	Isopropyl *N*-phenyl carbamate	Persistent; contact (sprout-depressant)
Proxan (sodium)	Sodium isopropyl xanthate	Semipersistent; contact
Sodium trichloroacetate...	Sodium trichloroacetate	Persistent; contact; systemic
DNC	2-Methyl-4,6-dinitrophenol	Semipersistent; contact
Dinoseb...............	2-(1-Methyl-*n*-propyl)-4,6-dinitro-phenol, or 2-*sec*-butyl-4,6-dinitrophenol, or 2,4-dinitro-6-*sec*-butylphenol	Semipersistent; contact
Dinex.................	2,4-Dinitro-6-cyclohexylphenol	Semipersistent; contact
Dinosam	2-(1-Methyl-*n*-butyl)-4,6-dinitro-phenol	Semipersistent; contact
Tar acids..............	Phenolic compounds obtained from coal-tar distillates	Semipersistent; contact
Petroleum oils	Distillates high in unsaturated hydrocarbons	Persistent

in an atomic ring; e.g.: N, O, S, Se, P, As. **h. compound.** A ring compound having atoms other than C in its nucleus; as:

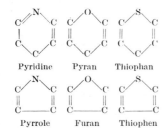

Pyridine   Pyran   Thiophan

Pyrrole   Furan   Thiophen

Antonym: homocyclic. See *ring compounds*.

heterogeneity. The state of being composed of particles or aggregates of different substances; hence, matter that is of dissimilar composition. Antonym: homogeneity.

heterogeneous. Opposed to homogeneous, q.v. Describes a substance that consists of more than one phase, and therefore is not uniform; as, colloids. **h. reaction.** A chemical change in which 2 or more reactions take place simultaneously.

heterogenesis. The derivation of a living thing from something unlike itself; e.g., of viruses from the complex cell.

hetero ion. An adsorption complex ion whose charge is due to an adsorbed simple ion, e.g., a protein complex with adsorbed OH⁻.

heterolysis (1) The dissolution of a cell by an external agent. Cf. *autolysis.* (2) The hemolytic action of the blood serum of one animal species on the blood corpuscles of another species. (3) A reaction in which a covalent bond is severed: $A:B \rightarrow A + :B$.

heterolyzate. The filtered liquid portion of the products of heterolysis.

heterometry. A form of turbidimetric titration in which nucleating chemical systems are studied by light-absorption measurements.

heterophase. Forming 2 or more states of aggregation. Cf. *phase.*

heteropolar. An unequal distribution of electric charges in a bond, so that one atom is more positive or negative than the other. Cf. *homopolar.*

heteropoly acids. The complex acids of heavy metals with phosphoric acids; as, phosphomolybdic a.

heteropoly blue. *Molybdenum* blue.

hetero sugars. *h* sugars. The structural isomers of the α and β mutarotation forms of a sugar, e.g., γ sugars.

heterotopes. Elements having different atomic numbers and therefore, occurring in different parts of the periodic table. Antonym: isotopes. **heterobaric-** H. having different atomic weights. **isobaric-** H. having the same atomic weight. Cf. *isobars.*

heterotype. A compound which differs in properties from compounds of a similar type.

hetoform. Bismuth cinnamate.

hetol. Sodium cinnamate.

322

hetralin. $C_6H_{12}N_6 \cdot C_6H_6O_2$ = 278.20. Dioxybenzolhexamethylenetetramine. Colorless needles, decomp. 155, soluble in water; a substitute for hexamethylenetetramine.

heulandite. $CaAl_2Si_6O_{15}$. A zeolite.

heuristic. Describing an approach to scientific problems based on finding out knowledge for oneself.

Heusler alloys. Strongly ferromagnetic alloys, containing no Fe but a mixture of Mn, Cu, and Al.

Hevea. See *rubber*.

Hevesy, George de (von). 1885–1966. Hungarian-born German chemist, codiscoverer of hafnium. Nobel Prize winner (1943).

hex. Hexamethylenetetramine.

hexa- Prefix (Greek) denoting 6.

hexaatomic. (1) Hexavalent. (2) Describing a molecule of 6 atoms.

hexabasic. Describing a compound in which 6 H can be replaced by basic radicals.

hexabiose. Hexobiose.

hexaborane. B_6H_{10} = 71.31. A boron hydride, q.v.

hexabromide number. An analytical value of fats. indicating their content of acids with 3 (or more) double bonds; the number of milligrams of Br needed to brominate 100 gm fat.

hexabromo- Prefix indicating 6 Br atoms. **h. ethane.** C_2Br_6 = 403.8. Yellow needles, decomp. 210, slightly soluble in water. **h. silicoethane.** Silicon tribromide.

hexachloro- Prefix indicating 6 Cl atoms. **h. benzene.** C_6Cl_6 = 284.7. Colorless needles, m.229, insoluble in water. Used in organic synthesis, in airfield flares, and in waterproofing dopes. Cf. *benzene* hexachloride. **h. ethane.** C_2Cl_6 = 236.8. Carbontrichloride, hexoram. White rhombic crystals, m.184, insoluble in water. Has an inherent tendency to agglomerate; so additives used to improve flow and stability. Used in organic synthesis; the manufacture of explosives and fireworks, smoke screens, and disinfectants. Cf. *H.C.*

hexachlorophane. Hexachlorophene (B.P.).

hexachlorophene. $C_{13}H_6O_2Cl_6$ = 406.93. 2,2′-Methylenebis(3,4,6-trichlorophenol). Hexachlorophane. White crystals with phenolic odor, m.161–167, insoluble in water; an anti-infective and detergent (U.S.P.).

hexacontane. $C_{60}H_{122}$ = 843.3. A saturated methane hydrocarbon. Colorless crystals, m.102.

hexacosane. $C_{26}H_{54}$ = 366.42. A saturated methane hydrocarbon. Colorless crystals, m.57.

hexacosanic acid. $C_{26}H_{52}O_2$ = 396.4. White solid, m.83, in peanut oil and in the wax from tubercle bacilli.

hexacyan. C_6N_6 = 180.5. A ring polymer of cyan.

hexad. (1) An element or radical having a valency of 6. (2) In crystallography, showing 6 similar faces on rotation of the crystal around its axis of symmetry.

hexadecane. $C_{16}H_{34}$ = 226.3. Dioctyl, cetane. A saturated methane hydrocarbon. White leaflets, m.18, insoluble in water.

hexadecanoic acid. Palmitic acid. **11-hydroxy-** Jalapinolic acid. **16-hydroxy-** Juniperic acid.

hexadecanol. Cetyl alcohol.

hexadecene. Cetene.

hexadecenoic acid. Zoomaric acid.

hexadecine. $C_{16}H_{30}$ = 222.2. Hexadecyne. An isomer of cetenylene, b.280.

hexadecoic acid. Palmitic acid.

hexadecyl. Cetyl. The radical, $-C_{16}H_{33}$, from hexadecane. **h. alcohol.** Cetyl alcohol. **h. amine.** Cetylamine.

hexadecylene. Cetene.

hexadiene. C_6H_{10} = 82.1. An unsaturated hydrocarbon with 2 double bonds. **1,4-** CH_2:·CH·CH_2·CH:CHMe **1,5-** Diallyl. **2,4-** (MeCH:·CH—)$_2$. Bipropenyl, dipropylene. Colorless liquid, b.82. **2,5-dimethyl-** $(Me_2C:CH—)_2$ = 101.11 Diisocrotyl. Colorless liquid, b.102.5.

hexadienedioic acid, 2,4-. Muconic acid.

hexadienic acid. Sorbic acid.

hexadienoic acid, 2,4-. Sorbic acid.

hexadiine. Bipropargyl.

hexadiyne. Bipropargyl.

hexaethylbenzene. C_6Et_6 = 246.3. Colorless monoclinic crystals, m.129, insoluble in water.

hexafluorodisilane. Disilane.

hexagalloyl mannite. $C_{48}H_{38}O_{30}$ = 1094.45. A brown tanning powder, soluble in water.

hexagon. A plane figure with 6 sides, and 6 angles. **h. tester.** An electrically heated device for determining the flash and fire points of oils.

hexagonal crystal system. A crystal system made up of 4 axes; 3 equal and intersecting in one plane at 60°, and one of a different length in a plane at right angles.

hexagonite. $CaMg_3(SiO_3)_4Mn$. A mineral from Edwards, N.J.

hexahydrate. Containing 6 molecules of water.

hexahydric. Containing 6 atoms of replaceable hydrogen.

hexahydro- Prefix indicating 6 more H atoms than are normally present. **h. anthracene.** $C_{14}H_{16}$ = 184.2. White leaflets, m.63, insoluble in water. **h. anthraquinone.** Rufigallol. **h. benzene.** C_6H_{12} = 84.1. Cyclohexane hexamethylene. Saturated benzene. A hydrocarbon in Austrian and Caucasian petroleum. Colorless liquid, d.0.76, b.79, insoluble in water. **h. benzodipyrazolone.** Dipyrazolone. **h. benzoic acid.** Naphthenic acid. **h. cumeme.** C_9H_{18} = 126.2. Trimethylcyclohexane. Colorless liquid, d.0.787, b.139, insoluble in water. **h. cymene.** $C_{10}H_{20}$ = 140.3. *p*-Hexahydrocymol. Colorless liquid, d.0.802, b.156, insoluble in water. **h. diphenyl.** Phenylcyclohexane. **h. mellitic acid.** $C_6H_6(COOH)_6$ = 348.2. Colorless crystals, decomp. by heat, soluble in water. **h. mesitylene.** $C_6H_9Me_3$ = 126.2. Trimethylhexahydrobenzene. Colorless liquid, b.136. **h. naphthalene.** $C_{10}H_{14}$ = 134.2. Colorless liquid, d.0.924, b.208. **h. naphthinoline.** $C_{16}H_{16}N_2$ = 236.2. Colorless crystals, m.128. **h. phenol.** Cyclohexanol. **h. pyrazine.** Piperazine. **h. pyridine.** Piperidine. **h. salicylic acid.** $C_6H_{10}OH(COOH)$ = 144.1. Colorless crystals, m.110, soluble in water. **h. thymol.** Menthol. **h. toluene.** $C_6H_{11}Me$ = 98.2. Colorless liquid, d.0769, b.101, insoluble in water. **h. xylene.** C_8H_{16} = 112.2. *meta*- Colorless liquid, d.0.771. b.118, insoluble in water. *para*- Colorless liquid, d.0.769, b.121, insoluble in water.

hexahydroxy- Prefix indicating 6 OH groups. **h. benzene.** Triquinoyl. **h. hexahydrobenzene.** Inositol.

hexaiodo- Prefix indicating 6 I atoms in a molecule.

hexakontaine. Hexacontane.

hexal. Hexamethyleneamine sulfosalicylate; a sedative compound of salicylic acid and urotropine.

Hexalet. Trade name for hexamethylenetetramine salicylsulfonic acid.

Hexalin. Trademark for cyclohexanol*.

hexalite. An explosive of high detonating velocity. Used to describe: (1) Hexanitromannite. (2) RBX. Cyclotrimethylene trinitramine mixed with beeswax. (3) Hexanitrodiphenylamine. (4) Dipentaerythritol hexanitrate. Cf. *hexolite.*

hexamethonium tartrate. $C_{20}H_{40}O_{12}N_2 = 500.61$. Vergolysen-T (B.P.C.), hexamethylenebistrimethylammoniumdi(hydrogen tartrate). White powder with acidic taste, soluble in water; used to treat hypertension.

hexamethylated. Describing an organic compound containing 6 Me groups.

hexamethylbenzene. $C_6Me_6 = 162.2$. Colorless rhombs, m.164, soluble in alcohol.

hexamethyldisilicane. $Si_2(CH_3)_6 = 146.26$. White solid, m.13.

hexamethylenamine. Hexamethylenetetramine.

hexamethylene. Cyclohexane*. **amido-** C_6H_{11}-$NH_2 = 99.11$. Aminohexahydrobenzene. Colorless liquid, b.133. **diketo-, triketo-** q.v.

h. amine. Hexamethylenetetramine. **h. diamine.** (1) Triethylenediamine. (2) See *diamine.*

hexamethyleneamine. Hexamethylenamine.

hexamethylenetetramine. $C_6H_{12}N_4 = 140.2$. Hexamethyleneamine, hexine, urotropine, hexamine, formin, aminoform, hex, naphthamine, uriton. Colorless rhombs, m.280, soluble in water; used as a urinary antiseptic, a reagent for metals and alkaloids, a rubber accelerator, a solid portable fuel (hexamine), in the manufacture of synthetic resins, and as an absorbent for phosgene in gas masks.

h. alliodide. A condensation product of h. and allyl iodide; a reagent for cadmium. **h. bromethylene.** Bromalin. **h. camphorate.** $(CH_2)_6N_4$·$C_8H_{14}(COOH)_2$. Amphotropine. A molecular combination of camphoric acid and hexamethylenamine. Colorless crystals, soluble in water. **h. methylenecitrate.** $C_7H_6O_7(CH_2)_6N_4 = 342.3$. Helmitol. White crystals, m.165. Used in place of hexamethylenamine. **h. quinate.** Quinotropine. **h. salicylate.** Saliformin. **h. salicylsulfonic acid.** Hexalet. White, crystalline powder, soluble in water; a diuretic. **h. sulfosalicylate.** Hexal. **h. tannin.** Tannopin. **h. tetraiodide.** $(CH_2)_6N_4I_4 = 647.6$. Siomine. Red powder, decomp 138; used in place of iodides.

hexamethylparafuchsin. Crystal violet.

hexamethylviolet. Crystal violet.

hexamine. Hexamethylenetetramine.

hexanal. Caproaldehyde.

hexanamide. Caproamide.

hexanaphthene. Cyclohexene.

hexane. $Me_2(CH_2)_4 = 86.14$. (1) Normal hexane, caproyl hydride, hexyl hydride. Colorless liquid, d.0.658, b.69, highly flammable, insoluble in water; a solvent. (2) $Me(CH_2)_2CHMe_2$. Ethylisobutane. Colorless liquid, d.0.701, b.62, soluble in alcohol. (3) $Me_2(CH_2)_2Me_2$. Diisopropane. Colorless liquid, d.0.67, b.58, soluble in alcohol. (4) Me_3CEt. Trimethylethylmethane. Colorless liquid, b.44,

soluble in alcohol. **amino-** Hexylamine. **bromo-** Hexyl bromide. **chloro-** Hexyl chloride. **1,2,3,4,5,6-hexachlorocyclo-** See *benzene* hexachloride. **neo-** A highly branched C_6 hydrocarbon used in high-octane fuels.

h. carboxylic acid. Heptoic acid. **h. dial.** Adipaldehyde. **h. diamide.** Adipamide. **h. dicarboxylic acid.** Suberic acid. **h. dioic acid.** Adipic acid. **h. diol.** Hexamethylene glycol. **h. dioyl chloride.** Adipyl chloride.

hexanitrin. Mannitol nitrate.

hexanitro- Prefix indicating 6 nitro groups. **h. diphenylamine.** $C_{15}H_5N_7O_{12} = 439.10$. Dipicrylamine, $[2,4,6-(NO_2)_3C_6H_2]_2NH$. Yellow crystals; a high explosive. **h. mannitol.** A misnomer for mannitol nitrate. **h. phenyl sulfide.** $[C_6H_2-(NO_2)_3]_2S = 466.0$. A high explosive.

hexanoic acid. Caproic acid.

hexanol*. (1) Hexyl alcohol. (2) Hexan-3-ol. See *hexyl alcohol* (3).

hexanone*. Ethyl propyl ketone.

hexaphenyl. (1) Sexiphenyl. (2) 6 phenyl radicals. **h. ethane.** Ph_3C—$CPh_3 = 486.24$. The dimer of a free radical, q.v. **h. tin.** Ph_3Sn·$SnPh_3 = 699.62$. White crystals, m.233.

hexasaccharose. A polysaccharide of the general type $(C_6H_{10}O_5)_6$·H_2O.

hexatomic. (1) Consisting of 6 atoms. (2) Hexavalent.

hexavalent. (1) Sexavalent. Describing an element or radical having 6 valence electrons; as, Os. (2) A compound containing 6 replaceable H atoms or OH groups.

hexecontane. Hexacontane.

hexenal*. $PrCH:CH·CHO = 98.08$. $α,β$-Hexenic aldehyde, propylacrolein. An oil $b_{17mm}48$, in green leaves.

hexene*. (1) $C_6H_{10} = 82.1$. Tetrahydrobenzene. Colorless crystals, m.83. (2) Hexylene.

hexenic*. See *hexenoic*.

hexenoic acid. $C_6H_{10}O_2 = 114.08$. Hexenic acid. **α-** or **1,2-** $MeCH_2CH_2CH:CH·COOH$. Prophylacrylic acid. White solid, m.32. **β-** or **2,3-** $MeCH_2CH:CHCH_2COOH$. Hydrosorbic acid. White solid, b.208. Cf. *pyroterebic acid.*

hexenoic aldehyde. Hexenal*.

hexenyl. The unsaturated radical C_6H_{10}—, from hexylene. **h. alcohol.** $C_6H_{11}OH = 100.1$. Colorless liquid, d.0.891, b.137, soluble in water.

hexestrol. $HO·C_6H_4(C_2H_5)CH·CH(C_2H_5)·C_6H_4·OH$. Dihydrodiethylstilbestrol. An estrogenic hormone.

hexine. (1) Hexyne*. (2) Hexadiene. (3) Hexamethylenetetramine.

hexinic acid. $C_6H_{10}O_3 = 130.1$. $α$-Propyltetronic acid. Colorless crystals, m.126.

hexitols. $C_6H_{14}O_6 = 182.11$. Hepatomic alcohols, as dulcitol, from hexoses.

hexobarbitone. Evipal, evipan, cyclural, hexobarbital; the $5-Δ^1$-cyclohexenyl-5-methyl-N-methylbarbituric acid; a sedative and anesthetic.

hexobiose. A carbohydrate (disaccharide) consisting of 2 hexoses; e.g., sucrose, lactose, maltose.

hexodiose. Hexobiose.

hexogen. Cyclotrimethylenetrinitramine. A constituent of high explosives.

hexoic. The radical —$CO(CH_2)_4Me$. **h. acid.** Caproic acid. *pentahydroxy-* Galactonic acid. **h. aldehyde.** Caproaldehyde.

hexokinase. A yeast enzyme; converts hexoses to hexosephosphates in presence of a magnesium salt catalyst.

hexolite. A high explosive prepared from nitrated cyclic compounds (U.S. usage). Cf. *hexalite, hexonit.*

hexon(e). $Me_2CH \cdot CH_2 \cdot COMe$ = 100.08. Methyl isobutyl ketone. Colorless liquid, b.118, insoluble in water; a solvent. **h. bases.** Histon bases. Organic bases containing 6 C atoms, formed by hydrolysis of proteins and histons, e.g., lysine.

hexonic acids. Acids obtained by the oxidation of hexoses: $C_5H_5(OH)_6 \cdot COOH$. Cf. *gluconic acid.*

hexonit. Nitroglycerin containing 10% hexogen; a high-explosive. Cf. *hexolite.*

hexoran. Hexachloroethane.

hexosans. Hemicelluloses which are hydrolyzed to hexoses. Cf. *glucosans.*

hexose. A carbohydrate (monosaccharide) containing 6 C atoms; as, dextrose. Widely distributed in plants and animals; each has 3 optical isomers: *d-, l-,* and *i-.*

hexotriose. A carbohydrate (trisaccharide) consisting of 3 hexoses, e.g., raffinose.

hexoylene. 2-Hexyne*.

hexuronic acid. $CHO(CHOH)COOH$ = 116.04. A tetrahydroxy aldehyde acid obtained by oxidation of hexoses; as, glucuronic acid.

hexyl. Enanthyl. The radical $Me(CH_2)_5-$, from *n*-hexane. **h. acetate.** $AcOC_6H_{13}$ = 144.2. Colorless liquid, d.0.890, b.169, insoluble in water. **h. acetylene.** Caprylidene. **h. alcohol.** $C_6H_{14} \cdot$ O = 102.2. Hexanol*, capryl alcohol. (1) Nor- (1) $Me(CH_2)_5OH$. Normal hexyl alcohol, amylcarbinol, hexan-1-ol. Colorless liquid, d.0.820, b.158, slightly soluble in water. (2) MeCH- $(OH)(CH_2)_3Me$. Methylbutylcarbinol, hexan-2-ol. Colorless liquid, d.0.833, b.137, slightly soluble in water. (3) $Et(CHOH)(CH_2)_2Me$. Ethylpropylcarbinol, hexan-3-ol. Colorless liquid, d.0.834, b.134, slightly soluble in water. (4) $Me_2C(OH) \cdot (CH_2)_2Me$. Dimethylpropylcarbinol. Colorless liquid, d.0.830, b.115, soluble in alcohol. (5) $Me_2C(OH)CHMe_2$. Dimethylisopropylcarbinol. Colorless liquid, d.0.836, b.112, soluble in water. (6) $Et_2C(OH)Me$. Diethylmethylcarbinol. Colorless liquid, b.120, soluble in alcohol. (7) $Me_3C \cdot CH(OH)Me$. Pinacolyl alcohol, tetramethylethanol. Colorless liquid, d.0.835, b.120, soluble in alcohol. **h. aldehyde.** Caproaldehyde. **h. amine*.** $C_6H_{15}N$ = 101.2. Aminohexane. A poisonous (ptomaine) base obtained by autolysis of protoplasm. **h. bromide.** $Me(CH_2)_4CH_2Br$ = 165.02. 1-Bromohexane*. Colorless liquid, d.1.1705, b.156. **h. caine(-Cl).** Cyclaine. An anesthetic. **h. chloride.** $Me(CH_2)_5Cl$ = 120.56. 1-Chlorohexane*. Colorless liquid, d.0.8741, b.132. **h. formate.** $HCOOC_6H_{13}$ = 130.2. Colorless liquid, d.0.898, b.153, miscible with alcohol. **h. iodide.** $C_6H_{13}I$ = 212.1. Iodohexane*. Colorless liquid, d.1.453, b.70. **h. methyl ketone.** $C_8H_{16}O$ = 128.12. 2-Octanone. A liquid, d.0.818, b.173. **h.resorcinol.** $C_6H_{13} \cdot C_6H_3(OH)_2$ = 194.28. Caprokol. White crystals, m.64, soluble in alcohol; a urinary antiseptic and anthelmintic (B.P.). (Phenol coefficient 45.0–55.0). Cf. *dihydranol.*

hexylene. $CH_2:CH(CH_2)_3Me$ = 84.1. (1) *n*-

Hexylene, hexene*. Colorless liquid, d.0.683, b.68, insoluble in water (2) $MeCH:CH(CH_2)_2Me$. Δ^2-Hexylene. (3) $MeCH_2CH:CHCH_2Me$. Δ^2-Hexylene, diethylethylene. **h. glycol.** Pinacone. **h. iodide.** $C_6H_{12}I_2$ = 337.8. Diiodohexane. Yellow liquid, decomp. by heat, d.2.024.

hexylic acid. Caproic acid.

hexyne*. $Me(CH_2)_3C:CH$ = 82.08. **1-** *n*-Butylacetylene, 1-hexine. Colorless liquid, d.0.712, b.71.5. **2-** $MeC:CPr$. Methylpropylacetylene. Colorless liquid, d.0.7377, b.84.

Heyrovsky, Jaroslav. 1890–1967. Czechoslovak chemist, codiscoverer of rhenium (1925), and inventor of the polarograph, q.v. Nobel Prize winner (1959).

Hf. Symbol for hafnium.

h.f. Abbreviation for high frequency.

Hg. Symbol for mercury (hydrargyrum).

hg. Abbreviation for hectogram (100 gm).

Hi. Symbol for hiburnium.

hiburnium. Thorium-Ω. A supposed radioactive element, at. no. approx. 40, in the black mica of Ytterby; half-life period 10^{16} years (Joly, 1922).

hibiscus. Musk seed.

Hickman pump. A borosilicate glass diffusion pump for producing high vacuum, containing butyl phthalate instead of mercury. Cf. *vacuum pump.*

hiddenite. An emerald-green gem variety of spodumene.

hidrotic. A substance that causes sweating; as, a diaphoretic.

hielmite. Hjelmite. A calcium, iron, manganese, and yttrium tantalate and stannate (Sweden). Black rhombs, d.58, hardness 5.

hierro. Spanish for iron.

Hi-flash. Trade name for an oil having a high flash point.

high. Above the average; great. **h. cranberry** Cramp bark. **h. explosive.** See *explosive.* **h. flash point.** Describing a substance as, an oil, that ignites at high temperatures only. **h. frequency.** Describing a rapidly alternating electric current. **h.f. spectrum.** An X-ray spectrum, produced by a h.f. current. **h. furnace.** A blast furnace. **h. grade.** Describing: (1) a pure substance; (2) a concentrated substance; (3) a rich ore. **h. speed steel.** A tool steel rich in carbon. Cf. *ferrotungsten.*

Hildebrand, Joel Henry. b. 1881. American chemist. **H. electrode.** A platinum electrode in a bell-shaped tube, through which hydrogen passes; used as a hydrogen electrode, being partly immersed in the solution and partly exposed to the gas. **H. rule.** The molal entropy of vaporization is a function of the molal concentration of the vapor involved. Cf. *Trouton's rule.*

Hillebrand, William Francis. 1853–1925. American chemist noted for work on mineral analysis.

Hilt's law. In a vertical section (e.g., of coal seams) the deeper seams are of higher rank than the upper.

hindrance. A retarding factor. **steric-** See *steric.*

Hinman tube. A glass apparatus for determining ammonia in illuminating gas.

hinokitol. $C_{12}H_{12}O_2(?)$. A constituent of the coloring matter of certain Japanese woods.

H· ion. Hydrogen ion. **H-ion concentration.** Hydrogen-ion concentration.

Hipersil. Trademark for a Fe–Si alloy having magnetic properties of special use in electric transformers.

hippocastanum. The seed and bark of the horse chestnut, *Aesculus hippocastanum* (Sapindaceae); a tonic, narcotic, and febrifuge.

hippol. $C_{10}H_9O_3N = 191.1$. Methylene hippuric acid. Colorless prisms, m.151, soluble in water; an antiseptic.

hippurate. A salt of hippuric acid, containing the radical $PhCONHCH_2COO—$.

hippuric acid. $PhCONHCH_2COOH = 179.1$. Benzoylglycine, benzaminoacetic acid. Colorless crystals, d.1.371, m.188 (decomp.), soluble in hot water; an antirheumatic.

hippuryl. The radical $PhCONHCH_2C:O—$, from hippuric acid. **h. hydrazine.** $Ph·CO·NH·CH_2·CO·NHNH_2 = 193.1$. Colorless crystals, m.162.

hiptagenic acid. $C_3H_5O_4N = 119.05$. Nitropropionic acid. A hydrolysis product of hiptagin.

hiptagin. $C_{10}H_{14}O_9N_2 = 306.2$. A glucoside from *Hiptage madablata*. Colorless, silky needles, m.112.

hiragashira oil. An oil from the livers of *Scoliodon lacticaudus*, containing scoliodinic acid.

hiragonic acid. $C_{16}H_{26}O_2 = 244.2$. A liquid, unsaturated fatty acid from sardine oil.

hirathiol. Ammonium sulfoichthyolate. Brown syrup of empyreumatic odor, soluble in water; a mild antiseptic.

hircine. (1) A strongly odorous fossil resin. (2) The odorous principle in the suet of goats.

hirudine. The active principle of a secretion from the buccal glands of leeches. It prevents the coagulation of blood.

hirudo. The leech *Sanguisuga medicinalis*.

histamine. $C_3H_9N_2·CH_2·CH_2·NH_2 = 111.1$. Ergamine, β-iminazolylethylamine. An amine derived from histidine in ergot. A powerful uterine stimulant, which lowers the blood pressure. **h. hydrochloride.** The soluble hydrochloride of histamine. **h. phosphate.** $C_5H_9N_3·2H_3PO_4 = 307.15$. Colorless prisms, m.129, soluble in water. A diagnostic aid for gastric secretions (U.S.P., B.P.).

histazarin. 2,3-Dihydroxyanthraquinone.

histidine. $C_6H_9O_2N_3 = 155.2$. An amino acid derived from the protamin of fishes, or by the action of sulfuric acid on ptomaines. *d-* White scales, m.288, soluble in water. *dl-* Tetragonal prisms, m.285, soluble in water. *l-* Colorless leaflets, m.277. **thiol-** A constituent of proteins.

histo- Prefix (Greek) denoting tissue.

histochemistry. The chemistry of the histological structures of the body.

histogram. Frequency curve.

histology. The study of the structure of tissues. **normal-** The study of healthy tissues. **pathological-** The study of diseased tissues. **phyto-** The science of plant tissues. **zoo-** The science of animal tissues.

histolysis. The disintegration or liquefaction of tissues.

histon. (1) See *hexon(e)* bases. (2) A protein from cell nuclei, soluble in water, coagulated by heat.

histoplasmin. A liquid concentrate of the soluble growth products of *Histoplasma capsulatum*. A clear amber liquid miscible with water; a diagnostic aid (U.S.P.).

Hittorf, Johan Wilhelm. 1824–1914. German physicist and discoverer of the cathode rays. **H. cell.** Transference cell. **H. number.** Transport number. **H. tube.** A modified Crookes tube.

hjelmite. Hielmite.

hl. Abbreviation for hectoliter (100 liters).

hm. Abbreviation for hectometer (100 meters). **hm².** Abbreviation for square hectometer (10,000 sq meters). **hm³.** Abbreviation for cubic hectometer (1,000,000 cu meters).

HMT. Hexamethylenetetramine.

Ho. Symbol for holmium.

hoangnan. The bark of *Strychnos malaccensis* (Loganiaceae); an arrow poison.

hoarhound. Horehound.

Hoff, Jacobus Hendricus van't. See *van't Hoff*.

Hoffman, Friedrich. 1660–1742. German physician and professor of chemistry. **H. clamp.** A clamp with one V-shaped and one flat jaw. **H. drops.** A mixture of alcohol and ether. **H. electrolytic apparatus.** Two inverted burets with platinum electrodes, with an overflow tube and bulb, to demonstrate the decomposition of water.

Hofmann, August Wilhelm von. 1818–1892. German chemist, founder of the coal-tar industry. **H. reaction.** The shortening of C chains by eliminating carbon monoxide by addition of bromine to an alkaline solution of an acid amine. The amine of the shorter C chain is formed: $R·CONH_2 + Br_2 + 3NaOH = R·NH_2 + Na_2CO_3 + NaBr + H_2O$. **H. sodium press.** An iron barrel, piston, and screw used to make sodium wire or ribbon.

Hofmeister series. The order in which anions and cations may be arranged according to their powers of coagulation of an emulsoid, in neutral, acid, or alkaline solutions. Cf. *lyotropic series*.

hog bane. Hyoscyamus.

hogbomite. $MgO(AlFe)_2·TiO_2$. A mineral from the Cameroons.

hoggin. A natural deposit of gravel held together with a little clay.

hog gum. Kuteera gum, gum hogg. A variety of Bassora gum from *Sterculia urens*; used in marbling paper.

hogshead. hhd. A measure: 52.5 imperial gal (238.5 liters). (2) A cask of capacity 100–140 gal (U.S.); 50–100 gal (U.K.). **Irish-** 52 gal. **United Kingdom-** 54 gal.

hogweed. Scoparius.

holadin. An extract of the pancreas containing its enzymes. Gray, hygroscopic powder, partly soluble in water; used in medicine. Cf. *pancreatic juice*.

holarsol. Dichlorophenarsine hydrochloride, q.v.

Holborn-Kurlbaum pyrometer. An instrument for determining high temperatures in furnaces.

holder. A device for retaining or holding objects in a definite position. **animal-** A wire net or metal tube, used to secure small animals for biological experiments. **buret-** A clamp to hold burets. **clamp-** Boss. Iron screws to attach clamps to supports. **crucible-** A wire clamp or frame for holding crucibles. **culture dish-** A wire frame for holding petri dishes together in a sterilizer. **gas-** Gasometer. **plate-** A light tight box for holding photographic plates. **watch glass-** A pair of circular wire springs for holding 2 watch glasses together.

hole. See *excitonic.*

hollander. An early form of beater, q.v.

hollyhock. (1) Althaea. (2) The flowers of *Althaea rosea* (Malvaceae); an emollient.

holmia. (1) A mixture of the oxides of holmium and dysprosium. (2) Holmic oxide.

holmic. A compound of the trivalent Ho atom. **h. oxide.** $Ho_2O_3 = 375.0$. Gray powder, insoluble in water.

holmium. Ho $= 164.93$. A rare-earth metal, at. no. 67, in gadolinite, discovered (1879) by Cleve. Valency 3. Its salts are slightly yellow. **eka-Einsteinium,** q.v.

h. chloride. $HoCl_3 = 269.8$. Holmic chloride. Colorless powder, soluble in water. **h. oxalate.** $Ho_2(C_2O_4)_3 = 591.0$. Colorless powder, insoluble in water. **h. oxide.** Holmic oxide.

holo- Prefix (Greek) indicating the whole or entirety.

holocaine. $C_{18}H_{22}O_2N_2 = 298.3$. Ethenyl-*p*-diethoxydiphenylamidine, phenacaine. Colorless crystals, m.189, slightly soluble in water; a local anesthetic. **h. hydrochloride.** $MeC:(NC_6H_4OEt)$-$(NHC_6H_4OEt)\cdot HCl$. Phenacaine chloride. The soluble form of h.

holocellulose. The total carbohydrate constituents of wood.

holography. A method of photography in which the light waves, emanating from an object in all dimensions, are frozen on the plate and revived by illumination.

holohedral. A crystal which has the full number of faces required for the maximum and complete symmetry of the system. Cf. *hemihedral.*

Holopon. Trade name for a preparation said to contain all the alkaloids of opium.

holosiderite. Meteoric iron.

Holtz, Wilhelm. 1836–1913. German physicist. **H. machine.** An induction machine.

homarine. $C_7H_7NO_2 = 137.1$. The methyl-betaine of picolinic acid, in shellfish, *Arbatia pustulosa.* Cf. *trigonelline.*

homatropine. $C_{16}H_{21}O_3N = 275.2$. An alkaloid condensation product of tropine and mandelic acid: tropine mandelate. Colorless prisms, m.97, slightly soluble in water. **h. hydrobromide.** $C_{16}H_{21}O_3N\cdot HBr = 356.28$. Homotropine hydrobromide. A very poisonous, soluble form of h. Colorless prisms, m.213, soluble in water. Used in opthalmology (U.S.P., B.P.). **h. hydrochloride.** $C_{16}H_{21}O_3N\cdot HCl = 311.20$. Homotropine hydrochloride. A soluble form of h.; white crystals, m.216, soluble in water; used in ophthalmology. **h. methyl bromide.** $C_{17}H_{24}O_3NBr = 370.30$. White powder, m.195, used similarly to h. hydrobromide (U.S.P.).

homeopathic. Pertaining to homeopathy. **h. dose.** An extremely small amount. **h. vial.** An elongated bottle for h. tablets.

homeopathy. A system of medicine employing extremely small doses of agents, which if administered in health, would produce symptoms similar to those for the relief of which they are given.

homilite. $FeCa_2B_2Si_2O_{10}$. A native borosilicate, d.3.0–3.28, hardness 5.5.

homo- (1) Prefix (Greek) indicating similarity. (2)

In names of organic compounds it indicates a difference of —CH_2—, but an otherwise similar structure.

homoantipyrine. $C_{12}H_{14}ON_2 = 202.2$. 1.2.3-Phenylethylmethylpyrazolone. Colorless crystals, m.73.

homoarecoline. $C_9H_{15}O_2N = 169.2$. Ethoxy-arecaidine. Yellow liquid, soluble in water. **h. hydrobromide.** $C_7H_{10}EtO_2N\cdot HBr$. Colorless crystals, m.118, soluble in water; an anthelmintic.

homoatomic ring. Homocycle.

homoatropine. Homatropine.

homocamphoric acid. $C_{11}H_{18}O_4 = 214.1$. An acid, similar to camphoric acid, but having a —CH_2— bridge. Distillation of its calcium salts yields camphor.

homocentric. Having the same center. **h. rays.** Light rays that are parallel or have a common focus.

homochelidonine. $C_{21}H_{21}O_5N = 367.2$. An alkaloid from the seeds of *Chelidonium majus* and sanguinaria. Colorless crystals, slightly soluble in alcohol.

homochemical. Describing a compound or molecule which consists of 2 types of atoms only, e.g., a binary compound.

homochromic. Possessing the same color, but having a different molecular composition.

homochromoisomers. Substances having similar absorption spectra, but different molecular compositions.

homocycle, homocyclic. Pertaining to compounds which contain a closed chain or ring of atoms of the same type, usually C atoms; e.g., benzene.

homodetic. Describing polypeptides rings consisting of amino acid residues (IUPAC).

homogeneity, homogeneous. Of uniform or similar nature throughout. Antonym: heterogeneous.

homogentisic acid. $(HO)_2C_6H_3\cdot CH_2COOH = 168.06$. 2,5-Dihydroxytoluic acid. Colorless crystals, m.147; an intermediate in the oxidation of tyrosine and phenylalanine.

homoisohydric. Having the same ions and a constant hydrogen-ion concentration in a solution.

homolog, homologue. Member of a series of compounds whose structure differs regularly by some radical, e.g., $=CH_2$, from that of its adjacent neighbors in the series.

homologous. Of similar structure. **h. lines.** A pair of spectrum lines, the relative intensities of which are independent of the electrical discharge producing them. **h. series.** A series of organic compounds which differ by CH_2 or some similar multiple. Cf. *methane series.*

homology. The similarity of organic compounds and their gradation of properties, as shown by a homologous series.

homolysis. Describing a reaction in which a covalent bond is severed according to the reaction A:B → A: + B. Cf. *heterolysis.*

homometric. Having the same X-ray pattern.

homonataloin. $C_{22}H_{24}O_9 = 332.21$. 1,2,8-Trihydroxymethylanthraquinone. A constituent of Natal aloes.

homophase. Forming a single and similar state of aggregation. Cf. *phase.*

homopolar. (1) Having an equal distribution of electric charges between 2 (generally C) atoms, neither of which becomes negative or positive; hence, a bond in which both atoms share the electron pair equally. (2) Covalent.

homopyrocatechol. $Me \cdot C_6H_3 \cdot (OH)_2 = 124.1$. 3,4-Dihydroxytoluene. Colorless prisms, m.51, soluble in water. Cf. *orcinol*.

homopyrrole. Methylpyrrole.

homoquinone. $C_{19}H_{22}N_2O_2 \cdot 2H_2O$. A crystalline alkaloid from cinchona bark.

homorenon. $(HO)_2C_6H_3CO \cdot CH_2 \cdot NHMe = 301.1$. Ethylaminoacetocatechol. A white powder.

homosalicylic acid. $C_8H_8O_3 = 152.1$. Cresotic acid. A compound containing a —COOH, —OH, and CH_3— group attached to the benzene ring; 10 possibilities.

homosaligenin. Salicyl alcohol.

homotaraxasterol. $C_{25}H_{40}O = 356.31$. A sterol, m.164, from dandelion.

homotope. An element in a vertical group of the periodic system; thus Br is a h. of Cl, Tl a h. of Ga.

homotropine. Homatropine.

homozyme. Vitagen.

Honduras bark. Cascara amarga.

hone. A mounted stone used for sharpening razors and knives. Mel.

honey. Mel. **h. dew.** A sugary, sticky excretion from certain leaf-sucking insects; toxic to bees and a contaminant of honey.

honeystone. $Al_2C_{12}O_{18} \cdot 18H_2O$. Aluminum mellate, mellite. A natural hydrocarbon-aluminum derivative (Germany). Yellow resinous mineral, d.1.6, hardness 2.

Hönigschmid, Otto. 1878–1945. German chemist noted for inorganic work.

honing guide. A device for keeping a dissecting knife at the proper angle while honing.

hood. A glass-enclosed ventilator shaft or flue in the laboratory which carries away fumes.

hoof and horn meal. A fertilizer (11–15 % N) made by processing, drying, and grinding hoofs and horns.

Hooke, Robert. 1635–1703. English philosopher. **H.'s law.** The stress applied to stretch or compress a body is proportional to the strain, or alteration in length, so produced; so long as the limit of elasticity is not exceeded.

hoolamite. A mixture of pumice, iodine pentoxide, and fuming sulfuric acid used as absorbing agent and reagent for carbon monoxide. It changes from white through blue-green to violet-brown.

hopcalite. (1) A mixture of cobalt, copper, silver, and manganese oxides, used in gas masks as a catalyst to oxidize carbon monoxide. (2) A mixture of manganese dioxide and cupric oxide (3:2), prepared by heating hydrated manganese oxide and copper carbonate.

Höpfner process. A method of recovering copper by electrolysis.

Hopkins, Sir Frederick Gowland. 1861–1947. British chemist, discoverer of the importance of vitamins in diet. Nobel Prize winner (1929).

Hopogan. Trade name for magnesium peroxide.

hop oil. A green, odorous oil from hops. Its chief constituents are terpenes, humulene, and geraniol; a flavoring. Cf. *humulene*. **Spanish-** Origanum oil.

hopper. A funnel-shaped trough, or trap inlet.

Hoppe-Seyler, Ernst Felix Immanuel. 1825–1895.

German physiologist noted for the development of biochemical analysis.

hopred. $C_{38}H_{26}O_{15} = 722.2$. A hydrolytic split product of the coloring matter, phlobabene, from hops.

hops. Humulus. The dried spikes or strobiles of *Humulus lupulus* (Urticaceae, Moraceae). They contain tannin, humulon, and lupulin, and have a bitter aromatic taste; used as an aromatic bitter and stomachic, and in beer as a flavoring and preservative. **h. oil.** See *hop oil.* **h. substitutes.** Bitter principles; as, quassia or camomile.

horbachite. A native sulfide of gold, iron, and nickel.

hordein. A protein of barley, the seeds of *Hordeum sativum.*

hordeine. Hordenine.

hordenine. $C_{10}H_{15}ON = 165.2$. Hordeine, ephedrine. An alkaloid, m.118, from malted barley; used to cure diarrhea and dysentery.

hordeum. Barley.

horehound. The dried leaves and flowering tops of *Marrubium vulgare*; an expectorant and stimulant. Cf. *marrubiin.*

hormone. A substance produced by the internal secretion of glands. It acts as an accelerating or retarding catalyst in metabolism and other internal reactions. Hormones are chemical messengers, which circulate in the bloodstream and coordinate the functions of organs by exciting them to activity. **food-** Vitamin. **plant-** A h. which promotes growth of plants, particularly by root formation; as, indole.

horn. A substance composed mostly of keratin and containing insoluble mineral salts, particularly calcium phosphate. **h. fiber.** See *fiber, vulcanized.*

hornblende. $Ca(MgFe_3) \cdot (SiO_3)_4$. An amphibole in colors ranging from black through green and olive to white.

horn lead. Phosgenite.

horn quicksilver. Native mercurous chloride.

horn silver. Argentum cornu.

horse chestnut. The seeds of *Aesculus hippocastanum*; a tonic, astringent, and febrifuge. **h.c. bark.** The bark of *A. hippocastanum*; used medicinally. **h.c. tannin.** $C_{26}H_{24}O_{11} = 528.2$. A tannin from the h.c.

horsehair. The hair from the mane or tail of horses; used for mattresses and fabrics. **vegetable-** Spanish moss. The fibers of *Tillandsia usneoides* (Bromeliaceae), America; used for pillows and mattresses.

horsemint oil. Monarda oil. A brown essential oil, from the leaves and stems of *Monarda punctata*; used in the preparation of liniments. Cf. *monarda.*

horsenettle. See *solanum.* **h.n. berries.** Solanum.

horse oil. Yellow oil from horse fat; used in soap manufacture.

horsepower. A unit of power or the rate of doing work. 1 hp = 33,000 ft-lb/min = 550 ft-lb/sec = 76 kg-meter/sec = 745.8 watts. **continental-** 1 hp = 736 watts. **metric-** Pferdekraft (German). 75 kg/sec.

horseradish. The root of *Cochlearia armoracia* (Cruciferae); a condiment stomachic, stimulant, and diuretic. It contains potassium myronate.

horsetail. See *aconitic acid, Equisetum.*

horsfordite. Cu_6Sb. A native copper-antimony ore.

Hortvet cryoscope. An apparatus for determining

the freezing point. **H. tube.** A graduated glass centrifuge tube for determining the volume of a sediment.

Horwood process. A method of flotation of partly roasted sulfides of Fe, Cu, Pb, and Zn, to separate the zinc.

Hoskin furnace. An electric heating device for metallurgical and dental laboratories.

hot. (1) Having or producing the sensation of heat. (2) A colloquialism describing material that is producing a dangerous degree of radioactivity. **h. air sterilizer.** See *sterilizer*. **h. bed.** A h. mass of fermenting material, used to accelerate plant growth. **h. water funnel.** See *funnel*. **h. wire gage.** Gage.

houdriforming reaction. A dehydration or isomerization reaction which requires group IV precious metals on an acidic support as catalyst.

hour. The unit of time, 60 min, $\frac{1}{24}$ of a civil day.

Howard chamber. A microscope slide with a small counting chamber, used for yeast cells, molds, etc. **H. pan.** A jacket and coil type of vacuum evaporating kettle, used to concentrate sugar juice.

Howe, Harrison Estell. 1881–1942. American chemist, noted for his development of industrial chemistry.

howlite. $2CaO \cdot 5B_2O_3 \cdot 2SiO_2 \cdot 5H_2O$. A mineral from Long Beach, Calif.

hp. Abbreviation for horsepower.

H.T.P. High-test hydrogen peroxide (more than $75\% \ H_2O_2$ by weight.)

huantajayit. A native sodium–silver chloride.

huanuco bark. Cinchona bark.

Hübl number. Iodine number. **H. solution.** A solution of iodine and mercuric chloride used to determine iodine numbers of unsaturated compounds.

hübnerite. $MnWO_4$. A native ferruginous tungstate occurring in western U.S. Red crystals, d.7.17. Cf. *ferberite*.

Hudson, Claude Silbert. 1881–1952. American chemist, noted for work on enzymes and carbohydrates. **H. rule.** To assign α and β to a sugar in comparison with their molecular rotation, R_α and R_β, select names so that $R_\alpha - R_\beta$ is equal to and of the same sign as the difference for the 2 corresponding forms of glucose.

hue. A property of color, q.v.

Huff separator. An electrostatic concentrator for crushed ores.

huile. French for oil.

Hulett, George Augustus. 1867–1955. American physical chemist. **H. still.** A device for distilling mercury.

hülsneride. $FeWO_4$. A native ferrous tungstate.

humatin. The sulfate of paromomycin, q.v.

humboldite. A variety of melilith.

Humbold penetrometer. A device for testing asphalt by measuring its resistance to the pressure of a needle.

humectant. A hygroscopic substance (e.g., glycerol) used to ensure the absorption of a certain amount of atmospheric moisture by the material to which it is added. Cf. *plasticizer*.

Hume-Rothery rule. The majority of elements in the B subgroups of groups IV, V, VI, and VII of the periodic table have $(8 - N)$ near neighbors in the solid state, where N is the number of the group to which the element belongs.

humic acid. A general term for acids derived from humus.

humicolin. An antibiotic from *Aspergillus humicola* from cave soils. A weakly acidic, yellow oil, which inhibits spore germination of many common fungi.

humidity. Dampness, hygrometric state. The amount of water vapor in the air. **absolute-** The weight of water vapor in a unit of moist air, in grams per cubic meter. **equivalent-** The relative h. of the air in contact with a particular substance when it neither gains nor loses moisture. **relative-** The weight of water vapor contained in a given volume of air expressed as a percentage of the weight that would be contained in the same volume of saturated air at the same dry-bulb temperature. See *dew point*.

humidor. A compartment whose atmosphere is kept saturated with water vapor.

huminite. A native hydrocarbon from Sweden.

humite. Chondrodite. A basic magnesium fluosilicate.

hummer. A microphone used in conductivity measurements, to determine a point at which no current is passing by the absence of hum.

humoceric acid. $C_{19}H_{34}O_2 = 294.26$. An acid from peat wax.

humulene. $C_{15}H_{24} = 204.19$. A sesquiterpene from hop oil. Colorless liquid, b.265.

humulic acid. $C_{15}H_{22}O_4 = 266.2$. A compound product of the action of alkali on humulon.

humulin. Lupulin.

humulon. $C_{21}H_{30}O_5 = 362.2$. A bitter constituent, m.66, of the soft resin of hop lupulin. Cf. *lupulon*.

humulo tannin. $C_{25}H_{24}O_{13} = 532.2$. A white amphoteric powder from hops. It loses water at 130 and forms a phlobaphen.

humulus. Hops.

humus. (1) The top layer of the soil, containing the organic decomposition products of vegetation (leafmold, etc.). (2) The decayed products of plant life. Cf. *gainic acid*.

Hund's rules. (1) Electrons tend to avoid the same space orbit. (2) Two electrons, each singly occupying 2 equivalent states, tend to have parallel spins in the lowest state.

Hünefeld solution. A reagent for blood: alcohol 25, glacial acetic acid 1.5, chloroform 5, turpentine 15 ml.

Huntington mill. An ore crusher: steel rollers are pressed by centrifugal force against a heavy encasing steel ring.

Huppert's reagent. A 10% aqueous solution of calcium chloride, used to detect biliary pigments in urine.

huttonite. $ThSiO_4$. A monoclinic mineral, d.7.18, in New Zealand beach sands.

Huygens, Christian. 1629–1695. Dutch physicist, noted for the development of optical instruments, and a wave theory of light. **H. ocular.** Negative ocular. A magnifying eyepiece lens on a microscope or telescope: 2 convex lenses mounted convex sides down. Cf. Ramsden *ocular*.

hyacinth. (1) A transparent red gem variety of zircon. (2) Erroneously applied to light-colored garnet, to red spinel from Brazil, and to red quartz. **Ceylon-** Garnet. **false-** Garnet. **oriental-** Corundum (rose-colored).

hyacinthozontes. A sapphire-blue gem beryl.

hyaenasic acid. Hyenic acid.

hyaline. Resembling glass.

hyalite. A clear, colorless gem opal.

hyalophane. $(K_2,Ba)Al_2(SiO_3)_4$. A barium feldspar.

hyalosiderite. A deep olive-green gem olivine.

hyaluronic acid. A viscous, highly polymerized mucopolysaccharide in mammalian joint fluids.

hyaluronidase. A mucolytic enzyme from mammalian testes; used to limit the spread of fluid in the tissues.

hybrid. An organism, usually a plant, obtained by crossbreeding.

hybridization. (1) Producing a hybrid. (2) A process in which electrons are raised from a lower to a higher energy state, and which lowers the total energy.

Hycar. Trademark for an oil-resistant synthetic rubber.

hychlorite. Antiformin.

Hycoloid. Trade name for a cellulose nitrate plastic.

hydantoic acid. $NH_2CONHCH_2COOH = 118.1$. Carbamidoacetic acid, glycoluric acid. Colorless prisms, m.171, slightly soluble in water. **iso-** $NH_2 \cdot C(:NH) \cdot O \cdot CH_2 \cdot COOH$. **phenylthio-** $NH_2 \cdot C(:NPh)S \cdot CH_2 \cdot COOH = 210.07$. (1) ϕ-Iminocarbimin thioglycolic acid. White needles, m.150, insoluble in water. (2) *ortho-* $PhNH \cdot C(:NH) \cdot S \cdot CH_2 \cdot COOH$. White crystals.

hydantoin. $\overline{CH_2 \cdot NH \cdot CO \cdot NH \cdot CO} = 100.1$. Glycolylurea, imidazoledione. Colorless needles, m.216, soluble in hot water or alcohol. Cf. *barbituric acid*. **5-carbamido-** Allantoin. **ethylphenyl-** Nirvanol.

hydnocarpic acid. $C_{16}H_{28}O_2 = 252.22$. κ-Δ^2-Cyclopentenylundecylic acid. White crystals, m.60, from the oil of *Hydnocarpus* species; used to treat leprosy. Cf. *chaulmoogric acid*.

Hydnocarpus. A genus of trees (Bixaceae) whose seeds yield oils used to treat leprosy; as, kavatel oil, maroti oil. Cf. *chaulmoogra oil*. **h. oil.** An oil of *H. wightiana*, d.0.947, m.21–24. Cf. *Moogrol*.

hydr- Prefix (Greek) indicating water or hydrogen.

hydracetamide. $(MeCH)_3N_2 = 112.2$. Yellow powder, soluble in water.

hydracetin. Pyrodin.

hydracid. An acid without O atoms, as HCl.

hydracrylic acid. $CH_2OH \cdot CH_2COOH = 90.1$. β-Hydroxypropionic acid, 3-hydroxypropanoic acid*. Colorless crystals, decomp. by heat. **amino-** Serine. **phenyl-** Tropic acid.

hydracrylo. The radical $HOCH_2 \cdot CH_2 \cdot C\equiv$. **h. nitrile.** $HO(CH_2)CN = 71.05$. 3-Hydroxypropanenitrile*. Colorless liquid, d.1.059, b.221, soluble in water.

hydragog(ue). A cathartic producing a watery stool, e.g., jalap.

hydrallazine hydrochloride. $C_8H_8N_4 \cdot HCl = 196.61$. 1-Hydrazinophthalazine hydrochloride. White, bitter powder, m.275, soluble in water; a vasodilator (B.P.).

Hydralo. Trade name for an activated alumina desiccant.

hydramine. A hydroxyalkylamine or glycol in

which an OH group is replaced by NH_2 radical: $HO \cdot R \cdot NH_2$.

hydramyl. Pentane.

hydrangea. Seven barks. The dried roots of *H. arborescens* (Saxifragaceae); a cathartic and diuretic.

hydrangin. $C_{34}H_{25}O_{11} = 609.39$. A glucoside from hydrangea.

hydranthranol. Hydroanthranol.

hydrargillite. $Al(OH)_3$. (U.K. usage.) Gibbsite (U.S. usage.) A native aluminum hydroxide. Colorless needles.

hydrargotin. Mercurous tannate.

hydrargyrol. $C_6H_4OH \cdot SO_3Hg = 373.7$. *p*-Phenylmercury thionate; an antiseptic.

hydrargyrum. Latin for mercury.

hydrastin. A concentrate containing the principles of golden seal.

hydrastine. $C_{21}H_{21}O_6N = 383.3$. An alkaloid from *Hydrastis canadensis*, golden seal. White prisms, m.132, slightly soluble in water; an alterative and uterine hemostatic. **h. hydrochloride.** $C_{21}H_{21}O_6N \cdot HCl = 419.77$. The soluble hydrochloride of h. Colorless, hygroscopic powder, soluble in water.

hydrastinine. $C_{11}H_{13}O_3N = 207.1$. A decomposition product of hydrastine. Colorless crystals, m.116, slightly soluble in water. **h. hydrochloride.** $C_{11}H_{11}O_2 \cdot N \, HCl = 242.6$. Yellow crystals, m.210, soluble in water; an astringent and hemostatic.

hydrastis. Golden seal, yellow pucoon, orange root, turmeric root. The dried roots of *H. canadensis* (Ranunculaceae); a bitter tonic and astringent. **h. alkaloids.** Compounds of the isoquinoline group; as, hydrastine.

hydratated. Combined with water in the form of a hydrate. Cf. *hydrated*.

hydrate. (1) A substance containing water combined in the molecular form, as $H_2SO_4 \cdot H_2O$. (2) Aqua compound. A crystalline substance containing one or more molecules of water of crystallization; as, $Na_2SO_4 \cdot 7H_2O$; sodium sulfate heptahydrate. (3) Hydroxide. (4) A solvate, q.v. **carbo-** See *carbohydrate*.

hydrated. Combined with water. Cf. *hydrate solvate*. **h. ion.** An ion surrounded by oriented water molecules. **h.lime.** Dry calcium hydroxide.

hydration. Combination with water, but not necessarily in the form of a hydrate. **heat of-** The energy difference between anhydrous and hydrous compounds (in calories).

hydratisomery. Isomerism depending on the structure of hydrated crystals. Thus, $CrCl_3 \cdot 6H_2O$, chromic chloride hexahydrate occurs as:

Grayish-blue	$[Cr(H_2O)_6]Cl_3$
Grayish-green	$[Cr(H_2O)_5Cl]Cl_2 \cdot H_2O$
Green	$[Cr(H_2O)_4Cl_2]Cl \cdot 2H_2O$

hydratropic acid. $Ph \cdot CH \cdot MeCOOH = 150.1$. α-Phenylpropionic acid, α-methyl-α-toluic acid. Colorless crystals, m.265, soluble in water. **hydroxy-** Atrolactic acid.

hydraulic. Pertaining to liquids, especially water. **h. cement.** A cement that sets under the action of water, instead of atmospheric carbon dioxide and moisture. **h. lime.** Limestone which, on burning, yields a quicklime that will set or harden under water. Cf. *hydrated* lime. **h. mining.** Excavation by means of a strong jet of water. **h. mortar.** A mortar that hardens under water. **h. press.** An extraction press of great force with water to transmit the pressure.

hydraulics. Hydromechanics. The study of the mechanical properties of liquids.

hydrazi- Prefix indicating the —NH·NH— group whose valencies both belong to the same atom. Cf. *hydrazo-*.

hydrazide. An acyl hydrazine of the type R·CO·-NH·NH₂. Hydrazides are metamers of diureides. Cf. *malein hydrazide*. **acet-** See *acethydrazide*. **carbo-** See *carbohydrazide*. **oxy-** See *oxyhydrazide*.

hydrazidine. (1) A compound containing the —NH·N:C·NH₂ group. (2) The theoretical compound, NH₂·N:CH·NH₂.

hydrazido mesoxalamide. NH₂·N:C(CONH₂)CO-NH₂ = 130.2. Colorless crystals, m.175.

hydrazimethylene. The theoretical compound, CH₂·NH·NH, from which the hydrazi compounds are derived. **benzoylphenyl-** NH·NH·CPh-(COPh). Colorless crystals, m.151. **diphenyl-** (NH·NH·CPh)₂. Colorless crystals, m.147.

hydrazine. H₂N—NH₂ = 32.1. Diamine, diamidogen. Colorless liquid, d.1.08, m.1.4, b.113, soluble in water. Used as a reducing agent in organic synthesis; and in liquid ammonia solution, as a nitridizing agent, analogously to the oxidizing action of hydrogen peroxide in aqueous solution. It gives the radicals:

H₂N·NH— .... Hydrazino, hydrazyl
H₂N·H=.............. Hydrazono
—HN·NH— .... Hydrazo, hydrazi
=N·N= .... Azo, diazo

Cf. *hydrazinium*, *hydrazidine*. **tetrafluoro-** See *difluoroamino-*.
h. carbamide. Diurea. **h. carboxamide.** Semicarbazide. **h. carboxylic acid.** Carbazic acid. **h. dicarbamide.** Biurea. **h. chloride**, **h. dihydrochloride.** N₂H₄·2HCl = 105.5. Colorless crystals, m.198, soluble in alcohol; used in organic synthesis. **h. formate.** N₂H₄·2HCOOH = 124.08. Cubic crystals, m.128, soluble in water. **h. hydrate.** N₂H₄·H₂O = 50.07. Colorless, fuming liquid, b.119. **h. nitrate.** HN₂·NH₂·NO₃. White crystals; a high explosive. **h. sulfate.** N₂H₄·H₂SO₄ = 130.1. Colorless scales, m.254, soluble in water; a reagent for separating copper.

hydrazines. Compounds from hydrazine: *methylhydrazine*, MeNH·NH₂; *phenylhydrazine*, PhNH·-NH₂. They are analogous to peroxides. **acyl-** Hydrazides. **alkyl-** Compounds of the type RNH·NH₂, R₂N·NH₂, or RNH·NHR, in which the H is replaced by an alkyl radical. **aryl-** Organic compounds from hydrazine, in which the H is replaced by an aryl radical.

hydrazinium. Hydrazonium. The monovalent radical H₂N·NH₃—, or the bivalent radical —NH₃·NH₃—, from hydrazine and containing respectively 1 and 2 pentavalent N atoms. **h. salt.** A compound of hydrazine and an acid, analogous to the ammonium salts derived from ammonia; as, H₂N·NH₃Cl, h. chloride.

hydrazino. The radical H₂N·NH—, from hydrazine. **h. acids.** Organic compounds, derived from hydrazine, of the general type H₂N·NH·R·COOH.

hydrazo- Prefix indicating the bivalent —NH·NH— or the tetravalent =N·N= group. The latter is more correctly called the azo group. Cf. *hydrazi-*. **h. amine.** Triazane. **h. benzene.** C₁₂H₁₂N₂ = 184.2. *1,1-*1,1-Diphenylhydrazine*. *1,2-* (Ph·-NH)₂ = 184.22. 1,2-Diphenylhydrazine*, N-bianiline. Colorless scales, m.132, slightly soluble in water; an intermediate in the manufacture of benzidine. **h. benzoic acid.** See *benzoic acid*. **h. compounds.** Compounds of the general formula RNH·NHR. **h.dicarbonamide.** (NH₂·CO·NH)₂ = 118.3. Hydrazoformamide. Colorless leaflets. m.245, soluble in water. **h. dicarbonimide.** Urazole. **h. formamide.** H. dicarbonamide. **h. toluene.** MeC₆H₄NH·NHC₆H₄Me = 212.2. Dituluylhydrazine. *1,2-* or *ortho-* Colorless leaflets, m.156 (decomp.), soluble in water. *1,3-* or *meta-* Colorless crystals, soluble in alcohol. *1,4-* or *para-* Monoclinic, colorless crystals, m.130, insoluble in water.

hydrazoate. A compound from hydrazoic acid, NH·N:N.

hydrazoic acid. NH—N=N = 43.03. Hydronitric acid, azoimide, diazoimide, from which the unstable hydrazoates are derived. Explosive liquid, b.37; a strong protoplasmic poison.

hydrazoin. A compound containing the radical —CH:(N₂)=.

hydrazone. (1) A condensation product containing the —NH·N:C— group, resulting from the action of hydrazines with aldehydes or ketones. (2) A phenylhydrazone, q.v. **diphenyl-** Osazone.

hydrazonic acid. A compound of the general type R·C(OH):N·NH, metameric with amidoximes and tautomeric with acethydrazides.

hydrazonium. Hydrazinium.

hydrazono. The radical =N·NH₂, from hydrazine. Cf. *hydrazido*.

hydrazyl. A free radical of the type R₂N·NAc—, from the hydrazino group.

hydride. A compound of hydrogen with: (1) a more positive element containing the anion H⁻; as, sodium hydride, NaH; (2) a member of the phosphorus group; (3) a radical, RH; as, methylhydride (methane). **antimony-** Stibine. **arsenic-** Arsine. **phosphorus-** Phosphine.

hydrin. The hydrogen acid ester of a polyatomic alcohol (as, glycerol) of the type HO—R—X.

hydrindene. C₉H₁₀ = 118.1. Indan(yl) (U.K. usage).

hydrindone. Indone.

hydrine. Hydrin.

hydriodic acid. HI = 127.9. A 57% solution of hydrogen iodide in water; a reagent for nitrites, methoxyl, and general reducing purposes.

hydriodide. A compound (usually an alkaloid) combined with hydrogen iodide.

hydrion. (1) Hydrogen ion. (2) A proton: the positive nucleus of an atom (Soddy).

hydro- (1) Prefix (Greek) indicating water or hydrogen. (2) Abbreviation for hydroextractor.

hydroacridine. C₁₃H₁₁N = 181.16. Colorless crystals, m.169, insoluble in water.

hydroalium. An alloy resistant to alkalies: Al 90–92, Mg 7–9, Si and Mn 0.2–0.6%.

hydroangelic acid. α-Methylbutyric acid.

hydroanthracene. Dihydroanthracene.

hydroanthranol. $C_{14}H_{12}O = 196.1$. Hydranthranol. Colorless needles, m.76, soluble in hot water. Cf. *oxanthrol*.

hydroaromatic. Naphthene.

hydroatropic acid. MeCHPhCOOH $= 150.1$. α-Phenylpropionic acid, hydratropic acid. Colorless liquid b.264, soluble in water; an isomer of hydrocinnamic acid.

hydrobenzamide. $C_{41}H_{18}N_2 = 298.2$. Tribenz-aldiamine. Colorless prisms, m.101, insoluble in water.

hydrobenzoin. $(Ph \cdot CHOH)_2 = 214.2$. Benzylene glycol, diphenyldihydroxyethane. Colorless leaflets, m.136, slightly soluble in water.

hydroberberine. $C_{20}H_{21}NO_4 = 339.17$. White crystals, m.167, insoluble in water.

hydrobilirubin. Urobilin.

hydroboration. The addition of a compound containing a B—H bond to an organic compound containing C with multiple bonds; e.g., the reaction of a carbonyl with diborane.

hydroboron. See *boron hydrides*.

hydrobromic acid. HBr $= 80.9$. A 40% solution of hydrogen bromide in water. Colorless liquid, d.1.38; a reagent.

hydrobromide. Hydrogen bromide. A salt of an organic base (e.g., an alkaloid) and hydrobromic acid. Cf. *bromide*.

hydrocaffeic acid. See *caffeic acid*.

hydrocarbobase. See *base*.

hydrocarbon. A compound consisting of only C and H. The number of hydrocarbons is very large. **aliphatic-** A compound consisting principally of C atoms in chains. **aromatic-** A compound consisting principally of C atoms in a ring. **cyclic-** Aromatic. **normal-** A h. without side chains. **saturated-** A h. in which all 4 valencies of the C atoms are satisfied. **unsaturated-** A h. with one or more double or triple bonds between the C atoms. **h. black.** Lampblack. **h. burner.** An oil stove with vaporized kerosene as fuel. **h. nomenclature** (U.S. usage):

Hydrocarbons—compounds containing only H and C.

Saturated hydrocarbons—with C atoms joined by single bonds, the unshared C valencies being fully saturated with H.

Unsaturated hydrocarbons—in which 2 or more C atoms are joined by bonds other than single bonds.

Paraffinic hydrocarbons (alkanes, paraffins)—saturated, open-chain; with type formula C_nH_{2n+2}.

Naphthenic hydrocarbons (naphthenes, cyclo-alkanes, cycloparaffins)—saturated; containing at least one ring.

Olefinic hydrocarbons (olefins, alkenes)—unsaturated; containing at least one double bond which is not in an aromatic ring.

Acetylenic hydrocarbons (acetylenes, alkynes)—unsaturated; containing at least one triple bond.

Aromatic hydrocarbons (arenes)—unsaturated; containing at least one benzene nucleus.

h. radical. A group of atoms of C and H, with one or more free bonds. Cf. *organic radicals*. **h. series.** A group of hydrocarbons arranged as

HYDROCARBON SERIES

	Formula
Alkanes, paraffins, or methane series	C_nH_{2n+2}
Alkenes, olefins, or ethylene series	C_nH_{2n}
Alkynes, acetylenes, or ethine series	C_nH_{2n-2}
Alkones or terpenes	C_nH_{2n-4}
Benzenes and diacetylenes	C_nH_{2n-6}
Phenylene series	C_nH_{2n-8}
Indene series	C_nH_{2n-10}
Naphthalene series	C_nH_{2n-12}
Diphenyl series	C_nH_{2n-14}
Stilbene series	C_nH_{2n-16}
Anthracene series	C_nH_{2n-18}
Fluoranthene series	C_nH_{2n-20}
Pyrene series	C_nH_{2n-22}
Chrysene series	C_nH_{2n-24}
Dinaphthyl series	C_nH_{2n-26}
Perylene series	C_nH_{2n-28}

homologs, which generally differ by $:CH_2$. Cf. *hydronitrogen*. See table.

hydrocarbostyril. $C_9H_9ON = 147.2$. Colorless prisms, m.163, soluble in water.

hydrocarpic. Misnomer for hydnocarpic.

hydrocellulose. $C_{12}H_{22}O_{11} = 342.2$. A compound obtained from cellulose by prolonged treatment with concentrated acids.

hydrocerulignone. $C_{16}H_{18}O_4 = 274.22$. A solid, m.190, soluble in water.

hydrochelidonic acid. $CO:(CH_2 \cdot CH_2COOH)_2 = 174.12$. Acetone diacetic acid, 4-oxoheptanedioic acid*. Crystals, m.142, soluble in water.

hydrochinone. Hydroquinone.

hydrochlorate. Incorrect term for hydrochloride.

hydrochloric acid. HCl $= 36.5$. Muriatic acid. A solution of hydrogen chloride gas in water. **concentrated-** Not less than 35% HCl. A clear, colorless, fuming liquid, d.1.18, used extensively as a reagent and in organic synthesis. **dilute-** A solution of about 20% HCl. **fuming-** A solution of about 37% HCl, d.1.19. **nitro-** Aqua regia.

hydrochloride. A salt of hydrochloric acid and an organic base, especially an alkaloid, usually more soluble than the base. It differs from chlorides in retaining the H atom; as, *alk*-HCl.

hydrochlorothiazide. $C_7H_8O_4N_3ClS_2 = 297.70$. White powder, m.267 (decomp.), insoluble in water; a diuretic (U.S.P., B.P.).

hydrocinnamic acid. $C_9H_{10}O_2 = 150.1$. β-Phenylpropionic acid. Colorless needles, m.49, slightly soluble in water. **amino-** Phenylalanine. **aminohydroxy-** Tyrosine. **hydroxy-** *alpha*- Phenyllactic acid. *ortho*- Melilotic acid. *para*- Phloretic acid. **methylene-** Benzylacrylic acid.

hydrocinnamic aldehyde. $C_9H_{10}O_3 = 134.1$. β-Phenylpropionic aldehyde. Colorless liquid, b.208, insoluble in water; used in organic synthesis.

hydrocollidine. A ptomaine from putrefying fish.

hydrocoridine. $C_{10}H_{17}N = 151.2$. A ptomaine produced by *Bacillus allii* or *Bacterium album* in agar cultures.

hydrocortisone. $C_{21}H_{30}O_5 = 362.47$. White crystals, m.214, insoluble in water. An adrenocortical hormone; used as the h. acetate and h. sodium succinate (U.S.P.). **h. acetate.** $C_{23}H_{32}O_6 = 404.51$. White crystals, m.220, insoluble in water; used similarly to h. (U.S.P., B.P.).

hydrocotarnine. $C_{12}H_{15}O_3N$ = 221.12. An alkaloid from opium. Colorless crystals, m.53, insoluble in water; a hypnotic.

hydrocotoin. See *cotoin*.

hydrocoumaric acid. $C_9H_{10}O_3$ = 166.1. β-Phenylpropionic acid. **ortho-** Meliliotic acid. **para-** Monoclinic, colorless crystals, m.128, soluble in water.

hydrocoumarone. C_8H_8O = 120.1. Colorless fragrant liquid, b.188.

hydrocupreine. $C_{19}H_{24}N_2O_2$ = 312.2. An alkaloid from cuprea bark. **ethyl-** Optochine. **methyl-** Hydroquinine.

hydrocyanic acid. HCN = 27.06. Prussic acid, hydrogen cyanide, formonitrile. Colorless, very poisonous gas, with an almond odor; d.0.697, b.25, soluble in water. Used as a poison gas, disinfectant; in metallurgy and mining (cyanide process), agriculture (insecticide and fumigation), and organic synthesis. **h. cyanogen chloride.** Softifume. A mixture of sodium cyanide and sodium chlorate, used for fumigation by adding to 50% hydrochloric acid solution.

hydrocyanide. The salt of an organic base with hydrocyanic acid, containing the HCN molecule.

hydrodiffusion. Diffusion into water.

hydrodynamics. The study of the mechanical properties of liquids, especially water.

hydrodynamometer. An instrument for measuring the velocity of a fluid in motion.

hydroextractor. Hydro. A rapid centrifuge for drying or dehydrating crystals, textiles, etc.

hydroferricyanic acid. Ferricyanic acid.

hydrofluogermanic acid. Fluogermanic acid.

hydrofluomethazide. $C_8H_8O_4N_3F_3S_2$ = 331.33. White crystals, m.271, slightly soluble in water; a diuretic (B.P.).

hydrofluoric acid. HF = 20.0. Phthoric acid. A solution of hydrogen fluoride in water. A colorless liquid which must be kept in paraffin, rubber, or plastic bottles. Used to etch glass, and as a reagent. Its salts are the fluorides.

hydrofluoride. A salt of hydrogen fluoride and an organic base, usually an alkaloid. Cf. *fluoride*.

hydrofluosilicic acid. Fluosilicic acid.

hydroforming. The cold forming of metal objects by pressure.

hydrofranklinite. Chalcophanite.

hydrogel. A gel produced by the coagulation of a colloid with the inclusion of water, e.g., coagulated silicic acid.

hydrogen. (1) History: H was probably first discovered in the 16th century by Paracelsus, and first investigated in 1766 by H. Cavendish, who later showed that water is produced when this gas burns (Greek $\bar{\nu}\delta\omega\rho$, water, and $\gamma\epsilon\nu\nu\alpha\omega$, to produce) Liquid and solid H were first prepared by Dewar in 1898. (2) H_2 = 2.0160. The simplest element, at. no. 1. Hydrogen gas. Colorless, inflammable gas, m.—256.5, b.20.379°K, slightly soluble in water, alcohol, or ether. Used to fill balloons; as fuel in torches for cutting metals, welding, and melting; in the production of synthetic stones or gems, annealing of steel, in the "limelight," in the hydrogenation of oils, the cracking of hydrocarbons, and the production of synthetic ammonia. (3) H = 1.00797. Hydrogen atom, the basis of the valence system, being taken as unity. Elements combining directly with H atoms have a negative valence number; elements replacing H have a positive valence number. (4) Constants of H atom and molecule:

Mass of atom = 1.662×10^{-24} gm

Radius of molecule = 10^{-8} cm

Mean free path of molecules at 760 mm pressure and 0°C = 1.6×10^{-5} cm/sec

Average velocity at 760 mm and 0°C = 1.70×10^{-6} cm/sec

1 cu meter weighs 89.87 gm (Regnault value)

1 liter at 760 mm and 0°C weighs 0.08987 gm

(5) Isotopes of H are protium, H^1 or H^a mass 1.00756; deuterium (diplogen), H^2, H^b or D, mass 2.0136; tritium, H^3, H^c or T, mass 3.0221. These form 6 possible molecules with molecular weights 2.015–6.04. Cf. *h. molecule*. (6) Compounds of H: 3 types: (a) Nonmetallic, e.g., SbH_3, in which H is the positive part, often gaseous and volatile. (b) Salts or hydrides, e.g., NaH, in which the H is the negative part; transparent crystals. (c) Metallic (H alloys), e.g., PdH_x, in which the H is alloyed with, occluded in, or absorbed in the metal. For other types of H compounds see: hydrocarbons, hydronitrogens, silanes, stannanes, boron hydrides. **activated-** Atomic. **arseniuretted-** Arsine. **atomic-** H gas subjected to a strong electromagnetic field, and whose molecules are thought to be torn apart. Used in certain blowpipes to obtain extremely high temperatures. **excited-** H gas subjected to a high potential at low pressure to emit characteristic radiations. **heavy-** The H isotope of mass 2: deuterium or diplogen. **labelled-** Deuterium. **nascent-** Freshly generated H, which is supposed to owe its greater chemical activity to its atomic form. **ortho-, para-.** See *h. molecule*. **phosphoretted-.** Phosphine. **proto-** See *protohydrogen*. **sulfuretted-** H. sulfide. **telluretted-** H. telluride. **triatomic-** H_3 = 3.02. A modification of H obtained by exposure to: (1) α rays, (2) vacuum discharge, (3) corona discharge, (4) a glass-tube ozonizer, (5) high-frequency Tesla discharge. It is very unstable; reduces S, As, Hg, and N; can be condensed by liquid air, and decomposed (to H_2) by Pt, Ni, Co, etc. **trivalent-** Misnomer for triatomic.

h. acid. Hydracid. An acid containing no oxygen; as HX. **h. bomb.** Deuterium bomb (more correctly). An atomic bomb in which a powerful explosion results from the 3 reactions of 2 atoms of deuterium; thus:

$$H^2 + H^2 \rightarrow H^3 + H^1 + \quad 4.0 \text{ Mev}$$
$$H^2 + H^2 \rightarrow He^4 + n + \quad 3.3 \text{ Mev}$$
$$H^2 + H^3 \rightarrow He^4 + n + \quad 17.6 \text{ Mev}$$

The fuse for the reaction is a powerful fission bomb. *dry h.b.* A h.b. in which the main charge is solid lithium deuteride made from Li^6. First exploded 1954. *wet. h.b.* A h.b. in which the main fuel is liquefied deuterium. First exploded 1952. **h. bromide.** HBr = 80.91. (1) Hydrobromic acid gas. Colorless gas, $d_{air=1}$2.71, b.—68.7, soluble in water. Used as a reagent, in organic synthesis, and forms salts (bromides). (2) Hydrobromide. Cf. *bromide*. **h. calomel cell.** An electrolytic cell comprising a h. gas electrode and calomel electrode, for conductivity and pH measurements. **h. cell.**

An electrolytic cell with h. gas electrodes. **h. chloride.** HCl = 36.46. (1) H. chloride gas, hydrochloric acid gas. Colorless gas, $d_{air=1}1.268$, b.—83.1, very soluble in water; used as a reagent and in organic synthesis. (2) A compound of an organic base (alkaloid) with HCl; usually more soluble in water than the base. **h. clay.** See *clay*. **h. cyanide.** Hydrocyanic acid. **h. dioxide.** H. peroxide. **h. electrode.** A gas electrode whose potential is set up between finely divided metal saturated with h., and the h. ions of the solution in which it is placed. It depends on the pH value of the solution. **h. equivalent.** The number of replaceable H atoms in a molecule of an acid; or the number of replaceable OH groups in the molecule of a base. **h. fluoride.** HF = 20.0. Hydrofluoric acid gas, phthoric acid. Colorless, poisonous gas, $d_{air=1}0.713$, b.19.4, soluble in water; used to etch glass. **h. iodide.** HI = 127.9. Hydroiodic acid gas. Colorless gas, $d_{air=1}4.38$, b.34, soluble in water; used as a reagent and in organic synthesis. **h. ions.** The electrically charged h. nucleus, H⁻ or H⁺, present in all acids. Cf. *hydrogen ion*. **h. line.** The spectrum lines due to h. Cf. *Bohr atom*. **h. molecule.** The simplest molecule, consisting of 2 H atoms. With 3 isotopes, H, D and T, the following 6 molecules are possible: HH, DD, TT, HD, HT, DT. H_2 consists of 2 types, ortho- and para-, which differ slightly in physical properties due to the different spins of the 2 nuclei. At 20°C, h. consists of ortho- 25, para- 75%. *ortho-, symmetrical-,* or *alpha-* Has even rotation quantum numbers: 0,2,4, ... *para-, antisymmetrical-,* or *beta-* Has odd numbers: 1,3,5, . . !. **h. overvoltage.** The electric charge needed to liberate h. at a metallic surface forming one of a pair of electrodes in a solution; e.g.: Pt 0, Ag 0.33, Pb 0.45, Zn 0.70. **h. oxide.** Water. **h. peroxide.** H_2O_2 = 34.016. H. dioxide, oxygen, auricome, perhydrol, peroxide of h. Clear, colorless liquid with a faint odor of nitric acid, d.1.458, m.—2, b.85, soluble in water. Marketed as a 3 or 6% solution, designated according to the number of volumes of oxygen they evolve, viz. as "10 volumes" and "20 volumes," respectively (cf. *perhydrol, c.c. test*). In the solid state it is explosive, in solution it decomposes into water and oxygen; this action is accelerated by alkalies, and retarded by acids. It can act as a reducing or oxidizing agent; a fuel, reagent, disinfectant, antiseptic, antichlor, and bleach. It occurs in traces in natural waters exposed to the sun. 100 vol. h.p. is 30.36% (by vol.), or 27.52% (by wt.). H.p. forms 2 eutectics with water: 45% H_2O_2 at —53.5, and 60% at —55°C. During World War II, stable 410-vol. (90%) h.p. was produced in the U.K. The Germans used 85% h.p. in their V weapons, as a high-energy propellant. Made electrolytically; or by successively catalytically reducing 2-ethylanthraquinone with h., and reversing the oxidation with atmospheric oxygen (autoxidation). **H.T.P. h.p.** See *H.T.P.* **h. peroxide hydrates.** $H_2O_2 \cdot H_2O$, $H_2O_2 \cdot 2H_2O$. They are stable if pure, but otherwise decompose explosively. **h. peroxide of crystallization.** Compounds which crystallize with one or more molecules of H_2O_2. **h. persulfide.** —H_2S_2—H_2S_3 = 165.04. Yellow oil, decomp. by alcohol into sulfur and h.

sulfide; bleaches litmus. **h. phosphide.** Phosphine. **h. selenide·** H_2Se = 81.2. Colorless poisonous gas, b.—42; very soluble in water. **h. sulfate.** Sulfuric acid. **h. sulfide.** H_2S = 34.1. Sulfuretted h., hydrosulfuric acid, hepatic gas. Colorless gas having the odor of rotten eggs, b.—59.6, $d_{air=1}1.189$; very soluble in water; a reagent for precipitation of metals. **h. sulfide water.** An aqueous solution of H_2S. Colorless liquid of characteristic odor, used as a reagent in qualitative analysis, for the precipitation of heavy metals, and as an antichlor. **h. telluride.** H_2Te = 129.52. A combustible gas or liquid, b.9; soluble in water with decomposition. **h. thermometer.** An instrument measuring temperatures from the pressure exerted by a confined volume of H gas.

hydrogenate. (1) To introduce H into a molecule; as, the saturation of unsaturated compounds. (2) To reduce. Cf. *oxidation*.

hydrogenated. Treated or saturated with H.

hydrogenation. The process of causing combination with H; e.g.: (1) saturation of aliphatic unsaturated compounds with H in the presence of Ni or Pd as catalyst; or (2) cracking higher hydrocarbons to gasoline by H under pressure. **h. apparatus.** A heavy copper retort with stirrer, used to transform liquid into solid fats by H.

hydrogen ion. H· or H⁺. A positively charged H atom constituent of aqueous solutions of acids. All acids dissociate, to some extent, into this ion, HCl = H⁺ + Cl⁻; and the strength or "acid" character (sour taste, change of color of indicator, reaction with metals, etc.) depends on the extent of this dissociation, which varies inversely with the concentration of the acid within certain limits. **h.i. concentration.** pH, P_H or p_H. Potential of hydrogen, "momentary," true, actual, or active acidity. The amount of H⁺ per unit volume (moles per liter, [H⁺] or C_H^+) of an aqueous solution. It denotes the true acidity or alkalinity of such solutions, and is expressed by the pH value (potential of hydrogen) which is the reciprocal logarithm of the number of gram ions of hydrogen per liter, $p_H = \log_{10} 1/C_H$. Pure water contains 10^{-7} gram ion of H per liter. Since there is an equal number of OH⁻ ions, pH(7.0) + pOH(7.0) = constant(14.00). Accordingly, pH values 0–7 indicate an acid solution; pH 7 neutrality; pH 7–14 an alkaline solution. **h.i. conversion.** If h.i. concentration $C_H^+ = a \times 10^{-b}$, pH = b — log a. If pH = x·yz, C_H^+ = [antilog (1 — yz/100)] × $10^{-(x+1)}$. **h.i. determination apparatus.** (1) Electrometric: Measures the potential of a H electrode (which depends on the pH of the solution) against a standard calomel electrode. (2) Colorimetric: Compares the color of an indicator added to the solution with its color in a solution of known pH. **h.i. indicator.** A dye that has definite colors at different pH values. See *indicators*. **h.i. recorder.** An automatic potentiometer for recording and controlling the acidity and alkalinity of solutions; used in industry.

hydrogenite. A mixture: silicon 25, sodium hydroxide 60, slaked lime 15%; ignites on burning to give 270–370 liters of hydrogen gas per kg.

hydrogenium. A volatile, metallic element of which H is the supposed vapor.

hydrogenize. To hydrogenate.

hydrogenolysis. The cleavage of a C—C or C—O bond accompanied by the addition of H_2; as, $R \cdot R' + H_2 \rightarrow RH + R'H$. Cf. *hydrogenation*.

hydrogenomonas. The first genus of bacteria occurring in the soil and oxidizing hydrogen gas to form water by catalytically reducing carbon dioxide:

$$CO_2 + H_2 \rightarrow HCHO + O$$
$$HCHO + O_2 \rightarrow H_2O + CO_2.$$

hydrogenylase. An enzyme which promotes liberation of molecular hydrogen.

hydroginkolic acid. Cyclogallipharic acid.

hydrohaeterolite. The mineral $2ZnO \cdot 2Mn_2O_3 \cdot H_2O$.

hydrohalic. Composed of hydrogen and halogens.

hydrohematite. $2Fe_2O_3 \cdot H_2O$. A crystalline, hydrated mineral.

hydrohydrastine. $C_{11}H_{13}O_2N$ = 191.1. An alkaloid, from hydrastine, m.66, soluble in alcohol.

hydrokinetics. The science of the motion of fluids under a force.

hydrol. See *hydrone theory*.

hydrolase. An enzyme or ferment that causes hydrolysis.

hydrolith. Calcium hydride.

hydrolysis. A decomposition reaction caused by water, $AB + H_2O = AOH + HB$, which, in its ionic form, $H_2O = H^+ + OH^-$, is the reverse reaction of neutralization. Cf. *hydrogenolysis*.

hydrolyst. A catalyst causing hydrolysis; as, a hydrolase.

hydrolyte. A substance that undergoes hydrolysis.

hydrolytic. Pertaining to hydrolysis. **h. condensation.** An erroneous term applied to condensations in which water is eliminated. **h. dissociation.** (1) Ionization. (2) Hydrolysis. **h. enzymes.** See *enzymes* A.

hydrolyze. To cause hydrolysis.

hydromagnesite. $3MgCO_3 \cdot Mg(OH_2) \cdot 3H_2O$. A chalk-like magnesium carbonate from Lodi, N.J.

hydromechanics. Hydraulics.

hydromel. A fermented (mead) or unfermented mixture of water and honey.

hydrometallurgy. The reduction of ores by leaching (wet processes).

hydrometer. Aerometer. A device to measure the specific gravity of liquids. Usually a graduated hollow weighted glass tube which sinks in the liquid to a certain depth; which, read on the scale, indicates the density of the liquid. **Sikes-** A hydrometer in which 1 degree equals a mean density interval of 0.002.

h. scales. Any of the conventional graduations on a h.; as, Baumé, Twaddle, Beck, Brix, Balling, and Sikes. Conversion of:

°Bé to D: $\quad D = \dfrac{144.3}{144.3 - \text{Bé}}$

°Tw to D: $\quad D = 1 + \dfrac{Tw}{200} = 1 + 0.005T$

°$Brix$ to D: $\quad D = 1 \pm \dfrac{400}{\text{Brix}}$ at 12.5°R

°$Balling$ to D: $\quad D = 1 \pm \dfrac{200}{\text{Balling}}$ at 17.5°C

$(D = \text{density})$

The U.S. petroleum industry uses the following conversion for liquids lighter than water: Bé = $(141.5/D) - 131.5$.

hydromycin. $C_{25}H_{47}O_{15}N_5(?)$. A low-toxicity antibiotic from *Streptomyces paucisporogenes*.

hydronal. Polychloral, viferral. A polymerized product of pyridine and chloral; a hypnotic.

hydronaphthoquinone. $C_{10}H_8O_2$ = 160.1. **1,2-** Colorless leaflets, m.60, soluble in water. **1,4-** Colorless needles, m.175, soluble in water.

hydrone. (1) An alloy: Na 35, Pb 65%; used to make hydrogen gas by the action of water. (2) The active molecule H_2O. **h. theory.** Water is a complex mixture of active molecules: *hydrone*, H_2O, *hydrol*, H_4O_2, and inactive or associated molecules, *polyhydrones*, $H_{2n}O_n$.

hydronitric acid. Hydrazoic acid.

hydronitrogen. A compound of hydrogen and nitrogen in which the H is generally replaceable by a hydrocarbon radical. **h. series.** A group of homologous compounds differing by NH; many exist only as derivatives. E.g.: saturated hydronitrogens: N_nH_{2n+2} (hydrazine); unsaturated hydronitrogens: N_nH_{2n} (triazene); N_nH_{2n-2} (hydrazoic acid); N_nH_{2n-4} (octazone).

hydronitrous acid. Nitroxylic acid.

hydronium ion. The solvated hydrogen ion, $H^+ \cdot (H_2O)$, considered to be present in all acids. Cf. *protophilia*.

hydroperoxide. A compound containing an —OOH group, e.g., as formed in the oxidation of rubber. Hydroperoxides have oxidizing properties.

hydrophane. A transparent opal.

hydrophil(e). Lyophile. A substance, usually a colloid or emulsion, which is wetted by water.

hydrophilic. (1) Lyophilic. Describing a substance that absorbs or adsorbs water. Antonym: hydrophobic. (2) Protophilia. **h. colloid.** Finely divided particles forming stable suspensions in water. Antonym: hydrophobic colloid.

hydrophilite. $CaCl_2$. Native calcium chloride (chlorocalcite), occurring as white incrustations on Mt. Vesuvius.

hydrophobe. Lyophobe. A substance, usually colloidal, which is not wetted by water.

hydrophobic. Describing a substance that does not adsorb or absorb water. Antonym: hydrophilic. **h. colloid.** Finely divided suspended particles in water which precipitate readily.

hydropirin. Sodium acetyl salicylate.

hydroponics. Tank culture. The cultivation of plants in aqueous solutions of inorganic salts, without soil.

hydropyrine. Lithium acetylsalicylate.

hydroquinine. $C_{20}H_{26}O_{22} \cdot 2H_2O$ = 362.3. Methylhydrocupreine. White crystals; a quinine substitute in malaria, developer in photography, and reducer in chemical analysis.

hydroquinol. $C_6H_4(OH)_2$ = 110.1. Hydrochinone, *p*-dioxybenzene, *p*-hydroxyphenol. Cf. *quinol*. White leaflets, m.169, soluble in water; an antiseptic and photographic developer. **ethyl-** H. ethyl ether. **hydroxy-** 1,2,4-Trihydroxybenzene. **tetrachloro-** Chloranol.

h. carboxylic acid. Gentisic acid. **h. dimethyl ether.** $C_6H_4(OMe)_2$ = 138.1. Dimethylhydrochinone. Colorless leaflets, m.55, insoluble in water; an antiseptic. **h. ethyl ether.** HOC_6H_4-OEt $= 138.1$. Ethylhydrochinone, p-ethoxyphenol. Colorless leaflets, m.66, soluble in water; an antiseptic and reducing agent.

hydroquinone. Hydroquinol.

hydroscopic. Hygroscopic.

hydrosilicofluoric acid. Fluosilic acid.

hydrosilicon. See *silanes.*

hydrosol. A colloidal suspension in water.

hydrosorbic acid. Hexenic acid.

hydrosphere. The liquid portion of the earth's surface, as the oceans, lakes, rivers, etc. Cf. *lithosphere, atmosphere.* Principal constituents: oxygen 85.8, hydrogen 10.7, chlorine 2.1, sodium 1.1%. Distribution, in million cubic kilometers: oceans 1,330, lakes 0.25, rivers 0.02, ice 4.0, groundwater 0.25.

hydrostatics. The study of liquids in equilibrium.

hydrosulfate. An addition combination of an organic base, usually an alkaloid, with sulfuric acid, without replacement of the hydrogen of the acid.

hydrosulfides. Sulfhydrates, sulfhydryls, thio-alcohols, thiols, sulfur alcohols, mercaptans. (1) A compound containing the radical SH^-, analogous to hydroxides (oxygen is replaced by sulfur). (2) Erroneous term for sulfide.

hydrosulfite. (1) Hyposulfite. A salt containing the radical $=S_2O_4$. (2) Erroneous term for sodium hyposulfite.

hydrosulfuric acid. (1) Hydrogen sulfide. (2) Dithionic acid.

hydrosulfurous acid. Hyposulfurous acid.

hydrotaxis. The motion of organisms or cells toward water.

hydrotetrazone. An aromatic compound containing 4 consecutive N atoms in the molecule, e.g., dibenzaldiphenyldihydrotetrazone, $PhCH:N\cdot NPh\cdot NPh\cdot N:CHPh$. Cf. *tetrazone.*

hydrotherapy. The treatment of disease by water.

hydroumbellic acid. β-2,4-Dioxyphenylpropionic acid.

hydrous. Containing water. Cf. anhydrous. **h. salt.** A salt containing water of crystallization.

hydroxamic acid. An organic compound containing the radical $-C(:O)\cdot NH\cdot OH$, isomeric with hydroximic acid. **iso-** Hydroximic acid.

hydroxamino. The radical $-NH\cdot OH$. Cf. *hydroxylamine.*

hydroxamphetamine hydrobromide. $C_9H_{13}ON\cdot HBr$ $= 232.13$. White crystals, m.191, soluble in water; an adrenergic (U.S.P.).

hydroxides. Compounds containing the OH^- group. In general, the h. of metals are bases; those of nonmetals are acids.

MOH . . . . Bases
NOH . . . . Acids
ROH . . . . Alcohols, phenols
RCO·OH . . . . Organic acids

alkyl- Alcohols. **aryl-** Phenols. **inorganic-** Bases.

hydroxidion. Hydroxyl ion. The basic ion OH^-.

hydroximic acid. An organic compound of the type, $R\cdot C(:NOH)\cdot OH$, isomeric with hydroxamic acids. **acet-** $CH_3C(OH):NOH$. Colorless crystals, m.59. **di-** $HON:C(OH)—C(OH):NOH$.

hydroximino. Isonitroso.

hydroxocobalamin. $C_{62}N_{89}O_{15}N_{13}COP = 1,346.30$. Vitamin B_{12a} or B_{12b}. The $—CN$ in vitamin B_{12} is replaced by $—OH$. Red crystals, soluble in water; used to treat megaloblastic anemia (B.P.).

hydroxonium. Hydronium.

hydroxy- Hydroxyl- Prefix indicating the OH group in an organic compound analogous to acids of the lactic series. Preferred to oxy-. **h. acetic acid.** Glycolic acid. **h. acetophenone.** C_6H_4-(OH)COMe $= 136.10$. *ortho-* $b_{10mm}97$. *meta-* m.95. *para-* m.110. **h. acetophenonecarboxylic acid.** Acetylhydroxybenzoic acid. **h. acid.** An organic compound containing both the hydroxyl and carboxyl radicals: $HO\cdot R\cdot COOH$. See *lactic acid series.* **h. amides.** Oxyamides. **h. amino-benzoic acid.** $NH_2\cdot C_6H_3(OH)COOH = 153.0$. Aminosalicylic acid. *3-* or *1,2,3-* Colorless crystals, m.235. *4-* or *1,2,4-* m.220. *5-* or *1,2,5-* m.283, soluble in water. **h. anthraquinone.** $C_{14}H_8O_3 = 224.1$. *1-* or α- m.190. *2-* or β- Yellow leaflets, m.302, slightly soluble in water. **h. azobenzene.** $C_{12}H_{10}ON_2 = 198.2$. *ortho-* Colorless needles, m.83, slightly soluble in water. *para-* Colorless prisms, m.152, slightly soluble in water. **h. benzaldehyde.** $C_7H_6O_2 = 122.2$. *ortho-* Colorless liquid, d.1.159, b.197, slightly soluble in water. *meta-* Colorless needles, m.104, soluble in water. *para-* Colorless needles, m.116, soluble in water. **h. benzamide.** $C_7H_7O_2N = 137.1$. *ortho-* Yellow leaflets, m.140, soluble in water. *meta-* Colorless leaflets, m.167, soluble in water. *para-* Colorless needles, m.162, soluble in water. **h. benzene.** Phenol. **h. benzoic acid.** $C_7H_6O_3 = 138.1$. *ortho-* Colorless needles, m.158, slightly soluble in water. *meta-* Rhombic crystals, m.200, slightly soluble in water. *para-* Colorless monoclinic crystals, m.201, slightly soluble in water. **h. benzyl alcohol.** $C_7H_8O_2 = 124.1$. *ortho-* Saligenin. Colorless rhombs, m.85 (sublimes), slightly soluble in water; an antiseptic. *meta-* Colorless needles, m.67, slightly soluble in water. *para-* Colorless needles, m.120, soluble in water. **h. butyric acid.** $C_4H_8O_3 = 104.1$. *alpha*-1-Hydroxybutyric acid. Colorless crystals, m.43, soluble in water. *beta-* $CH_3CHOHCH_2COOH$. *gamma-* $CH_2OH(CH_2)_2COOH$. Acetonic acid. **h. caffeine.** See *caffeine.* **h. caproic acid.** $C_6H_{12}O_3 = 132.1$. *alpha-* 1-Hydroxycaproic acid. Colorless crystals, m.60, slightly soluble in water. **h. chloroquinone sulfate.** $\cdot C_{18}H_{26}ON_3Cl\cdot H_2SO_4 = 433.92$. White, bitter crystals, m.198 or 240, soluble in water; an antimalarial and antiarthritic (B.P.). **h. choline.** Muscarine. **h. cinnamic acid.** Coumaric acid. **h. citric acid.** $C_6H_8O_8 = 208.2$. Colorless liquid, soluble in water; found in sugar beets. **h. Δ^2-10-decenoic acid.** $A(C_{10}H_{18}O_3)$. An optically inactive acid comprising the major portion of the ether-soluble fraction of royal jelly, q.v.; stated to have anticarcinogen properties. **h. ethylamine.** $NH_2(CH_2)_2OH = 61.06$. Colorless liquid, d.1.022, b.171, produced by the putrefaction of kephalin and serin. **h. formic acid.** Carbonic acid. **h. glutamic acid.** $NH_2(OH)C_3H_4(COOH)_2 = 163.08$. *beta-* Obtained by extraction of protein hydrolysate in butane. **h. imino.** Isonitroso. The radical $HON=$. **h. isobutyric acid.** Acetonic acid. **h. isophthalic acid.** $C_8H_6O_5 = 182.1$. *a-* 2-Hydroxy-1,3-isophthalic acid. Colorless needles, m.243, slightly soluble in water. *s*- 5-Hydroxy-1,3-isophthalic acid. Colorless needles, m.288, slightly soluble in water. *r*- 4-Hydroxy-1,3-isophthalic acid. Colorless needles m.305, slightly soluble in water. **h. peucedanin.** $C_{16}H_{14}O_5(?)$. A lactone, m.142, from *Peucedanum officinale*, and *Imperatoria osthruthium*. **h. phenylacetic acid.** *p*-HO·C_6H_4·CH_2COOH = 152.06, m.148; produced from tyrosine by intestinal putrefaction. **h. phthalic acid.** $C_8H_6O_5$ = 182.1. *a*-4-Hydroxy-1,2-phthalic acid. Colorless rosettes, decomp. 181, soluble in water. *v*- 3-Hydroxy-1,2-phthalic acid. Colorless prisms, decomp. by heat, soluble in water. **h. propanone.** Acetol. **h. propionic acid.** Lactic acid. **h. pyridine.** Pyridone. **h. quinol.** 1,2,4-Trihydroxybenzene. **h. quinoline.** 2- Carbostyril. 4- Kynurin. 8- C_9H_7NO = 145.03. A precipitant for aluminum, magnesium, and zinc. **h. quinolinecarbonic acid.** 4- Kynurenic acid **h. succinic acid.** Malic acid. **h. terephthalic acid.** $C_8H_6O_5$ = 182.1. 2-Hydroxy-1,4-dicarboxylbenzene. Colorless powder, slightly soluble in water. **h. toluene.** Cresol. **h. toluic acid.** $C_8H_8O_3$ = 152.1. Methylhydroxybenzoic acid, cresotic acids: 10 possibilities, according to the positions of the Me, COOH, and OH groups. Colorless needles, soluble in alcohol; some are used in organic synthesis. **h. urea.** NH_2CONHOH = 76.1. Colorless needles, m.130, soluble in water. **h. valeric acid.** *alpha*- $MeCH_2CH_2$CHOHCOOH = 118.1. Colorless needles, m.31, soluble in water.

hydroxyl. The —OH group. Its H is replaceable by positive elements (K, Na, etc.); the entire group by halogens. **h. group.** The radical —OH. **h. ion.** The OH⁻ ion, present in excess in all alkaline or basic solutions; and in smaller quantities than the hydrogen ion in all aqueous acids.

hydroxylamine. NH_2OH = 33.1. Oxyammonia. Colorless crystals, decomp. 130 (explode), m.33, soluble in water. Used as a reducing agent, and in the manufacture of synthetics. **aminonitrosophenyl-** Cupferron. **di-** The hypothetical compound, HO·NH·OH. **h. hydrochloride.** HCl·NH_2OH = 69.6. Colorless crystals, soluble in water; a reducing agent, for the detection of acetone, sulfonic acids, etc.

hydroxyl amines. Organic compounds containing the NH_2O— group (α-hydroxyl amines), or the —NHOH group (β-hydroxyl amines). **alpha-** An organic compound derived from hydroxylamine by substituting the OH hydrogen by an aryl or alkyl radical: NH_2OAr (aroxylamine) or NH_2OAk (alkoxylamine). **beta-** An organic compound derived from hydroxylamine by substituting the NH_2 hydrogen by an alkyl or aryl radical: NHR—OH. **nitroso-** See *nitrosohydroxyl amines*. **h. hydrochloride.** NH_2OH·HCl = 69.5. Oxammonium hydrochloride. Colorless crystals, m.151 (decomp.), soluble in water. Used as a reagent in determining gold, silver, copper, acetone, glucose, or colchicine; in organic synthesis; as a reducing agent (developer); and as an antiseptic. **h. hydrosulfate.** $(HN_2OH)_2H_2SO_4$ = 164.2. Oxammonium sulfate, hydroxylaminsulfate. Colorless crystals, m.140, soluble in water; a reagent and reducing agent.

hydroxylamino. The radical —NH·OH, amidoxyl, from hydroxylamine.

hydroxylammonium. See *quaternary amines*.

hydroxylation. Oxidation as opposed to hydrolysis, by which hydroxy groups are formed in an organic molecule.

hydroxylimide. A metamer of amidoximes of the type (R·NH)(OH)·C:NH.

hydroxylin. A product of the acid hydrolysis of lignin.

hydroxynaphthalene. Naphthol.

hydroxyphenol. Prefix indicating the HOC_6H_4— group.

hydroxytryptamine. A substance of potent biological activity in animals and plants, e.g., in venoms.

hydrozincite. $ZnCO_3$·$2Zn(OH)_2$. Zinc in bloom. Massive or fibrous incrustations in zinc mines.

hyenanchin. $C_{15}H_{18}O_7$ = 310.14. A crystalline poison from the seeds of *Hyaenanche globosa* (*Toxicodendron capense*) hyena poison, boesmansgif (Euphorbiaceae), S. Africa; decomp. 234. **iso-** Decomp. 299.

hyenic acid. $Me(CH_2)_{23}$COOH = 382.5. Tricosylacetic acid, m.78.

hygric acid. $C_6H_{11}O_2N$ = 129.09. Cf. *nipecotic acid*. **4-hydroxy-** $C_6H_{11}O_3N$·H_2O = 163.09. A crystalline, toxic principle from *Croton goubuga*, Transvaal croton bark (Euphorbiaceae), S. Africa.

hygrine. $C_8H_{15}ON$ = 141.2. An alkaloid from coca leaves. A liquid, d.0.935, b.195. **cusco-** $C_{13}H_{24}ON_2$ = 226.19. An alkaloid, $b_{23mm}170$, from coca leaves.

hygrol. Colloidal mercury.

hygrometer. A device for measuring the amount of moisture in the atmosphere. See *psychrometer*. **chemical-** A hygroscopic mixture of chemicals which indicates atmospheric moisture by a change of color (cobalt salts) or the formation of crystalline precipitate (camphor solutions). **physical-** A dry- and wet-bulb thermometer. The difference between the readings gives the humidity from tables. **whirling-** A physical h. attached to a handle so that it may be whirled around rapidly, thereby producing rapidly circulating air around the thermometer bulbs.

hygrometric. Pertaining to humidity. **h. paper.** A filter paper impregnated with a solution of cobalt chloride 4, sodium chloride 2, acacia 1, water 11, glycerin 1 pts. The amount of moisture is indicated by colors ranging from red (moist) to blue (dry). **h. scale.** Erroneous term for hydrometric scale. **h. state.** Humidity.

hygrometry. The measurement of the moisture content of the atmosphere.

hygroscopic. Becoming moist; as of a substance that absorbs water from the atmosphere; e.g., calcium chloride or phosphorus pentachloride. See *desiccants, deliquescence*.

hygroscopy. Hygrometry.

hygrosterol. A dextrorotary phytosterol from the roots of *Hygrophylia spinosa*, m.194.

hylergography. The study of the influence of foreign matter on living cells.

hylogenesis. The theory of the formation of matter (ύλη = hyle, Greek for matter).

hylon. The positive nucleus of the atom (obsolete).

hylotropic. Describing a substance that can undergo a change in phase (e.g., be melted), without change of composition.

hylotropy. Having a constant melting or boiling point. Cf. *azeotropy.*

hymolal salts. The salts of sulfuric esters of monohydric alcohols of high molecular weight, e.g., sodium lauryl sulfate; detergents.

hyoscine. $C_{17}H_{21}O_4N$ = 303.17. Scopolamine. A levorotatory alkaloid from Solanaceae. Colorless syrup, soluble in alcohol; its salts are hypnotics. Cf. *scopoline.* **inactive-** Atroscine.
h. hydrobromide. $C_{17}H_{21}O_4N \cdot HBr \cdot 3H_2O \cdot$ = 438.28. Scopolamine hydrobromide. Atroscin. Kwells. Colorless crystals, m.196 (anhydrous), soluble in water; a hypnotic (twilight sleep), (B.P.), an antitravel-sickness remedy. **h. hydrochloride.** $C_{17}H_{21}O_4N \cdot HCl \cdot 2H_2O$. Scopolamine hydrochloride. Colorless crystals, m.200, soluble in water; a hypnotic, anodyne, and antispasmodic. **h. hydroiodide.** $C_{17}H_{21}O_4N \cdot HI$ = 417.13. Scopolamine hydroiodide. Colorless prisms, soluble in water. **h. hydrosulfate.** $(C_{17}H_{21}O_4N)_2 \cdot H_2SO_4$ = 676.49. Scopolamine sulfate. Colorless crystals, soluble in water. **h. sulfate.** Hyoscine hydrosulfate.

hyoscyamine. $C_{17}H_{23}O_3N$ = 289.3. Daturine. An alkaloid from *Hyoscyamus niger* and other solanaceous plants, isomeric with atropine. Colorless needles, m.107, slightly soluble in water; a hypnotic, sedative, and antispasmodic. **h. bromide.** H. hydrobromide. **h. chloride.** H. hydrochloride. **h. hydrobromide.** $C_{17}H_{23}O_3N \cdot HBr$ = 370.2. Colorless prisms, m.152, soluble in water; a hypnotic. **h. hydrochloride.** $C_{17}H_{23}O_3N \cdot HCl$ = 325.7. Colorless crystals, soluble in water; a hypnotic. **h. hydroiodide.** $C_{17}H_{23}O_3N \cdot HI$ = 417.3. Colorless crystals, soluble in water; a hypnotic. **h. hydrosulfate.** $(C_{17}H_{23}O_3N)_2 \cdot H_2SO_4$ = 676.6. H. sulfate. Colorless crystals, m.199, soluble in water. **h. salicylate.** $C_{17}H_{23}O_3N \cdot C_7H_6O_3$ = 427.3. Colorless crystals, soluble in water; a hypnotic. **h. sulfate.** H. hydrosulfate.

hyoscyamus. Henbane, poison tobacco, hog bane. The dried leaves and tops of *H. niger* (Solanaceae), which should contain not less than 0.065% alkaloids (hyoscine, hyoscyamine, etc.); a sedative, analgesic, and antispasmodic (B.P.).

Hypalon. Trademark for a rubbery material obtained by the chlorination and sulfonation of polyethylenes.

hypaphorine. $C_{13}H_{17}O_2N$ = 203.15. Trimethyltryptophane, an alkaloid from the seeds and bark of *Hypaphorus subrumbrans* (Solanaceae). Colorless crystals, soluble in water.

hyper- Prefix (Greek) indicating an excess; e.g., hyperoxide or peroxide.

hyperchromic. Describing a radical that increases the intensity of a coloring material.

hyperchromicity. The change in spectral absorption due to a chemical reaction; e.g., the increase in ultraviolet absorption on the hydrolysis of polynuclear chains.

hypergolic. Describing propellants that are not self-igniting, usually comprising 2 constituents, e.g., hydrogen peroxide with kerosene or hydrazine.

hypericin. $C_{30}H_{16-18}O_8$. The red coloring matter from St. John's wort.

hypericism. Sensitivity to light in animals caused by eating plants of the genus *Hypericum.* Restlessness and irritation result, because of the hypericin present.

hyperol. Ortizon.

hypersonic. Exceeding 6 times the speed of sound. Cf. *supersonic.*

hypersthene. $(FeMg)O \cdot SiO_2$. A brown or green ferruginous, orthorhombic, pyroxene mineral resembling enstatite.

hypertensin Renin.

hypertonic. Describing a solution having a higher osmotic pressure than blood, or another solution with which it is compared. Cf. *isotonic, hypotonic.*

hypnacetine. $PhCO \cdot CH_2OC_6H_4 \cdot NHCOMe$ = 269.2. Hypnoacetine. Colorless crystals, m.160, slightly soluble in water; an antiseptic and hypnotic.

hypnal. $C_{13}H_{13}O_2N_2Cl_3$ = 335.5. Chloral hydrate antipyrine. Colorless crystals, m.67, soluble in water; a hypnotic, antipyretic, and analgesic.

hypnoacetine. Hypnacetine.

hypnone. Acetophenone.

hypnotic. An agent that produces sleep, e.g., sulfonal. Cf. *soporific, somnifacient.*

hypo- (1) Prefix (Greek) indicating below or under. (2) Common name for sodium hyposulfite, used as a photographic fixing agent.

hypoborate. A hypothetical, unstable reducing agent of the type MH_3BO, probably identical with a borohydride, MBH_4. Made by passing diborane into an aqueous alkali.

hypobromite. A compound derived from hypobromous acid containing the radical —BrO. **h. nitrogen.** The nitrogen which can be liberated from organic compounds by hypobromites.

hypobromous acid. $HBrO$ = 96.93. An unstable compound of monovalent bromine, b.40 (in vacuo).

hypochlorite. (1) A compound containing the radical —ClO. (2) The hypochlorites of sodium, potassium, calcium, or magnesium, used in bleaching.

hypochlorous acid. $HClO$ = 52.5. An oxyacid of chlorine containing monovalent chlorine; readily oxidized to chlorous acid or reduced to free chlorine.

hypochlorous ion. The ClO^- ion.

hypodermic. Beneath the skin; as, an injection.

hypogaeic acid. $C_{15}H_{29}COOH$ = 254.3. 7-Hexadecenoic acid*. A fatty acid in tallow and some oils (notably arachis). Colorless needles, m.33, insoluble in water. Cf. *physetoleic acid.*

hypoglycin-A. $C_7H_{11}O_2N$ = 141.03. The amino acid, $CH_2{=}C{\diagup}^{CH_2}_{\diagdown}CH \cdot CH_2 \cdot CH \cdot (NH_2)COOH$. A hypoglycemic agent from unripe "ackee" fruit of the W. Indies.

hypoiodous acid. HIO = 143.9. A hypothetical acid. **ammono-** H_2IN = 142.9. A solution of iodine in liquid ammonia; a nitridizing agent.

hypomagnesemia. Grass staggers. A magnesium deficiency disease of crops and cattle.

hypon. A hypothetical noble gas, at. no. 118 (obsolete).

hyponitrite. A compound containing the radical NO— or $N_2O_2{=}$; general type, MNO or $M_2N_2O_2$; used in chemical synthesis.

hyponitrous acid. $H_2N_2O_2$ = 62.2. An oxyacid of monovalent nitrogen, isomeric with nitrous acid, decomp. to nitrous oxide; an active reducing and oxidizing agent.

hypophamine. The hormone of the posterior lobe of the pituitary gland. **alpha-** Oxytocin, pitocin. The uterus-contracting principle. White powder, soluble in water (1 mg has an antidiuretic activity of 1 U.S.P. pituitary unit.) **beta-** Vasopressin, pitressin. The blood pressure–raising principle. White powder, soluble in water, and 80 times as potent as Standard Powdered Pituitary.

hypophorine. $C_{14}H_{18}N_2O_2$ = 246.11. Trimethyl-tryptophan. An amino acid, decomp. 255, from the proteins of erythrina seeds; it causes tetanus in frogs.

hypophosphate. A compound containing the radical $\equiv PO_2$ or the acid radical $-HPO_3$.

hypophosphite. A salt of hypophosphorus acid, containing the radical $-H_2PO_2$.

hyphosphoric acid. H_2PO_3 = 66.05. An oxy-acid of monovalent phosphorus. m.17.4, decomp. to phosphine and phosphoric acid.

hypophosphorous acid. A 30% aqueous solution of $HP(OH)_2$.

hypophysis. Desiccated pituitary body. The cleaned, dried, and powdered posterior lobes of the pituitary body of cattle. Yellow powder of characteristic odor, slightly soluble in water; a stimulant and hemostatic.

hyposochromic. Describing a change in color to a longer wavelength.

hyposulfate. (1) Dithionate. (2) Thiosulfate.

hyposulfite. (1) A compound containing the radical $=S_2O_4$. (2) Hypo or antichlor. Sodium thiosulfate used in bleaching and as a photographic fixing bath. **h. process.** Extraction of roasted ores with sodium hyposulfite solution and precipitation of the silver with sodium sulfide.

hyposulfuric acid. Dithionic acid.

hyposulfurous acid. Hyposulphurous acid. Sulfoxylic acid. Formerly applied incorrectly to dithionous acid.

hypothesis. A theory which has not been fully proved by experiment. Cf. *theory, law.*

hypotonic. Describing a solution having a lower osmotic pressure than blood (less than 6.6 atm.). Cf. *hypertonic, isotonic.*

hypovitaminosis. Vitaminosis.

hypoxanthine. $C_5H_4ON_4$ = 136.1. Sarkine, 6-oxy-purine, xanthoglobulin. Colorless needles, decomp. 150, insoluble in water. Cf. *purines.*

hypsochrome. A radical which when introduced into a colored compound intensifies the color by making it more violet; e.g., the $-CF_3$ group introduced into certain azo dyestuffs. Cf. *hyperchromic.*

hyptolide. $C_{18}H_{26}O_8$ = 370.3. The bitter principle of the leaves of *Hyptis pectinata* (Labiaceae). Colorless needles, soluble in hot water.

Hyraldite. Trade name for a bleaching preparation consisting principally of sodium thiosulfate and formaldehyde.

hyrax. A synthetic resin mounting agent for microscopic work (refractive index 1.75).

hyrgol. A colloidal solution of mercury, used to treat syphilis.

hyssop. The dried leaves of *Hyssopus officinalis*; an aromatic stimulant, carminative, and tonic. **hedge-** See *gratiolin.* **wild-** Verbena. Cf. *ysopol.* **h. oil.** Colorless oil from hyssop, d.0.932, soluble in alcohol; a flavoring.

hystazarin. $C_{14}H_8O_4$ = 240.1. 2,3-Dihydroxyanthraquinone. Orange needles, m.260, soluble in alcohol; a dye.

hystarzine. Hystazarin.

hysteresis. (1) The magnetic lag, or retention of the magnetic state of iron in a changing magnetic field. (2) The retardation of a chemical system from reaching equilibrium.

Hytor compressor. A rotary pump or blower employing a centrifuged liquid to obtain suction or pressure.

hyzone. Triatomic hydrogen. Cf. *ozone.*

I

I. Symbol for: (1) iodine; (2) moment of inertia; (3) ionic strength; (4) electric current; (5) light intensity. **I-, I'.** Symbols for the iodide ion.

i. (1) Abbreviation for inactive (optically inactive = *dl*). (2) Abbreviation for iso-. (3) The van't Hoff factor.

IATM. International Association for Testing Materials.

iatrochemists. A 16th century school of medicine based on the principles of Paracelsus.

iatrol. $PhNH \cdot O_2EtOI_2$ = 423.2. Oxyiodoethyl anilide. Gray powder, insoluble in water; an antiseptic.

ibit. Bismuth oxyiodotannate. Gray powder, insoluble in alcohol; a bactericide and disinfectant.

ibogaine. $C_{26}H_{32}O_2N_2$ = 404.26. An alkaloid, m.152, from the roots of *Tabernanthe iboga*, a narcotic arrow poison (Congo).

-ic. (1) Suffix indicating a higher valency, as compared with -ous. Thus: ferrous 2 and ferric 3. (2) A termination of acids generally. Cf. *-ate* (the salt).

icaroscope. An instrument for observing the sun from the afterglow of its image projected on a phosphorescent screen.

ice. Frozen or solid water. Transparent colorless solid, d.0.92, m.0. **Dry-** Trademark for solid carbon dioxide; a refrigerating packing material. **salt-** Frozen brine, m. − 21. A 2.5-lb eutectic mixture has the same cooling effect as 1 lb solid carbon dioxide (Dry Ice). **i. flowers.** Water flowers. Negative i. crystals produced in a slab of i. by exposure to heat rays. **i. point.** The m. of i. on the Kelvin temperature scale: 273.15°K. **i. ton.** The theoretical number of heat units required to melt one ton of i. at 0°C to water of 0°C; 284,000 BThU per 2,000-lb ton. **i. water mixture.** A mixture of pure water and crushed i.; used to maintain a constant temperature of 0°C.

Iceland agate. An obsidian from Iceland. **I. moss.** Cetraria. The dried lichens *Cetraria islandica*; gray white, brown, or red plant bodies. Cf. *cetraric acid, cetrarin, lichen, stearic acid.* **I. spar.** A transparent double-refracting calcite used in nicol prisms.

ichthalbin. Ichthyol albuminate. Gray powder, insoluble in water; an antiseptic.

ichthammol. The ammonium salts of the sulfonated oily substance resulting from the destructive distillation of bituminous schist or shale. Black viscous liquid with a strong odor, soluble in water; used in bacteriostatic ointments (B.P.). Cf. *ichthyol.*

ichthargan. Ichthyol silver, silver sulfoichthyolate. Brown powder: Ag 30, S 15%, soluble in water; an antiseptic and astringent.

ichthulin. A glycoprotein, q.v., from the eggs of the carp.

ichthylepidin. A protein of fish scales, intermediate between collagen and keratin.

ichthyocolla. Isinglass.

ichthyoform. Ichthyol formaldehyde. Brown powder, insoluble in water; an intestinal antiseptic.

ichthyol. $C_{28}H_{36}S_3O_6(NH_3)_2 \cdot 2H_2O$ = 634.40. Ammonium ichthyol sulfonate, anysin. Brown syrup of empyreumatic odor and burning taste, obtained by distillation of bituminous shale; soluble in water; an antiseptic, alterative, and astringent. Cf. *ichthammol.* **i. albuminate.** Ichthalbin. **i. formaldehyde.** Ichthyoform. **i. silver.** Ichthyolate. **i. sulfonic acid.** $C_{28}H_{38}O_5S_3$. The dibasic acid, from ichthyol. Cf. *sulfoichthyolic acid.*

ichthyolate. A compound containing the radical $=C_{28}H_{36}S_3O_6$.

ichthyophthalmite. A gem variety of apophyllite.

I.C.I. Imperial Chemical Industries, Ltd.

iconoscope. Electric eye emitron. An instrument in which invisible radiations, e.g., X rays, are rendered visible by impact on a luminescent screen.

icosane. Eicosane.

icosinene. $C_{26}H_{38}$ = 278.4. A liquid hydrocarbon from ozocerite.

I.C.T. coefficient. A numerical expression of the activity of an insecticide. The ratio of the average percent paralysis of a test insect over a given insecticide concentration range to that of a standard. I = insect; C = carrier; T = toxicant.

-id, -ide. Suffix indicating: (1) the presence of an anion; a compound derived from a negative or nonmetallic element and usually a binary compound, as chloride, oxide; (2) a glyceride.

idalin. An anthocyanin from bilberries.

-idene. Suffix indicating a bivalent radical attached to a single atom; thus: $R \cdot CH_2 \cdot CH_2 \cdot R$ (R-ethyl*ene*) and $CH_3 \cdot CH \cdot R_2$ (R-ethyl*idene*).

idioblast. A hypothetical unit of the living cell; a biophore.

idiosyncrasy. Abnormal, constitutional, or personal reaction to the effects of certain substances. Cf. *allergy.*

idite, iditol. $C_6H_{14}O_6$ = 182.1. A hexatomic *d*- and *l*-alcohol.

-ido. Suffix denoting ammonia derivatives substituted in an acid group; e.g., amido-, $CONH_2$.

idocrase. A gem variety of vesuvianite.

idonic acid. $C_6H_{12}O_7$ = 196.1. A monobasic, pentahydroxy acid, from idite.

idoplatinic acid. Platinic acid.

idosaccharic acid. $C_6H_{10}O_8$ = 210.1. A dibasic tetrahydroxy acid, from idite.

idose. $C_6H_{12}O_6$ = 180.1. Pentahydroxyhexanal.

A hexose of aldose sugar, isomeric with glucose; osazone m.156.

idrialene. $C_{22}H_{14} = 278.11$. A hydrocarbon from asphalt.

idryl. Fluoranthene.

I. G. Abbreviation for Interessen Gemeinschaft q.v.

Igamid. Trade name for superpolyamide synthetic fibers.

Igepon. Trademark for a series of anionic surfactants used as detergents, wetting agents, emulsifiers, dispersants, and foaming agents; including esters of sodium isethionate and oleic acid, and sulfoamides derived from *N*-methyltaurine or *n*-cyclohexyltaurine and fatty acids.

ignatia. Saint-Ignatius's-bean. The dried ripe seeds of *Strychnos ignatia* (Loganiaceae). It contains 2 % alkaloids, mainly strychnine and brucine.

igneous. Plutonic. Describing rocks formed from a molten state. Cf. *sedimentary rocks*.

ignis. A fire.

ignite. (1) To heat a substance at a high temperature until no more loss in weight occurs. (2) To set fire to a reaction mixture.

ignition. Combustion burning, or setting on fire. In analysis: (1) Complete oxidation of an organic compound by heating in oxygen gas. (2) Heating an inorganic compound until all volatile matter has been driven off. (3) Placing a flame directly or indirectly in contact with a reaction mixture until the reaction starts and continues to completion. **pre-** See *knock*.

    i. point. Kindling temperature. The temperature at which a substance begins to burn. Cf. *flash point*.

ihlenite. $Fe_2(SO_4)_3 \cdot 12H_2O$. A native sulfate.

ilang-ilang. Ylang-ylang.

Iletin. Trademark for a brand of insulin.

Ilex. A genus of shrubs and trees (Aquifoliaceae), including the hollies. Cf. *ilexanthin*.

ilexanthin. $C_{17}H_{23}O_{11} = 403.2$. The yellow coloring matter of *Ilex aquifolium*, holly. Yellow needles, m.198, insoluble in cold water.

ilicic alcohol. $C_{30}H_{50}O = 426.5$. α-Amyrin, m.185, prepared from *Ilex* species; a constituent of birdlime.

ilicin. A bitter principle from holly, *Ilex aquifolium*.

ilicyl alcohol. $C_{22}H_{38}O = 318.29$. A wax, m.139.

ilium, -ilium. (1) An alloy of Ni, Cr, Mn, Mo, Cu, and Fe. (2) Suffix indicating tetravalent oxygen. Cf. *pyrylium*. Cf. *-inium*.

illicium. Star *anise*.

illinium. Early name for promethium, q.v.

illinum. An acid-resistant alloy of Ni, Cr, Co, W, Al, Mn, Ti, B and Si.

-illion. Suffix which refers to successive powers of 10^6 (European usage).

illipé. (1) The fat of *Bassia latifolia* or *B. longifolia*. (2) Borneo tallow (a misnomer). See *tallow*.

illipene. $C_{64}H_{106} = 874.7$. An unsaturated hydrocarbon from the unsaponifiable matter of illipé.

illuminant. An agent that produces light.

illuminating gas. A gas mixture used for illuminating purposes: H 50, CH_4 28, C_nH_{2n} 4.5, CO 2, N 2, O 6%. Cf. *gas, natural gas*.

illumination. (1) The act of lighting up. (2) The quantity of light thrown on an object: $I = F/S$, where I is the intensity of illumination, F the flux density, and S the surface area; measured in meter-candles, footcandles, photo, or lux. **axial-** Light passing in the direction of the axis of a microscope. **dark-ground-** Light passing at right angles to the direction of the axis of a microscope. **direct-** Light falling directly on an object on the stage of a microscope from above. **indirect-** Dark-ground i. Cf. *ultramicroscope*.

ilmenite. $FeTiO_3$. Menaccanite, geikielite. A native, black titanate; a gem.

ilmenium. A supposed element, which proved to be a mixture of niobium and tantalum.

ilvaite. $CaFe_2Fe(OH)(SiO_4)_2$. Yenite. A native silicate, sometimes used as a gem.

im- Prefix indicating the $>NH$ group.

image. (1) The likeness or a reproduction of an object. (2) The picture of an object formed by rays of light after passing through an optical system. **real-** An image formed where rays of light meet or converge. **virtual-** An apparent image, formed in the direction from which rays enter the eye. The rays do not converge where the image is seen, but would do so if extended backward.

image stone. A gem variety of pyrophillite.

imasatic acid. Isamic acid.

imasatin. The lactam if isamic acid, q.v.

imazine. An organic compound containing the radical $=C:N \cdot CH:N—$.

imbibition. Absorption of a liquid by a solid or gel.

Imelon. Trade name for a polyamide synthetic fiber.

Imhoff sludge. A fertilizer made from sewage sludge settled with the aid of anaerobic bacteria: N 2-3.3, P 1%.

imid. Imide.

imidazole. $C_3H_4N_2 = 68.1$. 1,3-Diazole, glyoxaline. The ring compound

$$HC \overset{\displaystyle N:CH}{\underset{\displaystyle CH}{<}}{>}NH$$
$$(4) \qquad\qquad (1)$$

Cf. *glyoxaline*. **2,4,5-triphenyl-** Lophine.

imidazoledione. Hydantoin.

imidazoleethylamine. Histamine.

imidazoletrione. Parabanic acid.

imidazolone. $C_3H_4ON_2 = 84.1$. Iminazolone. Glyoxalone. Colorless needles, m.105. Cf. *creatinine*.

imidazolyl. The radical $C_3H_3N_2—$, from imidazole; 4 isomers. **i. ethylamine.** Histamine. **i. mercaptan.** $C_3H_3N_2SH = 100.2$. *meta-* Colorless crystals, m.222.

imide. (1) A compound containing the $>NH$ group, or a secondary amine, R_2NH, in which R is an acyl radical. (2) A compound from acid anhydrides in which O is replaced by NH; thus: OC:NH, carbimide. (3) Suggested synonym for polypeptide. **acid-** A compound of the type $R \cdot C:NH \cdot OH$. Cf. *imino bases*. **cyclic-** A ring formed by replacing 2 —OH groups by $>NH$; as, maleinimide. **di-** See *diimide*.

    i. chloride. A compound containing the radical —C(:NH)·Cl, formed by the action of hydrochloric acid on nitriles. **i. group.** Imido.

imido. The radical $>NH$. Cf. *imino, imide*. **acet-** The radical $MeC(:NH)—$.

    i. carbamide. Guanidine. **i. carbonic acid.**

$(HO)_2C:NOH$. **i. esters.** A compound of the type $R·C(:NH)·OR$, obtained as hydrochloride by the action of hydrochloric acid on a mixture of a nitrile and alcohol. **i. ethers.** A group of compounds, from i. carbonic acid; of the general type $R·C(:NOH)·OR$. **i. hydrogen.** The H of the NH group, which is replaceable by metals, such as K.

idodiphenyl. Carbazole.

idogen. Imido group.

imidoxanthin. Guanine.

iminazolone. Imidazolone.

imine. Describing a substance which contains the structure $>C=N—$, as in the imino ethers, $R_1·C(:NH)·OR_2$.

imineazole. Glyoxaline.

imino. The $=NH$ group attached to 1 or 2 C atoms; as, $=C:NH$ or $—C·NH·C—$. **i. acetic acid.** $NH(CH_2COOH)_2$ = 133.1. Colorless rhombs, m.225, soluble in water. **i. acetonitrile.** $NH(CH_2CN)_2$ = 95.1. Colorless leaflets, m.75, soluble in water. **i. bases.** Compounds containing the $=C:NH$ group, as guanidine. **i. ethanol.** $NH(CH_2CH_2OH)_2$ = 105.1. Colorless crystals, m.28, soluble in water. **i. ethyl alcohol.** Iminoethanol. **i. nitrogen.** See *ammonia nitrogen.* **i. urea.** Guanidine.

imipramine. Tofranil. *N*-(Dimethyl aminopropyl) imidodibenzyl hydrochloride. A tranquilizer. **i. hydrochloride.** $C_{19}H_{24}N_2·HCl$ = 316.86. White crystals, burning taste, m.170, soluble in water; used to treat psychotic depression (B.P.).

immersion. Submersion in a liquid. **oil-** Connecting an object and objective of a microscope with oil. **water-** Connecting an object and objective of a microscope with water.

　i. electrode. An electrode that can be lifted from the liquid and immersed at will. **i. objective.** See *objective.*

immiscible. Describing liquids that will not mix. **i. solvent.** A liquid that dissolves a solute from a solution with which it does not mix. See *partition coefficient.*

immune. Completely resistant to a disease. **i. body.** Ambiceptor, q.v. **i. serum.** The serum from the blood of an actively immunized animal, containing the antibodies for a certain disease.

immunity. The resistance of an organism to infection. **acquired-** I. acquired by a previous attack of the disease, or by inoculation with bacterial preparations. **active-** I. in which the cells of the organism manufacture antibodies, stimulated by bacterial preparations or a slight attack of the disease. **natural-** I. with which an individual is born. **passive-** I. that depends solely on inoculated immunizing sera. **theory of-** See *Ehrlich's side-chain theory.*

immunization. The process of enabling an organism to withstand the harmful effects of micro-organisms, to endure the metabolic products of the invader without injury, and to destroy the parasite.

immunochemistry. The study of the chemical phenomena of immunity.

immunology. The study of immunity.

immunotherapy. Treatment by vaccines.

impact. Sudden collision. **atomic-** Collisions between electrons and protons; as, in the bombardment of a gas with cathode rays. **molecular-**

Collisions between molecules, which are essential for the progress of a reaction.

imperatorin. $C_{16}H_{16}O_4$ = 272.2. Peucedanin. A crystalline principle from masterwort, the root of *Imperatoria ostruthium* (Umbelliferae). Colorless prisms, m.98, soluble in alkalies. Cf. *osthruthin.*

imperialine. $C_{35}H_{60}O_4N$ = 558.6. A colorless crystalline alkaloid, decomp. 254, from *Fritillaria imperialis* (Liliaceae).

imperial jade. A green aventurine gem quartz (China). **i. yu stone.** I. jade.

impermeable. Not permitting a passage.

impervious. Impenetrable, nonabsorbent.

impinger. An apparatus for sampling dust (q.v.) in air by drawing it at high velocity through a glass tube onto a wet glass plate on which microscopic counts are made.

implant. A foreign substance (e.g., organ, tissue, or drug) which is introduced surgically (e.g., subcutaneously) into the tissues of the body. **hypodermic-** An i. introduced subcutaneously, through an incision, in a sparingly soluble form. The slow release of the drug obviates repeated injections.

implosion. Explosion inward; as, the collapse of the walls of a vessel under internal vacuum.

impregnate. To saturate or charge with a gas or liquid.

impregnation. Saturation with a material having special properties; as, waterproofing. Cf. *introfaction.*

improver. (1) A mixture of starch and salts (as, phosphates) added to flour to stimulate the yeast and improve the rising properties. (2) Bleaching or whitening agents (as, persulfates) added to flour to remove or mask the color due to carotene.

I.M.S. Industrial methylated spirit.

in. (1) An inscription on a pipe or measuring vessel indicating that it is to be used to contain (not to deliver) its nominal volume (U.K. usage). Cf. *ex.* (2) Abbreviation for inch, q.v. $in.^2$ Square inch. $in.^3$ Cubic inch. **in-** Prefix indicating: (*a*) within; (*b*) not, e.g., *in*organic. **-in** Suffix indicating: (*a*) a neutral carbohydrate, as, insulin; (*b*) glucoside, as, amygdalin; (*c*) protein, as albumin; (*d*) a glyceride, as, palmitin.

In. Symbol for indium.

inactivate. To destroy activity.

inactivation. Destruction of activity (as, of a catalyst or a serum) by chemical or physical means.

inactive. Describing a compound having an asymmetric C atom but no optical activity. **divisibly-** Capable of being resolved into 2 optically active substances or racemic compounds. **indivisibly-** Incapable of being resolved into its optically active components.

incandescence. A state of glowing with intense brilliance.

incandescent. Emitting heat and/or light or both by virtue of being at a high temperature. **i. light.** An electric light bulb producing light by the passage of an electric current at a low pressure through a fine metallic element.

incaparina. A protein-rich food for children developed under the auspices of the World Health Organization in Central America. Composition: cottonseed flour 38, ground corn 29, sorghum 29,

Torula yeast 3, calcium carbonate 1, protein 27.5%, vitamin A 45 units per gram.

Inca stone. A gem pyrite.

incendiary. An agent that causes combustion. Classes: (1) Spontaneously inflammable solids, as, phosphorus; (2) metallic powders, as, thermite; (3) oxidizing combustible mixtures, as, potassium nitrate; (4) flammable material, as, carbon disulfide.

inch. A unit of length in the English system. 1 inch = 1/12 foot = 1/36 yard = 1/63,300 mile = $\frac{1}{4}$ hand. In accordance with an agreement between English-speaking countries (1959):

$$1 \text{ in.} = 2.54 \text{ cm}$$
$$1,000 \text{ in.} = 25.4 \text{ meters (the round factor)}$$
$$\text{U.S. in.} = 1/12 \text{ U.S. ft, q.v.}$$
$$\text{British in.} = 1/12 \text{ imperial standard ft}$$

cubic- in.^{3} or cu in. A unit of volume in the English system. 1 in.^{3} = 0.0005787 ft^3 = 16.387 cm^3. **micro-**10^{-6} in. = 254 Å. **square-** in.^{2} or sq in. A unit of area in the English system. 1 in.^{2} = 0.006944 ft^2 = 6.452 mm^2.

inchi grass oil. An oil from *Cymbopogon caesius* containing borneol, terpineol, camphene, and limonene; a substitute for palmarosa oil.

inch-pennyweight. The product of the gold content, in pennyweights per ton, of a gold reef, and the width, in inches, of the reef. A measure of the value of a reef in the S. African mining industry; 500 is a high figure.

incidence. The striking contact of one body with another. **angle of-** The angle made with the normal by a beam of light striking a surface.

incineration. Cremation. The process of burning to ashes. **i. dish.** A flat dish for reducing substances to ash in analysis.

incipient. Beginning. **i. red heat.** Beginning to glow. Cf. *color scale.*

inclination. Deviation. The angle of an object above the horizon.

inclinator. A stand for large bottles or carboys so that they can easily be tipped for emptying.

inclusion. A state of being enclosed in or surrounded by a substance; as, suspended foreign matter in a crystal.

incompatibility. Inability to be mixed without impairing the original properties. **chemical-** Describing substances which, when mixed, react with each other. **physical-** The property of repellent substances; as, water and oil. **physiologic-** Describing drugs that have a mutually antagonistic effect. **therapeutic-** Describing drugs that have opposite therapeutic effects.

incompatible. Applied to a substance which for chemical, physical, or physiological reasons cannot be mixed with another without a change in the nature or effect of either.

incomplete. Not carried to its greatest possible extent. **i. equilibrium.** Equilibrium that has not reached a balance. **i. reaction.** Reversible *reaction.*

incompressibility. Not compressible. Ability to resist pressure without change of form or volume.

incompressible volume. That part of a gas which is not uniformly compressed according to the gas laws: the quantity b of van der Waals' equation q.v.

Inconel. Trademark for a corrosion-resisting alloy containing 76 Ni, 15 Cr, and 9% Fe; m.400, d.8.51.

increment. The augmentation of the quantity of substance, e.g., during crystallization.

incrustation. Formation of a crust or scale.

incubation time. The period between implanting an infection in a culture medium or organism and the first signs of growth.

incubator. A chamber or box at a definite temperature (usually 37°C), in which bacterial cultures are grown.

indaconine. $C_{27}H_{47}NO_9$ = 529.37. An alkaloid, m.94, from aconite.

indaconitine. $C_{34}HN_{47}O_{10}$ = 629.37. Acetylbenzoyl-ψ-aconine. An alkaloid from aconite, m.202.

indamine. $HN:C_6H_4:N\cdot C_6H_4NH_2$ = 197.3. Phenylene blue. Obtained by oxidation of *p*-phenylenediamine and aniline.

indamines. Dyestuffs derived from indoaniline and containing the =NH group instead of the quinone oxygen; as, in indamine.

indan. C_6H_{10} = 118.1. Hydrindene, 2,3-dihydroindene. The bicyclic hydrocarbon $C_6H_4(CH_2)_2\cdot CH_2$. Colorless liquid, b.176, insoluble in water.

indandione. $C_9H_6O_2$ = 146.05. Diketohydrindene. **1,2-** White crystals, m.107. **1,3-** White crystals, m.130.

indanone. Indone.

indanyl. The radical, C_9H_9—, from hydrindene; 4 isomers.

indazole. (1) $C_7H_6N_2$ = 118.06. Benzopyrazole, 2,1-benzodiazole. Colorless crystals, m.146; 2 isomers:

Indazole (2,1-)   Isindazole (1,2-)

(2) A compound containing the i. nucleus; as: **α-phenylis-** $C_6H_4\cdot(N\cdot PH)(CH):N$. Colorless crystals, m.142.

Indema. Trade name for *phenylindanedione.*

indene.   (ϕ)

The Greek letters indicate the positions at which substitution may take place. Colorless liquid, d.1.040, b.188, soluble in alcohol. **dihydro-** Hydrindene. **iso-** See *isoindene.* **1-methylene-** Benzofulvene.

indenone. Indone.

indenyl. The radical C_9H_7—, from indene; 7 isomers.

indeterminable. That which cannot be determined.

indeterminate. That which cannot be predicted, but which (when it happens) can be determined.

indeterminism. See *Heisenberg's principle.*

index. (Pl. indexes or indices.) (1) Mathematical: the power to which a quantity is raised. (2) Physical: a numerical ratio of measurement in comparison with a fixed standard. (3) Bibliographical: a classified list; as subjects or patent numbers. **i. compound.** The parent substance, q.v., under which derivatives are listed.

Decennial I. A collective i. published at 10-year intervals by: (1) Chemical Abstracts of the

American Chemical Society; (2) The Chemical Society Abstracts (U.K.); (3) The Society of Chemical Industry (U.K.).

Indian. **I. agate.** A gem moss agate. **I. arrowroot.** Euonymus. **I. balm.** Trillium. **I. balsam.** Peru balsam. **I. barley.** Sabadilla. **I. bel.** Bael. **I. cannabis.** Cannabis. **I. corn.** Maize. **I. fig.** Prickly pear. **I. ginger.** Asarum. **I. gum.** (1) Ghatti gum, gummi indicum. The exudation of *Anogeissus latifolia* (India). Yellow tears, soluble in water; a mucilage. (2) Sterculia gum. **I. hemp.** Cannabis. **I. hippo.** Gillenia. **I. laburnum.** Cassia. **I. licorice.** Abrus root. **I. ocher.** A native ferric oxide war paint (N. American Indians). **I. physic.** Gillenia. **I. pink.** Spigelia. **I. poke.** Veratrum. **I. red.** (1) Red ocher from Ormus (Persian Gulf); an early coloring material. (2) I. ocher. **i. rubber.** Rubber. **I. saffron.** Turmeric. **I. sage.** Eupatorium. **I. shot.** Cannabin. **I. tobacco.** Lobelia. **I. topaz.** A saffron-yellow topaz. **I. turnip.** The corn of *Arisaema triphyllum*; an expectorant and diaphoretic. **I. yellow.** (1) Purree. A yellow I. pigment, containing the magnesium salt of purreic acid. (2) Azoflavin. (3) Cobalt and potassium nitrite. (4) Euxanthone.

india rubber. Rubber.

indican. (1) $C_{14}H_{17}NO_6$ = 295.14. A glucoside from woad, *Isatis tinctoria* (Cruciferae); also from indigo, *Indigofera* species (Leguminosae). Colorless leaflets, m.57, soluble in water; hydrolyzing to glucose and indoxyl; also formed from indole in the intestine during putrefaction. (2) $C_8H_6N \cdot SO_4K$ = 251.2. I. of urine, indoxyl sulfate. A normal constituent of urine. **i. meter.** A device for estimating the quantity of i. in urine. **i. test.** To 5 ml urine add a few drops of Obermayer's reagent (q.v.), shake, and add chloroform. The chloroform separates with a blue color if i. is present.

indicarmine. Indigo carmine.

indicator. (1) A substance that changes in physical appearance, e.g., color, at or approaching the end point of a chemical titration, e.g., on the passage between acidity and alkalinity. **absorption-** A substance that indicates the end point of a precipitation reaction by being released from the adsorbed state; as, rhodamine on silver chloride. **achromatic-** A mixture of 2 indicators or of an i. and dye which produces at the end point a color complementary to that of the i. at its transition point. The mixture thus appears colorless or gray at its end point; e.g., methyl red 0.125, methylene blue 0.0825%. **acid-base-** Hydrogen ion. **ammono system-** An i. that indicates the presence of an ammono acid or ammono base in a liquid ammonia solution; e.g., hydrazobenzene, yellow and red, respectively. **aquo system-** Hydrogen ion. **chelatometric-** Metal i. **Clark and Lubs-** Phthalein i., q.v., covering the pH range 1.0–9.0. **complexometric-** Metal i. **compound-** A mixture of indicators; as, universal i. **external-** Outside. **fluorescent-** A substance that indicates an end point or pH value by a change of fluorescence, intensity, or color; as, quinine sulfate. **hydrogen ion-** A substance that indicates by its color the approximate hydrogen-ion concentration of a solution. **inorganic-** Metallic salts used in

titrations; as, potassium chromate or ferrocyanide. **inside-, internal-** An i. added to a liquid to be titrated; as, litmus in neutralization titrations. **metal-** A chelating dyestuff which changes color with increase or decrease in metal ion concentration by forming metal-dye complexes; e.g., Eriochrome Black-T, used in complexometric titrations. **metallochromic-** An i. that is a complexing agent for the metal ion being treated, and changes in color at a titration end point. **neutralization.** An i. that shows the end point of an acid-alkali neutralization reaction. **one-color-** An i. that changes from colored to colorless, e.g., phenolphthalein. **outside-** External. An i. to which a drop of the titrated liquid is added on a porcelain plate. **oxidation-reduction, redox-** A substance that indicates the state of oxidation by its color; as, compounds of Mn. E.g.: At pH 7.0 the potentials are:

Indigo disulfonate	−0.121
Methylene blue	+0.011
o-Chlorophenol indophenol	+0.233
Ferrocyanide	+0.40

phthalein- Synthetic phthalein dye, used as an i. See table. **radioactive-** q.v. **redox-** Oxidation-reduction. **screened-** An i. mixed with another coloring matter (not necessarily an i.) to make the color change sharper. Cf. *achromatic-*. **turbidity-** A semicolloid which flocculates at a certain pH value (isoelectric point) and so indicates when this point has been reached in volumetric analysis. **two-color-** An i. that changes from one color to another. **universal-** A mixture of indicators covering a wider pH range than each individual i. E.g.: a solution of methyl orange 0.1, methyl red 0.4, bromthymol blue 0.4, α-naphtholphthalein 0.32, phenolphthalein 0.5, and cresolphthalein 1.6 gm in 100 ml 70% alcohol.

Red	3.0	Greenish blue	9.0
Yellow-orange	5.0	Blue	10.0
Yellow	6.5	Reddish violet	12.0
Green	8.0		

vegetable- An i. coloring matter, from plants. **i. exponent.** The pH value at which the color change of an i. is most rapid; theoretically the midpoint of the i. range. **i. paper.** A paper impregnated with an i. and dried. See *test paper*. **i. range.** The pH values over which the color of an i. changes. See table. **i. yellow.** The chromophore of rhodopsin, q.v.

indicolite. A blue gem tourmaline.

indigo. $C_{16}H_{10}O_2N_2$ = 262.2. I. tin, synthetic i., $\Delta^{2,2}$-bis-ψ-indoxyl. Dark blue rhombs, d.1.35, sublime 300, decomp. 390, insoluble in water, alcohol, or ether; soluble in hot aniline or hot chloroform; used in dyeing, and as a reagent. **chinese green-** A dye from the bark of *Rhamnus chlorophora* (China); used to dye silk. **leuco-** I. white. **natural-** I. blue. **soluble-** I. white or I. carmine.

i. blue. The blue color obtained by fermentation from various species of *Indigofera* (Leguminosae); used in dyeing and printing inks. **i. carmine.** $C_{16}H_8N_2O_2(SO_3Na)_2$ = 466.4. Soluble i., sodium indigotin sulfonate, sodium coerulin sulfate, i.

COMMON INDICATORS

Alphabetical List

Alizarin blue	Cochineal	Methyl red
Alizarin red	Congo red	Methyl violet
Alizarin yellow	o-Cresolphthalein	α-Naphtholphthalein
Alkali blue	m-Cresol purple	α-Naphthylamineazosulfanilic acid
Aminoazobenzene	Cresol red	Neutral red
Amphomagenta	Crystal violet	Nile blue
Aurin	Curcumin	p-Nitrophenol
Azolitmin	Dimethylaminoazobenzene	Nitrophenolsulfophthalein
Benzeneazobenzylaniline	Dinitrophenol	Phenacetolin
Benzeneazonaphthylamine	Diphenylaminoazobenzene	Phenolphthalein
Benzopurpurin	Erythrosin	Phenol red
Brilliant green	Ethyl violet	Poirrier's blue
Brilliant yellow	Fuchsin, acid	Propyl red
Bromchlorphenol blue	Fuchsin, basic	Purpurin
Bromcresol green	Hematoxylin	Rosolic acid
Bromcresol purple	Iodine green	Thymol blue
Bromphenol blue	Lacmoid	Thymolphthalein
Bromphenol purple	Malachite green	Trinitrobenzene
Bromphenol red	Metanil yellow	Tropeolin 0
Bromthymol blue	Methyl blue	Tropeolin 00
Carminic acid	Methyl green	Tropeolin 000
Chlorphenol red	Methyl orange	Xylenol blue

PROPERTIES OF COMMON INDICATORS

Name	Common name	pH range	Titration end point, K_{Ind}	Color change		Solvent	Concentration, %	Volume of 0.05 NaOH per 100 mg	Drops added to 10 ml of sample
				Acid	Alkaline				
Thymolsulfonephthalein....	Thymol blue	1.2–2.8	2.3	Rose	Yellow	Water	0.04	4.3	4
		8.0–9.6	8.8	Yellow	Blue				
Tetrabromophenolsulfone-phthalein..............	Bromphenol blue	3.0–4.6	4.1	Yellow	Purple	Water	0.04	3.0	4
Dibromo-o-cresolsulfone-phthalein..............	Bromcresol purple	5.2–6.8	6.1	Yellow	Purple	Water	0.02	3.7	4
Dibromothymolsulfone-phthalein..............	Bromthymol blue	6.0–7.6	6.9	Yellow	Blue	Water	0.04	3.2	6
Phenolsulfonephthalein.....	Phenol red	6.8–8.4	7.7	Yellow	Purple	Water	0.02	5.7	4
o-Cresolsulfonephthalein....	Cresol red	7.2–8.8	8.2	Yellow	Purple	Water	0.02	5.3	4
m-Cresolsulfonephthalein ...	m-Cresol purple	0.5–2.5	1.5	Red	Yellow	95% alcohol	0.02	...	4
		7.6–9.2	8.4	Yellow	Purple				
Tetrabromo-m-cresolsulfonephthalein	Bromcresol green	3.2–5.8	4.8	Yellow	Blue	Water	0.02	...	4
Dichlorophenolsulfone-phthalein..............	Chlorphenol red	5.0–6.0	5.5	Yellow	Red	Water	0.04	...	4
Dibromophenolsulfone-phthalein..............	Bromphenol red	5.4–7.0	6.2	Yellow	Red	Water	0.04	...	4
2,6-Dinitrophenol.........	....	1.7–4.4	...	Colorless	Yellow	Water	0.10		
2,4-Dinitrophenol.........	....	2.0–4.7	...	Colorless	Yellow	Water	0.10		
2,5-Dinitrophenol.........	....	4.0–6.0	...	Colorless	Yellow	Water	0.10		
p-Nitrophenol.............	....	5.0–7.6	...	Colorless	Yellow	Water	0.50		
m-Nitrophenol	....	6.5–8.5	...	Colorless	Yellow orange	Water	0.50		
	Alizarin yellow	10.0–12.0	...	Pale yellow	Orange	Water	0.10		
Tropeolin 00	Orange IV	1.3–3.2	...	Red	Yellow	Dilute alcohol	0.5	...	2
	Methyl orange	3.1–4.8	...	Red	Orange yellow	Water	0.02	...	6
	Methyl red	4.2–6.3	5.1	Red	Yellow	60% alcohol	2.0	...	3
	Neutral red	6.8–8.0	...	Red	Yellow	Water	1.0	...	3
	Litmus	5.0–8.0	...	Red	Blue	60% alcohol	2.0	...	15
Turmeric.................	Curcuma	7.8–9.2	...	Yellow	Brown	Dilute alcohol	1.0		4
Phenolphthalein...........	....	8.2–10.0	9.7	Colorless	Red	70% alcohol	1.0		10
Tropeolin 0	....	11.0–13.0	...	Yellow	Orange	Dilute alcohol	1.0	...	7

extract. Blue powder or paste, soluble in water. Used as a dye, and clinically in the function test of the kidneys (U.S.P., B.P.). **i. copper.** $CuSO_3$. Covellite. A native copper sulfite. **i. disulfonate.** An oxidation-reduction and pH indicator, changing at 12.5 from blue (acid) to yellow (alkali). **i. extract.** I. carmine. **i. red.** Indirubin. **i. white.** $C_{16}H_{12}O_2N_2$ = 264.2. Biindoxyl, leuco indigo, soluble indigo. Colorless powder, insoluble in water, oxidized to i. blue; used for vat dyeing of textiles with indigo.

indigotin. (1) Indigo. (2) The heterocyclic compound, diindogen or $\Delta^{2,2}$-bis-ψ-indoxyl. Cf. *indigo*. **dibromo-** Murex. **iso-** $C_{16}H_{10}O_2N$ = 262.2. Bioxindol. Cf. *isatan, isatide*.

indin. $C_{16}H_{10}O_2N_2$ = 262.18. An isomer of indigo, soluble in water. **chloro-** Chlorindin.

indirubin. $C_{16}H_{10}O_2N_2$ = 262.18. Indigo red, oxindole-$\Delta^{3,2}$-ψ-indoxyl. A red isomer of indigo in urine.

indium. In = 114.82. A ductile metal element of the aluminum subgroup, at. no. 49. Silver crystalline masses, d.7.362, m.115, b.1450, insoluble in water, soluble in acids. Discovered by Reich and Richter (1863), and named from the indigo blue lines of its spectrum. It is usually trivalent, but may be di- or monovalent; it forms low-melting alloys. **i. bromide.** $InBr_3$ = 354.5. I. tribromide. Yellow powder, soluble in water. **i. chloride.** InCl. I. monochloride. $InCl_2$. I. dichloride. $InCl_3$. I. trichloride. **i. cyanide.** $In(CN)_3$ = 192.8. Colorless poisonous powder, soluble in water. **i. dichloride.** $InCl_2$ = 185.7. Yellow liquid, decomp. by water into the trichloride and i. **i. hydroxide.** $In(OH)_3$ = 165.8. Colorless powder, insoluble in water. **i. iodide.** InI_3 = 495.8. Yellow hygroscopic crystals, soluble in water. .**i. nitrate.** $In(NO_3)_3 \cdot 3H_2O$ = 354.9. White crystals, soluble in water. **i. oxide.** In_2O_3 = 277.6. Yellow powder, insoluble in water. **i. sulfate.** $In_2(SO_4)_3$ = 517.6. Gray powder, hygroscopic, poisonous, and soluble in water. **i. sulfhydrate.** $In(SH)_3$ = 213.8. Yellow powder, precipitated from aqueous i. salt solutions by hydrogen sulfide. **i. sulfide.** In_2S_3 = 325.6. Red powder, insoluble in water. **i. trichloride.** $InCl_3$ = 221.2. I. chloride. White, hygroscopic, poisonous crystals, sublime 500, soluble in water; an external antiseptic.

indoform. Salicylic acid methylene acetate. White, astringent powder, sparingly soluble in water; used to treat gout.

indogen. The radical $C_6H_4(NH) \cdot CO \cdot C =$. **di-**Indigo. **pseudo-** Isatin.

indogenide. A compound containing the indogen radical.

indoldione. ψ-Isatin.

indole. $C_6H_4 \cdot (NH) \cdot CH : CH$ = 117.11. 1-Benzazole, ketole, benzopyrrole. Colorless leaflets, m.52, soluble in water. Occurs in oil of jasmine, clove oil, and in intestinal putrefaction, and has a fecal odor. Used as a microchemical reagent for cellulose and diluted, in orange blossom perfume. Cf. *indyl*. **dihydrodiketo-** Isatin. **dihydroketo-** Oxindole. **hydroxy-** Indoxyl. **iso-** 2-Benzazole. **α-methyl-** C_9H_8N = 130.1. Methyl ketol. Colorless crystals, m.59, soluble in water. **β-methyl-**

Skatole. **n-nitro-** $C_8H_7N_2O_2$ = 163.2. Colorless crystals, m.172. **pseudo-** Indolenine.

indolol. Indoxyl.

indolone. 1(3)- Phthalimidine. **2(3)-** Oxindole. **3(2)-** ψ-Indoxyl. Cf. *indolinone*.

indone. C_9H_8O = 132.1. Indanone, hydrindone. **alpha-** Rhombic leaflets, m.41, slightly soluble in water. **beta-** Colorless crystals, m.61.

indophenine. $C_{12}H_7ONS$ = 213.19. Colorless powder, insoluble in water.

indophenol. $CO(CH:CH)_2 \cdot CN \cdot C_6H_4 \cdot OH$ = 199.08. Hydroxyphenylimino benzenone. Used to synthesize sulfur dyes.

Indopol. Trademark for a range of moisture-resistant polybutenes, mol.wt. 300–1,900.

indoxyl. $C_6H_4 \cdot NH \cdot CH \cdot C(OH)$ = 133.1. **alpha-** 3-Hydroxyindole. Yellow crystals, m.85, soluble in water; used in organic synthesis. **ψ- or pseudo-** 3-Ketoindoline. An intermediate in the synthesis of indigo. **i. potassium sulfate.** Indican.

indoxylic acid. $C_9H_7O_3N$ = 177.11. An oxidation product of indoxyl, b.122 (sublimes and decomp.), soluble in water.

induced. Caused or produced indirectly. **i. current.** A high-frequency current produced by an induction coil. **i. radioactivity.** Radioactivity produced by the bombardment with neutrons, protons, or other particles, q.v. See *radioelements*. **i. reaction.** Sympathetic reaction: (1) If a slow reaction between substances A and C is hastened by promoting a fast reaction between A and B, then A is the *actor* or *donor* (usually an oxidizing or reducing agent), B the *inductor*, and C the *acceptor*. (2) An enzyme which removes an element from a compound and leaves the remainder free to react; acts as an acceptor in an induced reaction. Cf. *induction (4)*.

inducer. Inductor.

inductance. See *dielectric constant*.

induction. (1) A process of inference by which one passes from particular data to general principles. Cf. *deduction*. (2) The production of an electric or magnetic phenomenon by the influence of a neighboring electric or magnetic field; as, magnetizing by proximity to a magnet. Units:

1 international henry = 1.00052 absolute henry
1 absolute henry = 1 practical emu
= 10^9 emu
= 1.1124×10^{-12} esu

(3) See *induced reaction*. (4) A change (produced by radiation) in the energy of a molecule, due to interaction with another molecule, which is at a distance from it greater than the diameter of the molecule. Cf. *collision*. **chemical-** See *induction (4)*. **electromagnetic-** See *induction (2)*. **mutual-** See *mutual induction*. **photochemical-** See *photochemical induction*. **self-** See *self-induction*. **i. coil.** Electric transformer. A wire spool inside another, used to obtain high-frequency alternating currents from a continuous current passed through the primary (inner) coil. **i. furnace.** See *furnace*.

inductive capacity. Dielectric constant.

inductivity. Dielectric constant.

inductor. See *induced reaction*.

indulines. Blue or black dyestuffs, from the tricyclic ring

$$HN = C_6H_3 \begin{matrix} N \\ \diagdown \\ NR \end{matrix} C_6H_4$$

Substitution is usually at the N atom indicated. **benz-** Aposafranine. **naphth-** Dyestuffs of the type

$$HN = C_{10}H_5 \begin{matrix} N \\ \diagdown \\ NR \end{matrix} C_{10}H_6$$

ros- Dyestuffs of the type

$$HN = C_{10}H_5 \begin{matrix} N \\ \diagdown \\ NR \end{matrix} C_6H_4$$

indurated. Hardened, as in the firing of clays.
indyl. The radical C_8H_6N-, from indole. **iso-** See *isoindyl*.
-ine. Suffix indicating: (1) a halogen, as chlorine; (2) a hydrocarbon of the acetylene series, as butine; (3) an alkaloid or nitrogen base, as morphine. Cf. *-in*.
inert. Sluggish; having little or no chemical action. **i. elements.** The noble gases of the "zero" group of the periodic system which have no valency and do not combine with other elements. **i. substance.** A substance that is resistant to chemical or physical action.
inertia. The tendency of a physical body to remain in an unchanged condition, either in a state of uniform motion, or at rest. **moment of i.** A factor in the mathematic treatment of the rotation of a body in terms of mass and squares of the linear dimensions. Cf. *momentum*.
infection. Transmission of disease by contact, due to the successful invasion and growth of bacteria or parasites in the tissues of an organism. Cf. *contamination*. **aerial-** I. caused by dust particles in air. **focal-** I. in which the bacterial growth is restricted to a small area of the organism. **mixed-** I. caused by more than one kind of bacterium.
infectious disease. A pathological condition produced by invasion and growth by microorganisms (bacteria or protozoa).
infiltration. (1) The deposition of minerals from solution in the pores of a rock. (2) The slow diffusion of injected solutions into the tissues of an organism.
infinitesimal. Smaller than any assigned quantity. Negligible.
inflammable. Flammable. **i. air.** The original name for hydrogen.
infra. Beyond. **i. luminescence.** Luminescence whose wavelengths are in the infrared region. **i. phonic.** Vibrations in air of wavelength too high to be audible. **i. photic.** Radiations of a wavelength too long to be visible; as, i. red. **i. red.** Ultrared. The invisible part of the spectrum from 10^{-4} to 10^{-1} cm, which overlaps a portion of the visible spectrum. Cf. *radiations-long-* I.r. rays from 14,000 to 150,000 Å. *near-* or *short-* I.r. rays from 7,200 to 14,000 Å. Sources: see table. **i. röntgen rays.** Grenz rays. **i. sonic.** I. phonic.

	Infrared rays, %	Visible rays, %
Sunlight	60	34
Incandescent lamp . . .	95	4.8
Carbon arc	80	15
Resistance wire	99	0.5

infundibuliform. A funnel-shaped bacterial growth.
infusible. Not capable of being fused. **i. white precipitate.** Mercuridiammonium chloride.
infusion. Infusum. A solution obtained by steeping vegetable drugs in water below its boiling point, and straining. Cf. *decoction*.
infusoria. A class of protozoa. Erroneously applied to diatoms (protophyta).
infusorial earth. Diatomaceous earth, tripolite, kieselguhr. A light, earthy, sedimentary rock consisting of empty shells of diatoms and other protophyta. Used as a filtration aid, and adsorbent.
infusum. Infusion.
ingluvin. An enzyme from hen gizzards used to treat dyspepsia.
ingredient. Any constituent of a mixture. Cf. *constituent*.
inhaler. (1) A device to administer vapors or gases. (2) A device to filter dust from air to be breathed. Cf. *respirator*.
inhibin. The testicular hormone that prevents overdevelopment of the pituitary gland.
inhibition. A restraint or encumbrance.
inhibitor. A substance that arrests a chemical action. **vapor-phase-** An organic compound which is solid at ordinary temperatures, and which evolves a vapor which surrounds a metal article in a closed container and produces on its surface an invisible protective film; e.g., nitrites of nitrogen bases. Cf. *vapor*.
inhibitory phase. Protective *colloid*.
initiator. Trigger. Cf. *promoter*.
-inium. -ium. **i. compound.** Compounds of organic nitrogen bases with acids in which N is assumed to be pentavalent; as, pyridinium. Cf. *-ilium*.
injection. The administration of a substance into a part of an organism: intravenously (into the bloodstream), intramuscularly (into muscular tissue), subcutaneously (under the skin). **i. needle.** A hypodermic needle. **i. syringe.** A graduated glass tube, with piston, used to inject liquid into an organism.
ink. (1) A colored liquid, used for writing. (2) A colored paste or liquid used for printing. **aniline-** A solution of an aniline dye in a volatile solvent or dilute gum; used for printing in bright colors or at high speeds, e.g., by the gravure process. **canceling-** A suspension of lampblack in oil, used for stamp pads. **Chinese-** India i. **copying-** An iron-tannic acid i. **diamond-** A mixture of barium sulfate and hydrofluoric acid, used for writing on glass. **flexographic-** Aniline i. **fugitive-** An i. that disappears on treatment with water or bleaching chemicals. Used for printing checks. **india-** Finely divided lampblack suspended in water or gum. **invisible-** Secret i., sympathetic

i. An i. normally invisible to the human eye, but rendered visible by heat (lemon juice), light (soap solution in ultraviolet light), water (cobalt salts), or chemicals (iodine vapor on a starch i.). **long-** Free-flowing (printing) i. **marking-** A solution of silver nitrate, used to write indelibly on paper, textiles, laundry, etc. **printing-** Four types: (1) A suspension of a pigment (usually carbon black) in a mineral oil, which dries by absorption of oil into the paper; used for high-speed letterpress printing. (2) A suspension of a pigment in a drying oil (e.g., linseed oil), which dries by formation of a protective layer of hard linseed oil varnish over the pigment; used for general lithographic and letterpress work. (3) An aniline i., q.v., which dries mainly by evaporation. (4) A warm molten resinous pigment which dries by simple solidification. **secret-** Invisible i. **short-** Tacky (printing) i. **sympathetic-** Invisible i. **writing-** (1) Blue-black i. Normally, a slightly acidic solution containing principally an iron salt, a tannin, and a blue aniline dye (provisional color) to render the i. visible while it is being used. Oxidation of the iron-tannin compound produces a permanent blue-black color. (2) A solution of an aniline dye in a dilute gum; used for fountain pens, and for colored inks. (3) Ball-point. A solution of a dye in a waxy medium.

    i. transfer coefficient. The ratio of the amount of i. on the paper to that on the printing surface in a printing process.

innocuous. Describing a harmless substance.
innoxious. Harmless. Antonym: toxic or noxious.
-ino A suffix denoting substitution by one of the groups, NH_2, NHR, NR_2, NH, or NR. Cf. *amino.*
inoculation, innoculation (U.K. usage). (1) The insertion of a virus or virulent vaccine into a wound or scratch in the skin. (b) The planting of bacteria on a culture medium.
inoculum, innoculum (U.K. usage). The substance to be inoculated.
inorganic. (1) Unorganic. Pertaining to chemicals that do not contain carbon (carbonates and cyanides excepted). Cf. *organic.* (2) Devoid of an organized structure. **i. chemistry.** Chemistry which deals with inorganic or polar compounds, which do not contain carbon as a principal element.
i. compound. A substance containing an electropositive element or radical and an electronegative element or radical.
inose. Inositol.
inosin. $C_{10}H_{12}N_4O_6$ = 284.1. Hypoxanthin riboside. White needles, m.218, soluble in hot water.
inosinic acid. $C_{10}H_{13}N_4O_8P$ = 348.13. Inosinphosphoric acid. A nucleotide from adenylic acid of nucleoproteins.
inosite. Inositol.
inositol. $C_6H_6(OH)_6 \cdot 2H_2O$ = 216.2. (1) Generic name for 9 stereoisomeric cyclohexane hexols. (2) Muscle sugar, *1,2,3,4,5,6-cyclohexanehexanol**, dambose, inose, hexahydroxybenzene, Bios I, nucite, phaseomannite. Found in barley, peas, beans, and animal flesh, in the form of its phosphoric acid ester (phytin). Optically inactive white crystals, m.200 (decomp.), soluble in water; part of the vitamin B complex, q.v. **dextro-** Colorless crystals, m.247. **levo-** Colorless crystals m.238.
    i. hexaphosphoric acid. Phytic acid.

inquartation. Quartation.
insecticide. An agent used to destroy insects, generally by dusting or spraying on plants. Cf. *fumigant.* Classes: (1) Contact i., which corrode the surface of soft-bodied insects; as, kerosene. (2) Stomach i., which poison through the intestinal tract, as arsenicals. (3) Gaseous i., used as fumigants, as, hydrocyanic acid. (4) Systemic i., carried in the sap stream of plants, thereby rendering such plants poisonous to insects; as, selenium compounds. See table, pp. 348–351.
insect powder. Pyrethrum flowers, q.v. The powdered flowerheads of *Chrysanthemum* species, (Compositae); a stimulant, local irritant, and insecticide. **Dalmatian-** Obtained from *Chrysanthemum cinerariae folium.* **Persian-** Obtained from *Chrysanthemum roseum.*
insect wax. Chinese wax.
insemination. The introduction of semen into the reproductive organs of an animal. Cf. *telegenesis.*
insipid. Tasteless.
insipin. $(C_{20}H_{23}O_2N_2)OCH_2CO \cdot H_2SO_4 \cdot 3H_2O$. Quinine diglycol sulfate. An almost tasteless quinine substitute.
in situ. In the normal, or natural place or position.
insol. Abbreviation for insoluble.
insolation. Solarization, irradiation. Exposure to the sun's rays.
insolubility. The quality of being immiscible with, or insoluble in a liquid.
insoluble. Incapable of dissolving in a liquid.
inspirator. (1) Respirator. (2) A device for controlling automatically the proportions of the constituents of a mixture of gases.
inspissation. Thickening a liquid by evaporation.
inspissator. An evaporator.
instantizing. A process for manufacturing milk powder of improved wettability and pourability.
instrument. A mechanical device, apparatus, or appliance.
insuccation. Soaking a material with water.
insufflation. A fine powder for introduction into body cavities, openings, or wounds.
insulation. Mechanically placing apart or separating a physical system. **electrical-** Preventing the escape of electricity. **heat-** Preventing the escape of heat.
    i. value, k. The amount of heat that an insulator will conduct, expressed in BThU per hour per degree Fahrenheit of temperature difference, per square foot of substance 1 in. thick. Examples:

Sulfur dioxide	0.005
Oxygen	0.015
Air	0.015
Expanded plastics	0.20–0.28
Cork slab	0.27
Glass fiber	0.30
Vermiculite	0.45
Wood	1.1
Asbestos cement sheets	2.0
Concrete	6.7
Glass	5.8–14.0
Brick	9.0
Iron and steel	320

insulator. A protective and separating agent; a nonconductor. **electrical-** A device to prevent the

INSECTICIDES

Common name or code number	Chemical name	Type of commodity treated	Persistence and site of action
A. Halogenated Hydrocarbon Compounds			
BHC (mixed isomers) γ-BHC	1,2,3,4,5,6-Hexachloro-cyclohexane. Benzene hexachloride. γ isomer of the above	Stored products, growing plants, livestock, seeds, soil, ground baits: U.K. and overseas	Persistent: surface contact, stomach poison, fumigant
DDT...................	A complex chemical mixture in which pp'-DDT predominates	Stored products, growing plants, livestock, soil: U.K. and overseas	Persistent: surface contact, stomach poison,
pp'-DDT	1,1,1-Trichloro-2,2-di-(p-chlorophenyl)-ethane	Stored products, growing plants, livestock, soil: U.K. and overseas	Persistent: surface contact, stomach poison
TDE..................	1,1-Bis(p-chlorophenyl)-2,2-dichloroethane	Growing plants, livestock: overseas	Persistent: surface contact, stomach poison
Methoxychlor	1,1,1-Trichloro-2,2-di-(4-methoxyphenyl)-ethane	Growing plants, livestock: overseas	Persistent: surface contact, stomach poison
Dieldrin	Contains not less than 85% of 1,2,3,4,10,10-hexachloro-6,7-epoxy-1,4,4a,5,6,7,8,8a-octahydro-1,4,5,8-dimethano-naphthalene, and not more than 15% of insecticidally active related compounds	Growing plants, soil: overseas	Persistent: surface contact, stomach poison
Aldrin.................	Contains not less than 95% of 1,2,3,4,10,10-hexachloro-1,-4,4a,5,8,8a-hexahydro-1,4,-5,8-dimethanonaphthalene, and not more than 5% of of insecticidally active related compounds	Growing plants, soil, ground baits: overseas	Persistent: surface contact, stomach poison, fumigant
Toxaphene..............	Chlorinated camphene (67–69% chlorine)	Growing plants, livestock, ground baits: U.K. and overseas	Persistent: surface contact, stomach poison
Chlordane	2,3,4,5,6,7,10,10-Octachloro-4,7,8,9-tetrahydro-4,7-endomethyleneindan	Growing plants, livestock, soil ground baits: overseas	Persistent: surface contact, stomach poison
K.6451	4-Chlorophenyl-4-chlorobenzene sulfonate	Growing plants: overseas	Persistent: surface contact
PCPBS.................	4-Chlorophenylbenzene sulfonate	Growing plants: U.K.	Persistent: surface contact
88-R	2-(p-tert-Butylphenoxy)iso-propyl 2-chloroethyl sulfite	Growing plants: overseas	Persistent: surface contact
Carbon tetrachloride	Carbon tetrachloride	Stored products, soil: U.K. and overseas	Nonpersistent: fumigant
Methyl bromide	Methyl bromide	Stored products, soil: U.K. and overseas	Nonpersistent: fumigant
Ethylene dibromide.......	Ethylene dibromide	Stored products, soil: U.K. and overseas	Nonpersistent: fumigant
Ethylene dichloride.......	Ethylene dichloride	Stored products, soil: U.K. and overseas	Nonpersistent: fumigant

INSECTICIDES   (*continued*)

Common name or code number	Chemical name	Type of commodity treated	Persistence and site of action
A. Halogenated Hydrocarbon Compounds			
Tetrachloroethane	Tetrachloroethane	Growing plants: U.K.	Persistent
DD....................	1,2-Dichloropropane, 1,3-dichloropropylene in approximately equal proportions	Soil: U.K. and overseas	Semipersistent
Methyl allyl chloride	Methyl allyl chloride	Stored products: overseas	Nonpersistent: fumigant
Dichloroethyl ether	Dichloroethyl ether	Stored products: overseas	Nonpersistent: fumigant
Chloropicrin..............	Chloropicrin	Stored products, soil: U.K. and overseas	Nonpersistent: fumigant
Dichloronitroethane.......	Dichloronitroethane	Stored products: overseas	Persistent
B. Organophosphorus Compounds			
TEPP (HETP)...........	Tetraethyl pyrophosphate	Growing plants: U.K. and overseas	Nonpersistent: surface contact
Parathion...............	O,O-Diethyl o,p-nitrophenyl thion phosphate	Growing plants, soil: U.K. and overseas	Semipersistent: surface contact, stomach poison
Paraoxon...............	Diethyl-p-nitrophenyl phosphate	Growing plants: U.K.	Semipersistent: stomach poison, systemic
E.838	Diethylthiophosphoric acid ester of 7-hydroxy-4-methylcoumarin	Growing plants: overseas	Semipersistent: surface contact, stomach poison
Malathion	O,O-Dimethyl dithiophosphate of diethyl mercaptosuccinate [formerly known as S-(1,2-dicarboxyethyl)-O,O-dimethyl dithiophosphate]	Growing plants: overseas	Semipersistent: surface contact
Schradan...............	Bisdimethylaminophosphonous anhydride or octamethyl-pyrophosphoramide	Growing plants: U.K. and overseas	Semipersistent: systemic
Dimefox................	Bis(dimethylamino)fluoro-phosphine oxide	Growing plants: U.K. and overseas	Semipersistent: systemic
Mipafox................	Bis(monoisopropylamino)fluoro-phosphine oxide	Growing plants: U.K. and overseas	Semipersistent: systemic
Systox	Diethylthiophosphoric ester of β-ethyl mercaptoethanol	Growing plants: overseas	Semipersistent: systemic
EPN...................	O-Ethyl o,p-nitrophenyl benzene thiophosphate	Growing plants: overseas	Semipersistent: surface contact, stomach poison
C. Nitrophenol Compounds			
DNC...................	2-Methyl-4,6-dinitrophenol	Dormant trees: U.K. and overseas	Semipersistent: surface contact
Dinoseb	2-(1-Methyl-n-propyl)-4,6-dinitrophenol or 2-sec-butyl-4,6-dinitrophenol or 2,4-dinitro-6-sec-butylphenol	Dormant trees: U.K. and overseas	Semipersistent: surface contact

INSECTICIDES   *(continued)*

Common name or code number	Chemical name	Type of commodity treated	Persistence and site of action
D. Compounds of Vegetable Origin			
Nicotine..............	3-(1-Methyl-2-pyrrolidyl)-pyridine	Stored products, growing plants: U.K. and overseas	Nonpersistent: surface contact, stomach poison, fumigant
Pyrethrum............	Mixture of pyrethrins I and II and cinerins I and II extracted from pyrethrum flowers	Stored products, growing plants, livestock: U.K. and overseas	Semipersistent: surface contact
Derris................	Mixture of rotenone and related compounds extracted from roots of *Derris, Lonchocarpus,* and *Tephrosia* spp.	Growing plants, livestock: U.K. and overseas	Semipersistent: surface contact, stomach poison
E. Inorganic Compounds			
Lead arsenate...........	Diplumbic hydrogen arsenate	Growing plants, soil: U.K. and overseas	Persistent: stomach poison
Basic lead arsenate	Mixture of ill-defined basic arsenates	Growing plants, soil: U.K. and overseas	Persistent: stomach poison
Calcium arsenate	Calcium arsenate	Growing plants, soil: U.K. and overseas	Persistent: stomach poison
Paris green	Copper acetoarsenite	Soil, ground baits: U.K. and overseas	Persistent: stomach poison
Sodium fluorosilicate......	Sodium fluorosilicate	Growing plants, ground baits: U.K. and overseas	Persistent: stomach poison
Cryolite	Sodium fluoroaluminate	Growing plants, ground baits: U.K. and overseas	Persistent: stomach poison
Barium fluosilicate........	Barium fluosilicate	Growing plants, ground baits: U.K. and overseas	Persistent: stomach poison
Calomel	Mercurous chloride	Soil, seed: U.K. and overseas	Persistent: stomach poison

passage of electricity from a conductor. **thermal-** A packing that is nonconductive to heat.

insulin. $C_{45}H_{69}O_{14}N_{11}S \cdot 3H_2O$. Iletin, glucokinin. White, levorotatory crystals, m.233. A protein hormone secreted by the islets of Langerhans in the pancreas; a deficiency results in diabetes. Each unit is one-third of the amount required to lower the blood sugar in a normal rabbit for a given time. **globin-** A clear aqueous solution containing 80 units of i. in combination with a blood globin and a little zinc. Its effects are more lasting and controllable than are those of ordinary i.

    i. zinc suspension. A sterile aqueous suspension of i. with added zinc chloride such that the solid phase consists of 70% crystalline and 30% amorphous i.; an intermediate-acting i. (U.S.P.). *extended-* Long-acting i. zinc suspension having a crystalline solid phase. *prompt-* Rapid-acting i. zinc suspension whose solid phase is amorphous (U.S.P.).

intaglio. A process of printing from plates which

have been etched slightly in recess; the ink filling these is absorbed by the paper. See *rotogravure.*

intarvin. $C_3H_5(C_{16}H_{33}COO)_3 = 848.7$. Margarin, glycerol trimargarate. A fat used to treat diabetes, to produce an increase of sugar, but not of β-hydroxybutyric acid.

integration. (1) Assimilation or synthesis, as opposed to disintegration. (2) The summation of a series of values of a continuously varying quantity. Cf. *calculus.*

intensification. (1) A process of concentrating force. (2) In photography, to increase the density of a photographic image.

intensity. The strength or amount of energy per unit space. **acid-** Hydrogen-ion concentration. **color-** The (1) brilliance or (2) saturation of a color. Cf. *Beer's law.* **electric-** The electric moment per unit volume. **electric field-** The electric field which exerts a force of one dyne on a unit positive charge. **heat-** Temperature. **light-** Brightness. **magnetic field-** The magnetic field which exerts a

INSECTICIDES (*continued*)

Common name or code number	Chemical name	Type of commodity treated	Persistence and site of action
	F. Miscellaneous Compounds		
Carbon disulfide	Carbon disulfide	Stored products, soil: U.K. and overseas	Nonpersistent: fumigant
Prussic acid..............	Hydrogen cyanide	Stored products, soil, growing plants: U.K. and overseas	Nonpersistent: fumigant
Calcium cyanide..........	Calcium cyanide	Stored products, soil, growing plants: U.K. and overseas	Nonpersistent: fumigant
Ethylene oxide...........	Ethylene oxide	Stored products: U.K. and overseas	Nonpersistent: fumigant
Azobenzene	Azobenzene	Growing plants: U.K. and overseas	Semipersistent: fumigant
Azoxybenzene............	Azoxybenzene	Growing plants: U.K. and overseas	Semipersistent: fumigant
Allethrin	*dl*-2-Allyl-4-hydroxy-3-methyl-2-cyclopenten-1-one ester of a mixture of *cis*- and *trans-dl*-chrysanthemum monocarboxylic acid	Stored products, livestock: overseas	Semipersistent: surface contact
Piperonyl butoxide	(3,4-Methylenedioxy-6-propylbenzyl)(butyl)-diethylene glycol ether	Synergists for pyrethrins: U.K. and overseas	Semipersistent: surface contact
Tar oil	Phenolic compounds obtained from coal-tar distillates	Dormant trees: U.K. and overseas	Semipersistent: surface contact
Petroleum oil (summer)..............	Highly refined light petroleum oil	Growing plants: U.K. and overseas	Persistent: surface contact
Petroleum oil (winter)	Partially refined light petroleum oil	Dormant trees: U.K. and overseas	Persistent: surface contact

From "Toxic Chemicals in Agriculture" (London: H.M. Stationery Office, 1953). Cf. *fungicides, herbicides, rodenticides.*

force of one dyne on a unit magnetic pole (gauss). **magnetization-** The magnetic moment per unit volume. **sound-** Degree of loudness.

   i. factor. Of acidity, pH; of redox, rH.

inter- Prefix (Latin) indicating between.

interenin. A hormone from the suprarenal gland, containing 30% chlorine.

Interessen Gemeinschaft. I.G. A cooperative organization of large German chemical industries. Dissolved after World War II, and succeeded by one of its component companies, Badische Anilin und Soda Fabrik, A.G.

interface. Interphase. The boundary between 2 phases. Cf. *zone.*

interference. A conflict between 2 agencies which produces a retardation effect, or a waste of energy. **light-** The effect produced by 2 sets of light waves which annul each other and produce darkness. **sound-** The effect produced by 2 sets of sound waves which annul each other and produce silence.

   i. colors. Complementary *colors.*

interferometer. An instrument to determine the wavelength of light from interference by waves of known lengths. Cf. *fringes.*

interferon. A protein, mol. wt. approx. 63,000, from the dead virus infection of certain vertebrates.

It interferes with the growth of other viruses, especially in cells of species from which it is derived.

intermediate. A chemical used in organic synthesis; in the production of pharmaceuticals, dyes, or other artificial products; usually a derivative of "crudes" or raw materials.

intermetallic. Describing compounds of 2 or more metals (as distinct from alloys); e.g., NiAl or $CrBe_2$. **i. compound.** A compound of metals in stoichiometric proportions. Cf. *alloy.*

intermolecular. Referring to action between molecules. Cf. *intramolecular.*

internal. Pertaining to the inside. **i. anhydride.** A compound formed by elimination of water from the atoms of a molecule. **i. compensation.** The property of an optically inactive molecule that contains 2 asymmetric C atoms, one dextro-, the other levorotatory. **i. reaction.** A reaction within a molecule due to atomic rearrangement. **i. salt.** An organic compound formed by the union of a basic and acid radical within the molecule. **i. standard.** The principal line in spectrum analysis, by the logarithmic sector method, q.v.

international. Agreed upon between nations. **i. atomic weights.** Values for atomic weights selected by the I. Union of Pure and Applied Chemistry, q.v. **i. catalogue.** A pre-1914 reference index of the scientific literature of the world. **I. Organization for Standardization.** I.S.O. An association of 50 countries concerned with the standardization of technical data, nomenclature, specifications, and testing methods. **i. practical temperature scale.** See *temperature*. **i. temperature scale.** See *temperature*. **I. Union of Pure and Applied Chemistry.** I.U.P.A.C. An organization which standardizes chemical nomenclature, notation, symbols, data, atomic weights, etc. Its current reports are dated 1957 (inorganic and organic *nomenclature*) and 1959 (physicochemical *symbols* and terminology), q.v. Published by Butterworth Scientific Publications, London. Reports for 1961 onward are published in a *Journal*. A similar organization exists for physics. **i. unit.** (1) See *unit*. (2) I. U. A measure of the vitamin potency of a substance. See *vitamin units*.

interphase. Interfacial *zone*.

interpolation. The deduction of a value of a variable quantity, from values already known, by the use of arithmetical or graphical methods.

interruptor. A device for breaking an electric current.

interstice. A small space or capillary in a structure or tissue. **atomic-** The distance between the atoms in a molecule.

intertraction. Barophoresis. The increase in density of a colloidal solution (e.g., albumin) placed on a salt solution of nearly equal density, due to the rapid diffusion of the solute.

intolerance. Inability to withstand the effects of a drug.

intoxication. Poisoning by a drug.

intra- Prefix (Latin) indicating within.

intra-annular. Within the ring. **i. tautomerism.** The redistribution of double bonds within a ring. Cf. *intranuclear*.

intra-atomic. Pertaining to atomic structure. **i. matter.** Matter from which atoms are assumed to be constructed, e.g., electrons and positive nuclei.

intramine. $[C_6H_4(NH_2)S—]_2 = 248.1$. o,o'- Dithiobisaniline, contramine; an antiseptic.

intramolecular. Pertaining to the inside of molecules or to molecular structure. Cf. *internal, intermolecular*. **i. action.** A reaction occurring within the individual molecule. **i. condensation.** Ring formation. A reaction in which the atoms of an organic compound combine or rearrange and form a condensation (usually a ring) compound and another (usually binary) compound. **i. oxidation and reduction.** An internal oxidation and reduction reaction; as, $C_6H_4 \cdot CH_3 \cdot NO_2 \rightarrow C_6H_4 \cdot COOH \cdot NH_2$.

intramuscular. Inside muscular tissue; as of an injection.

intranuclear. (1) Within an atomic nucleus. (2) Within a molecular ring system. **i. tautomerism.** The shifting of a double bond within one or more rings.

intraval sodium. Thiopentone sodium.

intravenous. Within blood vessels, e.g., an injection.

intravital. Within the living organism.

introduction. Causing the entry of a different type of atom into an organic molecule, e.g., chlorination.

introfaction. A change in the fluidity and specific wetting properties of an impregnating material, due to an introfier.

introfier. Impregnation accelerator. A substance that speeds up the penetrating power of fluids; as: **sulfur-** Naphthalene or its derivatives which, when added to molten sulfur, accelerate its penetration into fiberboards.

intrusion. Forcing a material into the cavities or pores of a substance.

intumescence. (1) Swelling up, especially of certain crystals on heating. (2) Popping, puffing. The violent escape of moisture on heating.

inula. Elecampane, alant root, elfwort, horseheal, helenium. The dried rhizome of *Inula helenium*, (Compositae), U.S., Europe, and Central Asia; an expectorant and stimulant. **i. camphor.** Helenin.

inulase. Inulinase. A hydrolytic enzyme from fungi and other plants, which changes inulin to levulose.

inulenin. $(C_6H_{10}O_5)_x \cdot 2H_2O$. A carbohydrate associated with inulin. Colorless needles, soluble in water.

inulic acid. Alantic acid.

inulin. $C_{36}H_{62}O_{31} = 990.8$. Alant starch, alantin, dahlin, sinistrin. A carbohydrate from the rhizome of *Inula helenium* or *Dahlia variabilis*. White powder, m.160 (decomp.), soluble in hot water; a culture medium. **pseudo-** $(C_7H_{10}O_5)_6$. A polysaccharide; irregular granules, soluble in hot water.

inulinase. Inulase.

in vacuo. In a vacuum, q.v.

Invar. Trademark for the ferronickel: Ni 36, steel 64% (carbon content 0.2%), d.8.0, m.1500. It has a low coefficient of heat expansion; used for precision instruments.

inversion. (1) The turning of a levo to a dextro compound, or vice versa. (2) The change of an isomeric compound to its opposite, as a cis to a trans compound. (3) The hydrolysis of an optically active disaccharide to 2 optically active monosaccharides; e.g., the hydrolysis of cane sugar to dextrose and levulose by dilute acids, alkalies, or enzymes, resulting in a change in the direction and degree of rotation of polarized light. Cf. *Walden i., Clerget i.* (4) In an emulsion of 2 immiscible liquids, the interchange of the internal and external phases. **i. point.** The temperature at which i. takes place.

invertase. Now officially β-fructofuranosidase. Saccharase, sucrase, raffinase, invertin. A carbohydrase of the pancreatic juice and of yeast, which converts cane sugar into invert sugar.

invertin. Invertase.

invert soap. A cationic surface-active detergent, so-called because it ionizes oppositely to soap; e.g., quaternary ammonium or sulfonium compounds.

invert sugar. Approximately 50% dextrose and 50% levulose obtained by the acid hydrolysis of cane sugar. It is slightly levorotatory, fermentable, reduces Fehling's solution; used in brewing.

in vitro. Describing a biological reaction which can be performed outside the living organism in a test tube. Cf. *in vivo*.

in vivo. Describing a reaction which takes place within the living organism. Cf. *in vitro.*

inyoite. $2CaO\cdot3B_2O_3\cdot13H_2O.$ A native borate (S. California).

iod- See *iodo-, iodi-.*

iodacetanilide. $C_6H_4INHCOMe = 260.9.$ Iodantifebrin. Colorless crystals, m.182, insoluble in water; an antipyretic.

iodacetone. $CH_2I\cdot CO\cdot CH_3 = 184.1.$ Iodoacetone, monoiodoacetone. Colorless crystals; used to treat carbuncles.

iodagol. A colloidal antiseptic iodine preparation.

iodal. $C_2I_3OH = 421.77.$ A hypnotic liquid resembling chloral.

iodalbin. A red compound of blood albumen and iodine, of molasses-like odor.

iodalphionic acid. $C_{15}H_{12}O_3I_2 = 494.08.$ White crystals, m.162 (decomp.), insoluble in water; a radiopaque medium (U.S.P.).

iodaniline. Iodoaniline.

iodanisole. $C_6H_4IOMe = 234.2.$ Orthoiodanisole. Yellow liquid, d.1.80, b.240, insoluble in water; an antiseptic and local irritant.

iodantifebrin. Iodacetanilide.

iodate. A salt of iodic acid, containing the radical IO_3—.

Iodatol. Trade name for an injection of iodized oil.

iodeikon. Sodium tetraiodophenolphthalein; an X-ray contrast medium.

iodeosin. $C_{20}H_8O_5O_4 = 835.4.$ Erythrosin, tetraiodofluorescein. A red indicator powder, soluble in alcohol (alkalies—rose-red, acids-yellow). **i. solution.** A 0.0002% solution of iodeosin in ether. This is added to dilute alkali and titrated until the rose tint passes from the ether into the aqueous solution.

iodi- See *iodo-.*

iodic acid. $HIO_3 = 175.93.$ Colorless rhombs, m.110, soluble in water. Used as an oxidizing agent; reagent for alkaloids, biliary pigments, naphthol, sulfocyanides, and guaiacol; in organic synthesis; and for volumetric solutions. **dimeso**–$H_4I_2O_9.$ **i. anhydride.** Iodine pentoxide.

iodide. MI. A binary compound of iodine with a metal. **i. ion.** The I^- ion.

iodimetry. Iodometry.

iodinated (I^{131}) serum. A sterile solution of human serum albumin, treated with I^{131} and freed from iodide; used to diagnose circulatory system complaints (B.P.).

iodine. $I_2 = 253.81,$ or $I = 126.90.$ Iodum. A nonmetallic element, at. no. 53, of the halogen group. Rhombic, bluish black lustrous plates or scales, d.4.948, m.114, b.184, slightly soluble in water, soluble in alcohol or iodide solutions. Discovered by Courtois (1811) and named after its purple vapors (Greek: iodes, the violet, and ion, similar). Obtained from the mother liquor of Chile saltpeter and seaweed ash, and widespread in nature. World production (1966) 19 million lb. Valency: usually 1 (iodides); or 3 (iodonium) or 5 (iodates). Used as a reagent in volumetric analysis, in organic synthesis, in the manufacture of iodides, iodates, and iodine preparations, and as an alterative, antiseptic, and caustic. **eka-**Eline. **fluoro-** Fluoroiodine. **solution of-** (1) Lugol solution. (2) Colorless: Lugol solution decolorized with sodium thiosulfate. (3)

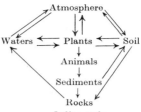
Iodine cycle.

Iodine water, q.v. **tincture of-** An alcoholic 7% iodine solution in 5% potassium iodide solution.

i. acetate. $I(C_2H_3O_2)_3 = 304.00.$ A solid prepared from chlorine dioxide and i. in glacial acetic acid. **i. bromides.** $IBr,$ i. monobromide; $IBr_3,$ i. tribromide; $IBr_5,$ i. pentabromide. **i. chlorides.** $ICl,$ i. monochloride; $ICl_3,$ i. trichloride. **i. cyanide.** $ICN = 152.9.$ Cyanogen i. Colorless crystals, m.146, soluble in water. Used as an animal poison and preservative for insect and mammal collections. **i. dioxide.** $IO_2 = 158.93$ or $I_2O_4 = 317.86.$ Yellow powder, decomp. into its elements at 130. **i. disulfide.** Sulfur iodide. **i. green.** A phenolphthalein dye pH-indicator, changing at 1.0 from yellow (acid) to blue-green (alkaline); also stains liquefied xylem in plant tissues. **i. fluoride.** See *i. pentafluoride* and *i. fluoriodide.* **i. monobromide.** $IBr = 206.8.$ Purple crystals, m.36, soluble in water (decomp.). Used in analysis (iodine numbers) and in organic synthesis. **i. monochloride.** $ICl = 162.4.$ Brown oil, d.3.182, b.101 (decomp.), decomp. by water; used in analysis and organic synthesis. **i. number.** I. absorption value, Hübl number, Wijs number. The quantity of i., in milligrams, absorbed by 1 gm fat or oil under specified conditions; it indicates the amount of unsaturated acids present. *hydro-* The number of parts of hydrogen (calculated as the equivalent amount of I) absorbed by 100 parts of a fat. **i. oxide.** (1) I. dioxide. (2) I. pentoxide. (3) $I_4O_9(?) = 651.73.$ A green supposed oxide of i. **i. pentabromide.** $IBr_5 = 526.7.$ Brown liquid, decomp. by water; a reagent. **i. pentafluoride.** $IF_5 = 221.93.$ A compound of pentavalent i., b.97. **i. pentoxide.** $I_2O_5 = 333.9.$ Iodic anhydride. White crystals, soluble in water; an oxidizing agent. **i. sulfate.** $I_2(SO_4)_3 = 542.07.$ Yellow crystals, soluble in water. **i. tincture.** See *tincture of i.* **i. tribromide.** $IBr_3 = 366.7.$ Tribromoiodine. Brown liquid, soluble in water; an antiseptic. **i. trichloride.** $ICl_3 = 233.3.$ Yellow, deliquescent crystals, decomp. 25, soluble in water; an antiseptic and disinfectant. **i. value.** I. number. **i. water.** An aqueous 0.02% solution of i.; a reagent.

iodinin. A purple-bronze antibiotic pigment from *Chromobacterium iodinum.*

iodipamide methylglucamine. $C_{34}H_{48}O_{16}N_4I_6(?)$ Yellow liquid; a radiopaque (B.P.).

iodipin. An iodine addition product of the fatty acids of sesame oil; an alterative and X-ray contrast medium.

iodite. A salt of the hypothetical iodous acid containing the $=IO_2$ radical. **hypo-** MOI. A salt of hypoiodous acid.

iodized. Admixed with iodine or an iodide. **i. oil.** Iodatol. A sterile iodine addition product of vegetable oils, usually made by treating poppyseed oil with hydriodic acid (38–42% of organically combined iodine). A viscous oil, used as a radiopaque medium (B.P.). **i. salt.** Common salt containing about 0.3% of potassium iodide.

iodo- Prefix indicating an iodine atom in an organic compound. Cf. *iodoso.*

iodoacetanilide. Iodacetanilide.

iodoacetic acid. $CH_2ICOOH = 185.95$. Carboxymethyl iodide. Yellow crystals, m.82 (decomp.), insoluble in water.

iodoaniline. $C_6H_4INH_2 = 219.0$ Aminoiodobenzene. **ortho-** Colorless needles, m.57. **meta-** Colorless leaflets, m.25. **para-** Colorless needles, m.63. Insoluble in water.

iodobenzene. $C_6H_5I = 204.0$. Colorless liquid, b.188, insoluble in water.

iodocasein. A compound of milk casein and 18% iodine. Brown powder, insoluble in water.

iodochlorhydroxyquin. $C_9H_5ONClI = 305.50$. 3-Chloro-7-iodo-8-quinolinol. Spongy, yellow powder, darkens in light, m.180, insoluble in water; a local anti-injective (U.S.P.).

iodocrase. $Ca_6[Al(OH·F)],Al_2(SiO_4)_3$. Vesuvianite.

iodocresine, iodocresol. Traumatol.

iodocrol. Carvacrol iodide.

iodoethylene. $CH_2:CHI = 153.9$. Vinyl iodide. Colorless liquid, b.56, slightly soluble in water.

iodoform. $CHI_3 = 393.8$. Triiodomethane, methenyl iodide, formyl triiodide. Iodoformum. Yellow hexagons, sublime 119 (decomp.), slightly soluble in water or alcohol; an antiseptic, alterative, and antituberculant.

iodogorgoic acid. $HO·C_6H_2I_2·CH_2CH(NH_2)COOH = 432.92$. 3,5-Diiodotyrosine. An amino acid from proteins. **dl-** Rectangular prisms, m.204. **d-** White needles, m.194.

iodohydromol. Thymol iodide.

iodol. $C_4HI_4N = 570.74$. Tetraiodopyrrole. Brown powder, m.150 (decomp); an antiseptic.

iodoleine. Iodized poppy-seed oil, used medicinally. Cf. *iodized oil.*

iodomethane. Methyl iodide.

iodometric. Iodimetric. Pertaining to iodometry. **i. acid value.** Acidity determined in terms of the amount of iodine liberated from an iodide-iodate mixture.

iodometry. Iodimetry. A method of volumetric analysis, by titration of a standard iodine solution and standard sodium thiosulfate solution: $I_2 + Na_2S_2O_3 \leftrightarrows 2NaI + Na_2S_4O_6$. Starch solution is indicator. Used to determine halogens, halides, hydrogen sulfide, sulfur dioxide, arsenic salts, manganese dioxide, ferrous salts, etc.

iodonium. The iodine atom $\equiv I$ in an organic compound. **i. hydroxide.** The radical $=I-OH$, as in Ph_2IOH. **i. iodide.** The radical $=I-I$, as in $Ph_2I·I$.

iodopanoic acid. Iopanoic acid.

iodophen. Nosophen.

iodophor. A bactericidal complex of iodine and a nonionic surface-active agent, which releases iodine in water.

iodophosphonium. Phosphonium iodide.

iodophthalein sodium. $C_{20}H_8O_4N_2I_4·3H_2O = 919.95$. Blue crystals, with a saline, astringent taste, decomp. in air, soluble in water; radiopaque medium (U.S.P.).

iodopropionic acid. $C_3H_5O_2I = 200.0$. **alpha-** $MeCH_2ICOOH$. Colorless prisms, m.45, soluble in water. **beta-** CH_2ICH_2COOH. Colorless leaflets, m.82, soluble in water.

iodopyracet. $C_{11}H_{16}O_5N_2I_2 = 510.08$. Diodone. The diethanolamine salt of 3,5-diodo-4-pyridone-N-acetic acid. Colorless liquid, d.1.19.

iodoso. The radical —IO, from iodonium hydroxide. **i. benzene.** $C_6H_5IO = 220.0$. Colorless powder, explodes 210, soluble in water.

iodosol. Thymol iodide.

iodous acid. The hypothetical acid H_2IO_2, known as its salts. **hypo-** The unstable acid HIO; decomposes to HI and HIO_3.

iodotannic acid. Iodotannin. Brown powder obtained from iodine and tannic acid; an alterative and astringent.

iodothyrin. $C_{11}H_{10}O_3NI_3 = 584.89$. The iodine compound of the thyroid glands.

iodotoluene. $C_7H_7I = 218.0$. Methyliodobenzene. **ortho-** Colorless liquid, b.211. **meta-** Colorless liquid, d.1.70, b.204. **para-** Colorless leaflets, m.35. All insoluble in water.

iodoxy. The radical —IO₂. **i. benzene.** $C_6H_5IO_2 = 236.0$. Colorless needles, m.167, explode 230, soluble in water.

iodoxyl. $C_8H_3O_5NI_2Na_2 = 492.92$. Neiopax, uroselectan-B, disodium iodomethamate. White powder, m. (free acid) 171 (decomp.), soluble in water; an injection radiopaque.

iodstarin. $Me(CH_2)_{10}·CI_2(CH_2)_4COOH$, 5,5-Diiodoheptadecanoic acid*, decomp. by light to tariric acid, q.v.

iodum. The pharmaceutical name for iodine.

iodylin. Bismuth iodosalicylate; an iodoform substitute.

iodyrite. AgI. A native silver iodide.

iolanthite. A jasper from Oregon.

iolite. $Mg_4Al_8O_6(SiO_3)_{10}$. Cordierite, dichroite, water sapphire. A blue orthorhombic magnesium aluminum metasilicate, hardness 7, d.2.65; a gem.

ion. An electrically charged (1) atom, (2) radical, or (3) molecule. If positively charged, it is called a *cation* (or *posion*); if negative, an *anion* (or *negion*). Ions travel in solution to the cathode (posode) and anode (negode), respectively. Cf. *ionic theory.* Classification: (1) Positive atoms (K⁺). (2) Negative atoms (Cl⁻). (3) Positive radicals (NH₄⁺). (4) Negative radicals (NO₃⁻). (5) Positive molecules (H₂⁺). (6) Negative molecules (N₂⁻). **acid-** Anion. **amphoteric-** Zwitter i. **aquated-** An i. surrounded by oriented water molecules. Cf. *solvated.* **basic-** Cation. **colloidal.** Micelle. **hydrogen-** See *hydrogen.* **hydroxyl-** See *hydroxyl.* **molecular-** A positive or negative gaseous i., e.g., produced under the influence of radiation. Cf. *activation, excitation.* **negative-** Anion. **positive-** Cation. **solvated-** An i. surrounded by oriented molecules of solvent. **zwitter-.** Amphoteric. An i. having both a negative and positive charge; as, ⁺NH₃RCOO⁻. See table, pp. 356–357.

i. burn. I. spot. A defect produced in cathode-ray tubes, believed to be due to ions issuing from the thermionic cathode. **i. exchange column.** A vertical tube filled with an i. exchange resin. See *resins, zeolite.* Used to separate mixtures into their constituents, e.g., by percolating a solution down the column. **i. product.** Solubility product. **i. retardation.** The slowing down of the passage of ions through a gel or resin in ion exchange, due to weak ionic associations. **i. spot.** I. burn. **i. states.** (1) Solid i., surrounded by oppositely charged ions; as in a polar crystal. (2) Liquid i., surrounded by oriented molecules of the solvent; as in a solution. (3) Gaseous i., with kinetic motion overcoming electrostatic charge; as in an ionized gas.

ionene. $C_{13}H_{18}$ = 174.14. 1,2,3,4-Tetrahydro-1,1,6-trimethyl naphthalene. A hydrocarbon formed on dehydration of ionone. Cf. *irene*.

ionic. Pertaining to electrically charged atoms, radicals, or molecules. **i. charge.** The unit electric charge carried by the hydrogen ion, e = 4.77×10^{-10} esu, or 1.59×10^{-20} emu. The i. charge of an element is denoted by a suffix superscript, thus, S^{++}. **i. conductivity.** The passage of a current in solution by means of ions. **i. migration.** The passage of ions toward the anode or cathode; as, in electrolysis. **i. mobility.** (1) The motion of ions in a solution, expressed numerically by the velocity under a gradient of 1 volt/cm. It is a periodic function of the atomic weight: H^+, 3.25×10^{-4}; OH^-, 1.78×10^{-4}; K^+ 6.5×10^{-4} cm/sec. (2) The velocity of ions under the influence of an electric current. **i. number.** The number of extranuclear electrons of an ion. It equals the atomic number plus or minus the valence electrons. **i. potential.** Assuming the ion in a crystal to be a charged sphere of definite extension, then the i.p. = valence/radius of ion. Cf. *ionization potential*. **i. radius.** The distance in angstroms from the periphery of the effective sphere from the center of a charged atom or group of atoms. **i. reactions.** Reactions characteristic of an ion; as, the precipitation of Cl^- by Ag^+. **i. theory.** Electrolytes dissociate into component ions when dissolved in water. **i. velocity.** The product of the mobility of an ion and the actual potential gradient. Cf. *migration*.

ionidine. $C_{19}H_{25}O_4N_4$ = 373.5. An alkaloid from the California poppy, *Eschscholtzia californica*.

ionise. Ionize.

ionium. Io = 230.5. A radioactive isotope, at. no. 90 (renamed thorium), formed by the disintegration of uranium X. It emits β- and γ-rays and is transformed into radium.

ionization, ionisation. (1) Electrolytic dissociation. The breaking up of a molecule into 2 or more negatively and positively charged components (ions); usually when a polar compound is dissolved in water. Cf. *solvation*. (2) The removal of one or more outer electrons from an atom or molecule, by which gases become electrically charged under the influence of a strong electrostatic field or radioactive rays: $H_2 \rightarrow H_2^+ + e$. Cf. *excitation.*, *i. potential*. **degree of-** The percentage of molecules that become ionized at a given temperature and concentration of solution, to those that remain un-ionized. Measured by the ratio of the equivalent conductivity under the conditions concerned to that of the solution at infinite dilution. Cf. *activity coefficient*, *pH value*.

i. constant. The analog of the dissociation constant, $k = [H^+][X^-]/[HX]$, in the application of the law of mass action to i. **i. gage.** See *gage*.

i. potential. The energy, in volts, to remove an electron from an atom in its normal state = 12.345/λ, where λ is the wavelength of a radiation in angstroms. Cf. *orbits, quantum*. **second i. potential.** The energy to remove a second electron completely; it is greater because of the positive charge on the ion. Cf. *ionic potential*.

ionize. To dissociate into ions or to become electrically charged.

ionized, ionised. (1) Describing a molecule that is separated into oppositely charged atoms or radicals, the sum of positive and negative charges being zero. (2) Describing a molecule or atom from which electrons have been removed, whereby it becomes positively charged. **non-** or **un-** Remaining in the molecular condition; not dissociated.

ionizing. The process of ionization, q.v. **i. potential.** Ionization potential. **i. solvent.** A liquid that facilitates ionization, e.g., water, or liquid sulfur dioxide. Organic liquids are generally non-ionizing.

ionogenic. A little-used term for ionic.

ionomer. A polymer having covalent bonds between the constituents of the long-chain molecules, and ionic bonds between the chains.

ionone. $Me_3C_6H_6CH:CHCOMe$ = 192.2. A ketone terpene, and isomer of irone. **alpha-** Colorless liquid, d.0.934, b.120. **beta-** Colorless liquid, d.0.949, b.135. Both slightly soluble in water; used in artificial extract of violets.

ionophoresis. The separation of ions by *electrophoresis*, q.v.

ionosphere. The radio-reflecting part of the Kennelly-Heaviside layer of the upper atmosphere, consisting of changing areas of ionized molecules.

iontophoresis. Migration of ionic medication through unbroken skin under the influence of a direct electric current.

ionotropy. The existence of tautomeric ions, a positive or negative atom or group becoming detached from an unsaturated molecule, thus leaving a − or + charge on the residual ion resulting in isomeric ions in dynamic equilibrium. When the detached atom is positive (H^+) the phenomenon is called *cationotropy*; when it is negative (OH^-), *anionotropy*; in the special case of H^+, *prototopy* (cf. *pseudo acid*), and in the case of OH^-, *pseudobasicity* (cf. *pseudo base*).

iopanoic acid. $C_{11}H_{12}O_2NI_3$ = 570.96. Creamy powder, insoluble in water, m.156 (decomp.); radiopaque medium (U.S.P.).

iopax. Uroselectan. Sodium-2-oxo-5-idopyridine-N-acetate. Used in pyelography.

iophendylate. $C_{19}H_{29}O_2I$ = 416.35. A sterile mixture of the isomers of ethyliodophenyldecylate. Yellow liquid with ethereal odor, slightly soluble in water, ref. index 1.5230–1.5260; a radiopaque medium (U.S.P., B.P.).

Iosol. Trademark for a series of organic solvent-soluble dyes for plastics and lacquers.

iothalamic acid. $C_{11}H_9O_4N_2I_3$ = 613.92. White powder, slightly soluble in water (B.P.).

iothion. Diiodohydroxypropane, diiodopropyl alcohol. Yellow oil, d.2.4, insoluble in water; used in external iodine ointments.

Ipatiev reaction. The catalytic reduction of ketones to alcohols, with nickel oxide under pressure.

Ipatiew. Ipatiev.

LIST OF NAMES FOR IONS AND RADICALS

(In organic chemistry substitutive names are seldom used, but the organic chemical names are shown to draw attention to certain differences between organic and inorganic nomenclature.)

Atom or group	As neutral molecule	As cation or cationic radical	As anion	As ligand	As prefix for substituent in organic compounds
H.........	Monohydrogen	Hydrogen	Hydride	Hydro	
F.........	Monofluorine	....	Fluoride	Fluoro	Fluoro
Cl	Monochlorine	Chlorine	Chloride	Chloro	Chloro
Br	Monobromine	Bromine	Bromide	Bromo	Bromo
I	Monoiodine	Iodine	Iodide		
I_3.........	....	....	Triiodide		
ClO........	....	Chlorosyl	Hypochlorite	Hypochlorito	
ClO_2	Chlorine dioxide	Chloryl	Chlorite	Chlorito	
ClO_3	....	Perchloryl	Chlorate	Chlorato	
ClO_4......	....	....	Perchlorate		
IO........	....	Iodosyl	Hypoiodite	....	Iodoso
IO_2.......	....	Iodyl	....	....	Iodyl or iodoxy
O.........	Monoöxygen	....	Oxide	Oxo	Oxo or keto
O_2........	Dioxygen	....	$O_2^=$: peroxide O_2^-: superoxide	Peroxo	Peroxy
HO	Hydroxyl	....	Hydroxide	Hydroxo	Hydroxy
HO_2	Perhydroxyl	....	Hydrogen peroxide	Hydrogen peroxo	Hydroperoxy
S	Monosulfur	....	Sulfide	Thio (sulfido)	Thio
HS	Sulfhydryl	....	Hydrogen sulfide	Thiolo	Mercapto
S_2	Disulfur	....	Disulfide	Disulfido	
SO.........	Sulfur monoxide	Sulfinyl (thionyl)	....	....	Sulfinyl
SO_2........	Sulfur dioxide	Sulfonyl (sulfuryl)	Sulfoxylate	....	Sulfonyl
SO_3........	Sulfur trioxide	....	Sulfite	Sulfito	
HSO_3	....	....	Hydrogen sulfite	Hydrogen sulfito	
S_2O_3	....	....	Thiosulfate	Thiosulfato	
SO_4......	....	....	Sulfate	Sulfato	
Se	Selenium	....	Selenide	Seleno	Seleno
SeO	....	Seleninyl	....	....	Seleninyl
SeO_2	....	Selenonyl	....	....	Selenonyl
SeO_3	Selenium trioxide	....	Selenite	Selenito	
SeO_4	....	....	Selenate	Selenato	
Te	Tellurium	....	Telluride	Telluro	Telluro
CrO_3	....	Chromyl			
UO_2	....	Uranyl			
NpO_2	....	Neptunyl			
PuO_2	....	Plutonyl			
AmO_3	....	Americyl			

ipecac. Ipecacuanha, ipecac root. The dried root of *Cephaelis ipecacuanha*, Rio ipecac, or *Cephaelis acuminata*, Carthagena ipecac (Rubiaceae). It contains 1.75% alkaloids (emetine, cepheline, etc.); an emetic, antiamebic, stomachic, and expectorant (U.S.P., B.P.). **American-** Gillenia. **Goanese-** Naregamine.

ipecacuanhic acid. $C_{14}H_{18}O_7 = 298.12$. Brown powder from the roots of *Psychotria ipecacuanha*.

I.P.K. International Prototype kilogram.

I.P.M. International Prototype meter.

ipoh. Malayan arrow poisons from Strychnos species. Cf. *upas*.

ipomic acid. Sebacic acid.

ipomoea. (1) Mexican scammony root. The dried root of *I. orizabensis* (Convolvulaceae). (2) A genus of Convolvulaceae, yielding jalap and turpeth; a cathartic.

ipomoein. A globulin from the sweet potato, *Ipomoea batatas*.

Ipral. $Ca(C_9H_{13}O_3N_2)_2 \cdot 3H_2O$. Trademark for the calcium salt of ethylisopropylbarbituric acid. Colorless crystals, m.202, soluble in water; a hypnotic.

ipsilene. A gaseous disinfectant made by heating ethyl chloride and iodoform under pressure.

LIST OF NAMES FOR IONS AND RADICALS (*continued*)

Atom or group	As neutral molecule	As cation or cationic radical	An anion	As ligand	As prefix for substituent in organic compounds
N.........	Mononitrogen	....	Nitride	Nitrido	
N_3......	....	....	Azide	Azido	
NH......	....	....	Imide	Imido	Imino
NH_2......	....	....	Amide	Amido	Amino
NHOH....	....	....	Hydroxylamide	Hydroxylamido	Hydroxylamino
N_2H_3......	....	....	Hydrazide	Hydrazido	Hydrazino
NO......	Nitrogen oxide	Nitrosyl	....	Nitrosyl	Nitroso
NO_2......	Nitrogen dioxide	Nitryl	....	Nitro	Nitro
O·NO.....	....	....	Nitrite	Nitrito	
NS.......	....	Thionitrosyl			
$(NS)_n$.....	....	Thiazyl (e.g., trithiazyl)			
NO_3......	....	....	Nitrate	Nitrato	
N_2O_2......	....	....	Hyponitrite	Hyponitrito	
P.........	Phosphorus	....	Phosphide	Phosphido	
PO.......	....	Phosphoryl			
PS.......	....	Thiophosphory			
PH_2O_2....	....	....	Hypophosphite	Hypophosphito	
PHO_3....	....	....	Phosphite	Phosphito	
PO_4......	....	....	Phosphate	Phosphato	
AsO_4......	....	....	Arsenate	Arsenato	
VO.......	....	Vanadyl	....		
CO........	Carbon monoxide	Carbonyl	....	Carbonyl	Carbonyl
CS........	....	Thiocarbonyl	Methanolate	Methoxo	Methoxy
CH_3O......	Methoxyl				
C_2H_5O.....	Ethoxyl	....	Ethanolate	Ethoxo	Ethoxy
CH_3S......	....	....	Methanethiolate	Methanethiolato	Methylthio
C_2H_5S......	....	....	Ethanethiolate	Ethanethiolato	Ethylthio
CN.......	....	Cyanogen	Cyanide	Cyano	Cyano
OCN......	....	....	Cyanatae	Cyanato	Cyanato
SCN......	....	....	Thiocyanate	Thiocyanato and Isothiocyanato	Thiocyanato and Isothiocyanato
SeCN.....	....	....	Selenocyanate	Selenocyanato	Selenocyanato
TeCN.....	....	....	Tellurocyanate	Tellurocyanato	
CO_3......	....	....	Carbonate	Carbonato	
HCO_3.....	....	....	Hydrogen carbonate	Hydrogen carbonato	
$CH_3 \cdot CO_2$....	....	....	Acetate	Acetato	Acetoxy
$CH_3 \cdot CO$....	Acetyl	Acetyl	....	....	Acetyl
C_2O_4......	....	....	Oxalate	Oxalato	

From "Handbook for Chemical Society Authors." 1960.

ipuanine. Artificial *emetine*.

ipuranol. $C_{23}H_{38}O_2(OH)_2$ = 380.31. An alcohol from buphane, m.290.

I.R. (1) Insoluble residue (in analysis). (2) Infrared.

Ir. Symbol for iridium.

iradiation. Irradiation.

iregenone. $MeEtC_6H_3 \cdot CMe_3$ = 176.20. A terpene-like hydrocarbon in the roots of Iris species.

irene. $C_{14}H_{20}$ = 188.17. 1,2,3,4-Tetrahydro-1,1,2,6-tetramethylnaphthalene. A white solid hydrocarbon. Cf. *irone, ionene*.

iretol. $MeO \cdot C_6H_2(OH)_3$ = 156.1. 1,2,3-Tri-hydroxy-5-methoxybenzene, 5-methoxypyrogallol. Colorless crystals, m.186; used in perfumery.

Iridaceae. A family of plants that yield drugs; e.g.: *Iris florentina* (orris), *I. versicolor* (iris).

iridane. 1,2-Dimethyl-3-isopropylcyclopentane. A derivative of linalool.

Iridaz. Trademark for a fluorescent white rayon yarn.

iridescence. Rainbow colors on a surface, as, opals.

iridescent. Describing a surface colored like that of nacre (mother of pearl); usually due to very thin films of air or other material which cause light-ray interference. **i. quartz.** A gem rock crystal with fine interstices, containing air films, which produce combinations of colors.

iridic. Describing a compound of tetravalent iridium. **i. bromide.** $IrBr_4$ = 512.9. Iridium tetrabromide. Hygroscopic, brown powder, or blue crystals, soluble in water. **i. chloride.** $IrCl_4 = 334.9$. Red crystals, soluble in water. **i. iodide.** $IrI_4 = 700.8$. Hygroscopic, black powder, soluble in water. **i. sulfide.** $IrS_2 = 257.3$. Black powder, insoluble in water.

iridin. $C_{24}H_{26}O_{13} = 522.3$. A glucoside from *Iris* species; a cholagogue.

iridious. Iridous.

iridium. $Ir = 192.2$. A metallic element, at. no. 77, of the platinum family; discovered by Tennant (1804). White, brittle, lustrous metal, d.22.42, m.2350, soluble in aqua regia. Used mainly, as alloys with the noble metals, to coat hydrogen electrodes and harden platinum for jewelry (10% Ir); also as catalyst, and with Os, for pen tips and compass bearings. **i. compounds.** Valency 2: irido-, as, IrO. Valency 3: iridous-, as, $IrCl_3$. Valency 4: iridic-, as, IrO_2. **i. sodium chloride.** $Na_2IrCl_6,12H_2O = 691.02$. Sodium iridichloride. Yellow crystals, m.50.

irido- Prefix for divalent iridium: $Ir<$.

iridosmine. Osmiridium.

iridous. Describing a compound of trivalent iridium, $Ir\equiv$. **i. oxide.** $Ir_2O_3 = 434.2$. Iridium trioxide, iridium black. Black powder, soluble in hydrochloric acid; a ceramic pigment.

iris. (1) An iridescent quartz or other mineral. (2) Blue flag. The dried rhizome of *I. versicolor* or *I. caroliana*; as purgative, emetic, or diuretic. (3) A genus of plants (Iridaceae), q.v.

Irish diamond. A gem quartz crystal from Ireland. **I. moss.** Carragheen, killeen. The red seaweeds *Chondrus crispus* and *Gigartina stellata*. The dried thallus of kelps (Ireland, N. America); a demulcent, and a clarifying agent in brewing.

irisin. An extract from *Iris versicolor*, blue flag.

irisoid. The combined principles from *Iris versicolor*, blue flag; a cathartic and alterative.

Irium. Trade name for sodium lauryl sulfate; a detergent.

iron. $Fe = 55.85$. Ferrum. A metallic element, at. no. 26, in the eighth group of the periodic system. Black, lustrous, cubic, magnetic metal, d.7.85, m.1530, b.3200. Compounds: see table below.

Valence	In acid solution	In alkaline solution
2	Fe^{++} ferrous (green)	$HFeO_2^-$ hypoferrite
3	Fe^{3+} ferric (brown or yellow)	FeO_2^- ferrite
4	FeO^{++} ferryl	$HFeO_3^-$ hypoferrate
6	....	$FeO_4^=$ ferrate (purple)

The many modifications of metallic i., (wrought, cast, steel, reduced i.) consist chiefly of its allotropes. **alibated-** I. covered with a protective layer of aluminum. **bicyclopentadienyl-** Ferrocene. **cast-** The molten i. from blast furnaces. Gray masses, m.1275–1505. **ingot-** The malleable i. from the Bessemer process. **malleable-** Wrought. **meteoric-** q.v. **native-** Meteorites. **passive-** I. rendered insoluble in dilute acids, e.g., by immersion in fuming nitric acid or hydrogen peroxide, or by making it the anode in electrolysis. This property is lost by mechanical shock. **pig-** Cast i. **Que-**

vennes- Reduced i. **reduced-** Finely powdered metallic i. obtained by heating ferric oxide in hydrogen. **specular-** Specularite. **steel-** A gray metal, m.1375. See *steel.* **white-** (1) Cast i. containing only combined carbon. (2) Marcasite. **wrought-** Cast i. heated and hammered. A gray metal, d.7.86, m.1505. Pure i. melts at 1535, and pure cementite, Fe_3C, containing 6.67% carbon at 1850. The solid solutions and compounds formed depend on the carbon content and are: α = ferrite; β = beta iron; γ = austenite, a solid solution of carbon in gamma iron; δ = delta iron (stable between 1400 and 1539); Fe_3C = cementite; $\alpha + Fe_3C$ = pearlite. *α-ferrite.* The chief constituent of wrought i., stable below 760, soft, and magnetic; it dissolves little i. carbide. *β-ferrite.* A nonmagnetic i. produced at 760; it dissolves i. carbide. *γ-ferrite.* A nonmagnetic i. produced at 900; it forms solid solutions with i. carbide. α- and β-ferrite are now classed as α-ferrite, the difference in magnetic properties being ignored. Irons contain up to 0.005, steels 0.008–1.7, and cast irons 1.7–5% carbon.

i. acetate. Ferric acetate. **i. alginate.** Ferric alginate. **i. alloys.** See *steel, ferrimanganese, silicon alloys.* **i. alum.** See *alum.* **i. albuminate.** Ferric albuminate. **i. ammonium bromide.** Ferroammonium bromide. **i. ammonium chromate.** Ferriammonium chromate. **i. ammonium chloride.** Ferriammonium chloride. **i. ammonium citrate.** Ferriammonium citrate. **i. ammonium citrate.** See *ammonium ferrocyanide, ammonium ferricyanide.* **i. ammonium oxalate.** Ferriammonium oxalate. **i. ammonium sulfate.** (1) Ferriammonium sulfate. (2) Ferroammonium sulfate. **i. ammonium tartrate.** Ferriammonium tartrate. **i. arsenate.** (1) Ferric arsenate. (2) Ferrous arsenate. **i. benzoate.** Ferric benzoate. **i. black.** Finely divided antimony. **i. brass.** A brass containing 1–9% i. **i. bromide.** (1) Ferric bromide. (2) Ferrous bromide. **i. buff.** Nanking yellow, ferric hydroxide. **i. cacodylate.** Ferric cacodylate. **i. camphorate.** Ferric camphorate. **i. carbide.** (1)$Fe_3C=179.52$. Regular, gray crystals, d.7.07, insoluble in water. (2) $FeC_4 = 103.84$. A gray crystalline mass. **i. carbonate.** (1) Ferric carbonate. (2) Ferrous carbonate. **i. carbonyl.** (1) $Fe(CO)_5 = 195.84$. I. pentacarbonyl. Yellow, viscous liquid, b.103, decomp. 180. (2) $Fe_2(CO)_9 = 363.68$. Diferrocarbonyl. Orange crystals, decomp. by heat. (3) $Fe(CO)_4 = 167.84$. I. tetracarbonyl. Green crystals. **i. chloride.** (1) Ferric chloride. (2) Ferrous chloride. **i. chromate.** Ferric chromate. **i. citrate.** Ferric citrate. **i. citrate green.** Ferriammonium citrate. **i. cyanides.** See *ferric* and *ferrous ferricyanides* and *ferrocyanides.* **i. dextran.** A sterile, aqueous, colloidal solution of a complex of ferric hydroxide with partly hydrolyzed dextran. A hematinic (U.S.P.). **i. dinitrosothiosulfates.** $M[Fe(NO)_2S_2O_3]H_2O$, where M is K or Rb. **i. disulfide.** $FeS_2 = 120.0$. Yellow rhombs, m.1171, produced by the precipitation of ferric salts with hydrogen sulfide. **i. family.** See *iron period.* Cf. *periodic system.* **i. flint.** An opaque variety of quartz, containing i. **i. fluoride.** Ferrous fluoride. **i. formate.** Ferric formate. **i. founding.** Making a facsimile of a pattern by running molten i. into a mold of the pattern. **i. froth.** A fine, spongy variety of hematite. **i. glycerophosphate.** Ferric glycerophosphate. **i. glance.** Hematite. **i. hydroxide.** (1) Ferric hydroxide. (2) Ferrous hydroxide. **i. hypophosphite.** (1) Ferric hypophosphite. (2) Ferrous hypophosphite. **i. hyposulfite.** Ferrous hyposulfite. **i. iodate.** Ferric iodate. **i. iodide.** (1) Ferrous iodide. (2) Ferric iodide. **i. lactate.** (1) Ferric lactate. (2) Ferrous lactate. **i. liquor.** A solution of ferrous acetate. **i. magnesium citrate.** Ferrimagnesium citrate. **i. magnesium lactate.** Ferromagnesium lactate. **i. magnesium sulfate.** Ferromagnesium sulfate. **i. malate.** Ferric malate. **i. manganese chloride.** Ferromanganous chloride. **i. manganese citrate.** Ferrimanganic citrate. **i. manganese iodide.** Ferromanganous iodide. **i. manganese lactate.** Ferromanganous lactate. **i. manganese sulfate.** Ferromanganous sulfate. **i. manganese tartrate.** Ferrimanganic tartrate. **i. minerals.** I. is, after aluminum, the most abundant metal in minerals. E.g.: meteorites, Fe; hematite, Fe_2O_3; pyrite, FeS_2; siderite, $FeCO_3$. **i. mordant.** (1) Ferric sulfate. (2) Ferrous nitrate. **i. nitrate.** (1) Ferric nitrate. (2) Ferrous nitrate. **i. nitride.** Fe_4N. A catalyst for the synthesis of ammonia. **i. nucleinate.** Ferric nucleinate. **i. oleate.** (1) Ferric oleate. (2) Ferrous oleate. **i. oxalate.** Ferric oxalate. **i. oxide.** (1) FeO. Ferrous oxide. (2) Fe_2O_3. Ferric oxide. (3) Fe_3O_4. Ferriferrous oxide. *black-* Ferric oxide. *magnetic-* Ferrous oxide. *red-* Ferric subcarbonate. **i. paranucleinate.** Triferrin. **i. pentacarbonyl.** See *i. carbonyl.* **i. peptonate.** Ferric peptonate. **i. perchlorate.** Ferric perchlorate. **i. perchloride.** Ferriferrous chloride. **i. period.** The central part of the third period in the periodic system, consisting of the elements Cr, Mn, Fe, Co, Ni, and Cu. All form colored salts and ions, and 2 or more series of compounds. **i. persulfate.** Ferriferrous sulfate. **i. phenolate.** Ferric phenate. **i. phosphates.** (1) Ferric phosphate. (2) Ferrous phosphate. **i. phosphide.** FeP = 86.86. Black powder, d.5.2. Also: Fe_2P, Fe_2P_3, Fe_3P, Fe_3P_4. **i. potassium citrate.** Ferripotassium citrate. **i. potassium cyanide.** (1) Potassium ferricyanide. (2) Potassium ferrocyanide. **i. potassium oxalate.** Ferripotassium oxalate. **i. potassium tartrate.** Ferropotassium tartrate. **i. protocarbonate.** Ferrous carbonate. **i. protochloride.** Ferrous chloride. **i. protosulfide.** Ferrous sulfide. **i. putty.** A mixture of ferric oxide and boiled linseed oil, used for pipe joints. **i. pyrite.** Pyrites. **i. pyrophosphate.** Ferric pyrophosphate. **i. pyrosulfate.** Ferric pyrosulfate. **i. pyrothioarsenate.** (1) Ferric pyrothioarsenate. (2) Ferrous pyrothioarsenate. **i. quinine citrate.** Brown-green, water-soluble scales. A pharmaceutical preparation containing 15% quinine, and not more than 11% water. **i. rhodanate.** Ferric thiocyanate. **i. rust.** $2Fe_2O_3 \cdot 3H_2O$. Hydrated ferric oxide. See *ferrous, ferric.* **i. sand.** See *sand.* **i. sesquichloride.** Ferric chloride. **i. sesquioxide.** Ferric oxide. **i. sesquisulfate.** Ferric sulfate. **i. sodium benzoate.** Ferrisodium benzoate. **i. sodium citrate.** Ferrisodium citrate. **i. sodium oxalate.** Ferrisodium oxalate. **i. sodium pyrophosphate.** Ferrisodium pyrophosphate. **i. sodium sulfate.**

Ferrisodium sulfate. **i. spar.** Siderite. **i. sponge.** Ferric oxide. **i. stearate.** Ferric stearate. **i. stone.** Siderite. **i. subcarbonate.** Ferric subcarbonate. **i. subsulfate.** Ferric subsulfate. **i. succinate.** Ferric succinate. **i. sulfate.** (1) Ferrous sulfate. (2) Ferric sulfate. **i. sulfide.** (1) FeS. I. monosulfide. See *ferrous sulfide.* (2) FeS_2. I. disulfide. See *pyrites.* (3) Fe_2S_3. I. trisulfide. See *ferric sulfide.* (4) Fe_3S_4. I. tetrasulfide. See *ferriferrous sulfide.* **i. sulfite.** Ferrous sulfite. **i. sulfocyanate.** Ferric thiocyanate. **i. tannate.** Ferric tannate. **i. tantalate.** Tantalite. **i. tartrate.** (1) Ferric tartrate. (2) Ferrous tartrate. **i. tersulfate.** Ferric sulfate. **i. thiocyanate.** Ferric thiocyanate. **i. trichloride.** Ferric chloride. **i. trioxide.** Ferric oxide. **i. tungstate.** See *ferberite, reinite, wolframite.* **i. valerianate.** Ferric valerianate. **i. vanadate.** Ferric vanadate.

irone. $C_{14}H_{22}O$ = 206.1. Iron. A terpene from orris root, and isomer of ionone. Colorless liquid, d.0.939, $b_{16mm}144$, slightly soluble in water; used in violet perfume.

irradiation. Exposure to: (1) radiation. More specifically to: (2) ultraviolet radiation, especially wavelengths of 250–300 mμ. I. is measured by Eder's solution, q.v.

irregular. Not according to rule.

irreversible. Describing a reaction that cannot be reversed, and usually proceeds to completion in one direction.

irritant. (1) An agent that produces inflammation or irritation; as, mustard oil. (2) The metals Ni, Mn, Cr, W and Si, which in iron alloys are i. to carbon.

Irvine, Sir James Colquhoun. 1887–1952. British chemist noted for research on carbohydrates.

isabellin. An alloy of Al, Mn, and Cu; used for standard electrical resistances.

isaconic acid. Itaconic acid.

isamatic. Isamic.

isamic acid. $C_{16}H_{13}N_3O_4$ = 311.1. Red prisms, m.164.5, slightly soluble in water; obtained from isatin.

isanic acid. $C_{13}H_{19}COOH$ = 220.15. A fatty acid from the oil of tsano nuts. Colorless crystals, m.41.

isano oil. Tsano oil.

isaphenic acid. $C_{17}H_{11}NO_3$ = 277.1. White leaflets, m.295, insoluble in benzene.

isapiol. $C_{12}H_{14}O_4$. An isomer of apiol.

Isarol. Trademark for ammonium sulfoichthyolate obtained by distilling bituminous slate, sulfiting the distillate, and combining it with ammonia. Brown, sticky liquid, soluble in water; an antiseptic, analgesic, and antipyretic.

isatic acid. $NH_2 \cdot C_6H_4CO \cdot COOH$ = 165.1. Isatinic acid, aminophenylglyoxylic acid, amidobenzoylformic acid. White powder, decomp. by heat, soluble in water.

isatide. $C_{16}H_{12}N_2O_4$ = 296.11. Dihydroxybioxindol, isatin-3,3′-pinacol. Colorless crystals, m.237, insoluble in water.

isatin. $C_6H_4 \cdot N : C(OH) \cdot CO$ = 147.1. 2-Hydroxy-3-pseudoindolone, *o*-aminobenzoylformic acid, lactam of isatinic acid. Red needles, m.198, soluble in hot water; used in the manufacture of dyestuffs.

β-imino- Imesatin. **pseudo-** $C_6H_4\cdot CO\cdot CO\cdot NH =$
147.10. Indoldione. The lactim form of isatin.
i. anilide. $C_{14}H_{10}N_2 = 222.17$, m.120. **i. chloride.**
$C_8H_4ONCl = 165.5$. Brown needles, decomp.
180, insoluble in water, used in the manufacture of
dyestuffs.

isatinic acid. Isatic acid.

isatoxime. $C_8H_6O_2N_2 = 162.10$. Nitrosoindoxyl.
Yellow needles, m.202 (decomp.), slightly soluble
in water.

isatropic acid. $C_{18}H_{16}O_4 = 296.12$. 1,2,3,4-Tetra-
hydro-1-phenyl-1,4-naphthalenedicarboxylic acid,
m.237, soluble in water. Cf. *atropic acid*.

isatropylcocaine. $C_{19}H_{22}O_4N = 328.3$. An alkaloid
from coca leaves.

isazol. $CH:N\cdot O\cdot CH:CH = 69.1$. A heteroatomic
pentacyclic isomer of oxazole.

ischidrotic. An agent that causes retention or
suppression of perspiration.

isentropic. Involving no change in entropy.

iserite. A sand rich in titanium and iron.

isethionate. $CH_2OH\cdot CH_2\cdot SO_3M$. A salt of 2-
hydroxyethane sulfonate; used in surfactant
synthesis.

isethionic acid. $CH_2OH\cdot CH_2\cdot SO_2OH = 126.1$.
Ethylenehydrinsulfonic acid, oxyethylsulfonic acid,
from which taurine is derived. A syrupy liquid.
With oleic acid it forms detergents, igepons.

ishkyldite. $H_{20}Mg_{15}Si_{11}O_{47}$. A structural variety of
chrysotile (Volga district).

isindazole. Isoindazole.

isinglass. (1) Fish glue, ichthyocolla. A pure
gelatin from the swimming bladders of fishes
(*Acipenser*); an adhesive and clarifying agent. (2)
Mica in thin sheets, used for windows in ovens and
goggles. **Japanese-** Agar. **vegetable-** Agar.

Isle of Wight diamond. A quartz crystal from the
Isle of Wight, sometimes used as a gem.

Isle Royal greenstone. Chlorastrolite.

iso- Prefix (Greek "equal"), indicating a similarity.
In organic compounds it is generally abbreviated
to *i-*; listed under the corresponding normal
compound.

ISO International Organization for Standardization.

isoaconitic. Isaconitic.

isoallyl. Propenyl.

isoamoxy. The radical $Me_2CH(CH_2)_2O-$.

isoamyl. The radical $Me_2CH\cdot CH_2\cdot CH_2-$. See *isoamyl*.

isoamylene. Pental.

isoanthraflavic acid. $C_{14}H_8O_4 = 240.13$. 2,7-
Dihydroxyanthraquinone. Yellow crystals, m.330,
soluble in alcohol.

isobar. (1) A line drawn through points on a chart
which have the same barometric pressure at a
given time. (2) Any one of 2 or more atomic species
having the same atomic weight and not necessarily
the same atomic number.

isobaric. Pertaining to atoms having the same
weight. Cf. *isobar*. **i. isotopes.** Those atomic
species which have the same atomic weights and
the same atomic numbers. Cf. *isobar*, *isotopes*.

isobenzofurandione. Phthalic anhydride.

isobenzofuranone. Phthalide.

isobestic point. The wavelength at which the extinc-

tion coefficients of 2 substances, one of which can
be converted into the other, are equal.

isobutane. See iso-*butane*.

isobutenyl. The radical $Me_2C:CH-$, from isobutylene.

isobutoxy. The radical $Me_2\cdot CH\cdot CH_2O-$, from isobutyl alcohol.

isobutyl. The radical $Me_2\cdot CH\cdot CH_2-$, from
isobutane.

isobutyryl. The radical $Me_2C\cdot CHCO-$, from isobutyric acid.

isocarb. A line in a diagram showing equal carbon
contents.

isocatalysis. See isomeric *catalysis*.

isocetic acid. Pentadecanoic acid*.

isocholine. Amantine (2).

isochore. The curve obtained by plotting the
pressure and temperature of a gas at constant
volume. See *reaction* isochore.

isochromatic. Having the same color throughout.

isochrone. A line joining points of equal stability
(expressed as log gelation time) on triangular
diagrams; used to express the stability of colloids.

isochronism. (1) Occurring at equal intervals of time.
(2) Lasting for equal periods of time.

isochronous. Occurring in the same period of time
at equal intervals.

isocorybulbine. $C_{21}H_{21}O_4N = 351.3$. An alkaloid
from *Corydalis cava*.

isocrotonic acid. $C_4H_6O_2 = 86.04$. *cis*-α-Butenic
acid, β-crotonic acid, q.v. Colorless liquid,
d.1.0252, m.14.6, decomp. 171.

isocyanate. Carbimide. A compound containing
the radical $-N=O$.

isocyanide. Isonitrile, carbylamine. A compound
containing the radical $-N=C$ or $-N \equiv C$.

isocyanin. A member of a group of dyes used as
photographic sensitizers. Cf. *carbocyanin*.

isocyano. The radical $C:N-$ or $C:N-$. Cf.
isocyanide.

isocyanuric acid. The heterocyclic ring compound
$HN:(CO\cdot NH)_2:CO$.

isocyclic. (1) Describing a closed-chain compound
containing the same number of atoms as the
compound with which it is i.; e.g.: the benzene
ring (6 C atoms) is i. with the pyridine ring (5 C
atoms and 1 N atom). (2) Homocyclic (erroneous).

isodecanol. A mixture of branched-chain primary
alcohols, used in the manufacture of plasticizers.

isodigitoxigenin. $C_{23}H_{34}O_4 = 374.2$. Lustrous,
white crystals, m.271, from digitalis.

isodimorphism. Isomorphs which have 2 crystalline
forms in common. Cf. *isomorphism*.

isodisperse. Dispersible in solutions having the
same pH value.

isodulcite. Rhamnose.

isodurene. $C_6H_2Me_4 = 134.11$. 1,2,3,5-Tetramethyl
benzene. Colorless liquid, b.197. **amino-** Isoduridine.

isodurenol. $C_6HMe_4OH = 150.1$. 2,3,4,6-Tetra-
methylphenol. White crystals, m.80.

isoduridine. $Me_4C_6H\cdot NH_2 = 149.13$. 2,3,4,6-Tetra-
methylaniline. White crystals, m.23.

isodurylic acid. $C_{10}H_{12}O_2 = 164.09$. Trimethyl-
benzoic acid. α or **3,4,5-** Needles, m.215. β or
2,4,6- White scales, m.152. γ or **2,3,5-** White
plates, m.147. All slightly soluble in water.

isodynamic. (1) Having equal force. (2) Generating

or liberating the same amount of energy (calories).

isoelectric point. The point of electric neutrality; the pH value at which a substance (protein, etc.) is neutral. At a lower or higher pH value it acts either as a base or acid, respectively. Coagulation of colloids occurs at or near the i. point. Typical values: see table.

pH	Protein
4.4	Serum globulin
4.6	Ovalbumin
4.7	Gelatin, casein, serum albumin
5.3	Fibrinogen
5.5	Edestin, serum albumin, pseudoglobulin
6.8	Hemoglobin, oxyhemoglobin
8.1	Globin

isoelectronic. Describing atoms that resemble one another in all but mass and nuclear charge. Cf. *isostere.*

isoerucic acid. Brassidic acid.

isoferulic acid. Hesperitinic acid.

isofluorophate. $C_6H_{14}O_3FP = 184.15$. Yellow, irritant liquid, d.1.05, insoluble in water; a parasympathomimetic (U.S.P.).

isogam. A map that shows contours of equal differences in gravity.

isogamous. Having morphologically identical male and female gametes.

isohemagglutinin. Isonin. A constituent of blood serum responsible for agglutination in blood-group tests.

isohexane. See iso-*hexane.*

isohydric. Describing a neutralization, during which the pH value does not change. Cf. *buffer.* Hence a set of solutions of similar H^+ concentration. **homo-** See *homoisohydric.*

isoindoledione. Phthalimide.

isoindyl. The radical C_8H_6N—, from isoindole; 4 isomers.

isokom. A line drawn through a diagram to connect points of equal viscosity.

isolate. (1) To separate or prepare an element or compound. (2) That which is isolated.

isoleucine. $NH_2 \cdot CH \cdot (CH \ EtMe)COOH = 131.11$. 2-Amino-3-methylpentanoic acid*. **dl-** Rhombic or monoclinic plates, m.292, slightly soluble in water. **d-** Greasy leaflets, m.283.

isoleucyl. The radical $MeCH_2 \cdot CHMe \cdot CHNH_2 \cdot CO$—.

isolog, isologue. A member of a series of compounds of similar structure, but having different atoms of the same valency and usually of the same periodic group.

isologous series. A set of isologs; e.g.; Water: H_2O, M_2O, R_2O, M_2S, M_2Se, M_2Te; hydroxylamine: R_2NOH, R_2POH, R_2IOH, R_2TlOH; methane: CH_4, CR_4, SiR_4, SnR_4, PbR_4.

isomalic acid. See *malic acid.*

isomer. One of a pair of or more compounds having the same composition, but different properties. Cf. See *metamers, dimers.*

isomeric. Pertaining to isomerism.

isomeride. One of a set of compounds that have similar structural groups but not necessarily the same number of atoms; thus, anabasine is an *isomer* of nicotine, but nornicotine is an *isomeride.*

isomerism. The property of having the same percentage composition as another compound,

yet differing in the relative positions of the atoms within the molecule, from which result different physical and chemical properties. Three types:

1. Structural: as, chain i. (propane and isopropane), place i. (1-chloropropane and 2-chloropropane), meta-i. (Δ^1-butylene and Δ^2-butylene), ring i. (*o-, m-, p-, v-, s-,* and *a-* positions)

2. Geometrical: as, cis-trans i., syn-anti i.

3. Stereo: or i. due to the presence of an asymmetric C atom which gives optically active dextro and levo compounds. **dynamic-** Tautomerism.

isomery. Isometry. The general phenomena of isomerism, tautomerism, and pseudomerism of organic compounds: 4 factors determine it:

P = arrangement of the atom in the molecule
T = type of the resulting compound
V = the valency of the principal atom
L = the linkage between the atoms

An organic molecule may show the following differences, (d), or similarities, $(-)$,:

P	T	V	L	
d	—	—	—	= isomerism and stereoisomerism
d	d	—	—	= metamerism ⎫ dynamic
—	d	—	d	= desmotropism ⎬ isomerism
d	d	—	d	= tautomerism ⎭
—	—	d	—	= pseudomerism

isometric. Of the same dimension. **i. crystal.** See *crystal systems.*

isometry. Isomery.

isomorph. One of a set of similarly shaped crystals having different compositions; e.g.; Na_2SO_4, Na_2SeO_4.

isomorphic. Pertaining to similar crystalline forms.

isomorphism. The crystallization of different compounds in the same form. These elements and radicals can replace one other without causing any essential alteration in crystalline form. See *isomorphs.*

isomorphous mixture. A mixture of isomorphs usually found in minerals and represented in the formula in parenthesis; as, $(Fe,Mn)CO_3$, which indicates that Mn and Fe are interchangeable and that each behaves as the equivalent weight of either element.

isomorphs. The elements arranged in the order of periodic groups and according to their isomorphism.

1. Cl, Br, I, F, Mn; as $KMnO_4$ and $KClO_4$.

2. S, Se, Te, as sulfides and tellurides; Cr, Mn, Te, as K_2RO_4; As, Sb, as MR_2 (glances).

3. As, Sb, Bi; N (as element), P, V, (in salts); N, P (in organic compounds).

4. K, Na, Rb, Cs, Li; Tl, Ag.

5. Ca, Sr, Ba, Pb; Fe, Mn, Zn, Mg; Ni, Co, Cu; Ce, La, Pr, Nd, Er, Y, with Ca; Cu, Hg, with Pb. Cd, Be, In, with Zn; Tl, with Pb.

6. Al, Fe, Cr, Mn; Ce, U, in oxides M_2O_3.

7. Cu, Ag (as monovalent compounds), Au.

8. Pt, Ir, Pd, Rh, Ru, Os; Au, Fe, Ni; Sn, Te.

9. Cd, Si, Ti, Zr, Th, Sn; Fe, Ti.

10. Ta, Nb.

11. Cr, Mo, W.

isoniazid. $C_6H_7NO_3 = 137.15$. Mybasan. Isonicotinhydrazine. White, crystalline powder, m.172, slightly soluble in water; a tuberculotic antibacterial (U.S.P., B.P.).

CLASSIFICATION AND EXAMPLES OF ISOMERY

A. Isomerism
1. Structural isomerism:

$$CH_3 \cdot CH_2 \cdot CH_2 \cdot CH_3 \quad \text{and} \quad \begin{matrix} CH_3 \\ CH_3 \end{matrix}\!\!>\!\!CH \cdot CH_3$$

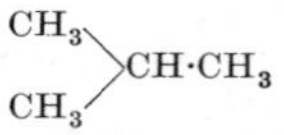

Nuclear or chain isomerism

$$CH_3 \cdot CH_2 \cdot CH_2Cl \quad \text{and} \quad CH_3CHCl \cdot CH_3$$

Position or place isomerism

$$CH_3 \cdot CH_2 \cdot CH:CH_2 \quad \text{and} \quad CH_3 \cdot CH:CH \cdot CH_3$$

Metamerism or meta isomerism

2. Geometrical isomerism:

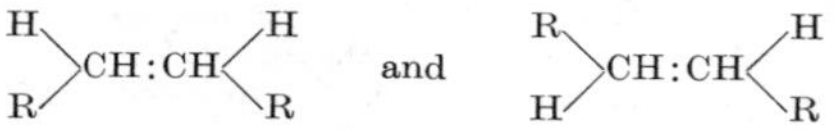

$$\begin{matrix} H \\ R \end{matrix}\!\!>\!\!CH:CH\!\!<\!\!\begin{matrix} H \\ R \end{matrix} \quad \text{and} \quad \begin{matrix} R \\ H \end{matrix}\!\!>\!\!CH:CH\!\!<\!\!\begin{matrix} H \\ R \end{matrix}$$

cis and trans isomerism

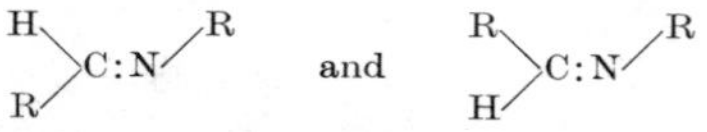

$$\begin{matrix} H \\ R \end{matrix}\!\!>\!\!C:N\!\!<\!\!\begin{matrix} R \\ \end{matrix} \quad \text{and} \quad \begin{matrix} R \\ H \end{matrix}\!\!>\!\!C:N\!\!<\!\!\begin{matrix} R \\ \end{matrix}$$

anti and syn isomerism

3. Stereo- or optical isomerism:

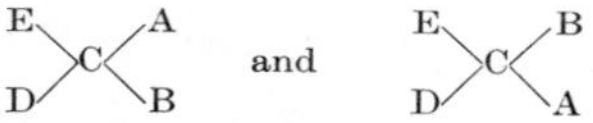

$$\begin{matrix} E \\ D \end{matrix}\!\!>\!\!C\!\!<\!\!\begin{matrix} A \\ B \end{matrix} \quad \text{and} \quad \begin{matrix} E \\ D \end{matrix}\!\!>\!\!C\!\!<\!\!\begin{matrix} B \\ A \end{matrix}$$

A, B, D, and E are different atoms or radicals.

B. Metamerism

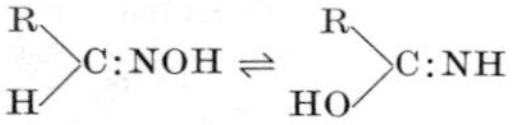

$$\begin{matrix} R \\ H \end{matrix}\!\!>\!\!C:NOH \rightleftharpoons \begin{matrix} R \\ HO \end{matrix}\!\!>\!\!C:NH$$

Oxime   Acid imide

C. Desmotropism

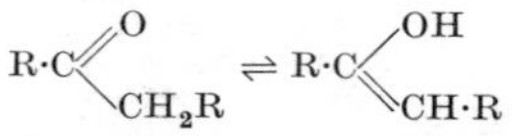

$$R \cdot C\!\!\begin{matrix} O \\ CH_2R \end{matrix} \rightleftharpoons R \cdot C\!\!\begin{matrix} OH \\ CH \cdot R \end{matrix}$$

Ketone form   Enol form

$$R \cdot C\!\!\begin{matrix} O \\ NH_2 \end{matrix} \rightleftharpoons R \cdot C\!\!\begin{matrix} OH \\ NH \end{matrix}$$

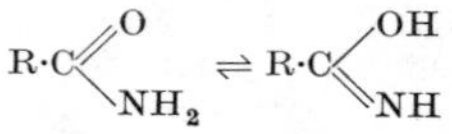

Acid amide   Acid imide

D. Tautomerism

$$R \cdot O \cdot N:C \rightleftharpoons R \cdot NO_2$$

Nitrite   Nitro compound

E. Pseudomerism

$$R \cdot OC \vdots N \qquad R \cdot C \vdots N \cdot O$$

Cyanate   Isocyanate

F. Coordination Isomerism
The different arrangement of radicals around the 2 nuclei in combination:

and $\quad \begin{matrix} [Cr(NH_3)_6] \cdot [Cr(SCN)_6] \\ [Cr(NH_3)_4(SCN)_2] \cdot [Cr(NH_3)_2(SCN)_4] \end{matrix}$

G. Hydration Isomerism
The formation of aquo compounds from ionizable halides in the nucleus.

H. Coordination Polymerism

and $\quad \begin{matrix} [Cr(NH_3)_3(SCN)_3] \\ [Cr(NH_3)_5(SCN)_3]_3 \cdot [Cr(SCN)_6]_2 \end{matrix}$

---

isonicotinhydrazine. Isoniazid.

isonin. Isohemagglutinin.

isonitramine. The radical —N·O·N·OH.

isonitrile*. Isocyanide. ⌐‿⌐

isonitro. Acinitro.

isonitroso. Hydroxyimino.

isontic. Being equal. Applied or relating to any line or surface points that are equal in some respects; as, isobar.

isoöctenyl alcohol. A mixture of 2 isomeric primary allyllic alcohols, used as a solvent and source of plasticizers.

isopentane. See *i-pentane.*

Isopestox. Trade name for bisisopropylamine fluorophosphine oxide. Solid, m.60; an insecticide, twice as toxic as DDT.

isophane. A sterile, aqueous suspension of crystals of protamine and zinc, used as an injection (U.S.P.), or as i. insulin (B.P.).

isophthalal. The group $C_6H_4(CH)_2 \cdot$ ‖‖

isophthalidene. Isophthalal.

isopiestic. Isotonic.

isoporous. Describing the equally spaced, cross-linked chemical structure of certain polymers; as, polystyrene; responsible for ion-exchange properties.

isopral. $CCl_3 \cdot CMeH \cdot OH = 163.44$. Trichloroisopropanol. White prisms, m.49, soluble in water; a hypnotic.

isoprenaline sulfate. $C_{11}H_{17}O_3N \cdot O \cdot 5H_2SO_4 \cdot H_2O = 278.30$. Isupren. White, astringent crystals, m.128 (decomp.), soluble in water; a sympathomimetic (B.P.).

isoprene. $CH_2:CMe \cdot CH:CH_2 = 68.1$. 2-Methylbutadiene-1,3. A distillation product of india rubber, d.0.679, b.34; the unit structure of terpenes, carotenoids, phytol, and rubber. Cf. *duprene.* **di-** The geraniol and linalool chain. **tri-** The farnesol and nerolidol chain. Cf. *vinyl compounds.*

isopropanol. $Me_2CH \cdot OH = 60.1$. Isopropyl alcohol, 1-methyl ethanol. Colorless liquid, d.0.780, b.82, soluble in water; a germicide (B.P.), denaturant, and perfume additive.

isopropenyl. The radical $CH_2:CMe$—, from isoprene.

isopropoxy. The radical $Me_2CH \cdot O$—, from isopropyl alcohol.

isopropyl. The radical Me_2CH—, from isopropane. **i. alcohol.** Isopropanol. **i. benzene.** Cumene. **i. carbinol.** Butanol-2. **i. ether.** $(Me_2CH)_2O = 102.11$. Colorless liquid, d.0.7247, b.69; a solvent for waxes, fats, and resins. **i. metacresol.** Thymol. **i. toluene.** Cymene.

isopropylidene. The radical $Me_2C=$, from isopropane.

isoproterenol hydrochloride. $C_{11}H_{17}O_3N \cdot HCl$ = 247.42. Bitter, white crystals, m.169, soluble in water; an adrenergenic (U.S.P.).

isopyknoscopy. Determination of the end point of a volumetric reaction from the specific gravity of the solution containing the reactants. Cf. *pyknometer.*

isopyre. An impure gem variety of opal.

isoquinoline. $C_6H_4 \cdot CH:N \cdot CH:CH$ = 129.1.

Leucoline, 2-benzazine. **i. alkaloids.** Alkaloids, q.v., from 1-benzyl-*N*-methyltetrahydroisoquinoline; e.g.: the papaverine, corydine, corydaline, morphine, dicentrine, hydrastine, cryptopine, berberine, and protopine groups.

isorhamnetin. A glucoside from the pollen of ragweed and bulrush.

isorheic. Describing liquids that have equal viscosity.

isosmotic. Isotonic; having the same osmotic pressure.

isostere. One of 2 or more atoms or atomic groups having an analogous arrangement of electrons and similar physical properties. Cf. *ionic number, isoelectronic.*

isosteric. Pertaining to similar electronic arrangements. **i. properties.** The physical properties due to electronic arrangements. See *isosterism.*

isosterism. Describing the similarity in physical properties of elements, ions, or compounds due to their similar or identical electronic arrangements.

isotachiol. Silver silicofluoride.

isotactic. See *polymers, polyvinyl chain.*

isoteniscope. An instrument for the static determination of vapor pressure from the change in level of a liquid in a U tube.

isotherm. An expression of equal temperature for a number of points, systems, or phases. Cf. *reaction isotherm.*

isothermal. Having a uniform or constant temperature. **i. change.** The change in volume of a gas under such conditions that the temperature remains constant. Cf. *adiabatic.* **i. distillation.** See *micro*diffusion. **i. line.** Isotherm.

isothermals. A group of curves that pass through regions having the same temperature at a given time; as, on a climatic chart.

isothermic. Isothermal.

isothiocyanate. Sulfocarbimide. A compound of the type R·NCS. Cf. *mustard oil.*

isothiocyanato (preferred usage), **isothiocyano.** The radical —N:C:S.

isothyanic acid. $HS.N:C$ = 59.1. Sulfocarbimide. It yields isothiocyanates.

isotoma. The dried herb *Isotoma longiflora* (Lobeliaceae), E. and W. Indies.

isotomine. An alkaloid from isotoma.

isotone. One of a number of atomic species having an equal number of neutrons in their nuclei.

isotonic. (1) Isosmotic. (2) Describing a solution that has the same osmotic pressure as blood serum. Cf. *hypertonic, hypotonic.* **i. salt solution.** Normal *saline.* **i. water.** A natural water: the sum of its mineral constituents amounts to about 300 millimols per liter, which corresponds with an osmotic pressure of 7.7 atm, and a freezing-point

depression of $-0.57°C$. If lower, the water is *hypotonic;* if higher, *hypertonic.*

isotopes. Atomic species differing in atomic weight, but having the same atomic number. The atomic weights are preferably shown as suffixes thus: Cl^{35}, Cl^{37}, etc.; but sometimes thus: Cl-35, Cl-37, etc. (1) Originally i. indicated radioactive disintegration products which occupied an identical place in the periodic system. (2) The term now applies to all other elements that consist of 2 or more atomic species as revealed by their high-frequency or mass spectra; e.g., chlorine is made up of the isotopes Cl^{35} and Cl^{37}, and its atomic weight of 35.5 is the resultant of the isotopic weights 35 and 37. Certain i. are produced by gamma-ray irradiation; e.g.; I^{131} from Te^{130}, and K^{42} from K^{41}. Used in medicine (e.g.; C^{14}) and tracer elements, q.v. **heterobaric-** I. of different atomic weights: as, the products of different disintegration series. Cf. *radioactive elements.* **isobaric-** I. of the same atomic weight, produced by expulsion successively of an α- and β-particle in a different order; as RaD and RaC₂. Cf. *isobars.* **metastable-** Represented, e.g., Ba^{137m}. See *metastable.*

isotopic. Pertaining to an element that occurs as more than one atomic species. **i. number.** The number N, which probably indicates the number of neutrons in the atomic nucleus: N = A.W. — 2A.N. or I.W. — 2A.N., where A.W. is the atomic weight, I.W. the isotopic weight, and A.N. the atomic number. **i. reaction.** Chemical change which involves isotopes; as, $H^1H^2O + NH_3^1$ = $H_2^1O + NH_2^1H^2$. **i. weight.** I.W. The atomic weight of an isotope. This was considered to be an integer, but more accurate measurements with the mass spectrograph indicate small deviations from whole numbers. See *packing fraction.*

isotropic. Having similar properties in every direction. Cf. *anisotropic.*

isourea. Pseudo-*urea.*

isovaleric acid. See iso-*valeric acid.* **amino-** Valine.

isovaleryl. The radical $Me_2CH \cdot CH_2 \cdot CO—$, from isovaleric acid.

isovaline. $C_5H_{11}O_2N$ = 117.09. Aminoisovaleric acid. An amino acid, q.v., of protein.

isovanillin. $C_5H_8O_3$ = 152.1. 3-Hydroxy-4-methoxybenzaldehyde. Colorless crystals of aromatic odor, m.116.

isovol. A line joining points corresponding with the same content of volatile matter; used on coal survey maps.

Isovyl. Trade name for a polyvinyl chloride synthetic fiber.

isoxazolyl. The radical $C_3H_2ON—$, from isoxazole; 5 isomers.

isoxozonide. $R_2 \cdot C(O)O \cdot O(O)C \cdot R_2$. A stabler rearrangement product of an oxozonide. Cf. *isezonide, oxozonide.*

isoxylic acid. $Me_2C_6H_3 \cdot COOH$ = 150.07. *p*-Xylic acid, 2,5-dimethylbenzoic acid. White needles, m.132, soluble in alcohol.

isozingiberene. $C_{15}H_{24}$ = 204.15. 1,7-Dimethyl-4-propenyloctahydronaphthalene. An isomer of zingiberene.

isozonide. A stable rearrangement product of an

COMMON ISOTOPES

Atomic number		Isotopic weight*
1	Hydrogen	1, 2 (3)
3	Lithium	7, 6
4	Beryllium	9, 8
5	Boron	11, 10
6	Carbon	12, 13
7	Nitrogen	14, 15 (16)
8	Oxygen	16, 18, 17
10	Neon	20, 22, 21
12	Magnesium	24, 25, 26
14	Silicon	28, 29, 30
16	Sulfur	32, 33, 34
17	Chlorine	35, 37
18	Argon	40, 36
19	Potassium	39, 41
20	Calcium	40, 44, 42
22	Titanium	48, 50
24	Chromium	52, 53, 50, 54
26	Iron	56, 54
28	Nickel	58, 60
29	Copper	63, 65
30	Zinc	64, 66, 68, 69, 65, 70, 63
31	Gallium	69, 71
32	Germanium	74, 72, 70, 73, 75, 76, 71, 77
34	Selenium	80, 78, 76, 82, 77, 74
35	Bromine	79, 81
36	Krypton	84, 86, 82, 83, 80, 78
37	Rubidium	87, 85
38	Strontium	88, 86, 87
40	Zirconium	90, 94, 92, 96
42	Molybdenum	90, 96, 95, 92, 94, 97, 100

Atomic number		Isotopic weight*
44	Ruthenium	102, 101, 104, 100, 99, 96, 98
46	Palladium†	102, 104, 106, 108, 110
47	Silver	107, 109
48	Cadmium	114, 112, 110, 113, 111, 116
50	Tin	120, 118, 116, 124, 119, 117, 122, 121, 112, 114, 115
51	Antimony	121, 123
52	Tellurium	130, 128, 126
54	Xenon	129, 132, 131, 134, 136, 128, 130
56	Barium	138, 137, 136, 135
58	Cerium	140, 142
60	Neodymium	142, 144, 146
62	Samarium	152, 154, 149, 148, 147, 144
63	Europium	151, 153
64	Gadolinium†	155, 156, 157, 158, 160
66	Dysprosium	161, 162, 163, 164
68	Erbium	166, 168, 167, 170
70	Ytterbium	174, 172, 173, 176, 171
74	Tungsten	184, 186, 182, 183
76	Osmium	192, 190, 189, 188, 186, 187
78	Platinum	196, 195, 194, 192
80	Mercury	202, 200, 199, 198, 201, 204, 196
82	Lead	208, 206, 207, 204, 209, 210, 203, 205, 212, 214
81–92	Radioactive series.	

* Arranged in the order of the intensities of the mass-spectrum lines, which indicates the order of abundance. Those in parenthesis are uncertain.

† Indicates order unknown.

ozonide, having the formula $R_2C(O) \cdot O \cdot (O) \cdot CR_2$. Cf. *isoxozonide, ozonide.*

Issoglio test. A test for water-soluble or steam-volatile substances characteristic of rancid fats.

Isupren. Trade name for isoprenaline sulfate.

istizin. 1,8-Dihydroxyanthraquinone. A spot reagent for Li, Mg, and Al (red color).

itaconic acid. $CH_2:C(COOH)CH_2COOH = 130.1$. 2,3-Dicarboxypropene, methylenebutanedioic acid*, m.161 (decomp.). Cf. *fumaric acid.*

itakolumite. An elastic sandstone from Brazil; used in refractories to minimize thermal fracture.

itamalic acid. $CH_2OH \cdot CH \cdot COOH \cdot CH_2COOH = 148.09$. Colorless, deliquescent solid, m.64 (decomp.), soluble in alcohol. Cf. *citramalic acid.*

-ite. Suffix indicating: (1) the salt of an *-ous* acid, e.g., sulfite (sulfurous acid). (2) A mineral.

itrol. Silver citrate.

I.U. International unit. See *vitamin* units.

-ium. Suffix denoting: (1) the presence of a metal or nonmetal in a salt-forming capacity (cf. *-onium*); (2) a Latin derivation (cf. *-ilium, -inium*); (3) many elements, generally metals; as, sodium, vanadium.

IUPAC Abbreviation for International Union of Pure and Applied Chemistry.

ivaine. $C_{24}H_{42}O_5 = 410.2$. An alkaloid obtained from *Achillea moschata* (Compositae).

iva oil. A green oil, distilled from the flowering tops of *Achillea* species; used in flavoring extracts.

ivaol. $C_{10}H_{20}O = 156.1$. An alcohol in iva oil. Yellow, bitter oil of pleasant odor.

ivory. The bonelike substance from the tusks of animals. **vegetable-** Corajo.

  i. black. Animal charcoal prepared by calcining the refuse from i. working; a decolorizing agent and filtering medium.

ivy. The climbing plant *Hedera helix* (Araliaceae); the leaves and berries are a stimulant and diaphoretic. **American-** Virginia creeper, wood vine. The bark and twigs of *Vitis hederacea* (Vitaceae); a tonic and astringent. **ground-** Gill-go-over-the-ground. The herb of *Glechoma hederacea* (Labiatae); a diuretic and tonic. **poison-** *Rhus toxicodendron.*

I.W. Abbreviation for isotopic weight.

iztac chalchihuitl. A white or green gem variety of Mexican onyx.

J

J. Abbreviation for: (1) joule; (2) yellow (French jaune): cf. *colors*; (3) gram-equivalent weight. **J. acid.** 6-Amino-1-naphthol-3-sulfonic acid. **J phenomenon.** The absorption of X rays by a substance varies discontinuously with a change in wavelength λ; thus certain λ excite the characteristic radiation of the adsorber.

J. Symbol for current density.

jaborandi. See *Pilocarpus.* **j. oil.** Yellow oil distilled from j. leaves, d.0.865, b.220, insoluble in water; used in pharmacy.

jaboridine. $C_{10}H_{12}O_3N_2 = 208.2$. An alkaloid from jaborandi leaves.

jaborine. $C_{22}H_{32}O_4N_4 = 416.6$. An alkaloid from jaborandi leaves. Yellow syrup, insoluble in water; an atropine substitute in ophthalmology.

jaboty fat. White tallow from Brazilian kernels of *Erisma calcaratum* and *E. uncinatum* (Vochysiaceae), m.42; a substitute for cacao butter.

jacinth. Hyacinth.

jack. Sphalerite.

jacket. (1) The false or double wall of a container by means of which it may be cooled or heated. (2) The iron sheath of a furnace. (3) The brick covering of a boiler.

Jackson, Sir Herbert. 1863–1936. British chemist noted for chemical research applied to industry.

jacobine. $C_{18}H_{23}O_5N = 333.3$. An alkaloid from *Senecio jacobaea*, ragwort (Compositae); the cause of Winton's disease of grazing animals.

jaconecic acid. $C_{10}H_{16}O_6(?)$. The acid hydrolysis product of jacobine.

jacutinga. A Brazilian ore containing approximately: hematite 98, chalcedony 0.9, manganous oxide 0.25%; a source of iron.

jade. (1) $3MgO \cdot CaO \cdot 2SiO_2$. True j., nephrite. A silica mineral, q.v., of the amphibole group. A fusible green or flaked gem (China, Siberia), d.3.0, hardness 6.0. See *imperial j.* (2) $NaAlO_2 \cdot 2SiO_2$. Jadeite, greenstone. A silica mineral, q.v., of the pyroxene group resembling j.

jadeite. Jade (2).

jaggery sugar. A crude sugar from the date palm. Cf. *gur.*

jaipurite. CoS. A native cobaltous sulfite.

jalap. The dried root of *Exogonium* or *Ipomoea purga* (Convolvulaceae), Mexico and W. Indies. It should contain not less than 7% of resins, and is a hydragogue cathartic.

jalapic acid. $C_{17}H_{30}O_9 = 378.23$. An acid, m.120, from jalap.

jalapin. $C_{34}H_{56}O_{16} = 700.3$. Orizabin. A resinous glucoside, m.150, from jalap. Cf. *convulvulin.*

jalapinolic acid. $Me(CH_2)_3CHOH(CH_2)_{10}COOH = 272.25$. *d*-11-Hydroxyhexadecanoic acid*, from jalap resin.

jalapoid. The combined principles from extracted jalap. A cathartic and diuretic.

jamaica dogwood. The bark of *Ichthyomethia piscipula* or *Piscidia erythrina*; an anodyne and hypnotic. **j. wood.** Hematoxylon.

jamaicine. A bitter principle from the bark of the cabbage tree, *Andira inermis* (Leguminosae), Jamaica. It resembles berberine.

jamboo. (1) Jambu. The seeds of *Piper jaborandi* (Piperaceae). (2) Jambul.

jambosine. $C_{10}H_{15}O_3N = 197.2$. A crystalline alkaloid from the root of *Jambosa vulgaris* (Myrtaceae), the rose apple of the tropics. Used to treat dysentery and leucorrhea.

jambul. The bark of *Eugenia jambolanum*, the Java plum tree (Myrtaceae), E. Indies; a stomachic astringent. **j. seeds.** The seeds of *E. jambolanum*; a carminative and stomachic. Cf. *antimellin.*

jambulol. $C_{16}H_8O_9 = 344.1$. A dibasic, pentahydroxy acid found in the seeds of *Eugenia jambolanum* (Myrtaceae), Java. It resembles ellagic acid.

jamesonite. $Pb_2Sb_2S_5$. Feather ore. A native sulfide.

James powder. Pulvis antimonialis. Antimoniated calcium phosphate. **J. tea.** Labrador tea.

Jamin effect. A capillary tube filled with alternate air and water bubbles sustains a finite pressure, due to oily contamination on the glass surface, which prevents complete wetting.

Janus green. A green dye intravital stain.

japaconine. $C_{26}H_{41}O_{10}N = 527.4$. An amorphous alkaloid, m.97, from Japanese aconite.

japaconitine. $C_{34}H_{49}NO_{11} = 647.39$. Acetylbenzoyljapaconine. An alkaloid, m.204, from Japanese aconite.

japan. A varnish for metallic and wooden articles. Cf. *stove.* **j. camphor.** Camphor. **j. clay.** Montmorillonite. **j. tallow.** J. wax. **j. wax.** A glyceride containing palmitic acid and small amounts of eicosanic and heneicosanic acids; from the berries of *Rhus succedanea* and other species of sumach tree. Yellow wax, d.0.970, m.53, soluble in benzene; used in the manufacture of candles, wax, and leather dressing.

japanic acid. $C_{22}H_{44}O_4 = 372.34$. A dibasic acid from japan wax, m.117; probably a mixture of eicosanic and heneicosanic dicarboxylic acids.

japanning. Varnishing by successive applications of a lacquer and heating in an oven.

japonic acid. A tannic acid from catechu.

japopinic acid. $C_{14}H_{22}O_2 = 222.17$. A monobasic acid from Japanese turpentine.

jar. A small earthen vessel, without spout or handle. **bell-** Bell glass. **Leyden j.** An electric condenser; a glass vessel lined internally and externally with tinfoil. **Naples-** See *Naples.*

jara jara. β-Naphthyl methyl ether.

jargon, jargoon. Zircon.

jargonia. Zirconia.

jargonium. A supposed element discovered by Sorby (1869): probably impure hafnium.

jasmine oil. A colorless essential oil from the flowers of *Jasminum grandiflorum* (Oleaceae). It contains benzyl acetate, linalol, linalyl acetate, and indole, d.1.008, soluble in alcohol; used in perfumery.

jasper. Touchstone, Lydian stone, bloodstone, Lydian stone. A gem variety of chalcedony. Formerly used to estimate the gold content of an alloy by comparing the color of the streak made on it with streaks made by standard alloys. **porcelain-** Porcellanite.

jateorhiza. Calumba.

jatrophine. $C_{14}H_{20}O_6N = 298.17$. An alkaloid from *Jatropha gossipifolia*. Yellow powder, soluble in cold water; acid solutions are fluorescent; used to treat stomach disorders.

jaune. French for yellow. **j. brillant.** Cadmium sulfide. **j. d'or.** Martius yellow.

javancin. $C_{15}H_{14}O_7(?)$. An antibiotic, weakly acidic pigment from cultures of *Fusarium javanicum*. Red plates, m.212.

Java pepper. Cubeb. **J. plum.** Jambul. **J. tea.** Orthosiphonin.

javelle. Eau de javelle.

javellization. The sterilization of water supplies by hypochlorites.

jaw oil. An oil from the jaws of the black fish, *Globicephalus melas*; a lubricant for fine machinery.

Jeans, Sir James. 1877–1946. British mathematician, astronomer, and physicist, noted for his correlation of the physical theories of the structure of matter with cosmic science.

jecolein. A glyceride from cod-liver oil.

jecorin. $C_{105}H_{186}O_{46}N_5SP_3$. A protein in the liver, spleen, and brain.

jel. See *gel*.

jelletite. A green variety of andradite. See *garnet*.

jellose. A carbohydrate plant constituent, related and having similar properties to fruit pectins, and composed of glucose, galactose, and xylose.

jelly. A soft, usually transparent colloidal system, q.v.: liquid suspended in a solid; as, water in gelatin. **mineral-** or **petroleum-.** See *vaselin*. **royal-** A secretion of the pharyngeal glands of nursing bees, *Apis mellifica*, and the sole food of queen larvae. It is believed to have anticarcinogenic properties by virtue of its principal constituent, 10-hydroxy-Δ^2-decenoic acid.

jellying power. The capacity of substances to solidify in solution; as, gelatin.

jelutong. The exudate from *Dyzra costulata* (Apocynaceae); used in chewing gum. Cf. *pontianac*.

Jena ware. Heat-resistant glassware, from Jena, Germany.

jenkolic acid. $CH_2[SCH_2CH(NH_2)COOH]_2 = 226.2$. Djenkolic acid from djenkol beans. *Pithecalobium lobatum* (Leguminosae).

Jenner stain. A 2-solution microscope stain for white blood corpuscles: (1) 0.5 % eosin in methanol; (2) 0.5 % methylene blue in methanol.

jeppel oil. Bone oil.

jequiritin. Abrin.

Jersey tea. The dried roots of *Ceanothus americanus* (Rhamnaceae); an astringent, sedative, and expectorant.

jervine. $C_{26}H_{37}O_3N = 411.1$. An alkaloid from *Veratrum* species (Liliaceae). White prisms, m.240, insoluble in water.

jesaconitine. $C_{40}H_{51}NO_{12} = 735.35$. An aconite alkaloid, q.v.

Jesuits' balsam. Copaiba balsam. **J. bark.** Cinchona bark.

jet. A dense, black, polished lignite, or cannel coal rendered black by fossilization; sometimes used for jewelry.

Jetspun. Trade name for a viscose synthetic fiber.

Jew's pitch. Asphalt.

jig. A vibrating screen submerged in water for ore concentration.

jigger. Jig.

Jimson weed. Stramonium.

johannite. Uranvitriol.

johimbine. $C_{23}H_{32}O_4N_2 = 400.4$. An alkaloid from the bark of *Corynanthe yohimbehe*, an African tree. Cf. *yohimbine*.

Joint Codex Alimentarius Commission. A United Nations organization formulating health and purity criteria; and standards of quality, appearance, and packaging of food.

jojoba. The shrub *Simmondsia Californica* (Buxaceae), California and Mexico. **j. oil.** The oil from the nuts of j., resembling whale sperm oil.

Joliot, Frédéric, 1900–1958, and his wife, **J., Irène Curie,** 1897–1956, daughter of Pierre and Marie Curie. French physical chemists and Nobel Prize winners (1935) for their work on induced radioactivity.

Jolly balance. A spring balance for determining the specific gravity of a solid by weighing it alternately in air and water.

Jones reagent. A bath of molten zinc in which a metal to be etched is immersed. **J. reductor.** A glass tube filled with amalgamated, granulated zinc or zinc wire spirals, used for reducing solutions of Fe, Ti, Mo, V, Cr, and U, before their volumetric determination by oxidation-reduction methods.

jordanite. $AsS_3 \cdot 4PbS$. A native sulfide.

Jorissen test. A pinch of phloroglucinol is added to a solution of the sample in hydrochloric acid. If the solution is made alkaline, a red or orange color results in presence of formaldehyde or acetaldehyde.

joseite. Bi_3Te. A bismuth telluride.

josephinite. A native iron and nickel alloy from Oregon.

Joule, James Prescott. 1818–1889. (Pronounced jool.) English physicist noted for work on energy transformations. Cf. *joule*. **J. effect.** (1) The change in length of a ferromagnetic material along the axis of the applied magnetic field, when the field strength is changed. (2) Heat effect. **J. equivalent.** The mechanical equivalent of heat; or the quantity of energy which is equivalent to unit quantity of heat: 4.185×10^7 ergs = 1 Calorie (20°). In absolute units, q.v.: $J = L^2T^{-2}\theta^{-1}$, or $JH = JM\theta = ML^2T^{-2}$. In 1948 the j. was adopted internationally as the unit of heat in place of the calorie. The Royal Society recommended (1950) that the value in calories should also be given in parentheses while it is still in common use. Cf. *calorie*, *BThU*. **J.-Kelvin effect.** The fall in temperature of a gas forced at high pressure through a small orifice which is proportional to the difference in pressure on the two sides; used in the Linde-Hampson process of liquefying gases. **J.-Thomson effect.** J.-Kelvin effect. **J's. law.** (1) The heat produced by a current $I = RI^2t$, where t is the time during which the current flows. (2) The internal energy of a volume of gas does not vary with temperature, if the volume remains constant. (3) The molecular heat of a solid compound is the sum of the atomic heats of its constituents. **J. unit.** J. equivalent.

joule. The unit of work. One j. equals 10^7 units of work (ergs) in the cgs system, and is practically equivalent to the energy expended in one second by one ampere passing through one ohm of resistance. Hence:

$$\text{Joule} = \text{amp}^2 \times \text{ohms} \times \text{sec} =$$
$$\text{watts} \times \text{sec}$$
$$= (\text{volts}^2 \times \text{sec})/\text{ohms} = 10^7 \text{ ergs}$$
$$1 \text{ joule} = 1 \text{ volt-coul} = 0.24 \text{ cal}$$
$$= 0.1020 \text{ kg-m} = 0.7376 \text{ ft-lb}$$
$$1 \text{ cal} = 4.1850 \text{ joules}$$
$$= 0.04337 \text{ volt-electron}$$
$$3,600 \text{ joules} = 1 \text{ kelvin} = 1 \text{ whr}$$

juar. Sorghum.

Juerst ebullioscope. A device for determining small percentages of alcohol from the boiling point of the liquid, which varies directly with the percentage of alcohol.

juglandin. A resinoid from the root bark of juglans. Brown powder, slightly soluble in alcohol; a cathartic.

juglandoid. The combined principles from the root bark of juglans, or butternut.

juglans. Butternut bark, white walnut. The dried inner bark from the roots of *Juglans cinera* (Juglandaceae); a cathartic and antiperiodic. Cf. *nucite.*

juglansin. A globulin from walnuts and butternuts.

juglone. $C_{10}H_6O_3 = 174.1$. 5-Hydroxynaphthoquinone, nucin. Brown prisms, m.153, insoluble

in water; from the bark of the European walnut, *Juglans regia.*

juice. (1) A fluid from a vegetable or animal tissue. (2) A colloquial term for electric current.

jumble beads. Abrus.

Jungius, Ioachim. 1587–1657. German alchemist, and forerunner of Boyle in showing the importance of observation and experiment.

juniper. The tree *Juniperus communis* (Coniferae) of temperate zones. **gum-** Sandarac.
    j. berries. The dried, ripe fruits of j.; a diuretic. **j. berry oil.** An essential oil distilled from j. berries. Yellow liquid, d.0.865, b.120, soluble in alcohol; a stimulant diuretic, and flavoring. It contains pinene, cadinene, and j. camphor. **j. tar.** Cade oil.

juniperic acid. $C_{16}H_{32}O_3 = 272.25$. *o*-Hydroxypalmitic acid, 16-hydroxyhexadecanoic acid*. A monobasic acid, m.95, from savin, *Juniperus sabina,* and arborvitae.

juniperin. A bitter principle from juniper, *Juniperus communis.*

juniperus. (1) The dried tops, wood, and berries of juniper; used as a source of an essential oil, and in fumigation. (2) A genus of Coniferae yielding berries, oils, and wood: *J. communis,* juniper; *J. sabina,* savin.

junket. Curds and whey, a food prepared by coagulating milk with rennet.

jurubeba. *Solanum insidiosum.*

jute. The bast fiber of *Corchorus* species (Tiliaceae), E. Indies and S. America; used in gunnysacks and twine. **China-** The fiber of *Abutilon avicenna* (Malvaceae), China. **medical-** The fibers of *Corchorus olitorius,* used in surgical dressings.

juvenile water. A water of magmatic or deepseated origin, supposed to come for the first time to the earth surface, e.g., artesian wells. Antonym: vadose water.

K

(See also under C)

K. (1) Symbol for potassium (kalium). **K⁺**, **K˙**. Potassium ion. **K*.** Excited potassium atom. **K₂⁺.** Ionized potassium molecule. **K₂*.** Excited potassium molecule. (2) Abbreviation for Kelvin. °K. Degrees on the absolute temperature scale. (3) Abbreviation for kaiser. **K acid.** 1-Amino-8-naphthol-4,6-disulfonic acid.

K. Symbol for chemical equilibrium constant. See law of *mass action*. **K₈.** Symbol for solubility product. **K electrons.** The 2 electrons in the innermost shell or orbit of the atom. **K line.** (1) One of a group of lines having the shortest wavelength that are visible when *K* radiations pass through an X-ray spectrograph. (2) The Fraunhofer line, λ3933.7, due to calcium. **K orbit.** The innermost path of electrons around the atomic nucleus. Cf. *atom, orbit.* **K radiation.** The homogeneous X rays emitted by metals used as an anticathode in an X-ray tube; assumed to originate from the excitation of the *K* electrons. Cf. *energy levels.* **K region.** The region of the 9,10-phenanthrene double bond. **K series.** The spectral lines produced by *K* radiations. Cf. *Moseley spectrum.* **K spectrum.** The spectrum produced by *K* radiations. The frequency of any line is approximately proportional to $A(N - b)^2$, where N is the atomic number, A and b are constants. The atomic number $N = Q_K + 1 = Q_L + 7.4$, where Q_K and Q_L express the frequencies of the K and L series of radiations, respectively.

k. Symbol for: (1) a constant; (2) Boltzmann's constant; (3) thermal conductivity; (4) velocity constant of chemical reactions.

ϰ. Greek kappa.

K.A. An aluminum alloy similar to duraluminum.

kabaite. A native hydrocarbon in meteorites.

kæ- See *kae-, ke-.*

kaempferide. $C_{16}H_{12}O_6$ = 300.1. Kaempferyl-4-methyl ether. A constituent of galangal, m.225, soluble in sulfuric acid (blue fluorescence) and in alkali (yellow color).

kaempferol. $C_{15}H_{10}O_6$ = 286.08. A cyclic alcohol, m.274, from *Indigofera erecta.*

kaf(f)ir. Sorghum. **k. corn.** Durra, the grain of sorghum.

kafirin. A protein from sorghum.

Kahle's solution. See *fixative.*

kahweol. $C_{19}H_{26}O_3$ = 302.2. A highly unsaturated alcohol, m.143, from coffee bean oil.

kainit. Synthetic kainite, containing 30% potassium sulfate.

kainite. $MgSO_4 \cdot KCl \cdot 3H_2O$. A native potassium magnesium sulfate associated with carnallite, from Stassfurt (Germany) and Poland; made synthetically; used as a potash fertilizer, and in water treatment. The AOAC defines it as potassium and sodium chloride sometimes with magnesium sulfate, containing not less than 12% potassium oxide.

kairine. $C_{10}H_{13}ON$ = 163.2. Methyloxytetrahydroquinoline. A quinine substitute, usually marketed as the hydrochloride. **k. hydrochloride.** $C_{10}H_{13}ON \cdot HCl$ = 199.6. Gray crystals, soluble in water; an antipyretic, and quinine substitute. Cf. *thalline.*

kairoline. $C_{10}H_{13}N$ = 147.2. Methyltetrahydroquinoline. Colorless liquid, $b_{720mm}245$, soluble in alcohol; an antipyretic.

kaiser. K. Reciprocal centimeter, cm.⁻¹ A little-used unit of length.

Kaiserling solution. A solution for preserving tissues, consisting of 3 gm potassium acetate, 1 gm potassium nitrate, 75 ml water, and 30 ml formaldehyde.

kakodyl. Cacodyl.

kakoxene. The mineral $2Fe_2O_3 \cdot P_2O_5 \cdot 12H_2O$.

kaladana. The dried seeds of *Ipomoea hederacea*; a purgative and anthelmintic. **k. resin.** A purgative resin from kaladana.

kalaite. A turquoise containing copper and iron. Cf. *callaite.*

kali. German for potassium hydroxide. **k. ammonsalpeter.** A mixture of potassium chloride and ammonium nitrate used as fertilizer (nitrogen 16, potassium oxide 27%).

kalicrete. A portland cement, containing iron, which is resistant to alkali soils.

kalimeter. Alkalimeter.

kalinite. $K_2Al_2(SO_4)_4 \cdot 24H_2O$. A native sulfate.

kaliophylite. $KAlSiO_4$. A nephelite silica mineral, q.v.

kalium. Latin and German for potassium.

kalk. German for lime. **k. ammon.** A mixture of ammonium chloride and calcium chloride used as fertilizer. **k. ammon salpeter.** Calnitro.

kallaite. Kalaite.

Kalle acid. 1-Naphthylamine-2,7-disulfonic acid.

kallekrein. Padutin. A circulatory hormone, which regulates the capillaries and small vessels.

kalmia. Mountain laurel, sheep laurel, lambkill. The leaves of *K. latifolia* (Ericaceae); a cardiac sedative and astringent.

kalsilite. $2KAlSiO_4$. A polymorph mineral resembling nepheline; minute grains in volcanic rocks of high potassium oxide content (Uganda).

kamacite. A component of meteoric iron-nickel alloys, present only when the nickel content is less than 6.5%.

kamala. Glandulae Rottlerae. A light granular powder which consists of the glands and hairs from the capsules of *Mallotus philippinensis* (Euphorbiaceae); a purgative.

kamalin. $C_{22}H_{20}O_6$ = 380.1. Rottlerin. The

bitter principle of kamala. Brown powder, m.200, soluble in alcohol; an anthelmintic.

kamarezite. A native basic copper sulfate, in green compact masses.

kambi. An aromatic gum, resembling elemi, from *Gardenai lucida* (Rubiaceae), India.

Kamerlingh-Onnes, Heika. 1853–1926. Dutch physicist and Nobel Prize winner (1913), noted for experiments at very low temperatures.

kampometer. An instrument for measuring heat radiations. Cf. *kapnometer.*

kanamycin. A basic antibiotic from *Streptomyces kanamyceticus,* consisting of two amino sugars linked glucosidally to 2-deoxystreptamine, related chemically to neomycin, and similar in properties to streptomycin. Injected into the urinary tract to treat tuberculosis. **k. sulfate.** $C_{18}H_{36}O_{11}N_4\cdot$ H_2SO_4 = 582.59. White crystals, soluble in water; an antibacterial (U.S.P.).

Kanebain. Trade name for a polyvinyl alcohol synthetic fiber.

kanerol. $C_{30}H_{50}O$ = 426.5. An alcohol from the roots of *Kanher nerium* (India). Colorless crystals, m.185, insoluble in water.

kanirin. Trimethylamine oxide.

kanyl alcohol. $C_{10}H_{18}O_2$ = 170.14. An alcohol from the liver oil of tarabakani, *Paralithodes camtschatica* (Japan Sea).

kaoliang oil. Koryan oil.

kaolin. $Al_2O_3\cdot2H_2O\cdot2SiO_2$. China clay, porcelain clay, bolus alba, terra alba, white bole, argilla. Derived from Kao-ling (Chinese: high ridge) the original site. A gray, fine, inert powder used in ceramics, as filler for paper and textiles, and for pencils. It is official in some pharmacopoeias. Three types: kaolinite (by weathering), dickite (by moderate heating), nakrite (by hypogene processes). Cf. *atalpo, fuller's earth, kaolinite.* **Georgia-** K of. enhanced brightness, produced by heating at 900–1000°C. **light-** K. containing not more than 0.5% of coarse particles (B.P.).

kaolinite. $Al_2O_3\cdot2SiO_2\cdot2H_2O$. Clay substance. The chief constituent of kaolin or clay; heated above 1100°C, it breaks down to mullite and cristobalite. White, fine powder, used medicinally as an absorbent and dusting powder, and as a clarifying agent.

kaolinization. Natural rock disintegration and formation of clay from the feldspars of decomposed granite (orthoclase).

Kapilon. Trade name for acetonaphthone.

kapnometer. An instrument for measuring the density of smokes. Cf. *kampometer.*

kapok. The Malay name for the cottonlike down from the seedpods of *Eriodendron anfractuosum,* (Sterculiaceae); used in mattresses and lifesaving jackets. **k. oil.** Yellow oil, expressed from k. seeds, d.0.923, soluble in alcohol; used in soap and edible fats manufacture.

kappa. κ. The tenth letter of the Greek alphabet. Symbol for: (1) kata position. (2) The tenth carbon atom. **k. number.** The number of milliliters of 0.1 N potassium permanganate consumed by one gram of dry cellulose pulp under specified conditions. It measures bleachability.

Kappoxan. Trade name for menaphthone.

Kapron. Trade name for a polyamide synthetic fiber.

karabin. $C_{21}H_{49}O_6$ = 397.5. A resinous substance from *Nerium oleander* (Apocynaceae).

karakin. $C_{10}H_{14}O_9N_2$ = 306.12 A crystalline glycoside from the berries of the karaka tree, *Corynocarpus laevigata,* m.122; a stereoisomer of hiptagenic acid.

karat. U.S. usage for carat, q.v.; the unit of gold fineness, as distinct from the unit of gem weight.

karaya gum. An Indian gum similar to tragacanth, used in toothpastes.

Karbogel. Trade name for a porous, solid, granular desiccant made from coal. It can be reactivated at 100°C, and does not readily disintegrate.

karitene. $C_{32}H_{56}$ = 440.4. A solid hydrocarbon, m.64, from shea fat.

Karl Fischer reagent. A solution of iodine and sulfur dioxide in methyl alcohol and pyridine, used to determine water by titration. In presence of water, the iodine passes into the combined state, and the end point is shown by the presence of excess iodine.

karpholite. The mineral $(Mn,Fe)O\cdot(Fe,Al)_2O_3\cdot$ $SiO_2\cdot2H_2O$.

karyokinesis. The phenomena of cell division or mitosis, during which the protoplasm of the cell and its nucleus undergo a series of changes which merge into one another.

kata- Cata-. Greek prefix indicating down or below. **k. position.** $\varkappa$- (1) The 1,7-substitution in naphthalene, q.v. (2) On the tenth C atom of a chain. **k. thermometer.** An instrument that measures the cooling effect of airflow as distinct from the temperature of the air: used to evaluate ventilation conditions.

katabolism. Catabolism.

katalase. Catalase.

katalysis. Catalysis.

kataphoresis. Cataphoresis.

katchung. Chinese for peanuts. (Kachang = Malay.) **oil of-** Peanut oil.

katharometer. An instrument for the analysis of a gas mixture by the changes in its thermal conductivity.

kathode. Cathode.

katine. $C_{10}H_{18}ON_2$ = 182.2. An alkaloid from the leaves of African tea, *Catha edulis* (Celastraceae). Cf. *celastrine, cathine.*

kation. Cation.

katode. Cathode.

kauri. Kauri gum, kauri resin. A resin exuded from the kauri tree, *Agathis australis,* a conifer (New Zealand), and dug from the soil. It contains a parent substance of the catechins, 1-leucomaclurinyl glycol. Amber-like resin, d.1.05, m.180–230, insoluble in water; used in varnishes. **k. gum.** Kauri. **k. oil.** An oil obtained by distilling peat from prehistoric kauri forests.

kaurinic acid. $C_{10}H_{16}O_2$ = 168.2. An acid constituent (about 1.5%) of kauri.

kaurinolic acid. $C_{17}H_{34}O_2$ = 270.3. An acid constituent (about 15%) of kauri.

kaurolic acid. $C_{12}H_{20}O_2$ = 196.2. The principal constituent (50%) of kauri.

kauronolic acid. $C_{12}H_{34}O_2$ = 200.2. A constituent (10%) of kauri.

kautchin. Terpene.

kava. Kavakava. Ava. The dried rhizome of

Piper methysticum (Piperaceae), Polynesian islands; mild diuretic and stimulant. **k. resin.** A resin derived from kava, containing kavaic acid.

kavaic acid. $C_{13}H_{12}O_3 = 216.1$. An acid derived from kava. Yellow crystals, m.165.

kavain. $C_{14}H_{14}O_3 = 230.02$. Methysticin, kawain. A principle from kava. White needles, m.102, soluble in alcohol.

kavatel oil. An oil obtained from the seeds of *Hydnocarpus Wightiana*; used in place of chaulmoogra oil.

kawa. Kava.

Keen tester. An instrument to determine hardness of metals by the impact-ball method.

kefir. Kephir, kephyr. A fermentation product of goat's milk produced by the *Bacillus caucasicus*; a nutritious food. Cf. *koumiss*. **k. milk.** A beverage made from cow milk and kefir powder. **k. powder.** White irregular bodies containing a yeast fungus and several bacteria; used to make kefir and kefir milk.

keilhauite. A native titanate and silicate of aluminum, calcium, iron, and the rare-earth metals. Cf. *sphene*.

Kekulé, Friedrich August. 1829–1896. German chemist noted for work on the constitution of carbon compounds. **K. ring.** See *benzene ring*.

Kelene. Trade name for ethyl chloride.

Kelheim. Trade name for a viscose synthetic fiber.

kellin. A glucoside from the fruit of *Ammi visnaga*.

kelp. (α) Varec. The large seaweeds (*Laminaria*) near the shores of the Pacific and Atlantic. (2) Kelp ashes (preferred usage). **dried-** A fertilizer containing nitrogen 1.6–3.3, phosphoric oxide 1–2, potassium oxide 15–20%. Cf. *algin*. **k. ashes.** Kelp. The ashes of k., formerly used to prepare potassium salts and iodine.

Kelvin, William Thompson (Lord Kelvin). 1824–1907. British physicist, pioneer in electrical science. **K. bridge.** A set of coils for accurate resistance measurements. **K. galvanometer.** An elliptical coil round a magnetic needle suspended on a fine wire with mirror attached, to detect small electric currents. **K. scale.** °K. An absolute temperature scale, a measure of kinetic energy. The freezing point of water is 273.15°K, the boiling point 373.13°K. Hence °K = °C + 273.15 (if above 0°C); and °K = 273.15 − °C (if below 0°C).

kemfert. Trona potash. A potassium chloride from the waters of Searles Lake, California.

kemp. A coarse, low-grade wool fiber, which resists dyeing and lacks the characteristic epidermal scales of the normal wool fiber.

kenaf. *Hibiscus cannabinus*. A S. African jute substitute.

Kendall, Edward Calvin. b. 1886. American chemist; isolated thyroxin from the thyroid gland. **K., James.** b. 1889. British inorganic and physical chemist. **K. compound.** Cortisone.

Kenithal sodium. Trade name for thiobarbitone sodium.

Kennelly-Heaviside layer. A stratum of electrons, 100–200 miles above the earth's surface created by solar rays. It is impenetrable by radio waves, and is the seat of the aurora. Cf. *ionosphere*.

kepayang oil. An oil resembling chaulmoogra oil, from the seeds of Pokok kepayang.

kephalin. (1) Cephalin, brain lipoid. A lecithin phosphatid from spinal and brain tissue of mammals. The constituent choline is replaced by cholamine. Yellow solid, of characteristic odor, slightly soluble in alcohol. Cf. *cuorin*. (2) A group of phosphatides from white brain substance resembling lecithin (q.v.) in structure, but with aminoethyl alcohol in place of the choline residue. White, brittle, very hygroscopic solids, forming colloidal solutions in water; hydrolyzed slowly to stearic acid and a mixture of unsaturated fatty acids.

kephaloidin. A constituent of the buttery substance of brain, q.v.

kephyr. Kefir.

ker. A Polish synthetic rubber, made from alcohol.

keracyanin. An anthocyanin from cherries.

kerasin. $C_{48}H_{93}O_8N = 881.7$. A cerebroside associated with phrenosin in the brain tissue. White powder, m.180 (decomp.), insoluble in water.

kerasol. $C_{20}H_{10}O_4I_4 = 821.8$. Tetraiodophenolphthalein. The soluble sodium salt renders the gallbladder visible in X rays (nosophen, antinosin).

keratin. $C_{41}H_{71}O_{14}N_{12}S$. A protein in horns, feathers, shells, fingernails; used to coat pills; resistant to digestion by pepsin and trypsin and insoluble in water. Believed to exist in a folded chain form, converted into a straight chain by simultaneous steaming and stretching. **meta-** The compound formed when the —SH groups in k. are oxidized to the —S—S— form.

keratoelastin. A protein from the eggshells of fishes, reptiles, and monotremes.

keratolytic. A substance that dissolves keratin or skin, e.g., salicylic acid for the treatment of corns.

kerenes. That portion of kerotenes which is insoluble in organic solvents.

kerites. The naturally occurring kerotene bitumens and protobitumens.

kermes. The dried insects, *Coccus ilicis*, from the leaves of Oriental oak species; an ancient red textile dye. **k. mineral.** Kermesite.

kermesite. Sb_2S_2O. Lyrostibnite. A native, red antimony sulfide pigment.

kern. German for ring and nucleus, especially the benzene ring.

kernel. An atom stripped of its valence electrons; the positively charged atomic nucleus surrounded by its proper numbers of electrons in their respective orbits, with the exception of the outermost. Cf. *periodic system, isostere, nucleus*.

kernite. $Na_2B_4O_7\cdot4H_2O$. A sodium borate from Kern County, Calif. Colorless monoclinic crystals, d.1.908, hardness 2.5.

kerocain. Procaine hydrochloride.

kerogen. $(C_6H_8O)_n$. The resinous chief organic constituent of shale oils; insoluble in most solvents containing solid hydrocarbons, sulfur, nitrogen, and oxygen. At 400°C, it yields fuel oil and gas. Cf. *oil shale*.

kerokaine. Procaine.

keroles. That portion of kerotenes which is soluble in pyridine, but insoluble in chloroform.

kerols. That portion of kerotenes which is soluble in both chloroform and pyridine.

kerones. That portion of kerotenes which is insoluble in organic solvents.

kerosine. Coal oil, astral oil, kerosene, paraffin (U.K. usage). A mixture of hydrocarbons, b.150–280; the fraction in the distillation of petroleum between gasoline and the oils; an illuminant and cleanser.

kerotenes. That portion of bitumen which is insoluble in carbon disulfide. Cf. *carboids, kerenes.*

Kerr constant. If L is the difference in wavelength between the ordinary and extraordinary rays, λ the wavelength of the light, v the potential, and d the distance between the poles; $L = k\lambda v^2/d^2$, where k is the Kerr constant. **K. effect.** Electrical birefringence. The elliptical double refraction of light by liquids in an electric field.

kesso oil. Japanese valerian oil. An essential oil from the roots of *Valeriana officinalis.* Green, liquid, d.0.996, insoluble in water; used in pharmacy.

kessyl alcohol. $C_{14}H_{24}O_2$ = 224.19. Wrongly called kersyl alcohol, m.85, $b_{11mm}156$, from kesso oil.

Kestner, Paul. b. 1864. Swiss chemist, noted for work on refractories and filters.

ketal. (1) Obsolete term for the $>CO$ group; as, dimethyl ketal (= acetone). (2) $R_1 \cdot R_2 \cdot C \cdot (OR_3) \cdot (OR_4)$. Ketone acetates prepared by condensation of alkyl orthoformates with ketones in presence of alcohols.

ketazin. $C_6H_{12}N_2$ = 112.2. Colorless liquid, d.0.836, b.131, soluble in water.

ketazine. Bisazimethylene. A compound containing the radical $>C:N—N:C<$.

ketene. $CH_2:CO$ = 42.0. Ketoethylene, ethenone, carbomethene. The simplest ketone. Colorless gas of penetrating odor, b.—56, decomp. by water; an acetylation agent. **k. diacetal.** $CH_2:C \cdot (OEt)_2$ = 116.0. Ethoxyethylene. Colorless liquid, b.125; reacts with water to form ethylacetate, and polymerizes to a white solid.

ketenes. $R_2C:CO$. A group of reactive organic compounds; 2 types: **aldo-** $R \cdot H \cdot C:CO$. Colorless, polymerized by pyridine and incapable of autooxidation. Cf. *aldoketenes.* **keto-** $R_2C:CO$. Colored, readily auto-oxidized and forming additive compounds. Both are homologs of ketene. Cf. *ketoketenes, ketenes.*

ketimide. $R_2:C:NX$ where X is an acyl radical. Cf. *ketimine.*

ketimine. An organic compound containing the $>C:NH$ group. Cf. *ketone, imine.*

ketine. $C_6H_8N_2$ = 108.2. 2,5-Dimethylpyrazine. Colorless liquid, d.0.990, b.153, soluble in water.

ketines. $R \cdot C:CH \cdot N:CR \cdot CH:N$, derived from ketine. Cf. *ketenes.*

keto- Oxo- Prefix indicating the keto or carbonyl group, $>C:O$, in an organic compound. Cf. *ketone.* **k. acid.** See *ketone acid.* **k. enol.** See *tautomerism.*

ketoamine. $R:CNH_2CO \cdot R$. An organic compound containing the keto and amino group, formed by the action of ammonia on ketones. Cf. *polypeptide.*

ketocoumaran. $C_6H_4 \cdot (O) \cdot CO \cdot CH_2$ = 134.1. Ketodihydrocoumarone. Colorless crystals, m.97.

ketodestrin. Estrone.

ketohexose. A monosaccharide of 6 C atoms, with a keto group instead of the usual aldehyde group, e.g., fructose.

ketohydroxyestrin. $C_{18}H_{22}O_2$ = 270.1. A hormone from the urine of pregnant women and mares; an anhydride of trihydroxyestrin. Cf. *sterols.*

ketoimine. A compound containing an imino and keto group.

ketoindole. Oxindole.

ketoketenes. $R_2C:CO$. The dialkylated homologs of ketene. They are colored, readily auto-oxidized, and form additive compounds with tertiary amines. Cf. *aldoketenes.*

ketol. Ketone alcohols. A compound containing a keto and hydroxy group. **alpha-** A compound containing the $R—CO \cdot CH_2OH$ group. **beta-** A compound containing the $R—CO \cdot CH_2 \cdot CH_2OH$ group. **saturated-** An α- or β-ketone alcohol. **unsaturated-** Acivinyl alcohols. A compound containing the unsaturated $R—CO \cdot CH:CHOH$ group.

ketole. Indole.

ketone. $R \cdot CO \cdot R$. An organic compound containing the ketone group, $>C:O$. Nomenclature: naming the 2 radicals before the term *ketone* (as dimethyl ketone) or attaching the suffix *-one* to the hydrocarbon: $CH_3 \cdot CO \cdot CH_3$ is dimethyl ketone or propanone (acetone). Classification: (1) Aliphatic, saturated: acetone, propanone*, $Me \cdot CO \cdot Me$. (2) Aliphatic, unsaturated; Δ^3-2-butenone, $MeCOCH:CH_2$. (3) Aliphatic, diketones: biacetyl, 2,3-butanedione*, $MeCOCOMe$. (4) Cyclic: cyclobutanone, $CO \cdot CH_2 \cdot CH_2 \cdot CH_2$. (5) Quinones: quinone, $CO \cdot CH_2 \cdot CH_2 \cdot CO \cdot CH_2 \cdot CH_2$. (6) Aromatic: acetophenone, $Ph \cdot COMe$. **acid-** Ketone acid. **aldehyde-** A compound containing the $=CO$ and —CHO groups. **amino-** Ketoamine. **amyl ethyl-** 3-Octanone. **amyl methyl-** 2-Heptanone*. **butyl methyl-** 2-Hexanone*. **di-** A compound containing 2 k. groups; e.g.: **alpha-** $R \cdot CO \cdot CO \cdot R$. **beta-** $R \cdot CO \cdot CH_2 \cdot CO \cdot R$. **gamma-** $R \cdot CO \cdot CH_2 \cdot CH_2 \cdot CO \cdot R$. **dibutyl-** 5-Nonanone*. **diethyl-** 3-Pentanone*. **diheptyl-** 8-Pentadecanone*. **dimethyl-** Acetone. **dipropyl-** 4-Heptanone*. **ethyl methyl-** 2-Butanone*. **ethyl propyl-** 3-Hexanone*. **methyl propyl-** 2-Pentanone*. **mixed-** A k. with 2 different radicals attached to the k. group, e.g., $Me \cdot CO \cdot Et$, methyl ethyl k. **nitroso-** A compound containing the k. and nitroso groups. **olefine-** A k. of the olefine series. **paraffin-** A k. of the paraffin series. **simple-** A k. with the same 2 radicals attached to the k. group. **tri-** $R \cdot CO \cdot CO \cdot CO \cdot R$. A compound containing 3 k. groups.

k. acid. A compound containing the radicals $>CO$ and —COOH. *alpha-* A compound containing the radical —CO·COOH, e.g., pyruvic acid. *beta-* A compound containing the radical —CO·CH_2·COOH, e.g., acetoacetic acid. *gamma-* A compound containing the radical —CO·CH_2·CH_2·COOH, e.g., levulinic acid. *delta-* A compound containing the radical —CO·CH_2·CH_2·CH_2·COOH, e.g., acetobutyric acid. **k. alcohol.** See *ketol.* **k. base.** Tetramethyldiaminobenzophenone. **k. color.** An artificial color containing the k. group, e.g., alizarin. **k. form.** See *ketonic ester type.* **k. group.** The $>C:O$ group; it usually confers reducing powers.

ketonic. Pertaining to a ketone. **k. ester type.**

An isomer of an enolic ester type compound:

$$
\begin{array}{cc}
\text{R.C} = \text{O} & \text{R.C} - \text{OR}'' \\
| & \| \\
\text{HCR}'' \rightleftharpoons \text{HC} \\
| & | \\
\text{COOR}' & \text{COOR}'
\end{array}
$$

Ketonic ester type   Enolic ester type

Cf. *desmotropism*.

ketose. A sugar containing a ketone group. Cf. *aldose*.

ketoside. A glucoside which yields a ketose on hydrolysis.

ketosis. The excretion of acetone bodies.

ketotriazole. Triazolone.

ketoxime. (1) Acetoxime. A compound containing the =C:NOH group, e.g. Me₂C:N·OH, acetoxime. (2) A compound containing the —HC·NO— group. Cf. *Beckmann rearrangement*. (3) See *dioxines*. **tetra-** See *diphenyltetraketoxime*.

Kevidon. Trademark for *thalidomide*.

key. A mechanical device for switching on or off, or reversing an electric current. **k. atom.** (1) An atom in a chain whose change in electronic structure induces corresponding changes in the other atoms of the chain. (2) An atom in a ring whose oscillations cause a shift of bonds. Cf. *porphin ring*.

kg. Abbreviation for kilogram.

kgf. Abbreviation for kilogram force.

kharasch-1408. A derivative of *N*-(1-carboxyacyl-aminoethylthiomethyl), used to treat tuberculosis.

kharophen. Acetarsol.

kharsivan. British-made salvarsan.

khat. Cafta, Arabian tea. The dried leaves of *Catha edulis*; a tea.

khelin. Khellin. A synthetic dimethoxymethyl-furanochromone derivative, used for its specific coronary vasodilatory activity. Also obtained from the seeds of the wild Mediterranean plant, *Ammi visnaga*, Lam.

Khotinsky, Achilles de. 1850–1933. Russian born American instrument designer. **de K. cement.** A cement for glass and porcelain; insulating, covering, and connecting electric wires, glass, rubber, wood, etc.; resistant to ordinary solvents.

kibbled. Broken up into small lumps of about 1 cm diameter.

kidney. A mammalian organ which eliminates urea, chlorides, and creatinine from the blood, and filters the noncolloidal material from blood plasma.

kidney ore. Red *hematite*.

kies. General term for sulfide ores.

kieselguhr. Diatomite. Tripoli powder. Guhr. A diatomaceous or infusorial earth. Used as an absorbent for nitroglycerin (dynamite), for filtering, insulating, and as an abrasive in soaps.

kieserite. MgSO₄·H₂O. A native magnesium sulfate. White compact masses in the Stassfurt salt beds.

Kikuchi lines. The black and white lines which appear when a stream of electrons is scattered by a crystal surface. Cf. electron *microscope*.

killeen. Irish moss.

Killiani, Heinrich. German chemist. **K. reaction.** The synthesis of a higher homolog by forming a nitrile, followed by hydrolysis, e.g., pentose to hexose: R·CHO → R·CHOH·CN → R·CHOH·COOH → R·CHOH·CHO.

kiln. (1) A potter's oven for baking bricks. (2) A furnace for calcining or drying coarsely broken ore or stone. (3) A building for drying malt.

kilo-, kilo. (1) Greek prefix indicating 1,000 units. (2) Kilogram.

kilocalorie. Cal. A great (or large) calorie: 1 Cal = 1000 calories.

kilocycle. A frequency of 1000 vibrational cycles per second.

kilodyne. 1,000 dynes (0.9806 gm).

kilogram. A unit of weight in the metric system; intended to be the mass of 1 cubic decimeter of water at 4°C. 1 kg = 1,000 gm = 15,432.25 grains = 2.2046 lb av. = 35.27 oz av. = 32.1507 oz troy = 2.679 lb apoth. Cf. *liter, yard, cubic centimeter*. **International Prototype-** I.P. Kg. A cylinder of platinum-iridium alloy; the standard k. weight.

kilogram-meter. A unit of energy in the metric system: the energy to raise one kilogram one meter. 1 kg-m = 7.233 ft-lb.

kilojoule. A unit of heat: a large joule, J. 1000 joules = 239.1 gm-cal.

kiloliter. Stere. 1 kl = 1,000 liter = 35.371 ft³ = 2641.7 U.S. liquid gal.

kilometer. A unit of length in the metric system. 1 km = 1,000 meters = 3280.83 ft = 1093.61 yd = 0.62137 mile. (1 mile = 1.609 km.)

kilonem. A unit of nutrition equivalent to 667 cal; supplied by a liter of milk.

kilostere. A unit of volume. 1 kilostere = 1,000 cubic meters = 1,000 kl.

kilowatt. A unit of electric power. 1 kw = 1,000 watts = 1000 joules/sec = 1.341 hp = 238.7 cal/sec. (1 hp = 746 watts.) **k. hour-** A commercial unit of electric energy. 1 kwhr = 1,000 whr = 3,600,000 joules/sec = 1 BThU.

kilurane. A suggested unit of radioactivity. 1 ku = 1,000 uranium units (uranes).

kimberlite. Blue ground. An igneous mineral in which diamonds occur.

kinase. Zymoexcitor. A substance in living tissues, which activates or transforms a zymogen into an active enzyme. **entero-** See *enterokinase*.

kinematics. The science of motion, apart from the forces that produce it.

kinetic. (1) Pertaining to motion. (2) Dealing with forces that influence the motion of bodies. **k. chemicals.** Gases used as refrigerants. **k. energy.** The force possessed by a body due to its motion = $mv^2/2$, where m is the mass and v the velocity. **k. theory.** The hypothesis that all molecules are in motion, which is most rapid in gases, less rapid in liquids, and very slow in solids, and is a function of temperature. $PV = \frac{1}{3}nmv^2 = RT$, where n is the number of molecules. See *Brownian motion, gas laws*.

kinetin. Zeatin.

kineurine. Quinine glycerophosphate.

king's yellow. Orpiment.

kinic acid. Quinic acid.

kino. Kino gum. The dried juice of *Pterocarpus marsupium* (Leguminosae), tropical Africa. Brown, brittle fragments, soluble in water; used as an intestinal astringent, and in the tanning and textile industries. **African-** Kino. **American-** The dried juice of *Coccoloba uvifera*; a k. substitute. **marri-** A red gum from *Eucalyptus calophylla* (Myrtaceae).

kinoin. $C_{14}H_{12}O_6 = 276.1$. A resin from kino.

kinovin. Quinovin.

Kipp generator. A 3-compartment apparatus for generating gases, generally hydrogen sulfide, from a solid reagent in the middle and a liquid reagent in the lower compartment.

Kirchhoff, Gustav Robert. 1824–1887. German physical chemist noted for development of the spectroscope. **K. equation.** $\log p = A + B/t + C \log t$, where p is the vapor pressure of a gas at the absolute temperature t; and A, B, and C are constants.

kish. Crystalline graphite deposited in iron furnaces from molten iron.

kisidwe oil. A hard, white fat from the nuts of *Allanblackia* species (Ghana); used in soap manufacture.

kitol. Vitamin A_3.

kittel plates. A device used in a fractionating column to ensure rapid renewal of the contacting surface between the liquid being distilled and its vapor.

kittool fiber. Kittul. A fiber from the leaves of a Ceylon palm, *Caryota urens*; used in brushes.

kittul. Kittool.

Kjeldahl, Johan. 1849–1900. Danish analytical chemist. **K. apparatus.** An arrangement for distilling ammonia from an organic compound. **K. flask.** A pear-shaped flask of heat- and acid-resistant glass with a long neck. **K. method.** A method to determine nitrogen in an organic compound by digesting with concentrated sulfuric acid and distilling the ammonia from the ammonium sulfate formed into a measured quantity of standard sulfuric acid.

kl. Abbreviation for kiloliter = 1,000 liters.

Klaproth, Martin Heinrich. 1743–1817. German chemist, who discovered uranium, titanium, and zirconium.

klaprotholite. $Cu_6Bi_4S_9$. A native copper bismuth sulfide.

Kleinenberg mixture. A mixture of cacao butter, spermaceti, and castor oil; a microscope embedding material.

kleinite. $HgCl_2 \cdot 3HgO$. A native mercury oxide and chloride.

Klein's liquid. A saturated solution of cadmium borotungstate, d.3.28; used to separate minerals.

klydonograph. A device to record automatically a temporary excess voltage by a spark passing through a moving film. The resulting Lichtenberg diagram indicates the nature of the current.

klystron. An electronic device for producing microwave (radio-type) oscillations of frequency 3,000–300,000. A beam of electrons is shot through a cavity, and repelled back through it by a reflector electrode.

km. Abbreviation for kilometer = 1,000 meters.

k.m.f. Abbreviation for the keratin-myosin fibrinogen system, a major group of proteins.

knallgas. The mixture of hydrogen, 2 vol., and oxygen, 1 vol., produced by electrolysis of water.

knap. To break up, e.g., lumps of ore.

knead. To work together a number of ingredients, usually by hand.

knock. The nearly instantaneous and high-pressure explosion of a compressed mixture of fuel and air in an internal-combustion engine. Much of the energy is absorbed by the walls of the cylinder as radiant energy, thus reducing the available mechanical energy. **anti-** A substance added to a liquid fuel which slightly retards the explosion and thereby reduces the energy wasted. *Antiknock gasoline* contains 0.05% of tetraethyllead. See *Ethyl* gasoline.

knock compound. Antiknock. A substance which when added to gasoline, reduces the knock.

Knop, Johann Ludwig Wilhelm. 1817–1871. German agricultural chemist. **K.'s solution.** A nutrient for plants: potassium nitrate 1, monobasic potassium phosphate 1, magnesium sulfate 1, calcium nitrate 4 pts., and a trace of ferric phosphate in 1,000 pts. water.

knoppern. Galls. A tan produced on oaks by insects.

Knorr, Ludwig. 1859–1921. German chemist, discoverer of antipyrine. **K. alkalimeter.** A device for determining carbon dioxide.

knot. The speed of 1 nautical mile = 6,082.66 ft/hr.

knotgrass. **English-** The herb of *Polygonum aviculare* (Polygonaceae); an astringent. **Russian-** The herb of *P. erectum*; an astringent.

knoxvillite. $CrSO_4$. A native chromous sulfate.

kobold. Early name for cobalt.

Koch, Robert. 1843–1910. German bacteriologist, discoverer of the tubercle bacillus. **K.'s acid.** Naphthylamine-3,6,8-trisulfonic acid. **K. bacillus.** The tuberculosis bacillus. **K. flask.** A pear-shaped flask used for growing bacterial cultures.

koechlinite. $Bi_2O_3 \cdot MoO_3$. A native molybdenum oxide.

kogi. An enzyme used to produce miso, q.v.

Kohlrausch, Friedrich. 1840–1910. German hpysicist. **K. law.** The conductivity of an electrolyte is the sum of the conductivities of its component ions when complete ionization occurs. **K. bridge.** A Wheatstone bridge type instrument to measure the conductivity of an electrolite.

koilin. A scleroprotein lining of birds' gizzards.

koilonychia. A dermatitis affecting the fingers of those working with alkaline cements.

kojic acid. $C_6H_6O_4 = 142.05$. 3-Hydroxy-5-hydroxymethyl-γ-pyrone, m.153; formed from glucose by certain molds, e.g. *Aspergillus oryzae*. Cf. *ascorbic acid*.

kok-saghyz. Russian dandelion from the Ukraine; the roots yield 10–20% of a rubber constituent.

kola. Cola, kola nuts. The dried seeds of *Cola* species (Sterculiaceae) of Africa; it contains 2–3% caffeine. Used as a nervine and cardiac stimulant, and in beverages.

kolanin. $C_{40}H_{56}O_{21}N_4 = 928.7$. A glucoside from kola, which hydrolyzes to caffeine, glucose, and kolared.

kolared. $C_{14}H_{13}(OH)_5 = 266.2$. A red coloring matter from kola nuts.

kollagraph. An instrument to measure the jointing capacity of a soldering system in terms of the surface and interfacial characteristics of the fluxed joint.

kolm. A radioactive asphaltic mineral: 0.45–0.027% Pb.

komanic acid. Pyrone-α-carboxylic acid.

komplexon. German for complexone.

konel. The alloy: ferrotitanium 8, cobalt 17, nickel 73%; a platinum substitute for radiotube filaments.

koniogravimeter. An instrument to determine dust in air.

kontrastin. Zirconium oxide contrast medium for X-ray examinations.

Kopp, Hermann. 1817–1892. German physical chemist. **K.'s law.** Every element has the same specific heat in its solid free state as in its solid compounds. Thus, the molecular heat is the sum of the atomic heats of the component atoms.

Koppeschaar solution. A 0.1 N bromine solution. Cf. *potassium bromate*.

koppite. $(Ca,Ce,Fe,Hg,Na_2)O·NbO_2·H_2O$. A vitreous brown mineral.

koprosterol. Coprosterol.

Koresin. Trade name for a plastic made by the reaction of acetylene with *p-tert*-butylphenol in presence of zinc naphthenate. Used to render synthetic rubber tacky.

kornerupine. A rare Indian magnesium aluminum borosilicate.

Koroseal. Trademark for a vinyl chloride plastic; proof against water, but not against water vapor.

korotin. Chlorionic gonadotropin.

koryan oil. Kaoliang oil. An oil from *Andropogon sorghum*, koryan corn (Manchukuo), d.0.926, iodine no. 121.

kosam seeds. The fruits of *Brucea sumatrana* (Simarubaceae), China; used to treat dysentery and diarrhea.

kosin. Koussin.

koso. Kousso.

kosotoxin. $C_{26}H_{34}O_{10} = 506.3$. A yellow, amorphous principle from kousso.

Kossel lines. Diffracted X-ray used in X-ray analysis. **K. press.** A metal syringe for making sodium wire.

kotoin. Cotoin.

Köttstorfer number. Saponification number.

koumiss. A beverage prepared by fermentation of mare's milk with kefir yeast.

kounidine. $C_{21}H_{24}N_2O_5 = 384.18$. An alkaloid from Chinese *Gelsemium* species; produces muscular and respiratory weakness.

Kourbatoff's reagents. Four etching agents for steel: A. 4% nitric acid in isoamyl alcohol. B. Equal parts of 20% hydrochloric acid in isoamyl alcohol and a saturated solution of nitroaniline in alcohol. C. Equal parts of 4% nitric acid in acetic acid, methanol, ethanol, and isoamyl alcohol. D. 3 pts. of saturated nitrophenol in alcohol and 1 pt. 4% nitric acid in alcohol.

koussein. A yellow, anthelmintic, amorphous principle from kousso.

koussin. $C_{51}H_{38}O_{10} = 570.4$. Kosin. Kussin. A resin from kousso; an anthelmintic.

kousso. Cusso, brayera. The dried flowers of *Brayer anthelmintica*, (*Hagenia Abyssinica*) (Rosaceae); an anthelmintic. Cf. *brayerin*.

kovar. A group of alloys (e.g., Fe 53.8, Ni 29, Co 17, Mn 0.2%) which show a sharp change in coefficient of expansion at certain temperatures; used for all-metal radio tubes and thermostats, and to cement glass in vacuum apparatus.

Kr. Symbol for krypton.

K. radiation. See under *K*.

kraft paper. A strong (German: kraft = force) wrapping paper made from wood pulp prepared by the sulfate process.

krameria. Rhatany root, payta. The dried root of *K. triandra*, Peru, or *K. argentia*, Brazil (Polygalaceae); an astringent and tonic.

krantzite. A variety of retinite.

Kraut's reagent. A microchemical reagent for ephedrine made by mixing *A* and *B* and diluting to 100 ml. *A*: 8 gm bismuth nitrate in 20 ml concentrated nitric acid. *B*: 27.2 gm potassium iodide in 50 ml water.

kreatine, kreatinine. See *creatine, creatinine*.

Krebs cycle. See *citric* acid cycle.

Kreis test. A test for 3C-chain unsaturated aldehydes, characteristic of rancid fats. A red color develops in the aqueous layer after an ethereal solution of fat has been treated with hydrochloric acid and phloroglucinol solution.

kremersite. $KCl·NH_4Cl·FeCl_3·1\frac{1}{2}H_2O$. A native iron chloride.

krennerite. (1) $(Ag, Au)Te_2$. A native telluride. (2) Bunsenite.

kreosol. Cresol.

kreotoxin. A meat ptomaine formed by bacteria.

kresatin. $MeCOOCH_2C_6H_4OH = 166.2$. *m*- Cresyl acetate. Colorless oil; an antiseptic.

krilium. The sodium salt of hydrolyzed polyacrylonitrile; it stimulates the effect of humus in aggregating soil particles and improving soil structure.

krinosin. $C_{38}H_{79}O_5N(?)$. A lipin from brain substance.

krith. Crith. The weight of one liter of hydrogen, at 0°C and 760 mm = 0.0896 gm. A term sometimes used to express the density of a gas with reference to hydrogen; thus the density of chlorine is 35.5 kriths.

krocodylite. Crocidolite.

krügite. $MgSO_4·K_2SO_4·4CaSO_4·2H_2O$. A native sulfate.

Krupp's disease. Fragility shown by steels after tempering and reheating.

Kryofine. $EtO·C_6H_4·NHCO·CH_2OMe = 209.12$. Trademark for cryofine, methoxyacet-*p*-phenetidine. Colorless needles, m.98; soluble in water; an antipyretic.

kryogenin. (1) See *cryogenin*. (2) $NH_2CO·C_6H_4NH··NH·CONH_2 = 194.1$. Colorless, bitter powder, soluble in water; an antipyretic and antiseptic.

kyroscopy. (1) Determination of the molecular weight of a substance from the lowering of the freezing point of its solutions. See *cryoscopy*. (2) In general, the production of low temperatures. (3) The study of the phenomena occurring during the cooling of molten alloys.

kryptidine. $C_{11}H_{11}N = 157.1$. 2,4-Dimethylquinoline. A homolog of quinoline.

krypto- See *crypto-*.

kryptocyanin. $C_{25}H_{25}N_2I = 480.0$. 1,1'-Diethyl 4,4'-carbocyanin iodide. A sensitizer for the infrared; used for photography through haze.

kryptol. A granular mixture of graphite, Carborundum, and clay; used as a resistance in electric furnaces.

krypton. $Kr = 83.80$. Colorless, inert, noble gas and element, at. no. 36, in the atmosphere (1 per 1,000,000); $d_{air}=13.708$, m.—169, b.—152.9. It forms no known chemical compound, and consists of at least 6 isotopes: at. wts. 84, 86, 82, 83, 80, 78.

kryptoxanthin. $C_{40}H_{55}OH$ = 552.4. Caricaxanthin. A yellow, carotinoid pigment from the pods of *Physalis* species, *Carica papaya*, and yellow corn. Cf. *carotene*.

K.S.K. Ethyl iodoacetate.

Kufasa. Trade name for a cuprammonium synthetic fiber.

kuh-seng. A Chinese drug, the dried roots of *Sophora flavescens* (Leguminosae). Its chief alkaloid is matrine.

kukersite. An Esthonian shale oil containing 43% organic matter (kerogen).

kukoline. An alkaloid from *Cucullus diversifolius* (Asclepiadaceae).

kumyss. Lac fermentatum. Sweetened cow's milk, fermented with yeast; a nutrient. Cf. *koumiss*.

Kundt, August. 1839–1894. German physicist. **K.'s constant.** (1) See *K'.s rule*. (2) A value obtained by dividing Verdet's constant by the magnetic susceptibility of the substance. **K. effect.** The rotation of the plane of polarized light in certain vapors and gases under the influence of magnetic forces. **K.'s rule.** An increase in refractive index produces a shift in the absorption bands of a solution toward the red, to an extent defined by K.'s constant. **K.'s tube.** A horizontal tube containing a light powder. On sounding a note at the open end, the sand assumes heaps whose distance apart measures the velocity of sound in the gas and hence its specific heat.

Kunkel, Johann. 1638–1703. German alchemist who published, under the pseudonym "Baron von Lowenstjern," a chemical textbook "Laboratorium Chymicum."

kunzite. $LiAl(SiO_3)_2$. A native, pink variety of spodumene.

kupfernickel. Niccolite.

kupferron. Cupferron.

kupramite. A preparation used in gas masks to absorb ammonia.

Kuralon, Kuravilon. Trade names for polyvinyl alcohol synthetic fibers.

kurchi. The root of *Holarrhena antidysenterica* (Apocynaceae); a febrifuge and antidysenteric.

kurchine. An alkaloid obtained from kurchi, q.v.

Kurehalon. Trade name for a mixed-polymer synthetic fiber.

Kuremona. Trade name for a polyvinyl alcohol synthetic fiber.

kurrajong oil. A thick, red oil from the seeds of *Brachychiton populenum*.

Kurrol's salt. $(KPO_3)_4$. Potassium polyphosphate, having ion-exchange properties. A long-chain metaphosphate made by slowly cooling and seeding molten potassium metaphosphate; mol.wt. exceeds 100,000, m.838.

kusamba. A narcotic obtained by macerating opium with rose water.

kussin. Koussin.

kuteera gum. Hog gum.

kvar. Wattless current. A term expressing the ratio of kilovolt-amperes to kilowatts.

kwells. Hyoscine hydrobromide.

*k***X.** The absolute measurement for the wavelengths of X rays. $kX \times 1.00202 = 1$ angstrom.

kyanite. Cyanite.

kyanizing. The preservation of wood by mercuric chloride solution.

kyanol. Early name for aniline.

kymograph. An instrument to record variations of blood pressure.

kynurenic acid. $C_6H_4 \cdot C \cdot OH \cdot C \cdot COOH \cdot CH : N$ =

189.09. 4- or γ-Hydroxyquinolinecarboxylic acid. A decomposition product of tryptophane in dog's unine; prisms, m.289, soluble in hot water.

kynuric acid. $C_9H_7O_5N$ = 209.1. Oxalylanthranilic acid, carbostyrilic acid. Colorless crystals, m.288.

kynurin. C_9H_7ON = 145.06. 4- or γ-Hydroxyquinoline. Colorless crystals, m.201, soluble in water.

kyrine. A basic substance from the hydrolysis of proteins.

kytoplasm. Cytoplasm.

L

L. Symbol for: (1) the abstract unit of length; L^2, of area; L^3, of volume; (2) latent heat per mole; (3) solubility product. **L electrons.** The electrons in the second shell or orbit of the atom, $Ne = 8$. **L lines.** (1) The group of lines following the K lines, q.v. (2) The Fraunhofer lines λ 3,820 to λ 3,858, due to iron. **L orbit.** The second series of paths of electrons around the atomic nucleus, and outside the innermost K orbit. **L radiations.** The second series of homogeneous X rays characteristic of the metal used as anticathode, and analogous to the K radiations, q.v. **L shell.** The second layer of electrons in the static atom (Lewis-Langmuir). **L spectrum.** The spectrum due to L radiations. Cf. K *spectrum, Moseley spectra.*

l. Abbreviation for liter.

l. Symbol for (1) latent heat per gram, (2) length, (3) ionic mobility, (4) mean free molecular path.

l- Abbreviation for levo- or levorotary; $l(d)$-levo- (or dextro-); ld- levo- and dextro- ($=$ meso).

λ. Greek lambda. Symbol for: (1) microliter $=$ 0.001 ml, (2) latent heat of reaction, (3) wavelength, (4) lithium nucleus.

Λ. Greek capital lambda. Symbol for equivalent conductivity.

La. Symbol for lanthanum.

lab. Lab ferment, rennase. The ferment of rennet, which coagulates milk.

Labarraque, Antoine Germaine. 1777–1850. French apothecary. **L. solution.** A solution of sodium hypochlorite (minimum 2.4% available Cl); a disinfectant and deodorant.

labdanum. A stimulant and expectorant resin from *Cistus* species.

labeling. Rendering a substance identifiable by means of a radioactive isotope; e.g., C^{14} is used to identify many organic compounds into which it is introduced. **specific-** L. of one particular atom in a molecule; e.g., C^{14} in $(CH_3)C^{14}OOH$. **uniform-** L. of all atoms of the same kind in a molecule, e.g., $C^{14}(H_3)C^{14}OOH$. Ref.: I. and E. Mellan, "Encyclopedia of Chemical Labeling" (U.S. usage).

LaBel tube. A distilling tube with 2 or more bulbs and return tubes, used for fractional distillation.

Labiate. Mint family, aromatic herbs that yield important essential oils; e.g., herbs: *Mentha piperita*, peppermint; *Lavandula spica*, lavender; *Thymus serpyllum*, wild thyme; *Monarda punctata*, horsemint; leaves: *Salvia officinalis*, sage; *Rosmarinus officinalis*, rosemary; *Thymus vulgaris*, thyme; *Ocimum basilicum*, sweet basil; flowers: *Lavandula vera*, lavender; rhizomes: *Collinsonia canadensis*, stoneroot.

labile. Unstable. **l. acid.** See *acid*. **l. state.** Temporary stability.

laboratory. The chemical working place.

Labrador tea. James tea, marsh tea, wild rosemary.

The leaves of *Ledum palustre* (Ericaceae) used as tea in Labrador; an expectorant. It contains ledum camphor, ericinol, and ericulin.

labradorite. Saussurite. An iridescent lime-soda feldspar.

laburnine. An alkaloid from *Cytisus laburnum* (Leguminosae). Cf. *cytisine.*

lac. (1) Lacca, resina lacca, lacca gum, lakh. A resin exuding around twigs of *Croton* species (Euphorbiaceae) and *Ficus* species (Moraceae), E. Indies; caused by the bite of the female insect, *Coccus lacca.* (2) The bodies of *Coccus lac*; a red dye. (3) Milk; as *lac sulfuris*, milk of sulfur. **alpha-** Suggested name for the insoluble portion of shellac. **seed-** L. broken from the twigs. **shel-** Shellac, q.v. Prepared by melting and straining seed l. **stick-** The crude red l. as taken from the tree.

lacca. See lac, shellac. **l. coerula.** Litmus.

laccaic acid. $C_{16}H_{12}O_8 = 332.1$. Laccainic acid. Red crystals in lac, decomp. 180.

laccase. (1) An oxidizing enzyme of the sap of plants (lac tree). (2) A class of oxidases which act on phenols.

lacceroic acid. $C_{31}H_{63}COOH = 480.29$. Dotriakontanic acid. A fatty acid, m.95, in waxes. Cf. *psyllic acid.*

lacerate. To cut or tear an edge or point irregularly.

lachesine chloride. $C_{20}H_{26}O_3NCl = 363.92$. β-Benzilyloxyethyldimethylethylammonium chloride. White bitter powder, m.214 (decomp.), soluble in water. A mydriatic, used similarly to atropine in ophthalmology.

lachry- See *lacri-.*

L acid. 1-Naphthol-5-sulfonic acid.

lacmoid. $C_{12}H_9O_4N = 231.1$. Resorcinol blue. Violet scales, soluble in water; an indicator: blue (pH 6.4) in alkaline, red (pH 4.4) in acid solution. **l. tincture.** A solution of 0.5 gm lacmoid in 100 ml each of water and alcohol; an indicator.

lacmus. Litmus.

lacquer. (1) A varnish, natural or containing shellac. (2) A solution of a resin which dries by evaporation of the solvent, and leaves a protective covering. (3) A solution of a cellulose ester in a solvent. **acetate-** A relatively nonflammable solution of cellulose acetate in carbon tetrachloride. **bronzing-** A solution of nitrocellulose in amyl acetate with suspended aluminum or bronze powder. **brush-** A l. applicable with brushes. **Burmese-** A natural l. exuding from the stems of *Melanorrhea usitata* (Anacardiaceae), which blackens on exposure. **cellulose-** Lacquer (3). **Chinese-** Japanese- **collodion-** See *collodion.* **dip-** A l. for coating by immersion. **glyptal-** A solution of the synthetic resins made from glycerol and organic acids. **Japanese-** The resinous sap of *Rhus vernicifera* (Anacardiaceae), Japan and China; often colored by pigments and thinned with camphor oil or turpentine. **nitrocellulose-** A l., containing cellulose nitrate in an organic solvent.

l. solvent. Organic liquids which dissolve resins, gums, or nitrocellulose; used in the manufacture of lacquers, varnishes, and rayon. See *solvents.*

lacri- Prefix indicating tears.

lacrimation. An excessive secretion of tears.

lacrimator(y). A tear-producing substance; as, ethyl iodoacetate. Cf. *dacryagogue.* **l. gas.** A poison gas used to produce tears; as, benzyl bromide.

lacry- Lacri-.

lactalbumin. The albumin of milk.

lactam. Lactan. An organic compound containing the —NH—CO— group in a ring formed by the elimination of water from —COOH and —NH₂ groups. Cf. *lactim.*

lactamic acid. Alanine.

lactamide. Me·CHOH·CONH₂ = 89.1. Lactic acid amide, 2-hydroxypropanamide*. Colorless crystals, m.74, soluble in water.

lactamine. Alanine.

lactan. Lactam.

lactase. An enzyme in intestinal juice, which hydrolyzes lactose to dextrose and galactose.

lactasidase. A zymase which converts lactose to lactic acid.

lactate. (1) A salt of lactic acid containing the radical Me·CHOH·COO—; used as flour conditioners and food emulsifiers. (2) To produce milk.

lactation. The secretion of milk.

lactazam. A compound containing the —NH·NH·-CO—group in its ring; as, 3-methylpyrazolon. Cf. *phenyllactazam.*

lactazone. Lactoxime.

lactic acid. C₃H₆O₃ = 90.08. 2-Hydroxypropanoic acid*, ethylidenelactic acid, acid of milk, fermentation l. acid. A fermentation acid from milk or carbohydrates. Colorless liquid, d.1.240, m.18, b₁₂ₘₘ119, soluble in water. Used as a reagent to detect glucose and pyrogallol; in organic synthesis; in leather, textile, and tanning industries; in pharmacy (U.S.P., B.P.); and to substitute citric and tartaric acids; 2 tautomers:

$$H\diagdown C\diagup COOH \qquad H\diagdown C\diagup OH$$
$$HO\diagup \diagdown CH_3 \quad and \quad HOOC\diagup \diagdown CH_2$$

l- or levo-   d- or dextro-

dextro- L. acid produced in muscle tissues by splitting glucose, or by the action of *Micrococcus acidi paralactici.* A solid, m.25. **levo-** L. acid formed by the action of *Bacillus acidi levolactica.* **para-** See *dextro-.* **sarco-** See *dextro-.* The aqueous solution of l. acid consists of an equilibrium of 4 forms:

$$MeCH(OH)COOH \rightleftharpoons MeCH(OH)CO\diagdown_O$$
$$HOOC·MeCH\diagup$$

Normal   Anhydride

$$\Updownarrow \qquad \Updownarrow$$

$$MeCH·C·(OH)_2 \rightleftharpoons O·CHMe·CO$$
$$\underset{O}{\llcorner\lrcorner} \qquad | \qquad |$$
$$OC·CHMe·O$$

Ethylene oxide   Lactide
form or sarco-
lactic acid

l. acid series. CₙH₂ₙ(OH)COOH. Monobasic hydroxy acids; e.g.: carbonic (hydroformic) acid, HO·COOH; lactic acid, hydroxypropionic acid, HO·C₂H₄·COOH.

lactic anhydride. (MeCHOCHO)₂O = 162.1. L. acid anhydride, 2-hydroxypropanoic anhydride. White powder, m.250, soluble in water.

lactide. CO·O·MeCH·O·CO·CHMe = 144.1. 3,6-
⌊_____⌋
Dimethyl-2,5-*p*-dioxandione. Monoclinic crystals, m.128, slightly soluble in water. Cf. *lactides.*

lactides. R₂C·O·CO·CR₂·CO·O. Compounds formed
⌊_____⌋
by the condensation of 2 α-hydroxy acids or their anhydrides.

lactim. Lactin. An organic compound containing the —N:COH— group in its ring. Lactims are isomeric with lactams, but differ in that they are formed by the elimination of the 2 H of the NH₂ group and the O of the CO group:

$$—NH \qquad\qquad —N$$
$$| \qquad\qquad\qquad ||$$
$$—CO \quad and \quad —C·OH$$

Lactam   Lactim
(ketol type)   (enol type)

lactin. (1) Lactose. (2) Lactim.

Lactobacillus. A bacillus which causes lactic acid fermentation of milk.

lactobiose. Lactose.

lactochrome. C₆H₁₈O₆N = 200.2. A coloring matter isolated from milk.

lactocrit. Lactokrit. An instrument to determine the amount of fat in milk.

Lactofil. Trade name for a synthetic protein fiber.

lactoflavin(e). Riboflavin(e).

lactoglobulin. C₁₈₆₄H₃₀₁₂N₄₆₈O₅₇₆S₂₁(?). A globulin from milk.

lactol. (1) MeCHOHCOOC₁₀H₇ = 216.1. Lactonaphthol, naphthyl lactate. Colorless crystals, insoluble in water: an intestinal antiseptic. (2) The cyclic form of hydroxy aldehydes (aldolactols) and hydroxy ketones (ketolactols); as, γ-valerolactol.

lactolactic acid. Dilactic acid.

lactolide. The ether of a lactol; as,
O·CHMe·CH₂·CH₂·CHOMe,
⌊_____⌋
methyl-γ-valerolactolide.

lactometer. A hydrometer to determine the specific gravity of milk.

lactonaphthol. Lactol.

lactone. An anhydro ring compound produced by intramolecular condensation of an oxyacid with the elimination of water; e.g.: γ- or *gamma*-, the commonest and most stable type. The pentatomic ring, R·CH·CO·O·CH₂·CH₂. The nomenclature of
⌊_____⌋
lactones is derived by adding (1) -olid to the hydrocarbon, or (2) lactone to the acid; as, butanolid, or γ-butyrolactone. **l. isomerism.** The shift from lactone to aldehyde acid; as,

$$C_6H_4\diagdown^{CO}_{CHOH}\diagup O \rightleftharpoons C_6H_4\diagdown^{COOH}_{CHO}$$

lactonic acid. Galactonic acid.

lactonitrile. Me·CHOH·CN = 71.05. 2-Hydroxy-propanenitrile*. Colorless liquid, d.0.992, b.183.

lactoprene. A copolymer of acrylic acid containing small proportions of other monomers. A rubber substitute which resists oils, oxygen, and aging.

lactose. $C_{12}H_{22}O_{11}\cdot H_2O$ = 360.32. Milk sugar, sugar of milk, lactobiose, glucose galactoside. A disaccharide in milk. Colorless rhombic crystals, d.1.525, m.203 (decomp.), slightly soluble in water. Used in pharmacy (for tablets), medicine (as nutrient), and industry (U.S.P., B.P.). **l.-litmus-agar.** A culture medium for growing certain bacteria: lactose 10, agar-agar 15, peptone 10 gm; bouillon stock 100 ml; neutralized to azolitmin with sodium hydroxide to a pale blue color.

lactoxime. Lactazone. An unsaturated lactam containing the —CH=N—O—CO— group in the ring.

lactucarium. The dried juice of *Lactuca virosa*, wild lettuce (Compositae); a mild narcotic and sedative.

lactucerol. $C_{18}H_{30}O$ = 262.23. α-Lactucol, taraxasterol. An alcohol from *Lactuca* species. Cf. *sycoceryl alcohol.*

lactyl. The acyl radical CH_3·CHOH·CO—, from lactic acid. **l. lactate.** Dilactic acid. **l. urea.** $C_4H_6O_2N_2, H_2O$ = 132.11. Colorless rhombs, m.145, soluble in water.

ladanum. Labdanum. **l. oil.** An essential oil from the resin of *Cistus creticus* (Cistaceae), Mediterranean islands. Yellow oil, d.1.01, insoluble in water; used in perfumery.

Ladenburg, Albert. 1842–1911. German chemist. **L. flask.** A distilling flask, with several bulbs in its long neck, used for fractional distillation. **L. formula.** See *benzene structure.* **L. law.** The velocity of a photoelectron is proportional to the square root of the voltage exciting it.

ladle. A vessel or pot with handle, for holding, transporting, and pouring molten metal.

lady's slipper. Cypripedium.

læ- See *lae-, le-.*

laevo- Levo-.

laevulinic acid. Levulinic acid.

laevulose. Fructose.

Lafayette mixture. Mixture copaiba.

lag. (1) To drag or follow behind. (2) To bind a pipe conducting steam with a nonconducting material (as asbestos), to keep it hot. **magnetic-** See *hysteresis.* **nitrogen-** See *nitrogen.*

lagam balsam. A balsam resembling copaiba.

lagoriolite. $3Na_2O\cdot Al_2O_3\cdot 3SiO_2$. A mineral of the garnet group.

lake. An adsorption compound of a coloring matter with a metallic oxide (mordant) produced by coprecipitation. Lakes are usually bright in color and insoluble, but the same dye can give different shades with different mordants.

lakh. (1) Lac. (2) In India: 100,000.

laking. Hemolysis.

lamb. Abbreviation for lambert.

Lamb, Arthur Becket 1880–1952. American chemist, noted for research in inorganic chemistry.

lambda. The Greek letter Λ or λ (L, l). **l. phenomenon.** The rapid loss of entropy of helium, q.v., at below 2.8°K, which accounts for its unusual properties in the liquid state.

lambert. Lamb. Unit of brightness of a perfectly diffusing surface, which radiates or reflects one lumen per square centimeter. 1 lamb. = 1 phot = 1 lumen/cm² = 0.3183 candle/cm² = 2.054 candles/in.²

Lambert's law. $I = I_0 e^{al}$, where I_0 and I are the intensities of the incident and emergent radiations, respectively, of rays of light of a wavelength λ; *l* is the thickness of the transmitting medium in centimeters; and *a* the absorption coefficient, q.v., of the medium for the wavelength λ.

Lambrecht's polymeter. A meteorological instrument; a hygrometer and thermometer with humidity conversion scales.

lambswool. A fabric made from the wool of sheep of up to 8 months old.

lamella. (1) A medicated disk or wafer. (2) Lamina.

lamina. A thin, flat plate or scale; as in mica.

Laminaria. Tangle, sea girdle. A genus of *Phaeophyaceae* or algae of the brown seaweed type (Laminariaceae). Cf. *kelp.*

laminaribiose. A glucose disaccharide derived from laminarin.

laminarin. A glucose polymer in the form of a spiral chain of 1,3-glucopyranose units typical of polysaccharides in seaweeds. It comprises approximately 33% of the fronds of brown seaweed and certain algae.

laminated. Split, or in thin layers.

lamine. An alkaloid from the blossoms of *Lamium album*, dead nettle (Labiatae).

laminography. The radiography of a thin layer of a thick specimen. The radiation source and recording film are rotated, during exposure, around the plane of the specimen under investigation.

lamp. A device for obtaining light or heat. **alcohol-** A vessel with wick, for burning alcohol. **arc-** See *arc.* **blast-** See *burner.* **carcel-** See *carcel unit.* **electric-** A device for transforming an electric current into light. **filament-** A device for heating a thread of carbon, tantalum, or tungsten to incandescence in an evacuated glass bulb. **gas-filled-** (1) Vacuum l. (2) A filament l. which contains a small quantity of gas, e.g., N_2 or A. **halide-** See *halide* lamp. **Harcourt-** A l. to burn a definite quantity of pentane at a definite rate; a standard of brightness. **Hefner-** A standard l. used in photometry. **mercury-** An evacuated quartz envelope containing mercury vapor. On the passage of an electric current it emits an intense bluish light rich in ultraviolet rays; used in spectroscopy, photography, and fluorescence analysis. **microscope-** A point source of light for microscopes. **miner's-** q.v. **neon-** A vacuum type l. containing a trace of neon. **Nernst-** An electric l. with metal oxide filament, which becomes a conductor when heated, and emits infrared rays on passage of an electric current. **pentane-** Harcourt l. **quartz-** Mercury l. **spectrum-** A device for coloring a nonluminous flame with vapors, sprays, or solid particles; used in spectroscopy of metals. **vacuum-** A vacuum tube, variously shaped, through which passes an electric current. Different residual gases in the tubes produce different colors.

lampblack. Carbon black. Paris black. Finely divided carbon obtained by burning gas or oil under a slowly rotating metal cylinder; a paint, ink, and paper pigment. Cf. *soot.*

lamprobolite. A basaltic hornblende.

lana. Wool. Flannel.

lanain, lanalin. Lanolin.

lanarkite. $PbSO_4 \cdot PbCO_3$, derived from $PbSO_4 \cdot PbO$. A native lead sulfate.

lanatoside. Digilanid.

lanaurin. A porphyrin-type coloring matter in suint.

lancet. A small pointed knife with two edges, used in surgery.

Landmark process. The synthesis of ammonia by passing steam over TiN_2 and carbon, and the recovery of TiN_2:

(1) $2TiN_2 + 2C + H_2O \rightarrow 2TiN + CO + 2NH_3$
(2) $N_2 + 2TiN \rightarrow 2TiN_2$

Landolt, Hans Heinrich. 1831–1910. Swiss physical chemist, noted for work on optical refractivity.

land plaster. Gypsum.

Landsberger apparatus. An apparatus to determine molecular weights from the rise in boiling point of a solution.

landsbergite. Ag_3Hg_4. Argental. A native silver amalgam.

langbeinite. $K_2SO_4 \cdot 2MgSO_4$. A native sulfate.

Lange solution. A colloidal solution of gold.

Langevin, Paul. 1872–1946. French physical chemist. **L. formula.** The activity coefficient (or coefficient of combination) of ions is: $\alpha = \Lambda_0 / \kappa$, where Λ_0 is the equivalent conductivity and κ the dielectric constant per volt.

langley. A unit for the timing of exposure tests on fabrics or plastics; 1 calorie of solar radiant energy per square centimeter of exposed area.

Langmuir, Irving. 1881–1957. American physical chemist noted for experiments on atomic hydrogen, low-pressure and high-vacuum reactions, and development of theories of isosterism and atomic structure. Nobel Prize winner (1932). Cf. *Lewis-Langmuir theory.* **L. theory.** (1) Electrons occupy positions in imaginary shells around the atom. See *orbit. periodic system.* (2) In the solid state secondary valencies supplant the effect of primary valences.

lanigerin. $C_{17}H_{14}O_5 = 298.12$. A red coloring matter from insects of the Coccidae group. Cf. *cochineal.*

lanital. An artificial wool formerly produced from casein. Cf. *Aralac.*

lanoceric acid. $C_{30}H_{60}O_4 = 484.46$. A dibasic fatty acid, m.105, from wool grease.

lanolin. Lanum, lanain, lanalin, lanesin, lanichol, laniol, adeps lanae hydrous, hydrous wool fat. Used as an external excipient and in cosmetics. **anhydrous-** Adeps lanae, wool fat. Yellow fat from sheep's wool, consisting of cholesterol esters of higher fatty acids, m.38–42, soluble in alcohol.

Lanon. Trade name for a polyester synthetic fiber.

lanopalmic acid. $C_{15}H_{30}O_3 = 358.2$. A fatty acid from wool grease.

lanosterol. $C_{30}H_{50}O(?)$. Isocholesterol. Lanostadienol. A triterpenoid. An unsaturated sterol closely related to cholesterol, m.140 (approximately 25% in wool wax).

Lansil. Trademark for a continuous-filament acetate yarn.

lantanine. An alkaloid from *Lantana brasiliensis* (Verbenaceae), Brazil; an antiperiodic, antipyretic, and quinine substitute. Cf. *yerba sagrada.*

lanthanide series. A series of elements having the same electronic structure as lanthanum, e.g., the rare earths. Cf. *lanthanons.*

lanthanite. $La_2(CO_3)_3 \cdot 9H_2O$. A dull, infusible mineral.

lanthanons. The rare-earth series of elements, at. nos. 57–71.

lanthanum. La $= 138.91$. A rare-earth metal, valency 3, at. no. 57, discovered (1839) by Mosander. A gray lustrous metal, d.6.15, m.810, in rare-earth minerals (cerite, samarskite, lanthanite, and gadolinite). It decomposes water slowly. Forms pyrophoric alloys and is a catalyst in ashing biological material. **l. acetate.** $La(CH_3COO)_3 \cdot 1\frac{1}{2}H_2O = 343.01$. White crystals, soluble in water. **l. carbonate.** $La_2(CO_3)_3 \cdot 8H_2O = 602.1$. White crystals, insoluble in water. **l. chloride.** $LaCl_3 \cdot 7H_2O = 371.4$. White, triclinic crystals, soluble in water. **l. nitrate.** $La(NO_3)_3 \cdot 6H_2O = 433.1$. White, deliquescent crystals, m.40, soluble in water; used as an antiseptic, and in incandescent gas mantles. **l. oxalate.** $La_2(C_2O_4)_3 = 451.8$. White crystals, insoluble in water. **l. oxide.** $La_2O_3 = 325.8$. Infusible, white powder, d.6.41, insoluble in water; used in incandescent gas mantles and limelights. **l. sulfate.** $La_2(SO_4)_3 \cdot 9H_2O = 727.9$. Colorless needles, d.2.81, decomp. by heat, slightly soluble in water. **l. sulfide.** $La_2S_3 = 374.02$. Yellow powder, d.4.997, m.2300–2350, insoluble in water.

lanthionine. $S(CH_2 \cdot CH \cdot NH_2 \cdot COOH)_2 = 180.28$. From wool, hair, and certain antibiotics, e.g., subtilin. White crystals, decomp. 294, slightly soluble in water.

lanthopine. $C_{20}H_{25}O_4N = 343.20$. Lantol. A colorless, crystalline alkaloid of opium, m.200.

lantol. Lanthopine.

Lanum. Trademark for lanolin.

Lanusa. Trade name for a viscose synthetic fiber.

lapacho bark. The bark of *Avicennia nitida*, black mangrove; a tan. **l. wood.** The heartwood of *A. tomentosa* (Verbenaceae), the tropics.

lapachoic acid. Lapachol.

lapachol. $C_{15}H_{14}O_3 = 242.11$. Lapachoic acid, targusic acid, 2-hydroxy-3-amylene-α-naphtho-quinone. A constituent of lapacho wood, m.141.

lapis. (1) Latin for stone. (2) An alchemical term for a nonvolatile substance. **l. albus.** A native calcium silicofluoride. Emery. **l. amiridis.** Emery. **l. calaminaris.** Calamine. **l. causticus.** Fused sodium or potassium hydroxide. **l. divinus.** Cuprammonium. **l. imperalis.** Silver nitrate. **l. lazuli.** (1) A mixture of minerals, usually calcite, pyrite, lazulite, sodalite, and häyenite; the ancient source of ultramarine. (2) A native copper silicate. Blue, green, or purple compact masses; a semiprecious stone. **l. lunaris.** Fused silver nitrate.

lappa. Burdock, clotbur, bardana. The dried roots of *Arctium lappa* (Compositae); a diuretic and diaphoretic.

lappaconitine. (1) $C_{32}H_{44}O_8N_2 = 584.32$. An alkaloid of *Aconitum septentrionale* (Ranunculaceae), m.205. (2) $C_{32}H_{42}N_2O_9 = 598.34$. An alkaloid, m.223.

larch. The bark of *Larix Europaea* (*Pinus larix*), (Coniferae); an astringent and diuretic. **American-** or **black-** Tamarac. **European-** Larch.

l. agaric. Agaric. **l. extract.** An extract of the bark of *Pinus larix*; a tan.

lard. Adeps. The purified abdominal fat from the hog (excluding unbleached hog grease). White, granular mass, m. not below 25, insoluble in water; used in cooking and pharmaceutical preparations. **l. benzoinated.** Adeps benzoinatus. L. containing 1% benzoin; an antiseptic. **l. oil.** A colorless oil, chiefly triglycerides of oleic acid, pressed from l., d.0.915, soluble in alcohol; a lubricant and illuminant.

lardacein. A wax, d.0.6969, m.55, from the scale of *Ceroplastens rubens*, an insect from tea and citrus trees.

lardine. A substitute for lard prepared by hydrogenating cottonseed oil.

largactil. Chlorpromazine hydrochloride.

large calorie. Great calorie. The amount of heat required to raise the temperature of 1 kg water from 14.5 to 15.5°C. See *calorie*.

Larix. A genus of Coniferae yielding timber, oils, and resins; e.g., *L. americana*, tamarac; *L. europaea*, larch.

larixine. $C_{10}H_{10}O_5 = 210.1$. Larixinic acid. A principle from larch bark, *Larix europaea* (Coniferae). White, empyreumatic, astringent crystals, m.153, soluble in water.

larkspur. Delphinium. **l. seeds.** The dried seeds of *Delphinium* species; an antiparasitic and diuretic.

Larmor, Sir Joseph. 1857–1942. British physicist. **L. theorem.** The angular velocity of an electrified particle moving at right angles to the direction of a magnetic field of constant strength is independent of the linear speed of the particle. Cf. *cyclotron*.

larocaine. 3-Diethylamino-2,2′-dimethyl-propyl-*p*-aminobenzoate.

Larodon. $C_{14}H_{18}N_2O = 240.18$. Trademark for 1-phenyl-2,3-dimethyl-4-isopropylpyrazolone; an analgesic and antipyretic.

Larosan. Trademark for a compound of casein and calcium oxide; used to treat infantile nutritional diseases.

larvicide. An agent that destroys larva, the first stage of development of insects.

Lasché unit. A unit of diastatic activity: the time in minutes required by an infusion of 0.55 gm malt to convert 5 gm soluble starch in 100 ml at 62.5°C.

laser. Abbreviation for light amplification by stimulated emission of radiation. A beam of light of uniform wavelength, traveling in phase in a series of parallel lines. It can be focused accurately to produce a high-energy concentration. On exposure for short intervals to ordinary light, ruby emits l. Cf. *maser*.

latensification. The intensification of a latent photographic image by preexposure; due to the fact that most photographic materials disobey the Bunsen-Roscoe law of photochemical equivalence.

latent. Not manifest or readily available. **l. energy, l. force.** Potential energy. **l. heat.** The amount of heat required to change the state of a body from solid to liquid at its melting point, or from liquid to gas at its boiling point. Likewise the heat liberated if a gas changes to a liquid, or a liquid to a solid, at the condensation or freezing point, respectively. **l. h. of fusion.** The number of gram calories required to convert 1 gram of a substance from solid into liquid, without a change of temperature. **l. h. of vaporization.** The number of gram calories required to convert 1 gram of substance from liquid into vapor without a change of temperature. **l. image.** The change produced on a photographic plate by exposure to light, made visible by developing.

lateral chain. See *chain*.

laterite. Murram. A natural hydrated oxide of iron and aluminum, and sometimes titanium (cf. bauxite), which occurs as a brown surface earth, and is used for building roads.

lateritiin. $C_{26}H_{46}O_7N_2 = 498.44$. An antibiotic pigment produced by the growth of *Fusaria*, m.121.

latex. The milky juice or exudation of plants obtained by tapping the trunk. **rubber-** A colloidal emulsion, d.0.983, pH 7.0–7.2, containing: water 60, rubber 36, sterols 1, proteins 0.3, quebracho 1.5, sugars 0.25, ash 0.5%. Cf. *lutoid*, *rubber*.

lather. A foam or froth of soap and water.

lat. ht. Abbreviation for latent heat.

latices. Plural of *latex*.

lattice. See *space lattice*.

laucaniline. Paraleucoaniline.

laudanidine. $C_{20}H_{25}NO_4 = 343.3$. Tritopine, *l*-laudanine. An alkaloid from opium. Hexagonal prisms, m.166.

laudanine. $C_{20}H_{25}O_4N = 343.3$. An alkaloid from opium. **dl-** Colorless prisms, m.166, insoluble in water; a strychnine substitute. **l-** Laudanidine.

laudanosine. $C_{21}H_{27}O_4N = 357.3$. *N*-Methyltetrahydropapaverine. An alkaloid from opium. Yellow crystals, m.89, insoluble in water.

laudanum. Tincture of opium. A brown solution of opium in alcohol; a powerful anodyne.

Laue, Max Theodor Felix von. 1880–1960. German physicist, noted for research on subatomic phenomena. Nobel Prize winner (1914). **L. diagram.** L. pattern. **L. equation.** An expression of the conditions to be obeyed simultaneously for a crystal to show diffraction. **L. method.** The diffraction of X rays by means of a crystal. **L. pattern.** The photographic record produced when X rays are diffracted by a crystal.

laughing gas. Nitrous oxide.

laumonite. $CaOAl_2O_3·4SiO_2·2H_2O$. A vitreous mineral. Cf. *lawsonite*.

Lauraceae. Laurel family: aromatic shrubs or trees, all parts of which yield an essential oil; e.g.: *Cinnamomum camphora*, camphor; *C. cassia*, cassia; *Laurus nobilis*, sweet bay.

lauraldehyde. Lauric aldehyde.

laurane. $C_{20}H_{42} = 282.32$. An isomer of eicosane in laurel fat, m.69.

laurel. Laurus, sweet bay, bayberry, noble berry. The dried leaves and berries of *Laurus nobilis*, used for making laurel oil. **cherry-** See *prune*. **ground-** Arbutus. **mountain-** Kalmia. **New Zealand-** See *pukateine*.

l. berries oil. An essential oil from the fruits of l., soluble in alcohol, and containing pinene, cineol, eugenol, and methylchavicol. **l. camphor.** Camphor. **l. fat.** Bay oil, l. oil. A buttery fat, m.32–36, obtained by pressing l. leaves; used in veterinary work. **l. leaves, oil.** Bay leaves oil. Yellow oil distilled from laurel, d.0.924, insoluble in water; a flavoring. **l. oil.** (1) L. fat. (2) L. leaves oil. **l. tallow.** undung. **l. wax.** (1) Myristin. (2) Bayberry wax.

laureline. $C_{17}H_{17}NO_3 = 283.1$. An apomorphine alkaloid from *Laurelia novae zealandicae* (Monimiaceae).

laurene. Pinene.

Laurent, Auguste. 1807–1853. French organic chemist, discoverer of aniline, caffeine, naphthalene, and their derivatives. Noted for his theory of types and radicals. **L. acid.** 1,5-Nitronaphthalenesulfonic acid.

lauric acid. $Me(CH_2)_{10}COOH = 200.3$. Decylacetic acid, dodecanoic acid*. Colorless needles, m.47, insoluble in water. **hydroxy-** Sabinic acid.

lauric aldehyde. $C_{12}H_{24}O = 184.3$. Dodecanal*. Colorless leaflets, m.44.4, insoluble in water.

laurin. $C_3H_5 \cdot (C_{12}H_{23}O_2)_3 = 638.57$. Trilaurin, laurostearin, glyceryl laurate, in the seeds of laurel, palms, coconuts. White needles, m.47; used in medicinal soaps.

laurite. RuS_2. A native sulfide.

lauroleic acid. $C_{12}H_{22}O_2 = 198.2$. Dodecenoic acid*. An unsaturated acid, $b_{2mm}90$, from the head oil of the sperm whale.

laurolene. $CMe:CMe \cdot CHMe \cdot CH_2 \cdot CH_2$ = 110.11.

1,2,3-Trimethyl-1-cyclopentene. Colorless liquid, d.0.800, b.121. **iso-** $CMe_2 \cdot CMe:CH \cdot CH_2 \cdot CH_2$.

1,1,2-Trimethyl-2-cyclopentene. Colorless liquid, d.0.791, b.109.

laurone. $(C_{11}H_{23})_2CO = 338.35$. 1,2-Tricosanone*. Colorless crystals, d.0.789, m.69.

lauronolic acid. $C_9H_{14}O_2 = 154.11$. Laurolene-3-carboxylic acid. Colorless liquid, d.1.016, m.6.

laurostearin. Laurin.

laurotetanine. $C_{19}H_{21}O_4N = 345.2$. A strychnine-like alkaloid from the bark of *Litsea latifolia* (Lauraceae), S. Asia. Cf. *glaucine*.

lauroyl. See *lauryl* (2).

laurus. Laurel.

lauryl. (1) The radical $C_{12}H_{25}$—, from dodecane. (2) The group $Me(CH_2)_{10}CO$—, from lauric acid, more properly termed lauroyl. **l. alcohol.** $Me(CH_2)_{11}OH = 186.20$. 1-Dodecanol*, n-dodecyl alcohol. White leaflets, m.23, insoluble in water. **l. bromide.** $Me(CH_2)_{11}Br = 249.11$. 1-Bromododecane*. Colorless liquid, $b_{45mm}177$. **l. chloride.** $Me(CH_2)_{11}Cl = 218.64$. 1-Chlorododecane*, dodecyl chloride, Colorless liquid, $b_{18mm}145$.

laurylene. (1) $C_{12}H_{24} = 168.2$. An unsaturated hydrocarbon in mineral oils. (2) $C_{10}H_{16} = 136.12$. A terpene from laurel oil.

Lauseto. Trade name for an insecticide containing DDT and related phenyl halogen ethanes. **L. neu.** Trade name for chlorophenylchloromethylsulfone. Compared with DDT, it is more toxic to lice and bedbugs, but less soluble in oils.

lautal. A hard aluminum alloy containing Cu 4–5, Si 1.5–2, Fe 0.4–0.7%.

Lauth's violet. Thionine.

lava. Liquid rock which has reached the earth's surface and is ejected from volcanoes. Cf. *magma*.

lavandula. Lavender.

lavender. The dried flowering tops of *Lavandula latifolia*; a tonic, carminative, and stimulant. **l.**

flower oil. Colorless essential oil from lavender flowers, d.0.885, insoluble in water; used in perfumery. **l. spike oil.** An essential oil distilled from the herb *L. officinalis*. Colorless liquid, d.0.905, insoluble in water; used in pharmaceutical preparations.

Lavoisier, Antoine Laurent. 1743–1794. French chemist, regarded as the founder of modern chemistry by virtue of his study of the role of oxygen in combustion. He formulated the theory of the conservation of matter, and laid the basis for chemical nomenclature. He was unjustly accused and executed during the French revolution.

law. A generalized statement of facts or principles. **empirical-** A l. which is the result of experience without theoretical considerations. **natural-** The formulation of systematized experience on the workings of nature. **periodic-** (1) A l. that expresses a periodic variation. (2) See *periodic system*.

lawang oil. An oil from the bark of an E. Indian plant, resembling mace oil.

Law cell. An electric cell (1.37 volts): a zinc anode, and carbon cathode in a 15% solution of ammonium chloride.

lawrencium. Lr = ?. An isotope of element 103. The natural element decayed out of existence shortly after the birth of the universe. Formed by bombarding californium with B^{10} nuclei in a heavy-ion linear accelerator by Ghiorso and coworkers, University of California (1961).

lawsone. $C_{10}H_6O_3 = 174.1$. Hydroxynaphthoquinone. The coloring matter of henna leaves, *Lawsonia alba*. Red needles, m.194.

lawsonite. $CaO \cdot Al_2O_3 \cdot 2SiO_2 \cdot 2H_2O$. A vitreous, colorless mineral. Cf. *laumonite*.

laxative. A mild cathartic; as, petrolatum.

layer. A mass of uniform thickness covering an area. **molecular-** A film of single molecules alongside one another over a surface. Cf. *zone*.

lazulite. $(MgFeCa) \cdot (AlOH)_2P_2O_8$. A blue, vitreous mineral.

lazurite. $2NaAlSiO_4 \cdot Na_2S$. A mineral from Ovalle, Chile.

lb. Abbreviation for pound(s). **lb. ap.** Abbreviation for apothecary's pound. **lb. av.** Abbreviation for avoirdupois pound. **lb. f.** Abbreviation for pound force. **lb. t.** Abbreviation for troy pound.

LD 50. The dose of a pesticide which kills 50% of the animal population tested.

leaching. Washing or extracting the soluble constituents from insoluble materials.

lead. Pb = 207.19. Plumbum. A metallic element, at. no. 82. A gray, soft, monoclinic or regular crystalline metal, d.11.34, m.327, b.1470, insoluble in water, soluble in nitric acid; principal ore, galena. L. was known to the Romans (plumbum nigrum). Used for chemical apparatus, in electrotechnics, as a solder, and in low-melting-point alloys. It forms 3 series of compounds and has valencies of 2 (plumbous) and 4 (plumbic). L. salts are poisonous. Metallic l. consists of several isotopes of different atomic weights. See table and *radioactive elements*. World production (1965), 3.2 million tons. **actinium-** Actinium D· **antimonial-** See *antimonial*. **argentiferous-** (1) PbAgS. (2) An alloy of silver and lead obtained in the cupellation process. **black-** Graphite. **brown-** Vanadinite. **horn-** Phosgenite. **pyrophoric-** Finely divided l. which oxidizes spontaneously on exposure to air. **radio-** The natural radioactive mixture of l. isotopes. **red-** L. tetroxide. *Siberian-* Crocoisite. **secondary-** L. recovered from scrap. **thorium-** Thorium D. **uranium-** (1) Radium G. (2) A conduit or vein which is being followed. **white-** L. carbonate.

ISOTOPIC COMPOSITION OF LEAD

Isotopic weight	%	Isotopic weight	%
203	0.04	207	20.20
204	1.50	208	49.55
205	0.03	209	0.85
206	27.75	210	0.08

l. accumulator. A reversible voltaic storage cell (2.2 volts: an anode of l. and a cathode of l. dioxide, suspended in sulfuric acid (d.1.1). **l. acetate.** $Pb(C_2H_3O_2)_2 \cdot 3H_2O = 379.3$. L. sugar, sugar of l., plumbous acetate. Colorless, efflorescent crystals, m.75, soluble in water. Used as a reagent, in manufacture of l. salts, as a mordant in dyeing, in the tanning industry, in preparation of white l. paints, and as an astringent lotion for bruises (B.P.). *basic-* L. subacetate. **l. acetotartrate.** Colorless crystals, soluble in water; an astringent and antiseptic. **l. alkyls.** Organic compounds of tetravalent l. and alkyl radicals; as, l. tetraethide, $PbEt_4$. Some are antiknock compounds. **l. alloys.** Usually have low melting points. Cf. *type metal, solder, carbox metal, pewter, linotype metal.* **l. antimoniate.** $Pb_3(SbO_4)_2 = 993.1$. Naples yellow, plumbous stibnate, giallioline. Orange powder, insoluble in water; a pigment for paint, ceramics and glass. **l. arsenate.** $Pb_3(AsO_4)_2 = 899.6$. Colorless, poisonous crystals, insoluble in water; an insecticide. **l. aryls.** Organic compounds of tetravalent l. and aryl radicals; as, l. tetraphenyl, $PbPh_4$. **l. azide.** $Pb(N_3)_2 = 291.27$. L. azoimide, l. nitride. Colorless crystals made from sodium azide with l. acetate, explodes 350; a detonating agent. **l. azoimide.** L. azide. **l. benzoate.** $Pb(C_7H_5O_2)_2 = 449.3$. Colorless crystals, soluble in water. **l. bichromate.** $PbCr_2O_7 = 423.2$. Red powder, insoluble in water; a pigment. **l. bioxide.** L. peroxide. **l. bitannate.** L. tannate. **l. black.** Graphite. **l. borate.** $Pb(BO_2)_2 \cdot H_2O = 311.2$. L. drier. White powder, insoluble in water; a paint drier. **l. borosilicate.** A mixture of the borate and silicate of l.; used in optical glass. **l. bromate.** $Pb(BrO_3)_2 = 463.2$. Colorless crystals, slightly soluble in hot water. **l. bromide.** $PbBr_2 = 367.0$. Colorless, rhombs, m.380, insoluble in water. **l. butyrate.** $Pb(C_4H_7O_2)_2 = 381.2$. Colorless scales, m.90, insoluble in water. **l. carbolate.** L. phenate. **l. carbonate.** $PbCO_3 = 267.2$. White powder, decomp. by heat, insoluble in water; a pigment. Occurs naturally as cerrusite. Cf. *Dutch process.* *basic-* $2PbCO_3 \cdot Pb(OH)_2 = 775.6$. Plumbous subcarbonate, basic l. carbonate, white l., ceruse, cerussa, l. flakes. White, heavy powder, decomp. by heat, insoluble in water; a pigment, putty, and constituent of ointments for burns.

l. chamber. See *sulfuric acid manufacture.* **l. chlorate.** $Pb(ClO_3)_2 = 374.1$. White, monoclinic crystals, decomp. 230, soluble in water. Cf. *Thiel*-Stoll solution. **l. chloride.** $PbCl_2 = 278.1$. Colorless rhombs, m.501, insoluble in water; a reagent for silver, alkaloids, and carbonates; and mixed with l. oxides, a pigment. **l. chromate.** $PbCrO_5 = 323.2$. Leipzig yellow, paris yellow, "chrome" yellow. Fusible, yellow monoclinic crystals, insoluble in water; a reagent and pigment. *basic-* $PbCrO_4 \cdot PbO = 546.4$. Plumbous subchromate. Red crystals, insoluble in water; a pigment. **l. citrate.** $Pb_3(C_6H_6O_7)_2 = 1001.76$. Colorless crystals, soluble in water. **l. cyanate.** $Pb(CNO)_2 = 291.24$. Colorless crystals, decomp. by heat, insoluble in water. **l. cyanide.** $Pb(CN)_2 = 259.2$. Colorless crystals, insoluble in water, soluble in potassium cyanide solution; used as an insecticide and in metallurgy. **l. dichromate.** L. bichromate. **l. dioxide.** L. peroxide. **l. dish.** A container for corrosive liquids and hydrofluoric acid; as, in glass etching. **l. dithiofuroate.** $(C_4H_3 O \cdot CS_2)_2Pb$. Furac III. Red powder; a vulcanizing accelerator. **l. drier.** L. borate. **l. dust.** Finely powdered metallic l.; used in l. plasters (B.P.). **l. ethyl sulfate.** $Pb(C_2H_5SO_4)_2 \cdot H_2O = 475.46$. Colorless liquid, soluble in water; used in organic synthesis. **l. ferrocyanide.** $Pb_2Fe(CN)_6 = 626.5$. Yellow powder, insoluble in water. **l. flake.** L. carbonate basic. **l. fluoride.** $PbF_6 = 245.2$. Fusible white powder, insoluble in water. **l. fluosilicate.** $PbSiF_6 = 349.28$. L. silicofluoride. *dihydrate-* $(2H_2O)$. White monoclinic prisms, soluble in water. *tetrahydrate-* $(4H_2O)$. Monoclinic crystals, soluble in water. **l. flux.** A reducing and desulfurizing agent used in the assay of gold and silver, and consisting of: sodium bicarbonate 16, potassium carbonate 16, flour 8, borax glass 4 pts. **l. formate.** $Pb(CHO_2)_2 = 297.2$. Plumbous formate. Lustrous rhombic needles, d.4.63, decomp. 190, soluble in water; a reagent. **l. hydrate.** See *l. hydroxide.* **l. hydroxide** (1) $Pb(OH)_2 = 241.2$. L. hydrate. White powder, m.145 (decomp.), soluble in water. (2) $3PbO \cdot H_2O = 687.6$. White cubic crystals. **l. hypophosphite.** $Pb(H_2PO_2)_2 = 337.2$. Hygroscopic, white powder, soluble in water. **l. hyposulfate.** $PbS_2O_6 = 367.2$. Colorless crystals, soluble in water. **l. hyposulfite.** $PbS_2O_3 = 319.2$. Plumbous hyposulfite, plumbous thiosulfate, l. thiosulfate. White crystals, darkening with age (due to formation of l. sulfide), insoluble in water, soluble in alkali thiosulfate solutions; used in inorganic synthesis. **l. iodate.** $Pb(IO_3)_2 = 557.0$. Colorless crystals, insoluble in water. **l. iodide.** $PbI_2 = 461.0$. Plumbi iodidium. Yellow hexagons, m.375, insoluble in water. Used as an astringent and resolvent; and technically, for bronzes, mosaic gold, printing and photography. **l. lactate.** $Pb(C_3H_5O_3)_2 = 385.2$. White powder, soluble in water. **l. laurate.** $(C_{12}H_{23}O_2)_2Pb = 605.58$. White powder, m.105, insoluble in water. **l. linoleate.** $Pb(C_{18}H_{31}O_2)_2 = 765.7$. Yellow paste, insoluble in water; used in ointments and varnishes. **l. malate.** $Pb(C_4H_4O_5) \cdot 3H_2O = 393.3$. Plumbous malate. White powder, slightly soluble in water. **l. minerals.** See *galena, massicot, cerussite, anglesite, crocoite, wulfenite.* Cf.

brongniardite, carminite, caryinite, lanarkite, plagionité, zinkenite. **l. molybdate.** $PbMoO_4 = 367.2$. Yellow powder, insoluble in water; a reagent. **l. monosulfide.** L. sulfide. **l. monoxide.** L. oxide (yellow). See also *massicot*. **l. myristate.** $(C_{14}H_{27}O_2)_2Pb = 661.64$. White powder, m.109, insoluble in water. **l. naphthalene sulfonate.** $Pb(C_{10}H_7SO_3)_2 = 621.45$. White crystals, insoluble in water. **l. nitrate.** $Pb(NO_3)_2 = 331.2$. Colorless octahedra, decomp. 223, soluble in water. Used as a reagent, astringent, deodorant, and detergent; a mordant in the dye and textile industries; an oxidizing agent in organic synthesis; a sensitizer in photography; and in the manufacture of l. salts, matches, and pyrotechnic toys. **l. nitride.** L. azide. **l. nitrite.** $Pb(NO_2)_2 = 299.2$. Yellow crystals, soluble in acids. **l. oleate.** $Pb(C_{18}H_{33}O_2)_2 = 769.8$. White, fatty granules, insoluble in water; used in medicine for ointments, and varnishes. **l. oxalate.** $PbC_2O_4 = 295.2$. White crystals, decomp. 300, insoluble in water, **l. oxide.** (1) *L. suboxide*, $Pb_2O = 430.4$. Black powder, decomp. by heat, insoluble in water. (2) *Yellow monoxide*, $PbO = 223.2$. Litharge, massicot, l. protoxide. Yellow rhombs, m.888, insoluble in water. Used as a reagent, pigment, and rubber filler; in ointments and manufacture of glass and pottery; and for acid-resisting cements and putty. (3) *Red monoxide*, $PbO = 223.2$. Plumbous oxide. Red hexagons, insoluble in water. (4) *L. sesquioxide*, $Pb_2O_3 = 462.4$. L. trioxide, plumbous plumbite, l. metaplumbate. Red powder; a pigment. Probably l. metaplumbate, since it is decomposed by acids into $PbO + PbO_2$. (5) *L. oxide red*, $Pb_3O_4 = 685.6$. Plumbous plumbate, l. orthoplumbate, red l. oxide, minium, sandix, orthoplumbate, l. tetroxide, plumbous-plumbic oxide. Heavy, orange powder, d.9.07, decomp. 500, insoluble in water. Used as a reagent and pigment, for ointments and cements, and in ceramics. Probably l. orthoplumbate, $2PbO·PbO_2$. (6) *L. peroxide*, $PbO_2 = 239.2$. Plumbous peroxide, l. dioxide, brown l. oxide, l. superoxide. Brown hexagons, d.8.91, decomp. by heat, insoluble in water; an oxidizing agent. It forms salts, PbX_4, and plumbates, X_2PbO_2. **l. oxychloride.** (1) $PbCl_2·PbO = 501.3$. White, tetragons, insoluble in water. (2) $PbCl_2·2PbO = 724.5$. Brown solid, m.693. **l. palmitate.** $(C_{16}H_{31}O_2)_2Pb = 717.70$. White powder, m.112.3, insoluble in water. **l. pentasulfide.** See *l. sulfide*. **l. pernitrate.** Colorless hygroscopic crystals, soluble in water. **l. peroxide.** L. oxide (6). **l. phenate.** $Pb(OH)OPh = 317.2$. L. phenolate, l. carbolate. Yellow powder, insoluble in water; used in ointments. **l. phenolate.** L. phenate. **l. phenolsulfonate.** $Pb(C_6H_4(OH)SO_3)_2·5H_2O = 643.52$. White needles, soluble in water; an astringent antiseptic. **l. phosphate.** (1) $Pb_3(PO_4)_2 = 811.7$. L. orthophosphate. White powder, insoluble in water. (2) $Pb(PO_3)_2 = 365.27$. L. metaphosphate. White crystals. (3) $Pb_2P_2O_7$. L. pyrophosphate, q.v. (4) $PbHPO_4 = 303.26$. L. acid phosphate. White crystals. **l. phosphite.** $PbHPO_3 = 287.2$. White powder, decomp. by heat, insoluble in water. **l. picrate.** A very sensitive explosive. **l. plaster** A medicinal plaster containing chiefly l. linoleate and glycerol.

l. plumbate. *ortho-* L. oxide (5). *meta-* L. oxide (4). **l. poisoning.** Plumbism, saturnism. Anemia and colic produced by frequent contact with l. **l. propionate.** $Pb(C_3H_5O_2)_2 = 353.2$. Colorless crystals, soluble in water. **l. protoxide.** L. oxide (1). **l. pyrophosphate.** $Pb_2P_2O_7·H_2O = 606.5$. Plumbous pyrophosphate. Colorless rhombs, decomp. by heat, insoluble in water. **l. resinate.** $Pb(C_{20}H_{29}O_2)_2 = 809.2$. Yellow paste, insoluble in water; a paint drier. **l. rhodanate.** L. thiocyanate. **l. saccharate.** A compound of saccharose with l. oxide. White powder, insoluble in water, used in medicine. **l. salicylate.** $Pb(C_7H_5O_3)_2·H_2O = 499.3$. White crystals, soluble in water. **l. selenate.** $PbSeO_4 = 350.4$. White powder, insoluble in water. **l. selenide.** $PbSe = 286.18$. Brown powder. *colloidal-* A suspension used in cancer therapy. **l. sesquioxide.** Pb_2O_3. L. oxide (5). **l. silicate.** $PbSiO_3 = 283.3$. White crystals, insoluble in water; used in ceramics, l. glass, paints, enamels, and for fireproofing fabrics. **l. silicofluoride.** $PbSiF_6·H_2O = 367.3$. Colorless crystals, soluble in water. **l. stearate.** $Pb(C_{18}H_{35}O_2)_2 = 773.8$. Yellow fat, m.116, insoluble in water; used in paint driers and varnishes. **l. stibnate.** L. antimoniate. **l. styphnate.** The l. salt of trinitroresorcinol; used in primings for gun ammunition. **l. subacetate.** $2Pb(C_2H_3O_2)_2·Pb(OH)_2 = 891.77$. Basic acetate of l. White powder, soluble in water. **l. subacetate solution.** Colorless liquid (189.5 gm/liter), d.1.24; a reagent and clarifier. Cf. *l. water, Goulard's extract*. **l. subcarbonate.** L. carbonate, basic. **l. suboxide.** L. oxide (1). **l. sugar.** L. acetate. **l. sulfate.** $PbSO_4 = 303.3$. White rhombs, m.1170, insoluble in water; a pigment and paint drier. *acidic-* $Pb(HSO_4)_2·H_2O = 419.4$. Crystals, decomp. by heat. *basic-* $PbSO_4·PbO = 526.5$. White powder, insoluble in water, decomp. by heat. **l. sulfide.** (1) $PbS = 239.3$. Galena, galenite. Dark gray crystals, m.1120, insoluble in water; used in ceramics and as a decolorizer. (2) $PbS_5 = 367.57$. L. pentasulfide. An unstable yellow powder. **l. sulfite.** $PbSO_3 = 287.3$. White granules, insoluble in water; an antiseptic and astringent. **l. sulfocyanide.** L. thiocyanate. **l. superoxide.** L. oxide (6). **l. tannate.** A compound of tannin and l. Brown powder, soluble in water; an astringent and antiseptic. **l. tartrate.** $PbC_4H_4O_6 = 355.3$. White powder, insoluble in water. **l. tetrachloride.** $PbCl_4 = 349.0$. Plumbic chloride. Yellow oil, $d_0 3.18$, decomp. by water and at 105. **l. tetraethide, l. tetraethyl.** Tetraethyl *plumbane*. **l. thiocyanate.** $Pb(CNS)_2 = 323.4$. L. rhodanate. Yellow, monoclinic crystals, soluble in water. **l. thiosulfate.** $PbS_2O_3 = 319.2$. L. hyposulfite. White powder, decomp. with age, insoluble in water; a dusting powder for rhus poisoning. **l. tree.** The branching crystalline growth of l. precipitated from its solution by more positive metals. **l. tungstate.** $PbWO_4 = 455.2$. L. wolframate, raspite, stolzite. Yellow powder, insoluble in water; a pigment. **l. vanadate.** $Pb(VO_3)_2 = 405.1$. Yellow powder, insoluble in water; a pigment. **l. water.** A 1% solution of l. subacetate. **l. white.** L. carbonate, basic. **l. wire.** (1) A wire made from l. (2) A chromelalum or other alloy wire of a thermocouple of a pyrometer. **l. wolframate.** L. tungstate. **l. yellow.** L. chromate.

Leadate. Trade name for dimethyl dithiocarbamate, a rubber accelerator.

leadhillite. $Pb(OH)_2 \cdot PbSO_4 \cdot 2PbCO_3$. A native sulfate of lead, from Leadhill, Scotland.

leaf. (1) See *leaves*. (2) A thin metal sheet or foil; as, gold l.; used for ornamenting.

lean. Deficient. Cf. *fat*. **l. clay.** A clay of poor plasticity. **l. coal.** A low gas-content coal. **l. ore.** A low metal-content ore.

leather. A tanned skin. **mountain-** Paligorskite. **l. tankage.** A fertilizer made from l. scraps by digestion with steam, drying, and grinding.

leatheroid. Vulcanized *fiber*.

leaves. The stem appendages of a plant, containing chlorophyll and possessing respiratory openings. Some are used in pharmacy; e.g.: belladonna, eucalyptus, tobacco.

LeBel, Jules Achille. 1847–1930. Alsatian capitalist who discovered the asymmetric carbon atom, (independently of van't Hoff) in 1874; and prepared the first optically active compound of asymmetric nitrogen.

LeBlanc, Nicolas. 1742–1806. French chemist, and founder of the alkali industry. **L. soda process.** The manufacture of sodium carbonate by treatment of salt cake (Na_2SO_4) with carbon and limestone.

lecanoric acid. $C_{16}H_{14}O_7 = 318.1$. Diorsellinic acid. Colorless crystals, decomp. by hot water to orsellinic acid. **l. monomethyl ether.** Evernic acid.

LeChâtelier, Henry Louis. 1850–1936. French chemist, noted for the law of chemical equilibrium and work on metallurgy.

lecithin. (1)Monoaminomonophosphatide. A group of substances of the general composition:

$$CH_2 \cdot OOCFA$$
$$|$$
$$CH \cdot OOCFA$$
$$|$$
$$CH_2O{-}PO_4{-}N{-}R$$

FA is a fatty acid; R an alkyl radical. They are the esters of oleic, stearic, palmitic, or other fatty acids with glycerophosphoric acid and choline. Cf. *kephalin.* (2) $C_{42}H_{84}NPO_9 = 777.93$. Brown wax in animal and vegetable tissues and egg yolk, decomp. by heat, insoluble in water; a tonic and nutrient. **animal-** Contains P 3.9–4.0, N 1.8–2.0%. **plant-** Contains P 3.3–3.7, N 1.5–1.7%. **soya-** L. derived from soybean; equal parts of true l. and kephalin.

Leclanché cell. A voltaic cell (1.46 volts); an anode of amalgamated zinc, and a cathode of carbon suspended in a solution of ammonium chloride, with manganese dioxide as a depolarizer.

leditannic acid. $C_{15}H_{20}O_8 = 328.2$. A tannin from *Ledum* species (Ericaceae).

ledixanthin. $C_{33}H_{34}O_{13} = 602.3$. A red coloring matter from *Ledum* species.

Leduc effect. Thermomagnetic difference of temperature: the effect of a magnetic field on the distribution of heat.

ledum camphor. A stearoptene from *Ledum palustre*, wild rosemary (Ericaceae). Cf. *Labrador tea*.

lees. The albuminoid sediment of fermented liquids, e.g., wine.

Leeuwenhoek, Anton van. 1632–1723. A lens maker of Delft, Holland, who discovered bacteria microscopically (1675).

legume. The pod of a leguminous plant.

legumelin. An albumin from peas and beans.

legumin. A globulin from leguminous plants. Cf. *avenin.*

Leguminosae. Pulse family: a group of plants with edible seeds; some contain drugs. Roots: *Glycyrrhiza glabra*, Spanish licorice; barks: *Acacia mimosa*, mimosa bark; woods: *Haematoxylon campechianum*, logwood; leaves: *Cassia acutifolia*, senna; herbs: *Megicago sativa*, alfalfa; fruits: *Cassia fistula*, purging cassia; seeds: *Arachis hypogoea*, peanut; plant products: *Acacia senegal*, gum arabic.

lehrbachite. HgPbSe. A mercury ore.

Leibnitz, Gottfried Wilhelm Freiherr von. 1646–1716. German mathematician and philosopher.

Leipzig yellow. Lead chromate pigment.

leishmaniasis. Diseases due to protozoan infections, e.g., kala azar.

lemco. A commercial meat extract, used to prepare beef broth media.

Lémery, Nicolas. 1645–1715. French physician and chemist, noted for his chemical textbook.

lemon. The ripe fruit of *Citrus limonum* (Rutaceae). Cf. *lime*. **l. balm.** Melissa. **l. chrome.** Barium chromate. **l. grass.** See *lemongrass*. **l. juice.** Lime juice. **l. oil.** Oleum limonis, oil of l. A fragrant, yellow oil, from fresh l. peel, d.0.849–0.855, $[\alpha]D + 57$–65, insoluble in water; a flavoring (U.S.P., B.P.). **l. peel** (U.S.P.), **dried l. peel** (B.P.). Cortex limonis. The outer rind of fresh ripe fruits of *Citrus medica*, lemon (Rutaceae); a tonic (U.S.P., B.P.) and flavoring. **l. yellow.** (1) Lead chromate. (2) Barium chromate.

lemon balm. Melissa.

lemongrass oil. Indian melissa oil. Yellow oil from *Cymbopogon* or *Andropogon citratus*, a grass of the E. Indies; d.0.89, insoluble in water; a flavoring and perfume. It contains citral, geranial, and methyl heptenone. Cf. *citronella oil, melissa oil*.

Lenard, Philipp. 1862–1947. German physicist. Nobel Prize winner (1905). **L. rays.** Long blue streamers produced when cathode rays penetrate thin sheets of aluminum or gold.

length. The shortest distance between 2 points, measured in the cgs system by the meter, q.v., which was supposed to be one ten-millionth of the distance from the equator to the pole. Some magnitudes are given in the table. The smallest accurate determination of length is 0.000,03 mm (Fizeau's interference method). The largest accurate measurement of length (for the purpose of determining the velocity of light) is the distance between Mt. Wilson and Mt. San Antonio, Calif. = 35,426.3 meters.

Lenigallol. Trade name for pyrogallol triacetate.

lenirobin. Chrysarobin tetracetate. Yellow powder, used to treat skin diseases.

lens. A piece of glass or other transparent material, with one or both faces curved, which converges, or diffuses light. The principal focus of a l. $= 1/f_1 + 1/f_2$, where f_1 and f_2 are conjugate focal distances, or the distances of the object and of the image.

Distance or size	Magnitude in:	Meters
	Light years[a]	
Einstein universe....................	2,000,000,000	1.9×10^{25}
Farthest spiral nebula	140,000,000	1.3×10^{24}
Milky Way diameter.................	50,000	4.7×10^{20}
Sirius from sun	8.9	8.4×10^{16}
	Kilometers[b]	
Solar system diameter	10,000,000,000	1×10^{13}
Earth from sun	149,000,000	1.5×10^{11}
Sun radius	692,000	6.9×10^{8}
Moon from earth....................	384,000	3.8×10^{8}
Earth equator	40,070	4×10^{7}
Earth radius........................	6,337	6.3×10^{6}
Moon radius........................	1,740	1.7×10^{6}
	Meters[c]	
Denver above sea level..............	1,638	1.6×10^{3}
Steamer Queen Elizabeth, length......	310	3.15×10^{2}
Lowest sound wave..................	16	1.6×10^{1}
	Centimeters	
Man, average height.................	172	1.72
	Millimeters[d]	
Longest sound wave.................	17	1.7×10^{-2}
	Microns[e]	
Smallest visible particle.............	50	5×10^{-5}
Cells of Drosophila	7–25	2.5×10^{-5}
Coccus bacteria	2	2×10^{-6}
	Millimicrons[f]	
Red blood corpuscle.................	800	8×10^{-7}
Red light wave	770	7.7×10^{-7}
Smallest microscopic particle	300	3×10^{-7}
Shortest ultraviolet wave.............	13	1.3×10^{-8}
Thickness of oil film	5	5×10^{-9}
Ultramicroscopic particle.............	4	4×10^{-9}
Molecules	0.2–5	5×10^{-9}
Gas molecule, distance...............	1	1×10^{-9}
	Micromicrons[g]	
Atoms..............................	100–600	6×10^{-10}
Silver atoms, distance................	400	4×10^{-10}
Electron orbit in hydrogen	53	5.3×10^{-11}
Hard X-ray wave	19	1.9×10^{-11}
Shortest gamma ray.................	2	2×10^{-12}
Longest cosmic ray..................	0.6	6×10^{-13}
Shortest cosmic ray.................	0.04	4×10^{-14}
Electron diameter...................	0.038	3.8×10^{-15}
Nucleus of gold atom................	0.0004	4×10^{-17}
Nucleus of hydrogen atom............	0.00002	2×10^{-18}

[a] 1 parsec = 3.08×10^{13} km = 3.1×10^{16} m.
  1 light year   9,462,700,000,000 km = 9.5×10^{15} m.
[b] 1 kilometer = 1,000 m = 1,000,000 mm = 10^3 m.
[c] 1 meter = 1,000 mm = 1,000,000 μ = 10^{-3} km = 1 m.
[d] 1 millimeter = 1,000 μ = 1,000,000 mμ = 10^{-6} km = 10^{-3} m.
[e] 1 micron = 1,000 mμ = 1,000,000 $\mu\mu$ = 10^{-6} m.
[f] 1 millimicron = 1,000 $\mu\mu$ = 10^{-9} m.
[g] 1 angström = 100 $\mu\mu$ = 1000 mÅ = 10^{-10} m.
  1 micromicron = 10 × units (λ) or mÅ = 10^{-12} m.

achromatic- A l. corrected for chromatic aberration to bring different spectral rays to one focus. **aplanatic-** A l. corrected for spherical aberration to bring rays into focus in the same plane. **apochromatic-** A system of lenses which corrects for chromatic and spherical aberration by bringing the 3 principal spectral regions to one focus. **biconcave-** A l. with a concave surface on each side:) (. **biconvex-** A l. with a convex surface on each side: ( ). **bifocal-** A double l., each portion of which has its own focus. **compound-** Two or more lenses

combined in series. **concave-** A l. in which the center is thinner than the periphery:) |. **convex-** A l. in which the center is thicker than the periphery: (|. **convex-concave-** A l. with both a concave and a convex surface:)). **electron-** See *electron optics.* **planoconcave-** A l. with both a plane and concave surface: | (. **planoconvex-** A l. with both a plane and convex surface: (|. **quartz-** A l. made of quartz, used with ultraviolet rays, to which glass is relatively opaque. **rocksalt-** A l. made of salt, which permits the passage of many ultraviolet rays to which glass and quartz are opaque.

lenticular. Having the shape of a lentil or lens.

lentine. $C_6H_4(NH_2)_2\cdot2HCl$ = 181.0. *m*-Diamino-benzene hydrochloride. Colorless crystals which turn pink with age; used as a reagent for nitrites in water, and to treat diarrhea.

leometer. Dynamic *meter*.

leonardite. A naturally oxidized lignitic coal.

leonite. $MgSO_4\cdot K_2SO_4\cdot4H_2O$. A Stassfurt salt.

leontin. Caulosaponin.

leonurus. Motherwort.

lepargylic acid. Azelaic acid.

lepathinic acid. $C_{20}H_{18}O_{14}$ = 482.2. A crystalline principle from the roots of *Rumex* species (Polygoniaceae).

lepidene. $C\cdot Ph(CPh)_3\cdot O$ = 372.2. Tetraphenylfurfurane. Colorless crystals, m.175.

lepidine. $C_{10}H_9N$ = 143.2. γ-Methylquinoline, cincholepidine. An alkaloid from cinchona bark. Colorless oil, d. 1.086, b.266, slightly soluble in water; used in organic synthesis. **aminophenyl-** Flavaniline. **oxy-** Dibenzoyl*stilbene*.

lepidolite. $(Li,Na,K)_2Al_2(SiO_3)_3(F,OH)_2$. Lithium mica.

lepidometer. An instrument to measure the scaliness of animal fibers in terms of the maximum tension developed when the fibers are suspended, roots downward, and rubbed between rubber surfaces.

lepidone. $C_{10}H_9ON$ = 159.1. Hydroxylepidine, γ-methyl-α-oxyquinoline. Colorless crystals, m.223, slightly soluble in water.

lepinine. 4-Methyl quinine.

leprocidal. Describing compounds used to cure leprosy, e.g., chaulmoogric acid.

leprotin. $C_{40}H_{54}$ = 534.4. A carotenoid red pigment from chromomycobacteria, m.199; a provitamin A.

leptandra. Culver's root. The dried rhizomes and roots of *Veronica (Leptandra) virginica* (Schrophylariaceae); a cathartic and tonic.

leptandrin. Yellow crystals from the roots of *Veronica (Leptandra) virginica*; an alterative and purgative glucoside.

leptandroid. An extract containing the combined principles of *Leptandra*; a tonic laxative, and alterative stimulant.

leptazol. $C_6H_{10}N_4$ = 138.20. Metrazol. 1,5-Pentamethylenetetrazole. Colorless, bittersweet crystals, m.58, soluble in water; a respiratory and vasomotor stimulant.

leptokurtosis. Describing a histogram, q.v., which is more peaked in the middle and rather longer in the tail than corresponds with a normal frequency distribution.

leptology. The study of the fine structure of matter.

leptometer. A device to compare the viscosity of 2 liquids simultaneously.

lepton. A fundamental particle of mass equal to or less than that of a muon; e.g.; a muon, electron, neutrino, and photon.

leptynol. Palladous hydroxide suspended in water; used medicinally.

lerp. A variety of manna found on the Australian shrub, mallee, *Eucalyptus dumosa*.

Lessing. Rudolf. 1878–1964. English fuel chemist. **L. ring.** Contact ring: a ¼-in. metal tube, split

and bent; used as packing material in gas-absorption towers and fractionating columns.

lethal. Fatal or deadly. **l. dose.** The minimum quantity of a substance that causes death. **l. gas.** Hydrocyanic acid.

Lethane. Trademark for a very active synergistic pesticide, e.g., for bedbugs, having no toxic effects on human beings.

lethridrone. Nalorphine hydrobromide.

letterpress. Printing by direct impression from inked projecting type.

leucacene. $C_{54}H_{32}$ = 680.2. A pyrolytic product of acenaphthene containing 12 hexatomic and 4 pentatomic rings. Silky crystals, m.250, insoluble in water.

leucaniline. $CH(C_6H_5\cdot NH_2)_3$ = 289.3. Triaminotriphenylmethane, methenyltrianiline; 3 isomers exist. **para-** Colorless leaflets, m.148, insoluble in water; used in organic synthesis. Cf. *leucoaniline*. **tetramethyl-** See *tetramethyl*.

leucaurine. $CH(C_6H_4OH)_3$ = 292.2. Trihydroxytriphenylmethane, triphenylolmethane, derived from aurine. *o*-**methyl-** Leucorosolic acid.

leucic acid. Leucinic acid.

leucicidin. A toxin formed in cultures of *Staphylococci*, very similar in properties to the lysins.

leucine. $C_2H_{13}O_2N$ = 131.1. Aminoisocaproic acid, α-aminocaproic acid. A constituent of many proteins (27% in zein). Colorless leaflets, decomp. 283, slightly soluble in water; used in organic synthesis; 2 optically active isomers exist. Cf. *leucyl*. **iso-** See *isoleucine*. **nor-** See *norleucine*.

leucinic acid. $C_5H_{10}(OH)COOH$ = 132.13. 2-Hydroxy-4-methylpentanoic acid*; m.77 (racemic), m.82 (active), soluble in alcohol.

leucinimide. $C_{12}H_{22}O_2N_2$ = 226.2. The imide of leucylleucine. A dipeptide formed by reaction of the amino and carboxyl groups of 2 leucine molecules.

Leucippus of Elea. A contemporary of Zeno, Empedocles, and Anaxagoras (about 450 B.C.); the founder of the Ancient Greek atomistic theory, later developed by Democritus.

leucite. $K_2O\cdot Al_2O_3,1\cdot4SiO_2$. A vitreous, white or gray crystalline mineral in lava. Cf. Lucite, lewisite.

leuco- Prefix meaning white, and indicating the presence of a triphenylmethane group.

leucoaniline. $(NH_2C_6H_4)_2\cdot CH\cdot C_6H_3(NH_2)Me$ = 303.4. Triaminotriphenylmethane. Colorless crystals, m.100, insoluble in water; used in organic synthesis. Cf. *leucaniline*. **para-** See *para-*.

leuco bases. Leuko bases. A group of colorless derivatives of triphenylmethane produced by the reduction of dyes which, on oxidation, are reconverted into the dye.

leucocyte. Leukocyte; white blood corpuscle. A colorless, ameba-like cell mass wandering through the tissues.

leucocytosis. The dissolution of leucocytes.

leucodendron. Kienabossie, langbeen. The plant *L. concinnum* (Proteaceae), S. Africa; malaria remedy.

leucodrin. $C_{15}H_{16}O_8$ = 324.12. Proteacin. A crystalline, bitter principle, m.212, from leucodendron.

leucoglycodrin. $C_{27}H_{44}O_{10}$ = 528.32. An amorphous, white glucoside from leucodendron.

leucoindigo. Indigo white.

leucoline. Quinoline.

leucomaclurin glycol. The parent substance of the catechins, from kauri gum. It forms acacin and anacardin by removal of water.

leucomaines. A group of poisonous nitrogen compounds, formed in animal tissues by metabolic activities; generally of the uric acid or creatinine type.

leucomalachite green. $Ph \cdot CH \cdot (C_6H_4NMe_2)_2 = 330.3$. Didimethylaminophenylphenylmethane. Colorless crystals, m.93, insoluble in water, which give malachite green on oxidation.

leucone. $SiH(OH)_3 = 80.09$. Orthosilicoformic acid.

leuconic acid. $CO \cdot (CO)_3 \cdot CO = 140.0$. Pentaketo-cyclopehtane. Colorless needles, produced by strong oxidation of croconic acid.

leucopyrites. $FeAs_2$. A silvery mineral.

leucorosolic acid. $C_{20}H_{19}O_3 = 307.2$. p_3-Trioxy-o-methyltriphenylmethane. Colorless crystals, from rosolic acid.

leucoscope. (1) An optical pyrometer. (2) A photometer for the study of colored light.

leucosin. An albumin from wheat, rye, and barley embryos.

leucotaxine. A polypeptide of low molecular weight formed by the action of vesicants on the skin. It produces increased permeability and accumulation of leucocytes.

leucotrope. Phenyldimethylbenzylammonium chloride.

leucyl. (1) The group $-NH \cdot CH(C_4H_9) \cdot CO-$, from the aminoacid leucine. (2) The group NH_2-$C_5H_{10}CO-$. **l. leucine.** The dipeptide: NH_2-$CH(C_4H_9) \cdot CO-NH \cdot CH(C_4H_9) \cdot COOH$.

leukemia. A disease of the blood produced *inter alia* by exposure to radioactive fallout, especially Sr^{90}. It is characterized by an excessive proportion of white corpuscles and by changed structure of the red corpuscles.

leuko- Leuco-.

leukomaines. Leucomaines.

leukonic acid. Leuconic acid.

leukonin. A commercial name for sodium antimoniate; used in enamels.

leukotine. $C_{21}H_{20}O_6 = 368.2$. A crystalline substance in paracoto bark.

leunaphos. A fertilizer: diammonium phosphate and ammonium sulfate (N 20, P_2O_5 25%).

leunaphoska. A fertilizer: diammonium phosphate, ammonium sulfate, and potassium chloride (N 13, P_2O_5 10, K_2O 13%).

leuna saltpeter. A fertilizer from Leuna, Germany: ammonium sulfate 165, ammonium nitrate 100 pts.

levallorphan tartrate. $C_{19}H_{25}ON \cdot C_4H_6O_6 = 433.44$. N-Allyl-3-hydroxymorphinan tartrate. White, bitter crystals, m.176, soluble in water; an anti-analgesic (B.P.).

levan. A soluble polysaccharide in the leaves of certain grasses, made up of repeating units of fructofuranose.

Levant wormseed. Santonica.

levarterenol bitartrate. $C_8H_{11}O_3N \cdot C_4H_6O_6 \cdot H_2O = 337.29$. White crystals, darkening on exposure, m.103, soluble in water; a sympathomimetic (U.S.P.).

leveler. A liquid added to a lacquer solvent to adjust volatility and/or viscosity.

leveling bulb. A glass vessel connected by rubber tubing to a buret; used in gas analysis to equalize the pressure in both containers.

lever. A mechanical device for increasing the speed or force of a source of power.

leverierite. $Al_2O_3 \cdot 2SiO_2 \cdot nH_2O$. A pearly, brown clay, resembling kaolin.

levigation. The reduction of a substance to a powder by grinding in water, followed by fractional sedimentation, to separate the coarse particles.

levo-, laevo- Prefix indicating that a substance rotates the plane of polarized light to the left (counterclockwise); abbreviation: l-.

levogyric. Levorotatory.

Levol's alloy. The alloy: Ag 71.9, Cu 28.1%.

levophed. Noradrenaline acid tartrate.

levorotatory. Rotating the plane of polarized light from right to left (counterclockwise). Cf. *optical activity*.

levorphanol. $C_{17}H_{23}ON = 257.24$. Levorphan, 3-hydroxy-N-methylmorphinan. White, bitter crystals, m.116, soluble in water; a narcotic analgesic. **l. tartrate.** (B.P.).

levulic acid. Levulinic acid.

levulin. Synanthrose.

levulinamide. $MeCOCH_2CH_2CONH_2 = 115.1$. Colorless crystals, m.107.

levulinic acid. $MeCOCH_2CH_2 \cdot COOH = 116.1$. Levulic acid, β-acetopropionic acid. Colorless leaflets, m.33, soluble in water, **dimethyl-** Mesitonic acid. **methyl-** Homolevulinic acid. **phenylhydrazine-** Antithermin. **l. aldehyde** $C_5H_8O_2 = 100.1$. b-Acetopropionaldehyde. Colorless liquid, d.1.016, decomp. 187, soluble in water. **l. hydrazide.** $MeCO \cdot CH_2 \cdot CH_8$-$CO \cdot NHNH_2 = 131.2$. Colorless crystals, m.82. **l. oxime.** $MeC:NH \cdot CH_2 \cdot CH_2 \cdot COOH = 115.1$. Colorless crystals, m.95.

levulosans. See *fructosans*.

levulose. Fructose.

levymite. $Ca(Al_2Si_4O_{12}) \cdot 6H_2O$. A zeolitic ion-exchange material.

Levy unit. A unit of penicillinase activity. 1 L. u. inactivates 35.6 μg of penicillin in one hour.

Lewis, Gilbert Newton. 1875–1946. American chemist, noted for thermodynamic theories applied to chemistry and atomic structure. **L.-Adams formula.** An expression relating the fundamental constants (q.v.) h, c, and e: $hc/2\pi e^2 = 8\pi(8\pi^5/15)^{\frac{1}{4}}$. The numerical values are 137.29 and 137.348. **L.'s atom.** The static concept of the atom, based on crystallography; as opposed to the dynamic Bohr atom, q.v. The electrons were thought to oscillate or vibrate around definite centers located at the corners of a cube (cubical atom) or in pairs at the corners of a tetrahedron (tetrahedral atom). **L. color theory.** Color is produced by the absorption of certain rays by those electrons of a molecule which vibrate with the same frequency. **L.-Langmuir theory.** The atom is built up of successive shells which hold 2, 8, 18, 32, 18, and 8 electrons as their maximum capacities. **L. symbols.** Illustrating bonds by indicating electrons as dots. Cf. *octet, formula, bond*. **L. theory.** A chemical bond is *polar* when an electron passes from one atom to another; *nonpolar* when 2 atoms share a pair of electrons equally.

lewisite. $Cl \cdot CH : CH \cdot AsCl_2$ = 207.28. 1-Dichloro-arsino-2-chloroethylene. An irritant liquid, d.1.89, b.190 (decomp.); a vesicant poison. Cf. *leucite, Lucite.* **British anti-** $C_3H_8OS_2$ = 124.41. Dithiol (U.S. usage). BAL. 2,3-Dimercaptopropanol. An antidote for l. and other arsenical poisons.

Lexan. Trademark for a thermoplastic polycarbonate condensation product of bisphenol-A and phosgene.

ley. (1) The mixture of salts 10–20 and glycerol 6–8% formed by saponification of crude fats by sodium hydroxide in soap manufacture. (2) Describing a system of farming of crops in rotation, interspersed with ploughing. Cf. *lye.*

Leyden jar. See *jar.*

li. Abbreviation for link.

Li. Symbol for lithium.

liatris. Deer's-tongue. The dried leaves of *Liatris odoratissima* (Compositae); used for flavoring and in tobacco.

Libavius, Andreas. 1540–1616. German alchemical writer and pioneer in blowpipe analysis.

liberation. The act of setting free, as the formation of carbon dioxide from chalk.

libration. A real or apparent oscillating motion. Usually applied to the movement of the moon relative to the earth.

licanic acid. A gelling fatty acid in drying oils used for paints.

lichen. Algae and fungi which live symbiotically, i.e., 2 primitive plants, one with, the other without chlorophyll, which live together; e.g., Iceland moss. They yield coloring matter (litmus, orchil, zearin), acids (e.g., orsellic acid), carbohydrates, and depsides. **l. starch.** Lichenin. **l. stearic acid.** $C_{14}H_{14}O_3$ = 230.1. A crystalline dibasic acid from Iceland moss, m.120, insoluble in water. **l. sugar.** Erythrite.

licheniformin. An antibiotic from *Bacillus licheniformis.*

lichenin. $(C_6H_{10}O_5)_n$ = $(162.11)_n$. [n = 80–160.] Lichen starch, moss starch. A β-glucopyranose carbohydrate derived from Iceland moss, *Cetraria islandicus,* which is digested by invertebrates only. White powder, soluble in hot water, m.10.

lichenol. $C_9H_9O_4 \cdot C_2H_5$ = 210.1. The ethyl ester of evernesic acid, from the oil of oak moss, *Evernia prunastri.* Cf. *sparassol.*

Lichtenberg figures. The pattern formed by an electric spark passing through a thin layer of insulator; as, sulfur. Cf. *klydonograph.*

licorice. Glycyrrhiza (U.S. usage). Cf. *liquorice.* **Indian-** Abrus. **Spanish-** Glycyrrhiza.

lidocaine. Lignocaine.

Lieben solution. A solution of iodine in potassium iodide.

Liebermann, Carl. 1842–1914. German chemist noted for the synthesis of alizarin (with Gräbe). **L. reaction.** Sodium nitrite in concentrated sulfuric acid gives a brown color, changing to blue, in presence of a phenol. The mixture poured into water gives a red solution, which changes to blue on addition of alkali, (formation of p-nitrosophenol.)

Liebig, Justus Freiherr von. 1803–1873. German chemist, founder of agricultural chemistry. **L. condenser.** A glass tube, surrounded by a wider

tube through which water circulates. **L. extract.** A meat extract used as a nutrient for making biological bouillon. **L. potash bulb.** A triangularly bent glass tube with 2 or more bulbs filled with potassium hydroxide; used in gas analysis.

lien siccus. The dried and powderized spleen of cattle; used medicinally.

Liesegang, Raphael Edward. 1869–1947. German chemist. **L. rings.** A periodic precipitation, formed as bands in gelatin, by the gradual diffusion towards one another of 2 mutually precipitating ions.

life. (1) The vital force: the principle underlying the phenomena of organized beings. It depends on the *protoplasm,* which exercises the function of *metabolism, growth, reproduction, adaptation,* and *evolution,* q.v. (2) An inappropriate synonym for "time" or "time period"; as: **damping l.** See *damping period.* **half l.** See *half-life* and *radioactivity.* **lingering l.** See *lingering period.* (3) Colloquially, but inappropriately, the period of usefulness of a device, machine, or other inanimate object.

l. elements. The bioelements (q.v.) necessary for an organism. **l. everlasting.** The dried herb of *Gnaphalium obtusifolium* (*Antennaria dioica*) (Compositae); a diuretic and astringent. **l. root.** Senecio.

ligand. A group of atoms around a central metallic ion in a complex compound; e.g.: CN^- and F^- are the ligands in $[Fe(CN)_6]^{4-}$ and $[SiF_6]^=$, respectively. **l. field theory.** The study of the effect of light on the energy level of a metal ion when a l. approaches it to form a complex.

ligasoid. A disperse colloidal system, consisting of a liquid phase suspended in a gaseous phase; as, a fog.

light. (1) A form of radiant energy. Cf. *radiation, spectrum.* In particular, electromagnetic waves of the visible spectrum: red, orange, yellow, green, blue, violet; or radiations which, when stopped by an object, render it visible by transformation into visible rays. The average velocity of l. in air is 299,711 km/sec; in a vacuum 299,776 km/sec. The ratios, (velocity in vacuo)/(velocity in medium) are shown in the table. The *intensity* of l. is measured

Medium	Violet λ 4200	Red λ 6500
Air	1.000297	1.000292
Water	1.3420	1.3320
Diamond. . . .	2.4570	2.4108

in phots, the *quantity* in lumens, the *quality* as colors. (2) Not heavy; as, l. metals. **absorbed-** Those radiations which are influenced by matter. **actinic-** Radiations that are rich in ultraviolet rays; and affect a photographic plate. Cf. *irradiation.* **artificial-** A gas-filled lamp operated at a color temperature of 2848°K; adopted as the *normal* artificial l. by an International Commission (1931). **axial-** The rays passing through the optic axis of a system. **diffracted-** L. that has undergone diffraction, q.v. **diffused-** L. that has been scattered or reflected. **Finsen-** Sunlight passed through a copper sulfate solution, which absorbs the yellow, red, and infrared rays. **monochromatic-** L. consisting of apparently one wavelength only, as the sodium flame which, however, is made up of several wavelengths. Absolutely monochromatic l. is obtained only by screening a spectrum. **polarized-** L. whose vibrations are all in the same plane, and parallel to one another, and change uniformly; as, circularly- or elliptically-polarized l., q.v. Polarized light can be obtained by reflection, or by passage through certain minerals; as Iceland spar. **reflected-** L. that is turned back from a smooth surface; as a mirror. **refracted-** L. that passes at an angle through a transparent medium, gas, liquid, or solid, and thereby changes its direction; as in lenses. **scattered-** See *scattering, Raman effect, Tyndall effect.* **transmitted-** L. that has passed through a medium, without absorption. **ultraviolet-** See *radiations, rays.* Wood's- See *Wood's.*

l. **filter.** Color screen. l. **metal.** A metallic element with a density below 4. In particular, the alkali, earth-alkali, and earth metals; characterized by a single valence (1, 2, or 3), a simple spectrum, strong electromotive force (positive), and colorless compounds. Cf. *periodic system.* Antonym: Heavy metals, nonmetals. l. **oils.** A fractional distillate from coal tar, b.110–210; a source of benzene, toluene, and xylenes. l. **pipe.** A tube or rod of plastic which transmits l. internally around corners. l. **scattering.** See *scattering.* l. **standard.** The international standard (1957) is a ceramic tube cavity irradiator immersed in a crucible of melted platinum. During solidification, the temperature is constant for a short time at the freezing point of platinum, and the radiator then has, by definition, a luminescence of 60 candelas/cm^2. l. **titration.** See *titration.* l. **unit.** 161 lux hours. Cf. *lux.* l. **year.** A unit of astronomical distance: the distance that l. travels in one year at the rate of 299,800 km/sec $= 9.5 \times 10^{12}$ km $= 5.9 \times 10^{13}$ miles.

lightning. The electric flash associated with thunderstorms; or artificially produced. l. **jar.** Leyden jar.

lignasan. Ethyl mercuric chloride. A wood preservative.

lignin. Generic name for an amorphous highly polymerized product which forms the middle lamella of many plant fibers (especially woods), and cements the fibers together by means of an intercellular layer surrounding them; insoluble in water; soluble in sodium sulfite solution, or dioxan. It contains OMe groups in proportions depending on the plant species (e.g., there are more in hardwoods than in softwoods); and 4 condensed molecules of coniferol. It occurs in woodpulp digester liquor wastes; a source of vanillin and plastics. **alkali-** L. obtained by acidification of an alkaline extract of wood. **Klason-** L. obtained from wood after the wood has been extracted with 72% sulfuric acid. **native-** L. obtained by direct extraction of wood with ethanol. **Willstätter-** L. obtained from wood after it has been extracted with fuming hydrochloric acid.

lignite. A brown coal, in which the original structure of the wood is still recognizable (25–45% C). See *jet, hartite.*

lignocaine hydrochloride. $C_{14}H_{22}ON_2 \cdot HCl \cdot H_2O =$ 288.72. Xylocaine, lidocaine. White, bitter crystals, m.77, soluble in water; a local anesthetic, which is more potent, lasting, and toxic than procaine hydrochloride.

lignoceric acid. $C_{23}H_{47}COOH = 368.50$. Tetracosanic acid*. A wood acid, m.81, soluble in alcohol. Δ^{14}-. Nervonic acid. **α-hydroxy-** $C_{22}H_{45}CHOH \cdot COOH$. An acid from phrenosin.

lignoceryl alcohol. $C_{24}H_{49}OH = 354.40$. An isomer of carnaubyl alcohol in tall oil.

lignone. A substance derived from wood: C 50.1, H 5.82, O 44.08%. l. **sulfonate.** The waste liquor from the sulfite process of paper pulp making.

lignose. A substance derived from wood: C 46.1, H 6.09, O 47.81%.

lignosulfin. Lignosulfite.

lignosulfite. Lignosulfin. A liquid by-product in the manufacture of sulfite cellulose; used for inhalations in pulmonary tuberculosis, and as a tan.

lignum. Latin for wood. l. **benedictum.** The wood of guaiac. l. **cedrum.** Cedarwood. l. **nephriticum.** Wood from *Pterocarpus indicus*, Philippines, or *Eysenhardtia polystachia*, Mexico. They give highly fluorescent infusions. l. **rhodium.** The wood of *Amyris balsamifera*, tropical America. l. **sanctum,** l. **vitae.** Guaiac.

ligroin. Ligroine. The fourth fraction petroleum distillation product. d.0.707–0.722, b.90–120; a solvent.

ligustrin. Syringin.

ligustron. A crystalline principle from the bark of *Ligustrum vulgare.* Colorless crystals, m.105.

Ligustrum. A genus of oleaceous shrubs, the privets.

lilac. The dried leaves and fruits of *Syringa vulgaris*; a bitter tonic.

lilacin. Syringin.

Liliaceae. Lily family, a group of herbs with flowering stems, from bulbs or corms, with parallel nerved leaves. Some yield drugs; d.g.: *Smilax china*, chinaroot; *Schoenocaulon sabadilla*, sabadilla; *Allium sativum*, garlic; *Aloe vera, ferox,* etc., aloes.

Liliiflorae. An order of phanerogamous plants (Junaceae, Liliaceae, Amaryllidaceae, Iridaceae, Dioscoraceae, and Bromeliaceae).

Lilion. Trade name for a polyamide synthetic fiber.

liliquoid. A dispersed or colloidal 2-liquid-phase system; as emulsions.

lilolidine. $C_{11}H_{12}N = 159.11$. Tetrahydrolilole. Colorless liquid, $b_{15mm}156$.

lily of the valley. Convallaria.

limanol. A preparation of salt-marsh mud used to treat rheumatism.

lime. (1) Calcium oxide, calx, quicklime, burnt l. (2) The fruit of *Citrus acida* (Rutaceae); an antiscorbutic. (3) The linden or l. tree, *Tilia Europaea* (Tiliaceae). Cf. *linden.* **burnt-** Calcium oxide. **chloride of-, chlorinated-** Bleaching powder. **fat-** Calcium oxide. **hydrated-** Calcium hydroxide. **quick-** Calcium oxide. **slaked-** A dry white powder chiefly calcium hydroxide, obtained by treating quicklime with sufficient water to satisfy its chemical affinity. **sulfurated-** Calcium sulfide. **unslaked-** Calcium oxide.

l. **juice.** Succus Citri. The expressed sap from lemons, the ripe fruits of *Citrus medica, C. limonum,* or *C. acida* (Rutaceae); an antiscorbutic and antiseptic. l. **nitrate.** Commercial calcium nitrate as fertilizer. **l. oil.** (1) An essential oil expressed from the rinds of the fruit of *Citrus limetta* (Rutaceae), containing citral and limonene; a flavoring and perfume. (2) An essential oil distilled from citron, b.175–215, containing *d*-limonene. **l. water.** Liquor calcis. A saturated solution of calcium hydroxide in water; a reagent and antiacid.

limelight. Illumination produced by heating lime to brilliant white heat with an oxyhydrogen flame.

limene. $C_{12}H_{24} = 204.2$. A sesquiterpene from lime oil.

limestone. A pulverized rock consisting mainly of calcium carbonate; used in fertilizers, concrete mixtures, and in metallurgy. **magnesian-** q.v.

limettin. A constituent of lime oil.

liminal. (1) Barely perceptible by the senses. (2) The lowest or minimal quantity. **l. value.** That fraction of a normal solution (in moles per liter) of a drug which produces a definite physiological effect; e.g.: for monacetin 0.5, for sulfonal 0.006. Cf. *schwellenwert.*

liming material. A medium for the application of lime or limestone in agriculture, e.g., burnt lime mixed with marl.

limit. A border or boundary. **l. of elasticity.** The smallest stress which produces a permanent alteration.

limiting curve. A line on a graph which represents a boundary between 2 phases.

limnology. The study of lakes and inland seas.

limonene. $C_{10}H_{16} = 136.2$. $\Delta^{1,8(9)}$-*p*-Menthadiene, q.v. A terpene of lemon odor. Colorless liquid, d.0.853, b.176, insoluble in water; 3 isomers: **dextro-** Citrene, carvene, hesperidene, in the essential oils from citrons and dill. **dl-** or **-i** Inactive limonene. **levo-** In oil of fir cones.

limonite. Bog ore. A hydrated ferric oxide, 60–70%, with some carbonate, from Rotorua, New Zealand; a cure for bush sickness and source of iron.

Linaceae. Flax family: a group of herbaceous (sometimes woody) plants, yielding drugs and fibers; as, *Linum usitatissimum*, linen, flaxseed, linseed oil.

linaloe oil. An essential oil from a Mexican wood. Colorless, fragrant liquid, d.0.88, insoluble in water; used in the manufacture of linalool.

linalool. $Me_2C:CH(CH_2)_2CMeOHCH:CH_2 = 154.2$. Coriandrol, dimethyloctadiene-2,7-ol-6. A terpene of bergamot-like odor in coriander and linaloe oils. Colorless liquid. **dextro-** d.0.875, b.198. **levo-** d.0.866, b.195, slightly soluble in water. Both used in perfumery.

linalyl. The radical $C_{10}H_{17}$—. 2,6-Dimethylocta-2,7-dienyl, from linalool. **l. acetate.** $Me_2C:CH(CH_2)_2CMe(OCOMe)CH:CH_2 = 196.2$. Linaloolacetic ester. Colorless liquid, d.0.91, b.220, slightly soluble in water; used in perfumery.

linamarin. $C_9H_{13}NO_7 = 247.14$. An acetone cyanhydrin glucoside, m.141, from flax and *Phaseolus lunatus.*

linarin. A glucoside from toadflax, *Linaria vulgaris* (Scrophulariaceae).

linarite. $PbSO_4 \cdot Cu(OH)_2$. A basic lead sulfate.

lindane. Official (U.S.) name for the gamma isomer of benzene hydrochloride, of purity not less than 99%; an insecticide.

Lindemann, Frederick, Alexander (Lord Cherwell).

1886–1957. British physicist noted for work on aeronautics and atomic energy; personal scientific advise to Winston Churchill.

linden. A tree of genus *Tilia* (Tiliaceae.) **American-** Basswood, American lime, *T. americana*, which yields l. oil. **European-** *T. europaea*, yielding tilia and lime (3). **l. flowers.** See *lime (3).* **l. oil.** Basswood oil. An oil from l. flowers and seeds, which resembles cottonseed oil.

Linderström-Lang, Kaj Ulrik. 1896–1959. Danish biochemist, from the Carlsberg Laboratory, Copenhagen.

lindgrenite. $2CuMoO_4 \cdot Cu(OH)_2$. A Chilean mineral. Transparent, green, biaxial holohedra.

Lindol. Trademark for tricresyl phosphate.

line, lines. (1) The dimension of extension which possesses length but neither breadth nor thickness. (2) The $\frac{1}{12}$ part of an inch. (3) A narrow streak or strip. See *spectroscope.* **absorption-** A l. corresponding with light which has been absorbed on its passage through a medium. **bright-** The emission l. characteristic of an element. **C-** The dark Fraunhofer l. of $\lambda 6562.8$ which corresponds with the hydrogen l., H_α. **calcium-** The characteristic l. of calcium, especially the Fraunhofer l. *G, H,* and *K.* D_1-, D_2- The yellow light of the sodium flame; $\lambda 5895.9$, $\lambda 5890.0$, respectively. **dark-** Absorption or Fraunhofer l. **emission-** The bright l. characteristic of an element. **Fraunhofer-** A dark l. in the solar spectrum caused by the absorption of light passing through incandescent vapor. Cf. *solar spectrum.* **hydrogen-** See *H. line.* **hyperfine-** L. close together, due to nuclear moments. **K-** See *K line.* **metallic-** L. due to metallic elements. **nebular-** L. characteristic of nebulae. Cf. *nebulium.* **solar-** See *solar spectrum.*

l. of force. The direction in which a force acts; as: **electric-** The curves radiating from a positive toward a negative charge. **magnetic-** The curves or l. made visible by small iron filings in the field of force of a magnet. **l. spectrum.** A spectrum of l., each corresponding with a wavelength of the rays comprising the source of light. L. are caused by excited atoms and ions; bands are due to molecules.

linear. Pertaining to one dimension: length. **l. expansion.** The lengthwise expansion of materials under the influence of heat. Cf. *cubical expansion.* **l. measures.** The units of measuring length.

linen. A textile manufactured from the fibers of the flax stem.

linhay. A concrete platform, on which china clay is stored before shipment.

liniment. An oily liquid used medicinally for external application.

linin. (1) Oxychromatin. A morphological or structural element of the cell (linin network). (2) The active principle of purging flax, *Linum catharticum* (Linaceae), Europe. Colorless, bitter crystals; a purgative.

lining. (1) The inside portion of a furnace. (2) A thin coating. **acid-** L. of silica bricks. **basic-** L. of magnesite bricks. **neutral-** L. of coal or chrome bricks.

link. li. An obsolete linear measure used in surveying. 1 li = 0.66 ft.

linkage. Lines used in structural formulas to represent valency connections between atoms. Produced by a pair of electrons, one from each atom. See *bond, polar.* **cross-** Networks of bonds between linear polymers; associated in plastics with reduced solubility and high softening temperature.

linnaeite. $(Co,Ni)_3S_4$. Linnaetite. Cobalt-nickel pyrite.

linnaetite. Linnaeite.

linoleate. $C_{17}H_{31}COOM$. A compound of a metal and linoleic acid where M is a monovalent metal. If M is replaced by an alcohol radical, a fat results.

linoleic acid. $Me(CH_2)_4CH:CH\cdot CH_2\cdot CH:CH\cdot (CH_2)_7\cdot COOH = 280.2$. Linolic acid, 9,12-octadecadienoic acid*. A fatty-acid glyceride in all drying oils. Yellow oil, d.0.921, b.230, insoluble in water. **l. acid series.** $C_nH_{2n-4}O_2$. A group of unsaturated aliphatic acids; as linoleic acid, $C_{18}H_{32}O_2$.

linolenic acid. $C_{17}H_{29}COOH = 278.2$. 9,12,15-Octadecatrienoic acid*. Colorless liquid, d.0.922, insoluble in water.

linoleum. Canvas coated with a mixture of linseed oil, powdered cork, and pigment. Cf. *oilcloth.*

linolic acid. Linoleic acid.

linotype metal. The alloy: Pb 83.5, Sb 13.5, Sn 3.0%; used for printing type.

linoxyn. Solid, oxidized linseed oil, used in the manufacture of linoleum.

linron. Trade name for bleached stabilized linen fiber.

linseed. The dried seeds of flax, *Linum usitatissimum* (Linaceae,); a demulcent and emollient. **l. cake, l. meal.** The solid residue of l. after removal of the oil; a cattle feed. **l. oil.** Flaxseed oil, oleum lini (B.P.). Yellow oil from linseed, d.0.932, m.—27, sapon. val. 188–195, iodine val. 170–192, insoluble in water, soluble in organic solvents. Used in paints, varnishes, lacquers, rubber substitutes, linoleum, and leather. *boiled-* A l. oil which has been thickened by boiling, and dries rapidly on exposure to air; used in varnishes and driers.

lint. Charpie byssus. A soft and flexible linen for dressing wounds. **cotton-** An inferior short fiber from the cotton plant.

linter. A machine for removing cotton linters from the seed.

linters. The short cotton fibers left after ginning; a source of pure cellulose for explosives or paper.

linum. Latin for linseed (flax).

lionite. Impure native tellurium.

lion's-tooth. Taraxacum.

liothryonine sodium. $C_{15}H_{11}O_4NI_3Na = 673.01$. White solid, insoluble in water; a thyroid hormone (B.P.).

lipase. (1) A ferment in the liver, pancreas, and other digestive organs, which splits neutral fats into glycerin and fatty acids. (2) A ferment that splits fats into fatty acids and alcohol. **gastric-** A l. of the stomach. **pancreatic-** Steapsase. **vegetable-** A l. in many plants.

lipide(s). Proposed name for lipins. **complex-** A l. that contains P and/or N. Cf. *lipoid.* **tertiary-** A l. that contains neither P nor N.

lipins. A generic term for fats and lipoids, the alcohol-ether-soluble constituents of propoplasm, which are insoluble in water. They comprise the fats, fatty oils, essential oils, waxes, sterols, phospholipins, glycolipins, sulfolipins, aminolipins, chromolipins (lipochromes), and fatty acids.

Lipiodol. Trademark for an injection of iodized oil.

lipochondria. Golgi apparatus.

lipochrome. A fatty pigment or coloring matter in natural fats, such as egg yolk and butter. See *carotenoids.*

lipoclastic. Lipolytic.

lipoid, lipoidic. Having the character of a lipid.

lipoids. A group of nitrogenous fats (lecithins, cholesterol, and phosphatides).

Lipoiodine. $C_{21}H_{39}I_2COOEt = 618.1$. Trademark for ethyldiiodobrassidate. White needles, m.37, insoluble in water; a substitute for iodides in medicine.

lipolutin. Progesterone.

lipolysis. The decomposition or dissolution of a fat: the reverse of saponification.

lipolytic. Lipoclastic. An agent that decomposes a fat into its alcohol (glycerin) and fatty acid.

lipoprotein. A complex of a simple protein with a higher fatty acid.

Lipowitz' alloy. The alloy: Bi 50, Pb 27, Sn 13, Cd 10%; m.71.7; used in automatic fire sprinklers.

lippia. Yerba dulce. The dried leaves and inflorescence of *Lippia dulcis,* (Verbenaceae); a demulcent or expectorant. **l. citriodora.** Lemon-scented verbena. The dried leaves of *Aloysia citriodora,* (Verbenaceae); a sedative.

lippianol. A monohydric alcohol from the essential oil of *Lippia species* (Verbenaceae).

Lippmann, Edmond Oskar von. 1857–1940. German organic chemist, noted for work on the sugar industry. **L. electrode.** Capillary electrode. An early form of standard mercury dropping electrode, q.v. **L. electrometer.** Capillary electrometer.

liq. Abbreviation for liquid.

liquation. The extraction of metals from ores by heating on an inclined hearth and collecting the molten metal.

liquefaction. The change to liquid form, especially the condensation of gases to a liquid.

liquefon. A unit of the starch-liquefying power of enzymes: $\log_{10} L = (S - 1078) 0.000565$, where $L = $ liquefons per 10 cc infusion, $S = $ milligrams of starch liquefied in one hour.

liquescent. Tending to become fluid or liquid.

liqueur. A strongly flavored and sweetened alcoholic beverage.

liquid. A state of matter intermediate between a solid and a gas, shapeless and fluid, taking the shape of the container and seeking the lowest level. Cf. *solvent, parachor.* **anomalous-** A fluid that is not a true liquid; e.g., paste. Cf. anomalous *viscosity.* **associated-** Polar. A l. in which the molecules form groups (probably coordinate bonds, q.v.), and in which K of the Ramsay-Shields or Morgan equation increases linearly with temperature to a maximum at t_c. **Newtonian-** A true l. which does not alter in viscosity on stirring. Cf. *thixotropy.* **nonassociated-** Normal. **normal-** Nonpolar. A l. consisting of independent molecules, with no coordinate bonds or unshared electrons in the octet, and in which $K = 2.12$ ergs/deg. **polar-** Associated l. **semipolar-** A l. intermediate between associated and normal; as, alcohol.

    l. acetylene. Acetylene gas compressed into steel cylinders containing infusorial earth and acetone; used in welding. **l. air.** Clear, colorless l., intensely cold, and giving off oxygen and nitrogen vapors which freeze the moisture of the surrounding air; kept in open Dewar vessels. Used to produce low temperatures; medicinally, in the treatment and relief of poison oak and poison ivy eruptions. **l. ammonia.** Ammonia gas liquefied under pressure in steel cylinders. For uses. see *ammonia*. **l. carbon dioxide.** Carbon dioxide gas compressed in steel cylinders. Used as a refrigerant, for producing pressure in carbonated drinks, for blowing up tires of automobiles, etc. See *carbon dioxide*. **l. chlorine.** L. chlorine compressed in steel cylinders; used in bleaching. See *chlorine*. **l. ethylene.** Ethylene gas compressed in steel cylinders; used as an anesthetic in welding, to ripen citrus fruits and in the synthesis of ethanol. See *ethylene*. **l. gold.** A solution of gold sulforesinate in essential oils, sometimes containing Bi and Rh, used to give a gold surface glaze to ceramics after firing. **l. helium.** Helium gas compressed in steel cylinders; used for filling dirigibles. **l. hydrogen.** Hydrogen gas compressed in steel cylinders; used in welding, production of high temperatures, filling balloons and dirigibles, hydrogenation of oils, and cracking of petroleum. See *hydrogen*. **l. hydrogen sulfide.** Hydrogen sulfide gas compressed in steel cylinders; used in chemical industry, and as a reagent. **l. nitrous oxide.** Nitrous oxide gas compressed in steel cylinders; used as a dentist's anesthetic, as a substitute for oxygen in jewelers' blowpipes, as a preservative. **l. oxygen.** Oxygen gas compressed in steel cylinders; used in welding, anesthesia, mine rescue work, and for blasting. See *oxygen*. **l. silver.** A mixture of silver powder and platinic chloride suspended in essential oils, used to give a silver surface glaze to ceramics after firing. **l. smoke.** The first distillate in the fractional distillation of wood, which contains acetic acid, tar, and phenol compounds (pyroligneous acid); used in the preservation or "smoking" of meat. **l. sulfur dioxide.** Sulfur dioxide gas compressed in glass bottles; a reducing agent and reagent. See *sulfur dioxide*.

liquidambar. Copal balsam, copalin. The balsamic exudates of *Liquidambar styraciflua* (Hamamelidaceae), N. America; used to treat coughs. Cf. *storax*.

liquidated. Describing the surface of an ingot or casting which shows exudations or protuberances due to inverse segregation.

liquidus. A curve relating to a liquid phase of a 2-component solution. See *solidus*.

liquor. An aqueous solution. **l. ammoniae.** Ammonium hydroxide. **l. calcis.** Limewater. **l. of flints.** A solution of silica in potash (potassium silicate). **l. trinitrin.** A 1% solution of glyceryl trinitrate in alcohol.

liquorice. Glycyrrhiza (B.P.). Cf. *licorice*.

liroconite. $Cu_9Al_4(OH)_{15}(AsO_4)_5 \cdot 20H_2O$. A native, hydrated arsenate.

lisoloid. A disperse or colloidal system consisting of a liquid phase surrounded by a solid phase; as, a jelly.

Lissajou's figure. The pattern produced by a spot of light reflected from 2 mirrors, mounted on the ends of two tuning forks vibrating at right angles.

Lissapol C. Trade name for sodium oleylsulfate; a

wetting agent. **L.NX.** Trade name for an octyl cresol condensation product with ethylene oxide; an anionic surfactant.

lissephen. Mephenesin.

Lister, Baron Joseph. 1827–1912. English surgeon who founded antiseptic surgery.

Listerine. Trademark for an antiseptic solution containing boric acid, benzoic acid, thymol, and essential oils of *Eucalyptus, Gaultheria,* etc.

liter, litre. The metric unit of volume or capacity. (1) The volume of a decimeter cube (Système International, 1964). (2) Formerly the volume occupied by 1 kg of pure water at 4°C and 760 mm pressure. It was originally intended to be 1,000 cc. 1 liter = 1,000 ml = 1,000.028 cc = 0.264178 gal = 33.8174 fl oz. One mole of any gas occupies 22.4 liters at 0°C and 760 mm. **micro-** μl or λ, lambda. One-millionth part of a liter. $1\lambda = 10^{-6}$ liter. **milli-** ml. One-thousandth part of a liter; 1 ml = 10^{-3} liter = approximately 1 cc. **Mohr-** An obsolete unit of volume: the volume of 1 kg of water at 15°C weighed in vacuo (1,000.91 cc).

litharge. Lead oxide, yellow.

lithate. Urate.

lithia. Lithium oxide. **l. mica.** Lepidolite. **l. water.** A solution of lithium bicarbonate.

lithic acid. Uric acid.

lithii. Latin designation for salts of lithium (U.S.P.).

lithionite. A lepidolite containing ferrous iron. Silvery scales from Cornwall, England.

lithiophyllite. A native lithium-manganese phosphate.

lithium. Li = 6.94. An element, at. no. 3, the first member of the alkali metals in group 1 of the periodic system; valency 1. Silver-gray metal, d.0.524, m.186, b.1400, reacting with water (stored in kerosene). L. is widely distributed, in small quantities; e.g.: in amblygonite, lepidolite, petalite, spodumene, and mineral waters. Discovered (1817) by Arfvedson, and named from the Greek lithos (stone). It forms one series of compounds, all soluble in water. Used as "scavenger" in purifying metals; as deoxidizer in copper alloys. Traces of Li added to Al increase hardness; with Pb it produces a bearing metal. L. salts are used in soaps, lubricants, and medicine; as rubber stabilizers; and in Ni-Co batteries; l. deuteride and l. tritide as hydrogen bomb boosters. **l. acetate.** $Li(C_2H_3O_2) \cdot 2H_2O$ = 102.0. White rhombs, m.70, soluble in water; a diuretic and antirheumatic. **l. acetyl salicylate.** $C_2H_3O \cdot OC_6H_4 \cdot COOLi$ = 186.06. Hydropyrine, apyron, tyllithin, litmopyrine, grifa; a diuretic. **l. agaricinate.** White powder, soluble in water; an anhidrotic. **l. amide.** $(LiNH_2)_n$ = $(22.96)_n$. Colorless cubes, m.390, decomp. in water; used as catalyst. **l. arsenate.** $Li_3AsO_4 \cdot \frac{1}{2}H_2O$ = 168.8. White powder, soluble in water; an antiarthritic. **l. benzoate.** $LiC_7H_5O_2$ = 128.0. White powder of cool taste, soluble in water; a diuretic, urinary antiseptic, and sedative. **l. benzosalicylate.** White crystals, soluble in water; a urinary antiseptic. **l. bicarbonate.** $LiHCO_3$ = 68.0. White powder, slightly soluble in water (lithia water). **l. bichromate.** $Li_2Cr_2O_7$ = 229.9. Orange crystals, soluble in water. **l. bitartrate.** $LiC_4H_5O_6 \cdot H_2O$ = 174.1. Tartarlithine. Colorless crystals, soluble in water; used to treat gout. **l. borate.**

$Li_2B_4O_7 \cdot 5H_2O$ = 259.2. White powder, soluble in water; used as an antiseptic and in dental cements. *meta-* $LiBO_2$ = 49.76. White powder, soluble in water. **l. borocitrate.** $Li_2HC_6H_5O_7 \cdot$ $2HBO_3 \cdot 2H_2O$ = 359.4. White powder, soluble in water; a urinary antiseptic. **l. bromide.** LiBr = 86.9. Colorless, hygroscopic powder, m.442, soluble in water; a nerve sedative. **l. cacodylate.** $LiMe_2AsO_2 \cdot H_2O$ = 162.1. White powder, soluble in water; used to treat anemia. **l. caffeine sulfonate.** Symphorol. **l. carbide.** Li_2C_2 = 37.89. White powder. **l. carbonate.** Li_2CO_3 = 73.9. Colorless prisms, m.700, slightly soluble in water; an antacid. *acid-* L. bicarbonate. **l. chlorate.** $2LiClO_3 \cdot H_2O$ = 198.82. A deliquescent solid, m.50. *per-* L. perchlorate. **l. chloride.** $LiCl(+2H_2O)$ = 42.4. Colorless octahedra, m.606, soluble in water; an antirheumatic, and pyrotechnic (red fires). **l. chromate.** $Li_2CrO_4 \cdot$ $2H_2O$ = 166.1. Yellow, hygroscopic crystals, soluble in water. **l. citrate.** $Li_3C_6H_5O_7 \cdot 4H_2O$ = 281.9. White, hygroscopic powder; sometimes used medicinally to treat gout. **l. dichromate.** L. bichromate. **l. dithiosalicylate.** $(LiC_7H_4O_3S)_2$ = 350.1. Gray powder, soluble in water; an antirheumatic. **l. fluophosphate.** $LiF \cdot Li_3PO_4 \cdot$ H_2O = 169.8. Colorless crystals, soluble in water; a ceramic flux. **l. fluosilicate.** $Li_2SiF_6 \cdot$ $2H_2O$ = 191.97. L. silicofluoride. White monoclinic crystals, d.2.33, soluble in water. **l. fluoride.** LiF = 26.0. White crystals, soluble in water; a ceramic enamel. **l. formate.** HCOOLi = 52.1. Colorless crystals, soluble in water; used to treat gout. **l. germanate.** Li_2GeO_3 = 134.48. Colorless powder, m.1239, soluble in water. **l. glycerophosphate.** $Li_2C_3H_7O_6P$ = 184.1. White crystalline powder, soluble in water; used to treat gout. **l. hippurate.** $LiC_9H_8O_3N$ = 185.1. White powder, slowly soluble in hot water; used for uric acid diathesis. **l. hydride.** LiH = 7.95. White solid, m.680, decomp. in water to H_2 and l. hydroxide. **l. hydroxide.** LiOH = 24.0. White crystals, soluble in water; a reagent. **l. iodate.** $LiIO_3$ = 182.0. White powder, soluble in water. **l. iodide.** $LiI(+3H_2O)$ = 133.86. White, hygroscopic crystals, m.720, soluble in water; used as a diuretic and alterative, and in artificial mineral waters. **l. lactate.** $LiC_3H_5O_3$ = 96.0. Colorless crystals, soluble in water; a diuretic. **l. laurate.** $C_{12}H_{23}O_2Li$ = 206.12. White solid, m.230. **l. mercuric iodide.** Mercuric l. iodide. **l. metaborate.** $LiBO_2$ = 49.8. White powder, soluble in water. **l. myristate.** $C_{14}H_{27}O_2Li$ = 234.15. White solid, m.224. **l. nitrate.** $LiNO_3$ = 69.0. Colorless rhombohedra, m.253, soluble in water; used in pyrotechnics (red fires), and in artificial mineral waters **l. nitride.** Li_3N = 34.83. A catalyst in ammonia synthesis. **l. nitrite.** $LiNO_2 \cdot H_2O$ = 70.96. Colorless needles, soluble in water. **l. oxalate.** $Li_2C_2O_4$ = 102.0. Colorless crystals, soluble in water. **l. oxide.** Li_2O = 29.9. Lithia. Colorless caustic powder, sublimes 600, soluble in water; used to manufacture l. salts. **l. palmitate.** $C_{16}H_{31}O_2Li$ = 262.18. White solid, m.225. **l. perchlorate.** $LiClO_4 \cdot 3H_2O$ = 160.45. Deliquescent solid. **l. phenate.** $LiC_6 \cdot$ H_5O = 100.0. L. carbolate, l. phenylate, phenol-lithium. Colorless powder, which turns pink with

age, soluble in water; an antiseptic. **l. phenol sulfonate.** $LiC_6H_5SO_4 \cdot H_2O$ = 198.1. L. sulfocarbolate. White crystals, soluble in water; used to treat uric acid diathesis. **l. phosphate.** $Li_3PO_4 \cdot H_2O$ = 133.9. Colorless rhomboids, m.857, soluble in water. **l. platinichloride.** $Li_2 \cdot$ $PtCl_6 \cdot 6H_2O$ = 529.9. Yellow crystals; used in analysis. **l. quinate.** Urosine. **l. rhodanate.** L. thiocyanate. **l. salicylate.** $LiC_7H_5O_3$ = 144.0. White, hygroscopic powder, soluble in water; an antirheumatic and intestinal antiseptic. **l. salol orthophosphite.** $C_6H_5 \cdot COO \cdot C_6H_4 \cdot OPO(OH) \cdot OLi$. Salvosal lithia, the l. salt of salol orthophosphorous acid. Colorless crystals, decomp. in hot water; used to treat influenza and gout. **l. silicate.** Li_2SiO_3 = 89.94. White rhombs, m.1201, insoluble in water. *basic-* Li_4SiO_4 = 119.82. White crystals, m.1256, insoluble in water. **l. silicide.** Li_6Si_2 = 97.76. Blue crystals, decomp. by heat or water. **l. silicofluoride.** L. fluosilicate. **l. sozoiodolate.** $C_6H_2(OH)I(SO_3Li)$ = 304.97. Yellow leaflets, soluble in water; an antirheumatic. **l. stearate.** $C_{18}H_{35}O_2Li$ = 290.21. White solid, m.221. **l. succinate.** $Li_2C_4H_4O_4 \cdot$ $3H_2O$ = 184.1. Colorless crystals, soluble in water; an antiseptic. **l. sulfate.** Li_2SO_4 $(+H_2O)$ = 110.0. Colorless, monoclinic crystals, m.843, soluble in water; a diuretic and antirheumatic. Used for red fires, and in artificial mineral waters. **l. sulfide.** Li_2S = 46.0. Colorless powder, soluble in water. **l. sulfite.** $Li_2SO_3 \cdot H_2O$ = 111.96. Soluble needles. **l. sulfocarbolate.** L. phenol sulfonate. **l. sulfocyanide.** L. thiocyanate. **l. sulfoichthyolate.** Tarry liquid; an ichthyol substitute. **l. tartrate.** $Li_2C_4H_4O_6 \cdot H_2O$ = 180.1. White crystals, soluble in water; an antirheumatic. **l. thallium tartrate.** $C_4H_4O_6LiTl \cdot 2H_2O$ = 396.39. Triclinic crystals. **l. thiocyanate.** LiCNS = 65.0. L. rhodanate. Colorless, hygroscopic crystals, soluble in water; a reagent. **l. urate.** $C_5H_3O_3 \cdot$ N_4Li = 174.04. A soluble salt of lithium used to treat gout. **l. valerate.** $LiC_5H_9O_2$ = 108.1. White crystals of valerian-like odor, soluble in water; an antirheumatic and sedative. **l. vanadate.** $LiVO_3 \cdot H_2O$ = 123.9. Yellow crystals, soluble in water.

litho- Prefix (Greek "stone"); as, lithography. **l. oil.** Stand oil.

lithocholic acid. $C_{24}H_{40}O_3$ = 376.32. An acid from bile. Cf. *choline, sterols.*

lithofellic acid. $C_{20}H_{36}O_4$ = 340.28. Microscopic crystals, m.206, insoluble in water.

lithoform. A zinc phosphate coating for protecting of zinc from corrosion.

lithography. A method of printing in which the design is drawn transversely inverted on a stone with a greasy ink, and treated in succession with water, and a printing ink which is accepted only by the greasy design; the stone is then used for printing on paper. In modern l. the design is produced photographically on a zinc plate from which it is transferred on a rotary machine to a rubber blanket, which is brought into contact with the paper (offset process).

lithology. Petrology.

lithol red. Sodium 2-hydroxynaphthaleneazonaphthalene-1-sulfonate. A red dye used in cosmetics.

lithomarge. $K_2O \cdot Al_2O_3 \cdot 6SiO_2 \cdot xH_2O$. A mottled hydrated aluminosilicate clay from Germany.

lithopone. Lithophone, Griffith white, Orr white, Charlton white. A stoichiometric mixture of zinc sulfide and barium sulfate; used as a white pigment in paints, in the rubber industry, for oil cloth manufacture, and as a filler. **cadmium-** A red or yellow pigment analogous to l., in which the zinc sulfide is replaced by cadmium sulfide.

lithosphere. The solid earth crust as compared with the liquid (hydrosphere) and gaseous (atmosphere) layers of the earth surface. See *abundance.*

lithuric acid. $C_{15}H_{19}NO_9 = 357.15$. White crystals, m.205, from bladder stones.

litmin. **azo-** See *azolitmin.* **erythro-** See *erythrolitmin.*

litmocydin. An antibiotic from *Proactinomyces cyaneus.*

litmopyrine. Lithium acetyl salicylate.

litmus. Lacmus, turnsole, lacca coerulea. A purple coloring matter from lichens (*Roccella* and *Dendrographa* species). Blue powder, usually mixed with calcium carbonate and compressed into small cubes; it contains azolitmin and lecanoric acid. An indicator for volumetric analysis. **l. milk.** Milk colored with l. and used in bacteriology as a culture medium, to detect production of acidity. **l. paper.** Filter paper impregnated with l. solution (neutral, pH 7.0—purple; alkaline, pH 8.0—blue; acid, pH 6.0—red). **l. tincture.** A saturated solution of l. in alcohol and/or water; used as an indicator and for culture media.

Litol process. Trade name for a process to produce benzene from coke-oven light oil by a single catalytic hydrogenation step (to remove most impurities), followed by dealkylation.

litre. Liter.

Little, Arthur Dehon. 1863–1935. American chemist noted for developments in chemical engineering.

littorol. See *pelagic.*

Littrow prism. A glass spectrograph prism with 90°, 60°, and 30° angles, which reflects light internally from one surface. Cf. *Cornu prism.*

liver. (1) A gland of mammals which forms glycogen from the maltose of veinous blood, and secretes bile. It also stores glycogen, aids the formation and destruction of blood corpuscles, and converts nitrogeneous matter into urea. (2) A natural sulfide mineral. **l. extract.** A concentration of the antianemic principle of mammalian l.; stimulates erythrocyte formation in bone marrow (U.S.P.). **l. of sulfur.** The result of fusing together potassium carbonate and sulfur. It contains chiefly potassium sulfide and polysulfides; used to treat skin diseases. **l. ore.** Cinnabar. **l. sugar.** Glycogen.

Liverpool test. A method for evaluating commercial caustic soda by titration. The at. wt. of Na is taken as 24; on this basis a sodium hydroxide content of 97.5% is reported as 100%.

liverwort. The dried herb of *Hepatica triloba* (Ranunculaceae); a mild astringent. **English-** Lichen caninus, ground liverwort. The lichen, *Peltigera canina*; a mild purgative.

livetin. A protein from egg yolk.

livingstoneite. $2Sb_2O_3 \cdot HgO$. Antimonite containing mercury.

lixiviation. The extraction and separation of a soluble substance from insoluble matter.

lixivium. The extract obtained by lixiviation

LL.30. A Novocaine substitute. The thirtieth preparation of L. Lundquist (1944).

llama. An animal textile fiber similar to, but coarser than alpaca.

lm. Abbreviation for lumen.

ln. Abbreviation for natural logarithm.

loading. A heavy substance, usually of mineral nature, (clay, gypsum, etc.) added to textiles, papers, rubber, etc., to give weight or smoothness. Cf. *filler.*

loadstone, lodestone. Magnetite.

Loalin. Trade name for a polystyrene plastic.

loam. Clay mixed with sand in nature.

loban. Indian name for gum benzoin.

lobate. Describing a growth of bacteria, in which the borders of the cultures show lobes, deep undulations, or fissures.

lobelia. Indian tobacco. The dried leaves and flowering tops of *Lobelia inflata* (Lobeliaceae); an antispasmodic and expectorant.

lobeline. $C_{18}H_{23}O_2N = 285.3$. Inflatine. An alkaloid from lobelia seeds. Yellow syrup, insoluble in water; an antispasmodic and sedative. **l. hydrochloride.** $C_{18}H_{23}O_2N \cdot HCl = 321.8$. Yellow crystals, soluble in water; an antispasmodic. **l. sulfate.** $(C_{18}H_{23}O_2N)_2 \cdot H_2SO_4 = 668.6$. Yellow, hygroscopic crystals, soluble in water. A relaxant and antispasmodic, used to treat the tobacco habit.

lobeloid. The combined principles of Indian tobacco; an expectorant and relaxant.

lobinine. $C_{22}H_{27}NO_2 = 335.2$. An alkaloid from *Lobelia inflata.*

lobinol. The principal dermatitant of poison oak, *Rhus diversiloba.*

locabiotal. Fusafungine.

locamphen. Brown, viscous liquid, insoluble in water; an antiseptic. Obtained by the interaction of iodine 10, phenol 20, camphor 70 pts.

Locke's solution. An artificial, protein-free blood serum: sodium chloride 9.0, calcium chloride 0.2, potassium chloride 0.4, sodium bicarbonate 0.2, glucose 0.25 gm, in 1,000 ml water. Cf. *Ringer's solution.*

Lockyer, Sir Joseph Norman. 1836–1920. English astronomer who discovered (with Frankland) helium in the sun's chromosphere.

locust bean. Carob bean. **l. tree.** The tree *Robinia pseudacacia* of semidesert N. America, which yields robin.

lode. A vein of metallic deposit in a rock fissure. **mother-** The great gold vein of Central California.

lodestone. Magnetite.

Lodge, Sir Oliver Joseph. 1851–1940. English physicist, noted for his work in electrical science. **L.-Cottrell process.** An industrial process for the electrostatic precipitation of smokes and fog, widely used in industry. Cf. *Cottrell.*

Loeb, Jacques. 1859–1924. American physiologist, noted for his work on the effects of ions on protoplasm. **L. collection.** A collection of elements and compounds in the United States National Museum.

Loeffler. See *Löffler.*

Loew theory. All substances acting on aldehyde or amino groups are poisonous to the living tissue, as they change the dynamic equilibrium of the protoplasm.

Löffler, Friedrich A. J. 1852–1915. German bacteriologist, noted for his bacterial stains. **L. methylene blue.** A bacteriological dye prepared by dissolving 0.5 gm methylene blue in 40 ml alcohol, 2 ml $N/10$ potassium hydroxide, and 98 ml water. **L. mixture.** A culture medium for the growth of bacteria: glucose bouillon 250, horse- or beef-blood serum 750 ml.

log. Abbreviation for logarithm. **log$_{10}$.** Common logarithm. **log$_e$** or **ln.** Natural logarithm.

Loganiaceae. Logania family. A group of herbs, shrubs, or trees, many poisonous; e.g., seeds: *Strychnos nux vomica*, nux vomica; bark: *Strychnos malaccensis*, hoang-nan; rhizomes: *Gelsemium sempervirens*, gelsemine; extractive: *Strychnos castelnaeana*, curare.

loganin. $C_{25}H_{34}O_{14}$ = 558.26. A glucoside from nux vomica, m.215.

logarithm. The logarithm (log) of a number n is the power x to which the logarithmic base a must be raised to give that number. $n = a^x$. $x = \log_a n$. **common-** L. whose base is 10. Abbreviated log or log$_{10}$. **Napierian-** Natural. **natural-** Napierian. L. whose base is e, q.v., or 2.71828.... Abbreviated, log$_e$ or ln. **l. conversion:** $\ln ( ) = 2.3026 \log ( )$, where ln is the natural, and log the common logarithm.

logarithmic. Pertaining to logarithms. **l. sector method.** Quantitative spectroscopy based on the difference in length between 2 tapering wedges, produced by photographing the 2 spectra concerned after passage of the incident light through a wedge-shaped aperture in a disk which rotates in front of the spectrograph.

logwood. Haematoxylon. **l. crystals.** Hematoxylin. **l. extract.** Reddish-blue paste made by extracting l.; used in dyeing textiles and leather and for the manufacture of haematoxylin. **l. paste.** Hematoxylin paste. Cf. *brazilwood, fustic, sappan.*

-logy. Suffix derived from the Greek λογος (word), indicating a science or doctrine; as, pathology.

loiponic acid. $C_{17}H_{11}NO_4$ = 173.1. Piperidine-3,4-dicarboxylic acid. An oxidation product of meroquine and quinine.

lokav. Chinese blue.

loliin. A volatile constituent of the seeds of *Lolium* species.

lolium. Poisonous darnel. A grass, *L. temulentum*, found in wheat and oat fields during wet seasons.

Lomonósov, Michájlo Vasílievič. 1711–1765. Russian scientist noted for theories of molecular structure and conservation of energy and matter.

London clay. A tough, compact, lower Eocene clay formation, red-brown at the surface and blue-gray below. **L. paste.** A mixture of quicklime and caustic soda moistened with alcohol. **L. purple.** An insecticide: arsenic trioxide 43, aniline 12, lime 21, ferrous oxide 1 pts.

longitudinal. Lengthwise, or parallel to the longer axis of a body. Antonym: latitudinal.

longitude. See *coordinates*.

lookafor. An instrument to locate faults in telephone lines. It measures electrically the time for an electric impulse to travel at a known speed from a given point to the fault, and return.

looking-glass ore. Fe_2O_3. A lustrous, variety of hematite.

loomite. A short-fibered variety of talc.

looseness. The extent to which a dyestuff may be removed by friction.

lophine. $C_{21}H_{16}N_2$ = 296.27. 2,4,5-Triphenylimidazole. Colorless needles, m.275, insoluble in water; a fluorescent neutralization indicator.

lophophorine. $C_{13}H_{17}O_3N$ = 235.2. Methoxyanhalonine. An alkaloid from mescal buttons, the buds of *Anhalonium lewinii*, a cactus of Mexico. It is similar to anhalonine and mescaline, and produces hallucinations.

lopion. G2949. A gold-thiourea preparation, used to treat tuberculosis.

Loramine. Trademark for a class of foaming agents based on fatty-acid ethanolamines.

lorandite. $TlAsS_2$. A native sulfoarsenide.

lorenit. $C_9H_6O_4NSI$ = 351.04. An isomer of loretin; an iodoform substitute.

Lorentz, Hendrik Antoon. 1853–1928. Dutch pioneer of the electron theory. **L.-Lorenz equation.** The molecular refractivity $R = M(n^2 - 1)/d(n^2 + 1)$, where M is the molecular weight, d the density, and n the refractive index.

loretin. $C_9H_4IN \cdot OH \cdot SO_3H$ = 351.05. 7-Iodo-8-hydroxyquinoline-5-sulfonic acid, yatren. Yellow crystals, soluble in water; a reagent for copper, a substitute for iodoform, and a specific amebicide in dysentery.

loretinates. The metal salts of loretin, e.g., bismuth loretinate (loretin bismuth); antiseptic wound dressings.

Lorexane. Trademark for γ-benzene hexachloride.

loriodendrin. A bitter principle from the bark of the tulip tree, *Liriodendron tulipifera* (Magnoliaceae). White scales, m.82, insoluble in water. Cf. *tulipiferine.*

Lorol. Trademark for: (1) a surfactant containing principally sodium lauryl sulfate; (2) a mixture of aliphatic alcohols formed by the high-pressure hydrogenation of coconut oil.

Loschmidt number. The number of gas molecules per cubic centimeter at 0°C and 760 mm pressure = 2.705×10^{19}. Cf. *Avogadro number.*

losophan. $C_6HI_3(OH)Me$ = 485.6. Triiodometacresol. Colorless crystals, insoluble in water; an external antiseptic.

lotase. An enzyme of *Lotus arabicus*, converting lotusin into hydrocyanic acid and lotoflavin.

loth. An obsolete German metallurgical unit of weight. 1 loth per centner = 1 part per 3,200.

lotion. A liquid washing and rinsing preparation; usually an antiseptic. **black-** A solution of calomel in limewater; a parasiticide and antiseptic. **yellow-** A solution of corrosive sublimate in limewater.

lotoflavin. $C_{15}H_{10}O_6$ = 286.08. A yellow coloring matter from *Lotus arabicus*. Cf. *lotusin.*

lotusin. $C_{28}H_{31}NO_{16}$ = 637.3. A glucoside from the leaves of *Lotus arabicus* (Leguminosae). Yellow crystals, hydrolyzed to lotoflavin.

lotus metal. The bearing alloy: Pb 75, Sb 15, Sn 10%.

loudness. The intensity of sound expressed in bels, q.v. Common conversation is about 60 decibels. Cf. *phon.*

loup. A simple magnifying lens.

louver, louvre. A ventilator of sloping boards which keep out rain, but not air.

lovage. Sea parsley, levisticum, ligusticum, Chinese tang-kui, man-mu. The dried herb of *Levisticum officinale* (Umbelliferae); an aromatic and carminative. Cf. *eumenol.* **Scotch-** The root of *Ligusticum scoticum,* a chewing tobacco. **l. oil.** A colorless, fragrant oil from l., insoluble in water; used in perfumery.

Lovibond tintometer. A colorimeter for comparing the color of a liquid with a standard series of tinted glass slides.

low. Weak or poor. **l. carbon.** A steel of low carbon content. **l. explosives.** Unstable chemicals and mixtures (carbon, sulfur, and nitrates) such as black gunpowder, blasting powder. Antonym: high explosives.

löweite. $2MgSO_4 \cdot 2Na_2SO_4 \cdot 5H_2O$. A vitreous, yellow, or white, fusible mineral.

Lowenstjern. See *Kunkel.*

Lowig process. The production of caustic soda from soda ash by heating at low red heat with ferric oxide, and hydrolyzing the resulting sodium ferrite with water.

lox. A mining explosive consisting of liquid oxygen. With fuses it explodes like gunpowder; with detonators it detonates like dynamite.

loxa bark. Cinchona bark.

lozenge. A medicated tablet, usually for throat diseases.

LSD. Lysergic acid diethylamide. A psychedelia used to treat nervous diseases. **LSD 25.** Lysergic acid diethylamide. A hallucinogenic drug.

Lu. Symbol for lutecium.

luargol. $(C_{12}H_{12}O_2N_2As)_2 \cdot AsBr \cdot SbO(H_2SO_4)_2$. 3,3'-Diamino-4,4'-hydroxyarsenobenzene silver bromide antimonyl sulfate. A remedy for sleeping sickness.

lubanol. Coniferol.

luboil. Lubricating oil.

lubricant. An agent that reduces friction between moving surfaces. **liquid-** An oil or semiliquid grease. **solid-** A l. such as graphite, talc, soap, or sulfur.

lubricating oil. A heavy distillate of petroleum used for lubricating machinery.

lubrication. Making smooth or slippery. **boundary-** The type of l. which occurs when the frictional effect is influenced by the nature of the underlying surface as well as by the chemical constitution of the lubricant; e.g., with thin l. films. **dry-** A solid (e.g., polytetrafluoroethylene) impregnant for the metal surface of valve plugs. See tribology.

lubricator. Lubricant.

lucalox. A strong, transparent refractory, made by the high-temperature firing of compressed fine alumina. Also used for gem bearings and as an electrical insulator.

lucanthone hydrochloride. $C_{20}H_{24}ON_2S \cdot HCl = 376.95$. Bitter, yellow powder, m.197, soluble in water; an antischistosomal (U.S.P.).

Lucas, Howard Johnson. b. 1885. American chemist. **L. theory.** In an organic compound the substituting radical affects the electronic orbits of a carbon atom by pulling the electronic pair toward the substituting radical if it has a high electron attraction, or vice versa.

lucerne. Alfalfa.

Lucidol. Trademark for organic peroxides, especially benzoyl peroxide.

luciferase. An enzyme in a luminous mollusk, *Pholas dactylas,* which is luminescent in cold but not hot aqueous solutions.

luciferin. A water-soluble protein from a luminous mollusk, *Pholas dactylus,* or the firefly, *Cypridina hilgendorfi.*

luciferinase. An enzyme associated with the production of luciferin.

lucigenin. Methyl acridilium nitrate.

lucinite. $Al_2O_3 \cdot P_2O_5 \cdot 4H_2O$. A native phosphate.

Lucite. Trademark for plastic based on polymerized methyl methacrylate resin, widely used for the enclosures of airplanes. Cf. *leucite, lewisite.*

Lucitone. Trademark for methyl methacrylate resins used in making dentures.

lucium. A supposed chemical element, discovered in 1896, which proved to be a mixture of rare-earth metals.

Lucretius. 98–55 B.C. The earliest scientific writer who conceived an atomic theory.

lucumin. A glucoside from the bark of *Lucuma glycyphloea.* Colorless needles. See *monesia.*

ludlamite. $Fe_3(PO_4)_2$. A green mineral.

Ludolf's number. The ratio of the circumference of a circle to its diameter;

$$\pi \text{ or pi} = 3,14159,26535,89793,23846.$$

Ludwig effect. Soret effect.

ludwigite. $3MgO \cdot B_2O_3Fe_3O_4$. A blue or green mineral.

ludyl. $C_{30}H_{26}O_8N_4S_2As_4Na$. Sodium salt of benzene-*m*-33'-disulfaminobis(3-amino-4,4'-dihydroxybenzene); used to treat syphilis.

luetin. An extract from killed cultures of *Treponema* bacteria; used in skin tests for syphilis.

luffa. Vegetable sponge, gourd towel, washrag sponge, loofah. The fibrous skeleton of the fruits of *Luffa cylindrica* (Cucurbitaceae).

Lugol solution. A solution containing iodine 5 and potassium iodide 10 (U.S.P.) or 7.5 (B.P.) gm per 100 ml.

lukabro oil. An oil from *Hydnocarpus anthelmintica,* Siam, similar to hydnocarpus oil, $d_{30°}0.943–0.950$.

Lully, Raymond. 1235–1315. Ramon Lull, Raymundus Lullus. Spanish alchemist who prepared nitric acid, aqua regia, alcohol, and potassium carbonate.

Lumarith CA. Trademark for a cellulose acetate plastic. **L. EC.** Ethocel. **L. Vn.** Koroseal.

lumbang oil. Candlenut oil. A colorless oil expressed from the seeds of *Aleurites moluccana,* candlenut, d.0.923, iodine val. 155–160, insoluble in water; used as an illuminant, and in soap manufacture and paints.

lumen. (1) lm. A unit of luminosity (luminous flux), the light emitted by a point source of one candlepower: 1 lumen = 0.001496 watt = 0.07958 spherical candlepower. 1 lumen emitted per square foot has a brightness of 1.076 millilamberts. (2) The bore of a small tube; e.g., the cavity of a thermometer tube, blood vessel, etc. **new-** A revised unit of luminosity based on the new candle, q.v.

lumiere Wood. An early international term for Wood's light.

Luminal. Trademark for phenobarbital. **L. sodium.** Sodium phenyl ethyl barbiturate. Cf. *luminol*.

luminescence. Emission of light at room temperature under the influence of various physical agents; as mechanical (tribo-l.), electrical (electro-l.), radiant (photo-l.), thermal (thermo-l.), or chemical (chemo-l.) means. Cf. *baro-l.*, *cando-l.*, *fluorescence*, *phosphorescence*. **chemo-** Emission of light by slow chemical reaction without appreciable temperature increase; as, by phosphorus. Cf. *phosphorescence*. **crystallo-** Emission of light during crystallization; as, arsenous acid from hydrochloric acid solution. **electro-** (1) Emission of light due to passage of electricity through gases at low pressure and temperature; as, in vacuum tubes. (2) L. produced by a phosphor-treated surface in contact with an electrically conducting surface, e.g., conductive glass, to which an electric potential is applied. Used for electric signs. **photo-** Emission of light on exposure to invisible radiations, by transfer from one wavelength into another; as, ultraviolet into visible rays. **radio-** Emission of light by radioactive substances. **thermo-** Emission of light after slight heating; as, by chlorophane. **tribo-** Emission of light by friction or other mechanical means without temperature rise; as, quartz.

luminiferous. Giving off light without a rise in temperature. Cf. *incandescent*.

luminizing. Rendering luminous by treatment with radioactive substances.

luminoflavin. A luminescent substance in urine and plant products having a blue fluorescence produced by the irradiation of flavin with ultraviolet light.

luminol. $NH_2 \cdot C_6H_3 \cdot (CO \cdot NH)_2 = 170.04$. 3-Aminophthalic acid cyclic hydrazide. White crystals, m.320, soluble in water. The alkaline solution becomes brightly luminescent when treated with hydrogen peroxide and potassium ferricyanide. Cf. *Luminal*. **l. reaction.** An analytical test in which l. in alkaline solution is used to produce a fluorescence.

luminophore. (1) A substance which emits light at room temperature. (2) An organic radical which produces or increases the luminescence of a compound.

luminosity. (1) The ratio of the luminous flux to the radiant energy flux (U.S. usage). (2) The quantity of visible rays or light emitted by a body, measured in lumens (U.K. usage). (3) Luminescence.

luminous. Pertaining to luminescence. **l. flux.** The radiant power of a substance in lumens. **l. heater.** A device to burn coal gas without a supply of excess air. It burns silently, without soot formation and is hotter than ordinary gas burners. **l. intensity.** The unit of brightness: candlepower. **l. paint.** A pigment which glows in the dark after exposure to light, usually sulfides of calcium, barium, and zinc, with a radioactive substance; used for watch dials.

lumisterol. Irradiated ergosterol. Cf. *calciferol*. *cholane*, vitamin D_1.

lumophore. Luminophore.

lunar caustic. Fused silver nitrate. **l. cornea.** Fused silver chloride.

Lunge, Georg. 1839–1923. German chemist, noted for work on technological analytical methods. **L. nitrometer.** Nitrometer.

lupanine. $C_{15}H_{24}ON_2 = 248.3$. An alkaloid from the seeds of *Lupinus angustifolius* (Leguminosae). Yellow syrup with green fluorescence in water. **iso-** Matrine.

luparenol. $C_{15}H_{24}O = 220.2$. An unsaturated alcohol from the higher-boiling fraction of hop oil, $b_{3mm}125-128$.

luparol. $C_{16}H_{26}O_2 = 250.20$. A phenolic ether derived from luparone. Colorless liquid, d.0.9170, $b_{2mm}123$.

luparone. $C_{13}H_{22}O = 194.17$. A ketone derived from the higher-boiling fractions of hop oil. Colorless liquid, d.08861, $b_{3mm}75$.

lupetazin. $C_6H_{14}N_2 = 11.42$. Dimethylpiperazine. White crystals, insoluble in water; an antirheumatic.

lupetidine. $C_7H_{15}N = 113.2$. 2,6-Dimethylpiperidine. Colorless oil.

lupin(e). *Lupinus*. A genus of leguminous plants; some are poisonous, others are forage plants. **l. alkaloids.** The alkaloids from *Lupinus* species; as, lupinine.

lupinidine. (1) $C_8H_{15}O_2N = 157.2$. An alkaloid from the seeds of *Lupinus luteus* and *L. niger*. Yellow syrup. (2) Sparteine. **l. hydrosulfate.** $(C_8H_{15}O_2N)_2 \cdot H_2SO_4 = 412.4$. Colorless crystals, soluble in water; used in medicine.

lupinin. $C_{29}H_{32}O_{16} = 636.3$. A glucoside from *Lupinus* species. Yellow crystals, hydrolyzed to glucose and lupigenin. Cf. *lupinine*.

lupinine. $C_{21}H_{40}N_2O_2 = 352.33$. An alkaloid from the seeds of *Lupinus* species. Colorless crystals, m.67, insoluble in water. Cf. *lupinin*. **anhydro-** $C_{10}H_{17}N$. **dimethyl-** $C_{10}H_{17}ONMe_2$. **methyl-** $C_{10}H_{18}ONMe$.

lupulin. Humulin. Brown granules, of hop taste, consisting of the glandular trichomes from the strobiles of *Humulus lupulus*, hops; a sedative and stomachic.

lupulinic acid. $C_{32}H_{50}O_7 = 546.5$. The bitter principle of hops. Rhombic prisms of hop flavor.

lupulon. $C_{26}H_{38}O_4 = 414.3$. A constituent of the soft resin of lupulin. Cf. *humulon*,

lupulus. Hops.

lupus lapidis. Stone disease. Deterioration of stonework attributed to microorganisms.

Lurgi process. The complete gasification of coal of high ash and moisture contents in producers at 25 atm in a continuous stream of oxygen and superheated steam. Benzole, tar, oils, and ammonia are by-products.

lusec. Liter-microns per second. A measure of small gas volumes.

luster. The reflection from the fractured surface of a rock, metal, or crystal.

Lustron. Trademark for a polystyrene plastic.

lustrus. Tygan.

lute. A mixture of fireclay and water used to seal cracks in crucibles.

lutein. (1) $C_{40}H_{50}O_2 = 568.4$. The carotenoid (q.v.) coloring matter of egg yolk: xanthophyllin 70, zeaxanthin 30%. (2) A yellow pigment from the fully developed corpora lutea of the hog. **l. solution.** A solution of the water-soluble extractives of l.; used in gynecology.

luteo- Prefix (Latin), indicating orange-yellow.

luteo compounds. $[M(NH_3)_6]X_3$ and $[M(NH_3)_6]X_2$.

Yellow cobaltiammonium compounds, e.g., [Co-$(NH_3)_6]Cl_3$, hexammincobaltic chloride.

luteol. Oxychlordiphenylquinoxaline. A sensitive indicator and reagent for ammonia; yellow in alkali and colorless in acid solutions.

luteole. A carotene in yellow corn grain.

luteolin. $C_{15}H_{10}O_6 = 286.08$. Isofisetin. Tetrahydroxyflavone. A flavone derivative coloring matter of weld, *Reseda luteola*, an ancient dye. Yellow crystals, m.328, insoluble in water; a dye and diuretic.

luteo salts. See *luteo compounds*.

luteostal. Progesterone.

luteosterone. Progesterone.

lutetium (lutecium). Lu = 174.97. A rare-earth metal, at. no. 71, valencies 3 and 4. Discovered (1905) by Auer von Welsbach and named cassiopeium; and (1907) by Urbain and named after Lutetia (= Paris). **l. chloride.** $LuCl_3 = 281.5$. White crystals, soluble in water. **l. oxide.** $Lu_2O_3 = 398.0$. White powder, insoluble in water.

lutidine. $C_7H_9N = 107.07$. Dimethylpyridine*. **α-** or **1,2-** Colorless liquid, soluble in water. **β-** or **1,3-** Colorless liquid; an antispasmodic. **2,4-** Colorless liquid, b.157, soluble in water. **2,6-** The commonest lutidine, obtained from tar and bone oils. Colorless liquid, d.0.942, b.142, soluble in water. **3,6-** Colorless liquid, b.163, soluble in water. **dihydro-** See *dihydrolutidine*. **hexahydro-** Lupetidine.

lutidinic acid. $C_7H_5O_4N,H_2O = 185.07$. 1,3-Pyridinedicarboxylic acid*. Colorless crystals, m.249, soluble in water.

lutidone. $C_7H_9ON = 123.1$. 2,4-Dimethyl-3-oxypyridine. Colorless crystals, m.225.

Lutocyclin. Lutoform, lutogyl. Trademark for Progesterone. **L. oral.** Ethisterone.

lutoid. A yellow, nonrubbery constituent of rubber latex, comprising 6–8% of the total solids. L. contains 85% water with proteins, salts, and lipoids; they make the latex resistant to photooxidation and mechanically stable, but reduce thermal stability.

lutol. Aluminum borotannate.

lutren. Progesterone.

luvitherm. A German thermoplastic film of high softening point, made from unplasticized polyvinyl chloride.

lux. lx. A unit of illumination: 1 lux = 1 lumen/$m^2 = 0.0001$ phot = $\frac{1}{1}$ footcandle. **new-** A unit based on the new lumen, q.v.

l. hour. The light emitted by a Hefner standard candle in 1 hour at 1 meter distance. A measure of the intensity of light exposure.

Clear sun	1,000,000 lux
Dull sun	300
Average room lighting	70
Bright moonlight	0.3
Lower limit of vision	0.000006

lx. Abbreviation for lux.

lyaconine. Acolytine.

lyate ion. A solvent molecule minus a proton, as OH^- from water.

lycetol. $C_{10}H_{20}O_6N_2 = 264.3$. Lupetazin tartrate,

dimethylpiperazine tartrate. Colorless crystals, m.243, soluble in water; used medicinally.

lychnin. A poisonous glucoside from *Lychnis* species (Caryophyllaceae).

lycine. $C_5H_{11}O_2N = 117.1$. An alkaloid from the leaves of *Lycium halimifolium* (Solanaceae). White, hygroscopic, crystals, soluble in hot water. Cf. *lysine*.

lycoctonine. $C_{27}H_{41}O_9N = 523.4$. An alkaloid from the roots of *Aconitum lycoctonum* (Ranunculaceae). White crystals, m.100, insoluble in water.

lycopene. $C_{40}H_{56} = 536.4$. Licopin. An unsaturated hydrocarbon and carotenoid (q.v.) pigment from many plants; as, tomato. Red crystals, m.168, isomeric with carotene.

lycopersicin. A fungistatic principle from the tomato plant.

lycopodium. Vegetable sulfur. Yellow powder, the flammable spores of *Lycopodium clavatum*, a club moss. A dusting powder, microscope reagent, pill coating, and (formerly) a stage flashlight.

lycorine. $C_{16}H_{17}O_4N = 287.2$. Narcissine. An alkaloid from the bulbs of *Lycoris radiata* (Amaryllidaceae). Colorless polyhedra, decomp. 250, slightly soluble in water; a substitute for emetine. **dimethylhydroxy-** Sekisanine.

Lycra. Trade name for an elastomeric synthetic fiber.

lyddite. An explosive containing principally picric acid.

lydian stone. Jasper.

lye. (1) The alkaline solution obtained by leaching wood ashes. (2) A solution of sodium or potassium hydroxide. Cf. *ley*.

lygosin. $CO(CH:CH\cdot C_6H_4ONa)_2 = 436.2$. Sodium lygosinate. Green crystals, soluble in water with a red color; a bactericide.

Lyman series. The first group of spectrum lines of hydrogen. Cf. *Balmer, Paschen series*.

lymph. A transparent, slightly alkaline liquid, permeating the animal organism and resembling blood serum.

lymphocyte. A white blood corpuscle with a single nucleus. Lymphocytes constitute about 25% of the white blood corpuscles.

lynoral. Ethinylestradiol.

lyochromes. A group of natural, water-soluble plant pigments. Cf. *carotenes*.

lyogel. A gel which contains a large proportion of the dispersion medium used.

lyonium ion. A solvent molecule plus a proton, as H_3O^+ from water. Cf. *hydronium*.

lyophil(e), lyophilic. Attracting liquids. Describing a colloidal system in which the dispersed phase is a liquid and attracts the dispersing medium. Cf. *hydrophile*.

lyophilized biological. A biological substance (as blood plasma) prepared in dry form by rapid freezing and dehydration, in the frozen state under high vacuum. It is made ready for use by addition of sterile, distilled water. Cf. *cryochem, desivac, lyovac*.

lyophobe, lyophobic. Repelling liquids. A colloidal system in which the dispersed solid phase has no attraction for the dispersion medium; hence it tends to separate. Cf. *hydrophobe*.

lyosorption. The adhesion of a liquid to a solid; as the adsorption of a solvent film on suspended particles. Cf. *adsorption*.

lyotrope. (1) An ion or radical of a lyotropic series. (2) A readily soluble substance.

lyotropic series. The arrangement of ions, radicals, or salts in the decreasing order in which they salt out or coagulate colloids by their dehydrating effect. The following salts usually appear in the same order: Potassium ferrocyanide > sodium citrate > sodium hydrogen phosphate > sodium fluoride > sodium sulfate > sodium tartrate > sodium thiosulfate > sodium acetate > sodium formate. Cf. *Hofmeister series.*

lyovac process. A process of freezing and dehydrating aqueous preparations.

lysatine. $C_6H_{13}O_2N_3$ = 159.2. A crystalline alkaloid from casein.

lysergic acid. $C_{16}H_{16}N_2O_2$ = 270.14. A monobasic acid from ergot. **l. acid diethylamide** (1) LSD. (2) LSD 25.

lysidine. $N:CMe \cdot NH \cdot (CH_2)_2$ = 84.1. Ethylene

ethenyldiamine, methyldihydroimidazol. Red, hygroscopic crystals, m.105, soluble in water. **l. solution.** A 50% aqueous solution of l.; a solvent for uric acid. **l. tartrate.** Colorless crystals, soluble in water.

lysimeter. A device for determining approximate solubility; or the water content of soils.

lysin. An antibody which dissolves cells formed in *Staphylococci* cultures; as, hemolysin.

lysine. $NH_2 \cdot (CH_2)_3 \cdot CHO_2 \cdot CHNH_2 \cdot COOH$ = 146.32. Diaminocaproic acid. An isolog of ornithine in many proteins. White needles, m.224, soluble in water; from casein. Cf. *lycine, lysin.*

lysis. (1) The dissolution of a substance by the action of a lysin; as, hemolysis. (2) The decomposition of a substance; as, electrolysis. (3) The cleavage of a bond with addition of: H—OH, hydrolysis; H—NH₂, ammonolysis; HO—C_2H_5, alcoholysis; H—H, hydrogenation.

lysitol. Lycetol.

lysivane. Ethopropazine hydrochloride.

lysogen. A substance that produces or generates a lysin.

Lysol. Trademark for a cresylic disinfectant and antiseptic.

lysozyme. An enzyme in body secretions which dissolves certain airborne bacteria by lysis.

lytic. Pertaining to: (1) lysins, e.g., hemolytic; (2) lysis, e.g., hydrolytic.

lyxose. $C_5H_{10}O_5$ = 150.1. A pentatomic monosaccharide; 2 optically active isomers: dextro- and levo-. $(CHOH)_3 \cdot O \cdot CH \cdot CH_2OH$.

M

M. (1) Symbol for metal. (2) Abbreviation for mega, or million. **M acid.** 1-Amino-5-naphthol-4-sulfonic acid.

M. Symbol for: (1) mass, (2) molal, (3) molecular weight, (4) the mathematical constant $\log_e 10 = 0.43429,44819$. M^{-1} The mathematical constant $\log_e 10 = 2.30258,50930$. **M electron.** The electron of the M shell or M orbit, q.v. **M orbit.** The third layer or energy level, in which electrons move around the proton in the dynamic atom. **M. radiation.** A series of homogeneous X rays characteristic of the metal used as anticathode, and fainter than the K and L series. **M series.** The spectral lines produced by the M radiations on diffraction through a crystal grating. Cf. *Moseley spectra.* **M shell.** The third layer or energy level, in which electrons oscillate in the static atom.

m. Abbreviation for: (1) meter, (2) milli-, or one-thousandth part. **m².** Abbreviation for square meter. **m³.** Abbreviation for cubic meter. Cf. *mm, mmm.*

m. Symbol for: (1) meta position, (2) metastable state.

♏. Abbreviation for minim.

μ. Greek mu. (1) Abbreviation for: (*a*) icron, (*b*)m micro-, or one-millionth of a unit. (2) Symbol for: (*a*) meso position, (*b*) magnetic permeability. Cf. mμ, $\mu\mu$.

Ma. Symbol for masurium.

ma. Abbreviation for milliampere.

Mac. See also *Mc.*

macassar oil. Yellow fat from the seeds of *Schleichera trijuga*, India and Malaysia.

mace. Macis. The dried covering tissues of the seeds of *Myristica fragrans;* a condiment. **m. oil.** An essential oil from mace. Colorless liquid, d.0.91; a flavoring.

macene. $C_{10}H_{18} = 138.1$. A terpene from mace oil.

maceral. General name for the microscopic structures of the mineral constituents of coals.

macerate. To break up a solid by soaking in a liquid.

Mache, Heinrich. Austrian physicist. born, 1876. **m. unit.** M.E. The quantity of radioactive emanation which produces a saturation current of one-thousandth of an electrostatic unit. 1 curie $= 2.8 \times 10^9$ maches. 1 mache $= 3.64 \times 10^{-10}$ curie/liter $= 3.64$ eman.

machine steel. A steel containing less than 0.3% carbon; easily machined.

macht metal. A forging alloy containing Cu 60, Zn 38, Fe 2%.

Mach unit. A unit of velocity, expressed as a percentage of the velocity of sound at sea level.

mackay bean. The dried seeds of *Entada scandens* (Leguminosae), Queensland; a coffee substitute.

mackenite metals. A group of heat-resisting Ni–Cr or Ni–Cr–Fe alloys.

Mackenzie amalgam. An amalgam made by grinding together the solid alloys Hg–Bi and Pb–Hg.

Mackey test. A test of the autoxidation fire hazards of oils.

maclayine. $C_{17}H_{32}O_{11} = 412.26$. An alkaloid from *Illipe maclayana* (Sapotaceae), the tropics.

macle. (1) A variety of andalusite. (2) A twin crystal.

MacLeod, John James Rickard. 1876–1935. Scottish-Canadian biochemist, awarded Nobel Prize (with Banting) in 1923 for share in discovery of insulin.

macleyine. Protopine.

maclurin. $C_6H_3(OH)_2CO.C_6H_2(OH)_3 = 280.1$. Pentahydroxybenzophenone, osage orange (q.v.), moringatannic acid. Yellow crystals from the wood of *Maclura aurantiaca*, m.200, soluble in hot water; a dye.

macro- Prefix (Greek $\mu\alpha\kappa\rho\acute{o}\varsigma$ = broad), indicating "large."

macroaxis. The long axis in orthorhombic or triclinic crystals.

macrobacterium. A large bacterium.

macrocarpine. An alkaloid from *Thalictrum macrocarpum* (Ranunculaceae). Yellow crystals, soluble in water.

macrochemistry. (1) The chemistry of reactions that are visible to the unaided eye. Cf. *microchemistry.* (2) Chemical operations on a large scale.

macrocyclic. Containing rings of more than 7 C atoms.

macrodome. See *dome.*

macrofarad. Megafarad.

macrograph. Photomacrograph.

macrolide. A substance having a macrocyclic lactone structure; as, streptomycin.

macromolecular chemistry. The study of the preparation, properties, and uses of substances containing large and complex molecules: i.e., mol. wt. exceeding 1,000. Cf. *polymer.*

macroscopic. Describing objects visible to the naked eye. Cf. *microscopic.*

macrotin. Cumicifugin.

macrotoid. The combined principles from the root of *Cimicifuga racemosa;* an antispasmodic.

macrotys. Cimicifuga.

maculanin. Potassium amylate.

madder. Turkey red, q.v. Garance. The root of *Rubia tinctorum* species. It contains glucosides which yield, on fermentation, alizarin and purpurin; a dye and pigment in lakes.

Maddrell salt. A long-chain, high-molecular-weight sodium metaphosphate, made by heating sodium metaphosphate at 300; soluble in potassium salt solutions.

mafic. A rock-forming material, mainly magnesium and iron silicates.

mafurite. A mineral association of kieserite and augite, q.v.

magdala red. $C_{30}H_{21}N_4Cl$. Naphthalene red. A safranine dye of the naphthalene series.

magenta. Fuchsin.

magma. (1) Geology: a liquid molten rock from which igneous rocks are formed. It is known as m. only while it is below the earth's surface. Cf. *lava, migma.* (2) Pharmacy: a suspension of a fine precipitate in water, e.g., magnesia m. Cf. *milk.*

magnalite. An aluminum piston alloy containing Cu 4, Ni 2, Mg 1.5%.

magnalium. An alloy of Al with Mg 2–10 and sometimes Cu 1.5–2.0%; used in aircraft, balances and, automobiles.

magnefen. A dead-burned dolomite.

magnesia. Magnesium oxide. **calcined-** Magnesium oxide obtained by heating the carbonate. **cream of-** *Magnesium* hydroxide mixture. **fluid-** A solution of magnesium bicarbonate: 2.65 gm/100 ml. **milk of-** See *milk.* **ponderous-** Heavy magnesium oxide.

m. alba. A hydrated magnesium carbonate. Cf. *milk* of m. **m. alba levis.** $4MgCO_3.Mg(OH)_2.$-$5H_2O$. *m. alba ponderosa.* $MgCO_3.Mg(OH)_2.$-$4H_2O$. **m. cement.** A cement made by heating hydrated magnesium chloride to redness and adding water. Used to coat pipes with asbestos insulation. **m. glass.** Glass containing 3–4% magnesium oxide, used for electric light bulbs. **m. magma.** Milk of m. A suspension containing 7–8.5% magnesium hydroxide; an antacid and cathartic (U.S.P.). **m. mixture.** Colorless liquid made by dissolving 55 gm hydrated magnesium chloride and 70 gm ammonium chloride in 650 ml water and adding 350 ml 10% ammonium hydroxide. Used in analysis to precipitate phosphates and arsenates. **m. niger.** An early name for pyrolusite. **m. usta.** Magnesium oxide, made by prolonged calcining of magnesium carbonate at a low temperature.

magnesian limestone. Limestone containing about 10% magnesite.

magnesioferrite. $MgFe_2O_4$. A spinel.

magnesite. $MgCO_3$. A refractory lining for furnaces and substitute for plaster of paris.

magnesium. Mg = 24.32. An alkaline-earth metal element, at. no. 12, valency 2. Silver metal, d.1.74, m.651, b.1120, insoluble in water, decomp. by acids. Occurs native in magnesite and dolomite (carbonates); serpentine, asbestos, talcum, biotite and meerschaum (silicates); in Stassfurt salts and mineral waters; and in seawater. M. was first obtained by electrolysis (1830) by Liebig and Bunsen; it forms only one series of compounds yielding the Mg^{++} ion in aqueous solutions. M. in bars, sheets, ingots, ribbons, wire, and powder is used in electric batteries, aircraft construction, flashlight powders, and pyrotechnics; as a deoxidizer in making brass, and for Thermit. **m. acetate.** $Mg(_2H_3O_2)_2.4H_2O$ = 214.4. Colorless monoclinic crystals, soluble in water. **m. acid citrate.** $MgHC_6H_5O_7.5H_2O$ = 304.4. Citresia. White crystals, soluble in water; a laxative. **m. alkyl compounds.** MgX_2, where X is an alkyl radical. **m. alkyl condensation.** Grignard reaction. **m. aluminate.** $MgAl_2O_4$ = 142.26. Spinel. Colorless cubes, m.2135, insoluble in water; a refractory. **m. ammonium arsenate.** $MgNH_4$-$AsO_4.6H_2O$ = 289.4. Colorless tetragons, soluble

in water. **m. ammonium chloride.** $MgCl_2.$-$NH_4Cl.6H_2O$ = 254.4. White crystals, soluble in water; used in magnesia mixture. **m. ammonium phosphate.** $MgNH_4PO_4.6H_2O$ = 245.6. Colorless, tetragons, decomp. by heat into m. pyrophosphate; soluble in water. **m. ammonium sulfate.** $MgSO_4(NH_4)_2SO_4.6H_4O$ = 360.4. Colorless crystals, soluble in water. **m. arsenide.** Mg_3As_2 = 222.88. Decomp. by water. **m. aryl compounds.** MgX_2, where X is an aryl radical. **m. benzoate.** $Mg(C_7H_5O_2)_2$ = 266.4. White powder, soluble in water; an antiseptic. **m. bicarbonate.** A solution of m. carbonate in carbonated water. **m. bichromate.** $MgCr_2O_7$ = 240.3. Brown, hygroscopic crystals, soluble in water. **m. biphosphate.** $MgH_4(PO_4)_2$ = 218.4. Acid m. phosphate. Yellow crystals, insoluble in water; a laxative. **m. bisulfate.** $MgH_2(SO_4)_2$ = 218.3. Acid m. sulfate. Colorless crystals, soluble in water; a cathartic. **m. borate.** $Mg(BO_2)_2$ = 109.9. Antifungin. White powder, soluble in water; an antiseptic. **m. boride.** Insoluble powder of doubtful composition. **m. borocitrate.** $Mg_2(BO_2)C_6$-H_5O_7 = 280.6. Colorless powder, soluble in water; an antiseptic. **m. bromate.** $Mg(BrO_3)_2.$-$6H_2O$ = 388.3. Colorless crystals, soluble in water, decomp. by heat. **m. bromide.** $MgBr_2.$-$6H_2O$ = 292.25. Colorless heaxgons, decomp. by heat, soluble in water; used for the electrolytic preparation of m. and as a sedative. **m. butyrate.** $Mg(C_4H_7O_2)_2$ = 198.4. Colorless, hygroscopic crystals, soluble in water. **m. cacodylate.** Mg-$(AsMe_2O_2)_2$. White powder, soluble in water. **m. calcium chloride.** Tachhydrite. **m. carbide.** (1) MgC_2 = 48.32. (2) MgC_3 = 60.32. **m. carbonate.** $MgCO_3$ = 84.32. Magnesite, dolomite, heavy m. carbonate. Colorless rhombs, decomp. 350, soluble in water. Used to prepare m. salts, fireproofing compositions, and toothpaste. *basic-* $4MgCO_3.Mg(OH)_2.5H_2O$ = 485.7. Magnesia alba levis, light m. carbonate, magnesii carbonas (U.S.P., B.P.). White powder, slightly soluble in water, soluble in ammonia; a dusting powder, antacid, and laxative. *heavy-* Magnesia alba ponderosa. A gastric antacid (B.P.). *light-* Basic m. carbonate. **m. chlorate.** $Mg(ClO_3)_2.6H_2O$ = 299.2. Hygroscopic, colorless crystals, m.40, soluble in water; used in skin ointments. **m. chloride.** $MgCl_2$ = 95.21. Fused m. chloride. White crystals, m.708, soluble in water. Used to manufacture metallic magnesium; for fireproofing; for magnesia cements, composition flooring, and artificial stones. *hydrated-* $MgCl_2.6H_2O$ = 203.3. Crystallized m. chloride. Colorless, bitter, hygroscopic crystals, m.100, soluble in water. Used as a saline cathartic; for disinfecting, fireproofing, and dressing fabrics. **m. chromate.** $MgCrO_4.7H_2O$ = 266.4. Orange crystals, m.100, soluble in water. **m. citrate.** $Mg_3(C_6H_5O_7)_2.14H_2O$ = 703.1. Colorless scales, soluble in water; used in pharmacy. *effervescent-* A granular mixture of m. citrate, sodium bicarbonate, citric acid, and sugar; a saline laxative. **m. copper alloy.** An activator for the Grignard reaction. **m. dioxide.** M. peroxide. **m. dust.** Finely powdered m. metal used in pyrotechnics, for photographic flashlights, and as a chemical reagent. **m. ethide.** $Mg(C_2H_5)_2$ = 82.4.

Colorless liquid. **m. ethyl bromide.** EtMgBr = 133.23. Grignard's reagent; used in organic synthesis. **m. fluoride.** MgF_2 = 62.3. White powder, m.1396, insoluble in water; used as an antiseptic, and in ceramics and glass. **m. fluosilicate.** $MgSiF_6$ = 166.6. M. silicofluoride. White powder; used in ceramics. *hexahydrate*- $6H_2O$ = 274.38. Trigonal crystals, soluble in water. **m. formate.** $Mg(CHO_2)_2 \cdot 2H_2O$ = 150.3. Colorless prisms, soluble in water. **m. glycerinate.** $Mg(C_3H_5O_4)_3$ = 339.4. White powder, soluble in water. **m. glycerinophosphate.** $Mg(C_3H_7O_2)$-PO_4 = 194.4. M. glycerophosphate. White powder, soluble in water; used to treat anemia. **m. glycerophosphate.** M. glycerinophosphate. **m. halides.** RMgX, where R is an aryl or alkyl radical, and X a halogen. **m. hydrate.** M. hydroxide. **m. hydrosulfide.** $Mg(HS)_2$ = 90.44. A compound which, on warming, yields pure hydrogen sulfide. **m. hydroxide.** $Mg(OH)_2$ = 58.34. M. hydrate. Brucite. White, rhombohedra, decomp. by heat, insoluble in water; used to manufacture m. oxide, milk of magnesia, and sugar. **m. hydroxyphosphate.** $Mg_3(PO_4) \cdot Mg(OH)_2$ = 165.94. A constituent of boiler scale. *m. h. mixture.* Cream of magnesia. An aqueous suspension ($\equiv 8.25\%$ m. hydroxide), made from a mixture of m. sulfate, sodium hydroxide, and light m. oxide. An antacid (B.P.). **m. hypophosphite.** $Mg(H_2PO_2)_2 \cdot 6H_2O$ = 262.5. Colorless crystals, soluble in water; a tonic. **m. hyposulfite.** M. thiosulfate. **m. iodate.** $Mg(IO_3)_2$, $4H_2O$ = 446.22. Crystals, decomp. by heat, soluble in water. **m. iodide.** MgI_2 = 278.2. Colorless powder, decomp. by heat, soluble in water. *hydrated*- $MgI_2 \cdot 8H_2O$ = 422.33 Colorless, hygroscopic crystals, soluble in water. **m. lactate.** $Mg(C_3H_5O_3)_2 \cdot 3H_2O$ = 256.4. White crystals, soluble in water; a laxative. **m. lactophosphate.** M. phospholactate. White powder soluble in water. **m. laurate.** $Mg(C_{12}H_{23}O_2)_2$ = 422.68. Colorless crystals, m.150. **m. lime.** Quicklime containing less than 20% m. oxide. **m. magma.** An aqueous suspension of 7–8.5% m. hydroxide, with a flavoring agent. Cf. *milk of magnesia.* **m. malate.** $MgC_4H_4O_5$ = 156.3. Colorless crystals, soluble in water; a laxative. **m. minerals.** M. is abundant in rocks (olivines, micas, pyroxenes, silicates, and amphiboles). **m. molybdate.** $Mg MoO_4$ = 184.3. Colorless crystals, soluble in water. **m. myristate.** $(C_{14}H_{27}O_2)_2Mg$ = 478.74. White powder, m.132. **m. nitrate.** $Mg(NO_3)_2 \cdot 6H_2O$ = 256.4. Colorless, monoclinic or triclinic crystals, m.90, soluble in water; used as a reagent and in pyrotechnics. **m. nitride.** Mg_3N_2 = 100.98. Yellow amorphous mass, decomp. by water. **m. nitrite.** $Mg(NO_2)_2 \cdot 2H_2O$ = 152.31. Colorless hygroscopic crystals, soluble in water; a reagent. **m. oleate.** $Mg(C_{18}H_{33}O_2)_2$ = 587.0. M. oleinate. Yellow oil, insoluble in water; a varnish drier. **m. oxalate.** $Mg(OOC)_2 \cdot 2H_2O$ = 148.4. Colorless crystals, soluble in water. **m. oxide.** MgO = 40.3. Magnesia, calcined magnesia, periclase, ponderous magnesia, magnesia usta. White hexagons, m.1900, insoluble in water. Used commercially in heat insulations, refractories, rubber and paper manufacture; as a dusting powder, antacid, and laxative. *heavy*- Amorphous m. oxide, obtained by heating

basic m. carbonate, d.3.58. (U.S.P., B.P.). *light*- Crystalline m. oxide obtained by heating m. carbonate d.3.36 (B.P.). See also *m. peroxide.* **m. palmitate.** $Mg(C_{16}H_{31}O_2)_2$ = 535.0. White soap, m.120, insoluble in water; a varnish drier. **m. peptonate.** Yellow powder, soluble in water, used to treat stomach disorders. **m. perborate.** MgB_4O_7 = 179.6. White powder, soluble in water, used in driers. **m. perchlorate.** $Mg(ClO_4)_2$ = 223.23. Anhydrone. White granules; a regenerable desiccant. **m. perhydrol.** M. peroxide. **m. permanganate.** $Mg(MnO_4)_2 \cdot 6H_2O$ = 370.3. Blue granules, soluble in water; an antiseptic. **m. peroxide.** MgO_2 = 56.3. M. superoxide, m. dioxide. White powder containing 25% MgO_2 and 75% MgO, insoluble in water. Used to detect bilirubin; for gastric disturbances; and for bleaching silk and wool. **m. phosphate.** $Mg_3(PO_4)_2 \cdot 4H_2O$ = 179.6. Tribasic or normal m. phosphate. Monoclinic crystals, insoluble in water. *acid*- $MgHPO_4 \cdot 7H_2O$ = 246.5. Dibasic or m. orthophosphate. Colorless hexagons, insoluble in water; an alterative and antirheumatic. *dibasic*- Acid m. phosphate. *monobasic*- M. biphosphate. *pyro*- $Mg_2P_2O_7 \cdot 3H_2O$ = 276.77. Colorless crystals, insoluble in water. *tribasic*- M. phosphate. See also *m. ammonium phosphate.* **m. phosphide.** Mg_3P_2 = 135.01. Black powder, decomp. by water. **m. phosphite.** $MgHPO_3$ = 104.3. Colorless crystals, soluble in water. **m. phospholactate.** M. lactophosphate. **m. propionate.** $Mg(C_3H_5O_2)_2$ = 170.4. White powder, soluble in water. **m. pyrophosphate.** See *m. phosphate.* **m. rhodanate.** M. thiocyanate. **m. salicylate.** $Mg(C_7H_5O_3) \cdot 4H_2O$ = 233.4. White crystals, soluble in water; an antirheumatic and intestinal antiseptic. **m. silicate.** $MgSiO_4$ = 116.6. White powder, insoluble in water; used as an astringent, and in rubber. **m. silicides.** (1) Mg_2Si = 76.70. (2) MgSi = 52.38. (3) Silicon m. **m. silicofluoride.** M. fluosilicate. **m. stearate.** $(C_{18}H_{35}O_2)_2Mg$ = 590.86. Dolomol. White, soapy powder, m.132. M. stearate containing the equivalent of 7–8% m. oxide is used for tablet making (U.S.P., B.P.). **m. succinate.** $MgC_4H_4O_4$ = 140.3. White powder, soluble in water. **m. sulfate.** (1) $MgSO_4$ = 120.4. Anhydrous m. sulfate. White powder, soluble in water. (2) $MgSO_4 \cdot 2H_2O$ = 156.4. *Dihydrate*, desiccated m. sulfate. White powder, soluble in water. (3) $MgSO_4 \cdot 7H_2O$ = 246.5. *Heptahydrate*, crystallized m. sulfate, Epsom salt (U.S.P.), Epsom salts (B.P.). Magnesii sulfas, bitter salt. Colorless tetragonal or monoclinic crystals, decomp. by heat, soluble in water. Used as a reagent, a constituent of bleaching solutions, and a refrigerant; as a saline cathartic and anticonvulsant (U.S.P.); for loading and warp-sizing cotton goods and textiles, and for fireproofing; in mineral waters, in the paper and leather industries, and in electric batteries. (4) $MgSO_4 \cdot H_2O$ = 138.4. Kieserite. d.2.3. *dried*- Anhydrous m. sulfate (B.P.). **m. sulfide.** MgS = 56.4. Brown cubes, decomp. by heat, soluble in water. **m. sulfite.** $MgSO_3 \cdot 6H_2O$ = 212.4. White crystalline powder, m.260, soluble in water; an antiseptic and cathartic. **m. sulfocyanide.** M. thiocyanate. **m. tartrate.** $C_6H_4O_6Mg \cdot 5H_2O$ = 262.43. White monoclinic crystals, soluble in water. *acid-* MgH$_2$(C$_4$H$_4$O$_6$)$_2$·4H$_2$O = 394.46. White rhombs, soluble in water. **m. thiocyanate.** Mg(CNS)$_2$ = 140.3. M. rhodanate. Colorless, hygroscopic crystals, soluble in water; a reagent. **m. thiosulfate.** MgS$_2$O$_3$·6H$_2$O = 244.4. M. hyposulfite. Colorless crystals, soluble in water; an antiseptic. **m. trisilicate.** 2MgO·-3SiO$_2$ = 260.91. White, hygroscopic powder, with indefinite water of crystallization. An antacid (U.S.P., B.P.). **m. tungstate.** MgWO$_4$ = 272.3. M. wolframate. Colorless crystals, insoluble in water; used for fluorescent screens and luminous paints. **m. urate.** MgC$_5$H$_2$O$_3$N$_4$ = 190.3. White powder, insoluble in water. **m. valerate.** Mg(C$_5$H$_9$O$_2$)$_2$ = 226.4. White powder, soluble in alcohol; a sedative. **m. wolframate.** M. tungstate.

Magnesol. Trademark for an acid silicate of magnesium, used in chromatographic columns.

magneson. *p*-Nitrobenzeneazoresorcinol. **m. II.** *p*-Nitrobenzeneazo-α-naphthol.

magnesyl. The radical —MgX. Cf. Grignard reagent.

magnet. A lodestone: iron that attracts iron. **bar-** A bar of magnetized soft iron. **electro-** Iron rendered temporarily magnetic by an electric current passing through a coil around it. **horseshoe-** A magnetized bar of iron bent into U shape.

magnetic. Pertaining to or possessing magnetism. **m. declination.** The deviation of the compass needle from the true axis of the earth, due to the m. pole not being coincident with the geographic poles. **m. deflection.** The deflection of radioactive rays or particles by a field, according to the sign and magnitude of their charges. **m. elements.** The elements of the iron family, all of which are m.; other elements have only slight magnetism. **m. field.** The lines of force in the space around the m. poles of a magnet. *atomic-* The m. region around an atom. **m. flux.** μH, where μ is the m. permeability, and H the intensity of the field of force. **m. force.** The force F on a m. pole depends on the strengths of the pole and the field. The intensity of a m. field H at a point is equal to the number of dynes m that act on a unit m. pole at the point; hence, $F = m \times H$. **m. guard.** A mask of magnetized steel wire gauze, used to protect workers from iron dust. **m. induction.** The m. flux per unit area taken perpendicularly to the direction of the m. flux. Cf. *induction*. **m. intensity.** The m. moment per unit volume. **m. iron ore.** Magnetite. **m. meridian.** The direction registered by a compass needle at any place. **m. moment.** Pole strength × length of magnet. **m. optic.** See *magneto-optic*. **m. ore.** (1) Magnetite. (2) A m. ore. **m. permeability.** The value of the total m. induction in a unit field μ. It is a measure of the force F of repulsion between 2 rigid magnetized poles, m and m', a distance r apart: $F = \mu(m \cdot m')/r^2$. Cf. *magnetic flux*. **m. polarization.** The optical activity acquired by substance in a m. field. **m. pole.** The point on which m. lines of force converge. *m. pole strength.* See *m. units*. **m. potential.** Magnetomotive force. **m. pyrite.** Pyrrhotite. **m. reluctance.** The ratio: magnetomotive force/flux. **m. rotation.** M. polarization. *specific-* The ratio of the m. rotation of a substance to that of water

under the same conditions. **m. separator** A device, usually a powerful electromagnet, for separating magnetic from nonmagnetic minerals. **m. spectrum.** The pattern (lines of force) produced by iron filings scattered on a plane surface in a m. field. See *m. field*. **m. susceptibility.** (1) The susceptibility of a substance to magnetism. (2) The m. intensity produced in a substance compared with the intensity of the m. field which produces it. **m. units.** (1) Quantity: a unit pole is the quantity of magnetism that repels another unit pole with a force of one dyne. (2) Intensity: the intensity of magnetization, or pole strength per unit area. (3) Field strength: the number of lines of force which cross a unit area in normal direction; a unit for one line per unit area = gauss. (4) Magnetic flux: unit—the maxwell.

magnetism. (1) The property of substances (as iron) which under certain conditions attract or repel each other or a like substance. (2) The science of magnetic phenomena. **electro-** M. due to induction currents. **ferro-** M. due to iron and independent of an electric current. **meta-** Describing the property of loss of m. at high and low temperatures. **photo-** See *photomagnetism*.

magnetite. FeO·Fe$_2$O$_3$. Magnetic iron ore, hercules stone, lodestone. A black, dense magnetic mass. Cf. *ferriferrous oxide*.

magnetization. The act of rendering magnetic. **specific-** See *specific m.*

magnetochemistry. The application of magnetic susceptibilities to chemical problems.

magnetoelectricity. A current of electricity produced by magnetism. Cf. *magnetism*, electro-.

magnetometer. A device to measure magnetic force.

magnetometric titration. Volumetric analysis in which changes in paramagnetism of an ion on addition of a complexing agent are followed by means of a magnetic-resonance spectrometer.

magnetomotive force. mmf. The amount of work required to bring a unit quantity of positive (attractive) magnetism from zero to a certain potential.

magneton. (1) μ. The unit of magnetic moment of a subatomic particle; unity for an electron. (2) A ring of negative electricity, assumed to consist of an electron traveling in a circle with the velocity of light. **nuclear-** μN. The magnetic moment per unit electron mass, i.e., $\mu/1{,}830$.
   m. theory. A theory of atomic structure (Parsons), in which magnetons form octets.

magneto-optic effect. A characteristic time lag in m. rotation used in qualitative analysis. **m. rotation.** Magnetic rotation, magnetic polarization. The rotation of polarized light passing through a magnetic field depends on the strength of the field, the wavelength of light, and the nature of the substance. Cf. *Verdet's constant*.

magnetophone. An instrument that records sound on a magnetic film of iron powder.

magnetostriction. The reversible change in dimensions of certain ferromagnetic materials in a magnetic field. Cf. *Joule* effect, *Villari* effect.

magnification. An apparent increase in size, *e.g.*, produced by a microscope.

magnifier. A lens used to read scales on instruments.

magnifying power. The ratio of the actual size of an object to its amplified image. Cf. *auxiometer*.

magnitude. A measurement of an object. Cf. *units*. **astronomical-** The size of a star, measured in the terms of its brightness.

magnochromite. A variety of chromite containing magnesium.

Magnoliaceae. A family of trees and shrubs including *Illicium*, staranise, and *Magnolia*, magnolin.

magnolin. A crystalline glucoside from the fruit of *Magnolia tripetala* (Magnoliaceae); insoluble in water.

magnolite. Hg_2TeO_4. A white mineral.

magnolium. The alloy: Pb 90, Sb 10%.

Magnus, Albertus. 1193–1280. Albrecht, Graf von Bollstädt. German philosopher, the founder of the European school of alchemists.

Magnus, Heinrich Gustav. 1802–1870. German chemist. **M. rule.** Each metal has a specific voltage at which it is deposited from a solution containing a mixture of metallic salts. **M. salt.** $Pt(NH_3)_4PtCl_4$. Tetraminplatotetrachloroplatinate. Green needles, soluble in water (Magnus, 1828).

Maillard reaction. The reaction between amino acids and reducing sugars which occurs in foods in hot conditions; a brown color, as in toasted cereals.

main cell. An amalgamated zinc cathode and a lead dioxide anode in sulfuric acid (2.5 volts).

maisin. A protein from maize.

maize. Indian corn. The seeds of *Zea mays*, a cereal. Cf. *zea, corn starch*. **m. oil.** Corn oil. Yellow oil, d_{25}0.915–0.920 (B.P.).

maizolith. An insulating material: cornstalks and corncobs pressed into sheets.

majolica. Lustrous pottery enameled with tin oxide.

makrolan. A polycarbonate (mol. wt. exceeds 200,000), made by reacting carbonyl chloride with diphenylolpropane.

malabar tallow. Fat from the seeds of *Valeria indica*, used in chocolate manufacture and to size yarn.

malachite. $Cu_2(OH)_2CO_3$. Dense smaragd or emerald green masses, which may be polished. **azur-** Bluish green m. from Arizona. **blue-** Azurite. **pseudo-** $Cu_3(PO_4)_2 \cdot H_2O$. Phosphochalcite. A green, native copper phosphate. **m. green.** (1) Pulverized malachite; a pigment. (2) $C_{23}H_{25}N_2Cl = 364.66$. Victoria green, benzal green. A triphenylmethane dye. Green crystals, soluble in water. A reagent for detecting sulfites in presence of thiosulfates; bacteriological stain. It is a pH indicator, changing at 1.0 from yellow (acid) to blue-green (alkaline). **leuco-** See *leuco-malachite*.

malacolac. An ether-soluble, soft lac resin from shellac.

malacolite. Augite.

malacon. An impure zircon.

Malaguti, Faustino Jovita. 1802–1878. Italian-born French chemist, noted for his work on the mass action of salts.

malakin. $EtO \cdot C_6H_4 \cdot N : CH \cdot C_6H_4(OH) = 225.2$. Salicylal-*p*-phenetidine. Yellow needles, m.92, insoluble in water; an antirheumatic.

malakograph. An apparatus to measure the rate of softening of wax by means of a falling weight attached to an indicator arm.

malamide. $NH_2CO \cdot CH_2 \cdot CHOH \cdot CONH_2 = 132.2$. 2-Hydroxybutanediamide*, malic amide. Colorless crystals, m.156. Cf. *malonamide*.

malarin. $EtO \cdot C_6H_4N = CMe \cdot C_6H_4Me = 253.15$. Acetophenonephenetidine. Yellowish crystals; an antipyretic.

malariol. Trade name for a blend of creosote and furnace oils, used as a spray mosquito repellent.

malate. A salt of malic acid, which contains the radical $—OCO \cdot CH_2 \cdot CHOH \cdot COO—$.

Malathion. Trade name for an insecticide containing the grouping $(RO)_2 \cdot PS.S.CH(COOOEt)_2$.

Malay camphor. *d*-Borneol.

malchite. A diorite containing quartz feldspar, hornblende, and biotite.

maldonite. Au_2Bi. A pink native alloy.

maleamic acid. $NH_2CO \cdot CH : CH \cdot COOH = 115.1$. Aminomaleic acid. Colorless crystals, m.152.

maleate. A salt of maleic acid which contains the radical $—OCO \cdot CH : CH \cdot COO—$.

male fern. Aspidium. The powder and extract used to expel tapeworms and liver flukes. **m. f. oil.** An essential oil from the rhizome of *Dryopteris filix-mas*. Colorless liquid, d.0.85, b.150; a flavoring.

male hormone. See *androsterone*.

maleic acid. $HOOC \cdot CH : CH \cdot COOH = 116.1$. Ethylenedicarboxylic acid, *cis*-butanedioic acid*. Colorless prisms, m.130 (decomp.), soluble in water; an isomer of fumaric acid. See *malenoid*. Used to adjust acidity in pharmaceutical preparations (B.P.). **amino-** Maleamic acid. **methyl-** Citraconic acid. **m. anhydride.** $(HC \cdot CO)_2 : O = 98.04$. *cis*-Butenedioic anhydride*. Colorless, trimetrical crystals, m.56, insoluble in water; used to manufacture polyester resins, alkyd resins, fungicides, and plasticizers. **m. hydrazide.** A growth retarder in agriculture. **m. hydrazine.** $C_4H_4O_2N_2 = 112.2$. Colorless crystals, m.250.

maleinamic acid. Maleamic acid.

malenoid. The cis form of geometrical isomerism as compared with the trans form (fumaroid):

$$
\begin{array}{cc}
HC \cdot CR & RC \cdot CH \\
\| & \| \\
HC \cdot CR & HC \cdot CR \\
cis & trans
\end{array}
$$

maletto tannin. $(C_{19}H_{20}O_9)_n$. Brown powder, from the bark of *Eucalyptus occidentalis*, soluble in water.

maleyl. The radical $C_4H_2O_2=$, from maleic acid.

malic acid. $OH \cdot H \cdot C \cdot COOH \cdot CH_2 \cdot COOH = 134.07$. Oxyethylenesuccinic acid, hydroxybutanedioic acid*. An intermediate in metabolism which exists in unripe fruit; 3 isomers. **dextro-** *d*-. Colorless needles, m.133, soluble in water. **inactive-** *dl*-. Colorless crystals, m.129, decomp. by heat, soluble in water. **iso-** Methyltartronic acid. White solid, m.160 (decomp.), soluble in water. **levo-** *l*-. Common m. Colorless crystals, m.100, decomp. 140. Cf. *aceric acid*. **β-hydroxy-** Tartaric acid. **methyl-** Citramalic acid. **m. amide.** Malamide.

mallardite. $MnSO_4 \cdot 7H_2O$. A vitreous, fusible, yellow or white mineral.

malleability. The ability to withstand hammering or rolling without fracture or return to the original shape.

malleable. Having malleability. **m. casting.** A small iron casting, made m. by heating.

mallee bark. The bark of *Eucalyptus occidentalis*, source of a commercial grade of eucalyptus oil.

Mallet, John William. 1832–1912. Irish-born American chemist, noted for atomic weight determinations.

mallophene. $Ph \cdot N : N \cdot C_5H_2N(NH_2)_2 \cdot HCl = 249.6$. Phenylazo-$\alpha$-diaminopyridine hydrochloride. Red powder, soluble in water; an antiseptic. Cf. *mellophanic acid*.

mallotoxin. Rottlerin.

mallow. Malva. The dried leaves of *Malva sylvestris* and *M.* species; herb teas. **marsh-** Althaea.

malol. Ursolic acid.

malonaldehydic acid. $CHO \cdot CH_2 \cdot COOH = 88.03$. Formylacetic acid; an isomer of peruvic acid.

malonamic acid. $COOH \cdot CH_2 \cdot CONH_2 = 103.03$. The half-amide of malonic acid.

malonamide. $NH_2CO \cdot CH_2 \cdot CONH = 102.1$. Propanediamide*, malonic diamide. Colorless crystals, m.170. Cf. *malamide*.

malonate. $M_2C_3H_2O_4$. A salt of malonic acid.

malonic acid. $CH_2(COOH)_2 = 104.1$. Propanedioic acid*, methane dicarboxylic acid*, occurring in many plants. Colorless triclinic crystals, m.132 (decomp.), soluble in water. **allyl-** See *allylmalonic acid*. **bromo-** $CHBr(COOH)_2 = 183.01$. Colorless needles, decomp. 112, soluble in water. **butyl-** $CHBu(COOH)_2 = 160.09$. *n-* White crystals, m.101.5. *iso-* m.107. *sec-* m.76. **cetyl-** $C_{19}H_{36}O_4 = 328.29$. White solid, m.121. **chloro-** $CHCl(COOH)_2 = 138.48$. Colorless crystals, m.133. **diethyl-** $CEt_2(COOH)_2 = 160.09$. White powder, m.121. **dimethyl-** $CMe_2(COOH)_2 = 132.06$. Colorless crystals, m.193. **ethyl-** $CHEt(COOH)_2 = 132.06$. White crystals, m.111.5, decomp. 160. Cf. *pyrotartaric, glutaric acid.* **ethylene.** Vinaconic acid. **hydroxy-** Tartronic acid. **keto-** Mesoxalic acid. **methyl-** Iso*succinic acid.* **nitril-** Cyanacetic acid. **oxo-** Mesoxalic acid. **oxy-** Tartronic acid.

    m. amide. $CH_2(CONH_2)_2 = 168.1$. Colorless needles m. 170, soluble in water. **m. anhydride.** $CH_2 : (CO)_2 : O = 87.1$. **m. dinitrile.** Malononitrile. **m. ester.** $CH_2(COOEt)_2 = 160.08$. Diethyl malonate. Colorless liquid, d.1.055, b.198. Its sodium compounds react with alkyl halides, yielding homologs of m. ester (m.e. synthesis).

malon oil. Blackfish oil. An oil from the pilot whale, *Globicephalus melas.*

malononitrile. $CH_2(CN)_2 = 66.1$. Propanedinitrile*, methylene cyanide. White powder, m.30, soluble in water, used in organic synthesis.

malonurea. Veronal. Cf. *malonyl urea.*

malonyl- The radical $-OC \cdot CH_2 \cdot CO-$, from malonic acid. **m. urea.** Barbituric acid. Cf. *malonurea.*

malourea. Barbital.

malt. Maltum. The grain of *Hordeum distichum* or *H. sativum* (barley), partly germinated, then dried. Yellow grains of biscuit odor and taste; used as a nutritive and digestant, and in the manufacture of malt extract, and beer. **m. extract.** Extractum malti. A dark syrup obtained by evaporating an infusion of m.; used as a tonic,

starch digestant, emulsifying agent, and vehicle for cod-liver oil. **m. liquor.** An alcoholic beverage derived from fermented infusions of m.; as beer.

maltase. Genease. An enzyme in yeast and body fluids which hydrolyzes maltose to dextrose; used in brewing.

maltha. A tar from the oxidation of petroleum. Dark asphalt-like masses, insoluble in water.

malthenes. Petrolenes.

maltobionic acid. $C_{12}H_{22}O_{12} = 358.2$. An oxidation product of maltose.

maltoboise. Maltose.

maltodextrin. Amylöin. A polysaccharide, constitutionally between dextrin and maltose, and produced from the starch in barley during the manufacture of malt. Its composition depends on the relative amounts of maltose and dextrin.

maltol. 3-Hydroxy-2-methyl-pyran-4-one. A microchemical reagent, especially for vanadium.

maltonic acid. Dextrogluconic acid.

maltosazone. $C_{12}H_{14}O_7(:N \cdot NHPh)_4$. The osazone of maltose, used in the synthesis of $C_{220}H_{142}O_{58}N_4I_2 = 4021.0$. Heptatribenzoylgalloyl-*p*-iodophenylmaltosazone; one of the largest molecules synthesized (Emil Fischer).

maltose. $C_{12}H_{22}O_{11} \cdot H_2O = 360.2$. Malt sugar, glucose-$\alpha$-glucoside. A dextrodisaccharide from malt and starch. Colorless crystals, + $[\alpha]p138°$, soluble in water. A sweetening agent and fermentable intermediate in brewing. **iso-** Gentiobiose.

malt sugar. Maltose.

maltum. Malt.

malva. Shallow.

Malvaceae. Mallow family, a group of mucilaginous plants, e.g., *Malva sylvestris*, mallow.

malvidin. The blue aglucone of the glucoside malvin in wild mallow.

malvin. A glucoside and anthocyan pigment from mallow.

malvon. $C_{29}H_{36}O_{20} = 704.3$. An oxidation product of malvin and the glucoside of a dideipside sugar ester.

mammagen. The factor responsible for the growth and development of the mammary gland.

mammary gland. The dried m. gland of the sheep. Yellow powder, partly soluble in water; used to treat menorrhagia.

man. The highest living organism of the third group of living beings. See *life.* Elementary composition of the human body: O 66.0, C 17.6, H 10.1, N 2.5, Ca 1.5%.

manaca. The dried root of *Brunfelsia hopeana* (Solanaceae), Brazil; a diuretic and diaphoretic.

manacine. Vegetable mercury. An alkaloid from manaca; a diuretic and diaphoretic.

Manchester brown. Triaminoazobenzene.

mancona bark. Erythrophloeum.

mancophalic acid. $C_{10}H_{30}O_2 = 184.3$. An amorphous resin from manila copal.

mandarine. (1) The reddish yellow fruit of *Citrus nobilis.* (2) $C_{10}H_6(OH)N : NC_6H_4SO_3H$. Orange II, β-naphtholorange. A monoazo dye. **m. oil.** The essential oil from m., b.175–179.

M. and B. 693. The 693rd experiment of May and Baker, which produced the first of the sulfapyrimidine drugs.

mandelic acid. $H \cdot OH \cdot C \cdot COOH \cdot Ph = 152.1$. Phenylglycolic acid, amygdalic acid, α-hydroxy-α-toluic acid, benzoylglycolic acid; 3 isomers.

inactive- *dl-*. Colorless rhombic crystals, m.118, soluble in water. **levo-** *l-*. The natural form, from amygdala, m.133. **para-** Inactive. **amino-** Hydrindic acid. **methyl-** Atrolactic acid. **phenyl-** Benzilic acid.

Mandelin's reagent. A reagent for alkaloids: 0.5 gm. vanadium chloride in 100 ml. concentrated sulfuric acid.

mandelonitrile. $Ph \cdot CH(OH)CN$ = 133.06. *dl-* Benzaldehyde cyanohydrin. Yellow oil, d.1.124, b.170 (decomp.), insoluble in water; used in organic synthesis.

mandioc. Tapioca.

mandragorine. $C_{17}H_{23}O_3N$ = 289.2. An alkaloid from the seeds and roots of *Mandragora officinalis* (Solanaceae), the Orient. Colorless, deliquescent crystals, m.78; a narcotic and sedative.

mandrake. Podophyllum.

mandrel. A handle or shaft in which a rotating tool is held.

manelemic acid. A constituent of elemi. **alpha-** $C_{37}H_{56}O_4$. **beta-** $C_{44}H_{80}O_4$.

mangabeira. *Hancornia speciosa*, Gom. A plant from Bahia, the latex of which is a source of rubber.

mangal. A noncorrosive aluminum alloy containing 1.5% manganese.

mangan. Manganese. **m. blende.** MnS. A native manganese sulfide.

manganate. A salt containing the radical $MnO_4=$. **per-** A salt containing the radical MnO_4-.

manganese. Mn = 54.93. A metallic element, at. no. 25. A grayish pink, lustrous, brittle metal, d.7.2, m.1260, b.1900, reacts with boiling water, soluble in acids. Discovered (1774) by Scheele, isolated (1789) by Gahn, and named from the Greek manganidso (purify) in allusion to its use to neutralize the green iron color in the manufacture of glass. Valencies: see table. **black-** Pyrolusite. **dvi-** Rhenium. **eka-** Masurium. **red-** (1) Rhodonite. (2) Rhodochrosite.

Valence no.	Compounds	Ions	Color of compound	Oxide
2	Manganous	Mn++	Slightly pink	MnO
3	Manganic	Mn³⁺	Slightly green	Mn_2O_3
4	Manganites	$MnO_3=$	Green	MnO_2
6	Manganates	$MnO_4=$	Dark green	
7	Permanganates	MnO_4-	Dark purple	Mn_2O_7

m. acetate. Manganous acetate. **m. binoxide.** M. dioxide. **m. blende.** MnS. A native m. sulfide. **m. boride.** MnB_2 = 76.6. Black powder, insoluble in water. **m. boron.** A manganese bronze: Cu 88, Sn 10, Mn 2%. **m. carbide.** Mn_3C = 177.1. Black crystals. **m. chloride.** See *manganic, manganous*. **m. copper.** M. bronze. **m. dioxide.** MnO_2 = 86.93. M. peroxide, pyrolusite, battery m. Black powder, decomp. 390, insoluble in water. Used as an oxidizing agent; in halogen manufacture; in electric dry cells; in paints and varnishes; as a black or purple color

for glass and ceramics; for making ferromanganese and manganese compounds, in the rubber industry; as a tonic and alterant. **m. green.** Barium manganate. **m. heptoxide.** Mn_2O_7 = 221.86. Permanganic acid anhydride. Green liquid, rapidly decomp. to m. dioxide; a powerful oxidizing agent. **m. minerals.** Principal ores: pyrolusite, MnO_2; braunite, Mn_2O_3; manganite (manganese spar rhodochrosite), MnO(OH); mangan blende, MnS. **m. nitrides.** Mn_5N_2 = 302.67. Mn_3N_2 = 192.81. **m. oxides.** (1) MnO. Manganous oxide. (2) Mn_3O_4. Manganic manganous oxide. (3) Mn_2O_3. Manganic oxide. (4) MnO_2. M. dioxide. (5) MnO_3. M. trioxide. (6) Mn_2O_7. M. heptoxide. **m. peroxide.** M. dioxide. **m. protoxide.** Manganous oxide. **m. sesquioxide.** Manganous manganic oxide. **m. silicate.** Mn_2SiO_4. See *braunite, rhodonite, tephroite*. **m. spar.** (1) Rhodonite. (2) Rhodochrosite. **m. steel.** An extremely hard and ductile steel containing 12% Mn. **m. sulfate.** See *manganic, manganous*. **m. tetrachloride.** $McCl_4$ = 196.77. Green solid. **m. tetrafluoride.** MnF_4 = 130.93. Brown solid. **m. titanium.** An alloy of m. and titanium, used in the steel industry. **m. trioxide.** MnO_3 = 102.93. An acidic oxide, which forms manganates. **m. tungstate.** See *hübnerite*.

manganesium. Manganesum. An early name for manganese.

manganic. Describing compounds of trivalent manganese; generally unstable and yield the green Mn^{3+} ion, which readily decomposes to the stable, Mn^{2+} state (manganous). **m. acid.** H_2MnO_4 = 120.9. An acid known only as salts of the type M_2MnO_4, manganates. *per-* $HMnO_4$ = 119.9. Red unstable liquid; forms salts of the type $MMnO_4$, permanganates. **m. chloride.** $MnCl_3$ = 161.3. An unstable compound which forms more stable double salts; soluble in water, and decomposes to $MnCl_2$ and Cl_2. **m. hydroxide.** $Mn(OH)_3$ = 106.1. An unstable hydroxide, which forms brown MnO(OH); a pigment for textiles. **m. manganous oxide.** Mn_3O_4 = 228.79. Manganomanganic oxide. Red. insoluble crystals. **m. metaphosphate.** $Mn_2(PO_3)_6 \cdot 2H_2O$ = 620.13. Pink crystals. **m. oxide.** Mn_2O_3 = 157.9. Manganese trioxide, m. sesquioxide, black m. oxide, braunite. Black powder, insoluble in water. *hydrated-* $Mn_2O_2(OH)_2$ = 175.88. Black powder. **m. sulfate.** $Mn_2(SO_4)_3$ = 398.1. Green crystals, decomp. by water or at 160; a powerful oxidizing agent.

manganiferous. Containing or carrying manganese.

manganin. An alloy: Mn 12, Cu 84, Ni 4%, m.910; used in electric heating elements.

manganite. $Mn_2O_3 \cdot H_2O$. Acerdese. A native manganic oxide hydrate.

manganites. A series of compounds derived from tetravalent manganese and its hydroxide, $Mn(OH)_4$, by replacement of the hydrogen.

manganomanganic oxide. Manganic manganous oxide.

manganosite. MnO. A native, emerald-green manganous oxide.

manganostilbite. A mineral: manganous oxide with orpiment and antimonous sulfide.

manganotantalite. A mineral: manganous oxide, and tantalum oxide, tin, and tungsten.

manganous. Describing the manganese salts containing the Mn^{++} ion; usually colorless or slightly pink, soluble in water. **m. acetate.** $Mn(C_2H_3O_2)_2 \cdot 4H_2O = 245.0$. Pink, monoclinic crystals, soluble in water. **m. ammonium phosphate.** $MnNH_4PO_4 \cdot H_2O = 186.0$. Manganese ammonium phosphate. Colorless crystals, soluble in water. **m. ammonium sulfate.** $Mn(NH_4)_2(SO_4)_2 = 283.1$. M. alum. Pink crystals, soluble in water; a reagent. **m. arsenate.** $MnHAsO_4 = 195.0$. Manganese arsenate. Pink powder, soluble in water; a hematinic, nutritive, and alterative tonic. **m. benzoate.** $Mn(C_7H_5O_2)_2 = 297.1$. Manganese benzoate. Colorless scales, soluble in water. **m. borate.** $Mn_2B_4O_7 = 265.1$. Manganese borate, manganese siccative. White powder, soluble in water; a paint drier. **m. bromide.** $MnBr_2 = 214.8$. Manganese bromide. Pink crystals, soluble in water. **m. butyrate.** $Mn(C_4H_4O_2)_2 = 229.2$. Manganese butyrate. Pink crystals, soluble in water; used to treat acute streptococcal infection. **m. cacodylate.** $Mn(Me_2AsO_2)_2 = 329.1$. Manganese cacodylate. Pink crystals, soluble in water; a tonic. **m. carbonate.** $MnCO_3 = 114.9$. Manganese carbonate, native as dialozite and rhodochrosite. Pink rhombs, decomp. by heat, insoluble in water; used to treat anemia. **m. chloride.** *anhydrous-* $MnCl_2 = 125.9$. Pink crystals, m.650, soluble in water. *hydrous-* $MnCl_2 \cdot 4H_2O = 197.7$. Pink, monoclinic crystals, m.87, soluble in water. Used to treat chlorosis; as an antiseptic (gargles), mordant, and disinfectant; and in the manufacture of manganese salts and the glass industry. **m. chromate.** $MnCrO_4 = 171.1$. Brown powder, partly soluble in hot water. **m. citrate.** $MnHC_6H_5O_7 = 245.1$. White powder, soluble in water; a tonic and astringent. **m. dithionate.** M. hyposulfate. **m. ferrocyanide.** $Mn_2Fe(CN)_6 = 322.0$. Green powder, insoluble in water, soluble in cyanide solutions. **m. fluoride.** $MnF_2 = 93.0$. Pink powder, soluble in water. **m. fluosilicate.** $MnSiF_6 \cdot 6H_2O = 305.08$. Pink hexagonal prisms, soluble in water. **m. formate.** $Mn(OOCH)_2 \cdot 2H_2O = 180.98$. Rhombic, red crystals, soluble in water. **m. glycerinophosphate.** $MnC_3H_7O_3PO_3 = 225.0$. Pink crystals, soluble in water; a tonic. **m. glycerophosphate.** M. glycerinophosphate. **m. hydrate.** M. hydroxide. **m. hydroxide.** $Mn(OH)_2 = 89.0$. Native as pyrochroite. White hexagons, decomp. by heat, insoluble in water. **m. hypophosphite.** $Mn(H_2PO_2)_2 \cdot H_2O = 203.0$. Pink crystals, soluble in water; used to treat anemia and chlorosis. **m. hyposulfate.** $MnS_2O_6 = 215.1$. Colorless needles, soluble in water. **m. iodide.** $MnI_2 \cdot 4H_2O = 183.8$. Pink, monoclinic crystals, decomp. by heat, soluble in water; an antiseptic, tonic, and alterant. **m. lactate.** $Mn(C_3H_5O_3)_2 \cdot 3H_2O = 287.1$. Pink crystals, soluble in water; a tonic. **m. lead resinate.** A mixture of lead and manganese resinates; a drier in varnishes and paints. **m. linoleate.** $Mn(C_{18}H_{31}O_2)_2 = 613.1$. Brown, fatty mass, insoluble in water; used in paint driers. **m. metaphosphate.** M. phosphate. **m. nitrate.** $Mn(NO_3)_2 \cdot 6H_2O = 287.1$. Pink, monoclinic crystals, m.26, soluble in water; a reagent. **m. oleate.** $Mn(C_{18}H_{33}O_2)_2 = 617.6$. Brown, granular, fatty mass, insoluble in water;

used in ointments, and as a drier for varnishes. **m. oxalate.** $Mn(OOC)_2 \cdot 2\frac{1}{2}H_2O = 188.0$. White, crystalline powder, decomp. 150; slightly soluble in water; a drier. **m. oxide.** $MnO = 70.9$. Manganese protoxide. Green powder, insoluble in water, soluble in acids. *manganic-* $Mn_3O_4 = 228.8$. Manganomanganic oxide, m. manganate. Brown powder; a reagent in chemical analysis. **m. peptonate.** Brown powder, soluble in water; a nutritive and tonic. **m. phosphate.** (1) *ortho-* $Mn_3(PO_4)_2 \cdot 7H_2O = 481.0$. Normal manganese phosphate. Red powder, insoluble in water; A reagent and tonic. (2) *meta-.* $MnHPO_4 = 150.97$. Pink crystals, soluble in water; used in analysis. (3) *pyro-.* $Mn_2P_2O_7 = 283.9$. White powder, d.3.58, insoluble in water. **m. propionate.** $Mn(C_3H_5O_2)_2 = 201.0$. Pink powder, slightly soluble in water. **m. pyrophosphate.** Manganese phosphate. **m. salicylate.** $Mn(C_7H_5O_3)_2 = 329.1$. White crystals, soluble in water; a tonic and antirheumatic. **m. silicate.** $MnSiO_3 = 131.2$. Pink crystals, m.1218, insoluble in water; used in ceramics and glass. **m. succinate.** $MnC_4H_4O_4 = 171.0$. White crystals, soluble in water. **m. sulfate.** (1) *anhydrous-* $MnSO_4 = 151.0$. Native as mallardite. Red crystals, soluble in water. (2) *tetrahydrate-* $MnSO_4 \cdot 4H_2O = 223.1$. Labile, pink prisms, slightly hygroscopic, m.30, soluble in water. Used as a tonic and carthartic; in the ceramic and glass industries; as a mordant in the textile industry. (3) *pentahydrate-* $MnSO_4$, $5H_2O = 241.08$. Stable at 8–27. (4) *heptahydrate-* $MnSO_4 \cdot 7H_2O = 277.10$. Red prisms, d.3.1, m.542. **m. sulfide.** $MnS = 87.0$, or $MnS \cdot H_2O = 105.0$. Manganese sulfide, native as alamandite and mangan blende. Gray, pink, or brown fusible powder, insoluble in water; a pigment. **m. sulfite.** $MnSO_3 = 135.0$. Gray crystals, insoluble in water; used medicinally. **m. sulfophenate.** $Mn(C_6H_4OH \cdot SO_3)_2 = 401.1$. Manganese phenolsulfonate. Pink crystals, soluble in water or alcohol; an antiseptic and tonic. **m. tannate.** A compound of Mn and tannin. Brown powder, insoluble in water. **m. tartrate.** $MnC_4H_4O_6 = 203.1$. White crystals, slightly soluble in water. **m. valerate.** $Mn(C_5H_9O_2)_2 \cdot 2H_2O = 293.2$. Brown powder, slightly soluble in water; a tonic.

manganum. Latin for manganese.

mangiferin. $C_{19}H_{18}O_{11} = 422.2$. Euxantogen. A principle from the leaves of *Mangifera indica;* thin, yellow needles, m.271.

mango. The tree *Mangifera indica* (Anacardiaceae), India. **m. gum.** An amber-colored or red-yellow resin from the m. tree.

mangrove. An extract from the bark of *Rhizophora mucronata,* containing 30–35% tannin; used in tanning. Cf. *cutch.*

Manihot. A group of S. American shrubs and herbs (Euphorbiaceae) which yield cassava, Brazilian arrowroot, cassareep, and ceara rubber.

Manila copal. A resin from *Agathis dammara,* a conifer of the Philippine Islands; contains 80% mancophaolic acid. **M. hemp.** Abaca. **M. paper.** A strong paper, correctly made from old M. rope (M. fibers).

manioc. Cassava.

manioca. Tapioca.

manna. The dried saccharine exudation of *Fraxinus ornus* (Oleaceae), the Orient. It contains mannite, and forms a yellowish white mass of sweet, slightly acrid taste. It can be compressed into tacky lumps for storage and subsequent purification and consumption, and is said to have been the food of the Israelites; a mild cathartic. **Armenian-** glucose. A m. from oak trees, containing glucose. **Australian-** A m. from the eucalyptus species, containing melitose. Cf. *lerp.* **yeast-** Yeast gum.

mannan. A glucoside constituent of yeast gum, and manna, analogous to araban.

Mannich reaction. The condensation of an amine and an aldehyde with a compound containing an acidic H atom attached to a C or N atom.

mannide. $C_6H_{10}O_4 = 146.08$. An anhydride of mannitol, b.317. **iso-** A solid, m.87, b.274.

mannitan. $C_6H_{12}O_5 = 164.3$. An anhydride of mannitol. A syrupy liquid, m.100; or crystals, m.137.

mannite. Mannitol.

mannitol. $C_6H_{14}O_6 = 182.2$. Mannite. A hexatomic alcohol from manna and many plants (larch, sugarcane, *Viburnum, Syringa,* and *Fraxinus* species), or, by electrolysis, from glucose. Two isomers: dextro and levo. Colorless· needles, m.166, soluble in water. A mild laxative (B.P.), and a reagent for detecting glucose. **m. nitrate.** $C_6H_8(ONO_2)_6 = 452.15$. Hexanitrin, MHN, nitromannite, m.108; a substitute for mercury fulminate in high explosives.

mannitose. Mannose.

mannoheptitol. Perseitol.

mannoheptonic acid. $C_7H_{14}O_8 = 226.11$. White solid, decomp. 175, soluble in water.

mannoheptose. $C_7H_{14}O_7 = 210.11$. A heptose m.134, in the avocado fruit of *Persea gratissima,* (Lauraceae).

mannolite. Chlorazene.

mannosans. $(C_6H_{10}O_5)_n$. Polysaccharides, which hydrolyze to mannose.

mannose. $CH_2OH(CHOH)_4CHO = 180.1$. A hexose or fermentable monosaccharide and isomer of glucose from manna; 2 optically active forms. **dextro-** Seminose. Colorless prisms, m.132, soluble in water.

mannoside. A glucoside which yields mannose. Cf. *rhamnomannoside.*

mannotriose. $C_{18}H_{32}O_{16} = 504.25$. Glucose galactose galactoside. A trisaccharide from manna, indigestible by man.

manocryometer. A device to determine the melting point under pressure.

manometer. An instrument to measure the pressure of gases or liquids. **gas-** See *gage, McLeod steam gage.* **mercury-** A U tube filled with mercury; the difference in the heights in the arms indicates the pressure. **photo-** A m. adapted for a photographic record of changes in level and thus of pressure. **sphygmo-** An instrument for measuring blood pressure. **spring-** An instrument constructed from a coiled tube into which the gas or steam passes and, according to its pressure, uncoils and records on the dial. Cf. *McLeod.* **water-** A U tube filled with water, with one end open and the other connected to the gas container. The difference in the heights of the water columns indicates the gas pressure. Classification of m.:

Ionization gage	$0.0001–0.1\ \mu$ Hg
Pyrometric gage	$0.001–1\ \mu$ Hg
McLeod gage	$0.01–1,000\ \mu$ Hg
Micromanometer	0.01–10 mm
U tube.	1–1,000 mm
Single tube	2–2,000 mm
Spring manometer.	0.5–10 lb
Diaphragm	0.5–200 lb
Carbon pile	50–2,000 lb
Crystals	100–20,000 lb
Steel tube spiral	1,000–10,000 lb

manool. The starting point for the synthesis of ambergris perfumes. A diterpene alcohol from the oil of the New Zealand yellow pine, *Dacrydium biforme.*

manoscopy. Gas-volumetric analysis.

mantle. The outer wall of a furnace. **filter-** Berkefeld filter. **gas-** Welsbach mantle.

Manucol. Trademark for an alginate thickening agent.

manure. Refuse, e.g., excreta, straw, etc.; used as fertilizer. Average composition: nitrogen 0.6, phosphorus pentoxide 0.3, potassium oxide 0.6 %. **m. salt.** A potassium salt (chiefly chloride) containing 20–30 % potash.

manzoul. A narcotic mixture of hashish and muscat nut.

Mapharsen. Trademark for arsphenoxide, mapharside, neohalarsine. The hemialcoholate of oxophenarsine hydrochloride, q.v.

mapharside. Mapharsen.

maple. The tree *Acer saccharum* (U.S.) or *A. campestris* (U.K.). **red-** The bark of *A. rubrum,* swamp m.; used by American Indians to cure sore eyes. **m. sugar.** Brown mass, chiefly sucrose with glucose, coloring matter, and proteins, from evaporated m. syrup. **m. syrup.** The concentrated sap of *A. Saccharum* (2–4 lb per tree).

MAR. Abbreviation for microanalytical reagent.

mar-aging. Maraging. Modification of the martensitic structure of steel by heating at 450–500°C for 3 hours, followed by air cooling without quenching. It produces high strength, impact, and ductility values.

Maranta. Arrowroot.

marble. $CaCO_3$. Native limestone recrystallized under the influence of heat and/or pressure, in many forms and colors.

marc. (1) The residual vegetable tissue and mucilage after expression of oil from a plant or nut kernel. (2) The cellular tissue left after complete extraction of the juice from the sugar beet or sugarcane. Cf. *bagasse.*

marcasite. FeS_2. Coal brass, white iron, spear, binarite, coxcomb, radiated pyrites. Yellow, orthorhombic crystals.

Marcet, Alexander. 1770–1822. Swiss physician, who became an English chemist and noted lecturer-demonstrator. **M., Jane Haldemand.** 1769–1858. Swiss exponent of popular science ("Conversations on Chemistry").

Marchand, Richard Felix. 1813–1850. German chemist, noted for atomic weight determinations. **M. tube.** A U-shaped, calcium chloride tube, with bulb and side-tube attached.

marcitine. $C_8H_{19}N_3$ = 157.1. A basic substance from putrid pancreas.

marennin. Green pigment in certain French oysters, derived from the chlorophyll of microorganisms present.

maretin. $MeC_6H_4NH·NH·CONH_2$ = 165.11. *m*-Tolyl semicarbazide. Colorless crystals, m.184, insoluble in water; an antirheumatic.

marfacing. Mar-aging, q.v., to produce a hard-faced deposit.

Marfanil. $NH_2·CH_2·C_6H_4·SO_2NH_2$ = 186.48. Mesudan, sulfabenzamine. Trade name for 4-aminomethylbenzene sulfonamide; a local antiseptic. It differs from the common sulfonamides in that the amino group is separated from the benzene ring by a methyl group.

margaric acid. $C_{17}H_{34}O_2$ = 270.4. Heptadecanoic acid*, daturic acid. A saturated fatty acid occurring in lichens (also synthesized). Colorless mass, m.60, insoluble in water.

margarine. A butter substitute; a solid emulsion of fats in milk serum. Named after its inventor, Mège-Mouries, 1870. **oleo-** The liquid fat from which m. is made by hydrogenation, which saturates the double bond.

margarite. $CaH_4Al_4H_2Si_2O_{12}$. Lustrous, pearly, monoclinic masses of various shades.

margaron. $(C_{16}H_{33})_2O$ = 466.7. Dihexadecyl ether. White powder from beef suet; an ointment base.

margaronitrile. $Me(CH_2)_{15}CN$ = 251.27. Heptadecane nitrile*, cetyl cyanide. White crystals, m.53.

Marggraf, Andreas Sigismund. 1709–1782. German chemist, founder of the beet sugar industry.

margosa oil. Neem oil, veepa oil, veppam fat, oil of azedarach, from the seeds of *Melia azedarach*, the bead tree, Indian lilac, cape syringa or china tree (Meliaceae), Asia and Africa.

margosic acid. $C_{22}H_{40}O_2$ = 336.4. A fatty acid from margosa oil; probably impure oleic acid.

marialite. $2NaCl.2Na_2O.3Al_2O_3.18SiO_2$. A vitreous, green mineral.

Mariana's trench. The ocean's deepest area (35,800 ft).

Marie Davy cell. Amalgamated zinc in dilute sulfuric acid, as anode; carbon, in a paste of mercurous sulfate, as cathode (1.5 volts).

Marignac, Jean Charles Galissard de. 1817–1894. Swiss chemist, noted for determinations of atomic weights, and investigations of rare-earth metals. **M. salt.** Potassium stannosulfate.

marigold. Calendula.

marihuana. Hashish.

marinating. Pickling in brine.

Mariotte, Edme. 1629–1684. A French prior. **M. law.** The product of volume and pressure of a gas is constant (1676). Cf. *Boyle's law.*

marjoram. The herbs *Origanum* (Labiatae). **sweet-** The herb and leaves of *O.major;* a tonic and emmenagogue. **wild-** The herb of *O. vulgare;* a stimulant. It yields origanum oil.
  m. oil. An essential oil from *Origanum majorana* (Labiatae). Odorless liquid, d.0.9, insoluble in water; a perfume. Cf. *origanum oil.* **French-** The essential oil of *Calamintha nepeta* (Labiatae) containing calaminthone.

marker. An electric instrument for registering small time intervals on smoked papers.

marking. Branding. **m. apparatus.** A microscope objective, used to make small circles on the cover glass, marking fields for reference. **m. ink.** A solution of silver nitrate; used to mark textiles in laundries. **m. nut.** Semecarpus.

Markownikoff's rule. (1) In the addition reaction of 2 organic molecules at *low* and *high* temperatures, the least hydrogenated C atom of one will combine with the most negative and positive elements of the other, respectively. (2) When the additive agent adds as H and R, the latter goes to the C atom with the smaller number of H atoms.

marl. (1) A soil consisting of clay, sand, and chalk; used as a fertilizer. (2) An earthy or soft rock deposit rich in calcium carbonate.

Marlex. Trademark for a high-density polyethylene synthetic fiber.

Marlspun. Trade name for a cellulose acetate synthetic fiber.

marmatite. A native zinc, iron, and manganese sulfide.

Marme's reagent. A solution of potassium iodide 6 and cadmium iodide 3 gm, in 18 ml water. A reagent for alkaloids (white or yellow precipitate).

Marmite. (1) Trade name for a food prepared by treating dried yeast with an acid under pressure, and neutralizing the product. (2) (not cap.) An earthenware vessel for boiling large volumes of bouillon or media.

Marne,N.H. Johann Bernhard Herrmann. German phlogistic chemist who attempted the first classification of elements (1786).

maroti oil. Fatty oil, d.0.96, expressed from the seeds of *Hydnocarpus wightiana*, (Flacourtiaceae).

marri-kino. Red gum from *Eucalyptus calophylla* (Myrtaceae); used in tooth powders.

marrubiin. $C_{21}H_{28}O_4$ = 344.22. The active principle from the leaves of *Marrubium vulgare* (Labiatae). Colorless scales, m.155, slightly soluble in water; a tonic.

marrubium. Horehound.

Marsh, James. 1789–1846. English chemist. **M. test.** Marsh-Berzelius test for arsenic. The substance is added to pure zinc, and pure hydrochloric acid is slowly added; the evolved hydrogen with any arsenic hydride, AsH_3, is passed through a long tube which is heated at the end so that arsenic is deposited; or the escaping hydrogen is ignited, and a cold porcelain dish is held above the flame. The arsenic deposits on it as a black mirror that can be dissolved in potassium hypochlorite solution, while any antimony deposit does not dissolve.

Marshall apparatus. A device for the determination of urea in blood.

marsh gas. The gaseous products, chiefly methane, formed from decaying, moist organic matter in marshes. Cf. *firedamp.* **m. mallow.** Althaea. **m. mint.** Wild mint. The herb, *Mentha sativa* (Labiatae); an emetic and stimulant. **m. ore.** Bogore. **m. tea.** Labrador tea.

marshmallow. Althaea.

Martens densitometer. An optical device to measure the density of the silver deposit on photographic plates. **M. illuminator.** A photometer to determine illumination efficiency. **M. spectroscope.** A direct-vision spectroscope. **M. test.** The determination of the temperature at which the free end of a testpiece, subjected to a specified bending stress at a gradually increasing temperature, first shows signs of deflection.

martensite. Normally, a solid solution of 2% carbon in iron, present in quenched steel. On slow cooling it decomposes into iron and iron carbide. **alpha-** The tetragonal form of normal (beta-) martensite.

martial ethiops. Magnetic ferric oxide.

Martin's flask. A culture flask, consisting of a glass bulb with 3 long necks; used to manufacture toxins. **M.'s centrifuge.** A small laboratory centrifuge driven by waterpower. **M.'s filter.** A Berkefeld filter with a funnel, for filtering toxins.

martite. A native ferric oxide. See *hematite*.

Martius yellow. The calcium salt of naphthalene yellow.

Marvinol. Trademark for a polyvinyl rubber substitute.

marzipan. A mixture of sugar, ground almonds, and starch, used in confectionery.

mascagnine. A mineral ammonium sulfate.

maser. Abbreviation for microwave amplification by stimulated emission of radiation. An ultra-sensitive amplifier based on the use of a synthetic crystal at $-452°F$, so that the thermal motion of the atoms present does not interfere with reception of very weak radio signals. Cf. *laser*.

mash. A warm mixture of malted barley and water used to prepare brewer's wort, q.v.

masked. Hidden; concealed. **m. element.** An element combined in an organic compound so that its properties are subdued or hidden, and it does not give the usual reactions; e.g., iron is masked in hemoglobin. **m. group.** An atomic group present in an organic compound, but combined so that its usual properties are subdued. **m. radical.** M. group.

maslin. A mixture of grains, especially wheat and rye.

masonite. Gun fiber. Trade name for a wood fiber constructional and insulating material. **M. process.** Chips of wood are placed in autoclaves (guns) and subjected to steam of 1,000 psi pressure for 5 seconds. The sudden release explodes the chips, which are then recombined as slabs, etc.

mass. (1) *M.* A definite quantity of matter, q.v., which offers resistance to change of motion. The physical quantity of an electron, atom, molecule, or an assembly of these, e.g., mole. Unit: milligram, gram, or kilogram. Unlike weight, q.v., mass is unchangeable; e.g., 1 gm water always contains the same number of molecules. **active-** The number of moles (gram molecules) in unit volume (1 liter). Cf. *atomic mass*. (2) Pharmacy: a homogeneous solid or semisolid mixture; as: **blue-** A preparation of fine metallic mercury, suspended in honey or syrup. **copaiva-** Copaiva solidified with magnesium oxide. **ferrous carbonate-** Vallet's mass. A paste containing 33% ferrous carbonate; a hematinic. **mercury-** Blue mass. **Vallet's-** Ferrous carbonate mass.

m. action. A law of chemical reaction: In a homogeneous system, the product of the molar concentrations of the participating substances on one side of the equation, when divided by the product of the molar concentrations of the substances on the other, is constant (k) for each temperature. It applies to both direct and reverse reactions (Guldberg and Waage). Hence,

MAGNITUDES OF MASS

Grams

Einstein universe	8×10^{78}
Galaxy (Milky Way system)........	2.3×10^{55}
Large stars	1×10^{36}
Sun 331,950 × earth	1.99×10^{33}
Earth 1.0 earth	5.99×10^{26}
Mercury 1/25 × earth	2.5×10^{25}
Moon 1/81.56 × earth	7.5×10^{24}
Hydrosphere 1,335,000,000,000 million tons	1.3×10^{24}
Atmosphere 5,633,000,000 million tons	5.6×10^{21}
Average asteroid 1,000,000,000 million tons	1×10^{21}
Steamship Queen Mary 72,000 tons	7.2×10^{10}
Meteorites, annual fall 40,000 tons	4×10^{10}
1 ton = 1,000 kg (2,205 lb)	
Man, average weight 76 kg (166 lb)..	7.5×10^{4}
Vitamin A, effective dose 3 γ	3×10^{-9}
Microbalance sensitivity 0.4 γ	4×10^{-10}
Sodium by flame test 0.07 γ	7×10^{-11}
Mercaptan by odor 0.002 γ	2×10^{-12}
Colloid particle	2×10^{-18}
Protein molecule 100,000 × H	1×10^{-18}
Oil film (0.000,000,2 cm square)....	2×10^{-21}
Cane-sugar molecule 342 × H	5.7×10^{-22}
Water molecule 18 × H	3×10^{-23}
Hydrogen atom 1 × H	1.663×10^{-24}
Electron 1/1,845 of H	9.01×10^{-28}

the velocity of a chemical reaction is proportional to the active masses (molar concentrations) of the reacting substances. *m.a. constant.* The constant k in the equation which applies to other equilibria, e.g., ionization. **m. conservation.** A law of physics: matter cannot be destroyed or created; all changes of matter are transformations (analogous to the law of energy conservation). Cf. *energy, matter.* **m. energy cycle.** The transformation of matter into energy, and vice versa. Cf. *Einstein's theory, materialization.* **m. law.** (1) M. conservation. (2) M. action. **m. number.** The nearest integer to the number expressing the m. of the corresponding neutral atom in terms of chemical oxygen as 16; denoted by a suffix superscript; as, S^{32}. Cf. *isobars.* **m. spectra.** Aston spectra. Spectra of isotopes. The separation of an element into its isotopes by making it the anode in a vacuum discharge tube. The canal rays (formed behind the perforated cathode), when exposed to a magnetic field, are deviated from a straight path proportionally to their mass, and made visible by a fluorescent screen or photographic plate. **m. spectrogram.** The photographic images produced when positive rays, deflected by a magnetic or electric field, fall on a photographic plate. **m. spectrograph, m. spectrometer.** An apparatus to produce m. spectra.

massecuites. A mixture of syrup and crystals of cane sugar, used in the sugar industry.

massicot. A native lead monoxide, d.9.3, m.600.

mastic. (1) Mastiche. The concrete resinous exudations from *Pistacia lentiscus* (Anacardiaceae),

Mediterranean. Yellow or green, transparent resin, insoluble in water, soluble in alcohol. Used in lacquers, incense, plasters, dental cements, chewing gum; and as a styptic and carminative. (2) A mixture of finely powdered rock and bituminous material, used for highway construction. (3) A mortar for plastering walls; finely ground limestone, sand, litharge, and linseed oil. **m. oil.** An essential oil from m., d.0.858–0.868, b.155–160, containing d-pinene.

mastic acids A group of resinous acids obtained from mastic; e.g.: mastichic acid, $C_{20}H_{32}O_2$ (α-resin); masticin, $C_{20}H_{31}O$ (β-resin).

mastication. The stage of chewing food, in which it is mixed with the salivary enzymes, and amylolytic changes begin. Cf. *digestion*.

masticatory. An agent to increase the secretion of saliva, e.g., chewing gum.

mastix. Mastic (1).

masurium. Ekamanganese. Ma = 98(?). An element of the manganese family, at. no. 43, discovered (1925) by Noddack from the X-ray spectra of platinum ores, gadolinite, and columbite. Now known as technetium, Tc. Cf. *nipponium*.

masut. Mazout. The residue remaining after the distillation of benzine and kerosene from Russian petroleum: C 87, H 12, O 1%; a fuel; burns at about 100°C.

mat. Matte (2).

match. A small strip of wood, paper, or wax tipped with a pyrophoric mixture. **lucifer-** A m. tipped with a paste of scarlet or yellow phosphorus or P_4S_3, gum, red lead, and sometimes potassium chlorate; ignites when rubbed on sandpaper. **safety-** A m. tipped with a mixture of antimony sulfide 24, potassium chlorate 22, potassium dichromate 12, red lead 22 pts., and gum and coloring pigments; ignites when rubbed on paper coated with red phosphorus, glass powder, and gum.

maté. Paraguay tea, yerba, Jesuit tea, Brazil tea, yerba mate. The dried leaves of *Ilex paraguayensis* (Aquifoliaceae), S. America. Its infusion is a beverage. **Zapek-** Maté leaves which have been heated.

materialization. The production of matter, e.g., electrons and positrons, by the transformation of γ rays. Cf. *mass-energy* cycle.

Materia Medica. (1) Knowledge of the natural history, physical characters, and chemical properties of drugs. (2) Pharmacy. (3) Pharmacology. (4) Therapeutics.

matesterin. $C_{23}H_{40}O_3(?)$. A dihydroxy sterol from maté. White needles, m.270.

matico. The dried leaves of *Piper angustifolium*, (Piperaceae); genito-urinary stimulant. **m. camphor.** $C_{12}H_{16}O$ = 176.1. A terpene from matico. **m. oil.** An essential oil from m., d.0.930–1.130, soluble in alcohol.

matildite. $AgBiS_2$. A silver ore.

matlockite. $PbO.PbCl_2$. A lead mineral from Matlock, England.

matrass. Distilling flask (obsolute).

matricaria. German chamomile. The dried flower heads of *M. chamomilla* (Compositae); a febrifuge and tonic.

matrine. (1) $C_{15}H_{24}ON_2$ = 248.20. Isolupanine. The chief alkaloid of kuh-seng; 4 isomers: **alpha-** Needles, m.77. **beta-** Rhombic prisms, m.87.

gamma- A liquid, d.1.088, b.223. **delta-** Prisms, m.84. All soluble in water. (2) $C_{15}H_{26}N$ = 220.2. A liquid alkaloid from *Sophora angustifolia*.

matrix. (1) Groundmass; rock or earth which contains a metallic ore or mineral. (2) The impression left in a rock by a fossil or crystal. (3) The material surrounding a precious stone. (4) A conventional arrangement of numbers in horizontal rows and vertical columns, the latter being the more numerous; used to interpret quantum numbers. Cf. *Pauli's principle*. **m. theory.** The spectral line which corresponds with a transition from one quantum state to another is expressed by an amplitude or intensity factor and a frequency or energy factor. Cf. *quantum theory*.

matte. (1) The crude metal, obtained by smelting sulfide ores, which still contains some sulfur. (2) (2) A roughened surface which diffuses light.

matter. Any body subject to gravitation; hence any substance, that occupies space. Cf *mass*. **annihilation of-** The theory that m. is destroyed in the interior of a star by the transformation of mass into radiations. Cf. *energy, mass-energy cycle*. **conservation of-** See *mass conservation*. **creation of-** The assumption that the diffuse gaseous nebulosities absorb radiation and transform it into m. Cf. *energy, mass-energy cycle*. **destruction of-** See *annihilation of-* and *disintegration of-*. **disintegration of-** The radioactive transformations by which m. of one kind is transformed into m. of another with liberation of energy. Cf. *radioactivity*. **transformation of-** Chemical changes; reactions.

Matthiessen's rule. The product of specific resistance and mean temperature coefficient of resistance is constant.

matt salt. Acid ammonium fluoride.

Maumené, Edme Jules. 1818–1891. French chemist. **M. number.** The rise in temperature occurring in the M. test. **M. test.** 50 gm is added to 10 ml concentrated sulfuric acid; if the rise in temperature exceeds 70°C, drying oils are present.

mauvein. $C_{27}H_{24}N_4$ = 404.4. Aniline purple, Perkin's mauve. A violet dye of the phenyl safranine group; the first aniline dye (Perkin, 1856).

max. Abbreviation for maximum.

maximal. Having attained the greatest value. **m. work.** The greatest amount of energy obtainable from a process or reaction.

maximum. The largest quantity or value. **m. boiling-point mixture.** That mixture of 2 or more liquids which has the highest boiling point. **m. temperature.** The temperature above which the growth of bacteria does not take place.

maxipen. See *penicillin* V.

maxite. Leadhillite.

maxivalence. The highest valency of an element; it generally corresponds with the group number in the periodic system.

Maxton screen. A rotating screen.

Maxwell, James Clerk. 1831–1879. Scottish physicist. **M.-Boltzmann distribution law.** An expression, based on the theory of probability, for the number of moles in a gas at equilibrium n_i which have a certain energy ϵ. $n_i = C \cdot e^{-\epsilon/kT}$, where C is a constant and k is Boltzmann's constant. **M. demon.** A means by which molecules of different velocities may be separated. **M. law.** If μ is the refractive index of a medium, and k the inductivity of a medium: $k = \mu^2$, provided the frequencies of the electrical and light vibrations are the same.

maxwell. A unit of magnetic quantity or flux:

1 international maxwell = 1.00043 absolute
maxwells = 1 line = 10^{-8} volt-sec
1 international maxwell/cm^3 = 6.452 maxwells/in.
1 absolute maxwell = 0.99957 international maxwell

Absolute dimensions: $L^{\frac{1}{2}}M^{\frac{1}{2}}k^{-\frac{1}{2}}$ esu units or
$L^{\frac{3}{2}}M^{\frac{1}{2}}T^{-1}u^{\frac{1}{2}}$ emu units

may apple. Podophyllum.

Mayer, Julius Robert von. 1814–1878. German physicist, who originated the mechanical theory of heat and conservation of energy and matter. Cf. *Meyer*.

mayer. My. A unit of heat capacity. The heat capacity of a body which is raised 1°C by 1 joule (4.18 My for 1 gm water at 20°C).

Mayer's hemalum. A stain: 1 gm hematein, 50 ml 90% alcohol, 50 gm alum, 0.5 gm thymol, and 1,000 ml water. **M.'s reagent.** A solution of mercuric chloride 1.35 and potassium iodide 5 gm, in 100 ml water, gives a white precipitate with alkaloids.

maysin. A globulin in corn meal (0.25%), which coagulates at 70°C.

Mayow, John. 1643–1679. English chemist who discovered that the atmosphere consists of gases, one supporting life and combustion.

mazout. Masut.

McBain, James William. 1882–1953. Canadian-born American physical chemist, noted for his conception of the colloid micelle. **McB.-Baker balance.** A silica spring balance enclosed in heavy glass tubing, for the study of sorption under pressure. **McB. centrifuge.** An ultracentrifuge, q.v., consisting of a spinning top driven by and floating on air.

McCance reagent. A solution containing silver nitrate and gelatin acidified with sulfuric acid; an etch to detect sulfur in iron or steel.

mcg. Abbreviation for microgram (U.S.P.).

McGill metals. A group of Al bronze casting alloys containing 2% Fe.

McLaurin process. A low-temperature carbonization method for coal.

McLeod gauge. A device for measuring low gas pressures (0.2–0.0005 mm) in a high-vacuum system by trapping a known volume of gas and compressing it to a measurable pressure. Cf. *MacLeod*.

MCPA. Methoxone. Common name for 2-methyl-4-chlorophenoxyacetic acid. A herbicide.

Mc/sec (U.S.), **mc/sec** (U.K.). Abbreviation for megacycles per second.

Me. Abbreviation for methyl, CH_3—.

mead. Hydromel.

Meadol. Trade name for a lignin plastic prepared from soda wood black liquors.

meadow anemone. Pulsatilla. **m. crocus.** Colchicum. **m. lily.** The bulb of *Silium candidum* (Liliaceae); a mucilaginous emulsion. **m. saffron.** *Colchicum autumnale.* **m. sweet.** Queen-of-the-meadow. The herb of *Spiraea ulmaria* (Rosaceae); a diuretic. **m. saffron.** Colchicum.

mean. Average. **arithmetic-** The quotient obtained

by dividing the sum of n numbers by n; hence, $(a + b + c + d)/4$ = arithmetic mean of a, b, c, and d. **geometric-** The nth root of n numbers multiplied by one another; hence, $\sqrt[4]{abcd}$ = geometrical mean of these 4 numbers. **harmonic-** The quotient obtained by dividing n by the sum of $1/n$ numbers. **proportional-** The quotient obtained by dividing $ma + nb + oc + \cdots$ by $m + n + o + \cdots$; thus the atomic weight is the proportional mean of the isotopic weights (multiplied by the percentages present). **quadratic-** The square root of the quotient obtained by dividing the sum of n^2 numbers by the number of added numbers; as, $\sqrt{(a^2 + b^2 + c^2 + d^2)/4}$. Numerical values follow the order: quadratic (highest), arithmetic, geometric, harmonic (lowest).

m. free path. The average distance molecules are supposed to travel without collision. **m. refractive index.** The average refractive index of a substance for the extreme red and violet rays.

means. The second and third term in the mathematical expression $a:b::c:d$, where b and c are the means, a and d the extremes: $a/b = c/d$.

measure. A device to determine a physical quantity, generally length, diameter, volume, and capacity; e.g., rules, calipers, graduates, etc. For units, see *metric system*.

meat. The edible portion of animal flesh, excluding fish; a major source of Sr^{90} radioactivity. **m. bases.** An arbitrary analytical number of m. foodstuffs: (Total nitrogen — insoluble and coagulable nitrogens, proteoses, peptones, and gelatin) $\times$ 3.12. **m. extract.** A partly evaporated bouillon, used for culture media. **m. meal.** A fertilizer consisting of cooked, dried, and powdered m., with little bone. It contains nitrogen 10–11.5, phosphorus pentoxide 1–5%. **m. sugar.** Inositol.

Mebaral. Trademark for phemitone, q.v.

mecamylamine hydrochloride. $C_{10}H_{21}N \cdot HCl$ = 203.78. 3-Methylaminoisocamphene hydrochloride. White crystals, m.246 (decomp.), soluble in water; a ganglionic blocking agent (B.P.).

mecaprine. See *atebrin, quinacrin*.

Mecca balsam. Balm of Gilead.

mechanical. Pertaining to the physical forces of masses and their control. **m. analysis.** Analysis by mechanical as distinct from physical or chemical means, e.g., sedimentation. **m. antidote.** The use of the stomach pump to remove a poison from an organ. **m. equivalent.** Joule. The quantity of energy which, transformed into heat, yields 1 calorie of heat = 4.8×10^7 ergs (at 20°C). **m. pulp.** A pulp obtained by the wet grinding of wood and used to manufacture cheap grades of paper, e.g., newsprint.

mechanics. The study of forces or bodies (solid, liquid, or gaseous) which involve no change in state or composition: e.g., machines (levers, wheels, screws), hydraulics, and pneumatics. **quantum-** See *quantum theory*. **soil-** The application of statistical methods to data deduced from the measured properties of geological sediments. **wave-** See *wave mechanics*.

mechanism. A machine or instrument which transforms or transmits mechanical force.

mecholyl. Acetyl-β-methylcholine. **m. chloride.** Methacholine chloride.

meclozine hydrochloride. $C_{25}H_{27}N_2Cl\cdot2HCl$ = 463.91. White crystals, m.224 (decomp.); an antihistaminic (B.P.).

mecocyanin. $C_{27}H_{30}O_{16}$ = 610.23. An anthocyanin from the poppy.

meconate. A salt of meconic acid, containing the radical $C_5H_2O_3(COO)_2=$.

meconic acid. $C_7H_4O_7\cdot3H_2O$ = 254.12. Hydroxypyrocomanedicarboxylic acid, from opium. White crystals, soluble in water. Cf. *comenic acid*.

meconidin. $C_{21}H_{23}NO_4$ = 353.19. Yellow amorphous powder, m.58, insoluble in water.

meconin. $C_{10}H_{10}O_4$ = 194.1. Opianyl. 5,6-Dimethoxyphthalide. The lactone of meconinic acid, derived from opium. Colorless crystals, m.102, soluble in water.

meconinic acid. $C_6H_2(OMe)_2(CH_2OH)COOH$ = 212.1. 1,2-Methoxy-3-carboxyl-4-methanolbenzene. It exists only as its salts and its lactone, meconine.

media. Plural of medium.

median. See *frequency*.

medical. Pertaining to the diagnosis and treatment of disease. **m. jurisprudence.** Legal *medicine*.

medicine. (1) The science and art of healing. (2) A drug or substance administered to the body to correct a disturbance of its normal function. **clinical-** The study of disease by practical methods. **forensic-** Legal medicine. Science applied to the detection of crime. **patent-** A m. or drug protected by letters patent. **preventive-** A branch of medical knowledge which aims to prevent disease. **veterinary-** The application of medical knowledge to the treatment of diseases of animals.

Medinal. Trademark for a brand of barbital sodium.

Mediolanum. Trademark for a urea-casein xanthate synthetic fiber.

medium. (1) A substance that acts as the transmitter of a force. (2) See *culture* medium. (3) an average or mean.

medroxyprogesterone acetate. $C_{24}H_{34}O_4$ = 386.54. White crystals, insoluble in water, m.204; a progestin (U.S.P.).

medullarin. A secondary hormone; the sex differentiator of the germ cell, which is responsible for maleness. Cf. *cortexin*.

meerschaum. $H_2Mg_2(SiO_3)_3\cdot H_2O$. Sepiolite. A common, porous rock-forming silicate, d.2.

Mees, Charles Edward Kenneth. 1882–1960. British-born American chemist, noted for his pioneer work in photographic science.

mega- (1) M. Prefix (Greek) for large. (2) One million times. (3) A unit of activity of penicillin preparations; million Oxford units.

megabar. A unit of pressure: 1 megabar = 1,000,000 bars = 0.987 atm. It is equivalent to the pressure of one megadyne per square centimeter. (Sometimes used erroneously for millibar.)

megabarye. Megabar.

megacycle. Mc. One million cycles.

megadyne. A unit of work: 1 megadyne = 1,000,000 dynes (about 1 kg).

megaerg. A unit of force: 1 megaerg = 1,000,000 ergs.

megafarad. Macrofarad. A unit of electrical quantity: 1 megafarad = 1,000,000 farads.

megaloblast. The parent cell in the normal development of the red blood corpuscles (U.S. usage).

megameter. 1,000,000 meters.

megarrhizin. A glucoside from the root of *Megarrhiza californica* (Cucurbitaceae).

megaton. A measure of explosive power, equivalent to 1 million tons of TNT.

megavolt. One million volts.

megestrol acetate. A derivative of progesterone used in oral contraceptives.

meglumine iothalamate. $C_{18}H_{26}I_3N_3O_9$ = 809.14. Yellow, viscous liquid; a radiopaque (U.S.P., B.P.).

meiler. A pit or heap of wood covered with soil, for the manufacture of charcoal.

meinorite. A vitreous, white, translucent, native calcium aluminum silicate.

Meissner, Paul Traugott. 1778–1850. Austrian pharmaceutical chemist, noted for his "Handbuch."

MEK. Abbreviation for methyl ethyl ketone.

Meker burner. A bunsen burner with metal screen in an enlarged opening. The gas and air are intimately mixed and thus produce a high temperature (about 1700°C).

mekonine. Meconin.

Mekralon. Trade name for a polypropylene synthetic fiber.

mel. Honey. The saccharine substance deposited by the honeybee, *Apis mellifera*, rich in fructose. Cf. *nectar, ceromel, hydromel, oxymel*.

melaconite. CuO. A native, black copper oxide.

melam. $C_6H_9N_{11}$ = 235.21. White powder, obtained with melamine, by heating potassium thiocyanate and ammonium chloride in intimate contact; insoluble in water. See *albene melem*.

Melamac. Trademark for a melamine-formaldehyde resin.

melamine. $N:C(NH_2)\cdot N:C(NH_2)\cdot N:C(NH_2)$ = 126.7 Cyanurotriamide cyanuramide 2,4,6-triamino-s-triazine. Colorless crystals, slightly soluble in water, insoluble in organic solvents, sublimes 350; forms a plastic with formaldehyde, used to give wet strength to paper.

melaminylphenylarsonic acid. $C_9H_{11}O_3N_6As$ = 326.11. Used, as its disodium salt (melarsen), to treat sleeping sickness.

melampsporin. $C_{23}H_{28}O_{15}$ = 544.34. A glucosidal coloring matter of galls, from *Melampsora goepporriana*. Yellow crystals, m.235.

melampyrine. Dulcitol.

melampyrite. Dulcitol.

melan. Brown oil from *Melilotus coeruleus* (Leguminosae); used to treat burns and ulcers.

melaniline. Diphenylguanidine.

melanin(e). $C_{77}H_{98}O_{33}N_{14}S$ = 1779.2. Black coloring matter (chromoprotein) from certain insects, hair, and dark skins; soluble only in alkali. Cf. *tyrosinase*.

melanite. A black andradite. See iron *garnet*.

melanoidins. Dark-colored substances formed by the interaction of reducing sugars and amino acids when heated; largely responsible for the color of molasses.

melanosis. Diffused pigmentation, usually of the face, caused by shock.

melanterite. $FeSO_4\cdot7H_2O$. A native ferrous sulfate.

melanuric acid. See *isocyanurimide*.

melarsen. See *melaminylphenylarsonic acid*.

melarsoprol. $C_{12}H_{15}ON_6AsS_2$ = 398.31. Creamy,

bitter powder, m.217 (decomp.), insoluble in water; used to treat trypanosomiasis (B.P.).

Melasol. Trade name for an antiseptic emulsion of titrol.

meldola blue. New blue. Naphthol blue. A methylene blue type dye.

melee. A diamond for glass cutting, weighing less than a quarter carat.

melem. $(C_6H_6N_{10})_x$ = 218.2. An amide of cyanuric acid, obtained with melam by heating ammonium thiocyanate.

melene. $C_{30}H_{60}$ = 420.6. Triacontylene. An unsaturated hydrocarbon from beeswax. Colorless fat, d.0.89, m.62, insoluble in water.

meletin. Quercetin.

melezitose. $C_{18}H_{32}O_{16}$ = 504.3. Melicitose. A trisaccharide from manna or the sap of conifers and poplars, which hydrolyzes to glucose and turanose (glucose-fructose). Cf. *melizitose.*

melibiase. An enzyme in bottom (but not top) yeasts, which ferments raffinose.

melibiose. $C_{12}H_{22}O_{11}$ = 342.17. Glucose-α-galactoside. A disaccharide$[α]_D$ + 143°, from Australian manna, yellow mallow, and by hydrolysis of raffinose.

melicitose. Melezitose.

meligrin. A condensation product of dimethyloxyquinine and methylphenylacetamide; used to treat neuralgia.

melilite. (1) Anhydrous calcium-aluminum silicates in igneous rocks. (2) (Al, Fe)$_2$(Ca, Mg)$_3$Si$_2$O$_{10}$.

melilith. Ca$_4$Si$_3$O$_{10}$. A melilite.

melilot. Melilotus, sweet yellow clover. The leaves of *Melilotus officinalis* (Leguminosae) which contains coumarin, coumaric and melilotic acid; a mild anodyne.

melilotic acid. $C_9H_{10}O_3$ = 166.08. o-Hydrocoumaric acid, oxyhydrocinnamic acid, β-phenolpropionic acid from *Melilotus* species. Colorless crystals, m.81 (forms a lactone). **m. lactone.** $C_9H_8O_2$ = 148.06. m.25.

Melinex. Trademark for a polyester synthetic film; it is stretched and heated during manufacture to improve strength.

melinite. A high explosive of the lyddite type.

melissa. The dried leaves and tops of balm, *Melissa officinalis* (Labiatae); a carminative and febrifuge. **m. oil.** Verbena oil. **East Indian-** Lemongrass oil.

melissic acid. $C_{30}H_{60}O_2$ = 452.6. A monobasic, fatty acid from beeswax. Colorless scales, m.90, insoluble in water. **m. alcohol.** Myricyl alcohol. **m. palmitate.** Myricin.

Melissos of Samos. 470–410 B.C. Greek philosopher famous for the statement: "Nothing can come from nothing."

melissyl alcohol. $C_{30}H_{62}O$ = 438.65. Colorless crystals, m.88.

melitic. Mellitic.

melitose. $C_{12}H_{22}O_{11}$ = 342.2. A disaccharide from Australian manna.

melitriose. Raffinose.

melizitose. A sugar from *Alhagi maurorum* (Leguminosae), yielding manna. Cf. *melezitose.*

mellisic. Melisic.

mellite. (1) Pharmacy: medicated honey. (2) Mineralogy: honeystone.

mellitene. $C_6(CH_3)_6$ = 162.1. Hexamethylbenzene. Colorless scales, m.164, insoluble in water.

mellitic acid. $C_6(COOH)_6$ = 342.1. Hexacarboxylbenzene. Colorless needles, m.287, soluble in water. Its aluminum salt occurs in peat as honeystone. **m. imide.** Euchroic acid.

mellitoxin. A poisonous constituent of certain honeys (New Zealand).

melloene. Describing a process for increasing the gluten tenacity of flour by treatment with sulfur dioxide and water vapor.

mellon(e). C_9H_{13} = 121.1. A hydrocarbon obtained, with melam and melem, on igniting mercuric thiocyanate. See *Pharaoh's serpents.*

mellophannic acid. $C_{10}H_6O_8$ = 254.05. Colorless crystals, m.238. Cf. *mallophene, pyromellitic acid.*

Mellor, Joseph William. 1869–1938. English chemist, noted for his handbook of inorganic chemistry.

mellorite. A complex garnet-type lime–ferric oxide silicate.

Mellot's metal. D'Arcet metal.

melon. $(C_6H_3N_9)_x$. An amide of cyanuric acid, obtained with and similar to melem, q.v.

melonite. (1) Ni$_2$Te$_3$. Tellurnickel. Red granules. (2) Ca$_4$Al$_6$Si$_6$O$_{25}$. A silica mineral of the scapolite group.

melting. Fusing. The transformation of a solid into a liquid by means of heat. **m. point.** The temperature at which a solid changes to a liquid; and the liquid and solid phases are in equilibrium under a pressure of 1 atm. The highest known m.p. is 4200°C (a mixture of hafnium carbide 25 and tantalum carbide 75%). The lowest is that of helium. *American m.p.* See *American. m.p. tube.* A capillary tube attached to a thermometer bulb and heated in both until the contents fuse. Cf. *Thiele tube.* **m. salt.** See *salt.*

Melubrin. $C_{12}H_{14}O_4N_2SNa$ = 305.2. Trademark for sodium-1-phenyl-2,3-dimethylpyrazolone sulfonate. Colorless crystals, soluble in water; a nontoxic antipyretic and analgesic.

membrane. A thin, enveloping or lining substance, which divides a space or an organ. **animal-** A skinlike tissue obtained from animal tissues (parchment), used for dialyzing. **semipermeable-** A tissue that permits the passage of certain substances, e.g., water or crystalloids, but prevents the passage of others, e.g., colloids. Classification:
1. Sieves: as such, or coarse filter paper
2. Cell filters: very fine filter paper
3. Bacterial filters: kieselguhr
4. Colloidal filters: parchment or collodion
5. Molecular sieves: copper ferrocyanide

menachanite. Menaccanite, menacanite, menacconite. A titaniferous magnetic iron oxide from Cornwall. Cf. *ilmenite.*

menadiol sodium phosphate. $C_{11}H_8O_8Na_4P_6,6H_2O$ = 530.20. Pink hygroscopic powder with characteristic odor, soluble in water; a prothrombogenic (U.S.P.).

menadione. $C_{11}H_8O_2$ = 172.18. Menaphthone (B.P.). 2-Methylnaphthoquinone. Davitamon-K. Vitamin K$_3$.

MENDELYEEV'S PERIODIC TABLE

Series	Period	0	I R_2O	II RO	III R_2O_3	IV RO_2 RH_4	V R_2O_5 RH_3	VI RO_3 RH_2	VII R_2O_7 RH	VIII
1			H							
2	1	He	Li	Be	B	C	N	O	F	
3	2	Ne	Na	Mg	Al	Si	P	S	Cl	
4	3	A	K	Ca	Sc	Ti	V	Cr	Mn	Fe Co Ni
5			Cu	Zn	Ga	Ge	As	Se	Br	
6	4	Kr	Rb	Sr	Y	Zr	Cb	Mo	Ma	Ru Rh Pd
7			Ag	Cd	In	Sn	Sb	Te	I	
8	5	Xe	Cs	Ba	La	Ce				
9					Rare earths					
10	6					Hf	Ta	W	Re	Os Ir Pt
11			Au	Hg	Tl	Pb	Bi	Po	El	
12	7	Rn	Ve	Ra	Ac	Th	Pa	U		

Yellow crystals, m.106, insoluble in water. A prothrombogenic; an antibleeding supplement for pregnant women. Also used as its sodium bisulfite compound (U.S.P.). On absorption it is converted into vitamin K.

menaphthone. Menadione. Vitamin K_3.

menaphthyl. The methyl naphthyl radical $C_{10}H_7$·-CH$_2$—.

Mendel(y)eev, Dmitri Ivanovitch. Mendeléeff, Mendelejeff. 1834–1907. Russian chemist, one of the discoverers of the periodic law (see *Meyer, Lothar*), and predictor of several *eka* elements. **M. chart.** Periodic table. **M. group.** A vertical group of the periodic table. **M. law.** Periodic law. **M. system.** Periodic system.

mendelevium. Md. An actinide group element, at. no. 101, discovered (1952) by Ghiorso and co-workers by bombarding Es^{253} (einsteinium) with helium accelerated in a cyclotron, to give Md^{256}. Named for Mendeleyev. It forms trivalent positive ions; its isotopes are radioactive.

mendozite. White, fibrous sodium–aluminum sulfate.

meneghinite. $4Pb_2SbS_2$. A native sulfide.

Menformon. Trademark for a brand of female sex hormone; cf. *Theelin*.

menhaden. The fish *Brevoortia tyrannis*, used to make oil and fertilizer.

meniscus. The flat or crescent shaped surface of a liquid in a tube, either concave (when the liquid wets the material of the container, as water and glass), or convex (when liquid does not wet, as mercury and glass). **m. reader.** (1) A colored

streak placed behind a buret to enable the m. to be read more exactly. It is customary to read the lowest point. (2) A lens or clamp and card attached to the buret.

Menispermaceae. Moonseed family, a group of woody, climbing tropical plants; as, *Anamirta paniculata*, cocculus indicus. Cf. *cucoline, deyamittin, diversine sinomenine*.

menispermine. $C_{18}H_{24}N_2O_2 = 300.3$. An alkaloid from *Cocculus indicus* (*Anamirta paniculata*) and *Menispermum canadense*. Colorless crystals.

menispermoid. The combined principles from *Menispermum canadense*.

menispermum. Yellow parilla, moonseed. The dried roots of *M. canadense*; used similarly to sarsaparilla.

menoform. Estrone.

menstruum. A solvent for the extraction of drugs.

mensuration. The act of measuring. **m. formula(e,s).** The mathematical equations by which plain cubical, or spherical figures or bodies are measured.

mentha. (1) Mint, e.g., peppermint. (2) A genus of Labiatae; e.g.: *M. crispa*, spearmint oil; *M. piperita*, peppermint oil; *M. spicata*, spearmint. **m. camphor.** 1-Menthol. **m. viridis.** Spearmint.

menthadiene. A group of terpenes with 2 double bonds, derived from menthane, e.g., $\Delta^{1.8(9)}$-*m*- or 1,8(9) *m*- Sylvestrene. 1,3-*p*- α-Terpinene. 1,4(8)-*p*- Terpinolene. 1,5-*p*- α-Phellandrene. 1(7)2-*p*- β- Phellandrene. 1,8(9)-*p*- Limonene. **m. dione.** Thymoquinone. **m. one.** Carvone.

menthane. $C_{10}H_{20} = 140.2$. Terpane. 4-Isopropyl-1-methylcyclohexane, hexahydrocymene, menthonaphthene. A saturated hydrocarbon parent substance of many terpenes:

$$CH_3 (7)$$
$$CH$$
$$(6) H_2C (1) CH_2 (2)$$
$$(5) H_2C (4) CH_2 (3)$$
$$CH$$
$$CH_3—CH—CH_3$$
$$(9) (8) (10)$$

Colorless liquid, d.0.807, b.169, insoluble in water. **amino-** Menthylamine. **dihydroxy-** Terpine. **epoxy-** Cineole. **3-hydroxy-** Menthol. **m. diol.** Terpinol.

menthanol. A hydroxy derivative of menthane. **2-** Carvomenthol. **3-** Menthol.

menthanone. A keto derivative of menthane, e.g.: **3-** Menthone.

menthe. A peppermint liqueur (crème de menthe), prepared from menthol and alcohol.

menthene. $C_{10}H_{18} = 138.2$. Δ^3-Menthane. Colorless liquid, d.0.814, b.167, insoluble in water. **carvo-** Carvomenthane.

menthenol. A hydroxy derivative of menthene. **3-** Pulegol.

menthenone. A keto derivative of menthene. **3-** $\Delta^{4(8)}$- Pulegone; **3-**$\Delta^{8(9)}$- Isopulegone. Δ^1- Piperitone. Δ^2- Carvenone.

menthol. $C_{10}H_{20}O = 156.27$. Peppermint camphor. 3-hydroxymenthane, menthacamphor. A dextrorotatory terpene alcohol, in many essential oils. Colorless crystals, m.42, slightly soluble in water. Used in perfumery, flavoring extracts, confectionery; for headache, toothache, colds, skin diseases; and as an anodyne, anesthetic, and antispasmodic (U.S.P., B.P.). **m. salicylate.** Salimenthol. **m. valerate.** Validol.

menthonaphthene. Menthane.

menthone. $C_{10}H_{18}O = 154.2$. Δ^3-Hydroxymenthene, 3-terpanone. A dextrorotatory, colorless liquid, d.0.896, b.207, soluble in water. **levo-** Apinol. **ethyl-** The radical 3-menthanyl, C_{10}-H_{19}—, from menthane.
    m. amine. $C_{10}H_{19}NH_2 = 155.1$. 3-Aminomenthane. Colorless liquid, b.205. *carvo-* See *carvomenthylamine.* **m. borate.** $BO_3(C_{10}H_{19})_2$. Estoral Colorless crystals, used in medicine. **m. camphorate.** White powder, insoluble in water; used to treat tuberculosis.

menyanthes. Marsh trefoil, buckbean. The dried leaves of *M. trifoliata* (Gentianaceae); an aromatic bitter.

menyanthin. $C_{33}H_{50}O_{14} = 670.4$. Celastin. A bitter glucoside from the leaves of the buckbean; soluble in water.

menyanthol. $C_7H_{11}O_2 = 111.09$. A split product of menyanthin.

mepacrine. Quinacrine. **m. hydrochloride.** C_{23}-$H_{30}ON_3 \cdot 2HCl \cdot 2H_2O = 508.92$. Metoquin. Yellow, bitter crystals, soluble in water; used to treat malaria (B.P.). **m. methane sulfonate.** Used as m. hydrochloride (B.P.).

mephenesin. $C_{10}H_{14}O_3 = 182.22$. Myanesin. White, bitter crystals, m.72, soluble in water, a muscle relaxant.

mephentermine. Mephine. Trimethyl-β-phenylethylamine. Used as: **m. sulfate.** $(C_{11}H_{17}N)_2 \cdot H_2SO_4,2HO = 460.64$. White crystals, soluble in water; a sympathomimetic (U.S.P., B.P.).

mephitic. Obsolete term for foul, noxious, or poisonous. **m. air.** Black damp, choke damp. Obsolete name for: (1) carbon dioxide, (2) nitrogen.

mephobarbital. Phemitone, q.v.

meprobamate. $C_9H_{18}O_4N_2 = 218.26$. 2,2-Di-(carbamoxymethyl)pentane. White crystals, m.-105, soluble in water; a sedative (B.P.).

mepyramine maleate. $C_{17}H_{23}ON_3 \cdot C_4H_4O_4 = 401.50$. White, bitter powder, m.100, soluble in water; an antihistamine (B.P.).

mer. A monomeric unit.

mer-, mere-, meri- Prefix (Greek) indicating a part.

meralluride. A mixture of methoxyhydroxymercuripropylsuccinylurea and urea theophylline in molecular proportions. Yellow powder, slightly soluble in water; a diuretic (U.S.P.).

merbaphen. $C_{16}H_{19}N_2O_6ClNaHg = 592.1$. Novasurol. A mercury derivative of barbital; a diuretic.

Mercadium. Trademark for an orange- to maroon-colored pigment: principally mercury and cadmium sulfides in a common crystal lattice.

mercaptal. Thioacetal. A compound formed from mercaptans and aldehydes in the presence of hydrochloric acid; $R' \cdot CHO + 2HSR'' = H_2O + R' \cdot CH(SR'')_2$. Cf. *mercaptol.*

mercaptan. (1) Ethyl mercaptan. (2) A hydrosulfide or compound containing the radical —SH; indicated by the prefix *mercapto-* and the suffix *-thiol.*

mercaptan acid. A compound containing the radicals —SH and —COOH, e.g., $HS \cdot CH_2 \cdot COOH$, thioglycolic acid.

mercaptide. R—SM. Metal mercaptan. A derivative of mercaptans, in which the sulfur hydrogen is replaced by a metal; thus, R is an aryl or alkyl radical, and M a metal.

mercapto- Prefix indicating a thiol group, —SH. **m. succinic acid.** Thiomalic acid. **m. sulfothiobiazole.** Bismuthiole.

mercaptol. $R_2C(SR')_2$. Mercaptans and ketones combine in the presence of acid to form mercaptols. Cf. *mercaptal.*

mercaptomerin sodium. $C_{16}H_{25}O_6NSHgNa_2 = 606.04$. White, hygroscopic powder, soluble in water; a diuretic (U.S.P.).

mercaptophenyl- Prefix indicating the presence of the radical $HS \cdot C_6H_4$—. **m. dithiodiazolone.** $C_8H_6N_2$-$S_3 = 226.05$. White crystals. A reagent for bismuth (red precipitate). Cf. *bismuthiole.*

mercaptopurine. $C_5H_4N_4S \cdot H_2O = 170.23$. Yellow crystals, m.300 (decomp.), insoluble in water; an antimetabolite (B.P.).

mercaptothiazole. The hypothetical ring compound $CH:CH \cdot N \cdot C(SH) \cdot S$.

Mercer, John. 1791–1866. English cotton printer who invented the mercerization process (1850); developed practically (1889) by Horace Arthur Lowe. **M. process.** Mercerization.

mercerization. Treatment of cotton with 25% caustic soda, causing it to shrink and become stronger, denser, and acquire a milky luster; it then becomes unshrinkable and easily dyed.

mercur- Prefix indicating a mercury compound. **m. ammonium.** Mercurammonium. **m. diammonium.** The radical $Hg(NH_3)_2=$. **m. diammonium chloride.** $Hg(NH_3Cl)_2 = 305.9$. An infusible, white precipitate obtained from Hg^{++} and Cl^- in the presence of NH_4^+.

mercurammonium- Prefix indicating NHg_2X, where X is a halogen, and Hg_2 has replaced the H_4 of ammonium; as, m. bromide, NHg_2Br. Cf. *mercuriammonium*.

mercuration. Mercurization.

mercurial. A drug containing mercury. **m. oil.** Grey oil.

mercurialine. A supposed alkaloid of *Mercurialis annua* (Euphorbiaceae); probably methylamine.

mercurialis. The dried herb of *M. perennis*.

mercuriammonium. Mercuric ammonium. A double salt of NHg_2X with 1 or 3 molecules of NH_4X: as, $2HgNH_2Cl$. Cf. *mercurammonium*.

mercuric. A compound of mercury, containing the $Hg=$ atom. **m. acetate.** $Hg(C_2H_3O_2)_2 = 318.7$. White crystals, soluble in water; a reagent, antisyphilitic, and cosmetic. *m.a. pyridyl.* An antiseptic, used in water treatment. **m. acetylide.** $3C_2Hg \cdot H_2O = 691.8$. Explosive, white powder, insoluble in water. **m. amidosuccinate.** $Hg(C_4H_7N_2O_3)_2$. Colorless needles, insoluble in water; an antisyphilitic. **m. aminophenyl arsenate.** M. atoxylate. **m. ammonium chloride.** $HgNH_2Cl = 251.8$. Mercuriammonium chloride, white precipitate, ammoniated mercury. White powder, insoluble in water, soluble in ammonium carbonate solutions; an antiseptic and alterant. **m. ammonium propionate.** $HgNH_2C_3H_4O_2 = 288.6$. Mercuriammonium propionate. White needles, soluble in water; an antisyphilitic. **m. anilinate.** $Hg(C_6H_4NH_2)_2 = 384.3$. White microcrystals, insoluble in water; an antisyphilitic. **m. arsenate.** $Hg_3(AsO_4)_2 = 879.7$. Yellow powder, insoluble in water; an antisyphilitic. **m. atoxylate.** $C_{12}H_{14}O_6N_2As_2Hg$. M. *p*-aminophenyl arsonate, asiphyl, aspirochyl, atoxylmercury. White powder, insoluble in water; an antisyphilitic. **m. benzoate.** $Hg(C_7H_5O_2)_2 \cdot 2H_2O = 478.6$. Colorless crystals, insoluble in water; an antysyphilitic and used to treat skin diseases. **m. bichromate.** $HgCr_2O_7 = 416.5$. Red, crystals, insoluble in water. **m. borate.** M. pyroborate. **m. bromide.** $HgBr_2 = 360.4$. Mercury dibromide. Colorless, rhombs, m.235, soluble in water; an antisyphilitic. **m. cacodylate.** $Hg(Me_2AsO_2)_2$. M. methyl arsenate. White crystals, soluble in water; used in ampul medication. **m. carbolate.** M. phenolate. **m. carbonate.** $HgCO_3 = 260.3$. White powder, insoluble in water. Known chiefly as its basic salts, $HgCO_3 \cdot 2HgO$, and $HgCO_3 3HgO$. **m. chloride.** $HgCl_2 = 271.5$. Corrosive sublimate, sublimate, corrosive mercury chloride, mercury bichloride. Poisonous white rhombs (antidote: 10 % sodium thiosulfate solution), m.287, soluble in water. Used to preserve wood and museum specimens; as an insecticide, rodenticide, mordant, antiseptic, caustic, and reagent; and in tanning, embalming, purification of gold, photography, textile printing, etching of steel and iron, and dyeing furs. **m. chloroiodide.** $HgCl_2 \cdot HgI_2 = 725.8$. Red crystals, soluble in alcohol; an antisyphilitic. **m. chromate.** $HgCrO_4 = $

316.4. Yellow crystals, insoluble in water. **m. cyanide.** $Hg(CN)_2 = 252.6$. Colorless tetragons, decomp. by heat, slightly soluble in water. Used in photography and in manufacturing cyanogen; as an antiseptic, antisyphilitic, and tonic; and a reagent for palladium. **m. diiodosalicylate.** $Hg(C_7H_3I_2O_3)_2$. Yellow powder, insoluble in water. **m. ethyl chloride.** Colorless scales, soluble in water; an antisyphilitic. **m. ferrocyanide.** $Hg_2Fe(CN)_6 = 612.8$. Brown powder, insoluble in water. **m. fluosilicate.** $HgSiF_6 \cdot 6H_2O = 450.76$. Rhombohedra. **m. fulminate.** $Hg(ONC)_2 \cdot \frac{1}{2}H_2O = 293.6$. Colorless, rhombs, explode on detonating or at 175°C, slightly soluble in water; a detonator. **m. gallate.** $[C_6H_2(OH)_3 COO]_2Hg$. Dark green powder, insoluble in water; an antisyphilitic. **m. halides.** The divalent halogen compounds of mercury, HgX_2. *alkyl-* $RHgX$, where R is an aliphatic or alkyl radical. *aryl-* $RHgX$, where R is an aryl or aromatic radical. **m. hydroxide.** $Hg(OH)_2 = 234.6$. White powder, insoluble in water. **m. hydroxides.** Compounds of the type $RHgOH$. **m. iodate.** $Hg(IO_3)_2 = 550.4$. White powder, insoluble in water. **m. iodide.** $HgI_2 = 454.4$. *red-* Mercury biniodide. Red tetragons, m.241, insoluble in water; an alterative, antiseptic, and antisyphilitic. *yellow-* Yellow rhombs, m.241, insoluble in water. **m. lactate.** $Hg(C_3H_5O_3)_2 = 378.4$. White, crystals, slightly soluble in water; an antisyphilitic. **m. lithium iodide.** $HgI_2 \cdot 2LiI = 722.4$. Mercuricide. Yellow powder, soluble in water; an antisyphilitic. **m. naphtholate.** $Hg(C_{10}H_7O)_2 = 486.6$. β-Naphtholmercury. Yellow powder, insoluble in water; an antiseptic. **m. nitrate.** $Hg(NO_3)_2 = 324.6$. White, hygroscopic powder, m.79 (decomp.), soluble in water; a reagent and antisyphilitic. *basic-* (1) $2Hg(NO_3)_2, 2H_2O = 685.29$. Deliquescent, colorless crystals. (2) $2Hg(OH) \cdot NO_3 \cdot H_2O = 577.27$. (3) $Hg(NO_3)_2 \cdot 2HgO \cdot H_2O = 775.87$. White, unstable powder. **m. oleate.** $Hg(C_{18}H_{33}O_2)_2 = 763.0$. Yellow or red solution of m. oxide in oleic acid, insoluble in water; an antiseptic and antisyphilitic. **m. oxalate.** $HgC_2O_4 = 288.61$. White powder, insoluble in water. **m. oxide.** $HgO = 216.6$. *red-* Hydrargyri oxydum rubrum, red mercury oxide. Red, monoclinic prisms, decomp. by heat, insoluble in water. Used in the manufacture of mercury salts, paints and pigments for ship keels, ceramics; and as a stimulant, caustic, and parasiticide. *yellow-* Hydrargyri oxydum flavum, yellow precipitate. Orange tetragonal crystals, insoluble in water; a parasiticide. **m. oxycyanide.** $HgO \cdot Hg(CN)_2 = 469.2$. White crystals, soluble in water; an antiseptic. **m. phenolate.** $Hg(C_6H_5O)_2 = 386.7$. Mercury phenolate, m. carbolate, phenol mercury. Gray or pink powder, insoluble in water; an antiseptic and antisyphilitic. **m. phenyl acetate.** $HgC_6H_5 \cdot C_2H_3O_2 = 336.7$. Colorless prisms, m.149, soluble in alcohol. **m. phosphate.** $Hg_3(PO_4)_2 = 791.9$. White powder, insoluble in water. *acid-* $HgHPO_4 = 296.3$. White powder, insoluble in water; an antisyphilitic. **m. potassium cyanide.** $HgK(CN)_3 = 317.7$. Potassium mercury cyanide. Colorless crystals, soluble in water; used in the manufacture of mirrors, and as an antiseptic. **m. potassium iodide.**

$HI_2 \cdot 2KI = 786.5$. Mayer's reagent. Yellow, deliquescent crystals, soluble in water; a reagent for alkaloids. Cf. *Toulet's* solution. **m. potassium thiosulfate.** $3Hg(S_2O_3)_2 \cdot 5K_2S_2O_3$. Colorless crystals, soluble in water; an antisyphilitic. **m. pyroborate.** $HgB_4O_7 = 355.9$. Mercuric tetraborate. Brown powder, insoluble in water. **m. rhodanate.** Mercuric thiocyanate. **m. salicylate.** $Hg(C_7H_5O_3)_2 = 474.6$. White powder, insoluble in water; an antiseptic, antisyphilitic, and alterant. **m. santonate.** $Hg(C_{15}H_{19}O_4) = 463.5$. Colorless powder. **m. silicofluoride.** $Hg_2SiF \cdot_6 2H_2O = 579.3$. Prismatic crystals, soluble in water; an antiseptic. **m. stearate.** $Hg(C_{18}H_{35}O_2)_2 = 767.0$. Yellow, granules, soluble in alcohol; used in ointments. **m. subsulfate.** $HgSO_4 \cdot 2HgO = 729.9$. Basic m. sulfate, turpeth mineral, Queen's yellow; powder, insoluble in water. **m. succinate.** $Hg(C_4H_4O_4) = 316.6$. Colorless crystals, insoluble in water. *imido-* M. succinimide. **m. succinimide.** $Hg[C_2H_4(CO)_2N]_2 = 372.5$. M. imidosuccinate. White crystals, soluble in water; an antiseptic and antisyphilitic. **m. sulfate.** $HgSO_4 = 296.7$. M. bisulfate, m. persulfate. Yellow powder, decomp. by heat, soluble in water. Used to manufacture calomel; in the extraction of gold and silver, in electric batteries; and as an antisyphilitic. *basic-* M. subsulfate. *hydrous-* (1) $HgSO_4 \cdot 2H_2O = 332.71$. (Erroneously called "basic.") Yellow crystals, soluble in water. (2) $3HgO \cdot SO_3 \cdot 4H_2O = 962.10$. Yellow powder. **m. sulfide.** $HgS = 232.7$. *black-* Black mercury sulfide, metacinnabarite. Black powder, insoluble in water; a pigment. *red-* Red mercury sulfide, artificial cinnabar, vermilion, cinnabar. Red rhombohedra, sublimes 446, insoluble in water; a pigment and fumigant. **m. sulfite.** $HgSO_3 = 280.6$. White powder, becomes pink with age, soluble in water. **m. sulfocyanide, m. thiocyanate.** $Hg(CNS)_2 = 316.6$. M. rhodanate, m. sulfocyanate. White powder, usually pressed into sticks, decomp. by heat. When ignited it glows and forms a voluminous, cohesive, and light ash (Pharaoh's serpent, q.v.), insoluble in water; used in photography. **m. urate.** $HgC_5H_2O_3N_4 = 366.6$. Yellow powder, insoluble in water. **m. xanthates.** $R \cdot HgS \cdot CS \cdot OR$. R is an aliphatic or aromatic radical.

mercuricide. Mercuric lithium iodide.

mercurides. R_2Hg. R is a hydrocarbon radical. See *mercury methide*, and *ethide*.

mercurification. Amalgamation. Cf. *mercurization*.

mercurimetry. The determination of a substance by precipitating it with a mercury salt and ascertaining the mercury in the precipitate.

mercuriovegetal. Manaca.

mercuripapain. $(RS)_2Hg(?)$. A compound of papain (RSH) and mercuric chloride.

mercurius. Mercury. **m. praecipitatus.** The "red precipitate," HgO, of the Latin alchemist Geber. **m. vitae.** Antimony oxychloride.

mercurization. The introduction of mercury into the formula of an organic compound.

mercuroammonium. $HgNH_3X$. Mercurous ammonium. A double salt. **m. chloride.** $HgNH_3Cl$. Black powder.

Mercurochrome. $C_{20}H_8O_6Na_2Br_2Hg$. Trademark for disodium dibromohydroxymercurifluorescein.

Iridescent, green crystals, soluble in water (red color); a genitourinary antiseptic, less irritating than tincture of iodine. Cf. *apagallin*.

mercurol. Mercury nucleinate. A compound of mercury and nucleic acid made from yeast (20% Hg). Brown powder, soluble in water; an astringent, antisyphilitic, and antipyretic.

mercurophen. Sodium hydroxymercury *o*-nitrophenolate. Red powder, soluble in water; a germicide.

mercurophylline. A molecular mixture of sodium β-ethoxy-γ-hydroxymercuripropylaminetrimethyl-cyclopentanonedicarboxylic acid and theophylline, soluble in water. A diuretic (U.S.P.).

mercurous. A compound of monovalent mercury, $Hg-: Hg_2X_2$, where X is a monovalent acid radical. **m. acetate.** $HgC_2H_3O_2 = 259.6$. Colorless, crystals, soluble in water; an antisyphilitic. **m. arsenite.** $Hg_3AsO_3 = 724.8$. Brown powder, insoluble in water; a parasiticide. **m. benzoate.** $HgC_7H_5O_2 = 321.3$. Colorless crystals, insoluble in water; an antiseptic. **m. bitartrate.** $HgHC_4H_4O_6 = 349.3$. Colorless crystals, insoluble in water. **m. bromide.** $HgBr = 280.5$. Yellow tetragons, sublime 350, insoluble in water; a substitute for calomel. **m. carbonate.** $Hg_2CO_3 = 461.2$. Yellow powder, slowly decomp., insoluble in water. **m. chloride.** $HgCl = 236.1$. Hydrargyri chloridum mite, calomel, m. monochloride, mild m. chloride, m. subchloride, m. protochloride; native as horn quicksilver. Colorless rhombs or tetragons, sublimes 303, insoluble in water. Used as a reagent, cathartic, intestinal antiseptic, alterative, green pyrotechnic; and in ceramics, for gold colors. **m. chromate.** $Hg_2CrO_4 = 517.2$. Red powder, insoluble in water, decomp. by heat. **m. citrate.** $Hg_3C_6H_5O_7 = 790.8$. Colorless powder, slightly soluble in water. **m. diammonium acetate.** $Hg(NH_2)_2(C_2H_3O_2)_2 \cdot H_2O = 370.74$. White rectangular plates, soluble in water. **m. fluosilicate.** $Hg_2SiF_6 \cdot 2H_2O = 579.29$. Colorless prisms. **m. formate.** $H \cdot COOHg = 245.62$. White scales, soluble in water. **m. iodide.** $HgI = 327.5$. Yellow m. iodide, hydrargyri iodidum flavum m. protiodide, m. monoiodide. Yellow tetragons, m.290, insoluble in water; an alterative and antisyphilitic. **m. iodobenzene-p-sulfonate.** Anogen. Yellow crystals, insoluble in water; an antisyphilitic. **m. lactate.** $HgC_3H_5O_3 = 289.3$. White, crystals, soluble in water; an antisyphilitic. **m. nitrate.** $HgNO_3 \cdot 2H_2O = 298.6$. Colorless monoclinic crystals, decomp. by heat, soluble in water; a reagent, antiseptic, caustic, and antisyphilitic. **m. oxalate.** $HgC_2O_4 = 489.22$. White powder, insoluble in water. **m. oxide.** $Hg_2O = 417.2$. Black powder, insoluble in water. *Hahnemann's-* $Hg_2O \cdot Hg_2NH_2NO_3 = 896.4$. Black precipitate, mercurius solubilis, Hahnemann's mercury. Black powder, insoluble in water; an antisyphilitic. **m. phosphate.** $Hg_3PO_4 = 681.2$. Colorless powder, insoluble in water. **m. potassium tartrate.** $HgKC_4H_4O_6 = 387.74$. White crystals, insoluble in water. **m. protoxide.** Black m. oxide. Native as montroydite. **m. santonate.** $HgC_{15}H_{19}O_4 = 463.5$. White powder, insoluble in water. **m. sulfate.** $Hg_2SO_4 = 497.3$. White, monoclinic crystals, decomp. by heat, soluble in water; used for batteries and standard cells. **m. sulfide.** $Hg_2S = 433.3$. Black powder, insoluble in water. **m. tannate.** $Hg_2OH(C_{14}H_9O_9)_3$. Hydrargotin. Gray powder; an antisyphilitic. **m. tartrate.** $Hg_2C_4H_4$-$O_6 = 549.25$. Yellow crystals, insoluble in water. *acid*- $HgHC_4H_4O_6 = 349.65$. M. bitartrate. White crystals, insoluble in water.

mercuroxyammonium. $NH_2Hg_2O \cdot X$. A double salt: e.g., m. chloride, $NH_2Hg_2O \cdot Cl$.

mercury. Hg $= 200.61$. Hydrargyrum. Quicksilver, mercurius, liquid silver. A liquid metal element, at. no. 80. Silver-white, metallic liquid, d.13.595, freezing at -38.8, b.357.2, insoluble in water, soluble in nitric acid. M. occurs in nature chiefly as sulfide (cinnabar). It forms mercurous (valency 1) and mercuric (valency 2) compounds. Used as a catalyst (Kjeldahl nitrogen determination); for filling thermometers and apparatus and for silvering mirrors; in electric cells, amalgams with gold and silver, electric rectifiers, and vacuum-tube lights; and in explosives manufacture. **ammoniated-** $NH_2HgCl = 252.09$. Sal alembroth, white precipitate, hydrargyrum ammoniatum, mercury and ammonium chloride. White powder, insoluble in water; an antiparasitic (U.S.P.). **aryl-** Phenyl m. used in foliage sprays. **biphenyl-** M. biphenyl. **repurified-** Redistilled m. used for dental amalgams or electrodes. **soluble-** See *soluble*. **vegetable-** Manacine.

m. acetate, m. acetylide, etc. See *mercuric and mercurous*. **m. alkylides.** HgR_2. R is a monovalent alkyl radical, e.g., m. ethide. **m. alloys.** Mixtures of m. with other metals. If liquid or semiliquid they are termed amalgams. **m. amalgams.** See *m. alloys*, and *amalgams*. **m. arc.** An electric arc between m. electrodes. **m. arylides.** Organic compounds of m. and an aryl radical, e.g., m. phenide. **m. bichloride** (U.S.P.). M. chloride. **m. biiodide.** Mercuric iodide. **m. biphenyl.** Hg-$(C_6H_4Ph)_2 = 506.75$. Colorless crystals, m.216. **m. boiler.** A power plant using m. vapor instead of steam. **m. cathode.** (1) See dropping *electrode*. (2) The positive electrode in a rectifier or a m. vacuum-tube lamp. Cf. *polarograph*. *m. c. cup.* A glass cylinder with fused-in platinum electrode; used for the electrolytic determination of m. **m. chloride.** See *mercuric chloride* (sublimate), and *mercurous chloride* (calomel). *corrosive-* Mercuric chloride. *mild-* Mercurous chloride. *ethyl m.c.** $C_2H_5HgCl = 265.11$. Ethylmercuric chloride. White, iridescent crystals, m.193. *methyl m.c.** $CH_3HgCl = 251.09$. Silver crystals, m.170. *phenyl m.c.** $C_6H_5HgCl = 313.11$. Chloromercury benzene. White leaflets, m.251. *p-tolyl m.c.** $Me \cdot C_6H_4HgCl = 327.12$. *p*-Chloromercury toluene. Silky crystals, m.233, insoluble in water. **m. cup.** (1) A small tray containing m. into which wires are dipped to make electric contact. (2) The glass bulb of a thermometer containing m. **m. dibenzyl.** $Hg(C_7H_7)_2 = 382.72$. Long needles, soluble in alcohol. **m. dibutyl.** $Hg(C_4H_9)_2 = 314.75$. Colorless liquid, d.1.835, b.205. **m. diethyl.** M. ethide. **m. dimethyl.** M. methide. M. **dinaphthyl.** M. naphthide. **m. diphenyl.** (1) M. phenide. (2) M. biphenyl. **m. dipropyl.** $Hg(C_3H_7)_2 = 286.72$. Colorless liquid, b.190, insoluble in water. **m. ditolyl.** $Hg(C_7H_7)_2 = 382.72$. White powder, m.107. **m. dropping**

electrode. See *electrode*. **m. ethide.** $HgEt_2 = 258.7$. M. diethyl. Colorless liquid, b.159, insoluble in water. **m. furnace.** A retort for distilling m. from cinnabar. **m. gatherer.** A stirrer for collecting m. from amalgams and rock material. **m. helide.** $HgHe_{10}$. A supposed compound. **m. mass.** See *mass*. **m. mercaptide.** $Hg(SEt)_2 = 322.8$. Colorless leaflets, m.86, insoluble in water. EtSHgCl also exists. **m. methide.** $HgMe_2 = 230.66$. M. dimethyl. Colorless liquid, b.96, insoluble in water. **m. minerals.** The chief ores of m. are native m. and its sulfide: cinnabar, HgS; and montroydite, HgO. **m. naphthide.** Hg-$(C_{10}H_7)_2 = 454.71$. Dinaphthylmercury. White powder, m.188. **m. nitrate.** See *mercuric and mercurous*. **m. nucleinate.** Mercurol. **m. ointment.** Blue *mass*. **m. ore.** (1) Native m. (2) Cinnabar. **m. oxide.** See *m. peroxide, mercuric*, and *mercurous oxide*. *black-* Mercurous oxide. *red-* Mercuric oxide. *yellow-* Mercuric oxide. **m. periodide.** $HgI_6 = 962.20$. Brown unstable powder. **m. peroxide.** $HgO_2 = 232.61$. Red powder, stable in absence of water. **m. phenide.** $HgPh_2 = 354.4$. White powder, m.120, insoluble in water. **m. phosphate.** See *mercuric, mercurous*. **m. potassium iodide solution.** See *Toulet's solution*. **m. protiodide.** Mercurous iodide. **m. protochloride.** Mercurous chloride. **m. protoxide.** Mercurous oxide. **m. pump.** Sprengel pump. **m. rhodanate, m. rhodanide.** Mercuric thiocyanate. **m. saccharate.** Mercury 1, sugar 2 pts.; a vermifuge. **m. subchloride.** Mercurous chloride. **m. subsulfate.** Mercuric subsulfate. **m. sulfuret.** See *mercuric or mercurous sulfide*. *black-* Mercurous sulfide. *red-* Mercuric sulfide. **m. thiocyanate reagent.** A solution of mercuric chloride and ammonium thiocyanate in water gives crystals of characteristic shape with copper, cobalt, and zinc solutions. **m. trap.** M. well. A box used in amalgamators to prevent the escape of m. **m. vapor lamp.** An evacuated glass tube containing some m. which is vaporized and gives an intense blue light in an electric discharge; used in photography and as an ultraviolet light source.

mergal. Mercuric cholate 1, albumin tannate 2 pts.; an antisyphilitic.

meridian. A geographical unit: 4 quadrants or 40,000,000 meters.

merino. Botany; a fine animal textile fiber from m. sheep.

Merinova. Trade name for a synthetic protein fiber.

meriquinone. A compound whose electronic constellation resembles that of a quinone but which contains no oxygen; as, *Wurster's red*.

merit number. A numerical expression of the quality of a steel: ultimate strength, psi $\times$ elongation, in.

merochrome. A chromoisomeric crystal having 2 isomeric forms.

merotropy. Desmotropy. Cf. *tautomerism*.

merperidine hydrochloride. $C_{15}H_{21}O_2N \cdot HCl = 283.81$. White crystals, m.187, soluble in water; an analgesic (U.S.P.).

merron. Proton.

mersalyl. $C_{13}H_{16}O_6NHg = 505.88$. White, bitter crystals, soluble in water; a diuretic (U.S.P., B.P.).

Mersolate. Trade name for alkyl sulfonate detergents prepared by the sulfochlorination of Fischer-Tropsch paraffins.

Mersolite. Trademark for mercury phenyl salicylate; a disinfectant.

Merthiolate. $C_2H_5 \cdot HgS \cdot C_6H_4 \cdot COONa$. Trademark for thiomersal. Sodium ethyl mercury thiosalicylate. Colorless crystals, soluble in water; a germicide.

merwinite. $3CaO \cdot MgO \cdot 2SiO_2$. An orthosilicate in refractory bricks and blast-furnace slags, m. (approx.) 1590; formed when the mixed oxides of calcium, magnesium, and silica are heated at 1500.

mes-, meso- Prefix (Greek) meaning middle or intermediate.

mesaconic acid. $C_5H_6O_4 = 130.1$. Methylfumaric acid. Unsaturated, dibasic acid and isomer of citraconic acid. Colorless needles, m.202, soluble in water. Cf. *fumaric acids*.

mesantoin. Trademark for methoin.

mescal. An intoxicating spirit distilled from pulque, the fermented juice of *Agave* (Mexico).

mescal buttons. The dried buds or young leaves of *Anhalonium lewinii*, q.v.; a cardiac tonic and narcotic. Cf. *lophophorine, pellotine*.

mescaline. $(3,4,5-)MeO \cdot C_6H_2 \cdot CH_2CH_2NH_2(-1) = 211.2$. 3,4,5-Trimethoxyphenylethylamine. An alkaloid from *Anhalonium lewinii*, a cactus species of Central America; related to adrenaline.

mesembrene. $C_{28}H_{56} = 392.45$. An unsaturated hydrocarbon from *Mesembryanthemum expansum* (Ficoidaceae or Aizoaceae).

mesembrine. $C_{16}H_{19}NO_4 = 289.15$. An alkaloid from *Mesembryanthemum tortuosum*, the kougoed of channa (Aizoaceae), S. Africa.

mesh. The number of openings per unit area in a sieve. See *particles*.

mesicerin. $C_6H_3(CH_2OH)_3 = 168.1$. Mesitylene-glycerol. Colorless, viscous liquid.

mesidine. $C_9H_{13}N = 135.1$. 2,4,6-Trimethylaniline. Colorless liquid, d.0.963, b.233.

mesitene lactone. Dimethyl *coumalin*.

mesitic acid. Uvitic acid.

mesitilol. Mesitylene.

mesitine spar. Mesitite.

mesitite. $2MgCO_3 \cdot FeCO_3$. Mesitine spar. A native carbonate.

mesitol. $Me_3C_6H_2OH = 136.1$. Mesitylene alcohol, 2,4,6-trimethylphenol. Colorless crystals, m.69.

mesiton. See *pyridostigmine* (B.P.).

mesityl. The radical $C_6H_3Me_2CH_2-$, from mesitylene. **m. alcohol.** Mesitol. **m. chloride.** Chloromesityl. **m. oxide.** $MeCO \cdot CH:CMe_2 = 98.11$. 4-Methyl-$\Delta^3$-2-pentenone. Colorless liquid, d.0.858, b.131.

mesitylene. $C_6H_3Me_3 = 120.2$. Mesitylol, *sym-* or 1,3,5-trimethylbenzene. Colorless liquid, d.0.86, b.164, insoluble in water. **chloro-** Chloromesitylene. **dihydroxy-** Mesorcinol. **hexahydro-** 1,3,5-Hexahydrocumene. **hydroxy-** Mesitol. **m. alcohol.** Mesitol. **m. carboxylic acid.** 2,4,6-Trimethylbenzoic acid. **m. glycerol.** Mesicerin. **m. lactone.** Dimethyl *coumalin*.

mesitylenic acid. Mesitylinic acid.

mesitylinic acid. $Me_2C_6H_3COOH = 150.13$. Mesitylenic acid, *sym*-dimethylbenzoic acid. White monoclinic crystals, m.166, slightly soluble in water. **hydroxy-** See *phenol acids*.

mesitylol. Mesitylene.

mesityl oxide. See *mesityl*.

meso- Prefix indicating between.

mesocolloid.. Particles 250 to 2500 Å long, consisting of 100 to 1,000 molecules; between *hemicolloids* and *eucolloids*.

mesoform. Mesomer. An optically inactive isomer containing asymmetric C atoms with internal compensation of the optical rotation; one C atom is dextrorotatory, the other levorotatory. Cf. *racemic* mixture.

mesohydry. A form of tautomerism which assumes divided valencies or oscillating bonds, especially between hydrogen and other atoms.

mesomer. Meso form.

mesomeric. Pertaining to the meso form.

mesomerism. (1) Desmotropism. (2) Resonance.

mesomethylene carbon. The 7th C atom in the camphane or menthane structure, which forms a bridge in the ring system.

mesomorphic. The anisotropic liquid crystal shape, intermediate in properties between the true liquid and the crystal states.

mesomorphous. See *turbostratic*. Cf. *mesomorphic*.

meson. (1) In general, a particle of mass intermediate between that of a proton and an electron. (2) A subatomic particle of mass 200 electron units. A $+$m. is emitted when a proton changes to a neutron. **π-m.** A positively or negatively charged particle having a mass 285 (π-m.) or 215 (μ-m.) times that of an electron. π-mesons have a mean life of 2×10^{-8} sec., and decay into $+\mu$-m. **β-m.** A negatively charged π-m. which, when captured by a nucleus, activates a photographic emulsion. **ρ-m.** A negatively charged μ-m. which does not affect a photographic emulsion. ρ-mesons occur in cosmic rays, and represent different stages of radioactive decay. **μ-m.** Muon.

mesonin. A protein constituent, 25% of wheat gluten.

mesoparaffins. See *paraffin*.

mesophilic. Describing organisms of optimum growth at temperature 25–40°C. Cf. *psychrophilic, thermophilic*.

mesophyll. The cellular structure of a leaf, through which water vapor passes.

meso position. (1) That of a substituting radical attached to a C atom between the 2 hetero atoms in a ring; indicated by the Greek letter μ. (2) The 5- or 10-position in the anthracene ring. (3) The 10-position in phenanthridine.

mesorcin. Mesorcinol.

mesorcinol. $C_9H_{12}O_2 = 152.1$. A homolog of resorcinol: mesorcin, 2,4,6-trimethylresorcinol. Colorless, lustrous scales, m.150, insoluble in water.

mesotan. $C_6H_4(OH)COOCH_2OMe = 182.1$. Ericin, methyloxy methyl salicylate. Yellow liquid, d.1.2, soluble in water; an anodyne.

mesotartaric acid. $C_4H_6O_6 \cdot H_2O = 168.1$. Colorless scales, m.140, soluble in water. See *tartaric acid*.

mesothorium. MsTh. A radioactive isotope of radium formed from thorium. See *radioactive elements*. Produced technically from thorium minerals; used in luminous pigments, and medicinally, for its radium emanations (250 times as active as radium). **m.1.** $MsTh_1$. An isotope of element 88, at. wt. 228, average life 9.7 years. **m.2.** $MsTh_2$. An isotope of element 89, at. wt. 228, average life 8.84 hours. **m. mud.** Barium carbonate containing m. and radium carbonates; a source of m.

mesotomy. The separation of optically inactive, isomers into equal parts of dextro- and levo-rotatory compounds. Cf. *inversion, resolution.*

mesoxalate. A salt of mesoxalic acid.

mesoxalic acid. $COOH \cdot C(OH)_2 \cdot COOH = 136.1$ Propandioldiacid, dioxymalonic acid, oxomalonic acid, oxopropanedioic acid*. Hygroscopic, colorless needles, m.120, soluble in water. **anhydrous-** $COOH \cdot CO \cdot COOH$. Oxymalonic acid, from which the mesoxalyl radical is derived.

mesoxalyl. The radical $CO(COO) =$, from anhydrous mesoxalic acid.

mesoxalylurea. Alloxan.

mesozoic. An era of geologic (q.v.) time, between the paleozoic and cenozoic eras.

mesquite gum. Brown resin from *Prosopis juliflora* (Leguminosae), New Mexico, Texas; resembling gum arabic.

mestinon. Pyridostigmine bromide.

mesudan. Marfanil.

mesulphen. $C_{14}H_{12}S_2 = 244.43$. Mitigal. Dimethylthianthrene. Yellow oil, insoluble in water; used to treat scabies and acne (B.P.C.).

met-, meta Prefix (Greek: beyond, over, or after), indicating: (1) the 1,3-position of benzene (cf. *ortho-*); (2) a transformation; as, in petrology; (3) a polymeric compound, e.g., metaldehyde; (4) a less hydrous acid, e.g., metaphosphoric acid; (5) a derivative of a complex compound, e.g., a meta-protein.

metaacetaldehyde. Metaldehyde.

metaacetone. Diethyl ketone.

metaaluminates. Aluminates.

metaarsenate. A salt of the type $MAsO_3$.

metaarsenic acid. See *arsenic acid.*

metaarsenite. A salt of the type $MAsO_2$.

metabolic. Pertaining to metabolism.

metabolism. The result of chemical reactions in a living cell or organism, by which food is transformed into living protoplasm, reserve materials are stored up, and waste materials are eliminated. **analytic-** Catabolism, or destructive m. The conversion of complex into simpler compounds; as, proteins to aminoacids. **basal-** The energy m. of an individual at rest. **constructive-** Anabolism, or synthetic m. The processes which build complex from simpler compounds. **destructive-** Analytic m. **energy-** The heat liberated by a living organism. **synthetic-** Constructive.

metabolite. A product of biological activity of importance in metabolism. **anti-** A substance that opposes metabolic reactions.

metaborate. A salt of the type MBO_2.

metaboric acid. See *boric acid.*

metacasein. An intermediate protein in the digestion of caseinogen to casein by pancreatic juice.

metacellulose. An isomer of cellulose (fungi and lichens), insoluble in cuprammonium.

metacenter. The center of gravity of that portion of a floating body which is not submerged. For stable flotation it should be as high as possible above the centre of gravity of the body.

metacetaldehyde. Metaldehyde.

metacetin. Methacetin.

metacetone. Diethyl ketone.

metacetonic acid. Propionic acid.

metachemistry. See *chemistry.*

metachromatic. Describing the property of certain substances which appear in different colors according to the wavelength of the light in which they are viewed.

metacinnabarite. HgS. A black, native sulfide.

metacompound. A derivative of benzene obtained by substitution of the first and third atoms.

metacresol. See *cresol.* **m. purple.** Cresol purple. **m. sulfonphthalein.** A pH indicator, changing at pH 2 from red (acid) to yellow (alkaline); and at pH 8.5 from yellow (acid) to purple (alkaline).

metacrolein. $(C_3H_4O)_3 = 168.1$. Colorless crystals, m.45.

metacryotic. Describing the liquid which separates gradually from frozen fruit juices.

metadiazine. Pyrimidine.

metadyne. A machine utilizing the principles of both the dynamo and electric motor to produce rapid acceleration and braking.

metaelement. A hypothetical substance, intermediate between an element and a protyl.

metafiltration. Edge filtration through super-imposed metallic strips with beveled edges, involving a change from coarse filtration (due to the strips) to fine filtration (due to the filter bed formed in their interstices).

metaformaldehyde. Trioxymethylene.

metafuel. Metacetaldehyde tablets; a fuel for alcohol lamps.

metaiodate. A salt of the type MIO_3.

metaiodic acid. See *iodic acid.*

metaisocymophenol. Carvacrol.

metaisomerism. A form of isomerism, q.v., due to the shifting of a double bond.

metakliny. An intramolecular transfer of groups. See *pinacole conversion.*

metal. (1) An electropositive chemical element characterized by ductility, malleability, luster, conductivity of heat and electricity, which can replace the hydrogen of an acid and forms bases with the hydroxyl radical. Recent work suggests that metals and nonmetals differ in lattice structure, each atom being surrounded by 8–12 or 1–4 other atoms, respectively. Cf. *nonmetal, periodic system.* (2) An alloy. **alkaline-** The elements of the first group in the periodic table. **alkaline earth-** The elements of the second group of the periodic table: Mg, Ca, etc. **basic-** Base m. A m. that is readily oxidized. **earth-** The elements of the third group of the periodic system: Al, etc. **fine-** White. **fusible-** A m. or alloy of relatively low melting point, e.g., Na, Pb, Sn. **heavy-** A m. with a density above 4, located in the lower half of the new periodic table, q.v. **"ideally pure"-** A m. that consists of atoms of only one element having the isotopic abundance ratios of the International Commission on Atomic Weights. **light-** A m. with a density below 4, located in the right upper part of the new periodic table. **noble-** A m. that is not readily oxidized or dissolved in acid, e.g., a member of the Au or Pt family. **primary-** A m. used for the first time. Cf. *secondary m.* **rare-** An element that occurs only in small quantities. **rare earth-** An element of the third long period: at. no.57–72. **respiratory-** Fe, Mn, Cu, V. **secondary-** A m. recovered from waste and scrap. **sensitized-** M. treated with light-sensitive material, so that designs can be photographed on it directly. Used in the mass production of metallic articles. **type-** See *type*. **virgin-** Primary. **white-** (1) Fine m. The almost pure cuprous sulfide obtained in the Welsh process for smelting Cu. (2) Alloys containing large proportions of Pb or Sn, e.g., pewter.

    m. bath. A fusible metal (as lead), used to obtain a high temperature. **m. compounds.** Intermetallic compounds, usually present in alloys.

metalammine. An ammine, q.v., of a metal.

metalammonia compound. Metalammine.

metalbumin. Paralbumin. A protein from ovarian cysts.

metalceramics. Powder metallurgy.

metaldehyde. (1) $(C_2H_4O)_3$ = 132.2. Metacetaldehyde. Colorless needles, sublime 112, insoluble in water; a sedative. (2) $(C_2H_4O)_4$ = 176.12. A polymer of acetaldehyde, b.150. Cf. *aldol, paraldehyde*.

metalepsis. An early term (Dumas, 1834) to indicate a substitution.

metalepsy. Substitution.

metalignitious. Noncaking; as, of coals.

metallic. Pertaining to metals in their uncombined forms. **m. carbonyls.** Compounds of carbon monoxide with metals; as, nickel carbonyl $Ni(CO)_4$. **m. nitroxyls.** Compounds of nitrogen peroxide with metals, e.g., cuprous nitroxyl, $Cu_2(NO_2)$. **m. soap.** See soap.

metalliferous. Describing an ore that contains a metal.

metallify. (1) To convert into a metal. (2) To extract a metal from its ore. (3) To give metallic properties.

metalline. Resembling a metal.

metallization. A process by which a surface is coated with a metal.

metallocene. Cyclopentadienylide. A metal derivative of cyclopentadiene existing uncharged (as ferrocene) or as charged ions; used in organic synthesis.

metallochrome. A tint imparted to metal surfaces by metallic salts.

metallogenic map. A map showing the distribution of mineral deposits in relationship to geological formation and tectonic features.

metallography. (1) The science of metals and of their ores, production, properties, and uses. (2) The microscopic study of the etched surfaces of metals and alloys. Cf. *mineralography, crystallography*.

metalloid. (1) Having the physical properties of metals and the chemical properties of nonmetals, e.g., As. (2) A nonmetal (incorrect usage).

metallurgy. The science of preparing metals from their ores. Cf. *siderurgy*. **electro-** The electrical preparation of metals. **hydro-** The preparation of metals by leaching processes. **powder-** The working of compressed metal powders, e.g., obtained by reducing the corresponding oxides. They are thus formed into solid masses by heat and pressure, and forged or drawn into wire. **pyro-** The preparation of metals by smelting, roasting, or furnace methods.

metalorganic. Pertaining to a metal in organic combination. **m. compound.** R_xM. Organometallic compound. A compound of organic radicals, R, with a metal, M; e.g., dimethylzinc.

metamerie. Early name for metamerism.

metamerism. Isomerism between 2 compounds which contain the same number and kind of atoms, but with the radicals in different positions; as: $CH_3 \cdot CH_2 \cdot CH_2 \cdot CO$ H, an aldehyde, and $CH_3 \cdot CH_2 \cdot CO \cdot CH_3$, a ketone. Cf. *isomery*.

metamers. Metameric compounds. Substances that exhibit metamerism, q.v.

metamorphism. In geology, a change in the texture and composition of a rock due to the external agencies (heat, wetness, etc.).

metamorphosis. (1) Biology: a change of form or structure, as during embryonic development. (2) Geology: a change in the crystalline structure of a mineral. **thermo-** Thermometamorphism.

metanilic acid. $NH_2 \cdot C_6H_4 \cdot HSO_3$ = 173.19. *m*-Aminobenzenesulfonic acid, aniline-*m*-sulfonic acid. An intermediate in dyestuff manufacture, decomp. 280.

metaniline yellow. Metanil yellow.

metanil yellow. Metaniline yellow, sodium phenylamidobenzene metasulfonate. A yellow dye used for wool and paper, for counterstaining tissues, and as an indicator, changing at pH 2.5 from red (acid) to yellow (alkaline).

metantimonate. A salt of the type $MSbO_3$.

metantimonic acid. The monobasic acid $HSbO_3$, from which the metantimonates are derived.

metapeptone. A digestive product of peptone.

metaperiodic acid. Periodic acid.

Metaphen. $CH_3 \cdot C_6H_4 \cdot ONO_2Hg$ = 783.0. Trademark for the anhydride of 4-nitro-5-hydroxymercury-*o*-cresol. Yellow powder insoluble in water; a germicide.

metaphenylene. The radical $C_6H_4 =$, from benzene with substitution in the 1- and 3-positions. **m. diamine.** $C_6H_4(NH_2)_2$ = 108.1. 1,3-Diaminobenzene. **m. diamine hydrochloride.** $C_6H_4(NH_2)_2 \cdot 2HCl$ = 181.0. Metadiaminobenzene hydrochloride. White crystals, soluble in water; a reagent to detect nitrites in water.

metaphosphate. A salt of the type MPO_3. See *phosphates*.

metaphosphinic acid. (1) $[PN(OH)_2]_n$. A group of nitrogen-phosphor acids. (2) $PN(OH)_2$. **hepta-** $7PN(OH)_3 \cdot H_2O$. **tetra-** $4PN(OH)_3 \cdot 2H_2O$.

metaphosphoric acid. The monobasic acid, HPO_3. See *phosphoric acids*.

metaposition. The 1- and 3-positions in the benzene ring.

metaprotein. A hydrolytic split product of proteins.

metarchon. A substance used to mask odor.

metaraminol(bi)tartrate. $C_9H_{13}NO_2 \cdot C_4H_6O_6$ = 317.30. White crystals, soluble in water, m.173; an adrenergic (U.S.P., B.P.).

metargon. An isotope of argon, at. wt. 38.

metarsenic acid. Metaarsenic acid.

metartrose. $C_{315}H_{504}O_{106}N_{90}S$. A product obtained on digestion of the proteins of wheat.

metasilicic acid. The dibasic acid H_2SiO_3, from silicic acid.

metasomatism. Natural enrichment of ores by chemical reaction with external substances.

metasomatosis. Chemical alteration of a mineral, to form a new mineral.

metasome. An individual mineral which has developed within another mineral.

metastable. An unstable condition which changes readily, to a more or a less stable condition. Indicated by the prefix *m*- in the case of isotopes, q.v. **m. electron.** An electron moving in an excited orbit. **m. phase.** The existence of a substance as a solid, liquid, or vapor under conditions in which it is normally unstable in that state.

metastannate. A salt of the type $M_2Sn_5O_{11}$.

metastannic acid. See *stannic acid.*

metastasic electron. (1) An electron which transfers from one atom to another. (2) An electron which changes its position in the atom during a radio-active change.

metastasis. Radioactive disintegration, in which an α-particle is thrown off and 2 electrons pass from the valence shell into inner orbits of the atom.

metastructure. A structure having a dimension between that of the molecule and the smallest structure visible microscopically. Cf. *colloid.*

metastyrene. $(C_8H_8)_x = (104.10)_x$. Metastyrolene. Fatty liquid, d.1.054, b.320. (decomp.), insoluble in water.

metastyrolene. Metastyrene.

metasulfite. Pyrosulfite. A salt of the acid $H_2S_2O_5$ (see *sulfur* acids); few are known.

metatenomeric change. The irreversible tautomeric transformation of nitrogen compounds; as,

Nitrate   Hydroxynitrite

Hydroxynitroso

metathesis. A chemical reaction (as, neutralization) in which there is an exchange of elements or radicals according to the general equation: $\overset{+\,-}{AB} + \overset{+\,-}{CD} = \overset{+\,-}{AD} + \overset{+\,-}{BC}$.

metathiazole. Thiazole.

metatorbernite. $Ca(UO_2)_2P_2O_8 \cdot 8H_2O$. A natural alteration product of torbernite, q.v.

metavanadate. A salt of the type MVO_3, from metavanadic acid.

metavanadic acid. HVO_3. A monobasic, hypothetical acid; exists only as metavanadates.

metazoa. A multicellular animal. Cf. *protozoa.*

Metchnikoff. See *Metshnikoff.*

meteoric. Pertaining to meteorites. **m. iron.** The metallic iron in meteorites; usually contains nickel. **m. stone.** A meteorite, mainly of aluminum silicates. **m. water.** Water reprecipitated as rain, snow, etc., that has entered the lithosphere from the earth's surface.

meteorite. Aerolite. A stony or metallic body that has fallen to the earth from outer space. Cf. *chondrite.* Three types: siderite (meteoric iron), siderolite (meteoric iron and stone), aerolite (meteoric stone). See *abundance.* **micro-** A cosmic particle of diameter less than 1 mm, which loses heat by radiation and does not burn up. The earth collects 10 million tons per year.

meteorograph. An apparatus that automatically records atmospheric pressure, temperature, humidity, and wind velocity.

meteorology. The study of climatic conditions.

meter, metre. (1) A unit of length: (*a*) Originally supposed to be 1/10,000,000th of the distance from the pole to the equator. (*b*) Now defined as the length of a platinum-iridium bar in Paris, with copies in the principal capitals. (*c*) Also defined as 1,553,164.13 times the wavelength of the red cadmium line. Cf. *yard.* (*d*) It has been internationally agreed (1961) that the m. be defined as 1,650,763.73 times the wavelength in vacuo of the orange-red radiation corresponding with the transition between the energy levels $2p_{10}$ and $5d_5$ of the Kr^{86} atom.

$$1 \text{ meter} = 100 \text{ cm} = 1,000 \text{ mm} = 0.001 \text{ km}$$
$$= 39.37011 \text{ in.} = 0.198838 \text{ rods}$$

See *magnitudes.* **atom-** Angström unit. **centi-** One-hundredth of a meter. **dynamic-** The gain in potential of 10^5 ergs/gm in a hypothetical place where $g = 1,000$ cm/sec^2. See *specific energy.* **fast-** A measure of the volume of a stack of wood (approx. 35 ft^3, voids excluded). Cf. *cord, cunit, board foot.* **international-** Prototype meter. The platinum-iridium bar taken as the standard meter. **kilo-** One thousand meters. **leo-** Dynamic m. **micro-** μm. Micron (preferred term, U.K. usage). **milli-** One-thousandth of a meter. **tenth-** Angström unit, i.e. 10^{-10} meter.

   m. angle. The angle of vision on viewing a point 1 meter distant. **m. bridge.** A slide-wire resistance 1 meter long, used in electrical resistance measurements. **m. candle.** The intensity of illumination of a candle 1 meter distant; or the luminosity of a white surface at 1 meter from a standard candle. **m. kilogram.** The force necessary to lift 1 kg 1 meter.

meter. (2) A measuring device for determining a quantity, e.g., of matter, flow, or force. **electro-** See *electrometer.* **gas-** A device for determining the quantity of gas passing through a pipeline. **gaso-** Gasholder. **photo-** See *photometer.* **ureo-** See *ureometer.* **Venturi-** A pipeline m. for liquids.

meth- Prefix indicating methyl, e.g., methoxy.

methacetin. $MeOC_6H_4NHCOMe = 165.1$. *p*-Methoxyacetaminophenol, *p*-acetanisidine, *p*-methoxyacetanilide. Colorless needles, m.127, soluble in water; an antipyretic and analgesic.

methacholine chloride. $C_8H_{18}O_2NCl = 195.70$. White deliquescent crystals, m.172, soluble in water; a parasympathomimetic (U.S.P.).

methacrylic acid. $CH_2{=}CMeCOOH = 86.07$. Δ^1-Methyl-1-propionic acid, d.1.015, b.160. Isomeric with vinylacetic, crotonic, and isocrotonic acids.

methadone hydrochloride. $C_{21}H_{27}ON \cdot HCl = 345.92$. Colorless crystals, m.235, soluble in water; an analgesic (U.S.P., B.P.).

methal. Myristic alcohol.

methallyl chloride. $CH_2CMe \cdot CH_2Cl = 90.0$. Colorless liquid, d$_{20}$0.925, b.72, from petroleum hydrocarbons; an insecticide.

methamphetamine hydrochloride. $C_{10}H_{15}N \cdot HCl = 185.70$. Methedrine. White crystals, soluble in water, m.172; a central stimulant (U.S.P.).

methanal*. Formaldehyde.

methanamide*. Formamide.

methandienone. $C_{20}H_{28}O_2 = 300.34$. White crystals, m.165, insoluble in water; an androgen (B.P.).

methane*. $CH_3 \cdot H = 16.04$. Methyl hydride. Cf. *marsh gas, firedamp.* The simplest saturated hydrocarbon. Colorless, flammable gas, $d_{air=1}$-0.558, m.-184, b.-161, slightly soluble in water. One of the chief constituents of illuminating and fuel gas, and formed in the decomposition of organic matter. Pure m. is obtained from aluminum carbide and water; used in the manufacture of formaldehyde and in organic synthesis. For most of its compounds see: *methyl-* CH_3—; *methylene,* —CH_2—; *methenyl,* =CH—. **m. d.** Deuteromethane, diplogen m. The isotopic compounds $CH_3D, CH_2D_2, CHD_3,$ and CD_4. **azi-** Diazomethane*. **bromo-*** Methyl bromide. **chloro-*** Methyl chloride. **cyano-** Acetonitrile. **diazo-*** Diazomethane. **dibromo-*** Methylene bromide. **dichloro-*** Methylene chloride. **dichlorodifluoro-*** Dichlorodifluoromethane. **dimethoxy-*** Formal. **dimethyl-** Propane*. **dimethylethyl-** Isopentane. **diphenyl-** Diphenylmethane. **diphenylene-** Fluorene. **fluoro-*** Methyl fluoride. **hydroxy-** Methanol. **iodo-*** Methyl iodide. **methoxy-*** Methyl ether. **methyldithio-*** Methyl disulfide. **methyl thio-*** Methyl sulfide. **nitro-*** $CH_3NO_2 = 61.03$. Colorless liquid, d.1.130, b.102, soluble in water. **phenyl-** Toluene. **tetrabromo-*** Carbon tetrabromide. **tetrachloro-*** Carbon tetrachloride. **tetrahydroxy-** *o*-Carbonic acid. **tetramethyl-** *tert*-Pentane. **tribromo-*** Bromoform. **trichloro-*** Chloroform. **trichloronitro-*** Chloropicrin. **trifluoro-*** Fluoroform. **triiodo-*** Iodoform. **trimethyl-** Isobutane.

m. acetic acid. Gentaric acid. **m. acid.** Formic acid. **m. alcohol.** Methanol. **m. aldehyde.** Formaldehyde. **m. amide.** Formamide. **m. arsonic acid.** Methylarsinic acid. **m. base.** Tetramethyldiaminodiphenylmethane. **m. chloride.** Methyl chloride. **m. dicarboxylic acid.** Malonic acid. **m. disulfonic acid.*** Methionic acid. **m. phosphonic acid.** Methylphosphinic acid. **m. series.** C_nH_{2n+2}. Paraffins, alkanes. A group of hydrocarbons denoted by the suffix *-ane*. Tetracontaine, $C_{40}H_{82}$, has 62,491,178,805,831 possible isomeric forms. **m. siliconic acid.** MeSiOOH $= 76.09$. Silicoacetic acid. White powder, insoluble in water. **m. stannonic acid.** MeSnOOH $= 106.73$. Methylstannic acid, stannoacetic acid. White, infusible powder, insoluble in water. **m. sulfonic acid.** Methylsulfonic acid. **m. sulfonyl chloride*.** $MeSO_2Cl = 114.54$. Colorless liquid, d.1.51, b.160. **m. thial*.** Thioformaldehyde. **m. thiol*.** $CH_3SH = 48.09$. Methylmercaptan. Colorless liquid or gas, d.0.868, b.7.6. **m. triacetic acid.** Centaric acid.

methano- Prefix indicating a —CH_2— bridge in a ring compound.

methanoic acid*. Formic acid.

methanol*. $CH_3OH = 32.04$. Methyl alcohol, carbinol, wood alcohol, pyroxylic spirit, wood spirit, wood naphtha, columbian spirit, colonial spirit, methyl hydroxide. Colorless liquid, d.0.810, b.64.7, flammable, soluble in water or ether; a solvent for varnishes, paints, organic compounds; a fuel; used to manufacture formaldehyde, in organic synthesis, and for denaturing. For derivatives, see *carbinol,* —CH_2OH.

methanoyl. Formoyl.

methantheline bromide. $C_{21}H_{26}O_3NBr = 420.36$. White, bitter powder, m.176, soluble in water; a parasympatholytic (U.S.P.).

methapyrilene hydrochloride. $C_{14}H_{19}N_3S \cdot HCl = 297.86$. White crystals, m.160, soluble in water; an antihistaminic (U.S.P.).

methazolamide. $C_5H_8N_4O_3S_2 = 236.27$. Yellow crystals, slightly soluble in water, m.213; a carbonic anhydrase inhibitor (U.S.P.).

methazonic acid. Metazonic acid.

methedrine. Methamphetamine hydrochloride. See *desoxyephedrine*

methemoglobin. A product derived from oxyhemoglobin, having the same composition as hemoglobin but with its oxygen more firmly bound. It contains Fe^{3+}; occurs in transudates containing blood, and in urine after hematuria. Mol. wt. 16,666. Cf. *porphin*.

methenamine. $C_6H_{12}N_4 = 140.19$. Hexamethylenetetramine. White, crystals, slightly soluble in water; a urinary anti-infective (U.S.P.). **m. mandelate.** $C_6H_{12}N_4 \cdot C_8H_8O_3 = 292.34$. White crystals, soluble in water, m.129; a urinary antibacterial (U.S.P.).

methene. Methylene. The group —CH_2—. Cf. *methano-.* **m. disulfonic acid.** Methionic acid.

methenyl. (1) The radical $C_{10}H_{17}$—. (2) Formylene, methine. The radical HC≡. Methylidene (U.K. usage). **di-** Acetylene.

   m. bromide. Bromoform. **m. chloride.** Chloroform. **m. iodide.** Iodoform.

methethyl. A mixture of ethyl and methyl chlorides; a local anesthetic.

methicillin sodium. $C_{17}H_{19}O_6N_2SNa \cdot H_2O = 420.40$. White crystals, soluble in water; an antibiotic (B.P.).

methide. A methyl compound of a metal; as, $MgMe_2$.

methimazole. $C_4H_6N_2S = 114.17$. Yellow powder, m.145, soluble in water; a thyroid inhibitor (U.S.P.).

methine. Methenyl: HC≡.

methiodal sodium. $NaCH_2O_3 \cdot NaIS = 243.99$. Sodium iodomethane sulfonate. White crystals with a saline taste, soluble in water; a radiopaque (U.S.P.).

methionic acid. $CH_2(SO_3H)_2 = 176.3$. Methenedisulfonic acid. Colorless, hygroscopic crystals.

methionine. $MeS \cdot CH_2 \cdot CH_2 \cdot CHNH_2COOH = 149.15$. 2-Amino-4-methylthiobutanoic acid*, from many proteins, e.g., casein; m.283 (decomp.).

methionyl. The radical —$SO_2 \cdot CH_2 \cdot SO_2$—.

metho- Prefix indicating a methyl group attached to a C atom of a side-chain or to a ring N atom.

methoestrol. Promethoestrol.

methohexitone (sodium). $C_{14}H_{17}N_2NaO_3 = 284.26$. White powder, soluble in water; a general (injection) anesthetic (B.P.).

methoin. $C_{12}H_{14}O_2N_2 = 218.32$. Mesantoin. Colorless plates, m.137, soluble in water; an anticonvulsant (B.P.).

methonal. $Me_2CSO_2Me_2 = 136.1$. Dimethylsulfone dimethylmethane. Colorless crystals, soluble in water; a hypnotic.

methopterin-A. An analog of folic acid, with a NH_2— and OMe— group replacing an —OH and

H atom, respectively. It inhibits the growth of malignant cells.

methose. $C_6H_{12}O_6$ = 180.09. A carbohydrate synthesized by the polymerization of formaldehyde in presence of magnesia. Cf. iso*fructose*.

methoxamine hydrochloride. $C_{11}H_{17}O_3N \cdot HCl$ = 247.73. White plates, m.214, soluble in water; a sympathomimetic (U.S.P.).

methoxide. Methylate.

Methoxone. Trade name for agroxone. MCPA. 4-Chloro-2-methylphenoxyacetic acid. A plant hormone growth substance; a selective weedicide.

methoxy- Prefix indicating a methoxy group, —OCH_3. **m. group.** The radical CH_3O—.

methoxybenzoic acid. $C_8H_8O_3$ = 152.1. **ortho-** 2-Methoxybenzoic acid. Colorless, monoclinic scales, m.98, soluble in water. **meta-** 3-Methoxybenzoic acid. Colorless needles, m.167, soluble in water. **para-** Anisic acid.

methoxyl. Methoxy. **m. amine.** Methylhydroxylamine.

methoxyphenyl (U.K. usage). Anisyl. **m. acetic acid.** $C_{18}H_{20}O_6$ = 332.18. A gravimetric reagent for Na, with which it forms an insoluble acid salt. **m. acetone.** Anisacetone.

methyl. The CH_3— radical. **m. acetamide.** C_3H_7ON = 73.1. $Me \cdot CO \cdot NHMe$. Exalgin. **m.** **acetate.** $MeCOOMe$ = 74.0. Colorless liquid with apple odor, d.0.924., b.45, soluble in water; a solvent and flavoring. **m. acetic acid.** Propionic acid. **m. acetoacetate.** $MeCOCH_2COOMe$ = 116.03. Colorless liquid, b.170. **m. acetone.** A mixture of methyl acetate and acetone; a rubber solvent. **m. acetyl.** Acetone. **m. acetylene.** Allylene. **m. acetyl salicylate.** $C_6H_4(O \cdot CO \cdot Me)_2$ = 194.08. Colorless crystals, m.54, isomeric with dimethyl phthalate. **m. acrylic acids.** See *acrylic acids*. **m. alcohol.** Methanol. **m. aldehyde.** Formaldehyde. **m. allyl ether.** Allyl m. ether. **m. allylphenol.** Anethol. **m. amidophenol.** Anisidine. **m. amine*.** CH_3-NH_2 = 31.1. Aminomethane. Colorless gas, soluble in water. Formed on distillation of wood and bones, putrefaction of fats and fish; a constituent of mercurialis. **m. p-aminophenol.** $MeNH—C_6H_4OH$ = 123.1. Rhodol. Used as its hydrochloride or hydrosulfate, as a photographic developer. **m. amphetamine hydrochloride.** $C_{10}H_{15}HCl$ = 185.92. White bitter crystals, m.173, soluble in water; a nerve stimulant (B.P.). **m. amyl ketone.** $MeCOC_5H_{11}$ = 114.11. A constituent of oils of cloves and of cinnamon. **m. aniline.** C_6H_5-$NHMe$ = 107.12. d.0.986, b.194. **m. anthranilate.** $NH_2 \cdot C_6H_4 \cdot COOMe$ = 151.08. M. *o*-aminobenzoate. Colorless crystals, m.25, soluble in alcohol; a perfume (orange). **m. arsenic acid.** *mono-* Arrhenic acid. *di-* Cacodylic acid. Cf. *m. arsinic acid.* **m. arsenious oxide.** CH_3AsO = 105.98. The anhydride of arrhenic acid, $Me \cdot As:O$, m.95. **m. arsine.** See *arsine*. **m. arsine dichloride.** CH_3AsCl_2 = 160.90. Volatile liquid, d.1.858, b.136. **m. arsinic acid.** $MeAsO(OH)_2$ = 139.97. White monoclinic leaflets, m.161, soluble in water. Cf. *m. arsenic acid.* **m. azide.** CH_3N-(N_2) = 57.1. Azoimidemethane, methyl azoimide. A hypothetical compound, known from its derivatives. **m. benzene.** Toluene. **m. ben-**

zoate. $PhCOOMe$ = 136.1. Essence niobe. Colorless fragrant liquid, d.1.094, b.198, insoluble in water; used in perfumery. **m. benzoic acid.** Toluic acid. **m. bismuthine.** $MeBiH_2$ = 226.04. Colorless liquid, d.2.30, b.110, insoluble in water. **m. blue.** A pH indicator changing at 11 from blue (acid) to brown (alkali). **m. borate.** B-$(OMe)_3$ = 104.0. Trimethoxyboron. It imparts a green color to a flame, and is used to test for borates. **m. bromide.** CH_3Br = 95.0. Bromomethane*. Colorless liquid, d.1.732, b.4.5, insoluble in water. Used in organic synthesis, in refrigerators, and as an antiseptic. **m. butex.** Methylhydroxybenzoate. **m. butyl.** Pentane. **m. butyl carbinol.** Hexyl alcohol. **m. butyrate.** $C_3H_7COOCH_3$ = 102.08. Used in perfumes. **m. Capri blue.** An oxidation-reduction indicator. **m. carbamate.** Urethylan. **m. carbimide.** CH_3-NCO. Methyl ψ-cyanate. **m. carbinol.** Ethanol. **m. carbonate.** See *carbonic acid esters*. **m. carbylamine.** CH_3NC = 41.1. Methyl isocyanide acetoisonitrile, d.0.76. Volatile liquid of unpleasant odor, b.60, soluble in water. **m. catechol.** Guaiacol. **m. Cellosolve.** See *Cellosolve*. **m. cellulose.** A cellulose m. ether (26–33% —OMe). White, fibrous powder, swelling in water to a viscous colloidal solution, insoluble in alcohol; a bulk laxative (U.S.P., B.P.). **m. chloride.** CH_3Cl = 50.5. Chloromethane*. Artic, arctic. Colorless gas, b.—23.7, soluble in water; an external anesthetic and refrigerant. **m. chlorofluoride.** Dichlorodifluoromethane. **m. chloroform.** $MeCCl_3$ = 133.4. Trichlorethane, ethenyl chloride. Colorless liquid of pungent odor, d.1.346, b.74; an anesthetic. **m. cinnamate.** C_8H_7COOMe = 162.08. White crystals, m.36, insoluble in water; an insect bait. **m. cocaine.** Cocainidine. **m. crotonic acids.** See *tiglic* and *angelic acids*. **m. cyanate.** $N\equiv COCH_3$ = 57.04. Cf. *m. isocyanate*. **m. cyanide.** Acetonitrile. **m. cyclohexane.** Hexahydrotoluene. **m. diphenyl.** Phenyltoluene. **m. disulfide.** $MeS \cdot SMe$ = 94.19. Methyldithiomethane*. **m. ene.** Methylene. Colorless liquid, b.112. **m. ergometrine (maleate).** $C_{20}H_{25}N_3O_2 \cdot C_4H_4O_4$ = 455.50. White powder, soluble in water with fluorescence; a uterine stimulant (B.P.). **m. ergonovine maleate.** C_{20}-$H_{25}N_3O_2 \cdot C_4H_4O_4$ = 455.52. Pink, bitter crystals, slightly soluble in water; an oxytocic (U.S.P.). **m. ether.** $MeOMe$ = 46.06. Dimethyl ether, methoxymethane*, A gas, b.—25, soluble in alcohol; a refrigerant. **m. ethyl ketone.** Me-$COEt$ = 72.1. Butanone, MEK. Colorless, flammable liquid, d.0.808, b.80, soluble in water; used in organic synthesis, as a solvent, and to manufacture colorless plastics. **m. fluoride.** CH_3-F = 34.02. Fluoromethane*. Colorless gas, b.—78. **m. formate.** $HCOOMe$ = 60.1. Methylformic acid ester. Colorless liquid, d.0.973. b.32, soluble in water; used to manufacture cellulose acetate. **m. gadenine.** $C_8H_{19}NO_2$ = 161.16. A poisonous oxygenated ptomaine from fish. **m. gallate.** Gallicin. **m. gallium dichloride.** $GaMeCl_2$ = 155.66. White crystals, m.75, decomp. in water. **m. glycine.** Sarcosine. **m. glycosine.** Sarcosine. **m. glyoxal.** Pyruvic aldehyde. **m. glyoxalidine.** Lysidine. **m. green.**

$(Me_2N-C_6H_4)_2C=C_6H_4=NMe_2Cl$. A triphenylmethane dye; used to dye silk and stain mitochondria; and as pH indicator changing from yellow (acid) through blue green to colorless (alkaline). **m. guanidine.** $MeN:C(NH_2)_2 = 73.06$. A ptomaine formed from creatine or arginine. **m. heptenone.** $Me_2C:CH(CH_2)_2COMe = 126.11$. Colorless liquid, b.167, in essential oils. **m. heptine carbonate.** Heptine methyl carbonate. **m. heptyl ketone.** 2-Nonanone*. **m. Hexalin.** Trademark for m. cyclohexanol. **m. hexane.** Heptane. **m. hexyl ketone.** Hexyl m. ketone. **m. hydrate.** Methanol. **m. hydrazine.** MeNH-$NH_2 = 46.07$. A liquid, b.745mm87. **m. hydrazone.** $MeCH=NNH_2$. **m. hydroxide.** Methanol. **m. hydroxybenzene.** (1) Cresol. (2) Hydroxybenzyl alcohol. **m. hydroxybenzoate.** $C_8H_8O_3 = 152.15$. M. butex. M. paraben (U.S.P.). White crystals with a burning taste, m.126, slightly soluble in water; a preservative (B.P.). **m. hydroxylamine.** See *hydroxylamine*. **m. indole.** Skatole. **m. iodide.** $CH_3I = 142.0$. Iodomethane*. Colorless liquid, d.2.28, b.44, insoluble in water; a local anesthetic. **m. isocyanate.** CONMe $= 57.04$. b.45. Cf. *m. cyanate.* **m. isocyanide.** $CH_3NC = 41.03$. M. carbylamine, m. isonitrile. Colorless liquid d.0.756, b.60. **m. isophthalic acid.** 4- Seylidic acid. **5-** Uvitic acid. **m. isothiocyanate.** M. *mustard oil*. **m. mercaptan.** Methane thiol. **m. mercuric chloride.** MeHgCl = 251.09. White crystals with a disagreeable odor, m.170. **m. mercuric iodide.** MeHgI = 342.55. Pearly leaflets, m.145, insoluble in water. **m. methacrylate.** $CH_2:CMe\cdot COOMe = 100.06$. A source of polymers used for transparent sheet material and laminated safety glass. **m. morphine.** Codeine. **m. nitramine.** $Me\cdot NH\cdot NO_2 = 76.0$. **m. nitrate.** $Me-O-NO_2 = 77.04$. Explosive liquid, $d_5O1.2$, soluble in water. **m. nitrite.** Me$-O-$NO $= 61.04$. A gas, d.0.99, b.-12. **m. nitrobenzene.** Nitrotoluene. **m. nitrolic acid.** Formoxime. **m. nonyl ketone.** 2-Hendecanone*. **m. orange.** $Me_2NC_6H_4N:NC_6H_4SO_2Na$. The sodium salt of p-dimethylaminobenzenesulfonic acid. Yellow powder, soluble in water; an indicator (alkalies—yellow, acids—red; pH 3.1–4.4). **m. oxide.** M. ether. **m. oxyaniline.** Anisidine. **m. paraben.** U.S. usage for m. hydroxybenzoate. **m. pentose.** $C_6H_{12}O_5$. A sugar containing 6 carbons but only 5 hydroxy groups; as, fucose. **m. phenate.** Anisole. **m. phenidine.** See *phenacetin*. **m. phenylacetamide.** Exalgin. **m. phenyl ether.** Anisole. **m. phosphate.** $MePO_2(OH)_2 = 112.09$. m.105. **m. phosphine.** $MePH_2 = 48.09$. A gas, b.-14, soluble in water. **m. phosphinic acid.** $CH_3PO(OH)_2 = 96.06$. Methanephosphonic acid. Colorless crystals, m.105. **m. prednisolone.** $C_{22}H_{30}O_5 = 374.45$. White, bitter crystals, m.243 (decomp.), insoluble in water; an adrenocortical steroid (B.P.). **m. propionate.** EtCOO-Me $= 88.06$. M. propanoate. Colorless liquid, d.0.9148, b.79.9, soluble in water; used in perfumes. **m. propyl ether.** MeOPr = 74.77. Colorless liquid, d.0.738, b.39. **m. propyl ketone.** $Me\cdot CO\cdot Pr = 86.77$. Acetylpropane, 2-pentanone*. Colorless liquid, d.0.812, b.102. **m. propyl phenol.** Thymol. **m. pyridine.** Picoline. **m.**

pyruvate. MeCOCOOMe $= 102.05$. A liquid, d.1.154, b.137; a solvent for resins. **m. quinolines.** *alpha-* Quinaldine. *gamma-* Lepidine. **m. red.** $Me_2NC_6H_4N:NC_6H_4COOH = 269.3$. p-Dimethylaminoazobenzenecarboxylic acid. Red powder, insoluble in water; an indicator (alkalies—yellow, acids—violet red; pH 3–6). **m. resorcinol.** Orcinol. **m. rhodanate, m. rhodanide.** M. thiocyanate. **m. rosaniline hydrochloride.** U.S.P. term for crystal violet. **m. rubber.** Early name for synthetic rubber made by polymerization of dimethylbutadiene. **m. salicylate.** $C_6H_4\cdot$ (OH)·COOMe $= 152.15$. Artificial wintergreen oil, methylic salicylas, betula oil, gaultheria oil, sweet birch oil. Colorless liquid, d.1.183, b.222, insoluble in water. Used as a flavoring, antipyretic, antiseptic; and in antirheumatic liniments (U.S.P., B.P.). **m. selenide.** Selenium dimethyl. **m. silicane.** $SiH_3\cdot CH_3 = 46.11$. Colorless gas, b.-57. **m. stannic acid.** MeSnOOH = 166.73. White powder, insoluble in water. **m. styryl ketone.** Benzylidene acetone. **m. succinic acid.** Pyrotartaric acid. **m. sulfate.** $Me_2SO_4 = 126.1$. Dimethyl sulfate. Colorless liquid, d.1.352, b.188, slightly soluble in water. A poison gas; used for methylating. **m. sulfide.** $Me_2S = 62.1$. M. thiomethane, m. thioether. Colorless liquid, d.0.845, b.37, insoluble in water. **m. sulfocyanide.** M. thiocyanate. **m. sulfonal.** Trional. **m. sulfonic acid.** $Me-SO_2-OH = 96.1$. Methanesulfonic acid*. A syrup, decomp. 130. **m. tartronic acid.** Iso*malic acid.* **m. telluride.** $(CH_3)_2Te = 157.1$. Yellow liquid with garlic odor, b.82. **m. testosterone.** $C_{20}H_{30}O_2 = 302.46$. Metandren, Neo-Hombreol-M, Oreton-M. The 17-methyl derivative of testosterone, q.v. White hygroscopic crystals, m.164, insoluble in water; an androgenic hormone (U.S.P., B.P.). **m. theobromine.** Caffeine. **m. thiocyanate.** $CH_3CNS = 73.1$. M. rhodanate. Colorless liquid, d.1.088, b.133, soluble in alcohol. **m. thionine chloride.** Methylene blue. **m. thiophen.** Thiotolene. **m. thiouracil.** $C_5H_6ON_2S = 142.18$. White crystals, m.330 (decomp.), soluble in water; a thyroid inhibitor (U.S.P., B.P.). **m. tin bromide.** CH_3-$SnBr_3 = 373.47$. White needles, m.54, soluble in water. **m. tin chloride.** $CH_3SnCl_3 = 240.09$. Colorless crystals, m.43, soluble in water. **m. tin iodide.** $CH_3SnI_3 = 514.48$. Yellow needles, m.87, soluble in water. **m. toluidine.** Xylidine. **m. urea.** See *urea*. **m. urethane.** Urethylan, **m. violet.** Crystal violet, pyoktanin blue. A mixture of the hydrochlorides of pentamethyl-p-rosaniline and hexamethyl-p-rosaniline. Green crystals, soluble in water; a reagent, indicator, and textile dye (alkalies—violet, acids—yellow; pH 2.0–3.1).

methylal. Formal.

methylamine. See *methyl*.

methylamino- Prefix indicating the radical —NHMe.

methylate. (1) The substitution of a methyl group for an atom or radical. (2) CH_3OM. Methoxide. A compound of a metal with the methoxy group, e.g., sodium m., $NaOCH_3$. (3) Denaturate. To add methanol to alcohol to render it unpotable.

methylated ether. Ethyl ether made from m. spirit instead of from pure ethanol. **m. spirit.** Rectified spirit, q.v., denatured by addition of crude wood spirit 10, mineral naphtha or pyridine 0.4%, and a purple coloring matter. Cf. *ethanol. power m.s.* Official British term for alcohol denatured for power purposes.

methylene. Methene. Now preferably called carbene. The radical —CH_2—, from methane. Cf. *di-, tri-,* etc., *methylene.* **meso-** See *mesomethylene.* **trioxy-** Paraformaldehyde.

    m. blue. $C_{16}H_{18}N_3SCl\cdot3H_2O = 373.90$. Tetramethylamidophenthiazinium chloride, methylthionine chloride, methylthioninae chloridum (U.S.P.); a dye of the thiazine group. Green crystals, soluble in water. Used as a redox indicator, a bacteriological stain, an antidote to cyanide poisoning, an anodyne, antiperiodic, and week antiseptic (B.P.); and a textile dye. *alkaline-*A stain: m. blue 5, sodium percarbonate 5 gm per liter of water. **m. bromide.** $CH_2Br_2 = 174.0$. Dibromomethane*. Yellow liquid, d.2.59, b.98, insoluble in water. **m. chloride.** $CH_2Cl_2 = 85.0$. Dichloromethane*, methylbichloride, carrene. Colorless liquid, d.1.377, b.41, soluble in alcohol; an anesthetic, solvent, degreaser, and refrigerant. **m. cyanide.** Malonitrile. **m. dicotoin.** Fortoin. **m. dioxy.** The radical —OCH_2O—. **m. disulfonic acid.** Methionic acid. **m. ditannin.** Tannoform. **m. glycol.** $CH_2(OH)_2 = 48.0$. Hydrated formaldehyde in its aqueous solutions. **m. imine.** See *methylenimine.* **m. iodide*.** $CH_2I_2 = 267.86$. Diiodomethane. Yellow liquid, d.3.335, b.180, insoluble in water; used to determine density of mineral mixtures and water-soluble substances. **m. triol.** Phloroglucitol.

methylenimine. $H_2C:NH = 29.01$. Azomethine.
methylic. Methyl (obsolete). **m. acid.** Formic acid.
    m. alcohol. Methanol.
methylidyne. U.K. usage for methenyl.
methylin. A lignin extracted from plants by ethylene glycol monomethyl ether.
methyloic- Prefix indicating a carboxyl group as a side chain, e.g., $Et_2CH\cdot COOH$, pentane-3-methyloic acid. Cf. *ethyloic.*
methylol. Hydroxymethyl. The radical $HO\cdot CH_2$—. See *carbinol.*
methyne. The radical —CH=, attached to 2 different C atoms.
methyprylon. $C_{10}H_{17}O_2N = 183.24$. White bitter crystals, m.76, soluble in water; a sedative (B.P.).
methysticin. Kavain.
methysticum. Kava.
Metol. Trademark for methyl-*p*-aminophenol sulfate; a photographic developer. **M. poisoning.** A misnomer for dermatitis caused by alkali; or by *p*-dimethyldiaminobenzene, formerly an impurity of Metol.
Metopon. Methyldihydromorphinone. A narcotic and analgesic; used to treat cancer.
metoquin. Mepacrine hydrochloride.
metozine. Antipyrine.
Metrazol(e). $C_5H_{10}N_4 = 126.1$. Trademark for pentamethylenetetrazole, cardiazol(e), leptazol, phrenazol. White, monoclinic crystals, m.58. soluble in water; a heart stimulant.
metre. Meter.
metric. (1) Pertaining to measure. **gravi-** Analysis involving the use of the balance. **volu-** Analysis

carried out by measuring volumes with pipet and buret. (2) Pertaining to the *m. system.*
    m. carat. See *carat.* **m. count.** A measure of the fineness of a fiber; the length (in meters) of 1 gram. **m. slug.** See *slug.* **m. system.** Weights and measures based on the meter, from which all other scientific units are derived. The multiples and fractions of units are uniformly prefixed with the Greek and Latin terms, respectively:

Greek

mega =	1,000,000 =	10^6
myria =	10,000 =	10^4
kilo =	1,000 =	10^3
hekto =	100 =	10^2
deka =	10 =	10^1

Latin

deci = 0.1	=	10^{-1}
centi = 0.01	=	10^{-2}
milli = 0.001	=	10^{-3}
micro = 0.000001	=	10^{-6}

Units commonly used:

Length = meter = m; km, cm, mm, μ (10^{-6} m), $m\mu$, $\mu\mu$

Area = square meter = m^2; are = 100 m^2

Volume = liter = 1; cc (cubic centimeter) and λ (10^{-6} l)

Mass = gram = gm; kg, mg, and γ (10^{-6} gm)

m. ton. 1,000 kilograms = 2204.6 pounds.
metrication. Conversion to the metric system.
metronidazole. $C_6H_9O_3N_3 = 171.20$. White, bitter crystals, m.161, soluble in water; used to treat trichomoniasis (B.P.).
metronome. An instrument to denote short time intervals, usually a mechanically driven pendulum.
metrotonin. An ergot substitute: epinephrine, acetylcholine, and other amines.
-metry. Suffix indicating measurement and measuring.
Metshnikoff, Elie. Metchnikoff. 1845–1918. Russian physiologist, discoverer of phagocytosis.
metso. Sodium metasilicate; a scouring agent.
metycaine. Neothesin, hydrochloride of γ-(2-methylpiperidino)propyl benzoate. White powder; a local anesthetic.
metyrapone. $C_{14}H_{14}N_2O = 226.28$. Yellow crystals, insoluble in water; a diagnostic aid (U.S.P.).
Mev, MEV. Abbreviation for million electron volts.
mevalonic acid. 3,5-Dihydroxy-3-methyl-*n*-valeric acid, involved in the biosynthesis of cholesterol.
Mewlon. Trade name for a polyvinyl alcohol synthetic fiber.
Mexican poppy oil. Brown oil from the seeds of prickly poppy, *Argemone mexicana*; used in soap manufacture. **M. onyx.** A variety of calcite, used in interior decorations. **M. scammony root.** Ipomoea.
Meyer, Lothar Julius. 1830–1895. German chemist, discoverer of the periodic system. Cf. *Mendeleev.* **M., Victor.** 1848–1897. German chemist. **M.'s formula.** (1) See *molecular free path.* (2) An equation connecting viscosity, q.v., and temperature. **M.'s law.** Law of *esterification.* **M.'s theory.** Anesthetics and narcotics are generally substances which diffuse rapidly. See *liminal value.* **M.'s tube.** An absorption tube for carbon dioxide, filled with barium hydroxide; used in

steel analysis. **M.'s value.** Liminal value. Cf. *Mayer*.

meyerhoffite. $2CaO \cdot 3B_2O_3 \cdot 7H_2O$. A native borate.

meymacite. $WO_3 \cdot H_2O$. Native, hydrated, brown, resinous masses.

mezcal. Mescal.

mezcaline. Mescaline.

mezereon. Mezereum, dwarf bay, paradise plant, wild pepper, spurge flax. The dried bark of *Daphne mezereum*, a European shrub; a diaphoretic. Cf. *daphnin*.

mezereum. Mezereon.

mezquit. *Prosopis juliflora* of Mexico and the S. W. United States. Its gum resembles gum arabic.

MF resin. Melamine-formaldehyde resin.

Mg. Symbol for magnesium.

mg. Abbreviation for milligram. **mg-%.** Mg/ 100 ml.

mho. A unit of electrical conductivity (the reciprocal of ohm, the unit of resistance) One mho conductance per centimeter cube with a potential of one volt allows the passage of one ampere current per square centimeter of area.

miamine. Chlorazene.

miargyrite. $AgSbS_2$. A silver sulfide ore.

miasma, miasm. Noxious vapors from swamps.

miazines. Metadiazines or pyrimidines. Heterocyclic compounds having 2 N atoms in the meta position; as, pyrimidine. Cf. *piazines*.

micas. (1) A group of laiminated silica minerals (q.v.); viz: biotite, muscovite, phlogopite, zinnwaldite. None has fixed properties. (2) $3Al_2O_3 \cdot K_2O \cdot 6SiO_2 \cdot 2H_2O$. Isinglass, muscovy glass. A native, hydrous silicate, which can be split into very thin transparent sheets. Used as an electrical insulator; as windows in furnaces and refracting instruments; and, ground, as a lubricant. (3) Geology: Prefix to describe rocks containing m; as mica basalt. **amber-** Phlogopite. **lithia-, lithium-** Lepidolite. **potash-** $KH_2Al_3(SiO_4)_3$. Potassium metasilicate. **ruby-** Muscovite. **m. black.** See *hibernium*.

micell(e). (1) An electrically charged colloidal particle or ion, consisting of oriented molecules. Cf. *zone*. (2) An oriented arrangement of a number of molecules; as in cellulose. Cf. *liquid, association*. (3) An aggregate of a number of molecules held loosely together by secondary bonds. Cf. *bonds*.

Michael's reaction. An organic addition reaction in which the sodium salts of acetocetic acid or malonic esters disrupt the double bond to form unsaturated compounds of the type, $R—CH:CH—X$, where X is a carbonyl or cyanogen radical.

Michler's hydrol. $(Me_2NC_6H_4)_2CH_2OH = 270.19$. *p*-Tetramethyldiaminobenzohydrol. White crystals, m.96; used in organic synthesis. **M.'s ketone.** $(Me_2NC_6H_4)_2CO = 268.3$. $4:4'$-Bisdimethylaminothiobenzophenone. Colorless plates, m.172, insoluble in water; used in the synthesis of dyestuffs and auramine derivatives and as a microreagent for metals (blue color with Hg).

micra. A little-used plural form for *micron*.

micrinite. An opaque material in coal durains, q.v.; and intermediate between fusain and vitrain.

micro- (1) Prefix (Greek,) indicating small. (2) The one-millionth part of a unit; as, μ = micrometer, λ = microliter and γ = microgram. **sub-** See *analysis*.

microampere. One-millionth of an ampere.

microanalysis. The identification of substances by examination with the microscope. Cf. *microchemistry, microreaction*.

microbalance. A balance to weigh micro quantities. See *McBain balance*.

microbe. A microorganism of animal or vegetable nature; generally causing disease; as, bacteria and pathological protozoa.

microbic. Pertaining to microorganisms.

microbicide. An agent that destroys microorganisms.

microbiology. (1) The study of microorganisms. (2) Synonym for bacteriology.

microbiotic. Any antibiotic produced by organisms.

microburner. A small bunsen burner.

microcalorie. See small *calorie*.

microchemical. (1) Pertaining to reactions observed under the microscope (2) Pertaining to chemical reactions in miniature apparatus with small quantities. **m. analysis.** The qualitative or quantitative analysis of small amounts of substances, e.g., 10 mg or less. Qualitative m.a. is based on spot, color, or microscope tests, q.v.; quantitative methods are usually small-scale adaptations of existing macro methods.

microchemistry. (1) Chemical investigation by means of the microscope, especially the performance of chemical reactions on a microscope slide requiring only minute quantities of substances. (2) Qualitative and quantitative reactions performed with small quantities (micrograms and microliters), using miniature apparatus.

microcidin. A surgical antiseptic; sodium β-naphtholates and phenates.

microcline. Amazonite.

micrococcus. A minute spherical or round bacterium.

microcosmic salt. $NaNH_4HPO_4 \cdot 4H_2O$. Phosphor salt. Acid sodium ammonium phosphate in blood and natural waters; used in blowpipe analysis for bead tests, q.v.

microcoulomb. One-millionth of a coulomb.

microcrith. The weight of a hydrogen atom (obsolete).

microcrystalline. Cryptocrystalline. Crystallizing in minute crystals. **m. wax.** A mixture of solid, mineral-origin hydrocarbons, e.g., precipitated during the deoiling of petroleum crude oil distillates and fractionally crystallized. White to pale amber, m. not less than 71, iodine val. not exceeding 4.0. It should conform to the B.P. test for sulfur compounds in liquid paraffin. Used in chewing gum and to make paper water- and vaporproof.

microdiffusion analysis. Isothermal distillation. An analytical method (milligram scale) based on the gaseous diffusion of a volatile substance from sample to reagent; e.g., of ammonia liberated from an ammonium salt to a standard acid. It is usually effected by the use of 2 petri dishes, one inside the other and both covered, each containing a reactant.

microfarad. One-millionth of a farad.

microfiche. A microfilm system $(148 \times 104$ mm$)$ used by the National Lending Library (U.S.) for making scientific papers available.

microfilm. A photographic film reproducing printed matter on a greatly reduced scale and read by projection on a screen.

microfractography. The microscopical study of the fracture surfaces of metals.

microgram. μg, mcg (U.S.P. usage). Gamma, γ. One-millionth of a gram.

micrography. (1) Photomicrography. (2) The measurement of physical properties with the microscope.

microhm. One-millionth of an ohm.

microlamp. (1) An illuminator lamp for microscopes. (2) A small source of artificial light.

microline. $K_2O,Al_2O_6,6SiO_2$. A vitreous, yellow mineral.

microliter. Lambda, λ, μl. One-millionth of a liter. $\lambda 1 = 1 \text{ mm}^3$.

microliths. Very small crystals, microscopic sections of rocks and slags.

micromanipulator. Attachments to the microscope stage (controls and levers) to manipulate an object under observations, e.g., for dissections.

micromerol. $C_{33}H_{52}O_2 = 480.43$. A monobasic alcohol from *Micromeria chamissonis* (Labiatae).

Micromet. Trademark for a mixed sodium and calcium phosphate boiler-water conditioner.

micrometer. (1) Micron. (2) An instrument for measuring small lengths under the microscope. **m. caliper.** An instrument for measuring with an accuracy of 0.01 mm.

micromicron. $\mu\mu$ (mu-mu) = one-millionth of a micron = 10^{-12} meter = 10^{-9} mm = 10λ = 10 X units. See *magnitudes*.

micromillimeter. Micron.

micromonosporin. An antibiotic produced by *Micromonospora* species of actinomycetes.

micron. Micrometer. (1) μ (mu). One millionth of a meter. Cf. *micra*. **micro-** See *micromicron*. **milli-** See *millimicron*. See *magnitudes*. (2) A colloidal particle:

Micron...... 10 to 0.2 μ; 10^{-3} to 2×10^{-3} cm
Submicron... 0.2 μ to 5 mμ; 2×10^{-5} to 10^{-7} cm
Amicron .... Less than 5 mμ; 10^{-7} cm

m. of mercury. The pressure exerted by a column of Hg 1 μ high; 1 μ Hg = 0.001 mm.

micronaire value. A measure of the fineness and general quality of a fiber. A known weight of fiber is compressed to a plug of known volume, and the flow of air forced through it is measured.

micronize. To reduce particles to a size below 5 μ.

microorganism. A minute animal or plant, visible only through a microscope.

microphone. An electrical instrument to intensify or transmit sound.

microphotogram. The record made by a microphotometer.

microphotograph. (1) A photograph reduced in scale. Cf. *photomicrograph*. (2) Microphotogram.

microphotometer. An instrument to measure and record the intensity of spectral lines by determining the density of their photographic images over small areas by means of a photoelectric cell.

microporous. Having openings or cavities of microscopic size. **m. rubber.** See *mipor rubber*.

micropolariscope. A microscope with polariscope attached; used to study minerals and crystals.

microreaction. A qualitative chemical reaction performed under the microscope with minute reagents Cf. *spot analysis*.

microsal. A disinfectant mixture of copper carbonate and crude sulfonephenolic acids.

microscope. An optical instrument consisting of objectives and eyepiece that magnifies minute objects for visual inspection or photographic record by direct illumination. Normal lower limit of visibility 0.10 μ. **binocular-** A m. having two eyepieces, which used simultaneously, produce a perspective effect. **compound-** An ordinary m., enlarging 30 to 1,000 diameters. **electron-** A device analogous to an ordinary m., in which a beam of electrons replaces the source of light and magnetic condensers replace the lenses. The image is rendered visible by projection on a fluorescent screen. Magnifications of over 100,000 are obtainable. **fluorescence-** A m. in which the illumination is filtered ultraviolet light; used to study fluorescence (q.v.) phenomena. Cf. *ultraviolet m*. **ion-** The most powerful m. (magnification $2 \times 10^6\times$). The image is produced on a fluorescent screen by the ions accelerated from a metal specimen. **polarizing-** A m. in which the object is on a rotating stage between crossed nicols. **ultra-** A m. in which the object is indirectly illuminated; e.g., a thin layer of a colloidal solution is illuminated at right angles to the line of sight, and the colloidal particles appear as bright points on a dark field. Lower limit of visibility 5 mμ. **ultraviolet-** A high-power m., in which an almost monochromatic ultraviolet ray is the illuminator. Objects may be enlarged by 1,000 to 6,000 diameters. Lower limit 30 $\mu\mu$. Cf. *fluorescence m*. **m. test.** Microreaction.

microscopic. Visible only under the microscope. Lower limit about 0.10 μ. **a-** Invisible under the ordinary microscope. **sub-** Amicroscopic. **ultra-** Visible under the ultramicroscope. Lower limit about 5 mμ. Cf. *micron*.

microscopy. (1) The study of the optical enlargement of objects, and their photography. (2) The application of the microscope to useful ends. **fluorescence-** See *fluorescence*. **phase contrast-** See *phase*.

microspectroscope. A microscope with spectroscope attached; used to study absorption spectra and the structure of spectral lines.

microtome. An instrument for cutting thin sections of materials for microscopic examination.

microtopography. The study of the fine structure of surfaces.

micro unit. A unit of small measurement, usually one-millionth part. It is characterized by a Greek letter; as, γ, λ, σ for microgram, microliter, microsecond, respectively.

microvolt. One-millionth of a volt.

microwave. Usually a wave, q.v., of wavelength less than 1 cm. High-frequency oscillation of very short wavelength generated by radio-frequency power tubes from high-voltage direct current. Used industrially and domestically to produce rapid internal heating by intramolecular friction and agitation.

micrurgy. The study of surgery by microscopical methods.

midrol. Iodomethylphenylpyrazolone, mydrol. Colorless crystals soluble in water; a mydriatic.

miemite. $CaCO_3\cdot MgCO_3$. A vitreous, brown mineral.

Miers, Sir Henry. 1858–1942. British chemist, noted for his work on mineralogy and crystallography.

Miescher pipet. A small tube for diluting blood specimens for hemacytometers.

migma. A stage in the formation of granites, when the rock material is fluid. Cf. *magma.*

mignonette oil. Reseda oil.

Migrainin. A proprietary headache mixture: antipyrine 85, caffeine 9, citric acid 5%.

migration. A change of position, as the m. of ions in an electric cell. **atomic-** See *rearrangement.*   **m. tube.** An H-shaped glass vessel with electrodes containing a salt solution and indicator. On passing an electric current, the m. of the ions is illustrated by the color. **m. velocity.** The velocity with which ions move through a solution during electrolysis. See *transport numbers.* Absolute velocity $= 10^8 \times$ migration velocity$/96,000$. Cf. *mobility.*

mikro- Micro-.

mikrobe. See *microbe.*

mikrobin. Sodium *p*-chlorobenzoate. A preservative.

mil. (1) Milliliter, ml. 1/1,000 of a liter = 1.000028 cc. This term now is used in the U.S.P. and B.P. (2) A measure of thickness, especially of wire: 1 mil = 1/1,000 in. = 25.4001 microns.

milammeter. Milliammeter.

milarite. $HKCa_2Al_2(SiO_3)_{12}$. Green, brittle, hexagonal prisms.

mile. A measure of length: 1 mile = 1.60935 km = 5,280 ft = 80 chains. **admiralty-** 6,080 ft. **nautical-** 1.853 km = 6082.66 ft = 80 fathoms. **geographical-** Nautical mile.

milk. (1) The opaque secretion of the mammary glands. A white emulsion, d.1.029–1.039, containing (averages, in $10\times$ %):

Origin	Water	Proteins	Fat	Sugar	Salts
Dog	754.4	99.1	95.7	31.9	7.3
Cat.	816.3	90.8	33.3	49.1	5.8
Goat	869.1	36.9	40.9	44.5	8.6
Sheep.	835.0	57.4	61.4	39.6	6.6
Human	875.5	12.5	35.0	75.0	2.0
Cow	871.7	35.5	36.9	48.8	7.1
Mare	900.6	18.9	10.9	66.5	3.1
Ass.	900.0	21.0	13.0	63.0	3.0
Pig.	823.7	60.9	64.4	40.4	10.6
Elephant. . .	678.5	30.9	195.7	88.5	6.5

A major source of Cs^{137} radioactivity. **acid of-** Lactic acid. **butter-** Milk from which the fat has been removed. **certified-** M. which has been chemically and bacteriologically tested, and contains few bacteria. **condensed-** Milk from which some water has been removed and sugar added. **dried-** M. from which water has been removed to produce a dry and relatively stable powder. **fermented-** Kumyss. **homogenized-** M. that has been reemulsified, e.g., after pasteurization, or treated so that the fats do not separate into cream. **modified-** A cream diluted with lactose solution for infant feeding. **pasteurized-** M. heated at 60°C for 30 minutes. **reconstituted-** The m. obtained by adding the appropriate quantity of water to dry m. **skimmed-** M. from which the separated cream has been removed.

sterilized- M. that has been heated at 100°C for 45–60 minutes. **UHT-** Ultra-heat-treated, m. clarified, heated to 270–280°F, for 2 sec, homogenized, and cooled. It keeps unchanged for considerable periods in sterile containers. **vegetable-** An emulsion of fats from the soybean, used extensively in China for bean cakes or cheeselike foods.

   m. extract. Condensed m. whose casein has been partly peptonized. **m. fat.** The total fats from milk. **m. powder.** A milk that has been evaporated and powdered. **m. scale.** A white opal strip along the length of a buret, to facilitate accurate meniscus readings. **m. serum.** Whey. **m. stone.** (1) A flint, whitened by fire. (2) A hard casein-containing scale produced in dairies, due to hard water for cleaning. **m. sugar.** Lactose. **m. test bottle.** A graduated centrifuge tube, used to determine the fat content of m. **m. weed.** Silkweed.

milk. (2) Magma. An emulsion or suspension. **m. of almonds.** An emulsion of 6% almond oil with acacia, in water; used in pharmaceutical preparations and cosmetics. **m. of asafoetida.** An emulsion of 4% asafoetida in water; a sedative and carminative. **m. of barium.** A suspension of barium hydroxide in water. **m. of bismuth.** Magma bismuthii, bismuth magma. A suspension of bismuth subnitrate in water; used medicinally. **m. of lime.** A suspension of calcium hydroxide in water. **m. of magnesia.** Magma magnesia. A suspension of 7% magnesium hydroxide in water; an antacid. **m. of sulfur.** Precipitated sulfur.

milky. A flat white or opaque appearance. **m. quartz.** Quartz with a milklike color and greasy luster.

mill. (1) A crushing, grinding, or pulverizing apparatus. (2) An establishment for reducing ores by mechanical means. (3) An establishment for grinding, crushing, powdering, or other processing, as paper mill, flour mill, etc. (4) The equipment of a rolling (steel) mill. **assay-** A small mechanical laboratory crusher. **ball-** A grinding apparatus with iron or quartz balls for powdering. **drug-** A laboratory apparatus for grinding drugs or seeds. **pebble-** Ball mill. **porcelain-** A laboratory machine for grinding wet or dry chemicals or bacteriological materials.

   m. iron. A pig iron suitable for puddling or for the basic open-hearth process.

millboard. Board made from wastepaper. Cf. *board.*

Miller, William Lash. 1866–1940. Canadian chemist, noted for his study of bios and physical chemistry. **M. indices.** See *atomic planes.*

millerite. NiS. Nickel pyrites. A native sulfide.

millet. A small-grain, edible cereal, cultivated on dry, sandy soils, *Setaria italica* (Gramineae).

milli- Prefix (Latin) indicating one-thousandth.

milliammeter. An amperemeter for measuring 0.001 ampere.

milliampere. ma. One-thousandth of an ampere.

milliangström. λ. One-thousandth of an angström unit: $1\lambda = 1/1,000$ Å $= 0.1$ $\mu\mu = 10^{-11}$ cm.

milliard. One thousand millions, 10^9 (U.K. usage). Cf. *billion.*

millibar. Vac. One-thousandth of a bar, q.v.

milligram. mg. A unit of weight: 1 mg = 1/1,000 gm = 0.01543 grain. **m. atom.** mg. at. The number of milligrams of an element, divided by its atomic weight. **m. per cent.** mg %. The concentration of a solution expressed in milligrams per 100 ml.

Milligramage. The amount of radioactive exposure produced by 1 mg radium in 1 hour.

milligram-hour. Milligramage.

Millikan, Robert Andrews. 1868–1954. American physicist, noted for his researches on electrical phenomena. Nobel Prize winner (1923). **M.'s rays.** Cosmic rays. A high-frequency radiation from interstellar space, which penetrates the atmosphere and upper crust of the earth. Cf. *mass-energy cycle.*

millilambert. A unit of illumination: 0.929 lumen/ft^2.

milliliter. Mil. In the U.K., the m. is accepted as a standard metric measure, and has been legal for use in trade since August, 1959. Cf. *cc*, *SI*.

millimeter. mm. One-thousandth of a meter.

millimicron. mμ. Nanometer, nm (European usage). 1 mμ = 1/1,000,000 mm = 1/1,000 μ. Cf. *micromicron*, uu.

millimole. mM. Molecular weight expressed in milligrams: 1/1,000 gm molecule (mole).

milling. The operation of crushing, grinding, or powdering. **chemical-** The removal of metal (especially aluminum) by controlled chemical reaction to produce a given shape or finish, e.g., by acid-etching unmasked areas.

millinormal. Describing a solution having 1/1,000 of the concentration of a normal solution.

million. 10^6 or 1,000,000.

milliphot. A unit of illumination: 1 milliphot = 1/1,000 phot = 0.929 ft-candle.

Millon's base. HO(Hg$_2$O)NH$_2$·H$_2$O or (HOHg)$_2$-NH$_2$OH. Yellow powder, produced from a solution of mercuric oxide in ammonium hydroxide. **M.'s reagent and test.** A reagent for the detection of proteins made by dissolving mercury in twice its weight of concentrated nitric acid and diluting with twice the volume of water (1849). Red color with proteins.

millstone. Buhrstone. A hard stone used for grinding cereals; it usually consists of a coarse sandstone with fine quartz inclusions.

milo. A cattle food containing crude protein.

milone. A beverage obtained by the fermentation of whey (about 0.8 % vol. of alcohol).

Milontin. Trademark for phenosuccimide (B.P.).

milorganite. An organic fertilizer prepared in Milwaukee by the dehydration of sewage. Brown granules, free from bacteria and seeds: nitrogen 5.4, phosphoric acid 3%.

Milori blue. A pigment similar to soluble prussian blue, but having a red tint; prepared by the oxidation of a paste of potassium ferrocyanide and ferrous sulfate.

Miltown. Trademark for meprobamate (B.P.).

mimetite. PbCl$_2$·3Pb$_3$(AsO$_4$)$_2$. Mimetisite. A native lead arsenate.

mimosa bark. The dried bark of *Acacia mimosa*, (Leguminosae); a tan.

mimosine. A toxic principle in the tropical leguminous shrub, *Leucaena glauca*, which causes cattle to lose hair.

min. Abbreviation for: (1) minute, (2) minim. ♏.

mina. The Sumerian unit of weight; one imperial pound.

mine. Subterranean workings for minerals, coal, or ores. Cf. *outcrop.*

mineral. A native, nonorganic or fossilized organic substance having a definite chemical composition and formed by inorganic reactions. **Ethiops-** Black mercuric sulfide with some free Hg and S. **m. acid.** An inorganic acid. **m. adhesive.** Sodium silicate. **m. alkali.** An inorganic base, e.g., sodium hydroxide. **m. blue.** (1) A mixture of ferriferrocyanide with calcium sulfate or barium sulfate. (2) A blue copper or tungsten ore. **m. butter.** Antimonous chloride. **m. caoutchouc.** Alaterite, helenite, bitumen elastic. A plastic bitumen. **m. carbon.** Graphite. **m. chameleon.** Potassium permanganate. **m. charcoal.** Amorphous coal with a vegetable structure, as thin layers in bituminous coal. See *coal* (fusain). **m. coal.** Fusain. **m. cotton.** M. wool. **m. dye.** An inorganic pigment. **m. fat.** Petrolatum. **m. green.** Copper carbonate. **m. jelly.** A semisolid mixture of hydrocarbons; as, petrolatum. **m. oil.** Paraffin oil, or its homologs. **m. oils.** An oil obtained from inorganic matter, as petroleum. **m. paint.** A pigment derived from a colored m. **m. pigment.** A native colored ore; or an artificial inorganic color. **m. pitch.** Asphalt. **m. purple.** A red, iron oxide pigment, or ocher. **m. resin.** A hydrocarbon mineral; as, asphalt, copal. **m. rubber.** Gilsonite. **m. separating fluid.** See *density fluid.* **m. spirit.** White *spirit.* **m. streak.** The characteristic colored streak produced when certain minerals are rubbed on a porcelain plate. **m. tallow.** Hatchettenine. **m. water.** A natural water containing sufficient salts or gases in solution to give it certain properties and taste. See *water.* *artificial-* A solution of certain salts in carbonated or distilled water. **m. wax.** Ozocerite. **m. white.** Pearl hardening. Pure natural calcium sulfate; used as a loading in paper, etc. **m. wool.** M. cotton. Finely interlaced filament produced by suddenly cooling molten slag; a filler for walls and coverings for steam pipes. **m. yeast.** A nonsporing yeast of the *Torula utilis* type; a contaminant of pressed yeast. On fermentation it gives high protein and low alcohol yields. **m. yellow.** Lead oxychloride.

mineralization. The replacement of organic constituents by inorganic matter, e.g., in fossilized plants. Cf. *petrifaction.*

mineralize. Petrify.

Minerallac. Trade name for an asphalt solution; used to insulate cable joints.

mineralography. (1) The descriptive branch of mineralogy. (2) The study of minerals by microscopic methods, and the photography of thin sections of the polished and etched minerals.

mineralogy. The study of the occurrence, description, mode of formation, and uses of minerals. **topo-** The m. of a particular region.

miner's inch. The quantity of water that flows through 1 in.^{2} in a 2-in. plank, the water standing 6 in. above the top of the hole = 2,274 ft^3/24 hr = 1.5 cfm.

miners' lamp. Davy's lamp. An oil lamp enclosed

in wire gauze which passes sufficient air for combustion, but conducts the heat of the flame away, thereby preventing explosion.

minetisite. Mimetite.

minim. ℳ = min. A unit of volume in the English system: 1 minim = 0.0616 ml = $\frac{1}{60}$ fluid dram. **U.S.-** 0.9606 imperial m. = 0.9483 grain water at 62°F.

minimal. Smallest quantity.

minimum. The smallest amount or lowest value.

mining. The processes by which useful minerals are obtained from the earth's surface (quarries) and underground (mines). **m. engineering.** The study of excavating, working, and controlling the technical processes of mines.

minioluteic acid. $C_{16}H_{26}O_7$ = 330.2. A dibasic acid from the mold fungus *Penicillium minioluteum*.

minium. Pb_3O_4. Red *lead oxide*. Originally cinnabar; now applied to its chief adulterant, red lead. Cf. *sandix*.

minivalence. The lowest valency of an element.

mink fat. The soft fat from *Putorius lutreula*. White solid, d.0.941, m.36.5, n_D1.4608.

mint. Mentha, q.v. **horse-** Monarda. **marsh-** Marsh mint. **mountain-** Calaminth. **pepper-** Peppermint. **spear-** Spearmint.

minulite. $KAl_2(OH,F)(PO_4)_2 \cdot 3.5H_2O$. A mineral from W. Australia.

minute. (1) Describing a particularly small object. (2) A unit of time: 1/60th hour. **m. glass.** An 8-shaped sealed glass vessel with fine sand which flows, in a given time, from the upper to the lower compartment.

Miocene. See *geologic* era.

miosis. Constriction of the eye pupil.

miostagmin reaction. Ascoli reaction. The lowering of the surface tension of dilute blood serum which results from the antigen-antibody reaction.

miotic. Myotic.

Mipolam. Trade name for a copolymer of vinyl chloride and acrylic nitrile; low-voltage dielectric.

mipor. Microporous. **m. rubber.** A soft rubber, with pores of about 0.0004 mm average diameter. **m. scheider.** A diaphragm of m. rubber used in accumulators.

mirabilite. $Na_2SO_4 \cdot H_2O$. A native sulfate.

miramint. A tungsten-molybdenum alloy, used in cutting tools.

mirbane oil. Nitrobenzene.

Mirlon. Trade name for a synthetic polyamide fiber.

mirror. A highly polished surface that reflects light, made of polished metal or glass. **concave-** A)-shaped mirror. **convex-** A (-shaped mirror. **plane-** A flat mirror.

mirrorstone. (1) Mica. (2) Muscovite.

misce. Latin for mix.

mischmetal(l). (1) A mixture of rare-earth metals. (2) Commercial cerium (40–75% Ce) with La, Nd, Pr, etc., and sometimes 1–5% Fe; used for pyrophoric alloys. Cf. *Auer metal*.

mischzinn. (German: mixed tin.) The alloy: Sn 54.4, Pb 41.9, Sb 3.6%; used to prepare solders.

miscibility. The ability of certain liquids to mix in all proportions. **m. gap.** The temperature range in which certain normally miscible liquids will not mix.

miscible. Capable of mixing or dissolving in all proportions. **im-** Not able to mix.

miso. An edible fermented soybean paste. Cf. *kogi*.

mispickel. $FeS_2 \cdot FeAs_2$. A native iron ore.

mist. Fog. Cf. *colloidal systems*. **m. tree.** Chionanthus.

mistletoe. The leaves and young twigs of *Phoradendron flavescens*; an antispasmodic and narcotic. Cf. *viscum*.

mistura. Latin for mixture; used in pharmacy.

mitigal. Mesulphen.

mitochondrion. A double-membrane structure in the living cell, which plays a role in the chemical changes involved in respiration.

mitogenic. Describing radiations supposed to be emitted by living humans; associated with religious hysteria. Cf. *scotography*.

mitosis. Karyokinesis.

mitragynine. $C_{22}H_{31}O_5N$ = 389.25. Mitragyne. An alkaloid, m.106, from *Mitragyna speciosa* (Rubiaceae).

mitraversine. $C_{22}H_{36}O_4N_2$ = 392.30. An alkaloid, m.237, from *Mitragyne diversifolia* (Rubiaceae).

Mitscherlich, Eilhardt. 1794–1863. German chemist. **M. desiccator.** A desiccator, with side tubes for evacuation. **M. eudiometer.** A closed glass buret, with platinum electrodes at one end and a glass stopcock at the other. **M. law.** (1) The law of isomorphism, q.v., which is not rigidly correct: The same number of atoms of similar elements combined in the same way produce an identical crystalline structure. (2) The spectra of isomorphous substances are similar. **M. pulp.** A strong sulfite wood pulp. Wood chips are digested for 70–80 hr at 45 psi pressure, the cooking liquors being circulated and heated outside of the digester.

mitsubaene. $C_{15}H_{24}$ = 204.19. A sesquiterpene from *Cryptotaenia japonica*, mitsuba-zeri (Umbelliferae), Japan.

mix. (1) To intermingle. (2) A physical mixture of substances, applied to rubber, etc.

mixed crystal. A crystal of 2 isomorphous substances, which crystallize in the same system. **m. ester.** An ester R—COO—R', in which the 2 radicals, R and R', are different. **m. ether.** An R—O—R' ether, in which the radicals, R and R', are different. **m. infection.** The invasion by and growth of 2 or more microorganisms in the animal body. **m. ketones.** A ketone of the type R—CO—R'. **m. salt.** A salt derived from a polyvalent acid, in which the H atoms are replaced by different metals, as $KNaNH_4PO_4$. **m. vaccine.** A suspension of 2 or more microorganisms, as bacteria in water.

mixer. Equipment for incorporating one or more material into another; a steel bowl, with revolving mixing arms moving in opposite directions. Cf. *mill*.

mixite. $Cu_2O \cdot As_2O_3 \cdot xH_2O$ with 13% Bi_2O_3. An emerald mineral.

mixture. (1) Substances that are mixed, but not chemically combined. Mixtures are nonhomogeneous, and may be separated mechanically. **A.C.E.-** An anesthetic m.: alcohol 1, chloroform 2, ether 3 pts. **constant boiling-** A m. of 2 liquids which, at a given pressure, distils unchanged, the boiling point remaining constant. Cf. *azeotropy*. **electrostatic-** A m. obtained by using electric energy to accelerate conducting particles or ions in a nonconducting medium, and so to impart rapid and violent motion to the dispersed particles. Used to desulfurize fuel oils. **freezing-** A m. of salts with water or ice which produces low temperatures. **law of-** Law of *alligation*.

mixture. (2) Mistura. A pharmaceutical preparation. **m. copaiba.** Lafayette m. A solution of copaiva 15 and acacia 30 minims in 1 fluid ounce water.

mks system. Meter-kilogram-second system. A technical system of measurements recommended by the International Electrotechnical Commission (1938) as simpler than the cgs system.

ml. Abbreviation for mil or milliliter (B.P., U.S.P.).

mM. Abbreviation for millimole.

mm. Abbreviation for millimeter = 1/1,000 meter.

mm^2. Abbreviation for square millimeter.

mm^3. Abbreviation for cubic millimeter.

mμ. Abbreviation for millimicron, 10^{-9} m.

$\mu\mu$. Abbreviation for micromicron, 10^{-12} m.

mmf. Abbreviation for magnetomotive force.

mmm. An abbreviation for millimicron

Mn. Symbol for manganese.

Mo. Symbol for: (1) molybdenum, (2) monium.

(Mo.) Abbreviation for morphine.

m.o. Abbreviation for *molecular* orbital.

mobile. Changing position; moving.

mobility. (1) The motion of atoms, molecules, ions, or colloidal particles. The mobility, α, of an ion in a liquid: $\alpha = 1.037 \times 10^{-5}\lambda n$, where λ is the equivalent conductivity, and n the transport number of the ion. (2) The visible motion of colloidal particles and microorganisms. Cf. *Brownian motion*.

mobilometer. A viscometer in which the time is noted for a disk to fall through a column of the liquid under investigation; used for oils and liquid foods.

mocha. See *coffee*. **m. stone.** Moss agate.

mochyl alcohol. $C_{26}H_{46}O = 374.35$. An alcohol, m.234 from mochi (Japanese birdlime).

mock gold. Iron pyrites. **m. lead.** Zinc blende. **m. ore.** Sphalerite. **m. silver.** Britannia metal. **m. vermilion.** Lead chromate.

mock-up. A nonworking model of an apparatus or plant intended to show the layout and method of operation.

mode. The actual composition of a substance, e.g., rock, as compared with its norm, q.v.

model. An arrangement from which an idea or concept can be visualized. **space lattice-** A group of wire nets and balls to show the arrangement of atoms in a crystal or molecule. Cf. *space lattice*.

moderator. A substance used in an atomic-pile to maintain a chain reaction by bringing the energies of the neutrons into the thermal region.

modification. (1) A slight alteration or change. (2) The conversion of cereal starch into a form in which it is readily acted on by proteolytic or amylolytic enzymes, as in malting barley.

modified soda. A mixture of sodium carbonate and bicarbonate; a cleanser.

Modrella. Trademark for a continuous-filament semimatt rayon yarn.

modulus. The measure of a force or properties of mass or their effects. **bulk-** An approximate value, in dynes per square centimeter, between the limit

of elasticity and the breaking strength of a material. **wet-** See *fiber*. **Young's-** The force (longitudinal elasticity), in dynes per square centimeter, required to stretch a metal wire a length proportional to FL/al, where F is the whole force, a the area, L the entire length of wire, and l the extension.

m. of elasticity. The ratio of the magnitude of the stress to that of the corresponding strain. (1) If the strain is volume, originally V, and the stress is pressure P, the m. of elasticity of volume (bulk m.) is PV/v, where v is the change in volume. (2) If the strain is a shear, the m. of elasticity is T/θ (shear modulus), where T is the shearing stress, and θ the corresponding shear. **m. of rigidity.** M. of elasticity (2).

mohair. A long, lustrous textile fiber from the Angora goat.

moho. Mohorovicic discontinuity. The boundary between the earth's inner mantle and the assorted surface rocks, 10–20 miles beneath the surface.

Mohr, Karl Friedrich. 1806–1879. German chemist and physicist. **M. condenser.** A modified Liebig condenser. **M. liter.** G.W.A. The space occupied by an amount of water at 17.5°C having an apparent weight in air (brass weights) of 1,000 gm. 1,000 G.W.A. = 1,002 ml. **M. pipet.** A small buret with tap, used as a pipet. **M. salt.** $(NH_4)_2Fe(SO_4)_2 \cdot 6H_2O$. Ferrous ammonium sulfate; a standard in volumetric analysis.

Mohs, Friedrich. 1773–1839. German mineralogist. **M. scale of hardness.** The hardness of a mineral is gaged by its ability to scratch or be scratched by one of ten standard minerals:

1. Talc	6. Orthoclase
2. Gypsum	7. Quartz
3. Calcite	8. Topaz
4. Fluorite	9. Corundum
5. Apatite	10. Diamond

Each mineral is scratchable by all below it. Cf. *abrasives*.

Moissan, Ferdinand Frédéric Henri. 1852–1907. French chemist, noted for the production of artificial diamonds and the isolation of fluorine. Nobel Prize winner (1906). **M. furnace.** A high temperature electric furnace. **M. process.** The reduction of chromic oxide with carbon in an electric furnace lined with calcium chromite.

moistness. The amount of liquid, generally water, held by a solid or gas. Cf. *wetting, absorption*.

moisture. The wetness or dampness of a substance; the percentage of water contained in a substance.

mol. Abbreviation for (1) molecule; (2) molecular. (3) Formerly used for *mole*.

molal. (1) Molar. Gram-molecular; pertaining to moles; the molecular weight expressed in grams. (2) Moles per weight, as in m. solution. **m. conductivity.** The conductivity between electrodes 1 cm apart of a solution containing 1 gm molecule/liter. **m. latent heat.** Molecular heat of vaporization. The quantity of heat (calories) required per molecular weight to transform a substance from the liquid to the gaseous state. **m. surface.** The area of a sphere of one mole of a substance. **m. solution.** Concentration expressed in moles of solute per 1,000 gm of solvent. Cf. *molar solution*. **m. volume.** The volume occupied by one mole of a substance: 22.4146 ± 0.0008 liter for an ideal gas under standard conditions. **m. weight.** The molecular weight expressed in grams; a mole.

molality. M. Concentration expressed in moles per 1,000 gm of solution. Cf. *molal, molar solution.*

molar. (1) Molal. (2) Referring to molecules in bulk. Cf. *molecular* (single molecules), *molal* (a definite quantity), *normal solutions.* (3) Moles per volume, as in *m. solution.* **m. solution.** A solution that contains 1 mole of substance in 1,000 ml of solution $= M$. Thus: 1.0 M NaCl solution contains 58.5 gm/liter.

molarity. M. The concentration of a substance in 1,000 cc of solution, expressed in moles. Cf. *molar, molal solution.*

molasses. Treacle. The uncrystallizable syrup obtained on boiling down raw cane- or beet-sugar solution (70% of sugars). Cf. *affination.*

mold. Mould. (1) A receptacle in which a molten or liquid mass solidifies. (2) To shape or form. (3) The loose earth on the upper surface of cultivated soil. (4) A variety of fungoid growth, usually filamentous, which grows Hypomycetes, found on damp vegetable material, e.g. *Penicillium.* **slime-** Myxomycetes.

moldavium. Virginium.

mole. Mol. (1) An amount of a substance, of specified chemical formula, containing the same number of formula units (atoms, molecules, ions, electrons, quanta, or other entities) as there are in exactly 12 gm of the pure nuclide ^{12}C. (2) A gram molecule; a formula weight in grams. The quantity of matter weighing M grams, where M is the molecular weight. Thus, 1 mole water weighs 18 gm. **milli-** See *milli.*

molecular. Pertaining to single molecules. Cf. *macromolecular.* **m. association.** Two or more molecules held by coordinate bonds. **m. colloid.** See *colloid.* **m. combination.** See *combination.* **m. compound.** Double salt. **m. conductivity.** Molal conductivity. **m. conversion.** See *rearrangement.* **m. depression.** The lowering of the freezing point of a solution. See *Raoult's Law.* **m. diagrams.** Drawings to scale of a view of the m. model. They resemble structure symbols, but show the ionic and effective radii and the shape of the molecule. **m. diameter.** The diameter of a molecule calculated from (1) Sutherland's equation, (2) van der Waals' equation, (3) the heat of conductivity, (4) the specific heat at constant volume; e.g., in angström units:

	(1)	(2)	(3)
Hydrogen	2.40	2.34	2.32
Helium	1.90	2.65	2.30
Oxygen	2.98	2.92	
Nitrogen	3.18		

m. dispersion. M. rotation. **m. elevation.** The raising of the boiling point of a solution. See *Raoult's Law.* **m. equation.** See *chemical equation.* **m. field.** See *field.* **m. film.** A monomolecular layer; as produced by adsorption. **m. flow.** See *flow.* **m. formula.** A combination of chemical symbols from which the m. weight of a substance is obtained by addition of the atomic weights of the constituents. Cf. *formula.* **m. free path.** The average free path of a molecule in a solution or gas, calculated from (1) Boltzmann's equation $\mu(0.3592\rho\Omega)$ or (2) Meyer's formula,

$\mu(0.3097\rho\Omega)$, where μ is the viscosity, ρ the density of the medium, and Ω the molecular velocity. **m. frequency.** The ratio $v = k(T_s/M\gamma^{\frac{2}{3}})^{\frac{1}{2}}$, where v is the molecular frequency, T the absolute temperature of the melting point of the substance, M the molecular weight, γ the molecular volume, and k a constant whose empirical value (Nernst) is 3.08×12^{12}. **m. heat.** Specific heat $\times$ molecular weight. **-of vaporization.** Molal latent heat. **m. number.** (1) A number, analogous to the atomic number, obtained by arranging molecules according to their molecular frequencies. (2) The sum of the atomic numbers of the elements of a molecule; in a compound it is *even*, in a free radical it is *odd.* Cf. *combination.* **m. orbital.** m.o. The region, for a given electronic state, over which the electrons in a molecular are distributed. **m. rays.** A stream of molecules moving uniformly in one direction, obtained by the escape of vapor through an orifice into a vacuum, screening, and condensing the vapor on the wall of the vessel. Velocity $= \sqrt{2RT/M}$ (about 2×10^4 cm for hydrogen at 20°C), where M is the m. weight. **m. rearrangement.** See *rearrangement.* **m. rotation.** Specific rotation $\times$ molecular weight. **m. sieve.** A zeolite having an open-network structure, used to separate hydrocarbon and other mixtures by selective occlusion of one or more of the constituents; e.g., gmelinite adsorbs methane but not isoparaffins. **m. solution.** A true solution, in which single molecules of the solute move in the solvent. *m.s. volume.* The difference between the volume of a solution containing 1 mole substance per liter, and that of 1 liter of solvent. **m. velocity.** The mean velocity with which the molecules move, proportional to the mean kinetic energy: $19,300\sqrt{(T/m)}$ cm/sec, where T is the absolute temperature, and m the molecular weight. **m. volume.** Mol. wt./density. See *parachor.* **m. weight.** M. The relative mass of a molecule in relation to that of a H atom. Obtained by adding together the atomic weights indicated by the formula of the substance; or determined by chemical or physical methods; as, lowering of freezing point, vapor pressure, conductivity, or vapor density.

molecule. The chemical combination of 2 or more like or unlike atoms. The smallest quantity of matter that can exist in the free state and retain all its properties. In noble gases and metals the m. is identical with the atom, i.e., monatomic. Other gaseous molecules usually consist of 2 atoms; as, O_2, Cl_2. **activated-** A m. with one or more excited atoms; having one or more electrons moving at a higher energy level. **biatomic-** (1) A m. of 2 atoms. (2) An isosteric m. having 2 atoms other than H; as, CH_3OH. **compound-** A m. consisting of different types of atoms. **elementary-** A m. consisting of one type of atoms. **excited-** Activated. m. **gram-** Mole. **homopolar-** Homonuclear m. A diatomic m. composed of 2 similar atoms, e.g., H_2. **isosteric-** One of a group of molecules having the same number of electrons, the same sum of atomic numbers, and, sometimes, the same molecular weight; as, CO_2 and N_2O. **nonpolar-** q.v. **oriented-** A m. having directional properties. Cf. *anisotropy.* **saturated-** A m. in which all valencies are satisfied. **symmetric top-** A m. with an n-fold axis of symmetry, where n exceeds 2; e.g., $CHCl_3$. **spherical top-** A m. having two axes of symmetry, e.g., CH_4. *tetratomic-* (1) A m. having 4 atoms. (2) An isosteric m. with 4 atoms, excluding H; as, $(CH_3)_3N$. **triatomic-** (1) A m. having 3 atoms. (2) An isosteric m. having 3 atoms, excluding H; as, C_3H_8. **unsaturated-** A m. in which there are double and/or triple bonds between certain of the atoms.

molecules (constants). (1) Avogadro's number. The number of molecules per gram molecule (mole) is $N = 6.06 \times 10^{23}$ (mean). (2) Loschmidt number. The number of molecules of a gas per milliliter at 0°C and 760 mm pressure is $n = 2.70 \times 10^{19}$. (3) Calculated constants:

Constant	H_2	O_2
Molecular weight	2	32
Velocity, meters/sec at 0°C. . . .	1,859	465
Mean free path, mm $\times$ 10^7	965	560
Collisions, millions/sec	17,750	7,646
Diameter, mm $\times$ 10^7	5.8	7.6
Mass, gm $\times$ 10^{25}	46	736
Number per ml $\times$ 10^{-19}	3.8	3.8

Typical molecular weights:

Insulin	12,000
Hemoglobin.	66,700
Tobacco seed globulin	300,000
Hemocyanin	6,800,000
Tomato bushy stunt virus. .	10,000,000

molions. The supposed negatively charged atomic groups of an ionized inert gas.

moloxide. An unisolated primary autoxidation product of one or more molecules of oxygen, added to an unsaturated organic compound.

molybdaenum, molybdan. Early names for both native molybdenum sulfide and graphite, which were frequently confused.

molybdate. A salt of molybdic acid. Simple salts; $M_2(MoO_4)$, or, $M_2Mo_2O_7$, corresponding with the chromates and bichromates, respectively. Complex salt: $M_6Mo_7O_{24}$.

molybdenic. Molybdic.

molybdenite. MoS_2. A white or green mineral.

molybdenous. A salt of divalent molybdenum, $Mo=$.

molybdenum. Mo = 95.95. A heavy metal, at. no. 42, of the chromium group of the periodic system. Gray metal, d.10.2, m.2620, b.3700, insoluble in water or alkalies. It occurs in molybdenite, molybdite, wulfenite, and other rare minerals; and its presence in soil is important for the growth of grasses and vegetables. The metal is cast with difficulty and is used for crankshafts and connecting rods; as a resistor in heating devices and radio apparatus; as wire for vacuum tubes and contacts. Valency 2, 3, 4, 5, or 6; but the commoner compounds are derived from divalent (molybdenous), trivalent (molybdic), and hexavalent (molybdate) molybdenum. **m. blue.** $MoO_2 \cdot 4MoO_3 \cdot H_2O$. Heteropoly blue. A mixture of m. dioxide and trioxide. **m. chlorides.** *di-*

$MoCl_2$ = 166.9. Molybdenous chloride. Yellow, insoluble powder. *tri-* $MoCl_3$ = 202.4. Molybdic chloride. Red needles. *tetra-* $MoCl_4$ = 237.8. Brown crystals. *penta-* $MoCl_5$ = 273.3. Black crystals, m.194. **m. hexacarbonyl.** $Mo(CO)_6$ = 264.0. Colorless crystals. **m. hydroxide.** (1) $Mo(OH)_3$. Black, insoluble powder. (2) $Mo(OH)_5$. Brown, insoluble powder. **m. minerals.** Principal ores: molybdenite, MoS_2; molybdite, MoO_3; wulfenite, $PbMoO_4$. **m. orange.** Pigments formed by the coprecipitation of lead molybdate, lead chomate, and lead sulfate in various proportions. **m. oxides.** *di-* MoO_2. Blue prisms; a textile pigment. *sesqui-* Mo_2O_3 = 240.0. Yellow to black mass, soluble in acid. *tri-* MoO_3 = 144.0. Molybdic anhydride. The most common oxide; white rhombs, soluble in alkalies; a reducing agent, and reagent for phosphorus pentoxide, arsenic oxide, hydrogen peroxide, aromatic oxy compounds, phenols, and alcohols. **m. sulfides.** *di-* MoS_2 = 160.1. Molybdenite. Black crystals, insoluble in water. A dry lubricant for metal bearings. *tri-* MoS_3 = 192.2. Red crystals. *tetra-* MoS_4 = 224.3. Brown crystals.

molybdenyl. (1) The radical $MoO_2=$. (2) The radical $MoO\equiv$. **m. dichloride.** $MoO(OH)_2Cl_2$ or $MoO_2Cl_2 \cdot H_2O$. **m. trichloride.** $MoOCl_3$. Green, soluble crystals.

molybdic. Describing a salt of trivalent or hexavalent molybdenum. **m. acid.** H_2MoO_4 = 162.0. M. hydroxide. Colorless needles. *hydrous-* $H_2MoO_4 \cdot 4H_2O$ = 234.08. Yellow, monoclinic crystals, soluble in ammonia; a reagent. **m. anhydride.** MoO_3. See *molybdenum oxides.* **m. ocher.** Molybdite.

molybdite. MoO_3. Molybdenum trioxide, molybdic ocher. Native as yellow, earthy or capillary tufted forms.

molybdoena. An obsolete term applied in confusion to both graphite and molybdenum sulfide.

molybdyl. Molybdenyl.

molysite. An incrustation of ferric chloride in lava and near volcanoes.

moment. The power to overcome resistance. **magnetic-** The strength of a magnetic pole multiplied by its length. **m. of force.** Torque. The effectiveness of a force in producing rotation around a center, in dyne-centimeters (force $\times$ distance from center). **m. of inertia.** See *inertia, momentum.*

momentum. The force effect of a moving body: velocity = $MV = MLT^{-1}$, where M is mass, V velocity, L length, and T time. **angular-** Spin.

momordicin. Elaterin.

mon-, mono- Prefix (Greek) indicating "one."

monacetin. $CH_2OH \cdot CHOH \cdot CH_2OOCCH_3$ = 134.1. Glyceryl monoacetate. Colorless liquid, d.1.221, $b_{2-3mm}131$, soluble in water; a solvent for basic dyes.

monacid. A compound having one OH group that can replace the H atom of an acid; as, monacid alcohol, MeOH.

Monacrin. Trade name for 3-aminoacridine.

monad. A monovalent element, radical, atom, or atomic group; e.g.: Na—, NH_4—, CH_2—, or —COOH. Cf. *dyad.*

monamide. An amide containing one amido group.

monamine. An amine containing one amino group.

monamycin. $C_{22}H_{37}N_4O_5(?)$. A stable basic antibiotic from the soil microorganism *Streptomyces jamaicensis*, m.126. It is active against organisms causing banana disease, which resist penicillin.

monarda. American horsemint, bee balm. The dried herb of *Monarda punctata* (Labiatae). **m. oil.** An essential oil from m., of thyme odor, d.0.930–0.940, containing thymol and cymol.

monardin. A thymol-like terpene from horsemint oil.

monascin. $C_{24}H_{30}O_6 = 414.2$. A red pigment produced by the growth of the fungus *Monascus purpureus* on rice, m.137, insoluble in water.

monastral blue. A phthalocyanin, q.v., containing a Cu atom. A blue pigment which has a great resistance to light, heat, and reagents.

monatomic. (1) Monad. Describing: (2) a molecule consisting of one atom; (3) an atom or atomic group having one free valency.

mona wax. Peat wax. Wax extracted from peat and used in making emulsions.

monazite. A native rare-earth phosphate sand, especially containing Ce, La, and Th (India, Brazil). Used in the manufacture of Welsbach burners and pyrophoric alloys.

Mond, Ludwig. 1839–1909. German-born English chemist. **M. gas.** Fuel gas made by the passage of superheated steam over coal. **M. process.** Separation of nickel and copper by carbon monoxide. Volatile nickel carbonyl, $Ni(CO)_4$, is formed and subsequently decomposed by heat. Cf. *Oxford process.*

Monel metal. Trademark for a native alloy containing normally Ni 67, Cu 28, Mn 1–2, Fe 1.9–2.5%; d.8.82, m.1160–1360. Very resistant to corrosion, and used in chemical plant.

monesia bark. The bark of *Chrysophyllum glyciphloeum* (Brazil); a tonic and astringent.

monesin. $C_{32}H_{54}O_{16} = 694.5$. A saponin-like glucoside from monesia bark.

mongol. Describing low mentality associated with facial characteristics (though not with the race) of Mongols.

monistic. Pertaining to singleness. **m. compound.** A substance that does not ionize in solution; as, sugar. Cf. *nonpolar.*

monitor. To guide or give warning. In particular, to follow the course of a process by radioactivity tests.

monitron. A device for the automatic monitoring of a radioactive area; it sounds an alarm when the intensity of the radiation exceeds the tolerance value.

monium. Victorium, q.v. A supposed rare-earth element (discovered 1898) which proved to be a mixture of rare-earth metals.

monkshood. Aconite.

mono- Mon-.

monoacetin. Monoacetin.

monoacid. A base or alcohol with one OH which can replace one H atom of an acid.

monoamino acid. An organic acid of the type, $NH_2 \cdot R \cdot COOH$.

monoatomic. Describing: (1) a base or alcohol containing one replaceable OH group; (2) an acid containing one replaceable H atom; (3) a molecule consisting of one atom.

monobasic. Describing an acid having one H atom replaceable by a metal or positive radical.

monobromated. A compound having one Br atom. **m. camphor.** See *camphor.*

monobromethane. (1) Ethyl bromide. (2) Methyl bromide.

monobromo- Describing a compound which contains one Br atom. **m. acetanilide.** Antisepsin. **m. isovaleryl urea.** Bromural.

monobutyrin. $C_3H_7COOC_3H_5(OH)_2 = 162.1$. Glycerol monobutyrate. Colorless liquid, d.1.008, b.271, produced by lipolysis.

monochloro- Describing a compound having one Cl atom. **m. amine.** $NH_2Cl = 51.5$. An intermediate product in the preparation of hydrazine from chlorine and ammonia; an unstable, pungent liquid. **m. ethane.** Ethyl chloride. **m. methane.** Methyl chloride.

monochroic. Monochromatic.

monochromatic. Monochroic. A substance having one color, represented by one wavelength only. **m. analysis.** The measurement of color by mixing white light with light of a pure spectral hue; only the hue and whiteness vary. **m. illuminator.** M. lamp. **m. lamp.** (1) A gas flame colored yellow with sodium compounds. (2) A spectrum apparatus with a narrow slit for isolating a radiation of one wavelength; a source of light for polarimetry, spectroscopy, or irradiation.

monochromatism. A rare form of color vision abnormality which enables the subject to match 2 colors merely by adjusting their intensities. Its frequency of occurrence in males is 0.003%.

monoclinic. See *crystal systems.*

monocon. An electrostatically focused cathode-ray tube used as an electron gun.

monoethan. Ethanolamine.

monoethanol. A compound having one ethanol radical, $-CH_2 \cdot CH_2OH$. **m. amine.** See *ethanolamine.*

monoethyl. A compound containing one ethyl radical.

monoethylin. See *ethylin.*

Monofil. Trade name for single-thread nylon, used in toothbrushes.

monofilm. Monolayer.

monoformin. $C_3H_5(OH)_2 \cdot COOH = 120.1$. Glycerylformate. An oil, b.165.

monogenetic. (1) Biology: pertaining to nonsexual reproduction. (2) Industry: pertaining to dyestuffs which produce only one color on textiles. Cf. *polygenetic dyes.*

monoglyceride. A glyceride, q.v., containing one acid molecule.

monohydrate. A crystal containing one molecule of water of crystallization. **m. crystals** $Na_2CO_3 \cdot H_2O$. Sodium carbonate; a cleansing agent.

monohydric. Describing a compound or acid containing one replaceable H atom.

monolayer. Monofilm. A monomolecular surface film, e.g., of octadecyl alcohol; used to retard the evaporation of large areas of water. Cf. *adsorption.*

monoleate. A combination of a base with one oleic acid radical.

monolupine. $C_{16}H_{22}N_2O = 258.2$. An alkaloid from *Lupinus caudatus* (0.45%). Yellow glass. $b_{4mm}257$, soluble in alcohol; related to anagyrine.

monomer. A substance composed of molecules which can polymerize with like or unlike molecules.

monometric. Isometric.

monomolecular. Pertaining to one molecule. **m. layer.** A layer one molecule thick. Cf. *adsorption.* **m. reaction.** A reaction concerning one molecule only; as, intramolecular rearrangements. Cf. *reaction order.* **m. zone.** See *zone.*

monomorphous. Occurring in one crystal form only. Cf. *dimorphic.*

mononitraniline. See *nitraniline.*

mononuclear. Describing (1) an aromatic compound having one ring of atoms; (2) a cell having one nucleus.

monoolein. $C_{17}H_{31}COOCH_2 \cdot CHOH \cdot CH_2OH =$ 354.30. Glycerol-1-monooleate. White crystals, m.35, insoluble in water; synthesized from fats by pancreatic lipase.

monopalmitate. An ester, especially of glycerol, containing one palmitic acid radical.

monopalmitin. $C_{15}H_{31}COOCH_2CHOHCH_2OH =$ 330.3. **alpha-** Glycerol 1-monopalmitate. White leaflets, m.77, soluble in alcohol. **beta-** $C_{15}H_{31}$-$COOCH(CH_2OH)_2$. Glycerol 2-monopalmitate.

monophosphate. A salt containing one phosphate radical.

monopole soap. A soap of highly sulfonated fatty acids.

monorefringent. Describing an isotropic solid or mineral.

monosaccharide. A hexose or pentose; in general, an aldehyde-alcohol or ketone-alcohol. Cf. *carbohydrates.*

CLASSIFICATION OF MONOSACCHARIDES

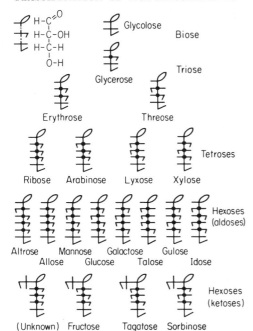

monose. Ose. A hexose or pentose. See *saccharides.*

monosilane. Silane.

monostearin. $C_{17}H_{35}COOCH_2 \cdot CHOH \cdot CH_2OH =$ 358.3. **alpha-** Glycerol 1-monostearate. White needles, m.74, insoluble in water. **beta-** $C_{17}H_{35}$-$COOCH(CH_2OH)_2$. Glycerol 2-monostearate. White solid, m.80.

monosulfide. Containing one divalent S atom, e.g., FeS. **m. equivalent.** A value of lime-sulfur solutions determined by titration with iodine to disappearance of the yellow color, giving the S of calcium sulfide, as distinct from polysulfides.

monotropic. Describing a substance occurring in one crystalline form. **pseudo-** Describing a substance that occurs in one stable form.

monotropitoside. A primeveroside of methyl salicylate from *Monotropa hypopitys*, yellow bird's nest (Pyrolaceae).

monotype metal. The alloy: Pb 80, Sb 15, Sn 5%; used for printing type.

monovalent. Describing an atom or radical having a valency of 1.

monovinylacetylene. Vinylacetylene.

Monox. Trademark for a mixture of silicon monoxide and dioxide; a thermal and electrical insulator, scale preventive, and corrosion inhibitor.

monoxide. A binary compound containing one oxygen atom; as PbO.

Monsel salt. Ferric subsulfate. **M. solution.** Liquor ferri subsulfatis. A brown styptic liquid containing about 15% iron.

montanic acid. $C_{29}H_{58}O_2 = 438.46$. A monobasic acid, m.87, from montan wax.

montanin. A disinfectant consisting chiefly of hydrofluosilicic acid.

montanite. $Bi_2O_3 \cdot TeO_3 \cdot 2H_2O$. A rare bismuth tellurate from Montana.

montan wax. A native hydrocarbon extracted from lignites. Brown or white masses, soluble in chloroform or benzene; used as a substitute for carnauba wax.

montanyl alcohol. $C_{29}H_{60}O = 424.26$. Nonacosanol*. White crystals, m.84.5, from beeswax, and *Parosela barbata* (Leguminosae).

monte-acid. An acid elevator or acid pump for raising acids to the tops of towers by means of air pressure.

montejus. An apparatus for raising liquids by air pressure (acid egg or monte-acid).

month. The twelfth part of a year; the period of revolution of the moon around the earth. **anomalistic-** = 27.5546 days, or the time of revolution of the moon from one perihel to another. **nodical-** = 27.2122 days, or the time of revolution of the moon from a node to the same node again. **sidereal-** = 27.32166 days, or the time of revolution of the moon from a distant star back to that star. **synodic-** = 29.5306 days, or the time elapsing from new moon to new moon. The ordinary month.

Monthier blue. $FeNH_4(FeCy_6)$. A blue pigment formed by the reaction of a ferrocyanide and ferrous ammonium sulfate.

monticellite. $MgO \cdot CaO \cdot SiO_2$. A native, calcium, magnesium silicate, belonging to the olivine group, and occurring in limestone in colorless or gray crystalline masses.

montmorillonite. $(Mg \cdot Ca)O \cdot Al_2O_3 \cdot 4SiO_2 \cdot nH_2O$. Japan clay. A rose-red mineral and acidic clay constituent, active in base exchange. When activated by treatment with acids, m. is used to catalyze the polymerization of unsaturated styrenes; for cracking petroleum, separating hydrocarbons, and adsorbing dyestuffs. The action is believed to be linked with the formation of colloidal silica by the acid treatment. **calcium-** Fuller's earth. **sodium-** Bentonite.

montroydite. HgO. Native mercury protoxide.

Moogrol. Trade name for the ethyl esters of hydnocarpus oil.

moonmilch. A pasty calcite formation found in caves where the air is saturated with moisture.

moonstone. A gem variety of feldspar with delicate, opalescent colors.

mora. Mowrah.

Moraceae. Urticaceae, q.v., yielding rubber, lac, hemp, timber, etc.

moradeine. An alkaloid from the bark of the tree *Pogonopus febrifugus* (Rubiaceae), S. America. Colorless prisms, m.195, soluble in alcohol; a quinine substitute.

morbific. Producing disease.

mordant. A chemical used for fixing colors on textiles by adsorption; as, soluble salts of aluminum, chromium, iron, tin, antimony. **m. dye.** An artificial or natural color for fibers which usually forms an insoluble metal compound (lake) with metallic salts (mordant). **m. rouge.** Aluminum acetate.

morenosite. $NiSO_4 \cdot 7H_2O$. Nickel vitriol.

Morgan, Sir Gilbert Thomas. 1872–1940. British industrial and research chemist; first Director of the Chemical Research Laboratory. **M., John Livingston Rutgers.** 1872–1935. American physical chemist, noted for research on the liquid state. **M. equation.** A modification of the Ramsay-Shields equation: $w(M/D) = k(t_c - t - 6)$, where w is the weight of the drop of liquid, M molecular weight, D density, and t_c critical temperature. Used to determine M. Cf. *stalagmometer*.

morin. $C_{15}H_{10}O_7 = 302.1$. $2',3,4',5,7$-Pentahydroxyflavone. A flavone, yellow coloring matter of the wood of *Morus tinctoria*, m.285. A wool dye and reagent for aluminum (green fluorescence).

morindone. $C_{15}H_{10}O_5 = 270.1$. Trihydroxymethylanthraquinone. A red coloring matter, similar to morin, from morus.

Morley, Edward W. 1838–1923. American chemist, noted for work on water and gases.

morograph. An instrument that records the death point of vegetable tissues.

-morphous, -morphous. Suffix (Greek), meaning form. See *amorphous, isomorph, monomorph, polymorph*.

morphia. Morphine.

morphina. Morphine.

morphine. (*Mo.*) $C_{17}H_{19}O_3N \cdot H_2O = 303.3$. Morphina, morphinum, morphia, morphium. An alkaloid derived from opium. Colorless crystals, decomp. 230, slightly soluble in water; a narcotic. **apo-** Apomorphine. **benzyl-** Peronine. **dehydro-** See *dehydromorphine*. **diacetyl-** Heroine. **dimethyl-** Thebaine. **ethyl-** Codethyline. **para-** Thebaine. **methyl-** Codeine.

m. acetate. (*Mo*)$C_2H_4O_2 \cdot 3H_2O = 399.36$. Yellow powder, soluble in water; a narcotic. **m. anisate.** (*Mo*)$C_6H_8O_3 = 413.35$. The salt of morphine and anisic acid. Colorless crystals,

soluble in water; a narcotic. **m. benzoate.** (*Mo*)-$C_7H_6O_2 = 407.33$. The salt of morphine and benzoic acid. White prisms, soluble in water; a narcotic. **m. borate.** The salt of m. and boric acid. Used in ophthalmology and for hypodermic injections. **m. bromide.** See *m. hydrobromide*. **m. chloride.** See *m. hydrochloride*. **m. citrate.** (*Mo*)$_3C_6H_8O_7 \cdot H_2O = 1065.92$. Colorless crystals, soluble in water; a narcotic. **m. hydrobromide.** (*Mo*)$HBr \cdot 2H_2O = 402.24$. Colorless needles, soluble in water; used for hypodermic injections (U.S.P., B.P.). **m. hydrochloride.** (*Mo*)$HCl \cdot 3H_2O = 375.8$. Colorless needles, soluble in water; a narcotic. **m. hydrosulfate.** M. sulfate. **m. lactate.** (*Mo*)$C_3H_6O_3 = 375.33$. Colorless prisms, soluble in water. **m. meconate.** (*Mo*)$_2C_7H_4O_7 \cdot 5H_2O = 575.5$. The natural form of m. in opium. Yellow crystals, soluble in water; a narcotic. **m. methyl bromide.** Morphosane. **m. phthalate.** (*Mo*)$_2C_8H_6O_4 = 736.4$. Colorless crystals, soluble in water; used for hypodermic injections. **m. saccharinate.** (*Mo*)$\cdot C_7H_4ON(SO_2) = 467.2$. Colorless crystals. **m. salicylate.** (*Mo*)$C_7H_6O_3 = 423.2$. Colorless crystals. **m. stearate.** (*Mo*)$C_{17}H_{35}COOH = 569.57$. Colorless crystals, soluble in water; a narcotic. **m. sulfate.** (*Mo*)$_2H_2SO_4 \cdot 5H_2O = 858.86$. Colorless needles, decomp. 250, soluble in water (U.S.P.); a narcotic (B.P.). **m. tartrate.** (*Mo*)$_2C_4H_6O_6 \cdot H_2O = 738.4$. Colorless crystals, soluble in water; used in hypodermic injections. **m. valerate.** (*Mo*)$C_5H_{10}O_2 = 387.36$. Colorless crystals, soluble in water; a narcotic.

morphinone. $C_{17}H_{17}NO_3 = 283.05$. The ketoform of morphine. **dihydro-** Dilaudide.

morphinum. Morphine.

morphol. $C_{14}H_{10}O_2 = 210.1$. 3,4-Dihydroxyanthracene. White needles, m.143, insoluble in water.

morpholine. $O \cdot (CH_2)_2 \cdot NH \cdot (CH_2)_2 = 87.1$. Tetrahydro-*p*-oxazine. Colorless liquid, d.0.9998, b.128, soluble in water; a reagent for Zn or Cu, and a corrosion inhibitor. **pheno-** See *phenomorpholine*.

morphology. The study of the form and structure of the living organism:

Internal:
- Cytology = the structure of cells
- Histology = the structure of cell aggregates (tissues)
- Anatomy = the structure of tissue aggregates (organs)

External: Taxonomy = the arrangement of organisms

morphosane. Morphine methylbromide; a narcotic.

-morphous. See *-morph*.

morrenine. An alkaloid from *Morrenia brachystephana*, Argentine milkweed. Colorless crystals, m.106.

morrhua. The codfish, *Gadus morrhua*; source of cod-liver oil.

morrhuic acid. An acid from the saponification of cod-liver oil. Its salts are used to treat tuberculosis and varicose veins.

morrhuin. $C_{19}H_{27}N_3 = 297.3$. A liquid ptomaine in some cod-liver oils.

morrhuol. The active principle of cod-liver oil; contains S, I, and P. Brown liquid, d.0.94, insoluble in water; a cod-liver oil substitute.

Morse, Harmon Northrup. 1848–1920. American chemist noted for osmosis experiments. **M. buret.** A capillary buret holding one cubic centimeter. **M. equation.** An approximate formula for the potential energy of a diatomic molecule as a function of nuclear separation.

mortar. (1) A cavity shaped container of glass, iron, agate, or brass; used for powdering materials with a pestle. (2) A building material: slaked lime and sand, sometimes mixed with plaster of paris or cement. Cf. *pozzolana*. **ballistic-** A m. closed with a tightly fitting steel projectile, used to test explosives by measuring the angle of recoil when the explosive is fired inside the m.

morus. Latin for mulberry. **m. tinctoria.** Yellow brazilwood, old fustic. The yellow wood from *M. tinctoria* (Moraceae); used to make morin and dye textiles.

Morveau. See *Guyton*.

moryl. Carbachol.

mosaic gold. (1) SnS$_2$. A pigment stannic sulfide. (2) A yellow alloy of copper and zinc. **m. silver.** An amalgam of tin and bismuth.

Mosander, Carl Gustav. 1797–1858. Swedish discoverer of some rare-earth metals.

mosandrium. A rare-earth metal isolated from samarskite and later separated into samarium and gadolinium.

Moseley, Henry Gwyn Jeffreys. 1887–1915. English physicist, noted for his work on X-ray spectra. **M. formula.** The frequency ν is related to Rydberg's constant ν_0 and atomic number N by $\nu = \frac{3}{4}\nu_0(N-1)^2$. **M. law.** All elements can arranged according to the frequencies of their X-ray spectra, in one continuous series which corresponds generally with the order of their atomic weights. **M. number.** Atomic number. **M. series.** An arrangement of elements according to increasing atomic numbers, as determined from the square root of the frequency of the principal line in their X-ray spectra. Cf. *periodic chain*. **M. spectrum.** The characteristic lines produced when the X rays from an anticathode of the metal under examination are diffracted through a crystal. Cf. *crystallogram*.

moslene. C$_{10}$H$_{16}$ = 136.12. A terpene from *Mosla japonica* (Labiatae).

moss. A cryptogamic plant, order *Musci*. **Ceylon-** See *agar*. **Iceland-** Cetraria. **Irish-** Chondrus. **m. agate.** Mocha stone. A gem variety of chalcedony, or an agate containing dark, mossy dendritic forms due to infiltration of iron and manganese salts. **m. gold.** Native gold in mosslike form. **m. silver.** Native silver in mosslike form. **m. starch.** Lichenin.

Mössbauer effect. The recoilless emission and resonant reabsorption of γ rays arising from nuclear excited states (lifetime 10^{-6}–10^{-10} sec); used to study chemical phenomena spectroscopically.

mote. A solid particle, e.g., dust, in a gas, which acts as a nucleus of condensation, causing the black fog of the modern city.

mother. A progenitor. **m. cell.** A single cell that divides into 2 daughter cells. **m. of coal.** Fusain. **m. liquor.** The residual saturated liquid which remains after the crystallization of a liquid. **m. lode.** The principal vein of a metallic deposit

passing through a district. **m. of pearl.** Nacre.

motherwort. The herb of *Leonurus cardiaca*; a bitter tonic and antispasmodic.

motile. Possessing motion.

motility. The phenomena of motion, especially as observed under the microscope (Brownian motion); or detected by chemical or physical means (ionic motion).

motion. Change of position. **laws of-** (Newton). (1) A body left to itself will continue in its state of rest or of motion. (2) The rate of change of momentum of a body is proportional, to the impressed force acting on it.

motor. An agent that produces motion or mechanical power (muscle or machine). **hot air-** An apparatus in which a current of hot air drives a set of propellers. **m. fuel.** A liquid (as gasoline) used in internal-combustion engines. Manufactured from coal by high- or low-temperature carbonization; Bergius process; gasification and conversion into methanol and other liquid combustibles; cracking processes. Cf. *diesel, petroleum.* **synthetic-** Methanol or synthol obtained from hydrogen and carbon monoxide subjected to 150–250 atm at 300–425°C (oxide of Zn, Cr, V, Mn, W, Pb, or Bi as catalyst).

mould. Mold.

mountain ash. Sorbus. **m. balm.** Eriodictyon. **m. blue.** Azurite. **m. butter.** A hydrated fibrous aluminum sulfate. **m. cork.** An elastic form of asbestos. **m. crystal.** Rock crystal. **m. flax.** (1) A silky variety of asbestos. (2) Purging flax. The herb of *Linum catharticum*; a laxative and cathartic. **m. grape.** Oregon grape. The root of *Berberis aquifolium*; an alterative and tonic. **m. green.** Malachite. **m. laurel.** Kalmia. **m. leather.** A tough asbestos, occurring in thin, flexible sheets. **m. milk.** A soft, spongy calcite. **m. mint.** Calamint. **m. soap.** An unctuous halloysite. **m. tallow.** Hatchettenine. A waxy hydrocarbon. **m. tobacco.** See *Arnica*. **m. wood.** A brown, compact, fibrous asbestos.

mounting. The preparation of specimens for microscopic study.

Moureu, Charles Léon Francois. 1863–1929. French chemist noted for research in catalysis, rubber chemistry, and autoxidation.

mouse jar. A glass jar with an iron screen top, to hold small animals. **m. factor.** A supposed vitamin, the absence of which causes blindness in mice.

Movil, Movyl. Trade name for a polyvinyl chloride synthetic fiber.

moving bed process. A process for the recovery of uranium and other metals by ion exchange, in which the separate stages of absorption, backwash, and elution are carried out in separate columns, the resin moving from one stage to the next.

mowrah. Mora, mowa. The seeds of *Bassia butyraceae* (Sapotaceae), India. **m. fat.** A soft mass expressed from m., used in soapmaking. **m. meal.** The dried and ground residue of m. seeds, after expression of the fat. It contains saponin and is unfit for animal food, but is used as fertilizer (2.7% N).

m.p. Abbreviation for melting point.

M radiations. See *M*.

ms. Abbreviation for *meso-*

M. S. or **M. Sc.** Abbreviation for Master of Science.
MTS. Trade abbreviation for sodium ethylmercuriosalicylate, a germicide.
mu. (1) Greek letter μ. (2) A unit of microscopical length: micron or micromillimeter.
muava. Muavi. The dried bark from a leguminous tree of Madagascar, used locally as an arrow poison.
muavine. An alkaloid from muava bark, an E. African tree of *Erythrophloeum* species (Leguminosae). Yellow powder, soluble in water; a digitalin substitute.
mucic acid. COOH(CHOH)$_4$COOH = 210.5. 2,3,-4,5-Tetrahydroxyhexanedioic acid. Colorless crystals, decomp. 224, insoluble in water; formed by the oxidation of *d*-galactose. Three of the other 10 isomers are named from mucic acid, namely *allo*-m. from *l*-galactose and *d*- and *l-talo*-m. from *d*- and *l*-talose, respectively.
mucicarmine. A stain for mucin: carmine 2, aluminum chloride 1, distilled water 4 pts.
mucilage. (1) A paste usually prepared from dextrin or gum. (2) In pharmacy, a solution of acacia, chondrus (Irish moss), tragacanth, or starch.
mucilaginous. Slimy or adhesive.
mucin. A glycoprotein; the chief constituent of mucus, the slimy secretion of organs or organisms. Soluble in water, precipitated by alcohol. Cf. *chitosan, mucoid*. **frog egg-** M. from frog eggs; it yields galactosamine on hydrolysis. **m. sugar.** Fructose.
muck. (1) A soil composed largely of highly decomposed organic matter, showing little of the original plant structure. Cf. *humus*. (2) Peat. (3) The miners' term for loose rock and ore.
muckite. C$_{20}$H$_{28}$O$_6$. A resin found in some coal beds.
mucoid. A group of glycoproteins, differing from the mucins in solubility and precipitated by acetic acid; in bone, tendon, cartilage, the cornea, white of egg, and ascitic fluids. **chondro-** M. from cartilage yielding chondroitin sulfuric acid. **cornea-** M. from the cornea. **ovo-** M. that does not coagulate; forming 10% of the solids of egg white. **serum-** M. from blood serum, forming 0.5–1% of its proteins.
mucolactonic acid. C$_6$H$_6$O$_4$ = 142.0. Colorless crystals, m.122, soluble in water.
mucolipoid. A compound that contains a fatty-acid residue bound to a carbohydrate residue, e.g., Wassermann antigens.
muconic acid. COOH·CH:CH·CH:CH·COOH = 142.0. 2,4-Hexadienedioic acid. Colorless crystals, m.260, decomp. 272, soluble in water.
mucopolysaccharide. A compound of low protein content, whose chemical reactions are primarily those of a carbohydrate; e.g., skin.
mucoprotein. (1) A compound of relatively high protein or peptide content, whose chemical reactions are predominantly those of a protein; e.g., plant globulins. (2) Glucoprotein (obsolete).
mucorin. A protein from plant molds.
mucous. Mucus.
mucus. (1) Slimy. (2) The saliva. (3) A slimy secretion from an organ or organism. **vegetable-** Tragacanthin.
mud. red- Bauxite sludge from the Bayer process for the manufacture of aluminum.

mudaric acid. C$_{30}$H$_{46}$O$_3$ = 454.37. An acid from mudar, *Calotropis gigantea* (Asclepiadaceae).
mudat. A low-grade opium; the refuse from yenshee, q.v.
Muencke pump. A glass filter pump attached to a water faucet.
muffle. A semicylindrical container of Alundun, fireclay, porcelain or silica, that protects substances placed in it from fuel gases and sudden temperature changes when heated. **m. furnace.** A fireclay container with resistance wires or other means of heating, which produces high temperatures rapidly, owing to reflection of the heat from the walls.
mugwort. Felon herb. The leaves of *Artemisia vulgaris* (Compositae); an emmenagogue and diaphoretic.
muirapauma. The dried stems and roots of *Dulacia ovata*, Brazil; an aphrodisiac or nervine.
muirapuamine. An alkaloid obtained from muirapuama wood (Olacaceae), Brazil.
mukogen. C$_{18}$H$_{15}$N$_2$O$_2$Cl = 326.5. Dimethylphenyl-*p*-ammonium-β-oxynaphtoxazime chloride. Green crystals, insoluble in water; a cathartic.
mullein. The dried flowers or leaves of *Verbascum thapsus* (Scrophulariaceae); a demulcent.
mullen. An instrument used to evaluate the bursting strength of paper from the pressure required to force a glycerin-inflated rubber diaphragm through the clamped sample.
muller. (1) A stone pestle for grinding pigments. (2) An instrument for grinding glass.
Müller's glass. Hyalite.
Mulliken, Samuel Parsons. 1864–1934. American chemist. **M.'s classification.** An arrangment of organic compounds based on their qualitative (*genus*) and quantitative (*order*) reactions:

Order I—Compounds containing:
    (1) Carbon and hydrogen
    (2) Carbon, hydrogen, and oxygen
Order II—Compounds containing:
    (1) Carbon and nitrogen
    (2) Carbon, nitrogen, and hydrogen
    (3) Carbon, nitrogen, and oxygen
    (4) Carbon, nitrogen, hydrogen, and oxygen
Higher Orders—Compounds containing any combination of the elements found in Orders I and II, with an additional element; as, halogen, sulfur, etc.

mullite. 3Al$_2$O$_3$·2SiO$_2$. An orthorhombic homogeneous solid solution of alumina in sillimanite, from the Island of Mull, or artificially made by heating andalusite, sillimanite, or cyanite. The only compound of Al and Si that is stable at high temperatures. Formed in fireclay above 1060°C, does not deform under loads at 1800°C, is resistant to corrosion, and has a low coefficient of expansion. Used as a refractory.
mulls. Pharmaceutical ointments of high melting point, spread on soft muslin ("mull").
mulser. An emulsifying machine.
multi- Prefix (Latin), indicating many. Cf. *poly-*.
multifrequent. Describing different wavelengths, e.g., those comprising a heterogeneous beam of light.
multiple proportions. Dalton's law. The chemical elements always combine in a definite ratio by

weight, or in multiples of that ratio. **m. tube burner.** Three or more bunsen burners mounted close together, and supplied from one connection.

multiplet. A spectral line, which on close examination is found to consist of 2 (doublet), 3 (triplet) or more single lines close together.

multipolar. Having more than 2 poles.

multirotation. Birotation.

multivalent. Having a valency of 3 or more. Cf. *polyvalent*. **m. vaccine.** A suspension of 2 or more species or varieties of the same microorganism.

mumeson. Muon.

Mumetal. Trademark for an alloy: approximately Ni 74, Fe 20, Cu 5.3, Cr 2, Mn 0.7%. It has a high magnetic permeability and low hysteresis; used for electric cables.

mundic. Iron pyrites. **white-** Arsenical iron pyrites.

mung. Green gram. The mung bean, *Phaseolus mungo* (*Ph. aureus*), E. Asia; it is rich in vitamin B.

mungo. A low-grade shoddy.

Munktell paper. A brand of filter paper.

Muntz metal. Yellow brass. The alloy: Cu 60, Zn 40%. It can be rolled hot or cold, and corrodes less than copper.

muon. Mumeson. A fundamental particle occurring in the atmosphere. It has a mass 206 times that of the electron, a negative charge, and a mean lifetime of 2×10^{-6} sec.

murex. $C_{16}H_8O_2N_2Br_2 = 419.87$. Tyrian purple. 6:6′-Dibromoindigotin. A dyestuff used by the aristocracy of the ancient world. A secretion from *M. brandaris*, a Mediterranean rock whelk; which develops color on exposure to light.

murexan. Uramil.

murexide. $C_8H_4O_6N_5NH_4 \cdot H_2O = 302.2$. Ammonium purpurate. Purple carmine. A purple coloring matter produced from uric acid by the action of nitric acid, followed by neutralization with ammonia. Brown crystals, green in reflected and red in transmitted light, soluble in water; a dye.

muriacite. Anhydrite.

muriate. Obsolete term for chloride. **m. of potash.** Potassium chloride. **m. of soda.** Sodium chloride.

muriatic acid. Obsolete term for hydrochloric acid. **oxygenated-** Early name for chlorine.

murram. See *laterite*.

muscarine. $MeCH_2 \cdot CHOH \cdot CH(NMe_3OH)CHO = 177.11$. Hydroxycholine. A very poisonous alkaloid resembling pilocarpine, from mushrooms, *Amanita muscaria*, and a ptomaine of decaying fish. Cf. *amanitine*. **m. effect.** See *m. wirkungs einheit*. **m. hydrochloride.** $Me_3NCl \cdot CH_2 \cdot CH(OH)_2 \cdot HCl = 277.5$. Colorless crystals, soluble in water. **m. nitrate.** $Me_3C(OH) \cdot CH_2 \cdot CH(OH)_2 \cdot HNO_2 = 198.14$. An oxidation product of choline. Brown, hygroscopic crystals, soluble in water. **m. sulfate.** $C_5H_{15}O_3N \cdot H_2SO_4 = 238.1$. *artificial-* An oxidation product of choline. Yellow, deliquescent needles, soluble in water. *natural-* A salt from the alkaloid of *Amanita* (toadstool). Brown syrup, soluble in water; a cardiac sedative. **m. wirkungs einheit.** M.W.E. A unit of poison effect; the amount which, in Ringer solution, reduces the activity of an isolated frog heart by $25 \pm 5\%$.

muscarufin. (1) $C_{25}H_{16}O_9 = 460.15$. An orange dyestuff, m.275.5, from *Amanita muscaria*. (2) $C_{25}H_{16}O_5 = 396.15$. A glucoside from *Amanita muscaria*.

musci. Mosses. A division of Bryophyta.

muscicide. An agent that destroys flies.

muscle fibrin. Syntonin. **m. sugar.** Inosital.

muscone. $C_{16}H_{30}O = 238.2$. Muskine. 3-Methylcyclopentadecanone, from musk. A thick liquid, b.328; used in perfumery.

muscovite. $KH_2Al_2(SiO_4)_3$. Phengite. A potashmica constituent of granite.

musenine. Mussanine.

musennin. An acid resin from the bark of mussena, *Albizzia anthelmintica* (Leguminosae); a tenifuge.

mushroom. (1) A toadstool fungus (q.v.), e.g., *Amanita, Boletus.* (2) The edible m., *Agaricus campestris*.

musical notes. A succession of sharp regular impulses at regular intervals of time. Cf. *sound, phonic*. **m. scale.** Sound vibrations in a harmonic series, the frequency of vibration of successive notes being fixed ratios for a particular scale. The scientific diatonic scale is based upon $C_3 = 256$ vibrations/sec; the musical even-tempered chromatic scale, on $A_3 = 435$ vibrations/sec.

musk. Moschus, deer musk, tonquin musk. The dried secretion from the follicles of *Moschus moschiferous*, the musk deer of Central Asia. Dark, shiny grains of penetrating odor, soluble in water; used in perfumery, and as an antispasmodic. Natural m. lost its scent all over the world in 1914. **artificial-** $Me_2C_6(NO_2)_3CMe = 295.1$. Trinitro-*tert*-butylxylene. A m. substitute. Colorless prisms, m.96, soluble in water. **vegetable-** M. seed.

m. root. Sumbul. **m. seed.** The seeds of *Hibiscus abelmoschus* (Malvaceae); used to clarify sugar.

muskeg. The vegetable cover over water-bearing soils.

muskine. Muscone.

Muspratt, James Sheridan. 1821–1871. Irish chemist, and founder (1848) of the College of Chemistry of Liverpool.

mussanine. Musenine. An alkaloid from *Acacia anthelmintica*.

must. (1) Most. The expressed, unfermented juice of grapes. (2) Any juice freshly expressed from fruits.

mustard. A condiment made by grinding the seeds of *Brassica* (*Sinapis*) species. **black-** The finely ground seeds of *B. nigra*. It contains a fixed oil; a pungent, irritant, essential oil (chiefly allyl thiocyanate); an enzyme myrosin; and a glucoside sinigrin. Cf. *sinamine*. **brown-** M. from the seeds of *B. nigra*, Linn. (Koch), and/or *B. juncea*, Linn. (Czernj and Cosson). **French-** Table m. **table-** A semi-liquid mixture of white mustard, salt, sugar, and vinegar. **white-** Yellow m. English m. The finely ground seeds of *Sinapis alba*, having the same constituents as black m. except that sinalbin is present. A condiment, counterirritant, and stimulant.

m. gas. $H \cdot S \cdot (CH_2Cl \cdot CH_2)_2S = 158.9$. 2,2′-Dichlorodiethylsulfide, yperite. An oil, d.1.28 m.14, b.215; used in World War I as a vesicant; it blisters the skin by penetrating the tissues and

forming hydrochloric acid. **m. meal.** The dried and ground residue of m. seeds after extraction of the oil: nitrogen 5, phosphorus pentoxide 1, potassium oxide 1%; a fertilizer. **m. oil.** (1) A fixed oil from m. seeds, d.1.1014, m. −17; used in medicine. (2) Oleum sinapis volatile. A volatile or essential oil obtained by distillation of macerated m. seeds. Its chief constituents are allyl isothiocyanate and allyl thiocarbimide. Colorless, pungent liquid, d.1.018, b.148, soluble in alcohol; used in medicine. (3) $CH_2:CH\cdot CH_2\cdot$
$\overline{N:CS}$ = 99.0. Allyl isothiocyanate. Allyl m. oil. Colorless liquid, d.1.017, b.151; used in World War I as a poison gas. (4) Acrinyl isothiocyanate. (5) A group of isothiocyanic esters. *artificial-* M. oil (3). *black-* M. oil (2). *essential-* M. oil (2). *fixed-* M. oil (1). *synthetic-* M. oil (3). *volatile-* M. oil (2). **m. seed.** The dried, ripe seed of *Brassica nigra;* a source of m. oil

mustard oils. Isothiocyanates, isosulfocyanic esters, sulfocarbimides. Compounds containing the radical —N:C:S: (*a*) MeNCS. Methyl m. oil, m. isothiocyanate. Colorless crystals, m.34, b.119. (*b*) EtNCS. Ethyl m. oil. Colorless liquid, b.133. (*c*) PrNCS. Propyl m. oil. Colorless liquid, b.153. (*d*) Me₂CHNCS. Isopropyl m. oil. Colorless liquid, b.137. (*e*) $CH_2:CHCH_2NCS$. Allyl m. oil. See *mustard oil* (3).

mustine hydrochloride. $MeN(C_2H_4Cl)_2\cdot HCl$ = 192.52. White, hygroscopic, vesicant, crystals, soluble in water. A cytotoxic agent used to treat leukemia (B.P.).

mutamer. A compound showing dynamic isomerism. See mutarotation.

mutamerism. The phenomenon of changing from one newly dissolved isomer to another, and establishing an equilibrium between the two. See *mutarotation.*

mutarotation. Birotation. A change of optical rotation occurring in newly prepared solutions of reducing sugars. Thus α-*d*-glucose solution has at first $[\alpha]_D$ +110° which drops to +87° in 25 minutes, to +52.5° in 6 hours, and then remains constant (β-*d*-glucose).

mutatochrome. A constituent of provitamin A. Cf. β-*carotene oxide.*

Muthman liquid. Acetylene tetrabromide.

mutterlauge. German for *mother liquor.*

mutual induction. The change of current in a circuit produced by a change of current in a neighboring circuit.

M.W., m.wt. (U.K. usage). Abbreviations for molecular weight.

Myanesin. Trade name for mephenesin.

mybasan. Isoniazid.

mycelioid. A bacterial growth that resembles the radiated filamentous appearance of molds.

mycelium. A mass of protoplasmic, colorless threads, constituting the plant body of mushrooms, toadstools, and certain molds (spawn).

Mycoban. Trademark for a product containing sodium propionate; used to prevent bread mold.

Mycoderma. Torula.

mycodextran. $C_6H_{10}O_5$(?). An unbranched polyglucose produced by certain molds, e.g., *Aspergillus niger.* It reduces Fehling's solution only after acid hydrolysis, and gives a light blue color with iodine.

mycogalactan. $(C_6H_{10}O_5)_n$. A polysaccharide from from the fungus *Aspergillus niger.*

mycoin. An antibacterial substance, probably identical with notatin.

mycophenolic acid. $C_{17}H_{20}O_6$ = 320.2. An acid antibiotic, antifungal, and antibacterial from the mold fungus, *Penicillium brevicompactum.*

mycoporphyrin. Penicilliopsin.

mycoprotein. The albuminous material of bacteria.

mycose. $C_{12}H_{22}O_{11}\cdot 2H_2O$ = 360.17. A carbohydrate occurring in manna, several fungi, and in ergot of rye. Cf. *trehalose.*

mycostatin. Hystatin (B.P.).

mycosterol. $C_{30}H_{48}O_2$ = 440.37. A sterol, m.160, from fungi and lichens.

mycoxanthin. A biologically active carotinoid, from algae.

mydaleine. A ptomaine from putrefied viscera.

mydatoxin. $C_6H_{13}O_2N$ = 131.1. A ptomaine from decaying flesh.

mydine. $C_9H_{11}O_2N$ = 165.1. A ptomaine in cultures of typhoid bacillus and putrefied flesh.

mydriatic. An agent that causes dilation of the eye pupil, as atropine.

mydrol. Midrol.

myelin. (1) A soft, yellow kaolin. (2) A doubly refractive lipoid from organic tissues. It forms a semifluid viscous covering around nerves. **m. forms.** The cylindrical excrescences which develop when lecithin swells in water.

mykonucleic acid. $C_{36}H_{52}O_{14}N_{14}\cdot 2P_2O_5$ = 1192.5. A nucleic acid from yeast.

Myleran. $Me\cdot SO_2\cdot O(CH_2)_4\cdot O\cdot SO_2\cdot Me$ = 246.41. Trademark for 1,4-dimethanesulfonyloxybutane; a drug used in the therapy of chronic human granulocytic leukemia.

mylonite. A rock deformed by earth movements, so as to lose all its original structure.

myocardiograph. An apparatus for recording movements of the heart muscles.

myocide. Phenyl mercury acetate.

myocrisin. Sodium aurothiomalate.

myodil. Ethyliodophenylundecanoate.

myogen. An albumin in muscle juice, soluble in water and salt solutions.

myoglobin. The principal red pigment of meat; similar to hemoglobin.

myokinase. A protein from milk, stable to heat and acidity.

myology. The study of muscles.

myosin. A globulin forming the clot in muscle press juice, insoluble in water, coagulated by heat, and converted into santonin by acids. Cf. *actomyosin, myogen.*

myotic. Miotic. An agent that contracts the eye pupil; as, eserine.

myoxanthim. A lipochrome, m.118, from the unsaponifiable matter of *Rivularia nitida.*

myrbane oil. Nitrobenzene.

myrcene. $C_{10}H_{16}$ = 136.1. 2-Methyl-6-methylene-2,7-octadiene*. An isomer of ocimene and a constituent of bay oil and other essential oils. Colorless liquid, d.1.467, b.67.

Myrcia. Tropical trees (Myrtaceae), related to the tree myrtles. **m. oil.** The essential oil of *Pimenta acris* (Myrtaceae), W. Indies.

myria- Prefix (Greek) indicating 10,000.

myrialiter. Ten thousand liters.

myriameter. Ten thousand meters.

myrica. Bayberry, wax myrtle, candleberry. The dried bark of *M. cerifera*, U.S. **m. leaves.** The leaves of *M. acris*, from which bay rum is prepared. **m. oil.** Bay oil.

myricetin. $C_{15}H_{10}O_8$ = 318.1. Oxyquercetin. A ketone and yellow pigment from the bark of Myrica species.

myricetrin. A glucoside resembling quercitrin.

myricin. $C_{30}H_{61}O_2C_{16}H_{31}$ = 676.9. Myricyl palmitate. A fatty ester (wax) and crystalline principle from beeswax; or from the bark of *Myrica*.

myricoid. The combined principles of *Myrica cerifera*; an alterative and hepatic stimulant.

myricyl. The radical $C_{30}H_{61}$—. **m. alcohol.** $C_{30}H_{61}OH$ = 438.7. Melissic alcohol. A constituent of carnauba and beeswax. Colorless needles, m.85, insoluble in water. **m. palmitate.** Myricin.

myriocarpin. A neutral resinous substance, insoluble in water, from the fruit of *Cucumis myriocarpus*, wild cucumber (Cucurbitaceae).

myristamide. $Me(CO_2)_{12}CONH_2$ = 227.23. Tetradecanamide*. White leaflets, m.103.

myristica. Nutmeg, nux moschata. The kernels of the ripe fruits of *M. fragrans*; a condiment. Cf. *mace, otoba*. **m. oil.** Oleum myristicae, oil of nutmeg. The essential oil of m.; d.0.880–0.910, n_D1.4690–1.4880 according to origin (E. or W. Indies) (U.S.P.).

myristic acid. $C_{13}H_{27}COOH$ = 228.29. Tetradecanoic acid*, from human subcutaneous fat (1%). Colorless leaflets, m.54, insoluble in water.

myristicene. $C_{10}H_{14}$ = 134.1. An eleoptene from the essential oil of nutmeg.

myristicin. $C_{11}H_{12}O_3$ = 192.1. 3-Methoxy-4,5-methenedioxypropenylbenzene, from myristica oil. Yellow liquid, d.1.1425, b_{15mm}149.5.

myristicol. $C_{10}H_{16}O$ = 152.1. A stearoptene from the essential oil of nutmeg.

myristin. $(C_{14}H_{27}O_2)_3C_3H_5$ = 722.9. Trimyristin, glyceryl myristate, laurel wax, myrtle wax. A fat in nutmeg butter, spermaceti, and other fats. Colorless needles, m.55, insoluble in water.

myristoleic acid. $C_{14}H_{26}O_2$ = 226.2. Tetradecenoic acid*, from fish oils. Δ^9-. Colorless liquid, b_{2mm}135. The Δ^5 isomer also exists.

myristone. $(C_{13}H_{27})_2:CO$ = 394.57. Myristic ketone. A solid, m.75.

myrobalan. Terminalia. The dried fruits of *Terminalia (Myrobalanus) chebula* (Combrataceae), Asia, containing 30% tannin. Cf. *beda nuts, chebulinic acid*.

Myrol. Trade name for a mixture of methyl nitrate with 33 vol. % of alcohol. An explosive.

myronic acid. $C_{10}H_{19}NS_2O_{10}$ = 377.3. An acid in sinigrin, the glucoside of black mustard, which is hydrolyzed to mustard oil.

myrosase. Myrosin.

myrosin. Myrosase. An enzyme of white and black mustard, which hydrolyzes the glucosides sinalbin and sinigrin to allyl mustard oil, glucose, and potassium sulfate.

myroxin. $C_{23}H_{36}O$ = 328.31. A principle from Peru balsam.

myrrh. A resinous gum exuded from the stems of *Commiphora myrrha* (Burseraceae), Ethiopia. It contains the resin myrrhin, a volatile oil, and a gum (brown tears of balsamic odor). Used medicinally as an astringent or carminative; and in dentistry for carious teeth. **m. oil.** An essential oil distilled from myrrh. Colorless liquid d.0.998, b.220–235, insoluble in water; used in perfumery. Cf. *myrrholic acid*.

myrrhin. A resin from myrrh.

myrrholic acid. $C_{17}H_{22}O_5$ = 306.17. An acid from myrrh.

Myrtaceae. The bay or eucalyptus family, which usually have pungent and fragrant leaves, fruits, and seeds, that yield essential oils and spices; e.g., roots: *Eucalyptus globulus*, (eucalyptus); leaves: *Pimenta (Myrcia) acris* (bay leaves); flowers: *Eugenia aromatica* (cloves); fruits and seeds. *Pimenta officinalis* (pimenta).

myrtenal. $C_{10}H_{14}O$ = 150.11. Myrtenic aldehyde: Colorless liquid, d.0.988, b_{10mm}90.

myrtenic acid. $C_{10}H_{14}O_2$ = 166.2. An acid from myrtol.

myrtenol. $C_{10}H_{16}O$ = 152.12. An alcohol, d.0.976, b.224, the chief constituent of myrtol.

myrtilin. An aqueous extract of myrtle; an insulin substitute.

myrtillidin. The aglucone of an anthocyan glucoside from the rose.

myrtillin. $C_{22}H_{22}O_{12}$ = 478.17. An anthocyanin from bilberry, *Vaccinium myrtillus* (Ericaceae); an indicator. **m. chloride.** (1)$C_{22}H_{23}ClO_{12}$ = 514.67. An anthocyanin from whortleberries, *Vaccinium uliginosum*. (2) A plant extract from *Vaccinium* with insulin-like properties.

myrtle. The dried leaves of *Myrtus communis*; an antiseptic. **m. oil.** (1) Yellow oil from m. leaves, which contains eucalyptole, *d*-pinene, and dipentene, d.0.90. insoluble in water; used in vapor inhalations. (2) Myrtol. **m. wax.** Bayberry wax.

myrtol. The essential oil of *Myrtus communis*; used to treat bronchial and pulmonary affections, and as an antiseptic. Cf. *myrtenal, myrtenol*.

mystin. A preservative mixture of sodium nitrite and formaldehyde.

mytilite. Mytilitol.

mytilitol. $C_6(OH)_5OMe$ = 194.11. Mytilite, pentahydroxymethoxybenzene, methyl inositol, from the mussell, *Mytilus edulis*. Rhombohedra, m.186. Cf. *inositol*.

mytilotoxin. $C_6H_{15}O_2N$ = 133.2. A leucomaine from mussels, rendered harmless by canning alkaline.

mytolin. $C_{234}H_{360}O_{70}N_{60}S(?)$. A protein obtained from muscles.

mytolon. Common name for 2,5-bis(3-diethylaminopropylamino)benzoquinonebisbenzyl chloride. Red crystals, similar in action to curare. It relaxes nerve muscles and renders deep anesthesia unnecessary.

myvizone. Thiacetazone.

myxo- Prefix indicating mucus or mucoid. **m. xanthinophyll.** $C_{40}H_{56}O_7$ = 648.6. The characteristic pigment of certain freshwater algae.

myxobacteria. Slimy moldlike organisms having an ameboid stage, as distinct from the common bacteria (eubacteria).

Myxomycetes. Mycetozoa, Myxogastres slime molds. A group of thallophytes comprising microorganisms having both vegetable and animal characteristics.

N

N. (1) Abbreviation for newton. (2) Symbol for nitrogen. **N*.** Excited nitrogen atom. **N₂.** Nitrogen molecule. **N₂*.** Excited nitrogen molecule. **NI.** Ionized nitrogen atom. **NII.** Doubly ionized nitrogen atom.

N. Symbol for: (1) normal, (2) normal solution, (3) Avogadro's number. **N electron.** The electron of the N shell or orbit; there are 8 in the third, 18 in the fourth, and 32 in the fifth period. **N orbit.** The fourth layer of energy level, in which electrons move around the proton in the dynamic atom. **N rays.** Nonluminous radiation whose wavelength is lower than that of visible light (Blondlet, 1903); emitted by a Welsbach burner, an X-ray tube, or the sun. They increase the luminosity of phosphorescent bodies. **N shell.** The fourth layer of energy level in which electrons oscillate in the static atom.

N-. In chemical names: the radical prefixed by N- is attached to the nitrogen atom.

n. (1) Any unknown number; as in C_nH_{2n}. (2) Symbol for index of refraction. (3) The number of molecules in 1 cc of gas. (4) Transport number.

n-. In chemical names: normal, as distinguished from isomeric, thus, n-butane.

ν. Greek nu. Symbol for frequency.

η. Greek eta. See E.

Na. Symbol for sodium (natrium).

naal oil. An essential oil distilled from naal grass, *Cymbopogon nervatus*, a Sudanese grass. Yellow liquid, d.0.954, insoluble in water. Chief constituents: *l*-limonene and perilla alcohol.

nabam. Official name (U.S., U.K.) for disodium ethylenebisdithiocarbamate; a fungicide.

Nacconol. Trademark for a group of surface-active sodium alkyl aryl sulfonates.

nacre. Mother of pearl. The hard, iridescent inside layer of oyster and other seashells.

nadi reagent. A reagent for cytochrome oxidase, e.g., in milk powders: dimethyl-*p*-phenylenediamine hydrochloride 0.02 and α-naphthol 0.1 gm are dissolved successively in 1 ml water. The blue color developed is a rough measure of the degree of oxidation.

nadorite. $PbClSbO_3$. An Algerian antimoniate. Brown orthorhombic crystals.

naehrsalz. (German for nutrient salt.) A mixture of sodium and ammonium phosphates.

naftolens. $(C_3H_4)_n$. A group of unsaturated, vulcanizable hydrocarbons, b.200–380, from acid-tar by-products of mineral oil refining; extenders for rubber.

nagelschmidtite. 7–9 CaO, P_2O_5, 2–3 SiO_2. The principal phosphatic phase in open-hearth steel furnace slags.

nagyagite. Tellurium glance. Lead sulfotelluride which contains gold and antimony.

nahcolite. Native sodium bicarbonate.

Nailon. Trade name for a polyamide synthetic fiber.

nakrite. $Al_2O_3 \cdot 2SiO_2 \cdot H_2O$. A gray clay.

nalorphine hydrochloride. $C_{19}H_{21}O_3N \cdot HCl = 347.85$. *N*-Allylnormorphine hydrochloride. White crystals, darkening on exposure, m.262, soluble in water; respiratory stimulant and antidote to morphine (U.S.P., B.P.).

nandinine $C_{19}H_{19}O_3N = 309.2$. A diisoquinoline alkaloid from the root bark of nanten, *Nandina domestica* (Berberidaceae), Japan. Cf. *domesticine.*

nandrolone phenyl propionate. $C_{27}H_{34}O_3 = 406.30$. White crystals, m.97, insoluble in water; an androgen (B.P.).

nano. The unit of 0.000,000,001.

Nanogen. A pesticide standardized in nanograms per microlitre.

nanometer. nm. Millimicron (European usage).

nantokite. CuCl. A native cuprous chloride.

napalin. An aluminum soap of lauric and naphthenic or oleic acids. A thickening agent for gelled gasoline fuels for incendiary bombs.

napalite. C_6H_4. Red wax, m.42, from near Napa, Calif.

napelline. $C_{26}H_{35}O_7N(OH)_4 = 541.3$. Benzaconine. An alkaloid from aconite.

naphazoline nitrate. $C_{14}H_{14}N_2 \cdot HNO_3 = 273.32$. White, bitter crystals, m.168, soluble in water; a vasoconstrictor (B.P.).

naphsultam acid. $C_{10}H_7O_2NS = 205.1$. The ring compound, O_2S—NH—$C_{10}H_6$. Cf. *naphsultone.*

naphsultone. $C_{10}H_6O_3S = 206.1$. Naphthosultone. Colorless crystals, m.154, soluble in water.

naphthalin. Naphthalene.

naphtha. (1) Oils of the C_nH_{2n+2} series, b.95–150, from the distillation of petroleum, coal tar, and shale oil. World production (1966), 20 million tons. (2) Gasoline. (3) A bitumen, q.v. **boghead-** Photogen. **coal tar-** Mainly benzene and its homologs. **petroleum-** Mainly paraffins and naphthenes distilled from crude oil. **shale-** Ligroin. It contains olefins and paraffins. **solvent-** A coal-tar distillate. **wood-** Mainly methyl alcohol and acetone, obtained by the distillation of wood; a solvent and denaturant for alcohol.

naphtha aceti. Ethyl acetate.

naphthacetol. 4-Acetamido-1-naphthol.

naphthacridine. $C_{10}H_6 \cdot N \cdot C_{10}H_6 \cdot CH = 279.1$. Dibenzacridine; 6 isomers. **di-** Dinaphthacridine. **fluoren-** Fluorenaphthacridine. **pheno-** Benzacridine.

naphthal. The radical $C_{10}H_7CH=$, from naphthoic aldehyde.

naphthaldehyde. $C_{10}H_7CHO = 156.1$. Naphthalene carbonal. **alpha-** Colorless liquid, b.291. **beta-** Colorless crystals, m.59.

naphthalene. $C_{10}H_8 = 128.1$. Naphthalin, naphthene, tar camphor. A hydrocarbon from coal-tar distillates:

Colorless, monoclinic crystals, $d_4^{\circ}1.152$, m.80, b.218, insoluble in water, soluble in alcohol or ether. Used as raw material for aniline dyes; as insecticide (mothballs), introfier, and antiseptic; for enriching illuminating gas and gasoline (albocarbon); and in the manufacture of indigo and lampblack. **acetyl-** Naphthyl methyl ketone. **amino-** Naphthylamine. **azo-** See *azonaphthalene.* **azoxy-** See *azoxynaphthalene.* **benzyl-** See *benzylnaphthalene.* **bi-** See *binaphthalene.* **bromo-** $C_{10}H_7Br = 206.97$. α- or *1-* Colorless crystals, m.5. β- or *2-* Colorless crystals, m.59. **chloro-** $C_{10}H_7Cl = 162.51$. α- or *1-* Colorless liquid, b.258, immiscible with water. β- or *2-* Colorless crystals, m.56. Used in organic synthesis and added to gasoline to lubricate the valve stems of internal-combustion engines (Halowax). **chlorinated-** C.K. wax. **decahydro-** Dekalin. **di-** Binaphthalene. **diamine-** Naphthylenediamine. **diazoamine-** See *diazoaminonaphthalene.* **dichloro-** $C_{10}H_6Cl_2 = 196.96$. Colorless solids, insoluble in water. *1,2-* m.37. *1,3-* m.61. *1,4-* m.68. *1,5-* m.107. *1,6-* m.48. *1,7-* m.62. *1,8-* m.88. *2,3-* m.120. *2,6-* m.135. *2,7-* m.114. **dihydro-** $C_{10}H_{10} = 130.08$. Dialine. Colorless liquid. *ortho-* or *1,2-* $b_{16mm}84.5$. *para-* or *1,4-* b.212, m.16. **dihydroketo-** Naphthoquinone. **dihydroxy-** Naphthalenediol. **dimethyl-** $C_{12}H_{12} = 156.09$. *1,4-* Colorless solid, b.264. *2,3-* b.266. *2,6-* m.111- **dinitro-** Dinitronaphthalene. **ethoxy-** Bromelia. **ethyl-** $C_{12}H_{12} = 156.09$. α- or *1-* Colorless liquid, d.1.064, b.258. β- or *2-* b.251. **ethylene-** Acenaphthene. **fluoro-** $C_{10}H_7F = 146.05$. α- or *1-* b.216. β- or *2-* m.59. **hexahydro-** $C_{10}H_{14} = 134.11$. Colorless liquid, b.205. **hydrazo-** Hydrazonaphthalene. **hydroxy-** Naphthol. **isopropylmethyl-** Eudalene. **methyl-** $C_{11}H_{10} = 142.08$. α- or *1-* Colorless liquid, d.1.025, b.243. β- or *2-* Colorless crystals, m.35. **methylisopropyl-** Eudalene. **monoxy-** Naphthol. **nitro-** Nitronaphthalene. **para-** Anthracene. **phenyl-** Phenylnaphthalene. **phenyldihydro-** Atronene. **tetrahydro-** Tetralin. **tetrahydrotetramethyl-** Irene. **tetrahydrotrimethyl-** Ionene. **tetranitro-** See *tetranitronaphthalene.* **trimethyl-** Sapotalene. **trinitro-** See *trinitronaphthalene.*

n. aldehyde. Naphthoic aldehyde. **n. carbonal.** Naphthaldehyde. **n. carboxylic acid.** Naphthoic acid. **n. diamine.** Naphthylenediamine. **n. 2,1-diazo oxide.** $C_{10}H_6N_2O = 170.1$. Colorless crystals, m.76. **n. dicarboxylic acid.** $C_{10}H_6(COOH)_2 = 216.12$. *1,5-* Colorless crystals, m. exceeds 286. *1,8-* Naphthalic acid. **n. diol.** See naphthalenediol. **n. disulfonic acid.** $C_{10}H_6(SO_3H)_2 = 288.2$. Armstrong acid. *amphi-* or

2,6- Colorless needles, soluble in water; used in organic synthesis. *pros-* or *2,7-* Colorless leaflets, soluble in water. **n. picrate.** m.153. **n. red.** Magdala red. A red dyestuff derivative of n. **n. sulfinic acid.** $C_{10}H_7SO_2H = 192.13$. Colorless solid. *alpha-* m.85. *beta-* m.105. **n. sulfonic acid.** $C_{10}H_7SO_3H \cdot H_2O = 226.15$. α- or *1-* Colorless crystals, m.90, soluble in water. β- or *2-* Colorless crystals, m.102, soluble in water. **n. sulfonic chloride.** $C_{10}H_7SO_2Cl = 194.6$. *alpha-* Colorless tablets, m.67, insoluble in water. *beta-* Colorless tablets, m.77, insoluble in water. **n. thiol.** Thionaphthol. **n. yellow.** $C_{10}H_5(NO_2)_2-OH = 234.2$. Dinitro-α-naphthol. Its calcium salt is martius yellow.

naphthalenediol. $C_{10}H_8O_2 = 160.1$. Dihydroxynaphthalene. A group of naphthols: **1,2-** m.60. **1,3-** m.125. **1,4-** m.176. **1,5-** m.258. **1,6-** m.138. **1,7-** m.178. **1,8-** m.140. **2,3-** m.159. **2,6-** m.216. **2,7-** m.190.

naphthalenedione. Naphthoquinone.

naphthalic acid. **α-** or **1,8-** (1) $C_{10}H_6(COOH)_2 = 216.1$. Naphthalenedicarboxylic acid. Colorless needles, soluble in water; used in organic synthesis. (2) $C_{10}H_6O_3 = 174.05$. Yellow needles, m.190 (anhydride).

naphthalic acid lactone. $C_{10}H_6(CO \cdot O)_2 = 214.1$. Colorless crystals, m.169, soluble in water.

naphthalide. (1) A compound of the type $MC_{10}H_7$, as, $Hg(C_{10}H_7)_2$, mercury naphthalide. (2) A compound of the type $RNHC_{10}H_7$; as, acetnaphthalide.

naphthalidine. Naphthylamine.

naphthalimido. The radical $C_{10}H_7(CO)_2 \cdot N-$, from naphthalic acid amide.

naphthalin. Naphthalene.

naphthalize. To enrich a gas or liquid with naphthalene.

naphthalol. $C_6H_4(OH)COOC_{10}H_7 = 264.0$. Betol, salinaphthol, naphthyl salicylate. Colorless powder, insoluble in water; an intestinal antiseptic.

naphthamide. $C_{10}H_7CONH_2 = 171.1$. Naphthalene carbonamide. **alpha-** Colorless leaflets, m.202, soluble in water. **beta-** Colorless crystals, m.192, soluble in alcohol.

naphthamine. Hexamethylenamine.

naphthane. Dekalin.

naphthanthracene. Benzanthrene.

naphthaquinone. Naphthoquinone.

naphthathiourea. See *ANTU.*

naphthazin(e). $C_{10}H_6:(N \cdot N):C_{10}H_6 = 280.2$. Anthrapyridine. Colorless crystals, m.273.

naphthazole. $C_{12}H_9N = 167.1$. Naphthindole.

peri- $C_{11}H_8N = 154.1$.

$$N = CH - C_{10}H_6$$

naphthenes. (1) C_nH_{2n}. Cyclic hydrocarbons, also termed hydroaromatics, cycloparaffins, or hydrogenated benzenes, from Caucasian and Californian petroleums. Polycyclic n. occur in the higher-boiling fractions. (2) The naphthalene ring system. **mentho-** Menthane.

naphthenic acid. (1) $C_6H_{11}COOH$ = 128.1. Hexahydrobenzoic acid. Colorless crystals, m.38 soluble in water. (2) $R \cdot (CH_2)_nCOOH$. Monocarboxylic acids of the naphthene hydrocarbons; R is a cyclic nucleus of 1 or more rings. They occur in crude mineral oils and are used in lubricants, paints, preservatives, and as industrial catalysts.

naphthenics. The undesirable constituents of lubricating oil, which have steep viscosity-temperature curves.

naphthenyl. The radical $C_{10}H_7C\equiv$.

naphthieno. The radical $-C_{10}H_6 \cdot S-$, attached to 2C atoms of another ring.

naphthindene. $C_{13}H_{10}$ = 166.1. The aromatic hydrocarbon,

(1)   (2)

$$C_{10}H_6 \underset{CH}{\overset{CH_2}{\diagdown}} CH \qquad C_{10}H_6 \underset{CH}{\overset{CH_2}{\diagdown}} CH$$

(2)   (3)
alpha-   beta-

Cf. *indene.*

naphthinduline. $C_{27}H_{18}N_2$ = 370.2. A crystalline coloring material, m.250. Cf. *induline.*

naphthionic. $NH_2 \cdot C_{10}H_6 \cdot SO_3H \cdot \frac{1}{2}H_2O$ = 232.2. **ortho-** 1-Naphthylamine-2-sulfonic acid. **para-** 1,4-Naphthylaminesulfonic acid. Colorless needles, decomp. by heat, soluble in water; used in the synthesis of dyestuffs and pharmaceuticals.

naphthisodiazine. $C_{12}H_8N_2$ = 180.1. Ring compounds derived from phenanthrene by replacement of 2 C atoms by 2 N atoms. The 10 different structural possibilities are named according to the positions of the 2 N atoms in the ring:

naphthisotetrazine. $C_{10}H_6N_4$ = 182.2. The ring compound derived hypothetically from phenanthrene (see *naphthisodiazine*) by replacing 4C atoms by 4N atoms.

naphthisotriazine. $C_{11}H_7N_3$ = 181.2. The ring compounds derived from phenanthrene by replacing 3C atoms ring by 3N atoms.

naphtho- Prefix indicating relationship to the naphthalene ring.

naphthodianthrene, meso-. $C_{28}H_{14}$ = 350.1. An octocyclic hydrocarbon,

naphthodiazine. $C_{12}H_8N_2$ = 180.1. The ring structures derived hypothetically from anthracene by replacing 2 C atoms by 2 N atoms.

naphthofluorene. $C_{21}H_{14}$ = 266.2. A hydrocarbon and ring compound:

$$C_{14}H_8 \underset{CH_2}{\overset{CH_2}{\diagdown}} C_6H_4 \qquad C_{14}H_8 \underset{CH_2}{\overset{}{\diagdown}} C_6H_4$$

2,3-β-   2,3-γ-

naphthoic acid. $C_{10}H_7COOH$ = 172.1. Naphthalenecarboxylic acid. **alpha-** Colorless crystals, m.160, soluble in water. **beta-** Colorless crystals, m.184, soluble in water. **nitro-** See *nitronaphthoic acid.* **oxy-** See *oxynaphthoic acid.*

naphthoic aldehyde. $C_{10}H_7CHO$ = 156.1. Naphthalene aldehyde. **alpha-** Colorless liquid, b.292, insoluble in water. **beta-** Colorless leaflets, m.60, soluble in water.

naphthol. $C_{10}H_7 \cdot OH$ = 144.1. Hydroxynaphthalene, naphthyl hydroxide or alcohol. **alpha-** Colorless monoclinic crystals, m.94, soluble in water; an antiseptic. **beta-** Colorless leaflets, m.122, soluble in water; an antiseptic. **acetamino-** See *acetaminonaphthol.* **amino-** $NH_2 \cdot C_{10}H_6 \cdot OH$ = 159.08. 3-β- White crystals, m.234. 7-β- m.163. **aminoazobenzene-** Sudan red. **anilineazo-** Sudan yellow. **benzoyl-** N. benzoate. **diiodo-** Thymol iodide. **dinitro-** See *dinitronaphthol.* **lacto-** Lactol. **nitro-** See *nitronaphthol.* **nitroso-** See *nitrosonaphthol.* **sulfo-** See *sulfonaphthol.* **thio-** $C_{10}H_7SH$ = 160.12. 2-Naphthalenethiol*, β-naphthyl mercaptan. White scales, m.81, soluble in water.

n. antipyrine. Naphthopyrine. **n. aristol.** Diiodo-β-naphthol. **n.AS.** β-Hydroxynaphthoic acid anilide. **n. benzoate.** $PhCOOC_{10}H_7$ = 248.09. Benzoylnaphthol, benzonaphthol, naphthyl benzoate. White crystals. *alpha-* m.56. *beta-* m.110. Soluble in water. **n. bismuth.** Bismuth β-naphtholate. **n. blue.** Meldola blue. **n. disulfonic acids.** See *sulfonic acids.* **n. ethyl ether.** Nerolin. **n. green B.** $C_{20}H_{10}O_{10}N_2S_2 \cdot FeNa_2$ = 604.2. The disodium ferrous salt of nitroso-β-naphtholsulfonic acid. Green powder, soluble in water. **n. lactate.** Lactol. **n. methyl ether.** Jara-jara. **n. orange.** Tropaeolin. **n. phthalein.** A pH indicator changing from slight pink (pH 7.3) to green (pH 8.7), for titrating weak acids in alcoholic solution. **n. salicylate.** Naphthyl salicylate. **n. sulfonic acid.** $HO \cdot C_{10}H_6 \cdot SO_3H$ = 224.2. Acid intermediates for dyestuffs. *ortho-* or *1,2-* Colorless tablets, m.250, soluble in water. *amphi-* or *2,6-* Schäffer's acid. Colorless leaflets, m.122, soluble in water. *1,4-* Neville-Winther's acid. Colorless crystals, m.170 (decomp.), soluble in water. *1,5-* Cleves' acid. Colorless hygroscopic crystals, soluble in water. *2,7-* Casella acid. Colorless crystals, m.89, soluble in water. **n. yellow.** $(NO_2)_2C_{10}H_4(OH)SO_3H$ = 314.2. 2,4- Dinitro-α-naphtholsulfonic acid, S yellow. Yellow crystals. **n. yellow S.** $C_{10}H_4 \cdot O_8N_2SNa$ = 412.21. Citronin. The potassium salt is a dye for wool, silk, and food and an oxidation-reduction and pH indicator, changing from colorless (acid) to yellow (alkali).

naphtholate. A compound derived from naphthol by replacing the hydroxyl-hydrogen by a base.

naphtholbenzein. $C_{54}H_{38}O_5$ = 766.3. Brown powder, soluble in alcohol; an indicator in volumetric analysis (alkalies—green, acids—orange).

naphthonitrile. $C_{10}H_7CN$ = 153.1. Naphthyl cyanide, naphthalene carbonitrile*. **alpha-** Colorless needles, m.34, insoluble in water. **beta-** Colorless leaflets, m.66, insoluble in water.

naphthophenanthrene. Dibenzanthrene.

naphthoquinaldine. $C_{13}H_8N\cdot CH_3$ = 193.17. **alpha-** A liquid, b. exceeds 300. **beta-** m.82, soluble in water.

naphthoquinoline. $C_{13}H_9N$ = 179.1. **alpha-** Colorless crystals, m.52, soluble in water. **beta-** Colorless crystals, m.93, soluble in water. **octohydro-** *alpha-* 1,2,3,4,7,8,9,10-Octohydro-α-naphthoquinoline. Colorless crystals, m.48. *beta-* 1,2,3,4,5,6,7,8-Octohydro-β-naphthoquinoline. Colorless crystals, m.325. **tetrahydro-** *alpha-* 1,2,3,4. Tetrahydro-α-naphthoquinoline. Colorless crystals, m.46. *beta-* Colorless crystals, m.63.

naphthoquinone. $C_{10}H_6O_2$ = 158.1. Dihydrodiketonaphthalene. α- or *1,4-* Yellow crystals, m.125, soluble in water. *β-* or *1,2-* Red needles, decomp. 115, soluble in water; a reagent for resorcinol and thalline. *amphi-* or *2,6-* Orange crystals, changing to gray at 130–135.
n. dioxime. $C_{10}H_8O_2N$ = 174.1. Derivatives of naphthoquinone formed by replacing the =CO by =CN·OH groups; α-compound, m.207. *5-hydroxy-* Tuglone.

naphthoquinoxaline. 1,4-Naphthisodiazine.

naphthoresorcinol. $C_{10}H_8O_2$ = 160.0. 1,3-Dihydroxynaphthalene, naphthalenediol*. Colorless crystals, m.124, soluble in water; a reagent for aldehydes, sugars, and uronic acids.

naphthosalol. Betol.

naphthosultone. See *naphsultone*.

naphthotetrazines. $C_{10}H_6N_4$ = 182.2. Ring structures derived theoretically from anthracene by replacing 4 C atoms by 4 N atoms.

naphthothiazoles. $C_{11}H_7NS$ = 185.2. Ring compounds similar in structure to the corresponding naphthoxazoles, whose O is replaced by an S atom.

naphthotriazines. $C_{11}H_7N_3$ = 181.2. Ring compounds similar to the naphthodiazines, but having one more N atom in place of a C atom.

naphthoxanthene. Benzoxanthene.

naphthoxazine. Phenoxazine.

naphthoxy. Naphthoyloxy. The radical $C_{10}H_7O$—, from naphthol. **n. acetic acid.** A yield and growth stimulant for strawberries.

naphthoyl. The radical $C_{10}H_7CO$—, from naphthoic acid. **n. oxy.** Naphthoxy.

naphthyl. The radical $C_{10}H_7$—, from naphthalene. **di-** See *dinaphthyl*.
n. acetate. $CH_3COOC_{10}H_7$ = 186.1. *alpha-* Colorless needles, m.130, soluble in water. *beta-* Colorless needles, m.142, insoluble in water. **n. acetic acid.** $C_{10}H_7CH_2COOH$ = 186.1. *alpha-* Colorless crystals, m.131. *beta-* Colorless crystals, m.139. **n. alcohol.** Naphthol. **n. acetylene.** $C_{12}H_8$ = 152.1. *alpha-* b$_{25mm}$143. *beta-* White crystals, m.36, soluble in alcohol. **n. aldehyde.** Naphthoic aldehyde. **n. amine.** See *naphthylamine*. **n. benzene.** An indicator, changing at pH 8.0 colorless (acid) to blue (alkaline). **n. benzoate.** Naphthol benzoate. **n. carbinol.** C_{10}-

$H_7\cdot CH_2OH$ = 158.1. Naphthobenzyl alcohol. *alpha-* Colorless crystals, m.60, soluble in alcohol. *beta-* Colorless crystals, m.80. **n. cyanide.** Naphthonitrile. **n. ether.** $(C_{10}H_7)_2O$ = 270.2. N. oxide, naphthoxynaphthalene*. α- or *1,1-* Colorless crystals, m.110, insoluble in water. *β-* or *2,2-* Colorless crystals, m.105, insoluble in water. **n. ethyl ether.** *alpha-* See *ethyl naphthyl ether*. *beta-* Bromelia. **n. hydrazine.** $C_{10}H_7\cdot NHNH_2$ = 158.1. *alpha-* Colorless leaflets, m.117. *beta-* Colorless leaflets, m.125. Both soluble in water. The hydrochlorides are reagents for sugars. **n. hydroxide.** Naphthol. **n. isocyanate.** $C_{10}H_7$·NCO = 169.0. Colorless crystals; a reagent for hydroxy and amino compounds. **n. ketone.** $(C_{10}H_7)_2CO$ = 282.1. α,β- Colorless needles, m.135, insoluble in water. **n. lactate.** Lactol. **n. mercaptan.** $C_{10}H_7SH$ = 160.17. Thionaphthol. A liquid, decomp. 285, insoluble in water. **n. methyl ether.** $C_{10}H_7\cdot O\cdot CH_3$ = 158.1. Methoxynaphthalene*. α- Colorless liquid, b.258. β- Yara-yara, nerolin. Colorless powder of fruity odor, m.78, insoluble in water; used in perfumery. **n. methyl ketone.** $C_{10}H_7\cdot CO\cdot Me$ = 170.1. *alpha-* Acetonaphthone. Colorless crystals, m.34, soluble in alcohol. **n. salicylate.** *alpha-* Alphol. *beta-* Betol.

naphthylamine. $C_{10}H_7NH_2$ = 143.1. Naphthalidine. **alpha-** Colorless needles, m.50, soluble in water. Used in the manufacture of Martius yellow, magdala red, and other dyestuffs; and as a reagent for nitrites and nitrates. **beta-** Colorless leaflets, m.111, soluble in water; used to manufacture azo dyes. **acet-** Acetnaphthalide. **dimethyl-β-** $C_{10}H_7NMe_2$ = 171.11. Colorless crystals, m.46. **ethyl-α-** $C_{10}H_7NHEt$ = 171.11. Colorless liquid. b.303. **methyl-α-** $C_{10}H_7NH$-Me = 157.10. Colorless liquid, b.293. **nitro-** See *nitronaphthylamine*. **nitroso-** q.v. **phenyl-** q.v. **tetrahydro-** q.v. **thiophenyl-** Benzophenothiazine.
n. brown. Acid brown. 4-Sulfo-α-naphthaleneazo-α-naphthol. An indicator for the pH range 6.0 (orange) to 8.4 (pink). **n. hydrochloride.** $C_{10}H_7N_2H\cdot HCl$ = 179.6. *alpha-* Colorless needles, soluble in water; an intermediate in organic synthesis. *beta-* Colorless leaflets, soluble in water; used in organic synthesis. **n. sulfonic acid.** A compound derived from naphthalene by substitution of one H by —NH$_2$, and another H by —SO$_2$OH. There are 13 isomeric monosulfonic acids $C_{10}H_6\cdot(NH_2)SO_3H$; 20 isomeric disulfonic acids $C_{10}H_5(NH_2)(SO_3H)_2$; and 10 isomeric trisulfonic acids, $C_{10}H_4(NH_2)(SO_3H)_3$. See *naphthionic*, *Baden*, *Brönner's*, *Dahl's*, and *Bayer* acids.

naphthylene. (1) The radical $C_{10}H_6$=, from naphthalene. (2) Obsolete name for cyclohexene. **di-** Perylene. **periethylene-** Acenaphthene.
n. diamine. $C_{10}H_6(NH_2)_2$ = 158.1. Diaminonaphthalene. Colorless crystals. *1,2-* m.98. *1,3-* m.95. *1,4-* m.120. *2,3-* m.191.

naphthylidene. The radical $CH:CH\cdot CH_2\cdot C_6H_4\cdot C$=.

naphthylmercuric. The radical $C_{10}H_9Hg$—. **n. acetate.** $CH_3COOHgC_{10}H_9$ = 388.70. Colorless needles, m.154, insoluble in water. **n. chloride.** $C_{10}H_9HgCl$ = 356.14. Silky, quadratic crystals, m.188, insoluble in water.

naphthyloxy. Preferred term for naphthoxy.

naphthyridine. $C_8H_6N_2$ = 130.06. 1,8-Benzo-diazine, q.v., 1,8-pyridopyridine.

octohydro- $C_8H_{14}N_2$ = 138.2. Colorless crystals, m.227.

naphtol. Naphthol.

Napier, John. 1550–1600. Scottish inventor of logarithms.

Napierian logarithms. The exponent of the power to which the quantity e (= 2.71828) must be raised in order to produce a given number. See *logarithms, e.*

napiform. Turnip-shaped cavities in culture media liquefied by bacteria.

Naples jar. A glass jar for staining microscope slides. **N. yellow.** Lead antimoniate.

napoleonite. Corsite.

naptha. Naphtha.

narceine. $C_{23}H_{27}O_8N\cdot3H_2O$ = 499.4. An alkaloid from opium. Colorless prisms, m.170, soluble in water; a hypnotic and sedative. **ethyl-** Narcyl. **n. hydrochloride.** $C_{23}H_{27}O_8N\cdot HCl$ = 535.7. White granules, m.190, soluble in water; a hypnotic. **n. meconate.** $C_{23}H_{27}O_8N\cdot C_7H_4O_7$ = 699.4. Yellow needles, m.126, soluble in hot water. **n. sodium salicylate.** Antispasmin. **n. sulfate.** $C_{23}H_{27}O_8N\cdot H_2SO_4$ = 595.3. Yellow crystals, soluble in water. **n. valerate.** $C_{23}H_{27}O_8N\cdot C_5H_{10}O_2$ = 601.5. Green powder, decomp. on ageing, soluble in hot water.

narcine. Narceine.

narcissine. Lycorine.

narcophine. A double salt of morphine and narcotine meconate.

narcosan. A solution of the lipids from soybeans, the nonspecific proteins from alfalfa seeds, and the water-soluble vitamins from plant seeds; used to treat nervous disorders and drug addiction.

narcotic. A drug that produces stupor, complete insensibility, or sleep; as: opium group, producing sleep; belladonna group, producing illusions and delirium; alcohol group, producing exhilaration. Cf. *Meyer's theory.* **n. poison.** A n. that produces stupor or delirium.

Narcotic Act. See *Harrison Narcotic Act.*

narcotine. $C_{22}H_{23}O_7N$ = 413.3. Noscapine. Opianine. An alkaloid from opium. Colorless needles, m.176, insoluble in water; an antipyretic, tonic, and cough suppressant (B.P.); little narcotic effect. Cf. *cotarnine.*

narcyl. $C_{25}H_{31}O_8N\cdot HCl$ = 509.7. Ethylnarceine hydrochloride. Colorless crystals, slightly soluble in water.

narcylene. An anesthetic grade of acetylene.

naregamine. An alkaloid from *Naregamia alata,* Goanese ipecac; used as an emetic.

nargol. Silver nucleinate.

naringenin. $C_{15}H_{12}O_5$ = 272.09. 4,5,7-Trihydroxyflavanone. A synthetic flavone.

naringin. $C_{21}H_{26}O_{11}$ = 454.2. Aurantium. A crystalline glycoside from the flowers of *Citrus decumana,* the grapefruit or pomelo tree. Yellow prisms, soluble in hot water.

narki metal. An acid-resistant alloy of iron and silicon.

nascency. In the nascent state.

nascent. Describing a chemical substance, especially a gas, at the moment of its formation when it is most chemically active. See *status nascendi.*

nasrol. Symphorol N.

naszogen process. The production of oxygen from a mixture of a chlorate, an inert substance (as kieselguhr), and an exothermic compound.

natalite. An alcohol and ether mixture; fuel for internal-combustion engines.

nataloin. $C_{34}H_{38}O_{15}$ = 686.3. A principle derived from Natal aloes. Cf. *aloin.*

National Physical Laboratory. A British Government institution which certifies scientific glassware, weights, and measuring instruments having a specified high degree of accuracy, and carries out physical research. Certified articles bear a monogram NPL.

National Research Council. Established in 1916 by the National Academy of Sciences in Washington, D.C., for the better coordination of research in industrial problems.

native. Describing a substance occurring in nature. Used: (1) to indicate an uncombined element; as, native mercury; (2) to distinguish natural from artificial substances. **n. coke.** Carbonite. **n. compound.** A chemical compound that occurs in nature. **n. element.** A chemical element that occurs uncombined in nature. **n. metal.** A metal that occurs uncombined in nature. **n. paraffin.** Ozocerite. **n. prussian blue.** Vivianite. **n. soda.** Natron.

natrine. An alkaloid from *Solanum tomatillo,* (Solanaceae).

natrium. The Latin and German for sodium. Symbol Na. It is "official" in certain E. European pharmacopoeias.

natrocalcite. Gaylussite.

natrolite. $Na_2O\cdot Al_2O_3\cdot3SiO_2\cdot2H_2O$. Needle stone. Sodium aluminum silicate. A yellow zeolite. Cf. *radiolite.*

natron. $Na_2CO_3\cdot10H_2O$. A native sodium carbonate from the Egyptian desert; hence the term *natrium* (sodium). Cf. *trona, urao.*

natronkalk. Soda lime.

natrum. Early (Arabic) name for trona. Cf. *natrium.*

natural. Not artificial or synthetic. **n. bases.** Alkaloids. **n. changes.** (1) Reactions produced by decay, fermentation, or putrefaction of organic compounds. (2) Reactions produced by decomposition, corrosion, oxidation, and hydrolysis of inorganic compounds. **n. dyes.** Coloring materials derived from the vegetable or animal world; as, indigo. **n. gas.** (1) A mixture of hydrogen 20, methane gas 70%; or a mixture of simple hydrocarbon homologs found near oil fields. It is collected at the oil fields, and piped to the cities to be used as fuel. World reserves (1967), 28×10^{12} cu m. (2) Helium. **n. immunity.** The resistence of species or races to certain infectious diseases. **n. logarithm.** Napierian logarithm. **n. philosophy.** The interpretation of natural phenomena by theories and abstract concepts. **n. science.** Knowledge of the phenomena of nature, as opposed to abstract or philosophical science. **n. ventilation.** The ventilation of a mine by natural means.

naucleine. $C_{21}H_{26}O_4N_2$ = 370.2. An alkaloid obtained from *Nauclea excelsa*, Japan; a cure for the opium habit.

nauli gum. An oleoresin from *Canarium commune*, Solomon Islands. **n. oil.** An essential oil of anise odor, distilled from n. gum. Cf. *elemi*.

naumannite. $(Ag_2Pb)Se$. Large cubes with metallic luster.

nauseant. An agent that produces sickness.

nautical mile. A measure of distance: 1.15136 statute miles. **n. speed.** See *knot*.

naval brass. The alloy: Cu 61, Zn 38, Sn 1%. **n. stores.** (1) Group name for the materials originally used by builders of wooden ships; as, tar, rosin, turpentine, asphalt, pine oil. (2) Products obtained from rosin; e.g., turpentine, pine oil.

Navashin's solution. A fixative for plant tissues: equal parts of (1) chromium trioxide 1.5, acetic acid 10, water 80%; (2) formaldehyde 40, water 60 ml.

Nb. Symbol for niobium (columbium).

NCR. No carbon required. Trade name for a coated paper containing chlorinated diphenyl, which produces smudgeproof copies without the use of an interleaving carbon paper.

Nd. Symbol for neodymium.

Ne. Symbol for neon.

neat's-foot oil. Oleum bubulum. An oil obtained by boiling calves' and sheep's feet and shinbones. Yellow oil, d.0.916, soluble in alcohol; a lubricant and leather dressing.

nebulium. A hypothetical light element, at. wt. 1.31. It is assumed (from spectroscopical evidence) to exist in nebulas, but its characteristic lines are due to doubly and triply ionized oxygen and doubly ionized nitrogen. Cf. *coronium, aurorium*.

nebulization. The transformation of a liquid into a fine spray.

nebulizer. An instrument for nebulization.

necic acids. The acid products of hydrolysis of senecio alkaloids.

necines. The basic products of hydrolysis of senecio alkaloids.

necrocryptoxanthol. A provitamin A in yellow corn grain.

nectandrine. $C_{20}H_{23}O_4N$ = 341.3. An alkaloid from the bark of *Nectandra rodiaei* (Lauraceae). White powder resembling bebeerine in action.

nectar. The sugary juice of flowers; the source of honey.

needle. (1) A sharp pointed rod of metal for puncturing or sewing. (2) A n. shaped crystal. (3) A magnetic n. **astatic-** See *astatic*. **compass-** A magnetized n., mounted to move freely horizontally. **dipping-** A magnetized n., mounted to move freely vertically. **hypodermic-** A hollow n., for the injection of solutions beneath the skin.

n. ore. (1) An iron ore, which occurs in long fibrous filaments. (2) Aikenite. A native sulfide of lead, bismuth, and copper. **n. spar.** Aragonite. **n. stone.** Natrolite. **n. valve.** A screw valve with a long tapering point instead of a disk, for high-pressure gas cylinders.

neem bark. Azadarach. **n. oil.** Margosa oil, nim oil. An oil from the seeds of *Melia azadirachta*, containing sulfur compounds; an anthelmintic and alcohol denaturant. Cf. *margosa* oil, *margosic* acid.

Nefa, Nefalon. Trade names for a polyamide synthetic fiber.

negative. (1) Having a charge due to electrons, e.g., a n. ion. (2) The absence of a reaction, property, or phenomenon, e.g., n. catalysis. (3) The opposite of positive; as, a photographic n. **n. catalysis.** The retardation of a chemical reaction by means of a catalyst. **n. cotton.** A low-nitrated cellulose, soluble in ether or alcohol, used for photographic plates. **n. crystal.** A birefractive crystal in which the refractive index of the ordinary ray exceeds that of the extraordinary ray. **n. electrode.** Cathode. **n. element.** An acid forming element or an atom with 4–7 valency electrons, as C = 4, N = 5, O = 6, Cl = 7. It tends to attract additional electrons and form a stable system of 8. **n. group.** (1) An acid radical. (2) A radical, which causes an organic compound to become more n., and so enables the H atoms to be replaceable by metals; as, carboxyl, phenyl, and thionyl groups. **n. ion.** An atom charged with one or more n. electrons; an anion. **n. plate.** A photographic plate whose image is inverted: light appears black, and shadows white. **n. radical.** An acid radical. **n. test.** A reaction or test which indicates the absence of the substance sought.

negatron. Proposed name for a negative electron. Cf. *positron*.

negion. Proposed name for cation. Cf. *posion*.

negode. Proposed name for cathode, q.v.

neiopax. Iodoxyl.

nemalite. Brucite.

nematic. Pertaining to threadlike liquid crystals. Cf. *smectic*.

nematocide. A substance that kills worms.

Nembutal. Trademark for pentobarbitol sodium.

neo- Prefix (Greek) indicating new or recent.

neoantergan maleate. Mypyramine maleate.

neoarsaminol, neoarsenobenzol, neoarsphenamine. Neosalvarsan.

neoarsycodyl. Sodium methyl arsenate.

neobrucidine. $C_{23}H_{26}N_2O_4$ = 394.2. An isomer of brucidine.

neobrucine. $C_{23}H_{26}N_2O_4$ = 394.2. An isomer of brucine.

neocaine. Procaine hydrochloride.

neocalamine. Prepared neocalamine. A mixture: zinc oxide 93, red ferric oxide 3, yellow ferric oxide 4%; used to treat skin diseases.

neocerotic acid. $C_{25}H_{50}O_2$ = 382.4. A fatty acid from beeswax, m.77.8.

neocianite. The blue mineral CuO,SiO_2.

neocid. See DDT.

neocinchophen. Novatophan. A cincophen derivative used similarly to that compound.

neocryl. Succinanilomethylamide-*p*-arsonic acid. Used to treat syphilis and sleeping sickness.

neocupferron. The homologous naphthyl derivative of cupferron, q.v.; a reagent for iron.

neocuproine. $C_{14}H_{12}N_2$ = 208.34. 2,9-Dimethyl-1,10-phenanthroline. A specific reagent for copper; it forms a colored compound extractable in isoamyl alcohol.

neocyanine. A dyestuff derivative of cyanine; a photographic sensitizer for infrared rays.

neodiarsenol. Neosalvarsan.

neodrenal. Isoprenaline sulfate.

neodymia. Neodymium oxide. See also *didymia*.

neodymium. Nd = 144.24. A rare-earth metal, at. no. 60, discovered by Auer v. Welsbach (1885). Cf. *rare* earths. Yellow metal, d.6.96, m.840, tarnishes slowly. It occurs in cerium and lanthanum minerals, and forms salts that are generally purple-colored and fluorescent. Valency 3. **n. acetate.** $(CH_3COO)_3Nd \cdot H_2O$ = 339.36. Pink crystals, soluble in water. **n. acetyl acetonate.** $Nd(MeCOCH_2COO)_3$ = 441.43. Violet crystals, m.122, soluble in water. **n. chloride.** $NdCl_3$ = 250.65. Rose crystals, soluble in water. **n. hydroxide.** $Nd(OH)_3$ = 195.29. Pink powder, insoluble in water. **n. iodide.** NdI_3 = 525.07. Purple crystals, soluble in water. **n. oxalate.** $Nd_2(C_2O_4)_3$ = 732.70. Rose crystals, insoluble in water. **n. oxide.** Nd_2O_3 = 336.54. Blue powder, insoluble in water. **n. phosphate.** $NdPO_4$ = 239.29. Red powder; an amethyst coloring for porcelain. **n. sulfide.** Nd_2S_3 = 384.72. Green powder, m.2200.

neoepinene. Isoprenaline sulfate.

neogen. A silver-white alloy: Cu 58, Zn 27, Ni 12, Sn 2, Al 0.5, Bi 0.5%.

neohexane. 2,2-Dimethylbutane*.

Neo-Hombreol. Trademark for testosterone propionate. **N.-H.M.** Methyltestosterone.

neohydriol. An injection preparation of iodized oil.

Neokharsivan. Trade name for a brand of neosalvarsan.

neolactose. An isomer of lactose.

neoline. $C_{23}H_{39}O_6N$ = 425.2. An alkaloid obtained by hydrolysis of neopelline.

neolite. A green, fibrous aluminum-magnesium silicate.

neolithic. Late Stone Age. Pertaining to the epoch of the beginning of agriculture, discovery of fire, and better implements of stone and bone. It was preceded by the paleolithic age and followed by the copper and bronze ages.

neomycin. An antibiotic from the genus *Streptomyces*, similar in effect to streptomycin. Commercial n. contains 2 isomers, **n.A** (predominating) and **n.B.** **n. sulfate.** White, hygroscopic crystals, soluble in water; an antibiotic (U.S.P., B.P.).

neon. Ne = 20.179. A rare, noble gaseous element, at. no. 10, discovered in the atmosphere (1898) by Ramsay and Travers. Colorless gas, $d_{H=1}9.96$, m.−253, b.−243. It occurs in the air (1 in 55,000) and consists of 2 isotopes (at. wt. 20 and 22). It forms no chemical compounds, and is used as a residual gas in vacuum tubes and incandescent lamps. **n. lamp, n. light, n. tube.** A vacuum tube containing a trace of n. It emits an intense red light of great fog-penetrating power, used for advertising signs and beacons.

Neonal. $C_{10}H_{16}O_3N_2$. Trademark for 5-*n*-butyl-5-ethylbarbituric acid; a hypnotic.

neonicotine. Anabasine.

neopelline. $C_{32}H_{45}O_8N$ = 571.36. An alkaloid from *Aconitum napellus*, aconite.

neopentane. 2,2-Dimethylpropane.

Neophrin. Trade name for phenylephrine hydrochloride.

neoplasm. A new growth of an abnormal character, e.g., cancer.

neoprene. $[-CH_2 \cdot CH:C(Cl)CH_2]_x$. Polychloro-

prene. Generic name for synthetic rubber made by polymerization of 2-chloro-1,3-butadiene (prepared by the action of hydrogen chloride on monovinylacetylene). Neoprene vulcanizates are markedly resistant to oils, chemicals, sunlight, ozone, and heat.

neosalvarsan. $C_{12}H_{11}O_2N_2As_2(CH_2)O \cdot SONa$ = 466.2. Neoarsaminol, neoarsphenamine, neodiarsenol, Ehrlich no. 914, novarsenobenzol, sodium-3,3'-diamino-4,4'-dihydroxyarsenobenzolmethanalsulfoxylate. A product of salvarsan and formaldehyde sodium sulfoxylate discovered by Ehrlich and Bertheim (1912). Orange powder, with characteristic odor, very soluble in water; used for intravenous and intramuscular injections.

neosine. A nitrogenous base from muscle.

neostibosan. The diethylamine salt of stibanilic acid; similar in action, but preferable to stibosan, q.v.

neostrychnine. $C_{21}H_{22}N_2O_2$ = 334.15. An isomer of strychnine.

neostygmine bromide. $C_{12}H_{19}O_2N_2Br$ = 303.22. White, bitter, crystalline powder, m.167 (decomp.), soluble in water; a parasympathomimetic (U.S.P., B.P.). **n. methyl sulfate.** m.143; used similarly (U.S.P., B.P.).

Neo-Synephrine. $C_9H_{13}NO_2$ = 167.1. Trademark for levo-α-hydroxy-β-methylamino-3-hydroxyethylbenzene. White crystals; a vasoconstrictor.

neothesine. $PhCOO(CH_2)_3N \cdot (CH_2)_4CHMe \cdot HCl$ = 297.7. γ-(2-Methylpiperidino)propyl benzoate hydrochloride. White crystals, m.172, soluble in water; a local anesthetic. Cf. *procaine*, *cocaine*. **n. base.** Yellow oil, insoluble in water.

neotype. Alstonite.

neovaricaine. Ethanolamine.

neoytterbium. Ytterbium.

Neozone. Trademark for phenylnaphthylamine derivatives; used as antioxidants in rubber manufacture.

nepalin. $C_{17}H_{14}O_4$ = 282.11. A crystalline constituent from the *Rumex* species (Polygonaceae). Cf. *nepodin*.

nepheline. A granular rock, which consists chiefly of nephelite and pyroxene.

nephelite. (1) An orthosilicate rock of sodium, potassium, and aluminum: aluminum potassium silicate 20, aluminum sodium silicate 75, albite 5%. (2) $NaAlSiO_4$. Elaeolite. A silica mineral, q.v., typical of a group.

nephelometer. A photometric or other optical device to determine the amount of suspended matter in a solution by comparison of the amount of light scattered by the suspended particles with that scattered by a standard suspension. Used to determine any substance that can be precipitated in a finely divided form. Cf. *turbidimetry*.

nephelometry. Quantitative analysis by determining the degree of light scattered from a fog or suspension. Cf. *turbidity*.

nephrite. Jade.

nepodin. $C_{18}H_{16}O_4$ = 296.12. A principle, m.158, from *Rumex nepalensis* (Polygoniaceae). Cf. *nepalin*.

neptunium. (1) Np = 239. An element, at. no. 93, obtained by bombarding ordinary uranium with neutrons (Abelson and McMillon, 1940); and as an impurity in plutonium formed by double-electron capture in U^{235}. It has valencies of 3, 4 (unstable), and 5. It transforms into plutonium. It has a half-life of 2 million years, and its most stable isotope has mass no. 237. (2) A supposed element of at. wt. 118, which proved to be a mixture of tantalum and niobium.

neptunyl. The NpO_2 ion.

Neradol. Trade name for a synthetic tanning agent.

Neral. Trade name for β-citral.

neriantin. A crystalline glucoside from the leaves of *Nerium oleander*.

neriin. A glucoside from the leaves of *Nerium oleander* (Apocynaceae), soluble in water; it resembles strophantin and has a digitalis-like action. Cf. *oleandrin*.

neriodorin. A glucoside from the bark of *Nerium odorum*.

nerium. Oleander.

Nernst, Walther Hermann. 1864–1941. German physical chemist. Nobel Prize winner (1921). **N. effect.** The thermomagnetic difference in potential observed on passing a current through a metallic plate placed between 2 magnetic poles. **N. heat theorem.** The entropy of a condensed, chemically homogeneous substance vanishes at the zero of absolute temperature. **N. lamp.** See *lamp*. **N. law.** Partition law. Distribution law, Nernst theorem. A substance in contact with 2 immiscible liquids and soluble in both, will dissolve in the 2 liquids in fixed proportions, providing no molecular association or electrolytic dissociation occurs. **N. theory.** (1) The electric stimulus to the tissues of an organism is due to the dissociation of the salts surrounding the cell membranes. (2) The theory of electrolytic solution pressure, q.v., which is set up by the tendency of a metal to dissolve and form ions. **N. unit.** A measure of flow, liters per second.

nerol. $C_{10}H_{18}O$ = 154.14. A primary alcohol derived from neroli oil. Colorless liquid, d.0.881, b.226.

nerolidol.. $C_{15}H_{26}O$ = 222.20. Peruviol, 3,7,11-trimethyldodecatriene-1,6,10-ol-3, from neroli oil and Peru balsam, d.0.880, b.277; used in perfumery.

nerolin. (1) $C_{10}H_7 \cdot O \cdot C_2H_5$ = 172.1. β-Naphthyl ethyl ether. (2) $C_{10}H_7 \cdot O \cdot CH_3$ = 158.1. β-Naphthyl methyl ether. Colorless crystals with a fruity odor, m.72, insoluble in water; a substitute for nerol.

neroli oil. A brown, essential oil distilled from orange blossoms, *Citrus bigardia* and *C. aurantium*, d.0.87, containing nerol, geraniol, and limonene; used in perfumery.

nerve. A fibrous whitish cord, which transmits impulses to and from the central nervous system. **n. sedative.** An agent that reduces the activity of sensory nerves; as, bromides. **n. stimulant.** An agent that increases the activity of sensory nerves; as, strychnine.

nervon. $C_{48}H_{91}NO_8$ = 809.74. A brain galactoside, m.61, containing nervonic acid, sphingosine, and galactose. Cf. *cerebroside*.

nervonic acid. $Me(CH_2)_7CH:CH(CH_2)_{13}COOH$ = 366.36. Selacholeic acid, 6,15-tetracosanic acid. White crystals, m.41, insoluble in water; in fish-liver oils and sphingo myelin.

nesquehonite. $MgCO_3 \cdot 3H_2O$. A native magnesium carbonate.

Nessler, Julius. 1827–1905. German analytical chemist. **N. reagent.** Dissolve (A) 3.5 gm potassium iodide in 10 ml water, and (B) 1.7 gm. mercuric chloride in 30 ml water. Slowly add B to A until a permanent precipitate occurs; then dilute with 20% sodium hydroxide to 100 ml. Again add B, until a permanent precipitate forms, settle, decant, and keep solution in the dark. **N.'s test.** A delicate test for detecting ammonia, aldehydes, and hexamethylenamine. N. reagent gives a brown precipitate with ammonia; or with traces, a yellow tint due to NHg_2I. Used for colorimetric determination: 1 pt. per 100,000,000. **N. tube.** A glass cylinder with a flat base; used to compare colors in colorimetric analysis.

nesslerize. To treat with Nessler reagent.

nether. An early (Egyptian) name for trona.

netoric acid. $C_{12}H_{14}O_5$ = 218.08. A monocarboxylic acid, m.92, derived from rotenol.

netropsin. $C_{18}H_{26}O_3N_{10}(?)$. An antibiotic from the genus *Streptomyces*.

nettle. Urtica. **horse-** *Solanum carolinense*, q.v.

Neuberg ester. Fructose-6-monophosphate, produced in the fermentation of sugar by yeast. Cf. *Robison ester*, *sugar phosphates*.

neudorfite. $C_{18}H_{28}O_2$ = 276.2. A resinous oxidized hydrocarbon in Bavarian coal beds.

neumandin. Isoniazid.

neuraminic acid. 5-Amino-3,5-dideoxy-D-glycero-D-galactononulosonic acid. A lipid component.

neuridin. $C_5H_{14}N_2$ = 102.2. A ptomaine in decaying animal matter.

neurine. $Me_3 \colon N(OH) \cdot CH \colon CH_2$ = 103.4. Amatine. Trimethylvinylammonium hydroxide. A poisonous quaternary amine, in decaying proteins from fishes, fungi, and brain substances. **oxy-** Betaine.

neurodin. $C_6H_4(OCOCH_3)_2NHCOOEt$ = 282.12. Acetyl-*p*-oxyphenylurethane. Colorless crystals, soluble in water; an antineuralgic and antipyretic.

neurodine. $C_5H_{19}N_2$ = 107.1. A ptomaine in decomposing flesh.

neurolecithin. An ester of fatty acids with glycerophosphoric acid and choline, prepared from the brain and spinal cord of healthy animals; a lecithin preparation.

neuron. A nerve cell.

neuronal. $NH_2 \cdot COCBrEt_2$ = 194.0. Diethylbromoacetamide. Colorless crystals, m.66, soluble in water; a somnifacient.

neurosin. Calcium glycerophosphate.

neurotic. An agent acting on the nervous system.

neusilber. *Nickel* silver.

neustab. Thiacetazone.

neuton. The theoretical zero element, consisting of neutrons, $_0n^1$, having at. no. 0 and mass no. 1. Cf. *neutron*.

neutral. (1) Neither acid nor basic. Cf. *amphoteric*. (2) Having no free electric charge. Cf. *neutron*. **n. atom.** An atom in which the nuclear positive charge is balanced by negative electrons, in *excited* or *normal* orbits. **n. compound.** A compound that has neither acid nor basic reaction. **n. element.** A member of the zero group of the periodic system; the rare gases: He, Ne, A, Kr, Xe, and Rd. **n. molecule.** A system of 2 ions (cation and anion) in a solvent. **n. oil.** Light petroleum, d.30–32°Be., flash point, 290–320°F, sometimes mixed with animal or vegetable oils. **n. point.** The point at which H^+ ions from an acid and OH^-

ions from a base give practically undissociated water, i.e., pH = 7.00. **n. principle.** The nonacid and nonbasic constituents of plants; as, glucosides. **n. reaction.** A reaction that is neither acid nor basic. **n. red.** $C_{14}H_{16}N_4$ = 240.13. Toluylene red, dimethyldiaminotoluphenazine hydrochloride. Green powder, soluble in water (red color). Used as a dye, to test the function of the stomach, and as an indicator, changing at pH 7.5 from blue (acid) to magenta (alkaline), and at pH 8 to orange-yellow. **n. salt.** A salt that does not react acidic or basic. It differs from the normal salt which may be neutral, acid, or basic. **n. salt effect.** The reduction of the ionization of a weak acid or base by addition of an ionizable salt containing one of the ions already present. Cf. *buffer solutions.* **n. solution.** A solution at the n. point, q.v. **n. violet.** $C_{14}H_{15}N_4Cl$. A compound similar to n. red, with H in place of a methyl group.

neutrality. The state of being neither acid nor basic in reaction.

neutralization. (1) The process of making a solution neutral by adding a base to an acid solution or an acid to an alkaline or basic solution. The fundamental reaction of n. is: Acid + Base $\rightleftharpoons$ H_2O + Salt. The reverse is hydrolysis. **heat of-** The amount of heat liberated during the n. of a strong acid and a strong base in equivalent quantities of dilute solutions equals about 13.7 large calories. (2) Proton reaction. The transfer of a proton, H^+, from an acid to a base, producing a weaker acid and a weaker base; as, $HCl + H_2O \rightleftharpoons H_3O^+ + Cl^-$; $H_3O^+ + Ac^- \rightleftharpoons HAc + H_2O$.

n. ratio. The ratio of the concentration of the anion of an acid to the total concentration of the undissociated acid.

neutralize. To make neutral.

neutralizer. Any agent that produces neutrality.

neutrapen. Approved common name for penicillinase.

neutrino. A hypothetical nuclear particle with no charge and small mass, 6×10^{-30} gm, emitted with an electron in radioactive and similar changes, e.g. β decay. Suggested by Pauli (1927) to satisfy the conservation laws, of spin, momentum, and energy. Cf. *neutron.*

neutron. n or $_0n^1$. (1) A proton and electron in immediate contact; a "building stone" of the atomic nucleus. Each isotope contains in its atom $(I - A)$ neutrons, where I is the isotopic weight and A the atomic number. (2) An electrically neutral particle, with the mass of 1.006, which does not ionize air, produced from elements by bombardment with α particles. Cf. *nuclear reactions, neutrino, neutron.* **anti-** An electrically neutral particle differing from a n. in that its magnetic moment is parallel with its spin angular momentum: antiproton + proton = neutron + antineutron.

n. activation analysis. The detection of traces of elements by activation with high-flux n. bombardment, and measuring the resulting emission-energy decay rate.

Neville acid. 1,4-α-Naphtholsulfonic acid.

nevyanskite. A native alloy of iridium and osmium with allied metals.

new blue. (1) Meldola blue. (2) Prussian blue. **n. fuchsin.** $C_{22}H_{23}N_3 \cdot HCl$ = 367.8. Soluble fuchsin. A bluish red dye obtained by oxidation of diamino-*o*-ditolylmethane.

Newlands, John Alexander Reina. 1838–1898. British chemist; pioneer in the development of the periodic system, q.v., from his conception of "octaves."

Newton, Sir Isaac. 1642–1727. English mathematician and philosopher, originator of the law of universal graviation. **N.'s alloy.** Bi 20, Sn 30, Pb 50%; m. 202°F. **N.'s law.** The attractive force between 2 bodies is proportional to their masses. **N.'s rings.** Colored rings produced when plane and convex glass surfaces are pressed together, due to interference between the beams of light reflected from the two surfaces.

newton. N. A unit of pressure in the international system: the force required to accelerate 1 kg mass at 1 meter/sec²; 1 psi = 6,895 N/in.² Cf. *SI Units.*

newtonian fluid. See *fluid.*

newtonium. Name given by Mendelyeev to his hypothetical protoelement.

N.F. Abbreviation for National Formulary, a supplement to the U.S. Pharmacopoeia.

ngai camphor. Borneol.

Ni. Symbol for nickel.

niacin. Nicotinic acid, q.v.

niacinamide. Nicotinamide, q.v.

Niagara blue. Trypan blue.

nialamide. $C_{16}H_{18}N_4O_2$ = 298.36. Bitter, white crystals, slightly soluble in water, m.152; an antidepressant (B.P.).

nicamide. Nikethamide.

niccolic. Nickelic (international usage).

niccolite. NiAs. Copper nickel, arsenical nickel. A red, native nickel arsenide.

niccolous. Nickelous (international usage).

niccolox. $C_4H_{12}O_4N_8(?)$. An oxamide dioxime reagent for nickel.

niccolum. Latin for nickel.

Nichols, William Henry. 1852–1930. American industrial chemist. **N. medal.** A prize for achievement in industrial chemistry.

Nicholson, William. 1753–1815. English physicist and chemist, a pioneer in electrolyzing water.

nicholsonite. $CaCO_3$. Aragonite, containing zinc.

Nichrome. Trademark for a high-melting-point alloy: Ni 60, Fe 25, Cr 15%; used in electric heaters and acid-resisting apparatus. **N. wire.** A wire: Ni 80, Cr 20%; used as a platinum substitute (for bead and flame tests), and for heating elements and electrical resistances.

nickel. Ni = 58.71. An element of the iron group, at. no. 28. A silver-white metal, d.8.8–8.9, m.1455, b.2900, insoluble in water, dilute acids or alkalies. It occurs in niccolite, Monel metal, kupfernickel, nickel glance, and nickel blende. Isolated (1751) by Cronstedt. N. has the common valencies of 2 (nickelous) and 3 (nickelic); but it can possess all 5 oxidation states from 0 to +4; e.g., $Ni(CO)_6$ to K_2NiF_6. Used as a hydrogenation catalyst (margarine manufacture); for galvanic coating of other metals (stainless steel); for acid-resisting alloys, chemical apparatus, coins and medals, electric apparatus, surgical and dental instruments; and in manufacture of n. salts. World production (1966) 8.3 million lb (W. bloc). **Admiralty-** Adnic. **arsenical-** Niccolite. **emerald-** Zaratite. **Raney-** q.v. **super-** q.v.

n. acetate. Nickelous acetate. **n. alloys.** Non-corroding alloys; as, nickeline, ferronickel. Some are harder than steel and are used for surgical instruments. Melting points (in °C) are:

with	90 %Ni 10 %	80 %Ni 20 %	70 %Ni 30 %	60 %Ni 40 %	50 %Ni 50 %
Cu	1440	1430*	1410†	1380‡	1335§
Sn	1380	1290	1200	1235	1290

*Nickeline. †Corronel, Monel.
‡Constantan. §Alpro, Copel.

See also Mumetal 74, permalloy 30–80, Nichrome 60–80, Monel 67, permivar 45, nickel silver 30% Ni; and table, at bottom of page, on composition and hardness. **n. alumide.** High-purity aluminum powder particles with a n. coating, m. exceeds 1,500. Used for spray-coating ceramics. *Cf. cermet.* **n. ammonium chloride.** Ni(NH₄)Cl₃·6H₂O = 291.2. Nickelous ammonium chloride. Green rhombs, soluble in water; used in n. plating. **n. ammonium nitrate.** Ni(NO₃)₂(NH₃)₄(H₂O)₂ = 286.9. Nickeloaminnitrate. Green crystals, soluble in water; used in n. plating. **n. ammonium sulfate.** Ni(NH₄)₂(SO₄)₂·6H₂O = 395.0. Nickelous ammonium sulfate. Green crystals, soluble in water; used in n. plating and as a reagent. **n. arsenate.** Nickelous arsenate. **n. benzoate.** Nickelous benzoate. **n. black.** N. peroxide. **n. blende.** NiS. A native n. sulfide. **n. bloom.** Annabergite. **n. borate.** Nickelous borate. **n. brass.** An alloy used in British coinage, q.v. **n. bromide.** Nickelous bromide. **n. carbide.** Ni₃C = 188.07. A black solid. **n. carbonate.** Nickelous carbonate. **n. carbon oxide.** N. carbonyl. **n. carbonyl.** Ni(CO)₄ = 170.7. N. carbon oxide. A poisonous gas. Colorless liquid, d.43, insoluble in water. Used for hypodermic injections; and in the Mond process for the isolation of n. If pure it explodes at 60: Ni(CO)₄ = Ni + 2CO₂ + 2C. **n. chloride.** Nickelous chloride. **n. chrome steel.** An alloy: Fe 95, Ni 3, Cr 1.5, C 0.5%.; used for heat- and acid-resistant machinery. **n. chromium triangle.** A triangle made of Nichrome wire; used to heat small laboratory utensils. **n. citrate.** Nickelous citrate. **n. cyanide.** Nickelous cyanide. **n. dimethyl glyoxime.** Ni(C₄H₇N₂O₂)₂ = 288.7. Red crystals, used to determine n.; sublimes at 120.

n. fluosilicate. NiSiF₆6H₂O = 308.84. Green trigonal crystals, d.2.109, soluble in water. **n. glance.** Ni₂AsS. A native arsenide and sulfide of n. **n. gymnite.** Genthite. A gymnite, in which part of the magnesium is replaced by n. **n. iodide.** Nickelous iodide. **n. minerals.** N. is associated with cobalt and iron in meteorites; with chromium in olivine; and as sulfide, arsenide, and silicates. E.g.: bunsenite, NiO; polydymite, Ni₄S₅; niccolite, NiAs; smaltite, (NiCoFe)As₂; white nickel ore, NiAs₂; nickel ocher, Ni₃(AsO₄)₂·8H₂O. **n. monoxide.** Nickelous oxide. **n. nitrate.** Nickelous nitrate. **n. ocher (ochre).** Annabergite. **n. oleate.** Ni(C₁₈H₃₃O₂)₂. A waxy n. soap, a compound of n. with oleic acid; used in ointments. **n. oxalate.** Nickelous oxalate. **n. oxides.** NiO, nickelous oxide; Ni₂O₃, nickelic oxide; Ni₃O₄, nickelous nickelic oxide; NiO₂, nickel peroxide; NiO₄, nickel superoxide. **n. phosphate.** Nickelous phosphate. **n. plating.** The deposition, usually of pure nickel on copper, or on steel coated with copper, from saturated n. ammonium sulfate. **n. pyrites.** Millerite. **n. salipyrine.** A green salt of nickel, salicylic acid, and antipyrine; an antiseptic. **n. sesquioxide.** Nickelic oxide. **n. silver.** German silver, neusilber, argentan, albata, British plate (U.K. usage). White alloys: copper 46–63, nickel 6–30, zinc 18–36%; used for resistance coils and cutlery. **n. steel.** A very tough alloy: Fe 96.5, Ni 3.5%. **n. stibine.** Ullmannite. **n. sulfate.** Nickelous sulfate. **n. sulfide.** Nickelous sulfide. **n. superoxide.** NiO₄ = 122.69. A black oxide produced by electrolysis. **n. tetracarbonyl.** N. carbonyl. **n. vitriol.** Morenosite. **n. yellow.** *Nickelous phosphate.*

nickelic. Niccolic. Describing compounds of trivalent nickel, which are all strong oxidizing agents, and readily reduced to the more stable nickelous compounds. **n. hydroxide.** Ni₂(OH)₆ = 219.41. Niccolic hydroxide. A black powder, rapidly decomp. by heat; used in the manufacture of n. compounds. **n. nickelous sulfide.** Ni₃S₄. Native as polydymite. **n. oxide.** Ni₂O₃ = 165.4. Nickel sesquioxide, niccolic oxide, nickel tetroxide, black nickel oxide. Black powder, reduced to nickelous oxide at 600°C, insoluble in water; used in storage batteries. **n. sulfide.** Ni₂S₃. Native as beyrichite, q.v.

Alloy	Composition, per cent								Brinell hardness
	Ni	Cu	Cr	Fe	Si	Mn	C	Other elements	
A nickel	99.6	—	—	0.05	0.02	0.25	0.07	—	196—cold–drawn
Duranickel..........	93.8	—	—	0.12	0.58	0.38	0.20	Al 4.5, Ti 0.4	235—cold–drawn
Monel...............	66.0	31.2	—	1.41	0.14	1.05	0.19	—	235—cold–drawn
K Monel.............	65.5	29.1	—	0.96	0.12	0.60	0.15	Al 3.0, Ti 0.5	340—aged
Inconel.............	78.5	—	14.5	6.40	0.20	0.23	0.07	—	262—cold–drawn
Inconel X	72.9	—	15.0	6.77	0.42	0.59	0.04	Al 0.9, Ti 2.4, Nb 1.0	340—aged
17–7 P.H. stainless ...	6.7	—	17.2	Bal.	0.36	0.64	0.07	Al 1.0, P 0.02	436—hardened
G nickel	94.2	—	—	0.5	1.5	0.80	1.5	—	131
S nickel	90.0	—	—	2.0	6.0	0.78	0.68	—	241
Colmonoy 6	65–75	—	13–25	—	—	—	—	B2.7—4.7	—
Waukesha 88	Bal.	—	12.0	—	0.20	0.80	—	Sn 4, Mo 3, Bi 3.5	127
Leaded bronze	0.46	79.9	—	—	—	—	—	Sn 6.3, Pb 10.1, Zn 2.1	69
Neveroil 21	32.3	64.5	—	—	—	—	—	Sn present	17

nickeline. (1) An alloy: Cu 80, Ni 20%. (2) An alloy: Cu 56, Ni 31, Zn 13%; used in high-resistance apparatus.

nickelous. Describing compounds containing divalent Ni^{++}. The anhydrous salts are yellow; the hydrous salts green. **n. acetate.** Ni(C$_2$H$_3$O$_2$)$_2$·4H$_2$O = 248.8. Green crystals, soluble in water. **n. arsenate.** Ni$_3$(AsO$_4$)$_2$·8H$_2$O = 598.2. Green powder, insoluble in water. **n. benzoate.** Ni(C$_7$H$_5$O$_2$)$_2$·H$_2$O = 318.7. Green powder, soluble in ammonium salt solutions. **n. borate.** Ni(BO$_2$)$_2$·2H$_2$O = 180.7. Green powder, insoluble in water. **n. bromide.** NiBr$_2$ = 218.52. Yellow scales, decomp. by heat, soluble in water. *ammonia-* NiBr$_2$·6NH$_3$ = 320.73. Purple crystals, soluble in water. *hydrous-* NiBr$_2$·3H$_2$O = 272.57. Green, deliquescent needles, soluble in water; an antiseptic and nerve tonic. **n. carbonate.** NiCO$_3$ = 118.7. Green rhombs, insoluble in water; used in electroplating. *basic-* 2NiCO$_3$·3Ni(OH)$_2$·4H$_2$O = 587.5. Green powder, insoluble in water; used in nickel plating. **n. chloride.** NiCl$_2$ = 129.6. Yellow scales, soluble in water or ammonium hydroxide. It sublimes, and is used as a reagent for sulfocarbonates, as an absorbent in gas masks, for nickel plating, and in sympathetic ink. *ammonia-* NiCl$_2$·6NH$_3$ = 231.8. Nickeloammonia chloride. Purple crystals, soluble in water. Cf. nickelous *ammonium chloride*. *hydrous-* NiCl$_2$·6H$_2$O = 237.7. Green hexagons, soluble in water or alcohol. **n. citrate.** Ni$_3$(C$_6$H$_5$O$_7$)$_2$·8H$_2$O = 698.2. Green, hygroscopic crystals, soluble in water; used in nickel plating. **n. cyanide.** Ni (CN)$_2$·4H$_2$O = 182.8. Apple-green powder-insoluble in water, soluble in cyanide solutions; used in electroplating and metallurgy. **n. formate.** (HCOO)$_2$Ni·2H$_2$O = 184.74. Green crystals, soluble in water. **n. hydroxide.** Ni(OH)$_2$ = 92.7. White powder, insoluble in water. *hydrous-* 4Ni(OH)$_2$·H$_2$O = 388.8. Green powder, insoluble in water; used in the manufacture of nickelous salts. **n. iodide.** NiI$_2$ = 312.5. Black scales, m.57, soluble in water. **n. nickelic oxide.** Ni$_3$O$_4$ = 240.0. Nickel tetroxide. Gray powder, insoluble in water. **n. nitrate.** Ni(NO$_3$)$_2$ = 182.7. Yellow powder, soluble in water (green color). *ammonia-* Ni(NO$_3$)$_2$·6NH$_3$ = 284.7. Nickeloammonia nitrate. Blue crystals, soluble in water; used with tannic acid, to stain hair and fur. *hydrous-* Ni(NO$_3$)$_2$·6H$_2$O = 290.8. Nickeloaquanitrate. Monoclinic, deliquescent crystals, m.57, soluble in water; used as a reagent and in nickel plating. **n. oxalate.** NiC$_2$O$_4$ = 146.7. Green powder, insoluble in water. **n. oxide.** NiO = 74.7. Nickel monoxide, nickel protoxide, green nickel oxide, insoluble in water; used in green ceramic pigments. **n. phosphate.** Ni$_3$(PO$_4$)$_2$·7H$_2$O = 492.2. Normal nickel (ortho) phosphate. Green powder, insoluble in water. Used in nickel plating and in the manufacture of nickel yellow. **n. silver.** *Nickel* silver. **n. sulfate.** NiSO$_4$ = 154.8. Regular yellow crystals, decomp. 830, soluble in water. *hydrous-* (1) NiSO$_4$·7H$_2$O = 280.86. Nickeloaquasulfate. Green rhombs, dehydrated at 100, soluble in water. Used in nickel plating, for blackening brass and zinc, as a textile mordant, a tonic and sedative, and a reagent for glucose and albumose. (2) NiSO$_4$·6H$_2$O = 262.84. Green crystals, soluble in ammonia. **n. sulfide.** NiS = 90.8. Black hexagons, m.797, slightly soluble in water; used in ceramics. **n. tartrate.** NiC$_4$H$_4$O$_6$·5H$_2$O = 296.9. Green powder, insoluble in water. **n. thallous sulfate.** NiSO$_4$·Tl$_2$SO$_4$·6H$_2$O = 767.6. A double salt; green crystals, soluble in water.

Nicol, William. 1766–1851. British physicist noted for optical devices. **N.'s prism.** See *nicols*.

nicoline. C$_3$H$_4$O = 56.0. A constituent of *Lonchocarpus rufescens* (Leguminosae), Guiana; used to stupefy fishes.

nicols. Nicol's prism. Two prisms of Iceland spar cemented together; used as polarizer and analyzer in polariscopes. Cf. *polaroids*.

nicopyrite. A pyrite containing nickel.

nicoteine. C$_{10}$H$_{12}$N$_2$ = 160.11. A mixture of nornicotine and anabasine from Kentucky tobacco.

nicotiana. Tobacco.

nicotianine. A volatile, fragrant principle from tobacco.

nicotinamide. C$_5$H$_4$N·CONH$_2$ = 122.12. Niacinamide. Nicotinic acid amide, vitamin PP. White crystals, m.129, soluble in water. A B-complex vitamin (U.S.P., B.P.); used to treat pellagra.

nicotine. C$_{10}$H$_{14}$N$_2$ = 162.2. Pyridyl-β-N-methyl-pyrrolidine. A diacid alkaloid from the leaves of *Nicotiana tabacum*. Yellow liquid, d.1.01, b.247, soluble in water; an antiparasitic, insecticide, and antitetanic. **dihydroxy-** Pilocarpidine. **neo-** Anabasine. **nor-** Nornicotine.

n. group. Alkaloids derived from pyridine and pyrrolidine: 1. Nicotine and pilocarpine and derivatives. (2) sparteine, oxalethyline, and lobeline; (3) coniine; (4) pyridine bases. **n. hydrochloride.** C$_{10}$H$_{14}$N$_2$·2HCl = 235.1. Colorless hygroscopic crystals, soluble in water. **n. salicylate** C$_{10}$H$_{14}$N$_2$·C$_7$H$_6$O$_3$ = 300.3. Colorless plates, m.117, soluble in water; used in skin ointments. **n. tartrate.** C$_{10}$H$_{14}$N$_2$·(C$_4$H$_4$O$_6$)$_2$·2H$_2$O = 494.4. Red crystals, soluble in water; an antitetanic and strychnine antidote.

nicotinic acid. C$_5$H$_4$NCOOH = 123.12. Niacin. β-Pyridinecarboxylic acid*. Colorless, bitter needles, m.236 (sublimes), slightly soluble in water; a peripheral vascoconstrictor and B-complex vitamin (U.S.P., B.P.). Cf. *vitamin B$_5$*. **iso-** 3-Pyridinecarboxylic acid. Colorless crystals, m.304, soluble in water. **tetrahydro-1-methyl-** Arecaidine.

nicotyrine. N-methyl-2-(pyrid-3-yl)pyrrole. a drug used similarly to nicotine.

nicouic acid. 2,4-(COOH)$_2$3-(OH)·C$_6$H$_2$OCMe$_2$·COOH = 284.08. From rotenone and deguelin.

nicoulin. A resin from nekoe or stinkwood, *Gustavia ocotea*; a Malayan arrow poison.

nicouline. Rotenone.

niello silver. Russian tula, blue silver. A bluish alloy of silver, copper, lead, and bismuth.

Nierenstein, Max. b. 1877. English chemist, noted for organic synthesis. **N. reaction.** The synthesis of ketones by diazomethane: R·COCl + CH$_2$N$_2$ → R·COCH$_2$Cl + N$_2$. Cf. *Schlotterbeck reaction*.

Nieuwland, Father Julius Arthur. 1878–1936. A Jesuit American chemist, noted for the synthesis of acetaldehyde, vinylacetylene, and synthetic rubber from acetylene.

nigella. Black caraway, black cumin, small fennel. The dried seeds of *Nigella sativa*; a condiment.

nigelline. An alkaloid in the seeds of *Nigella sativa* (Ranunculaceae).

nightshade. Plants of the Solanaceae. **deadly-** Belladonna. **garden-** *Solanum nigrum.* **woody-** Bittersweet.

nigraniline. Nigrosine.

nigre. A dark-colored layer, formed in the soap pan, between the neat soap and the lye; an isotropic solution containing a higher concentration of soap than lye, a fairly high concentration of salts, and colored impurities.

nigrite. A variety of asphalt.

nigrium. Alleged new element discovered by Church (1869); probably impure hafnium.

nigrometer. An instrument to evaluate the color of carbon blacks.

nigrosine. $C_{38}H_{27}N_3 = 525.3$. Aniline black. Pure nigrosine obtained by oxidation of aniline; a microscopic stain.

nigrosines. Black or deep blue aniline dyes obtained by oxidation of aniline or its homologs; used in the manufacture of inks and shoe polishes, and in dyeing.

nigrotic acid. 3,6-Dihydroxy-2,7-sulfonaphthoic acid.

Ni-Hard. Trademark for an abrasion-resistant cast iron containing Ni 4.5, Cr 1.5, Mn 1.5%.

nihil album. Zinc oxide.

nikethamide. $C_{10}H_{14}ON_2 = 178.24$. Coramine. Nicotinic acid diethylamide. Niacamide, niketharol, *N,N*-Diethyl-3-pyridinecarboxamide. Yellow liquid, congeals 22–24, miscible with water; a stimulant (U.S.P., B.P.).

niketharol. Nikethamide.

Nikiforoff stain. (1) A borax-carmine solution acidified with acetic acid; used to stain nuclei. (2) An alkaline concentrated methylene blue counter-stain.

nile blue. $C_{20}H_{19}ON_3 = 317.2$. A blue aniline dye, insoluble in water. Used as a pH indicator, changing from yellow (acid) through blue to magenta (alkaline). **n. blue sulfate.** An oxidation-reduction and pH indicator, and vital stain.

nilodin. Lucanthone hydrochloride.

nilvar. An alloy similar to Invar: 36% Ni. It has a low temperature coefficient, below 100°C.

nimbicitin. $C_{15}H_{10}O_6 = 286.09$. A compound similar to kaempferol, from *Melia azadirachter*, m.272.

nimbin. $C_{29}H_{36}O_9 = 528.12$. A carboxymethyl steroid from the bark of *Melia azadirachter*, m.204.

nimbiol. $C_{18}H_{24}O_2 = 272.02$. A ketophenolphenanthrene derivative from *Melia azadirachter*.

nimonic alloys. A range of alloys having good resistance to oxidation and to creep at high temperatures. They contain Ni, with Cr 18–21, Fe 5–11, Si 1.0–1.5, Ti 0.2–2.0, C 0.08–0.15%, and sometimes Al and/or Cu.

Ninhydrin. $C_6H_4 \cdot (CO)_2 \cdot C \cdot (OH)_2 = 178.09$. Trade name for triketohydrindene hydrate, ninidrine. Colorless crystals; a reagent in the Abderhalden test for proteins and amino acids (blue color) in diagnosing pregnancy and for developing fingerprints.

ninidrine. Ninhydrin.

niobate. Columbate. A salt of the type $MNbO_3$ or

$M_2O \cdot Nb_2O_5$; e.g. $NaNbO_3$, sodium n.; they often form complexes.

niobe oil. Methyl benzoate.

niobic. Columbic. Describing a compound containing pentavalent niobium, Nb^V. **n. acid.** $HNbO_3 = 142.10$. (1) An insoluble white powder derived from Nb_2O_5; soluble in alkalies to form complex niobates. (2) The compound $3Nb_2O_5 \cdot 4H_2O$, which gives the acid $H_8Nb_6O_{19}$. **n. anhydride.** Nb_2O_5. Columbic anhydride.

niobite. $(Fe, Mn)O \cdot (Nb, Ta)_2O_3$. Native in black crystals.

niobium. $Nb = 92.91$. A metallic element, at. no. 41, discovered (1801) by C. Hachette in the mineral columbite, named in honor of America. In 1802, A. G. Ekeberg isolated a new metal from yttrotantalite whose elemental nature was not realized until 1844, H. Rose (1844) isolated from Bavarian columbite 2 metals, niobium (named after Niobe, daughter of Tantalus, since it resembled Ta) and peloponium. Niobium proved to be an element, and peloponium a mixture of tantalum and niobium. Niobium was known as columbium until 1944, when its name was changed officially. A gray shining metal, d.8.4, m.1950, made by the hydrogen reduction of the pentachloride. It forms niobus (valency 3) and niobic (valency 5) compounds and belongs to the 5th subgroup of the periodic system. Nb is used as a reactor fuel element and in heat-resistant structures. **n. bromide.** $NbBr_5 = 492.68$. Purple crystals, decomp. by water. **n. chloride.** (1) $NbCl_3 = 199.47$. Niobus chloride. Violet crystals, soluble in water. (2) $NbCl_5 = 270.30$. Niobic chloride. Yellow hygroscopic crystals, m.194, decomp. in air or water, to form hydrochloric acid. **n. fluoride.** $NbF_5 = 188.11$. Niobic fluoride. Colorless monoclinic crystals, m.72, hydrolyzed by water. **n. hydride.** $NbH = 91.40$. Black powder, decomp. by heat. **n. minerals.** Nb occurs with Ti and usually the rare-earth metals, e.g., columbite, niobite (q.v.), tantalite, samarskite. **n. oxalate.** $Nb(HC_2O_4)_5 = 538.34$. Colorless, monoclinic crystals, decomp. by water. **n. oxides.** (1) $NbO = 219.10$. Insoluble in water. (2) $Nb_2O_3 = 454.23$. Insoluble in all solvents except hydrofluoric acid. (3) $NbO_2 = 125.10$. Black insoluble powder. (4) $Nb_2O_5 = 265.82$. See *n.* pentoxide. **n. oxybromide.** $NbOBr_3 = 348.85$. Niobyl bromide. Yellow crystals, hydrolyzed by water. **n. oxychloride.** $NbOCl_3 = 215.47$. Niobyl or nioboxy chloride. Colorless needles, sublime 400, hydrolyzed by water. **n. pentoxide.** $Nb_2O_5 = 265.82$. Niobic acid, niobic oxide, columbium pentoxide. White crystals, m.1520 (yellow when hot), insoluble in water. **n. potassium fluoride.** $NbOF_3 \cdot 2KF \cdot H_2O = 300.32$. Nioboxy potassium fluoride. White scales, soluble in water.

nioboxy. Columboxy. Niobyl. Describing a compound of pentavalent niobium, containing the radical $NbO\!\equiv$.

niobus. Columbus. Describing a compound of trivalent niobium, $Nb\!\equiv$.

niobyl. Nioboxy.

nioform. Bioform.

Ni-O-Nel. Trademark for an alloy resistant to acids; Ni 40, Fe 31, Cr 21, Mo 3, Cu 1.75%, and traces of Mn, Si, and C.

nioxime. 1,2-Cyclohexanone dioxime, m.195–200 (decomp.), slightly soluble in water. A reagent for nickel (1 pt. in 5×10^6 gives a purple-red color).

nipagin. $HO \cdot C_6H_4COOMe = 152.06$. Solbrol, methyl-$p$-hydroxybenzoate. An isomer of methyl salicylate; a preservative.

nipasol. $C_{10}H_{12}O_3 = 180.18$. Propyl p-hydroxybenzoate. White powder; a preservative.

nipecotic acid. $C_5H_{10}N \cdot COOH = 129.09$. 3-Piperidinecarboxylic acid. An isomer of hygric and nicotinic acids.

Niplon. Trade name for a Japanese polyamide synthetic fiber.

nipponium. Element no. 43 (Ogawa); not verified. See *technetium*.

niranium. An alloy for dental castings: Cr 64, Co 29, Ni 4.3, W 2, C 0.2%, with traces of Si and Al.

ni-resist. A heat-resistant, nonmagnetic, weldable alloy of Fe, with Ni 12–15, Cu 5–7, Cr 1.5–4%; used in glass-annealing furnaces and in manifold valves of automobile engines.

nirvanine. $Et_2N \cdot CH_2CONH \cdot C_6H_5(OH)COOMe = 280.2$. Diethylglycine methyl 2-hydroxy-5-aminobenzoate. A cocaine alkaloid. Colorless prisms, m.185, soluble in water; a local anesthetic.

nirvanol. $C_{11}H_{12}O_2N_2 = 204.11$. 5,5-Phenylethylhydantoin. White powder; a hypnotic. Cf. *Luminal*.

Nisalpin. Trademark of commercial nisin, an antibiotic produced by strains of *Streptococcus lactis*; occurs in milk and inhibits food spoilage bacteria.

nisin. A polypeptide antibiotic produced by *Streptococcus lactis*; a permitted preservative for canned food (U.K. usage). Cf. *Reading unit*.

nisinic acid. $C_{24}H_{36}O_2 = 356.29$. A highly unsaturated acid from fish-liver oils.

nital. A solution of 1–5 ml nitric acid (d.1.42) in 100 ml of 95% alcohol. An etching reagent for iron and steel.

niter, nitre. Potassium nitrate. **Chile-** or **cubic-** Sodium nitrate. **Norwegian-** Calcium nitrate. **rough-** Magnesium chloride. **spirit of-** Spirit of *ethyl nitrite*.

> **n. air.** See *oxygen*. **n. cake.** Crude sodium sulfate containing some bisulfate and nitrate; a by-product in the manufacture of nitric acid by the retort process.

nitinol. Generic name for nickel-titanium intermetallic compounds used in spacecraft construction, e.g., Ti–Ni. They have high ductility and impact resistance at low temperatures.

Nitionol. Trademark of a series of Ti-Ni alloys, used in nonmagnetic tools.

niton. Nt. (1) The element, at. no. 86, which consists of the isotopes radon, actinon, and thoron (1898, Mme. Curie). (2) Radon.

nitracetanilide. $C_8H_6O_2N_2 = 180.12$. Nitro-acetanilide. Colorless crystals. **ortho-** m.92. **meta-** m.151. **para-** m.210.

nitracidium ion. $H_2NO_3^+$. Nitriacidium ion. $OH \cdot N : O(OH)$. Believed to be responsible for the nitration of organic compounds by nitric acid according to the ionization equilibrium: $2HNO_3 \rightleftharpoons H_2NO_3^+ + NO_3^-$.

nitragin. A nitrifying bacterial ferment from the root tubercles of leguminous plants.

nitralising. A process for the preparation of steel sheets for enameling by degreasing, pickling, and immersion in fused potassium nitrate at 500°C. Blister formation is thereby minimized.

nitralloy. Cr-Al steels containing 0.2–0.6% C, surface-hardened by nitridation.

Nitram. Trade name for prills of ammonium nitrate fertilizer, with a deliquescence-preventing additive.

nitramide. $NH_2NO_2 = 62.1$. Colorless crystals, m.75. **phenyl-** $C_6H_5NH \cdot NO_2 = 138.1$. Colorless crystals, m.46, soluble in water.

nitramides. A group of compounds derived from nitramide and differing from nitramines by the presence of a radical —COO—; as, $NO_2 \cdot NH \cdot COOH$, nitrocarbamic acid.

nitramine. (1) An organic compound containing the radical —$NH \cdot NO_2$ or =$N \cdot NO_2$. (2) Picryl methyl n. An indicator, changing at pH 10.5 from colorless (weakly alkaline) to brown (strongly alkaline). **diethyl-** $Et_2N \cdot NO_2 = 118.1$. Colorless liquid, b.206. **dimethyl-** $Me_2N \cdot NO_2 = 90.1$. Colorless crystals, m.58, soluble in water. **ethyl-** $EtNH \cdot NO_2 = 90.1$. Colorless liquid, m.3. **iso-** A compound containing the radical

$$-N-O-N \cdot OH.$$

phenyl- $NHPh \cdot NO_2 = 138.1$. Colorless crystals, m.46, soluble in water. **phenyl methyl-** $MeNPh \cdot NO_2 = 152.2$. Colorless crystals, m.39, soluble in water. **propyl-** $PrNH \cdot NO_2$. Colorless liquid, b.140.

nitramino. The radical NO_2NH—. **n. acetic acid.** $C_2H_4O_4N_2 = 120.2$. A homolog of nitrourethane. Colorless crystals, m.103, soluble in water (strongly acid).

nitranilic acid. $C_6H_2O_6N_2 = 230.07$. Dinitrodihydroxybenzoquinone, m.100, decomp. 170, soluble in water.

nitranilide. $C_6H_5N : NO \cdot OH = 138.1$. Diazobenzene acid. Phenylisonitramine. An isomer of phenyl nitramine. Colorless crystals, m.46, soluble in water.

nitraniline. $NH_2 \cdot C_6H_4 \cdot NO_2 = 138.1$. **ortho-** or **1,2-** Colorless needles, m.71, soluble in water. **meta-** or **1,3-** Yellow needles, m.114, slightly soluble in water. **para-** or **1,4-** Yellow needles, m.146, soluble in water. All used in organic synthesis and as indicators for strong acids. **di-** See *dinitroaniline*.

nitranilines. Compounds derived from benzene by the substitution of 2 or more H atoms by one or more NH_2— and NO_2— radicals. The higher-nitrated anilines are powerful explosives.

nitrate. (1) A salt of nitric acid, or compound containing the radical —NO_3. (2) Nitration. **n. ion.** The NO_3^- ion, colorless, and forming no insoluble precipitates with metallic ions. **n. of lime.** Calcium n. **n. of potash.** Potassium n. **n. of soda.** Sodium n. **n. of soda-potash-** A crude Chilean saltpeter: sodium nitrate 75, potassium nitrate 25%; a fertilizer.

nitrated. Describing an organic compound containing the —NO_2 group.

nitratine. A mineral form of sodium nitrate.

nitration. The introduction of the NO_2 group into an organic compound, usually by means of a mixture of sulfuric and nitric acids.

nitrato- Prefix indicating an organic compound containing the radical —$O \cdot NO_2$. Cf. *nitrito-*.

nitrator. A vessel, usually double-jacketed, with

heating or cooling coils and stirring device, used for nitration.

Nitrazine Paper. Trademark for a filter paper, impregnated with sodium dinitrophenyl azonaphthol disulfonate; used to indicate pH values: yellow 4.5, olive green 6.2, blue 7.0. **N. yellow.** An indicator dye (pH 6.5: yellow—acid to blue-green—alkaline).

nitre. Niter. **n. air.** See *oxygen*.

nitrenes. Compounds of the type $R_2C:NR:CR_2$.

nitriacidium ion. Nitracidum ion.

nitric acid. HNO_3 = 63.02. Colorless liquid, d_0 1.53, m.−40.3, b.86, soluble in water; used extensively as its aqueous solutions: (1) Fuming: 86% HNO_3 with some N_2O_4. Brown-red fuming liquid, d.1.48–1.5; an energetic oxidizing agent in chemical analysis and synthesis. (2) Concentrated: 65% HNO_3. Aqua fortis, azotic acid. Faintly yellow liquid, d.1.40–1.42. Used as a solvent for metals and an oxidizing agent; in etching and many chemical operations; and to nitrate organic compounds. (3) 32–34% HNO_3. d.1.20. (4) Dilute: 10% HNO_3. Colorless liquid, d.1.06; a reagent, solvent, and acidifying agent. **chloro-** See *chloro-*. **per-** HNO_4. An acid of doubtful existence.

n. anhydride. Nitrogen pentoxide. **n. hydrate.** $HNO_3 + 32\% H_2O$. $d_{15.5}$ 1.414, b.121.

nitric ether. Ethyl nitrate.

nitric oxide. NO = 30.0. N_2O_2 = 60.0. Nitrogen dioxide. Colorless gas, $d_{air=1}$ 1.0366, b.−153, soluble in water. Formed in the electric arc from air; oxidizes readily to nitrogen peroxide.

nitridation. (1) Formation of metallic nitrides by heating metals in nitrogen to increase hardness. Cf. *nitration*. (2) De-electronation in the ammonia system, analogous to oxidation in the water system. Cf. *nitridizing agent*.

nitride. A binary compound of nitrogen and a metal. The alkali and earth-alkali nitrides are readily hydrolyzed: $Mg_3N_2 + 6H_2O = 3Mg(OH)_2 + 2NH_3$.

nitridizing agent. A substance that furnishes nitrogen or causes an exchange of electrons in liquid ammonia; as, hydrazoic acid (ammononitric acid), HN_3; analogous to nitric acid, HNO_3, as oxidizing agent.

nitrifiable. Desibing a nitrogen compound that can be transformed into nitrates by soil bacteria.

nitrification. Oxidation of the nitrogen in ammonia to nitrous and nitric acid or salts.

nitrifiers. Soil bacteria which oxidize ammonia and its derivatives to nitrites (as nitromonas) or to nitrates (as nitrobacter).

nitrifying. To cause the oxidation of ammonia or atmospheric nitrogen to nitrites and nitrates, e.g., by n. bacteria and n. catalysts.

nitrilase. A catalase that converts aldehydes to cyanohydrins, $R\cdot CHOH\cdot CN$.

nitrile. A cyanide prepared from an acid amide, $R\cdot CONH_2 - H_2O = R\cdot CN$; on hydrolysis they yield the corresponding acid and evolve ammonia. **n. group.** The negative $\equiv N$ from ammonia after substitution of its 3 H atoms. **n. rubber.** q. v.

nitriles. Cyanides. Organic compounds containing the radical —CN. **acid-** Nitrile. A name indicating the relation of n. with the —COOH group: —C(:O)·OH → —C(:O)·NH_2 → —C:N. **basic-** NR_3. A tertiary amine having 3 different C atoms attached

to the same N. **di-** Dicyanide. A compound containing 2 —CN radicals. **mono-** A compound containing one —CN radical.

nitrilo- Prefix indicating a triple-bond nitrogen atom, $\equiv N$.

Nitrilon. Trade name for a polyacrylonitrile synthetic fiber.

nitrine. N_3 = 42.02. A hypothetical allotropic form of nitrogen analogous to ozone, O_3. See *active nitrogen*.

nitrite. A salt of nitrous acid, or a compound containing the radical —NO_2. The inorganic nitrites of the type MNO_2 are all insoluble, except the alkali nitrites. The organic nitrites or nitrito compounds may be isomeric, but not identical with the corresponding nitro compounds.

nitrito- Describing an organic compound containing the radical —$O\cdot N:O$ (oxynitroso). **n. cobalomin.** Vitamin B_{12c}. The vitamin produced by replacing the —CN group of vitamin B_{12} by a —NO_2 group.

nitro- (1) A prefix which denotes the presence of the radical —NO_2 or —$N\diagdown_O^O$. Nitro compounds are usually yellow in color, and differ from the less stable, isomeric nitrito compounds. Cf. *nitroxyl*, *nitrite*, *nitrito*. (2) A misnomer for nitrate; as, nitroglycerin (glyceryl nitrate). **aci-** Isonitro-. The radical HOON=. **iso-** See *isonitro-*.

nitroacid. A compound containing both the radicals —COOH and —NO_2; as: $NO_2\cdot CH_2\cdot COOH$, nitroacetic acid; $NO_2\cdot CH_2\cdot CH_2\cdot COOH$, nitropropionic acid.

nitroalizarin. $C_{14}H_5O_2(OH)_2NO_2$ = 285.1. **α-** or **4,1,2-** Yellow crystals, decomp. 290. **β-** or **3,1,2-** Alizarin orange. Orange-yellow crystals, decomp. 244, slightly soluble in water, soluble in alcohol; used as dye, and as an intermediate in organic synthesis.

nitroamine. Nitramine.

nitroanisole. $C_6H_4(OMe)NO_2$ = 153.1. **ortho-** 1-Methoxy-2-nitrobenzene. Yellow liquid, d.1.268, m.9, b.265. **meta-** m.38, b.258. **para-** Colorless or yellowish plates, d.1.233, m.54, b.258. Insoluble in water, soluble in alcohol or ether.

nitroanthracene. $C_{14}H_9NO_2$ = 223.2. Nitrosoanthrone. Yellow needles, m.146, insoluble in water, soluble in benzene or chloroform.

nitroanthraquinone. $C_6H_4(CO)_2C_6H_3NO_2$ = 253.1. **α-** or **1-** Yellow needles, m.228, subliming when heated, insoluble in water, soluble in alcohol or ether. **β-** or **2-** Yellow needles, m.184, subliming when heated, insoluble in water, soluble in alcohol or ether.

n. sulfonic acid. A reagent for sugars.

Nitrobacter. A soil bacterium or other microorganism that oxidizes ammonia and its derivatives, or atmospheric nitrogen, to nitrites or nitrates.

nitrobacteria. Soil bacteria; as, Nitrobacter, Nitrosococcus, or Nitrosomonas.

nitrobarite. $Ba(NO_3)_2$. A native barium nitrate.

nitrobenzaldehyde. $C_6H_4(NO_2)CHO$ = 151.1. **ortho-** Yellow needles, m.44, slightly soluble in water. **meta-** Colorless needles, m.58. **para-** Colorless prisms, m.106, soluble in water; used in indigo synthesis.

nitrobenzamide. $NO_2 \cdot C_6H_4 \cdot CONH_2$ = 166.1. **ortho-** Colorless needles, m.174, soluble in water. **meta-** Yellow needles, m.140. **para-** Colorless needles, m.198, soluble in water.

nitrobenzanilide. $NO_2 \cdot C_6H_4 \cdot CONHPh$ = 242.2. **meta-** 3-Nitro-1-benzamidobenzene. Colorless leaflets, m.143, insoluble in water.

nitrobenzene. $C_6H_5NO_2$ = 123.08. Nitrobenzol, oil of mirbane, phenyl nitrite, essence of mirbane, artificial oil of bitter almonds. Yellow liquid, d_{20}1.198, b.210, slightly soluble in water. A reagent for sulfur, calcium oxide, and glucose; a substitute for almond oil; and a raw material for aniline and derivatives. **amino-** Nitraniline. **chloro-** $C_6H_4ClNO_2$ = 157.50. Colorless crystals. *ortho-* m.33. *meta-* m.44. *para-* m.84. **dimethyl-** Nitroxylene. **methyl-** Nitrotoluene. **tetra-** q.v. **tri-** q.v.

n. azoresorcinol. Magneson; a reagent for magnesium (blue color). **n. reduction.** The reduction of nitrobenzene to aminobenzene (aniline) in alkaline solutions. The following are produced: nitrobenzene (2 moles), azoxybenzene, azobenzene, hydrazobenzene, aniline (2 moles). **n. sulfonyl chloride.** A reagent for amines.

nitrobenzoic acid. $NO_2 \cdot C_6H_4 \cdot COOH$ = 167.1. **ortho-** Yellow crystals, m.148, soluble in water; a reagent. **meta-** Yellow leaflets, m.141, soluble in water. **para-** Nitrodracylic acid. Yellow crystals, m.242, soluble in water; used in organic synthesis.

nitrobenzol. Nitrobenzene.

nitrobenzonitrile. $NO_2 \cdot C_6H_4 \cdot CN$ = 148.1. **ortho-** 2-Nitro-1-cyanobenzene. Colorless needles, m.109, soluble in hot water. **meta-** Colorless needles, m.115, soluble in water. **para-** Colorless leaflets, m.149, insoluble in water.

nitrobenzophenone. $NO_2 \cdot C_6H_4 \cdot CO \cdot C_6H_5$ = 227.1. **ortho-** Colorless needles, m.105, soluble in alcohol. **meta-** Colorless leaflets, m.95, soluble in alcohol. **para-** Colorless needles, m.138, soluble in alcohol.

nitrobenzoquinone. $C_6H_3O_2NO_2$ = 153.1. Yellow crystals, decomp. 206, slightly soluble in water.

nitrobenzoyl. The radical, $NO_2 \cdot C_6H_4 \cdot CO-$, from nitrobenzoic acid. **n. chloride.** $C_7H_4O_3NCl$ = 185.5. *ortho-* A solid, m.75. *meta-* m.34. *para-* m.72. **n. formate.** $CO \cdot COOH$ = 195.09. *ortho-* A solid, m.123, soluble in warm water.

nitrobenzyl. The radical $NO_2 \cdot C_6H_4 \cdot CH_2-$, from nitrotoluene; 3 isomers. **n. alcohol.** $NO_2C_6H_4 \cdot CH_2OH$ = 153.1. *ortho-* Colorless needles, m.74, soluble in water. *meta-* Rhombic crystals. m.27. *para-* Colorless needles, m.93. **n. bromide,** $C_6H_4NO_3CH_2Br$ = 215.95. A reagent for hydroxy compounds. **n. chloride.** $C_6H_4NO_2 \cdot CH_2Cl$ = 171.55. *ortho-* m.48. *meta-* m.46. *para-* m.71. **n. cyanide** $NO_2C_6H_4CH_2CN$ = 162.1. *ortho-* Colorless needles, m.83, soluble in hot water. *meta-* Colorless prisms, m.115, insoluble in water. *para-* Colorless crystals, m.110, soluble in alcohol.

nitrobromoform. NO_2CBr_3 = 297.78. Bromopicrin. Colorless liquid, d.2.81, m.10, insoluble in water.

nitrocaptax. 6-Nitro-2-mercaptobenzothiazole. A reagent for alkyl halides.

nitrocarbamate. A salt or ester of nitrocarbamic acid

or a compound containing the radical $NO_2 \cdot NH \cdot COO-$. **ethyl-** Urethane.

nitrocarbol. Nitromethane.

nitrocarbonitrate. Ammonium nitrate sensitized with carbonaceous materials, e.g., diesel oil; an explosive.

nitrocellulose. $C_6H_7O_5(NO_2)_3$ = 2972. (1) An ester of nitric acid and cellulose; as, pyroxylin (11.2–12.4% N) and guncotton (12.4–13% N). Cf. *rayon, viscose.* Yellow granules used in Celluloid and collodion; mixed with picrates as an explosive; and in lacquers. (2) Also applied to other nitrates of cellulose.

nitrochalk. A fertilizer (10% available N); ammonium nitrate and calcium carbonate. Cf. *calnitro.*

nitrochlorobenzene. $NO_2C_6H_4Cl$ = 157.6. **ortho-** Colorless crystals; used in organic synthesis.

nitrochlorobenzol. Nitrochlorobenzene.

nitrochloroform. Chloropicrin.

nitrocinnamic acid. $NO_2C_6H_4CH:CHCOOH$ = 193.1. **ortho-** Colorless scales, m.240, insoluble in water. **meta-** Yellow needles, m.196, soluble in water. **para-** Colorless prisms, m.285, insoluble in water.

nitrococcus. Nitrosococcus.

nitrocolors. Colored compounds containing the nitro group; as, picric acid.

nitrocompound. A compound containing the $-NO_2$ group.

nitrocotton. Guncotton.

nitrocresol. $CH_3 \cdot C_6H_3 \cdot NO_2 \cdot OH$ = 153.10. Yellow solid, m.54, insoluble in water.

nitrocumene. $C_6H_4 \cdot NO_2 \cdot CHMe$ = 165.14. Colorless liquid, b.224 (decomp.).

nitrocymene. Nitroisopropylmethylbenzene.

nitrodiethylaniline. $NO_2C_6H_4NEt_2$ = 194.2. **ortho-** Soluble oil, b.290. **para-** Colorless needles, m.77, soluble in hot alcohol.

nitrodimethylamine. NO_2NMe_2 = 114.1. Colorless crystals, m.57, soluble in water.

nitrodimethylaniline. $NO_2C_6H_4NMe_2$ = 166.14. **ortho-** A liquid, b_{32mm}151. **meta-** Red prisms, m.60, insoluble in water. **para-** Yellow needles, m.164, insoluble in water.

nitrodiphenyl. $NO_2C_6H_4Ph$ = 199.14. **ortho-** Colorless leaflets, m.37, insoluble in water. **meta-** Yellow solid, m.61. **para-** Colorless needles, m.114, insoluble in water.

nitrodracylic acid. *p*-Nitrobenzoic acid.

nitrodye. A dyestuff nitrocolor.

nitroerythrite. Nitroerythrol.

nitroerythrol. $C_4H_6(NO_3)_4$ = 302.11. Butine tetranitrate, erythrol tetranitrate, tetranitroerythritol. Large plates, m.61, exploding on percussion or heating, slightly soluble in water; explosives.

nitroethane. $C_2H_5NO_2$ = 75.04. A colorless liquid, b.114, slightly miscible with water. Cf. *ethyl nitrite.*

nitroform. $CH(NO_2)_3$ = 151.1. Trinitromethane. Colorless crystals, m.15 (explode), soluble in water.

nitrofurantoin. $C_8H_6O_5N_4$ = 238.16. Yellow, bitter crystals, slightly soluble in water; a urinary antiseptic (B.P.).

nitrogelatin. Dynamite.

nitrogen. N = 14.007. A gaseous element in the atmosphere, at. no. 7. Colorless gas, d_{air}=0.967, m.−210, b.−77 to −35°K, slightly soluble in water or alcohol. First produced by Rutherford

(1772) from air ("mephitic air"). Priestley (1780) called it "phlogisticated air," and Cavendish (1785) produced nitric acid from air and called it nitrogen (niter-producing). N. occurs in many minerals, e.g., saltpeter, KNO_3. Its principal valencies are 3 and 5, but it forms several oxides and series of compounds, all fairly unstable (explosives, proteins). Used to manufacture nitric acids, nitrates, cyanamides, ammonia, nitrides, and cyanides. World consumption (1966), 24,952 million tons. **activated-** Excited n. **active-** Chemically active n., analogous to ozone, N_3. It has a characteristic afterglow. **alloxuric-** N. in organic tissues bound in purine bases. **alpha-** See *n. molecule.* **ammonia-** The n. of ammonium salts. **atmospheric-** See *atmosphere.* **beta-** See n. molecule. **carboxyl-** α-Amino acid n. **excited-** N. rendered luminous by exposure to radiations and low pressure. **fixed-** See *n. fixation.* **formol-** The n. of amino acids. See *formol* titration. **hydro-** See *hydronitrogens.* **ionized-** N. atoms or molecules ionized at low pressures; they produce lines in the spectra of aurora, corona, nebulas and stars. **ortho-** See *n. molecule.* **oxides of-** See *nitrous oxide* (N_2O), *nitric oxide* (NO), *nitrogen peroxide* (N_2O_4), *nitrogen pentoxide* (N_2O_5). **para-** See *n. molecule.* **radio-** A short-lived isotope (mass 13) obtained by bombardment of n. with α particles. Cf. *radioelements.* **soil-** The n. in soil nitrates or nitrites. **urea-** N. eliminated as urea.

n. balance. The ratio of n. intake (proteins) to n. output (urea, uric acid) of the human body. In the normal adult it is unity. **n. benzide.** Azobenzene. **n. cycle.** The passage of n. from the atmosphere to the soil by means of gaseous n. compounds, e.g., produced by thunderstorms; through bacteria to the plant; from the plant to the animal body; and back to the soil as excreta. **n. degradation.** 'The annual loss of n. from the soil by crop production. **n. dioxide.** Nitric oxide. **n. equilibrium.** The balance between the n. in the food and in the excreta. **n. equivalent.** 1 gm nitrogen $\equiv$ 6.25 gm protein. **n. fixation.** The conversion of atmospheric n. into a compound (in U.S.):

1. Natural processes:
   (a) Nonsymbiotic fixation: direct conversion of atmospheric nitrogen into nitrates by soil bacteria
   (b) Symbiotic fixation: gradual conversion of atmospheric nitrogen into nitrates by the intermediate formation of ammonia and nitrites
2. Artificial processes:
   (a) The electric arc at 2800–3300°C
   (b) Furnace process (Hausser process)
   (c) Direct catalytic union of nitrogen and hydrogen to form ammonia at 200–900 atm pressure at 600°C
   (d) Formation of metallic nitrides: $Al_2O_3 + 3C + N_2 = 2AlN + 3CO$ at 1750°C.
   (e) Formation of calcium cyanamide from calcium carbide and nitrogen at 1100°C

n. iodide. $N_2H_3I_3 = 411.80$. Red explosive compound, soluble in water. **n. lag.** The time between protein intake and appearance of an equivalent amount of nitrogen compounds in the urine. **n. molecule.** Normal N_2 is a mixture of 1 pt. ortho-N or β-N with odd rotational quantum numbers and 2 pts. para-N or α-N with even rotational quantum numbers. **n. monoxide.** Nitrous oxide. **n. oxychloride.** $NOCl = 65.5$. Nitrosyl chloride. Yellow or red gas, b.—5, decomp. by water; a constituent of aqua regia. **n. partition.** The distribution of the total nitrogen in urea, ammonia, uric acid, etc. **n. pentoxide.** $N_2O_5 = 108.0$. Nitric acid anhydride. Colorless crystals, b.46 (decomp.), soluble in water (nitric acid). **n. peroxide.** N_2O_4 or $NO_2 = 46.0$. An isomer of n. tetroxide. Colorless crystals, b.22; or brown, irritant gas. **n. sulfides.** (1) $N_4S_4 = 184.28$. Orange crystals, m.179, decomp. 185 or by water, sublimes 135. (2) $N_2S_5 = 188.32$. N. pentasulfide. Red liquid, m.10–11, decomp. by heat. **n. sulfochloride.** N_3S_4Cl. Thiazyl chloride. **n. tetroxide.** $N_2O_4 = 92.0$. An isomer of n. peroxide. Colorless crystals, m.—9. **n. tribromide.** $NBr_3 = 253.77$. Red, volatile, explosive oil. **n. trichloride.** $NCl_3 = 120.39$. Agene. Dark liquid, explodes 95. **n. trifluoride** $NF_3 = 71.01$. A liquid m.—200. **n. trioxide.** $N_2O_3 = 76.0$. Green liquid, b.3.5, soluble in water.

nitrogenated. Containing nitrogen. **n. oil.** An oil containing N compounds, e.g., oil of bitter almonds.
nitrogenium. Latin for nitrogen.
nitrogenization. The operation of (1) combining with nitrogen; or (2) impregnation with nitrogenous compounds.
nitrogenous. Describing a compound containing N; or N compounds. **n. tankage.** Process tankage. A fertilizer made by digesting n. waste (wood, felt, leather, hair, feathers) with steam under pressure, sometimes with sulfuric acid, and then drying and grinding.
nitroglucose. $C_6H_9O_5NO_2 = 207.2$. Yellow crystals; an arterial stimulant.
nitroglycerin. $C_3H_5(ONO_2)_3 = 227.1$. Glyceryl nitrate, glycerin trinitrate nitroglycerol, trinitrin, agioneurosin, nitric ester of glycerin, glonoin, trinitroglycerin, propenyl trinitrate, nitroleum, blasting oil, piroglycerina (early name). Yellow oil, d.1.60, m.13, explodes 260, insoluble in water. Used in the preparation of explosives; and as a vasodilator (U.S.P.).
nitroglycerol. Nitroglycerin.
nitroglycol. Ethylene dinitrate.
nitro group. Nitryl. The —NO_2 group.
nitroguanidine. $NO_2 \cdot NH \cdot CNH \cdot NH_2 = 104.1$. Colorless needles, m.230 (decomp.), slightly soluble in water.
nitrohydrochloric acid. Aqua regia.
nitroic acids. Compounds containing the radical —$NO(OH)_2$.
nitroleum. Nitroglycerin.
nitrolevulose. Levulose nitrate, dextrose nitrate. Yellow crystals, explode when heated.
nitrolic acid. A compound of the type $R \cdot C(NOH) \cdot (NO_2) \cdot$. The solutions are deep red.
nitrolim(e). Calcium cyanamide.
nitrols. Compounds of the type $R \cdot C(NO)(:NO)_2$ or $R \cdot CH(NO)_2$. The solutions are deep blue.
nitromagnesite. $Mg(NO_3)_2 \cdot xH_2O$. A native nitrate.
nitromannite. Mannitol nitrate.
nitrometal. An addition compound (nitroxyl) of nitric oxide and metallic oxides, e.g., Cu_2NO_2.

Nitrometals form nitrites and nitric oxide with water.

nitrometer. A glass apparatus for measuring gases evolved by a chemical reaction; essentially a eudiometer with a 2-way stopcock connecting the air or a funnel to a buret in which the gas is liberated.

nitromethane. $CH_3NO_2 = 27.0$. Nitrocarbol. Colorless liquid, d.1.14, b.101, slightly soluble in water.

Nitromonas. A soil bacterium that converts ammonium salts into nitrites and nitrates, but will not grow in organic media.

nitromuriatic acid. Aqua regia.

nitron. (1) $N:C(NPh)_2 \cdot CH \cdot NPh = 312.39$. 1,4-Diphenyl-3,5-endoanilino-4,5-dihydro-1,2,4-triazole, 4,5-dihydro-1,4-diphenyl-3,5-phenylimino-1,2,4-triazole. Yellow needles, insoluble in water; reagent for nitrates. (2) Trona; early (Greek) name. Cf. *nitrone*. **n. nitrate.** $C_{20}H_{16}N_4 \cdot HNO_3 = 375.3$. An insoluble precipitate formed by nitrates and nitron.

nitronaphthalene. $C_{10}H_7NO_2 = 173.1$. **alpha-** Yellow crystals, m.61, insoluble in water. Used in organic synthesis, and to remove fluorescence from oils. **beta-** Colorless, needles, m.79, insoluble in water; used in organic synthesis.

nitronaphthoic acid. $C_{10}H_6(NO_2)COOH = 217.1$. Colorless prisms, slightly soluble in water. **1,2-** or **1-β-** m.103. **2,1-** or **2-α-** m.218. **3,1-** or **3-α-** m.168. **4,1-** or **4-α-** m.164. **5,1-** or **5-α-** m.171. **5,2-** or **5-β-** m.147. **6,2-** or **6-β-** m.158. **8,1-** or **8-α-** m.215. **8,2-** or **8-β-** m.145.

nitronaphthol. $C_{10}H_6(NO_2)OH = 189.1$. **1,2-** Yellow crystals, m.103. **1,5-** Yellow needles, m.171. **2,1-** Colorless leaflets, m.128. **3,1-** m.168. **4,1-** Yellow needles, m.164. **5,2-** Yellow needles, m.147. **6,2-** m.158. **8,2-** Yellow needles, m.144. Used in organic synthesis.

nitronaphthylamine. $C_{10}H_6(NO_2)NH_2 = 188.1$. **1,2-** Orange needles, m.126. **1,4-** m.191. **1,5-** m.118. **1,8-** m.97. **2,1-** Yellow prisms, m.144. **5,2-** Red needles, m.142. **8,2-** Red needles, m.103. Used in organic synthesis.

nitrone. (1) The radical $=C:NO—$; as in phenyl nitrone. Cf. *nitron*. (2) $CH_2:NH:O$.

nitronic acid. A group of compounds containing the radical $=N(:O) \cdot OR$.

nitronitroso- See *pseudonitrols*.

nitronium ion. The positively charged NO_2^+ ion, believed to be formed from nitric acid.

nitropentaerythrol. $C_5H_{11}O_4 \cdot NO_3 = 165.09$. An explosive.

nitrophenetol. $C_2H_2O \cdot C_6H_4NO_2 = 167.08$. **ortho-** Yellow crystals m.2.1. **meta-** Yellow crystals m.34. **para-** Yellow crystals, m.57.8.

nitrophenol. $C_6H_4(NO_2)OH = 139.05$. **ortho-** Yellow prisms, m.45, soluble in water. **meta-** Yellow tablets, m.96, slightly soluble in water. **para-** Colorless monoclinic crystals, m.114, slightly soluble in water. Used to manufacture rhodamine dyestuffs, phenolphthalein, etc. *p*-Nitrophenol is an indicator for alkalimetry, and for blood and seawater; changing at pH 6 from colorless (acid) to yellow (alkaline). **chloro-** $Cl \cdot C_6H_3(OH)NO_2 = 173.50$. Chloronitrohydroxybenzene. The first number indicates Cl, the second NO_2; OH is the

1-position: *2,3-* m.120. *2,4-* m.111. *3,4-* m.133. *4,2-* m.87. *4,3-* m.127. *5,2-* m.38.9. *5,3-* m.147. *6,2-* m.70. *6,3-* m.118.

nitrophenols. Compounds, derived from phenol by the substitution of one or more nuclear H atoms by the nitro group.

nitrophenyl diethyl phosphate. The para compound is parathion.

Nitrophoska. Trademark for a fused, ternary mixture of KNO_3, NH_4Cl and $(NH_4)PO_4$; a fertilizer.

nitrophthalic acid. $C_6H_3(NO_2)(COOH)_2 = 211.1$. **3-** Yellow, monoclinic crystals, m.220, slightly soluble in water. **4-** Colorless needles, m.161, soluble in water.

nitrophthalide. $C_6H_4 \cdot CO \cdot O \cdot CHNO_2 = 179.2$. Colorless needles, m.141, insoluble in water.

nitropropane. $C_3H_7NO_2 = 89.1$. Colorless liquid, d.1.01, b.131, slightly soluble in water.

nitroprussiate. Nitroprusside.

nitroprusside. Containing the radical $[Fe(NO)(CN)]_5=$.

nitroquinoline. $C_9H_6N \cdot NO_2 = 174.1$. **5-** Colorless needles, m.72, soluble in water. **6-** Colorless needles, m.150, soluble in water. **7-** Colorless needles, m.132. **8-** Colorless needles, m.88, insoluble in water; a reagent for palladium.

nitrosalicylic acid. $C_6H_3(NO_2)(OH)COOH = 183.1$. **meta-** or 3- (3,2,1-) White needles, m.144, slightly soluble in water. **asym-** or 5- (5,2,1-) Colorless needles, m.230, slightly soluble in water. Used in organic synthesis.

nitrosalol. $C_6H_4(OH)COOC_6H_4NO_2 = 259.08$. Yellow powder, m.148, insoluble in water.

nitrosamines. (1) Yellow organic compounds containing the radical $=N \cdot NO$, obtained by the action of nitrous acid on secondary amines. Cf. *nitrosoamines* which contain the radicals $—NH_2$ and $—NO$. E.g.; **diethyl-** $Et_2N \cdot NO$. Nitrosodiethyline, b.177. **dimethyl-** $Me_2N \cdot NO$. Nitrosodimethyline, b.148. **diphenyl-** $Ph_2N \cdot NO$. **phenylethyl-** $PhEtN \cdot NO$. **phenylmethyl-** $PhMeN \cdot NO$. (2) Compounds containing the radical $—NH \cdot NO$; as: **ethyl-** $EtNHNO$. **methyl-** $MeNHNO$. **phenyl-** $PhNHNO$.

nitrosates. Compounds containing the $=C(ONO_2) \cdot C(:NOH)—$ group.

nitrose. A solution of nitrosylsulfuric acid in sulfuric acid, made by passing NO_2 and NO into sulfuric acid.

nitrosites. Compounds containing the $=C(ONO) \cdot C(:NOH)—$ group.

nitroso. Oximino, hydroximino. The radical $—NO$ (trivalent N). **iso-** The radical $—N:OH$. **oxy-** Nitrito. **n. R. salt.** $C_{10}H_4OH \cdot NO(SO_3Na)_2$; gives a blue color with cobalt and iron only.

nitrosoacetophenone, iso- Benzoylformoxime.

nitrosoamines. Compounds containing both the radicals $—NH_2$ and $—NO$; as, nitrosoaniline. Cf. *nitrosamines*.

nitrosoaniline. $C_6H_4(NO)NH_2 = 122.1$. **para-** Steel-blue needles, m.174, insoluble in water.

Nitrosobacter. A rodlike nitrifying bacterium.

nitrosobacteria. Nitrifying bacteria. See *Nitromonas*.

nitrosobenzene. $C_6H_5NO = 107.1$. Blue, monoclinic needles, m.68.

nitrosobenzoic acid. $C_6H_4(NO)COOH = 151.1$. **ortho-** Colorless crystals, decomp. 210, soluble in water.

nitrosocobalamin. Vitamin B_{12c}.

Nitrosococcus. A round, nitrifying soil bacterium; converts ammonia to nitrites. Cf. *Nitrosomonas*.

nitrosodiethylamine. $(C_2H_5)_2N \cdot NO = 102.1$. Nitrosodiethyline, diethylnitrosamine. Yellow oil, d.0.951, b.177, soluble in water.

nitrosodiethylaniline. $C_6H_4(NO)NEt_2 = 178.2$. **para-** Colorless needles, m.84, slightly soluble in water.

nitrosodimethylamine. $(CH_3)_2N \cdot NO = 74.1$. Nitrosodimethyline, dimethylnitrosamine. Yellow oil, b.148, soluble in water.

nitrosodimethylaniline. $C_6H_4(NO)NMe_2 = 150.1$. **para-** Green scales, m.88, slightly soluble in water. **n. hydrochloride.** $C_6H_4(NO)NMe_2 \cdot HCl = 186.45$. Yellow needles, soluble in water; used in the manufacture of dyes.

nitroso dyes. Dyestuffs derived from quinone oxime, which contains the chromophore

$$=C-O$$
$$\quad | \quad |$$
$$=C-N.OH$$

nitrosoethane. $C_2H_5NO = 59.1$.

nitrosohydroxylamines. Compounds containing the radical $-N(NO) \cdot (OH)$.

nitrosoketones. Compounds containing the $-CO \cdot C(:NOH)-$ group.

Nitrosomas. A soil bacterium of Europe, Asia, and Africa; converts ammonia into nitrites. Cf. *Nitromonas, Nitrosococcus*.

nitrosonaphthol. $C_{10}H_6(NO)OH = 173.1$. **α,α-** 4-Nitroso-2-hydroxynaphthalene. Yellow crystals, m.194, insoluble in water. **α,β-** 1-Nitroso-2-hydroxynaphthalene. Yellow prisms, m.110, soluble in water. **β,α-** 2-Nitroso-1-hydroxynaphthalene. Yellow needles, m.162, soluble in water; used in organic syntheses, and as reagents for cobalt.

nitrosonaphthylamine. $C_{10}H_6(NO)NH_2 = 172.1$. **α,β-** 1-Nitroso-2-aminonaphthalene. Green needles, m.150, soluble in hot water.

nitrosonitric acid. Fuming nitric acid.

nitrosonium. The NO^+ ion. It forms salts with anions, e.g., $NOClO_4$.

nitrosophenol. $C_6H_5O_2N = 123.1$. $OH \cdot C_6H_4 \cdot NO$. A solid, m.140 (decomp.), soluble in water. Cf. *quinone monoxime*, its tautomeric form.

nitrosophenyldimethylpyrazole. $C_{11}H_{11}O_2N_3 = 217.2$. A reaction product of antipyrine and nitrites in acid solution. Green needles, explode 200; an antipyretic and diuretic.

nitrososulfuric acid. Nitrosyl sulfate.

nitrosotoluene. $C_6H_4(NO)CH_3 = 121.1$. **ortho-** Yellow needles, decomp. 120, soluble in water.

nitrostarch. $[C_{12}H_{12}O_{10}(NO_2)_3]_n$. Starch nitrate. Orange powder, soluble in alcohol or ether. A nitrated starch used in the manufacture of explosives.

nitrostyrene. $NO_2C_6H_4 \cdot CH:CH_2 = 149.1$. Nitrostyrolene. **ortho-** Colorless oil, m.12 (decomp.), insoluble in water. **meta-** Colorless liquid, b.235, soluble in ether. **para-** Colorless prisms, m.58, soluble in hot ether.

nitrostyrolene. Nitrostyrene.

nitrosubstitution. The result of nitration.

nitrosulfamide. $H_2N \cdot SO_2 : NHNO = 125.2$. Colorless liquid; the silver salt is a detonator.

nitrosulfonic acid. Nitrosyl sulfate.

nitrosulfuric acid. Nitric acid 1, sulfuric acid 2 vol.; a nitrating agent. Cf. *nitrosylsulfuric acid*.

nitrosyl. The nitroso radical, NO—, when attached to a strongly electronegative element or group, as, Cl—. **n. bromide.** $NOBr = 109.93$. Brown liquid, decomp. —2. **n. chloride.** $NOCl$. Nitrogen oxychloride. **n. fluoride.** $NOF = 49.01$. A gas, b.—56. **n. perchlorate.** $NOClO_4 = 129.47$. An unstable liquid. **n. sulfate.** $NO \cdot HSO_4 = 111.1$. Nitrososulfuric acid, chamber crystals, nitrosulfonic acid, n. sulfuric acid, nitrose. Colorless crystals, m.75 (decomp.); formed in the lead chambers during the manufacture of sulfuric acid. **n. sulfuric acid.** N. sulfate. **n. sulfuryl chloride.** $ClSO_4ONO = 177.54$. Crystals, produced from sulfur trioxide and nitrosyl chloride.

nitrothiophen. $NO_2 \cdot C_4H_3S = 129.1$. Colorless crystals, m.44, insoluble in water.

nitrotoluene. $Me \cdot C_6H_4 \cdot NO_2 = 137.1$. **ortho-** Yellow liquid, d.1.168, b.218, insoluble in water. **meta-** Yellow crystals, m.16, insoluble in water. **para-** Yellow crystals, m.54, insoluble in water. All are used in organic synthesis. **di-** q.v. **tri-** See *trinitrotoluene*.

nitrotoluidine. $C_6H_3(NO_2)(NH_2)CH_3 = 152.12$. A series of nitroaminomethylbenzenes, used in the synthesis of dyestuffs. They are usually slightly soluble in water; soluble in alcohol, ether, or benzene. According to the positions of the 3 groups in the benzene ring there are:

NO_2	NH_2	CH_3	Description
			ortho-
	2	1	Orange prisms, m.92
4	2	1	Yellow, monoclinic crystals, m.104
5	2	1	Yellow needles, m.127
6	2	1	Yellow leaflets, m.92
			meta-
2	3	1	Yellow needles, m.53
4	3	1	Yellow leaflets, m.109
5	3	1	Orange needles, m.98
6	3	1	Yellow needles, m.138
			para-
2	4	1	Yellow, monoclinic crystals, m.77
3	4	1	Red prisms, m.114

nitrourea. $NH_2 \cdot CO \cdot NHNO_2 = 105.1$. White crystals, decomp. by heat, slightly soluble in water.

nitrourethane. $NO_2 \cdot NH \cdot COO \cdot C_2H_5 = 134.1$. Colorless leaflets, m.64, b.140(decomp.), soluble in water.

nitrous. (1) Describing nitrogen compounds containing positive trivalent nitrogen. Their ammonia compounds contain negative trivalent nitrogen. (2) A compound of nitric acid (obsolete). **n. acid.** $HNO_2 = 47.0$. An aqueous solution of nitrogen trioxide, N_2O_3. **n. anhydride.** Nitrogen trioxide. **n. ether.** $C_2H_5NO_2 = 75.04$. (1)

Ethyl nitrite. (2) Nitroethane. **n. oxide.** $N_2O =$ 44.1. Nitrogen monoxide, laughing gas, dental gas. Colorless gas, b.-88.4, soluble in water; an anesthetic (U.S.P., B.P.) and preservative. **n. vitriol.** A solution of oxides of nitrogen and sometimes of sulfur dioxide in strong sulfuric acid formed during the manufacture of sulfuric acid, q.v.

nitrousacidum. The ion $OH \cdot N : OH$.

nitroxanthic acid. Picric acid.

nitroxyl. The radical $-NO_2$, when attached to a strongly electronegative group, as F; or to a metal, as $Cu_2(NO_2)$. **n. chloride.** $NO_2Cl = 81.47$. Yellow liquid. **n. fluoride.** $NO_2F = 65.0$. Colorless gas, b.-64, decomp. by water.

nitroxylene. $Me_2 \cdot C_6H_3 \cdot NO_2 = 151.1$. **1,2,3-** Yellow liquid, b.250. **1,2,4-** or **ortho-** Yellow crystals, m.29. **1,3,2-** or **meta-** Yellow liquid, b.225. **1,3,4-** A liquid, b.238. **1,3,5-** m.74. **1,4,2-** or **para-** Yellow liquid, b.239. All are insoluble in water and used in organic synthesis.

nitroxylic acid. $H_2NO_2 = 48.0$. Hydronitrous acid. Cf. *nitroxyls*.

nitrum. An early (Latin) name for trona.

nitryl. (1) Nitro group. The radical $-NO_2$, from nitrous acid, HNO_2. (2) Vinylidene dinitrile. See *plastics*. **n. fluoride.** Nitroxyl fluoride.

nivalic acid. $C_{20}H_{26}O_6 = 362.22$. An acid from the lichen, *Cetraria nivalis*.

nivaquin. Chloroquine sulfate.

nivenite. Uranite with a large proportion of rare earths.

Nizin. Trademark for zinc sulfanilate.

nm. Abbreviation for nanometer.

No. (1) Symbol for nobelium. (2) At. no.; also Z (German: zahl). **No. 606.** Salvarsan. **No. 914.** Neosalvarsan.

Nobel, Alfred Bernhard. 1833–1896. Swedish chemist, the inventor of several explosives and artificial rubber; founder of the Nobel Prize. **N.'s explosive.** A high explosive: nitroglycerin 25–80, guncotton 0.5–7, liquid nitro-body 0.4–9, wood meal 0.9–10, potassium or sodium nitrate 6–45%. **N. oil.** Nitroglycerin. **N. Prize.** An annual award divided among 5 scientists who have been outstanding in physics, chemistry, physiology, medicine, and world peace.

nobelium. No. Element 102. Discovered (1957) by joint researches, in the U.S., U.K., and Sweden, on exposing Cm^{244} on thin foil to cyclotron bombardment with accelerated carbon ions.

Noble, Alfred. 1844–1914. American civil engineer who founded the **Noble Prize** for the best technical engineering paper. Cf. *Nobel Prize*.

noble gas. A member of the zero group of the periodic system: He, Ne, A, Kr, Xe, and Rn. Cf. *atmospheric gases*. **n. laurel.** Laurel. **n. liverwort.** Liverwort. **n. metal.** A metal that is not readily oxidized; as, the gold, platinum, and palladium family of the periodic system.

noctal. $C_{10}H_{13}BrN_2O_3 = 189.00$. Nostal, isopropyl-$\beta$-bromoallylbarbituric acid. White powder, m.178; a narcotic.

nodakenin. $C_{20}H_{24}O_9 = 408.15$. A glucoside from nodake, *Pellecedanum decursivium* (Umbelliferae), Japan.

node. (1) The point at which a curve or wave motion intersects a fixed plane. (2) A knot or protuberance.

nodule. A small round lump, as of a mineral.

noil. Short-staple, wool-fiber combings used in worsteds.

noise. See *loudness, sound, decibel*.

nomenclature. The systematic terminology of chemical compounds. Rules of chemical n. are formulated by the International Union of Pure and Applied Chemistry (IUPAC) in collaboration with the corresponding body for physics (IUPAP); and they are continually being extended and revised in the light of current international usage. Most, but not all, of the rules are accepted by the U.S. (American Chemical Society) and U.K. (Chemical Society). Where IUPAC rules do not exist there are usually agreements between the U.S. and U.K. chemical societies (e.g., for carbohydrates and organophosphorus compounds); Except where otherwise stated, the general IUPAC rules are used in this dictionary. See "Definitive Rules for Inorganic Nomenclature,"; "Definitive Rules for Organic Nomenclature,"; "Handbook for Chemical Society Authors,"; B.P. Commission, "Approved Names"; British Standard 2474: 1965, "Recommended Names for Chemicals used in Industry"; *atomic weights, elements, ion, notation, organic, radicals, symbols*.

Geneva- Rules adopted at the International Conference on Chemical Nomenclature (Geneva, 1892). They referred mainly to organic compounds and have since been superseded. Principal rules for inorganic nomenclature:

Binary compounds:

Positive element (metal) named first, followed by electronegative element (nonmetal).

Metal suffixes:

-ous indicates the lower valence; as, ferr*ous*.

-ic indicates the higher valence; as, ferr*ic*.

Nonmetal suffixes:

-ide; as, ox*ide*, chlor*ide*.

Tertiary compounds:

Acids:

-ous acid, indicating a lower valency; as sulfur*ous* acid.

-ic acid, indicating a higher valency; as, sulfur*ic* acid.

If there are more than 2 stages of oxidation, then:

hypo- -ous, the acid of lowest valency; as, *hypo*chlor*ous* acid.

per- -ic, the acid of highest valency; as, *per*chlor*ic* acid.

Salts:

-ite, when derived from an *-ous* acid; as, sulf*ite*.

-ate, when derived from an *-ic* acid; as, sulf*ate*.

nomogram. Nomograph.

nomograph. Nomogram. Alignment chart. Graphical scales, used for the rapid calculation and solution of complicated equations.

nomography. The representation of analytical or other correlations by means of charts and graphs, which eliminate calculations.

non- (1) Prefix (Latin) indicating not. (2) Prefix (Greek) for nine.

nonacosane*. $C_{29}H_{60} = 408.5$ A hydrocarbon in beeswax and the fat of cabbage leaves. Colorless wax, m.63.

nonacosanol*. $C_{29}H_{59}OH = 304.5$. **1-** Montanyl alcohol. **9-** White solid, m.75.4. **10-** m.75. **12-** m.74. **14-** m.79. **15-** m.84.

nonacyclic. (1) Having 9 rings; as violanthrole. (2) Not acyclic.

nonadecane*. $C_{19}H_{40}$ = 268.42. Enneadecane, enndecane. A solid, m.32.

nonadecanoic acid*. $C_{18}H_{37}COOH$ = 298.30. Nonadecylic acid. White leaflets, m.67.

nonadecanol*. $C_{19}H_{39}OH$ = 284.31. Nonadecyl alcohol. Opaque crystals, m.62.

nonadecanone*. $(C_9H_{19})_2CO$ = 282.30. 10-Caprinone, dinonyl ketone. Colorless leaflets, m.58, insoluble in water.

nonadecyl alcohol. Nonadecanol.*

nonadecylic acid. Nonadecanoic acid.*

nonaldehyde. Pelargonaldehyde.

nonane*. C_9H_{20} = 128.2. Colorless liquid, d.0.718, b.149, insoluble in water. n. carboxylic acid. Capric acid. n. dioic acid*. Azelaic acid.

nonanediol*. $CH_2OH \cdot (CH_2)_7 CH_2OH$ = 160.16. Nonamethylene glycol. Colorless liquid, b.149, slightly soluble in water.

nonanenitrile*. $Me(CH_2)_7 CN$ = 139.14. Pelargononitrile. Colorless liquid, d.0.8331, b.224, insoluble in water.

nonanoic acid*. Pelargonic acid.

nonanol*. $C_9H_{20}O$ = 144.16. 1- n-Nonyl alcohol. 2- $Me(CH_2)_6 CHOHMe$. Heptylmethylcarbinol. Colorless liquid, b.193, insoluble in water. 3- $Me(CH_2)_5 CHOHEt$, Ethylhexylcarbinol. Colorless liquid, b.194. 4- $Me(CH_2)_4 CHOHPr$. Amylpropylcarbinol. Colorless liquid, b.192. 5- $[Me(CH_2)_3]_2 CHOH$. Dibutylcarbinol. Oily liquid, b.194.

nonanone*. $C_9H_{18}O$ = 142.14. 2- $Me \cdot CO(CH_2)_6$-Me. Methyl n-heptyl ketone. A constituent of rue and clove oils. Colorless liquid, b.195. 3- $Et \cdot CO(CH_2)_5 Me$. Ethyl n-hexyl ketone, b.190. 5- $[Me(CH_2)_3]_2 CO$. Dibutyl ketone. Colorless liquid, b.187.

nonanoyl*. Pelargonyl. The radical $Me(CH_2)_7$-CO—, from nonanoic acid. n. chloride. C_9H_{17}-OCl = 176.59. Pelargonyl chloride. Colorless liquid, b.215, decomp. by water.

nonconductor. A substance that does not transmit electricity, heat, or light. Cf. insulator.

nondecylic acid. Nonadecanoic acid.*

nondrying oil. A liquid fat that remains fluid on exposure; contains olein and glycerides of unsaturated fatty acids. E.g., castor oil.

nonene*. Nonylene.

nonferrous. Other than iron.

nonine. Nonyne*.

nonmetal. An electronegative element in the upper left half of the periodic system. Nonmetals are generally polyvalent (except O and H), and exist in several stages of oxidation. Their oxides form acids.

nonoic acid. Pelargonic acid.

Nonox. Trade name for aldolnaphthylamine derivatives; rubber antioxidants.

nonvalent. Inert, having zero valency; as, the noble gases.

nonyl. The radical $-C_9H_{19}$, from nonane. n. alcohol. $C_9H_{19}OH$ = 144.2. Colorless liquid, b.213, insoluble in water. For other isomers see nonanol*. n. aldehyde. Pelargonaldehyde. n. amine. $C_9H_{19}NH_2$ = 143.17. Colorless liquid, b.195. n. cyanide. Caprinitrile.

nonylene. C_9H_{18} = 126.15. Nonene*, b.147.

nonylic acid. Pelargonic acid.

nonylone. 9-Neptadecanone.

nonyne*. $Me(CH_2)_6 C \vdots CH$ = 124.12. n-Heptylacetylene, nonine. Colorless liquid, b.160, insoluble in water.

nootkatin. $C_{15}H_{20}O_2$ = 432.18. A troplone, m.95, having one additional double bond.

nootkatone. A sesquiterpene ketone flavoring in grapefruit.

Nopco. Trademark for a group of surface-active agents.

nopinene. $C_{10}H_{16}$ = 136.12. β-Pinene, 7,7- dimethyl-2-methylenenorpinane. A terpene (30 %) in the oil of Ferula galbanifiua (Russia). Cf. galbanum.

nor- Prefix indicating: (1) a change from the trivial name of a branched-chain compound into that of a straight-chain compound, as norvaline (preferred use, IUPAC); (2) a lower homolog.

noradrenaline acid tartrate. $C_{12}H_{17}O_9N \cdot H_2O$ = 337.36. Bitter, white crystals, m.102, soluble in water; used similarly to adrenaline but, unlike it, reduces the flow of blood in muscles (B.P.).

noratropine. An alkaloid from various Solanaceae species, allied to atropine.

Norbide. B_6C. Trademark for boron carbide, formed by heating coke and boric acid in an electric furnace. Second to diamond in hardness; used for grinding, deoxidizing steel, and as an abrasion-resistant.

norcamphane. C_7H_{12} = 96.09. [1.2.2]Bicycloheptane, the parent compound of many terpenes. dimethyl- Camphenilane. dimethylmethylene- Camphene. trimethyl- Camphane.

norcamphanyl. The radical C_7H_{11}—, from norcamphane.

norconidendrin. An antioxidant for fats and oils, made by the methylation of a constituent of sulfite waste liquor from the pulping of western hemlock.

nordenskioldine. (Swedish.) $CaSnB_2O_6$. A tin ore.

Nordhausen acid. Oleum.

nordmarkite. A ferromagnesian–feldspathic soda syenitic rock, from Norway.

Nore- Prefix indicating a product of the Northern Regional Laboratory, Peoria, Ill.; e.g., Noreseal.

norephedrine. $Ph \cdot C(OH)NH_2 \cdot Et$ = 151.11. α-Aminoethyl benzyl alcohol; used similarly to ephedrine.

norepol. Agripol.

Noreseal. Trade name for a whipped-up mixture of glue, glycerin, glucose, peanut hulls, saponin, water, and formaldehyde; a cork substitute.

norethandrolone. $C_{20}H_{30}O_2$ = 302.45. White crystals, m.135, insoluble in water; an androgen (B.P.).

norethisterone. $C_{20}H_{26}O_2$ = 298.35. White crystals, m.203, insoluble in water; a progestational steroid (B.P.).

norethynodrel. Enovid.

Norge saltpeter. A Norwegian calcium nitrate fertilizer.

Norgine. Algin. Trade name for an adhesive made by boiling seaweed with alkali and precipitating the filtered solution with acid.

noric. The division of the Triassic system containing the limestones and dolomites with some clays and sandstones. n. steel. Steel from the region of Austria south of the Danube.

Norit. Trademark for purified charcoal made from birch; used to decolorize and deodorize syrup, oils or pharmaceutical products.

norium. A supposed rare-earth element from zircon; actually a mixture of rare-earth metals.

norleucine. $C_6H_{13}O_2N$ = 131.1. Caprine, glycoleucine, α-amino-n-caproic acid, α-amino-α-butylacetic acid, 2-aminohexanoic acid*. An amino acid from the leucine fractions of proteins of the brain and of casein.

norm. A theoretical standard. **n. system.** In mineralogy, a system of classification of rocks based on their theoretical chemical compositions. Cf. *mode*.

normal. (1) One plane or line perpendicular to another. (2) A fixed standard or an established type, as a solution. (3) Prefix indicating: (*a*) a neutral salt with all the available H atoms replaced; (*b*) an organic compound in its "normal" (as distinct from its "iso") form. (4) Average or mean. **n. atom.** An atom in the unexcited state. Cf. *neutral* atom. **n. benzine.** Benzine of d.0.695–0.705, b.65–95. **n. element.** A cell, used as standard of electromotive force. See *Weston element, cadmium cell*. **n. glass.** A glass whose composition can be represented by a definite chemical formula; as, $6SiO_2 \cdot CaO \cdot Na_2O$. **n. hydrocarbon.** An aliphatic hydrocarbon with a straight carbon chain in its molecule and no sidechains; as, n-pentane. **n. pressure.** Atmospheric pressure, atmosphere. The pressure of a column of mercury 760 mm high at sealevel (approximately 14.7 psi). **n. saline,** q.v. **n. salt.** A salt in which all the hydrogen atoms of the acid have been replaced by a metal, or all the hydroxide radicals of a base replaced by an acid radical. E.g., Na_2CO_3 (normal salt); $NaHCO_3$ (acid salt). **n. solution.** A solution that contains one equivalent of the active reagent in grams, in one liter of the solution. The equivalent in grams is that quantity of the active reagent which contains, replaces, unites with, or in any way, directly or indirectly, brings into reaction 1 gm of H.

1 N HCl = 36.5 gm HCl/liter = 1 M HCl
1 N H_2SO_4 = 49 gm H_2SO_4/liter = 0.5 M H_2SO_4
Weaker or stronger solutions are indicated thus: 0.5 N, 2 N, etc., the prefix being the normality. Cf. *centinormal, millinormal, supernormal*. **n. temperature.** Room temperature: 20°C or 68°F. Cf. *standard temperature* (0°C). **n. thermometer.** A standardized thermometer.

normality. See *normal solution*.

normalization. (1) The process of restoring normality. (2) The treatment of milk after pasteurization to disperse the fat homogeneously throughout it.

normalizing. The treatment of metals (especially aluminum alloys), with a molten mixture of sodium and potassium nitrates at 500°C.

normenthane. Isopropylcyclohexane.

Normocytin. Trademark for a concentrate of vitamins B_{12b} and B_{12}, used to treat pernicious anemia.

nornicotine. $C_9H_{12}N_2$ = 136.11. An isomer of nicotine in Kentucky tobacco.

noropianic acid. $C_8H_6O_5$ = 182.1. 5,6-Dihydroxyphthalaldehyde acid. Colorless crystals, m.171, soluble in alcohol.

norpinane. C_7H_{12} = 96.09. [1.1.3]Bicycloheptane. Cf. *nopinic acid*. **dimethylmethylene-** Nopinene.

norpinic acid. $C_8H_{10}O_4$ = 170.08. 2,2-Dimethyl-1,3-cyclobutanedicarboxylic acid. Cf. *truxillic acid, nopinic acid*.

Norris, Flack James, 1871–1940. American chemist, noted for organic research.

norsolanellic acid. Biloidanic acid.

Northylen. Trade name for a polythene synthetic fiber.

nortropinone. $C_7H_{11}ON$ = 125.09. A ketone derived from tropine by oxidation. Colorless powder, m.70.

nortryptaline hydrochloride. $C_{19}H_{21}N \cdot HCl$ = 299.78. Bitter, white crystals, soluble in water, m.218; an antidepressant (B.P.).

norvaline. $C_5H_{11}O_2N$ = 117.1. α-Aminovaleric acid. A protein aminoacid, m.291.

Norwegian saltpeter. Norge saltpeter.

noscapine. Narcotine.

nosean. An aluminum sodium silicate containing gypsum.

noselite. $Al_3Na_5SSi_3O_{16}$. A silicate mineral, q.v., of the sodalite group.

nosepiece. A revolving disk on a microscope, into which the objectives are screwed.

nosology. The classification of disease.

nosophen. $(C_6H_2I_2OH)_2(CO)_2C_6H_4$ = 821.5. Tetraiodophenolphthalein, iodophen. Yellow powder, m.225, slightly soluble in ether; an iodoform substitute. **bismuth-** Eudoxin. **mercury-** Apallagin. **sodium-** Antinosin.

nostal. Noctal.

nostrum. A cure-all, or quack medicine.

notalin. Citrinin.

notatin. An antibiotic from *Penicillium* species, identical with corylophilline and penicillin B.

notation. A system of numerals and symbols which indicate the structural characteristic of an organic compound. Principal symbols:

a	Asymmetric, or alpha position
α	Ana position, alpha position (first C atom)
β	Beta position (second C atom)
c	Cyclic, or cis type
d	Dextrorotatory
dl	Racemic
δ	Fourth C atom
ϵ	Epi position (fifth C atom)
γ	Gamma position (third C atom)
i	Iso or inactive
κ	Kata position
l	Levorotatory
m	Mesa position, or meso isomer
μ	Meso position
n	Normal, or nitrogen substitute
o	Ortho position, or oxygen substitute
ω	Substitution in the side chain or on the C atom farthest from a functional group
p	Para position, or primary
π	Peri position
r	Racemic
ρ	Pros position
s	Syn type, symmetric, secondary, or sulfur substitute
t	Trans type, or tertiary
v	Vicinal position

ψ Pseudo
φ Amphi position
Δ Double bond, as Δ^2, a double bond between the second and third C atoms, and $\Delta^{2(4)}$, a bond between the second and fourth C atoms of a ring.
T Triple bond
See "Rules," I.U.P.A.C. Notation for Organic Compounds," 1961. Cf. *formula, nomenclature.* See also first definition(s) under each letter.

International Chemical-, Dysonian- A tentative method for delineating the structures of organic compounds independently of national languages; published and recommended by the International Union of Pure and Applied Chemistry, 1958. It uses a cipher or line of capital letters, numbers, stops, or symbols, each feature of the formulas being described as a distinct operation separated from the others by stops. Thus, unsaturation is denoted by E, with (e.g.) $E3$ for a triple bond; methane is C.

noumeite. Garnierite.

novaculite. Razor stone. A fine-grained, abrasive rock.

Novadelox. Trade name for a mixture: benzoyl chloride 1, calcium phosphate 3 or 5 pts.; formerly used to bleach flour.

novain. Carnitine.

Novaldin. Trademark for dipyrrole.

Novamat. Trade name for a viscose synthetic fiber.

novargan. A silver proteinate (10% Ag). Yellow powder, soluble in water; an astringent and bactericide.

novarsenobenzol. Neosalvarsan.

novaspirin. $O : (OCH_2)(CO) : C : (CH_2COOC_6H_4\cdot\text{-} COOH)_2 = 444.1$. Methylenecitrylsalicylic acid, salictrin. White powder, insoluble in water; an antirheumatic and antiseptic.

novasurol. Merbaphen, the double salt of sodium mercury chlorophenoxy acetate and diethyl-malonylurea. White crystals, soluble in water; a diuretic and antisyphilitic.

Novatophan. Trade name for neocinchophen.

novatropine. $C_{16}H_{21}NO_3\cdot MeBr$. Homoatropine methyl bromide. White powder; an antispasmodic.

novobiocin. $C_{31}H_{35}O_{11}N_2(?)$. An antibiotic from *Streptomyces niveus;* used as the sodium or calcium salt (B.P.).

Novocain. Trademark for procaine hydrochloride.
N. oxide. $C_{12}H_{22}N_2O_4 = 274.2$. A genalkaloid anesthetic produced by the action of hydrogen peroxide on procaine.

Novodur. Trade name for a polyamide synthetic fiber.

novolak. A plastic of the resole type, q.v., but formed under acid conditions. Novolaks are fusible and soluble, and unlike the resoles, will not condense with like molecules without addition of a hardening agent.

noxious. Harmful. **n. gases.** A poisonous gas, or gas of strong odor.

Noyes, Arthur Amos, 1866–1936. American chemist, noted for development of thermodynamics. **N., William Albert,** 1859–1941. American chemist, noted for organic synthesis and atomic weight determinations.

Np. Symbol for neptunium.

NPK. Abbreviated description of a fertilizer containing nitrogen, phosphates, and potassium.

NPL. Abbreviation for National Physical Laboratory (U.K.).

Nt. Symbol for niton (now radon, Rn).

NTP. Abbreviation for normal temperature (0°C) and pressure (760 mm).

nu. Greek letter ν. Symbol for frequency.

nuces. The Latin plural of "nut"; as, nuces nucistae = nutmeg.

nucin. Juglone.

nucite. $C_6H_{12}O_6 = 180.09$. A carbohydrate resembling inositol, from the leaves of *Juglans cinera,* white walnut. Cf. *juglans.*

nuclear. Pertaining to a nucleus, q.v. **n. activation analysis.** Analysis for minute quantities of metals in very small samples, from the nature and magnitude of the radioactivity of the isotopes produced on irradiation with neutrons in a nuclear reactor.
n. chemistry. The branch of chemical physics dealing with the changes in the atomic nucleus.
n. equation. An expression indicating the changes occurring in the nucleus during a n. reaction. The sum of the atomic numbers (= *positive charges*) and of the isotopic weights (= *mass*) must be equal on both sides of the equation. **n. halogen.** A term erroneously applied to a halogen attached to a ring. **n. magnetic resonance.** The absorption of electromagnetic radiation by atomic nuclei which do not have even numbers of protons and neutrons, under the influence of a magnetic field. The variations in line width, magnitude, and spectral position of the absorption are used as a nondestructive method of structural analysis. Cf. *electron spin resonance.* **n. particles.** The building units of the atomic nucleus. See *atomic structure.*
n. reactions. The disruption of an atomic nucleus by bombardment with protons, deuterons or α particles, accompanied by the emission of neutrons, protons, α particles, positive or negative electrons; and formation of excited states or radioelements.
n. structure. (1) Each isotope consists of Z half particles (p_2e) and $I - 2Z$ neutrons (pe), where Z is the atomic number, I the isotopic weight, p a proton with one positive charge, and e an electron. (2) An isotope containing Z protons and $I - Z$ neutrons. **n. symbols.** The symbol for an element, X, is prefixed by its atomic number Z as subscript and followed by its isotopic weight I as superscript. Thus: $_ZX^I$; e.g.: $_4Be^9$, $_2He^4$.

nuclease. A bacteriolytic enzyme that digests the nucleoproteins of bacteria.

nucleate. A salt of nucleic acid.

nuclei. Plural of nucleus.

nucleic acids. Nucleinic acids. A group of compounds in which one or more molecules of phosphoric acid are combined with carbohydrate (pentose or hexose) molecules, which are in turn combined with bases derived from purine (as adenine) and from pyrimidine (as thymine). They commonly occur, conjugated with proteins, as nucleoproteins. The molecules of the most common nucleic acids are comprised of 4 phosphoric acid, 4 carbohydrate and 2 basic molecules each from purine and pyrimidine and are therefore tetranucleotides. Cf. *nuclein.* E.g.; from salmon $(C_{40}H_{56}N_{14}O_{26}P_4)$, from yeast $(C_{38}H_{49}N_{15}O_{29}P_4)$. **desoxyribo-** q.v. **ribo-** A n.a. which yields d-ribose on hydrolysis. **syn-** See *polynucleotide.* **thymus-** Desoxyribonucleic acid.

nucleid. A metal compound of nuclein.

nucleidic mass. The atomic weight, q.v., of an element based on .its dominant natural isotope.

nuclein. Nucleic acid.

nuclein. $C_{29}H_{49}O_{22}N_9P_3 = 968.7$. A nucleinate phosphoprotein in the nuclei of cells, obtained by peptic digestion or acid hydrolysis of albumins. Gray powder, slightly soluble in water; a bactericide and alterative. **cell-** True n. **pseudo-** Nucleoalbumin.

nucleinate. A salt of nucleic acid and a base.

nucleinic acid. Nucleic acid.

nucleoalbumin. Paranuclein, phosphoglobulin, pseudonuclein. A combination of nucleic acid and albumin.

nucleogen. A compound of iron, nuclein, and arsenic; used in medicine.

nucleolus. Plasmosone. A spot in the center of the nucleus of a cell which contains chromosomes, usually those determining sex.

nucleons. A collective term for neutrons and protons.

nucleonic(s). The study of the phenomena associated with atomic nuclei. **n. gage.** A device for measuring and recording automatically and continuously variations in thickness of a moving web, e.g., of paper, which passes between a radioactive source and a detector e.g., an ionization chamber.

nucleophilic. Electrophilic.

nucleoplasm. (1) The protoplasm of the cell nucleus. (2) The liquid portion of the cell nucleus.

nucleoprotein. A compound of a simple protein with nuclein and a hexose (in animals) or a pentose (in plants), containing $0.5-3.0\%$ P. White powders, soluble in weak alkalies and precipitated by acids. **ribo-** RNP. A complex of nucleic acid and protein involved in the synthesis of proteins in the living cell, and in the production of antibodies associated with the protein portion of the r.n., released after the nucleic acid portion has been destroyed.

nucleoside. A glucoside-like complex of a base (cytosine etc.) and a carbohydrate (as pentose) contained in a nucleotide, e.g., cytidine. A nucleotide, q.v., without the phosphoric acid.

nucleosin. A thymine from the spermatozoa of salmon.

nucleothymic acid. Thymic acid.

nucleotides. (1) Originally the phosphate esters of certain nitrogen glycosides of nucleosides (purine and pyrimidine bases) obtained by hydrolysis of nucleic acids. (2) The phosphates of nitrogen glucosides of heterocyclic bases, including the nucleic acids (polynucleotides). Cf. *nucleoside.*

nucleus. A kernel or central part. **acyclic stem-** A hydrocarbon chain, thus $CH_3 \cdot CH_2 \cdot CH_3$ is the a.s.n. of $ClCH_2 \cdot CH_2 \cdot CONH_2$. **alicyclic-** A saturated carbon ring. **atomic-** Proton. The positively charged center of an atom, with I positive charges and $(I - N)$ negative charges, where I is the isotopic weight, and N the atomic number. The positive charges are assumed to be hydrogen kernels or protons. The n. of an atom can be adequately specified by the 2 parameters atomic and mass number. Cf. *nuclear reactions, particles.* **benzene-** The 6C ring of benzene. **cell-** The central part of protoplasm which is darker than the remainder, and contains structural elements (chromosomes). **condensed-** A carbocyclic or heterocyclic compound; 2 or more rings joined by at least 2 C atoms, as in naphthalene. **heterocyclic-** A ring compound with an atom other than C in the ring. **homocyclic-** A ring compound of C atoms only. **projection-** A misnomer for the graphic representation of a part of an optically active C ring (as, terpenes), by projecting the asymmetric C atoms. **stem-** The hydrocarbon obtained by replacing all atoms except C, H, and heterocyclic atoms by H. All organic compounds can then be classified as derivatives of aci-, iso-, and hetero-.

nugget. A water-worn piece of native gold.

Nujol. Trademark for a heavy medicinal paraffin oil.

null instrument. An instrument indicating an end point, or point of balance between 2 effects, because it is not actuated at that point, e.g., the galvanometer in a Wheatstone bridge circuit.

Numal. Trademark for allonal.

number. A definite value. **magic-** The number of protons (20, 50, or 82) or neutrons (20, 50, 82, or 126) in a nucleus which produce a particularly stable state owing to the completion of the energy levels; e.g., Sn (at. no. 50) has 10 isotopes. **oxidation-** A n. indicating the state of oxidation of the atom it follows, as vitamin B_{12}, cyanocob (I)alamin. **preferred-** (Renard). An industrial standard for the increase in size of a commodity. **wave-** See *wave.*

numerate. Qualified in and familiar with the sciences; analog of literate.

numoquin. Optochine.

Nupercaine. Trademark for cinchocaine hydrochloride.

nupharine. $C_{18}H_{24}O_2N_2 = 300.3$. An alkaloid from the bulbs of (pond lily) *Nuphar luteum* (Nymphaeaceae).

nutgall. Galls, galla. The excrescence of *Quercus infectoria* (Cupuliferae) and allied species, produced by the deposited eggs of *Cynips tinctoria*, a gallfly. Nutgalls contain tannic acids, and are astringents.

nutmeg. Myristica. **n. butter.** Myristica oil. **American-** Otoba wax. **n. oil.** Myristica oil.

nutriant. A drug that modifies the nutritive processes of the body.

nutrient. A food for a body, organism, or cell.

nutrilite. A nutrient.

nutriment. Nourishment.

nutrition. The study of consumed food values.

nutrose. Sodium caseinate, with milk as a nutrient.

nux. A nut. **n. moschata.** Myristica. **n. vomica.** Poison nut, quaker nuts, quaker buttons. The dried seeds of *Strychnos nux vomica* (Loganiaceae), Ceylon, India, N. Australia; 25% alkaloids, principally strychnine and brucine; a tonic and stimulant (B.P.).

NVM. Abbreviation for nonvolatile matter.

NW acid. Neville and Winther's acid.

nyctanthin. $C_{28}H_{27}O_4 = 331.22$. A crystalline principle from the tree of sadness, *Nyctanthes arbortristis* (Oleaceae).

Nydrazid. Trademark for isoniazid.

Nylander, Claes Wilhelm. 1835-1902. Swedish chemist. **N. reagent.** A solution of potassium-sodium tartrate 4, sodium hydroxide 10, bismuth subnitrate 2 gm, in 100 ml water. **N. test.** Add 1 pt. N. reagent to 10 pts. urine. A black color or precipitate indicates sugar.

Nylenka. Trade name for a polyamide synthetic fiber.

nylon. Generic term for any long-chain synthetic polymeric amide which has recurring amide groups as an integral part of the main polymer chain, and can be formed into a filament whose structural elements are oriented in the axis direction. N. is characterized by high strength, elasticity, and resistance to water and chemicals. A single figure suffix (x) denotes derivation of the repeating unit from a C_x aminocarboxylic acid; a double figure suffix, $(x \cdot y)$ describes the combination of a linear (C_x) diamine and a linear (C_y) carboxylic acid. World production (1966), 1.5 million tons. Cf. *CIL-n.*, *Monofil.* **n.6.** Polycaprolactam. **n.11.** Rilsan. **n.12.** Vestamid. **n.66.** Polyhexamethylene.

Nymo. Trade name for a polyamide synthetic fiber.

nystagmus. An involuntary oscillatory movement of the eyeballs; an occupational disease, e.g., of miners, due to inadequate light.

nystatin. Mycostatin. An antibiotic produced by *Streptomyces noursei*; used to treat fungal infections (B.P.).

nytril. A copolymer of vinyl acetate and vinylidene dinitrile. Cf. *Darlan.*

O

O. (1) Symbol for oxygen. (2) Abbreviation for orange. See *colors*.

O orbit. The fifth shell. Cf. *periodic system.* **O shell.** See *atomic structure.*

O- Prefix indicating a radical attached to an oxygen atom.

o- Abbreviation for ortho-, the 1,2-position.

Ω. Greek capital omega. Symbol for: (1) ohm; (2) the ultimate disintegration products of a radioactive series.

ω. Greek omega. (1) Prefix indicating substitution in a side chain of an aromatic compound. (2) Symbol for: (*a*) angular velocity; (*b*) solid angle.

oak. A genus of trees, *Quercus* (Cupuliferae), which yield cork, nutgalls, quercin, and tans. **poison-** See *poison oak.* **white-** Quercus. **o. bark.** The bark of oak, *Q. robur*, containing 25% tannin; a tan and astringent. **o. red.** $C_{28}H_{22}O_{11} = 534.2$. A coloring matter obtained by hydrolysis of quercitannic acid. **o. tannin.** (1) Quercin (2) Quercitannic acid.

oakum. Fiber made by untwisting old hemp ropes. Used as a medicinal dressing and padding, and (impregnated with tar) for caulking.

oat. Avena.

oatmeal. Coarse flour from oats.

Obermayer, Friedrich. 1861–1925. Austrian physician. **O.'s reagent.** A 0.4% solution of ferric chloride in dilute hydrochloric acid. **O.'s test.** Equal parts of urine and chloroform shaken with 3 drops of O.'s reagent. The intensity of the blue color of the chloroform indicates the amount of indican present.

Obermüller's test (for cholesterol). The substance is melted in a test tube, and 3 drops of propionic aldehyde added; on cooling, the mass becomes successively blue, green, orange, and brown-red.

Oberphos. A dry, granular superphosphate fertilizer.

objective. (1) The lens of the microscope nearest to the object. (2) The lens of a photographic camera. **achromatic-** A compound lens to correct chromatic aberration. **immersion-** An o. dipped into a drop of cedar oil or similar liquid covering the object, to establish a continuous film between object and microscope. **tele-** A lens of long focus, for photographing distant objects.

oblivon. $CH:C(Me \cdot OH) \cdot CH_2Me = 98.09$. Methylpentynol. A short-duration drug to induce sleep and allay apprehension.

obs. Abbreviation for observed.

obsidian. A volcanic glass rock used by Indians for spearheads and implements.

occlude. To retain in pores; to adsorb.

occluded. Mechanically adhering to or enclosed in some other substance.

occlusion. The adhesion of a gas or liquid on solid particles or inside a solid mass; as, hydrogen on palladium, solvent on precipitates, or air in crystals.

oceanic sediments. (1) Mechanical deposits from rivers. (2) Remains of marine animals. (3) Substances formed by chemical action on the ocean floor. See table.

Classification	Fathoms	% calcium carbonate
Red clay	2,790	6.7
Radiolarian ooze.....	2,894	4.0
Diatom ooze	1,477	22.96
Globigerina ooze.....	2,049	64.5
Ptoropod ooze.......	1,044	79.2

oceanium. Hafnium.

ocher. Paint rock, mineral purple, yellow earth. Powdered iron oxide, usually with clay. A yellow (limonite), red (hematite), or brown pigment in paints, varnishes, linoleum, papermaking and oilcloth manufacture. **antimony-** Stibiconite. **bismuth-** Bismite. **brown-** Bogore. **Indian-** q.v. **molybdic-** Molybdite. **nickel-** Annabergite. **plumbic-** Brown lead oxide. **red-** A hematite. **Roman-** A deep orange o. **synthetic-** An artificial o. obtained by precipitating ferrous sulfate with soda and lime. **telluric-** Tellurite. **tungstic-** Tungstite. **uranic-** Uraconite. **yellow-** Selwynite. A mixture of ferric oxide and clay.

ocherous deposit. The accumulation of precipitated ferric hydroxide and calcium carbonate from mineral waters, due to escape of carbon dioxide.

ochre. Ocher.

ocimene. $C_{10}H_{16} = 136.12$. 2,6-Dimethyl-1,5,7-octatriene*. A terpene, d.0.799, $b_{21mm}74$, from the oil of sweet basil, *Ocimum basilicum.*

octad. An element or radical of valency 8. Cf. *octet.*

octadecane. $C_{18}H_{38} = 254.4$. $d._{20}°0.7668$, m.30, b.306. Cf. *anthemane.*

octadecanoic acid. Stearic acid.

octadecanol. $Me(CH_2)_{16}CH_2OH = 270.30$. Octadecyl alcohol. White leaflets, m.59, in spermaceti, whale, and linseed oils.

octadecenic acid. **epsilon-** Petroselinic acid. **theta-** Oleic acid.

octadecyl. The radical $Me(CH_2)_{17}$—. **o. alcohol.** Octadecanol.

octadecylic acid. Stearic acid.

octadiene. $C_8H_{14} = 110.11$. Conylene. Colorless liquid, d.0.770, b.130. **dimethylcyclo-** $C_{10}H_{16} = 136.1$. 1,5-Dimethylcyclooctadiene $(\Delta^{1,5})$. A major constituent of rubber. **methyl-, methylene-** Myrcene.

octahedral. Describing a crystal with 8 surfaces. **o. iron ore.** Magnetite.

octahedrite. TiO_2. Anatase. Native titanium dioxide. Dark blue or black tetragons.

octahedron. An isometric crystal with 8 surfaces, each having equal intercepts on all 3 axes; i.e., the faces are equilateral triangles.

octane*. C_8H_{18} = 114.2. Dibutyl. A colorless oil in petroleum, d.0.706, b.125, insoluble in water. **amino-** Octylamine*. **chloro-** Octyl chloride. **2,7-dimethyl-*** $[Me_2CH(CH_2)_2—]_2$ = 142.17. Biisoamyl. Colorless liquid, b.100. **iodo-*** Octyl iodide. **iso-** 2,2,4-trimethylpentane. See o. number. **100-** The standard against which antiknock values of fuels are evaluated; mainly iso-. See o. number.

o. carboxylic acid. Pelargonic acid. **o. dicarboxylic acid.** Sebacic acid. **o. number.** The percentage of 2,2,4-trimethylpentane, by volume, which must be mixed with n-heptane to reproduce the knocking characteristics of the gasoline being tested.

octanoic acid. Caprylic acid.

octanol*. Octyl alcohol.

octanone*. 2- Mexyl methyl ketone. 3- Amyl ethyl ketone.

octavalent. Having a valency of 8.

octaverine. A derivative of phenylisoquinoline; a spasmodic less toxic than papaverine.

octazone. $HN:N\cdot NH\cdot N:N\cdot NH\cdot N:NH$. A hypothetical compound known only in its derivatives. Cf. *hydronitrogens.*

Octel. Trade name for an antiknock compound containing tetraethyllead.

octene. C_8H_{16} = 112.12. Octylene, caprylene. Alkenes in bergamot and lemon oils, as: **1-**, **n-**, or Δ^1- $Me(CH_2)_5CH:CH_2$. Colorless liquid, d.0.722, b.123. **2-**, **iso-** or Δ^2- $Me(CH_2)_4CH:CHMe$. **3-** or Δ^3- $Me(CH_2)_3CH:CHEt$.

octet. A chemically inert group of 8 valence electrons. Cf. *polar bond.* **o. theory.** Lewis' theory.

Octin. $C_9H_{19}N$ = 141.15. Trademark for 2-methyl-amino-6-methylheptene-5. White powder, used to treat convulsions.

octine. Octyne*.

octivalent. Octavalent.

octo- Prefix indicating 8.

octodeca- Prefix indicating 18. **o. peptide.** An artificial protein containing 19 amino acids or 18 peptide groups. Cf. *polypeptide.*

octodecane. Octadecane.

octoic acid. Caprylic acid. **o. alcohol.** Octyl alcohol.

octoil. Ethyl hexyl phthalate, used for vacuum pumps, q.v.

octopeptide. An artificial peptide with 9 combined amino acids and 8 peptide groups.

octosan. Acetylated cane sugar. A bitter denaturant.

octyl. The radical $—C_8H_{17}$ (capryl), from octane. **o. acetate.** $CH_3COOC_8H_{17}$ = 172.15. Capryl acetate. Colorless liquid, d.0.885, b.210. **o.alcohol.** $C_8H_{17}OH$ = 130.2. Octanol*, heptylcarbinol, octylic alcohol, caprylic alcohol. Isomers: **n-** $Me(CH_2)_6CH_2OH$. 1-Hydroxyoctane. Colorless liquid, b.195, soluble in water. **d-sec-** $Me(CH_2)_5$-$CHOH\cdot Me$. 2-Hydroxyoctane. Colorless liquid, $b_{20mm}86$. **l-sec-** b.178.

o. aldehyde. $C_7H_{15}CHO$ = 128.2. Caprylic aldehyde. Colorless liquid, d.0.821, insoluble in water. **o. amine.** $C_8H_{17}NH_2$ = 129.3. *normal-* Colorless liquid, b.186, soluble in water, or alcohol. *secondary-* $Me\cdot CH\cdot NH_2\cdot C_6H_{13}$. b.174. **o. chloride.** $C_8H_{17}Cl$ = 148.64. *normal-* b.180. *secondary-* b.175. **o. cresol.** A mixture containing principally m- and p-cresols; a germicide. **o. formate.** $HCOOC_{18}H_{17}$ = 158.2. The formic acid ester of octane. Colorless liquid, d.0.893, b.198, insoluble in water. **o. gallate.** $C_{15}H_{22}O_5$ = 282.28. Octyl-3,4,5-trihydroxybenzoate. White powder, m.101, insoluble in water; an antioxidant (B.P.). **o. iodide.** $C_8H_{17}I$ = 240.0. *secondary-* $MeCHIC_6H_{13}$. Colorless, oil, d.1.31, decomp. 200, insoluble in water.

octylene. Octene.

octylic acid. Caprylic acid. **o. alcohol.** Octyl alcohol.

octyne*. $CH:C(CH_2)_5Me$ = 110.11. Octine, caprilydene, hexylacetylene. Colorless liquid, b.125.

ocular. The eyepiece of an optical instrument, **compensating-** An eyepiece that corrects the axial aberration of the objective. **Huyghenian-** q.v. **Ramsden-** An eyepiece to increase definition; 2 planoconvex lenses, with their convex surfaces facing. **stereoscopic-** Two eyepieces giving a stereoscopic effect.

oculin. A glycerin extract of the corpus ciliariae of the eye.

ocymene. Ocimene.

od. Od-rays. The luminescence of living organisms. Cf. *scotography.*

odallin. A glucoside from *Cerebera odollam.* Cf. *cerberin.*

odor, odour. The volatile portion of a substance perceptible by the sense of smell. Classification: (1) Aromatic (eugenol); (2) sweet (nitrobenzene); (3) citric (citral); (4) floral (citronellol); (5) fragrant (coumarin); (6) pungent (heliotropine); (7) ethereal (ether); (8) esteric (amyl acetate); (9) resinous (turpentine); (10) camphoric (terpineol); (11) heavy (chloroform); (12) empyreumatic (aniline); (13) tarry (phenol); (14) narcotic (pulegone); (15) fecal (skatole); (16) caprylic (valeric acid); (17) fishy (trimethylamine); (18) garlic (phosphine). **ammoniacal-** An o. resembling ammonia. **aromatic-** See (1). **balsamic-** An aromatic o. resembling balsam. **burnt-** An o. resembling tar or burnt organic matter. **camphorous-** An o. resembling camphor (10). **caprylic-** See (16). **citric-** See (3). **delicate-** A faint, agreeable o. **empyreumatic-** An o. resembling burnt animal or vegetable matter (12). **esteric-** See (8). **ethereal-** A delicate fruity or flowery o. (7). **fecal-** See (15). **fishy-** See (17). **floral-** See (4). **flowery-** The o. of flowers and blossoms. **foul-** See (15–18). **fragrant-** See (5). **garlic-** See (18). **heavy-** See (11). **narcotic-** See (14). **pungent-** A strong o. (6). **putrefactive-** The o. of decaying animal matter. **resinous-** An o. resembling rosin or turpentine (9). **spicy-** An o. resembling spices, like anise, cinnamon, cloves (1–3). **sweet-** See (2). **tarry-** An o. resembling tar (13).

o. intensity. The strength of an odor. Cf. *olfacty.* Various odors are used as a warning for miners, or for the detection of leaks in pipelines or boilers. The o. intensity is determined (cf. *olfacty*) in terms of the minimum perceptible concentration; as shown in the table:

Odor	mg/liter of air
Musk................	0.00004
Iodoform	0.018
Diamyl sulfide........	0.001
Propyl mercaptan	0.006
Butyric acid	0.009
Amyl isovalerate	0.012
Valeric acid	0.029
Oil of peppermint	0.03
Methyl salicylate	0.1
Acetic ether	0.68
Chloroform	3.3

o. permanency. The persistence of an o., measured by placing a definite quantity of the oil on a filter paper, exposing it to air, and comparing its o. after certain time intervals. Some of the most persistent odors, in decreasing order of permanence, are: patchouli oil, sandalwood oil, cinnamon oil, cassia oil, citronella oil, origanum oil, thyme oil, neroli oil. **o. theory.** The assumption that o. sensation is due to the combination of chemical radicals (*osmophoric* groups) of the odorous substance, with certain substances of the nasal membrane (*osmoceptors*), on analogy with Ehrlich's side-chain theory of immunity. Some of the osmophoric groups are supposed to be the radicals OH, CHO, CO, and COOH.

odorator. An atomizer or nebulizer for diffusing liquid perfumes.

odoriferous. Giving off odor; fragrant.

odorimetry. Olfactometry. The measurement of the intensity and permanency of odors.

odoriphore. Osmophore.

odorometer. An apparatus for measuring the intensity of odors and stenches for industrial purposes.

odorous. Having an odor. **o. principle.** A terpene, essential oil or balsam.

oe- See *e-*.

oenanthal. Enanthaldehyde.

oenanthe. Five-finger root, water dropwort, dead tongue. The dried herb of *O. crocata*, a highly poisonous umbelliferous plant.

oenanthic acid. Heptoic acid.

oenanthotoxin. $C_{17}H_{22}O_2 = 258.18$. A conjugated trienediyne alcohol, m.87. A convulsant poison in *Oenanthe crocata* (Umbelliferae), W. Europe; isomeric with circutoxin. **o. benzoate.** $C_{25}H_{28}$-$O_3 = 376.56$. Estradiol benzoate (U.S.P.), Dimenformon, estrone, Ovocyclin. Colorless crystals, m.192, insoluble in water; used similarly to o. (U.S.P.).

oenanthyl. Enanthyl.

oenidin, oenin. Anthocyanins from grapes.

oenology. The study of wine.

oenotannin. A tannin in wine.

Oersted, Hans Christian. 1777–1851. Danish physicist who discovered electromagnetism (1819) by passing a current of electricity through a wire in the same plane as a suspended magnetic needle.

oerstedite. Hydrated zircon containing titania.

oestradiol. Estradiol.

oestrane. Estrane.

oestrin. Estrone.

oestriol. Estriol.

oestrone. Estrone.

official. Pertaining to or listed in a pharmacopoeia.

officinal. (1) For sale in an apothecary shop or drugstore. (2) Official.

O.G. Abbreviation for original gravity.

Ohm, Georg Simon. 1787–1854. German physicist. **O.'s law.** $C = E/R$. The strength or intensity of an unvarying electric current C is directly proportional to the electromotive force E, and inversely proportional to the resistance R of the circuit concerned.

ohm. Ω. A unit of electrical resistance; the primary practical unit of electricity. **international-** The resistance of a column of mercury at 0°C, 14,4521 gm in mass, of constant cross section and 106.300 cm long. 1 international ohm = 1.00049 absolute ohms = 10^9 emu = $1/9 \times 10^{-11}$ esu = 1.01367 B.A. ohms = 1.06292 Siemens ohms. **legal-** (1884,) 0.9972 international ohm (obsolete). **mego-** A million ohms. **micro-** A millionth of an ohm. **reciprocal-** Mho, or ohm^{-1}. A unit of electrical conductivity; the reciprocal of resistance. **true-** The resistance of a column of mercury 106.25 cm long at 0°C, of 1 mm^2 cross section; experimentally determined (10^9 emu).

ohm^{-1}. See reciprocal *ohm*.

ohmammeter. A combined ohm- and ampere-meter.

ohmmeter. An instrument to measure electrical resistance in ohms.

ohmoil. A mineral oil with agerite (aldol-α-naphthylamine) to prevent decrease in electrical resistance on prolonged heating.

oiazines. Orthodiazines. A group of heterocyclic compounds having 2 nitrogens in the ortho position; as, pyridazine. Cf. *miazines*.

-oic. Suffix indicating the —COOH group, e.g., ethyloic, —CH$_2$·COOH.

-oid. Suffix indicating: (1) resemblance or likeness, as alkaloid; (2) the concentrated active principles of a drug, as echinacoid.

oil. (1) A liquid not miscible with water, generally combustible, and soluble in ether:

(*a*) Fixed oils—fatty substances of vegetable and animal organisms—contain esters (usually glycerol esters) of fatty acids.

(*b*) Volatile or essential oils—odorous principles of vegetable organisms—contain terpenes, camphors, and related compounds.

(*c*) Mineral oils, fuel oils, and lubricants—hydrocarbons derived from petroleum and its products. (2) Natural oil, q.v. **aniline-** Crude aniline. **acetone-** See *acetone*. **blown-** A fixed o. oxidized by a current of air. **boiled-** See *linseed* oil. **compounded-** A mixture of essential oils for flower perfumes. **crude-** Petroleum. World production (1966) 1,550 million tons. **distilled-** Essential. **drying-** See *drying oil*. **edible-** A fixed oil food or food accessory. **essential-** The volatile or distilled oils of plants, leaves, flowers. They contain aromatic hydrocarbons, aldehydes, alcohols, ethers, acids, terpenes, or camphors. **ethereal fruit-** A mixture of aromatic substances resembling fruit in odor. **expressed-** Fatty o. **fatty-** The nonvolatile oils of plants and animals; mixtures of fatty acids and their esters (usually triglycerides), subdivided into solid (mainly stearin), semisolid (mainly palmitin), and liquid (mainly olein). **fish-** See *fish* oils. **fixed-** Fatty o. **flower-** See *essential*, or *synthetic oil*. **green-** Heavy creosote. See also *green.* **liquid-** A fatty o.; contains chiefly olein and solidified by hydrogenation. **lubricating-** A mineral lubrication o. **mineral-** An o., mainly hydrocarbons derived from inorganic matter; as, petroleum. Recent work suggests primeval biological processes as partly responsible for their formation. **natural-** A mixture of hydrocarbon oils with their oxidation products; as, crude petroleum. **nondrying-** See *nondrying oil.* **quintessential-** A highly aromatic substance from a natural essential o.; as, anethole from anise o. **red-** See *red.* **residual-** An o. that does not distil in refining processes. **semisolid-** A fixed o., m. ca. 20, consisting chiefly of palmitin. **solid-** A fat that consists chiefly of stearin. **stand-** A drying o. which has been polymerized, i.e., thickened by heating in an inert atmosphere, without addition of a drier. **straight-cut-** A mineral o. fraction having a relatively small difference between the initial and final boiling points. **synthetic drying-** SDO. An amber, viscous liquid which polymerizes on drying to a hard chemically resistant protective coating. **tall-** See *tall.* **volatile-** Essential o.

o. of absinthe. Wormwood o. **o. of ajava.** Ajowan o. **o. of albahaca.** Tolu o. **o. of almond, artificial.** Benzaldehyde. **o. analysis.** The identification and evaluation of an o. in terms of: moisture content, foots content, color, specific gravity, boiling point, optical rotation, refractivity, congealing or melting point, flash point, solubility, unsaponifiable matter, saponification value, ester value, iodine value, acid value. **o. of anthos.** Rosemary o. **o. of ants.** Furfural. **o. of apple.** Amyl valerate. **o. of arachis.** Peanut o. **o. of aspic.** Spike o. **o. of badian.** Star *anise* o. **o. of bananas.** Amyl acetate. **o. bath.** A metal container filled with o. (rapeseed o.); used to heat glass apparatus to 100–200°C. **o. of bay.** Laurel o. **o. of bayberry.** Myrcia o. **o. of benne.** Sesame o. **o. of brazil nuts.** Castanhao o. **o. cake.** A compact mass of crushed seeds, from which o. has been expressed or extracted. It contains proteins 20–40; carbohydrates, salts, and residual oil 7–10%; a cattle food and fertilizer. **o. of candlenuts.** Lumbang o. **o. of caoutchouc.** Terpene. **o. of checkerberry.** Gaultheria o. **o. of chinawood.** Tung o. **o. of chinese beans.** Soybean o. **o. of chinese cinnamon.** Cassia o. **o. cloth.** Linoleum. Canvas coated with a mixture of linseed o. and pigments. **o. of cognac.** Enanthic ether. **o. of cuscus.** Vetiveria o. **o. of dogfish.** Shark o. **o. of dolphin.** Porpoise o. **o. of earthnuts.** Peanut o. **o. of fir.** Pine o. **o. of flaxseed.** Linseed o. **o. of Florence.** Olive o. **o. of garlic.** Allyl sulfide. **o. gas.** Combustible hydrocarbon gases; as, Blau gas. **o. of gingelly.** Sesame o. **o. of glonoin.** Nitroglycerin. **o. of goosefoot.** Chenopodium o. **o. of gourd.** Cucumber o. **o. of groundnuts.** Peanut o. **o. of gynocardia.** Chaulmoogra o. **o. of hoofs.** Neat's-foot o. **o. of illicium.** Star-*anise* o. **o. of katchung.** Peanut o. **o. of lemon.** Lemon o. **o. length.** An indication of the oil-resin ratio in a varnish medium; 1:1 is a short, 3:1 a long, oil varnish. **o. of maize.** Corn o. **o. of melissa.** Balm o. *East Indian-* Lemongrass o. **o. of mignonette.** Reseda o. **o. of mirbane.** Nitrobenzene. **o. of monarda.** Horsemint o. **o. of**

mosoi flowers. Ylangylang o. **o. of mustard. artificial.** Allyl isothiocyanate. **o. of mirbane,** Neroli o **o. of orange.** Orange o. **o. of origanum.** Wild *marjoram* oil. **o. of palmarosa.** Turkish *geranium* oil. **o. of pears.** Amyl acetate. **o. of pennyroyal.** Hedeoma o. **o. of pineapple.** Ethyl butyrate. **o. of ricinus.** Castor o. **o. seed cake.** O. cake. **o. of shale.** Compact, sedimentary rock yielding 12–60 gal oil per ton on distillation, and much ash (silica 30–50, ferric oxide 12–67%). Occurs in Scotland, Australia, Nevada, Colorado, Wyoming. Cf. *kerogen.* **o. of snakeroot.** Asarum o. **o. of sperm.** Whale o. **o. stone.** A fine-grained stone for sharpening knives and scalpels in o. **o. sugars.** Oleosaccharia. A trituration of 2 ml essential oil with 100 gm sugar; used medicinally and for flavoring. **o. supply.** World production of principal vegetable oils and fats (1966) 21.6 million tons. **o. of tar.** An empyreumatic o. obtained by distillation of pine tar. **o. of theobroma.** Cacao butter. **o. thief.** A tubular apparatus for taking samples of o. from the top, center, and bottom of tankcars or storage vessels. **o. of verbena.** *East Indian-* Lemongrass o. *Singapore-* Citronella o. **o. of vitriol.** Concentrated commercial sulfuric acid. **o. of wintergreen.** Gaultheria o. *artificial-* Methyl salicylate. *synthetic-* Methyl salicylate.

Oildag. Trademark for a colloidal dispersion of graphite in petroleum oil. Cf. *graphite, Dag, Aquadag.*

ointment. Unguentum. A salve or fatty preparation for external medicinal or cosmetic use. **basilcon-** 26% resin with beeswax, olive oil, and lard. **blue-** Mercury o. **boric acid-** An antiseptic mixture: boric acid 10, white petrolatum 85, paraffin 5%. **brown-** Mother's salve: a mixture of camphorated brown plaster, suet, and olive oil. **camphor-** A mixture of 22% camphor with lard and white wax; an anodyne and antipyretic. **carbolized-** Phenol o. **iodine-** A mixture of iodine 4 and potassium iodide 4%, with glycerin and benzoinated lard. **iodoform-** A mixture of 10% iodoform with benzoinated lard. **mercury-** Mercurial o.: an emulsion of finely divided mercury 50 in lard 10 and suet 35%. *diluted-* Blue o.: an emulsion: mercury 30 in lard 25 and suet 45%; an antiparasitic. **phenol-** A wound antiseptic o. containing 2% phenol. **simple-** White o. **sulfur-** A mixture of sublimed sulfur 20 and potassium carbonate 10% with benzoinated lard; an antiparasitic. **white-** Unguentum: a mixture: white wax 5 and white petrolatum 95%; a pharmaceutical base (U.S.P.). **yellow-** Unguentum flavum: a mixture: yellow wax 5 and petrolatum 95% (U.S.P.). **zinc oxide-** A mixture of 20% zinc oxide with white petrolatum or benzoinated lard; an antiseptic and astringent.

oiticica oil. A white fat from the nuts of the n. Brazilian tree *Licania rigida* (Rosaceae). It resembles Chinese wood oil, and contains coupeic acid.

okonite. (1) $CaH_2Si_2O_6$. A native calcium silicate in compact fibrous masses. (2) An insulating material obtained by vulcanizing a mixture of ozokerite and resin with rubber and sulfur.

-ol. Suffix indicating a hydroxyl group in organic compounds; as, phenol. Cf. *-ole.*

-ole. Suffix denoting: (1) a substance, not an alcohol, to which an ending -ol was originally given; as, indole; (2) an aromatic ether; as, anisole.

Oleaceae. Olive family of trees and shrubs: *Olea europaea*, olive oil; *Fraxinus ornus*, manna; *Jasminium grandiflorum*, jasmine oil; *Syringa vulgaris*, syringin.

oleaginous. Oily or greasy.

oleander. Nerium. Subtropical, poisonous shrubs (Apocyanaceae), which yield essential oils, karabin, neriin, pseudocurarine, and oleandrin.

oleandrin. $C_{31}H_{48}O_9 = 270.2$. A glucoside from *Nerium oleander*. Yellow powder, m.70–75, insoluble in water. Cf. *neriin*.

oleanol. $C_{29}H_{48}O = 412.2$. Needles, m.216–230, derived from caryophyllin, and sometimes used as its synonym.

oleanolic acid. Caryophyllin.

oleastene. $C_{21}H_{36} = 288.4$. A hydrocarbon from olive oil.

oleasterol. $C_{20}H_{34}O = 290.26$. A phytosterol from olive oil.

oleate. A compound of an alkaloid or a metal with oleic acid. Used medicinally for external applications; technically, in soaps and paints.

olefiant gas. Ethylene.

olefin(e). A unsaturated hydrocarbon of the type C_nH_{2n}, indicated by the suffix *-ene*; as, ethylene. See *ethylene series*. **o. acid.** An unsaturated hydrocarbon acid of the type $C_nH_{2n-1}COOH$. See *acrylic acids*. **o. alcohol.** An unsaturated alcohol of the type $C_nH_{2n-1}OH$; as, CH_2:CH·OH, vinyl alcohol. **o. aldehyde.** An unsaturated aldehyde of the type $C_nH_{2n-1}CHO$; as, CH_2:CHCHO, acrolein. **o. ketone.** An unsaturated ketone of the type $C_nH_{2n}CO$: as, MeCH:CH·CO·Me, ethidene acetone.

oleic acid. $Me(CH_2)_7·CH:CH(CH_2)_7COOH = 282.4$. Oleinic acid, 9-octadecanoic acid*, red oil. Colorless needles, m.14, insoluble in water. It occurs in many (nondrying) oils, and is hydrogenated to stearic acid (by catalysis with nickel); used to prepare soap (U.S.P., B.P.). **7-hydroxy-** Ricinoleic acid. **iso-** Elaidic acid, *trans*-oleic acid, rapinic acid, vaccenic acid.

 o. series. Acrylic acids.

olein. $(C_{18}H_{33}O_2)_3C_3H_5 = 885.1$. (1) Triolein, glyceryl trioleate. The glyceride of oleic acid. Colorless oil, m.−6, insoluble in water; the main constituent of olive and many other oils. (2) Oleine. A mixture of the fatty acids obtained by steam or vacuum distillation of the products of acid hydrolysis of fats. (3) A glyceride of oleic acid, as, monoolein.

oleinic acid. Oleic acid.

oleite. Sodium sulforicinoleate.

oleo- Prefix indicating oil. **o. creosote.** Creosote oleate. **o. guaiacol.** Guaiacol oleate. **o. oil.** A yellow oil of olein expressed from tallow; used to make oleomargarine.

oleomargarine. (1) Margarine. A butter substitute made from a mixture of hydrogenated fatty oils; colored with aniline dyes. (2) The liquid fat from which margarine is made by hydrogenation.

oleometer. A hydrometer for oils.

oleoptene. See *stearoptene*.

oleoresin. (1) A natural combination of resins and essential oils occurring in or exuded from plants,

e.g., benzoin. (2) A pharmaceutical preparation or ethereal extract of drugs. **o. aspidium.** Oleoresina aspidii, o. of male fern. A thick, green liquid from the male fern, which contains filicic acid; an anthelmintic. **o. capsicum.** Oleoresina capsica, o. of red pepper, cayenne pepper. Brown soft mass from acetone extraction of the fruit of capsicum species; used in external plasters, and as a gastric stimulant and spice. **o. cubeb.** Oleoresina cubeba. An alcohol extract from the fruits of *Piper cubeba*, insoluble in water; an expectorant. **o. ginger.** Oleoresina zingiberis. An acetone extract from Jamaica ginger, the rhizome of *Zingiber officinale*; a carminative. **o. lupulin.** An alcohol extract from the seeds of *Humulus lupulus*; a bitter tonic. **o. male fern.** O. aspidium. **o. parsley.** Oleoresina petroselini, liquid apiol. Green, semi-liquid mass obtained by alcohol extraction of parsley seeds, insoluble in water; an emmenagogue. **o. pepper.** Oleoresina piperis. An acetone extract of pepper seeds, insoluble in water; a carminative.

oleoresina. Latin for oleoresin. **o. aspidii.** Oleoresin aspidium. **o. capsici.** Oleoresin capsicum. **o. cubeba.** Oleoresin cubeb. **o. petroselini.** Oleoresin parsley. **o. piperis.** Oleoresin pepper. **o. zingiberis.** Oleoresin ginger.

oleosacchara. Oil sugar.

oleostearin. Beef stearin. An edible solid fat from fatty tissues of the cow.

oleovitamin A. A solution in marine liver oil or edible vegetable oil of natural or synthetic vitamin A alcohol, $C_{20}H_{29}OH$, or its esters. Brown, unstable oil, insoluble in water; an antixerophthalmic vitamin (U.S.P.). **o. D.** A solution of calciferol or activated 7-dehydrocholesterol in edible vegetable oil. Yellow oil, insoluble in water; an antirachitic vitamin (U.S.P.).

oleum. (1) Latin for oil. (2) Nordhausen acid, fuming sulfuric acid. A solution of sulfur trioxide in conc. (97–99%) sulfuric acid; a reagent in chemical industry. **o. alchitri.** Juniper oil. **o. amygdalae amarae.** Bitter almond oil. **o. anisi.** Anise oil. **o. anonae.** Ylang-ylang oil. **o. anthemidis.** Chamomile oil. **o. arachis.** Peanut oil. **o. auranthii.** Orange-peel oil. **o. bubulum.** Neat's-foot oil. **o. cadinum.** Cade oil. **o. cajeputi.** Cajeput oil. **o. calcis.** A solution of calcium chloride, produced by exposing the solid to air. **o. cari.** Caraway oil. **o. caryophylli.** Clove oil. **o. cassiae.** Cassia oil. **o. chaulmoograe.** Chaulmoogra oil. **o. chenopodii.** Chenopodium oil. **o. cinnamoni.** Cinnamon oil. **o. copaibae.** Copaiba oil. **o. coriandri.** Coriander oil. **o. crotonis.** Croton oil. **o. cubebae.** Cubeb oil. **o. cupressi.** Cypress oil. **o. eucalypti.** Eucalyptus oil. **o. foeniculi.** Fennel oil. **o. gaultheriae.** Wintergreen oil. **o. gossypii seminis.** Cottonseed oil. **o. graminis citrati.** Lemongrass oil. **o. hippoglossi.** Pharmaceutical name for halibut-liver oil. **o. juniperi.** Juniper berry oil. **o. lavendulae.** Lavender flower oil. **o. limonis.** Lemon oil. **o. lini.** Linseed oil. **o. menthae piperitae.** Peppermint oil. **o. menthae viridis.** Spearmint oil. **o. morrhuae.** Cod-liver oil. **o. myristicae.** Nutmeg oil. **o. olivae.** Olive oil. **o. phosphoratum.** Phosphorated oil. **o. picis liquidae.** Tar oil. **o.**

pimentae. Pimenta oil. **o. pini.** Pine needle oil. **o. pini pumilionis.** Pine oil. **o. pulegii.** Pennyroyal oil. **o. ricini.** Castor oil. **o. rosae.** Rose oil. **o. rosemarini.** Rosemary oil. **o. sabinae.** Savine oil. **o. santali.** Sandalwood oil. **o. sassafras.** Sassafras oil. **o. sesami.** Sesame oil. **o. sinapis volatile.** Mustard oil. **o. terebinthinae.** Turpentine oil. *rectificatum-* Turpentine oil, rectified. **o. theobromatis.** Cacao butter. **o. thymi.** Thyme oil. **o. tiglii.** Croton oil.

oleyl. The radical, $C_{17}H_{33}CO—$, from oleic acid. **o. alcohol.** 9,10-Octadecanol.

olfactie. Olfacty.

olfactometry. Odorimetry.

olfacty. A unit of intensity of odor: the minimum perceptible concentration, in grams per milliliter, multiplied by $6.06 \times 10^{21}/M$, where M is molecular weight, gives the number of molecules per milliliter: e.g.: ethyl disulfide 15×10^6, vanillin 20×10^6, valeric acid 47×10^6.

olibanoresin. $C_{14}H_{22}O = 206.1$. A neutral resin from olibanum.

olibanum. Frankincense, gum thus. A gum resin from incisions in trees, e.g., *Boswellia carteri* and other species from Sudan. Yellow tears or red fragments; perfume, incense, and emmenagogue. Cf. *boswellic acid*. **o. oil.** An essential oil from olibanum containing pinene, dipentene, and phellandrene, d.0.895, insoluble in water; used to treat bronchial affections.

-olid. Suffix indicating a lactone.

olifiant gas. Ethylene.

oligo- Prefix, meaning few.

oligoclase. A silica mineral of the feldspar group.

oligodynamic. (1) Small but powerful. (2) Describing the inhibition of fermentation or growth of bacteria by metals, e.g., iron containers.

oligodynamics. The bactericidal action of metals; as, Ag and Cu.

oligomer. A polymer comprising 2, 3, or 4 monomer units.

oligonite. $FeMn(CO_3)$. A native carbonate.

oligosaccharide. A carbohydrate that yields on hydrolysis a small number of monosaccharose molecules, e.g., disaccharides. Cf. *polysaccharide*.

olistomerism. Describing reactions in which the same substrates yield the same final products, but via different intermediate stages.

olive. The fruit of *Olea europaea* (Oleaceae), a food and source of olive oil. **o. oil.** A fixed oil expressed from the olive. Pale yellow liquid, d.0.91, m.—6, insoluble in water; contains olein and palmitin. Used as a food, in pharmaceutical preparations as an emollient, and in the manufacture of soap (U.S.P., B.P.). World production (1966) 1,060,000 tons. **o. kernel oil.** Yellow oil extracted or expressed from olive kernels, d.0.918, insoluble in water; used as food, a lubricant, and in soap manufacture.

olivenite. $CuO \cdot As_2O_3 \cdot H_2O$ Wood copper. A native copper arsenate.

olivine. (1) See *olivines*. (2) $(Mg,Fe)_2SiO_4$. Peridot, chrysolite. Green, orthorhombic crystals; a gem and refractory. Cf. *chrysotile, peridotite*. **o. diabase.** A diabase containing o. crystals.

olivines. A group of silica minerals, generally the sulfates of divalent metals.

olivomycin. A fluorescent antitumour antibiotic comprising a crystalline aglucone, olivin, and 4 sugars.

Olsen's testing machine. An apparatus to measure the tensile strength of cement. An arrangement of levers and 2 heavy forceps, between which the specimen is placed and torn apart.

oly. The scum on molten metal.

O.M. Abbreviation for organic matter.

omal. Trichlorophenol.

omega. Greek letter ω or Ω. See O. **o. chrome.** Eriochrome.

ommochrome. An animal pigment produced by the metabolism of tryptophan; 180,000 silkworm eyes yielded 100 mg.

-on. Little-used suffix indicating a ketonic grouping. Cf. *-one*.

önanthol. Enanthol.

onchocerciasis. A disease of meat due to filaria (*Onchocircia volvulus*), a worm of W. and Central Africa, which causes tumors.

-one. Suffix indicating: (1) a ketone; (2) a substance related to the starches and sugars; (3) an alkone, C_nH_{2n-4}. Cf. *hydrocarbons*.

-onic. Suffix usually denoting an acid produced by oxidation of an aldehydic group.

onion. The edible bulb of *Allium cepa* (Lilaceae); a condiment and food. **o. oil.** Yellow oil of penetrating odor (mainly allyl propyl disulfide), d.1.04, insoluble in water; a flavoring.

-onium. Suffix indicating a complex cation, e.g., oxonium $[H_3O]^+$. **o. compound.** RXH_y. An organic isolog of ammonium containing the element X in its highest positive valency; as, phosphonium, $X \cdot PH_4$; sulfonium, $X \cdot SH_3$; iodonium, $X \cdot IH_2$. O. compounds may also be considered as addition compounds. Cf. *oxonium, carbonium, stibonium, -inium, -ylium*.

onocerin. $C_{26}H_{42}(OH)_2 = 388.3$. Onocol. A secondary bivalent alcohol, m.232, from the root of *Onomis spinosa* (Leguminosae).

onocol. Onocerin.

onofrite. $Hg(S, Se)$. A native mercury sulfoselenide.

ononid. $C_{18}H_{22}O_8 = 366.2$. A neutral principle from the root of *Ononis spinosa* (Leguminosae), Europe. Yellow powder, soluble in water.

ononin. $C_{25}H_{26}O_{11} = 502.2$. A glucoside from the root of *Ononis spinosa*. White crystals, m.201, slightly soluble in hot water.

onychograph. A sphygmograph to record variations in blood pressure of the finger tips.

onyx. Calcareous sinter. A gem variety of agate (chalcedony quartz) in white and black strata. **o. marble.** Mexican o. A calcite resembling o.; an ornamental stone.

oöcyanin. Blue coloring matter from certain bird eggs.

oöcyte. A female egg before maturation.

oögenesis. The formation and maturation of an egg.

oölite. Peastone. Small, round granular concretions, usually of limestone containing silica or iron oxide, cemented together to form a compact mass. **o. limestone.** A calcareous o. used for building purposes.

oömeter. An instrument which grades egg by size.

oöplasm. The cytoplasm of an egg.

oöporphyrin. The pale brown pigment of eggshells.

oösperm. A fertilized egg.

oösphere. An unfertilized egg.

oöspora. Molds of the order Moniliales (Fungi Imperfecti).

oöze. o. leather. Leather made from calfskins by vegetable tanning, with a suede finish on the flesh side.

ooze. (1) The slime at the bottom of lakes and oceans. Cf. *oceanic sediment, diatoms*. (2) Slow exudation of liquid.

O.P. Abbreviation for overproof; see *proof spirit*.

Opaceta. Trademark for an acetate synthetic fiber.

opacifier. A substance which when added to a transparent substance makes the latter opaque, e.g., titanium dioxide when added to paper.

opacin. Iodophthalein.

opacity. The property of being impervious to light rays; not transparent or translucent. Cf. *opaque*.

opal. $SiO_2 \cdot xH_2O$. An amorphous form of silica containing a variable amount of water. Vitreous, transparent to translucent masses of rainbow colors, which reflect light after refracting it. agate- An o. of agatelike structure. cacholong- An opaque, blue-white or pale yellow o. fire- A red to yellow o. with red reflections. girasol- A blue-white, translucent o. with red reflections in strong light. harlequin- An o. having a variegated play of colors on a red background. hydrophan- A white, opaque o. that becomes transparent in water. jasp- O. containing iron. lechosos- O. with deep green flashes of color. moss- O. with mosslike inclusions of manganese oxide. pearl- An opaque, bluish white, lustrous o. semi- A native form of silica. tabasheer- An amorphous, opal-like silica in the joints of bamboo. Cf. *hydrophane, hyalite, isopyre*. wood- Wood that has become silicified into o.

o. flashes. The bright colors of an o. in certain positions, due to the refraction of light by thin layers. o. glass. A milky white glass. o. jasper. A form of silica resembling jasper.

opalescence. Milky, iridescent light reflected from a mineral or colloidal solution.

opalescent. (1) Resembling an opal in appearance. (2) Having a milky turbidity.

opalescin. A milk albumin which forms opalescent solutions.

opalized wood. A petrified wood resembling opal.

opaque. Nontransparent and nontranslucent. Cf. *opacity*.

open chain. Noncyclic. Describing a carbon chain that does not close and form a cyclic compound. o. hearth. A reverberatory furnace used in the manufacture of steel; hot producer gases are passed over a large open crucible containing iron ore, scrap iron, and pig iron.

ophelic acid. $C_{13}H_{20}O_{10} = 336.16$. An amorphous split product of chiratin in *Swertia (Ophelia) chirata* (Gentianaceae); soluble in water.

ophiolite. Serpentine containing calcium carbonate.

ophiotoxin. $C_{17}H_{26}O_{10} = 390.2$. A poison from the venom of the E. Indian cobra, *Naja tripudians*.

ophioxylin. $C_{16}H_{13}O_6 = 301.1$. A glucoside from the root of *Ophioxylon serpentinum* (Apocynaceae), India. Yellow crystals, m.72; an anthelmintic and snakebite antidote.

ophitron. A small lightweight microwave generator, based on an electron stream with an undulating path.

ophthalin. Vitamin A (obsolete).

ophthalmo- Prefix (Greek) indicating eye.

ophthalmoleukoscope. An instrument to test color sensitivity by polarized colors.

ophthalmoscope. An instrument to examine the interior of the eye.

opianic acid. $C_6H_2(OMe)_2 \cdot CHO \cdot (COOH) = 210.13$. 5,6-Dimethoxyphthalaldehydic acid. Colorless prisms, m.150, soluble in hot water.

opianine. (1) Narcotine. (2) $C_{66}H_{72}O_2N_3 = 938.7$. An opium alkaloid resembling morphine physiologically.

opianyl. Meconine.

opiate. A narcotic drug.

opium. The air-dried milky juice of the unripe capsules of the poppy *Papaver somniferum*. Brown masses, containing inert matter and alkaloids (see below). Used as a narcotic, and to prepare o. alkaloids. See *kusamba, meconine, chandoo, yenshee, mudat*. Pharmaceutical o. (U.S.P., B.P.) contains not less than 9.5% morphine. camphorated- A tincture containing 0.05% wt./vol. of morphine, with benzoic acid, camphor, and anise oil (B.P.).

o. alkaloids. A series of alkaloids obtained from or related to opium: e.g.: (1) Morphine group: morphine, chelidonine; (2) codeine group: papaverine, codeine, laudanosine, narcotine, hydrocotarnine, thebaine, hydrastine; (3) protopine group: protopine, cryptopine; (4) miscellaneous: chelerythrine, thebenine. o. vinegar. Black drops. A preparation containing 10% o.

opopanax. An oleoresin from the roots of *Pastinaca opopanax* (Umbelliferae), the Orient; an incense, perfume, and antispasmodic. o. oil. An oil, d.0.87–0.90, b.250–300 from *Commiphora katof* (Burseraceae). Cf. *balm of Gilead*.

oppanol. $[Me_2C:CH_2]_x$. A polymer of isobutylene; a rubber substitute.

opsogens. See *opsonigenous substances*.

opsonic index. The ratio of the opsonin content of the blood of a diseased person to that of a normal individual.

opsonigenous substances. Aggressins, opsogens. Substances produced by the metabolism of bacteria. Cf. *endotoxin*.

opsonin. A substance of the blood serum that renders invading microorganisms more susceptible to digestion by the phagocytes of the body. common- Normal. immune- Specific opsonins. Substances formed in the blood on the stimulation by bacterial poisons (opsonigenous substances). normal- The protective substances of the blood present in normal uninfected individuals. specific- Immune.

opsonization. Inoculation of opsonins into an organism.

optical. (1) Pertaining to sight. (2) Pertaining to light. o. activity. O. rotation, opticity. The power of a substance or solution to rotate the plane of vibration of polarized light to the left or right. It is characteristic of compounds containing an asymmetric atom (usually C); measured by the polariscope and used in quantitative analysis. Cf. *enantiomorph, birotation, mutarotation.* **o. bench.** A rail with holders to carry lenses and mirrors, whose distances apart may be varied and measured and whose o. axes are in the same straight line. Used for o. experiments. **o. contact.** Close contact between two plane surfaces, such that no interference lines are produced. **o. density.** Log I_0/I, where I_0 is the intensity of the incident ray, and I the intensity of the transmitted ray. Cf. *extinction coefficient.* **o. isomerism.** See *isomery.* **o. pyrometer.** An instrument for measuring high temperatures optically. A calibrated filament is heated by an electric current of known strength until the glow matches that of the furnace. **o. rotation.** O. activity. **o. telephone.** A telephone, the receiver diaphragm of which is connected to a mirror, so that its vibrations are magnified as bands of light of varying size.

opticity. Optical activity. A term used in the sugar and brewing industries.

optics. Photics. The study of visible radiations (light). Cf. *dioptrics.*

optimal. Describing the most favorable, suitable, or best factor or condition.

optimum. Best, most favorable. **o. temperature.** The temperature at which an enzyme or bacterium is most active.

optochine. $C_{21}H_{28}O_2N_2 = 340.35$. Numoquin, ethylhydrocupreine. A levorotatory quinine alkaloid; a specific for pneumococcic invasions. **o. hydrochloride.** Colorless crystals, soluble in water, used medicinally.

optophone. An instrument to enable ordinary print to be read by the blind. A selenium cell, telephone and illuminating device transform light waves into sound waves. Cf. *photophone.*

oraluton. Ethisterone.

orange. (1) A color intermediate between red and yellow. (2) The edible yellow fruit of *Citrus* species (Rutaceae), q.v. (3) A group of pH indicators changing from purple or magenta (acid) to orange (alkaline). **bitter-** Curacao or Seville o. The fruit of *Citrus bigararia.* Cf. *o. peel.* **sweet-** China or Portugal o. The fruit of *Citrus aurantium.* **o. blossom odor.** See *indole.* **o. dye.** Tropeolin. **o. flower oil.** Neroli oil. **o. oil.** Oleum aurantii (U.S.P.). An essential oil expressed from the peel or rind of oranges. Yellow liquid, d.0.84–0.85, insoluble in water; a flavoring, perfume, and pharmaceutical additive (U.S.P.). *bitter-* Curacao o. oil, Seville o. oil. The oil from the rinds of o. peels of *Aurantii amara* (*Citrus vulgaris*). *sweet-* The oil from sweet o. peels, *Aurantii dulcis* (*Citrus bigararia*). **o. mineral.** Sandix. **o. peel.** The dried rinds from oranges (U.S.P.). *bitter-* From the fruits of *Citrus vulgaris* = Seville o., curacao o.; or *Citrus aurantium* (B.P.). *sweet-* From the fruits of *Citrus bigararia* = Portugal o., China o. **o. peel oil.** O. oil. **o. pigments.** See *antimony orange, chrome orange,* etc. **o. red.** Sandix. **o. root.** Hydrastis. **o. syrup.** A solution of 60 ml o. tincture in 940 ml syrup (B.P.). **o. tincture.** A tincture prepared from 50% o. peel in alcohol (B.P.).

orangite. An orange variety of thorite.

orarsan. Acetarsol.

oraviron. Methyltestosterone.

Orbenin. See *penicillin.*

orbit. The path of an electron moving around the atomic nucleus (Bohr's dynamic concept of the atom). Orbits correspond with the shells of the static atom (Lewis' model), in which the electrons are assumed to oscillate about certain positions at different distances from the nucleus. Orbits are described by quantum numbers n_k; n is the magnitude or size corresponding with different energy levels. Thus, for the K, L, M, and N levels, n is 1, 2, 3, and 4, respectively; k indicates the quantum state; $k = n$, circular o.; $k < n$, elliptical o.

orbital. Pertaining to motion around a center. **o. state.** See *state.*

orcein. $C_{28}H_{24}O_7N_2 = 500.2$. A coloring matter of orchil, synthesized from orcin and ammonia. Brown crystals, insoluble in water, soluble in acid (red color) and alkalies (violet color); a microscope stain, antiseptic, and reagent.

Orchidaceae. Orchis family, a group of perennial herbs, some epiphytic, with showy flowers; e.g., *Orchis* species, salep.

orchil. Archil, orseille extract, cudbear, persio. Purple liquid with ammoniacal odor. A coloring matter obtained from lichens by treatment with ammonia and exposure to air. Contains orcein, orcin, and litmus; a coloring for pharmaceutical preparations. Cf. *orcein.*

orcin. Orcinol.

orcinaurine. Homofluorescein. Red dyestuff with green fluorescence, obtained by the action of chloroform and alkali on orcinol; a fluorescent indicator for pH values 6.5–8.0.

orcinol. $C_6H_3(CH_3)(OH)_2 = 124.0$. Orcin. 5-methyl-1,3-benzenediol, dimethylresorcinol. White crystals, reddens with age, m.107, soluble in water. It occurs in lichens and forms orcein with ammonia; an antiseptic, reagent for pentoses, and stain. **methyl-** Xylorcinol. **trinitro-** See *trinitroorcinol.*

ordeal bark. (1) Poisonous bark used in trial by ordeal. (2) Casca bark. Cf. *Erythrophloeum.* **o. bean.** Poisonous fruits used in ordeals; e.g., *physostigma, tanghinia.*

order. A grade in scientific classification, particularly zoology. **o. of compounds.** (1) An arrangement of types of compounds according to their complexity:

1st order: binary compounds; as, NaCl.
2nd order: tertiary compounds; as, $Al(OH)_3$.
3rd order: addition or coordinate compounds; as, $NiSO_4 \cdot 6NH_3$.

(2) See *Mulliken's classification.* **o. of reaction.** See *reaction.*

ordinal. Pertaining to a sequence or order. **o. number.** Rydberg's number, indicating position in the periodic system; superseded by atomic number. **o. test.** A reaction which determines qualitatively the elements of an organic compound.

ordinary. Common. **o. iron.** Cast iron. **o. ray.** The ray of light normally reflected or refracted in a polariscope; the extraordinary ray is not.

ordinate. The y coordinate in the cartesian system of graphical representation. Cf. *coordinates.*

ordination number. Atomic number.

ore. A natural mineral from which useful substances are obtained; found mixed with earthy matter (matrix or gangue). The principal ores are oxides, carbonates, silicates, sulfides, arsenides, antimonides, and halides usually of metals. Cf. *flotation, roasting, smelting.* **mock-** Sphalerite. **pay-** An o. that can be worked with profit. **positive-** q.v. **possible-** q.v. **raw-** An o. in its natural, but crushed, untreated condition.

    o. band. A zone of rock rich in ores; a vein. **o. bed.** A zone of o. between sedimentary deposits. **o. body.** A solid, continuous mass of o. **o. crusher.** A machine for the preliminary disintegration of ores. **o. dressing.** The refining or cleaning of o. by mechanical means; as, jigging, cobbing, etc. **o. mill.** A concentrator or stamp mill. **o. pocket.** An isolated occurrence of a rich deposit of o. **o. separator.** A mechanical device in which o. is separated from rock, as a cradle or jigging machine.

oreodaphene. A hydrocarbon oil of California laurel, *Umbellularia californica* (Lauraceae). Colorless oil, d.0.894, b.175.

oreodaphnol. An alcohol in the oil of California laurel. Colorless, pungent liquid.

Oreton. Trademark for testosterone propionate.

O.-M. Methyltestosterone.

orexin. $C_6H_4 \cdot CH_2N \cdot CHN \cdot C_6H_4 = 207.1$. Phenzoline, cedrarine, phenyldihydroquinazoline. White powder, soluble in hot water; a stomachic. **o. tannate.** The tannate of o. Yellowish powder, insoluble in water; a stomachic.

Orfila, Mathieu Joseph Bonaventura. 1787–1853. Spanish-born Frenchman; founder of toxicology.

organ. Any tissue or part of an organism that has a distinct function.

organellae. Substances within organic cells composed of lipoids.

organic. Pertaining to an organ or a substance derived from an organism. **o. acid.** A compound containing one or more carboxyl radicals, —COOH; e.g.: $C_nH_{2n+1} \cdot COOH$, acetic acid series; $C_nH_{2n}(COOH)_2$, oxalic acid series; $C_nH_{2n-8}(COOH)_2$, phthalic acid series. **o. analysis.** The qualitative or quantitative determination of o. compounds. See *analysis.* **o. bases.** The amines and alkaloids. **o. chemistry.** The study of carbon (nonpolar) compounds. Originally restricted to compounds from organisms, but the synthesis of many of them makes division into organic and inorganic chemistry of convenience only. Elements having o. combinations, in order of importance, are: C, H, O, N, Cl, Br, I, F, S, P, Al. Cf. *inorganic chemistry.* **o. combustion.** See *combustion.* **o. compounds.** Nonpolar compounds, which generally consist of carbon and hydrogen, with or without oxygen, nitrogen, or other elements, except those in which carbon plays no important part, e.g., carbonates. Many may be classified into aliphatic and aromatic compounds, q.v. *heavy-* O. compounds, mainly synthetic, used as primary industrial raw materials and in bulk; as, detergents. **o. radicals.** A group of atoms that normally passes unchanged from one molecule of a carbon compound to another (defined under their respective headings). See "Handbook for Chemical Society Authors," 1960; also *radicals, nomenclature, structure symbols, formulas,* and *notation.* **o. symbols.** Structure symbols.

CLASSIFICATION OF ORGANIC COMPOUNDS BY CLASS AND TYPE

The *Class* (or *Division* of Beilstein, cf. *stem nucleus*) is based on the fundamental structure of the compound; thus:

	Chain compound	Ring compound
Homogeneous	Class 1	Class 3
Heterogeneous	Class 2	Class 4

Class 1. A homogeneous chain compound, in which the C atoms form a continuous or a branched chain (hydrocarbons, ketones, acids, alcohols). Division I, Beilstein.

Class 2. A heterogeneous chain compound, in which the C atoms are interrupted by the atoms of other elements (ethers, esters, peptides). No division, Beilstein.

Class 3. A homogeneous ring compound, in which the C atoms form a closed ring (benzene, phenols, anilines). Division II, Beilstein.

Class 4. A heterogeneous ring compound, in which the atoms of the ring are other than of C. Division III, Beilstein.

Each class is subdivided into compounds containing:
(*a*) No double or triple bonds (saturated).
(*b*) One or more double bonds.

The *Type* (or *Functionary Class* of Beilstein, cf. *functioning group*) is based on the presence of one or more radicals to which are due the characteristic reactions of the compound; as, —OH, alcohols or phenols.

---

organism. A living complex, undergoing dynamic changes, which exists in a colloidal protoplasmic medium and has a definite pattern and function. Any animal, plant, or human body. Cf. *life.*

organoferric. Describing masked iron.

organoleptic. Referring to sensation; as, smell.

organolite. An organic base-exchange material.

organomagnesium halides. See *Grignard reagent.*

organometallic. Pertaining to the carbon-metal linkage. **o. compounds.** A class of compounds of the type R—M, where R is an alkyl or aryl radical and M a metal; e.g., $PbEt_4$, tetraethyllead. Cf. *Grignard reagent, organolite.*

organosol. A sol whose essential constituent is organic.

organotherapeutic extracts. Pharmaceutical preparations obtained from animal organs. Thus: brain (*cerebrine*), liver (*hepar siccatum*), lungs (*pulmones sicci*), kidney (*renes siccum*), spleen (*lien siccus*), bronchial gland (*glandula bronchis*), ciliary body (*corpus ciliare*), mammary gland (*mammae siccatae*), ovaries (*corpus luteum*).

organotherapy. The treatment of disease by dried organs or organ extracts.

organotin compounds. Used as preservatives, plastics stabilizers, and in lubricants.

organotropic. A substance that acts specifically on an organism, and not on parasites. See *parasitotropic.*

organzine. Warp silk. The reeled-off fibers from a number of silk cocoons.

oriental agate. A translucent gem variety of agate. **o. amethyst.** A native purple alumina. **o. cashew nut.** Semecarpus. **o. emerald.** A green corundum. **o. garnet.** Garnet. **o. hyacinth.** A rose-colored corundum. **o. powder.** A mixture of gamboge with potassium nitrate; a firework explosive. **o. ruby.** A red corundum. **o. sapphire.** A blue corundum. **o. sweet gum.** Styrax. **o. topaz.** A yellow corundum.

orientation. (1) The structural arrangement of radicals in a compound in relation to one another and to the parent compound. (2) The determination of crystal structure. (3) The direction or position assumed by a molecule, due to an electric charge, adsorption, or other cause. Cf. *zone*. **preferred-** The principal orientation which the crystal units of a metal assume when the metal is deformed.

origanum oil. (1) Spanish hop oil. An essential oil from *Origanum vulgare* (Labiatae), wild marjoram; used in veterinary medicine and in liniments. (The oil of *O. marjorana* is marjoram oil.) (2) An essential oil distilled from *Thymus vulgaris* (French usage).

orizabin. Jalapin.

orlean. Annatto.

Orlon. Trademark for a polyacrylonitrile (polyvinyl cyanide) continuous synthetic filament.

Orlovius flask. A flask similar to a wash bottle, used for handling of blood samples under sterile conditions.

ormolu. Mosaic gold. An alloy of equal parts of copper and zinc, used for cheap jewelry and ornaments.

ormosine. An alkaloid from the seeds of *Ormosia dasycarpa* (Leguminosae), Brazil. Colorless crystals, m.80, soluble in alcohol; a hypnotic and sedative.

ormosinine. $C_{20}H_{33}N_2 = 315.28$. An isomer of ormosine, m.205.

ornithine. $C_5H_{12}O_2N_2 = 132.11$. 2,5-Diaminopentanoic acid*. An amino acid from the excrements of birds. N^α-**guanyl-** Isoarginine. N^δ-**guanyl-** Arginine.

o. cycle. The theory that o. citrulline and arginine are intermediate stages in the synthesis of urea in the mammalian liver; the o. behaves as a catalyst.

oroberol. $C_{18}H_{14}O_8 = 358.1$. A chromogen from the leaves of *Orobus tuberosus*, m.290.

orobol. $C_{15}H_{10}O_6 = 286.1$. Dihydroxytetrahydroflavone, m.271, obtained by hydrolysis of oroboside.

oroboside. A glucoside from the leaves of *Orobus tuberosus* (*Lathyrus*)(Leguminosae), yielding orobol. White crystals, m.250.

orogen. The mobile belt of the earth's crust, in which mountain chains are formed.

orogenic. Describing the large-scale tangential compressive forces responsible for geological fractures.

Oronite. Trademark for a variety of chemical products.

Oropon. Trademark for a tryptic puering material.

orotic acid. $C_5H_6N_2O_5 = 174.05$. Isouracylcarboxylic acid. An acid from milk. White crystals, m.259.

oroxylin. $C_{19}H_{14}O_6 = 338.11$. A bitter principle from the bark of *Oroxylon indicum*. Yellow crystals, m.225, soluble in water.

Orphol. Trade name for bismuth β-naphtholate.

orpiment. As_2S_3. Kings' yellow, auripigment. Yellow crystalline masses; a pigment and depilatory. **red-** Arsenic disulfide.

orris. The dried rhizome of Florentine iris, *Iris florentina*. Creamy powder, insoluble in water; a dentifrice and perfume. **o. oil.** An essential oil from the rhizome of *Iris florentina*. Yellow oil, m.44, insoluble in water; used in cosmetics and perfumery.

Orr white. Lithopone.

Orsat apparatus. A portable gas analysis apparatus: a measuring buret and 3 or 4 gas-absorption pipets connected by a manifold.

orseille, orselle. Orchil.

orseillic acid, orseillinic acid. Orsellic acid.

orsellic acid. $MeC_6H_2(OH)_2COOH = 168.0$. Orsellinic acid, orseillic acid, 2,4-dihydroxy-6-methylbenzoic acid. A split product of lecanoric acid and a constituent of many lichens, m.176 (decomp.).

orsellin, orseillin. Roccellin. A constituent of orchil.

orsellinic acid. Orsellic acid.

orsudan. Sodium 3-methyl r-acetyl aminophenyl arsenate. Yellow crystals; an antisyphilitic and antiprotozoan.

orthanilic acid. $C_6H_7O_3NS = 173.17$. *o*-Aminobenzenesulfonic acid. An isomer of sulfanilic acid, used in organic synthesis.

Orthene. Trademark for tetrachlorodiphenylethane; a parasiticide.

orthin. $C_6H_3(OH)COOH(NH\cdot NH_2) = 168.1$. 4-Hydroxy-2-hydrazybenzoic acid. Colorless crystals; an antipyretic.

orthite. Allanite.

ortho- o- (1) Prefix indicating the neighboring or 1,2-position. Cf. *meta-*, *para-*. (2) Prefix indicating the most hydroxylated acid known in the free state or as salts or esters, e.g., *orthosilicic acid*. Cf. *pyro-*. (3) Prefix indicating an odd rotational quantum number; as, orthohydrogen. **o. acid.** (1) An organic acid having the carboxyl group in the ortho position. (2) An organic acid containing one additional molecule of water in chemical combination, as $H\cdot COOH$, formic acid, and $HC(OH)_3$, orthoformic acid. (3) An inorganic acid containing the stoichiometric amount of water; as, H_3PO_4, orthophosphoric acid. **o. compound.** A benzene derivative containing 2 substitution radicals in neighboring positions. See under the name of the compound. **o.-hydrogen.** See *hydrogen molecule*. **o.-nitrogen.** See *nitrogen molecule*. **o. position.** See *o. compounds*.

orthoacetic acid. $CH_3\cdot C(OH)_3$, known only in its esters.

orthoaluminic acid. The tautomer of aluminum hydroxide: $Al(OH)_3 \rightleftharpoons H_3AlO_3$. It forms aluminates.

orthocarbonic acid. $C(OH)_4$ or $H_2O\cdot H_2CO_3$. Tetrahydroxymethane, esters of which are known; as, $C(OEt)_4$.

orthoclase. $KAlSi_3O_8$. Sunstone, potash feldspar. The commonest silicate, a constituent of many rocks. White, gray, or pink monoclinic crystals.

orthoform. $C_6H_3(COOCH_3)OH(NH_2) = 167.1$. Orthocaine. Methyl-3-amido-4-hydroxybenzoate. White powder, m.143, soluble in water; an antiseptic and local anesthetic. **new-** Orthoform.

old- Methyl-4-amido-3-hydroxybenzoate. White crystals, m.118.; an antiseptic.

orthoformic acid. $HC(OH)_3$, known only as its esters, $H(COEt)_3$.

orthohydrogen. See *hydrogen molecule.*

orthokinetic coagulation. Coagulation due to motion of particles in one direction. Cf. *perikinetic.*

orthonitric acid. The hypothetical compound $O=N-(OH)_3$.

orthophosphate. A salt of the type M_3PO_4.

orthophosphoric acid. See *phosphoric acid.*

orthorhombic system. A prismatic, rhombic, or trimetric system. Crystal forms derived from a prism having 3 axes of different lengths intersecting at right angles (see figure).

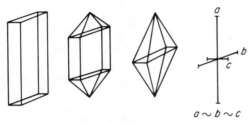

$a \sim b \sim c$

Orthorhombic system.

orthosilicate. A salt containing the radical $\equiv SiO_4$.

orthosilicic acid. Silicic acid.

orthosiphonin. A glucoside from the leaves of Java tea, *Orthosiphon stamineus* (Labiatae); a diuretic.

orthotaxy. Crystalline structure forming long parallel columns.

Orth stain. Lithium carmine. An aqueous solution of lithium carbonate 1 and carmine 3%, usually with picric acid; a nuclear stain.

Ortix. Trade name for a nonwoven fiber base; a blend of Terylene and polypropylene fibers, cemented with a rubber-type resin, and coated with a porous under a nonporous polyurethane layer.

ortizon. $CO(NH_2)_2 \cdot H_2O_2 = 94.07$. A colorless, crystalline compound of hydrogen peroxide and urea; an antiseptic, reagent, and bactericide.

ortnithine. Ornithine.

oryza. Rice.

oryzamin. (1) An extract from rice bran. (2) An antineuritic vitamin from rice bran or yeast. See *vitamin B_1.*

Os. Symbol for osmium.

osage orange. The bark of *Maclura aurantiaca* (N. America). It contains a yellow coloring material and tannin; used in the textile and leather industries. **o. o. wood.** The wood of *Maclura pomiferum*; a yellow coloring matter and fustic substitute.

osamine. A compound derived from sugars by replacing an OH group by NH_2.

Osann, Gottfried Wilhelm. 1797–1866. German chemist noted for his work on platinum metals.

osazone. $R \cdot C : N \cdot NHPh$. Diphenylhydrazone. A yellow or orange crystalline insoluble compound obtained by heating a polyhydroxy aldehyde or ketone (aldose or ketose sugar) with phenylhydrazine hydrochloride, and sodium acetate.

o. test. The identification of sugars by the microscopical examination and melting-point determination of their o. precipitates.

Osborne, Thomas Burr. 1859–1935. American biochemist, noted for work on vegetable proteins.

oscillation. A vibratory to-and-fro motion.

oscillograph. Oscillometer. A device for recording the waveforms of high-frequency currents, e.g., by cathode-ray discharge of frequency 10^{-5} sec.

oscillometer. Oscillograph.

oscillometry. See high-frequency *titration.*

oscine. The 3,7-anhydride of 6,7-dihydroxytropine.

-ose. Suffix indicating: (1) a carbohydrate, particularly a monose; (2) the substance produced by enzymic digestion of a protein, e.g., albumose.

oshaic acid. An acid from the osha root, *Ligusticum filicinum* (Umbelliferae); an expectorant.

Oslo unit. A vitamin unit, q.v.

osmate. A salt containing the radical $OsO_4 =$.

osmic. A compound of tetravalent osmium. **o. acid.** $OsO_4 = 254.9$. O. anhydride, osmium tetroxide, perosmic anhydride, perosmic oxide. Yellow crystals of irritating odor, m.20, soluble in water, depositing black o. hydroxide. Used as a reagent for adrenaline and indican, a microscope stain, in photography, and for Welsbach mantles. **o. acid anhydride.** O. acid. **o. anhydride.** O. acid. **o. hydroxide.** $Os(OH)_4 = 258.9$. A black precipitate from o. acid solutions.

osmics. The study of odors.

osmiridium. Iridosmine. An alloy: osmium 17–50, iridium 77%, with other platinum metals; occurs native in platinum deposits. Insoluble in aqua regia; used to prepare osmium and its salts, and for pen-nib points.

osmium. $Os = 190.2$. A hard, white metallic element of the platinum group, d.22.48, m.2700, insoluble in water or acids; at. no. 76. Used as a catalyst, in platinum alloys, for incandescent lamps, and penpoints. Valencies: 2 (green); 3, 4 (orange); 8 (orange). It is found native as an alloy: nevyanskite. **o. dichloride.** $OsCl_2 = 261.8$. Green, hygroscopic needles, soluble in water. **o. dioxide.** $OsO_2 = 222.9$. Copper-red powder, insoluble in water. **o. disulfide.** $OsS_2 = 255.0$. Yellow powder, slightly soluble in water. **o. fluoride.** $OsF_8 = 342.9$. Colorless crystals, m.34.5. OsF_6, b.203, is also known. **o. hydroxide.** (1) $Os(OH)_3$. Orange, insoluble powder. (2) $Os(OH)_4$. Black, insoluble powder. **o. monoxide.** $OsO = 206.9$. Black powder, insoluble in water. **o. potassium chloride.** $K_2OsCl_6 = 481.7$. Red octahedra, soluble in water. **o. sesquioxide.** $Os_2O_3 = 429.8$. Black powder, insoluble in water. **o. sodium chloride.** $Na_2OsCl_6 = 449.5$. Red rhombs, soluble in water. **o. tetrachloride.** $OsCl_4 = 332.7$. Yellow needles, slightly soluble in water. **o. tetrasulfide.** $OsS_4 = 319.2$. Black powder, insoluble in water. **o. tetroxide.** Osmic acid. **o. trichloride.** $OsCl_3 = 297.3$. Brown crystals, soluble in water.

osmoceptor. An atomic grouping which holds osmophore. Cf. *odor theory.*

osmometer. A device for measuring osmotic pressure.

Osmond iron. A high-grade iron made in an Osmund furnace, q.v.

osmondite. A solid solution of iron carbide in α iron.

osmophore. Odoriphore, aromatophore. Atomic linkages which cause odor, e.g., —CHO; and sulfides.

osmoscope. An osmometer, or device to demonstrate osmosis.

osmose. Osmosis.

osmosis. The diffusion of a liquid or gas through a semipermeable membrane, due to osmotic pressure, q.v. **reverse-** A desalination process; seawater is forced under pressure through a thin plastic membrane, which is selectively permeable to water but not salt.

osmotaxis. The movement of cells due to osmotic pressure.

osmotic. Pertaining to osmosis. **o. cell.** A container separated from another by a semipermeable membrane or a finely porous wall. **o. equivalent.** The ratio between the amount of water and the amount of solute passing in opposite directions through a semipermeable membrane. **o. pressure.** The force exerted by dissolved substances on a semipermeable membrane which separates a solution from the pure solvent. The force of the molecular attraction between solute and solvent. It is proportional to the number of molecules in solution (concentration). Phenomena due to o. pressure are the rise of sap in plants, the expanding force of roots, and the absorption and secretion of food and waste materials.

Osmund furnace. A high forge or primitive blast furnace. **O. iron.** Osmond iron.

osone. A ketone-aldehyde formed from an osazone by hydrolysis with concentrated hydrochloric acid. Reduction forms a ketone-alcohol, so that the original aldose can be changed to an isomeric ketose: $X \cdot CH(OH) \cdot CHO \rightarrow X \cdot C(:N \cdot NHPh) \cdot CH:N \cdot HNPh; X \cdot CO \cdot CH_2OH \leftarrow X \cdot CO \cdot CH:O$.

osotriazole. $\underset{|}{N}:(CH)_2:\underset{|}{N} \cdot NH = 69.1.$ 1,2,3-Triazole, pyrro(a,a')diazole. The heterocyclic compound. Colorless liquid, b.204, soluble in alcohol. **n-phenyl-** 1-Phenylosotriazole. Colorless liquid, b.224. **n-phenyl-c-amido-c-methyl-** 2-Phenyl-5-amino-4-methylosotriazole. Colorless crystals, m.83.

osram. An alloy of osmium and tungsten. **O. lamp.** Trade name for an incandescent lamp having a tungsten filament coated with osmium.

ossalin. Adeps ossium. A gray fat with tallow odor from ox bone marrow; used in ointments.

ossein. Collagen. The albumenoid material (bone marrow) which remains after treating bones with dilute hydrochloric acid; it is hydrolyzed by boiling water to glue and gelatin.

ossification. Formation of, or conversion into, bones, e.g., as of cartilage.

osso-albumin. A protein from ossein.

ossomucin. The substance that holds bone tissue together.

osteogenin. A factor of unknown composition involved in bone growth.

osteolite. An impure apatite or calcium phosphate.

osthole. A methoxycoumarin derivative, the active principle of Hseh tsuang (Umbelliferae), China.

ostranite. Zircon.

ostrole. $C_{15}H_{16}O_3 = 244.1.$ A substance like coumarin, m.84 from masterwort, the rhizome of *Imperatoria ostruthium*.

ostruthin. $C_{18}H_{20}O_3 = 284.2.$ A crystalline substance from the root of masterwort, *Imperatoria ostruthium* (Umbelliferae). Yellow crystals, m.119, insoluble in water, Cf. *imperatorin*.

Ostwald, Wilhelm. 1853–1932. German chemist. Nobel Prize winner (1909). **O. equation.** The degree of ionization of a solution of an electrolyte at a given concentration is $\Lambda/(1a + 1c)$, where Λ is the actual electrical conductivity, and $1a$ and $1c$ are the mobilities of the anion and cation, respectively, at infinite dilution. **O. indicator theory.** The color changes of indicators are due to their existence as weak acids or bases, one ionic radical having a different color from the undissociated molecule. **O. law.** Dilution law. In a solution of an electrolyte, (moles ionized)^2/(moles unionized) varies directly with the dilution. Cf. *activity.* **O. rule.** If a substance can exist in more than one modification, the least stable is formed first, and changes ultimately into the more stable.

osyritin. $C_{27}H_{30}O_{17} = 626.23.$ Yellow glucoside from *Osyris abyssinica*, Cape sumach or bergbas (Santalaceae), S. Africa; a tan.

otavite. A native cadmium carbonate, usually hydrated.

otoba butter. O. wax. **o. wax.** O. butter, American nutmeg butter, American mace butter. The fat from the fruits of *Myristica otoba* or *M. fragrans*, m.38, having a nutmeg odor. Cf. *mace, myristica.*

otobain. $C_{20}H_{20}O_4 = 342.16.$ The active constituent of otoba wax, m.137, soluble in hot alcohol. Used in S. America to treat skin diseases.

otobite. A white crystalline solid, m.133, from otoba wax.

otolith. Ear stone. A concretion of calcium carbonate formed in the ear.

otto of roses. Attar of roses.

ouabain. $C_{29}H_4O_{12} \cdot 8H_2O = 728.80.$ Uabain. Crystallized strophanthin, strophanthin G. A very poisonous glucoside from the seeds of *Strophanthus gratus*. Colorless, quadratic crystals, m. approx 200, soluble in hot water; a cardiotonic (U.S.P.) and constituent of Zulu arrow poison. Cf. *acocantherin, wabain.*

ounce. A measure of weight in the English system. **apothecary's-** 1 ap. oz = $\mathfrak{Z}$ = 1 troy oz = $\frac{1}{12}$ lb = 8 drams ($\mathfrak{Z}$) = 24 scruples ($\mathfrak{Z}$) = 480 grains (gr). 1 ap. oz = 31.1035 gm. **avoirdupois-** 1 av. oz = $\frac{1}{16}$ lb = 7.2916 drams = 18.229 pennyweights (dwt) = 21.875 scruples = 437.5 grains. 1 av. oz = 28.3502 gm = 28,350.2 mg = 138.449 carats = 142.045 metric carats. **fluid-** 1 fl. oz = $\frac{1}{16}$ lb = 0.05 pint = 0.25 gill = 480 minims ($\mathfrak{M}$) = volume of 1 av oz distilled water at 62°F = 29.5729 ml (U.S. usage), 28.412 ml (U.K. usage). See *fluid.* **troy-** 1 oz t. = 20 pennyweights = 480 grains = 31.10348 gm = 1.09712 av. oz.

ouroboros A symbol of Greek alchemy; viz., a snake seizing its own tail.

-ous. Suffix indicating the lower valence of an element or radical; as, ferrous.

outcrop. A mineral deposit that comes to the surface of the earth.

output. The total amount produced in a given time.

ouvarovite. Uvarovite.

ovalbumin. An albumin from egg white.

ovalene. $C_{32}H_{14} = 398.43$.

Orange needles, m.473 (sublimes), insoluble in water; the most compact configuration of benzene rings known.

ovarian substance. The dried and powdered entire ovaries of the hog. Yellow powder of peculiar odor, slightly soluble in water. Cf. *corpus luteum*.

ovarin. The dried and powdered ovaries of the cow, used medicinally.

oven. A compartment in which substances are heated. Cf. *furnace*.

overburden. The top layer of soil or waste which has first to be removed in mining or quarrying.

overcooled. Supercooled.

overgrowth. The growth of a crystal over the surface of a crystal of a different, but usually isomorphous, substance.

overheated. (1) Superheated. (2) Heated excessively.

overpotential. The difference in volts between the back potential of an electrode and that of a saturated calomel electrode, immediately after electrolysis. Cf. *overvoltage, undervoltage*.

oversaturated. Supersaturated.

Overton coefficient. Distribution coefficient.

overvoltage. (1) Overpotential. (2) Supertension. The excess voltage above the normal reversible electrode potential of a metal electrode required to decompose a solution or cause deposition on the electrode; used for the graded electrolytic deposition of metals from a mixed solution. Cf. *polarization*.

ovo. An egg. **o. flavin.** Vitamin B_2. **o. globulin.** A protein of egg white precipitated by dialysis. **o. keratin.** The membranous lining of birds' and sharks' eggs.

Ovoco classifier. A double-screw continuous conveyor to separate ores.

Ovocyclin. Trademark for estradiol. **O.B.** Estradiol benzoate. **O.P.** Estradiol dipropionate.

ovoflavin. Vitamin B_2.

ovomucin. A water-insoluble globulin from egg white.

ovomucoid. A non-heat-coagulable glycoprotein in egg white.

ovostab. Estradiol benzoate.

Owen process. A flotation process, in which the ores are agitated in water containing 2 oz eucalyptus oil per ton.

oxa- Prefix indicating an oxygen bridge; as, $-CH \cdot O \cdot CH-$.

oxacid. Oxyacid.

Oxacillin. Trademark for prostaphin.

oxalacetic acid. $COOH \cdot CO \cdot CH_2 \cdot COOH = 132.03$. Oxysuccinic acid, oxobutanedioic acid*. An unstable liquid whose methyl ester forms colorless crystals, m.74. **o. (ethyl) ester.** $EtOOC \cdot CO \cdot CH_2 \cdot COOEt = 188.14$. Colorless liquid, b.131.

oxalaldehyde. Glyoxal.

oxalamide. Oxamide.

oxalanilide. Oxanilide.

oxalate. A salt of oxalic acid containing the $(COO)_2 =$ radical. Only those of the alkalies and magnesium are soluble in water. **acid-** or **bi-** A salt containing the radical HC_2O_4-. **neutral-** Oxalate.

oxaldehyde. Glyoxal.

oxalene. The tetravalent group: $-N:C-C:N-$.

oxalethyline. Diethyl oxamide.

oxalic acid. $HOOC \cdot COOH = 126.1$. Dicarboxylic acid, ethanedioic acid*. Colorless, monoclinic, poisonous crystals, m.99, soluble in water. Occurs in many plants, and is prepared by passing carbon monoxide into concentrated sodium hydroxide or by heating cellulose (sawdust) with sodium hydroxide. Used as a reagent, in synthesis, as a precipitant in purifying glycerin and an ink eradicator, and in bleaching, photography, and the dye and textile industries. **chlor-** $C_2HO_4Cl = 127.5$. **diethyl-** Diethoxalic acid.

o. acid series. General formula: $(CH_2)_n(COOH)_2$. **o. aldehyde.** Oxaldehyde. **o. dianilide.** Oxanilide. **o. monoamide.** Oxamic acid. **o. monoanilide.** Oxanilic acid. **o. monoureide.** Oxaluric acid.

oxalium. Potassium bioxalate.

oxalmethylin. $(CONHMe)_2 = 116.08$. Dimethyloxamide. White crystals, m.210.

oxaluramide. $NH_2 \cdot CO \cdot NH \cdot CO \cdot NH_2 = 131.1$. Oxalan, oxamic acid ureide, m. exceeds 310.

oxalyl. The radical $-CO \cdot CO-$. **o. chloride.** $COCl \cdot COCl = 126.93$. Ethandioyl chloride*. Colorless liquid, b.64, decomp. by water. **o. diacetophenone.** $PhCOCH_2CO \cdot COCH_2COPh = 294.2$. Colorless crystals, m.180. **o. urea.** Parabanic acid.

oxam. Oxomonocyanogen.

oxamethane. $C_2O_2NH_2(C_2H_5O) = 117.09$. Acetyloxamide, ethyl oxamate. Colorless crystals, m.115.

oxamic acid. $HOOC \cdot CONH_2 = 89.1$. Oxaminic acid, oxalic acid monoamide. Colorless crystals, decomp. 210, slightly soluble in water. **carbamyl-** Oxaluric acid. **phenyl-** Oxanilic acid.

oxamide. $(CONH_2)_2 = 88.1$. Ethane diamide*. Colorless crystals, decomp. 417, insoluble in water.

oxamides. Compounds derived from oxamide by replacing the hydrogen atoms by alkyl or aryl radicals; e.g., $(CONHMe)_2$, dimethyl oxamide, m.210.

oxamidine. Amidoxime.

oxamido. The radical $H_2NCO \cdot CONH-$.

oxaminic acid. Oxamic acid.

oxamyl. The radical $H_2NCO \cdot CO-$.

oxane. Ethylene oxide.

oxanilic acid. $HOOC \cdot CONHPh = 165.1$. Phenyloxamic acid, oxalic acid monoanilide. Colorless rhombs, m.149, slightly soluble in hot water.

oxanilide. $(CONHPh)_2 = 240.2$. Colorless scales, m.245, insoluble in water; used in organic synthesis.

oxanthranol. $C_6H_4(COH)_2C_6H_4 = 210.1$. Anthrahydroquinone. Yellow needles, m.180.

oxatyl. Carboxyl.

oxazetidine. An organic fluorine compound containing the $-N-O-C-C-$ group; e.g., $CF_3 \cdot NO \cdot CFCl \cdot CF_2$. The $-N:O-$ group behaves like a $=C:C=$ group in the formation of polymers.

oxazine. C_4H_5ON = 83.1. A series of 13 heterocyclic compounds: e.g.,

1,2-[4], O·N:CH·CH$_2$·CH:CH.

The remaining are designated as 1,2-[2], 1,2-[3], 1,2-[5], 1,2-[6], 1,3-[2], 1,3-[3], 1,3-[4], 1,3-[5], 1,3-[6], 1,4-[2], 1,4-[3], and 1,4-[4]; the first and second numerals indicate the positions of O and N, and the numeral in brackets the position of the additional H (as CH$_2$ or NH group). Cf. *thiazine*, *benzoxazine*. **naphth-** Phenoxazine. **par-** 1,4-[2]-Oxazine. **phen-** Phenoxazine.

oxazole. C_3H_3ON = 69.1. Furo(*b*)-monazole. **dihydro-** Oxazoline. **tetrahydro-** Oxazolidine. **triphenyl-** Benzilam.

oxethyl. Ethylol. The radical CH$_2$OH·CH$_2$—. Cf. *ethoxy*.

oxetone. $C_7H_{12}O_2$ = 128.1. The heterocyclic spiro compound,

H$_2$C——O   O——CH$_2$
| C |
H$_2$C—CH$_2$ CH$_2$—CH$_2$

Oxford process. The separation of nickel from copper by means of sodium sulfide. Cf. *Mond process*. **O. unit.** An expression of the strength of a penicillin preparation. Cf. *mega*, *penicillin*.

oxgall. Bile from the gallbladder of oxen; used in the textile and printing industries.

oxid. Oxide.

oxidase. An oxidizing enzyme in living tissue.

oxidation. Originally, o. meant combining with oxygen; later it indicated also combination with electronegative elements. Now it has a broader meaning: an augmentation of the valence number of an ion or atom as the result of the loss of negative charges as electrons, thereby making it more electropositive. Cf. *electronation*, *hydroxylation*, *oxidoreduction*. **o. number.** The numerical charge on the ions of an element. Cf. *valency*. **o. process.** A reaction that increases the proportion of oxygen or acid-forming elements or radicals in a compound. **o. reaction.** Electronation reaction. A reaction accompanied by a correlated reduction in the valence number of another element. **o.-reduction indicators.** See *indicators*. **o.-reduction potential.** r_H, rH. Redox potential. The potential acquired by an inert electrode, e.g., platinum, immersed in a reversible oxidation-reduction system, e.g., Fe^{++}/Fe^{3+}; measured by the ratio of the oxidized and reduced forms. rH = log 1/pH$_2$, where pH$_2$ is the hydrogen gas pressure in atmospheres. **o. value.** A constant of oils. The degree of unsaturation (as grams of I per 100 gm sample) when a fat dissolved in carbon tetrachloride is oxidized by potassium dichromate in glacial acetic acid.

oxidative coupling. The formation of a high-molecular-weight polymer when an organic compound with activated hydrogens reacts catalytically with an oxidizing agent.

oxide. A binary compound of oxygen generally with a metal, M_2O (basic), or nonmetal, NO_x (acidic), containing the anion O$^=$. **acid-** An oxygen compound of nonmetals; as, SO$_2$, P$_2$O$_5$, which give oxyacids with water. **amphoteric-** An oxygen compound of the heavy metals; as, ZnO, Fe$_2$O$_3$,

which may form weak acids and weak bases. **basic-** An oxygen compound of metals; as, Na$_2$O, Al$_2$O$_3$, which give bases with water. **hydrous-** An amorphous colloidal substance, which is neither a definite hydroxide nor a definite crystalline hydrate. **inert-** An oxygen compound which forms neither acid nor basic compounds, as CO, N$_2$O. **metal-modified-** A refractory made by adding small amounts of refractory metals to refractory oxides. **neutral-** Hydrogen oxide (water). **per-** A binary compound containing the peroxide group, —O·O—, as H$_2$O$_2$, which yields hydrogen peroxides with acids. Cf. *dioxides*. **primary-** q.v. **prot-** The o. with the fewest O atoms of a series of oxides. **sub-** An o. lower than the commonest of a series.

oxidimetry. The use of an oxidizing agent in volumetric analysis.

oxidize. To cause to unite with oxygen; to increase the proportion of electronegative elements or radicals.

oxidizer. Oxidizing agent.

oxidizing. The act of oxidation. **o. agent.** A substance that: (1) yields oxygen readily, (2) removes hydrogen from a compound, or (3) attracts negative electrons; e.g.: the · common oxidizing agents are: O$_2$, O$_3$, Cl$_2$, KMnO$_4$, K$_2$Cr$_2$O$_7$, KClO$_3$, HNO$_3$, H$_2$O$_2$. **o. flame.** The outer zone of a gas flame containing an excess of air. Cf. *reducing flame*. **o. reaction.** See *oxidation*.

oxidoreduction. See *oxidation-reduction*.

oxime. A compound (syn- or anti-) containing the radical —CH(:N·OH); a condensation product of aldehydes or ketones with hydroxylamine. See *aldoxime*. **acet-** Acetoxime. **ald-** Aldoxime. **amid-** Amidoxime. **di-** Ketoxime. A compound containing 2 o. radicals; 3 types: syn-, anti-, and amphi-. **dimethyldi-** Dimethylglyoxime. **form-** See *nitrolic acid*. **glucose-** See *glucose*. **lact-** See *lactoxime*. **pent-** See *pentoxime*.
o. group. The radical >N·OH.

oximide. (CO)$_2$:NH = 71.1. The imide of oxalic acid. Colorless prisms obtained from oxamic acid by dehydration. **cyan-** See *cyanoximide*.

oximido. Hydroxyimino. **o. compounds.** Compounds containing the radical —NH·CHO or its derivatives.

oximinoketone. A compound of the type R·CO·-C:NOH, which gives a blue color with ferrous iron.

oxin(e). 8-Quinolinol. **thio-** 8-Mercaptoquinoline.

oxindole. $C_6H_4(NH·CH_2)CO$ = 133.1. α-Indolinone, 2-ketoindoline. Colorless needles, m.126, soluble in hot water. Cf. pseudo-*indoxyl*. **bi-** Indigotin. **imino-** Imestin. **methyl-** Atroscine.

oxirane. (1) Epoxide. Describing the oxygen atom of the epoxide ring, —C——C—. (2) Ethylene oxide. **methyl-** Propylene oxide.

oxirene. CH:CH·O. **methyl-** 1,2-Epoxypropene*.

oxo- Prefix indicating the keto group; as, oxo-malonic acid, HOOC·CO·COOH. **o. acid.** An acid containing an oxygen atom. **o. compounds.** Compounds having a keto group, excluding carboxylic acids. **o. process, o. reaction.** The manufacture of alcohols by catalytically reacting an olefin with water-gas under pressure and reducing the resulting aldehyde: $C_2H_4 \rightarrow CH_2 \cdot CHO \rightarrow CH_3 \cdot CH_2 \cdot CH_2OH$. If carbon monoxide and water are used, an acid results.

oxomalonic acid. Mesoxalic acid.

oxomonocyanogen. $CNO = 42.14$. Oxam. A gas prepared by heating cyanogen in oxygen.

Oxone. Trademark for a bleaching preparation, whose active constituent is potassium monopersulfate.

oxonite. An explosive: picric acid dissolved in nitric acid.

oxonium compounds. An addition or double compound of an organic oxide with strong acids or their salts; as, $[(CH_3)_2O] \cdot HCl$. **o. ion.** OH_3^+. Believed to represent the hydrogen ion more accurately.

oxophenarsine hydrochloride. $C_6H_3 \cdot AsO \cdot (NH_2) \cdot (OH) \cdot HCl = 235.49$. 3-Amino-4-hydroxyphenylarsine oxide hydrochloride. White powder, soluble in water, an antisyphilitic and antitreponemal (U.S.P.). See *Mapharsen*.

oxophenic acid. Catechol.

oxozone. O_4. A supposed modification of oxygen. Cf. *ozone*.

oxozonides. $R_2C(O:O) \cdot (O:O)CR_2$. Unstable compounds formed by the addition of 4 O atoms to the double bonds of an unsaturated organic molecule. Cf. *ozonide*.

oxy- (1) Prefix, infix, or suffix indicating oxygen in a molecule. (2) Prefix for the grouping —C—O— —C—. Cf. *keto-*, *ether*. (3) Misnomer for hydroxy. **o. acetylene.** A mixture of oxygen and acetylene gases used in a blowpipe to obtain high temperatures (6000°F); used to cut armor plate and weld. **o. hydrogen.** See *oxyhydrogen*. **o. muriatic acid.** Obsolete term for hydrochloric acid.

oxyacanthine. $C_{19}H_{21}O_3N = 311.17$. Vinetine. An alkaloid from the root of *Berberis vulgaris*, barberry. White crystals, m.210, soluble in alcohol. **o. hydrochloride.** $C_{19}H_{21}NO_3 \cdot HCl \cdot 2H_2O = 383.67$. White needles, soluble in water.

oxyacetone. Acetol.

oxyacid. An acid containing oxygen. **inorganic-** A tertiary compound of an acid radical with hydrogen; as, H_3PO_4. **organic-** An organic compound containing a —COOH and —OH group; as, $MeCOH \cdot COOH$, lactic acid.

oxyalizarin. Purpurin.

oxyamides. Hydroxyamides. Compounds containing the radicals —CONH_2 and —OH; as, $CHOH \cdot CONH_2$, glycol amide.

oxyammonia. Hydroxylamine.

oxyammonium compounds. Hydroxylammonium compounds. See *quaternary* amines.

oxyanthracene. Anthrol.

oxyazide. A compound containing the radicals —N_3 and —OH; e.g.: $HO \cdot CH_2 \cdot CO—N=N_2$, glycolazide.

oxyazo- Prefix indicating the —N:N— and —OH groups. **o.benzene.** $C_6H_5 \cdot N:N \cdot C_6H_4OH = 198.2$. Orange crystals. **o. compounds.** $R \cdot N:N \cdot C_6H_4OH$. Obtained by the action of diazo compounds on phenols in alkaline solution. They form dyes.

oxybenzene. Misnomer for phenol.

oxybenzoic. Misnomer for hydroxybenzoic (salicylic).

oxybenzoxazole. $C_6H_4(O \cdot N):C \cdot OH = 135.1$. Carbonylamidophenol. Colorless crystals, m.137.

oxybenzyl. Misnomer for hydroxybenzyl. **o. alcohol.** Misnomer for salicylic alcohol.

oxybiazole. 1,3,4-Oxydiazole.

oxybromide. (1) An organic compound containing the —OH and —Br groups. (2) The radical —OBr.

oxybutyric acid. See *butyric acid*. **o. aldehyde.** Aldol.

oxycamphor. $C_8H_{14} \begin{cases} CHOH \\ | \\ CO \end{cases} = 168.1$. Colorless crystals, m.204, soluble in water; used medicinally. See *oxaphor*.

oxycanthine. Oxyacanthine.

oxychloride. A compound that contains the radicals —OH and —Cl or the radical —OCl.

oxycholine. Muscarine.

oxychromatin. Linin (1).

oxyconiine. Conhydrine.

oxydase. Oxidase.

oxydation. Oxidation.

oxydizing. Oxidizing.

oxyfisetin. 3,3',4,5-Tetrahydroxyflavanol.

oxyfluorenone. $C_6H_4 \begin{cases} \\ CO \end{cases} C_6H_3OH = 196.1$. o-Oxydiphenylene ketone. Colorless crystals, m.115.

Oxygal. Trade name for sodium peroxide.

oxygen. $O = 15.9994$. Oxygenium, vital air, sauerstoff. A gaseous element, at. no. 8, free in the atmosphere as O_2 (23.2% by weight) and combined in many substances (50% of the earth crust). It was Hooke's *nitre air*, isolated August 1, 1774, by J. Priestly (*dephlogisticated air*) and in 1773 (but not published until 1777) by K. W. Scheele (*fine air*). Its name (oxy, acid; gennao, I form—Greek) is due to A. L. Lavoisier, who developed the theory of combustion. Colorless gas, $d_{air}=1.1053$, m.-227, b.90.18°K, slightly soluble in water. It occurs as 3 isotopes: masses 16, 17, and 18, in the proportions of 10,000:1:8. Prepared by fractional distillation of liquid air, or by electrolysis of water, and shipped in steel cylinders. Oxygen is the basis of atomic weights ($O = 16$), the valency system ($O = 2$), and the acid and base system. Used medicinally (U.S.P., B.P.) in pulmonary diseases and anemia; with nitrous oxide, ethylene, or other anesthetics; and with hydrogen, acetylene, or illuminating gas for producing high temperatures for welding, and melting metals. **active-** Ozone, O_3. **allotropic-** Ozone, oxozone. **hydroxyl-** The oxygen of the hydroxyl group. **ketonic-** The oxygen of the >CO group. **liquid-** See *liquid o*. **radio-** A short-lived isotope obtained by bombardment of o. with α particles. See *radioelements*. **o. absorbent.** A substance that removes gaseous oxygen from a gas mixture, as an alkaline solution of pyrogallic acid, or chromous sulfate.

o. carrier. A catalytic substance that absorbs O_2 molecules and splits off O as atoms. **o. difluoride, o. fluoride.** $OF_2 = 54.00$. Yellow liquid, b.147.

oxygenase. An enzyme that enables atmospheric oxygen to be utilized by an organism or system.

oxygenate. To enrich with oxygen.

oxygenated water. Water saturated with oxygen gas.

oxygenation. Saturation with oxygen.

oxygenium. Latin for oxygen.

oxygenize. (1) Oxygenate. (2) Oxidize.

oxyhematoporphyrin. A pigment from oxyhemoglobin; closely allied to urohematoporphyrin sometimes found in urine.

oxyhemocyanin. Oxidized hemocyanin.

oxyhemoglobin, oxyhaemoglobin. Hematoglobulin, hematocrystallin. Mol. wt. 16,669. The red pigment of blood corpuscles; it carries the oxygen to the individual cells of the body, and removes the carbon dioxide later.

oxyhydrase. An enzyme in vegetable and animal secretions that decomposes water to H^+ and OH^-.

oxyhydrazides. Compounds which contain the —OH group and —$NHNH_2$ radical; e.g., $HOCH_2 \cdot CON \cdot HNH_2$, glycolhydrazide.

oxyhydrogen. An explosive mixture of oxygen and hydrogen. **o. blowpipe.** A burner with a jet of oxygen inside a jet of hydrogen, ensuring complete combustion of both gases and an extremely hot flame. **o. flame.** A blowpipe flame obtained by burning hydrogen with oxygen (5000°F). **o. light.** The "lime" light produced by heating calcium oxide with the o. blowpipe.

oxyhydroquinone. $C_6H_3(OH)_3$ = 126.1. 1,2,4-Trihydroxybenzene, 2,4-dihydroxyphenol, α-hydroxyhydroquinol. Colorless crystals, m.140.

-oxyl. Suffix denoting the RO— group; as, methoxyl, MeO—. Cf. *hydroxyl*.

oxylactone. A lactone containing a —OH radical.

oxylan. Diphenan.

oxylepidine. Dibenzoyl*stilbene*.

oxyleucotin. $C_{34}H_{32}O_{12}$ = 632.2. A crystalline principle from paracoto bark.

oxylith. A mixture of sodium peroxide and bleaching powder, used to generate oxygen for welding purposes.

oxymalonic acid. Tartronic acid.

oxymel. A medicated honey: clarified honey 80, acetic acid 10, water 10%.

oxymethoxyallylbenzene. Eugenol.

oxymethylconiferin. Syringenin.

oxymethylcresoltannin. Cretaform.

oxymethylene. Formaldehyde. **o. diphosphoric acid.** See *diphosphoric acid*.

oxymorphine. Dehydromorphine.

oxymuriate. Chlorate.

oxymuriatic acid. Chloric acid.

oxyn. A crystalline dihydroxy peroxide glyceride in tung oil.

oxynaphthoic acid. $C_{10}H_6(OH)COOH$ = 188.1. α-Naphtholcarbolic acid. Colorless crystals, m.186, soluble in water; a disinfectant and antizymotic.

oxynaphthoxazime. Mukogen.

oxynarcotine. $C_{22}H_{23}NO_8$ = 429.14. White needles, soluble in alcohol.

oxyneurine. Betaine.

oxynicotinic acid. $C_5H_3N \cdot OH \cdot COOH$ = 139.1. 2-Hydroxypyridine-5-carboxylic acid. Colorless crystals, m.303. Cf. *oxyquinolinic* acid.

oxynitrilase. An enzyme decomposing hydroxynitriles to aldehydes.

oxynitriles. Compounds containing the radicals —OH and —CN; e.g., $HO \cdot CH_2 \cdot CN$, ethanolnitrile.

oxynitroso. Nitrito.

oxyphenarisine hydrochloride. $C_6H_6O_2NAs \cdot HCl$ = 235.50. White crystals, soluble in water; an antitrypanosomal (U.S.P.).

oxyphenazone. Resorufin.

oxyphencyclimine hydrochloride. $C_{20}H_{28}N_2O_3 \cdot HCl$ = 380.91. Bitter, white powder, soluble in water, m.230 (decomp.); an antispasmodic (B.P.).

oxyphenoxazone. Resorufin.

oxyphenyl. Hydroxyphenyl, the radical $HO \cdot C_6H_4$—. Cf. *phenoxy*.

oxyphile. (1) Describing an element which does not occur in the native state but which forms minerals containing oxygen (e.g., mineral oxides); as uranium. (2) A cell structure that can be stained with acid dyes.

oxyphor. Oxycamphor.

oxyphthalic acid. α-Hydroxyphthalic acid.

oxypicolinic acid. $C_6H_5O_3N$ = 139.1. 4-Hydroxypyridine-2-carboxylic acid. Colorless crystals, m.250. See *oxynicotinic acid*.

oxyproline. $C_5H_9O_3N$ = 131.1. γ-Hydroxy-α-pyrrolidinecarboxylic acid. An amino acid from proteins.

oxypurinase. An enzyme that oxidizes purine bodies.

oxypyridine. Pyridone.

oxyquercetin. Myricetin.

oxyquinaseptol. Diaphtherin.

oxyquinazoline. Quinazolone.

oxyquinoline. $C_9H_6N \cdot OH$ = 146.1. A hydroxy derivative of quinoline. **o. carboxylic acid.** Kynurenic acid. **o. potassium sulfate.** Chinosol. **o. sulfate.** $(C_9H_7ON)_2H_2SO_4$ = 390.2. Yellow crystals of saffron odor, m.175, soluble in water; an antiseptic for eyewashes and gargles, **o. sulfonic acid.** Diaphthol.

oxyquinolinic acid. $C_6H_5O_3N$ = 139.1. 2-Hydroxypyridine-5,6-dicarboxylic acid. See *oxynicotinic acid*.

oxyquinones. Derivatives of $CO \cdot CH : CH \cdot CO \cdot CH : C\text{-}H$, in which one or more H atoms is replaced by an OH, OMe, or OEt group.

oxysalt. A salt of an oxyacid.

oxysparteine. $C_{15}H_{24}ON_2$ = 248.4. An oxidation product of sparteine. Colorless crystals, m.49, soluble in water; a heart stimulant.

oxysuccinic acid. Malic acid.

oxytetracycline. $C_{22}H_{24}O_9N_2 \cdot 2H_2O$ = 496.48. Yellow crystals, darkening in light, insoluble in water; used (also as the hydrochloride) as an antibiotic (U.S.P.).

oxythiazole. C_3H_3ONS = 101.2. μ-Hydroxymetathiazole. **methyl-** β-Methyl-μ-oxythiazole, 5-methyloxythiazole. Colorless crystals, m.160, soluble in water. **phenyl-** α-Phenyl-μ-oxythiazole, 4-phenoloxythiazole. Colorless crystals, m.204. soluble in water.

oxy-Tobias acid. 2-Naphthol-1-sulfonic acid.

oxytocic. A drug that increases the expulsive power of the uterus, as ergot.

oxytocin. α-Hypophamine. A food for humans obtained from the posterior lobe of the pituitary body of domestic animals (U.S.P., B.P.). The first polypeptide hormone to be synthesized. Cf. *hypophamine, vasopressin*.

oxytoluol. Cresol.

oxytoxin. An oxidation product of a toxin. Cf. *oxytocin*.

oxytropism. The response of living cells to oxygen.

oz. Abbreviation for ounce(s). **oz ap.** Abbreviation for apothecaries' ounces = ℥. **oz av.** Abbreviation for avoirdupois ounce. **oz fl.** Abbreviation for fluid ounce. **ozt.** Abbreviation for troy ounce.

ozamin. Benzopurpurin.

ozocerite. Mineral wax, native paraffin, fossil wax. A native mixture of hydrocarbons. Brown to green mass, soluble in carbon disulfide. Used as an insulator, for paints, polishes, candles. **purified-** Ceresin.

ozogen. Hydrogen peroxide.

ozokerite. Ozocerite.

ozonation. Impregnation or saturation with ozone. Cf. *ozonidation.*

ozonator. Ozonizer. A device to generate ozone.

ozone. $O_3 = 48.000$. A modification of oxygen gas produced usually by a silent electric discharge in air or oxygen. Faint blue gas, of intense odor, $d_{air=1}1.658$, b.-119, decomp. 270, soluble in water. Used as an antiseptic, bactericide, and oxidizing agent; and for bleaching oils, fats, textiles, and sugar solutions. Cf. *oxozone.* **o. paper.** A filter paper impregnated with potassium iodide and starch, or with indigo solution, which turns blue on exposure to ozone. Cf. *thallium ozone paper.*

ozonidation. To convert into an ozonide. Cf. *ozonization.*

ozonides. Thick oily unstable compounds of ozone with unsaturated organic compounds containing a double bond: $=C\diagdown_{O_3}\diagup C=$. Cf. *oxozonide, isozonide.*

ozonization. Treatment or sterilization with ozone. Cf. *ozonidation.*

ozonizer. (1) An apparatus for applying ozone to wounds. (2) Ozonator.

ozonolysis. The treatment of hydrocarbons with ozone.

ozotetrazone. Vicinal *tetrazine.*

P

P. Symbol for phosphorus.

P. Symbol for: (1) pressure: P_T at constant temperature, P_V at constant volume; (2) principal series of spectrum lines; as, ^1P, ^2P; (3) the sixth shell or orbit of electrons in the atom; cf. *Bohr's theory*; (4) parachor.

P. Symbol for: (1) para; (2) the electrons responsible for the principal series of lines in the spectrum; (3) potential.

π, Π. Greek pi. Symbol for: peri-, q.v.; (2) the mathematical constant 3.1416; see *radius*.

φ, φ, Φ. Greek phi. Symbol for phenol.

ψ, Ψ. Greek psi. Symbol for: (1) pseudo; (2) the electric field of Schrödinger's atom.

Pa. Symbol for protoactinium.

pabestrol. Silbestrol.

pachnolite. $NaF \cdot CaF_2 \cdot AlF_3 \cdot H_2O$. A mineral.

pachyrhizid. $C_{30}H_{24}O_{10} = 544.22$. A glucoside from *Pachyrhizus angulatus*.

pacite. Arsenopyrite.

pack fong. Nickel silver.

packing. (1) A filling material. (2) Crowding together. **atomic-** The crowding of atoms which have lost electrons and can approach one another more closely; as in certain stars, which have a density of up to 50,000. Cf. *spectral classification*. **nuclear-** The crowding of hydrogen and helium nuclei and electrons within the atomic nucleus. **p. effect.** Loss of mass due to crowding of protons and electrons in atomic nuclei; as, in the hypothetical case $4H \rightarrow He$, where the atomic weight drops from 4.032, to 4.002. Cf. *mass-energy cycle*. **p. fraction.** The deviation per unit mass of the isotopic weight from whole numbers, in parts per 10,000. It measures the forces holding electrons and protons together.

paddy. Threshed rice.

padutin. Kallikrein.

pae, pæ-. See *pe-*.

paeonine. Peonine.

paeonol. Peonol.

pagodite. $2Al_2O_3 \cdot K_2O \cdot 3H_2O \cdot 5SiO_2$. Pinite. A mineral.

paint. A suspension of finely ground white pigment (as white lead or zinc oxide) with added colored pigments if required, in a vehicle (linseed oil, varnish, or turpentine). **luminous-** A suspension of zinc sulfide or barium sulfide in nitrocellulose lacquer. **water-** An aqueous mixture of pigment and adhesive, e.g., casein. **p. mill.** A mill that grinds to 200-mesh. **p. oil.** An oil for thinning paints; as, linseed oil. **p. rock.** Ocher. **p. thinner.** Turpentine or its substitutes.

paired electrons. An electron couple. A nonpolar bond between 2 atoms, each atom furnishing one of the electrons of the pair. Cf. *twin electrons*.

palaeontology. Paleontology.

palau. General name for Pd-Au alloys. A platinum

substitute where resistance to heat and chemicals is not important.

paleontology. The science of prehistoric life as revealed by fossil remains.

palev. A product resembling ice cream, but containing no milk product.

palicourine. A crystalline alkaloid from *Pali courea* species (Rubiaceae).

paligorskite. Mountain leather. An asbestos substitute from the blue limestone fractures of Alaska. Average composition: MgO 8.1, Al_2O_3 14.3, SiO_2 49.5, Fe_2O_3 2.6, CaO 3.3%.

Palissy, Bernard. 1499–1589. French leader in chemical technology and forerunner of Boyle.

palite. $ClCOOCH_2Cl = 128.9$. Chloromethyl chloroformate. A poison gas used during World War I. **super-** Superpalite

palladic. Describing a compound containing tetravalent palladium; as, p. dioxide.

palladichloride. M_2PdCl_6 or $2MCl \cdot PdCl_4$.

palladious. Palladous.

palladium. Pd = 106.4. A noble metal of the platinum group, at. no. 46, discovered (1803) by Wollaston. A silver-white, ductile, malleable metal, d.12.16, m.1553, b.2200, insoluble in water or acids; occurs native and alloyed with platinum metals. Used in alloys with gold or platinum in dentistry and jewelry; and with copper or silver in watches, pens, mirrors, and surgical instruments; as Pd sponge as a catalyst and hydrogen absorbent. Compounds: palladous (valency 2) and palladic (valency 4). **allo-** A hexagonal or cubic variety of p., formerly confused with potarite. **p. asbestos.** Asbestos coated with metallic p.; used to absorb hydrogen. **p. black.** Black finely divided p.; a catalyst in oil hydrogenation. **p. bromide.** $PdBr_2 = 266.5$. Brown powder, insoluble in water. **p. chloride.** $PdCl_2 \cdot 2H_2O = 213.7$. Brown, hygroscopic crystals, soluble in water; used as a local germicide and a reagent for malic acid, cocaine, iodine, mercury vapor, and carbon monoxide; and for photographic toning, porcelain prints, marking inks, and coating instruments. **p. cyanide.** $Pd(CN)_2 = 158.7$. Yellow solid, unstable to heat. **p. dioxide.** $PdO_2 = 138.7$. Palladic oxide. Black powder, decomp. 200, insoluble in water. **p. disulfide.** $PdS_2 = 170.8$. Brown powder, insoluble in water. **p. family.** The elements Ru, Rh, and Pd of group 8 of the fourth period of the periodic table. **p. gold.** Porpezite. Native gold containing up to 10% Pd. **p. hydroxide.** $Pd(OH)_2 = 140.7$. Brown powder, insoluble in water **p. iodide.** $PdI_2 = 360.5$. Black powder, m.100, insoluble in water. **p. monosulfide.** PdS = 138.8. Black powder, insoluble in water. **p. monoxide.** PdO = 122.7. Black powder, decomp. 875, insoluble in water. **p. nitrate.** $Pd(NO_3)_2 = 230.7$. Brown

485

rhombs, hydrolyzed in dilute solutions; a reagent for ptomaines and for separating of Cl and I. **p. oxides.** See *p. monoxide, p. dioxide.* **p. potassium chloride.** See *potassium palladi-* and *pallado- chlorides.* **p. sodium chloride.** $Na_2PdCl_4 = 294.6$. Red hygroscopic crystals, soluble in water; a reagent for gases (methane, carbon monoxide). **p. sponge.** A gray spongy mass of finely divided p.; a gas absorbent and catalyst for hydrogenation. **p. subsulfide.** $Pd_2S = 245.5$. Insoluble gray solid. **p. sulfate.** $Pd(SO_4)\cdot 2H_2O = 238.8$. Brown crystals, soluble in water. **p. tube.** A glass tube filled with p. asbestos or p. sponge.

pallado. Palladous.

palladous. Palladious. Describing compounds containing divalent palladium.

pallamine. Colloidal palladium.

pallas. An alloy of gold, palladium, and platinum; harder than platinum.

pallasite. A meteorite: Ni-Fe sponge enclosing olivine.

palm. (1) See *Palmae.* (2) The obsolete unit: 1 palm = 3 in. **p. butter.** P. oil. **p. grease.** P. oil. **p. kernel cake.** The residue after expressing p. nut oil; a cattle food. **p. kernel oil.** P. nut oil. **p. nut oil.** P. kernel oil. Yellow oil from the crushed fruits of W. African oil palm, d.0.952, m.26–36; consists of the glycerides of palmitic, oleic, and stearic acids. Used to manufacture soap, chocolate, and pharmaceuticals. World production(1966) 260,000 tons. **p. oil.** Oleum palmae, p. butter, p. grease, expressed from the crushed and fermented fruit of the W. African oil palm, *Elaeis guineensis.* It consists of the glycerides of palmitic, oleic, and stearic acids and free palmitic acid; d.0.859–0.870, sapon. val. 196–205, m.33–46. Used to manufacture soap, candles, and lubricants. World production (1966) 600,000 tons. **p. wax.** A yellow wax from *Ceroxylin andicola,* a palm of Ecuador; a beeswax substitute.

Palmae. Palm family of tropical trees; e.g.: *Areca catechu,* areca nut; *Copernicia cerifera,* carnauba; *Elaeis guineensis,* palm oil; *Cocos nucifera,* coconut oil. See also, *raffia, coyol, date palm, sago.*

palmarosa oil. Pamorusa oil. An essential oil d.0.885–0.896, from ginger grass, *Andropogon schoenanthus,* S. Africa; an adulterant for oil of rose. It contains perilla alcohol, geraniol, and esters.

palmellin. The red coloring, resembling hemoglobin, from the fresh water algae, *Palmella cruenta.*

palmetto. The fruit of *Serenoa serrulata* (Florida); a leather tan.

palmic. Palmitic.

palmierite. $K_2Pb(SO_4)_2$. A mineral from Italy.

palmin. Purified coconut fat for the manufacture of butter substitutes.

palmitamide. $C_{16}H_{33}ON = 255.27$. Palmitic acid amide, hexadecanamide*. Colorless solid, m.93.

palmitate. Hexadecanate*, cetylate. A salt of palmitic acid, which contains the radical $C_{15}H_{31}\cdot COO—$.

palmitic acid. $C_{15}H_{31}\cdot COOH = 256.3$. Hexadecanoic acid*, palmic acid, cetylic acid, ethalic acid. A saturated, fatty acid in many vegetable fats and oils. Colorless needles, m.62 (decomp.), insoluble in water; used in soap manufacture.

hydroxy- Juniperic acid. **p. cyanide.** Palmitonitrile.

palmitin. (1) $C_3H_5(C_{15}H_{31}COO)_3 = 807.1$. Tripalmitin. Tripalmitic acid ester of glycerin, which occurs in many vegetable fats and oils. Colorless fat, m.61, insoluble in water; used in soap manufacture. (2) A glyceride of palmitic acid; as, monopalmitin.

palmitinic acid. Palmitic acid.

palmitoleic acid. Zoomaric acid.

palmitolic acid. $C_{15}H_{27}COOH = 252.3$. 7-Hexadecynoic acid*. An unsaturated fatty acid, in oils and japan wax. Colorless needles, m.47, insoluble in water.

palmitone. $C_{31}H_{62}O = 450.65$. 16-Hentriacontanone*. The ketone of palmitic acid.

palmitonitrile. $C_{15}H_{31}CN = 237.3$. Palmitic cyanide, hexadecanenitrile*. Colorless scales, m.30, insoluble in water.

palmityl. The radical $C_{15}H_{31}CO—$, from palmitic acid. **p. alcohol.** Cetyl alcohol. **p. chloride.** $Me(CH_2)_{14}COCl = 274.70$. Hexadecanoyl chloride*. Colorless liquid, m.11.

palmoil. Palm oil.

Palmquist apparatus. A portable gas analysis apparatus for the determination of carbon dioxide in air.

palmyra. The palm, *Borassus flabellifer* (S. Asia). The wood is used for structures, the leaves for thatch and mats, the fruits for food, the sap for toddy and jaggery sugar, the fiber for brushes; and the young seedlings are ground to edible flour.

Paludrine. $C_{11}H_{16}N_5Cl = 254.61$. Trademark for plasmoquin(e). Proguanil. *N-p-*chlorophenyl-*N*-isopropylbiguanide. A synthetic antimalarial free from the undesirable effects of quinine and acridine-type drugs; probably a mixture of 3 tautomers.

palustrol. $C_{15}H_{26}O = 222.02$. A sesquiterpene oil from *Ledum palustre,* d.0.9544.

palygorskite. Attapulgite (U.S.S.R. usage).

palynology. The study of spores and pollen.

pamaquin(e). $C_{19}H_{28}N_2O = 300.2$. Pamaquine naphthoate, plasmochin, aminoquin, 8-dimethylaminoisoamyl-6-methoxyquinoline. Yellow powder, insoluble in water; an antimalarial.

PAN. Trade name for a polyamide synthetic fiber.

pan- Prefix indicating all, or the whole.

panabase. Tetrahedrite.

panacea. A universal remedy, generally applied to a quack medicine.

panacon. $C_{22}H_{19}O_8 = 317.2$. Colorless crystals from ginseng, the roots of *Aralia* or *Panax quinquefolium.*

Panama bark. Quillaja.

panaquinol. $C_{12}H_{25}O_9 = 313.2$. A bitter principle from ginseng, the root of *Panax quinquefolium.* Yellow powder, soluble in water. Cf. *panacon.*

panax. (1) Ginseng. (2) A genus of araliaceus plants.

panchromatic. Sensitive to light of all colors. Cf. *pantachromatic.*

panchromium. Early name for vanadium.

panclastite. Nitrogen tetroxide dissolved in a combustible liquid; as, carbon disulfide. An explosive.

pancreas. A gland below the stomach of mammals.

pancreatic juice. The secretions of the pancreas containing the digestive enzymes and ferments:

pancreatin, trypsin, amylopsin, steapsin, rennin, and invertin.

pancreatin. Pancreatinum. A mixture of enzymes from the fresh pancreas of the hog or ox. Cream powder of meatlike taste, slowly and partly soluble in water; it should convert 25 times its weight of starch into water-soluble products. Used to aid digestion (B.P.). Cf. *holadin.* **p. powder.** A peptonizing powder.

pandermite. $Ca_2B_6O_{11}\cdot 3_2HO$. A native source of boric acid.

Paneth, Friedrich Adolf. 1887–1958. German physicist. **P.'s rule.** A radioelement will be adsorbed by a solid substance if its electronegative radical can form a relatively insoluble compound with the adsorbing substance.

pangamic acid. Vitamin B_{15}.

paniculatine. $C_{29}H_{35}O_7N$ = 509.28. An alkaloid, m.263, from the seeds of *Panicularia* (*Glyceria*) (Gramineae), N. America.

pannic acid. $C_{11}H_{14}O_4$ = 210.1. A constituent of rhizoma pannae. Colorless crystals, m.192. Cf. *pannol.*

pannol. $C_{11}H_{14}O_4$ = 210.1. A constituent of *Aspidium athamanticum* (Filiceae). Cf. *pannic* acid.

panose. A nonfermentable trisaccharide produced from maltose by an enzyme from *Aspergillus niger.*

panscale. Calcium sulfate produced in salt manufacture by evaporation.

pansupari. A mixture of betel and areca nuts and lime, used for chewing in India.

pansy. The dried herb of *Viola tricolor*; an expectorant and alterative.

pantachromatic. Existing in 2 or more colored forms; entirely achromatic. Cf. *panchromatic.*

pantal. A corrosion-resistant aluminum alloy containing Cu 4.2, Mn 0.3–0.6, Mg 0.5–0.9%.

pantocaine. $Me(CH_2)_3NH\cdot C_6H_4\cdot COO(CH_2)_2NMe$ = 249.1. A local and spinal anesthetic, similar to procaine.

pantochromic. Pantachromatic.

pantogen. Protyl.

pantograph. A device for copying diagrams, etc., to any scale: a set of adjustable levers connect a pencil with a tracing guide or stylus.

pantomorphism. The perfect symmetry displayed by crystals.

pantopaque. $C_{19}H_{29}O_2I$ = 416.20. Ethyl iodophenyl undecoate. Yellow liquid, $b_{0.5mm}219$; injected to render body cavities visible in X rays.

Pantopon. Trademark for a brand of purified opium alkaloids. Yellow powder, soluble in water; an opiate or narcotic.

pantothenic acid. $CH_2\cdot OH\cdot CMe_2\cdot CHOH\cdot CO\cdot NH_2\cdot$ $CH_2\cdot CH_2\cdot COOH$ = 219.21. Vitamin B_3. α,α-Dihydroxy-β,β-dimethylbutyryl-β'-alanide. Colorless liquid, soluble in water. See *vitamin B_3.*

pantothenol. A derivative of pantothenic acid in which an Me group is substituted by OH; activity 86% (pantothenic acid 100%).

paoferro. The inner bark of the ironwood tree of Brazil; an antidiabetic.

paopereira. The bark of a Brazilian tree; a febrifuge.

papain. Papayotin, caricin, carase, vegetable pepsin, from the fruit of the papaw, *Carica papaya* (S. America). Gray powder, soluble in water; an active ferment for proteins.

Papase. Trademark for a protective enzyme from *Carica papaya*; an anti-inflammatory agent. Cf. *papain.*

Papaveraceae. Poppy family: herbs with a milky, narcotic juice, containing alkaloids; e.g.: *Papaver somniferum*, opium; *Papaver rhoeas*, rhoeadine; *Glaucium flavum*, glaucine.

papaveric acid. $C_{16}H_{13}NO_7$ = 331.11. Rhoeadic acid, m.233 (decomp.).

papaverine. $C_{20}H_{21}O_4N$ = 339.3. Tetramethoxy-benzylisoquinoline. An alkaloid from opium. White, rhombic prisms or needles, m.148, insoluble in cold water; a narcotic. Cf. *lodal.* **p. hydrochloride.** $C_{20}H_{21}O_4N\cdot HCl$ = 375.86. Colorless crystals, soluble in water; a muscle relaxant (U.S.P., B.P.).

papaveroline. $C_{16}H_{13}O_4N$ = 283.2. Tetrahydroxy-benzylisoquinoline. A derivative of papaverine: the MeO groups are replaced by OH groups.

papaw. (1) The edible fruit of papaya. (2) Erroneously applied to pawpaw, q.v.

papaya. Papaw, melon tree. The tropical *Carica papaya* (Passifloraceae), which yields fruit and juice containing proteolytic enzymes (papain), a milk-curdling ferment, caricin, myrosin, and carpain. Used locally to tenderize meat. Cf. *papayotin.*

papayotin. The dried milky juice of papaya; contains papain.

paper. A sheet or continuous web of material formed by the deposition of vegetable, mineral, animal, or synthetic fibers, or their mixtures, with or without the addition of other substances, from suspension in a gas, vapor, or liquid, in such a way that the fibers are intermeshed together to form a thin but compact whole. P. may be coated, impregnated, printed, or otherwise converted without necessarily losing its identity. The usual raw materials are wood pulp, rag, straw, esparto grass, and bagasse. World production (1966) 107 million tons. **art-** A p. coated on one or both sides with a mixture of a white or colored pigment (e.g., satin white) and an adhesive (e.g., casein), and dried and calendered to a high finish. Used for fine-screen printing. Cf. *chromo- p.* **asbestos-** An asbestos board or a tissue made from asbestos fibers. **azolitmin-** A substitute for litmus p. **bank-, bond-** A thin, strong writing p. **blueprint-** q.v. **carbon-** q.v. **chromo-** An art p., usually with a duller finish. **congo blue-** q.v. **coordinate-** q.v. **dahlia-** q.v. **dialyzing-** A parchment p. used for dialyzing. **drying-** An absorbent p. **emery-** A p. coated with abrasive material. **filter-** A porous, unsized p. used as an absorbent and filter. **glass-** p. coated with fine glass powder; an abrasive. **glazed-** A p. coated with a filler (e.g., barytes) and highly calendered. Its shiny surface is used for transferring precipitates. **imitation art-** A p. with a high finish, obtained by addition of a high proportion of loading and calendering. Cf. *art p.* **lens-** A soft tissue p. for wiping lenses. **linen-** A p. made from linen rags. **linen-faced-** A p. embossed with linen, an impression of which is retained on its surface. **litmus-** A filter p. impregnated with red or blue litmus solution used as a test paper for acids and alkalies. **niter-** A p. impregnated with saltpeter. **ozone-** See *ozone.* **paraffined-** A p. saturated with hot paraffin, used for electrical insulation and waterproofing. **parchment-** P. prepared by intensive beating of the fibers to imitate the characteristics of parchment. Cf. *parchment.* **polarity-** q.v. **sand-** q.v. **silver nitrate-** q.v. **starch-** q.v. **test-** A filter p. impregnated with an indicator solution. **turmeric-** A filter p. dipped in turmeric solution; used to identify boric acid (red color). **vegetable parchment-** See *parchment.* **vulcanized-** See *vulcanized, fiber.* **wax-** A p. made waterproof by treating it with molten paraffin wax.

p. analysis. See *Herzberg's stain.* **p. board.** A thick sheet of p. pulp mixed with size and filling materials. Cf. *board, pasteboard, millboard.* **p. chromatography.** Chromatographic analysis, q.v., with p. as the selective absorbent, e.g., as strips hung in the solution of the sample, or as circles in the center of which is placed the solution to be tested. **p. coal.** Brown coal in thin layers. **p. colors.** Aniline dyes used for coloring p. **p. filter.** A filter pulp cone or thick filter p. **thimble.** **p. pulp.** The mixture of fibers and water from which p. is deposited by drainage on wire mesh. Cf. *chemical-, mechanical-, soda-, sulfite-,* and *sulfate-pulp, Herzberg's stain.* **p. sizes.** International series. Writing and general printing. Based on A0 = 841 × 1,189 mm (= 1 sq meter); A1 is $\frac{1}{2}$ A0, or 594 × 841 mm; and A2, etc., each $\frac{1}{2}$ its predecessor. Also B (large printings) and C (envelope) series. **p. spar.** Calcite, in thin plates.

papier maché. Molded articles, made by boiling old paper with water and glue and soaking the semi-dried product in linseed oil.

papilloma. A nonmalignant wart, which sometimes precedes skin cancer.

Papreg. Trade name for paper which has been impregnated with a plastic, e.g., for lamination.

paprika. Ground red pepper used as a spice, rich in ascorbic acid.

para- Prefix (Greek "beyond" or "opposite") indicating (1) the 1,4-position (para compounds) of the benzene ring; (2) an even rotational quantum number, as in parahydrogen; (3) polymerization, as, paraformaldehyde; (4) the amount of water, as, paraperiodic acid; (5) a relationship, as, paracasein. **p. compounds.** See under the parent compound.

para arrowroot. Tapioca.

parabanic acid. $CO \cdot NH \cdot CO \cdot NH \cdot CO$ = 132.07. Oxalylurea, imidazoletrione, oxalic acid ureid. Colorless plates, m.227 (decomp.), soluble in water. **dimethyl-** Cholestrophan.

parabituminous. Describing a good caking gas-coal.

parabola. A plane curve, each point of which is equidistant from a straight line (axis) and a central point (focus). It resembles a circle at some points, a straight line at others.

paraboloid. The surface traced by a parabola when its vertex is always on another parabola. **p. condenser.** A spherical microscope mirror having an elongated focus.

parabuxin. $C_{24}H_{48}ON_2$ = 380.4. An alkaloid in common garden box, *Buxus sempervirens* (Euphorbiaceae).

paracasein. Casein digested with rennin.

paracellulose. Cellulose from the parenchyma or pith of plants (obsolete).

Paracelsus. 1493–1541. Philippus Aurelius Theophrastus Paracelsus Bombastus von Hohenheim. Swiss physician and alchemist, advocate of chemical as opposed to vegetable remedies. Cf. *iatrochemistry.*

paracetamol. $C_8H_9O_2N$ = 151.12. Acetaminophen. 4-Acetamidophenol. White, bitter crystals, m.171, soluble in water; an analgesic and antipyretic (B.P.).

parachor. $P = M\gamma^{1/4}/(D - d) = 0.78 \times V$, where V is the critical volume, γ is surface tension, M the molecular weight, and D and d the densities of a compound in the liquid and vapor state, respectively, at the same temperature. A comparison of the P of liquids is equivalent to a comparison of their molecular volumes at temperatures of equal surface tensions. P is an additive constant for saturated compounds and is used to determine chemical constitution.

Paracon. Trade name for an oil- and heat-resistant synthetic rubber consisting of chain esters of sebacic or succinic acid and ethylene or propylene glycols.

paraconic acid. $O \cdot CH_2 \cdot CH(COOH) \cdot CH_2 \cdot CO$ = 130.0. Itamalic acid γ-lactone, tetrahydro-5-oxo-3-furancarboxylic acid. Colorless crystals, m.58. Cf. *citraconic acid.* **dimethyl-** Terebic acid. **phenyl-** Phenyl paraconic acid.

paraconiine. $C_8H_{15}N$ = 125.1. An alkaloid obtained by heating butyric aldehyde with ammonia. Colorless liquid with stupefying odor, b.170.

paracoto. The dried bark of an unidentified tree of N. Bolivia; a substitute for coto bark, q.v.

paracotoin. $C_{12}H_8O_4$ = 216.1. An active principle from paracoto. Yellow crystals, m.150.

paracyanogen. $(CN)_5$ = 156.12. (1) An insoluble solid, sublimes if heated. (2) More correctly the water-insoluble polymer, $(CN)_x$, of unknown molecular weight. Brown powder converted into cyanogen when heated above 860° in absence of air. Produced by prolonged pyrolysis of cyanogen at 300°.

paradiazine. Pyrazine.

paradichlorobenzene. See *benzene.*

paradimethylaminobenzaldehyde. $C_6H_4(CHO) \cdot NMe_2$ = 149.1. A reagent for indole, skatole pyrrole. **paradioxybenzene.** Hydroquinone.

paraffin. (1) See *paraffins.* (2) Hard p. (B.P.). White wax, d.0.890, m.47–65, insoluble in water, soluble in organic solvents. P. is a mixture of hydrocarbons occurring native in ozocerite, peat, and bituminous coal, and is a constituent of petroleum from which it is distilled. Used in the manufacture of candles, ointments (U.S.P., B.P.), waxed paper, matches, lubricants, oil crayons; and for waterproofing wood and cork. Cf. kerosine. **liquid-** (B.P.) Petrolatum. **white soft-, yellow soft-** m.38–56; used in ointments (B.P.). **p. bath.** Molten paraffin. **p. oil.** Petrolatum. **p. scale.** A crude paraffin. **p. wax.** Paraffin (2).

paraffins. (1) Alkanes. (2) C_nH_{2n+2}. Saturated aliphatic hydrocarbons of the methane series, **iso-** An aliphatic saturated hydrocarbon containing one —CHMe— group or a side chain. **neo-** An aliphatic saturated hydrocarbon containing one —CMe₂— group. **normal-** An aliphatic saturated hydrocarbon containing only CH_3— and —CH_2—

groups. **meso-** An aliphatic saturated hydrocarbon containing 2 —CMe₂— groups.

paraffinum. Paraffin (2).

paraform. Paraformaldehyde.

paraformaldehyde. $O \cdot CH_2 \cdot O \cdot CH_2 \cdot O \cdot CH_2 = 90.04$.

Paraformaldehydum, paraform, triformol, trioxymethylene, trioxin. Colorless powder, m.150, soluble in water, in which it has the properties of formaldehyde; an antiseptic and preservative (forbidden in food). Cf. *paraldehyde.*

parafuchsin. $(C_6H_4NH_2)_2:C:C_6H_4:NH \cdot HCl$. Pararosaniline chloride. A dye. Cf. *pararosaniline.*

paragenesis. The passage of minerals through successive stages of chemical composition during the cooling of the earth's crust.

paraglobulin. Fibroplastin, serum globulin. A globulin from blood serum and lymph, precipitated as a white amorphous substance by carbon dioxide.

paragonite. $Al_3NaH_2Si_3O_{12}$. A mica-type silica mineral, q.v.

Paraguay tea. Maté.

parahemoglobin. Crystalline hemoglobin.

parahiston. A sulfur rich protein from thymus.

parahydrogen. See *hydrogen molecule.*

paralactic acid. Sarcolactic acid.

paralbumin. A protein from ovarian cysts.

paraldehyde. $(C_2H_4O)_3 = 132.16$. A polymer of acetaldehyde or a mixture of hydrated linear formaldehyde polymers having the type formula $OH(CH_2O)_nH$. Cf. *trioxane.* Colorless liquid of pungent odor, d.0.992, m.11, b.125, soluble in water; a reagent for alkaloids and fuchsin, and a hypnotic and sedative (U.S.P., B.P.). Cf. *metaldehyde, aldol.*

paraldol. $(C_4H_8O_2)_2 = 176.12$. A polymer of aldol, m.82.

parallax. The apparent displacement of an object due to a change in the position of the observer, e.g., errors in buret meniscus readings.

parallel. (1) Having the same direction, but separated by equal distances. (2) Electric connections such that like poles of a number of units are connected to one another. Cf. *series.*

parallelosterism. The relationship between isomorphous groups and their chemical compositions or physical properties.

paralyser. Paralyzer.

paralysol. $Me \cdot C_6H_4 \cdot OK$. A mixture of cresol and potassium cresolate. Colorless crystals, m.146, insoluble in water; an antiseptic.

paralyst. Paralyzer.

paralyzant. A substance that causes paralysis.

paralyzer. An agent that prevents a chemical reaction; a catalytic poison.

param. $N:C \cdot NHC(:NH)NH_2 = 84.2$. Cyanoguanidine. A condensation product of cyanamide, formed at 150, m.204, soluble in water.

paramagnetic. A substance that has magnetic properties stronger than those of air (as iron); i.e., a magnetic permeability over 1.

paramagnetism. The property of being attracted by a magnet. Cf. *diamagnetism.*

paramecium. A genus of unicellular animals or protozoa.

paramethadione. $C_7H_{11}NO_3 = 157.17$. Colorless liquid, slightly soluble in water; an anticonvulsant (U.S.P.).

paramide. Mellimide.

paramisan sodium. Sodium aminosalicylate.

paramorph. A crystal that has undergone paramorphism.

paramorphine. Thebaine.

paramorphism. (1) The physical change of a mineral from one modification to another, without a change of chemical composition. (2) A rearrangement of molecular structure.

paramucic acid. $C_6H_{10}O_8 = 210.1$. An isomer of mucic acid.

paramucosin. $C_{12}H_{23}O_{10}N = 341.3$. A salivary protein.

paramyelin. $C_{38}H_{75}O_9NP = 720.7$. White solid from brain and nerve substance.

paramylum. $C_5H_{10}O_5 = 162.1$. A carbohydrate from certain protozoa.

paranaphthalene. Anthracene (obsolete).

paranephrine. Adrenaline.

paranitraniline. $NO_2 \cdot C_6H_4 \cdot NH_2 = 138.2$. Yellow crystals, m.148, soluble in alcohol; a reagent and intermediate.

parapectic. $C_{24}H_{34}O_{23} = 690.3$. An oxyacid produced from pectose by the ripening of fruits.

parapeptone. Syntonin.

paraplasm. (1) The fluid portion of cell protoplasm. (2) The nonliving part of protoplasm.

paraquat. Common name for compounds containing the cation 1:1′-dimethyl-4,4′-bipyridylium; a herbicide for coarse grasses.

Paraquay tea. Maté.

paraquinanisol. $C_{10}H_9ON = 159.1$. A synthetic antipyretic alkaloid.

paraquinoid. Quinoid.

para red. A red aniline dye obtained from *p*-nitraniline.

pararosaniline. $(NH_2C_6H_4)_3C \cdot OH = 305.3$. Triaminotriphenylcarbinol. An organic base forming red salts. Colorless leaflets, m.188, insoluble in water; a dye. **hexamethyl-** Methyl violet. **p. chloride.** Parafuchsin. **p. dyes.** Dyestuffs derived from pararosolic acid; e.g., pararosaniline.

pararosolic acid. Aurin.

parartrose. $C_{120}H_{192}O_{40}N_{30}S$. A proteose obtained by digestion of wheat.

parasite. An organism that obtains its nourishment from another living organism. Cf. *saprophyte, epiphyte.* Classification: *Phyto*parasites, *vegetable* parasites (bacteria and fungi); *Zoö*parasites, *animal* parasites (protozoa and metazoa, worms, etc.). Each of these is subdivided into occasional, temporary, or obligate; and constant, stationary, or facultative.

parasiticide. An agent that destroys parasites, e.g. sulfur.

parasitotropic. A compound that acts specifically or protozoa.

parasorbic acid. $C_6H_8O_2 = 112.1$. Hepenolactone An acid from the berries of mountain ash, sorbus

Parasporin. Trademark for a bacterial insecticide the principal active ingredients of which are spore and paraspores of *Bacillus thurungiensis*, Berliner Used to combat alfalfa caterpillars.

paratartarics. Racemic forms.

parathesin. Benzocaine.

parathion. $C_{10}H_{14}O_5NP = 259.16$. E605. *o,c* Diethyl *o,p*-nitrophenyl thiophosphate. Yellow oil, d.1.26, approx. b.375; an insecticide.

parathormone. The hormone of the parathyroid. It maintains the normal level of calcium in the blood, and so antagonizes the action of vitamin D.

Parathyrin. Trademark for the active principle of the parathyroid gland.

parathyroid. One of the small glands associated with the thyroid. **p. gland.** The dried exterior p. gland of the ox, free from fat. Yellow powder, slightly soluble in water; a nervine.

paraxanthine. $C_7H_8O_2N_4$ = 180.2. 1,7-Dimethylxanthine, urotheobromine, a leucomaine in urine. Colorless crystals, m.298, soluble in water; an isomer of theobromine. **amine-** Paraxine.

Paraxin. Trademark for paraxine.

paraxine. $C_7H_{10}O_2N_5$ = 196.2. Dimethylamino-p-xanthine. White crystals, m.226, soluble in water; a diuretic.

paraxylene. See *xylene.*

Parchfoil. Trade name for an odor-resistant wrapping for fatty foods made by laminating aluminium foil to vegetable parchment.

parchment. A specially prepared animal skin. **imitation-** See *paper.* **vegetable-** P. paper. A paper treated with concentrated sulfuric acid to produce grease resistance, high wet strength, and some water resistance. Used to wrap fatty foods, for lampshades, and as a dialysis membrane.
  p. paper. Vegetable parchment.

paregoric. A flavored camphorated tincture of opium, for cough mixtures.

pareira. Perieira. The dried root of *Chondrodendron tomentosum* (Menispermaceae), S. America, which contains the alkaloid bebeerine.

pareirine. Pereirine.

parenchyma. The principal constituent of the thin cell-wall tissue of vegetable matter.

parent name. That part of a name from which the specific name is derived; e.g. ethane is the p.n. of ethanol. **p. substance.** Index substance. A compound yielding derivatives or substitution products.

parhelium. A form of helium in which both electrons move in one orbit; it gives the principal spectral line, 20.528 angström units.

pariantite. An asphalt from the pitch lake in Trinidad.

Paricin. Trademark for a group of alkylhydroxy and acetoxy stearates.

paricine. $C_{16}H_{18}ON_2$ = 254.3. An amorphous alkaloid from cinchona bark.

paridin. $C_{16}H_{28}O_7$ = 332.3. A glucoside from *Paris quadrifolia* (Liliaceae). Cf. *paristyphnin.*

parietic acid. Chrysophanic acid.

parietin. Physcion.

paraglin. Smilacin.

parillic acid. Parillin.

parilla. Sarsaparilla. **yellow-** Menispermum.

parillin. $C_{40}H_{70}O_{18}$ = 838.6. Parillic acid. A glucoside from the sarsaparilla root. Colorless needles or scales. Cf. *smilacin.*

parinaric acid. $C_{18}H_{28}O_2$ = 276.22. An unsaturated acid from the kernel fat of *Parinarium laurinum* (Rosaceae).

paris, plaster of- See *plaster.*
  p. black. Lampblack. **p. blue.** Ferric ferrocyanide. **p. green.** $Cu(C_2H_3O_2)_2 \cdot 3Cu(AsO_2)_2$. Emerald green, Schweinfürth green, copper aceto-arsenite. A green pigment insecticide. **p. red.**

(1) Colcothar. (2) Minium. **p. violet.** Methyl violet. **p. yellow.** Lead chromate.

parisite. A native fluoride and carbonate of the cerium metals. Brown hexagonal pyramids.

paristyphnin. $C_{38}H_{64}O_{18}$ = 808.6. A glucoside in the root of *Paris quadrifolia*, one-berry. Cf. *paridin.*

Parkerizing. Trademark for a process of forming by chemical reaction, a protective phosphate film on metal (especially cadmium) surfaces.

Parkes, Samuel. 1761–1825. English technical chemist. **P. process.** The refining of argentiferous lead by liquation, followed by addition of zinc to the molten mass, and skimming the surface crust (silver and zinc). The silver is isolated by distilling the zinc, and the lead purified by electrolysis.

parkesine. An early plastic made by Alexander Parkes (1813–1890), from a "dough" of nitro-cellulose in mixed alcohol and ether.

parkine. An alkaloid from the seeds of nitta tree, *Parkia biglandalosa* (Leguminosae), Africa.

Parma blue. A triphenylrosaniline dye. **p. violet.** Rosaniline violet.

paromomycin. An antibiotic produced by *Streptomyces rimosus forma paromomycinus.* **p. sulfate.** Humatin. Mixed sulfates of the antibiotics from *Streptomyces rimosus paromomycinus.* Yellow powder; an antibiotic (B.P.).

paroxazine. 1,4[2]Oxazine.

Parr, Samuel Wilson. 1857–1931. American chemist. **P. apparatus.** A device to determine the total carbon in fuels by means of a calorimeter and gas burets.

parsec. pc. The distance of a star whose annual parallax is 1 second of an arc. 1 parsec = 3.08×10^{13} km = 19.2×10^{12} miles = 3.26 light years = 206,265 astronomical units (distance of earth to sun). The SI unit, q.v., of length.

parsley. The umbelliferous plant *Carum (Apium) petroselinum* or *Petroselinum sativum.* It contains an essential oil and a camphor (apiol). Cf. *petroselinum.* **p. camphor.** Apiol. **p. fruit.** P. seeds. **p. leaves oil.** An essential oil from the leaves of p., d.0.900–0.925, greenish yellow and of strong parsley odor; it contains apiol. **p. oil.** An oil distilled from p. seeds. Colorless liquid, insoluble in water. **p. root.** Petroselini radix. The dried root of p.

Parsons, Charles Lathrop. 1867–1954. American chemist noted for his work on education, uranium minerals, and nitrogen fixation.

parthenicine. Parthenine.

parthenine. An alkaloid from *Chrysanthemum (Parthenium) hysterophorum* (Compositae), W. Indies; an antipyretic.

parthenogenesis. Development of the egg without previous fertilization by a male agency. Cf. *agamy.*

partial. Fractional. A proportion of the whole. **p. pressure.** The fraction of the total pressure due to each constituent of a gas mixture. The p. pressures are proportional to the concentrations of the individual gases in a mixture. See *Dalton's law.* **p. valence.** An excess valence of a compound, responsible for the formation of addition compounds. Cf. *coordinate valence.*

particle. A very small quantity of matter. **alpha-** Helium nucleus. **beta-** Electron. **colloidal-** See *colloids.* **elementary-, fundamental-** The simplest unit of matter not as yet shown to be subdivisible. At present 32 elementary particles have been identified or are believed to exist; e.g.: baryon, lepton, meson, photon. **gamma-** A misnomer for cathode rays. **nuclear-** See *subatomic p.* **subatomic-** Nuclear p. A "building stone" of matter. Fundamental characteristics: mass (units of proton mass), charge (electron units), spin (unit, $h/2\pi$), magnetic moment (Bohr magnetons), process of generation, destruction, and interconversion. Subatomic particles are shown in the table.

Charge	Mass of 1/1,800 H	Mass of 1 H
-1	Electron (negatron) e^- or $-$	Negative proton
0	Neutrino (photon) $_0n^0$	Neutron $_0n^1$
$+1$	Positron (oreston) e^+ or $+$	Proton p or $_1H^1$

Also the deuteron (diplon) of mass 2, and the particle of mass 4. Cf. *electron, neutron, neutrino, meson, photon, positron, proton.*

    p. board. A panel material made essentially from particles of wood and/or other lignocellulosic material (as, sawdust, flax shives) bonded with an organic binder. **p. distribution.** See *Perrin equation.*

parting. In assaying, the dissolution of silver from gold by means of nitric acid. **p. acids.** Nitric acid of graded strengths used in the stages of parting.

partinium. An alloy of tungsten and aluminum.

partition. The distribution of a substance or ions between 2 immiscible liquids, or between a liquid and a gas. **p. chromatography.** See *chromatography.* **p. coefficient.** Distribution coefficient. See *Perrin equation.* **p. function.** A thermodynamic function expressing the sum of the energy levels of an atomic system; $f = \Sigma e^{-E/TK}$, where E is the energy of the J level, K is Boltzmann's constant, and T is the absolute temperature. **p. law.** *Nernst's law.*

partridge berry. (1) Squaw vine. (2) Gaultheria.

Partz cell. An anode of amalgamated zinc in a solution of magnesium sulfate, and a cathode of carbon in a solution of potassium dichromate (2.06 volts).

parvoline. $C_9H_{13}N = 135.2.$ **alpha-** 2-Ethyl-3,5-dimethylpyridine. A ptomaine from decaying fish or meat. Amber oil, with odor of hawthorn blossoms, b.188. **beta-** See *parvuline.*

parvuline. $C_9H_{13}N = 135.2.$ *v*-Tetramethylpyridine, β-parvoline. A homolog of pyridine, and an isomer of parvoline in coal tar. Amber liquid, b.228.

PAS. Common name for *p*-aminosalicylic acid. See *salicylic.*

Pascal, Blaise. 1623–1662. French scientist and philosopher. **P.'s law.** The pressure applied to a liquid at any point is transmitted equally in all directions.

Paschen, F. 1865–1947. German physicist. **P. galvanoscope.** A sensitive milliamperemeter. **P.**

series. The spectrum lines produced when electrons fall from an outer orbit to the third ring. Cf. *Balmer* and *Lyman series, energy levels, Bohr theory.*

pasque flower. Pulsatilla.

passiflora. Passionflower.

Passiflorinae. A plant order comprising the families: *Passifloraceae, Caricaceae,* and *Begoniaceae.*

passionflower. Passiflora. The dried herb of *Passiflora incarnata* (Passifloraceae), N. America; a sedative. The fruit juice is a beverage.

passive. Not active. **p. immunization.** The process by which the blood serum of an actively immunized animal is injected into another animal, for protection against bacterial invasions. **p. metal.** Metal rendered noncorrodible by treatment with heat or strong acids. This property is sometimes lost by mechanical shock. **p. state.** See *passivity.*

passivity. The inertness of certain substances under conditions in which chemical activity is expected; e.g.: certain metals dissolve in acids of low, but not high, concentration, owing to the formation of a thin layer of peroxide, oxygen, or salt, which prevents direct contact of acid and metal. Mechanical shock can destroy this layer. Cf. *zone.*

paste. (1) A tenacious cementing substance. (2) A pharmaceutical preparation containing antiseptics for external use. (3) A poison preparation for exterminating vermin and rats. (4) A mixture of clay and water for making stoneware or porcelain. (5) A matrix in which minerals are embedded. **dextrin-** A 40% solution of dextrin in water, containing glucose 2, glycerin 2, alum 0.6, formaldehyde 0.16%. **London-** A mixture of equal weights sodium hydroxide and slaked lime, moistened with alcohol. **phosphorus-** A rat poison made of phosphorus and flour. **vienna-** A mixture of sodium hydroxide and slaked lime, moistened with water.

    p. blue. Prussian blue. **p. board.** Cardboard formed by pasting high-grade outer layers of paper (a pasting) on to a lower-grade middle layer or layers. It differs from ordinary board, which is formed directly without an adhesive.

Pasteur, Louis. 1822–1895. French chemist who established the connection between bacterial growth and disease, and laid the foundation of immunology. **P. effect.** P. reaction. Cells of yeast and other organisms which can ferment sugar, irrespective of the presence of oxygen, are more active in this respect in the absence of oxygen. **P. filter.** See *filter.* **P. flask.** A glass flask for bacterial cultures with a long neck bent downward and upward with constrictions and expansions. Opposite the neck is a tubular outlet. **P. reaction.** P. effect.

pasteuring. Pasteurizing.

pasteurization. Partial sterilization of organic fluids by heating at 65°C for not less than 30 min. Cf. *Stassanization.* **flash-** Continuous p. by passing the liquid through a coil surrounded by live steam. **H.T.S.T.-** Abbreviation for high-temperature, short-time p. The liquid, e.g., milk, is held at not less than 72.5°C for not less than 15 sec. and then cooled at once to 12.5°C.

pasteurized milk. Milk that has been partly sterilized by heating at 63 to 66°C at least 30 min, and then immediately cooled to 12°C.

pasteurizer. A machine for pasteurization.

pastil, pastille. A lozenge, sugared confection, or aromatic mass burnt as incense or fumigant.

pasting. See *pasteboard*.

patchoulene. $C_{15}H_{24} = 204.19$. A sesquiterpene, d.0.930, b.256, from patchouli oil.

patchouli. Patchouly. The herb *Pogostemon patchouli* (Labiatae), India, used in perfumery. **p. oil.** An essential oil from the leaves of patchouli. Yellow, aromatic oil, d.0.970, insoluble in water. It contains cadinene, eugenol, cinnamic aldehyde; used in perfumery.

patchoulin. $C_{15}H_{26}O = 222.2$. A terpene from patchouli oil. Colorless crystals, m.59.

patchouly. Patchouli.

patent. (1) A grant conveying public lands from the government. (2) Letters (of) patent. Any process, method, or device that has been accepted as new by the Patent Office and is, thereby, protected under the patent laws for a number of years. (3) Evident, not hidden. **provisional-** An official application for a patent, which gives temporary protection at relatively small cost until the final patent is granted. **p. blue.** A phenylated rosaniline disulfonic acid; a redox indicator. **p. yellow.** $PbO \cdot PbCl_2$. Mineral yellow. A yellow pigment.

Patera process. A method of producing silver by chloridizing the ore, roasting, and leaching successively with water and sodium hyposulfite solution, which dissolves the silver; precipitation with sodium sulfide follows, and finally heating the resulting silver sulfide.

path. (1) Orbit. (2) The course or track along which electrons, ions, or molecules move. See *Wilson method*. **free-** The average distance between collisions in the travel of a molecule in a gas or liquid.

pathochemistry. Chemical pathology. The study of the chemical changes of the living organism in a diseased condition.

pathogen. Any microorganism, bacterium, or protozoon that produces disease.

pathogenic. Describing an agent that produces disease.

pathologic. Pertaining to a diseased condition. **p. reaction.** A chemical test to diagnose disease.

pathology. The study of the nature of disease; especially the functional (physiological) and structural (morphological) changes produced. **experimental-** The study of artificially produced disease. **phyto-** The study of plant diseases.

patina. The thin and often multicolored coat of oxides formed on metallic surfaces. Cf. *brochanite*.

patronite. V_2S_3. A native sulfide.

pattern. (1) A design or arrangement of symbols or figures. (2) A model from which a cast is made. **crystal-** A space lattice of crystal structure, q.v. **Laue-** See *Laue diagram*.

Pattinson process. A former separation of silver from lead, by fractional crystallization and removal of the molten, silver-free lead crystals. Superseded by the Parkes process, q.v.

patulin. $(C_7H_{60}O_4)_x$. Anhydro-3-hydroxymethylenetetrahydro-γ-pyrone-2-carboxylic acid. An antibiotic from certain molds, e.g., *Penicillium patulum*, m.111. A suggested cure for the common cold. It behaves similarly to gram-positive and gram-negative organisms. Believed to be identical with clavacin.

paucine. $C_{27}H_{38}O_5N_5 = 512.3$. An alkaloid from the seeds of pauco nuts. Yellow scales, m.126, insoluble in ether. $C_{27}H_{39}O_5N_5 \cdot 2HCl \cdot 6H_2O = 693.4$. Colorless needles, m.245, slightly soluble in water.

pauco nuts. Graine d'owala. The fruits of *Pentaclethra macrophylla* (Leguminosae), Africa, which contain paucine.

Pauli, Wolfgang. 1900–1958. Austrian physicist. Nobel Prize winner (1945). **P.'s principle.** Exclusion principle. The number of electrons in a shell or orbit is limited. No 2 electrons can have, simultaneously, all 4 quantum numbers the same. Cf. *correspondence principle*. **P. rule.** The atomic nucleus has alternately odd and even numbers of α particles.

Pauling, Linus C. b. 1901. American chemist. Nobel Prize winner (1954). **P. structure.** A structure of the benzene molecule based on an electronic conception of the interatomic bonds. Each bond results from 2 electrons moving in orbits around the 2 nuclei of the atoms they join.

paullinia (paullinio) tannin. $C_{38}H_{36}O_{29} = 800.2$. Guaranatannin. White crystals from the seeds of *Paullinia cupana* (Sapindaceae) Brazil, used similarly to cacao.

pavemal. The phenyl ethyl barbiturate of papaverine; a hypnotic.

pavine. $C_{20}H_{23}O_4N = 341.2$. 2,4-Dihydropapaverine. White needles, m.201, soluble in chloroform.

Pavy's solution. (A) 4.158 gm copper sulfate in 500 ml water. (B) 20.4 gm sodium potassium tartrate, 20.4 gm potassium hydroxide, 300 ml strong ammonia, and water to make 500 ml. Mix in equal parts. To determine sugars, titrate into boiling P. solution until the blue color vanishes. Cuprous oxide is not precipitated as with ordinary Fehling's solution, q.v.

pawpaw. The seeds of the edible fruit of *Asimina triloba* (Anonaceae), E. United States; an emetic. Cf. *papaw*.

Payen, Anselme. 1795–1871. French chemist noted for industrial processes (decolorizing with charcoal).

Payne's process. Paynization. Making wood fireproof by successive treatments with ferrous sulfate and calcium chloride solutions.

paynize. To treat wood by Payne's process.

pay ore. An ore, rock, earth, or gravel that can be worked with profit.

payta. Krameria.

paytine. $C_{21}H_{24}ON_2 = 320.2$. An alkaloid, m.156, from cinchona bark.

Pb. Symbol for lead.

p.c.e. Abbreviation for pyrometric (q.v.) cone equivalent.

p.d. Abbreviation for potential difference.

Pd. Symbol for palladium.

pdl. Abbreviation for poundal.

pe- A syllable indicating a higher degree of saturation or of hydrogenation; as, pyridine and piperidine

peach. The edible fruit of *Prunus persica* (Rosaceae). **p. aldehyde.** γ-Undecalactone. **p. bark.** The bark of p.; a sedative. **p. kernel oil.** Persic oil (U.S.P.). Yellow liquid, d.0.915, m.—15, sapon. val. 189–192, iodine val. 93.5, insoluble in water; an adulterant for almond oil, and flavoring. **p.**

leaves. The dried leaves of the p. tree; a diuretic and stimulant.

peacock copper. Bornite.

peanut. The edible seeds of *Arachis hypogoea* (Leguminosae), of the temperate zones. It contains the globulins arachin and conarachin, q.v. Cf. *ardil.* **p. hull meal.** Ground p. shells; a fertilizer (1.5–2.5 % nitrogen). **p. oil.** Arachis oil, groundnut oil, earthnut oil, oil of katchung. Yellow oil expressed from peanuts, d.0.916, sapon. val. 188–196, iodine val. 103–104, insoluble in water. Used as a vehicle in pharmacy (U.S.P.), an adulterant of olive oil, and in poor-grade soap. Cf. *Bellier's test.* **p. ore.** Wolframite.

pearl. A calcareous secretion from various species of mollusks, chiefly oyster. **artificial-** (1) Culture p. (2) Synthetic p. **culture-** A natural p. produced by artificial stimulation of the oyster; as, insertion of a grain of sand. **imitation-** An imitation of natural pearls that produces only the outside appearance; as, alabaster coated with p. essence. **synthetic-** A p. made by slow precipitation from a gelatinous solution of certain salts.

    p. alum. Aluminum sulfate for paper manufacture. **p. ash.** Impure calcined potassium carbonate, made from potash. **p. essence.** A product obtained from fish scales, e.g., of European minnow, the principal constituent being guanine; used to obtain a highly lustrous coating, as, on imitation pearls. **p. grain.** 0.25 meter-carat. A unit of weight for pearls. **p. hardening.** Gypsum used as a paper filler. **p. mica.** Margarite. **p. opal.** A bluish white, lustrous opal. **p. powder.** A form of bismuth oxychloride; a cosmetic. **p. sinter.** A modification of silica. **p. spar.** Brown spar. A dolomite with pearly luster. **p. stone.** Perlite. **p. white.** (1) Lithopone. (2) Calcium sulfate for the paper industry. (3) $Bi(OH)_2 \cdot NO_3$. A form of bismuth subnitrate used medicinally, and formerly as a cosmetic.

pearlite. (1) A eutectic mixture: soft α-ferrite 87, hard cementite 13%, containing 0.9% carbon, formed during the slow cooling of molten steel. (2) Perlite, q.v.

pear oil. An alcoholic flavoring solution of amyl acetate.

peastone. Oolite.

peat. Dark soil produced by the decomposition of plants in moist places: water 25, ash 3, woody fiber 50, humus acids 22, nitrogen 1.5–2.5 %. A fuel, mud bath, and fertilizer. Cf. *dopplerite, ulmic acid.* **p. coal.** A soft coal, intermediate between p. and lignite. **p. coke.** A carbonized p. produced by destructive distillation. **p. gas.** A hydrocarbon gas obtained by distilling p. **p. tar.** A tar obtained by distilling p. **p. wax.** Mona wax. A black wax extracted by alcohol from p.; a substitute for montan wax.

pebble. A small stone, worn round by the action of water. **Brazilian-** A rock crystal or quartz, from which lenses are cut.

    p. mill. A power-driven, rotating steel cylinder with a porcelain lining, or steel, and partly filled with flint pebbles, porcelain, or metal balls for pulverizing or mixing materials. Cf. *ball mill, agate mill.* **p. powder.** Gunpowder pressed into large cubical grains.

PeCe. Trade name for a series of polyvinyl chloride synthetic fibers.

peck. Pk. A dry measure or unit of capacity in the U.S. and U.K. systems: 1 peck = 0.25 bushel = 2 gallons.

pectase. A nitrogeneous ferment in fruits, that converts pectin into pectic acid; used to clarify fruit juices.

pectate. A salt of pectic acid.

pectenine. A tetanic poison alkaloid from the cactus *Cereus poespitosus* or *C. pecten* (Mexico).

pectic acid. $C_{17}H_{24}O_{16} = 484.2$. A dibasic acid obtained from ripe fruit or vegetable pectin by enzyme action or long boiling with alkali. It forms a jelly with calcium salts (as in the setting of jams and fruit preserves). **para-** See *parapectic acid.*

pectinase. An enzyme that coagulates pectins by converting them to pectic acid.

Pectinol. Trademark for pectase.

pectinose. Arabinose.

pectins. Compounds formed from the protopectin of unripe fruits, whose function in ripe fruits is the cementation of individual cells. P. are (usually methyl) esters of polygalacturonic acid, and on hydrolysis form pectic acid in overripe fruits, which gives the juice the property of jelling.

pectization. Gelatinization.

pectocellulose. A substance from raw flax, which yields pectic acid and cellulose.

pectograph. The pattern obtained by drying a film of colloidal solution on a glass plate.

pectolinarigenin. $C_{13}H_{14}O_6 = 314.1$. 5,7-Dihydroxy-6,4'-dimethoxyflavone. Yellow needles, m.-215, slightly soluble in alcohol. Cf. *pectolinarin.*

pectolinarin. $C_{29}H_{34}O_{15} = 622.3$. A glucoside from the flowers of *Linaria vulgaris*, Linn., m.240 (decomp.), hydrolyzed to pectolinarigenin.

pectolite. $4CaO \cdot Na_2O \cdot 6SiO_2 \cdot H_2O$. Ratholite. A native hydrated acid silicate.

pectolysis. The clearing of fruit juices by the decomposition of pectin by pectase.

pectosase. An enzyme that separates the middle lamella of plants from the cell walls. Cf. *pectase.*

pectose. A polysaccharide in fruits and vegetables, from which pectins are formed on ripening.

pectosinic acid. $C_{32}H_{23}O_{31} = 903.2$. An amorphous acid derived from pectose by treatment with alkali. It forms gelatinous salts.

pedesis. Brownian movement.

pedology. The science of the soil.

peganine. Vasicine.

peganite. Variscite.

Peganum harmala. The commonest weed of the Russian and Siberian steppes. Its seeds contain harmaline and harmine, used in the Orient to prepare turkey-red dye.

pegmatite. Giant granite. An igneous rock of coarse-grained quartz, feldspar, muscovite, tourmaline, and biotite. Some pegmatites are a source of lithia minerals, rare earth, tin, tungsten, tantalum, or uranium minerals.

pegnin. A mixture of milk sugar and rennet; used to treat stomachic disturbances.

pegu catechu. Catechu.

pelagic. Pertaining to the deep sea. Cf. *littoral.*

pelagite. $xMnO_2 \cdot yFe_2O_3 \cdot 2H_2O$. A mineral.

pelargonaldehyde. $C_8H_{17}CHO = 142.1$. Nonanal*, *n*-nonylicaldehyde, in citron oil; used in perfumes.

pelargone. 9-Heptadecanone*.

pelargonic acid. $C_8H_{17}COOH = 158.2$. Nonanoic acid*, nondecylic acid, octanecarboxylic acid. An oxidation product of oleic acid, and a constituent of oil of *Pelargonium roseum*. Colorless leaflets, m.12, soluble in water; a flavoring.

pelargonidin. $C_{15}H_{10}O_5 \cdot HCl = 306.53$. An anthocyanidin from the flowers of *Pelargonium* species (Geraniaceae.)

pelargonin. Pelargonidin glucoside. An anthocyan from dahlia, geranium, and other flowers. Cf. *callistephin*. **p. chloride.** $C_{27}H_{31}O_{15}Cl \cdot 4H_2O = 702.7$. A pigment closely allied to that from scarlet pelargonium.

pelargononitrile. Nonane nitrile*.

pelargonyl. Nonanoyl*. The radical $C_8H_{17}CO$—, from pelargonic acid. **p. chloride.** Nonanoyl chloride*.

pelidisi. $10W/cm^3$, where W is the weight in grams and cm the sitting height in centimeters of a person; used in the calculation of normal diets.

Péligot, Eugène Melchior. 1811–1872. French chemist. **P. blue.** A hydrated copper oxide pigment. **P. salt.** Probably the potassium salt of the unknown chlorochromic acid, $K(CrO_3Cl)$, obtained by heating potassium dichromate with hydrochloric acid. **P. tube.** A calcium chloride tube or U tube with a bulb in each arm, and in the bend.

pelitic. Describing rocks essentially of clay origin, e.g., slate.

pellagra. Lesions of the mucous membrane due to deficiency of certain vitamins.

Pelletan, Pierre. 1782–1845. French chemist noted for his *Dictionnaire de Chimie* (1821).

Pelletier, Pierre Joseph. 1788–1842. French pharmacist who discovered toluene and several alkaloids (with Caventou). Cf. *Peltier*.

pelletierine. $C_8H_{15}ON = 141.1$. Punicine. A pyrrolidine alkaloid obtained from the root bark of pomegranate, *Punica granatum*. Brown oil, insoluble in water; an anthelmintic. **iso-** An alkaloid which occurs with pelletierine. **pseudo-** $C_9H_{15}ON = 153.2$. Yellow crystals, soluble in water.
    p. hydrochloride. Brown syrup, soluble in water; used medicinally. **p. sulfate.** Brown syrup, soluble in water; a teniacide. **p. tannate.** Brown mass, slightly soluble in water; an anthelmintic.

pellicle. (1) A thin skin. (2) The crust forming on the surface of a saturated solution during evaporation.

pellitory root. Pyrethrum.

pellote. (Mexican "peyotl.") Mescal buttons.

pellotine. $C_{13}H_{19}O_3N = 237.2$. An alkaloid from pellote, the dried cactus *Anhalonium williamsi* (Mexico). Colorless crystals, m.110, slightly soluble in water; a hypnotic. Cf. *mescaline*. **p. hydrochloride.** $C_{11}H_{13}ON(OMe)_2 \cdot HCl = 273.6$. Colorless crystals, soluble in water; a hypnotic.

pelopium. Impure niobium. A supposed element, isolated by Rose (1846) from tantalite.

peloponium. Columbium.

pelosine. Bebeerine.

pelotherapy. Treatment by external application of natural products; as, mud.

Peltier, Jean Charles Athanase. 1785–1845. French watchmaker and experimenter. Cf. *Pelletier*. **P. effect.** If a current passes through a circuit containing a thermocouple, heat is evolved at one junction and adsorbed at the other. Cf. *Kelvin* and *Joule effect*.
    coefficient of- The ratio of the quantity of heat applied to a thermocouple to the quantity of electricity obtained from it.

pemphigus alcohol. $C_{34}H_{70}O_2 = 510.5$. A solid, m.100–105, from the wax of the insect *Pemphigus xylostei*.

pemphigic acid. $C_{33}H_{66}(OH)COOH = 524.5$. From the wax of the insect *Pemphigus xylostei*; m.101.

pempidine. $C_{11}H_9N = 155.82$. 1,2,2,6,6-Pentamethylpiperidine; used to treat hypertension, as the tartrate (B.P.).

penagar. A 0.5% aqueous solution of agar containing penicillin; used for the inhalation of penicillin as an aerosol.

penatin. Notatin.

Penbritin. See *penicillin*.

pencil. (1) A roll or stick that contains an active substance in its center; as, a litmus p., wax p. (2) An aggregation of light rays meeting in a point.

pencil stone. Pyrophyllite.

penetration. (1) Entering or piercing. (2) The hardness or consistency of a material expressed as the distance that a standard needle passes vertically into it under conditions of loading (100 gm), time (5 sec) and temperature (25°C). (3) The focal distance or depth of a lens. (4) The passage of radiations through materials.

penetrometer. A device to measure penetration (2) or (4), q.v. Cf. *gelometer*.

Penex process. The catalytic isomerization of light naphthas.

penicidin. An antibiotic from a species of *Penicillium*.

penicillamine. $C_6H_{11}O_4N \cdot HCl(?)$. β,β-Dimethylcysteine. An optically inactive product of penicillin.

penicillanic acid. 6-amino- $C_8H_{12}O_3N_2S = 216.33$. An antibiotic less potent than penicillin, isolated (1959) from strains of *Penicillium chrysogenum*. White crystals, m.208 (decomp.).

penicillic acid. $C_8H_{10}O_4 = 170.1$. The γ-keto-β-methoxy-δ-methylene-Δ-α-hexenoic acid, an antibiotic from *Penicillium puberulum*.

penicillin. (1) Originally a thermostable substance isolated from the mold *Penicillium luteum purpurogenum*, which inhibits the production of citric acid by *Aspergillus niger* (Palei and Osuicheva, 1936). (2) Penicillin G. (3) Now describes the antibiotic principle of certain molds, *Penicillium notatum* in particular, having a selective bacteriostatic effect on certain gram-positive bacteria in high dilutions, and used widely in medicine. Cf. *notatin*. There are at least 11 penicillins; 5 are commercial products. They differ according to the nature of the group R in the formula,

$$
\begin{array}{c}
\text{S} \\
\text{H} \cdot \text{C} \qquad \text{CMe}_2 \\
R \cdot \text{CONH} \cdot \text{H} \cdot \text{C} \quad \text{N} \text{—CH} \cdot \text{COOH} \\
\text{C:O}
\end{array}
$$

U.S. common name	U.K. common name	Chemical name	R group
P. G	P. II	Benzyl-p.	$C_6H_5 \cdot CH_2-$
P. K	P. IV	n-Heptyl-p.	$Me(CH_2)_5CH_2-$
P. X	P. III	p-Hydroxybenzyl-p.	p-$OH \cdot C_6H_4 \cdot CH_2-$
P. F	P. I	2-Pentenyl-p.	$Me \cdot CH_2CH : CH_2-$
Dihydro-p. F	Dihydro-p. I	n-Amyl-p.	$Me(CH_2)_3CH_2-$
	P. V	Phenoxymethyl-p.	$CH_2 \cdot O \cdot C_6H_5-$

Official penicillins (1967) are: *U.S.P.*, *B.P.*: benzyl p.G., benzathine p., procaine p., phenoxymethyl p., potassium phenoxymethyl p.; *B.P.*: calcium phenoxymethyl p. The unit of p. activity is 0.0005988 mg. of the dry crystalline salt = 1,670 units/mg (B.P.); it almost equals the oxford unit, q.v. **benzathine p.G.** $C_{16}H_{20}N_2(C_{16}H_{18}O_4N_2S)_2 =$ 909.20. A white powder containing not less than 1,200 units of p. activity per mg, slightly soluble in water; used similarly to p. injection (B.P.). **p.G.** Benzyl-p. **benzyl-p.** $C_{17}H_{17}O_4N_2S = 344.42.$ White, birefringent particles, which exist as the sodium or potassium salt, soluble in water; used similarly to p. (B.P.). P. derivatives are now manufactured synthetically under the following principal trade names:

Brocillin. Potassium propicillin or potassium α-phenoxypropylpenicillin. Well absorbed orally and gives blood levels considerably higher than those achieved with penicillin G or potassium penicillin V.

Broxil, Maxipen. Potassium phenethicillin, potassium α-phenoxyethylpenicillin. Has a spectrum of antibacterial activity similar to that of penicillins G and V, but being better absorbed orally, gives considerably higher blood levels.

Celbenin. Sodium methicillin or sodium 6-(2,6-dimethoxy)benzamidopenicillanate monohydrate. The first penicillin to be effective against resistant staphylococci.

Orbenin. Sodium cloxacillin or 3-o-chlorophenyl-5-methylisoxazolylpenicillin sodium salt monohydrate. Stable to acid and to staphylococcal penicillinase; highly active against sensitive staphylococci and other gram-positive organisms.

Penbritin. Ampicillin or D($-$)d-aminobenzylpenicillin. Has greater activity than the tetracyclines and chloramphenicol against a wide range of organisms; it is bactericidal but free from side effects associated with other antibiotics.

penicillinase. Neutrapen. An enzyme from cultures of *Bacillus cereus*; it hydrolyzes benzylpenicillin to penicilloic acid.

penicillinum. Official B.P. name for penicillin.

penicilliopsin. $C_{30}H_{24}O_8 = 512.2.$ Mycoporphyrin. A pigment from the mycelia of molds. Orange needles, m.330.

Penicillium. A genus of Ascomycetes, fungi of the mildew group. **P. glaucum.** Blue mold. The common mold, e.g., of bread. It excites alcoholic fermentation and separates d- and l-tartrates from racemic mixtures, since the d isomer is acted on faster than the l.

penillic acid. $C_{14}H_{22}O_4N_2S = 314.42.$ A product of the catalytic hydrogenation of penicillin. Thick, d-rotatory rods, m.182, with blue fluorescence.

pennine. Penninite.

penninite. Pennine. A green crystalline chlorite from the Pennines, England.

pennone. $CMe_3 \cdot CMe_2 \cdot CO \cdot Me = 142.1.$ Tetramethyl pentanone. Colorless crystals, m.63.

pennyroyal. (1) *Hedeoma pulegoides* of N. America; (2) *Mentha pulegium* of Europe. **p. oil. American-** The essential oil of *Hedeoma* species (Labiatae), d.0.920–0.935, containing pulegone and hedeomol. **European-** The essential oil of *Mentha pulegium*, d.0.930–0.960.

pennyweight. (dwt). A unit of weight in the English system: 1 pennyweight = 24 grains = 0.05 troy ounce = 1.5552 grams.

Pensky-Martens apparatus. An instrument for determining flash points.

penta(a)- Prefix (Greek) indicating five.

pentaamino- Prefix indicating 5 amino groups in an organic compound. See *pentamino-*.

pentaatomic. Pentatomic.

pentabasic. Describing a compound that has 5 H atoms replaceable by bases or metals.

pentaborane. B_5H_9 or B_5H_{11}. Cf. *boron hydrides*.

pentabromo- Describing a compound that has 5 Br atoms in its molecule. **p. benzene.** $C_6HBr_5 =$ 472.6. Colorless needles, m.159, insoluble in water.

pentacarboxylic. Describing a compound containing 5 carboxyl groups.

pentacetate. A mixture of amyl alcohol 20 and amyl acetate 80%, b.128–148.

pentachloro- Indicating a compound containing 5 Cl atoms. **p. aniline.** $C_6Cl_5NH_2 = 265.33.$ Colorless needles, m.232; soluble in alcohol. **p. benzene.** $C_6HCl_5 = 250.3.$ Colorless needles, d.0.769, m.85, insoluble in water. **p. ethane.** $CCl_3CHCl_2 = 202.3.$ Colorless liquid, d.1.834, b.161, insoluble in water; a solvent. **p. phenol.** $C_6Cl_5OH = 266.51.$ Gray flakes, with phenolic odor, m.191; a pesticide.

pentacosamic acid. Cerebronic acid.

pentacosane. $C_{25}H_{52} = 352.4.$ A hydrocarbon from beeswax, m.54, insoluble in water.

pentacyclic. Describing a molecule with (1) 5 atomic rings; or (2) a ring of 5 atoms.

pentad. An element or radical having a valency of 5.

pentadecane*. $C_{15}H_{32} = 212.3.$ Normal pentadecane, in the oil from the rhizomes of *Kampheria galanga*. Colorless liquid, d.769, b.270, insoluble in water. **p. carboxylic acid.** Palmitic acid.

pentadecanoic acid. $C_{14}H_{29}COOH = 242.23.$ Isocetic acid, n-pentadecylic acid. Colorless solid, m.54, $d_{m100m}257$, occurring in agaricus.

pentadecanol*. $C_{15}H_{31}OH = 228.25.$ Pentadecyl alcohol. Colorless crystals, m.44.

pentadecanone*. $C_{15}H_{30}O = 226.23.$ **2-** Methyl tridecyl ketone. **3-** Ethyl dodecyl ketone. **8-** $[Me(CH_2)_6]_2CO.$ Diheptyl ketone, caprylone. Colorless crystals, m.40, soluble in alcohol.

pentadecyl. The radical $C_{15}H_{31}$— from pentadecane. **p. alcohol.** Pentadecanone.

pentadiene*. $C_5H_8 = 68.06$. **1,2-** CH_2:C:$CH·CH_2$-CH_3. Ethylallene. Colorless liquid, b.45. **1,3-** CH_3:$CH·CH$:$CH·CH_3$. α-Methyl bivinyl, piperylene. Colorless liquid, d.0.696, b.43. **1,4-** (CH_2:-$CH)_2CH_2$. Colorless liquid, d.0.6594, b.26. Cf. *pentinene*. **p. carboxylic acid.** Sorbic acid.

pentadienone. (CH_2:$CH)_2CO = 82.05$. Divinyl ketone. **diphenyl-** Styryl ketone.

pentadigalloylglucose. $C_{72}H_{52}O_{46} = 1,700.4$. A tannin from Chinese nutgalls. **alpha-** Brown mass, soluble in water. **beta-** Less soluble in water.

pentaerythrite. $C(CH_2OH)_4 = 136.12$. A liquid, b.161.

pentaerythritol. $C_5H_{12}O_4 = 136.12$. An isomer of pentaerythrite. Colorless solid, m.261. It forms polyesters with organic acids; used in plastics manufacture, and as a vasodilator (B.P.). **p. tetranitrate.** $C(CH_2NO_3)_4 = 316.13$. Penthrite. Colorless crystals, m.141; a powerful explosive.

pentaethylbenzene. $C_6HEt_5 = 218.2$. Colorless liquid, d.0.89, b.277, insoluble in water.

pentagalloyl glucose. $C_{41}H_{32}O_{26} = 940.2$. A yellow tannin soluble in water.

pentaglucose. Pentose.

pentaglycol. $Me_2C·(CH_2OH)_2 = 104.12$. A solid, m.129, soluble in water.

pentahydro- Prefix indicating 5 H atoms, or 5 additional H atoms; as, pentahydropyrane.

pentahydroxy- Prefix indicating 5 hydroxy groups. **p. pentane.** $C_5H_7(OH)_5 = 152.12$. A liquid, b.102.

pentaiodo- Prefix indicating 5 iodine atoms in the molecule.

Pental. Me_2C=$CHMe = 70.1$. Trademark for trimethylethylene; β-isoamylene. Colorless liquid, d.0.678, b.38, insoluble in water; a hypnotic and anesthetic; used in the manufacture of *tert*-amyl alcohol.

pentaline. Pentachloroethane.

pentamethyl- Prefix indicating 5 methyl groups in the molecule. **p. benzene.** $C_6HMe_5 = 148.0$. Colorless crystals, m.56, insoluble in water. **p. benzoic acid.** $Me_5C_6COOH = 192.2$. Colorless needles, m.210, soluble in water. **p. phenol.** $Me_5C_6OH = 164.1$. Colorless needles, m.125, insoluble in water.

pentamethylen- Prefix indicating 5 methylene groups in a molecule.

pentamethylene. (1) The radical —$CH_2(CH_2)_3CH_2$—. (2) $(CH_2)_5 = 70.1$. Tetrahydrocyclopenten, cyclopentane, cyclopentamethylene. Colorless liquid, b.50, insoluble in water; a constituent of Russian petroleum. **hydroxy-** Cyclopentanol*. **keto-** Cyclopentanol*.

p. amine. Piperidine. **p. bromide.** 1,5-Dibromopentane. **p. diamine.** Cadaverine. **p. oxide.** Tetrahydropyran. **p. tetrazole.** See *Metrazol*.

pentamidine isothionate. $C_{19}H_{24}O_2N_4·2C_2H_6O_4S = 592.69$. White, hygroscopic crystals, m.190, soluble in water; used to treat trypanosomiasis.

pentamino- Prefix indicating 5 amino groups in the molecule. **p. benzene.** $C_6H(NH_2)_5 = 153.1$. Colorless needles, soluble in water.

Pentamul. Trade name for a group of emulsifiers.

pentane*. $C_5H_{12} = 72.12$. Amylhydride. A saturated methane hydrocarbon. Colorless liquid, d.0.634, b.36, insoluble in water; an anesthetic, refrigerant, and thermometer filling. **amino-** Amylamine. **bromo-*** Amyl bromide. **chloro-*** Amyl chloride. **ethoxy-*** Amyl ethyl ether. **iodo-*** Amyl iodide. **iso-** Me_2CHCH_2Me. Secondary p. Dimethylethylmethane, 1,1,2-trimethylethane. Colorless liquid, d.0.622, b.30. **methoxy-*** Amyl methyl ether. **normal-** Pentane. **secondary-** Isopentane. **tertiary-** CMe_4. Tetramethylmethane. Colorless liquid or gas, b.10; a constituent of coal oil and gas. **tetrahydro-** Cyclopentane.

p. carboxylic acid. Caproic acid. **p. diamine, 1,5-** Cadaverine. **p. dicarboxylic acid*.** Pimelic acid. **p. dioic acid*.** Glutaric acid. **p. dione*.** Acetyl acetone. **p. lamp.** A photometric source of illumination. Cf. *Harcourt lamp*. **p. thermometer.** A low-temperature thermometer filled with colored p.

pentanediol*. $C_5H_{12}O_2 = 104.09$. **1,2-** $Me(CH_2)_2$-$CHOH·CH_2OH$. α-n-Amylene glycol. Colorless liquid, d.0.980, b.212. **1,4-** $MeCHOH(CH_2)_2CH_2$-OH. γ-Pentylene glycol. Colorless liquid, d.0.9954, b$_{20mm}$131. **1,5-** $CH_2OH(CH_2)_3CH_2OH$. Pentamethylene glycol. An oil, d.0.994, b.239. **2,3-** $MeCH_2(CHOH)_2·Me$. Methyl ethyl ethylene glycol, β-n-amylene glycol. Colorless liquid. d.0.9945, b.187.

pentanethiol*. $Me(CH_2)_4SH = 104.15$. Amyl mercaptan. Colorless liquid, d.0.857, b.126, insoluble in water.

pentanoic acid*. Valeric acid. **γ-keto-** Levulinic acid.

pentanol*. Amyl alcohol.

pentanone. A ketone derived from pentane; as, 2-pentanone (methyl propyl ketone). **phenyl-** Butyl phenyl ketone. **tetramethyl-** Pennone.

pentase. An enzyme that ferments pentoses.

Pentasol. Trademark for a mixture of amyl alcohols b.116–136.

pentasulfide. A compound containing 5 sulfur atoms; as, K_2S_5.

pentatomic. Describing: (1) a molecule consisting of 5 atoms; (2) a compound with 5 atoms in a ring; as, cyclopentane; (3) an acid with 5 replaceable H atoms; (4) a base, alcohol, or phenol with 5 hydroxyl groups.

pentatriacontane. $Me(CH_2)_{33}Me = 492.56$. White crystals, m.75.

pentavalent. An atom or group of atoms of valency 5.

pentazane. Pyrrolidine.

pentazdiene. A compound derived from HN:N-$NH·N$:NH.

pentazyl. The radical —N:N:N·N:N.

pentene. (1) Amylene. (2) Cyclopentane.

pentenedioic acid. Glutaconic acid.

pentenic acid. $C_5H_8O_2 = 100.06$. Pentenoic acid. **α-** or **1,2-** $EtCH$:$CHCOOH$. Propilideneacetic acid, γ-methylcrotonic acid. Colorless liquid, d.0.990, b.201. **β-** or **2,3-** $MeCH$:$CH·CH_2COOH$. Ethylidenepropionic acid. Colorless liquid, d.0.987, b.194. **γ-** or **3,4-** CH_2:$CH(CH_2)_2COOH$. Allylacetic acid. Colorless liquid, d.0.984, b.189. **dimethyl-** See *teracrylic* acid. **iso-** See *angelic* acid. **methyl-** See *pyroterebic* acid.

pentenoic acid. Pentenic acid.

pentenol. $C_5H_{10}O$ = 86.06. **1-p.-3.** CH_2:CH·· CHOH·CH_2·Me. 1-Penten-3-ol, ethylvinylcarbinol. Colorless liquid, d.0.840, b.114. **3-p.2.** Me·CHOH·CH:CHMe. Dimethylpropenylcarbinol. Colorless liquid, d.0.834, b.112. **4-p.-1.** CH_2-OH$(CH_2)_2$CH:CH_2. β-Allyl ethyl alcohol. A liquid, d.0.863, b.140. **4-p.-2.** Me·CHOH·CH₂·CH:CH_2. Allylmethylcarbinol. A liquid, d.0.834, b.116.

pentenyl. Describing a series of radicals derived from amylene; as, Δ^1. —CH:CH$(CH_2)_2$Me.

pentevalent. Pentavalent.

penthrite. Pentaerythritol tetranitrate.

pentine. Pentyne*. **p. dioic acid.** Glutinic acid.

pentinic acid. $C_6H_8O_3$ = 128.1. α-Ethyltetronic acid. Colorless crystals, m.128.

pentite. Pentitol.

pentitol. CH₂OH(CHOH)₃CH₂OH. Pentite: 5 isomers derived from the pentoses; 2 are optically active. See *arabite, xylite.* **methyl-** Rhamnite.

pentlandite. (Fe, Ni)S. A native sulfide.

pentobarbital. $C_{11}H_{18}N_2O_3$ = 226.1. Nembutal, pentabarbitone, ethyl-1-methylbutylbarbituric acid. White crystals, m.129; a hypnotic (U.S.P., B.P.). **p. sodium.** Used similarly to p. (U.S.P., B.P.).

pentobarbitone. Pentobarbital (B.P. usage).

pentoic acid. Valeric acid.

pentol. Cyclopentadiene.

pentolinium tartrate. $C_{23}H_{42}O_{12}N_2$ = 538.58. White, acidic powder, m.203 (decomp.), soluble in water; a central stimulant (U.S.P., B.P.).

pentonic acid. CH₂OH(CHOH)₃COOH. A series of pentavalent monobasic acids. See *arabonic acid.*

pentosans. A group of gums or resins (*hemi-* or *pseudocelluloses*) which hydrolyze to pentoses; as, araban. They are constituents of cell membranes of plants. **methyl-** Gums that yield methyl pentoses on hydrolysis.

pentose. $C_5H_{10}O_5$ = 150.08. Pentaglucose. A monosaccharide sugar containing 5 C atoms, fermented by yeast. See *arabinose, xylose.* **methyl-** See *rhamnose.*

pentoside. A·OP$(OH)O_2B$. A nuclein; A is a purine, B a pentose.

pentostam. Sodium stibogluconate.

Pentothal. Trademark for thiopentone sodium.

pentoxazol. 1,3[4]-Oxazine.

pentoxide. A binary compound containing 5 atoms of oxygen; as, nitrogen pentoxide, N_2O_5.

pentrite. C(CH₂O·NO₂)₄ = 316.0. Tetranitroerythrite. A high explosive.

pentyl. Amyl. The radical Me·$(CH_2)_3$·CH_2—. **p. acetate.** Amyl acetate. **p. amine.** Amylamine.

pentylene. Pentadiene. **p. tetrazol.** $C_6H_{10}N_2$ = 138.18. White, bitter crystals, m.177, soluble in water; a central stimulant.

pentylidene. Amylidene.

pentyne*. C_5H_8 = 68.06 HC:C$(CH_2)_2$Me. **1-** *n*-Pentine, propylacetylene. Colorless liquid, d.0.722, b.40. **2-** Me·C:C·Et. Ethylmethylacetylene, 2-pentine. A liquid, d.0.687, b.56. **p. dioic acid.** Glutinic acid.

Penzold's reagent. A solution of diazobenzosulfuric acid and potassium hydroxide; reagent for sugar in urine.

peonin. Aurine.

peonine. An alkaloid from the rhizome of peony, *Paeonia officinalis* (Ranunculaceae); an antispasmodic.

peonol. $C_9H_{10}O_3$ = 166.1. An aromatic ketone from the root of *Paeonia montana* (Japan). Colorless needles, of aromatic odor, m.50.

pepo. Pumpkin seed.

pepper. Piper. The dried fruit of tropical *Piper* species. **black-** The dried unripe fruits of *Piper nigrum* (Piperaceae), containing piperine, chavicine, essential oils, and a resin; a condiment and source of p. oil. **cayenne-** Red p. **Jamaica-** Pimenta. **long-** The dried, unripe fruit of *P. longum*; a carminative. **red-** The dried, ground unripe fruits of *Capsicum frutescens* (Solanaceae); a condiment. **Spanish-** Red p. **white-** Black p. without the outer skin; milder than black p. **wild-** Mezereon.

p. oil. An oil from the fruits of *Piper nigrum.* Yellow liquid, d.0.87–0.91, insoluble in water; contains cadinene, phellandrene, and dipentene.

peppermint. Mentha piperita. The dried leaves and flowering tops of *Mentha piperita* (Labiatae). Used for flavoring (U.S.P., B.P.), and to manufacture oil and menthol. **p. camphor.** Menthol. **p. oil.** An essential oil distilled from p. Colorless liquid of strong odor, d.0.91, insoluble in water (50–90% menthol). Grades: American, Chinese, English, Italian, Japanese, and Spanish; a flavoring, stimulant, antispasmodic (U.S.P., B.P.), and perfume. **p. water.** A saturated solution of p. oil in water; a carminative (U.S.P., B.P.).

pepsase. Pepsin, peptase, peptidase.

pepsin. Pepsase. Acid-proteinase. An enzyme of gastric juice that hydrolyzes proteins to proteases, peptones, and peptides, preferably in acid solution. Obtained from pigs' stomachs, as fine, white grains, slightly hygroscopic and soluble in water or dilute acid; a digestive. **vegetable-** Papain.

pepsinogen. The mother substance (zymogen) of pepsin in the cells of the stomach glands.

peptase. Pepsase.

peptidase. Pepsase.

peptide. A compound of amino acids. See *polypeptide.* **p. group.** The radical —CHR·CO·· NH—.

peptization. The change from a jelly to a liquid other than by melting.

peptolysis. The hydrolysis of peptone to amino acids.

peptolytic. An agent that splits peptones.

peptones. Simple mixtures of proteoses and amino acids, soluble in water, diffusible through parchment, not coagulated by heat; formed by the action of pepsin on albuminous bodies. Cf. *gastric digestion.* **beef-** Meat p. **casein-** Milk p. **gelatin-** P. obtained by digestion of gelatin. **meat-** An extract from fresh, lean beef treated with the digestive juices of the pancreas. Brown powder, soluble in water; a nutrient and culture medium. **meta-** A digestion product of p. **milk-** Brown powder obtained by digestion of casein, soluble in water; a nutrient for convalescents. **para-** Syntonin. **silk-** P. from silk; used in biochemical tests. **true-** Tryptone.

peptonization. The conversion of proteins into peptones.

peptonize. To change into peptone.

peptonizing powder. Pancreatin powder. **p. tube.** A parchment tube for dialyzing proteins.

peptotoxine. A ptomaine from decomposing proteins.

per- Prefix (Latin "per" = through) indicating: (1) very or more than ordinary, as, peracidity; (2) above or beyond, as, permanganate.

perabrodil. Diodone injection. **p. forte.** A mixture of the diethanolamine and diethylamine salts of 3,5-diiodo-4-pyridone-N-acetic acid; used similarly to p.

peracetic acid. $Me \cdot CO \cdot O \cdot OH = 76.03$. An isomer of methyl acetate, made by the action of hydrogen peroxide on acetic acid. Used to bleach textiles and as a selective oxidant in the formation of epoxides from olefins.

peracid, per- -acid. (1) A member of a group of inorganic acids containing peroxide oxygen, or an element in its highest valency; as, perboric acid. (2) Organic peracids containing the hypothetical radical, $-CO \cdot O \cdot OH$. True peracids give hydrogen peroxide with dilute sulfuric acid, and sometimes ozone with concentrated sulfuric acid. Cf. *hydrogen peroxide of crystallization, peri acid.*

peracidity. Excessive acidity.

Peractivin. Trade name for p-toluene sulfomonochloride; mild oxidant in textile bleaching.

Perandren. Trademark for testosterone propionate.

perborate. A salt of a perboric acid containing the radical BO_3- or $B_4O_8=$. Usually an oxidizing agent resembling hydrogen peroxide; used for bleaching and disinfecting. **meta-** A salt of the type MBO_3.

perboric acid. HBO_3. The hypothetical metaperboric acid, source of perborates. True p. acid is the parent of the salt $Na_2B_4O_8 \cdot 10H_2O$.

Perbunan. Trade name for a copolymer of butadiene and styrene. Cf. *buna.*

Perbutan. Trade name for a copolymer of butadiene and acrylic nitrile. Cf. *buna.*

Percaine. $C_{19}H_{28}O_2N_3 = 330.22$. Trademark for α-butyloxycinchoninic acid, diethyl ethylene diamide, cincaine, Nupercaine. Colorless crystals, m.97, soluble in water; a spinal analgesic.

percarbide. A binary compound of carbon containing excess of carbon.

percarbonate. A salt of the hypothetical percarbonic acid containing the radical $C_2O_6=$; decomp. in aqueous solution to hydrogen peroxide and carbonates.

percarbonic acid. $H_2C_2O_6$. The hypothetical acid, source of the percarbonates.

percentage. Parts in 100 parts by weight or volume.

perch. Rod.

perchlorate. A salt of perchloric acid containing the radical ClO_4-.

perchlorethane. Hexachlorethane.

perchlorether. $(C_2Cl_5)_2O = 418.6$. Decachlorethyl ether. Colorless scales, m.69, decomp.

perchlorethylene. Tetrachlorethylene.

perchloric acid. $HClO_4 = 100.5$. Colorless liquid, d.1.12, $b_{60mm}39$; contains 20% $HClO_4$ in water. Used as an oxidizing agent, in electroanalysis, for the destruction of organic material; and reagent for potassium. **p. anhydride.** Cl_2O_7. Chlorine heptoxide. **p. dihydrate.** $HClO_4 \cdot 2H_2O = 136.51$. A liquid oxidizing agent (72.4% p. acid), b.203. **p. ether.** Ethylperchlorate. **p. hydrate.** $HClO_4, H_2O = 118.49$. Explosive solid, m.50.

perchloride. A chloride that contains more chlorine than the corresponding normal chloride.

perchromate. A salt from perchromic acid: viz., $MCrO_5$ (deep blue) or M_3CrO_8 (deep orange-brown); rapidly decomposed in aqueous solution.

perchromic acid. $HCrO_3 = 101.1$ and H_3CrO_8, $2H_2O$, or $(OH)_4Cr(O \cdot OH)_3 = 219.06$. Two acids containing heptavalent chromium, formed by addition of hydrogen peroxide to a chromate solution (blue color); decomp. rapidly. Below $-15°C$ the H_3CrO_8 forms deep blue crystals.

percin. A ptomaine from perch and pike (78% arginine).

percolate. (1) To strain, or pass through fine interstices. (2) To extract soluble matter by the passage of water through a powdered drug. (3) The solution obtained by percolation.

percolater. Percolator.

percolator. A conical, long glass vessel, with tubulated bottom, for the extraction of drugs. **p. bottle.** A wide-mouthed graduated bottle in which the percolate is collected.

Percorten. Trademark for deoxycortone acetate.

percrystallization. The crystallization of a solute from a solution dialyzing through a membrane.

percussion. Striking a sharp blow. **p. cap.** A detonator or primer. **p. figure.** Strike figure. The radiating lines formed in certain minerals by striking them with a sharp hammer. **p. powder.** Fulminating powder. An explosive that ignites by p.

perdistillation. Distillation through a dialyzing membrane. Cf. *pervaporation.*

pereira. Pareira.

pereirine. $C_{19}H_{24}ON_2 = 296.2$. Pareirine. An alkaloid from the root of *Geissospermum laeve* (tropical America). Brown powder, m.119, insoluble in water; a quinine substitute. Cf. *geissine, vellosine.*

pereiro bark. The bark of *Geissospermum laeve* (tropical America); a tonic and antipyretic.

perezol. A 0.5% alcoholic solution of pipitzahoic acid; an indicator (acids—colorless, alkalies—deep orange).

perezon. Pipitzahoic acid.

perferrate. (1) Misnomer for ferrate, M_2FeO_4. (2) A green unstable compound of hepta- or octavalent iron, $MFeO_4$.

perforated plate. A porcelain plate with small holes; usually inserted in a funnel and covered with filter paper for rapid filtration.

perfume. A volatile, fragrant substance resembling a natural odoriferous substance in odor: (1) *natural*, if obtained by extraction of flower, herb, blossom, or plant; (2) *artificial*, if a mixture of natural oils or oil constituents; (3) *synthetic*, if a mixture of synthetically produced substances. Cf. *essential oils, odors, terpenes, flavors.*

perfusion. The passage of a fluid through spaces.

pergamyn. An artificial parchment paper (German). **echte-** Vegetable parchment (German).

pergenol. Solid hydrogen peroxide. A mixture of sodium perborate and bitartrate which, with water, gives hydrogen peroxide.

perhydrate. (1) Ortizon. (2) Peroxyhydrate.

perhydrol. (1) A 30% solution of hydrogen peroxide. Known as "100 volumes" or (inaccurately) "100%" hydrogen peroxide, q.v., because it evolves 100 times its volume of O_2. (2) A supposed combination of 2 hydroxyl groups with an inert element or compound; as, $N:N(OH)_2$.

peri- π. Prefix (Greek) meaning around. **p. acid.** 1-Naphthylamine-8-sulfonic acid. **p. bridge.** A bond between the first and eighth carbon atom of naphthalene. **p. position.** The 1,8-position of the naphthalene ring, q.v.

periclase. MgO. Native in aggregates of small cubes.

pericline. Albite.

pericyclivine. $C_{20}H_{22}N_2O_2 = 322.20$. An alkaloid from *Gabunia odoratissimi* (Apocyanoaceae).

pericyclo- Prefix describing a bond or valency that extends partly around a ring; as,

$$\begin{array}{c} O \diagdown \text{CH} \diagdown \\ \text{HC} \quad \text{CH} \\ \| \quad \| \\ \text{HC} \quad \text{CH} \\ O \diagup \text{CH} \diagup \end{array}$$

peridote. A gem variety of olivine.

peridotites. A group of crystalline, igneous rocks; chiefly olivine.

perifringens. A gas-gangrene antitoxin.

perigee. The point in the moon's orbit at which it is nearest the earth. Cf. *apogee*.

perihelion. The point of the orbit of a heavenly body at which it is nearest to the sun. Cf. *aphelion*. Applied to the electron in relation to the nucleus.

perikinetic. Concerning Brownian motion. Cf. *orthokinetic*.

perilla alcohol. $C_{10}H_{16}O_4 = 200.12$. Colorless solid from palmarosa and naal oils. Cf. *parilla*.

perilogic series. The allologic series of pyrene: C_{10}-H_8, $C_{16}H_{10}$, $C_{22}H_{12}$, etc.

perimeter. The sum of the lengths of the bounding lines of a figure.

perimidyl. Eight isomeric radicals, $C_{11}H_7N_2$—, from perimidine.

perimorph. A mineral that encloses another. Cf. *endomorph*.

perinaphthodiazine. $C_{12}H_8N_2 = 180.1$. *N*-naphthodiazine. A group of isomers of naphthodiazine and naphthisodiazine (1,2-, 1,3-, 1,4-).

perinaphthotriazole. $C_{10}H_7N_3 = 169.2$. π-Naphthotriazole. A series of compounds isomeric with naphthotriazole and naphthisotriazole (α- or 1,2,3-; β- or 2,1,3-).

period. (1) A regular interval between recurring phenomena. (2) A set of elements in the periodic system, q.v. (3) A family of closely related elements with consecutive atomic numbers; as, 24Cr–29Cu. (4) A geologic measure. See *geologic era*. **damping-** See *damping-*. **decay-** See *p. of decay*. **gold-** The elements Os, Ir, Pt, Au. **half-, half-life-** See *p. of decay*. **incubating-** The time necessary for the full development of a bacterial culture. **iron-** Iron family. The elements Mn, Fe, Co, Ni, forming the central portion of the third p. of the periodic system. **life-** (1) P. of decay. (2) The time during which an atom or molecule is in the activated or excited state. See *damping p.*, *lingering p.* **long-** The third, fourth, or fifth p. of the periodic system. **platinum-** The elements Os, Ir, Pt, Au, and Hg; part of the fifth p. of the periodic system. **rare earth-** The

elements with at. nos. 58–72, Ce to Hf; the center of the fifth p. of the periodic system. **short-** Either of the first or second periods of the periodic system. **silver-** The elements Ru, Rh, Pd, Ag, and Cd; the center of the fourth p. of the periodic system. **transitional-** (1) One of the trios of the eighth p. group. (2) One of the 3 series of elements from Ti to Ni, Zr to Pd, or Hf to Au. **uranium-** The sixth p. of the periodic system (the radioactive elements).

p. of decay. The time for the disintegration of 50% of a radioactive element into its next transmutation product. See *radioactive element*.

periodate. A salt of periodic acid, containing the IO_4— radical.

periodic. (1) Pertaining to a regularly recurring event, phenomenon, or characteristic. (2) Pertaining to the highest valency of iodine, as *p. acid*. **p. acid.** $HIO_4 \cdot 2H_2O$ or $H_5IO_6 = 228.0$. Colorless, monoclinic crystals, m.130 (decomp.), soluble in water. **p. chain.** An arrangement of chemical elements according to increasing atomic weight or number in a continuous sequence. It is divided into 6 sections (periods), and each subdivided into subperiods. If valencies are plotted, against atomic weights, a characteristic curve results. See table. Cf. *ionic number*. **p. law.** (1) Mendeléeff law. The properties of the elements change periodically when the elements are arranged in increasing order of atomic numbers. (2) Moseley's law: The properties of the elements are a p. function of their atomic numbers. **p. precipitation.** *Liesegang rings*. **p. properties.** Those properties of elements, which when plotted against atomic weights show the relationship exemplified in the periodic table; as, valency, atomic volumes, atomic heats, wavelengths of X-ray spectra, compressibilities. **p. spiral.** Helix Chemica. A graphical representation of the periodic system. **p. system.** A classification of elements into one system, from which their properties can be deduced and unknown elements and their properties were predicted. Represented: unidimensionally, as a chain; two-dimensionally, as a spiral or helix so that elements with similar properties come together; three-dimensionally, as a spatial model. **p. table.** An arrangement of the p. system, developed independently (1869) by D. Mendeléeff and (1870) by Lothar Meyer and, in a crude form, by Newlands, q.v.

periodicity. (1) The occurrence of a phenomenon at regularly recurring intervals. See *periodic properties*. (2) The occurrence of similar properties in a group of chemical elements in the periodic system.

peripheral. Situated near or at the surface, or on the circumference of a curvilinear figure. **p. speed.** The velocity of a point on the circumference of a rotating circular object: p.s. $= x \cdot \pi \cdot y$ fpm, where x is the rate of rotation in rpm, and y the diameter in feet.

periphery. The surface or outer part; in particular, a circumference.

periplocin. $C_{30}H_{48}O_{12} = 600.5$. A glucoside from the bark of *Periploca graeca* (Asclepiadaceae). Yellow powder, m.205, soluble in water; a heart tonic.

periscope. Altiscope. An arrangement of lenses and mirrors enabling an observer to see over intervening obstacles.

Period†	At. no.	Name	Distribution of electrons in K, L, M, N, O, P, Q orbits‡	−			+
	1	Hydrogen	1	1		H	1*
	2	Helium	2.0			He	
Ia	3	Lithium.	2.1			Li	1*
.	4	Beryllium	2.2			Be	. 2*
.	5	Boron	2.3		3	B	. . 3*
t	6	Carbon.	2.4	4		C	. . . 4*
.	7	Nitrogen.	2.6		3* 1	N	1 2 3 4 5
.	8	Oxygen	2.6		2*	O	
Ib	9	Fluorine	2.7		1*	F	
T	10	Neon	2.8.0			Ne	
IIa	11	Sodium	2.8.1			Na	1*
.	12	Magnesium	2.8.2			Mg	. 2*
.	13	Aluminum.	2.8.3			Al	. . 3*
t	14	Silicon	2.8.4	4		Si	. . . 4*
.	15	Phosphorus.	2.8.5		3*	P	1 . 3 4 5
.	16	Sulfur	2.8.6		2*	S	. 2 . 4 . 6
IIb	17	Chlorine.	2.8.7		1*	Cl	1 . 3 . 5 . 7
T	18	Argon	2.8.8.0			A	
IIIa	19	Potassium.	2.8.8.1			K	1*
.	20	Calcium.	2.8.8.2			Ca	. 2*.
.	21	Scandium	2.8.8.3			Sc	. 2 3*
t	22	Titanium	2.8.8.4			Ti	. 2 3 4*
.	23	Vanadium.	2.8.10.3			V	. 2 3*4 5
.	24	Chromium.	2.8.11.3			Cr	. 2 3*4 . 6
.	25	Manganese	2.8.13.2			Mn	. 2*3 4 . 6 7
.	26	Iron	2.8.13.3			Fe	. 2 3*. . 6 7
III'	27	Cobalt.	2.8.15.2			Co	. 2*3 4
.	28	Nickel	2.8.16.2			Ni	. 2*3
.	29	Copper.	2.8.17.2			Cu	1 2*
.	30	Zinc	2.8.18.2			Zn	. 2*
.	31	Gallium.	2.8.18.3			Ga	. . 3*
t	32	Germanium.	2.8.18.4	4		Ge	. . . 4*
.	33	Arsenic	2.8.18.5		3*	As	1 . 3 . 5
.	34	Selenium	2.8.18.6		2*	Se	. 2 . 4 . 6
IIIb	35	Bromine	2.8.18.7		1*	Br	1 . 3 . 5 . 7
T	36	Krypton	2.8.18.8.0			Kr	
IVa	37	Rubidium.	2.8.18.8.1			Rb	1*
.	38	Strontium	2.8.18.8.2			Sr	. 2*
.	39	Yttrium.	2.8.18.8.3			Y	. 2 3*
t	40	Zirconium.	2.8.18.8.4			Zr	. 2 3 4*
.	41	Niobium	2.8.18.10.3			Nb	. 2 3*4 5
.	42	Molybdenum	2.8.18.10.4			Mo	. 2 3 4*5 6
.	43	Technetium	2.8.18.12.3			Tc	. 2 3*4 . 6 7
.	44	Ruthenium	2.8.18.12.4			Ru	. 2 3 4*. 6 7 8
IV'	45	Rhodium.	2.8.18.14.3			Rh	. 2 3*4 . 6
.	46	Palladium.	2.8.18.16.2			Pd	. 2*. 4
.	47	Silver.	2.8.18.18.1			Ag	1*2
.	48	Cadmium.	2.8.18.18.2			Cd	. 2*
.	49	Indium	2.8.18.18.3			In	. . 3*
t	50	Tin.	2.8.18.18.4	4		Sn	. 2 . 4*
.	51	Antimony.	2.8.18.18.5		3	Sb	. . 3 . 5*
.	52	Tellurium	2.8.18.18.6		2*	Te	. . . 4 . 6
Ivb	53	Iodine	2.8.18.18.7		1*	I	. . 3 . 5 . 7

Period†	At. no.	Name	Distribution of electrons in K, L, M, N, O, P, Q orbits‡	Valence or polar numbers of elements§		
					−	+
T	54	Xenon...............	2.8.18.18.8.0		Xe	
Va	55	Cesium..............	2.8.18.18.8.1		Cs	1*
.	56	Barium	2.8.18.18.8.2		Ba	. 2*
.	57	Lanthanum..........	2.8.18.18.8.3		La	. 2 3*
t	58	Cerium..............	2.8.18.18.8.4		Ce	. 2 3 4*
.	59	Praseodymium	2.8.18.20.8.3		Pr	. 2 3*
.	60	Neodymium	2.8.18.21.8.3		Nd	. 2 3
.	61	Promethium.........	2.8.18.22.8.3		Pm	. 2 3
.	62	Samarium...........	2.8.18.23.8.3		Sm	. 2 3
.	63	Europium	2.8.18.24.8.3		Eu	. 2 3
.	64	Gadolinium..........	2.8.18.25.8.3		Gd	. 2 3
V''	65	Terbium	2.8.18.26.8.3		Tb	. 2 3
.	66	Dysprosium	2.8.18.27.8.3		Dy	. 2 3
.	67	Holmium............	2.8.18.28.8.3		Ho	. 2 3
.	68	Erbium	2.8.18.29.8.3		Er	. 2 3
.	69	Thulium	2.8.18.30.8.3		Tu	. 2 3
.	70	Ytterbium...........	2.8.18.31.8.3		Yb	. 2 3
.	71	Lutecium	2.8.18.32.8.3		Lu	. 2 3
t	72	Hafnium	2.8.18.32.8.4		Hf	. 2 3 4*
.	73	Tantalum	2.8.18.32.8.5		Ta	. . 3 4 5*
.	74	Tungsten............	2.8.18.32.10.4		W	. 2 3 4*5 6
.	75	Rhenium............	2.8.18.32.12.3		Re	. 2 3 4 . 6 7
.	76	Osmium	2.8.18.32.12.4		Os	. 2 3 4*. 6 . 8
V'	77	Iridium	2.8.18.32.14.3		Ir	. 2 3 4 . 6 7
.	78	Platinum............	2.8.18.32.14.4		Pt	. 2 . 4*. 6
.	79	Gold................	2.8.18.32.16.3		Au	1 . 3*4
.	80	Mercury............	2.8.18.32.18.2		Hg	1 2*
.	81	Thallium............	2.8.18.32.18.3		Tl	1*. 3
t	82	Lead	2.8.18.32.18.4		Pb	. 2*. 4
.	83	Bismuth	2.8.18.32.18.5		Bi	1 . 3*. 5
.	84	Polonium	2.8.18.32.18.6		Po	. 2 . 4 . 6
Vb	85	Astatine	2.8.18.32.18.7		At	1 . 3 . 5 . 7
T	86	Radon...............	2.8.18.32.18.8.0		Rn	
VIa	87	Francium	2.8.18.32.18.8.1		Fr	1
.	88	Radium	2.8.18.32.18.8.2		Ra	. 2*
.	89	Actinium............	2.8.18.32.18.8.3		Ac	. 2 3
.	90	Thorium	2.8.18.32.18.8.4		Th	. 2 . 4*
.	91	Protactinium	2.8.18.32.18.11.2		Pc	. 2 3 . 5
.	92	Uranium	2.8.18.32.18.12.2		U	. 2 . 4 5 6*
.	93	Neptunium..........	2.8.18.32.18.13.2		Np	
.	94	Plutonium...........	2.8.18.32.18.14.2		Pu	

† Roman numerals indicate the period or number of orbits of the atoms. Small letters indicate subperiods: i.e., *a*, electropositive elements (light metals); *b*, electronegative elements (nonmetals). *T* indicates the terminals of a period (noble gases); *t* the transitional elements (carbon group). Single prime (′) indicates heavy metals; double prime (″) the rare-earth metals.

‡ The passage of an electron between orbits gives rise to the corresponding radiations.

§ To the left, the number of electrons which that particular atom captures to form the octet; to the right, the number of electrons which the atom can give up. Numbers with asterisks following are the principal valencies.

periscopic. Applied to lenses having a concave-convex surface.

perisphere. The "atmosphere" around a molecule, ion, or radical in which its influence is felt. Cf. *molecular diagram.*

peristalsis. The rhythmic contractions of the intestines by which their contents are propelled through, mixed with digestive enzymes, and partly absorbed.

peristaltic. A substance that increases intestinal movements. **p. pump.** Rollers on a flexible plastic tube which propel the contents by p. motion. Used in automatic chemical analysis to take successive samples of liquid of determined quantity.

Peristaltin(e). $C_{14}H_{18}O_8$ = 314.2. Trademark for a glucoside from the bark of *Rhamnus purshiana*, cascara sagrada. Brown, hygroscopic crystals, soluble in water; a peristaltic.

periston. A colloidal solution containing polymerized vinylpyrrolidone (hemodyn) and inorganic salts; used to raise blood pressure temporarily, and (in Germany during World War II) as a blood substitute.

Perkin, Sir William Henry. 1838–1907. English chemist, who made the first synthetic dye, mauvein (1856). **P.'s mauve.** Mauvein. **P.'s reaction.** The formation of unsaturated acids of the cinnamic type by the condensation of aromatic aldehydes with fatty acids in presence of acetic anhydride: $Ar \cdot CHO + CH_3COONa = Ar \cdot CH = CH \cdot COONa + H_2O$. **P.'s violet.** Mauvein.

perlite. A volcanic glass. Cf. *pearlite.*

Perlofil. Trade name for a polyamide synthetic fiber.

perloline. $C_{36}H_{22}O_3N_4$ = 730.3. An alkaloid from perennial ryegrass (*Lolium perenne* L.), soluble in water. Solutions in chloroform are golden, with a green fluorescence visible in concentration $1:5 \times 10^6$.

Perlon. Trademark for a polyamide synthetic fiber. **P.-U.** Trademark for a polyurethane synthetic fiber.

permafrost. Describing areas of permanently frozen ground, *e.g.*, 33 % of Canada.

permalloy. A magnetic alloy of nickel (30–80%) and iron.

Permalon. Trade name for a mixed-polymer synthetic fiber.

permanent. Everlasting, fixed, enduring. **p. gas.** A gas that cannot be liquefied or condensed by pressure alone. **p. set.** The deformation that an object retains after removal of the deforming force. **p. white.** Precipitated barium sulfate.

permanganate. $MMnO_4$. A salt of permanganic acid. Purple in color. Good oxidizing agents, many permanganates are disinfectants. **p. ion.** The negatively charged radical MnO_4- which produces a purple color in solution.

permanganic acid. $HMnO_4$ = 120.0. An acid derived from heptavalent manganese, stable only in dilute solutions; decomp. to manganese dioxide and oxygen.

permanganyl. The radical MnO_3-. **p. chloride.** MnO_3Cl = 138.39. The green-brown acid chloride of permanganic acid which emits purple fumes in moist air and explodes if heated. **p. fluoride.** MnO_3F = 121.93.

permeability. (1) The ability to pass or penetrate a substance or membrane. (2) The quantity of air flowing through a body in unit time under standard conditions of area, thickness, and pressure. Cf. *porosity, osmosis.* **magnetic-** See *magnetic permeability.*

permeable. Pervious or porous. **semi-** Allowing the passage of some substances but not others; as, a semipermeable membrane.

permeate. To pass through the pores of a body without rupture of its parts.

Perminal. Trade name for a sodium alkylnaphthalene sulfonate wetting agent.

permittivity. Dielectric constant.

permivar. An alloy: Ni 45, Co 25, Fe 30%, which has a high magnetic permeability and low hysteresis loss; used in the cores of loading coils for telephone circuits.

permonosulfuric acid. Caro's acid.

permutation. (1) Substitution, *e.g.*, of radicals. (2) Transmutation.

Permutit. Trademark for a group of cation and anion exchangers.

permutite. $Na_2Al_2H_6Si_2O_8$. An artificial zeolite obtained by melting aluminum silicate, sodium carbonate, and sand together; used for water softening (p. process). Regenerated by a strong solution of sodium chloride: (1) hard water + sodium-permutite = soft water + calcium-permutite. (2) Calcium-permutite + sodium chloride = calcium chloride solution + sodium-permutite. **natural-** A zeolite mineral, boronite or refinite, used for water softening. Cf. *regeneration.* Also used for estimating ammonia in blood and urine.

permutoid reaction. A reaction of double decomposition between a soluble and insoluble substance. Cf. *permutite.*

pernambuco. Lima wood, Nicaragua wood. The red wood from *Caesalpinia echinata* (Leguminosae); a dye.

pernitric acid. HNO_4. An acid of doubtful existence.

pernocton. Pernoston.

pernoston. $C_{11}H_{15}O_3N_2Br$ = 303.03. β-Bromo-allyl-*sec*-butylbarbituric acid, pernocton. Colorless solid, m.132, soluble in alcohol; a hypnotic preanesthetic.

Pernot furnace. A reverberatory puddling furnace with a circular inclined hearth, used in making steel.

peroffskite. $CaTiO_3$. Perovskite.

peronine. $C_{24}H_{25}O_3N \cdot HCl$ = 411.8. Benzyl-morphine hydrochloride. Colorless powder, soluble in water; a narcotic.

perosis. Displacement of the ankle joint of chickens, due to manganese deficiency.

perosmic. A compound of octavalent osmium. **p. acid.** See *osmic acid.*

Pérot lamp. A mercury-vapor lamp light source for optical instruments.

peroxidase. (1) An enzyme of vegetable origin that splits hydrogen peroxide into water, or metal peroxides into the corresponding oxide and oxygen. (2) A substance that activates peroxides. Cf. *catalase.*

peroxide. (1) Superoxide. A derivative of hydrogen peroxide or a compound containing the —O—O—

or $=O_2$ group, in which 2 O atoms are singly linked. They liberate hydrogen peroxide with acids and are strong oxidizing agents; as, H_2O_2. (2) Used loosely for dioxides, q.v., which liberate oxygen with acids. **acid-** A compound of the type $(RCO)_2O_2$. **hydro-** See *hydro*.

p. of hydrogen. Hydrogen peroxide. **p. value.** A measure of the degree of deterioration by oxidation of oils and fats, determined analytically.

peroxo- Preferred term for peroxy-. Prefix indicating an acid or its salt derived by substitution from hydrogen peroxide.

peroxydisulfuric acid. Persulfuric acid.

peroxydol. Sodium perborate.

perparaldehyde. $CHMe \cdot O \cdot CHMe \cdot O \cdot O \cdot CHMe \cdot O$ =
148.1. A thin oil, $b_{12mm}45$, insoluble in water.

perphenazine. $C_{21}H_{26}ON_3ClS$ = 404.02. White bitter crystals, m.98, insoluble in water; a tranquilizer and antiemetic (B.P.).

perphosphoric acid. $H_4P_2O_8$ = 194.03. Crystalline solid.

perrhenate. $MReO_4$. Colorless, and (except those of Ag, Tl, K, Rb, and Cs) soluble in water.

perrhenic acid. $HReO_4$ = 251.32. Colorless, stable powder.

Perrin, Jean B. 1870–1942. French chemist and physicist. Nobel Prize winner (1926). **P. equation.** The distribution of particles in a colloidal system = $1.33\pi r^3 g(D-d)h = (RT/N) \ln (n_1/n_2)$, where r is the radius of the particles, D their density, d the density of the medium, g the gravitational acceleration, n_1 and n_2 the number of particles per unit volume in 2 layers of liquid a distance h apart, N Avogadro's number, R the gas constant, and T the absolute temperature.

perry. A fermented beverage made from pear juice. Cf. *cider*.

persalt. A salt having the highest valence number of an acid-forming element; as, perchromate.

perseite. Perseitol.

perseitol. $CH_2OH(CHOH)_5CH_2OH$ = 212.2. Perseite, from *Laurus persea* (Lauraceae), a tropical tree. Colorless needles, m.188, soluble in water; occurs as *l* and *d* compounds.

perseulose. $C_7H_{14}O_7$ = 210.11. A ketoheptose, m.110, produced by sorbose bacteria from perseitol.

Pershbecker furnace. A rotating furnace, heated by wood, for roasting mercury ores.

Persian flowers. Pyrethrum. **P. red.** Indian red.

persic oil. Peach kernel nut oil (U.S.P.).

persilicic. Describing an acid or acidic rock containing more than 60% Si.

persimmon. The fruit-bearing trees *Diospyros virginiana*, N. America; and *D. kaki*, China, Japan (Ebenaceae).

persio. Orchil.

personal equation. Differences in reading instruments or in making chemical operations, due to temperamental or other inherent qualities or habits of the observers.

persorption. The intimate and almost molecular mixture of a gas and solid due to absorption. Cf. *sorption*.

Persoz, Jean François. 1805–1869. French technical chemist. **P.'s solution.** 10 gm zinc chloride, 10 ml water, 2 gm zinc oxide; dissolves silk but not wool.

Perspex. Trademark for a transparent polymerized methyl methacrylate plastic; made from acetone, methyl alcohol, hydrogen cyanide, and sulfuric acid. It is light in weight, a good dielectric, and can "pipe" light round bends.

perstoff. Diphosgene.

persulfate. A salt derived from persulfuric acid, which contains the radical $=S_2O_8$; made by the electrolysis of sulfate solutions.

persulfide. A sulfide containing more S than is required by the normal valency of the element; as, Na_2S_2.

persulfuric acid. $H_2S_2O_8$ = 194.14. An acid in lead accumulators obtained by electrolyzing sulfuric acid; a strong oxidizing agent.

perthio. The radical $=S=S$.

perthiocarbonates. M_2CS_4. Salts formed from a solution of carbon disulfide in alkali disulfides.

pertusarene. $C_{60}H_{100}$ = 820.78. A solid hydrocarbon from the lichen *Pertusaria communis*.

pertussis vaccine. A sterile suspension of killed p. bacilli in normal saline. An immunizing agent for whooping cough (U.S.P., B.P.).

Peru apple. Stramonium. **P. balsam.** Indian balsam. A reddish brown balsam from *Myroxylon (Toluifera) pereirae* (Leguminosae), tropical America; a local irritant (U.S.P.).

peruol. Benzyl benzoate.

peruscabin. Benzyl benzoate.

Peruvian balsam. Peru balsam. **P. bark.** Cinchona.

peruvin. Cinnamic alcohol.

peruviol. Nerolidol.

pervaporation. The evaporation of a liquid through a dialyzing membrane; as, parchment.

pervesterol. A sterol, q.v., isolated from the fat of algae.

pervious. Allowing the passage of fluids.

pervitine. Desoxyephedrine, q.v.

perylene. $C_{10}H_6=C_{10}H_6$ = 252.2. $\alpha,\alpha,\alpha',\alpha'$-Dinaphthylene, m.274.

peryllartine. $C_6H_8 \cdot CMe \cdot CH_2 \cdot CHNOH$ = 165.1. Perillaldehyde–α-antialdoxime; 2,000 times sweeter than sugar. Cf. *perillaldehyde*.

pessary. Pharmaceutical term for a medicated solid body for vaginal insertion.

pesticide. General term for a substance that is toxic to objectionable insect pests. Cf. *insecticide*, *rodenticide*. The world loss of crops due to pests is estimated as $1,000 million per annum. For ISO nomenclature, see British Standard 1831.

pestle. A blunt, rounded instrument, for pounding drugs or chemicals in a mortar, or ores in a stamp mill.

petalite. $Li_2O \cdot Al_2O_3 \cdot 8SiO_2$. Found in S. W. Africa, and used in ceramics to produce resistance to high varying temperatures.

petalon. The hypothetical disk-shaped nucleus of helium.

pethidine. The ethyl hydrochloride of 1-methyl-4-phenylpiperidine-4-carboxylic acid. An aspirin substitute and analgesic. **p. hydrochloride.** Demerol, dolantal.

Petit, Alexis Thérèse. 1791–1820. French physicist. Cf. *Dulong-Petit Law*.

petitgrain oil. An essential oil distilled from the leaves and fruits of *Citrus bigardia*. Yellow liquid, d.0.887–0.90, insoluble in water. Used in perfumery to adulterate neroli oil; contains linalool, limonene, and esters. **p. citronier oil.** The essential oil from the unripe fruits of *Citrus medica*, d.0.869–0.878; contains citral and esters of linalool.

petrichor. An oil believed to be responsible for the odor of damp earth.

petri dish. A flat, shallow, circular glass dish for bacterial cultures.

petrifaction. Mineralization, silification. The process of changing organic matter into stonelike substances by the gradual infiltration and replacement of the tissues by mineral matter.

petrified wood. Fossil wood that has been gradually changed into stone by the slow infiltration of silica, details of its structure being preserved.

petrochemical. A chemical product derived from petroleum. E.g.: Chemical and hydrocarbon solvents, synthetic detergents, plastics and resins, agricultural chemicals (pesticides), ammonia and nitrogenous fertilizers, synthetic rubbers, synthetic fibers, glycerin, glycols, and other esters.

Petroff equation. The coefficient of friction f of a shaft revolving in a lubricating oil of absolute viscosity z, at N rpm and p psi of projected area $= \pi^2 z N R / 30 p C$, where R is the shaft radius and C the radial clearance. **P. reagent.** A sulfonic acid of nonparaffinic hydrocarbons. A by-product of the refining of petroleum oils with fuming sulfuric acid; a catalyst in fat manufacture (Twitchell's method).

petrograd standard. A measure of the volume of sawed softwood: 165 ft^3 (U.K. usage).

petrographical. Pertaining to the description of rocks and stones.

petrography. The study of rocks and stones as aggregates of minerals. Cf. *petrology*.

Petrohol. Trademark for isopropyl alcohol synthesized by hydration of propylene from petroleum cracking stills.

petrol. (1) Motor spirit or gasoline. The fraction of crude petroleum, 40–150°C; chiefly C_6H_{14}, C_7H_{16}, and C_8H_{18}. (2) Petroleum ether.

petrolate. A general term for products derived from petroleum, q.v.

petrolatum. Petroleum jelly, Vaseline, paraffin ointment, cosmolin, fossolin, adeps mineralis, yellow petrolatum. A purified mixture of semisolid hydrocarbons from petroleum; a yellow jelly, d.0.82–0.85, m.34–54, soluble in alcohol or chloroform; an ointment base, lubricant, cleanser, rust preventive, and leather dressing (U.S.P.). **heavy-** Liquid p. **hydrophilic-** A mixture of p. with cholesterol, stearyl alcohol, and white wax, used in ointments (U.S.P.). **light-** d.0.830–0.870. **liquid-** Heavy p. Colorless, nonfluorescent, odorless, tasteless mixture of liquid hydrocarbons from petroleum, d.0.860–0.905 (U.S.P.), 0.870–0.890 (B.P.); an internal lubricant. **white-** Albolene. A decolorized p. ointment base. Cf. *protosubstance*. **yellow-** Petrolatum.

    p. albumin. White p. **p. jelly.** Petrolatum. **p. liquidum.** Liquid p.

Petrolene. (1) Trademark for malthene, the oily or soft constituents of bitumen, soluble in petroleum spirit. (2) (not cap.) Asphalt.

petroleum. (1) Mineral oil, rock oil, coal oil, earth oil, seneca oil, crude oil, naphtha. A native mixture of gaseous, liquid, and solid hydrocarbons. Thick, brown or yellow oil, obtained from wells, springs, and lakes, d.0.78–0.97 (extreme limits 0.65–1.07); insoluble in water, soluble in organic solvents. (2) The fraction of crude p. distilling at 150–300°C. Classification:

A. Paraffin base: mainly C_nH_{2n+2} (C_4H_{10} to $C_{35}H_{72}$); small amounts of C_nH_{2n} ($C_{21}H_{42}$ to $C_{26}H_{52}$) and C_nH_{2n-x}. Sulfur occurs as thiophanes, $C_nH_{2n}S$.

B. Naphthene base (or asphalt base): mainly C_nH_{2n} (naphthenes and olefins); moderate amounts of C_nH_{2n-x}, where x is 2, 4, 6, 8, etc., up to 20; also some aromatic hydrocarbons, little or no C_nH_{2n-2}.

World production (1967) 2,350 million tons. Estimated reserves: see table. **p. asphalt.** The

PETROLEUM RESERVES

Area	Million tons
Asia—Middle East ...	23,250
Asia—Far East	1,280
U.S.A.	4,770
Canada	485
Mexico	345
Caribbean	2,480
Argentina	140
West Europe........	200
East Europe........	200
Africa	540
U.S.S.R.	3,525
Other countries	125
World total......	37,340

residues from Trinidad p. **p. coke.** The residue from the distillation of p.; used in metallurgical processes, carbon pencils, and dry batteries. It may contain petrolatum or paraffin wax. **p. ether.** See *petroleum* fractions. **p. fractions.** See table. **p. furnace.** An oil burner. **p. jelly.** Petrolatum. **p. naphtha.** Benzine. **p. ointment.** Petrolatum. **p. pitch.** Asphalt. **p. refining.** The industrial separation of the constituents of p., including cracking, decolorizing, distilling, filtering, and skimming. **p. spirit.** Ligroin.

petroline. A paraffin obtained by distillation of Indian petroleum.

petrology. Lithology. A branch of science dealing with the origin (petrogeny), structure, and composition (petrography) of rocks.

petromortis. Garage poison.

petroselic acid. Petroselinic acid.

petroselinic acid. $Me(CH_2)_{10}CH:CH(CH_2)_4COOH =$ 282.37. ϵ-Octadecenic acid. An isomer of oleic acid, in parsley seeds.

petroselinum. (1) Parsley. The dried herb of *Petroselinum sativum* (Umbelliferae); used medicinally and in cooking. (2) Parsley seeds, q.v.

petrosilane. $C_{20}H_{42} = 282.5$. A saturated hydrocarbon, m.69, in the unsaponifiable matter of parsley oil.

petrosilex. Chert. A hard, siliceous rock or flint; used for grinding.

petrous. Hard or stonelike.

petrox. Petroxolin.

PETROLEUM FRACTIONS

Product	Temperature, °C	Composition
	Boiling point	
Cymogen	0	C_4H_{10}
Rhigolene........	18–21	C_4H_{10}, C_5H_{12}
Petroleum ether ..	40–60	C_5H_{12}, C_6H_{14}
Gasoline........	60–200	C_6H_{14} to $C_{10}H_{22}$
Naphtha........	70–90	C_6H_{14} to C_7H_{18}
Ligroin.........	90–120	C_7H_{16} to C_8H_{18}
Benzine	120–150	C_8H_{18} to C_9H_{20}
Kerosine, coal oil, photogene ..	150–300	C_9H_{20} to $C_{16}H_{34}$
Lubricating oils ..	Over 300	
Light		C_{12} to C_{20}
Medium		C_{16} to C_{22}
Heavy		C_{18} to C_{26}
Paraffin oil liquid petrolatum, Albolene, Stanolax, Nujol, etc...	300	C_{10} to C_{18}
	Melting point	
Vaseline petrolatum, petroleum jelly	38–50	C_{20} to C_{22}
Paraffin, Parowax, Cerolene......	45–65	C_{23} to C_{25}
Paraffin wax.....	50–80	C_{27} to C_{30}

In practice, however, the fractions ("cuts") are:

Fraction	%
1. Below 200°F at 1 atm, gasoline or naphtha......................	2–80
2. 200–275°F at 1 atm, kerosine or coal oil ..	3–25
3. All vacuum fractions to 40 mm, gas oil ... (η below 50 sec)*	7–50
4. Light lubricating oil .... (η = 55–99)	2–15
5. Medium lubricating oil .... (η = 100–199)	3–20
6. Viscous lubricating oil................. (η exceeds 199)	0–22

* η = Saybolt viscosity in seconds.

petroxolin. Petroxolinum liquidum, liquid petrox, petrolatum saponatum liquidum. Paraffin oil saponified with ammonium oleate. Brown liquid, insoluble in water; used medicinally in external preparations.

Pettenkofer, Max von. 1818–1901. German chemist. **P. test.** (1) On adding urine to a mixture of sugar and sulfuric acid, a crimson color indicates the presence of bile acids. (2) The determination of carbon dioxide in air by absorption in a known volume of standard baryta solution, and titration of the excess with alkali.

petzite. $(Ag, Au)_2Te$. A native telluride.

peucedanin. $C_{16}H_{16}O_4$ = 272.1. Imperatorin. A principle derived from the root of hog fennel, *Peucedanum officinale* (Umbelliferae); a diuretic.

pewter. (1) A gray alloy: Sn 83–75, Pb 0–20, with sometimes Sb 0–7 and Cu 0–4%. The lead is omitted from p. household utensils. (2) Calcined tin used for polishing marble. (3) A p. pot.

PF. Abbreviation for phenol-formaldehyde plastic.

Pfeilring reagent. A fat-splitting catalyst made by the action of sulfuric acid on aromatic hydrocarbons and castor oil. Cf. *Twitchell.*

pferdekraft. A metric unit of horsepower: 75 kg/sec.

Pfeufer's green. Blue-green dye from the fungus *Chlorospenium aeruginosum.*

pfund. German for pound.

pH, pH, pH, pH, p_H. Symbol for the logarithm of the reciprocal of the hydrogen-ion concentration, C_H or H⁺; hence pH = log $(1/C_H{}^+)$. **international standard scale-** pH = pH (standard) + $F\, dE$- $\div 2 \times 3RT$.

p-H. Parahydrogen. See *hydrogen molecule.*

Ph. Abbreviation for phenyl, C_6H_5—.

phacolite. Chabazite.

phacometer. An instrument to measure the refractive index of a lens.

phaeo-, phæo-. See *pheo-.*

phage. An ultramicroscopic organism, which destroys bacteria. Often used synonymously with *bacteriophage.*

phagocytes. Cells that envelop and digest invading microorganisms or harmful cells. **fixed-** P. located in the connective tissue (endothelial cells). **motile-** P that move in the blood and lymph (leukocytes).

phagocytolysis. The destruction of phagocytes by microorganisms.

phagocytosis. The destruction of microorganisms, by phagocytes. Cf. *Metschnikoff.*

phagolysis. The destruction of phagocytes.

phallin. A toxic hemolytic protein from *Amanita phalloides*, a poisonous mushroom.

phanerogamia. The large group of flowering plants which produce seeds.

Phanodorn. $C_{12}H_{16}N_2O_3$ = 236.2. Trademark for cyclobarbitone, cyclohexenylethylbarbituric acid. White crystals, m.171–174, soluble in water; a hypnotic.

phanquone. $C_{12}H_6O_2N_2$ = 210.00. 7-Phenanthroline-5,6-quinone. Orange crystals, slightly soluble in water; an antiamebiatic (B.P.).

phantastica. Generic name for drugs producing visionary states in normal humans; as, cocaine.

pharaoh's serpents. A stick of mercuric thiocyanate, q.v. When ignited, it glows and swells during its formation to a voluminous ash that resembles a moving serpent. It liberates N_2, CS_2, and Hg vapor and leaves a gray residue of *mellon*, q.v.

Phar. D. Abbreviation for Doctor of Pharmacy.

Phar. M. Abbreviation for Master of Pharmacy.

pharmaceutic. Pertaining to drugs. **p. chemistry.** The analysis of drugs and isolation of their active constituents.

pharmacist. An apothecary or druggist.

pharmacodynamics. The study of the effects of drugs on living organisms.

pharmacognosy. The study of the identification, properties, and quality of crude drugs.

pharmacolite. $CaHAsO_4\cdot2H_2O$. A native arsenate.

pharmacology. The study of drugs, their origin and composition (*pharmacy*), identification (*pharmacognosy*), and effects on living organisms (*pharmacodynamics*).

pharmacopoeia, pharmacopeia. Official lists of drugs and chemicals issued by many countries. A p.

contains a description of each drug, its composition, tests for identification and purity, and its medicinal doses. Substances listed are called "official" or "officinal," and must have the specified purity for medical use.

Ph. Arg.: Farmacopeia Nacional Argentina
Ph. Aust.: Pharmacopoeia Austriaca.
Ph. Bras.: Pharmacopeia dos Estados Unidos do Brasil
Ph. Brit.: British Pharmacopoeia. B.P.
Ph. Eg.: Egyptian Pharmacopeia (English text). Eg.P.
Ph. Espan.: Farmacopea oficial Española
Ph. Fr.: Codex Medicamentarius Gallicus
Ph. Germ.: Deutsches Arzneibuch. D.A.
Ph. Helv.: Pharmacopoeia Helvetica
Ph. Hisp.: Farmacopoeia Hispanica
Ph. Ital.: Farmacopoeia ufficiale del regno d'Italia
Ph. Japon.: Pharmacopoeia Japonica
Ph. Mex.: Farmacopea Nacional de México
Ph. Ndl.: Pharmacopoeia Nederlandica
Ph. Norw.: Pharmacopoeia Norvegica
Ph. Port.: Pharmacopoeia Portugezá
Ph. Svec.: Svenska Farmacopen
U.S.P.: United States Pharmacopoeia
In addition to the official lists there are in use:
N.F.: National Formulary (U.S.A.)
N.N.D.: New and Nonofficial Drugs (American Medical Association)
B.P.C.: British Pharmaceutical Codex
E.P.: The Extra Pharmacopoeia (British)
The principal pharmacopoeias in use in other countries are: British Commonwealth: B.P.
Central America: Ph. Fr., Ph. Hisp., Ph. Mex., Ph. Port., Ph. Bras.
China: Locally, the old encyclopedia Pen-tsao-kang-mu; otherwise, the relevant foreign pharmacopoeia
Cuba: Ph. Fr., U.S.P.
Peru: Ph. Fr., U.S.P., Ph. Hisp.
Turkey: Ph. Fr., Ph. Germ.
Cf. *dispensatory, formulary.*

pharmacophore. An organic radical supposed to be the active group of a drug and to combine with a group of the protoplasm. See *glucophore, chromophore.*

pharmacosiderite. A native arsenate of iron.

pharmacotherapy. The treatment of disease with drugs.

pharmacy. The art of preparing drugs for medicinal use.

phase. (1) A solid, liquid, or gaseous homogeneous substance, that exists as a distinct and mechanically separate portion in a heterogeneous system. Cf. *colloid, zones, micelle.* (2) The succession of electrical impulses of an alternating current. (3) A stage in the growth of microorganisms. (4) A subdivision of the changes occurring in protoplasm during karyokinesis, q.v. **activatory-** The active stage or rapid growth of organisms, especially bacteria. **continuous-** External or enclosing p. The surrounding (dispersion) medium in a heterogeneous mixture. See *colloids.* **discontinuous-** Dispersed p. **dispersed-** Internal or enclosed p. The solute or insoluble part of a colloidal solution, as distinct from the solvent. **dispersion-** Continuous p. **enclosed-** The discontinuous or separated medium in a heterogeneous mixture.

enclosing- Continuous p. **inhibitory-** The passive stage or slow growth of an organism. **oriented-** Misnomer for zone, q.v. **suspended-** Enclosed p.

p. contrast microscopy. When light waves pass through an object whose refractive index is greater than that of its surroundings, they are retarded and emerge out of p. with those forming the background. If the p. difference is half the wavelength, the two sets of waves will cancel each other, and the object will appear dark. Used to improve visibility in microscopical work. **p. converter.** A device for changing the phases of an alternating electric current. **p. reversal.** The change of the components of an emulsion; thus, an emulsion of oil in water, converted into an emulsion of water in oil. **p. rule.** Gibbs: A mathematical generalization of systems in equilibrium: $V = C + 2 - P$, where P is the number of phases, V the variance or degrees of freedom, C the number of components. V is $0 =$ nonvariant (a *point* on a diagram), V is $1 =$ monovariant (a *line* on a diagram), V is $2 =$ divariant (an *area* on a diagram). Thus, for water:

Solid $\rightleftharpoons$ liquid $\qquad C = 1,\ P = 2,\ V = 1$
Solid $\rightleftharpoons$ liquid $\rightleftharpoons$ vapor $\qquad C = 1,\ P = 3,\ V = 0$

phaselin. An enzyme from the bean of *Dilkas mexicana*, resembling papain.

phaseolin. The chief protein of the navy bean, *Phaseolus vulgaris.*

phaseoline. An alkaloid obtained from string beans, *Phaseolus vulgaris.*

phaseolunatin. $C_{10}H_{17}NO_6 = 247.14$. A cyanogenetic glucoside, m.144, from *Phaseolus lunatus*, lima bean (Leguminosae).

phaseomannite. Inositol.

phasine. A group of vegetable proteins from seeds, that agglutinate the red blood corpuscles.

phasotropy. Dynamic isomerism in which the H atom of azoamino compounds, amidines, and formazyl derivatives oscillates from one nitrogen to the other:

$$
\begin{array}{cc}
\mathrm{H-NR'} & \mathrm{H\ \ NR'} \\
| & |\ \ \| \\
\mathrm{R.N=CH} & \mathrm{R.N-CH}
\end{array}
$$

Ph.B. Abbreviation for British Pharmacopoeia. (B.P.)

Ph.C. Abbreviation for Pharmaceutical Chemist.

Ph.D. Abbreviation for Doctor of Philosophy.

phellandrene. $C_{10}H_{16} = 136.1$. $\Delta^{1.5}$-*p*-Menthadiene, 3-isopropyl-6-methylenecyclohexene. A terpene from the seeds of water fennel, *Phellandrium aquitanium* (Umbelliferae); constituent of certain eucalyptus oils, elemi oil, and oil of water hemlock. Colorless, *l*-rotatory liquid, b.176. **p. tetrabromide.** $C_{10}H_{16}Br_4 = 455.81$. A crystalline *d*-rotatory derivative of p., m.111.

Phemerol. Trademark for *p-tert*-octylphenoxyethoxyethyldimethylbenzylammonium chloride, a cationic detergent and antiseptic.

phemitone. $C_{13}H_{14}O_3 = 218.13$. Mebara, mephobarbital, prominal, *N*-methyl-5-phenyl-5-ethyl-barbituric acid. Used to treat epilepsy, and as a substitute for barbitone.

phen- (1) Prefix derived from phenol, indicating a benzene derivative. (2) A suffix. See *-fen.*

phenacaine. Holocaine.

phenacetein. Phenacetolin.
phenacethydrazine. Pyrodin.
phenacetin. $C_{10}H_{13}O_2N$ = 179.17. Acetophenetidin (U.S.P.). White bitter scales, m.135, insoluble in water; used to reduce temperature in fever (B.P.). **methyl-** $C_{11}H_{15}O_2N$ = 193.1. Colorless crystals, soluble in alcohol; an antipyretic. **p. urethane.** Thermodin. Cf. *phenocoll, phesin.*
phenacetol. Phenoxy acetone.
phenacetolin. $C_{15}H_{12}O_2$ = 236.1. Phenacetein. An indicator (alkalies—red, acids—yellow).
phenacite. Be_2SiO_4. A native gem silicate.
phenacyl. The radical $PhCOCH_2$—. **p. alcohol.** See *hydroxyacetophenone.* **p. bromide.** $PhCOCH_2$-Br. White powder, a reagent for hydroxy compounds.
phenacylidene. The radical $PhCOCH=$.
phenacylidin. $C_6H_4(OMe)NH \cdot CH_2COPh$ = 241.2. Colorless powder, insoluble in water; an antipyretic in veterinary medicine.
phenalgin. $C_6H_5NH_3$ = 94.1. Ammoniophenylacetanilide. Colorless crystals, soluble in alcohol; an antipyretic.
Phenamine. Brand name for direct dyestuffs, for cotton and paper.
phenanthrahydroquinone. $C_{14}H_8(OH)_2$ = 210.15. 9,10-Dihydrophenanthrene. A solid, m.146, soluble in water.
phenanthraquinone. Phenanthrenequinone.
phenanthrene. $C_{14}H_{10}$ = 178.1. Phenanthrine. An isomer of anthracene from coal tar:

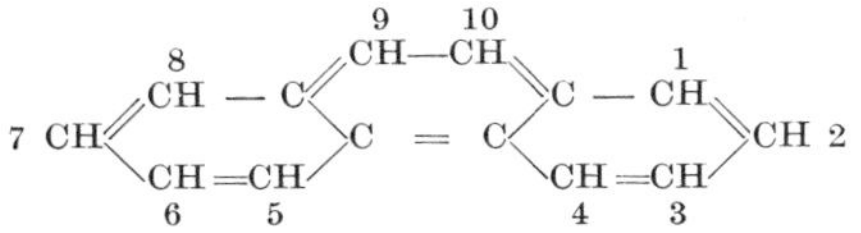

Colorless scales or leaflets, d.1.063, m.99, insoluble in water; used in the synthesis of dyes and drugs. **benzo-** Chrysene. **dihydroxy-** Phenanthrahydroquinone. **hydroxy-** Phenanthrol. **methylisopropyl-** Retene. **tetrahydro-** Tetranthrene. **p. dione.** Phenanthrenequinone. **p. hydroquinone.** Phenanthrenequinone.
phenanthrenequinone. $C_{14}H_8O_2$ = 208.1. Phenanthrenehydroquinone, dioxyphenanthrene. An oxidation product of phenanthrene. Orange needles, m.205, insoluble in water. **p. dioxime.** $C_{14}H_{10}O_2N_2$ = 238.2. A compound derived from phenanthraquinone by replacement of the two =C=O groups by two =C=N·OH radicals. **p. dioxime anhydride.** $C_{14}H_8ON_2$ = 220.1. A furazane derivative. Colorless crystals, m.181. **p. monoxime.** $C_{14}H_9O_2N$ = 223.1. A compound derived from phenanthrenequinone by the replacement of one =CO group by =C=N·OH. Colorless crystals, m.158; used in organic synthesis.
phenanthrenol. Phenanthrol.
phenanthrenone. Phenanthrone.
phenanthridine. $C_{13}H_9N$ = 179.1. The heterocyclic compound 3,4-benzoquinoline. Colorless crystals, m.104, soluble in alcohol. **dihydroketo-** Phenanthridone.
phenanthridinum 1553. Dimidium bromide, 2,7-diamino-9-phenyl-10-methylphenanthridinium bromide. A synthetic trypanosomicide.
phenanthridone. $C_{13}H_9ON$ = 195.07. The heterocyclic compound dihydroketophenanthridine.

Colorless crystals, m.293, soluble in alcohol; used in organic synthesis.
phenanthrine. Phenanthrene.
phenanthrol. $C_{14}H_9OH$ = 194.1. Hydroxyphenanthrene. Colorless crystals, m.112, soluble in water; used in organic synthesis.
phenanthrolines. $C_{12}H_8N_2$ = 180.2. Heterocyclic compounds derived from phenanthrene by substituting 2 N atoms for 2 CH groups in the ring. **batho-** 4,7-Diphenyl-1,10-phenanthroline. A sensitive, specific reagent for iron (red color). **dihydroxy-** Snyder's reagent. Cf. *bathocuproine, neocuproine.* **ortho-** 1,10-Compound; an oxidation-reduction indicator, and reagent for copper (brown color, soluble in isoamyl alcohol), iron, and cobalt. **meta-** or **pseudo-** 2,9-Compound. **para-** or **iso-** 3,8-Compound.
phenanthrone. $C_6H_4 \cdot C_6H_4 \cdot CH_2 \cdot CO$ = 194.15. Solid, m.148, soluble in water.
phenanthrophenazine. $C_{20}H_{12}N_2$ = 280.10. α,γ Dibenzophenazine.

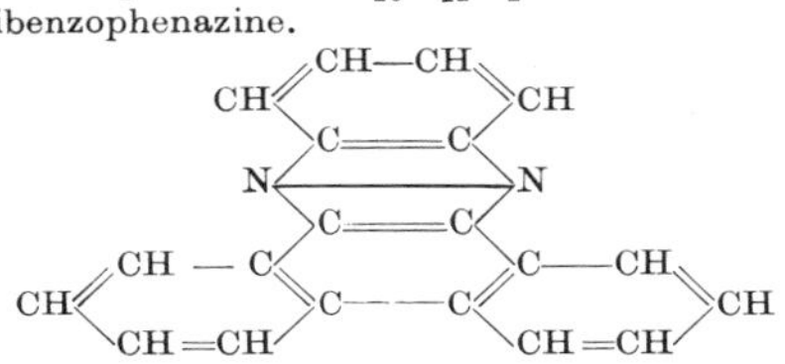

Colorless crystals, m.217, soluble in alcohol; used in organic synthesis.
phenanthryl. Describing a group of 5 isomeric radicals, $C_{14}H_9$—, from phenanthrene.
phenanthrylene. The radical $C_{14}H_8$—, from phenanthrene.
phenaphthacridone. Phenonaphthacridone.
phenarsen. Dichlorophenarsine hydrochloride, q.v.
phenate. C_6H_5OM. Phenoxide, carbolate. A derivative of phenol; M is a monovalent metal; as, sodium, potassium.
phenazine. $C_6H_4 \cdot NC_6H_4 \cdot N$ = 180.1. Dibenzoparadiazine, azophenylen, 5,6-naphthodiazine. Yellow needles, m.170, soluble in water; used in the manufacture of dyes. **benzo-** See *benzophenazine.* **dibenzo-** Phenanthrophenazine. **dibenzyl-** See *dibenzophenazine.* **naphtho-** Benzophenazine. **phenanthro-** See *phenanthrophenazine.*
phenazone. (1) $C_{12}H_8N_2O$ = 196.2. A heterocyclic compound. Green prisms, m.156, soluble in alcohol. (2) A former name for antipyrine.
phenazonium. Derivatives of phenazone in which one N atom is pentavalent. Cf. *flavinduline.*
phendioxin. Dibenzodioxin.
phene. Synonym for the benzene ring.
phenedin. Phenacetin.
phenegol. $Hg(PhONO_2 \cdot SO_3K)_2$. Mercury potassium nitro-*p*-phenol sulfate. Brown antiseptic powder. See *egol.*
phenelzine sulfate. $C_6H_5 \cdot (CH_2)_2 \cdot NH \cdot NH_2 \cdot H_2SO_4$ = 234.31. Phenethylhydrazine sulfate. Pearly plates, m.166, soluble in water; used to treat psychotic depression (B.P.).
phenenyl. The radical $C_6H_3\equiv$.
Phenergan. Trademark for promethazine hydrochloride.
phenethicillin. Common name for α-phenoxyethyl-penicillin. An antibiotic similar in origin and

properties to penicillin. **p. potassium.** $C_{17}H_{19}$-O_5N_2KS = 402.52. Bitter, white powder, soluble in water; an antibiotic (B.P.).

phenethyl. The radical $PhCH_2CH_2$—. Cf. *phenetyl.* **p. alcohol.** Benzylcarbinol.

phenethylamine. $PhCH_2CH_2NH_2$. **alpha-** Colorless liquid, d.0.9395, b.182, insoluble in water, alcohol, or ether. **beta-** Colorless liquid, d.0.9580, b.198, soluble in water. Each is a local anesthetic and narcotic. **p-hydroxy-** Tyramine. **p-hydroxy-N-dimethyl-** Nordenine.

phenethyl benzyl ketone. $PhCH_2CH_2\cdot CO\cdot CH_2Ph$ = 224.2. Colorless liquid, b.324, soluble in alcohol.

phenethylene. Styrene.

phenetidine. $NH_2\cdot C_6H\cdot_4OEt$ = 137.14. Amino-ethoxybenzene, ethoxyaniline, aminophenetole, *p*-aminophenol ethyl ether. **aceto-** Phenacetin. **aceto-phenone.** Malarin. **N-acetyl-** Phenacetin. **acon-ityl-** Apolysin. **ethyl carbonate-** Eupyrine. **meta-** Colorless liquid, b$_{100mm}$180, soluble in water. **methoxyacet-** Kryofine. **monocitryl-** Apolysin. **ortho-** Colorless liquid, b.228, soluble in water. **para-** Colorless liquid, b.224, soluble in water; used to manufacture phenacetin. **phenylglycol-** Amyg-dophenin. **propionyl-** Triphenin. **salicyl-** Sali-phen. **salicylal-** Malakin. **valeryl-** Valeridin.

p. camphorate. Colorless crystals; a febrifuge. **p. salicylate.** Phenosal. **p. tartrate.** Vinopyrine.

phenetidines. Synthetic drugs derived from phenetidine.

phenetidino. The radical $EtOC_6H_4NH$—.

phenetole. $Ph\cdot O\cdot Et$ = 122.1. Phenyl ethyl ether, ethoxybenzene*. Colorless liquid, d.0.892, b.172, insoluble in water. **acetamido-, acetylamino-** Phenacetin. **amino-** Phenetidine. **azo-** See *azo-phenetole.*

phenetyl. Ethoxyphenyl. The radical $EtOC_6H_4$—. Prefix indicating the presence of both phenyl and ethyl groups. Cf. *phenyl.* **p. urea.** Sucrol.

phengite. Muscovite.

phenglutarimide hydrochloride. $C_{17}H_{24}N_2O_2\cdot HCl$ = 324.87. Saline, white crystals, soluble in water, m.177 (decomp.); a parasympatholytic (B.P.).

phenic acid. Phenol. **di-** See *diphenic acid.*

phenicate. (1) Phenate. (2) To sterilize or disinfect with phenol.

phenidine. Phenacetin.

phenil. Phenyl.

phenin. Phenacetin.

phenindamine tartrate. $C_{19}H_{19}N\cdot C_4H_6O_6$ = 411.46. White, bitter powder, m.161, soluble in water; an antihistaminic (U.S.P., B.P.).

phenindione. $C_{15}H_{10}O_2$ = 222.19. Pheniodone. White crystals, m.150, soluble in water; an anti-coagulant (B.P.).

pheniodol. $C_{15}H_{12}O_3I_2$ = 494.08. White powder with characteristic taste, m.160, soluble in water; a radiopaque.

pheniodone. Pheniodol.

phenixin. Carbon tetrachloride.

phenkaptone. *S*-(2,5-Dichlorophenylthiomethyl)-*O,O*-diethylphosphorothiolothionate. A persistent ovicidal acaricide.

phenmethyl. The radical $PhCH_2$—.

phenmethyltriazine. $C_6H_4\cdot N:N\cdot C(Me):N$ = 145.2.

Colorless crystals, m.89, soluble in alcohol.

phenmetrazine hydrochloride. $C_{11}H_5ON\cdot HCl$ = 213.71. White crystals, soluble in water, m.174; an appetite suppressant (B.P.).

phenmiazin. Quinazoline.

phenobarbital. $C_{12}H_{12}O_3N_2$ = 232.24. Phenyl-ethylmalonylurea. Luminal. Phenobarbitone. White crystals, m.174, soluble in water; an anti-convulsant, used as the sodium salt (U.S.P., B.P.). Cf. *barbital.*

phenobarbitone. Phenobarbital.

phenocoll. $C_6H_4(OEt)\cdot NH\cdot CO\cdot CH_2\cdot NH_2$ = 194.12. Amidoaceto-*p*-phenetidine, glycocoll-*p*-phenetidide. Colorless needles, m.100, soluble in water; an anti-pyretic. **p. salicylate.** Salocoll.

phenodin. Hematin.

Phenodoxone. Trade name for *dl*-6-morpholino-4,4-diphenylheptan-3-one, an analgesic.

phenoiazine. **alpha-** Cinnoline. **beta-** Phthalazine.

phenol. (1) See *phenols.* (2) $C_6H_5\cdot OH$ = 94.1. Carbolic acid, hydroxybenzene, phenyl hydroxide, phenic acid, phenylic acid. Colorless needles, d.1.072, m.42, b.182, slightly soluble in water, soluble in alcohol or glycerol. Used as an anti-septic and disinfectant (U.S.P., B.P.), and in the manufacture of dyes and synthetic drugs, plastics, and insulating materials. **acetamino-** q.v. **aceto-** Hydroxyacetophenone. **allyl-** Chavicol. **allyl-methoxy-** Eugenol. **amino-** See *aminophenols.* **aminodinitro-** Picramic acid. **aminoethyl-** Tyr-amine. **amyl-** See *amylphenol.* **arsenobis-** Ar-senophenol. **benzoylamino-** Hydroxy*benzanilide.* **betel-** Chavicol. **bis-** See *bis.* **bromo-** See *brom-phenols.* **chloro-** A halogenated derivative of p. E.g.: (*a*) $OH\cdot C_6H_4\cdot Cl$. Chlorophenic acid, mono-chlorophenol. *ortho-* m.7. *meta-* m.33. *para-* m.37. (*b*) $HO\cdot C_6H_3\cdot Cl_2$. Chlorophenesic acid, dichlorophenol. (*c*) $HO\cdot C_6H_2\cdot Cl_3$. Chlorophenisic acid, trichlorophenol. (*d*) $HO\cdot C_6H\cdot Cl_4$. Chloro-phenosic acid, tetrachlorophenol. (*e*) $HO\cdot C_6Cl_5$. Chlorophenasic acid, pentachlorophenol. **diamino-** See *aminophenols.* **dichloro-** See *chloro-*. **di-methyl-** Xylenol. **dimethylaminoethyl-** Hordenine. **dinitro-** Dinitrophenol. **ethyl-** Phlorol. **hexa-hydro-** Cyclohexanol. **hydroxy-** Dihydroxy*benzene.* **iodized-** A mixture of iodine 20, phenol 60, glycerol 20%; an antiseptic. **iodo-** An iodized derivative of p. E.g.: (*a*) $OH\cdot C_6H_4\cdot I$. Iodophenic acid, monoiodophenol. *ortho-* m.40. *meta-* m.40. *para-* m.94. (*b*) $OH\cdot C_6H_3\cdot I_2$. Iodophenesic acid, diiodo-phenol. (*c*) $OH\cdot C_6H_2\cdot I_3$. Iodophenisic acid, triiodophenol. **2,4,6-** m.156. **isopropylmethyl-** Thymol. **liquefied, liquid-** P. containing 10% (U.S.P.), or 20% (B.P.) of water. **metheny-lamido-** Benzoxazole. **methoxy-** Guaiacol. **methoxymethyl-** Creosol. **methyl-** Cresol. **methallyl-** Anethol. **methyl-*p*-amino-** Metol. **monobrom-** C_6H_4BrOH = 173.1. Brown oil; an antiseptic. **monochlor-** C_6H_4ClOH = 128.6. Color-less liquid; an antiseptic. **nitro-** See *nitrophenol.* **nitroso-** Quinone monoxime. **propenyl-*p*.** Anol. **propyl-** Thymol. **seleno-** Selenophenol. **sulfo-** Aseptol. **tetrahydro-** Cyclohexanol. **thio-** See *thio-*. **triamino-** See *aminophenols.* **trichloro-** See *chloro-*. **trimethyl-** 2,3,5-Isopseudocuminol. 2,4,6-Mesitol. **trinitro-** Picric acid. **vinylenlbis-** Stilbenediol.

p. acids. Compounds having a hydroxy and a carboxyl group attached to a ring. E.g.- Hydroxybenzoic acids (salicylic acid, $HO \cdot C_6H_4 \cdot COOH$); hydroxyphthalic acids, $HO \cdot C_6H_3(COOH)_2$. **p. bismuth.** Bismuth carbolate. **p. blue.** $C_{14}H_{14}N_2O = 226.13$. Dimethylaminophenylimide. A blue indicator dye. **p. camphor.** A germicide mixture of phenol and camphor. **p. coefficient.** Antiseptic power compared with phenol as unity. Cf. *Rideal-Walker test.* **p. derivatives.** See *phenols.* **p. ethers.** Ph—O—R. **p. formaldehyde resin.** A synthetic resin formed by the condensation of p., or a p. with formaldehyde. Cf. *plastics.* **p. glycerin.** A 16% solution of p. in glycerin (B.P.). **p. phthalein.** Phenolphthalein. **p. red.** Phenolsulfonephthalein. **p. sulfophthalein.** Phenol-*sulfonphthalein.* **p. tricarboxylic acid.** $OH \cdot C_6H_2 \cdot (COOH)_3 = 226.09$. A solid, decomp. 245.

phenolase. An enzyme that oxidizes phenols.

phenolate. (1) To disinfect with phenol. (2) Phenate.

phenolic. Pertaining to phenol.

phenology. The study of bird migrations, with special reference to climate.

phenoloid. Algoid and similar plant substances, which contain compounds similar to phenol.

phenolphthalide, phenothalin. $C_{20}H_{14}O_4 = 318.33$. Dihydroxydiphenylphthalide, dioxydiphenylphthalide, p_2-phthalein, phenolax, dioxytriphenylcarbinolcarboxylic acid anhydride. White triclinic crystals, m.258, slightly soluble in water, soluble in alcohol; used as an indicator (acids—colorless, alkalies—deep red), a cathartic (U.S.P.), and in dye synthesis. Cf. *phenolphthaline.* **bismuthtetraiodo-** Eudoxine. **mercurytetraiodo-** Apagallin. **sodiumtetraiodo-** Antinosin. **tetrabromo-** An indicator. **tetraiodo-** Nosophen. *bismuth-* Eudoxine. *mercury-* Apagallin. *sodium-* Antinosin.

phenolphthalide. $Ph \cdot CO \cdot OCR_2$, in which R is an aromatic radical. Compare *fluorescein.*

phenolphthaline. $(C_6H_4OH)_2 : CH \cdot C_6H_4 \cdot COOH = 320.23$., m.225; a reagent for copper and blood. Cf. *phenolphthalein.*

phenolquinine. Quinine carbolate.

phenols. (1) Aryl hydroxides; as, phenol and derivatives. (2) In particular, hydroxy benzenes. Compounds containing one or more hydroxyl group attached to an aromatic or carbon ring. Classification:
A. Monoatomic (hydroxy benzenes); e.g.: phenol, phenyl hydroxide, C_6H_5OH.
B. Diatomic (diphenols or dihydroxy benzenes); e.g.: catechol, resorcinol, quinol, $C_6H_4(OH)_2$.
C. Triatomic (triphenols or trihydroxy benzenes); e.g.: pyrogallol, phloroglucinol, $C_6H_3(OH)_3$.
D. Polyatomic (polyphenols or polyhydroxy benzenes); e.g.: pentahydroxybenzene, quercitol, $C_6H(OH)_5$.
Cf. *phenol acids.* **di-** A p. containing two —OH groups. **poly-** A p. containing four or more —OH groups. **sulfurized-** Syntans. **tri-** A p. containing three —OH groups.

phenol sulfonate. $HO \cdot C_6H_4 \cdot SO_3M$. Sulfophenylate, sulfocarbolate. A salt of phenolsulfonic acid.

phenolsulfonephthalein. $(OH \cdot C_6H_4)_2 : C \cdot C_6H_4 \cdot SO_2 \cdot O$

$= 354.39$. Phenol red. A sulfuric acid derivative of phenolphthalein, generally marketed as the monosodium salt. Bright red crystals, slightly soluble in water. Used as a test for the secreting power of the kidneys (U.S.P., B.P.), and as a pH indicator changing at 7.7 from yellow (acid) to red (alkaline).

phenolsulfonic acid. $C_6H_4(OH)SO_3H = 174.14$. Three isomers, soluble in water, obtained by heating phenol with concentrated sulfuric acid. **ortho-** Aseptol.

phenolsulfuric acid. Phenylsulfuric acid.

phenomena. Plural of *phenomenon.*

phenomenon. An event or manifestation; that which is apparent, as distinct from that which merely exists.

phenonaphthazine. Benzophenazine.

phenones. $Ph \cdot CO \cdot R$. A series of ketones; as, propiophenone, $Ph \cdot CO \cdot Et$.

phenophenanthrazine. Dibenzophenazine.

phenopiazine. Quinoxaline.

phenopyrine. Antipyrine carbolate. Colorless oil, insoluble in water; as antipyretic and analgesic.

phenoquinone. $C_6H_4O_2 \cdot 2C_6H_6O = 296.22$. A solid, m.71, soluble in water.

phenoresorcin. Resorcinol carbolate. A mixture of phenol and resorcinol; used to treat skin diseases.

phenosafranine. $C_{18}H_{15}N_4Cl = 322.62$. 3,6-Diaminodiphenyl phenazine chloride. An aniline dye used in photography to prevent fogging. Green needles, soluble in water with a red color; an oxidation-reduction indicator. Cf. *aposafranine.*

phenosal. $EtO \cdot C_6H_4 \cdot NH \cdot CO \cdot CH_2O \cdot C_6H_4 \cdot COOH = 315.2$. Phenetidine salicylate. Colorless crystals, soluble in water; an antirheumatic.

phenosalyl. An antiseptic mixture of phenol, salicylic acid, menthol, and lactic acid.

phenose. $C_6H_6(OH)_6 = 180.1$. Hexahydroxyhexahydrobenzene. Colorless, deliquescent powder, soluble in water. Cf. *inositol.*

phenosolvan. A mixture of esters of higher aliphatic alcohols, b.130. A scrubbing agent in the recovery of phenols from effluents.

phenostal. $(COOPh)_2 = 242.1$. Diphenyl oxalate, diphenyloxalic ester; a germicide.

phenosuccin. Pyrantin.

phenothalin. Phenolphthalin.

phenothiazine. $C_6H_4 \cdot S \cdot C_6H_4 \cdot NH = 199.1$. Thiodiphenylamine, phenthiazine. Colorless rhombs, m.180, soluble in water; used to manufacture dyes, and as an insecticide.

phenoxarsine. $C_{12}H_9AsO = 243.9$. A compound similar to phenoxazine, but with AsH in place of NH.

phenoxaselenin. $C_{12}H_8OSe = 238.3$. A compound analogous to phenothioxin, with Se in place of S.

phenoxatellurin. $C_{12}H_8OTe = 296.6$. A compound analogous to phenothioxin, with Te in place of S.

phenoxazine. $C_6H_4 \cdot O \cdot C_6H_4 \cdot NH = 183.1$. Naphthoxazine. Colorless leaflets, m.150, soluble in alcohol.

phenoxetol. Phenoxyethanol. Ethyleneglycolmonophenyl ether. An antibacterial for stomach infections.

phenoxides. Phenates.

phenoxin. Carbon tetrachloride.

phenoxthine. Phenothioxin.

phenoxy*. (1) The radical PhO—, from phenol. Cf. *oxyphenol*. (2) Generic name for a polyhydroxy ether synthetic thermoplastic. **p. acetaldehyde.** $PhOCH_2CHO$. **p. acetone.** $PhOCH_2COMe$. Phenacetol. **p. benzamine hydrochloride.** $C_{18}H_{22}$-$ONCl\cdot HCl = 340.32$. White crystals, m.139, slightly soluble in water. **p. benzene*.** Phenyl ether. **p. caffeine.** $C_8H_9O_2N_4(OPH) = 286.11$. Colorless crystals, m.145, soluble in water; an analgesic. **p. methylpenicillin potassium.** $C_{16}H_{17}$-$O_5N_2KS = 388.48$. White crystals, soluble in water; an antibiotic (B.P.) Also used as, **p.m. calcium. p. propandiol.** $CH_2\cdot OPh\cdot CHOH\cdot CH_2$-$OH = 168.1$. Antodyne, glycerin monophenyl ether. Colorless crystals, m.69, soluble in water; an analgesic.

phenpiazine. Quinoxaline.

phensuximide. *N*-Methyl-α-phenyl succimide. Milontin.

phenthiazine. Phenothiazine.

phenetetrol. Apionol.

phenthiol. Thiophenol.

phentolamine hydrochloride. $C_{17}H_{19}ON_2\cdot HCl = 317.83$. White crystals, m.240, soluble in water; a sympatholytic (U.S.P., B.P.).

phentriazine. $C_6H_4\cdot N\!:\!N\cdot N\!:\!CH = 131.2$. 1,2,3-Benzotriazine. Colorless crystals, m.75, soluble in alcohol; used in organic synthesis. **phenyl-** Phenphenyltriazine.

phenyl. Ph. The radical C_6H_5—, from benzene or phenol. **hydroxy-** The radical —C_6H_4OH, from phenol. Cf. *phenoxy*.

phenyl acetaldehyde. $PhCH_2CHO = 120.1$. Colorless liquid, b.205, soluble in water; a perfume (hyacinth odor).

phenylacetamide. Acetanilide.

phenylacetanilide. See *acetanilide*.

phenyl acetate. $Me.COOPh = 136.1$. Colorless liquid, d.1.093, b.196, slightly soluble in water; used in organic synthesis.

phenylacetic acid. α-Toluic acid. **p. anhydride.** $(C_6H_5CH_2CO)_2\!:\!O = 254.2$. A solid, m.73. **p. nitrile.** Benzyl cyanide.

phenyl acetyl chloride. $C_8H_7OCl = 154.6$. Colorless fuming liquid.

phenylacetylene. $PhC\!:\!CH = 102.19$. Colorless liquid, d.0.937, b.139; insoluble in water.

phenylalanine. $C_9H_{11}O_2N = 153.10$. Aminohydrocinnamic acid, a constituent of proteins.

phenyl aldehyde. Benzaldehyde.

phenylamine. Aniline.

phenyl amines. A group of aromatic amino compounds: primary phenyl amines ($Ar\cdot NH_2$), e.g., aniline; secondary phenyl amines (Ar_2NH), e.g., diphenylamine; tertiary phenyl amines (Ar_3N), e.g., triphenylamine.

phenylaniline. ar- Biphenylamine. **N-** Diphenylamine.

phenylarsonic acid. Benzenearsonic acid.

phenylate. (1) Phenate. (2) MOPh. A compound of a metal and phenol.

phenylation. Introduction of the phenyl group into a molecule.

phenylazide. $C_6H_5N_3 = 119.06$. Triazobenzene. Colorless liquid, d.1.098, $b_{24mm}74$.

phenylazo. The radical PhN:N—. **p. aniline.** See *aminoazobenzene*.

phenylbenzamide. Benzanilide.

phenylbenzene. Diphenyl.

phenylbenzhydryl. The radical $Ph\cdot C_6H_4\cdot CHOH$—.

phenyl benzoate. $PhCOOPh = 198.1$. Benzophenid, phenol benzoate, benzocarbolic acid. Colorless monoclinic crystals, m.68, soluble in water.

phenylbenzoyl. The radical $Ph\cdot C_6H_4CO$—. **p. benzoic acid.** $PhC_6H_4COC_6H_4COOH = 302.11$. Diphenylphthaloic acid, 4-phenylbenzophenone-2-carboxylic acid; used in the synthesis of dyes. **p. carbinol.** Benzoin.

phenylbenzyl. The radical $Ph\cdot C_6H_4\cdot CH_2$—. **p. amine.** $PhNHCH_2Ph = 183.2$. Colorless crystals, m.32, soluble in alcohol; used inorganic synthesis. **p. ketone.** See phenyl*propiophenone*. **p. tin chloride.** $Ph\cdot C_6H_4CH_2SnCl_2 = 357.71$. Colorless needles, m.83.

phenylborine. $PhBH_2 = 89.8$. An isolog of aniline.

phenyl bromide. $C_6H_5Br = 156.96$. Bromobenzene*, Colorless liquid, d.1.497, b.156.2.

phenylbutazone. $C_{19}H_{20}O_2N_2 = 308.36$. White crystals, m.107, insoluble in water; an analgesic and antipyretic (B.P.).

phenylbutyric acid. $C_{10}H_{12}O_2 = 164.1$. **alpha-** $Ph(CH_2)_3COOH$. Colorless crystals, m.42, soluble in water. **beta-** $MeCHPh\cdot CH_2\cdot COOH$. Colorless crystals; 3 isomers: *dextro-* m.156. *levo-* m.157. *racemic-* m.270. Soluble in water; used in organic synthesis.

phenyl carbamate. $PhCOONH_2 = 137.1$. Colorless leaflets, m.141, slightly soluble in water.

phenylcarbamido. The radical PhNHCONH—.

phenylcarbinol. Benzyl alcohol.

phenylcarbylamine. Phenyl isocyanide.

phenylchinaldine. $C_{16}H_{13}N = 219.1$. Phenylquinaldine, methylquinol. Colorless crystals, soluble in water; an antimalarial.

phenylchinoline. Phenylquinoline.

phenyl chloride. $C_6H_5Cl = 112.50$. Chlorobenzene*, Colorless liquid, d.1.107, b.132.

phenyl chloroform. $C_6H_5CCl_3 = 195.4$. Benzotrichloride. Colorless liquid.

phenylcinchoninic acid. Atophan.

phenylcyanamide. $PhNH\cdot NC = 118.1$. Cyananilide. A solid, m.47, soluble in water.

phenyl cyanide. Benzonitrile.

phenylcyclohexane. $C_{12}H_{16} = 160.25$. Hexahydrodiphenyl. Colorless oil, $b_{13mm}107$.

phenyldicarbinol. Xylyl alcohol.

phenyl diethyl aminoethyl nitrobenzoate. A precipitant for nitrates and perchlorates.

phenyldihydrochinazolin. Orexin.

phenyldihydronaphthalene. Atronene.

phenyldimethylpyrazolone. Antipyrine.

phenyldiphenylcarbinol. Benzaurine.

phenyl disulfide. $Ph\cdot S\cdot S\cdot Ph = 218.3$. Phenyldithiobenzene*. Colorless needles, m.60, insoluble in water.

phenylene. The radical $C_6H_4=$, derived from benzene by replacement of 2 H atoms. Its compounds yield 3 isomers: ortho, meta, and para compounds. **p. blue.** Indamine. **p. diacetic acid.** $C_6H_4(CH_2COOH)_2 = 194.1$. *ortho-* m.150. *meta-* m.190. *para-* m.244. **p. diamine.** $C_6H_4(NH_2)_2 = 108.08$. Diaminobenzene, benzenediamine.

ortho- or *1,2*- m.104. *meta*- or *1,3*- m.63, *para*- or *1,4*- Ursol. m.140. Used to dye hairs and furs, as an indicator, and reagent for nitrogen. **methyl-** Tolylenediamine. *phenylazo*-Chrysoidine. **p. diazosulfide.** $C_6H_4 \cdot S \cdot N \cdot N$ = 136.1. Colorless crystals, m.35, soluble in alcohol. **p. dimercaptan.** $C_6H_4(SH)_2$ = 142.18. Benzenedithiole. *meta*- or *1,3*- Dithioresorcinol. Colorless crystals, m.27. *para*- or *1,4*- Dithiohydroquinone. Colorless crystals, m.98. **p. disazo.** The radical $-N:NC_6H_4N:N-$. **p. sulfourea.** $C_6H_4 \cdot NH \cdot C:S \cdot NH$ = 50.2. Thiobenzimidazoline,

p. urea. Colorless crystals, m.298, soluble in alcohol; used in organic synthesis.

phenylephrine hydrochloride. $C_9H_{13}NO_2 \cdot HCl$ = 203.67. Bitter, white crystals, soluble in water m.142; an adrenergic (U.S.P.).

phenylethane. Ethyl*benzene*.

phenylethanol. Benzylcarbinol. **p. amine.** C_8H_{11}-NO = 137.10. White powder, related and similar in action to adrenaline.

phenyl ether. $(C_6H_5)_2O$ = 170.1. Phenoxybenzene. Diphenyl oxide. Colorless, monoclinic crystals, or oil, d.1.073, almost insoluble in water; a heat-transfer agent.

phenylethyl. The radical $Ph \cdot CH_2 \cdot CH_2-$. **p. alcohol** Benzylcarbinol. **p. barbituric acid.** Luminal. **p. ether.** Phenetole. **p. hydantoin.** Nirvanol. **p. ketone.** Ethyl phenyl ketone.

phenylethylene. Styrene.

phenylformamide. Formanilide.

phenylformic acid. Benzoic acid.

phenyl gamma acid. *2-Phenylamino-8*-naphthol-*6*-sulfonic acid.

phenylglucosazone. $C_{18}H_{22}O_4N_4$ = 358.3. A condensation product of phenylhydrazine and glucose. Yellow needles, soluble in water. **alpha-** m.205. **beta-** m.145.

phenylglycine. $PhNHCH_2COOH$ = 151.2. Phenylglycocoll, m.127, soluble in water; used in the synthesis of indigo.

phenylglycocoll. Phenylglycine.

phenylglycolic acid. Mandelic acid.

phenylglycol. Cinnamic alcohol.

phenylglyoxal. Benzoyl formaldehyde.

phenylglyoxylic acid. Benzoylformic acid.

phenyl group. Ph. The radical C_6H_5-, from benzene.

phenyl hydrate. Phenol.

phenyl hydrazide. A derivative of phenylhydrazine of the type $Ph \cdot NH \cdot COR$ or $Ph \cdot N(COR)NH_2$: β (symmetric) or α- (asymmetric).

phenylhydrazine. $PhNHNH_2 \cdot \frac{1}{2}H_2O$ = 117.1. Hydrazobenzene. Colorless liquid, d.1.097, b.243, slightly soluble in water; a reagent for aldehydes and ketones. **acetyl-** Pyrodin. **ethyl-** See *ethylphenylhydrazine*. **phthalyl-** Phthalylphenylhydrazine. **salicyl-α-methyl-** Agathin. **p. hydrochloride.** $Ph \cdot NH \cdot NH_2 \cdot HCl$ = 144.6. Colorless crystals, m.200, soluble in water; a reagent for glucose, formaldehyde, and urea. **p. levulinic acid.** Antithermin. **p. urea.** Diphenylcarbazide.

phenyl hydrazone. $Ph \cdot NH \cdot N:CH_2$ = 120.1. **acetone-** See *acetone phenyl hydrazone*.

phenyl hydrazones. $Ph \cdot NH \cdot N:CHR$ or $Ph \cdot NH \cdot N:CR_2$. Formed by the action of phenylhydrazine on aldehydes or ketones.

phenyl hydroxide. Phenol.

phenylhydroxylamine. $PhNHOH$ = 109.1. Colorless needles, m.80, soluble in water; used in organic synthesis.

phenylic. Pertaining to phenol or the phenyl radical. **p. acid.** Phenol. **p. alcohol.** Phenol.

phenylid. Aniline.

phenylidene. The radicals

$$CH \begin{array}{c} CH:CH \\ \diagdown \\ CH \cdot CH_2 \end{array} C= \quad and \quad CH_2 \begin{array}{c} CH:CH \\ \diagdown \\ CH:CH \end{array} C=$$

ortho- para-

phenylindanedione. $C_{15}H_{10}O_2$ = 222.21. Dindevan. 2-Phenylindane-1,3-dione. White crystals, m.150, soluble in water; a blood coagulant (U.S.P.).

phenylindazole. See *indazole*.

phenyl isocyanate. $PhNCO$ = 119.1. A lachrymatory, d.1.096, b.163; a reagent for hydroxy and amino compounds.

phenyl isocyanide. $PhNC$ = 103.1. Phenylcarbylamine isocyanobenzene. Colorless liquid, d.0.978, b.165, decomp. by water.

phenylisonitramine. Nitranilide.

phenyl ketone. Benzophenone.

phenyllactazam. $C_6H_4 \cdot CPh:N \cdot NPh \cdot CO$ = 298.2. Colorless crystals, m.181, soluble in alcohol.

phenyl mercaptan. Thiophenol.

phenylmercuric. The radical C_6H_5Hg-. **p. acetate.** $CH_3COOHgPh$ = 336.67. Rhombic, colorless crystals, m.149. **p. chloride.** $PhHgCl$ = 313.11. Leaflets, m.251. **p. cyanide.** $PhHgCN$ = 303.66. White prisms, m.204. **p. nitrate.** $PhHgNO_3$ = 339.66. Rhombic scales, m.180, soluble in water. The basic compound (m.190, decomp.) is a nonirritant, low-toxicity antibacteriostatic (B.P.); a preservative for urine in alcohol tests.

phenylmethane. Toluene.

phenylmethylether. Anisole.

phenyl methyl ketone. Acetophenone.

phenyl mustard oil. C_6H_5NCS = 135.1. Phenyl isothiocyanate, thiocarbanil, phenylthiocarbonimide. Colorless liquid, d.1.138, b.221, insoluble in water; used in organic synthesis.

phenylnaphthalene. $C_{10}H_7Ph$ = 204.2. **alpha-** Colorless liquid, b.324, soluble in alcohol. **beta-** Colorless scales, m.102, soluble in alcohol.

phenylnaphthylamine. $C_{10}H_7 \cdot NH \cdot Ph$ = 219.2. **alpha-** Colorless needles, m.60, insoluble in water. **beta-** Colorless leaflets, m.107, insoluble in water; an anti-aging agent for rubber.

phenylnaphthylcarbazole. Benzonaphthindole.

phenyl naphthyl ketone. $C_{10}H_7 \cdot CO \cdot Ph$ = 232.2. **alpha-** Colorless rhombs, m.76, insoluble in water. **beta-** White needles, m.82, insoluble in water.

phenylnitramine. $Ph \cdot NH \cdot NO_2$ = 138.1. An isomer of diazoic acid. Colorless leaflets, m.46, explodes 98, soluble in water.

phenylo. Phenyl. **p. boric acid.** $C_6H_5B(OH)_2$ = 121.9. White powder, sparingly soluble in water; a germicide. Cf. *borophenylic acid*. **p. salicylic acid.** $C_6H_4(OH) \cdot C_6H_4COOH$ = 214.2. Hydroxydiphenylcarboxylic acid, o-oxydiphenylcarboxylic acid. White powder, soluble in water; a germicide.

phenylogic series. The hydrocarbon series; C_6H_6, $C_{12}H_{10}$, $C_{18}H_{24}$. Cf. *diphenyl*.

phenylon. Antipyrine.

phenyloxalate. Diphenyl oxalate.

phenyloxydisulfide. $Ph_2S_2O_2$ = 250.26. A solid, m.45, soluble in ether.

phenylparaconic acid. $C_{11}H_{10}O_4$ = 206.2. An aromatic lactone. Colorless crystals, m.109, soluble in alcohol.

phenyl-paraffin alcohols. Aromatic alcohols with an —OH radical in the side chain; as, $Ph·CH_2OH$, benzyl alcohol.

phenyl-peri acid. Phenyl-1-naphthylamine-8-sulfonic acid.

phenylphenol. $Ph·C_6H_4·OH$ = 170.08. **meta-** m.78. **ortho-** White crystals, m.56, soluble in water; phenol coefficient 38. A preservative for glues, and (with certain legal limitations) for noncitrus fruits. **para-** m.165.

phenylphosphine. $PhPH_2$ = 110.0. Phosphaniline. Colorless liquid, b.160, obtained by the action of hydriodic acid and phosphorus on phenyl chloride.

phenylphosphinic acid. $Ph·PO·(OH)_2$ = 158.13. A solid, m.158, soluble in water.

phenylpropiolic acid. $PhC \vdots C·COOH$ = 146.1. Needles, m.136, soluble in water; used in organic synthesis.

phenylpropionic acid. alpha- Hydratropic acid. **beta-** Hydrocinnamic acid.

phenylpropiophenone. See phenyl *propiophenone*.

phenyl propyl ketone. Butyrophenone.

phenylpyridine. $C_6H_5·C_5H_4N$ = 155.14. **alpha-** Colorless liquid, b.269, insoluble in water. **beta-** Colorless oil, b.270, insoluble in water. **gamma-** Colorless scales, m.77, soluble in water.

phenylquinaldine. Phenylchinaldine.

phenylquinoline. $C_{15}H_{11}N$ = 205.2. Phenyl chinoline. **alpha-** White needles, m.84, soluble in water; used to treat malaria.

phenyl salicylate. $C_6H_4(OH)COOPh$ = 214.14. Salol, phenylis salicylas. Colorless crystals, m.42, soluble in water; an intestinal antiseptic.

phenylsalicylic acid. $C_{13}H_{10}O_3$ = 214.14. The isomer of salol, insoluble solid, m.160.

phenyl semicarbazide. $Ph·NH·NH·CO·NH_2$ = 151.1. White scales, m.172, soluble in water; used in organic synthesis.

phenyl stannane. Sn_nPh_{2n+2}. An organic compound of tervalent tin; Sn_5Ph_{12}.

phenyl sulfate. $PhOSO_3M$. A salt of phenylsulfuric acid.

phenyl sulfhydrate. Thiophenol.

phenyl sulfide. $(C_6H_5)_2S$ = 186.2. Phenylthiobenzene. Colorless liquid, d.1.119, b.296, insoluble in water.

phenyl sulfone. Ph_2SO_2 = 218.14. Phenylsulfonylbenzene, diphenyl sulfone. White needles, m.128.

phenyl sulfonyl. The radical $PhSO_2$—. **p. benzene.** Phenyl sulfone.

phenylsulfuric acid. $C_6H_5OSO_3H$ = 174.1. A phenolester of sulfuric acid. An unstable acid whose salts are sometimes found in urine.

phenylthiocarbonimide. Phenyl mustard oil.

phenylthiohydantoic acid. $PhN\!:\!C(NH_2)S·CH_2·CO-OH$ = 210.1. Phenyliminocarbaminthioglycolic acid. White powder, m.150, insoluble in cold, soluble in hot water; a reagent for copper and cobalt. **ortho-** $PhNH·C(:NH)S·CH_2·COOH$. Insoluble in water.

phenyl thioisocyanate. Phenyl mustard oil.

phenylthiourea. $CSNH_2(NH)·Ph$ = 152.18. m.154. soluble in water.

phenyltin. The radical $C_6H_5Sn\!\equiv\!$. **p. bromide.** $PhSnBr_3$ = 435.49. Colorless liquid, $b_{25mm}185$. **p. chloride.** $PhSnCl_3$ = 302.11. Colorless liquid, $b_{25mm}143$. **p. tribenzyl.** $PhSn(CH_2Ph)_3$ = 468.90, Colorless liquid, $b_{5mm}290$; soluble in organic solvents except alcohol.

phenytoin. $C_{15}H_{11}O_2N_2Na$ = 274.32. Diphenylhydantoin sodium. White powder, soluble in water; an anticonvulsant (B.P.).

phenyltoluene. $Ph·C_6H_4·Me$ = 168.1. Diphenylenmethane, methyldiphenyl, phenyltolyl; 3 isomers: **meta-** Colorless liquid, d.1.031, b.272, insoluble in water. **ortho-** Colorless liquid, b.260, insoluble in water. **para-** Colorless liquid, d.1.015, b.263, insoluble in water.

phenyltolyl. Phenyltoluene.

phenyl tolyl ketone. $Ph·CO·C_6H_4·Me$ = 196.2. Tolyl phenyl ketone. **meta-** Colorless liquid, d.1.088, b.314, insoluble in water. **ortho-** Colorless liquid, b.315, soluble in alcohol. **para-** Colorless, monoclinic crystals, m.59, insoluble in water.

phenylurea. $PhNH·CO·NH_2$ = 136.2. Colorless, monoclinic crystals, m.146, slightly soluble in water.

phenylureido. Phenylcarbamido.

phenylurethane. $Ph·NH·COO·Et$ = 165.1. Euphorin, ethyl phenyl carbamate, carbamilic ether. White crystals of clove odor and taste, m.51, slightly soluble in water; an antirheumatic.

phenyl vinyl ketone. Acrylophenone.

phenzoline. Orexin.

pheochrome. Cellular tissue stained dark by chromium salts.

pheophorbide. $C_{31}H_{31}N_4(COOH)_2COOMe$ = 608.6. A split product of chlorophyll obtained by saponification of pheophytin.

pheophytin. $C_{31}H_{31}N_4(COOH)COOMe(COOC_{20}H_{39})$ = 870.6. A split product of chlorophyll obtained by treatment with oxalic acid.

pheoretin. $C_{14}H_8O_7$ = 288.1. A resinous principle from rhubarb root. Brown powder, soluble in alkalies.

pheromone. A chemical substance which acts as a medium of communication between living bodies. e.g., a perfume, or the external secretion of termites.

pheron. The colloidal carrier of an enzyme responsible for catalytic activity. Cf. *agon*.

phesin. $C_6H_3(OC_2H_5)SO_3Na(NH·COCH_3)$ = 259.2 Acetphenetidine sodium sulfonate. A sulfo derivative of phenacetin. Brown powder, soluble in water; an antipyretic.

Ph.G. Abbreviation for Graduate of Pharmacy.

phi. Greek letter φ, ϕ, Φ. Symbol for: (1) phenyl; (2) fluidity; (3) amphi position in the naphthalene ring; (4) the benzene ring in indone; (5) phlogiston.

phial. A vial, or small bottle.

philippium. A supposed rare-earth metal obtained from samarskite, shown to be mixed terbium and yttrium.

phillipite. $Fe_2Cu(SO_4)_4·12H_2O$. A native copper sulfate. Blue masses.

phillipsite. A complex clay containing Na, K, and Ca.

phillyrin. $C_{27}H_{34}O_{11}$ = 534.2. A glucoside from *Phillyrea* species. Colorless crystals; an antipyretic.

philosopher's stone. An imaginary substance supposed by the alchemists to transform base metals into gold, and, if taken internally, to prolong life; identical with the "elixir" of the iatrochemists, and the alkahest. **p. wool.** Zinc oxide.

philosophy. An appreciation of the many branches of science in one system of correlated and generalized knowledge. It differs from true science, q.v., in its more imaginary and speculative viewpoint.

phlobabene. $C_{50}H_{46}O_{25}$ = 1046.4. A glucoside from various tree barks and hops; yields glucose and hopred on hydrolysis.

phlobaphen. A series of resinous oxidation products of tannin materials, formed by boiling them with acids. Yellow or brown substances, soluble in dilute alkali.

phlobatannin. Catechol tannin. The coloring matter in the rinds of many fruits.

phlogistic. (1) Inflammatory. (2) Pertaining to burning or fire. **de-** Oxygen.

phlogisticated air. Priestley's term for nitrogen.

phlogiston. ϕ. The hypothetical component of flammable substances (Stahl). **p. theory.** (Becher, 1669.) An all-pervading substance, phlogiston, was supposed to be the combustible principle and to escape during combustion or oxidation in the form of heat and smoke. Cf. *antiphlogistic theory, phlogisticated.*

phlogopite. $K_2(Fe^{++}Mg)_6 \cdot Al_2Si_6O_{20} \cdot (OH,F)_4$. Rhombic mica. A natural mica, used as an electrical insulator. **fluoro-** $K_2Mg_6Al_2Si_6O_{20}F_4$. A synthetic industrial mica.

phlogosine. A ptomaine in cultures of staphylococcus.

phlolaphenes. Pyrocatechol esters of aliphatic C_{16-22} acids made by pyrolysis of pine bark; used as plasticizers.

phloretic acid. $C_6H_4OHCHMeCOOH$ = 166.13. 3-*p*-Hydroxyphenylpropionic acid, *p*-hydroxyhydrocinnamic acid, α,β-dihydrocoumaric acid, m.128, soluble in alcohol.

phloretin. $C_{15}H_{14}O_5$ = 274.2. A colorless crystalline split product of phlorizin, in fruit seeds, m.1259 (decomp.), soluble in ether.

phlorhizin. Phlorizin.

phloridzin. Phlorizin.

phlorizein. $C_{21}H_{30}O_{13}$ = 490.3. A red oxidation product of phlorizin.

phlorizin. $C_{21}H_{24}O_{10} \cdot 2H_2O$ = 472.3. Phlorhizin, phloridzin. A glucoside from the bark and root of hard fruit trees. White needles, m.110, soluble in water; an antimalarial and tonic. Cf. *rufin.*

phlorobenzophenone. Benzophloroglucinol.

phloroglucin(e). Phloroglucinol.

phloroglucinol. $C_6H_3(OH)_3 \cdot 2H_2O = 162.11$. Phloroglucine, 1,3,5-trihydroxybenzene, 1,3,5-benzenetriol*, 3,5-dihydroxyphenol. Yellow crystals, m.217, soluble in water. A reagent for hydrochloric acid in gastric juice; pentoses, lignin, and pentosans; hydrated chloral, etc.; and lignin in groundwood fiber. Tautomeric forms:

phenol form   ketone form

benzo- See *benzophloroglucinol.* **hexahydro-** Phloroglucitol. **triamido-** $C_6H_9O_3N_3$ = 171.2. 2,4,6-Triamino-1,3,5-trihydroxybenzene. **trinitro-** $C_6H_3-O_9N_3$ = 261.1. 2,4,6-Trinitro-1,3,5-trihydroxybenzene. **p. phthalein.** Gallein.

p. test. Add hydrochloric acid and a fragment of phloroglucinol, and heat; a cherry-red color and precipitate indicate pentoses or lignified fibers.

phloroglucite. Phloroglucitol.

phloroglucitol. $C_6H_{12}O_3$ = 132.1. Methylenetriol, cyclohexane-1,3,5-triol, hexahydrophloroglucinol, phloroglucite. Colorless crystals, m.184, soluble in water.

phlorol. $C_6H_4(OH)Et$ = 122.1. *o*-Ethylphenol. Colorless oil obtained from cresols, b.211, soluble in alcohol.

phlorone. $(CH:CMe \cdot CO)_2$ = 136.06. *p*-Xyloquinone. Colorless crystals, m.125. Cf. *phorone.*

phlorose. α-Glucose.

phloxin. Tetrabromodichlorofluorescein. An aniline-dye pH indicator changing at 3.5 from colorless (acid) to magenta (alkaline).

phocenic acid. Valeric acid.

phocenin. $C_3H_5(OOC \cdot C_4H_9)_3$ = 324.2. Trivalerin. The valeric acid ester of glycerol.

phoe- See *pho-*.

phoenicochroite. $PbCrO_4$. A native lead chromate.

pholcodine. $C_{23}H_{30}O_4N_2 \cdot H_2O$ = 416.44. Morphine 2-morpholinoethyl ether. White, bitter crystals, m.99, soluble in water; a cough suppressant (B.P.).

phon. The international unit of loudness. When a sound is n decibels greater than corresponds with 10^{-6} watt/cm^2, then the loudness is n phons; 1 p. is approximately the minimum loudness change that the human ear can detect.

phonene. A group of similar sounds.

phonic. Pertaining to sound. **infra-** The inaudible air vibrations of wavelengths longer than that of sound. **ultra-** The inaudible air vibrations shorter in wavelength than sound.

phonochemical. A reaction induced or produced by sound. Cf. *ultrasonic.*

phonolite. A variety of feldspar.

phonometer. Sonometer.

phonosensitive. Affected by sound.

-phore. Suffix indicating to carry, bear, or bring forth: as, in chromo- color. Cf. *chromogen.*

phoretic. See *electron.*

phorone. $Me_2C:CH \cdot CO \cdot CH:C:Me_2$ = 138.2. Diisopropilideneacetone. Yellow prisms, m.28, insoluble in water. Cf. *phlorone.*

phoronomy. The study of motion, time, and relativity.

phoryl resins. Resins made by the reaction of phenols with an excess of phosphorus oxychloride with calcium chloride as catalyst, and reacting the resulting aryloxyphosphoryl dichloride with a dihydroxyphenol. Colorless, glassy plastics, $n_D1.55$–1.63, mol.wt. approx. 15,000, resistant to mineral acids and many chemical reagents. Used as paint undercoats, to ensure adhesion to metals.

phosgene. Carbonyl chloride. **di-** Trichloromethylchloroformate. **thio-** Thiophosgene.

phosgenite. $PbCl_2 \cdot PbCO_3$. Horn lead. An ore.

phosphagen. Guanidinophosphoric acid, phosphocreatinine. A compound of phosphorus and creatinine, involved in muscle contraction.

phospham. $PN_2H = 60.0$. A white infusible phosphorazide.

phosphamic acid. Amidophosphoric acid.

phosphamide. $PO \cdot NH \cdot NH_2 = 78.07$. White powder, insoluble in water.

phosphaniline. Phenylphosphine.

phosphatase. An enzyme from body fluids or organs that splits carbohydrate-phosphate combinations. **p. test.** Active p. in raw milk liberates phenol from sodium diphenyl phosphate, which is determined colorimetrically.

phosphate. (1) A salt of phosphoric acid containing the radical $PO \equiv_4$; as:

M_3PO_4 . . . . Normal or tertiary phosphate
M_2HPO_4 . . . . Monoacid, monohydric, dibasic, or secondary phosphate
MH_2PO_4 . . . . Diacid, dihydric, monobasic, or primary phosphate
$(M, M')PO_4$ . . . . Double phosphate
$(M, M', M'')PO_4$ . . . . . Triple phosphate

(2) A salt of one of the phosphoric acids; as: $M_4P_2O_6$, *hypo*phosphate; M_3PO_4, *ortho*phosphate; MPO_3, *meta*phosphate; $M_4P_2O_7$, *pyro*phosphate. World production (1966), 19.2 million tons (as P_2O_5). **acid-** A mono- or dihydric p.; as, M_2HPO_4, MH_2PO_4, or $M_2H_2P_2O_7$. **alkaline-** A p. of sodium or potassium. **bone-** Calcium p. **dibasic-** A compound of the type M_2HPO_4. **dihydric-** A compound of the type MH_2PO_4. **disodic-** Sodium acid p. **earthy-** A p. of the alkaline-earth metals. **hypo-** A salt of hypophosphoric acid, $M_4P_2O_6$. **meta-** A salt of metaphosphoric acid, MPO_3. **monobasic-** An acid phosphate, MH_2PO_4. **monohydric-** An acid phosphate, M_2HPO_4. **normal-** A salt in which all H atoms of the acid have been displaced; as, Na_3PO_4. **ortho-** A salt of orthophosphoric acid, M_3PO_4. **poly-** A compound having the general formula $M_{x+2}P_xO_{3x+1}$, where M is an alkali metal. Made by fusing together $NaPO_3$ and $Na_4P_2O_7$ in the desired proportions; used for water softening by double decomposition. **pyro-** A salt of pyrophosphoric acid, $M_4P_2O_7$. **stellar-** Calcium p. occurring in star-shaped crystals. **super-** See *fertilizer, superphosphate*. **triple-** (1) A salt of the type $MM'M''PO_4$; as, NH_4KNaPO_4. (2) A calcium, magnesium, and ammonium p. sometimes occurring in urine.

p. of lime. Apatite. **p. rock.** A sedimentary rock containing calcium p.

phosphated, phosphatic. Containing phospates.

phosphatides. Phospholipins. Phospholipids. Lipoid substances that occur in cellular structures and contain esters of phosphoric acid; as, cephalin. **amino-** Lecithins.

phosphatins. Organic phosphates in animal tissues.

phosphazide. A compound of the type $R_3P : N \cdot N : NR$.

phosphazine. A compound of the type $R_3P : N \cdot N : CR_2$.

phosphazo. The radical $-N : P-$.

phosphazote. Phosphonitrogen.

phosphene. $CH : (CH)_2 : CH \cdot PH = 84.1$. Phosphurane. Cf. *pyrrole*.

phosphenyl. The radical $>PC_6H_5$. **p. chloride.** $C_6H_5PCl_2 = 179.0$. An unstable liquid d.1.319, b.225. **p. oxychloride.** $C_6H_5OPCl_2 = 194.98$. A liquid, d.1.375, b.258.

phosphenylic acid. $C_6H_5 \cdot H_2PO_3 = 158.1$. Phenylphosphorus acid. A crystalline solid, m.158 (decomp.), soluble in alcohol.

phosphide. A binary compound of phosphorus which contains trivalent P; as, Na_3P. **hydrogen-** Phosphorus hydrides.

phosphine. $PH_3 = 34.1$. See *phosphorus hydrides*. **p. oxide.** An organic derivative containing the $\equiv PO$ group; as, Et_3PO. **p. sulfide.** An organic derivative containing the $\equiv PS$ group; as, Et_3PS.

phosphines. Compounds derived from phosphine by the replacement of H atoms: $RPH_2 = $ primary p., e.g., $MePH_2$, methylphosphine. $R_2PH = $ secondary p., e.g. Me_2PH, dimethylphosphine. $R_3P = $ tertiary p., e.g., Me_3P, trimethylphosphine. $R_4POH = $ quaternary p. Cf. *phosphonium compounds*.

phosphinic acid. An organic derivative of hypophosphorous acid containing the radical $-H_2PO_2$ or $=HPO_2$; as, $Me \cdot HPO \cdot OH$, methylphosphinic acid; $Me_2 : PO \cdot OH$, dimethylphosphinic acid. Cf. *phosphonic acid*.

phosphinimine. A compound of the type $R_3P : NR$.

phosphino. The H_2P- group.

phosphinoborine. $R_2BPR'_2$. An inorganic polymer, q.v.

phosphinoso. (1) The $(OH)_2M-$ group. (2) The $HO \cdot P = $ group. Cf. *phosphonoso*.

phosphite. A salt of phosphorous acid containing the radical $\equiv PO_3$: e.g., Na_3PO_3, *normal* sodium phosphite. **p. esters.** Compounds of the type $P(OR)_3$, where R is an aryl or alkyl group.

phospho. (1) Indicating the presence of phosphorus. (2) The O_2P- group. **p. acid.** An organic derivative of asymmetric phosphorous acid:

$$P(OH)_3 \qquad = \qquad H-P : O(OH)_2$$
Symmetric   Asymmetric

which contains the radical $-PO(OH)_2$. **p. albumin.** An albuminous substance containing phosphorus. **p. globulin.** Nucleoalbumin. **p. lipin.** An ester of a fatty acid containing nitrogen and phosphorus radicals. **p. nitrogen.** Phosphazote. A fertilizer: urea solution and phosphate rocks. **p. protein.** See *phosphoprotein*.

phosphoaminolipid. A complex lipid containing phosphorus and amino radicals. Cf. *phospholipid*.

phosphobenzene. Phosphorbenzene.

phosphocalcite. Pseudo*malachite*.

phosphocarnic acid. Nucleol.

phosphocerite. Rhabdophane.

phosphochalcite. Pseudo*malachite*.

phosphoglobulin. Nucleoalbumin.

phosphogypsum. A gypsum produced in the manufacture of phosphoric acid and used in cement.

phosphoinositide. A lipid containing radicals derived from inositol and phosphoric acid.

phospholeum. A mixture of a phosphate or a phosphoric acid with soap, used to prevent precipitation of the latter in hard water.

phospholipid. A proposed name for phosphatide, q.v. Cf. *phosphoaminolipid*.

phospholipin, phospholipoid. Phosphatide.

phosphomolybdic acid. $H_3PO_4 \cdot 12MoO_3 \cdot 12H_2O = 2042.3$. Yellow solid; a reagent.

phosphonic acid. $RO \cdot P \cdot (OH)_2$; as, $C_6H_5O \cdot P(OH)_2$, phenylphosphonic acid. Cf. *phosphinic acid, phospho acid*.

phosphonitrogen. See *phospho-*.

phosphonitryl. The radical $=PN$. **p. bromide.** Phosphorus bromonitride. **p. chloride.** $PNCl_2 = 115.9$. Formed by the action of ammonium chloride on phosphorus chloride. It readily polymerizes at 260°C to a substance resembling rubber.

phosphonium. The radical PH_4—, analogous to ammonium. Cf. *-onium*. **p. bromide.** PH_4Br. Bromophosphonium. **p. chloride.** PH_4Cl. Chlorophosphonium. **p. compounds.** Quaternary phosphines. Compounds derived from phosphonium hydroxide by replacement of its H atoms: e.g., $R_4P(OH)$, tetra-*R*-phosphonium hydroxide. **p. hydroxide.** PH_4OH. **p. iodide.** PH_4I. Iodophosphonium.

phosphono. The radical, $(HO)_2PO$—. Cf. *phosphonic acid*.

phosphonoso. (1) The $HO \cdot OPH$— group. (2) The $HO \cdot OP=$ group. Cf. *phosphinoso*.

phosphoprotein. A group of conjugated proteins consisting of a simple protein combined with an unidentified phosphorous compound other than nucleic acid or lecithin.

phosphor. (1) German for phosphorus. (2) A substance which phosphoresces when stimulated by external radiation. Thus, sodium iodide activated with thallium iodide is used to detect and measure γ radiation from the fluorescence produced. **p. bronze.** Cu 82–94, Sn 9.5–10.8, Zn 1.0–2.0, P 0.01–0.1, impurities 0.30%. Used for suspension threads for galvanometer mirrors. **p. hydrogen compounds.** See *phosphorus hydrides*. **p. salt.** Microcosmic salt. **p. tin.** A white alloy of phosphorus and tin, m.370.

phosphorate. An organic compound, analogous to a nitrosate, containing the radical $=P_2O_4$; as, $C_6H_{10}P_2O_4$, cyclohexane phosphorate.

phosphorated. Containing phosphorus; as, p. oil.

phosphorbenzene. $P_4(C_6H_5)_4 = 432.15$. Phosphobenzene, phosphorobenzene. PhP:PPh. Yellow solid, m.150, of high thermal stability; insoluble in water.

phosphorescence. (1) The continuous emission of light from a substance, without apparent temperature rise, after exposure to a heat, light, or electric discharge. (2) The luminosity of a living organism; as, glowworms. (3) In particular, the faint green glow of white phosphorus in air, due to slow oxidation. Cf. *luminescence, fluorescence, scattering*.

phosphorescent paint. A luminous paint.

phosphoret(t)ed hydrogen. (1) Phosphorus hydrides. (2) Phosphine.

phosphoric. Containing pentavalent phosphorus. **p. acid.** $H_3PO_4 = 98.1$. Orthophosphoric acid. Colorless crystals, m.38, soluble in water. Marketed as: 85%—colorless oil, d.1.7, miscible with water; 10%—dilute p. acid, colorless liquid, d.1.057. A reagent; and stimulant of secretion of gastric juices (B.P.). *di-* Pyrophosphoric acid. *hypo-* See *hypophosphoric acid*. *meta-* $HPO_3 = 80.1$. Clear, viscous liquid. "Glacial metaphosphoric acid, sticks" contains 17–18% sodium oxide. *ortho-* P. acid. *pyro-* $H_4P_2O_7 = 178.11$. Colorless crystals, m.61, soluble in water. The p. acids are derived from phosphorus oxide by addition of water.

$P_2O_5 + H_2O = 2HPO_3$, metaphosphoric acid.
$P_2O_5 + 2H_2O = H_4P_2O_7$, pyrophosphoric acid.
$P_2O_5 + 3H_2O = 2H_3PO_4$, orthophosphoric acid.

p. anhydride. Phosphorus pentoxide.

phosphorimetry. Analysis based on the spectrophotometric examination of the phosphorescence excited in the sample by ultraviolet light.

phosphorite. (1) Apatite. (2) An organic compound analogous to a nitrosite, containing the radical $=P_2O_3$; as, $C_6H_{10}P_2O_3$, cyclohexane phosphorite.

phosphoro. The —P:P— group.

phosphorobenzene. Phosphorbenzene.

phosphorometer. An instrument, in which the duration of a phosphorescence phenomenon is measured in terms of the rate of rotation of radiometer vanes.

phosphoroso. The OP— group.

phosphorous. (1) Phosphorescent. (2) Describing a compound of trivalent phosphorus. **p. acid.** $H_3PO_3 = 82.1$. Orthophosphorous acid. Yellow crystals, m.70, soluble in water; a reagent and reducing agent. *ethyl-* Ethyl phosphite. *hypo-* $H_3PO_2 = 66.1$. Colorless liquid, d.1.493, m.27 (decomp.), soluble in water. Its salts are hypophosphites.

phosphorus. P = 30.97, $P_4 = 123.92$. A nonmetallic element of the nitrogen group, at.no. 15. Allotropic modifications:

(1) *Ordinary, yellow, white,* or *regular* p. Regular white crystals, usually compressed into yellow waxlike sticks, d.1.82, m.44, b.200, insoluble in and stored under water protected from light (which changes it into the red form). Three forms of yellow p. are α-, β-, and γ-.

(2) *Red, "amorphous"* p. Red rhombohedra, d.2.2, m.72, b.350, insoluble in water or carbon disulfide. Formed by heating yellow p. to 240; nonpoisonous and nonluminous.

(3) *Violet* p. Crystalline solid, d.2.4, m.590.

(4) *Metallic, rhombohedral,* or α-*black* p. Black powder, d.2.34, obtained by heating p. in a sealed tube with molten lead; a nonconductor of electricity.

(5) *Black,* or β-black p. Black powder, d.2.7, m.588; conducts electricity.

P. was discovered in 1669 by the alchemist H. Brandt of Hamburg, and was prepared independently by Boyle and Kunkel. It forms 3 main series of compounds, derived from tri- and pentavalent P, as shown in the table on top of next page. **amorphous-** See (2). **Baldwin's-** A phosphorescent form of commercial fused calcium nitrate. **black-** (a) See (4). (b) See (5). *Bologna-* Luminescent barium sulfide. **Canton-** q.v. **Homberg's-** Phosphorescent calcium chloride, made by heating lime and ammonium chloride. **metallic-** See (4). **ordinary-** See (1). **radio-** The isotope of mass 32; a radioactive indicator. **red-** See (2). **regular-** See (1). **rhombohedral-** See (4). **salt of-** Acid ammonium phosphate; used for bead tests. **scarlet-** Scarlet powder, intermediate in activity between red and yellow p.; used for matches. **violet-** See (3). **vitreous-** See (1). **white-** See (1). **yellow-** See (1).

p. bromides. PBr_3, p. tribromide; PBr_4, p. tetrabromide; PBr_5, p. pentabromide. **p. bromonitride.** $PNBr_2 = 204.86$. Phosphonitrile bromide. Rhombic crystals, m.190. **p. chloride.** See

Valency	Compounds
−3.....	PH₃, phosphine

$-3.....PH_3$, phosphine
$\quad$ (PH₄X, phosphonium)
$+1.....P_2O$, p. monoxide
$\quad$ (M₃PO₂, hypophosphite)
$+3.....P_2O_3$, p. trioxide
$\quad$ (M₃PO₃, phosphite)
$\quad$ PX₃, phosphorous-
$\quad$ (MPO₂, metaphosphite)
$+4.....P_2O_4$, p. tetroxide
$\quad$ (M₄P₂O₆ or M₂PO₃, hypophosphate)
$+5.....P_2O_5$, p. pentoxide
$\quad$ (H₃PO₄, phosphoric acid)
$\quad$ PX₅, phosphoric-
$\quad$ (HPO₃, metaphosphoric acid)
$\quad$ POX₃, phosphoryl-
$\quad$ (M₃PO₄, phosphate;
$\quad$ MPO₃, metaphosphate;
$\quad$ M₄P₂O₇, pyrophosphate)

p. dichloride, trichloride, pentachloride. **p. dichloride.** $P_2Cl_4 = 203.85$. Oily, fuming liquid, decomp. by water. **p. diiodide.** $P_2I_4 = 569.76$. Red solid, m.110, soluble in carbon disulfide. **p. group.** Sixth group of the periodic system, composed of the elements N, P, As, Sb, and Bi. **p. halides.** The halogen compounds of p. **p. hydrides.** *gaseous-* $PH_3 = 34.1$. Phosphine, phosphoreted hydrogen, hydrogen phosphide. Colorless, poisonous gas of characteristic odor, b.− 86, slightly soluble in water. *liquid-* $P_2H_4 = 66.1$. Colorless liquid, d.1.01, b.51, insoluble in water. *solid-* $P_{12}H_6 = 378.5$. Colorless crystals, decomp. by heat, insoluble in water. **p. monoxide.** $P_2O = 78.05$. White solid. **p. oxides.** P_2O, p. monoxide; P_2O_3, p. trioxide; P_2O_4, p. tetroxide; P_2O_5, p. pentoxide; P_4O, p. suboxide (doubtful). **p. oxychloride.** Phosphoryl chloride. **p. pentabromide.** $PBr_5 = 430.6$. Yellow crystals, m.100, decomp. by water; used in organic synthesis. **p. pentachloride.** $PCl_5 = 208.34$. More correctly, $[PCl_4]^+[PCl_6]^-$. Yellow rhombs, fuming in air, b.160 (sublimes), decomp. by water; a reagent and chlorinating agent. **p. pentafluoride.** $PF_5 = 126.1$. Colorless, irritant gas, b.−75. **p. pentaselenide.** $P_2Se_5 = 458.08$. Black solid, decomp. by heat. **p. pentasulfide.** $P_2S_5 = 222.4$. Yellow or gray crystals, m.270, decomp. by water. **p. pentoxide.** $P_2O_5 = 142.1$. White powder, d.2.38, soluble in water (forms metaphosphoric acid); a dehydrating agent for gases, and a reagent. **p. suboxide.** P_4O. Probably a mixture of red p. and $P_{12}H_6$. **p. tetroxide.** $P_2O_4 = 126.1$. Colorless, orthorhombic crystals, m.100, soluble in water. **p. tribromide.** $PBr_3 = 270.8$. Colorless, fuming liquid, d.2.88, b.175, decomp. by water. **p. trichloride.** $PCl_3 = 137.4$. Clear, fuming, poisonous liquid, d.1.613, b.76, decomp by water. **p. triiodide.** $PI_3 = 411.8$. Red prisms, m.61, decomp by heat or water. **p. trioxide.** $P_2O_3 = 110.1$. Phosphorous anhydride. Colorless, monoclinic crystals, m.23, soluble in water. **p. trisulfide.** $P_2S_3 = 158.3$. Yellow crystals, m.290, decomp. by water.

phosphoryl. The radical ≡P:O. **thio-** The radical ≡PS. **p. bromide.** $POBr_3 = 286.8$. m.55.

decomp. by water. **p. chloride.** $POCl_3 = 153.42$, Phosphorous oxychloride. Colorless fuming liquid, d.1.711, b.110; a reagent and catalyst in chlorination and dehydration. **p. fluoride.** $POF_3 = 104.03$. Colorless, fuming liquid, b.−40. **p. nitride.** $PON = 61.05$. Insoluble white solid. **p. triamide.** $PO(NH_2)_3 = 95.12$. Insoluble white solid, decomp. by heat.

phosphotungstate. Phosphowolframate. A salt of phosphotungstic acid.

phosphotungstic acid. $WO_3·2H_3PO_4 = 428.2$. Phosphowolframic acid. Green crystals, soluble in water; a reagent for alkaloids (Scheibler's reagent), and for albumin (Salkowski's reagent).

phosphovitin. A nonlipoid phosphoprotein, N 12, P 10%, in egg yolk.

phosphowolframate. Phosphotungstate.

phosphowolframic acid. Phosphotungstic acid.

phosphurane. Phosphene.

phosphuranolite. $(UPb)O·P_2O_5·xH_2O$. A mineral.

phosphuret(t)ed. Containing phosphorus in its lowest stage of oxidation. **p. hydrogen.** (1) See *phosphorus hydrides*. (2) Phosphine.

phostonic acid. A compound of the type $R·CH(O)·PO·OH$.

phot. A unit of intensity of illumination: 1 phot = 1 lumen/cm² = 10,000 lux = 1,000 milliphots.

photic. Pertaining to radiations.

photics. Synonym for optics.

photo- Pertaining to light.

photoactinic. Emitting visible and ultraviolet rays having photochemical activity.

photobacteria. A light-producing or phosphorescent vegetable microorganism.

photobiotic. Pertaining to organisms that live habitually in the light.

photocatalysis. The acceleration of certain reactions by light.

photocatalyst. A substance that aids photochemical reactions; as, chlorophyll.

photochemical. Pertaining to the chemical effects of light. **p. activation.** See *irradiation*. **p. catalysis.** The acceleration of a reaction by light. Cf. *p. reaction*. **p. dissociation.** The splitting of a molecule by the influence of light, low pressure, and low temperature; as, $H_2 \rightarrow 2H$. Cf. *p. excitation*. **p. effect.** Chemical changes produced by light. **p. equivalent.** The one quantum of energy, $h\nu$, which excites one molecule; hence, total radiation $E = nh\nu$, for n activated molecules. **p. excitation.** Dissociation of excited atoms; as, $H_2 \rightarrow 2H^*$. Cf. *p. dissociation*. **p. induction.** Draper effect. The period between exposure to light and the p. reaction which results. **p. processes.** A reaction in which light energy is stored as chemical energy; as, in photosynthesis. **p. reaction.** A reaction influenced by light.

photochemistry. The study of the relations between radiant and chemical energy. Cf. *photosynthesis, irradiation*.

photochromism. The property of changing color reversibly on exposure to ultraviolet or near-visible radiation.

photoconductivity. The property of a substance of conducting electricity when illuminated.

photodeposition. The formation of a thin polymer film on a surface by exposure to ultraviolet light in a monomer gas which reacts with the surface.

photodynamic. Describing a substance that fluoresces in light; as, chlorophyll.

photoelectric cell. Generic term for a device which produces changes in an electric circuit by the action of light. (1) Photoconductive (see *selenium cell*). (2) Photoemissive (e.g., the alkali cell), in which an emission of electrons occurs in a vacuum or across a gas-filled space. (3) Photovoltaic (e.g., the rectifier cell) which depends on contact between a metal and a semiconductor (as selenium). **p. effect.** Hallwach's effect. The discharge of electrons from the surface of a metal under the influence of light, leaving the metal positively charged.

photoelectricity. The transformation of light into electricity, e.g., the photoelectric effect.

photoelectrometer. Photogalvanometer.

photoelectrons. Electrons emitted from a surface under the influence of light.

photoflavins. A group of 9-alkylated alloxazins.

photofluorimeter. Fluorometer.

photofluoroscope. A fluorescent screen used to make X rays visible, e.g., coated with zinc sulfide.

photogalvanometer. A recording mirror galvanometer to measure minute quantities of light falling on a photosensitive cell. Cf. *microphotometer*.

photogen. Boghead naphtha. A constituent of vegetable or animal organisms that causes their luminescence.

photograph. A picture or image produced and fixed on a chemically sensitive surface. **micro-, microscopic-** A p. that shows the object in a size much smaller than normal. Cf. *photomicrograph*.

photographic. Pertaining to methods of recording or reproducing images by the action of light on light-sensitive surfaces. **p. brightness.** See *spectral classification*. **p. chemicals.** Chemicals for developing, fixing, toning, and sensitizing. **p. developer.** An organic reducing agent, as pyrocatechol or metol, used to develop an image by the reduction of light-exposed silver salts to metallic silver. **p. film.** A transparent, flexible sheet of cellulose coated with a light-sensitive emulsion. **p. filter.** See *color filter*. **p. intensifier.** A substance used to intensify an image; as, mercuric chloride. **p. negative.** An image in which black appears white, and white black. **p. paper.** Paper coated with a light-sensitive chemical; as, silver salts. **p. plate.** A glass plate coated with a light-sensitive emulsion. See *chromatic*. **p. positive.** An image copied from a p. negative, in which the light values appear in their true shades. **p. reducer.** A substance that reduces or bleaches the density of an image; as, ferrocyanides. **p. screens.** See *color filter*. **p. sensitizer.** A dye which increases sensitivity toward certain wavelengths of light. See *photosensitizer*. **p. spectrum.** The range of wavelengths, in 0.1 Å, that can be recorded by photography. The *ordinary* range, for glass lenses and ordinary plates or films, extends from ultraviolet (300) to yellow (550); the *extended* range, for quartz lenses and plates or films sensitized by dyes, extends from extreme ultraviolet (210) to infrared (920).

photography. The study of recording visible objects by light-sensitive plates or films, and copying them on light-sensitive papers or other media. **color-** The production of colored images by physical or chemical technique other than hand coloring.

photogravure. See *gravure*.

photohalide. A halogen salt sensitive to light.

photohyalography. Etching glass by a photomechanical process.

photoisomeric change. The transformation of one isomer into another by light.

photolysis. Decomposition or chemical action due to the action of light on a substance in solution: (1) photolyte alone is active: e.g., decomposition of hydrogen sulfide in hexane; (2) photolyte reacts with solvent: e.g., decomposition of hydrogen sulfide in water.

photolyte. A substance decomposed by light.

photolytic. Pertaining to the decomposition or dissociation of a substance by radiant energy.

photomacrograph. Macrograph. A magnified photograph. Cf. *photomicrograph*.

photomagnetism. Describing magnetic phenomena produced by light.

photometer. A device to measure light intensity. Cf. *nephelometer, colorimeter, actinometer*. **micro-** See *microphotometer*. **spectro-** A device for measuring the intensity of spectral lines, generally from the densities of their photographic images.

photometric. Pertaining to the measurement of light intensity. **p. curve.** See *photomicrograph*. **p. standards.**
1 standard English sperm candle = 1 candle.
1 standard Hefner lamp, burning amyl acetate, = 0.9 candle.
1 standard Carcel lamp, burning colza oil = 9.6 candles.
1 standard pentane lamp, burning pentane (International candle) = 10.0 candles.

photometry. (1) The measurement of light intensity. (2) The measurement of brightness from the density of photographic images.

photomicrograph. (1) Micrograph. The magnified photograph of a microscopic object obtained by means of a camera attached to a microscope. (2) Photometric curve. The line made by a beam of light reflected from the mirror of an electroscope, onto a photosensitive surface; as in a spectrophotometer. Cf. *photomacrograph*.

photon. (1) A corpuscle or particle of light analogous to the electron and magneton; mass 0, charge 0, spin 1 unit. Light or X rays consists of a stream of energy quanta, each quantum having energy $h\nu$ and momentum $h\nu/c$. (2) A structure in which the electron revolves around the proton at a distance equal to the electron radius; photon (*quantum*) = proton + electron. Cf. *neutron, neutrino*.

photoperiodism. The rhythmic changes in the composition of plant sap, due to light.

photopone. An instrument that transforms radiant energy into sound waves by means of selenium, which alters its electrical resistance on exposure to light. Cf. *optophone*.

photophoresis. The motion of small particles under the influence of light. Cf. *radiation pressure*.

photopic. See p. *spectrum*.

photopolymerization. A condensation reaction of molecules due to light.

photoproduct. A substance synthesized in a living organism by light. Cf. *precursor*.

photoreaction. A chemical reaction that occurs under the influence of light.

photosensitivity. (1) The capacity of an organ or organism to be stimulated by light. (2) The absorption of a certain portion of the spectrum by a chemical system. Cf. *irradiation*.

photosensitizer. A dyestuff (as aurine) which, when added to the substance of a photographic plate, increases the plate sensitiveness by absorbing the light of the wavelengths to which it best responds.

A. Halogenated fluoresceins, as

Eosin . . . . Yellow-green
Erythrosin . . . . Yellow-green

B. Derivatives of pyridine, quinoline, and acridine:

1. Isocyanins:

Pinaflavole . . . . Green
Pinachrome . . . . . . Orange
Ethyl red . . . . Orange-red, λ 6,500 Å

2. Carbocyanins:

Pinacyanole . . . . . . Red, 6,800
Naphthocyanole . . . Deep red, 7,500
Kryptocyanin . . . . . Extreme red, 8,000
Dicyanin . . . . Infrared, 9,000
Neocyanin . . . . Infrared, 10,000

Cf. *photographic spectrum, chromatic plates, cyanin*.

photosphere. The outer radiating surface of the sun, probably composed of incandescent clouds in a less luminous medium (cf. *chromosphere*): the source of the luminous portion of the solar spectrum.

photostable. Describing a substance that is not changed by light.

photosynthesis. (1) Synthesis caused by light. (2) The important reaction of all green plants in synthesizing glucose, and thence starch, from carbon dioxide and water by the catalytic action of chlorophyll and absorption of light and heat.

photosyntometer. A device to demonstrate photosynthesis of plants.

phototaxis. Phototropism. The response of cells or organisms to light; as, phototropism.

phototronic cell. Photoelectric cell.

phototropism. (1) The color change undergone by certain compounds, e.g., titanium dioxide, on exposure to light of certain wavelengths, followed by reversion to the original color in the dark or on irradiation with light of a different wavelength; attributed to impurities present. (2) The movement of living organs toward light.

phototropy. (1) A reversible change of color induced by colored light; as, in fulgides. (2) The change in or loss of color of dyestuffs in light of a specific wavelength.

photovoltaic effect. A change in potential of an electrode due to light.

phrenazol. Metrazol. Leptazol.

phrenosin. $C_{48}H_{93}NO_9 = 827.72$. A cerebroside from brain substance; hydrolyzed to sphingosine, phrenosinic acid, and galactose.

phrenosinic acid. $Me(CH_2)_{21} \cdot CHOH \cdot COOH = 384.38$. Cerebronic acid, neuro stearic acid. A hydroxy acid in phrenosin, which combines with bacterial toxins.

Phrilon. Trade name for a polyamide synthetic fiber.

Phrix. Trade name for a viscose cellulose synthetic fiber.

phrynin. A poisonous protein from the skin secretions of toads. See *bufonin*.

phthalal. The radical $=CH \cdot C_6H_4 \cdot CH=$.

phthalaldehyde. Phthalic aldehyde.

phthalaldehydic acid. $C_6H_4(CHO)COOH = 150.1$. *o*-Aldehydebenzoic *o*-formylbenzoic acid. Colorless crystals, m.97. **5,6-dimethoxy-** Opianic acid. **5,6-dioxy-** Noropianic acid.

phthalamic acid. $C_6H_4(CONH_2)COOH = 165.1$. Phthalaldehyde acidamide, *o*-carbamylbenzoic acid. Colorless crystals, m.148, soluble in alcohol. **phenyl-** Diphenamic acid.

phthalamide. Phthaldiamide.

α-phthalamidoglutarimide. $C_{13}H_{10}O_4N_2 = 258.38$. Distaval. Kevidon. Thalidomide. A tranquilizer drug. When used by pregnant women, it can result in deformed children.

phthalanil. $C_6H_4 : (CO)_2 : N \cdot Ph = 223.1$. *N*-Phenylphthalimide. **sym-** Colorless crystals, m.220, soluble in alcohol. **asym-** m.208 (sublimes).

phthalanone. Phthalide.

phthalate. A salt of phthalic acid containing the radical $C_6H_4(COO)_2=$; used for buffers (q.v.), standard solutions, and in vacuum pumps. **diamyl-** $C_6H_4(COOC_5H_{11})_2 = 306.2$. Colorless liquid, d.1.023, b.340, insoluble in water; a plasticizer (B.P.). **dibutyl-** $C_{16}H_{22}O_4 = 278.4$. Colorless liquid, d.1.046, b.340; a plasticizer and insect repellent, particularly for clothing (B.P.). **diethyl-** $C_{12}H_{14}O_4 = 222.2$. Colorless liquid, d.1.119, b.290; a plasticizer.

phthalazine. $C_6H_4 \cdot CH : N \cdot N : CH = 130.1$. β-Benzo-*o*-diazine, β-phenodiazine, 2,3-benzodiazine. Colorless crystals, m.91, soluble in alcohol. **benzo-** See *benzophthalazine*. **dihydroketo-** Phthalazone. **oxy-** Phthalazone. **tetrahydro-** $C_8H_{10}N_2 = 134.1$. The 1,2,3,4-tetrahydro derivative of phthalazine.

phthalazone. $C_8H_6ON_2 = 146.06$. 1-Oxyphthalazine, dihydroketophthalazine. Colorless crystals, m.183, soluble in alcohol. **benzyl-** Benzylphthalazone.

phthaldiamide. $C_6H_4(CONH_2)_2 = 164.2$. Phthalamide, phthalic diamide. Crystals, m.220 (decomp.), insoluble in water.

phthaleins. Colored compounds derived from phthalophenone by the substitution of its H atoms by OH or NH_2 groups; related to the colorless leuko compounds (phthalines). Cf. *phthalein indicators*. **cresolsulfon-** See *cresol red*. **phenol-** See *phenolphthalein*. **phenolsulfon-** Phenol red. **phloroglucinol-** Gallein. **resorcinol-** Fluorescin. **thymolsulfon-** Thymol blue.

phthalic acid. $C_6H_4(COOH)_2 = 166.1$. Alizarinic acid, 1,2-benzenedicarboxylic acid*, *o*-benzenedicarboxylic acid. Colorless rhombs, m.213, soluble in water; used in dye manufacture. **dimethoxy-** Hemipinic acid. **dimethyl-** Cumidic acid. **homo-** See *homophthalic acid*. **hydroxy-** See *hydroxyphthalic acid*. **hydroxymethyl-** Coccinic acid. **iso-** Meta-. Colorless needles, m.300 (sublimes). **meta-** Isophthalic acid. **methyl-** See *xylidic* and *uvitic acid*. **ortho-** Ordinary p. acid. **para-** Terephthalic acid. **tere-** Para-. Terephthalic acid.

p. a. series. $C_nH_{2n-8}(COOH)_2$. Cf. *aromatic acids*. **p. aldehyde.** $C_6H_4(CHO)_2 = 134.09$. Phthalaldehyde, 1,2-benzenedicarbonal*. *iso-* m.89. *ortho-* m.52. *tere-* m.116. **p. amide.** Phthaldiamide. **p. anhydride.** $C_6H_4 : (CO)_2 : O = 148.07$. Phthalandione, obtained by heating p. acid. White prisms, m.128, slightly soluble in water; used extensively in organic synthesis. *dimethoxy-* Hemipinic anhydride. **p. diamide.** Phthaldiamide. **p. nitrile.** Phthalonitrile.

phthalide. $C_6H_4 \cdot CO \cdot O \cdot CH_2 = 134.09$. Isobenzofuranone, 1-phthalanone. Colorless crystals, m.68, soluble in alcohol. **acetoxy-** See *acetoxyphthalide.* **benzal-** See *benzalphthalide.* **benzilidene-** Benzalphthalide. **bisbihydroxyphenyl-** Phenolphthalein. **bisbihydroxytolyl-** Cresolphthalein. **diindyl-** Indophthalein. **dimethoxy-** Meconin. **xanthilidene-** Fluoran.

phthalidene. The radical $C_6H_4 \cdot CO \cdot O \cdot C =$.

phthalidylidene. The radical $= C \cdot O \cdot CO \cdot C_6H_4$. U.K. usage for phthalidene.

phthalimide. $C_6H_4 \cdot CO \cdot NH \cdot CO = 147.1$. *o*-Phthalic imide, 1,3-isoindoledione. Colorless crystals, m.228 (sublimes). *iso-* A tautomer of p.

phthalimidine. $C_6H_4 \cdot CO \cdot NH \cdot CH_2 = 133.1$. 1-Isoindolinone. Colorless crystals, m.150, soluble in alcohol. **benzyl-** See *benzylphthalimidine.*

phthalimido. The radical $CO \cdot C_6H_4 \cdot CO \cdot N$—.

phthalines. $C_6H_4 \cdot (CHR_2) \cdot COOH$. Colorless compounds which, on reduction, form phthaleins.

phthalizine. Phthalazine.

phthalocyanin(e)s. Colored compounds containing 4 isoindole rings linked in a 16-membered ring of alternate C and N atoms around a central atom, usually a metal (Cu or Fe). Blue to green pigment dyestuffs, very stable to light, and to dilute acids and alkalies. Cf. *porphyrin, monastral blue.*

phthalonic acid. $COOH \cdot C_6H_4CO \cdot COOH \cdot 2H_2O = 194.1$. Carbobenzoylformic acid, *o*-carboxyphenylglyoxylic acid. White crystals, m.140, soluble in water. Cf. *terephthalonic acid.* **p. anhydride.** $C_9H_4O_4 = 176.03$. A solid, m.186.

phthalonitrile. $C_6H_4(CN)_2 = 128.05$. Dicyanobenzene. **homo-** Cyanobenzyl cyanide. **iso-** Meta-. **meta-** Isophthalic nitrile. Colorless crystals, m.161. **para-** Terephthalic nitrile. Colorless crystals, m.222. **tere-** Para-.

phthaloperine. The ring structure

phthalophenone. $C_6H_4 \cdot C : (Ph)_2 \cdot O \cdot CO = 286.21$. Benzoylbenzophenone, diphenylphthalein. The anhydride of the hypothetical triphenylcarbinol-*o*-carboxylic acid, and parent substance of the phthaleins and phthalins. Colorless leaflets, m.115., slightly soluble in water; used in organic synthesis. **dihydroxy-** Phenolphthalein.

phthaloyl. The radical $C_6H_4 \cdot CO \cdot O \cdot C =$, from phthaleins or phthalophenone.

phthaluric acid. $C_{10}H_7O_4N = 205.1$. Colorless crystals, m.192.

phthalyl. The radical $C_6H_4(CO)_2 =$, from phthalic acid. **di-** See *diphthalyl.*
p. alcohol. 1,2-Xylenediol. **p. chloride.** $C_6H_4 \cdot (COCl)_2 = 202.99$. 1,2-Benzenedicarbonyl chloride*. *ortho-* Colorless oil, b.276, soluble in ether. *meta-* m.41. *para-* m.77. **p. hydrazine.** $C_6H_4 \cdot CO \cdot (NH)_2 \cdot CO = 162.1$. Colorless crystals, m.200. **p. hydroxamic acid.** $C_6H_4 \cdot (CO)_2 \cdot N \cdot OH = 163.05$. Colorless crystals, m.230, soluble in water. **p. phenylhydrazide.** $C_6H_4(CO \cdot NH \cdot NHPh)_2 = 346.3$. Colorless crystals, m.161. **p. phenylhydrazine.** $C_6H_4 \cdot (CO)_2 \cdot N \cdot NHPh = 238.10$. *alpha-* Colorless crystals, m.178, soluble in alcohol. *beta-* Colorless crystals, m.210. **p. sulfathiazole.** $C_{17}H_{13}O_5N_3S_2 = 403.45$. Sulfathalidene. White crystals, m.275 (decomp.), insoluble in water; an antibacterial (U.S.P., B.P.).

phthioic acid. $C_{26}H_{52}O_2 = 396.35$. Phthoic acid, 3:13:19-trimethyltricosanoic acid. A saturated, branched-chain, fatty acid, m.48, from the lipoids of human and avian tuberculi bacilli, believed to be the specific cellular stimulant responsible for the tubercle.

phthoic acid. Phthioic acid.

phthoric acid. Obsolete name for hydrofluoric acid.

phtiocol. A pigment associated with carotene, q.v.

phycinic acid. An acid from the alga *Protococcus vulgaris.* White needles, m.136, insoluble in water.

phycite. Erythritol.

phycobilins, Photosynthetically active, blue or red plant pigments having a tetrapyrrole structure; as, seaweeds.

phycocerythrin. A globulin.

phycochrome. A chlorophyll-like pigment in freshwater algae.

phycocyanin. A blue pigment in blue-green algae (Cyanophyceae); active in photosynthesis.

phycoerythrin. The red pigment of brown algae (Florideae); active in photosynthesis.

phycology. The study of seaweeds or algae.

Phycomycetes. An order of thallophytes, algal fungi.

phycophaein. The brown pigment of certain algae.

phyllanthin. $C_{30}H_{37}O_8 = 525.3$. A glucoside from *Phyllanthus niruri* (Euphorbiaceae). Colorless needles, insoluble in water.

phyllins. The derivatives of chlorophyll

phyllite. Chloritoid

phylloerythrin. A split product of chlorophyll in the stomachs of herbiverous animals; identical with the porphyrin of human feces. Cf. *chlorophyll-a.*

phylloporphyrin. $C_{16}H_{18}ON_2 = 254.2$. A split product of chlorophyll. See *porphyrin, porphin ring.*

phyllopyrrole. $C_9H_{15}N = 137.1$. A pyrrole fragment of the porphin ring, q.v. White plates, m.69.

phylloquinones. See *vitamin K.*

phyllyrin. $C_{24}H_{34}O_{11} = 498.3$. Colorless leaflets; an antipyretic.

phylo- See *phyllo-.*

phylology. The study of seaweeds.

phylum. A primary division of the animal or plant kingdoms, which have 12 or 4 phyla, respectively.

physalin. $C_{72}H_{116}O_4 = 1,045.0$. A carotinoid pigment found in the sepals of *Physalis alkekengi* and *Ph. franchetti*, winter cherry. Yellow powder, soluble in water.

physalite. The mineral $Al_2O_3 \cdot SiO_2$.

physarsterol. $C_{30}H_{52}O_3$(?). An unsaturated trihydroxysterol isolated, as white crystals, from the slime mold *Physarum polycephalum*.

physcic acid. Physcion.

physcion. $C_{16}H_{12}O_5$ = 284.09. Physcic acid, chrysophyscin, parietin. A crystalline principle, m.207, from the lichen *Parmelia (Physcia) parietina*.

physeptone. Methadone hydrochloride.

physeteric acid. $Me(CH_2)_7CH:CH(CH_2)_3COOH$ = 226.2. 5,6-Tetradecenoic acid*. A constituent of sardine and whale oils.

physetoleic acid. $C_{15}H_{29}COOH$ = 254.24. Hypogaeic acid. A white, waxy constituent of tallow, m.30, insoluble in water.

physic. (1) Medicine. (2) Cathartic. Purgative. (3) Puddling or working molten iron in order to remove impurities. **p. nut.** *Jatrophan ureas* L. (Madagascar). Its oil, $d_{15}0.9228$, n_D 1.4733, iodine value 93–109, is used for soap manufacture and has purgative properties and fuel value.

physical. Pertaining to the energy relations of substances. **p. analysis.** Testing or determining the p. properties of a material. **p. chemistry.** A branch of science that employs experimental or theoretical p. methods to solve chemical problems. Subdivisions: Electrochemistry, thermochemistry, and thermodynamics; optical methods; radiochemistry and photochemistry. **p. properties.** Properties that can change without involving a change in chemical composition; as, melting point. **p. solution.** A solution from which the solute can be recovered chemically unchanged. **p. test.** A mechanical test to determine mechanical properties; as, hardness.

physicochemical. Pertaining to physical chemistry.

physics. The science of energy. The study of the phenomena due to forces acting on matter, and changes that do not involve a change in the composition of the material. Subdivisions: Mechanics, heat, electricity, magnetism, light, and radioactivity. **classical-** The branch of p. dealing with the mechanical, thermal, optical, and electrical properties of matter. **modern-** The branch of p. dealing with the relations among atoms, electrons, photons, quanta, and radiation.

physiochemical. Biochemical.

physiography. Physical geography. The study of the general properties of the earth and its atmosphere.

physiological. Pertaining to the functions and activity of living organisms (plant, animal, and human), especially in their normal condition, as opposed to their diseased (pathological) state. **p. action.** The effect of a substance on living organisms. **p. chemistry.** A branch of science that studies the chemical changes in normal living organisms. **p. salt solution.** (1) Normal saline. An isotonic solution of sodium chloride in water, usually 0.9%. (2) A solution remembling the salts of normal blood serum: calcium chloride 0.25, potassium chloride 0.10, sodium chloride 9.00 gm; water 1,000 ml.

physiology. The study of the functions and biological activities of living organisms; as, respiration. **animal-** The functions of the animal organism and its parts. **human-** The functions of the human organism, apart from its mental aspect. **phyto-** Plant p. **plant-** The functions of plants and their organs. **zoo-** Animal p.

physite. Erythrol.

physostab. Chlorionic gonadotrophin.

physostigma. Calabar bean. The seeds of *Physostigma venenosum* (Leguminosae), Africa, which contain the alkaloids, physostigmine, eseridine, and calabarine; an antineuralgic and antitetanic.

physostigmine. $C_{15}H_{21}N_3O_2$ = 275.35. White crystals, turning pink, slightly soluble in water; a cholinergic (U.S.P.). **p. benzoate.** $C_{23}H_{27}O_6N_3$ = 441.4. Eserine benzoate. Hard, white crystals, soluble in water. **p. borate.** Eserine borate. White crystals, soluble in water; used in ophthalmology. **p. citrate.** $(C_{15}H_{21}O_2N_3)_3 \cdot C_6H_8O_7$ = 1,017.66. Eserine citrate. White crystals, soluble in water. **p. hydrochloride.** $C_{15}H_{21}O_2N_3 \cdot HCl$ = 311.8. Eserine hydrochloride. Colorless powder, soluble in water. **p. salicylate.** $C_{15}H_{21}O_2N_3 \cdot C_7H_6O_3$ = 313.48. Eserine salicylate. The common form of p. Yellow crystals, m.186, soluble in water; a miotic, antitetanic, and peristaltic (U.S.P., B.P.). **p. sulfate.** $(C_{15}H_{21}O_2N_3)_2 \cdot H_2SO_4$ = 648.6. Eserine sulfate, physostigminae sulfas. Yellow crystals, m.140, soluble in water; a miotic.

phyt-, phyto- Prefix (Greek), indicating plant or vegetable.

phytalbumin. A vegetable albumin.

phytane. $C_{20}H_{42}$ = 282.28. A saturated hydrocarbon obtained by reduction of phytol. Colorless liquid $b_{10mm}169$, insoluble in water.

phytase. An enzyme from rice bran that hydrolyzes phytin to inositol and phosphoric acid.

phytelephas. The negrito palm, *P. macrocarpa* (Ecuador), whose fruit yields corajo or vegetable ivory. Cf. *tagud nut*.

phyterythrin. The red coloring matter of plants, especially of leaves in autumn.

phytic acid. $C_6H_6O_6(H_2PO_3)_6$ = 660.42. Inositolhexaphosphoric acid. A powder, m.214, slightly soluble in water. A metabolic intermediate in plant seeds. See *sugar phosphates*.

Phytin. Trademark for the calcium salt of phytic acid (calcium inositolhexaphosphoric ester), from hemp and other seeds; a nutrient for rickets, anemia, and tuberculosis.

phytochemistry. The study of chemical changes occurring in plants.

phytochrome. General name for the coloring matters of plants necessary for their synthetic metabolism; as, chlorophyll.

phytohormone. Auxin (2).

phytol. $C_{20}H_{39}OH$ = 296.3. 3,7,11,15-Tetramethyl-2-hexadecen-1-ol*. A colorless oil from chlorophyll, d.0.864, $b_{10mm}203$; a polymer of isoprene.

phytolacca. Pokeroot. The dried root of *P. decandra* (Phytolaccaceae); an alterative and emetic. **p. berries.** Pokeberries.

phytolaccic acid. An acid from pokeberries. Brown gum, soluble in water.

phytolaccin. A neutral principle from the seeds of *Phytolacca* species. Needles, insoluble in water; an alterative and laxative.

phytolaccine. An alkaloid obtained from the roots of *Phytolacca* species.

phytolaccotoxin. $C_{24}H_{38}O_8$ = 454.29. A toxic principle from *Phytolacca americana*, S. Africa and America.

phytomenadione. Phytonadione (B.P.).

phytonadione. $C_{31}H_{46}O_2$ = 450.71. Vitamin K_1. Phytomenadione (B.P.). 2-Methyl-3-phytyl-1,4-naphthoquinone. Yellow liquid, d.0.963, insoluble in water; a prothrombogenic (U.S.P.).

phytopathology. The study of diseased plants.

phytopharmacy. The study of fungicides and insecticides.

phytopyrrole. See *chlorophyll*.

phytosterin. Phytosterol.

phytosterol. (1) $C_{26}H_{44}O \cdot H_2O$ = 390.37. Phytosterin. An isomer of cholesterol, m.135–144. Its presence in all vegetable fats (0.5–1%) distinguishes them from animal fats which contain cholesterol. (2) Any sterol derived from plants. See *cholane derivatives*. **p. test.** To distinguish vegetable from animal fats: Treat the ether extract of the saponified fats with glacial acetic acid. The melting points are: phytosterol acetate, m.125–127; cholesterol acetate, m.114.

phytosterolin. $C_{34}H_{56}O_6$ = 560.0. A glucoside m.275–288, that yields phytosterol on hydrolysis.

phytyl. Indicating the presence of a hexahydro-tetraprenyl side chain.

pi. Greek letter π. (1) A mathematical constant which expresses the ratio of the circumference of a circle to its diameter: 3.1416. See *Ludolf's number*. (2) Symbol for peri-, q.v.

piaselenole. $C_6H_4 \cdot (N_2) \cdot Se$ = 183.3. Isobenzoselenodiazole, m.76. **iso-** Benzoselenodiazole. **tolu-** Tolupiaselenole.

piassaba. A fiber from *Leopoldina piasoaba*, Brazil; used for ropes. **Bahia-** A fiber from *Attalea funifera*, Brazil.

piazines. *p*-Diazines. Heterocyclic compounds having N atoms in the para position; as, pyrazine. Cf. *miazines, oiazines*.

piazothiole. $C_6H_4 \cdot (N)_2 \cdot S$ = 136.2. Colorless crystals, m.44. **iso-** Benzothiodiazole.

picamar. $C_6H_2(OMe)_2(OH)(C_3H_7)$ = 196.13. Propyl pyrogallol dimethyl ether, 1-propyl-2-hydroxy-3,4-dimethoxybenzene. Colorless liquid, b.245, used in perfumery.

picein. $C_{14}H_{18}O_7$ = 298.2. The β-glucoside of *p*-hydroxyacetophenone from the leaves of the Norway spruce, *Picea excelsa*, and bark of *Salix nigra*, willow (Salicaceae). White powder, m.194, soluble in water. Cf. *piceoside*.

picene. $C_{22}H_{14}$ = 278.2. Dibenzo[ai]phenanthrene. An aromatic, high-melting hydrocarbon from coal tar. Blue, fluorescent leaflets, m.364, insoluble in water.

picene perhydride. $C_{10}H_{16}$—CH₂—CH₂—$C_{10}H_{16}$ = 300.3. Doeikosinhydropicene. Colorless crystals, m.175, insoluble in water.

picenic acid. $C_{21}H_{14}O_4$ = 298.11. Colorless solid, solid, m.201.

piceoside. Salinigrin ameliaroside. A glucoside of *p*-hydroxyacetophenone in species of *Coniferae*, *Rosaceae*, and *Salicaceae*. Cf. *picein*.

pichi. The woody and resinous branches of *Fabiana imbricata* (Solanaceae), Chile; a tonic and diuretic. Cf. *fabiana*.

pichurim beans. Sassafras nuts. The seeds of

Nectandra puchury (Lauraceae), Brazil and Venezuela; an aromatic. **p. camphor.** $C_{12}H_{24}O_2$ = 200.2. An aromatic resembling laurel camphor, from p. beans. **p. fat.** The fatty matter of p. beans (30% laurostearin and p. camphor); a flavoring.

pickeringite. $MgAl_2(SO_4)_4 \cdot 22H_2O$. A native magnesia alum. Long, fibrous masses.

pickle. (1) Dilute acids, used to remove oxides, carbonates, or other scales. (2) A fruit or vegetable preserved in spiced vinegar. **p. inhibitor.** A substance added to p. (1) to restrain its corrosive action.

pickling. To clean metal by immersion in a pickle containing an inhibitor.

pico. Abbreviation for the unit 0.000,000,000,001.

picoampere. 0.001 milliampere.

picoline. $C_5H_4N \cdot Me$ = 93.1. Methylpyridine. Homologs of pyridine, from the dry distillation of bones and coal. **alpha-** Colorless liquid, d.0.952,

HC═N—CCH₃ ... HC═N—CH

Alpha-or 2,-   Beta-or 3,-
2-methylpyridine   3-methylpyridine

HC═N—CH

Gamma-or 4,-
4-methylpyridine

b.128, soluble in water; a nerve sedative. Cf. *picolinic acid, uvitonic acid*. **beta-** (1) Colorless liquid, b.144, soluble in alcohol; used to produce nicotinic acid. (2) A coal-tar base fraction containing 2,6-lutidine and β- and γ-picolines. **gamma-** Colorless liquid, d.0.974, b.147, soluble in water. **tetrahydro-** $C_5H_8N \cdot CH_3$ = 97.1. Colorless liquid, b.132. Cf. *uvitonic acid*.

picolinic acid. $C_5H_4N \cdot COOH$ = 123.1. Pyridinecarboxylic acid*. Colorless needles, m.136, soluble in water.

picolyl. The radical $C_5H_4NCH_2$—, from picoline.

picotite. The mineral $MgO \cdot Al_2O_2$, with iron and 7% chromium trioxide.

picraconitine. Picroaconitine.

picradonidin. A digitalis-like glucoside from *Adonis* species (Ranunculaceae).

picramic acid. $(NO_2)_2(NH_2)C_6H_2(OH)$ = 199.1. Dinitrophenamic acid, 2-amino-4,6-dinitrophenol*, 4,6,2,1-dinitroaminophenol, 1-hydroxy-2-amino-4,6-dinitrobenzene. Colorless crystals, m.168, insoluble in water.

picramide. $C_6H_2(NH_2)(NO_2)_3$ = 228.1. 1,2,4,6-Trinitroaniline, picrylamine. Yellow leaflets, m.186, insoluble in water. **methylnitro-** Tetryl.

picramnine. An alkaloid from the bark of *Picramnia antidesma* (Simarubaceae), Honduras bark.

picranisic acid. Picric acid.

picrasmine. $C_{35}H_{46}O_{10}$ = 626.5. From the wood of *Picrasma quassioides* (Simarubaceae), Himalayas.

picrate. $(NO_2)_3C_6H_2OM$. Explosive salts of picric acid. Carbazotate.

Picratol. Trademark for organic salts of silver.

picric acid. $CNO_2:CH\cdot CNO_2:C(OH)\cdot CNO_2:CH$ = 229.1. 2,4,6-Trinitrophenol*, picranisic acid, picronitric acid, chrysolepic acid. Yellow leaflets, m.122 (explode), soluble in water. Used as a reagent and to manufacture explosives and dyes. Cf. *lyddite*.

picrin. A bitter principle from *Digitalis purpurea* (Scrophylariaceae). **bromo-** Nitrobromoform.

picrite. Describing propellant action based on picric acid.

picro- Prefix (Greek) indicating bitter.

picroaconitine. $C_{31}H_{45}O_{10}N$ = 591.4. Picraconitine. A bitter principle from the bulbs of *Aconitum napellus* (Ranunculaceae).

picroadonidine. A bitter principle from *Adonis* species.

picrocarmine. A microscope stain: carmine 1, ammonia 5, water 50, saturated picric acid solution 50 pts.

picrocrocin. (1) $C_{38}H_{66}O_{17}$= 794.49. Saffron bitter. A glucoside from saffron. (2) $C_{10}H_{14}O$ = 150.11- A ketone, b.209, from saffron involved in the action of the hormone *fertilizin*, q.v. Cf. *pikrococin*.

picroerythrin. $C_{12}H_{16}O_7\cdot 3H_2O$ = 344.2. Bitter crystals, m.158, soluble in water, insoluble in alcohol.

picrol. $C_6H_3O_2I_2SO_3K$ = 479.7. Diiodoresorcin potassium monosulfonate. Colorless crystals, soluble in water; an antiseptic.

picrolonic acid. $C_{10}H_8N_4O_5$ = 264.1. 3-Methy-4-nitro-1-*p*-nitrophenyl-5-pyrazolone. A microreagent for calcium (rectangular crystals).

picromerite. The mineral $(K_2Mg)SO_4\cdot xH_2O$.

picronigrosin(e). An alcoholic solution of picric acid and nigrosine; a microscope stain.

picronitric acid. Picric acid.

picropodophyllin. A crystalline principle from *Podophyllum* species. Cf. *podophyllin*.

picroroccellin. $C_{27}H_{29}O_5N_3$ = 475.3. Bitter crystals from *Rocella tinctoria*.

picrosclerotine. An alkaloid from ergot.

picrotin. $C_{15}H_{18}O_7$ = 310.1. A decomposition product of picrotoxin, m.240.

picrotone. $C_{14}H_{16}O_3$ = 232.1. A ketone derived from picrotoxin.

picrotonol. $C_{14}H_{16}O_4$ = 248.1. An α-ketol, degradation product of picrotoxin.

picrotoxin. $C_{30}H_{34}O_{13}$ = 602.6. A neutral principle from the fruit of *Anamirta paniculata* (or *Cocculus, indicus*), fishberries, resembling strychnine in action. White needles, soluble in water; a respiratory stimulant and convulsant (B.P.).

picrotoxinin. $C_{15}H_{16}O_6\cdot H_2O$ = 310.2. A decomposition product of picrotoxin. Colorless crystals, m.201, soluble in water.

picryl. The radical $C_6H_2(NO_2)_3$—, from picric acid. **p. amine.** Picramide. **p. chloride.** $ClC_6H_2(NO_2)_3$ = 247.54. (1) 1-Chloro-3,5,2-trinitrobenzene. Yellow prisms, m.81, insoluble in water; used to manufacture explosives. (2) 1-Chloro-2,4,5-trinitrobenzene, m.116.

Pictet, Amé. 1857–1937. Swiss chemist noted for his work on vegetable alkaloids. **P. Raoul.** 1842–1929. Swiss chemist who liquefied oxygen, nitrogen, hydrogen, and carbon dioxide at $-140°C$. **P. crystals.** $SO_2\cdot xH_2O(?)$. White crystals formed when liquid sulfur dioxide evaporates.

Pictol. Trademark for monomethyl-*p*-aminophenol sulfate; a photographic developer.

picylene. Picenefluorene.

piedmontite. The mineral $4CaO\cdot 3(AlMn)_2\cdot O_3\cdot 6SiO_3\cdot H_2O$.

pieso- Piezo-.

pieze. The uniform pressure which spread over a surface of one square meter, produces a force of 1 sthene (French usage). **hecto-** Bar.

piezo- Prefix (Greek) indicating pressure.

piezochemistry. The study of chemical reactions under high pressure.

piezocontrol. The maintenance of a definite radio frequency with a quartz oscillator. Cf. *piezoelectricity*.

piezocrystallization. Crystallization under great pressure. See *diamond*.

piezoelectricity. An electric current produced by pressure exerted on certain crystals; as, quartz. Cf. *electrostriction, quartz oscillator*.

piezoelectron. A supposedly disk-shaped electron pressed between 2 petalons.

piezometer. An instrument to determine compressibility.

pig. A cast metal bar or brick. **p. iron.** An iron p., molded in sand.

pigment (1) A fine insoluble white, black, or colored material; used, suspended in a vehicle, as a paint, or ink. E.g.: mineral pigments, as ocher; animal pigments, as carmine; vegetable pigments, as madder lake; synthetic or artificial pigments, as phthalocyanines. (2) A coloring matter in the tissues of plants or animals; as, the chromoproteins. **carotenoid-** See *carotenoids*. **p. dye.** An insoluble dye, which does not form lakes. **p. green.** A green color prepared from an iron salt and nitroso-β-naphthol.

pigmentation. A deposit of coloring matter in a living organism.

pigmentolysis. The dissolution or destruction of pigmentation.

pikrococin.
$(C_6H_{10}O_5)\cdot CH\cdot CH_2\cdot CMe_2\cdot C(CHO):CMe\cdot\cdot CH_2$ = 313.2.

A glucoside of safranal in saffron. Cf. *picrocrocin*.

pilchardine. A commercial blend of oils from pilchard, sardine, and grayfish.

pile. A bundle or stack. **galvanic-** Voltaic p. **Hanford-** A p. in which short rods of U are loaded in cylindrical channels in a graphite medium. **thermo-** Sheets or bars, of 2 or more metals, that produce an electric current when heated at their junctions of contact. **uranium-** Uranium-graphite containing active uranium metal (U^{235}, q.v.) in a thick ferroconcrete casing. It emits heat by producing plutonium by radioactive decomposition of the U^{235}. The graphite damps down the action and enables the heat to be utilized. Cf. *chain* reaction, atomic *fission, moderator*. **voltaic-** A series of metallic disks, forming a galvanic battery.

pilewort. Lesser celandine, *Ranunculus ficaria*; used as ointment.

piliganine. $C_{15}H_{24}ON_2$ = 248.3. An alkaloid from piligan, *Lycopodium saururus*, S. American club moss. Yellow powder, insoluble in water.

pill. (1) A small round mass of a mixture of an active drug and inert material; used in medicine.

Cf. *tablets.* (2) A pellet of cesium "flashed" in a vacuum tube to remove all oxygen.

pilocarpidine. $C_5H_4N\cdot CMe(NMe_2)\cdot COOH$ = 194.2. An alkaloid from the leaves of *Pilocarpus.* Colorless syrup, insoluble in water. **p. nitrate.** $C_{10}H_{14}$-$N_2O_2\cdot HNO_3$ = 257.2. Colorless crystals, soluble in water.

pilocarpine. $C_{11}H_{16}O_2N_2$ = 208.2. An alkaloid from jaborandi. See *pilocarpus.* Colorless needles, m.34, soluble in water; it increases saliva and sweat, constricts pupils, and decreases intraocular tension. **p. hydrochloride.** $C_{11}H_{16}O_2N_2\cdot$-HCl = 244.73. Colorless, hygroscopic needles, m.202, soluble in water (U.S.P.). **p. nitrate.** $C_{11}H_{16}O_2N_2\cdot HNO_3$ = 271.3. Pilocarpinae nitras. Colorless crystals, m.178, soluble in water (U.S.P., B.P.). **p. phenate.** $C_{11}H_{16}O_2N_2\cdot C_6H_5OH$ = 302.2. Aseptolin. Colorless oil, soluble in water. **p. salicylate.** $C_{11}H_{16}N_2O_2\cdot C_7H_6O_3$ = 346.20. White crystals, m.120, soluble in water. **p. sulfate.** $(C_{11}H_{16}N_2O_2)_2\cdot H_2SO_4$ = 514.33. Colorless crystals, m.133.

pilocarpus. Jaborandi. The dried leaflets of *Pilocarpus pennatifolius* (Rutaceae), tropical America; a diaphoretic (0.6% alkaloids).

pilocereine. Pilocerine.

pilocerine. $C_{30}H_{44}O_4N_2$ = 496.5. An alkaloid from a cactus, *Cereus pilocereus.*

pilosine. $C_{16}H_{18}N_2O_2$ = 286.16. An alkaloid from pilocarpus. White crystals, m.187.

pilosinine. $C_9H_{12}N_2O_2$ = 180.11. An alkaloid from pilocarpus. White crystals, m.79.

pilot burner. A small burner, permanently alight, attached to a larger burner for relighting purposes.

pilot plant. An experimental assembly of manufacturing equipment to test a new process on the semilarge scale.

pimanthrene. $C_{16}H_{14}$ = 206.1. 1,7-Dimethylphenanthrene. A hydrocarbon from copal and pimaric acid.

pimaric acid. $C_{20}H_{30}O_2$ = 302.3. An optically active acid from burgundy pitch and galipot resin. Crystals, m.148 (inactive), soluble in hot alcohol. See *abietic acid.* **dextro-** m.210. **levo-** m.145.

pimelic acid. $CH_2(CH_2CH_2\cdot COOH)_2$ = 160.12. 1,5-Pentanedicarboxylic acid, heptanedioic acid*. The 6th member of the oxalic series, m.105, soluble in alcohol.

pimelinketone. Cyclohexanone*.

pimelite. A native green nickel-iron silicate, similar to meerschaum.

pimenta. Allspice, Jamaica pepper. The fruit of *Pimenta officinalis* (Myrtaceae), the tropics. A condiment and stimulant. **p. oil.** Allspice oil. Yellow oil from the pimenta of the W. Indies, d.1.05, insoluble in water; a perfume and flavoring.

pimpinella. The roots of *Pimpinella saxifraga* (Umbelliferae); a diuretic.

pimpinellin. $C_{13}H_{10}O_5$ = 246.1. A bitter crystalline principle from pimpinella. Colorless needles, insoluble in water. **iso-** A constituent of lime juice.

pin. An obsolete unit of volume; 4.5 gallons.

Pinaceae. Pines: trees and shrubs with a resinous juice and awl- or needle-shaped leaves. Used to manufacture wood pulp, especially kraft cellulose. Some yield drugs; e.g.: *Abies balsamea* (Canada fir), Canada balsam; *Juniperus oxycedrus,* cade oil;

Pinus sylvestris (Scotch fir), wood tar; *Thuja occidentalis* (arborvitae), thuja. Cf. *Abies.*

pinachrome. $C_{26}H_{29}IN_2O_2$ = 528.2. *p*-Ethoxyquinaldine *p*-ethoxyquinoline ethyl cyanine. An indicator, pH 5.8–7.8, (acids—colorless, alkalies—red violet).

pinacoid. See *pinakoid.*

pinacol. $Me_2C(OH)\text{---}C(OH)Me_2$ = 118.14. Tetramethylethylene glycol, pinacone, 2,3-dimethyl-2,3-butanediol*. Colorless crystals, m.38, soluble in water. **p. condensation.** Two aldehydes or ketones are reduced and linked together; as in the formation of pinacol from acetone: $2Me_2CO +$ $H_2O = Me_3COH\text{---}COHMe_3$. **p. conversion.** An intramolecular transfer of a $CH_3\text{---}$ group from 1 C atom to another; as in the change from pinacol to pinacoline: $Me_2C(OH)\text{---}C(OH)Me_2 \rightarrow Me_3C\cdot\text{-}COCH_3$.

pinacolin. $Me\cdot CO\cdot CMe_3$ = 100.1. *tert*-Butyl methyl ketone, 3,3-dimethyl-2-butanone*. Colorless oil of peppermint odor, b.106, slightly soluble in water.

pinacolines. Ketones containing a tertiary alkyl group, $R\cdot CO\cdot CR_3$.

pinacolone. Pinacolin.

pinacols. $R_2C(OH)\cdot C(OH)R_2$. Diatomic alcohols or glycols.

pinacolyl alcohol. $CMe_3\cdot CHOH\cdot Me$ = 102.11. 3,3-Dimethyl-2-butanol*, methyl-*tert*-butylcarbinol. Colorless liquid, d.0.812, b.121, soluble in water.

pinacone. Pinacol.

pinacones. See *pinacols.* **p. rearrangement.** See *pinacol conversion.*

pinacyanol. $C_{25}H_{25}N_2I$ = 480.9. A carbocyanine dye for sensitizing photographic plates to red; a histological stain.

pinaflavole. An isocyanine dye; a photosensitizer for green.

pinakoid. A prism crystal face intersecting one axis of the system, and parallel to the other 2. **brachy-** A p. intersecting the brachy (broad) axis. **macro-** A p. intersecting the macro (long) axis.

pinakryptol. A green dye; a photographic desensitizer.

pinalic acid. Valeric acid.

pinan(e). $C_{10}H_{18}$ = 138.2. Bicyclo[2′4]heptane. A terpene hydrocarbon in many essential oils. Cf. *pinene.*

pinang. *Areca* nut.

pinaverdol. $C_{22}H_{21}IN_2$ = 440.0. 1,6,1′-Trimethyl isocyanine iodide. An isocyanine dye for sensitizing plates to the orange of the spectrum.

pinch. An approximate measure: 1–2 grams.

pinchbeck. A yellow alloy: Cu 83, zinc 17%; imitation gold for jewelry.

pinckneyin. A glucoside from the bark of *Pinckneya pubens* (Rubiaceae).

pine. A general name for coniferous trees that yield turpentine, resin, tar, pitch, and cellulose (especially kraft) pulp. **p. camphor.** Pinol. **p. cone oil.** Turpentine. **p. leaf oil.** An essential oil distilled from p. needles. **p. needle oil.** Oleum pini. An essential oil distilled from fresh p. needles, the leaves of *Pinus pumilio.* Yellow liquid, d.0.865–0.875, b.165, containing pinene, limonene, and bornyl acetate; an inhalant. **p. oil.** Crude turpentine from distillation of pinewood: chiefly γ-terpinene, cineol, fenchyl alcohol, borneol, and α-terpineol. **p. tar.** Wood tar. **p. tar oil.** Red distillate from p. tar, d.0.97, insoluble in water; used in ore flotation.

pineal gland. The dried and powdered brain glands of young cattle; used medicinally.

pineapple. The fruit of *Ananas sativus* (Bromeliaceae), q.v. Cf. *bromelin.*

pinene. $C_{10}H_{16}$ = 136.2. Australene, laurene. 2,7,7-trimethyl-Δ^2-bicyclo[1.1.3]heptene. A terpene constituent in oils of turpentine, savine, and fir. Colorless aromatic liquid, d.0.859, b.155, slightly soluble in water. **beta-** Nopinene.

p. hydrochloride. $C_{10}H_{16}HCl$ = 172.65. Insoluble solid, m.134.

pinguin. Alantol.

pinicortannic acid. $(C_{16}H_{18}O_{11})_2 \cdot H_2O$. A brown tannin from the bark of Scotch fir, *Pinus sylvestris*. Cf. *cortepinitannic acid.*

pinipicrin. $C_{22}H_{36}O_{11}$ = 476.4. A bitter principle from the needles of *Thuja occidentalis* and *Pinus sylvestris* (Pinaceae).

pini-pini. The dried bark of *Jatropha urens* (Euphorbiaceae), Brazil; used medicinally.

pinitannic acid. $C_{14}H_{16}O_8$ = 312.2. A brown tannic acid from the wood of *Pinus sylvestris*.

pinite. (1) $C_6H_{12}O_5$ = 164.1. Hexahydropentahydroxybenzene. Colorless solid, m.150, in the resin from *Pinus lambertiana*. Cf. *quercitol*. (2) Pagodite. **methoxy-** Quebrachitol.

pinking. See *knock*.

pinkroot. Spigelia.

pink salt. $(NH_4)_2SnCl_6$ = 367.5. Tin-ammonium chloride, ammonium hexachlorostannate. Pink crystals; a textile mordant.

pinnoite. MgB_2O_4. A native borate.

pinol. $C_{10}H_{16}O$ = 152.13. Sobrerone, pine camphor, 6(8)-methoxy-1-*p*-menthene. A terpene, from pine needles: *d*- and *l*- forms. Colorless liquid, b.0.952, b.183, insoluble in water. **p. hydrate.** $C_{10}H_{16} \cdot O \cdot H_2O$ = 170.14. Sobrerol. The terpene Δ^6-*p*-menthanediol-2,8. m.150, soluble in water.

pinoline. Rosin spirit.

pinone. $C_{10}H_{16}O$ = 152.2. 6-Oxypinol. A terpene ketone constituent of many essential oils; isomer of α-thujone, camphor, fenchone, and carone.

pinonic acid. $C_{10}H_{16}O_3$ = 184.12. An oxidation product of pinene. *d(l)-* m.99. *dl-* m.105. A wetting agent for mercerizing processes. Cf. *umbellonic acid, nopinic acid.*

pinosylvin. $C_{14}H_{12}O_2$ = 212.1. *trans*-3,5-Dihydroxystilbene. A constituent of the heartwood of the tree *Pinus sylvestris*, m.156, slightly soluble in water, soluble in alcohol (violet fluorescence).

pint. A measure of volume, dry and liquid. **United States-** 1 pint = 0.5 quart = 0.125 gal = 4 gills = 16 fl. oz = 28.875 in.³ = 128 fluid drams = 7,680 minims = 0.473167 liter. **British-** Imperial p. **dry-** 1 dry pint = 0.5506 ml. **imperial-** British.

1 pint = 20 fl. oz = 34.6593 in.³ = 568.25 ml. **Scotch-** 1 Scotch pint = 3.0065 imperial pints.

pinte. An early French measure of capacity; renamed *liter*, without change of volume.

Pintsch gas. A fuel gas made by spraying oil into a hot retort.

Pinus. An important genus of Coniferae, q.v., which yield turpentine, galipot resin, pitch, tar, combopinic acid, ceropic acid, pinite, pinipicrin. Cf. *Pinaceae, Abies.*

Piobert effect. The surface markings on polycrystalline iron and soft steel at or near the yield point.

pipanol hydrochloride. Benzhexol hydrochloride. 1-Phenyl,1-cyclohexyl,3-piperidyl,1-propano-(trihexylphenidyl) hydrochloride. An antispasmodic, free from the glaucomatic effects of atropine.

pipe. A 115-gallon cask of wine (U.K. usage).

pipe clay. A fine, grayish white clay, similar to kaolin, used for heat-resisting apparatus, and as a whitening.

pipecoline. $C_6H_{13}N$ = 99.1. Methylpiperidine. **N-** or **1-** Colorless liquid, d.0.818, b.107. **α-** or **2-** Colorless liquid, d.0.844, b.117. **β-** or **3-** Colorless liquid, d.0.845, b.124. **γ-** or **4-** Colorless liquid, d.0.867, b.127.

pipecolinic acid. $C_6H_{11}NO_2$ = 131.2. Piperidine-2-carboxylic acid,

Colorless crystals, m.261, soluble in alcohol; occurs widely, e.g., in malt wort.

piper. (1) Pepper. (2) A genus of Piperaceae, q.v.

Piperaceae. The pepper family, a group of shrubs, or climbing tropical plants, containing aromatic substances; e.g.: *Piper betle*, betel leaf; *Piper nigrum*, black, white pepper; *Houttuynia californica*, yerba mansa.

piperamide. $C_{12}H_{11}NO_3$ = 217.1. The amide of piperic acid.

piperazidine. Piperazine.

piperazine. $C_4H_{10}N_2 \cdot 6H_2O$ = 194.3. Diethylenediamine, piperazidine, hexahydropyrazine, arthriticine, dispermin(e). Glassy leaflets, m.104, soluble in water; used in medicine. **dimethyl-** Lupetazin. **p. adipate.** $C_{10}H_{20}O_4N_1$ = 232.32. White crystals, m.250 (decomp.), soluble in water; used to treat threadworm (B.P.). **p. citrate.** Used similarly to p. adipate (B.P.). **p. dione.** NH·(CH₂·CO)₂·NH = 114.06. Diketopiperazine, glycine anhydride. The anhydride of the dipeptide glycylglycine, from silk fibroin. **p. phosphate.** $C_4H_{10}N_2 \cdot H_3PO_4 \cdot H_2O$ = 202.24. White powder, soluble in water; used to treat threadworm (B.P.). **p. quinate.** Sidonal. White crystals, soluble in water; used to treat gout and neurasthenia.

piperic acid. $C_{12}H_{10}O_4$ = 218.14. Piperinic acid, 5-(3,4-methylenedioxyphenyl)-2,4-pentadienoic acid*, piperonilidene crotonic acid, β-(3,4-methylenedioxystyryl)acrylic acid. An unsaturated monobasic acid, from piperonal. Yellow needles, m.216, slightly soluble in water.

piperidic acid. $NH_2(CH_2)_3COOH$ = 103.1. γ-Aminobutyric acid. Colorless crystals, m.183, soluble in water. **homo-** $NH_2(CH_2)_4COOH$ = 117.1.

δ-Aminovaleric acid. Colorless crystals, m.158, soluble in water.

piperidine. $CH_2 \cdot (CH_2)_2 \cdot NH \cdot CH_2 \cdot CH_2 = 85.1$. Hexahydropyridine. Pentamethylene imine. Colorless liquid, d.0.862, b.106, soluble in water; a vasodilator and a part of the structure of many alkaloids. **dimethyl-** Lupetidine. **ethylmethyl-** Copellidine. **methyl-** Pipecoline. **piperyl-** Piperine. **propyl-** Conine. **tetramethyl-N-methylbenzoxy-** Eucaine. **vinyl-** Meroquinene.
   p. carboxylic acid. Nipecotic acid. **p. dione.** Glutarimide.

piperidinium. The radical $C_5H_{10}NH_2-$, from piperidine, with pentavalent N. **p. compounds.** Derivatives of p.; as, $C_5H_{10}NH(CH_3)I$.

piperidinoethanol. $C_7H_{15}NO = 129.21$. A tertiary aliphatic amine. Yellow liquid, d.0.973, b45mm116; an intermediate in the manufacture of drugs and plastics.

piperidyl. The radical $C_5H_{10}N-$, from piperidine.
   p. urethane. $C_5H_{10}N \cdot CO \cdot OC_2H_5 = 157.2$. Colorless liquid, b.211.

piperine. $C_{17}H_{19}O_3N = 285.3$. Piperylpiperidine. An alkaloid from black pepper. Colorless, monoclinic crystals, m.129, slightly soluble in water, soluble in alcohol or ether; an antipyretic.

piperinic acid. See *piperic acid.*

piperocaine hydrochloride. $C_{16}H_{23}O_2N \cdot HCl = 297.83$. White crystals, m.173, soluble in water; a local anesthetic (U.S.P., B.P.).

piperolidine. $C_8H_{15}N = 125.13$. Octahydropyrrocoline, δ-coniceine. Colorless liquid, d.0.904. **dl-** b.161. **l-** b.158.

piperonal. $CH_2 : O_2 : C_6H_3 \cdot CHO = 150.1$. Heliotropin, 3,4-methylene dioxybenzaldehyde, piperonyl aldehyde; from piperine, having a heliotrope odor. Colorless needles, m.37, slightly soluble in water.

piperonilidene. The radical $(CH_2O_2)C_6H_3 \cdot CH-$, from piperonal. Cf. *piperic acid.*

piperonoyl. Piperonyloyl.

piperonyl. The radical $(CH_2O_2)C_6H_3 \cdot CH_2-$, from piperine. **homo-** See *homopiperonyl.* **p. alcohol.** $C_8H_8O_3 = 152.10$. 3,4-Methylene dioxybenzyl alcohol. A solid, m.51, slightly soluble in water. **p. aldehyde.** Piperonal.

piperonylic acid. $C_8H_6O_4 = 166.1$. Methyleneprotocatechuic acid, methylenedioxybenzoic acid, heliotropic acid; from paracoto bark, m.229.

piperonyloyl. Piperonoyl. The radical $-CO \cdot C_6H_4 : O_2CH_2$.

piperovatine. $C_{16}H_{21}O_2N = 259.3$. An alkaloid from the fruits of *Piper ovatum* (Piperaceae), Trinidad. Colorless crystals, insoluble in water; used medicinally.

piperyl. = The radical $CH_2 : O_2 : C_6H_3 \cdot CH : CH \cdot CH : - CH \cdot CO-$, from piperic acid.

piperylene. $CH_2 : CH \cdot CH : CH \cdot CH_3 = 68.1$. Pentadiene*, Δ-1,3-amenylene; from piperidine. A liquid, b.40.

piperylhydrazine. $C_5H_{12}N_2 = 100.2$. Piperidylamine. Colorless liquid, b.146, soluble in alcohol.

pipestone. Catlinite.

pipet. A graduated open glass tube used for measuring or transfering definite quantities of liquids. See *automatic, Babcock, capillary, counting, gas, Mohr p.* **auswaschen-** A micropipet which

contains a specified volume of liquid, as distinct from *delivering* it; and must be washed out with water after it has drained.

pipette. Pipet.

pipi root. The dried root of *Petiveria alliacea* (Phytolaccaceae); a stimulant, expectorant, and diaphoretic.

pipitzahoac. The dried roots of *Perezia* species (Compositae), Mexico.

pipitzohoic acid. $C_{15}H_{20}O_3 = 248.2$. Perezon. Aurum vegetabile. Yellow needles from pipitzahoac, m.103, soluble in water. See *perezol.*

pipitzahoin. A colored principle from the roots of *Perezia adnate* (Compositae); an indicator.

pipsissewa. Chimaphila.

piquia fat. A fat from the kernels of *Caryocar villosum* (Caryocaraceae), Brazil (souari or butternut); it resembles palm oil.

piroglycerina. An early name (due to the discoverer, Soluero) for nitroglycerin.

pisang. Malay for banana. **p. wax.** A wax from the leaves of the Java banana tree, *Musa paradisiaca* (Musaceae), containing pisangceryl alcohol.

pisangceric acid. Pisangcerylic acid.

pisangceryl alcohol. $C_{13}H_{28}O = 200.2$. A saturated alcohol, m.78.

pisangcerylic acid. $C_{24}H_{48}O_2 = 368.37$. A monobasic acid, m.71, from pisang wax.

pisanite. (Fe, Cu)$SO_4 \cdot 7H_2O$. A native sulfate.

piscidia. Jamaica dogwood. The dried bark of *P erythrina*; a W. Indies fish poison, and narcotic analgesic.

piscidic acid. $C_{11}H_{10}O_7 = 254.2$. A dibasic acid obtained from piscidia. Colorless needles, m.183, soluble in water.

piscidin. $C_{29}H_{24}O_8 = 500.3$. A neutral principle from piscidia (dogwood); an anodyne.

piscose. Allulose.

pisolite. A hard compact form of aragonite.

pistacite. Epidote.

pistil. Modified leaves forming the central part of a flower.

pistomesite. $MgCO_3 \cdot FeCO_3$. A native carbonate.

pitayamine. An alkaloid from the bark of *Cinchona pitayensis* (Rubiaceae).

pitch. (1) A heavy liquid or dark residue obtained by distillation of tar. See *rosin.* (2) To add yeast, with or without sugar, in order to start fermentation. (3) The distance between the threads of a screw. (4) The vibration frequency of the keynote of a tune. **archangel-** (1) Originally, pine tar p. from Archangel. (2) A blend of pine pitch with various oils, used to caulk boats (U.S. usage). **black-** Naval p. **Burgundy-** (1) Principally the solid resin obtained by heating and straining the air-dry solid resin exuded by Norway spruce *Picea excelsa*, and European silver fir, *Abies pectinata*. (2) A mixture made by heating rosin with certain fixed oils; used for adhesive plasters. **Canada-** The resin from *Tsuga* species. **earth-** Asphalt. **Jew's-** Asphalt. **mineral-** (1) Asphalt. (2) Bitumen. **naval-** The dark solid residue from the distillation of various tars. **petroleum-** Asphalt. **Trinidad-** Asphalt.
   p. blende. Impure uranite, q.v., in which radium was discovered. Cf. *bröggerite.* **p. coal.** Specular coal. **p. stone.** A dark-colored igneous rock, similar to obsidian.

pithecolobine. An alkaloid from the bark of *Pithecolobium saman* (Leguminosae), E. Indies. Brown oil, insoluble in water.

pitocin. Hypophamine.

pitot tube. A vertical U tube with a movable scale, closed at one end and containing a liquid to record differences in pressure; an anemometer.

pitressin. β-Hypophamine.

Pitrowsky test. Biuret reaction.

pittacol. Eupittonic acid.

pitticite. Scorodite.

pituitary. Hypophysis sicca. The dried, cleaned, and powdered posterior lobe of the pituitary gland of the ox; used in medicine. **posterior-** Gray powder prepared from the clean, dry posterior lobe of the p. body of domestic animals; a snuff and source of mixed hormones (U.S.P.).

p. liquid. A standardized solution of the active principle of the anterior or the posterior lobe of the p. gland (hypophysis cerebri) of the ox. See *hypophamine*.

pituitrin. An extract of the pituitary, containing pitocin and pitressin; a vasoconstrictor. Cf. *hypophamine*.

pituri. The powdered leaves and twigs of the p. plant, *Duboisia hopwoodii* (Solanaceae), Australia. Used locally as a narcotic stimulant.

piturine. $C_{10}H_{16}N_2 = 164.2$. An alkaloid from pituri. Brown oil resembling nicotine.

piuri. Indian yellow.

pival aldehyde, $CMe_3CHO = 86.08$. Trimethyl acetaldehyde, 2,2-dimethylpropanal*. Colorless liquid, d.0.793, m.3, b.75; used in organic synthesis.

pivalic acid. $CMe_3COOH = 102.1$. Trimethylacetic acid, *2,2-dimethylpropanoic acid**, Colorless crystals, m.35, soluble in water. Cf. *valeric acid*.

pivalyl. The radical $CMe_3 \cdot CO-$.

pix. Latin for pitch; as, pix burgundica (Burgundy pitch). **p. liquida.** Wood tar.

pK. Symbol for the logarithm of the reciprocal of the dissociation constant of an electrolyte: $pK = \log(1/K)$.

pk. Abbreviation for peck.

placebo. A pharmaceutical preparation which is prescribed for psychological rather than for therapeutical reasons.

place isomerism. The isomerism of chemical substances of similar compositions, which differ in structure by the positions of radicals; as, ortho-, meta-, and para-.

placement. A method of applying fertilizer in pockets or continuous narrow bands near to the seed at sowing time.

placentin. An extract from the placenta, used in Abderhalden's test.

placer. An alluvial or glacial deposit of sand or gravel containing gold or other precious minerals and metals. **p. mining.** The extraction of precious metals from sand by washing.

plagioclase. General name for triclinic feldspars. Cf. *gabbro*.

plagionite. $5PbS \cdot 4Sb_2S_3$. Cf. *lead minerals*.

plague vaccine. A sterile suspension in isotonic salt solution of killed *Pasteurella pestis*; a specific plague vaccine (U.S.P., B.P.).

Planck, Max Karl Ernst Ludwig. 1858–1947. German physicist. Nobel Prize winner (1918). **P. constant.** The universal constant, $h = \pm 0.008$

$\times 10^{-27}$ erg-sec. Thence, energy $= h\nu$, and momentum $= h\sigma$, where ν is frequency, and σ the wave number. See *quantum theory*. **P.'s element of action.** P. constant. **P.'s formula.** The energy radiated from a black body at wavelength λ microns $= C\lambda^{-5}/[e^{c/\lambda T} - 1]$, where e is the base of napierian logarithms; C a constant (9.226×10^3 when energy is expressed in gramcalories per second per square centimeter, and 3.86×10^4 when energy is expressed in watts per square centimeter); c a constant equal to 14,350; T the absolute temperature. **P.'s unit.** P. constant.

plane. A surface, imaginary or real, which is level with itself in all directions. **p. symmetric-** The cis or maleinoid form of a geometric isomerism. **p. symmetric isomerism.** Geometrical *isomerism*. **p. of symmetry.** An imaginary p. passing through a crystal so that, for each face or angle of the crystal, there is a similar face or angle on the opposite side of the p., a line joining the two faces being perpendicular to the p.

planet. A celestial body moving around the sun in a nearly circular orbit. Cf. *meteoric*.

planetary. Pertaining to a planet. **p. atmosphere.** The gases surrounding a planet; Mercury, none; Venus, CO_2; Earth, N_2; Mars, H_2O.

plangi. A form of reserve dyeing used in the Far East, in which patterned areas of cloth are brushed up and tied in small bundles, so that the cloth below is unaffected by the dye bath.

planocaine. Procaine hydrochloride.

planoform. Butylaminobenzoate.

plant. (1) The machinery and implements used in manufacturing processes. (2) A living organism of the vegetable kingdom, which generally contains chlorophyll and photosynthesizes food; hence (unless a parasite or saprophyte) it requires for life only inorganic substances. Cf. *animal*. Plants are grouped into 4 phyla and consist of 2 systems:

A. Protective system:
  1. The surface: epidermis, cork, bark
  2. The skeleton: bast fibers, collenchyma, sclerotic parenchyma

B. Nutritive system:
  1. Absorbing tissues: epithelium of roots, root hairs, etc.
  2. Assimilating tissue: chlorophyll parenchyma
  3. Conducting tissue: conducting parenchyma, vascular bundles, latex cells
  4. Storage tissue: reserve tissue of seeds, bulbs, tubers, and water tissues
  5. Aerating system: intercellular spaces, stomata, and lenticels
  6. Receptacles for secretions and excretions: glands, oil, resin and mucus canals, crystal sacs

p. acids. The organic acids in vegetable organisms; as, citric acid (lemons). **p. elements.** The elements known to be essential to p. growth: C, H, O, N, S, P, K, Ca, and Mg; traces of Fe, Na, Si, Al, Cl, Mn, Zn, B, and F may be essential. **p. food.** An artificial fertilizer containing the carbonates, nitrates, phosphates, or sulfates of potassium, calcium, magnesium, or iron. **p. pigments.** The coloring matter of plants, chiefly:
1. Chlorophyll pigments: the green and reddish colors of leaves. Cf. *porphin ring*.

2. Carotenoids, q.v.: the lipochromes or fatty pigments of plants.

3. Flavones and flavanols, q.v.: the fairly soluble pigments of blossoms and fruits. Cf. *antho-cyanin*.

plantain. (1) The dried leaves of *Plantago major* (Plantaginaceae); a diuretic. (2) The herbaceous tree *Musa sapientum paradisiaca* (Scitamineae); its fruit is the Adam's apple. Cf. *banana*.

plantose. An albuminous substance from rapeseed.

Plaskon. Trademark for a urea- or melamine-formaldehyde plastic.

plasma. (1) A green mottled variety of chalcedony. (2) A flame created by passing a gas through a concentric high-frequency field; it has 20 times the penetrating powers of conventional gas cutters toward steel. (3) The liquid part of the blood, containing fibrinogen; used to prepare antitoxins. **normal human-** Sterile p. obtained by pooling approximately equal volumes of the liquid portions of citrated whole blood from not less than 8 adult humans; a blood volume replenisher (U.S.P.). **proto-** Protoplasm.

p. torch. A very hot flame produced by passing a gas (as argon or nitrogen) through a continuous electric discharge between a rod and a nozzle electrode. It occurs in lightning; used in welding and metal spraying.

plasmin. An active fibrinolytic and proteolytic enzyme in human blood plasma.

plasminogen. The inactive precursor of plasmin.

plasmochin. Pamaquine.

plasmolysis. Dissolution of the protoplasm of a cell which occurs when it is bathed in water or a salt solution.

plasmoquin(e). Pamaquine.

Plasmosan. Trade name for a sterile 3.5% solution of polyvinylpyrrolidone with the chlorides of Na, Mg, K, and Ca in proportions similar to those in blood plasma. It is isotonic with blood; a substitute for blood plasma.

plasmosome. Nucleolus.

plastein. A substance formed when peptic digests of certain proteins (e.g., insulin) are concentrated and treated with more pepsin under slightly acid conditions.

plaster. (1) In pharmacy, a mixture having pressure-sensitive adhesive properties, spread evenly on fabric, the back of which may be coated with a water-repellent film (U.S.P.). (2) In general, a paste for coating surfaces or making molds. **adhesive-** A mixture of rosin and wax, for coating paper or textiles. **hard burnt-** An insoluble anhydrite. **lead-** See lead.

p. of paris. $CaSO_4$ to $3CaSO_4 \cdot 2H_2O$. A zeolite-type of hydrated calcium sulfate, made by heating gypsum. It quickly solidifies in the presence of water; used to make molds for taking impressions of objects.

plastic. Soft or moldable, pliable. Cf *plastics*.

plasticity. Capability of being formed or shaped in any desired way.

plasticization. The conversion of hard, glassy polymers into a soft, rubbery solid by the action of an organic compound, usually an ester.

plasticizer. A liquid having a low vapor pressure at room temperatures. Used to: (1) modify flow properties, as of synthetic resins; (2) reduce

evaporation rate, as of a paint solvent; (3) impart flexibility and toughness to a plastic, paint, or varnish film, e.g., phthalates in lacquers. Cf. lacquer *solvents*.

plastics. A group of organic materials which, though stable in use at ordinary temperatures, are plastic at some stage of manufacture and then can be shaped by application of heat and/or pressure. Synthetic rubber and certain inorganic materials, e.g., glass, comply with this definition but are not usually regarded as p. World production (1967) 16.2 million tons (66% thermoplastics). Cf. *elastomer, polymer.* See table. **ABS-** P. of improved impact strength obtained by dispersing an elastomer into a rigid styrene-acrylonitrile copolymer; as, Galalith. **cellulose-** P. made from nitrocellulose and camphor; as, Celluloid. **contact-pressure-** P. that form laminates at a pressure of 1 atm or less. **ethenoid-** P. comprising the acrylic, vinyl, and styrene types. **phenol-** P. made by condensation of phenol and formaldehyde; as, Bakelite. **rosin-** Phenol p. **thermoplastic-** P. that become moldable when treated; as, vinyl polymers. **thermosetting-** P. that harden when heated; as, phenol-aldehyde (Bakelite).

plastisol. (1) A plastic used as a solution or emulsion e.g., for coating. (2) The product resulting from plasticization.

Plastofilm. Trade name for a plastic made from reclaimed Pliofilm.

plastometer. (1) An instrument to measure the hardness of rubber from the depth of indentation of a hard body. Cf. *Brinell* test. (2) A device to measure the plasticity of a material by timing its flow through successive increments of length of a capillary tube.

plate. A thin sheet of metal, glass, etc., with a flat surface, e.g., silver-, or p. glass. **black-** P. for tinning, in the untinned state. **photographic-** A glass p. coated with an emulsion containing light-sensitive silver salts. Cf. *chromatic* p.

p. amalgamation. A method of extracting gold from finely crushed ore by floating it over a copper surface coated with mercury.

Platforming Process. Patented process for the catalytic upgrading of low-octane gasoline from natural gas or crude petroleum.

platina. Native platinum, often containing Ir, Rh, Ru, Os, Au, and Ag.

platinammines. Compounds of tetravalent platinum, which contain 4 molecules of ammonia.

platinammonium. The radical $Pt(NH_3)_2\equiv$.

plating. (1) A process by which a surface is coated with a metal; as, silver plating. (2) Infecting a culture medium with a bacterial suspension. **close-** A nonelectrolytic process in which sheets of metal are soldered to the surface to be plated. **electro-** Coating with a metal by electrodeposition.

platinibromide. Bromoplatinate. A salt containing the radical $PtBr_6 =$.

platinic. Describing a substance containing quadrivalent platinum; as, platinic chloride, $PtCl_4$. **p. acid.** $H_2PtO_3 = 245.2$. White powder, soluble in alkalies (forming platinates) and acids (forming platinic compounds). **chloro-** $H_2PtCl_6 \cdot 6H_2O = 518.1$. Brown crystals, soluble in water. Used as a reagent for separation of potassium from

CLASSIFICATION OF PLASTICS

Some of the principal trade names are given in parentheses. In many cases there are separate definitions under the name headings.

Acrylics (Lucite, Perspex, Plexiglas, Rhoplex). Glass substitutes.

Alkyds. Polyalcohol-phthalic anhydride esters, resinoids, resins and resin mixtures (Amberlac, Dulux, Duraplex, Esterol, Glyptal, Rezyl, Teglac), used in hardened forms, *e.g.*, for electrical insulation and cements.

Allyls (Allymer). Similar to alkyds.

Aniline-Formaldehyde (Cibanite). Heat-hardening.

Bituminous (Cetec, Thermoplax). Cold molding.

Caffelite. From coffee beans.

Casein (Galalith). Billiard balls and ivory substitute.

Cellulose (Cellophane). Transparent film and fibers.

Cellulose Acetate (Bakelite C.A.I, Lumarith, Textolite).

C.A.-Butyrate (Hercose C).

C.A.-Propionate (Hercose A.P.).

Cellulose Nitrate (*Pyroxylin*) (Celluloid, Fiberlac, Nitron). Inflammable film and solid articles.

Cellulose Propionate (Forticel).

Chlorinated Diphenyl (Arochlor).

Chlorinated Rubber (Parlon). Acid-resistant coatings.

Copal Esters (Kopal).

Coumarone-(Cumarone-)Indene (Brofo, Cumar, Paradene).

Cyclohexanone-Formaldehyde.

Epoxy, Epichlorhydrin-Diphenylolpropane (Epikote). Coatings and varnishes.

Ethyl Cellulose (Ethocel, ethylcellulose, Lumarith E.C.).

Formaldehyde-Sulfonamide (Santolite).

Furanes (Duralon).

Hydrogenated Rosin (Staybelite).

Lignin (Benalite, Lignolite, Meadol). Mainly a diluent for other plastics.

Melamines (Catalin, Melamine). Wet-strengthening agent for paper.

Methylcellulose (Methocel).

Phenol-Aldehydes (Aerolite, Albertol, Amberlite, Bakelite, Catalin, Formalite, Formica, Indurite, Micarta, Mouldrite, Phenolite, Textolite). Heat-hardening moldings or coatings; oil-soluble resins for use in varnishes, enamels, paints, and lacquers; adhesives for lamination.

Phenol-Copal (Beckopol).

Polyamide (nylon). Principally fibers, filaments, and bristles.

Polyamide-Aldehyde (Melopar).

Polyethylenes (Epolene, polythene) and *Polypropylene* (Propathene). Transparent film and moldings and extrusion material.

Polystyrene (Lustron, Styron).

Rubber Hydrochloride (Pliofilm, Plioform).

Sulfonamide-Aldehydes (Santolite).

Terpenes (Piccolyte, Rezinel).

Tetrafluoroethylene (Teflon).

Urea-Aldehyde (Aldur, Beatl, Beetle, Melamac, Plaskon, Pollopas, Uformite). Heat-hardened moldings.

Vinyl Polymers.

V. acetate (Alvar, Vinylite).

V. acetate and vinylidene dinitrile, or nytril, (Darvan).

V. alcohol (P.V.A., Vinal).

V. aldehyde (Formvar).

V. butyral (Vinylite X).

V. chloride (Chloroprene, Geon, Korolac, Plioflex, Tygon).

V. chloride and acetate (Elastiglas, Vinyon).

Polyvinylidenes (Saran).

Rubber substitutes, phonograph disks.

---

sodium; for platinization; in photographic toning; in ceramics, for metallic lusters; and in catalysts, q.v. **p. bromide.** $PtBr_4 = 514.9$. Platinum tetrabromide. Brown crystals, soluble in water. **p. chloride.** (1) Chloro*platinic acid.* (2) $PtCl_4 = 336.6$. Brown crystals, soluble in water. **p. hydroxide.** $Pt(OH)_4 = 263.2$. Brown powder, decomp. by heat, insoluble in water. **p. iodide.** $PtI_4 = 702.9$. Platinum tetraiodide. Brown powder, insoluble in water, soluble in iodide solutions. **p. oxide.** $PtO_2 = 227.2$. Platinum dioxide. Black powder, m.430 (decomp.), insoluble in water. **p. sodium chloride.** Sodium platinichloride. **p. sulfate.** $Pt(SO_4)_2 = 387.2$. Platinum sulfate. Green-black, deliquescent crystals, soluble in water; a microchemical reagent. **p. sulfide.** $PtS_2 = 259.3$. Platinum disulfide. Black needles, decomp. by heat, insoluble in water, soluble in ammonium sulfide solution.

platinichloride. Chloroplatinate. A salt of chloroplatinic acid containing the radical $PtCl_6 =$. Platinichlorides are double salts of platinic and another chloride.

platiniferous. An ore or substance containing platinum.

platiniridium. A native alloy of Pt and Ir, often containing Rh, Ru, and Cu.

platinize. To coat with metallic platinum.

platinized asbestos. Asbestos impregnated with a solution of a platinum salt and ignited, so that metallic platinum results; a catalyst.

platinochloride. Chloroplatinite. A salt of chloroplatinous acid containing the radical $PtCl_4 =$. Platinochlorides are double salts of platinous and another chloride.

platinocyanide. Cyanoplatinite. A double salt of platinous and another cyanide; as, $K_2Pt(CN)_4$. Used in photography and for fluorescent X-ray screens.

platinoid. The alloy Cu 61, Zn 24, Ni 14, W 1-2%; used for electrical-resistance coils.

platinous. Describing a compound containing divalent platinum, $Pt =$. **p.bromide.** $PtBr_2 = 355.0$.- Platinum dibromide. Brown, deliquescent crystals, decomp. 200, insoluble in water. **p. chloride.** $PtCl_2 = 266.1$. Platinum dichloride. Brown crystals, insoluble in water, soluble in chloride solutions. **p. cyanide.** $Pt(CN)_2 = 247.22$. Platinum dicyanide. Yellow powder, insoluble in water, soluble in cyanide solutions. **p. hydroxide.** $Pt(OH)_2 = 229.2$. Black powder, decomp. by heat, insoluble in water. **p. iodide.** $PtI_2 = 449.0$. Platinum diiodide. Black powder, decomp. 325, insoluble in water, soluble in acids. **p. oxide.**

THE PLATINUM METALS

Year of Discovery	Metal		Symbol	At. no.	At. wt.	Discoverer
1741..........	Native platina		....	....	....	Wood
1750..........	Platinum		Pt	78	195.2	Watson
	Palladium group	Platinum group				
1803..........	....	Osmium (trace)	Os	76	190.9	Smithson-Tenant
1803..........	....	Iridium (1–55%)	Ir	77	193.1	Smithson-Tenant
1804..........	Rhodium (0.2–4%)	....	Rh	45	102.9	Wollaston
1804..........	Palladium (0.1–21%)	....	Pd	46	106.7	Wollaston
1845..........	Ruthenium	....	Ru	44	101.7	Claus
1924..........	Masurium (trace)	....	Ma	43	98	Noddack
1924..........	....	Rhenium (trace)	Re	75	188	Noddack

PtO = 211.1. Platinum monoxide. Violet to black powder, decomp. by heat, insoluble in water. **p. sodium chloride.** Sodium platinochloride. **p. sulfide.** PtS = 227.3. Platinum monosulfide. Black powder, decomp. by heat, insoluble in water, soluble in ammonium sulfide solution.

platinum. Pt = 195.09. A noble metal of the fourth period, at. no. 78, described (1741) by Wood. Silver gray, d.21.37, m.1773.5, b.4300, insoluble in water, alcohol, acids, or bases; soluble in aqua regia. Used as a catalyst, foil, wire powder (p. black), gauze, or gray sponge; and for acid-proof containers, electrodes, and jewelry. P. forms 2 series of compounds: platinous (valency 2) and platinic (valency 4), each having many double salts. **p. alloy.** An alloy of p. with another noble metal; as, gold. **p. black.** A black powder of finely divided p.; a catalyst. **p. chloride.** (1) Commercial chloroplatinic acid. See *platinic acid*. (2) Platinic chloride. (3) Platinous chloride. **p. dibromide.** Platinous bromide. **p. dichloride.** Platinous chloride. **p. dicyanide.** Platinous cyanide. **p. diiodide.** Platinous iodide. **p. dioxide.** Platinic oxide. **p. disulfide.** Platinic sulfide. **p. iridium.** An alloy: Pt 90, Ir 10%. **p. metals.** A group of noble metals that occur together in nature, and form 2 groups in the periodic system. See table. **p. minerals.** P. occurs in nature alone or associated with the other metals of the group, e.g., platiniridium, Pt·Ir. See also *cooperite, platina*. **p. monosulfide.** Platinous sulfide. **p. monoxide.** Platinous oxide. **p. oxyfluoride.** PtOF₄ = 287.23. Red solid, sublimes 150 (orange vapor). **p. pentafluoride.** PtF₅ = 290.23. The only known pentavalent p. compound. Red solid, reacts with water to form the fluoroplatinate. **p. sponge.** Gray, spongy, porous, metallic p. mass, obtained by reduction of chloroplatinic acid; a catalyst. **p. sulfide.** Platinic sulfate. **p. tetrachloride.** Platinic chloride. **p. yellow.** An alkaline chloroplatinate coating for fluorescent X-ray screens.

platinum cladding. The bonding of a layer of platinum to a bar of other metal, and working down to a desired thickness; for laboratory ware.

platize. Platinize.

platosammine. Pt(NH₃)₂X₂. A compound of divalent platinum which contains 2 molecules of ammonia.

Plato unit. The weight (grams) of total solids in 100 grams of wort.

Plattner, Karl Friedrich. 1800–1858. German mineralogist. **P.'s process.** The extraction of gold as trichloride by passing chlorine gas through the gold-bearing pulp.

plattnerite. PbO₂. A native oxide.

Plausen mill. A colloid mill.

Plavia. Trade name for a viscose cellulose synthetic fiber.

plazolite. 3CaO·Al₂O₃·2(SiO₂·CO₂)·2H₂O. A Californian silicate. Colorless crystals.

pleiad. A group of isotopes (obsolete).

pleio- See *pleo*.

pleochroic. Pleochromatic.

pleochroism. Pleochromatism.

pleochromatic. Pleochroic. Showing more than one color; as, a fluorescent solution.

pleochromatism. Pleochroism. The capacity of certain optically biaxial crystals to transmit polarized light, so that a complementary color is seen at right angles to the direction of the ray. Cf. *dichroism*.

pleomorphic. Occurring in more than one form.

pleomorphism. The capacity to crystallize in 2 or more different crystal systems.

pleonast. The mineral (Mg·Fe)O·(Al·Fe)₂O₃.

plessite. Gersdorffite.

Plessy's green. Chromic phosphate.

pleurisy foot. Asclepias.

plevacol. A compound of aminobenzoyleugenoltricresol and Formalin. Yellow crystals, m.155, soluble in alcohol; a dental filling.

Plexiglas. Trademark for a methyl acrylate plastic.

pliers. Pincers with long jaws for holding, bending, or cutting. **button-** A circular disk with a round hole, used to hold assay buttons during polishing.

plinol. A hydroxy derivative of iridane, q.v.

Pliny the Elder. Cajus Secundus Plinius, 23-79. Roman soldier noted for his scientific observations and writings (*Historia naturalis*).

Pliofilm. Trademark for rubber hydrochloride. Cf. *Plastofilm*.

Pliolite. Trademark for resinous materials obtained when rubber is cyclized with agents such as tin tetrachloride. Used to produce water resistance, e.g., coated paper.

pliowax. Pliolite, q.v., containing 60% paraffin wax; a hot-melt coating, e.g., for paper.

plodding. Compression of warm soap into shape in a screw compressor.

Plotnikow effect. The longitudinal scattering of (especially infrared) rays by solid objects or fluids. Cf. *Raman effect*.

plotting. To make a graph representing a relationship between 2 unknowns, by determining a number of pairs of values that satisfy the relation, and representing them in terms of the lengths of 2 lines at right angles (coordinates).

Plucker tube. A glass tube with 2 electrodes, containing a gas under reduced pressure; used in spectroscopy.

plumbagin(e). $C_{11}H_8O_3$ = 188.1. Methyljuglone, 5-hydroxy-2-methyl-1,4-naphthoquinone. Yellow crystals, m.79, from the root of *Plumbago europea*, *P. zeylonica*, and *P. rosea*, (Plumbaginaceae).

plumbago. Native graphite. Black lead. Used to manufacture "lead" pencils, crucibles, etc.; and as a lubricant. See *Dag*.

plumbane. (1) PbR_4. An organic compound of lead, e.g., tetramethyllead, $PbMe_4$. (2) $Pb(C_2H_5)_4$ = 323.2. Tetraethyllead*, lead tetraethide. Colorless liquid; an antiknock compound for gasoline. Cf. *ethyl gasoline*.

plumbates. Salts derived from lead hydroxide, $Ph(OH)_4 \rightleftharpoons H_4PbO_4$. metaplumbates, M_2PbO_3; orthoplumbates, M_4PbO_4.

plumbic. Describing a compound of tetravalent lead. **p. ocher.** Brown *lead oxide*.

plumbiferous. A material containing lead.

plumbism. Poisoning by lead.

plumbite. $MHPbO_2$ or M_2PbO_2. Salts derived from lead hydroxide, $Pb(OH)_2$.

plumbocalcite. Lead containing calcite.

plumbogummite. A native aluminum and lead phosphate.

plumbosolvency. The degree of solubility of lead in a liquid.

plumbous. Describing a compound of divalent lead. **p. compounds.** See *lead*.

plumbum. Latin for lead. **p. candidum.** Early name for tin. **p. cinereum.** Early name for bismuth. **p. nigrum.** Early name for lead.

plumiera. Sucuuba bark. The dried bark of *Plumiera sucuuba* (Apocynaceae); an anthelmintic.

plumieric acid. $C_{20}H_{24}O_{12}$ = 456.2. A crystalline principle from plumiera.

plumierin. $C_{21}H_{26}O_{12} \cdot H_2O$ = 488.3. Agoniadin, asonidin. A glucoside from the bark of *Plumiera*. White crystals, m.155 (decomp.), soluble in water; used to treat gonorrhea.

plumose. Having a fleecy or feathery appearance. **p. growth.** A fleecy, feathery growth of bacteria on a culture medium. **p. mica.** A muscovite resembling asbestos.

plural gel. A gel formed by the simultaneous gelification of a mixture of 2 or more sols.

pluranium. An alleged new element discovered by Osann (1828) in a platinum ore: probably mixed titanium dioxide, silica, and zirconium oxide.

plutonic. Igneous. General name for rocks that have crystallized below the earth's surface; as, granite.

plutonium. (1) Pu. An element, at. no. 94, at. wt. 239, obtained by bombarding ordinary uranium with neutrons (Seaborg, etc., 1940); named after the planet Pluto. It is a transformation product of neptunium, q.v.; has positive valencies 1 to 4; and its stablest isotope has a mass no. 239. **trans-** An isotope of Pu produced by bombarding it with α particles in a cyclotron; used in connection with atomic bombs. See uranium *pile*. (2) Early name for native barium oxide.

pluviometer. An instrument to measure rainfall.

pneumatic. (1) Pertaining to air. (2) Pertaining to gases. Cf. *aerodynamics*. **p. drill.** A drill operated by compressed air. **p. jig.** A device for separating minerals by an air blast. **p. trough.** A vessel of water containing an inverted cylinder, filled with water, for the collection of gases.

pneumatics. The study of the mechanical properties of gases.

pneumatology. (1) The science of respiration. (2) The science of gases.

pneumatolysis. The production of ore deposits by liberation of gases or vapors during solidification of igneous rocks.

pneumin. Methylene creosote. Yellow powder, insoluble in water; used medicinally.

pneumo(no)coniosis. General name for pulmonary diseases due to inhalation of dust. Cf. *silicosis*.

pneumokoniosis. Pneumoconiosis.

pockeling. The development of circular patches on fresh surfaces of certain solutions, e.g., soap.

pocket. (1) A sac-shaped cavity or hole. (2) A small body of ore. (3) An enlargement of an ore vein. (4) A unit of measure, e.g., for hops.

poco oil. The essential oil from *Mentha aquatica*, rich in linalool acetate.

podophyllic acid. $C_{15}H_{16}O_7$ = 308.13. A monobasic acid derived from podophyllin by hydrolysis.

podophyllin. A resin obtained from podophyllum; contains podophyllic acid, podophyllotoxin, and picropodophyllin. Yellow powder, insoluble in water, soluble in alcohol; a purgative (U.S.P., B.P.). **picro-** $C_{12}H_{14}O_6$. An internal anhydride of podophyllic acid.

podophyllotoxin. $C_{15}H_{16}O_5$ = 290.1. The active principle of podophyllin. Yellow powder, insoluble in water.

podophyllum. Mandrake, May apple. The dried rhizome of *Podophyllum peltatum* (Berberidaceae) which contains 3% podophyllin. Used medicinally as the fluid extract (U.S.P.). **p. resin.** Podophyllin (U.S.P., B.P.).

podzol, podsol. A soil that has undergone podzolization.

podzolization, podsolization. The division of soil into 3 layers by continual leaching with rainwater. The top layer contains decaying organic matter; the center layer the material out of which silica, iron oxide, and alumina have been washed; and the bottom layer redeposited extractives.

Poggendorff, Johann Christian. 1796–1877. German physicist. **P. cell.** An amalgamated zinc anode and carbon cathode in a solution of potassium dichromate 12, sulfuric acid 25, water 100 pts. (2.01 volts.) **P. compensation method.** The determination of the potential of a cell by comparing the potential required to balance it with that required to balance a standard, in terms of the length of a resistance wire. Cf. *Wheatstone bridge.*

Pohl's commutator. An electrical-contact key that enables the direction of current to be reversed instantaneously; used in physiology.

poi. See *taro.*

poidometer. A rapid-action industrial weighing machine.

poikilothermism. The ability of living organisms, especially lower forms, to adapt themselves to temperature.

point. (1) That which has position but not magnitude. (2) A minute spot. (3) A numerical value on a scale. (4) A unit of weight used by jewelers. 1 p. = 0.01 carat. **boiling-** The minimum temperature at which a liquid changes rapidly to the vapor state. **condensation-** The maximum temperature at which a vapor changes to the liquid state. **critical-** The temperature above which a gas cannot be liquefied by pressure only. **dew-** The temperature at which the moisture of the air condenses. **end-** In titration: the stage at which one drop of solution completes the reaction. **freezing-** The maximum temperature at which a liquid changes to the solid state. **isoelectric-** See *isoelectric point.* **liquefaction-** (1) Melting p. (2) Condensation p. (3) Critical p. **melting-** The minimum temperature at which a solid becomes liquid. **quadruple-** The temperature at which all 4 phases in a 2-component system can exist. **refraction-** The spot on a surface at which a ray of light is refracted. **slip-** The minimum temperature at which a fat or wax slips downward in a vertical capillary tube, as distinct from melting completely. **triple-** See *triple point.*

pointage test. P. titration. The control of zinc phosphating baths from the volume of 0.1 N sodium hydroxide to neutralize (to phenolphthalein) a 10-ml aliquot of the bath.

poise. (1) The cgs unit of dynamic viscosity, q.v.: 1 dyne/(sec)(cm^2); or 1.45×10^{-5} lb-sec/ft^2; or stoke unit/density. Cf. *reyn, stoke, Poiseuille's law.* (2) To balance or maintain an oxidation-reduction equilibrium; as, a poising agent.

poised. Describing a system that resists oxidation or reduction. Cf. *buffer.*

Poiseuille's law. See *viscosity.*

poising agent. Poiser. A substance that stabilizes an oxidation-reduction equilibrium. Cf. *buffer.*

poison. (1) A substance that causes the disturbance, disease, or death of an organism. Classification: A. Chemical (according to composition):
1. Inorganic (alkalies, acids, metals, volatile nonmetals)
2. Organic (acids, glucosides, alkaloids, volatile substances, bacteria, animals)

B. Physiological (according to effect):
1. Irritants and corrosives
2. Neurotics (cerebro-): narcotics (spinal), tetanics (cerebrospinal), depressants, deliriants, asthenics.

(2) A substance that impairs the quality of a metal or alloy. (3) A substance that destroys or diminishes the action of a catalyst or enzyme. **acrid-** Irritant. **arrow-** See *arrow.* **bacterial-** P. produced by bacteria; as, ptomaines. **corrosive-** A substance that destroys tissue locally; as, acids. **cumulative-** A p. retained and gradually accumulating in the body. **fish-** A substance used to stupefy fish. **narcotic-** A p. that produces stupor or delirium. **true-** A p. that is absorbed and causes disease or death.

p. ash. Chioanthus. **p. effect.** See table. **p. gas.** See *p. vapor gas.* **p. ivy.** *Rhus toxicodendron.* **p. nut.** Nux vomica. **p. oak.** (1) The fresh leaflets of *Rhus toxicodendron* (Anacardiaceae), U.S. Atlantic States. Cf. *poison ivy.* (2) *Rhus diversiloba,* U.S. Pacific Coast. Both produce highly irritant skin inflammations. **p. vapors.** See table. **p. vine.** *Rhus toxicodendron.*

Poison vapor	(1) Fatal percent	(2) Tolerated percent
Acrolein	0.001*	0.00033
Ammonia	0.3	0.03
Aniline	. . . .	0.00004
Arsine	0.05*	0.001
Benzene	. . . .	0.0005
Bromine	0.1*	0.004
Carbon dioxide	30.0*	2–3
Carbon disulfide	0.001	0.0001
Carbon monoxide	0.5*	0.04
Carbon tetrachloride	0.03*	0.001
Chlorine	0.10*	0.0001
Chloroform	0.03*	0.001
Chloropicrin	0.05*	0.0001
Dichlorodiethyl sulfide	. . . .	0.002
Dioxan	. . . .	0.02
Hydrochloric acid	0.5*	0.005
Hydrocyanic acid	0.048*	0.002
Hydrogen sulfide	0.06*	0.01
Iodine	. . . .	0.0001
Mercury	. . . .	0.00012†
Nitrobenzene	. . . .	0.00002
Nitrogen monoxide	0.07*	0.0033
Phosgene	0.02*	0.0001
Phosphine	0.2*	0.01
Phosphorus trichloride	0.00035	0.0000004
Sulfur dioxide	0.2*	0.01
Sulfur trioxide	0.001*	0.0002
Toluidine	. . . .	0.0001

(1) *Percentage in air fatal in 30 min. Others dangerous after 30 min.
(2) Maximum safe concentration in air for humans for 1 hr.
†Exposure for 2–3 months causes poisoning

poisoning. The diseased condition produced by a poison. **acute-** A morbid condition caused by a single large dose of poison. **chronic-** A morbid condition caused by many small doses of poison. **garage-** A morbid condition due to inhalation of carbon monoxide from an internal-combustion motor.

poisonous dose. The amount that produces marked pathological conditions.

Poisson's ratio. The ratio of lateral contraction to longitudinal extension for a bar under a stress parallel to its length.

poivrette. Ground olive stones; an adulterant for pepper.

poke. Phytolacca. **Indian-** Veratrum. **p. berries.** The fresh fruits of *Phytolacca decandra*; an emetic, narcotic, and indicator. **p. root.** *Phytolacca.*

Polaises reaction. See *Grignard reaction.*

Polan. Trade name for a polyamide synthetic fiber.

polar. Pertaining to a pole. **p. bond.** The electrostatic union of 2 atoms established by the passage of one or more electrons from one to the other. *non-* The electromagnetic union of 2 atoms established by sharing in common one or more pairs of electrons. **p. compound.** An electrolyte: a compound that can ionize when dissolved or fused; as inorganic acids, bases, and salts. The atoms are supposed to be held in electrostatic union. *non-polar-* A nonelectrolyte: an organic compound the atoms of which are supposed to be held in electromagnetic union by sharing a pair of electrons. **p. formula.** See *formula.* **p. number.** See *polar number.* **p. zone.** See *zone.*

polarimeter. Polariscope. A device for measuring the rotation of polarized light. Between 2 nicol prisms is placed a column of polarizing liquid. By rotating the prism nearest to the eye until the intensity of the light passing through the liquid equals the intensity of the comparison field, the new plane of vibration of the light can be read from the scale in degrees. See *rotation.*

polarimetry. Polariscopy. Measurement of the rotation of polarized light by the polariscope.

polarisation. Polarization.

polariscope. Polarimeter.

polariscopy. Polarimetry.

polariser. Polarizer.

polarising. Polarizing.

polarity. Describing a body having 2 poles, or different properties at terminal points. **atomic-** The loss or gain of one or more electrons by an atom. See *polar bond.* **chemical-** Describing a molecule that has an acid and a basic radical; as, an aminoacid. **electrical-** The positive and negative terminal, pole, or electrode of an electrical device. **magnetic-** The north or south pole of a magnet. **molecular-** The distribution of electric charges in a molecule. See *polarization (3).* **p. formula.** A formula which shows the distribution of electric charges in the molecule. Cf. *formula, molecular diagram, structure symbols.* **p. paper.** A paper used to distinguish the positive and negative poles of a direct electric current. E.g., a filter paper saturated with sodium chloride and phenolphthalein is colored red at the positive terminal, due to the liberation of hydroxyl ions.

polarization. (1) The ability of certain substances to polarize light passing through them. (2) The stoppage or reversal of the voltaic current from an electrolytic cell due to the accumulation of dissociation products at the electrodes. See *overvoltage.* Cf. *p. potential.* (3) The orientation of a molecule in an electric field: e.g., the positive nucleus toward the negative pole; the electron cloud toward the positive pole. $P. = 3R/4N$, where R is molecular refractivity, and N Avogadro's number. $P. = el/I$, where e is the charge,

l the distance, and I the intensity of the field. Cf. *molecular refractivity.* **cell-** The accumulation of hydrogen bubbles on the negative electrode of a battery. **circular-** Polarized light in circular vibrations. **elliptic-** Polarized light in elliptical vibrations. **plane-** Polarized light, the vibrations of which are parallel and in one plane.

p. curve. (1) The current-voltage curve obtained when the intensity of an electrolytic current is plotted against the polarizing electromotive force. (2) Polarogram. **p. potential.** The reverse potential of an electrolytic cell, tending to oppose the direct potential effecting electrolytic decomposition in the cell; due to p. (2). Cf. *overvoltage.*

polarize. To produce polarization.

polarized light. A composite of 2 types of rays whose vibrations are in 2 directions at right angles: the ordinary and extraordinary rays. The ordinary ray is "lost" in the polarimeter by total reflection, and the extraordinary ray emerges as light polarized in one plane only. Optically active substances rotate this plane. Cf. *radiation, Verdet.*

polarizer. A device for polarizing light; as, a nicol prism through which light vibrating only in one plane passes. The p. acts as a filter by transmitting only parallel vibrations, thus ‖‖‖, which, on passing through an optically active substance, are rotated either ///// or \\\\\. Cf. *analyzer.*

polarizing. Causing polarization. **p. angle.** See *Brewster's law.* **p. disk.** Polaroid. A cellulose film containing oriented iodoquinine sulfate crystals, mounted between 2 glass plates; a substitute for nicol prisms in polarimeters; and used in microscopes, reading glasses, and windshields to prevent glare.

polar number. Valence number. The mathematical expression of valence by assigning to each atom in a compound a positive or negative integer: H is $+1$, O is -2. Cf. *oxidation, reduction, valence.*

polarogram. Polarization curve. The current-voltage curve produced by a polarograph. It indicates the quantity and purity of substances electrolytically reduced at specific cathode potentials.

polarograph. An instrument that records photographically, minute changes in the intensity of a current resulting from a gradually increasing applied voltage, in electrolysis with a dropping mercury cathode. Used to measure deposition or reduction of cations and anions, overvoltage, ionic complexity and equilibria, solubility; and for qualitative and quantitative microanalysis. Cf. *Heyrovsky, tastpolarograph.*

polaroid. A polarizing disk, q.v. **p. vectograph.** Aerial photography in which the p. is used to obtain stereoscopic effects.

polaron. An electron produced in an aqueous medium by radiation. It is associated with one or more water molecules, and it polarizes the surrounding medium.

Polathene. Trade name for a polythene synthetic fiber.

poldine methylsulfate. $C_{22}H_{29}O_7NS = 451.45$. White, bitter crystals, m.139, soluble in water; a parasympatholytic (B.P.).

pole(s). (1) Rod. (2) The points at the opposite ends of an axis; 2 points that have opposite physical properties. **negative-** The cathode: an electric terminal charged with electrons. (**magnetic**) **north-** That point toward which a freely suspended magnetic needle will point. **positive-** The anode: an electric terminal that becomes positively charged by loss of electrons.

Polenské number. The number of milliliters of 0.1 normal alkali (less the blank) to neutralize an alcoholic solution of the water-insoluble volatile fatty acids liberated on acidification of the soap made by saponification of 5 grams of a fat. Cf. *Reichert number.*

polianite. Pyrolusite.

policeman. A device to remove precipitates from the walls of glass vessels in quantitative analysis. **platinum-** A platinum-iridium alloy claw that fits over a glass rod, to hold a quantitative filter during ignition. **rubber-** A small piece of rubber tubing fitting snugly over the end of a glass rod.

polishing. Rubbing or smoothing metal or glass surfaces. **electrolytic-** Smoothing a metal surface by making it the anode in a suitable electrolyte (usually phosphoric acid and glycerin). The high current density produced on the small projecting portions results in their preferential dissolution.

polishing slate. Gray or yellow slate used for polishing.

Pollack's cement. A stiff paste of equal weights of red lead and litharge, in gelatin, for jointing metal and/or glass: slow-setting but strong.

pollantin. An antitoxin obtained by inoculating horses with pollen extract; used for immunization.

pollen. The male sex cells or fertilizing grains of a flowering plant, which contain glucosides; e.g.: ragweed p., quercitin; timothy p. (*Phleum pratense*), dactylin. Cf. *stamen.* **p. extract.** A solution of proteins from the pollens of plants believed to cause hay fever; used for immunization. **fall-** An extract of the proteins of ragweed, goldenrod, and maize. **spring-** An extract of the proteins of rye, timothy, orchard grass, redtop grass, and sweet vernal grass; used for immunizing to hay fever.

Pollopas. Trade name for a glasslike transparent plastic; a glass substitute.

pollucite. $Cs_2O \cdot Al_2O_3 \cdot 5SiO_2 \cdot H_2O$. Pollux. A rare, native silicate, in pegmatite (Island of Elba).

pollution. (1) Contamination. (2) The introduction of a deleterious substance into a water supply.

pollux. Pollucite.

polonium. Po = 218.2. Radiotellurium, dvitellurium. The radioactive element RaF, at. no. 84, formed by disintegration of radium, and belonging to the sixth group of the periodic system; the first radioactive decomposition product, discovered by Madame Curie (1898).

poly- Prefix (Greek) meaning many. (Latin: multi-.)

polyacetylenes. Unbranched carbon chain compounds, sometimes part of a ring structure, C_{10} to C_{13} predominating; formed by plants (hydrocarbons) and microorganisms (alcohols and acids).

polyacid base. A compound that yields 2 or more hydroxyl ions; as, $Ca(OH)_2$.

polyactivation. Activation e.g., of fluorescence, by more than one substance.

polyad. An element or radical with a valency greater than 2, e.g., triad.

polyadelphite. A brown to green manganese garnet.

polyalkane. A hydrocarbon polymer of long-chain molecules containing only saturated atoms in the main chain.

polyallomers. Plastics having a highly crystalline and stereoregular structure, and consisting of chains of polymerized crystalline segments of each of the constituent olefinic monomers. Specially suitable for blow-molding and extrusion processes, e.g., propylene-ethylene p.

polyamide. A polymer, usually of a carboxylic acid (e.g., adipic acid) and its aminated derivative, in which the structural units are linked by amide or thioamide groupings; many have fiber-forming properties. Cf. *nylon.*

polyargyrite. A native silver-antimony sulfide.

polyatomic. (1) Describing a molecule with 3 or more atoms (2) Polybasic. (3) Polyacidic. (4) Describing an organic compound containing 2 or more hydroxyl groups; as, glucose.

polybasic acid. A compound that yields 2 or more H ions per molecule in aqueous solution; as, H_2SO_4.

polybasite. Ag_9SbS_6. A native sulfide, containing copper.

polybutylenes. Polybutenes. Polymers of butylene, ranging from viscous to rubbery substances.

polycaprolactam. Nylon 6. A polyamide synthetic fiber.

polycarbonates. Thermoplastic linear polyesters of carbonic acid, made by the polymeric condensation of bisphenols with a phosgene or its derivatives. Used for injection molding, especially where clarity is important.

Polycarpeae. A group of families of Phanerogams (Nymphaeaceae, Ranunculaceae, Magnoliaceae, Myristicaceae, Menispermaceae, Berberidaceae, Lauraceae).

polyceptor. An amboceptor that binds different complements.

polychloral. Hydronal.

Polychol. Trademark for surfactant condensation products of polyoxethylene and wood alcohols.

polychrom. Esculin.

polychromatic. Showing more than one color, particularly if viewed by polarized light. **pseudo-** Pseudodichromatic, pseudodichroic. Showing more than one color when viewed by polarized light, but otherwise colorless.

polychromatophile. Describing a cell or tissue that can be stained differentially with dyes.

polycondensation. A form of polymerization in which recurring structural units are formed from simpler molecules by elimination of a simple substance, e.g., water.

polycrase. Euxenite.

polycyclic. Polynucleated. Describing a molecule that contains 2 or more atomic rings; as, naphthalene. Cf. *ring systems.*

polydymite. $(Ni, Co)_4S_5$. A native sulfide.

polyelectrolyte. A polymer producing large chaintype ions in solutions, that can carry positive or negative groups along the polymer chain; used as industrial flocculants.

polyene. A compound containing many double bonds; as, the carotenoids. **p. grouping.** A system of double bonds associated with color reactions; as, in carotene.

polyester. A polymer having structural units linked by ester groupings; obtained by condensation of carboxylic acids with polyhydric alcohols.

polyether. A polymer containing the $-(CH_2-CHR-O-)_n$ linkage in the main chain or side chain.

polyethylene (U.S. usage). Polythene (U.K. usage); (strictly) polymethylene. A member of a series of straight-chain paraffin hydrocarbons of high molecular weight (18,000–20,000), made by polymerizing ethylene at very high pressures, e.g., 30,000 psi, under controlled conditions, m.110–115. Polyethylenes are thermoplastic and can be extruded or molded by injection or compression. World production (1965) 2.8 million tons. **p. glycol.** A polyglycol derived from ethylene glycol. *p.g.—400.* $H(OCH_2CH_2)_nOH$. A condensation product of ethylene oxide and water, where n is 8–10. Colorless, hygroscopic liquid, miscible with water; used in ointments (U.S.P.). *p.g.—4000.* Similar to p.g.—400, where n is 70–85. A wax, m.54; used in ointments (U.S.P.).

polygalic acid. Polygalin.

polygalin. $C_{32}H_{54}O_{18} = 726.6$. Polygalic acid. An active principle from *Polygala senega.* Cf. *senega.*

polygamarin. A crystalline bitter principle from *Polygala amara* (Polygalaceae).

polygarskite. Attapulgite (U.S. usage). A hydrated, aluminum-magnesium silicate from Attapulgus, Decatur, Ga., and Ukraine; a drilling mud, fungicide base, and filler.

polygen. An element that forms 2 or more series of compounds; as, chlorine (chlorides, chlorites, and chlorates).

polygenetic. Producing more than one phenomenon. **p. dye.** A coloring material that gives different shades with different mordants. Cf. *monogenetic.*

polyglycol. A dihydroxy ether formed by dehydration of 2 or more glycol molecules, e.g., diethylene glycol.

polygon. A plane figure bounded by 3 or more sides.

Polygonaceae. The buckwheat family of herbs or woody plants; e.g.: *Rheum* species, rhubarb; *Rumex crispus,* rumex *Polygonum bistorta,* bistort.

polygonatum. Solomon's seal.

polygonin. $C_{21}H_{20}O_{10} = 432.15$. A glucoside from *Polygonatum cuspidatum* (Lilaceae), Japan.

polygraph. A device to record arterial and venous pulse waves simultaneously; used as a lie detector.

polyhalite. $K_2SO_4\cdot MgSO_4\cdot 2CaSO_4\cdot 2H_2O$. A native hydrated sulfate.

polyhydrate. A compound containing more than 2 molecules of water.

polyhydric. A compound containing more than 2 hydroxyl groups.

polyhydrone. $(H_2O)_x$. A polymer of hydrone, q.v.

polymer. Polymere, polymeride (obsolete). A member of a series of polymeric compounds. A substance composed of very large molecules, which consist essentially of recurring long-chain structural units, which distinguish polymers from other types of organic molecules, and confer on them tensile strength, deformability, elasticity, and hardness. Some 50 units (*monomers*), largely derived from coal and oil, are used to build up such polymers. Considerable modification of properties results on introducing a second type of monomer (B) into the main structure (monomer A), producing a *copolymer,* in which the units A and B are arranged completely at random. Alternatively, the A and B units may be arranged in order of long segments, e.g., $\sim$A–A–A–A–B–B–B–B–B–A–A–A–A$\sim$ (*block p.*). There are also *branched* polymers, in which the B units branch from the A units; and *crosslinked* polymers, in which 2 A chains are joined by one or a block of B units. Polymeric molecules are classified below (after Pinner). Examples of *high* polymers are plastics, fibers, rubber, human tissue. Cf. *macromolecular chemistry, elastomer.*

alloy- A p. produced by the simultaneous polymerization of 2 substances. Cf. *silicone alloy.* **blocked-** See above. **branched-chain-** See above. **co-** A composite p. prepared by the polymerization of a mixture of 2 or more monomers, or of a monomer and p. of low molecular weight. Cf. *alloy p. block c.p.* A p. built of linearly linked polymeric units. *random c.p.* A p. having 2 or

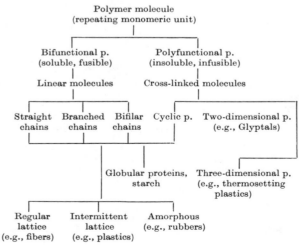

Polymer molecule
(repeating monomeric unit)

Bifunctional p. — Polyfunctional p.
(soluble, fusible) — (insoluble, infusible)

Linear molecules — Cross-linked molecules

Straight chains — Branched chains — Bifilar chains — Cyclic p. — Two-dimensional p. (e.g., Glyptals)

Globular proteins, starch — Three-dimensional p. (e.g., thermosetting plastics)

Regular lattice (e.g., fibers) — Intermittent lattice (e.g., plastics) — Amorphous (e.g., rubbers)

more types of units combined in random succession in a linear chain structure. **crosslinked-** See above. **electron-exchange-** Redox p. A polymeric structure having several sites capable of accepting or donating electrons. Thus, modified cellulose with redox properties is used as a catalyst to remove oxygen from water to obtain anaerobic conditions. **graft-** A p. produced by grafting a monomer onto a straight-chain p. to produce a branched-chain p. Thus, a fluorocarbon p. is heated sufficiently to form free radicals on its surface and then dipped into a monomer, e.g., styrene, to produce a graft p. having a printable surface. **high-** A p. of high molecular weight, e.g., containing a large number of structural units. **high-trans-** A rubbery p. in which a large proportion of the C atoms are arranged in a definite pattern that repeats itself consistently in the chain; as, natural rubber. **homo-** A p. having only a single type of repeating unit. **inorganic-** Inorganic structures that form polymers on heating or by catalytic action; as, mica, silicones, inorganic rubber. **isostatic-** A crystalline p. made from α-olefins, in which the substituents in the asymmetric C atoms all have the same configuration relative to the main chain. **linear-** A p. in which the molecules are essentially in the form of long chains. **organized-** A p. having a regular macroscopic structure, without necessarily showing microcrystallinity. Cf. *polyallomers.* **orientated-** A p. film that has been stretched mechanically in 2 directions at right angles to improve its strength properties. **redox-** Electron-exchange p. **super-** A p. in which the polymerized molecules have an average molecular weight exceeding 10,000.

    P.R. Trade name for a polyamide synthetic fiber.

polymeric. Related molecularly to an isomeric compound, but having a multiple of its molecular weight; as, acetylene and benzene. See *polymerism.* **p. dialdehyde.** See dialdehyde *starch.*

polymericular weight. The molecular weight of a polymerized molecule of an element.

polymeride. Polymer.

polymerisation. Polymerization.

polymerism. The property of certain organic compounds which have the same percentage composition, but different molecular weights, the heavier being multiples of the lighter. Thus, C_2H_2, C_4H_4, C_6H_6, C_8H_8 are polymeric compounds. See *polymerization.*

polymerization. Describing a reaction in which 2 or more molecules of the same substance combine to form a compound, from which the original substance may or may not be regenerated. Cf. *molecular association, hydrone.* **aromatic-** The formation of an aromatic compound from two or more molecules of an aliphatic compound; as, benzene from acetylene. **carbohydrate-** The formation of monosaccharides from formaldehyde: $6HCHO = C_6H_{12}O_6$. See *photosynthesis.* **co-** The structural arrangement, e.g., of rubber, in which 2 or more different monomers or types of group are present in alternate sequence in a chain. **condensed-** P. in which atomic displacement occurs. See *aldol condensation.* **degree of-** (1) The number of times a structural unit occurs in the molecule of a polymer. (2) D.P. A measure of the chain

length and molecular weight of cellulose derivatives; determined from the viscosity of the cellulose in cuprammonium solution; e.g.: cellulose acetate 150–250, regenerated cellulose 100–250, sulfite wood pulp 230–310, ramie cellulose 1,000, cotton 750. **photo-** See *photopolymerization.* **true-** P. in which the atoms remain in similar relative positions; as, hexaphenylethane from triphenyl methyl.

polymers. Compounds having the same percentage composition, but containing different numbers of the same atoms.

polymeter. (1) A device to measure 2 or more different physical properties simultaneously. (2) A hygrometer, thermometer, and barometer mounted together.

polymethylene. See *cycloparaffins, polythene.* **p. glycols.** A polyglycol derived from methylene glycol, $CH_2(OH)_2$, or from its anhydride (formaldehyde); as, dimethylene glycol. **p. tetrasulfide.** Thiokol.

polymignite. A native lime-niobium oxide containing numerous metallic oxides.

polymixin. An antibacterial polypeptide from *Bacillus polymyxa,* having a unique specificity for gram-negative bacteria. It contains threonine and a branched C_9 fatty acid. Used medicinally as the sulfate (U.S.P., B.P.). **p.A.** Aerosporin. An antibiotic from *B. aerosporus,* similar to p. but containing also *d*-leucine.

polymorph. A substance that occurs in 2 or more different forms.

polymorphism. Ability to crystallize in 2 or more different systems. See *dimorphism, isomorphism.*

Polynosic. (From "polymer d'un glucose".) Trademark for viscose rayon fibers having a fibrillar structure.

polynucleated. Polycyclic.

polynucleotide. A complex nucleotide of high molecular weight, e.g., nucleic acids.

polyol. General name for a polyhydroxy compound of the sorbitol type.

polyoxy- Prefix indicating more than 3 oxygen atoms. **p. methylene.** $(CH_2O)_x$. A condensation product of formaldehyde. Cf. *paraformaldehyde.*

polyoxyl-40-stearate. Polyoxyethylene stearate. The monostearate of the condensation product, $H(OCH_2 \cdot CH_2)_n \cdot O \cdot CO \cdot C_{16}H_{32}Me$, where n is 40. Waxy solid, m.40, soluble in water; used in ointments (U.S.P.).

polypeptides. Compounds of 2 or more amino acids, which contain one or more peptide groups, —CO·NH—. E.g.: dipeptides:
NH_2—R—CO·NH—R—COOH (as, carnosine); tripeptides:
NH_2—R—CO·NH—R—CO·NH—R—COOH (as, glutatione); tetrapeptides:
NH_2—R—CO·NH—R—CO·NH—R—CO·NH—R—COOH (as, triglycylglycine).
The higher polypeptides resemble the peptones and proteins. A synthetic octodecapeptide (18 molecules of amino acids) has been prepared; theoretically 6,402,373,705,728,000 are possible.

polyphase. Having more than one phase; as, an alternating electric current.

polyphosphides. M_2P_n. Compounds of monovalent metals; as, K_2P_n.

Polyporaceae. A genus of 2,000 species of spore-forming fungi; as, the edible *Boletus*.

polyporin. An acidic, nontoxic, nonhemolytic substance formed during the growth of *Polyporus* species.

polypropylene. Propathene. A polymer derived from propylene with an organometallic catalyst. Similar in chemical and electrical properties to polythene, but light, d.0.90, and stronger, m. above 150; it retains its shape in boiling water; **p. tetramer** has detergent action.

polypyknotic. Consisting of 2 independent components of different densities.

polyquinoyl. Describing an organic compound containing 4 or more $=CO$ groups; e.g., diquinoyl, $C_2H_2(CO)_4$.

polyric oil. A mixture of polymerized α-methylstyrene and castor oil in proportions having a refractive index 1.515 at 20°C; less viscous than cedarwood oil, and used to substitute it for oil-immersion lenses.

polysaccharides. Polysaccharoses. Carbohydrates containing more than 3 molecules of simple sugars; as, $(C_6H_{10}O_5)_x$, polyhexoses, and $(C_5H_8O_4)_x$, polypentoses. They are theoretically derived from mono-, di-, or trisaccharides by abstraction of water. E.g., starch, dextrin, glycogen, and inulin, which hydrolyze to monosaccharides in steps (staircase reaction). See *sugars, carbohydrate*.

polysaccharose. Polysaccharide.

polysilicate. See *silicate*.

polysorbate-80. Sorethytan. A complex mixture of polyoxyethylene ethers of mixed partial oleic esters of sorbitol anhydrides. Yellow, bitter oil, d.1.08, soluble in water; used in ointments (U.S.P.).

polystichalbin. $C_{22}H_{26}O_9 = 434.3$. A constituent of filix extract, insoluble in water.

polystichin. $C_{22}H_{24}O_9 = 432.3$. An acid from the roots of *Aspidium* or *Polystichum* species (Filices).

polystichoflavin. $C_{24}H_{30}O_{11} = 494.2$. A constituent of the rhizome of *Aspidium spinulosum*. Cf. *polystichum*.

polystichum. The dried roots of *Polystichum (Aspidium) spinulosum* and *Filix mas* (male fern); an anthelmintic.

polystyrene. Polymerized styrene, q.v., derived from petroleum. White solid; a basis for synthetic rubber of outstanding insulating properties. P. resins have base-exchange properties.

polysulfide. A binary sulfur compound containing more sulfur than is required by the normal valency of the metal; Na_2S is the normal sulfide; and $Na_2S_2, Na_2S_3, Na_2S_4$ and Na_2S_5 the polysulfides of sodium. **p. ion.** An ion that contains 2 or more S atoms; as, AsS_2-.

polyterpenes. $(C_{10}H_{16})_x$. Compounds containing 2 or more terpene molecules.

polytetrafluoroethylene. $(CF_2\cdot CF_2)_n$. Teflon (U.S.). Fluon (U.K.). A plastic in which the hydrogen of polyethylene is replaced by fluorine; insoluble in all mineral or organic solvents, heat-resisting (up to 350), and has a low power factor and dielectric constant. Used for corrosion-resistant gaskets, and on cooking vessels, calendars, and dryers.

polythene (U.K. usage). Polyethylene, q.v. (U.S. usage).

polythionate. $M_2S_xO_6$. A salt of a polythionic acid in which x is 2–5.

polythionic acid. $H_2S_xO_6$. Thionic acid. A sulfur acid in which x is 2–6.

polytrophic. A bacterium or microorganism that produces 2 or more different types of fermentation.

polytropy. A form of polymorphism, q.v.

polyurethanes. A group of synthetic materials characterized by the methane group $-NH\cdot CO\cdot O-$; used to produce a wide range of fibers, lacquers, adhesives, and foams. World output (1966) 165 million pounds.

polyurohide. A substance that yields one or more uronic acids on hydrolysis.

polyvalent. Having more than one valency. Cf. *multivalent, polygen*. **p. vaccine.** A suspension of 2 or more species of the same microorganism in a liquid.

polyvinyl. Describing a compound containing a number of vinyl, $-CH:CH_2$, groups in a polymerized form. **p. acetate.** $(CH_2\cdot CHOOC\cdot Me)_n$. A transparent, thermoplastic solid, insoluble in water or mineral oils, soluble in most organic solvents; a heat-sealable adhesive, binder, plastic, and size. **p. alcohol.** $(CH_2:CHOH)_n$. Cream-colored powder, soluble in water, insoluble in most organic solvents; an adhesive, emulsifier, and sizing agent. **p. chain.** The structure $-(CH_2\cdot CHX)_2-$. It is isotactic, syndiotactic, or atactic, according as the configurations of the tertiary C atoms are identical, regularly alternating, or at random. **p. chloride.** An addition polymer of the type $-CH_2\cdot CHCl\cdot CH_2\cdot CHCl$, first suggested for the manufacture of synthetic fibers in 1913. A finely divided powder made by heating vinyl chloride under pressure with azodiisobutyronitrile. P. chloride fibers and film are resistant to chemicals, microorganisms, water, and ignition, but are decomp. by heat. P. chloride forms important copolymers with vinylidene chloride (Saran). World production (1966) 2.1 million tons.

Polyzime. Trademark for a malt extract containing the enzyme constituents in an active state.

pomace. The pressed residue after the extraction of apple juice in cider manufacture; a cattle food.

pomade. (1) A perfumed ointment, especially for the hair. (2) See *enfleurage*.

pomegranate. Granatum. The dried bark of the stems and roots of *Punica granatum* (Punicaceae), containing pelletierine alkaloids; an anthelmintic and teniafuge. Cf. *coccon, granatine*. **p. tannin.** Ellagitannic acid.

Pompey red. Ferric oxide.

Ponder's stain. A solution of 0.02 gm toluidine blue in glacial acetic acid 1, absolute alcohol 2, and water 97 ml.

ponite. Rhodochrosite containing iron.

pontanin. $C_{23}H_{18}O_5 = 544.3$. A glycosidal coloring matter of galls, produced by *Pontiania proxima*. Orange needles, m.284.

pontianac. A resin of the copal type, used in paint. Cf. *jelutong*.

Pontocaine. Trademark for tetracaine hydrochloride.

pontol. A mixture of secondary and tertiary alcohols; a denaturant for ethanol.

poonahlite. A hydrated calcium-aluminum silicate (Poonah, India).

poor gas. A group of combustible gases from the blast furnace (Siemen's and Martin's furnace); also Mond gas and regenerator gas.

Pope, Sir William Jackson. 1870–1939. English chemist noted for his work on crystallography and organic chemistry.

poplar buds. Balm of Gilead buds. The air-dried. winter-leaf buds of *Populus nigra* (Salicaceae); an aromatic. **p.b. oil.** An essential oil from p., d.0.895–0.905, b.255–265, soluble in alcohol and containing humulene, sesquiterpenes, and a paraffin.

poplox. A sodium silicate. See *intumescence.*

poppy. Maw seed. The plant *Papaver somniferum* (Papaveraceae). **California-** Eschscholtzia. **red-** Corn p., corn rose. The flower petals of *Papaver rhoeas*; an anodyne expectorant. **p. capsules.** Papaveris fructus. The fruit of *Papaver somniferum* (Papaveraceae). **p. seed oil.** Yellow oil from *Papaver* species, m.5, insoluble in water; lubricant for fine machinery.

populin. $C_{13}H_{17}O_7 \cdot C_7H_5O \cdot 2H_2O = 426.3$. Benzoyl salicin. A glucoside from the bark of aspen species. White powder, m.180, soluble in water; an antipyretic.

populoid. The combined principles from the bark of *Populus tremuloides* (American aspen) or *P. tremula* (European aspen); a bitter tonic, astringent, and mild antipyretic.

porcelain. A white, semiopaque, dense, waterproof substance obtained by strongly heating and sintering a mixture of kaolin, feldspar, and quartz; m. 850–1400. Used for domestic and laboratory utensils, and in dentistry (teeth). Cf. *sillimanite.* **high fusing-** m.1340 (2440°F). **low fusing-** m.930 (1700°F). **medium fusing-** m.1260 (2300°F). (All melting points are approximate.) **p. clay.** Kaolin. **p. color.** A pigment used to color p.; as a metal oxide. **p. glaze.** See *glaze.* **p. jasper.** *Porcellanite.* **p. mill.** A mill made of p., for wet or drying grinding. **p. utensils.** See *casserole, crucible, combustion boat, evaporating dish, funnel, mortar, retort, spatula.*

porcellanite. Porcelain jasper. A sintered clay and shale, on the borders of burned coal seams.

pore. A minute opening on a surface.

porosimeter. An instrument to determine porosity from the volume of liquid absorbed, or air transmitted, in a given time.

porosity. The state of a solid body penetrated by minute open spaces filled with liquid or gas. P. is expressed as the percentage of open space in the total volume. Cf. *permeability.* **apparent-** The volume of open-pore space per unit total volume. **true-** The volume of both open and sealed pore spaces per unit total volume.

porous. Penetrated by small open spaces.

porpezite. Palladium gold.

porphin ring. A heterocyclic structure of 4 pyrrole rings united by methylene groups, in the center of which may be a metal (Fe or Mg). It is a structural part of chlorophyll and hemoglobin. **aza-** See *tetraaryl-.*

p. derivatives.

Chlorophyll Group:
$C_{31}H_{34}N_4Mg$, etiophyllin
$C_{31}H_{34}N_4O_2$, pyrroporphyrin
$C_{32}H_{34}N_4O_3$, rhodoporphyrin
$C_{43}H_{36}N_4O_4$, phylloporphyrin
$C_{33}H_{34}N_4O_3$, phylloerythrin
$C_{34}H_{32}N_4O_5Mg$, chlorophyllin (?)
$C_{55}H_{72}N_4O_5Mg$, chlorophyll *a*

$C_{55}H_{07}N_4O_6Mg$, chlorophyll *b*

Hemoglobin Group:
$C_{30}H_{30}N_4O_4$, deuteroporphyrin
$C_{30}H_{30}N_4O_4FeCl$, deuterohemin
$C_{32}H_{38}N_4$, etioporphyrin III
$C_{34}H_{32}N_4O_4FeCl$, hemin
$C_{34}H_{32}N_4O_4FeO$, hematin
$C_{34}H_{32}N_4O_4FeOH$, protohematin
$C_{34}H_{34}N_4O_4$, protoporphyrin
$C_{34}H_{36}N_4O_4FeCl$, mesohemin
$C_{34}H_{38}N_4O_6$, hematoporphyrin
$C_{34}H_{38}N_4O_4$, mesoporphyrin IX
$C_{36}H_{38}N_4O_8$, coproporphyrin
$C_{38}H_{38}N_4O_{16}$, uroporphyrin
$C_{38}H_{38}N_4O_{16}Cu$, turacin

Bile Pigments:
$C_{33}H_{36}N_4O_6$, bilirubin (protoporphyrin in which the alpha —CH= group is replaced by —OH and O=).

porphyric acid. Euxanthone.

porphyrilic acid. $C_{16}H_{10}O_7 \cdot C_6H_{11}NH_2 \cdot H_2O = 431.23$. A sparingly soluble constituent of crustaceous lichens, m.274–278 (decomp.).

porphyrin. An iron-free decomposition product of hematin; as, hemoporphyrin, $C_{16}H_{18}N_2O_3$; or a magnesium-free decomposition product of chlorophyll; as, phylloporphyrin, $C_{16}H_{18}N_2O$ (q.v.)

porphyrine. $C_{21}H_{25}O_2N_3 = 351.2$. An alkaloid from the bark of *Alstonia constricta* (Apocynaceae). Colorless substance, m.97, soluble in acids (blue fluorescence). Cf. *alstonine.*

porphyrite. A coarse-grained igneous rock.

porphyrization. Pulverization.

porphyropsin. The pigment of the eyes of freshwater fish.

porphyroxine. $C_{19}H_{23}O_4N = 329.19$. An alkaloid of opium, m.135.

porphyry. An igneous rock with large red crystals set in a finer grained or glassy dark red mass.

porpoise oil. A yellow fixed oil from porpoises.

porporino. (1) Hematoporphyrin. (2) A decorative imitation of gold; an alloy of mercury, tin, and sulfur.

portland cement. A hydraulic cement, obtained by burning a mixture of lime and clay and pulverizing the clinker. A greenish gray powder of basic calcium silicates, calcium aluminates, and calcium ferrites. When mixed with water, it solidifies to an artificial rock, similar to portland stone. See *cement.*

portland stone. Yellowish limestone from the Isle of Portland.

Portsmouth accelerator. POTG. Phenyl-*o*-tolylguanidine; an accelerator for the vulcanization of rubber.

posion. Proposed name for anion. Cf. *negion.*

positive. (1) Not negative. (2) Greater than zero. **p. crystal.** A crystal whose refractive index for the extraordinary ray is greater than that for the ordinary ray. **p. electron.** Positron. **p. element.** A light-metal element of the upper right and lower left of the periodic table, which can yield valence electrons to another element and become positively charged. **p. group.** A positively charged and base-forming group of atoms; as, NH_4^+. **p. nucleus.** The center of an atom, assumed to be composed either of tightly packed electrons, hydrogen or helium kernels; or of IZ neutrons, $2Z$

protons, and Z electrons, where I is the isotopic weight and Z the atomic number; thought to be responsible for atomic weight, atomic number, and radioactive properties. Suggested names: *proton* (Rutherford), *hydrion* (Soddy), *centron* (Lodge), *ambron, merron, uron, prime, hylon,* and *prouton.* **p. ore.** An ore that has been exposed and properly worked on four sides. Cf. *possible ore.* **p. radical.** An atom or group of atoms that has lost one or more electrons and so becomes positively charged. **p. ray analysis.** See *mass spectrograph.* **p. rays.** A stream of positively charged molecules shooting from the anode to the cathode of a discharge tube. If the cathode is perforated, the rays are made visible on a fluorescent screen behind it. See *canal rays.* **p. reaction.** A reaction that produces the effect sought.

positon. Positron.

positron. Positon, oreston, positive electron. A subatomic particle and a fundamental "building stone" of matter, having a positive charge and a mass 1/1,800 of that of an H atom; magnetic moment $+1$ magneton; spin $\frac{1}{2}$. Cf. *particle, nucleus.*

positronium. The bound electron-positron system formed under certain conditions before the annihilation of both particles. **ortho-p.** A p. in which the spins of the electron and positron are parallel; mean life 1.4×10^{-7} sec. **para-p.** A p. in which the spins of the electron and positron are antiparallel; mean life 10^{-10} sec. See *spin.*

posode. Proposed name for anode. Cf. *negode.*

posologic. Pertaining to medicinal doses.

posology. The study of the form, quantity, and frequency of administering medicines.

possible ore. An ore that may exist out of sight, or below the lowest workings of a mine. Cf. *positive ore.*

postulate. An assumption not capable of proof: (1) An indisputable prerequisite; (2) a stipulated condition; (3) a demand. Cf. *axiom.*

potable. Drinkable without injury to health. Cf. *brackish, water.*

potarite. A native compound of palladium and mercury. Cf. *allopalladium.*

potash. (1) Potassium hydroxide. (2) Potassium carbonate. (3) An early name (pot ash) for wood ash used as a source of potassium carbonate. World production (1966) 14.9 million tons (as K_2O). **black-** A commercial grade of caustic *soda:* 5% NaOH with iron oxide and sodium carbonate impurities. **caustic-** Potassium hydroxide. **salvosal-** Potassium salol orthophosphite. **sulfurated-** A mixture of potassium thiosulfate and potassium polysulfides containing not less than 12.8% sulfur as sulfide. Brown lumps, changing to green-yellow, with odor of hydrogen sulfide and acrid taste, soluble in alcohol; an astringent lotion (U.S.P.).
 p. alum. Kalinite. **p. bulb.** Variously shaped glass bulbs, filled with potassium hydroxide solution; for the absorption of carbon dioxide in chemical analysis. **p. feldspar.** Orthoclase. **p. glass.** See *glass.* **p. mica.** Muscovite. **p. value.** Incorrect synonym for saponification value or acid value. **p. water.** Potassic water. See water *glass.*

potassa. Potassium hydroxide. **p. sulfurata.** Potassium sulfide.

potassamide. $NH_2K = 55.2$. White (if pure) or brown (if impure) flammable solid, m.271, sublimes 400.

potassic. Containing potassium. **p. water.** Potash water. An aerated mineral water in which the potassium ions exceed the sodium ions.

potassii. Official Latin for "of potash."

potassium. $K = 39.102$. Kalium. An alkali-metal element, at. no. 19. Silver-white, soft substance, d.0.87, m.62, b.720, which reacts violently with water, and rapidly oxidizes in air; stored under a layer of coal oil. It occurs abundantly in its salts, as sylvenite, kainite and carnallite in Stassfurt (Germany) and Alsace and in smaller quantities in feldspars, rocks, and soils. First prepared (electrolytically) in 1807 by Davy. Its salts are all soluble in water and yield the colorless p. ion, K^+; valency 1. Used as a reagent and reducing agent in many chemical reactions, and in the metallic state emits weak β radiation. **p. acetate.** $CH_3COOK = 98.1$. Potassii acetas, diuretic salt. White, deliquescent powder, m.292, soluble in water; used as a reagent, in buffer solutions, and medicinally. *acid-* $KH(C_2H_3O_2)_2 = 158.2$. Colorless needles, m.148. **p. acetotungstate.** A double salt of p. acetate and tungstate; a photographic toning. **p. acetyl salicylate.** $KC_9H_7O_4 \cdot 2H_2O = 254.19$. White crystals, m.65. **p. acid carbonate.** P. bicarbonate. **p. acid chromate.** P. dichromate. **p. acid phthalate.** $C_6H_4 \cdot (COOH)(COOK) = 204.15$. P. phthalate. White crystals; a buffer. **p. acid sulphate.** P. bisulfate. **p. acid tartrate.** P. bitartrate. **p. alloys.** Liquid or semi-solid mixtures of potassium with sodium:

K	Na	m.
90	10	17
80	20	-10
70	30	-3
60	40	5
50	50	11

p. aluminate. $K_2Al_2O_4 \cdot 3H_2O = 250.5$. Colorless crystals, soluble in water. **p. aluminum sulfate.** $KAl(SO_4)_2 \cdot 12H_2O = 474.4$. Potash alum. kalinite. Large, colorless rhombs, soluble in water; a mordant. **p. aminochromate.** $CrO_2(OK) \cdot NH_2 = 155.13$. Red crystals. **p. aminonaphthol.** Helthin. **p. ammonium tartrate.** $K-NH_4C_4H_4O_6 = 205.17$. White powder, soluble in water. **p. amyl sulfate.** $KC_5H_{11}SO_4 = 206.2$. White granules, soluble in water. **p. anthranilate.** $C_6H_4(NH_2)COOK = 175.2$. White crystals, soluble in water. **p. antimonate.** $KSbO_3 = 207.3$. P. stibnate. White crystals, soluble in water. *pyro-* See *p. stibnate.* **p. antimonyl tartrate.** $KSbOC_4H_4O_6 \cdot \frac{1}{2}H_2O = 332.3$. Tartar emetic. Colorless octahedra, soluble in water. **p. argentocyanide.** $KAg(CN)_2 = 199.00$. A constituent of solutions of silver cyanide in potassium cyanide solution, used for silver plating. **p. arsenate.** $K_3AsO_4 = 256.3$. Normal p. arsenate. Colorless crystals, soluble in water; a reagent for tannic acid and opium alkaloids. *acid-* $KH_2AsO_4 = 180.1$. Colorless crystals, m.228, soluble in water; an alterative and reconstructive. **p. arsenite.** $KAsO_2 = 146.1$. Gray powder, soluble in water; a reagent for Ceylon cinnamon oil, a tonic and stomachic, and a reducing agent in the manufacture of mirrors. **p. aurate.** $AuO·OK, 3H_2O = 322.4$. Soluble yellow needles. **p. aurichloride.** $AuCl_3,KCl, 2H_2O = 414.2$. Soluble plates. **p. auricyanide.** $Au(CN)_3KCN, H_2O = 358.4$. Soluble, colorless solid. **p. aurocyanide.** $2KAu(CN)_6·3H_2O = 734.28$. Colorless solid, soluble in water; used for gold plating. **p. benzoate.** $C_6H_5·COOH·3H_2O = 214.2$. White crystals, soluble in water; a mild antiseptic. **p. benzodisulfonate.** $C_6H_4(SO_3K)_2 = 314.3$. Colorless crystals, soluble in water; used in organic synthesis. **p. biborate.** P. tetraborate. **p. bicarbonate.** $KHCO_3 = 100.1$. Acid p. carbonate, potassii bicarbonas, saleratus (*sal aeratus*). Colorless, transparent, monoclinic crystals, decomp. by heat, soluble in water. Used as a reagent in titrating arsenous and antimonous oxides; in the manufacture of potassium salts and inorganic synthesis; in foam-type fire extinguishers; and as an antacid (U.S.P.). **p. bichromate.** P. dichromate. **p. bifluoride.** See *p. fluoride, acid-*. **p. biiodate.** See *p. iodate, acid-*. **p. binoxalate.** P. bioxalate. **p. bioxalate.** $KHC_2O_2 = 96.1$. P. binoxalate, salt of sorrel, salt of lemons, salt acetosella. White crystals, soluble in water. Used as a reagent, in stain removers, and in medicine and photography. **p. biphosphate.** See *p. phosphate.* **p. bisaccharate.** $(CHOH)_4(COOH)COOK = 248.1$. Yellow crystals, soluble in water. **p. bismuth tartrate.** $KBi_3C_4H_2O_9·4H_2O$. White granules, soluble in water; an antiluetic. **p. bisulfate.** $KHSO_4 = 136.2$. Potassii bisulfas, p. acid sulfate, sal enixum. Colorless crystals, m.197 (decomp.), soluble in water; used as a reagent and in effervescent drinks. **p. bisulfite.** $KHSO_3 = 120.17$. P. acid sulfite. White crystals, decomp. 190, soluble in water; an antiseptic and disinfectant. **p. bitartrate.** $KHC_4H_4O_6 = 188.1$. Potassii bitartras, cream of tartar, depurated tartar. Colorless crystals, soluble in water; a reagent, refrigerant, and diuretic (B.P.). **p. black.** Suint ash. **p. borates.** $K_2B_2O_4$, p. metaborate; $K_2B_4O_7$, p. tetraborate. **p. borofluoride.** $KBF_4 = 126.0$. White crystals, soluble in alcohol. **p. borohydride.** $KBH_4 = 54.04$. White crystals, stable to heat, soluble in water; a strong reducing agent, and nonpyrophoric specific hydrogenation catalyst. **p. borotartrate.** A mixture of p. metaborate and p. bitartrate. White crystals, soluble in water; an antiseptic and photographic-developer retardant. **p. bromate.** $KBrO_3 = 167.0$. Colorless rhombohedra, m.434, soluble in water; a reagent (Koppeschaar solution) for titrating phenol and oxalic acid, and standard in iodometry. **p. bromide.** $KBr = 119.0$. Potassii bromidum. White, regular crystals, m.740, soluble in water; a reagent, photographic chemical, nerve sedative, and antispasmodic. **p. bromo-o-oxybenzoate.** P. bromosalicylate (B.P.). **p. bromosalicylate.** $C_6H_3Br(OH)COOK = 255.1$. P. bromo-o-oxybenzoate. White crystals, soluble in water; a hypnotic and antirheumatic. **p. butyrate.** $C_3H_7COOK = 126.1$. White, deliquescent crystals, soluble in water. **p. cacodylate.** $Me_2AsO_2K = 194.1$. White crystals, soluble in water; a tonic.

p. camphorate. $K_2C_{10}H_{14}O_4 = 276.3$. Colorless, deliquescent crystals, soluble in water; an antiseptic. **p. carbonate.** $K_2CO_2 = 138.2$. Potassii carbonas, sal tartar, potash. Colorless, monoclinic crystals or hygroscopic powder, d.2.2, m.900 (decomp.), soluble in water, insoluble in alcohol; a reagent, flux for silicates and insoluble sulfates, neutralizing agent, and antiacid and mild caustic *acid-* See *p. bicarbonate*. **p. carbonyl.** $K_6(CO)_6 = 402.60$. Gray or red explosive crystals. **p. chlorate.** $KClO_3 = 122.6$. Potassii chloras, p. oxymuriate. Colorless monoclinic crystals, m.357, decomp. 400, soluble in water, slightly soluble in alcohol. Used as a reagent for alkaloids, phenols, indican; a diuretic and cardiac stimulant; and in mouthwashes, toothpastes, and the manufacture of explosives, fulminators, and pyrotechnics. **p. chloraurate.** $KAuCl_4,2H_2O = 774.3$. **p. chloraurite.** $KAuCl_2 = 307.3$. **p. chloride.** $KCl = 74.6$. Potassii chloridum. White, regular crystals, m.776 (sublimes), soluble in water. Used as a reagent (determination of fluosilicic acid), in fertilizers and explosives, and to prepare saline injections (U.S.P., B.P.). **p. chlorochromate.** $KClCrO_3 = 174.7$. Red crystals, decomp. by water; an oxidizing agent. **p. chloroplatinate.** $K_2PtCl_6 = 486.2$. Platinic p. chloride. Yellow regular crystals, decomp. by heat, slightly soluble in water; a reagent. **p. chloroplatinite.** $K_2PtCl_4 = 415.24$. Platinous chloride. Red crystals, soluble in water. **p. chromate.** $K_2CrO_4 = 194.2$. Yellow rhombohedra, m.971, soluble in water; a reagent and volumetric indicator, mordant, and oxidizing agent. *acid-* P. dichromate. *chloro-* P. chlorochromate. **p. chromic sulfate.** $KCr(SO_4)_2·12H_2O = 499.42$. Chrome alum, chromium p. sulfate. Red or green, cubic or octahedral crystals, m.89, soluble in water; a mordant. **p. chromicyanide.** $K_3Cr(CN)_6 = 325.4$. Yellow, insoluble solid. **p. cinnamate.** $KC_9H_7O_2 = 186.1$. White crystals, soluble in water. **p. citrate.** $K_3C_6H_6O_7·H_2O = 325.27$. Potassii citras. Colorless crystals, decomp. 230, soluble in water; a diaphoretic and diuretic (B.P.). *monobasic-* $KH_2(C_6H_5O_7) = 230.15$. White crystals, soluble in water. **p. cobalticyanide.** $K_3Co(CN)_6 = 332.36$. A solid, decomp. by heat, soluble in water. **p. cobaltinitrite.** $K_3Co(NO_2)_6 = 452.33$. Cobaltic p. nitrite. Yellow tetragons, decomp. 200, soluble in water; a reagent and pigment. Cf. *aureolin yellow.* **p. cobalt malonate.** $KCo(C_3H_2O_4)_2 = 341.17$. Pink crystals, soluble in water. **p. cobalt sulfate.** $K_2SO_4·CoSO_4,6H_2O = 437.4$. Soluble plates. **p. copper lead nitrite.** $K_2CuPb(NO_2)_6 = 645.00$. Rectangular black crystals, produced by the triple nitrite reaction for p. **p. cuprocyanide.** $KCu(CN)_2 = 154.69$. A solution of copper cyanide in p. cyanide solution, used for copper plating. **p. cyanate.** $KCNO = 81.12$. Colorless needles, soluble in water. **p. cyanide.** $KCN = 65.12$. White, regular crystals or sticks, soluble in water. Used as a reagent and insecticide, for gold extraction (*cyanide process*), and in photography and medicine. **p. dichromate.** $K_2Cr_2O_7 = 294.2$. P. bichromate, p. acid chromate. Yellowish red triclinic or monoclinic crystals, d.2.692, m.396 (decomp.), soluble in water, insoluble in alcohol. Used as a reagent, general oxidizing agent, bactericide, caustic, and astringent; in cleansing solutions with sulfuric acid, and in electric batteries, photography, and the dye, textile, tanning, printing, bleaching, and oil industries. **p. dihydrogen phosphate.** KH_2PO_4. See *p. phosphates*. **p. disulfate.** $K_2S_2O_7 = 254.32$. White needles, m.210 (decomp.), soluble in water. **p. dithionate.** P. hyposulfate. **p. dithiooxalate.** $K_2C_2O_2S_2 = 198.32$. A solid reagent for nickel. **p. ethyl sulfate.** $KC_2H_5SO_4 = 164.1$. Monoclinic, white crystals, soluble in water. **p. ethyl xanthate.** $KC_3H_5OS_2 = 160.28$. White powder; a collector in flotation. **p. ferrate.** $K_2FeO_4 = 198.05$. P. perferrate. Purple solid, rapidly decomp. in acid solution. **p. ferric ferrocyanide.** $KFe'''Fe''(CN)_6 \cdot H_2O$. Prussian blue. Blue, insoluble precipitate from ferric ion and ferrocyanide. **p. ferric oxalate.** $K_3Fe(C_2O_4)_3 \cdot 3H_2O = 491.19$. Brown crystals, decomp. 230, slightly soluble in water. **p. ferric sulfate.** $K_2SO_4, Fe_2(SO_4)_3, 24H_2O = 1006.60$. Iron alum. Soluble violet crystals. **p. ferricyanide.** $K_3Fe(CN)_6 = 329.1$. Red prussiate of potash, ferric p. cyanide. Red, monoclinic crystals, decomp. by heat, soluble in water or alcohol. Used as a reagent for ferrous salts, a reducing agent and indicator; and in light-sensitive papers, manufacture of prussian blue, and the textile industry. **p. ferrite.** $K_2Fe_2O_4 = 253.90$. Yellow solid. **p. ferrocyanide.** $K_4Fe(CN)_6 \cdot 3H_2O = 422.4$. Yellow prussiate of potash, ferrous p. cyanide. Yellow, monoclinic crystals, soluble in water. Used as a reagent; for hardening steel; and in electroplating, photography, the textile industry, and manufacture of prussian blue. **p. ferrous ferricyanide.** $K_2Fe''Fe'''(CN)_6 = 357.9$. White precipitate from ferrous sulfate and a cold neutral solution of p.ferrocyanide; oxidized to β-soluble prussian blue.**p. fluorescein.** $K_2C_{20}H_{10}O_5 = 408.3$. Yellow-red powder, soluble in water (pink solution, green fluorescence). **p. fluoride.** $KF \cdot 2H_2O = 94.1$. Colorless, hygroscopic crystals, m.860, soluble in water. Used as a preservative and disinfectant; and in ant powders and etching glass. *acid-* $KF \cdot HF = 78.1$. P. bifluoride, Fremy's salt. Colorless crystals, soluble in water; used as an antiseptic, antizymotic, and in etching glass. **p. fluosilicate.** $K_2SiF_6 = 220.5$. Colorless hexagons, insoluble in water. **p. formate.** $H \cdot COOK = 84.2$. Colorless, deliquescent crystals, m.197, soluble in water. **p. glycerinate.** $KC_3H_5O_4 = 144.1$. White deliquescent powder, soluble in water. **p. glycerophosphate.** $K_2C_3H_7O_3 \cdot PO_3 = 264.4$. White, hygroscopic crystals, soluble in water, marketed as a 50–75% solution; a nerve tonic and reagent. **p. hippurate.** $KC_9H_8O_3N \cdot H_2O = 235.2$. Colorless crystals, soluble in water. **p. hydrate.** P. hydroxide. **p. hydride.** $KH = 40.11$. White, volatile needles, from p. heated in hydrogen. **p. hydrogen phosphate.** $K_2HPO_4 = 174.25$. Large crystals; a buffer. See *p. phosphates*. **p. hydrogen sulfide.** P. hydrosulfide. **p. hydrosulfide.** $KSH = 72.1$. Colorless, hygroscopic crystals m.455, soluble in water. **p. hydrotartrate.** P. bitartrate. **p. hydroxide.** $KOH = 56.11$. Potassii hydroxidum, potash, p. hydrate, caustic potash, kalilauge. White rhombohedral crystals or deliquescent sticks, d.2.044, m.360 (sublimes), soluble in water, alcohol, or ether;

absorbs carbon dioxide from air. Used as a reagent; for neutralization; and in the manufacture of soft soap (U.S.P., B.P.), oxalic acid, and glass. Cf. *lapis causticus, vienna caustic*. **p. hypochlorite.** $KClO = 90.6$. Colorless crystals, decomp. by heat, soluble in water. Cf. *eau de javelle*. **p. hypophosphite.** $KH_2PO_2 = 104.1$. Potassii hypophosphis, diacid p. phosphate. White, opaque plates or deliquescent powder, soluble in water; a nerve tonic. **p. hyposulfate.** $K_2S_2O_6 = 238.3$. P. dithionate. Colorless crystals, decomp. by heat, soluble in water. **p. hyposulfite.** $K_2S_2O_3 = 190.3$. P. thiosulfate. Colorless, hygroscopic crystals. **p. indigosulfate.** $K_2C_{16}H_8O_3N_2(SO_3)_2$. Blue powder, soluble in water; used in dyeing textiles. **p. indigosulfonate.** P. indigosulfate. **p. indoxylsulfonate.** Indican (2). **p. iodate.** $KIO_3 = 214.02$. Colorless, regular, deliquescent crystals, m.560 (decomp.), soluble in water, a volumetric reagent and antiseptic. *acid-* $KHI_2O_2 = 389.8$. P. biiodate. Colorless crystals, soluble in water; used in volumetric analysis. **p. iodide.** $KI = 166.02$. Potassii iodidum. Colorless, regular crystals, m.680, soluble in water; a volumetric reagent, solvent for iodine and iodides, antiseptic and alterative (U.S.P., B.P.), and photographic chemical. *tri-* See *p. triiodide*. **p. iodohydrargyrate.** Mercuric p. iodide. **p. iodotetrachloride.** $KICl_4 = 307.86$. **p. ion.** K^+. The positively charged p. atom. **p. lithium tartrate.** $KLi(C_4H_4O_6) \cdot H_2O = 221.09$. White, monoclinic crystals, soluble in water; an antirheumatic. **p. magnesium chloride.** $KCl \cdot MgCl_2 \cdot 6H_2O = 277.90$. Colorless solid, decomp. by heat. **p. manganate.** $K_2MnO_4 = 197.13$. Green rhombohedra, decomp. 190, soluble in water. *per-* See *p. permanganate*. **p. manganic sulfate.** $K_2SO_4 \cdot Mn_2(SO_4)_3 \cdot 24H_2O = 1004.8$. Mangan alum. Green crystals, soluble in water. **p. mercuric iodide.** Mercuric p. iodide. **p. mercuric thiosulfate.** Mercuric p. thiosulfate. **p. metabisulfite.** $K_2S_2O_5 = 222.32$. P. pyrosulfite. White, soluble plates, decomp. by heat. **p. metaphosphate.** KPO_3. See *p. phosphates*. **p. metasilicate.** K_2SiO_3. See *p. silicates*. **p. molybdate.** $K_2MoO_4 \cdot 5H_2O = 328.10$. White microcrystals, soluble in water. **p. monosulfide.** P. sulfide. **p. myronate.** $KC_{10}H_{18}O_{10}NS_2 = 415.2$. Sinigrin. Colorless, crystalline, glucoside salt from black mustard seeds, decomp. by myrosin into glucose, p. bisulfate, and allyl thiocyanate; soluble in water. **p. nitranilate.** $K_2C_6O_8N_2 = 306.22$. P. dinitrodihydroxybenzoquinone. Yellow crystals, slightly soluble in water. **p. nitrate.** $KNO_3 = 101.1$. Saltpeter, potassii nitras, niter, sal prunella. Colorless prisms or rhombohedra, d.2.109, m.337 (decomp.), soluble in water, insoluble in alcohol or ether. Used as a reagent, oxidizing flux, diaphoretic, and diuretic (U.S.P., B.P.); and in pyrotechnics, gunpowder, fertilizers, and preservatives. **p. nitrite.** $KNO_3 = 85.1$. Colorless, deliquescent prisms or sticks, d.1.915, soluble in water. Used as a reagent (e.g., for cobalt, amino acids, phenols, and iodine); reducing agent, heart tonic; and in the manufacture of dyes. Cf. *Indian yellow*. **p. nitrosohydroxylamine sulfonate.** $K_2SO_3N(OH)NO = 218.24$. **p. oleate.** $KC_{18}H_{33}O_2 = 320.5$. Yellow mass, soluble in water; a soap. **p. osmate.** $K_2OsO_4\cdot2H_2O$ = 369.3. P. perosmate. Purple crystals, decomp. in warm, moist air, soluble in water; a reagent for nitrogen, and a sedative. **p. oxalate.** $K_2C_2O_4\cdot H_2O$ = 184.2. Colorless, monoclinic crystals, decomp. by heat, soluble in water; used as a reagent, and in photography and stain removers. *acid-* KHC_2O_4 = 128.11. Monoclinic crystals, slightly soluble in water. *acid-* (*hemihydrate.*) $KHC_2H_4\cdot\frac{1}{2}H_2O$ = 137.12. Trimetric crystals. *acid-* (*monohydrate.*) $KHC_2H_4\cdot H_2O$ = 146.2. Rhombic crystals. *tetraacid-* $KH_3(C_2O_4)_2\cdot2H_2O$ = 254.15. Triclinic crystals, d.1.836. **p. oxide.** K_2O = 94.2. Burnt potash, calcined potash. Colorless octahedra, soluble in water; used extensively as a reagent and in the manufacture of p. salts. Cf. *p. peroxide.* **p. oxymuriate.** P. chlorate. **p. palladichloride.** K_2PdCl_4 = 397.7. Palladiopertassium chloride. Red, crystals solid, decomp. by heat. **p. palladochloride.** K_2PdCl_4 = 326.7. Palladous p. chloride. Brown prisms, soluble in water, decomp. by heat. **p. parawolframate.** P. tungstate. **p. pentasulfide.** K_2S_5 = 238.50. Yellow granules, m.220, soluble in water. **p. perborate.** KBO_3 = 98.0. A soluble solid. **p. percarbonate.** $K_2C_2O_6\cdot H_2O$ = 216.3. Colorless powder, decomp. by water (to bicarbonate and oxygen) and acids (to hydrogen peroxide and carbon dioxide). Used as a reagent, in microscopy, photography (antihypo), and bleaching. **p. perchlorate.** $KClO_4$ = 138.6 Colorless rhombs, m.610, slightly soluble in water. Used as a reagent, oxidizing agent, pyrotechnic, antipyretic, sedative (B.P.), and source of oxygen. **p. perferrate.** P. ferrate. **p. periodate.** KIO_4 = 230.0. Colorless rhombs, m.582, slightly soluble in water; a volumetric reagent. **p. permanganate.** $KMnO_4$ = 158.0. Potassii permanganas, p. hypermanganate. Purple, rhombic needles, d.2.703, decomp. 240, soluble in water. Used as a volumetric and oxidizing agent, antiseptic and disinfectant (U.S.P., B.P.); for mordants; and in bleaching and photography. **p. permanganate.** P. osmate. **p. peroxide.** K_2O_2 = 110.2 or K_2O_4 = 142.2. Yellow powder, decomp. in air and moisture, soluble in alcohol; an oxidizing agent. **p. persulfate.** KSO_4 = 135.2, or $K_2S_2O_8$ = 270.4. Anthion. Colorless prisms, decomp. by heat, soluble in water. Used as a strong oxidizing agent and disinfectant, and in photography (anthion). **p. phenol sulfonate.** $KC_6H_4(OH)SO_3\cdot H_2O$ = 230.2. P. sulfocarbolate. *ortho-* Colorless crystals, m.400, soluble in water; an intestinal antiseptic. *para-* Rhombic crystals. **p. phenylate.** PhOK = 132.1. P. phenate. Colorless crystals, soluble in water; an antiseptic. **p. phosphates.** (1) K_3PO_4 = 212.3. Normal ortho- or tribasic p. phosphate. Colorless rhombs, soluble in water. (2) K_2HPO_4 = 174.3. P. hydrophosphate, dipotassium phosphate, monoacid phosphate. Colorless crystals, soluble in water. (3) KH_2PO_4 = 136.2. Monobasic p. phosphate, dihydrophosphate, Sörensen's p. phosphate. Colorless tetragons, d.2.338, m.96, decomp. by heat, soluble in water; a reagent and pH buffer. (4) $K_4P_2O_7\cdot3H_2O$ = 306.27. P. pyrophosphate. Colorless crystals, soluble in water. (5) KPO_3 = 118.14. P. metaphosphate. Colorless crystals, insoluble in water. **p. phosphide.** K_2P_5 =

233.2. Unstable yellow solid. **p. phosphite.** (1) K_2HPO_3 = 158.0. White powder, decomp. by heat, soluble in water. (2) K_3PO_3. Normal phosphite. (3) KH_2PO_3. Monobasic or dihydrophosphite. **p. phthalate.** (1) $C_6H_4(COOK)_2$. (2) See *p. acid phthalate.* **p. picrate.** $C_6H_2(NO_2)_3\cdot OK$ = 267.1. P. trinitrophenate. Yellow crystals, soluble in water; used in explosives. **p. platinichloride.** P. chloroplatinate. **p. platinobromide.** K_2PtBr_4 = 593.0. An unstable solid. **p. platinochloride.** P. chloroplatinite. **p. platinocyanide.** $K_2Pt(CN)_4,3H_2O$ = 431.5. An unstable solid. **p. plumbate.** $K_2PbO_3,3H_2O$ = 387.45. Colorless crystals; soluble in water. **p. pyroantimonate.** P. stibnate. **p. pyroborate.** P. tetraborate. **p. pyrophosphate.** See *p. phosphates* (4). **p. pyrosulfate.** $K_2S_2O_7$ = 254.3. White crystals, soluble in water. **p. pyrosulfite.** P. metabisulfite. **p. rhodanate.** P. thiocyanate. **p. salicylate.** $KC_7H_5O_3$ = 176.2. White crystals, soluble in water; an antirheumatic and antipyretic. **p. salol o-phosphite.** $C_6H_4(COOC_6H_5)\cdot OPO(OH)OK$ = 332.2. Salvosal potash. Colorless crystals, soluble in cold water; used to treat influenza and gout. **p. silicate.** K_2SiO_3 = 154.5, or $K_2Si_2O_5$ = 214.3. Potash–water glass. Glassy mass, soluble in water. Cf. *p. tetrasilicate.* **p. silicate solution.** Potash–water glass. An aqueous syrup of p. silicate 30–38 Bé, miscible with water. Used as a cement, for fireproofing, and in bleaching and soap manufacture. **p. silicofluoride.** K_2SiF_6 = 220.5. White powder, soluble in water. **p. sodium tartrate.** $KNaC_4H_4O_6$ = 210.1. $+4H_2O$ = rochelle salt. $+3H_2O$ = Seignette salt. Colorless crystals, soluble in water; a reagent (in Fehling's solution) and depilatory. **p. sorbate.** A water-soluble fungistatic for food, similar in action to sorbic acid. **p. sozoiodol.** $C_6H_2I_2(SOH)OK$ = 431.8. P. diiodo-*p*-sulfonic acid phenate; a desiccant for eczema. **p. sozoiodolate.** $C_6H_2I_2(SOK)OH$ = 431.8. P. diiodo-*p*-phenol sulfonate. Colorless crystals, soluble in water; a dusting powder. **p. stannate.** K_2SnO_3 = 244.9. Colorless crystals, soluble in water; a mordant. **p. stannosulfate.** $K_2Sn(SO_4)_2$ = 388.8. P. stannous sulfate, Marignac salt. Colorless crystals, soluble in water; a reagent for mercury and bismuth salts. **p. stibnate.** (1) $K_2H_2Sb_2O_7\cdot6H_2O$ = 543.8. P. pyroantimonate. White granules, slightly soluble in water; a reagent for sodium salts. (2) P. antimonate. **p. succinate.** $K_2C_4H_4O_4$ = 194.3. White powder, soluble in water; used medicinally. **p. sulfate.** K_2SO_4 = 174.3. Potassii sulfas, normal p. sulfate, tarcanum, sal de duobus, tartarus vitriolatus. White rhombs or hexagons, d.2.663, m.1076 (sublimes), soluble in water. Used as a reagent, medicinally in place of saline, and in fertilizers and artificial mineral waters. *acid-* $KHSO_4$ = 136.2. Monobasic or monoacid p. sulfate. Colorless, monoclinic or rhombic crystals, d.2.24, m.200, soluble in water. *pyro-* See *p. pyrosulfate.* **p. sulfide.** K_2S = 110.3. P. monosulfide. Brown crystals, soluble in water. **p. sulfides:** K_2S, K_2S_2, K_2S_3, K_2S_4, K_2S_5. Commercial "p. sulfide" contains some or all of these. **p. sulfite.** $K_2SO_3\cdot2H_2O$ = 194.3. White crystals, decomp. by heat, soluble in water;

a reagent, mordant, antiseptic, and laxative. *acid-* $KHSO_3 = 120.2$. P. bisulfite. Colorless needles, decomp. by heat; soluble in water. **p. sulfocarbolate.** P. phenyl sulfonate. **p. sulfocarbonate.** $K_2CS_3 = 186.2$. Orange, hygroscopic crystals, soluble in water; used to treat skin diseases. **p. sulfocyanate.** P. thiocyanate. **p. sulfocyanide.** P. thiocyanate. **p. sulfophenylate.** P. phenyl sulfonate. **p. tartrate.** *d-* $K_2C_4H_4O_6 \cdot \frac{1}{2}H_2O = 235.3$. Tartarus, soluble tartar, sal vegetal, normal p. tartrate. Colorless, monoclinic crystals, d.1.9715, soluble in water; a reagent, medicinal refrigerant, and laxative. *d-acid-* $KHC_4H_4O_6 = 188.14$. Rhombic crystals, d.1.956. *dl-* $K_2C_4H_4O_6 = 226.23$. Monoclinic crystals, d.1.984. *dl-acid-* Monoclinic crystals, d.1.954. *sodium-* P. sodium tartrate. **p. tellurite.** $K_2TeO_3 = 253.3$. Colorless powder, soluble in water; a selective antibiotic, especially to organisms unaffected by penicillin. **p. tetraborate.** $K_2B_4O_7 \cdot 5H_2O = 324.3$. P. borate. Colorless hexagons, soluble in water. **p. tetraoxalate.** $(COOH)_3COOK \cdot 2H_2O = 254.1$. Colorless prisms, soluble in water; a volumetric standard. **p. thiocyanate.** $KCNS = 97.2$. P. sulfocyanide, p. rhodanate. Colorless deliquescent prisms, m.162, soluble in water. Used as a reagent for ferric (red), copper (blue), and silver (white) salts. **p. thiocyanide.** P. thiocyanate. **p. triiodide.** $KI_3 = 419.86$. Prismatic crystals, m.45 (decomp.), soluble in p. iodide solution. **p. tungstate.** $3K_2O \cdot 7WO_3 \cdot 6H_2O = 2,015.0$. P. parawolframate. White crystals, soluble in water. **p. valerate.** $KC_5H_9O_2 = 140.2$. White crystals, soluble in water; a nerve sedative. **p. wolframate.** $K_2WO_4 \cdot 5H_2O = 416.4$. White, hygroscopic crystals, soluble in water; used for bronzing solutions. **p. xanthate.** $SC(SK)OEt = 160.28$. Yellow prisms, decomp. 200, soluble in water, decomp. by acids to alcohol and carbon disulfide; a flotation agent, soil flumigant, and reagent for the separation of nickel and cobalt. **p. zincate.** $K_2ZnO_2 = 175.7$. Colorless powder, soluble in alkalies.

potato. The rhizome of *Solanum tuberosum*. **sweet-** The rhizome of *Ipoemoea batatus*.

p. culture. A slice of p. used as culture medium for bacteria. **p. gum.** Euphorbia gum. **p. spirit.** Fusel oil. **p. starch.** See *starch*.

potency. (1) Mathematical: magnitude—the number of times a number is multiplied by itself; e.g., $10^3 = 1,000$; $10^{-2} = 0.01$. (2) Therapeutic: the activity of a drug. (3) Homeopathic: the degree of dilution of a remedy by a neutral medium, corresponding with the mathematical potency.

potential. (1) Stored-up energy capable of performing work. (2) Voltage: low, below 301; medium, 301–651; high, above 651. **absolute-** See *mercury cathode*. **chemical-** A measure of the tendency of a chemical reaction to take place. The increase in internal energy on adding an infinitesimally small quantity of substance to a system, the entropy and volume being constant. **electric-** Electromotive force. **electrolytic-** See *electroaffinity*. **half-wave-** The p. of a standardized dropping mercury electrode at the point on the current-voltage curve where the current is 50% of its limiting value. It is a characteristic property of electroreducible substances, and is independent of their concentrations. Cf. *polarograph*. **hydrogen-** See *pH*. **ionic-** See *ionic*. **magnetic-** Magnetomotive force. **oxidoreduction-** See *rH*. **pseudo-** The electrokinetic potential set up between ions adsorbed on the surface of a solid immersed in a liquid, and those in the liquid. **sedimentation-** The vertical electric field set up when suspended particles settle. **streaming-** The p. set up between the ends of a capillary when an electrolyte is forced through it. **super-** Overvoltage.

p. alcohol. The amount of alcohol that can be produced in practice by fermentation of a sugar solution of definite specific gravity. **p. difference.** The difference in voltage between the electrodes of a battery, vacuum tube, or thermocouple. See *electrode* potential. **p. energy.** (1) The heat capacity of a compound. (2) The latent energy of a body due to its position (as water in a high tank). **p. mediator.** A substance used to accelerate equilibrium in measurements of oxidation-reduction potentials. Cf. *poiser*.

potentiation. The activity induced in one insecticide by another used with it.

potentiometer. A low-resistance instrument for the accurate determination of small differences in electric potentials by Poggendorff's method, q.v. Cf. *galvanometer, hydrogen-ion recorder*.

potentiometric titration. Volumetric analysis in which the potential of an electrode immersed in the solution to be titrated is continually determined; a rapid change corresponds with the end of the reaction. Cf. *conductometric analysis*. **chrono-** The analysis of a solution of several electrolytes having different reduction potentials, by means of a stepped potential-time curve.

potentiostat. An electrical device to control the potential of an electrochemical system, e.g., in electrodeposition.

P.O.T.G. Portsmouth accelerator.

pothole. A deep, natural cavity in the earth surface, often filled with a deposit of salts; as, sodium carbonate; it may be formed by the grinding action of pebbles in a stream.

potstone. Talc.

potter's clay. A pure, plastic clay, free from iron. Cf. *pipe clay*. **p. lead.** Alquifou. **p. ore.** Alquifou.

pottery. Ware made from clay, molded while soft and moist, and hardened by heat; e.g.: (1) earthenware—relatively soft and fusible, and (a) unglazed, (b) glazed, (c) lustrous, (d) enameled; (2) stoneware—hard, infusible, and containing more silica. See *porcelain*.

pounce. Powdered chalk, charcoal, or (more usually) cuttlefish bones; formerly used to dry ink.

pound. lb, ♯. A unit of weight in the fps system. The weight in vacuo of a platinum cylinder known as the imperial standard pound. Cf. *pfund*.

1 imperial standard p.	= 0.453,592,338 kg
1 U.S. p.	= 0.453,592,4277 kg
1 Canadian p.	= 0.453,592,43 kg
1 international p. (1965)	= 0.453,592,37 kg

The U.S. and Canadian p. are defined in terms of

the international prototype *kilogram*, q.v. **apoth-ecaries'-** = 12 oz = 96 drams = 288 scruples = 5,760 grains = 0.37 kg. **avoirdupois-** = 16 oz = 7,000 grains = 0.453 kg = 16 fluid oz. **gee-**Slug. **troy-** (for gold and silver, etc.) = 5,760 grains = 16 oz.

  p. per square inch. A unit of pressure. See *atmosphere*. **p.-mole.** The number of pounds of a gas numerically equal to its molecular weight: 359 cubic feet.

poundal. pdl. The unit of force in the fps system. The force to accelerate 1 pound 1 foot per second each second = 13,825.5 dynes.

pour. The flow of a liquid under gravity. **p. point.** (1) The lowest temperature of flow under standard conditions. (2) The temperature at which an alloy is cast.

powder. (1) An aggregation of loose small solid particles. (2) Discrete particles of dry material, the maximum diameter of which is less than 1,000 microns (British Standards Institution, 1958) (3) An explosive used in blasting or gunnery. **algaroth-** Precipitated antimonous oxychloride. **baking-** See *baking powder*. **bleaching-** See *bleaching*. **dusting-** see *dusting*. **effervescent-** A mixture of salts that develops carbon dioxide in water. **flameless-** An explosive that produces little or no muzzle flash. **insect-** (1) See *insect powder*. (2) An insecticidal mixture of drugs. **Seidlitz-** A mixture of rochelle salt, sodium bicarbonate, and tartaric acid, used to make an effervescent saline water. **smokeless-** An explosive producing little or no smoke.

  p. cutting. The use of pyrophoric iron in a flame for cutting metals to increase temperature and eroding power.

powellite. $CaMoO_4 \cdot CaWO_4$. Yellow tetragons.

powellizing. Hardening wood by impregnation with a saccharin solution.

power. (1) Potency. (2) The time rate of doing work: $WT^{-1} = ML^2T^{-3}$, where W is work, T time, and M and L are the absolute units of mass and length. (3) See *diopter*. **p. factor.** That proportion of the total electric power flowing in an a-c circuit which is actually delivered to the load. It measures the ratio of watts dissipated to volt-amperes used. **p. transmission.** Methods: (1) mechanical, or direct; (2) hydraulic, by water columns; (3) pneumatic or compressed air; (4) steam in pipes; (5) electricity, through wires. **p. units.** See *watt, horsepower*.

poyok oil. A drying oil from a Nigerian tree, whose fatty acid contains licanic acid 41, eleostearic acid 31%; used in paints.

pozzolana. (1) Puzzolane, q.v. (2) A substance mixed with lime mortar to increase its strength. **artificial-** Burnt clay, granulated slag, certain clinkers and burnt oil shale. **natural-** Volcanic ash and celite.

pozzolanic action. Chemical action which forms insoluble compounds in cement.

P.P. Abbreviation for: (1) the pellagra-preventing factor of vitamin B, q.v.; (2) purified protein derivative. See *protein*.

PPD. Piperidine pentamethylene dithiocarbonate; a rubber vulcanization accelerator.

ppm. Abbreviation for parts per million. Cf. *epm*.

ppt(n). Abbreviation for precipita(te) -tion.

Pr. (1) Symbol for praseodymium. (2) Abbreviation for propyl: Pr$^\alpha$, *n*-Pr—α-propyl (normal propyl). Prβ, *i*-Pr—β-propyl (isopropyl).

praequine. Pamaquin.

Prager-Jacobson classification. The system of grouping organic compounds in 4,877 divisions, used in Beilstein's Handbuch.

pragilbert. The ratio of watts to intensity of magnetic current. Cf. *gilbert*.

pragmoline. Acetylcholine bromide.

Prandtl number. Specific heat at constant pressure × kinematic viscosity/thermal conductivity. Cf. *Reynolds number*.

prase. (1) Greenish. (2) A gray-green chalcedony.

praseodymia. The earth corresponding with the element praseodymium.

praseodymium. Pr = 140.91. A rare-earth metal, at. no. 59. Green metal, d.6.48, m.940, slowly decomp. in water. Separated (1885) by Auer von Welsbach from the earth didymia, and occurs in cerite and rare-earth minerals. Principal valency 3. **p. acetate.** $Pr(C_2H_3O_2)_3 \cdot 3H_2O$ = 372.04. Green needles, soluble in water. **p. chloride.** $PrCl_3$ = 247.3. Green needles, m.818; soluble in water. **p. oxalate.** $Pr_2(C_2O_4)_3 \cdot 10H_2O$ = 726.00. Green crystals, insoluble in water. **p. oxides.** (1) Pr_2O_3 = 329.8. P. trioxide. Yellow-green powder. (2) Pr_2O_4 = 345.8. P. tetroxide. Black powder. (3) Pr_2O_5 = 361.8. P. peroxide. **p. peroxide.** P. oxide (3). **p. phosphate.** $PrPO_4$ = 235.9. Green powder for coloring ceramics. **p. sulfate.** $Pr_2(SO_4)_3 \cdot 8H_2O$ = 714.2. Green crystals, soluble in water. **p. sulfide.** Pr_2S_3 = 378.0. Brown powder, decomp. by heat, insoluble in water.

praseolite. A green alteration product of iolite.

preboarding. The setting of hosiery fibers by the combined actions of steam and pressure.

precalciferol. See *calciferol*.

precancerous. Describing a growth which develops into a cancer.

precious. Valuable, rare. **p. garnet.** Almandite. **p. metals.** The noble metals: gold, platinum, and silver. **p. opal.** An opal exhibiting a play of delicate colors. **p. stone.** A mineral used as a gem.

precipitable. Describing that which can be precipitated.

precipitant. A substance which, when added to a solution, causes the formation of an insoluble substance. **group-** A reagent that will precipitate several related substances; as, hydrogen sulfide or ammonia. See *qualitative analysis*.

precipitate. ppt. (1) To cause a substance to be precipitated. (2) The deposit of an insoluble substance in a solution as a result of a chemical reaction after the addition of a precipitating reagent. Cf. *policeman, schwellenwert*. **banded-** Periodic p. **black-** Mercurous oxide. **group-** The p. formed by a group precipitant consisting of substances of related properties. See *qualitative analysis*. **periodic-** See *periodic precipitate*. **red-** Red *mercuric oxide*. **white-** Ammoniated *mercury*. **yellow-** Yellow *mercuric oxide*.

precipitated. Settled out; rendered insoluble. **p. bone.** A by-product in the manufacture of glue from bones; chiefly dicalcium phosphate. **p. chalk.** Calcium carbonate produced by precipitation. **p. phosphate.** Dicalcium phosphate obtained from phosphate rock or processed bone.

p. vapor. The deposit of solid particles from gases or vapors on the walls of a container.

precipitation. The process of producing a precipitate. **co-** The simultaneous p. of more than one substance. Cf. group *precipitate.* **electrostatic-** The use of an electric potential to cause the p. of the charged moisture globules of a fog, or the dust particles of a smoke. See *Lodge-Cottrell process.* **fractional-** The separation of substances by precipitating them in increasing order of solubility.

precipitin. An immunizing substance formed in the blood serum of animals or humans, that can precipitate the bacteria whose cultures have been employed in the immunizing treatment.

precipitinogen. A substance which, on injection, causes the formation of precipitins.

precipitum. The deposit of bacteria formed by the action of precipitins.

precision. The degree of reproducibility or scatter of results of an experiment or method, as distinct from its accuracy (U.S. usage). **p. instrument.** A graduated measuring instrument, certified by the manufacturer, but not tested at a government bureau, and differing from certified instruments, q.v.

precursor. (1) A substance synthesized in the dark by an organism, and decomposed by light. Cf. *photoproduct.* (2) A substance that forms the raw material for the synthesis of protoplasm in the living animal body. (3) A substance that precedes the formation of another compound. Cf. *provitamin.*

predissociation. A spectral phenomenon by which a molecule dissociates at a lower level than its dissociation energy.

prednisolone. $C_{21}H_{28}O_5 = 360.55$. Sterane. White, bitter crystals, m.229 (decomp.), soluble in water; a cortisone substitute, as it has fewer side effects (B.P.). **p. sodium phosphate.** $C_{21}H_{27}O_8NA_2P = 484.40$. Bitter, white powder, soluble in water; an adrenocortical steroid (B.P.).

prednisone. $C_{21}H_{26}O_5 = 358.44$. White, bitter crystals, insoluble in water; used similarly to prednisolone (B.P.).

preform. Material produced in a state ready for molding to a desired shape, e.g., plastic-impregnated wood pulp for molded panels.

Pregl, Fritz. 1868–1930. Austrian chemist, noted for his development of quantitative microanalysis Nobel Prize winner (1923).

pregnane. $C_{21}H_{36} = 288.2$. A tetracyclic hydrocarbon, cholane derivative, q.v. **p. diol.** $C_{21}H_{36}$-$O_2 = 320.2$. A sterol, m.233, from the urine of pregnant women. **p. dione.** $C_{21}H_{32}O_2 = 316.2$. A ketone derivative of p. diol.

pregnanolone. $C_{21}H_{34}O_2 = 318.2$. A corpus luteum hormone. Cf. *cholane derivatives.*

pregnene. $C_{21}H_{34} = 286.2$. $\Delta^{5:6}$-pregnane. A cholane derivative, q.v. **p. diol.** $C_{21}H_{32}O_2 = 316.2$. A corpus luteum hormone.

pregneninolone. Ethisterone.

Pregnyl. Trademark for chlorionic gonadotrophin.

pregrattite. A variety of muscovite from Tyrol.

prehnite. $H_2Ca_2Al_2(SiO_4)_3$. A hydrous silicate.

prehnitene. $C_{10}H_{14} = 134.2$. Prenitol, 1,2,3,4-Tetramethylbenzene*. Colorless liquid, b.204, insoluble in water.

prehnitic acid. $C_{10}H_6O_8 = 254.05$. 1,2,3,4-Benzenetetracarboxylic acid*. Colorless crystals, decomp. 237. Cf. *mellophanic acid.*

prehnitilic acid. 2,3,4-Trimethylbenzoic acid*.

preignition. See *knock.*

preimpregnate. A substance used to hold the ingredients of a mix together, before resin impregnation and molding, e.g., polyester resins.

premier alloy. The heat-resisting alloy: Ni 61, Fe 25, Cr 11, Mn 3%.

premier jus. The edible oils obtained by rendering the tissues surrounding the kidneys of the cow. Cf. *dripping.*

prenitic acid. Prehnitic acid.

prenitol. Prehnitene.

prenyl. 3-Methylbut-2-en-iso-yl. Indicating the presence of an isoprene unit.

prep. Abbreviation for preparation.

preparation. (1) A chemical process for the production of a chemical compound. (2) A chemical compound. (3) The treatment of ores; as, dressing. (4) A pharmaceutical product. **p. dish.** A glass dish with glass cover, for microscope slides or cover glasses. **p. jar.** A large glass jar with glass cover, for museum specimens. **p. of salts.** See *salts.*

prescription. A written direction for compounding or administering a drug. **p. balance.** A delicate scale used to weigh small quantities: less sensitive than an analytical balance.

preservative. A substance that prevents decay and decomposition of organic liquids or foods, including sulfites, fluorides, benzoates, salicylates, borates, and formaldehyde. This use is limited or prohibited in many countries. **histological-** P. used for biological specimens; as, Zenker's solution. **wood-** P. used for lumber; as, creosote.

press. A device that applies pressure. **cork-** A corrugated wheel rotating in a corrugated elliptical frame, for softening corks by pressure. **filter-** See *filter.* **plant-** A piston in a perforated cylinder, to express juices from plants.

pressing paper. A coarse filter paper for drying specimens.

presspahn. Wallboards, made by hydraulic pressure from wood pulp.

pressure. Strain or stress produced by the meeting of opposite forces; as, compression. Barometric units of p. are (in order of preference):

Basic unit = 1 dyne/cm^2

1 millibar (mb) = 1,000 dynes/cm^2

Millimeters Hg at 0°C and standard gravity = 980.665 cm/sec^2

Inches Hg at 0°C and standard gravity = 980.665 cm/sec^2

atmospheric- The p. exerted by the gasous envelope on the earth surface, measured in atmospheres: 1 atm = 14.7 psi = 1,012,630 dynes/cm^2 = 760 mm Hg. **critical-** The p. required to condense a gas at the critical temperature. **disruptive-** See *disruption.* **electrical-** Electromotive force. **fugitive-** The variations of atmospheric p. in the vicinity of explosions. **high-** A p. above one atmosphere. **low-** A p. below one atmosphere. **negative-** Suction. A p. less than one atmosphere. **normal-** One atmosphere. **osmotic-** See *osmosis.* **partial-** The p. exerted by a single gaseous constituent of a gas mixture. See *Dalton's law.* **radiation-** See *radiation.* **solution-** The molecular force of a solid that tends to dissolve; a measure of the attractive forces (coordinate bonds) between the molecules of solute and solvent. **standard-** See *normal-*. **total-** The sum of the partial pressures of the constituents of a gas mixture. **ultrahigh-** A p. exceeding 100,000 atm. Produced by the force exerted on a tetrahedral crystal of pyrophyllite by 4 tapered anvils, one on each face. P. on the anvils is transmitted hydrostatically to a specimen container midway between 2 opposite edges of the tetrahedron.

p. blower. A device to produce a current of air. **p. bottle.** A heavy-walled glass container. **p. filter.** (1) A porous porcelain cylinder through which the solution to be filtered is pumped. (2) A filter press. **p. gage.** A device to measure the p. of gases or liquids; as, mechanical instruments (coiled tubes or diaphragms) or hydrostatic devices (mercury columns). Cf. *manometer*. **p. packing.** See *Aerosol*. **p. tubing.** Thick-walled rubber tubing used for vacuum pumps.

Prest-O-Lite. Trademark for acetylene gas, compressed in small cylinders, for soldering and brazing.

Prestone. Trademark for ethylene glycol antifreeze.

Preventol. Trademark for dihydroxydichlorodiphenylmethane. A fungicide, bactericide, and preservative for adhesives.

Prezenta. Trade name for a viscose cellulose synthetic fiber.

prezymogen. The substance of a living cell that forms the zymogens.

pribramite. (1) A variety of sphalerite from Bohemia (2) A variety of göthite.

priceite. $3CaO \cdot 4BO_3 \cdot 6H_2O$. A mineral from Death Valley, Calif.

prickly ash bark. Xanthoxylum.

prickly ash berries. Xanthoxyli fructus. The fruits of *Xanthoxylum* species (Rutaceae); used as a carminative and alterative.

prickly pear. Opuntia, Indian fig. The fruit of a cactus species, *Opuntia;* a source of alcohol for motor fuel.

Priestley, Joseph. 1733–1804. English-born American chemist, noted for his discovery of oxygen and gas experiments.

prill. A small globule or button of material, e.g., of metal formed in assays.

primaquine phosphate. $C_{15}H_{21}ON_3 \cdot 2H_3PO_4 = 455.36$. Bitter, orange crystals, m.203, soluble in water; an antimalarial (U.S.P., B.P.).

primary. The first, simplest form. **p. alcohol.** An organic compound characterized by the —CH_2OH group. **p. amine.** An organic compound characterized by the —CH_2NH_2 group. **p. battery.** A voltaic cell producing a potential as a result of chemical changes undergone by its constituents. **p. carbon atom.** A C atom attached to one other C atom only. **p. color.** One of a number of simple colors, combinations of which are supposed to produce all others possible. See *Helmholtz' theory*. **p. current.** The inducing current of an induction coil, q.v. **p. flash distillate.** A very light petroleum oil fraction, which can be hydrolyzed to produce benzole and/or town gas. **p. nucleus.** An organic, cyclic compound with only H atoms attached to the ring. **p. oxide.** A hypothetical unstable oxide formed during an oxidation reaction, and having the characteristics of a peroxide which loses oxygen. See *induced reactions*. **p. reaction.** The principal or fastest reaction in a composite system of reactions. **p. valence.** See principal *valence*.

primer. (1) Detonator, percussion cap. (2) An explosive cartridge containing the detonator.

primeverose. $C_{11}H_{20}O_{10} = 312.15$. A disaccharide from the glucosides of cowslips and primrose.

primeverosidase. An enzyme that hydrolyzes primrose glucoside to primeverose.

primidone. $C_{12}H_{14}O_2N_2 = 218.34$. Bitter, white crystals, m.281, slightly soluble in water or organic solvents; an antiepileptic (B.P.).

priming. (1) Escape into the condenser of a liquid being distilled, due to splashing, bumping, etc. (2) P. sugar. **p. powder.** Fulminating powder. **p. sugar.** Glucose or invert sugar added to beer to impart body or briskness as a result of afterfermentation. **p. tube.** Primer.

primula. Cowslip. The dried herb of *Primula officinalis* (Primulaceae).

primulaverin. A glucoside from the root of primula. Cf. *primverin*.

primulin. (1) A crystalline substance from the root of *Primula officinalis*. (2) A primrose-colored azo dye; the alkali salts of primulin bases. **p. bases.** A group of sulfur dyes obtained by heating *p*-toluidine and sulfur with amines.

primulite. Volemitol. A crystalline sugar from the roots of *Primula officinalis*.

primverase. An enzyme from the root of *Primula officinalis*.

primverin. A glucoside from the root of *Primula grandiflora*. Cf. *primulaverin*.

primycin. $C_{19}H_{37}O_7N = 391.53$. An actinomycetic antibiotic from the larvae of the wax moth *Galeria melonella*. White crystals, m.167 (decomp.), sparingly soluble in water.

Prince Rupert drops. Pear-shaped droplets of glass, formed when molten glass falls into water. They shatter explosively into fine powder when the tips are broken.

Prince's metal. The brass: Cu 75, Zn 25%.

principal. The main or chief function, leading or first; as, p. valence. Cf. *principle*. **p. axis.** (1) The optical axis of a crystal. (2) The longest axis of a crystal. **p. series.** A type of spectrum that contains the strongest lines. See *Rydberg equation*, *Bohr's atom*. **p. valence.** That valence of an element for which it has the largest number of stable compounds.

principle. (1) A theory or assumption; a fundamental concept; as, the p. of LeChâtelier. Cf. *principal*. (2) A substance on which the characteristic effect of a vegetable drug or mixture depends. **acid-** The organic acids of a vegetable drug. **active-** The substance on which the physiological effect of a drug depends; as, tannins. **basic-** Alkaloid. **bitter-** Amaroids. **neutral-** A glucoside, salt, ester, or essential oil. **odorous-** Essential oil, **proximate-** Active p. **resinous-** Resin. **sweet-** Glucoside. **toxic-** The poisonous constituent of a drug.

printer's ink. See *ink*.

printer's liquor. A solution of ferrous acetate.

printing. The mechanical reproduction of reading

matter or designs. See *gravure, letterpress, lithography*.

Priodax. Trademark for pheniodol.

Priscol. Trademark for tolazoline hydrochloride.

prism. (1) A crystal or solid figure whose faces are parallelograms parallel to the axis, and whose ends are triangular or polygonal faces parallel and similar to one another. They may belong to the tetragonal, hexagonal, orthorhombic, monoclinic, or triclinic systems. (2) A triangular glass rod or hollow glass vessel, used to produce a spectrum. **hollow-** A p.-shaped glass or quartz container for measuring the refractive index of or obtaining a more dispersed spectrum from highly refractive liquids. **nicol-** Two similar triangular pieces of Iceland spar cemented together to form a prism. It splits a ray of light into 2 portions, polarized and reflected, and is used in polarimeters to obtain polarized light. **spectrum-** A polished triangular glass rod used in spectroscopes.

prismatic. Formed or shaped like a prism. **p. colors.** Rainbow colors. The monochromatic tints produced by the unequal refraction of the constituent rays of light passing through a prism. See *spectrum*.

pristane. $C_{18}H_{38} = 254.3$. Isooctadecane, from shark-liver oil.

pristimerin. $C_{27}H_{34}O_4 = 422.33$. A quinonoid antibiotic (to gram-positive cocci) from the roots of *Pristimera indica* (Wilhd.), m.219, soluble in light petroleum; used to treat throat infections.

Privine. Trademark for naphthazole. (2-(1-Naphthylmethyl)imidazoline nitrate; a vasoconstrictor.

proactinomycin. An antibiotic substance from *Nocardia gardneri* (Actinomycetes).

proagglutinoid. An agglutinoid that has greater attraction for the agglutinogen than the agglutinin.

probability. A mathematical treatment of data to find the limits or error. Let M be the total number of cases in a series, m the number in one group, and n the number in another. Then $n + m = M$, and $(m/M):(n/M)$ is the proportion of the parts to the whole. The probability $= m/M + 2\sqrt{2mn/M^3}$; e.g.: if in 100 observed cases (M), there are 25 cases (m) of one type, and 75 cases (n) of the other, then in any other series of similar experiments there may be observed as many as 37 or as few as 13 cases of m. Correspondingly, there will be 63 to 87 cases of n.

probe. electron- An electron beam less than 1 micron in diameter. It excites the X-ray characteristics (photons) of the elements in the area on which it is focused, enabling them to be determined.

probenecid. $C_{13}H_{19}O_4NS = 285.37$. 4-(Di-*n*-propylsulfamoyl)benzoic acid. Bitter, white crystals, m.199, insoluble in water; used to treat gout (B.P.).

procainamide hydrochloride. $C_{13}H_{21}ON_3 \cdot HCl = 271.80$. Pronestyl. White crystals, m.167, soluble in water; a cardiac depressant (U.S.P., B.P.).

procaine. $NH_2 \cdot C_6H_4 \cdot COOCH_2CH_2 \cdot NEt_2 \cdot HCl = 272.7$. Novocaine, *p*-aminobenzoyl diethylaminoethanol hydrochloride, ethocaine, kerocaine, syncaine, neocaine. Colorless crystals, m.155, soluble in water; a local anesthetic (U.S.P., B.P.). Cf. *Percaine*. **p. base.** $C_{13}H_{20}N_2O_2 = 236.7$. Novocaine base. β-diethylaminoethyl *p*-aminobenzoate.

White granules, m.61, insoluble in water. **p. hydrochloride.** Planocaine. Pharmacopoeial name for procaine. **p. nitrate.** Colorless crystals, m.100, soluble in water. **p. penicillin.** The monohydrate of the p. salt of benzyl penicillin. White powder, soluble in water. Administered intramuscularly to create a depot from which *p.* is released slowly into the blood (B.P.).

procellose. $C_{18}H_{32}O_{16} = 504.25$. Procellulose. Cellotriose. A trisaccharide from cellulose, m.210.

process. A method used in the manufacture or treatment of substances. **type-** The principal operations involved in a chemical plant. **unit-** (1) A single chemical operation carried out on a non-laboratory scale. (2) One of the successive individual operations necessary for the production of a definite compound; as, crushing, grinding, separating, leaching, dissolving, concentrating, evaporating, distilling, mixing. **p. tankage.** A fertilizer made from nitrogenous waste material by the action of acid or alkali and pressure. Cf. *nitrogenous tankage*.

prochlorite. A mineral containing pennine and chlorite.

prochlorperazine. $C_{20}H_{24}N_3ClS \cdot 2C_4H_4O_4 = 606.12$. Yellow crystals, m.201, insoluble in water; a tranquilizer and antiemetic (B.P.). Also used as p. methanesulfonate (B.P.).

Procion. Trade name for a class of fast, soluble azo dyestuffs for cellulose fibers, of the dichlorotriazinyl type. P. are unique in that they are fixed to the fibers by esterification of one or more OH groups of the cellulose molecule.

procyclidene hydrochloride. $C_{19}H_{29}ON \cdot HCl = 323.91$. Bitter, white crystals, m.226, slightly soluble in water; used to treat Parkinson's disease (B.P.).

Prodag. Trademark for a semicolloidal suspension of graphite in water; a mold wash in metal casting and rubber curing. Cf. *Aquadag*.

prodorite. An acid-resisting concrete which contains pitch.

producer. An apparatus producing illuminating and fuel gas, by passing air over red-hot coke. **p. gas.** A combustible mixture of nitrogen, carbon monoxide, and small quantities of carbon dioxide, hydrogen, and methane obtained by passing steam and air over coal at 1,000°C.

product. The substance manufactured. **reaction-** Reactant. The compound formed by a reaction. **split-** A decomposition product. **substitution-** A derivative, q.v.

proenzyme. The substance of the living cell that produces enzymes.

Profax. Trademark for polypropylene.

proferment. The substance of the living cell that produces ferments. See *zymogen*.

profile paper. Coordinate paper.

profilogram. A diagram showing the variation of a property over a relative flat surface; as the roughness of paper.

proflavine. $C_{13}H_{11}N_3SO_4 = 307.1$. Common name for 2,8-diaminoacridine. Brown crystals, soluble (with fluorescence) in water; used as an antiseptic and to treat sleeping sickness. **p. hemisulfate.** $(C_{13}H_{11}N_3)_2 \cdot H_2SO_4 \cdot H_2O = 534.58$. Bitter, hygroscopic crystals, soluble in water; an antiseptic (B.P.).

progallin-P. Propyl gallate.

progesterone. $C_{21}H_{30}O_2 = 314.47$. Progestin. Proluton. Luteosterone C, luteal hormone, from corpus luteum. White crystals, insoluble in water; 2 isomers: **alpha-** m.128. **anhydrohydroxy-** q.v. **beta-** m.131. They produce progestational changes in the uterus (U.S.P., B.P.). See *cholane*.

Progestin. Trademark for α- and β-progesterone, secreted by the corpus luteum; used to treat disorders of pregnancy and menstruation.

progestogen. Generic name for drugs used to maintain pregnancy and to treat uterine bleeding.

Progestoral. Trademark for ethisterone.

progression. Series. A series of related increasing or decreasing numbers; e.g.: **arithmetic-** 1,2,3,4, ... **geometric-** 1,2,4,8, ... **harmonic-** $\frac{1}{2}, \frac{1}{3}, \frac{1}{4}$, ... Q.v.

proguanil hydrochloride. $C_{11}H_{16}N_5Cl \cdot HCl = 290.18$. Paludrine hydrochloride. Bitter, white crystals, m.245, soluble in water; an antimalarial (B.P.).

Progynon. (1) Brand name for estrone. **P.-DP.** Estradiol dipropionate. (2) German for Theelin.

proidonite. SiF_4. A mineral.

projection nucleus. See *nucleus*.

prokayvit. Menaphthone. **p. oral.** Acetomenaphthone.

pro-knock. A substance that induces knocking in an internal-combustion engine. Cf. *antiknock*.

prolactin. A hormone from the anterior pituitary which causes mammary glands of mammals and crop glands of pigeons to secrete milk.

prolamine. A group of proteins from cereals; insoluble in water, soluble in dilute alcohol. **p. from oats.** Contains cystidine and histidine. **p. from sorghum.** Contains no tryptophane.

prolan. Chlorionic gonadotrophin.

Prolene. Trademark for a polypropylene synthetic textile fiber.

proline. $\underset{\underline{\hspace{3em}}}{NH \cdot (CH_2)_3 \cdot CH \cdot (COOH)} = 115.1$. **alpha-** 2-Pyrrolidinecarboxylic acid. An amino acid, protein split product, which does not react with nitrous acid or ninhydrin.

prolon. A synthetic protein fiber, analogous to rayon, e.g., Ardil.

Proluton. Brand name for progesterone.

prolyl. The radical $\underset{\underline{\hspace{3em}}}{NH \cdot (CH_2)_3 \cdot CH \cdot (COO—)}$, from proline.

promazine hydrochloride. $C_{17}H_{20}N_2S \cdot HCl = 320.86$. 10-(3-Dimethylaminopropyl)phenothiazine hydrochloride. Bitter, white, hygroscopic crystals, m.179; a tranquilizer (B.P.).

promethazine chlorotheophyllinate. Avomine. Used to prevent travel sickness. **p. hydrochloride.** $C_{17}H_{20}N_2S \cdot HCl = 320.90$. Bitter, yellow crystals, m.223, slightly soluble in water; an antihistaminic (B.P.).

promethium. Pm. Accepted name for illinium, q.v., rare-earth element of at. no. 61. A product of the fission of U^{235}; does not occur in nature; stablest isotope, mass no. 147. Cf. *florentium*.

Promin. Trademark for *p,p'*-diaminodiphenylsulfone *n*-didextrose sulfonate. Bitter, yellow, hygroscopic solid, soluble in water; used to treat leprosy and said to be active against tubercle bacilli in guinea pigs.

prominal. Methophenobarbitone.

Promizole. Trademark for 4,2'-diaminophenyl-5'-thiazolesulfone; a possible remedy for human tuberculosis.

promoter. (1) Catalyst accelerator. (2) In flotation: see *collector*.

pronethalol hydrochloride. $C_{15}H_{19}NO \cdot HCl = 265.80$. Bitter, white powder, soluble in water; an anti-adrenalinitic (B.P.).

prontosil. The sulfonamide of chrysoidine. An internal antiseptic whose activity is due to the aminobenzene sulfonamide group; an antistreptococcal. Cf. *sulfa* drugs.

proof gallon. U.S.: 1.8927 liters at 60°F, U.K.: 2.5926 liters at 15°C, of ethyl alcohol. **p. spirit.** (1) Dilute aqueous ethyl alcohol containing 50% C_2H_5OH by volume at 60°F (U.S. and Netherlands usage). (2) Dilute aqueous ethyl alcohol which at 51°F weighs exactly $\frac{12}{13}$ of an equal measure of distilled water. At 60°F it contains 49.28% by weight or 57.10% by volume of C_2H_5OH; d.0.91984 (U.K. usage). **overproof-** *x* overproof describes a spirit, 100 volumes of which when diluted to $(100 + x)$ volumes, gives proof spirit. **underproof-** A spirit that is *x* underproof contains in 100 volumes $(100 — x)$ volumes of proof spirit.

propadiene*. $H_2C=C=CH_2 = 40.0$. Allene, dimethylenemethane. **dioxo-** Carbon suboxide.

propaesin. $NH_2C_6H_4 \cdot COOC_3H_7 = 179.11$. Propesin, propyl *p*-aminobenzoate. White crystals, m.76, slightly soluble in water; a sedative.

propalanine. Aminobutyric acid.

propaldehyde. Propionaldehyde.

propamidine. $NH:C(NH_2) \cdot C_6H_4O \cdot (CH_2)_3 \cdot O \cdot C_6H_4 \cdot (NH_2)C:NH$. 4,4'-Diamidino-1,3-diphenoxypropane; a surgical antiseptic.

propanal*. Propionaldehyde. Cf. *propenal*, *proponal*. **2,2-dimethyl-*** Pivaldehyde. **2-methyl-*** Isobutyraldehyde.

propanamide*. Propionamide. **2-hydroxy-*** Lactamide.

propane*. $C_3H_8 = 44.1$. The third member of the methane series. Colorless gas, $d_{air=1}1.558$, b.—39, slightly soluble in water; a fuel for internal-combustion engines. **acetyl-** Propyl methyl ketone. **bromo-*** Propyl bromide. **chloro-*** Propyl chloride. **diamino-** P. diamine*. **dihydroxy-*** Propanediol. **epoxy-*** Propylene oxide. **hydroxy-** Propanol. **imino-** Propylenimine. **iodo-*** Propyliodide. **methoxy-*** Methyl propyl ether. **nitroso-** Propyl pseudonitrol. **phenyl-** Cumene. **trichloro-*** Trichlorohydrin. **trihydroxy-** Glycerol. **p. carboxylic acid.** Butyric acid. **p. diamide*.** Malonamide. **p. diamine*.** $NH_2(CH_2)_3NH_2 = 74.09$. Trimethylenediamine, propylenediamine. A ptomaine from beef-broth cultures of coma bacillus. Colorless liquid, b.136; a reagent for mercury. **p. dicarboxylic acid.** Glutaric acid. **p. dinitrile*.** Malononitrile. **p. dioic acid*.** Malonic acid. **p. tricarboxylic acid.** Tricarballylic acid.

propanediol*. $C_3H_8O_2 = 76.1$. Dihydroxypropane. **α-** or **1,2-** $MeCHOH \cdot CH_2OH$. Propylene glycol. Colorless liquid, b.188. **β-** or **1,3-** $CH_2OH \cdot CH_2 \cdot CH_2OH$. Trimethylene glycol. A liquid, b.215, soluble in water. **3-chloro-*** α-Chlorohydrin.

propanedione*. 1,2-Pyruvaldehyde.

propanetriol*. Glycerol.

propanoic acid*. Propionic acid.

propanol*. $C_3H_8O = 60.1$. **normal-** $CH_3 \cdot CH_2 \cdot CH_2 \cdot OH$. 1-Propyl alcohol. Colorless liquid, d.0.799, b.97, soluble in water. **iso-** $CH_3 \cdot CHOH \cdot CH_3$. 2-Propyl alcohol. Colorless liquid, d.0.780, b.82, soluble in water. **chloro-*** Propylene chlorhydrin. **diethoxy-*** See *diethylglycerol*, *diethyline*. **diiodo-*** Iothion. **epoxy-*** Glycidol. **methyl-** Butyl alcohol. **phenyl-** Phenetyl alcohol. **trichloromethyl-** Chloretone.

propanone*. Acetone. **dihydroxy-** Dihydroxy acetone. **diphenyl-** Benzyl ketone. **hydroxy-** Acetol.

propantheline bromide. $C_{20}H_{30}O_3NBr = 448.42$. Bitter, white powder, m.158, soluble in water; used similarly to atropine (B.P.).

propargyl. (1) The radical $HC \equiv C \cdot CH_2$—, from propargyl alcohol. (2) Prop-2-enyl. **bi-** or **di-** Bipropargyl.

propargyl acetate. $MeCOOC_3H_3 = 98.1$. Colorless liquid, d.1.005, b.124.

propargyl alcohol. $CH \vdots C \cdot CH_2OH = 56.1$. Propinol. Colorless liquid, d.0.972, b.114, soluble in water.

propargylic acid. Propiolic acid.

propäsin. Propaesin.

Propathene. Trade name for polypropylene.

propellant. An explosive material which generates a large volume of hot gas at a predetermined rate. Propellants may be solid (plasticized cellulose nitrate) or liquid (concentrated hydrogen peroxide). **bi-** A p. whose action depends on the interaction of 2 substances, one of which is an oxidant. **mono-** A p. whose action is due to a single substance. See table.

Propellant	*Specific impulse*
Hydrogen peroxide, hydrogen nitrate, or dinitrogen tetroxide with alcohols, petroleum fuels, or hydrazine hydrate	210–250
Liquid oxygen with ethanol, kerosene, liquid ammonia, liquid acetylene, or liquid hydrogen	240–345
Liquid ozone with kerosene or liquid hydrogen	275–370
Liquid fluorine with kerosene, liquid ammonia, hydrazine, or liquid hydrogen	265–355
Perchlorates with organic polymers	180–245
Cordite	190–235
Hydrogen peroxide (90%), ethylene oxide, hydrazine, propyl nitrate, nitromethane	135–220

propenal. Acrolein. Cf. *propanal*, *proponal*.

propene*. $C_3H_6 = 42.1$. **1,2-** or $\Delta^{1(2)}$- Propylene. **1,3-** or $\Delta^{1(3)}$- Cyclopropane. **bromo-*** Allyl bromide. **chloro-*** Allyl chloride. **dichloro-*** Allylene dichloride.

p. dicarboxylic acid. Glutaconic acid. **p. oxide.** Propylene oxide. **p. thiol*.** Allyl mercaptan. **p. tricarboxylic acid.** Aconitic acid.

propenol. Allyl alcohol. **phenyl-** Cinnamic alcohol.

propenyl. (1) Prop-1-enyl. The group, $CH_3 \cdot CH \vdots CH$—, derived from propylene. (2) Glyceryl. **p. benzene.** Allyl benzene. **p. hydrate.** Glycerol. **p. phenol.** Anol. **p. trinitrate.** Nitroglycerin.

prop-2-enyl. Preferred term for propyl.

propenylidene. The radical $CH_3 \cdot CH \vdots C =$, from propylene.

propeptone. Hemialbumose.

properties. The characteristics of a substance. **additive-** (1) P. that depend on the quantity of matter; as, mass. (2) P. of a molecule which can be calculated from those of constituent atoms; as, molecular weight. Cf. *constitutive-*. **atomic-** P. depending on atomic characteristics; as, spectrum lines. Cf. *molecular-*, *molar-*. **chemical-** The chemical reactions of a substance. Cf. *physical-*. **constitutive-** (1) P. that depend on the quality of matter; as, melting point. (2) P. due to constitution; as, optical rotation. Cf. *additive-*. **extensive-** P. depending on quantity; as, momentum. Cf. *intensive-*. **general-** P. inherent in all matter; as, gravity. Cf. *special-*. **intensive-** P. depending on quality; as, solubility. Cf. *extensive-*. **mechanical-** The general physical p. of a substance; as, density. **molal-** P. depending on the amount of substance; as, m. boiling-point elevation. **molar-** P. depending on size, form, or weight; as, mechanical p. Cf. *atomic-*, *molecular-*. **molecular-** P. depending on molecules; as, isomerism. Cf. *atomic-*, *molar-*. **physical-** Physical phenomena which remain unchanged so long as there is no change in molecular composition; e.g., mechanical p. **radiant-** The light and color characteristics of a substance. **special-** P. exhibited to varying extents by some but not all matter; as, color. Cf. *general-*. **thermal-** The p. of a substance due to absorption or liberation of heat; such as, melting and boiling.

Prophem. Trade name for isopropyl *N*-phenylcarbamate, $C_6H_5 \cdot NH \cdot COOCHMe_2$; a herbicide.

prophetin. $C_{20}H_{36}O_7 = 388.4$. A glucoside from *Ecballium officinale* and *Cucumis prophetarum* (Cucurbitaceae), soluble in water.

prophoretin. $C_{20}H_{30}O_4$. An amorphous, resinous split product of prophetin.

prophylactic. A preventive, particularly of disease.

prophylaxis. Preventive treatment.

propilidene. Propylidene.

propine. Allylene. **p. dicarboxylic acid.** Glutinic acid.

propinol. Propargyl alcohol.

propinyl. The radical —C_3H_3.

propiolaldehyde. $CH \vdots C \cdot CHO = 54.0$. Propynal*. Oily liquid, b.61.

propiolic acid. $CH \vdots C \cdot COOH = 70.0$. Carboxyacetylene, propargylic acid, acetylenecarboxylic acid, propynoic acid*. Colorless liquid, b.144, soluble in water. **methyl-** Tetrolic acid. **phenyl-** Ph·$C \vdots C \cdot COOH$. Colorless crystals, m.136, soluble in water.

p. acid series. See *acetylene acids*. **p. alcohol.** $CH \vdots C \cdot CH_2OH = 56.05$. 2-Propyn-*1*-ol, b.114, soluble in water.

propiolyl. The radical $HC \vdots C \cdot CO$—, from propiolic acid.

propion. (1) Propione. (2) Propionyl. **p. aldoxime.** $EtCH \vdots NOH = 73.1$. Propionic aldoxime. Colorless crystals, m.21. **p. amide.** $EtCONH_2 = 73.1$. Propionic amide, propionylamine, propanamide*. Colorless leaflets, m.79, soluble in water. **p. anilide.** $EtCONHPh = 149.1$. Propionylaniline. Colorless leaflets, m.104, soluble in water.

propionaldehyde. $MeCH_2CHO = 58.1$. Propanal*, propaldehyde, propyl aldehyde. Colorless liquid, d.0.807, b.48, soluble in water. **dihydroxy-** Glyceraldehyde. **dimethyl-** Pivaldehyde.

propionamide. Propion.

propionate. C_2H_5COOM. A salt or ester of propionic acid.

propione. $EtCOEt = 86.1$. Propion, 3-pentanone*, diethyl ketone. Colorless liquid, b.101, soluble in water; a hypnotic.

propionic acid. $MeCH_2COOH = 74.1$. Carboxyethane, propanoic acid*, pseudoacetic acid. Colorless liquid, d.0.987, b.141, soluble in water. **acetyl-** Levulinic acid. **amino-** Alanine. **aminohydroxy-** Serine. **aminohydroxyphenyl-** Tyrosine. **aminoindyl-** Tryptophane. **benzoyl-** Benzoylpropionic acid. **carbamyl-** Succinamic acid. **dihydroxy-** Glyceric acid. **dimethyl-** Pivalic acid. **dioxyphenyl-** Hydrocaffeic acid. **epoxy-*** Glycidic acid. **hydroxy-** (1) Lactic acid. (2) Hydracrylic acid. **keto-** Pyruvic acid. **β-nitro-** Hiptagenic acid. **phenol-** Hydrocoumaric acid. **phenyl-** (1) Hydratropic acid. (2) Hydrocinnamic acid. **p. aldehyde.** Propionaldehyde. **p. anhydride.** $(MeCH_2CO)_2O = 130.11$. Propionyl oxide, propanoic anhydride*. Colorless liquid, d.1.017, b.168, decomp. by water.

propionitrile. Ethyl cyanide.

propiono. Propionyl.

propionyl. Propiono. The radical $MeCH_2CO$—, from propionic acid. **p. chloride.** $C_2H_5 \cdot COCl = 92.52$. Propanoyl chloride*, b.80. **p. phenetidine.** Triphenin. **p. salicylic acid.** $C_6H_4(OOC \cdot CH_2Me) \cdot COOH = 194.1$. White scales, m.95, insoluble in water; an antirheumatic.

propiophenone. $MeCH_2COPh = 134.1$. **β-phenyl-** $PhCH_2COPh = 196.09$. Phenyl benzyl ketone, α-benzylacetophenone. Colorless solid, m.60; used in organic synthesis.

proponal. $(C_3H_7)_2C:(CONH)_2:CO = 212.2$. Diisopropylbarbituric acid. Colorless crystals, m.145, soluble in water; a hypnotic. Cf. *propanol*.

proportion. A ratio; a numerical comparison of a part to the whole. **definite-** Proust's law of definite proportions: the same compound always consists of the same elements combined together in the same proportions by weight. **equivalent-** Compounds of elements A and C contain m atoms of A and n atoms of C. Compounds of elements B and C contain x atoms of B and y atoms of C. Compounds of elements A and B contain p atoms of A and q atoms of B. m, n, x, y, and p, q are whole numbers, usually small. Hence p, q equal either m, x or whole multiples of them, usually small. **multiple-** Law of multiple proportions. If 2 elements combine in more than one p., the molecules of one compound must be formed by adding a whole number of atoms of one or both elements to one or more molecules of the other compound. **p. limit.** The least p. of a substance that can be detected in another specified substance.

propoxy. The radical $MeCH_2CH_2O$—, from propanol.

propoxyphene hydrochloride. $C_{22}H_{29}O_2N \cdot HCl = 375.94$. White crystals, m.163, soluble in water; an analgesic (U.S.P.).

propyl. Pr. $MeCH_2CH_2$—. Prop-2-enyl. Propargyl. α-Propyl (Pr^α), normal propyl (n-Pr, or Pr^nO). **iso-** The radical Me_2CH—, from isopropane. β-Propyl (Pr^β). Isomeric propyl (i-Pr or Pr^i).

p. acetate. $MeCOOPr = 102.1$. Colorless liquid, d.0.891, b.102; soluble in water. **p. acetylene.** $PrC:CH = 68.1$. Colorless liquid, b.48, insoluble in water. **p. alcohol.** Propanol.* **p. aldehyde.** Propionic aldehyde. **p. amine.** $C_3H_9N = 59.1$. *normal-* $PrNH_2$. Propaneamine*. Colorless liquid, b.49, soluble in water; a sedative. *iso-* Me_2CHNH_2. b.32, soluble in water. **p. amine hydrochloride.** $PrNH_2 \cdot HCl = 95.6$. Colorless, deliquescent crystals, soluble in water; used medicinally. **p. amine sulfate.** $(PrNH_2)_2 \cdot H_2SO_4 = 216.2$. Colorless crystals, soluble in water; used medicinally. **p. aniline.** $PhNHPr = 135.2$. Colorless liquid, b.222, soluble in water. **p. benzene.** $PhPr = 120.14$. Phenylpropane. Colorless liquid, b.158, insoluble in water. **p. benzoate** $PhCOOPr = 164.2$. Colorless liquid, b.229, sparingly soluble in water. **p. benzoic acid.** $C_6H_4PrCOOH = 164.2$. *ortho-* Colorless leaflets, m.58, soluble in water. *para-* Colorless crystals, m.140, soluble in water. **p. bromide.** $C_3H_7Br = 123.0$. Bromopropane*. Colorless liquid, b.71, soluble in water. **p. butex.** P. hydroxybenzoate. **p. butyrate.** $PrCOOPr = 130.2$. Colorless liquid, b.143, soluble in alcohol. **p. carbamate.** $NH_2-COOPr = 103.1$. Colorless prisms, m.53, soluble in water. **p. carbinol.** 1-Butanol*. **p. carbylamine.** *iso-* $Me_2CHNC = 69.09$. A liquid, b.87. **p. chloride.** $C_3H_7Cl = 78.53$. *normal-* $MeCH_2-CH_2Cl$. 1-Chloropropane*. Colorless liquid, b.46, soluble in water. *iso-* $MeCHClMe$. 2-Chloropropane, secondary, or propyl 2-chloride. Colorless liquid, b.37, soluble in water. **p. cyanide.** $C_4H_7-N = 69.1$. *normal-* $PrCN$. Butyronitrile. Colorless liquid, b.118, soluble in water. *iso-* $Me_2CHCN = 69.1$. A liquid, b.107. **p. ether.** $Pr_2O = 102.1$. Propyl oxide, propoxypropane*. Colorless liquid, b.90.7, soluble in water. *iso-* Isopropyl oxide. Colorless liquid, b.68, insoluble in water; a solvent for gums, waxes, and asphalt. **p. formate.** $HCO-OPr = 88.1$. Colorless liquid, b.81, soluble in water. **p. gallate.** $C_{10}H_{12}O_5 = 212.10$. 3,4,5-Trihydroxybenzoate. White crystals, m.147, slightly soluble in water; a preservative (B.P.) **p. 4-hydroxybenzoate.** $C_{10}H_{12}O_3 = 180.12$. White crystals, m.97, slightly soluble in water; a preservative (B.P.). **p. hydroxylamine.** $C_3H_9-ON = 75.1$. *alpha-* $PrONH_2$. *beta-* $PrNHOH$. **p. iodide.** $C_3H_7I = 170.0$. 1-Iodopropane*. Colorless liquid, d.1.748, b.102, sparingly soluble in water; used in organic synthesis. **p. isocyanide.** *normal-* $PrNC$. *iso-* Me_2CHNC. **p. ketone.** Butyrone. **p. mercaptan.** $PrSH = 76.1$. Hydrosulfopropane, propyl hydrosulfide. Colorless liquid, b.67, soluble in water. **p. nitramine.** $Pr-NHNO_2 = 104.1$. Colorless liquid, b.130, soluble in water. **p. nitrate.** $C_3H_7NO_3 = 105.1$. Colorless liquid, b.119, soluble in alcohol. **p. nitrite.** $C_3H_7NO_2 = 89.1$. Colorless liquid, b.57, soluble in alcohol. **p. nitrolic acid.** $MeCH_2C(NO_2) \cdot NOH = 118.08$. m.74, soluble in water. **p. phenyl ketone.** Butyrophenone. **p. pyridine.** $C_3-H_7 \cdot C_5H_4N = 121.14$. *alpha-* b.166, *beta-* b.158, *gamma-* b.177. **p. sulfide.** $Pr_2S = 118.2$. Propyl thioether, 1-propylthiopropane*. Colorless liquid, b.141, insoluble in water. **p. thiocyanate.** *iso*-$C_3H_7NCS = 101.15$. P. mustard oil, b.137. **p. thioether.** See *p. sulfide*. **p. urea.** $NH_2 \cdot CO \cdot NHPr = 102.1$. Colorless crystals, m.107, soluble in water.

propylen. The radical $CH_3CH:CH—$, from propylene. **p. aldehyde.** Acetonic aldehyde.

propylene. $C_3H_6 = 42.1$. (1) $MeCH:CH_2$. Propene*. A homolog of ethylene and isomer of cyclopropene. Colorless gas, soluble in water. (2) The radical $—CHMe \cdot CH_2—$. Cf. *propylidene*. (3) The radical $CH_2 \cdot CH:CH—$. Cf. *propylen*. **poly-** See *polypropylene*.
p. aldehyde. Crotonaldehyde. **p. bromide.** $C_3H_6Br_2 = 201.89$. 1,2-Dibrompropane*. Colorless liquid, b.131, soluble in water. **p. chloride.** $C_3H_6Cl_2 = 113.0$. 1,2-Dichloropropane*. Colorless liquid, d.1.166, b.97, soluble in water; an insecticidal food fumigant. **p. chlorohydrin.** $C_3H_7ClO = 94.52$. (1) $Me \cdot CHOH \cdot CH_2Cl$. Chloroisopropyl alcohol, 1-chloro-2-propanol*. Colorless liquid, b.126. (2) $Me \cdot CHCl \cdot CH_2OH$. 2-Chloropropyl alcohol. Colorless liquid, b.134. **p. diamine.** Propanediamine*. **p. dichloride.** P. chloride. **p. ether.** $C_3H_6O = 58.06$. A liquid, b.35, soluble in water. **p. glycol.** $C_3H_8O_2 \cdot CH_3 \cdot CHOH \cdot CH_2OH = 76.10$. Propanediol. Colorless, hygroscopic, viscous liquid, d.1.036, b.188, soluble in water; used in hydrophilic ointments (U.S.P., B.P.). **p. oxide.** $C_3H_6O = 58.1$. Propene oxide. *1,2*- $Me \cdot CH(O) \cdot CH_2$. Epoxypropane*. Colorless liquid, m.35, soluble in water. *1,3*- $CH_2:(CH_2)_2:O$. Trimethylene oxide.

propylhexedrine. $C_6H_5CH_2C(Me) \cdot H \cdot NHMe = 155.29$. Colorless liquid, with fishy odor, d.0.849, b.205, soluble in water; an inhalant (U.S.P.).

propylidene. Propilidene. The radical $MeCH_2CH=$, from propane. **p. bromide.** 1,1-Dibrompropane*. **p. chloride.** 1,1-Dichloropropane*.

propyliodone. $C_{10}H_{11}O_3NI_2 = 447.02$. White crystals, m.188, insoluble in water; a contrast medium for bronchography (B.P.).

propyloic- Prefix indicating the radical $—CH_2 \cdot CH_2 \cdot COOH$ on a side chain. Cf. *methyloic-*.

propylparaben. $C_{10}H_{12}O_3 = 180.21$. Propyl *p*-hydroxybenzoate. White powder, m.90, insoluble in water; a fungistatic (U.S.P.).

propylthiouracil. $C_7H_{10}ON_2S = 170.24$. Bitter powder, m.220, slightly soluble in water; a thyroid inhibitor (U.S.P., B.P.).

propynal*. Propiolaldehyde.

propyne*. Allylene. **bromo-*.** Propargyl bromide.

propynoic acid*. Propiolic acid.

propynol*. Propargyl alcohol.

propyrin. Pyrenol.

propytal. 5,5-Propylbarbituric acid.

prorennin. Rennase.

pros- Prefix (Greek) indicating by, near, or at. **p. position.** The 2,3-position of the naphthalene ring.

prosapogenin. $C_{50}H_{80}O_{14}(?)$. A nonsugar hydrolysis product of saponin, decomp. 208, hydrolyzing to endosapogenin.

prosopite. A native, hydrated calcium aluminum fluoride.

prospecting. Searching for ore deposits.

prostaglandins. Non-nitrogenous carboxy acids in body fluids causing vasodilation.

prostaphin. Oxacillin. Common name for sodium-5-methyl-3-phenyl-4-isoxazolylpenicillin; an oral antibiotic.

prostate. A gland at the neck of the male bladder. **p. powder.** Dried, powdered p.

prosthesis. Replacement or substitution.

prosthetic group. (1) A complex protein containing a simple protein; as, the chromophoric group. (2) The group formed by an organic radical not derived from an amino acid, in the complex molecule of a conjugated protein.

Prostigmin. Trademark for neostigmine.

protactinium (preferred usage). Pa = 230. Protoactinium. Brevium. A radioactive disintegration product between uranium and actinium; an isotope of ekatantalum, at. no. 91; the genetic link between the uranium and actinium series. Discovered (1918) by Hahn and Meitner. Half-life 32,000 years.

protagon. $C_{160}H_{303}O_{35}N_5P$. A crystalline substance from red blood corpuscles and brain matter. Cf. *pseudocerebrin*.

protamin. Simple proteins in the sex cells of fishes; as, salmine.

protamine. $C_{16}H_{32}O_2N_9 = 382.35$. An amine from spermatozoa and fish spawn. **p. sulfate.** A heparin antagonist (B.P.), used as an injection and prepared from the sperm of certain fishes.

Protan. Trademark for sodium formate. A masking agent, neutralizer in wool dyeing, and solubilizer and buffer in the chemical industry.

protanope. A dichromat, q.v., insensitive to long wavelengths.

Protargol. Trade name for a compound of silver and albumin. Brown powder (8.3% Ag), soluble in water; a bactericide.

protargyl. Protyle.

proteacin. Leucodrin.

protean. A group of derived proteins, q.v.

protease. An enzyme that splits proteins to proteoses and peptones. **gastric-** Pepsin. **pancreatic-** Erepsin. Trypsin. **vegetable-** Bromelin. Papain.

protective colloid. A covering envelope for colloidal particles, stabilizing them against coagulation by electrolytes. Cf. *cone*.

proteid. Protein (obsolete).

proteidin. An immunizing bacterial solvent developed from complex proteins and bacteriolytic enzymes.

protein(s). Nitrogenous organic compounds, mol. wt. 34,000–200,000, in vegetable and animal matter. P. yield amino acids on hydrolysis and are foods assimilated as amino acids and reconstructed in the protoplasm. Cf. *polypeptide*, *proteinate*, *p. salt*. **alcohol-soluble-** Prolamines. Gliadins. **bacterial-** A toxic p. formed by bacteria. **bitterness-** A muco-p. containing 33% carbohydrate and forming complexes with sugars, mol. wt. 166,000–175,000; responsible for bitter flavors. **coagulated-** A simple p. rendered insoluble by heat or chemical agents. **compound-** Conjugated p. **conjugated-** Complex p. containing a protein and a nonprotein molecule. **defensive-** A p. formed in an organism as a protection against bacteria. See *immunity*. **derived-** A decomposition product of p., in complexity of structure between proteins and amino acids. **gamma-** A mixture: approx. protein 50 (often from soybeans), starch 50%; a paper size.

CLASSIFICATION OF PROTEINS

I. U.S. Usage
  A. Simple Proteins: Substances that yield only
     α-amino acids or their derivatives on hydrol-
     ysis:
     1. Albumins: soluble in water or dilute salt
        solution, and coagulable by heat; as, oval-
        bumin
     2. Globulins: insoluble in water, soluble in
        salt solutions, and coagulated by heat; as,
        edestin from hemp seed
     3. Glutelins: insoluble in neutral solvents,
        soluble in dilute acids or bases, and
        coagulated by heat; as, glutenin
     4. Prolamines (gliadins): soluble in 80%
        alcohol, insoluble in water, absolute
        alcohol, or neutral solvents; as, zein
     5. Albuminoids: insoluble in all neutral
        solvents; as, elastin
     6. Histones: soluble in water, or dilute acids,
        precipitated by ammonia, not coagulated
        by heat; as, globin
     7. Protamines: soluble in water, uncoagulable
        by heat; as, salmine
  B. Conjugated Proteins: Protein combined with
     another (prosthetic) substance:
     1. Nucleoproteins: compounds of one or more
        proteins with a nucleic acid; as, nucleo-
        histones
     2. Glycoproteins: compounds of protein with
        carbohydrates; as, mucins
     3. Phosphoproteins: compounds of proteins
        with a phosphorus compound other than
        lecithin or nucleic acids; as, casein
     4. Chromoproteins (hemoglobins): compounds
        of proteins with a chromophoric group; as,
        hemoglobin
     5. Lecithoproteins: compounds of proteins
        with lecithins
     6. Lipoproteins: compounds of proteins with
        fatty acids

I. U.S. Usage (*continued*)
  C. Derived Proteins: Primary and secondary
     split products of proteins:
     1. Proteans: insoluble products from the
        action of water or enzymes; as, myo-
        san
     2. Metaproteins: from the action of acids or
        bases
     3. Coagulated proteins: from the action of
        heat or alcohol
     4. Proteoses: from further hydrolysis; soluble
        in water, not coagulated by heat, and
        precipitated in saturated solution by
        ammonium or zinc sulfate
     5. Peptones: soluble in water, noncoagulable
        by heat, not precipitated by ammonium
        sulfate
     6. Peptides: compounds of amino acids con-
        taining peptide groups
II. U.K. Usage (References in parentheses are to
    U.S. usage)
  A. Simple Proteins:
     1. Protamins (*A*7)
     2. Histones (*A*6)
     3. Albumins (*A*1)
     4. Globulins (*A*2)
     5. Glutelins (*A*3)
     6. Alcohol-soluble proteins (*A*4)
     7. Scleroproteins (*A*5)
     8. Phosphoproteins (*B*3)
  B. Conjugated Proteins:
     1. Glucoproteins (*B*2)
     2. Nucleoproteins (*B*1)
     3. Chromoproteins (*B*4)
  C. Hydrolysis Products:
     1. Infraproteins (*C*2)
     2. Proteoses (*C*4)
     3. Peptones (*C*5)
     4. Polypeptides (*C*6)

---

hemo- Hemoglobin p. **purified-p. derivative.**
P.P.D. Official name for purified tuberculin p., by
growing a pure culture of tubercule bacilli on a p.
medium. **synthetic-** See *polypeptide.* **X-** A globulin-
type p. in blood serum having a low sedimentation
rate; of physiological importance in lipid transport.
  p. error. A change in the color of an acid-base
indicator due to the amphoteric nature of p. present.
p. salt. A compound of a p. with an acid; as,
casein hydrochloride. Cf. *proteinate.*
proteinase. An enzyme that hydrolyzes proteins.
  acid- Pepsin. **alkali-** Trypsin.
proteinate. A compound formed from a protein and
a base; as, sodium caseinate. Cf. *protein salt.*
proteoclastic. Proteolytic.
proteolysis. The conversion of proteins into soluble
peptones by decomposition or hydrolysis.
proteolytic. Proteoclastic.
proteoses. A group of derived proteins, q.v.
protheite. A variety of pyroxene.
prothesis. The replacement of human organs by
synthetic materials, e.g., in plastic surgery.
prothrombin. A factor in blood plasma responsible
for the clotting of blood. Cf. *menaphthone.*

protiodide. An iodide that contains the minimum
amount of iodine. Cf. *biniodide.*
protista. The most primitive forms of life: single-cell
organisms, part plant, part animal in nature.
protistology. The study of unicellular organisms.
protium. The hydrogen isotope, mass 1.0. Cf.
deuterium, tritium.
proto- Prefix (Greek) indicating first. **p. salt.**
A compound that contains the smallest amount of
the negative radicals or atoms of the same positive
element; as, HgI, mercurous iodide or mercury
protoiodide (obsolete).
protoactinium. Protactinium (preferred usage).
protobastite. A variety of enstatite.
protobitumen. A partially reduced carbohydrate,
which on further reduction yields oil; as, algarose
(synthetic) and algarite (natural).
protocatechol. (1) Catechol. (2) Pyrocatechol.
protocatechualdehyde. $C_6H_3(OH)_2CHO$ = 138.1.
Dihydroxybenzaldehyde, dihydroxybenzenecar-
bonal*, protocatechoic aldehyde. Colorless leaflets, m.153, soluble in water. **methyl-** Vanillin.
methylene- Piperonylic acid.
protocatechuic acid. $C_6H_3(OH)_2COOH$ = 154.03.

3,4-Dihydroxybenzoic acid, from the oil of shepherd's purse. Colorless crystals, decomp. 199, soluble in water; a photographic developer. **p. alcohol.** Protocatechuyl alcohol. **p. aldehyde.** Protocatechualdehyde.

protochloride. A compound containing less chlorine than normal (obsolete).

protocotoin. $C_{16}H_{14}O_6 = 302.2$. A principle from paracoto bark. Cf. *cotein.*

protocurarine. An alkaloid from curare.

protofluorine. An element, at. wt. 2.1, assumed to exist in nebulae, and between hydrogen and helium in the periodic table. Cf. *coronium, nebulium.*

protohydrogen. An element, assumed to exist in bright stars and nebulae, of atomic weight less than that of hydrogen.

protolysis. A reaction in which a proton is transferred from an acid to a base.

protomorph. A particulate substance in cellular juices; an intermediate state between the organized cell and the disorganized juice.

proton. Prouton, uron. (1) Originally the positive nucleus, q.v., of an atom (Rutherford, Bohr). (2) The nucleus of the H atom, e.g., the hydrogen ion, H^+. (3) A particle of mass one and one positive charge; spin $\frac{1}{2}$; magnetic moment 2.8 nuclear electrons; a "building stone" of atomic nuclei. Thus, a *proton* and *electron* in immediate contact make a *neutron*; if at a distance equal to that of the electron radius, a *photon*. **anti-** Negative-p. The analog of the positron, produced by collision of high-velocity p. with a copper target.
   p. acceptor. A substance that gains a hydrogen ion; as, a base. **p. bombardment.** The production by fast-moving protons of an excited isotope which yields γ rays. Cf. *radioactivity.* **p. donor.** A substance yielding a hydrogen ion; as an acid. **p. number.** The whole-numbered isotopic weight, assumed to be the number of hydrogen nuclei or protons and neutrons. Cf. *atomic structure.* **p. reaction.** (1) Neutralization. Cf. *prototropy.* (2) Nuclear reactions.

protones. A group of hydrolyzed products of protamines.

protophile. A weak base which unites with a proton. Cf. *acid* (3).

protophilia. Hydrophilia. The tendency of a molecule to unite with hydrogen ions (protons). See *hydrogenium ions.*

protophyllin. Chlorophyll hydride, a colorless substance that changes to green chlorophyll by the action of carbon dioxide.

protophyta. A single-celled plant; as, yeasts. Cf. *diatoms.*

protopine. $C_{20}H_{19}O_5N = 353.2$. Macleyine, fumarine. An alkaloid from opium, chelidonium, and corydalis species. Colorless crystals, m.207.

protoplasm. Protoplasma bioplasm. A viscid colloidal material, the physical basis of all life. Living p. consists of an interreacting system of proteins, fats, and carbohydrates, as a gel, with water as the continuous phase, in which occur a network (spongioplasm); a more fluid portion (hyaloplasm); a nucleus with nucleoplasm, chromatin, and linin. See *cell, micelle, paraplasm.*

protoplasma. Protoplasm.

protoporphyrin. A constituent of hemoglobin and the brown pigment of eggshells, having a nucleus of 4 pyrrole rings. Cf. *phylloporphyrin.*

protoproduct. A diesel fuel obtained from wood waste by "controlled internal combustion."

protosal. $C_{11}H_{12}O_6 = 240.1$. Glycerin salicylic formic ester. Colorless oil, d.1.344, insoluble in water; an antirheumatic.

protosubstance. The gel-forming constituent of natural petrolatum, of unknown chemical composition.

protosulfate. A sulfate containing the smallest amount of SO_4 radical.

prototropic. Pertaining to reactions influenced by protons.

prototropy. Pseudoacidity, mobile H-tautomerism, mobile proton tautomerism. Ionotropy in which a detached H atom causes a molecule to exist as tautomeric ions. Cf. *aci-, anionotropy, pseudomolecule.*

prototype. An original type, model, or measure: e.g., the international *meter.*

protoveratrine. $C_{32}H_{51}O_{11}N = 625.5$. An alkaloid, m.247, from the rhizome of *Veratrum album* (Liliaceae); physiologically more active than veratrine.

protovitamin. A precursor to a vitamin. **p.A.** Carotene. See β-carotene oxide, *mutatochrome.* **p.D.** Sterols, e.g., ergosterol, converted into vitamin D by exposure to ultraviolet or cathode rays. **p.D₃.** See 7-dehydrocholesterol. Cf. β-carotene.

protoxide. That oxide of a metal containing the least number of O atoms.

protozoon. (Pl. protozoa.) A unicellular animal: the lowest class of the animal kingdom; as, ameba. Cf. *protophyta.*

protractor. An instrument to measure angles.

protuberance. A projecting part. **solar-** The giant streamers of incandescent gases on the sun's surface. Cf. *coronium, corona.*

protyl. Propargyl. The radical —$CH_2 \cdot C : CH$.

protyle. Archyl, protargyl, pantogen, urstoff. The hypothetical substance from which all chemical elements are derived.

Proust, Louis Joseph. 1755–1826. French chemist. **P.'s law.** The law of constant *proportions.*

proustite. Ag_3AsS_3. Ruby silver. Native, red hexagons.

Prout, William. 1785–1850. English physician. **P. hypothesis** (1815). All elements are multiples of a protyle or of hydrogen. Cf. *atomic structure, radioelements.*

prouton. Suggested name for proton.

proxam. Common name for isopropyl xanthate. **sodium-** $S \cdot C \cdot (SNa) \cdot (OCHMe)_2$. A herbicide.

proximate. The nearest approach. **p. analysis.** Quantitative analysis rationally interpreted. **p principle.** The active principle of a drug; as an alkaloid.

prozane. Triazane(2).

prulaurasin. $C_{14}H_{17}NO_6 = 295.19$. A racemic mandelonitrile glucoside, m.122, from cherry laurel, *Prunus laurocerasus.*

prunasin. $C_{14}H_{17}NO_6 = 295.19$. A d-mandelonitrile glucoside, m.147, from *Prunus padus.*

prune. Prunus. The partly dried fruit of *Prunus domestica* (Rosaceae); a food and mild laxative.

prunetol. Genistein.

prunicyanin. An anthocyanin from plums.

prunol. Ursolic acid.

prunus. Prune. **p. amygdalus.** Almond. **p. domestica.** Prune. **p. spinosa.** Blackthorn. **p. virginiana.** Wild cherry.

prussian blue. Complex salts formed by oxidation of the white precipitate obtained from solutions of ferrous sulfate and potassium ferrocyanide. A blue coloring for inks and paper. **insoluble-** Turnbull's blue. **native-** Vivianite. **α-soluble-** $4FeK[Fe(CN)_6]\cdot7H_2O$. True b. plue, α-potassium ferric ferrocyanide. Blue powder, a colloidal solution with water. **β-soluble-** β-Potassium ferric ferrocyanide. $FeK[Fe(CN)_6]\cdot H_2O$. **x-soluble-** A stabler β variety. Cf. *milori blue*.

prussian red. Colcothar.

prussiate. (1) Cyanide. (2) Ferrocyanide. (3) Ferricyanide. **red-** Potassium ferricyanide. **yellow-** Potassium ferrocyanide.

prussic acid. Hydrocyanic acid.

prussine. Cyanogen.

ps. Abbreviation for pseudo.

pseud-, pseudo- *ps-* or *ψ-*. Prefix (Greek) indicating false or similar to. Indicating derivation from a hypothetical parent substance or tautomeric form (Baeyer).

pseudacetic acid. Propionic acid.

pseudaconitine. $C_{36}H_{51}O_{12}N = 689.4$. Acetylveratryl-ψ-aconine. A crystalline alkaloid, m.211, from *Aconitum ferox*.

pseudo acid. (1) An organic compound that forms salts, but has no carboxyl radical. The acid character is due to a hydroxyl group attached to an N atom; as, isonitroso compounds, $R\cdot CHN(:O)O^-$. (2) The hydroxy form of an acid; as, $O:Pt(OH)_2$. Cf. *prototropy*.

pseudoaconitine. Pseudaconitine.

pseudoallyl. Isopropenyl.

pseudoalum. $MAl_2(SO_4)_4\cdot24H_2O$, where M is divalent as Mn, Fe = Mg. Cf. true *alum*.

pseudoasymmetry. Optical isomerism in which a C atom becomes asymmetric, owing to the presence of *d*- and *l*-asymmetric groups; as,

$$l\text{-}x \diagdown \quad \diagup A$$
$$\qquad C$$
$$d\text{-}x \diagup \quad \diagdown B$$

pseudobase. An organic compound that becomes basic in presence of acids. Cf. *amphoteric*.

pseudobrookite. $2Fe_2O_3\cdot3TiO_3$. A vitreous mineral.

pseudobutylene. 2-Butene*.

pseudocellulose. Hemicellulose.

pseudocholestene. $C_{27}H_{46} = 370.4$. The hydrocarbon corresponding with allocholesterol.

pseudoconhydrine. See *conhydrine*.

pseudocumene. $C_6H_3Me_3 = 120.14$. Cumol, *asym*- or 1,2,4-trimethylbenzene. Colorless liquid, b.170, insoluble in water. **hexahydro-** See *hexahydrocumene*.

pseudocumidine. $C_6H_2(NH_2)Me_3 = 135.2$. 2,4,5-Trimethylaniline, 1-amino-2,4,5-trimethylbenzene. Colorless needles, m.66, soluble in water.

pseudocumyl. The radical, $Me_3C_6H_2$—, from pseudocumene; as, *asym*- or 2,3,5-; *sym*- or 2,4,5; *vic*- or 2,3,6-.

pseudocurarine. A nonpoisonous alkaloid in *Nerium oleander* (Apocynaceae).

pseudocyanate. A compound having the radical —ONC. Cf. *fulminate*.

pseudocyanic acid. The acid HONC. Cf. *pseudoisocyanic acid*.

pseudodichroism. Pseudopolychroism.

pseudogalena. Sphalerite.

pseudoindoxyl. See *indoxyl*.

pseudoindyl. C_8H_6N—. Isomeric (7) radicals, from pseudoindole.

pseudoisatin. Isatin.

pseudoisocyanic acid. The acid HOCN. Cf. *pseudocyanic acid*.

pseudoisomerism. Isomerism between 2 molecules containing the same number and kind of atoms, but having different atomic linkages and valencies; as, cyanide and isocyanide. See *isomerism*.

pseudoisotope. A radioactive element resembling an isotope in its reactions, but having a different atomic number.

pseudomalachite. See *malachite*.

pseudomerism. Dynamic isomerism, in which a molecule reacts under different conditions according to one or another of its isomeric structures.

pseudomonads. Motile, gram-negative rod organisms from soil and food, giving a positive oxidase test and often forming pigment. They decompose food and pharmaceuticals.

pseudomonotropy. Allotropy in which the transition temperature is below the melting point.

pseudomorph. A crystal having the general outline of one crystal system, but actually an aggregation of minute crystals of another system. **chemical-** A p. produced by chemical substitution or alteration. **physical-** A p. produced by a change in allotropic form.

pseudonarcissine. An alkaloid from the bulbs of *Narcissus pseudonarcissus* (Amarylladaceae).

pseudonitrol. $R_2\cdot C(NO)\cdot(NO_2)$.

pseudonitrosite. Organic nitronitroso compounds in which the 2 radicals are attached to different C atoms: —C(NO)—C(NO₂)—. Cf. *nitrols*.

pseudonuclein. Nucleoalbumin.

pseudopelletierine. $C_9H_{15}NO\cdot2H_2O = 189.16$. N-Methylgranatanine. An alkaloid from the root of the pomegranate. Prisms, m.48, soluble in water. Cf. *pelletierine*.

pseudophenanthroline. 4,7-Naphthisodiazine.

pseudophysostigmine. $C_{15}H_{21}O_3N_2 = 277.19$. An alkaloid from calinuts or false calabar beans. White crystals, soluble in alcohol.

pseudopolychroism. See *polychromatic*.

pseudoraceme. A crystal composed of equal mixtures of dextro and levo compounds.

pseudosolution. A colloidal suspension or emulsion.

pseudotannin. Tannin split products unable to convert hide into leather.

pseudotropine. See *tropine*.

pseudoviscosity. See *viscosity*.

pseudowavellite. A hydrous calcium-aluminum phosphate (Florida) containing 8–9% phosphorus pentoxide and sand; a fertilizer.

pseudoxanthine. (1) An isomer of xanthine. (2) A leucomaine from muscle tissue, resembling xanthine in properties but not composition.

pseudozoogloea. A clump of living bacteria resembling a protozoon microscopically.

psi. Greek letter ψ, Ψ. (1) Symbol for: (a) pseudo; (b) specific function, or the electric field in Schrödinger's atom. (2) Abbreviation for pounds per square inch.

psicaine. $(COOH \cdot CHOH)_2 NMe \cdot C_7 H_{10}(COOMe)O \cdot OPh$ = 453.23. d-ψ-Cocaine bitartrate. White crystals, soluble in water; a local anesthetic.

psilomelane. $(Ba \cdot H_2 O)_2 Mn_5 O_{10}$. A hydrated pyrolusite (Saxony, Germany).

psoraline. Caffeine.

PSP. Phenolsulfonephthalein.

psychedelic. A mind-expanding drug; as LSD.

psychomimetic. Describing drugs that produce hallucinations.

psychotrine. $C_{28}H_{36}O_4N_2$ = 464.4. An alkaloid in ipecac.

psychrometer. See *hygrometer.* **sling-** Whirling hygrometer, q.v.

psychrometric chart. A chart showing the drying temperature plotted against the weight of water vapor removed per unit weight of dry air.

psychrophilic. Describing organisms of optimum growth at temperature 4–10°C. Cf. *mesophilic.*

psylla alcohol. Psyllic alcohol. **p. wax.** A solid wax from the leaf louse, *Psylla alni.*

psyllic acid. $C_{32}H_{65}COOH$ = 492.51. Psyllostearylic acid, m.95, from psylla wax. Cf. *lacceroic acid.* **p. alcohol.** $C_{33}H_{67}OH$ = 480.53. Psyllostearyl alcohol, m.70, from psylla and beeswax.

psyllostearyl alcohol. Psyllic alcohol.

psyllostearylic acid. Psyllic acid.

pt. Abbreviation for: (1) pint; (2) part.

pteridine. $C_6 H_4 N_4$ = 132.11. A diaminopyrimidine derivative. Yellow plates, m.140, soluble in water (violet fluorescence).

Pteridophyta. A main division of Cryptogamia, as Filices (ferns), Equisetaceae (horsetails), Lycopodiaceae (club mosses).

pterin. A yellow purine pigment from mammalian tissues. Cf. *rhodopterin.*

pterocarpine. An alkaloid from red sandalwood, *Pterocarpus santalidus* (Leguminosae).

pterygospermin. The antibacterial principle from *Moringa pterygosperma*, Gaertn.

pteryolglutamic acid. Folic acid.

ptomaine. Animal, cadaveric, or putrefactive alkaloid. Amino compounds that result from the decomposition of proteins by microorganisms; e.g.: aminovaleric acid (meat), cadaverine (animal tissues), diethylamine (fish), morrhuic acid (cod-liver oil), mydine (human tissue), tetanine (cultures of tetanus bacillus), tyrotoxicone (dairy foods).

ptyalase. Salivary amylase, ptyalin, salivin. Hydrolyzes starch to dextrin, maltose, and glucose; sucrose to dextrose and levulose. Cf. *amylase, diastase.* **p. unit.** The quantity of p. that will digest 1 gm starch at 37°C in 30 min at pH 6.7, in presence of 0.05% sodium chloride.

ptyalin. Ptyalase.

Pu. Symbol for plutonium.

puberonic acid. Puberulonic acid.

puberulic acid. $C_8 H_6 O_6$ = 198.0. An antibiotic. Colorless crystals, m.317.

puberulonic acid. $C_9 H_4 O_7$ = 224.04. An antibiotic from *Penicillium puberulum.* Yellow prisms, m.298.

pucherite. $BiVO_4$. A mineral.

puchiin. A specific antibiotic from the tubers of the Chinese water chestnut, *Eleocharis tuberosa.*

puddle, puddling. (1) The conversion of cast iron into wrought iron by fusion in a reverberatory furnace, in contact with the haematite lining of the furnace,

where oxidation of carbon to carbon monoxide occurs. (2) Clay, moistened and well-worked.

puering. Bating. The cleaning of depilated leather hides, by the action of tryptic enzymes.

pukateine. $C_{17}H_{17}O_3N$ = 283.3. An aporphine alkaloid found in *Laurelia novae zealandiae.* Cf. *laureline.*

pulegium. The Labiatae *Hedeoma pulegoides* (American p.) and *Menthae pulegium* (European p.).

pulegol. $C_{10}H_{18}O$ = 154.2. 3-Menthenol. An aromatic alcohol in the essential oils of *Mentha pulegium* (Labiatae).

pulegone. $C_{10}H_{16}O$ = 152.2. 3-$\Delta^{4(8)}$-Menthenone. An aromatic ketone in oil of hedeoma. Colorless liquid, d.0.932, b.221, insoluble in water; causes fatty infiltration of liver, heart, and kidney.

Pulfrich refractometer. A refractometer, especially for oils and fats.

pulmoform. $CH_2(C_6H_3 \cdot OMe \cdot OH)_2$ = 260.0. Methylenediguaiacol. Yellow powder, insoluble in water; an antiseptic.

pulmones sicci. The dried and powdered lungs of animals, used medicinally.

pulp. Any soft mixture of solid particles and liquids as, *paper pulp.*

pulpwood. A raw material for paper manufacture, generally debarked conifer trunks.

pulque. The fermented sap of an *Agave* species (Mexico). Cf. *mescal.*

pulsatilla. Pasque flower. The dried herb of *Anemone pulsatilla* (Ranunculaceae); an alterative and sedative.

pulse. The edible seeds of leguminous plants; as, peas.

pulverization. The reduction of a substance to a powder.

pulverizing. Powdering.

pulvic acid. $C_{18}H_{12}O_5$ = 308.1. The monolactone of diphenylketipic acid. Colorless crystals, m.214. Cf. *pulvinic acid.*

pulvinate. (1) Convex- or cushion-shaped; as a colony of bacteria. (2) A salt of pulvinic acid.

pulvinic acid. $C_{18}H_{12}O_5$ = 308.1. 2,3-Dihydroxy-1,4-diphenylmuconic acid γ-lactone. Cf. *pulvic acid.* **p,p'-dihydroxy-** Atromentin.

pulvis. Latin for powder.

pumice (stone). A light porous stone of volcanic origin, which consists of the silicates of aluminum, sodium, and potassium; an abrasive and catalyst base.

pump. A machine for drawing or forcing liquids or gases from one container or level into another. **acid-** See *acid.* **air-** See *air.* **backing-** A low-power p. to produce a partial vacuum in preparation for a high-power p. **filter-** A low-power p. operated by a water faucet. **Hickmann-** See *vacuum p.* **mercury-** See *Sprengel p.* **suction-** Filter p. **Töpler-** A p. that removes air by entrainment between drops of mercury falling in a tube. **vacuum-** See *vacuum.*

pumpkin seed. Pepo. The seeds of varieties of *Cucurbita pepo*; an anthelmintic.

punctiform. Describing a bacterial colony, near the limit of natural vision.

pungent. Sharp or biting, as a p. odor.

punicic acid. $C_{18}H_{32}O_2$ = 280.27. An isomer of eleostearic acid, m.44, from the seed oil of *Punica granatum*, pomegranate (Punicaceae).

punicine. (1) Pelletierine. (2) A purple oxidation product of colorless shellfish juices.

pure. Free from contamination. **bacteriologically-** Containing no live bacteria. **chemically-** Containing no other substance. Cf. *chemicals*.

purgatin. Purgatol.

purgative. An agent that causes the evacuation of the bowels; as, castor oil.

purgatol. $C_{14}H_5O_2(OH)(C_2H_3O_2)_2 = 340.1$. Purgatin, anthrapurpurin diacetate. Orange crystals, m.177, insoluble in water; a purgative.

purine.

$$\begin{array}{c} 1 \quad 2 \\ N{-}CH \\ 6 \ HC \diagdown \quad \diagup N\ 7 \\ C{=}C \\ = 120.1. \\ 3\ HN \diagup \quad \diagdown N\ 9 \\ CH \\ 8 \end{array}$$

Colorless needles, m.212, soluble in water. **endogenous-** q.v. **exogenous-** q.v. **p. alkaloids.** Purine bases. **p. bases.** The alkaloids derived from purine; as, theobromine, caffeine. **p. body.** A compound derived from purine by the substitution of its H atoms; as, 2,6-dioxypurine (xanthine), 2,6,8-trioxypurine (uric acid). Many p. bodies are hydrolytic products of nucleoproteins, and occur in animal waste products. **p. dione.** Xanthine. **p. ring.** The heterocyclic arrangement of the atoms in the molecule of purine, q.v. **p. skeleton.** The p. ring. **p. trione.** Uric acid.

Purinethol. Trademark for mercaptopurine.

purinometer. A small buret with a glass stopcock having a closed bore to form a small compartment; for estimating purine bodies in urine.

purinone. Hypoxanthine.

Purkinje (Purkyně), Jan Evangelista. 1787–1869. Czech physiologist. **P. effect.** Optical sensation increases with increasing intensity of light more rapidly for the red than for other spectral colors.

purone. $C_5H_8O_2N_4 = 156.1$. 2,8-Dioxy-1,4,5,6-tetrahydropurine. A reduction product of uric acid produced by electrolysis.

purple. A reddish blue coloring matter of the purple snail. **antique-** 6,6′-Dibromoindigo. A blue vat dye. **tyrian-** Murex. **visual-** The photosensitive material of the retinal rods of the eye. It sensitizes the eye to dim light, and contains vitamin A. Cf. *rhodopsin*.

p. carmine. Murexide. **p. of cassius.** Red, colloidal tin oxide with adsorbed gold, formed on adding alkali to a mixture of solutions of stannous, stannic, and gold chlorides; used in the manufacture of ruby glass and red enamels. **p. copper.** Bornite.

purpureo. Describing metal amines of tetra-, tri-, or bivalent metals with NH_3 molecules and negative radicals; as, chloropentammine, $[Co(NH_3)_5 X]X_2$; and chlorotetrammine, $[Co(NH_3)_4X_2]X$, where X is a halogen or other negative radical. There are also double salts; as, chloropentammine cobaltinitrate, $[Co_2(NH_3)_{10}Cl_2](NO_3)_4$.

pupuric acid. $C_8H_4N_5O_6 = 266.2$. An oxidation product of uric acid, related to alloxantin. Cf. *murexide*.

purpurin. $C_{14}H_8O_5 = 256.1$. Trihydrooxyanthraquinone, oxalizarin 6, 1,2,4-trihydroxy-5,10-dioxyanthracene, from the glucoside of madder, or obtained synthetically. Red needles, m.256 (de-

comp.), soluble in water. **anthra-** See *anthrapurpurin*. **flavo-** See *flavopurpurin*.

purpurogallin. $C_{11}H_8O_5 = 220.07$. A tetrahydroxy constituent or hydrolysis product (with glucose) of many galls. See *dryophantin*, *eriophyesin*, *pontanin*.

purpuroxanthene. Xanthopurpurin.

purpuroxanthic acid. $C_{15}H_8O_6$. A substance in madder.

purree. *Indian* yellow.

purreic acid. (1) $C_{19}H_{16}O_{10}\cdot3H_2O = 458.2$. A monobasic acid from Indian yellow. Yellow crystals of first sweet, later bitter, taste, soluble in water. (2) Euxanthic acid.

purrenone. Euxanthone.

purrone. Euxanthone.

pus. A liquid from infected wounds, consisting of leukocytes with microorganisms and serum. **blue-** Blue p. produced by the *Bacillus pyocyaneus*. Cf. *cyopin*.

pustulant. An agent that produces small inflammations of the skin (pustules); as, croton oil. Cf. *vesicant*.

putrefaction. Putrescence. The progressive chemical decomposition of organic matter, especially proteins, generally by anaerobic bacteria. See *decay*.

putrefactive alkaloids. Ptomaines.

putrescence. Putrefaction.

putrescent. Undergoing putrefaction.

putrescine. $NH_2CH_2\cdot CH_2\cdot CH_2\cdot CH_2NH_2 = 88.1$. Tetramethylenediamine, butylenediamine, 1,4-butanediamine*. A ptomaine from the decay of animal tissues and the action of certain bacteria. Colorless liquid with unpleasant odor.

putrid. Putrefactive.

putrine. $C_{16}H_{21}N_2O_3 = 234.2$. A base in putrid pancreas.

putty. A mixture: chalk 11, raw linseed oil 3, with or without basic lead carbonate 5 pts.; used for setting glass and filling holes and cracks. **iron-** See *iron*. **p. powder.** A polishing powder made by heating tin in air, removing the dross, and igniting the product of the action of nitric acid on the residue; used in white enamel and opal glass.

puzzolane. A native, silicate-rich, lime-poor cement (Puzzuoli, Italy); used by the Romans. Cf. *pozzolana*.

PVA. Abbreviation for polyvinyl alcohol (or acetate) plastics.

PVC. Abbreviation for polyvinyl chloride. See *plastics*.

pwt. Abbreviation for pennyweight. See *troy* measure.

Py. Abbreviation for the pyridine ring.

pycazide. Isoniazid.

pycnometer. Pyknometer.

pycnosis. The agglomeration by colchicine of the chromatin constituents of leukocytes.

pydine. $C_7H_{13}NO = 127.1$. A bicyclic combined piperidine and pyrane ring:

$$\begin{array}{c} 1 \\ 8\ CH_2{-}CH{-}CH_2\ 2 \\ |\quad\quad |\quad\quad | \\ 7\ NH\quad CH_2\quad O\quad 3 \\ |\quad\quad |\quad\quad | \\ 6\ CH_2{-}CH{-}CH_2\ 4 \\ 5 \end{array}$$

pyelectan. Iodoxyl.

pyelography. A branch of radiography in which organs are made opaque to X rays. See *radiopaque.*

pyelosil. Diodone injection.

pyknometer. A graduated glass vessel of definite volume with a glass stopcock, with or without a thermometer, used to weigh a definite volume of liquid in order to determine its specific gravity, W/V, where W = weight, V = volume.

pylumbrin. Diodone injection.

pyo- Prefix (Greek) indicating pus.

pyoctanin. Pyoktanin.

pyocyanase. A mixture of antibiotics produced by the growth of *Bacillus pyocyaneus*; to treat anthrax and diphtheria.

pyocyanin(e). A blue antibiotic pigment from *Pseudomonas aeruginosa.*

pyogenic. A microorganism that produces pus, especially in wounds.

pyogenin. $C_{16}H_{128}O_{19}N_2(?)$. A substance from pus cells.

pyoktanin. Dahlia violet. Methyl violet, methyl aniline violet; an antiseptic **p. blue.** Methyl violet. **p. yellow.** Auramine.

pyoluene. $C_5H_9O_2SN = 133.2$. Oxymethyl allyl sulfocarbamide; a bactericide.

pyosin. $C_{57}H_{110}O_{15}N_2(?)$. A protein from pus cells, m.238.

pyr- See *pyro-.*

pyracetic acid. Pyroligneous acid.

pyracin. A lactone of an acid produced from pyridoxin, in α and β forms. It prevents anemia in chicks.

pyraconitine. $C_{32}H_{41}NO_9 = 583.32$. An alkaloid, m.171, from aconite.

pyramid. A polyhedron whose base is a polygon and whose faces are triangles, with a common vertex and the sides of the polygon as bases. Cf. *crystal systems.*

Pyramidon. $C_{13}H_{17}ON_2 = 217.2$. Trademark for dimethylaminoantipyrine, 1-phenyl-2,3-dimethyl-4-dimethylamino-5-pyrazolone, amidopyridine. Colorless crystals, m.108, sparingly soluble in water; an antipyretic. The α and β forms have different solubilities.

pyran. $C_5H_6O = 82.1$. The group of compounds:

benzo- See *benzopyran.* **dibenzo-** See *dibenzopyran.*
diketo- Glutaconic anhydride. **keto-** Pyrone.
naphtho- See *naphthopyrane.*
　　p. dione. Glutaconic anhydride.

pyranil black. A black sulfur dye.

Pyranol. (1) Trademark for dielectric material, principally of the askarel type. (2) (not cap.) Sodium acetyl salicylate. (3) (not cap.) Chlorinated diphenyl.

pyranone. Pyrone.

pyranose. The cyclic form of glucose, e.g.:

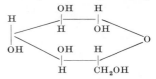

pyranoside. A glucoside having a pyran ring; as, adenosine. Cf. *furanoside.*

pyranthrene. $C_{30}H_{16} = 376.2$.

pyrantin. $EtO\cdot C_6H_4\cdot N(COCH_2)_2 = 219.2$. *p*-Ethoxyphenylsuccinimide, phenosuccin. Colorless needles, m.155, soluble in water; an antipyretic.

pyranyl. A group of radicals: C_5H_5O-, from pyran.

pyrargyrite. $3Ag_2S\cdot Sb_2S_3$. Acrosite, aerosite. A red ore.

pyrathiazine hydrochloride. $C_{18}H_{20}N_2S\cdot HCl = 332.90$. White powder, darkening in light, m.200, soluble in water; an antihistaminic (U.S.P.).

pyrazine. $CH\cdot CH\cdot N\colon CH\cdot CH\colon N = 80.1$. Paradiazine, piazine, 1,4-diazine, q.v. An isomer of pyrimidine and pyridazine. Colorless crystals, m.47, soluble in water. **dimethyl-** Ketine. **hexahydro-** Piperazine. **tetraphenyl-** Amaron.

pyrazole. $CH\colon CH\cdot NH\colon CH = 68.1$. α-Pyrromonazole-1,2-diazole. Colorless needles, m.70, soluble in water. **dihydro-** Pyrazoline. **iso-** 1,2-Isodiazole. **tetrahydro-** Pyrazolidine.

pyrazolidine. $C_3H_8N_2 = 72.1$. Tetrahydropyrazole. Does not occur in the free state. **keto-** Pyrazolidine. **phenyl-** N-Phenylpyrazolidine. Colorless liquid, b.160.

pyrazoline. (1) $CH\colon N\cdot NH\cdot CH_2\cdot CH_2 = 70.1$. Dihydropyrazole. Colorless liquid, b.144, soluble in water. (2) Antipyrine. **keto-** Pyrazolone.

pyrazolinium. A pyrazoline with pentavalent nitrogen.

pyrazolones. $C_3H_6ON_2 = 84.13$. Ketopyrazolines.

3-　NH·NH·CO·CH:CH

4-　NH·N:CH·CO·CH₂

5-　NH·N:CH·CH₂·CO

5- Solid, m.165 (sublimes), soluble in water.
iodomethylphenyl- Midrol. **3-methyl-** Butyrolactazam. **phenyldimethyl-** Antipyrine. **phenyldimethyl-5-salicylate-** Salipyrine. **phenyldimethyl-4-amidomethane sulfonate-** Melubrin. **phenyldimethylamino-** Pyramidone.

pyrazolyl. The radical $C_3H_3N_2$—, from pyrazole; 4 isomers.

Pyrene. (1) Trade name for a carbon tetrachloride fire extinguisher. Cf. *Pyrex.* (2) (not cap.) $C_{16}H_{10} = 202.2$. Benzo[def]phenanthrene. A tetracyclic hydrocarbon from coal tar:

Colorless monoclinic crystals, m.148, insoluble in water.

pyreneite. A grayish black andralite. Cf. *iron garnet.*

pyrenite. Tetryl.

pyrenoids. Large, spherical structures in the chloroplasts of certain algae.

pyrenol. Pyrenum, propyrin, sodium thymol benzoate. A mixture of thymol with sodium benzoate and salicylate. White crystals, soluble in water; an expectorant, antispasmodic, antipyretic, and antineuralgic.

pyrenum. Pyrenol.

pyrethrin. Dalmatian flowers. Insect flowers. Persian flowers. The active principle of pyrethrum: **p.I.** The chrysanthemin monocarboxylic ester of pyrethrolone. **p.II.** The chrysanthemin dicarboxylicmonomethyl ester of pyretholone.

pyrethrol. $C_{21}H_{34}O = 302.3$. Pyretol. An alcohol from the leaves of *Chrysanthemum cinerariaefolium* (insect powder). White needles, m.222, insoluble in water.

pyrethrolone. A complex mixture of keto alcohols, whose esters are the active principles of pyrethrum flowers.

pyrethrone. A ketone from pyrethrum, which forms pyrethrol.

pyrethrum. (1) Insect powder. (2) Pellitory root. The dried root of *Anacyclus pyrethrum* (Compositae); local irritant. Active principles: pyrethrins I and II and cinerins I and II. **p. camphor.** $C_{10}H_{16}O = 152.1$. A terpene from the essential oil of *Chrysanthemum parthenium* (Compositae). **p. extract.** An extract of p. containing 25 % by weight of pyrethrin, with petroleum as diluent. See *synergism.*

pyretol. Pyrethrol.

Pyrex. (1) Trademark for a variety of chemical, cooking, and other glassware, including low-expansion, heat-resistant or chemically resistant glasses. **P.EC.** P. glass permanently bonded with a thin, transparent, electrically conducting metal film, used to heat the glass. (2) Trade name for a carbon tetrachloride fire extinguisher. Cf. *Pyrene.*

pyridazine. $CH:CHN:NCH:CH = 80.05$. 1,2- or o-Diazine, q.v. Colorless liquid, b.206, soluble in water.

pyridazinone. $(CH_2)_2 \cdot CH:N \cdot NH \cdot CO = 98.1$. A dihydroketopyridazine. Colorless liquid, b.170, soluble in alcohol.

pyridinole. $C_6H_4 \cdot (NH) \cdot C_5H_3N = 168.1$. A group of heterocyclic compounds.

pyridine. $C_5H_5N = 79.1$. The heterocyclic compound

in coal tar, bone oil, and vegetable distillation products (tobacco smoke). Colorless liquid, $d_{15}0.9893$, m.—42, b.115, soluble in water or ether; an antiseptic, denaturant for alcohol, solvent for rubber and paint, and reagent for acetone and blood. **allyl-** See *allylpyridine.* **benzyl-** See *benzylpyridine.* **dihydroketo-** Pyridone. **dimethyl-** Lutidine. **ethyldimethyl-** Parvoline **ethylmethyl-** (1) Aldehydine. (2) Collidine. **hexahydro-** Piperidine. **hydroxy-** See *oxynicotinic acid.* **methyl-** Picoline. **methylethyl-** Aldehydine. **oxy-** Pyridone. **propyl-** Conyrine. **tetramethyl-** Parvoline. **trimethyl-** Collidine.

p. bases. The homologs of pyridine, $C_nH_{2n-5}N$; as: picolines, lutidines, collidines. parvulines, rubidine, viridine. **p. carboxylic acid.** α- or *1*-Picolinic acid. β- or 2- Nicotinic acid. γ- or 3-Isonicotinic acid. **p. dicarboxylic acid.** *1,2*-Quinolinic acid. *1,3*- Lutidinic acid. *1,4*- Isocinchomeronic acid. *1,5*- Dipicolinic acid. *2,3*-Cinchomeronic acid. *2,4*- Dinicotinic acid. **p. pentacarboxylic acid.** $C_5N(COOH)_5 = 299.10$. ($+ 2$- or $3H_2O$.) Soluble acid, decomp. 220. **p. sulfonic acid.** $C_5H_4NSO_3H = 159.1$. Colorless needles, soluble in water; used in organic synthesis. **p. thiocyanate reaction.** The precipitation of certain metals, e.g., Zn, Ni, Co, by pyridine and ammonium thiocyanate; used in analysis. **p. tricarboxylic acid.** $C_5H_2N(COOH)_3 \cdot 2H_2O = 247.12$. *1,2,3,4*- Carbocinchomeronic acid. *1,2,3,5*- m.323. *1,2,3,6*- m.71, b.130. *1,2,4,5*- m.235. *1,2,4,6*- m.277 (decomp.). *1,3,4,5*- Berberonic acid.

pyridinium. Describing compounds derived from pyridine, in which the heterocyclic N atom is pentavalent. Cf. *piperidinium.*

Pyridium. Trademark for phenylazodiaminopyridine; a urinary antiseptic.

pyridol. Hydroxypyridine. The hydroxy form of pyridone: $HO \cdot C_5H_4N \rightarrow O:C_5H_5N$.

pyridone. $C_5H_5ON = 95.1$. Ketopyridine, oxypyridine, pyridol; a group of heterocyclic ketones or quinones; e.g., 1-oxypyridine, m.106.

pyridopyridine. $C_8H_6N_2 = 130.06$. 1,5-Naphthyridine, 1,5-benzodiazine. An isomer of cinnoline, quinazoline, and quinoxaline.

pyridoquinoline. $C_{12}H_8N_2 = 180.1$; and $C_{12}H_{11}g$ $N = 169.1$. Heterocyclic compounds containing 1 or 2 N atoms in a quinoline and pyridine ring fused together, as

2.5-Pyridoquinoline

Pyridose. Trademark for pyridylmercuric acetate; used to sterilize water.

pyridostigmine. 3-Dimethylcarbamoyloxy-1-methyl-pyridinum. **p. bromide.** $C_9H_{13}O_2N_2Br = 261.12$. Mestinon. White, bitter, deliquescent crystals, m.154, soluble in water; an anticholinesterase.

pyridotropolone. $C_{10}H_7O_2N = 173.07$. Pale yellow needles, m.168.

pyridoxal. $C_8H_{11}O_3N = 169.10$. Vitamin B_6, An oxidation product of pyridoxine. Colorless crystals, m.160, soluble in water.

pyridoxin(e). Adermin, vitamin B_6. 2-Methyl-3-hydroxy-4,5-di(hydroxymethyl)pyridine. Its need in human nutrition has not been established. **pseudo-** A growth factor for microorganisms, derived from p.

   p. hydrochloride. $C_8H_{11}NO_3 \cdot HCl = 205.65$. Adermin. Vitamin B_6 hydrochloride. White crystals, darkening in light, m.206 (decomp.), soluble in water. The commercial form of p. (U.S.P., B.P.).

pyridyl. The radical C_5H_4N—, from pyridine. **C-pyridyl.** P. with substitution on the C atom of the ring. **N-pyridyl.** P. with substitution on the N atom of the ring. **ter-** q.v.

   p. amine. Aminopyridine.

pyridylidene. The radical $C_5H_5N=$, from pyridine.

pyrilamine maleate. $C_{17}H_{23}N_3O \cdot C_4H_4O_4 = 401.47$. White crystals, m.100, soluble in water; an antihistaminic (U.S.P.).

pyrimidine. $CH{:}CH{\cdot}CH{:}N{\cdot}CH{:}N = 80.05$. **1,3-**

m-Diazine, q.v., metadiazine, miazine. An isomer of pyrazine and pyridazine. Colorless crystals of pungent odor, m.22, soluble in water. **dihydro-keto-** Pyrimidone. **2,6-dioxy-** Uracil. **methyl-dioxy-** Thymine. **2-oxy-6-amino-** Cytosine. **2,-4,6-trioxy-** See barbituric acid.

   p. bases. Compounds in nucleoproteins: E.g.: dioxy- Uracil. trioxy- Barbituric acid. **p. dione.** Uracil. **p. tetrone.** Alloxan. **p. trione.** Barbituric acid.

pyrimidone. $C_4H_6N_2O = 98.06$. Dihydroketopyrimidine. **4-amino-** Cytosine.

pyrimidyl. The radical $C_4H_3N_2$—, from pyrimidine.

pyrite. (1) FeS_2. Brassil, fool's gold. Yellow, shining crystals. (2) Native iron sulfide.

pyrites. Generic name for sulfide minerals; as, tin pyrite (stannite). **arsenical-** Mispickel. **arseno-** Arsenopyrite. **auriferous-** A p. containing gold. **capillary-** Millerite. **cobalt-** Smaltite. **copper-** The yellow ore, $CuFeS_2$. **coxcomb-** Marcasite. **iron-** Pyrite. **magnetic-** Pyrrhotite. **nickel-** Millerite. **radiated-** Marcasite. **spear-** Marcasite. **tin-** Stannite. **white iron-** Marcasite.

pyro(-) (1) Pyr- Prefix (Greek) indicating heat or fire; as, pyrometer. (2) Pyroxylin.

pyroacetic acid. Crude acetic acid from wood distillation. **p. spirit.** Acetone.

pyroacid. An acid produced by the loss of 1 mole of water from 2 moles of an orthoacid, q.v.; e.g., by heat. Cf. pyrophosphoric acid.

pyroantimonate. A salt derived from pyroantimonic acid; as, $K_2H_2Sb_2O_7$.

pyroantimonic acid. $H_4Sb_2O_7$. A hypothetical acid; its sodium salt is insoluble.

pyroarsenate. A salt of pyroarsenic acid.

pyroarsenic acid. $As_2O_3(OH)_4 = 266.1$. Diarsenous acid; obtained by heating arsenic acid to 180.

pyrobitumen. A constituent of shale oil; converted to bitumen by heat.

pyroborate. A salt of pyroboric acid; as, borax, $Na_2B_4O_7$.

pyroboric acid. $H_2B_4O_7$.

pyrocatechin. Pyrocatechol.

pyrocatechoic acid. 2,3-Dihydroxybenzoic acid.

pyrocatechol. (1) $C_6H_6O_2 = 110.08$. Catechol, pyrocatechin, o-dihydroxybenzene, 2-hydroxy-phenol, 1,2-benzenediol*. Colorless leaflets, m.105, soluble in water; an antiseptic, antipyretic, and photographic developer. Cf. hydroquinol. (2) Protocatechols. Diatomic phenols derived from catechol; as, homopyrocatechol, $C_6H_3Me \cdot (OH)_2$.

pyrocatechu aldehyde. $(HO)_2C_6H_3 \cdot CHO = 138.05$. **ortho-** 2,3-Dihydroxybenzaldehyde. White crystals, m.108.

Pyoceram. Trademark for a hard, thermal-shock-resistant, homogeneous composite having the properties of both glass and a ceramic.

pyrochlore. $(CaFe, Ce)O \cdot (Nb, Ti, Th)O_2 \cdot H_2O$. A blue, vitreous mineral.

pyrochroite. $Mn(OH)_2$. An amorphous mineral.

pyrochromate. Dichromate.

pyroclastic. Describing volcanic ash deposits that are partly igneous and partly sedimentary in origin.

pyrocoll. $C_{10}H_6O_2N_2 = 186.2$. Pyrrolecarboxylic acid anhydride. Yellow leaflets, m.269, insoluble in water.

pyrocomane. 1,4-Pyrone.

pyrocondensation. A union of molecules due to heat; as, formation of biuret from urea.

pyrodextrin. A brown, tasteless heat-decomposition product of starch, involving the linkage of linear chains from amylose with branched chains from amylopectin.

pyrodin. $Ph \cdot NH \cdot NH \cdot OCMe = 150.2$. Hydracetin, phenacethydrazine, acetylphenylhydrazine. Colorless crystals, m.130, soluble in water; an antipyretic and analgesic.

pyroelectricity. Thermal deformation. The property of crystals which are electrically charged by heat.

pyrogallate. A salt or ether of pyrogallol.

pyrogallic acid. Pyrogallol.

pyrogallol. $C_6H_6O_3 = 126.1$. Pyrogallic acid, 1,2,3-triphydroxybenzene, 1,2,3-benzenetriol*. White needles or leaflets, m.133, decomp. 293, very soluble in water or ether; a reagent (absorbs oxygen), weak reducing agent, photographic developer, and antiparasitic. **acetyl-** Gallacetophenone. **methylmethoxy-** Iridol. **propyl-p-dimethyl-** Picamar. **trimethoxy-** $C_6H_3(OMe)_2 = 168.1$. Pyrogallol trimethyl ether. Colorless crystals, m.47, soluble in alcohol.

p. carboxylic acid. 2,3,4-Trihydroxybenzoic acid. **p. monoacetate.** $CH_3COO \cdot C_6H_3(OH)_2 = 168.1$. Eugallol. Yellow syrup, soluble in water; used to treat skin diseases. **p. phthalein.** Gallein. **p. red.** P. sulfonphthalein. An indicator for chelatometric titration. **p. salicylate.** Saligallol. **p. triacetate.** $(CH_3COO)_3C_6H_2 = 252.1$. Lenigallol. White, insoluble, antiseptic powder.

pyrogen. (1) An impurity in a drug which when injected into the bloodstream produces fever. (2) In particular, a heat-stable polysaccharide having this effect.

Pyrogen(e) dye. Trademark for a sulfur dye.

pyrogenic. Describing a reaction induced by heat.

pyrogram. The result of applying gas chromatography to the hydrolysis products of a compound.

pyrographitic oxide. $C_{22}H_2O_4 = 330.02$. Grayblack powder produced by heating graphitic acid; used for crucibles, and formerly to coat electric bulb filaments.

pyrokomane. 1,4-Pyrone.

pyroligneous. Pertaining to wood distillation. **p. acid.** Wood vinegar. Pyracetic acid. Impure acetic acid from the destructive distillation of pine tar and wood. **p. alcohol.** Methanol. **p. spirit.** Methanol.

pyroluminescence. Luminescence produced by low-temperature flames. Cf. *candoluminescence.*

pyrolusite. MnO_2. Polianite. Cf. *psilomelane.*

pyrolysis. Decomposition of organic substances by heat.

pyrolythic acid. Cyanuric acid.

pyromagnetic. Pertaining to heat and magnetism.

pyromellitic acid. $C_6H_2 \cdot (COOH)_4 \cdot H_2O = 272.12$. Benzene-1,2,4,5-tetracarboxylic acid*. Colorless tablets, m.275, soluble in water. Cf. *mellophanic acid.*

pyrometallurgy. The study of metallurgical heat treatment.

pyrometer. An instrument to measure high temperatures. **electrical-** A thermocouple to measure the current produced at a metal-metal junction. **mechanical-** A thermocouple (lever system) that magnifies the heat distortion of 2 joined metal strips. **optical-** A p. to measure the intensity of light emitted by a hot body by comparison with a standard. **radiation-** A p. to measure heat radiated by a hot body, e.g., by a thermocouple. **resistance-** A thermometer to measure the change in resistance of a heated conductor.

pyrometric. Pertaining to high temperature. **p. cone.** Seger cone. **p.c. equivalent.** A measure of refractoriness in terms of the softening temperature of a Seger cone. **p. gage.** See *gage.*

pyrometry. The study of the measurement of high temperatures.

pyromorphite. $3Pb_3(PO_4)_2 \cdot PbCl_2$. Green lead ore (apatite group).

pyromucic acid. $C_4H_3O \cdot COOH = 112.1$. Furan-2-carboxylic acid, furoic acid. Colorless, monoclinic crystals, m.132, soluble in water. Cf. *furoates.* **beta-** Fucusoic acid.

pyromucyl. 2-Furoyl. The radical $O \cdot CH:CH \cdot CH:C \cdot$

$\quad \overline{}$

$CO—$, from pyromucic acid. Cf. *furoyl.* **bi-** Furil. **p. chloride.** $C_4H_3O \cdot COCl = 130.48$. Furoyl chloride, 2-furan carbonyl chloride. Colorless liquid, b.60.

pyrone. $O \cdot CH:CH \cdot CO \cdot CH:CH = 96.1$. Pyroco-

$\quad \overline{}$

mane, pyrokomane, γ-pyrone. Colorless crystals, m.32. **benzo-** *1,2-* Coumarin. *1,4-* Chroman. **dibenzo-** Xanthone. **hydroxy-** Kojic acid. **p. α-carboxylic acid.** $C_5H_3O_2 \cdot COOH = 140.06$. Komanic acid. A soluble solid, derived from chelidonic acid, decomp. 250. **p. dicarboxylic acid.** Chelidonic acid.

pyrones. Heterocyclic compounds derived from α- or γ-pyrone, in numerous natural coloring materials, and synthetic dyes and drugs. See *coumalin, glutaconic anhydride, pyronone.* **benzo-** Chromones. **dibenzo-** Xanthones.

pyronine dyes. Aniline dyes containing the chromo-

phore, $=R \diamondsuit R=$.

pyronone. $C_5H_4O_3 = 112.0$. α,γ-Pyrone. An isomer of glutaconic anhydride. See *pyrones.* **methylaceto-** Dehydroacetic acid.

pyrope. Aluminum garnet.

pyrophore. A pyrophoric substance.

pyrophoric. Producing sparks when rubbed, or burning spontaneously in air, e.g., finely divided metals. **p. alloy.** A Cr–Ce–Fe alloy, used in gas lighters. **p. lead.** The pyrophoric Pb–C mixture obtained on heating lead tartrate. **p. reaction.** A reaction that produces flame.

pyrophosphorus. Pyrophoric.

pyrophosphate. A salt of pyrophosphoric acid; as, $M_4P_2O_7$ and $M_2H_2P_2O_7$.

pyrophosphite. A salt of pyrophosphorous acid; as, $M_4P_2O_5$ and $M_2H_2P_2O_5$.

pyrophosphoric acid. $H_4P_2O_7 = 178.1$. Colorless crystals, m.61, soluble in water.

pyrophosphorous acid. $H_4P_2O_5 = 146.03$. A tetrabasic acid of trivalent phosphorous. Colorless needles, m.38, decomp. in water.

pyrophosphoryl. The radical $\equiv P_2O_3$, from pyrophosphoric acid. **p. chloride.** $(Cl_2PO)_2O = 251.86$. Colorless, fuming liquid b.250, hydrolyzed by water to orthophosphoric and hydrochloric acids.

pyrophyllite. $Al_2O_3 \cdot 4SiO_2 \cdot H_2O$, resembling talc and montmorillonite; its melting point is raised from 1315 to 2093 by pressure. Used as filler for paper, paint, rubber, and textiles; a polishing agent for foods; in lubricants and toilet preparations; and to produce ultrahigh pressures, q.v. Cf. *image stone.*

pyroracemamide. $MeCO \cdot CO \cdot NH_2 = 87.1$. Colorless crystals, m.124.

pyroracemic acid. Pyruvic acid.

pyroracemic aldehyde. Pyruvic aldehyde.

Pyro-Sal. Trade name for salipyrine.

pyrosine. Erythrosin.

pyrostilbnite. Kermesite.

pyrosulfate. $M_2S_2O_7$, or MHS_2O_7. A salt of pyrosulfuric acid.

pyrosulfuric acid. $H_2S_2O_7 = 178.0$. Disulfuric acid. Fuming crystals obtained by freezing Nordhausen acid.

pyrosulfuryl. The radical $=S_2O_5$, from pyrosulfuric acid. **p. chloride.** $S_2O_5Cl_2 = 215.06$. Sulfur pentoxydichloride. A fuming liquid, d.1.844, $b_{730mm}150.7$, decomp. by water.

pyrotartaric acid. $MeCH(COOH)CH_2COOH = 132.1$. Methylsuccinic acid, methylbutanedioic acid*, pyrovinic acid. Colorless, triclinic crystals, m.112, soluble in water. Cf. *ethylmalonic acid*. *n-*Glutaric acid. **hydroxy-** Citramalic acid.

p. aldehyde. Pyrotartar aldehyde.

pyrotechnics. The manufacture of fireworks.

pyroterebic acid. $Me_2C:CH\cdot CH_2COOH = 114.08$. 4-Methyl-2-pentenoic acid*. Colorless crystals, m.207.

pyrothioarsenate. $M_4As_2S_7$.

pyrotritaric acid. Uvic acid.

pyrouric acid. Cyanuric acid.

pyrovanadic acid. $H_4V_2O_7$. Cf. *vanadic acid*.

pyrovinic acid. Pyrotartaric acid.

pyroxene. $CaO\cdot MgO\cdot 2SiO_2$. A white, green, or black silicate.

pyroxenite. Websterite.

pyroxylic spirit. Methanol.

pyroxylin. Pyroxylinum, soluble guncotton, collodion cotton, trinitrocellulose, collodium, colloxylin. A solution of nitrated cellulose in a solvent of high boiling point; it consists of cellulose trinitrate, $C_6H_7O_5(NO_3)_3$, and tetranitrates, C_6H_6-$O_5(NO_3)_4$. Used as an artificial skin collodion (U.S.P.), and in the manufacture of artificial silk, leather, cloth, and lacquers. See *rayon*.

pyrrhosiderite. Göthite.

pyrrhotine. Pyrrhotite.

pyrrhotite. Fe_6S_7 or $Fe_{11}S_{12}$. Pyrrhotine. Natural or synthetic magnetic pyrite; the former usually contains nickel.

pyrrilium. Pyrylium.

pyrrole*. $CH:CH\cdot NH\cdot CH:CH = 67.1$. Azole.

Colorless liquid from bone oil, $d_{20}0.9481$, b.130, insoluble in water, soluble in alcohol or ether; its derivatives are antiseptics. Cf. *porphin ring*. **cyan-** See *cyanopyrrole*. **dibenzo-** Carbazole. **dihydro-** Pyrroline*. **dimethylethyl-** Kryptopyrrole. **tetrahydro-** Pyrrolidine*.

p. α-carboxylic acid. $C_4H_4N\cdot COOH = 111.08$. A solid, decomp. 191, soluble in water.

pyrrolidine. $CH_2\cdot CH_2\cdot NH\cdot CH_2\cdot CH_2 = 71.1$. Pentazane, butylene imide, tetramethyleneimine, tetrahydropyrrole. Colorless liquid, b.88, soluble in water. **keto-** Pyrrolidone. **methyldiketo-** Succinimide. **pyridylmethyl-** Nicotine.

p. alkaloids. See *nicotine group*. **p. carboxylic acid.** Proline. **p. dione.** Succinimide.

pyrrolidinium. A derivative of pyrrolidine containing pentavalent nitrogen. Cf. *piperidinium*.

pyrrolidyl. The radical C_4H_8N—, from pyrrolidine.

pyrroline. $C_4H_7N = 69.1$. Dihydropyrrole. Colorless liquid, b.90, soluble in water.

pyrrolinium. A derivative of pyrroline containing pentavalent nitrogen. Cf. *piperidinium*.

pyrroloindole. $C_{11}H_9N = 155.1$ and $C_{10}H_6N_2 = 154.0$. A compound with a benzene ring and 2 pyrrole rings.

pyrrolopyridine. $C_7H_5N_2$ or C_8H_7N. A compound with a fused hexa- and pentatomic ring, each having one N. **2,4-** Pyrindole. **8-** Pyrrocoline.

pyrroloquinoline. (1) A tricyclic system containing a quinoline and a pyrrole ring. (2) $C_{11}H_9N = 155.1$. A heterocyclic compound.

pyrrolylene. Bivinyl.

pyrromonazole. **alpha-** Pyrazole. **beta-** Glyoxaline.

pyrrotriazole. $N:CH\cdot NH\cdot N:N = 70.2$. Colorless crystals, m.156.

pyrroyl. The radical $CH:CH\cdot CH:CH\cdot N\cdot CO$—, from pyrrolecarboxylic acid.

pyrryl. The radical C_4H_4N—, from pyrrole. **C-pyrryl.** The substituting radical is attached to a C atom. **N-pyrryl.** The substituting radical is attached to the N atom. **alpha-** $C_4H_4N\cdot CO\cdot Me$. Colorless crystals, m.90.

pyruric acid. Cyanuric acid.

pyruvaldehyde. Pyruvic aldehyde.

pyruvic acid. $Me\cdot CO\cdot COOH = 88.1$. Pyroracemic acid, ketoacetic acid, acetylformic acid, 2-oxopropanoic acid*, 2-hydroxypropenoic acid*. Colorless crystals, or liquid, d.1.288, m.14, b.165 (decomp.), soluble in water; an intermediate product in the metabolism of proteins, fats, and carbohydrates.

pyruvic aldehyde. $Me\cdot CO\cdot CHO = 72.1$. Pyroracemic aldehyde, ketoacetaldehyde, methyl glyoxal, 2-oxopropanal*. Yellow, pungent liquid, b.72, polymerizes to a glassy mass.

pyruvonitrile. $CH_3COCN = 69.03$. Acetyl cyanide, 2-oxopropane nitrile*. Colorless liquid, b.93, decomp. in water.

pyrvinium panoate. $C_{75}H_{70}N_6O_6 = 1151.43$. Orange crystals, insoluble in water; an anthelmintic (U.S.P.).

pyrvolidine. An alkaloid from the leaves of the wild carrot, *Daucus carota* (Umbelliferae).

pyrylium. $CH:CH\cdot CH:O(R)\cdot CH:CH$. Describing compounds derived from pyran, having a supposedly 4-valent O.

pyx. (1) Trial of the pyx. The annual independent testing of coins issued by the British Mint, for composition and weight, since the 13th century. (2) Pix. **p. liquida.** Wood tar.

Q

Q. (1) Describing the seventh and outermost shell or orbit of electrons in the atom. Cf. *periodic system*. (2) Symbol for quantity of electricity. (3) A unit of energy equivalent to 1 million billion (10^{15}) BThU.

q. Symbol for heat entering a system.

qt. Abbreviation for quart.

Qu. Abbreviation for quinine.

quadrant. (1) The quarter of a circle. (2) The distance from the pole to the equator = 10^7 meters = 0.25 meridian. (3) See *henry*.

quadratic. A cubical tetragon. Cf. *crystal systems*.

quadri- Prefix (Latin) indicating 4 or fourfold. Cf. *tetra-*.

quadribasic. Describing a compound that has 4 H atoms replaceable by a base or metal; as, H_4SiO_4. **q. acid.** An acid requiring 4 molecules of a monatomic base for neutralization.

quadrilateral. Describing a 4-sided figure.

quadrimolecular. Pertaining to 4 molecules. **q. reaction.** A reaction involving 4 similar molecules.

quadrine. d,l-α-amino-N-butyric acid. **iso-** d,l-α-aminoisobutyric acid.

quadrivalent. Having 4 different valences; as, bromine (1, 3, 5, 7). Cf. *tetravalent*.

quadroxalate. MOOC·COOH. Bioxalate (obsolete).

quadroxide. A binary compound of oxygen having 4 O atoms.

quadruple point. The temperature at which 4 phases are in equilibrium, e.g., a saturated solution containing excess of solute. Cf. *triple point*.

quaker buttons. Nux vomica.

qualitative. Pertaining to the kind or type. **q. analysis.** The methods by which the constituents of a substance are detected. **q. reaction.** A reaction that detects one substance in a mixture.

quality. The purity of a substance; e.g.:
C.P.: chemically pure, tested, analyzed
U.S.P. or B.P.: conforming to the tests of the respective pharmacopoeia
A.R.: analytical reagent
pure: the best commercial grade
technical: a somewhat impure grade
crude: an unrefined grade

quanta. Plural of quantum.

quantitative. Pertaining to an amount. **q. analysis.** The methods by which the amount of a constituent is determined. **q. reaction.** (1) A reaction of q. analysis. (2) A reaction that proceeds wholly or almost to completion

quantity. The amount, active mass, or concentration of a substance. **physical-** The numerical value of a phenomenon: *Extensive* when the quantity has an additive effect; as, mass. *Intensive* when the quantities added increase the intensity of a property; as, temperature.

q. of electricity. The amount of electricity to produce at unit distance (1 cm) a repulsion of unit force (1 dyne) in a vacuum = 1 international coulomb = 1/3,600 ampere-hour = 1/96,500 faraday = 3×10^9 electrostatic units.

quantivalence. The combining power of an element or radical, expressed in terms of the number of H atoms with which it will unite. See *valence*.

quantivalent. Describing an atom that can combine with 2 or more H atoms. Cf. *multivalent*.

quantization. A change from a normal to an excited atom, in which electrons are raised to a higher energy level by the absorption of energy. Cf. *quantum notation*.

quantum. (Pl. quanta.) (1) Ergon. The unit amount of energy ϵ set free or bound during the emission or absorption of radiations: $\epsilon = h\nu$, where ν is the atomic frequency number of the radiation, and h is Planck's constant, 6.55×10^{-27} erg-sec. Cf. *energy level, Compton effect, Raman effect*. **q. efficiency.** The number of molecules transformed in a photolytic reaction per q. of actinic light absorbed. **q. group.** A number that defines spectroscopic terms as a resultant of the orbital numbers of an atom. Cf. *Stoner quanta*. **q. mechanics.** See *wave mechanics*. **q. notation.** Normal energy levels are indicated by a q. number, and a given spectrum line is indicated by the change from one energy level to another; thus $K-L_{22}$ or $L_{22}-M_{33}$. **q. number.** The integer n, which indicates the energy level of the electron orbit or the number of quanta: $n = E/h\nu$, where E is the total radiation. Cf. *Bohr's atom, Rydberg's equation, hydrogen atom*. **q. relation.** See table. **q. state.** See *energy levels*. **q. theory.** Energy changes occur in continuous pulsations, not gradually, and always in multiples of a definite quantity, the q. of energy, ϵ. **q. unit.** Planck's constant.

QUANTUM RELATION OF RADIATION AND ENERGY

Type	λ	ν	$h\nu$	Q
Red	7,500	400	2.62	37.8
Yellow	5,900	508	3.33	48.6
Blue	4,900	612	4.01	57.9
Violet	4,550	659	4.32	62.3
Ultraviolet	3,950	759	4.97	71.8

λ = wavelength, angströms
ν = frequency ($\times 10^{12}$ per sec)
$h\nu$ = quantum per molecule ($\times 10^{-12}$ erg)
Q = quantum energy of 1 mole of matter, kcal ($9.06 \times 10^{23} h\nu$)

quarentoxide. M_4O. An oxide of a divalent metal.

quarry. An open or surface working for minerals, as limestone. Cf. *mine, outcrop*.

quart. Qt. 0.25 gallon = 0.946333 liter. **dry-** The equivalent of 1.1012 liters. **imperial-** The equivalent of 1.13586 liters, or 69.3185 in.³; 2.5 lb distilled water occupies 1 qt. **liquid-** The equivalent of 0.946 liter. **Winchester-** q.v.

quartation. Inquartation. Winchester. Separation (parting) of silver from gold by dissolving the silver in nitric acid; it is quantitative for Au 25, Ag 75%, and, if necessary additional silver must be added for separation.

quarter. (1) One-fourth part. (2) An English measure of capacity, generally for grain: 8 bushels. **q. wave plate.** A transparent plate, e.g., mica, used in petrological determinations of refractive index; it produces a phase difference of $\frac{1}{4}$ wavelength of light between 2 emergent beams.

quartering. A method of sampling, e.g., coal, by dividing a heap into approximately equal quarters, mixing opposite quarters, redividing the mixture into quarters, and continuing these operations until a sample of suitable size results.

quartile. See *frequency*.

quartz. SiO_2. Silicon dioxide, silica. (1) Glassy or crystalline, native silica; or massive in veins; as, rose or milky q. (2) Prepared artificially by seeding an aqueous solution of sodium hydroxide with small q. crystals, and autoclaving. Pure q. occurs in colorless hexagons, d.2.66, hardness 7, mean refractive index 1.55. It occurs in α and β forms (transition point 573), is stable below 870, and changes to cristobalite above 1,200. See *silica*. Many colored varieties are semiprecious stones. Native varieties: amethyst (red-violet, transparent), catalinite (green, red, and brown mottled), cat's-eye (green and brown), citrine (yellow), milky quartz (opalescent), rock crystal (colorless hexagons), rose quartz (pale rose), smoky quartz (gray). Q. is very resistant to acids, m.1715, and is used for chemical apparatus: rock crystals (transparent to ultraviolet rays) for optical apparatus; threads for delicate suspensions. **q. apparatus.** Chemical utensils, transparent and highly resistant to sudden temperature changes, made from fused rock crystal. **q. lamp.** Mercury-vapor lamp. **q. lens.** (1) A rock crystal lens transparent to ultraviolet rays. (2) A fused quartz lens. **q. oscillator.** A section cut from a q. crystal; used to tune radio circuits, as it shows sharply tuned resonance. **q. resonator.** Q. oscillator. **q. rock.** Quartzite.

quartzite. A yellow impure quartz.

quasar. The most distant type of astronomical object, believed to be formed by explosion in the center of a galaxy. A quasi-stellar source of radio waves in space.

quasichemical. Having the attributes of a chemical compound, but not conforming to the law of constant proportions.

quassia. Bitterwood, bitter ash. The dried wood of *Picrasma excelsa*, Jamaica q., or *Quassia amara*, Surinam q. (Simarubaceae); a bitter tonic, hop substitute, and vermicide. **q. wood.** Quassia.

quassic acid. $C_{30}H_{38}O_{10} = 558.30$. A glucoside from quassia.

quassin. $C_{10}H_{12}O_3 = 180.1$. A bitter principle from quassia (0.03%). Colorless crystals, m.210, slightly soluble in water; a tonic.

quassoid. The total bitter principles of quassia; a febrifuge and bitter tonic.

quaternary. (1) The last geologic epoch, q.v. (2) A compound containing 4 different elements (types of

atoms); as, $NaHSO_4$. **q. amines.** Organic derivatives of NH_4OH in which the hydroxyl group and the 4 H atoms are replaced by radicals; as, NMe_4I. **q. carbon atom.** A C atom linked to 4 other C atoms.

quebrachamine. An alkaloid from quebracho. Colorless crystals, m.142, insoluble in water.

quebrachine. $C_{21}H_{26}N_2O_3 = 354.3$. An alkaloid from quebracho bark. Yellow crystals, m.214, insoluble in water, soluble in hot alcohol; an antiperiodic and tonic. **hypo-** $C_{21}H_{26}O_2N_2 = 338.26$. Brown powder from quebracho bark, insoluble in water. **q. hydrochloride.** $C_{21}H_{26}O_3N_2 \cdot HCl = 390.7$. Colorless crystals, soluble in water; used to treat asthma.

quebrachite. Quebrachitol.

quebrachitol. $C_7H_{14}O_6 = 194.11$. Methoxypinite, *l*-inosite methyl ether, quebrachite, bornesitol. Colorless crystals, m.191. Cf. *pinite*.

quebracho, quebracho blanco. Aspidosperma. The dried bark of *Aspidosperma quebracho blanco*, (S. America); a tonic and antiasthmatic. It contains tannins and a number of alkaloids. **q. colorado.** The dried wood of *Schinopsis* species, which contains fisetin. **q. extract.** A tanning extract from the heartwood of q. (35–65% tannin). **q. gum.** The dried juice of *Schinopsis lorentzii* (Anacardiaceae), Argentina; a tan.

quebrachomine. An alkaloid from quebracho.

queen of the meadow. (1) The dried root of *Eupatorium purpureum* (Compositae), an astringent and diuretic. Cf. *euparin*. (2) Meadowsweet.

queen's delight. Stillingia. **q.'s root.** Stillingia. **q.'s yellow.** Mercuric subsulfate.

queen substance. A substance secreted by queen honeybees, which inhibits queen rearing and the development of ovaries in workers. Its principal constituent is related to the 10-hydroxy-Δ^2-decenoic acid present in royal jelly.

quenching. (1) Cooling suddenly, as in tempering steel. (2) Producing a diminution, e.g., of fluorescence.

quercetagetin. $C_{15}H_{10}O_8 = 318.08$. Yellow crystals, m.318, from African marigold. See *flavone*.

quercetin. $C_{15}H_{10}O_7 = 302.16$. Meletin, sophoretin, quercetinic acid, flavin, tetrahydroxyflavanol. Yellow dye obtained by decomposition of q., m.312, soluble in water. **hydroxy-** Myricetin. Cf. *rhamnetin*.

quercetinic acid. Quercetin.

quercic, quercinic acid. Quercin (2).

quercimetin. Quercitrin.

quercin. (1) $C_6H_{12}O_6 = 180.1$. Bitter crystals, from oak bark and acorns. (2) $C_{15}H_{12}O_5 \cdot 2H_2O = 308.1$. Quercic acid, quercinic acid, oaktannin. Brown powder from the wood of *Quercus* species. Cf. *quercitannic acid*.

quercitannic acid. $C_{28}H_{28}O_{14} = 588.22$. A tannin from oak bark; hydrolyzed to oak red.

quercite. Quercitol.

quercitin. (1) A glucoside in ragweed pollen. (2) Quercetin.

quercitol. $CHOH \cdot (CHOH)_2 \cdot CH_2 \cdot (CHOH)_2 = 164.1$.

Cyclohexanpentol*, quercite, acorn sugar, pentahydroxycyclohexane. Colorless, sweet crystals in oak bark, m.224 (decomp.), soluble in water.

quercitrin. $C_{21}H_{22}O_{12} \cdot 2H_2O = 502.3$. Quercimetin, quercitrinic acid. A rhamnoside of quercitron bark, oak bark, tea leaves, hops, horse chestnut. Yellow crystals, m.160–200, insoluble in water; hydrolyzed by acids to isodulcitol and quercetin, and used in their manufacture.

quercitrinic acid. Quercitrin.

quercitron. The coarse, powdered bark (25% tannin) of *Quercus tinctoria* (Cupuliferae), N. America; a tan and dye.

quercus. The dried bark of *Quercus alba*, white oak (Cupuliferae); an astringent and tan.

Quevenne's iron. Reduced iron.

quickening liquid. A solution of mercuric nitrate or cyanide, used in electroplating.

quicklime. Calcined limestone; chiefly calcium oxide or hydroxide in natural association with magnesium oxide.

quicksilver. Mercury. **horn-** A native mercurous chloride.

quick-vinegar process. Vinegar manufacture by passing weak alcohol slowly through wood shavings covered with *Bacterium aceti*.

quillaia. Quillaya, quillaja, soapbark, Panama bark. The bark of *Quillaja saponaria* (Rosaceae), S. America, containing saponins; a foam producer, emulsifier, and sternutatory (B.P.).

quillaic acid. $C_{19}H_{30}O_{10} = 418.3$. A saponin from the bark of *Quillaja saponaria*.

quina. Cinchona bark.

quinacetine. $C_{27}H_{31}N_3O_2 = 429.4$. An alkaloid from cinchona bark. **q. sulfate.** $(C_{27}H_{31}N_3O_2)_2$-$H_2SO_4 \cdot H_2O = 974.8$. Colorless powder, soluble in water; an antipyretic and anodyne.

quinacridine. $C_{20}H_{12}N_2 = 280.2$. Pentacyclic compounds of 3 benzene rings and 2 pyridine rings; as,

quinacridone. Quin(2,3-b)-acridone-7,14(5,12)dione, C.I. Pigment Violet 19. A red pigment which can be converted into other red and a blue pigment.

quinacrin(e). $C_{23}H_{30}ClN_3O = 401.98$. Mepacrine, atebrin(e), 2-chloro-5-[ω-diethylamino-α-methylbutylamino]-7-methoxyacridine. **q. hydrochloride.** $C_{23}H_{30}ClN_3O \cdot 2HCl \cdot 2H_2O = 508.94$. Bitter, yellow crystals, soluble in water; an anthelmintic, antiprotozoan, and antimalarial (U.S.P.).

quinalbarbitone sodium. $C_{12}H_{17}O_3N_2Na = 260.33$. Bitter, white hygroscopic powder, soluble in water; used similarly to barbitone (B.P.).

quinaldic acid. $C_{20}H_{12}O_2N_2 = 312.13$. Orthorhombic crystals, prepared by the action of potassium cyanide on quinoline-2-aldehyde. **hydroxy-** Kynurenic acid.

quinaldine. $C_6H_4 \cdot CH:CH \cdot CMe:N = 143.13$. α-Methylquinoline. Colorless liquid, d.1.186, b.244, soluble in water; used medicinally. **naphtho-** See *naphthoquinaldine*. **oxy-** See *oxyquinaldine*. **phenyl-** See *phenylquinaldine*.

quinaldinium compounds. Derivatives of quinaldine in which the N atom is pentavalent.

quinalizarin. $C_{14}H_{12}O_2 = 212.1$. 1,2,5,8-Tetrahydroanthraquinone. A reagent for beryllium; the violet alkaline solution becomes blue.

quinamine. $C_{19}H_{24}N_2O_2 = 312.3$. A crystalline alkaloid from cinchona bark. Cf. *apoquinamine*.

quinanaphthol. $C_{20}H_{24}N_3O_2(OHC_{10}H_6SO_3H)_2 = 786.49$. Quinaphthol, chinaphthol, quinine β-naphthol monosulfate. Yellow crystals, m.185, soluble in water.

quinane. $C_{20}H_{24}N_2 = 292.21$. Desoxyquinine. The heterocyclic reduction product of quinine.

quinaphthol. Quinanaphthol.

quinaseptol. Diaphthol. **q. silver.** Argentol.

quinate. A salt of quinic acid. **q. of urotropine.** Quinotropine.

quinazerin. Quinizarin.

quinazine. Quinoxaline.

quinazoline. $C_6H_4 \cdot N:CH \cdot N:CH = 130.06$. Phenmiazine, benzopyrimidine, 1,3-benzodiazine. Colorless crystals, m.48. **dihydroketo-** Quinazolone. **diketotetrahydro-** Benzoyleneurea. **ketodihydro-** Quinazolone. **methyl-** $C_9H_8N_2 = 144.1$. 2-Methylquinazoline. Colorless crystals, m.35. **oxy-** Quinazolone.

quinazolone. $C_8H_6N_2O = 146.1$. Oxyquinazoline, ketodihydroquinazoline. Cf. *quinoxalone*.

quince seeds. The dried seeds of *Pyrus cydonia* (Rosaceae). Used medicinally, as the mucilage, as a demulcent.

quinene. $C_{20}H_{22}N_2O$. Koenig's term for the heterocyclic parent compound of the quinine alkaloids.

quinetum. A mixture of the alkaloids of cinchona bark in the proportions in which they occur in nature. Cf. *quinium, quinoidine*.

quinhydrone. $C_6H_4O_2 \cdot C_6H_4(OH)_2 = 218.14$. A compound of quinone and hydroquinone dissociating in solution. Green powder, m.171 (sublimes), soluble in hot water. **q. electrode.** A platinum wire in a saturated solution of q.; used as a reversible electrode standard in pH determinations: $pH = 2.03 + E/0.0577$, where E is the electromotive force against a saturated calomel electrode at 18°C.

quinhydrones. Intermediate reduction products of quinones.

quinia. Quinine.

quinic acid. $C_6H_7(OH)_4 \cdot COOH = 192.1$. Kinic acid, hexahydrotetrahydroxybenzoic acid, in cinchona bark. Colorless, monoclinic crystals, m.162 (decomp.), soluble in water; used to treat gout.

quinicine. $C_{20}H_{24}N_2O_2 = 324.20$. An amorphous cinchona bark alkaloid, m.60, isomeric with quinine.

quinidine. $C_{20}H_{24}N_2O_2 = 324.2$. An alkaloid from cinchona bark: the *d* isomer of quinine. Colorless prisms, m.168, insoluble in water, soluble in alcohol, ether or chloroform. Used as a cardiac rhythm regulator, and similarly to quinine. **q. gluconate.** $C_{20}H_{24}N_2O_2 \cdot C_6H_{12}O_7 = 520.58$. Bitter, white powder, soluble in water; a cardiac depressant (U.S.P.). **q. hydrochloride.** $C_{20}H_{24}N_2O_2 \cdot HCl = 360.8$. White prisms, soluble in water. **q. sulfate.** $(C_{20}H_{24}O_2N_2)_2H_2SO_4 \cdot 2H_2O = 789.97$. Bitter, colorless needles, soluble in water; a cardiac depressant (U.S.P., B.P.), and quinine substitute.

quinine. $C_{20}H_{24}O_2N_2 = 324.3$. Quinina, quinia, chinine. *Qu*. A levorotatory alkaloid from the bark of *Cinchona* species. Colorless needles, m.175, slightly soluble in water, soluble in alcohol or ether; a stimulant and antimalarial, usually as its salts: QuHCl·2H₂O (B.P.); (QuH₂SO₄)₂·2H₂O (U.S.P., B.P.); QuH₂SO₄·7H₂O (B.P.); Qu2HCl (B.P.). Its *d* isomer is quinidine. **desoxy-** Quininone. **eu-** Q. ethyl carbonate. **salicyl-** Saloquinine.

q. acetate. $QuC_2H_4O_2 = 384.3$. White crystals, soluble in water; a diuretic and antimalarial. **q. acetyl salicylate.** $Qu\cdot CH_3COOO\cdot C_6H_4\cdot COOH$. Q. aspirin, xaxaquin. White crystals, used medicinally. **q. aesculinate.** Escoquinine. Yellow powder, insoluble in water; used medicinally. **q. albuminate.** Yellow scales; a tonic. **q. alkaloids.** Alkaloids from cinchona bark, related to q. Q. contains 4 asymmetric C atoms (in bold type):

R′ R″	*l* isomer	*d* isomer
H *(1)*	Cinchonine	Cinchonidine
H *(2)*	Hydrocinchonidine	Hydrocinchonine
OH *(1)*	Cupreine	Cupreidine
OH *(2)*	Hydrocupreine	Hydrocupreidine
OCH₃ *(1)*	Quinine	Quinidine
OCH₃ *(2)*	Hydroquinine	Hydroquinidine
OCH₃ *(3)*	Ethylquitenine	Ethylquitenidine
OC₂H₅ *(2)*	Optochine	Optochinidine
OC₅H₁₁ *(2)*	Eucupine	(Eucupidine)
OC₈H₁₇ *(2)*	Vuzine	(Vuzidine)

(1) is —CH:CH₂; *(2)* is —CH₂·CH₃; *(3)* is —COOC₂H₅

q. anisate. $Qu_2C_{10}H_{12}O\cdot 2H_2O = 832.7$. Anetholquinine. Colorless crystals, soluble in alcohol. **q. antimonate.** $QuH_3SbO_4 = 513.2$. Q. stibnate. White powder, insoluble in water; an antirheumatic. **q. arrhenate.** $Qu_2AsO(OH)_2CH_3 = 788.7$. Q. methyl arsenate. Colorless crystals, m.140, insoluble in cold, slightly soluble in hot water. **q. arsenate.** $Qu_2H_3AsO_4\cdot 8H_2O = 934.3$. Colorless crystals, soluble in hot water; a tonic. **q. arsenite.** $Qu_2H_2AsO_3 = 773.6$. White powder, slightly soluble in water. **q. aspirin.** Q. acetyl salicylate. **q. benzoate.** $QuC_7H_6O_2 = 446.3$. Colorless crystals, slightly soluble in water;

used medicinally. **q. borate.** $QuH_3BO_3 = 386.3$. White crystals, soluble in water. **q. bromate.** $QuHBrO_3 = 453.3$. Colorless crystals, soluble in water. **q. camphorate.** $QuC_{10}H_{16}O_6 = 556.4$. White powder, insoluble in water. **q. carbolate.** Phenolquinine. White powder, slightly soluble in water. **q. carbonate.** $QuH_2CO_3\cdot H_2O = 404.4$. Colorless needles, soluble in water. **q. chlorate.** $QuHClO_3 = 408.8$. White crystals, soluble in water, explodes when heated. **q. chromate.** $Qu\cdot H_2CrO_4\cdot 2H_2O = 478.4$. Yellow needles, insoluble in water. **q. cinnamylate.** $QuC_9H_8O_2 = 472.3$. White crystals, soluble in water. **q. citrate.** $Qu_2\cdot C_6H_8O_7\cdot 7H_2O = 966.7$. Colorless crystals, soluble in water. **q. eosolate.** $Qu_2C_9H_7O_{12}S_3 = 1,051.7$. Q. trisulfoacetyl creosote; used medicinally. **q. ethyl carbonate.** $QuEt_2CO_3 = 442.3$. Euquinine. Needles, m.89, slightly soluble in water; a tasteless. q. substitute. **q. ferricyanide.** $QuH_3Fe(CN)_6 = 539.6$. Yellow crystals, slightly soluble in water. **q. ferrosulfate.** Brown powder, slightly soluble in water; a tonic. **q. formate.** $QuCH_2O_2 = 370.3$. White needles, soluble in water. **q. glycerophosphate.** $Qu_2H_2PO_4C_3H_7O_2\cdot 4H_2O = 892.6$. Kineurine. White powder, soluble in hot water; a tonic. **q. hydrochloride.** $QuHCl = 360.8$. Needles, m.156, soluble in water (B.P.). **q. hydroiodide.** $QuHI = 452.2$. Yellow powder, soluble in alcohol. **q. hypophosphite.** $QuHPO_2\cdot 2H_2O = 424.3$. White needles, decomp by heat (forms phosphine), soluble in water. **q. iodate.** $QuHIO_3 = 500.2$. Colorless needles, slightly soluble in water. **q. ligosinate.** Yellow powder, insoluble in water. **q. nitrate.** $QuHNO_3 = 387.4$. Colorless crystals, soluble in water. **q. phenol sulfonate.** $QuC_6H_4(OH)SO_3H = 498.4$. Q. sulfocarbolate. Yellow mass, soluble in water. **q. quinate.** $Qu\cdot C_7H_{12}O_6\cdot 2H_2O = 552.4$. Yellowish crystals, soluble in water. **q. salicylate.** Saloquinine. **q. santonate.** $QuC_{15}H_{20}O_4 = 588.5$. Yellow powder, soluble in alcohol. **q. stearate.** $QuC_{18}H_{36}O_2 = 608.6$. Colorless crystals, soluble in alcohol; used to treat sunburn. **q. stibnate.** Q. antimoniate. **q. succinate.** $Qu_2C_4H_6O_4\cdot 8H_2O = 910.8$. Colorless needles, slightly soluble in water. **q. sulfate.** $Qu_2H_2SO_4\cdot 7H_2O = 872.8$. The commonest q. salt. Colorless silky needles, m.205, slightly soluble in water; soluble in alcohol, ether, or very dilute acids; an antipyretic, antiperiodic, and antimalarial. *iodo-.* Herapathite. **q. sulfate periodide.** Herapathite. **q. sulfoguaiacolate.** Sulfoguaiacin. Yellow leaflets, soluble in water; an antiseptic. **q. sulfoiodoiodate.** $Qu_2(H_2SO_4)_3(HI)_2I_4\cdot 3H_2O = 1,760.26$. Dichromatic crystals which polarize light. **q. synthesis.** Skraup's reaction. **q. tannate.** $Qu(C_{14}H_{10}O_9)_3\cdot 8H_2O = 1,434.7$. Yellow powder, partly soluble in alcohol. **q. trisulfoacetyl creosote.** Q. eosolate. **q.-urea hydrochloride.** $C_{20}H_{24}N_2O_2\cdot HCl\cdot CH_4N_2O\cdot HCl\cdot 5H_2O = 547\cdot 48$. Bitter, translucent prisms, darkening, soluble in water; a sclerosing injection (U.S.P.). **q. valerate.** $QuC_5H_{10}O_2\cdot H_2O = 444.4$. White crystals, slightly soluble in water.

quininic acid. $MeO\cdot C_9H_5N\cdot COOH = 203.14$. Yellow prisms, m.280 (decomp.), slightly soluble in water; used in quinine organic synthesis.

quininone. $C_{20}H_{22}N_2O_2 = 322.3$. The ketone of quinine, q.v.; R‴ is CO, R″ is CH:CH₂, and R′ is OCH₃.

quinisatin. $C_9H_5NO_3$ = 175.1. The heterocyclic lactam or lactim of quinasitinic acid:

$$C_6H_4 \underset{NH}{\overset{CO \cdot CO}{<}} CO \qquad C_6H_4 \underset{N}{\overset{CO \cdot CO}{<}} C \cdot OH$$

Colorless crystals, m.257.

quinite. Quinitol.

quinitol. $C_6H_{12}O_2$ = 116.1. Quinite, 1,4-cyclohexanol, cyclohexanediol. Diatomic alcohols occurring in several cis and trans forms, as colorless crystals. **cis-1,2-** m.75. **trans-1,2-** m.100. **cis-1,3-** Resorcitol. m.65. **trans-1,3-** m.89. **cis-1,4-** m.102. **trans-1,4-** m.140. **iso-1,4-** Colorless liquid, b.220.

quinium. Crude quinine containing alkaloids of cinchona bark. Amorphous, white mass; used to prepare quinine and its salts. Cf. *quinetum, quinoidine.*

quinizarin. $C_{14}H_8O_4$ = 240.13. 1,4-Dihydroxyanthraquinone, quinazerin. Colorless solid, m.280, insoluble in water.

quinizine. Antipyrine.

quinoa. Dried seeds of *Chenopodium quinoa* (Chenopodiaceae), Peru and Chile; an edible, starchy flour.

quinochromes. Blue, fluorescent products of the oxidation of vitamin B_1. Cf. *thiochrome.*

quinogen. $R \cdot CO \cdot CO \cdot CH_2 \cdot C \cdot R \cdot (OH) \cdot CO \cdot CH_3$. An intermediate compound in the condensation of α-diketones to quinones.

quinoid. Paraquinoid. The chromophoric group,

$$=C\overset{C=C}{\underset{C=C}{<}}C=$$

Cf. *hemiquinoid.*

quinoidine. Brown mass of noncrystallizable alkaloids of cinchona bark; used medicinally. Cf. *quinium.*

quinol. $CO \cdot CH:CH \cdot CHOH \cdot CH:CH$ = 110.05. Hydroquinone, 4-hydroxy-*p*-benzenone. A tautomeric or ketoform of hydroquinol.

quinoline. C_9H_7N = 129.1. 1-Benzazine, chinoline. A decomposition product of quinine; a distillation product from bone oil and petroleum.

$$\begin{array}{c} \text{CH} \quad \text{N} \\ 7\text{HC} \diagup \quad \diagdown\text{C}\diagup \quad \diagdown\text{CH2} \\ | \quad \quad || \quad \quad | \\ 6\text{HC} \diagdown \quad \diagup\text{C}\diagdown \quad \diagup\text{CH3} \\ \text{CH} \quad \text{CH} \end{array}$$

Colorless, refractive oil, d_{20}1.0944, m.−20, b.238, aromatic odor, soluble in hot water or benzene; an antiseptic and solvent for resins, camphor, and terpenes. **amino-** Aminoquinoline. **aminophenyl-methyl-** Flavaniline. **benzo-** Benzoquinoline. **chloro-** Chloroquinoline. **dibenzo-** Phenanthroquinoline. **dimethyl-** Kryptidine. **hydroxy-** Quinolinol. **iso-** 2-Benzazine, leucoline. Colorless crystals, m.23, slightly soluble in water. **methoxy-** Plasmoquin. **methoxytetrahydro-** Kairine. **α-methyl-** Quinaldine. **γ-methyl-** Lepidine. **α-oxy-** Carbostyril. **tetrahydro-** $C_9H_{11}N$ = 133.1. 1,2,3,-4-Tetrahydroquinoline. Colorless liquid, b.244.

q. acids. $C_9H_6N \cdot COOH$ = 173.1.
ortho- 8-Quinolinecarboxylic acid, m.187.
meta- 7-Quinolinecarboxylic acid, m.249.

para- 6-Quinolinecarboxylic acid, m.291.
ana- 5-Quinolinecarboxylic acid, m.369.
alpha- 2-Quinoline(quinaldic acid), m.156.
beta- 3-Quinoline(quinaldic acid) m.171.
gamma- 4-Quinoline(cinchoninic acid) m.254.

q. aldehyde. $C_9H_6N \cdot CHO$ = 157.12. α- or 2-Colorless crystals, m.71, soluble in water. **q. alkaloids.** See *alkaloids.* **q. blue.** Cyanine. **q. dyes.** Dyestuffs, photographic sensitizers, and indicators containing the q. ring. See *cyanine.* **q. hydrochloride.** $C_9H_7N \cdot HCl$ = 165.6. Colorless crystals, m.94, soluble in water. **q. red.** $C_{26}H_{19}$-N_2Cl. 1,1′-Benzilidene 2,2′-quinocyanine chloride. A q. dye. **q. rhodanate.** Q. thiocyanate. **q. salicylate.** $C_9H_7N \cdot C_7H_6O_3$ = 267.2. White crystals, soluble in water; an antiseptic. **q. tartrate.** $(C_9H_7N)_3(C_4H_6O_6)_4$ = 987.5. White powder, m.125, soluble in water; an antiseptic. **q. thiocyanate.** $C_9H_7N \cdot HCNS$ = 188.2. Q. rhodanate. Yellow crystals, m.137, slightly soluble in water; a bactericide.

quinolinic acid. $C_5H_3N(COOH)_2$ = 167.1. Pyridine-2,3-dicarboxylic acid*. Colorless crystals, m.190 (decomp.), insoluble in water.

quinolinium compounds. Quinoline derivatives with pentavalent N, analogous to pyridinium and quinaldinium compounds.

quinolinol. C_9H_7NO = 145.06. Hydroxyquinoline. **2-** Carbostyryl. **4-** Kynurine. **5-** m.224. **6-** m.193, b.360. **7-** decomp. 238. **8-** Oxin, m.76; a precipitant for aluminum. **diiodo-** Diodoquin.

quinolizine. C_9H_9N = 131.1. Heterocyclic compounds of 2 pyridine rings, with a common N atom and one saturated C atom.

quinolone. Carbostyril.

quinolyl. Quinoyl. The radical C_9H_6N—, from quinoline; 7 possibilities of substitution. See *quinoline.*

quinondiimine. Quinone diimine. See *quinone.*

quinone. $O:C\overset{CH=CH}{\underset{CH=CH}{<}}C:O$ = 108.1. Benzoquinone, paradioxybenzene, benzenone, dihydrodiketobenzene. Gold prisms, m.116 (sublimes), slightly soluble in water, soluble in ether; a reagent, **anthra-** See *anthraquinone.* **benzo-** Quinone. **dimethyl-** Xyloquinone. **dinitrohydroxy-** Nitranilic acid. **hydro-** Quinol. **meri-** Meriquinone. **methyl-** Toluquinol. **naphtho-** Naphthoquinone. **semi-** The structure

$$\overset{H}{\underset{H}{>}}N\diagdown \diagup N\overset{H}{\underset{H}{<}}$$

tetrachloro- Chloranil.
q. chlorimide. C_6H_4ONCl = 141.53, m.116 (sublimes), soluble in water. **q. compounds.** Organic dioxy derivatives of q., usually yellow dyestuffs. **q. dichlorimide.** $C_6H_4N_2Cl_2$ = 175.0, m.164 (decomp.), soluble in water. **q. diphenylmethane.** Fuchsone. **q. imine.** Quinonimine. **q. monoxime.** $O:C \cdot CH:CH \cdot C(NOH) \cdot CH:CH$ = 123.1. Quinoxime. Cf. *nitrosophenol*, of which it is the stabler tautomeric form. **q. pigments.** See *quinones.*

quinones. Yellow compounds characterized by the quinone grouping; as, brasilin.

quinonoid. The quinone structure. Cf. *quinone compounds, quinoid.*

quinonyl. The radical $C_6H_3O_2$—, from quinone.

quinopyrine. Chinopyrine. A combination of antipyrine and quinine hydrochloride, soluble in water; an antimalarial (subcutaneous injection).

quinoquinoline. 1,10-Napthodiazine.

Quinoral. Trade name for chinoral.

quinosol. Chinosol, potassium oxyquinoline sulfate. Yellow powder, soluble in water; a preservative for anatomical specimens. Cf. *superol.*

quinotannic acid. $C_{14}H_{16}O_9$ = 328.12. Cinchonatannin. A tannin from cinchona bark. Yellow powder, soluble in water.

quinotropine. Urotropine quinate, chinotropine, hexamethylene amine quinate. A compound of urotropine and quinic acid, used medicinally.

quinovic acid. $C_{32}H_{48}O_6$ = 528.37. White crystals, soluble in chloroform.

quinovin. $C_{30}H_{48}O_8$ = 536.37. Kinocin, chinovin. A glucoside from cinchona bark, m.235

quinovose. A glucoside in cinchona bark; a stereoisomer of rhamnose.

quinoxaline. $C_8H_6N_2$ = 130.06. Benzo-*p*-diazine, quinazine, phenpiazine, 1,4-benzodiazine, q.v. Colorless crystals, m.305, slightly soluble in water; used in organic synthesis. **benzo-** See *benzoquinoxaline.* **naphtho-** Naphthisodiazine. **oxychlorodiphenyl-** Luteol. **tetrahydro-** $C_8H_{10}N_2$ = 134.2. 1,2,3,4-Tetrahydroquinoxaline. Colorless crystals,

m.97, soluble in alcohol. **q. dicarboxylic acid.** $C_8H_4N_2(COOH)_2$ = 218.2. *ab-* or *2,3-* Colorless crystals, m.190, soluble in water.

quinoxalyl. The radical $C_8H_5N_2$—, from quinoxaline.

quinoxime. Quinone monoxime.

quinoyl. Quinone group.

quinque- Quinqui-. Pertaining to 5.

quinquemolecular. Pertaining to 5 molecules. **q. reaction.** A reaction between 5 similar molecules.

quinquevalent. (1) Having 5 different valencies. (2) Pentavalent. **q. nitrogen.** See *-onium.*

quinqui- Quinque-.

quintal. (1) A unit of weight in the English system, equal to 100 pounds (av.). (2) A unit of weight in the metric system equal to 100 kilograms.

quintavalent. Quinquevalent.

quintenyl. Amyl.

quintessence. A concentrated extract; as, an essential oil.

quintuple point. The temperature of a system at which 5 phases exist in equilibrium. Cf. *triple-, quadruple point.*

quire. A number of sheets of paper (usually 144) of the same dimensions and weight per unit area.

quitenidine. $C_{19}H_{22}O_4N_2$ = 342.19. An oxidation product of quinidine. Cf. *chitenine.*

quotient. The numerical result of division. **albumen-** The ratio of blood albumen to total albumen. **D-** The ratio of glucose to nitrogen in urine.

q.v. Abbreviation for: (1) quantum viz—as much as you wish; and (2) quod vide—which see.

R

R. Symbol for organic radical, as R′ monovalent, R″ divalent, etc. **°R.** (1) Réaumur degrees. (2) Rankine degrees. **R acid.** 2-Naphthol-3,6-disulfonic acid. **2R acid.** 2-Amino-8-naphthol-3,6-disulfonic acid. **R salt.** Sodium salt of R acid.

R. Symbol for the gas constant: $R = 82.07$ (cm³)-(atm)/deg $= 1.9885$ cal/deg $= 8.316$ joules/deg.

r. Abbreviation for roentgen. **r$_H$, rH.** Symbol for oxidation-reduction potential, q.v.

r. Symbol for: (1) racemic, (2) radius.

ρ. Greek letter rho. Symbol for: (1) the mathematical constant 0.47693 62762; (2) the *pros-* or **2,3**-position of naphthalene; (3) *rhe*, the absolute unit of viscosity.

Ra. Symbol for radium.

ra. Abbreviation for radioactive; as *ra*Cl, radiochlorine.

rabble. An iron stirrer for molten metal; as, rabbling a charge of ore in a reverberatory furnace.

rabelaisin. A poisonous glucoside from *Rabelaisia philippinensis* (Philippines); a local arrow poison.

*ra*C. Radiocarbon.

RaC′. Radium C′.

racahout. Meal prepared from the edible acorn; used, with sugar and flavoring, as an invalid food.

racemate. A salt of a racemic acid; generally of *r*-tartaric acid.

racemation. Racemization.

raceme. A racemic compound.

racemic. *r*- or *dl*-. Inactive, but separable into dextro- and levorotatory compounds. **r. acid.** (1) HOOC·CHOH·CHOH·COOH = 150.05. Paratartaric acid. An optically inactive isomer of tartaric acid with which it occurs in nature. Colorless crystals, m.205, soluble in water. Cf. meso-*tartaric* acid. (2) An optically inactive equimolecular mixture of *d* and *l* acids. **r. compound.** A crystal that consists of an equal number of optically active *d* and *l* molecules, but can be separated into its active constituents. Cf. *meso form*. **r. mixture.** An optically inactive mixture of equal quantities of a *d* and *l* compound.

racemization. Racemation, racemisation. The transformation of optically active substances into optically inactive substances or mixtures. **auto-** Spontaneous r. **partial-** R. that affects only a few asymmetric groups.

racephedrine. Racemic ephedrine. **r. hydrochloride.** Ephetonin.

rackarock. An explosive that is made, as required, from a mixture of potassium chlorate and nitrobenzene, sometimes with picric acid.

racking. (1) Separation of ores by washing on an inclined plane (rack). (2) The final stage in brewing, when the liquor is clarified. (3) The almost complete separation of solid glycerides from cod-liver oil on cooling.

raCl. Radiochlorine.

rad. The unit dose of absorbed radiation: an energy absorption of 100 ergs per gram of tissue. Cf. *rem-roentgen, curie.*

radar. Radiolocation. The location of an object by means of the radiation reflected from it. Thus a vessel emitting radio waves can produce the image of an otherwise invisible object on a screen sensitized to the reflected waves.

raddle. Hematite.

radian. rad. (1) An arc of a circle that is as long as the radius. (2) The angle subtended at the center by the arc of a circle equal to the radius: $180°/\pi = 57.29578° = 1$ radian; $1° = 0.017453$ radian. The SI unit for plane angles.

radiant. Diverging from a common center in all directions. **r. energy.** A dynamic disturbance of the ether that diverges from a common center and manifests itself as heat, light, or electricity. **r. flux.** See *flux.* **r. heat.** Heat waves. **r. matter.** (1) The residual gas in a luminous vacuum tube. (2) Radioactive matter. **r. state.** (1) The condition of emitting light; as, incandescence, luminescence, fluorescence. (2) Crooke's fourth state of matter.

radiated. Describing a rosette-shaped arrangement of crystals. **r. pyrite.** Marcasite.

radiation. (1) Transmission of energy through space, unassociated with motion of material particles, and without loss or change; *electromagnetic r.* accounts for interference, diffraction, refraction, and polarization. (2) Emission of material particles moving at high velocity; *corpuscular r.* accounts for the photoelectric and Compton effects. (3) Sometimes, transfer or diffusion of energy through matter, as heat waves. Cf. *ray, irradiation.* **corpuscular-** A stream of particles; as, α rays, positively charged atomic nuclei; or β rays or cathode rays, negatively charged particles or electrons moving with the velocity of light. **cosmic-** A penetrating r. of very short wavelength from all directions of space, day and night. Its origin is probably the interstellar or intergalactic space, and it transforms matter into energy. **electromagnetic-** An electric field E oscillating at right angles to the direction of propagation, accompanied by a similar magnetic field H at right angles to the direction of both. See *Planck's constant.* **immaterial-** The vibratory disturbance of a medium; as, sound waves in air. **infraphotic-** See *electromagnetic-.* **K-, L-, M-** See under K, L, M, etc. **material-** Corpuscular-. **mechanical-** Those material radiations which cause a vibration of molecules; as, heat waves. **monochromatic-** A single colored r., which consists of waves of equal or approximately equal wavelength. **permissible-** The maximum dose of r. regarded as safe for factory workers in proximity to X rays, γ rays, β rays, electrons, or positrons; i.e., 20 rads in air at or near the hands, forearms, feet, and

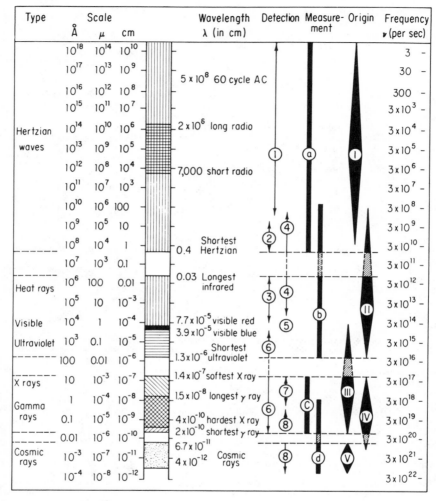

Electromagnetic radiations.

Detection:

1 Electric resonance in a receiving set (coherer, rectification and amplification)
2 Nichols' radiometer
3 Bolometer
4 Thermometer or thermocouples
5 Selenium cell
6 Photographic plate and phosphorescence
7 Photoelectric effect
8 Ionization of gas

Measurement:

a Quality of resonant electric circuit
b Interferometers or gratings
c Crystal diffraction
d Absorption coefficients

Origin:

I Coil rotating in magnetic field
II Oscillating triode valve, spark gap, etc.
III Spark-gap discharge
IV Heat radiations (chemical reactions)
V Radiation from hot bodies and ionized gases
VI Radiations from very hot bodies and ionized gases
VII Emitted by sudden stoppage of fast-moving electrons
VIII Emitted when atomic nuclei disintegrate (radioactivity)
IX Condensation of matter and transformation into energy

ankles, and 8 rads in air at or near other parts of the body (U.K. usage). **photic-** See *electromagnetic-, light.* **polarized-** An electromagnetic r. in which the direction of the electromagnetic field, i.e., the plane of the waves, is parallel. In *plane*-polarized r. the plane remains constant; in *circular*-polarized r. the plane rotates; in *elliptical*-polarized r. the plane rotates and also changes in quantity. **solar-** (1) The r. of the sun which reaches the surface of the earth; its intensity is the *solar constant*—the amount of energy per unit area and time: 1.938 cal/(min)/(cm^2) = 1.35 × 10^6 ergs/(sec)/(cm^2) = 1.81 hp/(min)/(m^2). (2) The total r. from the sun's surface: 3.79 × 10^{33} ergs/sec = 5.43 × 10^{27} cal/min = 5.08 × 10^{23} hp/min. **ultraphotic-** See *electromagnetic-*. See figure.

    r. constants. See *Planck's formula, Stefan-Boltzmann equation.* **r. effect.** The phenomena resulting when r. falls on matter or is intercepted by a body. The effects of r. may be physical (thermionic, photoelectric, fluorescent), chemical (photographic), or biological (photosynthetic). **r. hypothesis.** See *r. theory of chemical reaction.* **r. pressure.** The force exerted by light on particles that it strikes; as, radiometer. Sunlight has a r. pressure of 4.5 × 10^{-5} dyne. **r. temperature.** See *radiator.* **r. theory of chemical reaction.** The application of the quantum theory to chemical reactions. Before a molecule can react, the electrons of its constituent atoms become excited. The energy of activation may be calculated from the temperature coefficient of the reaction rate.

radiator. An incandescent body which emits an increasing amount of energy as the temperature is increased. **perfect-** Black body: a material absorbing all radiant energy (reflecting no light) and transforming it into heat. See *Stefan's law Wien's law.*

radical. (1) A group of atoms that behaves as a single atom in a chemical reaction; as (NH$_4$)$^+$. The nomenclature has been standardized by the International Union of Pure and Applied Chemistry in 1958 (inorganic) and 1957 (organic). Cf. *organic radicals, nomenclature, ion.* (2) A free r., q.v. **acid-** An electronegative group of atoms that remains intact in ordinary chemical reactions. **acyl-** Ac. An acid organic r. of the general type R.CO—. **alkyl-** Al. An aliphatic organic r.; as, Me. **aryl-** Ar. An aromatic organic r.; as, Ph or Bz. **bi-** A molecule having 2 separate unsatisfied valencies. **free-** In general, an unsaturated molecule, particularly a substance existing in equilibrium only with its compounds; as, methyl in equilibrium with tetramethyllead. Produced by the action of radiant energy on a diatomic gas (hydrogen) adsorbed on a platinum catalyst. **organic-** An unsaturated group of atoms which confers characteristic properties on a compound containing it, or which remains unchanged during a series of reactions; as, —COOH, carboxyl. See *organic radicals, structure symbols.*

    r. weight. The sum of the atomic weights of the elements in the r.

radio- Prefix (Latin) indicating rays or radiation. **r. chlorine.** raCl. See *chlorine.* **r. elements.** See *radioelements.*

radioactinium. RaAc. A radioactive disintegration product (at. wt. 226, at. no. 90) of actinium. It is an isotope of thorium, has a life period of 28.1 days, and then disintegrates to actinium X.

radioactive. Able to give off rays. **r. constant.** λ The life period of a r. element: $n = n_0 e^{-\lambda t}$, where n_0 is the number of atoms originally present, n the number of atoms present after time t, and e the base of natural logarithms. **r. decay.** The speed of disintegration: $n/n_0 = e^{\lambda t}$. **r. disintegration.** The breaking up of an atom of a r. element. *artificial-* or *synthetic-* The breaking up of an element by bombardment with particles (protons, neutrons, deutons, etc.). See *radioelements, nuclear reactions.* **r. earth.** Soil containing one microgram of radium per pound; used medicinally for external packs. **r. elements.** The elements of high atomic weight, which disintegrate spontaneously with emission of rays. There are 3 series beginning with U, Ac, and Th; and 3 types of radiation: (1) The emission of α particles, or helium nuclei, lowers the atomic weight by 4 and the atomic number by 2. (2) β particles, or negative electrons, increase the atomic number by 1. (3) γ rays, or X rays, are a secondary phenomenon caused by the β rays striking an obstacle. See *radioelements, nuclear reactions.* **r. equilibrium.** An equilibrium in a mixture of elements whose decay is balanced by the formation of fresh products; as in the transformation of radon into helium. **r. fallout.** Atmospheric radioactivity resulting from the explosion of nuclear bombs; the isotopes Sr^{90}, Cs^{137}, and C^{14} are principally responsible. It is believed to produce leukemia, bone cancer, and gene mutations resulting in hereditary changes. Cf. atmospheric *radioactivity.* **r. indicator.** Radiothor, r. tracer. A r. substance mixed in minute amounts with an isotope; the mixture behaves as a single chemical substance, although the indicator may always be detected by its radioactivity. **r. material** (Official U.K. usage). A substance containing an element specified below in such proportion that the number of millicuries per gram of substance is greater than the quantity specified (for solids): Ac, Pb, Po, Pa, Ra, Th, and U, all 10^{-5}; K, 9 × 10^{-4}; Ra (as gas or vapor), 10^{-6}. **r. tracer.** R. indicator. **r. units.** See *radium units.*

radioactivity. The spontaneous disintegration of elements with emission of rays. It is shown usually by elements of atomic weight over 207, and is unaffected by chemical or physical influences. **artificial-** Induced r. **atmospheric-** The r. of the atmosphere, which comprises r. due to natural sources (e.g., cosmic rays), medical and industrial uses of r., and radioactive fallout. When their relative proportions are 100:22:1, the r. is believed to be safe. **induced-** Artificial r., synthetic r. Temporary r. produced in an element of atomic weight below 207 by bombardment with particles. Cf. *radioelements, nuclear reactions.* **supra-** R. characteristic of hypothetical elements of atomic number over 92. Cf. *transuranium.* **synthetic-** Induced.

radioassay. Chemical analysis by means of radioactive indicators.

radiobiology. The study of the effects of radiations (especially light) on living organisms.

radiochemistry. The study of radioactive elements and their reactions. Cf. *nuclear chemistry.*

radiochromatography. Chromatography in which

identification of constituents of a separated mixture is aided by adding radioactive isotopes.

radioelements. (1) Elements of at. nos. 82–92, Pb to U. Other elements may be slightly radioactive; as, K. (2) Synthetic r., artificial r. Elements of low atomic number made temporarily radioactive by exposure to high-velocity protons, deuterons, neutrons, or α particles. Cf. *nuclear reaction.*

radiogenic. Produced by radioactive action; as, uranium lead.

radiogram. (1) Radiograph. Skiagraph. An X-ray photograph. (2) A telegram transmitted by radio. (3) A combination of a gramophone and radio receiver.

radiograph. Roentgenogram. (1) Exographs, taken with X rays. (2) Gammagraphs, taken with γ rays. **auto-** A r. produced by direct contact of a radioactive sample with a photographic negative.

radiography. Skiagraphy. Photography with X rays. **mass-** Routine examination by the reproduction on a reduced scale of an X-ray image on a fluorescent screen, on a photographic film; used in tuberculosis studies.

radiolead. (1) The natural radioactive mixture of lead isotopes in minerals. (2) Radium G, PbRa, RaΩ or Pb^{206}. A radioactive disintegration product of radium F and an isotope of lead.

radiolite. A variety of natrolite.

radiolocation. Radar.

radiology. The study of radioactivity and radioactive elements.

radiolucent. Offering resistance to the passage of X rays. Cf. *radiopaque.*

radioluminescence. Fluorescence caused by radioactive rays striking a screen treated with a suitable substance.

radiolysis. Decomposition by radiations, e.g., formation of formaldehyde from methanol.

radiometallography. The examination of the structure of metals by photography with radioactive substances and fluorescent screens.

radiometer. (1) An instrument measuring the penetrating power of radioactive rays. (2) An apparatus demonstrating the mechanical effect of light. (3) A bolometer. (4) A thermocouple. Cf. *radiator.*

radiometric titration. The use of a radioactive indicator to follow the transfer of material between 2 phases in equilibrium; e.g., the titration of Ag^{110}NO$_3$ against potassium chloride.

radiomicrometer. A delicate thermopile, to detect small changes in radiation intensity.

radion. A particle thrown off by a radioactive element (obsolete). Cf. *radon.*

radionitrogen. See *nitrogen.*

radiopaque. Impervious to the passage of X rays. Cf. *pantopaque, radiolucent, radioparent.*

radioparent. Allowing the free passage of X rays. Cf. *radiopaque, radiolucent.*

radioscope. An electroscope to detect radioactive substances.

radiosodium. See *sodium.*

radiostol. Viosterol.

radiotellurium. Polonium.

radiotherapy. Radium therapy.

radiothor. Radioactive indicator.

radiothorium. RaTh. A radioactive element, at. no. 90; disintegration product of mesothorium II;

an isotope of thorium, disintegrating to thorium X.

radiotronic. Heatronic. Describing a process operated by waves of radio frequencies.

radiovision. Transmission of pictures by wireless telegraphy. Cf. *television.*

radish. The root of Raphanus sativus (Cruciferae); a vegetable and source of an indicator color.

radium. Ra = 226.05. A radioactive element, at. no. 88, a disintegration product of ionium. It is a homotope of barium, and isotope of thorium X, actinium X, and mesothorium I; and it disintegrates to radon and helium. Discovered (1898) by Dr. and Mme. Curie. Gray powder, m.700, decomp. by water, and forms a series of salts; extremely toxic, and deposits in the bones of organisms. **RaA, RaB, etc.** See *radon.* **r. bath water.** Water containing 4 μg Ra per 200 ml, colored with fluorescein; used medicinally. **r. bromide.** RaBr$_2$ = 385.8. Colorless crystals, sublimes 900, soluble in water; used medicinally, usually mixed with barium bromide. **r. carbonate.** RaCO$_3$ = 286.0. White powder, insoluble in water; marketed mixed with barium carbonate. **r. chloride.** RaCl$_2$ = 296.5. Yellow crystals, m.1650, soluble in water; used medicinally mixed with barium chloride. **r. compress.** An oiled silk bag which contains finely ground radium ore and barium sulfate; used to treat rheumatism. **r. drinking water.** Distilled water containing 1 μg Ra per 30 ml; used medicinally. **r. emanation.** Radon. **r.F.** Polonium. **r.G.** Radiolead. **r. sulfate.** RaSO$_4$ = 322.0. White powder, insoluble in water; used mixed with barium sulfate. **r. therapy.** Curie therapy. The use of radioactive substances to treat disease. **r. units.** (1) Micrograms of Ra (0.001 mg). (2) Curies, q.v., millicuries, and microcuries; the emanation from 1 gm, 1 mg, and 1 μg Ra, respectively. (3) Mache units, q.v., a concentration of Ra emanation corresponding with 1/2,500 microcurie. Cf. *urane.*

radius. Any line from the center to the circumference of a circle: radius = 0.5 diameter = circumference/π.

radix. Latin for root. **r. sarsale.** Sarsaparilla.

radome. A solid shape produced by the electrophoretic deposition of a ceramic powder on an electrode, from which it is subsequently removed and consolidated by sintering.

radon. Rn = 222. Niton, actinon, radium emanation. The element of at. no. 86; the last of the series of inert gases. It is produced in radioactive minerals by radioactive disintegration. See *r. decay chain table.* Discovered by Mme. Curie in

RADON DECAY CHAIN TABLE

Chain member	Isotope	Half-life	Radiation
Radon	Radon-222	3.8 days	α
Radium-A	Polonium-218	3.1 min	α
Radium-B	Lead-214	26.8 min	$\beta\gamma$
Radium-C	Bismuth-214	19.7 min	$\beta\gamma$
Radium-C'	Polonium-214	160μ sec	α
Radium-D	Lead-210	19.4 yr	$\beta\gamma$
Radium-E	Bismuth-210	5.0 days	β
Radium-F	Polonium-210	138.4 days	α
Radium-G	Lead-206	Stable	

1898 (niton), and isolated by Dorn (1901). It has a life of 5.5 days, and liquefies -153 to a colorless liquid, b.-65, d.9.97, and glows with a blue light which turns orange at lower temperatures. **r. unit.** Curie.

rador. An early name for *radar*.

raestelin. $C_{23}H_{18}O_{15} = 534.02$. A glucoside, the coloring matter of galls produced by *Raestelia lucerta*. Green needles, m.243.

*ra***F.** Radiofluorine.

Ra F. Radium F.

raffia. Raphia.

raffinase. An enzyme that hydrolyzes raffinose, and is similar to invertase. Cf. *melibiase*.

raffinate. The purified product obtained by a refining operation. In particular, a refined oil from the fractionation of crude lubricating oils.

raffinose. $C_{18}H_{32}O_{16}\cdot 5H_2O = 594.4$. Melitriose, melitose. A carbohydrate from sugar beets, cottonseed, or eucalyptus; hydrolyzed to fructose, glucose, and galactose. Colorless needles, m.119, soluble in water.

Ra G. Uranium-lead.

Ragsky test. The toxicological detection of chloroform by the reaction: $6CHCl_3 \rightarrow C_6Cl_5 + 3Cl_2 + 6HCl$, whose products are deposited as white needles, detected by iodide-starch paper, and absorbed by silver nitrate solution, respectively.

ragweed. The dried leaves and flowers of *Ambrosia artemisiaefolia;* an astringent and styptic.

ragwort. Senecio.

raies ultimes. Ultimate lines. The strongest and most persistent lines of a spectrum from a given element, and used to identify it.

rainfall. The depth of water precipitated annually from the atmosphere onto a given area of the surface of the land, in a liquid or solid state: 1 in. r. $= 4.75$ gal/yd^2.

raised growth. A heavy bacterial growth, with abrupt or terraced edges.

raisin. The dried ripe fruit of grapes, *Vitis vinifera* (Vitaceae). **r. seed oil.** Grape-seed oil. Yellow oil, d.0.92–0.93. Used in foods, as a lubricant, and in soap making.

ralstonite. $3Al(OH,F)_3\cdot(Na_2,Mg)\cdot F_2\cdot 2H_2O$. A mineral.

Raman, Sir Chandrasekhara Venkata. b. 1888. Indian physicist, Nobel Prize winner (1930). **R. effect.** The scattering of monochromatic light with a change in wavelength, due to the absorption of energy by the scattering medium. Cf. *scattering, luminescence.* **R. lines.** The shift in wavelengths of the R. effect, indicating molecular structure and the type of atomic bonds. **R. spectrum.** The characteristic line patterns on a photograph taken at right angles through a substance illuminated with a quartz mercury lamp.

ramie. Rhea fiber. The bast fiber from the nettle *Boehmeria tenacissima;* used for weaving grass cloth or Canton linen, and for making Bible papers. **false-** China grass from *B. nivea*.

ramigenic acid. $C_{16}H_{20}O_6 = 308.2$. An acid produced by the mold fungus, *Penicillium Charelsii*.

rammelsbergite. NiAs$_2$, in nature.

Ramsay, Sir William. 1852–1916. British chemist, Nobel Prize winner (1904); discovered the noble gases and some radioactive elements. **R.-Shields equation.** $\gamma(MV)^{\frac{2}{3}} = K(t_c - t - 6)$, where γ is the surface tension, MV the molecular volume, t_e the critical temperature, t the temperature of the liquid; K is 2.12 ergs/deg for a normal liquid. Cf. *Morgan* equation. **R.-Young equation.** $p = kT - c$, where p is the pressure; T the absolute temperature of a gas or homogeneous liquid, the volume being constant; and k and c are constants. **R.-Young law.** $A/B = A'/B'$, where A is the boiling point of compound a, B the boiling point of b at pressure x, A' the boiling point of a, and B' the boiling point of b at pressure y.

Ramsden ocular. See *ocular*.

rancid. Having the peculiar tainted smell of oily substances that have begun to spoil, owing to formation of free fatty acids; as, rancid butter.

Raney's alloy. An alloy, Ni 30, Al 70%; used in place of Devarda's alloy, q.v., for the determination of nitrates by reduction to ammonia. **R. catalyst.** Ni$_2$H.(?) R. nickel. A highly active, finely divided nickel catalyst, prepared by dissolving the aluminum out of R. alloy by alkali; used for hydrogenating organic compounds.

Rankine scale. A thermometer scale based on absolute zero of the Fahrenheit scale: $-460°F = 0°R$. Cf. *Kelvin scale, Réaumur degree*.

rankinite. $3CaO\cdot 2SiO_2$. A natural silicate (Ireland); a constituent of high-lime blast-furnace slags.

Ranunculaceae. The crowfoot family; e.g.: *Helleborus niger*, black hellebore; *Anemone hepatica*, liverwort. Cf. *aconite alkaloids*.

ranunculine. An alkaloid cardiac poison from *Ranuncula* species.

Raoult, François Marie. 1830–1901. French chemist. **R.'s law.** The lowering of the freezing point or of the vapor pressure p of a solution is proportional to the amount of substance dissolved in the solution: $(p_0 - p)/p_0 = aM/bm$, where p_0 is the vapor pressure of the pure solvent, a the weight in grams of the solute of molecular weight m, and b the weight in grams of the solvent of molecular weight M. It is used to determine molecular weights. Cf. *Blagden's law, Coppet's law*.

*ra***P.** Radiophosphorus.

rapeseed oil. Colza oil, cole oil, rape oil. Brown oil from the seeds of rape, *Brassica napus* (Cruciferae). Unpleasant odor, d$_{25}$0.906–0.910, m.20, soluble in alcohol; used as a lubricant, and in the heat treatment of steel and manufacture of rubber substitutes.

raphanin. $C_{17}H_{26}N_3O_4S_5(?)$. An antibiotic anthocyanin from radishes, which prevents the germination of seeds. Yellow syrup, b$_{0.06mmHg}$135, soluble in water.

raphia. Raffia. A fiber from the leaves of the palm *Raphia pedunculata* (Madagascar), used for mats and basketry. **r. wax.** A wax from palm leaves; little used, as it has poor solubility in solvents.

raphides. Small crystals of calcium oxalate in plants.

rapic acid. Rapinic acid.

rapinic acid. $C_{18}H_{34}O_2 = 282.27$. An unsaturated, monobasic isomer of oleic acid (probably identical with petroselinic acid), in rapeseed oil.

rare. Not common. **r. earth metals.** The metallic elements, at. nos. 57–72. Two classes: ceria earths and yttria or gadolinite earths, which are similar in physical and chemical properties, forming the one group in the periodic system whose elements have consecutive atomic numbers. **r. earth minerals.**

The r. earth metals generally occur associated with one another as phosphates and silicates; e.g.: zircon, $ZrSiO_4$; monazite, $CePO_4$. **r. earths.** (1) The oxides of the r. earth metals; now known as the lanthanons. (2) In a wider sense, the oxides of Sc, Y, La, and even of Hf, Zr, Th.

rarefaction. Making less dense by increasing the volume without changing the amount of a gas; or decreasing the amount of gas in a certain volume.

rarefied. Describing a gas at pressure less than atmospheric.

rare gases. Noble gases.

rasmosin. A resin from the root of *Cimicifuga racemosa* (Ranunculaceae).

Rasorite. Trademark for sodium borate ore concentrates from California.

raspberries. The fruits of *Rubus idaeus* (Rosaceae); used as food and in pharmaceutical preparations.

raspberry leaves. The dried leaves of *Rubus* species. Used in pharmacy as a flavoring vehicle (U.S.P.) and astringent.

raster. A grid of narrow parallel beams used in the photoelectric scanning of letters and figures in electronic "readers."

rat. White rat, *Rattus norvegicus*, used in animal experiments. **r. unit.** (1) The minimum quantity of pituitary hormone injected subcutaneously that will cause the formation of one or more corpora lutea in the female white r. (2) The vitamin A potency of a substance in terms of its therapeutic effects on rats.

ratafia. A cordial prepared by steeping crushed fruit kernels.

ratany. Krameria.

rate. The relative degree of speed. **r. of decomposition, r. of formation.** The velocity of a chemical reaction expressed in moles per second per milliliter.

ratholite. Pectolite.

raticide. A rat-killing chemical.

ratio. Proportion.

ration. The daily allowance of food and drink.

rational. Based on reasoning and not on direct experience. **r. analysis.** The expression of analytical results so that the method of combination of the elements present is indicated; e.g., in water analysis. Cf. *ultimate analysis*. Thus, clay would be expressed in terms of calcium silicate, rather than as Ca, Si, and O. Cf. *ultimate*. **r. formula.** A combination of chemical symbols indicating the probable atomic links in the molecule. **r. units.** See *ultimate units*.

rattlesnake root. Senega. **r. venom.** The poisonous proteins from the fangs of *Crotalus* species. (Antidote: external application of potassium permanganate.)

Raulin's solution. A culture fluid for fungi.

rauwolfia alkaloids. Alkaloids from a variety of *Rauwolfia* species, particularly *R. serpentina*, Benth; e.g.: reserpine, rauwolfine, Δ-yohimbine.

rauwolfine. $C_{20}H_{26}N_2O_3 \cdot 2\frac{1}{2}H_2O = 387.2$. An alkaloid, decomp. 235, from the bark of *Rauwolfia caffra* (Apocynaceae).

raw. Crude, unrefined, or unfinished. **r. material.** A crude material from which useful substances can be made. **r. ore.** An ore in its natural state.

ray(s). A beam of light, heat, or rapidly moving particles. Cf. *radiation*. **absorbed-** A light r.

transformed into heat (molecular motion) on passing through matter. **actinic-** Chemically active (especially ultraviolet) light. **alpha-** α particles. Positively charged, high-velocity helium nuclei produced by the disintegration of radioactive elements. Cf. *canal r.* **Becquerel-** X rays produced by disintegration of radioactive elements. **beta-** Negatively charged, high-velocity electrons produced by the disintegration of radioactive elements. Cf. *cathode r.* **Blondlot-** n rays. **canal-** Positively charged particles produced by the electric discharge in an evacuated tube having a perforated cathode through which the particles pass. Cf. *alpha r.* **cathode-** High-velocity electrons moving at right angles to the cathode of a vacuum tube and producing X rays on striking a solid. **chemical-** Actinic. **cosmic-** Millikan, ultra-γ or ultra-X rays. Radiations of extremely short wavelengths coming from space. **extraordinary-** See *ordinary*. **gamma-** X rays produced by the impact against a solid of β rays from radioactive elements. **hard-** X rays of short wavelength and high penetrating powers. **heat-** See *infrared r.* **infrared-** Heat radiations beyond the red portion of the visible spectrum. **K-** See *K* radiations. **L-** See *L* radiations. **Lenard-** Residual cathode r. that pass through windows of thin metal foil in a vacuum tube. **M-** See *M* radiations. **Millikan-** See *cosmic r.* **molecular-** See *molecular.* **n-** Blondlot r. A nonluminous radiation from certain flames that produces fluorescence on striking certain substances. **negative-** Cathode or β rays. **od-** The radiations of living organisms. Cf. *scotography.* **ordinary-** See *ordinary.* **phonic-** Sound waves. **photic-** Visible light r. **positive-** Canal and α rays. **roentgen-** X rays. **secondary-** Radiation produced after a primary r. strikes matter. **soft-** Any X ray of long wavelength that has low penetrating powers. **ultimate-** See *raies ultimes.* **ultra-γ-** See *cosmic r.* **ultraviolet-** The radiations from beyond the violet end of the visible spectrum; they produce fluorescence. **UV-** Ultraviolet. **W-** Rays between UV and X rays. **X-** Roentgen r. Nonluminous radiation, usually produced by cathode r. striking a solid. Cf. *X rays.*

Rây, Sir Prafulla Chandra. 1861–1944. Hindu chemist, noted for his work on the organic nitrites and history of chemistry.

Rayleigh, (Lord) John William Strutt. 1842–1919. English physicist, Nobel Prize winner (1904); noted for the discovery of the noble gases, and determinations of the densities of gases. **R., (Lord) Robert John.** 1875–1947. English physicist, noted for his work on radioactivity and optics.

Rayolande. Trade name for a chemically modified viscose rayon synthetic fiber.

rayon. (1) Generic term applied to all textile fibers that do not occur naturally. (2) In particular, an artificial substance whose chief ingredient is cellulose or one of its derivatives. Cf. *prolon*. **acetate r.** The acetic ester of cellulose, prepared by treating the cellulose of cotton or wood pulp with acetic anhydride, acetic acid, and concentrated sulfuric acid in presence of a catalyst; precipitating with water; and dissolving in acetone, from which it is spun. Trade names: Celanese and Lustron. **cuprammonium r.** Cupra-r., r. glanzstoff, Pauly r. Made by dissolving cotton or wood pulp in an ammoniacal copper solution, which is ejected through fine orifices into a setting bath of dilute sulfuric acid. **nitrocellulose r.** (Chardonnet) is prepared by treating cotton with nitric and sulfuric acid, dissolving the resulting trinitrocellulose in alcohol and ether (collodion solution), and ejecting through fine nozzles into water or warm air. The flammable filaments are denitrated with sodium hydrosulfide. **seaweed r.** R. made by extruding an extract of seaweed in an aqueous alkali into acid. The alginic acid is precipitated as an alkali-insoluble filament, e.g., calcium alginate. **tang r.** A Norwegian textile made from staple fiber derived from r. and treated seaweed. **viscose r.** The commonest process of making r. involves soaking wood pulp or cotton linters in 18% caustic soda solution, treating the soda cellulose with carbon disulfide (xanthation), dissolving in caustic soda (viscose), and forcing the viscose through fine outlets into a setting and bleaching bath.

razor stone. Novaculite.

Rb. Symbol for rubidium.

R.B.C. Abbreviation for red blood corpuscles.

RBX. See *hexalite*.

r.d. Abbreviation for: (1) rod; (2) rutherford, q.v.

R.D.X. A high explosive of the tetranitrocellulose type.

Re. Symbol for rhenium.

Ré. Abbreviation for Réaumur.

react. To enter into a chemical combination.

reactants. Molecules that act with one another to form a new set of molecules (resultants).

reacting. Undergoing a reaction. **r. weight.** Equivalent weight.

reaction. (1) That force which tends to oppose a given force (Newton's laws). (2) The acidity or alkalinity of a solution. (3) A chemical change: the transformation of one or more molecules (reactants) into others. **acid-** A positive test for the presence of hydrogen ions (acidity); as, blue litmus turning red. **addition-** Molecules combine to form a more complex molecule. **aldol-** See *aldol condensation*. **alkaline-** A positive test for the presence of hydroxyl ions (alkalinity); as, red litmus turning blue. **amphoteric-** The r. of a substance that has both acid and alkaline properties. **analytic-** Decomposition r. **analytical-** A r. used to determine the quantity and/or quality of matter. **balanced-** A reversible r. that does not go to completion in either direction. **bimolecular-** A r. of the second order. **Bunsen-** See *Bunsen*. **catalytic-** A r. whose rate is accelerated by a catalyst. Cf. *induced r.* **chain-** See *chain, trigger*. **color-** A r. involving a change in color. **combination-** Elements unite to form a compound. **complete-** A chemical change that proceeds to completion; as, precipitation. **complex-, composite-** A chemical change in which more than one r. occurs simultaneously. **concurrent-** A chemical change consisting of a series of connected reactions that could not occur separately. **condensation-** A r. in which atoms are removed from 2 or more molecules, the residues combining to form a single molecule. **counter-** A reversible r. **coupled-** A concurrent r. **decomposition-** Molecules decompose into simpler molecules and/or atoms. **diazo-** See *diazotization*. **displacement-** An element molecule interacts with a compound molecule.

dissociation- A compound molecule splits into element molecules. **electron-** Oxidation-reduction r. **endothermic-** A r. in which heat is consumed. **esterification-** R·OH + HA = RA and H_2O, where R is an aryl or alkyl radical; a catalyst (as zinc chloride) is required. **etherification-** R·OH + HOR′ = R·OR′ + H_2O, where R and R′ are aryl and/or alkyl radicals. **exothermic-** A r. in which heat is liberated. **flame-** See *Bunsen*. **group-** A r. typical of a certain group of elements, as in qualitative analysis. **heat of-** See *heat*. **heterogen(e)ous-** A composite r. **hydrolysis-** The reversal of a neutralization r. by the action of water. **incomplete-** A balanced r. **induced-** A r. that is accelerated by an inductor or promoter. **ionic-** An instantaneous r. between ions in solution. **irreversible-** A r. that proceeds to completion and cannot be reversed. **main-** The principal r. **metathetic-** R. involving interaction of molecules. **micro-** See *micro*. **molecular-** In general, a slow r. between molecules and not ions. **monomolecular-** A r. of the first order. **negative-** The absence of r., e.g., in a colorimetric, qualitative analytical test. **neutral-** A r. that is neither acid nor basic. **neutralization-** q.v. **nuclear-** See *nuclear*. **opposing-** The reverse r. in a balanced r. **oxidation-reduction-, oxidoreduction-** See *oxidation-reduction*. **peritectic-** A r. between a solid phase (α) and a liquid phase producing a second solid phase (β). **photo-** See *photo*. **positive-** A r. that is definite, e.g., in a colorimetric, qualitative analytical test. **primary-** The principal or main r. that occurs in a composite system of reactions. **principal-** Primary r. **proton-** Neutralization r. **pyrogenic-** See *pyrogenic*. **qualitative-** q.v. **quantitative-** q.v. **restitution-** The reverse of substitution r. **reversible-** An incomplete r. A r. that under suitable conditions can proceed from right to left or left to right. **secondary-** Subsidiary r. **side-** A r. simultaneous with the principal r., occurring between the same reactants or their products, and usually forming different products. **simultaneous-** Side r. **staircase-** See *staircase*. **subsidiary-** A r. between the resultants of a r. **substitution-** An element molecule substitutes one of the elements in a compound molecule. **successive-** A r. made up of a number of component reactions which occur in succession, the reactants being in turn the resultants of the preceding r. **sympathetic-** Induced r. **synthetic-** Combination and addition r. **topochemical-** See *topochemistry*. **transfer-** Metathetical r. **trigger-** q.v.

r. control. (1) Speed of r. depends on amounts of substances present and energy (potential energy, electromotive force, and free energy). A r. can be accelerated mechanically (as by increasing the number of molecules coming in contact with one another, by increasing the surface by subdivision); thermally (by increasing the velocity of the molecules by heating); electrically (by electrolysis); optically (by irradiation). (2) R. acidity is controlled by buffer solutions. **r. equation.** See *chemical reaction, equation*. **r. isochore.** An equation relating temperature and the equilibrium constant K at constant volume (or pressure) of a gas: $d(\log_e K)/dT = -U/RT^2$; where T is absolute temperature, U the decrease in total energy or heat quantity, and R the gas constant. By integration the maximum work at any temperature can be determined. **r. isotherm.** An equation for ideal gases indicating the maximum external work or diminution in free energy obtainable from a chemical reaction at constant temperature and volume: $A = RT \log K - RT\Sigma v \log C$, where A is the decrease in free energy (affinity), and $RT\cdot\Sigma_v \log C$ represents the concentration. **r. law.** If a system in equilibrium undergoes a restraint, a change tends to take place, and partly annul the constraint. **r. order.** A classification of reactions:

First order: mono- or unimolecular reaction—in which only one molecule is involved. Velocity $= dx/dt = k(a - x)$, where a is the initial amount of substance, x the amount that has changed after time t, and k the velocity constant.

Second order: di- or dimolecular reaction—in which 2 molecules undergo a change: $2A$ or $A + B = 1$ or more products. Velocity $= k(a - x)(b - x)$.

Third order: tri- or termolecular reaction—in which 3 molecules undergo a change: $3A$ or $2A + B$ or $A + B + C = 1$ or more products. Velocity $= k(a - x)(b - x)(c - x)$.

r. promoter. Promoter. **r. sensitivity.** The dilution at which a r. still gives identifiable end products. **r. velocity.** Velocity constant. The rate at which molecules change in a chemical r. See *reaction order*.

reactivation. The rendering active again of a catalyst or serum which has become inactivated. Cf. *revivification*.

Reading unit. A measure of the activity of nisin.

reagent. (1) A chemical substance that reacts or participates in a reaction. (2) A substance used for the detection or determination of another substance by chemical or microscopical means; especially analysis. Types:

1. Precipitants—produce an insoluble compound.
2. Solvents—used to dissolve water-insoluble materials.
3. Oxidizers—used in oxidation.
4. Reducers—used in reduction.
5. Fluxes—used to lower melting points.
6. Colorimetric reagents—analogous to 1, but produce coloured soluble compounds.

See *volumetric solutions*. **r. solution.** The aqueous solution of a r. used in the laboratory; usually 10% concentration.

realgar. As_2S_2. Ruby sulfur, red arsenic, red orpiment. Orange prisms.

ream. A number of sheets of paper of the same kind, size, and weight per unit area; usually 500, but also 480, 1,000, etc., according to trade custom.

rearrangement. Intramolecular conversion, migration, or transposition, in which the atoms or atomic groups redistribute or arrange themselves in a different manner. Cf. *pinacol, enol form*.

reastiness. Describing the flavor produced in salt-preserved meat due to oxidation of the fats present.

Réaumur, René Antoine Ferchault de. 1683–1757. French natural philosopher, noted for his invention of a thermometer scale based on the freezing point $(0°R)$ and the boiling point $(80°R)$ of water. **R. degree.** °R or °Ré. $80°R = 100°C$. Cf. *Rankine scale*.

recalescence. An increase in the emission of visible light during the cooling of molten metals; explained by thermally excited electrons falling back to a lower energy level in the atom. Cf. *luminescence*.

recalescent point. The temperature at which evolution of heat occurs during the cooling of steel. It is lower than the decalescent point by an amount that is a measure of the hysteresis of steel.

recarbonize. To restore the carbon content of steel after decarbonizing.

recarburize. Recarbonize.

receiver. A vessel in which the products of a distillation are collected.

receptor. (1) A radical or atom on the surface of the protoplasmic, colloidal molecule that fixes drugs or poisons and thereby renders them effective. (2) A chemical group containing less than 12 atoms, which normally performs one of the metabolic duties of the living cell. Receptors are associated with the active group of an enzyme, and can be "blocked" (inactivated) by drugs. Cf. *Ehrlich side-chain theory*.

reciprocal. The quotient r obtained by dividing unity by a number n: $r = 1/n$. **r. ohm.** The unit of conductivity, mho. **r. salt pair.** Two salts which may act either as the reactants or resultants of a reaction; as, $NaNO_3 + KNO_3 \rightleftharpoons NaNO_3 + KCl$.

reciprocating motion. Motion to and fro in a straight line; as, a piston.

reciprocity failure. See *latensification*.

reciprocity law. Bunsen and Roscoe law.

recoil. Return motion. **r. atom.** The atom of a radioactive substance in the process of expelling an α particle; the high velocity causes a recoil. **r. radiation.** Radiation produced by bombarding gaseous atoms with α particles; its source is the action of the r. atom.

reconstituted (reconstructed) milk. A beverage obtained by emulsifying unsalted butter in a solution of skimmed milk powder. Gelatin is sometimes added as a stabilizer.

recovery. The extraction of a valuable constituent from a raw material, by-product, or waste product; as, silver from photographic wastes.

recryst. Abbreviation for recrystallization.

recrystallization. Repeated crystallizations for the purpose of purification.

recrystallize. To purify a substance by repeated crystallization.

rectification. (1) The redistillation of a liquid for purification. (2) The transformation of an alternating into a direct current. (3) The evaluation of the length of a curved line.

rectified spirit. Spirits of wine. Redistilled alcohol; 84% by weight of absolute alcohol, 50° over proof (O.P.), and a specific gravity 0.8382 at 60°F. Cf. *proof spirit*.

rectifier. A device to convert alternating to direct current, e.g., quartz r. **Dryr-** An asymmetric conductor consisting of a disk of lead sulfide waxed on one side, with tinfoil on both sides. **r. cell.** Photoelectric cell.

rectorite. A white aluminum silicate, similar to kaolinite.

recuperator. Regenerator.

red. The least refracted portion of the visible spectral colors. **natural-** See *carmine*.

r. **acid.** 1,5-Dihydroxynaphthalene-3,7-disulfonic acid. r. **antimony.** Kermesite. r. **arsenic.** Realgar. r. **bark.** R. cinchona. r. **bole.** R. ocher. r. **brass.** An alloy: Cu 78–83, Zn 7–9, Pb 6–10, Sn 4–2%. r. **cake.** Commercial sodium vanadate, used in the manufacture of ceramic colors and catalysts. r. **cedar.** Juniper. r. **chalk.** R. ocher mixed with clay. See *red hematite.* r. **chrome.** Lead chromate. r. **cobalt.** Erythrite. r. **copper ore.** Cuprite. r. **couch grass.** Carex. r. **hematite.** See *hematite.* r. **iron ore.** Hematite. r. **lead.** Lead tetroxide. r. **lead ore.** Crocoisite. r. **liquor.** A solution of aluminum acetate, used in dyeing. r. **manganese.** Rhodonite. Rhodochrosite. r. **mercury iodide.** Mercuric iodide. r. **mercury oxide.** Mercuric oxide. r. **metal.** A copper alloy. r. **mustard.** Sinapis nigra. r. **ochre.** Reddle, r. bole. A r. often impure hematite; a pigment. r. **oil.** Commercial oleic acid. r. **orpiment.** Realgar. r. **oxide.** Iron sesquioxide. r. **oxide of zinc.** Zincite. r. **pepper.** Capsicum. r. **phosphorus.** See *phosphorus.* r. **precipitate.** Mercuric oxide. r. **prussiate.** Ferricyanide. -*of potash.* Potassium ferricyanide. -*of soda.* Sodium ferricyanide. r. **root.** Sanguinaria. r. **sensitive plate.** A photographic plate with the emulsion made orthochromatic by addition of a sensitizer; as, neocyanine. r. **silver ore.** Pyrargyrite. Proustite. *dark-* Pyrargyrite. *light-* Proustite. r. **stone.** Ferric oxide. r. **vitriol.** Bieberite. r. **zinc ore.** Zincite.

reddingite. A native iron and manganese phosphate from Redding, California.

reddingtonite. A native chromium sulfate.

reddle. Hematite.

redistillation. Repeated distillation of a liquid, usually to purify it.

Redon. Trade name for a polyamide synthetic fiber.

Redonda phosphate. A phosphate ore (40% phosphorus pentoxide), W. Indies.

redox. Reduction-oxidation or electronation. r. **equilibrium.** Describing a reaction that is poised at a definite rH value. Cf. *oxidation-reduction potential.* r. **indicator.** See *indicator.* r. **polymer.** See electron-exchange *polymer.* r. **series.** Oxidizing and reducing reactions arranged in order of intensity.

redoxokinetic effect. The current-rectifying power of certain reversible electrodes. It depends on the kinetics of their redox reactions. Used for electrometric titration.

redruthrite. Cu_2S. A black mineral.

reduce. To add one or more electrons to an atom (electronate). Hence: (1) to decrease the valence number of an atom with a corresponding increase in the valence number of another atom (which is oxidized); (2) to deprive of oxygen; (3) to add hydrogen. Antonym: *oxidize.*

reduced. (1) Brought or restored to metallic form. (2) Brought to a lower stage of oxidation. r. **iron.** Finely powdered iron obtained by heating ferric oxide in a current of hydrogen. r. **oil.** Crude petroleum from which hydrocarbons of low boiling point have been removed by distillation or evaporation.

reducer. (1) Reducing agent. (2) A solution that decreases the intensity of a photographic image;

Reducer

as, equal volumes of sodium thiosulfate 10 and potassium ferricyanide 3% solutions. (3) A cast-iron kettle with a power-driven stirrer. **Jones-** An apparatus used in chemical analysis to reduce ferric iron to ferrous iron by passing the solution through granulated zinc. Cf. *reductor.*

reducible. Capable of being reduced.

reducin. $C_{12}H_{24}N_6O_9$. A leukomain from urochrome.

reducing agent. Reducer. A substance that is readily oxidized by reducing another substance; as, nascent hydrogen, stannous chloride, formaldehyde, and zinc dust. Cf. *oxidizing agents.* r. **flame.** The luminous portion or inner cone of the blowpipe or bunsen burner where an excess of unburnt carbon or hydrocarbon gas acts as a reducing agent on substances in it. r. **sugar.** A mono- or disaccharide (as, glucose or fructose) that reduces copper or silver salts in alkaline solutions. Cf. *Fehling's solution.*

reductase. An enzyme reducing agent.

reductic acid. See *reductones.*

reduction. (1) Making less or smaller. Converting to a fine state. Reproducing on a smaller scale. (2) A chemical reducing reaction; e.g.: (*a*) removal of oxygen; as, $CuO \rightarrow Cu$; (*b*) addition of hydrogen; as, $Mg \rightarrow MgH_2$; (*z*) change from a higher to lower valence; as, from the ferric to the ferrous state, viz.: $Fe^{3+} + 1(-) = Fe^{++}$, where the atom gaining the electron $(-)$ is reduced, and that losing it is oxidized. Cf. *oxidation, redox.* **Birch-** R. of organic compounds with sodium and liquid ammonia.

r. **intensity.** rH. See *oxidation-reduction potential.* r. **oxidation.** See *redox.* r. **potential.** The potential of a platinum electrode immersed in a solution containing an ion being reduced.

reductones. Apparent vitamin C. Reductic acid. Reducing substances present in certain processed foods which react similarly to ascorbic acid, and interfere with its determination.

reductor. (1) An apparatus for a reducing reaction, e.g., for determination of phosphorus in steel. See *Jones.* (2) A metal or metal amalgam which acts as a reducing agent.

Redwood number. A measure of oil viscosity in terms of rate of flow from a standard Redwood viscometer (U.K. standard).

Reech's theorem. The ratio of the adiabatic to the isothermal elasticity of a fluid equals the ratio of the specific heats at constant pressure and constant volume; equals 1.66 (for monatomic gases).

Reevon. Trade name for a polyethylene synthetic fiber.

refikite. $C_{20}H_{16}O_2$. A white resin, in lignite.

refine. To purify.

refinery. (1) A building or apparatus for refining. (2) A shallow hearth furnace for making wrought iron.

refining heat. The temperature 655°C, that imparts fineness of grain and toughness to steel.

reflection. The rebounding of an incident ray of light, heat, or sound from a surface, as a reflected ray having the same form, quality, and intensity.

reflux. Backward flow, return. **r. condenser.** A vertical or inclined condenser, from which the condensed liquid flows back into the distilling vessel. **r. valve.** A check valve.

Reformatzky reaction. A condensation reaction between ketones and α-bromoaliphatic acids in the presence of zinc or magnesium: $R_2CO + BrCH_2\text{-}COOR + Zn \rightarrow (ZnO\cdot HBr) + R_2C(OH)CH_2\text{-}COOR$.

reforming. The converse of cracking, q.v. The conversion, e.g., catalytically, of low-octane-value, long-chain paraffin hydrocarbons into isoparaffins, hydroaromatics, and olefins of the same boiling-point range.

refract. To change the direction, deviate, or bend (usually rays).

refraction. The change in direction of rays of light obliquely incident on, or traversing a boundary between, 2 transparent media, or a medium of varying density. Cf. *light, diffraction.* **atomic-** See *refractivity.* **double-** Birefringence. Having more than one refractive index, according to the direction of the traversing light. Occurs in all except isometric crystals; transparent substances with internal strains, e.g., glass; and substances with different structures in different directions, e.g., fibers. **electrical-** See *Kerr effect.* **index of-** See *refractive index.* **specific-** See *refractivity.*

refractive. Refringent. Pertaining to refraction. **r. constant.** The sum of the refractivities of the pure constituents of a solution, each multiplied by the ratio of its mass per unit volume of solution to its own density when pure. **r. index.** Symbol, *n.* The ratio of the velocities of light in a medium and in air under the same conditions. Measured by the ratio of the sines of the angles of incidence and refraction. Estimated by immersing a crystal in liquids of known *n* until one is found in which the crystal is invisible; e.g. (n_D at 23°C):

Methyl alcohol	1.3279
Water	1.3328
Acetone	1.3598
Hexane	1.3750
Heptane	1.3868
Ethylene chloride	1.4417
Chloroform	1.4430
Cineol	1.4552
Glycerol	1.4671
Decahydronaphthalene	1.4750
Iso-amyl phthalate	1.4870
Xylene	1.4957
Pentachloroethane	1.5006
Anisole	1.5150
Chlorobenzene	1.5218
Trimethylene bromide	1.5220
Ethylene bromide	1.5353
O-nitrotoluene	1.5440
Nitrobenzene	1.5506
Tri-o-cresyl phosphate	1.5560
O-toluidine	1.5700
Aniline	1.5840
Bromoform	1.5940
Quinaldine	1.6088
Iodobenzene	1.6168
Quinoline	1.6239
α-Chloronaphthalene	1.6318
α-Bromonaphthalene	1.6569
Methylene iodide	1.7400

absolute- The r. index in a vacuum: $n \times 1.0029$.

refractivity. The change in direction of light passing at an angle through media of different densities; expressed as refractive index minus 1. **atomic-** The specific r. of an atom multiplied by its atomic weight. **molecular-** The sum of the atomic refractivities of the atoms in a molecule. For molecules of normal structure, it equals specific r. times molecular weight. **specific-** The r. of a substance calculated from its r. index: $(n^2 - 1)/(n^2 + 2)d$, where n is the r. index and d the density. *specific r. power.* The expression $(n - 1)/d$, which is almost independent of temperature.

refractometer. An instrument to determine the refractive index of a substance at various temperatures.

refractories. Plural of refractory. See table on the facing page.

refractoriness. Resistance to softening on application of heat. Cf. *Seger cones.* **r. under load.** The resistance to deformation of a refractory subjected to stress at a definite temperature.

refractory. A material that is slow to soften and resists heat; as, brick. **r. cements.** Materials used to hold r. bricks together: *straight-* Fireclay, silica, magnesite, etc. which have high refractoriness (>1,650°C) but poor bonding strength. *synthetic-* (1) Vitrifying at about 9,000°C, as portland cement, glass, fusible clays, which have a good bonding strength; (2) air-setting mixtures of refractories and fluxes of good bonding strength.

refrigerant. (1) An agent that produces the sensation of cold; used medicinally. (2) An agent used to obtain a low temperature. See *freezing mixture.* **mechanical-** A noncorrosive liquid of suitable vapor pressure, used in refrigeration; it should be nontoxic and nonflammable; e.g.: carbon dioxide, ammonia, dichlorodifluoromethane.

Refractory	Formula	Temperature of failure under load, °C	Bulk density	Porosity, %	Fusion point, °C
Alundum..........	Al_2O_3	1550^c	2.6	...	1750–2000
Bauxite brick......	$Al_2O_3 \cdot TiO_3$	1350^a	1.6	46–50	1750–2000
Chrome brick......	$Cr_2O_3 \cdot Al_2O_3 \cdot MgO$	1450^b	2.8–3.2	...	1850–2050
Fireclay brick......	$SiO_2 \cdot Al_2O_3$	1500^a	1.7–2.1	20–30	1500–1750
Magnesite brick	MgO	1550^b	2–2.8	24–40	2150–2615
Silica brick	SiO_2	1600^b	2–2.2	18–43	1685–1800
Silicon carbide.....	SiC	1650^c	2.0–2.6	17–34	2200–2240
Zirconia brick......	ZrO_2	1510^a	3.4–4	19	2000–2600

^{a} softens, ^{b} shears, ^{c} no failure—under a load of 25 psi.

refrigeration. The production of cold; the lowering of the temperature of a body by conducting away its heat.

refrigerator. A machine to produce refrigeration by compressing a gas, cooling it, and expanding it into a low-pressure pipe system, where it absorbs the heat, and is pumped out and compressed again.

refringent. Refractive.

refuse. Waste, garbage, or sewage.

regelation. The fusion of ice under pressure, followed by solidification of ice particles into a solid mass.

regeneration. The repair or renewal to the original state; as, of an electric battery, or catalyst. Cf. *revivification, Weldon process.*

regenerative. Capable of being utilized anew. **r. furnace.** A furnace in which the incoming fuel gases are preheated by the waste gases.

regenerator. A series of checkerwork brick chambers through which the flue gases and fuel gases of a furnace are alternately directed.

Regnault, Henri Victor. 1810–1878. French chemist, noted for researches in physical chemistry. **R. cell.** An anode of amalgamated zinc and a cathode of cadmium in a solution of sulfuric acid 1, calcium sulfate 1, water 12 pts; yields 0.34 volt. **R. value.** The weight of a cubic meter of hydrogen: 89.87 gm. Cf. *krith.*

Reguir cell. An anode of copper and cathode of lead oxide in a solution of copper sulfate and sulfuric acid; yields 1.4 volts.

regular system. The cubic system of crystal forms.

regulator. (1) Buffer solution. (2) A substance used in flotation processes for pH control; as lime.

regulus. (1) A small compact mass of metal in the bottom of the crucible on reduction of ores. (2) A compound of one or more metals with sulfur; usually brittle and crystalline with a dull greasy luster.

Reich, Ferdinand. 1799–1882. German mining engineer; discoverer of indium (with Richter, 1863).

Reichert number. The number of milliliters of 0.1 N alkali required to neutralize the volatile, water-soluble acids liberated on acidification of the soap produced by saponification of 10 gm fat. **R.-Meissl number, R.-Wollny number.** Similar to the R. number, referred to 5 gm fat and determined according to specified procedures. Cf. *Polenské number.*

Reimer's reaction. A reaction of phenols and chloroform in alkaline solutions to form phenol aldehydes.

Reinecke's acid. $[Cr \cdot (NH_3)_2 \cdot (SCN)_4]H$. Tetrathiocyanodiammonochromic acid. A reagent in the isolation of organic bases, e.g., choline from proteins. **R. salt.** $[(NH_3)_2Cr(SCN)_4]NH_4 \cdot H_2O$. Used similarly to R.'s acid; also as reagent for mercury (a red color or precipitate).

reinforced. Made stronger. **r. concrete.** Concrete with a steel foundation, used in building. **r. wine.** Wine to which alcohol has been added.

reinite. $FeWO_4$. The native tungstate.

Reinsch test. The detection of a small quantity of arsenic by depositing it from solution as a black stain on metallic copper.

Rekylon. Trade name for a polyamide synthetic fiber.

relative. Dependent upon or connected with some other phenomenon. **r. weight.** Atomic weight.

relativity. Einstein's theory: the conception that matter, space, and time are relative and not absolute; that all physical phenomena depend upon position in or relation to the universe. **general-**Mass exerts an attraction on light; hence: (1) large bodies, as the sun, deflect light waves; and (2) spectral lines of atoms on the surface of very massive stars are shifted toward the red. **special-**Energy E has mass; hence mass M increases slightly when energy content is increased. $M = E/c^2$, where c is the velocity of light, an absolute constant of nature. Cf. *mass-energy cycle.*

relaxation effect. The time lag of the response of a chemical equilibrium reaction to a change in external conditions.

relay. (1) A sensitive electromechanical device which, when operated by a comparatively weak current (as from an photoelectric cell) will cause corresponding action in a more powerful circuit. (2) A substance of natural origin used as an intermediate in the course of a long synthesis.

relict(a). Residue(s).

rem. The absorbed dose of an ionizing radiation; has the same biological effect as 1 rad of X radiation. Cf. *roentgen.*

remanence. The permanence of a permanent magnet.

remedy. An agent that cures disease.

remolinite. Atacamite.

Remsen, Ira. 1846–1927 American chemist noted as teacher and writer.

renal. Pertaining to the kidneys. **r. test.** A diagnostic test of the functions of the kidneys by administering phenolsulfonephthalein and determining colorimetrically the quantity in the urine.

Renard number. Preferred *number.*

renature. To restore to a natural or original condition. Cf. *denature, fibroinogen.*

render. (1) To melt down; to clarify. (2) To remove fat from animal tissues by heat.

renes. An extract from the kidneys of sheep, pigs, or calves. **r. siccii.** Dried and powdered r.; used medicinally.

renin. Hypertensin. A pseudoglobulin in fresh kidneys after intravenous injection of saline extract; soluble in water. It maintains a normal blood pressure. **anti-** A substance of the same origin as, but opposite in effect to, r. Cf. *rennin*.

rennase. Rennin, prorennin, chymogen, caseinase, lab ferment, chymosin. An enzyme of the gastric juice from the fourth stomach of calves. It hydrolyzes caseinogen, coagulating milk with formation of curd and whey; used in cheese manufacture.

rennet. A preparation of the lining of the stomach of the calf; a source of rennase.

rennin. Rennase. Cf. *renin*.

renosine. A nucleoprotein in the kidney.

rensselaerite. A variety of talc.

rep. Abbreviation for roentgen equivalent. A measure of degree of exposure to radioactivity.

repand. Wrinkled; as a bacterial culture with an uneven surface.

repeatability. Describing the extent to which the same results can be obtained over and over again by the same operator, using the same apparatus. Cf. *reproducibility*.

repeating unit. The original structural unit of a polymer, which is repeated to form the polymer, e.g., the diene unit in a butadiene rubber.

repercolation. A repeated percolation.

replacement. (1) The substitution of an atom or radical by another atom or radical: $X + HA = HX + A$. (2) The change from one mineral to another by gradual substitution during geological ages.

replica. (1) A copy or reproduction taken from an original. (2) In microscopy, a technique in which a mold is made of a specimen, e.g., a fiber, in moist cellulose acetate, and then coated with a 0.001-mm layer of silver by evaporation in a high vacuum, as the basis for building up a solid copper replica by electrodeposition.

replicable. Describing results that are always the same, within experimental error, when obtained by tests on the replicate samples of the same substance. Cf. *reproducible*.

repp. A plain weave, in which one of the elements (usually the finer) covers and conceals the other.

reproducibility. Describing the extent to which results are always the same, within experimental error, when obtained by different operators using different sets of apparatus. Cf. *repeatability*.

reproducible. Describing results that are always the same, within experimental error, when obtained by successive tests on the same sample. Cf. *replicable*, *reproducibility*.

reprography. Collective term for all processes for reproducing texts or illustrations.

repulsion. The tendency of 2 bodies to move away from each other.

resacetophenone. $MeCO \cdot C_6H_3(OH)_2 = 152.06$. 2,4-Dihydroxyacetophenone. White needles, m.147. **methyl-** Peonol.

resaldol. $(OH)_2 \cdot C_6H_3 \cdot CO \cdot C_6H_4COOC_2H_5 = 286.11$. Resorcinol benzoyl carbonic acid ethyl ester, 2,4-

dioxybenzoyl o-benzoic acid ethyl ester. Yellow powder, insoluble in water; an intestinal antiseptic.

resalgin. $(C_{11}H_{12}O_4N_2)_2C_7H_6O_4 = 626.2$. Antipyrine resorcylate, antipyreticin. Colorless crystals, m.110, soluble in water; an antiseptic. **beta-** Resorcylalgin.

resazurin. $C_{12}H_7O_4N = 133.06$. Blue dyestuff used to test milk. Reduction to red resorufin, and eventually to colorless dihydroresorufin, occurs in presence of mastitis cells or of milk more than 24 hours old.

research. (1) Scientific investigation directed to the discovery or examination of a new or existing fact or phenomenon. (2) A literary search, followed by planned experimental investigation or verification. **operational-** The use of scientific methods, and particularly applied statistics, to provide a quantitative basis for policy decisions.

reseda oil. Mignonette oil. Fragrant oil, used as a flavoring and scent, extracted from plants of the *Reseda* genus, such as mignonette.

resenes. The constituents of resins, insoluble in alkalies. They contain O; but not as OH, COOH, lactone or ester. The most valuable varnish resins; as, dammar, copal, dragon's blood, are rich in r.

reserpine. $C_{33}H_{40}O_9N_2 = 608.70$. An alkaloid from the trees *Rauwolfia serpentina* (India), and *Alstonia conesticta* (Australia). Brown crystals, m.270 (decomp.), insoluble in water; used as the vegetable extract, as a tranquilizer, and to treat blood pressure and hypertension (B.P.).

reserve. Resist. A substance that will resist the dyeing of those portions of a fabric onto which it has been printed, e.g., wax. Cf. *batik*.

reservoir. A storage receptacle.

residual. That which remains. **r. affinity.** See *affinity*. **r. gas.** The small amount of gas that remains in an evacuated apparatus, e.g., a vacuum tube.

residue. That which remains as the ash after an ignition. **spray-** See *spray*.

resilience. The property of returning to the original shape after distortion within elastic limits. Measured by the work done per unit volume.

resilient. Elastic, rebounding.

resin(s). Flammable, amorphous, vegetable products of secretion or disintegration, usually formed in special cavities of plants. Generally insoluble in water and soluble in alcohol, fusible, and having a conchoidal fracture. They are the oxidation or polymerization products of the terpenes, and are mixtures of aromatic acids and esters. Some are official; as, *benzoin, guaiac*; others are nonofficial; as, *copal, sandarac*. Cf. *plastics, resinoid, rosin*. **alkyd-** R. made from phthalic anhydride and glycerol. **artificial-** See *plastics*. **gum-** R. containing gum which softens in water; as, olibanum, myrrh, gamboge, scammony. **ion-exchange-** A solid solution of an active electrolyte in a highly stable insoluble matrix (usually a synthetic r.). It exists in cation-active and anion-active forms, and can react with the ions present in (e.g.) water. See table on facing page. $R^\pm$ is the active r., M^+ a given metallic ion, and A^- an anion. The squared groups are insoluble r. complexes. The functional groups are:

Cation-exchange resins

(1) $\boxed{R^- Na^+} + M^+ A^- \rightleftharpoons \boxed{R^- M^+} + Na^+ A^-$ (Water softening)
(2) $\boxed{R^- H^+} + M^+ A^- \rightleftharpoons \boxed{R^- M^+} + H^+ A^-$ (Salt splitting)
(3) $\boxed{R^- H^+} + M^+ (OH)^- \rightarrow \boxed{R^- M^+} + H_2O$ (Neutralization)

Anion-exchange resins

(4) $\boxed{R^+ (OH)^-} + M^+ A^- \rightleftharpoons \boxed{R^+ A^-} + M^+ (OH)^-$ (Salt splitting)
(5) $\boxed{R^+ (OH)^-} + H^+ A^- \rightarrow \boxed{R^+ A^-} + H_2O$ (Neutralization)

Cation exchanges: Strong—sulfonic acid / Weak —carboxylic acid

Anionic exchanges: Strong—quaternary ammonium / Weak —amino

Used to demineralize water. **modified-** A mixture of a synthetic and natural r. e.g., colophony, which may be an extender or may confer special properties. **oil-reactive-** A synthetic phenol-formaldehyde r., soluble in oil to form a quick-hardening varnish. **oil-soluble-** R. not reacting with an oil but soluble in it. **oleo-** Balsams. A viscous mixture of r. with essential oils; as, Canada balsam, turpentine, pitch, storax, white dammar. **single-stage-** Resol. **synthetic-** A heterogeneous group of compounds produced synthetically from simpler compounds by polymerization and/or condensation. Upon them are based many plastics, q.v. The term was originally used to describe such synthetic substances having the properties of r., but is now used in a wider sense. **true-** A natural r. that is neither a gum nor oleo r.; as, colophony, kauri, sandarac, mastic, shellac, jalap, copal. **vinyl-** A synthetic polymerization product of vinyl compounds. Cf. *vinylite*.

r. acids. Organic acids derived from r.; as, pimaric acid. **r. of copper.** Cuprous chloride (obsolete).

resina. (1) Latin for resin. (2) Rosin.

resin amines. Insoluble, amorphous, solid bases from low-temperature tar, which fuse to glassy masses and are deposited from solution as tough films.

resinate. A salt of a resin acid mixture.

resinene. Generic name for neutral resins.

resineon. An essential oil, distilled from black tar oil, b.148; an antiseptic.

resinification. (1) The process of oxidation or polymerization of essential oils by which they become solid resins. (2) Artificial condensation polymerization, or similar processes, by which resin-like substances are formed. Cf. *plastics*.

resinite. A resinous constituent of coal.

resinoic acid. Generic name for acidic resins.

resinoid. A substance resembling a resin in physical properties, except that it changes to an insoluble and infusible solid on heating. Cf. *plastics*.

resinol. (1) Resole. (2) The noncrystalline constituents of tar, soluble in sodium hydroxide solution and precipitated from solution in an organic solvent by light petroleum. Cf. *resinotannol*.

resinotannol. A colored alcohol of resin esters which gives the tannin reaction. Cf. *resinol*.

resinous. Having properties of a resin.

resist. Reserve.

resistance. (1) Opposition to force or external conditions. (2) The reciprocal of conductance, measured in ohms; the opposition that a conductor offers to the passage of an electric current. See *ohm, mho*. **body-** See *immunity*. **external-** The opposition to the passage of an electric current outside the source of current; as in wires. **internal-** Electrical resistance within the generating device. **specific-** See *specific resistance*. **thermal-** The reciprocal of thermal conductivity, q.v.

r. box. An arrangement of rheostat coils in mounted rows in a container. By turning dials or inserting plugs, degrees of resistance may be obtained. **r. capacity.** The cell constant K: the ratio of the measured conductivity of a solution to its known specific conductivity. Used to correct for peculiarities in the shape of a conductivity cell. **r. coil.** A spool of wire for increasing the r. in a circuit. **r. gage.** See *gage*. **r. to infection.** See *immunity*. **r. thermometer.** See *pyrometer*. **r. wire.** Nichrome wire for heating units or r. devices having a definite r.

resistivity. The specific resistance, $\rho = Ra/l$, where R is the resistance, a the cross section, and l the length of the material.

resistor. A metal (as chromium) which becomes hot on the passage of an electric current; used in electric heaters. **age-** A rubber additive which inhibits oxidation, e.g., aromatic diamine antioxidants.

resocyanin. $C_{10}H_8O_3 = 176.1$. 4-Oxy-β-methylcoumarin, β-methylumbelliferone. Colorless crystals, m.185; used in perfumery.

resoflavin. $C_{14}H_3O_4(OH)_3 = 286.05$. Yellow dye, from resorcinol.

resol. A single-stage synthetic resin produced from a phenol and an aldehyde. Cf. *resole*.

resole. Resinol. A compound formed by the condensation of a phenol with an aldehyde in presence of a catalyst and alkali, and hardened by heat. Cf. *Bakelite, novolak*.

resolution. (1) Mesotomy. The separation of a racemic mixture into its optically active components. Cf. *racemization, inversion*. (2) The separation of spectral lines into a number of component lines by intense electric or magnetic fields. Cf. *Stark effect*.

resolving power. The power of a lens to produce a detailed and distinct image of an object at a certain distance.

resonance. (1) The vibrations set up by sound or electromagnetic waves in a material that is capable of vibrating with the same or a multiple frequency. (2) Rays emitted by an atom, of the same wavelength as those previously absorbed. (3) Mesomerism. The phenomenon that occurs when an atom takes up a spatial position intermediate between 2 other theoretically possible positions.

resonant. Producing sound.

resonator. (1) An instrument used to intensify sound waves or electromagnetic oscillations by resonance.

Cf. *quartz oscillator.* (2) A chromophoric or fluorophoric constellation, q.v., of electrons which absorbs rays of certain wavelengths.

resopyrine. A derivative of resorcinol and antipyrine. Rhombic crystals, insoluble in water; used medicinally.

resorcin. Resorcinol. **r. blue.** A microchemical stain.

resorcinol. $C_6H_4(OH)_2 = 110.11$. Resorcin, 1,3-benzenediol, metadihydroxybenzene. Colorless tablets, m.116, very soluble in water or ether. Used in the manufacture of fluorescein, eosin, and other dyes, synthetic drugs, and photographic developers; and as a reagent, reducing agent, external dehydrant, antiseptic, antiferment, and bactericide (U.S.P., B.P.). **acetamido-** Dihydroxyacetanilide. **dimethoxy-** $C_6H_4(OMe)_2 = 138.1$. Colorless liquid, b.214, soluble in water; used in organic synthesis. **dimethyl-** Xylorcinol. **dithio-** 1,3-Phenylene mercaptan. **hexahydro-** 1,3-Cyclohexanediol. **hexyl-** Hexylresorcinol. **methyl-** Orcinol. *p*-**nitrobenzeneazo-** $(HO)_2C_6H_3N:N\cdot C_6\cdot H_4\cdot NO_2$. A reagent for magnesium (0.1 mg in 5 ml gives a blue color). **propyl-** Divarinol. **trimethyl-** Mesorcinol. **trinitro-** Styphnic acid.

r. carbolate. Phenoresorcin. **r. monoacetate.** Euresol. **r. phenate.** Phenoresorcin. **r. phthalein.** See *fluorescein.* **r. yellow.** Tropeolin.

resorcitol. 1,3-Quinitol.

resorcyl. The radical $-C_6H_4\cdot OH$, of resorcinol (1,3-hydroxybenzene).

resorcylalgin. Resalgin, antipyrine resorcylate. An isomer of resalgin, m.115, soluble in water.

resorcylate. A salt of a resorcylic acid.

resorcylic acid. $C_6H_3(OH)_2COOH = 154.1$. Resorcinolcarboxylic acid, dihydroxybenzoic acid, in which the 2 OH groups are in the meta position. **propyl-** Divaric acid.

resorption. The absorption of excreted material; as, the products of inflammation.

resorpyrine. Resopyrine.

resorufin. $C_{12}H_7O_3N = 213.1$. Oxyphenazone, oxyphenoxazone. A heterocyclic compound; used to detect halogens, which destroy its intense fluorescence in alkaline solution. See *resazurin.*

respiration. The process of breathing, by which air is inhaled (inspiration) and expelled (expiration) by a living organism. In mammals r. depends on the chemical equilibrium between hemoglobin, oxygen, carbon dioxide, and sodium bicarbonate. In the lungs the hemoglobin is oxidized to oxyhemoglobin. In the tissues (where an excess of carbon dioxide exists) the oxyhemoglobin releases the oxygen and removes the carbon dioxide. The sodium bicarbonate is a buffer.

respirator. Inspirator, inhaler. A gas mask or screen of fire wire or gauze with or without adsorbing or chemical reagents, worn over the mouth or nose to protect the wearer from dust, smoke, poisonous or irritating gases.

respiratory. Pertaining to respiration. **r. metal.** The metals Fe, Mn, Cu, Zn, and Mg, which are constituents of chromoproteins. See *pigment.* **r. quotient.** The ratio of the volumes of inhaled oxygen to expelled carbon dioxide.

restitution. The reverse reaction of substitution, q.v.: an element is either oxidized or reduced to the free state.

restorative. An agent that aids, renews, or promotes a healthy physical condition.

resublimed. Purified by repeated sublimation.

resultants. The products of a chemical reaction: reaction products. Cf. *reactants.*

resuscitation. The restoration of consciousness or life in one apparently dead from asphyxiation or suffocation. **r. gas.** A mixture: approx. oxygen 93, carbon dioxide 7%; used for artificial respiration.

retamine. $C_{15}H_{26}ON_2 = 250.2$. An alkaloid from *Retama sphaerocarpa*; long needles, m.162, insoluble in water.

retardation. Slowing up of a chemical reaction; negative catalysis.

retarder. A substance added to a reacting mixture to prevent the reaction from becoming too vigorous; as potassium bromide in photographic developers prevents overdevelopment. Cf. *accelerator, catalytic poison.*

retene. $C_{18}H_{18} = 234.23$. Methylisopropylphenanthrene. A hydrocarbon from pine tar. Lustrous leaflets, m.98, slightly soluble in water.

retentate. Suggested term for the material retained by a semipermeable membrane. Cf. *dialyzate.*

retention. The holding or retaining of a substance or property.

Retger's law. The physical properties of mixed crystals vary in proportion to their percentage compositions.

reticulated. Retiform. Resembling a network.

reticulin. The protein of the fibers of reticular tissue not digested by pepsin or trypsin.

retiform. Reticulated.

retina. The portion of the eye on which the image is focused by the lens; bundles of sensitive rods and cones, which carry the sensation of vision to the brain.

retinene. A yellow protein pigment formed in the eye retina by the action of light on rhodopsin. It subsequently forms vitamin A, which forms more rhodopsin.

retinite. $C_{12}H_{18}O$. The amorphous, gray native substance. **r. resins.** Hard, brittle brown resins from brown coal. They contain no wax, and are derived from amber. Cf. *bituminous resins.*

retinol. $C_{32}H_{16} = 400.1$. Resinol, codol, resinoil, obtained by distilling pitch or rosin. Yellow liquid, b.280, insoluble in water; an antiseptic.

retonation. A wave propagated backward through the burned gases from the starting point of an explosion.

retort. A distilling vessel. Originally a flask with a bent neck (alembic).

retro- Prefix (Latin) indicating backward.

retrogression. A reversal; a reverse reaction.

retronecine. $C_8H_{13}NO_2 = 155.1$. A basic hydrolysis product of retrorsine.

retronecinic acid. $C_{10}H_{16}O_6 = 232.12$. An acid hydrolysis product of retrorsine.

retrorsine. $C_{18}H_{25}NO_6 = 351.2$. An alkaloid from *Senecio retrorsus* (Compositae).

retting. Loosening the fiber of vegetable materials by the action of moisture, enzymes, and/or bacteria. Cf. *coir. flax.*

retzbanyite. Native lead bismuth sulfide.

reussinite. A resin-like, reddish-brown hydrocarbon in certain coal deposits.

reverberatory. Flickering, blowing downward. **r. furnace.** An oven in which the flames, but not the fuel, come into contact with the material to be heated, by reflection from a sloping roof. Cf. *furnace.*

reversible. Capable of being restored to an original condition. **r. action.** The reestablishment of an original condition. **r. cell.** An electric cell which after discharge can be activated by an external current; as, an accumulator. **r. colloid.** See *colloid.* **r. electrode.** An electrode which owes its potential to ionic changes of a r. nature. See *electrode.* **r. reaction.** A reaction that establishes an equilibrium, and can proceed from right to left or from left to right: $A + B \rightleftharpoons C + D.$

revertose. $C_{12}H_{22}O_{11} = 342.2.$ A disaccharide produced by the action of maltase on glucose solution.

revive. (1) To restore original activity, e.g., of a catalyst. (2) To reduce a metallic ore or oxide to the metal.

revivification. The restoration of an active condition. **r. of carbon.** R. of spent carbon black by (1) burning in the absence of air; (2) washing with acids to remove its ash; (3) washing with an alkaline solution.

Rey, Jean. 1630. An alchemist who experimented with metallic oxides.

reyn. A unit of absolute viscosity: 1 r. = centipoises $\times 6.9 \times 10^6$. Cf. *Reynolds number.*

Reynolds foil. Waxed kraft paper laminated with asphalt to a lead sheet, the other side of which is laminated to a heat-sealing viscose film with a moisture-proof adhesive. A specialty wrapping. **R. number.** An expression of fluid flow in a pipe: (velocity of flow $\times$ diameter of pipe)/coefficient of kinematic viscosity of the liquid.

Rf value. In paper-strip chromatography, the proportion of the total length of climb of a solution that is reached by a spot characteristic of one of the constituents present.

RG acid. 1-Naphthol-3,6-disulfonic acid.

Rh. Symbol for rhodium. **Rh factor.** A dominant, agglutinable blood-group factor, associated with stillbirths. It has antigenic effects similar to those of the blood of *Rhesus* monkeys; it occurs in 85% of the cells of human blood, and is of importance in selecting blood for transfusion. Cf. *blood groups.*

rH or **r$_H$.** Symbol for oxidation-reduction potential: rH = log (1/pH²), where pH² is the hydrogen pressure in atmospheres. Cf. *pH.*

r.h. Abbreviation for relative humidity.

rhabdophane. $(Ce,Di,La)_3(PO_4)_2.$ Phosphocerite. A mineral.

Rhamnaceae. Buckthorn family; shrubs from which drugs are derived; as, *Rhamnus frangula,* frangula; *R. purshiana,* cascara sagrada. Cf. *cathartin.*

rhamnase. An enzyme from fungi that hydrolyzes rhamnose.

rhamnegin. $C_{12}H_{10}O_5 = 234.1.$ A glucoside from buckthorn berries.

rhamnetin. $C_{16}H_{12}O_7 = 316.1.$ A methyl ester of quercetin and a split product of xanthorhamnin; a yellow color.

rhamnicogenol. A pentahydroxymethylanthranol occurring as primeveroside in purgative buckthorn and other *Rhamnus* species.

rhamnicoside. $C_{26}H_{30}O_{15}\cdot4H_2O = 652.3.$ A glucoside from the stem bark of purgative buckthorn, *Rhamnus cathartica* (Rhamnaceae). Cf. *Chinese green.*

rhamnin. A fluid extract of *Rhamnus frangula* containing rhamnetin. **xantho-** Xanthorhamnin.

rhamninose. $C_{18}H_{32}O_{14} = 470.25.$ A trisaccharide from Persian berry, *Rhamnus infectoria,* which hydrolyzes to 2 rhamnose and 1 glucose residues.

rhamnite. Rhamnitol.

rhamnitol. $Me(CHOH)_4-CH_2OH = 166.14.$ A reduction product of rhamnose. Colorless crystals, m.121, soluble in water.

rhamnofluorin. A constituent of *Rhamnus* species.

rhamnogalactoside. Glucosides that are hydrolyzed to rhamnose and galactose; as robinin.

rhamnoglucoside. A glucoside that is hydrolyzed to rhamnose and glucose; as, rutin.

rhamnol. $C_{20}H_{36}O = 292.3.$ An alcohol, m.132, from cascara sagrada.

rhamnomannoside. A glucoside that is hydrolyzed to rhamnose and mannose; as baptisin.

rhamnose. $Me(CHOH)_4CHO\cdot H_2O = 182.1.$ Isodulcite. A methyl pentose from rhamninose and various glucosides. Colorless crystals. m.92, soluble in water. Cf. *quinovose.*

rhamnoside. (1) A glucoside that is hydrolyzed to rhamnose. (2) $C_{21}H_{20}O_9.$ A split product of rhamnoxanthin; occurs in *Rhamnus* species.

rhamnoxanthin. A crystalline glucoside from *Rhamnus frangula.*

Rhamnus. A genus of trees and shrubs; many have a purgative bark or fruit. **R. cathartica.** Buckthorn berries. The dried fruits of *Rhamnus cathartica.* **R. frangula.** See *frangula.* **R. purshiana.** See *cascara sagrada.*

rhatanin. $C_{40}H_{43}O_3N = 585.4.$ Geoffrayin, andirin. A glucoside of rhatany root; needles, m.280.

rhatany. Krameria.

rhe. The absolute unit of fluidity; the reciprocal of the unit of viscosity (centipoise).

rheadine. $C_{21}H_{21}O_6N = 383.18.$ An alkaloid from opium; white prisms, m.246.

rhea fiber. Ramie.

rheic acid. $C_{20}H_{16}O_9 = 400.1.$ A red powder. Cf. *chrysophanic acid.*

rhein. $C_{15}H_8O_6 = 284.1.$ Rheinic acid. 1,9-Dihydroxyanthraquinone-3-carboxylic acid. A monobasic diketonic acid from senna leaves, rhubarb, and lichens. Golden prisms, m.162.

rheinic acid. Rhein.

rhenate. $M_2ReO_4.$ **per-** $MReO_4.$ Rhenates are colorless, soluble in water (except the Ag, Tl, K, Rb, and Ce salts).

rhenic acid. $H_2ReO_4.$ A dibasic acid which changes to $HReO_4.$ **per-** $HReO_4$ formed on dissolving R_2O_7 in water.

rhenium. Re = 186.31. Dvimanganese. Bohemium, q.v., uralium. The element of at. no. 75, a noble metal of the platinum group discovered by Noddack (1924) by means of its X-ray spectrum, in platinum ores. Obtained as a by-product in the roasting of molybdenum sulfide. Silvery, d.21.0 g/ml, m.3180 (the highest of the elements, except W and C). Used in high-temperature technology, for electric contacts and acid-resistant chemical plant, and as a catalyst to dehydrogenate alcohols to aldehydes or ketones: 2 isotopes, mass

185 and 187; and valencies of 7, 6, 5, 4, and 3. **r. black.** A catalyst for selective hydrogenation reactions, prepared by the hydrogenation reduction of r. heptoxide in a solvent. **r. chloride.** (1) $ReCl_7$ = 434.8. R. heptachloride. Green volatile crystals, hydrolyzed in water. (2) $ReCl_6$ = 399.3. R. hexachloride. Brown volatile crystals. (3) $ReCl_4$ = 328.3. R. tetrachloride. Brown crystals. (4) $ReCl_3$ = 292.68. Hexagonal red crystals, soluble in water. **r. fluoride.** ReF_6 = 300.31. Yellow crystals, m.26. **r. oxides:** (1) Re_2O_8. R. peroxide. Bluish white solid, soluble in water. (2) Re_2O_7. R. heptaoxide. Yellow solid, m.200, soluble in water forming perrhenic acid. (3) ReO_3. Red solid, changes to Re_2O_7. (4) ReO_2. R. dioxide. Black powder formed by heating $NaReO_4$ in hydrogen. (5) Re_3O_8. Blue solid. **r. sulfide.** $Re_2S_7 \cdot H_2O$. R. heptasulfide. Black powder, insoluble in acids or alkalies, oxidized by nitric acid.

rheochrysin. $C_{22}H_{22}O_{10}$ = 446.2. A glucoside from rhubarb. Cf. *rheopurgin*.

rheoid. The combined principles from the root of *Rheum officinale*, rhubarb; a tonic and alterative.

rheology. The science of the deformation and flow of matter. Cf. *softener*.

rheometer. (1) A galvanometer. (2) An instrument to measure the velocity of the blood current.

rheopexy. A form of thixotropy, in which solidification occurs as the result of a regular gentle motion instead of vigorous shaking.

rheopurgin. A constituent of rhubarb which decomposes into 4 glucosides. Cf. *rhein*.

rheoscope. An instrument for detecting an electric current.

rheostan. The alloy: Cu 52, Zn 18, Ni 25, Re 5%; used for rheostats.

rheostat. An instrument to regulate electrical resistance.

rheotannic acid. $C_{26}H_{26}O_{14}$ = 562.2. Rhubarb tannin. Yellow powder, soluble in water.

rheotome. A current breaker.

Rheovot. Trade name for a mixed-polymer synthetic fiber.

rheum. Rhubarb.

rhigolene. The first condensation product of the fractional distillation of petroleum, b.21; consists mainly of butane and pentane. Used to produce coldness of the skin before surgical operations; also as a solvent.

rhinanthin. A glucoside from the seeds of *Alectorolophus hirsutus* or *Rhinanthus major* (Scrophulariaceae).

rhine metal. An alloy: Sn 97, Cu 3%; d.7.35, m.300.

rhinestone. Colorless, highly refractive glass; a semigem.

rhizobia. Soil bacteria which infect legumes, forming nodules that enable the plant to utilize atmospheric oxygen.

rhizocarpic acid. $C_{28}H_{23}O_6N(?)$. A yellow constituent of the lichen *Lecanora epanora*. Cf. *epanorin*.

rhizocholic acid. An oxidation product of cholic acid.

rhizoid. Describing an irregularly branched bacterial growth.

rhizome. An underground plant stem having the

functions of a root, and characterized by the presence of leaf bases. Some are used medicinally; as, arnica, hydrastis, valerian.

rhizonic acid. $C_{10}H_{12}O_4$ = 208.1. 6-Hydroxy-4-methoxyisoxylic acid. White crystals, m.232. **iso-** 4-Hydroxy-6-methoxyisoxylic acid. White crystals, decomp. 156, decomp. by boiling water.

rhizoplane. Soil particles adhering to roots.

rhizosphere. The zone of soil subject to the influence of plant roots; it supports a high biological activity.

rho. Greek letter ρ or P. **r. 1.** Theelin. **r. 2.** Progesterone.

rhodacene. $C_{30}H_{20}$ = 380.2. A pyrolytic product from acenaphthene. Violet crystals with green metallic luster, m.339, isomeric with chalcacene, into which it changes on strong illumination in dilute solution.

rhodalline. Allyl sulfocarbamide.

rhodamic acid. Rhodanine.

rhodamine. (1) $C_3H_4ON_2S$ = 116.1. Rhodamic acid, 4-keto-2-thiothiazolidine. (2) Red dyes closely allied to the fluoresceins, obtained by condensation of phthalic anhydride with p-alkylated aminophenols. **tetraethyl-** $C_{28}H_{30}N_2O_3$ = 442.2. Colorless, but its salts are red dyes with an oxonium or quinoid structure.

rhodan. The radical —SCN. See *thiocyanate*.

rhodanate. Thiocyanate.

rhodanic acid. (1) Rhodanine. (2) Thiocyanic acid.

rhodanide. Thiocyanate.

rhodanine. $CH_2 \cdot CO \cdot NH \cdot CS \cdot S$ = 133.1. Rhodanic

acid, 4-keto-2-thio-m-thiazolidine. **p-dimethylaminobenzilidene-** $(C_3HNOS_2):CH \cdot C_6H_4 \cdot NMe_2$. A reagent for silver (flocculent red precipitate).

rhodanizing. Plating with rhodium (especially on silver) to prevent tarnishing.

rhodanometry. (1) The use of free cyanogen to determine the absorption values of oils. Cf. *iodine number*. (2) Thiocyanometry. Titration with thiocyanate solutions to determine silver, mercury, etc.

rhodeite. Rhodeol.

rhodeol. $CH_3(CHOH)_4CH_2OH$ = 166.1. Rhodeite, rhodeitol; oxidized to rhodeose.

rhodeoretin. Convolvulin.

rhodeose. $C_6H_{12}O_5$ = 164.1. A methylpentose glucoside and isomer of fucose in jalap roots.

Rhode test. Concentrated sulfuric acid and dimethyl aminobenzaldehyde give a purple color with proteins.

Rhodia, Rhodiafil, Rhodialin. Trade names for cellulose acetate synthetic fibers.

rhodiene. $(C_{10}H_{16})_x$. A hydrocarbon from *Rhodium lignum*, rosewood.

rhodinol. $Me_2C:CH \cdot CH_2 \cdot CH_2 \cdot CHMe \cdot CH_2 \cdot CH_2OH$ = 156.2. 2,6-Dimethyloctene-2-ol-8. A constituent of citronella and geranium oils; used in perfumes.

rhodite. Rhodium gold.

rhodium. Rh = 102.91. A metal of the platinum group; at. no. 45; usual valency 3. Grayish white ductile metal, d.12.44, m.1920, insoluble in water. Occurs in the platinum ores and gold gravels of S. America. Discovered by Wollaston (1804). Used for plating (superior to chromium plating); and in alloys, thermoelements, and astronomical measuring instruments. **r. black.** Finely divided r. metal obtained by precipitation of r. salt solutions by formaldehyde; a catalyst. **r. cesium alum.** $Rh_2(SO_4)_3,Cs_2(SO_4),24H_2O = 128.10$. Yellow octagons, m.110, soluble in water. **r. chloride.** $RhCl_3 \cdot 4H_2O = 281.34$. R.sesquichloride. Brownish, deliquescent powder, decomp. 475, soluble in water. **r. gold.** Rhodite. A native alloy: Au 57–66, Rh 34–43%. **r. hydroxide.** $Rh(OH)_3 = 153.92$. Black powder, decomp. by heat, insoluble in water. **r. nitrate.** $Rh(NO_3)_3 \cdot 2H_2O = 325.0$. Red, deliquescent crystals, soluble in water. **r. oxides.** (1) $RhO = 118.9$. R. monoxide. Gray powder, insoluble in water. (2) $Rh_2O_3 = 253.8$. R. sesquioxide. Gray powder obtained by heating r. with barium peroxide; insoluble in water. (3) $RhO_2 = 134.9$. R. dioxide. Brown powder, insoluble in water. **r. sulfate.** $Rh_2(SO_4)_3 \cdot 12H_2O = 710.2$. Yellow crystals, soluble in water. **r. sulfide.** $RhS = 135.0$. Blue powder, decomp. by heat, insoluble in water.

rhodizite. White or green native calcium borate.
rhodizonic acid. $C \cdot OH : C \cdot OH \cdot (CO)_3 \cdot CO = 170.1$. A dihydroxydiquinone that acts as a dibasic acid. Its sodium salt is a reagent for barium and strontium (brown color).

rhodochrosite. $MnCO_3$. Red manganese. A native carbonate.
rhododendrin. $C_{16}H_{22}O_7 = 326.2$. A constituent of *Rhododendron chrysanthemum* (Ericaceae). Colorless crystals, m.187, soluble in hot water.
rhododendrol. $C_{10}H_{12}O_2 = 164.1$. A constituent of *Rhododendron chrysanthemum*. Colorless crystals, m.80.
rhodol. Methyl-*p*-aminophenol. Used as a photographic developer.
rhodolite. A variety of garnet.
rhodonite. $MnSiO_3$. Red manganese, manganese spar. A native manganese silicate.
rhodopsin. The protein pigment of the visual purple in the retina of the eye, associated with the mechanism of color vision. A rose-colored carotenin containing a prosthetic group which is liberated by light. Cf. *retinene*.
rhodopterin. A purple oxidation product of pterin.
rhodopurpurin. Rhodovibrene.
rhodotannic acid. $C_{14}H_6O_7 = 286.1$. A tannin from the leaves of *Rhododendron ferrugineum*.
rhodovibrene. Rhodopurpurin. A purple carotenoid pigment produced by bacteria.
rhodoviolascene. $C_{42}H_{60}O_2(?)$. A carotenoid pigment from purple bacteria.
rhodoxanthin. $C_{40}H_{50}O_2 = 562.35$. Thujorhodin. A carotenoid and red isomer of xanthophyll in the red berries of *Taxus baccata*, yew.
Rhoduline. Trademark for aniline dyes of the safranine type; used in textile printing.
Rhoeadales. An order of plants comprising the families: *Papaveraceae, Cruciferae, Resedaceae*.
rhoeadic acid. Papaveric acid.
rhoeadine. $C_{21}H_{21}O_5N = 383.2$. A crystalline alkaloid from *Papaver rhoeas* (Papaveraceae).
rhoeagenine. An isomer of rhoeadine.
rhoetzite. Kyanite.
Rhofil. Trade name for a polyamide synthetic fiber.
rhomb. A rhombic crystal. **r. spar.** A rhombic dolomite.
rhombic. Describing a crystal with 3 unequal axes, all at right angles; as, iodine. **r. dodecahedron.** A

crystal of the isometric system with 12 faces; each face is parallel to 1 axis and has equal intercepts on the other 2 neighboring faces. **r. mica.** Phlogopite. **r. quartz.** Feldspar (obsolete). **r. spar.** A form of dolomite. **r. system.** The orthorhombic crystal system.
rhombohedral. Describing a crystal of the trigonal system with a vertical axis of 3-fold symmetry and 3 horizontal axes of 2-fold symmetry. **r. system.** A modified trigonal system of crystals with 3 horizontal axes of 2-fold symmetry in place of the 3-fold symmetry of the hexagonal system.
rhombohedron. A crystal form bounded by 6 rhombic faces.
rhometer. An instrument to measure resistivity.
rhotanium. An alloy of palladium and rhodium.
Rhovyl. Trade name for a polyamide synthetic fiber.
rhubarb. Rheum. The dried rhizomes and roots of *Rheum palmatum*, and *Rheum* species (Polygonaceae). It contains rheopurgin, chrysophanic acid, rhein, tannic acid, and is a laxative and gastric tonic (B.P.). Cf. *aporhetin*. **r. tannin.** A rheotannic acid.
rhumbatron. A device to produce high-speed electrons for molecular bombardment. Cf. *cyclotron*.
Rhus. A genus of trees and shrubs of the cashew family (Anacardiacea). **R. aromatica.** A tonic and stimulant. **R. continus.** Fustic. **R. coriaria.** Sumac. **R. diversiloba.** The poison oak of the Pacific Coast. **R. glabra.** Sumac berries. An astringent. **R. toxicodendron.** Poison oak, poison ivy.
rhusin. Rhusoid. The combined powdered principles from *Rhus glabra*, used medicinally.
rhusoid. Rhusin.
rhythm. Occurrence at regular intervals, as wave motion.
rhythmic. Occurring at regular intervals. **r. deposition.** Precipitation or condensation in gas or vapor mixtures at periodic intervals; as produced from containers of hydrochloric acid and ammonia in a closed bell jar. **r. precipitation.** Periodic precipitation. Precipitation in bands or zones in a colloid. See *Liesegang's rings*.
ribichloric acid. $C_{14}H_8O_9 = 320.1$. An acid constituent from *Galium aparine*, goose grass. (Rubiaceae).
riboflavin. $C_{17}H_{20}N_4O_6 = 376.38$. Riboflavine (B.P.), lactoflavin, vitamin B_2, q.v., vitamin G. Bitter, orange crystals, m.280 (decomp.), slightly soluble in water (U.S.P.).
ribonic acid. $CH_2OH(CHOH)_3COOH = 166.1$; derived from ribose.
ribonucleoprotein. See *nucleo-*.
ribose. $CH_2OH \cdot (CHOH)_3 \cdot CHO = 150.1$. A pentose sugar constituent of some nucleic acids, existing in the furanoside and pyranoside forms. **deoxy-** See *desoxyribose*.
  r. ketohose. Allulose.
ribosome. Ribonucleoprotein particles; the main constituent of cytoplasm.
rice. The seeds or grains of *Oryza sativa*; mainly starch (rice flour). A food, and dusting powder.
rich. High in content; having a great percentage. **r. gas.** The second group of combustible gases obtained by the distillation of coal and coke; as, coke-oven gas. **r. iron.** Iron having a high silicon content.

Richards, Theodore William. 1868–1928. American chemist, Nobel Prize winner (1914); noted for his atomic weight and physical chemistry experiments.

richellite. A native iron, calcium phosphate from Richelle, Belgium.

richmondite. A heterogeneous mineral associated with galena, and containing: galena 36, antimonous sulfide 22, chalcocite 19, ferrous sulfide 14, sphalerite 6, argentite 2, manganous sulfide 0.5%, bismuth sulfide traces.

Richter, Jeremias Benjamin. 1762–1807. German chemist noted for his work on volumetric analysis and stoichiometry. **R.'s law.** Wenzel's law. Each equivalent weight of an acid will completely neutralize an equivalent weight of a base. **R., Victor von.** 1841–1891. German chemist, author of textbooks.

ricin. An albuminous toxin of castor-oil beans, *Ricinus communis*; it agglutinates red blood corpuscles.

ricinate. Ricinoleate. A salt of ricinoleic acid.

ricinic acid. Ricinoleic acid.

ricinine. $C_{12}H_{12}O_2N_2 = 216.1$. An alkaloid from the castor-oil plant, *Ricinus communis*.

ricinoleate. Ricinate. A salt of ricinoleic acid.

ricinoleic acid. $Me(CH_2)_6 \cdot CHOH \cdot CH : CH(CH_2)_7 \cdot COOH = 298.36$. Ricinic acid, 12-hydroxy-9-octadecanoic acid*, elaeodic acid. Yellow, fatty acid from castor oil, m.17, insoluble in water. Its alkali salts detoxify antigens.

ricinolein. $C_{57}H_{104}O_9 = 932.83$. Glyceryl ricinoleate, triricinolein, in castor oil (80%).

Ricinus. The castor-oil plant, *R. communis* (Euphorbiaceae), whose seeds yield castor oil and ricinine.

rickardite. Cu_3Te_3. A copper mineral.

Rideal-Walker test. The evaluation of an antiseptic from the amount required to prevent the growth of certain organisms (as *B. typhosus*) under standard working conditions. Phenol is the standard of comparison. **R-W. value.** Phenol coefficient. Cf. *germicide*.

riebeckite. A blue amphibole asbestos in ironstone seams (W. Australia); it contains about 6% crocodilite.

riffles. (1) Small waves. (2) A corrugated surface. (3) A sampler, q.v.

rigidity. The state of being inflexible or stiff. **r. modulus.** Modulus of elasticity.

Rilsan, Rilson. (1) Nylon 11. Trade names for a polyundecanolactam film, synthesized from castor oil, with 11 C atoms in each repeating molecular unit. (2) Trade names for polyamide synthetic fibers.

rimiform. Isoniazid.

rimnic acid. The chief constituent of rimu resin.

rimose. Describing a bacterial culture which shows fissures and cracks.

rimu resin. Red resin from the rimu (red pine), *Dacrydium cupressinum* (Coniferae), New Zealand.

ring. (1) A circular structure. (2) A closed chain of atoms. (3) A system of rings; as, the porphin r. See *r. structures*. **bacterial-** A growth of bacteria on the surface of a medium in a petri dish, which adheres to the glass forming a rim. **benzene-** See *benzene ring*. **fused-** 2 or more rings having at least 2 atoms each in common. Cf. *spirane*. **heterocyclic-** Misnomer for heteroatomic r. or heterocycle. See *r. structures*. **homocyclic-** Mis-

nomer for homoatomic or carboatomic r. or homocycle. See *r. structures*. **Liesegang's-** See *Liesegang, rhythmic precipitation*. **Newton's-** See *Newton*.

    r. breakage. Disruption of an atomic r.; changing an aromatic to an aliphatic compound. **r. closure.** R. formation. **r. compound.** A compound, the atoms of which form a r. or closed chain; as, a cyclic compound. **r. formation.** Exocondensation. The closing of an atomic chain; as, the change from an aliphatic to an aromatic compound. **r. reaction.** R. test. A chemical reaction (precipitate or color formation) at the boundary between one liquid superimposed as a layer on another. **r. structures.** The atomic arrangements in aromatic molecules which may contain one or more rings connected or joined by simple or double bonds or by a single atom (spiro compound). See *carbocyclic, heterocyclic*. **r. symbol.** A graphical representation of an atomic r., as skeleton symbols. **r. system.** An arbitrary representation on a plane surface of the geometrical arrangement of atoms. The American Chemical Society (Abstracts Index) lists 20 r. systems, the largest comprising the sequence $(C_4N)_4(C_6)_{16}$, i.e., naphthindolotrinaphthophenanthropyrolodicarbazole. **r. test.** Ring reaction.

Ringelmann smoke chart. A set of 6 cards, printed with straight lines at right angles, which are viewed at 50 ft from a chimney. The cards show progressive darkening from white to black and can be matched against the shades of the smoke.

Ringer, Sidney. 1835–1910. English physiologist. **R. fluid, R. solution.** An isotonic solution: sodium chloride 0.86, potassium chloride 0.03, calcium chloride 0.033%, in water; used in physiological experiments (U.S.P.). Cf. *saline*. **lactated-** R. solution containing not more than 330 mg sodium lactate per 100 ml (U.S.P.).

rinkite. $3NaF \cdot 4CaO \cdot 6(Ti,Si)O_2 \cdot Ce_2O_3$. A mineral.

Rinmann's green. $CoZnO_2(?)$. Green mass obtained by melting zinc compounds with a trace of cobalt salts. A blowpipe identification test for zinc compounds.

rinneite. $FeCl_2 \cdot 3KCl \cdot NaCl$. A Stassfurt salt.

rio arrowroot. Tapioca.

Rio Tinto process. The extraction of copper from its ores after atmospheric oxidation.

ripener. Ethylene gas used to ripen imported fruit (dates, persimmons, bananas, avocados) which are exposed to the gas (1:1,000).

ripening. (1) Progressive, enzymatic hydrolytic changes in fruit: the fruit becomes sweeter, tannins and organic acids disappear, proteins are hydrolyzed, starch changes to sugar and some sugars form esters, and characteristic flavors develop. The cell wall changes, and the color generally deepens. The term is applied similarly to cheese. (2) The gradual formation of light-sensitive centers in the emulsion of a photographic plate. (3) Fermentation, as of tobacco, in which organic catalysts produce maturity. (4) A stage in the manufacture of rayon in which the solution attains the necessary properties for successful spinning. **artificial-** Ripener.

ripidolite. $(Al,Cr)_2O_3 \cdot 5(Mg,Fe)O \cdot 3SiO_2 \cdot 4H_2O$. A green or white mica.

riptography. Analysis in which a solution is titrated

with a precipitating agent, and the properties of the clear layer are measured.

risic acid, rissic acid. $C_6H_2(OMe)_2COOH \cdot OCH_2CO \cdot OH = 256.09$. 2-Carboxy-4,5-dimethoxyphenoxy-acetic acid. A split product of rotenone; a lower homolog of derric acid. White crystals, m.262.

ristocetin. An antibiotic produced by *Nocardia lurida* (U.S.P.).

Ritz formula. The wave number of a line in a series of the spectrum: $A - N/[m + \mu + (d/m)^2]^2$, where M is the universal series constant; m is an integer; and A, μ, and d are constants.

rivanol. $C_{15}H_{15}ON_3 = 253.3$. 2-Ethoxy-6,9-diaminoacridine, ethodin. Yellow crystals; a local antiseptic for wounds.

rivotite. A native, basic copper antimony carbonate.

rms. Abbreviation for root mean square.

Rn. Symbol for radon.

RNP. Abbreviation for ribo*nucleoprotein*.

roan. Sheepskin tanned with sumach. Cf. *skiver*.

roast. (1) To heat in air. (2) The product obtained by heating substances, especially ores, in air. **r. gases.** The gases formed on roasting ores, especially sulfides; mainly sulfur dioxide, arsenious fumes, air and the gases of the fuel used.

roaster. Roasting furnace.

roasting. Oxidation of ores by heat in a current of air, to remove sulfur and arsenic, and make the ores more porous for chlorination or hyposulfitization. **r. furnace.** A long firebrick furnace; ore is fed into one end, raked toward the firebox, and removed after about 3 hours. **r. temperature.**

Deg C	Effects
100......	Water removed
250......	Ag_2O decomposes
350......	Sulfides begin to burn; $CuSO_4$ dehydrated
600......	$FeSO_4$ decomposes to Fe_2O_3
653......	$CuSO_4$ becomes basic
655......	Ag_2SO_4 melts
702......	Basic $CuSO_4$ decomposes to CuO
807......	Ag_2SO_4 decomposes
1050......	CuO forms Cu_2O
1100......	Fe_2O_3 forms Fe_3O_4

Robac. 2-Mercaptoimidazoline. Trade name for an accelerator for neoprene.

robin. A poisonous nucleoprotein from the bark of the locust tree, *Robinia pseudacacia* (Leguminosae), N. America; an emetic and purgative.

robinin. A coloring material from the heartwood of *Robinia pseudacacia*, locust.

robinose. $C_{18}H_{32}O_{14} = 472.2$. A trisaccharide in *Robinia* species; it hydrolyzes to 2 molecules of rhamnose and 1 of glucose.

Robinson, Sir Robert. b. 1886. British chemist, Nobel Prize winner (1947); noted for organic research.

Robiquet, Henri Edme. 1822–1860. French chemist noted for work on fermentation and photography. The son of **R., Pierre Jean.** 1780–1840. French chemist, noted as an analyst of vegetable materials.

Robison, Robert. 1884–1941. British biochemist noted for his work on sugar and fermentation. **R. ester.** Glucose-6-phosphoric acid, produced in the fermentation of sugar by yeast. Cf. *Neuberg ester*, *sugar phosphates*.

roburite. An explosive: ammonium nitrate 87, dinitrotoluene 11, chloronaphthalene 2%.

Roccal. Trademark for benzylalkonium chloride.

Roccella. A genus of lichens, as *R. tinctoria*, litmus plant.

roccellic acid. $C_{20}H_{20}O_7 = 372.15$. α-Methyl-α'-n-dodecylsuccinic acid. A dibasic acid from *Roccella fuciformis* and other fungi or lichens. Colorless scales, m.178, insoluble in water.

roccellin. Orseillin.

rochelle salt. Potassium sodium tartrate.

Rochleder, Friedrich. 1819–1874. Austrian chemist noted for his plant analyses.

rock. A natural aggregation of mineral matter in the earth crust. **basic-** See *basic*. **igneous-** See *igneous*. **primary-** R. that has not undergone weathering and disintegration. **secondary-** R. that has been altered by disintegration. **sedimentary-** q.v. **r. asphalt.** Sandstone or limestone impregnated with asphalt. **r. breaker.** A machine that crushes rock. **r. candy.** Crystallized sucrose. **r. cork.** A variety of asbestos. **r. crystal.** A transparent, colorless variety of quartz. **r. gas.** Natural gas. **r. meal.** Calcium carbonate deposited from water. **r. milk.** A fine-quality r. meal. **r. oil.** Petroleum. **r. quartz.** Quartz. **r. ruby.** A red variety of garnet. **r. salt.** Common table salt. Sodium chloride obtained solid by mining. Cf. *sea salt*. **r. sand.** The debris of abraded r. **r. silk.** A variety of fine asbestos. **r. tallow.** Hatchettenine. **r. tar.** A crude petroleum. **r. wool.** A fibrous substance made by blowing a jet of steam against a small stream of molten lime and siliceous r.; a heat insulator. Cf. *slag wool*.

rod. (1) Pole, perch. A unit of length in surveying: 1 rod = 25 links = $5\frac{1}{2}$ yards = $\frac{1}{4}$ chain = 5.02921 meters. Cf. *rood*. (2) A stick-shaped bacillus. **square r.** A unit of area in surveying (normally 1/160 acre).

rodenticide. A chemical substance used to destroy rodent pests; as, zinc phosphide, phosphorus, barium carbonate, thallium sulfate, arsenious oxide ("arsenic"), α-naphthylurea(ANTU), 3-α-acetonylbenzyl-4-hydroxycoumarin (warfarin), bacterial preparation cultures of *Salmonella enteritidis*. Cf. *insecticide*.

Rodinal. $NH_2C_6H_4 \cdot OH = 109.1$. Trademark for *p*-aminophenol; a photographic developer.

Roentgen. See *Röntgen*.

roentgen photograph. Skiagram. **r. rays.** X rays. **r. ray analysis.** X-ray analysis. **r. tube.** See *X-ray tube*. **r. unit.** An international unit of *X-ray intensity*, now replaced by the curie.

roentgenogram. Radiograph. An X-ray photograph.

roentgenography. Radiography.

roentgenology. The study of X rays.

Roese-Gottlieb method. The determination of fat in dairy products. The moist food is extracted with a mixture of ethyl ether and petroleum ether, and the separated ethereal layer evaporated in a weighed vessel.

Roesler's process. The separation of copper and silver from gold by fusion with sulfur or antimony sulfide to obtain copper and silver sulfides.

rogascope. An electromagnetic device to detect cracks in or variations of the diameter of wire threads.

rogitine. Phentolamine.

Roha salt. A mixture of 90.7% sodium bicarbonate with approximately equal amounts of sodium sulfate, calcium carbonate, and magnesium carbonate, with calamus and anise powder and some absinthe; used in pharmacy.

Rohrbach's solution. An aqueous solution, d.3.58, of barium and mercuric chlorides, for determining the density of minerals by the suspension method.

Röhrig tube. A separating device for fat extraction.

Roman cement. A cement made by heating clay and limestone. **R. ocher.** A native orange variety of ocher. **r. vitriol.** Cupric sulfate.

romanium. An alloy of aluminum with small amounts of tungsten, copper, and nickel.

romeite. $5CaO \cdot 3Sb_2O_5$. A native antimoniate.

Rongalite. $CH_2O \cdot NaHSO_2 \cdot H_2O$. Trademark for an addition product of formaldehyde; a substitute for sodium hyposulfite.

Röntgen, Wilhelm Konrad. 1845–1923. German physicist, Nobel Prize winner (1901); discoverer of X rays (1895).

röntgen. See *roentgen.*

rood. A survey measure: 1 rood = 1,210 square yards = 0.025 acre. Cf. *rod.*

root. An underground portion of a plant that conducts moisture and salts to the leaves. It maintains the plant in position, and stores reserve materials. Some are used medicinally; as, glycyrrhiza, rhubarb, sarsaparilla. Cf. *rhizome.*

Roozeboom, Hendrick Willem Bakhuis. 1854–1907. Dutch chemist noted for his practical application of the phase rule.

ropiness. Stickiness or stringiness of an organic liquid (also beer, milk, or bread) caused by microorganisms of the *B. mesentericus* group.

Rosaceae. Rose family of herbs, shrubs, or trees; several yield drugs and edible fruits; e.g.: *Prunus domestica,* prune; *P. amygdalus amara,* bitter almonds; *Quillaja saponaria,* soapbark.

rosaniline. $OH \cdot C \cdot (C_6H_4NH_2)_2 \cdot (C_6H_3Me \cdot NH_2)$. A triphenylmethane dye. Red needles, soluble in water. **r. hydrochloride.** Fuchsin.

Roscoe, Sir Henry Enfield. 1833–1915. English chemist.

roscoelite. A vanadium-mica ore (California).

Rose, Friedrich. 1839–1899. German chemist, noted for work on cobalt-ammonia compounds. **R., Gustav.** 1798–1873. German chemist noted for his system of crystallography. **R., Heinrich.** 1795–1864. German chemist, and originator of the use of hydrogen sulfide in qualitative analysis. Both were sons of **R., Valentin (the younger).** 1762–1807. German chemist, noted for analytical methods, son of **R., Valentin (the elder).** 1736–1771. German chemist who first prepared *rose metal.*

rose. The dried petals of *Rosa gallica* (Rosaceae); a tonic and perfume. **cabbage-** The petals of *Rosa centifolia,* used for rose water. **Christmas-** Black hellebore. **corn-** Red *poppy.* **dog-** The ripe fruit of *Rosa canina,* used for making pill masses. It contains invert sugar, citric and malic acids.

r. bengal(e). Diiodoeosin. A red adsorption indicator in the titration of chlorides by silver nitrate. **r. bengal sodium I[131] injection.** A sterile solution of r. bengal with I[131] in the molecular structure; a diagnostic aid (U.S.P.). **r. copper.**

Rosette copper. r. metal. Rose's metal. An alloy: Bi 2, Sn 1, Pb 1 pts., m.94. **r. oil.** (1) An essential oil perfume obtained by cold extraction of r. petals. (2) The volatile oil from flowers of Rosaceae; e.g.: *Rosa gallica* and *R. alba.* Yellow liquid with a r. odor, $d_{30}0.848$–0.863; a perfume and emollient (U.S.P.). **r. process.** Separation of gold from its ores by fusion of the zinc precipitates and aeration **to** oxidize the baser metals to removable borax-silica flux. **r. quartz.** A pink gem variety of quartz. **r. vitriol.** Cobaltous sulfate. **r. water.** Water saturated with the odoriferous principles of r. oil (U.S.P.).

rosein. Fuchsin.

roselite. A native hydrated oxide containing Ca, Co, Mg, and As.

rosellane. Rosite.

rosemary. Rosmarinus. **wild-** Labrador tea. **r. oil.** The volatile oil from the flowering tops of *Rosmarinus officinalis* (Labiatae). Yellow liquid, with characteristic odor and warm camphoraceous taste, d.0.895–0.910, insoluble in water; a flavoring.

Rosenstein process. [Ludwig R. b. 1886. American chemist.] A method of making hydrochloric acid from chlorine and water gas.

Rosensthiel's green. Barium manganate.

roseo compound. $Co(NH_3)_5X_3 \cdot H_2O$. A red cobalt ammine.

roseoquinine. A red color produced on adding fresh potassium ferricyanide solution to a solution of thalleoquinine.

rosette. A disk with a centrally arranged pattern of crystals. **r. copper.** A disk formed on the surface of molten copper by sudden cooling with water.

rosin. Colophony. The resin after distilling turpentine from the exudation of species of pine, e.g., *Pinus palustris.* It contains abietic acid (80–90%) and its anhydride. Yellow, brittle mass, insoluble in water, soluble in alcohol; used as an insulator, for sizing paper, and in plastics. **r. acetal.** A highly polymerized compound of repeating oxymethylene units. **r. ester.** Ester gum. **r. jack.** A yellow variety of sphalerite. **r. oil.** Blue fluorescent oil obtained by the destructive distillation of rosin and pitch. It contains complex hydrogenated retenes, phenols, and resin acids; a lubricant. Cf. *retinol.* **r. spirit** A hydrocarbon mixture from the destructive distillation of rosin. **r. tin.** A red variety of cassiterite.

rosindone. $C_{22}H_{14}N_2O = 322.12$. Rosindulone. Red crystals, m.224, soluble in water; a dye.

rosinduline. $C_{22}H_{15}N_3 = 321.26$. An aniline dye, m.199, soluble in water. **r. scarlet.** A red oxidation-reduction indicator.

rosindulone. Rosindone.

rosinoil. Retinol. Cf. *rosin oil.*

rosinol. Retinol.

rosinweed. The dried root of *Silphium laciniatum.* A tonic and expectorant.

rosite. Decomposed anorthite.

rosmarinus. The dried leaves and plants of *Rosmarinus officinalis,* rosemary (Labiatae); an aromatic.

rosolic acid. $C_{20}H_{16}O_3 = 304.2$. Corallin, trioxytrimethylphenylmethane. Red scales with a green luster, m.270 (decomp.), slightly soluble in water; an indicator and dyestuff intermediate. Cf. *aurin.*

rosterite. A light red variety of beryl.

rosthornite. $C_{24}H_{40}O = 344.3$. A native brown resin, d.1.076 (Carinthia).

rostone. A synthetic stone molded from finely ground shale mixed with slaked lime and moistened with 18–22% water.

rot. dry- Dry wood decay due to *Merulius lacrymans*. **wet-** Wet wood decay due to organisms other than *M. lacrymans*; commonly *Coniphora cerebella*.

rotamerism. Geometric *isomerism*.

rotameter. A nonrecording indicator of fluid flow.

rotary. (1) Rotatory. (2) Revolving. **r. kiln.** A long drum, usually inclined, which rotates and can be heated. **r. movement.** A circling or twining motion.

rotate. To turn or twist.

rotation. Turning around an axis, or with a circular motion. **magnetic-** The optical activity of a liquid between magnetic poles. **molecular-** The quotient of the molecular weight by specific rotation. **specific-** $[\alpha]_D^t = \alpha/l \cdot d$, where α is the observed angle of rotation, l the length of the layer of liquid in decimeters, d the grams of substance in one milliliter, and $[a]_D$ the specific rotation when the examination is made with the sodium flame (D line), at $t°C$. Cf. *polarimeter*.

rotational. Pertaining to rotation.

rotatory. Optically active; capable of turning the plane of polarized light. **r. dispersion.** The ratio of the specific rotations of a substance with lights of 2 different wavelengths. **r. power.** Specific rotary power.

rotaversion. The rearrangement of a cis to a trans isomer; or vice versa.

rotenic acid. $C_{12}H_{12}O_4 = 220.09$. Isotubaic acid. White crystals, m.182, derived from rotenone. Cf. *tubaic acid*.

rotenoid. Describing substances related structurally to rotenone, in leguminous fish poison plants.

rotenone. MeOC=COMe—CH = 394.15. Derrin.
$$\begin{array}{ccc} | & & \| \\ CH=C— & & C— \end{array}$$
Tubatoxin, nicouline. A crystalline, insecticidal principle, m.163, insoluble in water; from *derris root*, q.v., *cube root*, q.v., and *Cracca* (*Tephrosia*) *vogelii*. It is harmless to birds and mammals, but 30 times as toxic as lead arsenate (to silkworms), 25 times as toxic as potassium cyanide (to goldfish), and 15 times as toxic as nicotine (to aphids). It crystallizes with many organic solvents; as, rotenone-benzene, $C_{23}H_{22}O_6 \cdot C_6H_6$.

rothic acid. $C_{14}H_{12}O_7 = 292.1$. A split product of nucitannin.

rothoffite. A native, brown garnet, which contains magnesium, iron, and calcium.

rotogravure. A high-speed printing process, in which a rotating metal cylinder, etched to various depths corresponding with the shade gradations of an illustration, is inked with an ink prepared with a volatile solvent. The ink transfers from the etching to the paper in amounts corresponding with the depths. Cf. *intaglio*.

rotor. (1) The rotating portion of a piece of machinery, as distinct from the stationary stator around or inside which it revolves. (2) The spinning top of an ultracentrifuge.

rotoscope. A stroboscope for the observation of rapid mechanical motion. Cf. *chronoteine*.

rotten. The state resulting from natural decomposition. **r. stone.** (1) Terra cariosa. Light, friable fine grains of silica formed by the decomposition of siliceous limestone (Derbyshire); a polishing material. (2) Tripoli.

rottisite. A native, hydrated nickel silicate.

rottlera. Kamala.

rottlerin. $C_{22}H_{20}O_6 = 380.2$. Mallotoxin, kamalin. Yellow leaflets from kamala, m.200, soluble in ether or alkalies (red color).

Rotwyla. Trade name for a viscose synthetic fiber.

Rouelle, Guillaume François. 1703–1770. French chemist; the first physiological chemist.

rouge. (1) A cosmetic dye made from safflower mixed with talc. (2) A cosmetic that simulates flushed skin. (3) Colcothar. **jeweler's-** Colcothar.
　　r. flambé. A glaze containing copper, of Chinese origin.

roughage. Fibrous food material (usually cellulose), which stimulates the digestive and excretory organs by frictional contact with the alimentary tract.

round factor. See *inch*.

Roussin's salt. $K[Fe_4(NO)_7S_3]$. Dark-colored salts formed when nitric oxide is passed through a suspension of precipitated ferrous sulfide in potassium sulfide solution.

ROV. Refined oil of vitriol: 95–96% sulfuric acid.

Rowland, Henry Augustus. 1848–1901. American physicist. **R.'s value.** The wavelength of a Fraunhofer line in the solar spectrum.

rowlandite. A native silicate of yttrium, with cerium, lanthanum, and thorium.

Royal Society of London. A society founded in 1662 for furthering the natural and physical sciences.

Roylon. Trade name for a polyamide synthetic fiber.

Ru. Symbol for ruthenium.

rubber. $(C_5H_8)_x = (544)_x$. Caoutchouc, elastica, india r. An elastic substance obtained from the coagulated milky juice (latex) of *Hevea* (para r.) and *Ficus* (india r.) species. It contains the hydrocarbon unit $—CH_2 \cdot CMe:CH \cdot CH_2—$, and is a linear polymer: mol. wt. approx. 300,000. The main constituent is *cis*-1,4-polyisoprene, d.0.92, with varying quantities of oxidation products, resins 2–60, water and impurities 3–15%. Soluble in chloroform, carbon disulfide, ether, or benzene. On destructive distillation it yields isoprene, dipentene, and other hydrocarbons. World production (1966): natural r. 2.5 million tons; synthetic r. 3.2 million tons. Cf. *elastomer* and table. **butyl-** See *butyl, elastomer*. **cold-** Synthetic r. made by a cold process, e.g., at 41° instead of 122°, as with GR-S r., q.v. It has improved wearing properties. **cyclized-** A finely divided powder produced by heating a solution of pure natural r. with (e.g.) stannic chloride, and evaporating the solvent. The r. molecules are cross-linked to give a ring structure and good plastic properties; cf. *Pliolite*. **deuterio-** A synthetic r. of high strength and specific gravity made from a polyisoprene derivative in which all the H atoms are replaced by heavy H atoms. **fluorine-** See *elastomer*. **guayule-** Guayule. **hard-** Econite, vulcanite. **inorganic-** $(NPCl_2)_n$. Polymerized cyclic chlorophosphazene. An inorganic polymer. **microporous-** Micropor. **nitrile-** See elastomer. **silicone-** See *elastomer, silicone*. **stereo-** Synthetic r. made from stereopolymers.

TYPES OF RUBBER AND PRINCIPAL USES

Type of rubber	Principal uses	Qualities
SBR, styrene-butadiene	Tires, heels, soles, foamed products, mechanical goods, wire coatings, floorings	Resilience, tear strength, resistance to high and low temperatures and abrasion
Neoprene	Mechanical goods, wire coatings, heels and soles	Resistance to oil, ozone, abrasion, solvents
Butyl................	Auto-motor, body mountings, tubes, tire linings, mechanical goods, cable insulation	Shock absorption, sun and ozone resistance. Holds air. Incompatible with other rubbers unless chlorinated
Nitrile................	Coated paper, leather, and textiles	Oil resistance; resistance to abrasion, ozone, solvents, high and low temperatures; resilience
Polybutadiene	Blends with SBR in tires	Abrasion resistance, good oxidation and low temperature resistance, low hysteresis (low heat buildup). Poor skid resistance
Polyisoprene	Tires, adhesives, bathing caps, sneaker soles, dipped and proof goods, foamed products, rubber bands	Man-made duplicate of natural rubber
Ethylene-propylene	Wire and cable coatings, weather stripping, steam hose, automotive parts	Ozone and sunlight resistance, excellent electrical properties, resilience, abrasion resistance. Can be oil-extended
Natural...............	Truck tires, off-the-road tires, dipped and proof goods, textile backing, footwear, drug sundries, mechanical goods, latex, foamed products	Abrasion resistance, resilience, good high and low temperature performance, tear

synthetic- Elastomer. World production (1967), 3.3 million tons.
r. accelerators. See *accelerators*. **r. acid.** Sulfuric acid produced by the oxidizing action of water organisms on sulfur in rubber; the cause of deterioration of fire hose. **r. goods.** Articles prepared by mixing various substances with r. and subjecting to vulcanization, acceleration, and aging. **r. graft-** A blend of natural r. and a polymer, as styrene. **r. hydrochloride.** $C_{10}H_{18}Cl_2$. A reaction product of r. with dry hydrogen chloride at below 10°; used as an adhesive, waterproof wrapping (Plioform), and in paints. **r. sources:**

Euphorbiaceae:
Hevea brasiliensis	Para r.
Manihot	Ceara r., q.v.
Micrandra............	Venezuelan r.
Sapium	Bolivian r., Colombian r.

Moraceae:
Ficus elastica	India r.
Castilloa	Mexican r., W. Indian r.

Apocynaceae:
Funtumia	African r.
Landolphia............	Madagascar r.
Clitandra	Central African r.
Willoughbeia	Borneo r., Java r.
Hancornia	Mancabeira r.

Asclepiadaceae:
Asclepias	Milkweed r.

Compositae:
Parthenium argentatum..	Guayule r., q.v.

r. sulfide. A reinforcing substance formed in r. during vulcanization. **r. uses.** See table.
Rubbone. $C_{10}H_{16}O$ (approx.). Brand name for an orange viscous gum, produced by atmospheric oxidation of rubber. Used to accelerate the oxidation of polymerized linseed oil.
rubeane. $(NH_2 \cdot C:S)_2$ = 120.2. Rubeanhydride, carbon disulfhydrate, thioxalic acid diamide, obtained by heating hydrogen sulfide and cyanogen. Red crystals, soluble in water; a microreagent for copper.
rubeanhydride. Rubeane.
rubeanic acid. Rubeane.
rubefacient. An agent that produces redness of the skin, due to dilation of the blood vessels; as, mustard.
rubellin. $C_{36}H_{48}O_{16}(?)$. A glycoside from *Urginea rubella*, m.262; a cardiac rat poison.
rubellite. Tourmaline.
rubene. $C_{18}H_8R_4$. A compound that absorbs and regenerates oxygen; it contains the dibenzofulvene group. **diphenylditolyl-** $C_{44}H_{30}$ = 558.2. White crystals, m.375, violet fluorescence. **tetraphenyl-** Rubrene.
ruberite. Cuprite.
ruberythric acid. Rubianic acid.
ruberythrinic acid. Rubianic acid.
rubia. Madder. The root of dyer's madder, *Rubia tinctorium* (Rubiaceae).
Rubiaceae. The madder family of herbs, shrubs, or trees that yield drugs; e.g.: bark: *Cinchona* species, quinine alkaloids; herbs: *Mitchella repens*, squaw vine; roots: *Rubia tinctorium*, madder, alizarin;

seeds: *Coffea arabica*, coffee; extract: *Oruouiarpa gambir*, gambir.

rubianic acid. $C_{26}H_{28}O_{14} = 564.22$. Ruberythr-(in)ic acid. A glucoside from rubia, hydrolyzed to glucose and alizarin. Yellow prisms, m.259.

rubicelle. Spinel.

rubicene. $C_{26}H_{14} = 326.1$. Red needles, m.305, insoluble in water.

rubidine. $C_{11}H_{17}N = 163.14$. A pyridine base, q.v.

rubidium. Rb $= 85.47$. An alkali metal element, at. no. 37, discovered by Bunsen (1861). A soft, white metal, d.1.52, m.38, b.696, decomp. in water or alcohol, soluble in ether; occurs in Stassfurt salts, lepidolite, leucite, and mineral waters. **r. acetate.** $RbC_2H_3O_2 = 144.4$. Colorless crystals, soluble in water. **r. alum.** Aluminum rubidium sulfate. **r. ammonium bromide.** $RbBr \cdot 4NH_4Br = 545.4$. Yellow crystals, soluble in water; a hypnotic. **r. bichromate.** Rubidium dichromate. **r. bitartrate.** $RbHC_4H_4O_6 = 234.4$. Colorless prisms, soluble in water. **r. bromide.** RbBr $= 165.4$. Colorless, regular crystals, m.683, soluble in water; a nerve sedative. **r. carbonate.** $Rb_2CO_3 = 230.90$. Colorless, deliquescent crystals, m.837, soluble in water. **r. chloride.** RbCl $= 120.91$. Colorless crystals, m.710, soluble in water. **r. chromate.** $Rb_2CrO_4 = 286.9$. Yellow crystals, soluble in water. **r. dichromate.** $Rb_2Cr_2O_7 = 386.9$. Orange crystals, soluble in water. **r. fluoride.** RbF $= 104.4$. White crystals, soluble in water. **r. fluosilicate.** $Rb_2SiF_6 = 312.94$. White octahedra, soluble in water. **r. hydride.** RbH $= 86.45$. Colorless needles, decomp. 300. **r. hydroxide.** RbOH $= 102.5$. Gray, deliquescent powder, soluble in water; used in the manufacture of glass and rubidium salts. **r. iodate.** $RbIO_3 = 260.4$. Colorless prisms, soluble in water. **r. iodide.** RbI $= 212.4$. Colorless cubes, soluble in water; an alterative. **r. ion.** The cation, Rb^+. **r. nitrate.** $RbNO_3 = 147.5$. Colorless hexagons, soluble in water. **r. oxide.** $Rb_2O = 186.9$. Colorless octahedra, soluble in water. **r. perchlorate.** $RbClO_4 = 184.91$. Colorless crystals. **r. peroxide.** $Rb_2O_2 = 202.9$. Yellow needles, m.600, decomp. by water. **r. platinichloride.** $Rb_2PtCl_6 = 578.9$. Yellow crystals, soluble in water. **r. sulfate.** $Rb_2SO_4 = 266.96$. Colorless rhombs, m.1,051, soluble in water; a cathartic. **r. sulfide.** $Rb_2S \cdot 4H_2O = 275.0$. Colorless crystals, soluble in water. **r. sulfite.** $Rb_2SO_3 = 250.9$. Colorless crystals, soluble in water. **r. tartrate.** $Rb_2C_4H_4O_6 = 318.8$. Colorless crystals, soluble in water. *acid-* $RbHC_4H_4O_6 = 234.48$. White prisms, soluble in water.

rubijervine. $C_{26}H_{43}O_2N = 401.34$. An alkaloid from *Veratrum album* and *V. viride* (Liliaceae), m.236.

rubin. An anthocyanin from radishes.

rubine. Fuchsin.

rubitannic acid. $C_{14}H_{22}O_{12} \cdot \frac{1}{2}H_2O$. A tannin from the leaves of *Rubia tinctorium*.

rubixanthin. $C_{40}H_{55}OH = 552.4$. An orange carotinoid pigment from *Rosa rubiginosa*.

rubrene. $C_{41}H_{26} = 518.22$. Phenylethinyldiphenyl-methane, tetraphenyldibenzodifulvene. A red, fluorescent, solid hydrocarbon, m.331. When illuminated in air it forms *oxyrubrene*, $C_{41}H_{26}O_2$, which dissociates when heated, to $C_{41}H_{26}$ and O_2. This reversible oxidation is rare. Cf. *hemoglobin*,

rubene. **r. bromide.** A solid, m.500, the highest of any known organic compound.

rubrocyanine. Ruhrgasol.

rubrofusarin. An antibacterial red pigment from the mycelia of *Fusaria* cultures.

rubroglaucine. $C_{16}H_{12}O_5 = 284.0$. A red pigment related to auroglaucine, q.v.

rubrones. Substances prepared by bubbling air through a solution of rubber with cobalt linoleate as catalyst. Used in paints and varnishes, and for molding.

rubrum scarlatinum. Scarlet R.

Rubus. (1) A genus of shrubs and herbs of the family Rosaceae, q.v. (2) Blackberry, cloudberry, dewberry, fingerberry. The dried bark of the rhizomes of *Rubus* species, which contain tannin; used as an astringent: e.g., *Rubus idaeus*, raspberry.

ruby. Al_2O_3. A red, transparent corundum gem, similar to sapphire. **artificial-** A r. made by fusing chromium sesquioxide and powdered alumina. **r. alamandine.** Spinel. **r. arsenic.** Realgar. **r. balas.** Spinel. **r. blende.** A red variety of sphalerite. **r. copper.** Cuprite. **r. glass.** A dark red glass, colored by colloidal gold. Ordinary red glass is colored by selenium. **r. mica.** Goethite. **r. silver.** Proustite. **r. spinel.** Spinel. **r. sulfur.** Realgar.

Rudolfi's equation. The degree of ionization α, related to the dilution v: $\alpha^2/(1 - \alpha)\sqrt{v} = $ constant. See also *dilution law*, *Ostwald's law*.

rue. Ruta. The dried shrubby *Ruta graveolens*; a condiment containing rutic and rutinic acids. **r. oil.** Oleum rutae. An essential oil from the leaves of *Ruta graveolens*. Green liquid, d.0.837, b.230, insoluble in water.

rufianic acid. Quinizarinsulfonic acid, 1,4-dioxyanthraquinone-2-sulfonic acid. White crystals; a reagent for the separation of amino acids.

rufigallic acid. $C_{14}H_8O_8 \cdot 2H_2O = 340.16$. 1,2,3,5,-6,7-Hexahydroxyanthraquinone. Orange needles, sublime if heated, insoluble in water; a dye.

rufigallol. $C_{14}H_8O_8 = 322.2$. 1,2,3,6,7,9-Hexahydroxyanthraquinone. Red crystals.

rufin. $C_{21}H_{20}O_8 = 400.2$. A resinous mass obtained by heating phlorizin; soluble in alkalies (red color).

rufiopin. $C_{14}H_8O_6 = 272.13$. Tetrahydroxyanthraquinone. Orange crystals, soluble in alcohol.

rufol. $C_{14}H_{10}O_2 = 210.1$. 1,5-Dihydroxyanthracene, 1,5-anthradiol, 1,5-anthracendiol*. Yellow needles, decomp. 265, soluble in alcohol (blue fluorescence).

rugosimeter. An instrument to measure the roughness of a flat surface in terms of the resistance to airflow between it and a plane surface resting on it, under a standard pressure.

rugosity. Roughness, angularity. The ratio of measured specific surface to hypothetical surface area, of a particle, assumed to be spherical.

Ruhmkorff, Heinrich Daniel. 1803–1877. German electrician. **R. coil.** An induction or spark coil.

ruhrgasol. A mixture of CO_2, CO, H_2, N_2, and C_3- and C_4-aliphatic hydrocarbons (35% by vol. of C_3H_6) recovered from coke-oven gas; an autofuel in Germany.

rule. (1) An empirical relationship of physical and chemical properties; as, *Crum Brown rule*. Cf. *theory*, *law*, *hypothesis*. (2) A ruler. **phase-** See *phase* rule. **slide-** See *slide* rule.

rum. A distillation product from fermented molasses.
  bay- See *bay rum.*

rumex. Yellow dock, yellow jasmine. The dried roots of *Rumex crispus* (Polygonaceae); used medicinally.

Rumford, Count (Benjamin Thompson). 1753–1814. American scientist noted for his work on the nature of heat, and cofounder of the Royal Institution, London.

rumicin. $C_{15}H_{10}O_4$ = 254.08. Yellow crystals, m.182, from the roots of *Rumex crispus*. It resembles chrysophanic acid.

Runge, Friedlieb Ferdinand. 1795–1867. German chemist, discoverer of aniline. See *aniline.*

Rupert's drops. See *Prince Rupert's drops.*

Rupp's test. A test for chlorine in chemically sterilized milk. Yellow color with potassium iodide; little used.

Rush, Benjamin. 1745–1813. American physician and pioneer in chemical education, noted as the first American author and professor of chemistry.

russellite. $Bi_2O_3 \cdot WO_3$ = 698.0. A mineral, that occurs sparingly as yellow pellets, in concentrates of tungsten ores (Cornwall, England).

Russell-Saunders notation. See *quantum numbers.*

russium. Rs. Early name for the undiscovered ekacesium. Cf. *verium.*

rust. (1) Iron oxide mixed with hydroxides and carbonates, formed on the surface of iron exposed to moisture and air. (2) A red fungus on cereal grain. **white-** A form of corrosion of steel due to excess of chloride from the galvanizing operation.
  r. proofing. Plating a metal with a less corrodible metal; as, tin, cadmium, or zinc. See *galvanization, sherardizing.*

ruta. Rue.

Rutaceae. Rue family, yielding acrid resinous principles and essential oils; e.g.: *Galipea (Cusparia) officinalis,* angostura bark; *Pilocarpus jaborandi,* jaborandi leaves; *Aegle marmelos,* bael fruit.

ruthenate. M_2RuO_4. M is a monovalent metal. Red salts, soluble in water, derived from hexavalent ruthenium. **per-** $MRuO_4$, e.g., $NaRuO_4$. Dark green crystals, soluble in water.

ruthenic. Describing a compound derived from tetravalent ruthenium; as, $RuCl_4$.

ruthenious. Ruthenous. Describing a compound derived from divalent ruthenium: as, **r. chloride.** $(RuCl_2)_x$ = $(172.61)_x$. Ruthenium dichloride. Blue solid, insoluble in water.

ruthenium. Ru = 101.07. A rare metallic element of the platinum group, at. no. 44. Gray or silvery, brittle metal, d.12.06, melts in the electric arc; insoluble in water or acids. It can have every positive valency from 1 to 8, and forms coordination compounds and double salts. **r. bromide.** $RuBr_3$ = 341.7. Dark hygroscopic crystals; soluble in water:

+2	Ru^+	Ruthenious	Blue
+3	Ru^{3+}	Ruthenic	Gray
+4	$RuO_3^=$	Ruthenite	Yellow
+6	$RuO_4^=$	Ruthenate	Orange-red
+7	RuO_4^-	Perruthenate	Green
+8	$RuO_5^=$	....	Red

  r. carbonyl. $Ru(CO)_x$. Orange crystals. **r. chloride.** (1) *di-* Ruthenious chloride. (2) *tri-*

Ru_2Cl_6 = 416.2. Ruthenic chloride. R. sesquichloride. Deliquescent, brown crystals, soluble in water, decomp. by alcohol; an antiseptic and catalyst. (3) *tetra-* $RuCl_4$ = 196.70. Orange crystals, soluble in water. **r. fluoride.** RuF_5 = 196.70. Green crystals, m.101, decomp. in water. When heated with iodine, it is converted into r. trifluoride, q.v. **r. hydrochloride.** $RuCl_4 \cdot 2HCl$ = 320.6, or H_2RuCl_6. Chlororuthenic acid. Orange crystals, soluble in water. **r. hydroxide.** (1) $Ru(OH)_3$ = 192.8. Black powder, insoluble in water. (2) $Ru_2O_3 \cdot xH_2O$. Ruthenic hydroxide. Yellow powder, soluble in water. (3) $RuO_2 \cdot xH_2O$. R. tetrahydroxide. Black powder, insoluble in water. **r. minerals.** R. is associated with the platinum metals, and occurs as laurite, RuS_2, and the element. **r. nitrosotrinitrate.** $Ru(NO)(NO_3)_3 \cdot$ $4H_2O$. Deliquescent, red solid, decomp. by water (to nitric acid) and heat. **r. oxide.** (1) RuO_2 = 133.8. R. dioxide. Violet crystals, insoluble in water, formed by the action of oxygen on hot r. (2) Ru_2O_3 = 251.44. R. sesquioxide. Brown powder, insoluble in water. (3) RuO_4 = 165.7. R. tetroxide. Yellow crystals, m.25, insoluble in water. (4) Ru_2O_5 = 283.40. R. pentoxide. Black powder. (5) Ru_2O_9 = 550.80. R. monoxide. Black powder, insoluble in water. **r. oxychloride.** $Ru(OH)Cl_2$ = 189.63. R. red. Red powder. *ammoniated-* $Ru(OH)Cl_2 \cdot 3NH_3 \cdot$ H_2O = 258.75. Brown powder, soluble in water; a reagent for pectin, plant mucin, gums, and a microscope stain. **r. red.** R. oxychloride. **r. sesquichloride.** R. chloride. **r. sesquioxide.** R. oxide (2). **r. silicide.** $RuSi$ = 129.76. Metallic prisms, insoluble in water. **r. sulfide.** RuS_2 = 165.82. Laurite. Gray cubes, insoluble in water. **r. tetroxide.** R. oxide (3). **r. trifluoride.** RuF_3. Brown crystals, insoluble in water.

ruthenous. Ruthenious.

Rutherford, Daniel. 1749–1819. Scottish botanist who discovered nitrogen (1772). **R., Lord Ernest.** 1871–1937. British physicist (born New Zealand), Nobel Prize winner (1908); noted for research on the structure of the atom. **R. atomic theory.** An atom consists of a small positive nucleus with A free positive charges in its nucleus, surrounded by a system of A electrons (A is the atomic number). The nucleus contains equal numbers of positive and negative charges which balance.

rutherford. rd. A unit of radioactivity: 10^6 disintegrations/sec is taken as the comparison standard. Cf. *curie.*

rutherfordite. A mixed native phosphate of cerium, lanthanum, and didymium.

rutic acid. (1) $C_{10}H_{20}O_2$ = 172.15. A monobasic acid from rue. (2) Capric acid.

rutile. TiO_2. Dark tetragonal crystals; a source of titanium compounds.

rutin. (1) $C_{27}H_{32}O_{16}$ = 612.25. A hydroxyflavone glucorhamnoside from cowslip and other plants. Yellow needles m.190; used to treat capillary disorders. (2) Barosmin.

rutinic acid. $C_{25}H_{28}O_{15}$ = 568.3. The coloring material of rue, *Ruta graveolens.*

rutonal. $C_{11}H_{10}N_2O_3$ = 218.1. Phenylmethylbarbituric acid. White crystals, m.227.

Rydberg, Johannes Robert. 1854–1919. Swedish physicist. **R.'s formula.** The frequency vibration of a radiation $= k(1/n^2 - 1/n'^2)$, where n is the number of the inner, and n' that of the outer orbit in a given jump. **R. fundamental constant.** The value $N = 109678.8$, in the expression $N = V_0/c$, where c is the velocity of light and V_0 is R. frequency constant. **R. fundamental frequency constant.** The value $V_0 = 3.28880 \times 10^{15}$ sec^{-1} in the expression, $V_0 = cN$. Cf. *Ritz formula*. **R. number.** Ordinal number. **R. relation.** The atomic number A is related to the frequency, ν, of the characteristic radiation by $\nu = \frac{3}{4}V_0(A - n)^2$, where n is a constant nearly equal to unity.

rye. The grain of *Secale cereale*, used in making bread. **spurred-** Ergot.

S

S. Symbol for: (1) sulfur; (2) black (German: schwarz) in color names. **S acid.** 1-Amino-8-naphthol-4-sulfonic acid. **2S acid.** 1-Amino-8-naphthol-2,4-disulfonic acid. **S yellow.** Naphthol yellow.

S. Symbol for entropy.

s. Abbreviation for second.

s. Symbol for: (1) symmetrical, (2) secondary, (3) solubility. *s.* **state** *Orbital* state.

σ. Greek sigma. (1) Symbol for: (a) 1/1,000 second, (b) stopping power. (2) Prefix indicating the syn position.

Σ. Greek capital sigma. (1) Symbol for: summation. (2) Σ **reaction.** Wassermann test for syphilis.

∫. Symbol for integration. Cf. *f* = function.

Sa. Former symbol for samarium, Sm.

sabadilla. Cevadilla, Indian barley. The seeds of *Veratrum sabadilla* or *Schoenocaulon officinale* (Liliaceae), Mexico and Central America; a vermicide containing veratrine and sabadine.

sabadilline. $C_{34}H_{53}O_3N = 523.6.$ Cevadilline. An alkaloid from sabadilla. Cf. *cevilline.*

sabadine. $C_{29}H_{51}O_8N = 541.0.$ An alkaloid obtained from sabadilla and veratrum. Colorless needles, m.238.

sabadinine. $C_{27}H_{45}O_8N = 511.5.$ An alkaloid from sabadilla. Colorless needles, m.160, soluble in alcohol.

sabal. Saw palmetto berries. The partly dried, ripe fruit of *Serenoa serrulata* or *Sabal serrulata* (Palmacea); a tonic sedative. **s. fiber.** The split leaves from *Sabal palmetto*, thatch palm; used for matting.

sabalol. The active principle of sabal.

Sabatier, Paul. 1854–1941. French chemist, Nobel Prize winner (1912); pioneer in the hydrogenation of vegetable oils.

sabatrine. $C_{51}H_{86}O_{17}N = 984.9.$ An alkaloid from sabadilla seeds.

sabbatia. American centaury. The dried herb of *Sabbatia angularis* (Gentianaceae); a febrifuge.

sabbatin. A glucoside from *Sabbatia elliottii*, quinine flower.

sabin. Absorption unit (in acoustics), after W. C. Sabine.

sabina. Savine.

sabina oil. Savine oil.

sabinane. $C_{10}H_{18} = 138.14.$ A terpene based on the thujyl radical. **6-keto-** Thujone.

sabinene. $C_{10}H_{16} = 136.2.$ A hydrocarbon from savine oil. Colorless liquid, d.0.840, b.163, insoluble in water.

sabinic acid. $HO(CH_2)_{11}COOH = 216.3.$ *λ*-Hydroxylauric acid, 12-hydroxydodecanoic acid*; from savine and juniper oils.

sabinol. $C_{10}H_{16}O = 152.2.$ 6-Hydroxysabinene. An alcohol from savine oil.

sabromin. $Ca(C_{22}H_{41}O_2Br_2)_2 = 1034.41.$ Calcium dibrombehenate. White powder, insoluble in water; a hypnotic.

saccharase. Invertase.

saccharate. Sucrate. (1) A salt of saccharic acid. (2) A compound of a saccharide and a metallic oxide; as, $CaO \cdot C_{12}H_{22}O_{11} \cdot H_2O.$

saccharetin. $(C_5H_7O_0)_n.$ The yellow crust of sugarcane; probably a phlobaphen.

saccharic acid. $(CHOH)_4 \cdot (COOH)_2 = 210.11.$ Tetrahydroxyadipic acid, obtained on oxidation of hexoses; very soluble in water. Cf. *saccharinic acid.*

saccharide. (1) A compound of an organic base with sugar; as, casein saccharide. (2) See *polysaccharide, sugars, carbohydrate.*

saccharification. (1) Conversion into sugar. (2) Impregnation with sugar solutions; as, in malting.

saccharify. To convert starches into sugar.

saccharimeter. A device to determine sugar in solution; as, a polarimeter. Cf. *saccharometer.*

saccharimetry. The determination of the sugar content of a solution from its optical activity.

saccharin, saccharine. $C_6H_4 \cdot (SO_2) \cdot (CO) \cdot NH = 183.19.$ Gluside, sykose, benzosulfimide, benzoylsulfonic imide, saccharinose, sulfobenzoic acid imide, saccharinol, glucid, saccharol, sulfinid, guarantose, saxin, agucarina, 1-benzosulfonaxol-2(1)-one. White crystals, m.228 (decomp.), soluble in water and 400 times sweeter than cane sugar; a sugar substitute (U.S.P., B.P.). **soluble-** $C_7H_4N \cdot NaO_3S \cdot 2H_2O = 241.21.$ The sodium salt of s.; often s. mixed with $NaHCO_3.$

s. sodium. (1) Soluble s. (U.S.P., B.P.). (2) A lactone of a saccharic acid.

saccharinic acid. $C_6H_{12}O_6 = 180.09.$ Acids obtained by oxidation of sugars; 24 possible isomers. **gluco-** $CH_2OH \cdot (CHOH)_2 \cdot CHMe \cdot COOH.$ Glucosaccharic acid, obtained from glucose and fructose; 8 isomers. **iso-** $CH_2OH \cdot CHOH \cdot CH_2 \cdot COH(CH_2-OH) \cdot COOH$, from milk sugar and cellulose; 4 isomers. **meta-** $CH_2OH(CHOH)_2CH_2 \cdot CHOH \cdot CO-OH$; 8 isomers. **para-** $CH_2OH \cdot CH_2 \cdot COH(COOH) \cdot CHOH \cdot CH_2OH$, from galactose and milk sugar; 4 isomers. All form lactones when their aqueous solutions are evaporated. Cf. *saccharonic acid.*

saccharobiose. Sucrose.

saccharol. Saccharin.

saccharolactic acid. Mucic acid.

saccharometer. A fermentation tube.

Saccharomyces. Yeasts, q.v., which ferment sugar. **S. unit.** S.U. A unit of vitamin H activity.

saccharon. $C_6H_8O_6 = 176.1.$ The lactone of saccharonic acid.

saccharonic acid. $HOOC \cdot CMeOH \cdot (CHOH)_2 \cdot COOH = 194.1.$ Obtained by oxidation of sucrose. Colorless crystals, soluble in water.

saccharose. Sucrose.

Saccharum officinarum. Sugarcane. **S. saturnii.** Early name for an aqueous lead acetate solution.

SAE classification (Society of Automotive Engineers). The grouping of steel alloys by numbers which indicate the alloying metal or type of steel, percentage of the principal alloying metal, and percentage of carbon. A similar classification used by the U.S. War Department is abbreviated W.D.

SAE number. A measure of the relative viscosity of lubricating oils, related to the Saybolt universal viscosity.

Safa. Trade name for a polyamide synthetic fiber.

safety. Avoidance of hazards, q.v. **s. lamp.** Miner's lamp. **s. tube.** A device to oppose the effects of sudden pressures or sudden flows of liquids.

safflorite. $(Fe, Co)As_2$. A native, rhombic arsenide.

safflower. Carthamus.

saffron. Crocus. The stigmas of *Crocus sativus* (Iridaceae), containing the glucoside crocetin. A yellow food coloring, carminative, and emmenagogue. **American-, bastard-, false-** Carthamus. **Indian-** Turmeric. **meadow-** Colchicum. **s. bronze.** Orange *tungsten*. **s. glucoside.** Crocetin. **s. of mars.** Ferric subcarbonate. **s. substitute.** Dinitrocresol.

safranal. $C_{10}H_{14}O = 150.1$. An aldehyde occurring in saffron as the glucoside pikrococin: $CHO\cdot C:CMe\cdot CH:CH\cdot CH_2\cdot CMe_2$.

safranine. $C_{18}H_{14}N_4 = 286.1$. Phenosafranine. A phenazine dye used as a stain in microscopy and the textile industry.

safraninol. $C_{18}H_{13}ON_3 = 287.2$. A derivative of safranine, in which the :NH group is replaced by the keto-oxygen, :O.

safrene. $C_{10}H_{16} = 136.1$. A terpene from sassafras oil.

safrole. $C_6H_3(OCH_2O)\cdot CH_2\cdot CH:CH_2(3:4:1) = 162.13$. Allyl pyrocatechol methylene ether, shikimol, 1-allyl-3,4-methylenedioxybenzene; in sassafras oil. Colorless oil, m.10, insoluble in water; an anodyne and perfume. **iso-** $C_6H_3(OOCH_2)\cdot CH:CH\cdot CH_3$. A liquid, b.251, insoluble in water.

safron. Saffron.

safrosin. $C_{22}H_8O_5Br(NO_2)_2$. A scarlet textile dye, chiefly dinitrodibromofluorescein.

sagapenum. A gum resin from *Ferula persica* (Umbelliferae).

sage. Salvia. **s. brush.** Artemisia. **s. oil.** The essential oil of *Salvia officinalis*, d.0.915–0.925, soluble in alcohol; contains cineol.

sagenite. Silica containing rutile.

sago. (1) An edible starch from the pith of palms, chiefly *Metroxylon rumphii* (India and E. Indian islands). (2) The pith of several palms and tree ferns; as, Palmaceae, q.v.; Cyatheaceae, tree ferns; and Cycadaceae.

Sahli's stain. A solution of borax and methylene blue in water; a stain for nerve tissues and cell nuclei.

sahlite. Augite containing iron.

Sainte-Claire Deville, Etienne Henri. 1818–1881. French chemist noted for mineralogical and inorganic research.

Saint Ignatius bean. Ignatia.

Saint John's bread. Carob beans.

saiodine. Sajodin.

sajodin. $Ca(C_{22}H_{42}O_2I)_2 = 974.1$. Calcium monoiodobehenate. Yellow powder, insoluble in water; used medicinally.

saké, saki. Japanese beer prepared from rice, water, tané-koji, and saké yeast; a yellow, aromatic liquid with pleasant taste: ethyl alcohol 13–14, sugar 0.9%.

Sakurai, Joji. 1858–1939. Japanese chemist noted for organic research. **S.-Landsberger apparatus.** A device for rapidly determining approximate molecular weights by the vapor-pressure method.

sakuranin. $C_{22}H_{24}O_{10} = 448.19$. A glucoside, m.212, from sakura, the Japanese cherry tree.

sal. Latin for salt. **s. acetosella.** Potassium binoxalate. **s. aeratus.** Potassium bicarbonate. **s. alembroth.** Ammoniated mercury. **s. amarum.** Magnesium sulfate. **s. ammoniac.** Ammonium chloride. **s. carolinum facticum.** An artificial Carlsbad salt. **s. communis.** Sodium chloride. **s. de duobus.** Potassium sulfate. **s. enixum.** Potassium bisulfate. **s. epsom.** Magnesium sulfate. **s. ethyl.** Ethyl salicylate. **s. fossile.** Sodium chloride. **s. glauberi.** Sodium sulfate. **s. marinum.** Sodium chloride. **s. mirabile.** Sodium sulfate. **s. perlatum.** Sodium phosphate. **s. prunella.** A concentrated, refined saltpeter, made by fusion to remove moisture and molded into a cake; used for meat curing. **s. rupium.** Rock salt. **s. sapientiae.** Mercuric ammonium chloride. **s. sedatirum.** Borax. **s. sedative.** Boric acid. **s. soda.** Sodium carbonate. **s. tartari.** Potassium carbonate. **s. volatile.** Ammonium carbonate.

salacetol. $C_6H_4(OH)COOCH_2COMe = 194.1$. Salantol, salicylacetol, acetosalicylic ester. Colorless needles, m.71, soluble in water; a substitute for salol.

salamandaridine. An alkaloid from the poisonous skin secretion of the salamander species. Cf. *samandaridine*.

salamander. A truncated cone of plumbago, for heating a crucible uniformly.

salamanderine. $C_{34}H_{60}O_5N_2 = 576.5$. A poisonous alkaloid from the skin of the salamander species. Cf. *samandarine*.

salamide. Salicylamide.

salantol. Salacetol.

salazolon. Salipyrine.

saldanine. An alkaloid from *Datura arborea*, a Mexican shrub; a local anesthetic.

salep. The tubers of *Orchis mascula*, *O. latifolia*; demulcents and a food. Cf. *arrowroot*.

saleratus. Potassium bicarbonate (sal aeratus).

sal ethyl. Ethyl salicylate.

sal hypnone. $C_6H_4(OCOPh)COOCH_3 = 256.1$. Benzoyl methyl salicylate. Colorless needles, m.113, insoluble in water; a mild antiseptic.

salic. Containing alumina. **s. minerals.** Igneous rocks that contain more alumina than iron. Cf. *alferric*.

salicin. $C_{13}H_{18}O_7 = 286.2$. Saligenin. A glucoside from the bark of *Populus tremula*, American aspen; *Spiraea* and *Salix* species, willows. Colorless leaflets, m.201 (decomp.), soluble in water; a tonic, antipyretic, and reagent for nitric acid. **benzoyl-** Populin.

salicoside. Salicin.

salicoyl. Salicyloyl.

salicyl. The radical $HO \cdot C_6H_4$—, from salicylic acid. Cf. *salicylyl.* **s. fluorone.** 2,6,7-Trihydroxy-9-(*o*-hydroxyphenyl)fluorone. A color reagent for rare-earth elements.

salicylacetol. Salacetol.

salicylal. (1) Salicylaldehyde. (2) The radical $1,2\text{-}C_6H_4(OH)CH\!\!=\!\!\!.$

salicyl alcohol. $C_6H_4(OH)CH_2OH = 124.1$. Saligenin, saligenol, *o*-hydroxybenzyl alcohol. A hydrolysis product of salicin. Colorless needles, m.86, soluble in water; an antipyretic. **p-amino-** Edinol.

salicylaldehyde. $C_6H_4(OH)CHO = 122.1$. Salicylic aldehyde, salicylal, *o*-hydroxybenzaldehyde. Colorless, aromatic liquid, b.197, slightly soluble in water; a reagent for acetone, and used in perfumery. **methoxy-** Vanillin. **s. glucose.** Helicin.

salicylamide. $C_6H_4(OH)CONH_2 = 137.1$. Salamide, *o*-hydroxybenzamide. Colorless leaflets, m.138, slightly soluble in water; an antipyretic and analgesic. **salicylic-** Disalicylamide.

salicylanilide. $C_6H_4 \cdot OH \cdot CONHC_6H_5 = 213.11$. Salifebrin. A compound of salicylic acid and acetanilide. Colorless powder, insoluble in water; an antipyretic and, formerly, a crop fungicide.

salicylase. An enzyme that oxidizes salicylaldehyde to salicylic acid.

salicylate. $C_6H_4(OH)COO \cdot M$. A salt of salicylic acid: M is a monovalent metal.

salicylic acid. $C_6H_4(OH)COOH = 138.1$. *o*-Hydroxybenzoic acid. Colorless needles, m.158, slightly soluble in water. A reagent for ferric salts, nitrites, formaldehyde; a preservative; and antirheumatic (U.S.P., B.P.). **acetamidoethyl-** Benzacetin (1). **acetamidomethyl-** Benzacetin (2). **acetyl-** See *acetyl.* **o-amino-** $C_6H_3(NH_2)OH \cdot CO \cdot OH = 153.1$. 1-Amino-2-hydroxy-3-benzoic acid. Gray powder, insoluble in water; an antirheumatic. **p-amino-** $C_7H_7NO_3 = 153.15$. PAS. Bulky powder, darkening in air, with acetous odor, slightly soluble in water; a tuberculostatic antibacterial (U.S.P.). **arsino-** See *arsino.* **homo-** Cresotic acid. **5-hydroxy-** Gentisic acid. **meth-oxymethyl-** Everninic acid. **methyl-** Cresotic acid. **methylcarboxyl-** Spiracin. **nitro-** Nitrosalicylic acid. **phenyl-** q.v. **phenylo-** q.v. **propionyl-** q.v. **salicylo-** Diplosal. **sulfo-** q.v.
    s.a. anhydride. Salicylide. **s.a. collodion.** A mixture of 100 grams s.a. with sufficient flexible collodion to make 1 liter; a keratolytic (U.S.P.).

salicylic aldehyde. Salicylaldehyde.

salicylic amide. Salicylamide.

salicylic glycerinformaldehyde. Protosal.

salicylide. $C_{28}H_{16}O_8 = 480.2$. Tetrasalicylide, an anhydride of salicylic acid. Colorless crystals, m.260.

salicylol. $C_7H_8O_2 = 124.06$. Colorless, fragrant liquid from various plants; used in perfumery.

salicylonitrile. $C_6H_4(OH)CN = 119.1$. *o*-Hydroxybenzylnitrile. Colorless crystals, m.98, soluble in water.

salicylosalicylic acid. Diplosal.

salicyloyl. Salicoyl. The radical $o \text{-} CO \cdot C_6H_4 \cdot OH$.

salicyl-p-phenetidine. Saliphen.

salicylquinine. Saloquinine.

salicylresorcinol. $C_6H_4(OH) \cdot CO \cdot C_6H_3(OH)_2(1:2:4)$

$= 230.1$. The ketone of salicylic acid and resorcinol, trihydroxybenzophenone. Colorless leaflets, soluble in water; an antipyretic and antiseptic.

salicylyloyl. The radical $1,2\text{-}C_6H_4(OH)CO$—, Cf. *salicyl.*

salifebrin. Salicylanilide.

saliformine. $C_6H_{21}N_4 \cdot C_6H_4(OH)COOH = 278.16$. Urotropine salicylate, hexamethylene salicylate, formine salicylate. White crystals, soluble in water; an antiseptic and uric acid solvent.

salify. To form a salt.

saligallol. Pyrogallol salicylate. A resin used externally in acetone solution.

saligenin. (1) Salicyl alcohol. (2) Salicin. **homo-** Methylhydroxybenzene.

saligenol. Salicyl alcohol.

salimenthol. $C_6H_4(OH)COOC_{10}H_{19} = 276.2$. Samol, menthol salicylate. Colorless liquid, insoluble in water; a local anodyne and analgesic.

salimeter. A hydrometer to determine the density of salt solutions. Cf. *salinimeter.*

salinaphthol. Betol.

saline. (1) Saltlike. (2) A salt spring or well. (3) The taste of common salt. (4) Containing sodium chloride. **normal-** A sterilized 0.9% solution of common salt in water. **s. solution.** A 0.6% solution of sodium chloride; a physiological salt solution.

salines. Salt springs; salt lands.

salinigrin. $C_{13}H_{16}O_7 = 284.2$. A glucoside from the bark of *Salix nigra*, willow; probably identical with piceoside.

salinimeter. An hydrometer for determining the salt content of brine or seawater. Cf. *salimeter.*

salinity. (1) A comparative indication of the concentration of salts in natural waters. (2) The number of grams of salt in 1 kg seawater, when bromides and iodides are converted to chlorides, the carbonates to oxides, organic matter destroyed, and the mass heated at 450°C for 72 hours. $S = 0.03 + 1.805$ Cl content.

salinometer. An instrument which uses the electrical conductivity of water to control its salt content. Cf. *salinimeter.*

saliphen. $C_6H_4(OEt)NHC_6H_4(OH)CO = 257.2$. Saliphenin, salicyl-*p*-phenetidine. Colorless crystals, m.140, insoluble in water; an antifebrile and antipyretic.

saliphenin. Saliphen.

salipyrine. $C_{11}H_{12}ON_2 \cdot C_6H_4(OH)COOH = 326.2$. Antipyrine salicylate, salpyrin, pyrosal, tyrosal, salazolon. White hexagons, m.91, slightly soluble in cold water; an antipyretic and antiseptic.

saliretin. $C_{14}H_{14}O_3 = 230.2$. A yellow resin from salicin.

saliseparin. Smilacin.

salit. Borneol salicylate.

salitannol. $C_{14}H_{10}O_7 = 290.1$. A condensation product of salicylic acid and gallic acid. White powder, insoluble in water; an antiseptic.

saliter, salitre. Sodium nitrate.

salithymol. $C_6H_4(OH)COOC_{10}H_{13} = 270.2$. Thymol salicylate. Colorless crystals, insoluble in water; an antiseptic.

saliva. The alkaline secretion of the mouth glands; contains digestive enzymes (ptyalin), salts (potassium thiocyanate), proteins (albumin). The composition depends on the diet and can cause tartar formation on teeth. Cf. *sputum.*

salivin. Ptyalin.

Salix. The willows (Salicaceae) whose bark yields salicin. **S. alba.** The European or white willow. **S. fragilis.** The brittle willow, snap willow. Its bark is an astringent and febrifuge. **S. nigra.** The pussy willow (American, black, or swamp willow). Its bark is a tonic, antipyretic, and sedative.

Salkowski's solution. A solution of phosphotungstic acid; used to test for albumose in urine.

Salle index. See *germicide*.

salmak. Ammonium chloride.

salmiac. Ammonium chloride.

salmine. $C_{30}H_{57}O_6N_{14} = 709.9$. A protamine from salmon spermatozoa.

salmonellosis. Food poisoning, which can be fatal, due to organisms of the *Salmonella typi-murium* type, especially in frozen eggs.

salochinine. Saloquinine.

salocoll. $C_6H_4(OC_2H_6)NHCOCH_2\cdot CH_2C_7H_6O_3 = 331.2$. Phenocoll salicylate. Colorless needles, soluble in hot water; an antirheumatic.

salol. Phenylsalicylate. **acetamido-** Salophen. **acetyl-** Spiroform. **acetylamino-** q.v. **chloro-** q.v. **nitro-** q.v. **tribrom-** Cordol.

salolphosphinic acid. Salvosal.

salophen. $C_6H_4(OH)COOC_6H_4NH\cdot(COCH_3) = 271.1$. Acetyl-*p*-amidosalol, acetamidosalol, acetyl-*p*-aminophenyl salicylate, phenetsal. White scales, m.188, soluble in hot water; an intestinal antiseptic and antipyretic.

saloquinine. $C_6H_4(OH)COOC_{20}H_{23}ON_2 = 444.24$. Salicylquinine, salochinine, quinine salicylate. Colorless crystals, m.130, almost insoluble in water; used medicinally.

salosalicylide. Disalicylide.

salpyrine. Salipyrine.

salseparin. Smilacin.

salseparisin. Parillin.

salsoline. $C_{11}H_{15}NO_2 = 193.12$. An alkaloid from *Salsola Richteri* (Cactaceae). Cf. *carnegine*.

salt. (1) See *salts*. (2) Common s., halite, or sodium chloride. **air-** See *air*. **baker's-** Ammonium carbonate. **bay-** Sodium chloride from seawater. **bitter-** Magnesium sulfate. **carlsbad-** A mixture of sodium and potassium sulfates, sodium bicarbonate, and sodium chloride. **common-** Sodium chloride. **diuretic-** Potassium acetate. **epsom-** Magnesium sulfate. **Everitt's-** Potassium ferricyanide. **glauber-** Sodium sulfate. **green-** Uranium tetrafluoride. **Gregory-** See *Gregory*. **Homberg's-** Boric acid. **iodized-** Sodium chloride, with a trace of iodide, for table use. **melting-** A s., e.g., the carbonate and phosphate of sodium, added to and melted with cheese during processing to improve emulsification and texture. **microcosmic-** NaNH₄·HPO₄·5H₂O. Sodium ammonium acid phosphate. **Mohr's-** Ferrous ammonium sulfate. **Monsel's-** Ferric subsulfate. **pepetic-** A mixture of sodium chloride and pepsin. **phosphor-** Microcosmics. **Plimmer's-** Sodium antimony tartrate. **Preston's-** An aromatized ammonium carbonate; a smelling s. **rochelle-** Potassium sodium tartrate. **rock-** Sodium thioantimonate. **sea-** Sodium chloride from seawater. **Seignette's-** Potassium sodium tartrate. **solar-** S. produced by evaporation of seawater by the sun. **Sorrel-** Potassium bioxalate. **spirits of-** Commercial hydrochloric acid. **Stassfurt-** See *Stassfurt s*. **sweet-** Sodium chlorite. **table-** Sodium chloride.

s. of amber. Succinic acid. **s. cake.** (1) Impure sodium sulfate by-product of the Leblanc soda process. (2) A synthetic s. cake made by fusing sulfur and sodium carbonate together in the correct proportions. **s. deposits.** Saline residues. The accumulation of salts from the evaporation of natural waters, as at Strassfurt, q.v., and in the desert. Chiefly carbonates, chlorides, sulfates, and borates of sodium potassium, calcium, and magnesium. **s. glaze.** See *glaze*. **s. hydrates.** The solid phases, salt and water; hence any crystal with one or more molecules of water of crystallization. **s. ice.** Frozen brine, m. −21. **s. of lemon.** Potassium binoxalate. **s. peter.** See *saltpeter*. **s. of phosphorus.** Sodium ammonium acid phosphate. **s. solution.** Saline solution. **s. of sorrel.** Potassium bioxalate. **s. of tartar.** Acid potassium tartrate. **s. of tin.** Stannous chloride. **s. of vitriol.** Zinc sulfate. **s. of wormwood.** Potassium carbonate.

salting. Treating with salt. **s. in.** The mutual increase in the solubilities of an electrolyte and an organic compound added to the same solvent. **s. out.** Aiding liquid-liquid extraction by addition of an electrolyte. Separation of a substance from its solution by adding soluble salts; as, precipitation of proteins by salts.

saltpeter, saltpetre. Potassium nitrate. **Chile-** Sodium nitrate. **German-** Ammonium nitrate. **Norge-** or **Norway-** Calcium nitrate.

salts. Substances produced from the reaction between acids and bases; a compound of a metal (positive) and nonmetal (negative) radical: M·OH (base) + HX (acid) = MX (salt) + H₂O (water). **acid-** S. containing unreplaced H atoms from the acid; as, NaHSO₄. **acidic-** S. having an acid reaction. **alkaline-** S. having a basic reaction. **amphoteric-** S. having both acid and basic reactions. **basic-** S. containing unreplaced hydroxyl radicals of the base; as Bi(OH)Cl₂. **binary-** A compound of 2 bases and one acid radical; as, NaKSO₄. **complex-** S. made up of more than one simple acid or metallic radical, but which ionize in solution into only 2 types of ions. Thus potassium ferrocyanide: K₄Fe(CN)₆ ⇌ 4K⁺ + Fe(CN)₆⁴⁻. Cf. *Werner's theory*. **double-** A molecular combination of 2 s.; as, alums: M₂SO₄·M₂(SO₄)₃·24H₂O. Cf. *complex salts*. **ethereal-** An ester. **mixed-** S. of 2 or more metals; as, NaKSO₄. **neutral-** S. having a neutral reaction, as potassium chloride. **normal-** A compound of a base and acid that have completely neutralized each other. **oxy-** Compounds of a base with an oxy-acid radical. **triple-** S. containing 3 metals; as, triple chloride.

salubrol. $C_{23}H_{24}O_2N_4Br_4 = 708.4$. Methylene diantipyrine tetrabromide. Orange powder, m.155, insoluble in water; a dusting powder.

salufer. Sodium silicofluoride.

salumin. Aluminum salicylate.

Salvarsan. A German brand of *arsphenamine*.

salve. See *ointment*.

salvia. Sage, save. The dried leaves of *Salvia officinalis* (Labiatae). It contains an essential oil, resin, tannin, and bitter principles; a spice. Cf. *sclareol*. **s. oil.** Sage oil.

salvianin. Monardein. A coloring matter from *Salvia coccinea*.

salviol. $C_{10}H_{16}O = 152.1$. Thujone. An eleoptene

from the essential oil of *Salvia*. Colorless liquid, b.201, insoluble in water.

salvosal lithia. Lithium salol-*o*-phosphite. **s. potash.** Potassium salol-*o*-phosphite.

Salyrgan. Trademark for mersalyl.

sama condition. Sama-zustand. A temperature difference in complete equilibrium; as, gases at low pressures in a gravitational field.

samandaridine. $C_{20}H_{31}ON = 301.3$. An alkaloid from *Salamandra maculosa*, a salamander. Cf. *salamandaridine*.

samandarine. $C_{52}H_{80}O_2N_4 = 792.8$. An alkaloid from the skin secretion of salamanders. Cf. *salamanderine*.

samaric. Pertaining to trivalent samarium. **s. bromide.** $SmBr_3 \cdot 6H_2O = 498.27$. Green crystals, soluble in water. **s. chloride.** *anhydrous-* $SmCl_3 = 256.80$. Green crystals, m.686, soluble in water. *hydrate-* $SmCl_3 \cdot 6H_2O = 364 \cdot 89$. Green, trigonal crystals, soluble in water. **s. hydroxide.** $Sm(OH)_3 = 201.45$. Colorless powder, insoluble in water. **s. nitrate.** $Sm(NO_3)_3 \cdot 6H_2O = 444.55$. Yellow prisms, soluble in water. **s. oxalate.** $Sm_2(C_2O_4)_3 \cdot 10H_2O = 745.02$. Colorless crystals, insoluble in water. **s. sulfate.** $Sm_2(SO_4)_3 \cdot 8H_2O = 733.18$. Yellow, monoclinic crystals, slightly soluble in water. **s. sulfide.** $Sm_2S_3 = 396.8$. Yellow powder, m.1900.

samarium. $Sm(Sa) = 150.35$. A rare-earth metal and element, at. no. 62, discovered by Boisbaudran (1879). Gray metal, d.7.7, m.1350, soluble in acids. Valency 2 or 3; green and pink salts. Cf. *samaric*, *samarous*. **s. oxide.** $Sm_2O_3 = 348.8$. White powder, insoluble in water.

samarous. Pertaining to bivalent samarium. **s. chloride.** $SmCl_2 = 221.33$. Brown needles, m.740; soluble in water, evolving hydrogen. **s. sulfate.** $SmSO_4 = 246.4$. Orange powder, insoluble in water.

samarsiite. Black, native columbate and tantalate of uranium, cerium, and yttrium metals, including samarium.

sambucinin. $C_{24}H_{42}O_7N_2 = 470.40$. An antibiotic from sambucus.

sambucus. Elder flowers. The dried flowers of *Sambucus* species, elder. **s. juice.** Elderberry juice. An extract from the fruit of *Sambucus* species; a diuretic and alterant.

sambunigrin. $C_{14}H_{17}NO_6 = 295.14$. A glucoside, m.152, from the leaves of *Sambucus nigra;* hydrolyzes to glucose and *l*-mandelonitrile.

samin. $C_{13}H_{14}O_5 = 250.1$. A hydrolysis product of sesamolin. Colorless needles, m.103.

samneh. Rendered butterfat (Israel).

samol. Salimenthol.

samphire. Common name for. *Crithmum maritimum* (Umbelliferae), an English herbal; a pickle.

sample. A representative portion of a substance, systematically taken for the purpose of judging its quality by analysis.

sampler. Riffles. A device for automatically splitting aggregates of ore, coal, cement, etc, for analysis.

sand. Particles of disintegrated siliceous rock; quartz. **black-** Ilmenite. **calais-** An extremely fine s. (Calais), used to polish platinum ware. **iron-** Titanomagnetite: Fe 60, Ti 5%. **silver-** Fine s.,

washed with hot acids and water, for grinding substances before their extraction.

s. bath. A heating vessel filled with s., to obtain a uniform distribution of heat; used similarly to the water bath. **s. blast.** A stream of s. projected by compressed air or steam; used as an abrasive, metal cutter, or for frosting glass. **s. paper.** An abrasive made by coating stout paper or thin cloth with glue, and dusting fine s. on it.

sandalwood. White s., santalum, white sanders. The heartwood of *Santalum album* (Santalaceae); a diuretic and antiseptic, and source of s. oil and incense. **red-** Red sanders, ruby wood. The heartwood of *Pterocarpus santalinus* (Leguminosae); a coloring. See *santalin*. **yellow-** Yellow sanders. A yellow s.; a coloring. **s. oil.** *East Indian-* The essential oil of white s., d.970–0.985, containing santalol, santalin, and its esters. *West Indian-* The essential oil from *Amyris balsamifera* (Rutaceae).

sandarac(h). Gum juniper, sandarach. The resin from *Callitris quadrivalvis* (*Thuja articulata*), a pine of N.W. Africa.

Sanderit. Trade name for a polyamide synthetic fiber.

sandix. Orange mineral. A pale orange, native lead oxide; a pigment.

Sandmeyer's reaction. The transformation of diazo compounds into halogen compounds in presence of cuprous halogen salts: $Ph \cdot N_2Cl \rightarrow PhCl + N_2$.

sandoptal. $C_{11}H_{16}N_2O_3 = 224.2$. 5-Allyl-5-isobutylbarbituric acid. Colorless crystals, soluble in water; a hypnotic.

sandstone. A sedimentary rock, of coherent grains of sand.

sang de boeuf. Red pottery glaze produced by reduction of copper oxide.

sanguinaria. (1) Bloodroot, redroot, tellerwort. The dried rhizomes of *Sanguinaria canadensis* (Papaveraceae). It contains the alkaloids, sanguinarine, homochelidonine, protopine, and chelerythrine (see *opium alkaloids);* an emetic and expectorant (2) A green bloodstone with red spots. (3) Hematite.

sanguinarine. $C_{20}H_{15}O_4N = 333.2$. An alkaloid from the root of *Sanguinaria canadensis* and *Stylophorum diphyllum*. White needles, m.213, soluble in alcohol (red color). Cf. *argemonine*. **s. nitrate.** $C_{20}H_{15}O_4N \cdot HNO_3 = 396.2$. Orange crystals, soluble in water; a cardiac stimulant. **s. sulfate.** $(C_{20}H_{15}O_4N)_2H_2SO_4 = 764.4$. Red crystals, soluble in water.

sanguis draconis. Dragon's blood.

sanicle. Sanicula.

sanicula. Wood march, sanicle. The herb and root of *Sanicula europaea* (Umbelliferae); an astringent.

sanidine. A glassy orthoclase.

Sankey diagram. A diagram depicting the flow of a process; the quantities involved are shown by double lines of proportional widths.

sanocrysin. $Au(S_2O_3)_2Na_3$ (37.4% Au). Used to treat pulmonary tuberculosis.

sanoform. $C_6H_2I_2(OH)COOMe = 404.0$. Methyl diiodosalicylate. Colorless crystals, m.110, insoluble in water; a dusting powder.

sansa. The residue after pressing oil from olives.

santal. Santalenic acid. **oil of-** Sandalwood oil.

santalene. $C_{15}H_{24} = 204.19$. A terpene. **alpha-** b.252. **beta-** $b_{7mm}126$. **gamma-** $b_{10mm}120$.

santalenic acid. $C_{15}H_{24}O_5 = 274.1$. Santalic acid, Santalin. The coloring of red sandalwood, m.104. insoluble in water.

santalic acid. Santalenic acid.

santalin. Santalenic acid.

santalol. (1) $C_{15}H_{24}O = 220.2$. Terpenes from sandalwood. Colorless liquids.

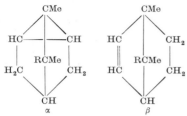

$$(\text{R is } -CH_2 \cdot CH_2 \cdot CH : CHMe \cdot CH_2OH.)$$

alpha- Arheol, d.0.979, b.300. **beta-** d.0.973, b.309; used to treat urethritis. (2) Santyl. **s. methyl ester.** Thyresol.

santalum. Sandalwood.

santalyl. The radical $C_{15}H_{23}$—. **s. carbonate.** Carbosant. **s. chloride.** $C_{15}H_{23}Cl = 238.64$. Colorless liquid, $b_{10mm}155$. **s. salicylate.** Santyl.

santene. $C_9H_{14} = 122.11$. A liquid, b.142.

santenol. $C_9H_{16}O = 140.2$. 1,4-Methylene-2,2-dimethylcyclohexene-2. Colorless crystals, m.98.

santiganine. $C_{19}H_{24}ON_2 = 296.23$. An alkaloid from *Adenocarpus;* an optical isomer of adenocarpine. **s. hydrochloride.** m.241.

Santobrite. $C_6Cl_5ONa = 288.3$. Trademark for pentachlorophenate. A preservative and pesticide.

Santochlor. Trademark for *p*-dichlorobenzene.

santol. $C_8H_6O_3 = 150.0$. Colorless crystals, from red sandalwood.

Santomerse. Trademark for an alkylated aryl sulfonate preparation having surface-active properties.

santonica. Levantwormseed, cina, xantholine, semen cinae. The dried flower heads of *Artemisia* (Compositae); contains santonin, artemisin, essential oils, resins, and gums; a vermifuge and diuretic.

santonic acid. $C_{13}H_{18}O_8 = 302.14$. An acid from santonica, m.171. **apo-** $C_{14}H_{20}O_3 = 236.14$. White crystals, m.164. **hydroxy-** $C_{14}H_{20}O_6 = 284 \cdot 14$. Colorless crystals, decomp. 215. **s. lactone.** Santonin.

santonin. $C_{15}H_{18}O_3 = 246.22$. Santoninic acid lactone. A neutral, nonglucosidal bitter principle from santonica. Colorless leaflets, m.172 (sublimes and decomp.), insoluble in water; an anthelmintic (B.P.). Cf. *myosin*. **oxy-** Artemisin.

santoninic acid. $C_{15}H_{20}O_4 = 264.2$. Santonic acid. Colorless crystals, m.179.

santoninoxime. $C_{15}H_{18}O_2(NOH) = 261.2$. White needles, m.217, slightly soluble in water; an anthelmintic.

santyl. $C_6H_4(OH)COOC_{15}H_{23} = 340.3$. Santalyl salicylate, santalol. Yellow oil, d.1.07, $b_{22mm}126$, insoluble in water; a urinary antiseptic. **s. methyl ester.** Thyresol.

s.ap. Abbreviation for apothecaries' scruple = ℈.

sap. (1) The circulating plant juices that assist growth. (2) The surface of a rock softened by weathering.

Sapamine. Trademark for trimethyl-β-oleoamido-ethylammonium sulfate, a wetting agent.

Sapindales. An order of plants (families Anacardiaceae Aquifoliaceae, Aceraceae, Sapindaceae).

sapine. $C_5H_{14}N_2 = 102.2$. A nontoxic isomer of cadaverine.

sapiphores. The groups in an organic compound that produce a sweet or bitter taste according to their combination. Cf. *glucophores*.

sapo. A soap from olive oil and sodium hydroxide.

sapogenin. $C_{14}H_{22}O_2 = 222.2$. Sapogenol. A decomposition product of saponin. Colorless needles, m.257, insoluble in water.

sapogenol. Sapogenin.

saponaretin. Vitexin.

saponaria. Soaproot, soapwort, bruisewort, *S. officinalis* (Caryophyllaceae) which contains saponin and sapotoxin.

saponarin. $C_{21}H_{24}O_{12} = 468.19$. A glucoside, m.232, from saponaria.

saponification. The conversion of an ester into an alcohol and acid salt; as fats into soaps by an alkali: $(R \cdot COO)_3G + 3NaOH = 3R \cdot COONa + G(OH)_3$. G = glycerol. **s. equivalent.** The quantity of fat in grams saponified by one liter of normal alkalies = 56,108/sap. no. **s. number, s. value.** The quantity of potassium hydroxide in milligrams to saponify 1 gm of fat.

saponin. $C_{32}H_{54}O_{18} = 726.5$. A glucoside from soapwort, quillaia, and especially the heartwood of *Mora excelsa* (British Guiana), which contains 4–5%. White powder, soluble in water; a toxic foam producer and antiseptic. **sasanqua s.** $C_{73}H_{11}O_{22} \cdot 3H_2O$. A glucoside from the seeds of *Camelia sasanqua* (Theaceae), decomp. 222; hydrolyzes to pentose, galactose, and prosapogenin.

saponins. Amorphous glucosides that produce foaming solutions in *Saponaria* species (Hippocastanaceae).

saponite. A native, hydrous silicate of magnesium and aluminum.

sapota. The dried fruit of the bully tree, *Achras sapota* (Sapotaceae), S. America; an antiperiodic. Cf. *chicle*.

Sapotaceae. Tropical shrubs, many of which bear edible berries, and are sources of saponin; as, *Mimuseps globosa*, balata, chicle. Cf. *butternut, illipe, maclayine, sapotin*.

sapotalene. $C_{13}H_{14} = 170.1$. 1,2,7-Trimethylnaphthalene. Colorless crystals, insoluble in water.

sapotin. $C_{29}H_{52}O_{20} = 720.5$. A glucoside from the seeds of *Achras* or *Sapota sapotilla*. Colorless crystals, m.240.

sapotoxin. $C_{17}H_{26}O_{10} = 390.3$. A toxin from the bark of quillaia.

sappanwood. Sibucao. The wood of *Caesalpini sappan* (Leguminosae); a dye.

sapphire. Al_2O_3. A native, blue gem corundum. **Brazilian-** Tourmaline. **water-** Iolite.

saprine. $C_5H_{14}N_2 = 102.2$. A ptomaine from decaying meat.

sapropel. A submarine deposit formed by the sedimentation of dead algal colonies.

sapropelic coal. A coal that contains microscopic oil-bearing algae.

sapropelitic. Resembling coal or asphalt.

saprophyte. A vegetable microorganism in air, soil,

or water, which feeds on dead or decaying animals or plants. Cf. *parasites*.

Saran. Trade name for a vinyl chloride–vinylidene chloride copolymer; used as a chemical-resistant lining for piping; in filament form, to make rot-proof fabrics; and to render fabrics flameproof and water-vapor-resistant.

Sarcina (pl. **Sarcinae**). A genus of *Coccaceae* (Schizomycetes) which forms bale-like packs. Cf. *bacteria*.

sarcine. Hypoxanthine.

sarcocol. A gum resin from *Penaea sarcocolla* (Penaeaceae), Africa.

sarcolactate. A salt of sarcolactic acid, which contains the radical MeCHOH·COO—.

sarcolactic acid. Me·CHOH·COOH = 90.1. *p*-Lactic acid. Colorless liquid, soluble in water. See *lactic acid.*

sarcolite. A melilitic aluminum silicate, which contains lime and sodium.

sarcoma. A malignant tumor formed by cells of connective tissue. **Rous-** A s. produced by the injection of cell-free filtrates of tumor tissues.

sarcosine. MeNH·CH$_2$·COOH = 89.08. Methylglycine, sarkosine, methylaminoacetic acid. Colorless rhombs, m.210, soluble in water; an antirheumatic. **dimethyl-** Betaine.

sard. A brown sardonyx.

sardinianite. PbSO$_4$. A monoclinic anglesite.

sardonyx. A brown, translucent chalcedony; a semiprecious stone. Cf. *sard.*

Sarelon. Trade name for a protein synthetic fiber.

sarkine. Hypoxanthine.

sarkokaulin. C$_{13}$H$_{24}$O$_2$ = 212.19. An alcohol, m.78, from the wax of the candle bush, *Sarcocaulon burmin* (Leguminosae), S. Africa.

sarmentogenin. C$_{23}$H$_{34}$O$_5$ = 420.25. A steroid glycone from the seeds of *Strophanthus sarmentosus;* a heart poison used in the synthesis of cortisone.

sarracenine. An alkaloid from the roots of *Sarracenia* species, flytrap or pitcher plant. White needles, soluble in alcohol.

sarsapsarilla. Radix sarsae. The dried root of *Smilax medica* (Liliaceae). It contains glucosides (smilacin, parillin), resin, saponins, and essential oils; a tonic. **American-, false-** The root of *Aralia nudicaulus* (Araliaceae). **Indian-** The root of *Hemidesmus indicus* (Asclepiadaceae). **Jamaica-** Sarsaparilla.

sarsasaponin. A glucoside from sarsaparilla or smilax; an emetic and expectorant.

sarverogenin. C$_{23}$H$_{32}$O$_7$ = 420.25. A steroid glycone found with and similar to sarmentogenin, q.v.

SAS. Abbreviated trade name for the sodium salt of an alkane sulfonic acid. The sulfonate groups are randomly distributed along a straight hydrocarbon chain. Used in the manufacture of soft detergents.

sasanqua See *saponin.*

sassafras. The dried bark of the root of *Sassafras variifolium* (lauraceae), N. America. It contains an essential oil, resin, tannin, and wax; a carminative. **Australian-** Atherospermine.

s. nuts. Pichurim beans. **s. oil.** Oleum sassafras, An essential oil from the bark of *S. officinalis,* d.1.065–1.095, containing safrole, eugenol, camphor, pinene, and phellandrene. **s. pith.** The dried pith of sassafras. White, spongy pieces; used to treat inflammations of the air and digestive passages.

sassa gum. A red gum from *Albizzia fastigiata* (Leguminosae), Ethiopia.

sassoline. Sassolite.

sassolite. B(OH)$_3$. Sassoline. A native boric acid; occurs in triclinic scales at the fumaroles.

sassy bark. Mancona bark, casca bark, doom bark. The bark of *Erythrofloeum guinense* (Leguminosae), W. Africa; a local ordeal poison, cardiac tonic, and narcotic.

satin spar. A smooth compact variety of calcite. **s. white.** A mixture of calcium sulfate and aluminum hydroxide, produced by the coprecipitation of lime and aluminum sulfate in presence of water; a pigment for coating paper.

saturate. (1) To link up all the atomic bonds in a molecule so that only single bonds exist. (2) To dissolve sufficient substance in a solution, so that no more can be dissolved. (3) Abbreviation for saturated hydrocarbon.

saturated. Completely satisfied. **super-** See *supersaturated.* **s. compound.** An organic compound with no free valence, with neither double nor triple bonds. **s. hydrocarbons.** Paraffins. **s. solution.** A solution that contains so much dissolved substance that no more will dissolve at a given temperature.

saturation. (1) Complete neutralization of an acid or base. (2) Complete or maximum absorption of a substance by a solvent. (3) Complete satisfaction of the valency bonds in a molecule. (4) A property of color, q.v. **super-** See *supersaturation.* **s. current.** The maximum current that can pass as a silent discharge through a gas or vapor without decomposing it. **s. isomerism.** Isomerism between 2 compounds, one of which is saturated, and the other unsaturated; as, acetone, CH$_3$·CO·CH$_3$, and allyl alcohol, CH$_2$:CH·CH$_2$OH. **s. point.** (1) The concentration at which a solution is saturated with a particular substance. (2) In color printing, the stage at which one color becomes dominant at the expense of the others.

saturnism. Lead poisoning.

saturnus. The alchemical name for lead.

saunders. Sandalwood.

saussurite. An impure labradorite.

save. Salvia.

savine. Sabina. The fresh tops of *Juniperus sabina*, containing essential oil, tannin, and resin; a diuretic, vermifuge, and aromatic. Cf. *juniperic acid.* **s. oil.** Oleum sabinae. An essential oil from *Juniperus sabina.* Yellow liquid, d.0.903, which contains pinene, cadinene, sabinene, and sabinol.

savorquin. Diiodohydroxyquinoline.

savory. The herb *Satureia hortensis* (summer s.) and *S. montana* (winter s.); an aromatic and carminative.

saw palmetto berries. Sabal.

saxicoles. A group of lichens.

saxifrage. Pimpinella.

Saxin. A brand of saccharin.

Saybolt seconds. A relative unit of viscosity; the time necessary for a specified volume of a liquid to flow through the orifice of a S. viscosimeter at a definite temperature. Cf. *Engler, centipoises, SAE number, rhe.*

Sb. Symbol for antimony (from Latin, stibium).

SBR. See *GR-S.*

Sc. Symbol for scandium.

scagliola. A 19th century imitation marble made from colored plaster.

scalar. Describing a quantity that has magnitude but no direction, e.g., density. Cf. *vector*.

scale. (1) A thin, flaky leaflet. (2) A crust of oxides formed on the surface of metals. (3) Boilerstone. The incrustation of insoluble salts formed by the evaporation of water. (4) Markings at regular intervals, on instruments, drawings, and graphs. (5) A balance used for relative rough weighings. **conversion-** A graph of 2 or more parallel scales, used for the rapid solution of proportional problems. Cf. *nomograph*.
  s. copper. Copper in thin flakes. **s. stone.** Wollastonite.

scaling index. A measure of the degree of corrosion of a metal in a liquid; the gain in weight in milligrams per square centimeter under specified conditions.

scalpel. A small, curved dissecting knife.

scammonin. $C_{34}H_{56}O_{16}$ = 720.5. A glucoside derived from scammony.

scammony. The dried root of *Convolvulus scammonia* (Convolvulaceae), Asia Minor. It contains the glucoside scammonin, a gum, and a resin; a cathartic and anthelmintic. **Mexican-** Ipomoea.

scandia. Scandium oxide.

scandium. Sc = 44.96. A rare metal of the aluminum group, at. no. 21. Predicted by Mendeleev (as ekaboron), and discovered (1879) by Nilson; obtained from thortveite. Gray metal with pink tinge, m.1550, soluble in acids; valency 3. **s. acetyl acetonate.** $Sc(MeCOCHCOMe)_3$ = 342.26. White plates, m.187, soluble in water. **s. chloride.** $ScCl_3$ = 151.5. Colorless flakes, sublimes 800, soluble in water. **s. hydroxide.** $Sc(OH)_3$ = 96.12. Colorless powder, insoluble in water. **s. oxalate.** $Sc_2(C_2O_4)_3 \cdot H_2O$ = 448.28. White crystals, m.140, insoluble in water. **s. oxide.** Sc_2O_3 = 138.2. Scandia. Colorless powder, insoluble in water. **s. sulfate.** $Sc_2(SO_4)_3$ = 378.41. Colorless crystals, soluble in water.

scapolite. Wernerite. A powder or green calcium, aluminum, sodium silicate containing chlorine.

scarlet. $MeC_6H_4N:NC_6H_3MeN:NC_{10}H_{15}OH$. Scarlet R, Biebrich red, aminoazotoluolazo-β-naphthol. Brown powder, insoluble in water; used in ointments and as a dye.

scatol. Skatole.

scattering. (1) Dispersing. (2) The splitting of molten metals on pouring. **light-** The emission of light from a particle or molecule under illumination, due to resonance and excitation; e.g.: *Tyndall effect*, where the initial and final state of the scattering medium and the incoming and scattered quantum remain unchanged, except for a new direction of motion; *fluorescence*, where the scattered light is of shorter or longer frequency as compared with the incident light; *Raman effect*, where only a portion of the incoming quanta are used for excitation; *Compton effect*, where a quantum of high frequency (X rays) dislodges an electron from the scattering substance. Cf. *luminescence*.

scavenger. A purifying substance; as, metallic lithium which removes impurities from alloys.

Schäffer's acid. $HSO_3 \cdot C_{10}H_6 \cdot OH$. Armstrong's acid. β-Naphtholsulfonic acid, 2-hydroxynaphthalene-6-sulfonic acid; used in organic synthesis.

schapbachite. $PbS \cdot Ag_2S \cdot Bi_2S_3$. A native sulfide.

schappe. Silk waste.

Schardinger dextrin. α-Dextrin.

Scheele, Carl Wilhelm. 1742–1786. Swedish apothecary noted for his discovery of oxygen, chlorine, ammonia, manganese, and barium. **S.'s green.** $CuHAsO_3$. An acid copper arsenite used as pigment.

scheelite. $CaWO_4$. A native calcium tungstate.

scheelium. Tungsten (obsolete).

scheererite. A mineral hydrocarbon, m.45, b.92.

Scheibler, Carl. 1827–1899. German chemist noted for developments in the sugar industry. **S.'s reagent.** A solution of phosphotungstic acid; yellow precipitate with sulfates of the alkaloids.

Schick test. A test for susceptibility to diphtheria in which intracutaneous injection of a toxin produces a local reaction.

schieferspar. A flaky variety of calcite.

Schiff, Hugo. 1834–1915. German organic chemistry. **S. bases.** $R \cdot N:CHR$. Condensation products of aromatic amines and aliphatic aldehydes: $PhNH_2 + OCH \cdot Ph = PhN:CHPh + H_2O$. **S. reagent.** Thioacetic acid. **S. solution.** A solution of 0.2 gm rosaniline and 15 ml sulfurous acid in 200 ml water; a test for aldehydes which restore the red color.

schiller spar. Bronzite.

schinus oil. An essential oil from the pepper tree, *Schinus molle* (Anacardiaceae), N. America, d.0.850, containing phellandrene, pinene, and carvacrol.

schist. A crystalline rock that can be split into scales or flakes.

schistic. Not aschistic, q.v.

schistosomiasis. Bilharziasis.

Schizomycetes. Schizophyta, fission fungi, bacteria, q.v. Plant microorganisms of the chlorophyll-free, fungi class. Family 1: Coccaceae, round or spherical in shape:
  Genus I: Streptococci, beadlike chains.
  Genus II: Micrococci, grapelike clusters.
  Genus III: Sarcina, bale-like packs.
  Genus IV: Planococci, like II but mobile.
  Genus V: Planosarcina, like III but mobile.
  Family 2: Bacteriaceae, cylindrical or rodlike in shape.
  Family 3: Spirillaceae, curved or S-like in shape.

Schizophyta. Schizomycetes.

schlempe. Vinasse.

schlieren. Describing the region of changing refraction in an otherwise optically homogeneous medium, e.g., heat waves seen over a hot surface.

Schlippe, Carl Friedrich von. 1799–1874. German-born Russian chemist. **S.'s salt.** $Na_3SbS_4 \cdot 9H_2O$. Sodium sulfantimonate.

Schlotterbeck reaction. The synthesis of ketones from aldehydes: $R \cdot CHO + CH_2N_2 \rightarrow R \cdot CO \cdot CH_3 + N_2$. Cf. *Nierenstein reaction*.

Schmidt test. A test for glue; white precipitate with a solution of ammonium molybdate.

Schmoluchowski's equation. The average length in microns of the path of a particle in a dispersed system: $2.37 \sqrt{K \cdot R \cdot T \cdot t / N \eta r}$, where R = gas content, N = Avogadro's number, T = absolute temperature, t = period of vibration of the particle, η = viscosity of the medium, r = radius of the particle.

schneebergite. $CaSbO_3$. A native antimonite.

Schneider's furnace. A retort for the distillation of zinc from zinc-lead ores.

schoe- See *Schoe-*.

Schoenbein, Christian Friedrich. 1799–1868. German chemist noted as discoverer of ozone and for work on catalysis.

Schoenherr process. A nitrogen fixation method in which the air circulates spirally around a 6-meter electric arc.

schöenite. $K_2SO_4 \cdot MgSO_4 \cdot 9H_2O$. A Stassfurt salt, q.v.

Schöllkopf's acid. (1) 1-Naphthol-4,8-disulfonic acid. (2) 1-Naphthylamine-4,8-disulfonic acid. (3) 1-Naphthylamine-8-sulfonic acid.

schorl. Tourmaline.

Schörlemmer, Carl. 1834–1900. German chemist, noted for his textbooks.

schorlomite. A titanium garnet, q.v.

Schötten, Carl. 1853–1910. German organic chemist noted for his organic synthesis methods. **S. reaction.** Acylation in alkaline solution with benzoyl chloride.

schou oil. A gelatinous product of the oxidation of soybean oil; an emulsifying agent in the margarine industry.

schradan. Common name for octamethylpyrophosphoramide, a systemic insecticide.

schraufite. $C_{11}H_{16}O_2$. A fossil resin in Carpathian sandstone.

schreibersite. $(FeNiCo)_3P$. A mixed phosphide, in certain meteorites.

schreinering. Reduction of the fiber interstices of a knitted fabric to give a tighter structure and higher density.

Schrödinger, Erwin. 1887–1961. Austrian physicist, Nobel Prize winner (1933); noted for his atomic concepts. Much of his work was done in the U.S. and U.K. **S. atom.** Pulsating or fluctuating atom. The atom is regarded as a sphere of electricity which may vary slightly in its density, but which may pulsate, with absorption or liberation of radiation. **S. equation.** Wave equation. The differential equation which determines the statistical charge density. Cf. *Heisenberg principle*.

schroeckingerite. Dakerite.

Schroeder's paradox. Polymers swell more in a liquid than in its vapor, owing to small temperature differences.

Schrötter apparatus. Calcimeter.

Schultz number. The classification number of a dyestuff as given in "Farbstofftabellen," by Gustav Schultz. Cf. *Color Index*.

Schulze's rule. The precipitating effect of an ion varies with its valency.

Schumann rays. The extreme ultraviolet portion of the spectrum which affects a photographic plate. Cf. *ultraviolet*.

Schütz-Borrisow rule. Enzyme activity; $x = tK\sqrt{c}$, where x is the amount of substance digested; t the reaction time, e.g., 24 hours; K a constant, and c the concentration of the enzyme.

Schwarza. Trade name for a viscous synthetic fiber.

schwatzite. A tetrahedrite containing mercury.

Schweinfurt green. Cupric subacetate.

Schweitzer, Mathias E. 1818–1860. German chemist. **S.'s reagent.** An ammoniacal solution of cupric hydroxide, which dissolves cellulose.

schwellenwert. Liminal value, threshold value.

The minimum quantity of electrolyte required to precipitate a colloidal solution.

sciadopitene. $C_{20}H_{32} = 272.3$. A diterpene, m.96, from the wood oil of *Sciadopitys verticillata*, the parasol pine, or umbrella fir of Japan.

sciagraph, sciagram. Skiagram.

science. Systematized and verifiable knowledge reached by observation, measurement, and/or experiment. Science describes, measures, and coordinates facts, but does not explain their ultimate cause. Cf. *philosophy*.

Formal science:
  Logic: ideas and concepts
  Mathematics: numbers and magnitudes
  Geometry: space and extension
  Phoronomy: motion, time, and relativity

Natural science:
  Physics: energy transformations
  Chemistry: matter transformations
  Astronomy: the universe
  Geology: the earth

Biological science:
  Botany: structure and functions of plants
  Zoology: structure and functions of animals
  Anthropology: man
  Psychology: human behavior
  Economics: human relationship
  Sociology: human society.

scientific. Based on systematized and verifiable facts or experience. Cf. *empiric*.

scilla. Squill.

scillain. (1) An amorphous glucoside obtained from the bulbs of *Scilla maritima*, squill. (2) Scillipicrin.

scillarabiose. $C_{12}H_{22}O_{10} = 326.1$. A disaccharide hydrolyzed to rhamnose and *d*-glucose. Cf. *scillaren*.

scillaren. $C_{37}H_{54}O_{13} = 706.4$. A glucoside from squill, *Scilla maritima*. Yellow powder, m.230–240, hydrolyzed to scillaradin and scillarabiose; a cardiac tonic and diuretic. **s. B.** A mixture of glucosides of greater physiological activity than s.

scillaridin. $C_{25}H_{32}O_3 = 380.0$. A cardiac glucoside related to scillin. **s. A.** A cholane (q.v.) diglycone.

scillin. A yellow, crystalline glucoside from the bulbs of *Scilla* species.

scillipicrin. Scillain. Yellow, amorphous glucoside from the bulbs of *Scilla maritima;* a diuretic.

scillitin. $C_{17}H_{25}O_6 = 325.19$. A brown bitter principle, m.154, from the bulbs of *Scilla maritima*, squill; a diuretic.

scillitoxin. Brown, amorphous glucoside from squill; used medicinally.

scintillascope. Spinthariscope.

scintillation. (1) Burning with brilliant sparks, as an iron wire in oxygen. (2) The emission or production of sparks; as, in a spinthariscope.

scission. (1) The splitting of a molecule. (2) Ring breakage. The opening of an atomic ring. (3) Fission, the division of a living cell. See *cell division*.

Scitaminaceae. The Musaceae or banana family, a group of tropical plants from which drugs are obtained: as, *Zingiber officinale*, ginger; *Musa sapientum*, banana.

sclareol. $C_{54}H_{63}O_3 = 759.5$. A tertiary unsaturated polyhydric alcohol, the principal constituent of oil of sage and similar to sterols.

sclerethyrin. A red coloring matter in ergot.

sclero-, sklero- Prefix (Greek) indicating hard.

sclerolac. An ether-soluble, hard lac resin from shellac.

sclerometer. An instrument for determining the hardness of materials from the pressure on a moving diamond point necessary to produce a scratch.

scleron. A light, noncorrodible alloy of Al with Si, Cu, Fe, Mn, Zn, and Li.

scleroproteins. A group of proteins in animal skeletons.

scleroscope. An instrument for determining the hardness of substances from the extent to which a steel ball rebounds on being dropped from a certain height. Cf. *Shore hardness.*

sclerotic acid. Sclerotinic acid, ergotic acid. A brown substance from ergot.

sclerotin. An early name for pectin.

scolecite. $CaAl_2Si_3O_{10}\cdot3H_2O$. A white or yellow mineral.

scoline. Suxamethonium chloride.

scoliodonic acid. $C_{24}H_{38}O_2 = 358.3$. A highly unsaturated acid from hiragashira oil, q.v.

scombrin. A protamine from mackerel sperm: 88.8% arginine.

scombron. A histone from immature mackerel sperm.

scoparin. $C_{20}H_{20}O_{10} = 420.2$. A yellow crystalline principle from scoparius.

scoparius. Spartium. Broom tops. The dried tops of *Cytisus scoparius* (Leguminosae). It contains sparteine and scoparin; a diuretic and purgative.

scopine. $C_8H_{13}NO_2 = 155.1$. *2,3*-Epoxytropan. A product of hydrolysis of scopolamine, and isomer of scopoline.

scopola. The dried rhizome of *Scopola carniolica* (Solanaceae). It contains the belladonna alkaloids; used medicinally. Cf. *atroscine.*

scopolamine. *d*-Hyoscine. *l*-Atroscine. **s. hydrobromide.** $C_{27}H_{31}NO_4\cdot HBr\cdot3H_2O = 438.34$. White powder, m.197, soluble in water, an ophthalmological parasympatholytic (U.S.P.). **s. hydrochloride.** Hyoscine hydrochloride.

scopoleine. $C_{17}H_{21}O_4N = 303.2$. A crystalline alkaloid from several *Scopola, Duboisia,* and *Atropa* species.

scopoletin. $C_{10}H_8O_4 = 192.06$. Chrysatropic acid, gelsemic acid, 7-hydroxy-6-methoxycoumarin, *β*-methylesculetin. Colorless crystals, m.204.

scopoline. $C_8H_{13}O_2N = 155.1$. A decomposition product of scopolamine (hyoscine). Colorless crystals, m.110, soluble in water.

Scopomannit. Trademark for stable scopolamine. A solution of scopolamine hydrobromide in water containing 10% mannitol.

scopometer. An instrument with an optical wedge for visual measurement of turbidity by observing the disappearance of an illuminated target.

scopometry. A branch of nephelometry, q.v.; matching colors or turbidities by comparing an illuminated line against a field of constant intensity.

scorbutanin. Vitamin C.

scorification. The assay of ores by roasting, fusion, and oxidation of gold and silver ores with lead and borax glass in a shallow clay vessel in a muffle.

scorifier. A vessel for scorification.

scorodite. $Fe_2O_3\cdot As_2O_5\cdot4H_2O$. Pitticite. A native hydrated ferrous arsenate.

scorodites. $M_2O_3\cdot N_2O_5\cdot xH_2O$. *M* is ferric iron or aluminum, and *N* is arsenic or phosphorus.

scotogram. Scotograph.

scotograph. Skotogram, skiagraph. An image produced on a photographic plate in the dark by human radiations.

scotographic. Affecting a photographic plate in the dark.

scotography. Skiagraphy. The study of human radiations, radioactivity, aura, or od-rays, q.v.

scotoma. A spot in the visible field where there is no vision.

scouring. (1) Corroding; as by certain ores that attack furnaces. (2) Cleaning; as, removing the grease or stain from a vessel. **s. cinder.** A basic slag that attacks the lining of a shaft furnace. **s. rush.** Equisetum.

screen. (1) A sieve of wire cloth, textile, or perforated metal plates, used to sort particles according to size. (2) A prepared surface on which light or images are projected. (3) An apparatus with *circular* apertures as compared with a sieve (*square* apertures). **fluorescent-** A plate coated with calcium tungstate or barium thiocyanate; used to make ultraviolet rays, X rays, etc., visible to the eye. **revolving-** A steel cylinder, usually inclined, with round holes.

s. analysis. The separation of a material into particles of definite sizes, by screens of graded sizes.

screening effect. In any atom the inner-orbital electrons act as screens between the nucleus and the outer orbital electrons, and thus decrease the effective nuclear charge of the latter. Cf. *Pauling structure, Lucas theory.*

Scrophularia. Figwort, rose noble. The herb of *S. nodosa* (Scrophylariaceae); a diuretic and anodyne. **water-** Bishop's leaves. The leaves of *S. aquatica*; used externally for poultices.

Scrophulariaceae. Figwort family. Herbs and shrubs that contain glucosides and drugs; e.g.: leaves: *Digitalis purpurea,* digitalin; herbs: *Veronica officinalis* (speedwell), veronica; rhizomes: *Veronica (Leptandra) virginica,* leptandra.

scrubber. A device for washing or absorbing gases; used in chemical plants for purification dissolving, or reacting gases in or with liquids.

scrubbing. Removal of impurities by extraction from the separated phase in liquid-liquid extraction.

scruff. Surface dirt or impurities. Cf. *scurf.*

scruple. ℈. A unit of apothecaries' weight: 1 scruple = 20 grains = 1.295978 grams. ·

scullcap. Scutellaria.

scum. The impurities on the surface of molten materials. Cf. *oly, froth.*

scurf. Material that flakes off; dross. Cf. *scruff.*

Scutellaria. Scullcap, helmet flower. The dried plant of *S. lateriflora* (Labiatae), N. America. It contains scutellarin and an essential oil; an antispasmodic and tonic.

scutellarin. $C_{10}H_8O_3 = 176.1$. A nontoxic crystalline principle from the leaves of *Scutellaria.* Yellow needles, m.199, insoluble in water.

scyllitol. $C_6H_6(OH)_6 = 180.09$. An isomer of inositol and constituent of the soap plant, *Helinus ovata* (Rhamnaceae), S. Africa; used locally as an emetic.

SDO. Synthetic drying oil.

Se. Symbol for selenium.

seal. Water, mercury, wax, oil, or other substance placed around joints to prevent ingress or egress of

air. vacuum- The mercury surrounding joints or stopcocks.

sealing wax. A colored, scented mixture of resins and shellac; used for sealing.

seam. A stratum or bed of a mineral or ore.

sea salt. (1) Commercial sodium chloride from evaporated seawater. (2) The residual mixture of salts on evaporating seawater. **s. water.** See *hydrosphere*, *water*. **s. weed.** Kelp. **s. wrack.** Fucus.

sebacic acid. $COOH(CH_2)_8COOH = 202.19$. Ipomic acid, decanedioic acid*, 1,8-octanedicarboxylic acid. Colorless leaflets, m.133, soluble in water.

sec. (1) Abbreviation for: (*a*) second, a unit of time; (*b*) secondary. (2) Dry.

Secale cereale. Rye. **S. cornutum.** Ergot.

secaline. Trimethylamine.

secalonic acid. $C_{14}H_{14}O_6 = 278.1$. Yellow crystals, in ergot.

secalose. A carbohydrate from rye. White, hygroscopic powder. Cf. *trifructosan*.

Secchi, Angelo. 1818–1876. Italian Jesuit astronomer, noted for spectrum analysis and polaroscopic experiments.

sechometer. A hand-driven induction apparatus.

secobarbital sodium. $C_{12}H_{17}N_2NaO_3 = 260.28$. Bitter, white powder, soluble in water; a central depressant (U.S.P.).

secohm. A unit of self inductance: 1 ohm per second.

Seconal Sodium. Trademark for quinalbarbitone sodium. Sodium 5-allyl-5-(1-methylbutyl) barbiturate, a short-acting barbiturate.

second. sec. (1) The duration of 9,192,631,770 periods of the radiation corresponding to the transition between the two hyperfine levels of the fundamental state of the atom of cesium 133 (international agreement, 1967). (2) The fraction 1/31,556,925.975 of the length of the solar tropical year 1900. (3) More commonly, the $\frac{1}{60}$ part of a minute: 1/86,164.09 of a sidereal day; 1/(24 × 60 × 60) of a mean solar day. 1 second = 3.168876×10^{-8} year. **s. ionization constant.** See *ionization constant*.

secondary. (1) Second in order. (2) Next in importance. **s. alcohol.** An organic compound containing the radical =CHOH. **s. amine.** An organic compound containing the radical =NH. **s. carbon atom.** A carbon atom directly attached to 2 others. **s. metal.** Metal recovered from scrap, sweepings, skimmings, drosses, etc. Cf. *primary metal*. **s. reaction.** Subsidiary *reaction*. **s. X rays.** The characteristic scattered radiations emitted from a substance exposed to X rays; used for analytical purposes.

secretin. A polypeptide containing P from the intestinal mucosa of the pig, and from plants; slightly soluble in water. It acts on the secretion of the pancreas and liver, and excites peristalsis.

secretion. The separation of a substance, other than a waste material, from a living organism; as, resins from plants, serum from wounds.

section. A thinly cut piece of a substance for microscopic study. **histological-** A thin cut of a plant or animal tissue. **metallographic-** A thin cut of a metal.

sectrometer. A vacuum-tube titrimeter for potentiometric titrations; a cathode-ray tube replaces the microammeter, and the end point is a sudden permanent change in the shadow angle on a fluorescent screen. Cf. *titrimeter*.

securite. A mine explosive not ignited by firedamp; contains ammonium nitrate and oxalate, and dinitrobenzene.

sedanolid. $C_{12}H_{18}O_2 = 194.14$. The lactone of sedanolic acid, in celery seeds, *Apium graveolens*.

sedanonic anhydride. $C_{12}H_{18}O_3 = 210.14$. White powder from celery seeds.

sedatin. Valeridin.

sedatine. Antipyrine.

sedative. A calming agent that counteracts stimulation, irritation, or excitement; as, bromides. Cf. *stimulant*.

sediment. A deposit of an insoluble material, especially if settled by gravitation. Cf. *precipitate*.

sedimentary rock. A rock formed by the accumulation of grains or fragments of rock carried by water or air.

sedimentation. The precipitation or settling of insoluble materials from a suspension, either naturally (by gravity) or artificially (by a centrifuge). **free s.** S. in which the particles exert no mutual interference. Stokes' law then applies. **hindered s.** The opposite of free s. **rate of-** See *settling*, *Stokes' law*.

Sedormid. Trademark for allylisopropylacetylcarbamide, a sedative-hypnotic.

sedum. The herb of *Sedum acre* (Crassulaceae), which contains alkaloids, carbohydrates, and a mucilage; used externally for wounds.

see. Salt. **s. mixte.** A natural mixture of sodium chloride and magnesium sulfate ($7H_2O$), deposited in the salt lakes of the Volga regions, U.S.S.R.

Seebeck, Thomas Johann. 1770–1831. German physicist; discoverer of thermoelectricity and the magnetism of cobalt and nickel.

seed lac. See *lac*.

seeds. The product of fertilized and developed ovules of plants; usually rich in proteins, carbohydrates, and oils, and an important source of food e.g., those of Gramineae (grains) and Leguminosae (peas and beans). Some are official, medicinally. See *fruits*.

seekay wax. C.K. *wax*.

seepage. (1) The percolation of a fluid through a porous material. (2) The fluid that results from s. (3) The separation of 2 phases.

Sefström, Nils Gabriel. 1787–1845. Swedish chemist and mineralogist, discoverer of vanadium.

Seger, Hermann A. 1839–1893. German technologist noted for ceramic research. **s. cones.** Pyrometric cones. Small pyramids of various clay and salt mixtures; used to indicate the temperature of a furnace. Each cone softens at a definite temperature, ranging from 500 to 2000°C.

seggar. Clay boxes in which ceramics are kilned.

segregate. To separate.

sehta. CoAsS. Indian name for cobaltite; as used to make blue-enameled metalware.

Seidlitz powder. An effervescent mixture of potassium sodium tartrate, sodium bicarbonate, and tartaric acid; used in alkaline mineral waters.

seifert solder. See *solder*.

Seignette's salt. Potassium sodium tartrate.

seismometer. An instrument for recording earth shocks.

sekisanine. $C_{34}H_{34}O_9N_2 = 614.3$ Dimethylhydroxylycorine. A physiologically inactive alkaloid from the bulbs of *Lycoris radiata* (Amaryllidaceae). Colorless prisms. Cf. *lycorine*.

selacholeic acid. $Me(CH_2)_7CH:CH(CH_2)_{13}COOH = 366.3$, Nervonic acid, 6,15-tetracosenoic acid*; from shark-liver oil.

selachyl alcohol. $C_{18}H_{35}OC_3H_5(OH)_2 = 342.3$. A liquid glyceryl ether from shark liver oil. Cf. *batyl, chimyl*.

selection rules. Important rules of wave mechanics, which control the possible transitions that an electron can make between states.

selenate. M_2SeO_4. A salt of selenic acid.

selenic. A compound of tetravalent or hexavalent selenium. **s. acid.** $H_2SeO_4(xH_2O) = 145.2$. An isolog of sulfuric acid. Colorless prisms, m.58, soluble in water; forms selenates.

selenide. (1) M_2Se. A binary compound of divalent selenium. (2) An organic compound containing divalent selenium: $=Se$. **di-** $R·Se·Se·R$. Cf. *disulfide*. **hydro-** A compound containing the radical HSe—. Cf. *selenyl*.

seleninic acid*. An organic compound having a —SeO_2H radical; as, $PhSeO_2H$, benzeneseleninic acid. Cf. *selenonic acids*.

selinino. The radical (HO)OSe—, from selenious acid. Cf. *selenono*.

selenious. Selenous. A compound containing divalent or tetravalent selenium; as, $SeCl_2$, SeO_2. **s. acid.** $H_2SeO_3 = 129.2$. Colorless crystals, decomp. by heat, soluble in water; forms selenites. **s. oxide.** Selenium dioxide.

selenite. (1) M_2SeO_3. A salt of selenious acid. (2) $CaSO_4·2H_2O$. A native gypsum.

selenium. $Se = 78.96$, or $Se_8 = 631.68$. A non-metal element of the sulfur group, at. no. 34. Modifications: (1) *Metallic*. Gray hexagons, m.217. b.690, insoluble in water, soluble in ether. (2) *Crystalline*. Red monoclinic crystals, m.180–200, soluble in carbon disulfide. (3) *Amorphous*. Red powder, obtained by precipitation, m.100, soluble in carbon disulfide. (4) *Colloidal*. Red solution, slowly depositing amorphous s. S. was discovered (1817) by Berzelius in the lead chambers of a sulfuric acid plant. It burns with a blue flame and garlic-like odor to its dioxide, SeO_2. It has valencies of 2, 4, and 6, and forms ions: $Se=$, selenides; $SeO_3=$, selenites; $SeO_4=$, selenates. The electrical resistance of metallic s. decreases with increase in intensity of illumination; and it is used for s. cells, q.v., the optophone, q.v.; for making red glasses, enamels, and glazes; and in insecticides (selocide).

s. bromide. (1) $Se_2Br_2 = 318.2$. S. monobromide. Red liquid, m.—46. (2) $SeBr_2 = 239.0$. S. dibromide. Brown liquid. (3) $SeBr_4 = 398.8$. S. tetrabromide. Orange crystals, soluble in carbon disulfide. **s. cell.** An arrangement of metallic s. plates enabling electricity or sound to be transmitted by means of the variation of electrical resistance of the cell with light intensity. **s. chloride.** (1) $Se_2Cl_2 = 229.4$. S. monochloride. Brown crystals. (2) $SeCl_4 = 150.1$. S. dichloride, selenous chloride. Brown oil. (3) $SeCl_4 = 221.0$. S. tetrachloride, selenic chloride. Yellow crystals. **s. dibromide.** See *s. bromide*. **s. dichloride.** See *s. chloride*. **s. diethyl.** $SeEt_2 =$

137.3. Ethyl selenide. Colorless liquid, b.108, insoluble in water. **s. dimethyl.** $Se(CH_3)_2 = 109.3$. Methyl selenide. Colorless liquid, b.58, insoluble in water. **s. dioxide.** See *s. oxide*. **s. hydride.** Hydrogen selenide. **s. iodide.** (1) $Se_2I_2 = 412.2$. S. monoiodide. Brown solid, m.65, decomp. by water. (2) $SeI_4 = 586.9$. S. tetraiodide, selenic iodide. Green solid, m.77, decomp. by water. **s. monobromide.** See *s. bromide*. **s. monochloride.** See *s. chloride*. **s. monoiodide.** See *s. iodide*. **s. nitride.** $Se_2N_2 = 186.4$. Yellow solid, explodes 200, insoluble in water. **s. oxide.** $SeO_2 = 111.2$. S. dioxide, selenious acid anhydride. Colorless crystals, sublimes 260, m.390 (decomp.), soluble in water. **s. oxides.** Organic compounds that contain the radical $=SeO$; as, Me_2SeO. **s. oxychloride.** Selenyl chloride. **s. sulfide.** $SeS = 111.3$. Yellow solid, m.118, insoluble in water.

seleno. The divalent atom $=Se$. Cf. *sulfo*. **s. diphenylamine.** Phenoselenazine. **s. furan.** See *selenofuran*. **s. naphthene.** Benzoselenofuran.

selenocyano. The radical NCSe—.

selenofuran. $Se·CH:CH·CH:CH = 131.2$. Selenophene. Colorless liquid, b.110, insoluble in water; resembles thiophen and burns in air with a blue flame, forming selenium.

selenoid. Solenoid. A hollow cylinder, wound with resistance wire, used to produce fields of electric force.

selenole. See *piaselenole*.

selenomercaptan. R·SeH.

selenoic acids*. Organic compounds that contain the radical —SeO_3H, analogous to sulfonic acids. Cf. *seleninic acid*.

selenonium. Tetravalent selenium; as, $RSeH_3$. Cf. *-onium*.

selenono. The radical HO_3Se—, from selenic acid. Cf. *selenino*.

selenoyl. The radical —SeO_2—. Cf. *sulfuryl*.

selenophene. Selenofuran.

selenophenol. $C_6H_6Se = 157.25$. PhSeH. Colorless liquid, b.183.

selenophthalide. $C_6H_4·CO·Se·CH_2 = 197.2$. Colorless crystals, m.58.

selenopyronine. Selenoxanthene.

selenotungstate. A salt containing the green radical $=WSe_4$. **di-** A salt containing the red radical $=WSe_2O_2$.

selenous. Selenious.

selenoxanthone. 9-Ketoselenoxanthene.

selenuretted. A substance impregnated or combined with hydrogen selenide.

selenyl. (1) The radical HSe—. (2) The radical $=SeO$. **s. chloride.** $SeOCl_2 = 166.1$ Selenium oxychloride. Colorless liquid, m.10, decomp. by water.

self-inductance. The emf produced in a circuit by a unit rate of variation of the current passing through it.

self-induction. A change in the magnetic field of a conductor, produced by a variation in the current passing through it.

selinene. $C_{15}H_{24} = 204.2$. A sesquiterpene from celery seed oil. A colorless liquid, $b_{16mm}135$, soluble in alcohol.

sellaite. MgF_2. A native magnesium fluoride.

selocide. An insecticide made by dissolving selenium in potassium ammonium sulfide solution [30% $(KHN_4S)_5Se$].

selwynite. Yellow *ocher.*

semecarpus. Marking nut, Oriental cashew nut, acajou nut. The fruit of *S. anacardium* (Anacardiaceae), E. Indies; a black stain.

semen. The fecundating fluid of the male. See *Florence test.*

semi- Prefix (Latin) indicating half; hemi- (Greek); demi- (French).

semicarbazide. $NH_2 \cdot NH \cdot CO \cdot NH_2 = 75.1$. Hydrazine carboxamide, aminourea, carbamylhydrazine. An amide and hydrazide of carbonic acid. Colorless prisms, m.96, soluble in water; a reagent for aldehydes and ketones. **4-amino-** Carbohydrazide. **s. hydrochloride.** $CH_5ON_3 \cdot HCl = 111.5$. Amidourea hydrochloride. Colorless prisms, m.175, soluble in water; a reagent for aldehydes and ketones.

semicarbazido. The group $NH_2 \cdot CO \cdot NH \cdot NH-$.

semicarbazino. Semicarbazono.

semicarbazone*. $R_2C:N \cdot NH \cdot CO \cdot NH_2$. A condensation product of aldehydes or ketones and semicarbazide.

semicarbazono. Semicarbazino. The radical $=N \cdot NH \cdot CO \cdot NH_2$.

semicoke. Fuel made from coal by low-temperature carbonization at 594; smokeless, with little ash.

semiconductor. A substance that allows the passage of current in one direction only, e.g., galena. Button-size semiconductors are made from germanium or silicon in a glass or ceramic housing, and are amplifiers, rectifiers, or switches (transistors). A s. uses 1% of the power required for an electronic valve and lasts 40 times as long.

semidines. $R \cdot C_6H_4 \cdot NH \cdot C_6H_4 \cdot NH_2$. Aromatic amines ortho- or para- according to the position of the NH_2 group. **s. rearrangement.** A special type of benzidine rearrangement, q.v., in which only one-half the molecule rotates; as, $R \cdot C_6H_4 \cdot NH \cdot NH \cdot C_6H_4 \cdot R \rightarrow R \cdot C_6H_4 \cdot NH \cdot C_6H_3RNH_3$.

semidrying oils. Fatty oils that thicken slowly on exposure to light and air.

semimetal. An element midway in properties between metals and nonmetals, as arsenic (obsolete).

seminase. An enzyme in alfalfa.

seminose. *d*-Mannose.

semiopal. A native silica.

semipermeable. Permitting the passage of certain molecules, and hindering others. **s. membrane.** A diaphragm through which certain substances pass, while others are retained; as, a cell membrane. See *osmosis.*

semipervine. $C_{19}H_{16}N_2 = 272.17$. A brown alkaloid from Carolina jasmine, *Gelsemium sempervireus.*

semiprecious. Describing a decorative gem or metal which is inferior to the precious grades.

semisilica brick. A firebrick made from a siliceous clay, or a mixture of fireclay and ganister (80–92% silica).

semisolid. Soft and slowly flowing; as, asphalt.

semivalence. A monoelectronic link between 2 rigid systems, characteristic of unstable, intermediate addition compounds and less stable than the ordinary nonpolar bond (bielectronic link).

Semmler, Friedrich Wilhelm. 1860–1931. German organic chemist noted for work on the essential oils.

senarmontite. Sb_2O_3. A native antimony trioxide.

seneca oil. Petroleum.

senecifolidine. $C_{18}H_{25}NO_7 = 367.2$. An alkaloid from *Senecio latifolius.* Rhombic plates, m.212.

senecifoline. $C_{18}H_{27}NO_8 = 385.22$. An alkaloid from *Senecio latifolius* (Compositae), S. Africa. Colorless plates, m.194, soluble in ether. **s. hydrochloride.** $C_{18}H_{27}NO_8 \cdot HCl = 421.68$. White crystals, m.260, soluble in water.

senecine. An amorphous alkaloid from *Senecio vulgaris.*

senecio. Liferoot, ragwort, squaw-weed. The dried herb of *Senecio aureus;* a tonic and diuretic. **s. alkaloids.** Alkaloids from s.; as, jacobine, necine, retronecine, retrorsine, senecifoline, senecifolidine.

senecioic acid. $Me_2C=CH \cdot COOH = 100.06$. Isopropylidene acetic acid, β-methyl-α-butenoic acid, β-methylcrotonic acid. An isomer of tiglic acid.

senega. Senega snakeroot. Rattlesnake root. The dried root of *Polygala senega* (Polygalaceae); contains senegin and polygalin.

senegenin. $C_{26}H_{44}O_6 = 452.4$. Senegeninic acid. A dibasic acid hydrolysis product of senegin. Colorless powder, m.272.

senegeninic acid. Senegenin.

senegin. (1) $C_{32}H_{52}O_{17} = 708.4$. A saponin derived from senega. (2) $C_{20}H_{32}O_7 = 384.2$. A hydrolysis product of (1). Cf. *senegenin.*

seneski. A natural coke from the intrusion of igneous basaltic rock into a coal seam (20% ash); used to produce water gas.

senna. The dried leaflets of *Cassia acutifolia,* Alexandria s.; or *C. angustifolia,* India s., Tinnevelly s. (Leguminosae); contains glucosides, acids, and resins; a cathartic (B.P.). **American-** The leaves of *C. marilandica.* **wild-** See *globularesin.*

sensibilizer. (1) An agent that renders an enzyme active. (2) An amboceptor.

sensitive. (1) Responding readily to a test or force. (2) See *anaphylaxis.*

sensitiveness, sensitivity. (1) The degree of accuracy of a test or instrument. (2) The speed with which light acts on a photographic plate. (3) The property of exploding by mechanical shock.

sensitization. (1) Biochemistry: Rendering a cell sensitive to the action of a complement by treating it with a specific amboceptor. (2) Photography: (a) coating a surface with light-sensitive emulsions; as silver salts; (b) rendering the photographic emulsion more sensitive by addition of dyes which absorb certain portions of the spectrum. (3) Treatment of paper with chemicals so that ink writing cannot be eradicated without producing a telltale stain.

sensitizer. (1) A trace of substance, other than a catalyst, which promotes a catalytic action. (2) Biology: Amboceptor, opsonin, or tropin. A specific substance that occurs in small quantities in serum, and in larger quantities during immunization. Cf. *Ehrlich side-chain theory.* (3) Photography: An aniline dye that increases the sensitiveness of the emulsion to certain light waves. See *photosensitizer.*

sensor. Thermistor.

separator. A device or machine for separating materials of different densities by the aid of air or water. See *centrifuge.*

separatory funnel. A tap funnel or device for separating 2 immiscible liquids.

Sephadex. Trade name for a hydrophilic, insoluble molecular-sieve chromatographic medium, made by cross-linking dextran.

sepia. The dried, inky juice of a cuttlefish or squid; a dye.

sepiolite. $2MgO \cdot 3SiO_2 \cdot 4H_2O$. A very absorptive, native magnesium silicate; similar to meerschaum.

sepsine. $C_5H_{14}N_2O_2 = 134.1$. A ptomaine from decaying yeast.

sepsis. Poisoning produced by microorganisms or putrefaction. Cf. *asepsis.*

septavalent. Septivalent, heptavalent. Possessing a valency of 7; as, Cl in perchlorates.

septic. Pertaining to putrefaction.

septicemia. Blood poisoning. A morbid condition caused by the presence of pathogenic bacteria and their waste products in the blood.

septicum. A gangrene antitoxin.

septivalent. Septavalent.

septurit. A molecular compound of sulfanilamidine and hexamine; an antiseptic.

sequestering. The removal of a metal ion from a system by forming a complex ion which does not have the chemical reactions of the ion removed; e.g., the removal of Ca^{++} ions from water by means of Graham's salt. **s. agent.** A substance added to a system to preclude the normal ionic effects of the metals present.

sequestration. Chelation, complexing. The reversible reaction of a metallic ion with a molecule or ion to form a complex molecule which does not have all or most of the characteristics of the original metallic ion.

sequestric acid. $(CH_2 \cdot COOH)_2N(CH_2)_2 \cdot (CH_2 \cdot COOH)_2 = 292.21$. Ethylenediaminetetraacetic acid. White crystals, slightly soluble in water; forms soluble complexes with many metal ions especially Ca and Mg ions, liberating acid; a volumetric reagent for such ions.

sequiatannic acid. Sequoia tannin.

sequoia tannin. $C_{21}H_{20}O_{10} = 432.2$. A tannin from the cones of *Sequoia gigantea*, the mammoth tree of California. Brown powder, soluble in water.

Seraceta. Trade name for an acetate synthetic fiber.

seralbumin. The albumin of the blood.

serenoa. Sabal.

serge blue. Methylene blue.

sericin. $C_{15}H_{25}O_3N_5 = 323.5$. Silk gelatin, silk glue. An amorphous substance from silk, q.v.

sericite. A flaky muscovite, causing silicosis.

series. A succession of compounds, objects, or numbers, arranged systematically according to a rule. See *progression.* **aliphatic-** See *aliphatic compounds.* **alkane-** See *methane s.* **alkene-** See *ethylene s.* **alkine-** See *acetylene s.* **analogous-** See *analogs.* **aromatic-** See *aromatic compounds.* **Balmer-** The hydrogen lines, H_α, H_β, $H_\gamma \cdots$, which correspond with an electron transition from superior orbits to the second orbit. Cf. *hydrogen atom, Bohr theory.* **benzene-** See *benzene series.* **chemical-** See *s. of compounds.* **diffused-** The spectrum lines resulting from transition from the p state to the d state. **displacement-** q.v. **electrical-** (1) See *electromotive force.* (2) See *s. of cells.* **ethylene-** See *olefins.* **fatty-** See *methane series.*

fuzzy- The spectrum lines caused by transit from the outermost orbit, q.v. **galvanic-** See *galvanic battery.* **geologic-** See *geologic era.* **homologous-** Compounds differing by a definite radical or atomic group; as, CH_2. **homotopic-** The elements in a group or family of the periodic system. **isologous-** See *isologous.* **isotopic-** The isotopes of an element. See *isotopes.* **isomorphous-** See *isomorphism.* **isosteric-** See *isosteres.* **K-** See *K radiations.* **Lyman-** The hydrogen lines in the ultraviolet spectrum, due to transition of electrons from superior orbits to the first orbit. Cf. *energy levels.* **methane-** See *methane series.* **Paschen-** The hydrogen lines in the infrared spectrum, due to transition of electrons from superior orbits to the third orbit. Cf. *energy levels.* **periodic-** See *periodic system.* **principal-** The spectrum lines caused by transition from the p state to the lowest or s state. Cf. *Rydberg's formula.* **radioactive-** See *radioactive elements.* **sharp-** The spectrum lines produced by an electronic transition from the p state to the s state.

s. of cells. Electric cells arranged with the anode of one connected to the cathode of another. Cf. *parallel.* **s. of compounds.** Compounds of an element whose valency is the same throughout; e.g., iron forms the ferrous and ferric s. of salts. **s. of lines.** See *Balmer-, Lyman-, Paschen-s.* **s. notation.** See *quantum numbers.*

serine. $CH_2OH \cdot CHNH_2 \cdot COOH = 105.1$. α-Amino-β-hydroxypropionic acid, hydroxylalanine. Colorless crystals from sericin and horn. A constituent of many proteins, m.246 (decomp.), insoluble in alcohol.

seriplane test. A test for the evenness of yarn. The sample is wound on an inspection board in uniformly spaced panels, and assessed by comparison with photographs of standard yarns similarly wound.

seroden. Thiacetazone.

serogan. Serum gonadotrophin. The follicle-stimulating sex hormone from pregnancy urine.

serology. The study of reactions in or of sera.

seroreaction. A reaction that occurs in a serum as a result of immunization.

serotonoin. 5-Hydroxytryptamine. A protein in human blood.

serozyme. Thrombogen.

serpentaria. Virginia snakeroot. The dried rhizome and roots of *Aristolochia serpentaria* (Aristolochiaceae); a tonic and stimulant.

serpentine. $Mg_3Si_2O_7 \cdot 2H_2O$. Green, massive or lamellar oxides in rocks, often containing ferrous masses. Cf. *ophiolite.*

serum. (Pl. sera.) (1) The clear, liquid portion of a body fluid. (2) The clear, amber, alkaline fluid of the blood from which the cellular elements have been removed by clotting. It contains the salts, soluble proteins, and carbohydrates; used in biochemical and therapeutic work. See *immunity.* **milk-** Whey.

s. albumin. A protein, molecular weight 45,000, from s. and nephritic urine. **s. globulin.** A protein closely associated with s. albumin.

servo. A general term describing mechanisms which control automatically a changing physical condition, e.g., temperature. **s. mechanism.** A system whose output is compared with its input in order that the error between the two quantities may be controlled in a prescribed manner; e.g., speed-control systems.

sesame oil. Ben(n)e, gingelly, simsim, til, or ufuta oil. The oil extracted from the seeds of *Sesamum indicum* (Pedaliaceae), $d_{25}0.918$; an olive oil substitute (U.S.P., B.P.). Cf. *Villavecchia* test.

sesamin. $C_{18}H_{16}O_5 = 312.0$. An aromatic ether. Colorless crystals, m.123, slightly soluble in alcohol.

sesamol. $C_7H_6O_3 = 138.1$. A phenolic hydrolysis product of sesamolin; responsible for the Baudouin color test.

sesamolin. $C_{20}H_{18}O_7 = 450.1$. A substance in sesame oil (0.3%), m.94; hydrolyzes to sesamol and samin.

sesqui- Prefix (Latin) indicating $1\frac{1}{2}$, or proportion $3:2$.

sesquicarbonate. A compound of carbonic acid and a base in the proportion $3:2$. **s. of soda.** $NaHCO_3\cdot Na_2CO_3\cdot 2H_2O$. Sodium s. Snowflake crystals; used as a neutralizing agent, and in the manufacture of soap, glass, paper, and cleansers.

sesquichloride. A compound of chlorine and metal in the proportion $3:2$; as, Fe_2Cl_3.

sesquioxide. A compound of oxygen and a metal in the proportion $3:2$; as, Al_2O_3, Fe_2O_3.

sesquisalt. A compound of an acid and base in the proportion $3:2$; as, $Fe_2(SO_4)_3$.

sesquisoda. A molecular mixture of $NaHCO_3$ and Na_2CO_3.

sesquiterpenes. $C_{15}H_{24}$. Terpenes formed by the theoretical polymerization of 3 isoprene units; as, cadinene, clovene, santalene.

Setilose. Trade name for an acetate synthetic fiber.

setoff. Transfer of ink from a printed to an unprinted surface by direct contact, due to slow drying of the ink. Cf. *offset.*

setting. The hardening of semiliquid mixtures on crystallization (as cement) or organic condensation (as polymers).

settling. The precipitation of insoluble materials from suspension in a liquid, and their gradual sinking by gravitation. **hindered-** S. prevented by some factor other than specific gravity. **rate of-** The velocity of fall of particles in a liquid. If the particle is large and causes eddies, velocity $= k\sqrt{D(S-s)/s}$, where D is the diameter of the particle; S and s are the specific gravity of solid and liquid, respectively; and k is a constant (9.3 for spheres, 9.0 for irregular particles). Otherwise Stokes' law applies.

set up. The working arrangement of instruments, glassware, and other implements properly connected and ready for a chemical experiment.

sevicaine. Procaine hydrochloride.

Sevin. Trade name for 1-naphthyl-N-methylcarbamate; an insecticide.

sewage. The domestic waste from lavatories, kitchens, bathrooms, stables, and industrial plants.

sewerage. A system of pipes for carrying off excreta and waste materials.

sewer gas. The gases from decomposition of sewage.

sexiphenyl. $Ph(C_6H_4)_4Ph = 458.2$. Hexaphenyl, a hydrocarbon chain of 6 benzene rings. Colorless crystals, m.475, insoluble in water.

sexivalent. (1) Having 6 different valencies. (2) Hexavalent.

sextate. Methyl cyclohexanol acetic ester.

Sextol. Trademark for methylcyclohexanol.

seybertite. A complex hydrated native iron, calcium, aluminum silicate.

sfax. A variety of esparto, q.v., from near Sfax, N. Africa.

shadowgram, shadowgraph. Skiagram.

shadowing. A process to give an electron photomicrograph a 3-dimensional appearance by depositing on the specimen an opaque substance; e.g., metal is evaporated from an electrically heated filament at such a distance from the specimen that the metal ions reach it in almost parallel straight lines.

shale. A fine-grained sedimentary rock, with splintery uneven fractures. Cf. *slate.* **alum-** q.v. **oil-** q.v. **s. naphtha.** A petroleum from shale. **s. oil.** A crude oil from bituminous shales by destructive distillation; chief constituent, *kerogen.* Cf. *oil shale, gabianol.* **Esthonian-** Kukersite. **s. spirit.** The lower-boiling fractions from distilling oil.

shallu. Durra.

shearing. Side cutting or a lateral motion; as in grinding. Cf. *crushing.*

sheave. A grooved pulley wheel.

sheep. The herbiverous mammal *Ovis aries,* providing meat, wool, leather, and endocrine glands. **s. dip.** An antiseptic dipping fluid for sheep (arsenic or phenols and cresols). **s. laurel.** Kalmia. **s. oil.** Lanolin. **s. sorrel.** The dried herb of *Rumex acetosella;* a refrigerant and diuretic.

sheerness. The combined qualities of transparency, surface gloss, and smoothness, as of nylon hose.

Sheffield plate. Copper with a fused-on layer of sheet silver, rolled out and worked into articles of desired forms; displaced by electroplating (1837).

shell. (1) The husk of a fruit. (2) The calcareous or siliceous covering of marine invertebrates. (3) A projectile filled with explosives. (4) An area surrounding an atomic nucleus containing electrons. Cf. *Lewis atom.* **s. lime.** A fertilizer made by grinding mollusks containing 90% calcium (or magnesium) carbonate. **s. marl.** A fertilizer made by grinding natural deposits of shells containing not less than 80% calcium (or magnesium) carbonate.

shellac. The purified resin lac, q.v., obtained from plants by the incisions of an insect, *Laccifer lacca* (*Coccus lacca*). Brown leaflets, insoluble in water; used in varnishes, polishing materials, sealing wax, and pyrotechnics. It contains aleuritic acid 30, resin acid mixture 35–38%. **earth-** Acaroid resin.

shellane. (1) Trademark for a compressed natural gas, shipped in cylinders as fuel. (2) $C_{13}H_{22} = 178.1$. Proposed name for the saturated hydrocarbon corresponding with shellene.

shelloic acid. An acidic constituent of shellac, in which it occurs to the extent of less than 1%.

shellolic acid. $C_{15}H_{20}O_6 = 296.14$. 10-Hydroxy-shellene-*1,12*-dicarboxylic acid. Colorless crystals, m.200 (decomp.), soluble in hot water.

shepherd's purse. The freshly gathered green herb of *Capsella Bursa-pastoris;* a stimulant.

sherardize. To galvanize articles by covering them with zinc dust and heating in a tightly closed retort. Cf. *calorizing.*

sherbet. Sorbet. (1) An effervescing drink, sold in powder form, consisting of sugar, sodium bicarbonate, tartaric acid, and flavoring materials. (2) A frozen fruit juice used as a dessert.

shibuol. $C_{14}H_{20}O_9 = 332.15$. A phenol from kaki shibu, the unripe kaki fruit of Japan. Used in waterproofing paper.

shift. (1) A slight change in the wavelength of a spectral line caused by: (*a*) density (cf. *pressure*), (*b*) mass (cf. *relativity*), (*c*) motion (cf. *Doppler effect*), (*d*) absorption (cf. *Compton effect*), (*e*) reflection (cf. *Raman effect*). (2) A change of workers.

shikimol. Safrole.

shikonin. $C_{16}H_{16}O_5 = 288.11$. A principle from shikon, the dried root of *Lithospermum erythrorhizon* (Boraginaceae), Japan.

shilajatu. A mineral gum from India.

shirlacrol. A solution of phenolic tars and sodium hydroxide; used as a textile industry wetting agent.

Shirlan. Trademark for a mildew-preventive for textiles, 30 times as powerful as zinc chloride; evolved originally at the Shirley Institute, q.v.

Shirlastain. Trademark for a stain evolved by the Shirley Institute, q.v., for distinguishing various textile fabrics.

Shirley Institute. Headquarters of the British Cotton, Silk, and Man-made Fibres Research Association, Manchester.

shock. (1) A violent collision between bodies; (2) the concussion it occasions. (3) The effect of an electric discharge on the animal body.

shoddy. Wool waste recovered for reuse from knitted fabrics; a better grade than mungo.

shogaol. $C_{17}H_{24}O_3 = 276.19$. 4-Hydroxy-3-methoxyphenyl ethyl heptenyl ketone. A pungent constituent of ginger, resembling zingerone in having OH, OMe, and CO groups. Colorless liquid, $b_{15mm}235$, soluble in water.

Shore hardness. The height of rebound of a diamond-pointed hammer falling under gravity on an object; a high-carbon steel is taken as 100.

short circuit. An electric current that passes directly between leads which touch at a point between the source of current and its destination.

shorthand. See *structure symbols*.

shortite. $Na_2CO_3 \cdot 2CaCO_3$. A pyroelectric crystalline mineral from Wyoming.

shotgun pattern. The irregular points on a diagram which do not coincide with a theoretical curve.

shoyu. The aromatic, phenolic principle of fermented koji; a flavoring agent.

shunt. An alterable resistance in parallel with a galvanometer; used to control the current passing through it by diverting or "shunting."

SI. Abbreviation for Système International d'Unités, an extension and refinement of the metric system formally approved by 30 countries as the only legally accepted system. Main features are: Six basic units, the meter and kilogram in place of the centimeter and gram; the unit of force, the newton $(kg\ m\ s^{-2})$, is independent of the earth's gravitation; introduction of g into equations is unnecessary; the unit of all forms of energy is the joule (newton $\times$ meter), and of power the joule per second (watt) in place of calories, kilowatthour, BThU, and horsepower; electrostatic and electromagnetic units are replaced by SI electrical units; multiples of units and their fractions are normally restricted to steps of a thousand and a thousandth, respectively. See tables (from "Metrication in Scientific Journals," London; The Royal Society, 1968).

BASIC SI UNITS

Quantity	Name	Symbol
length	meter	m
mass	kilogram	kg
time	second	s
electric current	ampere	A
thermodynamic temperature ..	degree Kelvin	°K
luminous intensity	candela	cd

DERIVED SI UNITS

Quantity	Unit	Symbol	Definition
energy	joule	J	$kg\ m^2\ s^{-2}$
force	newton	N	$kg\ m\ s^{-2} = J\ m^{-1}$
power	watt	W	$kg\ m^2\ s^{-3} = J\ s^{-1}$
electric charge	coulomb	C	$A\ s$
electric potential difference ...	volt	V	$kg\ m^2\ s^{-3}\ A^{-1} = J\ A^{-1}\ s^{-1}$
electric resistance	ohm	Ω	$kg\ m^2\ s^{-3}\ A^{-2} = V\ A^{-1}$
electric capacitance	farad	F	$A^2\ s^4\ kg^{-1}\ m^{-2} = A\ s\ V^{-1}$
magnetic flux	weber	Wb	$kg\ m^2\ s^{-2}\ A^{-1} = V\ s$
inductance	henry	H	$kg\ m^2\ s^{-2}\ A^{-2} = V\ s\ A^{-1}$
magnetic flux density	tesla	T	$kg\ s^{-2}\ A^{-1} = V\ s\ m^{-2}$
luminous flux...............	lumen	lm	$cd\ sr$
illumination	lux	lx	$cd\ sr\ m^{-2}$
frequency	hertz	Hz	cycle per second
customary temperature, *t*	degree Celsius	°C	$t/°C = T/°K - 273.15$

FRACTIONS AND MULTIPLES

Fraction	Prefix	Symbol	Multiple	Prefix	Symbol
10^{-1}	deci	d	10	deka	da
10^{-2}	centi	c	10^2	hecto	h
10^{-3}	milli	m	10^3	kilo	k
10^{-6}	micro	μ	10^6	mega	M
10^{-9}	nano	n	10^9	giga	G
10^{-12}	pico	p	10^{12}	tera	T
10^{-15}	femto	f			
10^{-18}	atto	a			

UNITS ALLOWED IN CONJUNCTION WITH SI

Quantity	Name	Symbol	Definition
length	parsec	pc	30.87×10^{15} m
area	barn	b	10^{-28} m^2
	hectare	ha	10^4 m^2
volume	litre	l	10^{-3} m^3 = dm^3
pressure	bar	bar	10^5 N m^{-2}
mass	tonne	t	10^3 kg = Mg
kinematic viscosity, diffusion coefficient	stokes	St	10^{-4} m^2 s^{-1}
dynamic viscosity	poise	P	10^{-1} kg m^{-1} s^{-1}
magnetic flux density (magnetic induction)	gauss	G	10^{-4} T
radioactivity	curie	Ci	37×10^9 s^{-1}
energy	electronvolt	eV	$1.6021 = 10^{-19}$ J

TRADITIONAL UNITS WITH SI EQUIVALENTS

Physical quantity	Unit	Equivalent
length	ångström	10^{-10} m
	inch	0.0254 m
	foot	0.3048 m
	yard	0.9144 m
	mile	1.609 34 km
	nautical mile	1.853 18 km
area	square inch	645.16 mm^2
	square foot	0.092 903 m^2
	square yard	0.836 127 m^2
	square mile	2.589 99 km^2
volume	cubic inch	$1.638\ 71 \times 10^{-5}$ m^3
	cubic foot	0.028 316 8 m^3
	U.K. gallon	0.004 546 092 m^3
mass	pound	0.453 592 37 kg
	slug	14.593 9 kg
density	pound/cubic inch	$2.767\ 99 \times 10^4$ kg m^{-3}
	pound/cubic foot	16.0185 kg m^{-3}
force	dyne	10^{-5} N
	poundal	0.138 255 N
	pound-force	4.448 22 N
	kilogramme-force	9.806 65 N
pressure	atmosphere	101.325 kN m^{-2}
	torr	133.322 N m^{-2}
	pound (f)/sq in.	6894.76 N m^{-2}
energy	erg	10^{-7} J
	calorie (I.T.)	4.1868 J
	calorie (15°C)	4.1855 J
	calorie (thermochemical)	4.184 J
	BThU	1055.06 J
	foot poundal	0.042 140 1 J
	foot pound (f)	1.355 82 J
power	horsepower	745.700 W
temperature	degree Rankine	$\frac{5}{9}$ °K
	degree Fahrenheit	$t/°\text{F} = \frac{9}{5} T/°\text{C} + 32$

Si. Symbol for silicon.

sial. (Derived from Si and Al.) A hypothetical solid or semisolid rock substance on which the land masses of the earth are assumed to be supported. Cf. *sima*.

sialagogue. An agent that increases the flow of saliva.

sialic acid. *N*-Acylneuraminic acid.

siaresinolic acid. $C_3H_7 \cdot C_{26}H_{39}O_2 \cdot COOH = 470.4$. A resin acid, from Siamese benzoin gum, m.260.

sib(ling)s. Progeny having one or both parents in common.

sibucao. Sappan wood.

siccative. Drier. A solution of lead, manganese, or zinc salts of resin acids; a drying accelerator for varnish or paint.

side chain. A group of 2 or more similar atoms, generally C atoms, that branch off from a ring of atoms or a longer chain of atoms: 2 types:

$$CH_3$$
$$|$$
$$CH_2$$
$$|$$
$$-CH_2-CH_2-CH-CH_2-CH_2-$$

Branched side chain

True side chain

Cf. *chain*. **s. isomery.** The isomery of molecules that differ in structure by the arrangement of the side-chain atoms; as:

$$C_6H_4 \cdot CH_2 \cdot CH_2 \cdot CH_3 \quad \text{and} \quad C_6H_4 \cdot CH{\Large\langle}^{CH_3}_{CH_3}$$

Propylbenzene   Isopropylbenzene

s. substitution. A reaction in which substitution takes place in the side chain of a molecule. **s. theory.** See *Ehrlich's theory*.

side cut. A distillate obtained by fractional distillation.

siderazote. Fe_5N_2. A volcanic incrustation.

side reaction. A subsidiary reaction which occurs simultaneously with the main reaction.

sidereal. Pertaining to the fixed stars. Cf. *solar*, *lunar*. **s. day.** 86164.1 sec. **s. year.** 365 d, 6 hr, 9 min, 9 sec.

siderite. (1) $FeCO_3$. Clay ironstone, chalybite, spathose, spathic iron ore, a native iron carbonate. (2) An iron meteorite. A body of metallic iron with nickel, cobalt, etc., from outer space.

siderocyte. A blood cell containing iron.

siderography. (1) The study of the natural surface condition of siderites. (2) The etching of steel and iron, and its microscopic study.

siderolite. Mesoderite. A meteorite of spongy meteoric iron, with embedded grains of silicate minerals; as, olivine.

siderology. Siderurgy.

sideroplesite. A form of bruennerite.

siderosis. A pulmonary disease due to inhalation of iron dust. Cf. *byssinosis*.

siderostat. An instrument to transmit a beam of light along the optical axis of a fixed horizontal telescope.

siderotilate. $FeSO_4 \cdot 5H_2O$. A native sulfate.

siderurgy. Siderology. A branch of science that deals with the metallurgy of iron.

Sidgwick, Nevil Vincent. 1873–1952. British physical chemist, noted for his electronic theory of valency.

sidonal. Piperazine quinate.

Sidot's blende. An artificial zinc sulfide, which contains traces of copper; used in fluorescent screens for X rays or radioactive rays.

Siegbahn, Karl Manne George. b. 1886. Swedish physicist, Nobel Prize winner (1924); noted for his work on crystal structure. **S. notation.** See *quantum numbers*.

Siemens, Carl Friedrich von. 1872–1941. German industrialist. **S., Karl Wilhelm (Sir Charles William).** 1823–1883. German born, British chemist, inventor of the S. process. **S. furnace.** A. reverberatory furnace, heated by gas. **S.-Halske process.** A method of dissolving copper sulfides in a solution of ferrous sulfate and sulfuric acid, and obtaining metallic copper by electrolysis. **S.-Martin process.** A method for producing steel in a reverberatory furnace by adding scrap iron to iron ores. **S. ozonizer.** Two concentric glass tubes, the outer covered and the inner lined with tinfoil, which act as electrodes for a silent discharge passed through oxygen flowing between them. **S. process.** A method for making wrought iron directly from iron ores. **S. producer.** A furnace used to manufacture producer gas.

sienna. Raw sienna. Brown-yellow clay; a permanent pigment. It contains hydrated ferric oxide and manganic oxide. **burnt-** A burnt form of s., richer and brighter in color than raw s.

sieve. An apparatus with square apertures, to separate particles according to size. Cf. *screen* (round holes), *fineness*. See also *molecular* s.

sigma. Greek letter σ. The one-thousandth part of a second. **s. phenomenon.** Anomalous *viscosity*. **s. reaction.** Σ test: the Wassermann test for syphilis.

Sikes' hydrometer. See *hydrometer*.

sikimin. $C_{10}H_{16} = 136.1$ A terpene in the leaves of the sikimi plant *Illicium religiosum* (Magnoliaceae), Japan. Cf. *star anise*.

silage. A fodder made of finely cut green plants packed tightly in tanks (silos) and fermented.

silal. A heat-resisting iron containing 5% Si.

silandiol. A disubstituted chlorosilane of the type $R_2Si(OH)_2$. Silandiols can condense to form chain or ring structures.

silane. $R_{4-n}SiX_{4n}$, where R = Me or Ph, X = Cl or EtO, $n = 1, 2,$ or 3. The fundamental unit of silicones, which are formed by hydrolysis to a silanol and polymerization.

silanes. Silicans, q.v., silicohydrides, hydrosilicons. Compounds similar to hydrocarbons in which tetravalent Si replaces the C atom; as, SiH_4, monosilane, silicomethane. S. are very reactive, ignite in air, and form derivatives; as, $SiHCl_3$, trichlorosilane or silicochloroform. **methylchlor-** $CH_3ClSiH_2 = 80.40$. A volatile liquid, decomp. by water to silica; used to make textiles and paper water-repellent.

silanol. $R_{4-n}Si(OH)_n$. See *silane*.

silantriol. A hypothetical hydrolysis product of a monosubstituted chlorosilane of the type $R \cdot Si(OH)_3$. Silantriols condense to form 3-dimensional polymeric resins.

silanol. Silicol. The trivalent group $\equiv SiOH$.

Silastic. Trademark for a heat-stable silicone, q.v. Cf. *silicone rubber*

silavans. Group name for colorless, high-melting-point, strong polymers, containing silicon, carbon, and nitrogen.

silbamin. Silver fluoride.

Silberrad, Oswald John. 1878–1960. British chemist, noted for his work on explosives.

Silesia explosive. A high explosive: potassium chlorate 75, nitrated resin 25%.

silex. A heat- and shock-resistant glass (98% quartz). **liquid-** Water glass.

Sil-Fos. Trademark for an alloy, m.625–705: Cu 80, Ag 15, P 3%; used for brazing alloys containing copper.

silica. $SiO_2 = 60.1$. Silicon dioxide, silicic acid anhydride. Occurs abundantly in nature (12% of all rocks), and exists in 7 crystalline forms. Classification: (1) Phenocrystalline or vitreous minerals; see *quartz*. (2) Cryptocrystalline and amorphous minerals; see *chalcedony*. (3) Amorphous and colloidal minerals; see *opal*. **amorphous-** Colorless powder, m.1650, insoluble in water, soluble in hot alkalies or hydrofluoric acid; used for chemical glassware. **colloidal-** See *silicic acid*. **crystalline-** Colorless, transparent prisms, m.1760, insoluble in water, soluble in hydrofluoric acid. Used in optical instruments, kitchenware, and chemical plant. The main crystalline forms (quartz, tridymite, and cristobalite) have definite transition points (870 and 1470°C, respectively). **s. brick.** A firebrick containing over 92% s.; its crystalline phase is cristobalite and tridymite. **s. gel.** Gelatinous s. which, if activated, absorbs water; used to dry blast-furnace gases, air, and other gases. **s. minerals.** Rock-forming minerals comprising the groups, q.v.: amphiboles, andalusite, cancrinite, sodalite, chlorite, feldspar, garnet, iolite, leucite, melilite, mica, nephelite, olivine, pyroxene, scapolite, topaz, tourmaline, zeolite, zoisite; also beryl, quartz, serpentine, talc.

silicam. $Si(NH)_2 = 100.2$. White powder from heating silicon imide. Insoluble in water; forms silicon nitride, Si_2N_4, when further heated.

silicane. (1) A silane, i.e., a compound of the type Si_xH_y. (2) SiR_4. R is a hydrocarbon radical. (3) $SiH_4 = 32.08$. Monosilane, silicomethane, silicohydride. Colorless gas, b.−112. **bromo-** $SiH_3Br = 111.0$. Colorless gas, b.1.8. **chloro-** $SiH_3Cl = 66.54$. Colorless gas, b.−30. **di-** $Si_2H_6 = 62.16$. Silicoethane, a gas, m.−132. **dibromo-** $SiH_2Br_2 = 189.91$. Colorless liquid, d.2.17, b.66. **dichloro-** $SiH_2Cl_2 = 100.99$. Colorless gas, b.8.3. **dimethyl-** $Si_2H_2Me_2 = 60.12$. Dimethylmonosilane. Colorless gas, b.−20. **ether-** $(SiH_3)_2O = 78.17$. Disilane oxide. Colorless gas, b.15. **ethoxytriethyl-** $Et_3SiOEt = 160.22$. Triethylsilane ethyl oxide, triethyl silicol ethyl ether. Colorless liquid, b.153, insoluble in water. **hydroxy-** Silicol. **methyl-** $MeSiH_3 = 46.11$, Methylmonosilane. Colorless gas, b.−57. **tetra-** $Si_4H_{10} = 122.31$. Silicobutane. A gas, m.−94. **tetrabromo-** Silicon bromide.

tetrachloro- Silicon chloride. **tetraethyl-** $SiEt_4 = 144.25$. Silicon tetraethyl, silicononane. Colorless liquid, d.0.7682, b.153. **tetrafluoro-** Silicon fluoride. **tetraiodo-** Silicon iodide. **tetramethyl-** $SiMe_4 = 144.22$. Silicon tetramethyl. Colorless liquid, d.0.645, b.27. **tetraphenyl-** $Si(C_6H_5)_4 = 336.24$. Silicon tetraphenyl, tetraphenyl silicon. Colorless crystals, m.233. **tri-** $Si_3H_8 = 92.24$. Silicopropane. A gas, m.−117. **tribromo-** $SiHBr_3 = 268.82$. Silicobromoform. Colorless liquid, d.2.7, b.109. **trichloro-** Silicochloroform. **trichloroethyl-** $Si(C_2H_5)Cl_3 = 163.47$. Colorless liquid, d.1.239. **trichlorophenyl-** $Si(C_6H_5)Cl_3 = 211.47$. Colorless liquid, d.1.326, b.197, decomp. in water. **triethyl-** $(C_2H_5)_3SiH = 116.18$. Triethyl silicon, silicoheptane. Colorless liquid, d.0.751, b.107, insoluble in water. **trifluoro-** $SiHF_3 = 86.07$. Silicofluoroform. Colorless gas, b.−80. **triiodo-** $SiI_3H = 409.83$. Silicoiodoform. Red liquid, d.3.314, b.220.

silicate. A salt derived from silica or the silicic acids. Silicates form the largest group of minerals (see *silica*), and are derived from M_4SiO_4, *ortho*silicate, and M_2SiO_3, *meta*silicate, which may combine to form *poly*silicates. Except for the alkali silicates, they are insoluble in water. See *silica minerals*. **fibrous-** *Natural*: Asbestos. *Man-made*: Glass, silica, and aluminosilicate fibers, rock wool, slag wool. **s. cement.** See *dental* cement. **s. of soda.** Sodium silicate.

siliceous. Containing silica. **s. algae.** See *algae*. **s. deposit.** S. sinter. The solid accumulation of silica deposited from hot mineral springs. Cf. *geyserite*. **s. earth.** Silica of diatomite origin, purified by boiling with dilute acid, washing, and calcining; a filter medium (U.S.P.). **s. sinter.** S. deposit.

silicic. (1) Containing silicon. (2) Containing silicic acid. **s. acid.** $H_4SiO_4 = 96.3$. Orthosilicic acid. White powder, slightly soluble in water. **di-** $H_2Si_2O_5$ or $H_6Si_2O_7$. White, insoluble powder. **meta-** $H_2SiO_3 = 78.1$. White powder, insoluble in water. **tri-** $H_4Si_3O_8 = 216.3$. White, insoluble powder.

SILICIC ACIDS

$H_2Si_4O_9$	$= 4SiO_2 \cdot H_2O$, tetra-
$H_2Si_2O_5$	$= 2SiO_2 \cdot H_2O$, meta-di-
$H_4Si_3O_8$	$= 3SiO_2 \cdot 2H_2O$, meta-tri-
H_2SiO_3	$= SiO_2 \cdot H_2O$, meta-
$H_8Si_3O_{10}$	$= 3SiO_2 \cdot 4H_2O$, ortho-tri-
$H_6Si_2O_7$	$= 2SiO_2 \cdot 3H_2O$, ortho-di-
H_4SiO_4	$= SiO_2 \cdot 2H_2O$, ortho-

silicide. M_3Si. M is Fe, Ni, Co, Cr, Mn, Cu, or Mg.

silicification. The gradual replacement of rocks or fossils by silica (petrifaction).

silicified. Describing an organic material, e.g., wood, that has been petrified.

silicium. Silicon.

silico- Prefix indicating silicon, generally in organic compounds. **s. benzoic acid.** $PhSiOOH = 138.1$. m.92, insoluble in water. **s. bromoform.** $SiHBr_3 = 268.9$. Heavy, colorless liquid, d.2.7, b.116, decomp. by water. **s. butane.** See *silanes*. **s. calcium.** A product of the electric furnace used to deoxidize steel. **s. chloroform.** $SiHCl_3 = 135.36$

Colorless liquid, d.1.34, b.34, decomp. by water.
s. decitungstic acid. $SiO_2 \cdot 10WO_3 \cdot 4H_2O$. White powder; a reagent for cesium (insoluble salts).
s. ethane. See *silanes*. **s. fluorides.** Fluosilicate.
s. fluoric acid. Fluosilic acid. **s. formic acid.** See *leucone*. **s. heptane.** $Et_3SiH = 116.1$. Triethylsilane. Colorless liquid, d.0.751, b.107. **s. hydrides.** Silanes. **s. iodoform.** $SiHI_3 = 409.9$. Heavy, colorless liquid, d. 3.4, b.220, decomp. by water.
s. methane. Silane. **s. oxalic acid.** $HOOSi \cdot SiOOH = 122.2$. White, unstable solid. **s. tungstic acid.** S. decitungstic acid.
silicol. R_3SiOH. Hydroxysilane. **triethyl-** $Et_3SiOH = 132.18$. Silicoheptyl alcohol. Colorless liquid, b.154, insoluble in water.
silicon. Si = 28.09. Silicium. A nonmetallic element of the carbon group, at. no. 14. Allotropic modifications: (1) *Amorphous:* Brown powder, d.2.35. (2) *Crystalline:* Gray crystals, m.1500, insoluble in water. (3) *Graphitoidal:* Dense crystals, or graphite-like masses deposited from molten s. (4) *Adamantine:* Hard needles. Principal valency 4. S. forms many complex compounds in the earth surface (rocks). Used in alloys to impart hardness, and in transistors. See *silica minerals*. **ethyl-** The radical ≡SiEt. Cf. *silicane*. **methyl-** The radical ≡SiMe. **radio-** A s. isotope, mass 27. Cf. *radioelements*.
 s. alkyls. (1) Hydrogen compounds of s. corresponding with hydrocarbons; as, SiH_4, silane. (2) Organic compounds of s. and alkyl radicals; as, $SiMe_4$. See *silicanes*. **s. alloys.** Noncorrodible alloys of s. with metals; as, Duriron. Cf. *s. copper*.
s. borides. SiB_3, SiB_4, and SiB_6 exist. Black, irregular crystals, of high m.; very hard, and good conductors of electricity. **s. bromides.** (1) $SiBr_4 = 347.9$. S. tetrabromide. Colorless, fuming liquid, b.154, decomp. by water to silicic acid. (2) $Si_2Br_6 = 535.7$. S. tribromide. Colorless solid, b.240, decomp. by water. **s. bronze.** A noncorrodible alloy: Cu, Sn, with 1–4% Si. **s. carbide.** SiC = 40.1. Colorless plates, dissociates 2250; used in refractories and abrasives. **s. chlorides.** (1) $SiCl_4 = 170.0$. S. tetrachloride. Colorless, fuming liquid, d.1.524, b.58, decomp. by water to silicic acid. Used in electrotechnics, and mixed with ammonia vapors, in smoke screens. (2) $Si_2Cl_6 = 269.0$. S. trichloride, b.146, decomp. by water. (3) $Si_3Cl_8 = 367.8$. S. octachloride. White powder. **s. copper.** An alloy: Si 20–30, Cu 70–80%, used in metallurgy. **s. dioxide.** Silica. **s. disulfide.** $SiS_2 = 92.2$. White needles, sublime when heated, decomp. by water. **s. ethane.** See *silanes*. **s. ethyl.** Tetraethylsilicane. See *silicane*. **s. fluorides.** (1) $SiF_4 = 104.3$. S. tetrafluoride. Colorless, suffocating gas, $b_{1810mm} -65$, decomp. by water to fluosilicic acid, soluble in alcohol. (2) $Si_2F_6 = 170.6$. S. subfluoride. White powder. **s. hydrides.** See *silanes*. **s. iodides.** (1) $SiI_4 = 535.8$. S. tetraiodide. Colorless solid, m.121, insoluble in water. (2) $Si_2I_6 = 817.7$. S. subiodide. Colorless solid, m.250 (in vacuo), decomp. by water. **s. iron.** Ferrosilicon. Iron containing 2–15% Si; used in metallurgy. **s. magnesium.** $Mg_2Si = 76.7$. Magnesium silicide. Gray leaflets, decomp. by water to silanes. **s. methane.** Silane. **s. methyl.** $SiMe_4 = 88.3$. Colorless liquid, b.26. **s. nitride.** $Si_3N_4 = 140.2$.

White powder, insoluble in water, existing in 2 hexagonal phases stable below and above 1400–1450°C, respectively. Very resistant to thermal shock and chemical reagents; used as a support for catalysts and in stator blades of high-temperature gas turbines. **s. octachloride.** See *s. chlorides*.
s. oxide. Silica. **s. oxychlorides.** Si_2OCl_6(b.137); $Si_4O_3Cl_8$ (b.200); $Si_4O_3Cl_{10}$ (b.153); $Si_8O_{10}Cl_{12}$ (b.300); $Si_2O_3Cl_2$ (b.400); $Si_4O_7Cl_2$ (m.400). **s. steel.** Steel containing 2–3% Si; hard and brittle.
s. sulfide. S. disulfide. **s. tetrabromide.** See *s. bromides*. **s. tetrachloride.** See *s. chlorides*. **s. tetrafluoride.** See *s. fluorides*. **s. tetraiodide.** See *s. iodides*. **s. tetraphenyl.** Tetraphenyl silicon.
s. tungstic acid. Silicodecitungstic acid. **s. zirconium.** An alloy used to purify molten steel.
silicone. (1) S. rubber. An elastomer in which the C linkages of a polymerized hydrocarbon are replaced by Si—O linkages. It retains its elastic properties between −50 and +291, and can be kneaded; used for protective coatings on wires and for high-temperature lubricants. World production (1967), 55,000 tons. (2) Originally a compound having the empirical formula R_2SiO (contraction of silicoketone). (3)$H_3Si_3O_2 = 119.22$. Yellow solid. **s. alloy.** A compound produced by the simultaneous polymerization of 2 silicones; e.g., tetravinyl s. and methyl hydrogen siloxane give a s. alloy of high water repellency.
siliconic acid. $R \cdot SiOOH$, analogous to organic acids. Cf. *carbylic acid*.
silicono. The radical (HO)OSi—, derived from metasilicic acid.
Silicool. Trade name for a protein synthetic fiber.
silicosis. A form of pneumonoconiosis due to silica dust less than 10 microns in diameter.
silicotungstate. A salt of silicotungstic acid, especially with the alkaloids.
silicotungstic acid. $SiO_2 \cdot 12WO_3 \cdot 26H_2O$. Yellow crystals, soluble in water, used alkaloid analysis.
silicyl. (1) The radical H_3Si—, from silane. (2) The radical =SiO, from silicic acid. **di-** The radical $=Si_2O_5$. **s. oxide.** $(R_3Si)_2O$; as: *hexaethyl-*$(Et_3Si)_2O = 246.35$. Colorless liquid, b.231.
silicylene. The radical $H_2Si=$, from silane.
silk. (1) Fibroin, sericin. The fibrous envelope of the silkworm before the chrysalis state (cocoon). It consists of fibroin (the fiber protein) and sericin (the gummy protein). (2) A sieve for grading flour: no. 5 = 0.270, no. 8 = 0.190 mm aperture. (3) A series of parallel fine-line inclusions in certain gems (e.g., rubies) Cf. *asterism*. **"all-"** S. containing fillers, but no other fibers. **artificial-** Rayon. **net-** S. fabric made from yarns of continuous s. filament. **pure-** S. fibers without fillers **schappe-, spun-** Describing a fabric made from silk-waste staple fiber. **vegetable-** (1) The floss from the seeds of *Calotropis gigantea* (Asclepiadaceae), Asia. (2) Kapok.
silk warp. Organzine.
silkweed. Milkweed. The dried roots of *Asclepias syriaca;* a diuretic and tonic.
Silliman, Benjamin. 1779–1864. American chemist and geologist, who founded the American Journal of Science and Arts.
sillimanite. Al_2SiO_5. (1) Rhombic aluminum silicate m.1820; used for porcelain. Above 1545 it forms mullite and siliceous glass. See *cyanite*. (2)

Fibrolite. **s. ware.** Laboratory utensils resistant to mechanical and thermal shock.

Sillman bronze. An alloy: Cu 86, Al 10, Fe 4%.

silo. (1) A tank or channel for conveying solid material in small pieces. (2) A pit or chamber in which fodder is fermented. See *silage.*

Silon. Trade name for a polyamide synthetic fiber.

siloxicon. Si_2OC_2. A refractory obtained by heating quartz, carbon, and sawdust in the electric furnace. Cf. *fibrox.*

silphenylene. Trade name for heat-resistant laminating resins derived from silicones.

silumin. A noncorrodible alloy: Si and Al, sometimes containing 4–5% Cu.

silundum. Silicon carbide.

silva. Describing a lithographic printing process with zinc plates coated with silver halide emulsion instead of a dichromate. The silver image is converted into an ink image, enabling large-scale printing plates to be made from miniature negatives.

silvan. Sylvan.

silve. The volume of 1 cubic meter of wood calculated from the diameter of a tree and the known mean diameter-volume relationship.

silver. Ag = 107.8868. A metal of the gold family; element of at. no. 47. White, lustrous metal of regular crystalline structure, d.10.50, m.960.5, b.1950, soluble in nitric acid or hot conc. sulfuric acid, insoluble in hydrochloric acid, water, or cold sulfuric acid. Valency 1. Used in jewelry, coins, instruments; and in the manufacture of s. salts for photography and pharmacy. **antimonial-** Dyscrasite. **black-** Stephanite. **blue-** Niello. **coinage-** See *s. alloys, coinage.* **colloidal-** Collargol. **800-** The alloy: Ag 80, Cu 20%. **fulminating-** S. nitride. **german-** Nickel s. **horn-** Argentum cornu. **liquid-** Mercury. **moss-** Native s. in mosslike form. **nickel-** q.v. **niello-** q.v. **quick-** Mercury. **ruby-** Proustite. **Russian-** Mello. **sterling-** The alloy: Ag 92.5, Cu 7.5%. **s. acetate.** $AgC_2H_3O_2$ = 166.9. Colorless crystals, decomp. by heat, soluble in water; used in ophthalmia. **s. acetylide.** Ag_2C_2 = 239.88. S. carbide. An explosive white powder. **s. alloys.** Principally:

    Coinage:
        U.S.: Ag 90, Cu 10%
        U.K.: Ag 50, Cu 40, Ni 5, Zn 5%
    Jewelry:
        Ordinary: Ag 80, Cu 20%
        Hall-marked: Ag 92.5, Cu and/or Cd 7.5%

s. amalgam. $AgHg_2$ = 509.1. A silvery ,brittle solid. **s. ammonium chloride.** $AgCl \cdot NH_4Cl$ = 196.9. Colorless cubes, soluble in ammonium hydroxide; used medicinally. **s. ammonium nitrate solution.** A solution of 1 gm s. nitrate in 20 ml water, ammonia being added until the precipitate just dissolves, used to produce a s. mirror on heating with certain reducing agents. **s. antimonide.** S. stibide. **s. arsenate.** Ag_3AsO_4 = 462.6. Red powder, insoluble in water. **s. arsenide.** Ag_3As = 398.4. Black precipitate, decomp. when dried. **s. arsenite.** Ag_3AsO_3 = 446.60. Yellow powder, insoluble in water; an antiseptic in skin diseases. **s. arsphenamine.** A medicinal compound of s. and salvarsan. **s. atoxylate.** $NH_2C_6H_4AsO \cdot AgO \cdot OH$ = 323.8. Argatoxyl, s. *p*-aminophenyl

arsenate; a bactericide. **s. azide.** AgN_3 = 149.91. A curdy, white explosive powder. **s. benzamide.** See *benzamide.* **s. benzoate.** $AgC_7H_5O_2$ = 228.8. Colorless powder, soluble in hot water. **s. bichromate.** S. dichromate. **s. bolus.** See *bolus.* **s. borate.** $Ag_2B_4O_7$ = 371.0. Unstable white powder, soluble in cyanide solutions. **s. bromate.** $AgBrO_3$ = 235.8. Colorless tetragons, decomp. by heat, soluble in hot water. **s. bromide.** $AgBr$ = 187.80. Native as bromyrite and embolite. Yellow regular crystals, m.427, decomp. 700, insoluble in water, soluble in thiosulfate solution; a light-sensitive coating in photography. **s. carbide.** S. acetylide. **s. carbonate.** Ag_2CO_3 = 275.8. Heavy, yellow powder, d.6.0, decomp. 200, insoluble in water, soluble in cyanide solutions. **s. caseinate.** Argonin. **s. chlorate.** $AgClO_3$ = 191.3. Colorless tetragons, m.230, decomp. 270, soluble in water. **s. chloride.** $AgCl$ = 143.34. Lunar cornea. Native as horn s., cerargyrite, embolite. Colorless regular crystals, d.5.553, m.455, insoluble in water, soluble in ammonium hydroxide. Used as an antiseptic and nerve sedative; in the manufacture of pure s., and s. salts; for s. plating; and in photography and photometry. **s. chlorite.** $AgClO_2$ = 175.3. Yellow powder, slightly soluble in water. **s. chromate.** Ag_2CrO_4 = 331.8. Red crystals, d.5.623, insoluble in water, soluble in ammonium hydroxide. **s. cinnamate.** $AgC_9H_7O_2$ = 254.8. S. cinnamylate. Heavy, white powder, slightly soluble in water; an antiseptic. **s. cinnamylate.** S. cinnamate. **s. citrate.** $Ag_3C_6H_5O_7$ = 512.4. Itrol. White powder, insoluble in water; a dusting powder. **s. colloidal.** Collargol, argentum, colloidale. An allotrope of s., with a small percentage of albumin; black scales giving a fairly stable colloidal suspension with water. **s. cyanate.** $AgCNO$ = 149.9. Colorless powder, decomp. by heat, slightly soluble in water. **s. cyanide.** $AgCN$ = 133.90. White crystals, decomp. by heat, insoluble in water, soluble in cyanide solutions; an antipyretic and sedative. **s. dichromate.** $Ag_2Cr_2O_7$ = 431.76. Purple, triclinic crystals, decomp. by heat or alcohol, slightly soluble in water. **s. dithionate.** $Ag_2S_2O_6$ = 375.90. **s. eosolate.** $C_6H_5O \cdot CH_2O \cdot C_2H_3O \cdot Ag_2(SO_3)_3$. An antiseptic. **s. ferricyanide.** $Ag_3Fe(CN)_6$ = 535.5. Orange crystals, slightly soluble in water, soluble in ammonium hydroxide. **s. ferrocyanide.** $Ag_4Fe(CN)_6 \cdot H_2O$ = 661.4. Yellow crystals, insoluble in water. **s. fluoride.** $AgF \cdot H_2O$ = 144.90. Tachiol. Silbamin. Yellow, deliquescent tetragons, m.435, soluble in water; an antiseptic. **s. fluosilicate.** (1) Ag_2SiF_6 = 249.94. White powder. (2) $Ag_2SiF_6 \cdot 4H_2O$ = 366.94. Globular granules, slightly soluble in water. **s. fulminate.** $Ag_2C_2N_2O_2$ = 299.8. Colorless needles, explode when heated, slightly soluble in water; used in detonators. **s. gelatose.** Albargin. **s. glance.** S. glanz. Argentite. **s. hypochlorite.** $AgClO$ = 159.34. An unstable bleaching agent. **s. hypophosphate.** See *s. phosphates.* **s. iodate.** $AgIO_3$ = 282.80. Colorless, monoclinic crystals, decomp. by heat, insoluble in water; an astringent and antiseptic. **s. iodide.** AgI = 234.8. Native as iodyrite. Yellow hexagons, d.5.67, m.536, insoluble in water; soluble in cyanide, iodide, or thiosulfate solutions; used in photography, and as an alterative. **s. lactate.** $AgC_3H_5O_3 \cdot H_2O$ = 214.8. Actol. Colorless needles, soluble in water; an antiseptic and astringent. **s. laurate.** $AgC_{12}H_{23}O_2$ = 307.06. Colorless powder, m.213. **s. leaf.** Stillingia. **s. methylene blue.** A compound of s. and methylene blue. Blue powder, soluble in water; an internal antiseptic. **s. myristate.** $AgC_{14}H_{27}O_2$ = 335.09. White powder, m.211, insoluble in water. **s. nitrate.** $AgNO_3$ = 169.89. Argenti nitras. Colorless hexagons or rhombs, d.4.352, m.209 (decomp.), soluble in water. Used as a reagent (especially for halogens) and a local antiseptic (U.S.P., B.P.); for s. plating, permanent laundry-proof markings, and dyeing hair and fur; and in the manufacture of s. salts and photography. *fused-* Lunar caustic, molded s. nitrate. White, hard sticks; an external antiseptic. *toughened-* White, molded crystal masses, made by fusing s. nitrate 95 and potassium nitrate 5 pts., soluble in water; a caustic (U.S.P., B.P.). **s. nitrate paper.** A filter paper impregnated with a solution of nitrate and dried in the dark. A test for arsenic (yellow), phosphorus (black), chromates (red), and uric acid (brown). **s. nitride.** Ag_3N = 337.4. Fulminating s. Gray, explosive solid, insoluble in water. **s. nitrite.** $AgNO_2$ = 153.9. Colorless crystals, d.4.453, decomp. 150, slightly soluble in water; a reagent for standardizing permanganate solutions, determining nitrites, and differentiating alcohols. **s. nucleinate.** Nargol. A compound of nucleic acids and s.; used medicinally. **s. ores.** Silver is associated in nature with copper and gold minerals generally in binary compounds, as: native s., Ag; argentite, Ag_2S; proustite, Ag_3AsS_3; stromeyerite, AgCuS; bromyrite, AgBr; argentiferous lead, AgPbS. **s. oxalate.** $Ag_2C_2O_4$ = 303.8. White crystals, detonated by heat, insoluble in water. **s. oxide.** Ag_2O = 231.8. Brownish powder, d.7.521, decomp. 330, insoluble in water; an antiseptic and tonic. **s. oxyquinoline sulfonate.** Argentol. **s. palmitate.** $AgC_{16}H_{31}O_2$ = 363.12. White powder, m.209, insoluble in water. **s. perchlorate.** $AgClO_4$ = 207.3. White crystals, m.486, soluble in water. **s. period.** Heavy metals of the fourth subperiod in the periodic system, Ru, Rh, Pd, Ag, Cd, In. **s. permanganate.** $AgMnO_4$ = 225.8. Violet, monoclinic crystals, decomp. by heat, slightly soluble in water; an antiseptic. **s. peroxides.** (1) Ag_2O_2 = 247.76. Black insoluble solid, d.7.44, decomp. 110. (2) Ag_2O_4 = 279.76. An unstable solid. **s. phenolsulfonate.** $C_6H_4(OH)SO_3Ag$ = 280.9. S. sulfophenylate, s. sulfocarbolate. Colorless crystals, soluble in water; used in ophthalmology, an antiseptic. **s. phosphates.** (1) Ag_3PO_4 = 418.7. S. orthophosphate. Yellow powder, m.849, insoluble in water; used in photography. (2) $Ag_4P_2O_7$ = 605.60. S. pyrophosphate. White, insoluble solid, m.585. (3) Ag_2PO_3 = 294.76. S. hypophosphate. **s. phosphide.** AgP_2 = 169.88. Gray powder. **s. picrate.** $C_6H_2O(NO_2)_3Ag \cdot H_2O$ = 353.9. Picratol, s. trinitrophenylate. Yellow crystals, soluble in water: an antiseptic. **s. plate.** A metal article plated or covered with metallic s. See *Sheffield plate.* **s. plating.** The electrolytic deposition of s. on another metal. **s. potassium cyanide.** $KAg(CN)_2$ = 199.0. Potassium argentocyanide Colorless octahedra, soluble in water; an antiseptic, and used

in silvering and s. plating. **s. protein.** Brown hygroscopic powder (7.5–8.5 % Ag), made by the reaction of a s. compound and gelatin in presence of an alkali; an antibacterial. **s. quinaseptol.** Argentol. **s. salicylate.** $C_6H_4(OH)COOAg$ = 244.9. Pink crystals, soluble in water; an antiseptic. **s. salt.** Sodium anthraquinone β-sulfonate; used in stripping dyed rags by reducing agents. **s. selenide.** Ag_2Se = 187.0. Gray powder, insoluble in water. **s. silicofluoride.** Ag_2SiF_6 = 357.9. Isotachiol. Colorless powder, slightly soluble in water; used to sterilize drinking water. **s. silvinate.** S. sylvate. **s. sodium chloride.** $NaAgCl_2$ = 201.8. Colorless crystals, decomp. by water. **s. sodium cyanide.** Sodium argentocyanide. **s. sodium thiosulfate.** $Na_4Ag_2(S_2O_3)_3$ = 643.6 White crystals, soluble in water. **s. solder.** An alloy of 40, 50, or 60 % Ag with Cu, Zn, and Cd. **s. stearate.** $AgC_{18}H_{35}O_2$ = 391.15. White powder, m.205, soluble in water. **s. stibide.** Ag_3Sb = 443.6. S. antimonide. Black rhombs, insoluble in water. **s. sulfate.** Ag_2SO_4 = 311.82. Colorless, triclinic or rhombic crystals, m.651, soluble in water; a reagent and electroplating agent. **s. sulfides.** (1) Ag_2S = 247.83. Native as argentite and acanthite. Gray, regular crystals, m.676, insoluble in water; used in ceramic pigments. (2) Ag_2S_2 = 279.88. Black solid. **s. sulfite.** Ag_2SO_3 = 295.8. Colorless crystals, decomp. 100, slightly soluble in water. **s. sulfocarbolate.** S. phenol sulfonate. **s. sulfocyanide.** S. thiocyanate. **s. sulfoichthyolate.** Ichthargan. **s. sulfophenylate.** S. phenol sulfonate. **s. sylvate.** $AgC_{20}H_{29}O_2$ = 408.8. S. silvinate. Brown crystals, insoluble in water. **s. tartrate.** $Ag_2C_4H_4O_6$ = 363.6. White crystals, soluble in water. **s. telluride.** Ag_2Te = 343.1. Native as hessite. Black powder, insoluble in water. **s. thiocyanate.** $AgCNS$ = 166.0. White powder, decomp. by heat, insoluble in water, soluble in cyanide or ammonia solutions. **s. thiosulfate.** $Ag_2S_2O_3$ = 327.90. White solid, soluble in water, decomp. by heat. **s. tree.** Arbor Dianae. **s. trinitrophenolate.** S. picrate. **s. vanadate.** Ag_3VO_4 and $Ag_4V_2O_7$, m.385; a catalyst. **s. vitellin.** Argyrol.

silvering. Coating with metallic silver, chemically (reduction of silver salts), or electrolytically.

silverweed. Wild tansy. The herb of *Potentilla anserina* (Rosaceae); an astringent and tonic.

silvestrene. $C_{10}H_{16}$ = 136.1. Sylvestrene. A terpene from European turpentine. Colorless liquid, d.0.863, b.177.

silvinate. Sylvate.

silyl. The radical SiH_3, analogous to the methyl group CH_3.

sima. A contraction of silica and magnesia magma. Semiliquid rock on which the sial floats.

simaruba. Bitter damson. The dried root bark of *Simaruba amaris* or *S. officinalis* (Simarubaceae), tropical America; an astringent (contains quassin).

Simarubaceae. Tropical shrubs and trees; e.g.: *Picrasma excelsa*, Jamaica quassia; *Ailanthus glandulosa*, Chinese sumac; *Picramnaea antidroma*, cascara amarga.

simmer. Boil gently.

Simon's test. Acetaldehyde and sodium nitroprusside, added together, give a red and blue color with primary and secondary amines, respectively.

simple. Not complex, as s. spectrum; not mixed, as s. ether; not double, as s. salt.

simsin. Sesame.

simulator. A device that produces a token performance, e.g., of plant or apparatus, by means different from the plant itself.

simultaneous reaction. (1) Side reaction. (2) Secondary reaction. (3) One of 2 or more reactions that occur at the same time in the same reacting system.

sinactine. $C_{21}H_{20}NO_4 = 339.0$. l-Tetrahydroepiberberine. A diisoquinoline alkaloid from *Sinomenium actum*.

sinalbin. $C_{30}H_{41}O_{16}N_2S_2 = 722.27$. A glucoside from the seeds of *Brassica (Sinapis) alba*, white mustard seed (Cruciferae). Colorless crystals, hydrolyzed to sinapine, p-oxybenzyl mustard oil, and glucose.

sinamine. $C_4H_6N_2 = 82.1$. Allylcyanamide. An amine from black mustard seed. **thio-** Allylsulfocarbimide.

sinapic acid. $C_{11}H_{12}O_5 = 224.1$. An unsaturated oxyacid derived from sinapine.

sinapine. $C_{16}H_{25}O_6N = 327.3$. An alkaloid from sinalbin, the glucoside of white mustard; hydrolyzes to sinapic acid and choline.

sinapis alba. White *mustard*. **s. nigra.** Black *mustard*.

sinapolin. $C_{14}H_{12}O_2N_2 \cdot C_7H_{12}O_2N = 382.3$. Diallylurea, in mustard oil.

sine. The ratio of the length of the side opposite an angle of a right-angled triangle to that of the hypotenuse. Cf. *cosine*.

singular solution. A solution with a maximum or minimum on its vapor-pressure curve.

sinigrin. Potassium myronate.

sinistrin. $C_6H_{10}O_5 = 162.1$. A levorotatory carbohydrate from squill.

sinkaline. Choline.

sinomenine. $C_{19}H_{23}O_4N = 329.3$. An isoquinoline alkaloid from *Sinomenium acutum* (Menispermaceae). Colorless needles, m.182.

Sinox. Trademark for an aqueous paste of sodium dinitroorthotolyl oxide; a weedicide.

sinter. (1) Saline incrustations formed around mineral springs. (2) See *sintering*. **calcareous-** Tufa, travertine, or onyx. **iron-** Amorphous scorodite. **pearl-** A modification of silica. **siliceous-** (1) Geyserite. (2) Fluorite.

sintering. The coalescence by heat of crystalline or amorphous particles into a solid mass, due to the formation of allotropic crystals. Cf. *fritted*.

siomine. $(CH_2)_5N_4I_4 = 633.6$. Hexamethyleneamine tetraiodide. Colorless powder, insoluble in water.

sipalin. A plasticizing mixture of the cyclohexyl and methylcyclohexyl esters of adipic acid.

siphon. A ∩ shaped tube with one short leg which takes up liquid and delivers it, by atmospheric pressure, to a lower level.

sipylite. A negative columbate of erbium and other rare-earth metals.

Sirius. Trade name for a viscose synthetic fiber.

sirup. Syrup.

sisal. S. hemp. A fiber from the leaves of *Agave sisalana*, a cultivated plant of Mexico and E. Africa; used in making rope, twine, and sacking. Cf. *henequen*. **s. wax.** A hard wax from s. waste, m.63, decomp. 95, d.1.007, sapon. val. 55, I. val. 26.

sitostane. $C_{27}H_{46} = 370.4$. An isomer of cholane.

sitosterol. $C_{27}H_{45}OH = 386.4$. An isomer of cholesterol from wheat, corn, bran, and calabar beans; occurs in cigarette smoke. Cf. *cholane*. **beta-** $C_{29}H_{48}O = 412.4$. 22-Dihydrostigmasterol. **dihydro-** $C_{27}H_{48}O.H_2O = 406.37$. m. 140, from wheat, insoluble in water.

six hundred six (606). Salvarsan.

Six hundred sixty-six (666). (1) Trademark for a line of common cold remedies. (2) Trade name for γ-benzene hexachloride, an insecticide.

sizing. The dressing and preparation: (1) of textiles for printing, (2) of surfaces to receive paint, (3) of paper to prevent water or ink absorption due to capillary attraction. **fortified-** Rosin s. whose effect is enhanced by reaction with maleic anhydride, which produces 2 extra carboxyl groups. **tub-** See *tub*.

s. materials. Starch, gums, gelatin, rosin, tragacanth, albumin, casein, and plastics; used to size textiles or paper.

skatole. $C_9H_9N = 131.1$. Methylindole. Colorless leaflets with strong fecal odor, m.95, insoluble in water; a protein decomposition product.

skatoxyl. The radical $C_9H_8ON—$, from skatole.

skelgas. Pentane.

skep. A heat-resistant, Russian, synthetic rubber copolymer of ethylene and propylene.

skiadin viscous. Injection of iodized oil.

skiagenol. A vegetable radiopaque oil (20% iodine).

skiagram, skiagraph. (1) Radiograph. Skiogram. A photograph made by X rays. (2) Scotograph.

skiameter. A device to measure the intensity of X rays preparatory to a photographic exposure.

skimmianine. $C_{32}H_{29}O_9N_3 = 599.3$. An alkaloid from the Japanese plant, *Skimmia japonica* (Rutaceae).

skimming. Removing floating matter from the surface of a liquid.

skimmiol. Taraxerol.

skiogram. Skiagram.

skiver. A sheepskin, split, and tanned with sumach, Cf. *roan*.

sklero- See *sclero*.

skleron. An aluminum alloy containing Li, Cu, Zn, and Mn.

sklodowskite. $MgO.2UO_3.2SiO_2.7H_2O$. A radioactive mineral (Congo). Named for Mme. Curie (née Sklodowska).

skotography. Scotography.

Skraup, Zdenko Hans. 1850–1910. Polish chemist. S. synthesis. Quinoline synthesis. The ring formation, $C_6H_4 \cdot N:CH \cdot CH:CH$, obtained by heating an aromatic amine with a free ortho position (as aniline) with glycerin and concentrated sulfuric acid in presence of an aromatic nitro body (as nitrobenzene).

skullcap. Scutellaria.

skunk. The mammal *Mephitis mephitis;* it has an offensively odorous secretion. **s. bush.** Feverbush. The leaves of *Garrya Fremontii* (Cornaceae). California; a tonic containing garryine. **s. cabbage.** The rhizones of *Symplocarpus foetidus* (Araceae); a stimulant and antispasmodic.

skutterudite. $CoAs_3$. A native arsenide.

slack. (1) Slake. Quench with water. (2) Lumpy and damp, as lime exposed to air. (3) Loose. (4) Slow.

slacken. To mix ores with slag to prevent fusion of the nonmetallic portions.

slag. The vitreous mass which separates from fused metals during the melting of ores. **basic-** Thomas s. A slag of calcium phosphate and free lime, produced in the manufacture of steel by the basic hearth process; a fertilizer. **electro-** A homogeneous ingot produced from a consumable electrode of the material immersed in a pool of molten slag in a water-cooled mold which forms the other electrode. **soda-** q.v. **Thomas-** Basic s. **s. wool.** A fibrous packing material made by pouring molten s. into a pan with steam injection.

Slagceram. Trade name for a strong, chemical-resistant, glassy material produced by heating blast-furnace slag with sand, followed by addition of metal oxides.

slake. To slack or loosen.

slaked lime. Calcium hydroxide.

slashing. The stiffening of warp yarn, before spinning, with a solution containing an oil and starch. It reduces the abrasive action of the shuttle.

slat. A thin, flat piece of solid material.

slate. A dense, fine-textured rock whose mineral constituents are indistinguishable to the unaided eye. It has parallel cleavage planes and breaks into thin plates. Cf. *shale.* **polishing-** Gray or yellow shale, used for polishing.

slide. A plane glass plate. **film-** q.v. **lantern-** 80×80 mm for projection. **microscope-** 25×75 mm for observation. **s. rule.** A ruler with a medical s., and 2 scales graduated logarithmically; used for rapid calculations. *chemical-* A s. rule labeled for rapid chemical calculations.

slime. A fine powder suspension; as, ore crusher mud. **s. molds.** Myxomycetes.

slip. (1) A fluid suspension of clay, fluxing material, and water, used to coat ceramics before final heating to give a glaze; as, zinc oxide and clay. (2) The sliding of atoms over one another in a crystal. **s. direction.** The direction in which crystal slip occurs. **s. plane.** The plane in which crystal slip occurs.

sludge. A soft mud. **activated-** S. produced by bubbling air through sewage, to promote growth of aerobic bacteria; a fertilizer: nitrogen 4–6, phosphorus pentoxide 2.5–4%, dry basis. **Imhoff-** S. produced by the action of anaerobic bacteria; a fertilizer: nitrogen 1.5–2.5, phosphorus pentoxide 1%, dry basis. **s. acid.** The tarry sediment in oil refining tanks; impurities from the oil mixed with the strong sulfuric acid refining agent. **s. acid phosphate.** A superphosphate manufactured with s. acid. **s. gas.** See *gas.*

slug. (1) The mass that acquires an acceleration of 1 ft/sec² under the free weight of 1 lb. (2) A large tablet. **metric-** The mass that acquires an acceleration of 1 meter/sec² under a free weight of 1 kg = 0.45359237 kg.

slugging. The mechanical compression of powders to form oversize tablets, often with a binder; often as a preliminary to granulation. Cf. *spheronizing.*

sluice. A long, inclined trough with baffles for washing gold-bearing earth. **s. box.** A wooden box in which the gold accumulates on washing auriferous gravel.

slum. The insoluble oxidation products deposited from lubricating oil; eliminated by solvent extraction of the oil.

Sm. Symbol for samarium. See *Sa.*

smalls. Slack (of coal).

smalt. A blue glass or pigment of cobalt, potash, and silica.

smaltine. Smaltite.

smaltite. $CoAs_2$. Cobalt pyrites. Smaltine. A native diarsenide. Cf. *bismuthosmaltite.*

smaragd. A green gem variety of beryl.

smartweed. Water pepper.

smectic. Pertaining to liquid crystals of the soap type, having disk-shaped molecules.

smell. See *odors.*

smelt. (1) To obtain metals from their ores by a process that involves (*a*) roasting to remove volatile constituents; (*b*) reduction (smelting proper) in which the fused metals are separated from gangue; (*c*) purification of the metals. (2) The material obtained in (*b*).

smilacin. (1) $C_{18}H_{30}O_6 = 342.3$. Salseparin, pariglin. A glucoside from sarsaparilla. (2) $C_{26}H_{42}O_3 = 402.3$. A solid, decomp. 160.

Smilax. A genus of climbing plants (Liliaceae); as, sarsaparilla and chinaroot.

Smith, Edgar Fahs. 1854–1929. American chemist, noted for his writings and educational methods.

smithite. $AgAsS_2$. A native sulfide.

Smithson, James. 1765–1829. English chemist noted for his bequest for the foundation of the Smithsonian Institution.

Smithsonian Institution. A government establishment in Washington, D.C., created in 1846 according to the will of James Smithson "to increase and diffuse knowledge among men."

smithsonite. $ZnCO_3$. Calamine. A native yellow carbonate.

smog. A toxic haze or fog, resulting from geographical location and temperature inversions that prevent normal diffusion of air pollutants. Principal ingredients: carbon dioxide, carbon monoxide, sulfur dioxide and sulfuric acid, nitrogen oxides, ethylene and other olefins, formaldehyde and acrolein, and soot.

smoke. (1) The dispersed system of solid carbon in air escaping or expelled from a burning substance. (2) A colloidal solid phase suspended in a gaseous phase; also termed sogasoid, from so(lid) gas(eous). **dark-** See *Ringelmann* s. chart. **s. screen.** A s. or fog produced by chemical reaction, to screen objects from observation, e.g., vapors of silicon tetrachloride and ammonia. **s. stone.** Smoky quartz.

smokeless powder. An explosive consisting mainly of nitrocellulose.

smoky quartz. A smoky, gray or brown variety of quartz. **s. topaz.** S. quartz used for jewelry.

Sn. Symbol for tin (stannum).

snake. One of a large class of reptiles. **s. head.** Balmony, turtlebloom. The leaves of *Chelone glabra* (Scrophulariaceae); an anthelmintic, tonic, and detergent. Cf. *chelonin.* **s. lily.** Iris. **s. poison.** S. venom. **s. root.** Snakeroot. **s. venom.** The proteins secreted by certain snakes, which hemolyze the blood. **s. weed.** Bistort.

snakeroot. black- Cimifuga. **Canada-** Asarum. **Seneca-** Senega. **Texas-, Virginia-** Serpentaria.

sniol. Trade name for a polyvinyl chloride synthetic fiber.

snow. A crystalline, finely divided form of water. **carbon dioxide-** Dry Ice. Frozen carbon dioxide obtained by rapid evaporation of liquid carbon dioxide; temperature −110; a refrigerant, sometimes mixed with ether. **nitrous oxide-** The s. formed by the rapid evaporation of liquid nitrous oxide.

Snyder reagent. 4,7-Dihydroxy-1,10-phenanthroline. A reagent for ferrous iron (stable red compound).

soap. A salt of a higher fatty acid with an alkali or metal. Soaps exist in 2 microcrystalline forms, viz., hexagonal plates and curd fibers, and in 3 types of solution, viz., isotropic solutions (including lyes and nigre), and neat and middle soaps, the 2 latter being conic, anisotropic "liquid crystal" forms. **castile-** A s. made from sodium carbonate and olive oil. **essence of-** An alcoholic s. solution, used in pharmacy. **green-** S. liniment. **hard-** An ordinary s., made with soda, giving a poor lather. **invert-** q.v. **marine-** Salt water s. **medicinal-** Sapo mollis. A soft s. that yields not less than 44.0% fatty acids (U.S.P., B.P.). **metallic-** The salts of heavy metals with oleic, stearic, palmitic, erucic, and lauric acids. Used as paint and ink driers (Pb, Co, Mn), and fungicides (Cu, Hg); for decolorizing varnish (Zn, Fe, Ni, Co, Cr), and waterproofing textiles (Al, Mg), and leather. **middle-** A phase sometimes formed in s. boiling at concentrations intermediate between those of neat s. and isotropic solutions. A conic, anisotropic, plastic solution, darker in color than neat s. **neat-** The upper layer in the s. pan; an anisotropic solution (63% fatty acid for sodium, and 40% fatty acid for potassium, soaps). **potash-** A soft s. made with potassium hydroxide. **salt water-** S. containing caproic, caprylic, capric, and myristic acids. not readily precipitated by Ca++ and Mg++ ions; made from coconut oil. **soda-** A hard s. made with sodium hydroxide. **soft-** Potash s. **toilet-** S. containing 70% or more of fatty and resin acids. **transparent-** S. made transparent by adding methyl alcohol. **white curd-** S. made from tallow.

s. bark. Quillaia. **s. liniment.** Green s. A solution of soft s. in 70% alcohol, containing camphor and rosemary oil or lavender oil (U.S.P.). **s. root.** Saponaria. **s. tree.** Quillaia. **s. wort.** Saponaria.

soapstone. Talc.

sobita. Bismuth sodium tartrate.

Sobrero, Ascanio. 1812–1888. Italian discoverer of nitroglycerin (1847). Cf. *Nobel*.

sobrerol. Pinol hydrate.

sobrerone. Pinol.

soda. Sodium carbonate. **baking-** Sodium bicarbonate. **caustic-** Sodium hydroxide (solution). **chlorinated-** Sodium hypochlorite. Sal-sodium carbonate. **scotch-** An impure grade of sodium carbonate. **sesqui-** A molecular mixture of $NaHCO_3$ and Na_2CO_2. **washing-** Sodium carbonate.

s. alum. A double salt of aluminum and sodium sulfates. **s. ash.** Commercial anhydrous sodium carbonate (99% Na_2CO_3). Used widely in industry. World production (1966) 20.5 million tons. **s. feldspar.** Albite. **s. lime.** (1) See *sodium hydroxide with lime*. (2) A mixture of calcium and sodium hydroxides (U.S.P.). **s. mint.** Compound *sodium bicarbonate*. **s. niter.** Native

sodium nitrate. **s. powder.** B-powder. An early blasting powder made from Chile saltpeter glazed with graphite to prevent deliquescence. **s. process.** (1) A method of manufacturing sodium carbonate. See *Le Blanc*. (2) See *soda pulp*. **s. pulp.** Paper pulp obtained by digesting chipped wood with sodium hydroxide at about 7 atm pressure. **s. slag.** A slag obtained in the desulfurization of pig iron: chalcedony 35, sodium oxide 22, sulfur 7 pts.; used in bottle glass melts to oxidize the sulfides. **s. water.** A beverage made by injecting carbon dioxide into a solution of sodium carbonate Cf. aerated *waters*.

sodalite. $Na_4Al_3Si_3O_{12}Cl$. A silicate that contains salt.

sodamide. Sodium amide.

Soddy, Frederick. 1877–1956. British chemist, Nobel Prize winner (1921); noted for his researches on radioactive elements.

sodic. Containing sodium (obsolete).

sodii. Official Latin for "of sodium."

sodiomalonic. Sodium malonic.

sodion. Sodium ion: Na+.

sodium. Na = 22.990. Natrium. An alkali-metal element, at. no. 11. A tetragonal, crystalline, soft metal, silvery white when freshly cut; rapidly dulling in air; stored under coal oil. Becomes brittle at low temperature, d_{15}0.9732, m.97, b.880, decomp. by water, insoluble in alcohol or ether. Isolated by Davy (1807). Used as a dehydrating agent, flux, reactor coolant, reducing agent, conductor in cables; and in organic synthesis. **radio-** The isotope of mass 24, half-life 15.5 hours, formed from s. by bombardment with deuterons; decomposes to magnesium with emission of β rays (electrons).

s. abietate. $C_{20}H_{29}O_2Na(?)$. The s. salt of abietic acid, produced when rosin is saponified for use as a size for paper. See *colophony*. **s. abietinate.** S. sylvate. **s. acetate.** $CH_3COONa = 82.0$. Colorless, monoclinic crystals, m.58, soluble in water. Used as a mordant, reagent for alkaloids; for filling thermophores; and in photography, and the manufacture of acetic acid, acetic ether, and pigments. *hydrated-* $NaC_2H_3O_2·3H_2O = 136.07$.d Colorless, monoclinic crystals, m.58, soluble in water. **s. acetotungstate.** $Na_2(CH_3CO)WO_4 = 337.0$. S. acetwolframate. White crystals, soluble in water; a microscope reagent. **s. acetrizoate.** $C_9H_5NI_3NaNO_5$. A radiopaque, used as the injection (U.S.P., B.P.). **s. acetsulfanilate.** C_6H_4·$(SO_3Na)·NH·COMe = 223.0$. Cosaprin. Green crystals, soluble in water. **s. acetwolframate.** S. acetotungstate. **s. acetyl arsanilate.** $NaAsO_2$·$C_6H_4·NHCOCH_3 = 264.1$. Yellow crystals. **s. acetyl salicylate.** $C_2H_3O·OC_6H_4COONa = 202.06$. Hydropirin, Pyranol; used medicinally. **s. agaricinate.** Colorless powder, soluble in water; used medicinally. **s. alginate.** The sodium salt of alginic acid-; a protective colloid for pharmaceuticals and cosmetics. **s. alizarin sulfonate.** NaC_{14}·$H_5O_2(OH)_2SO_3 = 342.1$. Alizarin carmine. Orange powder, soluble in water; a dye, and indicator for strong acids (yellow) and strong alkalies (violet), except carbonates. **s. alum.** Aluminum s. sulfate. **s. aluminate.** $Na_2Al_2O_4 = 164.2$. Colorless powder, m.1850, soluble in water. **s. aluminum chloride.** $2NaCl,AlCl_3 = 383.7$. Colorless deliquescent solid, m.185. **s. amalgam.** A mercury amalgam (2–10% Na); a reducing agent. **s. amide.** NaNH$_2$ = 39.03. Sodamide. Colorless crystals, m.208, decomp. by water. Used similarly to s., but forms explosive products when exposed to air. **s. aminohippurate.** C$_9$H$_9$N$_2$O$_3$Na = 216.21. A diagnostic aid used as an aqueous injection (U.S.P.). **s. aminosalicylate.** C$_7$H$_6$O$_3$NNa·2H$_2$O = 211.16. Cream crystals, with sweet, saline taste, soluble in water (slow decomp.); a tuberculostatic antibacterial (U.S.P., B.P.). **s. aminosuccinate.** S. asparaginate. **s. ammonium acid phosphate.** S. ammonium phosphate. **s. ammonium phosphate.** NaNH$_4$HPO$_4$·4H$_2$O = 209.15. Microcosmic salt, triphosphate, acid ammonium phosphate. Colorless crystals, decomp. by heat, soluble in water; an analytical reagent; forms a molten bead which is colored characteristically by impurities. **s. ammonium sulfate.** NaNH$_4$SO$_4$ = 137.1. Colorless crystals, soluble in water. **s. amyl sulfate.** C$_6$H$_{11}$SO$_4$Na = 202.2. Colorless crystals, soluble in water. **s. amyl xanthogenate.** Me$_2$CH·CH$_2$·CH$_2$·O·CS$_2$Na = 186.1. Yellow crystals, soluble in water, a bactericide and insecticide. **s. amytal.** Isoamyl ethyl barbiturate. White powder, soluble in water; a basal hypnotic. **s. anhydromethylene citrate.** Citarin. **s. aniline sulfonate.** S. sulfanilate. **s. anisate.** C$_6$H$_4$(OMe)-COONa = 174.1. White crystals, soluble in water, an antipyretic and antirheumatic. **s. anoxynaphthonate.** C$_{26}$H$_{16}$O(SO$_3$Na)$_3$ = 695.58. Blue, hygroscopic powder; a dye used to investigate cardiac disease (B.P.). **s. anthranilate.** NH$_2$·C$_6$H$_4$·COONa = 159.1. Sodium orthoaminobenzoate. Gray powder, soluble in water; an antiseptic. **s. anthrarobinate.** Brown powder, soluble in water; an antiseptic. **s. antimonate.** 2NaSbO$_3$·7H$_2$O = 508.5. Colorless crystals, slightly soluble in water. *pyro-* See *s. pyroantimonate.* **s. antimonyl gluconate.** White powder (33.0–38.0% Sb), prepared by the action of alkali on antimony trichloride and gluconic acid, soluble in water; used to treat schistosomiasis (B.P.). **s. antimony tartrate.** Na(SbO)C$_4$H$_4$O$_6$. Plimmer's salt. Colorless, transparent crystals, soluble in water. **s. argentocyanide.** NaAg(CN)$_2$ = 182.90. S. silver cyanide. Yellow, soluble solid produced in the cyanide process for silver extraction. **s. arsanilate.** Na(AsO$_2$)C$_6$H$_4$NH$_2$ = 222.2. Colorless crystals, soluble in water. **s. arsenates.** *acid-* (1) Na$_2$-HAsO$_4$·12H$_2$O = 402.2. Dodecahydrate. Colorless, rhombic crystals, m.28, soluble in water. (2) Na$_2$HAsO$_4$·7H$_2$O = 312.2. Heptahydrate. Colorless prisms, m.57, soluble in water; a reagent, tonic, and antiseptic. (3) Na$_2$HAsO$_4$ = 186.0. Anhydrous. White powder, soluble in water; used in dyeing and printing textiles. *normal-* Na$_3$AsO$_4$·12H$_2$O = 424.2. Colorless crystals, m.85, soluble in water; a reagent. **s. arsenide.** Na$_3$As = 143.96. Black solid, evolves arsine in presence of water. **s. arsenite.** *ortho-* Na$_2$HAsO$_3$ = 170.0; *meta-* NaAsO$_2$ = 129.9. Gray powder, soluble in water; an antiseptic and parisiticide. **s. arsphenamine.** The s. salt of Salvarsan. **s. ascorbate.** C$_6$H$_7$O$_6$Na = 198.11. White crystals, soluble in water; an antiscorbutic vitamin (U.S.P.). **s. asparaginate.** HOOC·CH$_2$·CHNH$_2$·COONa = 155.1. S. aminosuccinate. Colorless needles, soluble in water. **s.**

auribromide. Gold s. bromide. **s. aurichloride.** Gold s. chloride. **s. aurosulfide.** NaAuS·4H$_2$O = 324.33. Colorless crystals. **s. aurothiomalate.** Yellow hygroscopic powder (44.5–46.0% Au) prepared by the action of gold iodide on s. thiomalate. Soluble in water; used to treat rheumatoid arthritis (B.P.). **s. azide.** NaN$_3$ = 65.1. A poisonous crystalline salt used to make explosives. **s. azo-α-naphthol sulfanilate.** Tropeolin. **s. barbitone.** Barbital s. **s. benzene sulfonate.** NaC$_6$H$_5$SO$_3$ = 180.1. S. sulfobenzene. Colorless crystals, soluble in water. **s. benzoate.** NaC$_7$H$_5$O$_2$ = 144.11. White crystals, soluble in water; an antiseptic and antipyretic (U.S.P., B.P.). **s. benzosulfinide.** NaC$_7$H$_4$O$_3$NS·2H$_2$O = 241.2. Soluble gluside, soluble saccharin. S. benzoyl sulfonate. Colorless crystals, soluble in water; an intestinal antiseptic. **s. benzosulfite.** Colorless crystals; antiseptic. **s. benzoyl sulfonate.** S. benzosulfinide. **s. biborate.** S. borate. **s. bicarbonate.** NaHCO$_3$ = 84.01. S. hydrogen carbonate, acid s. carbonate, baking soda. White powder, d.2.206, decomp. 270, soluble in water, insoluble in alcohol. Used as an antacid (U.S.P., B.P.) and reagent; in baking powders and pharmaceutically in effervescent mixtures; and to make volumetric solutions. *compound-* Soda mint. S. bicarbonate tablets containing peppermint oil; a flavoring (B.P.). **s. bichromate.** S. dichromate. **s. bifluoride.** NaF·HF = 62.0. Colorless crystals, soluble in water; used as an antiseptic, in ant powders, and for etching glass. **s. bilactate.** NaH(C$_3$H$_5$O$_3$)$_2$ = 202.1. Colorless liquid, soluble in water. **s. binoxalate.** NaHC$_2$O$_4$ = 112.0. Colorless, monoclinic crystals, soluble in water; a stain remover. **s. biphosphate.** See *s. phosphates.* **s. bipyrophosphate** (U.S.P.). See *s. pyrophosphate.* **s. bismuthate.** NaBiO$_3$ = 280.0. Fawn powder, used in manganese determinations. **s. bismuth thiosulfate.** Na$_3$Bi(S$_2$O$_3$)$_3$ = 614.42. Colorless crystals. **s. bisulfate.** NaHSO$_4$·H$_2$O = 138.1. Colorless crystals, m.300, soluble in water; a reagent, flux, and antiseptic. **s. bisulfite.** NaHSO$_3$ = 104.07. White crystals, soluble in water; a pharmaceutical (U.S.P.), reagent, disinfectant, bleach, and preservative. **s. bitartrate.** NaHC$_4$H$_4$O$_6$·H$_2$O = 190.08. Colorless crystals, soluble in water. Used as a reagent and in effervescent mixtures. **s. borates.** (1) *S. metaborate.* Na$_2$BO$_2$ = 66.0. Colorless prisms, m.966, soluble in water. (a) *tetrahydrate-* Na$_2$B$_2$O$_4$·4H$_2$O = 203.6. Colorless prisms, m.57, soluble in water; an antiseptic. (2) *S. tetraborate.* (a) *calcined-* Na$_2$B$_4$O$_7$·10H$_2$O = 381.42. Borax. White powder, soluble in water; a reagent. (b) *fused-* Na$_2$B$_4$O$_7$ = 202.0. Borax glass, anhydrous borax. Colorless, vitreous mass, m.741, slightly soluble in water, soluble in alcohol; used as a reagent and antacid and in ointments (U.S.P.). (c) *pentahydrate-* Na$_2$B$_4$O$_7$·5H$_2$O = 292.1. Colorless octahedra, slightly soluble in water or alcohol; a reagent. (d) *decahydrate-* Na$_2$B$_4$O$_7$·10H$_2$O = 382.2. Borax, sodii boras (U.S.P.), s. biborate, s. pyroborate. Colorless, monoclinic crystals, d$_{17}$1.72, m. red heat, slightly soluble in water, insoluble in alcohol; used as a reagent, flux, and preservative; and for borax beads. **s. borosalicylate.** Borsalyl, a reaction product of salicylic acid and sodium borate.

White powder, soluble in water; an antiseptic. **s. bromate.** $NaBrO_3 = 150.9$. Colorless crystals, m.384, soluble in water; an oxidizing agent. **s bromides.** (1) $NaBr = 102.91$. Colorless cubes, m.768, soluble in water; a reagent, alterative, and diuretic (U.S.P., B.P.). (2) $NaBr \cdot 2H_2O = 138.95$. Colorless, monoclinic crystals, soluble in water. **s. butyl sulfate.** $NaSO_4C_4H_9 = 176.1$. Colorless crystals, soluble in water. **s. butyrate.** C_3H_7-$COONa = 110.06$. Colorless, deliquescent crystals, soluble in water. **s. cacodylate.** $NaAsO_2$-$(CH_3)_2 = 160.02$ and $NaAsO_2Me_2 \cdot 3H_2O = 214.17$. White powder, soluble in water; a hematinic. **s. caffeine sulfonate.** Symphorol N. **s. calciumedetate.** The calcium chelate of the disodium salt of ethylenediaminetetracetic acid; used to treat lead poisoning (B.P.). Cf. *EDTA*. **s. camphorate.** $Na_2C_{10}H_{14}O_4 = 244.2$. White, deliquescent powder, soluble in water; an antiseptic. **s. cantharidate.** $Na_2C_{10}H_{14}O_6 \cdot 2H_2O = 312.2$. The s. salt of cantharides camphor, the active principle of *Cantharis vesicatoria*. White crystals, soluble in water; a tonic. **s. carbide.** $Na_2C = 58.0$. Gray powder, decomp. by water. **s. carbolate.** S. phenate. **s. carbonate.** Soda, washing soda. Cf. *Solvay process, ammonia soda process*. (1) *anhydrous*. $Na_2CO_3 = 106.0$. White powder, d.2.476, m.852 (decomp.), soluble in water; used as a reagent and in freezing mixtures. Cf. *sesquisoda, soda ash*. (2) *monohydrate*- $Na_2CO_3 \cdot H_2O = 124.0$. White crystals, soluble in water; an antacid (U.S.P.), reagent, and photographic chemical. (3) *decahydrate*- $Na_2CO_3 \cdot 10H_2O = 286.2$. Colorless, monoclinic crystals, d.1.458, m.34, soluble in water; a reagent, precipitant, neutralizer, and antacid. See *soda ash*. (4) $Na_2CO_3 \cdot 1\frac{1}{2}H_2O_2 = 157.01$. Formerly regarded as a peroxide. **s. carboxymethylcellulose.** S. cellulose glycolate, cellulose gum. White, odorless, bulky, tasteless solid made by the action of chloroacetic acid and alkali on sulfite wood pulp; used as a thickener, emulsifier, and stabilizer in pharmacy (U.S.P.); and in adhesives, paper manufacture, cosmetics, and confectionery. **s. carminate.** $Na_2C_{11}H_{10}O_6 = 284.1$. A red dye in microscopy. **s. cellulose glycolate.** S. carboxymethylcellulose. **s. chlorate.** $NaClO_3 = 106.5$. Colorless cubes or tetragons, m.250 (decomp.), soluble in water; a reagent, explosive (in pyrotechnics), and antiseptic. **s. chloride.** $NaCl = 58.5$. Table salt, common salt, rock salt, sea salt. colorless cubes, d.2.176, m.800, soluble in water, insoluble in alcohol. Used as a reagent and condiment; for freezing mixtures and producing chlorine; and widely in industry. The principal constituent, sometimes with dextrose (B.P.), of physiological salt solutions (U.S.P.). **s. chlorite.** $NaClO_2 = 90.5$. Colorless crystals, soluble in water; an oxidizing agent. **s. p-chlorobenzoate.** Mikrobin. **s. chloroplatinate.** S. platinichloride. **s. chloroplatinite.** S. platinochloride. **s. chlorosulfonate.** $NaClSO_3 = 138.7$. Fine crystals, readily hydrolyzed to hydrochloric acid; a reagent for sulfonation and chlorination. **s. cholate.** Bile salts. **s. chromate.** $Na_2CrO_4 \cdot 10H_2O = 342.2$. Yellow, triclinic crystals, m.20, soluble in water; a reagent and mordant. *Cr*-51. A sterile injection of radioactive s. chromate made from Cr^{51}, q.v. (B.P.). **s. chromite.** $Na_2CrO_3 = 146.1$. Green needles,

soluble in water. **s. cinnamate.** $NaC_9H_7O_2 = 170.1$. Hetol. White crystals, soluble in water. **s. citrate.** $C_6H_5O_7Na_3 \cdot 2H_2O = 294.11$. Sodii citras (U.S.P.). Colorless crystals, m.150, soluble in water; a reagent, antipyretic, refrigerant; and, with dextrose, a blood coagulant (U.S.P., B.P.). *s. acid citrate.* $C_6H_6O_7Na_2 \cdot 1 \cdot 5H_2O = 263.12$. White powder, soluble in water; a blood anticoagulant (B.P.). **s. cobaltic nitrite, s. cobaltinitrite.** $Na_3Co(NO_2)_6 \cdot \frac{1}{2}H_2O = 413.0$. Purple, hygroscopic crystals, soluble in water; reagent for potassium. **s. coerulin sulfate.** Indigo carmine. **s. colismethate.** $C_{49}H_{89}O_{23}N_{13}S_4Na_4 = 1432.55$. White powder, soluble in water; an antibacterial (U.S.P.). **s. copaivate.** $C_{20}H_{29}O_2Na = 324.24$. Yellow powder, soluble in water; an antiseptic. **s. corallinate.** Sodium rosolate. **s. cyanamide.** $Na_2NCN = 86.02$. **s. cyanaurite.** Aurous s. cyanide. **s. cyanide.** $NaCn = 49.01$. White, deliquescent crystals, soluble in water. Used as a reagent, parasiticide, and antiseptic; and in electroplating, case hardening, flotation, metal extraction (cyanide process), fumigation, and rubber accelerators. **s. cyclamate.** $C_6H_{12}O_3NSNa = 201.22$. White, sweet crystals, soluble in water; a sweeting agent (B.P.). **s. diatrizoate.** $C_{11}H_8O_4$-$N_2I_3Na \cdot 4H_2O = 708.00$. S. 3,5-diacetamido-2,4,-6-triiodobenzoate hydrate. White, saline powder, soluble in water; a radiopaque (B.P.). **s. dichromate.** $Na_2Cr_2O_7 \cdot 2H_2O = 298.0$. S. bichromate. Red, triclinic crystals, m. 320, soluble in water; an oxidizing agent and antiseptic. **s. diethyl barbiturate.** $NaC_8H_{11}O_3N_2 = 206.1$. Barbitalsodium. White crystals, soluble in water; a hypnotic. **s. diethyl dithiocarbamate.** $Et_2N \cdot CS \cdot SNa = 171.2$. Sensitive reagent for copper (brown color). **s. dihydrogen phosphate.** See *S. phosphates, monobasic.* **s. dimethylaminoazobenzene sulfonate.** Methyl orange. **s. dinitrocresolate.** Antinonnin. **s. dioxide.** S. peroxide. **s. diphenylhydantoin.** $C_{15}H_{11}O_2N_2Na = 274.26$. Hygroscopic, white powder soluble in water; an anticonvulsant (U.S.P.). **s. disulfate.** S. pyrosulfate. **s. dithionate.** S. hyposulfate. **s. dithiosalicylate.** Dithion. **s. divanadate.** $Na_2V_4O_{11} \cdot 9H_2O = 589.0$. S. tetravanadate. Orange crystals, slightly soluble in water; used in the manufacture of dyes and inks. **s. ethoxide.** S. ethylate. **s. ethylate.** $NaC_2H_5O = 68.0$. S. ethoxide. White hygroscopic powder; a reagent and escharotic. **s. ethylmercurithiosalicylate.** $C_9H_9O_2SHgNa = 404.81$. MTS. White crystals, m. approx. 230, soluble in water and lower alcohols, insoluble in liquid solvents; used to preserve plasma and to protect articles (especially optical instruments) against tropical conditions. **s. ethyl sulfate.** $NaC_2H_5SO_4 = 148.11$. S. sulfovinate. Colorless, deliquescent, crystals, soluble in water. **s. ferricyanide.** $Na_3Fe(CN)_6 \cdot H_2O = 298.93$. Red prussiate of soda. Red, hygroscopic crystals, soluble in water; used as a reagent, and in the manufacture of pigments and ferro-photobase paper. **ferric oxalate.** $2Na_3Fe(C_2O_4)_3 \cdot 10H_2O = 957.82$. Green, monoclinic crystals, dehydrated at 100 ($4H_2O$) and 200°C ($10H_2O$); soluble in water. **s. ferrite.** $Na_2Fe_2O_4 = 221.7$. Decomp. by water. **s. ferrocyanide.** $Na_4Fe(CN)_6 \cdot 12H_2O = 520.18$. Yellow prussiate of soda. Yellow prisms, soluble in water; used as a reagent in photography, and in pigment manufacture. **s. fluobenzoate.** C_6H_4-FCOONa = 162.0. White crystals, soluble in water; an antiseptic. **s. fluorescein.** Uranin. **s. fluoride.** NaF = 41.99. Colorless cubes, m.982, soluble in water; a reagent for blood, an antiferment in brewing, an antiseptic and dental prophylactic (U.S.P., B.P.). **s. fluosilicate.** Na_2SiF_6 = 188.05. S. silicofluoride, salufer. White crystals, slightly soluble in water, a by-product of superphosphate manufacture; a reagent, antiseptic, insecticide, and enameling and laundry chemical. **s. formaldehyde sulfoxylate.** $NaHSO_2 \cdot HCHO \cdot 2H_2O$. A reducing agent in dyeing. **s. formate.** $NaCHO_2$ = 68.0 or HCOONa. Colorless rhombs, decomp. by heat, soluble in water; an antiseptic, and reagent for arsenic and phosphorus. **s. fusidate.** $C_{31}H_{47}O_6$-$Na \cdot \frac{1}{2}H_2O$ = 547.70. The s. salt of fusidic acid; an antibiotic from *Fusidium coccineum* (B.P.). **s. germanate.** Na_2GeO_3 = 166.0. Colorless crystals, soluble in water, a hematinic. **s. glycerino-phosphate, s. glycerophosphate.** $Na_2C_3H_7PO_6$-xH_2O. Yellow, viscid liquid, soluble in water; a tonic, hematinic, and reagent for phosphatase. **s. gynocardate.** $NaC_{14}H_{23}O_2$ = 246.0. Yellow powder, soluble in water; an antiseptic. **s. halides.** The sodium salts of the halogen acids. **s. hydrate.** S. hydroxide. **s. hydride.** NaH = 24.01. Colorless crystals, decomp. by water or heat. **s. hydrogen carbonate.** S. bicarbonate. **s. hydrogen oxide.** S. hydroxide. **s. hydrogen peroxide.** (1) Sodyl hydroxide. (2) $2NaOH \cdot H_2O_2$ = 148.04. A white solid. **s. hydrogen phosphate.** See *s. phosphates.* **s. hydrogen phosphite.** See *s. phosphites.* **s. hydrogen sulfate.** S. bisulfate. **s. hydrogen sulfide.** S. hydrosulfide. **s. hydropyroantimonate.** S. metantimonate. **s. hydrosulfate.** S. sulfhydrate. **s. hydrosulfide.** $NaHS.2H_2O$ = 92.10. S. hydrogen sulfide. Deliquescent, colorless crystals, decomp. by heat. **s. hydrosulfite.** $Na_2S_2O_4 \cdot 2H_2O$ = 210.1. S. dithionate. Colorless crystals, decomp. red heat, soluble in water. **s. hydroxide.** NaOH = 40.01. S. hydrate, soda, caustic soda, sodii hydroxidum (U.S.P.). White, hygroscopic powder, or white flakes, plates, pellets, or sticks, d.2.13, m.318; very soluble in water, alcohol, or ether. Used extensively in chemistry, the chemical industry, metallurgy, photography, and in glycerin suppositories (U.S.P., B.P.). Commercial grades of purity: (1) reagent from sodium (for special analytical work; (2) reagent from alcohol (for general analytical work; (3) reagent, purified (for general chemical work); (4) for pharmaceutical work; (5) technical (fused or in flakes for industrial purposes). *s. hydroxide solution.* Commercial grades: 31%, d.1.34; 27%, d.1.30; 15%, d.1.17; 5%, d.1.06. *s. hydroxide with lime.* Soda lime. A mixture of s. hydroxide and calcium oxide. White granules, or porous mass; a reagent, and general absorbent for acid gases (U.S.P., B.P.). **s. hydroxylamine sulfonates.** *mono*-HO·NH(SO₃Na) = 135.40. *di*- HO·N·(SO₃Na)₂ = 237.16. **s. hypobromite.** NaOBr = 119.0. Colorless powder, soluble in water; an oxidizing agent. **s. hypochlorite.** NaOCl = 74.5. Colorless powder, decomp. by heat, soluble in water, decomp. by ether; an oxidizing and bleaching agent. Cf. *eau de javelle.* **s. hyponitrite.** $Na_2N_2O_2$ = 106.0 Colorless crystals, soluble in water. **s. hypophosphite.**

$NaH_2PO_2 \cdot H_2O$ = 106.1. Colorless, deliquescent prisms or white granules, soluble in water; a reagent in gas analysis, and a tonic. **s. hyposulfate.** (1) $Na_2S_2O_6 \cdot 2H_2O$ = 242.1 Transparent prisms, soluble in water. (2) S. thiosulfate. **s. hyposulfite.** (1) $Na_2S_2O_4$ = 174.1. S. hydrosulfite. Colorless crystals, soluble in water; used to recover silver from photographic waste. (2) S. thiosulfate. (3) S.bisulfite. **s. indigotin sulfonate.** Indigo carmine. **s. iodate.** $NaIO_3$ (+ $5H_2O$) = 197.9. White powder, decomp. by heat, soluble in water; a reagent. **s. iodide.** NaI = 149.9. Colorless cubes, m.664, soluble in water; a reagent, and alterant used in iodine tinctures (U.S.P., B.P.). *dihydrate.* $NaI \cdot 2H_2O$= 185.9. Colorless crystals, soluble in water. Cf. *s. radioiodide.* **s. iodipamide.** $C_{20}H_{12}O_6N_2I_6Na_2$ = 1183.73. A radiopaque medium, used as an aqueous injection (U.S.P.). **s. iodoeosin.** Erythrosin. **s. iodohippurate I-131.** A diagnostic aid containing radioactive I¹³¹ (U.S.P.). **s. iodomethamate.** $C_8H_3O_5NNa_2I_2$ = 492.92. White powder, soluble in water; a radiopaque (U.S.P.). **s. iodotheobromate.** Theobromine s. iodide. **s. ion.** The cation Na⁺. **s. iothalamate.** $C_{11}H_8O_4N_2I_3Na$ = 635.90. A radiopaque medium, used as an aqueous injection (U.S.P., B.P.). **s. iridichloride.** Iridium s. chloride. **s. iron pyrophosphate.** $Na_8Fe_2(P_2O_7)_3$ = 818.4. A catalyst in carbohydrate oxidation. **s. lacate.** $NaC_3H_5O_3$ = 112.06. A thick syrup, soluble in water; an electrolyte replenisher (U.S.P., B.P.), sometimes compounded with Ringer's solution (B.P.). **s. lauryl sulfate.** $NaC_{12}H_{25}SO_4$ = 288.3. Irium. White powder; a detergent, and emulsifier in pharmacy (U.S.P., B.P.) and toiletries. **s. lorinate.** Griserin. Yellow powder, soluble in water; used medicinally. **s. lygosinate.** The s. salt of diorthocumare ketone. See *lygosin.* **s. magnesium tartrate.** $Na_2Mg(C_4H_4O_6)_2 \cdot 10H_2O$ = 546.53. White powder, soluble in water. **s. malonic ester.** EtO(NaO)C:CH.COOEt = 182.1. Sodiomalonic ester. White needles. Formed, but not usually isolated, in the malonic ester synthesis. **s. manganate.** $Na_2MnO_4 \cdot 10H_2O$ = 345.1. Green, monoclinic crystals, decomp. by heat, soluble in water. **s. metabisulfite.** $Na_2S_2O_5$ = 190.14. White crystals, soluble in water; used in photography, and as an antioxidant (B.P.). **s. metaborate.** See *s. borates.* **s. metantimonate.** $Na_2H_2Sb_2O_5$ = 400.0. S. hydropyroantimonate. White granules, soluble in hot water. **s. metaphosphate.** $NaPO_3$ = 101.98. Two crystalline forms; one soluble in water (s. trimetaphosphate), the other insoluble. Melting either and quickly cooling gives a water-soluble glass (Graham's salt). **s. metasilicate.** See *s. silicates.* **s. metastannate.** $Na_2Sn_5O_{11} \cdot 4H_2O$ = 887.6. Crystals, insoluble in alcohol. **s. metavanadate.** $NaVO_3$ = 122.2. Green crystals, soluble in hot water; a reagent. **s. methicillin.** $C_{17}H_{19}O_6N_2SNa \cdot H_2O$ = 420.42. White crystals, soluble in water; an antibacterial (U.S.P.). **s. methyl arsenate.** See *methyl.* **s. methyl arsenite.** $Na_2CH_3AsO_3$ = 184.0. Disodium methyl arsonate, monomethyl disodium arsenate, arrhenal, arsynal, neoarsycodyl, stenosine. Colorless crystals, m.135, soluble in water; a cacodylate substitute. **s. methylate.** $NaCH_3O$ = 54.0. MeONa. White powder, decomp. by water.

s. molybdate. $Na_2MoO_4 \cdot 2H_2O = 242.0$. Colorless leaflets with pearly luster, soluble in water; a reagent. **s. monosulfide.** S. sulfide. **s. monoxide.** Na_2O. S. oxide. **s. morrhuate.** The sodium salt of a fraction of the fatty acids of cod-liver oil having a high iodine content; used to treat varicose veins (U.S.P.). **s. naphthionate.** S. naphthylamine sulfonate. **s. naphthol sulfonate.** $NaC_{10}H_7SO_4 = 246.1$. S. β-naphthol α-sulfonate. White tablets, soluble in water. **s. naphthoquinone sulfonate.** White powder; a reagent for nitrogen in amino acids. **s. naphthylamine sulfonate.** $NaC_{10}H_6 \cdot NH_2SO_4 = 261.1$. S. naphthionate. Colorless prisms, soluble in water; reagent for nitrous acid. **s. nipagin-M.** Soluble methylhydroxybenzoate. **s. nipagol-M.** Soluble propylhydroxybenzoate. **s. nitranilate.** $C_6(NO_2)_2O_2 \cdot (ONa)_2 = 274.02$. S. dinitrodioxyquinonate. Brown powder, soluble in water. **s. nitrate.** $NaNO_3 = 85.01$. Saliter. Soda niter, cubic niter, caliche, Chile saltpeter. Colorless rhombohedra, m.312, soluble in water. Used as a flux in metallurgy, an oxidant; in the manufacture of acids, fertilizers, explosives, and glass; and medicinally. **s. nitride.** $Na_3N = 83.01$. An unstable, explosive compound formed by passing an electric arc between a platinum cathode and a sodium anode in liquid nitrogen. **s. nitrite.** $NaNO_2 = 69.01$. Pale yellow crystals or yellow sticks, d2.167, m.271, soluble in water; a reagent in the manufacture of azo dyes and synthetics; a seasickness remedy, diuretic, and diaphoretic (U.S.P.). Cf. *mystin.* **s. 5-nitro-6-chlorotoluene-3-solfonate.** White powder; reagent for potassium. **s. nitroferricyanide.** $Na_2Fe(CN)_5NO \cdot 2H_2O = 297.8$. S. nitroprusside. Red, transparent crystals, soluble in water; reagent for alkali sulfides, acetone, formaldehyde, amino acids, and alkaloids. **s. nitroprussiate.** S. nitroferricyanide. **s. nitroprusside.** S. nitroferricyanide. **s. nitrosohydroxylamine sulfonate.** $ON \cdot N(ONa)SO_3Na = 186.09$. **s. nucleate.** S. nucleinate. **s. nucleinate.** S. nucleate. The s. salt of yeast nucleic acids. Gray powder, soluble in water; a tonic and antisyphilitic. **s. oenanthate.** $Me(CH_2)_5COONa = 152.1$. S. salt of n-heptylic acid. White crystals, soluble in water. **s. oleate.** $NaC_{18}H_{32}O_3 = 304.3$. Yellow, unctuous granules, soluble in water. **s. orthoaminobenzoate.** S. anthranilate. **s. orthovanadate.** See s. vanadate. **s. oxacillin.** $C_{19}H_{18}O_5N_3 \cdot SNa \cdot H_2O = 441.44$. White crystals, soluble in water; an antibacterial (U.S.P.). **s. oxalate.** $Na_2C_2O_4 = 134.0$. White crystals, soluble in water; a reagent, and stain remover. *acid*-$NaOOC \cdot COOH \cdot H_2O = 130.02$. Colorless, monoclinic crystals, soluble in water. **s. oxide.** $Na_2O = 62.0$. S. monoxide. Gray mass, sublimes and m. at red heat, decomp. by water (to s. hydroxide); a reagent and strong base. **s. paraperiodate.** $Na_3H_2IO_6 = 293.9$. An oxidizing agent. **s. pentasulfide.** See s. sulfides. **s. pentobarbital.** White powder, used to treat seasickness. **s. pentoxydichloride.** $Cl \cdot SO_2O \cdot SO_2Cl = 215.4$. Straw-colored liquid, b.150, slightly soluble in cold water, reacts violently with warm water. **s. perborate.** $NaBO_2 \cdot H_2O_2 \cdot 3H_2O = 154.1$. Peroxydol. White crystals, soluble in water. Used as reagent, oxidizing agent, antiseptic, deodorant, bleach; and

in dentifrices and detergents. **s. percarbonates.** (1) *normal*- $Na_2C_2O_6 = 166.00$. (2) *mono*- $Na_2CO_4 = 122.00$. Used in detergents, dentistry, photography, and for bleaching. **s. perchlorate.** $NaClO_4 = 122.5$. Colorless rhombohedra, m.482 (decomp.), soluble in water: a reagent and explosive. **s. periodate.** $NaIO_4 \cdot 3H_2O = 267.9$. Efflorescent hemihedra, dehydrated at 300. **s. permanganate.** $NaMnO_4 \cdot 3H_2O = 194.98$. Purple crystals, decomp. by heat, soluble in water; an oxidizing agent, and antidote to snakebites, morphine, and curare. **s. peroxide.** $Na_2O_2 = 78.0$. S. dioxide, s. superoxide. Pale yellow powder, d.2.805, decomp. by heat, in water produces heat, s. hydroxide, and hydrogen peroxide. Used as a flux for minerals; in bleaching and the preparation of calcium peroxide, s. perborate, and ferrate; and to oxidize organic matter in analysis. *Use with caution!* (it can ignite organic matter). **s. persulfate.** $Na_2S_2O_8 = 238.0$. White crystals, soluble in water; an antiseptic, bleaching agent, aperient; and reagent for indican and adrenaline. **s. phenate.** $NaC_6H_5O = 116.0$. S. carbolate. Colorless, hygroscopic powder; an antiseptic. **s. phenolphthaleinate.** $Na_2C_{20}H_{12}O_4 = 362.1$. Red syrup, soluble in water. **s. phenol sulfonate.** $C_6H_4(OH)SO_3Na = 196.1$. S. sulfocarbolate. Colorless crystals, soluble in water; an antiseptic and disinfectant. **s. phenyl ethyl barbiturate.** Luminal sodium, phenobarbital s. White, hygroscopic powder, m.147; a hypnotic. Pr·$C_6H_4 \cdot ONa = 192.1$. White powder; a glue preservative. Cf. *phenylphenol.* **s. phosphates.** *monobasic*-$NaH_2PO_4 \cdot H_2O = 138.1$. Monosodium orthophosphate, dihydrogen s. phosphate, s. biphosphate. Transparent rhombs, soluble in water; used (as $NaH_2PO_4 \cdot 2H_2O$) as a purgative (B.P.). *dibasic*-, *anhydrous*- $Na_2HPO_4 = 142.0$. Sörensen's s. phosphate, disodium orthophosphate. White, hygroscopic powder; a reagent and buffer. *dibasic*-, *hydrous*- $Na_2HPO_4 \cdot 12H_2O = 358.2$. Disodium orthophosphate, monohydrogen s. phosphate. Transparent rhombs, m.35, soluble in water; a reagent. *tribasic*- $Na_3PO_4 \cdot 12H_2O = 380.2$. S. orthophosphate. Colorless hexagons, m.77, soluble in water. *metaphosphate*- $NaPO_3 = 101.98$. Insoluble form, colorless crystals; soluble form, colorless crystals; m.627 (glass obtained by quenching melt). Cf. *s. metaphosphate. pyrophosphate*- $Na_4P_2O_7 \cdot 10H_2O = 446.24$. Colorless, monoclinic crystals, m.988, soluble in water; a reagent. *tetraphosphate*- $Na_6P_4O_{13} = 470.16$. Cf. *s. radiophosphate.* **s. phosphide.** $Na_3P = 100.04$. Red solid, evolves phosphine with water, decomp. by heat. **s. phosphites.** Na_3PO_3, Na_2HPO_3, NaH_2PO_3. $Na_2HPO_3 \cdot 5H_2O = 216.2$. Colorless rhombohedra, m.53, soluble water. **s. phosphomolybdate.** $Na_3PO_4 \cdot 10MoO_4 = 1764.0$. S. molybdophosphate. Yellow crystals, soluble in water; used as a reagent for alkaloids and vegetable fats, and in microscopy. **s. phosphotungstate.** $Na_4P_2O_7 \cdot 12WO_3 \cdot 18H_2O = 3374.0$. S. phosphowolframate. White granules, soluble in water; a reagent for alkaloids, potassium, ferrous salts, and uric acid. **s. phosphovanadate.** $Na_4P_2O_7 \cdot 6V_2O_5 \cdot 21H_2O = 1736.4$. Yellow crystals, soluble in water; a microscope reagent. **s. phosphowolframate.** S. phosphotungstate. **s. phthalate.** $C_6H_4(COONa)_2$

= 210.03. White powder, slightly soluble in water. **s. platinichloride.** $Na_2PtCl_6 \cdot 6H_2O$ = 562.1. S. platinic chloride. Red solid, m.100, soluble in water. **s. platinochloride.** Na_2PtCl_4 = 383.04. S. platinous chloride. Brown crystals. **s. platinocyanide.** Platinous s. cyanide. **s. plumbate.** $Na_2PbO_3 \cdot 3H_2O$ = 351.9. Yellow powder, decomp. by water. **s. polystyrene sulfonate.** Brown powder, insoluble in water; a cation-exchange resin (U.S.P.). **s. potassium carbonate.** $NaKCO_3 \cdot 6H_2O$ = 230.2. Colorless, monoclinic crystals, soluble in water. **s. potassium tartrate.** Potassium s. tartrate. **s. propionate.** Et·COONa = 96.04. White granules, soluble in water. **s. pyroantimonate.** $H_2Na_2Sb_2O_7 \cdot 6H_2O$ = 508.5. Colorless powder, slightly soluble in water. **s. pyroborate.** See *s. borates.* **s. pyrophosphate.** See *s. phosphates.* **s. pyrosulfate.** $Na_2S_2O_7$ = 284.2. S. disulfate. Colorless crystals, soluble in water. **s. pyrosulfite.** $Na_2S_2O_5$ = 190.1. Colorless crystals, soluble in water. **s. pyrovanadate.** $Na_4V_2O_7$ = 206.00. Gray crystals, slightly soluble in water. **s. radioiodide.** A sterile solution containing 95–105% of I^{131} as iodide. A diagnostic and therapeutic agent for oral use (B.P.) or injection (U.S.P.). **s. radiophosphate.** A sterile solution containing 95–105% P^{32} as phosphate; a diagnostic agent for oral use (B.P.) **s. rhodanate, s. rhodanide.** S. thiocyanate. **s. rosolate.** $NaC_{20}H_{15}O_3$ = 326.1. S. corallinate, the s. salt of trihydroxydiphenyltolylcarbinol. Red powder with green luster, soluble in water; a stain in microscopy. **s. saccharate.** $NaC_{12}H_{21}O_{11}$ = 364.2. White powder, soluble in water; used in ampul medication. **s. salicylate.** $NaC_7H_5O_3$ = 160.1. White scales, soluble in water; an antirheumatic and antipyretic (U.S.P., B.P.); and a reagent for free acid in gastric juice. **s. salicyl sulfonate.** S. sulfosalicylate. **s. santonate.** $NaC_{15}H_{19}O_4$ = 286.2. Colorless, hygroscopic powder; an anthelmintic. **s. santoninate.** $Na_{15}CH_{19}O_4 \cdot 3\frac{1}{2}H_2O$ = 353.1. Colorless crystals, soluble in water; an anthelmintic. **s. selenate.** $Na_2SeO_4 \cdot 10H_2O$ = 369.3. White crystals, soluble in water; a reagent, **s. selinite.** Na_2SeO_3 = 173.1. Colorless powder, soluble in water; used as a reagent in bacteriology, and in red glass. **s. sesquicarbonate.** See *sesquicarbonate of soda.* **s. silicate.** *liquid-* $Na_2Si_4O_9 \cdot xH_2O$ = 303.2 + 18x. Water glass, soluble glass. An amorphous powder or heavy liquid aqueous solution, soluble in water. *solid-* Na_2SiO_3 = 122.3. S. metasilicate. Colorless, monoclinic crystals, m.1056, soluble in water. Used as an adhesive (paper industry), binder (acid-proof cements), protective coating (concrete, wood), preservative (eggs), cleanser (bottles); and in the manufacture of soap and boiler compounds. *tetra-* See *s. tetrasilicate.* **s. silicofluoride.** Na_2SiF_6 = 188.3. S. fluosilicate, salufer. White granules, slightly soluble in water; a reagent, antiseptic, and germicide. **s. silver cyanide.** S. argentocyanide. **s. silvinate.** S, sylvate. **s. sozoiodolate.** $C_6H_2I_2(ONa)SO_3H$ = 447.7. Sozoiodole sodium. Colorless crystals, soluble in water; an antiseptic. **s. stannate.** $Na_2SnO_3 \cdot 3H_2O$ = 266.7. White hexagons, soluble in water; a dye mordant. **s. stannite.** $HSnOONa$ = 174.71 Known only in solution; analogous to s. formate. **s. stearate.** $NaC_{18}H_{35}O_2$ = 306.3. White, unctuous powder, soluble in

water; used (with s. palmitate) for suppositories (U.S.P.). **s. stibogluconate.** Colorless powder made by the action of antimony trichloride and gluconic acid in presence of alkali; it contains 30.0–34.0% Sb. Soluble in water, insoluble in alcohol or ether; used to treat leishmaniasis (B.P.). **s. succinate.** (1) $Na_2O_4H_4O_4$ = 162.2. Colorless powder, soluble in water. (2) $Na_2C_4H_4O_4 \cdot 6H_2O$ = 270.3. Colorless prisms, soluble in water. **s. sulfalizarate.** Alizarin red. **s. sulfanilate.** $Na_6C_6H_4(NH_2)SO_3 \cdot 2H_2O$ = 231.1. S. aniline sulfonate, s. *p*-aminobenzene sulfonate. Colorless flakes, soluble in water. **s. sulfantimonate.** $Na_3SbS_4 \cdot 9H_2O$ = 479.4. Schlippe's salt, s. thioantimonate. Colorless tetrahedra, decomp. by heat, soluble in water; a reagent for alkaloids. **s. sulfates.** *anhydrous-* Na_2SO_4 = 142.1. Salt cake, niter cake, native as thenardite. Colorless powder, d.2.673, m.884, soluble in water. *monohydrate-* $Na_2SO_4 \cdot H_2O$ = 160.1. Native as mirabilite. White powder, soluble in water. *heptahydrate-* $Na_2SO_4 \cdot 7H_2O$ = 268.2. Colorless rhombs or tetragons, soluble in water. *decahydrate-* $Na_2SO_4 \cdot 10H_2O$ = 322.2. Glauber's salt, ordinary s. sulfate. Colorless, monoclinic crystals, d.1.462, m.38, soluble in water, a reagent, precipitant, cathartic, and diuretic. Cf. *s. bisulfate.* **s. sulfhydrate.** NaHS = 56.0. S. hydrosulfide, s. hydrosulfate. Colorless crystals, soluble in water; a reagent. **s. sulfides.** (1) Na_2S = 78.1. Anhydrous s. monosulfide. Amorphous, pink powder, decomp. by heat, soluble in water. (2) $Na_2S \cdot 9H_2O$ = 240.3. Colorless, hygroscopic crystals, soluble in water; a reagent, instead of hydrogen sulfide. (3) Principal polysulfides: (*a*) Na_2S_2 = 110.1, disulfide; (*b*) Na_2S_3 = 142.2, trisulfide: (*c*) Na_2S_4 = 174.2, tetrasulfide; (*d*) Na_2S_5 (+ $8H_2O$) = 206.4, pentasulfide. **s. sulfites.** (1) Na_2SO_3 = 126.1. *anhydrous-* Colorless prisms, m.150 (decomp.), soluble in water; a reagent and reducing agent. (2) $Na_2SO_3 \cdot 7H_2O$ = 252.2. *heptahydrate-* Colorless prisms, m.100 (decomp.), soluble in water; a reagent, preservative, antiseptic, and antizymotic. **s. sulfocaffeinate.** Symphorol N. **s. sulfocarbolate.** S. phenol sulfonate. **s. sulfocarbonate.** Na_2CS_3 = 154.2. S. trithiocarbonate. Brown granules, soluble in water; an insecticide, antiseptic, and reagent for nickel and cobalt. **s. sulfocyanate. s. thiocyanate. s. sulfocyanide.** S. thiocyanate. **s. sulfooleate.** Thigenol. **s. sulfosalicylate.** $NaC_7H_5O_3SO_3$ = 240.0. S. salicyl sulfonate. White crystals; soluble in water; an antiseptic. **s. sulfovinate.** S. ethyl sulfate. **s. sulfoxylate formaldehyde.** $NaHSO_2 \cdot CH_2O \cdot 2H_2O$ = 154.11. White prisms, m.64, soluble in water; a reagent. **s. superoxide.** S. peroxide. **s. tartrate.** $Na_2C_4H_4O_6 \cdot 2H_2O$ = 230.1. White, trimetric crystals, soluble in water; a reagent, cathartic, and refrigerant. **s. taurocholate.** (1) $NaC_{26}H_{44}NSO_7$ = 537.5. Yellow powder, soluble in water, from the bile of carniverous animals; a diagnostic reagent. (2) B.P. Codex term for bile salts, q.v. **s. tellurate.** $Na_2TeO_4 \cdot 5H_2O$ = 327.6. White powders, soluble in water. **s. tellurite.** Na_2TeO_3 = 221.5. White powder, soluble in water; used in bacteriology. **s. tetraborate.** See *s. borates.* **s. tetraiodophenolphthalein.** Antinosin. **s. tetravanadate.** S. divanadate. **s. thioantimonate.** S. sulfantimonate. **s. thiocarbonate.**

$Na_2CS_3 = 154.21$. Brown oil; the sulfur analog of s. carbonate. **s. thiocyanate.** $NaSCN = 81.1$. S. sulfocyanate, s. sulfocyanide, s. rhodanate, s. rhodanide. White, deliquescent rhombs, m.287, soluble in water; a reagent, especially for ferric ions. **s. thiopentone.** See *thiopental* sodium. **s. thiophene sulfonate.** $NaC_4H_8O_3S_2 \cdot H_2O = 209.1$. White powder, soluble in water; an antiseptic. **s. thiosulfate.** $Na_2S_2O_2 \cdot 5H_2O = 248.20$. S. hyposulfite, s. subsulfite, antichlor. Colorless, monoclinic crystals, d.1.729, m.32–48, decomp. 220, soluble in water, A volumetric reagent, group precipitant instead of hydrogen sulfide, "antichlor" in bleaching, mordant, photographic fixing salt, solvent for lead and silver, and detoxicant for metal poisons. **s. thiotetraphosphate.** $Na_6P_4O_{10}S = 454.3$. A detergent. **s. thymol benzoate.** Porphyrin. **s. titanates.** $(Na_2O)_2Ti_2O_5$; $Na_2O \cdot Ti_2O_5$, and $Na_2O \cdot (Ti_2O_5)_2$. **s. trichloracetate.** $CCl_3COO-Na = 185.4$. Colorless crystals, soluble in water. **s. trichlorophenate.** $C_6H_2Cl_3ONa = 219.4$, Dowicide B. White crystals, soluble in water; antiseptic. **s. trithiocarbonate.** S. sulfocarbonate. **s. triticonucleinate.** The s. salt of wheat nucleic acids. Gray powder, soluble in water. **s. truxillate.** $Na_2C_{18}O_4 \cdot 10H_2O = 520.2$. White powder, soluble in water. **s. tungstate.** $Na_2WO_4 \cdot 2H_2O = 330.0$. S. wolframate. Colorless prisms, m.100, soluble in water; a reagent for alkaloids, bile pigments, and tannins; and waterproofing and fire-proofing agents. **s. uranate.** $Na_2UO_4 = 348.20$. Uranium yellow. Orange rhombs, soluble in water; used as a reagent, and in the manufacture of green glass and ceramic pigments. **s. valerate.** $NaC_5H_9O_2 = 124.1$. Colorless crystals, soluble in water; a sedative. **s. vanadate.** $Na_3VO_4 = 184.2$. S. orthovanadate. Colorless crystals, soluble in water; used as a reagent and in the manufacture of inks and dyes. *meta-* See *s. metavanadate. pyro-* See *s. pyrovanadate.* **s. versenate.** Versene. **s. wafarin.** $C_{19}H_{15}O_4Na = 330.32$. Bitter, white crystals, soluble in water; an anticoagulant (U.S.P.). **s. wolframate.** S. tungstate. **s. xanthogenate.** $NaS(OC_2H_5)C:S = 144.1$. Yellow powder, soluble in water; an antiseptic and germicide. **s. zincate.** $Na_2ZnO_2 = 143.6$. White powder, decomp. by water into zinc and sodium hydroxides.

sodos. A mixture of sodium dihydrogen phosphate and sodium bicarbonate; used medicinally.

sodyl. The radical NaO–. **s. hydroxide.** NaOOH $= 56.01$. White powder, explodes if heated.

soft. biologically- Having low resistance to biological decomposition. **s. acid.** Reverse of hard acid, q.v.; as lead. **s. base.** Reverse of hard base, q.v.; as sulfides. **s. sized paper.** Bibulous or blotting paper

softener. (1) A substance that increases plasticity: either a true s. or a lubricant; as, stearic acid or pine tar, respectively, for rubber. (2) See soft *water, permutite.* (3) A substance that improves pliability and softness. **anti-** A substance that stiffens; as, benzidine in rubber.

softening. (1) Making plastic. (2) Removing salts. **water-** See soft *water, permutite.* **s. temperature.** The point at which substances without a sharp melting point change from viscous to plastic flow.

softifume. A brick of sodium cyanide, sodium chlorate, and sand, used for fumigation by dropping it into hydrochloric acid to liberate hydrogen cyanide gas.

sogasoid. A dispersion of a solid phase in a gaseous phase; as, smoke.

soil. The surface layer of the earth; the weathered mineral and rock fragments with decomposed vegetable and animal matter. 1,000 million hectares of the s. of the world are used for agriculture.

SOILS

Lime	Sand	Clay	Type
Lime-poor:			
0–15	80–100	0	Flying sand
		10	Loose sand
		20	Clay sand
	30–50	30	Sandy loam
		40	Mild loam
		55	Strong loam
	0–30	65	Mild clay
		75	common clay
		90	Strong clay
Lime-rich:			
15–20	25–50	20–50	Loamy soil
	0–25	50–75	Clayey soil
15–60	40–80	....	Sandy soil
50–75	Little	....	Calcareous soil
75–95	Little	....	Lime soil

Type	Particles, mm diameter
Gravel	Over 2
Coarse sand	0.2–2.0
Fine sand	0.02–0.20
Silt.............	0.002–0.02
Clay	Below 0.002

Cf. *humus, subsoil.* See table. **s. amendment.** A material added to s. to improve it other than by plant nutrients, e.g., sand added to prevent hardening of clay. **s. bacteria.** Protophyta that enrich the s. by the ammonification and nitrification of nitrogen compounds, e.g., *Bacillus mycoides.* Cf. *Azobacter, Nitrobacter.* **s. horizon.** Layers of a s. profile which have become differentiated as a result of processes occurring in the s. mass. **s. mechanics.** See *mechanics.* **s. profile.** A section of s. showing the layers produced at different depths by geological or other causes. Cf. *s. horizon.* **s. science.** Pedology. The study of the earth surface layer.

soja. Soybean

sol. (1) A colloidal solution. (2) The liquid phase of a colloidal solution. (3) Abbreviation for soluble. **aero-** A colloidal system in which the surrounding phase is a gas, *e.g.,* fog. **collo-** Collosol. **electro-** Electrosol. **hydro-** A colloidal suspension in a water-liquid phase. See *gel.* **sulfo-** See *sulfosol.*

Solanaceae. Nightshade family. Herbs or shrubs with rank-scented, often poisonous foliage, and a colorless juice containing alkaloids; e.g., roots: *Atropa belladonna,* atropine; leaves: *Datura* *stramonium*, stramonium; branches: *Fabiana imbricata*, pichi; fruits: *Capsicum frutescens*, cayenne pepper. **S. alkaloids.** The alkaloids obtained from various species of s.; as: atropine, hyoscyamine, belladonine. Cf. *lycine, solandrine, solanine.*

solandrine. An alkaloid from *Solandra lavis*. It resembles hyoscine.

solanellic acid. $C_{23}H_{34}O_{12} = 502.2$. A hexabasic acid from oxidation of bile acids.

solanesol. A long-chain isoprenoid alcohol from tobacco.

solanidine $C_{27}H_{43}O_3N = 397.4$. A decomposition product of solanine. Colorless crystals, m.208, soluble in alcohol.

solanin. $C_{45}H_{73}O_{15}N = 867.7$. A glycoside from *Solanum nigrum*, potato and other species. Colorless microcrystals, m.280, soluble in water; a nerve sedative.

solanine. $C_{52}H_{91}O_{18}N = 1017.7$. An alkaloid in Solanaceae, decomp. 254. Potato s. can cause poisoning.

solanorubin. Licopene.

Solanum. Herbs and shrubs of the family Solanaceae; includes nightshades and potatoes. **S. carolinense.** Solanum, horse nettle, poison potato, sand brier, bull nettle. Air-dry ripe fruits (Southern States); a sedative. **S. dulcamara.** Bittersweet. **S. grandiflora.** S. yielding grandiflorine, q.v. **S. insidiosum.** Jurubeba. The root (Brazil) is a stomachic and diuretic. **S. melongena.** Eggplant. **S. nigrum.** The common garden nightshade. **S. tomatillo.** S. yielding natrine, q.v. **S. tuberosum.** The common potato.

solapson(e). $C_{30}H_{28}O_{14}N_2S_5Na_4 = 892.93$. Sulfetrone. White, amorphous powder, soluble in water; a bacteriostatic (B.P.).

solar. Pertaining to the sun. **s. constant.** 1.932 small calories: the amount of s. energy falling at normal incidence per square centimeter per minute on a body at the earth's mean distance from the sun. **s. pan, s. pond.** Flat areas surrounded by low dykes in which seawater is evaporated for salt. **s. radiation.** See *radiation.* **s. rays.** The visible and invisible radiations of the sun. **s. salt.** See *salt.* **s. spectrum.** The spectrum produced when sunlight is refracted by a prism or grating; characterized by Fraunhofer lines. **s. year.** The ordinary year.

solargentum. A compound of silver and gelatin. Black granules; used medicinally.

solarization. (1) Exposure to the sun; as in accelerated aging. Cf. *irradiation.* (2) A decrease in starch content following long exposure of plant leaves to light. (3) The partial inversion of a photographic negative into a positive by exposure to light during development; used to enhance shading effects.

solate. A liquefied gel.

solation. Liquefaction of a gel; the reverse of gelation.

solbrol. Nipagin.

solder. Braze. A fusing metal or alloy used to unite adjacent surfaces of less fusible metals. **brass-** Copper s. **copper-** An alloy: Sn 5, Pb 2 pts., with zinc chloride as flux. **fine-** Soft s. **fusible-** An alloy of Pb, Sn, and Bi, which melts in water; used in fire-spray extinguishers. **gold-** An alloy:

Au 10, Ag 6, Cu 4 pts. **hard-** A high-melting-point alloy used as s.; it fuses at red heat: e.g., Cu + Zn + Ag. **lead-** An alloy of equal parts of Pb and Sn, used for soldering lead. **plumber's-** An alloy usually containing approx. Pb 65, Sn 30%, with some Sb. **seifert-** A s. for aluminum, containing Sn 73, Zn 21, Pb 5%. **silver-** See *silver.* **soft-** A s. that fuses below red heat; as, Sn + Pb: *lead s., fusible s.* **zinc-** An alloy: Sn 5, Pb 3 pts.

soldering. (1) Uniting metallic pieces by heat with or without an alloy (solder) and flux (borax). (2) In commerce, soft (as distinct from hard) solders. S. differs from *brazing* and fusion *welding*, q.v. **autogenous-** Uniting metal surfaces by interfusion, without a more fusible alloy. **fusing-** uniting metal surfaces by filling all intervening space with a completely fused solder. **sweating-** S. in which the solder is heated near its melting point and adheres.

solenhofen stone. A fine-grained, porous limestone; contains clay.

solenoid. Selenoid. A hollow cylinder, wound with resistance wire, used to produce fields of electric force.

solfatara. A volcanic vent from which sulfur is obtained.

solferino. Fuchsin.

solid. (1) A substance of definite shape, and relatively great density, low internal heat content, and great cohesion of its molecules. It may be homogeneous (as crystals and solid solutions); or heterogeneous (as amorphous and colloidal substances). **s. solution.** (1) Sosoloid. A homogeneous, s. mixture of substance; as, glass. (2) A s. solution of a solid, liquid, or gas in a solid.

solidago. Goldenrod. The dried herb of *Solidago odora* (Compositae); a diaphoretic, stimulant, carminative, and diuretic.

solidify. To change into the solid state.

solidifying point. Freezing point.

solidus. In a temperature-concentration diagram for both solid and liquid solutions whose concentrations differ, the s. curve relates to the solid phase and the *liquidus* to the liquid phase. Cf. *diagram.*

soliquoid. Suspension. A dispersed system of a solid phase in a liquid phase.

soln. Abbreviation for solution.

solodization. Dealkalization. Removal of alkali from soils by degradation.

Solomon's seal. Polygonatum. The dried herb of *Polygonatum officinale* (Liliaceae); an astringent and antirheumatic.

Solozone. Trademark for a brand of hydrogen peroxide.

solubility. The extent to which a substance (solute) mixes with a liquid (solvent) to produce a homogeneous system (solution). **apparent-** The total amount of the nonionized and ionized portions of a substance dissolved in a liquid. **degree of-** The concentration of a saturated solution at a given temperature. S. generally increases with increase in temperature. **molar-** s/M, where s is the number of grams per liter, and M the molecular weight. **real-** The amount of nonionized solute in a liquid.

  s. curve. A graph obtained by plotting the amount of dissolved substance in a saturated solution against the temperature. **s. exponent.**

p or $p_s = \log 1/S$. Cf. *pH*. **s. product.** $S =$ $[M^+] \times [X^-]/[MX]$, where the brackets indicate the concentrations of the components of the ionization equilibrium: $MX \rightleftharpoons M^+ + X^-$. If $[M^+] \times [X^-]$ exceeds S, MX will precipitate; and vice versa. E.g., NaCl is precipitated from concentrated solutions by HCl gas.

soluble. Capable of mixing with a liquid (dissolving) to form a homogeneous mixture (solution). Cf. *solubility, solution.* **s. barbital.** Barbital sodium. **s. cotton.** Nitrocellulose. **s. glass.** Sodium silicate. **s. gluside.** Sodium benzosulfinide. **s. mercury.** $NH_2Hg_2NO_2 = 479.6$. Hahnemann's mercury. Black precipitate on adding ammonia to mercurous nitrate; used medicinally. **s. starch.** See *starch.* **s. tartar.** Ammonium potassium tartrate. **s. tartrate.** Potassium tartrate.

soluend. Solute (obsolete).

solum. A damp-resisting layer of material installed on the ground under a floor, e.g., bitumen.

solurol. $C_{30}H_{46}O_{16}N_4 \cdot 2P_2O_5 = 1002.5$. Thyminic acid, nucleotinphosphoric acid. Yellow powder, soluble in water; used medicinally. Cf. *nucleic acid.*

solustibosan. Sodium stibogluconate.

solute. A substance that mixes with or dissolves in a solvent to produce a solution.

solution. (1) Dissolution. The mixing of a solid, liquid, or gaseous substance (solute) with a liquid (the solvent), forming a homogeneous mixture from which the dissolved substance can be recovered by physical processes. (2) The homogeneous mixture formed by the operation of s. **anisotonic-** Any nonisotonic s.; as, a hypotonic or hypertonic s. **aqueous-** A s. in which water is the main solvent. **buffer-** A s. of acid or basic salts that can neutralize either acids or bases without appreciable change in hydrogen-ion concentration. **centinormal-** A s. containing 0.01 equivalent mole per liter. **chemical-** A s. in which solute and solvent react to form a compound that dissolves in the solvent and cannot be recovered by distillation. Cf. *physical s.* **colloidal-** A macroscopically homogeneous, microscopically heterogeneous system, of minute particles (colloid, dispersed phase) suspended in a liquid (continuous phase, medium). Cf. *colloid.* **concentrated-** A s. in which the solute content is relatively great. **decinormal-** A s. that contains 0.1 equivalent mole per liter. **dilute-** A s. in which the solute is relatively small in quantity. **grammolecular-** Molar s. **heat of-** See *heat.* **hypertonic-** A s. whose osmotic pressure is greater than that of blood serum. **hypotonic-** A s. whose osmotic pressure is less than that of blood serum. **ionic-** A s. whose ions of the solute are surrounded by oriented molecules of the solvent. **isotonic-** A s. having an osmotic pressure equal to that of blood serum; as, 0.6–0.7% sodium chloride s. **molal-** A s. containing 1 gm molecule (mole) of substance per 1,000 gm of s. **molar-** A s. containing 1 gm molecule of substance per liter. Cf. *normal s.* **molecular-** A true s. in which the molecules of solute are surrounded by the molecules of solvent. Cf. *colloidal-, ionic s.* **normal.** A s. containing 1 equivalent gm molecule per liter. **normal salt-** A s. containing 1 mole sodium chloride per liter. Cf. *physiological s.* **physical-** A s. in which solute and solvent mix but do not react chemically; the solute can be recovered on evaporation, the solvent by distillation. Cf. *chemical s.* **physiological-** Isotonic s. **saturated-** A s. that normally contains the maximum amount of substance able to be dissolved. **solid-** See *solid solution, sosoloid.* **standard-** A s. that contains a definite amount of substance dissolved; as, a molar. **standardized-** A s. adjusted to a known concentration. **supersaturated-** A s. that contains a greater quantity of solid than can normally be dissolved at a given temperature; on slow cooling, the excess precipitates under suitable conditions. **test-** T.S. A reagent s. **volumetric-** V.S. A standard analytical s., usually containing 1, $\frac{1}{2}$, or $\frac{1}{10}$ mole of a substance dissolved in 1 liter of water.

s. mining. Winning soluble salts (as potassium chloride) by pumping water into the formation and evaporating the resulting solution. Cf. *Frasch process.* **s. pressure.** The tendency of atoms or molecules to mix with a liquid, or to dissolve in it; measured by the osmotic pressure. **s. tension.** The tendency of atoms or molecules to dissolve in a liquid with ionization; measured by the electromotive force. See *Nernst's theory.* **s. theory.** See *Nernst's theory, Arrhenius' theory.*

solvate. A molecular or ionic complex of molecules or ions of solvent with those of solute; as $Cl(H_2O)_x^-$. The ions are surrounded by a zone of oriented water molecules. **crystalline-** A crystal containing solvent as part of its lattice. **s. theory.** The abnormalities of solutions are due to the formation of complexes between the ions or molecules of the solute and solvent. Cf. *hydration.*

solvation. A combination between solute and solvent; if the latter is water, hydrates or hydrated ions are formed, e.g., $M(H_2O)_x$.

solvatochromism. The formation, by molecular addition, of a colored complex (solvate) between colorless molecules of organic compounds and those of other compounds.

Solvay, Ernst. 1838–1922. Belgian industrial chemist. **S. process.** Making sodium carbonate and calcium chloride by treating sodium chloride with ammonia and carbon dioxide. The sodium bicarbonate produced is heated, and some carbon dioxide recovered; the ammonia is recovered by lime or magnesia.

solvent. (1) That component of a homogeneous mixture which is excess. (2) A liquid which dissolves another substance (solute), generally a solid, without any change in chemical composition; as, water containing sugar. (3) A liquid that dissolves a substance by chemical reaction; as, acids and metals. **acid-** A s. that acts as an acid by losing a proton to the solute. **aqueous-** Water. **associating-** A s. whose molecules form complexes; as water. Cf. *bond.* **basic-** A s. that acts as a base by gaining a proton from the solute. **chemical-** See (3). **ionizing-** See *polar-s.* **lacquer-** Organic liquids used to dissolve resins and nitrocellulose: *low-boiling-* b. below 100 (alcohol). *medium-boiling-* b. near 125 (toluene). *high-boiling-* b. 150–200 (xylene). *plasticizers and softeners-* b. near 300 (camphor). **molten-** Flux. **nonassociating-** A s. that does not form complexes between its molecules or ions and the solute; as, benzene. **nonaqueous-** A solvent other than water. **nonionizing-** Nonpolar. **nonpolar-** A s.

that does not conduct an electric current; as, hydrocarbons. **normal-** Nonassociating. **physical-** A s. that does not react chemically with the solute. **polar-** A s. that produces electrically conducting solutions (as, water), and causes dissociation of the solute into ions. **two-type-** A s. having 2 groups which confer s. properties; as alcohol-ethers, HO·R·O·R, e.g., Cellosolve. **universal-** Aqua regia. **s. action.** A process of making substances water-soluble

solvolysis. The effect of the acid or basic character of a solvent on the ionization of a salt dissolved in it.

solvolytic. Pertaining to solvation. **s. dissociation.** Ionization in a nonaqueous solution. Cf. *solvate* theory.

sombrerite. A "hard" mineral phosphate (35 % phosphorus pentoxide); a source of phosphorus.

Sommelet reaction. The production of benzaldehyde by the reaction between benzylamine and formaldehyde, preferably in presence of hexamine.

Sommerfeld, Arnold. 1868–1951. German physicist; developed the quantum theory of atomic structure. **S. notation.** See *quantum numbers.*

somnal. $C_7H_{12}NO_3Cl_3 = 264.49$. An ethyl derivative of chloral urethane; a hypnotic and diuretic.

somnifacient. A hypnotic, q.v.

Somnifene. Trademark for a soluble barbiturate sedative-hypnotic.

somnirol. $C_{32}H_{44}O_7 = 540.34$. A monohydric alcohol of *Withania* species (Solanaceae).

Somnitol. $C_{33}H_{46}O_7 = 554.32$. Trade name for a alcohol from *Withania* species (Solanaceae).

Somnol. $C_9H_{11}O_6Cl_9 = 518.2$. Trade name for chlorethanal alcoholate; a hypnotic.

Somnos. Trademark for chlorethanal alcohol.

soneryl. Neonal. Butobarbitone (neonal).

sonic. Phonic. Cf. *sound.*

Sonnenschein, Franz Leopold. 1819–1879. German forensic analyst. **S.'s reagent.** A solution of phosphomolybdic acid forms a yellow precipitate with the sulfates of alkaloids.

sonoluminescence. Luminescence induced by sound waves.

sonometer. Phonometer. An instrument to measure sound vibrations.

sonora gum. The exudations of the creosote bush, *Covillea tridentata* (Mexico).

soot. An impure black carbon containing oily and empyreumatic compounds from the incomplete combustion of resinous materials or wood. It contains hydrocarbons, and if derived from coal, ammonium sulfate. Cf. *lampblack.*

sophol. A yellow compound of silver and methylenenucleinic acid; used medicinally.

sophora. Coral bean. The poisonous seeds of *Sophora* species (Leguminosae), India. **S. tomentosa.** A leguminous shrub (Japan); a remedy for cholera and diarrhea.

sophorine. An alkaloid from *Sophora* species. Colorless liquid resembling cytisine and matrine. Cf. *kuhseng.*

soporific. An agent that produces deep sleep. Cf. *hypnotic.*

sorbet. Sherbet.

sorbic acid. Me·CH:CH·CH·CH·COOH $= 112.1$. Hexadienic acid, pentadienecarboxylic acid, 2,4-hexadienoic acid*, from the unripe berries of mountain ash, *Sorbus.* Colorless needles, m.134,

b.228 (decomp.), soluble in water; a selective fungistatic for certain foods. **hydro-** Hexenic acid*. **methylenedioxyphenyl-** Piperic acid. **para-** A lactone-like body forming sorbic acid when heated with acid or alkali.

sorbin. Sorbinose.

sorbinose. $C_6H_{12}O_6 = 180.1$. Sorbin, 1,3,4,5,6-pentahydroxy-2-hexanone*, sorbose. An optically active carbohydrate from the fruits of mountain ash, *Sorbus.* Colorless rhombs, m.154; slightly soluble in water.

sorbite. (1) Sorbitol. (2) A mixture of ferrite and cementite, with conglomerations of carbon in steel; a transition form between pearlite and troostite.

sorbitol. $C_6H_{14}O_6\cdot\frac{1}{2}H_2O = 191.1$. Sorbite, 1,2,3,4,5,6-hexanehexol*. An alcohol isomer of mannitol from *Sorbus aucuparia.* Colorless crystals, m.111, soluble in water. Used chiefly for the preparation of ascorbic acid (U.S.P.); also as a humectant and in surfactants, pharmaceuticals, foods and rigid polymethane foams.

Sorbol. $C_{34}H_{70}O = 494.5$. Trade name for an alcohol, m.78, from the wax of the berries of *Sorbus aucuparia.*

sorbose. Sorbinose.

sorbus. Rowan tree, mountain ash. The tree *Pyrus* (*Sorbus* or *Mespilus*) *aucuparia* (Rosaceae). A decoction of the bark contains sorbitol and sorbinose; used to treat diarrhea.

Sorel cement. $MgO\cdot MgCl_2\cdot 11H_2O$. A hard, quicksetting mixture of magnesium oxide and a concentrated solution of magnesium chloride. **S. dental cement.** A mixture of zinc oxide, zinc chloride, and fine sand. **S. floor cement.** A mixture of magnesium oxide, zinc chloride, and portland cement, used for floors; 10 % copper powder makes it waterproof.

Sörensen, Sören P. L. 1868–1939. Danish chemist. **S. indicators.** A group of hydrogen-ion-concentration indicators, q.v. **S. phosphate.** Dibasic sodium phosphate. **S. symbols.** See *pH.* **S. value.** Hydrogen-ion concentration.

Soret effect, S. principle. Ludwig phenomenon. When differences of temperature are maintained in a salt solution, the solute will concentrate in the coolest parts.

sorethytan. U.S.P. name for polysorbate-80.

sorghum. A cane, *Andropogon sorghum* or *Sorghum vulgare*, from which a sugar and Indian millet (African, durra) are obtained.

sorgo. *Sorghum vulgare.*

sorption. A reaction on a surface, especially *absorption*, q.v., or solution, *adsorption*, q.v., and *persorption* (permeation into a very porous solid). Cf. *monomolecular film.* **ab-** See *absorption.* **ad-** See *adsorption.* **re-** See *resorption.* Cf. *zone.*

sorrel. The leaves of *Rumex acetosa* (Polygonaceae); a refrigerant and diuretic. **s. salt.** Potassium bioxalate.

sosoloid. Solid solution. One solid phase dispersed in another. See *colloidal systems.*

Soubeiran, Eugène. 1797–1858. French apothecary; discoverer of chloroform.

sound. (1) Air oscillations or vibrations that affect the ear and are rendered audible. Cf. *musical notes.* (2) Vibrations in air or other medium which may or may not be audible; as, *infraphonic* (longer frequency than audible s.); *phonic* (audible); *ultraphonic* (shorter frequency than audible s.). (3) Free from defect. **s. intensity, s. loudness.** S. loudness as sensed by the human ear is related to intensity as follows:

Loudness	Intensity
10 decibels =	10
30 decibels =	1,000
50 decibels =	100,000
70 decibels =	10,000,000

Typical values in decibels are: pneumatic drill (at 10 ft) 100, motorcycle 82, automobile 75. Cf. *phon, loudness.* **s. velocity.** The speed with which s. vibrations travel in materials; e.g., in meters per second: air 331.9, water 1,460, iron 5,000. Cf. *Mach.* **s. waves.** Phonic waves. Mechanical radiations consisting of air vibrations. Cf. *sound.* (2), *noise, decibel.* The *highest pitched* s. produced has a wavelength of 33×10^{-6} mm; the *highest audible* s. 17 mm; the *lowest audible* s. 16 m.

sourwood. The leaves of *Oxydendrum arboreum*, N. America; used medicinally.

southern wood. *Abrotanum.*

sovprene. A polymerized chloroprene.

Soxhlet, Franz. 1848–1913. German food analyst. **S. apparatus.** A flask and condenser for the continuous extraction of alcohol- or ether-soluble materials.

soy, soya. Soybean.

soybean. Soja, soy, soya. The bean of *Soja hispida* (Leguminosae), China. An important local food, and source of many preparations; as, flour, sizing materials, bean cake, sauce, oil, cheese. Average composition: proteins 40, oils 18% (phosphatides 2%), urease, raffinose, stachyose, saponins, phytosterins, and isoflavone. **s. oil.** Colorless liquid oil expressed from s., $d_{15}°0.925$, free fatty acids (as oleic acid) 0.46%, sapon. val. 191.1, iodine val. 129.2; used in cooking. World production (1967) 5 million tons.

Soylon. Trade name for a protein synthetic fiber.

sozal. $Al_2[C_6H_4(OH)SO_3]_6 = 1093.4$. Aluminum *p*-phenolsulfonate, aluminum sulfocarbolate. Brown crystals, soluble in water; an iodoform substitute.

sozalbumin. A nontoxic defensive protein. Antonym: toxalbumin.

sozins. Defensive proteins which occur normally in the body. Antonym: toxosozins.

sozoidol. $C_6H_2I_2OH \cdot SO_3H = 425.94$. Sozoiodolic acid, soziodol, diodo-*p*-phenosulfonic acid. White crystals, decom. 200, soluble in water; an antiseptic.

sozoiodolate. A salt of sozoiodol. Those of Pb, Hg, K, Na, and Zn are antiseptics.

sozoiodolic acid. Sozoiodol.

sozolic acid. Aseptol.

sp. Abbreviation for: (1) spirit, (2) specific.

space. The three-dimensional concept of length, width, and height: L^3, where L is a unit of length. **Crookes'-.** Dark s. **dark-** A nonluminous region near the cathode of a vacuum tube, through which a high-frequency current is passing. **interatomic-** The region between the outermost orbits of 2 atoms. **intraatomic-** The region within the outer-

most orbit of an electron and the nucleus of an atom. It consists of the kernel and the orbits of the valence electrons.

s. group. A characteristic arrangement of atoms in a crystal. **s. lattice.** Bravais lattice. The characteristic pattern formed by the spatial distribution of atoms or radicals in a crystal In noncrystalline solids the s. lattice is distorted, and in truly amorphous solids there is no order. *homopolar-* A s. lattice in which the constituents are neutral atoms linked to a number of adjacent similar atoms by chemical valencies (electron sharing), e.g., diamond. *ionic-* A s. lattice in which each ion of a given charge is equidistant from a small number of ions of opposite charge, arranged equidistantly around it, e.g., the sodium chloride crystal. *metallic-* A s. lattice composed of atoms of a metal which have lost one or more valency electrons; these are thus free to produce conductivity. *molecular-* A s. lattice composed of a regular arrangement of molecules held together by van der Waals forces, the constituent atoms being held by valencies.

spalling. (1) The failure of a refractory material under stresses induced by temperature fluctuations. (2) The cracking or flaking of particles from a metal surface, e.g., wheels. (3) In general, splintering, cracking, or breaking due to heat.

Span. (1) Trademark for a group of sorbitan ester emulsifiers. (2) (not cap.) 9 inches. A little used unit of length in the English system.

spandex. Generic name (U.S. Textile Fiber Products Identification Act) for stretch fibers based on synthetic, elastomeric long-chain polymers. S. comprises at least 85% polyurethane (U.S. Federal Trade Commission), e.g., Vyrene. Monofilament s. fiber returns to its original length after being stretched several times that length.

Spanish broom. Spartium. **S. flies.** Cantharides. **S. hops.** Origanum. **S. moss.** Vegetable *horse-hair.*

spar. A transparent or translucent, readily cleavable, crystalline mineral of vitreous luster; as, fluorspar.

sparassol. $C_6H_2(COOMe)Me(OMe)OH = 196.09$. Methyl everninate. **1, 2, 4, 6-** An ester and ether from the oil of *Sparassis ramona*, a lichen. Colorless powder, m.68. Cf. *lichenol.*

spark. A flash of light produced chemically or physically; as, burning iron wire in oxygen, or an electric discharge in air. **s. spectrum.** An emission spectrum characteristic of the electrode metal, obtained from a high-voltage discharge between metallic electrodes. It is characterized by enhanced lines due to ionized atoms. Cf. *arc spectrum, isostere.*

sparking Producing electric sparks Cf. *arcing.* **s. potential.** The electric potential necessary to produce a spark in vapor or gas at ordinary temperature. It depends on the distance apart, shape, and size of the electrodes.

sparklet. A powder (similar to baking powder) for the generation of small quantities of carbon dioxide in the laboratory or household (for beverages).

spartalite. Native zinc oxide, usually pink in color due to Fe or Mn; found in New Jersey.

sparteine. $C_{15}H_{26}N_2 = 234.2$. Lupinidine. An alkaloid from *Spartium scoparium* or broom. Cf. *scoparius.* Colorless oil, d.1.02, b.328, soluble in water; a heart stimulant. Cf. *cytisine, anagyrine.*

s. bisulfate. S. sulfate. **s. hydriodide.** $C_{15}H_{26}N_2(HI)_2 = 490.09$. Colorless needles, soluble in water. **s. hydrochloride.** $C_{15}H_{26}N_2(HCl)_2 = 307.17$. Colorless crystals, soluble in water. **s. sulfate.** $C_{15}H_{26}N_2.H_2SO_4.5H_2O = 422.40$. S. bisulfate. Colorless, deliquescent crystals, m.136, soluble in water; a cardiac tonic and diuretic.

spartium. (1) Scoparius. (2) The fiber from *S. junceum*, Spanish broom (Leguminosae). Cf. *esparto*. **s. alkaloids.** A group of alkaloids derived from scoparius, e.g., sparteine, $C_{15}H_{26}N_2$.

spasmotin. $C_{20}H_{21}O_9 = 405.2$. Sphacelotoxin. A poisonous principle from ergot. Yellow powder, soluble in alcohol.

spathic. Describing a lamellar or foliated structure. **s. iron ore.** Siderite.

spathose. Siderite.

spatial. Pertaining to space.

spatula. A blunt knife for mixing or transferring small quantities of powders.

spavin. Warrant. A fireclay found underneath coal deposits; used for refractories.

spearmint. Mentha viridis. The dried leaves of *Mentha spicata* (Labiatae); a carminative and flavoring. **s. oil.** Oleum menthae viridis, from the flowering plant *Mentha spicata*. Colorless oil, d.0.917–0.934, soluble in alcohol; it contains carvone, linalol, pinene.

spear pyrites. Marcasite.

species. (1) Subdivision of a genus of plants or animals. (2) Latin for a tea. (3) A type; as, atomic s. **aromatic-** A mixture of thyme, peppermint, lavender, and cloves. **laxative-** St. Germain tea. A mixture of senna, elder flowers, fennel, anise, and potassium bitartrate. **pectoral-** Breast tea. A mixture of althaea, coltsfoot, licorice, anise, mullein, and orris.

specific. Pertaining to a particular kind of matter, microorganism, plant, or animal. **s. charge.** The ratio $e/m_0 = 1.760 \times 10^{17}$ emu/gm $= 5.276 \times 10^{71}$ esu/gm. **s. conductance.** *L*. Reciprocal of the resistance R of 1 cm^3: $L = 1/R$. **s. conductivity.** See *conductivity*. **s. energy.** See *energy*. **s. gravity.** The ratio of the density of a substance to that of another as standard: i.e., (weight of substance)/(weight of equal volume of standard). With solids and liquids the standard is usually water, and in metric units s. gravity = density. With gases the standards are oxygen, hydrogen, or air, and can be calculated from the molecular weight for ideal gases (see *equation of state*):

$$d_{O_2=1} = \text{mol. wt.} = M$$
$$d_{H_2=1} = \text{mol. wt.}/2$$
$$d_{air=1} = \text{mol. wt.}/28.95$$

See *hydrometers*. **s. heat.** The number of calories required to raise the temperature of 1 gm of material by 1°C. **s. inductive capacity.** Dielectric constant. **s. magnetization.** The susceptibility to a magnetic field, $\chi = I/Hd$, where I is the quantity of magnetization, H the intensity of the magnetic field, and d the density of the material. **s. reaction rate.** *k*. Rate of reaction at unit concentration: 1 mole/liter. **s. refraction.** Refractivity. The degree of deviation of light caused by a substance $= (n-1)/d$, where n is the refractive index, and d the density. **s. resistance.** Resistivity. The number of ohms offered at a particular temperature by 1 cm^3 of material = Ra/l ohm-cm, where R is the resistance in ohms, a the area of a cross section, and l the length of the body. Cf. *conductivity*. **s. rotation.** The angle of rotation produced by 1 cm^3 of material at standard temperature with sodium light: $[\alpha]_D^t = rv/nl$, where $[\alpha]_D^t$ is the s. rotation at t°C for the sodium line D, r the observed rotation in angular degrees, v the number of milliliters, n the number of grams dissolved, and l the length of the tube in centimeters. See *polariscope, rotation*. **s. rotatory power.** The rotation in angular degrees produced by a solution containing 1 gm/ml in a column 10 cm long, usually with the yellow sodium flame (D line of spectrum) and at room temperature (20°C); hence $[\alpha] = 100a/lc$, where $[\alpha]$ is the s. rotation, a the observed angle, l the length of the column in decimeters, and c the concentration in grams per 100 ml. **s. surface.** A/V. The ratio of the area A per unit volume V of a colloidal system. **s. volume.** The volume occupied by 1 gm of material; the reciprocal of density. **s. weight.** S. gravity.

specifics. Remedies that are exceptionally consistent in their action toward certain diseases; as, quinine for malaria, or mercury for syphilis.

specpure. Spectroscopically pure; e.g., as, a substance giving a pure spectrum, characteristic of itself only.

spectinomycin. Trobicin. An antibiotic produced by *Streptomyces spectabilis*.

spectra. Plural of spectrum. Classification: *Source* of light:

Arc s.	Solar s.	Vacuum arc s.
Explosion s.	Spark s.	Vacuum flash s.
Flame s.	Stellar s.	Vacuum spark s.
Flash s.		X-ray s.

Kind of spectrum produced:
Emission s. or absorption s.:
  Continuous s.:
    A hot solid body
  Discontinuous s.:
    Line s.—atoms
    Band s.—molecules
Mode of production:

Crystal-diffracted s.	Grating-refracted s.:
Grating-diffracted s.:	Primary
Primary	Secondary
Secondary	etc.
etc.	Prism-refracted s.

spectral. Pertaining to a spectrum. **s. analysis.** See *spectrum analysis*. **s. classification.** S. types. Harvard Star classification. A systematic arrangement of the stellar spectra in a continuous sequence of types, from bright line spectra to diffused band spectra. Of the stars examined 99% fall into the classes:

  A. Hydrogen lines
  B. Hydrogen and helium lines
  F. Hydrogen lines and faint metallic lines
  G. Many metallic lines, but no compounds
  K. Strong metallic lines, very weak bands
  M. Banded spectra of metallic oxides.

s. tube. An evacuated glass tube with 2 electrodes containing rarefied traces of gas which produce light of characteristic spectrum when an electric current is passed. **s. types.** (1) S. classification. (2) See *spectra*.

spectrochemical analysis. Spectroscopic analysis.

spectrochemistry. A branch of science that utilizes light waves for chemical analysis. See *spectrum analysis*.

spectrogram. The photographic record of a spectrum with a standard comparison spectrum.

spectrograph. (1) An instrument to produce a spectrogram, consisting of the slit, the lenses (collimator or camera), the dispersing system (photographic, thermal, or ionic). (2) Misnomer for a device to convert speech sound waves into electrical impulses which produce a graph (voiceprint) said to be characteristic of the individual. **quartz-** A s. used for wavelengths of 8000–2000 Å. **X-ray-** a device for obtaining crystallograms.

spectroheliograph. A device for photographing the sun's surface by means of a spectroscope employing a specific spectrum line.

spectrometer. A spectroscope with scales for measuring the angle of refraction and the wavelengths of lines or bands. **constant deviation-** A s. in which the collimator and telescope are fixed permanently at right angles, and the prism is rotated.

spectrometry. The measurement of the wavelengths of the lines or bands in a spectrum and their identification with the elements producing them

spectrophotometer. (1) A device to measure photometrically the quantity of light of any particular wavelength range absorbed by a colored solution. (2) A device to measure the intensity of the photographic image of a spectral line. **atomic absorption-** A s. for determination of elements from capacity to absorb light of characteristic frequency in the atomic state.

spectropolarimeter. An instrument to measure optical rotation for different wavelengths of light. Cf. *dispersion*.

spectroscope. (1) An instrument for analyzing light by separating it into its component rays. It consists essentially of a prism that refracts or a grating that diffracts the light, with a device for making the rays parallel (collimator) and an eyepiece for enlarging the spectrum. (2) A device by which radiations are separated into component parts; as, mass s. **abridged-** An absorptiometer used for restricted spectral ranges. **comparison-** A s. for comparing 2 spectra side by side. **direct-vision-** A low-dispersive s., with a crown-glass collimator along the axis of a single tube with the train of prisms and eyepiece. **grating-** A s. of high dispersive power in which a series of spectra is formed by either: (1) a reflection grating, a finely ruled piece of plane or concave (self-focusing) speculum metal; or (2) a cast of the original transmission grating. **mass-** A device for the separation of charged molecular species according to their mass-to-charge ratio (m/e) by subjecting them to electric and magnetic fields; used to determine the structure of organic compounds and in mixture and isotope analysis. Cf. *mass spectra*. **measuring-** A s. adapted to the measurement of the wavelengths of the component rays. **micro-** See *microspectroscope, spectrometer*. **nuclear-magnetic-resonance-** A s. that measures the absorption of energy by spinning nuclei in a strong magnetic field. The sample is subjected to radio-frequency radiations from an oscilloscope, and the energy absorption is measured over a wide

frequency range. **photographic-** A s. with the viewing telescope replaced by a camera; a *spectrograph*. **prism-** A s. whose dispersive power depends on one or more prisms, of glass, quartz, or rock salt. **reversion-** A s. that enables the same spectrum to be reproduced twice, but in reverse directions, thus doubling any displacement of absorption bands; used to determine carbon monoxide in blood. **X-ray.** See *X-ray spectrometer*.

spectroscopic. Associated with the spectroscope. **s. analysis.** Spectrum analysis, spectrochemical analysis. Minute quantities of elements may be detected by their characteristic spectral lines. Cf. *flame photometer*. Methods:

1. A flame (bunsen burner) colored with a small quantity of the substance (in millimicrons):
   Barium, green line 553, bands 534–524, etc.
   Calcium, orange band 620–618
   Cesium, blue line 455, 459
   Copper, green and blue lines and bands
   Indium, blue line 451, purple line 410
   Lithium, red line 671
   Potassium, red lines 766, 769; purple line 404
   Radium, red band 670–653
   Rubidium, purple lines 420, 421
   Sodium, yellow line 589
   Strontium, red bands 686–674–662, 606
   Thallium, green line 535
2. An electric spark passing through a cup containing a solution of the substance: for Mg, Fe, Mn, Zn, Co, Ni, Cr.
3. Examination of the spectrum after the light has passed through a solution of the substance (absorption spectrum); used especially for organic substances.

spectroscopically. Pertaining to spectroscopy. **s. pure.** Specure. A degree of purity enabling a substance to be identified s., the essential lines being apparent without interference by impurities.

spectroscopy. The study of the properties of light by means of the spectroscope.

spectrum. (1) A variously colored band of light showing in succession the rainbow colors or isolated lines or bands of colors; produced by refraction through a prism, or by diffraction by a grating. Cf. *spectra*. (2) A similar band of radiant energy, invisible to the eye and extending beyond the violet (ultraviolet) or red (infra-red) portions of the visible spectrum. See figure under *radiation*. **absorption-** The visible or invisible s. produced by a composite ray of light after it has passed through a colored solution or through a layer of vapor or gas, which absorbs one or more of the constituent rays. **arc-** A s. from a substance placed between the carbon poles of an arc. **Aston-** See *mass s*. **band-** Lines so close together that they appear as a continuous band; due to *molecular* vibrations. Cf. *line s*. **bright-line-** See *line-*, *flash-s*. **chemical-** That portion of the s. which contains the most chemically active wavelengths, as ultraviolet rays. **comparison-** A s. having sharp lines, as standard; usually photographed on the same plate above and below the spectrum of the sample, e.g., the arc or spark spectrum of titanium or iron. **continuous-** A s. in which no Fraunhofer lines are visible; there is an uninterrupted change from one color to another. **dark-line-** Reversal s.

A s. containing Fraunhofer lines. Cf. *absorption s.*
diffraction- A s. produced by means of a grating.
discontinuous- A combined line and bands. **electro-chemical-** See *electrochemical.* **electromagnetic-** See *radiations.* **electronic-** Visible and ultraviolet s. produced by the changes in the electronic state of molecules. **emission-** Bright lines from an incandescent source. **explosion-** A s. produced by exploding a metallic wire or a solution on an asbestos fiber by means of an electric current. It shows lines from excitation states above the spark s. **flame-** A s. with a bunsen flame as the source of excitation. **flash-** (1) Explosion s. (2) A s. showing bright Fraunhofer lines on a dark background; seen during a solar eclipse. **furnace-** A s. obtained with an electric furnace (3000°C) source; intermediate between the flame and arc s. **high-frequency-** An X-ray s. produced by high-frequency currents. **hyperfine-** Extremely thin lines close together; due to nuclear vibrations. Cf. *band s.* **infrared-** The thermal-ray region beyond the red end of the s. **invisible-** See *ultraviolet-, infrared-s.* **line-** Colored or bright lines on a dark background; due to atomic vibrations. Cf. *hyperfine s.* **magnetic-** See *magnetic.* **mass-** Aston s. The images produced when canal rays are subjected to electric and magnetic fields, which separate the ions according to their mass. Cf. *isotopic weight.* **molecular-** See *band s., molecular ray.* **Moseley-** See *X-ray spectrum.* **nebular-** A s. obtained by photographing gaseous, planetary, or spiral nebulae with telescope and spectrograph. **normal-** Diffraction s. A s. produced by a grating; it shows the rays of different wavelengths in proper relationship to one another, and less distorted than a prism. **photographic-** A s. that affects photographic emulsions. **photopic-** A s. bright enough to arouse color sensations in the human eye. Cf. *scotopic s.* **planetary-** A polarized solar s., produced by light reflected from planets. **primary-** The most prominent s. produced by a grating. **Raman-** See *scattering, Raman spectrum.* **reversal-** See *dark-line-* **roentgen-** X-ray s. **rotational-** A s. in the microwave region produced by changes in the rotational states of nonhomopolar molecules. **scotopic-** The s. seen by the dark-adapted human eye. Cf. *photopic s.* **secondary-** The second most prominent s. produced by a grating. **secondary-electron-** A very sensitive and nondestructive method of detecting substances on a surface by bombardment with low-energy electrons and measuring the energies of the secondary (Auger) electrons emitted which are characteristic of the atoms from which they originate. **solar-** A s. produced by the light of the sun; it shows Fraunhofer lines. **spark-** A s. produced by the excitation of a vapor by electric sparks; a characteristic s. is obtained for each electrode metal. **stellar-** A s. produced by the light of stars. **sunspot-** A s. obtained by passing the light from sunspots through a quarter-wave plate or nicol prism; it shows the Zeeman effect. **ultraviolet-** The dark portion beyond the violet end of the s.; chiefly chemically active rays. Cf. *irradiation.* **vibrational-** Infrared s. produced by changes in the vibrational state of nonhomopolar molecules. **X-ray-** Moseley s. Lines characteristic of the metal used as anticathode in an X-ray tube. The

X rays are diffracted by a crystal acting as a grating. The frequencies are proportional to the atomic number of the element used as anticathode. **s. analysis.** (1) The measurement of the intensity and frequency of s. lines. (2) Spectroscopic analysis. (3) The analysis of the structure of a spectrum, e.g., resolution into series or multiplets. **s. classes.** See (1) *spectra,* (2) *spectral classification.* **s. lamp.** See *lamp.* **s. lines, s. series.** A mathematical relationship existing between the lines or group of lines in the s. of an element: $\nu = 1/\lambda = L + BN/(m + \alpha + \beta/m^2)^2$, where

ν = wave number in vacuo, waves/cm
L = wave number of the limit of the series
N = Rydberg universal series constant
m = a variable integer corresponding with a definite line
α, β, B = constants

s. types.
1. Continuous; as, from an incandescent lamp, carbon arc, or hot, glowing body
2. Discontinuous:
   (a) *Bright-line* s.; as, incandescent gas, flame of sodium, arc of iron, or spark spectra
   (b) *Dark-line* s.; as, solar s., or continuous s. absorbed by a hot, gaseous envelope
   (c) *Bright-band* s.; as, comet s.
   (d) *Dark-band* s.; as, the absorption s. of dye solutions.

specular. Mirrorlike. **s. coal.** Pitch coal. A shining variety of coal. **s. hematite, s. iron.** Specularite. **s. metal.** Speculum metal.

specularite. Fe_2O_3. Specular hematite, specular iron, gray hematite. Native, disklike crystals, with metallic luster.

speculation. A conclusion drawn from incomplete knowledge of facts. Cf. *deduction, hypothesis.*

speculum metal. An alloy: Cu 66, Sn 33%, As trace; used in making mirrors.

speise. A usually fusible and brittle native arsenide.

speisequark. A German soft-curd cheese.

speiss cobalt. $(FeNiCO)As_2$. An impure smaltite.

speleology. The study of cave formation.

spelter. Commercial zinc used for galvanizing. **hard-** S. recovered from galvanizing-bath dross (10% iron).

Spencer, Leonard James. 1870–1959. British mineralogist.

Spergon. Trademark for tetrachloro-*p*-benzoquinone; a seed dressing to protect against smut disease.

sperm. A male reproductive cell. **s. oil.** The oil of the s. whale. **s. whale.** The mammal, *Physeter macrocephalus*, a source of spermaceti and ambergris.

spermaceti. Cetaceum. The solid fat from the head of the sperm whale, *Physeter macrocephalus*, Linné; chiefly cetyl palmitate. White, unctuous mass of faint odor, d. 0.94, m.45; used in ointments (U.S.P.), and standard candles.

spermin. $C_5H_{14}N_2 = 102.1$. A leucomaine constituent of spermatic fluid, sputum, and other animal substances. Colorless crystals, soluble in water; a nerve tonic.

sperrschicht cell. A photoelectric cell sensitive over the visual spectrum.

sperrylite. $PtAs_2$. A native arsenide.

spessartite. $3MgO.Al_2O_3.3SiO_2$. A red aluminum garnet (Germany).

sp. gr. Abbreviation for specific gravity.

sphacelic acid. An acid from ergot.

sphacelotoxin. Spasmotin.

sphaerite. A hydrous phosphate of aluminum.

sphalerite. ZnS. Pseudogalena. Zinc blende, cleiophane blende, rosin jack, blackjack, mock ore. An isometric, native zinc sulfide. Cf. *wurtzite*.

sphene. $CaTiSiO_5$. Titanite. A native, lustrous brown calcium silicotitanite, found in rocks.

sphenoid. A hemihedral crystal or half-crystal.

spherical. Bell-shaped or globular.

spherocobaltite. $CoCO_3$. A native carbonate.

spheroidal. Sphere-shaped.

spheroidization. The formation of rounded grains in alloys, generally during annealing.

spherometer. An instrument to determine surface curvature.

spheronizing. A process for converting fine particles of powder into pellets by maintaining them in turbulent motion against baffle bars and so forming agglomerates, e.g., for increasing the apparent density of carbon black.

spherulite. A spherical aggregation of outward radiating fibers, as from a solidifying polymer melt; gives a maltese cross in polarized light.

sphingoin. $C_{17}H_{35}O_2N = 285.3$. A brain leucomaine.

sphingolipid. A lipid containing a long-chain base.

sphingomyelin. $C_{46}H_{96}N_2O_6P = 1035.00$. A phospholipin from brain, hydrolyzing to phosphoric acid, choline, sphingosine, and cerebronic acid.

sphingosine. $C_{17}H_{35}O_2N = 285.32$. An unsaturated, aliphatic aminoalcohol split product of cerebrosides.

sp. ht. Abbreviation for specific heat.

sphygmograph. A device for recording the pulse.

sphygmomanometer. A device for recording heartbeats.

spice. A condiment or substance used to give flavor and distinctive taste to food; the majority contain essential oils.

spicular. Needle-shaped.

spider poison. Arachnolysin.

spiegel. (1) Spiegeleisen. (2) German for mirror.

spiegeleisen. Spiegel. A white cast iron (Mn 5–20%), obtained in the blast furnace; used to make manganese steel.

Spiegler Jolle's reagent. A solution of mercuric chloride 2, succinic acid 4, sodium chloride 4 gm in 100 ml water; a reagent for albumin in urine.

spigelia. Pinkroot, Indian pink. The dried roots of *Spigelia marilandica* (Loganiaceae); contains spigeline; a teniafuge.

spigeline. An alkaloid from *Spigelia* species.

spike. (1) Plantain. (2) Pepper. **s. nard.** See *spikenard*.

spikenard. The aromatic root of a herb, *Nardostachys Jatamansi* (Valerianaceae). **American-** Aralia.

spilanthol. $C_{14}H_{25}NO = 213.20$. Isisilli (local name). A liquid, from *Spilanthus acmella* (Compositae), S. Africa; a toothache remedy.

spin. Angular momentum; rotation around an axis, e.g., of an electron. **antiparallel-** The s. of 2 particles in opposite directions. **parallel-** The s. of 2 particles in the same direction.

spinacene. Squalene.

spinasterol. $C_{28}H_{46}O = 398.0$. A phytosterol from spinach; α, β, and γ isomers. Cf. *cholane*.

spindel oil. A mixture of fuel oil about 95 and wool fat 5%. used in the textile industry to preserve and lubricate raw fibers.

spindle. A hydrometer.

spindle tree. Euonymus.

spinel. $MgAl_2O_4$. Rubicelle, ruby alamandine, ruby balas. Variously colored isometric crystals, some used as gems.

spinels. $M''M'''_2O_4$. Rockforming aluminates or ferrates. M'' is magnesium, zinc, manganese, or ferrous iron; M''' is aluminum, chromium, ferric iron, or manganic manganese. They have a high hardness and refractive index; e.g.; gaehnite, $ZnAl_2O_4$; franklinite, $(Fe, Zn, Mn)Fe_2O_4$; chromite, $FeCr_2O_4$.

spinneret. (1) A platinum thimble with a flat base containing minute holes, through which rayon spinning solution is forced to form filaments. (2) The spinning organ of spiders.

spinning. (1) Revolving around its axis. (2) The production of a synthetic filament by extrusion of a liquid under pressure through fine holes in a spinneret. **dispersion-** S. in which a dispersion of fine particles of the material is made in a viscous medium. **dry-** S. in which a hot gas evaporates the solvent of the liquid. **melt-** S. in which the liquid is molten and solidifies into a filament on cooling. **reaction-** S. in which solidification is effected by polymerization. **wet-** S. in which the liquid is coagulated by a chemical precipitant. **s. electron.** The fourth motion of an electron in an atom. Cf. *Pauli's exclusion principle*. **s. power.** The property of a fluid which enables it to be drawn out into threads; as, egg white.

spinthariscope. Scintillascope. An instrument for detecting radioactive rays from the fluorescence of a needle tipped with a radioactive material (e.g., sodium iodide activated with thallium iodide) apparent as each α particle strikes a fluorescent screen behind the needle.

spinulosin. $C_8H_8O_5 = 184.1$. 3,6-Dihydroxy-4-methoxy-2,5-toluquinone. Purple-bronze plates, m.201; an antibiotic from cultures of the mold *Penicillium spinulosum* (cf. *penicillin*), and *Aspergillus fumigatus*.

spiracin. Methylcarboxylsalicylic acid. White crystals, insoluble in water; a substitute for salicylic acid.

spiraeic acid. Salicylic acid.

spirane structure. The atomic arrangement,

X is an atomic held in common by 2 rings, as in spiro compounds.

spirans. A spiro compound.

Spirillaceae. The third family of the Schizomycetes bacteria; with wave-shaped cells: *Spirosoma:* no organs of locomotion; *Microspira:* rigid cells, few polar flagella; *Spirillum:* rigid cells, many flagella; *Spirochetae:* flexible and mobile cells.

spirit. (1) Any distilled liquid. (2) A solution of a volatile substance in alcohol. (3) Ethanol. **cologne-** Ethanol. **colonial-, Columbian-** Methanol.

Libavius- Stannic chloride. **methylated-** q.v. **mineral-** White s. **motor-** Gasoline (U.S.) or petrol (U.K.). **potato-** A whisky distilled from fermented potatoes. **proof-** See *proof spirit.* **pyroacetic-** Acetone. **pyroligneous-, pyroxylic-** Methanol. **rectified-** 90% ethyl alcohol. **silent-** The alcoholic s. distillate from a spiritous liquor, before addition of denaturants. **white-** Mineral s. A solvent composed entirely of petroleum products, b.150–190, Abel's closed flash point 78 or over; a paint thinner and turpentine substitute. **wood-** Methanol.

    s. acid. Concentrated acetic acid obtained by distillation of 12% vinegar. **s. of alum.** Sulfuric acid. **s. colors.** Aniline dyes insoluble in water, soluble in alcohol; used as stains and to dye silk. **s. of copper.** Acetic acid obtained from copper acetate. **s. of ethyl nitrite.** Spiritus aethylis nitritis; s. of sweet niter. An alcoholic solution of ethyl nitrate: 3.5–4.5 (U.S. usage), 1.52–2.66% (U.K. usage); used in medicine. **s. of hartshorn.** Ammonium hydroxide. **s. of niter.** S. of ethyl nitrite. **s. of salt.** Hydrochloric acid. **s. of tin.** Stannic chloride. **s. of vitriol.** Concentrated sulfuric acid. **s. of wine.** Ethyl alcohol. **s. of wood.** Methanol.

spirit(u)ous. Having the character of spirit.

spirocid. Acetarsol.

spiro compounds. Spirans, spirocyclans. Organic compounds having 2 rings joined by a carbon atom common to both; as, spiroheptane. Cf. *ring structures.*

spirocyclans. Spiro compounds (Baeyer).

spiroform. $C_6H_4(OOCMe)COOPh = 256.10$. Vesipyrin, acetyl salol, acetyl salicyl phenyl ester, acetylphenyl-*o*-oxybenzoic acid. White powder, insoluble in water; an antirheumatic.

spirogyra. A filamentous alga: a green, feltlike mass or scum in fresh-water ponds or tanks.

spironolactone. $C_{24}H_{32}O_4S = 416.58$. Yellow crystals, insoluble in water, m.200; a diuretic (U.S.P.).

spirosal. $C_6H_4(OH)COOCH_2CH_2OH = 182.1$. Monoglycosalicylate, glysal. Colorless liquid, b.170, soluble in water; used medicinally.

spitting. Small explosions and scattering of materials when certain substances are dried and heated or brought together; as, with sulfuric acid and water. Cf. *decrepitation.*

splash head. A device between the flask and condenser of a distillation apparatus to prevent liquid from splashing over into the latter. Usually an open glass tube in a bulb, bent away from the direction of the flask.

split product. A decomposition product, e.g., of a hydrolyzed glucoside.

splitting. The breaking of a molecule into 2 or more individual atoms.

spodumene. $(Li,Na)_2Al_2Si_4O_{12}$. Triphane. The pink (kuntzite) and green (hiddenite) are used as gems. Some spodumene crystals are 47 feet long.

spoilage. Any detrimental change due to physical or chemical action.

spoilbank. Bing.

sponge. (1) A marine animal, *Euspongia officinalis* (Poriferae). (2) The flexible, fibrous skeleton of the animal, cut and dried. Yellow, porous masses of various shapes. (3) A metal in porous form, as platinum s. **gelatin-** A spongy, water-insoluble

form of gelatin, solubilized by pepsin; a local hemostatic (U.S.P.). **iron-** Ferric oxide. **platinum-** Platinized asbestos. **vegetable-** Tufa.

spongin. A scleroprotein from bath sponge; yields diiodotyrosine and bromine.

spontaneous. Sudden or voluntary, and without apparent external cause or incitement. **s. combustion.** Self-ignition of flammable material, caused by the accumulation of heat on slow oxidation.

sporangia. Cells containing spores.

spores. The resting state of microorganisms. Single cells capable of growth and reproduction.

spot analysis. (1) A microchemical identification test, made on a porcelain plate. (2) A reaction on impregnated filter paper.

spout. (1) A slightly projecting depression on the rim of a vessel through which the contents are poured. (2) The cylindrical projection of a teapot. (3) A trough to conduct molten metals.

spray. A stream of mixed air and finely divided liquid produced with an atomizer. **s. drying.** Rapid evaporation, in which a solution is heated in the atomized state so that the dissolved substance falls out of the spray in the solid state. **s. residue.** The amount of insecticide remaining on fruits, such as apples, pears, peaches, and grapes. Maximum amounts permitted in most foods: Cu 20, As 1, Pb 2 ppm, fluorides nil.

sprays. (1) Pharmaceutical preparations used as antiseptics for body cavities. The active substances are dissolved, usually in liquid. (2) Technical preparations used as pesticides

Sprengel pump. A high-vacuum mercury pump: 0.001 mm.

spring. A source of a natural water. **hot-** Water emerging from the soil at a temperature above 50°C.

spring balance. A device for measuring force by the extension it produces in a spring. See *Hooke's law.*

sprinkler. (1) A perforated plate near the top of a gas-scrubbing tower. It produces a rain of gas-absorbing liquid. (2) A bushing filled with a low-melting alloy, e.g., D'Arcet metal, which when heated, will release water from a pipe system.

sprudel effect. Emerging gas bubbles rising in a continuous stream, or s., from gas-jet electrodes.

sprue. A projection left on a casting, to be broken off for testing purposes.

Sprunstron. Trade name for a polypropylene staple fiber used for ropes.

spur feterita. Sorghum.

spurred rye. Ergot.

sputter. To produce finely divided metal by passing a high-potential discharge between 2 electrodes of the metal in a dielectric liquid or gas.

sputum. Saliva mixed with mucus and other secretions of the mouth or nose. Typical analysis, per cent:

Organic constituents		4.1–6.9
Fatty acids		0.02–0.97
Soaps		Traces–0.40
Cholesterol		Traces–0.16
Lecithin		Traces–0.15
Nuclein		Traces–0.48
Proteins		0.90–0.52
Inorganic constituents	0.3–0.9	
Water	93.0–95.0	

sp. vol. Abbreviation for specific volume.

sq. Abbreviation for square. **sq ch.** Square chain. **sq cm.** Square centimeter; cm². **sq in.** Square inch; in.² **sq ft.** Square foot; ft². **sq m.** Square meter; m². **sq mi.** Square mile. **sq yd.** Square yard. **sq rd.** Square rod.

squalene. $C_{30}H_{50} = 410.40$. Spinacene. An unsaturated hydrocarbon in the oils of the Elasmobranch (shark family) and, as its homologs, in many marine oils. Colorless oil, $d_{15}°0.8610$, $b_{25\,mm}284$. Cf. *carotene.*

square. A four-sided figure, whose sides are equal and whose angles are right angles. **s. centimeter.** cm². A unit of area 1/10,000 square meter: $1\,cm^2 = 0.155\,sq\,in.$ **s. foot.** ft² or sq ft. A unit of area in the English system $= 929\,cm^2$. **s. inch.** in.² or sq in. A unit of area in the English system $= 6.452\,cm^2$. **s. meter.** m². A unit of area in the metric system: $1\,m^2 = 10,000\,cm^2 = 10.7638$ ft² $= 24.7104$ sq links. **s. root.** That quantity which, when multiplied by itself, gives the original quantity. **s. yard.** yd², or sq yd. A unit of area in the English system $= 0.836\,m^2$.

squawroot. Caulophyllum.

squaw vine. Partridgeberry. The dried herb of the evergreen, *Mitchella repens,* a diuretic, astringent, and emmenagogue.

squaw-weed. Senecio.

squill. Scilla. The fleshy inner scales of the bulb of *Urginea maritima* (Liliaceae); contains scillin, scillitoxin, sinistrin; an emetic and expectorant.

Sr. Symbol for strontium.

St. Abbreviation for stoke.

S.T. Abbreviation for surface tension. **S.T.37.** A solution of hexylresorcinol in glycerol and water (surface tension 37 dynes); a rapidly penetrating germicide.

S.T.A. Abbreviation for softening temperature of ash; used in coal analysis.

stabile. Stable.

stabilizer. (1) A retarding agent, for a vigorous accelerator which preserves chemical equilibrium. (2) A substance added to a solution to render it more stable; as acetanilide to hydrogen peroxide.

stable. A balanced condition not readily destroyed; as, photo-s. **s. scopolamine.** Scopomannite.

stachydrine. $C_7H_{13}O_2N = 143.1$. A heterocyclic amino acid in many plant juices (as *Stachys* species) and in mussels (as *Arca noae*). Cf. *trigonelline.*

stachyose. $C_{24}H_{42}O_{21} = 666.4$. A nonreducing tetrasaccharide from the roots of soybean and *Stachy stuberifera* (Labiatae); hydrolyzes to fructose, glucose, and galactose.

stagonometer. Stalagmometer.

Stahl, Georg Ernst. 1660–1734. German physician and chemist; developed the phlogiston theory (1697).

stain. Dyes in solution for coloring materials such as wood, tissues, textiles. Cf. *paints.* **contrast-** q.v. **counter-** q.v. **microscope-** A dye used to stain preparations for microscopic examination; used for differentiating structural elements. **negative-** A s. that stains only the surroundings of a structure and so renders it more easily visible. Cf. *positive s.* **positive-** A s. that stains the structure itself. Cf. *negative s.*

s. jar. A small, square glass vessel used to stain microscopic slides.

staircase reaction. Chemical changes that proceed stepwise; as, the hydrolysis of starch to glucose, via α and β dextrins and di- and trisaccharides.

stalactite. A hanging column of calcite formed by the slow evaporation of carbonated mineral solutions dripping from the roof of a cavern.

stalagmite. A standing column of calcite formed by the slow evaporation of carbonated mineral solutions dripping onto the floor of a cavern.

stalagmometer. A device to obtain drops of liquid at definite intervals; e.g., Traube's s., used to calculate surface tension from the number of liquid drops passing an orifice in a given time; also used to determine molecular weight (cf. *Morgan equation*) and the degree of association of liquids.

stalagmometry. Measuring the progress of chemical reactions (as esterifications) from the change in surface tension.

stalagmones. Substances lowering the surface tension of urine; associated with certain diseases (as tuberculosis) and severe infections, but occurring normally in pregnancy.

Stalloy. Trademark for high-silicon steel sheets and laminations used in electrical transformers.

stamen. The male organ of a plant, in which the pollen is prepared. Cf. *pistil.*

stamp. (1) To break up or crush ore and rock by machinery. (2) A heavy mechanical pestle for crushing ore. **s. battery.** A group of pestles working mechanically in an iron mortar. **s. mill.** An establishment for crushing ores by s. batteries.

standard. (1) An established form of quality or quantity. (2) A substance used to establish the strength of volumetric solutions. **s. candle.** A spermaceti candle that burns 120 grains per hour. See *standard lamp.* **s. cell.** An electrolytic cell having a definite voltage; as, the Weston cell. **s. conditions.** In gas analysis an atmospheric pressure of 760 mm, and a temperature of 0°C, at latitude 45°; sometimes abbreviated STP (standard temperature and pressure). Cf. *NTP.* **s. deviation.** The square roots of the sum of the squares of the deviations between the variates and the mean of a series, divided by one less than the total number in the series, Cf. *error.* **s. error.** See *error.* **s. lamp.** A source of light of a known light intensity for photometric determinations; as: pentane 10.00, Hefner 0.9, Carcel 9.6, standard 1.0 international candles. **s. meter.** The length between 2 lines ruled on a bar of platinum-iridium at the International Bureau of Weights and Measures, Sèvres, Paris. **s. pressure.** Pressure equal to a column of 760 mm mercury at sea level in latitude 45°. **s. solution.** A solution of definite concentration. See *normal.* **s. substance.** A substance used to standardize volumetric solutions. It should be easily obtainable pure, unaltered in air and at moderate temperatures, neither hygroscopic nor efflorescent, readily soluble in water or alcohol; and have a high molecular weight (to reduce effects of error in weighing), produce no interfering product on titration, and be free from color before and after titration (to avoid interference with the indicator). **s. temperature.** 0°C (273°A). **s. volume.** The normal volume occupied by one mole of a gaseous substance: 22.4 liters. **s. wavelength.** The wavelength of the red cadmium line, observed in air at 15°C and 760 mm pressure. It is equal to 6438.4696 angstroms.

standardization. The procedure to bring a preparation to an established quality. **physiological-** Testing of drugs or biological products (which cannot be chemically analyzed) by their pharmacological action on a normal animal. Thus: digitalis, strophanthum—frog heart; ergot—rooster; aconite —guinea pig; cannabis, adrenaline—dog.

standardized. Describing a utensil, device, or preparation that has been tested, measured, and compared with a standard. See *Bureau of Standards* (B.S., U.S.A.), *National Physical Laboratory* or *British Standard* (N.P.L. or B.S., U.K.), *volumetric glassware.*

standards. The agencies establishing or defining s. in various countries are:

USASI . . . . United States of American Standards Institute; formerly;
ASA . . . . American Standards Association
BSI . . . . British Standards Institution
IRAM . . . . Instituto Argentino de Racionalizacion de Materiales (Argentina)
INDITECNOR . . . Instituto National de Investigaciones Tecnologicas y Normalizacion (Chile)
UPN . . . . Ura pro normalisaci (Czechoslovakia)
AFNOR . . . . Association Française de Normalisation (France)
DNA . . . . Deutscher Normenausschuss (Germany)
NEN . . . . Stichting Nederlands Normalisatie-Instituut (Holland)
MSH . . . . Office Hongrois de Normalisation (Hungary)
PKN . . . . Polski Komitet Normalizcyjny (Poland)
IGPAI . . . . Repartição de Normalização (Portugal)
Ods . . . . Officiul de Stat Pentru Standards (Rumania)
KSMIIP . . . . Komitet Standartov Mer i Izueritel'nyh Priborov pri Sovete Ministrov S.S.S.R. (U.S.S.R.)
SAA . . . . Standards Association of Australia
SOS . . . . Swedish Standards Society
SVMT . . . . Eidgen. Materialsprüfungs- und Versuchsanstalt für Industrie, Bauwesen und Gewerbe (Switzerland).
CESA . . . . Canadian Engineering Standards Association
ISO . . . . International Organization for Standardization

stand oil. Litho oil. An oil heated at 250–300 without addition of oxygen or driers, and allowed to settle to remove coagulated "mucilage" (foot).

stannanes. A group of organic compounds containing tetravalent tin; as: tetramethyltin, $SnMe_4$; tristannane, $H_3Sn \cdot SnH_2 \cdot SnH_3$.

stannate. M_2SnO_3. A salt of stannic acid. **sulfato-** $R_2H_2Sn(SO_4)_3$. Cf. *stannosulfate.* **sulfo-** M_2SnS_2. A salt. **thio-** M_2SnS_3. A salt.

stannated. Treated with tin salts. See *Gutzeit test.*

stannekite. $C_{20}H_{22}O_3$. A resinous hydrocarbon in coal deposits. Bohemia.

stannic. Describing compounds of tetravalent tin. **s. acids.** α- or *normal-* $H_2SnO_3 = 168.7$. White, amorphous powder, insoluble in water, soluble in alkalies. β- or *meta-* $H_{10}Sn_5O_{15} = 843.6$. $H_2Sn_5O_{11}$ or H_2SnO_3. White powder, insoluble in water, soluble in alkalies. **s. bromide.** $SnBr_4 = 438.4$. Colorless, fuming, caustic liquid, d.3.349, m.31, soluble in water, decomp. by alcohol; used as a mordant and in tinning. **s. chloride.** $SnCl_4 = 260.5$. Tin bichloride. Colorless, fuming, caustic liquid, d.2.2738, b.114, soluble in water; a mordant, reagent, and tinning agent. **s. chromate.** $Sn(CrO_4)_2 = 350.7$. Yellow crystals, soluble in water; a ceramic pigment. **s. ethide.** Tetraethyltin. **s. ethyl hydroxide.** Ethyltin hydroxide. **s. fluoride.** $SnF_4 = 194.7$. White, deliquescent crystals, b.705. **s. hydroxide.** $Sn(OH)_4 = 186.5$. White powder, insoluble in water. **s. ion.** The tetravalent cation Sn^{4+}. **s. iodide.** $SnI_4 = 626.4$. Tin tetraiodide. Red crystals, m.144, decomp. by water. **s. methide.** Tetramethyltin. **s. oxide.** $SnO_2 = 150.7$. Tin dioxide, tin ash, flowers of tin, stannic anhydride. White powder, d.6.95, m.1197, insoluble in water, soluble in alkalies. Used as a polishing material for steel, glass, and fingernails; and in opal glass. **s. phenide.** Tetraphenyltin. **s. sulfate.** $Sn(SO_4)_2 \cdot 2H_2O = 346.9$. Colorless rhombs, soluble in water. **s. sulfide.** $SnS_2 = 183.80$. Tin bisulfide, mosaic gold, tin bronze. Yellow hexagons, decomp. red heat, insoluble in water; used for bronzing and gilding.

Stannine. (1) Trade name for restrainers for the acid pickling of iron, steel, and ferrous alloys. (2) (not cap.) Stannite.

stannising. A process for tin-coating metal objects in a mixture of vapors of hydrogen and stannous chloride at 500–600°C.

stannite. $SnS_2 \cdot Cu_2S \cdot FeS$. Stannine, tin pyrites.

stannites. M_2SnO_2. Theoretically, salts of stannous acid derived from stannous hydroxide; actual composition: $MHSnO_2$ or $HSnOOM$.

stannonate. $RSnOOM$.

stannonic acids. $RHSnO_2$, or $R \cdot SnOOH$. **s. ester.** $RR' \cdot SnO_2$, or $RSnOOR'$.

stannonium. $RSnH_3$. An organic compound of tetravalent tin. Cf. *-onium, stannane, stannyl.*

stannosulfate. $M_2Sn(SO_4)_3$. A salt. Cf. *sulfatostannate.*

stannous. Describing a compound containing divalent tin, Sn^{++}. **s. bromide.** $SnBr_2 = 278.5$. Tin protobromide. Yellow crystals, m.215, soluble in water, decomp. by alcohol. **s. chloride.** $SnCl_2 = 189.6$. Tin salt, tin protochloride. White crystals, m.247, soluble in water. It absorbs oxygen to form an insoluble oxychloride; a reagent, reducing agent, and mordant. *hydrous-* $SnCl_2 \cdot 2H_2O = 225.7$. Colorless, triclinic crystals, m.38 (decomp.), soluble in water; a reagent. **s. chromate.** $SnCrO_4 = 234.6$. Brown powder; slightly soluble in water; a ceramic pigment. **s. citrate.** $SnC_6H_6O_7 = 308.5$. Tin citrate. White powder, soluble in water. **s. ethide.** Diethyltin. **s. fluosilicate.** $SnSiF_6 = 260.76$. S. silicofluoride. Colorless prisms, soluble in water. **s. hydroxide.** $Sn(OH)_2 = 152.7$. White powder, insoluble in water, soluble in fused alkalies (forms stannites). **s. iodide.** $SnI_2 = 372.5$. Red needles, m.316, soluble in water. **s. ion.** The cation Sn^{++}. **s. oxalate.** $SnC_2O_4 = 206.7$. White crystals, insoluble in water; used in dyeing. **s. oxide.** $SnO = 134.7$. Tin monoxide, t. protoxide. Brown powder, d.6.3, burns on heating, insoluble in water; a reducing agent. **s. sulfate.** $SnSO_4 = 214.8$. White crystals, soluble in water; a mordant. **s. sulfide.** $SnS = 150.8$. Brown crystals, m.882, insoluble in water. **s. tannate.** $SnC_7H_2O_5 \cdot H_2O = 302.7$. Brown crystals, insoluble in water. **s. tartrate.** $SnC_4H_4O_5 = 250.7$. White crystals; a mordant.

stannum. Latin for tin.

stannyl. The radical $H_3Sn—$.

staphisagria. Stavesacre seed. The ripe seeds of *Delphinium staphisagria* (Ranunculaceae); an external insecticide. **s. alkaloids.** See *delphinine, delphinoidine, delphisine, staphisagroine*.

staphisagrine. $C_{22}H_{33}O_5N = 391.3$. Staphisaine. An alkaloid from staphisagria.

staphisagroine. $C_{20}H_{24}O_4N = 342.20$. An alkaloid from staphisagria.

staphisaine. Staphisagrine.

Staphylococcus. (Pl. -cocci.) A genus of Coccaceae (Schizomycetes) forming grapelike clusters. Many are pathogenic and produce pus. See *bacteria*.

staphylotoxin. A poison from *Staphylococcus* cultures.

staple. The average length of the majority of the fibers in a textile. **s. fiber.** See *fiber*.

star. (1) Needle-shaped crystals that radiate from a common center. (2) A sunlike body outside the solar system. See *spectral classification*. (3) A burner attachment for holding small vessels. **blazing-** Aletris. **s. anise.** See *anise*. **s. grass.** Aletris.

starch. $(C_6H_{10}O_5)_x = (162.1)_x$. Amylum. carbohydrates or polysaccharides in many plant cells, and serving as their chief carbohydrate reserve. As extracted, s. is a white, amorphous powder, d.1.5, insoluble in cold water, alcohol, or ether; partly soluble in hot water; hydrolyzed to several forms of dextrin and to glucose. It consists of at least 2 fractions: (1) Amylose or α-amylose, a straight-chain of 1,4,α-glucopyranose units (chain length approx. 24 units), soluble in water without forming a paste, but reverting to a soluble form on storage; stained deep blue by iodine. (2) Amylopectin or β-amylose, which gels with water, and has little affinity for iodine with which it gives a violet color. It contains esterified phosphoric acid and may be associated with fatty acids. Waxy starches are almost pure amylopectin; starches from pea and lily contain up to 75% amylose. Amylose contents, per cent:

Corn (maize) 23–29
Potato 18–27
Rice 14–17
Tapioca 17–21
Wheat 24–32

alant- Inulin. Official in (1) U.S.P., (2) B.P. **allyl-** A soft, gummy mass prepared by the action of s. with allyl chloride in presence of strong alkali; a coating for wood, paper, or metal. **animal-** Glycogen. **cassava-** Tapioca. **corn-** Amylum. S. granules from the fruit of *Zea mays*,

Indian corn (U.S.P., B.P.). Used to starch fabrics, and as a dusting powder, food, antidote for iodine, reagent, and indicator for iodine. **lichen-** Lichenin. **nitro-** See *nitrostarch*. **rice-** Rice flour. The s. granules from the seeds of *Oryza sativa*, rice. Used as a nutrient and to starch fabrics. **soluble-** See *s. soluble*. **waxy-** S. containing amylopectins with little or no amylose; a thickener in the food, textile, and adhesive industries. **wheat-** The s. granules from the seeds of *Triticum vulgare*, wheat: used as a reagent and to starch fabrics (see illustration on facing page).

s. dialdehyde. Polymeric dialdehyde. The product of the periodate oxidation of s. This breaks the C_2—C_3 bond of the glucose units in the molecule, forming dialdehyde units. Used in adhesives and coatings, for textiles and wet-strengthening papers, and as a pretan for leather. **s. glycerin, s. glycerite.** A protective colloid freshly prepared by heating 1 pt. starch with glycerol and diluting to 100 pts. with water; an emollient (U.S.P.). **s. gum.** Dextrin. **s. iodide, s. iodized.** Dark blue, antiseptic powder (2% iodine), insoluble in water. Produced by the reaction of s. and iodine solution, and a test for either. **s. nitrate.** Nitrostarch. **s. phosphates.** Reaction products of s. and alkali-metal phosphates; thickeners or binders for foods, pharmaceuticals, and adhesives. **s. soluble.** $C_{36}H_{62}O_{31} \cdot H_2O$. Amylodextrin. A hexasaccharide. White powder obtained by heating s. with glycerin: yellow color with iodine solution; soluble in water; an indicator, emulsifying agent, and textile dressing. **s. sugar.** A dextrose obtained by heating s. with dilute sulfuric acid (dextrose 1, glucose 2 pts.); used as a syrup.

Stark effect. The separation of the lines of a positive-ray spectrum by action of an intense electric field.

starlite. A brilliant, light green or blue artificial gem. Blue zircon of Siam is burned 7 hours and treated with cobalt nitrate or potassium ferrocyanide. See *zircon*.

starter. A mixture of a culture of a suitable organism and nutrient medium, used to initiate large-scale fermentation; e.g.: lactic acid–producing streptococci is a s. for cheese making.

Stas, Jean Servais. 1813–1891. Belgian chemist, noted for atomic weight determinations. **S. pipet.** A pipet whose jet has parallel walls so that the level after free drainage is always at the same point.

stassanization. A method of sterilization. Milk is heated at 167°F for 15–20 sec, and then cooled rapidly to 40–45°F. Cf. *pasteurization*.

stassfurtite. A double salt of magnesium borate and chloride from Stassfurt.

Stassfurt salts. A large deposit of oceanic salts, mainly chlorides and sulfates, found in Magdeburg Halberstadt, N. Germany; principally rock salt and anhydrite, in layers under a top alluvial deposit and sandstone. Also present are gypsum, glauberite, kainite, sylvite, sylvine, and carnallite. Cf. *abraum salts*.

state. (1) A condition. (2) A form of aggregation or dispersion; as colloidal s. (3) Orbit, energy level. The condition of an electron in a neutral or ionized atom. **activated-** See *activation*. **amorphous-** Noncrystalline. Describing a homogeneous solid whose molecules are not symmetrically oriented. Cf. *crystal*. **change of-** See *change*.

1. Potato

2. Arrowroot

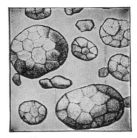

3. Oat

4. Wheat

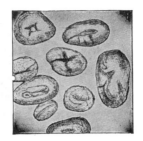

5. Pea

6. Bean

7. Rice

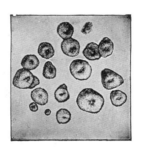

8. Maize (corn)

9. Buckwheat

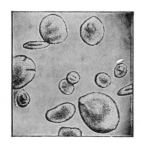

10. Rye

From Hawk and Bergeim, "Practical Physiological Chemistry."

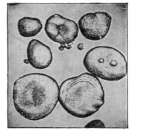

11. Barley

colloidal- Finely divided particles, surrounded by another medium. See *colloidal systems*. **crystalline-** A homogeneous, anisotropic solid, whose atoms are symmetrically oriented. **d-** See *orbital s*. **dissociated-** See *dissociation*. **dynamic-** The condition of the atoms in an ion. Cf. *static s*. **equation of-** See *equation, gas laws*. **excited-** See *excitation*. **f-** See *orbital s*. **fluid-** Molten, liquid, or gaseous s. **gaseous-** A condition in which the molecules are in rapid and irregular motion. See *gas*. **irradiated-** See *irradiation*. **liquid-** A condition between the solid and gaseous states. **luminescent-** See *luminescence*. **molten-** A liquid s. above melting-point temperature. **nascent-** The s. of a newly formed atom or molecule. Cf. *status nascendi*. **orbital-** The position toward which electrons fall during a quantum transition; final states: *s, p, d, f*. Cf. *orbit, series*. **p-** See *orbital s*. **quantum-** See *energy levels*. **radiant-** See *incandescence, luminescence, fluorescence*. **s-** See *orbital s*. **solid-** A condition in which the molecules are in slow motion as compared with the liquid s.; they are in relatively rigid positions, which may be symmetrical (crystalline s.) or nonsymmetrical (amorphous s.). **static-** The condition of atoms in a molecule. Cf. *dynamics*. **steady-** (1) A balance between the formation and decomposition of a substance. (2) If in a chain of reactions, $A \rightarrow B \rightarrow C$, the concentration of B remains constant, while that of A decreases, and that of C increases; then, B is in the steady s.

static. (1) The condition of rest or equilibrium as opposed to motion (dynamic). (2) The interference with radio radiations due to atmospheric electric charges or other sources of electricity.

s. atom. See *Lewis-Langmuir atom*. **s. electricity.** An electric charge at rest; often produced by friction.

statics. The study of matter and forces in equilibrium.

statistics. (1) The science of classifying numerical facts, judging collective numerical data, and determining probabilities from values obtained by enumeration or estimation. (2) In particular, the consideration of conditions and properties of matter (as the *average* normal value of a group of units) rather than the *actual* values of individual units. Cf. *histogram*.

stator. The stationary as distinct from the revolving portion of a machine. Cf. *rotor*.

status nascendi. Nascent state.

staubosphere. The dust of the atmosphere. (German: staub = dust.)

Staudinger, Hermann. 1881–1965. German chemist, Nobel Prize winner (1953); pioneer in the basic chemistry of synthetic plastics.

staurolite. Staurotide. An iron aluminum silicate gem.

staurotide. Staurolite.

stavesacre seed. Staphisagria.

Staybwood. Trade name for uncompressed wood, dimensionally stabilized by heat.

steam. Water vapor. **dry-** S. in which the drops of water have been evaporated. **flash-** S. at low pressure obtained from a boiler condensate. **superheated-** Water vapor heated under pressure to a temperature above 100°C. **wet-** S. containing drops of liquid water in suspension.

s. bath. A vessel surrounded by s. **s. black.** Hematoxylon. **s. distillation.** Distillation by blowing s. through the liquid, to obtain a distillate consisting of water and dissolved substance. **s. gage.** See *pressure gage*.

steapsase. Steapsin. A pancreatic juice lipase that hydrolyzes fats to glycerol and free acids.

steapsin. Steapsase.

stearaldehyde. $C_{17}H_{35}CHO = 268.28$. Octadecanal*. White scales, m.63.5.

stearamide. $Me(CH_2)_{16}CONH_2 = 283.3$. Octadecanamide*. White leaflets, m.109.

stearate. $C_{17}H_{35}COOM$. A salt or ester of stearic acid; M is a monovalent radical.

stearic acid. $CH_3(CH_2)_{16}COOH = 284.38$. Octodecanoic acid*, *n*-octodecylic acid; in many vegetable and animal fats. Colorless leaflets, m.69, insoluble in water. U.S.P. s.a. contains palmitic acid; used in glycerin suppositories. **s. aldehyde.** Stearaldehyde. **s. amide.** Stearamide.

stearin. (1) $C_3H_5(C_{17}H_{35}COO)_3 = 891.9$. Tristearin, glyceryl tristearate. Colorless crystals, the chief constituent of many fats, $d_{65^\circ}0.943$, m.71, insoluble in water. (2) *commercial-* A mixture of fatty acids, prepared by hydrolysis of fats; used in the manufacture of candles and solid alcohol. **lauro-** Laurin.

stearolic acid. $Me(CH_2)_7C \vdots C(CH_2)_7COOH = 280.3$. 9-Octadecynoic acid*. Colorless prisms, m.48, insoluble in water.

Stearone. $(C_{17}H_{35})_2CO = 506.74$. Trade name for 18-pentatriacontanone*. A solid, m.88, insoluble in water.

stearonitrile. $C_{17}H_{35}CN = 265.28$. Octadecane nitrile*. Colorless crystals, m.41.

stearoptene. Oleoptene. The oxygenated portions of an essential oil consisting chiefly of the solid part (camphor, as opposed to the liquid part; as, eleoptene).

stearoxylic acid. $Me(CH_2)_7CO \cdot CO(CH_2)_7COOH = 312.35$. 9,10-Dioxooctadecanoic acid*. A solid, m.86, insoluble in water.

stearyl. Octadecanoyl*. The radical $C_{17}H_{35}CO—$, from stearic acid. **s. alcohol.** $C_{18}H_{38}O = 270.03$. White flakes, m.58, insoluble in water; used in ointments (U.S.P.).

steatite. A variety of talc.

stechiometry. Stoichiometry.

steel. (1) Carbon s. A tough, elastic alloy of iron containing small quantities of carbon:

Mild or soft steel	Less than 0.15 % C
Medium steel	0.15–0.30 % C
Hard steel	More than 0.30 % C

See *iron*. World production (1966) 451 million tons. (2) Alloy steel. An alloy of iron whose properties are due to an element or elements other than carbon; as, Cr, Mn, Ni, W, Si. Cf. *SAE classification*.

alloy- Iron and other metal, fused together and cooled rapidly. **alloy-treated-** S. containing metals added during manufacture for curative purposes. Cf. *alloys*. **austenitic-** Acid-resisting s. containing Cr 18, Ni 8, Mo 1–4%. **bulletproof-** S. containing Mn 12, C 1, P or S less than 0.02%. **carbon-** An alloy of iron and carbon without the addition of other metals. **chrome-molybdenum-** A light alloy of iron, with Cr 0.8–1.1, Mn 0.4–0.6, Mo 0.15–0.25 C 0.25–0.35%. **chromium-nickel-** See *stainless s.* **high-speed-** An iron alloy containing C 0.65, Mn 0.2, Cr 4.7, Mo 8.5 (or W 17), V 5%; used for tools, and does not lose temper if heated. **nickel-** See *nickel.* **nickel-zirconium-** A tough alloy of iron with Ni 2, Zr 0.34, Mn 1, Si 15, C 0.4%; used for armor plates and helmets. **stainless-** A s. containing Ni and/or Cr; does not tarnish on exposure; used for high-grade kitchenware. **super-** A high-speed s. containing 4% Co. Cf. *Carboloy.*

Steele acid. An oxidizable form of abietic acid comprising 60–90% of the resin acids in tall oil. **S. microbalance.** A quartz beam with a small quartz ball, whose buoyancy is changed by increasing or decreasing the air pressure. Sensitivity 4×10^{-6} mg. Used to measure the density of 0.1 cu mm of radium emanation (Ramsay and Gray).

Steelon. Trade name for a polyamide synthetic fiber.

Steenbock unit. A *vitamin* unit, q.v.

Stefan-Boltzmann equation. The radiations per square centimeter per second radiated by a black body at absolute temperature T to surroundings at absolute temperature $t_0 = \sigma(T^4 - t_0^4)$. Cf. *Wien's equation.* **S. constant.** The constant σ (sigma) of the S.-B. equation: $\sigma = 5.72 \times 10^{-12}$ watt $\div$ (cm²)(deg). **S. law.** The total amount of energy E in ergs radiated from a black body (which is a perfect radiator) and due to heat alone $= \sigma T^4$, where σ is 5.72×10^{-5}, T is the absolute temperature.

Steffen waste. A by-product in the manufacture of sugar from beet; a source of amino acids, particularly *l*-glutamic acid.

steigerite. $Al_2O_3 \cdot V_2O_5 \cdot 6 \cdot 5H_2O$. A yellow mineral in Colorado uranium deposits.

stellar. (1) Pertaining to stars. (2) Star-shaped; as crystals. **s. evolution.** See *spectral classification.* **s. spectra.** See *spectral classification.*

stellate crystals. Stellar- or star-shaped crystals; as phenylglucosazone.

Stellite. Trademark for nonferrous alloys of cobalt, chromium, and tungsten; used for metal-cutting steels, wear-resistant castings, and hard-facing welding rods.

stem correction. The correction to a thermometer reading for the portion of the mercury column not in the liquid.

stench. (1) An obnoxious odor. (2) A group of malodorous gases used industrially (as in mine warnings); e.g., mercaptan.

stenocarpine. Gleditschine.

stenosation. A process for increasing tensile strength, e.g., of viscose fibers, by treatment with formaldehyde.

stenosine. Sodium methyl arsenate.

stephanite. $5Ag_2S \cdot Sb_2S$. A native sulfide.

stepwise decomposition. Staircase reaction. **s. dissociation.** A gradual dissociation.

steradian. sr. The solid angle subtended by a surface of a sphere equivalent to the square of the radius. The SI unit for solid angles.

steramide. Sulfacetamide.

sterandryl. Testosterone propionate.

Sterane. (1) Trade name for prednisolone. (2) (not cap.) Gonane.

stercobilin. $C_{33}H_{46}N_4O_6 = 594.5.$ The normal pigment of feces, m.236; allied to urobilin.

stercorite. $Na(NH_4)HPO_4.$ Native microcosmic salt.

stercorol. Coprosterol.

Sterculia. A genus of tropical plants, used for edible seeds and barks, cordage, and mats. **S. gum.** Indian tragacanth, Indian gum. A tragacanth-like exudation from *S.* species (India); a filler for ice cream. Cf. *hog* gum.

Sterculiaceae. Softwood trees or shrubs; as, *Cola acuminata*, kola nut; *Theobroma cacao*, cocoa.

stere. (1) A kiloliter or 1,000 liters (nearly 1 cubic meter). (2) A French unit of wood measurement: volume of logs 1 meter long in a cube of 1 meter side; for conifers, 1 s. $= 0.75\,\text{m}^3 = 26.48\,\text{ft}^3$ of wood.

stereo- (1) Prefix (Greek) indicating "solid" in structure or "three-dimensional." (2) Abbreviation for stereotype.

stereochemistry. Spatial or configurative chemistry. The study of the spatial arrangement of the atoms in a molecule.

stereoisomer. Stereomer. A compound containing the same number and kinds of atoms as another compound, but with the atoms grouped differently; optically active and contains asymmetric atoms (C, pentavalent N, S, Se, Sn, Cr, Co, or Pt).

stereoisomerism. The phenomenon shown by optically active compounds having different spacial arrangements of their atoms. See *isomery, allelotropism.* Types:

A. Geometrical (due to double bond)

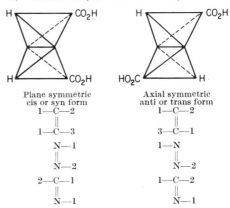

Plane symmetric   Axial symmetric
cis or syn form   anti or trans form

1—C—2	1—C—2
‖	‖
1—C—3	3—C—1
‖	‖
N—1	1—N
‖	‖
N—2	N—2
‖	‖
2—C—1	1—C—2
‖	‖
N—1	N—1

B. Optically active (due to asymmetric atom)

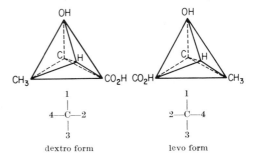

$$\begin{array}{c} 1 \\ | \\ 4—C—2 \\ | \\ 3 \end{array} \qquad \begin{array}{c} 1 \\ | \\ 2—C—4 \\ | \\ 3 \end{array}$$

dextro form   levo form

stereomer. See *stereoisomer*.

stereoscope. A device for viewing a pair of photographs simultaneously, each with one eye, to obtain a perspective effect.

stereoscopic photographs. Two adjacent photographs of the same object, taken on the same plate at the same time; used in a stereoscope.

stereoselectivity. The difference in properties of molecular stereoisomers.

stereoskiagraphy. The production of stereoscopic X-ray pictures to locate an opaque object in the body.

stereotyping. A printing operation in which the original type is used to emboss a plastic paper sheet (flong), which is then hardened and used to cast metal type for high-speed rotary letterpress machines.

steric. Pertaining to the spatial arrangement of atoms in the molecule. **s. hindrance.** The nonoccurrence of an expected chemical reaction, due to inhibition by a particular atomic grouping.

sterid. Steroid.

steride. A tertiary lipid in which the alcohol is a sterol.

sterile. Aseptic or free from microorganisms. **s. solution.** A solution made aseptic by the destruction or removal of all microorganisms.

sterilization. The destruction or removal of all living bacteria, microorganisms, and spores: physically (heat, sound, light, or other radiations, adsorption, filtration), or chemically (antiseptics). **cold-** S. by γ rays. They penetrate deeply, so that large packages may be treated intact without temperature rise.

sterilizer. An autoclave, steam or bake oven, for sterilizing.

sterilizing. Rendering free from all living microorganisms and their spores. Glass and metal utensils are heated in a hot-air oven or autoclave, in steam or boiling water. Solutions are treated similarly or are filtered through a stone, porcelain, or Alundum filter. **s. area.** A pressure-temperature-time diagram on which the thermal death points of all bacteria occur in a wedge-shaped area.

sternbergite. $Ag_2S \cdot Fe_4S_5$. A native sulfide.

sternutative. An agent that produces sneezing. **poison gas-** A s. used in explosive shells; on liberation, causes violent sneezing; as, diphenylchlorarsine.

sternutatory. Able to produce sneezing.

steroid. Sterid. Generic name for compounds comprising the sterols, bile acids, heart poisons, saponins, and sex hormones. Basic structure:

Cf. *bufanolide, cardanolide, estrane, gonane*.

sterols. Solid alcohols of vegetable origin; consist chiefly of high-atomic *monohydric* unsaturated alcohols; e.g.: farnesol, $C_{15}H_{26}O$ (acacia);

ergosterol, $C_{27}H_{46}O \cdot H_2O$ (yeast, animal tissues); cholesterol, $C_{27}H_{46}O$ (animal and plant tissues); sitersterol $C_{27}H_{46}O$ (wheat).

sterro metal. The alloy: Cu 56.5, Zn 40, Fe 1.5, Sn 1%; stronger than gunmetal or bronze.

sterule. An ampul or glass container for a sterile solution.

Stetefeldt furnace. A furnace for roasting silver and copper ores in chlorine gas.

steviol. The nonsugar component of stevioside.

stevioside. $C_{38}H_{60}O_{18} = 804.54$. A glucoside, 300 times as sweet as sugar, from the leaves of Kaa-ha-e, *Stevia rebaudiana* (Compositae), S. America; long prisms, m.238.

Stewart-Kirchhoff law. The light waves emitted by a hot gas can be absorbed by the same substance at a lower temperature. Cf. *Fraunhofer lines*.

sthene. The force which in 1 second communicates to a mass equal to 1 metric ton, an increase in velocity of 1 meter per sec (French usage).

sthenosage. The waterproofing of, e.g., fabrics by means of gelatin treated with formaldehyde (Eschalier process).

stibate, stibiate. Antimonate.

stibic. Antimonic.

stibiconite. $Sb_2O_3(OH)_2$. Antimony ocher. Stibite. A native hydroxide of antimony.

stibide. Antimonide, stibnide. A binary compound of antimony with hydrogen or a metal.

stibine. (1) Antimonous hydride. (2) SbR_3. An organic compound. **triphenyl-** $Sb(C_6H_5)_3 = 352.8$. Triphenylantimony. Colorless crystals, m.48. **s. hydroxide.** R_3SbOH. An organic compound.

stibino. The group H_2Sb—.

stibinoso. (1) The group $(OH)_2Sb$—. (2) The group $(OH)Sb=$.

stibious. Antimonous.

stibite. Stibiconite.

stibium. Antimony.

stibnate. Antimonate.

stibnic. Antimonic.

stibnide. Stibide.

stibnite. Antimony glance.

stibnous. Antimonous.

stibo. The group O_2Sb—.

stibonic acid. R_2SbO_2H. An organic compound.

stibonium. The radical SbH_4^+, analogous to ammonium. **s. compounds.** R_4SbX. Organic compounds derived from stibine and stibonium, in which antimony is pentavalent. **s. hydroxide.** R_4SbOH. **s. iodide.** R_4SbI.

stibono. The radical $(HO)_2Sb$—.

stibonoso. (1) The group $HO \cdot OSb \cdot H$—. (2) The group $HO \cdot OSb=$.

stibophen. $(NaO_3S)_2C_6H_2O_2 : SbOC_6H_2(ONa)(SO_3-Na)_2 \cdot 7H_2O = 895.26$. Fuadin, fouadin, neoantimosan. Sodium antimony−bispyrocatechol-3,5-sodium disulfonate. White crystals, darkening in light, soluble in water; used to treat trichinosis and trypanosomiasis (U.S.P., B.P.).

stibosan. $NH_2 \cdot C_6H_4 \cdot SbO(OH)ONa \cdot 5H_2O$. The antimony analog of atoxyl; used medicinally.

stiboso. The group OSb—.

stick. (1) A rod or cylinder, e.g., of dynamite. (2) Gummy or viscous; as, syrup. (3) A thick syrup obtained by evaporation of the water used in making tankage (1.5–10% N).

stick lac. See *lac*.

stictography. The photographic fixation on paper of an image left by radio waves.

Stieglitz, Julius Oscar. 1867–1937. American chemist noted for organic research.

stigmastane. $C_{29}H_{48} = 396.35$. A hydrocarbon derived from stigmastanol.

stigmastanol. $C_{29}H_{48}O = 412.3$. A hydrogenation product of stigmasterol.

stigmasterol. $C_{29}H_{46}O = 410.35$. A sterol, m.170, from calabar beans, soybeans, and vegetable oils. Cf. *cholane.*

stilbamidine. 4,4'-Diaminostilbenedi-β-hydroxyethane sulfonate; used to treat kala azar.

stilbene. $Ph \cdot CH : CH \cdot Ph = 180.17$. Diphenylethylene, toluylene, bibenzal. Colorless leaflets, m.124, insoluble in water. **diamino-** See *diaminostilbene.* **dibenzoyl-** $(Ph \cdot CH \cdot COPh)_2 = 390.16$. Acicular oxylepidine. **phenyl-**Triphenylethylene.

s. hydrate. $Ph \cdot CHOH \cdot CH_2 \cdot Ph = 198.2$. Toluylene hydrate. Colorless crystals, m.62, soluble in alcohol. **ar-** $PhCH : CHC_6H_4OH$. *ar-*Hydroxystilbene, styrylphenol.

stilb(o)estrol. $C_{18}H_{20}O_2 = 268.42$. Colorless crystals, m.170, slightly soluble in water; used to suppress lactation (B.P.). **diethyl-** q.v.

stilbite. $(Na_2 \cdot Ca)O \cdot Al_2O_3 \cdot 6SiO_2 \cdot 6H_2O$. A silicate of the zeolite group; pearly prisms.

still. An apparatus in which a substance is heated to the gaseous state and then condensed. See *distillation.* **column-** A s. for fractional distillation. **pot-** A distillation apparatus for potable spirits. **vacuum-** A device for distilling at a low temperature, under a reduced pressure. **water-** A s. for water.

s. head. Fractionating column. A device for selectively refluxing the less volatile components of mixtures under distillation, thus improving fractionation.

stillingia. Queen's-root, silver leaf, yawroot. The dried roots of *Stillingia sylvatica* (Euphorbiaceae), N. America; an alternative and expectorant. S. oil has drying properties.

stillingine. An alkaloid from stillingia.

stillingoid. The combined principles of the root of stillingia; used medicinally as an alternative.

stilpnomelane. $FeSiO_3$. A native metasilicate which contains Al, Ca, and Mg.

stimmi. Sb_2S_3. A black, native sulfide.

stimulant. An agent that excites or increases a functional activity. Cf. *sedative.*

stimulation. The acceleration of crystallization by addition of another crystal.

stinging nettles. Urtica.

stinkstone. Anthraconite.

stinkweed. Stramonium.

stipitatic acid. $C_8H_6O_5 = 182.05$. A diabasic acid metabolite in cultures of the mold *Penicillium stipitatum;* its sodium salt gives a deep yellow solution.

Stirling's approximation. A relationship of importance in statistical mechanics; viz., if N is large, then: $\log_e N! = N \cdot \log_e N - N$.

stirrer. A device for agitating liquids. **magnetic-** A piece of magnetic steel, in the liquid to be stirred, is rotated from outside by a rotating electromagnet.

stirring rod. (1) A glass rod suitably bent and mechanically driven, for agitating liquids. (2) A glass rod used for stirring. Cf. *policeman.*

stizolobin. A globulin from Chinese velvet beans, *Mucuna (Stizolobium) pruriens* (Leguminosae).

stoechiometry. Stoichiometry.

stoichiometric point. Equivalence point.

stoich(e)iometry. The study of the numerical relationship between elements or compounds (atomic weights), the determination of the proportions in which the elements combine (formulas) and the weight relations of reactions (equations).

stok(e). St. The unit of kinematic viscosity η as determined from Stokes' law. It equals dynamic viscosity in poises/density at the same temperature. Viscosity of water at 20°C = 1.0018.

Stokes, George Gabriel. 1819–1903. English mathematician. **S. law.** The rate of fall v of a spherical body of radius a under gravity $g = 2ga^2(\sigma - \rho)/9\eta$, where η is the viscosity of the medium in cgs units, and σ and ρ are the density of the substance and of the medium, respectively; used to calculate the charge on an electron (Millikan's method). For sedimentation, q.v., the formula is $v = gD(\sigma - \rho)/18\eta$, where D is the effective diameter of the particle of density σ in a liquid of density ρ. Cf. *settling.*

stolzite. $PbWO_4$. Native lead tungstate.

stomach. A pouch between the esophagus and the intestines, in which food is partly digested. **powdered-** The dried, defatted powdered wall of hog s., containing vitamin B_{12}; used to increase the number of red corpuscles in the blood in cases of pernicious anemia (U.S.P.). **s. enzyme.** Pepsin. **s. juice.** Gastric juice. **s. pump, s. tube.** A rubber syphon tube used to wash out or sample s. contents.

stomachic. An agent that stimulates the appetite or increases gastric secretions; as, gentian.

stone. (1) A standard British weight: 14 pounds. (2) Concrete mineral matter or pieces of rock. (3) A concretion or calculus, q.v. **blue-** Copper sulfate. **brass-** q.v. **gall-** Calculus. **Lydian-** Jasper. **precious-** Gem. **rotten-** See *rotten.* **touch-** See *touchstone.*

s. flax. Asbestos. **s. root.** Collinsonoid. **s. ware.** See *ceramics, earthenware, pottery.*

stonecrop. The herb of *Penthorum sedoides* (Crassulaceae); a laxative.

Stoner energy levels. See *S. quanta.* **S. quanta.** A modified Bohr theory, which deals with the distribution of electrons in different energy levels. The quantum number k of Bohr is divided into functions k_1 and k_2, from which a systematic relationship of the lines of x-ray spectra is found. Cf. *Pauli's principle.*

stoneroot. Richweed, knobweed, horse balm. The root of *Collinsonia canadensis* (Labiatae); a stomachic and diuretic. Cf. *collinsoid.*

stool. The discharge from the bowels; feces, q.v.

stopping power. The capacity of substances to absorb α particles, compared with air $= k \cdot N^{2/3}$, where N is the atomic number, and k a constant.

storax. Styrax. A semiliquid balsam from the wood of *Liquidambar orientalis* (Hamamelidiaceae), W. Asia. It contains styrol, styracin, and cinnamic acid; insoluble in water. **American-** Solid mass, softening when warmed. **Levant-** Red semiliquid. Both are used in benzoin tinctures (U.S.P.).

s. oil. The volatile oil of s., d.0.890–1.100,

b.150–300, containing styrene and cinnamic esters. Cf. *liquidambar*.

storesin. $C_{36}H_{55}(OH)_3 = 538.46$. A hard resin from storax. **alpha-** An amorphous mass, m.160–168. **beta-** A white flocculent mass, m.140–145.

stovaine. $MeCH_2C(PhCOO)Me \cdot CH_2 \cdot NMe_2 = 235.19$. Benzoyldimethylaminomethylpropanol hydrochloride. Lustrous scales, m.175, soluble in water; a local anesthetic.

stovarsol. Acetarsol.

stove. (1) A heating device whose flame is covered. (2) To heat a paint or varnish film on metal to convert it into a protective and/or decorative coating.

STP. Abbreviation for standard temperature and pressure: 0°C and 760 mm. Cf. *NTP*.

strain. (1) A deformation resulting from stress; the increase in length per unit original length. (2) To pass through a coarse filter. **s.-aging.** The increase in resistance to deformation which occurs in time after a metal has been deformed. It increases hardness and tensile strength. **s. theory.** Baeyer's theory. The assumption that the normal lines of force of the valency bonds of a C atom run from the center of a tetrahedron to each of the 4 corners.

stramonium. Thorn apple leaves, Jamestown weed, jimsonweed, stinkweed, apple of Peru. The dried leaves of *Datura stramonium* (Solanaceae), containing alkaloids; a nerve sedative and antispasmodic (B.P.). **s. seeds.** The seeds of stramonium, containing atropine, hyoscyamine, oil, resin, and proteins; a hypnotic and antispasmodic.

strata. Pl. of stratum, q.v. (1) The geological layers of rock on the earth surface. (2) The several layers of the atmosphere. (3) The seams of minerals.

stratification. The formation of layers, as in *Liesegang* rings.

stratiform. Describing a bacterial growth in a solid culture medium, characterized by liquefaction near the walls of the tube and downward.

stratometer. An instrument to determine the hardness of a soil from the distance it sinks under a given impact.

stratosphere. The atmosphere above approximately 7 miles; temperature about −55°C.

stratum. A geological layer. See *geologic era*.

streak. The colored line produced when a mineral is rubbed across unglazed porcelain. **s. test.** The approximate gold content of an alloy is determined by streaking a fine-grained silica stone, covered with charcoal, with the alloy, and comparing the streak with those produced by alloys of known compositions, before and after treatment with dilute aqua regia. Cf. *touchstone*.

streamline filtration. Edge filtration. Filtration with the filter in a plane perpendicular to the direction of motion (streamline) of the liquid; a pack of stout paper sheets held together in a press; the filtrate passes by pressure or suction between the sheets and emerges through holes running along the length of the pack. Cf. *filter press*.

Strecker reaction. Formation of amino acids by the action of ammonia on cyanohydrins.

strengite. $FePO_4 \cdot 2H_2O$. An ore.

streptococcus. (Pl. -cocci.) A group of round or spherical bacteria arranged in strings or rows.

streptoducin. A mixture of equal weights of the

sulfates of dihydrostreptomycin and streptomycin. An antibiotic (U.S.P.).

streptolin. An anticoliform antibiotic from species of *Streptomyces*.

streptolysin. A protein which, when activated by reducing enzymes, hemolyzes red blood corpuscles.

streptomycin. $(C_{25}H_{43}O_7N)_x$. An antibiotic from certain strains of *Streptomyces griseus*, especially from the soil. A bitter, macrocyclic lactone of amino acids. It inhibits the development of tuberculosis in pigs. **s. sulfate.** $(C_{21}H_{39}O_{12}N_7)_2 \cdot 3H_2SO_4 = 1457.44$. White powder, soluble in water. An antibiotic (U.S.P., B.P.). Cf. *streptoducin*.

streptonigrin. $C_{24}H_{20}O_8N_4 = 492.22$. An antibiotic from *Streptomyces flocculus*. Brown rectangular crystals; active against certain forms of cancer in rats.

streptothricin. An antibiotic from *Streptomyces lavendulae*. Similar in action to streptomycin.

stress. The force per unit area that tends to deform a body. Cf. *strain*.

striate. Striped; provided with lines.

string. A gold-plated quartz thread, 1.5–6 microns thick, for Einthoven galvanometers.

stripped atom. An atom from which one or more electrons have been removed; hence, the gaseous ion of an element. Cf. *ionization potential*.

stripping. (1) Back-extraction. Extracting a solute from a solvent which has already been used to extract it from another. (2) Removal of light fractions, e.g., of lubricating-oil distillates, by distillation with superheated steam. (3) Removal of dyestuffs from textiles by bleaching agents.

strobinin. $C_{30}H_{24}O_8 = 512.21$. A red pigment from black aphids.

stroboscope. Rotoscope. A mercury arc or neon lamp coupled with a periodically discharging capacitor. By regulating the frequency of the flashes (up to 2,000 per second) fast-moving machinery can be observed in apparent slow motion. **s. photography.** A moving picture of quick-moving objects illuminated by the stroboscope to reduce it to slow motion. Cf. *chronoteine*.

stroma. The granular background matrix of chloroplasts.

stromatin. A constituent of blood corpuscles; forms a loose compound with hemoglobin.

Stromeyer, Friedrich. 1786–1835. German apothecary, discoverer of cadmium (1817).

stromeyerite. $(Ag,Cu)_2S$. A native sulfide.

strontia. Strontium oxide.

strontianite. $SrCO_3$. A native strontium carbonate.

strontium. $Sr = 87.62$. An alkaline-earth metal and element, at. no. 38. Silvery crystals, d.2.54, m.900, b.1,000, slowly soluble in water forming the hydroxide. Occurs native as strontianite and celestite; forms one series of compounds: valency 2. The isotope Sr^{90} (s. ninety) is a constituent of radioactive fallout from atomic explosions. It is absorbed by foodstuffs, soil, vegetables, and especially milk; occurs in human bone, where an excess can cause leukemia; maximum permissible occupational level 10 micromicrocuries per gram of bone Ca. The acceptable daily intake, averaged over 1 year, is 200 micromicrocuries (U.S. Federation Radiation Council). Cf. *calcium* (Ca^{47}), *s. unit*. **common-** Sr as found in minerals having a high Sr : Rb ratio; e.g., celestite.

s. acetate. $Sr(C_2H_3O_2)_2 \cdot \frac{1}{2}H_2O = 214.7$. White crystals, soluble in water; an anthelmintic. **s. arsenite.** $Sr(AsO_2)_2 \cdot 4H_2O = 373.7$. White powder, soluble in water; an insecticide. **s. bromate.** $Sr(BrO_3)_2 \cdot H_2O = 361.5$. Colorless, deliquescent crystals, decomp. 240, soluble in water. **s. bromide.** $SrBr_2 = 247.5$. Colorless needles, m.630, soluble in water. *hydrous-* $SrBr_2 \cdot 6H_2O = 355.6$. Colorless, hygroscopic crystals, soluble in water; a tonic, **s. caffeine sulfonate.** Symphorol s. **s. carbonate.** $SrCO_3 = 147.6$. Native as strontianite. Colorless rhombs, d.3.62, decomp. 1155, insoluble in water; a source of s. salts. **s. chlorate.** $Sr(ClO_3)_2 = 254.6$. Colorless, rhombic or monoclinic crystals, m.290 (decomp.), soluble in water; a pyrotechnic for red fires. **s. chloride.** $SrCl_2 = 158.6$. Colorless crystals m.872, soluble in water. *hydrous-* $SrCl_2 \cdot 6H_2O = 266.6$. Colorless needles, m.112, soluble in water; a reagent and pyrotechnic. **s. chromate.** $SrCrO_4 = 202.7$. Yellow, monoclinic crystals, insoluble in water, soluble in acetic acid. **s. citrate.** $Sr_3(C_6H_5O_7)_2 = 640.8$. Colorless crystals, soluble in water. **s. dioxide.** S. peroxide. **s. dithionate.** $SrS_2O_6 \cdot 4H_2O = 319.81$. Plates, insoluble in alcohol. **s. fluoride.** $SrF_2 = 125.6$. Colorless octahedra, m.902, insoluble in water; an antiseptic. **s. fluosilicate.** $SrSiF_6 \cdot 2H_2O = 265.72$. S. silicofluoride. White, monoclinic crystals, soluble in water. **s. formate.** $Sr(OOCH)_2 = 177.6$. Colorless rhombs, m.72, soluble in water. *hydrated-* $Sr(OOCH)_2 \cdot 2H_2O = 213.68$. White powder, soluble in water. **s. glycerophosphate.** $SrC_3H_7 \cdot PO_6 \cdot (H_2O)_x$. White crystals, soluble in water. **s. hydroxide.** $Sr(OH)_2 = 121.7$. S. hydrate. Colorless powder, m.375, slightly soluble in water. *hydrous-* $Sr(OH)_2 \cdot 8H_2O = 265.8$. Colorless, deliquescent tetragons, slightly soluble in water; used to crystallize sugar from beet molasses. **s. hyposulfate.** $SrS_2O_6 \cdot 4H_2O = 319.6$. Colorless crystals, soluble in water. **s. hyposulfite.** S. thiosulfate. **s. iodide.** $SrI_2 = 341.5$. Colorless, hygroscopic plates, m.402, slightly soluble in water. *hydrous-* $SrI_2 \cdot 6H_2O = 449.6$. Colorless crystals, slightly soluble in water; a potassium iodide substitute. **s. lactate.** $Sr(C_3H_5O_3)_2 \cdot 3H_2O = 319.8$. White granules, soluble in water; a diuretic and antirheumatic. **s. monoxide.** S. oxide. **s. nitrate.** $Sr(NO_3)_2 = 211.7$. Colorless cubes or octahedra, m.645 (decomp.), soluble in water. The synthetic crystals are used as imitation diamonds. *hydrous-* $Sr(NO_3)_2 \cdot 4H_2O = 283.7$. Colorless, triclinic crystals, soluble in water; a pyrotechnic for red fires. **s. nitrite.** $Sr(NO_2)_2 = 179.8$. White powder, soluble in water. **s. oxalate.** $SrC_2O_4 \cdot H_2O = 193.7$. White crystals, decomp. by heat, insoluble in water; a pyrotechnic. **s. oxide.** SrO $= 103.63$. Strontia, s. monoxide. Colorless rhombs, m.3,000, decomp. by water; used in beet-sugar manufacture. **s. peroxide.** $SrO_2 = 119.62$. White powder, soluble in water; an antiseptic and bleaching agent. *hydrous-* $SrO_2 \cdot 8H_2O = 263.76$. White crystals, decomp. red heat. **s. phosphate.** $Sr_3(PO_4)_2 = 452.8$. White powder, insoluble in water; a tonic. *acid-* $SrHPO_4 = 183.7$. Colorless rhombs, insoluble in water. **s. platinocyanide.** Platinum cyanide. **s. saccharate.** $C_{12}H_{22}O_{11} \cdot 2SrO = 549.52$. An almost insoluble salt used to separate sugar from molasses. The sugar is isolated by precipitation of the s. as carbonate. **s. salicylate.** $Sr(C_7H_5O_3)_2 \cdot 2H_2O = 397.6$. Colorless crystals, soluble in water; used medicinally. **s. silicofluoride.** $SrSiF_6 \cdot 2H_2O = 265.8$. A soluble solid. **s. sulfate.** $SrSO_4 = 183.7$. Native as celestine. Colorless rhombs, decomp. white heat, insoluble in water; used in pyrotechnics. **s. sulfide.** $SrS = 119.7$. Colorless, regular crystals, soluble in water; a depilatory, and constituent of luminous paints. **s. sulfite.** $SrSO_3 = 167.7$. Colorless crystals, decomp. by heat, insoluble in water, soluble in sulfurous acid. **s. tartrate.** $SrC_4H_4O_6 \cdot 4H_2O = 307.6$. White crystals, soluble in water. **s. thiosulfate.** $SrS_2O_3 \cdot 5H_2O = 289.83$. S. hyposulfite. Colorless needles, soluble in water. **s. titanate.** $SrTiO_3 = 183.52$. Fabulite. An imitation diamond. **s. unit.** S.U. A measure of the Sr^{90} content of bones. 1 S.U. = 1 micromicrocurie of Sr^{90}. The provisional permissible industrial dose is 1,000 S.U. Cf. *radioactive fallout, strontium* (Sr^{90}).

strophanthic acid. $C_{23}H_{30}O_8 = 434.3$. A dibasic acid from strophanthin, decomp. 270, insoluble in water.

strophanthidin. $C_{23}H_{32}O_6 = 404.3$, or $C_{22}H_{38}O_7 = 474.29$. An aglucone from strophanthus, m.178.

strophanthin. $C_{31}H_{48}O_{12} = 612.5$. Methylouabain, chorchorin strophanthum. A mixture of glucosides (strophantidin, strophantobiose methyl ether, etc.) from the ripe seeds of strophanthus. Pale yellow, poisonous crystals, m.179, soluble in water; a heart tonic. **crystallized-** Ouabain. **G-** Ouabain. **K-** The glucosides from *Strophanthus kombé.*

strophanthobiose. $C_{12}H_{22}O_{11} = 326.17$. A disaccharide obtained by partial hydrolysis of strophanthin; hydrolyzes to mannose and rhamnose.

strophanthum. Strophanthin.

strophanthus. The dried ripe seeds of *Strophanthus kombé* (Apocynaceae), Africa and Asia; used to treat heart disease.

structural. Pertaining to the arrangement of atoms in a molecule. **s. formula.** A plane representation of the atomic arrangement of a molecule.

structure. (1) The mode of linkage of atoms in a molecule. It signifies manner of building or construction, as distinct from configuration, q.v. (2) The arrangement of nuclear particles, q.v. (3) The arrangement of electrons in the atom. **atomic-** Structure (3). Cf. *constellation.* **molecular-** Structure (1). Cf. *atomic distance, molecular models.* **nuclear-** Structure (2). Cf. *isotopes, radioactive elements.*

s. symbol. A geometrical representation of the arrangement of atoms in an organic molecule. Each line indicates a bond or a pair of electrons; with a H atom at the end of each line; and O, N, and C atoms at the junctions of 2, 3 or 5, and 4 lines, respectively. Atoms of other elements are represented by their symbols in their respective locations. *electronic-* A s. symbol showing the relative positions of electrons. See *bonds, molecular diagram.*

Strutt, John William. See *Rayleigh.*

struvite. $Mg_2(NH_4)_2(PO_4)_2 \cdot 12H_2O$. Guanite. White crystals; in canned fish.

strychnine. $C_{21}H_{22}O_2N_2 = 334.3$. Vauqueline. An alkaloid from various species of *Strychnos ignatia* and *S. nux vomica.* Colorless tetragons, m.268, slightly soluble in water; a tonic stomachic, and pest poison. **dimethoxy-** Brucine. **methyl-** Yellow powder, soluble in water.

s. acetate. (Str)$C_2H_4O_2$ = 394.3. Colorless crystals, soluble in water; used medicinally. **s. arsenate.** (Str)$H_3AsO_4(+2H_2O)$ = 476.3. Colorless crystals, soluble in water; used in ampul medication. **s. arsenite.** (Str)$HAsO_2$ = 442.4. Colorless crystals, soluble in water; used medicinally. **s. bisulfate.** (Str)H_2SO_4 = 432.3. Colorless needles, soluble in water. **s. cacodylate.** (Str)AsO_2Me_2 = 471.3. White powder, soluble in water. **s. citrate.** (Str)$C_6H_8O_7$ = 497.4. Colorless crystals, soluble in water. **s. glycerophosphate.** (Str)$C_3H_7PO_6$ = 504.3. Colorless crystals, soluble in water; used in ampul medication. **s. hydrobromide.** (Str)HBr = 415.3. Colorless needles, soluble in water; used medicinally. **s. hydrochloride.** (Str)$HCl·2H_2O$ = 406.92. Colorless, trimetric crystals, soluble in water; a nerve stimulant. **s. iodate.** (Str)HIO_3 = 510.2. Colorless crystals, soluble in water. **s. lactate.** (Str)$C_3H_6O_3$ = 424.4. White crystals, soluble in water. **s. nitrate.** (Str)HNO_3 = 397.3. Colorless needles, decomp. by heat, soluble in water; a tonic and stomachic. **s. phenol-sulfonate.** (Str)$PhOHSO_3$ = 508.4. White crystals, soluble in water. **s. phosphate.** (Str)$H_3PO_4·2H_2O$ = 468.5. Colorless crystals, soluble in water. **s. salicylate.** (Str)$C_7H_6O_3$ = 472.4. White crystals, soluble in water. **s. sulfate.** (Str)$_2H_2SO_4·5H_2O$ = 856.7. Colorless prisms, anhydrous at 200, soluble in water; a tonic and stomachic. **s. valerate.** (Str)$C_5H_{10}O_2$ = 436.4. Colorless crystals, soluble in water; a tonic and sedative.

strychninium. A strychnine containing pentavalent nitrogen. Cf. *piperidinium.*

Strychnos. A genus of tropical trees (Loganiaceae). They yield strychnine, nux vomica, ignatia, curare, and ipoh.

stucco. A mixture of calcium sulfate, sand, and lime; a decorative building material.

Stuffer law. Sulfones with 2 =SO_2 groups on adjacent C atoms are readily saponified.

stuffing. A dyeing process; textiles are passed through the color and then through a mordant. **s. box.** A box containing packing which fits around and seals the point where a moving rod passes through the side of a vessel.

stumpage. Merchantable standing timber for commercial use.

sturin. $C_{36}H_{69}O_7N_{10}$ = 753.65. A protein from the sperm of the sturgeon.

sturnutatory. Sternutatory.

Stutzer's reagent. A suspension of cupric hydroxide in aqueous glycerol used to separate proteins from other nitrogenous constituents of plants.

stylophorum. The herb of *Stylophorum diphyllum* (Papaveraceae). It contains the alkaloids, chelidonine, protopine, sanguinarine, and chelerythrine.

styphnic acid. $C_6H_3O_8N_3$ = 245.1. Trinitroresorcinol, 2,4-dihydroxy-1,3,5-trinitrobenzene. Yellow crystals, m.180; used in explosives.

styptic. An astringent that contracts blood vesssels and stops hemorrhage locally; as, alum.

stypticine. $C_{12}H_{15}O_4N·HCl$ = 273.5. Cotarnine hydrochloride. Yellow crystals, soluble in water; a styptic.

styptol. Cotarnine phthalate. Yellow crystals, soluble in water; a styptic.

styracin. $PhCH:CHCOOCH_2CH:CHPh$ = 264.2. Cinnamyl cinnamate. A solid constituent of liquidambar or styrax, m.44; used in perfumery.

styracol. $C_6H_4(OC_9H_7O·CH_3)$ = 238.1. Cinnamyl guaiacol. Colorless crystals, soluble in alcohol; an antiseptic.

Styrax. (1) A genus of trees and shrubs (Styraceae) that yield balsams; as, storax, benzoin. (2) Storax.

styrene. (1) $Ph·CH:CH_2$ = 104.1. Cinnamene, styrolene, phenethylene, styrol, vinylbenzene, phenylethylene. A constituent of storax, essential oils, and coal tar. Colorless, aromatic liquid, d.0.925, b.145, soluble in alcohol. Used in organic synthesis, and forms 2 types of derivatives; as, o-, m-, p-, aminovinylbenzene =$NH_2C_6H_4CH:CH_2$. ω-, p-phenylvinylamine =$C_6H_5CH:CHNH_2$. (2) The radical —$CHPh·CH_2$—.

styrilic acid. Cinnamic alcohol.

Styroflex. Trade name for a polystyrene synthetic fiber.

styrol. (1) Styrolene. (2) Colloidal silver.

styrolene. Styrene. **s. alcohol.** Cinnamic alcohol.

Styron. Trademark for polymerized styrene.

styrone. Cinnamic alcohol. **m-methoxy-p-oxy-** Coniferol.

styryl. The radical $PhCH:CH$—, from styrolene. **s. alcohol.** Cinnamyl alcohol. **s. amine.** C_8H_9N = 119.1. $PhCH:CHNH_2$. Colorless liquid, b.236, insoluble in water. **s. ketone.** $(Ph·CH:CH)_2$. CO = 210.1. Dibenzilideneacetone, 1,5-diphenyl-3-pentadienone*. Colorless crystals, m.112. **s. methyl ketone.** Benzilidene acetone.

S.U. *Saccharomyces* unit, q.v.

sub- Prefix (Latin), indicating below, almost, under, or near. It designates a lower form of oxidation or a basic compound, and a deficiency of the substance or radical it describes. Cf. *per-.*

subacetate. A basic acetate; as, lead subacetate.

subatomic. Pertaining to the structure of actual atoms as distinct from their function as parts of a molecule. **s. decomposition.** (1) Radioactive disintegration. (2) Phenomena in which an atom is split. Cf. *radioelement.* **s. particle.** See *particles.* **s. reaction.** A change in which an atom is disintegrated or transformed. See *nuclear chemistry.*

subatomics. The study of the structure of atoms and the role of electrons and nuclei in subatomic changes.

subcarbonate. A basic carbonate.

subcutaneous. Located beneath the skin. **s. injection.** The administration of a drug by injection under the skin.

subdural injection. The administration of a drug by injecting it into the outermost membrane of the brain or spinal cord.

suber. Cork

suberane. $(CH_2)_7$ = 98.1. Cyclophetane*, heptamethylene. Colorless liquid, b.117, soluble in alcohol.

suberic acid. $(CH_2)_6·(COOH)_6$ = 174.1. Octanedioic acid*, 1,6-hexanedicarboxylic acid. A homolog of oxalic acid, obtained by oxidation of cork. Colorless needles, m.140, soluble in water.

suberin. A polysaccharide constituent of wood bark.

suberol. $C_7H_{14}O = 114.1$. Cycloheptanol*. Colorless liquid, b.185.

suberone*. $(CH_2)_6{\cdot}CO = 112.1$. Cycloheptanone, ketoheptamethylene. Colorless oil obtained by distilling calcium suberate, b.180, slightly soluble in water.

suberyl. The cyclic radical $C_7H_{13}{-}$, from suberane. **s. alcohol.** Suberol.

subhalide. A compound of the type $Hal{\cdot}_2M{\cdot}MHal{\cdot}_2$; e.g., B_2Cl_4.

sublamine. $HgSO_4{\cdot}2C_2H_4(NH_2)_2{\cdot}2H_2O = 452.6$. Mercuric sulfate ethylenediamine. White crystals, soluble in water; a nonirritant germicide.

sublethal. Not quite fatal. **s. dose.** A quantity of drug below the fatal dose.

sublimate. (1) The deposit formed on heating substances which pass directly from the solid to the vapor phase and then back to the solid state. Cf. *distillate*. (2) Mercuric chloride. **corrosive-** Mercuric chloride.

sublimation. The production of a sublimate; used to purify substances; as, iodine.

submicron. A particle between 2×10^{-6} and 5×10^{-7} cm in diameter; visible only under the ultramicroscope. Cf. *amicron*.

subnitrate. A basic nitrate.

subnormal. Below normal.

suboxide. That oxide of an element which contains the lowest proportion of oxygen.

subsoil. The layer below the surface soil. It contains the rain-soluble organic portion of the soil.

subsonic. Describing a velocity less than that of sound.

substance. The material of which a body is composed; as, a chemical compound.

substantive dyeing. The coloring of fabrics with dyestuffs, without mordants.

substantive dyes. A group of coal-tar colors, chiefly for cotton, that dye without mordants; as, benzidine dyes.

substituent. The atom or radical that enters into the structure of a molecule by replacing another.

substitute. To replace one element or radical in a compound by a substituent.

substituted. Pertaining to a compound which has undergone substitution. **s. compound.** A compound obtained by substitution; a derivative, q.v.

substitution. (1) A reaction in which an atom or group of atoms in a (usually simple) molecule is exchanged for another. (2) A reaction in which an element or radical is oxidized or reduced, and a portion of it combines with the displaced element; as, $MN + 2X = MX + XN$.

substitutive derivative. A compound formed by the replacement of one atom or radical by another; as, $C_6H_6 \rightarrow C_6H_5Cl$. Cf. *additive derivative*; as, $C_6H_6 \rightarrow C_6H_6Cl_2$.

substrate. The material upon which an enzyme acts.

subsubmicron. Amicron.

subsulfate. A basic sulfate.

subtilin. An antibiotic polypeptide produced by *Bacillus subtilis*, especially from the fermentation of asparagus canning waste.

subultramicroscopic. Invisible in the ultramicroscope. Cf. *amicron*.

Sucaryl. Trademark for sodium cyclohexylsulfamate, a nonsugar sweetening agent.

succinaldehyde. $C_2H_4(CHO)_2 = 86.07$. Butanedial*.

alpha- b.169. **beta-** b.171. **gamma-** m.64. **delta-** m.135. **epsilon-** m.95 (decomp). **methyl-** Pyrotartaraldehyde.

succinamic acid. $COOHCH_2{\cdot}CH_2CONH_2 = 117.1$. Amidosuccinic acid, β-carbamylpropionic acid. White powder, soluble in water. **amino-** Asparagine.

succinamide. $(NH_2COCH_2)_2 = 116.1$. Butanediamide*. Colorless needles, m.242 (decomp.), soluble in water. **hydroxy-** Malamide.

succinamyl. The radical $-OC(CH_2)_2CONH_2$.

succinate. $C_2H_4(COOM)_2$. A salt of succinic acid.

succinelite. Succinic acid from amber.

succinic acid. $HOOC{\cdot}CH_2{\cdot}CH_2{\cdot}COOH = 118.1$. Ethylenedicarboxylic acid, amber acid, butanedioic acid*. Occurs in amber and other resins as colorless monoclinic prisms, m.184, slightly soluble in water; a reagent. **iso-** $CH_3{\cdot}CH{:}(COOH)_2$. A solid, m.130 (decomp.), soluble in alcohol. **α-amino-** Aspartic acid. **diamido-** Succinamide. **dihydroxy-** Tartaric acid. **ethyl-** See *ethylsuccinic acid*. **formyl-** Aconic acid. **hydroxy-** Malic acid. **keto-** Oxalacetic acid. **mercapto-** Thiomalic acid. **methyl-** Pyrotartaric acid. **methylene-** Itaconic acid.

s. aldehyde. Succinaldehyde. **s. anhydride.** $CH_2{\cdot}CO{\cdot}O{\cdot}CO{\cdot}CH_2 = 100.1$. Succinyl oxide, butanedioic anhydride*. Colorless needles, d.1.104, m.120, insoluble in water. **s. peroxide.** $(HOOC{\cdot}CH_2{\cdot}CH_2{\cdot}CO)_2O_2 = 234.2$. Alphozon, alphogen. White, fluffy powder, soluble in water; a germicide and mouthwash.

succinimide. $CH_2{\cdot}CO{\cdot}NH{\cdot}CO{\cdot}CH_2 = 117.1$. Butaneimide*. Colorless octahedra, m.124, soluble in water. **phenetyl-** Pyrantin.

succinite. (1) An amber-colored grossularite or aluminum garnet, q.v. (2) Baltic amber (4% succinic acid).

succinol. An oil obtained by distilling amber.

succinonitrile. Ethylene cyanide.

succinoresinol. $C_{12}H_{20}O = 180.2$. An alcohol from amber.

succinyl. Butanedioyl*. The radical $-OC{\cdot}CH_2{\cdot}CH_2{\cdot}CO{-}$, from succinic acid. **s. chloride.** $C_2H_4(COCl)_2 = 154.97$. S. dichloride, butanedioyl chloride*. Colorless, fuming, highly refractive liquid, d.1.412, b.190; used in organic synthesis. **s. choline chloride.** $C_{14}H_{30}O_4N_2Cl_2 = 361.31$. White crystals, soluble in water, m.161; a muscle relaxant (U.S.P.). **s. oxide.** Succinic anhydride. **s. sulfathiazole.** $C_{13}H_{13}O_5N_3S_2{\cdot}H_2O = 373.41$. Yellow crystals, slightly soluble in water; an antibacterial (U.S.P.).

succus cerasi. *Cherry* juice.

sucramine. The ammonium salt of saccharin.

sucrase. Invertase.

sucrate. A compound of sucrose.

sucroclastic. Describing a glycolytic enzyme.

sucrol. $NH_2{\cdot}CO{\cdot}NH{\cdot}C_6H_4OEt = 180.2$. Dulcin, p-phenetylurea, valzin, p-ethoxyphenylurea, p-phenetolcarbamide. Colorless needles, m.173, slightly soluble in water, soluble in alcohol or ether; a sweetening 200 times as sweet as cane sugar.

sucrolite. A formaldehyde-urea-type plastic in which most or all of the former is replaced by sugar or molasses; some are transparent.

sucrose. $C_{12}H_{22}O_{11}$ = 342.2. Cane sugar, saccharobiose, beet sugar, saccharose. A disaccharide, hydrolyzing to fructose and glucose, $[\alpha]_D^{20} + 66.5°$. Colorless, monoclinic crystals, d.1.588, m.160 (decomp.), soluble in water, slightly soluble in alcohol. Cf. *sugar refining.* Used as a food sweetening, and in pharmacy (U.S.P., B.P.) and explosives. **s. octaacetate.** White, bitter powder, m.69–72; a denaturant for rubbing alcohol (4.25 lb to 100 gal).

suction. The effect of sucking. Drawing a fluid into a pipe. **s. gas.** The coal gas in producer gas when coal replaces coke. **s. pump.** See *pump.*

sucuuba bark. Plumiera.

Suda. Trade name for a viscose synthetic fiber.

Sudan. Trademark for a series of dyestuffs. **S. I.** S. yellow. **S. II.** Xylidineazo-β-naphthol. A brown dye. **S. III.** S. red. **S. IV.** Scarlet Red. **S. brown.** A fat-soluble diazo dye, soluble in alcohol. **S. red.** $Ph\cdot N_2C_6H_4\cdot N_2C_{10}H_6OH$ = 352.3. Aminoazobenzeneazo-β-naphthol, S. III. Brown powder, insoluble in water; a microscope stain and fat coloring. **S. yellow.** $C_{12}H_{10}O_2N_2$ = 214.2. Aniline azo-β-naphthol, S. I. Red powder, insoluble in water; used to color oils and varnishes.

sudanite rock. A mixture of talc and magnesite.

sud cake. A fertilizer made from sewage sludge and waste textile fibers (10–15% oil).

sudermo. Mesulfen.

sudorific. A diaphoretic; produces sweat.

suet. Tallow. (1) The fat from the abdominal cavity of sheep: chiefly stearates and palmitates, with some oleates of glycerol. Colorless, unctuous mass, m.45–50, soluble in alcohol; used in ointments, cerates, and cooking. (2) The fat from beef. (3) The solid fat from any animal.

suffocating gases. Poison gases, q.v., that stop respiration; as, Cl_2 or $COCl_2$.

sugar. (1) $C_nH_{2n}O_n$ or $C_nH_{2n-2}O_{n-1}$. A sweet carbohydrate. Cf. *carbohydrates, monosaccharides, furanoside, pyranoside, sweetness.* (2) Generally sucrose. World production (1967) 54 million tons. **acorn-** Quercitol. **amorphous-** A hygroscopic form of s. produced by spray drying. Each particle is a hollow sphere. **avocado-** A mannoketoheptose from the avocado or alligator pear. **beechwood-** Xylose. **beet-** Sucrose from the s. beet, *Beta vulgaris.* **blood-** Glucose. **brain-** Cerebrose. **cabbage-** A triose from cabbage leaves. **cane-** A sucrose from sugarcane, *Saccharum officinalis.* **collagen-** Glycocoll. **corn-** Glucose. **diabetic-** Misnomer for saccharin. **fruit-** Fructose. **gelatin-** Glycocoll. **grape-** Glucose. **gum-** Arabinose. **heart-** Inositol. **invert-** See *invert sugar.* **larch-** Melezitose. **liver-** Glycogen. **malt-** Maltose. **maple-** A crude s., chiefly sucrose, of agreeable flavor made from the sap of certain maples (*Acer saccharum, A. nigrum,* etc.), native in eastern Canada and northeastern U.S. **meat-** Inositol. **milk-** Lactose. **muscle-** Inositol. **palm-** A sucrose from the toddy palm, *Caryota urens;* or the coconut palm, *Cocos nucifera.* Cf. *jaggery.* **priming-** See *priming sugar.* **reducing-** A s. that will reduce Fehling's solution at the boiling point; indicative of free aldehyde or keto groups. **sorghum-** A sucrose from s. millet, *Sorghum saccharatum.* **stonecrop-** A heptose in *Sedum spectabile.* **wood-** Xylose. **yeast-** A sulfur-containing s., found in small traces in yeast.

s. cane. *Saccharum officinarum,* the source of cane sugar. **s. carbonate.** A carbonic ester of sugars, e.g., glucopyranose carbonate. **s. chemicals.** Chemical products made commercially from cane s.; e.g.: detergents, cosmetics, pesticides, alcohol, s.-formaldehyde plastics, and plasticizers (e.g., sucrose benzoate). **s. granulation.** Crystallization in jams, due usually to sucrose or dextrose, caused by under- or overinversion, respectively. **s. of lead.** Lead acetate. **s. phosphates.** Metabolic intermediates formed in the assimilation and utilization of carbohydrates by plants, animals, or microorganisms; e.g.: fructose 6-phosphoric acid, $C_6H_{11}O_5\cdot PO_4H_2$ = 260.14; fructose 1,6-diphosphoric acid, $C_6H_{14}O_{12}P_2$ = 340.13; galactose 6-phosphoric acid, $C_6H_{11}O_5\cdot H_2PO_4$ = 260.14; glucose phosphoric acids, $C_6H_{11}O_5\cdot H_2PO_4$ = 260.14; inositol hexaphosphoric acid, $C_6H_{18}O_{24}\cdot P_6$ = 660.08 (cf. *phytic acid*); mannose 6-phosphoric acid, $C_6H_{11}O_5\cdot H_2PO_4$ = 260.14; 6-phosphogluconic acid, $C_6H_{13}O_{10}P$ = 276.14; ribose 5-phosphoric acid, $C_5H_9O_4\cdot H_2PO_4$ = 276.14. **s. refining.** The purification of beet or cane sugar by removal of vegetable proteins and salts, followed by decolorization and crystallization of pure sucrose.

suint. Greasy potassium salts of organic acids derived from dry sheep perspiration. **s. ash.** Potassium black. A source of potassium salts and fertilizer.

sulf-, sulph- Prefix indicating the presence of sulfur. See *thio-.*

sulfabenzamine. Marfanil.

sulfacetamide. $p\text{-}NH_2\cdot C_6H_4\cdot SO_2NH\cdot COMe$ = 214.25. White crystals with sour taste, m.182, soluble in water; an antibacterial (U.S.P.). **s. sodium.** The sodium salt of s.; used similarly (U.S.P., B.P.).

sulfacetimide. $NH_2\cdot C_6H_4\cdot SO_2\cdot NH\cdot MeCO$ ≒ 214.45. Albucid, sulamyd, *p*-aminobenzenesulfonacetamide. Used to treat urinary infections and meningitis.

sulfacid. (1) A thio acid. (2) A sulfonic acid.

sulfactol. Sodium thiosulfate used in sulfur therapy.

sulfadiazine. $NH_2\cdot C_6H_4\cdot SO_2\cdot NH\cdot C_4H_3N_2$ = 250.29. 2-Sulfanilamidopyrimidine, *p*-amino-*N*-2-pyrimidylbenzenesulfonamide. White powder, darkening in light, m.254, slightly soluble in water; an antibacterial (U.S.P., B.P.). **s. sodium.** The sodium salt of s., used similarly (U.S.P.).

sulfadimethoxine. $C_{12}H_{14}O_4N_4S$ = 310.31. Cream crystals, slightly soluble in water, m.201; a sulfonamide (B.P.).

sulfadimethylpyrimidine. Sulfamethazine.

sulfadimidine. $C_{12}H_{14}O_2N_4S$ = 278.31. White, bitter crystals, m.198, insoluble in water; a bacteriostatic (B.P.); also used as the sodium salt (B.P.).

sulfa drugs. Sulfonamide drugs which combat certain bacterial infections; as, sulfadiazine, sulfamerazine, sulfanilamide, sulfathiazole.

sulfafurazole. $C_{11}H_{13}O_3N_3S$ = 267.33. White crystals, m.196, insoluble in water; a sulfa drug (B.P.).

sulfaguanidine. $NH_2\cdot C_6H_4\cdot SO_2\cdot N\colon C(NH_2)_2\cdot H_2O$ = 232.31. Sulfanilylguanidine monohydrate, *p*-aminobenzenesulfonylguanidine monohydrate. White crystals, m.191, slightly soluble in water. Used to treat intestinal infections; poorly absorbed from the gastrointestinal tract.

sulfaldehyde. $Me\cdot CS\cdot H$ = 74.1. Thioaldehyde. Oily liquid; a hypnotic.

sulfamerazine. $C_{11}H_{12}O_2N_4S$ = 264.32. 2-Sulfanil-amido-4-methylpyrimidine, 4-methylsulfadiazine. White, bitter crystals, darkening in light, m.238, slightly soluble in water; an antibacterial, more soluble and rapidly absorbed than sulfadiazine (U.S.P.); used also as the sodium salt (U.S.P.).

sulfamethazine. $C_{12}H_{14}O_2N_4S$ = 278.34. Sulfamezathine. 2-Sulfanilamido-4,6-dimethylpyrimidine, dimethylsulfadiazine. White, bitter powder, m.197, slightly soluble in water; an antibacterial (U.S.P.).

sulfamethizole. $C_9H_{10}O_2N_4S_2$ = 270.41. White crystals, m.209, slightly soluble in water; a sulfa drug (B.P.).

sulfamethoxydiazine. $C_{11}H_{12}O_3N_4S$ = 280.29. Yellow crystals, insoluble in water, m.211; a sulfonamide (B.P.).

sulfamethoxypyridazine. $C_{11}H_{12}O_3N_4S$ = 280.25. White, bitter crystals, m.182, slightly soluble in water; a sulfa drug (B.P.).

sulfamic. The radical $=N\cdot SO_2—$. **s. acid** (1) $HSO_3\cdot\text{-}NH_2$ = 97.23. Aminosulfonic acid, sulfonamic acid, sulfamidic acid. White crystals, soluble in water, m. approx. 250; a cleaning agent. (2) $R_2N\cdot SO_2\cdot OH$. An organic acid.

sulfamide. $SO_2(NH_2)_2$ = 96.18. Sulfuric acid diamide, m.92, soluble in water. Cf. *sulfaminic acid*. **alkyl-** $R_2N\cdot SO_2\cdot NR_2$. An organic compound.

sulfamidic acid. Sulfamic acid.

sulfamidobarbituric acid. Thionuric acid.

sulfamine. Sulfonamide. The radical, $—SO_2NH_2$. Cf. *sulfa drugs*.

sulfaminic acid. $NH_2\cdot SO_2OH$ = 97.10. Amidosulfonic acid. Cf. *sulfamide*. Colorless crystals, soluble in water. **alkyl-** $R_2N\cdot SO_2\cdot OR$. An organic compound.

sulfamino, sulfoamino (preferred). The radical $HO_3SNH—$ or $—NHSO_2\cdot OH$, from sulfaminic acid.

sulfaminobenzoic acid. $NH_2SO_2\cdot C_6H_4\cdot COOH$ = 201.2. *o*-Sulfaminebenzoic acid. Colorless rhombohedra, m.165, soluble in water.

sulfamyl. The radical $NH_2SO_2—$.

sulfanilamide. $NH_2\cdot C_6H_4\cdot SO_2\cdot NH_2$ = 172.20. Sulfamidyl, prontylin, prontosil-album, streptozone, streptocide, stramid, lysococcine, *p*-aminobenzenesulfonamide; an antibacterial.

sulfanilate. A salt of sulfanilic acid.

sulfanilic acid. $NH_2\cdot C_6H_4\cdot SO_3H$ = 173.17. Sulphanilic acid, *p*-aminobenzenesulfonic acid. Colorless, efflorescent rhombs, decomp. 280, soluble in water. Used in microscopy, organic synthesis, the manufacture of azo dyes; and to detect nitrous acid and bile pigments.

sulfantimonate. M_3SbS_4. Obtained by dissolving antimonic sulfide in ammonium sulfide. **sodium-** *Schlippe's salt*.

sulfantimonide. $MS\cdot SbS$. A double salt of sulfide and antimonide.

sulfantimonite. M_3SbS_3. obtained by dissolving antimonous sulfide in ammonium sulfide.

sulfapyridine. $NH_2\cdot C_6H_4\cdot SO_2\cdot NH\cdot C_5H_4N$ = 249.28. Dagenan, eubasin, coccoclase, pyriamid, M&B 693. 2-Sulfanilylaminopyridine. White crystals, darkening in light, m.192, slightly soluble in water; an antibacterial, especially for dermatitis and pneumonia (U.S.P., B.P.). **s. sodium.** The sodium derivative of s.

sulfarsenate. M_3AsS_4, derived from the hypothetical sulfarsenic acid, H_3AsS_4.

sulfarsenide. $MAsS_2$. A double salt of sulfide and arsenide.

sulfarsenite. M_3AsS_3, derived from the hypothetical sulfarsenous acid, H_3AsS_3.

sulfarsphenamine. A compound similar to arsphenamine; less irritant but less efficient.

sulfasomidine. $C_{12}H_{14}O_2N_4S$ = 278.26. White crystals, m.240 (decomp.), soluble in water; a sulfa drug (B.P.).

Sulfasuxidine. Trademark for medicinal products containing succinylsulfathiazole, q.v. An antibacterial for stomach infections; hydrolyzed in the lower bowel to free sulfathiazole.

sulfate. M_2SO_4. A salt of sulfuric acid. **acid-** $MHSO_4$. **basic-** $M(OH)SO_4$. A subsulfate. **bi-** Acid s. **hydrogen-** Acid s. **hypo-** $M_2S_2O_6$. Dithionate. **neutral-, normal-** Sulfate. **pyro-** $M_2S_2O_7$. **thio-** $M_2S_2O_3$. Thionate.
    s. ion. The anion $SO_4^=$. **s. of lime.** Calcium s. **s. of potash.** Potassium s. **s. pulp.** Paper pulp obtained by digestion of wood in a solution of sodium hydroxide, containing some sodium sulfide, sulfate, and carbonate.

sulfathalidine. Phthalylsulfathiazole. An antibacterial similar to sulfasuxidine, but more effective.

sulfathiazole. $NH_2C_6H_4SO_2NHC_2H_2SN$ = 255.31. 2-Sulfanilylaminothiazole. Used to treat pneumonia, and for certain wounds. **s. sodium.** The sodium derivative of s.

sulfatide. Lipoid substances containing sulfuric acid esters.

sulfation. Conversion into sulfates; as, in the determination of ash content. Cf. *sulfonation*.

sulfatostannate. $R_2H_2Sn(SO_4)_3$. An organic compound. Cf. *sulfostannate*.

sulfazide. $R—NH\cdot SO_2—R$. An organic compound.

sulfetrone. $C_{30}H_{28}O_{14}N_2S_5Na_4$ = 889.45. Tetrasodium-4:4'-bis(γ-phenylpropylamino)diphenylsulfone-α:γ,α':γ'-tetrasulfonate. Solapsone. Used to treat tuberculosis.

sulfhydrate. Hydrosulfide.

sulfhydryl. Mercapto. The radical $—SH$.

Sulfidal. Trademark for colloidal sulfur.

sulfide. M_2S or R_2S. M is a monovalent metal; R a monovalent organic radical, named like the ethers, *thio-** replacing *oxy**, as methylthioethane*, MeSEt. **alkyl-** $R—S—R$. Thio esters. **di-** M_2S_2 or R_2S_2. **s. dye.** A dye used in a sodium s. bath. **s. ion.** The ion $S^=$. **s. sulfur.** The divalent, negative sulfur atom in sulfides, as distinct from tetra- or hexavalent positive sulfur.

sulfidion. See *sulfide ion*.

sulfilimine. $R_2S:NH$.

sulfime. A compound containing a $=C:N\cdot S—$ group; as, $R\cdot CH(:NSH)$. Cf. *oxime*.

sulfimide. (1) A compound containing the radical $—SO_2\cdot NH—$. (2) $(SO_2NH)_3$ = 239.7. A sulfuric acid imide.

sulfinate. (1) $R_2S\cdot CH_2\cdot CO\cdot O$. Thetines. (2) A compound having the grouping R_2SX_2. (3) $R\cdot OH\cdot S:O$. A salt of sulfinic acid.

sulfindigotic acid. $C_8H_5NOSO_3$ = 211.11. Obtained by the action of sulfuric acid on indigo. Cf. *thioindigo*.

sulfine. Sulfonium compound. An organic compound of the type R_3SX. See *sulfonium*.

sulfinic acid. $R-SO \cdot OH$; as, ethanesulfinic acid*, $EtSO_2H$. In derivatives it becomes the prefix sulfino-*.

sulfinid. Saccharin.

sulfino*. (1) The radical $-SO_2H$. Cf. *sulfinic acid*. (2) Prefix denoting a sulfinic functional group.

sulfinoxide. $R_3 \cdot S \cdot OH$. An organic compound.

sulfinpyrazone. $C_{23}H_{20}O_3N_2S = 404.5$. Bitter, white powder, insoluble in water, m.133; a uricosuric (B.P.).

sulfinyl. Thionyl.

sulfion. Sulfide ion: $S^=$.

sulfisoxazole. $C_{11}H_{13}O_3N_3S = 267.32$. White crystals, m.193, insoluble in water; an antibacterial (U.S.P.).

sulfite. M_2SO_3. A salt of sulfurous acid. **acid-** $MHSO_3$. **bi-, hydrogen-** Acids. **hypo-** (1) $M_2S_2O_4$. (2) Thiosulfate. **sub-** Thiosulfate.

s. ion. The anion $SO_3^=$. **s. cellulose liquor.** The waste liquor from the pulping of wood by the s. process: free SO_2 2–4, $SO_3^=$ 2–7, $SO_4^=$ 2–5, solids 80–90, ash 12–16%, with calcium compounds, carbohydrates, and lignin sulfonate. Used as a tanning, binding, or mordanting agent, or for fermentation. *s.c.l. lactone.* Tsugaresinol. **s. pulp.** Paper pulp obtained by the digestion of wood (generally coniferous) with calcium bisulfite containing free sulfur dioxide.

sulfivinyl. The radical $=SO$. A term preferred to thionyl, except for the thionyl halides (U.K. usage).

sulfo-, sulpho- Prefix indicating the presence of (1) divalent sulfur, or (2) the sulfo group, $-SO_3H$. Cf. *thio-*. **s. acid.** Sulfonic acid. **s. amino.** Preferred term for *sulfamino*. **s. group.** The $-SO_3H$ group. See *sulfonic acids*. **s. salt.** (1) A salt of an acid containing sulfur. (2) An ester of sulfonic acid.

sulfoacetic acid. $HSO_3 \cdot CH_2 \cdot COOH \cdot H_2O = 158.10$. Colorless tablets, m.86 (sublimes), soluble in water.

sulfoarsenide. Sulfarsenide.

sulfobenzide. $(C_6H_5)_2SO_2 = 218.2$. Diphenylsulfone. Colorless scales, m.123, insoluble in water.

sulfobenzoic acid. $HSO_3 \cdot C_6H_4 \cdot COOH = 202.12$. **ortho-** Colorless, triclinic crystals, m.134 (forming an anhydride above 125), soluble in water. **meta-** Colorless crystals, m.141, soluble in water. **para-** Colorless needles, m.260, soluble in water. Cf. *halazone*.

sulfobromophthalein sodium. $C_{20}H_8O_{10}Br_4Na_2S_2 = 833.06$. White, hygroscopic bitter crystals; a diagnostic aid for liver ailments (U.S.P., B.P.).

sulfocarbamide. Thiourea.

sulfocarbanilide. $Ph \cdot NH \cdot CS \cdot NH \cdot Ph = 228.24$. Thiocarbanilide, diphenylsulfourea. Colorless leaflets, m.153, insoluble in water.

sulfocarbazide. A compound containing the radical $-NH \cdot NH \cdot CS \cdot NH \cdot NH-$.

sulfocarbimide. Isothiocyanic acid.

sulfocarbodiazone. A compound containing the radical $-N:N \cdot CS \cdot N:N-$.

sulfocarbolate. A salt of phenolsulfonic acid.

sulfocarbolic acid. Phenolsulfonic acid.

sulfocarbonate. M_2CS_3. A salt derived from sulfocarbonic acid.

sulfocarbonic acid. $H_2CS_3 = 110.2$. Trithiocarbonic

acid. Brown oil, insoluble in water, readily decomposed; a reagent for nickel (as the K salt).

sulfochloride. $R \cdot SO_2 \cdot Cl$. The chloride of sulfonic acids.

sulfocyan. Thiocyanate.

sulfocyanate. Thiocyanate.

sulfocyanic acid. Thiocyanic acid.

sulfocyanide. Thiocyanate.

sulfoform. $(C_6H_5)_3 \cdot SbS = 384.8$. Triphenylstibine sulfide. Colorless needles, m.120; used to treat skin diseases. *crude-* Yellow liquid; a powerful reducing agent.

sulfo group. The $-SO_3H$ group. See *sulfonic acid*.

sulfoguaiacin. Quinine methyl sulfoguaiacate.

sulfohydrate. Hydrosulfide.

sulfoichthyolic acid. A compound obtained from bituminous shales; contains sulfur as sulfonate, sulfone, or sulfide.

sulfoid. Colloidal sulfur.

sulfolane. $C_4H_8O_2S = 120.26$. Tetramethylsulfone, tetrahydrothiophen-1,1-dioxide. Colorless solid, m.27, miscible with water; a selective solvent for hydrocarbons.

sulfoleate. A salt of sulfoleic acid.

sulfoleic acid. Obtained by mixing sulfuric acid with oils containing oleic acid.

sulfolipins. Fatty substances containing sulfur.

sulfonal. $Me_2C(SO_2Et)_2 = 228.3$. Sulphonal, sulfonmethane, diethylsulfonedimethylmethane. Colorless prisms, m.126, slightly soluble in water; a hypnotic. **methyl-** Trional.

sulfonamic. Sulfamic.

sulfonamide. Sulfamine.

sulfonamido. The radical $-NH \cdot SO_2-$. Cf. *sulfamino*, *sulfamyl*.

sulfonaphthalein. A compound similar to the phthaleins, but with a sulfone, instead of a carbonyl, group. Made by condensation of *o*-sulfobenzoic acid anhydride with phenols. Many are important indicators, q.v., and dyes; as, *o*-cresol s., cresol red.

sulfonaphthol. $HSO_3 \cdot C_{10}H_6 \cdot OH = 224.13$. Colorless powder; an antiseptic.

sulfonate. (1) To treat an aromatic hydrocarbon with fuming sulfuric acid. (2) A sulfuric acid derivative. (3) A sulfonic acid ester.

sulfonation. Substitution of H atom(s) by $-SO_3H$ group(s). **direct-** Treatment of an organic compound with fuming sulfuric acid. **indirect-** Treatment with acid sulfites.

sulfonator. A double-walled, cast-iron vessel with power-driven stirrer, for large-scale sulfonation.

sulfone. R_2SO_2 or $RSOOR$, obtained by oxidation of sulfides. In derivatives its prefix is sulfonyl*, Et_2SO_2. **s. methanes.** Compounds used to induce sleep; as, trional, q.v. **s. phthalein.** See *sulfonphthalein*.

sulfonethylmethane. Trional.

sulfonic acid*. An organic compound containing the radical $-SO_2OH$, derived from sulfuric acid by replacement of an $-OH$ group. Sulfonic acids are soluble in water and yield phenols when heated with potassium hydroxide. Used in the manufacture of dyes and synthetic drugs. **amino-** Sulfamic acid. **diamino-** Sulfamide. **nitro-** Nitrosyl sulfate.

sulfonium. Sulfine. The radical R_3S-. **s. compound.** R_3SX. Sulfine. R is an organic radical, and X an electronegative element (Cl) or radical

(OH). **s. hydroxides.** $R_3S \cdot OH$. Strong bases ionizing to R_3S^+ and OH^-. **s. iodide.** R_3SI. An organic compound.

sulfonmethane. Sulfonal.

sulfonyl. (1) Sulfuryl. The radical $-SO_2-$. (2) Prefix denoting a sulfone functional group.

sulfoparaldehyde. $(C_4H_4S_2)_3 = 448.5$. Trithioacetaldehyde. Colorless crystals, insoluble in water; a hypnotic.

sulfophenol. Aseptol.

sulfophenylate. (1) Phenol sulfonate. (2) Phenyl sulfate.

sulforhodanide. Thiocyanate.

sulfosalicylic acid. $C_6H_3(OH) \cdot (COOH) \cdot SO_3H = 218.1$. A soluble solid, m.120; a reagent for albumin.

sulfosalt. (1) A salt of an acid containing sulfur. (2) A sulfonic acid ester.

sulfoselenide. M_4SSe. A double salt.

sulfosemicarbazide. A compound containing the radical $NH_2 \cdot CSNH \cdot NH-$.

sulfosol. A colloidal system with sulfuric acid as the disperse phase.

sulfostannate. M_2SnS_3. Cf. *sulfatostannate.*

sulfostannite. M_2SnS_2.

sulfourea. Thiourea.

sulfovinic acid. Ethylsulfuric acid.

sulfoxide. The radical $=SO$.

sulfoxides*. $R \cdot SO \cdot R$. In derivatives they have the prefix sulfinyl*; as, methyl sulfoxide*, Me_2SO. Obtained by oxidation of mercaptans (analogous to the ketones).

sulfoxone sodium. $C_{14}H_{14}O_6N_2Na_2S_3 = 448.46$. White powder with characteristic odor, soluble in water; an antibacterial (U.S.P.).

sulfoxylate. $MHSO_2$, derived from sulfoxylic acid.

sulfoxylic acid. The hypothetical acid $S(OH)_2$, containing divalent sulfur; known as its salts, Na_2SO_2 and $NaHSO_2$. See *Rongalite.*

sulfur (U.S. usage), **sulphur** (U.K. usage). $S = 32.06$. Brimstone. Solid nonmetal element, at. no. 16. A yellow, brittle mass or transparent, monoclinic or rhombic crystals; but existing in a number of modifications: (1) Rhombic: $S_8 = 256.4$. Stable at ordinary temperatures, d.2.07, m.114, b.444.7. (2) Monoclinic: $S_8 = 256.4$. Stable above 96, forms transparent, yellow, monoclinic prisms, d.1.957, m.119, b.444.7. (3) Amorphous: S_x. Soft, pale yellow or fine, white powder (colloidal), d.2.046, m.120, b.444.7.

Deg C	Effect of heat
20	Rhombic, S_8.
96	Monoclinic, S_8.
114	Melts to thin, yellow liquid, S_8 or S_λ
160	Forms thick, brown liquid containing thiozon S_3, besides S_8.
220	Becomes dark brown and plastic, S_6 and S_8 or $S_{\lambda\mu}$.
250	Begins to burn if heated in air.
440	Forms thin, brown liquid, S_6 or S_μ.
447	Boils: reddish brown vapor of S_6; becomes lighter in color and larger in volume, until:
860	Colorless vapor of S_2, d.2.23.

S. is found native in Sicily and U.S., but its principal source is natural gas. It is insoluble in water; slightly soluble in alcohol or ether; soluble in carbon disulfide: solubility varies with the modification. Used in the manufacture of gunpowder, disinfectants, vulcanizing agents, sulfuric acid, sulfides, and pharmaceuticals. See *sulfur compounds*. World production (1967) 26 million tons (all forms). **colloidal-** Sulfidal, sulfoid. Finely divided s. obtained by passing hydrogen sulfide through a solution of a sulfite; used to treat skin diseases. **elastic-** S. mu. Amorphous, chemically pure s., 90–95% soluble in carbon disulfide; used in the rubber industry. **flowers of-** Sublimed s. **lac-** Precipitated s. obtained by adding sulfuric acid to a solution of a polysulfide (contains up to 45% calcium sulfate), used in pharmacy. **liver of-** A mixture of potassium sulfide and polysulfides. **milk of-, precipitated-** A suspension of finely divided s. obtained by precipitation of calcium pentasulfide or a thiosulfate with an acid (U.S.P.). **ruby-** Realgar. **sublimed-** Fine, yellow powder obtained by distilling s. **vegetable-** Lycopodium. **washed-** S. washed with ammonium hydroxide and water; used medicinally.

s. acids. See *sulfur acids, sulfuric acids.* **s. alcohols.** Hydrosulfides. **s. anhydride.** S. trioxide. **s. bromide.** $S_2Br_2 = 224.0$. S. monobromide. Yellow liquid, soluble in carbon disulfide. **s. chlorides.** (1) $S_2Cl_2 = 135.0$. S. monochloride. Brown, fuming liquid, b.138, decomp. by water, soluble in carbon disulfide. Used as a reagent; for s. solvents, war gases, vulcanized oils; and in vulcanizing rubber and sugar purification. (2) SCl_2. S. dichloride. (3) $S_3Cl_4 = 238.02$. Trisulfur tetrachloride. (4) SCl_4. S. tetrachloride *red-* Brown liquid: SCl_2 75, S_2Cl_2 25%; used for synthesis; and in the manufacture of varnishes, rubber pigments, and poison gas. *yellow-* Yellow, corrosive liquid, containing 5–9% S; used similarly to red s. **s. compounds.** S has a valency of 2, 4, or 6; and forms 4 series of compounds; as, hydrogen sulfide (valency -2), s. dichloride (valency 2), s. dioxide (valency 4), s. trioxide (valency 6). **s. cycle.** The transformation of s. compounds by living organisms:

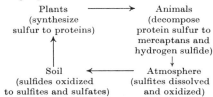

Plants   ⟶   Animals
(synthesize   (decompose
sulfur to proteins)   protein sulfur to
                        mercaptans and
                        hydrogen sulfide)

Soil   ⟵   Atmosphere
(sulfides oxidized   (sulfites dissolved
to sulfites and sulfates)   and oxidized)

s. dichloride. $SCl_2 = 104.1$. Brown liquid. b.69, decomp. by water or heat. Used as a s. solvent and for vulcanizing rubber and purifying sugar juices. Probably a mixture of the mono- and tetrachlorides. **s. dioxide.** $SO_2 = 64.1$. Sulfurous acid anhydride. Colorless gas, b.-10, soluble in water or ether. Marketed as liquid under pressure; a reagent, bleach, and preservative (U.S.P.). **s. dyes.** Pyrogenic dyes. Organic dyes containing s., obtained by heating amino or nitro compounds with alkali sulfides, insoluble in water, soluble in sodium sulfide solutions; permanent textile dyes. **s. ether.**

R_2S. See *thioethers*. **s. fluorescein.** Uranin. **s. fluoride.** $S_2F_2 = 102.1$. S. monofluoride. Colorless gas, readily hydrolyzed to hydrofluoric acid, s. dioxide, and s. **s. group.** The 6th group of the periodic system: S, Se, Te, O. **s. hexafluoride.** $SF_6 = 146.2$. A gas of high dielectric capacitance which captures electrons in an electric field; used in high-voltage switches and stabilizers. **s. hexaiodide.** $SI_6 = 793.8$. Green crystals, soluble in carbon disulfide, decomp. by water. **s. introfier.** See *introfier*. **s. iodide.** $S_2I_2 = 317.8$. Iodine disulfide, s. subiodide. Gray, lustrous, brittle crystals, insoluble in water; used in skin ointments. **s. monobromide.** S. bromide. **s. monochloride.** S. chloride. **s. monofluoride.** S. fluoride. **s. mu.** Elastic s. **s. oxides.** See *s. dioxide, s. trioxide*. **s. oxychlorides.** (1) $SO_2Cl_4 = 205.96$. Red liquid, b.100, decomp. by water. (2) $S_2O_3Cl_4 = 253.96$. White needles, m.57 (sublime), decomp. by water. (3) See *sulfuryl chloride*. **s. oxyfluoride.** $SO_2F_2 = 134.12$. Sulfuryl fluoride; an irritating vapor. **s. subbromide.** S. bromide. **s. subchloride.** S. chloride. **s. subiodide.** S. iodide. **s. tetrachloride.** $SCl_4 = 173.9$. Yellow liquid, m.−31; unstable, but forms stable compounds; as, $2Al_3 \cdot SCl_4$. **s. tetrafluoride.** $SF_4 = 108.20$. A toxic, gaseous fluorinating agent. **s. trioxide.** $SO_3 = 80.1$. Sulfuric acid anhydride. *gamma*- Liquid, b.44.8, obtained by distillation of oleum; rapidly polymerizes in moist air to the *beta*- (straight-chain) form, and then the *alpha*- (cross-linked) form, m.100. On heating, these revert to the gamma form, which may be stabilized by addition of 0.2% of boric oxide. *solid*- $(SO_3)_2$. Colorless prisms, m.15, b.46, rapidly decomp. by water to form sulfuric acid; soluble in concentrated sulfuric acid. **s. yellow.** Naphthol yellow.

sulfur acids. The following are known:

H_2S.	Hydrosulfuric acid or hydrogen sulfide.
H_2S_5.	Hydrogen pentasulfide.
H_2SO_3.	Sulfurous acid.
H_2SO_4.	Sulfuric acid.
$H_2SO_4 + SO_3$.	Oleum.
$H_2S_2O_3$.	Thiosulfuric acid.
$H_2S_2O_4$.	Dithionous acid.
$H_2S_2O_5$.	Caro's acid, metasulfuric acid.
$H_2S_2O_6$.	Dithionic acid.
$H_2S_2O_7$.	Pyrosulfuric acid.
$H_2S_2O_8$.	Persulfuric acid.
$H_2S_3O_6$.	Trithionic acid.
$H_2S_4O_6$.	Tetrathionic acid.
$H_2S_5O_6$.	Pentathionic acid.
$H_2S_6O_6$.	Hexathionic acid.

sulfurated, sulfuretted, sulphuretted. Combined with sulfur. **s. oils.** An essential oil containing sulfur compounds; as, mustard oil.

sulfuret. Sulfide (obsolete).

sulfuretted hydrogen. Hydrogen sulfide.

sulfuric. Pertaining to hexavalent sulfur. **s. acid.** See *sulfur acid, sulfuric acid*. **s. anhydride.** Sulfur trioxide. **s. chloride.** Sulfuryl chloride.

sulfuric acid. $H_2SO_4 = 98.1$. Oil (spirit) of vitriol, hydrogen sulfate. A dibasic acid from sulfur dioxide. See *sulfuric acid manufacture*.
(1) $H_2SO_4 = 98.1$. d.1.8542, m.10, b.316.
(2) $H_2SO_4 \cdot H_2O = 116.1$. Colorless prisms, d.1.788,

m.8, b.210, soluble in water, decomp. by alcohol.
(3) $H_2SO_4 \cdot 2H_2O = 134.1$. Colorless liquid, d.1.665, m.−38, b.170; soluble in water, alcohol, or ether.
(4) $H_2SO_4 \cdot xHO$. Concentrated acid, 94%, d.1.84.
(4a) Concentrated: U.S.P. 95.0–98.0% w./w.; B.P. 97.0% w./w.
(4b) Diluted: U.S.P. 5.7% v./v.; B.P. 10.4% w./w.
(5) $H_2SO_4 \cdot xSO_3$. Oleum (above 100%).
World production (1967) 60 million tons. Cf. *sulfaminic acid, sulfur acids, BOV, DOV, ROV*. **chloro-** See *chlorosulfuric acid*. **concentrated-** See (4), (4a). **dilute-** See (4b). **ethyl-** See *ethylsulfuric acid*. **fuming-** See (5). **glycerol-** q.v. **nitro-** q.v. **nitroso-** q.v. **Nordhausen-** Oleum. **phenol-** Phenylsulfuric acid.

sulfuric acid manufacture. (1) *Lead-chamber process*: Sulfur or pyrites are burned in furnaces, and the sulfur dioxide formed passes through the Glover tower, where it comes in contact with 65% s. acid from the lead chamber and the acid containing oxides of nitrogen from the Gay-Lussac tower. A portion of the sulfur dioxide is oxidized and dissolved. The remaining mixture of gases, consisting now principally of sulfur dioxide and nitric oxide, passes into the lead chamber, where the principal reaction occurs:

$$SO_2 + O_2 + NO \rightarrow SO_3 + NO_2 \rightarrow H_2SO_4(65\%)$$

The escaping nitrogen dioxide is passed through the Gay-Lussac tower, in which it is dissolved in strong sulfuric acid from the Glover tower. The acids collecting at the bottom of the lead chambers are finally concentrated in pans by heat. (2) *Contact process*: Sulfur or pyrites are burned in furnaces, and the sulfur dioxide formed passes through scrubbers. In some the gas is washed with water; in others it is dried with sulfuric acid. The dry gas enters the contact chamber in which a catalyst (generally platinum or iron oxide) oxidizes it to sulfur trioxide which, in turn, is passed through water and absorbed as sulfuric acid.

sulfuric ester. R_2SO_4. Sulfuric acid ester.

sulfuric ether. Commercial ether (a misnomer).

sulfuring. (1) Burning sulfur in barrels to disinfect them for wines, etc. (2) Dressing growing crops with flowers of sulfur to arrest mold growth. (3) Adding sulfur to hop kiln fires to liberate sulfur dioxide as preservative.

sulfurize. To combine with sulfur.

sulfurous. Pertaining to tetravalent sulfur. **s. acid.** $H_2SO_3 = 82.1$. An aqueous solution of sulfur dioxide (6% SO_2). Colorless liquid, d.1.03; a reducing agent and bleach. *ethyl*- See *ethylsulfurous acid*. **s. anhydride.** Sulfur dioxide. **s. esters.** R_2SO_3.

sulfuryl. Sulfonyl. The radical $=SO_2$, derived from sulfuric acid by subtraction of 2 —OH groups. **s. chloride.** $SO_2Cl_2 = 135.0$. Sulfuric chloride, chlorsulfuric acid. Colorless, pungent liquid, b.69, decomp. by water; a reagent. **s. diamide.** Sulfamide. **s. fluoride.** Sulfur oxyfluoride.

sulph-, sulpho-, sulphur, sulphuretted, sulphuric, etc. See *sulf-, sulfo-*, etc. (U.S. usage).

sultam. A derivative of 1,8-naphthylaminesulfonic acid.

sultone. A derivative of 1,8-naphtholsulfonic acid.

sulvanite. Cu_3VS_4. A vanadium mineral.

sumac(h). (1) Sicilian s., the shrub *Rhus coriaria* (Anacardiaceae), S. Europe; leaves used for tanning and dyeing (2) Any of the *Rhus* species. (3) Sumac. A tan (18–25% tannin) from the dried leaves of *Rhus* species. Cf. *fustic*. **American-** *R. copellina* and *R. metopium*. **Chinese-** Tree of heaven. The bark of *Ailanthus glandulosa* (Simarubiaceae); used as an astringent and antispasmodic, and for tanning. **curriers-** The plant *Coriaria myrtifolia* (Coraniaceae), containing coriamyrtin. **Indian-** *R. succedania*. **smooth-** S. berries. The dried ripe fruit of *R. glabra*; used as an astringent and tonic. **sweet-** Fragrant s. The bark of the root of *R. aromatica*, used as an astringent and diuretic. **Tizra-***R. pentaphylla*. **Venetian-** *R. cotinus*. **White-** *R. glabra*.

    s. bark. Sweet s. **s. berries.** Smooth s.

sumaresinol. $C_{30}H_{48}O_4 \cdot 4H_2O$ = 544.35. Sumaresinolic acid, m.298, from Sumatra gum benzoin.

sumbul. Muskroot. The dried rhizome of *Ferula sumbul* (Umbelliferae), Asia; a nerve stimulant and antispasmodic.

sump. An open channel or pit for collecting drainings for removal by pumping.

sun. The star nearest to the earth; mass 1.99×10^{33} grams, d.5.00, surface temperature 6000°C. Cf. *spectral classification, solar spectrum, earth constants*.

    s. atmosphere. H 92, He 3, O 3, metal vapors (mainly Mg, Fe, Si, Na) 3 vol. %. **s. light.** Intensity on a clear day: 100,000–125,000 lux.

sundew Drosera.

sunflower. Helianthus. The dried seeds of *Helianthus annuus* (Compositae); a diuretic. **s. oil.** A slow-drying oil from the seeds of s. (contain 32–45%). Consists mostly of the glycerides of oleic, linolic, and palmitic acids; used for margarine manufacture.

sunstone. Orthoclase.

sunt. An aqueous extract of *Acacia arabica* (Sudan); a brown preservative for tent canvas.

S.U.P. *p*-Benzoyl-*p*-aminobenzoyl-1-amino-8-naphthol-3,8-sodium sulfonate. A substance that supplies stabilizing electrons to colloidal particles.

super- Prefix (Latin) indicating above, beyond, or higher.

superacid. Excessively acid in reaction. **s. solution.** A solution in acetic or phosphoric acid.

superacidity. Increased acidity of the gastric juice.

Superayflex. Trade name for a viscose synthetic fiber.

superbine. A poisonous bitter principle from *Gloriosa superba* (Liliaceae), India and S. Africa; resembles the bitter principle of squill.

supercalender. A calender, q.v., which uses both steam and high pressure to obtain a high finish, e.g., on paper.

supercarbonate. Bicarbonate.

superchlorination. Sterilizing water by chlorinating in excess, and then adding an antichlor.

superconductivity. Supraconductivity. The property of certain metals of becoming good electrical conductors at low temperatures; e.g.: Pb 7.2, Hg 4.21, Sn 3.71, In 3.41, Tl 2.47°K. No other metal shows any change above 1.3°K. **s. motor.**

A device utilizing the s. of copper to produce considerable reductions in the size and weight of conventional electric motors.

supercooled. Over- or undercooled. Cooled below the freezing point of a liquid without the separation of solid matter.

superfluid. A fluid having exceptionally good heat-transfer and penetrating properties, e.g., liquid *helium*-II.

Supergas. Trade name for triptane.

superheated. Overheated. Describing a liquid or gas heated above its boiling point in the liquid state; as superheated steam (water vapor at above 100°C).

supermalloy. The alloy: Ni 75, Mo 5, Fe + Mn 20%. It has a high electrical permeability; used in transformer cores.

supernatant. Describing the liquid above a sediment or precipitate.

supernickel. The alloy: Cu 70, Ni 30%; retains its strength at high temperatures.

supernormal. A volumetric solution of concentration greater than normal.

superol. *o*-Hydroxyquinoline sulfate.

superoxide. Peroxide.

superpalite. A poison gas. Cf. *palite*.

superphosphate. (1) An acid phosphate. (2) A fertilizer mixture of calcium phosphate and calcium sulfate obtained by the action of concentrated sulfuric acid on phosphate minerals (apatite, phosphorite). **ammoniated-** A fertilizer containing s. or dissolved bone, or both, but no potash. **double-** A fertilizer made by the action of phosphoric acid on rock phosphate (40–50% phosphorus pentoxide).

superpolymer. A polymer, molecular weight exceeds 10,000.

superpotential. Overvoltage.

supersaturated. More than saturated. **s. solution.** A solution containing an excess of dissolved substance over that normally required for saturation at a particular temperature, obtainable by slowly cooling a saturated solution.

supersolubility. Supersaturation. **s. curve.** The curve relating the concentration of a supersaturated solution with the temperature; analogous to and parallel with the solubility curve, q.v.

supersonic. Describing speeds of velocity greater than that of sound. Cf. *ultraphonic*.

supersteel. A high-speed steel, q.v.

supertension. Overvoltage.

suppository. A plug impregnated with or containing a medicament, for insertion into a body aperture, e.g., the rectum.

suppurative. An agent that produces pus.

supra- Prefix (Latin) indicating above.

supracapsuline. Adrenaline.

supraconductivity. Superconductivity.

Supramid. Trade name for a polyamide synthetic fiber.

suprarenal. A gland above the kidney. **s. liquid.** An aqueous extract of the s. gland, used medicinally.

suprarenalin. Adrenaline.

Suprarenin. Trademark for the acid tartrate of epinephrine (adrenaline).

suprasterols. Sterols produced by irradiation of lumisterol.

Suprema. Trade name for a viscose synthetic fiber.

Supron. Trade name for a polyamide synthetic fiber.

suramin, sodium- $C_{51}H_{34}O_{23}N_6S_6$ = 1429.25. Bayer 205. Bitter, hygroscopic powder, insoluble in ether; a urea derivative, used to treat trypanosomiasis (B.P.).

surcharge. The sum of the errors involved in an assay.

surface. The outer part of a body having length and breadth but not thickness. **s. active.** See *surfactant*. **s. density.** The electric or magnetic charge per unit area on the surface of an electrode. Cf. *current density*. **s. energy.** The product obtained by multiplying surface tension by the two-thirds power of the molecular weight and specific volume. **s. tension.** The contractile surface force of a liquid which makes it tend to assume a spherical form, e.g., to form a meniscus. It also exists at the junction of 2 liquids. It is measured directly (grams per square centimeter, or dynes) or indirectly by determining the capillarity. The s.t. (at constant temperature) γ is in a constant ratio to the 4th power of the orthobaric densities of liquid, D, and gas, d; hence $\gamma\frac{1}{4} = K(D - d)$. Cf. *parachor*. **s. tension apparatus.** Tensiometer. A device for determining the s. t., based upon the flexibility of a wire. **s.t. 37.** See *S.T.37*.

surfactant. A surface-active substance, i.e., alters (usually reduces) the surface tension of water. Widely used in cosmetics, wetting agents, and detergents. Three types: nonionic (polyethylene oxides), anionic (sodium lauryl sulfate), and cationic (cetyl pyridinium chloride).

surfen. Bis(2-methyl-4-amino-6-quinoyl)melamine. An antibacterial.

surfusion. The unstable condition of a liquid cooled below its freezing point without solidifying. Cf. *supercooled*.

surpalite. Diphosgene.

surrogate. A substitute for another substance; as, margarine for butter.

surrosion. The increase in weight of a substance due to corrosion.

susceptible. (1) Sensitive. Readily capable of responding to an action or force; as, magnetic susceptibility. (2) See *immune*.

susotoxin. $C_{10}H_{26}N_2$ = 174.3. Sustoxin. A ptomaine from cultures of hog cholera bacillus.

suspension. (1) Suspensoid. (2) A thin thread on which the mirror and magnet of a galvanometer hang. **s. method.** The determination of the density of a solid by placing it in a solution of known density. See *density fluids*.

suspensoid. Suspension, soliquoid. Finely divided colloidal particles floating in a liquid, too small to settle, but kept in motion by Brownian movement, q.v.

sussexite. A native, hydrated magnesium manganese pyroborate.

sustoxin. Susotoxin.

Sutherland's equation. The diameter of a molecule = $[1.402/\sqrt{2}\pi NL(1 + C/T)]^{\frac{1}{2}}$, where N is the number of molecules per unit volume, L the mean free path in centimeters, and C Sutherland's constant. **S.-Einstein equation.** $D = RT/Nf$,

where D is the diffusion constant, R the gas constant, T the absolute temperature, N Avogadro's constant, and f the frictional force in dynes on each molecule having unit velocity.

suture. A stitch, or the operation of stitching, used in surgery. **absorbable-** A sterile s. prepared from the collagen of healthy animals (U.S.P.). **nonabsorbable-** A s. that resists enzyme digestion in living animal tissues, e.g., of metal.

suxamethonium bromide. $C_{14}H_{30}O_4N_2Br_2\cdot2H_2O$ = 486.32. Succinylcholine bromide. White, saline powder, m.225 (approx.), soluble in water; a muscle relaxant (B.P.). **s. chloride.** B.P. name for succinylcholine chloride (U.S.P.).

Sved. A unit of sedimentation rate.

Svedberg, The(odor). b. 1884. Swedish physical chemist, Nobel Prize Winner (1926); noted for research on colloids. **S.'s equation.** The amplitude A of Brownian movement of a particle is proportional to its vibration period t.

swage. To fashion metal, particularly iron, by drawing it into a groove, mold, or die having a desired shape.

Swan, Sir Joseph Wilson. 1828-1914. English chemist, pioneer in photography, electric carbon filament lamps, and electrodeposition of metals.

swan neck. A tube bent into the shape of an upright U joined to an inverted U; thus ∽.

swarf. The raw edge of a metallic object produced in casting metals, and removed for reuse.

Swarts, Frederic. Dutch chemist noted for organic research.

Swedenborg, Emanuel. 1688-1772. Swedish mineralogist (and later, theosophist) who invented mercury pumps.

sweetbirch oil. Methyl salicylate.

sweeten. (1) To remove substances of unpleasant odor (as mercaptans) from spirits, petroleum, etc., usually by oxidation. (2) To purify. (3) To add a sugar.

sweet flag. Calamus.

sweetness. The characteristic taste of sugars. Relative physiological response:

Peryllartine	2000
Saccharin	700
Sucrol	300
Cyclamates	300
Fructose	175
Invert sugar	123
Sucrose	100
Glucose	74
Xylose	40
Maltose, rhamnose, galactose	32
Raffinose	23
Lactose	16

Cf. *cyclamic acid, dulcigen, sapiphore*.

swell. The swelling of a canned food container due to the liberation of gas, e.g., hydrogen from the action of acidic fruit juices on the metal.

swelling. The adsorption of water by an amorphous substance, to form a jelly.

sycoceryl alcohol. $C_{18}H_{30}O$ = 262.23. Colorless crystals, m.90. Cf. *lactucerol*.

sydone. An aromatic compound having a ring structure of the type

$$Ar-N\left\langle\begin{array}{cc} CH-CO \\ | \quad | \\ N-O \end{array}\right.$$

e.g., the anhydro derivative of a *N*-nitroso-*N*-arylglycine.

syenite. A granular, igneous rock, chiefly orthoclase with or without albite, biotite, hornblende, microcline, or corundum.

Sykose. A brand of saccharin.

sylvan. $CH:CH\cdot O\cdot CMe:CH = 82.1.$ α-Methylfuran. A constituent of wood tar. Yellow liquid, b.63, soluble in alcohol.

sylvanite. $(Au,Ag)Te_2$. Graphic tellurium.

sylvanium. Tellurium.

sylvate. A salt of abietic acid.

sylvic acid. Abietic acid.

sylvic oil. Tall oil.

sylviculture. The study of forestry.

sylvine. An isomorphous, native mixture of sodium and potassium chlorides.

sylvinite. A sylvite, with rock salt (about 16% potassium oxide); a fertilizer.

sylvite. KCl. A native potassium chloride fertilizer from Stassfurt.

Sylvius, François. 1614–1672. (Dubois de la Boë.) German-born Dutch physician who considered that combustion, respiration, and similar physiological functions are based on chemical reactions.

sym- Abbreviation for symmetrical.

symbiosis. A partnership of 2 different living organisms, of mutual benefit to both. **antagonistic-** S. in which one species derives more benefit than the other. **conjunctive-** The living together of 2 organisms with bodily union; as, lichens, which consist of algae and fungi. **disjunctive-** An association of 2 living organisms that are not actually united.

symbiotic fixation. The conversion of atmospheric nitrogen to nitrates or nitrites by soil bacteria and leguminous plants. Cf. *nitrogen fixation.*

symbol. A mark which represents a substance, quality, or relation. **chemical-** A letter or a combination of letters that represents an atom of an element and its relative mass. Chemical symbols are used to indicate: (1) an atom, as, H; (2) an ion, as, H$^+$; (3) a molecule, as, H$_2$; (4) a gram atom or gram molecule: thus H= 1 gm hydrogen (see *mole*); (5) an excited atom (by an asterisk), as, H*; (6) an isotope by its isotopic weight or small letter showing its abundance, as, Cl^{35}; (7) an atomic nucleus by prefixing its atomic number as subscript, and its mass number as superscript; and suffixing its number of atoms per molecule as subscript, and ionic charge as superscript. Thus, $^{23}_{16}S_2^{2+}$ (international usage). In the U.S. it is customary to show the mass number at the right, as in this Dictionary. See *ion, nomenclature, radical, notation, formula, alchemistic* symbols. **mathematical-** A letter that indicates quantity; or a mark that indicates or forms part of an algebraic operation. **structure-** A graph that indicates the arrangement of atoms in an organic compound. See *structure symbols, units,* and table of symbols.

symmetric, symmetrical. Having constituent parts arranged in a definite pattern, and repeated continually in a definite direction of space; as, atoms in a crystal. (2) Describing a s. compound. **axial-** See *stereoisomerism.* **plane-** See *stereoisomerism.* **s. carbon atom.** See *asymmetric carbon.* **s. compound.** A benzene derivative with substitution of the 1-, 3-, and 5-hydrogen atoms.

symmetry. Being symmetrical. The s. of a crystal is determined by regularities in the positions of the similar faces or edges, and is defined by the number of elements of symmetry. See *crystal systems.* **axis of-** An imaginary axis through a symmetrical body. If this body is rotated, it occupies the same position in space more than once in a 360° turn. **center of-** A central point of a symmetrical body, around which like faces are arranged in opposite pairs. **elements of-** The number of planes, axes, and centers of s. of a symmetrical body. A cube has the largest possible number; viz.: 9 planes, 13 axes, and one center. **external-** The s. of the outside crystal form. Cf. *internal s.* **geometrical-** The external shape of a crystal, which resembles that of a geometrical figure. **internal-** The s. of the arrangement of the atoms inside a crystal. Cf. *external s.* **plane of-** An imaginary plane through a symmetrical body, which divides it into mirror-image halves. Cf. *projection nucleus.*

s. groups. The grouping of crystals according to the number and nature of their elements of s.; 32 groups exist, but 11 cover most common substances. See *crystal systems.*

sympathetic. Pertaining to or related to a mutual relationship. **s. ink.** An ink, visible only if heated (as cobaltous chloride solution) or when treated with a specific reagent. **s. reaction.** Induced *reaction.*

sympathin. A hormone produced in smooth muscle under sympathetic impulse, causing augmentation of blood pressure, heart rate, and salivary secretion. Cf. *sympathol*(2).

sympathol. (1) $C_9H_{13}O_2N\cdot HCl = 203.6.$ Methyl-δ-hydroxy-β-*p*-hydroxyphenylethylamine hydrochloride. Colorless crystals, m.184, similar to adrenaline in pharmacology. (2) $HO\cdot C_6H_4\cdot CMe\cdot OH\cdot NHMe = 167.1.$ *p*-Hydroxy-α-(methylaminomethyl)benzyl alcohol. Probably identical with sympathin.

sympathomimetic action. Stimulation of the sympathetic nervous system by drugs.

sympathomimetic amine. Wakeamine.

symphorol. Salts of caffeinesulfonic acid, used as diuretics; as, symphorol N (sodium–caffeine sulfonate, nasrol).

symphytum. Bruisewort, comfrey, blackwort. The dried root of *Symphytum officinale* (Boraginaceae), Europe and Asia; a demulcent.

symplesite. $Fe(AsO_4)_2\cdot 8H_4O.$ A mineral.

symplocarpus. Skunk cabbage.

syn- (1) Prefix (Greek "with" or "together") signifying union, association, or building up. (2) The syn position. **s. position.** $\sigma.$ The position occupied by 2 related radicals in that type of stereoisomerism in which they are closer together than in the corresponding antiposition; e.g., H and OH may split out and form water. See *stereoisomerism.*

synaldoxime. See *aldoxime.*

INTERNATIONALLY APPROVED SYMBOLS FOR PHYSICAL QUANTITIES[a]

Where two or more symbols separated by commas are given for a quantity, these symbols are regarded as alternatives for which no preference is expressed; where they are separated by a dotted line, the first is preferred. Letters of the Latin alphabet are generally printed in italic type except that boldface roman type may be employed for vector quantities.

A. Space and Time

angle (plane angle)	$\alpha, \beta, \gamma, \theta, \phi$, etc
solid angle	Ω, ω
length	l
breadth	b
height	h
thickness	d, δ
radius	r
diameter: $2r$	d
distance along path	s, L
generalized coordinate	q
rectangular coordinates	x, y, z
cylindrical coordinates	r, ϕ, z
spherical coordinates	r, θ, ϕ
position vector (radius vector)	$\boldsymbol{r}$
area	$A \ldots S$
volume	$V \ldots v$
time	t
angular velocity: $d\theta/dt$	ω
angular acceleration: $d\omega/dt$	α
velocity: ds/dt	u, v, w
acceleration: du/dt	a
acceleration of free fall	g
speed of light in a vacuum	c
Mach number	(Ma)

B. Periodic and Related Phenomena

period	T
relaxation time[b]	τ
frequency: $1/T$	v, f
rotational frequency[c]	n
angular frequency[c]: $2\pi v$	ω
wavelength	λ
wave number: $1/\lambda$	$\sigma \ldots \bar{v}$
wave vector	$\boldsymbol{\sigma}$
circular wave number: $2\pi\sigma$	k
circular wave vector	$\boldsymbol{k}$
damping coefficient[d]	δ
logarithmic decrement[d]: δ/v	Λ
attenuation coefficient[e]	α
phase coefficient[e]	β
propagation coefficient[e]: $\alpha + i\beta$	γ

C. Mechanics

mass	m
density (mass density): m/V	ρ
relative density: ρ_2/ρ_1	d
specific volume: V/m	v
reduced mass: $m_1 m_2/(m_1 + m_2)$	μ
momentum: mu	p
momentum (vector): $m\boldsymbol{u}$	$\boldsymbol{p}$
angular momentum	b, p_θ
angular momentum (vector): $\boldsymbol{r} \times \boldsymbol{p}$	$\boldsymbol{L}$
moment of inertia[f]	I, J
force	F

C. Mechanics (continued)

force (vector)	$\boldsymbol{F}$
weight	$G \ldots P, W$
bending moment	M
moment of force (vector): $\boldsymbol{r} \times \boldsymbol{F}$	$\boldsymbol{M}$
torque, moment of a couple	$\boldsymbol{T}$
pressure	$p \ldots P$
normal stress	σ
shear stress	τ
linear strain: $\Delta l/l_0$	ϵ, e
shear strain (shear angle)	γ
volume strain: $\Delta V/V_0$	θ
Young modulus: σ/ϵ	E
shear modulus: τ/γ	G
bulk modulus: $-p/\theta$	K
Poisson ratio	μ, v
compressibility: $-V^{-1} dV/dp$	κ
second moment of area[g]	I_a
second polar moment of area[h]	I_p
section modulus	Z, W
coefficient of friction	$\mu \ldots f$
viscosity (dynamic viscosity)	$\eta \ldots \mu$
fluidity: $1/\eta$	ϕ
kinematic viscosity: η/ρ	v
diffusion coefficient	D
surface tension	γ, σ
angle of contact	θ
work	W, A
energy	E, W
potential energy	E_p, V, Φ
kinetic energy	E_k, T, K
power	P
Hamiltonian function	H
Lagrangian function	L
gravitational constant	G
Reynolds number: $\rho ul/\eta$	(Re)

D. Thermodynamics

thermodynamic temperature (absolute temperature)	$T \ldots \Theta$
common temperature	t, θ
linear expansivity: $l^{-1} dl/dT$	α, λ
cubic expansivity: $V^{-1} dV/dT$	α, γ
heat, quantity of heat	q, Q
work, quantity of work	w, W
heat flow rate	$\Phi \ldots q$
thermal conductivity	$\lambda \ldots k$
heat capacity	C
specific heat capacity: C/m	c
specific heat capacity at constant pressure	c_p
specific heat capacity at constant volume	c_V
ratio c_p/c_V	γ, κ
thermal diffusivity: $\lambda/\rho c_p$	α

---

[a] From "Symbols, Signs and Abbreviations," The Royal Society, London, 1967.
[b] If F is a function of time t given by $F(t) = A + B \exp(-t/\tau)$. Also called time constant.
[c] Also called pulsatance.
[d] If F is a function of time t given by $F(t) = A \exp(-\delta t) \sin \{2\pi v(t - t_0)\}$.
[e] If F is a function of distance x given by $F(x) = A \exp(-\alpha x) \cos \{\beta(x - x_0)\}$.
[f] $I^2 = \int (x^2 + y^2) \, dm$. [g] $I_{a,y} = \int x^2 \, dx \, dy$. [h] $I_p = \int (x^2 + y^2) \, dx \, dy$.

INTERNATIONALLY APPROVED SYMBOLS FOR PHYSICAL QUANTITIES (*continued*)

D. *Thermodynamics* (*continued*)

entropy .... S
internal energy .... $U \ldots E$
enthalpy: $U + pV$ .... H
Helmholtz function: $U - TS$ .... $A \ldots F$
Gibbs function: $U + pV - TS$ .... G
Massieu function: $-A/T$ .... J
Planck function: $-G/T$ .... Y
specific entropy: S/m .... s
specific internal energy: U/m .... $u \ldots e$
specific enthalpy: H/m .... h
specific Helmholtz function: A/m .... $a \ldots f$
specific Gibbs function: G/m .... g
latent heat L
specific latent heat: L/m l
Joule–Thomson coefficient: $(\partial T/\partial P)_H$ .... μ, μ_{JT}
isothermal compressibility: $-V^{-1}(\partial V/\partial p)_T$ .. κ, κ_T
isentropic compressibility: $-V^{-1}(\partial V/\partial p)_S$ ...... κ_S
isobaric expansivity: $-V^{-1}(V\partial/\partial T)_p$ ...... α
thermal diffusion ratio .... k_T
thermal diffusion factor .... α_T
thermal diffusion coefficient .... D_T

E. *Electricity and Magnetism*

electric charge (quantity of electricity) .... Q
electric current: $\mathrm{d}Q/\mathrm{d}t$ I
charge density: Q/V .... ρ
surface charge density: Q/A .... σ
electric field strength .... E
electric potential .... V, ϕ
electric potential difference .... $U \ldots V$
electromotive force .... E
electric displacement .... D
electric flux .... Ψ
capacitance C
permittivity: $D = \epsilon E$ .... ϵ
permittivity of a vacuum .... ϵ_0
relative permittivity[i] .... ϵ_r
electric susceptibility: $\epsilon_r - 1$ .... χ_e
electric polarization: $D - \epsilon_0 E$ .... P
electric dipole moment .... $\mathbf{p} \ldots \mu$
electric current density .... J, j
magnetic field strength .... H
magnetic potential difference.................. U_m
magnetomotive force: $\oint H_s \, \mathrm{d}s$ .... F_m
magnetic flux density, magnetic
  induction .... B
magnetic flux .... Φ
magnetic vector potential.................... A
self inductance L
mutual inductance .... M, L_{12}
coupling coefficient: $L_{12}/(L_1 L_2)$ .... k
leakage coefficient: $(1 - k^2)$ .... σ
permeability of a vacuum .... μ_0
relative permeability ....μ_r
magnetic susceptibility: $\mu_r - 1$ .... χ_m
electromagnetic moment:
  $E_p = -m \cdot B$ .... m
magnetization: $B = \mu_0(H + M)$ .... M
magnetic polarization: $B - \mu_0 H$ .... J
electromagnetic charge density .... w
Poynting vector: $E \times H$ .... S
velocity of propagation of electromagnetic waves in vacuum c

E. *Electricity and Magnetism* (*continued*)

resistance .... R
conductance: $1/R$ .... G
resistivity: E/J .... ρ
conductivity: $1/\rho$ .... γ, σ
reluctance: U_m/Φ .... R, R_m
permeance: $1/R_m$ .... Λ
number of turns .... N
number of phases .... m
number of pairs of poles .... p
loss angle .... δ
phase displacement .... ϕ
impedance: $R + iX$ .... Z
reactance: $\mathrm{Im}\, Z$ X
resistance: $\mathrm{Re}\, Z$ .... R
quality factor: $|X|/R$ .... Q
admittance: $1/Z$ .... Y
susceptance: $\mathrm{Im}\, Y$ .... B
conductance: $\mathrm{Re}\, Y$ .... G
power, active .... P
power, reactive .... Q
power, apparent .... S

F. *Light and Related Electromagnetic Radiation*

The same symbol is often used for a pair of corresponding radiant and luminous quantities. Subscripts e for radiant and v for luminous may be used when necessary to distinguish these quantities.

velocity of electromagnetic waves
  in vacuum c
radiant energy .... Q, Q_e
radiant flux, radiant power .... $\Phi, \Phi_e \ldots P$
radiant intensity .... I, I_e
radiance .... L, L_e
radiant emittance .... M, M_e
irradiance .... E, E_e
emissivity ....
quantity of light .... Q, Q_v
luminous flux .... Φ, Φ_v
luminous intensity .... I, I_v
luminance .... L, L_v
luminous emittance .... M, M_v
illuminance, illumination .... E, E_v
light exposure: $\int E \, \mathrm{d}t$ .... H
luminous efficacy: Φ_v/Φ_e .... K
absorption factor, absorptance:
  Φ_a/Φ_0 .... α
reflection factor, reflectance:
  Φ_r/Φ_0 .... ρ
transmission factor, transmittance:
  $\Phi_{\mathrm{tr}}/\Phi_0$ .... τ
linear extinction coefficient .... μ
linear absorption coefficient .... a
refractive index .... n
refraction: $(n^2 - 1)V/(n^2 + 2)$ .... R
angle of optical rotation .... α

G. *Acoustics*

velocity of sound c
velocity of longitudinal waves .... c_l
velocity of transverse waves .... c_t
group velocity .... c_g
sound energy flux .... P
sound intensity .... I, J

---

[i] Also called dielectric constant, D, when it is independent of E.

INTERNATIONALLY APPROVED SYMBOLS FOR PHYSICAL QUANTITIES (*continued*)

G. Acoustics (*continued*)

reflection coefficient: P_r/P_0 .... ρ
acoustic absorption coefficient:
$\quad$ $(1 - \rho)$ .... $\alpha_d \ldots \alpha$
transmission coefficient: P_{tr}/P_0 .... τ
dissipation coefficient: $(\alpha_a - \tau)$ .... δ
loudness level .... L_N

H. Physical Chemistry

relative atomic mass of an
$\quad$ element (atomic weight)^j .... A_r
relative molecular mass of a substance
$\quad$ (molecular weight)^j .... M_r
amount of substance .... n
molar mass: m/n .... M
molar volume: V/n .... V_m
molar internal energy: U/n .... U_m
molar enthalpy: H/n .... H_m
molar heat capacity: C/n .... C_m
$\quad$ at constant pressure: C_p/n .... $C_{p,m}$
$\quad$ at constant volume: C_V/n .... $C_{V,m}$
molar entropy: S/n .... S_m
molar Helmholtz function: A/n .... A_m
molar Gibbs function: G/n .... G_m
(molar) gas constant .... R
compression factor: pV_m/RT .... Z
mole fraction of substance B .... x_B
mass fraction of substance B .... w_B
volume fraction of substance B .... ϕ_B
molality of solute B: (n_B
$\quad$ divided by mass of solvent) .... m_B
concentration (molarity) of
$\quad$ solute B: n_B/V .... $c_B, [B]$
chemical potential of substance
$\quad$ B: $(\partial G/\partial n_B)_{T,p,n_C}$ .... μ_B
absolute activity of substance
$\quad$ B: $\exp(\mu_B/RT)$ .... λ_B
partial pressure of substance B in
$\quad$ a gas mixture: $x_B^G p$ .... p_B
fugacity of substance B in a gas
$\quad$ mixture: $\lambda_B \lim_{p \to 0} (x_B^G p/\lambda_B)$ .... p_B^*
relative activity of substance B .... a_B
activity coefficient (mole fraction
$\quad$ basis .... f_B
activity coefficient (molality
$\quad$ basis) .... γ_B
activity coefficient (concentration
$\quad$ basis) .... y_B
osmotic coefficient .... g, ϕ
osmotic pressure .... Π
surface concentration .... Γ
electromotive force .... E
faraday constant .... F
charge number of ion i .... z_i
ionic strength: $\frac{1}{2}\Sigma_i m_i z_i^2$ I
velocity of ion i .... v_i
electric mobility of ion i: v_i/E .... u_i
electrolytic conductivity^k: J/E .... κ
molar conductance of electrolyte:
$\quad$ κ/c .... Λ
transport number of ion i .... t_i
molar conductance of ion i: $t_i\Lambda$ .... λ_i

H. Physical Chemistry (*continued*)

overpotential .... η
exchange current density .... j_0
electrokinetic potential .... ζ
intensity of light I
transmittance: I/I_0 .... T
absorption (extinction) coefficient:
$\quad$ $(-\ln T)/lc$ .... κ
absorbance (extinction)^l: $-\log_{10} T$ .... A
absorptivity (decadic absorption or
$\quad$ extinction coefficient): A/l .... a
molar absorptivity (molar decadic
$\quad$ absorption or extinction coefficient):
$\quad$ A/lc .... ϵ
angle of optical rotation .... α
specific optical rotary power:
$\quad$ $\alpha V/ml$............................ α_m
molar optical rotatory power:
$\quad$ α/cl .... α_n
molar refraction: $(n^2 - 1)V_m/(n^2 + 2)$......... R_m
stoichiometric coefficient of molecules
$\quad$ B (negative for reactants, positive
$\quad$ for products) .... ν_B
general equation for a chemical
$\quad$ reaction .... $0 = \Sigma_B \nu_B B$
extent of reaction: $d\xi = dn_B/\nu_B$ .... ξ
rate of reaction: $d\xi/dt$ .... ξ, J
affinity of a reaction: $-\Sigma_B \nu_B \mu_B$ .... A
equilibrium constant .... K
degree of dissociation .... α
rate constant of a reaction .... k
activation energy of a reaction .... E

I. Molecular Physics

Avogadro constant .... L, N_A
number of molecules .... N
number density of molecules: N/V .... n
molecular mass .... m
molecular velocity.............. $c(c_x, c_y, c_z)$,
$\quad\quad\quad\quad\quad\quad\quad\quad$ $u(u_x, u_y, u_z)$
molecular position .... $r(x, y, z)$
molecular momentum .... $p(p_x, p_y, p_z)$
average velocity .... $\langle c \rangle, \langle u \rangle, c_0, u_0$
average speed .... $\langle c \rangle, \langle u \rangle, \bar{c}, \bar{u}$,
most probable speed .... $\hat{c}, \hat{u}$
mean free path .... l, λ
molecular attraction energy .... ϵ
interaction energy between
$\quad$ molecules i and j .... ϕ_{ij}, V_{ij}
velocity distribution function:
$\quad$ $N/V = \int f \, dc_x \, dc_y \, dc_z$ .... $f(c)$
Boltzmann function..................... H
generalized coordinate .... q
generalized momentum .... p
volume in phase space .... Ω
Boltzmann constant .... k
$1/kT$ in exponential functions .... β
partition function .... Q, Z
grand partition function .... Ξ
statistical weight .... g
symmetry number .... σ, s
dipole moment of molecule .... p, μ

---

^{j} The ratio of the average mass per atom (molecule) of the natural isotopic composition of an element (the elements) to $1/12$ of the mass of an atom of the nuclide ^{12}C. The natural isotopic composition is assumed unless some other composition is specified.

INTERNATIONALLY APPROVED SYMBOLS FOR PHYSICAL QUANTITIES (*continued*)

I. Molecular Physics (continued)

quadrupole moment of molecule .... Θ
polarizability of molecule .... α
Planck constant .... h
Planck constant divided by 2π .... $\hbar$
characteristic temperature .... Θ
Debye temperature: $h\nu_D/k$ .... Θ_D
Einstein temperature: $h\nu_E/k$ .... Θ_E
rotational temperature: $h^2/8\pi^2 Ik$ .... Θ_r
vibrational temperature: $h\nu/k$ .... Θ_v
Stefan-Boltzmann constant:
$2\pi^5 k^4/15 c^2 h^3$ .... σ
first radiation constant:
$2\pi hc^2$ .... c_1
second radiation constant: hc/k .... c_2
rotational quantum number .... J, K
vibrational quantum number v

J. Atomic and Nuclear Physics

nucleon number, mass number .... A
atomic number, proton number .... Z
neutron number: $A - Z$ .... N
(rest) mass of atom .... m_a
unified atomic mass constant:
$m_a(^{12}C)/12$ .... m_u
(rest) mass of electron .... m_e
(rest) mass of proton .... m_p
(rest) mass of neutron .... m_n
elementary charge .... e
Planck constant .... $\hbar$
Planck constant divided by 2π .... h
Bohr radius: $\epsilon_0 h^2/\pi m_e e^2$ .... a_0
Rydberg constant: $m_e e^4/8\epsilon_0^2 h^3 c$ .... R_∞
magnetic moment of particle .... μ
Bohr magneton: $eh/4\pi m_e$ .... μ_B
nuclear magneton: $(m_e/m_p)\mu_B$ .... μ_N
gyromagnetic ratio: $2\pi\mu/Ih$ .... γ
g factor .... g
Larmor (angular) frequency:
$eB/2m_e$ .... ω_L
nuclear angular precession
frequency: $geB/2m_p$ .... ω_N
cyclotron angular frequency
of electron: eB/m_e .... ω_e
nuclear quadrupole moment .... Q
nuclear radius .... R
orbital angular momentum
quantum number .... L, l_i
spin angular momentum
quantum number .... S, s_i
total angular momentum
quantum number .... J, j_i
nuclear spin quantum number .... I, J
hyperfine structure quantum
number .... F
principal quantum number .... n, n_i
magnetic quantum number .... M, m_i
fine structure constant: $e^2/2\epsilon_0 hc$ .... α
electron radius: $e^2/4\pi\epsilon_0 m c^2$ .... r_e
Compton wavelength: h/mc .... λ_C
mass excess: $m_a - Am_u$ .... Δ
packing fraction: Δ/Am_u .... f
mean life .... τ
level width: $h/2\pi\tau$ .... Γ
activity: $-dN/dt$ .... A

J. Atomic and Nuclear Physics (continued)

specific activity: A/m .... a
decay constant: A/N .... λ
half-life: $(\ln 2)/\lambda$ .... $T_\frac{1}{2}, t_\frac{1}{2}$
disintegration energy .... Q
spin-lattice relaxation time .... T_1
spin-spin relaxation time .... T_2
indirect spin-spin coupling .... J

K. Nuclear Reactions and Ionizing Radiations

reaction energy .... Q
cross section .... σ
macroscopic cross section .... Σ
impact parameter .... b
scattering angle .... θ, ϕ
internal conversion coefficient .... α
linear attenuation coefficient .... μ, μ_1
atomic attenuation coefficient .... μ_a
mass attenuation coefficient .... μ_m
linear stopping power .... S, S_1
atomic stopping power .... S_a
linear range .... R, R_1
recombination coefficient .... α

L. Quantum Mechanics

complex conjugate of Ψ .... Ψ^*
probability density: $\Psi^*\Psi$ .... P
probability current density:
$(h/2\pi im)(\Psi^* \nabla\Psi - \Psi \nabla\Psi^*)$ ..... S
charge density of electrons: $-eP$ .... ρ
electric current density of
electrons: $-eS$ ....
expectation value of A .... $\langle A \rangle, \bar{A}$
commutator of A and B:
$AB - BA$ .... $[A, B], [A, B]_-$
anticommutator of A and B:
$AB + BA$ .... $[A, B]_+$
matrix element: $\int \phi_i^*(A\phi_j) d\tau$ .... A_{ij}
Hermitian conjugate of
operator A .... $A^\dagger$
momentum operator in coordinate
representation .... $+ (h/2\pi i)\nabla$
annihilation operators .... a, b, α, β
creation operators .... $a^\dagger, b^\dagger, \alpha^\dagger, \beta^\dagger$

M. Solid State Physics

Fundamental translations $\quad\{\ \boldsymbol{a, b, c};$
for lattice .... $\{\boldsymbol{a_1, a_2, a_3}$
Miller indices .... $h, k, l; h_1, h_2, h_3$
plane in lattice[m] .... $(h, k, l); (h_1, h_2, h_3)$
direction in lattice[n] ... $[h, k, l]; [h_1, h_2, h_3]$
fundamental translations $\quad\{\boldsymbol{a^*, b^*, c^*};$
in reciprocal lattice .... $\{\ \boldsymbol{b_1, b_2, b_3}$
vector in crystal lattice .... $\boldsymbol{r}$
distance between successive
lattice planes .... d
Bragg angle .... θ
order of reflection .... n
short-range-order parameter .... σ
long-range-order parameter .... s
Burgers vector .... $\boldsymbol{b}$
circular wave vector, propagation
vector (of phonons) .... $\boldsymbol{q}$

---

[k] Formerly, specific conductance.   [l] Formerly, optical density.   [m] Braces { } are also used.   [n] Angle brackets ⟨ ⟩ are also used.

INTERNATIONALLY APPROVED SYMBOLS FOR PHYSICAL QUANTITIES *(continued)*

M. Solid State Physics (continued)		*M. Solid State Physics (continued)*	
circular wave vector, propagation vector (of particles)	$\boldsymbol{k}$	Thomson coefficient	μ
effective mass of electron	m^*, m_{eff}	piezoelectric coefficient (polarization/stress)	d_{mn}
Fermi energy	$E_{\mathrm{F}}, \epsilon_{\mathrm{F}}$	characteristic (Weiss) temperature	$\Theta, \Theta_{\mathrm{W}}$
Fermi circular wave vector	$\boldsymbol{k}_{\mathrm{F}}$	Curie temperature	T_{C}
work function	Φ	Néel temperature	T_{N}
differential thermoelectric power	$S \ldots \Sigma$	Hall coefficient	R_{H}
Peltier coefficient	Π		

N. Molecular Spectroscopy

QUANTUM NUMBER:

of component of electronic orbital angular momentum vector along symmetry axis .... Λ, λ
of component of electronic spin along symmetry axis .... $\Sigma, \sigma^{\mathrm{i}}$
of total electronic angular momentum vector along symmetry axis .... $\Omega, \omega_{\mathrm{i}}$
of electronic spin .... S
of nuclear spin I
of vibrational mode v
of vibrational angular momentum (linear molecules) l
of total angular momentum (excluding nuclear spin) .... J
of component of $\boldsymbol{J}$ in direction of external field .... M, M_J
of component of $\boldsymbol{S}$ in direction of external field .... M_S
of total angular momentum (including nuclear spin: $\boldsymbol{F} = \boldsymbol{J} + \boldsymbol{I}$) ... F
of component of $\boldsymbol{F}$ in direction of external field .... M_F
of component of $\boldsymbol{I}$ in direction of external field .... M_I
of component of angular momentum along axis (linear and symmetric top molecules;
  excluding electron- and nuclear spin; for linear molecules $K = |\Lambda + l|$) .... K
of total angular momentum (linear and symmetric top molecules; excluding electron-
  and nuclear spin[o]: $\boldsymbol{J} = \boldsymbol{N} + \boldsymbol{S}$) .... N
of component of angular momentum along symmetry axis (linear and symmetric
  top molecules; excluding nuclear spin; for linear molecules[p]: $P = |K + \Sigma|$) ...... P
degeneracy of vibrational mode .... d
electronic term[q]: E_{e}/hc .... T_{e}
vibrational term: E_{vib}/hc .... G

COEFFICIENTS IN EXPRESSIONS FOR VIBRATIONAL TERM FOR:

diatomic molecule:
$$G = \sigma_{\mathrm{e}}(v + \tfrac{1}{2}) - x\sigma_{\mathrm{e}}(v + \tfrac{1}{2})^2 \quad \ldots \quad \sigma_{\mathrm{e}} \text{ and } x\sigma^{\mathrm{e}}$$
polyatomic molecule:
$$G = \Sigma_{\mathrm{j}}\sigma_{\mathrm{j}}(v_{\mathrm{j}} + \tfrac{1}{2}d_{\mathrm{j}}) + \tfrac{1}{2}\Sigma_{\mathrm{j}}\Sigma_{\mathrm{k}}x_{\mathrm{jk}}(v_{\mathrm{j}} + \tfrac{1}{2}d_{\mathrm{j}})(v_{\mathrm{k}} + \tfrac{1}{2}d_{\mathrm{k}}) \quad \ldots \quad \sigma_{\mathrm{j}} \text{ and } x_{\mathrm{jk}}$$
rotational term: E_{rot}/hc .... F
moment of inertia of diatomic molecule I
rotational constant of diatomic molecule: $8\pi^2 cI$ .... A
principal moments of inertia of polyatomic molecule ($I_{\mathrm{A}} \leqslant I_{\mathrm{B}} \leqslant I_{\mathrm{C}}$) .... $I_{\mathrm{A}}, I_{\mathrm{B}}, I_{\mathrm{C}}$
rotational constants of polyatomic molecule: $A = h/8\pi^2 cI_{\mathrm{A}}$, etc. .... A, B, C
total term: $T_{\mathrm{e}} + G + F$ .... T

Mathematical Operations on Physical Quantities

Addition and subtraction of two physical quantities are indicated by

$$a + b \quad \text{and} \quad a - b$$

Multiplication of two (scalar) physical quantities may be indicated in one of the following ways:

$$ab \quad a\,b \quad a.b \quad a \cdot b \quad a \times b$$

Division of one quantity by another quantity may be indicated in one of the following ways:

$$\frac{a}{b} \quad a/b \quad ab^{-1}$$

or in any of the other ways of writing the product of a and b^{-1}.

These procedures can be extended to cases where one of the quantities or both are themselves products, quotients, sums, or differences of other quantities.

Brackets should be used in accordance with the rules of mathematics.

---

[o] Case of loosely coupled electrons.   [p] Case of tightly coupled electrons.
[q] All energies are taken here with respect to the ground state as reference level.

synanthrose. $C_6H_{10}O_5$ = 162.1. Levulin. A carbohydrate isomeric with inulin, from the rhizomes of *Helianthus tuberosus* (Compositae).

synaptase. Emulsin.

synartesis. Stabilization of the transition state of an ionizing substance.

syncaine. Procaine.

synchronal. Occurring at the same time.

synchronism. The occurrence of 2 or more phenomena at the same time.

synchronizing. To produce synchronism; as, a speed controller for a number of current generators.

synchroton. A device based on the principle of the synchronous motor for accelerating charged particles to very high energy states. Cf. *cyclotron*.

syncortyl. Deoxycortone acetate.

Syncurine. Trademark for decamethonium iodide.

syncyanin. A blue pigment produced by the bacteria *B. syncyanus*, and *B. cyanogenus*.

Syndet. (1) Trade name for a detergent (U.K. usage). (2) (not cap.) Abbreviation for synthetic detergent (U.S.P.).

syndiazotate. See *diazotate*.

syndiotactic. See *polyvinyl* chain.

syndrome. A group of signs and symptoms that occur together and characterize a disease.

synephrin. $C_9H_{14}NO_2$ = 168.1. White crystals; a vasoconstrictor.

syneresis. The contraction of a clot or gel; as of blood.

synergism. The combined action of 2 distinct agencies, the sum of the effects of which is greater than the sum of the effects of each taken separately; e.g.: the addition of piperonyl butoxide to pyrethrin produces a mixture having an insecticidal toxicity greater than the sum of the effects of these ingredients used separately.

synergist. Booster. A noninsecticide which can partly replace one; e.g.: lethan, q.v., will partly replace pyrethrins.

synergy. A mechanism involving stepwise action, direct interaction, or complementary function of the components.

syngenite. $CaSO_4 \cdot K_2SO_4 \cdot H_2O$. A native potassium-calcium sulfate.

synonym. One of several names given to the same substance; e.g.: wood alcohol, methyl alcohol, and wood spirit are synonyms for methanol.

synourin oil. A paint drying oil produced by the chemical dehydration of certain glyceride molecules of castor oil.

syntactic. Describing a cellular polymer produced by dispersing rigid microscopic particles in a fluid polymer, and then stabilizing the system.

syntan. (1) A sulfurized phenol. (2) **alpha-** An artificial tan made by the sulfonation of hydrocarbons, e.g., naphtha. **beta-** A s. prepared by condensing pyrogallol or catechol with formaldehyde in presence of hydrochloric acid.

synthalin-A. $NH_2 \cdot C:NH \cdot NH(CH_2)_{12}NH \cdot C:NH \cdot NH_2$. The synthetic hydrochloric acid salt of decamethylene bisguanidine; a former oral insulin substitute, now known to be ineffective. **s.-B.** $NH_2 \cdot NH:C \cdot NH(CH_2)_{12}NHC:NH \cdot HCl$. Dodecamethylene bisguanidine hydrochloride.

synthesis. A reaction, or series of reactions, in which a complex compound is obtained from elements or simple compounds. Cf. *analysis*. **electro-** q.v.

organic- The production of dyestuffs and medicinals; the artificial production of a naturally occurring substance, e.g., indigo. **photo-** q.v.

synthesize. To produce a complex compound from simpler compounds.

synthetic. (1) Produced synthetically. (2) Produced by artificial means. However, certain polymers, e.g., some plastics, are not regarded as synthetic (U.K. usage). (3) An artificially produced organic compound used in medicine. **s. drying oil.** See *oil*. **s. resins.** (1) Plastics, q.v., produced by: (a) polymerization (polyolefins), (b) condensation (phenol aldehyde). (2) Polymers of organic compounds; as, (a) association polymers (viscose silk), (b) hemicolloidal polymers (warm styrene), (c) eucolloidal polymers (cold styrene).

Synthofil. Trade name for a polyvinyl synthetic fiber.

synthol. A synthetic motor fuel obtained from carbon monoxide and hydrogen (water gas) at 75–150 atm and 400–435°C with an iron and sodium carbonate catalyst. A mixture of higher alcohols, aldehydes, ketones, and higher fatty acids with aliphatic hydrocarbons; 8200 cal/kg.

synthovo. Hexestrol.

syntonin. Muscle fibrin, parapeptone, acid albumin. An acid albumin from albumose. Yellow powder, insoluble in water, produced in the body as an intermediate product of the gastric digestion of proteins, which eventually become peptones.

syphon. See *siphon*.

syr. Abbreviation for syrup.

syringa. The dried fruits of *Syringa vulgaris*, lilac bush (Oleaceae), America and Europe. It contains glucosides; bitter tonic.

syringe. An injection tube, usually glass, with a jet at one end and a small piston pump or bladder at the other.

syringenin. $C_{11}H_{14}O_4$ = 210.1. Oxymethyl coniferin. Red mass from syringa, insoluble in water; formed by hydrolysis of syringin.

syringetin. $C_{17}H_{14}O_6$ = 314.11. 3,4′,5,7-Tetrahydroxy-3′,5′-dimethoxyflavone, from lilac.

syringic acid. $C_9H_{10}O_5$ = 198.1. 4-Hydroxy-3,5-dimethoxybenzoic acid, obtained by hydrolysis of syringin.

syringin. $C_{17}H_{24}O_9 \cdot H_2O$ = 390.3. Lilacin, ligustrin. A glucoside from *Syringa vulgaris*, lilac (Oleaceae), *Ligusturum vulgare*, privet; *Robinia pseud-acacia*. White needles, m.212, soluble in water; an antipyretic and antiperiodic. Cf. *syrengenin*.

syrup. Sirup. A concentrated aqueous solution of a carbohydrate (as, cane sugar), with or without drugs. U.S.P. s. contains 85.0, and B.P. s. 66.7% w./w. of sucrose in water. **simple-** Syrupus simplex. An aqueous solution of cane sugar (83%).

s. acacia. A 10% solution of acacia in sucrose s.

system. (1) A combination of matter containing one or more phases. (2) An organized and related group of facts, phenomena, or ideas. **binary-** A s. involving 2 components (elements or compounds). **condensed-** A s. with no gaseous phase. **divariant-** A s. with 2 degrees of freedom (cf. *phase rule*), represented by an area on a diagram, q.v. **geological-** See *epochs*, *strata*. **heterogeneous-** A s. containing 2 or more phases or distinct regions, separated by definite boundaries. **homogeneous-**

A s. with no definite boundaries; its properties are the same at all parts, or vary gradually. **mobile-** A s. that responds readily to external conditions, as pressure. **monovariant-** A s. with one degree of freedom. Cf. *phase rule, line diagram.* **nonvariant-** A s. with no degree of freedom (cf. *phase rule*), represented by a point on a diagram, q.v. **periodic-** See *periodic system.* **quaternary-** A 4-component s. **ring-** See *ring system.* **stable-** A s. that does not respond readily to a changing environment. **tertiary-** A 3-component s. **thermodynamic-** A s. which may consist of matter, energy, or both, and is limited by a physical or imaginary boundary. **unstable-** See *mobile s.*

s. of compounds. See *notation, organic compounds.* **s. of elements.** See *periodic system.* **s. of stars.** See *spectral classification.*

systematic name. A name based on the systematic structure of a compound, e.g., pentane. Cf. *trivial name.*

Système International d'Unités. See *SI.*

systemic. Describing a fungicide which is absorbed by the plant and depresses the growth of the fungus by translocation through the plant tissues.

Szent-Györgyi hypothesis. A mechanism permits the energy of absorbed light or of a chemical reaction occurring in one part of a living system to be available, without degradation or distortion, for reactions in other parts of the system.

szomolnokite. $FeSO_4 \cdot H_2O$. A mineral.

T

T. Symbol for: (1) time; (2) absolute temperature; (3) transport number; (4) tera; (5) triple bond: thus T^3 = a triple bond between the third and fourth C atoms. Cf. *delta*.

t. Symbol for: (1) metric ton; (2) temperature (not absolute scale); (3) tertiary; (4) time. $t_{\frac{1}{2}}$. Symbol for half-life period.

τ. Greek letter tau. Symbol for quantum number: τ_1 = azimuthal; τ_2 = radial.

θ. Greek letter theta. Symbol for thermodynamic temperature.

Θ. Greek capital letter theta. (1) Symbol for the absolute temperature at which C_V is $\frac{3}{2}R$. (2) The absolute temperature of a transition point.

Ta. Symbol for tantalum.

tabacin. The toxic principle of tobacco. A yellow, waxy, hygroscopic, nitrogenous acid glucoside, decomp. 110.

tabacum. Tobacco.

tabashir. Tabashis.

tabashis. A secretion of bamboo containing lime and silica; a Hindi cure for tuberculosis.

table. (1) A lamella, or flat, scalelike crystal. (2) The flat surface of a precious stone. **t. salt.** Sodium chloride. *iodized-* Sodium chloride with 0.1% of potassium or sodium iodide. **t. spoon.** An empirical measure, about 15 ml.

tablet. Tabloid. A medicated disk made from a drug incorporated into a mixture of absorbents or adhesives. Moistening agents—water or alcohol. Absorbents—starch, milk sugar, magnesium carbonate, magnesium oxide, or licorice root. Adhesives—cane sugar, tragacanth, acacia, glucose, gelatin, dextrin, flour, boric acid. **effervescent-** A t. with an effervescent mixture incorporated to cause rapid disintegration in water. Cf. *pill*.

tabloid. A small tablet.

tabular crystal. A table-shaped or flattened crystal. **t. spar.** Wollastonite.

tabun. $C_2H_5O\cdot P(:O)\cdot CN\cdot NMe_2$. A tasteless, odorless gas that affects the nerves with rapidly fatal results; antidote, atropine.

tacamahac. (1) A resin from *Calophyllum tacamahaca* (Guttiferae). (2) A resin from *Populus balsamifera*, balsam poplar (Salicaceae).

TACE. Chlorotrianisene.

Tachenius, Otto. 17th century. German physician and chemist, the first to use distilled water and to suspect a hidden acid in oils and fats; author of *Epistola de famoso liquore alcahest* (1655) and *Hippocrates chymicus* (1674).

tachhydrite. $CaCl_2\cdot 2MgCl_2\cdot 12H_2O$. Yellow, very hygroscopic, native chloride.

tachia. Caferana. The dried root of *Tachia guianensis* (Gentianaceae), S. Africa and S. America; a glucosidal antimalarial and tonic. Cf. *tachinin*.

tachinin. A glucoside from tachia.

tachiol. Silver fluoride. **iso-** Silver silicofluoride.

tachogram. A curve indicating the speed of the blood current.

tachometer. (1) A device to record the speed of the blood current. (2) An instrument to record the angular speed of a revolving shaft.

tachylite. A dark, basic, volcanic glass.

tachymeter. A speed recorder.

tachyol. Tachiol.

tachysterol. An isomer of ergosterol; yields vitamin D on irradiation. Cf. *calciferol, cholane derivatives*.

tackiness. The property of stickiness; as of resins.

taconite. A low-grade ferruginous ore from Labrador and Venezuela; a source of iron if upgraded.

Tacryl. Trade name for an acrylic synthetic fiber.

tactile. Pertaining to touch.

tactole. A bird repellent. Strips of soft plastic which prevents birds from settling and breaks their roosting pattern.

tæ- *tae-, te-.*

tael. A Chinese bullion weight unit; $1\frac{1}{3}$ oz av.

taeniacide. Teniacide.

taeniafuge. Teniafuge.

taenite. A constituent of iron-nickel meteoric alloys (35–48% Ni).

tagatone. $C_{10}H_{18}O$ = 154.14. A ketone, related to myrcene, in the volatile oil of *Tagates glandulifera* (Compositae).

tagatose. $C_6H_{12}O_6$ = 180.09. The *d*-form, m.124, is an unfermentable ketohexose.

tagma. Corajo.

tagud nut. Vegetable ivory. The dried fruit of the negrito palm, *Phytelephas macrocarpa*.

tagulaway. Cebur. The dried bark of *Parameria vulneraria* (Apocynaceae), Philippine Islands; contains a resin and caoutchouc.

taka amylase. (Japanese, taka—strong.) Anamylolytic enzyme found with taka diastase. **T. diastase.** Trade name for a diastatic enzyme from a fungus growing on bran. **t. maltase.** An enzyme analogous to maltase found with taka diastase.

Talbot, William Henry Fox. 1799–1877. British archaeologist and inventor of photographic paper (1840) and plates. **T.'s law.** If the eye retina is excited with intermittent light recurring periodically, regularly, and sufficiently rapidly, a continuous impression will result; as, moving pictures.

talc. (1) $3MgO\cdot 4SiO_2\cdot H_2O$. Talcum, soapstone, rensselaerite, potstone, steatite, French chalk. Purified t. is used as a dusting powder, filtering material (U.S.P., B.P.), and in crayons. (2) Mica used for glazing (U.K. usage).

talcum. Talc (1).

talisai oil. An oil from the seeds of *Terminalia catappa*, country almond (Combretaceae).

talite. Talitol.

talitol. $CH_2OH(CHOH)_4CH_2OH$ = 182.1. Talite, obtained by reduction of talose; m.86.

tallate. A salt of the fatty acids of tall oil; used in paints.

tall oil. A by-product from sulfate wood pulp digestion, mainly resin acids and fatty acids; as linoleic, abietic (Steele acid); linolenic, and some oleic acid, with 2,2'-dihydrostigmasterol and lignoceryl alcohol. Used in soaps, varnishes, and fruit sprays. World production (1967) 785,000 tons.

tallois-desmi. Talmi.

tallol. Floating soap, finn oil, sylvic oil. An emulsifying agent from the waste black liquors of sulfate and soda–wood-pulp manufacture. Cf. *tall oil*.

tallow. A solid fat; as suet, q.v. **bone-** See *bone*. **Borneo-** Illipé butter (misnomer). A fat used in the chocolate industry, from shared fats. **japan-** See *japan wax*. **Malabar-** q.v. **mineral-** Hatchettinine.

Tallquist scale. Perforated sections of blotting paper with 10 printed shades of hemoglobin (10–100%). Used to estimate blood counts by matching a blot of blood with the color scale.

talmi. Talmi gold, tallois-desmi. Gold-plated brass used in jewelry.

talomucic acid. $COOH(CHOH)_4COOH = 210.07$. Derived from talose and altrose. White crystals, m.158, soluble in water; *d*- and *l*- forms. Cf. *mucic acid*.

talose. $CH_2OH(CHOH)_4CHO = 180.1$. An aldose or hexose; *d*- and *l*- forms.

tamarac. The dried bark of the hackmatack, *Larix laricina* or *L. americana*, larch, N. America; an astringent and stimulant.

tamarind. The preserved pulp of the fruit of *Tamarindus indica* (Leguminosae), India; a mild laxative.

tampicin. $C_{34}H_{54}O_{14} = 686.4$. An amorphous resin from tampico jalap, *Ipomoea simulans* (Convolvulaceae).

tanacetin. $C_{11}H_{16}O_4 = 212.1$. A bitter principle from tanacetum. A brown, amorphous, hygroscopic mass, soluble in water or alcohol, insoluble in ether.

tanacetone. $C_{10}H_{16}O = 152.13$. A ketone obtained from tansy oil, and similar to thujone. Colorless liquid, b.195.

tanacetum. Tansy. The dried leaves and tops of *Tanacetum vulgare* (Compositae), Asia, Europe, and N. America. **t. balsamita.** Costmary. The dried leaves of *T. balsamita;* a vermifuge. **t. oil.** An essential oil from t. It contains tanacetene, tanacetone, and borneol; an anthelmintic. Cf. *silverweed*.

tanekaha. The bark of *Phyllocladus trichomanoides* (Coniferae), pine tree of New Zealand; used in tanning and dyeing leather.

tané-koji. Brown powder from the mold *Aspergillus oryzae;* used to make saké.

tangent. The ratio of the side opposite the angle concerned to the base of the right-angled triangle in which it occurs.

tanghinia. The fruit of *Tanghinia venenifera* (Apocynaceae), Madagascar; an ordeal bean containing a cardiac poison, tanghinine.

tanghinine. $C_{10}H_{16}N = 150.1$. An alkaloid from tanghinia. Colorless scales, soluble in alcohol; a cardiac poison.

tang-kui. (1) Eumenol. (2) Lovage.

tangle. Laminaria.

tankage. The rendered, dried, ground by-products from animal carcasses; a fertilizer and feeding stuff: nitrogen 5–10, tricalcium phosphate 8–30%. **fish-** q.v. **garbage-** The rendered, dried, ground product of waste household food materials: nitrogen 2.5–3.5, phosphorus pentoxide 2–5, potassium oxide 0.5–1.0%. **gashouse-** A misnomer for "spent oxide," consisting of iron oxide and substances taken up in the purification of illuminating gas (N 5–10%). **hynite-** A t. with high N content. **process-** Hynite t.

tank culture. Hydroponics.

tannal. Aluminum tannate.

tannalbin. Tannin albumate. Brown powder, insoluble in water; an intestinal astringent.

tannase. An enzyme in tannin-bearing plants; it hydrolyzes tannins to gallic acid.

tannate. A salt of tannic acid.

tannic acid. (1) $COOH \cdot C_6H_2(OH)_2 \cdot COO \cdot C_6H_2(OH)_3 = 322.2$. Tannin. Gallotannic acid, digallic acid. Yellow powder or lustrous scales, m.200 (decomp.), soluble in water or glycerol, slightly soluble in ether. Used as a reagent and to treat burns and some forms of metal poisoning (B.P.). (2) $C_{76}H_{52}O_{46}$. Gallotannin, chinese tannin, turkish tannin. Brown powder from galls of oak and sumac, soluble in water or alcohol; probably a glucoside of polydigalloylgallic acids. **iodo-** See *iodotannic acid*.

tannigen. $C_{14}H_8(COMe)_2O_9 = 406.11$. Acetannin, tannogen, tannin diacetanilate. Gray powder, insoluble in water; an intestinal astringent.

tannin. (1) Tannic acid. (2)

$$CHOR \cdot CHOR \cdot CHOR \cdot CHO \cdot CHOR \cdot CH_2OR.$$

The glucoside, pentadigalloylglucose, from nutgalls. R is tannic acid less the carboxyl —OH. (3) See *tannins*. **acetyl-, condensed-** Catechol. **diacetyl-** Tannigen. **ellagi-** q.v. **iodo-** See *iodotannic acid*. **white-** The mixture of polyphenols extracted in ethyl acetate from aqueous infusions of green leaves.

t. albumate. Tannalbin.

tanning. Converting skins or hides into leather. **t. materials.** Vegetable preparations containing tannic acid. See table.

tannins. Astringent, aromatic, acidic glucosides, in various plants and trees. They precipitate alkaloids, mercuric chloride, and heavy metals; form blueblack solutions (ink) with ferric solutions; and their strongly alkaline solutions absorb oxygen rapidly. See *tannic acid*. Classification:

1. Hydrolyzable tannins, ester type, RCOOR:
   (a) Depsides or gallotannins, $(HO)_x RCOOR'$, $(OH)_y \cdot COOH$; as, di-β-resorcylic acid, $C_{14}H_{10}O_7$.
   (b) Glusides or galloyl sugars, $(HO)_x RCOOR'$-$(OH)_y$; as, digalloyl-*l*-glucosan.
   (c) Ellagitannins or diphenylmethylolids, $R(CO \cdot O)(O \cdot CO)R'$; as, ellagic acid, $C_{14}H_6O_8$.
2. Condensed tannins, keto type, R·CO·R:
   (d) Ketones, $HOR \cdot CO \cdot R'$; as, hydroxybenzophenone, $C_{13}H_{10}O_2$.
   (e) Catecholtannins or phlobatannins, $(HO)_x RCOOR'(OH)_y \cdot (COOH)$; as, the catechols.

Tanning material	% of tannin in:*
Pistacio, *Pistacia* species	g. 30–40
Sumac, *Rhus copollina*	l. 17–38
Chinese galls, *Rhus semialata*	g. 70
Quebracho, *Schinopsis* species	e. 35–65
White quebracho, *Aspidosperma* species .	l. 27–30
Minibari, *Alnus firma*	f. 25–28
Myrobalan, *Terminalia chebula*	n. 30–40
Thann, *Terminalia oliveri*	b. 30–35
Celery pine, *Phyllocladus* species	b. 28–30
Pentacme suavis	l. 12–24
White dammar, *Vateria indica*	f. 25
Cleistanthus collinus	b. 32–34
Amla, *Phyllanthus emblica*	f. 26–35
Valonia, *Quercus aegilops*	e. 30–65
Red oak, *Qu. rubra*	g. 35
Quercitron bark, *Q. tinctoria*	b. 25–30
Angica, *Acacia angica*	b. 20–25
Black wattle, *A. binervata*	b. 30
Cutch, *A. catechu*	e. 60
Wattle, *A. decurrens*	b. 20–51
Golden wattle, *A. pycnantha*	b. 40–50
Bengal kino, *Butea frontosa*	e. 30–40
Algarobilla, *Caesalpinia brevifolia*	p. 43–67
Cascalote, *C. cacolaco*	p. 40–55
Divi-divi, *C. coriaria*	p. 30–50
Tari, *C. digyna*	p. 40–50
Kino, *Pterocarpus* species	e. 45–60
Piagao, *Xylocarpus granatum*	b. 21–48
Ribbon gum, *E. amygdalina*	s. 58–65
Spotted gum, *E. maculata*	s. 45
Black mallet, *E. occidentalis*	b. 40–50
Mallet, *E. occidentalis*	b. 30–50
Messmate, *E. piperita*	s. 33–62
Red ironbark, *E. siderophloia*	s. 35–73
Yhva, *Eugenia* species	b. 44
Oak gum, *Spermolepsis* species	s. 43–80
Mangrove, *Rhizophora* species	b. 21–58
Guara, *Paullinia sorbilis*	f. 43–55
Tamarisk, *Tamarix* species	g. 26–58

* b. Bark   l. Leaves
   e. Extract   n. Nuts
   f. Fruit   p. Pods
   g. Galls   s. Secretion or sap

tannoform. $(C_{14}H_9O_9)_2CH_2$ = 656.2. Methylene-ditannin. A condensation product of formaldehyde and tannic acid. Pink powder, insoluble in water.

tannogen. Tannigen.

tannon. Tannopin.

tannopin. $(CH_2)_6N_4(C_{14}H_{10}O_9)_3$ = 1106.3. Hexamethylenetetraminetannin, tannon, urotropine tannin. Brown powder, insoluble in water; an intestinal antiseptic and disinfectant.

tannyl. The radical —$C_{14}H_9O_9$, from tannic acid. **t. acetate.** Tannigen.

tansy. Tanacetum. **wild-** Silverweed. **t. oil.** Tanacetum oil.

tantalate. $MTaO_3$. A salt of tantalic acid. **hexa-** $M_8Ta_6O_{19}$. **peroxy-** M_8TaO_8.

tantalic acid. $HTaO_3$ = 230.5. Colorless crystals, insoluble in water; forms complex salts, as, $Na_8Ta_6O_{19}$.

tantalite. $(FeMn)O·Ta_2O_4$. Black crystals, often found with niobium.

tantalites. $M(TaO_3)_2$. M is divalent iron, or manganese. Minerals usually mixed with the corresponding columbites.

tantalous. A compound of trivalent tantalum. **t. bromide.** See *tantalum bromide* (1). **t. chloride.** See *tantalum chloride* (1).

tantalum. Ta = 180.95. A rare metal of the vanadium family, and element, at. no. 73. Gray metal, d.16.6, m.2850, insoluble in alkalies or acids (except hydrofluoric acid). Occurs in tantalite and columbite; discovered (1802) by Ekeberg. Valencies 5 (principal) and 3. Resistant to corrosion, and a substitute for platinum; used for electric-light filaments, surgical instruments (it may be heat-sterilized without losing hardness), rayon spinnerets, jewelry, laboratory ware, bone repair; and as an electrode in current rectifiers, and a catalyst for producing synthetic diamonds. **beta-** A possible allotrope of Ta formed as a film by cathode sputtering; it has a higher resistivity, lower temperature coefficient of resistance, and becomes a superconductor at much lower temperature.

  t. bromides. (1) $TaBr_3$ = 421.5. Tantalous bromide. Yellow crystals, m.240, decomp. by water. (2) $TaBr_5$ = 581.1. Tantalic bromide. Colorless powder, decomp. by water. **t. carbide.** TaC = 192.9. A hard mixture: t. carbide 75, hafnium carbide 25%, m. exceeds 4200 (highest known). **t. chlorides.** (1) $TaCl_3$ = 287.88. Tantalous chloride. Yellow prisms, decomp. by water. (2) $TaCl_5$ = 359.0. Tantalic chloride. Yellow needles, m.211, decomp. in moist air to tantalic acid. **t. fluorides.** $(MF)_2TaF_5$, or, M_2TaF_7. M is a monovalent metal. **t. minerals.** Ta occurs in nature associated with Nb. Its principal ore is tantalite, $FeTa_2O_6$. **t. nitride.** TaN = 195.5. Colorless powder, soluble in mixed hydrofluoric and nitric acid. **t. oxide.** Ta_2O_5 = 443.0. Tantalic acid anhydride, t. pentoxide. White rhombs, d.7.53, insoluble in water, soluble in fused potassium bisulfate. **t. pentabromide.** See *t. bromide* (2). **t. pentachloride.** See *t. chloride* (2). **t. pentoxide.** See *t. oxide.* **t. potassium fluoride.** K_2TaF_7 = 392.7. White needles, soluble in water. **t. tribromide.** See *t. bromide* (1). **t. trichloride.** See *t. chloride* (1).

tantcopper. A copper alloy, analogous to tantiron.

tantiron. An acid-resistant alloy of iron containing silica, used for chemical equipment.

tantnickel. A nickel alloy analogous to tantiron.

tapioca. Cassava, manioca starch, Bahia arrowroot, Rio arrowroot, mandioc, from the root of cassava, *Jatropha manihot* (Euphorbiaceae), of Brazil; a food.

tar. A thick brown to black liquid mixture of hydrocarbons and their derivatives with distinctive odor, obtained by distillation of wood, peat, coal, shale, or other vegetable or mineral materials. **coal-** A t. from destructive distillation of bituminous coal or crude petroleum. It contains naphthalene, toluene, quinoline, aniline, cresols. Cf. *coal.* *prepared-* Pix carbonis prep. A product made by heating commercial c.t. at 50°C for 1 hour, with stirring. Used to treat skin affections (B.P.). **oil of-** T. oil. **pine-** Wood tar. **rock-** Crude petroleum. **Schroeter-** A "tar" produced by the action of aluminum chloride on tetrahydro-naphthalene, followed by distillation. It contains 3,4-benzpyrene, and is carcinogenic. **Stockholm- A** wood t. **wood-** Pix liquida, pine t. The empyreumatic syrup from distillation of the *Pinus* species: contains resins, turpentine and oils; used as a disinfectant and antiseptic, to treat forms of eczema (B.P.). On fractional distillation it yields an acid liquor (pyroligneous acid), empyreumatic oil (oil of t.), and a black residue (pitch). **t. camphor.** Naphthalene. **t. oil.** Oleum picis rectificatum. The volatile oil from pine t. rectified by steam distillation, d. 0.862–0.872.

tarapacaite. Native potassium chromate.

taraxacum. Dandelion, lion's tooth. The dried roots of *T. officinale* (Compositae); a tonic and laxative.

taraxanthin. $C_{40}H_{56}O_4 = 600.43$. A carotenoid from dandelion flowers, m.184; isomer of violaxanthin.

taraxasterol. Anthesterol, α-lactusterol, α-lactucol. A triterpene alcohol from chamomile.

taraxerol. $C_{30}H_{50}O = 426.05$. Skimmiol. An alkaloid from *Taraxacum officinale*, m.269.

tarchonyl alcohol. $C_{50}H_{102}O = 718.79$. A methanol alcohol, m.82, insoluble in water, from *Tarchonanthus camphoratus* (Compositae), Africa.

tare. (1) The weight of an empty container. (2) A counterweight used to balance a container. (3) A fodder plant of the vetch family. (4) Any weed among corn. (5) Waste cloth wrappings, usually jute, for paper manufacture.

target. (1) Anticathode. (2) A substance exposed to bombardment by particles. Cf. *rays.*

targusic acid. Lapachol.

tariric acid. $Me(CH_2)_{10}C \vdots C(CH_2)_4COOH = 280.3$. 5-Octadecynoic acid*. An isomer of linoleic acid, m.51; a glyceride in Guatemalan tarira, *Picramia* species.

tarnish. A surface film of contrasting color formed on an exposed surface of a metal or mineral; usually the oxide or sulfide.

taro. The rhizome of *Colocasia esculenta* (Araceae) of the tropics, whose poison is destroyed by fermenting, and then boiling to remove the hydrogen cyanide so liberated; a food (poi).

tarpaulin. Canvas rendered waterproof by tar.

tarragon. The plant *Artemisia tranunguloides* (Compositae); a spice. **t. oil.** Estragon oil.

tartar. (1) Tatar. A crude potassium bitartrate sediment in wine casks. (2) Calculus. A deposit of saliva proteins and calcium phosphate on teeth, causing pyorrhea. **cream of-** Potassium bitartrate. **oil of-** A saturated solution of potassium carbonate. **salt of-** Potassium carbonate.

tartaric acid. $C_4H_6O_6 = 150.1$. Dihydroxysuccinic acid, 2,3-dihydroxybutanedioic acid*. A dibasic, tetratomic acid; 4 isomers:

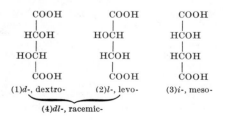

(1)*d*-, dextro-   (2)*l*-, levo-   (3)*i*-, meso-

(4)*dl*-, racemic-

The *d*-acid occurs in many vegetable tissues and fruits. **dextro-** or **levo-** Colorless, monoclinic crystals, m.168, soluble in water; used as a reagent, and in pharmacy to produce effervescence. **inactive-** Meso-. **levo-** See *dextro-.* **meso-** $+1H_2O$. Colorless scales, m.140, soluble in water. **racemic-** $+1H_2O$. A mixture of *d*- and *l*-tartaric acids, m.205.

tartarlithine. Lithium bitartrate.

tartarus. Potassium bitartrate. **t. stibiatus.** Potassium antimonyl tartrate. **t. tartarisatus.** Potassium tartrate. **t. vitriolatus.** Potassium sulfate.

tartrate. $M_2C_4H_4O_6$. A salt of tartaric acid. **acid-** or **bi-.** $MC_4H_5O_6$. **normal-** See *tartrate.* **pyro-** See *pyrotartrate.*

tartrazine. $Ph \cdot N \cdot CO \cdot C(:N \cdot NPh) \cdot C(COOH):N =$ 307.13 A yellow pyrazolone dye. Often used in foodstuffs.

tartronic acid. $CHOH \cdot (COOH)_2 \cdot 0.5H_2O = 129.1$. Oxymalonic acid, propanoldiacid, 2-hydroxy-propanedioic acid*. Colorless prisms, sublime 110, m.185 (decomp.), soluble in water. **benzyl-** See *benzyltartronic acid.* **methyl-** Isomalic acid.

t. a. series. Polyhydroxy acids formed from carbohydrates.

tartronyl. The radical —CO·CHOH·CO—. **t. urea.** Dialuric acid.

taste. The sensation caused by a soluble substance on the nerves of the tongue. Threshold values of taste stimulus, grams per 100 ml water: salty, 0.25 sodium chloride; sweet, 0.5 sugar; acidic, 0.007 hydrochloric acid; vanilla (coumarin), 0.0002; bitter, 0.00005 quinine.

tastpolarograph. A polarograph in which the current is measured only during a short time interval before the fall of each mercury drop, and at the same time the cell voltage is altered and the chart paper advanced. It eliminates distortion of the polarogram.

tatar. Tartar.

tau. Greek letter τ, q.v.

taurine. $NH_2 \cdot CH_2 \cdot CH_2 \cdot SO_3H = 125.14$. Amino-ethionic acid, aminoethylsulfonic acid. Prisms, m.240 (decomp.), soluble in water; formed in bile by the hydrolysis of taurocholic acid.

taurocholeic acid. $C_{27}H_{47}NO_6S = 513.45$. A bile acid, q.v., which hydrolyzes to choleic acid and taurine.

taurocholic acid. $C_{26}H_{45}O_7NS = 515.4$. Choleic acid, in bile. Colorless needles, m.180, soluble in water; hydrolyzes to taurine and cholic acid.

tauryl. The radical $NH_2 \cdot CH_2 \cdot CH_2 \cdot SO_2$—.

tauto- Prefix indicating a tautomeric form; as, tautohypoxanthine.

tautocyanate. $R \cdot N:CO$. An ester.

tautomeric. Capable of tautomerism.

tautomerism. Dynamic allotropy. Existing in a state of equilibrium between 2 isomeric forms, and able to react according to either; as, $R \cdot CN$ and $R \cdot NC$. The molecules may differ in L (the linkage, bond or connections between the atoms) and P (the position or distribution of these atoms in the molecule).

Tautomerism: L different, P different
Metamerism: L alike, P different
Desmotropism: L different, P alike

electrolytic- The property of an amphoteric substance in solution which produces hydroxyl ions in presence of acids, and hydrogen ions in presence of alkalies. **mesohydric-** T. involving the intramolecular sharing of H atom(s). **protropic-** T. of the keto-enol type.

tautourea. $NH_2 \cdot C : NH \cdot OH$, as distinct from $NH_2 \cdot CO \cdot NH_2$ (urea).

tautouric. See *uric acid*.

tawing. Tanning of hides with mineral substances; as, alum.

taxicatin. $C_{13}H_{22}O_7 \cdot 2H_2O = 326.2$. A crystalline glucoside from *Taxus*.

taxine. $C_{37}H_{51}O_{10}N = 669.4$. An alkaloid from *Taxus baccata*. White scales, m.80, slightly soluble in water.

taxis. The movement of a cell in response to an external stimulus; as, chemotaxis.

taxometer. An instrument to measure the feel of sheet materials, e.g., leather, in terms of bending length and flexural rigidity.

taxus. Yew, chinawood. The poisonous dried seeds of *Taxus baccata* (Taxaceae), Africa.

Taylor, Hugh Stott. b. 1890. English-born American chemist, noted for work in photochemistry and thermodynamics.

Taylor-White process. Toughening steel by heating almost to fusion, successively cooling in molten lead and hot oil, reheating to 400–600°C, and cooling in air.

tazettine. $C_{18}H_{21}NO_5 = 331.17$. Base VIII, ungernine. An alkaloid, m.206, from the dried corm of *Narcissus tazetta*, related to sekisanine.

TB. Abbreviation for tuberculin.

Tb. Symbol for terbium.

Tc. Symbol for technetium.

TDE. DDD.

Te. Symbol for tellurium.

tea. (1) A medicinal or beverage plant decoction or infusion. (2) The dried leaves of *Thea sinensis* and other species of China, Japan, India. Average composition: water 10, extractives 32.7, tannin 11.4, caffeine 1.9, ash 6.23, fibers 30–60%. World consumption (1966) 2,000 million pounds.

Paronychia species	Algerian t.
Melaleuca species	Australian t.
Chenopodium anthelminticum	Mexican t.
Monarda species	Oswego t.
Gaultheria species	Salvador t.
Capraria species	West Indian t.
Thea sinensis	Chinese t. (Pekoe, souchong, congou)
Catha edulis	Arabian t. (kat)
Stachy tarpheta species	Jamaica t.
Neea theifera	Caparrosa t.

Brazil- Maté. **James-** See *Labrador*. **Jesuit's-, Paraguay-** Maté.

   t. berries. Gaultheria. **t. cup.** About 120 ml or 4 fluid ounces. **t. root.** The root of *Ceanothus Americanus* (Celastraceae), an astringent. Cf. *ceanothine*. **t. spoon.** About 3.5 ml or 1 fluid drachm. **t. tree.** Cajeput.

teak. The extremely hard wood of *Tectona grandis* (Verbenaceae), S. Asia.

tear gases. Volatile lachrymatory compounds, usually halogenated ketones, $RCO \cdot CH_2X$, as chloroacetophenone, or halogenated cyanides, as $PhCHBrCN$, bromobenzyl cyanide. Cf. *poison gas*.

teas. (1) See *tea*. (2) See *species*.

tebelon. Isobutyl oleate.

Teb-x-cel. Trademark for fabrics treated with a sodium sulfatoethyl sulfonium compound to enable them to dry smooth, without drip drying.

Teca. Trade name for an acetate synthetic fiber.

technetium. Tc = 98.91. Masurium. Nipponium. The element of at. no. 43. A fission product of uranium, not occurring in nature; its stablest isotope has a mass no. 99 (Noddack, 1925). Obtained by the extraction of neutron-irradiated molybdenum in methyl ethyl ketone; valencies 2, 4, and 7; m.2200 ± 50.

technician. A technically qualified worker whose skill is based on some knowledge of science and mathematics, and who works under the general direction of a technologist. See *technology*.

technology. The application of science to manufacturing methods.

Teclu burner. A modified bunsen burner, with finely adjustable air and gas streams.

tecomin. Lapachol.

Tecsol. Trade name for a product of wood distillation; an alcohol denaturant.

tectite. Tektite.

tectonics. The study of the deformation of the structure of the earth's crust.

Tedion. Trademark for the acaricide 2,4,5,4′-tetrachlorodiphenyl sulfone.

Teflon. Trademark for polytetrafluoroethylene. **T.-100.** A fully fluorinated copolymer of hexafluoropropylene and tetrafluoroethylene. It resists chemical attack and has good electrical insulating properties.

Tegit. Trade name for molded asbestos and tar products used for electrical insulation.

Tego. Trademark for a kraft paper impregnated with a phenol-formaldehyde resin, used as a bonding agent in plywood manufacture.

Teichmann's crystals. See *hemin*.

teilungs koeffizient. Distribution coefficient.

tektite. Tectite. A mineral of high silica and alumina content, often glassy and always associated with sediments; produced by weathering of granite and basalt, followed by removal of iron and the alkaline earths by leaching.

telcomer. The product of a telomerization reaction.

tele- Prefix (Greek, "far off") indicating distance.

telegenesis. The artificial insemination of human beings.

teleidoscope. A television device in which a modulated cathode ray scans an image on a uniform liquid layer spread on a revolving glass disk. Each point takes the form of a minute lens, the curvature of which depends on the instantaneous change in that area produced by the cathode ray.

telekinesy. Action at a distance without contact.

Telepaque. Trademark for iopanoic acid.

telephotography. Transmission of black and white pictures by telegraphy or wireless.

telescope. An optical instrument for observing distant objects, and for reading measuring scales at a distance.

telfairic acid. Linoleic acid.

tellerwort. Sanguinaria.

tellurate. M_2TeO_4, or M_6TeO_6. A salt of telluric acid.

tellur(o)bismuth. Tetradymite. **t. nickel.** Melonite. **t. ocher.** Tellurium dioxide.

telluretted. Describing a compound containing divalent tellurium (obsolete). **t. hydrogen.** Hydrogen telluride.

telluric. (1) Of earthly (as opposed to meteoric, or solar) origin. (2) Referring to hexavalent tellurium. **t. acid.** $H_2TeO_4 = 193.5$. Allotelluric acid. Colorless powder, decomp. 160, insoluble in water. *soluble-* H_6TeO_6, or $H_2TeO_4 \cdot 2H_2O = 229.5$. White crystals, obtained by oxidation of tellurium dioxide. **t. bismuth.** Tetradymite. **t. lead.** Nagyagite. **t. lines.** The lines in the solar spectrum due to absorption of rays by the atmosphere; as, Fraunhofer lines A and B. **t. ocher.** Tellurite. **t. silver.** Hessite.

telluride. (1) M_2Te. A compound of divalent tellurium; as, hessite, Ag_2Te; tetradymite, Bi_2Te_3. (2) Weissite. (3) R_2Te. **di-, per-** $R_2Te \cdot Te \cdot R$.

tellurinic acid. $RTeO_2H$; as, methanetellurinic acid, $MeTeO_2H$. Cf. *telluronic acid.*

tellurious. Tellurous.

tellurite. (1) M_2TeO_3. A salt of tellurous acid. (2) TeO_2. Telluric ocher. Native tellurium dioxide.

tellurium. $Te = 127.60$. Sylvanium. A nonmetal and element, at. no. 52. Rhombic crystals, m.451, insoluble in water; a homolog of sulfur and selenium. Discovered by Müller (1782); occurs native as lionite in tellurite and tellurides. Inorganic compounds: see table. Organic compounds: R_2Te, R-telluride; R_2TeO, R-tellurium oxide. **black-** $(Pb,Au)(Te,S)$. A lead-gold mineral. **foliated-** Nagyagite. **graphic-** Sylvanite. **radio-** Polonium.

Name	Ion	Valency
Tellurides and tellurous.....	$Te^=$	-2
Tellurites.................	$TeO_3^=$	$+4$
Tellurates and telluric......	$TeO_4^=$	$+6$

t. bichloride. See *t. chloride.* **t. bromides.** (1) $TeBr_2 = 287.3$. Tellurous bromide. Gray needles, m.280, decomp. by water. (2) $TeBr_4 = 447.25$. Telluric bromide. White powder, hydrolyzed by water. **t. chlorides.** (1) $TeCl_2 = 198.4$. Tellurous chloride. Black crystals, m.175, decomp. by water. (2) $TeCl_4 = 269.3$. Telluric chloride. White crystals, m.224, decomp. by water. **t. dibromide.** T. bromide (1). **t. dichloride.** T. chloride (1). **t. diethyl.** $TeEt_2 = 185.6$, b.137. **t. dimethyl.** $TeMe_2 = 157.6$, b.182. **t. dioxide.** See *t. oxide.* **t. disulfide.** T. sulfide. **t. glance.** Nagyagite. **t. graphite.** $(AgAu)Te_2$. A native telluride. Cf. *sylvanite.* **t. hydride.** Hydrogen telluride. **t. hydroxides.** (1) R_3TeOH. (2) $TeO(OH)_2$. Basic tellurous acid. **t. iodide.** $TeI_2 = 381.3$. Black crystals, insoluble in water. **t. lead.** Lead containing 0.05% Te. It resists mechanical shock and stress reversal better than pure lead, and may be used with 77% or less of sulfuric acid. **t. monoxide.** See *t. oxide.* **t. nitrate.** $Te_2O_3(OH) \cdot NO_3$, derived from tellurous acid, $TeO(OH)_2$. **t. nitrates.** $R_2Te(NO_3)_2$. **t. oxides.** (1) $TeO = 143.5$. T. monoxide, a rare compound. (2) $TeO_2 = 159.5$. T. dioxide. Yellow octahedra,

m.700, slightly soluble in water. (3) $TeO_3 = 175.5$. T. trioxide. Orange powder, decomp. red heat, insoluble in water. (4) R_2TeO; as, dimethyltellurium oxide. **t. oxychloride.** $TeOCl_2$, derived from tellurous acid. **t. sulfate.** $Te_2O_3SO_4$, derived from tellurous acid, $TeO(OH)_2$. **t. sulfide.** $TeS_2 = 191.6$. Black powder, insoluble in water. **t. sulfite.** $(TeO_2)_2SO_3$, derived from tellurous acid. **t. sulfoxide.** $TeSO_3 = 207.5$; formed by treating tellurium with concentrated sulfuric acid. **t. trioxide.** See *t. oxide.*

telluro- Prefix indicating the atom Te^{2+}. Cf. *sulfo-.*

telluronic acid. $RTeO_3H$; as, methane telluronic acid*. Cf. *tellurinic acid.*

telluronium. $R \cdot TeH_3$. Cf. *selenonium.*

tellurous. Tellurious. Describing a compound of tetravalent tellurium. **t. acid.** $H_2TeO_3 = 177.5$. Tellurious acid. Colorless octahedra, decomp. 40, slightly soluble in water. Salts: M_2TeO_3, $M_2Te_2O_5$, $M_2Te_3O_7$, $M_2Te_4O_9$, also $TeO \cdot SO_4$, nitrate, oxychloride, and oxybromide. **t. bromide.** See *tellurium bromide.* **t. chloride.** See *tellurium chloride* (1).

telluryl. The radical $TeO=$, from tellurous acid.

telochrome. A television cathode-ray tube with 2 beams modulated by incoming signals to produce effects in 2 primary colors.

telomerization. A polymerization reaction between 2 substances providing respectively the terminal groups and internal linkages of the resulting telcomer molecule; e.g., a saturated compound (carbon tetrachloride) and a polymerizable substance (ethylene) produce low-molecular-weight vinyl polymers; as tetrachloralkanes, $Cl(CH_2 \cdot CH_2)_n \cdot CCl_3$.

telopsis. Early name for television.

TEM. Tretamine.

temp. Abbreviation for temperature.

temparin. Dicoumarol.

temperature. The international temperature scale (1948) was renamed international practical temperature scale in 1960, and is based on 6 defining points, zero being 0.01°C below the triple point of water. Temperatures on this scale are designated: °C (international, 1948); degrees Celsius (international practical, 1948), or t_{int}. International practical Kelvin t. are thence obtained by adding 273.15, and are designated °K (international) or T_{int}. For extremes of t. see table, Temperature Magnitudes. **absolute-** T. on the absolute scale, °A, which begins at -273°C. **color scale of-** See table, Color Scale of Temperatures. **critical-** The t. above which a gas cannot be condensed to a liquid by pressure alone. **critical solution-** See *critical.* **flame-** See *flame temperature.* **maximum-** The t. above which life or growth of bacteria ceases. **normal-** (1) Room t. (2) T. measured on the hydrogen thermometer. (3) Standard t. **optimum-** The t. most favorable for action or growth. **room-** About 20°C (U.S.), or 15.5°C (U.K.). **salt-** T. at which crystals begin to separate when a solution is concentrated by boiling. **standard-** T. of 0°C or 273°A. **transition-** q.v.

t. coefficient. A factor that indicates quantitatively the effect of t. on a property of matter; as, electrical conductivity, 2.5% per °C. **t. reaction.** See *Maumené number.* **t. recorder.** An electric device for recording temperature. **t. regulator.** Thermoregulator. **t. scale.** An internationally

TEMPERATURE MAGNITUDES, °C

Stellar interior..........	40,000,000
Mercury lamp	14,000
Solar surface (G star)....	6,000
Atomic hydrogen torch ..	4,200
Stellar surface (M star) ..	3,000
Tungsten, melting point..	2,970
Gas burner	1,700
Water, boiling point.....	100
Hottest climate (Tripoli).	58
Man, body temperature..	37
Ocean water (La Jolla) ..	25.7
Water, freezing point....	0
Coldest climate (Alaska) .	−63.3
Liquid air..............	−195
Lowest experimental temperature (1965)	-10^{-6} above abs. zero
Absolute zero..........	−273.13

COLOR SCALE OF TEMPERATURES

Color	Temperature	
	°C	°F
Red, visible in dark........	400	750
Red, visible in daylight.....	525	975
Dark red	700	1,290
Bright cherry	1,000	1,830
Orange-red...............	1,100	2,010
Yellow	1,200	2,190
White...................	1,450	2,500
Blue, dazzling............	1,600	2,910

accepted t. scale, the primary fixed points of which are, °C:

Boiling of oxygen	−182.970
Melting of ice (fundamental point)	0
Boiling of water (fundamental point) ...	100
Boiling of sulfur	444.600
Solidification of silver................	960.8
Solidification of gold.................	1,063.0

Cf. *thermometer scale*.

tempered. Subjected to successive heatings, of decreasing intensity. **t. steel.** A hardened steel that has been reheated at a lower temperature.

tempering. (1) The reheating and cooling of metal; especially hardening steel. (2) Rendering plastic materials (as clay) homogeneous. Cf. *annealing*. **t. oil.** A heavy, viscous oil used for cooling metals during tempering.

template. An outline (e.g., of wood, paper, or metal) of an article to be constructed; used as a pattern.

tempolabile. Describing a substance that changes with time.

temulentine. $C_{12}H_{42}O_{19}N$ = 504.3. An alkaloid from the seeds of *Lolium temulentum*, the darnel grass associated with wheat.

temuline. $C_7H_{12}ON_2$ = 140.1. An alkaloid from *Lolium*.

tenacity. Ability to hold fast. Cf. *tensile strength*.

tenaculum. A hook-shaped dissecting needle.

Tenasco. Trade name for a viscose synthetic fiber.

tenate. That portion of a liquid which is not separated by dialysis, diffusion, filtration, or distillation.

tendering unit. A measure of the tendering of fabrics by chemical attack (e.g., in laundering) in terms of the cuprammonium viscosity in reciprocal poises.

tenderometer. An instrument for measuring the ripeness of peas in terms of the force required to push them through a standard grid.

tengujo. Yoshino.

teniacide. An agent that kills tapeworms; as, aspidium.

teniafuge. An agent that expels tapeworms; as, spigelia, pomegranate.

Tenite. Trademark for a cellulose acetobutyrate plastic.

Tenith. Trade name for a cellulose acetate plastic.

Tennant, Charles. 1768–1838. Scottish industrial chemist; the original manufacturer of chloride of lime. **T., Smithson.** 1761–1815. English chemist, discoverer of iridium and osmium.

tennantite. $3Cu_2S \cdot As_2S_3$. A native sulfarsenide, associated with iron.

tenorite. CuO. A native black copper oxide.

tenside. Surface-active substance (collective name).

tensile. Rigid. **t. strength.** Tenacity. Resistance to pulling action, measured by the breaking stress in kilograms per square millimeter; e.g.: steel, 50–100; ramie fibers, 70–80; rayon, 60; copper, 20–50; silk fibers, 35–44; cotton fibers, 28–44; rubber, 15–20.

tensimeter. An instrument used to determine transition points from small vapor-pressure changes.

tensiometer. An apparatus for measuring surface tension.

tension. The stress caused by pulling; as, of rubber. **adhesion-** The degree of wetting of a solid by a liquid. **electric-** Electromotive force. **gaseous-** The elasticity of a gas. **surface-** The force exerted on the surface of a liquid, responsible for the formation of a meniscus or the absence of froth. **vapor-** See *vapor tension*.

tenter. A machine for drying woolen felts.

tenth-meter. 10^{-10} m; 1 angström unit.

tenth-normal solution. $N/10$ or 0.1 N, decinormal. A solution that contains 0.1 of the equivalent weight of a substance per liter.

tephigram. An entropy-temperature diagram, used for weather forecasting.

tephroite. Mn_2SiO_4. A native silicate.

tephrosia. (1) Devil's shoestring, Turkey pea. The dried leaves of *T. virginiana* (Leguminosae); a cathartic. (2) Fish bean, uwuwa, ombwe. The leaves of *T. vogelii* (Leguminosae), N. Rhodesia; a fish poison and parasiticide.

tephrosin. $C_{23}H_{22}O_7$ = 410.15. Hydroxydequelin. A crystalline principle from tephrosia, derris, and cube. Transparent prisms, m.198, insoluble in water.

ter- Prefix (Latin) indicating thrice. Cf. *tri-*.

tera. T. The unit of 1,000,000,000,000.

Teracol. Trade name for a polymethylene oxide having the properties of a rubber substitute.

teraconic acid. $Me_2C:C(COOH) \cdot CH_2COOH$ = 158.12. 2-Isopropilidenebutanedioic acid*. Crystals, m.162 (decomp.), soluble in water.

teracrylic acid. $C_7H_{12}O_2$ = 128.09. β,γ-Dimethylpentenic acid. A liquid, b.218.

teratolite. A mixed, native oxide of iron and manganese, with decomposed feldspar.

terbium, Tb = 158.92. A rare-earth metal and element, at. no. 65; discovered by Mosander in gadolinite. **t. chloride.** $TbCl_3 = 265.6$. Colorless crystals, soluble in water. **t. hydroxide.** $Tb(OH)_3 = 210.2$. Colorless powder, insoluble in water. **t. nitrate.** $Tb(NO_3)_3 = 345.2$. White powder, soluble in water, decomp. by heat to Tb_2O_3. **t. oxide.** $Tb_2O_3 = 366.4$. White powder, insoluble in water. **t. sulfate.** $Tb_2(SO_4)_3 = 606.5$. Colorless crystals, soluble in water.

terchloride. Trichloride.

terchoic acid. Polymers of phosphates of glycerol or ribitol, in which the units are joined through phosphodiester linkages; occur in the walls of certain bacteria.

terebene. $C_{10}H_{16} = 136.18$. A mixture of terpenes, made by the action of sulfuric acid on turpentine. Yellowish, fragrant liquid, b.160–172, insoluble in water. Used in disinfectant soaps. Cf. *terebine*.

terebenthene. Turpentine.

terebentylic acid. $C_8H_{10}O_2 = 138.12$. A liquid, b.160.

terebic acid. $O\cdot CMe_2\cdot CH(COOH)\cdot CH_2CO = 158.1$.

Terebinic acid, 2,2-dimethylparaconic acid. An oxidation product of turpentine. Colorless crystals, m.175. Cf. *terpenylic acid*. **pyro-** Pyroterebic acid.

terebine. A paint dryer, made by fusing rosin with a metallic acetate or oxide and thinning with white spirit.

terebinic acid. Terebic acid.

terebinthina. Turpentine.

terephthalal, terephthalyl. The radical $=CH\cdot C_6H_4\cdot CH=$.

terephthalic. Pertaining to *p*-phthalic acid. **t. acid.** $C_6H_4(COOH)_2 = 166.1$. Benzene-*p*-dicarboxylic acid. White powder, sublimes when heated, insoluble in water; used as a reagent for alkali in wool, and in the manufacture of plasticizers, and polyester fibers and films. **t. aldehyde.** $C_6H_4-(CHO)_2 = 134.1$. Benzene-*p*-dialdehyde. Colorless needles, m.116, soluble in water or alcohol. **t. nitrile.** $C_6H_4(CN)_2 = 128.1$. *p*-Dicyanobenzene. Colorless crystals, m.215, insoluble in water.

terephthalonic acid. Carboxyformylbenzoic acid.

terephthalyl alcohol. α,α'-*p*-Xylenediol.

teresantalic acid. $C_8H_{15}O_2 = 143.1$. A terpene acid in sandalwood oil.

Tergal. Trade name for a polyester synthetic fiber.

Tergitol. Trademark for a group of detergent sodium or amine salts of higher primary or secondary alkyl sulfates.

Terital. Trade name for a polyester synthetic fiber.

Terlenka. Trade name for a polyester synthetic fiber.

terlinguarite. Hg_2ClO. A native oxychloride from Terlingua, Tex.

term. A mathematical relation. **D-** The diffuse spectrum lines. **P-** The principal spectrum lines. **S-** The sharp spectrum lines. See *hydrogen atom, series*. **t. system.** See *quantum numbers*.

terminal. The end of an electric wire or electrode; or its binding post.

terminalia. Myrobalan.

terminology. (1) The study of the construction, definition, and arrangement of names and terms. (2) A nomenclature. **Geneva-** See *Geneva*. **organic-** See *organic compounds, structure symbols*.

termolecular. Trimolecular.

ternary. (1) Consisting of three. (2) Tertiary. **t. compound.** A molecule consisting of 3 different types of atoms. **t. steel.** A steel consisting of iron, carbon, and one other metal. **t. system.** A system of 3 components.

terne plate. Steel coated with an alloy of Pb 80–90, Sn 10–20 %.

ternitrate. Trinitrate.

teroxide. Trioxide.

terpadiene. A terpane (methane) derivative containing 2 double bonds.

terpadienone. A derivative of terpanone containing 2 double bonds; as, carvone.

terpane. Methane.

terpanone. $C_{10}H_{13}O$. A saturated ketone derived from terpenes; as, tetrahydrocarvone.

terpene(s). (1) $C_{10}H_{16}$. Hydrocarbons in essential oils, resins, and other vegetable aromatic products. Classification: monocyclic (limonene), bicyclic (camphene group), acyclic (aliphatic terpenes). Related to the terpenes are: hermiterpenes, C_5H_8 (isoprene); sesquiterpenes, $C_{15}H_{24}$ (caryophyllene); diterpenes, $C_{20}H_{32}$; polyterpenes, $n(C_{10}H_{16})$. (2) A derivative of the hydrocarbons, $C_{10}H_{14}$, $C_{10}H_{18}$, and $C_{10}H_{20}$; as, pinol, menthol, ionone. (3) $C_{10}H_{16} = 136.1$. Dipentene, *dl*-limonene, cinene, cajeputene, kautchin, diamylene, in the oils of bergamot, geranium, citronella, dill, caraway, wormseed. Colorless liquid, d.0.85, b.181, insoluble in water; a flavoring anthelmintic, antispasmodic, and anodyne. **t. dihydrochloride.** $C_{10}H_{16}\cdot 2HCl = 209.0$. Dipentene dihydrochloride. Colorless crystals, m.50, insoluble in water. **t. hydriodide.** $C_{10}H_{16}\cdot HI = 264.1$. Dipentene iodide, terpene iodide. Brown liquid, insoluble in water. **t. hydrochloride.** $C_{10}H_{16}\cdot HCl = 172.6$. Dipentene hydrochloride, pinene hydrochloride, artificial camphor, turpentine camphor. Colorless crystals, m.125, insoluble in water; an antiseptic.

terpenol. $C_{10}H_{17}OH$. Cyclic alcohols derived from the terpenes; as, carvestrol.

terpenone. $C_{10}H_{16}O$. Ketones derived from terpanones; as dihydrocarvone.

terpenylic acid. $C_8H_{12}O_4 = 172.1$. An oxidation product of turpentine. Colorless crystals, m. about 90. See *terebic acid*.

terpilene. $C_{10}H_{16} = 136.1$. Terpinylene, obtained by dehydrating a terpene dihydrochloride solution, b.176. **t. dihydrochloride.** Eucalyptole.

terpilenol. Terpineol.

terpin, terpine. $CH_2OH\cdot C_6H_{10}\cdot CH(Me)(CH_2OH) = 172.2$. Dipentene glycol, dihydroxymenthane. **cis-** m.104. **trans-** m.156.

t. hydrate. $C_{10}H_{20}O_2\cdot H_2O = 190.23$. Colorless rhombs, m.106, soluble in water, obtained by oxidation of turpentine; used to treat whooping cough.

terpinene. $C_{10}H_{16} = 136.27$. A hydrocarbon from turpentine in α and β forms. Colorless liquid, b.179, insoluble in water.

terpineol. $C_{10}H_{18}O = 154.2$. Lilacin, terpilenol. Colorless liquid. **alpha-** d.0.936, m.35, b.219.8. **beta-** d.0.923, m.33, b.210. **gamma-** d.0.936, m.70, b.218. Insoluble in water; lilac odor.

pharmaceutical t. A mixture of isomers in which the *dl*-α-t. predominates. Colorless, viscous liquid, d.0.933, b.214–224, slightly soluble in water; an antibacterial.

terpinol. A terpene mixture. Colorless oil, insoluble in water; an antiseptic, perfumery (hyacinth), and pharmaceutical.

terpinolene. $C_{10}H_{16}$ = 136.2. Colorless liquid, b.183, insoluble in water. Soluble in alcohol, ether, or glycerol. Cf. *citral.*

terpinylene. Terpilene.

Terposol. Trademark for solvents made by the catalytic etherification of pinene

terpyridyl. 2,6-Di-2′-pyridylpyridine. A solution in hydrochloric acid is a reagent for cobalt (orange color).

terra- Prefix indicating an earth or earthly origin **t. alba.** White clay; kaolin. **t. cariosa.** Rottenstone. **t. cotta.** A coarse clay, baked and used for decorative purposes or utensils. **t. japonica.** Pale catechu or gambir. **t. rossa.** A fossil red earth. **t. verde.** Green earth. A green disintegration product of hornblende minerals; used to fix basic dyes on textiles.

terracoles. A group of lichens.

Terramycin. Trademark for oxytetracycline, an antibiotic from cultures of *Streptomyces rimosus,* a soil organism. **T. hydrochloride.** Oxytetracycline hydrochloride.

terrein. $C_8H_{12}O_3$ = 154.0. A hydroxycyclopentanone produced by the mold *Aspergillus terreus.*

tersulfate. A sulfate containing 3 SO_4= radicals.

tert- Abbreviation and prefix indicating tertiary.

tertiary. Third in order or type. **di-** See *arsine.* **t. alcohol.** $R_3C \cdot OH$. **t. amine.** R_3N; as, trimethylamine. **t. carbon atom.** A C atom attached to 3 others. **t. epoch.** A geologic period, q.v., and system of strata deposited during the Cenozoic era. **t. lipid.** See *lipids.* **t. phosphate.** M_3PO_4. The normal phosphate.

tervalent. Having 3 different valencies.

Terylene. Trademark for a synthetic fiber made from a terephthalic acid polyester and ethylene glycol; very elastic, stable, and resistant to moisture and chemicals, and twice as strong as cotton. Structural unit:

$$— — —OC\!\!\big\langle\bigcirc\big\rangle\!\!CO—O—(CH_2)_2—O— — —$$

tesla. T. The unit of magnetic flux density; webers per square meter.

tesseral. Isometric. See *crystal system.*

test. (1) Qualitative trial, or reaction. (2) A physical experiment to determine a physical property. **biological-** A serum reaction. **generic-** q.v. **hot toddy-** An evaluation of: (a) *aroma:* treat 10 ml liquor with 40 ml hot water and smell in comparison with a standard; (b) *flavor:* sip and roll the liquid over the tongue without swallowing. **layer-** Ring t. **load-** Subjection to different pressures or weights and temperatures, and measurement of the resulting deformation. **negative-** q.v. **ordinal-** q.v. **ring-** A chemical reaction between 2 liquid layers, so that the reaction products form a zone between them. **slag-** An examination of refractories for their behavior toward slag penetration. **spalling-** The behavior of heated materials after repeated quenching. **spot-** q.v. **streak-** q.v. **t. glass.** T. tube. **t. meal.** A specially prepared food that is eaten, withdrawn from the stomach after a certain time, and analyzed. **t.**

paper. A filter paper impregnated with a reagent or indicator, q.v. Used with solutions that must not be contaminated by the reagent. **t. solution.** T.S. A solution of reagent. **t. tube.** A small cylindrical glass vessel of resistant glass; used for chemical reactions.

testa. A shell; as, testa ovi (eggshell).

testes. The dried substance of the testes of the steer; used to treat neurasthenia and diabetes.

testosterone. $C_{19}H_{28}O_2$ = 288.43. A male sex hormone from testis tissue, or synthesized. White crystals, m.154, insoluble in water. Cf. *androsterone.* **t. cypionate.** $C_{27}H_{40}O_3$ = 412.62. White crystals, insoluble in water, m.101; an androgen (U.S.P.). **t. propionate.** $C_{22}H_{32}O_3$ = 344.52. Testoviron. White crystals, m.120, insoluble in water; used similarly to t. (U.S.P., B.P.).

testoviron. Testosterone propionate.

tetan. Tetranitromethane.

tetanics. A spinal-cord poison producing spasmodic contractions of the muscles; as, nux vomica.

tetanine. $C_{13}H_{30}O_4N_2$ = 288.2. A ptomaine from cultures of the tetanus bacillus.

tetanotoxin. $C_5H_{11}N$ = 85.1. A ptomaine from cultures of the tetanus bacillus.

tetanthrene. $C_{14}H_{14}$ = 182.11. Tetrahydrophenanthrene, an aromatic hydrocarbon.

tetanus toxoid. (U.S.P.). **t. vaccine** (B.P.). A sterile solution of the formaldehyde-treated growth products of the tetanus bacillus, *Clostridium tetani;* used adsorbed on aluminum hydroxide or after precipitation with alum.

tetartohedral. A crystal form with only one-quarter of the full number of faces required by the symmetry of the system.

tethelin. A principle obtained from the anterior lobe of the pituitary body; supposed to control growth.

Tetmosol. Trademark for tetraethylthiuram monosulfide; an insecticide.

tetra- Quadri-. Prefix (Greek) indicating four. **t. arylazadipyrromethines.** Stable dyestuffs made by the progressive replacement of methine bridges in porphins to form azaporphins and finally phthalocyanines.

tetrabasic. Describing an acid that has 4 replaceable H atoms; as, H_4SiO_4.

tetrabenzyl- Prefix indicating 4 benzyl radicals. **t. tin.** $Sn(CH_2Ph)_4$ = 482.92. Colorless prisms, m.43, insoluble in water.

tetraborane. See *boron hydrides.*

tetraborate. $M_2B_4O_7$. A salt of tetraboric acid. See *borax.*

tetraboric acid. See *boric acid, pyro-.*

tetrabrom(o)- Prefix describing a compound containing 4 Br atoms in its molecule. **t. benzene.** 1, 2, 3, 5- or 1, 3, 4, 5- $C_6H_2Br_4$ = 393.73. m.99, insoluble in alcohol. **t. cresolsulfonphthalein.** Bromocresol green. **t. ethane.** $CHBr_2 \cdot CHBr_2$ = 345.8. Ethylene tetrabromide. Colorless liquid, d.2.972, m. −20, insoluble in water. **t. fluorescein.** Eosin. **t. phenolsulfonphthalein.** Bromophenol blue.

tetracaine hydrochloride. $C_{15}H_{24}O_2N_2 \cdot HCl$ = 300.84. Amethocaine hydrochloride, pontocaine, decicaine. The hydrochloride of 4-butylaminobenzoyl-β-dimethylaminoethanol. Bitter crystals, m.148, soluble in water; a local anesthetic (U.S.P.).

tetracarboxylic acid. A tetrabasic organic acid; as, dimalonic acid, $(CH)_2(COOH)_4$.

tetracarp. Tetrachloroethylene.

tetracene. $C_2H_8ON_{10} = 188.11$. Tetrazene. 1-Guanyl-4-nitrosoaminoguanyltetrazene. Yellow crystals, insoluble in water; a percussion primer.

tetracetate. $(CH_3COO)_4M$. A compound containing 4 acetate radicals.

tetrachlor(o)- Prefix describing a compound containing 4 Cl atoms in its molecule. **t. acetone.** $(CHCl_2)_2CO = 195.86$. Didichloromethyl ketone. Colorless crystals, m.48. **t. aniline.** $C_6HCl_4NH_2 = 230.9$. *2,3,4,5,-* 1-Aminotetrachlorobenzene. Colorless crystals, m.118, insoluble in water. *2,3,5,6-* m.106. **t. benzene.** $C_6H_2Cl_4 = 215.9$. *1,2,3,4,-* Colorless needles, m.45, insoluble in water. *1,2,4,5-* Colorless, monoclinic crystals, m.140, slightly soluble in water. *1,2,3,5-* White needles, m.50, insoluble in water. **t. ethane.** $C_2H_2Cl_4 = 167.87$. Acetylene tetrachloride, ethylene tetrachloride. *1,1,2,2-* or *α,α,β,β-* $CH_2Cl_2·CH_2Cl_2$. Colorless liquid, d.1.600, b.146, insoluble in water; a fat solvent, airplane dope, paint remover, spotting agent, and insecticide. *1,1,1,2-* or *α,α,α,β-* $CH_2Cl·CCl_3$. Colorless liquid, b.129. **t. ethylene.** $CCl_2:CCl_2 = 165.85$. Perchloroethylene. Colorless liquid, d.1.608, b.119, insoluble in water; a spotting and drying agent, soap and fat solvent, and anthelmintic (U.S.P., B.P.). **t. methane.** Carbon tetrachloride. **t. quinol.** Chloranil.

tetrachloride. A compound with 4 Cl atoms in its molecule.

tetracid. A base or alcohol with 4 OH radicals.

Tetracol. Trade name for carbon tetrachloride.

tetracosane. $C_{24}H_{50} = 338.4$. A paraffin hydrocarbon. Colorless crystals, m.51, insoluble in water.

tetracosanic acid*. $C_{24}H_{48}O_2 = 368.37$. A fatty acid, m.84, from peanut oil. **iso-** A fatty acid, m.80, from pine oil.

tetracycline. $C_{22}H_{24}O_8N_2 = 444.45$. Yellow crystals, insoluble in water; an antibiotic (U.S.P.), also used as the hydrochloride (U.S.P., B.P.).

tetrad. (1) An atom or group of atoms of valency 4. (2) A crystal showing 4 similar faces when rotated 360° about its axis of symmetry.

tetradecane*. $C_{14}H_{30} = 198.24$. A methane hydrocarbon. Colorless liquid, d.0.765, b.253, insoluble in water.

tetradecanoic acid*. Myristic acid.

tetradecoic acid. Myristic acid.

tetradecyl. The radical $-C_{14}H_{29}$, from tetradecane.

tetradymite. Bi_2Te_3. Tellurbismuth. A native telluride; usually contains sulfide.

tetraedrite. A native arsenic and copper sulfide, intermediate in composition between tennantite and tetrahedrite.

tetraethyl- Prefix describing a compound with 4 Et groups in its molecule. **lead-** See t. *plumbane* and t. *gas.* **t. ammonium hydroxide.** $NEt_4OH = 147.1$. Colorless, hygroscopic needles, m.50, soluble in water; an antirheumatic and uric acid solvent. **t. ammonium iodide.** $NEt_4I = 257.2$. Yellow crystals, soluble in water or alcohol. **t. benzene.** $C_6H_2Et_4 = 190.2$. An aliphatic-aromatic hydrocarbon. *1,2,3,4-* Colorless liquid, d.0.888, b.254, insoluble in water. *1,2,4,5-* Colorless liquid, d.0.887, b.250. **t. gas.** "Knockless" gasoline; contains tetraethyllead. **t. germanium*.** $GeEt_4 = 188.76$. Colorless liquid, b.163, insoluble in water.

t. lead*. T. *plumbane.* **t. tin*.** $SnEt_4 = 234.86$. Ethylstannane. Colorless liquid, b.181, insoluble in water. **t. urea-** $Et_2N·CO·NEt_2 = 172.18$. Colorless liquid, b.210, soluble in water.

tetragalloyl- Prefix indicating 4 $C_6H_2(OH)_3CO$—radicals, from gallic acid. **t. erythrite.** $C_4H_6O_4·[C_6H_2(OH)_3CO]_4 = 730.2$. White crystals, decomp. 308, soluble in water.

tetragonal. Describing a crystal having its 3 axes at right angles to one another: 2 of equal length, the third shorter or longer.

tetrahedrite. Cu_2SbS_3, or $3Cu_2S·Sb_2O_3$. Panabase, fahlerz, gray copper ore. Cf. *tetraedrite.*

tetrahedron. A structure in the isometric system, with 4 equal faces; as, a pyramid.

tetrahedronal. Tetrahedral. Resembling a tetrahedron. **t. atom.** A static atom in which the electron octet is divided into 4 pairs of electrons which oscillate around centers located at the 4 corners of a tetrahedron. Cf. *Lewis atom.* **t. carbon.** T. models of the C atom, to illustrate the bonds; as: single bond, touching on corners; double bond, touching on edge; triple bond, touching on face.

tetrahexahedron. A crystal of the isometric system with 24 equal faces, 4 on each face of the cube.

tetrahydro- Prefix describing a compound with 4 H atoms in excess of the formula indicated by its suffix name. **t. benzene.** $C_6H_{10} = 82.11$. $C_6H_6·H_4$. Colorless liquid, b.82. **t. benzoic acid.** See *benzoic acid.* **t. butene.** Tetramethylene. **t. furane.** Butylene oxide. **t. naphthalene.** Tetralin. **t. naphthol.** $C_6H_5·OH·(CH_2)_4 = 148.15$, m.69, soluble in water. **t. naphthylamine.** $C_{10}H_{11}·NH_2 = 147.2$. *alpha-* Aryl-. Colorless oil, b.277, soluble in alcohol. *beta-* Acyl-. Colorless liquid, b.251, soluble in alcohol. **t. phenol.** $C_6H_3·OH·H_4 = 98.11$, b.166, soluble in water. **t. quinoline.** $\overline{C_6H_4·NH·(CH_2)_3} = 133.1$. Hydrogenated quinoline. Colorless crystals or oily liquid, m.20, soluble in water. *iso-* $\overline{C_6H_4·CH_2·NH·(CH_2)_3}$. Yellow liquid b.232, soluble in water. **t. thiazoles.** Thiazolidines. **t. thiophene.** $\overline{CH_2·CH_2·CH_2·CH_2·S} = 88.12$. A liquid, b.121, immiscible with water; an odorant for hydrocarbon gases other than coal gas. **t. tubanol.** q.v.

tetrahydroform. Trimethylenimine.

tetrahydroxy- Prefix indicating 4 OH groups. **t. benzene.** (1:2:4:5) $C_6H_2(OH)_4 = 142.1$. Colorless leaflets, m.215, soluble in water. **t. benzoic acid.** $C_6H(OH)_4COOH = 186.1$, m.148. **t. stearic acid.** $C_{18}H_{36}O_6 = 348.4$. Sativic acid. A white purgative powder in strophanthus oil.

tetraiodo- Prefix indicating 4 I atoms. **t. ethylene.** $CI_2:CI_2 = 531.73$. Colorless crystals, m.187; an antiseptic. **t. phenolphthalein.** $C_{20}H_8I_4N_4Na = 834.63$. Bluish powder, soluble in water; a radiopaque medium. **t. pyrrole.** Iodol.

-tetraketone. Suffix indicating 4 =CO groups. Cf. *tetrone.*

tetrakis hexahedron. A form of the regular crystal system (4-faced cube).

Tetralin. $C_6H_4·C_4H_8 = 132.15$. Trademark for tetrahydronaphthalene. Colorless liquid, d.0.967, b.205, insoluble in water; a solvent and substitute for turpentine. Cf. *Dekalin.*

tetralite. Tetryl.
tetramethyl- Prefix indicating 4 Me groups. **t. ammonium.** $N(CH_3)_4X$. A group of organic compounds; as, $N(CH_3)_4Br$, **t.** bromide. **t. ammonium formate.** Forgenin. **t. ammonium hydroxide.** $NMe_4OH = 91.13$. Soluble solid, decomp. by heat. **t. benzene.** $C_6H_2Me_4 = 134.1$. *1,2,3,4-* Colorless liquid, d.0.882, b.204, insoluble in water; an isomer of prehenitol. *1,2,3,5-* Isodurene. *1,2,4,5-* Durene. *6,1,2,4-* Isodurene. **t. diaminobenzhydrol.** *Michler's hydrol.* **t. diaminobenzophenone.** See *Michler's ketone.* **t. diaminodiphenylmethane.** See *diphenylmethane.* **t. diaminotriphenylmethane.** Leucomalachite green. **t. lead*.** $PbMe_4 = 267.31$. Colorless liquid, d.1.995, b.110, insoluble in water. **t. oxamide.** $(CONMe)_2$. White crystals, m.80. **t. p-phenylenediamine.** Wurster's blue. **t. tin*.** $SnMe_4 = 178.79$. Colorless liquid, d.1.314, b.78, insoluble in water.
tetramethylene. (1) $CH_2 \cdot CH_2 \cdot CH_2 \cdot CH_2 = 56.06$.
Tetrahydrobutene. Cyclobutane, cyclotetramethylene. Derivatives include: amino-, $C_4H_7 \cdot NH_2$, b.81; hydroxy-, $C_4H_7 \cdot OH$, b.123; methyl-, $C_4H_7 \cdot Me$, b.39. (2) 1,4-Butylene. The radical $—CH_2 \cdot CH_2 \cdot CH_2 \cdot CH_2—$; as, in t. amine, $H(CH_2)_4NH_2$. (3) A compound containing 4 CH_2= radicals. **t. amine.** Aminobutane. **t. diguanidine.** Arcaine. **t. glycol.** 1,4-Butanediol. **t. imine.** Pyrrolidine. **t. oxide.** Butylene oxide. **t. sulfide.** Butylene sulfide.
tetramethyl ethylene ketone. Pinacone.
tetramethyl leucaniline. $(Me_2N \cdot C_6H_4)_2CH \cdot C_6H_4NH_2 = 345.25$. Lustrous crystals, m.151, soluble in alcohol; used in organic synthesis.
tetramethylmethane. $CMe_4 = 72.1$. *tert*-Pentane, 2,2-dimethylpropane. Colorless liquid, isomer of pentane.
tetramido- Prefix indicating 4 amino groups and 1 or more O atoms.
tetramine. An organic compound containing 4 amino nitrogens; as, hexamethylenetetramine, $(CH_2)_6(NH_4)$. Cf. *tetrammine, amines.*
tetramino- Prefix indicating 4 amino groups, $R(NH_3)_4$.
tetrammine. $M(NH_3)_4X_3$. M is a trivalent metal (as Co or Cr), and X a halogen. Cf. *tetramine, ammines.*
tetramolecular. Describing a reaction of the fourth order, in which 4 molecules undergo a change.
tetramorphism. Crystallizing in 4 different crystal systems; as, phosphorus.
tetrandrine. (1) $C_{19}H_{23}NO_3 = 313.19$. An alkaloid, m.217, from *Stephania tetrandra* (Menispermaceae). Cf. *codethyline.* (2) $C_{38}H_{42}O_6N_2 = 622.3$. An alkaloid from the Chinese drug hanfengchi.
tetrane. Butane.
tetranitrate. A compound containing 4 $—NO_3$ radicals; as, erythroltetranitrate.
tetranitro- Prefix indicating 4 $—NO_2$ radicals. **t. aniline.** $NH_2 \cdot C_6H(NO_2)_4 = 273 \cdot 06$. TNA. A high explosive, m.170, explodes 237. **t. anthraquinone.** Aloetic acid. **t. chrysazin.** Chrysammic acid. **t. diphenyl.** $C_{12}H_6(NO_2)_4 = 334.1$. Colorless crystals, m.140, insoluble in water; used in organic synthesis. **t. diphenylmethane.** $C_{13}H_8(NO_2)_4 = 348.2$. Yellow prisms, m.172, insoluble in alcohol; used in organic synthesis. **t. methane.** $C(NO_2)_4 = 196.1$. Tetan. Colorless

liquid, d.1.650, m.13, b.126 (decomp.), insoluble in water, soluble in alcohol; an explosive, and color reagent for unsaturation in organic compounds. **t. methylaniline.** Tetryl. **t. naphthalene.** $C_{10}H_4(NO_2)_4 = 308.12$. *1,3,5,8-* Yellow tetragons, m.194, soluble in water. *1,3,6,8-* Long needles, m.203 (explodes), insoluble in water. *1,4,5,8-* or α- Yellow rhombs, m.257 (explodes), slightly soluble in water. **t. phenol.** $C_6H(OH)(NO_2)_4 = 274.1$. 1-Hydroxy-2,3,4,6-tetranitrobenzene. Yellow needles, m.130 (explodes), soluble in water. **t. phenolsulfonphthalein.** An indicator (acids—yellow, alkalies—magenta).
tetranitrol. Erythrol tetranitrate.
tetranthera. The bark of *Tetranthera citrata*, (Lauraceae).
tetraphenyl. Describing a compound containing 4 phenyl groups $(—C_6H_5)_4$. **t. ethane.** $\alpha,\alpha,\beta,\beta$-$CHPh_2 \cdot CHPh_2 = 334.3$. Colorless needles, m.209, insoluble in water. **t. ethylene.** $Ph_2C:CPh_2 = 332.2$. Colorless, monoclinic crystals, m.221, insoluble in water. **t. lead*.** $PbPh_4 = 515.38$. White needles, m.228, soluble in benzene. **t. methane.** $CPh_4 = 320.15$. Colorless crystals, m.285. **t. silicon.** $C_{24}H_{20}Si = 336.2$. Colorless crystals, m.228, insoluble in water. **t. succinic acid.** $Ph_2C(COOH) \cdot C(COOH)Ph_2 = 422.2$. Tetraphenylethanedicarboxylic acid. Colorless crystals, m.261. **t. tin*.** $SnPh_4 = 426.86$. Tetragonal crystals, m.226, insoluble in water. **t. urea.** $Ph_2N \cdot CO \cdot NPh_2 = 364.17$. Colorless crystals, m.183, insoluble in water.
tetraphenylene. Describing a compound containing 4 phenylene groups, $(=C_6H_4)_4$.
tetraphosphorus monoselenide. $P_4Se = 203.34$. Insoluble solid, m.166.
tetrasaccharide. A carbohydrate that can be hydrolyzed to 4 monosaccharides; as lupeose.
tetrasilane. $SiH_3 \cdot SiH_2 \cdot SiH_2 \cdot SiH_3 = 122.32$. Unstable liquid, b.90.
tetrathionate. $M_2S_4O_6$, soluble in water.
tetrathionic acid. $H_2S_4O_6 = 226.0$. A polythionic acid obtained by the action of iodine on thiosulfates. When heated, it decomposes into sulfuric acid, sulfur dioxide, and sulfur; exists only in dilute solutions.
tetratomic. Describing: (1) a molecule consisting of 4 atoms, as, NH_3; (2) a compound with 4 hydroxyl groups in its molecule; as, $M(OH)_4$.
tetravalent. Indicating a valency of 4. Cf. *quadrivalent.*
tetrazane*. A derivative of bihydrazine, q.v. See *tetrazone, tetrazo-.*
tetrazene*. Tetracene. Cf. *tetrazane.*
tetrazine. $C_2H_2N_4 = 82.2$. Heterocyclic compounds. **asymmetric-** 1,2,3,5- **symmetric-** 1,2,4,5- Red prisms, m.99, insoluble in water. **vicinal-** 1,2,3,4- Ozotetrazone. Known only in its derivatives.
tetrazo- Bisazo, bisdiazo. Prefix indicating 2 azo groups, $(—N:N—)_2$; as, bisdiazoamine (tetrazoamine).
tetrazoles. $CH_2N_4 = 70.06$. **1,2,3,4-** $N:CH \cdot NH \cdot N:N$. **2,1,3,4-** $N:N \cdot CH:N \cdot NH$, m.156 (sublimes), soluble in water. Derivatives: C- When the substituting radical is on the C atom. N- When the substituting

radical is on the N atom. **azo-** q.v. **benzo-** q.v. **bis-** q.v. **diazo-** q.v. **phenyl-** q.v. **pyrro-** q.v.

tetrazolium. A tetrazole derivative in which one nitrogen atom is pentavalent.

tetrazone. $R_2N \cdot N : N \cdot NR_2$. Obtained by the action of yellow mercuric oxide on asymmetric dialkyl hydrazines. Tetrazones are strong reducing agents in acid solution. Cf. vicinal *tetrazine*.

tetrazotic acid. $(CH_2)N_4$. Known only in derivatives. Cf. *tetrazole, tetrazyl*.

tetrazyl. The radical —HCN_4, from tetrazole. **t. hydrazine.** $CN_4 \cdot NH \cdot NH_2 = 99.08$. Yellow crystals, m.199.

tetrinic acid. $CH_2 \cdot CO \cdot CHMe \cdot CO \cdot O = 114.05$. α-Methyltetronic acid. Colorless crystals, m.189. Cf. *pentinic acid*.

tetrodonine. A curare-like poisonous principle, fugin, from the roe of Japanese fishes: genus *Tetrodon*.

tetrole. Furan.

tetrolic acid. $MeC \vdots C \cdot COOH = 84.1$. Butynoic acid*. Colorless leaflets, m.76, soluble in water. **t.a. series.** See *acetylene acids*.

tetronal. $Et_2C(SO_2Et)_2 = 256.3$. Diethylsulfone-diethylmethane, 3,3-bisethylsulfonylpentane*. Lustrous leaflets, m.85, soluble in water; a hypnotic and sedative, but may produce hematoporphyrin in urine.

-tetrone. Suffix indicating 4 =CO groups. Cf. *-tetraketone*.

tetronerythrin. Red pigment from the feathers of birds.

tetronic. A class of detergents made by condensing ethylene oxide and ethylene diamines. **t. acid.** $CH_2 \cdot CO \cdot CH_2 \cdot CO \cdot O = 100.03$. Colorless crystals, m.141, soluble in alcohol. *ethyl-* Pentinic acid. *methyl-* Tetrinic acid. *propyl-* Hexinic acid.

Tetrophan. Trade name for dihydrobenzacridine-carboxylic acid.

tetrose. $C_4H_8O_4$—. Monosaccharides containing 4 C atoms. Isomers: *d-* and *l-*erythrose, *d-* and *l-*threose.

tetroxide. A binary compound containing 4 O atoms.

tetryl. $(NO_2)_3C_6H_2NMe \cdot NO_2 = 287.08$. Tetranitromethylaniline, methylnitropicramide, pyrenite, tetralite, 2,4,6-trinitrophenylmethylnitramine. Yellow powder, m.130, explodes 187; an explosive in detonators, and primer for less sensitive explosives.

teucrin. $C_{21}H_{24}O_{11} = 452.2$. A glucoside from germander, *Teucrium fruticans* (Labiatae); used to treat tuberculosis.

teucrium. (1) Cat thyme, Syrian mastic. The dried herb of *Teucrium marum* (Labiatae); contains an essential oil, camphor, resin, and glucoside. A sterilized extract is used in ampoul medication. (2) *T. chamaedris*. Germander, q.v. (3) *T. scordium*. Water *germander*.

tex. An international unit expressing the linear density of fiber yarns and threads: 1 t. = 1 gm/100 meters. Cf. *denier*.

textile. (1) A natural or man-made fibrous material suitable to be spun and made into a yarn. World production (1967) 16.2 million tons (66% cotton and wool). Cf. *fibers*. (2) An assembly of interlacing yarns or fibers in the form of woven, knitted or other structures. Cf. *fabric*.

textryl. Generic name for sheet structures prepared by papermaking processes from synthetic fibers, which are held together at their points of contact by fibrillated synthetic thermoplastic polymers (fibrids). Textryls are intermediate in character between paper and nonwoven fabrics (as, felts).

texture. Coarse structure, e.g., the arrangement of fibers in textiles.

tfol. An argillaceous earth containing gelatinous silica (N. Africa); a substitute for soap. **t. ointment.** A mixture of tfol 20, tar 100 pts.; an antiseptic paste.

t function. See standardized *error*.

Th. Symbol for thorium. **Th** Ω. Hibernium. **ThEm.** Thoron. **ThX.** See *radioactive elements*.

thalazole. Phthalylsulfathiazole.

thalenite. $2Y_2O_3 \cdot 4SiO_2 \cdot H_2O$. A mineral.

Thales of Miletus. 640–546 B.C. Greek philosopher noted for his attempt to find a single material cause for all things: "Moisture is the principle of all life."

thalictrine. $C_{20}H_{27}O_4N = 345.2$. An alkaloid obtained from *Thalictrum macrocarpum*, or *T. foliolosum* (Ranunculaceae). Colorless needles, m.208, insoluble in water; a cardiac poison and laxative.

thalidomide. $C_{13}H_{10}N_2O_4 = 258.10$. α-Phthalimidoglutarimide. A hypnotic, withdrawn because it produces fetal malformations when taken by pregnant women.

thalistatyl. Phthalylsulfathiazole.

thalleoquine reaction. A characteristic color is obtained with alkaloids on adding, in succession, chloroform, bromine water, and sodium hydroxide.

thallic. Describing a compound containing trivalent thallium, Tl^{3+}. **t. chloride.** Thallium chloride (2).

thalline. $C_9H_6N(OMe) \cdot H_4 = 163.2$. Tetrahydro-*p*-quinanisol, tetrahydro-*p*-methoxyquinoline. Colorless rhombs, m.40, soluble in water. It has a coumarin-like odor, and gives a deep green color with ferric chloride. **t. salicylate.** $C_{10}H_{13}ON \cdot C_7H_6O_3 = 301.2$. Red crystals, soluble in alcohol; an antiseptic and antipeptic. **t. sulfate.** $(C_{10}H_{13}ON)_2 \cdot H_2SO_4 \cdot 2H_2O = 460.4$. Colorless crystals, m.110, soluble in water; an antiseptic and antipyretic. **t. tartrate.** $C_{10}H_{13}ON \cdot C_4H_6O_6 = 313.2$. White crystals, m.155, soluble in water; an antipeptic.

thallium. $Tl = 204.37$. A rare metal of the gallium-indium family, and element, at. no. 81; the lightest element having naturally radioactive isotopes. Bluish-white, d.11.862, m.303.5, b.1280, insoluble in water, soluble in nitric acid. Discovered (1861) by Crookes and named from its green spectral line (Greek, thallein = green). Widely distributed in nature and obtained from lead-chamber sludge by precipitation with zinc. T. forms 2 series of compounds, and has valencies of 1 (thallous) and 3 (thallic). Its salts are all cumulative poisons. Chemically it is analogous to the alkali metals, lead, and aluminum. Used as a catalyst in the manufacture of azobenzene, an antiknock compound, a pesticide, and in optical glass. Principal sources: lorandite (59–60% Tl), $TlAsS_2$; vrbaite (29–32% Tl), $TlAs_2S_5$. **t. acetate.** $TlC_2H_3O_2 = 263.4$. Thallous acetate. Colorless, hygroscopic crystals, m.110, soluble in water. **t. alcoholate.** $TlOC_2H_5 = 249.4$. A saturated alcoholic solution of thallous oxide, d.3.55; the heaviest liquid known, excepting mercury. **t. alkyls.** R_2TlX; as, T. diethyl chloride, Et_2TlCl. **t. alum.** $Tl_2SO_4 \cdot Al_2(SO_4)_3 \cdot 24H_2O = 1279.64$. Soluble white crystals. **t. amalgam.** An alloy: Tl 8.5, Hg 91.5%; used in thermometers for low temperatures ($-60°C$). **t. bromides.** (1) $TlBr = 284.3$. Thallous bromide. Colorless, regular crystals, m.450, insoluble in water. (2) $TlBr_3 = 444.1$. Thallic bromide. Yellow needles, decomp. by heat, soluble in water. **t. carbonate.** $Tl_2CO_3 = 468.8$. Thallous carbonate. Colorless, monoclinic crystals, d.7.11, m.272 (decomp.), soluble in water. **t. chlorides.** (1) $TlCl = 239.5$. Thallous chloride. Colorless cubes d.7.02, m.429, soluble in water: a getter, q.v., in tungsten lamps. (2) $TlCl_3H_2O = 328.5$. Thallic chloride. Thallium sesquichloride. Colorless, deliquescent crystals, decomp. 100, occurring anhydrous or with 1, 4, and 7·5 moles of water. **t. chloroplatinate.** $Tl_2PtCl_6 = 816.54$. Yellow, sparingly soluble solid, analogous to potassium chloroplatinate. **t. ethyl.** $TlEt_3 = 291.39$. An antiknock compound. **t. fluosilicate.** $Tl_2SiF_6 \cdot 2H_2O = 382.48$. Hexagonal plates, soluble in water. **t. formate.** $HCO_2Tl = 249.39$. Thallous formate. Colorless liquid, used for mineralogical solutions. **t. formate-malonate.** A double salt, m.60, miscible with water. Cf. *Clerici's solution.* **t. glass.** A high-refractive-index flint glass in which lead is replaced by thallium. **t. hydroxides.** (1) $TlOH = 221.4$ ($+H_2O$). Thallous hydroxide. Yellow powder, decomp. 100, soluble in water; contains $1H_2O$ and is a strong base. (2) $Tl(OH)_3 = 255.4$, or $TlO\cdot(OH) = 237.4$. Thallic hydroxide. Orange powder, decomp. 100, insoluble in water or alkalies, soluble in acids. **t. iodides.** (1) $TlI = 331.31$. Thallous iodide. Yellow crystals, d.7.072, m.432, insoluble in water. (2) $TlI_3 = 585.15$. Thallic iodide. Yellow powder, slowly decomp. in air, soluble in alcohol. **t. ions.** The Tl^+ (thallous) or Tl^{3+} (thallic) ion. **t. mercurous nitrate.** A saturated solution, d.5.3, used for the separation of minerals. **t. nitrates.** (1) $TlNO_3 = 266.2$. Thallous nitrate. Colorless rhombs, m.205, soluble in water; a reagent, indicator, and pyrotechnic for green fires. (2) $Tl(NO_3)_3 + 3H_2O = 444.4$. Thallic nitrate. Colorless, deliquescent crystals, decomp. 100. **t. oxides.** (1) $Tl_2O = 424.8$. Thallous oxide. Black powder, m.870, soluble in water, used in the manufacture of flint glass, and artificial gems. (2) $Tl_2O_3 = 456.8$. Thallic oxide. Brown hexagons, m.759, insoluble in water. (3) TlO or $Tl\cdot O\cdot Tl:O$ and (4) Tl_3O_5 also exist. **t. oxysulfide.** Tl_2SO. A light-sensitive substance used in photoelectric (thalofide) cells. **t. ozone paper.** A filter paper impregnated with t. hydroxide; colored brown by ozone. **t. peroxide.** T. oxide(2). **t. phosphate.** $Tl_3PO_4 = 708.07$. Thallous phosphate. Colorless needles, soluble in water. **t. sesquichloride.** Thallic chloride. **t. sulfates.** (1) $Tl_2SO_4 = 504.8$. Thallous sulfate. Colorless prisms, m.632 (decomp.), soluble in water; a reagent. (2) $Tl_2(SO_4)_3,7H_2O = 823.1$. Thallic sulfate. Colorless crystals, decomp. by heat, soluble in water; forms double salts: $MTl(SO_4)_2$, not isomorphous with $TlAl(SO_4)_2$. A rodenticide and insecticide. **t. sulfides.** (1) $Tl_2S = 440.8$. Thallous sulfide. Black tetragons, m.448

(decomp.), insoluble in water. (2) $Tl_2S_3 = 505.0$. Thallic sulfide. Black mass, decomp. by heat, insoluble in water. **t. trioxide.** T. oxide (2).

thallochlor. The green coloring material of Iceland moss. Cf. *chlorophyll.*

thallofide cell. Thalofide cell.

thallophytes. Cryptogamous plants:

Peridineae	Flagellates
Cyanophyceae	Blue-green algae
Chlorophyceae	Green algae
Rhodophyceae	Red algae
Phaeophycetes	Brown algae
Diatomae	Diatoms
Schizomyces	Bacteria
Phycomycetes	Algal fungi
Myxomycetes	Slime molds
Eumycetes	Fungi
Characeae	Stoneworts

thallous. Describing a compound of monovalent thallium. **t. compounds.** See *thallium.* **t. formate.** See *thallium formate.*

thal(l)ofide cell. A photoelectric cell in which thallium oxysulfide is the light-sensitive material; the ohmic resistance decreases on illumination.

thalviol. Thujone.

thanatol. $C_6H_4(OEt)OH = 138.08$. Guaethol, ajacol, pyrocatechin monoethyl ether, ethoxyhydroxybenzene. An oil, b.215, insoluble in water; used medicinally.

Thanite. Trademark for isobornyl thiocyanoacetate.

thanmasite. $CaSiO_3 \cdot CaCO_3 \cdot CaSO_4 \cdot 15H_2O$. A mineral from Paterson, N.J.

thanomin. Ethanolamine.

thapsic acid. A fatty acid, m.124, from *Thapsia garganica* (Umbelliferae), insoluble in water.

thawing. (1) The liquefaction of ice by heat. (2) The softening of frozen dynamite.

thea. The Latin (pharmaceutical) term for tea.

theaflavin, thearubigin. Compounds formed by the oxidation of polyphenols in tea during fermentation; largely responsible for the characteristic flavor.

theamin. $C_7H_8N_4O_4 \cdot NH \cdot C_2H_4OH$. Theophylline ethanolamine. White powder; a diuretic and vasodilator.

thebaine. $C_{19}H_{21}O_3N = 311.3$. Paramorphine, dimethylmorphine. An alkaloid from opium. Very poisonous, colorless prisms, m.193, slightly soluble in water; used similarly to strychnine. **methyl-** $C_{20}H_{23}O_3N = 325.3$. An alkaloid from opium. Colorless crystals, insoluble in water. **t. hydrochloride.** $(Tbn)HCl \cdot H_2O = 365.7$. Colorless rhombs, soluble in water; used in ampul medication. **t. tartrate.** $(Tbn)C_4H_6O_6 \cdot H_2O = 479.36$. White crystals, soluble in water.

thebaol. $C_{16}H_{13}O_3 = 253.1$. 3,6-Dimethoxy-4-hydroxyphenanthrene. A phenol from thebaine.

thebenedine. The ring structure

Theelin. Trademark for oestrone.
Theelol. Trademark for oestriol.

theetsee. A black varnish obtained by tapping the stems or trunks of *Melanorrhoea usitata* (Anacardiaceae), Malaya.

theine. Caffeine.

thelophoric acid. $C_{20}H_{12}O_9 = 396.1$. Red pigment from the fungus *Thelophora*, or *Hydnum ferrugineum*.

ThEm. Symbol for thoron.

Thénard, Louis Jacques. 1777–1857. French chemist, noted for the isolation of elementary boron. **T.'s blue.** $Co(AlO_2)_2$. The blue cobalt aluminate obtained by heating alum moistened with cobalt nitrate, in the blowpipe test.

thenardite. Na_2SO_4. A native sodium sulfate.

thenyl alcohol. Thiophene carbinol. **t. diamine hydrochloride.** $C_{14}H_{19}N_3S \cdot HCl = 297.86$. White crystals, m.170, soluble in water; an antihistaminic (U.S.P.).

theobroma. (1) Cocoa. (2) Plants (Sterculiaceae) that yield cacao. **oil of-** Cocoa butter.

theobromine. $C_7H_8O_2N_4 = 180.1$. Cacaine, 3,7-dimethylxanthine, 3,7-dimethyl-2,6-dioxypurine. An alkaloid from the leaves and seeds of *Theobroma* species; an isomer of theophylline and paraxanthine. Microcrystals, m.337, soluble in water; a diuretic and nerve stimulant. **iodo-** T. sodium iodide. **methyl-** Caffeine. **uro-** Paraxanthine. **t. acetyl salicylate.** $(TBr)C_9H_8O_4 = 360.16$. White crystals, insoluble in water. **t. barium sodium salicylate.** Barutine. White powder. **t. hydrochloride.** $(Tbr)HCl = 215.6$. White crystals, soluble in water; a nerve stimulant. **t. lithium.** $C_7H_7LiO_2N_4 = 186.10$. Theobromose. Uropherin. Colorless needles, soluble in water. **t. lithium benzoate.** $C_7H_7LiO_2N_4 \cdot LiC_7H_5O_2 = 314.14$. Uropherin-B. White powder, soluble in water; used medicinally. **t. lithium salicylate.** $C_7H_7LiO_2N_4 \cdot LiC_7H_5O_3 = 330.14$. Uropherin-S. White powder, soluble in water. **t. salicylate.** $(Tbr)C_7H_6O_3 = 318.15$. White needles, soluble in water. **t. sodium acetate.** $C_7H_7NaO_2N_4 \cdot NaC_2H_3O_2 = 284.12$. Theonacet, aguirin. Hygroscopic, white powder; used medicinally. **t. sodium benzoate.** $C_7H_7NaO_2N_4 \cdot NaC_7H_5O_2 = 346.14$. White crystals, soluble in water. **t. sodium citrate.** $C_7H_7NaO_2N_4 \cdot Na_3C_6H_5O_7 = 460.40$. Urocitral. White powder, soluble in water. **t. sodium formate.** $C_7H_7NaO_2N_4 \cdot NaCHO_2 \cdot H_2O = 288.12$. Theophorin. White powder, soluble in water; used as a diuretic. **t. sodium iodide.** $C_7H_7NaO_2N_4 \cdot NaI = 352.02$. Eustenin, iodotheobromine, sodium iodotheobromate. White, hygroscopic powder, soluble in water.

theobromose. Theobrominelithium.

Theocine. A brand of synthetic theophylline.

Theoform. Trademark for theobromine sodium formate.

theogallin. $C_{14}H_{16}O_{10} \cdot 2H_2O(?)$. A polyphenol in unprocessed tea leaves.

theoline. $C_7H_{16} = 100.1$. An aromatic hydrocarbon from petroleum.

theonacete. Theobromine sodium acetate.

Theophorin. Trade name for theobromine sodium formate.

theophorine. Theobromine sodium formate.

theophylline. $C_7H_8O_2N_4 \cdot H_2O = 198.19$. 1,3-Dimethylxanthine, 1,3-dimethyl-2,6-dioxypurine. An isomer of theobromine; an alkaloid from tea leaves. Colorless needles, m.269, slightly soluble in water; a cardiac stimulant and diuretic (B.P.). **t. ethylenediamine.** Aminophylline. White crystals, soluble in water. **t. hydrate.** Used as for t. (B.P.). **t. sodium.** $C_7H_7NaO_2N_4 = 202.3$. Colorless crystals, soluble in water. **t. sodium formate.** $C_7H_7NaO_2N_4 \cdot NaCHO_2 \cdot H_2O = 288.12$. An isomer of theobromine sodium formate. White powder, soluble in water.

theorem. Theory.

theory. The reduction of data or facts to a principle, and the demonstration of their interrelations. **atomic-** See *atom*. **ionic-** See *ions, ionization*. **phlogiston-** See *phlogiston*. **quantum-** See *quanta, energy levels, orbits*. **side chain-** See *Ehrlich theory*. **valency-** See *valency*.

theotannin. A tannin prepared from freshly plucked green tea leaves.

therapeutic. Pertaining to the art of healing. **t. agent.** A remedy or substance used to alleviate disease, pain, or injury. **t. index.** The ratio: minimum fatal dose/minimum curative dose. **chemical-** The ratio: curative dose/tolerated dose.

therapeutics. The study of remedial measures.

therapy. A system of treatment, as: pharmacotherapy (drugs); specific chemotherapy (chemicals); immunotherapy (vaccines); organotherapy (glands); ray therapy (radiation), e.g., X rays, ultraviolet rays, infrared rays, radioactivity. Cf. *aerotherapy, atmotherapy, hydrotherapy, electrotherapy, radium therapy*.

therm. (1) A unit of heat: 1 t. = 100,000 BThU. (2) British Thermal Unit: 1 BThU = 252 gm-cal. (3) Large calorie. (4) Small calorie.

thermae. Natural warm springs.

thermal. Pertaining to heat or temperature. **t. analysis.** Analysis depending on a change in weight or condition due to heat. Cf. *thermometric*. **t. capacity.** The amount of heat necessary to change unit mass of a body 1°C = mass × specific heat. **t. conductivity.** The amount of heat that passes, in unit time, through a unit volume (1 cm^3) of a substance when the opposite faces of the cube differ by 1°C. The accepted unit of measurement is $(ft^2)(hr)(deg)/(BThU)(in.)$. Typical values, in $BThU/(hr)(ft^2)(°F)(in.$ thickness): glass, 8; stainless steel, 110; lead, 240; cast iron, 360; aluminum, 1440; copper, 2610. **t. constant.** The heat in calories evolved during a particular reaction. **t. death point.** The degree of temperature required to kill bacterial cultures in 10 minutes. **t. deformation.** Pyroelectricity. **t. energy.** Heat energy. **t. excitation.** The transition of an electron to an excited orbit, by an increase in temperature. The fraction Y of a gas which is excited at the absolute temperature T is log $Y/(1 - Y) = -5,048E$, where E is the excitation potential (Saha). **t. expansion.** The increase of volume due to heat; small for solids and liquids, large for gases. **t. intensity.** Temperature. **t. ionization.** The loss of an electron by an atom due to an increase in temperature. **t. radiations.** Heat radiations, q.v. **t. transmittance coefficient.** The number of BThU transmitted per hour through 1 ft^2 of insulator for 1°F difference in the temperature of the air on each side. **t. unit.** Therm.

thermel. Thermocouple.

thermic. Pertaining to heat.

thermifugin. $C_9H_8(CH_3N \cdot COONa)_3 = 404.1$. Sodium methyltrihydroxyquinoline carbonate. Yellow powder, soluble in water; an antipyretic.

thermil. The quantity of heat required to raise, by $1°C$, the temperature of a mass of 1 metric ton of a body having a specific heat equal to that of water at $15°C$, at the normal atmospheric pressure of 1.013 hectopieze (French usage).

thermin. $C_{10}H_{11}NH_2 \cdot HCl = 183.6$. Tetrahydro-$\beta$-naphthylamine hydrochloride. Rose crystals, m.237, soluble in water; a mydriatic.

thermionic effect. The loss of electrons from a heated body maintained at an electric potential; the basis of the thermionic valve.

thermions. The ions that carry current through a vacuum in a thermionic tube; positively charged atoms, or electrons.

thermistor. A sensory material or device which changes rapidly in electrical resistance with change in temperature.

Thermit. Trademark for a mixture of aluminum and ferric oxide (Fe_3O_4). If ignited by a primer (magnesium powder), it liberates heat and forms aluminum oxide and molten iron at about $3000°C$. **T. process.** Goldschmidt's process. Thermoreduction. (1) Obtaining a high temperature and molten iron by Thermit; used in welding steel, rails. (2) Obtaining metallic chromium or manganese by mixing their oxides with powdered aluminum and igniting the mixture with a primer.

thermo- Prefix (Greek) indicating heat.

thermobalance. A balance for weighing substances while they are being heated, e.g., during drying.

thermochemical standard. A substance of known heat of combustion used to standardize bomb calorimeters. Benzoic acid for this purpose is certificated by the National Bureau of Standards, Washington, D.C., and by the National Physical Laboratory, Teddington, England.

thermochemistry. The study of the relations of heat and chemical reactions. See *thermodynamics.*

thermochor. An expression of the relationship between the molecular volume and the temperature of a substance at the boiling point. Cf. *parachor.*

thermocouple. Thermopile, thermel, thermoelement, thermojunction. A device for measuring temperature by the production of a thermoelectric current at the junction of 2 different metallic wires embedded in porcelain. One wire is kept at constant low temperature, the other at the temperature to be measured. E.g.: copper-constantan, 25.54 mv (maximum 500°C); nickel-nickel chrome, 41.80 mv (maximum 1090°C). Cf. *pyrometer.*

thermocross. Thermocouple.

thermodin. $EtO \cdot C_6H_4 \cdot N(COMe)COOEt = 251.2$. Phenacetin urethane, acetyl-p-ethoxyphenylurethane. Colorless crystals, m.87, soluble in water; an antipyretic.

thermoduric. Describing organisms that resist the conditions used for milk pasteurization.

thermodynamic concentration. Activity. **t. potential.** Gibbs' function, thermopotential. "The differential coefficient of the energy with respect to the variable expressing the quantity of the substance." (Gibbs.)

thermodynamics. The study of the empirical relations between heat energy and other forms of energy. **first law of-** *Conservation of energy:* "Heat and work are equivalent." A definite quantity of heat gives a fixed amount of mechanical energy and vice versa. Since any change or transformation produced in a body is proportional to the *heat equivalent*, the change in energy content of a body depends only on the difference between the original and final states. The maximum net amount of work obtained from a given process, changing at constant temperature and pressure from a higher to a lower state, is the *free energy.* **second law of-** *Degradation of energy:* It is impossible, when unaided, to convey heat from one body to another at a higher temperature; therefore in all changes, the *entropy*, or amount of irreversible energy of the participating bodies, increases. **third law of-** Every substance has a finite positive entropy and, at absolute zero temperature, the entropy value is zero for pure crystalline substances. Cf. *entropy.*

thermoelectric. Pertaining to electricity produced by heat. **t. current.** An electric current produced from a thermocouple. **t. power.** The thermoelectromotive force produced at the junction of 2 metals by a temperature difference of 1°C.

thermoelectromotive force. Thermoelectric power.

thermoelement. (1) Thermocouple. (2) Thermopile.

thermogenesis. The spontaneous generation of heat by living bodies; e.g., by organisms in compost, or by germinating seedlings.

thermograph. A self-recording thermometer.

thermogravimetric analysis. Chemical analysis by measuring the weight changes of a system as a function of increasing temperature.

thermojunction. Thermocouple.

thermokalite. A mixture of trona, thenardite, thermonatrite, and sodium bicarbonate.

thermolabile. Decomposed or destroyed by heat.

thermoluminescence. Luminescence caused by a slight increase in the temperature of a body, without production of incandescence.

thermolysis. Dissociation or decomposition produced by heat.

thermomagnetic effect. A difference in magnetic properties caused by heat. See *Leduc effect, Nernst effect.*

thermometamorphism. A change in allotropic forms produced by heat.

thermometer. A device for determining temperature. (1) *Mechanical:* substance that expands and contracts with temperature changes. (2) *Electrical:* measures the change in or production of an electric current or resistance due to change of temperature; as, resistance thermometers. (3) *Optical:* evaluates the light of an incandescent body; as, optical pyrometer. **angle-** An L-shaped t. for insertion in the vertical side of a vessel. **armored-** A t. surrounded by a metal casing. **Beckmann-** See Beckmann. **kata-** q.v. **ultra-** Beckmann t.

t. conversion. (1) °C to °F: multiply the °C by 9, divide by 5, and add 32. (2) °F to °C: subtract 32 from the °F, multiply by 5, and divide by 9.

t. scales.

   (1) °C = degree centigrade or degree Celsius

$$t°C = \tfrac{9}{5}t + 32°F = \tfrac{4}{5}t°R = t + 273°A$$

   (2) °F = degree Fahrenheit

$$t°F = \tfrac{5}{9}(t - 32)°C = \tfrac{4}{9}(t - 32)°R$$

   (3) °R = degree Réaumur

$$t°R = \tfrac{5}{4}t°C = \tfrac{9}{4}t + 32°F = \tfrac{5}{4}t + 273°A$$

(4) °A = degree absolute
$t°A = t - 273°C$

(5) °K = degree Kelvin (practically the same as °A)

(6)°Ra = degree Rankine, absolute Fahrenheit (°F based on absolute zero) = $\frac{5}{9}$°K
$-459°F = 0°Ra$; $0°F = 459°Ra$; $212°F = 671°Ra$

thermometric titrimetry. Enthalpimetry. The use of temperature changes to indicate the end point of a volumetric reaction.

thermonatrite. $Na_2CO_3·H_2O$. A native carbonate.

thermoneutrality. The absence of a heat change when dilute solutions of neutral salts are mixed and no precipitate forms.

thermonuclear reaction. A reaction that proceeds at high temperatures, e.g., in a star, and transmutes elements by bombardment by particles, etc.

thermophilic. Describing organisms of optimum growth at temperature 60–80°C. Cf. *psychrophilic*.

thermophone. A device for converting a-c electricity into thermal (and some sound) waves, by supplying it to a platinum strip immersed in a true fluid.

thermophore. A device for retaining or holding heat.

thermopile. A thermoelement: soldered metal plates or bars arranged in series so as to produce a cumulative effect; on heating their junctions, an electric current results.

thermoplastic. Rendered soft and moldable by heat. Cf. *plastics*.

thermopotential. Thermodynamic potential.

thermoredress. The latent power of recovery from a strain applied to a solid, due to the action of heat.

thermoreduction. Thermit process.

thermoregulator. A device for mechanically regulating temperature by controlling the source of heat. See *thermostat*.

thermosetting. Rendered hard by heat; as, certain plastics, q.v.

thermostabile, thermostable. (1) Refractory, heat-resisting. (2) In biochemistry: not affected by temperatures above 55 or below 100°C.

thermostat. A device for regulating the heat of an apparatus automatically.

thermotaxy. (1) A form of orthotaxy, q.v., produced by heat. (2) The directional tendency of regular groupings in crystalline substances, due to heat.

thermotension. The subjection of a red-hot metal to high tensile stress during cooling.

thermothyrins. Temperature-regulating hormones of the thyroid: **t.**-*A*. $C_{20}H_{40}O(?)$, m.53. **t.**-*B*. $C_{26}H_{42}O(?)$, m.66.

thermotropic. Caloritropic. Stimulated by or responding to a change of temperature.

Thermovyl. Trade name for a polyvinyl chloride synthetic fiber.

thermsilid. An acid-resisting alloy: Fe 84, Si 16%.

theta. Greek letter θ, Θ. See under T.

thetine. Thiobetaine, sulfinate. Organic compounds derived from the heterocyclic compound,

$$CO \underset{CH_2}{\overset{O}{\diagdown}} S \underset{R}{\overset{R}{\diagup}}$$

e.g., dimethylthetine, where R is —CH_3.

theveresin. $C_{48}H_{70}O_{17} = 918.7$. White powder; a split product of thevetin.

thevetin. $C_{54}H_{48}O_{24} = 1100.5$. A crystalline glucoside from the seeds of yellow oleander, *Thevetia*

neriifolia (Apocynaceae), Central America. Colorless crystals, m.215, soluble in water. Cf. *theveresin*.

thiacetamide. Thioacetamide.

thiacetazone. $C_{10}H_{12}ON_4S = 236.33$. Amithiozone, myvizone. Yellow, bitter crystals, soluble in water; used to treat tuberculosis.

thiacetic. Thioacetic acid.

-thial*. Suffix for a thioaldehyde; as, ethanethial*, CH_3CHS.

thialdine. $C_6H_{13}NS_2 = 163.26$. Colorless crystals, m.43 (decomp.), soluble in water; heart stimulant.

thiambutosine. $C_{19}H_{25}ON_3S = 343.45$. White, bitter crystals, m.125, insoluble in water; used to treat leprosy (B.P.).

thiamide. R—C:S·(NH). **iso-** R—C:NH·(SH).

thiamin. Thiamine (obsolete).

thiamine. Vitamin B_1. **t. hydrochloride.** $C_{12}H_{17}ON_4S·HCl = 337.29$. White, hygroscopic needles with a yeasty odor and a salty nutty taste, m.247 (decomp.), soluble in water, insoluble in ether. a vitamin B complex (U.S.P.). **t. mononitrate.** $C_{12}H_{17}O_4N_5S = 327.37$. White crystals, soluble in water; used similarly to t. hydrochloride (U.S.P.).

thianthrene. $C_6H_4·(S_2)·C_6H_4 = 216.24$. Diphenylene disulfide, dibenzo-*p*-dithiin, m.159., insoluble in water.

thiazamide. Sulfathiazole.

thiazine. Sulfur-containing heterocyclic compounds. Cf. *benzothiazine, benzisothiazine, phenothiazine*. **t. dyes.** Aniline dyes derived from thiazines and containing the grouping S·R·N·R; as, in thionine, toluidine blue.

thiazole. $C_3H_3NS = 85.1$. Metathiazole, thio-[o]-monazole, vitamin T. Colorless liquid, b.117, insoluble in alcohol. **t. purple.** $C_{19}H_{17}BrN_2S_2$. 1,1'-Dimethylthiocarbocyanine bromide. A carbocyanine dye photographic sensitizer.

thiazoles. Organic compounds derived from:

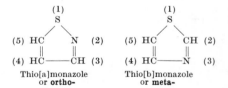

	(1)				(1)	
	S				S	
(5) HC		N (2)		(5) HC		CH (2)
(4) HC—CH (3)				(4) HC—N (3)		
Thio[a]monazole or **ortho-**				Thio[b]monazole or **meta-**		

The derivatives are named according to position; thus:

1—*s*—(sulfur)	1—*s*—(sulfur-)
2—*n*—(nitrogen)	2—*μ*—(median-)
3—*γ*—(gamma)	3—*n*—(nitrogen-)
4—*β*—(beta)	4—*β*—(beta-)
5—*α*—(alpha)	5—*α*—(alpha-)

dihydro- Thiazoline. **tetrahydro-** Thiazolidine.

thiazoline. $C_3H_5NS = 87.1$. Dihydrothiazoles. Organic compounds derived from the heterocyclic compound, $CH_2·CH_2·S·CH:N$; as:

μ-methylthiazoline, C_3H_4NSMe	b.145
μ-phenylthiazoline, C_3H_4NSPh	b.276

thiazyl. (1) The radical C_3H_2NS—, from thiazole. (2) The radical N_3S_4—.

thicken. (1) To evaporate to a high viscosity. (2) To expand the ends of a metal rod.

thickness. (1) The degree of viscosity or fluidity.

(2) The width of a plate. (3) The radius or gauge of a wire.

Thiele tube. A specially shaped test tube which, if heated at the base, ensures the circulation of the liquid in it, and thus, even distribution of heat. Used in melting-point determinations.

Thiele tube.

Thiel-Stoll solution. A saturated solution of lead perchlorate, d.2.6; used for determining specific gravity by the suspension method.

thienone. Thienyl ketone. **aceto-** Thienyl methyl ketone.

thienyl. The radical —C_4H_3S, from thiophen. **t. diphenylmethane.** $(C_4H_3S)CHPh_2 = 250.1$. Colorless crystals, m.63, soluble in alcohol. **t. ketone.** $(C_4H_3S)_2CO = 194.17$. Thienone, 2,2′-dithienyl-ketone. White needles, m.87, insoluble in water. **t. methyl ketone.** $(C_4H_3S)COMe = 126.1$. Colorless liquid, b.213. **t. phenyl ketone.** $(C_4H_3S)COPh = 188.1$. Colorless crystals, m.55, soluble in alcohol.

Thies process. Extraction of gold from crushed ores by adding chloride of lime and sulfuric acid.

Thigenol. Trademark for sodium sulfoöleate solution, an antiseptic used in dermatology and gynecology.

thimble. A porous cup of filter paper, fritted glass, or Alundum, used as a container for materials being extracted; e.g., in a Soxhlet apparatus.

thimerosal. Thiomersal.

thinner. A liquid used to dilute a paint, but not necessarily a solvent for it. Cf. *vehicle.*

thinolite. Tufa or native calcium carbonate, forming layers of interlaced crystals (Nevada and California).

thio- Prefix (Greek, "theion"—sulfur). It indicates the replacement of oxygen in an acid radical by sulfur having a negative valence of 2. Cf. *sulfo-.* **t. acid.** An organic compound in which divalent sulfur has replaced some or all of the oxygen atoms of the carboxyl group; as,

R·CO·SH........ Thiolic acids*
(carbothiolic acid*)
R·CS·OH........ Thionic acids*
(carbothionic acid*)
R·CS·SH .... Dithionic acids*
(carbodithioic acid*)

Thio acids differ from sulfo acids, in which sulfur is tetra- and hexavalent. See *polythionic acids, carbylic acid.*

thioacetal. Mercaptal.

thioacetaldehyde. $(CH_3·CHS)_3 = 180.31$. A solid, m.45, insoluble in water.

thioacetamide. $Me·C:S·NH_2 = 75.1$. Thiacetamide. Colorless leaflets, m.109, soluble in water. Its derivatives are thiamides.

thioacetanilide. $Me·CS·NHPh = 151.2$. A thiamide. Colorless needles, m.75 (decomp), insoluble in water; used in organic synthesis.

thioacetic acid. $MeCOSH = 76.1$. Thiacetic acid, thiolacetic acid. Colorless liquid, b.93, soluble in water.

thioacetin. $C_5H_{10}O_3S = 150.15$. Akcethin.

thioalcohol. Hydrosulfide.

thioaldehyde. Organic compounds containing the —CHS radical, with the suffix -thial*, q.v.

thioamides. $R·CS·NH_2$.

thioanhydride. An anhydride of a thioacid:

$$R\diagup^{CO}_{CO}\diagdown S \qquad R\diagup^{CS}_{CS}\diagdown O \qquad R\diagup^{CS}_{CS}\diagdown S$$

Thiolic anhydride   *Thionic* anhydride   *Dithionic* anhydride

thioanilide. Mercaptic 2-aminonaphthalide; a precipitation reagent for Cu, Ag, Hg, and Bi.

thioaniline. $(C_6H_4NH_2)_2S = 216.24$. E.g.: *p*-diamidodiphenyl sulfide, m.115; *o*-diamidodiphenyl sulfide, m.93.

thioantimonate. A salt of the unknown ortho-thioantimonic acid, H_3SbS_4 or $Sb_2S_5·3H_2S$. See *Schlippe's salt.*

thioantimonites. R_3SbS_3, $R_4Sb_2S_5$, and RSb_2. Salts known only in solution.

thioarsenate. M_3AsS_4.

thioarsenite. M_3AsS_3.

thiobacilli. Bacilli which oxidize many inorganic sulfur compounds to sulfuric acid. They require no organic food, and some tolerate 10% sulfuric acid. T. occur in soil and in deteriorating iron and concrete structures.

thiobacteria. Bacteria that reduce or oxidize sulfur compounds.

thiobenzaldehyde. $PhCHS = 122.14$. **alpha-** A solid, m.160 (decomp.), insoluble in water. **beta-** A solid, m.225.

thiobenzamide. $Ph·CS·NH_2 = 137.1$. Colorless crystals, m.116.

thiobenzanilide. $Ph·CS·NHPh = 213.2$. Colorless crystals, m.98.

thiobenzimidazolone. Phenylenethiourea.

thiobenzoic acid. $Ph·COSH·0.5H_2O = 147.15$. Colorless crystals, m.24, insoluble in water. Cf. *sulfobenzoic acid.*

thiobenzophenone. $Ph·CS·Ph = 198.14$. Colorless crystals, m.147.

thiobetaine. Thetine.

thiocacodylate. A salt of thiocacodylic acid containing the radical $Me_2AsOS—$.

thiocarbamic acid. $CS(NH_2)SH = 93.16$. Soluble in water. **t. ester.** $R_2N·CS·OR$. E.g., Diphenyl-thiocarbamic phenyl ester, $Ph_2N·CS·OPh$.

thiocarbamide. Thiourea.

thiocarbanilide. Sulfocarbanilide.

thiocarbimide. Isothiocyanic acid.

thiocarbin. A mercaptan prepared by boiling glycerol with sodium thiosulfate; a photographic emulsion ripening accelerator, and analytical reagent.

thiocarbonate. (1) M_2CS_3. A salt of trithiocarbonic acid. (2) A salt of a thiocarbonic acid.

thiocarbonic acids. (1) Thio acids derived from carbonic acid by substitution of oxygen atoms:

$CS(OH)_2$ .... Monothiocarbonic acid
(thioncarbonic acid)

$CO(SH)OH$ .... Carbonylmonothio acid
(thiolcarbonic acid)

$CO(SH)_2$ .... Dithiolcarbonic acid
(carbonyl-dithio acid)

$CS(SH)OH$ .... Dithiocarbonic acid
(see *xanthic* acid)

$CS(SH)_2$ .... Trithiocarbonic acid

(2) H_2CS_3 = 110.6. Insoluble liquid. Cf. *sulfocarbonic acid*. **ortho-** $C(SH)_4$. Known only in esters. **per-** H_2CS_4 = 142.2. Red oil, decomp. to carbon disulfide, hydrogen sulfide, and sulfur. **t. ester.** An ester of a thiocarbonic acid; as, diphenyl*thio*carbonic ester, $PhO \cdot CS \cdot OPh$.

thiocarbonyl. The radical $>CS$ (analogous to $>CO$).

thiocarbonyl chloride, thiocarburyl chloride. Thiophosgene.

thiochrome. A fluorescent quinochrome, q.v., which contains sulfur; an oxidation product of vitamin B_2, q.v.

thiochromene. 1,2-Benzothiopyran.

thiochromone. 1,4-Benzothiopyrone. **2,3-dihydro-** Thiochromanone. **3-hydroxy-** Thiochromonol. **2-phenyl-** Thioflavone. **2-phenyl-4-keto-** Thioflavone.

Thiocol. Trademark for a preparation containing orthopotassium guaiacol sulfonate. Used to treat disorders of the respiratory tract.

thiocoumarin. 1,2-Benzothiopyrone.

thiocresol. MeC_6H_4SH = 124.16. **ortho-** m.15. **meta-** A liquid. **para-** m.43. It stimulates cell proliferation and granulation of tissue.

thioctic acid. 6,8-Dithioöctanoic acid.

thiocumazone. C_6H_7ONS = 165.14. Benzodihydrothiometoxazine. Colorless crystals, m.142.

thiocumothiazone. $C_8H_7NS_2$ = 181.21. Benzodihydrothiothiazine. Colorless crystals, m.166.

thiocyanate*. A salt of thiocyanic acid, which contains the radical —SCN. The preferred term for thiocyanide, sulfocyanate, sulfocyanide, rhodanate, rhodanide.

thiocyanic acid. $HS \cdot C:N$ = 59.1. Sulfocyanic acid, rhodanic acid. Colorless liquid, decomp., 200, soluble in water. **t. ester.** R—SCN. An ester of thiocyanic acid, e.g., methyl thiocyanate, MeSCN.

thiocyanide. Thiocyanate.

thiocyano. The radical NCS—. **t. dyestuffs.** Dyestuffs produced from nuclear-substituted t. derivatives or aromatic amines and phenols; deeper in shade than the corresponding nonsubstituted compound.

thiocyanogen. NCS—SCN = 116.0. White rhombs, m. —2: unstable, particularly in light. **t. value.** An analog of the iodine number, q.v., in which the thiocyanate radical replaces iodine. Cf. *thiocyanometry*.

thiocyanometry. Rhodanometry. Volumetric analytical methods using thiocyanates; as in the determination of silver.

thiocyanuric acid. $C_3N_3S_3H_3$ = 177.25. Yellow needles, decomp. 200, soluble in alcohol.

thiodialkylamine. R_2NSNR_2; as, thiodiethylamine, $Et_2NSN \cdot Et_2$.

thiodiazolidine. $C_2H_6N_2S$ = 90.2. Tetrahydrothiodiazole. Heterocyclic compounds derived by saturating thiodiazoles.

thiodiazoline. $C_2H_4N_2S$ = 88.2. Dihydrothiodiazole. Heterocyclic compounds derived by partially saturating thiodiazoles.

thiodiglycolic anhydride. $O \cdot CO \cdot CH_2 \cdot S \cdot CH_2 \cdot CO$ = 132.10. Colorless crystals, m.103.

thiodiphenylamine. Phenothiazine.

thioether. R·S·R. Alkyl sulfide, sulfur ether. Obtained from alkyl halides and alkali sulfides, and forming colorless, volatile liquids that can be oxidized to sulfones, e.g., methyl sulfide, Me_2S. In mixed ethers the term thio* is used; thus, methylthioethane*, MeSEt.

thioform. Basic bismuth dithiosalicylate; a dental antiseptic.

thioformanilide. $Ph \cdot NH \cdot CSH$ = 137.14. Colorless crystals, m.137.

thiofuran. Thiophen.

thiogenic dyes. Sulfur dyes.

thioglycerol. $C_3H_8O_2S$ = 108.12. **1-** $CH_2SH \cdot CHOH \cdot CH_2OH$. Colorless liquid, decomp. by heat. **2-** $(CH_2OH)_2CHSH$. **1,2-** *di-* $C_3H_8OS_2$ = 124.19. Thick liquid, decomp. 130. *tri-* $C_3H_8S_3$ = 140.26. Heavy odorous liquid, d.1.391. All used to treat skin diseases.

thioglycolic acid. $HS \cdot CH_2COOH$ = 92.04. White crystals; a reagent for iron (1:10 million), and a setting agent in hair waving.

thiohydantoic. See *hydantoic*.

thiohydroquinone. $C_6H_4(SH)_2$ = 142.20, m.98.

thiohydroxy. Hydrosulfide, q.v. Cf. *thiol**.

thioindigo. $C_{16}H_8O_2S_2$ = 296.20. A permanent purple dye.

thioindigotic acid. Sulfindigotic acid.

thioketone. R_2CS; as 2-butanethione*, MeCSEt or $CH_3 \cdot CS \cdot CH_2 \cdot CH_3$. Suffix: -thione*.

Thiokol. Trademark for an oil-resistant synthetic rubberlike substance made from ethylene dichloride and sodium polysulfide.

Thiol. (1) Trade name for perchloromercaptan, used in the production of lubricant additives. Cf. *Thiovanic Acid*. (not cap): (2) The radical —SH. Cf. *hydrosulfide, thiols*. (3) Suffix, indicating the presence of a —SH group.

thiolacetic acid. (1) Thioacetic acid. (2) Thioglycolic acid (incorrect use).

thiolic acid. An organic compound containing the radical —CO·SH. **t. anhydride.** A compound of the type $R \cdot CO \cdot S \cdot CO \cdot R$.

thiols. R·SH. Mercaptans, hydrosulfides; as, methanethiol*, CH_3SH.

thiomalic acid. Mercaptosuccinic acid. A reagent for molybdenum (yellow complex).

thiomersal(ate). $C_9H_9O_2SHgNa$ = 404.81. Thimerosal. Sodium ethylmercurithiosalicylate. Creamy crystals, soluble in water; an antibiotic for skin sterilization (B.P.).

thion. Pertaining to divalent sulfur. Cf. *thione*. **t. dyes.** Sulfur dyes. **t. kudor.** A red-yellow solution of sulfur in boiling milk of lime; contains the calcium polysulfides, CaS_2 to CaS_7.

thionalid. Thioglycolic β-aminonaphthalide; a reagent.

thionamic acids. $R \cdot NH \cdot S : O \cdot OH$, in which sulfur replaces the carbon of the COOH group, e.g., ethylthionamic acid, $EtNH \cdot SOOH$. Cf. *carbamic acid*.

thionaphthene. $C_6H_4 \cdot S \cdot CH : CH = 134.1$. Benzothiophene, benzothiofuran. Colorless leaflets, m.31, soluble in water.

thionate. Thiosulfate. **di-** $M_2S_2O_6$. **penta-** $M_2S_5O_6$. **tetra-** $M_2S_4O_6$. **tri-** $M_2S_3O_6$.

-thione. The suffix for a thioketone; as, propanethione, $CH_3 \cdot CS \cdot CH_3$. Cf. *thion*.

thioneine. $C_9H_{16}N_3O_2S = 230.12$. Thionene, thiazine, ergothioneine, sympectothiene; in blood and certain plants. Cf. *histidine*.

thionic acid. (1) An organic compound containing the radical $-CS \cdot OH$. See *thio acids, polythionic acids*. (2) $H_2S_nO_6$, where n varies from 2 to 6. See *sulfuric acids*. **t. anhydride.** $R \cdot CS \cdot O \cdot CS$.

thionine. $C_{12}H_9N_3S = 227.2$. Lauth's violet, amidophenthiazine. Greenish-black powder of metallic luster, soluble in water with violet color; a nuclear stain in microscopy, and hydrogen-ion indicator. Cf. *methylene blue*.

thiono. The radical $=CS$. Cf. *thiocarbonyl, thione*.

thionyl. Sulfinyl. The group $=SO$, from sulfurous acid. Cf. *sulfoxide, thienyl*. **t. amines.** $R \cdot N : SO$. E.g.: thionylmethylamine, $MeN : SO$, b.58; thionylethylamine, $EtN : SO$, b.75. **t. aniline.** $PhN : SO = 139.1$. Colorless liquid, b.200; used in organic synthesis. **t. benzene.** $Ph_2SO = 202.1$. Diphenyl sulfoxide. Colorless crystals, m.70. **t. bromide.** $SOBr_2 = 207.91$. Red liquid, $b_{40mm}68$. **t. chloride.** $SOCl_2 = 118.9$. Colorless, pungent liquid, b.79; used in organic synthesis. **t. chlorobromide.** $SOClBr = 163.45$. Yellow liquid, b.115. **t. dialkylamine.** $R_2N \cdot SO \cdot NR_2$; as thionyldiethylamine, $(Et_2N)_2SO$, b.118. T. dialkyl amines are carbamides (ureas) with the C atom replaced by a tetravalent S atom. Cf. alkyl *sulfamide*. **t. fluoride.** $SOF_2 = 86.07$. Colorless gas, b.-32; forms with ammonia the compounds, $2SOF_2 \cdot 5NH_3$ and $2SOF_2 \cdot 7NH_3$. **t. hydrazine.** $R_2N \cdot N : SO$. thionyldiethylhydrazine, $Et_2N \cdot NSO$. **t. imide.** $SONH = 63.2$. Colorless liquid, m.-85, from the action of ammonia on t. chloride; polymerizes -70 to a yellow, transparent resin, soluble in alcohol, insoluble in water. **t. toluidines.** $Me \cdot C_6H_4N : S : - O = 153.1$. *ortho-* b.184. *meta-* b.220. *para-* m.7, b.224. Used in organic synthesis.

thio-oxamide. $(CSNH_2)_2 = 120.18$. A solid, decomp. by heat, soluble in alcohol.

thio-oxybiazoline. The heterocyclic compound, $O \cdot CS \cdot NH \cdot N : CH$, known only as its derivatives; as, n-naphthylamido-, $NH_2 - C_2ON_2S - C_{10}H_7$.

thio-oxydiphenylamine. Sulfaminol.

thioparamizone. Thiacetazone.

thiopental sodium. $C_{11}H_{17}O_2N_2NaS = 264.33$ Thiopentone sodium. Yellow crystals with characteristic odor, soluble in water. A barbiturate-type, general, short-acting anesthetic (U.S.P.), sometimes used with calcium carbonate (B.P.).

thiopentone sodium (B.P.). Thiopental sodium.

thiophanes. $C_nH_{2n}S$. Sulfurated hydrocarbons from crude petroleum.

thiophen(e). $CH : CH \cdot S \cdot CH : CH = 84.11$. Thiofuran. Colorless, benzene-like liquid, $d_{15}^\circ 1.071$, m.-37, b.84, insoluble in water; used in organic synthesis. Cf. *thienyl*. **amino-** Thiophenine. **benzo-** Thionaphthene. **methyl-** Thiotolene. **nitro-** q.v. **tetrahydro-** Butylene sulfide. **tetraphenyl-** Thionessal. **t. alcohol.** $C_4H_3S \cdot CH_2OH = 114.13$, b.207. **t. biniodide.** $C_4H_2I_2S = 336.0$. Thiophen diiodide. Yellow leaflets, m.40, insoluble in water; an iodoform substitute and antiseptic. **t. carboxylic acids.** Acids derived from thiophen. (1) $C_4H_3S \cdot COOH = 128.12$; 2-thiophencarboxylic acid, m.126. (2) $C_4H_2S(COOH)_2 = 172.2$; 2,4-thiophendicarboxylic acid, m.118. **t. sulfonate.** $C_4H_3S \cdot HSO_3 = 164.1$. Colorless crystals, insoluble in water. The sodium salt is an antiseptic. **t. tetrabromide.** $C_4Br_4S = 400.0$. Yellow crystals, m.112, insoluble in water, soluble in alcohol; an antiseptic.

thiophenine. $C_4H_3S \cdot NH_2 = 99.1$. Aminothiophen. Yellow liquid, insoluble in water.

thiophenol. $PhSH = 110.1$. Phenthiol, phenylmercaptan, phenylthiol*, phenyl sulfhydrate. Colorless liquid, b.168, insoluble in water; used in organic synthesis. **ethenylamino-** q.v.

thiophenyl. The radical, $PhS-$, from thiophenol. Cf. *phenoxy*. **t. acetone.** Colorless liquid, b.266, soluble in alcohol.

Thiophos. Trademark for *o,o*-diethyl-*o,p*-nitrophenol triophosphate; an insecticide.

thiophosgene. $CSCl_2 = 115.0$. Thiocarbonyl chloride, carbon thionyl chloride. Red liquid, b.73, insoluble in water.

thiophosphates. Compounds derived from phosphoric acids by substituting divalent sulfur for one or more oxygen atoms; as, monothiophosphates, M_3PO_3S.

thiophosphoric acid. $PS(OH)_3 = 114.12$. A solid, decomp. by water, soluble in alcohol. **t. anhydride.** Phosphorus pentasulfide.

thiophosphorous anhydride. Phosphorus trisulfide.

thiophosphoryl. The radical $PS \equiv$ derived from thiophosphoric acid. **t. bromide.** $PSBr_3 = 302.86$. Yellow solid, m.38, decomp. by water. **t. chloride.** $PSCl_3 = 169.5$. Colorless liquid, b.126, decomp. by water. **t. triamide.** $PS(NH_2)_3 = 111.18$. White solid, decomp. by heat or water.

thiophthalide. $C_6H_4 \cdot CO \cdot S \cdot CH_2 = 150.1$. Colorless crystals, m.60.

thiophthene. $C_6H_4S_2 = 140.10$. Bithiophene. Colorless liquid, b.225, insoluble in water, soluble in alcohol.

thiopyrophosphoryl bromide. $P_2S_3Br_4 = 477.94$. Yellow liquid, decomp. by water or heat.

thioresorcinol. $C_6H_4(SH)_2 = 142.19$. Yellow powder, m.27, insoluble in water; an antiseptic.

thioridazine hydrochloride. $C_{21}H_{26}N_2S_2 \cdot HCl = 407.00$. White, bitter crystals, m.161, soluble in water; a tranquilizer (B.P.).

Thiosa. Trade name for tetramethyl thiuram disulfide; a dip solution to control potato scurf.

thiosemicarbazide. $CH_5N_3S = 91.1$. $H_2N \cdot CSNH \cdot \cdot NH_2$. Colorless needles, m.181, soluble in water; used in organic synthesis, and as reagent for aldehydes and ketones.

thiosinamine. Allyl sulfocarbamide. **t. ethyl iodide.** $C_4H_8N_2S \cdot C_2H_5I = 272.1$. Tiodine. Colorless crystals, soluble in water; used in medicine.

thiostannates. M_2SnS_3. A salt of thiostannic acid.

thiostannic acid. $H_2SnS_3 = 216.9$. Yellow unstable crystals.

thiosulfate. $M_2S_2O_3$. A salt of thiosulfuric acid. Cf. *sodium t.*, *thionate.*

thiosulfuric acid. $H_2S_2O_3 = 114.0$. An unstable acid, decomp. readily to sulfur and sulfurous acid.

thiotepa. $P \cdot S \cdot [N(CH_2)_2]_3 = 189.22$. Highly poisonous, white flakes, soluble in water, m.55; an antineoplastic (U.S.P.).

thiotolene. $C_5H_6S = 98.13$. Methylthiophen. A homolog of thiophen. **α-** or **2-** m.13. **β-** or **3-** b.120.

thiouracil. $NH \cdot CS \cdot NH \cdot CO \cdot CH : CH = 128.25$. Used to treat hyperthyroidism.

thiouramil. $NH \cdot CO \cdot NH \cdot C \cdot SH : CH \cdot CO$.

thiourazole. $NH \cdot CO \cdot NH \cdot NH \cdot CS = 75.0$. Colorless crystals, m.177, soluble in alcohol.

thiourea. $NH_2 \cdot CS \cdot NH_2$ or $NH_2 \cdot CNH \cdot SH = 76.1$. Sulfourea, sulfocarbamide, thiocarbamide. Colorless prisms, m.180, slightly soluble in water or ether. Used in organic synthesis, and as reagent for bismuth. **allyl-** See *allyl sulfocarbamide.* **benzoyl-** q.v. **benzyl-** q.v. **diethyl-** q.v. **dimethyl-** q.v **diphenyl-** Sulfocarbanilide. **ethyl-** q.v. **glycol-** q.v. **phenyl-** q.v. **pseudo-** $NH_2 \cdot CNH \cdot SH$. Cf. pseudo-*urea.*

thioureido. The radical $NH_2 \cdot CS \cdot NH$—.

thiourethane. $NH_2 \cdot CO \cdot SEt = 105.14$, m.108 (sublimes), insoluble in water.

Thiovanic Acid. Trademark for vacuum-distilled thioglycolic acid (approximately 75 % with some dithioglycolic acid). Colorless liquid with faint sulfur odor, soluble in water; used as an analytical reagent, a depilatory, and in hair waving.

thioxanthene. $C_6H_4 \cdot S \cdot C_6H_4 \cdot CH_2 = 198.1$. Methylene diphenylene sulfide. Colorless crystals, m.128; used in organic synthesis.

thioxanthone. $C_6H_4 \cdot S \cdot C_6H_4 \cdot CO = 212.1$. Benzophenone sulfide. Colorless crystals, m.207.

thioxene. $C_4H_2Me_2S = 112.13$. Dimethylthiophen. **2,3-** b.136. **2,4-** b.138. **2,5-** b.135. **3,4-** b.145.

Thiozell. Trade name for a protein synthetic fiber.

thiozon. An allotrope of sulfur, q.v.

Thiram. TMT. TMTD. Trade name for tetramethyl thiuram disulfide, a seed-protectant fungicide.

third law of thermodynamics. See *thermodynamics, entropy.*

third order. See *reactions, tertiary.*

thiuram. (1) The radical $R_2N \cdot CS \cdot$—. (2) $(Me_2N \cdot CS \cdot S)_2 = 240.35$. Bis(dimethyl thiocarbamyl) disulfide. Yellow crystals, m.155. **ethyl-** $(Et_2 \cdot N \cdot CS \cdot S)_2 = 296.41$. Bis(diethyl thiocarbamyl) disulfide, tetraethyl thiuram disulfide. Yellow crystals, m.70. **t. disulfide.** $R_2N \cdot CS \cdot S \cdot S \cdot CS \cdot NR_2$. **t. monosulfide.** $R_2N \cdot CS \cdot S \cdot CS \cdot NR_2$. Cf. *xanthogenate.*

thiurea. Thiourea.

thiuret. $C_6H_7N_3S_2 = 185.2$. Colorless crystals, insoluble in water; an iodoform substitute.

thixotrope. A colloid whose properties are changed by mechanical treatment; as, clay.

thixotropic. Pertaining to thixotropy. **t. viscosity.** The anomalous viscosity of sols which are about to gel.

thixotropy. The property of certain gels of becoming fluid on agitation and coagulating again when at rest (as, a suspension of ferrous hydroxide); due to the mechanical destruction of the zones, q.v., of oriented molecules. **inverse-** Dilatancy.

thiylation. Introduction of S-containing groups into organic compounds.

Thomas, Sidney Gilchrist. 1850–1885. British technologist noted for his improvement of the Bessemer process. **T. meal.** Basic slag. **T. process.** The use of burned dolomite as a converter lining, which reacts with the phosphorus of pig iron. **T. slag.** The finely powdered phosphatic basic slag obtained in the T. process; a fertilizer.

Thompson, Benjamin. See *Rumford.*

Thompson process. Electric-arc welding with the metal to be welded as electrode.

Thomsen, Hans Peter Jürgen Julius. 1826–1909. Danish chemist, noted for his work in thermochemistry. **T. process.** The manufacture of soda and alumina by heating powdered cryolite with lime, leaching out the sodium aluminate, and decomposing it into aluminum hydroxide and sodium carbonate by means of carbon dioxide.

thomsenolite. $NaCaAlF_6 \cdot H_2O$. A native fluoride.

Thomson, Sir Joseph John. 1856–1940. British physicist, Nobel Prize winner (1906); noted for work in theoretical physics, discoverer of the electron. **T., Thomas.** 1773–1852. British chemist, noted for his textbooks. **T., William.** Lord Kelvin.

thomsonite. A gem variety of zeolite; a hydrous aluminum sodium calcium silicate.

thonzylamine hydrochloride. $C_{16}H_{22}ON_4 \cdot HCl = 322.85$. White crystals, m.174, soluble in water; an antihistaminic (U.S.P.).

thoria. Thorium oxide.

thorianite. A complex mineral; thorium oxide 70, uranium oxide 10–12 %, and rare earths.

thorin. Thoron(ol). APNS. 1-(*o*-Arsonophenylazo)-2-naphthol-3,6-disulfonic acid. A reagent for thorium (red precipitate in presence of dilute hydrochloric acid).

Thorite. (1) Trade name for a nonshrink patching mortar. (2) (not cap.) $ThSiO_4$. Freyalite. Orangite. A native thorium silicate, containing Ca, Fe, Mn, and V.

thorium. $Th = 232.04$. A radioactive metal and element, at. no. 90, in monazite and thorite; discovered (1828) by Berzelius. A gray, amorphous or crystalline, soft mass, readily burning in air to thorium oxide, d.11.3, m.1845; insoluble in water, alcohol, alkalies, or acids, soluble in aqua regia. Used to produce Th–Mg alloys and, as the nitrate, in gas mantles. Cf. *radioactive elements, isotopes.* **meso-** See *mesothorium.* **radio-** See *radiothorium.*

    t.-Ω. See *hibernium.* **t. anhydride.** T. oxide. **t. chloride.** $ThCl_4 = 374.2$. Colorless, deliquescent plates, m.820 (sublime), soluble in water, used

in incandescent burners. **t. dioxide.** T. oxide.
t. emanation. Thoron, Tn. A radioactive gas disintegration product of t. **t. hydroxide.** Th-$(OH)_4$ = 300.4. Colorless, gelatinous substance, insoluble in water. **t. lead.** ThD. See *radioactive elements.* **t. nitrate.** $Th(NO_3)_4·3H_2O$ = 534.2. White, hygroscopic crystals or granules, decomp. to t. oxide by heat; used in Welsbach mantles. **t. oxalate.** $Th(C_2O_4)_2$ = 408.12. White crystals, insoluble in water. *hexahydrate-* $Th(C_2O_4)_2·6H_2O$ = 516.21. White powder. **t. oxide.** ThO_2 = 264.1. Thoria, t. dioxide. White, infusible powder, insoluble in water; main constituent of the ash of incandescent gas mantles. A substitute for bismuth subnitrate in X-ray photography. **t. picrate.** $Th(C_6H_2N_3O_7)_4·10H_2O$ = 1324.43. Yellow powder, highly explosive. **t. series.** See *radioactive elements.* **t. sulfate.** $Th(SO_4)_2·4H_2O$ = 496.2. Colorless crystals, slightly soluble in water. **t. x.** ThX. A radioactive substance produced from t. via mesothorium I and II, and radiothorium. See *radioactive series.*

thorn apple. Stramonium.

Thornel. Trade name for continuous filaments of graphite. See *whiskers.*

thorogummite. $UO_2·3ThO_23SiO_2·6H_2O$. A native silicate.

thoron. (1) Tn = 220. Thorium emanation, ThEm. An isotope of radon, and member of the thorium series. See *radioactive elements.* (2) Thorin.

thoronol. Thorin.

thorotrast. A colloidal preparation of thorium oxide.

thoroughwort. Eupatorium.

Thorpe, Jocelyn Field. 1872–1940. British chemist noted for organic synthesis; co-editor of *Thorpe's Dictionary of Applied Chemistry,* the original author of which was: **T., Thomas Edward.** 1845–1925. British chemist noted for atomic weight determinations and studies on gold.

thortveitite. A mineral, chiefly scandium silicate $(37–42\% \; Sc_2O_3)$.

Thoulet's solution. A concentrated solution of potassium and mercuric iodides in water, d.3.17; used to determine density by the suspension method.

thread. (1) A string, q.v. (2) A unit of worsted yarn measure, 36 inches.

threo- Describing isomers of the type (*a*), as distinct from erythro- (*b*).

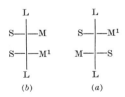

(*b*)   (*a*)

threonine. α-Amino-β-hydroxy-*n*-butyric acid. An amino acid essential for growth.

threose. $C_4H_8O_4$ = 120.1. A tetrose and isomer of erythrose, in *d* and *l* forms.

threshold. (German: Schwellenwert.) Liminal value. **t. treatment.** The process of stopping precipitation at the threshold of its occurrence. Thus certain phosphates, e.g., Graham salt, do not stop the formation of nuclei of calcium carbonate in water, but do inhibit growth of the nuclei. Used in water treatment.

thrombase. Thrombin.

thrombin. Thrombase, zymoplasm. The enzyme of the blood that transforms fibrinogen to fibrin, thus causing coagulation. T. from bovine blood is a local hemostatic (U.S.P.).

thrombocytes. Blood platelets.

thrombogen. Serozyme. A blood substance that gives the enzyme thrombase with thrombokinase (cytozyme).

thrombokinase. Thrombozyme. A blood substance that causes the formation of thrombase, and then the clotting of blood.

thromboplastin. An extract of cattle brain. Used, in physiological salt solutions, as a hemostatic.

thrombosis. The formation of clots in the blood vessels. Cf. *prothrombin.*

thrombozyme. Thrombokinase.

throwing power. The efficiency of an apparatus or electrolyte for the electrodeposition of metals. $(L - M)100/(L + M - 2)$; where L is the ratio of the distance between the anode and 2 half-cathodes in the liquid, and M is the ratio of the weights of metal deposited on the 2 half-cathodes.

THT. Tetrahydrothiophene. An oxidizing agent added to natural gas to render leaks apparent.

thuja. Thuya. Arbor vitae, white cedar, tree of life. The dried, young tops of *Thuja occidentalis* (Pinaceae), N. America and Europe. It contains an essential oil and tannin; a diuretic and sudorific. **t. oil.** Oil of white cedar. Sharp, camphor-like odor and taste, d.0.925, b.190, soluble in alcohol. It contains pinene, fenchene, thujone, and carvone.

thujene. $Me·C_6H_6·CHMe_2$ = 136.2. Tanacetene. A terpene obtained from thuja oil. **hydroxy-** Thujol.

thujetic acid. $C_{28}H_{22}O_{13}$ = 566.2. Obtained by heating thujin with barium hydroxide.

thujetin. $C_{14}H_{14}O_8$ = 310.1. Colorless crystals formed by hydration of thujigenin.

thujic acid. $COOH·C_6H_4·C·MeCH_2$ = 168.01. Dehydroperillic acid. An optically inactive acid from the heartwood of Western red cedar, *Thuja plicata.*

thujigenin. $C_{14}H_{12}O_7$ = 292.1. A decomposition product of thujin. Cf. *thujetin.*

thujin. $C_{20}H_{22}O_{12}$ = 454.18. A glucoside and coloring matter of thuja. Yellow crystals, insoluble in water.

thujoid. The combined principles of thuja; used medicinally.

thujol. $C_{10}H_{16}O$ = 152.2. Absinthol. Hydroxy-thujene. An alcohol in thuja oil.

thujone. $C_{10}H_{16}O$ = 152.2. Thalviol, 6-ketosabinane, salviol, tanacetone. A dextrorotatory, colorless liquid, d.0.913, b.203, from the essential oil of *Thuja* and *Salvia* species, insoluble in water.

thujorhodin. Rhodoxanthin.

thujyl. The radical $C_{10}H_{17}$—, from sabinane.

thulite. Zoisite.

thulium. Tm (or Tu) = 168.93. A rare-earth metal and element, at. no. 69, valency 3. Discovered by Cleve (1879) and independently by Soret. **t. chloride.** $TmCl_3$ = 275.8. Colorless crystals, soluble in water. **t. oxalate.** $Tm_2(C_2O_4)_3·6H_2O$ = 710.89. Greenish white precipitate, soluble in alkaline oxalate solutions. **t. oxide.** $Tm_2O_3 =$ 386.8. White powder, insoluble in water.

thuringite. $4(AlFe)_2O_3 \cdot 7FeO \cdot 6SiO_2 \cdot 9H_2O$. An amorphous mineral.

thus. Olibanum.

thuva. Thuja.

thylakoid. The pigmented lamellar membrane structure of chloroplasts.

Thylox process. Removal of sulfur dioxide from coal gas in ammonium thioarsenate solution, which is then warmed and aerated to precipitate the sulfur, which is purified by distillation.

thymacetin. $C_6H_2MeC_3H_7(OEt)NHC_2H_3O$. Thymol phenacetin. White crystals, slightly soluble in water; a hypnotic and analgesic.

thymamine. $C_{22}H_{40}O_5N_6 = 468.2$. A protamine from the thymus gland.

thyme. Thymus. The dried tops of *Thymus vulgaris*, garden thyme (Labiatae); an aromatic carminative and flavoring. **t. camphor.** Thymol. **t. oil.** d.0.894–0.930, soluble in alcohol; many grades.

thymegol. See *egol*.

thymene. $C_{10}H_{16} = 136.2$. A terpene from thyme oil. Colorless, aromatic liquid, d.0.868, b.160, insoluble in water; an antiseptic. Cf. *thymine*.

thymidol. Methyl propyl phenyl menthol. A condensation product of thymol and menthol; an antiseptic mouthwash.

thymine. $NH \cdot CO \cdot NH \cdot CH : CMe \cdot CO = 126.06$. 5-Methyluracil. Colorless crystals, decomp. 335; a constituent of nucleic acids, used to treat pernicious anemia. Cf. *thymene*.

thyminic acid. Solurol.

thymiodol. Thymol iodide.

thymipin. A dialyzate of *Thymus vulgaris*, *Drosera rotundifolia*, and *Pinguicula alpine*. Used to treat whooping cough.

thymodin. Thymol iodide.

thymoform. $CH_2 : (C_6H_3Me_3CH_7O)_2 = 312.3$. A condensation product of thymol and formaldehyde. Yellow powder, insoluble in water; an antiseptic dusting powder.

thymohydroquinone. $C_{10}H_{14}O_2 = 166.16$, m.140, soluble in water.

thymol. $Me \cdot C_6H_3OH \cdot CHMe_2 = 150.2$. Thyme camphor　*p*-propyl-*m*-cresol,　3-hydroxy-*p*-cymene. Colorless crystals, m.50, slightly soluble in water; a reagent for indican, an antiseptic, and anthelmintic (B.P.). **acetyl-** q.v. **diiodo-** T. iodide. **hexahydro-** Menthol.

t. blue. $C_{27}H_{30}O_5S = 466.23$. T. sulfonphthalein. Black powder; a pH indicator, changing from pink (1.5) to yellow (2.8–8) to blue (9.6). *brom-* See *indicators*. **t. carbamate.** $C_{10}H_{13}OCO \cdot NH_2 =$ 193.2. T. urethane, thymotal, tyratol, thymolcarbamic ether. Colorless crystals, soluble in water, decomp. by hydroxides; an intestinal antiseptic. **t. iodide.** $(C_{10}H_{13}OI)_2 = 552.22$. Diiodothymol, aristol, annidalin, thymotol, iodohydromol, iodosol, thymiodol, thymodin. Brown powder, obtained by the action of alkaline iodine on t., insoluble in water; an iodoform substitute. **t. phenacetin.** Thymacetin. **t. phthalein.** A pH indicator changing at 9.8 from colorless (acid) to blue (basic). **t. salicylate.** Salithymol. **t. sul-**

phonphthalein. T. blue. **t. urethane.** T. carbamate.

thymoquinone. $C_{10}H_{12}O_2 = 164.15$. Colorless crystals, m.46, soluble in water.

thymotal. Thymol carbamate.

thymotic acid. $C_6H_2(Me)C_3H_7(OH)COOH = 194.27$. Colorless crystals, m.127 (sublime), soluble in alcohol. **t. alcohol.** Methyl isopropyl benzyl alcohol. **t. anhydride.** $C_{11}H_{12}O_2 = 176.15$. Colorless crystals, m.174.

thymotol. Thymol iodide.

thymovidin. A hormone from thymus.

thymus. (1) Thyme. (2) A lymph gland in the neck and chest of an infant or young animal, which disappears before maturity is reached. Cf. *thymamine*. **t. histon.** A protein from t., mol. wt. = 6,000, which lowers the pressure and coagulability of blood.

thymyl. The monovalent radical,

$$HC : CMe \cdot CH : CH \cdot C(i\text{-}Pr) : C—,$$

from thymol.

thynnin. A protamine (75% arginine) from the sperm of *Thymnus thynnus*, the Pacific Ocean tunny fish.

thyraden. A dried extract of the thyroid gland; used to treat rickets and cretinism.

thyratron. A gas-filled, hot-cathode, grid-controlled valve rectifier and self-amplifier.

thyresol. $C_{15}H_{23}OMe = 234.21$. Santalol methyl ester. Colorless liquid; a santalol substitute in urethritis.

thyristor. A rectifier consisting of a thin plate of pure silica containing added trace elements with attached lead cathode mounted on a copper anode; used to control electronic drives.

thyroglobulin. A pseudoglobulin containing thyroxine and diiodotyrosine; a thyroid hormone.

thyroid. Thyroideum siccum. Dried thyroid glands. Yellow powder, slightly soluble in water; an alterative and hormone (U.S.P., B.P.). **t. gland.** A large gland in front and on either side of the windpipe of man and animals; it produces thyroxine and other hormones, e.g., iodothyronines.

thyroidectin. The dried blood of animals from which the thyroid gland has been removed; used to treat goiter.

thyroidine. A crystalline, iodine-free substance from thyroid.

thyroiodine. Thyroxine.

thyro-oxindole. Thyroxine.

thyrotrophin. The active principle of the anterior lobe of the pituitary gland; it acts on the thyroid gland.

thyroxine. $C_{15}H_{11}O_4NI_4 = 776.8$. Thyro-oxyindol, iodothyroglobulin, thyroiodine; a derivative of tyrosine, and the natural or synthetic active hormone of the thyroid gland. Colorless needles, m.250, insoluble in water. Used to treat goiter, cretinism, and myxedema. **t. sodium** is used similarly to t. (B.P.).

Ti. Symbol for titanium.

tiemannite. HgSe. Native mercurous selenide.

tiferron. Disodium-1,2-dihydroxybenzene-3,5-disulfonate. Colorimetric reagent for ferric iron.

tigaldehyde. $MeCH : CMe \cdot CHO = 84.06$. Guaiol,

tiglic aldehyde, 2-methyl-2-butenal*. Colorless liquid, b.117.

tiglic. Pertaining to tiglium. **t. acid.** $C_5H_8O_2$ = 100.1. Methylcrotonic acid, cevadic acid, *2-methyl-2-butenoic acid**. An unsaturated, monobasic acid, which occurs in 2 isomeric forms in croton oil and chamomile oil.

$$\begin{array}{cc} \text{Me—C—H} & \text{H—C—Me} \\ \| & \| \\ \text{Me—C—COOH} & \text{Me—C—COOH} \\ \text{cis- or } tiglic\ acid & \text{trans- or } angelic\ acid,\ \text{q.v.} \end{array}$$

Colorless prisms, m.64, slightly soluble in water. An isomer of angelic acid, q.v. **t. aldehyde.** Tiglaldehyde

tiglium. Croton seeds. The dried seeds of the croton oil plant, *Croton tiglium* (Euphorbiaceae), E. Indies and Philippines. It contains croton oil, tiglic acid, and crotonol; a drastic purgative.

tikitiki. Darak.

til. Sesame.

tile ore. Cuprite.

tilia. Linden flowers, lime flowers. The dried flowers of *Tilia europea* (Tiliaceae), Europe. It contains an essential oil; an antispasmodic and tonic.

Tillman's reagent. *2,6*-Dichlorophenol indophenol; a quantitative reducing agent for ascorbic acid.

timbo. The bark of *Serjania curassavica* (Sapindaceae), Brazil. It contains an alkaloid; used locally as a fish poison.

timbonine. An alkaloid from timbo.

time. (1) The fourth dimension: a measure of duration of an object, phenomenon, or event. The standard unit is the second, i.e., 1/86,400 part

MAGNITUDES IN TIME

		Seconds
Sun diminishing one-half its mass	. . . .	1.5×10^{19}
Uranium, average life	6,300,000,000 yr	1.9×10^{17}
Earth age (He in rocks)	2,000,000,000 yr	6×10^{16}
Earth, quaternary period	1,500,000 yr	4.6×10^{13}
Dawn of history . . .	6,000 yr	1.9×10^{11}
Birth of Christ	1,969 yr	6.2×10^{10}
Oxygen discovered .	195 yr	6.2×10^9
Man, average life . .	42 yr	1.3×10^9
Earth period around sun	365.2 days	3.1×10^7
Sun rotation	24.6 days	2×10^6
Earth rotation	23 hr 56 m 4 sec	8.6×10^4
1 hr		3.6×10^3
Radium A, average life	4.5 min	270
Sound vibration . . .		4×10^{-3}
1 σ		1×10^{-3}
Oscillograph		1×10^{-6}
High-frequency cycle		1×10^{-7}
Thorium C′, average life		1×10^{-9}
Cosmic-ray oscillation		1×10^{-22}

of a mean solar day: 1 sec = 1,000 σ. Sensitive measurements of time are made with a tuning fork (registers 1/1,000–1/5,000 sec). Longer periods are measured in days, q.v., and years, q.v. See table. (2) The theoretical basis of time is the natural resonant frequency of the cesium atom, used to calibrate quartz clock standards to within 0.0001 sec/day ($\pm$1 in 10^9). (3) The relative hour of a day, which depends on geographical longitude and the position of the earth relative to the sun. Cf. *year*.

ephemeral- The definition of the second based on the motion of the moon, as distinct from *physical* or *universal* t., based on the atomic frequency standards; e.t. is 3.5 sec greater than u.t.

t.-lapse photography. The cinephotography of very slowly moving or developing processes or objects (as bacteria), and subsequent projection at a higher speed.

tin. Sn = 118.69. Stannum. A metal and element, at. no. 50. Silver-white, rhombic or tetragonal metal, d.7.29, m.232, b.2270, insoluble in water, decomp. in dilute acids or concentrated alkalies. Crystalline forms:

$$\text{Sn}\beta \quad 18°C \quad \text{Sn}\alpha \quad 170°C \quad \text{Sn}\gamma$$

Gray tin,	$\rightleftharpoons$ Tetragonal,	$\rightleftharpoons$ Rhombic,
d.5.85,	d.7.29,	d.6.56,
brittle	malleable	brittle

T. has a valency of 2 or 4 and forms 2 series of compounds (see table). The t.–organic compounds are derived mainly from tetravalent t., and some are important insecticides. T. is used in alloys for t. foils, solders, utensils, type metal, dental alloys; and in the manufacture of t. salts. World production (1967) 211,000 tons. **alpha-** White t. **beta-** Gray t. **black-** A treated ore: 60–70% stannic oxide. **block-** Cassiterite. **butter of-** Stannic chloride. **cry of-** The sound heard on bending a stick of t. **flowers of-** Stannic oxide. **gray-** Beta t., β-tin. An enantiotropic form of white t. produced as a gray powder when white t. is cooled to −40°C; transition point 18°C. It is the cause of t. disease, q.v. **stream-** Tinstone, in an alluvial deposit. **tetraphenyl-** See *t. tetraphenyl*. **white-** Alpha-, ordinary-, α-tin. The usual form of malleable t.

Valency	Cations	Anions
2	Sn^{2+}, stannous	$SnO_2^=$, stannites
4	Sn^{4+}, stannic	$SnO_3^=$, stannates

t. acetate. Stannous acetate. **t. alkyls.** SnR_4. See *stannanes, t. tetraethyl, t. tetramethyl,* etc. **t. alloys.** See *aluminum, cobalt, lead, nickel, silver*; also *babbitt, britannia, pewter, rhine metal, solder*. **t. ammonium chloride.** Pink salt. **t. anhydride.** Stannic oxide. **t. ash.** Stannic oxide. **t. bath.** Molten t. in which metals are dip-coated. **t. bichloride.** (1) Stannic chloride. (2) Na_2SnCl_6. Sodium stannic chloride. **t. bisulfide.** T. disulfide. **t. bronze.** Stannic sulfide. **t. chlorides.** (1) Stannous chloride. (2) Stannic chloride. **t. chloride solution.** A solution of 5 pts. stannous chloride in 1 pt. hydrochloric acid. Yellow, refractive liquid; a reagent. **t. chromate.** See *stannic* or *stannous chromate*. **t. citrate.** Stannous citrate.

t. dichloride. Stannous chloride. **t. diethyl*.** $Sn(C_2H_5)_2 = 176.8$. Stannous ethide. An oil, d.1.654, decomp. by heat, insoluble in water. **t. dioxide.** Stannic oxide. **t. disease.** Transformation into gray t. with resulting brittleness and loss of metallic luster. **t. disulfide.** Stannic sulfide. **t. foil.** A thin sheet of t. or t. alloy; a wrapper. **t. glass.** (1) A glass that contains t.; as, certain flint glasses. (2) Bismuth (obsolete). **t. glaze.** opaque glaze formed on pottery by t. salts. **t. hydroxide.** Stannic hydroxide. *triphenyl-* A fungicide used to combat blight of root crops. **t. iodide.** Stannic iodide. **t. minerals.** Chiefly:

Cassiterite	....	SnO_2
Stannite	....	Cu_3FeSnS_4
Teallite	....	$PbSnS_2$

t. monosulfide. Stannous sulfide. **t. monoxide.** Stannous oxide. **t. mordant.** A t. salt used in dyeing; as, stannous chloride. **t. nickel.** The alloy: Sn 65, Ni 35%, hard, acid-resistant, with pink tinge; used to electroplate small precision machine parts. **t. oxalate.** Stannous oxalate. **t. oxide.** See *stannous oxide, stannic oxide.* **t. oxychloride.** Stannous chloride. **t. oxymuriate.** Commercial stannic chloride. **t. peroxide.** Stannic oxide. **t. pickling.** Immersing iron in dilute acid prior to a t. bath. **t. plate.** Steel sheet, covered with a film of t., usually about 1.5% t.; used for cans. World production (1967) 12 million tons. **t. protochloride.** Stannous chloride. **t. protoxide.** Stannous oxide. **t. pyrites.** Stannine. **t. salt.** Stannous chloride. **t. spar.** Cassiterite. **t. sponge.** Argentine. **t. stone.** Cassiterite. **t. sulfate.** Stannous sulfate. **t. tetraethyl*.** $Sn(C_2H_5)_4 = 234.9$. Stannic ethide. Colorless liquid, b.181, insoluble in water. **t. tetramethyl*.** $Sn(CH_3)_4 = 178.86$. Stannic methide. Colorless liquid, b.78, insoluble in water. **t. tetraphenyl*.** $Sn(C_6H_5)_4 = 426.86$. Stannic phenide. Colorless crystals, m.226, soluble in ether. **t. triethyl*.** $Sn_2(C_2H_5)_6 = 411.7$. Distannic ethide, Colorless liquid, b.270, insoluble in water. **t. triethyl hydroxide.** $Sn(C_2H_5)_3OH = 222.7$. Stannic ethyl hydroxide. Colorless crystals, m.66.

tincal. Borax.

tincture. A medicated liquid made by extraction of a drug; generally weaker than a fluid extract. **alcoholic-** A solution made by percolating 10 gm of a drug with 100 ml alcohol, or macerating in the case of a resinous drug. **aqueous-** An extract made with water.
  t. of iodine. A solution of iodine 7 and potassium iodide 5 gm, in 5 ml water, made up to 100 ml with alcohol; an antiseptic.

tinder. Flammable charred cloth or wood used for lighting furnaces.

tinevelly senna. India *senna.*

tinkal. Borax.

tinning. Coating with tin.

tinstone. Cassiterite.

tint. A pale shade of a color.

tintometer. A device for estimating the intensity of a colored solution by comparison with standard solutions, or colored glass slides; as, the Lovibond t.

tiodine. Thiosinamine ethyl iodide.

Tiolan. Trade name for a protein synthetic fiber.

tissue. In biology, a structure composed of cells and cell products.

titanate. A salt of titanic acid; as, M_2TiO_3—, metatitanate; M_4TiO_4—, orthotitanate.

titanellow. Yellow titanium oxide, used for making ivory shades in ceramics. Cf. *titan yellow.*

titania. Titanium dioxide.

titanic. Pertaining to tetravalent titanium. **t. acid.** (1) $H_2TiO_3 = 97.9$. *meta-* $TiO(OH)_2$. Colorless precipitate obtained by boiling titanium sulfate solution, insoluble in water, soluble in alkalies, to form salts. (2) $H_4TiO_4 = 115.9$. *ortho-*$Ti(OH)_4$. White precipitate on adding acids to metatitanates, soluble in excess of acid or alkali and forming with the latter, the titanyl radical. **t. anhydride.** Titanium oxide. **t. chloride.** Titanium tetrachloride. **t. hydroxide.** Titanic acid. **t. iron.** Ilmenite. **t. oxide.** Titanium dioxide.

titaniferous. Containing titanium. **t. iron ore.** Ilmenite.

titanite. Sphene.

titanium. Ti $= 47.90$. A metallic element of the carbon group, at. no. 22, discovered by Gregor (1789). Dark gray, amorphous metal, d.4.5, m.1800, insoluble in water, soluble in warm hydrochloric acid. Used (as ferrotitanium) as a cleaning and deoxidizing agent for molten steel; and in alloys with copper, bronze, and other metals. Cf. *konel.* It has a valency of 2, 3, and 4 and forms several ions:

Ti^{3+}	....	Titanous ion
Ti^{4+}	....	Titanic ion
$TiO_3^=$	....	*m*-Titanate ion
TiO_4^{4-}	....	*o*-Titanate ion
TiO^{2+}	....	Titanyl ion

t. bromide. $TiBr_4 = 367.8$. Orange crystals, m.39, decomp. by water. See *t. dichloride, t. trichloride, t. tetrachloride.* **t. dichloride.** $TiCl_2 = 119.0$. Titanous chloride. Black, hygroscopic powder, burns in air, decomp. by water. **t. dioxide.** $TiO_2 = 80.1$. Titania. Colorless to black tetragons or rhombs, d.3.70–4.26, m.1560, insoluble in water, soluble in alkalies or concentrated sulfuric acid. Used as an opaque white pigment for paint, inks, shoe polish, soap, plastics, rubber goods, ceramic glazes, and paper. World production (1962) 871,000 tons; U.S. 570,000, U.K. 217,000 tons. **t. hydroxide.** (1) $Ti(OH)_3 = 98.9$. Titanous hydroxide. Blue-black powder, insoluble in water. (2) $Ti(OH)_4 = 115.9$. Titanic hydroxide. White, insoluble solid. **t. iodide.** $TiI_4 = 555.8$. Titanic iodide. Red octahedra, m.150, soluble in water. **t. minerals.** T. is widely diffused in igneous and sedimentary rocks, chiefly as:

Ilmenite	....	$FeTiO_3$
Pseudobrookite	....	$Fe_4(TiO_4)_3$
Perofskite (perowskite)	....	$CaTiO_3$
Titanite	....	$CaTiSiO_5$
Rutile, brookite, anatase, octahedrite		TiO_2

t. nitrate. Titanyl nitrate. **t. nitride.** $Ti_2N_2 = 123.8$. Dark powder prepared from rutile and nitrogen in the electric furnace; used for dusting molds before casting steel. **t. oxalate.** $Ti_2(C_2H_4)_3 \cdot 10H_2O = 539.97$. Yellow prisms, soluble in water. **t. oxides.** See *t. sesquioxide, t. dioxide, t. trioxide.* **t. peroxide.** T. trioxide. **t. sesquioxide.** $Ti_2O_3 = 143.8$. Black powder, insoluble in water, **t. sulfates.** (1) $Ti(SO_4)_3 = 240.1$. Colorless crystals, soluble in water. (2) $Ti_2(SO_4)_3 = 384.0$. Green crystals, insoluble in water; an antiseptic. **t. tetrachloride.** $TiCl_4 = 189.9$. Titanic chloride. Colorless liquid, b.136, soluble in water; a mordant. **t. trichloride.** $TiCl_3 = 154.5$. Violet crystals, decomp. 440, soluble in water; a reducing agent. **t. trioxide.** $TiO_3 = $ Titanellow, q.v. **t. white.** White pigment: t. dioxide 26.5, barium sulfate 73.5%.

titanous. Pertaining to trivalent titanium. **t. chloride.** Titanium trichloride.

Titanox. Trademark for titanium-containing products, including pigments.

titan yellow. Clayton yellow, thiazol yellow. Yellow dye; used to detect caustic alkalies (red) and magnesium (red). Cf. *titanellow.*

titanyl. The radical $TiO=$. **t. nitrate.** $TiO(NO_3)_2 = 188.1$. Titanium nitrate. Colorless soluble crystals, in water. **t. sulfate.** $TiOSO_4 = 160.1$. White needles, soluble in acidic water; a mordant.

titer. (1) A standard test for oils and waxes in which the solidifying point (titer) of the fatty acids resulting from saponification is determined. (2) The number of milliliters per liter by which a normal solution differs from a standard. (3) The normality of a solution as determined by titration with a standard. (4) The number of grams of an element, radical, or compound in 1 ml of a standard solution.

titrant. A standard solution used for titration.

titrate. (1) To analyze by a volumetric method. (2) The solution being titrated.

titration. The volumetric determination of a constituent in a known volume of a solution by the slow addition of a standard reacting solution of known strength until the reaction is completed, as indicated by color change (indicators) or electrometrically. **chelatometric-** A complexometric t. involving the use of a chelating agent. **complexometric-** T. by means of a complexan and a metal indicator, q.v. **differential-** The t. of equal portions of test solution so that one always contains the same volume of titrating solution in excess of that in the other. At the end point the potential difference between the solutions in a maximum. **high-frequency-** Oscillometry. A method of following the chemical changes taking place in solution during t. from the changes in dielectric constant measured by an oscillator. It is sensitive, and does not involve contact between the test solution and the electrodes, e.g., the t. of beryllium compounds with sodium hydroxide.

    t. error. The ratio of the concentrations of active ions at the end point and initially. **t. level.** The order of concentration (normality) of a titrant.

titre. Titer.

Titrimeter. Trademark for a vacuum-tube device for potentiometric titrations, which is followed continuously and automatically on a microammeter. Cf. *potentiometer, sectrometer.*

titrol. Tea tree oil. The volatile oil of *Melaleuca alternifolia* (Myrtaceae), Australia; an antiseptic. Cf. *melasol.*

Tl. Symbol for thallium, at. no. 81.

Tm. Symbol for thulium, at. no. 69.

TMT, TMTD. Thiram.

Tn. Symbol for thoron, isotope of radon (at. no. 86).

tn. Abbreviation for ton.

TNA. Abbreviation for trinitroaniline.

TNB. Abbreviation for trinitrobenzene.

TNT. Abbreviation for trinitrotoluene. **alpha-** 2,4,6-Trinitrotoluene.

TNX. Abbreviation for trinitroxylene.

tobacco. Tabacum. The dried leaves of *Nicotiana tabacum* (Solanaceae). It contains nicotine, nornicotine, nicotianine, nicotelline, and other alkaloids; used for smoking, and as a relaxant and insecticide. **Indian-** Lobelia.

    t. stems. The ground waste products of t.; a fertilizer: nitrogen 1.2–3.3, potassium oxide 4–9%.

t. wax. A wax from the t. leaf and smoke, principally *n*-paraffinic hydrocarbons with *n*-hentricontane.

Tobias acid. 2-Naphthylamine-1-sulfonic acid; an intermediate.

Tobin Bronze. Trade name for the alloy: Cu 55, Zn 43, Sn 2%.

tocol. A precursor of vitamin E.

tocopherols. See *vitamins E.* α-, β-, γ-t. are now approved names.

toddy. (1) The fermented sap of the coconut and other palms. (2) A hot tea containing some spiritous liquor. **t. test.** See *test.*

Tofranil. Trademark for imipramine.

Toison solution. A stain for red blood corpuscles: 0.025 gm methyl violet (6B), 1.0 gm sodium chloride, 8.0 gm sodium sulfate, 30 ml glycerin, in 300 ml water.

tolamine. Chlorazene.

tolane. $C_6H_5C\!:\!CC_6H_5 = 178.2$. Bibenzyl, diphenylacetylene. Colorless leaflets, m.60, insoluble in water. **t. sulfide.** $C_6H_5 \cdot C\!:\!C\!\cdot\!S\!\cdot\!C_6H_5$. Tollalyl sulfide. Colorless crystals, m.174.

tolazoline hydrochloride. $C_{10}H_{12}N_2 \cdot HCl = 196.69$. Priscol. White crystals, m.173, soluble in water; a sympatholytic and vasodilator (U.S.P., B.P.).

tolbutamide. $C_{12}H_{18}O_3N_2S = 270.34$. *N*-Butyl-*N'*-toluene-4-sulfonylurea. White crystals, m.136, insoluble in water; an oral hypoglycemic (B.P.).

tolerance. (1) Capacity to withstand continued use of a drug. (2) The limit of error permitted in the graduation of measuring instruments, standardized products, or analytical evaluations.

tolidine. $NH_2MeC_6H_3 \cdot C_6H_3MeNH_2 = 212.22$. Dimethylbenzidine, 4,4'-diamino-3,3'-dimethyl diphenyl. **1,1',4,4'-** m.128; a reagent. **2,2',4,4'-** m.109. **3,3',4,4'-** Colorless scales, soluble in water. **t. sulfate.** $C_{14}H_{16}N_2 \cdot H_2SO_4 = 310.3$. White crystals, soluble in water.

tolite. Trinitrotoluene.

tollalyl sulfide. Tolane sulfide.

Tollens, Bernhard. 1841–1918. German agricultural chemist. **T. reagent.** An ammoniacal solution of silver oxide, used to test for aldehydes and ketones.

toloxy. Cresoxy. The radical MeC_6H_4O-, from cresol.

Tolserol. Trademark for mephensenin.

tolu. Balsam of Tolu. The resinous exudation of *Myroxylon balsamum* (Leguminosae) of tropical

America; a stimulant and stomachic (U.S.P., B.P.).
t. oil. Albahaca oil.

tolualdehyde. $C_8H_8O = 120.06$. Toluic aldehyde. **alpha-** $PhCH_2CHO$. Phenylacetaldehyde, b.194. **ortho-** $Me\cdot C_6H_4CHO$. Methylbenzaldehyde, b.196. **meta-** b.195. **para-** b.204.

toluamide. $C_8H_9ON = 135.1$. (1) $Me\cdot C_6H_4\cdot CO\cdot NH_2$. Carbamyltoluene. **ortho-** Colorless needles, m.139, soluble in water. **meta-** Colorless crystals, m.94, soluble in water. **para-** Colorless needles, m.158, soluble in water. (2) $C_6H_5CH_2CONH_2$. α-Phenylacetamide.

toluanilide. $PhNHCOCH_2Ph = 211.11$. α-Phenylacetanilide. Colorless crystals, m.117.

toluene. $C_6H_5\cdot CH_3 = 92.1$. Toluol, methylbenzene, phenylmethane. Colorless liquid, $d_{13}0.871$, m.−93.2, b.111, insoluble in water, soluble in alcohol or ether. Obtained from coal tar and used as a solvent, in organic synthesis, in the manufacture of benzoic acid derivatives, coal-tar products, and explosives. See *benzal, benzenyl, benzyl, benzylene, tolyl, tolylene*. **amino-** Toluidine. **aminohydroxy-** Cresidine. **bromo-** $MeC_6H_4Br = 171.1$. (1) *ortho-* Colorless liquid, b.182, soluble in alcohol. (2) *para-* Red crystals, soluble in alcohol. *alpha-* Benzyl bromide. **chloro-** $C_7H_7Cl = 126.6$. *alpha-* Benzyl chloride. *para-* Colorless liquid, b.161, soluble in alcohol. **cyano-** $CN\cdot C_6H_4Me = 117.1$. Toluic nitrile. (1) *ortho-* Brown liquid, b.203, soluble in alcohol. *alpha-* Benzyl cyanide. (2) *para-* Yellow crystals, m.28, soluble in alcohol. **diacetylamidoazo-** Dimazon. **dihydroketo-** Toluenone. **isopropyl-** Cymene. **nitro-** q.v. **nitroso-** $NO\cdot C_6H_4\cdot Me = 121.1$. *ortho-* m.72. *meta-* m.53. *para-* m.48. **oxy-** Cresol. **phenyl-** q.v. **trichloro-** Benzotrichloride. **trinitro-** q.v. **trinitro-*tert*-butyl-** Artificial musk.

t. sulfochloride. $MeC_6H_4SO_2Cl = 190.61$. A reagent for amines. **t. sulfonic acid.** $Me\cdot C_6H_4\cdot SO_2OH = 172.1$. Cf. *tosyl*. *ortho-* $2H_2O = 208.2$. Hygroscopic plates, decomp. 145. *meta-* $H_2O = 190.1$. An oil. *para-* $H_2O = 190.1$. Colorless leaflets, m.92, soluble in water. *hydroxy-* Cresolsulfonic acid. **t. sulfonic amide.** $Me\cdot C_6H_4\cdot SO_2NH_2 = 171.18$. *ortho-* m.155. *meta-* m.107. *para-* m.137. **t. sulfonyl chloride.** T. sulfochloride. *ortho-* m.10. *meta-* m.12. *para-* m.66.

toluenone. $CH:CMe\cdot CO\cdot CH_2\cdot CH:CH = 108.1$. A carbocyclic ketone.

toluenyl. The radical $C_6H_5CH=$. Cf. *toluylene, tolylene*.

toluic acid. $Me\cdot C_6H_4\cdot COOH = 136.10$. Methylbenzoic acid. *ortho-* Colorless needles, m.102, soluble in water. *meta-* Colorless prisms, m.110, slightly soluble in water. *para-* Colorless needles, m.176, soluble in water; used in organic synthesis. *alpha-* α-$Ph\cdot CH_2\cdot COOH$. Phenylacetic acid. Crystals, m.77. **o-carboxy-** Homophthalic acid. **dihydroxy-** α- Homogentisic acid. **α-hydroxy-α-** Mandelic acid. **methyl-** Xylic acid. **α-methyl-α-** Hydratropic acid.

t. aldehyde. α-Tolualdehyde. **t. anhydride.** $(Me\cdot C_6H_4CO)_2O = 254.2$. o-Toluic acid anhydride. Colorless crystals, m.36, soluble in water. **t. nitrile.** Cyano-*toluene*.

toluidide. A compound derived from the toluidines

by replacing an amino H atom by an acyl radical, e.g., $MeC_6H_4NHCOMe$, acetotoluidide.

toluidine. $Me\cdot C_6H_4\cdot NH_2 = 107.12$. Aminotoluene. *ortho-* Colorless liquid, b.198. *meta-* Colorless liquid, b.203. *para-* Colorless leaflets, m.43, slightly soluble in water; used in the synthesis of dyes and medicines. **acetyl-** Acetotoluide. **diethyl-** q.v. **methyl-** Xylidine. **nitro-** q.v. **thionyl-** q.v.

t. blue.

$$Me_2N\cdot C_6H_3 \underset{N}{\overset{S}{<\!\!\!>}} C_6H_2Me:NH\cdot HCl\cdot ZnCl_2.$$

A double salt of zinc chloride and dimethyltoluthionine. Green powder with blue luster, soluble in water; used to dye textiles. Cf. *methylene blue, thiazine dyes*. **t. hydrochloride.** $C_7H_9N\cdot HCl = 143.6$. Red crystals, soluble in water. **t. sulfate.** $C_7H_9N\cdot H_2SO_4 = 205.1$. Yellow crystals, soluble in water.

toluidino. Toluino. The radical $MeC_6H_4NH—$, from toluidine.

tolunitrile. Cyano*toluene*. **alpha-** Benzyl cyanide.

toluol. Commercial toluene.

toluoyl. *o*-Toluyl.

toluphenazine. $C_{13}H_{10}N_2 = 194.1$. Colorless crystals, m.117. **dimethyldiamino-** Neutral red.

tolupiaselenole. $C_7H_6N_2Se = 197.2$. Colorless crystals, m.73.

toluquinone. $MeC_6H_3:O_2 = 122.08$. m.67 (sublimes), insoluble in water. **methoxydihydroxy-** $CO\cdot CMe:COH\cdot CO\cdot COH:COMe = 184.0$. A pigment produced from glucose by the fungus *Penicillium spinulosum*.

toluresitannol. $C_{16}H_{14}O_3OCH_3OH$. A constituent of tolu balsam.

tolurhodin. A noncarotenoid pigment from rubra-type torulae.

tolurin. Vitamin B_1.

toluyl. The methylbenzoyl radical, $MeC_6H_4CO—$; 3 isomers: *ortho-, meta-, para-*. **alpha-** The radical $PhCH_2CO—$.

t. aldehyde. $MeC_6H_4CHO = 120.10$. *ortho-* A liquid, b.200. *meta-* A liquid, b.199. *para-* A liquid, b.204. **t. azo-β-naphthol.** Scarlet R.

toluylene. (1) Tolylene, cresylene; 6 isomers. The radical $CH_3C_6H_3=$, from toluene. (2) Stilbene. **t. blue.** An oxidation-reduction indicator, q.v. **t. diamine.** $CH_3C_6H_3(NH_2)_2 = 122.1$. *2,3-* Colorless scales, m.61, soluble in water. *2,4-* Asymmetric diaminotoluene. Colorless needles, m.99, soluble in water. *2,5-* m.64, b.273. *2,6-* m.104. **t. diamine indophenol.** An oxidation-reduction indicator. **t. hydrate.** Stilbene hydrate. **t. red.** Neutral red. **t. urea.** $CO(NH_2)_2:C_6H_3\cdot Me = 148.1$. Colorless crystals, m.290.

tolyantipyrine. Tolypyrine.

tolyl. The radical $CH_3\cdot C_6H_4—$, from benzene; 3 isomers: *ortho-, meta-, para-*. **alpha-** Benzyl. **t. acetic acid.** $CH_3\cdot C_6H_4\cdot CH_2COOH = 150.10$. *ortho-* Colorless needles, m.88, soluble in water. *para-* Colorless needles, m.91, soluble in water. **t. alcohol.** T. carbinol. **t. bromide.** Bromo*toluene*. **t. carbinol.** $CH_3\cdot C_6H_4\cdot CH_2OH = 122.1$. *ortho-* Colorless needles, m.34, soluble in water. *meta-* Colorless liquid, b.217, soluble in water. *para-* Colorless needles, m.59, soluble in water. **t.**

chloride. (1) Chloro*toluene*. (2) C_8H_9Cl. Xylyl chloride. **t.hydrazine.** $CH_3C_6H_4NHNH_2 = 122.08$. Hydrazomethylbenzene. *ortho-* Colorless leaflets, m.56, soluble in water. *meta-* b.245. *para-* Colorless tablets, m.65, soluble in water. **t. hydrochloride.** $C_7H_{10}N_2 \cdot HCl \cdot H_2O = 176.57$. *ortho-* Red crystals, soluble in water. *para-* Brown powder, soluble in water. **t. hydroxylamine.** $CH_3 \cdot C_6H_4 \cdot NHOH = 123.1$. *ortho-* Colorless leaflets, m.94, soluble in water. **t. mercuric chloride.** $C_7H_7HgCl = 327.12$. Rhombic crystals, m.233, insoluble in water. **t. mustard oil.** $CH_3 \cdot C_6H_4 \cdot NCS = 149.2$. Thiocyanomethylbenzene. *ortho-* Yellow liquid, b.238, insoluble in water. *para-* Colorless crystals, m.26, insoluble in water. **t. phenyl ketone.** Phenyl tolyl ketone.

tolylene. The radical $-C_6H_4 \cdot CH_2-$; 6 isomers. **alpha-** Benzal. Cf. *toluylene*. **t. diamine.** $C_7H_{10}N_2 = 122.09$. Isomeric compounds; as, diaminotoluene, $Me \cdot C_6H_3(NH_2)_2$.

tolypyrine. $MeC_6H_4N(NMe \cdot CMe:CH \cdot CO) = 202.2$. Tolyantipyrine, *p*-tolyldimethylpyrazole. Colorless crystals, m.136, soluble in water; an antipyretic. **t. salicylate.** Tolysal.

Tolysal. $CH_3 \cdot C_6H_4 \cdot N(CO \cdot CH:)NMe \cdot CMe = 202.2$. Trade name for tolypyrine salicylate. Colorless crystals, m.101, insoluble in water; an antipyretic.

tombak. A copper and zinc alloy.

ton. Unit of weight: 1 short ton = 2,000 lb = 907.18486 kg (U.S. usage). 1 long ton = 2,240 lb = 1,016.047 kg (U.K. and Commonwealth usage). 1 metric ton (tonne) = 0.9842 long tons = 1.1023 short tons = 1,000 kg (in use in Continental Europe and non-English-speaking world). **assay-** See *assay*. **deadweight-** The carrying capacity of a ship; about 66% of the gross t. **gross-** 100 cu ft of permanently enclosed space (shipping). **net-** Gross t. minus nonearning spaces on a ship. **refrigeration-** 288,000 BThU. The quantity of heat required to melt 2,000 lb of pure solid ice into water at 32°F.

tonalite. A group of quartz, orthoclase, and feldspathic rocks.

tonga. A mixture of the barks of *Rhaphidophora vitiensis* (Araceae) and *Premma taitensis* (Verbenaceae), from the Pacific Islands. It contains tongine and an essential oil; used to treat neuralgia. Cf. *tonka*.

tongine. An alkaloid from tonga.

tongs. A laboratory appliance for holding hot objects, such as crucibles, test tubes, or flasks. **remote-handling-** Tongs manipulated by a distant mechanism; used to handle radioactive substances.

tonic. An agent that increases or restores vigor; as, iron.

tonite. An explosive: wet guncotton pulp 54, barium nitrate 46%.

tonka. Tonka bean, snuff bean. The dried seeds of *Coumarona odorata* or *Dipteryx odorata* (Leguminosae), N. Brazil and Guiana; contains coumarin. A cardiac stimulant, ingredient of perfumery and flavorings, and source of coumarin. Cf. *tonga*.

tonnage. An evaluation of the capacity of ships. See deadweight *ton*.

tonne. Metric ton.

tonneau. A unit of volume (French wine industry): 1 t. = 200 gal (approx.).

tonquinol. $C_{11}H_{13}O_6N_3 = 283.13$. Colorless crystals, a musk substitute.

toot poison. Tutin.

topaz. $Al_2SiO_4F_2$. Colorless or varicolored crystals. The transparent, yellow variety is a precious stone. **false-** Quartz. **oriental-** Corundum.

topazolite. A yellow variety of iron garnet, q.v.

topochemical. Referring to: (1) localized reactions in the inner or outer fields of force of crystalline matter; as, the building of crystals on a limited surface by local supersaturation; (2) reactions occurring in zones.

topochemistry. The study of localized reactions; as in colloidal systems. Cf. *zone, protoplasm*.

topography. (1) The science of the accurate description or delineation of a locality or region. (2) In microscopy, the grouping, orientation, and situation of structures.

topomineralogy. See *mineralogy*.

tor(r). A unit of pressure used in German literature (named for Torricelli). 1 t. = 1 mm mercury = 133.332 newtons/m².

toramin. The ammonium salt of trichlorobutyl malonate; an opium substitute.

Toranomer. Trade name for a viscose synthetic fiber.

torbane. Torbanite.

torbanite. $C_{18}H_{30}O_{0.5}$. Black cannel coal, q.v., with a high ash, from Torbane Hill, Australia, d.1.3. Believed to be a high polymer of highly unsaturated organic esters and acids produced by the degradation of fatty matter from algoid deposits in lakes.

torbernite. $Cu(UO_2)_2P_2O_8 \cdot 12H_2O$. A green fluorescing, hydrated copper, uranium phosphate. Cf. *chalcophyllite*.

tori seed oil. Mustard-seed oil.

tormentil. Tormentilla, septfoil. The dried rhizome of *Potentilla tormentilla* (Rosaceae), Europe and N. Asia. It contains a red coloring matter, tormentil tannic acid, and quinovic acid; a tan and astringent. Cf. *five-finger glass*. **t. tannic acid.** $C_{26}H_{22}O_{11} = 510.2$. A constituent of tormentil; brown tanning powder.

Tornesite. Trade name for chlorinated rubber. White powder, turning brown at 150, and resistant to common solvents and reagents.

toroid. (1) A thick, solid ring. (2) Describing a burner in which some of the gases are sucked back into the center of the flame, thus giving a relatively small area of t. form having great stability and intensity. (3) A ring-shaped, hollow tube.

torque. The force of or resistance to a twisting motion.

torr. Tor.

Torricelli, Evangelista. 1608-1647. Italian assistant of Galilei, noted for construction of barometers, microscope, and telescope.

torsion. Producing a strain by twisting or rotating at right angles to the length.

torula. Mycoderma. A yeast (fungi imperfecti) having a chainlike cell formation, in milk and beer.

torulin. (1) Vitamin B_1. (2) A carotenoid pigment from rubra-type torulae.

torun metal. A bearing-metal alloy: Sn 90, Cu 10%.

tosate. Indicating the *p*-toluene sulfonate group.

tosyl. Abbreviation for the *p*-toluene sulfonyl radical.

totaquina. An antimalarial evolved by the Malaria Commission of the League of Nations; contains at least 75% crystallizable cinchona bark alkaloids (at least 15% quinine); much cheaper than quinine.

totaquine. A totaquina preparation having an antimalarial activity approximately equal to that of quinine.

touch. The sense of feeling. **hard-** A t. like that of crystals of inorganic salts. **slippery-** The touch produced by alkali hydroxides. **soft-** A t. like that of phthalic anhydride or beeswax. **unctuous-** A smooth, fatty feel due to substances such as soapstone or ointments.

touchstone. (1) Jasper. (2) A hard black stone, on which a streak is made with a gold alloy. It is treated with hydrochloric and nitric acids and water in succession, and the resultant streak compared with a standard gives an approximate value of the alloy. Cf. *streak test*.

Toulet's solution. A concentrated solution of mercury potassium iodide, d.3.17; used to separate minerals by flotation.

tourmaline. Brazilian sapphire, schorl, rubellite. Aluminum silicates in various colors containing boron and lithium. Cf. *silica minerals*. The red, blue, green, and colorless t. are gems. Tourmalines are mixtures of aluminum borate with alkali, magnesium, or iron silicates, and frequently contain chromium, manganese, calcium, and fluorine; doubly refractive and used in optical instruments (polariscopes). See *achroite, indicolite*. **artificial-** Herapathite.

tower. A tall structure used for absorption, scrubbing, cooling, or distilling.

towsagis. Mountain gum. A Russian plant source of rubber.

toxalbumin. A poisonous albumin, e.g., in cobra venom. Cf. *sozalbumin*.

toxamins. Antivitamins. Harmful substances of unknown chemical composition that exist in minute quantities in certain foods. Antonym: *vitamins*.

Toxaphene. $C_{10}H_{10}Cl_2(?)$. Trade name for a chlorinated camphene insecticide, m.65–90.

toxemia. Poisoning caused by substances produced by body cells or microorganisms.

toxic. Poisonous. **t. concentration.** Recommended maximum permissible concentration of gases and dusts in air, parts per million:

Ammonia	100
Arsine	0.05
Carbon dioxide	5,000
Carbon monoxide	100
Chlorine	1
Fluoride	2.5
Formaldehyde	5
Furfural	5
Hydrogen peroxide	1
Lead	0.2
Methylene chloride	500
Nickel carbonyl	0.001
Ozone	0.1
Petroleum	500
Phosphine	0.05
Pyrethrum	2
Pyridine	5
Stibine	0.1
Turpentine	100
Zinc oxide	15

t. dose. A dose that produces the characteristic symptoms of poisoning. **t. equivalent.** The smallest amount of a substance to kill an animal, divided by the weight of the animal.

toxicarol. (1) $C_{23}H_{22}O_7 = 410.19$. Yellow crystals, optically inactive, m.219, from the roots of *Tephrosia* (Cracca) *toxicaria*, S. America; a fish poison. (2) $C_{23}H_{22}O_6 = 394.19$. Unnamed. Green crystals, m.171, in derris, q.v., and cube, q.v. Cf. *rotenone*.

toxicity. The ratio between the smallest amount of a poison that will kill an animal and the weight of the animal (toxic equivalent). Cf. median lethal *dose* **t. unit.** See *LD 50*.

toxicodendron. The dried, poisonous leaves of *Rhus toxicodendron*, q.v.

toxicology. The study of the actions, detection, and treatment of poisons and poisonings.

toxigenes. Chemicals which, on injection into an animal, are not poisonous until modified by the vital activity of the cells; as, ptomaines. Cf. *toxins*.

toxin(e)s. Soluble substances produced during bacterial growth that stimulate the formation of antitoxins. Cf. *toxigenes*. **t. formation.** The production of poisonous substances from proteins of the living body by the action of bacteria: (1) *Phytotoxins* or *vegetable* t.; as, abrin. (2) *Zootoxins* or *animal* t.; as t. of the snake. (3) *Bacteriatoxins* or t. proper; as, t. produced by cholera. **t. immunity.** The production in the living body of antitoxins that counteract the effects of t.

toxisterol. A sterol produced by irradiation of calciferol.

toxoflavin. An antibiotic produced by *Bacterium cocovenenans*.

toxoid. A degenerated toxin deprived of its poisonous toxophore, and chemically modified to produce immunity, but not disease. See *Ehrlich*.

toxone. A toxin made less poisonous by partial combination with an antitoxin; a mixture of toxins with neutralized toxins (*toxoids*).

toxophore. The poisonous radical in a toxin molecule that reacts with the living protoplasm and forms a stable compound (*paraplasm*). Cf. *constellation*.

TPX. Trade name for a synthetic methylpentene polymer.

trabuk metal. A substitute for nickel silver: Sn 87.5, Ni 5.5, Sb 5.0, Bi 2.0%.

trace. A very small quantity: usually less than $5\,\gamma$ per gm.

tracer. A mixture of calcium resinate with magnesium, rare-earth nitrates, and glue; used in projectiles to make their path visible. **t. element.** Radioactive indicator.

tracheid. Fiber. An elongated cell from woody plants, containing various amounts of lignin, and characterized by bordered pits or discoid markings which vary in pattern according to origin.

trachoma. A chronic virus infection of the eye, frequently causing blindness; occurs principally in the Middle and Far East.

track. The path described by a particle, e.g., as, α or β rays, protons, electrons, ions, or molecules; made visible in a cloud chamber. Cf. *Wilson tracks*, *Brownian movement*.

tracking. Arc resistance. Creepage. Treeing. The path of an electric current when it short-circuits a faulty conductor. If sufficient heat is produced, the t. may be visible, e.g., with vulcanite.

tractive force. The power of pulling; as, of a magnet.

trademark. "A mark adopted in relation to any goods to distinguish in the course of trade any goods certified by any person in respect of origin, material, mode of manufacture, quality, accuracy, or other characteristics, from goods not so certified" (Trade Marks Act). Trademarks have capital initial letters.

tragacanth. Gum dragon. The gummy exudation from the stems of *Astragalus gummifer* and other Astragalae species (Leguminosae), Asia Minor. Contains bassorin, pectin, and starch; used as an emulsifier, suspending agent, and adhesive in pharmacy (U.S.P., B.P.), the textile industry, and by cigar makers. Cf. *bandoline.* **Indian-** Sterculia gum.

tragacanthin. The carbohydrate of tragacanth, a polysaccharide hydrolyzing to pentosans.

tragon. Locust kernel gum from carob beans.

train. A connected arrangement of several chemical instruments; as, combustion train.

trancyclopromine sulfate. $(C_9H_{11}N)_2 \cdot H_2SO_4 =$ 364.52. White crystals, soluble in water, an antidepressant (B.P.).

tranquilizer. A drug used to relieve mental stress, e.g., reserpine.

trans- Prefix (Latin) indicating across. **t. form.** An axially stereoisomeric form of a compound. Cf. *cis.*

```
    H—C—R              H—C—R
       ‖                  ‖
    R—C—H              H—C—R

    trans form          cis form
```

transaminase. An enzyme in yeasts and bacteria which catalyzes the transfer of the —NH_2 group of glutamic acid to the α position of oxalacetate.

transamination. The reversible transfer of amino groups by enzymes (transaminase) into ammodicarboxylic acids and keto acids.

transaudient. Permitting sound waves to pass.

transcalent. Permitting heat waves to pass.

transcrystallization. The formation of crystals with their principal axes perpendicular to the direction of heat flow.

transducer. Substitute: A device used to convert a pulsating electric potential into periodic vibrations at ultrasonic frequencies, e.g., a piezoelectric crystal. Cf. load *cell.*

transesterification. Direct conversion of an organic acid ester into another ester of the same acid; e.g., by treatment of a fat with the appropriate alcohol in presence of a catalyst.

transfer. Conveyance of matter or energy from one location to another. **t. number.** Transport number. **t. pipet.** A pipet with only one graduation mark, that measures one definite volume of liquid.

transference. Transfer. **t. cell.** Hittorf cell. An electrolytic cell with a detachable center portion; used to determine changes in concentration of an electrolyte during electrolysis. **t. numbers.** Transport numbers.

transformation. A change in form, structure, or internal arrangement of atoms. Cf. *nuclear reaction, radioelements.* **radioactive-** See *radioactivity.*

t. constant. The fraction of radioactive material that disintegrates each second. **t. series.** See *radioactive* disintegration. **t. theory.** Electromagnetic radiations have corpuscular aspects, e.g., Compton effect; and the motion of matter has undulatory aspects, e.g., electron scattering. Cf. *mass-energy cycle.*

transformer. A device for changing the nature of an electric current; as, *step-down* t. (higher to a lower potential), *step-up* t. (lower to a higher potential), change of phase, and conversion from alternating to direct, or the reverse. Cf. *rectifier.*

transistor. An amplifier or oscillator replacing the vacuum triode. It consists of large lapped crystals of germanium or silicon, and does not develop heat or noise. Cf. *semiconductor.* **optical-** A device using gallium arsenide to convert part of the energy of an incoming electric current into light, which is then absorbed and used to free electrons on the output side.

transition. A change from one state or form to another; as, melting. **t. elements.** The 3 trios of elements in the periodic table which connect the odd series 4, 6, and 8 with the following even series, viz.: (*A*) Fe, Co, Ni; (*B*) Ru, Rh, Pd; (*C*) Os, Ir, Pt. **t. interval.** The range of concentration of active ion in a titration over which the eye is able to perceive the change in appearance of the relevant indicator. **t. point, t. temperature.** The temperature at which an allotrope or polymorph is converted into another of its forms; e.g., the t. p. of rhombic into monoclinic sulfur is 95–96°.

transitron. An electrical oscillator used to produce alternating current of high and constant frequency. Cf. *transistor.*

translucent. Semitransparent. Cf. *radiolucent, transparent.*

transmissibility. Capacity to allow the passage of light, involving absorption of certain wavelengths. It may be qualitative (color screens) or quantitative (translucence).

transmutation. (1) The change of one element into another element; as, in radioactive disintegration. In the alchemical case t. was always a change from a base to a noble metal (gold). (2) Artificial. T. by bombardment with fast-moving protons, deuterons, or α particles. Cf. *radioelements, proton bombardment.*

transparency. The property of permitting the passage of radiations; e.g.:

Glass: transparent to visible light.

Rock salt: transparent to heat, visible and ultraviolet rays.

White fluorite: transparent to infrared, visible, and ultraviolet rays.

Paraffin: transparent to hertzian rays.

Thin metals: transparent to γ rays.

Cf. *opacity.*

transparent. Describing a substance which permits the passage of rays of the visible spectrum. Cf. *translucent.*

Transpex. Trade name for a transparent polymethyl methacrylate plastic.

transpiration. Exhalation of water vapor by a plant or animal through its surface tissue or skin. Cf. *respiration.*

transplutonium. See *plutonium.*

transport number. Transference number, Hittorf

number (n). The relative migration velocities of the anion and cation of an electrolyte. If these are u for the anion and v for the cation, then the corresponding transport numbers are: n(anion) $= v/(u + v)$; $(1 - n)$(cation) $= u/(u + v)$.

transposition. An atomic displacement within a molecule by which one atom changes place with another.

transudate. Liquid which has passed through a living tissue. Cf. *osmosis.*

transuranium elements. The elements of atomic weights, q.v., higher than that of uranium. They are believed to comprise about 98 % of the universe and to exist in the interior of stars. Cf. *hypon.* By bombardment of uranium, ekarhenium and ekaosmium, q.v., were synthesized (1935).

transvallin. $C_{36}H_{56}O_{14}(?)$. A glycoside from *Urginea burkei*, m.193; toxic to rats.

trapezohedron. A crystal of 6, 8, or 12 faces, having unequal intercepts on all the axes.

trass. A natural pozzolana, q.v.

Traube, Isidor. 1860–1943. German chemist. **T. stalagmometer.** A stalagmometer for determination of the surface tension of biochemical fluids. **T.'s rule.** The absorption of organic substances from aqueous solutions increases strongly and regularly in a homologous series with increasing number of C atoms.

traumatol. $CH_3C_6H_3I\cdot OH = 234.3$. Iodocresol, iodocresine. Purple powder; an iodoform substitute.

Trauzl test. A measure of the strength of an explosive from the increase in volume on firing a standard charge in a cavity in a lead cylinder, as compared with that from a standard explosive.

traversal. The path of a particle made visible by a track, q.v.

traversellite. Augite containing Al_2O_3.

travertine. $CaCO_3$. Calcareous sinter, onyx. A native calcium carbonate, usually banded similarly to marble. Cf. *tufa.*

Travis. Trade name for a viscose synthetic fiber.

treacle. Molasses.

Treadwell, Frederick P. 1857–1918. English chemist, noted for analytical methods.

treble. Triple.

treeing. Tracking.

trehalose. $C_{12}H_{22}O_{11} = 342.2$. A disaccharide from manna, yeast, mushrooms (trehala), and ergot. White crystals, m.210, $[\alpha]_D +197$. It hydrolyzes to glucose and is used to differentiate paratyphoid bacteria. Cf. *mycose.*

treibgas. Calorgas.

Trelon. Trade name for a polyamide synthetic fiber.

tremolite. $3MgO\cdot SiO_2\cdot CaSiO_3$. A white or green native amphibole.

trephone. Secretions from leucocytes which stimulate tissue repair in the healing of wounds.

trester. The residue after pressing grapes. **t. fermentation.** The fermentation of diluted grape residues.

tretamine. TEM. Generic name for 2,4,6-triethyleneimino-*s*-triazine, triethylenemelamine. A drug based on mustard gas, suggested for treating cancer.

Trevira. Trade name for a polyester synthetic fiber.

tri- Prefix (Latin) indicating three. See *ter-.*

triacetamide. $N\cdot(C_2H_3O)_3 = 143.11$. A solid, m.78, soluble in ether.

triacetate. A compound whose molecule contains 3 acetate radicals, $(CH_3COO\!-\!)_3$.

triacetin. $(MeCOO)_3C_3H_5 = 218.2$. Glyceryl triacetate. An oil from cod-liver oil, butter, and other fats, d.1.161, b.258, slightly soluble in water, soluble in alcohol or ether. Cf. *acetin.*

triacetone diamine. $(NH_2CMe_2\cdot CH_2)_2CO = 172.2$. 2,6-Diamino-2,6-dimethylheptanone-4. A reaction product of ammonia and acetone.

triacontane. $C_{30}H_{62} = 422.5$. A solid from the roots of *Oenanthe crocata* (Umbelliferae), m.66.

triad. (1) A group of 3 related elements or compounds; as, the triad Cl, Br, and I. (2) A trivalent atom or radical. (3) A crystal which shows 3 similar faces when rotated about its axis of symmetry through 360°.

triallylamine. $N(C_3H_5)_2 = 137.1$. A colorless oil.

triamido. Triamine.

triamine. $R(NH_2)_3$. Cf. tertiary amine.

triaminoazobenzene. $NH_2\cdot C_6H_4N:N\cdot C_6H_3(NH_2)_2 = 227.2$. Aniline brown, Manchester brown, vesuvin, Bismarck Brown. Brown powder, m.143, soluble in water. Used as a dye and bacteriological stain, and to determine the decolorizing power of charcoal.

triaminobenzene. $C_6H_3(NH_2)_3 = 123.1$. **1,2,3-** m.103, b.330. **1,2,4-** m. below 100, b.340. Very soluble in water, alcohol, or ether.

triamorph. A substance that crystallizes into 3 different types of crystals (trimorphous).

triamylamine. $N(C_5H_{11})_3 = 227.1$. White solid, used as an antioxidant and solvent, and for flotation.

triangle. A plane figure, bounded by 3 straight lines, pairs of which meet at 3 points. **reference-** See *diagram.*

triatomic. Describing: (1) a molecule consisting of 3 atoms; (2) an acid with 3 replaceable H atoms; (3) a base, alcohol, or phenol with 3 OH groups.

triazane. (1) Hydrazoamino. The radical —NH·NH·NH_2. (2) $NH_2\cdot NH\cdot NH_2$. Prozane. The H is replaceable by hydrocarbon radicals. Cf. *hydronitrogen.*

triazene. (1) The radical —NH·N:NR. (2) $NH_2\cdot N:NH$. Diazoamine. The H is replaceable by hydrocarbon radicals. Cf. *hydronitrogen.*

triazeno. The radical $NH_2N:N\!-$.

triazine. $C_3H_3N_3 = 81.03$. The heterocyclic compounds:

s(ymmetric)-   *a*(symmetric)-   *v*(icinal)-
(kyanidine)

t. triol. Cyanuric acid.

triazinyl. The radical $C_3H_2N_3\!-$, from triazine.

triazo. Azide. Trinitride. The group $N:N\cdot N\!-$. **t. benzene.** Phenyl azide.

triazole. $C_2H_3N_3 = 69.06$. Pyrrodiazole. *1,2,4-* Common t., pyrro-[*a,b''*]-diazole. Colorless needles, m.120, soluble in water. **benzo-** See *benzotriazole.* **diphenyl-** See *diphenyltriazole.*

triazolone. $CH:N\cdot CO\cdot(NH)_2 = 85.1$. Ketotriazole.

triazolyl. The radical $C_2H_2N_3\!-$, from triazole.

tribasic. Describing a molecule that has 3 replaceable H atoms, or produces 3 H ions in solution.

tribenzal. Indicating 3 benzal radicals, $Ph \cdot CH =$.
tribenzo-*p*-diazine. Naphthophenazine.
tribenzoylmethane. $(Ph \cdot CO)_3CH = 328.24$. Colorless crystals, m.225 (sublime), soluble in water.
tribenzyl. Indicating the presence of 3 benzyl radicals, $Ph \cdot CH_2-$. **t. amine.** $N(C_6H_5 \cdot CH_2)_3 = 287.28$, m.91, soluble in water. **t. ethyltin.** $EtSn(CH_2Ph)_3 = 420.90$. White crystals, m.31, soluble in organic solvents. **t. tin chloride.** $(PhCH_2)_3SnCl = 427.32$. White needles, m.142, insoluble in water. **t. tin hydroxide.** $(PhCH_2)_3 \cdot SnOH = 408.87$. Rhombic crystals, m.120, soluble in organic solvents.
tribenzylidene diamide. Hydrobenzamide.
tribo- Prefix (Greek) indicating friction or rubbing.
triboelectric series. Electrostatic series. A list of substances such that when any 2 are rubbed together, the higher and lower in the list acquire a positive and negative charge, respectively; e.g.: $(+)$ asbestos, rabbit fur, glass, nylon, wool, calcite, silk, cotton, paper, magnalium, wood, amber, slate, steel, ebonite, sulfur, Celluloid, rubber, polythene $(-)$.
tribology. The science of interacting surfaces in relative motion: in particular, lubrication.
triboluminescence. The light emission from substances, especially crystals, when crushed, rubbed, or mechanically pressed together. Cf. *luminescence*.
tribromide. A binary compound having 3 Br atoms in the molecule.
tribromo-, tribrom- Prefix indicating 3 Br atoms in a molecule. **t. acetaldehyde.** Bromal. **t. acetic acid.** $CBr_3COOH = 296.78$. Colorless leaflets, m.135, soluble in water; used in organic synthesis. **t. aniline.** $NH_2C_6H_2Br_3 = 329.83$. Aniline 2,4,6-tribromide. Small needles, m.119, insoluble in water; used medicinally to treat neuralgia. **t. benzene.** $C_6H_3Br_3 = 314.8$. *1,2,3-* m.87. *1,3,4-* m.44. *1,3,5-* or *sym-* Colorless needles, m.119, insoluble in water. **t. ethane.** $C_2H_3Br_3 = 266.77$. *1,1,2-* or **β-** $BrCH_2 \cdot CHBr_2$. A liquid, d.2.579, b.188. **t. ethanol.** $CBr_3 \cdot CH_2OH = 282.79$. Avertine. White, unstable crystals, m.80, soluble in water; a general anesthetic (U.S.P.). **t. ethylene.** $BrCH:CBr_2 = 264.76$, d.2.708, b.164. **t. hydrine.** Allyl tribromide. **t. methane.** Bromoform. **t. β-naphthol.** $C_{10}H_4Br_3OH = 380.9$. Gray crystals, soluble in alcohol; a disinfectant. **t. phenol.** $C_6H_3Br_3O = 330.8$ *2,4,6-*. Bromol. White needles, m.92 (sublimes), slightly soluble in water; a disinfectant and antiseptic. **t. phenol bismuth.** Xeroform. **t. phenyl salicylate.** Cordol. **t. resorcinol.** $C_6H(OH)_3Br_3 = 346.81$. Colorless needles, m.112, slightly soluble in water. **t. salol.** $C_6H_4 \cdot OHCOOC_6H_2Br_3 = 450.72$. Cordol, tribromophenyl salicylate. Colorless crystals, slightly soluble in water; an antiseptic.
tributylamine. $N \cdot (C_4H_9)_3 = 185.3$. Colorless liquid, d.0.778, b.216, insoluble in water. **iso-** $N(CH_2CH \cdot Me_2)_3$. Colorless liquid, d.0.766, b.191.
tributyrin. Butyrin.
tricalcium phosphate. See *calcium phosphate*.
tricaprin. $(C_9H_{21}COO)_3C_3H_5 = 560.48$. Glyceryl tricaprinate. Triclinic crystals, d.0.921, m.31, insoluble in water.
tricaproin. $(C_5H_{11}COO)_3C_3H_5 = 386.27$. Glyceryl

tricapronate. Colorless liquid, d.0.988, insoluble in water.
tricapryllin. $(C_7H_{15}COO)_3C_3H_5 = 470.39$. Glyceryl tricapryllate. Colorless liquid, d.0.954, m.8, insoluble in water.
tricarballylic acid. $CH_2COOH \cdot CHCOOH \cdot CH_2CO \cdot OH = 176.12$. Propanetricarboxylic acid. Colorless rhombs, in beet molasses, m.166 (decomp.), soluble in water. **β-hydroxy-** Citric acid.
Tricel. Trade name for a triacetate synthetic fiber.
tricetin. $C_{15}H_{10}O_7 = 302.1$. 5,7,3′,4′,5′-Pentahydroflavone. A pigment from wheat.
trichinae. A race of food parasites.
trichinella. An aqueous extract of the antigens of the larvae of *T. spiralis* from inoculated rodents; a dermal reactivity indicator (U.S.P.).
trichloride. Terchloride. A binary compound containing 3 Cl atoms in its molecule.
trichloro-, trichlor- Prefix indicating 3 Cl atoms in a molecule. **t. acetal.** $(EtO)_2CH \cdot CCl_3 = 221.5$. (1) Colorless liquid, d.1.288, b.197, soluble in water. (2) A solid, m.83. **t. acetamide.** $CCl_3 \cdot CONH_2 = 162.40$. Colorless, deliquescent leaflets, m.141, soluble in water; a caustic (U.S.P., B.P.). **t. acetic acid.** $CCl_3 \cdot COOH = 163.4$. Colorless rhombs, d_{60}1.630, m.57, soluble in water; a reagent for unsaturated compounds. **t. acetyl chloride.** $CCl_3 \cdot COCl = 181.8$. Colorless liquid, b.118, soluble in alcohol; used in organic synthesis. **t. aldehyde.** Chloral. **t. benzenes.** $C_2H_3Cl_3 = 181.43$. Colorless solids or liquids, insoluble in water. *1,2,3-* m.52. *1,2,4-* d_{100}(liq.)1.466, b.213. *1,3,5-* or *asym-* m.63. **t. butyl alcohol.** Chloretone. **t. butyl aldehyde.** Butyl chloral. **t. butyl malonate.** Toramin. **t. ethane.** $C_2H_3Cl_2 = 133.41$. *alpha-* $MeCCl_3$. Methyl chloroform. Colorless liquid, d.1.325, b.75, insoluble in water; an anesthetic. *beta-* $CHCl_2 \cdot CH_2Cl$. Colorless liquid, d.1.478, b.114, insoluble in water. **t. ethanol.** $CCl_3 \cdot CH_2OH = 149.4$. Trichloroethyl alcohol. Colorless tablets, m.18, slightly soluble in water. **t. ethyl alcohol.** Trichloroethanol. **t. ethylene.** $CHCl:CCl_2 = 131.40$. Trilene. 1-Chloro-2-dichloroethylene. Colorless liquid, d.1.459, b.87, insoluble in water, soluble in ether. Used as a refrigerant, inhalation anesthetic (U.S.P., B.P.); for the extraction of fats, caffeine, and nicotine; and in organic synthesis, dry cleaning, degreasing, perfumes, paints, and varnishes. **t. ethyl urethane.** Voluntal. **t. hydrin.** $CH_2 \cdot Cl \cdot CHCl \cdot CH_2Cl = 147.4$. Allyl trichloride, trichloropropane, glyceryl chloride, glyceryl trichlorohydrin. Colorless liquid, d.1.417, b.158, insoluble in water; a hypnotic and anesthetic. **t. hydroquinone.** $C_6H(OH)_2Cl_3 = 213.4$. Colorless prisms, m.134, soluble in water. **t. lactic acid.** $CCl_3 \cdot CHOH \cdot COOH = 193.42$, m.116, soluble in water. **t. methane.** Chloroform. **t. methyl chloroformate.** $C_3Cl \cdot COOCl = 197.8$. Diphosgene. Colorless liquid, b.127. A lung-irritant poison gas. **t. methylthio.** The group $-SCCl_3$, associated with fungicidal activity. Cf. *captan*. **t. phenol.** $C_6H_2 \cdot (OH)_3Cl_3 = 197.43$. 1-Hydroxy-2,4,6-trichlorobenzene. Colorless rhombs, m.68, soluble in water; an antiseptic and disinfectant. *1,2,3,5-* m.53, soluble in water, very soluble in alcohol or ether. **t. propane.** Trichlorohydrin. **t. quinone.** $CH:CCl \cdot CO \cdot CCl:CCl \cdot CO = 211.5$. Yellow leaflets,

m.165, insoluble in water. **t. toluene.** Benzotrichloride. **t. triethylamine.** $N(C_2H_4Cl)_3 = 204.5$. An irritant liquid, causing blisters.

trichodesmine. $C_{18}H_{27}NO_6 = 353.2$. An alkaloid, m.202 (decomp.), from *Trichodesma incanum* (Boraginaceae).

trichothein. $C_{15}H_{18}O_4(?)$. A neutral antibiotic from the fungus *Trichothecium roseum*. Colorless crystals, m.118. Slightly soluble in water.

trichroism. Having 3 different colors when viewed at different angles; as certain minerals and crystals.

trichromatic. Three colors, q.v. **t. analysis.** The matching of colors in terms of 3 primary components: red, green, blue.

tricin. $C_{17}H_{14}O_7 = 330.1$. 5,7,4-Trihydroxy-3',5'-dimethoxyflavone. A dimethyl ether of tricetin, a pigment in the leaves of wheat (especially khopli, *Triticum dicoceum*). Yellow needles, m.292, insoluble in water.

Triclene. Trademark for trichloroethylene.

triclinic. Anorthic, asymmetric. A crystal with 3 unequal, long axes at oblique angles. See *crystal system, prism*.

triclofos sodium. $C_2H_3O_4Cl_3PNa = 251.42$. 2,2,2-Trichloroethyl dihydrogen sodium phosphate. White, saline, hygroscopic powder; a hypnotic (B.P.).

tricosane. $Me(CH_2)_{21}Me = 324.37$. Crystals, m.48.

tricosanoic acid. See *cosanic acids*.

tricosanol. See *cosanols*.

tricosoic acid. $C_{22}H_{46}COOH$. A group of isomers. **n-** Tricosanoic acid.

tricot. A knitted fabric.

tricresol. A mixture of *o*-, *m*-, and *p*- cresols.

tricresyl. Indicating 3 cresol radicals. **t. phosphate.** $(C_6H_4Me)_3PO_4 = 368.19$. Tritolyl phosphate (preferred but little-used name). Lindol, tri-*p*-cresyl phosphate. Colorless liquid, d.1.18, m.77; a plasticizer, waterproofing, and softener for resins and rubber. It causes "ginger paralysis."

tricyanic acid. Cyanuric acid.

tricyano- Indicating the ring $\cdot C:N\cdot C:N\cdot C:N$, derived from cyano compounds by polymerization.

tricyanogen chloride. $C_3N_3C_3 = 184.4$. Cyanuric chloride. The heterocyclic polymer of cyanogen chloride. Colorless crystals, m.146, slightly soluble in water.

tricyclamol chloride. $C_{20}H_{32}ONCl = 337.90$. Bitter white crystals, soluble in water, m.167; an antispasmodic (B.P.).

tricyclic. Describing: (1) a molecule containing 3 rings of carbon; as anthracene; (2) a ring of 3 atoms.

tridecane. $C_{13}H_{28} = 184.3$. A saturated methane hydrocarbon. Colorless liquid, d.0.757, b.234, insoluble in water.

tridecanoic acid. $C_{12}H_{25}COOH = 214.20$. Tridecyclic acid, *n*-tridecoic acid, ficocerylic acid; in figs and coconuts. Colorless crystals, m.51.

tridecanol. Tridecyl alcohol.

tridecoic acid. An isomer of $C_{12}H_{25}COOH$. **n-** Tridecanoic acid. **cyclopentyl-** Chaulmoogric acid.

tridecyl. The radical $C_{13}H_{27}$—, from tridecane. **t. alcohol.** $C_{13}H_{27}OH = 200.22$. *n*-Tridecanol. Crystals, b.31. **t. amine.** $C_{13}H_{29}N = 199.23$. *n*-Aminotridecane. Crystals, m.27.

tridecylene. $C_{13}H_{26} = 182.3$. An unsaturated ethylene hydrocarbon. Colorless liquid, d.0.845,

b.233, insoluble in water, soluble in alcohol or ether.

tridecylic acid. Tridecoic acid.

Tridione. Trademark for trimethadione.

tridiphenylmethyl. $(Ph\cdot C_6H_4)_3C$. A "free radical" compound, in colorless crystals that form a colored solution.

tridymite. SiO_2. A native silica (quartz), d.2.26, stable below 1,470, having 3 crystalline forms. Also formed when quartz or cristobalite is heated at 870–1,470.

trieline. Trichloromethylene.

trien. Triethylenetetramine. A reagent for sulfates and copper.

-triene. Suffix indicating 3 double bonds.

trienol. A conjugated triene glyceride made from castor oil, and having the properties of tung oil.

triethanolamine. $N(C_2H_4OH)_3 = 149.12$. β,β',β''-Trihydroxytriethylamine. Colorless liquid, b$_{150mm}$227, soluble in water; a soap base, oil emulsifier, reagent for antimony and tin, and pharmaceutic aid (U.S.P.). T. (U.S.P.) is a mixture of t. with mono- and diethanol amines.

triethoxy. Indicating 3 ethoxy radicals, EtO—. **t. boron.** $B(OC_2H_5)_3 = 145.94$. Colorless liquid, b.120.

triethyl- Prefix indicating 3 C_2H_5 radicals in a compound. **t. amine.** $NEt_3 = 101.2$. Colorless liquid, b.89, soluble in water; a ptomaine in decaying fish. **t. arsine.** $AsEt_3 = 162.1$. Colorless liquid, b$_{735mm}$140, soluble in alcohol. **t. benzene.** *1,3,5-* $C_6H_3Et = 162.20$. Colorless liquid, b.218, insoluble in water. **t. bismuthine.** $BiEt_3 = 296.12$. Colorless liquid, b$_{79mm}$107, insoluble in water. **t. boron.** $BEt_3 = 97.94$. Colorless liquid, insoluble in water. **t. carbinol.** $CEt_3OH = 116.2$. Colorless liquid, b.141, soluble in water. **t. gallium.** $GaEt_3 = 156.85$. Colorless liquid, d.142.6, decomp. by water. **t. phosphine.** $PEt_3 = 118.2$. Colorless liquid, b.127, insoluble in water; a reagent for carbon disulfide. **t. phosphite.** $(C_2H_5)_3PO_3 = 166.2$. Colorless liquid, b.155, insoluble in water.

triethylenediamine. $(CH_2\cdot)_6N_2 = 112.15$. Hexamethylenediamine. A liquid, b.210. **t. glycol.** $(CH_2OH\cdot CH_2\cdot O\cdot CH_2—)_2 = 150.1$. Colorless liquid, b.276, soluble in water; a solvent for nitrocellulose.

triferrin. Iron paranucleinate. Red powder (Fe 22, P 2.5%), insoluble in water; a hematinic.

trifluoperazine hydrochloride. $C_{21}H_{24}N_3F_3S\cdot HCl = 480.40$. Creamy, bitter crystals, m.240, soluble in water; a tranquilizer and antiemetic (B.P.).

trifolium. Red clover blossoms of *T. pratense* (Leguminosae); an alterative.

triformol. Paraformaldehyde.

trifructosan. $C_{18}H_{13}O_{15} = 486.24$. Secalose, trifructose anhydride. White, sweet crystals from rye flour, used to detect its presence in other flours; insoluble in 70% alcohol.

trigalloyl. Three galloyl radicals, $C_6H_2(OH)_3CO$—, from gallic acid. **t. acetone glucose.** $C_{30}H_{28}O_{18} = 676.2$. Brown mass, soluble in water. **t. glucose.** $(C_7H_5O_4)_3C_6H_9O_6 = 636.15$. Yellow mass, soluble in water. **t. glycerol.** $(C_7H_5O_4)_3\cdot C_3H_5O_3 = 548.12$. Brown mass, soluble in water; a tanning agent.

trigemin. $C_{18}H_{30}O_3N_3C_{15} = 424.6$. Dimethylamidoantipyrine butyl chloral hydrate. White needles, m.85; an analgesic and sedative.

trigger. A substance that initiates a chain reaction, q.v.

triglyceride. See *glyceride*.

trigonal. Describing a crystal with 2 equal axes and a third shorter or longer axis, all at right angles. See *crystal systems*.

trigonelline. $C_7H_7O_2N = 137.1$. Nicotinic methylbetaine, in many plant seeds; sea urchin, *Arabacia pustulosa*; the Coelenterata, *Vella spirans*, jellyfish; and in urine, after taking nicotinic acid. Colorless crystals, m.218. Cf. *stachydrine*.

triguaiacyl. Indicating 3 guaiacyl radicals, MeO·C$_6$-H$_4$·O—. **t. phosphate.** $(C_7H_7O_2)_3P·OH = 416.19$. White crystals, m.98; a plasticizer. **t. phosphite.** $(C_7H_7O_2)_3P = 400.19$. White crystals, m.78; a plasticizer.

trihemellitic acid. Trimellitic acid.

trihexosan. A beer dextrin.

trihexylphenidyl. See *benzhexol*.

trihydrate. A compound containing 3 molecules of water of crystallization.

trihydric. Describing an alcohol with 3 OH groups.

trihydrocyanic acid. See *cyanidines*.

trihydrol. $H_2:O·H·O·H·O:H_2$. An assumed threefold polymer of water. Cf. *dihydrol*.

trihydroxy- Prefix indicating 3 OH groups. **t. anthraquinone.** See *anthragallol, purpurin*. **t. benzene.** *1,2,3-* Pyrogallol. *1,2,4-* $C_6H_3(OH)_3 = 126.1$. Hydroxyhydroquinone. White crystals, m.141, soluble in water. *1,3,5-* Phloroglucinol. **t. benzoic acid.** $C_6H_2(OH)_3COOH = 170.1$. *2,3,-4-* Pyrogallolcarboxylic acid. Colorless needles, m.110, soluble in water. *3,4,5-* Gallic acid. **t. benzophenone.** $C_{13}H_{10}O_4 = 230.2$, m.133. **t. oestrin.** Oestriol. **t. pyridine.** $C_5H_5O_3N = 127.08$. m.220–230 (decomp.), soluble in water. **t. stearic acid.** $C_{17}H_{32}(OH)_3COOH = 332.0$. White solid, m.146; a purgative.

triiodide. A binary compound containing 3 I atoms.

triiodo-, triiod- Prefix indicating 3 I atoms. **t. acetic acid.** $C_3I·COOH = 437.8$. Yellow scales, m.150, soluble in water. **t. benzene.** $C_6H_3I_3 = 455.81$. *1,2,3-* m.116 (sublimes). *1,2,4-* m.91. *1,4,5-* m.183. **t. cresol.** *meta-* Losophan. **t. methane.** Iodoform.

triketo- Prefix indicating 3 =CO groups in a molecule. **t. hydrinden hydrate.** Ninhydrin. **t. purine.** Uric acid.

triketones. Organic compounds containing 3 ketone groups; as, Me·CO·CO·CO·Me, pentanetrione.

Trilan. Trade name for an acetate synthetic fiber.

trilaurin. $C_3H_5(OOC·C_{11}H_{23})_3 = 638.7$. Glyceryl laurate. A crystalline glyceride from palm-nut, coconut, and bayberry oils.

Trilene. Trademark for trichloroethylene; an anesthetic.

trilinolein. $C_3H_5(OOC·C_{17}H_{30})_3 = 878.8$. Glyceryl linolate. A glyceride from linseed, sunflower, and hempseed oils.

trilite. Trinitrotoluene.

trillion. (1) 10^{18} (English and German usage = 1,000,000^3). (2) 10^{12} (American and French usage = 1,000,000^2).

trillium. Bethroot, Indian balm, ground lily. The dried rhizome of *T. erectum* (Liliacae); a tonic and alterative.

Trilon. Trade name for water-treatment compositions. Cf. *Calgon*. **T. A.** N(CH$_2$·CO$_2$Na). Sodium nitriloacetic acid. **T. B.** (CH$_2$·CO$_2$Na)$_2$N·-C$_2$H$_4$·N(CH$_2$·CO$_2$Na)$_2$. Sodium ethylenediaminotetramethyl carbonate. Cf. *EDTA*.

trimellitic acid. $C_6H_3(COOH)_3 = 210.1$. *1,2,4-* Benzenetricarboxylic acid. Colorless crystals, m.216, soluble in water.

trimer. A condensation product of 3 monomer molecules. Cf. *polymer*.

trimeric. Describing capacity to form threefold polymers. Cf. *trimetric*.

trimesic acid. Trimesitinic acid.

trimesitinic acid. $C_6H_3(COOH)_3 = 210.1$. Trimesic acid, 1,3,5-benzenetricarboxylic acid. Colorless crystals, m.348, soluble in water.

trimetaphan camphor sulfonate. $C_{22}H_{25}ON_2S·C_{10}H_{15}O_4S = 596.78$ White, bitter crystals, soluble in water; a ganglion blocking agent (B.P.).

trimethadione. $C_6H_9NO_3 = 143.14$. White crystals with camphor odor, m.46; soluble in water, an anticonvulsant (U.S.P.).

trimethano- Prefix indicating 3 —CH$_2$— bridges in a ring.

trimethoxy- Prefix indicating 3 methoxy groups, CH$_3$O—. **t. boron.** B(OMe)$_3 = 103.69$. Methyl borate. Colorless liquid, b.65.

trimethyl- Prefix indicating 3 methyl groups, CH$_3$, in a molecule. **t. acetaldehyde.** Pival aldehyde. **t. acetic acid.** Pivalic acid. **t. acetyl chloride.** Pivalyl chloride. **t. amine.** Me$_3$N = 59.1. Secaline. In leaves of *Chenopodium* species, blood (0.002%), and putrefying choline. Colorless gas, b.3.5, soluble in water. It is poisonous, has a fishy odor. **t. amine oxide.** Me$_3$NO = 75.08. Kanirin, m.96, in muscle, urine, Cephalapoda and Crustaceae. **t. amino hydrochloride.** C$_3$H$_9$N·HCl = 95.6. Colorless crystals, m.271, soluble in water. **t. arsine.** C$_3$H$_9$As = 120.1. AsMe$_3$. Colorless liquid, b.53, soluble in water. **t. benzene.** *1,2,3-* Hemimellitene. *1,2,4-* Pseudocumene. *1,3,5-* Mesitylene. **t. benzoic acid.** C$_6$H$_2$Me$_3$COOH = 164.1. *2,3,5-* Colorless needles, m.149, soluble in alcohol. *2,4,6-* Isodurylic acid. Colorless crystals, m.152, soluble in water. **t. bismuthine.** C$_3$H$_9$Bi = 254.07. BiMe$_3$. Colorless liquid, b.110. **t. boron.** BMe$_3$ = 55.89. White crystals, m.56. **t. carbinol.** CMe$_3$OH = 74.1. Colorless crystals, m.25, soluble in water. See *butanol*. **t. cyclohexane.** Hexahydrocumene. **t. cyclopentene.** Laurolene. **t. ethylene.** MeCH:CMe$_2$ = 70.1. β-Isoamylene. Colorless liquid, b.36, insoluble in water; an anesthetic. **t. gallium.** GaMe$_3$ = 114.79. Colorless liquid, b.56. **t. glycine.** See *betaine*. **t. naphthalene.** Sapotalene. **t. phosphate.** Me$_3$P O$_4$ = 140.1. Colorless liquid, b.197, soluble in alcohol. **t. phosphine.** Me$_3$P = 76.1. Colorless liquid, b.40, insoluble in water. **t. pyridine.** Collidine. **t. quinoline.** C$_{12}$H$_{13}$N = 171.17. *2,3,4-* m.65. *2,3,6-* m.86. *2,5,7-* m.43. *2,6,8-* m.45. **t. tin.** Sn$_2$Me$_6$ = 327.54. Colorless liquid, b.182, insoluble in water. Cf. *stannane*. **t. tin bromide.** Me$_3$SnBr = 243.69. White crystals, m.27. **t. tin chloride.** Me$_3$SnCl = 199.23. White crystals, m.37. **t. tin hydride.** Me$_3$SnH = 164.78. An oil, b.60. **t. tin hydroxide.** Me$_3$SnOH = 180.78. Colorless prisms, decomp. 118. **t. tin oxide.** (Me$_3$Sn)$_2$O = 343.54. White powder. **t. tin sulfide.** (Me$_3$Sn)$_2$S = 359.60. Yellow oil, m.6.

t. tryptophane. Hypophorine. **t. xanthine.** Caffeine. **t. urea.** MeNH·CO·NMe$_2$ = 102.1. Colorless crystals, m.75, soluble in water.

trimethylene. C$_3$H$_6$ = 42.1. (1) Cyclopropane, q.v. (2) Prefix indicating 3 methylene groups. (3) The radical —CH$_2$·CH$_2$·CH$_2$—. **acetyl-** C$_3$H$_5$·CO·Me = 84.1. Colorless liquid, b.113, insoluble in water. **benzoyl-** Benzoyl cyclopropane. **keto-** Cyclobutanone. **methyl-** C$_3$H$_5$Me = 56.0. Colorless gas, b.4, insoluble in water.

t. bromide. CH$_2$Br·CH$_2$·CH$_2$Br = 209.90. b$_{720mm}$160. **t. cyanide.** Glutaronitrile. **t. diamine.** 1,3-Propanediamine. **t. glycol.** 1,3-Propanediol. **t. group.** The radical —CH$_2$·CH$_2$·CH$_2$—.

trimetric. Orthorhombic. Cf. *trimeric*.

trimolecular. Pertaining to 3 different molecules. **t. reaction.** A third-order *reaction*, q.v.

trimorphism. Crystallization in 3 different systems.

trimorphous. Showing trimorphism.

trimyristine. Myristine.

trinitrate. A compound containing 3 nitrate radicals, (NO$_3$)$_3$.

trinitride. Triazo.

trinitrin. Nitroglycerin.

trinitro- Prefix indicating 3 nitro groups in a molecule. **t. aniline.** Picramide. **t. anisole.** MeO·C$_6$H$_2$(NO$_2$)$_3$ = 243.06. White crystals. *2,3,4-* m.155. *2,3,5-* m.104. *2,4,6-* m.68. *3,4,5-* m.120. *3,4,6-* m.107. High explosives. **t. benzene.** C$_6$H$_3$(NO$_2$)$_3$ = 213.1. TNB. *1,2,4-* Yellow crystals, m.57, slightly soluble in water. *1,3,5-* or *sym-* Yellow crystals, m.122, slightly soluble in water. **t. cellulose.** Pyroxylin. **t. cresol.** C$_6$HMe(OH)- (NO$_2$)$_3$ = 243.1. 1-Methyl-3-hydroxy-2,4,6-trinitrobenzene. Yellow needles, m.105, soluble in water; an antiseptic and explosive. **t. glycerin.** Nitroglycerin. **t. naphthalene.** C$_{10}$H$_5$(NO$_2$)$_3$ = 263.1. α- or *1,3,5-* Yellow, monoclinic crystals, m.122, slightly soluble in water. β- or *1,3,8-* Yellow needles, m.215, soluble in alcohol. γ- or *1,2,5-* m.113. δ- or *1,4,5-* Yellow needles, m.147, soluble in alcohol. Explosives. **t. orcinol.** C$_6$- (NO$_2$)$_3$Me(OH)$_2$ = 259.10, m.164, slightly soluble in water. **t. phenol.** HO·C$_6$H$_2$(NO$_2$)$_3$ = 229.05. α- or *2,4,6-* Picric acid. β- or *2,4,5-* m.96. γ- or *2,3,6-* m.117.5. δ- or *2,3,5-* m.120. All yellow crystals, soluble in water; explosives. **t. phenylmethyltetramine.** Tetryl. **t. resorcinol.** C$_6$H- (NO$_2$)$_3$·(OH)$_2$ = 245.08, m.176 (sublimes), soluble in water. **t. toluene.** C$_6$H$_2$Me(NO$_2$)$_3$ = 227.1. α- or *2,4,6-* Trotyl, tolit, trilite, triton, trinol, TNT, 1-methyl-2,4,6-trinitrobenzene. Yellow leaflets, d.1.654, m.81, slightly soluble in water; used similarly to picric acid in explosives. β- or *2,3,4-* Colorless leaflets, m.112, insoluble in water. γ- or *2,4,5-* Colorless crystals, m.104, insoluble in water. δ- or *3,4,5-* m.138. ε- or *2,3,5-* m.97. ζ- or *2,3,6-* m.80. High explosives. **t. triazidobenzene.** (NO$_2$)$_3$C(N$_3$)$_3$ = 336.0. Turek detonator. Yellow crystals, m.131 (forming hexanitrobenzene), insoluble in water; a detonating high explosive. **t. xylene.** C$_6$H(NO$_2$)$_3$Me$_2$ = 241.13. TNX. *2,3,5,1,4-* m.140. *2,4,6,1,3-* m.182.

trinitrol. Erythrol tetranitrate.

trinol. Trinitrotoluene.

-triol. Suffix indicating 3 hydroxy groups; as, propanetriol, C$_3$H$_5$(OH)$_3$, glycerol.

triolein. Olein.

trional. EtC(SO$_2$Et)$_2$Me = 242.3. Sulfonethylene methane. Colorless crystals, m.76, soluble in water; a hypnotic.

-trione. Suffix indicating 3 keto groups, =CO.

triose. C$_3$H$_6$O$_3$ = 90.1. Monosaccharides derived from glycerol; as, CHO·CHOH·CH$_2$OH.

trioxa- Prefix indicating 3 O bridges in a ring system; as, t. bicyclooctane. C$_5$H$_3$O$_2$ = 116.1.

(1)

(7) CH$_2$—CH—CH$_2$ (2)

| | |

O O (3)

| |

(6) O——CH—CH$_2$ (4)

(5)

trioxan(e). O:(CH$_2$·O)$_2$:CH$_2$ = 90.1. Paraformaldehyde. The heterocyclic trimer of formaldehyde. Cf. *paraformaldehyde*. Made by heating paraformaldehyde in a sealed tube with sulfuric acid, at 115°C. White crystals, m.61, soluble in water to form a constant-boiling mixture. It vaporizes without depolymerization, but is depolymerized by acid to give formaldehyde. A source of formaldehyde for organic syntheses and plastics manufacture.

trioxide. Teroxide. A binary compound containing 3 O atoms in the molecule, e.g., SO$_3$, sulfur trioxide.

trioxime. A compound containing 3 =NOH radicals.

trioximido- Prefix indicating 3 —CH:N·OH groups in a molecule. **t. propane.** HON:CH—C(:N-OH)—CH:NOH = 132.08. Colorless crystals m.171.

trioxin. Paraformaldehyde.

trioxy- (1) Prefix indicating 3 O atoms in a compound, generally as —C:O groups. (2) Trihydroxy. **t. methylene.** Paraformaldehyde. **t. purine.** Uric acid.

tripalmitin. Palmitin.

tripan roth. Trypan red.

tripelennamine hydrochloride. C$_{16}$H$_{21}$N$_3$·HCl = 291.38. White crystals, darkening in light, m.190, soluble in water; an antihistaminic (B.P.).

tripestone. A concretionary form of anhydrite.

triphane. Spodumene.

triphasic. Describing a system involving 3 phases.

triphen- Prefix indicating 3 benzene rings in a molecule.

triphenin. EtC$_6$H$_4$ONH(OC·CH$_2$·Me = 193.2). Propionyl phenetidine. Colorless crystals, m.120, soluble in water; an antipyretic.

triphenol. Triatomic phenol. A compound having 3 —OH groups in an unsaturated ring.

triphenyl- Prefix indicating 3 phenyl radicals in a molecule. **t. acetic acid.** CPh$_3$·COOH = 288.23. Colorless, monoclinic crystals, m.264 (decomp.), slightly soluble in water. **t. amine.** (C$_6$H$_5$)$_3$N = 245.22. Colorless prisms, m.127, slightly soluble in alcohol. **t. benzene.** C$_6$H$_3$Ph$_3$ = 306.26. *1,3,5-* Colorless rhombs, insoluble in water. **t. bismuthine.** BiPh$_3$ = 440.12. Bismuth triphenyl. White, monoclinic crystals, m.78, soluble in chloroform. **t. carbinol.** Ph$_3$C·OH = 260.22. Colorless prisms, m.159, insoluble in water; used to manufacture triphenylmethane dyes. *amino-* NH$_2$C$_6$H$_4$·CPh$_2$·OH = 275.2. meta-, m.155. para-, m.116. *diamino-* C$_{19}$H$_{14}$O(NH$_2$)$_2$ = 290.2. **t. ethane.** Ph$_2$CH·CH$_2$Ph = 258.15. Colorless crystals, m.54.

t. ethylene. $Ph_2C:CHPh = 256.4.$ α-Phenylstilbene. **t. guanidine.** $PhN:C:(NHPh)_2 = 287.17.$ *alpha-* Solid, m.143 (decomp), soluble in alcohol. *beta-* Solid, m.131, soluble in water. **t. methane.** $(C_6H_5)_3CH = 244.2.$ Colorless leaflets, m.92, insoluble in water; used to manufacture dyes. **t. methane dyes.** Dyes derived from triphenylcarbinol by the introduction of auxochromic groups.

(1) Fuchsin group:

$$(X \cdot C_6H_4)_2 = C = C \underset{CH=CH}{\overset{CH=CH}{<}} C=NH$$

(2) Aurin group:

$$(X \cdot C_6H_4)_2 = C = C \underset{CH=CH}{\overset{CH=CH}{<}} C=O$$

(3) Phthalein group:

$$(X \cdot C_6H_4)_2 = C \underset{O}{\overset{C_6H_4}{<}} CO$$

t. methyl. $Ph_3C = 354.3.$ A "free radical" compound. Colorless crystals, m.300. **t. phosphate.** $(C_6H_5O)_3PO = 182.06.$ Colorless needles, m.49, insoluble in water; a plasticizer, causing dermatitis with hypersensitive persons. **t. phosphine.** $Ph_3P = 262.3.$ Colorless, monoclinic crystals, m.15, insoluble in water. **t. pyridazine.** $PhC:N:N:\text{-}CPh \cdot CPh:CH = 308.15.$ Colorless crystals, m.171.

t. stibine. $Ph_3Sb = 352.9.$ **t. tin.** $SnPh_3 = 349.82.$ Tin triphenyl. White powder, m.232 (decomp.). **t. tin chloride.** $Ph_3SnCl = 385.27.$ White crystals, m.106, insoluble in water; a reagent for fluorides.

triphylite. $LiFePO_4.$ A native phosphate. Green-blue rhombs.

triple. Threefold. **t. bond.** $—C:C—.$ The acetylene linkage, indicated by the suffix *-yne** (replacing former *-ine*); as propyne* (propine). **t. chlorides.** $M_4'M''M_2'''Cl_{12}$, in which M' is Na, K, Cs, or NH_4; M'' is Zn, Cu, Hg, Ag_2, or Au_2; and M''' is trivalent; Au. **t. nitrite reagent.** A solution (120 gm sodium nitrite, 9.1 gm copper acetate, 16.2 gm lead acetate, 2 ml acetic acid, in 50 ml water), giving crystals of characteristic shape with potassium salts. **t. phosphate.** (1) A magnesium, calcium, ammonium phosphate, sometimes found in urine. (2) Treble superphosphate. A phosphate rock containing 3 times as much phosphoric acid as superphosphate. **t. point.** The conditions in which 3 phases can exist in equilibrium, e.g., in the system ice-water-water vapor, at 4.57 mm pressure and 0.0100°C. See *phase rule*. **t. salts.** Salts whose molecules consist of 3 cations and 1 anion; as, $Na_2CaCu(NO_2)_6.$

triplet. See *multiplet*. **t. state.** Describing the state of an atom or molecule having 2 electrons with parallel spin.

triplite. $(Fe,Mn)_2FPO_4.$ A greasy mineral.

tripod. A three-legged support for holding containers over a bunsen burner.

tripoli. Rottenstone. Decomposed limestone used for polishing; made from tripolite. **t. powder.** Kieselguhr.

tripolite. A native silica secreted by diatoms. Cf. *kieselguhr*.

trippkeite. A native copper arsenate.

triprolidine hydrochloride. $C_{19}H_{22}N_2 \cdot HCl \cdot H_2O = 332.9.$ Bitter, white crystals, soluble in water, m.120; an antihistamine (B.P.).

tripropyl- Prefix indicating 3 propyl radicals. **t. amine.** $(C_3H_7)_3N = 143.2.$ A tertiary amine. Colorless liquid, m.15, slightly soluble in water.

triptane. Supergas. Common name for 2,2,3-trimethylbutane, used to obtain high-octane-value petroleum.

triquinoyls. The oxidation products of hexahydroxybenzene: (1)$CO \cdot CO \cdot CO \cdot CO \cdot CO \cdot CO = 168.0.$ Hexaoxybenzene. (2) $C_6H_{16}O_{14} = 312.16.$ A solid, decomp. 95, slightly soluble in water.

triricinolein. Ricinolein.

trisaccharide. A carbohydrate that contains 3 monosaccharides in its molecule and hydrolyzes to 3 simple sugars, e.g., $(C_6H_{10}O_5)_3 \cdot H_2O$, raffinose.

Trisalyt. Trademark for a mixture of cyanides (sodium and zinc) with sodium sulfite; used in electroplating.

trisazo- Prefix indicating 3 azo groups, $—N:N—$, in a molecule.

trisilane. $Si_3H_8 = 92.2.$ An unstable, colorless liquid, b.53.

trisilicic acid. $H_4Si_3O_8 = 216.3.$ A white insoluble powder.

tristearin. $C_{57}H_{110}O_6 = 890.10.$ Stearin. Glyceryl tristearate. A constituent of animal and vegetable fats, e.g., cocoa butter, tallow. White powder, m.55, and again at 72, insoluble in water or ether; used in cosmetic creams and as an emulsifier.

tristimulus. Describing effects depending on the stimulation of the optical senses by the 3 primary colors, e.g., trichromatic colorimetry.

trisulfapyrimidines. A mixture of 30–37% each of sulfadiazine, sulfamerazine, and sulfamethazine; an oral antibacterial (U.S.P.).

trisulfide. A binary compound containing 3 S atoms in its molecule, e.g., Fe_2S_3, iron trisulfide.

tritartaric acid. Uvic acid.

triterium. Tritium.

trithioacetaldehyde. Sulfoparaldehyde.

trithiocarbonic acid. See *thiocarbonic acids*.

trithionic acid. $H_2S_3O_6.$ A sulfur acid, q.v.

tritiated. Having hydrogen in a molecule converted into tritium atoms.

triticum. (1) A genus of grasses which includes wheat. (2) Couch grass, dog grass. The dried rhizomes of *T.* or *Agropyron repens* (Gramineae), containing carbohydrates and malates; a diuretic.

tritium. T or $H^e = 3.00.$ Triterium. An isotope of hydrogen, q.v., having a mass of 3 and obtained with deuterium, q.v., by the electrolysis of water.

tritolyl phosphate. Tricresyl phosphate (preferred name).

Triton. Trademark for a line of synthetic organic surface-active agents. **T.-B.** Tetramethylammonium hydroxide. **T.-F.** Dimethyldibenzylammonium hydroxide. Used as solvents for cellulose, for saponifying fats, and in inorganic synthesis.

triton. Trinitrotoluene.

tritonope. A person who is blind to blue.

tritopine. $C_{42}H_{54}O_7N_2 = 698.4.$ An alkaloid from opium. Colorless scales, m.182.

triturate. To grind or rub to a powder (usually with a liquid) in a mortar.

trituration. Any finely powdered drug, or a mixture of milk sugar with a drug.

trityl. The radical triphenyl methyl, Ph_3C—, in ether groupings.

triuret. Carbonyldiurea.

trivalent. Tervalent. Describing an atom or radical of valency 3.

trivalerin. Phocenin.

trivial name. (1) A name that is not systematic, q.v. (2) The abbreviated name given to a chemical compound for convenience in general use, e.g., EDTA is the t. n. for ethylenediaminetetracetic acid.

trobicin. Spectinomycin.

troche. A tablet or medicated disk.

troctolite. A granitoid, crystalline, plutonic rock containing olivine and feldspar.

trogerite. A native hydrous uranium arsenate.

troilite. FeS. A native form.

tromexan. Ethyl biscoumacetate.

trommel. A cylinder of perforated steel plate revolving around an inclined central axis; for large-scale sifting.

Trommer's test. On warming urine with sodium hydroxide and copper sulfate, a yellowish red precipitate indicates sugar.

tron(a). $Na_2CO_3 \cdot NaHCO_3 \cdot 2H_2O$. Native sodium, carbonate and sodium bicarbonate. Cf. *natron*, *urao*. **t. potash.** Kemfert. A high-grade potassium chloride, Searles Lake, Calif. (58–62% potassium oxide); used in fertilizers.

troostite. (1) A native zinc-magnesium silicate. (2) A transition form of cementite, austenite, and ferrite. Cf. *steel*.

tropacocaine. $C_5H_9N \cdot CH_2 \cdot CH \cdot O \cdot COPh = 245.17$. Benzoyl pseudotropine. An alkaloid from coca leaves. Colorless crystals, m.49, slightly soluble in water; a local anesthetic. **t. hydrochloride.** $C_{15}H_{19}O_2N \cdot HCl = 281.62$. Colorless crystals, m.271, soluble in water; a local anesthetic.

tropaeolin. Tropeolin.

tropaic acid. Tropic acid.

tropan. $C_8H_{15}N = 125.1$. N-Methylnortropan. The hydrocarbon of tropine, q.v.

tropate. A salt of tropic acid.

tropeine. An ester of tropine and an organic acid, as atropine.

tropeolin. R—N_2—$C_6H_4 \cdot SO_3Na$. Hydroxyazodyes, the sodium salts of R-azobenzenesulfonic acids; as: T. D, methyl orange, p-dimethylaminoazobenzenesulfonic acid; R is $Me_2NC_6H_4$—.

T. O, yellow T, resorcinol yellow, resorcinolazobenzenesulfonic acid; R is $(HO)_2C_6H_3$—. A pH indicator, changing at 12.0 from yellow (acid) to brown (alkaline).

T. OO, diphenylamine orange, orange IV, phenylamineazobenzenesulfonic acid; R is $PhNH \cdot C_6H_4$—. A pH indicator, changing from red (1.3) to yellow (3.2).

T. OOO 1,α-naphthol orange, orange I; R is $HO \cdot C_{10}H_6$—.

T. OOO 2,β-naphthol orange, orange II; R is $HO \cdot C_{10}H_6$—.

tropic acid. $CH_2OH \cdot CHPh \cdot COOH = 166.1$. Phenylhydracrylic acid, tropaic acid, obtained by hydrolysis of atropine. **dextro-** m.127. **iso-** Colorless crystals, m.117 (decomp.), soluble in water. **levo-** m.123.

tropidine. $C_8H_{13}N = 123.1$. N-Methylnortropidine. An oil obtained by dehydration of tropine, d.0.95, b.162, insoluble in water. Cf. *nortropidine*.

tropilidene. $C_7H_8 = 92.1$. 1,3,5-Cycloheptatriene. An oil, d.0.903, b.117, prepared by distilling tropine with soda lime.

tropin. See *sensitizer* (2).

tropine.

$$CH \underset{CH_2-CH\ OH-CH_2}{\overset{CH_2-----CH_2}{\diagup\diagdown}} NMe \diagdown CH = 141.2.$$

Tropanol-3, 3-hydroxytropan. Colorless needles, m.62, soluble in water. **iso-** See *atropine*. **pseudo-** ψ-Tropine. An optically inactive isomer obtained by heating t. with phenyl amylate; a hydrolytic split product of Java coca plants. Colorless needles, m.108, soluble in water. **t. alkaloids.** See *atropine, cocaine, ecgonine*. **t. carboxylic acid.** Ecgonine. **t. sulfate.** $(C_8H_{15}ON)_2H_2SO_4 = 380.6$. White crystals, soluble in water.

tropomysin. An asymmetric protein component of muscle.

tropopause. The altitude at which the temperature of the atmosphere ceases to decrease with increase in height.

troposphere. The atmosphere below the stratosphere, q.v.

tropylium. The symmetrical, heptagonal salt-forming aromatic structure

t. ion. The C_7H_7— ion, from cycloheptatriene, C_7H_8.

trotyl. Trinitrotoluene.

Trouton, Frederick Thomas. British physicist. **T.'s rule.** The molal latent heat or heat of evaporation is equal to 20.22 times the (absolute) boiling point. Exceptions include water or alcohol. Cf. *Hildebrand's rule*. Also $T_{760mm} = T_p(1.648 - 0.255 \log p)$, where T_{760mm} is the boiling point at 760 mm, and p the pressure.

troxidone. B.P. name for trimethadione.

troy. A British system of weights and measures for jewelers. 1 oz troy = $\frac{1}{12}$ pound = 480 grains = 20 pennyweights = 1.09714 oz avoir. = 1 oz apoth. = 31.1035 gm. 1 pound troy = 5,760 grains = 240 pennyweights = 13.1667 oz avoir. = 0.82286 pound avoir. = 373.2509 gm. **t. weights.** The weight system used in reports on gold, silver, or precious metals.

Trubenizing. A process for permanently stiffening and shrinkage-resisting fabrics, by inserting a cellulose acetate thread between the cotton or linen and calendering with a cellulose acetate solvent.

truxelline. An alkaloid from coca leaves; an ester of ecgonine and truxillic acids.

truxillic acid. $C_{18}H_{16}O_4 = 296.1$. A dimer of cinnamic acid from coca leaves; 5 stereoisomeric compounds; the γ and δ isomer is *truxillic acid*. Cf. *norpinic acid*.

truxinic acid. $C_{18}H_{16}O_4 = 296.1$. An isomer of truxillic acid, q.v.

trypaflavin(e). 3,6-Diamino-10-methylacridine hydrochloride. Yellow dye, darkens on exposure; a bactericide. Cf. *acriflavine*.

trypan blue. $[(NaSO_3)_2C_{10}H_3(NH_2)OH \cdot N : N \cdot C_6H_3 \cdot Me—]$. Diamine blue, congo blue, Niagara blue, sodium tolidinedisazo-bi-1-amino-8-naphthol-3,6-disulfonic acid. Blue-gray powder; a dye, and an antiprotozoan for malaria and trypanosomiasis.

trypanosomiasis. Chaga's disease, sleeping sickness. A tropical disease of Africa and S. America due to *Trypanosoma* species; transmitted through the blood by the tsetse fly.

trypan red. Tripanroth. Brown powder, a dye and antiprotozoan agent.

tryparsamide. $NH_2 \cdot CO \cdot CH_2 \cdot NH \cdot C_6H_4AsO(OH)ONa = 296.01$. Sodium-*N*-phenyl cinnamide *o*-arsonate. White powder, soluble in water; used to treat sleeping sickness and neurosyphilis (U.S.P., B.P.). Cf. *acetarsone*.

trypsase. Trypsin.

trypsin. Trypsase. Alkali proteinase. An enzyme of pancreatic juice that hydrolyzes proteins to proteoses, and proteoses to true peptones (tryptones) and finally to leucine and tyrosine. Yellow powder, soluble in water; most efficient in slightly alkaline solution.

tryptachrome. $C_{17}H_{14}O_2N_3(?)$. A violet-pink indirubin compound produced by the action of an oxidizing agent, e.g., bromine, on tryptophane. It has an intense greenish orange fluorescence (test for tryptophane).

tryptic activity. The hydrolytic power of trypsin.

tryptones. True peptones produced by trypsin, as distinct from pepsin peptones.

tryptophan(e). $NH : (C_6H_4 \cdot CH) \vdots C \cdot CH_2 \cdot CH(COOH) \cdot NH_2 = 204.2$. Indylalanine, α-amino-β-indylpropionic acid, indolealanine. An aromatic amino acid protein split product from the seeds of *Erythrina hypaphorus* (Leguminosae). Colorless solid, m.289, soluble in water. **trimethyl-** Hypophorine.

tryptophyl. The radical $C_{11}H_{11}ON_2$—, from tryptophane.

T.S. Abbreviation for test solution.

tsano oil. Isano oil. A paint-drying oil from the nuts of a W. African tree.

tschermigite. A native ammonium alum.

Tschugajew's reaction. A scarlet-red precipitate forms on addition of dimethyl glyoxime to a weakly ammoniacal solution containing nickel.

T-stoff. See *xylyl bromides*.

tsugaresinol. $C_{20}H_{20}O_6 = 356.2$. *l*-Conidendrin. A lignin lactone in sulfite waste liquor, and in Japanese hemlock, *Tsuga sieboldii*. White crystals, m.250 (approx.).

T.T. Tuberculin-tested; as, milk from tuberculin-tested cows.

T.T.T. curve. S. curve, showing the progress of a reaction in terms of time and temperature. Applied particularly to mineralogical transformations, e.g., of austenite into pearlite.

Tu. Symbol for thulium.

tubacurarine. $C_{19}H_{26}N_2O = 298.21$. Amorphous brown alkaloid from curare.

tubaic acid. $C_{12}H_{12}O_4 = 220.09$. A constituent of derris root; q.v. **iso-** See *rotenic acid*.

tubain. A resin from derris root, q.v.

tubanol. $C_{11}H_{12}O = 160.0$. A split product of rotenone. **hydroxycarboxy-** Tubaic acid. **tetrahydro-** 2-Isoamylresorcinol.

tuba root. Derris root.

tubatoxin. Rotenone.

tube. A long and hollow device. **absorption-** q.v. **agglutination-** A small test t. **Arndt-** q.v. **arsenic-** A long glass t. with drawn-out tip bent at an angle of 120°. Cf. *Marsh test*. **Babcock-** q.v. **barometer-** A narrow t. closed at one end and more than 760 mm long. **Brown-** A potash bulb. **calcium chloride-** A glass t. of suitable shape, filled with calcium chloride; used to dry gases. **capillary-** A glass t. with bore less than 1 mm. **cathode-** q.v. **centrifuge-** A thick-walled glass container of appropriate shape, for use in a centrifuge. **colorimeter-** A flat-bottomed test t. of clear white glass. **combustion-** A glass t., resistant to heat. **comparison-** Colorimeter t. **condenser-** The inner t. of a condenser. **Coolidge-** An X-ray t. with electrically heated cathode. **Crookes-** A vacuum t. exhausted so that X rays are produced on the passage of an electric current. **culture-** A test t. for growing bacteria. **Dorn-Goetz-** A vacuum t. for spectroscopy. **drying-** A glass t., filled with a drying agent. **Emmerling-** An absorption t. **extraction-** See *Soxhlet apparatus*. **fermentation-** Saccharometer. An inverted test t. for collecting gases. **filter-** A glass t. for connecting filter crucibles to a source of suction. **funnel-** A long glass t. with conical top. **Geissler-** A t. containing gas at low pressure; produces the characteristic spectrum of the gas on passage of an electric current. **Giltner-** A t. for anaerobic cultures. **guard-** (1) A metal casing to protect glassware from mechanical injury. (2) See *guard*. **Hittorf-** A modified Crookes t. **Hortvet-** A centrifuge t. **melting point-** A thin-walled capillary t. **Nessler-** Colorimeter t. **Peligot-** Calcium chloride t. **Pitot-** A manometer t. **T-** A T-shaped t. for making 3-way connections. **test-** A glass t., closed at one end, made of heat- and acid-resistant glass. **thistle-** A funnel t. with bulb-shaped top. **U-** A U-shaped glass t. **vacuum-** A highly evacuated glass vessel; as, a Crookes t. **X-** A cross-shaped t. for 4-way connections. **X-ray-** See *X-ray tube*. **Y-** A Y-shaped t. for 3-way connections.

tuberculin. A therapeutic preparation obtained from tubercle bacillus by grinding with a solvent. Cf. purified *protein* derivative. **old-** T. Koch. **purified protein-** P.P.D. T. prepared in a medium from which free proteins have been removed by fractional precipitation with ammonium sulfate (U.S.P., B.P.). **t. Koch.** Old- T. prepared from *Mycobacterium tuberculosis* in glycerin and isotonic salt solution (U.S.P., B.P.).

tuberculostearic acid. $Me(CH_2)_7 \cdot CHMe(CH_2)_8 \cdot CO_2H = 298.21$. 10-Methylstearic acid, from bovine tubercle bacilli. Cf. *phthioic acid*.

tuberin. (1) A globulin from potato juice, representing about 50% of the total protein present. (2) A mixture of amino acids, chiefly leucines.

tubers. The underground stems of plants; they store reserve materials; as, aconite, jalap.

tubing. Glass, metal, or rubber tubes used in the

construction of chemical apparatus. **pressure-** Heavy-walled rubber hose for connecting pressure or vacuum lines. **silica-** A hollow silica rod for high-temperature combustion.

Tubize. Trade name for an acetate synthetic fiber.

tubocurarine chloride. $C_{38}H_{44}O_6N_2Cl_2 \cdot 5H_2O = 785.78$. White crystals, m.270 (decomp.), soluble in water; a skeletal muscle relaxant (U.S.P., B.P.).

tubomel. Isoniazid.

tub sizing. Passing high-class writing papers through a bath of gelatin and slowly drying air, to increase the strength and improve the writing surface.

tubule. A small tube or neck on a glass apparatus.

tufa. A calcareous sinter or sedimentary rock of calcium carbonate and silica, formed by chemical reaction from lake or groundwater; as, travertine. Cf. *tuff.*

tuff. A sedimentary rock of volcanic dust, ash, and cinders. Cf. *tufa.*

Tufton. Trade name for an acetate synthetic fiber.

tulipiferine. An alkaloid from the bark of *Liriodendron tulipifera* (Magnoliaceae).

tulip tree. The tree *Liriodendron tulipifera* (Magnoliaceae), N. America.

tumbago. An alloy of ancient origin (Columbia): Cu 55, Au 33, Ag 12%.

tundish. A refractory trough to prevent splash when ingot molds are poured.

tung oil. Chinese wood oil. A rapidly drying oil from the nuts of *Aleurites cordata* and *A. fordii* (Euphorbiaceae), China and Japan; now cultivated in Florida and elsewhere. Yellow jellifying liquid, d.0.936–0.942. It replaces linseed oil in paints and linoleum and gives a higher gloss and more water-resistant finish. Cf. *lumbang oil, trienol.* **t. pomace.** T. oil cake. The seeds after the t. oil is extracted: nitrogen 5–6, phosphorus 2, potassium oxide 1.3%; a fertilizer.

tungstate. M_2WO_4. Wolframite (international usage). A salt of tungstic acid. **meta-** A salt of metatungstic acid of the general type $M_2W_4O_{13}$; as, sodium metatungstate, $Na_2W_4O_{13}$. **para-** A salt of paratungstic acid of the general type $M_{10}W_{12}O_{41}$.

tungsten. $W = 183.85$. Wolfram (German usage), wolframium. A heavy metal and element, at. no. 74. Gray powder, d.19.3, m.3370, b.5900, insoluble in water, soluble in nitric acid and hot hydroxide solutions. Valencies 2, 4, 5, and 6. Occurs native in wolframite, scheelite, and tungstite; used (as ferrotungsten) in the manufacture of steel for high-speed tools, and metallic filaments (m.3100) for electric light bulbs. **ferro-** An alloy for high-speed tools; W 7–9, Cr 2–3%, and Fe. **orange-** $Na_2WO_4 \cdot W_2O_5$. Saffron bronze, tungsten-sodium tungstate. Gold scales, insoluble in ordinary solvents: a pigment. **violet-** $K_2W_3O_9 \cdot W_2O_5$. Potassium tritungstate. Blue-black powder; a pigment.

  t. alloy. See *ferrotungsten, steel, partinium.* **t. bronze.** An alkali-metal salt of polymerized tungstic acid; as orange t., violet t., q.v. **t. carbides.** (1) WC, d.15.7, m.2780. (2) W_2C, d.16.06, m.2880. (3) W_3C, m. above 2700. *cemented-* An extremely hard machine-tool alloy of WC embedded in tungsten with 5–15% Co, d.14–15, hardness, second to diamond. Cf. *Carboloy.* **t. chlorides.** See *t. dichloride, t. tetra-*

chloride, t. pentachloride, t. hexachloride. **t. dichloride.** $WCl_2 = 254.9$. Gray powder, decomp. by water. **t. dioxide.** $WO_2 = 216.0$. Brown rhombs, d.12.11, insoluble in water. **t. disulfide.** $WS_2 = 248.1$. Gray crystals, d.7.5. **t. fluoride.** $WF_6 = 298.0$. A gas. **t. hexachloride.** $WCl_6 = 396.8$. Blue cubes, d.13.3, m.275, slightly soluble in water, soluble in carbon disulfide. **t. minerals.** Chiefly: tungstenite, WS_2; wolframite (Fe, Mn), WO_4; scheelite, $CaWO_4$. **t. oxides.** See *t. dioxide, t. trioxide, t. pentoxide.* **t. oxychloride.** $WOCl_4 = 341.63$. Tungstyl chloride. Red crystals, m.209, decomp. by water. **t. pentachloride.** $WCl_5 = 361.3$. Black needles, m.248, decomp. in water. **t. pentoxide.** $W_2O_5 = 448.0$. Blue tungstic oxide. Blue powder, insoluble in aqua regia. **t. tetrachloride.** $WCl_4 = 325.8$. Gray crystals, decomp. by water or heat. **t. trioxide.** $WO_3 = 232.0$. Tungstic acid anhydride. Yellow rhombs, d.7.16, m. red heat, insoluble in water; used to make tungsten for lamp filaments. **t. trisulfide.** $WS_3 = 280.2$. Black powder, slightly soluble in water.

tungstic. Pertaining to pentavalent or hexavalent tungsten. **t. acid.** $H_2WO_4 \cdot (H_2O) = 250.02$. Yellow crystals, insoluble in water. **t. acids.** Acids derived from hexavalent tungsten by polymerization of tungstic acid:

Tungstic acid	$(WO_3 + H_2O)$,	H_2WO_4
Metatungstic acid..	$(4WO_3 + H_2O)$,	$H_2W_4O_{13}$
Paratungstic acid..	$(12WO_3 + 5H_2O)$,	$H_{10}W_{12}O_{14}$

t. ocher. Tungstite.

tungstite. Tungstic ocher. Wolframine. Native tungsten trioxide.

tungstosilicic acid. $H_8SiW_{12}O_{42}$. A compound isomeric with silicotungstic acid; forms hydrates.

tungstyl. The radical $\rangle\!\rangle$WO.

tunicin. Cellulose from animal tissues, similar to cotton cellulose but contains no pentoses; galactose and glucose units are present. Found in tunicates, e.g., *Phallusia mammillata.*

tuning fork. A forked-shaped metal instrument with 2 prolonged arms which may be set in rapid and sustained vibration at almost constant frequency, by means of a sharp blow, or electrically. Used to synchronize vibrations.

tuno gum. Chicle.

tupelo. A forest tree of N. America, *Nyssa aquatica*, or cotton gum tree (Cornaceae) of Mississippi. A commercial timber; the spongy wood of the roots is used for sponge tents.

turacin. A crimson pigment containing copper from the feathers of the turakoo, an African bird. Cf. *tetronerythrin.*

turaco-porphyrin. A chromophoric substance, similar to hematoporphyrin, from turacin.

turanose. $C_{12}H_{22}O_{11} = 342.18$. 3-Fructose-α-glucopyranoside. A disaccharide, consisting of glucose and fructose, formed by partial hydrolysis of melezitose.

turbid. Describing the slight cloudiness of a solution caused by fine suspended particles.

turbidimetry. Determination of the quantity of fine suspended particles in a liquid, by measuring the thickness of liquid that produces a reduction in visual transmission equivalent to that of a standard solution or a standard pattern. Cf. *nephelometry.*

turbidity value. The temperature at which a solution of an oil in a solvent, e.g., alcohol, shows the first signs of turbidity when cooled under specified conditions. Cf. *Valenta value.*

turbostratic. Describing a mesomorphous structure in which the layers of atoms, though parallel, are randomly displaced with respect to one another. Coke is t.; graphite is not.

Turek detonator. Trinitrotriazido benzene.

turgor pressure. The excess of diffusion pressure of a solute in an osmometer, over the diffusion pressure of the solute in the solution at atmospheric pressure.

turkey corn. Corydalis. **t. pea.** Tephrosia. **t. red.** (1) Harmala red. A color from the seeds of *Peganum harmala* (Rutaceae). (2) Madder. **t. red oil.** Obtained by the action of cold concentrated sulfuric acid on castor oil. Used as a wetting agent, and to prepare textiles for dyeing.

turmeric. Indian saffron, curcuma. The dried rhizomes of *Curcuma longa* (Scitaminaceae); a condiment and indicator. See *curcuma.* **t. paper.** Curcuma paper. **t. root.** Hydrastis.

turmeron. A pungent sesquiterpene constituent of curcuma.

Turnbull's blue. $Fe_3(FeC_6N_6)_2$. Insoluble prussian blue. Blue precipitate, obtained from excess of a ferrous salt and a solution of potassium ferricyanide.

turnsole. (1) Litmus. (2) A dye prepared from *Chrozophora tinctoria* (Euphorbiaceae) of the Mediterranean.

turpentine. Pine-cone oil. Terebenthene. Terebinthina. An oleoresin from the *Pinus* species. Yellow sticky masses of balsamic odor; a source of turpentine oil.

Aleppo	*Pinus halepensis*
Bordeaux	*Pinus maritima*
Canada	*Pinus maritima*
Carpathian	*Pinus cembra*
Common	*Pinus palustris, P. sylvestris*
Hungarian	*Pinus pumilio*
Larch	*Larix europaea*
Strassburg	*Abies pectinata*
Venice	*Larix europaea*

Cf. *colophony, terpinene.* **chinese-** The volatile oil from *Pistacia terebinthus* (Anacardiaceae). **t. oil.** An essential oil distilled from turpentine; contains pinene, sylvestrene, dipentene. Colorless, volatile liquid, d.0.869, insoluble in water, soluble in oils. A carminative, solvent, vehicle for paints and disinfectants, and with soap and camphor, a liniment (B.P.). See table.

COMPOSITION OF TURPENTINES
IN PERCENTAGES

Terpene	Gum	Wood	Sulfate pulp process
α-Pinene	60–65	75–80	60–70
β-Pinene	25–35	Nil	20–25
Camphene	—	4–8	—
Other terpenes . .	5–8	15–20	6–12

turpeth. The root of *Ipoemoea turpethum* (Convulvulaceae), India; a cathartic and jalap substitute. **t. mineral.** Mercuric subsulfate.

turquoise. Callaite, callainite. A hydrous gem phosphate of aluminum, colored blue by copper.

turtle oil. An oil from the muscles and genital glands of the giant sea turtle, d.0.9112, m.25, iodine no. 64.6; used as a cosmetic.

tussah. Tussore.

tussol. $C_{11}H_{12}N_2OPhCHOH\cdot COOH = 340.2$. Antipyrine mandelate, phenylglycolantipyrine. White crystals, soluble in water; used to treat whooping cough.

tussore. Tussah. Wild silk; coarser and darker than true silk. Cf. *anaphe.*

tutanag. Chinese spelter. An alloy of lead and tin used for tea chest linings.

tutia. Tutty. Zinc carbonate (obsolete).

tutin. $C_{17}H_{20}O_7 = 336.2$. A poisonous glucoside from the toot plant, a *Coriaria* species of New Zealand.

tutocaine. $Me_2N\cdot CH_2\cdot CHMe\cdot CHMe\cdot OCOC_6H_4NH_2\cdot$- HCl. Butamin, γ-D-methylamino-α,β-dimethyl-propyl-*p*-aminobenzoate hydrochloride. Colorless needles, m.214, soluble in water; a local anesthetic.

Tutton's salts. $M'M''(SO_4)_2\cdot 6H_2O$. Double salts, resembling the alums, q.v.; where M' is NH_4, K, Tl, etc.; M'' is Mg, Zn, Fe, etc.; and S can be replaced by Se.

tutty. Tutia.

tuyere. Tweer. A pipe inserted into the walls of a furnace through which an air blast is forced.

T value. A measure of the base-exchange capacity of a soil.

Tw. Abbreviation for degrees on the Twaddell hydrometer.

Twaddell. A technical hydrometer scale, q.v., named for the inventor. If the specific gravity is d, $Tw° = 200(d - 1)$.

Twaddle. Twaddell.

Tweens. Trademark for a group of surface-active agents.

tweer, twere. Tuyere.

twill. A fabric weave in which the warp and weft pass alternately over one and under two threads.

twin. One of a closely connected pair. **t. crystals.** A pair of crystals that have grown in contact, usually to form a symmetrical figure (a cross or star). **t. electrons.** A pair of electrons supposed to form a chemical bond, each atom providing one electron. See *polar bond.* **t. nuclei.** A bicyclic structure, e.g., 2 connected rings, as in naphthalene.

twinning. The plastic deformation of low-symmetry metals, e.g., hexagonal, as distinct from the slipping of cubic crystalline metallic structures. Each layer of atoms slips a constant amount over that below, so that the resulting twinned plane is the mirror image of the original lattice.

Twitchell reagent. $C_{18}H_{35}O_2\cdot C_{10}H_6SO_3H(?)$. A catalyst of fat hydrolysis, prepared by the action of sulfuric acid on oleic acid and naphthalene. **T. process.** The splitting of fats by steam catalyzed by about 0.5% T. reagent. Cf. *Pfeilring reagent.*

two-four-eight. Toxisterol: absorption spectrum maximum, 248 mμ.

Tygan. Lustrus. Trade name for a mixed-polymer synthetic fiber.

tyllithin. Lithium acetyl salicylate.

tylophorine. An alkaloid from *Tylophora asthmatica* (Asclepiadaceae), S. Asia; an emetic.

tylose. Methylcellulose.

tylosin. A mixture of antibiotics (desmycosin, macrocin, relomycin, and lactenosin) produced by *Streptomyces fradiae* growing on certain soils.

tympan. A thick paper, often impregnated with oil or glycerin, used for backing up sheets before printing, or for interleaving.

Tyndall, John. 1820–1893. British physicist. **T. cone effect, phenomenon.** The path of light through a heterogeneous medium is made visible by the solid particles; as, a sunbeam in air. Cf. *scattering ultramicroscope.*

tyndallimetry. The estimation of the suspended matter in a solution by measuring the intensity of the scattered light from a Tyndall cone. Cf. *turbidimetry.*

tyndallization. Sterilization, e.g., of media, by heating in stages.

Tynex. Trademark for a polyamide synthetic fiber.

type. A general or prevailing character. **t. of compounds.** (1) An arbitrary classification of organic compounds which groups together those obtainable from one another by substitution. (2) An indication of the presence of typical radicals; as, —OH. Cf. *classification.* **t. metal.** An alloy for making printers' type: Pb 7, Sb 2 pts., with small amounts of Sn, Bi, Ni, or Cu. **t. reaction.** A reaction common to a group of related substances.

Typel. Trade name for an acetate synthetic fiber.

typhasterol. A phytosterol from the pollen of *Typha orientalis* (Typhaceae). **alpha-** White powder, m.133.

typhotoxin. A ptomaine from cultures of Eberth's bacillus.

typhus vaccine. A sterile suspension of the killed rickettsial organisms of a strain of epidemic typhus (U.S.P., B.P.).

typical. Having a certain characteristic, property or standard. **t. compounds.** Fundamental compounds from which a number of others are derived by substitution; as, H_2O, HCl, NH_3, CH_4. **t. elements.** The most abundant element of each group of the periodic system.

tyramine. $NH_2 \cdot CH_2 \cdot CH_2 \cdot C_6H_4 \cdot OH = 137.1$. *p*-Hydroxyphenylethylamine, aminoethylphenol. An alkaloid obtained from ergot or by heating tyrosine. White crystals, soluble in water; a heart stimulant and vasoconstrictor. **t. hydrochloride.** $C_8H_{11}ON \cdot HCl = 173.5$. Colorless crystals, soluble in water; a substitute for pituitary extract.

tyratol. Thymol carbamate.

Tyrian purple. Murex.

tyrocidin(e). An antibiotic component of tyrothricin, q.v., from *Bacillus brevis;* salt of a polypeptide of mol. wt. approx. 1,260.

tyrolite. Copper froth.

tyrosal. Salipyrine.

tyrosinase. An enzyme in vegetable and animal tissues, that oxidizes tyrosine to homogentisic acid and melanin pigments.

tyrosine. $HO \cdot C_6H_4 \cdot CH_2 \cdot CH(NH_2) \cdot COOH = 181.14$. β-*p*-Hydroxyphenyl-α-aminopropionic acid. An amino acid occurring in *d*- (m.311) and *l*- (m.295) forms, obtained by hydrolysis of many proteins and old cheese. (Greek, tyros = cheese.) Silky needles, slightly soluble in water; an antidote for snake poisoning. Isomers: *ortho*- m.249; *meta*- m.280. Cf. *erythrosin.* **diiodo-** A source of iodine in bath sponges and coral.

tyrosol. $HO \cdot C_6H_4 \cdot (CH_2)_2OH = 138.1$. *p*-Hydroxyphenethyl alcohol. White rhombs, m.93, formed during putrefaction of tyrosine.

tyrosyl. The radical $HO \cdot C_6H_4 \cdot CH_2 \cdot CHNH_2 \cdot CO—$, from tyrosine.

tyrothricin. An antibiotic from cultures of the aerobic soil bacterium *Bacillus brevis.* White powder, m. approx. 240, insoluble in water (U.S.P.). Contains a soluble (gramicidin) and insoluble (tyrocidine) fraction.

tyrotoxicon. Tyrotoxin.

tyrotoxin. $PhN:N \cdot OH = 122.1$. Diazobenzene hydroxide. A ptomaine in stale milk or ice cream. Yellow needles, m.90, are produced with a solution of auric chloride.

tysonite. $(Ce,La,Di)F_3$. A native fluoride.

U

U. Symbol for uranium.
U. Symbol for intrinsic energy.
u. Abbreviation for unit.
u. Symbol for velocity component of ions.
ν. Greek letter upsilon.
ϒ. Greek capital letter upsilon.
ν. See *nu.*
μ. See *mu.*
uabain. Ouabain.
ubiquinone(s). (1) $C_{44}H_{66}O_3$. Coenzyme Q, 2,3-dimethoxybenzoquinones. A u. widely distributed in human and animal organs, m.34; associated with vitamin E deficiency (characteristic absorption at 272 mμ). (2) Compounds having the structure

R is —$(C_5H_8)_{6-10}H$.
ucuhuba fat. A fat extracted from the ground kernels of *Virola surinamensis* (Myristicaceae), tropical America; d.0.90, m.47, $[n]_D^{50}1.450$.
U effect. Generation of an alternating voltage by the mechanical vibration of a double layer in a glass capillary.
U-F. Abbreviation describing a urea-formaldehyde resin.
Uformite. Trademark for a urea-formaldehyde plastic.
ufuta. Sesame.
uintaite. Gilsonite.
ukambine. An alkaloid from African arrow poisons, similar to strophanthin in action.
ulexine. $C_{11}H_{14}ON_2 = 190.2$. An alkaloid from the seeds of *Ulex europaeus*, European gorse; a local anesthetic and powerful diuretic. Cf. *cytisine.*
ulexite. $NaCaB_5O_9\cdot8H_2O$. A hydrous borate (California).
ullage. The amount by which a container is short of being full.
ullmannite. NiSbS. A native sulfantimonide.
ulmic acid. $C_{20}H_{14}O_6 = 350.1$. Geic acid; from peat and elm bark.
ulmin. $C_{40}H_{16}O_{14} = 720.1$. A gum from the sap of *Ulmus fulva*, slippery elm (Ulmaceae). **amin-** A gum formed in coal and peat by the action of amino acids on carbohydrates.
ultimate. Fundamental or basic. **u. analysis.** Primary analysis. The determination of each element in a compound without regard to molecular combination. Cf. *proximate* and *rational analysis.* **u. lines.** See *raies ultimes.* **u. rational units.** URU. A suggested system of measurement based on the charge of an electron, $(4\pi e)^2$, which has the

dimension of energy times length, and from which all other units may be derived.
ultra- Prefix (Latin, beyond) indicating values outside certain limits.
ultracentrifuge. A high-speed centrifuge to determine the size and distribution of particles in amicroscopic colloids. **McBain's-** A spinning rotor driven by and suspended in air (350,000 rpm).
ultrafilter. See *filter.*
ultrafiltration. Filtration by suction or pressure through a colloidal filter or semipermeable membrane; used to prepare colloidal solutions and to determine particle size in terms of a standard ultrafilter.
ultra-gamma rays. Cosmic rays.
ultrahertzian waves. See *hertzian* waves.
ultramarine. $Na_3Al_3Si_3S_2O_{12}$. Artificial lapis lazuli. A blue pigment: sodium and aluminum silicates with sodium polysulfides. World production (1962) 20,000 tons. **genuine-** Lapis lazuli. **synthetic-** U. prepared by melting clay, soda, and sulfur or coal; used as a paper and textile pigment. **yellow-** Barium chromate.
    u. green. U. having a green shade.
ultramicron. A particle less than 0.25 micron in diameter; the smallest visible under the ultramicroscope.
ultramicroscope. A microscope in which the object is brightly illuminated at right angles to the optical axis, to detect particles smaller than 0.1 micron, which appear as dots of bright light. Cf. *Tyndall cone.*
ultramicroscopic. Beyond the range of microscopic visibility, but detectable by the ultramicroscope, q.v.
ultraphonic. Ultrasonic.
ultraphotic. The invisible rays of the ultraviolet and infrared regions.
ultraquinine. Homoquinine.
ultrared. Infrared.
ultrasonic. Ultraphonic. Describing high-frequency sound waves of the order of 200,000 cps, produced by applying alternating current to a quartz crystal, or by electromagnetic oscillation of a metal immersed in a liquid. Used in medicine similarly to X rays, to make emulsions, descale metals, sterilize milk, and depolymerize macromolecules Cf. *supersonic.*
ultrastructure. Structure as seen under the ultramicroscope.
ultrathermometer. Beckmann thermometer.
ultraviolet. That portion of the spectrum just beyond the violet on the short-wavelength side: generally 180–3,900 Å. See table. Emitted by sunlight; and the carbon, mercury-vapor, tungsten, and Kronmeyer lamps. **far-** 180–2,900 Å. **near-** 2,900–3,900 Å. **vital-** 2,900–3,100 Å. Cf. *radiation.*

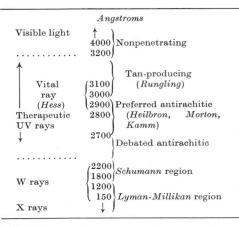

Angstroms

Visible light — 4000 } Nonpenetrating
.... 3200 }

Vital — 3100 } Tan-producing
ray — 3000 } (*Rungling*)
(*Hess*) — 2900 } Preferred antirachitic
Therapeutic — 2800 } (*Heilbron, Morton,*
UV rays — 2700 } *Kamm*)

Debated antirachitic

....

W rays — 2200, 1800 } *Schumann* region
— 1200, 150 } *Lyman-Millikan* region

X rays ↓

u. rays. Invisible rays that induce chemical activity, produce fluorescence, have therapeutic properties, and induce the formation of vitamins in sterols. Cf. *irradiation, fluorescence analysis.*

Ultrawets. Trade name for alkylated monosodium benzene sulfonate detergents and wetting agents.

ultra-X rays. Cosmic rays.

umangite. $CuSe \cdot Cu_2Se$. A native selenide. Cf. *berzelianite.*

umbellic acid. $(HO)_2C_6H_3CH:CH \cdot COOH = 180.00$. *p*-Hydroxycoumaric acid, obtained from umbelliferone by heating with alkali. Yellow powder, decomp. 125, soluble in water.

Umbelliferae. Parsley family, with hollow stems and umbrella-shaped flowers. Many seeds yield essential oils, spices, or drugs; e.g.: *Pimpinella anisum*, anise; *Angelica officinalis*, angelica root; *Conium maculatum*, hemlock leaves; *Ferula foetida*, asafetida resin. Cf. *hentriacontane, mitsubaene.*

umbelliferone. $OH \cdot C_6H_3 \cdot CH:CH \cdot CO \cdot O = 162.1$. 4-Hydroxycoumarin. A lactone in galbanum and umbelliferous plants. Colorless crystals, m.223 (sublime), slightly soluble in water. **methyl-** Resocyanine.

umbellulic acid. $C_{11}H_{22}O_2 = 186.17$. Colorless crystals, m.23, from California laurel. Cf. *cocinic acid.*

umbellulone. $C_{10}H_{14}O = 150.1$. A ketone from the oil of *Umbellularia californica* (Lauraceae). The chief constituent of California laurel oil, readily changed to thymol by heating under pressure.

umber. Raw umber. A native ferric hydroxide containing manganese dioxide and silicate; a brown pigment. **burnt-** A warm reddish brown pigment produced by heating raw u.

umbonate. Describing a bacterial culture that has a button-like raised center.

unary. Composed of molecules that are physically and chemically identical. Cf. *associated, dissociated.*

uncertainty principle. Heisenberg principle.

undecane. $Me(CH_2)_9Me = 156.2$. Hendecane*. Colorless liquid, $d_{15}0.74$, b.194, insoluble in water.

undecene. Hendecene*.

undecenoic acid. Undecylenic acid.

undecenyl. The radical $C_{11}H_{21}$—, from undecylene.

undecyl. Hendecyl. The radical $C_{11}H_{23}$—, from undecane.

undecylene. Hendecene*.

undecylenic acid. $CH_2:CH(CH_2)_8 \cdot COOH = 184.28$. Undecenoic acid* (B.P.). Yellow liquid, b.295, insoluble in water; a fungistatic.

undecylic acid. $Me(CH_2)_9COOH = 186.2$. Hendecanoic acid*. A constituent of castor oil. Colorless scales, m.28, soluble in water. Cf. *umbellulic acid, cocinic acid.* **cyclopentyl-** Hydnocarpic acid. **u. alcohol.** Hendecyl alcohol. **u. aldehyde.** Hendecanal*.

under. Below normal. **u. cooling.** Supercooling. **u. meter.** Venturi meter. **u. voltage.** The difference between the potential of a positive hydrogen electrode and that of a reversible hydrogen electrode. Cf. *overvoltage.*

undulate. Describing: (1) a regular wavelike motion; (2) a bacterial growth with wavy borders and surface.

undulation. (1) A wavelike motion. (2) Periodic expansion and contraction, as of steel rails.

undung. Laurel tallow. A vegetable fat from *Litsea* (*Tetranthera*) *laurifolia* (Lauraceae), tropical Asia.

unedol. The reducing aglucone of unedoside.

unedoside. A glucoside from *Arbutus unedo*; its reducing power is decreased by hydrolysis (unique for a glucoside).

ung. Abbreviation for unguentum.

unguentum. (1) Latin for an ointment. (2) A simple ointment.

unhairing. Depilating.

uni- Prefix (Latin) indicating one. Cf. *mono-.*

uniaxial. (1) Having only one axis; as, a crystal that does not doubly refract. (2) Having properties in one direction only, as along one crystal axis.

unicellular. Consisting of a single cell; as, protozoa.

unicorn. A plant of the genus *Martynia* (Pedaliaceae). **false-** (1) Aletris. (2) Chamaelirin. (3) Helonias.

unifrequent. Describing a homogeneous beam of light consisting of rays of similar wavelengths.

unimolecular. Monomolecular. See *reactions.*

union. A fabric having a flax warp and cotton weft; or vice versa.

un-ionized. Not ionized; in a non-dissociated molecular form.

unit. (1) A quantity used as a measure. (2) A standardized equipment comprising a definite arrangement of devices, considered as a whole; as in a unit process. **angström-** See *angström*. **Board of Trade-** q.v. **British Thermal-** q.v. **capacity-** Farad. **cgs-, CGS-** A metric u. expressed in terms of centimeter-gram-second. **derived-** q.v. **electrical-** q.v. **electromagnetic-** q.v. **electrostatic-** q.v. **emu-, EMU-** Electromagnetic u. **esu-, ESU-** Electrostatic u. **fertilizer-** Plant food u., 0.01 cwt/acre. **force-** Dyne. **fundamental-** q.v. **heat-** Calorie. **international-** q.v. **light-** See *candle, phot, lux.* **metric-** q.v. **mkh-, MKH-** A metric u. expressed in terms of meter-kilogram-hour. Cf. *cgs.* **quantum-** See *Planck's constant.* **repeating-** A group of atoms that occurs repeatedly in a chain molecule; as CH_2 in $X(CH_2)_nY$. Cf. *polymer.* **S.I.-** q.v. **ultimate-** q.v. **uru-, URU-** Ultimate rational unit based on electronic charge. **work-** The erg.

United States Adopted Names. A publication listing approved nonproprietary names for drugs (1965).

univalent. (1) Having only one valency and forming only one series of compounds; as, Na. Cf. *polyvalent*. (2) Monovalent.

universal. General; applicable in all cases. **u. indicator.** A pH indicator, q.v., which changes color over the whole range of pH values. **u. series constant.** Rydberg's constant. The value for N in the equations of the spectrum series.

unofficial. Describing a drug not authorized by a pharmacopoeia or formulary.

unorganic. Inorganic (obsolete).

unorganized. (1) Having no cellular or protoplasmic structure. (2) Amorphous. **u. ferment.** An enzyme active in sterile solutions and independent of cell life.

unsatisfied. Describing a hydrocarbon having one or more free valencies. Cf. *unsaturated*.

unsaturate. Abbreviation for unsaturated hydrocarbon.

unsaturated. (1) Describing a solution capable of dissolving more solute. (2) Describing an organic compound having double or triple bonds; as, ethylene.

unslaked lime. Calcium oxide.

unstable. Readily decomposing; as, hydrogen peroxide.

unsymmetrical. Not symmetrical; as, the 1,2,4-positions of the benzene ring.

U.P. Under proof. See *proof spirit*.

upas. A Javanese arrow poison containing strychnine (Malay, ipoh). **bohan-** A poisoning resin from the tree *Antiaris toxicaria* (Java). Cf. *antiarin*.

uperization. The sterilization of milk by very rapid heating to 150°C, followed by immediate cooling; more permanent in effect than pasteurization.

upsilon. Greek letter v, Υ (see *u*).

uptake. An exit pipe leading upward.

uracil. $HN \cdot CO \cdot NH \cdot CO \cdot CH : CH = 112.1.$ 2,4(1,3)-Pyrimidine dione. A pyrimidine base in nucleic acids, m.338. **methyl-** Thymine.

uraconite. Uranic ocher.

uralin. $CCl_3CH(OH) \cdot NH \cdot COOEt = 236.6.$ Chloral urethane. Colorless crystals, soluble in water; a hypnotic.

uralite. (1) A variety of amphibole (Ural Mountains). (2) Asbestos impregnated with sodium silicate and bicarbonate, and chalk; fireproof.

uralium. (1) A supposed element isolated by Guyard from platinum ores; identical with rhenium. (2) Chloral urethane.

uramido. Carbamido. **u. acetic acid.** Hydantoic acid.

uramil. $CO : (NH \cdot CO)_2 : CH \cdot NH_2 = 143.1.$ Dialuramide, aminobarbituric acid, murexan. Colorless crystals, soluble in water; used in organic synthesis. **thio-** See *thiouramil*.

uramine. Guanidine.

uramino. Carbamido.

uranalysis. Analysis of urine.

uranate. $M_2U_2O_7$. A salt of uranic acid.

urane. (1) A unit of radioactivity: 0.001 kilurane. (2) Uranium oxide. (3) Urethane.

uranediol. $C_{21}H_{36}O_2 = 330.04.$ A steroid urane (3) derivative from the urine of pregnant mares.

uranic. Indicating hexavalent uranium; as, uranium

fluoride. **u. acid.** $H_2UO_4 = 304.2.$ Yellow insoluble powder; u. oxide in various degrees of hydration. The salts are derived from the hypothetical acid, $2UO_3 \cdot H_2O$ or $H_2U_2O_7$. **u. ocher.** U_2O_3. Uraconite. Yellow, native uranium oxide, containing radium. **u. oxide.** $UO_3 = 286.2.$ Uranium trioxide. Orange powder, insoluble in water; used in ceramics, glass, paint, and textiles.

uranin. $Na_2C_{20}H_{10}O_5 = 376.2.$ Sodium fluorescein. Brown powder; a reagent.

uraninite. $UO \cdot U_2O_3$. Pitchblende. Native uranium oxide, a source of radium.

uranites. Mineral phosphates of uranium, with calcium or copper.

uranium. $U = 238.03.$ A heavy metal, the last stable element of the periodic system, at. no. 92. Cf. *transuranium, ekaosmium*. A hard, heavy, nickel-white metal, d.18.68, m. red heat, insoluble in water or alcohol, soluble in acids. It is radioactive, consists of the isotopes U^{238} and U^{235}, which occur in nature in the ratio 140:1. They can be disintegrated by fast and slow neutrons, respectively, and the latter are used to start the chain reaction which is the basis of the atomic bomb (u. pile). Cf. *radioactive disintegration*. U. is obtained from its ores by anion exchange of the complex $UO_2(SO_4)_3$. Cf. *moving-bed process*. Non-Communist world production (1958) 36,000 tons as U_3O_8 (U.S.A. and Canada, 26,000 tons). U. forms principally tetravalent (uranous) or hexavalent (uranic, uranyl, and uranate) compounds; valencies of 2, 3, 5, and 8 also exist. The yellow oxide, UO_3, is amphoteric, and forms uranates with bases, and uranyl salts with acids.

depleted- U. from which most of the fissile U^{235} has been removed. Used, as UF_6, as a source of U for nonnuclear purposes, e.g., alloys. **trans-** See *transuranium*. U_1, U_2, U_x, etc. See *radioactive elements*.

u. acetate. (1) Uranyl acetate. (2) Uranyl-sodium acetate. **u. ammonium fluoride.** Uranyl-ammonium fluoride. **u. barium oxide.** $BaU_2O_7 = 725.8.$ Barium diuranate. Orange powder, soluble in acids. **u. bromide.** $UBr_4 = 557.9.$ Uranous bromide. Black leaflets, soluble in water. **u. carbide.** (1) $UC_2 = 262.17.$ A solid, d.11.3, m.2260. (2) $U_2C_3 = 512.34.$ A solid, d.11.28, m.2400. **u. chloride.** (1) $UCl_4 = 380.0.$ Uranous chloride. Green cubes, soluble in water. (2) $UCl_3 = 344.51.$ U. trichloride. Purple, soluble crystals. **u. fluorides.** $UF_4 = 314.07.$ Green salt. $UF_6 = 352.07.$ Sublimes 56 (760 mm). Both are used to concentrate U^{235} by the diffusion process being more convenient than the volatile U compounds. **u. glass.** Yellow glass with green fluorescence; contains u. oxides. **u. hydroxide.** $U(OH)_4 = 306.15.$ Green, insoluble powder. **u. iodide.** $UI_4 = 745.9.$ Uranous iodide. Yellow, monoclinic crystals, m.500, soluble in water. **u. lead.** (1) Radium G (RaG). (2) A mixture of RaG and AcD. See *lead*. **u. minerals.** Numerous and complex, and contain the phosphates and vanadates of rare earths; carnotite, uraninite, becquerelite, and autunite are radioactive. **u. oxides.** Principally: dioxide UO_2 (uranous oxide); trioxide UO_3 (uranic oxide); tritaoctoxide U_3O_8 [which may be uranosic oxide $UO_2 \cdot 2UO_3$, uranyl uranate $(UO_2)_2UO_4$, or uranous uranate $U(UO_4)_2$]. Others are sesquioxide U_2O_3 (or hemitrioxide); pentoxide U_2O_5 (or hemipentoxide); tetroxide UO_4. **u. oxychloride.** Uranyl chloride. **u. pile.** See under *uranium.* **u. strontium oxide.** $SrU_2O_7 = 676.0$. Strontium uranate. Yellow powder; soluble in acids. **u. sulfate.** $U(SO_4)_2 \cdot 8H_2O = 574.5$. Native as uranvitriol and zippeite. Green prisms, m.300, decomp. by water. **u. sulfide.** $US_2 = 302.3$. Uranous sulfide. Gray powder, m.1100, insoluble in water. **u. tetrabromide.** U. bromide. **u. tetrachloride.** U. chloride. **u.X., u.Y.** See *radioactive elements.* **u. yellow.** Sodium uranate; a ceramic and glass pigment. **u.Z.** Isotope of ekatantalum, half-life period 9.7 hours. Cf. *protactinium.*

uranocircite. $(UO_2)_2BaP_2O_8$. A mineral. Cf. *autunite.*

uranophane. $U_2SiO_3 \cdot CaSiO_8$. A native silicate.

uranopilite. $CaO \cdot 8UO_3 \cdot 2SiO_2 \cdot 25H_2O$. A mineral from Colorado. **beta-** $CaO \cdot 8UO_3 \cdot 2SiO_3 \cdot 25H_2O$.

uranospathite. $(UO_2)_3(PO_4)_2 \cdot nH_2O$. A mineral.

uranospherite. $U_2O_7(BiO)_2 \cdot 3H_2O$. An orange, scaly mineral containing radium.

uranospinite. $(UO_2)_2CaAsO_8$. A native arsenate.

uranothallite. $2CaCO_3 \cdot U(CO_3)_2 \cdot 10H_2O$. A mineral from Bohemia.

uranous. Describing a compound containing tetravalent uranium. **u. chloride.** See *uranium chloride.* **u. oxide.** $UO_2 = 270.2$. Uranium dioxide. Black octahedra, d.10.95, m.2176, insoluble in water. **u. uranic oxide.** Uranyl uranate.

uranvitriol. Johannite. A mineral containing copper.

uranyl. The radical $UO_2=$, from UO_3; it forms many salts with acids, which ionize to UO_2^{++} (yellow in solution). **u. acetate.** $UO_2(C_2H_3O_2)_2 \cdot 2H_2O = 424.3$. Yellow crystals, soluble in water; a reagent. **u. ammonium carbonate.** $UO_2CO_3 \cdot 2(NH_4)_2CO_3 = 522.3$. Yellow crystals, soluble in water, used in ceramics and glass. **u. ammonium fluoride.** $UO_2F_2 \cdot 3NH_4F = 419.3$. Uranium ammonium fluoride. Green, fluorescent crystals, soluble in water; used in X-ray screens. **u. benzoate.** $UO_2(C_7H_5O_2)_2 = 514.3$. Uranium benzoate. Yellow powder, slightly soluble in water. **u. calcium phosphate.** $(UO_2)_2Ca(PO_4)_2 = 770.5$. Yellow crystals, soluble in water. **u. chloride.** $UO_2Cl_2 = 341.1$. Uranium oxychloride. Yellow, hygroscopic crystals, decomp. by heat, soluble in water. **u. ferrocyanide.** $(UO_2)_2Fe(CN)_6 = 752.25$. Uranyl hexacyanoferrate. Brown powder, insoluble in water. **u. formate.** $UO_2(HCO_2)_2 \cdot H_2O = 378.17$. Yellow octahedra, slightly soluble in water. **u. hydroxide.** $UO_2(OH)_2 = 304.19$. Uranic acid, H_2UO_4. White solid. **u. nitrate.** $UO_2(NO_3)_2 \cdot 6H_2O = 502.3$. Uranium nitrate. Yellow, deliquescent crystals, m.59, soluble in water; used as a reagent, indicator, antidiabetic; and in ceramics, glass, and photography. **u. oxalate.** $UO_2C_2O_4 \cdot 3H_2O = 412.2$. Uranium oxalate. Yellow powder, insoluble in water. **u. oxide.** Uranium trioxide. **u. phosphate.** $UO_2HPO_4 + 4H_2O = 438.3$. Yellow crystals, insoluble in water; an atomic reactor fuel. **u. potassium nitrate.** $UO_2(NO_3)_2 \cdot 2KNO_3 = 596.5$. Yellow crystals, soluble in water. **u. potassium sulfate.** $UO_2SO_4 \cdot K_2SO_4 = 540.5$. Yellow powder, soluble in water. **u. sodium acetate.** $UO_2(C_2H_3O_2)_2 \cdot$

$2NaC_2H_3O_2 = 552.3$. Yellow crystals, soluble in water; a reagent. **u. sodium sulfate.** $UO_2SO_4 \cdot Na_2SO_4 = 508.2$. Yellow crystals, soluble in water. **u. sulfate.** $2UO_2SO_4 \cdot 7H_2O = 858.6$. Yellow crystals, soluble in water. **u. sulfide.** $UO_2S = 302.3$. Brown powder, decomp. by heat, slightly soluble in water. **u. uranate.** $(UO_2)_2 \cdot UO_4 = 842.6$. Uranous uranic oxide. Green crystals, d.7.31, decomp. by heat, insoluble in water. **u. zinc acetate.** A solution of u. acetate and zinc acetate in acetic acid; gives crystals of characteristic shape with sodium salts.

urao. A native sodium carbonate and bicarbonate (S. America).

urari. Curare.

urase. Urease.

urasol. $CH_2[C_6H_3(COOH)OC_2H_3O]_2 = 372.1$. Acetylmethylenedisalicylic acid, afsal. Yellow powder, insoluble in water; an antiseptic.

urate. Lithate. A salt of uric acid.

urazine. $OC \cdot N(NH_2) \cdot CO \cdot (NH)_2 = 116.0$. Amino-

urazole. Cf. *diurea.*

urazole. $CO \cdot (NH)_2 \cdot CO \cdot NH = 101.2$. Hydrazodicarbonimide, diketotriazolidine. Colorless crystals, m.244, soluble in alcohol. **amino-** Urazine. **1-phenyl-** $C_2H_2O_2N_3Ph = 177.2$. Colorless crystals, m.263. **3-phenyl-** Colorless crystals, m.203, soluble in alcohol. **thio-** See *thiourazole.*

Urbain, Georges. 1872–1938. French chemist, noted for work on the rare earths.

Ure, Andrew. 1778–1857. Scottish chemist, author of "A Dictionary of Chemistry" (1821). **U. eudiometer.** A long U-shaped glass tube closed at one end, in which are 2 electrodes with a graduated scale to measure gases.

urea. $NH_2 \cdot CO \cdot NH_2 \rightleftharpoons NH_2 \cdot CNH \cdot OH$ (pseudo u.) $= 60.1$. Carbamide. Colorless tetragons, m.132 (decomp. to biuret and ammonia), soluble in water. The end product of mammalian protein metabolism, the chief nitrogenous constituent of urine, and the first organic compound synthesized (Wöhler, 1828). Used as a diuretic (U.S.P.), a reagent for lignin; and in pyrotechnics, organic synthesis, and plastics manufacture. Its derivatives have the prefix *ureido-** or suffix *-urea**; as, butylurea*, $C_4H_9NHCONH_2$; butyrylurea*, $C_4H_9 \cdot CONH \cdot CONH_2$. The radical $—NH \cdot CO \cdot NH—$ is urylene*. Cf. *ureide, uramido.* **ψ-** See pseudo *urea.* **acetonyl-** See *acetonylurea.* **acetyl-** See *acetylurea.* **alkene-** $RHN \cdot CO \cdot NHR$ (urylenes), or $R_2N \cdot CO \cdot NR_2$. **allylthio-** Allylsulfocarbamide. **amino-** Semicarbazide. **bi-** See *biurea.* **bromoethylbutyryl-** Adaline. **bromoisovaleryl-** Bromural. **carbamido-** Biurea. **carbamyl-** Biuret. **carbonyl-** Triuret. **cinnamyl-p-oxyphenyl-** Elbon. **di-** See (1) *diurea,* (2) *urazine,* (3) *uril.* **diamino-** Carbohydrazide. **diphenyl-** Carbanilide. **ethoxyphenyl-** Sucrol. **ethylene-** Oxazoline (μ-amido). **formaldehyde-** See *plastics.* **guanyl-** q.v. **imino-** Guanidine. **malonyl-** Barbituric acid. **mesoxalyl-** Alloxan. **methyl-** $C_7H_7ON_2 = 75.08$. White prisms, m.76, soluble in water. **oxalyl-** Parabanic acid. **phenetyl-** Sucrol. **phenylene-** Benzimidazolone. **phenylhydrazine-** Diphenylcarbazide. **propylene-** Oxazoline (μ-amido-α-methylene-). **pseudo-** $NH_2 \cdot C:NH \cdot OH$. The tautomer of u.

selen- Selenurea. **tartronyl-** Dialuric acid. **thio-** Thiourea.

u. acetate. A variable mixture of u. and acetic acid. **u. apparatus.** A device for the rapid determination of u. by the action of urease. **u. carboxylic acid.** Allophanic acid. **u. citrate.** $CH_4ON_2 \cdot C_6H_8O_7 = 252.2$. Colorless crystals, soluble in water. **u. form.** A solid u.-formaldehyde condensate with excess u.; a slow nitrogen-release fertilizer. **u. formaldehyde.** See *plastics.* **u. hydrochloride.** $CH_4ON_2 \cdot HCl = 96.6$. Colorless, deliquescent crystals; a local anesthetic (with quinine hydrochloride). **u. nitrate.** $CH_4ON_2 \cdot HNO_3 = 123.1$. Colorless scales, soluble in water. **u. oxalate.** $CH_4ON_2 \cdot C_2H_2O_4 = 150.1$. Colorless crystals, soluble in water. **u. quinate.** $(CH_4ON_2)_2 \cdot C_7H_{12}O_6 = 312.3$. Urol. Colorless prisms, m.107, soluble in water. **u. quinine.** Quinine and u. hydrochloride. **u. stibamine.** $NH_2 \cdot CO \cdot NH \cdot C_6H_4 \cdot SbO_3H \cdot NH_4$. White powder; used to treat kala azar.

ureameter. Ureometer. An apparatus to determine urea from the volume of nitrogen evolved. Cf. *urinometer.*

urease. Urase. A crystallizable protein enzyme in soybeans (its richest source), numerous fungi, and jack beans; converts u. into ammonium carbonate. White octahedra, soluble in dilute alkali, isoelectric point pH 5.05. It is inactivated by metals; used to determine u. Cf. *uricase.*

urechitin. $C_{28}H_{42}O_8 = 506.4$. A glucoside from *Urechites suberecta,* the Savannah flower, yellow nightshade (Apocynaceae).

urechitine. $C_{24}H_{42}O_8 \cdot H_2O = 476.4$. An alkaloid from *Urechites suberecta.*

ureide. (1) A derivative of urea; as, $NH_2 \cdot CO \cdot NHEt$, ethylurea. (2) A compound analogous to the amides, derived from carboxy acids and containing the radical $-NH \cdot CONH_2$. **cyclic-** A compound formed by replacement of one H of each NH_2 group by a dibasic acid; as, in alloxan. **di-** A compound containing 2 ureido radicals. **pseudo-** $NH_2 \cdot CNH \cdot OR$.

ureido. (1) The radical $-NH \cdot CO \cdot NH-$. (2) Carbamido (U.K. usage). (3) Prefix denoting a urea functional group.

ureometer. Ureameter.

ureous acid. Xanthine.

-uret. Suffix (obsolete) indicating a binary compound of sulfur, arsenic, phosphorus, carbon, etc., with some other element. Superseded by *-ide;* as, hydrogen sulfide.

urethan. (1) A derivative of urethane; as, adalin. (2) Urethane (U.S.P.).

urethan(e). $NH_2 \cdot CO \cdot OEt = 89.10$. Ethyl carbamate, urane ethylurethane. Colorless needles, m.49, soluble in water; a hypnotic (U.S.P., B.P.). **acetylethoxyphenyl-** Thermodin. **acetyloxyphenyl-** Neurodin. **amyl-** Amylcarbamate. **chloral-** Uralin. **ethyl-** Urethan. **ethylchloral-** Somnal. **ethylidene-** q.v. **phenacetin-** Thermodin. **phenyl-** q.v. **piperidyl-** q.v. **poly-** q.v. **thio-** q.v. **thymol-** Thymol carbamate. **trichloro-** Voluntal.

urethanes. In general, carbamic esters.

urethano. Carbethoxymino (U.K. usage).

urethylan. $NH_2 \cdot CO \cdot OMe = 75.05$. "Methylurethane," methyl carbamate. White crystals, m.52, soluble in water.

uric acid. $C_5H_4O_3N_4 = 168.1$. Triketopurine, 2,6,-8-trioxypurine.

Uric acid   Isouric acid

Tauto-uric acid

Colorless scales, d.1.85, decomp. by heat, slightly soluble in water. The end product of the purines of muscle and cell nuclei. **iso-** An isomer of u. a. **tauto-** A tautomer of u. a. **trimethyl-** Caffeine. Cf. *purine derivatives.*

uricase. An enzyme in animal tissues that splits uric acid to allantoin, urea, and glycocoll. Cf. *urease.*

uridin. $C_4H_3N_2O_2 \cdot C_5H_9O_4 = 244.13$. Uracil-*d*-riboside. A nucleoside, m.150, from nucleic acid. **u. phosphoric acid.** A nucleotide, m.202, from nucleoproteins.

uril. $RNH \cdot CO \cdot NH \cdot NH \cdot CO \cdot NHR$. See *biurea.*

urine. A fluid secreted by the kidneys and discharged from the bladder (1,250–1,500 ml per 24 hr). Normally a clear, slightly acidic, amber liquid, d.1.005–1.030. Composition: water 96, urea 2.3, sodium chloride 1.1, phosphates 0.2, sulfates 0.1%. *Abnormal constituents*: albumin, sugar, pus, blood, diacetic acid, indican, hydrogen sulfide. Cf. *Bang method, Benedict test, Ehrlich's solution, urinometer.*

urinoid. $CH_2 \cdot CH : CH \cdot CH_2 \cdot CO \cdot CH_2 = 96.1$. Cyclohexene-3-one. A constituent of urine, supposed to cause its characteristic odor.

urinometer. Urometer. A hydrometer for determining the specific gravity of urine. Cf. *ureameter.*

uriodone. Injection of iodone.

urobenzoic acid. Hippuric acid.

urobilin. $C_{32}H_{40}O_7N_4 = 592.36$. Hydrobilirubin. A bile pigment produced by the putrefaction of bilirubin in the gut and removed via the kidney or liver. Brown, resinous mass, soluble in alcohol; a reagent. Cf. *Ehrlich's solution.*

urobromohematin. $C_{68}H_{94}O_{26}N_8Fe_2$. A colored hemoglobin derivative in urine of lepers.

urocanic acid. $NH \cdot CH : C \cdot (CH : CH \cdot COOH)N : CH = 138.1$. Imidazoacrylic acid. A ptomaine from histidine, in dog's urine. White crystals, m.224, slightly soluble in water. Cf. *urocaninic acid.*

urocanin. $C_{11}H_{19}ON_4 = 223.19$. A base in dog's urine.

urocaninic acid. $C_6H_6O_2N_2 \cdot 2H_2O = 174.2$. An acid from dog's urine, decomp. by heat to carbon dioxide and urocanin. Cf. *urocanic acid.*

urochrome. $C_{43}H_{51}O_{26}N = 997.5$. A yellow coloring matter in urine.

urochromogen. A tissue substance oxidized to urochrome.

urocitral. Theobromine sodium citrate.

uroerythrin. An orange pigment in urine.

urol. Urea quinate.

urolith. A calculus in urine.

uromelanin. $C_{18}H_{43}O_{10}N_7 = 517.6$. A black pigment; sometimes occurs in urine as a decomposition product of urochrome.

urometer. See *urinometer, ureameter*.

uronic acids. $CHO\cdot(CHOH)_x COOH$. (1) Polyhydroxyaldehyde acids prepared by oxidizing hexoses or pentoses whose aldehyde group is blocked (as in glucosides); e.g., penturonic acids, $CHO(CHOH)_3\cdot COOH$; as, ribosuric acid. (2) Lactones of (1); as, ascorbic acid. **hept-** $CHO(CHOH)_5COOH$.

uropac. Iodoxyl.

uropepsin. Urinary pepsinogen.

urophan. A substance which passes chemically unchanged into the urine.

uropherine. Theobromine lithium. **u. benzoate.** Uropherine *B*. Theobromine lithium benzoate. **u. salicylate.** Theobromine lithium salicylate.

uropittin. $C_9H_{10}O_3N_2 = 194.1$. A resinous decomposition product of urochrome.

uroprotic acid. $C_{66}H_{116}O_{54}N_{20}S = 2085.1$. An acid protein from urine.

uropterin. A yellow pigment from the purine fraction of human urine.

uroselectan-B. Iodoxyl.

urosine. $C_6H_7(OH)_4\cdot COOLi = 198.09$. Lithium quinate; used to treat gout.

Urotropin. Hexamethylenetetramine. Trademark for a brand of urinary antiseptic. **U. quinate.** Quinotropine. **U. salicylate.** Saliformine. **U. tannin.** Tannopin.

uroxameter value. A measure of the intensity of ultraviolet light from the amount of oxalic acid decomposed on exposure for a given time in presence of uranyl acetate.

ursanic acid. $C_{30}H_{48}O_2 = 440.4$. Colorless acid, m.224, derived from methyl arsonate.

ursin. Arbutin.

ursol. *p*-Phenylenediamine.

ursolene. Gray wax, m.192, from cranberry skins. Above 200° it hardens and resembles montan wax.

ursolic acid. $C_{29}H_{46}(OH)COOH = 456.4$. Urson, malol, prunol, in the leaves of *Arctostaphylos uva-ursi*, bearberry; *Prunus serotina*, wild cherry; and the fruit of *Pyrus malus*, apple. Colorless powder, m.267, insoluble in water.

urson. Ursolic acid.

urstoff. Protyle.

urtica. Stinging nettle. The dried herb of *U. dioica* (Urticaceae), containing tannin and glucosides; a diuretic and hematinic.

Urticaceae. The nettle family (Moraceae, Ulmaceae, and Cynocrambaceae), a source of drugs; e.g.: *Ulmus campestris*, elm bark; *Humulus lupulus*, hops; *Cannabis sativa*, Indian hemp. See *fustic, morus, ramie*.

uru, URU. Abbreviation for ultimate rational units. Cf. *cgs, esu*.

urumbrin. Iodoxyl.

urunday. A vegetable tanning agent.

urusene. $C_{15}H_{28} = 208.20$. A hydrocarbon from urushi, Japanese lac, the secretion of *Rhus vernicifera* (Anacardiaceae). Cf. *rhus*.

urushic acid. $C_{23}H_{36}O_2 = 344.28$. Laccol. An acid from the juice of the Japanese lac tree.

urushiol. $C_6H_3(OH)_2C_{15}H_{27} = 316.3$. An oily catechol derivative, in *Rhus vernicifera*; induces sensitiveness to poisoning.

urycury oil. Rabassu oil.

urylene. The radical $-NH\cdot CO\cdot NH-$. See alkene *urea*.

USASI. Abbreviation for United States of America Standards Institute; formerly American Standards Association (ASA).

usnaric acid. $C_{20}H_{22}O_{15} = 622.18$. An acid from the lichen *Usnea barbata*.

usnic acid. $C_{18}H_{16}O_7 = 344.22$. Usninic acid, from the lichen *Usnea barbata*. Insoluble solid. **levo-** m.190. **dextro-** m.195.

U.S.P., U.S. Phar. Abbreviation for United States Pharmacopoeia (17th ed., 1965).

U.S.R.-604. Trade name for 2,3-dichloro-1,4-naphthoquinone; a seed disinfectant.

ustilago. Corn smut. A moldlike fungus parasitic on maize, and resembling ergot. It contains several alkaloids (secaline); an ergot substitute.

UV. Ultraviolet.

uva. Raisins. **u. ursi.** Bearberry leaves. The dried leaves of *Arctostaphylos uva-ursi* (Ericaceae), containing arbutine, ericoline, and urson; a tonic and diuretic.

uvarovite. $(CaO)_3Cr_2O_3Si_3O_6$. Uwarowite. A garnet.

Uverite. $7CaO\cdot CaF_2\cdot 6TiO_2\cdot 2Sb_2O_3$. Trademark for a synthetic mineral, used to opacify enamel.

uvic acid. $Me\cdot C:CH\cdot C(COOH):CMe\cdot O = 140.06$.

Pyrotritartaric acid, dimethylfuranecarboxylic acid, uvinic acid. Colorless needles, m.135, soluble in water; formed by dry distillation of tartaric acid.

uvinic acid. Uvic acid.

uviol. A glass that transmits ultraviolet light.

uvitic acid. $Me\cdot C_6H_3(COOH)_2 = 180.06$. Mesitic acid, 5-methylisophthalic acid. Colorless needles, m.287, insoluble in water. **iso-** m.175, insoluble in water.

uvitinic acid. $C_6H_3Me(COOH)_2 = 180.06$. Methylphthalic acid. White crystals, soluble in water.

uvitonic acid. $N:CMe\cdot CH:C\cdot COOH\cdot CH:C\cdot COOH = 181.1$. 2-Methylpyridine-4,6-dicarboxylic acid. Colorless crystals, m.244.

uvoflavin. Vitamin B_2.

uwarowite. Uvarovite.

uzara. The powdered root of an African plant (Asclepiadaceae); used to treat diarrhea and bacillary dysentery.

V

V. (1) Symbol for vanadium. (2) Abbreviation for volt.

V. Symbol for: (1) velocity: (2) volume: $V_p =$ at constant pressure; $V_t =$ at constant temperature.

v- Abbreviation for vicinal.

ν. See *nu*.

ʊ. See *upsilon*.

vac. Abbreviation for: (1) vacuum; (2) millibar.

vaccenic acid. $C_{18}H_{34}O_2 = 282.0$. *trans*-Octadecen-11-oic acid. An isomer of oleic acid, in meat or butter fats.

vaccine. (1) A bacterial suspension used to produce active immunization by injection or inoculation (U.S.P., B.P.). (2) The lymph from a cowpox vesicle.

vaccinium. Whortleberry, European huckleberry. The dried fruit of *Vaccinium myrtillus* (Ericaceae), containing quinic acid, myrtillin, and arbutin; a diuretic.

vacuum. (1) Strictly, a space that contains no fluid. (2) A space from which gas has been almost wholly removed. Measured in relation to air pressure (760 mm), in millimeters of mercury. See table. **high-** A v. of below 0.01 mm, as in X-ray tubes. **low-** A. v. of 50–1 mm. **Toricellian-** The v. in a barometric tube between the mercury and the closed top.

	mm Hg absolute
Water pump: $760 - 7 = 753$	
mm Hg relative	7.00
Sprengel mercury pump	0.001
Geryk oil pump	0.0002
Charcoal in liquid air	0.0000008
Gaede molecular pump	0.0000002
1 atm = 760 mm Hg = 1.013569 bars	

v. desiccator. An apparatus in which a substance is dried under reduced pressure. **v. distillation.** Distillation under reduced pressure; used to purify liquids or separate mixtures. **v. evaporation.** Evaporation in vacuo. **v. fan.** A surface fan. **v. filter.** A device for filtration under reduced pressure or by suction. **v. gases.** (1) The gases obtained by heating solids, e.g., metals, in a v. (2) The residual gas in a v. tube. **v. lamp.** See *lamp*. **v. pan.** A closed retort used in industry for v. distillation. **v. pump.** A suction pump that exhausts gases to a high v.; as one using mercury (Sprengel pump) or the phthalates (Hickman pump), e.g., 10^{-4}–10^{-7} mm Hg. **v. pump oil.** An organic liquid used in place of mercury in v. pumps; e.g.: *n*-butyl phthalate, 21×10^{-4}; benzyl phthalate, 1.2×10^{-7} mm Hg. **v. still.** A v. pan. **v. tar.** A tar obtained from coal by v. distillation, rich in hydrocarbons. **v. tube.** A sealed, glass vessel containing a gas at low pressure; used to produce luminous electric discharges; as, X-ray tube. **v. vessel.** Dewar flask.

vadose. Water just below the earth's surface; as ground- or rainwater. Cf. *juvenile* water.

vagival. Acetarsol.

vagusstoff. Acetylcholine.

vakerin. Bergenin.

valence, valency. (1) The capacity of one atom to combine with others in definite proportions. (2) Also applied, by analogy, to radicals and atomic groups. The combining capacity of a hydrogen atom is taken as unity. Thus, in: HCl, chlorine is monovalent; H_4C, carbon is tetravalent. Values are integers 1–8. See *periodic chain*. According to electronic concepts v. is due to "valence electrons" located in the outer shell of an atom. Cf. *bond*. A *positive* v. is the number of electrons that an atom can *give* up; thus, Be = 2. A *negative* v. is the number of electrons that an atom can *take* up; thus, O = 2. A *covalence* indicates the number of pairs of electrons that an atom can share with its neighbors. An element or its atom may exist in several stages of oxidation and thus form several corresponding series of compounds, e.g., ferrous and ferric. V. is represented thus:

Positive divalent, e.g., ferrous: Fe^{++}
Positive trivalent, e.g., ferric: Fe^{3+}
Negative divalent, e.g., sulfate: $SO_4^=$

(3) The term *valence* is frequently used to indicate the theory of bonding, as distinct from the number of bonds, *valency*. See *bond*. **active-** The commonest v. of an element. **auxiliary-** Covalence. **chief-** (1) The maximum v. of an element. (2) The v. shown by the greatest number of stable compounds. **co-** Auxiliary v. The pairs of electrons shared between 2 molecules; as, NH_3—H_2O. Cf. *electro-v.* **contra-** Co-v. **divided-** A bond that oscillates from one atom to another; represented thus —<. **electro-** q.v. **free-** The v. that appears to be unsatisfied, as in free radicals. **maximum-** The highest stage of oxidation of an element. **negative-** V. due to an atom taking up electrons; as of chlorine. **normal-** The v. based on the group of the periodic system. **null-** Zero v. No v., as in the case of the inert gases, which form no compounds. **partial-** An unsaturated or divided v. **positive-** V. due to an atom giving up electrons; as, sodium. **principal-** The normal v. of an atom or radical. **residual-** Supplementary v. The v. that enables complex compounds to be produced from apparently saturated molecules. **rotating-** V. supposedly due to oscillations of electrons between 2 atoms; as, the H between the 2 O atoms in —COOH. Cf. *bond*. **semi-** See *semivalence*. **supplementary-** Residual v. **zero-** Null v. The state of v. of an atom in a complex when it retains the electronic structure of its gaseous state; e.g., metal atoms in carbonyls.

v. bonds. A pair of electrons consisting of 1 electron from each of the 2 atoms they unite. Cf. *bond, polar.* **v. electrons.** The mobile electrons located outside the kernel or in the outer shell of an atom. Atoms that lose these electrons become positive ions, and atoms that gain these electrons become negative ions. **v. number.** Polar number. A negative or positive number that indicates the stages of oxidation of an element according to the number of electrons lost (positive) or gained (negative). **v. tautomerism.** A dynamic isomerism in which + and − charges produced by a moving double linkage are neutralized by the concomitant movement of a second double linkage, so that ions do not separate. Cf. *ionotropy.*

valencene. A sesquiterpene hydrocarbon flavoring in grapefruit.

Valenta value. The turbidity value, q.v., of an oil, with glacial acetic acid as solvent.

Valentine, Basil. See *Basil.*

valentinite. Sb_2O_3. White antimony. A mineral.

valeral. Valeraldehyde.

valeraldehyde. $C_4H_9 \cdot CHO = 86.11$. Valeral, amyl aldehyde, pentanal. **iso-** $Me_2CH \cdot CH_2CHO$. A liquid, d.0.8041, b.92, soluble in water. **normal-** $Me(CH_2)_3CHO$. Colorless liquid, b.103, slightly soluble in water.

valeramide. $Me(CH_2)_3CO \cdot NH_2 = 101.1$. Valeric amide, pentanamide. Colorless crystals, m.127, soluble in water.

valerate. $C_4H_9 \cdot COOM$. Valerianate. A salt of valeric acid.

valerene. Amylene.

valerian. The dried rhizome of *Valeriana officinalis* (Valerianaceae). It contains valerian, an essential oil, the bornyl ester of isovaleric and other fatty acids; a nervine, antispasmodic, and stimulant. **American-** Cypripedium. **Japanese-** Kesso oil. **v. oil.** The volatile oil of v. Green liquid, d.0.990–0.996, b.250–300, containing borneol, bornyl formate, b. acetate, pinene, and camphene.

valerianate. Valerate.

valerianic acid. Valeric acid.

valeric acid. $C_5H_{10}O_2 = 102.1$. Valerianic acid, pentanoic acid. Isomeric, fatty acids in valerian. **amino-** See *valine, norvaline.* **aminoguanido-** Arginine. **aminomethyl-** See *leucine.* **diamino-** Ornithine. **dl-, dextro-,** or **levo-** $MeCH_2 \cdot CHMe \cdot COOH$. **dl-** $EtCHMeCOOH$. Methylethylacetic acid. Colorless liquid, d.0.941, b.177, soluble in water. *trimethylacetic acid.* Pivalic acid, q.v. **iso-** or **common-** $Me_2CH \cdot CH_2 \cdot COOH$. Isopropylacetic acid, pentoic acid. Colorless liquid, d.0.942, b.186, soluble in water. Occurs in the essential oil of valerian; a perfume and flavoring. **keto-** Levulinic acid. **methyl-** Isocaproic acid. **normal-** $MeCH_2 \cdot CH_2 \cdot CH_2 \cdot COOH$. A liquid, b.185. **tetrahydroxy-** Arabic acid. **v. aldehyde.** Valeraldehyde. **v. anhydride.** $(C_4H_9CO)_2O = 186.2$. Pentanoic anhydride. Colorless liquid, b.205, decomp. by water to valeric acid.

valeridin. $EtO \cdot C_6H_4 \cdot NH \cdot OC \cdot C_4H_9 = 221.2$. Valeryl-*p*-aminophenetol, valerylphenetidine, sedatin, valerydin. Colorless needles, insoluble in water; a nervine and a sedative.

Valerius Cordus. 1515–1544. German author of the first legal pharmacopoeia: "Dispensatorium pharmacorum omnium" (1535).

valerol. $C_{18}H_{20}O_3 = 284.2$. A ketone from oil of valerian.

valerolactone. $MeCH \cdot (CH_2)_2CO \cdot O = 100.06$. Colorless liquid, b.220, in wood tar.

valerone. Diisobutyl ketone.

valeronitrile. Butyl cyanide.

valerydin. Valeridin.

valeryl. Pentanoyl. The radical $C_4H_9CO—$, from valeric acid. **v. chloride.** $Me_2 \cdot CH \cdot CH_2COCl = 120.53$. Isovaleryl chloride, pentanoyl chloride*. Colorless liquid, d.0.989, b.114, decomp. by water. **v. diethyl amide.** Valyl (2). **v. oxybutyrine.** Quietol. **v. phenetidine.** Valeridin.

valerylene. $MeC:CEt = 68.1$. Pentylene, 2-pentyne*, methylethylacethylene. An unsaturated hydrocarbon of the acetylene series; an isomer of pentinene, $Me_2C:C:CH_2$.

Validol. $C_{16}H_{28}O = 236.2$. Trade name for menthol valerate. Colorless liquid, insoluble in water; a nerve sedative and stomachic.

valine. $Me_2CH \cdot CHNH_2 \cdot COOH = 117.1$. Aminoisovaleric acid, 2-amino-3-methylbutanoic acid*. An amino acid from seeds and proteins; 2 stereoisomers: dextro- and levorotatory. **iso-** See *isovaline.* **nor-** See *norvaline.*

Vallets mass. Ferrous carbonate mass.

valonia. The acorn cups of *Quercus aegilops* (Fagaceae), Greece and Asia Minor; a tan.

value. A number expressing a property: as, iodine v.

valve. A device for controlling the motion of a fluid along a passage; arranged to close or open an outlet by the pressure of the fluid. **bunsen-** A piece of rubber tubing with a short slit in the side, and a glass rod inserted, so that steam or air can escape but not reenter. **Contat-Göckel-** A chemical v. used in the cooling of acid solutions, which are easily oxidized when hot. A solution of sodium bicarbonate is drawn into the flask as it cools, and the carbon dioxide evolved prevents the entry of an excess of alkali. **Fleming-** q.v. **radio-** See vacuum tubes. **v. effect.** Unilateral conductivity. The property of conducting a current in one direction only; i.e., of rectification.

valyl. (1) $MeCH_2CH_2CH_2CONEt_2 = 157.2$. Valeric acid, diethyl amide, valeryl diethyl amide. Colorless liquid, slightly soluble in water; a sedative and antispasmodic. (2) The radical $Me_2CH \cdot CHNH_2 \cdot CO—$, from valine.

valzin. Sucrol.

vanadate. M_3VO_4. A salt of vanadic acid. **meta-** MVO_3. **ortho-** M_3VO_4. Vanadate. **pyro-** $M_4 \cdot V_2O_7$.

vanadic. Describing a compound containing tri- or pentavalent vanadium; as, VCl_3 or V_2O_5. **v. acid.** $HVO_3 = 100.0$. *meta-* Golden scales, slightly soluble in water; an oxidizing agent and antiseptic. *ortho-* $H_3VO_4 = 118.0$. Yellow powder, slightly soluble in water. *pyro-* $H_4V_2O_7 = 218.0$. Brown powder, slightly soluble in water. **v. anhydride.** Vanadium pentoxide. **v. salts.** See *vanadium.*

vanadinite. $PbCl_2 \cdot 3Pb_3(VO_4)_2$. A native vanadate.

vanadite. (1) $M_2V_4O_9$. A salt of vanadous acid. (2) Vanadinite.

vanadium. $V = 50.94$. A rare metal and element, at. no. 23, discovered (1830) by Sefström; in the blood of ascidians. Light gray metal, d.5.96

m.1,710, insoluble in water, soluble in acids. Valencies 2, 3, 4, and 5. V. is amphoteric, giving basic salts (vanadyl compounds) and acid salts (vanadates). V. is used in metallurgy, and in catalysts. It resembles tantalum, and can be cold-worked into wire.

Valence number	Ion	Name	Color in solution
2	V^{++}	Vanadous	Violet
3	V^{3+}	Vanadic	Green
	VO^+	Vanadyl(ous)	Bluish gray
5	VO_4^{3-}	Orthovanadate	Yellow
	$VO_3^=$	Metavanadate	Yellow
	VO^{3+}	Vanadyl(ic)	Blue

v. bromide. $VBr_3 = 290.71$. Dark green powder, soluble (decomp.) in water. **v. carbides.** (1) $VC = 62.96$. Black crystals, d.5.36, m.2830; insoluble in acids, except nitric acid. (2) $V_4C_3 = 239.84$. **v. chlorides.** (1) $VCl_2 = 121.9$. Vanadous chloride. Violet hexagons, soluble in water. (2) $VCl_3 = 157.4$. Vanadic chloride. Green crystals, d.3.0, soluble in water. (3) $VCl_4 = 192.8$. V. tetrachloride. Red liquid, d.1.865, b.154, soluble in water. **v. dichloride.** See v. chloride (1). **v. difluoride.** See v. fluoride (1). **v. dioxide.** (1) $VO_2 = 82.95$ (or V_2O_4). V.tetroxide. Blue-black, hygroscopic solid, d.4.34, m.1967. (2) V_2O_2. See v. monoxide. **v. dioxymonochloride.** Vanadyl chloride. **v. disulfide.** $V_2S_2 = 166.05$. Black powder, d.4.2, insoluble in hydrochloric acid. **v. fluorides.** (1) $VF_2 = 89.0$. Vanadous fluoride. Insoluble, except in hydrofluoric acid. (2) $VF_3 = 107.96$. Vanadic fluoride. Green crystals, d.3.363, m. about 800, insoluble in water. (3) $VF_3 \cdot 3H_2O = 162.01$. Rhombohedra, readily soluble in water. (4) $VF_4 = 126.96$. V. tetrafluoride. Yellow, hygroscopic crystals, decomp. 325, soluble in water. **v. hydroxides.** (1) $VO \cdot xH_2O$, or $V(OH)_2$. Vanadous hydroxide. Violet-gray powder, insoluble in water, soluble in acids. (2) $V_2O_3 \cdot xH_2O$ or $V(OH)_3$. Vanadic hydroxide. Green powder, insoluble in water. **v. minerals.** V. is widely diffused in small quantities in rocks, clays, and coals; e.g.: vanadinite, $Pb_6V_3O_{12}Cl$; patronite, V_2S_3. Cf. roscoelite, volborthite. **v. monosulfide.** See v. disulfide. **v. monoxide.** $VO = 66.95$ (or V_2O_2). Gray-brown solid, d.5.6, soluble in acids or alkalies (lavender solution) with strong reducing action. **v. nitride.** $VN = 64.97$. A solid, d.5.63, m.2050, insoluble in water. **v. oxides.**

V_2O	V. suboxide
VO	V. monoxide, vanadous oxide
VO_2	V. dioxide
V_2O_3	V. trioxide, vanadic oxide v. sesquioxide
V_2O_4 or VO_2	V. tetroxide
V_2O_5	V. pentoxide, vanadic anhydride

Positive ions:

VO^{++}	Vanadyl(ous) or vanadyl
VO^{3+}	Vanadyl(ic) or pervanadyl
VO_2^+	Vanadol

v. oxybromide. Vanadyl bromide (1). **v. oxychloride.** Vanadyl chloride (2). **v. oxydibromide.** Vanadyl bromide (2). **v. oxydichloride.** Vanadyl chloride (3). **v. oxydifluoride.** Vanadyl fluoride (1). **v. oxyfluoride.** Vanadyl fluoride (2). **v. oxytribromide.** Vanadyl bromide (3). **v. oxytrichloride.** Vanadyl chloride (4). **v. pentafluoride.** V. fluoride (5). **v. pentasulfide.** $V_2S_5 = 264.2$. Vanadic sulfide. Green powder, soluble in alkalies. **v. pentoxide.** $V_2O_5 = 182.0$. Vanadic oxide, vanadic anhydride. Brown-black, hygroscopic solid (yellow if pure), soluble in hot acids; d.3.34, m.660; used as a catalyst, and in medicine, dyes, inks, and glass, a strong oxidizing agent. **v. sesquioxide.** V. trioxide. **v. sesquisulfide.** V. trisulfide. **v. silicides.** (1) $V_2Si = 129.98$. Silvery prisms, insoluble in water. (2) $VSi_2 = 107.08$. Metallic prisms, insoluble in water. **v. steel.** An alloy: Fe and 0.1-0.15% V; used in tool manufacture. **v. suboxide.** V_2O. Existence doubtful, but possibly the brown stain formed on v. in air. **v.sulfate.** Vanadyl sulfate. **v.sulfides.** (1) V_2S_2. V. disulfide. (2) V_2S_3. (vanadous) v. trisulfide. (3) V_2S_5. (vanadic) v. pentasulfide. **v.tetrachloride.** V. chloride (3). **v. tetrafluoride.** V. fluoride (4). **v. tetroxide.** $V_2O_4 = 165.9$. Vanadous acid. Indigo crystals, m. above 1,750, insoluble in water. **v. trichloride.** V. chloride (2). **v. trifluoride.** See v. fluorides (2) and (3). **v. trioxide.** $V_2O_3 = 149.92$. V. sesquioxide, vanadous oxide. Black, infusible crystals, m.1970, slightly soluble in water. It changes slowly in air to the indigo-blue oxide, V_2O_4; used as a catalyst, a mordant in dyeing, and in the manufacture of steel and of silver vanadate, Ag_3VO_4. **v. trisulfide.** $V_2S_3 = 198.2$. Vanadous sulfide. Red crystals, insoluble in water.

vanadol. The radical VO_2^+.
vanadous. Describing a compound containing di- or trivalent vanadium; as, VCl_2 or V_2O_3. **v. acid.** $H_2V_4O_9$. The hypothetical compound from which vanadites are derived. **v. chloride.** Vanadium chloride (1). **v. fluoride.** Vanadium fluoride (1). **v. hydroxide.** Vanadium hydroxide (1). **v. oxide.** Vanadium trioxide. **v. sulfide.** Vanadium trisulfide.
vanadyl. (1) The radical $VO\equiv$, vanadyl(ic), from pentavalent vanadium (vanadic). (2) The radical $VO-$, vanadyl(ous), from trivalent vanadium (vanadous). **di-** The tetravalent radical $V_2O_2\equiv$. **v. bromides.** (1) $VOBr = 146.87$. Vanadylous bromide, vanadium oxybromide. A solid, decomp. 480, slightly soluble in water. (2) $VOBr_2 = 226.79$. V. oxydibromide. Brown, hygroscopic powder, $VOBr_3 = 306.7$. V. tribromide, vanadium oxytribromide. Red liquid, soluble in water (decomp.). **v. chlorides.** (1) $V_2O_2Cl = 169.4$. V. semichloride, vanadium dioxymonochloride. Yellow crystals, insoluble in water. (2) $VOCl = 102.4$. V. monochloride, vanadylous chloride, vanadium oxymonochloride. Brown powder, insoluble in water. (3) $VOCl_2 = 137.8$. V. oxydichloride. Blue scales, deliquescent, slowly decomp. by water. (4) $VOCl_3 = 173.3$. Vanadium trichloride, vanadic chloride, vanadium oxytrichloride. Dark green syrup, b.127, soluble in water; a mordant. **v. dibromide.** V. bromide (2). **v. dichloride.** V. chloride (3). **v. difluoride.**

V. fluoride (1). **v. fluorides.** (1) $VOF_2 = 104.96$. V. difluoride, vanadium oxydifluoride. A solid, decomp. by heat, insoluble in water. (2) $VOF_3 = 123.96$. V. trifluoride, vanadylic fluoride, m.300, very soluble in water. **v. monobromide.** V. bromide (1). **v. monochloride.** V. chloride (2). **v. semichloride.** V. chloride (1). **v. sulfate.** $(VO)_2(SO_4)_3 = 422.2$. Blue crystals, soluble in water. di- $(V_2O_2)(SO_4)_2 = 326.0$. A double salt of v. sulfate. **v. tribromide.** V. bromide (3). **v. trichloride.** V. chloride (4). **v. trifluoride.** V. fluoride (2).

vanadylic. The radical $VO\equiv$. **v. bromide.** Vanadyl bromide (3). **v. chloride.** Vanadyl chloride (4).

vanadylous. The radical $-VO$. **v. bromide.** Vanadyl bromide (1). **v. chloride.** Vanadyl chloride (2).

vanaspati. (1) An Indian food; wholly hydrogenated vegetable oils containing 5 % sesame oil for identification purposes, and fortified (by law) with 700 I.U. per ounce of vitamin A. (2) Often applied specifically to groundnut oil. Cf. *ghee.*

vancomycin hydrochloride. An antibiotic produced by *Streptomyces orientalis.* Bitter, brown powder, soluble in water (U.S.P.).

van der Waals, Johannes Diderik. 1837–1923. Dutch physicist, Nobel Prize winner (1910). **v. d. W. constant.** The factors a and b in the equation of state, q.v. **v. d. W. equation.** A modification of the equation of state with 2 correcting factors: $(p + a/v^2)(v - b) = RT$, in which the volume factor b corresponds with 4 times the square root of the space occupied by the molecules themselves; the factor, a/v^2, expresses the mutual attraction of the molecules. See *corresponding states.* **v. d. W. forces.** The weak forces between atoms and molecules which cause crystallization of inert gases at low temperature, and the packing together of nonpolar organic compounds to form soft crystals of low melting point.

Vandura. Trade name for the first *prolon,* q.v., produced from gelatin by A. Miller (1894).

van Dyck brown. Vandyke. A mixture of ocher and lampblack.

van Helmont. See *Helmont.*

Vanier's tube. A potash bulb and drying tube, used to absorb the carbon dioxide evolved in the determination of carbon in steel.

vanilla. V. bean. The unripe fruit of *V. planifolia* (Orchidaceae) containing vanillin and vanillic acid; an aromatic (U.S.P.), flavoring, and perfume.

vanillal. The radical $(3,4)(MeO)(HO)C_6H_3$, $CH\equiv$, from vanillin.

vanillic acid. $MeO\cdot C_6H_3(OH)COOH = 168.1$. 3-Methoxy-4-hydroxybenzoic acid. Colorless needles, m.207 (sublimes), slightly soluble in water. **v. alcohol.** $MeO\cdot C_6H_3\cdot OH\cdot CH_2OH = 154.1$. 3-Methoxy-4-hydroxybenzylalcohol. Colorless needles, m.115 (decomp.), soluble in water.

vanillin. $MeO\cdot C_6H_3(OH)CHO = 152.15$. Methylprotocatechuic aldehyde, 3-methoxy-4-hydroxybenzaldehyde. An odorous principle from the vanilla bean, or prepared synthetically. Colorless needles, m.81 (sublimes), soluble in water; a reagent, flavoring agent, and vanilla substitute (U.S.P.). **ethyl-** $C_9H_{10}O_3 = 166.08$. m-Ethoxy-p-hydroxybenzaldehyde, bourbonal. A homolog of vanillin

4 times as strong in flavor. Cf. *ethyl vanillate.* **iso-** See *isovanillin.*

vanilloyl. The radical $(3,4)(MeO)(HO)C_6H_3CO-$, from vanillic acid.

vanillyl. The radical $(3,4)(MeO)(HO)C_6H_3CH_2-$, from vanillic alcohol. **v. alcohol.** Vanillic alcohol.

vanirom. Bourbonal

van Laar, J. J. b. 1860. Dutch coworker of van't Hoff and van der Waals.

vanning. Separation of constituents of an ore by washing away the lighter portions in a stream of water.

Van Slyke, Donald Dexter. b. 1883. American chemist. **V. S. apparatus.** Apparatus for the determination of aliphatic amino nitrogen in proteins. **V. S. method.** Determination of proteins from the nitrogen evolved from aromatic amino compounds and nitrous acid: $RNH_2 + HNO_2 \rightarrow R\cdot OH + N_2 + H_2O$.

Van Slyke, Lucius Lincoln. 1859–1931. American chemist noted for research on dairy products.

van't Hoff, Jacobus Henricus. 1852–1911. Dutch chemist noted for work on stereochemistry, Nobel Prize winner (1901). **v. H.'s factor.** The empirical factor i in the equation of state for solutions: $pv = iRT$, where p is osmotic pressure, v the volume. If d is the degree of ionization and n the number of ions into which a molecule is partly dissociated, $i = 1 + d(n - 1)$. **v. H.'s law.** The osmotic pressure exerted by a solute in solution equals that for the same solute in the state of an ideal gas occupying the same volume as the solution. **v. H. reaction.** *Reaction* isochore. **v. H. solution.** Calcium chloride 2, magnesium chloride 7.8, potassium chloride 2.2, magnesium sulfate 3.8, sodium chloride 100.2 gm in 1 liter of water. **v. H. theory.** Dissolved substances obey the gas laws.

vanthoffite. $MgSO_4\cdot 3Na_2SO_4$. A Stassfurt salt.

vapodust. An insecticidal spray consisting of vaporized petroleum oils; used as a fog, in orchards.

vapor, vapour. A gas, especially from a substance that at ordinary temperature is a solid or liquid; as, ether v. It forms when the v. pressure of a substance equals that of the atmosphere. **saturated-** A v. when liquid in it and from which it is derived cannot further evaporate. **unsaturated-** A v. in a space which contains insufficient liquid to saturate it.

   v. bath. Steam bath. **v. density.** The density of a gas compared with a standard gas: hydrogen or air $= 1$, or oxygen $= 16$. The relationship of these 3 standards is: $H = M/2$, $O = M$, air $= M/28.95$, where M is the molecular weight of the substance, the data being corrected for pressure and temperature by the equation of state. **v. phase chromatography.** See *chromatographic analysis.* **v. phase inhibitor.** A volatile substance enclosed in a package which protects the contents against corrosion by emitting a vapor which excludes air, e.g., cyclohexamine carbonate. **v. pressure.** The pressure at which a liquid and its v. are in equilibrium at a definite temperature. If the v.p. reaches the prevailing atmospheric pressure (1 atm), the liquid boils. Cf. *Clausius equation.* **-of air.** That portion of the total pressure of air due to the water v. present. *saturated-* The v.p. at a particular temperature when

the partial pressure exerted by it is a maximum.
v. tension. The tendency of a liquid to form a v. It depends on the equilibrium between the molecules in the gas and in the liquid, which depends on the prevailing temperature and pressure.

vaporimeter. An instrument to test the volatility of oils by heating them in a current of air.

vaporization. Volatilization. The change from the liquid to the gaseous state without change in the chemical composition of the molecule. Cf. *evaporation*. **heat of-** The number of calories required to transform one gram of liquid substance, at its boiling point, into its vapor. Cf. *Clausius equation*.

vaporize. (1) To change into a vapor, e.g., by heating a liquid. (2) To atomize, or subdivide a liquid into a fine spray.

vaporizer. (1) An atomizer. (2) A still.

varek. Kelp (French).

variability. The deviation from the normal. Cf. *variance*.

variable. (1) Not constant. (2) A factor that is variable.

variance. (1) *V*. The square of the standard deviation. (2) Degree of freedom. The number of external conditions that may be arbitrarily fixed; as, composition, temperature, and pressure. See *phase rule*.

variant. Pertaining to variable factors. **di-** An area in a diagram, q.v. **mono-** A line in a diagram. **non-** A point in a diagram. Cf. *phase rule*.

variate. A numerical value or result when used in statistical treatment.

variolation. Vaccination with serum from a human being having a mild attack of smallpox. No longer practiced.

variscite. $Al(OH)_2 \cdot H_2PO_4$. Peganite. A green gem mineral; it has been synthesized.

varnish. A solution of a resin or drying oil in a volatile solvent, e.g., turpentine. See *lacquer*.

varve. (1) A lamination in a deposit of natural clay. (2) A cycle.

vasculose. Early name for impure lignin.

vaselin. Fossolin. A mixture of hydrocarbons of the paraffin series obtained from petroleum residues. See *petrolatum*.

Vaseline. Trademark for a brand of petroleum jelly and certain similar products. Cf. *vaselin*.

vasicine. $C_{11}H_{12}N_2O = 188.11$. An alkaloid from *Peganum harmale* or *Adhatoda vasica* (Acanthaceae). White needles, decomp. 198; an insecticide.

vasoconstrictor. A vasomotor stimulant that increases arterial pressure by constriction of the blood vessels; as, cocaine.

vasodilator. A vasomotor depressant that lowers arterial pressure by dilation of the blood vessels; as, aconitine.

vasopressin. β-Hypophamine. The antidiuretic hormone. **v. injection.** A sterile solution in water of the pressor principle of the posterior lobe of the pituitary of healthy domestic animals used for human food. A source of pituitary hormones (U.S.P., B.P.).

vat. (1) A vessel or tub in which colors are dissolved, or ores are washed and chemically treated, or liquids are stored or fermented; as, indigo v., cyanide v. (2) The solutions used in these tubs. **v. dye.** A color that is applied with a mordant. See *dyes*.

vaterite. $CaCO_3$. A probable anisotrope of calcite.

Vaughan's cage. A collapsible, sterilizable iron-screen box for animal experiments.

Vauquelin, Louis Nicolas. 1763–1829. The French discoverer of chromium and organic compounds.

vauqueline. Strychnine.

vauquelinite. $2PbO \cdot CuO \cdot 2CrO_3$. A native mixed oxide.

vazadrine. Isoniazid.

V-board. A high-grade water-resistant kraft board for packaging service stores, used in World War II. The liners are laminated with asphalt and the centers with urea-formaldehyde plastic. Cf. *W-board*.

v.d. Abbreviation for vapor density.

veatchine. $C_{22}H_{32}O_2N = 342.01$. An alkaloid from *Garrya veatchii*, m.119. Cf. *garryine*.

vectograph. Stereoscopic photographs produced by forming 2 images in 2 layers of polarizing crystals crossed with respect to each other, and mounted on aluminum.

vector. A quantity; as, velocity, force, etc.; that has both magnitude and direction, and may be represented as a straight line of suitable length and direction. Cf. *coordinates*.

veepa oil. Margosa oil.

vegetable. Pertaining to plants, q.v. **v. dyes.** Coloring matter from plants; as, chromoproteins, indicators, cyanins, carotenes. **v. horsehair.** See *horsehair*. **v. parchment.** A grease-resisting imitation parchment of high wet strength, used to wrap foodstuffs; prepared by passing paper through sulfuric acid or zinc chloride solution. **v. potash.** A fertilizer made from distillery waste: 33% potassium oxide.

vegolysen. Hexamethonium bromide. **v.-T.** Hexamethonium tartrate.

vehicle. A usually inactive medium or carrier for an active substance; as, oil in paints. Cf. *thinner*.

vein. (1) A vessel that conveys blood toward the heart. (2) A lode or deposit of ores distinct from the surrounding rocks.

vellosine. $C_{23}H_{28}O_4N_2 = 396.3$. An alkaloid from the bark of *Geissospermum vellosii*, pareira bark. Yellow crystals, m.189, insoluble in water.

velocity. (1) The speed of travel, expressed as the distance covered in a unit of time. (2) The time

MAGNITUDES OF VELOCITY

Magnitude	cm/sec
Light	2.99×10^{10}
Sun, around hub of Milky Way	3×10^7
Earth around sun	2.95×10^6
Sound in iron (cf. *Mach unit*)	5×10^5
Hydrogen molecules at 0°C	1.8×10^5
Nitrogen molecules at 0°C	4.97×10^4
Earth rotation at equator	4.65×10^4
Sound in air	3.32×10^4
Moon around earth	1.63×10^4
Nerve impulse	3.9×10^3
Papermaking machine (newsprint)	2.5×10^2
Crystal growth (picric acid)	1.43
Gas diffusion (H into O)	0.69
Fastest plant growth	3×10^{-3}
Growth of beard	1×10^{-6}
Growth of eucalyptus tree	1×10^{-8}
Diffusion of gold into lead	4.6×10^{-9}

required for a phenomenon to take place; as, v. of reaction. See table. **angular-** q.v. **migration-** q.v. **molecular-** q.v. **reaction-** q.v. **terminal-** The v. acquired by a freely falling body when the resistance of the medium through which it falls balances the weight of the particle.

v. constant. See reaction *velocity*.

Velon. Trademark for a mixed-polymer synthetic fiber.

Velox. Trade name for photographic printing paper.

Velsicol. $C_{10}H_6Cl_8$. Trade name for a mixture of isomeric chlorinated hydrocarbons. Viscous colorless liquid; an insecticide.

venenation. Acovenoside.

venetian red. Fe_2O_3. A ferric oxide pigment. **v white.** A pigment mixture of equal parts of lead white and barium sulfate.

venom. The poison secreted by reptiles, amphibians, spiders, and insects.

vent. An outlet for fumes or gases.

ventriculin. A dry, granular powder from dessicated and defatted hog stomach; used to treat pernicious anemia.

venturi meter. Undermeter. A pipeline meter for measuring the quantity of liquid flowing past a certain point. The pressure across a streamline or constriction shows the velocity of flow.

venus crystals. Copper acetate.

Veral. Trade name for a copolymeric vinyl chloride-acrylonitrile synthetic fiber.

veratral. The radical $(3,4)(MeO)_2C_6H_3CH=$.

veratraldehyde. $(MeO)_2C_6H_3 \cdot CHO = 166.2$. 3,4-Dimethoxybenzaldehyde. White needles, m.43. **ortho-** 2,3-Dimethoxybenzaldehyde.

veratric acid. $3,4-(MeO)_2C_6H_3 \cdot COOH = 182.2$. Dimethoxybenzoic acid. An acid in sabadilla, m.181. **ortho-** 2,3-Dimethoxybenzoic acid. **formyl-** Opianic acid.

veratrum. A mixture of the alkaloids of veratrum; as veratrine, sabadine, sabadinine, jervine; a cardiac sedative and motor depressant. **amorphous-** Veratroidine. **crystalline-** Veratrine. **proto-** See *protoveratrine*.

veratrine. $C_{32}H_{49}O_9N = 591.5$. Cevadine. The chief alkaloid of veratrum. Colorless crystals. m.205, insoluble in water; used in ointments. See *veratroidine*. **proto-** See *protoveratrine*.

v. hydrochloride. $C_{32}H_{49}O_9N \cdot HCl = 627.9$. Colorless powder, soluble in water. **v. nitrate.** $C_{32}H_{49}O_9N \cdot HNO_3 = 654.5$. Colorless crystals, soluble in water. **v. sulfate.** $(C_{32}H_{49}NO_9)_2H_2 \cdot SO_4 = 1,280.80$. An amorphous, brittle mass, soluble in water.

veratroidine. $C_{37}H_{53}O_{11}N = 698.43$. Amorphous veratrine, q.v. When heated with potassium hydroxide, it hydrolyzes to cevine, $C_{27}H_{43}O_8N$, and 2 molecules of tiglic acid; veratrine gives 1 molecule of tiglic acid.

veratrole. $C_6H_4(OMe)_2 = 138.1$. Dimethoxypyrocatechol, dimethoxybenzene*. Colorless crystals m.23, soluble in water; an antiseptic and anodyne. **allyl-** Methyleugenol.

veratroyl. The radical $(3,4)(MeO)_2C_6H_3CO$—, from veratric acid.

veratrum. American hellebore, green or false hellebore, Indian poke. The dried roots of *V. viride* (Liliaceae). It contains the alkaloids veratrine, protoveratrine, rubijervine, pseudo-

jervine, veratravine, and veratroidine; a cardiac depressant and diaphoretic.

veratryl. The radical $(3,4)(MeO)_2C_6H_3CH_2$—, from veratryl alcohol.

verbascum. Mullein leaves. The dried flowers and herbs of *V. thapsus* (Schrophulariaceae); a demulcent and anodyne. Cf. *mullein*.

verbena. Blue vervain, wild hyssop. The dried overground portions of *V. hastata* (Verbenaceae); a tonic and diaphoretic. **v. oil.** The volatile oil from the leaves of *V. triphylla*, France and Spain (30% citral). Cf. *lippianol, andropogon oil*. *East Indian-* Lemongrass oil. *Singapore-* Citronella oil.

Verbenaceae. The vervain family of herbs and shrubs; some contain aromatic principles; as, *V. officinalis*, verbenaloside; *Premna taitensis*, tonga bark.

verbenalin. Verbenaloside.

verbenaloside. $C_{17}H_{25}O_{10} = 389.19$. Verbenalin. A crystalline, reducing glucoside from the flowering tops of *Verbena officinalis*, wild verbena; m.181, soluble in water.

Verdet's constant. *R*. The magnetic rotation of polarized light per centimeter, per unit magnetic field $= \alpha/H \cdot l$, where α is the rotation in minutes for the substance in a magnetic field of H gauss, and l the length of the light path parallel to the lines of force. Films of Fe, Co, and Ni are exceptions. **V.'s equation.** The magneto-optic rotation $= clH(r - \lambda \cdot dr/d\lambda)r^2/\lambda^2$, where c is a constant for the substance, l the length of the path of the polarized beam, H the intensity of the magnetic field, r the index of refraction of the substance, λ the wavelength of the light used.

verdigris. Basic cupric acetate. A blue to green pigment. **blue-** Cupric acetate.

verditer. (1) Bremen green, q.v. (2) Copper carbonate. **blue-** Blue copper carbonate. **green-** Green copper carbonate.

verdoflavin. A green reduction product of riboflavin.

verdoperoxide. A green enzyme in leukocytes (1–2%), having peroxidase activity.

verine. $C_{28}H_{45}O_8N = 523.5$. An alkaloid from sabadilla.

verium. Ve. A supposed rare alkali metal, like mercury, at. no. 87. d.2.5(?), m.17(?), b.610(?). It is the most electropositive metal, is not radioactive, has no visible spectrum. It is precipitated by silicotungstic acid and occurs in a few clays and alkali deposits of the western U.S., in some springs, and in the ocean. Cf. *francium, virginium*. **v. silicotungstate.** White prisms, insoluble in water.

vermeil. An early method of gilding by firing gold onto a silver surface.

vermicide. An agent that destroys intestinal parasites. Cf. *vermifuge, teniacide*.

vermiculite. $22MgO \cdot 5Al_2O_3 \cdot Fe_2O_3 \cdot 22SiO_2 \cdot 40H_2O$ (mean of 7 true U.S. v.). A gold-colored mineral (U.S. and S. Africa), m. approx. 1,370. Very light (5.8 pcf); used as a heat and sound insulator, filler for plastics, packing for corrosive and flammable materials; expands on ignition.

vermiform. Describing a bacterial growth resembling a mass of worms.

vermifuge. An agent that expels intestinal parasites; especially worms. Cf. *vermicide, teniafuge*.

vermilion. HgS. Red mercuric sulfide, cinnabar; a pigment and polish for lenses. Commercial grades may contain red lead and insoluble synthetic dyes. **mock-** Lead chromate.

vermilionette. A vermilion substitute; usually dyed chalk.

vermouth, vermuth. An aperitif; white wine flavored with wormwood. Cf. *absinthe.*

vernadite. H_2MnO_3. A natural "manganic acid" in dispersed, brown colloidal particles, or black masses.

vernalization. Bringing plants artificially to the spring state, by subjecting them to indoor temperature before planting.

vernier. A small, movable auxiliary scale attached to a larger scale, to increase the accuracy of the readings.

vernine. $C_{16}H_{20}O_8N_8 \cdot 3H_2O = 506.3$. An alkaloid from ergot and leguminous seedlings; as, clover or vetches.

vernonine. $C_{10}H_{24}O_7 = 256.2$. A glucoside from the batiator root, *Vernonia nigritiana* (Compositae), Africa. Hygroscopic white powder, soluble in water; a cardiac poison.

Veronal. Trademark for barbital.

veronica. Speedwell. The dried herb of *V. officinalis* (Scrophulariaceae); an alterative and tonic.

verrucose. Describing a growth of bacteria that resembles warts.

Versatic (911). Trademark for a mixture of cyclic and (mostly) tertiary acids containing 9–11 C atoms, made by the action of carbon monoxide and water on refinery olefins with an acid catalyst. Used in the manufacture of surface coatings, paint driers, and alkyd plastics.

Versene. Trademark for sodium versenate. The sodium salt of ethylenediaminetetraacetic acid, versenic acid; a reagent for gold (violet color), and for titrating the hardness of waters. See, *EDTA.*

versenic acid. See *ethylenediaminetetraacetic acid.*

vertivert oil. The volatile oil of *Andropogon muricatus,* d.1.015–1.030, soluble in water. Cf. *verbena oil.*

vervain. Verbena.

vesicant. An agent that blisters the skin; as mustard gas. Cf. *pustulant.*

vesicle. A small blister.

vesipyrin. Spiroform.

vesorcinol. Dihydroxytoluene.

vesotinic acid. Hydroxytoluic acid.

vessel. (1) A container; as, a beaker. (2) In biology a canal or tube for carrying a fluid such as blood.

Vestamid. Trade name for nylon-12; similar to nylon-6.

Vestan. Trade name for a polyvinyl chloride synthetic fiber.

vesuvianite. Iodocrase.

vesuvin. Triaminoazobenzene.

vesypin. Spiroform.

vetiveria. Cuscus, khuskhus. The Indo-Malayan grass *V. zizanioides* (Graminaceae) whose roots are woven into fragrant mats, fans, baskets. **v. oil.** A volatile oil distilled from v. Cf. *verbena oil.*

V-film. Trade name for a polyvinyl-type plastic.

viability. The capacity to live and grow, e.g., of plants.

vial. Phial. A small bottle. Cf. *ampoule.*

vibracone. An ore screen, with a vibrating conical surface.

vibration. Rapid to-and-fro motion. **atomic-** The

motion of the atoms of a molecule. **electronic-** The rapid v. of the electrons of the dynamic atom, causing emission of rays. Cf. *spinning* electron.

vibrator. A device that produces mechanical vibration, as screens.

vibrograph. An instrument to measure short time intervals; a rotating drum on which an electrically driven tuning fork records the time.

Viburnum. A genus of trees and shrubs (Caprifoliaceae). **V. opulus.** Cramp bark. Cranberry tree, guelder rose. The dried bark of *V. opulus;* contains viburnin, valeric acid, sugar, and tannins. A uterine antispasmodic and tonic. **V. prunifolium.** Black haw. The dried bark of *V. prunifolium;* contains viburnin, valerates, citrates, malates, and tannin. A uterine sedative and tonic.

vicalloy. An alloy for making very small magnets: Co 50, Fe 25–30, V 10–14%.

Vicara. Trademark for a fiber made by extruding a solution of zein in dilute alkali into formaldehyde. It resembles wool, but does not felt or shrink.

vicianin. A glucoside from the seeds of vetch, *Vicia sativa.*

vicianose. $C_{11}H_{20}O_{10} = 312.15$. A disaccharide (glucose and arabinose) obtained by hydrolysis of vicianin.

vicilin. A globulin from peas, beans, and lentils.

vicinal. The neighboring position of radicals, as the 1,2,3-positions of the benzene ring.

victor bronze. The alloy: Cu 58.5, Zn 38.5, Al 1.5, Fe 1.0, V 0.03 pts.

victoria blue. $C_{33}H_{31}N_3 \cdot HCl = 505.75$. Phenyltetramethyltriamido-α-naphthyldiphenylcarbinol hydrochloride. Bronze crystals, soluble in hot water; a textile dye. **v. green.** Malachite green. **v. orange.** $C_7H_5O_5N_2K = 236.3$. Aniline orange, potassium dinitro-*o*-cresol. Yellow dye for wool and silk. **v. yellow.** Antinnonin.

victorium. Vi = 117. Monium, Mo. A supposed metallic element discovered by Sir William Crookes (1898) in yttria minerals; proved later to be a mixture of rare earths.

vicuna. An expensive, fine, soft hair from a species of small llama.

vienna caustic. Potassium hydroxide mixed with lime.

Vierordt, Carl. 1818–1884. The German founder of quantitative spectrum analysis.

Vieth's ratio. For milk, ash:protein:sugar = 1:5:6. Revised to, ash:(nitrogen $\times$ 6.387):lactose hydrate = 2:9:13.

viferral. Hydronal.

Villari effect. The change in magnetization of a fluoromagnetic material under a stress. Cf. *Joule effect.*

Villavecchia test. An oil (5 ml) is shaken with 5 ml fuming hydrochloric acid and 2 drops of a 1% solution of furfural in alcohol (Baudouin's reagent); the bottom (acid) layer becomes rose-colored if sesame oil is present.

villose. Describing a bacterial growth with hairlike flimsy extensions.

vinaconic acid. $CH_2 \cdot CH_2 \cdot C(COOH)_2 = 130.05$. 1,1-Cyclopropanedicarboxylic acid*. White needles, m.175.

vinasse. Schlempe. The residue from the fermentation of molasses, or grapes; a fertilizer and source of potassium salts.

vinegar. (1) A weak (approx. 6%) solution of acetic acid containing coloring matter and other substances (esters, mineral matter etc.), formed by the fermentation of alcoholic liquids (as cider, wine) with an acetifying organism. Cf. *acetifier, acetimetry*. (2) Acetextracts, acetum. The strained liquid obtained by macerating a drug with dilute acetic acid; as, squill v. **artificial-** A v. substitute containing acetic acid, which is not wholly the product of alcoholic and subsequent acetous fermentation. **distilled-** The distillation product of v. **imitation-** Artificial v. **malt-** V. derived, without intermediate distillation, wholly from malted barley with or without addition of whole cereal grain, the starch of which has been saccharified by malt diastase. **nonbrewed-.** Artificial v. **spirit-** The product of a distilled alcoholic fluid, containing 4–15% (w./v.) of acetic acid. **wood-** Pyroligneous acid.

v. essence. A product made synthetically or by distillation of wood (12% acetic acid), and colored with an aniline dye or caramel. Cf. *spirit acid*.

vinesthine, vinethine. Vinyl ether.

Vinethene. Trademark for an anesthetic preparation consisting of vinyl ether.

vinetine. Oxyacanthine.

vinic acids. A group of organic compounds analogous to acid salts; as, $EtHSO_4$, ethylsulfuric acid or sulfovinic acid. **v. ether.** (Ethyl) ether.

vinifera palm oil. Bamboo oil.

Vinol. Trade name for polyvinyl alcohol.

vinometer. A hydrometer to measure the percentage of alcohol in wine.

vinopyrine. Phenetidine acid tartrate. Colorless crystals, decomp. by hot water; an antipyretic.

vinum. Latin for wine.

vinyl. Ethenyl*. The radical $—CH:CH_2$, from ethylene. Cf. *polyvinyl, vinylene*. **v. acetate.** $CH_3COOCH:CH_2$. **v. acetic acid.** β-Butenic acid **v. acetylene.** $CH_2:CH\cdot CH:CH = 52.05$. Butone, monovinylacetylene. A gas formed on passing acetylene into ammoniacal cuprous chloride solution; with hydrochloric acid it forms chloroprene, a source of artificial rubber. See *elastomer*. **di-** See *divinylacetylene*. **v. alcohol.** $CH_2:CH\cdot OH = 44.0$. Vinol, ethenol*. An unsaturated alcohol. **v. amine.** $C_2H_3NH_2 = 43.06$. Ethenylamine*. A liquid, b.56. **v.benzene.** Styrolene. **v. bromide.** $CH_2:CHBr = 106.95$. Ethenyl bromide, bromoethene*. Colorless liquid, b$_{750mm}$-16, insoluble in water. **v. carbazole.** See *green oil*. **v.chloride.** $C_2H_3Cl = 62.5$. Chloroethene*. Colorless gas, d$_{-13.9}$0.97, b.−13.9, soluble in alcohol or ether. **v. cyanide.** $CH_2:CH\cdot CN = 53.03$. Acrylonitrile, propenenitrile*. Colorless liquid, b.78. **v. ether.** $CH_2:CH\cdot O\cdot CH:CH_2 = 70.09$. Divinyl oxide, ethenyloxyethene*, vinesthine, vinethine. Colorless liquid, b.30, insoluble in water; a general anesthic (U.S.P., B.P.). **v. ethylene.** Bivinyl. **v.imine.** Dimethyleneimine. **v. iodide.** Iodoethylene. **v. ketone.** Pentadienone. **v. oxide.** Vinyl ether. **v. sulfide.** $CH_2:CH\cdot S\cdot CH:CH_2 = 86.13$. Ethenylthioethene*. Colorless oil, d.0.913, b.101, slightly soluble in water.

vinylation. Converting a phenolic group into a vinyl group, thus: $R\cdot OH + C_2H_2 \rightarrow R\cdot O\cdot CH:CH_2$, with potassium hydroxide at 120–180 as catalyst.

vinylene. The radical $—CH:CH—$, from ethylene. Cf. *vinyl*. **v. chloride.** Ethylene dichloride.

vinylidene. The radical $H_2C:C=$, from ethylene. Cf. *vinyl*.

Vinylite. Trademark for vinyl resins and plastics, polymers of vinyl acetate, vinyl chloride, vinyl butyral, and vinyl chloride–acetate. **V. A.** Colorless, thermoplastic resin, softening 40–60, soluble in ketones, esters, and hydrocarbons. **V. 80.** White powder, partly soluble in ketones. **V. N.** A 35% solution in toluene. Vinylites are used in the manufacture of dentures and phonograph records, and may be colored with dyes and pigments.

Vinylon. Trade name for a polyvinyl alcohol synthetic fiber.

Vinyon. Trademark for vinyl resins, fibers, and yarns; copolymers of vinyl chloride with acrylonitrile or vinyl acetate; in particular a filament copolymer of 90% vinyl chloride and 10% vinyl acetate, m.70. Cf. *Dynel*.

Vioform. $C_9H_4N(OH)ICl$. Nioform. Trademark for iodochlorohydroxyquinoline. Yellow powder m.177, insoluble in water; an iodine dusting powder.

Viola. The violet family, which includes violet and pansy (Violaceae). Cf. *violene*. E.g., *V. odorata*, sweet violet; *V. tricolor*, pansy or heartsease. **v. crystallina.** Crystal violet. Pure gentian violet, used to treat impetigo. **v. quercetrin.** Oxyritin.

violacein. An antibiotic produced by *Bacillus violaceum*.

violanthrole. $C_{34}H_{16}O_2 = 456.2$. Dibenzanthrole. A nonacyclic diketone; a purple dye for vegetable fibers.

violaquercitrin. $C_{27}H_{30}O_{16} = 610.3$. Osyritin. A glucoside found in various *Viola* species; it hydrolyzes to glucose, quercitrin, and isodulcitol.

violaxanthin. $C_{40}H_{56}O_4 = 600.5$. A carotenoid, m.207, from *Viola tricolor*, and orange hued.

violet. (1) A species of the Violaceae family. Cf. *Viola*. (2) A reddish blue shade. **anthracene-** Gallein. See *crystal* v. **crystal-** Methyl v. **Döbner's-** Aminofuchsin iminochloride. A triphenylmethane dyestuff reagent for aldehydes. Cf. *fuchsin*. **essence of-** Orris. **ethyl-** See *ethyl* v. **gentian-** q.v. **hexamethyl-** Methyl v. **Lauth's-** Thionine. **methyl-** q.v. **ultra-** q.v.

violine. An alkaloid from *Viola* species, resembling emetine in action.

violuric acid. $CO:(NH\cdot CO)_2:C:NOH\cdot H_2O = 175.09$.

5-Oxime alloxan, slightly soluble in water.

viomycin sulfate. The sulfate of an antibiotic from *Streptomyces griseus* var. *purpureus*. White, bitter, hygroscopic powder (B.P.).

viosterol. Vitamin D.

viprynium embonate. $C_{52}H_{56}N_6\cdot C_{23}H_{14}O_6 = 1151.4$. Orange crystals, insoluble in water, m.206 (decomp.); anti-threadworm agent (B.P.).

Virginia snakeroot. Serpentaria.

virginium. Vi (or Vm). Ekacesium. Element no. 87 discovered by Allison and Murphy (1930) by the magneto-optic method; occurs in traces in pollucite and lepidolite. Cf. *verium*.

viride nitens. Brilliant green.

viridin. $C_{20}H_{16}O_6(?)$. Colorless, levorotatory prisms from cultures of the mold *Trichoderma viride,* Pers.; decomp. 208–217, insoluble in ether; an antibiotic, existing as the α and β isomers, $[\alpha]_D$ $-213.4°$ and $-50.7°$.

Viridine. (1) Trade name for phenyl acetaldehyde dimethylacetal. (2) (not cap.) $C_{12}H_{19}N = 177.2$. A homolog of pyridine, distilled from coal tar and bone oil. (3) An alkaloid in *Veratrum viride.*

viridinine. $C_8H_{12}N_2O_3 = 184.1$. A monoacid base from putrid pancreas.

Virion. (1) Trade name for a viscose synthetic fiber. (2) (not cap.) The largest, freely existing infective unit that can be described as a single virus particle.

virosine. (1) $C_{12}H_3O_2N = 193.04$. An alkaloid from *Securinega virosa,* m.135. (2) A biologically active indole alkaloid from *Catharanthus roseus.*

virulence. Extreme toxicity.

virulent. Exceedingly poisonous or active in damaging protoplasm; as of bacteria.

virus. An animal poison that can transmit disease. A submicroscopic, obligately parasitic pathogen. Viruses are all chemically similar nucleoproteins with varying P and carbohydrate contents, but with widely different properties. **true-** A v. that multiplies only in living cells.

Visca. Trademark for a continuous, flat, monofilament rayon yarn.

viscid. Sticky, gummy, glutinous.

viscidity. Stickiness.

viscin. $C_{20}H_{48}O_8$ or $C_{20}H_{32}\cdot8H_2O = 416.5$. The glutinous constituent of mistletoe berries; the chief constituent of birdlime. See *viscum.*

viscoelastic. Plastically deformable.

viscometer. Viscosimeter.

viscose. An extremely viscous syrup obtained by treating cellulose with potassium hydroxide and carbon disulfide. On pressing this liquid through fine openings into dilute acids the cellulose separates as threads of viscose rayon. **v. silk.** See *rayon.*

viscosimeter. Viscometer. An instrument to determine the internal friction (fluidity) of a liquid from the number of revolutions of a vane immersed in the liquid in comparison with its speed in water (cf. *consistometer*); or its rate of flow through an orifice (cf. *Engler*). **torsion-** A v. based on the force required to twist a cylinder immersed in the liquid through a certain angle.

viscosimetry. Measuring fluidity.

viscosity. Internal fluid friction. The ratio of the shear stress to the rate of shear of a fluid. The property of being glutinous or sticky, i.e., offering a slight resistance to a change of form, due to intermolecular attraction. Poiseuille's formula for determining dynamic v. by the capillary-tube method is: $v = \pi p r^4 t / 8 l V$ poises, where p is the pressure difference between the 2 ends of the tube, r the radius of the tube, l its length, V the volume of liquid delivered in a time t. Antonym: fluidity. Cf. *poise, Engler degree, Redwood, Saybolt seconds, Arrhenius, Einstein, Meyer's formula.* **absolute-** Dynamic v. The tangential force per unit area of 2 parallel planes at unit distance apart, when the space between them is filled with the fluid in question and one plane moves with unit velocity in its own plane relative to the other. Cgs unit, the poise. **anomalous-** Sigma phenomenon. The v. of an anomalous liquid, q.v., which is greater than

the true v., and which decreases as the shear increases. **dynamic-** Absolute v. **intrinsic-** The limiting value at infinite dilution of the specific v. of a polymer, referred to its concentration. **kinematic-** The ratio of absolute v. to density of a fluid. Cgs unit, the stoke. **pseudo-** The v. of a thixotropic substance in its most viscous state. See *stoke.* **relative-** The ratio of the absolute v. of a solution of a given concentration to that of the pure solvent at the same temperature. Water (1.002 centipoises at 20°C) is the primary standard for the calibration of viscosimeters. **specific-** The relative v. of a polymer, minus 1. **Woolwich-** The time in seconds for a steel ball $\frac{1}{16}$ in. in diameter to fall 15 cm through a solution at 20°C.

  v. index. $100(L - V)/(L - H)$, where V is the v. at 100°F of a lubricating oil sample; and L and H are respectively the v. at 100°F of an oil of 0 and 100 v.i., having the same v. at 210°F as the sample (in centistokes). It expresses the effect of temperature on v. Cf. *SAE number.*

viscum. Mistletoe. The leaves and branches of *V. flavecens* (Loranthaceae). It contains viscin, bassorin, gum, and tannin; an antispasmodic and tonic.

visibility. Perceptibility to sight. The visibility K of a particular wavelength of light is the ratio of luminous flux F to the radiant power producing it. **mean-** The average visibility K_m over any range of wavelengths or the entire spectrum, $K_m = (F)/$(erg/sec), where (F) is the total luminous flux in lumens and (erg/sec), the total radiant energy in watts or ergs per second.

visible. Perceptible by the eye; as, v. light.

viskiosol-6. A viscous injection of diodone.

Vistanex. Trademark for a synthetic fiber produced by spinning a viscous solution of polyisobutylene in *n*-hexane. Cf. *Vinyon.*

Vistra. Trade name for a viscose synthetic fiber.

Vita. Trade name for a polyvinyl chloride–type plastic.

vitagen. A substance having vitamin activity, but also providing energy for life: e.g., choline and derivatives; as, betaine.

vitaglass. A colorless window glass transparent to ultraviolet light.

vital. Pertaining to life.

vitamer. One of 2 or more substances which have the same ability to cure single vitamin-deficiency symptoms; e.g., gadol and galol.

vitamin. Accessory (food) factor (Hopkins, 1906), vitamin e (essential to life, Funk, 1912), advitant, exogenous hormone, food hormone, vitol, biosterin, biotic. An organic substance which is essential in small quantities for maintaining the life of an animal, but which cannot be synthesized by the animal, and does not itself provide energy. Cf. *vitagen, bios, biocatalyst.* Antonym: toxamin. A deficiency results in characteristic disorders (avitaminosis); an excess of some vitamins may cause hypovitaminosis. Vitamins have been classified according to their solubility or the effects they produce, and were originally known by letters. A number have been synthesized, and what were formerly regarded as single vitamins are now known to consist of a "complex" of several vitamins, often having similar but different properties. The most important known and doubtful vitamins, the internationally accepted names (in capitals), and the commonest synonyms are given in the table. **anti-** Toxamin. A substance that offsets the action of a v., but usually similar in structure; its effect is roughly proportional to the amount present. Thus, sulfanilamide is an anti-v. to *p*-aminobenzoic acid. **antiallpecia-** *p*-Aminobenzoic acid. **antiberiberi-** V. B. **anticanitic-** *p*-Amino-

benzoic acid. **antiencephalitic-, antidermatitic.** V. B₃. **antihemorrhagic-** V. J. **anti-infection-** V. A. **antineuritic-** V. B₁. **antipellagric-** V. B₂. **anti-perosis-** V. Bₚ. **antipneumonia-** V. J. **anti-rachitic-** V. D. **antiscorbutic-** V. C. **antisterility-** V. E. **apparent-** A type of reductone, q.v. **deca-** q.v. **lactation-** Vitamins L. **pro-** See *provitamin*. **sunshine-** V. D. **weight-restoring-** V. B₃.

Original alphabetical classification	Deficiency effects	Synonyms, chemical names, and formulas
Fat soluble		
A	Eye (xerosis) and lung infections	Axerophthol. β-Carotene ($C_{40}H_{56}$). Vitamin A₁ ($C_{20}H_{30}$-O). Carenol
D	Rickets	Derivatives of 7-dehydrosterols
D₂	Rickets	Calciferol. ERGOCALCIFEROL. Viosterol. Vitamin L ($C_{28}H_{44}O$)
D₃	Rickets	CHOLECALCIFEROL. 7-Dehydrocholesterol. ($C_{27}H_{44}O$)
Water soluble		
B-complex	Beriberi	Folic acid (U.S.P., B.P.). ($C_{19}H_{19}O_6N_7$)
B₁	Beriberi	Aneurin. THIAMINE. ($C_{12}H_{17}ON_4SCl \cdot HCl$)
B₂	Angular stomatitis and cheilosis	Lactoflavin. RIBOFLAVIN. Vitamin G. ($C_{17}H_{20}O_6N_4$)
B₃	Chick dermatitis	Filtrate factor. PANTOTHENIC ACID. ($C_9H_{17}O_5N$)
B₄	Rat pellagra	Arginine and glycine. BIOTIN. Vitamin H. ($C_{10}H_{16}O_3N_2S$)
B₅	Pellagra	Niacinamide. NICOTINAMIDE. Nicotinic acid. U factor. Vitamin PP. ($C_6H_6ON_2$)
B₆	Rat dermatitis	Adermin. PYRIDOXIN ($C_8H_{11}O_3N$), and its derivatives, i.e., pyridoxal ($C_8H_9O_3N$), and pyridoxamine ($C_8H_{12}O_2N_2$)
B₇(?)	Pigeon digestion disturbances	Vitamin I
B₈(?)	Suppression of lactic bacteria	Adenylic acid
B₁₂	Suppression of lactic bacteria Anemia	COBALAMIN (group name). CYANOCOBALAMIN (pure substance). Animal protein factor
B₁₂ᵦ	As B₁₂	HYDROXYCOBALAMIN
B₁₂꜀	As B₁₂	NITROSOCOBALAMIN. Nitritocobalamin
B꜀	Chick anemia	Inositol
Bₚ	Perosis	
C	Scurvy	ASCORBIC ACID ($C_6H_8O_6$)
C₂	Pneumonia	Vitamin J
E	Sterility	ALPHA-TOCOPHEROL ($C_{29}H_{50}O_2$). BETA- and GAMMA-TOCOPHEROLS ($C_{28}H_{48}O_2$). Delta-Tocopherol ($C_{27}H_{46}O_2$)
F(?)	Scaliness of rat tails	Nutritionally essential fatty acids, e.g., arachidonic ($C_{20}H_{32}O_2$), linoleic ($C_{18}H_{32}O_2$), linolenic ($C_{18}H_{30}O_2$)
G: see B₂.		
H: see B₄.		
J: see C₂.		
K	Hemorrhage	Naphthoquinone derivatives, viz. K₁ ($C_{31}H_{46}O_2$), phytonadione; K₂ ($C_{41}H_{56}O_2$)
L: see D₂		
P(?)	Hemorrhage	Citrin, hesperidin ($C_{26}H_{34}O_{15}$), and related glycosides
PP: see B₅.		
M(?)	Mouse factor	
PARA-AMINO-BENZOIC ACID	Graying rat hair. An antibiotic	} $C_7H_7O_2N$. Antiallpecia-v.
Animal protein factor: see B₁₂.		
Choline	Fatty dog liver	$C_5H_{15}O_2N$. Cf. vitamin B-complex
FOLIC ACID	Anemia	Pteroyl glutamic acids, e.g., $C_{19}H_{19}O_6N_7$ Cf. vitamin B-complex

v. A. $C_{20}H_{30}O = 286.2$. Vitasterol A, biosterin A, v.A_2, ophthalin, anti-infection v. Trimethylcyclohexenyldimethyloctatetraenecarbinol,

$$CH_2 \cdot C(CH_3)_2 \cdot C \cdot [CH:CH \cdot C(CH_3):CH]_2 \cdot CH_2OH$$
$$CH_2—CH_2— C \cdot CH_3$$

A readily oxidized, fat- and solvent-soluble, water-insoluble alcohol: in butter, milk, egg yolk, green vegetables, fish livers (especially cod, halibut, mackerel), and in glandular fat; yellow isotropic plates, m.63. It is derived from carotene, q.v.; has epithelium-protecting and antixerophthalmic properties; and is essential to growth; a deficiency results in the common cold. Activity: 4.5×10^6 I.U./gm. It has a green fluorescence, and exists in 2 isomeric forms, trans v.A, and neo v.A. **v.A_1.** Gadol. Cf. *galol.* **v.A_2, v.A_3.** Vitamins similar to v. A, from fish oils. They are probably β-apo-5-carotinols. Cf. *cholane. concentrated v.A.* A solution containing 45,000–55,000 units of v. A (B.P.). *oleo v.A.* V. A rendered water-miscible by addition of a harmless dispersing agent (U.S.P.). *water-miscible v.A.* Oleo v. A. **v. A acid.** An acid synthesized from B-ionone, m.182; it has a strong v. A activity. **v. A alcohol.** The compound $C_6H_3Me_3 \cdot (CH_2:CH \cdot CMe:CH)_2CH_2OH$. **v. A aldehyde.** Axerophthol. **v. B.** A complex consisting of v. B_1. $C_{12}H_{17}ON_4SCl \cdot HCl = 337.2$. Thiamine (U.S. usage), aneurin(e) (European usage), oryzamin (Japanese usage), torulin, polyneuramin, betaxin, v.F (obsolete). **v. B_1.** Antineuritic v., antiberiberi v. The hydrochloride of the aminopyridinesulfonic acid. A heat-labile, antineuritic powder, m.234, soluble in water or alcohol, insoluble in ether; found in the outer coatings of grains, fruits, and vegetables (e.g., ripe peas and beans) and in yeast, often with riboflavin (see *v. B_2*); oxidized to thiochrome. Activity, 3,333,000 I.U./gm. **v. B_2.** $C_{17}H_{20}N_4O_6 = 376.2$. Riboflavin (U.S. usage), lactoflavin (European usage), uvoflavin, ovoflavin, hepatoflavin. **v. G.** Pellagra-preventing v. The heat-stable, lyochromic lactoflavin, q.v.

$$CH_2 \cdot (CHOH)_3 \cdot CH_2OH$$
$$CH_3 \cdot C:CH \cdot C \cdot N \cdot C:N \cdot CO$$
$$CH_3 \cdot C:CH \quad C \cdot N:C \cdot CO \cdot NH$$

Orange crystals, m.282 (decomp.), soluble in alkali, slightly soluble in water or alcohol (green-yellow fluorescence), insoluble in ether. Widely distributed in plant and animal cells, milk, and urine; and has pellagra-preventing properties. Activity, 400,000 Bourquin-Sherman units per gm. **v. B_3.** $C_{19}H_{17}O_5N = 339.2$. Pantothenic acid (Greek, everywhere), pantothen, antidermatosis factor, chick antidermatitis factor, yeast filtrate factor, chick A.P. (antipellagra) factor, liver factor 2. Yellow, viscous oil, $OH \cdot CH_2 \cdot CMe_2CHOH \cdot CO \cdot NH \cdot CH_2 \cdot COOH, [\alpha]_D^{25} + 37.5°$, soluble in water, slightly soluble in ether. It occurs in animal tissues, livers, and kidneys; a deficiency causes loss of weight; it has been identified with v. B_2 and B_4. Activity, 70,000–75,000 chick units per gm. **v. B_4.** Biotin, arginine, glycine (?). A v. that prevents pellagra in rats. **v. B_5.** Nicotinic acid

(q.v.), nicotinamide, niacin, niacinamide, P.P. factor, pellagramine, niamid. A v. from living cells, liver, and yeast, which prevents pellagra and lesions of the mucous membrane. **v. B_6.** $C_{18}H_{11} \cdot O_3N = 289.1$. Pyridoxin(e) (U.S.usage), adermin (European usage), rat antidermatitis factor, yeast eluate factor, factor 1, factor Y, v. H, complementary factor. 3-Hydroxy-4,5-di(hydroxymethyl)-2-methylpyridine. Colorless, bitter crystals m.160, soluble in water or alcohol, slightly soluble in ether. It occurs in yeast and rice polishings and in seed husks, and prevents dermatitis. **v. B_7.** V.I. A supposed v., which prevents digestive disturbances in pigeons. **v. B_8.** Adenylic acid. A supposed v., whose absence prevents development of lactic bacteria. **v. B_{12}.** $C_{63}H_{88}O_{14}N_{14} \cdot CoP = 1,355.42$ Cyanocobalamin. Castle's extrinsic X factor. A.P.A. A v. whose absence causes pernicious anemia, occurring in liver (15 mg/ton), and produced by the growth of *Streptomyces griseus*. It is the only v. containing a metal, and is believed to consist of 4 biologically active compounds (v.B_{12}, B_{12b}, B_{12c}, and B_{12d}), which are distinguished by their absorption spectra and partition coefficients. Red needles, m. exceeds 300, soluble in water or alcohol, insoluble in ether. Human requirement, 0.001 mg/day. See *corrin*. **pseudo v. B_{12}.** Adenine. **v. B_{15}.** Pangamic acid. A v. of doubtful existence. **v. B_c.** A supposed vitamin, which prevents anemia in chicks. **v. B_p.** Antiperosis v. A supposed v., which prevents the deformation of chicks' legs. **v. B_t.** Carnitine. A supposed v. from yeast, liver extract, or animal flesh, related to folic acid. Its absence reduces the activity of the common mealworm. **v. B_u.** V.H. **v. B_x.** $C_6H_8O_6 = 176.1$. *p*-Aminobenzoic acid. **v. C.** $OH \cdot C:C \cdot OH \cdot C:O \cdot O \cdot CH$. Ascorbic acid, hexuronic acid, cevitamic acid, antiskorbutin, scorbutamin. Colorless crystals, m.191, soluble in water, slightly soluble in ether. It occurs in citrus fruits and green vegetables, and its absence from a diet causes scurvy. Activity, 20,000 I.U./gm. **v. C_2.** See table. *apparent*- A constituent of walnut tissues, closely allied to v. C, but having no specific dye-reducing powers: probably 1,4,5-trihydroxynaphthalene. **v. D.** $C_{27}H_{42}O = 382.3$. Viosterol, vitasterol D, biosterin 2, antirachitic v., rachitamin, irradiated ergosterol, acterol. A fat-soluble v. from milk and fish (cod)-liver oils, produced by activation of provitamins D (q.v.) by ultra-violet light; its absence causes rickets; 5 constituents have been prepared: **v. D_1.** A mixture of v. D_2 and lumisterol, q.v. **v. D_2.** $C_{28}H_{43}OH = 396.6$. Activated ergosterol, califerol, viosterol, m.115–118; an isomer of ergosterol. **v. D_3.** $C_{27}H_{44}O = 384.6$. Activated 7-dehydrocholesterol, m.82. **v. D_4.** Activated 2,2-dehydroergosterol, m.107. **v. D_5.** Activated 7-dehydrositosterol. All are white crystals, soluble in fats or organic solvents, insoluble in water. **v. E.** Tocopherol (Greek, childbirth), antiencephalomalacin v., factor X, antisterility v., reproductive v., fertility v., sterilamin, vitasterol E, biosterin 3. It comprises: α-tocopherol, $C_{29}H_{50}O_2$; β-tocopherol, $C_{28}H_{48}O_2$; γ-tocopherol, $C_{28}H_{48}O_2$ (activities, 400, 200, and 200 rat units per gm, respectively). They occur principally in plants and vegetable oils. Eight

DAILY VITAMIN REQUIREMENTS

Subject	Vitamin A, 1,000 I.U.	Thiamine, mg	Riboflavin, mg	Niacin, mg	Ascorbic acid, mg	Vitamin D. I.U.
Man	5.0	1.2–2.0	1.6–2.6	12–20	75	
Woman	5.0–8.0	1.1–2.0	1.5–3.0	11–20	75–150	400–800
Adolescent	5.0–6.0	1.3–1.8	1.8–2.5	13–18	80–100	400
Child	2.0–4.5	0.6–1.2	0.9–1.8	6–12	35–75	400

tocopherols are known to exist in nature, chiefly in wheat bran. **v. F.** (1) V. B_1. (2) See *vitagens*. (3) A supposed anti-pernicious-anemia v. **v. G.** V. B_2. **v. H.** $NH \cdot CO \cdot NH \cdot CH \cdot CH_2 \cdot S \cdot CH_2 \cdot C(C-H_2)_4 \cdot COOH = 244.3$. Biotin, bios II, bios IIB, factor X, factor W, coenzyme R, skin factor. Occurs widely in nature, e.g., in vegetables and yeast. Its absence causes injury to white of egg, and prevents the growth of *Saccharomycetes* yeasts and rats. Activity, 27×10^6 rat units $= 25,000 \times 10^6$ S.U./gm; 1 S.U. = amount of v. H to increase cell growth of yeast by 100%. **v. I.** V. B_7. **v. J.** See table. **v. K_1, K_2**, ..., etc. α-, β-, ..., etc. Phylloquinones, coagulation v., antihemorrhagic v., prothrombin F. General formula:

O
CH$_3$
R
O

R varies according to the v. K. v. K_1R (phytyl), $C_{20}H_{39}(C_{31}H_{46}O_2)$, and v. K_2R, $C_{30}H_{49}(?)(C_{41}H_{56}O_2)$ are known for certain (in hog liver, leafy vegetables, and cereals); and their absence inhibits the clotting of blood. Cf. *menadione, menandone, menaphthone*. **v. M.** A supposed vitamin, whose absence causes anemia and loss in weight of monkeys, probably related to xanthopterin. **v. P.** (1) Citrin, permeability v. A crude extract from paprika, rose hips or citrus fruits, consisting principally of eriodictin (5,7,3',4'-tetraxhydroxy-flavanol) and hesperitin (4'-methyl eriodictin); believed to reduce the permeability of cells to albumin, but this was not substantiated and the name is now obsolete. (2) V. B_1. (3) V. B_2. (4) V. C_2. **v. T.** A supposed v., the absence of which promotes the growth of chicks. **v. units.** In 1942 international units (I.U.) were defined as the activities of:

V. A: $0.6 \mu g$ of pure β-carotene
V. B: $3 \mu g$ of pure anhydrous aneurin hydrochloride
V. C: $50 \mu g$ of pure ascorbic acid
V. D: $1 \mu g$ of a certain solution of crude, irradiated ergosterol
V. E: $1 \mu g$ of synthetic, racemic tocopheryl acetate

For v. C: 1 Sherman unit $= 0.5$–0.6 mg ascorbic acid = 1 minimum protective dose (guinea pig); formerly based on 1 ml fresh lemon juice.
For v. D: I.U. = 1 U.S.P. unit = 1 Medical Research Council unit = 1 Coward unit $= 0.025 \gamma$.

v. $D_2 = 1.66$ Oslo units $= 2.6$ prophylactic units $= 10^{-6}$ standard unit; 1 clinical unit = 12.5–17.1 I.U.; 1 Steenbock unit = 3.2 I.U.
See also under individual vitamins.
Pharmacopoeia terminology and units (1968):
v.A.—1 mg v.A (alcohol) = 3,333 U.S.P. units of v.A. B.P. unit, $0.344 \mu g$ of all-trans v.A acetate.
v.B_1—U.S.P., thiamine hydrochloride. B.P., aneurine hydrochloride.
v.B_2—U.S.P. and B.P., riboflavin.
v.B_6—U.S.P., pyridoxine hydrochloride.
v.B_{12}—U.S.P. and B.P., cyanocobalamin.
v.C—U.S.P. and B.P., ascorbic acid.
v.B complex—U.S.P. and B.P., folic acid.
v.D—B.P. unit, $0.025 \mu g$ of a standard preparation of v.D_3 (activated crystalline 7-dehydro-cholesterol); cholecalciferol (U.S.P.).
v.D_2—U.S.P., calciferol. $1 \mu g$ = 400 U.S.P. units. B.P., calciferol.
v.D_3—U.S.P. and B.P., activated 7-dehydro-cholesterol. $1 \mu g$ = 40 units.
v.K_1—U.S.P., phytonadione.
vitaminosis. Hypovitaminosis. The effect of overdosage with vitamins. Cf. *avitaminosis*.
vitasterol. Vitamins A, D, and E.
vitavel-K. Menaphthone. **v.K (oral).** Acetomenaphthone.
vitazyme. Homozyme. Ergon. A substance having the properties of a vitamin and an enzyme. Cf. *biocatalyst*.
vitellin. A globulin from egg yolk. Similar proteins occur in lentils, corn, and other cereals. **silver-Argyrol.**
vitellolutein. The yellow coloring matter of eggs.
vitexin. $C_{21}H_{20}O_{10}(?)$. Saponaretin. A flavonoid pigment from *Vitex lucens*, T. Kirk, m.246.
vitexine. $C_{21}H_{14}O_6 = 362.09$. A coloring matter and flavone glucoside in *Vitex litoralis* (Verbenaceae).
vitiatine. $C_5H_{14}N_6 = 158.07$. A meat base.
vitiglio. A skin disease related to leprosy, producing small, white, shining tubercles on the face and hands.
vitol. Vitamin.
Viton. Trademark for a synthetic rubber derived from the combination of vinylidene fluoride and hexafluoropropylene.
vitrain. A constituent of *coal*, q.v.
Vitreosil. Trademark for heat-resisting apparatus, made from a translucent variety of silica, prepared by fritting sand with a hot carbon plate.
vitreous. Glassy. **v. copper ore.** Redruthite. **v. enamel.** Metal with a fused-on glass surface. **v. silver ore.** Argentite.
vitrescence. The property of becoming hard and transparent like glass.
vitrification. The conversion of a material into a glass or glasslike substance, of increased hardness and brittleness.

vitrify. To sinter or melt to a glassy mass.

vitrinite. A uniform brown constituent of coal, with a low ash content; consists mainly of ulmin compounds. Cf. *vitrain*.

vitriol. A sulfate of a heavy metal; as:

Blue or roman... Copper sulfate (chalcanthite)
Green .... Ferrous sulfate (copperas)
Red or rose ..... Cobaltous sulfate (bieberite)
Uran .... Uranium sulfate (johannite)
White .... Zinc sulfate (goslarite)

Cypria- Copper sulfate. **nitrous-** Nitrososulfuric acid formed in the Gay-Lussac tower. **oil of-** Sulfuric acid. Cf. *BOV, DOV, ROV*. **salt of-** Zinc sulfate.

vitriolate. The sulfate of a metal (obsolete). **v. of soda.** Sodium sulfate. **v. of tartar.** Potassium sulfate.

vitriolum veneris. Copper sulfate.

vitro- Prefix (Latin, glass) indicating a mineral or rock of glassy texture; as, vitrophyric. Cf. *in vitro*.

vitrophyric. Describing an igneous rock having a glassy base.

vivianite. $Fe_3(PO_4)_2 \cdot 8H_2O$. Blue ocher, blue iron ore. A native ferrous phosphate which is white when freshly broken and becomes bluish on oxidation.

vivo. Pertaining to life. Cf. *in vivo*.

vobasine. $C_{21}H_{24}O_3N_2 = 362.21$. See acylindole *alkaloids*.

vocoder. An instrument for synthesizing speech and sound effects by electrical methods.

voiceprint. See *spectrograph*.

volatile. Evaporating rapidly. **v. alkali.** Ammonia. **v. oils.** Essential oils. **v. poisons.** Poisonous substances that form vapors:

Nonmetallic: bromine, chlorine, iodine, fluorine, phosphorus, hydrofluoric acid, arsine, antimonous hydride, bismuthine, phosphine, hydrogen sulfide.
Organic: Chloral, chloroform, ether, aniline, acetanilide, etc.

volatility product. The product of the concentrations of the constituent gases from a solid substance (as ammonium carbonate) which dissociates into 2 volatile gases when heated, is constant. Cf. *solubility product*.

volatilization. Vaporization: the conversion of a solid into a vapor or gas without chemical change.

volatilize. To convert into a gas or vapor.

volborthite. A native hydrous copper-calcium vanadate.

volcanic. Pertaining to molten rock or lava. **v. ash.** Tuff. **v. glass.** A volcanic, igneous rock; as, obsidian. **v. mud.** A mud of fine-grained ash or tuff and water.

volemite. Volemitol.

volemitol. $CH_2OH(CHOH)_5CH_2OH = 212.2$. Heptahydroxyheptane, heptaheptanol, volemite, α-sedoheptitol, m.150, $[\alpha]_D +2.25$-2.65, from *Lactarius volemus* and *Primula* species. Cf. *primulite*.

Volhard, Jakob. 1834–1910. German analytical chemist. **V.'s solution.** A decinormal solution of potassium thiocyanate. **V.'s volumetric method.** The determination of halogens by means of standard thiocyanate solutions.

Volidan. Trade name for an anti-ovulatory, oral contraceptive based on megestrol acetate, a derivative of progesterone.

volkonskoite. A magnesium chromium silicate (30% chromic oxide); a zeolite.

volt. A unit of electromotive force and potential difference. It is the potential or electrical pressure which, if steadily applied to a conductor of one ohm resistance, will produce a current of one ampere. 1 international volt $= 10^8$ emu $= 1/300$ esu $= 1.00034$ absolute volts. A Weston normal cell at 20°C gives 1.0183 international volts. **ampere-** Watt. **electron-** See *electron volt*. The SI unit, q.v., of energy.

Volta, Count Alessandro. 1745–1827. Italian physicist. **v. couple.** An electric cell having a zinc anode and copper cathode (potential 0.98 volt). **v. effect.** The change in the sign of the charge on a metal electrode after it has been heated. **v. series.** Displacement series.

voltage. Electromotive force (in volts). See *potential*.

voltaic. Pertaining to a direct electric current. **v. battery.** A number of v. cells. **v. cell.** An electric cell or device in which an oxidation-reduction reaction produces an electromotive force. See *bunsen, Daniell, Grove, Léclanché, Weston normal, cadmium, Clark cell; lead accumulator*. **v. couple.** A pair of metallic celectrodes producing a potential when set up as a cell. See *volta couple*. **v. electricity.** Galvanic electricity, chemical electricity. A continuous stream of electrons (direct current) caused by a chemical reaction. **v. pile.** A series of metallic disks forming a v. battery.

voltaite. The mineral $2(FeAl)_2O_3 \cdot 5(MgFeNa_2K_2) \cdot (OH)_2(SO_4) \cdot 14H_2O$.

voltameter. Coulometer. An apparatus for the electrolysis of water. The volume of the gases liberated measures the number of coulombs of current flowing in the circuit during the decomposition. Cf. *voltmeter*.

voltammeter. An instrument that indicates both volts and amperes.

volt-ampere. The equivalent of the watt power factor, q.v.; the product of a volt and ampere.

voltmeter. An instrument that indicates voltage. Cf. *voltammeter*.

voltoids. Small compressed tablets of ammonium chloride, used in voltaic (Léclanché) cells.

voltolise, voltolize. To subject to a silent electric discharge.

voltzite. Zn_5OS_4. A native oxysulfide.

volucrisporin. $C_{18}H_{12}O_4$(?). A red pigment from the fungus *Volucrispora aurantiaca*. A rare example of a naturally occurring terephenylquinone, monosubstituted with an —OH group in the *m*-position.

volume. The space occupied by a substance, generally expressed in cubic centimeters or liters according to the formula, $V = CL^3$, in which C is a constant depending on the shape of the space occupied (if a cube, $C = 1$) and L is the length. **atomic-** the quotient of the atomic weight and the specific gravity of a solid or liquid element. **critical-** The v. occupied by one gram of a gas at the critical temperature and pressure. See *parachor*. **co-** The quantity b in van der Waals' equation, q.v. **humid-** The v. of that quantity of moist air which contains 1 liter of dry air. **incompressible-** That which cannot be made smaller by pressure. **molecular-** The v. occupied by one gram molecule of a substance, i.e., molecular weight/density. It varies for solids and liquids according to their atomic volumes, but is 22.4 liters for gases at normal temperature and pressure. See *parachor*. **specific-** The v. occupied by one mole of a substance = molecular weight/density. **standard-** The v. occupied by one mole of gas at 0°C and 760 mm pressure = 22.4 liters.

v. susceptibility. The ratio of the intensity of magnetization of a medium to the strength (in gauss) of the magnetic field inducing it.

volumenometer. (1) An apparatus for the accurate determination of the volume of a known weight of substance, and thence its density. (2) Pyknometer (obsolete).

volumetric. Pertaining to measurements of volumes. **v. analysis.** The quantitative analysis of a known volume of a solution of unknown strength by adding a reagent of known concentration until the end point of the reaction has been reached. From the amount of reagent used the unknown strength can be calculated. An indicator is added to establish a definite end point. Methods: neutralization (alkalimetry, acidimetry); oxidation-reduction (oxidimetry, iodometry); precipitation (titration with a reagent that causes a precipitation.) **v. factor.** The amount of substance corresponding with 1 ml of normal, half-normal, or tenth-normal solution. **v. glassware.** The graduated glass utensils used to measure definite quantities of a solution; i.e.: burets, cylinders, flasks, and pipets. Cf. *standardized*. **v. solutions.** V.S. Solutions of known strengths used in v. analysis. See *normal solution*. **v. standards.** *primary-* When the composition is gravimetrically determined. *secondary-* When standardized against a weighed amount of reagent. *tertiary-* When one solution is titrated against another. **v. weight.** The amount of substance to be weighed in order that, on titration, the number of milliliters found will equal the percentage of unknown present.

voluminal. Pertaining to 3 dimensions. **v. expansion.** Cubical *expansion*.

voluntal. $NH_2COOCH_2 \cdot CCl_3$ = 192.39. Trichloroethylurethane. White crystals; an anesthetic.

volutin. A nucleoprotein from yeast.

vomicine. $C_{22}H_{24}N_2O_4$ = 382.2. An alkaloid from strychnos.

vomipyrine. $C_{15}H_{16}N_2$ = 224.04. An alkylated pyrroquinoline produced by the degradation of vomicine; m.107. Its ether solution has a blue-violet fluorescence.

votator. A concentric, double-tube heat exchanger, with a scraper in the central tube.

v.p. Abbreviation for vapor pressure.

VPI. Trademark for dicyclohexylammonium nitrite, a vapor-phase inhibitor, q.v.

vrbaite. $TlAs_2S_5$. A mineral source of thallium.

V.S. Abbreviation for volumetric solution.

vug. A cavity in a casting. **v. crystals.** The metallic crystals found inside v.

vulcanite. A hard rubber produced by heating caoutchouc or india rubber with sulfur. Cf. *ebonite*.

vulcanization. (1) The oxidation of rubber by reducing sulfur to sulfides. The rubber is mixed with a vulcanizing agent (as, sulfur), and heated at 110–140°C. The tacky, plastic mixture changes gradually to an elastic, rigid product. Accelerators are added to improve the quality. See *vulcanizing agent*. (2) The treatment of cellulose fibers with a quaternary ammonium base, e.g., cuprammonium, to produce oxygen bridges between the cellulose chains. Cf. *vulcanized fiber*.

vulcanize. To produce vulcanization.

vulcanized. Subjected to vulcanization. **v. fiber.** See *vegetable parchment*. **v. paper.** Horn fiber. A hard, resistant material made by impregnating paper with zinc chloride solution, followed by washing. Several layers may be laminated together; used for luggage. Cf. *vegetable parchment*, *Willesden goods*.

vulcanizing agent. A substance that vulcanizes (q.v.) rubber; e.g.: sulfur (chiefly), selenium, sulfur dichloride, *m*-dinitrobenzene, nitrogen compounds; as, di- and triphenylguanidine, tetramethylthiuram, and piperidine derivatives.

vulnerary. A substance used externally to treat wounds and bruises.

Vulpak. Trade name for a cellulose acetate–type plastic.

vulpic acid. $C_{19}H_{14}O_5$ = 322.11. Chrysopicrin. An acid from the lichen *Cetraria vulpina*.

vulpinite. An amorphous form of anhydrite.

vuzine. $C_{27}H_{40}N_2O_2$ = 424.3. Isooctylhydrocupreine. A levorotatory quinine (q.v.) alkaloid. Colorless powder, insoluble in water. **v. hydrochloride.** $C_{27}H_{40}N_2O_2 \cdot HCl \cdot 2H_2O$ = 533.44. Colorless crystals, soluble in water; a powerful bactericide for deep-seated wounds.

Vycor. Trademark for heat- and chemical-resistant glassware, including low-expansion glasses.

Vyrene. Trademark for a silicone-lubricated, polyester polyurethane, spandex monofilament.

W

W. (1) Symbol for tungsten (wolfram). (2) Abbreviation for: (*a*) work, (*b*) watt. **W rays.** The radiations intermediate between UV (ultraviolet, q.v.) and X rays.

w. Abbreviation for: (1) weight, (2) work.

Waage, Peter. 1833–1900. Norwegian chemist noted for developments in physical chemistry.

Waals. See *van der Waals.*

wabain. $C_{36}H_{46}O_{12} = 670.4$. A glucoside from the root of *Carissa schimperi* (Apocynaceae), the waba tree of Africa; a heart stimulant and local anesthetic. Cf. *ouabain.*

Wackenroder's reaction. The reaction between hydrogen sulfide and sulfur dioxide in aqueous solution to form polythionic acid.

wad. (1) Bog manganese. An earthy hydrate of pyrolusite, containing baryta. Cf. *psilomelane.* (2) Graphite.

Waelz process. Low-grade zinc ore is heated with fuel oil or powdered coal in a rotary kiln; volatilized zinc and zinc oxide result.

wafer. A thin, double layer of dried paste that encloses a medicament. **w. ash.** The bark of the root of *Ptelea trifoliata* (Rutaceae); a tonic and antiperiodic.

wagnerite. $Mg(MgF)PO_4$. A native fluophosphate. Cf. *adelite.*

Wagner's reagent. An aqueous solution of iodine and potassium iodide; a microchemical reagent for alkaloids.

wagofo. An African arrow poison, the dried juice of *Euphorbia* species.

wahoo. Euonymus.

wakeamine. Sympathomimetic amine. General name for amphetamine-type drugs used to delay the onset of fatigue.

Walden, Paul. 1863–1957. German organic chemist. **W. inversion.** A chemical reaction which reverses the rotatory power of an optically active compound. It indicates that the mechanism of substitution does not involve the simple replacement of one group by another, but a rearrangement of groups and atoms; e.g.: *d*-chlorosuccinic acid changes (on treatment with potassium hydroxide) to *l*-malic acid; while *l*-chlorosuccinic acid changes to *d*-malic acid and not to *l*-malic acid.

Wallach, Otto. 1847–1931. German chemist, Nobel Prize winner (1910); noted for research on the constitution of essential oils.

walnut. Juglans. **w. oil.** The clear, colorless oil of walnuts, $d_{25}0.923$, n_D^{25} 1.4750; an emulsifier in cosmetics.

warfare gas. See poison *gas.*

warfarin. (3-γ-Acetonebenzyl)-4-hydroxy-coumarin. A rodenticide which kills by producing hemorrhage, but is tasteless, odorless, and relatively safe to human beings and domestic animals. **w. sodium.** $C_{19}H_{15}$-$O_4Na = 330.32$. White crystals, m.162, soluble in water; an anticoagulant (B.P.).

warp. The threads of a woven fabric which are extended lengthwise in the loom. Cf. *weft.*

warrant. Spavin.

warringtonite. Domingite.

wash bottle. A glass or plastic flask or bottle fitted with a stopper and 2 unequally long tubes, so arranged that on forcing air by blowing or pressure through one, a stream of water emerges from the other. Used to wash precipitates on filters, and other chemical operations.

Washburn cell. A glass vessel with 2 electrodes for determining the electrical conductivity of solutions.

washing. Rubbing and rinsing with a liquid. **w. bottle.** See *wash bottle.* **w. soda.** Commercial crystalline sodium carbonate.

Wassermann, August von. 1866–1925. German biochemist. **W. reaction.** Σ test. A diagnostic reaction for syphilis, in which a series of blood samples is subjected to the action of various hemolytic sera. Cf. *complement fixation.*

water. (1) $H_2O = 18.016$. Hydrogen oxide. Colorless, tasteless liquid, forming the largest proportion of the earth surface, m.(freezes) 0, b.100; the commonest solvent. Regarded as an element by the alchemists; recognized as a combustion product of hydrogen by Cavendish (1781); as a compound of oxygen and hydrogen by Lavoisier (1783); and as a mixture of isotopes (1933). Probably a mixture of multiples of H_2O: as, H_4O_2, dihydrol; H_6O_3, trihydrol; etc. Cf. *heavy w., ice w., steam w.* W. is an essential constituent of all living organisms, and occurs as "water of crystallization" in many crystals and compounds. (2) Aqua. Potable w. (U.S.P.). See *potable.* (3) Aqua. Aromatic w. (B.P.). Pharmaceutically, a weak solution of a volatile substance in water; as, chlorine w. (4) The degree of transparency of a precious stone; as, diamond. **acidulous-** W. containing dissolved carbon dioxide (together with alkali bicarbonates and common salt) which is liberated with effervescence by warming, e.g., Appolinaris w. **aerated-** W. containing a gas; as air. **alkaline-** A mineral w. containing bicarbonates of Na and sometimes Li and K, e.g., Vichy w. **aromatic-** See (3). **bitter-** A mineral w. containing the sulfates of Na and Mg, e.g., Marienbad w. **bound-** That portion of a system, e.g., tissue that does not freeze at $-20°C$. **camphor-** A 0.1% solution of camphor in 0.2% alcohol; used in pharmacy. **capillary-** The w. of the soil held between rock interstices above the groundwater. **carbonated-** A drinking water containing carbon dioxide under pressure. **chalybeate-** Ferruginous w. A mineral w. containing ferrous carbonate held in solution as bicarbonate; as, Pyrmont w. **cologne-** A w. containing essential oils (as lavender); a household perfume. **conductivity-** A w. purified by repeated distillation through silver stills, or by treatment with synthetic resins; a solvent in electrolytic measurements. **crystal-** W. of crystallization. **distilled-** W. purified by distillation. **drinking-** W. that contains neither pathogenic organisms nor a large amount of organic matter, ammonia, nitrites, and nitrates. Maximum limits: total solids 1,000, Pb 0.1, Cu 0.2, Zn 0.5, Fe 0.3, Mg 100, Cl^- 250, $SO_4^=$ 250 ppm. See *w. analysis*. **ferruginous-** Chalybeate w. **free-** That portion of a system which freezes. Cf. *bound w.* **fresh-** W. other than sea or brackish w., irrespective of whether it is potable. **ground-** W. at a definite level beneath the soil. **hard-** W. that contains the carbonates and bicarbonates of calcium and magnesium; it forms insoluble compounds with soap and prevents lather formation. See *w. purification.* **heavy-** (1) D_2O or $H^b_2O = 20.0$. Deuterium oxide, q.v. The isotopic compound of hydrogen of mass 2 (deuterium, diplogen) with oxygen. For physical constants see table. (2) One of the other compounds of isotopic H or O; as, DOH, TOT, TOH, TOD, where D is hydrogen of mass 2, T hydrogen of mass 3 (tritium); or H_2O^b, H_2O^c, D_2O^b, D_2O^c, T_2O^b, T_2O^c, where O^b is oxygen of mass 17, and O^c oxygen of mass 18, or a combination of these (as, DO^bH). **hepatic-** A mineral w. containing hydrogen sulfide and alkali sulfides, e.g., Harrogate w. **ice-** Freshly molten w. containing smaller aggregates of $(H_2O)_x$ than w. at 4°C. Cf. *steam w.* **industrial-** W. that can be used for process work, but not necessarily potable. **injection-** Sterile, distilled w. without any added substance (U.S.P., B.P.). **juvenile-** W. of deep-seated origin, that is supposed to have reached the surface of the earth for the first time. **light-** Protium oxide. See *heavy w.* and table. **metabolic-** See *w. metabolism.* **meteoric-** W. from the atmosphere; as, rain. **mineral-** A natural, therapeutic w.; as: acidulous, chalybeate, hepatic, alkaline, bitter, siliceous w.; hot springs (may contain radium emanation). **natural-** A w. as it occurs in nature; as: rain, snow, river, spring, deep well, sea, and mineral w. Impurities may be suspended or dissolved solids and gases. **potable-** W. that is fit to drink; e.g.: nontyphoid, nonpolluted. Cf. *drinking w.* **purified-** W. that has been repeatedly distilled and subjected to purifying operations, e.g., with ion-exchange materials (U.S.P., B.P.). **sea-** Ocean w. that contains an average of dissolved solids 3.6% (sodium chloride 2.6%). See *hydrosphere, salinity.* **siliceous-** W. containing dissolved colloidal silica and alkali silicates, e.g., w. of the hot geysers of Yellowstone Park. **soda-** q.v. **soft-** (1) Rain w. or snow w., which is naturally free from Ca and Mg salts. (2) W. after removal of Ca and Mg salts. See *hard w., w. purification.* **steam-** Freshly condensed w. It

contains a different proportion of dihydrol and trihydrol to ice w. **sterilized-** W. free from living microorganisms. **sweet-** W. containing glycerin residues, from soap manufacture. **well-** Ground w.
　w. analysis. (1) Sanitary: The bacteriological and chemical determination of the harmful constituents of w.; e.g., determinations of: ammoniacal and albumenoid ammonia, nitrite and nitrate, nitrogen, oxygen consumed, total solids, alkalinity, hardness, halogens. Decaying vegetable and animal matter is indicated by the nitrogen. (2) Complete: The determination of all inorganic constituents. The results are expressed as oxides of elements present, as salts, or as ions and radicals. **w. bath.** A vessel of boiling w. used in the laboratory to evaporate liquids in a smaller vessel over it. **w. constants.** Cf. *heavy w.*

Density—greatest at 4°C; hence 1 ml w. at 4°C is the
　classical unit of mass = 1 gm
0°C . . . .　0.99987 gm
10°C . . . .　0.99973 gm
Heat of fusion. . . . .　79 cal/gm
Heat of vaporization . . . .　536 cal/gm
Specific heat . . . .　1.00477 at 5°C
　　　　　　　　　　　　　　　1.00000 at 15°C
　　　　　　　　　　　　　　　0.99829 at 50°C
　　　　　　　　　　　　　　　1.00645 at 100°C

H^- and OH^- ion concentration
　(each) . . . .　10^{-7} gm/liter
Critical temperature. . . . .　370°C
Critical pressure . . . .　195.5 atm
Critical volume . . . .　2.33
Degree of ionization. . . . .　10^{-7} mole/liter

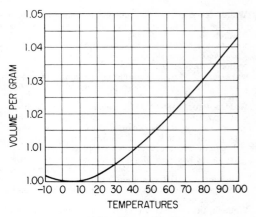

Specific volumes of water.

w. of constitution. W. that is chemically combined, as in hydroxides. **w. of crystallization.** W. that is a physical constituent of crystals or hydrated salts, and removed at 100°C. **w. culture.** A method of growing plants by using a nutrient 0.01 M solution of potassium nitrate, calcium sulfate, and magnesium hydrogen phosphate, with or without other salts or ions. Cf. *hydroponics, nutrient media.* **w. detection.** (1) Filter paper saturated with a solution of potassium lead iodide

Constant	Light (H₂O)	Heavy (D₂O)
d. (20°C)	0.9982	1.1056
m.	0°C	3.802°C
b.	100°C	101.42°C
Refractive index.	1.33293	1.3281
Viscosity	10.87	14.2
Surface tension.	72.75	67.8
Raman spectrum	3420 Å	2549 Å

in acetone turns yellow. (2) Anhydrous (white) copper sulfate turns blue. (3) The Karl Fischer reagent, q.v. **w. distillation.** The evaporation and condensation of w. To remove all dissolved material distil in a quartz or silver vessel first from an alkaline solution of permanganate, then from sulfuric acid. Cf. *conductivity w.* **w. divining.** Dowsing. The detection of underground w. supplies by means of, e.g., a bent hazel twig, which twists in the hands of the operator when he is over w. It is stated to arise from great sensitivity to electromagnetic radiations emitted by w. **w. flowers.** Ice flowers. **w. gas.** A mixture of hydrogen and carbon monoxide, obtained by the action of steam on glowing coal. **w. glass.** Sodium silicate. **w. of hydration.** *W. of crystallization,* or *w. of constitution.* Cf. *hydrates.* **w. metabolism.** The daily balance of w. in the human body. In 24 hr the intake from food, drink, and metabolic w. totals 2,200 ml. The output in urine 300, skin 700, lungs 600, feces 100 ml. **w. pollution.** The contamination of natural waters by wastes, q.v., from sewage or industry. **w. proof.** Rainproof. Impermeable to water. **w. pump.** See *filter pump.* **w. purification.** The removal of salts or organisms from natural waters; e.g., softening (partial removal of salts), distillation (complete removal of salts), filtration (partial removal of organisms and suspended matter), sterilization (complete destruction of organisms). **w. softening.** The removal of Ca^{++} or Mg^{++} by: (1) filtration through permutite or ion-exchange natural zeolites, in which calcium ions are replaced by sodium ions; (2) heating, which removes Ca^{++} as calcium carbonate (boiler scale); (3) chemical treatment, as with lime. **w. sterilization.** The destruction of bacteria and spores by heat, or their removal in porcelain filters. **w. still.** A device for the continuous production of distilled w.

water mint. The dried leaves of *Mentha aquatica* (Labiatae) containing essential oils and tannin; an antispasmodic and stimulant.

water pepper. Smartweed. The dried herb of *Polygonum punctatum* (Polygonacae); a stimulant and diuretic.

waterproofing. Making a substance impermeable to moisture.

Watt, James. 1736–1819. Scottish inventor of the first steam engine (1769).

watt. Ampere-volt, volt-ampere. A unit of power, or time rate at which work is done: 1 watt = 1 joule (10 million ergs) per second, or the energy expended per second by an unvarying current of 1 ampere under a potential of 1 volt.
Watts = volts × amperes = amperes² × ohms
1 watt = 1/746 hp
1 watthour = 3,600 joules = 1 kelvin
international watt- The energy expended per second by an unvarying electric current of 1 international ampere under an electrical pressure of 1 international volt. 1 I.W. = 1.00019 watts.

wattage. Amperage multiplied by voltage.

wattle gum. Australian gum, from *Acacia pycnantha* (Leguminosae), Australia and S. Africa.

Watts, Henry. 1815–1884. British chemist, author of "Dictionary of Chemistry."

wave. (1) A to-and-fro motion of the particles of a solid, liquid, or gas. (2) The harmonic curve

obtained on plotting distance and time for points representing centers of force in rhythmic motion. **longitudinal-** Forward and backward motion of particles in the direction in which the w. moves, as sound waves in air. **micro-** Electromagnetic w. similar to but of much shorter wavelength than the w. of television: namely, 30 cm to 3 mm (equivalent to 1,000 to 100,000 mc/sec); used for the rapid curing of plastics. **transverse-** Motion at right angles to the direction in which the w. moves. Cf. *electromagnetic* wave.

w. front. The surface of propagation, at right angles to the direction of motion, which passes through corresponding points of a number of waves. **w. function.** The factor ψ in Schrödinger's equation, q.v. **w. length.** The distance between corresponding points on 2 adjacent waves. Cf. kX, *angström, sound, spectrum,* and figure under *radiation.* **w. mechanics.** Quantum mechanics. A derivation of the velocity v and position p of electrons, one of which can be determined by predicting the probable range of values. The motion of each particle of mass m is associated with a wavelength $\lambda = h/mv$; $mc^2 = h\nu$, where c is the velocity of light; wave velocity $\mu = \lambda\nu$ (cf. *Heisenberg principle*); $\lambda = 12,336/V$; where V is the corresponding energy change in volts. **w. motion.** The progressive disturbance of particles in a medium. The speed of propagation is the velocity of the wave c; this depends on the wavelength λ, and the time period T, or on the frequency ν; hence $c = \lambda/T$, $= \nu\lambda$, and $\nu = c/\lambda$. **w. number.** The number of waves per unit length; for light, $n = 1/\lambda$ (if λ is measured in centimeters), or $n = 10^8/\lambda$ (if λ is measured in angstroms), where n is the number of waves per centimeter. Cf. *frequency, Ritz formula.* **w. theory.** Radiations comprise electric (E) and magnetic (M) fields at right angles, and moving in the direction of propagation. Cf. *quantum theory.*

wavellite. $Al_3(OH \cdot F)_3 \cdot (PO_4)_2$. A native phosphate, containing some fluorine.

wax. (1) An ester of a high-molecular-weight fatty acid with a high-molecular-weight alcohol other than glycerol. (2) An ester of high-molecular-weight fatty acid with a high-molecular-weight monohydric fatty alcohol. (3) A mixture of esters, fatty acids, high-atomic alcohols, and hydrocarbons. Cf. *sterols.* (4) Plastic substances obtained from plants or deposited by insects; consists of the esters of fatty acids with high-atomic alcohol radicals; e.g., beeswax, myricyl palmitate, $C_{30}H_{61} \cdot C_{16}H_{31}O_2$. (5) Modern usage: a substance having the properties: (*a*) crystalline to microcrystalline structure; (*b*) capacity to acquire gloss when rubbed (distinction from *greases*); (*c*) capacity to produce pastes or gels with suitable solvents or when mixed with other waxes; (*d*) low viscosity at just above the melting point (distinction from *resins* and *plastics*); (*e*) low solubility in solvents for fats at room temperature. Waxes differ from fats in that fats are the esters of trihydric, low-atomic alcohols; as, glycerol. See table. **bees-** q.v. **carnauba-** q.v. **chinese-** q.v. **C.K.-, Seekay-** Trade name for a chlorinated w., used for stopping deposition in selective electroplating. **coal-** A hard brittle, coal hydrocarbon, m.99; used in paper coatings. **cochineal-** Coccerin. **earth-** Ceresin.

Source	Examples	Composition
Mineral waxes ...	Paraffin	Straight-chain hydrocarbons, 26-30 C atoms/molecule
	Microcrystalline	Branched-chain hydrocarbons, 41-50 C atoms/molecule
	Oxidized microcrystalline	Hydrocarbons, esters, fatty acids
	Montan	Wax acids, alcohols, esters, ketones
	Hoechst waxes	Acids, esters (obtained by oxidizing montan)
	Ozokerite	Saturated and unsaturated high-mol.-wt. hydrocarbons
Vegetable waxes	Carnauba	Complex alcohols, hydrocarbons, resins
	Esparto	Mainly hydrocarbons
	Flax	Fatty-acid esters, hydrocarbons
	Sugarcane wax	Hydrocarbons, long straight-chain aldehydes, alcohols
	Candelilla	Hydrocarbons, acids, esters, alcohols, stearols, resins
Animal waxes....	Beeswax	Hydrocarbons, acids, esters, alcohols, lactones
Synthetic waxes..	Fischer-Tropsch	Saturated and unsaturated hydrocarbons, oxygen compounds
	Polyethylene	Hydrocarbon

fossil- Ozokerite. **insect-** Chinese w. **Japan-**,q.v. **Java-** Ceryl alcohol. **microcrystalline-** See *micro-*. **mineral-** Paraffin. **montan-** q.v. **palm-** q.v. **paraffin-** q.v. **peat-** q.v. **pisang-** q.v. **sealing-** q.v. **sugarcane-** Cerosin. **wasp-** A constituent of certain beeswaxes; it has a low saponification value (about 60). **white-** Cera alba. Bleached beeswax. **yellow-** U.S.P. for cera flava. Beeswax. Soft, yellow solid, obtained by melting and purifying the honeycombs of the bee; insoluble in water, soluble in ether or oils. Used in ointments (U.S.P.). **wool-** See *wool fat*.
   w. bean. Butter bean. **w. tailings.** The residue after destructive distillation of petroleum; contains the solid hydrocarbons, chrysene, picene; and resembles asphalt; used for waterproofing and as a filler in cheap greases.
W.B.C. Abbreviation for white blood corpuscles.
W-board. A low-grade of V-board.
weak. (1) Not strong. (2) Not ionizing greatly. **w. acid.** An acid that does not ionize greatly. **w. base.** A base that does not ionize greatly. **w. salt.** A salt that does not ionize greatly. Cf. *ionization*.
weathering. Chemical reactions which change the composition and disintegrate rocks; as, the effects of air, water, bacteria, heat, freezing.
weave. (1) To intertwine threads or fibers in a regular manner to form a continuous web of fabric. (2) The manner or system in which the threads are woven. See *faille, serge, tricot, twill*. **plain-** A w. in which the warp and weft threads pass alternately over and under the weft and wrap threads, respectively.

weber. (1) The unit of magnetic flux. (2) Coulomb.
Weber's law. A sensation is proportional to the natural logarithm of the stimulus.
Webril. Trademark for a bonded fiber web.
websterite. $Al_2SiO_6 \cdot 9H_2O$. A native silicate. Cf. *cecilose*.
weckamine. Generic name for amphetamine-type drugs.
wedge. A solid object with a triangular section, used to separate surfaces by the forcible introduction of the pointed end. **w. photometer.** A photometer in which the illuminations on 2 faces of a wedge are matched.
weedicide. A substance, usually a chemical, used to kill weeds selectively in agriculture and horticulture. Cf. *pesticide*.
weft. The threads of a woven fabric that cross from side to side of the web and interlace the warp, q.v.
Weigert effect. Dichroism shown by a colloidal suspension or gel.
weighing. Measuring gravitational attraction. **double-** W. independently of any variation in length of the 2 balance arms. If the object weighs *a* when placed on one pan, and *b* when on the other, then the weight is given by $\sqrt{ab}$.
   w. bottle. A small, stoppered, thin-walled, light glass vessel, used to weigh quantities of a substance for analytical purposes. **w. by substitution.** Measuring the weight of an object independently of the lengths of the arms of the balance. The object is counterpoised by lead shot, then removed, and the lead shot counterpoised by weights. **w. by swings.** A method in which the lack of sensitiveness of a balance is

compensated by noting the swings of the balance pointer, and the distances traversed to left and right.

weight. The degree of heaviness or the force with which a body is attracted by the earth; it varies with geographical location. Cf. *mass.* **atomic-** The relative weight of an atom of an element as compared with a hydrogen atom. **carrier-** The weight of substance, e.g., protein, which carries one gram equivalent of prosthetic groups. **combining-** Equivalent weight. **equivalent-** The weight of a substance that can combine with or displace one unit weight of hydrogen, or its equivalent of another substance. **isotopic-** The relative mass of an isotope, q.v. **molecular-** The sum of the atomic weights of the atoms contained in a compound. **specific-** See *specific gravity.*

w. buret. A small bottle with a tap and jet, which is weighed before and after titration to give the weight (instead of the volume) of titrating solution used. **w. concentration.** The number of grams of substance per kilogram of solution. **w. normality.** Normality expressed per kilogram instead of per liter. **w. strength.** A method of expressing the strength of an explosive per unit weight. Cf. *Trauzl* test, ballistic *mortar.*

weights. Units of weight in common use: *Metric*: 1 milligram = 0.001 gram = 10^{-6} kilogram = 10^{-9} ton. *Apothecaries'*: 20 grains troy = 1 scruple = 0.33 dram = 0.0417 ounce troy = 0.00347 pound = 1.296 grams. *Avoirdupois*: 27.347 grains troy = 1 dram = 0.0625 ounce = 0.0039 pound = 1.772 grams. *Troy*: 24 grains troy = 1 pennyweight = 0.05 ounce = 0.0042 pound = 1.555 grams. See *SI units.*

Weil-Felix reaction. An agglutination test for diagnosing typhoid fever.

weinschenkite. $(YEr)PO_4 \cdot 2H_2O$. A native rare-earth phosphate, resembling gypsum in structure.

weiss. A unit of atomic magnetic moment (P. Weiss, 1911). Cf. *Bohr, magneton.*

Weissenberg effect. The tendency of a viscous elastic liquid to climb up a vertical rod rotating in it; associated with the orientation of high-polymer molecules in flowing solutions.

weissite. Cu_5Te_3. Telluride. Lens-shaped crystals in veins of pyrites.

weld. To join metals by pressure at a temperature below that of complete fusion. **dyer's-** A yellow dye from *Reseda lutea.*

welding. (1) The joining of metals by heat; as: (*a*) *plastic-* united by pressure without a weld metal (forge, electrical-resistance heater, or Thermit); (*b*) *fluid-* united by a weld metal without pressure (torch, arc or Thermit). (2) Heating a metal to white heat and pressing the pieces together; or heating a metal to fusion and letting it flow into the joint without hammering or pressure (fusion w.). Cf. *Thermit* process. **cold-** Hammering metal foils together into a compact piece. **friction-** W. in which heat generated by 2 rotating rods in contact melts a metal layer on each rod. **sigma-** A process for welding carbon in an inert gas by a metallic arc. **spot-** Fluid w. at adjacent spots, which subsequently run together as a continuous weld. **ultrasonic-** W. by vibratory energy, usually having a frequency greater than that of sound waves.

Weldon, Walter. 1832–1885. British industrial chemist. **W. process.** The manufacture of chlorine from hydrochloric acid by the action of manganese dioxide, and the regeneration of the W. mud by lime, followed by reoxidation to manganese dioxide. **W. mud.** The slime of manganese and calcium manganites from the W. process.

Welsbach, Carl Freiherr Auer von. 1858–1929. Austrian chemist. **W. mantles.** Incandescent gas mantles. Cellulose impregnated with cerium and thorium nitrates is ignited, and a mixture of ceria 1 and thoria 99% remains.

Welter's rule. The heat of combustion of an organic compound is obtained approximately by subtracting the oxygen and hydrogen in the proportion of H_2O, and then adding the heats of combustion of the residual carbon and hydrogen atoms.

Welvic. Trademark for a polyvinyl-type plastic.

Wenzel's law. Richter's law.

Werner, Alfred. 1866–1919. Swiss chemist, Nobel Prize winner (1913). **W.'s theory.** The affinity of an atom is an attractive force toward the center of the atom evenly distributed over its spherical shell. In a combination of 2 atoms, the attractive force concentrates itself in a definite area, dependent on the nature of the combining atoms. Two combining molecules probably first form an association held together by residual valencies; the affinities then may redistribute themselves uniformly, with the formation of radicals. Hence the behavior of the Cl atoms in chloroplatinic acid, H_2PtCl_6. Cf. *coordination number, valence.*

wernerite. Scapolite.

Wesson tube. An absorption tube for carbon dioxide, containing soda lime and calcium chloride.

West, Clarence Jay. 1886–1953. American chemist noted for chemical literature.

Weston, Edward. 1850–1936. British-born American electrical engineer. **W. normal cell.** Cadmium cell.

Westphal balance. A beam balance for determining the specific gravity of liquids or solids.

Westron. Trade name for acetylene tetrachloride.

wet. Moist. **w. analysis.** Qualitative analysis by means of reagents in solution. Cf. *blowpipe analysis.* **w. bulb thermometer.** Psychrometer. **w. combustion.** A method of determining organic carbon by oxidation with chromic acid. **w. process.** An industrial method involving solutions; as, the extraction of ores by acids.

wetness. See *freeness.*

wettability. Degree of wetting, measured by the adhesion tension between a solid and liquid phase. Cf. *introfaction.*

wetting. The adhesion of a liquid to a surface, resulting in a tray-shaped meniscus. Cf. *flotation, adhesion, tension.*

whale. An aquatic mammal, order *Cetaceae.* **w. bone.** Baleen. The horny, elastic substance from the upper jaw of the Greenland w. **w. guano, w. meal.** A fertilizer made from dried and ground w. meat: nitrogen 6–8, phosphorus pentoxide 4–8%. **w. oil.** Blubber oil, d.0.92–0.93; a leather dressing, lubricant, illuminant, and source of soap. World production (1967) 65,000 tons. **w. shot.** Crude spermaceti.

wheat. The seeds of *Triticum* species (Gramineae);

a food. Chief varieties: *T. monococcum*, one-grained w.; *T. sativum*, common w.; *T. durum*, flint w.; *T. compactum*, dwarf w.

Wheatstone, Sir Charles. 1802–1875. British physicist. **W. bridge.** An instrument for the measurement of electrical resistance. A point on a graduated resistance wire is found such that no current flows from an accumulator connected to the ends of the wire, through a galvanometer joining a standard and the unknown resistance with a sliding contact on the wire. Then the ratio of the lengths of the 2 portions of the wire equals that of the 2 resistances.

whey. Milk serum. The watery residue after the fat and casein have been removed from milk.

whiskers. Microscopic, needle-shaped, single crystals of metal, ceramic, or a salt grown from vapor, molten material, or solutions, and free from grain boundaries and imperfections. W. have high tensile strength, e.g., 250,000 psi for glass. Produced by condensation from vapor or in eutectics; used to reinforce metals, ceramics, or plastics.

whisk(e)y. A grain spirit obtained from malted barley or other cereal by mashing and fermentation, followed by distillation and aging.

white. A color, q.v., produced by the reflection of all the visible rays, or of 2 complementary rays. **w. agate.** Chalcedony. **w. antimony.** Valentinite. **w. arsenic.** Arsenous oxide. **w. ash.** The dried bark of *Fraxinus americana* (Oleaceae); used medicinally. **w. bole.** Kaolin. **w. byrony.** Bryonia. The dried roots of *Bryonia alba*; a cathartic. **w. cedar.** Thuja. **w. coal.** Power obtained from hydroelectric plants. **w. lead.** A basic lead carbonate, a white pigment. **w. lead ore.** Cerussite. **w. lead paper.** A filter paper impregnated with lead carbonate. **w. lotion.** A solution of 40 gm each of zinc sulfate and potassium sulfide in 1,000 ml water; an astringent (U.S.P.). **w. mustard.** Sinapis alba. **w. nickel ore.** $NiAs_2$. A native nickel arsenide. **w. oak.** Quercus. **w. olivine.** Forsterite. **w. pigment.** An opaque, w. pigment; as, lead carbonate, sulfate, or oxychloride; barium sulfate; zinc sulfide; kaolin; lithopone or titanium oxide. **w. pine.** Pinus alba. The dried bark of *Pinus strobus* (Pinaceae); an expectorant. **w. pond lily.** The dried roots of *Castalia odorata* (Salicaceae); an astringent. **w. poplar.** The dried bark of *Populus tremuloides* (Nymphaceae); a tonic and febrifuge. **w. precipitate.** Ammoniated mercury. **w. vitriol.** Zinc sulfate. **w. wash.** A suspension of chalk in water, used for decorative purposes. **w. zinc.** Zinc oxide.

Whitfield's ointment. A mixture: benzoic acid 60, salicylic acid 30, polyethylene glycol ointment 910 pts.; a keratolytic.

whiting. Whitening. Washed chalk; a pigment for polishing or wall wash.

whitlockite. $Ca_3(PO_4)_2$. A late hydrothermal mineral in New Hampshire granite pegmatites.

Whitney, Willis Rodney. 1868–1958. American physicist, noted for work on colloids.

whitneyite. Cu_9As. A native copper arsenide.

whortleberry. Vaccinium.

widia. (German, *wie diamant*.) Cemented tungsten carbide.

Wiedemann, Gustaf Heinrich. 1826–1899. German physical chemist, editor of *Poggendorff's Annalen*.

W-Franz's law. The thermal and electrical conductivities of the metals follow the same order.

Wieland, Heinrich. 1877–1957. German chemist and Nobel Prize winner (1927), noted for biochemical research (bile acids, chlorophyll, and hemoglobin).

Wien, Wilhelm. 1864–1928. German physicist, Nobel Prize winner (1911). **W. equation.** The intensity of a radiation $= c_1\lambda^{-5} \exp(c^2/\lambda T)$, where λ is the wavelength, T the absolute temperature, and c_1, c_2 are W. constants ($c_2 = 1.4312$). **W. law.** With a perfect radiator, energy intensity is a maximum for a certain wavelength λ_m, depending on the absolute temperature T: $\lambda_m = 0.289/T$ cm.

Wifatite. Trade name for phenol-formaldehyde and amino plastics, used for water purification. Cf. *zeolite*.

Wijs, J. J. A. 1864–1942. Dutch analyst. **W. solution.** A solution of iodine monochloride in glacial acetic acid; used for the determination of iodine numbers. **W. value.** Iodine number.

wild. (1) Pharmacy: not cultivated (plants); not domesticated (animals). (2) Metallurgy: over-oxidized; as, steel which splits owing to the escape of gases. **w. cherry.** Prunus virginianica. The stem bark of *Prunus serotina* (Rosaceae); a sedative and expectorant (U.S.P.). **w. ginger.** Asarum. **w. hyssop.** Verbena. **w. indigo.** Baptisia. **w. licorice.** Abrus. **w. mint.** *Mentha canadensis*, a plant resembling pennyroyal. **w. rosemary.** q.v. **w. rue.** Harmel. **w. yam.** Dioscorea.

Wiley, Harvey Washington. 1844–1930. American chemist, noted for his work on food laws.

willemite. Zn_2SiO_4. A native zinc silicate.

Willesden goods. Articles made from vulcanized fiber, q.v.; as picnic plates, spoons, combs, traveling cases, which are hard and relatively water-resistant.

Williamson, Alexander Edward. 1824–1904. British chemist, founder of the molecule concept. **W. reaction.** The synthesis of ethers from sodium alcoholate and an alkyl iodide: $RI + NaOR' \rightarrow ROR' + NaI$. **W.'s. violet.** $KFe[Fe(CN)_6] \cdot 2H_2O$. Potassium ferric ferrous cyanide.

willow. A genus of trees (Salicaceae); the bark and leaves contain salacin.

Willstätter, Richard. 1872–1942. German chemist, Nobel Prize winner (1915), noted for research on plant pigments. **W. lignin.** See *lignin*.

wilnite. A green variety of grossularite. See aluminum *garnet*.

Wilson, Charles Thomson Rees. 1869–1959. British physicist, Nobel Prize winner (1927). **W. fog method.** To demonstrate the motions of atomic fragments from their paths in a low-pressure fog chamber (cloud-track apparatus). The charged ions or electrons cause condensation of the gaseous water molecules, as visible minute droplets. **W. tracks.** When α, β, γ, or X rays are shot into a low-pressure fog chamber, they cause condensation of single microscopic droplets, which appear as lines and can be photographed.

Winchester. A tall bottle of standard cylindrical shape, with a relatively small base. **W. bushel.** See U.S. *bushel*. **W. gallon.** Before 1886, 272.25 cubic inches; at present, 277 cubic inches. **W. quart.** A W. bottle: 2.25–2.5 liters (80 fluid ounces).

Windaus, Adolf. 1876–1959. German chemist,

Nobel Prize winner (1928) for his work on sterols.

wind gage. Anemometer.

wine. Naturally fermented grape juice, containing 6–22% alcohol; traces of oenanthic and other ethers; essential oils, grape sugar, glycerol; tannic, malic, phosphoric, and acetic acids; tartrates of potassium and calcium; coloring matters; and some proteins. **dry-** W. of low sugar content; as, burgundy. **fortified-** W. to which alcohol has been added. **medicated-** W. to which a medicament, e.g., meat extract, has been added. **sour-** W. which has begun to ferment to acetic acid. **spirit of-** Ethanol. **sweet-** W. of high sugar content; as, port.

w. gallon. See *gallon.* **w. glass.** An approximate liquid measure: 60 ml (2 fluid ounces). **w. lees oil.** Oil from the yeast of a fermenting w. and responsible for the characteristic bouquet. Principally ethyl pelargonate, with ethyl caprylate, the corresponding free acid, and about 0.4% decyl alcohol.

wing top. A triangular-shaped attachment for a bunsen burner, producing a long and narrow flame.

Winkler, Clemens Alexander. 1838–1904. German mineralogist; discovered uranium.

winterene. $C_{15}H_{24} = 204.2.$ A hydrocarbon in the essential oil of winter's bark.

wintergreen. Gaultheria. **bitter-** Chimaphilia. **w. oil.** The essential oil of *Gaultheria* species, d.1.175–1.187 (99% methyl salicylate). *artificial-* Methyl salicylate.

winterization. A process to prevent edible oils from clouding or setting at low temperatures, by cooling slowly to 45°C and filtering.

winter's bark. The dried bark of *Drimys winteri* (Magnoliaceae) containing an essential oil, tannin, and resin; an aromatic and stomachic. Cf. *drimin.*

wipla. (German, wie platin.) A chromium-nickel steel; a platinum substitute in dentistry.

wire. A drawn-out rod. **cross-** Two thin crossing wires in the objective of an optical instrument to fix the position of the object under examination.

wiring. An electric circuit.

Wislicenus, Johannes. 1835–1902. German chemist noted for his work on stereochemistry.

wismuth. Bismuth.

wistarin. A crystalline glucoside from *Wistaria chinensis* (Leguminosae).

witch hazel. Hamamelis.

Witcogum. Trademark for a rubbery elastomer obtained by polymerizing and condensing glycerides in presence of resins or nonelastic compounds.

withania. The plant geneesblaar, vimba, *W. somnifera* (Solanaceae), S. Africa, used locally as an antiseptic and hypnotic.

withanic acid. $C_{30}H_{46}O_8 = 534.35.$ A monobasic acid from withania.

withaniol. $C_{35}H_{34}O_5 = 534.25.$ A monohydric alcohol from withania.

witherite. $BaCO_3.$ A native carbonate, d.4.29–4.35, hardness 3–3.75; used in the glass, pyrotechnic and sugar industries.

witness. A tube of (usually) calcium chloride at the beginning or end of a gas train; it is weighed at the beginning and end of the experiment to indicate any loss of solvent. Cf. *guard tube.*

Witt's color theory. Certain (chromophoric) linkages in organic compounds induce color. If certain other (auxochromic) linkages are also present, a dyestuff (chromogen) results.

woad. An early blue dye or stain made from the ground, fermented leaves of *Isatis tinctoria* (Cruciferae), Mediterranean region. Used by the ancient Britons.

Woestyn's law. Joule's law.

Wöhler, Friedrich. 1800–1882. German chemist, noted for the isolation of aluminum and beryllium, discovery of isomerism, and the first synthesis of an organic compound (urea) in 1828. **W.'s law.** Dynamic deformation may occur as a result of vibrations, none of which attains the breaking limit; ultimately rupture may result.

wöhlerite. A native mixture of oxides of sodium, calcium, niobium, silicon, and zirconium.

Wohl's reaction. Boiling with ammoniacal silver nitrate hydrolyzes acetyl groups and eliminates hydrogen cyanide from the oxime of an acetylated sugar: $R \cdot CHOAc \cdot CN \rightarrow R \cdot CHOH \cdot CN \rightarrow R \cdot CHO + HCN.$

Wohwill process. The electrolytic refining of gold from a weak acid solution.

Wolacryl. Trade name for a polyamide synthetic fiber.

Wolcrylon. Trade name for a polyamide synthetic fiber.

Wolffram's salt $(PtCl)Cl_2 \cdot (H_2O)_2.$ A microchemical reagent.

Wolf process. A flotation process involving the use of sulfochlorated oils. **W. trap.** A device to suck atmospheric dust into a culture medium, where increase in turbidity or bacterial growth can be measured.

wolfram. (1) Tungsten (official nomenclature). (2) Wolframite. **w. ocher.** Tungstite.

wolframate. International usage for tungstate.

wolframine. Tungstite.

wolframites. $(Fe,Mn)WO_4.$ Tungstates, intermediate between ferberite, $FeWO_4$, and hübernite, $MnWO_4.$

wolframium. Tungsten.

wolfsbane. See *arnica flowers.*

wolfsbergite. (1) Chalcostibite. (2) Essonite.

Wollaston, William. 1766–1828. British chemist, discoverer of palladium and rhodium. **W. wires.** Platinum wires, 0.001 mm diameter, drawn inside a silver sheath, which is subsequently removed in nitric acid.

wollastonite. $CaSiO_3.$ Tabular spar, scale stone. A native triclinic pyroxene. **para-** Monoclinic w. **pseudo-** A third modification of w.

Wolpert's air tester. See *air tester.*

wood. The structural and supporting part of a tree or shrub; chief constituent, cellulose. Cf. *lignin, xylose.* Used in pharmacy; as, quassia, guaiacum, hematoxylon. Commercial woods are classified as: softwoods (conifers); hardwoods (as, poplar, oak); cabinet woods (as, mahogany). **w. alcohol.** Methanol. **w. ash.** The residue from burning w. (4% potassium oxide); a fertilizer. **w. cellulose.** Xylon. Cellulose obtained from w. **w. charcoal.** Carbo lignis. **w. flour.** W. meal, sawdust, pulverized w. Finely powdered w., generally white pine; a filler in moldings, linoleum, flooring, rubber, soap; and absorbent for nitroglycerin (dynamite). **w. free.** Describing a paper that contains no groundwood pulp, and usually contains only chemical w. pulp. **w. march.** Sanicula. **w. meal.** W. flour. **w. metal.** See *Wood's alloy.* **w. naphtha.** Methanol. **w. oil.** Tung oil. **w. opal.** Xylopal. Fossilized w., in which silica replaces the woody fibers. **w. pulp.** A mechanically ground or chemically digested w. used to manufacture paper or rayon. Cf. *pulpwood.* **w. spirit.** Methanol. **w. stone.** Xylolith. **w. sugar.** Xylose. **w. tar.** See *tar.* **w. vinegar.** See *pyroligneous acid.* **w. waste.** Products of lumber waste; as, w. pulp (paper, twine, yarn, rayon); w. flour (dynamite, linoleum, plastics); ethyl alcohol (motor fuels); cattle food, rosins, turpentine, pine oil, tar, tannin, fatty acids, dyes, and potash. **w. wool.** Narrow, thin shavings, used for packing.

Wood's alloy. A low-melting-point alloy (65.5°C): Bi 5, Pb 2.5, Sn 1.25, Cd 1.25 pts. **W. glass.** A glass that absorbs most of the visible spectrum but transmits waves in the ultraviolet. **W. light.** The filtered rays of the mercury-vapor lamp. wavelength 3340–3906 Å.

woodwardite. $CuSO_4 \cdot Al_2(SO_4)_2 \cdot H_2O$. Native copper aluminum sulfate.

Woodward rules. Rules for the correlation of ultraviolet spectra with substitution patterns in unsaturated organic compounds.

wool. The fibrous hair of lambs and sheep. It contains keratin (a characteristic odor on burning), and about 40% of a grease (chiefly cholesterol); similar in composition to horn. **blended-** Cloth containing not less than 50% w. **casein-** Lanital. **glass-** Fine glass threads used for filtering. **mineral-** See *mineral.*

w. alcohols. A constituent (with paraffin wax) of ointments, made by saponification of w. fat and separating the alcohol fraction. Contains not less than 28.0% cholesterol (B.P.). **w. fat.** (1) Anhydrous lanolin (U.S.P., B.P.). (2) Degras. The commercial wax alcohol extracted from pure w. fat. *hydrous-* W. fat containing 25–30% water (U.S.P., B.P.). **w. waste.** A fertilizer by-product of w. carding, consisting of sheep manure, seeds, and wool fibers, 3–6% N_2.

Woolon. Trade name for a mixed-polymer synthetic fiber.

Woolwich viscosity. See *viscosity.*

woorara. Curare.

work. W. is performed when a force moves its point of application; measured by the product of the force and the distance it is displaced in the direction of the force. Units: Fps system: 1 foot-pound, the work done when 1 pound is lifted 1 foot against gravity. Metric system: 1 centimeter-dyne = 1 erg. Gravitational unit: 1 gram and 1 centimeter = gram-dyne-centimeters = gram-ergs. Dimensions: $FL = ML^2T^{-2}$. For rate of work, see *power.* **w. of expansion.** The resistance offered by the molecules of an expanding gas, due to molecular attraction. **w. hardening.** Cold working. The modification of the physical properties of metals and alloys by cold (as distinct from heat) treatment.

wormseed. (1) Santonica. (2) Chenopodium. **w. oil.** *American*: The essential oil from *Cheno-podium ambrosioides*, d.0.960–0.980. *Levant*: The oil of *Artemisia maritima*, d.0.930, containing cineol.

wormwood. Absinthium. **salt of-** Potassium carbonate. **w. oil.** Absinthe oil. An essential oil from the herb of *Artemisia absinthium*. Green volatile liquid, d.0.925–0.955, soluble in alcohol; contains chiefly thujone, phenandrene, and thujyl alcohol.

worsted. A close woolen cloth, which can, however, contain up to 3% of inadvertent impurities, and up to 7% of material other than wool for decorative purposes or to facilitate processing.

wort. An infusion of a plant to be fermented; as, beer w.

Woulfe bottle. A 2- or 3-necked bottle used in chemical experiments, first described by Peter Woulfe (1727–1803) in 1784.

W rays. See *W.*

wrightine. Conessine.

Wright's stain. A microscopic stain for white blood corpuscles; 1 gm specially prepared methylene blue-eosin mixture in 600 ml methanol.

Wroblewski, Sigismund A. von. 1845–1888. Polish physicist, noted for the liquefaction of gases.

wrought. Describing a metal that has been worked into shape or condition, e.g., by hammering. Cf. *cast.* **w. iron.** A pure grade of iron with a low carbon content.

wt. Abbreviation for weight.

Wu, Lu-Chiang. 1904–1936. Chinese chemist, noted for historical research.

wulfenite. $PbMoO_4$. Yellow lead ore. A native molybdate.

Wulff net. A circle onto which are projected stereographically the longitudinal (meridional) and latitudinal (polar) lines of a globe; used in crystallographic analysis.

Wullner's law. The lowering of the vapor pressure of water by a solute is proportional to the concentration of the solute.

Wurster's blue. An oxidation product of tetramethyl-*p*-phenylenediamine; an indicator. **W. red.** A meriquinone oxidation product of *p*-aminodimethylaniline.

Würtz, Carl Adolphe. 1817–1884. French chemist, noted for organic research and his statement "*La chimie est une science française.*" **W. flask.** A distillation flask with a side arm in the neck. **W.'s reaction.** The synthesis of hydrocarbons by treating alkyl iodides in ethereal solution with sodium: $2MeI + 2Na = Me \cdot Me + 2NaI$.

wurtzite. ZnS. Aegerite. A hexagonal, native zinc sulfide. Cf. *sphalerite.*

wustite. A ferrite, often found in cements. Crystalline ferrous oxide with varying amounts of ferric oxide in solid solution.

Wynene. Trade name for a polyethylene synthetic fiber.

wyomingite. A porous rock in the Leucite Hills, S. Wyoming; potash (11% potassium oxide) is extracted by acid.

Wysor machine. A device for grinding and polishing metals for metallographic examination.

X

X. Symbol for: (1) xenon (Xe is preferred); (2) in a formula, a halogen or acid radical; as, HX. **X ray.** q.v. **X unit.** q.v.

x. Symbol for: (1) an unknown quantity; (2) molecular fraction.

ϰ. Greek letter chi.

ξ. Greek letter xi.

xanthaline. $C_{37}H_{36}O_9N_2$ = 652.4. An alkaloid, m.208, in opium.

xanthate. EtO·CS·SM or RO·CS·SM. Xathogenate. A salt of xanthic acid. M is a metal, and R an alkyl radical; as, potassium ethyl x., EtO·CS·SK. Cf. *viscoe.* **butyl-** MeCH₂·CHMeO·CS·SK. Potassium *sec*-butyl x. A flotation collector; 94% mineral recovery. **ethyl-** EtO·CS·SK. Potassium ethyl x. A flotation collector; 85% mineral recovery. **propyl-** MeCH₂CH₂O·CS·SK. A flotation collector; 90% mineral recovery.

xanthein. A yellow coloring matter of plants; a split product of chlorophyll.

xanthematin. A yellow coloring matter and split product of hemoglobin.

xanthene. $C_6H_4·CH_2·C_6H_4·O$ = 182.1. Methylene diphenylene oxide, diphenylene methane oxide. Colorless leaflets, m.105, slightly soluble in water. Cf. *xanthydrol.* **benzo-** See *benzoxanthene.* **dibenzo-** See *dibenzoxanthene.* **hydroxy-** Xanthydrol. **keto-** Xanthone. **thio-** Thioxanthene.

xanthenol. Xanthydrol.

xanthenone. Xanthone.

xanthic acid. EtO·CS·SH = 122.18. Xanthonic acid, xanthogenic acid, ethyloxydithiocarbonic acid. Unstable, colorless oil, insoluble in water, decomp. 24 to ethanol and carbon disulfide. **x. amide.** NH₂·CS·OEt = 105.14, m.38, soluble in water. **x. disulfide.** HO·CS·S·S·CS·OH = 186.3. Colorless crystals, m.28.

-xanthin. Suffix indicating yellow; as, co-xanthin.

xanthin(e). $C_5H_4O_2N_4$ = 152.1. 2,6-Dioxypurine. A purine base in blood, liver, urine, and some plants. Yellow crystals, m.360, soluble in water. **allo-** Alloxantin. **dimethyl-** *1,3-* Theophylline. *1,7-* Paraxanthine. *3,7-* Theobromine. **hetero-** $C_6H_6O_2N_4$ = 166.1. 7-Methyl-2,6-dioxypurine. **hypo-** $C_5H_4ON_4$ = 136.1. 6-Oxypurine. **imido-** Guanine. **methyl-** $C_6H_6O_2N_4$ = 166.1. 1-Methyl-2,6-dioxypurine. **para-** $C_7H_8O_3N_4$ = 196.2. 1,7-Dimethyl-2,6-dioxypurine, an isomer of theophylline. **pseudo-, tauto-** $C_5H_4O_2N_4$ = 152.1. 2,6-Dihydroxypurine. A tautomer of x. **tautohypo-** $C_5H_4ON_4$ = 136.1. A tautomer of hypoxanthine, q.v. **trimethyl-** Caffeine.

x. bases. Alloxuric bases, oxypurines, in vegetable and animal tissues, e.g., xanthine, hypoxanthine, uric acid, carnine, theophylline, caffeine, theobromine.

xanthium. Spiny clotbur, cocklebur. The herb of *Xanthium spinosum* (Compositae); a diuretic. Cf. *xanthostrumarin.*

xantho- Prefix (Greek, yellow) indicating the yellow color of a compound; as in xanthocobaltic.

xanthochelidonicacid. CO(CH₂·CO·COOH)₂ = 202.0. Acetonedioxalic acid. 2,4,6-Dioxypimelic acid. An unstable acid formed from chelidonic acid by treatment with excess alkali. Its salts are yellow.

xanthochromium. The divalent group Cr(NO₂)-(NH₃)₅ which forms salts; as, x. bromide, Cr(NO₂)(NH₃)₅Br₂.

xanthocobaltic. The divalent group, Co(NO₂)-(NH₃)₅, which forms yellow salts; as, x. bromide, Co(NO₂)(NH₃)₅Br₂.

xanthocreatinine. $C_5H_{10}ON_4$ = 142.1. A yellow, crystalline leukomaine resembling creatinine, in muscle tissues.

xanthogenate. (RO·CS·S—)₂. **diethyl-** EtO·CS·S·S·CS·OEt = 242.32. Bisethyl xanthogene. Yellow liquid, b.92; an antiparasitic.

xanthogene. A coloring material of plants, producing a yellow pigment with alkalies.

xanthogenic acid. Xanthic acid.

xanthoglobulin. Hypoxanthine.

xantholine. Santonica.

xanthone. $C_{13}H_8O_2$ = 196.1. Xanthene ketone, dibenzo-γ-pyrone xanthenone. Colorless crystals, m.173, slightly soluble in water. The nucleus of certain plant pigments, used in the synthesis of dyes, e.g., euxanthone, India yellow. **dihydroxy-** *1,7-* Euxanthone. *3,8-* Isoeuxanthone. **methoxydihydroxy-** Gentisin. **naphtho-** Naphthoxanthone. **thio-** See *thioxanthone.* **trihydroxy-** Gentisein.

xanthonic acid. Xanthic acid.

xanthophyll. $C_{40}H_{56}O_2$ = 568.4. Yellow plant pigment, m.192, similar to chlorophyll; a polymer of isoprene and related to carotene.

xanthophyllite. A native, hydrous silicate of calcium, magnesium, iron, and aluminum.

xanthopicrin. Yellow color from the bark of *Xanthoxylum cariboeum* (Rutaceae).

xanthoprotein reaction. A yellow color results on boiling proteins with nitric acid.

xanthopterin. The yellow pigment from the wings of the "brimstone" butterfly (Pieridae). Cf. *vitamin M.*

xanthopurpurin. $C_{14}H_6O_2(OH)_2$ = 240.13. 1,3-Dihydroxyanthraquinone, purpuroxanthene. A solid, m.263, soluble in alcohol.

xanthorhamnin. A glucoside hydroxyflavone from buckthorn berries, *Rhamnus cathartica.* Cf. *rhamnoxanthin.*

xanthorhodium. The group Rh(NO₂)(NH₃)₅, which forms yellow salts; as, x. bromide, Rh(NO₂)(NH₃)-Br₂.

xanthorrhiza. Yellowroot. The dried rhizome of *X. apiifolia* (Ranunculaceae); a bitter tonic.

xanthosiderite. $Fe_2O_3 \cdot 2H_2O$. Fine, yellow, stellate needles.

xanthostrumarin. A glucoside from *Xanthium strumarium*, cocklebur (Compositae). Cf. *xanthium*.

xanthotoxin. $C_{12}H_8O_4 = 216.01$. Ammoidin, from the powdered fruits of *Ammi majus* (*Fagera xanthoxyloides*), m.146; soluble in water; used to treat leukoderma.

xanthoxylene. $C_{10}H_{16} = 136.1$. Xanthoxylin. A terpene from the essential oil of *Xanthoxylum* species (Rutaceae).

xanthoxylin. (1) An alcohol extract of xanthoxylum. (2) Xanthoxylene.

xanthoxylone. $C_{10}H_{12}O_4 = 196.1$. A crystalline principle from *Xanthoxylum*.

xanthoxylum. Prickly ash, yellowwood, angelica tree. The dried bark of *X. americanum*, *X. officinalis* (Rutaceae), containing xanthoxylene, essential oils, tannin, and resin; a diaphoretic and stimulant. Cf. *angelica tree, artar root.*

xanthydrol. $C_{13}H_{10}O_2 = 198.08$. 9-Hydroxyxanthene. A reagent for urea. Cf. *xanthene.*

xanthyl. The radical $C_{13}H_9O—$, from xanthene; 5 isomers.

xanthylium. The radical $C_6H_4 \cdot CH_2 \cdot C_6H_4 \cdot O=$ containing tetravalent oxygen; derived from xanthene.

xaxa. Acetylsalicylic acid.

xaxaquin. Quinine acetyl salicylate.

xble. Abbreviation for crucible.

Xe. Symbol for xenon.

xenate. A salt of xenic acid, XeO_4^-; used in analysis.

xenene. Biphenyl.

xenol. $PhC_6H_4OH = 170.1$. Xenenol, phenylphenol. **ortho-** White solid; an antiseptic. **para-** White solid; used in plastics to increase resistance to high temperatures and hot water.

xenolite. An aluminum silicate resembling fibrolite.

xenon. $Xe = 131.30$. (X is obsolete.) A rare, heavy noble gas and element, at. no. 54; discovered by Ramsay and Travers (1898); Greek, $\xi\epsilon\nu o\varsigma$, strange. Occurs in the atmosphere (5/100,000 %), with 9 isotopes. Colorless gas, $d_{air} = {}_14.422$, m.—112, b.—107.1; insoluble water; used in vacuum tubes. **x. tetrafluoride.** $XeF_4 = 207.30$. Colorless solid, sublimes 20, formed by reaction of the elements at 400°C.

Xenophanes. B.C. 576–480. Greek philosopher of the Eleatic school, who suggested one of the earliest known theories of atomic structure which he believed to be continuous and completely filling space.

xenotime. YPO_4. A native yttrium phosphate, containing uranium and rare-earth metals.

xenyl. Diphenyl. The radical $Ph_6CH_4—$, from diphenyl. **x. amine.** $PhC_6H_4 \cdot NH_2 = 169.1$. *p*-Biphenylamine, *p*-phenylaniline, martylamine, commercial aniline. White leaflets, m.53. Cf. *diphenylamine.*

xeroform. $Bi_2O_3(C_6H_2Br_3OH) = 796.8$. Bismuth tribromophenyl. Yellow powder, insoluble in water; an intestinal antiseptic.

xerogel. (1) A gel containing little or none of the dispersion medium used. (2) An organic polymer which swells in suitable solvents to give particles containing a 3-dimensional network of polymer chains. See *molecular sieve.*

xerography. A rapid method of printing or photography in which an electrostatically charged paper attracts pigment powder to certain patterned areas on its surface. The pigment is then fused by heat, which fixes it.

xeroradiograph. A radiograph produced by xerography.

xestophanesin. $C_{23}H_{18}O_{15} = 554.37$. A glucosidal coloring matter from galls, produced by *Xestophanus potentillae*. Orange needles, m.281–287.

xi. Greek letter ξ or Ξ.

xiphidin. A ptomaine from the sperm of the swordfish (81.5% arginine).

xi-zero. A particle whose existence was deduced mathematically. It has no electric charge; has 2,570 times the weight of an electron, and a life of 10^{-9} second.

xonotlite. $5CaO \cdot 5SiO_2 \cdot H_2O$. A fibrous-structured constituent of boiler scales.

X protein. See *protein.*

X ray(s). Roentgen rays. A radiation, q.v., of short wavelengths (0.06–2 Å) produced in an X-ray tube, q.v., by cathode rays focused on a metal surface. They resemble the γ rays of radioactive substances, and are made visible by fluorescent screens or photographic plates. Their *quantity* is determined with Eder's solution; their *intensity* is expressed in roentgen units. Cf. *spectrum, radiations.* **hard-** X rays of relatively high penetration (wavelength 0.19–0.43 Å, which decreases as they traverse a medium). **heterogeneous-** Multifrequent. **homogeneous-** Monochromatic. **infra-** Grenz rays. **monochromatic-** Unifrequent, homogeneous. X rays of a single wavelength or a group of wavelengths, depending on the nature of the target. The shortest measured is 0.1075 Å for the K line of uranium; the longest 17.66 Å for the L_β line of iron. **multifrequent-, polychromatic-** Heterogeneous. X rays of many different wavelengths. **soft-** X rays of relatively low penetration (wavelength 11.9–13.6 Å, which increases as they traverse a medium). **ultra-** Cosmic rays. **unifrequent-** Monochromatic. **white-** Common X rays, consisting of a band of many different wavelengths. Their limit depends on the voltage applied, and not on the nature of the target: $Ve = h\nu_0 = hc/\lambda_0$, where V is the voltage, e the charge of an electron, h Planck's constant, c the velocity of light, λ_0 the maximum frequency, and ν_0 the minimum wavelength.

X-ray analysis. Determination of the internal structure of a material from the diffraction pattern formed when an X ray passes through it. Types: (1) *Corona* or diffuse fog, indicating the gaseous state. (2) *Halo*, indicating a liquid or amorphous substance; the molecules are distributed irregularly. (3) *Rings*, indicating a regular space lattice with the molecules in definite positions. (4) *Points*, indicating a crystal, in which the atoms, ions, or molecules are fixed in definite positions.

X-ray film. Skiagram.

X-ray intensity unit. (International standard, 1937.) The roentgen, r. The quantity of X or γ radiation such that the associated corpuscular emission per 0.001293 gm of air produces, in air, ions carrying 1 esu of electricity of either sign. Thus, 1 r produces 1.61×10^{12} ion pairs/gm of air. Cf. *angström, kX.*

X-ray photograph, X-ray picture, X-ray plate. Skiagram.

X-ray spectrogram. A photographic record produced by the spectrograph.

X-ray spectrograph. A spectrometer fitted with a camera. Cf. *spectrograph.*

X-ray spectrometer. An arrangement for diffracting X rays using the space lattice of a crystal as grating.

X-ray spectrum. Moseley spectrum, high-frequency spectrum. The spectrum (produced by a crystal-diffraction grating) of the characteristic radiations emitted by the metal used as anticathode in an X-ray tube. Each metal produces a few, strong, characteristic lines, the square roots of the frequencies of which are in direct proportion to the atomic number of the element; a means of analysis.

X-ray structure. The structural arrangement of atoms in a crystal as revealed by the Laue pattern and crystallograms, q.v., produced when X rays pass through the crystal and fall on a photographic plate.

X-ray tube. A highly evacuated tube containing a disk concentric with the tube as cathode; a heavy, inclined plane of high-melting-point metal as anticathode; and a small wire as anode. The cathode rays concentrate on the anticathode, which emits rays of very short wavelengths.

X unit. (1) A wavelength of 10^{-3} Å (10^{-11} cm). (2) More accurately, $1.00201 \times 10^{-3} \times$ (Craven).

xylan. A hemicellulose in many trees and industrial wastes; e.g., peanut shells; it hydrolyzes to xylose, q.v.

xylanbassoric acid. $C_{19}H_{28}O_{17} = 528.22$. A soluble hydrolysis product of bassorin from gum traganth; hydrolyzed to xylose.

xylene. $C_6H_4Me_2 = 106.12$. Dimethylbenzene*, xylol. **ortho-** or **1,2-** Colorless liquid, d.0.881, m.-28, b.144, insoluble in water; used in the manufacture of synthetic resins, pharmaceuticals, dyestuffs, and phthalic acid. **meta-** or **1,3-** Colorless liquid, d.0.866, m.-54, b.139, insoluble in water. **para-** or **1,4-** Colorless, monoclinic crystals, m.15, insoluble in water. See *xylol.* **bromo-** $Me_2C_6H_3Br = 184.99$. Cf. *xylyl bromide.* *4-ortho-* b.214. *2-meta-* b.206. *4-meta-* b.207. *5-meta-* b.204. *2-para-* b.206. **dihydroxy-** Xylenediol. **ethyl-** Dimethylethyl*benzene.* **hydroxy-** Xylenol. **nitro-** See *nitroxylene.*

x. sulfonic acid. $C_8H_{10}O_3S = 186.18$. (1,2,4)-$C_6H_3Me_2 \cdot SO_3H$, b.19.

xylenediol. $C_6H_4(CH_2OH)_2 = 138.1$. Xylylene alcohol, xylylol, phenyldicarbinol, benzenedicarbinol. **ortho-** or **α,α'-o-** Phthalyl alcohol, m.62. **meta-** or **α,α'-m-** m.46. **para-** or **α,α'-p-** Terephthalyl alcohol, m.112. All used in organic synthesis.

xylenol blue. 1,4-Dimethyl-5-hydroxybenzenesulfonphthalein. An indicator; changes from red (pH 1.2) to yellow (pH 2.8), and from yellow (pH 8.0) to blue (pH 9.6).

xylenols. $C_6H_3Me_2OH = 122.1$. Dimethyl phenols or hydroxydimethyl benzenes. Colorless crystals, soluble in water.

xylic acid. $Me_2C_6H_3COOH = 150.13$. Methyltoluic acid, dimethylbenzoic acid. **2,3-** α-Hemellitic acid, m.144. **2,5-** or **para-** *Iso*xylic acid, m.132. **3,5-** Mesitylinic acid, m.167.

xylidene. Xylidine.

xylidic acid. $C_6H_3Me(COOH)_2 = 180.1$. 4-Methylisophthalic acid. Colorless crystals. **1,2,3-** m.144 (decomp.). **1,2,4-** m.325 (sublimes). **1,2,5-** m.282. Cf. *uvitic acid.*

xylidine(s). $C_6H_3Me_2NH_2 = 121.1$. Xylidene. Methyl toluidines, dimethyl anilines, aminoxylenes. Aniline homologs in technical xylidine, slightly soluble in water; used in the synthesis of dyes.

xylidinic acid. Xylidic acid.

xylite. Xylitol.

xylitols. $CH_2OH(CHOH)_3CH_2OH = 152.1$. Xylite. Pentahydric alcohols derived from xylose.

xylo- Prefix (Greek, wood) indicating a relation to wood.

Xylocaine. Trademark for lignocaine.

xylochloral. A compound of choral and xylose. Colorless scales, m.132; a hypnotic.

xyloidine. $C_6H_9O_5(NO_2) = 207.1$. An explosive obtained by the action of nitric acid on starch or wood (Braconnot, 1842).

xyloketose. $C_5H_{10}O_5 = 150.1$. A pentose-ketose corresponding with xylose and lyxose.

xylol. A mixture of xylenes, q.v.; a solvent in microscopy.

xylolith. Woodstone. A mixture of magnesia, magnesium chloride, and sawdust which dries to an extremely hard mass; used for floors or laboratory tables.

xylon. Wood cellulose.

xylonic acid. $CH_2OH(CHOH)_3COOH = 166.1$. Obtained by oxidation of xylose. Cf. *pentonic acid.*

xylonite. Celluloid.

xylopal. Wood opal.

xyloquinone. $C_6H_2Me_2O_2 = 136.1$. Dimethylquinone, a homolog of quinol. Soluble solids. **2,3-** m.55 (sublimes). **2,5-** m.61 (sublimes). **2,6-** m.72. **3,5-** Phlorone.

xylorcinol. $C_6H_2Me_2(OH)_2 = 138.1$. **1,3,4,6-** Dimethylresorcinol, methylorcinol, a homolog of orcinol. White crystals, m.124, soluble in water.

xylose. $CH_2OH(CHOH)_3CHO = 150.1$. Wood sugar. A pentose obtained from xylan or vegetable fibers by heating with sulfuric acid. Colorless crystals, m.140, soluble in water; used in tanning, dyeing, and diabetic foods. Cf. *xylan.*

xylostein. A poisonous glucoside from the fruit of *Lonicera xylosteum* (Caprifoliaceae), a variety of honeysuckle.

xyloyl. The radical $Me_2C_6H_3CO$—, from xylic acid; 7 isomers.

xylyl. (1) The radical $CH_3C_6H_4CH_2$—, from xylene; ortho, meta, and para types. (2) Dimethylphenyl. The radical $Me_2C_6H_3$—. Cf. *tolyl.*

x. alcohol. (1) Xylenediol. (2) Tolylcarbinol. **x. bromides.** $MeC_6H_4CH_2Br = 184.99$. *ortho-* m.21. *meta-* b.215. *para-* m.38. The mixed isomers are a lachrymatory poison gas (T-stoff). Cf. bromo*xylene.* **x. chlorides.** $CH_3 \cdot C_6H_4 \cdot CH_2 \cdot Cl = 140.6$. Monochloroxylene, tolyl chloride. Colorless liquids, insoluble in water. *ortho-* b.197. *meta-* b.195. *para-* b.192. **x. hydrazine.** $C_6H_3 \cdot Me_2NH \cdot NH = 136.1$. Colorless needles, m.85, soluble in ether.

xylylene. The radical —$CH_2 \cdot C_6H_4 \cdot CH_2$—, from xylene; ortho, meta, and para types.

x. alcohol. Xylenediol. **x. amine.** X. diamine. **x. bromide.** $C_6H_4(CH_2Br)_2$. **x. carbinol.** $C_6H_3Me_2 \cdot CH_2 \cdot CH_2OH$. Dimethylphenylethanol. **x. chloride.** X. dichloride. **x. cyanides.** C_6H_4-$(CH_2CN)_2 = 156.13$. *ortho-* m.59. *meta-* m.28. *para-* m.98. **x. diamines.** $C_6H_4(CH_2NH_2)_2$ and $C_6H_2Me_2(NH_2)_2 = 136.2$. Diaminoxylene. Used in the manufacture of dyes. **x. dichlorides.** C_6H_4-$(CH_2Cl)_2 = 175.02$. Phthalyl chloride. *ortho-* m.55. *meta-* m.34. *para-* m.98. **x. glycol.** Xylenediol.

xylylenimine. $C_8H_9N = 119.1$. Dihydroisoindole. Yellow liquid, b.213.

xylylol. Xylenediol.

Xyptal. Trade name for an alkyd-type plastic made from xylitol. Cf. *Glyptal.*

xysmalobin. $C_{46}H_{70}O_{20} \cdot 5H_2O = 1032.59$. A crystalline glucoside from the root of *Xysmalobium undulatum*, wild cotton, milkbush, iShongwe (Asclepiadaceae), S. Africa; used locally as an emetic.

Y

Y. Symbol for yttrium.

y. The second dimension in coordinates, q.v.

Υ. See *upsilon*.

γ. See *gamma*.

yaba bark. Andira bark, cabbage tree bark. The bark of *Andira excelsa*. Cf. *andirin*, *goa*.

yabine. An alkaloid from yaba bark.

yacca gum. Acaroid resin.

yajeine. Harmine.

yajenine. An alkaloid from yajé (Apocynaceae), S. Colombia.

yam. The starchy tubers of *Dioscorea species*, q.v., cultivated for food in the tropics; as, **cush-cush-** The y. of *D. trifida*. **negro-** The y. of *D. cayennensis*. **white-** The y. of *D. alata*.

yara-yara. β-Naphthyl methyl ether.

yard. yd. A unit of length in the English system.
1 yard = 3 feet = 36 inches = 0.914 meter.

    U.S. y. = 0.914,401,83 m.

    Imperial standard y. = 0.914,397,2 m.

    Canadian y. = 0.9144 m.

National Physical Laboratory (U.K.) y. (based on the 1922 value of the Imperial standard y.) = 0.914,398,41 m.

International y. (accepted by U.S., U.K., Australia, Canada, New Zealand, S. Africa, in 1959) = 0.9144 m.

The Imperial standard y. is shrinking at about 0.0002 inch per year.

cubic- yd³ or cu yd = 764.535 cubic centimeters. **square-** yd² or sq yd = 836.13 square meters.

yarn. A thread. **filament-** See *filament*. **synthetic-** See *fiber*, *rayon*.

yarrow. The dried leaves and inflorescence of *Achillea millefolium* (Compositae); a tonic, alterative, and astringent.

yatren. Loretin.

yawroot. Stillingia.

Yb. Symbol for ytterbium.

yd. Abbreviation for yard.

year. A measure of time, q.v.; the period of the earth's revolution around the sun.

Anomalistic y.	365 days 6 hr 13 min 48 sec
Ordinary y.	365 days 5 hr 48 min 46 sec
Sidereal y.	365 days 6 hr 9 min 9 sec
Average civil y. . . .	365.2422 mean solar days = 3.155693 × 10⁷ sec

light- A unit of astronomical distance; the distance that light travels in one year, 5.9 × 10¹² miles or 9.4627 × 10¹² km. **solar-** Ordinary y. **tropical-** Ordinary y.

yeast. Cerevisiae. Unicellular vegetable organisms (fungi) of the family Saccharomycetaceae. They ferment sugars to carbon dioxide and alcohol by virtue of the enzymes (zymases) they contain.

They also contain invertase, an enzyme that inverts unfermentable sugars (as cane sugar) to fermentable sugars. **baker's-, beer-** Compressed y. The moist living cells of *Saccharomyces cerevisiae* compressed with some starchy or other absorbent material. Used in baking, brewing, and fermenting; and as a vitamin-rich nutrient. **bottom-** Low y. **brewer's-** High and low y. **compressed-** Baker's y. **copro-** A y. that contains a large quantity of coproporphyrin. **dried-** (1) Y. dried at a low temperature, for storage or transport, without greatly impairing its vitality. (2) Pharmacy: y. dried to contain not more than 7% water; a source of natural vitamin B complex (U.S.P.). **high-** Top y. It rises during fermentation; as in English beers; distinguished from low y. by absence of melibiase, which ferments raffinose. **low-** Bottom y. It falls to the bottom of the liquid it is fermenting; as in German beers. Cf. *high-*. **mineral-** q.v. **pressed-** Baker's y. **top-** High y. **wild-** A y. not grown as a pure culture, responsible for beer diseases.

y. food. A mixture of mineral substances (phosphates, etc.) added to stimulate the y. activity. **y. gum.** A mannan formed from a combination of the principal carbohydrates of the y. cells with glycogen. **y. nucleic acid.** A nucleic acid from the nucleoprotein of y.

yeatmanite. $(MnZn)_{16}Sb_2Si_4O_{29}$. A triclinic mineral from Franklin, N.J.

yellow. A primary color: between orange and green. **acid-** An aminoazo dye. **butter-** q.v. **chrome-** Lead chromate. **Eger's-** q.v. **fast-** An aminoazo dye. **indicator-** A pigment, yellow in acid, colorless in alkali; a light filter. **queen's-** Mercuric subsulfate.

y. acid. 1,3-Dihydroxynaphthalene-5,7-disulfonic acid. **y. arsenic.** Orpiment. **y. bark.** Cinchona. **y. brass.** Muntz metal. **y. cake.** Uranium oxide concentrate. **y. copper.** Chalcopyrite. **y. copperas.** Copiapite. **y. dock.** Rumex. **y. dyes.** See *dyes*. **y. earth.** Ocher. **y. fever vaccine.** The living virus of an attenuated strain of y. fever virus in chick embryo tissue (U.S.P., B.P.). **y. flag.** The root of *Iris pseudacorus*; an astringent. **y. jasmine.** Rumex. **y. lead ore.** Wulfenite. **y. ore.** Chalcopyrite. **y. parilla.** Menispermum. **y. pigments.** See *cadmium y.*, *chrome y.*, *gamboge*, *Indian y.*, *litharge*, *orpiment*, *ocher*. **y. precipitate.** Y. mercuric oxide. **y. prussiate of potash.** Potassium ferrocyanide. **y. prussiate of soda.** Sodium ferrocyanide. **y. puccoon.** Hydrastis. **y. resin.** Acaroid resin. **y. root.** Xanthorrhiza. **y. sandalwood, y. sanders.** See *sandalwood*. **y. ultramarine.** Barium chromate. **y. wax.** (1) A variety of beeswax. (2) A semisolid residue from the distillation of petroleum. **y. wood.** Xanthoxylum.

yenite. Ilvaite.

yenshee. Opium dross. Low-grade opium, consisting of dregs and carbonized opium after smoking (1-10% morphine). Cf. *chandoo, mudat.*

yerba. (1) Spanish for herb. (2) Maté. **y. buena.** Micromeria. The dried leaves of *Micromeria douglassi* (Labiatae), the Pacific Coast; an aromatic and carminative. **y. maté.** Maté. **y. reuma.** The dried herb of *Frankenia grandifolia* (Frankeniaceae); a mild astringent. **y. sagrada.** The dried herb of *Lantana braziliensis* (Verbenaceae); an antipyretic. Cf. *lantanine.* **y. santa.** Eriodictyon.

yerbine. An alkaloid from *Ilex paraguayensis*, which resembles caffeine.

yew. Taxus.

yield. (1) The percentage of finished material obtained from the raw material. (2) The percentage of finished material obtained, based on that obtainable theoretically.

yield point. The stress at which a marked and permanent increase in the deformation of a substance occurs without an increase in the load.

-yl. Suffix indicating: (1) a monovalent hydrocarbon radical; as, methyl; (2) the presence of oxygen in a radical; as, hydroxyl. Cf. *-ylene.*

ylangol. $C_{10}H_{18}O = 154.20$. An isomer of geraniol from ylang-ylang oil.

ylang-ylang. Ilang-ilang. A tree of the Philippine and Malayan Islands, *Cananga odorata* (Anonaceae); the flowers contain an essential oil: **y. oil.** Cananga oil, d.0.911-0.958; used in perfumery; contains linalool, geraniol, and pinene. Y. has been synthesized (trade name Gylan).

-ylene. Suffix indicating a bivalent hydrocarbon radical; as, methylene. Cf. *-yl, -ylium, -ene.*

-yne*. Suffix indicating: (1) an acetylene linkage (U.S. usage); (2) a triply unsaturated compound (U.K. usage). Cf. *-ine.*

yogurt, yoghurt, yoghourt. Soured milk, used as a beverage. Made by treating pasteurized milk with a standardized bacterial culture for 3 hours at 43.5°C. Cf. *kefir.*

yohimbehe. The bark of *Corynanthe johimbe* (Rubiaceae) of the Cameroons, containing alkaloids; an aphrodisiac.

yohimbenine. $C_{35}H_{45}O_6N_3 = 603.6$. Corynanthine. An alkaloid from yohimbehe.

yohimbic acid. $C_{20}H_{24}N_2O_3 = 340.15$. A monobasic acid; yohimbine is its methyl ester.

yohimbine. $C_{21}H_{26}O_3N_2 = 352.15$. Methyl yohimbate, corynine. An alkaloid from the bark of yohimbehe. White needles, m.234, slightly soluble in water. Cf. *aribine.* **y. hydrochloride.** $C_{22}H_{28}O_3N_2 \cdot HCl = 404.8$. Aphrodine. Colorless crystals, soluble in water; an aphrodisiac.

yolk. The yellow part of an egg, containing nutrient proteins and lecithins.

yoloy. A steel alloy containing small proportions of P, Ni, and Cu.

yoshino. Tengujo. Kodzu. A strong thin typewriter stencil paper, made in Japan from the fiber of the paper mulberry, *Broussonetia papyrifera.*

Youden square. A method of planning experiments under different conditions, for comparing batch-to-batch differences in a particular property.

Young, James. 1811-1883. British chemist noted for the development of the gas and oil industries.

Y., Sydney. 1857-1937. British chemist, noted for boiling-point laws. Cf. *Ramsay and Young equation.*

Young, Thomas. 1733-1829. British physicist, noted for: **Y.'s modulus.** Longitudinal elasticity. The force in dynes per square centimeter to permanently deform a material by stretching, bending, or twisting. Stretching modulus = stress/strain $= mgl/\pi r^2 s$, where s is the elongation produced by a weight m in a wire of length l and cross section of radius r.

yperite. Mustard gas.

ysopol. $C_{10}H_{18}O = 154.20$. A terpene alcohol from hyssop.

Yt. Symbol for yttrium (obsolete).

ytterbia. Ytterbium oxide.

ytterbite. Gadolinite.

ytterbium. Yb = 173.04. Neoytterbium, formerly supposed to be a mixture of aldebaranium and cassiopeium. A trivalent rare-earth metal and element, at. no. 70, discovered by Marignac (1878). **y. acetate.** $Yb(C_2H_3O_2)_3 \cdot 4H_2O = 422.63$. White plates, soluble in water. **y. bromide.** $YbBr_3 \cdot 8H_2O = 557.7$. Green, hygroscopic crystals. **y. chloride.** $YbCl_3 \cdot 6H_2O = 388.0$. Green rhombs, m.150, soluble in water. **y. oxalate.** $Yb_2(C_2O_4)_3 \cdot 10H_2O = 791.16$. White crystals, insoluble in water. **y. oxide.** $Yb_2O_3 = 395.2$. Ytterbia. White powder, insoluble in water. **y. oxychloride.** $YbOCl = 225.1$. White powder, insoluble in water. **y. sulfate.** $Yb_2(SO_4)_3 = 635.41$. Green crystals, decomp. 900, soluble in water.

Ytterby. A village in Sweden which gives its name to local rare-earth minerals; as, *ytterbium, yttrium.*

yttergranate. A calcium-iron garnet, containing yttrium compounds.

yttria. (1) Yttrium oxide. (2) Gadolinite. **y. group.** See *rare-earth metals.*

yttrialite. $Y_2O_3 \cdot 2SiO_2$. A green mineral, containing Fe and Th.

yttrium. Y or Yt = 88.91. A trivalent rare-earth metal of the aluminum group and element, at. no. 39, discovered by Gadolin (1794) in gadolinite, which was separated by Mosander (1843) into yttria, terbia, and erbia. Gray hexagons, m.1552, d.5.51, which decompose water and dilute acids; used in incandescent gas mantles. Removal of dissolved gases improves its ductility for use in atomic reactors and missiles. **y. acetate.** $Y(C_2H_3O_2)_3 \cdot 8H_2O = 410.1$. Colorless crystals, soluble in water. **y. bromide.** $YBr_3 = 328.8$. White, deliquescent powder. **y. carbonate.** $Y_2(CO_3)_3 \cdot 3H_2O = 411.8$. Pale red powder, insoluble in water. **y. chloride.** $YCl_3 \cdot 6H_2O = 303.2$. Pale red, hygroscopic prisms, m.160, soluble in water. **y. hydroxide.** $Y(OH)_3 = 139.7$. White powder, decomp. by heat, insoluble in water. **y. minerals.** Chiefly: gadolinite, rowlandite, thalenite, xenotime, yttrialite. **y. nitrate.** $Y(NO_3)_3 \cdot 6H_2O = 382.8$. Colorless crystals, soluble in water. **y. oxalate.** $Y_2(C_2O_4)_3 \cdot 9H_2O = 603.98$. White crystals, slightly soluble in water. **y. oxide.** $Y_2O_3 = 225.0$. Yttria. Colorless crystals, insoluble in water. **y. sulfate.** $Y_2(SO_4)_3 \cdot 8H_2O = 610.1$. Pale red crystals, decomp. 1000, slightly soluble in water. **y. sulfide.** $Y_2S_3 = 274.0$. Yellow powder, m.1900-1950, insoluble in water.

yttrocerite. A native mixed fluoride of yttrium, cerium, erbium, and calcium.

yttrotantalite. $Y_4(Ta_2O_7)_3$. A rare-earth tantalate containing Fe, Ca, and He.

yttrotitanite. A siliceous calcium titanate containing oxides of Y, Al, and Fe.

yucca. Adam's needle, Spanish bayonets, *Y. filamentosa* (Liliaceae), Southern California, Texas, and Mexico; the leaves yield a fiber.

Yukawa, Hideki. Japanese physicist, Nobel Prize winner (1949). **Y. particle.** Heavy electron.

yukon. Heavy electron; named in honor of Yukawa.

yulocrotine. $C_{19}H_{26}O_3N$ = 316.21. An alkaloid from *Julocroton Montevidensis* (Euphorbiaceae).

Z

Z. Symbol for: (1) atomic number (German, Atom Zahl); (2) gram-equivalent weight.

z. (1) The third dimension of coordinates, q.v. (2) Symbol for the valency of an ion.

zaffer, zaffre. A mixture of cobalt oxides and arsenates obtained by roasting cobalt ores; a raw material for the production of cobalt compounds.

zala. Borax.

zanaloin. The aloin from aloes of Zanzibar.

zaratite. $NiCO_3 \cdot 2Ni(OH)_2 \cdot 5H_2O$. Emerald nickel. A native nickel carbonate.

zea. (1) A genus of annual grasses to which Indian corn (maize) belongs. (2) Corn silk, the fresh styles and stigmas of *Zea mays*, the maize plant; a diuretic.

zearin. $C_{52}H_{88}O_4 = 776.8$. A colorless principle from lichens.

zeatin. Kinetin. An aminopurine factor in plant extracts, which induces cell division.

zeaxanthin. $C_{40}H_{56}O_2 = 568.4$. A carotenoid color, q.v., from maize, egg yolk, and plants; isomer of xanthophyll and lutein. Yellow leaflets, m.101, optically inactive.

zebromal. $Ph \cdot CHBr \cdot CHBr \cdot COOEt = 336.0$. Ethyl dibromocinnamate. White crystals, insoluble in water, soluble in oils; a sedative and hypnotic.

zedoary. The dried rhizomes of *Curcuma zeodaria* (Zingiberaceae), E. Indies; a stomachic and carminative. **z. oil.** The volatile oil of z., d.0.990–1.010, b.240–308, containing cineol.

Zeeman, Pieter. 1865–1943. Dutch physicist. **Z. effect.** A resolution of spectral single lines into 3 fine lines (triplet) when the source of light, as a flame, is placed in a strong magnetic field.

Zefran. Trademark for a synthetic-fiber copolymer of acrylonitrile and vinyl acetate, with vinyl pyrrolidine as acceptor.

Zehla. Trade name for a viscose synthetic fiber.

zein. A prolamine from maize; it contains no tryptophane, cystine, or lysine.

Zeise salt. $KCl \cdot PtCl_2C_2H_4 \cdot H_2O$. Cf. *π-complex*.

Zeisel reaction. The formation of methyl iodide from methoxy compounds and hydriodic acid:

$$(1)\ ROMe + HI = R \cdot OH + MeI$$
$$(2)\ MeI + AgNO_3 = AgI + MeNO_3$$

The silver iodide is weighted to give the MeO group content.

zelio paste. A rat poison containing thallium.

Zellner's paper. Fluorescein paper.

Zenker's solution. A fixative and preservative for biological specimens: potassium dichromate 2.5, sodium sulfate 1, mercuric chloride 5 gm; acetic acid 5 ml; water to 100 ml.

Z enzyme. An enzyme (probably β-glucosidase) in soya which promotes the hydrolysis of amylose to maltose.

zeolite. $Na_2O \cdot 2Al_2O_3 \cdot 5SiO_2$ and $CaO \cdot 2Al_2O_3 \cdot 5SiO_2$. Hydrated aluminum and calcium or sodium silicates, reacting in solution, by double decomposition, with salts of the alkali and alkaline-earth metals; used for water softening. Cf. *analcine, chabazite, natrolite, organolite.* **artificial-** Permutite. **organic-** A synthetic resin having the properties of a z.

Zephiran Chloride. Trademark for benzalkonium chloride; a cationic detergent and antiseptic.

zephirol. Early name for Zephiran Chloride.

zero. (1) The complete absence of a particular quantity. (2) The point at which a scale has the value of 0, e.g., zero degree centigrade. **absolute-** q.v.

Z. Gradient Synchotron. A device (Argonne, Illinois) to accelerate protons to 12.5 billion electron volts. **z. potential.** The potential across the Gouy layer, q.v., on a colloidal particle.

Zetec. Trade name for a mixed-polymer synthetic fiber.

zewaphosphate. A fertilizer, 30% phosphorus pentoxide, obtained by treating sulfite cellulose waste liquor with crude phosphates.

zeyherine. An alkaloid from the seeds of *Erythrina zeyheri* (Leguminosae), S. Africa.

zibet. Civet.

Ziegler catalyst. A mixture of aluminum triethyl monochloride (or similar compound) with titanium tetrachloride; used in the: **Z. process.** A low-pressure method of manufacturing high-density polymers and synthetic rubber.

Ziehl's stain. Carbolfuchsin.

zierone. $C_{15}H_{22}O = 218.02$. A sesquiterpene ketone from *Zieria macrophylla*.

Ziervogel process. Extraction of silver by roasting the sulfide to silver sulfate, leaching with water, and precipitating metallic silver with copper.

zinc. $Zn = 65.37$. A metal and element, at. no. 30, known to the Hindus, observed by Agricola, described by Paracelsus (1520). White, brittle metal, d.6.7–7.2, m.419, b.918, insoluble in water, soluble in acids or hot solutions of alkalies. Z. occurs in nature principally as sulfide, carbonate, and silicate. Used as a reducing agent (indigo vats), reagent for the production of hydrogen (arsenic test); and in alloys and the metal industry. World production (1962), excluding Eastern bloc, 3 million tons. Z. is normally divalent, but monovalent z. is known. **activated-** Z. granulated in presence of cadmium sulfate for the Marsh test, q.v. **butter of-** Z. chloride. **granulated-** Distorted granules prepared by pouring molten z. into water. **powdered-** Finely powdered z. used as a reagent. Cf. *z. dust.*

z. acetate. $Zn(C_2H_3O_2)_2 \cdot 3H_2O = 237.5$. Colorless plates, m.242, soluble in water. Used as a reagent, mordant, emetic; and in glaze manufacture and gargles and disinfectants. *fused-* $Zn(C_2H_3O_2)_2 = 183.4$. White, fused mass, soluble in water.

z. albuminate. A compound of albumin and z. Yellow scales, slightly soluble in water. **z. alkyl(s).** ZnR_2, in which R is an alkyl radical; as, z. methide. $ZnMe_2$. **z. alkyl condensation.** Frankland's synthesis of hydrocarbons. Z. is removed from a z. alkyl as hydrate or iodide: $2R_3CI + ZnMe_2 = 2R_3CMe + ZnI_2$. **z. alum.** Aluminum z. sulfate. **z. amalgam.** A mixture of z. and mercury, used as a reducing agent, and in electric batteries. **z. ammonium salts.** $Zn(NH_3)_4Cl_2 \cdot H_2O$, $Zn(NH_3)_5$-SO_4, etc., analogous to copper-ammonium salts. **z. arsenate.** $ZnHAsO_4 = 205.4$. White powder, slightly soluble in water. Cf. *adamite*. **z. arsenide.** $Zn_3As_2 = 346.06$. **z. arsenite.** $Zn(AsO_2)_2 = 279.4$. Colorless powder, insoluble in water. **z. ashes.** The oxidized z. from the surface of a galvanizing bath. **z. benzoate.** $Zn(C_7H_5O_2)_2 = 307.46$. White powder, soluble in water. **z. biborate.** Z. tetraborate. **z. bichromate.** Z. dichromate. **z. blende.** Sphalerite. **z. bloom.** Z. oxide. **z. borate.** $ZnB_4O_7 \cdot 7H_2O = 346.7$. White antiseptic powder. **z. bromate.** $Zn(BrO_3)_2 = 321.31$. White, hygroscopic powder, m.100; an antiseptic. **z. bromide.** $ZnBr_2 = 225.2$. Colorless, hygroscopic needles, m.394; a sedative and antispasmodic. **z. butter.** Z. chloride. **z. carbonate.** $ZnCO_3 \cdot H_2O = 143.40$. Tutia. White rhombs, decomp. 300, insoluble in water; an antiseptic. Cf. *zinc spar*. **z. chlorate.** $Zn(ClO_3)_2 \cdot 6H_2O = 340.4$. Colorless, hygroscopic crystals, m.60. **z. chloride.** $ZnCl_2 = 136.3$. Z. Butter. White, deliquescent octahedra, m.365. A reagent for alkaloids; solvent for cellulose; an antiseptic, astringent (U.S.P.), and escharotic; preservative in embalming; mordant, and soldering flux. **z. chloroiodide.** A mixture of z. iodide and chloride. The saturated solution is a microchemical reagent for cellulose (blue color) and tannin (violet color). **z. chloroiodide solution.** Naegeli's solution. A microchemical reagent prepared by decomposing hydrochloric acid with z. and saturating the solution with potassium iodide and iodine. Cf. *Herzberg's stain.* **z. chromate.** $ZnCrO_4 \cdot 7H_2O = 307.6$. Z. yellow, buttercup yellow. A soluble, yellow pigment. **z. citrate.** $Zn_3(C_6H_5O_7)_2 \cdot 2H_2O = 610.3$. White powder, soluble in water; an antiepileptic. **z. copper couple.** Sheet zinc coated with a black deposit of copper by immersion in an acid solution of copper sulfate. It liberates nascent hydrogen from acid solutions, and will reduce nitrates to ammonia. Used to determine nitrates in water. **z. cream.** A mixture of z. oxide, oleic acid, arachis oil, wool fat, and calcium hydroxide (B.P.). **z. cyanide.** $Zn(CN)_2 = 117.4$. Colorless prisms, decomp. by heat, insoluble in water; an insecticide, disinfectant, and anthelmintic. **z. dichromate.** $ZnCr_2O_7 = 281.6$. Z. bichromate. Orange powder, soluble in water. **z. diethyl*.** Z. ethide. **z. dimethyl*.** Z. methide. **z. dithiofuroate.** $(C_4H_3OCS_2)_2Zn$. Furac II. Brown powder; a rubber vulcanization accelerator. **z. dust.** (1) Finely divided z.; a reducing agent. (2) The flue dust of smelters, containing z., z. oxide, and impurities; a gray paint. **z. ethide.** $Zn(C_2H_5)_2 = 123.5$. Z. ethyl. Diethyl z. Colorless liquid, ignites in air, b.118, violently decomp. by water; used in organic synthesis. **z. ethyl.** Z. ethide. **z. ethyl sulfate.** $Zn(C_2H_5SO_4)_2 = 315.5$. Colorless, hygroscopic leaflets, soluble in water or alcohol.

z. ferrocyanide. $Zn_2Fe(CN)_6 \cdot 3H_2O = 396.7$. White powder, soluble in ammonia water; an antiseptic. **z. flowers.** Z. oxide. **z. fluoride.** $ZnF_2 = 103.4$. White powder, slightly soluble in water. **z. fluosilicate.** $ZnSiF_6 \cdot 6H_2O = 315.53$. Hexagonal prisms, very soluble in water. **z. foil.** Sheet z. prepared by heating z. at $100-150°C$ and rolling it. **z. formate.** $Zn(CHO_2)_2 = 155.4$. Colorless crystals, soluble in water; an antiseptic. *dihydrate-* $Zn(CHO_2)_2 \cdot 2H_2O = 191.43$. White, monoclinic crystals, soluble in water. **z. gelatin.** A smooth paste of zinc oxide, in a mixture of gelatin, glycerol, and water; a pharmaceutical protective (U.S.P., B.P.). **z. glycerophosphate.** $Zn(C_3H_7O_2)PO_4 = 235.44$. White powder, soluble in water; used medicinally. **z. hydroxide.** $Zn(OH)_2 = 99.4$. White prisms, decomp. by heat, insoluble in water. **z. hypophosphite.** $Zn(H_2PO_2)_2 \cdot H_2O = 245.4$. White, deliquescent crystals; an antiseptic and astringent. **z. iodate.** $Zn(IO_3)_2 = 415.1$. White crystals, slightly soluble in water. **z. iodide.** $ZnI_2 = 319.2$. Colorless octahedra, m.446, soluble in water; a reagent (detecting chlorine and narceine) alterant, and antiseptic. **z. iodide–starch paper.** Filter paper, impregnated with a z. iodide–starch solution; used to detect free chlorine, iodine, or ozone (blue color). **z. iodide–starch solution.** A solution of z. iodide and soluble starch; a test reagent and indicator for oxidizing agents. **z. isopropyl xanthate.** An accelerator for the vulcanization of rubber. **z. lactate.** $Zn(C_3H_5O_3)_2 \cdot 3H_2O = 297.5$. Colorless crystals, soluble in water; an antiepileptic. **z. malate.** $ZnC_4H_4O_5 = 197.4$. White crystals, soluble in water. **z. methide.** $Zn(CH_3)_2 = 95.43$. Z. dimethyl. Colorless liquid, ignites in air, $d_{10}° 1.39$, m.-40, b.46, decomp. by water or alcohol; used in organic synthesis. **z. methyl.** Z. methide. **z. minerals.** Chiefly: sphalerite (regular), ZnS; zincite, ZnO; franklinite, $ZnFe_2O_4$; smithsonite (zinc spar), $ZnCO_3$; willemite, Zn_2SiO_4. **z. monochloroacetate.** $Zn(C_2H_2ClO_2)_2 = 252.35$. Colorless powder, soluble in water; an antiseptic. **z. nitrate.** $Zn(NO_3)_2 \cdot 6H_2O = 297.50$. Colorless tetragons, m.36, soluble in water; a reagent, escharotic, and mordant. **z. nitride.** $Zn_3N_2 = 224.6$. Green powder, decomp. by water to z. oxide and ammonia. **z. oleate.** $Zn(C_{18}H_{32}O_2)_2 = 625.89$. White, greasy granules, insoluble in water; used in ointments, and as a varnish drier. **z. oxalate.** $ZnC_2O_4 \cdot 2H_2O = 189.4$. White powder, slightly soluble in water. **z. oxide.** $ZnO = 81.38$. Philosopher's wool. Amorphous powder or hexagons, d.5.42, insoluble in water, soluble in acids, alkalies, or ammonium salt solutions. Used as a reagent and neutralizing agent, in the manufacture of ointments, rubber goods, glass, pigments, cosmetics, and dusting powders; an antiseptic and sedative (U.S.P., B.P.). **z. oxide cement.** See *dental cement.* **z. paste.** A mixture of z. oxide, starch, and white petrolatum; an astringent (U.S.P., B.P.). **z. perborate.** $Zn(BO_3)_2 = 183.0$. White powder, insoluble in water; an oxidizing agent and antiseptic in cosmetics. **z. perhydrol.** Z. peroxide. **z. permanganate.** $Zn(MnO_4)_2 \cdot 6H_2O = 411.5$. Brown, deliquescent crystals; an oxidizing agent, astringent, and antiseptic. **z. peroxide.** $ZnO_2 = 97.4$. Z. perhydrol. Yellow, voluminous powder, insoluble in water; a bactericide. **z. phenate.** $Zn(C_6H_5O)_2$ = 251.46. Z. carbonate. White powder, slightly soluble in water; a dusting powder and antiseptic. **z. phenol sulfonate.** $Zn(C_6H_5SO_4)_2$ = 411.60. Z. sulfophenate, z. sulfocarbolate. Colorless prisms, soluble in water; an antiseptic. **z. phosphate.** $Zn_3(PO_4)_2$ = 386.2. White prisms, m. red heat, insoluble in water, soluble in ammonium salt solutions; a reagent, antiseptic, tonic, and astringent. *ortho-* Z. phosphate. *pyro-* $Zn_2P_2O_7$ = 304.8. White powder, insoluble in water. **z. phosphide.** Zn_3P_2 = 258.2. Gray powder, d.4.72, decomp. in moist air, insoluble in water; a phosphorus substitute, and a reagent in making hydrogen phosphide. **z. phosphite.** $ZnHPO_3$ = 145.4. White granules, soluble in water; a tonic and antiseptic. **z. picrate.** $Zn[C_6H_2O_2(NO_2)_2]_2$ = 489.47. Yellow, explosive crystals, used in hydrated form as an antiseptic. **z. potassium cyanide.** $K_2Zn(CN)_4$ = 247.7. Colorless crystals, soluble in water; a tonic. **z. potassium iodide.** K_2ZnI_4 = 651. Colorless crystals, soluble in water; a reagent. **z. potassium sulfate.** $K_2Zn(SO_4)_2$ = 335.7. Colorless, hygroscopic crystals. **z. pyrophosphate.** See *z. phosphate.* **z. rhodanide.** Z. thiocyanate. **z. salicylate.** $Zn(C_6H_4OHCOO)_2 \cdot 3H_2O$ = 393.5. Colorless needles, soluble in water. **z. silicate.** $ZnSiO_3$ = 141.3. White powder, insoluble in water. **z. silicofluoride.** $ZnSiF_6 \cdot 6H_2O$ = 315.4. Colorless crystals, soluble in water. **z. spar.** $ZnCO_3$. An important z. ore. **z. spinel.** Gahnite. **z. stearate.** $Zn(C_{18}H_{35}O_2)_2$ = 632.0. White, greasy granules, insoluble in water; an antiseptic, dusting powder (U.S.P.), a drier for paints. **z. succinate.** $ZnC_4H_4O_4$ = 181.4. White powder, insoluble in water. **z. sulfanilate.** $Zn(C_6H_4NH_2SO_3)_2 \cdot 4H_2O$ = 481.5. Nizin. Colorless powder, insoluble in water; an astringent and antiseptic. **z. sulfate.** $ZnSO_4$ = 161.45. *anhydrous-* Colorless crystals, soluble in water. *dihydrate-* $ZnSO_4 \cdot 2H_2O$ = 197.48. Fused sticks or white powder, soluble in water. *heptahydrate-* $ZnSO_4 \cdot 7H_2O$ = 287.56. Crystalline or common z. vitriol, white vitriol. White, rhombic, prismatic, or monoclinic crystals, d.2.015, m.50, soluble in water, alcohol, or ether. Used as a reagent (in volumetry and to precipitate proteins); an antiseptic, eyewash, gargle, and emetic; a mordant in dyeing and textile printing; a preservative for skins and woods; a weed killer; an ophthalmic astringent (U.S.P.); and in the manufacture of paints and varnishes. **z. sulfide.** ZnS = 97.4. Yellow hexagons or tetragons, m.1049, insoluble in water; a pigment, and reagent in testing the acidity of soils. Cf. *Sidot's blende.* **z. sulfite.** $ZnSO_3 \cdot 2.5H_2O$ = 190.49. White crystals, soluble in water; a preservative for anatomical specimens. **z. sulfocarbolate.** Z. phenol sulfonate. **z. sulfocyanate.** Z. thiocyanate. **z. sulfhydrate.** $Zn(SH)_2$ = 131.4. White powder, insoluble in water, decomp. when dry (therefore stored under water); an intestinal antiseptic. **z. tartrate.** $ZnC_4H_4O_6$ = 213.5. White powder, slightly soluble in water. **z. tetraborate.** ZnB_4O_7 = 220.7. Z. borate, z. biborate. White powder, insoluble in water; an antiseptic. **z. thiocyanate.** $Zn(CNS)_2$ = 181.5. Z. rhodanate. Z. sulfocyanate. White, deliquescent crystals. **z. undecylenate.** $[CH_2: - CH(CH_2)_8 \cdot CO_2]_2Zn$ = 431.93. Z. undecenoate.

White powder, insoluble in water; a fungistatic (U.S.P., B.P.). **z. valerate.** $Zn(C_5H_9O_2)_2 \cdot 2H_2O$ = 303.5. White crystals, soluble in water; an antispasmodic and astringent. **z. vitriol.** Z. sulfate. **z. white.** (1) Z. oxide. (2) A mixture of z. oxide 80, barium sulfate 20% (German usage). **z. yellow.** Commercial z. chromate; a pigment.

zincaloy. An alloy of zirconium with amounts of iron, nickel, chromium, tin, and not more than 0.5 ppm boron.

zincamide. $Zn(NH_2)_2$ = 97.43.

zincates. M_2ZnO_2. Salts of amphoteric zinc hydroxide. Z. form hydrated ions, in solution; as $Zn(OH)_2^-$, $Zn(OH)_3^=$.

zincic acid. The amphoteric form of zinc hydroxide: $H_2ZnO_2 \rightleftharpoons Zn(OH)_2$.

zincite. ZnO. A rare, red, native zinc oxide, hardness 4–4.4, d.5.4–5.7.

zincography. Process engraving. Reproduction on zinc plates, the surface of which is first coated with special wax, on which is drawn or photographed the subject to be printed. A strong acid dissolves the zinc not covered by the image, which is thus left in relief.

zineb. Pharmaceutical name for zinc ethylene bisdithiocarbamate; a fungicide.

zinethyl. Zinc ethide.

zingerone. $MeCOCH_2CH_2C_6H_3(OH)OMe$ = 194.1. 4-Hydroxy-3-methoxyphenylethyl (methyl) ketone. Colorless crystals, m.41, soluble in water; with a pungent taste, in ginger. Cf. *capsicin.*

zingiber. Ginger.

Zingiberaceae. See *Scitaminaceae.*

zingiberene. $C_{15}H_{24}$ = 204.19. 1-Methyl-4-propenylcyclohexane. A sesquiterpene from oil of ginger, d.0.872, b.279.

zingiberol. $C_{15}H_{26}O$ = 222.2. An alcohol, $b_{14mm}157$, from ginger.

zinin. Azoxybenzene.

zinkenite. $PbSb_2S_3$. A native antimonite.

zinkite. Zincite.

zinnkies. Cu_2FeSnS_4. Native sulfostannate.

zinnwaldite. $(K, Li)_3FeAl_3Si_5O_{16}F_2$. A pale violet, yellow, or brown lithia mica.

zippeite. $2UO_3 \cdot SO_3 \cdot H_2O$. A native uranium sulfate; less than 5% copper oxide.

ziram. Pharmaceutical name for zinc dimethyl dithiocarbamate; a fungicide.

Zircal. Trade name for the alloys: Zn 7.0–8.5, Mg 1.75–3.0, Cu 1–2, Cr 0.1–0.4, Mn 0.1–0.6, Fe + Si 0.7%. They are strong, light, and elastic, and may be rolled, drawn, or extruded.

zircon. $ZrSiO_4$. Ostranite. Jargon. A native zirconium silicate. Transparent, yellow crystals, d.4.68–4.70, hardness 7.5; a source of Zr compounds and gem (hyacinth, jargon). See *starlite, malacon, oerstedite.* **z. alba.** Zirconium oxide.

zirconate. M_2ZrO_3. A salt of amphoteric zirconium hydroxide.

zirconia. Zirconium oxide.

zirconic acid. Zirconium hydroxide. **z. anhydride.** Zirconium oxide.

zirconium. Zr = 91.22. A rare-earth metal and element of the carbon group, at. no. 40, discovered by Klaproth (1789). Silvery, crystalline or gray amorphous metal, d.4.15 (cryst.), 6.41 (amorph.), m.1900, insoluble in water or acids, soluble in aqua regia or molten alkalies. Valency 4; forms 3 series of compounds: normal, $Z^{4+}r$; basic, ZnO^{++} (zirconyl); $ZrO_3^=$ (zirconates). Used as a steel deoxidizer, denitrifier, and desulfurizer (in the form of silicon-zirconium or ferrosilicon-zirconium); a "getter" in radio tubes; an X-ray filter; a flash powder with 40% Mg; for wires and filaments in many alloys, for flash bulbs coated on aluminum foil, and for making cesium from cesium dichromate. **z. bromide.** $ZrBr_4 = 411.0$. Z. tetrabromide. White powder, decomp. violently by water to form zirconyl bromide. **z. carbonate.** Zirconyl carbonate. **z. chloride.** $ZrCl_4 = 232.8$. Z.tetrachloride. Colorless crystals, sublimes 350, decomp. by water to zirconyl chloride; used in organic synthesis (Friedel-Craft reaction). **z. dioxide.** Z. oxide. **z. fluoride.** $ZrF_4 = 167.2$. Colorless crystals m. red heat, insoluble in water. **z. hydroxide.** $Zr(OH)_4 = 159.2$. Colorless powder, insoluble in water, soluble in acids with formation of Zr^{4+} and ZnO^{++} ions, and in alkalies with formation of $ZrO_3^=$ ions. **z. iodide.** $ZrI_4 = 599.1$. Hygroscopic, brown crystals. **z. nitrate.** Zirconyl nitrate. **z. oxide.** $ZrO_4 = 123.2$. Zirconia, zircon alba, z. anhydride, z. dioxide, native as baddeleyite, zirkite, and becarite; 3 crystal forms. Heavy, white powder, m.2730, insoluble in water, soluble in hot acids. It is a durable refractory; an effective opacifier of fused enamels, glass, and glazes; also used in the manufacture of Welsbach mantles, in X-ray photography as a substitute for bismuth salts, and with silica and graphite for safe and vault walls. **z. oxybromide.** Zirconyl bromide. **z. oxychloride.** Zirconyl chloride. **z. silicate.** See *zircon, azorite.* **z. silicide.** $Zr_5Si_3 = 537.9$. A compound of very high molecular weight, analogous to z. stannide. **z. stannide.** $Zr_5Sn_3 = 809.1$. A compound of very high molecular weight analogous to z. silicide; m.2000. **z. sulfate.** $Zr(SO_4)_2 \cdot 4H_4O = 355.4$. Colorless crystals, soluble in water; a reagent for potassium. **z. tetrachloride.** Z. chloride.

zirconyl. The radical $ZrO=$. **z. bromide.** $ZrOBr_2 = 267.1$. Zirconium oxybromide. Colorless, deliquescent powder, decomp. in moist air. **z. carbonate.** $ZrOCO_3 = 167.22$. White powder, insoluble in water. **z. chloride.** $ZrOCl_2 = 178.14$. Zirconium oxychloride. Colorless, silky needles, soluble in water. **z. hydroxide.** $ZrO(OH)_2 = 141.24$. White powder, insoluble in water. **z. nitrate.** $ZrO(NO_3)_2 = 231.24$. White crystals, soluble in water; used in Welsbach mantles. **z. phosphate.** $(ZrO)_3(PO_4)_2 \cdot 8H_2O = 655.79$. Colorless powder, insoluble in water.

zirkite. ZrO_2. A native zirconia ore (Brazil); a firebrick, cement, and opacifier.

zirlite. $Al(OH)_3$. Yellow, native aluminum hydroxide.

Z.I.X. Trade name for zinc isopropyl xanthate.

Zn. Symbol for zinc.

zoisite. $Ca_2Al_3(OH)(SiO_4)_3$. Thulite. Gives its name to a group of silica minerals, q.v.

Zöller, Philipp. 1833–1885. German chemist, noted for agricultural and biochemical work.

zone. An area of interest; especially a region of oriented molecules. Cf. *orientation.* It differs from a phase in that it is heterogeneous with molecules oriented. **interfacial-** The layer of oriented A and B molecules between 2 phases A and B. **micellar-** A region of isolated or continuous

oriented molecules in a surrounding phase. **monomolecular-** A layer of oriented C molecules between 2 phases A and B. **polar-** A z. consisting of oriented dipoles; as in solvates, q.v.

z. leveling. The use of z. melting to produce a uniform distribution of one solid in another. **z. melting, z. refining.** A method of purification of metal ingots by heat, in which a molten zone is caused to pass along the length of the ingot (z. melting), thereby producing a change in the concentration of the impurities. Especially suitable for the purification of semiconductors and uranium.

zoo- Prefix (Greek) indicating animals.

zoochemistry. The study of the composition and reactions occurring in animal organisms.

zooglea, zoogloea. A firm mass of bacteria embedded in a jellylike matrix.

zoology. The study of the classification, structure, and function of animals.

zoom. Describing the property of an optical instrument, e.g., microscope, which enables sharp focusing to be obtained over a wide range of magnifications without change of objectives.

zoomaric acid. $Me \cdot CH:CH \cdot (CH_2)_{11} \cdot COOH = 240.22$. Hexadecenoic acid, from marine animal oils; probably identical with palmitoleic acid.

zoonic acid. An early name for acetic acid.

zoospore. A mobile spore (swarm spore) produced by fungi.

zoosterol. A sterol, q.v., of animal origin, e.g., cholesterol.

zootoxin. A poison derived from an animal; as, venoms.

Zosimos of Panopolis. Middle 5th century B.C. A Greek writer of Egypt, who wrote 20 chemical works, which show that the term "chemistry" is not of Arabic origin ($\pi\epsilon\rho\iota\ \tau\eta\varsigma\ \chi\pi\mu\epsilon\iota\alpha\varsigma =$ On Chemistry).

Zr. Symbol for zirconium.

Zsigmondy, Richard. 1865–1929. Austrian chemist, Nobel Prize winner (1925). **Z. filters.** A series of graded ultrafilters for separating ultramicroscopical particles or colloids from solutions, according to their sizes. They are semipermeable membranes of various compositions and permeabilities; used in analytical and physiological chemistry.

zuckerin. Saccharin.

zwitterion. A complex ion that is both positively and negatively charged; as, $X^- \cdot R \cdot Y^+$, e.g., $^+NH \cdot R \cdot SO_3^-$. Cf. *amphoteric.*

Zycon. Trademark for a protein synthetic fiber.

zygadenine. $C_{39}H_{63}O_{10}N = 705.5$. An alkaloid from the bulbs of *Zygadenus nuttalli* (Liliaceae), Rocky Mountains. It resembles veratrine.

zygograph. (Greek, zygon, a yoke.) A graphical relationship between the composition of a vapor and that of a liquid in equilibrium with it; used in distillation problems.

zygote. A fertilized cell. See *gamete.*

Zyklon. Trade name for hydrocyanic acid absorbed on wood pulp and used in fumigation.

zylonite. Celluloid.

zymamsis. Alcoholic fermentation.

zymase. An enzyme of yeast that splits sugar into alcohol and carbon dioxide. It retains its activity if separated from the yeast cell. Cf. *invertase.*

zyme. A disease-producing ferment of virus.

zymin. An acetone-dried yeast.

zymochemistry. The chemistry of fermentation.

zymoexcitor. A kinase that converts a zymogen into an active enzyme.

zymogen. The mother substance of an enzyme; a substance secreted from tissues or glands that is split into an active enzyme and protein by a kinase.

zymohexose. A monosaccharide that ferments readily; as, d-glucose.

zymohydrolysis. Zymolysis.

zymology. The study of the action and composition of ferments or enzymes.

zymolysis. Zymohydrolysis. A chemical reaction produced by an enzyme.

zymoplasm. Thrombase.

zymosis. Fermentation; reactions caused by enzymes.

zymosterol. $C_{27}H_{44}O = 384.3$. A sterol, q.v., from yeast, m.108, insoluble in water.

zymurgy. The study of the application of enzymes in brewing, distilling, or wine making. In its broader meaning it includes the processes of fermentation for manufacturing purposes, as in the tobacco, cheese, indigo, or leather industry.